American Casebook Series
Hornbook Series and Basic Legal Texts
Nutshell Series

of

WEST PUBLISHING COMPANY
P.O. Box 64526
St. Paul, Minnesota 55164–0526

ACCOUNTING

Faris' Accounting and Law in a Nutshell, 377 pages, 1984 (Text)

Fiflis, Kripke and Foster's Teaching Materials on Accounting for Business Lawyers, 3rd Ed., 838 pages, 1984 (Casebook)

Siegel and Siegel's Accounting and Financial Disclosure: A Guide to Basic Concepts, 259 pages, 1983 (Text)

ADMINISTRATIVE LAW

Davis' Cases, Text and Problems on Administrative Law, 6th Ed., 683 pages, 1977 (Casebook)

Gellhorn and Boyer's Administrative Law and Process in a Nutshell, 2nd Ed., 445 pages, 1981 (Text)

Mashaw and Merrill's Cases and Materials on Administrative Law–The American Public Law System, 2nd Ed., 976 pages, 1985 (Casebook)

Robinson, Gellhorn and Bruff's The Administrative Process, 3rd Ed., 978 pages, 1986 (Casebook)

ADMIRALTY

Healy and Sharpe's Cases and Materials on Admiralty, 2nd Ed., 876 pages, 1986 (Casebook)

Maraist's Admiralty in a Nutshell, 2nd Ed., 379 pages, 1988 (Text)

Schoenbaum's Hornbook on Admiralty and Maritime Law, Student Ed., 692 pages, 1987 (Text)

Sohn and Gustafson's Law of the Sea in a Nutshell, 264 pages, 1984 (Text)

AGENCY—PARTNERSHIP

Fessler's Alternatives to Incorporation for Persons in Quest of Profit, 2nd Ed., 326 pages, 1986 (Casebook)

AGENCY—PARTNERSHIP—Cont'd

Henn's Cases and Materials on Agency, Partnership and Other Unincorporated Business Enterprises, 2nd Ed., 733 pages, 1985 (Casebook)

Reuschlein and Gregory's Hornbook on the Law of Agency and Partnership, 625 pages, 1979, with 1981 pocket part (Text)

Selected Corporation and Partnership Statutes, Rules and Forms, 621 pages, 1987

Steffen and Kerr's Cases and Materials on Agency-Partnership, 4th Ed., 859 pages, 1980 (Casebook)

Steffen's Agency-Partnership in a Nutshell, 364 pages, 1977 (Text)

AGRICULTURAL LAW

Meyer, Pedersen, Thorson and Davidson's Agricultural Law: Cases and Materials, 931 pages, 1985 (Casebook)

ALTERNATIVE DISPUTE RESOLUTION

Kanowitz' Cases and Materials on Alternative Dispute Resolution, 1024 pages, 1986 (Casebook)

Riskin and Westbrook's Dispute Resolution and Lawyers, 223 pages, 1987 (Coursebook)

Riskin and Westbrook's Dispute Resolution and Lawyers, Abridged Ed., 223 pages, 1987 (Coursebook)

Teple and Moberly's Arbitration and Conflict Resolution, (The Labor Law Group), 614 pages, 1979 (Casebook)

AMERICAN INDIAN LAW

Canby's American Indian Law in a Nutshell, 2nd Ed., about 319 pages, 1988 (Text)

Getches and Wilkinson's Cases on Federal Indian Law, 2nd Ed., 880 pages, 1986 (Casebook)

List current as of July, 1988

I

LAW SCHOOL PUBLICATIONS—Continued

ANTITRUST LAW

Gellhorn's Antitrust Law and Economics in a Nutshell, 3rd Ed., 472 pages, 1986 (Text)

Gifford and Raskind's Cases and Materials on Antitrust, 694 pages, 1983 with 1985 Supplement (Casebook)

Hovenkamp's Hornbook on Economics and Federal Antitrust Law, Student Ed., 414 pages, 1985 (Text)

Oppenheim, Weston and McCarthy's Cases and Comments on Federal Antitrust Laws, 4th Ed., 1168 pages, 1981 with 1985 Supplement (Casebook)

Posner and Easterbrook's Cases and Economic Notes on Antitrust, 2nd Ed., 1077 pages, 1981, with 1984–85 Supplement (Casebook)

Sullivan's Hornbook of the Law of Antitrust, 886 pages, 1977 (Text)

See also Regulated Industries, Trade Regulation

ART LAW

DuBoff's Art Law in a Nutshell, 335 pages, 1984 (Text)

BANKING LAW

Lovett's Banking and Financial Institutions in a Nutshell, 2nd Ed., about 455 pages, 1988 (Text)

Symons and White's Teaching Materials on Banking Law, 2nd Ed., 993 pages, 1984, with 1987 Supplement (Casebook)

BUSINESS PLANNING

Painter's Problems and Materials in Business Planning, 2nd Ed., 1008 pages, 1984 with 1987 Supplement (Casebook)

Selected Securities and Business Planning Statutes, Rules and Forms, about 475 pages, 1987

CIVIL PROCEDURE

American Bar Association Section of Litigation—Reading on Adversarial Justice: The American Approach to Adjudication, edited by Landsman, 217 pages, 1988 (Coursebook)

Casad's Res Judicata in a Nutshell, 310 pages, 1976 (text)

Cound, Friedenthal, Miller and Sexton's Cases and Materials on Civil Procedure, 4th Ed., 1202 pages, 1985 with 1987 Supplement (Casebook)

Ehrenzweig, Louisell and Hazard's Jurisdiction in a Nutshell, 4th Ed., 232 pages, 1980 (Text)

Federal Rules of Civil-Appellate Procedure—West Law School Edition, about 600 pages, 1988

Friedenthal, Kane and Miller's Hornbook on Civil Procedure, 876 pages, 1985 (Text)

Kane's Civil Procedure in a Nutshell, 2nd Ed., 306 pages, 1986 (Text)

CIVIL PROCEDURE—Cont'd

Koffler and Reppy's Hornbook on Common Law Pleading, 663 pages, 1969 (Text)

Marcus and Sherman's Complex Litigation–Cases and Materials on Advanced Civil Procedure, 846 pages, 1985 (Casebook)

Park's Computer-Aided Exercises on Civil Procedure, 2nd Ed., 167 pages, 1983 (Coursebook)

Siegel's Hornbook on New York Practice, 1011 pages, 1978 with 1987 Pocket Part (Text)

See also Federal Jurisdiction and Procedure

CIVIL RIGHTS

Abernathy's Cases and Materials on Civil Rights, 660 pages, 1980 (Casebook)

Cohen's Cases on the Law of Deprivation of Liberty: A Study in Social Control, 755 pages, 1980 (Casebook)

Lockhart, Kamisar, Choper and Shiffrin's Cases on Constitutional Rights and Liberties, 6th Ed., 1266 pages, 1986 with 1988 Supplement (Casebook)—reprint from Lockhart, et al. Cases on Constitutional Law, 6th Ed., 1986

Vieira's Civil Rights in a Nutshell, 279 pages, 1978 (Text)

COMMERCIAL LAW

Bailey and Hagedorn's Secured Transactions in a Nutshell, 3rd Ed. about 390 pages, 1988 (Text)

Epstein, Martin, Henning and Nickles' Basic Uniform Commercial Code Teaching Materials, 3rd Ed., 704 pages, 1988 (Casebook)

Henson's Hornbook on Secured Transactions Under the U.C.C., 2nd Ed., 504 pages, 1979 with 1979 P.P. (Text)

Murray's Commercial Law, Problems and Materials, 366 pages, 1975 (Coursebook)

Nickles, Matheson and Dolan's Materials for Understanding Credit and Payment Systems, 923 pages, 1987 (Casebook)

Nordstrom, Murray and Clovis' Problems and Materials on Sales, 515 pages, 1982 (Casebook)

Nordstrom, Murray and Clovis' Problems and Materials on Secured Transactions, 594 pages, 1987 (Casebook)

Selected Commercial Statutes, about 1525 pages, 1988

Speidel, Summers and White's Teaching Materials on Commercial Law, 4th Ed., 1448 pages, 1987 (Casebook)

Speidel, Summers and White's Commercial Paper: Teaching Materials, 4th Ed., 578 pages, 1987 (Casebook)—reprint from Speidel, et al. Commercial Law, 4th Ed.

Speidel, Summers and White's Sales: Teaching Materials, 4th Ed., 804 pages, 1987 (Casebook)—reprint from Speidel, et al. Commercial Law, 4th Ed.

LAW SCHOOL PUBLICATIONS—Continued

COMMERCIAL LAW—Cont'd

Speidel, Summers and White's Secured Transactions—Teaching Materials, 4th Ed., 485 pages, 1987 (Casebook)—reprint from Speidel, et al. Commercial Law, 4th Ed.

Stockton's Sales in a Nutshell, 2nd Ed., 370 pages, 1981 (Text)

Stone's Uniform Commercial Code in a Nutshell, 2nd Ed., 516 pages, 1984 (Text)

Uniform Commercial Code, Official Text with Comments, 1155 pages, 1987

Weber and Speidel's Commercial Paper in a Nutshell, 3rd Ed., 404 pages, 1982 (Text)

White and Summers' Hornbook on the Uniform Commercial Code, 3rd Ed., Student Ed., about 1200 pages, 1988 (Text)

COMMUNITY PROPERTY

Mennell and Boykoff's Community Property in a Nutshell, 2nd Ed., 432 pages, 1988 (Text)

Verrall and Bird's Cases and Materials on California Community Property, 5th Ed., about 587 pages, 1988 (Casebook)

COMPARATIVE LAW

Barton, Gibbs, Li and Merryman's Law in Radically Different Cultures, 960 pages, 1983 (Casebook)

Glendon, Gordon and Osakive's Comparative Legal Traditions: Text, Materials and Cases on the Civil Law, Common Law, and Socialist Law Traditions, 1091 pages, 1985 (Casebook)

Glendon, Gordon, and Osakwe's Comparative Legal Traditions in a Nutshell, 402 pages, 1982 (Text)

Langbein's Comparative Criminal Procedure: Germany, 172 pages, 1977 (Casebook)

COMPUTERS AND LAW

Maggs and Sprowl's Computer Applications in the Law, 316 pages, 1987 (Coursebook)

Mason's Using Computers in the Law: An Introduction and Practical Guide, 2nd Ed., 288 pages, 1988 (Text)

CONFLICT OF LAWS

Cramton, Currie and Kay's Cases-Comments-Questions on Conflict of Laws, 4th Ed., 876 pages, 1987 (Casebook)

Scoles and Hay's Hornbook on Conflict of Laws, Student Ed., 1085 pages, 1982 with 1986 P.P. (Text)

Scoles and Weintraub's Cases and Materials on Conflict of Laws, 2nd Ed., 966 pages, 1972, with 1978 Supplement (Casebook)

Siegel's Conflicts in a Nutshell, 469 pages, 1982 (Text)

CONSTITUTIONAL LAW

Barron and Dienes' Constitutional Law in a Nutshell, 389 pages, 1986 (Text)

Engdahl's Constitutional Federalism in a Nutshell, 2nd Ed., 411 pages, 1987 (Text)

Lockhart, Kamisar, Choper and Shiffrin's Cases-Comments-Questions on Constitutional Law, 6th Ed., 1601 pages, 1986 with 1988 Supplement (Casebook)

Lockhart, Kamisar, Choper and Shiffrin's Cases-Comments-Questions on the American Constitution, 6th Ed., 1260 pages, 1986 with 1988 Supplement (Casebook)—abridgment of Lockhart, et al. Cases on Constitutional Law, 6th Ed., 1986

Manning's The Law of Church-State Relations in a Nutshell, 305 pages, 1981 (Text)

Marks and Cooper's State Constitutional Law in a Nutshell, about 300 pages, 1988 (Text)

Miller's Presidential Power in a Nutshell, 328 pages, 1977 (Text)

Nowak, Rotunda and Young's Hornbook on Constitutional Law, 3rd Ed., Student Ed., 1191 pages, 1986 with 1988 Pocket Part (Text)

Rotunda's Modern Constitutional Law: Cases and Notes, 2nd Ed., 1004 pages, 1985 with 1988 Supplement (Casebook)

Williams' Constitutional Analysis in a Nutshell, 388 pages, 1979 (Text)

See also Civil Rights, Foreign Relations and National Security Law

CONSUMER LAW

Epstein and Nickles' Consumer Law in a Nutshell, 2nd Ed., 418 pages, 1981 (Text)

Selected Commercial Statutes, about 1525 pages, 1988

Spanogle and Rohner's Cases and Materials on Consumer Law, 693 pages, 1979, with 1982 Supplement (Casebook)

See also Commercial Law

CONTRACTS

Calamari & Perillo's Cases and Problems on Contracts, 1061 pages, 1978 (Casebook)

Calamari and Perillo's Hornbook on Contracts, 3rd Ed., 904 pages, 1987 (Text)

Corbin's Text on Contracts, One Volume Student Edition, 1224 pages, 1952 (Text)

Fessler and Loiseaux's Cases and Materials on Contracts, 837 pages, 1982 (Casebook)

Friedman's Contract Remedies in a Nutshell, 323 pages, 1981 (Text)

Fuller and Eisenberg's Cases on Basic Contract Law, 4th Ed., 1203 pages, 1981 (Casebook)

Hamilton, Rau and Weintraub's Cases and Materials on Contracts, 830 pages, 1984 (Casebook)

LAW SCHOOL PUBLICATIONS—Continued

CONTRACTS—Cont'd

Jackson and Bollinger's Cases on Contract Law in Modern Society, 2nd Ed., 1329 pages, 1980 (Casebook)

Keyes' Government Contracts in a Nutshell, 423 pages, 1979 (Text)

Schaber and Rohwer's Contracts in a Nutshell, 2nd Ed., 425 pages, 1984 (Text)

Summers and Hillman's Contract and Related Obligation: Theory, Doctrine and Practice, 1074 pages, 1987 (Casebook)

COPYRIGHT

See Patent and Copyright Law

CORPORATE FINANCE

Hamilton's Cases and Materials on Corporate Finance, 895 pages, 1984 with 1986 Supplement (Casebook)

CORPORATIONS

Hamilton's Cases on Corporations—Including Partnerships and Limited Partnerships, 3rd Ed., 1213 pages, 1986 with 1986 Statutory Supplement (Casebook)

Hamilton's Law of Corporations in a Nutshell, 2nd Ed., 515 pages, 1987 (Text)

Henn's Teaching Materials on Corporations, 2nd Ed., 1204 pages, 1986 (Casebook)

Henn and Alexander's Hornbook on Corporations, 3rd Ed., Student Ed., 1371 pages, 1983 with 1986 P.P. (Text)

Jennings and Buxbaum's Cases and Materials on Corporations, 5th Ed., 1180 pages, 1979 (Casebook)

Selected Corporation and Partnership Statutes, Rules and Forms, 621 pages, 1987

Solomon, Schwartz' and Bauman's Materials and Problems on Corporations: Law and Policy, 2nd Ed., 1391 pages, 1988 (Casebook)

CORRECTIONS

Krantz's Cases and Materials on the Law of Corrections and Prisoners' Rights, 3rd Ed., 855 pages, 1986 with 1988 Supplement (Casebook)

Krantz's Law of Corrections and Prisoners' Rights in a Nutshell, 2nd Ed., 386 pages, 1983 (Text)

Popper's Post-Conviction Remedies in a Nutshell, 360 pages, 1978 (Text)

Robbins' Cases and Materials on Post Conviction Remedies, 506 pages, 1982 (Casebook)

CREDITOR'S RIGHTS

Bankruptcy Code, Rules and Forms, Law School Ed., 792 pages, 1988

Epstein's Debtor-Creditor Law in a Nutshell, 3rd Ed., 383 pages, 1986 (Text)

Epstein, Landers and Nickles' Debtors and Creditors: Cases and Materials, 3rd Ed., 1059 pages, 1987 (Casebook)

CREDITOR'S RIGHTS—Cont'd

LoPucki's Player's Manual for the Debtor-Creditor Game, 123 pages, 1985 (Coursebook)

Riesenfeld's Cases and Materials on Creditors' Remedies and Debtors' Protection, 4th Ed., 914 pages, 1987 (Casebook)

White's Bankruptcy and Creditor's Rights: Cases and Materials, 812 pages, 1985, with 1987 Supplement (Casebook)

CRIMINAL LAW AND CRIMINAL PROCEDURE

Abrams', Federal Criminal Law and its Enforcement, 882 pages, 1986 (Casebook)

Carlson's Adjudication of Criminal Justice, Problems and References, 130 pages, 1986 (Casebook)

Dix and Sharlot's Cases and Materials on Criminal Law, 3rd Ed., 846 pages, 1987 (Casebook)

Federal Rules of Criminal Procedure—West Law School Edition, about 500 pages, 1988

Grano's Problems in Criminal Procedure, 2nd Ed., 176 pages, 1981 (Problem book)

Israel and LaFave's Criminal Procedure in a Nutshell, 4th Ed., 461 pages, 1988 (Text)

Johnson's Cases, Materials and Text on Criminal Law, 3rd Ed., 783 pages, 1985 (Casebook)

Johnson's Cases on Criminal Procedure, 859 pages, 1987 with 1988 Supplement (Casebook)

Kamisar, LaFave and Israel's Cases, Comments and Questions on Modern Criminal Procedure, 6th Ed., 1558 pages, 1986 with 1988 Supplement (Casebook)

Kamisar, LaFave and Israel's Cases, Comments and Questions on Basic Criminal Procedure, 6th Ed., 860 pages, 1986 with 1988 Supplement (Casebook)—reprint from Kamisar, et al. Modern Criminal Procedure, 6th ed., 1986

LaFave's Modern Criminal Law: Cases, Comments and Questions, 2nd Ed., 903 pages, 1988 (Casebook)

LaFave and Israel's Hornbook on Criminal Procedure, Student Ed., 1142 pages, 1985 with 1987 P.P. (Text)

LaFave and Scott's Hornbook on Criminal Law, 2nd Ed., Student Ed., 918 pages, 1986 (Text)

Langbein's Comparative Criminal Procedure: Germany, 172 pages, 1977 (Casebook)

Loewy's Criminal Law in a Nutshell, 2nd Ed., 321 pages, 1987 (Text)

Saltzburg's American Criminal Procedure, Cases and Commentary, 3rd Ed., 1302 pages, 1988 with 1988 Supplement (Casebook)

LAW SCHOOL PUBLICATIONS—Continued

CRIMINAL LAW AND CRIMINAL PROCEDURE—Cont'd

Uviller's The Processes of Criminal Justice: Investigation and Adjudication, 2nd Ed., 1384 pages, 1979 with 1979 Statutory Supplement and 1986 Update (Casebook)

Uviller's The Processes of Criminal Justice: Adjudication, 2nd Ed., 730 pages, 1979. Soft-cover reprint from Uviller's The Processes of Criminal Justice: Investigation and Adjudication, 2nd Ed. (Casebook)

Uviller's The Processes of Criminal Justice: Investigation, 2nd Ed., 655 pages, 1979. Soft-cover reprint from Uviller's The Processes of Criminal Justice: Investigation and Adjudication, 2nd Ed. (Casebook)

Vorenberg's Cases on Criminal Law and Procedure, 2nd Ed., 1088 pages, 1981 with 1987 Supplement (Casebook)

See also Corrections, Juvenile Justice

DECEDENTS ESTATES

See Trusts and Estates

DOMESTIC RELATIONS

Clark's Cases and Problems on Domestic Relations, 3rd Ed., 1153 pages, 1980 (Casebook)

Clark's Hornbook on Domestic Relations, 2nd Ed., Student Ed., 1050 pages, 1988 (Text)

Krause's Cases and Materials on Family Law, 2nd Ed., 1221 pages, 1983 with 1986 Supplement (Casebook)

Krause's Family Law in a Nutshell, 2nd Ed., 444 pages, 1986 (Text)

Krauskopf's Cases on Property Division at Marriage Dissolution, 250 pages, 1984 (Casebook)

ECONOMICS, LAW AND

Goetz' Cases and Materials on Law and Economics, 547 pages, 1984 (Casebook)

See also Antitrust, Regulated Industries

EDUCATION LAW

Alexander and Alexander's The Law of Schools, Students and Teachers in a Nutshell, 409 pages, 1984 (Text)

Morris' The Constitution and American Education, 2nd Ed., 992 pages, 1980 (Casebook)

EMPLOYMENT DISCRIMINATION

Jones, Murphy and Belton's Cases on Discrimination in Employment, 1116 pages, 1987 (Casebook)

Player's Cases and Materials on Employment Discrimination Law, 2nd Ed., 782 pages, 1984 (Casebook)

EMPLOYMENT DISCRIMINATION—Cont'd

Player's Federal Law of Employment Discrimination in a Nutshell, 2nd Ed., 402 pages, 1981 (Text)

Player's Hornbook on the Law of Employment Discrimination, Student Ed., 708 pages, 1988 (Text)

See also Women and the Law

ENERGY AND NATURAL RESOURCES LAW

Laitos' Cases and Materials on Natural Resources Law, 938 pages, 1985 (Casebook)

Rodgers' Cases and Materials on Energy and Natural Resources Law, 2nd Ed., 877 pages, 1983 (Casebook)

Selected Environmental Law Statutes, about 650 pages, 1988

Tomain's Energy Law in a Nutshell, 338 pages, 1981 (Text)

See also Environmental Law, Oil and Gas, Water Law

ENVIRONMENTAL LAW

Bonine and McGarity's Cases and Materials on the Law of Environment and Pollution, 1076 pages, 1984 (Casebook)

Findley and Farber's Cases and Materials on Environmental Law, 2nd Ed., 813 pages, 1985 with 1988 Supplement (Casebook)

Findley and Farber's Environmental Law in a Nutshell, 2nd Ed., about 348 pages, 1988 (Text)

Rodgers' Hornbook on Environmental Law, 956 pages, 1977 with 1984 pocket part (Text)

Selected Environmental Law Statutes, about 650 pages, 1988

See also Energy Law, Natural Resources Law, Water Law

EQUITY

See Remedies

ESTATES

See Trusts and Estates

ESTATE PLANNING

Lynn's Introduction to Estate Planning, in a Nutshell, 3rd Ed., 370 pages, 1983 (Text)

See also Taxation, Trusts and Estates

EVIDENCE

Broun, Meisenholder, Strong and Mosteller's Problems in Evidence, 3rd Ed., about 420 pages, 1988 (Problem book)

Cleary, Strong, Broun and Mosteller's Cases and Materials on Evidence, 4th Ed., about 1050 pages, 1988 (Casebook)

Federal Rules of Evidence for United States Courts and Magistrates, 370 pages, 1987

LAW SCHOOL PUBLICATIONS—Continued

EVIDENCE—Cont'd

Graham's Federal Rules of Evidence in a Nutshell, 2nd Ed., 473 pages, 1987 (Text)

Kimball's Programmed Materials on Problems in Evidence, 380 pages, 1978 (Problem book)

Lempert and Saltzburg's A Modern Approach to Evidence: Text, Problems, Transcripts and Cases, 2nd Ed., 1232 pages, 1983 (Casebook)

Lilly's Introduction to the Law of Evidence, 2nd Ed., 585 pages, 1987 (Text)

McCormick, Sutton and Wellborn's Cases and Materials on Evidence, 6th Ed., 1067 pages, 1987 (Casebook)

McCormick's Hornbook on Evidence, 3rd Ed., Student Ed., 1156 pages, 1984 with 1987 P.P. (Text)

Rothstein's Evidence, State and Federal Rules in a Nutshell, 2nd Ed., 514 pages, 1981 (Text)

Saltzburg's Evidence Supplement: Rules, Statutes, Commentary, 245 pages, 1980 (Casebook Supplement)

FEDERAL JURISDICTION AND PROCEDURE

Currie's Cases and Materials on Federal Courts, 3rd Ed., 1042 pages, 1982 with 1985 Supplement (Casebook)

Currie's Federal Jurisdiction in a Nutshell, 2nd Ed., 258 pages, 1981 (Text)

Federal Rules of Civil-Appellate Procedure—West Law School Edition, about 600 pages, 1988

Forrester and Moye's Cases and Materials on Federal Jurisdiction and Procedure, 3rd Ed., 917 pages, 1977 with 1985 Supplement (Casebook)

Redish's Cases, Comments and Questions on Federal Courts, 878 pages, 1983 with 1988 Supplement (Casebook)

Vetri and Merrill's Federal Courts, Problems and Materials, 2nd Ed., 232 pages, 1984 (Problem Book)

Wright's Hornbook on Federal Courts, 4th Ed., Student Ed., 870 pages, 1983 (Text)

FOREIGN RELATIONS AND NATIONAL SECURITY LAW

Franck and Glennon's United States Foreign Relations Law: Cases, Materials and Simulations, 941 pages, 1987 (Casebook)

FUTURE INTERESTS

See Trusts and Estates

HEALTH LAW

See Medicine, Law and

IMMIGRATION LAW

Aleinikoff and Martin's Immigration Process and Policy, 1042 pages, 1985 with 1987 Supplement (Casebook)

IMMIGRATION LAW—Cont'd

Weissbrodt's Immigration Law and Procedure in a Nutshell, 345 pages, 1984 (Text)

INDIAN LAW

See American Indian Law

INSURANCE

Dobbyn's Insurance Law in a Nutshell, 281 pages, 1981 (Text)

Keeton's Cases on Basic Insurance Law, 2nd Ed., 1086 pages, 1977

Keeton and Wydiss' Insurance Law, Student Ed., about 1024 pages, 1988 (Text)

Wydiss and Keeton's Course Supplement to Keeton and Wydiss's Insurance Law, 425 pages, 1988 (Casebook)

York and Whelan's Cases, Materials and Problems on General Practice Insurance Law, 2nd Ed., about 811 pages, 1988 (Casebook)

INTERNATIONAL LAW

Buergenthal International Human Rights in a Nutshell, about 275 pages, 1988 (Text)

Buergenthal and Maier's Public International Law in a Nutshell, 262 pages, 1985 (Text)

Folsom, Gordon and Spanogle's International Business Transactions – a Problem-Oriented Coursebook, 1160 pages, 1986, with Documents Supplement (Casebook)

Folsom, Gordon and Spanogle's International Business Transactions in a Nutshell, 3rd Ed., about 484 pages, 1988 (Text)

Henkin, Pugh, Schachter and Smit's Cases and Materials on International Law, 2nd Ed., 1517 pages, 1987 with Documents Supplement (Casebook)

Jackson and Davey's Legal Problems of International Economic Relations, 2nd Ed., 1269 pages, 1986, with Documents Supplement (Casebook)

Kirgis' International Organizations in Their Legal Setting, 1016 pages, 1977, with 1981 Supplement (Casebook)

Weston, Falk and D'Amato's International Law and World Order—A Problem Oriented Coursebook, 1195 pages, 1980, with Documents Supplement (Casebook)

INTERVIEWING AND COUNSELING

Binder and Price's Interviewing and Counseling, 232 pages, 1977 (Text)

Shaffer and Elkins' Interviewing and Counseling in a Nutshell, 2nd Ed., 487 pages, 1987 (Text)

INTRODUCTION TO LAW STUDY

Dobbyn's So You Want to go to Law School, Revised First Edition, 206 pages, 1976 (Text)

LAW SCHOOL PUBLICATIONS—Continued

INTRODUCTION TO LAW STUDY—Cont'd

Hegland's Introduction to the Study and Practice of Law in a Nutshell, 418 pages, 1983 (Text)

Kinyon's Introduction to Law Study and Law Examinations in a Nutshell, 389 pages, 1971 (Text)

See also Legal Method and Legal System

JURISPRUDENCE

Christie's Text and Readings on Jurisprudence—The Philosophy of Law, 1056 pages, 1973 (Casebook)

JUVENILE JUSTICE

Fox's Cases and Materials on Modern Juvenile Justice, 2nd Ed., 960 pages, 1981 (Casebook)

Fox's Juvenile Courts in a Nutshell, 3rd Ed., 291 pages, 1984 (Text)

LABOR LAW

Gorman's Basic Text on Labor Law—Unionization and Collective Bargaining, 914 pages, 1976 (Text)

Grodin, Wollett and Alleyne's Collective Bargaining in Public Employment, 3rd Ed., (The Labor Law Group), 430 pages, 1979 (Casebook)

Leslie's Labor Law in a Nutshell, 2nd Ed., 397 pages, 1986 (Text)

Nolan's Labor Arbitration Law and Practice in a Nutshell, 358 pages, 1979 (Text)

Oberer, Hanslowe, Andersen and Heinsz' Cases and Materials on Labor Law—Collective Bargaining in a Free Society, 3rd Ed., 1163 pages, 1986 with Statutory Supplement (Casebook)

Rabin, Silverstein and Schatzki's Labor and Employment Law: Cases, Materials and Problems in the Law of Work, (The Labor Law Group), about 1000 pages, 1988 with Statutory Supplement (Casebook)

See also Employment Discrimination, Social Legislation

LAND FINANCE

See Real Estate Transactions

LAND USE

Callies and Freilich's Cases and Materials on Land Use, 1233 pages, 1986 (Casebook)

Hagman's Cases on Public Planning and Control of Urban and Land Development, 2nd Ed., 1301 pages, 1980 (Casebook)

Hagman and Juergensmeyer's Hornbook on Urban Planning and Land Development Control Law, 2nd Ed., Student Ed., 680 pages, 1986 (Text)

Wright and Gitelman's Cases and Materials on Land Use, 3rd Ed., 1300 pages, 1982, with 1987 Supplement (Casebook)

LAND USE—Cont'd

Wright and Wright's Land Use in a Nutshell, 2nd Ed., 356 pages, 1985 (Text)

LEGAL HISTORY

Presser and Zainaldin's Cases on Law and American History, 855 pages, 1980 (Casebook)

See also Legal Method and Legal System

LEGAL METHOD AND LEGAL SYSTEM

Aldisert's Readings, Materials and Cases in the Judicial Process, 948 pages, 1976 (Casebook)

Berch and Berch's Introduction to Legal Method and Process, 550 pages, 1985 (Casebook)

Bodenheimer, Oakley and Love's Readings and Cases on an Introduction to the Anglo-American Legal System, 2nd Ed., 166 pages, 1988 (Casebook)

Davies and Lawry's Institutions and Methods of the Law—Introductory Teaching Materials, 547 pages, 1982 (Casebook)

Dvorkin, Himmelstein and Lesnick's Becoming a Lawyer: A Humanistic Perspective on Legal Education and Professionalism, 211 pages, 1981 (Text)

Greenberg's Judicial Process and Social Change, 666 pages, 1977 (Casebook)

Kelso and Kelso's Studying Law: An Introduction, 587 pages, 1984 (Coursebook)

Kempin's Historical Introduction to Anglo-American Law in a Nutshell, 2nd Ed., 280 pages, 1973 (Text)

Murphy's Cases and Materials on Introduction to Law—Legal Process and Procedure, 772 pages, 1977 (Casebook)

Reynolds' Judicial Process in a Nutshell, 292 pages, 1980 (Text)

See also Legal Research and Writing

LEGAL PROFESSION

Aronson, Devine and Fisch's Problems, Cases and Materials on Professional Responsibility, 745 pages, 1985 (Casebook)

Aronson and Weckstein's Professional Responsibility in a Nutshell, 399 pages, 1980 (Text)

Mellinkoff's The Conscience of a Lawyer, 304 pages, 1973 (Text)

Pirsig and Kirwin's Cases and Materials on Professional Responsibility, 4th Ed., 603 pages, 1984 (Casebook)

Schwartz and Wydick's Problems in Legal Ethics, 2nd Ed., 341 pages, 1988 (Casebook)

Selected Statutes, Rules and Standards on the Legal Profession, 449 pages, 1987

Smith's Preventing Legal Malpractice, 142 pages, 1981 (Text)

Wolfram's Hornbook on Modern Legal Ethics, Student Edition, 1120 pages, 1986 (Text)

LAW SCHOOL PUBLICATIONS—Continued

LEGAL RESEARCH AND WRITING

Child's Materials and Problems on Drafting Legal Documents, 286 pages, 1988 (Text)

Cohen's Legal Research in a Nutshell, 4th Ed., 450 pages, 1985 (Text)

Cohen and Berring's How to Find the Law, 8th Ed., 790 pages, 1983. Problem book by Foster, Johnson and Kelly available (Casebook)

Cohen and Berring's Finding the Law, 8th Ed., Abridged Ed., 556 pages, 1984 (Casebook)

Dickerson's Materials on Legal Drafting, 425 pages, 1981 (Casebook)

Felsenfeld and Siegel's Writing Contracts in Plain English, 290 pages, 1981 (Text)

Gopen's Writing From a Legal Perspective, 225 pages, 1981 (Text)

Mellinkoff's Legal Writing—Sense and Non-sense, 242 pages, 1982 (Text)

Ray and Ramsfield's Legal Writing: Getting It Right and Getting It Written, 250 pages, 1987 (Text)

Rombauer's Legal Problem Solving—Analysis, Research and Writing, 4th Ed., 424 pages, 1983 (Coursebook)

Squires and Rombauer's Legal Writing in a Nutshell, 294 pages, 1982 (Text)

Statsky's Legal Research and Writing, 3rd Ed., 257 pages, 1986 (Coursebook)

Statsky and Wernet's Case Analysis and Fundamentals of Legal Writing, 3rd Ed., about 450 pages, 1988 (Text)

Teply's Programmed Materials on Legal Research and Citation, 2nd Ed., 358 pages, 1986. Student Library Exercises available (Coursebook)

Weihofen's Legal Writing Style, 2nd Ed., 332 pages, 1980 (Text)

LEGISLATION

Davies' Legislative Law and Process in a Nutshell, 2nd Ed., 346 pages, 1986 (Text)

Eskridge and Frickey's Cases on Legislation, 937 pages, 1987 (Casebook)

Nutting and Dickerson's Cases and Materials on Legislation, 5th Ed., 744 pages, 1978 (Casebook)

Statsky's Legislative Analysis and Drafting, 2nd Ed., 217 pages, 1984 (Text)

LOCAL GOVERNMENT

Frug's Cases and Materials on Local Government Law, about 1000 pages, 1988 (Casebook)

McCarthy's Local Government Law in a Nutshell, 2nd Ed., 404 pages, 1983 (Text)

Reynolds' Hornbook on Local Government Law, 860 pages, 1982, with 1987 pocket part (Text)

Valente's Cases and Materials on Local Government Law, 3rd Ed., 1010 pages, 1987 (Casebook)

MASS COMMUNICATION LAW

Gillmor and Barron's Cases and Comment on Mass Communication Law, 4th Ed., 1076 pages, 1984 (Casebook)

Ginsburg's Regulation of Broadcasting: Law and Policy Towards Radio, Television and Cable Communications, 741 pages, 1979 with 1983 Supplement (Casebook)

Zuckman, Gaynes, Carter and Dee's Mass Communications Law in a Nutshell, 3rd Ed., 538 pages, 1988 (Text)

MEDICINE, LAW AND

Furrow, Johnson, Jost and Schwartz' Health Law: Cases, Materials and Problems, 1005 pages, 1987 (Casebook)

King's The Law of Medical Malpractice in a Nutshell, 2nd Ed., 342 pages, 1986 (Text)

Shapiro and Spece's Problems, Cases and Materials on Bioethics and Law, 892 pages, 1981 (Casebook)

Sharpe, Fiscina and Head's Cases on Law and Medicine, 882 pages, 1978 (Casebook)

MILITARY LAW

Shanor and Terrell's Military Law in a Nutshell, 378 pages, 1980 (Text)

MORTGAGES

See Real Estate Transactions

NATURAL RESOURCES LAW

See Energy and Natural Resources Law

NEGOTIATION

Edwards and White's Problems, Readings and Materials on the Lawyer as a Negotiator, 484 pages, 1977 (Casebook)

Peck's Cases and Materials on Negotiation, 2nd Ed., (The Labor Law Group), 280 pages, 1980 (Casebook)

Williams' Legal Negotiation and Settlement, 207 pages, 1983 (Coursebook)

OFFICE PRACTICE

Hegland's Trial and Practice Skills in a Nutshell, 346 pages, 1978 (Text)

Strong and Clark's Law Office Management, 424 pages, 1974 (Casebook)

See also Computers and Law, Interviewing and Counseling, Negotiation

OIL AND GAS

Hemingway's Hornbook on Oil and Gas, 2nd Ed., Student Ed., 543 pages, 1983 with 1986 P.P. (Text)

Kuntz, Lowe, Anderson and Smith's Cases and Materials on Oil and Gas Law, 857 pages, 1986, with Forms Manual (Casebook)

Lowe's Oil and Gas Law in a Nutshell, 2nd Ed., about 402 pages, 1988 (Text)

See also Energy and Natural Resources Law

LAW SCHOOL PUBLICATIONS—Continued

PARTNERSHIP

See Agency—Partnership

PATENT AND COPYRIGHT LAW

Choate, Francis and Collins' Cases and Materials on Patent Law, 3rd Ed., 1009 pages, 1987 (Casebook)

Miller and Davis' Intellectual Property—Patents, Trademarks and Copyright in a Nutshell, 428 pages, 1983 (Text)

Nimmer's Cases on Copyright and Other Aspects of Entertainment Litigation, 3rd Ed., 1025 pages, 1985 (Casebook)

PRODUCTS LIABILITY

Fischer and Powers' Cases and Materials on Products Liability, 685 pages, 1988 (Casebook)

Noel and Phillips' Cases on Products Liability, 2nd Ed., 821 pages, 1982 (Casebook)

Phillips' Products Liability in a Nutshell, 3rd Ed., 307 pages, 1988 (Text)

PROPERTY

Bernhardt's Real Property in a Nutshell, 2nd Ed., 448 pages, 1981 (Text)

Boyer's Survey of the Law of Property, 766 pages, 1981 (Text)

Browder, Cunningham and Smith's Cases on Basic Property Law, 4th Ed., 1431 pages, 1984 (Casebook)

Bruce, Ely and Bostick's Cases and Materials on Modern Property Law, 1004 pages, 1984 (Casebook)

Burke's Personal Property in a Nutshell, 322 pages, 1983 (Text)

Cunningham, Stoebuck and Whitman's Hornbook on the Law of Property, Student Ed., 916 pages, 1984 with 1987 P.P. (Text)

Donahue, Kauper and Martin's Cases on Property, 2nd Ed., 1362 pages, 1983 (Casebook)

Hill's Landlord and Tenant Law in a Nutshell, 2nd Ed., 311 pages, 1986 (Text)

Kurtz and Hovenkamp's Cases and Materials on American Property Law, 1296 pages, 1987 with 1988 Supplement (Casebook)

Moynihan's Introduction to Real Property, 2nd Ed., 239 pages, 1988 (Text)

Uniform Land Transactions Act, Uniform Simplification of Land Transfers Act, Uniform Condominium Act, 1977 Official Text with Comments, 462 pages, 1978

See also Real Estate Transactions, Land Use

PSYCHIATRY, LAW AND

Reisner's Law and the Mental Health System, Civil and Criminal Aspects, 696 pages, 1985 with 1987 Supplement (Casebooks)

REAL ESTATE TRANSACTIONS

Bruce's Real Estate Finance in a Nutshell, 2nd Ed., 262 pages, 1985 (Text)

Maxwell, Riesenfeld, Hetland and Warren's Cases on California Security Transactions in Land, 3rd Ed., 728 pages, 1984 (Casebook)

Nelson and Whitman's Cases on Real Estate Transfer, Finance and Development, 3rd Ed., 1184 pages, 1987 (Casebook)

Nelson and Whitman's Hornbook on Real Estate Finance Law, 2nd Ed., Student Ed., 941 pages, 1985 (Text)

Osborne's Cases and Materials on Secured Transactions, 559 pages, 1967 (Casebook)

REGULATED INDUSTRIES

Gellhorn and Pierce's Regulated Industries in a Nutshell, 2nd Ed., 389 pages, 1987 (Text)

Morgan, Harrison and Verkuil's Cases and Materials on Economic Regulation of Business, 2nd Ed., 666 pages, 1985 (Casebook)

See also Mass Communication Law, Banking Law

REMEDIES

Dobbs' Hornbook on Remedies, 1067 pages, 1973 (Text)

Dobbs' Problems in Remedies, 137 pages, 1974 (Problem book)

Dobbyn's Injunctions in a Nutshell, 264 pages, 1974 (Text)

Friedman's Contract Remedies in a Nutshell, 323 pages, 1981 (Text)

Leavell, Love and Nelson's Cases and Materials on Equitable Remedies and Restitution, 4th Ed., 1111 pages, 1986 (Casebook)

McCormick's Hornbook on Damages, 811 pages, 1935 (Text)

O'Connell's Remedies in a Nutshell, 2nd Ed., 320 pages, 1985 (Text)

York, Bauman and Rendleman's Cases and Materials on Remedies, 4th Ed., 1029 pages, 1985 (Casebook)

REVIEW MATERIALS

Ballantine's Problems

Black Letter Series

SECURITIES REGULATION

Hazen's Hornbook on The Law of Securities Regulation, Student Ed., 739 pages, 1985, with 1988 P.P. (Text)

Ratner's Securities Regulation: Materials for a Basic Course, 3rd Ed., 1000 pages, 1986 (Casebook)

Ratner's Securities Regulation in a Nutshell, 3rd Ed., 316 pages, 1988 (Text)

LAW SCHOOL PUBLICATIONS—Continued

SECURITIES REGULATION—Cont'd

Selected Securities and Business Planning Statutes, Rules and Forms, 493 pages, 1987

SOCIAL LEGISLATION

Hood and Hardy's Workers' Compensation and Employee Protection Laws in a Nutshell, 274 pages, 1984 (Text)

LaFrance's Welfare Law: Structure and Entitlement in a Nutshell, 455 pages, 1979 (Text)

Malone, Plant and Little's Cases on Workers' Compensation and Employment Rights, 2nd Ed., 951 pages, 1980 (Casebook)

SPORTS LAW

Schubert, Smith and Trentadue's Sports Law, 395 pages, 1986 (Text)

TAXATION

Dodge's Cases and Materials on Federal Income Taxation, 820 pages, 1985 (Casebook)

Garbis, Struntz and Rubin's Cases and Materials on Tax Procedure and Tax Fraud, 2nd Ed., 687 pages, 1987 (Casebook)

Gelfand and Salsich's State and Local Taxation and Finance in a Nutshell, 309 pages, 1986 (Text)

Gunn and Ward's Cases and Materials on Federal Income Taxation, about 815 pages, 1988 (Casebook)

Hellerstein and Hellerstein's Cases on State and Local Taxation, 5th Ed., about 1060 pages, 1988 (Casebook)

Kahn and Gann's Corporate Taxation and Taxation of Partnerships and Partners, 2nd Ed., 1204 pages, 1985 (Casebook)

Kaplan's Federal Taxation of International Transactions: Principles, Planning and Policy, 635 pages, 1988 (Casebook)

Kragen and McNulty's Cases and Materials on Federal Income Taxation: Individuals, Corporations, Partnerships, 4th Ed., 1287 pages, 1985 (Casebook)

McNulty's Federal Estate and Gift Taxation in a Nutshell, 3rd Ed., 509 pages, 1983 (Text)

McNulty's Federal Income Taxation of Individuals in a Nutshell, 4th Ed., about 500 pages, 1988 (Text)

Pennell's Cases and Materials on Income Taxation of Trusts, Estates, Grantors and Beneficiaries, 460 pages, 1987 (Casebook)

Posin's Hornbook on Federal Income Taxation of Individuals, Student Ed., 491 pages, 1983 with 1987 pocket part (Text)

Rose and Chommie's Hornbook on Federal Income Taxation, 3rd Ed., 923 pages, 1988 (Text)

TAXATION—Cont'd

Selected Federal Taxation Statutes and Regulations, about 1400 pages, 1989

Solomon and Hesch's Cases on Federal Income Taxation of Individuals, 1068 pages, 1987 (Casebook)

TORTS

Christie's Cases and Materials on the Law of Torts, 1264 pages, 1983 (Casebook)

Dobbs' Torts and Compensation—Personal Accountability and Social Responsibility for Injury, 955 pages, 1985 (Casebook)

Keeton, Keeton, Sargentich and Steiner's Cases and Materials on Tort and Accident Law, 1360 pages, 1983 (Casebook)

Kionka's Torts in a Nutshell: Injuries to Persons and Property, 434 pages, 1977 (Text)

Malone's Torts in a Nutshell: Injuries to Family, Social and Trade Relations, 358 pages, 1979 (Text)

Prosser and Keeton's Hornbook on Torts, 5th Ed., Student Ed., 1286 pages, 1984, with 1988 pocket part (Text)

See also Products Liability

TRADE REGULATION

McManis' Unfair Trade Practices in a Nutshell, 2nd Ed., about 430 pages, 1988 (Text)

Oppenheim, Weston, Maggs and Schechter's Cases and Materials on Unfair Trade Practices and Consumer Protection, 4th Ed., 1038 pages, 1983 with 1986 Supplement (Casebook)

See also Antitrust, Regulated Industries

TRIAL AND APPELLATE ADVOCACY

Appellate Advocacy, Handbook of, 2nd Ed., 182 pages, 1986 (Text)

Bergman's Trial Advocacy in a Nutshell, 402 pages, 1979 (Text)

Binder and Bergman's Fact Investigation: From Hypothesis to Proof, 354 pages, 1984 (Coursebook)

Goldberg's The First Trial (Where Do I Sit?, What Do I Say?) in a Nutshell, 396 pages, 1982 (Text)

Haydock, Herr and Stempel's, Fundamentals of Pre-Trial Litigation, 768 pages, 1985 (Casebook)

Hegland's Trial and Practice Skills in a Nutshell, 346 pages, 1978 (Text)

Hornstein's Appellate Advocacy in a Nutshell, 325 pages, 1984 (Text)

Jeans' Handbook on Trial Advocacy, Student Ed., 473 pages, 1975 (Text)

Martineau's Cases and Materials on Appellate Practice and Procedure, 565 pages, 1987 (Casebook)

McElhaney's Effective Litigation, 457 pages, 1974 (Casebook)

Nolan's Cases and Materials on Trial Practice, 518 pages, 1981 (Casebook)

LAW SCHOOL PUBLICATIONS—Continued

TRIAL AND APPELLATE ADVOCACY—Cont'd

Sonsteng, Haydock and Boyd's The Trialbook: A Total System for Preparation and Presentation of a Case, Student Ed., 404 pages, 1984 (Coursebook)

See also Civil Procedure

TRUSTS AND ESTATES

Atkinson's Hornbook on Wills, 2nd Ed., 975 pages, 1953 (Text)

Averill's Uniform Probate Code in a Nutshell, 2nd Ed., 454 pages, 1987 (Text)

Bogert's Hornbook on Trusts, 6th Ed., Student Ed., 794 pages, 1987 (Text)

Clark, Lusky and Murphy's Cases and Materials on Gratuitous Transfers, 3rd Ed., 970 pages, 1985 (Casebook)

Dodge's Wills, Trusts and Estate Planning, Law and Taxation, Cases and Materials, 665 pages, 1988 (Casebook)

Kurtz' Cases, Materials and Problems on Family Estate Planning, 853 pages, 1983 (Casebook)

McGovern's Cases and Materials on Wills, Trusts and Future Interests: An Introduction to Estate Planning, 750 pages, 1983 (Casebook)

McGovern, Rein and Kurtz' Hornbook on Wills, Trusts and Estates including Taxation and Future Interests, about 924 pages, 1988 (Text)

Mennell's Wills and Trusts in a Nutshell, 392 pages, 1979 (Text)

Simes' Hornbook on Future Interests, 2nd Ed., 355 pages, 1966 (Text)

TRUSTS AND ESTATES—Cont'd

Turano and Radigan's Hornbook on New York Estate Administration, 676 pages, 1986 (Text)

Uniform Probate Code, Official Text With Comments, 578 pages, 1987

Waggoner's Future Interests in a Nutshell, 361 pages, 1981 (Text)

Waterbury's Materials on Trusts and Estates, 1039 pages, 1986 (Casebook)

WATER LAW

Getches' Water Law in a Nutshell, 439 pages, 1984 (Text)

Sax and Abram's Cases and Materials on Legal Control of Water Resources, 941 pages, 1986 (Casebook)

Trelease and Gould's Cases and Materials on Water Law, 4th Ed., 816 pages, 1986 (Casebook)

See also Energy and Natural Resources Law, Environmental Law

WILLS

See Trusts and Estates

WOMEN AND THE LAW

Kay's Text, Cases and Materials on Sex-Based Discrimination, 3rd Ed., about 979 pages, 1988 (Casebook)

Thomas' Sex Discrimination in a Nutshell, 399 pages, 1982 (Text)

See also Employment Discrimination

WORKERS' COMPENSATION

See Social Legislation

CRIMINAL LAW
Second Edition

By

Wayne R. LaFave

David C. Baum Professor of Law and
Professor in the Center for Advanced Study,
University of Illinois

and

Austin W. Scott, Jr.

Late Professor of Law,
University of Colorado

HORNBOOK SERIES
STUDENT EDITION

This book is an abridgement of LaFave and Scott's two volume "Substantive Criminal Law" in West's Criminal Practice Series.

WEST PUBLISHING CO.
ST. PAUL, MINN., 1986

This is an abridgement of LaFave & Scott's
Substantive Criminal Law, 2 volumes, Criminal Practice Series,
West Publishing Co., 1986.

West Publishing Co.
50 West Kellogg Boulevard
P.O. Box 64526
St. Paul, Minnesota 55164–0526

Printed in the United States of America

Library of Congress Cataloging in Publication Data

LaFave, Wayne R.
  Criminal law.

  (Hornbook series)
  Rev. ed. of: Handbook of criminal law. 1972.
  Includes index.
  1. Criminal law—United States. I. LaFave, Wayne R.
Handbook on criminal law. II. Title. II. Series.
  KF9219.L38 1986   345.73   86–15909
                          347.305

ISBN 0-314-26045-5

LaFave & Scott Crim.Law 2nd Ed.HB

1st Reprint—1989

TO LORETTA, JIM AND TERRI,
the source of my pyrrhonism
regarding Francis Bacon's
familiar apothegm: "He that
hath wife and children hath
given hostage to fortune, for
they are impediments to great
enterprises, either of virtue
or mischief."

     –W.R.L.

Preface

This text is intended primarily for use by law students during their study of substantive criminal law. There is, to be sure, no substitute for careful examination of the basic sources—the appellate opinions, statutes, and critical commentary which are to be found in the modern casebooks dealing with this subject. It is neither intended nor expected that the *Criminal Law* will be of particular use to the student who has not grappled with those materials. Rather, this book has been prepared on the assumption that the diligent student (particularly in the first year of law study) may find a textual treatment of the subject useful as he or she[1] undertakes the necessary process of reviewing and synthesizing the regularly assigned materials.

Criminal law casebooks currently in use vary considerably in their approach and coverage. It is unlikely that any two teachers of the subject could agree completely as to the objectives of the basic course in criminal law or the content which is most suited to achieving those objectives. This being the case, a brief explanation of the scope of and emphasis within this text is in order.

For one thing, this text is *not* an encyclopedia of crimes in which black-letter definitions of all common offenses—from abortion to vagrancy—may be found. The imparting of detailed information about many different crimes is not the goal of a basic course in criminal law, and thus the discussion of specific offenses herein is limited to certain crimes against the person (Chapter 7) and crimes relating to property (Chapter 8). Major emphasis is given to homicide and theft, two areas most teachers of criminal law have concluded are particularly suited to such tasks as: (a) evaluation of the criminal process as a technique for social control; (b) comparison and evaluation of the actual and potential contributions of courts (through the common law) and legislatures (through codification) in defining and grading crimes; (c) understanding the significance of history in the development of the law of crimes; (d) acquiring expertise in use of the case method and techniques of legal analysis.

The reach of the substantive criminal law is constantly expanding, and thus today's law student is much more likely than his counterpart of some years ago to find himself engaged to some extent in the practice of criminal law after graduation. This practice may involve the prosecution of or defense against charges of such familiar crimes as robbery, battery, and rape; it may instead or in addition be concerned with the

---

1. So that the sentence structure may be as short and direct as possible, the phrases "he or she" and "his or her" are generally not used in this Hornbook. Consistent with traditional rules of construction in statutes and legal texts, masculine pronouns should be read as referring to both male and female actors unless the context indicates otherwise.

increasing body of regulatory crimes which have been enacted in response to such contemporary concerns as consumer protection and environmental control. An adequate preparation for such practice requires an *understanding* of the fundamental bases of our system of substantive criminal law, rather than *knowledge* of the precise definitions of the growing list of crimes. Consequently, the major emphasis in this text is upon what is usually referred to as the "general part" of the criminal law; the basic premises of the criminal law (Chapter 3); responsibility (Chapter 4); justification and excuse (Chapter 5); inchoate crimes and accomplice liability (Chapter 6). Greater attention has been given to certain subjects—such as causation, insanity, and conspiracy—which experience has shown are particularly troublesome for beginning law students.

In American law schools, particularly during the first year of study, there has been an undue preoccupation with the decisions of appellate courts and the common law system. There is a growing realization that law students should be made equally aware of the actual and potential contributions of the legislative branch, and the course in substantive criminal law often has been found particularly suited to this purpose. At many schools, students enrolled in criminal law are required to work intensively with some actual or proposed criminal code; the intent is not to teach "local law," but rather to give the student a greater sense of the potentialities and limitations of legislative formulation. This development has been taken into account in the preparation of this text. Frequent reference is made to the Model Penal Code, which has "played an important part in the widespread revision and codification of the substantive criminal law of the United States that has been taking place in the last twenty years." [2] In addition, considerable attention is given to the matter of statutory interpretation and to the constitutional limits upon the federal and state legislative power to create crimes (Chapter 2).

Largely because of the tremendous growth in recent years of that body of law concerning the constitutional rights of persons suspected or accused of crime, the teaching of criminal procedure is today a separate

---

2. Wechsler, Foreword, in 1 American Law Institute, Model Penal Code and Commentaries (1985). This six-volume work should be consulted for more detailed treatment of the Code's impact.

No effort has been made in this Hornbook to document this legislative response with extensive citations to the statutes of the various jurisdictions on each point discussed. The assumption is that a law student will not have a need for such citations in the context in which this Hornbook will ordinarily be used. However, if a student is undertaking some research on a matter of substantive criminal law as to which statutory references are needed, two sources may be suggested. One is Professor Paul H. Robinson's excellent two-volume work on *Criminal Law Defenses*. The other is LaFave and Scott, *Substantive Criminal Law,* a two-volume treatise which follows the format of this Hornbook but also contains many citations to statutory sources, especially in the 36 jurisdictions which have adopted new criminal codes.

In this Hornbook, some attention is also given to the proposed new federal code of 1971, as drafted by the National Commission on Reform of the Federal Criminal Laws. Although Congress has not adopted that proposal or any other major revision of federal substantive law, the Commission's work is worth noting, especially as to certain innovative proposals and also certain divergences from the Model Penal Code which have occasionally been adopted in state law reform.

enterprise at most law schools. Consequently, this book concentrates upon the substantive criminal law, and no attempt has been made at a systematic or comprehensive treatment of criminal procedure.[3] Some aspects of criminal procedure have been discussed, however, when deemed essential to an adequate understanding of certain substantive provisions. For example, incompetency to stand trial, the manner of presenting the insanity defense, and the consequences of a finding of not guilty by reason of insanity are all dealt with in some detail because of their importance in gaining a full appreciation of the insanity defense. Similarly, it has obviously been necessary to take into account certain procedural matters in discussing such subjects as consolidation of theft offenses, abolition of the distinctions between parties to crime, and the peculiar problems raised by the crime of conspiracy. On a more general level, attention has been given to the relationship between discretionary enforcement and the content of the substantive criminal law, and to the burden and manner of proving the elements of crimes and defenses thereto.

It is truly fitting and proper that Austin W. Scott, Jr., is listed as the co-author of this edition, though it is being published twenty years after his untimely demise. The present work is an expanded and updated version of the *Criminal Law* Hornbook, first published in 1972. Austin began that text alone and worked diligently on the book for many years. Such was his dedication and courage that he continued with his research and writing even after he knew he would be unable to complete the project. I attempted to the best of my ability to see that book to completion in the manner I believe Austin contemplated. My hope was that those who were familiar with Austin and his work would sense his influence in every aspect of the final product.

I have undertaken this second edition in like fashion. I have added to and revised the text and footnotes at several points, but the basic structure and organization and approach is that originated by Austin. My effort throughout has been to maintain that quality of scholarship for which Austin was known. I regret that the circumstances were such that we could not be collaborators in the true sense of that word, for I know that I would have profited greatly from Austin's guidance and counsel.

With respect to my contribution to this book, I am greatly indebted to my secretary, Carol Haley, who has seen this project through from start to finish. I also wish to express my appreciation to George Clark, William Feurer, and (now Professors) Joseph Grano and John Nowak for their work on the first edition; and to Donald Driscoll and Christine

---

3. On criminal procedure, see W. LaFave & J. Israel, Criminal Procedure (1985).

Berry for assistance on the second edition. I must also acknowledge my debt to the great many writers in the field of criminal law whose ideas have given me direction. They are too numerous to be mentioned here individually, but I hope that the extent of my indebtedness is sufficiently apparent from the frequent citations to secondary sources throughout this book.

I would be remiss, however, were I not to make specific mention here of the one source to which reference is made on hundreds of occasions throughout this book. I refer, of course, to the Model Penal Code and accompanying commentary. The imaginative proposals contained in the Code constitute an outstanding contribution toward reform of the substantive criminal law, and thus an attempt has been made to put these proposals before the reader at all relevant points in this book. The extensive commentary by the Code draftsmen, succinctly setting forth the current law and the major policy issues, has independent value; it has served as my guide throughout this undertaking. (References to the Code herein are for the most part to the final version as adopted by the American Law Institute in 1962, though on occasion a specific reference is made to one of the thirteen Tentative Drafts which preceded it. With few exceptions, quotations from the commentary are taken from the more recently published revised version.)

WAYNE R. LaFAVE

July 1986

WESTLAW Introduction

Criminal Law offers a detailed and comprehensive treatment of criminal law. However, law students sometimes need to find additional authority. In an effort to assist with comprehensive research, preformulated WESTLAW references are included after sections and subsections of the text. These references are designed for use with the WESTLAW computer-assisted legal research service. By joining this publication with the extensive WESTLAW databases, the reader is able to move straight from this text into WESTLAW with great speed and convenience.

The preformulated references in this text provide illustrative searches for readers who wish to do additional research. The references are approximately as general as the material in the text to which they correspond. Readers should be cautioned against placing undue emphasis upon these references as final solutions to all possible issues treated in the text. In most instances, it is necessary to make refinements to the search references, such as the addition of other search terms or the substitution of different proximity connectors, to adequately fit the particular needs of an individual reader's research problem. The freedom, and also the responsibility, remains with the reader to "fine tune" the WESTLAW references in accordance with his or her own research requirements. The primary usefulness of the preformulated references is in providing a basic framework upon which further query construction can be built. Appendix A gives concise, step-by-step instruction on how to coordinate WESTLAW research with this book.

THE PUBLISHER

*

Summary of Contents

*

Table of Contents

*

Chapter 1

INTRODUCTION AND GENERAL CONSIDERATIONS

Table of Sections

1

---

§ 1.1 The Scope of Criminal Law and Procedure

The substantive criminal law is treated in this book. It is mostly concerned with what act and mental state, together with what attendant circumstances or consequences, are necessary ingredients of the various crimes. Criminal procedure, which is not covered in this book,[1] is concerned with the legal steps through which a criminal proceeding passes, from the initial investigation of a crime through the termination of punishment. Besides criminal law and procedure, the administration of criminal justice includes such matters as police organization and administration (how most effectively to detect and apprehend criminals),[2] prison administration,[3] and administration of probation and parole.[4]

(a) The Concern of Criminologists. There are, however, groups of people other than lawyers, policemen, probation and parole officers, and prison authorities whose professional work involves the problems of crime and criminals. In particular, criminol-ogists spend their professional lives studying crime and criminals and the administration of criminal justice. Criminologists have varying backgrounds, coming from the fields of sociology, social psychology, medicine (especially psychiatry), anthropology and biology. They are "concerned with the study of the phenomenon of crime and of the factors or circumstances—individual and environmental—which may have an influence on, or be associated with, criminal behavior and the state of crime in general."[5] Criminologists are trying to determine why people become criminals, not just to acquire knowledge for its own sake but for the practical ultimate purpose of eradicating the causes of crime and thus reducing if not eliminating crime. The cost of crime in this country is, of course, enormous—doubtless several billion dollars a year if we consider property losses, personal injury losses, the cost of law enforcement (including the cost of maintaining the police, the criminal courts and the prosecutor), the cost of maintaining prisons and parole agencies, and the loss of productive labor of criminals.[6] It is obvious

---

§ 1.1

1. Except insofar as certain aspects of procedure are very closely related to the substantive criminal law and must be understood to appreciate the significance of the substantive provisions. See, e.g., § 1.8 on burden of proof; § 4.4 on incompetency at time of criminal proceedings; § 4.5 on procedures for presenting the insanity defense; and § 4.6 on procedures after a finding of not guilty by reason of insanity.

2. See, e.g., A. Bouza, Police Administration: Organization and Performance (1978); C. Hale, Fundamentals of Police Administration (1977).

3. See, e.g., A. Briggs, Jail Administration and Procedures Manual (1977); R. Carter, D. Glaser & L. Wilkins, Correctional Institutions (2d ed. 1977).

4. See, e.g., G. Cavender, Parole: A Critical Analysis (1982); G. Killinger, H. Kerper & P. Cromwell, Probation and Parole (1976).

5. L. Radzinowicz, In Search of Criminology 168 (1962).

6. Although there is a lack of data on the economic costs of crime, an estimate of some years ago was that the cost runs above 21 billion dollars a year. President's Comm'n on Law Enforcement and Administration of Justice, The Challenge of Crime in a Free Society 33 (1967).

that if crime could be reduced, the savings would be great.

The modern criminologist's method of attacking the problem of crime and criminals is a scientific one, including the collection of statistics on crime and the making of case studies of individual criminals and group studies of criminal classes. What effect does heredity have on crime? What is the effect of environment? What is the effect of poverty, lack of education, unemployment, urban life, poor housing, broken homes, or evil companions? Is there a connection between physique and criminality, between mental defect and crime? Are some racial groups more prone to commit crimes than others? What is the effect of cultural influences—religion, newspapers, comic books, television and radio, moving pictures? In order to take effective steps to combat the crime problem, we must first know with some degree of certainty the answers to such questions. But the field of criminology as a science is new, and the answers are by no means yet certain.[7]

Criminologists are interested not only in the causes of crime and remedies to be taken to eliminate these causes, but also in the treatment to be given the criminal who is caught and convicted. How should we treat him in order to reduce his chances of committing subsequent crimes? It is in this area of criminology (termed penology) that criminologists have had their greatest influence on criminal law and procedure: in the classification of convicts into corrigibles and incorrigibles, and into professionals and casuals, for penal treatment; the establishment of procedures for probation and parole; the indeterminate sentence; the treatment of juvenile delinquency as non-criminal; and to some extent the treatment of alcoholics, drug

addicts and sex offenders as sick rather than criminal.

 WESTLAW REFERENCES

digest(criminolog*** penolog***)

(b) The Concern of Lawyers. Lawyers no less than criminologists are interested in preventing socially undesirable conduct. Their principal weapon in the war on crime is the criminal law. They too are interested in the question of what forms of anti-social conduct should be punished as criminal (i.e., what should be the scope of the substantive law of crimes). And they conceive of punishment for violation of the criminal law as a device for preventing such conduct—by deterring prospective offenders by threat of punishment and by preventing repetition by incapacitating and if possible reforming those who have already committed crimes.[8] But lawyers also play a part, outside of the criminal law, in the area of crime prevention through laws designed to improve social and economic conditions—those relating to public housing, zoning, public health, industrial working conditions, minimum wages, unemployment compensation and such matters.

In recent years particularly, lawyers have become more conscious of the need for law reform in the administration of criminal justice. This concern has been reflected in several ambitious projects sponsored by the organized bar and other professional groups or otherwise participated in by members of the legal profession.

In the realm of substantive criminal law, by far the most significant development has been the completion of the American Law Institute's Model Penal Code, to which frequent reference is made in this book.[9] The Code is

---

T. Flanagan & M. McLeod, Sourcebook of Criminal Justice Statistics—1982, reports that the costs directly to federal, state and local governments exceeded 27 billion dollars a year.

7. For a helpful account of the progress in the field, see L. Radzinowicz, supra note 5.

8. For a discussion of the theoretical bases of punishment, see § 1.5.

9. There are a total of 13 tentative drafts, consisting of proposed code sections and accompanying commentary,

dating from 1953 to 1961. The Code was approved by the American Law Institute in 1962 and published that year without commentary. Commencing in 1980, the Code was republished in seven volumes with expanded and updated commentary prepared by Professor R. Kent Greenawalt, Chief Reporter; Professors Malvina Halberstam and Peter W. Low, Reporters for Part I; Professor Sanford Fox, Associate Reporter for Articles 6 and 7; Professor Peter W. Low, Reporter for Part II: and Professor John Jeffries, Associate Reporter for Part II. These revised commentaries are an excellent source. All citations and references

organized into four main parts: (1) the general provisions, which set forth the basic principles that govern the existence and the scope of liability; (2) the definition of specific offenses; (3) provisions governing the processes of treatment and correction; and (4) provisions on the organization of correction. The commentary to the Code, prepared in a desire "to place the systematic literature of our penal law upon a parity with that of well-developed legal fields," [10] is in itself a major contribution.

It must be emphasized that the American Law Institute has produced a *model* code, not a *uniform* code. Uniformity is of less importance in penal law than in other fields, such as commercial law. It is appropriate that the several states should have significant variations in their penal laws, based upon differences in local conditions or points of view. The principal contribution of the Model Penal Code is that it represents a systematic reexamination of the substantive criminal law. It identifies the major issues which should be confronted by the legislature in the recodification process and articulates and evaluates alternative methods of dealing with these is-

sues. The intention was "to provide a reasoned, integrated body of material that will be useful in such legislative effort." [11]

Perhaps because of the lack of such guidance in earlier years, the criminal codes of most states long suffered from neglect. As one commentator noted in 1956: "Viewing the country as a whole, our penal codes are fragmentary, old, disorganized and often accidental in their coverage, their growth largely fortuitous in origin, their form a combination of enactment and of common law that only history explains." [12] In many codes, some of the most significant crimes (such as murder) were not defined, and it was not uncommon for basic doctrines concerning the scope of liability to have little or no reflection in the statutes. Prior to the time that the work on the Model Penal Code began to be circulated, only two states, Louisiana [13] and Wisconsin, [14] had accomplished over-all reform of their substantive criminal law. But now, largely stimulated by the labors of the American Law Institute, there are a total of thirty six states which have recently adopted new substantive criminal law codes. [15] Efforts directed toward similar reform are now under way in some

to the Model Penal Code and commentary in this book are to these volumes unless there is an indication to the contrary.

10. Wechsler, The Challenge of a Model Penal Code, 65 Harv.L.Rev. 1097, 1130 (1952).

11. Wechsler, The American Law Institute: Some Observations on Its Model Penal Code, 42 A.B.A.J. 321 (1956).

12. Ibid.

13. La.Stat.Ann.–Rev. Stat. 14:1 et seq. See Bennett, The Louisiana Criminal Code,—a Comparison with Prior Louisiana Criminal Law, 5 La.L.Rev. 6 (1942); Bennett, Louisiana's Criminal Code of 1942, 20 U.Kan.City L.Rev. 208 (1952); Morrow, The Louisiana Criminal Code of 1942—Opportunities Lost and Challenges Yet Unanswered, 17 Tulane L.Rev. 1 (1942); Smith, How Louisiana Prepared and Adopted a Criminal Code, 41 J.Crim.L. & Crim. 125 (1950).

14. Wis.Stat.Ann. 939.01 et seq. See Remington, Criminal Law Revision—Codification v. Piecemeal Amendment, 33 Neb.L.Rev. 396 (1954); Remington, A Proposed Criminal Code for Wisconsin, 20 U.Kan.City L.Rev. 221 (1952).

15. Ala.Code tit. 13A (effective 1980); Alaska Stat. tit. 11 (effective 1980); Ariz.Rev.Stat. tit. 13 (effective 1978); Ark.Stats. tit. 41 (effective 1976); Colo.Rev.Stat. tit. 18 (effective 1972); Conn.Gen.Stat.Ann. tit. 53a (effective 1971); Del.Code tit. 11 (effective 1973); West's Fla.Stat.

Ann. tit. 45 (effective 1975); Ga.Code tit. 26 (effective 1969); Hawaii Rev.Stat. tit. 37 (effective 1973); Ill.— S.H.A. ch. 38 (effective 1962); West's Ann.Ind.Code tit. 35 (effective 1977); Iowa Code Ann. tit. 35 (effective 1978); Kan.Stat.Ann. ch. 21 (effective 1970); Ky.Rev.Stat. chs. 500–534 (effective 1975); La.Stat.Ann.–Rev. Stat. tit. 14 (effective 1942); Me.Rev.Stat.Ann. tit. 17–A (effective 1976); Minn.Stat.Ann. ch. 609 (effective 1963); Vernon's Ann.Mo.Stat. ch. 28 (effective 1979); Mont.Code Ann. tit. 45 (effective 1974); Neb.Rev.Stat. ch. 28 (effective 1979); N.H.Rev.Stat.Ann. tit. 62 (effective 1973); N.J.Stat.Ann. tit. 2C (effective 1979); N.M.Stat.Ann. ch. 30 (effective 1963); N.Y.—McKinney's Penal Law (effective 1967); N.D. Cent.Code tit. 12.1 (effective 1975); Ohio Rev.Code tit. 29 (effective 1974); Or.Rev.Stat. tit. 16 (effective 1972); Pa. Cons.Stat.Ann. tit. 18 (effective 1973); S.D.Cod.Laws tit. 22 (effective 1977); Vernon's Tex. Code Ann., Penal Code (effective 1974); Utah Code Ann. tit. 76 (effective 1973); Va.Code tit. 18.2 (effective 1975); West's Rev.Code Wash. Ann. tit. 9A (effective 1976); Wis.Stat.Ann. chs. 939–953 (effective 1956); Wyo.Stat. tit. 6 (effective 1983).

On these recodifications, see the following (listed by state): Stern, The Proposed Alaska Revised Criminal Code, 7 U.C.L.A.—Alaska L.Rev. 1 (1977); Symposium on Arkansas Criminal Code, 30 Ark.L.Rev. 105 (1976); Dunahoo, The New Iowa Criminal Code, 29 Drake L.Rev. 237, 491 (1979); Symposium on Kansas Criminal Code, 19 Kan.L.Rev. 771 (1977); Symposium on Kentucky Criminal Code, 61 Ky.L.J. 620 (1972); Symposium on Maine Crimi-

other states,[16] and on the federal level.[17] (The Model Penal Code has also had a substantial impact upon the judiciary; courts have frequently relied upon provisions in the Code when formulating substantive criminal law rules.[18])

The legal profession has longer shown interest in the realm of criminal procedure. This is reflected in the fact that a number of efforts directed toward reform of criminal procedure antedated the Model Penal Code project. In 1930, the American Law Institute produced a procedure code.[19] The Federal Rules of Criminal Procedure were adopted in 1946, and they have since served as a model for procedure rules in a number of states. In 1952, the National Conference of Commissioners on Uniform State Laws published its Uniform Rules of Criminal Procedure.[20]

This is not to suggest, however, that meaningful reform came earlier in the area of criminal procedure. None of the procedure "models" mentioned above accomplished for the field of criminal procedure what the Model Penal Code has done for the substantive criminal law. The basic defect is that they did not identify and constructively deal with many of the major issues in criminal procedure. In part, this may be attributable to the fact that courts, particularly the United States Supreme Court, have played a leading role in certain procedural areas, such as search and seizure.[21] But, whatever the reason, one characteristic of all the earlier procedure "models" is that they tend to concentrate upon the formal, in-court procedures to the exclusion of other problems of equal or

nal Code, 28 Me.L.Rev. 148 (1976); Symposium on Missouri Criminal Code, 38 Mo.L.Rev. 361, 549 (1973); Luedtke, Nebraska Criminal Code Revision—A Decade of Legislative Perseverance, 11 Creighton L.Rev. 78 (1977); Knowlton, Comments Upon the New Jersey Penal Code, 32 Rutgers L.Rev. 1 (1979); Symposium on North Dakota Criminal Code, 50 N.Dak.L.Rev. 617 (1974); Symposium on Ohio Criminal Code, 33 Ohio St.L.J. 351 (1972); Symposium on Pennsylvania Criminal Code, 78 Dick.L.Rev. 208 (1973); Note on South Dakota Criminal Code, 22 S.Dak.L. Rev. 98 (1977); Symposium on Virginia Criminal Code, 59 Va.L.Rev. 1234 (1973); Symposium on Washington Criminal Code, 48 Wash.L.Rev. 1 (1972).

16. Revisions have been completed but not yet enacted in the District of Columbia, Massachusetts, Michigan, North Carolina, and West Virginia; revisions are under way in Rhode Island and South Carolina; and revision is contemplated in Mississippi. Revisions were completed but abortive in California, Idaho, Maryland, Oklahoma, Tennessee and Vermont, and no overall revision is planned in Nevada. American Law Institute, Annual Report 21 (1984).

For more on the problems of codification, see (in addition to items previously cited); Cohen, Criminal Law Legislation and Legal Scholarship, 15 J.Legal Ed. 253 (1964); Cohen, Reflections on the Revision of the Texas Penal Code, 45 Tex.L.Rev. 413 (1967); Gausewitz, Considerations Basic to a New Penal Code, 11 Wis.L.Rev. 346 (1936); George, Reform of State Criminal Law and Procedure, 41 Law & Contemp.Prob. 63 (1977); Hall, Proposal to Prepare a Model Penal Code, 4 J.Legal Ed. 91 (1951); Harno, Rationale of a Criminal Code, 85 U.Pa.L.Rev. 549 (1937); LaFave, Penal Code Revision: Considering the Problems and Practices of the Police, 45 Tex.L.Rev. 434 (1967); Quayle, Criminal Law Revision in Wisconsin and Minnesota, 40 J.Am.Jud.Soc'y 88 (1956); Remington & Rosenblum, The Criminal Law and the Legislative Process, 1960 U.Ill.L.F. 481; Wechsler, Revision and Codification of Penal Law in the United States, 7 Dalhousie L.J. 219 (1983); Symposium on the Model Penal Code, 63 Colum.L.Rev.

589 (1963). Symposium on the Model Penal Code, 63 Colum.L.Rev. 589 (1963); Symposium on the Politics of Criminal Law Reform, 21 Am.J.Crim.L. 21 (1973); Symposium on Recodification of the Criminal Laws, 4 U.Mich. J.L.Ref. 425 (1971).

17. See National Comm'n on Reform of Federal Criminal Laws, Final Report—Proposed New Federal Criminal Code (1971). The two-volume set of Working Papers, published in 1970, is a very valuable source, for it contains the various consultants' reports and staff memoranda which served as a basis for the proposed code. Over the past several years, many bills have been introduced into the Congress proposing recodification as recommended by the Commission or in other forms, but as yet without success. See, e.g., S. 1630, 97th Cong., reported with amendments by the Senate Judiciary Committee on Jan. 1, 1982; H.R. 1647, 4711, 5679 and 5703, 97th Cong., reported by Subcommittee on Criminal Justice of House Judiciary Committee, reintroduced as H.R. 2013, 98th Cong., and referred to House Judiciary Committee. There has been considerable comment on the proposals. See, e.g., Schwartz, Reform of the Federal Criminal Laws: Issues, Tactics and Prospects, 41 Law & Contemp.Prob. 1 (1977); Symposia, 47 Geo.Wash.L.Rev. 451 (1979); 72 J.Crim.L. & C. 381 (1981); 68 Nw.U.L.Rev. 173 (1973).

18. See, e.g., United States v. Brawner, 471 F.2d 969 (D.C.Cir.1972) (adopting Model Penal Code insanity test); State v. Toscano, 74 N.J. 421, 378 A.2d 755 (1977) (adopting Code position on duress defense).

19. American Law Institute, Code of Criminal Procedure (1930).

20. The rules appear in National Conference of Commissioners on Uniform State Laws, 1952 Handbook 307–56.

21. One explanation for the Court's movement into these areas, however, is that "our law-making bodies, federal, state, and local, have so far defaulted on that job." Packer, Policing the Police, The New Republic, Sept. 4, 1965, p. 17, at 18.

greater importance but of lower visibility.[22] More recently, however, efforts have been made to construct "models" dealing with these problems. One noteworthy effort is the American Law Institute's Model Code of Pre-Arraignment Procedure.[23] Another is the American Bar Association's Standards Relating to the Administration of Criminal Justice.[24] Yet another is the Commissioners' more recent version of Uniform Rules of Criminal Procedure.[25]

As noted earlier, essential to law reform are the identification of major issues and the articulation of alternative ways of dealing with those issues. This, in turn, can be accomplished only through careful scrutiny of existing practices. Such empirical research has been undertaken through the years, but it has been sporadic and sometimes misdirected. A flurry of crime surveys were published in the 1920's and 1930's,[26] and in 1931 a major national survey by the federal government was completed.[27] However, as one writer has aptly pointed out, "the early crime surveys did not produce any clear conception of the kinds of administrative problems which ought to be of greatest concern to legal research." [28]

More recently, there has been a renewed interest in the study of the actual processes of criminal justice administration for the purpose of uncovering and analyzing critical problems with which the law ought to be concerned. One of the most ambitious studies is the American Bar Foundation's Survey of the Administration of Criminal Justice in the United States.[29] The President's Commission on Law Enforcement and Administration of Justice also sponsored considerable research into the actual workings of our criminal justice systems.[30]

WESTLAW REFERENCES

digest("model penal code")

§ 1.2 Characteristics of the Substantive Criminal Law

The substantive criminal law is that law which, for the purpose of preventing harm to society, declares what conduct is criminal and prescribes the punishment to be imposed for such conduct. It includes the definition of specific offenses and general principles of liability.

---

22. See LaFave, Improving Police Performance Through the Exclusionary Rule—Part II: Defining the Norms and Training the Police, 38 Mo.L.Rev. 566, 568–79 (1965).

23. See Model Code of Pre-Arraignment Procedure (1975), containing the official draft and the reporters' commentary.

24. The ABA has published standards on the following subjects: Fair Trial and Free Press (1966); Post-Conviction Remedies (1967); Pleas of Guilty (1967); Appellate Review of Sentences (1967); Speedy Trial (1967); Providing Defense Services (1967); Joinder and Severance (1967); Sentencing Alternatives and Procedures (1967); Pretrial Release (1968); Trial by Jury (1968); Electronic Surveillance (1968); Criminal Appeals (1969); Discovery and Procedure Before Trial (1969); Probation (1970); The Prosecution Function (1970); The Defense Function (1970); The Urban Police Function (1972); The Function of the Trial Judge (1972). Each of these publications also contains useful commentary, and all the standards were published collectively without commentary, ABA Standards Relating to the Administration of Criminal Justice (1974). See Symposium on the ABA Standards, 12 Am.Crim.L.Rev. 251, 415 (1974, 1975). The standards were later revised and published in four volumes with updated commentary, ABA Standards for Criminal Justice (2d ed. 1980).

25. Uniform Rules of Criminal Procedure (Approved Draft, 1974).

26. E.g., Criminal Justice in Cleveland (1922); The Illinois Crime Survey (1929); The Missouri Crime Survey (1933).

27. Reports of the National Commission on Law and Enforcement (1931).

28. Remington, Criminal Justice Research, 51 J.Crim. L., C. & P.S. 7, 12 (1960).

29. For a description of practices in Detroit based upon the survey, see Law Enforcement in the Metropolis (D. McIntyre ed. 1967). For description and analysis of practices in Kansas, Michigan and Wisconsin, see: L. Tiffany, D. McIntyre & D. Rotenberg, Detection of Crime (1967); W. LaFave, Arrest (1965); F. Miller, Prosecution (1970); D. Newman, Conviction (1966); and R. Dawson, Sentencing (1969). Articles based in part upon the survey are listed in Law Enforcement in the Metropolis, p. x (D. McIntyre ed. 1967).

30. The basic document is President's Comm'n on Law Enforcement and Administration of Justice, The Challenge of Crime in a Free Society (1967). Task Force Reports were published on the following subjects: The Police; The Courts; Corrections; Juvenile Delinquency and Youth Crime; Organized Crime; Science and Technology; Assessment of Crime; Narcotics and Drugs; Drunkenness. Several research papers and consultants' papers were also published.

"Conduct" in the above statement is used in a broad sense to cover two distinct matters: (1) the act,[1] or the omission to act where there is a duty to act; and (2) the state of mind which accompanies the act or omission.[2] Thus the definition of a particular crime will spell out what act (or omission) and what mental state is required for its commission. Furthermore, as we shall see, the definition of a particular crime may require, in addition to an act or omission and a state of mind, something in the way of specified attendant circumstances; and with some crimes the definition also requires a specified result of the act or omission.[3] As the above definition of substantive criminal law implies, conduct cannot be called "criminal" unless a punishment is prescribed therefor.[4]

(a) Specific Crimes and General Principles. The substantive criminal law is to a large extent concerned with the definitions of the various crimes (whether defined by the common law or, far more commonly, by statute)—what conduct, including what state of mind, is necessary for guilt of murder, or rape, or burglary, etc. But it is concerned with much more than is found in the definitions of the specific crimes, for there are many general principles of the substantive criminal law which apply to more than a single crime—for instance, the principle that an insane person cannot be guilty of any

crime, or that one coerced into committing what would otherwise be criminal conduct cannot be guilty of most crimes.[5] Thus criminal battery is sometimes defined as "the intentional or reckless application of force to the person of another, directly or indirectly." The definition does not continue: ". . . by one who is not legally insane; not legally too young; not too intoxicated to have the necessary state of mind; who was not coerced by threat of immediate death or great bodily harm; and who was not justified because he acted in self-defense, or pursuant to domestic authority, or because the other person consented," and so on.

Besides the general principles of the type represented by insanity, infancy, coercion and self-defense (all of which have to do with *defenses to liability* which, if applicable, negative the commission of the specific crime), there are other general principles of criminal liability of an *affirmative-liability* sort, which cut across the various specific crimes and which therefore may properly be called "general principles." One type of affirmative-liability general principle concerns the three "inchoate crimes" of attempt, conspiracy and solicitation. Though these crimes are in one sense three specific crimes, yet in another sense they concern all the other specific crimes; thus with attempt the issue may be attempted murder or attempted rape or at-

---

§ 1.2

1. Sometimes a series of acts, rather than one single act, is required for a particular crime. Thus at common law and under some modern statutes burglary requires a breaking and an entering; larceny requires a taking and a carrying away.

The act may consist of physical activity, as in pulling the trigger of a gun in the homicide crimes, or merely of speech, as is usually the case with the crimes of false pretenses and perjury. Indeed, homicide may be committed by speech, as where one suddenly shouts "boo" at an enemy leaning over the edge of a precipice.

2. "State of mind" is here used rather loosely to include whatever element of blameworthiness, if any, a particular crime may require. We shall see that this may require, with regard to a particular crime, an *intention* to bring about some forbidden result; or *knowledge* of the existence of certain facts or laws; or *recklessness* in behavior or in producing a specified result; or *negligence* in doing so. See §§ 3.5, 3.6. And we shall see that some crimes may be committed without any bad intention or knowledge or recklessness or negligence—i.e., without any

blameworthiness at all—simply by doing something the criminal law forbids or by not doing something the criminal law requires. See § 3.8.

The word "conduct" is sometimes used to cover an act or omission, without also covering the accompanying mental state. Using "conduct" in that sense, it would have to be said that a particular crime consists of defined conduct, together with a defined state of mind, which the criminal law punishes. But Model Penal Code § 1.13(5) defines "conduct" in the double sense used in this book, i.e., an act (or omission) *and* its accompanying state of mind.

3. See § 1.2(c).

4. See § 1.2(d).

5. Some of these general principles apply to all crimes (e.g., insanity, infancy), some to most but not all crimes (e.g., coercion), some to a few crimes (e.g., consent, self-defense). But all apply to more than one crime, or we should not call it a general principle; we should instead incorporate it into the definition of the particular crime.

tempted burglary, etc.; and so with conspiracy to commit murder or to commit embezzlement, and with solicitation to commit any one of the many specific crimes. The second type of general principle of affirmative criminal liability concerns parties to specific crimes, including the liability of accessories as well as of principals—for instance, the liability for murder not only of the one who fired the fatal bullet, but of the other person who urged him to do it, or who supplied him with the gun.

The general principles of the substantive criminal law are taken up in chapters 4 through 6, and the definitions of some of the specific crimes in chapters 7 and 8.

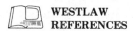

**WESTLAW
REFERENCES**

di criminal law

(b) Nature of Criminal Law—Basic Premises. In addition to the definitions of specific crimes and the general principles applicable to more than one specific crime, there exist some basic premises which underlie the whole of the Anglo-American criminal law.[6] (1) One such premise, based on a commonly accepted notion of fair play, is that there must be some advance warning to the public as to what conduct is criminal and how it is punishable—a fundamental principle sometimes expressed by the maxim *nullum crimen sine lege, nulla poena sine lege* (no crime or punishment without law). (2) Another is that there can be no criminal liability for bad thoughts alone; there is a requirement of some sort of action (or non-action when there is a duty to act) for criminal liability. This is sometimes expressed as a requirement of an *actus reus* (guilty act). (3) Conversely, action (or non-action) alone without a bad mind cannot be the basis of criminal liability; crime requires some sort of *mens rea* (guilty mind).[7] (4) Another basic premise is that the *actus reus* and the *mens rea* must concur. (5) There

is also a requirement of causation: where the definition of the crime requires that certain conduct produce a certain result (in murder, the defendant's conduct must produce a death; in arson, his conduct must cause a house to burn; in false pretenses, his conduct must cause the victim to hand over his property), it must be shown that the conduct caused the result. The difficult problems arise in connection with harmful results that differ from those results which the defendant intended, or that occur in a different way from the way which the defendant contemplated. (6) Lastly, there is the basic premise that, since the criminal law aims to prevent harm to the public, there can be no crime without harm.

These basic premises, more or less strictly observed in practice, have of course been extremely important in shaping the development of the substantive criminal law. They are discussed in greater detail in chapter 3 of this book.

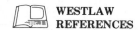

**WESTLAW
REFERENCES**

null** +1 crimen poena +1 "sine lege"

(c) Variations in Definitions of Crimes. The various crimes (whether they are statutory crimes or common law crimes) are of course variously defined as to what actions and states of mind are required for guilt. Here we may note that the definitions also often require, in addition, the presence or absence of attendant *circumstances,* and sometimes require that the necessary conduct produce certain *results.* For example, as to circumstances, burglary (at least at common law) requires night-time activity, receiving stolen property requires that the goods received be stolen goods, bigamy requires a previous marriage, statutory rape that the girl be under age, perjury that the witness be sworn, incest that the parties be related. In some

---

6. For a complete analysis of the basic premises, see J. Hall, General Principles of Criminal Law (2d ed. 1960). Professor Hall terms these basic premises "general principles."

7. Of all the basic premises, this is doubtless the one least adhered to in modern criminal law, which has often

created strict criminal liability based upon acts or omissions alone, and vicarious liability based upon another's acts or omissions. See §§ 3.8, 3.9. Some authorities contend that this type of liability should not be called "criminal" at all, or that nothing more than a fine should be imposed for this innocent-minded conduct.

cases the necessary circumstances may consist of the absence of something; thus in rape the victim must be someone who is not the wife of the rapist. Perhaps we might say that in criminal homicide and battery an attendant circumstance necessary for guilt is the absence of any justification or excuse.

In respect to the requirement of a result, some crimes are so worded that a bad result is needed for commission of the crime. For instance, criminal homicide requires the death of a human being, battery the injury of such a person, arson the burning of property, malicious mischief the injury or destruction of property, false pretenses the loss of title to property or money. On the other hand, many crimes are so defined that no bad result is required, it being the policy of the criminal law in these cases to punish activity likely to produce bad results if not nipped in the bud. Thus forgery may be committed although no one other than the forger ever saw the forged document; perjury may be committed although the false testimony was not believed and so did not affect the outcome of the matter in dispute; criminal assault although the bullet intended for the victim missed him; attempt and conspiracy although the crime attempted or agreed upon was never consummated. Similarly, a case holds that one may be guilty of the crime of transporting a woman across state lines for purposes of prostitution although the young lady in question, upon arrival at her destination, refused to perform as expected.[8]

The totality of these various items—conduct, mental fault, plus attendant circumstances and specified result when required by

the definition of a crime—may be said to constitute the "elements" of the crime.

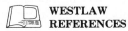

WESTLAW REFERENCES

headnote(definition /s crime (criminal +1 act***** conduct) /s element)

(d) Necessity for Prescribed Punishment. We have seen that a crime is made up of two parts, forbidden conduct and a prescribed penalty. The former without the latter is no crime.[9] The modern criminal penalties are: the death penalty, imprisonment with or without hard labor, and the fine.[10] In many cases the section of the statute which describes the forbidden conduct concludes with a statement of the punishment; or perhaps one section sets forth the forbidden conduct and the next section the punishment. Sometimes, however, the statute forbidding the conduct may refer to another statute for the punishment, such as the rather common statute which provides that whoever commits embezzlement (defining it) shall be punishable as if he committed larceny, and the larceny statute provides for a certain penalty of fine or imprisonment. Another method sometimes encountered is for the statute, after forbidding certain conduct, to conclude "shall be guilty of a felony" (or "misdemeanor"), without setting forth the penalty; but another catch-all statute provides that one who commits a felony (or a misdemeanor) not otherwise punishable shall be punished in a prescribed way. Similarly, the statute defining certain conduct as criminal may say that this crime is a felony or misdemeanor of a certain classification; another statute then indicates the permissible punishment for each classifi-

---

8. United States v. Sapperstein, 198 F.Supp. 14 (D.Md. 1961).

9. See cases cited note 13 infra.

10. In former times, especially in England, criminal punishment included, in addition to the above types of penalties: mutilation; whipping; the pillory; transportation (from England to the colonies) and its close relative, penal servitude. All of these, except possibly whipping, have now disappeared from the criminal scene in the Anglo-American legal system. In State v. Cannon, 55 Del. 587, 190 A.2d 514 (1963), whipping as a form of criminal punishment was held not to violate constitutional provi-

sions against cruel or unusual punishments. Compare Jackson v. Bishop, 404 F.2d 571 (8th Cir.1968) (Arkansas prison practice of beating prisoners with a leather strip was cruel and unusual punishment).

Somewhat closely related to the fine is the pecuniary penalty for violation of a statute, the penalty being recoverable by the injured party, or the state, or the informer, as the statute may provide. For the difficulties in determining whether such a penalty is a criminal or a civil penalty, see Note, 51 Harv.L.Rev. 1092 (1938); and § 1.7(d).

cation.[11] In all of these cases there is little difficulty in concluding that, since the statutes set forth both forbidden conduct and criminal penalty, the legislature has created a crime.[12]

But sometimes the legislature forbids conduct and then omits (in most cases unintentionally) to provide for a penalty; and there is no catch-all statute of the type mentioned above. In such a situation one who engages in the forbidden conduct is not guilty of a crime.[13] However, one case has held that prohibited conduct without a penalty can be punished by a state which has retained common law crimes [14] with the same penalty which such a state would impose for a common law crime.[15]

(e) Purpose of Criminal Law—Prevention of Harm. The broad aim of the criminal law is, of course, to prevent harm to society— more specifically, to prevent injury to the health, safety, morals and welfare of the public. This it accomplishes by punishing those who have done harm, and by threatening with punishment those who would do harm, to others.[16] Sometimes the harm to be prevented is physical: death or bodily injury to a human being in criminal homicide or battery; burning of a house in arson; loss of property in the theft crimes. Sometimes the harm is to some more intangible interest, as where it consists of the outraged feelings of the victim of indecent exposure. Sometimes the harm to be prevented is simply a mischievous situation, or situation of danger, as in the case of the crime of reckless driving or of the "inchoate" crimes of attempt, conspiracy and solicitation, where, when the defendant's conduct is over, no member of society may have suffered any damage (physical, property or intangible) at all.[17]

11. See, e.g., Ill.—S.H.A. ch. 38, ¶¶ 1005–8–1, 1005–8–3, setting out permissible sentences for class X, 1, 2, 3 and 4 felonies and class A, B and C misdemeanors.

12. Thus in State v. Deer, 80 Wash. 92, 141 P. 321 (1914), the game statute provided that deer-hunting with dogs is a gross misdemeanor and punishable as hereinafter provided; there was, however, no prescribed punishment contained in the game statute; but another statute provided that the penalty for a gross misdemeanor, if not otherwise set forth, is a maximum of one year's imprisonment or $1000 fine or both; *held,* deer-hunting with dogs is a punishable crime.

13. United States v. Evans, 333 U.S. 483, 68 S.Ct. 634, 92 L.Ed. 823 (1948) (Congress prohibited concealing an alien, but the penalty prescribed was too vague, so one who did the forbidden act committed no crime); Acunia v. United States, 404 F.2d 140 (9th Cir.1968) (federal statute re offenses in Indian country had no reference to state or federal law for the crime of incest; statute unenforceable as to that conduct for lack of both definition and penalty); State v. Mandel, 78 Ariz. 226, 278 P.2d 413 (1954) (statute provides that attempt is punishable by half the punishment for completed crime; punishment for first degree murder is death or life imprisonment, which cannot be halved; dictum that there is no crime of attempted first degree murder); Johnston v. State, 100 Ala. 32, 14 So. 629 (1894) (statute provided that stealing dogs is punishable as in other cases of larceny; statute did not say whether grand larceny or petit larceny; so penalty too uncertain; so stealing dogs no crime); State v. Ching, 62 Haw. 656, 619 P.2d 93 (1980) (statute proscribing business activity within street yard setback did not provide penalty, so conduct not criminal); State v. Fair Law Service Center, 20 N.J. 468, 120 A.2d 233 (1956) (violator of Sunday observance law cannot be convicted where no penalty provided); Commonwealth ex rel. Varronne v. Cunningham, 365 Pa. 68, 73 A.2d 705 (1950) (statute prohibiting driving overweight trucks on highways set forth four ways in which a truck might be overweight; the penalty clause set forth penalty for only one of the four ways; so the other three ways are not criminal); State v. Truax, 130 Wash. 69, 226 P. 259 (1924) (larceny statute provides imprisonment as only penalty; corporation was guilty of larcenous conduct; since corporation cannot be imprisoned, there is no penalty, so corporation has committed no crime).

Compare Olinyk v. People, 642 P.2d 490 (Colo.1982) (though statute imposing 55 m.p.h. speed limit contained no penalty, it may be enforced by use of penalties in preexisting statute which classifies speeding offenses generally by the number of miles by which speed limit exceeded; statutory penalty requirement "is based in part on the necessity of knowing that the legislature indeed intended to impose criminal sanctions for commission of an act," and such legislative intent clear here because maintenance of federal highway funding was contingent upon enactment of an enforceable 55 m.p.h. maximum).

14. See § 2.1.

15. State v. Bishop, 228 N.C. 371, 45 S.E.2d 858 (1947) (statute forbade conduct but provided no penalty; state retains common law crimes; *held,* conduct punishable as a misdemeanor). But compare Commonwealth ex rel. Varronne v. Cunningham, supra note 13 (statute forbade conduct but omitted to impose a penalty; state retains common law crimes; "Since no common law crime is involved, no penalty can be imposed by the Court unless the statute itself provides such a penalty").

16. For the theories of how punishment and the threat of punishment prevent harm, see § 1.5.

17. The extent to which the legislature may, under its police power, determine what conduct is harmful to the health, safety, morals or welfare of the public, is treated in § 2.12. Very occasionally a court has struck down a

Of course, not all harmful conduct is criminal. There is the basic requirement that harmful conduct, to be criminal, must be prohibited by law. And the legislatures have never succeeded in making criminal every sort of harmful conduct.[18]

WESTLAW
REFERENCES

headnote(purpose objective aim /3 "criminal law")

(f) Criminal Law and Morality. There is no doubt that society's ideas of morality, to the extent that they are held by those members of society who are legislators (in the case of statutory crimes) and judges (with common law crimes), have had much to do with formulating the substantive criminal law. The English judges of long ago shared the feelings of the English public that killing human beings without justification or excuse, and forcible sexual intercourse with a woman other than one's wife, and stealing other people's property were wrongful, and so they created the crimes of murder, rape and larceny to punish such behavior. In more modern times the legislatures of some American states have shared the feelings of the public of those states that it is immoral for gamblers to pay money to athletes to lose games (thus allowing the gamblers to bet on a sure thing), so the legislature has created a new statutory crime, bribery of athletes, to punish that sort of conduct. No doubt at times there are moral issues on which the public is sharply divided, as is true in some places concerning the sale of intoxicating liquor, in which case the side with the more effective lobby may carry the day in creating a crime or defeating its

creation. Doubtless too a good deal of criminal law is the result of pressure from narrow groups who are actually concerned with their own best interests much more than they are concerned with thoughts of morality. For instance, automobile dealers in the city, who cannot sell automobiles on Sunday by local city ordinance, have sometimes persuaded the legislature to punish as criminal the Sunday sale of cars anywhere in the state, in order to force the Sunday closing of the out-of-town car dealers, who have been doing a brisk Sunday business to the financial detriment of the city dealers.[19]

But immorality and criminality, though related, are not synonymous. A good deal of conduct that is ethically immoral is not criminal. For example, there are many situations where one has a moral duty to save another's life where it can be done with little danger or inconvenience or expense, but failure to take action to do so is not usually criminal.[20] In many states one may conjure up some novel and immoral way of injuring others, which the legislature has not yet thought of, and escape criminal liability because there is no criminal statute forbidding it. As we shall see, other states hold the threat of "common law crimes" in readiness for just such an emergency.[21]

On the other hand, some conduct which is not immoral may yet be criminal. As we shall see, a modern tendency in the substantive criminal law is to relax the old requirement that there cannot be a crime without a bad state of mind; today we find that many statutory crimes may be committed unintentionally but with negligence or even uninten-

---

criminal statute because the harm the legislature sought to prevent was not a harm at all, or because, though the harm it sought to prevent was real, the forbidden conduct had no tendency to bring about such a harm.

To the extent that there can be no crime without harm, the requirement of harm may be considered to be a "basic premise" of criminal law. See § 3.1.

18. E.g., Peebles v. State, 101 Ga. 585, 28 S.E. 920 (1897) (defendant put poison in victim's well with intent to kill him, but victim discovered the poison before he drank the water; at the time of defendant's act no statute made his conduct a crime; the closest crime was assault with intent to kill, but defendant committed no assault; a later statute, however, made it a crime to poison a well).

19. There is sometimes a question whether criminal legislation which is obviously specially designed to benefit a narrow group is constitutional. See § 2.12(b). (Of course, with criminal law not backed by a substantial portion of the public there are often difficulties in enforcement.)

There is also a question whether conduct which is immoral but not harmful can (or should) be made criminal. See § 2.12.

20. See § 3.3.

21. See § 2.1.

tionally without negligence, as in the case of strict-liability and vicarious-liability crimes.[22] As we shall also see, a good motive will not normally prevent what is otherwise criminal from being a crime.[23] Thus it is none the less murder that one intentionally kills a loved one suffering from a painful incurable disease, or larceny that one stole a rich man's money to give his impoverished family a better life. An honest religious belief in polygamy does not serve as a defense to the crime of bigamy.[24]

§ 1.3   Crimes and Civil Wrongs

The criminal law and the civil law have much in common. Criminal statutes have played a part in creating civil liability, while civil statutes have been important in the development of the substantive criminal law. There are, however, a number of differences between criminal law and civil law because of their different functions.

(a) Similarities and Differences. The substantive criminal law and the substantive civil law (such as the law of torts, contracts, and property) have much in common. Civil law, like criminal law, aims to shape people's conduct along lines which are beneficial to society—by preventing them from doing what is bad for society (as by imposing liability for damages upon those who commit torts or break contracts) or by compelling them to do what is good for society (as by decreeing specific performance of contracts for the sale of real property). Society has an interest in preventing killings and rapes; but it also wants to prevent automobile accidents and to discourage breaches of contracts. Civil law, like criminal law, is effective mainly because

of the sanctions which the law imposes, through the courts, upon those who commit violations. Even these sometimes do not differ greatly as between the civil and the criminal law. Paying damages (especially "punitive damages") for torts or contract breaches is not much different from paying fines for criminal violations.[1] Confinement of mental defectives in mental hospitals, of juvenile delinquents in reform schools, or of aliens awaiting deportation is not too far removed from imprisonment of criminals in penitentiaries or jails, especially those modern prisons devoted to principles of rehabilitation rather than of revenge and retribution.

Indeed, it has been argued with some force that the only real basis for distinction between crimes and civil wrongs lies in the moral condemnation which the community visits upon the criminal but not (at least not so powerfully) upon his civil wrongdoer counterpart.[2] Yet, even aside from differences in moral condemnation, it would seem that criminal punishment, with emphasis on imprisonment, is on the whole more drastic than the sanctions, with emphasis upon paying money, imposed by the civil law, even though in a particular case it may be that the civil sanction imposed is harder on the defendant than the counterpart criminal punishment would be.

WESTLAW REFERENCES

di civil

(b) Crimes and Torts.[3] Criminal law and the law of torts (more than any other form of civil law) are related branches of the law; yet in a sense they are two quite different mat-

---

22. See §§ 3.8, 3.9.

23. See § 3.6.

24. A good motive is, of course, sometimes relevant in criminal law, as where A shoots B for the motive of preventing B from killing A (at least under some circumstances) or where A shoots B for the motive of preventing B from committing a felony (similarly, under certain circumstances).

§ 1.3

1. For comparison of punitive damages in civil cases and criminal punishment, see Notes, 41 N.Y.U.L.Rev. 1158 (1966); 34 U.Chi.L.Rev. 408 (1967).

2. Hart, The Aims of the Criminal Law, 23 Law & Contemp.Prob. 401, 404–406 (1958), argues therefrom that the criminal law must not be permitted to create crimes out of conduct which lacks the blameworthiness deserving of such moral condemnation.

3. See J. Hall, Principles of Criminal Law, 240–46 (2d ed. 1960); W. Prosser & W. Keeton, Torts § 2 (5th ed. 1984); Epstein, Crime and Tort: Old Wine in Old Bottles, in Assessing the Criminal 231 (R. Barnett & J. Hagel eds. 1977).

ters. The aim of the criminal law, as we have noted, is to protect the public against harm, by punishing harmful results of conduct or at least situations (not yet resulting in actual harm) which are likely to result in harm if allowed to proceed further. The function of tort law is to compensate someone who is injured for the harm he has suffered. With crimes, the state itself brings criminal proceedings to protect the public interest but not to compensate the victim;[4] with torts, the injured party himself institutes proceedings to recover damages (or perhaps to enjoin the defendant from causing further damage).[5] With crimes, as we have seen, there is emphasis on a bad mind, on immorality. With torts the emphasis is more on "a fair adjustment of the conflicting interests of the litigating parties to achieve a desirable social result,"[6] with morality taking on less importance.[7]

Thus tort law requires pecuniary damage, with but minor emphasis on immorality; while criminal law emphasizes immoral behavior, but often does not require any actual damage.[8] The great difference in function between the two branches of law produces important differences between crimes and torts, even with respect to those crimes and torts which are rather closely related (e.g., tort of deceit, crime of false pretenses)—even, in fact, where they may bear the same name (e.g., assault, battery, libel).

So with assault: to shoot at and miss a sleeping man cannot be a civil assault, as there is no injury, even mental, to the sleeper; but such behavior is socially dangerous enough to constitute a criminal assault.[9] And with libel: a defamatory letter written to the one defamed but seen by no one else cannot be civil libel, because he can suffer no injury where no outsider sees it; but on the criminal side no such publication to a third person is needed, the evil which the crime is designed to prevent being the danger of a breach of the peace caused by the libel victim's anger on learning of the defamatory matter. Where one person by misrepresentation obtains something of value from another, an action for the tort of deceit will not lie if in fact the victim received all the value that he bargained for and has paid for; in such a case he has suffered no financial loss. But the crime of false pretenses may be committed even if the victim of the misrepresentations suffered no financial loss—in fact, where he got more value than he bargained for.[10] An innocent converter of another's property (e.g., a bona fide purchaser of stolen property) is liable in tort for conversion. But the crime of embezzlement requires more than simply a conversion; because of the criminal law's emphasis on immorality a "fraudulent" conversion is required.[11] Ordinary negligence is a common basis of tort liability, but more than ordinary

4. In spite of the theory that criminal law is not concerned with compensating the victim of crime, in practice restitution of property obtained by theft is sometimes, with or without statutory authority, made a condition of probation; the district attorney may decline to prosecute if the parties settle their problems; the victim may decline to appear and testify when the criminal settles up; several states by statute provide for mitigation of punishment if embezzled property is restored. See Note, 39 Colum.L.Rev. 1185 (1939). On the so-called restitutionary theory of justice and specific proposals to formalize the restitution function as part of the criminal process, see the various essays in Assessing the Criminal (R. Barnett & J. Hagel eds. 1977).

5. To the limited extent that tort law allows punitive damages, over and above actual damages, for aggravated torts, the law of torts does borrow one of the features of criminal law—that of punishing wrongdoing. See W. Prosser & W. Keeton, Torts § 2 (5th ed. 1984).

6. W. Prosser & W. Keeton, Torts § 3 (5th ed. 1984).

7. In State v. Bushey, 425 A.2d 1343 (Me.1981), upholding defendant's conviction of assault for her act in hitting an officer's chest several times but causing no injury, the court adopted an objective standard for proving offensive physical conduct, meaning there is an assault even when the defendant strikes an unusually insensible victim. The court explained this approach was justified by the fact that the criminal law focuses upon the "bad" behavior of the defendant rather than the pecuniary damage to the victim.

8. In the case of some torts the plaintiff is not required to prove actual damages: libel; slander where the spoken words are actionable per se; assault producing apprehension but not fear; malicious prosecution; trespass; nuisance. With most of these the reason may well be that pecuniary damages are apt to be substantial but hard to prove.

9. See § 7.16.

10. See § 8.7.

11. See § 8.6.

negligence is usually required in the criminal law.[12]

Turning to matters of defense, we find that in related matters there are differences in defenses to torts and defenses to crimes, because torts are wrongs to private individuals but crimes are wrongs to the public. Thus consent of the adult injured party is a defense to intentionally inflicted torts; but in analogous situations in the field of criminal law consent of the victim may not be a defense.[13] So the consent of the woman to an abortion may be a defense to a tort action for battery,[14] but it is not alone a defense to the criminal action. So too an injured party may condone the tort committed against him; but a victim of crime may not normally obliterate the commission of the crime by forgiving the criminal.[15] Contributory negligence is a well known defense to tort liability based upon negligence; but in the case of crimes based on negligence (e.g., criminal homicide, battery) the contributory negligence of the victim is no defense (although, as we shall see, the conduct of the victim is often important in determining whether the defendant was culpably negligent).[16]

There are fundamental differences in matters of responsibility as well. Infants are generally liable for their torts, because tort law is concerned more with compensating the injured party than with the moral guilt of the wrongdoer;[17] but, because of the greater interest of the criminal law in morality, infants below a certain age are deemed incapable of committing crimes.[18] Much the same thing may be said for the tort and criminal liability of insane persons, who are liable for many of their torts but never for crimes.[19]

In spite of the differences between tort law and criminal law, however, there are many ideas and concepts common to both branches of the law. Some crimes (e.g., felony-murder and misdemeanor-manslaughter) make use of the idea of "proximate cause,"[20] one of the important concepts of tort liability for negligence. We meet the phrase "intervening cause" in crimes as well as torts. Liability for failure to act where there is a duty to act may be criminal as well as civil, and duty for one purpose is duty for the other.[21] The defense of self-defense is about the same whether the defendant is defending against a suit for the tort of battery or against prosecution for criminal battery.[22]

Frequently the defendant's conduct makes him both civilly and criminally liable: *A* intentionally hits *B* with a baseball bat; or embezzles his property; or publishes defamatory matter about him; or intentionally destroys his watch or burns his house. In any such situation the civil suit need not await the outcome of the criminal proceedings by the modern weight of authority.[23]

On the other hand, sometimes the defendant's conduct renders him criminally but not civilly liable, as is the case with the crime of treason or the crimes of possessing counterfeiting implements or burglar's tools; driving too fast without an accident is a crime but not a tort; and forgery may be committed although no one has lost a cent on account of the forgery. And, conversely, his conduct may render him civilly but not criminally liable, as where he kills or injures another person with but ordinary negligence, or unintentionally commits a trespass, or innocently converts another's property.

12. See § 3.7.

13. See § 5.11(a).

14. See W. Prosser & W. Keeton, Torts § 18 (5th ed. 1984), pointing out there is an even split of authority on the matter.

15. See § 5.11(d).

16. See § 5.11(c).

17. W. Prosser & W. Keeton, Torts § 134 (5th ed. 1984).

18. See § 4.11.

19. See § 4.1.

20. See § 3.12.

21. See § 3.3.

22. See § 3.7.

23. See Hitchler, Crimes and Civil Injuries, 39 Dick.L. Rev. 23 (1934); Comment, 5 Okla.L.Rev. 242 (1952). The comment concludes that only a few states follow the English rule that public policy requires that the victim do his public duty to instigate prosecution before seeking private redress.

Criminal procedure and civil procedure, like the substantive law of torts and crimes, have much in common. A criminal trial, for instance, proceeds along a course greatly resembling that traveled by a civil trial. Most of the rules of evidence (e.g., the hearsay rule) apply equally to both types of cases. But still there are important differences between the two types of procedure, perhaps best illustrated by the requirement that in a civil case the party with the burden of proof must establish his claim "by a preponderance of the evidence," while in a criminal case the state must prove the defendant guilty "beyond a reasonable doubt."

Some substantive criminal law is made in the relatively quiet setting of a civil case. Thus some law of theft has been developed in suits on theft insurance policies, where the insured must show that his property was taken by theft. The law of murder must be considered in the constructive trust branch of the law of restitution which declares that an heir (or legatee, or insurance beneficiary) who obtains property by murdering his ancestor (or testator, or insured) is unjustly enriched if permitted to retain it. Since it is a defense to the tort of malicious prosecution that the plaintiff was actually guilty of the crime charged, these tort cases often go into the question of whether the plaintiff actually committed the crime for which the defendant initiated prosecution. Even federal tax cases have had to decide questions of criminal law because of the formerly-held peculiar notion that one is taxable on the income he derives from larceny or false pretenses or extortion or racketeering but not for what he embezzles.[24]

(c) Interaction of Criminal Law and Civil Law. Criminal statutes have played a part in creating civil liability and defenses to civil liability.[25] Statutes are expressions of public policy, and the common law is, after all, merely the courts' notion of what best promotes public policy. In the absence of any legislative expression of policy, the courts will seek it on their own; but where the legislature has expressed its ideas, the courts will naturally give those ideas great weight. Thus in tort law a criminal statute, designed to protect certain types of people from certain kinds of harms, sets up the standard of conduct of the reasonable man for purposes of negligence liability, so that it is negligence *per se* (or at least evidence of negligence) when a defendant, violating the statute, causes a person of that type to suffer that sort of harm.[26] In contracts law a criminal statute punishing gambling may not spell out that the winner may not sue the loser to recover his winnings, yet the loser has a defense to the civil action.[27] The criminal statute has disclosed a public policy which the courts in civil cases may further effectuate by using that policy in deciding the law in civil cases.

On the other hand, civil statutes have to some extent been important in the development of the substantive criminal law. Thus the common law rule that one cannot be guilty of larceny of his spouse's property (since husband and wife are one individual) has generally been done away with by judicial decision because Married Women's Property Acts (which do not speak of criminal liability at all) have made the wife, in property matters at least, an individual separate from her husband. The common law presumption of coercion, where a wife commits what would otherwise be a crime in her husband's presence, has generally fallen the same way, although the civil statutes freeing the wife from her husband's domination do not themselves

24. See Commissioner v. Wilcox, 327 U.S. 404, 66 S.Ct. 546, 90 L.Ed. 752 (1946) (embezzled money does not constitute taxable income to the embezzler in the year of embezzlement), which was overruled in James v. United States, 366 U.S. 213, 81 S.Ct. 1052, 6 L.Ed.2d 246 (1961).

25. See Lowndes, Civil Liability Created by Criminal Legislation, 16 Minn.L.Rev. 361 (1932); Morris, The Relation of Criminal Statutes to Tort Liability, 46 Harv.L.Rev. 453 (1933); Thayer, Public Wrong and Private Action, 27 Harv.L.Rev. 317 (1914). An example is found in Fitzgerald v. Pan American World Airways, 229 F.2d 499 (2d Cir. 1956).

26. W. Prosser & W. Keeton, Torts § 36 (5th ed. 1984).

27. 6A A. Corbin, Contracts § 1484 (1962). So too of other types of contracts, the making of which is a criminal offense. Id. part 8 (illegal bargains). Contracts law sometimes makes use of the distinction between crimes *mala in se* and *mala prohibita* in suits on illegal contracts.

directly deal with the matter of coercion as a criminal defense. The criminal law is slower to borrow from civil statutes than civil law is to borrow from criminal statutes, at least in the area of imposing criminal liability where none existed before. This is because of the basic premise of common law, expressed in the maxim *nulla poena sine lege*, that public policy alone (even when disclosed by civil statutes) is not sufficient to make conduct criminal, in the absence of a direct expression of advance warning from the legislature.

§ 1.4 Characteristics of Criminal Procedure

The subject of criminal procedure is not dealt with in this book.[1] It is appropriate, however, to consider at this point some of the basic characteristics of the criminal process in order to understand the significance of the substantive criminal law in terms of day-to-day criminal justice administration. Without such an understanding, the discussion of the substantive criminal law might prompt the inappropriate conclusion that the law of crimes is extremely severe and technical. While it is true that many of the nice technicalities of the substantive criminal law have continued to exist long after the reasons for their existence have disappeared, many of these technicalities (and the severity of them) are overcome through law and practice in the realm of criminal procedure.

Is the assumption underlying the substantive criminal law that all persons whose conduct reasonably appears to be criminal (utilizing the definitions of specific crimes and the general principles of liability) shall be subjected to the full array of criminal proceedings—investigation, arrest, charge, trial, conviction, sentence, and correctional treatment? Even apart from the obvious fact that only a portion of all criminal conduct is detected, the answer is clearly no. For one thing the law has always been concerned with the risk of innocent persons being subjected to criminal

proceedings, and thus certain evidentiary tests must be met at several points in the criminal process. The strictest test, that which requires evidence "beyond a reasonable doubt" for conviction, clearly rests upon the notion that it is better to allow some of the guilty to escape conviction than to risk conviction of an innocent person.

Secondly, our systems for criminal justice are pervaded by official discretion; many persons who are guilty of crimes (and who could be proved guilty) are not proceeded against because there appears to be some sound policy reason for such inaction. The authority of the prosecutor to decide on policy grounds whether to prosecute is well known, but there are several other officials who also exercise similar discretion. Finally, some of those who have engaged in criminal conduct are subjected to a part but not all of the criminal process. Sometimes this is done because of serious doubts as to whether the system can effectively deal with certain conduct which the courts or legislatures have declared criminal, while on other occasions the attempt is to reduce the burden upon the limited resources of the criminal justice system.

(a) The Evidentiary Tests. One helpful way of looking at the entire system for the administration of criminal justice is to view it as a series of critical decisions—critical to both the individual concerned and to society as a whole. Taken in their usual chronological order, the key decisions are whether and how to conduct an investigation, whether to arrest, whether to charge, whether to convict, what the sentence should be, and, finally, various decisions in the field of corrections. Although this is somewhat of an oversimplification, many of these decisions, when so ordered, result in what might be called a step profile of the criminal justice system; each succeeding decision point requires a higher degree of evidence of guilt than the immediate preceding decision. As the consequences to the individual being dealt with become

<hr/>

§ 1.4

1. On criminal procedure, see W. LaFave & J. Israel, Criminal Procedure (1984) (three volumes).

more serious, the decision-maker must have a higher quantum of evidence.

In the early stages of the criminal process, the police are limited in what they may do by several evidentiary tests. Some evidence (sometimes referred to as "reasonable grounds to suspect") must be present before an individual may be stopped and questioned.[2] Arrests are usually permitted only when the police have "reasonable grounds to believe" that the person to be arrested has committed a crime,[3] and searches require "probable cause."[4] Similarly, the prosecutor is limited as to whom he may charge with a crime. At least in serious cases, an individual may not be required to stand trial unless a magistrate has found "probable cause" at a preliminary hearing[5] or a grand jury has returned an indictment based upon "probable cause."[6] Certain correctional decisions, such as the revocation of probation or parole,[7] also must be based upon a required quantum of evidence.

The high point in the evidentiary profile referred to above is the conviction stage, for it requires admissible evidence which establishes guilt "beyond a reasonable doubt."[8] In a number of instances this means that the person on trial may not be convicted even though a layman, on the basis of all available facts, would reach the conclusion that the

individual in question has engaged in criminal conduct. For good reason, all available facts are not disclosed at trial. Some evidence, even if it conclusively establishes guilt, may be excluded from the trial because it was obtained in violation of the defendant's constitutional rights.[9] Also, "much evidence of real and substantial probative value goes out on considerations irrelevant to its probative weight but relevant to possible misunderstanding or misuse by the jury."[10] As to that evidence which is received in the case, the fact-finder (the jury in a jury trial, the judge in a trial without jury) is to apply a high standard of persuasion, namely, the reasonable doubt test. Although a completely satisfactory definition of this test has never been developed,[11] it is commonly said that there must be "an abiding conviction, to a moral certainty, of the truth of the charge."[12] (By comparison, in civil cases only a "preponderance of evidence" is required.[13]) There must be proof beyond a reasonable doubt of all the elements of the crime and of the defendant's participation or responsibility, but not of each evidentiary fact.[14]

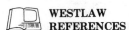 **WESTLAW REFERENCES**

synopsis,digest("probable cause" /p magistrate /p "preliminary hearing")

2. See Terry v. Ohio, 392 U.S. 1, 88 S.Ct. 1868, 20 L.Ed. 2d 889 (1968); Sibron v. New York, Peters v. New York, 392 U.S. 41, 88 S.Ct. 1889, 20 L.Ed.2d 917 (1969); discussed in LaFave, "Street Encounters" and the Constitution, 67 Mich.L.Rev. 40 (1968).

3. E.g., Draper v. United States, 358 U.S. 307, 79 S.Ct. 329, 3 L.Ed.2d 327 (1959).

4. E.g., Jones v. United States, 362 U.S. 257, 80 S.Ct. 725, 4 L.Ed.2d 697 (1960).

5. This is generally a requirement of state and federal law, but is not constitutionally compelled. Gerstein v. Pugh, 420 U.S. 103, 95 S.Ct. 854, 43 L.Ed.2d 54 (1975); Ocampo v. United States, 234 U.S. 91, 34 S.Ct. 712, 58 L.Ed. 1231 (1914).

6. This is a guarantee of the Fifth Amendment, but is one of a very few provisions in the Bill of Rights which has not been held applicable to the states. Hurtado v. California, 110 U.S. 516, 4 S.Ct. 111, 28 L.Ed. 232 (1884).

7. See R. Dawson, Sentencing chs. 5, 14 (1969).

8. This is a constitutional requirement under the due process clause. In re Winship, 397 U.S. 358, 90 S.Ct. 1068, 25 L.Ed.2d 368 (1970).

9. E.g., Mapp v. Ohio, 367 U.S. 643, 81 S.Ct. 1684, 6 L.Ed.2d 1081 (1961) (illegal search); Miranda v. Arizona, 384 U.S. 436, 86 S.Ct. 1602, 16 L.Ed.2d 694 (1966) (confession obtained in violation of privilege against self-incrimination).

10. Brinegar v. United States, 338 U.S. 160, 69 S.Ct. 1302, 93 L.Ed. 1879 (1949).

11. Rex v. Summers, [1952] 1 All E.R. 1059 ("I have never yet heard any court give a real definition of what is a 'reasonable doubt,' and it would be very much better if that expression was not used.") See 9 J. Wigmore, Evidence § 2497 (Chadbourne rev. 1981); McBain, Burden of Proof; Degrees of Proof: Degrees of Belief, 32 Calif.L.Rev. 242 (1944).

12. This is the oft-quoted language in Commonwealth v. Webster, 59 Mass. 295, 320 (1850).

13. 9 J. Wigmore, Evidence § 2498 (Chadbourne rev. 1981).

14. State v. Raine, 93 Idaho 862, 477 P.2d 104 (1970); State v. May, 292 N.C. 644, 235 S.E.2d 178 (1977).

(b) Corpus Delicti. Also deserving mention here is the often misunderstood concept of *corpus delicti* ("the body of the crime"). Wigmore explains it this way: every crime "reveals three component parts, *first* the *occurrence* of the specific kind of injury or loss (as, in homicide, a person deceased; in arson, a house burnt; in larceny, property missing); *secondly,* somebody's criminality (in contrast, e.g., to accident) as the source of the loss,— these two together involving the commission of a crime by *somebody;* and *thirdly,* the accused's *identity* as the doer of this crime." [15] By the great weight of authority, the first two without the third constitute the *corpus delicti*.[16] Although Wigmore has written in terms of those crimes which require not only bad conduct but also a bad result of conduct (as homicide requires a resulting death, arson a resulting burning and larceny a resulting loss of property in the sense that the property is moved out of the owner's possession), there are many crimes (e.g., attempt, conspiracy, perjury, forgery, reckless or drunken driving) which do not require the doing of any actual harm. Perhaps then it is more accurate to say that the *corpus delicti* embraces the fact that a crime has been committed by someone—i.e., that somebody did the required act or omission with the required mental fault, under the required (if any) attendant circumstances, and producing the required (if any) harmful consequence, without embracing the further fact (needed for conviction) that the defendant was the one who did or omitted that act or was otherwise responsible therefor.

The concept of *corpus delicti* in criminal law is principally used in connection with two rules, both of which are concerned with reducing the possibility of punishing a person for a crime which was never in fact committed: (1) the almost-universal American rule that, in order to convict the defendant of a crime on the basis of his extrajudicial (i.e., out of court) confession or admission, the confession or admission must be corroborated by some evidence (it need not be evidence beyond a reasonable doubt) of the *corpus delicti;* [17] and, (2) the rule of a few states that capital punishment cannot be imposed without direct proof of the *corpus delicti*.[18]

Most *corpus delicti* cases are homicide cases, where the difficulty may be either (a) that, the victim having simply disappeared, no dead body can be produced so as to make it absolutely certain that the victim will not later turn up alive and well, or (b) that, although a dead body is found conveniently lying about, examination of the body and the surrounding circumstances reveals that the death may have been caused as well by accident, suicide or natural causes as by someone's foul play.[19] But the principles concerning *corpus delicti* are equally applicable to other crimes, such as arson,[20] burglary,[21] driv-

15. 7 J. Wigmore, Evidence § 2072 (Chadbourne rev. 1978).

16. Ibid. But the *corpus delicti* in a homicide case is occasionally said to consist only of the first one of the three. See, e.g., State v. Ruth, 181 Conn. 187, 435 A.2d 3 (1980).

17. E.g., State v. Lucas, 30 N.J. 37, 152 A.2d 50 (1959).

18. L. Hall & S. Glueck, Criminal Law and Its Enforcement 454 (2d ed. 1958).

19. Perkins, The Corpus Delicti of Murder, 48 Va.L. Rev. 173 (1962). (a) In the no-body case of People v. Scott, 176 Cal.App.2d 458, 1 Cal.Rptr. 600, 348 P.2d 882 (1959), the defendant's conviction of the murder of his wife was affirmed on the basis of strong circumstantial evidence, though her body was never found and he never confessed. (b) The most common type of body-without-proof-of-criminality case involves the mother suspected of murdering her baby, at birth or later, but doctors cannot tell whether the baby died of foul play or from natural causes, e.g., In re Flodstrom, 134 Cal.App.2d 871, 277 P.2d 101 (1954)

(ordering mother's release on habeas corpus, when she was being held on murder charge on the basis of her confession of smothering her child, because of lack of corroboration of *corpus delicti*).

20. Bussey v. State, 474 S.W.2d 708 (Tex.Crim.App. 1972) ("To establish the corpus delicti, in arson cases, it is necessary to show (a) that the house was designedly set on fire, and (b) that the accused did it or was criminally connected therewith").

21. White v. United States, 300 A.2d 716 (D.C.App. 1973) ("The crime of burglary requires, *inter alia*, a breaking or an entry without a breaking, and the Government must establish this as part of the corpus delicti before an inference from the possession of recently stolen property may properly be indulged"); State v. Hale, 45 Haw. 269, 367 P.2d 81 (1961) (proof of intent to steal or commit felony is part of the *corpus delicti* of burglary; but circumstantial evidence *held* to prove it to extent necessary to corroborate confession; proof of nighttime conduct not part of *corpus delicti*, since burglary may be committed in

ing under the influence,[22] obtaining property by false pretenses,[23] incest,[24] larceny and robbery,[25] and statutory rape.[26]

 WESTLAW REFERENCES

synopsis,digest("corpus delicti" /p confess*** admissi!)

(c) The Exercise of Discretion. The substantive criminal law has been aptly described as "an island of technicality in a sea of discretion." [27] The substantive law is quite inflexible: if one moves another's property an inch one is guilty of larceny, where the other elements of larceny are present, but not if he fails to move the property; one who breaks and enters a dwelling-house of another at a certain hour may at common law be guilty of burglary, but if he does so a few minutes

earlier he is innocent. And so it is with all the various crimes.[28]

On the other hand, the procedural side of the administration of criminal justice is full of situations in which the exercise of discretion plays a large role in determining what happens to the offender.[29] Often the victim of the crime decides not to complain to the authorities.[30] Even if the crime becomes known to the police, they may decide not to seek out the identity of the offender or, if the offender is known, they may decide not to arrest him.[31] Similarly, the prosecutor may exercise his well-recognized discretion and decide that certain offenders should not be prosecuted,[32] or such a decision may be made by the magistrate at the preliminary hearing or by the grand jury. It is well known that juries sometimes refuse to convict persons who have been

daytime, and nighttime provision relates only to increased punishment).

22. See Kyle v. State, 208 Tenn. 170, 344 S.W.2d 537 (1961) (defendant, who confessed that he had driven the car, was found by police alone near the car and drunk shortly after an accident; while independent proof of *corpus delicti* is required, the circumstances here proved the *corpus delicti*, so conviction *held* affirmed).

23. See People v. Ranney, 153 Mich. 293, 116 N.W. 999 (1908) (defendant's confession to obtaining money by false pretenses by cashing a check which he knew to be worthless must be supported by independent evidence of the *corpus delicti*; but *held* that evidence of his conduct under the circumstances constituted such proof).

24. Marsh v. State, 170 Tex.Cr.R. 512, 342 S.W.2d 435 (1961) (defendant's confession of sexual intercourse with stepdaughter *held* not to support conviction for incest, when the only evidence from the girl was that she was his stepdaughter and there was no testimony that he had had intercourse with her).

25. People v. Brooks, 334 Ill. 549, 166 N.E. 35 (1929) (conviction of robbery *held* reversed, where evidence was that defendant and victim had fight, in which victim's shirt was torn, after which victim noticed his money in the shirt was missing; there was no confession by defendant; the evidence of *corpus delicti* was as consistent with accidental loss as with stealing).

26. Wistrand v. People, 213 Ill. 72, 72 N.E. 748 (1904) (defendant's confession that he, at age 44, had sexual intercourse with Eva, who was proved to be aged 13, *held* sufficient to support conviction in absence of some evidence outside his confession that he was over 16, a requirement for this crime; and the jury cannot decide the matter of his age by looking at him!). Consider also People v. Lett, 61 Ill.App.3d 467, 18 Ill.Dec. 744, 378 N.E.2d 208 (1978) (*Wistrand* distinguished; here crime of indecent liberties required defendant be over 13, defendant's out-of-court admission he 21 is not alone sufficient, but was sufficiently corroborated by descriptions of perpe-

trator as a "man" and an individual "in his 20's," and evidence defendant had valid driver's license and 1972 class ring).

27. L. Hall & S. Glueck, Criminal Law and Its Enforcement 3 (1st ed. 1951).

28. Id. at 2 points out: "A good many of the nice technicalities of the [substantive] criminal law have sprung from the fact that in the past (when the English law developed) many offenses were punished by death. It was therefore natural for lawyers and judges to indulge in fine-spun reasoning in order to avoid the serious consequences of conviction in borderline cases."

29. Pound defines discretion as "an authority conferred by law to act in certain conditions or situations in accordance with an official's or an official agency's own considered judgment and conscience. It is an idea of morals, belonging to the twilight zone between law and morals." Pound, Discretion, Dispensation and Mitigation: The Problem of the Indvidual Special Case, 35 N.Y.U.L. Rev. 925, 926 (1960). Judge Breitel defines it as "the power to consider all circumstances and then determine whether any legal action is to be taken. And if so taken, of what kind and degree, and to what conclusion." Breitel, Controls in Criminal Law Enforcement, 27 U.Chi.L. Rev. 427 (1960). A typical dictionary definition of discretion is the "ability to make decisions which represent a responsible choice and for which an understanding of what is lawful, right, or wise may be presupposed." Webster, Third International Dictionary 647 (1961).

30. In a national survey of crime victimization, it was found that the number of offenses reported to the survey per thousand residents 18 years or over ranged, depending on the offense, from 3 to 10 times more than the number contained in police statistics. President's Comm'n on Law Enforcement and Administration of Justice, The Challenge of Crime in a Free Society 21 (1967).

31. See W. LaFave, Arrest chs. 4–6 (1965).

32. See F. Miller, Prosecution chs. 9–11, 14–18 (1970).

proved guilty beyond a reasonable doubt,[33] and judges occasionally do likewise when the case is tried without a jury.[34] After the verdict or plea of guilty the trial court usually has some discretion as to probation,[35] the sentencing authority (court or jury) as to the length of sentence if probation is not granted,[36] the parole authority as to release on parole,[37] and the pardoning authority as to pardon or commutation.[38]

It is important to note that in large measure such discretion is exercised because of the scope and state of the substantive criminal law. Because no legislature has succeeded in formulating a substantive criminal code which clearly encompasses all conduct intended to be made criminal and which clearly excludes all other conduct, the exercise of discretion in interpreting the legislative mandate is necessary. In part the problem is the result of poor draftmanship and a failure to revise the criminal law to eliminate obsolete provisions,[39] but it also results from the inability of a legislature to envisage all of the day-to-day situations which may arise.[40]

This "administrative interpretation" of the substantive law, however, extends beyond the kind of statutory construction engaged in by courts under recognized principles of legislative interpretation.[41] For example, an unambiguous statute which appears to have been broadly drafted in order to ensure against

loopholes through which some offenders could regularly escape may be narrowed, for enforcement purposes, to exclude those persons not the object of real concern by the legislature.[42] Similarly, other penal statutes are not enforced because they are viewed as obsolete [43] or because they are thought to be only "state-declared ideals" rather than definitions of conduct which is to be routinely subjected to penal sanction.[44]

One obvious characteristic of the substantive criminal law is that even the most carefully drafted statute cannot anticipate every situation which might arise under it. Each of the several crimes is defined to encompass a category of activity which may differ from case to case, and even the principles of justification and excuse [45] must be stated in general terms. No more can be expected, as "a legal system which seeks to cover everything by a special provision becomes cumbrous and unworkable." [46]

The substantive criminal law, read literally, may thus appear unduly harsh, and for this reason too discretion is exercised because of the special circumstances of the individual case. As one judge has observed, "If every policeman, every prosecutor, every court, and every post-sentence agency performed his or its responsibility in strict accordance with rules of law, precisely and narrowly laid

33. See H. Kalven & H. Zeisel, The American Jury chs. 15–27 (1966).

34. See D. Newman, Conviction chs. 9–12, 14 (1966).

35. See R. Dawson, Sentencing ch. 3 (1969).

36. See id. at chs. 6–8.

37. See id. at ch. 11.

38. See Lavinsky, Executive Clemency: Study of a Decisional Problem Arising in the Terminal Stages of the Criminal Process, 42 Chi-Kent L.Rev. 13 (1965).

39. Wechsler, The Challenge of a Model Penal Code, 65 Harv.L.Rev. 1097, 1101 (1952); Remington & Rosenblum, The Criminal Law and the Legislative Process, 1960 U.Ill. L.F. 481, 483–87.

40. "No lawmaker has been able to foresee more than the broad outlines of the clash of interest or more than the main lines of the courses of conduct to which the law even of his own time must be applied." R. Pound, Criminal Justice in America 40 (1945).

41. On the latter, see, § 2.2.

42. Remington & Rosenblum, The Criminal Law and the Legislative Process, 1960 U.Ill.L.F. 481, 490–91.

43. Again, this is an "administrative interpretation"; a legislative enactment does not become inoperative by nonuse or obsolescence, nor is it repealed by a lack of enforcement. District of Columbia v. John R. Thompson Co., 346 U.S. 100, 73 S.Ct. 1007, 97 L.Ed. 1480 (1953). See Bonfield, The Abrogation of Penal Statutes by Nonenforcement, 49 Iowa L.Rev. 389 (1964).

44. On the enactment of statutes for this purpose, see R. Pound, Criminal Justice in America 67 (1945). "Most unenforced criminal laws survive in order to satisfy moral objections to established modes of conduct. They are unenforced because we want to continue our conduct, and unrepealed because we want to preserve our morals." T. Arnold, The Symbols of Government 160 (1935).

45. See ch. 5.

46. R. Pound, Criminal Justice in America 40–41 (1945).

down, the criminal law would be ordered but intolerable." [47]

Finally, the very scope of the substantive criminal law, as compared to the resources which have been allocated for its enforcement, dictate some selectivity in enforcement. Because state and local legislative bodies have not provided nearly enough funds to permit enforcement of all the criminal laws against all offenders, the boundaries of criminal law enforcement are determined more by the size of the appropriations made than by the definitions found in the substantive criminal law.[48] Precisely what crimes deserve priority under these circumstances is a matter on which there is not agreement, although it has been suggested that the maximum sentence authorized for the various offenses might be some guide.[49]

 WESTLAW REFERENCES

synopsis,digest(prosecutor*** (state district prosecuting +1 attorney) /6 discretion*** /s not +2 prosecute*)

(d) Use of Part of the Criminal Process. Brief mention should also be made of the fact that often certain informal accommodations are resorted to whereby those who have violated the substantive criminal law are subjected to only a part of what is usually viewed as the complete criminal process. These accommodations are resorted to because it is thought that desired objectives may be best

accomplished thereby, that subjecting the offender to the total process would be unduly costly in view of the minimal additional benefits to be expected, or that use of the total process is not possible even if desirable because of limited personnel and facilities. Here as well, then, the scope and coverage of the substantive criminal law has had an effect.

As we shall see later, there are constitutional limits on the power of legislatures to declare conduct criminal.[50] For example, the Supreme Court has held that narcotics addiction may not be made a crime.[51] But even within such limitations, legislatures and courts have made criminal certain conduct which those who administer our systems for criminal justice often believe cannot be effectively dealt with by the usual process of arrest, prosecution, conviction, and sentence. Illustrative is the offense of public drunkenness. Because of a belief that nothing is to be gained by convicting the drunk and imposing a fine or jail sentence on him, it is common practice for drunks to be arrested for their own safety and then released when they are sober.[52] Given this practice, perhaps the continued existence of public drunkenness as a crime in some jurisdictions can best be explained as an instance in which conduct is declared criminal so that the criminal justice process may perform social services not otherwise available.[53]

47. Breitel, Controls in Criminal Law Enforcement, 27 U.Chi.L.Rev. 427 (1960).

48. The necessity of discretionary enforcement on this basis has frequently received recognition, e.g., R. Pound, Criminal Justice in America 19–20 (1930); Breitel, Controls in Criminal Law Enforcement, 27 U.Chi.L.Rev. 427, 431 (1960); Hall, Police and Law in a Democratic Society, 28 Ind.L.J. 133, 149–50 (1953).

49. Goldstein, Police Discretion Not to Invoke the Criminal Process: Low-Visibility Decisions in the Administration of Criminal Justice, 69 Yale L.J. 543, 568 (1960).

50. See §§ 2.10–2.15.

51. Robinson v. California, 370 U.S. 660, 82 S.Ct. 1417, 8 L.Ed.2d 758 (1962).

52. For a detailed description of the practice, see W. LaFave, Arrest ch. 21 (1965).

53. Thus, the American Law Institute's Model Penal Code Advisory Committee favored deleting the section on

public drunkenness "so as to preclude the handling of non-disorderly drunks through the usual facilities of law enforcement, i.e., police station and jail, and to require that such persons be taken to their homes or to hospitals, where drunkenness can be differentiated from epileptic attacks or other pathological conditions," but a majority of the Council favored retaining the provision. By way of justification, it was stated: "In most cases, the drunk will have been guilty of some other category of disorderly conduct, but it seems necessary to provide a basis for police action for those who, for example, are in a drunken stupor but not otherwise making a nuisance of themselves." Model Penal Code § 250.11, Comment (Tent. Draft No. 13, 1961).

On the consequences of overloading the criminal justice system by using it as a device for the administration of social services, see Allen, The Borderland of the Criminal Law: Problems of "Socializing" Criminal Justice, 32 Social Serv.Rev. 107 (1958).

Another illustration of the use of less than the total criminal process is what is commonly referred to as the negotiated plea of guilty. Very few criminal cases result in a trial; about 90 per cent are disposed of by a plea of guilty, and a good many of these pleas are obtained in exchange for a promise by the prosecutor to seek some concessions for the defendant.[54] The offender may be permitted to plead guilty to an offense less serious than the one he actually committed; he may plead guilty to one of the offenses he has committed in exchange for the prosecutor's promise to drop or not bring other charges; or he may plead guilty in exchange for the prosecutor's promise to recommend a light sentence. Suffice it to note here that one of the explanations for this practice is the state of the substantive criminal law. Thus, when an offense carries a high mandatory minimum sentence, the trial judge may feel that by "accepting lesser pleas . . . [there may result] a finer adjustment to the particular crime and offender than the straight application of the rules of law would permit." [55]

 **WESTLAW**
REFERENCES

narcotic drug /3 addiction /s crim**** /p
   constitutional*** unconstitutional
plead*** /5 guilty /s less** /5 serious!

---

§ 1.5 Purposes of the Criminal Law— Theories of Punishment

The broad purposes of the criminal law are, of course, to make people do what society regards as desirable and to prevent them from doing what society considers to be undesirable. Since criminal law is framed in terms of imposing punishment for bad conduct, rather than of granting rewards for good conduct, the emphasis is more on the prevention of the undesirable than on the encouragement of the desirable.[1]

In determining what undesirable conduct should be punished, the criminal law properly aims more to achieve a minimum standard of conduct than to bring about ideal conduct (say, the conduct of a highly-principled, selfless, heroic person). It is a fine thing for a man, at the risk of his own life, to enter a blazing building in order to rescue a stranger trapped therein; but the law does not (and should not) punish a failure to live up to such a heroic standard of behavior. It is a virtuous thing for an engaged man and woman to refrain from engaging in sexual intercourse until they are married; but it does not follow that the law should punish a failure to adhere to such a highly moral standard of conduct.

The protections afforded by the criminal law to the various interests of society against harm generally form the basis for a classification of crimes in any criminal code: protection from physical harm to the person;[2] protection of property from loss, destruction or damage;[3] protection of reputation from injury;[4] safeguards against sexual immorality;[5] protection of the government from injury or destruction;[6] protection against interference with the administration of justice;[7] protec-

---

54. For a detailed discussion of the practice, see D. Newman, Conviction: The Determination of Guilt or Innocence Without Trial (1966).

55. Breitel, Controls in Criminal Law Enforcement, 27 U.Chi.L.Rev. 427, 432 (1960). See Ohlin and Remington, Sentencing Structure: Its Effects Upon Systems for the Administration of Criminal Justice, 23 Law and Contemp. Prob. 495, 503–07 (1958).

§ 1.5

1. To the limited extent that the law imposes criminal liability for omission to act, see § 3.3, criminal law does encourage good conduct.

2. Thus the crimes of murder, manslaughter, assault, battery, mayhem and kidnapping aim to safeguard this interest.

3. E.g., the crimes of larceny, embezzlement, false pretenses, burglary, robbery, bad checks, blackmail, extortion, receiving stolen property, arson, forgery, malicious destruction of property.

4. E.g., the crime of libel, which, however, originally at least, was also made criminal in order to protect against breaches of the peace, much as larceny was originally considered a crime to prevent breaches of the peace.

5. E.g., the crimes of rape, bigamy, adultery, fornication, sodomy, incest, obscenity.

6. E.g., treason, sedition, sabotage, bribery of government officials.

7. E.g., perjury; bribery of witnesses, judges and jurors.

tion of the public health;[8] protection of the public peace and order;[9] and the protection of other interests.[10]

The criminal law is not, of course, the only weapon which society uses to prevent conduct which harms or threatens to harm these important interests of the public. Education, at home and at school, as to the types of conduct that society thinks good and bad, is an important weapon; religion, with its emphasis on distinguishing between good and evil conduct, is another. The human desire to acquire and keep the affection and respect of family, friends and associates no doubt has a great influence in deterring most people from conduct which is socially unacceptable. The civil side of the law, which forces one to pay damages for the harmful results which his undesirable conduct has caused to others, or which in appropriate situations grants injunctions against bad conduct or orders the specific performance of good conduct, also plays a part in influencing behavior along desirable lines.

(a) **Theories of Punishment**. How does the criminal law, with its threat of punishment to violators, operate to influence human conduct away from the undesirable and toward the desirable? There are a number of theories of punishment, and each theory has or has had its enthusiastic adherents. Some of the theories are concerned primarily with the particular offender, while others focus

more on the nature of the offense and the general public. These theories are:

(1) Prevention. By this theory, also called *intimidation,* or, when the deterrence theory is referred to as general deterrence, *particular deterrence,* [11] criminal punishment aims to deter the criminal himself (rather than to deter others) from committing further crimes, by giving him an unpleasant experience he will not want to endure again. The validity of this theory has been questioned by many, who point out the high recidivism rates of those who have been punished.[12] On the other hand, it has been observed that our attempts at prevention by punishment may enjoy an unmeasurable degree of success, in that without punishment for purposes of prevention the rate of recidivism might be much higher.[13] This assumption is not capable of precise proof,[14] nor is the assertion that in some instances punishment for prevention will fill the prisoner with feelings of hatred and desire for revenge against society and thus influence future criminal conduct.

(2) Restraint. The notion here, also expressed as *incapacitation, isolation,* or *disablement,*[15] is that society may protect itself from persons deemed dangerous because of their past criminal conduct [16] by isolating these persons from society. If the criminal is imprisoned or executed, he cannot commit

8. E.g., stream pollution laws, food and drug laws, narcotics and liquor laws.

9. E.g., public drunkenness, disorderly conduct.

10. E.g., the crimes of gambling, cruelty to animals, bribery of athletes, and many others.

Sometimes a crime may threaten harm to two social interests, a situation that gives rise to some difficulty in the classification of crimes. Thus robbery is a crime both against property and against the person; arson is a property crime which also involves the danger of death or injury to the person; forcible rape is a crime both against sexual morality and against the person.

11. See J. Andenaes, Punishment and Deterrence (1974); F. Zimring & G. Hawkins, Deterrence 224–48 (1973); F. Zimring, Perspectives on Deterrence 97–107 (1971).

12. E.g., L. Hall & S. Glueck, Criminal Law and Its Enforcement 17 (2d ed. 1958).

13. Andenaes, General Prevention—Illusion or Reality?, 43 J.Crim.L.C. & P.S. 176, 181 (1952). Also, the rate of recidivism is not as high as is frequently presumed. D.

Glaser, The Effectiveness of a Prison and Parole System ch. 2 (1964).

14. "Taken as a whole, studies of recidivism estimate that those subjected to punishment for major crimes commit many more crimes after their release than other groups in the population, but fewer perhaps than they would if they had not been caught." F. Zimring, Perspectives on Deterrence 106 (1971).

15. See M. Ancel, Social Defense: A Modern Guide to Criminal Problems (1965); A. von Hirsch, Doing Justice ch. 3 (1976); National Counsel on Crime and Delinquency, Guides to Sentencing the Dangerous Offender (1969); Contemporary Punishment ch. 4 (R. Gerber & P. McAnany eds. 1972); Cohen, The Incapacitative Effect of Imprisonment: A Critical Review of the Literature, in Deterrence and Incapacitation: Estimating the Effects of Criminal Sanctions on Crime Rates 187 (A. Blumstein, J. Cohen & D. Nagin eds. 1978), and articles cited therein.

16. Indeed, under this theory it has even been argued that "society has a right to isolate, not only an actual criminal, but also, anyone who can be conclusively shown

further crimes against society.[17] Some question this theory because of doubts that those who present a danger of continuing criminality can be accurately identified.[18] It has also been noted that resort to restraint without accompanying rehabilitative efforts is unwise, as the vast majority of prisoners will ultimately be returned to society.[19] The restraint theory is sometimes employed to justify execution or life imprisonment without chance of parole for those offenders believed to be beyond rehabilitation.

(3) Rehabilitation. Under this theory, also called *correction* or *reformation,* we "punish" the convicted criminal by giving him appropriate treatment, in order to rehabilitate him and return him to society so reformed that he will not desire or need to commit further crimes. It is perhaps not entirely correct to call this treatment "punishment," as the emphasis is away from making him suffer and in the direction of making his life better and more pleasant. The rehabilitation theory rests upon the belief that human behavior is the product of antecedent causes, that these causes can be identified, and that on this basis therapeutic measures can be employed to effect changes in the behavior of the person treated. There has been more of a commit-

ment to the "rehabilitative ideal"[20] in recent years than to other theories of punishment. Yet, much of what is done by way of post-conviction disposition of offenders[21] is not truly rehabilitative, which is perhaps why the theory of reformation has not as yet shown very satisfactory results in practice.[22]

Some have questioned the rehabilitation theory on the ground that "it sees rule-breakers as lacking in dignity, and capable of manipulation."[23] Others have expressed skepticism about reliance upon this theory in practice on "two distinct but related grounds: first, the great uncertainty, indeed ignorance, that presently attends our efforts to reform offenders; second, the injustices, greatly increased by our uncertainty and ignorance, that may be done to offenders who are treated differently because of assumed differences in the needs to which their penal treatment is supposed to respond."[24]

(4) Deterrence. Under this theory, sometimes referred to as *general prevention,*[25] the sufferings of the criminal for the crime he has committed are supposed to deter others from committing future crimes, lest they suffer the same unfortunate fate.[26] The extent to which punishment actually has this effect upon the

to be a potential criminal." Wood, Responsibility and Punishment, 28 J.Crim.L. & Crim. 630, 639 (1938).

17. But "only execution incapacitates absolutely. All manner of crimes against persons occur in prisons, and few crimes against property are literally impossible in prison; so incapacitation is largely a matter of degree." J. Gibbs, Crime, Punishment and Deterrence 58 (1975).

18. A. von Hirsch, Doing Justice 21 (1976), concludes that "the ability to predict dangerousness has not lived up to such hopes. One reason for error has been that predicters—be they judges, psychiatrists, or correctional officials—seldom have taken the trouble to follow up their forecasts and check their accuracy, and thus learn from their mistakes. But even were forecasts verified systematically, that still would not yield the 'reasonable accuracy' of which the Model Sentencing Act speaks so optimistically. For a more fundamental problem is encountered: an inherent tendency to overpredict." On overprediction, see id. at 20–26.

19. L. Hall & S. Glueck, Criminal Law and Its Enforcement 17 (2d ed. 1958).

20. See Allen, Legal Values and the Rehabilitative Ideal, 50 J.Crim.L.C. & P.S. 226 (1959).

21. Including much done in the name of rehabilitation. Ibid.

22. L. Hall & S. Glueck, Criminal Law and Its Enforcement 18 (2d ed. 1958).

23. P. Bean, Punishment 194 (1981).

24. Packer, The Practical Limits of Deterrence, in Contemporary Punishment 102, 105 (R. Gerber & P. McAnany eds. 1972).

25. See J. Andenaes, Punishment and Deterrence (1974); P. Bean, Punishment 29–44 (1981); A. von Hirsch, Doing Justice ch. 5 (1976); F. Zimring & G. Hawkins, Deterrence 92–224 (1973); F. Zimring, Perspectives on Deterrence 32–97 (1971); Contemporary Punishment ch. 3 (R. Gerber & P. McAnany eds. 1972); Nagin, General Deterrence: A Review of the Empirical Evidence, in Deterrence and Incapacitation: Estimating the Effects of Criminal Sanctions on Crime Rates 95 (A. Blumstein, J. Cohen & D. Nagin eds. 1978); Walker, The Efficacy and Morality of Deterrents, 1975 Crim.L.Rev. 129.

26. "The theory of simple deterrence is that threats can reduce crime by causing a change of heart, induced by the unpleasantness of the specific consequences threatened. Many individuals who are tempted by a particular form of threatened behavior will, according to this construct, refrain from committing the offense because the pleasure they might obtain is more than offset by the risk of great unpleasantness communicated by a legal threat." F. Zimring, Perspectives on Deterrence 3 (1971). Of

general public is unclear; conclusive empirical research on the subject is lacking,[27] and it is difficult to measure the effectiveness of fear of punishment because it is but one of several forces that restrain people from violating the law.[28]

It does seem fair to assume, however, that the deterrent efficacy of punishment varies considerably, depending upon a number of factors. Those who commit crimes under emotional stress (such as murder in the heat of anger) or who have become expert criminals through the training and practice of many years (such as the professional safebreaker and pickpocket) are less likely than others to be deterred.[29] Even apart from the nature of the crime, individuals undoubtedly react differently to the threat of punishment, depending upon such factors as their social class, age, intelligence, and moral training.[30] The magnitude of the threatened pun-

ishment is clearly a factor, but perhaps not as important a consideration as the probability of discovery and punishment.[31]

(5) Education. Under this theory, criminal punishment serves, by the publicity which attends the trial, conviction and punishment of criminals, to educate the public as to the proper distinctions between good conduct and bad—distinctions which, when known, most of society will observe.[32] While the public may need no such education as to serious *malum in se* [33] crimes,[34] the educational function of punishment is important as to crimes which are not generally known, often misunderstood, or inconsistent with current morality.[35]

(6) Retribution. This is the oldest theory of punishment, and the one which still commands considerable respect from the general public. By this theory, also called *revenge* or *retaliation*,[36] punishment (the infliction of suf-

course, the "punishment is not itself the threat but a consequence of failure of the threat. Only when the threat has failed in a particular case do we apply punishment. When we do so, we say that in order to keep the threat credible we must punish those who break the law." Contemporary Punishment 93 (R. Gerber & P. McAnany eds. 1972).

27. J. Andenaes, Punishment and Deterrence 9 (1974). "The disagreement over the importance of general prevention is of course largely due to the fact that its effectiveness cannot be measured." For assessments of research on deterrence, see F. Zimring, Perspectives on Deterrence (1971); Deterrence and Incapacitation: Estimating the Effects of Criminal Sanctions on Crime Rates (A. Blumstein, J. Cohen & D. Nagin eds. 1978).

A particular area of dispute has been the significance of various studies on whether the death penalty deters. See Lempert, Desert and Deterrence: An Assessment of the Moral Bases of the Case for Capital Punishment, 79 Mich. L.Rev. 1177, 1196–1224 (1981), and sources cited therein.

28. As noted in P. Bean, Punishment 29 (1981), "it is a theory that has fostered and encouraged empirical inquiry—not with a great deal of success, I would add, for it is rarely possible to control the variables to complete a refined study."

29. J. Andenaes, Punishment and Deterrence 45–46 (1974), concludes that generally the deterrence function is more important as to malum prohibitum offenses.

30. J. Andenaes, Punishment and Deterrence 10 (1974): "Psychological attitudes vary markedly in the different categories of law-breaking, and they can also vary markedly in different groups and strata of the society."

31. Thus, it has been claimed that the deterrence theory has never been given a fair chance, in that we have mistakenly reacted to past failures by increasing the pen-

alties rather than increasing the certainty of punishment. E. Puttkammer, Administration of Criminal Law 16–17 (1953).

32. F. Zimring, Perspectives on Deterrence 4–5 (1971), notes that punishment may be viewed as "a teacher of right and wrong": "The association of forbidden behavior with bad consequences may lead individuals to view the behavior itself as bad. * * * Along a somewhat different tack, the threat and example of punishment by a legal system will communicate to the individual that the legal system views the threatened behavior as wrong, and this information will also affect the moral attitudes of the individual. * * * Finally, threat and punishment may aid moral education by serving as an attention-getting mechanism. The threat of punishment for stealing forces the individual to think about the moral quality of the act of stealing. Such reflections may lead to the conclusion that stealing is wrong because it causes other people to suffer and undermines the security of a system of private property."

33. See § 1.6(b).

34. But, it may sometimes appear that there is a need for public education on the principles of justification and excuse relating to serious crimes, as where the limits on the right to use force in the protection of property are not understood. See Regina v. McKay, [1957] Vict.L.R. 560.

35. H. Oppenheimer, The Rationale of Punishment 293–94 (1913).

36. See P. Bean, Punishment 12–29 (1981); T. Honderich, Punishment: The Supposed Justifications 1–39, 132–33 (1969); W. Moberly, The Ethics of Punishment (1968); A. Ross, On Guilt, Responsibility and Punishment (1975); A. von Hirsch, Doing Justice ch. 6 (1976); Assessing the Criminal (R. Barnett & J. Hagel eds. 1977); Contemporary Punishment ch. 2 (R. Gerber & P. McAnany eds. 1972); Gardner, The Renaissance of Retribution—An Examina-

fering) is imposed by society on criminals in order to obtain revenge, or perhaps (under the less emotional concept of retribution) because it is only fitting and just that one who has caused harm to others should himself suffer for it. Typical of the criticism is that this theory "is a form of retaliation, and as such, is morally indefensible." [37]

However, the retribution theory, when explained on somewhat different grounds, continues to draw some support. Some contend that when one commits a crime, it is important that he receive commensurate punishment in order to restore the peace of mind and repress the criminal tendencies of others.[38] In addition, it is claimed that retributive punishment is needed to maintain respect for the law and to suppress acts of private vengeance.[39] For this reason, even some critics of the retribution theory acknowledge that it must occupy a "minor position" in the contemporary scheme.[40]

Although retribution was long the theory of punishment least accepted by theorists, it "is suddenly being seen by thinkers of all political persuasions as perhaps the strongest ground, after all, upon which to base a system of punishment." [41] Today it is commonly put forward under the rubric of "deserts" or "just deserts" [42]:

> The offender may justly be subjected to certain deprivations because he deserves it; and he deserves it because he has engaged in wrongful conduct—conduct that does or threatens injury and that is prohibited by law. The penalty is thus not just a means of crime prevention but a merited response to the actor's deed, "rectifying the balance" in the Kantian sense and expressing moral reprobation of the actor for the wrong.[43]

Those who favor the theory claim it "provides an important check against tyranny, for a person is punished only when he deserves it; and the opposite is also true—that he is not punished if he does not deserve it." [44] They

tion of Doing Justice, 1976 Wis.L.Rev. 781; Mabbott, Punishment, 48 Mind 152 (1939).

37. Wood, Responsibility and Punishment, 28 J.Crim.L. & Crim. 630, 636 (1938).

38. "Similarly, retaliation can be regarded as a form of emotional compensation for both the victim and the general public. The satisfaction of resentment would operate directly to restore the balance of pleasure and pain in the lives of persons affected by the harm to a level closer to that obtaining prior to the offense, and also operate to make more tolerable the general distress felt as a result of the harm. * * * A final justification of a penalty structure which takes account of resulting harm can be based on the 'condemnatory' theory of punishment. This theory sees punishment as a symbolic statement that the conduct on which the punishment is based is strongly in conflict with societal norms. An important practical function of punishment, according to this view, is defining and preserving society's value system." Note, 78 Colum.L.Rev. 1249, 1257–59 (1978). See E. Puttkammer, Administration of Criminal Justice 9 (1953), for a criticism of this view.

39. J. Gibbs, Crime, Punishment and Deterrence 82–83 (1975); A. Goodhart, English Law and the Moral Law 92–93 (1953).

40. L. Hall & S. Glueck, Criminal Law and Its Enforcement 16 (2d ed. 1958).

41. Gardner, The Renaissance of Retribution—An Examination of Doing Justice, 1976 Wis.L.Rev. 781, 784.

42. N. Morris, The Future of Imprisonment 73–77 (1974); A. von Hirsch, Doing Justice 45–55 (1976); Hospers, Retribution: The Ethical Punishment, in Assessing the Criminal 181 (R. Barnett & J. Hagel eds. 1977).

A somewhat different characterization is the so-called restitutionary theory of justice. "Under a restitutionary theory of justice, the dominant concern of any criminal proceeding should be the fact that some person or persons have violated the rights, properly defined, of another. The settlement of this dispute using principles of justice may not achieve any independent social goals, but it will vindicate the rights of the aggrieved party and thereby vindicate the rights of all persons." Assessing the Criminal 25 (R. Barnett & J. Hagel eds. 1977).

43. A. von Hirsch, Doing Justice 51 (1976). It "is likely to include two principle assertions. First, the primary object of criminal sanctions is to punish culpable behavior. Although punishment may result in certain utilitarian benefits, notably the reduction of criminal behavior, the justification of punishment does not require such a showing; for it is moral and just that culpable behavior be punished. Second, the severity of the sanctions visited on the offender should be proportioned to the degree of his culpability." F. Allen, The Decline of the Rehabilitative Ideal 66 (1981).

44. P. Bean, Punishment 19 (1981). Compare Kaufman, Retribution and the Ethics of Punishment, in Assessing the Criminal 211, 227 (R. Barnett & J. Hagel eds. 1977): "My thesis that punishments can never be deserved also means that the notion of desert is a confused notion and that on closer examination we find that desert cannot be calculated."

Likewise, it is said that it ensures that punishment will be proportional. A. von Hirsch, Doing Justice 66 (1976). Compare Gardner, The Renaissance of Retribution—An Examination of Doing Justice, 1976 Wis.L.Rev. 781, 790: "But because desert establishes only rough boundaries of proportionality between offense and punishment, there is

are also likely to reject utilitarian approaches to punishment because of the view that punishment may not be inflicted upon a person in order to benefit the collective interests of others.[45]

WESTLAW REFERENCES

theory /2 punishment /s prevent! restraint rehabilitat*** deterren** retributi**

(b) Conflict Between the Theories. For many years most of the literature on the subject of punishment was devoted to advocacy of a particular theory to the exclusion of others. Those who espoused the rehabilitation theory condemned the rest, those who favored the deterrence theory denied the validity of all others, and so on. But in recent years the "inclusive theory of punishment" [46] has gained considerable support; there is now general agreement that all (or, at least most) of the theories described above deserve some consideration.[47]

This has given rise to another difficult problem, namely, what the priority and relationship of these several aims should be.[48] This problem must be confronted, as it is readily apparent that the various theories tend to

conflict with one another at several points.[49] The retribution, deterrence, and prevention theories call for presenting the criminal with an unpleasant experience; but the chances for rehabilitation are often defeated by harsh treatment. The rehabilitation theory would let the criminal go when (and perhaps *only* when [50]) he had been reformed. This may be a substantially shorter period of time (or a substantially *longer* period of time [51]) than can be justified under the deterrence and retribution theories, which would vary the punishment in accordance with the seriousness of the crime. Because of such conflicts, the legislators who enact the punishment clauses (generally with minimum and maximum provisions) for the various crimes, the judges (or, in some states as to some crimes, the juries) who must sentence the convicted defendant within the limits set forth in legislation, and the administrative officials (parole and pardoning authorities) who are empowered to release convicted criminals from imprisonment, must determine priorities.[52]

It is undoubtedly true that the thinking of legislators, judges and juries, and administrative officers who have a part in fixing punishment, as well as the thinking of the expert

---

no reason in principle why it cannot serve as a rationalization for those legislators and others who seek to impose capital punishment for the most serious offenses and long presumptive sentences for less serious crimes."

45. A. von Hirsch, Doing Justice 50 (1976): "Our difficulty is, however, that we doubt the utilitarian premises: that the suffering of a few persons is made good by the benefits accruing to the many. A free society, we believe, should recognize that an individual's rights—or at least his most important rights—are prima facie entitled to priority over collective interests."

That argument is rejected by Frankel, J., in United States v. Bergman, 416 F.Supp. 496 (S.D.N.Y.1976): "Each of us is served by the enforcement of the law * * *. More broadly, we are driven regularly in our ultimate interests as members of the community to use ourselves and each other, in war and peace, for social ends. One who has transgressed against the criminal laws is certainly among the more fitting candidates for a role of this nature. This is no arbitrary selection. Warned in advance of the prospect, the transgressor has chosen, in the law's premises, 'between keeping the law required for society's protection or paying the penalty.'"

46. J. Hall, General Principles of Criminal Law 308 (2d ed. 1960).

47. See L. Radzinowicz, Ideology and Crime 113–27 (1966); Contemporary Punishment ch. 6 (R. Gerber & P.

McAnany eds. 1972); Feinberg, Punishment, in Philosophy of Law 502 (J. Feinberg & H. Gross eds. 1975).

48. See Hart, The Aims of the Criminal Law, 23 Law & Contemp.Prob. 401 (1958).

49. See P. Bean, Punishment 44–46 (1981).

50. Unless we limit the rehabilitation theory by borrowing and changing somewhat the retribution theory notion that the punishment should fit the crime, and thus bar continued incarceration for purposes of rehabilitation after the criminal has served time commensurate with his crime. See Brandt, The Conditions of Criminal Responsibility, in Responsibility 106 (C. Friedrich ed. 1960).

51. "Surprisingly enough, the rehabilitative ideal has often led to increased severity of penal measures." F. Allen, The Borderland of Criminal Justice 34 (1964). "Rehabilitation can be weak and gentle, involving nothing more than a discussion with a friendly social worker, or it can be as strong and tough as the imposition of indeterminate sentences for relatively minor offences. It can also include aversive conditioning, chimotherapy and psychosurgery." P. Bean, Punishment 58 (1981).

52. Criminal codes rarely contain anything by way of an indication of the priorities to be followed. No statement of priorities was included in the Model Penal Code because of the view that these priorities would vary depending upon the particular context or situation. Model Penal Code § 1.02, Comment at 22 (1985).

criminologist and non-expert layman whose views tend to influence those officials, varies from situation to situation.[53] Sometimes the retribution theory will predominate; most of us share the common feeling of mankind that a particularly shocking crime should be severely punished. Where, for example, a son, after thoughtfully taking out insurance on his mother's life, places a time bomb in her suitcase just before she boards a plane, which device succeeds in killing the mother and all forty–two others aboard the plane, we almost all feel that he deserves a severe punishment, and we reach this result with little reflection about influencing future conduct. Likewise, when a less serious crime is involved and it was committed by a young person who might be effectively reformed, the rehabilitation theory rightly assumes primary importance. And the deterrence theory may be most important when the crime is not inherently wrong or covered by moral prohibition.[54] Illustrative are income tax violations, as to which deterrence is especially important because of our reliance on a system of self-assessment.[55]

Although allowance must be made for such variables, it is fair to say, as a general proposition, that for much of the present century the pendulum has been swinging away from retribution and deterrence and in the direction of rehabilitation as the chief goal of punishment; or, to put it differently, away from the philosophy that the punishment should fit the crime toward one that the punishment

should fit the criminal.[56] The tendency has been to move away from backward-looking and negative theories to the positive goal of influencing future conduct along desirable lines.[57] In part, this may be attributed to the fact that we still know very little about the deterrent effect of punishment on potential offenders,[58] while we have gained increased knowledge of the causes of human conduct as the result of scientific study in such fields as psychology, psychiatry, and criminology.

This emphasis upon rehabilitation is reflected in our criminal justice system in several ways.[59]

> Perhaps the most tangible evidences of the dominance of the rehabilitative ideal are found in its legislative expressions. Almost all of the characteristic innovations in criminal justice in this century are reflections of the rehabilitative ideal: the juvenile court, the indeterminate sentence, systems of probation and parole, the youth authority, and the promise (if not the reality) of therapeutic programs in prisons, juvenile institutes, and mental hospitals. * * * [I]t is remarkable how widely the rehabilitative ideal was accepted in this century as a statement of aspirations for the penal system, a statement largely endorsed by the media, politicians, and ordinary citizens.[60]

But skepticism regarding the rehabilitative model began developing in the mid-1960's,[61] and about ten years later there came "an explosion of criticism * * * calling for restructuring of the theoretical underpinnings

---

53. Hall, Reduction of Criminal Sentences on Appeal, 37 Colum.L.Rev. 521, 528–56 (1937), concludes that the theory of revenge and retribution predominates with crimes against the person; the prevention theory with crimes against property; and the deterrence theory with crimes not involving the person or property.

54. Andenaes, The General Preventive Effects of Punishment, 114 U.Pa.L.Rev. 949, 957–58 (1966).

55. Sentencing the Income Tax Violator, 26 F.R.D. 264 (1961).

56. See Williams v. New York, 337 U.S. 241, 69 S.Ct. 1079, 93 L.Ed. 1337 (1949), where the Court, speaking of the theory underlying the presentence investigation, the indeterminate sentence and parole, said: "Retribution is no longer the dominant objective of the criminal law. Reformation and rehabilitation of offenders have become important goals of criminal jurisprudence." Compare the

Court's earlier statement: "The great end of punishment is not the expiation or atonement of the offence committed, but the prevention of future offences of the same kind." Hopt v. Utah, 110 U.S. 574, 4 S.Ct. 202, 28 L.Ed. 262 (1884).

57. Hart, The Aims of the Criminal Law, 23 Law & Contemp.Prob. 401, 409 (1958).

58. B. Wootton, Crime and the Criminal Law 97–103 (1963), arguing that for this reason we should concentrate on the offender himself.

59. See P. Bean, Punishment 155–69 (1981).

60. F. Allen, The Decline of the Rehabilitative Ideal 6 (1981).

61. Dershowitz, Background Paper, in Report of the Twentieth Century Fund Task Force on Criminal Sentencing, Fair and Certain Punishment 98 (1976).

of the criminal sanction." [62] This rejection of rehabilitation, usually in favor of a "just deserts" theory, was prompted by several considerations. One was the concern with the wide disparity in sentencing which resulted from giving judges broad sentencing discretion to act according to the perceived rehabilitative needs in the particular case.[63] The "just deserts" model was seen as necessary "to counter the capricious and irresponsible uses of state power." [64] The existing system was perceived by many as being arbitrary because rehabilitative efforts were often unsuccessful.[65] When confidence was "lost in the rehabilitative capacities of penal programs and in the ability of parole boards and correctional officers to determine when reformation has been achieved, the rehabilitationist rationale for treatment differentials no longer serves, and the differences are seen as irrational and indefensible." [66] Finally, the retribution or "just deserts" theory, precisely because it "operates from a consensus model of society where the community * * * is acting in the right" and "the criminal is act-

ing in the wrong," [67] had appeal because it seemed to reaffirm our moral values at a time when they were under frequent attack.[68]

This trend is reflected by "a spate of legislative proposals, enacted or advocated throughout the country, that attack the statutory expressions of the rehabilitative ideal. The objects of this attack are sentencing discretion, the indeterminate sentence, the parole function, the uses of probation in cases of serious criminality, and even allowances of 'good time' credit in the prisons." [69] If this trend continues, then an increasing number of jurisdictions will adopt sentencing schemes which place the greatest emphasis upon the nature of the crime which was committed and comparatively little upon the characteristics of the particular offender.[70]

§ 1.6　Classification of Crimes

Crimes are classified for various purposes, the principal classification being that which divides crimes into felonies and misdemeanors. Other classifications are: crimes which are *mala in se* versus crimes *mala prohibita* ;

62. Gardner, The Renaissance of Retribution—An Examination of Doing Justice, 1976 Wis.L.Rev. 781. See, e.g., N. Morris, The Future of Imprisonment (1974); E. van den Haag, Punishing Criminals (1975); A. von Hirsch, Doing Justice (1976); J. Wilson, Thinking About Crime (1975); American Friends Service Committee, Struggle for Justice (1971); Report of the Twentieth Century Fund Task Force on Criminal Sentencing, Fair and Certain Punishment (1976).

63. "The most obvious drawback of allowing wide-open discretion in the name of 'individualization' is the disparity it permits. Judges whose sentencing decisions are unchecked by general standards are free to decide similar cases differently. A striking illustration emerged in a recent conference of federal trial judges of the Second Circuit, comprising New York, Connecticut and Vermont. The facts of numerous cases were selected from the files, and each of the fifty judges present was asked to state what sentences he would have imposed. The results, in some instances, were striking discrepancies. In one case, a crime that drew a three-year sentence from one judge drew a twenty-year term and a $65,000 fine from another. These discrepancies could not be attributed to differences in the cases being decided, since each judge was deciding on the identical set of assumed facts. A. von Hirsch, Doing Justice 29 (1976).

64. F. Allen, The Decline of the Rehabilitative Ideal 67 (1981).

65. A. von Hirsch, Doing Justice 13 (1976), argues that rehabilitation advocates may no longer say it had not been given a fair chance, as "during recent decades—especially

in California—serious thought-out and well-financed experimental programs have been tried. The results have not been encouraging." See id. at 14–18; Dershowitz, Background Paper, in Report of the Twentieth Century Fund Task Force on Criminal Sentencing, Fair and Certain Punishment 98, 137–38 n. 23 (1976).

66. F. Allen, The Decline of the Rehabilitative Ideal 73 (1981).

67. P. Bean, Punishment 17 (1981).

68. F. Allen, The Decline of the Rehabilitative Ideal 67 (1981).

69. Id. at 8. See Rubin, New Sentencing Proposals and Laws in the 1970's, 43 Fed.Prob. 3 (June 1979); Skrivseth, Abolishing Parole: Assuring Fairness and Certainty in Sentencing, 7 Hofstra L.Rev. 281 (1979); Glick, Mandatory Sentencing: The Politics of the New Criminal Justice, 43 Fed.Prob. 3 (March 1979); Zalman, The Rise and Fall of the Indeterminate Sentence, 24 Wayne L.Rev. 857 (1978).

70. This is because "the retributive theory holds that 'the primary justification of punishment is always to be found in the fact that an offense has been committed which deserves punishment, not in any future advantage to be gained by its infliction.' Such a description will fit most if not all the various formulations of retribution, since it emphasizes the following common features: that punishment should primarily view the offender rather than the sanction; and above all, that the offender must suffer because he is responsible for his evildoing, i.e., he could have done otherwise but chose not to." Contemporary Punishment 39 (R. Gerber & P. McAnany eds. 1972).

infamous crimes versus crimes which are not infamous; crimes involving moral turpitude versus those which do not involve moral turpitude; major crimes versus petty crimes; and common law crimes versus statutory crimes. It is important as to each classification to consider: (1) What is the distinction between the one class of crime and the other? (2) What difference does it make whether a crime is classified one way or the other?

(a) Felony and Misdemeanor. The most important classification of crime in general use in the United States is that of felony and misdemeanor.[1] In this country the distinction is usually spelled out by statute or (far less frequently) by the constitution. In the modern codes, it is sometimes provided that a crime punishable by death or imprisonment in the state prison (or penitentiary) is a felony, and that any other crime (i.e., any crime punishable only by fine or by imprisonment in a local jail or both) is a misdemeanor. The practical effect of that dividing line is usually such that these statutes indirectly state what the statutes in almost all other jurisdictions expressly declare: that any crime punishable by death or imprisonment for more than one year (or, occasionally, for one year or more) is a felony and that any other crime is a misdemeanor. The typical provision, in whichever of these two forms it may be found, uses the word "punishable" or the phrase "which may

be punished." Under a test so worded it is the possible sentence, not the actual sentence imposed, which controls, by the great weight of authority.[2] There is some authority to the effect that the sentence actually imposed governs,[3] and even a third view that a crime punishable either by imprisonment in the penitentiary or by a fine is a misdemeanor even though the sentence is actually imprisonment in the penitentiary.[4]

Thus in the United States most criminal statutes defining specific crimes do not themselves label as felonies or misdemeanors the crimes which they describe, leaving the matter to be determined by reference to the punishment provided (according to the place or to the length of confinement). Some statutes defining crimes provide that whoever is guilty of certain described conduct shall be guilty of a felony (or shall be guilty of a misdemeanor), sometimes without setting forth any punishment. There is generally to be found, however, some catch-all statute which provides for the punishment to be awarded for crimes which the statutes designate as felonies or misdemeanors but which do not themselves set forth the punishment to be awarded.

What difference does it make whether a particular crime is labeled a felony or misdemeanor? It may be important to make the distinction for purposes either (1) of the substantive criminal law, or (2) of criminal proce-

---

§ 1.6

1. In England the criminal law gradually developed over the centuries in such a way as to create a three-fold classification: treason, felony and misdemeanor. It was there important to distinguish between treason and felony because of the old land law that the lands of a traitor were forfeited to the King, whereas the lands of a felon escheated to his overlord. After the abolition of forfeiture for crime there was little need to keep the distinction between felony and treason, although the three-fold classification is still kept. In the United States the property of a felon or traitor has never been forfeited, so that here there is no need to differentiate between treason and felony. Hence in America treason is considered merely a part of that subdivision of crime called felony; it is not a separate classification of crime.

2. United States v. Schutte, 610 F.2d 698 (10th Cir. 1979) (even though statute described issuance of false warehouse receipts as misdemeanor, it is a felony since offender is subject to possible term of imprisonment of up to 10 years); Rivett v. State, 578 P.2d 946 (Alaska 1978) (person convicted of assault with dangerous weapon is a

felon whether sentenced to more or less than one year of imprisonment); State v. Nagel, 98 Idaho 129, 559 P.2d 308 (1977) (where offense punishable by imprisonment in state penitentiary, offense is a felony even if penalty actually imposed is of a lesser degree).

3. United States v. Houston, 547 F.2d 104 (9th Cir. 1976) (state offense of which defendant convicted only a misdemeanor where defendant only sentenced to 3 months in county jail, though possible punishment up to 15 years, as by state law sentence actually imposed governs); People v. Russell, 22 Cal.App.3d 330, 99 Cal.Rptr. 277 (1971) (because actual sentence was to county jail, crime only a misdemeanor).

4. United States v. Latham, 385 F.Supp. 57 (E.D.Ill. 1974), affirmed 519 F.2d 1404 (7th Cir.1975) (by virtue of state law, offense of intimidation which allows for penalties of a fine, imprisonment in a penitentiary, or both fine and imprisonment is a misdemeanor); People v. McGreal, 4 Ill.App.3d 312, 278 N.E.2d 504 (1971) (presence of alternative to serving penalty of imprisonment in place other than penitentiary makes offense a misdemeanor).

dure, or (3) of legal matters entirely outside the field of criminal law.

So far as the substantive criminal law is concerned, there are a number of crimes whose elements are defined, or whose punishment is stated, with reference to felonies as distinguished from misdemeanors. Burglary is defined at common law as breaking and entering another's dwelling house at night with intent to commit a felony (a misdemeanor will not do) therein.[5] An accidental death in the commission or attempted commission of a felony may constitute murder under appropriate circumstances, but an accidental death resulting from the commission of or attempt to commit a misdemeanor generally can constitute no more than manslaughter.[6] There exists a common law crime of compounding a felony, which is committed by one who for a consideration agrees not to prosecute for, or agrees to keep quiet about, a felony (but not a misdemeanor) he knows has been committed.[7] At common law parties involved in felonies are divided into principals and accessories, from which fact various consequences followed, whereas with misdemeanors all parties are considered principals.[8] The

punishment clauses of criminal statutes are not infrequently worded in terms of felony or misdemeanor; thus a criminal conspiracy (or attempt) statute may provide for one punishment in the case of a conspiracy (or attempt) to commit a felony, and a lighter punishment where there is a conspiracy (or attempt) to commit a misdemeanor. In that part of the substantive criminal law dealing with justifiable homicide, the rule of justification is sometimes worded in terms of felony as distinguished from misdemeanor.[9] Thus it may under appropriate circumstances be justifiable homicide (i.e., no crime at all) intentionally to kill as a last resort in order to prevent the commission of a felony (but not to prevent the commission of a misdemeanor),[10] or in order to effect the lawful arrest of, or prevent the threatened escape of, a felon (but not a misdemeanant).[11]

In the area of criminal procedure, many of the procedural rules depend upon whether the crime in question is a felony or a misdemeanor. A court's jurisdiction over a crime often depends upon whether the crime is classified as a felony or a misdemeanor.[12] The law of arrest distinguishes between arrest for

5. See § 8.13. Many modern statutes have broadened the scope of burglary in various ways—sometimes even to the extent of making it burglary to break, etc., with intent to commit a misdemeanor therein. To the extent this has been done, it may not be necessary to classify the intended crime as felony or misdemeanor. Some states, however, have accomplished an expansion of burglary by creating new types of or degrees of burglary, e.g., first degree burglary if an intended felony, second degree if an intended misdemeanor; under such a statutory scheme it is important still to distinguish felonies from misdemeanors.

6. See §§ 7.5, 7.13.

7. See § 6.9(c). Some modern statutes have, however, expanded the scope of this crime to include compounding any crime, including a misdemeanor. There is also the related common law crime of misprison of felony, a crime committed by one who, knowing of the commission of a felony (but not a misdemeanor) and the identity of the felon, yet fails to disclose this knowledge to the proper authorities. The crime of misprison of felony may not exist today, at least in its common law form punishing simple non-disclosure.

8. See § 6.6. Many states have by statute abolished the distinction between principals and accessories; others have kept the distinction but have to some extent by statute altered the consequences.

9. See ch. 5. In a majority of states, there are statutes setting forth circumstances under which homicide is justi-

fiable or excusable. In some states these circumstances of justification and excuse are left to the common law. Other states set forth some circumstances of excuse or justification, leaving the other circumstances to be determined by the general principles of the common law.

10. The modern rule, however, tends to limit this privilege to kill to the prevention of some felonies but not all felonies—perhaps felonies which threaten death or serious bodily harm, e.g., murder, voluntary manslaughter, mayhem, robbery, forcible rape, kidnapping and burglary; or, in vaguer terminology felonies which are "forcible" or "atrocious." In addition it may be justifiable homicide to kill in the suppression of a dangerous riot, though the crime of rioting may amount only to a misdemeanor.

11. Once again, there is some modern tendency to limit the privilege to kill-to-arrest-or-to-prevent-escape to the more serious felonies or to the dangerous felonies.

12. There are courts of limited criminal jurisdiction, which may try only misdemeanors, or some specific misdemeanors, or crimes with penalties not exceeding a certain maximum; and courts of general criminal jurisdiction, with power to try any criminal case (or, perhaps any felony case). A court with jurisdiction only over misdemeanors has no power to try a person for a crime amounting to a felony. Conversely, a court with jurisdiction only over felonies cannot try a person on a misdemeanor charge, although such a court may convict of a lesser

a felony and for a misdemeanor.[13] In some jurisdictions, felonies must be prosecuted upon a grand jury indictment, whereas an information will do for a misdemeanor.[14] An accused felon must generally be present at his trial, though a misdemeanant may agree to be tried in his absence.[15] A witness, including a criminal defendant who testifies in his own behalf, may be impeached on the ground of former conviction of felony, but not of misdemeanor, in some jurisdictions.[16] Habitual criminal statutes normally provide for increased criminal punishment where the defendant has a record of prior convictions of felonies (but not of misdemeanors).[17] The rules relating to probation and parole may differ depending upon whether the defendant has been convicted of a felony or a misdemeanor.

Even outside the area of substantive or procedural criminal law the distinction between felony and misdemeanor is frequently important. One convicted of a felony is in some jurisdictions disqualified from holding public office.[18] He may lose his right to vote or serve on a jury; he may be prohibited from practicing as an attorney.[19] Conviction of felony is often made a ground for divorce.[20] These by-products of conviction of a felony do not generally apply to conviction of a misdemeanor.

The above examples demonstrate that the classification of crime into the two great subdivisions—felony and misdemeanor—is an important one both within and outside the field of criminal law.

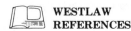 **WESTLAW REFERENCES**

disgest(felony misdemeanor /5 define* definition)

(b) Malum In Se and Malum Prohibitum. Crimes are divided for certain purposes into crimes *mala in se* (wrong in themselves; inherently evil) and crimes *mala prohibita* (not inherently evil; wrong only because prohibited by legislation).[21] The distinction, though an ancient one,[22] has survived down to the present time, especially in the area of criminal manslaughter and battery.

---

included misdemeanor on a felony charge. Pierce v. State, 96 Okl.Cr. 76, 248 P.2d 633 (1952).

13. Under the common law, arrest without an arrest warrant is permitted on "reasonable grounds to believe" that the person arrested committed a felony, Smith v. Hern, 102 Kan. 373, 170 P. 990 (1918), but a misdemeanor arrest without warrant is permissible only if the offense occurred in the officer's presence. State v. Merrifield, 180 Kan. 267, 303 P.2d 155 (1956). The early common law also required that the misdemeanor constitute a breach of the peace. 9 H. Halsbury, Laws of England, Criminal Law and Procedure § 117 (2d ed. 1933).

14. Several states also require indictment of serious misdemeanors. See 2 W. LaFave & J. Israel, Criminal Procedure § 15.1(b) (1984); Calkins, Abolition of the Grand Jury Indictment in Illinois, 1966 U.Ill.L.F. 423, 424 n. 6; Spain, The Grand Jury, Past and Present; A Survey, 2 Am.Crim.L.Q. 119 (1964).

15. This was the common law view, although many jurisdictions now permit a felony defendant in a noncapital case to waive his presence. See 3 W. LaFave & J. Israel, Criminal Procedure § 23.2(b) (1984).

16. C. McCormick, Evidence § 43 (E. Cleary 3d ed. 1984), pointing out that the legislation of the various states differs greatly. Some states allow impeachment for conviction of "infamous crimes"; others allow impeachment for "crimes involving moral turpitude"; others allow impeachment for "felony" crimes; still others allow impeachment for "any crime."

17. See Note, 60 Colum.L.Rev. 1134, 1157–58 (1960).

18. Some jurisdictions speak of conviction of "infamous crimes" or "crimes involving moral turpitude".

19. Once again, in some jurisdictions, the distinction is not between felony and misdemeanor; it may be between infamous crimes and non-infamous crimes, or between crimes involving moral turpitude and those which do not.

20. Here too in some jurisdictions the ground is worded in terms of conviction of an infamous crime or a crime involving moral turpitude.

21. A leading case defining these terms is State v. Horton, 139 N.C. 588, 51 S.E. 945 (1905): "An offense *malum in se* is properly defined as one which is naturally evil as adjudged by the sense of a civilized community, whereas an act *malum prohibitum* is wrong only because made so by statute."

22. 6 W. Holdsworth, History of English Law 218–19 (1927), mentions the use of this classification in a 1496 case dealing with the King's dispensing power (the power to give advance permission to disobey a criminal statute, to be distinguished from the King's power to pardon after the violation of criminal law). The case states that the King may use his dispensing power as to a crime *malum prohibitum* but not as to a crime *malum in se*. Y.B. 11 Henry VII, pl. 35, ff. 11, 12 (1496). The case classifies murder and fornication as *mala in se*; coining money and the violation of an embargo law as *mala prohibita*. The distinction may have originated even earlier in the area of ecclesiastical law: a priest who commits a wrong *malum in se* should be unfrocked; not so with a wrong only *malum prohibitum*.

Some difficulty has been encountered by the courts in putting particular crimes into one category or the other. Though courts tend to classify common law crimes as *mala in se* and statutory crimes as *mala prohibita,* such a test does not always work, for some statutory crimes have been held to be *mala in se.*[23] It has been said that a crime of which a criminal intent is an element is *malum in se,* but if no criminal intent is required, it is *malum prohibitum;*[24] and that generally a crime involving "moral turpitude" is *malum in se,* but otherwise it is *malum prohibitum.*[25] In a general way, it may be said that crimes which are dangerous to life or limb are likely to be classified as *mala in se,* while other crimes are more likely to be considered *mala prohibita.*[26]

Applying these various generalities to particular crimes, the courts have held these crimes to be *mala in se:* battery,[27] robbery,[28] grand or petit larceny,[29] malicious injury to property,[30] drunken driving (driving while intoxicated),[31] public drunkenness,[32] possession of drugs,[33] abortion,[34] and attempted suicide.[35] On the other hand, courts have held these crimes to be *mala prohibita:* driving over the speed limit,[36] failure to yield the right of way,[37] leaving the scene of an accident,[38] driving under the influence of intoxicants,[39] sale of intoxicating liquors,[40] public intoxication,[41]

---

23. See cases in the footnotes which follow. Perhaps common law crimes are necessarily *mala in se;* the judges who created these crimes thought them to be inherently evil and so undertook to punish them. Perhaps, though, the "sense of a civilized community" may change somewhat in the course of time, so that a court might find that conduct which constituted a common law crime is no longer *malum in se* although still prohibited by statute.

24. Compare State v. Smith, 17 Wn.App. 231, 562 P.2d 659 (1977) (delivery of narcotics is *malum in se,* but guilty intent shown notwithstanding professor's claim he acted to gain valuable research information to further his studies in Machiavellianism, as he failed to notify proper officials and profited from his sales); with Duncan v. Commonwealth, 289 Ky. 231, 158 S.W.2d 396 (1942) (sale of liquor to minor or to intoxicated adult or to habitual drunkard is *malum prohibitum,* so defendant's lack of bad intent is no defense). It hardly seems helpful to say that a crime which requires no bad intent is *malum prohibitum,* and that therefore no bad intent is required to commit the crime.

25. E.g., In re Pearce, 103 Utah 522, 136 P.2d 969 (1943) (conspiracy to maintain houses of prostitution is *malum in se,* and therefore is a crime involving "moral turpitude", so as to require disbarment of convicted attorney.) The trouble is that "moral turpitude" is just as vague an expression as "*malum in se*", so it helps very little to define one term by reference to the other.

26. R. Moreland, Law of Homicide 187 (1952), says that the early criminal law writers, Hale, Foster and East, used the terms in this way. In Dixon v. State, 104 Miss. 410, 61 So. 423 (1913), the court classified carrying a concealed weapon, public drunkenness and public shooting as *mala prohibita* because "not per se vicious or dangerous."

27. Gunter v. State, 499 S.W.2d 954 (Tenn.1973) (manslaughter case). Scuffling with a policeman to take his pistol, a battery, was held *malum in se* in Creel v. State, 186 Miss. 738, 191 So. 814 (1939) (manslaughter case).

28. Bell v. State, 394 So.2d 979 (Fla.1981); Gregory v. State, 259 Ind. 652, 291 N.E.2d 67 (1973).

29. United States ex rel. Chartrand v. Karnuth, 31 F.Supp. 799 (W.D.N.Y.1940) (deportation case); In re Henry, 15 Idaho 755, 99 P. 1054 (1909) (disbarment).

30. People v. Causley, 299 Mich. 340, 300 N.W. 111 (1941) (conspiracy case).

31. Baker v. State, 377 So.2d 17 (Fla.1979) (manslaughter); State v. Kellison, 233 Iowa 1274, 11 N.W.2d 371 (1943) (manslaughter); State v. Budge, 126 Me. 223, 137 A. 244 (1927) (manslaughter); King v. State, 157 Tenn. 635, 11 S.W.2d 904 (1928) (battery). Driving under the influence has been held to be *malum in se:* State v. Darchuck, 117 Mont. 15, 156 P.2d 173 (1945) (manslaughter); Grindstaff v. State, 214 Tenn. 58, 377 S.W.2d 921 (1964) (manslaughter); and, conversely, only *malum prohibitum:* State v. Budge, supra. Driving so as to endanger was said to be *malum in se* in District of Columbia v. Colts, 282 U.S. 63, 51 S.Ct. 52, 75 L.Ed. 177 (1930) (therefore not "petty offense" for purposes of trial by jury).

32. People v. Townsend, 214 Mich. 267, 183 N.W. 177 (1921) (manslaughter). Contra: Dixon v. State, 104 Miss. 410, 61 So. 423 (1913) (manslaughter).

33. Matter of Gorman, 269 Ind. 236, 379 N.E.2d 970 (1978). Contra: State v. Hartzog, 26 Wn.App. 576, 615 P.2d 480 (1980), affirmed in part, reversed in part on unrelated point 96 Wn.2d 383, 635 P.2d 694 (1981) (is *malum prohibitum*).

34. Peoples v. Commonwealth, 87 Ky. 487, 9 S.W. 509 (1888) (manslaughter).

35. Commonwealth v. Mink, 123 Mass. 422, 25 Am. Rep. 109 (1877) (manslaughter).

36. Commonwealth v. Adams, 114 Mass. 323, 19 Am. Rep. 362 (1873) (battery); Hurt v. State, 184 Tenn. 608, 201 S.W.2d 988 (1947) (manslaughter).

37. State v. Carty, 27 Wn.App. 715, 620 P.2d 137 (1980).

38. State v. Dyer, 289 A.2d 693 (Me.1972).

39. State v. Budge, 126 Me. 223, 137 A. 244 (1927) (manslaughter). Contra: Keller v. State, 155 Tenn. 633, 299 S.W. 803 (1927) (manslaughter).

40. United States v. Haynes, 81 F.Supp. 63 (W.D.Pa. 1948) (impeachment of witness); State v. Reitze, 86 N.J.L.

hunting without permission,[42] selling unregistered securities,[43] false notorization of a document,[44] carrying a concealed weapon,[45] shooting in a public place,[46] defacing the flag,[47] keeping slot machines,[48] and passing through a toll gate without paying the toll.[49]

It may be that the violation of a criminal statute can be considered *malum prohibitum* or *malum in se* depending upon the degree of the violation. Thus speeding a little over the limit may be *malum prohibitum*, but speeding at high speed *malum in se*. Or a violation of a statute prohibiting driving under the influence of liquor might be *malum prohibitum* if the defendant, though under the influence, was not actually intoxicated; but *malum in se* if intoxicated.[50]

What difference does it make whether a crime is classified as *malum prohibitum* or *malum in se?* In the field of substantive

criminal law, the principal use of the distinction is with respect to the crimes of manslaughter and battery.[51] One whose criminal conduct *malum in se* causes unintended death (or injury) may be guilty of manslaughter (or battery) without regard to the unlikelihood of that result; but if his conduct is only *malum prohibitum,* he is generally not as readily liable for manslaughter (or battery)—the principal view being that he is liable only if death (or injury) is the foreseeable consequence of his criminal act.[52] Courts which are faced with the statutory interpretation problem of whether a particular crime may be committed without any sort of bad intent sometimes utilize the distinction by stating that the crime is *malum in se* and so needs a bad intent, or is *malum prohibitum* and so does not.[53] The distinction also is sometimes used in criminal (or civil) procedure, as under a rule of evidence that a witness may be impeached on

---

407, 92 A. 576 (1914) (manslaughter); Ross-Lewin v. Johnson, 39 N.Y.Sup.Ct. 408 (1884) (civil action to recover purchase price of liquor); People v. Pavlic, 227 Mich. 562, 199 N.W. 373 (1924) (manslaughter).

41. Dixon v. State, 104 Miss. 410, 61 So. 423 (1913) (manslaughter). But see People v. Townsend, 214 Mich. 267, 183 N.W. 177 (1921) (voluntary intoxication is *malum in se* and has been so ever since the time of Noah).

42. State v. Horton, 139 N.C. 588, 51 S.E. 945 (1905) (manslaughter).

43. Hentzner v. State, 613 P.2d 821 (Alaska 1980).

44. Johnson v. State, 251 Ind. 17, 238 N.E.2d 651 (1968).

45. Potter v. State, 162 Ind. 213, 70 N.E. 129 (1904) (manslaughter); Dixon v. State, 104 Miss. 410, 61 So. 423 (1913) (manslaughter).

46. Dixon v. State, 104 Miss. 410, 61 So. 423 (1913) (manslaughter); Sparks v. Commonwealth, 66 Ky. 111 (1868) (manslaughter).

47. State v. Waterman, 190 N.W.2d 809 (Iowa 1971).

48. People v. Boxer, 24 N.Y.S.2d 628 (Sp.Sess.1940) (issue was whether bad intent an element of the crime).

49. Estell v. State, 51 N.J.L. 182, 17 A. 118 (1889) (manslaughter).

50. There is a suggestion of this idea in some cases: Silver v. State, 13 Ga.App. 722, 79 S.E. 919 (1913) (manslaughter case; *D* gave *V* morphine not on doctor's orders in violation of law, and *V* died; a small dose is *malum prohibitum;* a large dose may result in manslaughter liability); Thiede v. State, 106 Neb. 48, 182 N.W. 570 (1921) (manslaughter case; *D* gave *V* intoxicating liquor in violation of law, and *V* died; giving ordinary drink of liquor is *malum prohibitum*, but giving an extremely potent or a poisonous drink of liquor may result in manslaughter liability). In these two cases, however, the

courts did not actually label the larger violation *malum in se.*

51. It may be that the distinction between crimes *mala prohibita* and crimes *mala in se* has importance in the field of murder, too. As we shall see in § 7.5, an unintended killing in the commission of a felony may be murder; but there are generally some limits to murder liability. One such limit may be: for the rule to apply, the felony must be *malum in se*, not *malum prohibitum.* People v. Pavlic, 227 Mich. 562, 199 N.W. 373 (1924), a manslaughter case, suggests that this may be so for murder.

52. See § 7.13 (manslaughter), and § 7.15 (battery), for the various ways courts have treated manslaughter and battery liability for fatal or injurious results of criminal conduct *malum in se* or *malum prohibitum.*

53. Hentzner v. State, 613 P.2d 821 (Alaska 1980); State v. Smith, 17 Wn.App. 231, 562 P.2d 659 (1977). It hardly seems helpful, however, for a court to designate the crime at issue as *malum in se* or *malum prohibitum* in order to decide whether that crime requires a bad intent or not.

Perkins, The Civil Offense, 100 U.Pa.L.Rev. 832 (1952), suggests other instances where the substantive criminal law distinguishes between crimes *mala in se* and *mala prohibita.* Thus as to the problem of whether one can be guilty of a crime which his agent commits within the scope of his employment (vicarious liability), he suggests the answer is no if the crime is *malum in se*, yes if *malum prohibitum.* With conspiracy, agreement to commit a crime *malum in se* is a conspiracy even if the parties do not know that what they agree to do is a crime; but it is otherwise as to an agreement to commit a crime *malum prohibitum.* With the defense of condonation (forgiveness by the victim of a crime), condonation never is a defense to a crime *malum in se;* it is sometimes a defense to one *malum prohibitum.*

account of his prior conviction of a misdemeanor *malum in se*, but not *malum prohibitum*.[54] It is sometimes used in areas of the law outside the field of criminal law and procedure.[55]

When the issue involved in a case is the criminal manslaughter or battery responsibility of the defendant who unintentionally kills or injures another in the commission of some other crime, then, if the concept of crimes *mala in se* is used at all as a basis for liability, the term should be limited to crimes which involve danger of death or injury, and should not include crimes which may be considered morally wrong.　Danger and not morality should be the decisive factor here.　(Of course, when the issue in a case is disbarment, deportation, impeachment of a witness or the right to recover on an illegal contract, the emphasis ought to be on the morality of the crime in question.[56])　The difficulty of classifying particular crimes as *mala in se* or *mala prohibita* suggests further that the classification should be abandoned, at least in homicide and battery cases.[57]　Some cases quite sensibly ignore the distinction and yet reach proper conclusions as to liability on the basis of the danger of death or injury involved in the defendant's criminal conduct.[58]

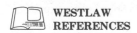

**WESTLAW
REFERENCES**

synopsis,digest(malum　+2　se prohibitum)

(c) Crimes Involving Moral Turpitude.
For some purposes crimes are divided into those involving moral turpitude, and those which do not.　Legislation in some jurisdictions has provided for the exclusion or deportation of aliens, or for the disbarment of attorneys or the revocation of the licenses of doctors, or for the impeachment of witnesses, who have been convicted of "crimes involving moral turpitude."[59]　These same unfortunate consequences (deportation, disbarment, etc.) do not, by such legislation, follow conviction of crimes not involving moral turpitude.　The distinction between crimes which do, and crimes which do not, involve moral turpitude is much the same as the distinction between crimes *mala in se* and crimes *mala prohibita;* so much so that courts often define one phrase in terms of its counterpart.[60]　Just as the courts have found it difficult sometimes to distinguish between the crimes which are *mala in se* and those *mala prohibita,* so have the courts been troubled by the vagueness of the phrase "moral turpitude."[61]　We have seen that the *malum prohibitum—malum in se* distinction may mean different things in different settings; so too the definition of the phrase "crimes involving moral turpitude" may depend somewhat on the setting in which the phrase occurs.[62]

54.　Price v. State, 546 P.2d 632 (Okl.Crim.1976).

55.　E.g., Price v. S.S. Fuller, Inc., 639 P.2d 1003 (Alaska 1982) (action to recover leased premises); Gates v. Rivers Constr. Co., 515 P.2d 1020 (Alaska 1973) (suit by employee to recover wages); Sarkco, Inc. v. Edwards, 252 Ark. 1082, 482 S.W.2d 623 (1972) (right to recover under contract).

56.　For this reason, cases in these areas of the law labeling a crime one way or the other should not be conclusive in a manslaughter or battery case.

57.　See Note, 30 Colum.L.Rev. 74, 86 (1930).

58.　E.g., Commonwealth v. Gallison, 383 Mass. 659, 421 N.E.2d 757 (1981); State v. Hallett, 619 P.2d 335 (Utah 1980).　See Wilner, Unintentional Homicide in the Commission of an Unlawful Act, 87 U.Pa.L.Rev. 811, 831 (1939).

59.　See Note, 43 Harv.L.Rev. 117 (1929).

60.　E.g., State v. Jenness, 143 Me. 380, 62 A.2d 867 (1948) (statute provided for impeachment of witness convicted of crime involving moral turpitude; witness convicted of illegal sale of liquor; *held,* no ground for impeachment, as sale of liquor is not *malum in se* and so does not "involve moral turpitude"); In re Pearce, 103 Utah 522, 136 P.2d 969 (1943) (statute provided for disbarment of attorney for conviction of crime involving moral turpitude; attorney convicted of conspiracy to maintain houses of prostitution; *held,* disbarred, as the crime is *malum in se* and so involves moral turpitude).

61.　See dissenting opinion in Jordan v. De George, 341 U.S. 223, 71 S.Ct. 703, 95 L.Ed. 886 (1951).　Note, 43 Harv. L.Rev. 117 (1929), collects cases showing that most theft crimes—grand larceny, embezzlement, false pretenses, receiving stolen property, burglary, bad check violations—as well as perjury, crimes involving intentionally giving false information to government officials, commercialized vice crimes, bigamy and rape have been generally held to involve moral turpitude; but that the cases are split as to assault with a deadly weapon, adultery, fornication, petit larceny and liquor law violations.

62.　Thus with a statute involving impeachment of witnesses, perhaps the emphasis can more properly be on the

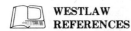

digest(crim**** /8 "moral turpitude")

(d) Infamous Crimes. Crimes are divided for some purposes into infamous crimes and those which are not infamous. Several American constitutions, including the United States Constitution, require that infamous crimes be prosecuted by indictment. In a number of states, statutes provide for certain consequences (e.g., disbarment of attorneys, disenfranchisement of voters, disqualification of jurors or public officeholders) which follow conviction of an infamous crime. At common law one who had been convicted of an infamous crime was incompetent to testify as a witness; today persons who have been convicted of crime are generally competent witnesses, but modern statutes usually permit impeachment on account of their convictions, sometimes, however, limited to infamous crimes.[63]

Once again, whether a particular crime is to be considered infamous or not may depend, to a large extent, on the purpose for which the distinction is to be made. Where the purpose was in former times to render a witness incompetent (or today to authorize the impeachment of the witness), the term "infamous" properly has reference to those crimes involving fraud or dishonesty or the obstruction of justice (sometimes called *crimen falsi*). Where the term is used in connection with disbarment or disqualification to hold office, vote or serve on a jury, it generally has a similar meaning. Under constitutional provisions relating to indictment, however, the factors of fraud and dishonesty are not especially

pertinent. The United States Supreme Court and several states have held that, in this connection, "infamous" refers, not to the nature of the crime, but rather to the kind of punishment which may be awarded. Thus "infamous crime" in the Fifth Amendment concerning indictment includes crime (even a misdemeanor) punishable by imprisonment at hard labor,[64] or in a prison or penitentiary.[65] The states whose constitutional provisions require indictments for infamous crimes generally equate the term "infamous crime" with felony, without emphasis on the hard labor aspects of possible punishment.[66]

digest("infamous crime")

(e) Petty Offenses. Crimes are for some purposes divided into major crimes and petty crimes. Generally speaking, petty offenses are a sub-group of misdemeanors; that is, a felony is necessarily a major crime, but a misdemeanor may be either a major crime or a petty offense depending upon the possible punishment. It is commonly a rule of criminal jurisdiction that petty offenses may be tried by a magistrate [67] summarily. Summary procedure means a trial without many of the usual paraphernalia required for criminal trials for the greater crimes—i.e., without a preliminary examination, without an indictment (or probably even on information; the defendant may generally be tried on the complaint) and usually without a jury. Aside from the question of summary jurisdiction of magistrates, the defendant may constitutionally be denied a jury trial for a petty offense

---

likelihood that one convicted of a certain crime will lie, than should be the case where the statute provides for disbarment.

63. The statutes differ in their wording, variously allowing impeachment for an "infamous crime" or a "crime involving moral turpitude" or a "felony" or "any crime."

64. United States v. Moreland, 258 U.S. 433, 42 S.Ct. 368, 66 L.Ed. 700 (1922) (misdemeanor); Ex parte Wilson, 114 U.S. 417, 5 S.Ct. 935, 29 L.Ed. 89 (1885) (felony). The cases show that the important factor is the punishment which *may* be awarded, not that actually awarded.

65. Mackin v. United States, 117 U.S. 348, 6 S.Ct. 777, 29 L.Ed. 909 (1886).

66. See Oppenheimer, Infamous Crimes and the Moreland case, 36 Harv.L.Rev. 299 (1923); State v. Arris, 121 Me. 94, 115 A. 648 (1922) (a felony is necessarily an infamous crime); Annot., 24 A.L.R. 1002, 1006 (1923). For a collection of cases on whether particular crimes are infamous for purposes of the requirement of a grand jury indictment, see id. at 1007–16.

67. This "magistrate" may be called a "justice of the peace" in rural areas, or a "municipal judge" in the urban centers; in the federal system he was formerly called a United States commissioner, but is now referred to as a magistrate. 18 U.S.C.A. § 3060.

even when tried in a regular court of record.[68] In many states the borderline between major crimes and petty offenses is not spelled out by statute, so that the courts themselves have had to draw the line.[69]

A special problem exists as to whether a minor offense which requires for its commission no bad intent and which involves only a light punishment should be classified as a "crime" at all, or whether instead it should not be called a "public tort" or a "civil offense" or by some other more pleasant name not involving the stigma inherent in the word "crime." Such strict-liability offenses are in most jurisdictions still considered crimes, however, in spite of the good arguments which have been made to the contrary.[70]

WESTLAW REFERENCES

digest("petty offense")

(f) Common Law Crimes and Statutory Crimes. Historically, the first step in the creation of crimes was taken by the courts, which invented a few important "common law" crimes, setting forth their definitions and providing for their punishments. Later, as the legislature came to sit more regularly and more often, that body took over more and more the task of creating, defining and punishing new crimes (by statute) and to some extent changing the scope of the old judge-made crimes, until today the law of crimes is mostly statutory law. One question remains to this day: to what extent may a court now create a new crime where the legislature has not done so?[71] Another modern problem concerns the way in which courts interpret stat-

utes defining crimes; the answer sometimes depends upon whether the crime in question involves a statutory definition of one of the old judge-made crimes or whether it concerns a definition of a crime which the legislature first created.[72] The classification is sometimes important in other areas of the criminal law.[73]

WESTLAW REFERENCES

di common-law crime
di crime

§ 1.7   Classification of Proceedings

Proceedings to determine the guilt or innocence of those accused of a "crime," as that word is used herein, must be distinguished from other related proceedings, such as those dealing with juvenile delinquency, sexual psychopathy, municipal ordinance violations, statutory penalties, and contempt of court. These other proceedings, though serving objectives not unlike many of the aims of punishment for crime, are usually said to be civil in nature, or perhaps quasi-criminal (or, in the case of criminal contempt, summary). One important reason why such classifications are significant is that those dealt with in other than regular criminal proceedings are not entitled to all of the constitutional and statutory protections provided for criminal defendants.

(a) Juvenile Delinquency. As we shall see, at common law and today generally by statute children under a certain age are deemed completely incapable of crime. Often there is also an age group beyond this age of

68. Duncan v. Louisiana, 391 U.S. 145, 88 S.Ct. 1444, 20 L.Ed.2d 491 (1968). In Baldwin v. New York, 399 U.S. 66, 90 S.Ct. 1886, 26 L.Ed.2d 437 (1970), the Court held that "no offense can be deemed 'petty' for purposes of the right to trial by jury where imprisonment for more than six months is authorized."

69. In some states the magistrate is given summary jurisdiction—perhaps not exclusive—over all misdemeanors; in such case the petty offense as a sub-type of misdemeanor may not be a relevant category.

70. See Gauzewitz, Reclassification of Certain Offenses as Civil Instead of Criminal, 12 Wis.L.Rev. 365 (1937); Perkins, the Civil Offense, 100 U.Pa.L.Rev. 832 (1952); Note, Public Torts, 35 Harv.L.Rev. 462 (1922).

Model Penal Code § 1.04(5) terms such an offense a "violation", for which no imprisonment may be awarded, while National Comm'n on Reform of Federal Criminal Laws, Final Report—Proposed New Federal Criminal Code § 109(s) (1971) uses the word "infraction" for this purpose.

71. See § 2.1.

72. See § 2.2.

73. E.g., People v. Pavlic, 227 Mich. 562, 199 N.W. 373 (1924), involving the felony-murder rule, where the court suggests, among other things, that accidental death in the commission of a felony is not murder if the felony is not a common law felony.

absolute incapability within which the prosecution must, to convict, prove that the child had the mental capacity to know right from wrong.[1] Aside from these rules concerning capacity to commit crime, every state and the District of Columbia have in modern times created a new type of misbehavior called "juvenile delinquency."[2] Those children under a certain age who commit what would be crimes if committed by adults are instead adjudicated as juvenile delinquents; this is a civil rather than a criminal matter, calling for treatment instead of punishment.[3]

Juvenile courts or family courts have been created by statute (either as separate courts or as branches of existing courts) to handle juvenile delinquency cases. These statutes also set the upper age limit for juvenile court jurisdiction[4] and determine the division of jurisdiction in these cases between the juvenile and criminal courts. Some statutes give the juvenile court discretion, in the case of all offenses which would be criminal if committed by adults, to determine whether to retain jurisdiction or to deliver the juvenile to the criminal courts. In some other states the juvenile court has exclusive jurisdiction, although it is common to except certain serious offenses. As to such exceptional crimes, the criminal courts may be allowed to transfer the case to juvenile court, or the juvenile court may be authorized to decide whether the juvenile should be dealt with as a criminal or a delinquent.

The typical juvenile delinquency statute indicates more or less specifically that juvenile delinquency proceedings are designed not for the punishment of the offender but for the salvation of the child. In other words, the proceedings are civil, not criminal. A long-standing consequence of this distinction was that youths proceeded against in juvenile court were not entitled to the many rights recognized for criminal defendants, such as those of confrontation of witnesses, counsel, and the privilege against self-incrimination. However, because of the decision of the United States Supreme Court in *In re Gault*[5] and subsequent developments, this has changed substantially.[6]

Juvenile courts are often given jurisdiction over offenses committed by adults against juveniles, such as contributing to the delinquency or neglect of children. Such proceedings are criminal in nature, and the ordinary rules of criminal procedure must be followed.[7]

WESTLAW REFERENCES

di delinquent child

(b) Sexual Psychopathy. About half of the states have enacted statutes establishing special procedures for dealing with the "sexual psychopath" or "sexually dangerous person."[8] These laws provide for the selection of certain persons, those who have committed sex offenses or who are believed likely to do

§ 1.7

1. See § 4.11.

2. M. Levin & R. Sarri, Juvenile Delinquency: A Comparative Analysis of Legal Codes in the United States 11 (1974).

3. A few jurisdictions have also provided for special treatment in the case of youthful offenders below age 21 but outside the limits of juvenile court jurisdiction. The federal government and several states have adopted the American Law Institute's Youth Correction Authority Act with some modifications. See S. Rubin, The Law of Criminal Correction 508 (2d ed. 1973).

4. The maximum age is 17 in most jurisdictions; in some others it is either 16 or 15. M. Levin & R. Sarri, supra note 2, at 13.

5. 387 U.S. 1, 87 S.Ct. 1428, 18 L.Ed.2d 527 (1967).

6. In *Gault,* the Court held the following rights applicable in juvenile court: (1) notice of the charges; (2)

counsel, including appointed counsel for the indigent; (3) confrontation and cross-examination of witnesses; and (4) the privilege against self-incrimination. In the case of In re Winship, 397 U.S. 358, 90 S.Ct. 1068, 25 L.Ed.2d 368 (1970), the Court held that delinquency must be proved beyond a reasonable doubt. Other courts have held other constitutional rights applicable, such as to exclusion of illegally seized evidence, State v. Lowry, 95 N.J.Super. 307, 230 A.2d 907 (1967), and jury trial, Peyton v. Nord, 78 N.M. 717, 437 P.2d 716 (1968). But in McKiever v. Pennsylvania, 403 U.S. 528, 91 S.Ct. 1976, 29 L.Ed.2d 647 (1971), the Court held that the due process clause does not require trial by jury in a state juvenile proceeding.

7. State v. Barilleau, 128 La. 1033, 55 So. 664 (1911); State v. Eisen, 53 Or. 297, 302, 99 P. 282, 100 P. 257 (1909).

8. For a survey of these laws, see Swanson, Sexual Psychopath Statutes: Summary and Analysis, 51 J.Crim. L.C. & P.S. 215 (1960).

so,[9] for special disposition, which involves their referral to special facilities and their continued custody until they are believed to pose no danger to the community. The sexual psychopath statutes appear to be based upon the assumptions that: (1) they are needed for the protection of society [10] (that is, that the regular processes of the criminal law are inadequate for this purpose); and (2) the designated individuals, more than the ordinary criminal, are susceptible to effective medical treatment. Both of these assumptions have been seriously questioned.[11]

The statutes vary considerably as to the basis for jurisdiction: most require that the person have been convicted of some crime or of a specific sex crime; several others require that the person be charged with some crime or a sex crime; while a few require neither charge nor conviction but only probable cause that the person is a sexual psychopath. Assuming a basis for jurisdiction, the statutes also are not in agreement as to whether the institution of proceedings by prosecutor or judge is discretionary or mandatory. If proceedings are initiated, they usually require a medical examination of the alleged sexual psychopath, which is followed by a judicial hearing. If the individual is found to be a sexual psychopath, then he is committed for an indeterminate term, and release usually comes only upon a finding that the individual no longer represents a danger to society.

The prevailing view is that sexual psychopath proceedings are civil and not criminal in nature.[12] One consequence of this is that it may not be viewed as double jeopardy subsequently to prosecute the individual for the crime which gave rise to the sexual psychopath proceedings (or, where these proceedings are undertaken after conviction, to now require him to serve the sentence for the criminal conviction),[13] although some jurisdictions by statute require termination of the criminal proceedings or give credit on the sentence for the previous confinement. Another consequence of the characterization of the proceedings as civil is that the alleged sexual psychopath may not be granted all of the procedural rights afforded a defendant in a criminal case. There is, however, increasing acceptance of the position that, because one found to be a sexual psychopath is deprived of his liberty as a result of the proceedings, many of the safeguards normal to criminal prosecutions must be followed.[14]

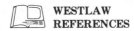 **WESTLAW REFERENCES**

digest(sexual** /5 psychopath!)

(c) Violations of Municipal Ordinances.[15] By the weight of authority, violations of the ordinances of local governmental organizations (municipalities or counties),[16] although resembling crimes, are not strictly criminal. Pursuant to authorization from the legislature, these local governmental units have the police power to regulate for the protection of the lives, health and property of their inhabitants and the preservation of good order and morals.[17] Thus in most states the typical city or town has passed numerous ordinances on local traffic matters—forbidding speeding, regulating parking, prohibiting careless and reckless driving, requiring stops at stop-signs, within municipal territorial lim-

---

9. The statutes vary considerably in the definition of persons covered , but usually refer to one lacking the power to control his sexual impulses or having criminal propensities toward the commission of sex offenses. Ibid.

10. See People v. Rancier, 240 Cal.App.2d 579, 49 Cal. Rptr. 876 (1966), taking the view that the California statute is primarily to protect society and only secondarily to rehabilitate.

11. E.g., S. Rubin, The Law of Criminal Correction 477–78 (2d ed.1973).

12. People v. Horton, 191 Cal.App.2d 592, 13 Cal.Rptr. 33 (1961); Williams v. Director, Patuxent Institution, 276 Md. 272, 347 A.2d 179 (1975); State v. Madary, 178 Neb. 383, 133 N.W.2d 583 (1965).

13. On this issue, see Swanson, supra note 8, at 222–23.

14. People v. Burnick, 14 Cal.3d 306, 121 Cal.Rptr. 488, 535 P.2d 352 (1975) (requiring proof beyond a reasonable doubt); People v. Olmstead, 32 Ill.2d 306, 205 N.E.2d 625 (1965).

15. For a more extended treatment of this topic, see O. Reynolds, Local Government Law (1982).

16. In this section the term "municipality" is used to cover the two principal units of local government: (1) municipalities (cities, towns, villages) and (2) counties.

17. E.g., People v. Hizhniak, 195 Colo. 427, 579 P.2d 1131 (1978).

its; and usually has passed ordinances covering local non-traffic matters as well—curbing dogs, cleaning sidewalks of snow and ice, requiring compliance with health and building regulations and regulating the disposal of trash and garbage. Not infrequently the ordinances forbid some of the same matters which state criminal laws forbid—driving while intoxicated, hit-and-run driving, assault and battery, petit theft.[18] Pursuant to authority from the state, these ordinances frequently provide for fines or imprisonment or both for their violation, although sometimes the power to imprison is limited to imprisonment for failure to pay a fine.[19] A municipal court (variously called municipal court, police court, city court, etc.) is generally created to exercise jurisdiction over cases involving municipal violations committed within the limited territorial jurisdiction of the municipality in question.

Just as a state statute may be invalid because the subject matter has been preempted by the federal government,[20] a municipal ordinance may likewise be held unenforceable because state legislation has occupied the field.[21] And in any event an ordinance is invalid if it is directly contrary to state law—either in purporting to permit that which state law proscribes [22] or in purporting to forbid that which state law expressly permits.[23] Absent preemption, it is not objectionable that a municipal ordinance parallels a state penal statute,[24] and this is so even though there is a difference in the applicable penalties.[25] Given the fact that state and municipal prosecution for the same conduct is impermissible,[26] the existence of such differences can give rise to state-local conflict.

The majority view is that the violation of a municipal ordinance constitutes a civil wrong against the municipality,[27] even though the ordinance authorizes imprisonment as a pen-

---

18. Successive municipal and state prosecutions for the same acts is impermissible, for it is in violation of the constitutional protection against double jeopardy. Waller v. Florida, 387 U.S. 387, 90 S.Ct. 1184, 25 L.Ed.2d 435 (1970).

19. See State ex rel. Keefe v. Schmiege, 251 Wis. 79, 28 N.W.2d 345 (1947), holding that the legislature cannot delegate to municipal or county authorities the power to treat violation of an ordinance as a misdemeanor and to impose penalties other than forfeitures and imprisonment to enforce forfeitures, and that the legislature cannot grant to municipalities or counties the power to pass ordinances which impose direct imprisonment as a penalty in a civil action. But courts are more likely to infer a power to impose a sentence of imprisonment. See, e.g., Dunn v. Mayor and Council of Wilmington, 59 Del. 287, 219 A.2d 153 (1966).

20. See § 2.15(b).

21. Lancaster v. Municipal Court, 6 Cal.3d 805, 100 Cal.Rptr. 609, 494 P.2d 681 (1972) (county ordinance making it a misdemeanor for a person to massage a member of the opposite sex as a commercial business is invalid, as "the state had adopted a general scheme for the regulation of the criminal aspects of sexual activity and * * * the state had occupied the field to the exclusion of all local regulation"); State by City of Rochester v. Driscoll, 118 N.H. 222, 385 A.2d 218 (1978) (ordinance on use of ambulance siren invalid; "because the legislature has undertaken the regulation of emergency vehicle sirens in several ways, it has clearly manifested an intent to preempt the field").

22. Hawes v. Dinkler, 224 Ga. 785, 164 S.E.2d 799 (1968) (where state law prohibits sale of liquor at certain times, sale at those times may not be permitted by local law).

23. Crackerneck Country Club v. Independence, 522 S.W.2d 50 (Mo.App.1974) (where state law permits sale of liquor by the drink in premises with state license, such sales may not be proscribed by local ordinance).

24. Aurora v. Martin, 181 Colo. 72, 507 P.2d 868 (1973).

25. The more typical situation is that in which the penalty for the ordinance violation is lower. See, e.g., State v. Suire, 319 So.2d 347 (La.1975) (ordinance which punishes aggravated battery as a misdemeanor is not unconstitutional as inconsistent with a state law punishing such conduct as a felony). But consider People v. Hizhniak, 195 Colo. 427, 579 P.2d 1131 (1978) (because regulation of traffic speeds on city streets is a matter of local concern and as such falls within the scope of the home rule amendment, city may impose penalty of imprisonment for speeding though under state statutes conduct punishable only by a fine). On the validity of ordinances with higher penalties than comparable state statutes, see Note, 20 U.Cin.L.Rev. 400 (1951).

26. See note 18 supra.

27. 9 E. McQuillin, Municipal Corporations § 27.06 (rev.3d ed. 1978). Examples are: Kansas City v. Waller, 518 S.W.2d 202 (Mo.App.1974); Commonwealth v. Dortort, 202 Pa.Super. 211, 208 A.2d 797 (1965); State v. County Court, 70 Wis.2d 230, 234 N.W.2d 283 (1975). It is sometimes said that the proceedings against an ordinance violator are in the nature of a civil action to recover a debt. Johnston v. Bloomington, 61 Ill.App.3d 209, 18 Ill. Dec. 538, 377 N.E.2d 1174 (1978), reversed on other grounds 77 Ill.2d 108, 32 Ill.Dec. 319, 395 N.E.2d 549 (1979).

alty for violation,[28] and even when the state criminal laws prohibit the same conduct as that prohibited by the ordinance.[29] The consequences of the view that municipal violations are civil wrongs, rather than criminal, arise mainly in determining the procedure to be followed in the proceedings against the violator. Thus it has been held that the prosecution need not be begun by warrant issued upon oath;[30] that the violator is not entitled to a jury trial (even though the offense is such that if it were prosecuted by the state as a crime a jury would be required);[31] that proof beyond a reasonable doubt is not necessary for conviction;[32] that (if there is a jury trial) the judge may direct a verdict of conviction;[33] that all the rules of evidence applicable in criminal trials need not be followed;[34] and that the municipality may appeal from an acquittal of the defendant.[35]

On the other hand, some states have taken the view that, at least where imprisonment is an authorized penalty, municipal violations are criminal, not civil, offenses.[36] Another position is that municipal violations are criminal if the conduct forbidden by the ordinance is also forbidden by a counterpart state statute.[37] Other states have stated that municipal violations are quasi-criminal, or partly criminal, and then they apply at least some of the principles of criminal procedure to prosecutions for ordinance violations,[38] especially where the ordinance in question prohibits the same conduct prohibited by the state criminal law (statutory law, or common law if applicable)[39] or where the ordinance provides for imprisonment as a punishment.[40]

The modern trend is away from the notion that municipal violations are civil offenses and in the direction of calling them criminal,[41] especially when violation is punishable by imprisonment as an end in itself, and not simply as a method of collecting a fine. It is perhaps possible to view the collection of a fine as a civil matter, but sixty days in jail is hardly an appropriate remedy for a civil wrong. Even the language of municipal violations is more nearly criminal than civil: the defendant is "prosecuted," he is asked to plead "guilty" or "not guilty," he is "convicted" or "acquitted," he is "sentenced" to fine or imprisonment. It would seem preferable frankly to label such violations as criminal and, as a consequence thereof, afford the defendant the same procedural safeguards to which he would be entitled in criminal cases of equal seriousness.[42]

 **WESTLAW REFERENCES**

synopsis,digest(violat*** penalty /s municipal + 1
    ordinance law regulation /s   civil criminal)

28. But see City of St. Paul v. Whidby, 295 Minn. 129, 203 N.W.2d 823 (1972) (must be treated as criminal if imprisonment may result).

29. But see Municipal Court v. Brown, 175 Colo. 433, 488 P.2d 61 (1971).

30. City of Nashville v. Baker, 167 Tenn. 661, 73 S.W.2d 169 (1934).

31. State v. Ketterer, 248 Minn. 173, 79 N.W.2d 136 (1956); State ex rel. Cole v. Nigro, 471 S.W.2d 933 (Mo. 1971); City of Brookings v. Thomsen, 84 S.D. 651, 176 N.W.2d 46 (1970).

32. City of Chicago v. Joyce, 38 Ill.2d 368, 232 N.E.2d 289 (1967); City of St. Paul v. Keeley, 194 Minn. 386, 260 N.W. 357 (1935).

33. Lloyd v. City of Canon City, 46 Colo. 195, 103 P. 288 (1909).

34. State v. Nelson, 157 Minn. 506, 196 N.W. 279 (1923) (rules requiring corroboration of the testimony of accomplice and requiring proof of corpus delicti aside from a confession).

35. City of Greeley v. Hamman, 12 Colo. 94, 20 P. 1 (1888); People v. Riksen, 284 Mich. 284, 279 N.W. 513

(1938); O'Haver v. Montgomery, 120 Tenn. 448, 111 S.W. 449 (1908); see Annot., 11 A.L.R. 4th 399 (1982).

36. State v. Walker, 265 N.C. 482, 144 S.E.2d 419 (1965); City of Akron v. Sabol, 2 Ohio App.2d 109, 206 N.E.2d 575 (1965).

37. City of Greenwood Village v. Fleming, 643 P.2d 511 (Colo.1982); City of Canon City v. Merris, 137 Colo. 169, 323 P.2d 614 (1958).

38. Donahey v. City of Montgomery, 43 Ala.App. 20, 178 So.2d 832 (1965); City of Danville v. Clark, 63 Ill.2d 408, 348 N.E.2d 844 (1976).

39. E.g., The President, etc., of the Village of Platteville v. McKernan, 54 Wis. 487, 11 N.W. 798 (1882).

40. E.g. see City of Newark v. Pulverman, 12 N.J. 105, 95 A.2d 889 (1953). But New Jersey does not actually require that there must be imprisonment or that the act must also constitute a state crime. See State v. Yaccarino, 3 N.J. 291, 70 A.2d 84 (1949).

41. The New Jersey cases, as illustrated by Newark v. Pulverman, supra note 40, point the way toward this trend.

42. See Note, 1 Vand.L.Rev. 262 (1948).

(d) Statutory Penalties.[43] Statutes, federal and state, not infrequently forbid certain conduct and then provide for pecuniary penalties for violations of the statute. Sometimes the pecuniary penalty is in lieu of the usual criminal penalty of fine or imprisonment, sometimes it is in addition to regular criminal punishment. Under some statutes the penalty may be recovered by the state; in others by an injured party or by an informer. Under some statutes the penalty is a fixed amount;[44] under others it is a percentage of an amount due as a result of the forbidden conduct[45] or a multiple of the damages caused by such conduct.[46] Sometimes the statute provides that the penalty is recoverable in a civil action; sometimes it provides for recovery by indictment or information; often the nature of the proceedings is not mentioned.

The question frequently arises as to whether the proceedings to recover statutory penalties are criminal or civil. Should the action be brought in a court of civil or of criminal jurisdiction? Is the civil or the criminal statute of limitations applicable? Is the defendant entitled to the rights of a criminal defendant at the trial—the right to a jury trial, to be confronted by witnesses, to refrain from taking the stand, to be convicted only on proof beyond a reasonable doubt—or to the rights of a defendant in a civil suit? Is it double jeopardy to sue for the penalty if the defendant had been tried criminally for his violation of the statute? If the verdict is against the suing party, may he move for a new trial or appeal, or is a second trial barred by the prohibition against double jeopardy?

The courts have generally considered that proceedings to recover statutory penalties are civil in nature, and therefore the rules governing civil procedure are applicable.[47] But a number of cases have held the proceedings under particular statutes to be criminal, therefore applying rules of criminal procedure; or to be quasi-criminal, therefore applying at least some of the criminal procedural rules.[48] Insofar as the proceedings are criminal, they are within the scope of this book.

43. See Comment, 51 Harv.L.Rev. 1092 (1938); Annot., 27 L.R.A. (N.S.) 739 (1910).

44. Thus a federal statute, 32 Stat. 1213 (1903), provided that it is unlawful to prepay the transportation of an alien into the United States to perform labor; for every violation the violator shall forfeit $1000, which may be sued for by the United States or by any person who shall first bring his action therefor in his own name. Hepner v. United States, 213 U.S. 103, 29 S.Ct. 474, 53 L.Ed. 720 (1909), held that a suit to recover this penalty was not so far criminal that the trial court could not under proper circumstances direct a verdict for the United States. In criminal cases, of course, there can be no directed verdict of guilty. See § 1.8(g).

45. Thus a federal tax statute, now 26 U.S.C.A. § 6653, provides that one who fradulently underpays his tax shall be assessed, in addition to the tax deficiency, a fraud penalty of 50% of the deficiency; this penalty is in addition to criminal punishment of fine or imprisonment for wilfully underpaying the tax. Helvering v. Mitchell, 303 U.S. 391, 58 S.Ct. 630, 82 L.Ed. 917 (1938), held that the penalty, being civil in nature, was not barred by double jeopardy because of taxpayer's acquittal on the criminal charge.

46. Thus the federal anti-trust law, 15 U.S.C.A. § 1 et seq. provides for criminal punishment for violation, id. § 1, and in addition provides that the injured party may recover triple damages, id. § 15.

See also the state statute upheld in Shevlin-Carpenter Co. v. Minnesota, 218 U.S. 57, 30 S.Ct. 663, 54 L.Ed. 930 (1910), making it a felony, punishable by fine or imprisonment, to cut timber on state land without a permit, and providing in addition for double (if unintentional trespass) or triple (if intentional trespass) damages to the state. The Court gave no opinion as to whether it would be double jeopardy both to prosecute criminally and sue for the penalty.

47. See Comment, 51 Harv.L.Rev. 1092 (1938); Annot., 27 L.R.A.(N.S.) 739 (1910).

48. Ibid. Various tests have been used to classify proceedings to recover statutory penalties. If the statute provides for recovery by indictment or information it is criminal; otherwise it is civil. If the state sues it is criminal; if a private person it is civil. If the penalty goes to the state it is criminal; if to a private party it is civil. If the statute uses the term "suit" or "action" or "as debts of like amount are recovered" it is civil; if it speaks in terms of "indictment" or "prosecution" it is criminal. If the statute also provides regular criminal punishment it is criminal; if not it is civil. See Comment, supra note 47, at 1096–97. The note, finding such tests somewhat unsatisfactory, suggests that the nature of the prohibited conduct (whether the sort normally considered criminal) and the seriousness of the penalty should have a bearing on the problem.

Consider also the common law criminal forfeiture, reestablished in the federal system by 18 U.S.C.A. § 1963. The forfeiture arises out of the criminal prosecution and conviction and, as at common law, the defendant is entitled to notice, trial and a special jury finding on the factual issues surrounding the declaration of forfeiture. See Fed.R.Crim.P. 7(c)(2), 31(e), 32(b)(2).

penalty /6 statut*** /s civil /3 proceeding
procedure

(e) Contempt of Court. Contempt of court is divided into (1) criminal contempt and (2) civil contempt, depending upon whether the purpose of the contempt proceeding is to punish or coerce.[49] It is also divided into (1) direct contempt and (2) indirect (or constructive) contempt, depending upon whether the contempt was in the presence of the court (and perhaps in the judge's view or hearing) or not.

Looking at contempt of court from the point of view of the purpose of the contempt proceeding, contempts may be divided into "two classes,—those prosecuted to preserve the power and vindicate the dignity of the courts, and to punish for disobedience of their orders; and those instituted to preserve and enforce the rights of private parties to suits, and to compel obedience to orders and decrees made to enforce the rights and administer the reme-

dies to which the court has found them to be entitled. The former are criminal and punitive in their nature, and the government, the courts, and the people are interested in their prosecution. The latter are civil, remedial, and coercive in their nature, and the parties chiefly in interest in their conduct and prosecution are the individuals whose private rights and remedies they were instituted to protect or enforce." [50]

Thus it is a civil contempt for one, after having been enjoined by a court from doing a certain act, to do it;[51] or conversely for one, ordered by the court to do some act, not to do it, at least if it is within his power to do it.[52] For his civil contempt he may be imprisoned until he purges himself by compliance with the order.[53] On the other hand, one is guilty of criminal contempt if, whether with good aim or bad, he throws a brickbat at the judge sitting on the bench;[54] or, whether an attorney, litigant, juror, witness or spectator, he behaves in a disrespectful or boisterous manner in court;[55] or refuses to obey a lawful order of the court;[56] or commits an assault or

---

49. See Beale, Contempt of Court, Criminal and Civil, 21 Harv.L.Rev. 161 (1908); Nelles, The Summary Power to Punish for Contempt, 31 Colum.L.Rev. 956 (1931).

50. Sanborn, J., in In re Nevitt, 117 F. 448 (8th Cir. 1902). This distinction continues to be drawn in the cases. See, e.g., Ventures Management Co. v. Geruso, ___ R.I. ___, 434 A.2d 252 (1981); State v. King, 82 Wis.2d 124, 262 N.W.2d 80 (1978).

It is said that the "line of demarcation in many instances is indistinct and even imperceptible." People ex rel. Chicago Bar Association v. Barasch, 21 Ill.2d 407, 173 N.E.2d 417 (1961). Perhaps this is because in a particular instance it serves both to coerce and to punish. See, e.g., People v. Denson, 59 Ill.2d 546, 322 N.E.2d 464 (1975).

51. In re Debs, 158 U.S. 564, 15 S.Ct. 900, 39 L.Ed. 1092 (1895) (injunction, issued by federal court during Pullman Strike of 1894, enjoined union officers from interfering with interstate movement of railroads by threats, force and violence; proceeding for violation is civil in nature).

52. United States v. Rylander, 460 U.S. 752, 103 S.Ct. 1548, 75 L.Ed.2d 521 (1983) (burden on defendant to show inability to comply); Duran v. District Court, 190 Colo. 272, 545 P.2d 1365 (1976) (contempt for failure to comply with support order improper where defendant unemployed and without funds). See Annots., 22 A.L.R. 1256 (1923), 31 A.L.R. 649 (1924), 40 A.L.R. 546 (1926), 76 A.L.R. 390 (1932), 120 A.L.R. 703 (1939).

53. When, however, a witness at a trial improperly refuses to testify and is imprisoned for civil contempt to coerce him into testifying, he must be released when the

trial is over. See Yates v. United States, 355 U.S. 66, 78 S.Ct. 128, 2 L.Ed.2d 95 (1957). So too imprisonment for civil contempt to coerce testimony before a grand jury terminates with the discharge of the jury. Howard v. United States, 182 F.2d 908 (8th Cir.1950), rev'd on other grounds, 340 U.S. 898, 71 S.Ct. 278, 95 L.Ed. 651 (1950). And imprisonment for civil contempt to coerce compliance with a no-strike injunction must cease when the labor matter is settle. State v. King, 82 Wis.2d 124, 262 N.W.2d 80 (1978).

54. Anonymous, 73 Eng.Rep. 416 (1631), a savage little case wherein a criminal defendant, convicted of a felony in a court presided over by the chief justice, threw a Brickbat at the judge upon which he was adjudged in contempt, his right hand (presumably because he threw right-handed) cut off and fixed to the gibbet, after which he was hanged in the presence of the court.

55. United States v. Sacher, 182 F.2d 416 (2d Cir.1950), affirmed 343 U.S. 1, 72 S.Ct. 451, 96 L.Ed. 717 (1952) (defense attorney directed many contemptuous remarks to judge, often refused to obey his orders); United States v. Hall, 176 F.2d 163 (2d Cir.1949), (defendants in criminal case stepped toward bench, shouted at judge, referring to "such monstrosity" and "kangaroo court.").

56. Cf. Johnson v. Virginia, 373 U.S. 61, 83 S.Ct. 1053, 10 L.Ed.2d 195 (1963) (refusal by a black to obey trial judge's order to sit in part of courtroom reserved for blacks—an unconstitutional order under 14th amendment outlawing segregation of public facilities—cannot be the basis of conviction of criminal contempt).

battery upon someone (judge, juror, attorney, litigant, witness, bailiff or marshal) in the courtroom.[57]

One who obstructs justice by committing perjury[58] or who procures or tries to procure another to commit perjury,[59] is guilty of criminal contempt. A litigant who tampers with the jury trying his case[60] or with a witness in his case,[61] is likewise guilty of criminal contempt. So too is a juror who is guilty of

misconduct in connection with the case he is trying.[62] A witness who, though ordered to do so by the court, refuses to appear in court[63] or to answer a proper question put to him in court or by a grand jury or administrative body,[64] or who refuses to produce before the appropriate body papers in his possession called for by a subpoena duces tecum,[65] is guilty of criminal contempt, unless of course his refusal is based upon a privilege properly invoked by him.[66] Disobedience of the court's

57. In re Terry, 36 F. 419 (C.C.N.D.Cal.1888) (when federal judge ordered U.S. marshal to remove Terry's wife from courtroom after she had refused to be silent during the reading of an opinion, Terry attacked marshal and drew a bowie-knife), habeas corpus denied in Ex parte Terry, 128 U.S. 289, 9 S.Ct. 77, 32 L.Ed. 405 (1888). Upon an earlier occasion the lively Mrs. Terry, when a litigant, committed a criminal contempt by pulling a pistol from her handbag during the examination of a witness, threatening to kill counsel for the other side. Sharon v. Hill, 24 F. 726 (C.C.Cal.1885). See Annots., 52 A.L.R.2d 1297 (1957); 55 A.L.R. 1230 (1928), for contempt committed by fighting in court. See Lewis, The Supreme Court and a Six-Gun: The Extraordinary Story of In re Neagle, 43 A.B.A.J. 415 (1957), for a short history of the turbulent feud between former California Supreme Court Justice David S. Terry and his former associate on that court, who became a U.S. Supreme Court justice, Stephen J. Field, which feud culminated in Terry's death at the hands of U.S. Deputy Marshal Neagle while Terry was in the act of making a murderous attack on Field during a breakfast stopover at a railroad station restaurant, In re Neagle, 135 U.S. 1, 10 S.Ct. 658, 34 L.Ed. 55 (1890) (federal police officer cannot be prosecuted for murder in state court for a killing committed by him in the course of his federal duties).

58. United States v. Appel, 211 F. 495 (S.D.N.Y.1913) (witness' answers of "I don't know" were transparently evasive; *held,* criminal contempt); Eykelboom v. People, 71 Colo. 318, 206 P. 388 (1922) (witness' manifestly false testimony appeared from own testimony; *held,* contempt); Blankenburg v. Commonwealth, 272 Mass. 25, 172 N.E. 209 (1930) (litigant's claim to estate as child of decedent shown by documentary evidence to be false; *held,* contempt.) See Annot., 89 A.L.R.3d 1258 (1963). Compare the situation where the judge believes but cannot be certain that the witness is lying: there can be no finding of contempt, but instead the witness should be prosecuted for perjury. Ex parte Hudgings, 249 U.S. 378, 39 S.Ct. 337, 63 L.Ed. 656 (1919). And if there was perjury but it did not obstruct the court in the performance of its functions, this in most jurisdictions does not amount to contempt. State v. Hill, 55 Wn.2d 576, 349 P.2d 210 (1960).

59. In re Estate of Melody, 42 Ill.2d 451, 248 N.E.2d 104 (1969) (defendant obtained services of lawyer to draw up will for person already dead and then obtained person to commit perjury re witnessing will; *held,* criminal contempt); Taylor v. State, 112 Neb. 259, 199 N.W. 509 (1924) (criminal defendant promised witness new dress if she would suppress evidence; *held,* criminal contempt). See Annot., 29 A.L.R.2d 1157 (1953).

60. Sinclair v. United States, 279 U.S. 749, 49 S.Ct. 471, 73 L.Ed. 938 (1929) (criminal defendant employed private detectives to shadow jurors; *held,* defendant guilty of contempt though detectives did not communicate with jurors and jurors may not have been aware of being shadowed). Compare United States v. Smith, 555 F.2d 249 (9th Cir.1977) (no contempt where it not shown spectator at trial knowingly or intentionally made remark to a juror). See Annot., 63 A.L.R. 1269 (1929).

61. State v. Goff, 228 S.C. 17, 88 S.E.2d 788 (1955) (litigant threatened to beat witness in a pending case, *held,* contempt); see Whitten v. State, 36 Ind. 196 (1871) (contempt forcibly to abduct witness in pending case to prevent his testimony).

62. Clark v. United States, 289 U.S. 1, 53 S.Ct. 465, 77 L.Ed. 993 (1933) (juror on voir dire concealed his past employment by defendant and falsely stated she had no bias; *held,* criminal contempt); People v. Rosenthal, 370 Ill. 244, 18 N.E.2d 450 (1938) (jurors, instructed by judge not to separate and not to communicate with outsiders, violated his instructions and agreed to hide their violations from judge; *held,* contempt). See Annot., 125 A.L.R. 1274 (1940).

63. Commonwealth v. Maurizio, 496 Pa. 584, 437 A.2d 1195 (1981).

64. Yates v. United States, 355 U.S. 66, 78 S.Ct. 128, 2 L.Ed.2d 95 (1957) (criminal-defendant witness testified in own defense, then refused on cross-examination to answer eleven questions; *held,* criminal contempt, but only one, not eleven, contempts); Piemonte v. United States, 367 U.S. 556, 81 S.Ct. 1720, 6 L.Ed.2d 1028 (1961) (witness before grand jury, ordered to answer by court, refused to answer self-incriminating questions when granted immunity, because of fear of gangland reprisals; *held,* criminal contempt). The grand jury itself has no power to punish a balky witness for contempt. Gendron v. Burnham, 146 Me. 387, 82 A.2d 773 (1951). When a witness will not answer, the witness is taken before the court, which rules on whether he must answer. If the court orders him to answer, and he refuses, he is then in contempt of court. As to witnesses before administrative bodies, see Davis, The Administrative Power of Investigation, 56 Yale L.J. 1111 (1947).

65. Nilva v. United States, 352 U.S. 385, 77 S.Ct. 431, 1 L.Ed.2d 415 (1957) (subpoena issued by court in connection with criminal trial).

66. Blau v. United States, 340 U.S. 159, 71 S.Ct. 223, 95 L.Ed. 170 (1950) (witness before grand jury refused to answer questions on the ground of self-incrimination;

order to a defendant on bail to surrender himself to begin serving his sentence is a criminal contempt.[67]

In the case of the criminal contempt, a fine or imprisonment for a definite term may be awarded as punishment.[68] One thus punished by a definite sentence for criminal contempt cannot purge himself of contempt by undoing the wrong he did, as in the case of civil contempt.

A single act or refusal to act in violation of a court order often constitutes both civil contempt and criminal contempt, for which he may be fined or imprisoned for the purpose of coercing him into doing the right thing, and in addition fined or imprisoned for the purpose of punishing him for having done the wrong thing;[69] and principles of double jeopardy do not stand in the way of applying both coercive and punitive sanctions.[70]

For purposes of the appropriate procedure to be used for dealing with civil and criminal contempts, contempts are divided into direct contempts and indirect (sometimes called constructive) contempts. A contempt which is

committed in the actual presence of the court[71] (in the courtroom or in chambers) or in its immediate vicinity, whether during a trial or during a recess in the trial, is a direct contempt generally punishable summarily.[72] An indirect contempt, one committed outside the presence or immediate vicinity of the court but which nevertheless improperly interferes with the work of the court, is punishable only after notice (by an indictment or information, or by an order to show cause) and hearing, with an opportunity to be heard in defense to the charge.[73]

It is a direct contempt, for instance, for lawyers or parties to talk disrespectfully to the judge on the bench[74] or to commit assaults or batteries during the course of the trial,[75] or for newspapermen to take surreptitious pictures in court when forbidden to do so.[76] On the other hand, it is an indirect contempt for a litigant or his attorney to tamper with a juror away from the courthouse,[77] to destroy evidence which might be used against the litigant,[78] or to go to the home or office of a prospective witness in a pending case, in order to bribe or intimidate

held, criminal contempt conviction reversed, since witness' claim of privilege was valid).

67. Green v. United States, 356 U.S. 165, 78 S.Ct. 632, 2 L.Ed.2d 672 (1958).

68. There is in many jurisdictions no statutory maximum sentence for criminal contempt, as there is for other crimes. See Piemonte v. United States, 367 U.S. 556, 81 S.Ct. 1720, 6 L.Ed.2d 1028 (1961), dissenting opinion n. 1, for some examples of definite sentences of 2 or 3 years imprisonment for criminal contempt.

If there is no statutory maximum, the defendant may not be imprisoned more than six months unless he is granted a jury trial. Cheff v. Schnackenberg, 384 U.S. 373, 86 S.Ct. 1523, 16 L.Ed.2d 629 (1966); Dyke v. Taylor Implement Mfg. Co., 391 U.S. 216, 88 S.Ct. 1472, 20 L.Ed. 2d 538 (1968); Bloom v. Illinois, 391 U.S. 194, 88 S.Ct. 1477, 20 L.Ed.2d 522 (1968).

69. United States v. United Mine Workers, 330 U.S. 258, 67 S.Ct. 677, 91 L.Ed. 884 (1947) (defendants, a labor union and its president, violated restraining order issued in a labor dispute; *held,* both criminal and civil contempt).

70. Yates v. United States, 355 U.S. 66, 78 S.Ct. 128, 2 L.Ed.2d 95 (1957).

71. This "extends beyond those places within the sight and hearing of the presiding judge" and covers every place set aside for use of the court, its officers, jurors and witnesses." Knox v. Municipal Court, 185 N.W.2d 705 (Iowa 1971).

72. But see Commonwealth v. Stevenson, 482 Pa. 76, 393 A.2d 386 (1978) (to justify summary procedure, contempt must be direct and in addition there must be a necessity for immediate action).

73. If a contempt committed in the presence of the court is not committed in the actual view or hearing of the judge, see note 71 supra, then the judge cannot punish summarily on his own knowledge, but he must inform the contemnor of the charge and give him a chance to defend. Gendron v. Burnham, 146 Me. 387, 82 A.2d 773 (1951). (On the other hand, a direct contempt is sometimes defined as requiring that the contempt be committed in the view of the judge, as well as in the presence of the court, e.g., Cooper v. People ex rel. Wyatt, 13 Colo. 337, 22 P. 790 (1889).) If the contempt occurred in view of the judge so that he could have proceeded summarily, but the matter is put into the hands of another judge, he must hear testimony and generally follow more elaborate procedures. Knox v. Municipal Court, 185 N.W.2d 705 (Iowa 1971).

74. United States v. Sacher, 182 F.2d 416 (2d Cir.1950); United States v. Hall, 176 F.2d 163 (2d Cir.1949).

75. Ex parte Terry, 128 U.S. 289, 9 S.Ct. 77, 32 L.Ed. 405 (1888); Knox v. Municipal Court, 185 N.W.2d 705 (Iowa 1971).

76. Ex parte Sturm, 152 Md. 114, 136 A. 312 (1927).

77. Sinclair v. United States, 279 U.S. 749, 49 S.Ct. 471, 73 L.Ed. 938 (1929).

78. Burtch v. Zeuch, 200 Iowa 49, 202 N.W. 542 (1925).

him concerning his testimony.[79] It is generally considered an indirect contempt for a newspaperman falsely to charge in an editorial that a court trying or hearing the appeal of a pending case has been bribed.[80]

It has been said that criminal contempt is a crime,[81] just as much as perjury or any other crime against the administration of justice; or that it is a quasi-crime; [82] or that it is no crime at all.[83] What these conflicting expressions seem to signify is that, on the substantive law side, criminal contempt is very much like an ordinary crime; but procedurally may be treated quite differently. Although it has been held that criminal contempt is a common law crime inherited from England and hence a crime, though no statute makes it so, in those American jurisdictions which recognize common law crimes,[84] yet even in those jurisdictions which do not recognize common law crimes, a power to punish for contempt exists.[85] In some jurisdictions, however, the legislature has enacted an ordinary statutory crime called contempt, sometimes varying the common law elements thereof.[86]

Criminal contempt, like most ordinary crimes, requires something in the way of a bad state of mind: there must be at least an intent to do the act constituting the contempt,[87] or possibly recklessly doing the act; [88] it is not necessary, however, that one do the act with any specific intent to be contemptuous or insulting.[89]

Conduct constituting a criminal contempt of court may, of course, also constitute one of the ordinary crimes, as where a disappointed

79. State ex rel. Huie v. Lewis, 80 So.2d 685 (Fla.1955).

80. People v. Wilson, 64 Ill. 195 (1872). See Annot., 69 A.L.R.2d 676 (1960).

81. Bloom v. Illinois, 391 U.S. 194, 88 S.Ct. 1477, 20 L.Ed.2d 522 (1968) (criminal contempt is "a crime in every fundamental respect"); Gompers v. United States, 233 U.S. 604, 34 S.Ct. 693, 58 L.Ed. 1115 (1914) ("If such acts are not criminal, we are in error as to the most fundamental characteristic of crimes as that word has been understood in English speech."); People v. Siegal, 400 Ill. 208, 79 N.E.2d 616 (1948) (criminal contempt "is a crime against the court and against the people and is a misdemeanor"); Ex parte Stephenson, 89 Okl.Cr. 427, 209 P.2d 515 (1949) (criminal contempt "is an offense against the public or society ∗ ∗ ∗. Direct contempt is a crime, and the punishment therein constitutes a sentence in a criminal case").

82. Hutton v. Superior Court, 147 Cal. 156, 81 P. 409 (1905) ("contempt proceedings are quasi criminal in their nature"); Knox v. Municipal Court, 185 N.W.2d 705 (Iowa 1971) (contempt considered "quasi-criminal").

83. State ex rel. Trotcky v. Hutchinson, 224 Ind. 443, 68 N.E.2d 649 (1946) (contempt of court "is neither civil, criminal nor equitable").

84. Dockerty v. People, 96 Colo. 338, 44 P.2d 1013 (1935) (because Colorado adopted the common law of England as it existed prior to 1607, criminal contempt, a crime in England before 1607, is a common law crime in Colorado).

85. United States v. Hudson & Goodwin, 11 U.S. (7 Cranch) 32, 3 L.Ed. 259 (1812) (although there are no federal common law crimes, federal courts have an inherent power to punish contempts); Knox v. Municipal Court, 185 N.W.2d 705 (Iowa 1971) (power to punish for contempt inherent in the nature and constitution of a court).

86. E.g., 18 U.S.C.A. § 401, defining, but limiting the definition of, contempt: (1) misbehavior of any person in the presence of or near the court, (2) misbehavior of officers of the court in their official transactions, and (3) disobedience or resistance to the lawful order or process of the court.

87. United States ex rel. Porter v. Kroger Grocery & Baking Co., 163 F.2d 168 (7th Cir.1947) (defendant sold goods at price above ceiling price in violation of court order, in the honest belief that sales price was below the ceiling; *held*, not criminal contempt); Uhler v. Superior Court, 117 Cal.App.2d 147, 255 P.2d 29 (1953) (an intent to commit a forbidden act is required); Petition of Boasberg, 286 App.Div. 951, 143 N.Y.S.2d 272 (1955) (attorney improperly excepted generally to judge's charge, though exception served no useful purpose; *held;* not criminal contempt, unless done with an intent to defy the authority of the court).

88. Many cases speak of "willful" violation; and "willful" sometimes includes recklessness.

89. But compare People v. Post Standard Co., 13 N.Y.2d 185, 245 N.Y.S.2d 377, 195 N.E.2d 48 (1963) (contempt by newspaper publishing a false or grossly inaccurate report of a judicial proceeding is not committed without an intent to assail the dignity and authority of the court), with In re San Francisco Chronicle, 1 Cal.2d 630, 36 P.2d 369 (1934) (contempt by newspaper publication of false or grossly inaccurate report of judicial proceeding; "good-faith" intent or motive of publisher is immaterial except in mitigation).

Thus a witness who politely violates an order to answer a question in court or before a grand jury is guilty of criminal contempt, though he bases his refusal on an honest but erroneous belief that he is privileged not to answer. Reina v. United States, 364 U.S. 507, 81 S.Ct. 260, 5 L.Ed.2d 249 (1960). But if the witness is misled into the honest but erroneous belief that he is privileged to be silent by an earlier opinion by the Supreme Court itself, he is not guilty of contempt until he has been afforded an opportunity to answer in the light of the new Supreme Court opinion denying the privilege: Murphy v. Waterfront Commission of New York Harbor, 378 U.S. 52, 84 S.Ct. 1594, 12 L.Ed.2d 678 (1964) (overruling earlier decision which gave witness privilege not to answer).

litigant hurls a missile at the judge (a battery if his aim is good, an assault if he misses), or where a witness, intending to obstruct the administration of justice, testifies falsely upon the witness stand (perjury). The fact that the conduct which constitutes criminal contempt is also an ordinary crime does not prevent its punishment as contempt.[90] Although there is authority that the rule against double jeopardy does not forbid punishment both for the criminal contempt and for the ordinary crime,[91] the recent cases are to the contrary.[92]

The procedures which are used to deal with a criminal contempt differ depending upon whether or not the contempt was committed in the actual view or hearing of the judge. If the contempt was committed within the presence of the court, it is then punishable by the judge at once, summarily, on his own knowledge, without a formal written accusation, arraignment, plea, proof, or other trappings of an ordinary criminal prosecution.[93] This is because of the "need for immediate penal vindiction of the dignity of the court." [94] Other forms of contempt, however, require more elaborate procedures, although not all of the safeguards of a criminal trial are necessary. There is no right to a grand jury indictment,[95] but the accused is entitled to fair notice of the charges,[96] and a reasonable opportunity to defend against them with the assistance of counsel,[97] the right to call witnesses,[98] and to confront and cross-examine the witnesses against him.[99] He cannot be compelled to testify against himself,[100] he must be proved

90. E.g., Green v. United States, 356 U.S. 165, 78 S.Ct. 632, 2 L.Ed.2d 672 (1958) (bail jumping in violation of federal court order to surrender constitutes criminal contempt, though bail jumping is a federal crime); Ex parte Terry, 128 U.S. 289, 9 S.Ct. 77, 32 L.Ed. 405 (1888) (battery on U.S. marshal in court constitutes contempt); Ex parte Hudgings, 249 U.S. 378, 39 S.Ct. 337, 63 L.Ed. 656 (1919) (perjury constitutes contempt).

91. United States v. Rollerson, 308 F.Supp. 1014 (D.D.C.1970), affirmed 449 F.2d 1000 (D.C.Cir.1971) (defendant summarily held in contempt for throwing water pitcher at judge could be prosecuted for assault; no double jeopardy violation because separate interests served and defendant not subjected to multiple proceedings); United States v. Mirra, 220 F.Supp. 361 (S.D.N.Y.1963) (during criminal trial defendant threw chair at prosecuting attorney; summary conviction of contempt with one year's imprisonment *held* not to bar prosecution for assault upon federal officer in the performance of his duties); State v. Smith, 97 Ohio App. 86, 121 N.E.2d 199 (1954) (if several persons riot in violation of a court injunction, they commit both contempt and crime of riot; and conviction of one will not bar prosecution for the other).

92. People v. Gray, 69 Ill.2d 44, 12 Ill. Dec. 886, 370 N.E.2d 797 (1977) (defendant, who struck his wife with a gun and then shot her, was held in contempt for violating a protective order in a divorce proceeding; this barred later prosecution for aggravated assault and attempted murder, as circumstances come within the same evidence test for double jeopardy, the "purpose of criminal contempt is identical with that of many other criminal laws, namely, to protect the institutions of government," and "the impact on the particular defendant is the same" as an ordinary criminal prosecution); People v. Colombo, 31 N.Y.2d 947, 341 N.Y.S.2d 97, 293 N.E.2d 247 (1972).

93. Sacher v. United States, 343 U.S. 1, 72 S.Ct. 451, 96 L.Ed. 717 (1952); Ex parte Terry, 128 U.S. 289, 9 S.Ct. 77, 32 L.Ed. 405 (1888).

But even if the judge proceeds immediately to deal with a direct contempt, the better view is that "the judge should give the offender notice of the charges and at least a summary opportunity to adduce evidence or argument relevant to guilt or punishment." 1 ABA Standards for Criminal Justice § 6–4.4 (2d ed. 1980). Some jurisdictions have adopted that view; see, e.g., State ex rel. Young v. Woodson, 522 P.2d 1035 (Okl.1974).

94. Cooke v. United States, 267 U.S. 517, 45 S.Ct. 390, 69 L.Ed. 767 (1925). But where the judge sees no need to act immediately, and thus finds the person in contempt only after the trial is completed, due process sometimes requires that another judge sit in judgment on the defendant's conduct. Mayberry v. Pennsylvania, 400 U.S. 455, 91 S.Ct. 499, 27 L.Ed.2d 532 (1971); Johnson v. Mississippi, 403 U.S. 212, 91 S.Ct. 1778, 29 L.Ed.2d 423 (1971).

95. Green v. United States, 356 U.S. 165, 78 S.Ct. 632, 2 L.Ed.2d 672 (1958).

96. Cooke v. United States, supra note 94; Marcisz v. Marcisz, 65 Ill.2d 206, 2 Ill. Dec. 310, 357 N.E.2d 477 (1976).

97. State v. Browder, 486 P.2d 925 (Alaska 1971); Commonwealth v. Crawford, 466 Pa. 269, 352 A.2d 52 (1976).

There may be a right to counsel, albeit not grounded in the Sixth Amendment, in civil contempt cases as well. See Sword v. Sword, 399 Mich. 367, 249 N.W.2d 88 (1976) (counsel should be appointed if case is complicated); Ferris v. State ex rel. Maass, 75 Wis.2d 542, 249 N.W.2d 789 (1977) (counsel required because "liberty is threatened").

98. Cooke v. United States, 267 U.S. 517, 45 S.Ct. 390, 69 L.Ed. 767 (1925).

99. Matusow v. United States, 229 F.2d 335 (5th Cir. 1956).

100. Gompers v. Buck's Store & Range Co., 221 U.S. 418, 31 S.Ct. 492, 55 L.Ed. 797 (1911); Marcisz v. Marcisz, 65 Ill.2d 206, 2 Ill.Dec. 310, 357 N.E.2d 477 (1976).

guilty beyond a reasonable doubt,[101] and the state or other party may not appeal.[102]

It was long the rule that there was no constitutional right to jury trial in a criminal contempt case.[103] In *Cheff v. Schnackenberg*,[104] however, the Court, in upholding a six-month jail sentence for contempt imposed without jury trial, intimated that the result would have been otherwise had the punishment not been within the "petty offense" exception to the right to jury trial in criminal cases. Finally, in *Bloom v. Illinois*[105] the Court expressly held that the Constitution requires jury trial for criminal contempt except for those in the "petty offense" category.[106] Moreover, the Court declined to create an exception for direct contempt cases; while the need "to quell a disturbance cannot attend upon the impaneling of a jury," the solution in such a case is summary punishment of not more than six months imprisonment.[107]

 **WESTLAW REFERENCES**

digest(contempt! /5 civil /10 direct indirect constructive)

§ 1.8 Burden of Proof; Directed Verdict

What are customarily referred to as the elements of crime—a specified act or omis-

sion, usually a concurring specified mental state, and often specified attendant circumstances and a specified harmful result caused by the conduct—are described and discussed herein both in general terms[1] and with respect to certain crimes against the person[2] and certain crimes relating to property.[3] Considerable attention is also given to the various defenses to crime, both those based upon an alleged lack of responsibility[4] and those based upon a claim of some justification or excuse.[5] One cannot appreciate the full significance of these elements and defenses without an understanding of the significance of their proof or lack of proof at the criminal trial. It is thus necessary to give some attention to certain matters which are procedural in nature, but which have a large substantive dimension: the burden of proof; and directed verdicts.

(a) Aspects of Burden of Proof. It is a basic policy of Anglo-American criminal law that, in view of the serious consequences which follow conviction of crime, the prosecution has the burden of proving beyond a reasonable doubt all the facts necessary to establish the defendant's guilt.[6] This burden of proof has two separate aspects: (1) The burden of producing evidence; and (2) the burden of persuading the fact-finder (jury; or judge

---

101. Ibid. In a civil contempt case, by contrast, "substantial evidence is all that is required." Matter of Graveley, 188 Mont. 546, 614 P.2d 1033 (1980).

102. State ex rel. Sanborn v. Bissing, 210 Kan. 389, 502 P.2d 630 (1972); Commonwealth v. Maruizio, 496 Pa. 584, 437 A.2d 1195 (1981). Compare Ventures Management v. Geruso, ___ R.I. ___, 434 A.2d 252 (1981) (contempt was partially civil and partially criminal, so appeal not totally barred).

103. See United States v. Barnett, 376 U.S. 681, 84 S.Ct. 984, 12 L.Ed.2d 23 (1965), citing over 50 prior decisions of the Court allowing disposition of contempt without jury trial.

104. 384 U.S. 373, 86 S.Ct. 1523, 16 L.Ed.2d 629 (1966).

105. 391 U.S. 194, 88 S.Ct. 1477, 20 L.Ed.2d 522 (1968), held to be prospective only as to the states in DeStefano v. Woods, 392 U.S. 631, 88 S.Ct. 2093, 20 L.Ed.2d 1308 (1968).

106. State law may go further. See State v. Browder, 486 P.2d 925 (Alaska 1971).

107. In Baldwin v. New York, 399 U.S. 66, 90 S.Ct. 1886, 26 L.Ed.2d 437 (1970), the Court held that a criminal

offense cannot be deemed "petty" for purposes of the right to jury trial where the *authorized* imprisonment is more than six months. This, however, must be considered with the holding in *Bloom* that in criminal contempt, where no legislative maximum has been fixed, it is the penalty actually imposed which governs. And see Frank v. United States, 395 U.S. 147, 89 S.Ct. 1503, 23 L.Ed.2d 162 (1969), holding that a sentence of three years probation on a criminal contempt charge may be imposed without jury trial, though if the defendant violates the terms of probation he cannot be sent to jail for more than six months.

§ 1.8

1. See ch. 3.

2. See ch. 7.

3. See ch. 8.

4. See ch. 4

5. See ch. 5.

6. The proof, of course, may be either by direct or by circumstantial evidence.

sitting without a jury).[7] Thus the prosecution must both produce evidencee of,[8] and persuade beyond a reasonable doubt of,[9] the existence of certain facts relating to defendant's guilt of the crime charged.

But a question of some difficulty is: what sorts of facts are meant? In a jury trial of *A* for the battery of *B,* for instance, the prosecution must certainly introduce evidence, and persuade the jury beyond a reasonable doubt, (1) that *A* did an act (fired a gun, threw a rock, swung a stick, drove a car), (2) which caused bodily injury to *B,* (3) which result was either intended by *A* or was within the risk which *A*'s reckless conduct created—these three items being the elements of the crime of battery.[10] But what about matters of defense which negative guilt, such as self defense, duress and insanity? Must the prosecution, while presenting its side of the case, produce evidence of facts showing that *A* did not act in self-defense, that *A* was not coerced, that *A* was sane, and so on; and must the prosecution convince the jury of the non-existence of facts giving rise to these defenses beyond a reasonable doubt? It would, of course, make the prosecution of *A* for the simple battery of *B* a rather cumbersome proceeding if the prosecution had to establish its case by proving, not only the existence of the three elements of the crime, but also the non-existence of every conceivable defense.

The rules which have developed concerning both the burden of production and the burden of persuasion cannot be satisfactorily explained on the basis of any single principle. The exceptional situation in which we place one or both burdens upon the defendant has sometimes been explained in terms of relieving the prosecution of the necessity of proving a negative or in terms of requiring the defendant to prove defenses which are not a part of the definition of the crime.[11] Neither is totally convincing. "What is involved seems rather a more subtle balance which acknowledges that a defendant ought not to be required to defend until some solid substance is presented to support the accusation, but beyond this perceives a point where need for narrowing the issues coupled with the relative accessability of evidence to the defendant warrants calling upon him to present his defensive claim."[12]

 WESTLAW REFERENCES

di burden of proof

(b) Elements of the Crime. It is everywhere agreed that the prosecution has the burden of proving each of the various elements of the offense[13] in both burden-of-proof senses: it must, to avoid a directed verdict of acquittal, produce evidence of each element; and it must, to secure a conviction, convince the trier of fact of the existence of each element beyond a reasonable doubt.[14] Because this was the law in all jurisdictions, the United States Supreme Court for many years never had occasion to hold explicitly that proof of

---

7. C. McCormick, Evidence, §§ 336–37 (E. Cleary ed. 3d ed. 1984). It is often stated that one accused of crime is presumed innocent until proved guilty. This is generally held to mean no more than that the prosecution has the two burdens of producing evidence and persuading the fact-finder (beyond a reasonable doubt). See § 1.8(f).

8. In order to avoid a directed verdict. See § 1.8(h).

9. In order to secure a conviction.

10. See § 7.15.

11. E.g., Rossi v. United States, 289 U.S. 89, 53 S.Ct. 532, 77 L.Ed. 1051 (1933).

12. Model Penal Code § 1.12, Comment at 194 (1985).

13. Again, the elements of a crime are its requisite (a) conduct (act or omission to act) and (b) mental fault (except for strict liability crimes)—plus, often, (c) specified attendant circumstances, and, sometimes, (d) a specified result of the conduct.

Generally, they are spelled out in the statute defining the crime; but sometimes a statute omits to state any of the elements of the crime (e.g., a statute which punishes simply "whoever commits murder," leaving it up to the common law of murder to furnish all the particular elements), or omits to state one of several elements (e.g., the statute involved in United States v. Carll, 105 U.S. 611, 26 L.Ed. 1135 (1881), held to include the three elements mentioned in the statute—(a) uttering (b) a forged obligation of the United States (c) with intent to defraud—plus a fourth element not so mentioned: (d) knowledge by the utterer that the document is a forgery.)

14. C. McCormick, Evidence, § 341 (E. Cleary ed. 3d ed. 1984). This proposition is sometimes stated in these terms: the prosecution has the burden of proof (in both senses) of the *corpus delicti* and of the defendant's responsibility therefor. E.g., Anderson v. State, 35 Ala.App. 557, 51 So.2d 257 (1951), cert. denied 255 Ala. 302, 51 So.2d 260 (1951) (prosecution must prove beyond a reasonable doubt

a criminal charge beyond a reasonable doubt was constitutionally required, although such view was frequently expressed in the Court's decisions.[15] But in the course of holding that due process required this burden of proof to be met in juvenile court cases, the Supreme Court in *In re Winship* explicitly held "that the Due Process Clause protects the accused against conviction except upon proof beyond a reasonable doubt of every fact necessary to constitute the crime with which he is charged." [16]

In the *Winship* opinion, the Court explained why the reasonable-doubt standard is indispensable in American criminal procedure. The basic point, of course, is that it is "a prime instrument for reducing the risk of convictions resting on factual error." There are several reasons, the Court noted, for reducing the margin of error in criminal cases in this way: (1) because the individual defendant has at stake an interest of immense importance, both in terms of the possibility that he will lose his liberty and that he would be stigmatized by the conviction; (2) because the moral force of the criminal law would be diluted if the public was in doubt whether innocent men were being convicted; and (3) because every individual going about his ordinary affairs should have confidence that the government cannot judge him guilty of a criminal offense without convincing the fact-finder of his guilt with utmost certainty.

The existence of certain facts may call for increased punishment—as under a statute, applicable to a single crime, punishing armed robbery more severely than simple robbery, or under habitual criminal statutes, applicable to many crimes punishing subsequent offenders more heavily than first offenders. The

prosecution has the burden of proving the aggravated-punishment facts, which may be considered to be, in a sense, elements of a principal crime.[17] Thus when the prosecution seeks, in connection with defendant's conviction of the crime charged, to impose habitual criminal punishment on account of former crimes committed by the defendant, the prosecution must produce evidence of the facts that these other crimes were committed and that the defendant committed them, and then persuade the fact-finder of these matters beyond a reasonable doubt.[18]

That the *Winship* principle also applies to elements which serve to distinguish a more serious crime from a less serious crime (as compared to elements which serve to distinguish criminal from noncriminal conduct) was settled by the Supreme Court in *Mullaney v. Wilbur*.[19] The defendant there had been convicted of murder in Maine despite his defense of provocation. Under Maine law, as the court explained,

> absent justification or excuse, all intentional or criminally reckless killings are felonious homicides. Felonious homicide is punished as murder—i.e., by life imprisonment—unless the defendant proves by a fair preponderance of the evidence that it was committed in the heat of passion on sudden provocation, in which case it is punished as manslaughter—i.e., by a fine not to exceed $1,000 or by imprisonment not to exceed 20 years.

Consequently, the trial judge instructed the jury that "if the prosecution established that the homicide was both intentional and unlawful, malice aforethought was to be conclusively implied unless the defendant proved by a fair preponderance of the evidence that he acted in the heat of passion on sudden provo-

that the crime charged was committed, and that defendant committed it). Once again, the prosecution's proof may be by either direct or circumstantial evidence.

15. E.g., Miles v. United States, 103 U.S. 304, 26 L.Ed. 481 (1880); Davis v. United States, 160 U.S. 469, 16 S.Ct. 353, 40 L.Ed. 499 (1895); Holt v. United States, 218 U.S. 245, 31 S.Ct. 2, 54 L.Ed. 1021 (1910).

16. 397 U.S. 358, 90 S.Ct. 1068, 25 L.Ed.2d 368 (1970).

17. Byler v. State, 16 Ohio App. 329, 157 N.E. 421 (1927) (former conviction one of elements of alleged subsequent offense).

18. State v. McCarty, 210 Iowa 173, 230 N.W. 379 (1930); State v. Livermore, 59 Mont. 362, 196 P. 977 (1921); People v. Brennan, 229 App.Div. 378, 242 N.Y.S. 692 (1930); Annots., 58 A.L.R. 20, 79 (1929), 19 A.L.R.2d 227, 261 (1951). If the former conviction is thus proved, however, it may be that the defendant has the burden of showing that the judgment did not become final, as where he claims that he won a reversal on appeal. People v. Logan, 358 Ill. 64, 192 N.E. 675 (1934).

19. 421 U.S. 684, 95 S.Ct. 1881, 44 L.Ed.2d 508 (1975).

cation." But the Supreme Court concluded this instruction was constitutionally infirm under *Winship,* and thus held "that the Due Process Clause requires the prosecution to prove beyond a reasonable doubt the absence of the heat of passion on sudden provocation when the issue is properly in a homicide case."

For one thing, the Court noted in *Mullaney,* this conclusion squares with two "important points" which emerged from its "historical review" of heat-of-passion voluntary manslaughter: (i) "the fact at issue here—the presence or absence of the heat of passion on sudden provocation—has been, almost from the inception of the common law of homicide, the single most important factor in determining the degree of culpability attaching to an unlawful homicide"; and (ii) "the clear trend has been toward requiring the prosecution to bear the ultimate burden of proving this fact." For another, this result gives proper recognition to the interests emphasized in *Winship;* considering the substantial differences in the penalty for murder as compared to that for manslaughter, both the individual and the societal interests in a solidly-grounded conviction were no less here than in *Winship.* Finally, the Court stressed it could "discern no unique hardship on the prosecution that would justify requiring the defendant to carry the burden of proving a fact so critical to criminal culpability." (The Court did not question, however, that the state could put the initial burden of production on the defendant, so that the state would not be required as a matter of course to prove absence of heat of passion in each and every murder prosecution.)

Just two years after *Mullaney* came *Patterson v. New York,*[20] where the Court held that the burden of proof could constitutionally be placed on the defendant to establish the affirmative defense of extreme emotional dis-

turbance. *Patterson* 's meaning in the affirmative defense context is discussed below; suffice it to note here that some commentators have found it impossible to reconcile *Patterson* with the *Mullaney* notion that the prosecution must *always* carry the burden of persuasion as to all offense elements. So the argument goes, if the state has it in its power to redefine the crime so as to transform an "element" into an "affirmative defense," then there is no reason—other than excessive formalism—to prohibit the state from instead leaving that particular in the statute as an element and merely assigning the burden of proof as to it to the defendant.[21]

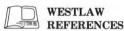

WESTLAW REFERENCES

winship /25 burden /2 proof prov***

(c) Affirmative Defenses. This book deals with a number of possible defenses which a criminal defendant may use to avoid conviction. Some of these are substantive law defenses which negative guilt by cancelling out the existence of some required element of the crime. For example, certain kinds of mistake of fact, mistake of law, intoxication, or insanity are properly viewed as proof that the defendant did not have the mental state required for the crime charged. Certain other defenses, such as self-defense and necessity, do not negative any of the elements of the crime but instead go to show some matter of justification or excuse which is a bar to the imposition of criminal liability. In addition to these defenses of general applicability, there are also substantive law defenses applicable to individual crimes, in which case the common practice is for the statute defining the crime to contain an exception or proviso setting forth the defense. Thus the typical bigamy statute, punishing one who, though married, marries again, continues with a proviso stating that it is not bigamy if his second marriage occurs after his first spouse has

20. 432 U.S. 197, 97 S.Ct. 2319, 53 L.Ed.2d 281 (1977).

21. See Allen, Structuring Jury Decisionmaking in Criminal Cases: A Unified Constitutional Approach to Evidentiary Devices, 94 Harv.L.Rev. 321 (1980); Allen, More on Constitutional Process-of-Proof Problems in Criminal Cases, 94 Harv.L.Rev. 1795 (1981); Jeffries & Ste-

phan, Defenses, Presumptions and Burden of Proof in the Criminal Law, 88 Yale L.J. 1325 (1979). For a contrary view, see Nesson, Rationality, Presumptions and Judicial Comment: A Response to Professor Allen, 94 Harv.L.Rev. 1574 (1981).

been absent for seven years and is not known by him to be living. An abortion statute, punishing the use of instruments or drugs on a woman to procure a miscarriage, may contain a provision exempting one who does the act on a doctor's orders to save the woman's life.[22]

There various substantive law defenses, whether of the general-principle or of the single-crime type, are often called (somewhat loosely) "affirmative defenses," although they are generally raisable upon a not guilty plea.[23] Who has the burden of proof in connection with these defenses—that is, who has the burden of production, and who has the burden of persuasion and by what measure?

As to the burden of production of evidence, it is uniformly held that the defendant is obliged to start matters off by putting in some evidence in support of his defense—e.g., evidence of his insanity, or of his acting in self-defense, or of one of the other affirmative defenses [24]—unless of course the prosecution, in presenting its own side of the case, puts in some evidence of a defense, in which case the matter of defense is properly an issue though the defendant himself produces nothing further to support it.[25] Experience shows that most people who commit crimes are sane and conscious; [26] they are not compelled to com-

mit them; and they are not so intoxicated that they cannot entertain the states of mind which their crimes may require. Thus it makes good sense to say that if any of these unusual features are to be injected into the case, the defendant is the one to do it; it would not be sensible to make the prosecution in all cases prove the defendant's sanity, sobriety and freedom from compulsion. Perhaps experience might show that homicides and battery are, as often as not, committed in self-defense; but even if this is so, it would still be wise (in the interests of simplifying issues and saving time which would be spent in presenting matters on which there is no dispute, and because the defendant normally has greater opportunity to know the facts) to place the burden of production on the defendant. Nothing in *Mullaney* or *Patterson* casts any doubt upon the constitutionality of so allocating the burden of production.[27]

What then of the burden of persuasion? Prior to *Mullaney,* the courts were split into different camps. One point of view was that the defendant has the burden of persuading the fact-finder by a preponderance of the evidence of the existence of facts giving rise to these defenses.[28] The other point of view was that, once the defendant has introduced some evidence of the defense, he need not persuade

22. In a sense too it is a "defense" to a crime that one or more of the required elements of the crime is missing— as where the defense to a murder prosecution is that the victim died accidentally or of natural causes or by suicide, or the defense to an abortion prosecution, under a statute punishing the use of instruments or drugs on a pregnant woman with intent to cause a miscarriage, is that the woman was not in fact pregnant at all. The matter of a missing element, not really an "affirmative defense" at all, Commonwealth v. Donough, 377 Pa. 46, 103 A.2d 694 (1954) (suicide), is treated under § 1.8(b).

23. In some jurisdictions, however, by statute the defense of insanity must be specially pleaded, not being available on a simple plea of not guilty. The real purpose of such a statute is to give the prosecution pretrial notice of the defense. See § 4.5.

24. E.g., Davis v. United States, 160 U.S. 469, 16 S.Ct. 353, 40 L.Ed. 499 (1895) (insanity); State v. McNamara, 252 Iowa 19, 104 N.W.2d 568 (1960) (self-defense); State v. Rosasco, 103 Or. 343, 205 P. 290 (1922) (statutory proviso); C. McCormick, Evidence, § 347 (3d ed. E. Cleary ed. 1984).

25. Davis v. United States, supra note 24.

26. Davis v. United States, supra note 24 (defense of insanity); Government of the Virgin Islands v. Smith, 278

F.2d 169 (3d Cir.1960) (defense of unconsciousness as result of epileptic seizure).

27. See Simopoulous v. Virginia, 462 U.S. 506, 103 S.Ct. 2532, 76 L.Ed.2d 775 (1983) (state not required to disprove medical necessity defense on abortion charge until defendant invoked the defense; placing burden of going forward on defendant permissible, as it did not negate element of the offense); United States v. Bailey, 444 U.S. 394, 100 S.Ct. 624, 62 L.Ed.2d 575 (1980) (Court without hesitation recognized the propriety of placing the burden of production on the defendant as to the necessity and duress defenses).

28. E.g., People v. Monk, 56 Cal.2d 288, 14 Cal.Rptr. 633, 363 P.2d 865 (1961) (insanity); State v. Clark, 34 Wash. 485, 76 P. 98 (1904) (insanity; the court says that, since insanity is "easily feigned and difficult to disprove," it is right on principle to impose the burden of persuasion of insanity on the defendant); Leland v. Oregon, 343 U.S. 790, 72 S.Ct. 1002, 96 L.Ed. 1302 (1952) (Oregon rule, later repealed, putting burden on defendant to persuade of his insanity beyond a reasonable doubt, *held* not to violate 14th Amendment due process); Commonwealth v. Donough, 377 Pa. 46, 103 A.2d 694 (1954) (dictum that defendant has burden of proving affirmative defenses of insanity, alibi and self-defense by a "fair preponderance of the

the fact-finder that the defense exists; instead the prosecution must persuade the factfinder beyond a reasonable doubt that the defense does not exist.[29] But *Mullaney* placed the former view in doubt, as that case could readily be interpreted as meaning that the prosecution now had the burden of persuasion with respect to many (if not all) the traditional affirmative defenses.[30] Indeed, some lower courts so held.[31]

That *Mullaney* did not go so far was first indicated in *Rivera v. Delaware,*[32] where the Court dismissed, as not presenting a substantial federal question, an appeal claiming a state statute burdening the defendant with proving insanity by a preponderance of the evidence was unconstitutional. Any lingering doubts were removed by *Patterson v. New York,*[33] upholding a New York murder conviction obtained in a case in which the jury was told the defendant had the burden of proof as to the affirmative defense of "extreme emotional disturbance," which if proved would reduce the crime to manslaughter. In one sense the *Patterson* circumstances were quite like those in *Mullaney,* for (as the Court conceded) New York's affirmative defense of extreme emotional disturbance was merely "a substantially expanded version of the older heat of passion concept" involved in *Mullaney.* But in another respect *Patterson* was quite different: the crime of murder was defined merely in terms of the defendant having intentionally caused the death of another, and thus the matter of emotional disturbance had nothing to do with any element of the crime but rather involved only an "affirmative defense." This, as it turned out, was a critical difference; the majority in *Patterson* concluded *Mullaney* meant only that "the Due Process Clause requires the prosecution to prove beyond reasonable doubt all of the elements included in the definition of the offense of which the defendant is charged."

Patterson makes some pragmatic sense for precisely the reasons noted by the majority. If the burden must be on the prosecution also to disprove affirmative defenses, then an understandable and likely response from the state legislatures would be to abolish those affirmative defenses which experience showed prosecutors had particular difficulty in disproving. The due process clause, as the Court saw it, does not put any state "to the choice of abandoning those defenses or undertaking to disprove their existence in order to convict for a crime which otherwise is within its constitutional powers to sanction by substantial punishment." *Patterson* thus recognizes that state legislative bodies are in a better position to engage in the "more subtle balancing of society's interests against those of the accused" which is involved in determining whether creation of a particular defense and then imposition of the burden of its disproof on the prosecution "would be too cumbersome, too expensive, and too inaccurate."

The trouble with *Patterson,* objected the dissenters, is that it "allows a legislature to shift, virtually at will, the burden of persuasion with respect to any factor in a criminal case, so long as it is careful not to mention the nonexistence of that factor in the statutory language that defines the crime." This means, they continued, that under *Patterson* a legislature could define murder simply as the causing of another's death and then leave it to the defendant to prove the affirmative defense that he lacked any culpable mens rea. But, unless a crime as serious as murder may constitutionally be made a strict liability of-

evidence"); State v. Baker, 246 Iowa 215, 66 N.W.2d 303 (1954) (alibi); State v. Sappienza, 84 Ohio St. 63, 95 N.E. 381 (1911) (duress); State v. Hairston, 222 N.C. 455, 23 S.E.2d 885 (1943) (intoxication); Commonwealth v. Chapman, 359 Pa. 164, 58 A.2d 433 (1948) (intoxication). See C. McCormick, Evidence, § 341 (E. Cleary ed. 3d ed. 1984).

29. E.g., Davis v. United States, 160 U.S. 469, 16 S.Ct. 353, 40 L.Ed. 499 (1895) (insanity); State v. McNamara, 252 Iowa 19, 104 N.W.2d 568 (1960) (self-defense); State v. Strawther, 342 Mo. 618, 116 S.W.2d 133, 120 A.L.R. 583

(1938) (defense of another); Government of the Virgin Islands v. Smith, 278 F.2d 169 (3d Cir.1960) (defense of no "acts"; unconsciousness because of epileptic seizure).

30. See Comment, 11 Harv.C.R.–C.L.L.Rev. 390 (1976).

31. E.g., Evans v. State, 28 Md.App. 640, 349 A.2d 300 (1975), affirmed 278 Md. 197, 362 A.2d 629 (1975).

32. 429 U.S. 877, 97 S.Ct. 226, 50 L.Ed.2d 160 (1976).

33. 432 U.S. 197, 97 S.Ct. 2319, 53 L.Ed.2d 281 (1977).

fense, which hardly seems likely,[34] this is not so. *Patterson*, as the majority explained, does not give the legislatures a free hand "to reallocate burdens of proof by labeling" elements as affirmative defenses. The "obvious constitutional limits" to which the majority referred are the various constitutional doctrines which presently exist[35] regarding the way in which crimes may be defined. Thus, if a crime defined by law as consisting of elements *X, Y* and *Z* is reformulated by the legislature so as to consist only of elements *X* and *Y*, with non-*Z* now an affirmative defense to be proved by the defendant, this is permissible under *Patterson* if and only if it is constitutionally permissible to make *X* plus *Y*, standing alone, a criminal offense.[36]

Most lower courts seem to have applied *Patterson* in essentially this way. Thus, based upon an element-versus-defense analysis of particular statutory schemes, it has been held that the burden of persuasion may properly be placed upon the defendant as to insanity,[37] extreme emotional disturbance,[38] intoxication,[39] duress,[40] self-defense,[41] and various other defenses.[42] But, it is essential to note that merely calling something an affirmative defense does not settle the issue; it must appear that the so-called defense does not in actuality negate any element of the crime.[43] Thus, the burden of proof as to the "defense" of alibi may not be placed upon the defendant, for alibi of necessity negates defendant's participation in the conduct defined as criminal.[44] Similarly, where the law of criminal homicide is defined in terms of an "unlawful" killing, the burden of proof as to the "defense" of self-defense may not be placed on the defendant, for a killing in self-defense is not unlawful.[45]

One way to assess the *Patterson* rule is in terms of what tasks it does and does not impose upon the courts. In praise of *Patterson*, it might be said that the majority there freed courts from the most difficult task of making individual judgments about various kinds of defenses in the manner apparently contemplated by the dissenters. (The *Patterson* dissenters would have permitted a shifting of the burden of persuasion to the defendant only as to "[n]ew ameliorative affirmative defenses," and thus would have required case-by-case determination of what

---

34. See § 3.8(b).

35. See, e.g., §§ 2.10–2.15.

36. This is not to suggest that it is sound to argue that if a matter could be entirely removed from a certain crime definition, then it is hardly objectionable that instead this matter is included in the form of an affirmative defense to be proved by the defendant. Some have forcefully contended the contrary. One concern is that selected, unpopular defendants may be denied the benefits of a defense if they must bear the burden of persuasion. Underwood, The Thumb on the Scales of Justice: Burdens of Persuasion in Criminal Cases, 86 Yale L.J. 1299, 1321–22 (1977). A more direct argument is that imposition of the burden of persuasion on the defendant by a greater-includes-the-lesser rationale "must be rejected because it permits the imposition of stigma without requiring the government to prove that there is a difference between greater and lesser offenders." Saltzburg, Burdens of Persuasion in Criminal Cases: Harmonizing the Views of the Justices, 20 Am. Crim.L.Rev. 393, 407 (1983).

37. Walker v. Butterworth, 599 F.2d 1074 (1st Cir. 1979); Spivey v. State, 253 Ga. 187, 319 S.E.2d 420 (1984); State v. Bertrand, 123 N.H. 719, 465 A.2d 912 (1983); Ward v. State, 438 N.E.2d 750 (Ind.1982); State v. McKenzie, 186 Mont. 481, 608 P.2d 428 (1980); Ybarra v. State, ___ Nev. ___, 679 P.2d 797 (1984); Navni v. State, 670 P.2d 126 (Okl.Crim.App.1983); State v. Smith, 117 Wis.2d 399, 344 N.W.2d 711 (1983).

38. Vasquez v. Vaughn, 454 F.Supp. 194 (D.Del.1978); State v. Elliot, 177 Conn. 1, 411 A.2d 3 (1979); State v.

Gratzer, ___ Mont. ___, 682 P.2d 141 (1984); State v. Dilger, 338 N.W.2d 87 (N.D.1983).

39. Hobby v. Housewright, 698 F.2d 962 (8th Cir.1983); Long v. Brewer, 667 F.2d 742 (8th Cir.1982); United States ex rel. Goddard v. Vaughn, 614 F.2d 929 (3d Cir.1980); Commonwealth v. Costello, 392 Mass. 393, 467 N.E.2d 811 (1984).

40. United States v. Mitchell, 725 F.2d 832 (2d Cir. 1983); United States v. Calfon, 607 F.2d 29 (2d Cir.1979); State v. Strickland, 307 N.C. 274, 298 S.E.2d 645 (1983).

41. Baker v. Muncy, 619 F.2d 327 (4th Cir.1980); Thomas v. Arn, 704 F.2d 865 (6th Cir.1983); State v. Davis, 8 Ohio App.3d 205, 456 N.E.2d 1256 (1982); McGhee v. Commonwealth, 219 Va. 560, 248 S.E.2d 808 (1978).

42. E.g., that a robbery gun was unloaded, Farrell v. Czarnetsky, 566 F.2d 381 (2d Cir.1977), or inoperable, Connolly v. Commonwealth, 377 Mass. 527, 387 N.E.2d 519 (1979); that a felony-murder defendant was unaware his accomplice was armed, State v. Gamboa, 38 Wn.App. 409, 685 P.2d 643 (1984); that possession of hypodermic syringes and needles was justified, Commonwealth v. Jefferson, 377 Mass. 716, 387 N.E.2d 579 (1979).

43. Holloway v. McElroy, 632 F.2d 605 (5th Cir.1980).

44. Adkins v. Bordenkircher, 674 F.2d 279 (4th Cir. 1982).

45. Holloway v. McElroy, 632 F.2d 605 (5th Cir.1980); In re Doe, 120 R.I. 732, 390 A.2d 920 (1978); State v. McCullum, 98 Wn.2d 484, 656 P.2d 1064 (1983).

statutory defenses could be properly so characterized.[46]) But, it appears that *Patterson* raises other, equally challenging questions for courts. For one thing, the majority's approach brings to the fore issues about constitutional limits on defining crime which otherwise would be unlikely to arise. Consider, for example, the defense of self-defense, the "major remaining area of uncertainty after *Patterson.*"[47] Even if the homicide statute in question does *not* express an "unlawful" killing element, there is certainly room for argument that self-defense nonetheless must be treated for burden-of-proof purposes as an element rather than as an affirmative defense. So the argument goes, to claim otherwise "is to assert that the State may punish a defendant with life imprisonment * * * for [murder] even if the killing was done in the purest self-defense," when in fact "both the Due Process Clause and the Eighth Amendment restrict the State's ability to so punish a defendant whose 'crime,' for example, consisted in an immediate response to a murderous attack upon him."[48]

Secondly, *Patterson* also appears to raise interesting but occasionally difficult questions about the relationship of (even traditional) defenses and the common elements of crimes. For example, if a defendant is charged with an offense which requires a particular mental state but the defendant interposes the defense

of voluntary intoxication, statutorily defined as a defense when it "negatives the existence of a state of mind essential to the crime," then must not the burden to disprove that defense be placed on the prosecution beyond a reasonable doubt because it raises the ultimate question of whether the mental state element of the crime existed in the particular case?[49] (Or, if it is thought that the question should be, as some have argued ought be the case,[50] whether the crime *could* constitutionally be defined without including the particular matter at issue, then cases such as this would require courts to resolve the difficult question of the due process limits on strict liability.)

Within the range of what is constitutionally permissible under *Mullaney* and *Patterson,* it remains for each jurisdiction to decide how to allocate the burden of proof in criminal cases as to so-called affirmative defenses. A few of the modern codes put the burden of persuasion on the prosecution as to virtually all issues, while a greater number allocate the burden to the defendant as to any matter which has been designated an "affirmative defense." But many jurisdictions have not adopted any general statutory rules on burden of proof, thus leaving the matter to be worked out by the courts on a defense-by-defense basis. This "seems an inappropriate approach given the lack of consensus on crite-

---

46. In a footnote they stated: "Numerous examples of such defenses are available: New York subjects an armed robber to lesser punishment than he would otherwise receive if he proves by a preponderance of the evidence that the gun he used was unloaded or inoperative. A number of States have ameliorated the usual operation of statutes punishing statutory rape, recognizing a defense if the defendant shows that he reasonably believed his partner was of age. Formerly the age of the minor was a strict liability element of the crime. The Model Penal Code also employs such a shift in the burden of persuasion for a limited number of defenses. For example, a corporation can escape conviction of an offense if it proved by a preponderance of the evidence that the responsible supervising officer exercised due diligence to prevent the commission of the offense. § 2.07(5) (Proposed Official Draft 1962)." The dissenters did not make it absolutely clear what places a defense into this category, except to distinguish those examples from defenses which "historically" were important in the sense of making "a substantial difference in punishment and stigma." Query whether historical credentials ought be the sole distinction or whether (as seems true of the specific examples given in

the language quoted above) it should also be relevant that it would be genuinely difficult for the prosecution to prove the contrary of the defense.

47. Note, 78 Colum.L.Rev. 655, 672 (1978). See also Melchir v. Jago, 723 F.2d 486 (6th Cir.1983) (an "open question"); Cherry v. Jago, 722 F.2d 1296 (6th Cir.1983) (noting "confusion" on this point).

48. Moran v. Ohio, ___ U.S. ___, 105 S.Ct. 350, 83 L.Ed. 2d 285 (1984) (Brennan and Marshall, JJ., dissenting from denial of certiorari). See also Jeffries & Stephan, Defenses, Presumptions, and Burden of Proof in the Criminal Law, 88 Yale L.J. 1325, 1366–79 (1979).

49. Yes, the court concluded in State v. Schulz, 102 Wis.2d 423, 307 N.W.2d 151 (1981). See also State v. Charlton, 338 N.W.2d 26 (Minn.1983), reaching the less convincing conclusion that the defense of duress is inconsistent with the required mental state of intent, defined as a conscious desire and purpose to bring about a criminal result, and that consequently the burden must be on the state to disprove duress.

50. See note 48 supra.

ria for allocating the burden," for it "invite[s] inconsistency in allocation between similar offenses." [51]

But if the matter were confronted as one of legislative policy, it would seem that imposition of the burden of persuasion upon the defendant is an especially attractive alternative in some circumstances. Just when this should be the choice is difficult to define, though in general it may be said that such allocation is appropriate as a compromise of divergent views on substantive issues. That is, creation of the defense with the burden on the defendant sometimes can be fairly seen to be a sensible middle position between a much broader statute or a strict-liability-type of statute, on the one hand, and, on the other, a statute recognizing the defense and placing an impossible burden on the prosecution to establish the existence of facts within the special knowledge of the defendant. An illustration of such a defense from the Model Penal Code is that which provides for exculpation of a corporation on a showing of due diligence by supervising officers to prevent the commission of the offense. [52] It is quite obviously of the "fair compromise" variety, for it is desirable that corporations not be held liable where there was such due diligence, but equally desirable that the prosecution not have to prove an absence of due diligence by every corporate defendant. [53]

51. 1 P. Robinson, Criminal Law Defenses § 5(b)(2) (1984).

52. Model Penal Code § 2.07(5).

53. Of this and similar situations, it is said: "These were characteristically situations where the defense did not obtain at all or as broadly under antecedent law and the Code sought to introduce a mitigation. Resistance to the mitigation, often based upon the prosecution's difficulty in obtaining evidence, would presumably be lowered if the burden of persuasion were imposed on the defendant. Where the prosecution's problem appeared genuine and there was something to be said against allowing the defense at all, shifting the burden was believed to be acceptable." Model Penal Code § 1.12, Comment at 188 (1985).

54. See §§ 2.10–2.15.

55. People v. Albrecht, 145 Colo. 202, 358 P.2d 4 (1960) (defendant, accused of the crime of charging a fee more than the statutory maximum for employment agencies, pleaded not guilty, admitting the alleged acts but "by way of defense" asserting the unconstitutionality of the statute).

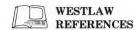

WESTLAW REFERENCES

topic(110) /p "affirmative defense" /p burden /2 proof prov*** persuasion

(d) Unconstitutionality of a Criminal Statute. Later in this book there is a discussion of the various constitutional limitations upon the powers of the state and federal government to create crimes. [54] If this power is exceeded, then the defendant may defend on the ground that the statute which defines the crime with which he is charged is invalid, and this may also be thought of as a "defense" to the prosecution. [55] The constitutionality of criminal statutes sometimes hinges upon the existence or nonexistence of underlying facts. [56] It has been held that the burden of proving facts showing unconstitutionality is upon the defendant, partially at least because there is a presumption of validity and a reluctance on the part of courts to strike down legislation as unconstitutional. [57]

WESTLAW REFERENCES

burden /2 proof prov*** /s statut*** /3 crim**** /s unconstitutional***

(e) Rebuttable Presumptions, Case Law and Statutory. [58] Courts have created some rebuttable presumptions in favor of the prosecution in criminal cases—e.g., the presumption from recent exclusive unexplained possession of stolen property that the possessor

56. Thus a state statute, enacted as a safety measure, making it unlawful to operate interstate passenger trains over fourteen cars, and interstate freight trains over seventy cars, in length, was attacked on the ground that the act burdens interstate commerce without promoting the interests of safety. Southern Pacific Co. v. State of Arizona ex rel. Sullivan, 325 U.S. 761, 65 S.Ct. 1515, 89 L.Ed. 1915 (1945). The railroad defendant at the trial proved as facts that the act (1) burdened interstate commerce and (2) did not promote safety; and so the act was held unconstitutional. See also People v. Albrecht, supra note 57, holding the employment-agency-fee statute unconstitutional on the basis of evidence of facts showing the statute to be unreasonable and confiscatory and so in violation of due process.

57. E.g., Thiele v. City & County of Denver, 135 Colo. 442, 312 P.2d 786 (1957) (dog leash ordinance upheld over dog owner's contention that it was not within the police power of the municipality to enact).

58. As to the constitutionality of statutory presumptions in criminal law, see § 2.13.

stole it, and the presumption from the intentional use of a deadly weapon upon another human being that the user intended to kill his victim with it. In addition, the legislatures have created a great variety of statutory presumptions which aid the prosecution in criminal cases.[59] Often these criminal statutes make proof of a physical fact (or group of facts) "presumptive evidence" or "prima facie evidence" of a mental fact necessary for a conviction [60]—as where, in connection with a crime of receiving stolen property knowing it to be stolen, the statute makes the fact of receiving the stolen property prima facie evidence that the receiver knew it to be stolen.[61] Less frequently, the statutes provide that proof of one physical fact (or group of facts) is prima facie (or presumptive) evidence of another physical fact which is required for conviction—as where a statute makes it a crime to deface the manufacturer's marks on firearms, and then provides that possession of a firearm on which the marks have been defaced is prima facie evidence that the possessor has defaced it.[62]

The question which now arises is: what is the effect of these case-law and statutory rebuttable presumptions upon the burden of proof, using that term in both its senses—the burden of production and the burden of persuasion? The generally accepted rule is that once the prosecution has proved the underlying fact (or facts) to which the presumption attaches, the case must go to the jury (i.e., there will be no directed verdict for the defendant); [63] but the jury is not compelled, even in the complete absence of rebuttal evidence by the defendant, to find the ultimate fact required for conviction (i.e., the "presumption" is a "permissive" rather than a "mandatory" [64] one).[65] Thus the defendant does not, strictly speaking, have the burden of production to overcome the presumption; yet, as a practical matter, he may well be convicted in some circumstances if he does not do so. As to the burden of persuasion, it is generally held that the defendant is entitled to be acquitted if there is a reasonable doubt in the minds of the jury (or other fact-finders); [66] the burden of persuasion is not shifted by the presumption to the defendant.[67]

59. See C. McCormick, Evidence §§ 342–348 (E. Cleary ed. 3d ed. 1984), and sources cited therein.

60. The statute may be worded this way: the mental fact "shall be presumed" from the physical fact.

61. Other examples: a bad-check statute, which punishes the giving of a bad check with intent to defraud, providing that non-payment of the check within 5 days after it is dishonored is prima facie evidence of an intent to defraud; or a burglar-tools statute, making it a crime to possess burglar tools with intent to use them to commit burglary, providing that the fact of possession of burglar tools by one previously convicted of a felony is presumptive evidence of an intent to use the tools to commit burglary.

State v. Thomas, 58 Wash.2d 746, 364 P.2d 930 (1961), involved a statute, applicable to crimes of violence generally, which provided that the fact that the defendant was armed with a pistol for which he had no license is prima facie evidence of an intent to commit a crime of violence.

62. E.g., United States v. Gainey, 380 U.S. 63, 85 S.Ct. 754, 13 L.Ed.2d 658 (1965): a federal statute makes it a crime to carry on the business of an illegal distiller; and it provides that the defendant's unexplained presence at the site of an illegal still authorizes the fact-finder to convict of carrying on such business. The Court upheld the constitutionality of this statutory presumption.

63. Cf. United States v. Gainey, supra note 64 (the statute, providing that unexplained presence at illegal still constitutes sufficient evidence to authorize conviction

of carrying on business of illegal distiller, construed as not requiring court to submit case to jury where only evidence against defendant is his unexplained presence at the illegal still).

64. The word "presumption" by itself is ambiguous without the accompanying adjective, for it may mean either that the jury *must,* or that it *may,* find the presumed fact from the proved fact. So doubtless a better single word for the permissive sort of presumption is "inference." See Barfield v. United States, 229 F.2d 936 (5th Cir.1956) (reversing conviction for interstate transportation of stolen car knowing it to be stolen, because the trial court charged jury that unexplained possession of recently stolen property raises "presumption" of guilty knowledge; it was held this might have misled the jury into belief that it must, not may, find guilty knowledge; the proper word is "inference").

65. See County Court of Ulster County v. Allen, 442 U.S. 140, 99 S.Ct. 2213, 60 L.Ed.2d 777 (1979).

66. Brosman, Statutory Presumptions, 5 Tulane L.Rev. 17, 199–200 (1930). Thus in United States v. Gainey, supra note 64, the trial court instructed the jury that unexplained presence at the still was not enough to convict; the jury must believe the defendant conducted the business of an illegal distiller beyond a reasonable doubt; the Supreme Court, approving the instruction, upheld the constitutionality of the presumption.

67. Some cases which seem to shift the burden are explained by Brosman, supra note 68, at 199.

**WESTLAW
REFERENCES**

topic(110) /p rebuttable /2 presumption /s
  permissive mandatory

**(f) Meaning of "Beyond a Reasonable
Doubt" and "Presumption of Innocence".**
The expression "beyond a reasonable doubt"
appears most often in the trial court's instructions to the jury, which is generally told: the
defendant is presumed to be innocent; the
mere fact that he has been charged with a
crime is not to be taken as any evidence of his
guilt; and the prosecution must prove, beyond
a reasonable doubt, all the elements of the
crime charged.[68] While some courts have undertaken to define the term "reasonable
doubt," [69] other courts have thought that the
words themselves are sufficiently clear not to
require any embellishment.[70]

The so-called "presumption of innocence" is
actually not a presumption at all in the legal
sense discussed above,[71] that, once an underlying fact has been proved, another (ultimate)
fact may (or must) be taken as proved. It is
not even a presumption in the popular sense
of a thing which is more likely to be true than

not, for statistically more people who are
charged with crime are convicted as guilty
than are acquitted as innocent. It is more
properly said that the innocence of the defendant is assumed,[72] which is generally taken to
mean no more than that the prosecution has
the two burdens of proof discussed in this
section: the burden of producing evidence of
guilt in order to avoid a directed verdict; and
of persuading the fact-finder of guilt beyond a
reasonable doubt in order to secure a conviction.[73] However, the customary statement to
the jury when the trial court gives instructions is that the defendant is presumed innocent, that the mere fact of accusation is no
evidence of his guilt, and that the prosecution
must prove guilt beyond a reasonable doubt.[74]

**WESTLAW
REFERENCES**

di beyond a reasonable doubt

di presumption of innocence

(g) No Directed Verdict of Guilty. After
the evidence is in, the trial court may not, on
motion of the prosecution, direct a verdict of
guilty, no matter how conclusive the evidence
of guilt.[75] Nor may the court, without going

---

68. See Goldstein, The State and the Accused: Balance
of the Advantage in Criminal Procedure, 69 Yale L.J.
1149, 1153 (1960).

69. The most famous definition is that of Shaw, C.J.,
instructing the jury in Commonwealth v. Webster, 5 Cush.
295, 320, 52 Am.Dec. 711 (Mass.1850): "[R]easonable doubt
* * * is a term often used, probably pretty well understood, but not easily defined. It is not a mere possible
doubt; because everything relating to human affairs, and
depending on moral evidence is open to some possible or
imaginary doubt. It is that state of the case, which, after
the entire comparison and consideration of all the evidence, leaves the minds of the jurors in that condition
that they cannot say they feel an abiding conviction, to a
moral certainty, of the truth of the charge."

70. Miles v. United States, 103 U.S. 304, 26 L.Ed. 481
(1880) ("Attempts to explain the term 'reasonable doubt'
do not usually result in making it any clearer to the
minds of the jury"); State v. Sauer, 38 Minn. 438, 38 N.W.
355 (1888) ("The term 'reasonable doubt' is almost incapable of any definition which will add much to what the
words themselves imply"). See 9 J. Wigmore, Evidence
§ 2497 (Chadbourne rev. 1981); C. McCormick, Evidence
§ 341 (E. Cleary ed. 3d ed. 1984); McBaine, Burden of
Proof: Degrees of Belief, 32 Calif.L.Rev. 242 (1944).

"The Code does not define 'reasonable doubt,' in the
view that definition can add nothing helpful to the
phrase." Model Penal Code § 1.12, Comment at 190
(1985).

71. See § 1.8(e).

72. Model Penal Code § 1.12; National Comm'n on
Reform of Federal Criminal Laws, Final Report—Proposed
New Federal Criminal Code § 103 (1971).

73. C. McCormick, Evidence § 342 (E. Cleary ed. 3d ed.
1984).

74. In Kentucky v. Whorton, 441 U.S. 786, 99 S.Ct.
2088, 60 L.Ed.2d 640 (1979), the Court, 6–3, held that "the
failure to give a requested instruction on the presumption
of innocence does not in and of itself violate the Constitution." The majority stressed that Taylor v. Kentucky, 436
U.S. 478, 98 S.Ct. 1930, 56 L.Ed.2d 468 (1978), reversing a
conviction where the trial judge refused to give such an
instruction, "focused on the failure to give the instruction
as it related to the overall fairness of the trial considered
in its entirety." In *Taylor*, the trial judge's instructions
were Spartan, the prosecutor improperly referred to the
indictment and otherwise made remarks of dubious propriety, and the evidence against the defendant was weak.
See Fox, The "Presumption of Innocence" as a Constitutional Doctrine, 28 Cath.U.L.Rev. 253 (1979).

75. United Brotherhood of Carpenters & Joiners of
America v. United States, 330 U.S. 395, 67 S.Ct. 775, 91
L.Ed. 973 (1947); Rowan v. People, 93 Colo. 473, 26 P.2d
1066 (1933).

Cf. State v. Godwin, 227 N.C. 449, 42 S.E.2d 617 (1947)
(suggesting that in rare instances a verdict may be directed for the prosecution).

quite so far as to direct a finding of guilty, direct the jury to find against the defendant on one of the several elements of the crime, even though the prosecution's evidence concerning the evidence is uncontradicted.[76] The notion is that for the court to decide that all elements, or that a single element, of the crime exist would improperly invade the province of the jury,[77] which in fact if not in theory has the power to disregard the applicable law given it by the court by finding, in favor of the defendant, that an element does not exist even when it knows very well that it does exist.[78]

 WESTLAW REFERENCES

di directed verdict

(h) Directed Verdict of Acquittal. If in its opening statement the prosecution omits to state some essential element of its case, the defendant's motion for a directed verdict of acquittal will not be granted without first giving the prosecution an opportunity to embellish its opening statement by adding any missing parts.[79] In a rare case, however, the prosecution's opening statement may affirmatively show that it cannot make out a successful case against the defendant, in which case the court will direct a verdict of acquittal then and there.[80]

In most jurisdictions,[81] the trial court has the power and duty, on the defendant's motion or even on its own motion,[82] after the evidence on either side is closed, to direct a verdict for the defendant [83] if the evidence is insufficient to support a conviction.[84] The prosecution may have proved all of the required elements of the crime except one, but a lack of proof concerning one element requires a directed verdict. Thus a verdict of acquittal is properly directed: in a prosecution for receiving stolen property, where there is no evidence that the defendant knew the proper-

See Annot., 72 A.L.R. 899 (1931).

76. United States v. Hayward, 420 F.2d 142 (D.C.Cir. 1969); United States v. Manuszak, 234 F.2d 421 (3d Cir. 1956).

77. United States v. Johnson, 718 F.2d 1317 (5th Cir. 1983) (on trial of defendant for interstate transportation of a falsely made security, judge improperly instructed jury that document in question was a "security"; notwithstanding trial judge's characterization of this as an issue of law rather than fact, it is a disputed issue that cannot be taken from the jury).

78. The judge may not even submit special interrogatories to the jury, at least when the effect is to confront the jury with "a progression of questions each which seems to require an answer unfavorable to the defendant." United States v. Spock, 416 F.2d 165 (1st Cir.1969). On the other hand, the defendant is not entitled to a jury instruction to the effect that the jury has the power to acquit even if the defendant is clearly guilty. United States v. Dougherty, 473 F.2d 1113 (D.C.Cir.1972); United States v. Moylan, 417 F.2d 1002 (4th Cir.1969).

79. Rose v. United States, 149 F.2d 755 (9th Cir.1945); People v. Gomez, 131 Colo. 576, 283 P.2d 949 (1955).

80. See Rose v. United States, 149 F.2d 755 (9th Cir. 1945). Thus in United States v. Dietrich, 126 Fed. 676 (C.C.Neb.1904), in which the defendant was prosecuted for receiving a bribe while serving as "a member of Congress," and the prosecution in its opening stated facts which showed that the defendant, on the date of the alleged bribe, though he had been elected to the U.S. Senate, was not yet "a member of Congress," the court was bound to direct a verdict of not guilty.

81. In some states it is provided by statute that the trial judge may not take a case from the jury, reflecting the view that directed verdicts make abuse by the courts possible and that they prejudice the prosecution by an unappealable acquittal. Winningham, The Dilemma of the Directed Acquittal, 15 Vand.L.Rev. 699, 718 (1962). But there is a growing tendency for courts to ignore these statutes and rule that it is the duty of the trial judge to direct a verdict if the evidence is insufficient. Snow v. State, 325 P.2d 754 (Okl.Crim.App.1958). This is a salutary development. The risk of abuse is not great, and statistics show that directed verdicts are not granted in a large number of cases. H. Kalven & H. Zeisel, The American Jury 508 (1966). Moreover, withholding relief until the appeal places an undue burden on the defendant and transfers the issue from the judge who actually heard the evidence to others who must determine it solely upon the basis of the record.

82. E.g., Fed.R.Crim.P. 29(a) providing for what is there called a "motion for judgment of acquittal" by the defendant or the court.

83. In a few jurisdictions this procedure is called by some other name—e.g., a demurrer to the evidence, or a motion for a judgment of acquittal, or a motion to exclude the prosecution's evidence, or a motion to dismiss the prosecution, or a motion to nonsuit the prosecution.

84. Jackson v. Virginia, 443 U.S. 307, 99 S.Ct. 2781, 61 L.Ed.2d 560 (1979); France v. United States, 164 U.S. 676, 17 S.Ct. 219, 41 L.Ed. 595 (1897).

See Annot., 17 A.L.R. 910 (1922), collecting cases. The power of trial judges to direct verdicts is a comparatively recent development, having been first asserted in Syderbottom v. Smith, 1 Strange 649, 93 Eng.Rep. 759 (K.B.1725) (civil case).

ty was stolen;[85] or false pretenses, where there is no evidence that the victim relied on the defendant's falsehoods;[86] or for burglary, where there is no evidence of a breaking.[87] Stated more broadly, a verdict should be directed for the defendant if there is no evidence of the *corpus delicti* or, if there is such evidence, there is no evidence connecting the defendant with the crime.[88] In a jurisdiction which adopts the rule that there can be no conviction on the uncorroborated testimony of an accomplice, a verdict must be directed where such corroboration is missing from the prosecution's case.[89]

If the prosecution introduces insufficient evidence to support a conviction, so that the defendant's motion for a directed verdict, made at the close of the prosecution's case, is erroneously denied, but then the defendant, in presenting his own case, himself fills the gap in the prosecution's case, the defendant's renewed motion for a directed verdict, made at the close of his case, is properly denied.[90] This means that a defendant who believes that the prosecution failed to prove a prima facie case is presented with a hard choice. He may present no evidence in his own behalf and thus preserve for appeal the question of whether the trial judge's ruling was erroneous, or else abandon the point by putting in evidence on his side of the case. It has been

argued that this rule comes perilously close to compelling the defendant to incriminate himself,[91] and a few courts have declined to follow it.[92]

A defendant is not entitled to a directed verdict at the close of his side of the case just because defense testimony of facts which, if true, would constitute a defense is plausible and uncontradicted by the prosecution, for there is no rule that an unimpeached witness must be believed.[93]

A comparatively modern procedural device in use in civil as well as criminal cases allows a defendant, who has unsuccessfully moved for a directed verdict at the close of all the evidence, to move again, after a jury verdict against him, for a judgment in accordance with his earlier motion for a directed verdict.[94] This motion is popularly known, perhaps a little loosely, as a motion for judgment notwithstanding the verdict ("judgment n.o.v."). A trial judge who has reserved decision on the earlier motion, and who now believes that it would have been proper to have directed a verdict of acquittal at that time, may now enter a judgment of acquittal notwithstanding the jury's verdict of guilty. The question to be determined is exactly the same as that raised by the defendant's motion for a directed verdict of acquittal at the close of all the evidence.[95]

85. Mullins v. State, 15 Okl.Cr. 347, 176 P. 765 (1918).

86. State v. Miller, 47 Or. 562, 85 P. 81 (1906).

87. Green v. State, 68 Ala. 539 (1881).

88. But if the motion is made at the conclusion of the prosecution's case and the failure in the proof was clearly inadvertent, the court in its discretion may permit the prosecution to reopen its case. United States v. Hinderman, 625 F.2d 994 (10th Cir.1980).

89. Reynolds v. State, 14 Ariz. 302, 127 P. 731 (1912). Cf. Black v. State, 59 Wis. 471, 18 N.W. 457 (1884) (in this state, where a conviction may be had on uncorroborated testimony of accomplice, there is no duty to direct a verdict for the defendant when an accomplice's testimony is uncorroborated).

90. United States v. Lopez, 625 F.2d 889 (9th Cir.1980); State v. Blue, 225 Kan. 576, 592 P.2d 897 (1979). A defendant, by introducing evidence after the denial of his motion for directed verdict at the close of the prosecution's evidence, is generally held to waive his right to appeal on the ground that it was error to deny the motion. The result is that he must renew the motion at the end of all the evidence.

91. Note, 70 Yale L.J. 1151 (1961).

92. E.g., Cephus v. United States, 324 F.2d 893 (C.A. D.C.1963).

93. Commonwealth v. McNeese, 156 Mass. 231, 30 N.E. 1021 (1892); Annot., 62 A.L.R.2d 1191, 1210 (1958).

94. See Fed.R.Civ.P. 50(b); Fed.R.Crim.P. 29(c). Prior to the 1966 amendment of rule 29, it was assumed that a motion at the close of all the evidence was a prerequisite to a motion after discharge of the jury, Mosca v. United States, 174 F.2d 448 (9th Cir.1949), but the amendment makes it clear that this is not the case. However, it "would be a rash defense counsel who waited to make such a motion until after the verdict, in view of the impact a guilty verdict is likely to have on the court's determination of the motion." Reznick, The New Federal Rules of Criminal Procedure, 54 Geo.L.J. 1276, 1313 (1966).

95. United States v. Sutton, 426 F.2d 1202 (D.C.Cir. 1969); State v. Summers, 62 Haw. 325, 614 P.2d 925 (1980).

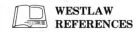

WESTLAW REFERENCES

digest("directed verdict" /2 acquit!)

(i) Test for Passing on Motion. There is some doubt as to how best to express the question which the court must answer when the defendant moves for a verdict of acquittal. Asking whether the prosecution's "evidence is insufficient to sustain a conviction" [96] is quite vague. Some earlier cases took the view that the motion should be granted unless the evidence was sufficient to "exclude every other hypothesis" except guilt.[97] However, this is unsound, for it would seem to mean that the judge would have to be convinced of guilt beyond doubt before he could submit the issue to the jury, and thus the judge would be preempting the functions of the jury.[98] Under another approach, "the standard of evidence necessary to send a case to the jury is the same in both civil and criminal cases," [99] which means that the judge must submit the case to the jury if there is substantial evidence in support of the charge.[100] This view has been rightly criticized [101] and has attracted little support.

The proper test has been stated in the following terms: "If the evidence is such that

reasonable jurymen must necessarily have [a reasonable] doubt, the judge must require acquittal, because no other result is permissible within the fixed bounds of jury consideration. But if a reasonable mind might fairly have a reasonable doubt or might fairly not have one, the case is for the jury, and the decision is for the jurors to make." [102] Although there once was some authority to the contrary,[103] the established rule now is that the test previously quoted is also applicable to cases based upon circumstantial evidence.[104]

It must be kept in mind that a defendant may be found guilty of a lesser offense necessarily included in the offense charged. This means that on a motion for a directed verdict the court must consider whether the evidence would be sufficient to sustain a conviction of some lesser offense, for if it would be then the issue of defendant's guilt of the lesser offense should be submitted to the jury.[105]

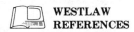

WESTLAW REFERENCES

digest("directed verdict" /2 acquit! /p reasonab!)

---

96. Fed.R.Crim.P. 29(a).

97. Isbell v. United States, 227 F. 788 (10th Cir.1915); Lombardi v. People, 124 Colo. 284, 236 P.2d 113 (1951); Commonwealth v. Shea, 324 Mass. 710, 88 N.E.2d 645 (1949); People v. Foley, 307 N.Y. 490, 121 N.E.2d 516 (1954).

98. Curley v. United States, 160 F.2d 229 (D.C.Cir. 1947).

99. United States v. Feinberg, 140 F.2d 592 (2d Cir. 1944), later rejected in United States v. Taylor, 464 F.2d 240 (2d Cir.1972).

100. United States v. Consolidated Laundries Corp., 291 F.2d 563 (2d Cir.1961).

101. Goldstein, The State and the Accused: Balance of Advantage in Criminal Procedure, 69 Yale L.J. 1149, 1152–72 (1960).

102. Curley v. United States, 160 F.2d 229 (D.C.Cir. 1947), characterized as "the prevailing criterion for judging motions for acquittal in federal criminal trials" in Jackson v. Virginia, 443 U.S. 307, 99 S.Ct. 2781, 61 L.Ed. 2d 560 (1979). See Comment, 65 Iowa L.Rev. 799 (1980).

103. E.g., Riggs v. United States, 280 F.2d 949 (5th Cir. 1960), rejected in United States v. Burns, 597 F.2d 939 (5th Cir.1979).

104. United States v. Burns, 597 F.2d 939 (5th Cir. 1979); United States v. Scott, 578 F.2d 1186 (6th Cir.1978); Early v. United States, 394 F.2d 117 (10th Cir.1968), so construing Holland v. United States, 348 U.S. 121, 75 S.Ct. 127, 99 L.Ed. 150 (1954).

105. Austin v. United States, 382 F.2d 129 (D.C.Cir. 1967); United States v. Kelly, 119 F.Supp. 217 (D.D.C.1954).

Chapter 2

SOURCES AND GENERAL LIMITATIONS

Table of Sections

---

§ 2.1   Common Law Crimes

Today we find the substantive criminal law in several forms: (1) mostly in statutes; (2) not infrequently in administrative regulations passed pursuant to legislative delegation of authority to an administrative agency;[1] (3) occasionally in constitutions;[2] and (4) sometimes in the common law of crimes.[3] Since historically the substantive criminal law began as common law for the most part, and only later became primarily statutory, it will be well to begin with common law crimes, with a view especially to determining the place of such crimes in modern criminal law.

(a) The Problem. On the civil side of the law we are used to the idea of judges deciding cases where there is no applicable statutory law. If *A*'s dog bites *B,* and *B* sues *A,* the judge who must decide whether a dog-owner is liable to one bitten by the dog may find that no statute covers the situation; but there may well be one or more dog-bite decisions in the reported cases of his state; or if not there may be some cases from other states, as well as from other jurisdictions in the Anglo-American system. He may follow these prior cases, or distinguish them, or choose between them; but he does use precedents to help him decide what the law is.

The situation may be a new one. Perhaps the city has hired a rainmaker to fill its empty reservoirs; the rainmaker seeds the clouds above the mountains where the water for the reservoirs collects; the rain falls; the reservoirs fill up; but a hotel owner in a mountain resort suffers a financial loss when his guests depart because of the dreary weather conditions. When the hotelman sues the city or the rainmaker for damages, what is the law to be applied? The judges who have to decide the law may well find no statute governing rainmaking, no reported case in the state, nor in any other American state, nor any federal case, nor any English, Canadian, Australian, etc., case. Yet the judges do not throw up their hands and say the case cannot be decided; they decide it. Maybe they can utilize some settled law in an analogous situation—perhaps the law of liability for seeping or collapsing dams may point the way. Even if there is no available analogy or if there are competing analogies, the judges will make (some prefer to say discover) the law to apply to the new situation. The new law will be decided according to the judges' ideas (ideas they acquire as members of society) of what is moral, right, just; of what will further sound public policy, in the light of the customs and traditions of the people of which the judges are members.[4]

A modern theory of jurisprudence suggests, somewhat loftily, that judges select between alternative solutions in order to "satisfy a maximum of human wants with a minimum of sacrifice of other wants * * * [and thus achieve] elimination of friction and waste, economizing of social effort, conservation of social assets, and adjustment of the struggle of individual human beings to satisfy their overlapping individual claims in life in civilized society, so that if each may not get all

---

§ 2.1

1. See § 2.6.

2. E.g., U.S. Const. art. III, § 3, defining treason. However, the federal and state constitutions contain much more on criminal procedure than on the substantive law of crimes.

3. Sometimes spoken of as "unwritten law"—perhaps not quite accurately, as the common law may be found in earlier decided (written) cases, unless we take the view that case law is only "evidence" of the common law—or "non-statutory law," using "statute" in a broad sense to include constitution and administrative regulation.

4. In Slutsky v. City of New York, 197 Misc. 730, 97 N.Y.S.2d 238 (Sup.Ct.1950), the court refused to enjoin rainmaking operations at the suit of the hotel operator. That was the first reported case on the subject.

that he demands, he may at least obtain all that is reasonably practicable in a wise social engineering." [5]

The question in the criminal law field is whether judges can create (or discover) new crimes for which to punish the ingenious fellow who conceives and carries out a new form of anti-social conduct not covered by the criminal code. Today the criminal law of any particular jurisdiction is contained in an imposing mass of statutory material, punishing conduct ranging all the way from murder down to defacing billboards. But it is hard for the legislature in advance to conceive of all possible anti-social behavior that ought to be criminal. If someone intentionally or by chance finds a loophole, may the courts create a new crime to plug that gap?

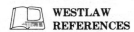

WESTLAW REFERENCES

di jurisprudence

(b) Common Law Crimes in England. In the beginning, at least, that is exactly what the English judges did. Although there were some early criminal statutes, in the main the criminal law was originally common law. Thus by the 1600's the judges, not the legislature, had created and defined the felonies of murder, suicide, manslaughter, burglary, arson, robbery, larceny, rape, sodomy and mayhem; and such misdemeanors as assault, battery, false imprisonment, libel, perjury, and intimidation of jurors. [6] During the period from 1660 (the Restoration of the monarchy of Charles II after Cromwell) to 1860 the process continued, [7] with the judges creating new crimes when the need arose and punishing those who committed them: blasphemy (1676), conspiracy (1664), sedition (18th century), forgery (1727), attempt (1784), solicitation

(1801). From time to time the judges, when creating new misdemeanors, spoke of the court's power to declare criminal any conduct tending to "outrage decency" or "corrupt public morals," or to punish conduct *contra bonos mores;* thus they found running naked in the streets, publishing an obscene book, and grave-snatching to be common law crimes.

Of course, sometimes the courts refused to denote as criminal some forms of anti-social conduct. At times their refusal seemed irrational, causing the legislature to step in and enact a statute; thus false pretenses, embezzlement, incest and other matters became statutory crimes in England. [8] Doubtless the English judges would have declared some other forms of conduct to be criminal but never had the chance because the legislature declared them criminal before the first case arose; such matters might still be considered "common law crimes" even though no court ever declared them so. [9] Some immoral conduct, mostly of a sexual nature (such as private acts of adultery or fornication, and seduction without conspiracy), was punished by the ecclesiastical courts in England. The common law courts never punished these activities as criminal, and thus they never became English common law crimes.

At the same time that judges were developing new crimes, they were also developing new common law defenses to crime, such as self-defense, insanity, infancy, and coercion.

About the middle of the nineteenth century the process of creating new crimes almost came to a standstill in England, and the foremost English criminal law commentator of the time predicted that the era of new common law crimes was over. [10] *Rex. v. Manley* [11] thus caused quite an uproar in legal circles in England in the 1930's. A woman falsely told

---

5. Pound, The Theory of Judicial Decision, 36 Harv.L. Rev. 940, 954 (1923). Such a philosophy may not automatically decide a particular case, but a judge armed with a philosophy of the purposes of law will do better than one without. B. Cardozo, The Growth of the Law 99–103 (1924).

6. See Jackson, Common Law Misdemeanors, 6 Camb. L.J. 193 (1937).

7. J. Hall, General Principles of Criminal Law 53 (2d ed. 1960).

8. For a brief history of English common law crimes, see Jackson, supra note 6, and G. Williams, Criminal Law: The General Part § 189 (2d ed. 1961).

9. See State v. Schleifer, 99 Conn. 432, 121 A. 805 (1923); Commonwealth v. McHale, 97 Pa. 397 (1881).

10. 3 J. Stephen, A History of the Criminal Law of England 359–60 (1883).

11. [1933] 1 K.B. 529 (1932).

the police that she had been robbed—with the result that valuable police time was wasted on a futile search for the non-existent robber, and innocent persons were subjected to suspicion. No statute made such a false report criminal, and no precise common law precedent existed. Yet the judges held that this constituted a common law misdemeanor (the court called the offense "public mischief") and convicted the woman of this new crime.[12]

At the present time it is clear that a new offense will be created by the courts only rarely in England, and any new offense created will be a misdemeanor and not a felony.[13]

 WESTLAW REFERENCES

110k13 & "common law" /s engl***
di common law

(c) **Common Law Crimes in the United States.** The original colonists in America who emigrated from England brought with them the English common law with its then existing statutory modifications, both civil and criminal, so far as applicable to conditions in America. After the American Revolution the thirteen states retained the English common law where applicable to local conditions. As new states joined the union the common law with statutory modifications generally became the basis of their law, sometimes by an express constitutional or statutory provision to that effect, and sometimes without the aid of such a provision. The rule, whether embodied in a "reception statute" or

not, is that the English common law of a general nature, together with the English statutory law in aid of the common law, existing at the time of the founding of the American colonies,[14] if applicable to local conditions, is the law of the state unless repealed expressly or impliedly by statute.[15]

Thus it was that most of the states in the beginning had common law crimes. The states soon began to enact criminal statutes; and in the nineteenth century a number of states undertook to enact comprehensive statutory criminal codes, covering most of the common law crimes as well as new crimes unknown to the common law. Some of these codes expressly provided that there should be no crimes except as found in the code (or, if the code was not meant to be completely comprehensive, except as found in the code or some other statute). Other states without such an express provision held that the comprehensive code by implication abolished common law crimes. In other states common law crimes were retained either by an express "reception statute" or without the aid of any statute. But in recent years a great many states have enacted comprehensive new criminal codes,[16] and in the process they have usually but not always abolished common law crimes.

It has long been settled that there are no federal common law crimes; if Congress has not by statute made certain conduct criminal, it is not a federal crime.[17] In spite of this

---

12. For English reaction, see Stallybrass, Public Mischief, 49 L.Q.Rev. 183 (1933); Jackson, Common Law Misdemeanors, 6 Camb.L.J. 193 (1937).

13. In Shaw v. Director of Public Prosecutions, [1962] A.C. 220, (1960) the House of Lords affirmed the defendant's conviction of conspiracy to effect a public mischief, and left open the question whether, if the conspiracy aspect had been absent, the defendant could have been convicted of a common law crime on these facts: the defendant published and sold a booklet called the "Ladies' Directory" which contained the names, addresses, telephone numbers, and, in some cases, the nude photographs of, and, in some cases, references to the specialized services of, various London prostitutes (who, no longer allowed to solicit business on the streets, found this to be a good way to procure employment). The case is noted at 75 Harv.L.Rev. 1652 (1962), and is discussed in detail in Brownlie & Williams, Judicial Legislation in Criminal Law, 42 Can.B.Rev. 561 (1964).

14. Jamestown, founded in the fourth year of James I, 1607, was the first English colony.

15. Some states use the date 1775, when the colonies broke away from England, instead of 1607, when the first colony was established. See Pope, The English Common Law in the United States, 24 Harv.L.Rev. 6 (1910). A few states name no date. A few states undertook to compile a statutory list of all the English statutes modifying the common law in force in those states. Some states with a civil law background (i.e., originally settled by French or Spanish settlers) did not take over the English law; yet even some of these states enacted statutes recognizing common law crimes.

16. See § 1.1(b).

17. In United States v. Hudson and Goodwin, 11 U.S. (7 Cranch) 32, 3 L.Ed. 259 (1812), the defendants, having falsely written in a newspaper that the President and Congress had secretly voted two million dollars to Napole-

general proposition, Congress has provided for common law crimes in the District of Columbia,[18] and Congress has provided that state criminal law (and this would include state criminal law of the common law variety in the states retaining common law crimes) applies (in the absence of a federal criminal statute) in those "federal enclaves", or islands of federal territory (e.g., army posts, naval bases), located within states.[19]

 WESTLAW REFERENCES

110k11 /p "common law"

topic(110) /p "common law" /p "district of columbia"

(d) The Common Law in Jurisdictions Abolishing Common Law Crimes.
Some of the states which have abolished common law

crimes nevertheless have catch-all criminal statutes almost broad enough to bring in the various common law misdemeanors.[20] Moreover, the states rejecting common law crimes often use common law terms in their statutes without defining them, in which case resort must be had to the common law for definition.[21]

Jurisdictions which have abolished common law crimes have not necessarily also abolished common law defenses to crime, such as self-defense, prevention of crime, insanity, infancy, coercion and necessity, especially if their statutes do not expressly provide for these defenses.[22] (The reason why common law defenses may exist where common law crimes have been abolished is to be found in the rationale underlying the abolition of such crimes, discussed below.) So also, the com-

---

on, were indicted for criminal libel; no federal statute made libel a crime; *held*, libel is no crime, for there are no federal common law crimes. The proposition was affirmed soon thereafter in United States v. Coolidge, 14 U.S. (1 Wheat.) 415, 4 L.Ed. 124 (1816). See also Liparota v. United States, ___ U.S. ___, 105 S.Ct. 2084, 85 L.Ed.2d 434 (1985): "The definition of the elements of a criminal offense is entrusted to the legislature, particularly in the case of federal crimes, which are solely creatures of statute."

As an original proposition, United States v. Hudson and Goodwin was probably wrong. See Warren, New Light on the History of the Federal Judiciary Act of 1789, 37 Harv. L.Rev. 49, 73 (1923). But the proposition is too well settled now for argument. See also Note, 22 Ky.L.J. 152 (1933).

18. See, e.g. United States v. Davis, 167 F.2d 228 (D.C. Cir. 1948) (crime of negligently permitting prisoner to escape). The statute has also been interpreted as incorporating into D.C. law common law doctrines such as transferred intent. United States v. Sampol, 636 F.2d 621 (D.C. Cir.1980); O'Connor v. United States, 399 A.2d 21 (D.C. App.1979).

19. 18 U.S.C.A. § 13. The federal government owns almost half a billion acres, 23% of the total land area of the continental United States. Note, 101 U.Pa.L.Rev. 124 (1952). See Notes, 18 Geo.Wash.L.Rev. 500 (1950); 58 Yale L.J. 1402 (1949).

20. New York formerly punished as a misdemeanor "any act which seriously injures the person or property of another, or which seriously disturbs or endangers the public peace or health, or which openly outrages public decency, for which no other punishment is expressly prescribed." N.Y.Penal Law of 1909, § 43. On other such statutes, see Note, 47 Colum.L.Rev. 1332, 1333 (1947).

21. Thus in State v. Dailey, 191 Ind. 678, 134 N.E. 481 (1922), and in State v. Moore, 196 La. 617, 199 So. 661 (1940), where the statute punished "murder," the common law year and a day rule of murder was applied as a matter

of interpretation. In State v. De Wolfe, 67 Neb. 321, 93 N.W. 746 (1903), where the statute punished "any nuisance," the court looked to common law to find that exposing others to a contagious disease was a common law nuisance and hence came under the statute. In Turner v. State, 1 Ohio St. 422 (1853), where the robbery statute punished the taking of property by force or fear "from the person" of another, it was held robbery to take "from the presence" of another as at common law. In State v. Potts, 75 Ariz. 211, 254 P.2d 1023 (1953), and State v. Anthony, 179 Or. 282, 169 P.2d 587 (1946), where a statute punished "sodomy or the crime against nature," without defining it, the common law definition applied. In Sneed v. State, 61 Okl.Cr. 96, 65 P.2d 1245 (1937), where the statute used "steal" without definition, the court looked to the definition of larceny at common law.

As to federal criminal law, see In re Greene, 52 Fed. 104, 111 (C.C.S.D.Ohio 1892): "When congress * * * adopts or creates common-law offenses, the courts may properly look to that body of jurisprudence for the true meaning and definition of such crimes, if they are not clearly defined in the act creating them."

If, on the other hand, the statute departs from the common law in clear language, there is no occasion to look to the common law. "Resort to common-law rules is proper but only to aid in statutory construction * * *; e.g., where the language of a statute based on the common law is doubtful." State v. Forsman, 260 N.W.2d 160 (Minn. 1977).

22. A comprehensive criminal code might purport to contain a complete listing of all defenses. But more commonly it sets forth some defenses and leaves open the possibility of other defenses. Even without such an express provision incorporating the common law defenses by reference, it would seem that such defenses would apply. Thus, although not all states have a general statutory provision giving the defense of necessity, this defense is a common law defense which doubtless all states would apply where justice required it.

mon law of criminal procedure is not abolished in those states which have rejected the substantive common law crimes.

 WESTLAW REFERENCES

110k21 /p "common law"

topic(110) /p "common law" /p insan*** /p statut!

(e) What the Common Law of Crimes Encompasses in States Retaining Common Law Crimes. In the United States the following conduct has been held criminal, although no statute made it so: conspiracy;[23]

23. State v. Cawood, 2 Stew. 360 (Ala.1830); State v. Dalton, 168 N.C. 204, 83 S.E. 693 (1914) (conspiracy to injure business of another through lies); State v. McFeely, 25 N.J.Misc. 303, 52 A.2d 823 (Ct.Quar.Sess.1947) (conspiracy to intimidate and harass police).

24. Nider v. Commonwealth, 140 Ky. 684, 131 S.W. 1024 (1910); Commonwealth ex rel. Swisher v. Ashe, 145 Pa.Super. 454, 21 A.2d 479 (1941). But see People v. Dolph, 124 Colo. 553, 239 P.2d 312 (1951) (since criminal attempt did not become a common law crime in England until after 1607, it is not a common law crime in Colorado).

It has been held that attempted suicide is not a common law crime, although suicide itself is an English common law crime. Commonwealth v. Dennis, 105 Mass. 162 (1870); May v. Pennell, 101 Me. 516, 64 A. 885 (1906).

A few states by statute make attempted suicide a crime, see May v. Pennell, supra. But see State v. La Fayette, 15 N.J.Misc. 115, 188 A. 918 (1937) (attempted suicide a common law misdemeanor).

25. State v. Schleifer, 99 Conn. 432, 121 A. 805 (1923) (labor leader orally addressed strikers against the New Haven Railroad: "You will never win the strike with soft methods * * *. Don't use eggs; use coal * * *. Break foremen's windows * * *. Watch the scabs when they come from work, lay for them * * *. Take them in a dark alley and hit them with a lead pipe * * *. Don't forget to bump off a few now and then * * *," with further exhortations to derail trains and put sand in the journal boxes of the engines.); Commonwealth v. Flagg, 135 Mass. 545 (1883) (solicitation to burn a barn); Commonwealth v. Randolph, 146 Pa. 83, 23 A. 388 (1892) (solicitation to commit murder with offer of money), distinguishing Smith v. Commonwealth, 54 Pa. 209, 93 Am. Dec. 686 (1867) (solicitation to commit fornication or adultery, both misdemeanors; *held* no common law crime to solicit a misdemeanor. See Annot., 35 A.L.R. 961 (1925).

26. Bell v. State, 31 Tenn. 42 (1851) (defendant publicly spoke of having had sexual intercourse with sundry ladies and contracting a disease from one); Commonwealth v. Mochan, 177 Pa.Super. 454, 110 A.2d 788 (1955) (obscene language over party telephone line).

27. State v. Bradbury, 136 Me. 347, 9 A.2d 657 (1939) (an act highly indecent, hence *contra bonos mores*). In England Stephen, J., held in Regina v. Price, 12 Q.B.D.

attempt to commit a crime;[24] solicitation to commit a crime;[25] uttering grossly obscene language in public;[26] burning a body in the cellar furnace;[27] keeping a house of prostitution;[28] maliciously killing a horse;[29] blasphemy;[30] negligently permitting a prisoner to escape;[31] discharging a gun near a sick person;[32] public drunkenness;[33] offenses against the purity of elections;[34] libel;[35] being a common scold;[36] indecent assault;[37] misprision of felony;[38] creating a public nuisance;[39] eavesdropping;[40] and violations of international law by individuals.[41] This is by no means a

247 (1884), that cremation of a body, although offensive (mostly on religious grounds) to the majority of the population, does not constitute a common law crime.

28. Lutz v. State, 167 Md. 12, 172 A. 354 (1934) (statute punishing the offering or receiving of the body for sexual intercourse for hire *held* not to repeal common law crime of keeping bawdy house).

29. Respublica v. Teischer, 1 Dall. 335 (Pa.1788).

30. E.g., Ex parte Delaney, 43 Cal. 478 (1872), and cases cited in Annot., 14 A.L.R. 880 (1921).

31. State ex rel. Farrior v. Faulk, 102 Fla. 886, 136 So. 601 (1931); United States v. Davis, 167 F.2d 228 (D.C.Cir. 1948).

32. Commonwealth v. Wing, 26 Mass. (9 Pick.) 1 (1829).

33. Willard v. State, 174 Tenn. 642, 130 S.W.2d 99 (1939).

34. Commonwealth v. McHale, 97 Pa. 397 (1881) (ballot-box stuffing); Commonwealth v. Slome, 147 Pa.Super. 449, 24 A.2d 88 (1942) (obtaining signatures on nomination papers by false pretenses).

35. See State v. Pulle, 12 Minn. 164, 12 Gil. 99 (1866).

36. Commonwealth v. Mohn, 52 Pa. 243 (1866).

37. Commonwealth v. De Grange, 97 Pa.Super. 181 (1929).

38. State v. Biddle, 32 Del. 401, 124 A. 804 (Gen.Sess. 1923) (misprision of felony is the criminal neglect to prevent a felony or to bring the felon to justice, but without such previous concert with or subsequent assistance to the felon as would make him an accessory).

39. State ex rel. Maples v. Quinn, 217 Miss. 567, 64 So. 2d 711 (1953) (fish reduction plant discharged nauseating vaporous waste matter into atmosphere; *held,* injunction granted, to abate the common law crime of public nuisance).

40. State v. Williams, 2 Tenn. (Over.) 108 (1808).

41. Ex parte Quirin, 317 U.S. 1, 63 S.Ct. 1, 87 L.Ed. 3 (1942) (wartime enemies, in civilian dress, passed through American military lines for purpose of engaging in sabotage); Respublica v. De Longchamps, 1 Dall. 111 (Pa.1784) (threatening bodily harm to secretary of the French Legation).

complete list of all the cases upholding common law crimes.[42]

We have seen that some activities of a sexual nature were considered offenses against religion not punishable as common law crimes; for instance, private acts of fornication or adultery, and seduction. In general these activities are held not to constitute common law crimes in America.[43]

There are several problems which have arisen in connection with common law crimes:

1. There is the problem of the extent of the punishment which may be imposed on one convicted of such a crime. Normally a statute defining a crime states the punishment therefor, but by hypothesis there is no statute creating the common law crime. Most, if not all, states have general statutes providing for a certain punishment for felonies and misdemeanors where no punishment is otherwise declared. A few have statutes providing punishment for common law crimes. The problem then is to determine whether the common law crime in question is a felony or misdemeanor. As to offenses derived from English precedents, the precedent will generally determine this.[44] As to new offenses not found in English precedents, it would seem that the court should treat the new crime as a misdemeanor. In some of the common law crime states it is theoretically possible to create common law felonies,[45] but it seems that

this should be done only if the crime involved was one of the few serious crimes which were common law felonies. Some states by statute provide that all nonstatutory crimes are misdemeanors.[46] (Of course, when a common law crime is enacted into a statute which states the punishment therefor, the punishment prescribed is exclusive.)[47]

2. Another problem in the states retaining common law crimes concerns the effect on the common law of criminal statutes relating more or less directly to the same subject matter: does the statute take over (preëmpt) the field and thus abrogate the common law crime?[48] Thus a state anti-trust statute makes criminal certain conspiracies in restraint of trade, but it does not mention conspiracy to injure rival businesses by telling lies. Does such a statute abrogate the common law crime of conspiracy to injure the business of another by systematic falsehood?[49] A state statute on conspiracy punishes unlawful agreements to accomplish four or five listed bad things, but at common law the list was greater. Does such a statute abrogate common law conspiracy to produce a result within the common law, but not within the statutory, list?[50] A state statute on conspiracy requires not only an unlawful agreement but also an overt act in furtherance of such an agreement. Does such a statute modify the common law definition of conspira-

---

42. A more complete list may be found in 1 F. Wharton, Criminal Law §§ 18–24 (12th ed. 1932), where three categories of common law crimes are listed: (1) those which tend to provoke a public disturbance, (2) those involving injury to another's property in such a way as to invite violent retaliation, (3) those constituting public scandal or public indecency. The Model Penal Code § 1.05, Comment at 78–79 (1985) states: "The preservation of the common law has its largest practical importance in the residual area of common law misdemeanors, public mischief and indecency offenses."

43. Adultery and fornication: Crouse v. State, 16 Ark. 566 (1855); Richey v. State, 172 Ind. 134, 87 N.E. 1032 (1909); State v. Brunson, 2 Bailey 149 (S.C.1831); Anderson v. Commonwealth, 26 Va. 627 (1826). Contra: Grisham v. State, 10 Tenn. 589 (1831). These cases indicate, however, that open fornication or adultery is a common law crime. Seduction: Anderson v. Commonwealth, supra (seduction of girl over 16).

44. See § 2.1(b). Thus burglary is a common law felony, solicitation a common law misdemeanor. The so-called "public mischief" and indecency offenses are considered misdemeanors.

45. Note, 47 Colum.L.Rev. 1332, 1333 (1947).

46. Ibid.

47. Bentley v. Commonwealth, 269 S.W.2d 253 (Ky. 1954).

48. The common law persists only in so far as statutes have not expressly or impliedly repealed it. The statute seldom if ever expressly repeals the common law. The difficulty lies in the scope of "implied repeal."

49. State v. Dalton, 168 N.C. 204, 83 S.E. 693 (1914), held no.

50. State v. McFeely, 25 N.J.Misc. 303, 52 A.2d 823 (Ct. Quar.Sess.1947); State v. Dalton, 134 Mo.App. 517, 114 S.W. 1132 (1908). Both cases held no; the statute was not meant to cover the entire field of conspiracy.

cy?[51] Does a state statute making prostitution (defined as the offering or receiving of the body for sexual intercourse for money) a criminal offense impliedly repeal the common law offense of keeping a house of prostitution?[52] Does a state statute, defining bribery as giving or offering compensation to a witness on his agreement that his testimony shall be influenced thereby, impliedly abrogate common law bribery, which does not require that the witness agree?[53] The problem is similar to that of implied repeal of statutes, where the courts are apt to say that repeals by implication are not favored, but that the earlier statute is repealed by a later statute if the two are so repugnant that they cannot stand together, or if the later statute is such a revision of the entire subject as to manifest a legislative intention to substitute the later for the earlier. So here the courts say that statutes in derogation of the common law are not favored, will be strictly construed, and will not repeal the common law beyond their terms, unless they are clearly repugnant to the common law or unless they constitute such a revision of the whole subject-matter as to evince an intention by the legislature to substitute statute for common law.[54]

3. The next problem is that of determining what sorts of conduct constitute common law crimes. How does a court determine whether something the defendant has done amounts to a common law crime? Does this mean that the court must find an English case or statutory precedent in point dated before 1607?

May the court use post-1607 precedents? What if there is no precedent to be found?

If the court finds an English case directly in point decided before 1607 (or, in some states, 1775),[55] holding that the activity in question constituted a common law crime, clearly this would qualify as a common law crime in a state in this country which recognizes such crimes. A more generally used technique, however, is to look at books by recognized writers on English crimes, especially Blackstone, to determine the existence and definition of a common law crime.[56] To some extent courts look to the case law of other states which retain common law crimes.[57]

The principal difficulty has to do with conduct not covered by any English case law (or statute) dated prior to 1607 (or 1775), the cutoff date in the typical reception statute or reception rule. Perhaps no English case or statute before 1607 can be found punishing false entries in election books because elections were unknown or infrequent in England before that time. Perhaps no English case or statute before 1607 punished the making of false reports to the police because England never got around to dealing with the problem until 1933, being delayed by the fact that it was not until recent times that England had a regular police force. Blackstone could not have mentioned these specific crimes for obvious reasons. Does it therefore follow that these cannot be common law crimes?

Of course, on the civil side of the law we are used to the idea that the common law can

---

51. State v. Dalton, 134 Mo.App. 517, 114 S.W. 1132 (1908), holds yes.

52. Lutz v. State, 167 Md. 12, 172 A. 354 (1934), holds no.

53. State v. Benson, 144 Wash. 170, 257 P. 236 (1927), holds yes.

54. E.g., Reddick v. State, 219 Md. 95, 148 A.2d 384 (1959). See also State v. Reese, 283 Md. 86, 388 A.2d 122 (1978) ("where a statute has been enacted covering the crime of forgery, common law forgery subsists to the extent that the statute was not intended to preempt the entire field or repeal the common law"); Commonwealth v. Bellis, 497 Pa. 323, 440 A.2d 1179 (1981) (if defendant's conduct falls within a common law and a statutory crime with different elements, he may be convicted of either or both).

55. See note 15 supra.

56. E.g., Commonwealth v. McHale, 97 Pa. 397 (1881), holding it a common law crime to make false entries in election books, stating that the "highest authority upon this point is Blackstone," and also citing Bishop and Wharton and cases in point from other states in America. State ex rel. Farrior v. Faulk, 102 Fla. 886, 136 So. 601 (1931), referred to Blackstone, Hawkins and Hale. Similar cases are Ex parte Delaney, 43 Cal. 478 (1872) (blasphemy; Blackstone and Bishop); State ex rel. Maples v. Quinn, 217 Minn. 567, 64 So.2d 711 (1953) (nuisance; Blackstone). A more recent tendency is to look at modern encyclopedias. Thus in Lewis v. Commonwealth, 184 Va. 69, 34 S.E.2d 389 (1945), the court, holding that disorderly conduct was not a common law crime, took as conclusive 27 C.J.S. 277: "At common law there was no offense known as 'disorderly conduct.'" State ex rel. Maples v. Quinn, supra, referred to Am.Jur. and C.J.S.

57. E.g., Commonwealth v. McHale, 97 Pa. 397 (1881).

grow to meet new situations and to accommodate changing customs and sentiments,[58] but there are difficulties on the criminal side, bound up with the notion, discussed more fully below, that the public is entitled to fair warning of what conduct is criminal.

In one case the defendant was prosecuted for the crime of attempting to obtain property by false pretenses in Colorado, a state which then retained common law crimes by virtue of a reception statute accepting the English common law as it existed in 1607. Colorado had no general statute punishing attempt, so the question was whether attempted false pretenses was a common law crime. The court could find no English case earlier than 1625 so holding, and that case was eighteen years too late to qualify this as a common law crime.[59] An older Kentucky case did much the same thing with the common law crime of conspiracy, the precise question being whether an agreement between competitors to maintain prices constituted such a crime. The court found that as of 1607 common law conspiracy was limited to agreements to promote false indictments and stir up litigation; agreements to do other bad things came later; hence an agreement to maintain prices was not a common law crime.[60]

Most other courts which discuss the problem do not limit themselves to pre-1607 precedents. They may be classified, however, into two groups: (1) those bold spirits willing to create a new crime in the absence of any precedent; and (2) those less bold but willing to follow post-1607 (or post-1775, in some states) English precedents (or perhaps precedents from other American states) but not willing to create a new crime in the absence of all precedent.[61] Illustrative of the first view, it has been held a common law crime to make false entries in election books even though there is no precedent in point from England. "The test is not whether precedents can be found in the books, but whether [defendant's activities] injuriously affect the public policy and economy," and "it is not so much a question whether such offences have been so punished as whether they might have been."[62] As an example of the second point of view, a court held that enticing away a sixteen year old girl for purposes of intercourse did not amount to a common law crime in the absence of any precedent; "it is too late now to assume jurisdiction over a new class of cases, under the idea of their being *contra bonos mores*."[63] Where the question was whether it is a common law crime to burn a body in the furnace (the criminal statute on dead bodies being limited to disinterring, indecently exposing, and abandoning such a body), the court relied on an 1840 English case[64] and on the general principle that "the common law gives expression to the changing

58. See the discussion of the rainmaker case, supra note 4 and accompanying text.

59. People v. Dolph, 124 Colo. 553, 239 P.2d 312 (1951). Actually the 1625 English case cited in *Dolph* does not seem to be in point, and apparently the English courts did not formulate the crime of attempt until much later. Cf. Chilcott v. Hart, 23 Colo. 40, 45 P. 391 (1896), where the same court consulted post-1607 English decisions to determine the common law rule against perpetuities which applies in Colorado.

60. Aetna Ins. Co. v. Commonwealth, 106 Ky. 864, 51 S.W. 624 (1899).

But see Chicago, W. & V. Coal Co. v. People, 114 Ill.App. 75 (1904) (agreement to maintain prices constitutes a common law conspiracy).

61. Of course the cases which are decided on the authority of a post-1607 precedent are not conclusive on whether the court would have decided as it did in the absence of all precedent.

62. Commonwealth v. McHale, 97 Pa. 397 (1881), citing Commonwealth v. Hoxey, 16 Mass. 385 (1820). In the

Hoxey case defendant was charged with disturbing a town meeting with intent to prevent an election of selectmen; *held*, although no statute makes this a crime, and although town meetings are not known in England, this is a common law offense.

See Means v. State, 125 Wis. 650, 104 N.W. 815 (1905), involving sodomy: "There is sufficient authority to sustain a conviction in such a case, and, if there were none, we would feel no hesitancy in placing an authority upon the books." (Wisconsin has since abolished common law crimes.)

63. Anderson v. Commonwealth, 26 Va. 627 (1826), conceding, however, "that if something peculiar in our situation had given rise to a class of cases *contra bonos mores*, as in regard to our slaves, which could not have existed in England, we might be justified in applying the rule in the absence of all precedent."

64. Pope, supra note 15, points out that the American cases on the common law of England to be applied generally draw no distinction between pre-1607 and post-1607 English cases.

customs and sentiments of the people" whereby such common law crimes have been created as blasphemy, open obscenity and similar indecent offenses against religion and morality which are *contra bonos mores*.[65] The many cases finding that solicitation, attempt and conspiracy (other than conspiracy to indict or stir up litigation) are common law crimes [66] show that pre-1607 English case law is not a prerequisite, since these crimes were developed in England after 1607.[67]

If one takes the view that common law is unwritten law and decided cases serve only to illustrate the law, the existence of common law crimes without early precedent is easy enough. The Anglo-American notion that case law operates retroactively points to the same result. And it is often difficult to tell what the common law of England before 1607 is "without regard to later decisions which have in fact settled the law as, theoretically, it always was." [68] It has been pointed out as a historical fact that in colonial times, when the colonists were applying the common law of England, they did not usually refer to English decisions (doubtless there were few libraries available), but rather to general principles.[69]

It has been said that American courts have no right to invent new crimes but only to declare the common law.[70] Most states accepting common law crimes, however, would agree that the common law can expand to meet a new situation hitherto unknown; and this process is not one of inventing new crimes but of applying common law principles.[71]

4. Another problem concerns the applicability of English criminal statutes in the United States. Such statutes have played a distinctly minor role in American common law crimes. An English criminal statute enacted before 1607, if applicable to our conditions, becomes part of our American common law.[72] Some states have also adopted English statutes enacted after 1607 and before 1775.[73]

5. A final problem concerns whether, if the court finds whatever common law precedent or principle would be necessary in order to recognize a certain common law crime, the court is then obligated to do so. It is possible, of course, that the legislature may have left the courts of the state with no discretion in this regard.[74] But if that is not the case, then the court might well decline to recognize the common law crime if it is deemed not "compatible with our local circumstances and situation and our general codes and jurisprudence." [75] In particular, a court might decline to declare a particular common law crime as the law of the state because of concerns with the due process right to fair warning,[76] or because of a perceived risk that the

---

65. State v. Bradbury, 136 Me. 347, 9 A.2d 657 (1939).

66. See notes 23–25 supra.

67. See Jackson, supra note 6.

68. Pope, supra note 15, at 17. Ray v. Sweeney, 77 Ky. 1 (1878), suggests a possible compromise: to accept pre-1607 English law without regard to its soundness in principle but to accept post-1607 law only if sound. But no court should blindly accept without regard to its soundness a pre-1607 English common law crime; and of course as to post-1607 common law crimes the court would naturally concern itself with soundness in principle.

69. Pope, supra note 15, at 15–16.

70. State v. Schleifer, 99 Conn. 432, 121 A. 805 (1923), holding that solicitation to kill, rob and destroy property constituted a common law crime.

71. Thus in State v. Schleifer, supra note 70, the court quotes a statement that "acts in violation * * * of the rules prescribing the duties of individuals to the state and to each other, as settled by universal acceptance, are offenses. Where these rules are not formulated by statute, they may be declared by courts; and a 'common law' is developed in the process."

See also Commonwealth ex rel. Lord v. Sherman, 34 Erie 27 (C.P.Erie County Pa.1950), to the effect that, though a common law crime has no name, it is still a crime.

72. E.g., Nider v. Commonwealth, 140 Ky. 684, 131 S.W. 1024 (1910) (statute enacted in reign of Elizabeth I, who immediately preceded James I, part of common law in this state.)

73. E.g., State v. McMahon, 49 R.I. 107, 140 A. 359 (1928) (English statute punishing false pretenses, enacted in 1757, is part of the common law of the state).

74. In State v. Egan, 287 So.2d 1 (Fla.1973), where a statute declared that the common law "shall be of full force in this state where there is no existing provision by statute on the subject," the court concluded: "When the common law is clear we have no power to change it."

75. Pope v. State, 284 Md. 309, 396 A.2d 1054 (1979).

76. In Pope v. State, 284 Md. 309, 396 A.2d 1054 (1979), declining to recognize the common law crime of misprision of felony, the court emphasized the ambiguity of the crime on such significant points as how strong a suspicion of criminality would give rise to a duty to report matters to

crime would infringe upon some other constitutional guarantee, such as the privilege against self-incrimination [77] or the equal protection clause.[78]

**WESTLAW
REFERENCES**

110k27 /p conspira! /p "common law"

topic(110) /p "common law" /p conspir! attempt!
    assault! solicitat! obscen! /p punish! sentenc! /p
    statut!

110k13 /p "common law" /p conduct element
    act***

(f) The Pros and Cons of Common Law Crimes. Finally, there is the question whether it is wiser to retain or wiser to abolish common law crimes. The advantage of retaining such crimes is that there are no gaps. So the argument goes, if something ought to be a crime, but the legislature forgot to declare it a crime, the courts can step in and make it a crime. It is useful to have a reservoir of substantive criminal law to plug loopholes left by the legislative branch. "It is impossible to find precedents for all offences. The malicious ingenuity of mankind is constantly producing new inventions in the art of disturbing their neighbors. To this invention

must be opposed general principles, calculated to meet and punish them." [79]

The principal argument against common law crimes is expressed in the maxim *nullum crimen sine lege,* the basis of which is that the criminal law ought to be certain, so that people can know in advance whether the conduct on which they are about to embark is criminal or not. "Although it is not likely that a criminal will carefully consider the text of the law before he murders or steals,[80] it is reasonable that a fair warning should be given to the world in language that the common world will understand, of what the law intends to do if a certain line is passed. To make the warning fair, so far as possible the line should be clear." [81] To require one who intends to tread close to the line of criminality (yet remaining on the side of legality) to study the criminal statutes (and the cases construing those statutes) may be fair enough; but to make him read the English and American cases on common law crimes and speculate on their scope is worse; and it is even more unfair (so the argument runs) to make him guess at his peril as to what a court will hold in a new situation never before encountered by the courts.[82] It is true also that the due

the authorities. In State v. Palendrano, 120 N.J.Super. 336, 293 A.2d 747 (1972), the court concluded that the charge of being a common scold was "unconstitutionally vague and therefore unenforceable."

77. Pope v. State, 284 Md. 309, 396 A.2d 1054 (1979) (common law crime of misprision of felony, consisting merely of concealing a felony).

78. State v. Palendrano, 120 N.J.Super. 336, 293 A.2d 747 (1972) (common law crime of common scold, defined as a habitually quarrelsome woman).

79. Commonwealth v. Taylor, 5 Binn. 277, 281 (Pa. 1812) (common law crime to enter another's dwelling house secretly at night and make terrifying noises therein with intent to disturb the peace; here it caused a miscarriage).

80. But see: "In federal court in New York City Thursday, before Judge Irving Kaufman, the Barra Brothers— Joseph and 'Mickey Mouse'—long hunted by the FBI, pleaded guilty to postage stamp forgery. In Mickey's apartment was found a locked drawer which contained his prized possessions, fake stamps, lottery tickets and a decision by Judge Learned Hand detailing the circumstances under which a counterfeiter may be acquitted." Syndicated column "The Lyons Den," Denver Post, Mar. 26, 1950.

81. Holmes, J., in McBoyle v. United States, 283 U.S. 25, 51 S.Ct. 340, 75 L.Ed. 816 (1931). Although this case

deals with interpretation of ambiguous statutes rather than the wisdom of common law crimes, the principle of fair warning is equally applicable to both subjects. People v. Brengard, 265 N.Y. 100, 191 N.E. 850 (1934), states: "[T]he abolition of all common-law crimes was accomplished not alone for the advantage of those individuals who might be charged with offenses, but also for the benefit of the people of the State. The bar, the courts, society in general, as well as each private person, were to be specifically informed concerning acts which are criminal and the nature and degrees of particular crimes as defined." The case held that the comprehensive code of New York abolished the year-and-a-day rule for murder.

82. As stated in State v. Palendrano, 120 N.J.Super. 336, 293 A.2d 747 (1972): "All that the average person has to guide his conduct is * * * a catch-all statute which tells him that if * * * his conduct would have been indictable at common law (i.e., pre-1776), he is a criminal. One can scarcely conceive of anything more vague or indefinite. To know the criminal risks he might run, the average citizen would be obliged to carry a pocket edition of Blackstone with him."

Compare State v. Egan, 287 So.2d 1 (Fla.1973), concluding it is not objectionable that "the statute imposes the duty upon the reader thereof to ascertain for himself what the common law is."

process requirement of definiteness in criminal statutes and the policy underlying the ban on *ex post facto* criminal statutes are analogies militating against common law crimes. The fact that Nazi Germany, and Soviet Russia until recently, adhered to the policy of punishing as criminal activity which no statute expressly covered tends to make Americans wonder about the democratic basis of common law crimes.[83]

As to the argument that it is necessary to plug loopholes, it has been noted that because of the proliferation of criminal statutes in all American jurisdictions there cannot be very many gaps; "By comparison with lack of discovery of criminal conduct, lack of detection, lack of complaint, and inefficiency in administration, the failure to punish the guilty resulting from gaps in the penal law is an almost trivial defect." [84] Furthermore, whenever a loophole is discovered, the modern legislature can and usually does act quickly to plug it.[85]

To a great extent, a decision on whether it is better to retain or to abolish common law crimes depends upon one's view of the theories of punishment. If punishment is imposed primarily for revenge or retribution, common law crimes punishing anti-social conduct of novel sorts are justified. Likewise, if the primary purpose is to jail and therefore disable for a time persons dangerous to society, or to reform those with anti-social tendencies, it makes greater sense to recognize common law crimes. But if the primary purpose is to deter future offenders through fear of punish-

ment, it has been suggested that new kinds of bad conduct should not be punished, "for if the first wrongdoer had no certain foresight that he would be punished, the threat of punishment could not deter him, and the punishment would be useless." [86] It could be argued, however, that certainty of punishment is not necessary to the deterrent theory (as, indeed, one must recognize from the fact that although many who commit statutory crimes escape punishment for one reason or another, many of us are deterred), and that a substantial chance that punishment will be inflicted for new forms of bad conduct will still deter.

It was only natural that judges should create crimes from general principles in medieval England, because such legislature as there was sat only infrequently and legislation was scanty. Today in the United States, as in modern England, the various legislatures meet regularly. The principal original reason for common law crimes has therefore disappeared.[87] And thus it is not surprising that as more and more states have enacted comprehensive new criminal codes in place of the miscellaneous collection of uncoordinated statutes, they have generally abolished common law crimes.

 **WESTLAW REFERENCES**

topic(110) /p "common law" /p vague! "fair warning"

topic(110) /p "common law" /p punish! sentenc! & theor*** /p retribut! reform! rehabilitat! deter!

---

83. For the abolition by Russia of crime by analogy, see Grzybowski, Soviet Criminal Law Reform of 1958, 35 Ind.L.J. 125 (1960). The principle of analogy is still applied in Comrades' Courts. See Berman & Spindler, Soviet Comrades' Courts, 38 Wash.L.Rev. 843 (1963).

84. J. Hall, General Principles of Criminal Law 50–51 (2d ed. 1960).

85. There are no common law crimes in California, and thus it was decided in Keeler v. Superior Court, 2 Cal.3d 619, 87 Cal.Rptr. 481, 470 P.2d 617 (1970), that the courts of the state were not empowered to broaden the definition of murder so as to include the killing of an unborn but viable fetus. A few months later, the California legislature amended West's Ann.Cal.Penal Code § 187 so that it now defines murder as "the unlawful killing of a human being, or a fetus, with malice aforethought."

86. G. Williams, Criminal Law: The General Part § 134 (1953).

87. The importance of a regularly-sitting legislature on the problem of crimes-without-statutes is well pointed up in Note, 47 Colum.L.Rev. 613–14 (1947), by reference to two statements by Justice Jackson as chief prosecutor of Nazi war criminals. He castigated the Nazis for punishing as criminal acts not forbidden by statute (a weapon used to achieve a police state); but as to whether international law made aggressive war-making criminal in the absence of statute he had said one year earlier: "International law * * * is not capable of development by legislation for there is no continuously sitting international legislature. * * * It grows, as did the common-law, through decisions reached from time to time in adapting settled principles to new situations. Hence, I am not disturbed by the lack of precedent" for the crime of launching aggressive war. For full discussion of the legal aspects of the war trials, see Glueck, The Nuernberg Trial and Aggressive War, 59 Harv.L.Rev. 396 (1946).

§ 2.2   Interpretation of Criminal Statutes

Statutes creating crimes are not immune to that malady which so often afflicts legislation of all types—ambiguity.[1] Courts are frequently faced with the problem of the criminal statute which is unclear as applied to the particular fact situation in question. Sometimes the letter of the statute covers the fact situation, but as so applied the statute seems harsh, unjust or even senseless; could the legislature have meant what it seems to have said? In the case of the "administrative crime" it may be that the administrative regulation, the violation of which the legislature has made a crime, is ambiguous.[2]

(a) Use of Canons of Construction. When interpreting[3] an ambiguous statute the court will seek to find the intention of the legislature.[4] At times it is clear that the legislature never thought of the particular fact situation now in question, in which case "intention of the legislature" may mean simply "intention the legislature would have had if it had thought of this problem," to be determined from a consideration of the general purpose the legislature had in mind in enacting the statute.[5] In order to help solve the often difficult problem of the legislature's intention, the courts have a large assortment of rules and maxims at their disposal.[6]

There is something of a dispute among those who like to speculate on the workings of the judicial mind as to whether courts first decide how a defective statute ought to be interpreted and then display whatever canons of statutory construction will make this interpretation look inevitable, or whether the courts actually first use the applicable canons and second reach the result.[7] Doubtless the truth lies somewhere in between—some judges are apt to do it one way, some the other; some cases lend themselves to one technique, some to the other. It is no doubt true that, as applied to a particular fact situation, several rules of interpretation may often be referred to, some looking in one direction and some in the opposite direction. It is also true that most of the rules are stated in a way which ends with the exception that the rule does not apply if the meaning of the statute is clear, but a good deal of discretion remains in the courts as to when a statute is clear and when it is ambiguous. At all events, because rules of statutory interpretation sometimes do decide cases and because even in other cases judges must find some applicable rules, one who deals with criminal law (which is, of course, largely statutory) must know something of the techniques of statutory interpretation.

§ 2.2

1. For some thoughts on why ambiguity exists, see Note, 36 A.B.A.J. 321 (1950): (1) words are imperfect symbols to express ideas; (2) situations unforeseen by the legislature are inevitable; (3) uncertainties may be added in the course of enactment.

2. E.g., North American Van Lines v. United States, 243 F.2d 693 (6th Cir.1957) (I.C.C. administrative regulation ambiguous, so court applied the maxim that criminal statutes should be strictly construed in favor of the defendant; as so applied, conviction reversed). See § 2.6 on administrative crimes.

3. In this section of the book the terms "interpret" and "construe" are used interchangeably.

4. See, e.g., United States v. Agrillo-Ladlad, 675 F.2d 905 (7th Cir.1982); State v. Hooper, 57 Ohio St.2d 87, 386 N.E.2d 1348 (1979). Similarly, when interpreting an ambiguous will, the court looks for the "intention of the testator"; when interpreting an ambiguous contract, it seeks "the intention of the parties"; an ambiguous trust provision, "the intention of the settlor"; and so on with other ambiguous written documents or even oral agreements.

5. The word "intention" itself is somewhat ambiguous. It sometimes is used as a synonym of "meaning," but it can also mean "purpose." See Landis, A Note on "Statutory Interpretation," 43 Harv.L.Rev. 886 (1930).

At all events, in interpreting statutes, including criminal statutes, the purpose of the statute ("the evil to be cured"), whether it is discovered by a study of the written legislative history of the statute or simply known to the court as a matter of judicial knowledge, is of great importance in deciding what the legislature would have thought of a particular fact situation if it had had its attention directed to that situation. E.g., United States v. Shirey, 359 U.S. 255, 79 S.Ct. 746, 3 L.Ed.2d 789 (1959), and the quotation from L. Hand, J., therein that the art of statutory interpretation is "the proliferation of purpose."

6. Most of these same rules and maxims are available to courts seeking to interpret wills, contracts and other written documents of private persons.

7. This is perhaps but a part of a larger question: Do courts decide cases first and then unearth reasons which make the decision look good; or do they reason first and then come to their conclusions from these reasons?

di legislative intent

"fair warning" /s criminal penal /s statute law
     ordinance

(b) Plain Meaning Rule.[8] Courts often express this thought: "Where the language [of a statute] is plain and admits of no more than one meaning the duty of interpretation does not arise, and the rules which are to aid doubtful meanings need no discussion";[9] or that if the language is plain and its meaning clear, courts must give effect to it, regardless of what it thinks of its wisdom. This plain meaning rule, it has been noted, "reaffirms the preeminence of the statute over materials extrinsic to it."[10]

The courts, of course, are on even firmer ground in applying the plain meaning rule if they can think of some good reason which the legislature might have had in mind in providing what it literally seems to have provided. On the other hand, courts sometimes conclude that what seems to be clear language is so harsh or foolish or devoid of sense that it is ambiguous after all, and they then proceed to find that the legislature did not mean what it literally said.[11]

---

8. See R. Dickerson, The Interpretation and Application of Statutes, 229–33 (1975); 2A C. Sands, Sutherland on Statutory Construction § 46.01 (4th ed. 1975).

9. Caminetti v. United States, 242 U.S. 470, 37 S.Ct. 192, 61 L.Ed. 442 (1917). The Mann Act prohibits transportation of a girl from one state to another "for the purpose of prostitution or debauchery, or for any other immoral purpose." Defendant transported a willing girl to another state for the purpose of having personal sexual relations with her. The majority thought it too plain for argument that his purpose was an "immoral purpose." There was a dissent which found the word "immoral" to be so broad as to be ambiguous; and it found some legislative history that the Mann Act was aimed at "commercialized vice," not at private acts of sexual immorality.

10. R. Dickerson, supra note 8, at 229.

11. E.g., Church of the Holy Trinity v. United States, 143 U.S. 457, 12 S.Ct. 511, 36 L.Ed. 226 (1892). A federal statute forbade (and provided for a monetary penalty for violation) the importation of aliens into the country under a contract to perform "labor or service of any kind." A church imported a foreign minister to preach. Literally a minister surely performs "labor or service" of some kind. But the Court, instead of finding that the language was clear, found it hard to believe that Congress meant to

"plain meaning rule" /s statute law ordinance

(c) Implied Exceptions[12] **and Obvious Mistakes.** As noted above, courts sometimes do not follow statutes which, though apparently plain, are also harsh or foolish. Courts sometimes speak of an "implied exception" in the statute when they do not wish to apply it literally. Thus a federal statute makes it a crime "knowingly and wilfully to obstruct the passage of the mail." Defendant policeman, with a warrant for the arrest of a mail carrier for murder, arrested the mailman on his appointed rounds. The Supreme Court held this was not an obstruction of the mail under the statute; statutes, even plain statutes, should not receive a construction leading to "injustice, oppression, or an absurd consequence. It will always, therefore, be presumed that the legislature intended exceptions to its language, which would avoid results of this character."[13] Similarly, a state criminal statute punishing speeding impliedly excepts a police officer reasonably speeding, in the discharge of his duties, after a fleeing criminal.[14] We shall later see that, generally speaking, a good motive will not excuse criminal conduct,[15] as where a man shoots his beloved but dying wife to end her suffering. This is per-

---

cover ministers, and therefore found the language ambiguous; and then it discovered in the legislative history of the statute a purpose to keep out *manual* laborers. So it was held that ministers were not covered by the statute.

In People v. Clark, 242 N.Y. 313, 151 N.E. 631 (1926), a statute made it a felony, with a maximum punishment of ten years imprisonment, for a public officer to receive any emolument not authorized by law. Defendant received an unauthorized emolument believing it authorized. Under the literal wording of the statute he was guilty. But the court concluded, in view of the severe penalty, that the legislature must have meant to cover only those who *knew* the emolument was unauthorized.

12. See R. Dickerson, supra note 8, at 198–200.

13. United States v. Kirby, 74 U.S. (7 Wall.) 482, 19 L.Ed. 278 (1869). Probably the Court did not need to talk in terms of implied exceptions; it could have decided that under the circumstances defendant did not "wilfully" obstruct the mail.

14. State v. Gorham, 110 Wash. 330, 188 P. 457 (1920); Annot., 9 A.L.R. 367 (1920). A similar principle should apply to speeding ambulances and fire trucks.

15. See § 3.6.

haps but a way of saying that implied exceptions are not readily to be made for forbidden conduct springing from good motives.[16] There is a general defense, to be dealt with later, called "necessity,"[17] whereby one who in an emergency situation commits what would otherwise be a crime may be excused, as where one who is starving takes food belonging to another to save his own life. Most of the cases on "implied exceptions" could more properly be treated under such a principle.[18]

In the area of entrapment, an implied exception in a criminal statute has been used to explain the defendant's nonliability where the police entrap him into violating the literal terms of a criminal statute—as where a policeman persuades the other to sell him liquor, in violation of a statute forbidding the sale of liquor. One commonly-used explanation of the liquor seller's nonliability is that the liquor statute impliedly excepts the situation where the policeman entraps the other into the act of selling.[19]

Sometimes a criminal statute is quite obviously worded erroneously—perhaps containing too much, perhaps containing too little.

Suppose a health statute makes it a crime for a hotel proprietor to permit someone to sleep in a "hotel, dining room or restaurant." Defendant, a hotel proprietor, lets a guest sleep in his hotel. Literally, the statute makes him a criminal. Quite obviously, however, a comma was erroneously inserted between "hotel" and "dining room"; as the statute is thus corrected by the court, the defendant would not be guilty. Courts are less likely to correct obvious mistakes where the statute's error is in favor of the defendant,[20] though even here courts sometimes interpret statutes to read as they were obviously meant to read.[21]

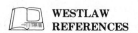 **WESTLAW REFERENCES**

"implied exception" /s statute law ordinance 361k200

(d) Strict Construction of Criminal Statutes.[22] Most of the rules of statutory interpretation which are utilized in construing ambiguous criminal statutes are rules which apply as well to civil statutes, but there is one rule which is specifically applicable to the former: criminal statutes must be strictly construed in favor of the defendant.[23] The

---

16. Thus in Commonwealth v. Gardner, 300 Mass. 372, 15 N.E.2d 222 (1938), a criminal statute forbade the sale or gift of a contraceptive; defendant doctor gave his patient a contraceptive with the good motive of protecting her health; *held,* the statute is plain and covers this situation; there is no implied exception here.

17. See § 5.4.

18. Thus State v. Gorham, 110 Wash. 330, 188 P. 457 (1920), involving the speeding policeman, does speak in terms of "necessity."

19. See § 5.2(c), pointing out, however, that another explanation is that, although the defendant who is entrapped by the police is in fact guilty of the crime in question (for there is really no implied exception), nevertheless he is not to be punished for his crime, for it is more important to deter the police from such conduct than to punish this defendant.

20. E.g., United States v. Evans, 333 U.S. 483, 68 S.Ct. 634, 92 L.Ed. 823 (1948). Here a federal statute, forbidding persons to bring into the U.S. an alien not entitled to enter, was later amended by forbidding them also to conceal such an alien; but the penalty clause was unamended and read that the violator should be punished by a certain fine or imprisonment "for * * * every alien so * * * brought in"; in amending the statute Congress probably forgot to amend the penalty clause by adding "or so concealed." *Held,* one who conceals an alien cannot be punished. Courts cannot add to the statute what Congress forgot to add, at least here where it is uncertain that

Congress would have provided the same penalty for concealing as for bringing in.

Consider also State v. Archuletta, 526 P.2d 911 (Utah 1974), where the statute said that an aggravated assault consisted of an "assault as defined in section 76–5–101" plus certain aggravated circumstances. The cited section contained only a definition of the word "prisoner"; assault was defined in section 76–5–102. The court concluded that the statute "simply does not state a crime, and we are not empowered to state one for the legislators simply because it seems certain that they intended to state one themselves."

21. E.g., Haworth v. Chapman, 113 Fla. 591, 152 So. 663 (1933), where the statute forbade certain conduct and provided that whoever did it should be "fined not more than $10,000 and ten years in the state penitentiary." Defendant, who violated the statute, received a sentence of seven years imprisonment, and then sought release on habeas corpus, on the theory that the statute nowhere authorized imprisonment but only a fine. The court read into the statute the obviously omitted words, "imprisoned for" before the phrase "ten years," and so denied habeas corpus.

22. See R. Dickerson, supra note 8, at 201–11; 3 C. Sands, Sutherland on Statutory Construction ch. 59 (4th ed. 1975).

23. The rule is often expressed: "penal statutes must be strictly construed", and "penal" may include some statutes which might properly be called civil—e.g., a mu-

rule grew out of conditions during the period in England before the 19th Century when hundreds of crimes, many relatively minor, were punishable by death.[24] With the decline in the severity of punishment, the rule nonetheless continued in effect in England and in this country. As the Supreme Court has put it, "ambiguity concerning the ambit of criminal statutes should be resolved in favor of lenity."[25] One modern reason for the rule of strict construction is said to be that criminals should be given fair warning, before they engage in a course of conduct, as to what conduct is punishable and how severe the punishment is.[26] Another is that the power to define crimes lies with the legislatures rather than the courts.[27]

Consistent with these reasons are the now generally accepted limitations upon the rule

of strict construction. For one thing, there is no occasion to construe a penal statute strictly or otherwise if the statute is devoid of ambiguity.[28] For another, a statute is "not to be construed so strictly as to defeat the obvious intention of the legislature"[29] or "to override common sense."[30] And in any event, strict construction should not be carried to extremes; it is not necessary that the statute be given its "narrowest meaning"[31] or a "forced, narrow or overstrict construction."[32]

In a number of states legislation has been enacted to abrogate the common law rule of strict construction of criminal statutes.[33] This has very often (but not always) occurred in connection with the adoption of a comprehensive new criminal code.[34] Such legislation has doubtless had an effect on courts in some

nicipal ordinance, or a statute providing for a money penalty for certain conduct. See § 1.7 for a discussion of how these matters may be civil in nature although probably "penal" too. Note also an analogous rule applicable to civil as well as criminal statutes to the effect that statutes in derogation of the common law should be strictly construed.

24. Hall, Strict or Liberal Construction of Criminal Statutes, 48 Harv.L.Rev. 748, 750 (1935). In those days the English courts often went to great lengths to find an ambiguity that could be given a strict interpretation, in order to relieve a defendant from the death penalty. Id. at 751.

25. Rewis v. United States, 401 U.S. 808, 91 S.Ct. 1056, 28 L.Ed.2d 493 (1971). See also Liparota v. United States, ___ U.S. ___, 105 S.Ct. 2084, 85 L.Ed.2d 434 (1985); United States v. United States Gypsum Co., 438 U.S. 422, 98 S.Ct. 2864, 57 L.Ed.2d 854 (1978); United States v. Bass, 404 U.S. 336, 92 S.Ct. 515, 30 L.Ed.2d 488 (1971); Bell v. United States, 349 U.S. 81, 75 S.Ct. 620, 99 L.Ed. 905 (1955).

26. R. Dickerson, supra note 8, at 209; United States v. Bass, 404 U.S. 336, 92 S.Ct. 515, 30 L.Ed.2d 488 (1971); State v. Stockton, 97 Wn.2d 528, 647 P.2d 21 (1982). As Holmes, J., stated in McBoyle v. United States, 283 U.S. 25, 51 S.Ct. 340, 75 L.Ed. 816 (1931): "Although it is not likely that a criminal will carefully consider the text of the law before he murders or steals, it is reasonable that a fair warning should be given to the world in language that the common world will understand, of what the law intends to do if a certain line is passed. To make the warning fair, so far as possible the line should be clear."

The principle that prospective criminals should be given fair warning is the underlying basis of other important rules of criminal law: (1) the rule that vague criminal statutes violate due process, see § 2.3; (2) the federal and state constitutional prohibitions against ex post facto laws, see § 2.4; and (3) the decision of the courts or legislatures of a number of states and of the federal

government that there are no common law crimes, see § 2.1.

27. United States v. Bass, 404 U.S. 336, 92 S.Ct. 515, 30 L.Ed.2d 488 (1971); State v. Jewell, 345 So.2d 1166 (La. 1977).

28. United States v. Culbert, 435 U.S. 371, 98 S.Ct. 1112, 55 L.Ed.2d 349 (1978); State v. Dean, 357 N.W.2d 307 (Iowa 1984).

29. Barrett v. United States, 423 U.S. 212, 96 S.Ct. 498, 46 L.Ed.2d 450 (1976). See also State v. Millett, 392 A.2d 521 (Me.1978).

30. United States v. Moore, 423 U.S. 122, 96 S.Ct. 335, 46 L.Ed.2d 333 (1975); Dover v. State, 664 P.2d 536 (Wyo. 1983).

31. United States v. Moore, 423 U.S. 122, 96 S.Ct. 335, 46 L.Ed.2d 333 (1975); Dover v. State, 664 P.2d 536 (Wyo. 1983).

32. State v. Carter, 89 Wn.2d 236, 570 P.2d 1218 (1977).

33. The legislation may specifically abolish the common law rule, followed by a statement that criminal statutes shall be "construed according to the fair import of their terms," or, without an express abolition, providing for "liberal" construction or providing that no distinction in construing statutes shall be made between civil and criminal statutes. See Hall, supra note 24, at 752–56; State v. Maggio, 432 So.2d 854 (La.1983).

34. Model Penal Code § 1.02(3) calls for construction "according to the fair import of their terms but when the language is susceptible of differing constructions it shall be interpreted to further the general purposes stated in this Section and the special purposes of the particular provision involved." Thus, while the rule of strict construction is not preserved as such, one of the "general purposes" referred to is "to give fair warning" of the nature of the conduct declared criminal and the nature of the sentences which may be imposed. Model Penal Code § 1.02(1)(d), (2)(d).

jurisdictions,[35] but in others the rule of strict construction seems to be an attitude of mind that is not readily changed by legislation.[36] No doubt some criminal statutes deserve a stricter construction than others. Other things being equal, felony statutes should be construed more strictly than misdemeanor statutes;[37] those with severe punishments more than those with lighter penalties; those involving morally bad conduct more than those involving conduct not so bad; those involving conduct with drastic public consequences more than those whose consequences to the public are less terrible; those carelessly drafted more than those done carefully.[38]

Numerically, most crimes today are crimes which were unknown to the common law;[39] even the great common law crimes (e.g., murder, manslaughter, rape, mayhem, burglary, robbery, larceny, sodomy, conspiracy, attempt) are reduced to statutory form today in most Anglo-American jurisdictions. But courts construe statutes which spell out common law crimes differently from statutes which create new crimes. As the Supreme Court stated, when the legislature "borrows terms of art in which are accumulated the legal tradition and meaning of centuries of practice, it presumably knows and adopts the cluster of ideas that were attached to each borrowed word in the body of learning from which it was taken and the meaning its use will convey to the judicial mind unless otherwise instructed."[40] Thus courts interpret common law terminology in statutes according to its common law meaning[41] rather than its everyday meaning, with the result that language which might at first blush seem ambiguous or vague takes on a quite definite meaning. For instance, a statute making it involuntary manslaughter to kill another person by doing a lawful act "without due caution or circumspection" (language which literally sounds almost exactly like the ordinary negligence term "lack of due care") should be interpreted to require a high degree of negli-

National Comm'n on Reform of Federal Criminal Laws, Final Report—Proposed New Federal Criminal Code § 102 (1971), calls for construction to achieve certain stated objectives, one of which is "to give fair warning of what is prohibited and of the consequences of violation." Language in the Tentative Draft explicitly rejecting the strict construction rule was not carried over to the Final Report, and this has been explained as follows: "The purpose of the change is to make clear that arbitrary application of the strict construction rule is disavowed, while not explicitly abrogating the rule. The concerns militating against an explicit repudiation of the rule include the following: (a) it might be read to permit an improper delegation of authority to define crime to the judiciary; (b) it might be read to obviate the necessity for the sort of precision in the drafting of criminal legislation which should, particularly for a new Code, be sought; and (c) it might result in an increase in the number of undesirable and unnecessary constitutional confrontations." 1 National Comm'n on Reform of Federal Criminal Laws, Working Papers 9 (1970).

35. E.g., Commonwealth v. Davis, 75 Ky. (12 Bush.) 240 (1876).

36. See R. Dickerson, supra note 8, at 221 (noting statutes abolishing the rule "have languished in near oblivion"); J. Hall, General Principles of Criminal Law 48 (2d ed. 1960) (noting that such legislation is largely ineffective because the "fair warning" principle is so firmly embedded in Anglo-American criminal law); Note, 25 Loyola L.Rev. 417 (1979) (criticizing State v. Muller, 365 So.2d 464 (La.1978), where, notwithstanding a statutory direction to construe statutes "according to the fair import of their words," the court relied upon the strict contruction rule to hold that indecent exposure in a supermarket was not within a statute proscribing such exposure "in any location or place open to the view of the public").

37. State v. Millett, 160 Me. 357, 203 A.2d 732 (1964); State v. Lauritsen, 178 Neb. 230, 132 N.W.2d 379 (1965).

38. The modern tendency in criminal law is to create new crimes punishing conduct without an express requirement of any sort of bad intent or even negligence. Courts sometimes read some sort of *mens rea* requirement into the statute, at least if the punishment is severe, the consequences of the conduct are not too drastic to the public, etc. See § 3.8(a).

39. There were relatively few common law crimes, although those few crimes remain among the most important crimes today. See § 2.1.

40. Morissette v. United States, 342 U.S. 246, 72 S.Ct. 240, 96 L.Ed. 288 (1952).

41. United States v. Bell, 505 F.2d 539 (7th Cir.1974) (the assault with intent to rape statute covers the situation in which the victim was not in apprehension because of mental illness, as one type of common law assault was attempted battery, and "when a federal criminal statute uses a common law term without defining it, the term is given its common law meaning"); Keeler v. Superior Court, 2 Cal.3d 619, 87 Cal.Rptr. 481, 470 P.2d 617 (1970) (phrase "human being" in murder statute does not include viable fetus, as it may be presumed when legislature "couches its enactment in common law language, that its intent was to continue those rules in statutory form"); State v. Rusk, 289 Md. 230, 424 A.2d 720 (1981) (terms "force," "threat of force," "against the will" and "without the consent" in rape statute are not defined and thus will be given common law meaning).

gence or recklessness rather than ordinary negligence, in view of the common law requirements of manslaughter.[42] The statute is merely an inartistic legislative attempt to spell out the elements of common law manslaughter, not an attempt to change the negligence element from greater negligence or recklessness to ordinary negligence.

This is not to suggest that common law terms in a statute must inevitably be taken to have their common law meaning, for it may appear that the legislature intended otherwise. Such intent may be discerned by the context within which the term is used [43] or by the fact that the statute has quite clearly expanded upon the common law in other, related respects.[44]

Another rule of statutory interpretation, which may perhaps be considered a special application of the rule of strict construction, is that "where a statute is susceptible of two constructions, by one of which grave and doubtful constitutional questions arise and by the other of which such questions are avoided, [the court's] duty is to adopt the latter." [45]

An *ambiguous* criminal statute will often be narrowly construed but, as so construed, upheld by the courts. A *vague* criminal statute is another matter. A criminal statute, federal or state, so vague "that men of common

intelligence must necessarily guess at its meaning and differ as to its application" [46] is unconstitutional.[47] No doubt there is no exact borderline which can be drawn between a statute which is merely ambiguous and one which is unconstitutionally vague.

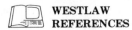 **WESTLAW REFERENCES**

di strict construction
crim! penal /s strict** /s constru! /s statute law ordinance

(e) Legislative History.[48] With a federal statute, whether civil or criminal, there is often a good deal of "legislative history" to aid in finding the intention of the legislature.[49] The history of a federal statute from the time a bill is introduced until final enactment is generally quite thoroughly recorded in writing. After a bill is introduced by a member of Congress (say the House of Representatives) it is assigned to a House committee for study and recommendations. The committee holds hearings on the bill, listening to arguments pro and con, which are reduced to writing. The committee makes a written report to the entire House, expressing its thoughts and recommendations. A debate thereafter takes place on the floor of the House, which debate is taken down verbatim in the Congressional Record. Perhaps an

---

42. People v. Penny, 44 Cal.2d 861, 285 P.2d 926 (1955).

43. Perrin v. United States, 444 U.S. 37, 100 S.Ct. 311, 62 L.Ed.2d 199 (1979) (phrase "bribery ✻ ✻ ✻ in violation of the laws of the State in which committed" in 18 U.S.C.A. § 1952 not to be given common law meaning limited to bribery of public officials, as when this law passed most state bribery laws not so limited); Appeal No. 180, 278 Md. 443, 365 A.2d 540 (1976) (word "solicit" not limited to meaning re common law solicitation, as it used in soliciting-for-prostitution statute, a type of statute as to which word has a broader common meaning).

44. Bell v. United States, 462 U.S. 356, 103 S.Ct. 2398, 76 L.Ed.2d 638 (1983) (federal Bank Robbery Act, 18 U.S.C.A. § 2113(b), by using common law term "takes and carries away," was not thereby limited to larceny and inapplicable to obtaining by false pretenses, as the crime clearly extends beyond common law larceny in several other respects and thus reflects a broad "congressional goal of protecting bank assets").

45. United States ex rel. Attorney General v. Delaware & Hudson Co., 213 U.S. 366, 29 S.Ct. 527, 53 L.Ed. 836 (1909). This canon of statutory construction is used in interpreting civil as well as criminal statutes.

46. Connally v. General Constr. Co., 269 U.S. 385, 46 S.Ct. 126, 70 L.Ed. 322 (1926).

47. See § 2.3 infra. Once again, a statute using common law terminology is not void for vagueness where the common law can give otherwise vague language a sufficiently definite meaning.

48. See R. Dickerson, supra note 8, at ch. 10; 2A C. Sands, supra note 8, at ch. 48. For discussion of how to find this history, see M. Cohen & R. Berring, How to Find the Law ch. 10 (8th ed. 1983); G. Folsom, Legislative History (1972).

49. See, e.g., Perrin v. United States, 444 U.S. 37, 100 S.Ct. 311, 62 L.Ed.2d 199 (1979) (word "bribery" in 18 U.S.C.A. § 1952 not limited to common law bribery of public officials, as legislative history shows intent to deal with organized crime beyond capacity of local officials, and organized crime involved in other forms of bribery).

The intention of the legislature is never determined by asking individual members of the legislature what intention they had in mind when they voted for the statute. Thus in State v. Partlow, 91 N.C. 550 (1884), the court refused to consider the testimony of the statute's sponsor as to what the statute meant.

amendment is offered and adopted or voted down. The House passes the bill and sends it on to the Senate, where hearings are held by a Senate committee, written reports are made to the Senate as a whole, debate on the bill is recorded for posterity, and the bill is voted upon and passed. Often the Senate votes a bill with somewhat different provisions from the House bill, in which case a "conference committee" of House and Senate members may meet to iron out differences, often writing a report upon the joint product.

The testimony before the committees will often throw light on "the evil to be cured"— the bad situation which required legislative correction—and thus give an indication of the scope of the statute.[50] The committee reports will also usually spell out the existing situation which the legislation is designed to cure; and they may state more or less specifically what the committee thinks the bill means, perhaps giving examples of fact situations coming within or without the statute. Of course, courts are after the intent of Congress, not the intent of a committee of Congress, but it is generally considered that as to details Congress adopts the committee's intent.[51] Courts naturally pay little or no attention to what a single legislator during debate on the floor states he thinks the statute means, unless he happens to be the sponsor of the bill or perhaps a member of the committee which reported on the bill. But resort may be had

to the debates to determine a common understanding indicated by many legislators as to what the bill means. If during debate an amendment is offered but voted down, that is generally a clear indication that Congress did not want that provision in the law.[52]

At times a comparison of the wording of an earlier draft with the language of the statute as enacted may throw some light on the meaning of an ambiguous statute. Suppose a state statute makes it bigamy for one already married to remarry; excepting, however, one who marries again after his spouse, whom he does not know to be alive, has been absent for seven years. Defendant's wife leaves on a sea voyage and is reliably reported by shipwreck survivors to have gone down with the ship; so defendant marries a new wife at the end of five years. Thereafter the old wife turns up. It might be argued, though not without some difficulty, that, as a matter of statutory interpretation, it is a defense to bigamy to remarry within seven years honestly and reasonably believing the spouse is dead.[53] But suppose it is found that an earlier draft, otherwise like the statute as enacted, contained a second exception, expressly providing that remarriage after one year in the reasonable belief the spouse is dead is also a defense. The absence of this clause, struck out in the course of enacting the statute, shows pretty clearly a legislative intent that remarriage before seven years is no defense, however

---

50. Thus in Church of the Holy Trinity v. United States, 143 U.S. 457, 12 S.Ct. 511, 36 L.Ed. 226 (1892), where a federal statute provided for a monetary penalty for importing aliens into the U.S. under a contract to perform "labor or service of any kind," the Court held that the statute did not apply to a church which imported an alien minister, one reason being that the evil to be cured, "as it was pressed upon the attention of the legislative body," was the depressing effect upon American laborers of the importation of foreign *manual* laborers. Foreign ministers did not contribute to the bad conditions which led to the statute.

51. L. Hand, J., in SEC v. Robert Collier & Co., 76 F.2d 939 (2d Cir.1935), stated: "It is of course true that members [of Congress] who vote upon a bill do not all know, probably very few of them know, what has taken place in committee * * *. But courts * * * recognize that while members deliberately express their personal position upon the general purposes of the legislation, as to the details of its articulation they accept the work of the

committees; so much they delegate because legislation could not go on in any other way."

52. E.g. Gossnell v. Spang, 84 F.2d 889 (3d Cir.1936), where the Business Census Act was on its face somewhat ambiguous as to whether veterans had preference to employment for which the Act provided. The legislative history, however, disclosed that a Senator on the Senate floor during debate offered an amendment that veterans should have preference. The sponsor of the bill opposed the amendment, and it was voted down. *Held,* veterans do not have preference. In a rare case it might be that the proposed amendment was turned down, not because it was undesirable, but because the bill already covered it; if the legislative history disclosed this reason, the court would doubtless decide the other way.

As to later unsuccessful efforts to amend the statute, see the *International Minerals* case, note 55 infra.

53. So held in Regina v. Tolson, 23 Q.B.D. 168 (1889).

reasonable the belief in the spouses' death.[54] (In a similar fashion, it is often useful to compare the wording of a law as originally enacted with that law as it was subsequently amended.[55])

The use of legislative history as an aid to statutory interpretation has its limits. While a good deal of legislative history can be mined for a federal statute, most state legislatures, although they may go through much the same motions as Congress, do not keep as good a written record of their work. Elaborate committee reports are seldom made, and it is rare for a record to be kept of legislative debates.[56] One incidental benefit to be derived from the complete recodification of a state's criminal code is that the draftsmen (probably not legislators) will often prepare commentary for each section, which will be used by the courts to determine the legislative intent.[57] In the absence of such written evidence, state courts have to ascertain the "evil to be cured" from other sources.[58]

It should be noted also that not all judges are enamored of the use of legislative history in interpreting ambiguous statutes.[59] And in any event, legislative history is less likely to be controlling in construing criminal statutes than civil statutes. If one purpose of a criminal statute is to warn the public of what conduct will get them into criminal trouble—that is, if prospective criminals are entitled to fair warning—then the public should be able to ascertain the line between permitted and prohibited conduct from the statute itself. It is too much to expect the public to delve studiously into drafts of bills, committee hearings and reports and debates on the bill in order to understand the statute. In other words, the rule that criminal statutes should be strictly construed to some extent limits the use of legislative history in the case of criminal statutes.

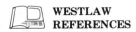

WESTLAW REFERENCES

361k217.4 /p intent***
361k217.4 /p interpret!

---

54. Commonwealth v. Mash, 48 Mass. (7 Metc.) 472 (1844), was substantially the above situation, except that there the legislature refused to enact a proposed recommendation of the statute revision commissioners to give this second defense.

55. Bell v. United States, 462 U.S. 356, 103 S.Ct. 2398, 76 L.Ed.2d 638 (1983) (though federal Bank Robbery Act, 18 U.S.C.A. § 2113(b), was originally limited to robbery, it was expanded beyond that later, reflecting "congressional goal of protecting bank assets," and thus extension not limited to what was common law larceny); Barnes v. United States, 412 U.S. 837, 93 S.Ct. 2357, 37 L.Ed.2d 380 (1973) (by amendment the word "so" deleted from phrase "knowing the same to have been so stolen" in possession of articles stolen from mails statute, showing defendant need not know from where objects possessed were stolen); State v. Morris, 331 N.W.2d 48 (N.D.1983) (amendment deleting "intentionally or knowingly" from possession of marijuana statute shows intent to impose strict liability); LaBarge v. State, 74 Wis.2d 327, 246 N.W.2d 794 (1976) ("or other serious bodily injury" phrase following list of extreme harms not limited by *ejusdem generis* rule to others equally extreme, as that language added by amendment of the law for express purpose of broadening the statute).

An attempt to amend an existing statute may also be relevant. See United States v. International Minerals & Chemical Corp., 402 U.S. 558, 91 S.Ct. 1697, 29 L.Ed.2d 178 (1971).

56. "But if you have to work with state law few legislatures have transcripts of proceedings comparable to those that are available at the federal level. The problem of

legislative intent as such seems to me to involve as much in the way of possibility of being misled as almost anything one can get into. There are bits of legislative record that are devised peculiarly by congressmen or senators for the purpose of misleading judges. And sometimes it is difficult to know which of those you are looking at." Leflar, Statutory Construction: The Sound Law Approach (remarks at Federal Appellate Judges Conference, Federal Judicial Center, Washington, D.C., May 13, 1975).

57. E.g., People v. Miller, 55 Ill.App.2d 146, 204 N.E.2d 305 (1965), reversed in part and vacated in part, but not on this point 35 Ill.2d 62, 219 N.E.2d 475 (1966): "The Criminal Code of 1961 was adopted by the Legislature following a long period of study by eminent lawyers and legal scholars. The published comments regarding the various Articles and Paragraphs thereof, of those who drafted the legislation and presented it to the Legislature, deserve consideration in the interpretation of the intent contained in the Code."

58. E.g., Caspar v. Lewin, 82 Kan. 604, 109 P. 657 (1910), involving a factory safety statute, which the court interpreted in the light of its purpose to reduce the appalling rate of human injury in factories. The court seemed to take a sort of judicial notice of this purpose, rather than find it in any specific aspect of its legislative history. Sometimes a statute expresses its purpose in its preamble, where of course the court can readily find and use it as an aid to interpretation.

59. See Jackson, J., concurring, in Schwegmann Bros. v. Calvert Distillers Corp., 341 U.S. 384, 71 S.Ct. 745, 95 L.Ed. 1035 (1951).

(f) Title of the Statute.[60] Sometimes a statute's title throws some light on the meaning of an ambiguous statute.[61] Thus, suppose a criminal statute makes it larceny for a chattel-mortgagor to injure, destroy or conceal mortgaged property, with intent to defraud the mortgagee, or to sell or dispose of the same without the mortgagee's written consent. Defendant sells the mortgaged property with the mortgagee's oral consent. Though the result seems harsh, by the literal wording of the statute the defendant is guilty, in spite of his lack of any fraudulent intent, since "intent to defraud" does not go with "sell or dispose." The court, however, thought the statute ambiguous enough in view of the heavy penalty and the fact the crime was labeled "larceny" to warrant a look at the title, which stated: "An act relating to chattel mortgages, providing punishment for selling, destroying or disposing of chattel-mortgaged property, with intent to defraud." Since the title coupled "dispose" and "intent to defraud", the body of the statute was interpreted to require a fraudulent intent to convict a mortgagor who sold or disposed of mortgaged property.[62]

WESTLAW REFERENCES

361k211

(g) "Striking Change of Expression." When courts interpret wills, contracts, trust instruments and other private documents, they generally look first at the ambiguous word or phrase or clause or sentence which must be construed, and then at the instrument as a whole, to see what light the other parts of the document may throw on the ambiguous portion. So too with statutes,[63] including criminal statutes. If the legislature uses quite different language in two parts of the same statute, that is often an indication of a different legislative intention as to the two parts. Thus in the chattel-mortgage larceny statute, referred to above, comparison of the "injure, destroy or conceal, with intent to defraud" clause with the "sell or dispose without written consent" clause indicates a legislative intent that no fraudulent intent is required for a sale of, as distinguished from an injury to, mortgaged property.[64]

A "striking change in expression"[65] in two different parts of the same statute indicates "a deliberate difference of intent." If the court can in addition think of a good reason why the legislature might want to make the distinction (was there a special danger in the sale situation that did not apply to the injury situation?), this conclusion is almost inevitable.

The change of expression may appear in the comparison of the statute as it used to read with the statute as it reads now after its amendment. For example, a "blue sky" statute, which formerly made it a felony "knowingly" to make a false statement to the Secretary of State in connection with the registration of securities is later amended by striking out "knowingly," thus making it a felony to make a false statement to the Secretary. The defendant thereafter made an untrue statement honestly believing it to be true. The court interpreted the statute to mean that an honest belief in the truth of statement is no defense; by comparing the old and the new it is apparent that the legisla-

---

60. See 2A C. Sands, supra note 8, at § 47.03.

61. See Marshall, C.J., in United States v. Fisher, 6 U.S. (2 Cranch) 358, 2 L.Ed. 304 (1804), on the influence which the title ought to have in construing statutes: Though the title cannot control plain words in the body of the statute, it may assist in removing ambiguities. "Where the mind labors to discover the design of the legislature, it seizes everything from which aid can be derived; and in such case, the title claims a degree of notice, and will have its due share of consideration."

62. State v. Miller, 74 Kan. 667, 87 P. 723 (1906).

63. Marshall, C.J., in United States v. Fisher, 6 U.S. (2 Cranch) 358, 2 L.Ed. 304 (1804), speaks of the "well-

established principle in the exposition of statutes, that every part is to be considered, and the intention of the legislature to be extracted from the whole."

64. We saw that actually the court went the other way, because of the harsh penalty, the "larceny" name and the title. But compare an almost identically-worded statute (except that it carries a three-year penalty, and calls it a misdemeanor, and has no similar title), construed to cover a mortgagor who sold with oral permission of his mortgagee, in Bank of New South Wales v. Piper, [1897] A.C. 383.

65. The phrase is that of L. Hand, J., in SEC v. Robert Collier & Co., 76 F.2d 939 (2d Cir.1935).

ture purposely omitted the word "knowingly" so as to catch persons who make honest mistakes.[66]

The "striking change" technique is most applicable when the problem is one of comparing two clauses side by side in the same sentence, as is the case in the above-discussed statute on chattel-mortgages. It is slightly less applicable perhaps when the comparison is between two adjoining sentences of the same section of the statute; still less if the sentences do not adjoin; still less if the sentences are to be found in different sections of the same statute (though passed as two parts of a statute enacted as a whole at the same time); and still less where the two sections were enacted at different times, though dealing with the same subject-matter.[67] So too, the technique is not as apt to be applied by comparing the wording of two statutes dealing with different subjects. But though the rule grows weaker as the two parts to be compared become more remote (as to location, date of enactment and subject matter) from one another, the rule may still be applicable. Thus in the case of the previously mentioned "blue sky" statute which makes it a crime to "make any false statement" in connection with the *registration* of securities, where the question of interpretation was whether the statute required that the maker know the statement to be false, the court discovered that quite another section of the "blue sky" law, dealing with the *sale* of securities, makes it a crime for the seller to "knowingly make any false * * * statements" about the security. The court said that this shows the

legislature knew how to use appropriate language for giving the defense of innocent mistake, yet it failed to use the appropriate language in the section on registration of securities; so the statute covers those who innocently make untrue statements.[68]

An invitation to compare the language of two statutes on the same subject, which may point up different expressions indicating different intentions, is given by the following rule of statutory construction: statutes dealing with the same subject-matter are *in pari materia* and must be construed together.

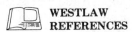 **WESTLAW REFERENCES**

opinion(expression /s change /s statute law ordinance)
di in pari materia

(h) Ejusdem Generis.[69] Sometimes criminal (or civil) statutes (or written documents of private persons) list some specific items followed by a general catch-all phrase, usually introduced by the words "or other." The general phrase may be construed to be limited to things "of the same kind" (*ejusdem generis*) as the specific items. Thus a federal criminal statute makes it a felony for one to transport in interstate commerce an "automobile, automobile truck, automobile wagon, motor cycle, or any other self-propelled vehicle not designed for running on rails" which he knows to be stolen. Defendant flies an airplane he knows to be stolen from one state to another. Is an airplane a "self-propelled vehicle not designed for running on rails"? Literally, it would seem to be. But the Supreme Court

66. State v. Dobry, 217 Iowa 858, 250 N.W. 702 (1933). Compare State v. Johnston, 149 S.C. 195, 146 S.E. 657 (1929), similarly involving a statute making it a crime for a corporate officer to "make any false statement" to shareholders. The court interpreted the word "false" to mean more than "incorrect"; it means "incorrect, and known by the speaker to be incorrect." There was no history, however, of the legislature's striking out a word like "knowingly," as in State v. Dobry, supra. See other cases in note 55 supra.

67. Even though the two parts are enacted at different times, the technique of comparison of expression may still be used, on the theory that the legislature had the old statute before it when it passed the new statute on the same subject. State v. Gerhardt, 145 Ind. 439, 444 N.E. 469 (1896).

68. State v. Dobry, 217 Iowa 858, 250 N.W. 702 (1933). The court's other reason for affirming the conviction—comparing the wording of the old statute with the new—is discussed at note 66 supra.

Another useful illustration is provided by State v. Bradley, 215 Kan. 642, 527 P.2d 988 (1974). In concluding that the crime of assault "committed against a uniformed or properly identified * * * law enforcement officer" did not require knowledge by defendant of the victim's status, the court noted that at the same session of the legislature a related statute was adopted making it a crime to "knowingly and intentionally" assault a fireman, deemed to indicate that scienter was not also intended as to the police officer statute.

69. See 2A C. Sands, supra note 8, at §§ 47.12–47.22.

held that an airplane was not covered by the quoted phrase. The theme of the specific objects listed (automobiles, trucks, motorcycles) is vehicles which run on land, so that "other self-propelled vehicles" is limited to land-vehicles, and airplanes are excluded.[70] Similarly, a statute proscribing destruction of property by "use of bombs, dynamite, nitroglycerine or other kind of explosives" was held not to cover igniting a firecracker in a telephone coin return slot, as the named items are all distinguishable from fireworks by being designed to produce an explosion of extreme effect.[71]

The *ejusdem generis* rule is deemed to be "especially applicable to penal statutes"[72] because of the need for fair warning. But it is to be utilized only when uncertainty exists and not to defeat the obvious purpose of the legislation being construed.[73] For example, if the general language was later added to the statute for the express purpose of broadening its reach beyond the kinds of things specifical-

ly enumerated, then clearly the *ejusdem generis* approach is not warranted.[74]

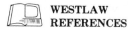 **WESTLAW REFERENCES**

di ejusdem generis

(i) Expressio Unius, Exclusio Alterius.[75] Another maxim of statutory interpretation sometimes used in construing criminal statutes (as well as other types of statutes and documents of private parties) is that the expression of one thing is the exclusion of another (in Latin, *expressio unius, exclusio alterius*). Thus, for instance, a criminal statute which sets forth one exception (or several listed exceptions) to liability impliedly excludes other exceptions. A typical bigamy statute makes it a crime for one who has a living spouse to remarry; provided, however, that one who marries more than seven years after his spouse, whom he does not know to be alive, has disappeared is not guilty. The question which sometimes arises is whether remarriage, after less than seven years' ab-

---

70.   McBoyle v. United States, 283 U.S. 25, 51 S.Ct. 340, 75 L.Ed. 816 (1931). *Ejusdem generis* was only one reason for the decision. "Criminals should receive fair warning" is another. See supra note 26. The Court also thought that the word "vehicle" by itself imports a thing moving on land. Compare Cleveland v. United States, 329 U.S. 14, 67 S.Ct. 13, 91 L.Ed. 12 (1946), where the Court said that though "prostitution" is a word indicating commercialized vice, "debauchery" has no such connotation, so that "prostitution, debauchery or other immoral purpose" is not, by *ejusdem generis,* limited to commercialized vice.

No doubt if the specific listed items contained all possible land vehicles and then concluded "or other self-propelled vehicles not designed for running on rails," so that, if the quoted clause means anything, it must mean things that do not go on land, the result would have been different. Thus, in Kidwell v. State, 249 Ind. 430, 230 N.E.2d 590 (1967), where the statute covered attempted rape "while armed with a pistol, revolver, rifle, shotgun, machine gun or any other firearm or any dangerous or deadly weapon," the court held that a knife was included in the last phrase, the reason being that the phrase would have no meaning unless it went beyond the previous designation of "any other firearm."

Cf. Gooch v. United States, 297 U.S. 124, 56 S.Ct. 395, 80 L.Ed. 522 (1936) (the phrase "or otherwise" in the federal kidnapping statute forbidding interstate kidnapping "for ransom or reward or otherwise" was construed to cover a kidnapping to prevent arrest, though no financial gain was involved); Crump v. State, 625 P.2d 857 (Alaska 1981) (kidnapping defined as abducting another who defendant "holds for ransom, reward or other unlawful reason," latter not limited to other pecuniary motives).

71.   State v. Lancaster, 506 S.W.2d 403 (Mo.1974). See also State v. Hooper, 57 Ohio St.2d 87, 386 N.E.2d 1348 (1979) (statute providing no person "shall insert any instrument, apparatus or other object into the vaginal or anal cavity of another" by force or threat did not include finger, as only inanimate objects named); State v. Stockton, 97 Wn.2d 528, 647 P.2d 21 (1982) (statute on obtaining "property or services" by threat and defining services as including such things as "professional services, transportation services, electronic computer services" did not cover case in which sexual favors obtained, as services listed are those for which compensation usually received).

72.   State v. Kahalewai, 56 Haw. 481, 541 P.2d 1020 (1975). See also Giant of Maryland, Inc. v. State's Attorney, 274 Md. 158, 334 A.2d 107 (1975).

73.   United States v. Powell, 423 U.S. 87, 96 S.Ct. 316, 46 L.Ed.2d 228 (1975) (18 U.S.C.A. § 1715, making it a crime to mail "pistols, revolvers, and other firearms capable of being concealed on the person" covers sawed-off shotgun); United States v. Alpers, 338 U.S. 680, 70 S.Ct. 352, 94 L.Ed. 457 (1950) (statute making illegal interstate shipment of any "obscene * * * book, pamphlet, picture, motion picture film, paper, letter, writing, print, or other matter of indecent character" not limited to objects comprehensible by sight only and thus extended to obscene phonograph record). See also the *Gooch* and *Crump* cases, note 70 supra, also explainable on this basis.

74.   LeBarge v. State, 74 Wis.2d 327, 246 N.W.2d 794 (1976).

75.   See 2A C. Sands, supra note 8, at §§ 47.23–47.25.

sence but with the affirmative belief that the spouse is dead, is a defense. Many jurisdictions answer no; the statute gives one exception; that impliedly excludes all other exceptions.[76]

The *expressio unius* canon is not limited to questions concerning possible defenses. Illustrative is a case holding that a felony-murder statute permitting conviction where death occurs in the perpetration of an "arson" by the defendant did not extend to a case where the death resulted from the malicious burning of a car. Because the arson statute named only one type of conveyance, "trailer coaches," this indicated it was not intended to cover other vehicles.[77]

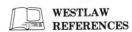

WESTLAW REFERENCES

"expressio unius"   &   topic(110)

(j) The Special Controls the General, the Later Controls the Earlier. At times courts are faced with the problem of fitting together two statutes (perhaps criminal, perhaps civil) which deal with the same subject matter but which face in opposite directions.[78] One state statute may punish whoever within the state fishes without a license. Another statute permits fishing without a license in Oxbow Lake, which is located within the state. Neither statute refers to the other. Defendant is tried for fishing in Oxbow Lake without a license.

A general rule of interpretation of apparently inconsistent statutes is that the special statute controls the general. Putting the two statutes together, then, the result is that fishing without a license anywhere except in Oxbow Lake is a crime. Another such rule is that, with two inconsistent statutes on the same subject, the later statute controls the earlier. If the general fishing statute was passed in 1940, the Oxbow statute in 1950, then *a fortiori* the fisherman in question is not guilty; the Oxbow statute is surely an exception to the general statute, since a later-special statute controls an earlier-general statute.[79] The greater difficulty comes in fitting together an earlier-special statute and a later-general statute. If the Oxbow statute is dated 1940 and the general statute 1950, the question is whether the 1950 statute impliedly repealed the 1940 statute, or whether, though not so worded, it covers all places except the Oxbow Lake, leaving that situation untouched. Here the court might well exhibit another maxim of statutory construction, that "repeals by implication are not favored," and hold that the earlier-special statute controls the later-general statute, in the absence of a legislative intent to cover the subject of fishing entirely in the new statute. This is especially so if the earlier-special statute is in favor of a criminal defendant.[80]

---

76. Thus the great weight of authority in the United States is that honest and reasonable belief that the spouse is dead is no defense to bigamy as so defined by the typical statute. See § 5.1(b). On the other hand, the great English case of Regina v. Tolson, 23 Q.B.D. 168 (1889), reached the opposite result. The court dealt with the *expressio unius* argument, but concluded that it did not apply because: (1) the legislature by expressing one defense (seven years absence without knowledge one way or the other as to whether the spouse is alive) could not have intended to deprive the defendant of what should even more clearly be a defense (positive evidence that spouse is dead, though disappearance less than seven years); (2) anyway, the statute did not purport to list all possible exceptions, such as insanity, infancy, duress, and *expressio unius* should not apply where the one listed exception was obviously not meant to be the only exception. (The answer to # 2 is that statutes defining particular crimes never set out defenses like insanity, etc.; but special defenses to particular crimes—like seven years absence in bigamy—would naturally be set forth; so that *expressio unius* is applicable.)

77. People v. Nichols, 3 Cal.3d 150, 89 Cal.Rptr. 721, 474 P.2d 673 (1970).

78. Once more, courts are invited to look at both statutes by the maxim that statutes *in pari materia* should be construed together, in the light of one another.

79. State v. Collins, 55 Wash.2d 469, 348 P.2d 214 (1960) (1854 manslaughter statute; 1937 statute on negligent homicide by motor vehicle).

80. Compare Simpson v. United States, 435 U.S. 6, 98 S.Ct. 909, 55 L.Ed.2d 70 (1978) (where 18 U.S.C.A. § 2113, the bank robbery statute, has an enhancement provision where robbery is by "use of a dangerous weapon or device," and a later enactment, 18 U.S.C.A. § 924(c), covers whoever "uses a firearm to commit any felony for which he may be prosecuted in a court of the United States," defendant may not be sentenced under both statutes; "our result is supported by the principle that gives precedence to the terms of the more specific statute where a general statute and a specific statute speak to the same concern, even if the general provision was enacted later"); Ex parte Chiapetto, 93 Cal.App.2d 497, 209 P.2d 154 (1949)

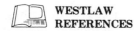

361k223.4 /p earlier /p later

(k) Administrative Interpretation.[81] The written interpretations given to a statute by the administrative officials charged with administering the statute, or even the unwritten administrative practices of those public officials, are sometimes looked to by courts for assistance in the interpretation of ambiguous statutory language.[82] With criminal statutes the interpretation placed thereon by the administrators of the criminal law (attorneys general on a state level; district attorneys on a local level) is similarly entitled to some weight. Thus suppose a statute punishes adultery, without spelling out the detail of whether an unmarried man who has sexual relations with a married woman is an adulterer. A bachelor enjoys such a relationship with a married lady. Though the constant practice in the past has been to prosecute such a man for the lesser crime of fornication, this particular bachelor is tried for adultery. The court interpreted the ambiguous statute so as not to apply to unmarried men, in view of this constant past practice.[83]

(where earlier-special statute provided that the misdemeanor of contributing to the delinquency of a minor was punishable by a maximum of two years imprisonment in the county jail and later-general statute provided that no person should be sentenced to the county jail for more than one year, the latter statute impliedly repeals the two-year provision of the former).

81. See 2A C. Sands, supra note 8, at § 49.09.

82. Thus the interpretation put upon the federal tax statutes by the Treasury Department in its Treasury Regulations is given some weight by the courts when interpreting a tax statute, especially if the statute in question has been reenacted in its original language after its administrative interpretation.

83. Respublica v. Roberts, 1 Yeates 6 (Pa.1971). Of course, the constant practice of not prosecuting for a crime on the books can not effect a repeal. District of Columbia v. John R. Thompson Co., 346 U.S. 100, 73 S.Ct. 1007, 97 L.Ed. 1480 (1953). But see United States v. Elliott, 266 F.Supp. 318 (S.D.N.Y.1967), noting that "in some situations a desuetudinal statute could present serious problems of fair notice."

The situation discussed here should be distinguished from the cases in which the defendant raises a mistake of law defense based upon erroneous advice given to him by an administrative official. See § 5.1(e)(3).

LaFave & Scott Crim.Law 2nd Ed.HB—5

Where a criminal statute has been construed by a court or by the appropriate administrators and thereafter the statute is reenacted without change, it may be argued that the legislature placed its stamp of approval upon (and therefore adopted) the interpretation given by that court or those administrators. This, however, requires an assumption, which may or may not be true, that the legislature knew of the construction placed upon the language by the court or administrators.[84] It has even sometimes been argued that judicial or administrative interpretation, if known to the legislature, followed by long legislative silence (rather than by legislative reenactment) indicates legislative approval of the interpretation.[85]

congress! legislat! +3 silen** /p interpret! constru!
   /s statut! law

(l) Borrowed Statutes.[86] At times one state borrows a statute (criminal or civil) word for word, or nearly so, from another state. It may even borrow a whole criminal code.[87] It has often been held that, when the legislature borrows a statute, it also borrows the prior interpretations placed on the statute

84. L. Hand, J., rejected this argument in Fishgold v. Sullivan Drydock & Repair Corp., 154 F.2d 785 (2d Cir. 1946), affirmed 328 U.S. 275, 66 S.Ct. 1105, 90 L.Ed. 1230 (1946), where it was very doubtful that Congress actually knew of the prior interpretations placed upon the statute.

85. Thus there was a sequel to Caminetti v. United States, 242 U.S. 470, 37 S.Ct. 192, 61 L.Ed. 442 (1917), discussed above, in Cleveland v. United States, 329 U.S. 14, 67 S.Ct. 13, 91 L.Ed. 12 (1946), which involved the applicability of the Mann Act to a member of a Mormon sect who transported his second wife across state lines for the purpose of living with her in the second state. Rutledge, J., concurring in the view that *Caminetti* applies, discussed the contention that Congressional silence after *Caminetti* indicates Congressional approval of the *Caminetti* interpretation, so that the Court cannot overrule *Caminetti* now even though it now thinks *Caminetti* was wrong. He considered the contention to be weak.

86. See R. Dickerson, supra note 8, at 131–36; 2A C. Sands, supra note 8, at § 52.02.

87. E.g., when Colorado first set up a government, and naturally needed a criminal code, its legislative body adopted almost intact the Illinois criminal code as it then existed.

by the courts of the state from which the statute is borrowed;[88] though there is always a safety valve: the foreign interpretation is not to be followed if the court thinks it to be quite wrong.[89]

The states which have received, into their criminal law, common law crimes[90] have also adopted those English criminal statutes in aid of the common law which were enacted before 1607 (or, in some states, 1775). The interpretation put upon these English statutes by the English courts before 1607 (1775) is generally adopted along with the statute.

Courts themselves cannot very well borrow criminal statutes from other jurisdictions, in the absence of any legislative borrowing. Thus if every state but one has a statute making it a crime to bribe an athlete to throw a game, the courts of that one state could not very well make such bribery a crime, unless it has the power to create new common law crimes,[91] in which case it might point to these statutes as indicating such a strong public policy against such conduct that it ought to be criminal. But courts might more readily look to statutes from other jurisdictions giving a criminal a defense, or might look to such statutes when interpreting its own not-borrowed statutes.[92]

A legislature might "borrow" a particular statutory formulation from some other source,

in which case a court construing the enactment will understandably place considerable reliance upon authoritative pronouncements concerning the intended meaning of the source formulation. Not at all uncommon these days is a court's reliance upon the Model Penal Code commentary when interpreting a statute following rather closely a section in the Model Penal Code.[93] Similarly, if a state has enacted a criminal statute following the language of a section of the original proposal for recodification of the federal criminal law, then the Working Papers which accompanied that undertaking are an especially relevant source.[94]

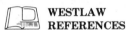

WESTLAW REFERENCES

statute law /s borrow** /p prior previous /s interpret! constru!

(m) Stare Decisis In Interpreting Criminal Statutes. Sometimes a court, having earlier construed a criminal statute strictly in favor of the defendant, later decides that its earlier construction was wrong. Thus, for instance, a state supreme court, in the case of *State v. X*, interprets its false pretenses statute in such a way as to give the defense to the defendant *X*, who obtained property from his victim by false pretenses, that the victim himself was also engaged in some criminality.[95] The great weight of Anglo-American authori-

---

88. State v. Elliot, 177 Conn. 1, 411 A.2d 3 (1979); State v. Milano, 167 N.J.Super. 318, 400 A.2d 854 (1979), affirmed 172 N.J.Super. 361, 412 A.2d 129 (1980). The rule is weaker, and perhaps disappears, where the interpretation is by an administrative agency or by a court other than the highest appellate court.

See Note, 43 Harv.L.Rev. 623 (1930). The rule does not apply where the Oregon interpretation *follows* the Alaska enactment, though even here the Oregon interpretation would—like any other decision in point by a foreign court—be "persuasive."

89. E.g., State v. Chaplain, 101 Kan. 413, 166 P. 238 (1917) (borrowed statute rule is not to be used "where the foreign interpretation is too severe a shock to the intelligence of the courts of the adopting state").

90. See § 2.1.

91. See § 2.1.

92. State v. Hooper, 57 Ohio St.2d 87, 386 N.E.2d 1348 (1979) (in concluding that a finger is not an "object" within the meaning of a statute saying no person "shall insert any instrument, apparatus or other object into the vaginal or anal cavity of another" by force or threat, court

in rejecting dictionary definition of "object" as anything tangible emphasizes that 19 other jurisdictions prohibit penetration by something other than the sex organ and 12 use the term "object" and clearly exclude parts of the body); State v. Mellenberger, 163 Or. 233, 95 P.2d 709 (1939) (on the question of whether it is a defense to false pretenses that the victim himself had a criminal mind, court in holding that it is no defense derived some comfort from fact that the legislature of New York, which state formerly had allowed the defense, had abolished the defense by statute).

For the argument that courts should make use of statutes from other jurisdictions in determining its own case law, see Landis, Statutes and the Sources of Law, Harvard Legal Essays 213 (1934).

93. Commonwealth v. Mumma, 489 Pa. 547, 414 A.2d 1026 (1980).

94. People v. Frysig, 628 P.2d 1004 (Colo.1981); State v. Sadowski, 329 N.W.2d 583 (N.D.1983).

95. Perhaps the defendant induces the victim to pay for what the defendant misrepresents to be a counterfeit-

ty, however, is that the criminality of the victim is no defense; and on principle the majority view is sound.[96] Now the case of *State v. Y* is before the state supreme court, and *Y*'s defense is that, under the false pretenses statute as formerly interpreted, the victim was himself a rogue (though of course not so clever a rogue as *Y*). The court now recognizes that its earlier decision was wrong. Can it now overrule its earlier decision and hold that criminality of the victim is no defense? Obviously, other things being equal, courts should interpret statutes correctly, regardless of past mistakes. On the other hand, it may not be fair to *Y*, who may have relied on the decision in the *X* case before he engaged in his scheme to defraud his victim,[97] to change the rule now. The difficulty lies in the Anglo-American theory of precedents that case law operates retroactively, and in particular that case law which overrules earlier precedents operates retroactively.[98] When faced with this very problem—that of overruling or following an earlier erroneous interpretation of the false pretenses statute—the New

York court felt obliged in the *Y* case to follow the *X* case precedent, with an invitation to the legislature to change the rule for the future;[99] but the Oregon court made bold to overrule the *X* case even though it meant that *Y*, who may have relied on the *X* case, went to jail.[100] The Oregon court made a distinction between crimes *mala in se* (e.g., false pretenses) and crimes only *mala prohibita;* a person who commits a crime with "a consciousness of wickedness" in doing it has no right to the benefits of *stare decisis*.[101]

The choice, however, is not necessarily between following the precedent (thus letting the defendant off but perpetuating a bad decision) and retroactively overruling it (thus eliminating a bad precedent but putting the defendant behind bars). There are two techniques by which the defendant may go free even if the precedent is overruled. It is not impossible for a court to overrule for the future only, letting the defendant go but stating in the opinion that anyone who from now on conducts himself the way this defendant did will be guilty of the crime.[102] The second

---

ing machine; the victim plans to get rich by counterfeiting money with the machine.

96. Thus in analogous situations it is no defense that defendant stole property from another thief, or that he murdered another murderer, or that he raped a prostitute, the bad character of the victim being irrelevant.

97. Courts seldom ask in *stare decisis* cases whether the defendant actually had read or heard of the precedent and did in fact rely on it. The chance that he did seems to be enough.

Compare LaBarge v. State, 74 Wis.2d 327, 246 N.W.2d 794 (1976) (new broad interpretation of phrase "or other serious bodily injury," though contrary to that court's 1959 interpretation consistently followed by lower courts, is applicable in instant case, as there was no showing of reliance by the defendant upon the prior interpretation when he stabbed the victim).

98. One of the beauties of law created by legislation, as opposed to law created by cases, is that legislation can be made to operate prospectively only, where the legislature so provides, expressly or by implication.

99. People v. Tompkins, 186 N.Y. 413, 79 N.E. 326 (1906), following McCord v. People, 46 N.Y. 470 (1871). The rule was later changed by the legislature. See N.Y.—McKinney's Penal Law § 155.05.

100. State v. Mellenberger, 163 Or. 233, 95 P.2d 709 (1939), overruling State v. Alexander, 76 Or. 329, 148 P. 1136 (1915).

101. The court intimates also that it may be easier to overrule a single precedent than a series of precedents.

102. E.g., State v. Jones, 44 N.M. 623, 107 P.2d 324 (1940) (former case held theatre "bank night" not within definition of criminal "lottery"; this case overrules former case as to conduct in the future but lets Jones go free); State v. Bell, 136 N.C. 674, 49 S.E. 163 (1904), following the precedent case (which wrongly gave the defendant a certain defense) as far as defendant Bell is concerned, but stating that the proper interpretation of the statute does not permit this defense, and warning that "the construction now put upon the statute will be applied to all future cases." "Future cases" must mean cases arising out of future conduct, not cases which reach the courts in the future arising from past conduct.

The technique of "overruling for the future" is also used sometimes in civil cases, and in civil or criminal cases not involving statutory interpretation. E.g., Mutual Life Ins. Co. v. Bryant, 296 Ky. 815, 177 S.W.2d 588 (1943) (involving interpretation of a clause in an insurance policy); Durham v. United States, 214 F.2d 862 (D.C.Cir.1954) (involving common law doctrine of criminal law-insanity rather than interpretation of a criminal statute).

Also, in recent years the United States Supreme Court has declared many of its decisions broadening the constitutional rights of criminal defendants to be prospective only. The defendant in that case, of course, receives the benefit of the broadened constitutional doctrine, and this has contributed to some inconsistency as to what other persons are covered. See United States v. Johnson, 457 U.S. 537, 102 S.Ct. 2579, 73 L.Ed.2d 202 (1982), and cases cited therein.

method is to overrule the erroneous precedent but to give the defendant the defense of mistake of law induced by an appellate court. Mistake as to the interpretation of a criminal statute is generally no defense. Thus a defendant is ordinarily guilty of burglary if he enters a house by opening wider a partly open window in order to squeeze through to steal the silverware in the house, even though he honestly but mistakenly believes there can be no burglary unless he opens a window entirely shut. But if the state supreme court had previously held that the burglary element of "breaking" is absent in the wider opening of an already partly open window, and the defendant relied on it, he would have the defense of mistake of law.[103] Some courts have even gone so far as to say that the adoption by a court of a new interpretation of an old statute is forbidden by *ex post facto* constitutional provisions if the new interpretation is harder on the defendant than the old.[104]

We have been speaking of the *stare decisis* problem involved when the court decides that its previous interpretation of a criminal statute was too favorable to the defendant. If it decides that its earlier interpretation was too hard on the defendant, it would have no trouble in overruling the earlier case, since the present defendant could not have relied on it to his disadvantage.[105]

WESTLAW REFERENCES

di stare decisis

"stare decisis" /p interpret! understand*** /s
   criminal penal /s statute law ordinance

§ 2.3 Unconstitutional Uncertainty— The Void-for-Vagueness Doctrine

At common law, it was the practice of courts to refuse to enforce legislative acts deemed too uncertain to be applied.[1] A similar approach was taken by the United States Supreme Court in some early cases where the separation of powers doctrine was invoked to support the proposition that Congress, by the enactment of an ambiguous statute, could not pass the law-making job on to the judiciary.[2] The Court has also reversed convictions under uncertain criminal laws on the basis that the accused was denied his right to be informed "of the nature and cause of the accusation" as guaranteed by the Sixth Amendment.[3] However, today it is the void-for-vagueness doctrine which prevails:[4] the due process clauses of the Fifth Amendment (when a federal statute is involved) and the Fourteenth Amendment (when a state statute is involved) re-

State courts may, without violating 14th Amendment due process, elect either to give retroactive effect, or prospective effect only, to an overruling decision. See Great Northern Ry. v. Sunburst Oil & Ref. Co., 287 U.S. 358, 53 S.Ct. 145, 77 L.Ed. 360 (1932). For a discussion of many of the problems in this area, see Schaefer, The Control of "Sunbursts": Techniques of Prospective Overruling, 42 N.Y.U.L.Rev. 631 (1967).

103. See § 5.1(e)(2). In State v. O'Neil, 147 Iowa 513, 126 N.W. 454 (1910), a defendant who violated the Iowa liquor laws, having been misled by the Iowa Supreme Court into thinking the laws unconstitutional, was held to have the defense of mistake of law.

104. E.g., State v. Longino, 109 Miss. 125, 67 So. 902 (1915).

See § 2.4(c).

105. Even here the court might overrule for the future only, as occurred in the famous case on the test for insanity, Durham v. United States, 214 F.2d 862 (D.C.Cir. 1954), adopting a new test generally considered to be more favorable to the defendant than the old test.

§ 2.3

1. Aigler, Legislation in Vague or General Terms, 21 Mich.L.Rev. 831 (1923). And thus the Supreme Court, in

early cases, overturned federal convictions under vague statutes without reference to any particular constitutional proscription, e.g., United States v. Brewer, 139 U.S. 278, 11 S.Ct. 538, 35 L.Ed. 190 (1891).

2. James v. Bowman, 190 U.S. 127, 23 S.Ct. 678, 47 L.Ed. 979 (1903); United States v. Reese, 92 U.S. 214, 23 L.Ed. 563 (1876). The Court also appears to have taken this approach more recently in United States v. Evans, 333 U.S. 483, 68 S.Ct. 634, 92 L.Ed. 823 (1948).

3. Yu Cong Eng v. Trinidad, 271 U.S. 500, 46 S.Ct. 619, 70 L.Ed. 1059 (1926); United States v. L. Cohen Grocery Co., 255 U.S. 81, 41 S.Ct. 298, 65 L.Ed. 516 (1921).

4. On this subject, see: Amsterdam, Federal Constitutional Restrictions on the Punishment of Crimes of Status, Crimes of General Obnoxiousness, Crimes of Displeasing Police Officers, and the Like, 3 Crim.L.Bull. 205, 216–33 (1967); Aigler, supra note 1; Collings, Unconstitutional Uncertainty—An Appraisal, 40 Cornell L.Q. 195 (1955); Freund, The Use of Indefinite Terms in Statutes, 30 Yale L.J. 437 (1921); Scott, Constitutional Limitations on Substantive Criminal Law, 29 Rocky Mt.L.Rev. 275, 287–89 (1957); Note, 109 U.Pa.L.Rev. 67 (1960); Note, 62 Harv.L. Rev. 77 (1948); Note, 23 Ind.L.J. 272 (1948).

quire that a criminal statute be declared void when it is so vague that "men of common intelligence must necessarily guess at its meaning and differ as to its application."[5]

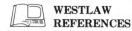 **WESTLAW REFERENCES**

di void for vagueness

(a) In General. Undue vagueness in the statute will result in it being held unconstitutional, whether the uncertainty goes to the persons within the scope of the statute,[6] the conduct which is forbidden,[7] or the punishment which may be imposed.[8] (While most of the cases have involved statutes,[9] the same principle applies to common law crimes [10] and to administrative regulations which carry penal sanctions.[11]) Ordinarily, a challenge to the statute in this regard is raised in the context of a criminal prosecution, but under limited circumstances an injunction may be obtained barring a prosecution under an unconstitutionally uncertain statute.[12] In any event, the statute is not tested "on its face," but rather with its "judicial gloss," that is, as it has been authoritatively construed by state courts.[13]

The Supreme Court has said that "[n]o one may be required at peril of life, liberty or property to speculate as to the meaning of penal statutes. All are entitled to be informed as to what the State commands or forbids." [14] And the Court has frequently emphasized that a statute is unduly vague when it gives neither the person subject thereto nor the jury which would try him a basis upon which to safely and certainly judge the result.[15] Nonetheless, it is obviously unrealistic to require that criminal statutes define offenses with extreme particularity. For one thing, there are inherent limitations in the use of language; few words possess the precision of mathematical symbols.[16] Secondly, legislators cannot foresee all of the variations of fact situations which may arise under a statute. While some ambiguous statutes are the result of poor draftsmanship, it is apparent that in many instances the uncertainty is merely attributable to a desire not to nullify the purpose of the legislation by the use of specific terms which would afford loopholes through which many could escape. And thus the Supreme Court has held that statutes are not invalid as vague simply because it is difficult to determine whether certain marginal offenses fall within their language.[17] If the general class of offenses to which a statute is directed is plainly within its terms, the stat-

5. Connally v. General Constr. Co., 269 U.S. 385, 46 S.Ct. 126, 70 L.Ed. 322 (1926).

6. E.g., Lanzetta v. New Jersey, 306 U.S. 451, 59 S.Ct. 618, 83 L.Ed. 888 (1939).

7. E.g., Colautti v. Franklin, 439 U.S. 379, 99 S.Ct. 675, 58 L.Ed.2d 596 (1979); Interstate Circuit, Inc. v. City of Dallas, 390 U.S. 676, 88 S.Ct. 1298, 20 L.Ed.2d 225 (1968); Winters v. New York, 333 U.S. 507, 68 S.Ct. 665, 92 L.Ed. 840 (1948).

8. E.g. United States v. Evans, 333 U.S. 483, 68 S.Ct. 634, 92 L.Ed. 823 (1948). Compare the *Batchelder* case discussed in note 52 infra.

9. The discussion herein concerns criminal statutes. While vague civil statutes may likewise violate due process, the standard of certainty in criminal statutes is higher than for those depending upon civil sanctions for enforcement. Winters v. New York, supra note 7.

10. Ashton v. Kentucky, 384 U.S. 195, 86 S.Ct. 1407, 16 L.Ed.2d 469 (1966). It is rare that a common law crime is held to be vague because the Court usually finds that the terms used at common law have taken on a certain meaning over the years. In *Ashton,* a problem arose because the common-law meaning would have rendered the statute unconstitutional and the state courts had not as yet given the common law crime a new definition.

11. United States v. Mersky, 361 U.S. 431, 80 S.Ct. 459, 4 L.Ed.2d 423 (1960); M. Kraus & Bros. v. United States, 327 U.S. 614, 66 S.Ct. 705, 90 L.Ed. 894 (1946).

12. See § 2.10(b).

13. Winters v. New York, supra note 7. Appropriate construction by the state court may remove the vagueness objection. Ward v. Illinois, 431 U.S. 767, 97 S.Ct. 2085, 52 L.Ed.2d 738 (1977); Wainwright v. Stone, 414 U.S. 21, 94 S.Ct. 190, 38 L.Ed.2d 179 (1973); Fox v. Washington, 236 U.S. 273, 35 S.Ct. 383, 59 L.Ed. 573 (1915). As to the problem of relying upon such a construction when it occurs subsequent to the defendant's conduct, see § 2.4(c).

14. Lanzetta v. New Jersey, 306 U.S. 451, 59 S.Ct. 618, 83 L.Ed. 888 (1939).

15. E.g., Cline v. Frink Dairy Co., 274 U.S. 445, 47 S.Ct. 681, 71 L.Ed. 1146 (1927).

16. "Condemned to the use of words, we can never expect mathematical certainty from our language." Grayned v. City of Rockford, 408 U.S. 104, 92 S.Ct. 2294, 33 L.Ed.2d 222 (1972).

17. United States v. National Dairy Products Corp., 372 U.S. 29, 83 S.Ct. 594, 9 L.Ed.2d 561 (1963).

ute will not be struck down because hypothetical cases could be put where doubt might arise.[18]

As the above suggests, there is no simple litmus-paper test for determining whether a criminal statute is void for vagueness. This had led some to question whether there is a thread of consistency running through the Supreme Court's decisions on this subject,[19] although it is probably fair to conclude that a reasonable level of consistency appears once the underlying bases of the void-for-vagueness doctrine are identified.[20] These bases are reflected in three questions often considered by the Supreme Court: (1) Does the statute in question give fair notice to those persons potentially subject to it? (2) Does it adequately guard against arbitrary and discriminatory enforcement? and (3) Does it provide sufficient breathing space for First Amendment rights?

 **WESTLAW
REFERENCES**

void /4 vague! /s "common intelligence"

(b) Fair Warning. One rationale underlying the void-for-vagueness doctrine is that of fair warning to persons potentially subject to a statute; the Supreme Court has frequently stressed that everyone is entitled to be informed what the law commands or forbids.[21] Although the Court has said that the law must be clear to the "average man," [22] to "men of common intelligence," [23] and to "ordinary people," [24] such language cannot be accepted at face value. Words of a statute which otherwise might be considered unduly vague may be considered sufficiently definite because they have a well-settled meaning in the common law,[25] or because of their usage in other legislation.[26] These sources of clarification are not likely to occur to the average person. This suggests that the requirement of fair warning is satisfied if a statute suggests the need to seek legal advice and if the statute's meaning might reasonably be determined through such advice.[27]

The language quoted above is somewhat misleading in another respect, as there is no need for legislation to give fair warning except to those potentially subject to it. For this reason, if a penal statute is addressed to those in a particular trade or business, it is sufficient if the terms used have a meaning well enough defined to enable one engaged in that trade or business to apply it correctly.[28]

---

18. United States v. Harriss, 347 U.S. 612, 74 S.Ct. 808, 98 L.Ed. 989 (1954).

19. Collings, supra note 4.

20. This is the conclusion reached in Note, 109 U.Pa.L. Rev. 67 (1960).

21. E.g., Lanzetta v. New Jersey, supra note 6.

22. Cline v. Frink Dairy Co., 274 U.S. 445, 47 S.Ct. 681, 71 L.Ed. 1146 (1927).

23. Connally v. General Constr. Co., 269 U.S. 385, 46 S.Ct. 126, 70 L.Ed. 322 (1926). See also Village of Hoffman Estates v. Flipside, Hoffman Estates, Inc., 455 U.S. 489, 102 S.Ct. 1186, 71 L.Ed.2d 362 (1982) ("person of ordinary intelligence").

24. Kolender v. Lawson, 461 U.S. 352, 103 S.Ct. 1855, 75 L.Ed.2d 903 (1983).

25. Connally v. General Constr. Co., 269 U.S. 385, 46 S.Ct. 126, 70 L.Ed. 322 (1926).

26. Omaechevarria v. Idaho, 246 U.S. 343, 38 S.Ct. 323, 62 L.Ed. 763 (1918).

27. "In general, it would seem fair to charge the individual with such knowledge of a statute's meaning and applicability as he could obtain through competent legal advice, provided that the statute gives him enough warning that he ought reasonably to see the need of obtaining such advice." Note, 62 Harv.L.Rev. 77, 80 (1948).

This rationale is more convincing under some circumstances than others. Compare the *Hoffman Estates* case, supra note 23 (upholding ordinance requiring license to sell certain items, and declaring that "economic regulation is subject to a less strict vagueness test because its subject-matter is often more narrow, and because businesses, which face economic demands to plan behavior carefully, can be expected to consult relevant legislation in advance of action" and "may have the ability to clarify the meaning of the regulation by its own inquiry, or by resort to an administrative process"); with Papachristou v. City of Jacksonville, 405 U.S. 156, 92 S.Ct. 839, 31 L.Ed. 2d 110 (1972) (vagrancy ordinance void for vagueness; Court stresses that the "poor among us, the minorities, the average householder are not in business and not alerted to the regulatory schemes of vagrancy laws; and we assume they would have no understanding of their meaning and impact if they read them").

28. Hygrade Provision Co. v. Sherman, 266 U.S. 497, 45 S.Ct. 141, 69 L.Ed. 402 (1925) ("kosher" meat).

See also United States v. Vuitch, 402 U.S. 62, 91 S.Ct. 1294, 28 L.Ed.2d 601 (1971), where the Court rejected the contention that an abortion statute was vague because of the "necessary for the preservation of the mother's life or health" exception for doctors, noting that "whether a particular operation is necessary for a patient's physical or mental health is a judgment that physicians are obvi-

It follows that a statute with uncertain language is more likely to be declared void for vagueness if it is addressed to the general public or to a substantial group of persons who have not voluntarily chosen to subject themselves to a particular regulatory scheme.[29]

One consequence of the fair-warning rationale is that a defendant's chances of mounting a successful vagueness challenge are greater when he can establish an appealing claim to clear notice of the boundaries of the statute in question. This is reflected in the fact that the Supreme Court has given consideration to whether the defendant's conduct is particularly evil [30] and whether the ambiguity being urged appears to be merely a pretext for evading the law.[31] Similarly, while the vagueness objection may be raised in court by one who was totally unaware of the statute prior to his conduct,[32] it should be noted that most of the cases reaching the Supreme Court in which the void-for-vagueness doctrine has been successfully invoked have been those in which it is likely the defendant actually consulted the statute book in advance and was confounded.[33]

Not infrequently the Supreme Court, in passing upon a statute claimed to be unconstitutional for vagueness, has concluded that the statute gives fair warning because scienter is an element of the offense.[34] That is, the statute is upheld because it requires that the prohibited act have been done "intentionally," "knowingly," or "willfully." *Boyce Motor Lines, Inc. v. United States*,[35] although it involves an administrative crime, is illustrative. The company was charged with violating an Interstate Commerce Commission regulation which required drivers of vehicles transporting explosives or inflammables to avoid "so far as practicable, and where feasible," congested thoroughfares and tunnels. The Court upheld the indictment because the statute under which it was brought punished only knowing violation of an I.C.C. regulation; the regulation was not vague, the Court concluded, because it would apply only in cases where the defendant was aware of a safer route and deliberately took the more dangerous one or where he willfully neglected to make inquiry about a safer alternate route. But as Justice Jackson correctly pointed out in his dissent, scienter—at least as it has been traditionally

ously called upon to make routinely whenever surgery is considered."

29. Amsterdam, supra note 4, at 218.

30. Hygrade Provision Co. v. Sherman, 266 U.S. 497, 45 S.Ct. 141, 69 L.Ed. 402 (1925); Miller v. Strahl, 239 U.S. 426, 36 S.Ct. 147, 60 L.Ed. 364 (1915).

An excellent illustration is provided by Rose v. Locke, 423 U.S. 48, 96 S.Ct. 243, 46 L.Ed.2d 185 (1975). Though the state "crime against nature" statute had never been expressly held to extend to defendant's conduct, forcible cunnilingus, it was not deemed vague simply because this possible interpretation was unresolved, as "there was nothing to indicate, clearly or otherwise, that respondent's acts were outside the scope" of the statute. In other words, while if the statute had been clear and narrow defendant might have had a valid retroactive expansion argument, see § 2.4(c), here the statute was uncertain as to a specific type of conduct deemed evil, in which case it is sufficient, as the Court put it, that defendant had notice "that his conduct might be within its scope." Compare the commonly-asserted objection to vague statutes: "Uncertain meanings inevitably lead citizens to ' "steer far wider of the unlawful zone" * * * than if the boundaries of the forbidden area were clearly marked.' " Grayned v. City of Rockford, 408 U.S. 104, 92 S.Ct. 2294, 33 L.Ed.2d 222 (1972).

31. United States v. Korpan, 354 U.S. 271, 77 S.Ct. 1099, 1 L.Ed.2d 1337 (1957); United States v. Five Gam-

bling Devices, 346 U.S. 441, 74 S.Ct. 190, 98 L.Ed. 179 (1953); United States v. Kahriger, 345 U.S. 22, 73 S.Ct. 510, 97 L.Ed. 754 (1953).

32. It has sometimes been questioned whether this should be so. Comment, 53 Mich.L.Rev. 264, 270 (1954) asks "whether or not a person should be allowed to assert vagueness as a defense without some indication that he actually consulted the statute with a view toward compliance." If fair warning were the only concern, this question would have more relevance, but as noted herein there are other important considerations underlying the void-for-vagueness doctrine.

33. Note, 109 U.Pa.L.Rev. 67, 87 n. 98 (1960).

34. United States v. National Dairy Products Corp., 372 U.S. 29, 83 S.Ct. 594, 9 L.Ed.2d 561 (1963); Boyce Motor Lines, Inc. v. United States, 342 U.S. 337, 72 S.Ct. 329, 96 L.Ed. 367 (1952); Screws v. United States, 325 U.S. 91, 65 S.Ct. 1031, 89 L.Ed. 1495 (1945); United States v. Ragen, 314 U.S. 513, 62 S.Ct. 374, 86 L.Ed. 383 (1942); Gorin v. United States, 312 U.S. 19, 61 S.Ct. 429, 85 L.Ed. 488 (1941); Omaechevarria v. Idaho, 246 U.S. 343, 38 S.Ct. 323, 62 L.Ed. 763 (1918). Compare Colautti v. Franklin, supra note 7 (vagueness in abortion statute deemed compounded by liability without fault aspect of the law).

35. 342 U.S. 337, 72 S.Ct. 329, 96 L.Ed. 367 (1952).

defined—cannot cure vagueness in a statute or regulation. One "knowingly" commits an offense when he knows that his acts will bring about certain results (those defined in the statute in question),[36] and whether he knows that deliberately causing such results is proscribed by statute is immaterial.[37] Because it is knowledge of the consequences of one's actions and not knowledge of the existence or meaning of the criminal law which is relevant, it seems clear that uncertain language in a statute is not clarified by the addition of a scienter element. Stated in the context of the *Boyce* case, the fact that a conviction may be had only if it is found that the driver willfully failed to take or discover a safer route "so far as practicable, and where feasible," does not require proof of actual knowledge or understanding of the quoted language and thus does not serve to clarify that language.[38] Or, to put it yet another way, it is possible willfully to bring about certain results and yet be without fair warning that such conduct is proscribed.[39]

As noted earlier,[40] it is often difficult to determine whether the uncertain language in a statute renders it ambiguous, so that it may be narrowly construed and thus remain valid, or whether the language makes the statute vague, so that it is void. Consideration of the fair-warning underpinnings of the void-for-vagueness doctrine may be helpful in this regard. If the language of the statute is rather uncertain, but a person potentially subject to the statute could (perhaps with legal advice) reasonably foresee the limited alternative meanings which might be given the statute, then perhaps there is sufficient fair warning to justify subsequent construction and validation of the statute.[41] On the other hand, if the statute is so uncertain that the means by which it might be rehabilitated cannot reasonably be foreseen, then it seems appropriate to invalidate the statute for vagueness.[42]

While the fair-warning principle is one important aspect of the void-for-vagueness doctrine it does not provide a complete rationale of the cases in this area. Particularly because some of the decisions cannot be squared with the notion of fair warning,[43] it may be that the two factors discussed below are more likely to be controlling.

 **WESTLAW REFERENCES**

fair** /3 warn*** /s void /4 vague!

(c) Arbitrary and Discriminatory Enforcement. The decisions of the United States Supreme Court on the void-for-vagueness doctrine also reflect concern with statutes which are so broad that they are susceptible to arbitrary and discriminatory enforcement.[44] Although most of these cases have also reflected a fair-warning concern, the Court recently declared a statute void because of the unlimited discretion given to juries even though no problem of fair warning was present.[45] The objection to a vague statute, then, is akin to a claim of denial of equal

36. See § 3.5.

37. Ellis v. United States, 206 U.S. 246, 27 S.Ct. 600, 51 L.Ed. 1047 (1907).

38. See Collings, supra note 4, at 227–31; 26 Minn.L. Rev. 661 (1942).

39. The Supreme Court decisions on this point might also be criticized in terms of the risk of arbitrary and discriminatory enforcement, as even if it is required that the defendant know what he is doing, it is nonetheless possible that the police, prosecutor, court, and jury will be arbitrary in determining whether his conduct is within the statute.

40. See § 2.2.

41. Consider, in this regard, the case of Rose v. Locke, discussed in note 30 supra.

42. Dombrowski v. Pfister, 380 U.S. 479, 85 S.Ct. 1116, 14 L.Ed.2d 22 (1965), supports this conclusion, as the

Court there would not afford the state court an opportunity to narrow the statute because there was no readily apparent construction which suggested itself as a vehicle for rehabilitating the statute in a single prosecution. Cf. J. Hall, General Principles of Criminal Law 41–44 (2d ed. 1960).

43. For example, those cases in which the Supreme Court has taken account of "judicial gloss" added to the statute subsequent to the defendant's conduct. See § 2.4(c).

44. See Amsterdam, supra note 4, at 220–24; Lewis, The Sit-In Cases: Great Expectations, 1963 Supreme Court Rev. 101, 110; Note, 109 U.Pa.L.Rev. 67, 80–85, 89–96 (1960).

45. Giaccio v. Pennsylvania, 382 U.S. 399, 86 S.Ct. 518, 15 L.Ed.2d 447 (1966).

protection in law enforcement,[46] although it may more appropriately be said to rest upon the notion that the language of the statute is so uncertain that arbitrariness in its enforcement might not be detected.[47]

This risk of abuse in the administration of the law is present in two forms when the meaning of a criminal statute is unclear. One risk is that the law may be arbitrarily applied by police and prosecution officials, which the Court has recently characterized as "the more important aspect of vagueness doctrine."[48] The Supreme Court has voided statutes which give the police unlimited discretion,[49] and has evidenced equal concern about laws which furnish convenient tools for discriminatory enforcement by prosecuting officials.[50] The other risk is that the law may be so unclear that a trial court cannot properly instruct the jury. A statute is unconstitutionally vague when it leaves judges and jurors free to decide, without any legally fixed standards, what is prohibited and what is not in each particular case.[51]

This is not to say, however, that a penal statute is void merely because it grants some discretion to those who administer the law.[52] The criminal law is full of instances in which the legislature has passed on to the administrators some responsibility for determining the actual boundaries of the law, as with the frequent occasions when a jury is asked to determine whether the defendant acted "reasonably" in some respect. Account must be taken of what has been called the 'principle of necessity":[53] when the concern is with whether the statute provides some opportunity for arbitrary enforcement, it is relevant to ask whether some alternative formulation not carrying this risk reasonably suggests itself.[54] Uncertain statutory language has been upheld when the subject matter would not allow more exactness[55] and when greater specificity in language would interfere with practical administration.[56] On the other hand, statutes which appear to be the result of poor draftsmanship are more likely to be struck down.[57]

46. The latter contention may be more difficult to mount successfully. See § 2.11.

47. Thus, in Interstate Circuit, Inc. v. City of Dallas, 390 U.S. 676, 88 S.Ct. 1298, 20 L.Ed.2d 225 (1968), the Court, after declaring the ordinance void for vagueness, noted that its vices were "the lack of guidance to those who seek to adjust their conduct and to those who seek to administer the law, as well as the possible practical curtailing of the effectiveness of judicial review."

Some risk of arbitrary enforcement is present, however, even with the most carefully drafted statute. See Remington & Rosenblum, The Criminal Law and the Legislative Process, 1960 U.Ill.L.F. 481, 488–89.

48. Kolender v. Lawson, 461 U.S. 352, 103 S.Ct. 1855, 75 L.Ed.2d 903 (1983).

49. E.g., Kolender v. Lawson, supra note 48 (statute requiring lawfully stopped person to provide "credible and reliable" identification vague because it confers virtually complete discretion on the police); Palmer v. City of Euclid, 402 U.S. 544, 91 S.Ct. 1563, 29 L.Ed.2d 98 (1971). Shuttlesworth v. City of Birmingham, 382 U.S. 87, 86 S.Ct. 211, 15 L.Ed.2d 176 (1965).

50. Thornhill v. Alabama, 310 U.S. 88, 60 S.Ct. 736, 84 L.Ed. 1093 (1940).

51. Giaccio v. Pennsylvania, supra note 45; United States v. L. Cohen Grocery Co., 255 U.S. 81, 41 S.Ct. 298, 65 L.Ed. 516 (1921).

But, an obscenity statute is not unconstitutionally vague merely because of "the possibility that different

juries might reach different conclusions as to the same material." Smith v. United States, 431 U.S. 291, 97 S.Ct. 1756, 52 L.Ed.2d 324 (1977).

52. A prime example is United States v. Batchelder, 442 U.S. 114, 99 S.Ct. 2198, 60 L.Ed.2d 755 (1979) (though two different statutes make it criminal for a felon to receive a firearm, one carrying a 2-year maximum and one a 5-year maximum, there is no vagueness here, as though the defendant may be uncertain of which statute he will be prosecuted under, he does know the maximum possible penalty and is no more in doubt than when a single statute permits alternate punishments).

53. Note, 109 U.Pa.L.Rev. 67, 95 (1960).

54. The Court has often noted that "the Constitution does not require impossible standards." E.g., United States v. Petrillo, 332 U.S. 1, 67 S.Ct. 1538, 91 L.Ed. 1877 (1947).

55. For example, in United States v. Petrillo, supra note 54, where the Lea Act made it a crime to compel a broadcaster to employ "persons in excess of the number of employees needed," the Court said the statute embodied as much exactness as the subject matter permitted.

56. United States v. Kahriger, 345 U.S. 22, 73 S.Ct. 510, 97 L.Ed. 754 (1953); Waters-Pierce Oil Co. v. Texas, 212 U.S. 86, 29 S.Ct. 220, 53 L.Ed. 417 (1909).

57. United States v. Cardiff, 344 U.S. 174, 73 S.Ct. 189, 97 L.Ed. 200 (1952); United States v. Evans, 333 U.S. 483, 68 S.Ct. 634, 92 L.Ed. 823 (1948).

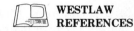
**WESTLAW
REFERENCES**

arbitrar! /s void /4 vague!

(d) Breathing Space for First Amendment Rights. In some of the cases on the subject of unconstitutional indefiniteness, the legislature has not extended its regulation via enactment of criminal statutes into areas protected by the Constitution, but has merely left uncertain exactly what is regulated. That is, even giving the vague statute a most generous reading, it is clear that the legislature could (had it used clear language) proscribe all such conduct. The vice is not legislative overreaching, but merely the lack of fair warning to the public and the lack of standards for those who must enforce and apply the law.

By contrast, in other cases the legislature has undertaken regulation in a "danger zone," in that there are substantive due process limits on how far it may go in regulating conduct without infringing upon, for example, constitutionally protected free speech. If the statute is unclear, there are again likely to be present the two vices of insufficient warning and inadequate enforcement standards. But—of particular importance when the defendant is not in a position to object on either of these two grounds [58]—there is another evil as well: the indefiniteness in the statute, or in the "judicial gloss" placed upon the statute in an attempt to overcome the claim that it prohibits constitutionally protected conduct,[59] may inhibit the exercise of constitutional rights. That is, "there is the danger that the state will get away with more inhibitory regu-

lation than it has a constitutional right to impose, because persons at the fringes of amenability to regulation will rather obey than run the risk of erroneous constitutional judgment." [60]

It is for this reason that the United States Supreme Court has repeatedly applied strict standards of permissible statutory vagueness to legislation in the area of First Amendment rights.[61] "Because First Amendment freedoms need breathing space to survive, government may regulate in the area only with narrow specificity." [62] This bolstering of the void-for-vagueness doctrine by the "breathing space" argument, it should be noted, is somewhat different than a direct attack upon a statute on the ground that it violates constitutional guarantees of the First Amendment. Criminal statutes, of course, may be attacked on the latter basis as well,[63] but the circumstances in which this may be successfully done are in some respects more limited. Thus, when a statute is challenged on this basis it is generally required that the party making the challenge establish that the statute actually infringes upon his own constitutional rights.[64] This is not so when it is alleged that the statute is vague and that it thus does not afford sufficient "breathing space." Such an attack is permitted even though the person making the attack fails to demonstrate that his own conduct could not be regulated by a statute drawn with the requisite narrow specificity.[65] In appraising a vague statute's inhibitory effect upon First Amendment rights, the Court will take into

58. See NAACP v. Button, 371 U.S. 415, 83 S.Ct. 328, 9 L.Ed.2d 405 (1963).

59. E.g., Winters v. New York, supra note 7.

60. Note, 109 U.Pa.L.Rev. 67, 80 (1960).

61. Hynes v. Mayor and Council of Borough of Oradell, 425 U.S. 610, 96 S.Ct. 1755, 48 L.Ed.2d 243 (1976); Interstate Circuit, Inc., v. City of Dallas, 390 U.S. 676, 88 S.Ct. 1298, 20 L.Ed.2d 225 (1968); Ashton v. Kentucky, 384 U.S. 195, 86 S.Ct. 1407, 16 L.Ed.2d 469 (1966); NAACP v. Button, supra note 58; Smith v. California, 361 U.S. 147, 80 S.Ct. 215, 4 L.Ed.2d 205 (1959); Winters v. New York, supra note 7, Herndon v. Lowry, 301 U.S. 242, 57 S.Ct. 732, 81 L.Ed. 1066 (1937); Stromberg v. California, 283 U.S. 359, 51 S.Ct. 532, 75 L.Ed. 1117 (1931).

62. NAACP v. Button, 371 U.S. 415, 433, 83 S.Ct. 328, 338, 9 L.Ed.2d 405, 418 (1963).

63. See § 2.14.

64. E.g., McGowan v. Maryland, 366 U.S. 420, 81 S.Ct. 1101, 6 L.Ed.2d 393 (1961). As stated in Village of Hoffman Estates v. Flipside, Hoffman Estates, Inc., 455 U.S. 489, 102 S.Ct. 1186, 71 L.Ed.2d 362 (1982), if the law "implicates no constitutionally protected conduct," then a court "should uphold the challenge only if the enactment is impermissibly vague in all of its applications. A plaintiff who engages in some conduct that is clearly proscribed cannot complain of the vagueness of the law as applied to the conduct of others."

65. Plummer v. City of Columbus, 414 U.S. 2, 94 S.Ct. 17, 38 L.Ed.2d 3 (1973); Dombrowski v. Pfister, 380 U.S. 479, 85 S.Ct. 1116, 14 L.Ed.2d 22 (1965); Thornhill v. Alabama, 310 U.S. 88, 60 S.Ct. 736, 84 L.Ed. 1093 (1940).

account possible applications of the statute in other factual contexts.[66]

 WESTLAW REFERENCES

"breathin space" /p narrow /3 specificity

---

§ 2.4 Ex Post Facto Laws and Bills of Attainder

The United States Constitution forbids both the federal government and the states to enact any ex post facto law or bill of attainder.[1] Many state constitutions also contain one or both of the same two provisions. While bills of attainder and ex post facto laws overlap to some extent, they do not always mean the same thing and thus are treated here under separate headings.

(a) Ex Post Facto Laws.[2] The Supreme Court long ago gave this much-quoted list of ex post facto laws: "1st. Every law that makes an action done before the passing of the law, and which was innocent when done, criminal; and punishes such action. 2d. Every law that aggravates a crime, or makes it greater than it was, when committed. 3d. Every law that changes the punishment, and inflicts a greater punishment, than the law annexed to the crime, when committed. 4th. Every law that alters the legal rules of evidence, and receives less, or different testimony, than the law required at the time of the commission of the offense, in order to convict the offender."[3] The first three are restrictions as to the substantive criminal law, while the fourth—dealing with retroactive changes in the law of evidence—is a limitation on procedural law. And later cases have included procedural changes other than changes in the rules of evidence when the accused is thereby deprived of a substantial right.[4] The subject of ex post facto laws will, however, be treated as a whole in this section rather than divided into its substantive and procedural parts, as the principle underlying the ex post provision applies equally to its substantive and procedural law applications.

The ex post facto prohibition has been recognized by the Supreme Court as furthering two important purposes. For one thing, it serves "to assure that legislative acts give fair warning of their effect and permit individuals to rely on their meaning until explicitly changed."[5] Moreover, the prohibition "also restricts governmental power by restraining arbitrary and potentially vindictive legislation."[6] A third basis has sometimes been stated, namely, that it "assures the legislature can make recourse to stigmatizing penalties of the criminal law only when its core purpose of deterrence could thereby possibly be served."[7]

The ex post facto prohibition is concerned with legislative acts (federal or state), rather than with judicial decisions.[8] It applies only to criminal matters,[9] although retroactive civ-

---

66. NAACP v. Button, supra note 58; Thornhill v. Alabama, supra note 65; Winters v. New York, supra note 7.

§ 2.4

1. U.S. Const. art. I, §§ 9 (federal) and 10 (state).

2. See Black, Statutes of Limitation and the Ex Post Facto Clauses, 26 Ky.L.J. 41 (1937); Crosskey, The True Meaning of the Constitutional Prohibition of Ex Post Facto Laws, 14 U.Chi.L.Rev. 539 (1947); Field, Ex Post Facto in the Constitution, 20 Mich.L.Rev. 315 (1922); Hochman, The Supreme Court and the Constitutionality of Retroactive Legislation, 73 Harv.L.Rev. 692 (1960); McAllister, Ex Post Facto Laws in the Supreme Court of the United States, 15 Calif.L.Rev. 269 (1927); Slawson, Constitutional and Legislative Considerations in Retroactive Lawmaking, 48 Calif.L.Rev. 216 (1960); Note, 73 Mich.L.Rev. 1491 (1975).

3. Calder v. Bull, 3 U.S. (3 Dall.) 386, 1 L.Ed. 648 (1798). It would seem that items # 2 and # 3 are really different ways of expressing a single idea.

4. E.g., People v. Edenburg, 88 Cal.App. 558, 263 P. 857 (1928).

5. Weaver v. Graham, 450 U.S. 24, 101 S.Ct. 960, 67 L.Ed.2d 17 (1981).

6. Weaver v. Graham, 450 U.S. 24, 101 S.Ct. 960, 67 L.Ed.2d 17 (1981).

7. Warren v. United States Parole Comm'n, 659 F.2d 183 (D.C.Cir.1981).

8. Ross v. Oregon, 227 U.S. 150, 33 S.Ct. 220, 57 L.Ed. 458 (1913) (the Court states that legislative acts include constitutional provisions, statutes, ordinances and administrative regulations and orders). See § 2.4(c) for further discussion of judicial decisions as ex post facto laws.

9. Calder v. Bull, supra note 3, holding that a retroactive state statute affecting civil, not criminal, rights and remedies is not an ex post facto law. Thus deportation, disbarment and criminal sexual psychopath proceedings, not being "criminal" matters, do not involve the ex post facto prohibition. Galvan v. Press, 347 U.S. 522, 74 S.Ct.

il statutes have sometimes been held unconstitutional on some other ground, usually as a taking of property rights without due process of law.

The clearest sort of an ex post facto law is one which creates a new crime and applies it retroactively to conduct not criminal at the time committed. This is so obviously true that legislation seldom if ever has attempted to accomplish this result. The same result would follow from a statute that eliminated a former element of the offense (e.g., omitting the word "knowingly" in a statutory crime or the phrase "in the nighttime" in a burglary statute), or which took away a defense formerly available, such as self-defense in battery or lack of pregnancy in abortion.[10]

More difficult problems are frequently encountered under the second aspect of the ex post facto prohibition, which forbids the retroactive application of an increase in the punishment for a crime which carried a lesser penalty when committed. (A lessening of the punishment is not prohibited, and thus a change from the death penalty to life imprisonment may be applied retroactively.)[11] If a statute making grand theft punishable by one to five years imprisonment is amended to increase the punishment to from two to ten years, the amendment would be ex post facto

as applied to theft committed before the amendment.[12] And a statute changing the punishment from life imprisonment or death to a mandatory death penalty is ex post facto as applied to a past crime,[13] as is a statute changing the punishment from a fine or imprisonment to a fine *and* imprisonment.[14] In *Dobbert v. Florida,*[15] the Supreme Court held that a defendant's sentence of death did not violate the ex post facto prohibition where it was imposed pursuant to valid procedures superceding those which had existed at the time of his crime and which had been thereafter declared unconstitutional. The majority, stressing the fair warning function, deemed it sufficient that the law at the time of defendant's conduct revealed what the legislature wanted to accomplish. The dissenters in *Dobbert,* on the other hand, stressed that at the time of defendant's crime there existed no valid means of imposing a death sentence in Florida.[16]

Although some earlier cases took the view that any change in the kind or manner of punishment is ex post facto as to prior offenses,[17] today it is generally accepted that such a change is permissible if it does not increase the punishment, as with a change in the procedures for arriving at [18] or carrying out [19] a sentence of death. It is not always

737, 98 L.Ed. 911 (1954) (deportation); In re Craven, 178 La. 372, 151 So. 625 (1931); State ex rel. Sweezer v. Green, 360 Mo. 1249, 232 S.W.2d 897 (1950) (sexual psychopath). That interpretation has been questioned; see Crosskey, supra note 2.

10. See Beazell v. Ohio, 269 U.S. 167, 46 S.Ct. 68, 70 L. Ed. 216 (1925).

11. People ex rel. Lonschein v. Warden, 43 Misc.2d 109, 250 N.Y.S.2d 15 (1964); Commonwealth v. Vaughn, 329 Mass. 333, 108 N.E.2d 559 (1952); McGuire v. State, 76 Miss. 504, 25 So. 495 (1899).

12. As to whether such an amendment operates to repeal the old statute so as to free the defendant from liability, see § 2.5.

13. See Lindsey v. Washington, 301 U.S. 397, 57 S.Ct. 797, 81 L.Ed. 1182 (1937).

14. Flaherty v. Thomas, 94 Mass. 428 (1866).

15. 432 U.S. 282, 97 S.Ct. 2290, 53 L.Ed.2d 344 (1977).

16. "The majority dismissed this argument summarily, but the point seems well taken because the ability to revise an invalid punishment and apply it to persons whose identities or characteristics are already fixed and knowable by the law makers can be readily abused. The

basic principle of the clauses would seem to deny a legislative power to design sentences for application to such persons." 2 R. Rotunda, J. Nowak, & J. Young, Treatise on Constitutional Law § 15.9(b) (1986).

17. E.g., Shepherd v. People, 25 N.Y. 406 (1862).

18. In Dobbert v. Florida, 432 U.S. 282, 97 S.Ct. 2290, 53 L.Ed.2d 344 (1977), where defendant was sentenced to death by the judge notwithstanding the jury's recommendation of mercy, defendant invoked the ex post facto clause because between the time of his crime and sentencing the law was changed so that a jury's recommendation of mercy was advisory rather than binding. In rejecting that claim the Court reasoned: (1) that this change was "ameliorative" and that it could only be speculated what the jury would have done under the old law, as a jury might be less likely to recommend mercy if that would be final; and (2) that this change must be considered together with many other changes in death penalty sentencing procedures produced by the same legislation, as "the new statute affords significantly more safeguards to the defendant than did the old."

19. Malloy v. South Carolina, 237 U.S. 180, 35 S.Ct. 507, 59 L.Ed. 905 (1915) (change to electrocution); Hernandez v. State, 43 Ariz. 424, 32 P.2d 18 (1934) (to gas).

easy, however, to tell whether the new punishment is greater than or the same as or less than the old.[20] A statute delaying execution for three months has been held not to be ex post facto,[21] but a new law providing for solitary confinement before execution is not valid as to past capital crimes.[22]

An amendment which lowers the maximum punishment but raises the minimum punishment is viewed as increasing the punishment.[23] Likewise, the better view is that the same is true as to a change which reduces the statutory minimum sentence but increases the time which must be served before parole may be granted,[24] although some of the older cases reach the contrary result by viewing

release on parole as an act of grace and not a right.[25] A statute reducing the amount of "good time" which can be earned in prison to reduce the sentence imposed is also ex post facto if applied to the sentence on a prior crime; this is so even if "good time" is technically not a part of the sentence, as the change "substantially alters the consequences attached to a crime already completed, and therefore changes 'the quantum of punishment.' "[26] In all such instances, one may object to an ex post facto law which increases the punishment for a past offense even if he actually received a punishment within the old limits.[27]

---

20. Strong v. State, 1 Black. 193 (Ind.1822), held the change from up to 100 lashes to a year and a day's confinement did not increase the punishment.

21. Rooney v. North Dakota, 196 U.S. 319, 25 S.Ct. 264, 49 L.Ed. 494 (1905). But a statute shortening the time within which an execution may take place is void as to prior offenses. People v. DeMoss, 5 Cal.2d 612, 55 P.2d 489 (1936).

22. In re Medley, 134 U.S. 160, 10 S.Ct. 384, 33 L.Ed. 835 (1890).

23. Commonwealth v. McDonough, 95 Mass. 581 (1866).

24. In re Griffin, 63 Cal.2d 757, 408 P.2d 959, 48 Cal. Rptr. 183 (1965) (statutory penalty changed from 10 years to life to 5 years to life, but parole eligibility changed from 3 years and 4 months to 5 years).

Compare Heirens v. Mizell, 729 F.2d 449 (7th Cir.1984) (statute enacting new parole criteria, including whether release "would deprecate the seriousness of his offense or promote disrespect for the law," could be applied to prisoners convicted of earlier crimes, as previously the board had "broad discretion" and "could consider principles of general deterrence and retributive justice," and thus the legislation "merely codified prior law").

25. Zink v. Lear, 28 N.J.Super. 515, 101 A.2d 72 (1953).

26. Weaver v. Graham, 450 U.S. 24, 101 S.Ct. 960, 67 L.Ed.2d 17 (1981). The Court rejected the state court's position that this was not so because the "good time" was not a "vested right," declaring: "Critical to relief under the Ex Post Facto Clause is not an individual's right to less punishment, but the lack of fair notice and governmental restraint when the legislature increases punishment beyond what was prescribed when the crime was consummated. Thus, even if a statute merely alters penal provisions accorded by the grace of the legislature, it violates the Clause if it is both retrospective and more onerous than the law in effect on the date of the offense."

Consider also Beebe v. Phelps, 650 F.2d 774 (5th Cir. 1981), where the new law instead said previously-earned good time would be forfeited by conviction of another crime while on parole. The court concluded that the "practical effect is a statutory increase in punishment for

the first offense, enacted subsequent to the commission of the offense," rather than punishment for the second offense, as in the cases in notes 28 and 29 infra, so that the law was ex post facto.

Distinguishable from *Weaver* is Warren v. United States Parole Comm'n, 659 F.2d 183 (D.C.Cir.1981), concerning a statute providing for use of parole guidelines in place of unlimited discretion. In finding no ex post facto violation, the court emphasized that the changes made were not necessarily disadvantageous to those in defendant's position, and that the guidelines existed prior to his new offense which prompted parole revocation (so that the situation was like that in the cases in notes 28 and 29 infra).

27. Lindsey v. Washington, 301 U.S. 397, 57 S.Ct. 797, 81 L.Ed. 1182 (1937) (former indeterminate sentence statute provided for judge to fix a minimum punishment at between 6 months and 5 years and a maximum at some figure 15 years or less; new indeterminate sentence statute provided that judge must fix maximum at 15 years, after which parole board fixes the actual term the convict must serve; *held,* ex post facto as applied to past offenders even though the judge under old law *might* have given a maximum term of 15 years, the term he *must* give under the new law). The *Lindsey* case also holds that when a state statute is before the United States Supreme Court involving the federal question of whether the statute violates the federal Constitution, the Court will decide the question whether the new punishment is greater than or less than the old one, not being bound by the state court decision on the question.

In Dobbert v. Florida, 432 U.S. 282, 97 S.Ct. 2290, 53 L.Ed.2d 344 (1977), defendant objected that the sentencing law had been changed so that a person receiving a life sentence was not eligible for parole until he had served 25 years. In concluding this defendant, who had been sentenced to death, could not object to that change, the Court took *Lindsey* "to mean that one is not barred from challenging a change in the penal code on ex post facto grounds simply because the sentence he received under the new law was not more onerous than that which he might have received under the old. It is one thing to find an ex post facto violation where under the new law a

Some ex post facto questions of the increased-punishment type have arisen in connection with the passage of habitual criminal laws, which impose enhanced penalties for later offenses if the defendant has previously been convicted of one or more crimes. If the defendant commits crime *A* at a time when there is no habitual criminal statute, then such a statute is passed imposing increased punishment for a second offense, and then the defendant commits crime *B*, it is not within the ex post facto prohibition to apply the habitual criminal statute to crime *B*. No additional punishment is prescribed for crime *A*, but only for the new crime *B*, which was committed after the statute was passed.[28] Similarly, it is permissible to define a crime as limited to certain conduct engaged in by persons who have theretofore been convicted of some other offense and to apply the statute to one whose earlier offense and conviction predated the enactment of this statute.[29]

Another aspect of the ex post facto prohibition is concerned with retroactive changes in evidence and procedure which operate to the disadvantage of the criminal defendant by making conviction easier.[30] Thus a statute which changes the burden of proof on the prosecution from the usual rule of beyond a reasonable doubt to one of the preponderance of the evidence is ex post facto if retroactive.[31] A retroactive statutory change in the rules of evidence is ex post facto, whether it excludes formerly-admissible evidence which is favorable to the defendant [32] or, as more frequently is the case, admits formerly-inadmissible evidence which is favorable to the prosecution.[33]

On the other hand, statutory changes in rules of evidence that admit evidence, formerly inadmissible, which may be used by criminal defendants as a group to show their innocence as well as by prosecuting attorneys as a group to show guilt, are not within the ex post facto ban even though, in a particular case, the new rule is applied to help the prosecution's side of the case. Thus a statute changing the law of evidence relating to identification of disputed handwritings from a rule prohibiting the use of handwriting appearing in letters of a defendant to his wife to a rule allowing the use of any genuine handwriting

---

defendant *must* receive a sentence which was under the old law only the maximum in a discretionary spectrum of length; it would be quite another to do so in a case, such as this, where the change has had no effect on the defendant in the proceedings of which he complains."

28. McDonald v. Massachusetts, 180 U.S. 311, 21 S.Ct. 389, 45 L.Ed. 542 (1901); Finley v. State, 282 Ark. 146, 666 S.W.2d 701 (1984); State v. Holloway, 144 Conn. 295, 130 A.2d 562 (1957). The result would of course be different if the sequence of events was as follows: *D* commits crime *A*, then he commits crime *B*, then the habitual criminal statute is passed, then *D* is convicted of crime *A*, then he is convicted of crime *B*. To apply the habitual criminal statute to crime *B* would be ex post facto. People v. d'A Philippo, 220 Cal. 620, 32 P.2d 962 (1934).

29. Smith v. United States, 312 F.2d 119 (10th Cir. 1963) (federal Firearms Act makes it an offense for one previously convicted of a crime of violence to transport a pistol across state lines; no ex post facto violation when applied to one convicted of such a crime before the Act was passed); State v. Williams, 358 So.2d 943 (La.1978) (same result as to state law on possession of firearm after felony conviction).

Compare Gasby v. State, 429 A.2d 165 (Del.1981) (where defendant on parole committed new crime of which he then convicted, change in law occurring after first crime but before second crime which said unexpired time on first sentence to be consecutive rather than concurrent with new sentence could not be applied to defendant). It seems that the court in *Gasby* might have concluded

instead that the change really affects how long the second sentence really will be, so that the increased punishment is for subsequent conduct.

30. Calder v. Bull, supra note 3, mentions changes in the rules of evidence but not other procedural changes; other cases have, however, recognized that some procedural changes other than those involving evidence may come under the ex post facto ban.

31. See Thompson v. Missouri, 171 U.S. 380, 18 S.Ct. 922, 43 L.Ed. 204 (1898).

32. Since the trend in the law of evidence has been to extend the scope of admissible evidence, rather than to restrict it, there is a dearth of authority on this point.

33. E.g., Walker v. State, 433 So.2d 469 (Ala.1983) (repeal of law making inadmissible statement by child while in custody of law enforcement officers); Plachy v. State, 91 Tex.Crim.R. 405, 239 S.W. 979 (1922) (change from a rule requiring corroboration of the testimony of an accomplice to one abolishing the corroboration requirement is ex post facto as to past offenses); State v. Johnson, 12 Minn. 476, 12 Gilf. 378 (1867) (change from a rule requiring conviction only on direct evidence to one allowing conviction on either direct or circumstantial evidence).

Compare Murphy v. Commonwealth, 652 S.W.2d 69 (Ky. 1983) (abolition of accomplice corroboration requirement only removes impediment to witness, as in *Hopt*, infra note 35, so no ex post facto violation).

of the defendant, is not ex post facto if retroactive.[34] The new rule is not necessarily disadvantageous to criminal defendants as a class, for the rule may be used by the defendant to show that the disputed handwriting is not his, as well as by the prosecution to show that it is. Similarly a statute enlarging the class of persons competent to testify is not ex post facto as applied to past offenses, for the new rule may be used either for or against criminal defendants as a class.[35] The same is true of a statute which broadens the rules of admissibility as to evidence in aggravation *and* mitigation for purposes of sentencing, even though it operates to the disadvantage of a defendant in a particular case.[36]

As to procedural changes other than changes in the rules of evidence, the Supreme Court has stated the test in this way: a procedural change which does not injuriously affect a substantial right to which the accused was entitled as of the time of his offense is not ex post facto though retroactive; but it is otherwise if it does deprive him of a substantial right.[37] However, it is not always easy to place a particular procedural change in one category or the other. Among the procedural changes which have been held to be substantial are: reduction of the number of trial jurors;[38] reduction of the number of jurors which must agree to a verdict;[39] abolition of jury trial;[40] and creation of the power to convict for lesser included offenses.[41] The following changes have been held to be not substantial (or as some courts put it, to "merely relate to the mode of procedure"): shifting of sentencing responsibility from the judge to the jury;[42] lengthening of the statute of limitations before it has run;[43] altering the grounds for challenging prospective jurors;[44] granting more peremptory challenges to the prosecution or less to the defendant;[45] and changes in the venue law[46] or the jurisdiction of courts,[47] and shortening of the time in which to seek a suspended sentence.[48] There is a split of authority on some other changes, such as allowing prosecution by information rather than indictment[49] and changing the number of grand jurors.[50]

 WESTLAW REFERENCES

di ex post facto law

"ex post facto" /p "fair warning"

death /3 sentenc*** penalty punish! /p "ex post facto"

34. Thompson v. Missouri, 171 U.S. 380, 18 S.Ct. 922, 43 L.Ed. 204 (1898).

35. Hopt v. Utah, 110 U.S. 574, 4 S.Ct. 202, 28 L.Ed. 262 (1884) (old law, in effect when defendant committed the crime, forbade testimony by convicted felons; new law, repealing old, allowed convicted felons to testify).

36. People v. Ward, 50 Cal.2d 702, 328 P.2d 777 (1958).

37. Kring v. Missouri, 107 U.S. 221, 2 S.Ct. 443, 27 L.Ed. 506 (1883) (old law, in effect at time of offense, provided that on a charge of first-degree murder a guilty plea of second-degree murder operated as an acquittal of first-degree murder, even if the plea is later set aside; new law, passed after offense, provided that if the plea is set aside, new trial may be had for first-degree murder; *held,* ex post facto, as the change deprives defendant of a substantial right); Beazell v. Ohio, 269 U.S. 167, 46 S.Ct. 68, 70 L.Ed. 216 (1925) (old law provided for separate trials of jointly indicted defendants as matter of right; new law for separate trials in judge's discretion; *held,* not ex post facto, as not affecting substantial rights). See People v. Edenburg, 88 Cal.App. 558, 263 P. 857 (1928).

38. Thompson v. Utah, 170 U.S. 343, 18 S.Ct. 620, 42 L.Ed. 1061 (1898).

39. State v. Ardoin, 51 La.Ann. 169, 24 So. 802 (1899).

40. State ex rel. Sherburne v. Baker, 50 La.Ann. 1247, 24 So. 240 (1898).

41. People v. Cox, 67 App.Div. 344, 73 N.Y.S. 774 (1901).

42. People v. Dusablon, 16 N.Y.2d 9, 261 N.Y.S.2d 38, 209 N.E.2d 90 (1965).

43. Clements v. United States, 266 F.2d 397 (9th Cir. 1959).

44. Stokes v. People, 53 N.Y. 164 (1873).

45. South v. State, 86 Ala. 617, 6 So. 52 (1889); State v. Ryan, 13 Minn. 370, 13 Gilf. 343 (1868).

46. Cook v. United States, 138 U.S. 157, 11 S.Ct. 268, 34 L.Ed. 906 (1891).

47. Duncan v. Missouri, 152 U.S. 377, 14 S.Ct. 570, 38 L.Ed. 485 (1894).

48. State v. Theodosopoulous, 123 N.H. 287, 461 A.2d 100 (1983).

49. Wells v. Maxwell, 174 Ohio St. 198, 188 N.E.2d 160 (1963) (not ex post facto); Putty v. United States, 220 F.2d 473 (9th Cir.1955) (ex post facto).

50. United States v. London, 176 F. 976 (E.D.Okl.1909); United States v. Haskell, 169 F. 449 (E.D.Okl.1909) (both ex post facto); Hallock v. United States, 107 C.C.A. 487, 185 F. 417 (1911); State v. Carrington, 15 Utah 480, 50 P. 526 (1897) (not ex post facto).

(b) Date of Offense for Ex Post Facto Purposes. With those crimes which consist of both conduct and the result of conduct, as is the case with criminal homicide (a blow with a resulting death is needed), there may arise a question as to the time of the offense for purposes of applying the ex post facto clause. Thus, if the defendant delivers the mortal blow on April 1, a new homicide statute becomes law on April 10, and the victim dies from his wounds on April 20, can the new statute, if disadvantageous to the defendant, constitutionally be applied to his situation? If the theory behind the prohibition on retroactivity is that of giving fair warning, it seems clear that for ex post facto purposes the date of the blow should be the date of the offense.[51]

The problem of determining the date of the offense for ex post facto purposes may also be present when the offense is of a continuing nature, as with an ongoing conspiracy or where the offense is defined in terms of allowing a certain condition to continue or is based upon omissions by the defendant. If the conduct, condition, or failure to act continues after the enactment or amendment of the statute in question, this statute may be applied without violating the ex post facto prohibition. Thus, a statute increasing the penalty with respect to a conspiracy may be applied to a conspiracy which commenced pri-

or to but was carried on and continued beyond the effective date of the new act.[52] Similarly, if a certain condition existed prior to the enactment of a statute making the permitting of such a condition a crime, this does not bar prosecution for the continuance of the condition thereafter.[53] However, if the basis of the prosecution is an omission by the defendant, it must be determined whether the duty to act existed subsequent to the new statutory enactment.[54]

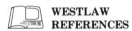
WESTLAW REFERENCES

date /3 offense /p "ex post facto"

(c) Ex Post Facto Judicial Decisions. It is clear that the ex post facto prohibition in the federal constitution applies only to legislative acts and not to judicial decisions.[55] At the same time, it is obvious that the rationale behind the ex post facto prohibition—whether it be stated as a concern for adequate notice to the defendant or as a concern with the exercise of unfettered power by public officials[56]—is relevant in the situation where a judicial decision is applied retroactively to the disadvantage of a defendant in a criminal case. And thus the United States Supreme Court has said that the due process clause bars an appellate court from doing what the ex post facto clause prohibits a legislature from doing.[57] Actually, the proposition can-

---

51. State v. Detter, 298 N.C. 604, 260 S.E.2d 567 (1979) (where defendant's murderous acts committed at time when maximum penalty was life, sentence of death violated ex post facto clause even though victim did not die until death penalty statute enacted).

52. United States v. Shackelford, 180 F.Supp. 857 (S.D. N.Y.1957); United States v. Ogull, 149 F.Supp. 272 (S.D. N.Y.1957).

53. Of course, statutes sometimes allow a grace period if considerable effort will be needed to change the condition, and if the statute does not expressly provide for a grace period the courts may take the view that a reasonable time to comply must be allowed. City of Louisville v. Thompson, 339 S.W.2d 869 (Ky.1960).

54. In State v. Masino, 216 La. 352, 43 So.2d 685 (1949), the majority held that the defendant's failure to encase gas pipes with concrete (the cause of an explosion resulting in deaths) was an omission which occurred only prior to the enactment of the negligent homicide law, while a dissenting judge was of the view that the omission continued up to the time of the explosion, subsequent to the passage of the law. Compare People v. Jones, 329 Ill.App.

503, 69 N.E.2d 522 (1946), holding that a statute which made it an offense "to permit any well * * * to remain unplugged, after such well is no longer used for the purpose for which it was drilled" could be applied to a defendant who gave up drilling a well and abandoned it unplugged two years before the statute was enacted.

55. See Marks v. United States, 430 U.S. 188, 97 S.Ct. 990, 51 L.Ed.2d 260 (1977). Ross v. Oregon, supra note 8; Frank v. Mangum, 237 U.S. 309, 35 S.Ct. 582, 59 L.Ed. 969 (1915). In view of the fact that the ban against ex post facto laws appears in U.S. Const. art. I (dealing with legislative power) and not in art. III (judicial power), this result seems to be sound.

56. See J. Hall, General Principles of Criminal Law 63 (2d ed. 1960).

57. Bouie v. City of Columbia, 378 U.S. 347, 84 S.Ct. 1697, 12 L.Ed.2d 894 (1964): "If a state legislature is barred by the Ex Post Facto Clause from passing such a law, it must follow that a State Supreme Court is barred by the Due Process Clause from achieving precisely the same result by judicial construction."

not be applied that broadly, as all case-law, including that interpreting criminal statutes, operates retroactively, and such retroactivity is an essential part of our legal system.[58] It is fair to conclude that: (1) the prohibition of retroactive judicial decisions is not as extensive as the prohibition of ex post facto statutes; and (2) the law regarding the former is not as clearly developed as that concerning the ex post facto clause.

Perhaps the easiest case is that in which a judicial decision subsequent to the defendant's conduct operates to his detriment by overruling a prior decision which, if applied to the defendant's case, would result in his acquittal. For example, the later decision may overrule a prior ruling that the statute under which the defendant was prosecuted is unconstitutional.[59] Or, it may disallow a defense permitted in an earlier case,[60] or interpret a criminal statute as covering conduct previously held to be outside this statute.[61] Under such circumstances, the overruling decision (whether on appeal of the defendant's case or in another case decided subsequent to his conduct) is not applied retroactively,[62] at least where the defendant's conduct is not *malum in se*.[63] This result has been explained on various grounds—as required by the ex post facto prohibition,[64] by the prohibition on cruel and unusual punishment,[65] by "principles of justice," [66] or by the due process clause.[67] If the defendant was actually aware of the prior decision and relied upon it, then the basis of decision may be that the defendant has the defense of mistake of law as a result of being misled as to the existence or interpretation thereof by the highest court of the jurisdiction.[68]

More difficult are those cases in which the appellate court in interpreting a statute which is not unconstitutionally vague or overbroad, decides a question of first impression in that jurisdiction concerning the meaning and scope of that statute.[69] For example, may a state supreme court hold for the first time that the felony-murder statute covers instances in which death is caused by a shot

---

58. J. Hall, General Principles of Criminal Law 61 (2d ed. 1960).

59. State v. O'Neil, 147 Iowa 513, 126 N.W. 454 (1910); State v. Stout, 90 Okl.Cr. 35, 210 P.2d 199 (1949).

60. State v. Bell, 136 N.C. 674, 49 S.E. 163 (1904); State v. Mellenberger, 163 Or. 233, 95 P.2d 709 (1939).

61. State v. Longino, 109 Miss. 125, 67 So. 902 (1915); State v. Jones, 44 N.M. 623, 107 P.2d 324 (1940). Cf. Marks v. United States, 430 U.S. 188, 97 S.Ct. 990, 51 L.Ed.2d 260 (1977) (where defendants' conduct, giving rise to a transportation of obscenity charge, occurred before Supreme Court decision in Miller v. California, announcing a new standard regarding what material is protected under the First Amendment, the *Miller* standard may not be applied retroactively to them, as it produced "expanded criminal liability" and the defendants "had no fair warning that their products might be subjected to the new standards").

62. See cases cited notes 59–61 supra. See also von Moschzisker, Stare Decisis in Courts of Last Resort, 37 Harv.L.Rev. 409, 426 (1924); Snyder, Retrospective Operation of Overruling Decisions, 35 Ill.L.Rev. 121 (1940); Note, 42 Yale L.J. 779 (1933).

It would appear that the decision of Bouie v. City of Columbia, 378 U.S. 347, 84 S.Ct. 1697, 12 L.Ed.2d 894 (1964), now requires such a result as a matter of due process. See State v. Saylor, 6 Ohio St.2d 139, 216 N.E.2d 622 (1966), where the court, citing *Bouie*, expressed serious doubt that it could overrule a prior decision that the word "possession" in an obscene materials statute meant possession with intent to sell, and then apply the new rule retroactively.

63. In State v. Mellenberger, supra note 60, the defendant was prosecuted for receiving money by false pretenses. He defended on the basis of the particeps criminis doctrine, which the state supreme court had held applicable in an earlier, similar case so as to require acquittal when the defendant's victim is guilty of illegal conduct. The court overruled the prior decision, and then held that the new decision could be applied retroactively because the defendant's conduct was malum in se.

The nature of the defendant's conduct has also been a consideration in other cases. See note 78 infra.

64. State v. Stout, supra note 59.

65. State v. Longino, supra note 61.

66. State v. Jones, supra note 61.

67. Bouie v. City of Columbia, supra note 57.

68. State v. O'Neil, supra note 59. See § 5.1(e)(2).

69. Sometimes courts experience difficulty in determining whether the most recent decision changes or merely adds to the law. In Bouie v. City of Columbia, supra note 57, the Court did not speak clearly on this point, although an examination of the prior state decisions shows that none were actually overruled by the case which held that the trespass statute also covered instances in which a person refuses to leave the land of another after being ordered to do so. But, in United States ex rel. Almeida v. Rundle, 255 F.Supp. 936 (E.D.Pa.1966), aff'd 383 F.2d 421 (3d Cir.1967), the court distinguished *Bouie* by saying that there the state supreme court had adopted a new rule directly contrary to their prior decisions.

fired by someone other than the felon, and then apply this interpretation to conduct which occurred prior to that holding?[70] May an appellate court do so when deciding, as a matter of first impression, that the word "arson" in the felony-murder statute must be read to incorporate not only the arson statute (limited to the burning of dwellings) but also the malicious burning statute (dealing with the burning of other buildings)?[71] Is it permissible for a state supreme court to affirm a trespass conviction, based upon a statute which forbids entry upon lands after notice prohibiting same, by resort to a decision subsequent to the defendant's conduct which interprets the statute as also covering failure to leave the property of another after being ordered to do so?[72]

Sometimes the application of appellate decisions on matters of first impression to prior conduct is justified on the ground that nothing in the way of retroactivity is involved because the court has merely decided what the criminal statute has meant from the time of its enactment (and thus prior to the defendant's conduct.)[73] But, even if it may be said that the judicial decision has only explained the statute and not amended it, an element of unfairness may be present if the construction

given the statute is one which could not have been reasonably anticipated. Thus, the United States Supreme Court, in *Bouie v. City of Columbia*,[74] reversed the conviction in the trespass case described above because the judicial construction of the statute was "unexpected and indefensible by reference to the law which had been expressed prior to the conduct in issue."[75] Although this standard reflects a concern with fair warning (by the reference to the "unexpected" construction) and also with arbitrary official action (by the reference to the "indefensible" construction), it obviously cannot be applied with ease because it requires a difficult evaluation of "the actual quality of the adjudication"[76] in the case of first impression.[77] For example, if extension-by-analogy is "unexpected" and "indefensible" when a trespass statute, dealing with entry after notice prohibiting same, is held also to cover refusal to leave after notice, why is it not equally so when the word "arson" in a felony-murder statute is held also to cover other malicious burning? Perhaps it is because some defendants have a greater claim to fair warning than others; in *Bouie* the Court noted that the defendants' conduct could not be deemed improper or immoral.[78]

70. See United States ex rel. Almeida v. Rundle, supra note 69, holding yes.

71. See Chavez v. Dickson, 280 F.2d 727 (9th Cir.1960), holding yes.

72. See Bouie v. City of Columbia, supra note 57, holding no.

73. Chavez v. Dickson, supra note 71.

74. 378 U.S. 347, 84 S.Ct. 1697, 12 L.Ed.2d 894 (1964).

75. Id., quoting J. Hall, General Principles of Criminal Law 61 (2d ed. 1960).

76. The phrase is Professor Hall's. Ibid.

77. If the statute is very precise, as it was in *Bouie*, that may in a sense strengthen the argument that extension of it by analogy was "unexpected and indefensible." Compare Rose v. Locke, 423 U.S. 48, 96 S.Ct. 243, 46 L.Ed. 2d 185 (1975), upholding defendant's conviction by a first-time application of the state's "crime against nature" statute to cunnilingus. Because some other states had applied such statutes to that conduct and because this state had already extended the statute beyond common law sodomy by applying it to fellatio, the Court concluded there had been sufficient warning that the statute might be further extended by analogy to cunnilingus. That is, defendant Locke, unlike the defendants in *Bouie*, had not

been put in a situation which might "lull 'the potential defendant into a false sense of security * * *.'"

78. By comparison, in United States ex rel. Almeida v. Rundle, supra note 69, the court emphasized that Almeida's conduct as a robber was "improper, illegal and immoral." This may also have been a factor in Rose v. Locke, 423 U.S. 48, 96 S.Ct. 243, 46 L.Ed.2d 185 (1975), upholding defendant's conviction for forcible cunnilingus under a state "crime against nature" statute which until defendant's case had not been held to extend to such conduct.

Query whether this is why the Supreme Court in Ginzburg v. United States, 383 U.S. 463, 86 S.Ct. 942, 16 L.Ed. 2d 31 (1966), felt free to apply retroactively an expanded definition of obscenity which takes account of the defendant's pandering. In has been argued, however, that "the emphasis in the decisions since *Roth* upon the materials themselves may be regarded as so misleading in light of the Court's new emphasis upon context that in a realistic sense the defendants were not afforded 'fair warning.'" The Supreme Court, 1965 Term, 80 Harv.L.Rev. 125, 193 (1966).

Compare with *Ginzburg* the case of Marks v. United States, supra note 55; and Rabe v. Washington, 405 U.S. 313, 92 S.Ct. 993, 31 L.Ed.2d 258 (1972) (where on defen-

There is yet another situation in which a judicial decision may appear to operate retroactively to the detriment of a criminal defendant. The language of a statute defining a crime, as yet without any limiting judicial gloss, may be unduly vague or broad and thus unconstitutional unless clarified or narrowed by judicial interpretation. May a defendant's conviction be affirmed on the basis of such a limiting construction which occurs subsequent to his conduct? That is, is it consistent with the fair-warning principle to charge the defendant with knowledge of the scope of a subsequent, saving interpretation? The United States Supreme Court has assumed that it is,[79] and thus in a number of cases has allowed these statutes the benefit of whatever clarifying gloss state courts may have added in the course of litigation after defendant's conduct.[80] The thrust of these cases seems to be that prospective defendants are not entitled to warning as to the precise way in which the statute will be construed to bring it within the Constitution. In some cases this result

is not shocking, as where a defendant is prosecuted for sale of obscene literature and on his appeal the statute is saved by reading in a requirement that the sale be with knowledge of the obscene character of the literature.[81] It has been suggested, however, that this kind of judicial decision should have retroactive effect only when "the limiting construction is a relatively simple and natural one,"[82] that is, when there is some warning as to the actual reach of the statute because the way in which it will be construed can be reasonably foreseen. In the *Bouie* case, the Supreme Court intimated it might go at least this far.[83]

 **WESTLAW REFERENCES**

di malum in se

bouie +5 columbia /p "ex post facto"

(d) Bills of Attainder.[84] The Supreme Court has given this definition: "A bill of attainder is a legislative act which inflicts punishment without a judicial trial."[85] More recently, the Court defined such bills more

---

dant's appeal from obscenity conviction court indicated obscenity determination possible only by taking into account the "context" of the exhibition, i.e., that the film was shown in an outdoor theatre, conviction could not stand, as neither the statute nor prior interpretations had "given fair notice that the location of the exhibition was a vital element of the offense").

Compare with *Almeida* the approach taken in Keeler v. Superior Court, 2 Cal.3d 619, 87 Cal.Rptr. 481, 470 P.2d 617 (1970), where the court concluded that in light of *Bouie* the California murder statute could not be retroactively interpreted as to cover the killing of an unborn but viable fetus. Although the defendant's conduct was clearly "immoral" and "improper," the court emphasized that "the guarantee of due process extends to violent as well as peaceful men."

79. "We assume that the defendant, at the time he acted, was chargeable with knowledge of the scope of subsequent interpretation." Winters v. New York, 333 U.S. 507, 68 S.Ct. 665, 92 L.Ed. 840 (1948).

80. See Note, 109 U.Pa.L.Rev. 67, 73–74 (1960), discussing the cases. Illustrative is United States v. Vuitch, 402 U.S. 62, 91 S.Ct. 1294, 28 L.Ed.2d 601 (1971), where the Court relied upon lower court constructions of the D.C. abortion statute occurring subsequent to the defendant's conduct.

81. People v. Finkelstein, 11 N.Y.2d 300, 183 N.E.2d 661, 229 N.Y.S.2d 367 (1962).

82. Freund, The Supreme Court and Civil Liberties, 4 Vand.L.Rev. 533, 540 (1951).

83. The Court quoted from the Freund article, supra note 82, and supported its holding by saying that such a

result follows from the proposition that a vague statute could not be cured retrospectively by ruling of either the trial court or appellate court. In a later case, Ashton v. Kentucky, 384 U.S. 195, 86 S.Ct. 1407, 16 L.Ed.2d 469 (1966), the Court held that an indefinite definition of a common law offense by the trial court could not be cured by a subsequent limited construction by the appellate court. Cf. Shuttlesworth v. Birmingham, 394 U.S. 147, 89 S.Ct. 935, 22 L.Ed.2d 162 (1969) (conviction for conducting a parade without a permit cannot stand though, on defendants' appeal, the state supreme court "performed a remarkable job of plastic surgery upon the face of the ordinance" so that "as now authoritatively construed [it] would pass constitutional muster," as it "would have taken extraordinary clairvoyance for anyone to perceive that this language meant what the Supreme Court of Alabama was destined to find that it meant more than four years later").

84. See Davis, United States v. Lovett and the Attainder Bogey in Modern Legislation, 1950 Wash.U.L.Q. 13 (1950); Norville, Bill of Attainder—A Rediscovered Weapon Against Discriminatory Legislation, 26 Ore.L.Rev. 78 (1947); Reppy, The Spectre of Attainder in New York, 23 St. John's L.Rev. 1 (1948); Schuman, "Bill of Attainder" in the Seventy-Eighth Congress, 37 Am.Pol.Sci.Rev. 819 (1943); Wormuth, Legislative Disqualifications as Bills of Attainder, 4 Vand.L.Rev. 603 (1951); Comments, 18 Geo. Wash.L.Rev. 541 (1950); 63 Yale L.J. 844 (1954); Note, 72 Yale L.J. 330 (1962).

85. Cummings v. Missouri, 71 U.S. (4 Wall.) 277, 18 L.Ed. 356 (1867), pointing out that the term "bill of attainder" as used in the Constitution includes punishment less than death, even though originally a "bill of attainder"

broadly as "legislative acts, no matter what their form, that apply either to named individuals or to easily ascertainable members of a group in such a way as to inflict punishment on them without a judicial trial." [86] Thus, a statute, federal or state, providing that any public official found guilty of misconduct in office by his superiors should be fined or imprisoned, would be unconstitutional as a bill of attainder.[87]

Actually, most of the cases which have found legislative acts to be bills of attainder have involved punishment in a much broader sense than criminal; thus denial of the right to practice one's profession,[88] or of the right to government or private employment,[89] has been held to be "punishment" within the meaning of the definition of bills of attainder, and this is so whether the legislature's aim was to punish past conduct or to discourage future conduct which it dislikes.[90]

A statute might provide that a named individual (or named individuals, or an identifiable group of individuals), who had in the past done something which the legislature thought to be bad but which was not criminal, should be fined or imprisoned. Such a statute would, of course, be a bill of attainder. But it would also be an ex post facto law and thus doubly unconstitutional. The two constitutional

prohibitions do tend to overlap somewhat, though they are clearly not identical.

§ 2.5 Repeal or Amendment of Statute

What becomes of the criminal liability of a person, who has violated a criminal statute when that statute was in force, if the statute in question is later repealed? Does the repeal operate retroactively so as to let him go free? Or does the repeal operate only as to future conduct, leaving past conduct to be governed by the law in effect at the time of such conduct? Does it make a difference whether the person in question has been convicted before the repeal, or whether his prosecution is then pending, or whether prosecution has not yet been commenced at the time of repeal? The same questions may be asked, though the answers may be different, in the situation where the criminal statute in question has been amended, rather than repealed, as where the amendment alters the punishment or changes the scope of the statute's coverage.

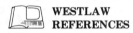 **WESTLAW REFERENCES**

110k15

(a) Common Law Rule. The common law rule is that, in the absence of an effective saving provision, the outright repeal of a criminal statute operates to bar prosecutions

---

was a legislative act punishing by death, while a legislative act providing for punishment less than death was known as a "bill of pains and penalties." The historical background of bills of attainder is given in the *Cummings* case, supra; United States v. Lovett, 328 U.S. 303, 66 S.Ct. 1073, 90 L.Ed. 1252 (1946); United States v. Brown, 381 U.S. 437, 85 S.Ct. 1707, 14 L.Ed.2d 484 (1965).

86. United States v. Brown, 381 U.S. 437, 85 S.Ct. 1707, 14 L.Ed. 484 (1965) quoting United States v. Lovett, 328 U.S. 303, 66 S.Ct. 1073, 90 L.Ed. 1252 (1946). In Nixon v. Administrator of General Services, 433 U.S. 425, 97 S.Ct. 2777, 53 L.Ed.2d 867 (1977), the Court held that a statute providing for governmental custody of President Nixon's presidential papers was not a bill of attainder. The law was nonpunitive and merely set the policy that historical papers should be preserved, and did not become a bill of attainder because only Nixon was named; he was a legitimate class of one because the papers of past presidents were already safely housed.

87. See Jones v. Slick, 56 So.2d 459 (Fla.1952), holding unconstitutional a city ordinance declaring that any city official found guilty of violation of city laws by two-thirds vote of the city council should be fined or imprisoned or both, and removed from office.

88. Cummings v. Missouri, supra note 85, invalidating a Missouri constitutional provision requiring clergymen and priests, as a condition of practicing their profession, to make oath they had not opposed the Union in the Civil War. Ex parte Garland, 71 U.S. (4 Wall.) 333, 18 L.Ed. 366 (1867), invalidating a federal statute forbidding law practice in federal courts by attorneys failing to swear they had not opposed the United States in the Civil War. Though Congress and the states may properly prescribe qualifications for the practice of professions, the Supreme Court in the two cases held that sympathies during the Civil War bore no relationship to fitness to practice the professions of religion and law.

89. United States v. Lovett, supra note 86 (invalidating a federal statute depriving three named men forever of their right to work for the federal government for compensation); United States v. Brown, supra note 86 (invalidating a federal statute making it a crime for one who is, or within five years preceding has been, a Communist Party member to serve as a labor union officer).

90. United States v. Brown, supra note 86.

for earlier violations of the statute, whether the prosecutions are pending, or not yet begun, at the time of the repeal, on the theory that the legislature by its repeal has indicated an intention that the conduct in question shall no longer be prosecuted as a crime.[1] But such a repeal does not operate to set free a person who has been prosecuted and convicted and as to whom the judgment of conviction has become final before the statute is repealed.[2] This doctrine has been criticized by some as lacking any reasonable basis,[3] and praised by others because it "provides a judicially fashioned rule of statutory construction based upon a reasonable presumption of legislative intent." [4]

The same rules apply where the criminal statute has not been taken off the books, but has been rendered ineffective by other legislation which makes what was criminal a right. Thus, absent an effective saving provision, the passage of a state public accommodations law bars prosecution for trespass of those seeking service in public accommodations and requires release of those convicted for such trespass if their convictions have not become final.[5] And in the controversial case of *Hamm v. City of Rock Hill*,[6] the United States Supreme Court held that, under the supremacy

clause of the Constitution, the federal Civil Rights Act of 1964 abated nonfinal state prosecutions for conduct rendered nonpunishable by that Act.[7]

Sometimes the criminal statute is amended to provide a more severe punishment than before. Of course it is clear that the greater punishment cannot be applied to one who violated the statute before the amendment.[8] But if there is no applicable saving provision, does the amendment impliedly repeal the old statute so to prevent further prosecutions thereunder, under the common law rule discussed above that repeals operate to bar further prosecutions in the absence of saving provisions? Some cases have so held,[9] but it seems clear that the legislature can hardly have intended by its amendment that the conduct in question should no longer be prosecuted (the rationale of the common law rule of repeal); so other states adopt the better view that the old statute is still available for prosecution of those who violated it before its amendment.[10]

Where, as sometimes happens, the amendment reduces rather than increases the punishment, it is generally held that an offender who violated the statute at the time it carried the heavier penalty may be punished under

§ 2.5

1. United States v. Chambers, 291 U.S. 217, 54 S.Ct. 434, 78 L.Ed. 763 (1934) (repeal of prohibition laws by U.S. Const. amend. XXI); United States v. Tynen, 78 U.S. (11 Wall.) 88, 20 L.Ed. 153 (1871); Spears v. Modoc County, 101 Cal. 303, 35 P. 869 (1894) (repeal of ordinance); Robertson v. Circuit Court, 121 Fla. 848, 164 So. 525 (1935); People v. Scott, 251 Mich. 640, 232 N.W. 349 (1930); State v. Spencer, 177 S.C. 346, 181 S.E. 217 (1935); Wharton v. State, 45 Tenn. 1 (1868). In some of these cases the repeal was express, in others the repeal was by implication; that distinction made no difference.

2. This question, left open in United States v. Chambers, supra note 1, was so decided in Rives v. O'Hearne, 73 F.2d 984 (D.C.Cir.1934), indicating, however, that probably the legislature, repealing a criminal statute, could expressly provide for amnesty for all who had theretofore been convicted and were serving terms under the repealed statute; but in the absence of such amnesty final judgments are not affected by the repeal.

3. Levitt, Repeal of Penal Statutes and Effect on Pending Prosecutions, 9 A.B.A.J. 715, 716 (1923).

4. Comment, 121 U.Pa.L.Rev. 120, 122 (1972).

5. In Bell v. Maryland, 378 U.S. 226, 84 S.Ct. 1814, 12 L.Ed.2d 822 (1964), the United States Supreme Court

remanded such a case to the state court for a determination of the applicability of the state general saving clause statute in this situation. The Court viewed the convictions in question as not being final, notwithstanding the fact they were affirmed by the state court of appeals prior to the enactment of the public accommodations law, because the judgments were on direct review to the United States Supreme Court. The state court held that the saving clause statute was applicable and affirmed the convictions. Bell v. State, 236 Md. 356, 204 A.2d 54 (1964).

6. 379 U.S. 306, 85 S.Ct. 384, 13 L.Ed.2d 300 (1964).

7. Four Justices dissented on the ground that the federal saving statute dictated a contrary result for federal prosecutions and that the doctrine of abatement could not be applied to affect the existing legislation of another jurisdiction.

8. See § 2.4.

9. E.g., Flaherty v. Thomas, 94 Mass. 428 (1866); People v. Lowell, 250 Mich. 349, 230 N.W. 202 (1930). See Annot., 167 A.L.R. 845, 853–64 (1947).

10. E.g., Sekt v. Justice's Court, 26 Cal.2d 297, 159 P.2d 17 (1945); City of Kansas City v. Griffin, 233 Kan. 685, 664 P.2d 865 (1983); Ex parte Mangrum, 564 S.W.2d 751 (Tex. Crim.App.1978); Annot., 167 A.L.R. 845, 867–874 (1947).

the amended law;[11] here too the amendment does not serve to free him from all punishment.

There is also a generally recognized simultaneous-repeal-and-reenactment exception to the common law rule. Under this exception, if what was criminal under the repealed statute is also encompassed within the new law, which perhaps carries a different offense label, then prosecution under the repealed statute is permissible.[12] Here as well the result accords with what in all likelihood was the legislature's intent.

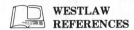
**WESTLAW
REFERENCES**

110k15 & repeal** amend! /s statute law /p
  prosecut! punish!

110k15 & 1 +4 109 /p penalty punish!

110k1206(5)

(b) Saving Provisions. The common law rule that repeal of a criminal statute bars further prosecution against earlier offenders, being based on the legislature's presumed intent, may of course be changed by an expression of legislative intent that earlier violations may still be prosecuted.[13] So the repealing statute may itself contain a saving clause, or there may be applicable a general saving statute or constitutional provision. Thus most states and the federal government have statutes or constitutional provisions (often applicable to civil statutes as well as criminal) providing in effect that repeal (or either repeal or amendment) of a statute shall not affect prior liability thereunder unless the repealing act expressly so provides.[14] And in the enactment of a new comprehensive criminal code and repeal of prior substantive criminal laws, there is usually included a saving provision to the effect that crimes committed prior[15] to the effective date of the new code are subject to prosecution and punishment under the law as it existed at the time.

Although there is in the jurisdiction a general saving provision, it may be that it is not worded broadly enough to cover the particular repeal situation, in which case the common law applies. Thus when the federal prohibition law was repealed by the Twenty-first Amendment to the Constitution, it was held that the federal saving provision[16] was not applicable to a repeal accomplished by constitutional amendment rather than an act of Congress, with the result that prohibition law violators whose prosecutions were pending at the time of the repeal came under the common law rule and so went free.[17] It was argued before the Supreme Court that the fact that most jurisdictions have expressed dissatisfaction with the common law rule by the enactment of general saving provisions,

---

11. See Sekt v. Justice's Court, supra note 10, and cases cited therein; State v. Hamilton, 289 N.W.2d 470 (Minn.1979); Attletweedt v. State, 684 P.2d 812 (Wyo. 1984). Here there is of course no ex post facto difficulty in applying the amended statute.

12. State v. Babbitt, ___ R.I. ___, 457 A.2d 1049 (1983) (where rape statute repealed without saving clause when sexual assault statute enacted, prosecution under the former not barred, as "every element needed to prove a violation under the old statute for rape is also needed to prove first-degree sexual assault"); Ex parte Mangrum, 564 S.W.2d 751 (Tex.Crim.App.1978) (prosecution permissible under repealed welfare fraud statute, as it repealed at time of enactment of new theft statute, and "the constituent elements of the offense are substantially the same"). Compare State v. Souza, ___ R.I. ___, 456 A.2d 775 (1983) (prosecution barred, as new sexual assault statute not mere reenactment of old indecent assault statute, as new law but not old requires purpose of sexual gratification).

13. See, e.g., State v. Matthews, 131 Vt. 421, 310 A.2d 17 (1973); State v. Fenter, 89 Wn.2d 57, 569 P.2d 67 (1977); State ex rel. Miller v. Bordenkircher, ___ W.Va. ___, 272 S.E.2d 676 (1980).

14. See Comment, 121 U.Pa.L.Rev. 120, 127 n. 51 (1972), citing general saving statutes applicable to criminal prosecutions in 42 states; and 1 U.S.C.A. § 109: "The repeal of any statute shall not have the effect to release or extinguish any penalty, forfeiture, or liability incurred under such statute, unless the repealing Act shall so expressly provide, and such statute shall be treated as still remaining in force for the purpose of sustaining any proper action or prosecution for the enforcement of such penalty, forfeiture or liability."

15. Some statutes specify that the offense is prior to the new law if any element occurred before the law was enacted.

16. See note 14 supra.

17. United States v. Chambers, supra note 1. Similarly, the Florida constitutional saving provision, that repeal or amendment of a criminal statute shall not affect prosecution for crimes theretofore committed, was held inapplicable when repeal was accomplished by a constitutional amendment, and so the common law rule applies: Robertson v. Circuit Court, supra note 1. See Annot., 89 A.L.R. 1514 (1934), on repeals effected by constitutional amendment.

constitutional or statutory, should persuade the Court to abolish the common law rule even in the absence of an applicable saving provision. The argument was rejected: it took legislation to change the common law rule in other jurisdictions; therefore in the absence of legislation the common law prevails.[18] Similarly, in a more recent case the Supreme Court took the view that the federal saving statute would not apply in the case of a prosecution for prior acts now protected by the Civil Rights Act of 1964; the savings statute was read as being limited to instances of repeal or amendment and not extending to a case in which a new statute substitutes a right for a crime.[19]

There is some variation in these saving provisions.[20] Some declare that a legislative change in a statute will not extinguish penalties or liabilities accrued or incurred under the old law, and others (addressed specifically to criminal cases) state that offenses under the old law shall be punished as if the repeal or amendment had not occurred. Only in a few jurisdictions are the saving statutes expressly limited to the repeal-followed-by-reenactment or changed penalty situations, though it is quite common for the saving statute or some other law to provide that if the penalty is reduced the defendant is entitled to be sentenced[21] (or at least to seek to be

sentenced[22]) under the new penalty provisions.[23]

When these saving provisions are applied in instances in which there has been an amendment increasing the penalty or a repeal and substantial reenactment, they produce a sound result. In such circumstances, "the statutes have clearly and consistently been used to prevent unintentional and unwarranted legislative pardons."[24] But the broader provisions have often been applied literally in other situations as well. As a consequence, defendants have been convicted of crimes which no longer existed in any form at the time of their prosecution[25] and have been subjected to penalties more severe than those more recently declared sufficient by the legislature.[26]

When applied to these latter circumstances, it is to be doubted that the saving statutes represent either sound policy or the actual intention of the legislature.[27] "A legislative mitigation of the penalty for a particular crime represents a legislative judgment that the lesser penalty for different treatment is sufficient to meet the legitimate ends of the criminal law. Nothing is to be gained by imposing the more severe penalty after such a pronouncement; the excess in punishment can, by hypothesis, serve no purpose other than to satisfy a desire for vengeance."[28] And if the conduct has been decriminalized

---

18. United States v. Chambers, supra note 1.

19. Hall v. City of Rock Hill, 379 U.S. 306, 85 S.Ct. 384, 13 L.Ed.2d 300 (1964). Similarly, in Bell v. Maryland, 378 U.S. 226, 84 S.Ct. 1814, 12 L.Ed.2d 822 (1964), the Court speculated that because a state saving statute was limited to "repeal" and "amendment" it would not be read as covering the case in which a new statute made a right of what was previously a crime. On remand, the state court took the contrary view, holding that the new public accommodation law constituted an implied amendment of the trespass law because the two statutes were inconsistent; thus the saving statute did apply. Bell v. State, 236 Md. 356, 204 A.2d 54 (1964).

20. See Comment, supra note 4, at 128–30, discussing the variations in greater detail.

21. See State v. Saxton, 30 Utah 2d 456, 519 P.2d 1340 (1974) (remand for resentencing because of noncompliance with provision defendant to have benefit of new, lower penalty provisions); State ex rel. Arbogast v. Mohn, ___ W.Va. ___, 260 S.E.2d 820 (1979) (habeas writ granted, as no showing defendant given statutory right to opt for penalties under new law).

22. State v. Buck, 275 N.W.2d 194 (Iowa 1979) (provision that upon defendant's request and approval of the court defendant to be sentenced under new law).

23. Some saving statutes also or instead declare that the defendant may elect any defense available under the new law.

24. Comment, supra note 4, at 142.

25. E.g., State v. Tracy, 64 N.M. 55, 323 P.2d 1096 (1958).

26. E.g., State v. Dosztal, 135 Ariz. 485, 662 P.2d 450 (1983); Turner v. State, 273 Ind. 627, 407 N.E.2d 235 (1980).

27. "It is so easy to show that the statute, when applicable, has often been overlooked by lawyers and judges that it is hard to believe that legislators have always had it in mind." People v. Bilderback, 9 Ill.2d 175, 137 N.E.2d 389 (1956).

28. People v. Oliver, 1 N.Y.2d 152, 151 N.Y.S.2d 367, 134 N.E.2d 197 (1956).

entirely because "a new social view decides that certain conduct is no longer to be punished," then again it is anomalous that the saving statute "steps in and imposes the punishment fixed by an earlier generation." [29] Some appellate courts have consequently given seemingly broad saving statutes a narrow reading in order not to deprive the defendant before them of the benefit of a prior legislative judgment that the conduct should not be criminal [30] or should be subjected to lesser punishment.[31]

Although in some jurisdictions violation of a local ordinance may not be a criminal offense, the same principles applicable to the repeal or amendment of a criminal statute apply to the repeal or amendment of an ordinance.[32]

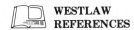

WESTLAW REFERENCES

di saving clause

110k15 & "saving clause"

topic(110) & saving /3 clause provision /s sentenc***

topic(110) & saving /3 clause provision /s common-law

§ 2.6 Administrative Crimes

Sometimes the legislature by statute invites an administrative agency to play a part in

formulating substantive criminal law. Thus, Congress may provide that the Interstate Commerce Commission may issue regulations for the safe transportation of certain substances, and further that any violation of the regulations shall be punishable by fine or imprisonment.[1] Or, a state statute may authorize the state food board to issue regulations concerning the importation of food stuff into the state, with the further provisions that a violation of such regulations is a misdemeanor (or, perhaps, that it is a misdemeanor if the regulations so provide). The term "administrative crime" has been applied to define this type of substantive criminal law, and just as administrative law in general is a growing field of law, the administrative crime is becoming more and more important.

As to these administrative crimes, there are three principal questions: (1) May the legislature authorize an administrative agency to issue regulations, the violation of which is punishable as a crime by virtue of penalties set by statute? (2) May the legislature go further and authorize the agency to determine whether criminal penalties should be provided for violation of the rules or to determine what criminal penalties are appropriate? [2] (3) May the legislature go still further and permit the agency to adjudicate individual cases and thus determine guilt?

29. People v. Bilderback, 9 Ill.2d 175, 137 N.E.2d 389 (1956).

30. People v. Rossi, 18 Cal.3d 295, 134 Cal.Rptr. 64, 555 P.2d 1313 (1976) (where consensual oral copulation among adults no longer criminal, broad saving statute construed as not allowing prosecution); State v. Babbitt, ___ R.I. ___, 457 A.2d 1049 (1983) (where transportation for purposes of prostitution no longer criminal unless "for pecuniary gain," application of saving statute to allow prosecution under old, broader law would be inconsistent with legislative intent).

31. In re Estrada, 63 Cal.2d 740, 48 Cal.Rptr. 172, 408 P.2d 948 (1965) (notwithstanding broad language of saving statute, it intended to reach situation in which no punishment otherwise possible because the penalty had been raised, and thus not intended to change common law rule that defendant has benefit of mitigation of penalty); State v. Macarelli, 118 R.I. 693, 375 A.2d 944 (1977) (broad saving statute, when read with another statute declaring legislation to be construed consistent with intent of legislature, not applicable to case where reduction in penalties).

32. City of Kansas City v. Griffin, 233 Kan. 685, 664 P.2d 865 (1983). Thus Spears v. Modoc County, supra note 1, involved the repeal of an ordinance, and in the absence of a saving provision applied the common law rule to a pending case for ordinance violation. A general saving provision covering repeal of a "statute" has been held not applicable to repeal of an ordinance: Moore v. Village of Ashton, 36 Idaho 485, 211 P. 1082 (1922); Denning v. Yount, 62 Kan. 217, 61 P. 803 (1900).

§ 2.6

1. See United States v. International Minerals & Chemical Corp., 402 U.S. 558, 91 S.Ct. 1697, 29 L.Ed.2d 178 (1971).

2. This subject is thoroughly covered in Schwenk, The Administrative Crime, Its Creation and Punishment by Administrative Agencies, 42 Mich.L.Rev. 51 (1943), and is also treated in 1 K. Davis, Administrative Law Treatise ch. 3 (1978).

(a) **When Statute Fixes the Penalty.** As to question (1), the leading American case is *United States v. Grimaud,*[3] holding that Congress may constitutionally delegate to an administrative agency the power to issue regulations the violation of which is punished by statute as a criminal offense. The defendant argued that the statute delegated the power to create new crimes, a power reserved to the legislature, but the Court responded that the violation of the rules had been made a crime by Congress rather than by the agency.[4] Thus, if we consider a crime as being composed of two matters—the elements of the offense (act and mental state) and the penalty—it may be said that Congress may delegate to an administrative agency the task of filling in the elements if Congress itself fixes the penalty.[5] The majority of state courts which have considered the problem have followed the lead of the federal courts in this matter.[6]

This is not to suggest, however, that any such delegation will pass muster, for it is commonly asserted that for the delegation to be valid the legislature must provide sufficient standards to guide the agency. But,

while the Supreme Court back in 1935 invalidated congressional delegations for lack of sufficient standards,[7] in more recent times the Court has been much less demanding and, indeed, has upheld standards "so vague as to be almost meaningless."[8] The declaration by one federal court that it will now suffice "if Congress clearly delineates the general policy"[9] seems, if anything, an overstatement of current limitations on the federal level.

It is difficult to generalize about the situation on the state level, as there still exists some variation from state to state on the matter of what will be tolerated by way of delegation of the crime-defining function. In some states the wholesale delegation to an administrative agency of power to adopt rules and regulations in a certain area, punishable as the legislature has specified, is deemed an unlawful delegation.[10] But the prevailing view is that such delegation is permissible even with minimal guidelines from the legislative branch; the rationale is that such delegation is necessary to assure the flexibility and expertise needed to deal with certain subject matter.[11]

Much less likely to be successfully challenged is a delegation to an administrative agency of responsibility to ascertain certain particulars with respect to a specific criminal

3. 220 U.S. 506, 31 S.Ct. 480, 55 L.Ed. 563 (1911). Here a statute dealing with national forests authorized the Secretary of Agriculture to make regulations on the use and occupancy of the forests in order to carry out the purposes of the statute, i.e., to preserve the forests from destruction; the statute itself provided the punishment for violation of the regulations. The Secretary issued regulations for grazing sheep in the forests, requiring sheep grazers to obtain a permit prior to grazing. Defendant grazed sheep in a national forest without a permit, for which he was indicted. *Held,* demurrer to the indictment should have been overruled. Accord: McKinley v. United States, 249 U.S. 397, 39 S.Ct. 324, 63 L.Ed. 668 (1919); Yakus v. United States, 321 U.S. 414, 64 S.Ct. 660, 88 L.Ed. 834 (1944).

4. "Today we would probably say that Congress and the officer together make the crime, the officer acting within the intelligible limits established by Congress." L. Jaffe, Judicial Control of Administrative Action 110 (1965).

5. Schwenk, note 2 supra, at 57–59.

6. See, e.g., State v. Dube, 409 A.2d 1102 (Me.1979); State v. King, 257 N.W.2d 693 (Minn.1977); State v. Smith, 539 P.2d 754 (Okl.Crim.App.1975).

7. Panama Refining Co. v. Ryan, 293 U.S. 388, 55 S.Ct. 241, 79 L.Ed. 446 (1935); Schechter Poultry Corp. v. United States, 295 U.S. 495, 55 S.Ct. 837, 79 L.Ed. 1570 (1935). Defendants who today rely upon those decisions will usually be met with the response that they are no longer controlling. See, e.g., United States v. Barron, 594 F.2d 1345 (10th Cir.1979).

8. 1 K. Davis, Administrative Law Treatise § 3:5 (1978).

9. United States v. Barron, 594 F.2d 1345 (10th Cir. 1979).

10. Howell v. State, 238 Ga. 95, 230 S.E.2d 853 (1976) (statute declaring that any person who violates any of the rules or regulations promulgated by the Department of Natural Resources is guilty of a misdemeanor constitutes an unlawful delegation in violation of the state constitution).

11. State v. Smith, 539 P.2d 754 (Okl.Crim.App.1975).

statute.[12] Illustrative is the situation in which the legislature declares it a crime to swim in an area not authorized for swimming and then delegates to the Game and Parks Commission the responsibility to designate the no swimming areas,[13] and that where the legislature makes the possession of controlled substances a crime and then delegates to the State Board of Pharmacy the responsibility to keep current the list of drugs which belong in that classification.[14] But even here there is not agreement as to just what constitutes adequate legislative guidelines.[15] Those court decisions upholding delegation of either type typically emphasize that the problems being dealt with are such as to require more expert or more intense scrutiny than the legislature itself could reasonably be expected to provide.[16]

Although a jurisdiction which adopts the rule that all crimes must be statutory may

consistently allow administrative crimes of the sort discussed,[17] in one sense the problem discussed above is similar to that of whether common law crimes should be recognized. One argument against administrative crimes is similar to the argument used against common law crimes: fair warning to the public of what constitutes criminal conduct is a necessary requirement of fair play, and for the most part administrative regulations are not published.[18] Perhaps the best way of dealing with this difficulty would be to give the defendant a mistake-of-law defense when he believed his conduct to be noncriminal and the administrative regulation defining the offense was not reasonably made available.[19]

While administrative crimes are generally valid where the statute fixes the penalty, the due process requirement that statutes must set forth a reasonably definite standard of conduct [20] applies with equal force to adminis-

12. To be distinguished from the enactment of a vague statute by the legislature with directions that those to whom the state is directed should seek clarification from a particular administrative agency. See D'Alemberte v. Anderson, 349 So.2d 164 (Fla.1977) (statute prohibiting public officials from accepting gifts "that would cause a reasonably prudent person to be influenced in the discharge of his official duties" is unconstitutionally vague, and provision that public official unsure of the law's application may obtain an advisory opinion from the Commission on Ethics is an impermissible delegation).

13. State v. Cutright, 193 Neb. 303, 226 N.W.2d 771 (1975).

14. State v. King, 257 N.W.2d 693 (Minn.1977).

15. Compare Sundberg v. State, 234 Ga. 482, 216 S.E.2d 332 (1975) (unlawful delegation where depressant and stimulant drugs include any substance the State Board of Pharmacy "shall determine to be habit-forming because of its stimulant effect on the central nervous system or any drug which the State Board shall determine to contain any quantity of a substance having a potential for abuse because of its depressant or stimulant effect on the central nervous system or its hallucinogenic effect," as this means "a depressant or stimulant drug is anything the State Board of Pharmacy says it is without any real guidelines"); with State v. Boyajian, 344 A.2d 410 (Me. 1975) (similar delegation upheld; "Pharmacists certainly understand what is meant by 'central nervous system stimulants or depressants,' and by training and experience are familiar with the effects which may flow from improper use of such medicinal substances").

16. State v. King, 257 N.W.2d 693 (Minn.1977) (delegation regarding what are controlled substances permits "precisely that type of expert analysis that an administrative board composed mainly of pharmacists is best able to provide"); State v. Cutright, 193 Neb. 303, 226 N.W.2d 771

(1975) (delegation of power to determine where swimming illegal proper; it "would be a physical impossibility for the Legislature to visit all the state lakes personally, and make its own determination of where swimming shall be permitted"); Sheriff, Clark County v. Luqman, __ Nev. __, 697 P.2d 107 (1985) (delegation re what are controlled substances, court stresses "board's role as a fact finder" in determining, as to each new drug which becomes available, "the medical propriety of the drug and its potential for abuse"); State v. Reed, 14 Ohio App.3d 63, 470 N.E.2d 150 (1983) (delegation re what are controlled substances permits "ongoing adjustments with the marketing of new drugs and the increased knowledge of the nature of existing drugs"); State v. Smith, 539 P.2d 754 (Okl.Crim. App.1975) (delegation of authority to make rules and regulations regarding hunting and wildlife proper "so that a full-time body of persons particularly aware of the problems of wildlife conservation could govern and regulate those areas to which the Legislature has little insight").

17. E.g., the leading jurisdiction abolishing common law crimes is the federal government, but the leading authority upholding the administrative crime is the United States Supreme Court, United States v. Grimaud, supra note 3. Compare State v. Maitrejean, 193 La. 824, 192 So. 361 (1939) (since all crimes must be statutory, delegation is invalid).

18. Federal regulations are now required to be published in the Federal Register. Many states do not require publication. Schwenk, supra note 2, at 52. But in some jurisdictions a lawful delegation requires not only standards but also adequate procedural safeguards to guard against "insufficient notice of the promulgation of a rule." In re Powell, 92 Wn.2d 882, 602 P.2d 711 (1979).

19. See § 5.1(e)(1).

20. See § 2.3.

trative regulations having the effect of law.[21] Likewise, administrative rules in the criminal law field are strictly construed in the same fashion as criminal statutes.[22]

The typical delegation statute provides, expressly or by implication, that violations of *valid* regulations are criminal. In such a case, an administrative crime may be invalid (although the statute prescribed sufficient standards, and the regulation definitely set forth the forbidden conduct) because the regulation exceeded the authority set out in the statute.[23] However, a defendant in a criminal prosecution may be foreclosed from raising the invalidity of the regulation as a defense because he failed to take advantage of other established procedures for challenging the regulation.[24]

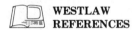 **WESTLAW REFERENCES**

grimaud /p agency administrat! /p crime (crim**** penal /s sanction penalty)

(b) When Regulations Fix the Penalty. The second problem is the constitutionality of a statute which not only authorizes an administrative agency to issue regulations, but also delegates to the agency the question of whether criminal penalties should be provided for violation of the regulations or the question of what the criminal penalties should be for

such a violation. For example, assume that a statute, setting forth proper standards to guide the agency, provides that the agency shall issue regulations and that violation of the regulations shall be a misdemeanor "if the regulation so provides." This type of statute has been held unconstitutional as an invalid delegation of the legislative power to define a crime.[25] If, as in the *Grimaud* case, it is permissible for the agency to determine the elements of a crime, then why is it not permissible for the agency to decide which of its rules are to have criminal penalties attached to them? There is no obvious distinction between the two situations, but it may be that in the latter case the real problem is that the legislature has given no guidance on when a penal sanction should be used.[26]

The kind of statute described above must be distinguished from a statute which makes the violation of every rule adopted under it criminal but delegates to the agency, within fixed statutory limits, the power to set the criminal penalties for each rule. For example, the statute may give the agency authority to issue regulations, all of which are criminal, and then provide that the agency may set penalties for the regulations "not to exceed $500, or six months imprisonment, or both." The courts are not in agreement as to the validity of such a statute,[27] although the chances of

---

21. See Boyce Motor Lines v. United States, 342 U.S. 337, 72 S.Ct. 329, 96 L.Ed. 367 (1952) (I.C.C. regulation forbade driving trucks containing inflammables and explosives through crowded streets, tunnels, dangerous crossings; defendant drove truck loaded with inflammables through Holland Tunnel; *held,* regulation valid.)

22. M. Kraus & Bros., Inc. v. United States, 327 U.S. 614, 66 S.Ct. 705, 90 L.Ed. 894 (1946). See § 2.2(d).

23. Schwenk, supra note 2, concludes that the cases generally take a narrow view of the area which regulations may cover. United States v. Eaton, 144 U.S. 677, 12 S.Ct. 764, 36 L.Ed. 591 (1892); Reims v. State, 17 Ala.App. 128, 82 So. 576 (1919); State v. Retowski, 36 Del. 330, 175 A. 325 (1934); Bloemer v. Turner, 281 Ky. 832, 137 S.W.2d 387 (1939).

24. Yakus v. United States, supra note 3, holding that it was not a violation of due process to deprive petitioners of an opportunity to attack the validity of a price regulation in a prosecution for its violation, where Congress had provided another means for determining the validity of price regulations.

25. People v. Grant, 242 App.Div. 310, 275 N.Y.S. 74 (1934), affirmed per curiam, 267 N.Y. 508, 196 N.E. 553

(1935); State v. Curtis, 230 N.C. 169, 52 S.E.2d 364 (1949); Note, 43 Colum.L.Rev. 213 (1943). The United States Supreme Court so intimated in United States v. Grimaud, supra note 2.

The same result has been reached where the statute allows the agency to decide whether the regulation shall be treated as a crime and also sets a maximum penalty. Gilgert v. Stockton Port Dist., 7 Cal.2d 384, 60 P.2d 847 (1936).

26. L. Jaffe, Judicial Control of Administrative Action 110 (1965).

27. Holding such a statute valid: Smallwood v. District of Columbia, 17 F.2d 210 (D.C.Cir.1927); Commonwealth v. Diaz, 326 Mass. 525, 95 N.E.2d 666 (1950). Invalid: Gilgert v. Stockton Port Dist., 7 Cal.2d 384, 60 P.2d 847 (1936); State v. Gallion, 572 P.2d 683 (Utah 1977) (statute allowed attorney general to determine what should be controlled substances and on which schedule particular substances should be listed; since statute set different penalties for different schedules, this is an impermissible delegation of the power to fix the penalty).

such a delegation being upheld appear to be greater when it appears that the range of penalties allowed is reasonable, considering the nature of the regulations.[28] Likewise, such a delegation probably is not valid if the statute fails to set any maximum penalty.[29]

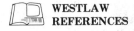

WESTLAW REFERENCES

topic(15a) /p crim**** penal /p penalty sanction punish

(c) Delegation of Power to Adjudicate. The problems described above must be distinguished from yet another issue regarding delegation which, although basically a question of procedure and not substantive law, should be briefly noted here. May the legislature delegate to an administrative agency the power of adjudication (that is, the authority to determine guilt or innocence in individual cases) when the proceedings are criminal in nature? The answer clearly is no; as the Supreme Court declared, "[c]ivil procedure is incompatible with the accepted rules and constitutional guaranties governing the trial of criminal prosecutions."[30]

What is not clear, however, is the precise significance of this rule, for the dividing line between criminal penalties and civil or remedial penalties is an uncertain one.[31] Administrative agencies frequently do impose penalties, such as the revocation or suspension of licenses, the withdrawal of privileges (such as second-class mailing privileges), the denial of benefits, or the confiscation of property. Penalties have been held to be civil notwithstanding their severity,[32] and there are a number of

cases upholding the power of administrative agencies to levey fines.[33]

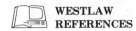

WESTLAW REFERENCES

15ak329
15ak758

(d) Administrative Orders. Although administrative bodies often issue rules and regulations setting forth general rules of conduct within the delegated spheres of action, sometimes they issue specific orders as to particular persons (e.g., an order to deport X, or an order for Y to report for induction into the armed services), the violation of which is criminal. Thus, there is a federal criminal statute which provides that an alien who has been ordered deported by the administrative body, and who thereafter wilfully fails to depart or to apply for permission to depart, is guilty of a crime.[34] Another statute provides that one ordered to report for induction by his local selective service board who wilfully fails to do so is guilty of a criminal offense.[35] The administrative agency, by issuing an order to deport or to report for induction, in a sense sets the stage for a violation of the substantive criminal law by establishing one of the elements of the crime.

There is no doubt that such administrative action is valid. A problem may arise, however, as to whether the invalidity of the order is a defense to criminal prosecution.[36] Surely this is a defense if the statute reads "ordered by a valid order of deportation (or induction)." Even without such wording the defense may be allowed as a matter of implied intent of the legislature.[37] But where the legislature

---

28. See Commonwealth v. Diaz, supra note 27.

29. Schwenk, supra note 2, at 75.

30. Helvering v. Mitchell, 303 U.S. 391, 58 S.Ct. 630, 82 L.Ed 917 (1938).

31. 1 K. Davis, Administrative Law Treatise § 3:10 (1978).

32. E.g., Wright v. SEC, 112 F.2d 89 (2d Cir.1940), where the petitioner was expelled from membership in five national securities exchanges and thus deprived "for all time of any opportunity to pursue his calling in a lawful manner."

33. E.g., Oceanic Steam Navigation Co. v. Stranahan, 214 U.S. 320, 29 S.Ct. 671, 53 L.Ed. 1013 (1909); W.J.

Dillner Transfer Co. v. Pennsylvania Pub. Util. Comm'n, 191 Pa.Super. 136, 155 A.2d 429 (1959). Contra: Tite v. State Tax Comm'n, 89 Utah 404, 57 P.2d 734 (1936).

34. 8 U.S.C.A. § 1252.

35. 50 U.S.C.A.App. § 462.

36. See Schwartz, Administrative Law and the Sixth Amendment: "Malaise in the Administrative Scheme," 40 A.B.A.J. 107 (1954).

37. Estep v. United States, 327 U.S. 114, 66 S.Ct. 423, 90 L.Ed. 567 (1946), allowing defendant, prosecuted for violation of order for induction, to show that he was a minister of religion and therefore exempt. "We cannot believe that Congress intended that criminal sanctions

makes it clear that a wilful violation of an administrative order, whether valid or invalid, is criminal, the defense of invalidity is probably not available.[38]

WESTLAW REFERENCES

di administrative order

topic(15a) /p administrat! agency /s order /p crim**** penal

topic(15a) & estep /p crim**** penal

---

§ 2.7   Criminal Jurisdiction—In General

The word "jurisdiction" is used in two quite different senses in the field of criminal law: (1) the power to create criminal law, and (2) the power to enforce the criminal law thus created. The two meanings sometimes coincide: thus a state or nation which has no power to make certain conduct criminal has no power to enforce such conduct. But the power to create crimes is not always co-extensive with the power to enforce: thus a state or nation which has the power to enact a law making certain conduct criminal may lack the power in a particular situation to enforce that criminal law.

Jurisdiction in the first sense—the power to prescribe rules of conduct and to provide the punishment for violating those rules—is properly a subject to be dealt with in this book, as it is actually the power to create substantive criminal law. Jurisdiction in the second sense—the power to enforce rules of conduct (to hear and decide cases involving violations of these rules and to award punishment therefor)—is more properly viewed as a matter of criminal procedure, and this is not covered in this book. We are therefore concerned here with the necessary prerequisite to criminal law enforcement that the *sovereign* (nation or state) which is prosecuting the defendant for crime have jurisdiction to create the crime, but not the requirement that the particular *court* which is trying the defendant have jurisdiction over the offense,[1] nor the requirement that the court have jurisdiction over the *defendant* as well as over the offense.[2]

WESTLAW REFERENCES

sy(jurisdiction power /s sovereign state nation /s pr*scrib! defin! enact! /s crime criminal /s

---

were to be applied to orders issued by local boards no matter how flagrantly they violated the rules and regulations which define their jurisdiction." But defendant is not entitled to a jury trial on the issue of the validity of the order. Cox v. United States, 332 U.S. 442, 68 S.Ct. 115, 92 L.Ed. 59 (1947).

38. See United States v. Spector, 343 U.S. 169, 72 S.Ct. 591, 96 L.Ed. 863 (1952); Yakus v. United States supra note 3. The *Yakus* case shows that where Congress has not set up machinery for the appeal of administrative orders (e.g., induction orders) there is more sense in concluding Congress meant to allow the validity issue to be brought up in the criminal trial than there is where Congress has set up such machinery (e.g., regulations of the O.P.A. as to ceiling prices of meat). It may be argued that a statute not setting up such machinery and not allowing the defense in the criminal trial would be unconstitutional. See Jackson, J., dissenting in United States v. Spector, supra. Perhaps the problem is not too different from that of the validity of a statute making it a criminal offense to escape from jail. If the statute is worded so that it is no defense that the authorities wrongfully jailed the defendant, surely depriving defendant of the defense of the invalidity of the incarceration does not render the statute unconstitutional. So also a statute making it a crime to resist a police officer who is making an arrest might constitutionally provide that the invalidity of the arrest should not be a defense.

§ 2.7

1. Generally, a court with jurisdiction only over misdemeanors has no power to try a person for a crime amounting to a felony, and conversely a court with jurisdiction only over felonies cannot try a person on a misdemeanor charge. But see Pierce v. State, 96 Okl.Crim. 76, 248 P.2d 633 (1952), to the effect that a court with felony jurisdiction only might properly convict, on a felony charge, of a lesser included misdemeanor. Here the charge was aggravated battery, a felony, and conviction was of simple battery, a misdemeanor.

2. The court will not have jurisdiction over the defendant if he has not been arrested or summoned, Thiem v. Commonwealth, 269 S.W.2d 195 (Ky.1954), unless the defendant voluntarily appears and goes to trial without objection. People v. Halling, 203 Misc. 428, 122 N.Y.S.2d 543 (1953).

A court does not lack jurisdiction over the defendant because the defendant was illegally arrested, State v. Ryan, 48 Wash.2d 304, 293 P.2d 399 (1956), because of an irregularity in the extradition proceedings, In re Greenough, 116 Vt. 277, 75 A.2d 569 (1950), or even because the defendant's presence was obtained by forcible abduction from another state or country. Frisbie v. Collins, 342 U.S. 519, 72 S.Ct. 509, 96 L.Ed. 541 (1952); 1 W. LaFave, Search and Seizure § 1.7 (1978); Scott, Criminal Jurisdiction of a State Over a Defendant Based Upon Presence Secured by Force or Fraud, 37 Minn.L.Rev. 91 (1953).

conduct act acti**)

(a) The Power to Create Crimes. Jurisdiction in the sense of power to create crimes [3] is not a matter which involves the United States (the nation and the states) alone, or even the Anglo-American world alone, for it depends in large part upon international law, and thus it involves all nations. Quite obviously, the United States cannot properly claim power under international law to prescribe rules of conduct in foreign countries or in other areas (such as on the high seas) outside the United States without recognizing reciprocal power in foreign nations; likewise, it cannot claim jurisdiction over its own nationals abroad without recognizing that other nations have similar jurisdiction over their nationals here.[4]

The situation in the United States is somewhat complicated by the fact that governmental power (including the power to create and enforce criminal law) is divided between two sets of sovereign powers—the national government and those of the fifty states—and by the added fact that, so far as state power is concerned, each state is a separate sovereign power.[5] Under the United States Constitution, as interpreted by the Supreme Court, the national government possesses only those powers of government which the Constitution expressly or impliedly grants to it; the states have reserved to themselves all other powers which the Constitution does not expressly deny to them.[6] The power of the national government to create crimes is the subject of the next section; the power of a state of the United States to do so is covered by the following section.

The principal bases of jurisdiction to prescribe criminal law, whether it be the jurisdic-

tion of a nation under international law or of a state within a nation under domestic law, are (1) territory and (2) nationality or citizenship.[7] Thus a nation or a state has jurisdiction to make rules governing conduct taking place within its territory, and a nation or state has jurisdiction to make rules as to the conduct of its nationals or citizens outside its territory. In addition (3) a national or state government may have jurisdiction of a limited sort to make criminal certain conduct by non-nationals or non-citizens acting outside its territory, which conduct threatens the interests of that government. There is some question whether the same principle applies to conduct which threatens the interests of the citizens of that government rather than the interests of the government itself. Furthermore, (4) it is a well-settled principle of international law that any nation may make piracy a crime and punish its commission without regard to territory or citizenship. There is no "universal" jurisdiction, however, to make criminal any conduct by anyone anywhere irrespective of territory, nationality or citizenship or the limited extensions of jurisdiction just mentioned.

There is often a gap between what a sovereign (state or nation) *may* do in the way of creating criminal law and what it actually *does* do in this regard; in America the federal government and the states have not always legislated as to crimes to the full extent of their power to do so.

 **WESTLAW REFERENCES**

jurisdiction power /s sovereign state /s pr*scrib! defin*** definition enact! /s crime criminal! /s conduct acti*** /s territor! nation! citizen!

---

3. And, indeed, jurisdiction in the other sense—power to enforce criminal law.

4. For a clear analysis of the problem of jurisdiction of nations to prescribe and enforce rules of conduct (including but not limited to criminal rules), see Restatement (Second) of the Foreign Relations Law of the United States §§ 6–93 (1965). Although this Restatement obviously does not purport to cover jurisdiction of states, as distinguished from nations, many of the principles involved are similar.

5. A few other governments have somewhat similar problems of federalism involving divisions of governmen-

tal power between national and local government, e.g., Canada, Australia, Switzerland, but not England.

6. U.S. Const. amend. X; see 1 R. Rotunda, J. Nowak, & J. Young, Treatise on Constitutional Law ch. 3 (1986); McCulloch v. Maryland, 17 U.S. (4 Wheat.) 316, 4 L.Ed. 579 (1819).

7. The word "nationality" is an appropriate word to use with respect to the jurisdiction of a nation, "citizenship" with respect to the jurisdiction of a state within a nation.

crime criminal! /p piracy hi-jack terroris! /p
   jurisdiction!

(b) Proof of Jurisdiction. At least when
the matter has been put into issue by the
defendant,[8] whether the prosecuting government actually has criminal jurisdiction over
the conduct of the defendant is a matter to be
determined by the trier of fact. There is not
unanimity, however, as to the prosecution's
burden of proof in this regard.

It has sometimes been held that it is sufficient that jurisdiction of the state to prosecute
is established by a clear preponderance of the
evidence.[9] But the more recent cases have
quite consistently held that jurisdiction is a
matter which must be proved beyond a reasonable doubt.[10] Even if this result is not
compelled under *In re Winship* [11] because jurisdiction is not one of "those facts essential
to establishing criminality of the defendant's
conduct," [12] it is nonetheless sound. Use of
the beyond a reasonable doubt standard mini-
mizes the possibility that a defendant will be
tried in one state for a crime actually committed elsewhere.[13] Moreover, it makes it more
likely that other states will afford full faith
and credit to decisions regarding criminal jurisdiction,[14] even though they are not constitutionally required to do so.[15] There is also
the practical consideration that using a lesser
standard for a portion of the prosecution's
case and the beyond a reasonable doubt standard for the rest would doubtless create confusion in the minds of jurors.[16]

Problems of proof can be especially difficult
in homicide cases, where there is unavailable
a victim to testify about the location of the
critical events. As we shall see, the common
law view was that jurisdiction over homicide
was grounded in the victim's presence in that
state's territory when he was struck, without
regard to the location of the defendant at that
time or the location of the victim when he
finally died.[17] Some modern statutes also provide for jurisdiction based upon the place of
death or the place where the defendant acted,[18] which overcomes some but not all of the
difficulty. If, for example, a decayed body is
found in Illinois, there may be absolutely no
way to establish where the person died, where
he was hit, or where his assailant was when
he inflicted the harm. To deal with that
problem, some states have adopted the Model
Penal Code provision that "if the body of a
homicide victim is found within the State, it
is presumed that such result occurred within
the State." [19]

**WESTLAW
REFERENCES**

situs locus /s crime criminal! /p proof prove eviden!
   /p jurisdiction!

crime criminal! /s situs locus /p "common law"

§ 2.8 Criminal Jurisdiction—The Fed-
eral Government

The power of the national government of
the United States to create crimes falls main-

---

8. See Commonwealth v. Bighum, 452 Pa. 554, 307
A.2d 255 (1973) (failure to instruct jury on the jurisdiction
issue not reversible error where defendant never disputed
jurisdiction below and did not ask for such an instruction).

9. People v. Cavanaugh, 44 Cal.2d 252, 282 P.2d 53
(1955) (on issue of territorial jurisdiction as between California and Mexico).

10. People v. Holt, 91 Ill.2d 480, 64 Ill.Dec. 550, 440
N.E.2d 102 (1982); State v. Baldwin, 305 A.2d 555 (Me.
1973); State v. Batdorf, 293 N.C. 486, 238 S.E.2d 497
(1977).

11. 397 U.S. 358, 90 S.Ct. 1068, 25 L.Ed.2d 368 (1970).

12. State v. Baldwin, 305 A.2d 555 (Me.1973). But the
holding in *Winship* was that due process protects "against
conviction except upon proof beyond a reasonable doubt of
every fact necessary to constitute the crime with which he
is charged," which might well be read as extending to the
matter of jurisdiction, at least in some circumstances. In
Baldwin, though there was a question as to whether the

rape occurred in Maine or New Hampshire, at least it was
clear that the conduct was criminal no matter in which
state it occurred.

13. State v. Batdorf, 293 N.C. 486, 238 S.E.2d 497
(1977).

14. State v. Baldwin, 305 A.2d 555 (Me.1973).

15. Thompson v. Whitman, 85 U.S. (18 Wall.) 457, 21
L.Ed. 897 (1873).

16. Model Penal Code § 1.13, Comment (Tent. Draft
No. 4, 1955). Thus the Code provides that "each element
of such offense" must be proved beyond a reasonable
doubt and that "element of an offense" includes conduct,
attendant circumstances or results which "establishes jurisdiction." Model Penal Code §§ 1.12(1), 1.13(9)(e).

17. See § 2.9(a).

18. See § 2.9(b).

19. Model Penal Code § 1.03(4).

ly into two broad categories: (1) its power, rather extensive as to subject matter, over conduct in federally owned or controlled territory (on land, on water, or in the air) not within the jurisdiction of any state of the United States, and over conduct of American citizens outside the jurisdiction of the states; and (2) its power, much more limited as to subject matter, over conduct taking place within the borders of the United States but also within the territory occupied by the states.

In the first category, where the federal government must shoulder the entire burden of criminal law without help from the states, the federal government may be said to have a broad "police power" to regulate conduct (prescribing criminal penalties for violations) in the interest of public health, safety, morals and welfare. Within this category falls (a) conduct in federal land areas not located within the states, such as the District of Columbia and the Territories; (b) conduct in federal enclaves (islands of federal territory located within the states), such as army posts, naval bases, post offices and national parks; (c) conduct on ships and aircraft of American nationality when outside the jurisdiction of the states, as on the high seas or even in foreign waters; and (d) conduct by United States citizens which takes place outside the jurisdiction of any state of the Union, as on the high seas or in foreign lands. The basis for all such power is either territoriality or nationality. In addition, under the first category, there is limited power in the federal government to protect its interests against harmful conduct by aliens in foreign lands—the "protective principle" of jurisdiction—a

power which is not based on territory or nationality.

In the second category—federal power to regulate conduct occurring within the United States but also taking place within the states—there is no such broad "police power" to regulate and prescribe punishment. In this area of law, governmental power in the United States is divided up between the nation and the states; the national government can exercise only those powers expressly, or (more often) impliedly under the "necessary and proper" clause, granted to it by the Constitution.[1]

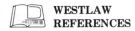

WESTLAW REFERENCES

di police power

(a) Federal Power as to Conduct Outside State Jurisdiction—Territorial Jurisdiction

(1) Territories. The federal government has the power to make criminal almost any anti-social conduct committed in the District of Columbia and the Territories.[2] Rather obviously, a complete criminal code, from murder down to minor crimes, is needed for these land areas.

(2) Enclaves. The United States government has territorial jurisdiction over those islands of federally owned and controlled lands located within the borders of the various states—military posts, navy yards, the service academies, arsenals, post offices, federal court houses, federal prisons, national parks, and the like.[3] In these enclaves it is also important to have a complete criminal code from murder down to minor crimes.

---

§ 2.8

1. U.S. Const. art. I, § 8: "The Congress shall have Power: * * * to make all Laws which shall be necessary and proper for carrying into Execution the foregoing [express] Powers, and all other Powers vested by this Constitution in the Government of the United States."

2. See U.S. Const. art. I, § 8, for the District of Columbia; art. IV, § 3, for Territories.

"In the Territories of the United States, Congress has the entire dominion and sovereignty * * * and has full legislative power over all subjects upon which the legislature of a State might legislate within the State; and may, at its discretion, intrust that power to the legislative

assembly of a territory": Simms v. Simms, 175 U.S. 162, 20 S.Ct. 58, 44 L.Ed. 115 (1899).

Congress has enacted a criminal code for the District of Columbia.

3. See, e.g., United States v. Cassidy, 571 F.2d 534 (10th Cir.1978). U.S. Const. art. I, § 8, gives Congress exclusive legislative power over places purchased from the states for "Forts, Magazines, Arsenals, Dock-Yards and other needful Buildings." Congress has acquired exclusive jurisdiction over enclaves sometimes as the result of purchase from the states, sometimes as the result of reservation when granting federal land to a new state. See 18 U.S.C.A. § 7, including such enclaves in the "spe-

Congress has provided expressly for a few particular crimes applicable in federal enclaves—murder, manslaughter, assault and battery, rape, mayhem, arson, robbery, larceny, receiving stolen property—but for the rest Congress has incorporated by reference the criminal laws of the state in which the enclave lies.[4]

(3) Ships and Aircraft. The federal government has the power (called its "maritime ju-

risdiction") to prescribe criminal law governing conduct aboard American ships and aircraft—conduct either by American citizens or aliens—when the ship or aircraft is on or over the high seas,[5] or even in (or over) foreign waters or ports.[6] In addition, the United States exercises maritime jurisdiction over crimes committed on vessels (of whatever nationality) in its internal waters[7] and territorial seas,[8] where the sea or waterway is not

cial * * * territorial jurisdiction of the United States." Sometimes state jurisdiction over federal lands is reserved in the transfer of the land or conferred by statute. See, e.g., Bruce v. State, 268 Ind. 180, 375 N.E.2d 1042 (1978); State v. Stewart, 175 Mont. 286, 573 P.2d 1138 (1977). As to crimes within "Indian country," it may generally be said that the federal government has exclusive jurisdiction over offenses committed by Indians, but the state has jurisdiction over offenses committed therein by non-Indians. 18 U.S.C.A. § 1153. See United States v. John, 437 U.S. 634, 98 S.Ct. 2541, 57 L.Ed.2d 489 (1978). Even if this results in an Indian being convicted of an offense (e.g., felony-murder) which a non-Indian could not because nonexistent under state law, there is no violation of due process. United States v. Antelope, 430 U.S. 641, 97 S.Ct. 1395, 51 L.Ed.2d 701 (1977). Nor is it objectionable that the Indian was previously proceeded against in a tribal court for the same conduct; the tribe in so acting is a separate sovereign, see § 2.8(d), and thus there has been no double jeopardy violation. United States v. Wheeler, 435 U.S. 313, 98 S.Ct. 1079, 55 L.Ed.2d 303 (1978). The statute was amended to require six states to assume exclusive criminal jurisdiction and to permit other states to do so (six others did), and then was amended again to require tribal consent in the future. See Clinton, Criminal Jurisdiction Over Indian Lands: A Journey Through a Jurisdictional Maze, 18 Ariz.L.Rev. 503 (1976); Washington v. Confederated Bands and Tribes of the Yakima Indian Nation, 439 U.S. 463, 99 S.Ct. 740, 58 L.Ed.2d 740 (1979).

4. 18 U.S.C.A. § 13, known as "The Assimilative Crimes Act." The present act, enacted in 1948, incorporates by reference state criminal laws in force at the time of the defendant's conduct, rather than (as formerly) in force at the time of the enactment of the Assimilative Crimes Act. This act was held constitutional in United States v. Sharpnack, 355 U.S. 286, 78 S.Ct. 291, 2 L.Ed.2d 282 (1958), as applied to a crime created by the state after the enactment of the 1948 Assimilative Crimes Act.

The proposed new federal code would replace 18 U.S.C.A. § 13 with a provision which would limit the grading for assimilated crimes to misdemeanors. National Comm'n on Reform of Federal Criminal Laws, Final Report—Proposed New Federal Criminal Code § 209 (1971). This is explained on the ground that the new code will itself define all serious crimes, and that it is desirable "to minimize the consequences of the wholesale purchase of * * * grossly disparate existing state laws and penalties." Id. at § 209, Comment. See also the consultant's report by Professor Norman Abrams, in 1 National Comm'n on Reform of Federal Criminal Laws, Working Papers 77 (1970).

5. U.S. Const. art. I, § 8, authorizes Congress to define and punish piracy and felonies committed on the high seas. 18 U.S.C.A. § 7 defines federal maritime jurisdiction to include the high seas or other waters outside the jurisdiction of the states, vessels belonging to the U.S. or to American citizens or to American corporations when the vessel is out of the jurisdiction of the states, and vessels of U.S. registry on voyage on the Great Lakes or its connecting rivers. An amendment to § 7, covering aircraft belonging to the U.S. or its citizens or its corporations, in flight over the high seas or other waters outside the jurisdiction of the states, was added in 1952 after United States v. Cordova, 89 F.Supp. 298 (E.D.N.Y.1950), disclosed a loophole, as to crimes committed on American aircraft over the high seas. In 1981 § 7 was further amended to include U.S. spacecraft "from the moment when all external doors are closed on Earth following embarkation until the moment when one such door is opened on Earth for disembarkation." For more on criminal jurisdiction in outer space, see Comment, 23 Santa Clara L.Rev. 627 (1983).

6. United States v. Flores, 289 U.S. 137, 53 S.Ct. 580, 77 L.Ed. 1086 (1933) (murder on U.S. vessel at anchor in Congo River in Belgian Congo 250 miles inland); United States v. Rodgers, 150 U.S. 249, 14 S.Ct. 109, 37 L.Ed. 1071 (1893) (assault on U.S. vessel in Detroit River within Canadian limits and outside the jurisdiction of any state). England applied the same principle in Regina v. Anderson, 11 Cox C.C. 198 (1868) (homicide by American on British ship in French waters). Doubtless the foreign country involved has jurisdiction also. The matter of competing jurisdiction is often regulated by treaty, a distinction usually being made in the treaty between crimes disturbing only those aboard the ship and those disturbing the peace and dignity of the foreign country.

7. That is, rivers, lakes and canals within its land area and areas of sea on the landward side of the baseline of its territorial seas. Restatement (Second) of the Foreign Relations Law of the United States § 13 (1965).

8. In brief, a strip three nautical miles from the shore. For a more accurate definition, see Restatement (Second) of the Foreign Relations Law of the United States §§ 14, 15 (1965). Some recent legislation is broader. See, e.g., 21 U.S.C.A. § 955a, discussed in United States v. Romero-Galue, 757 F.2d 1147 (11th Cir.1985), asserting jurisdiction as to possession of marijuana with intent to distribute which occurs "within the customs waters of the United States," statutorily defined as waters within 12 miles of the coast plus vessels on the high seas pursuant to treaty or other arrangement between a foreign government and the United States.

within the jurisdiction of any state.[9] The United States has also asserted jurisdiction over stateless vessels on the high seas.[10]

Though there is no doubt that a nation has jurisdiction over the airspace above its territory,[11] there is some question as to precisely when the federal or state government has jurisdiction as to the airspace above a state of the United States.[12] Congress has undertaken to make the following conduct criminal when committed on vessels or aircraft within the federal maritime jurisdiction: [13] murder, manslaughter, assault and battery, rape (including statutory rape), mayhem, larceny, receiving stolen property, false pretenses, robbery, arson, misconduct by officers of vessel causing loss of life, and seduction by a seaman of a lady passenger.[14]

It is something of a question whether to place the above maritime jurisdiction under the territorial principle of jurisdiction (an American ship or airplane has sometimes been considered a floating or flying island of American territory), or under the nationality principle (America has power to regulate conduct of its nationals abroad, and its "nationals" may be said to include American ships and planes as well as American individuals).[15] At all events, whatever the proper jurisdictional principle involved, the federal government does have jurisdiction over American ships and aircraft as described above.

(4) Situs of the Crime. Sometimes, with federal crimes of the type where jurisdiction is based on the principle of territoriality, there arises the problem of determining the situs (or locus) of the crime where the crime is committed partly in federal territory, and partly outside of such territory. The problem becomes important because of the common law limitation on territorial jurisdiction: every crime has but one situs, and, in the absence of a statute enlarging its jurisdiction to cover crimes only partly committed within its territorial boundaries, only the sovereign within whose territory the situs exists has jurisdiction to make the bad conduct a crime.[16] Generally, it may be said that the situs of a crime is where the defendant's acts take effect, even though the acts occurred elsewhere or the ultimate consequences happen elsewhere.[17] Thus where a murderer shoots his victim in the District of Columbia, but the victim later dies in New Jersey, the federal courts of the District have jurisdiction to try the murderer.[18] Where *A* by shooting murders *B* aboard an American vessel in a foreign port, the federal courts have jurisdiction to try *A* for murder; [19] but if *C*, on the same ship in the same port, fires his shot into *D* standing aboard a nearby foreign ship, the

---

9. 18 U.S.C.A. § 7. Murray v. Hildreth, 61 F.2d 483 (5th Cir.1932) (offense between low water mark of Florida coast and three miles off Florida coast). While it is clear that a nation has jurisdiction over a three mile strip from its shores, it is not so clear whether the jurisdiction of the state also extends three miles from its shores. See Cooper, Crimes Aboard American Aircraft: Under what Jurisdiction are they Punishable, 37 A.B.A.J. 257 (1951). The United States has no jurisdiction to punish as crimes acts (except piracy) committed on foreign vessels outside the territorial seas of the United States (unless perhaps committed by U.S. citizens; see § 2.8(b)(1).

10. 21 U.S.C.A. § 955b, discussed in Note, 25 Wm. & Mary L.Rev. 313 (1983). See, e.g., United States v. Henriquez, 731 F.2d 131 (2d Cir.1984).

11. See, e.g., 49 U.S.C.A. § 1508 (federal government assertion of "exclusive sovereignty").

12. See Marsh v. State, 95 N.M. 878, 620 P.2d 878 (1980) (Federal Aviation Act did not deprive states of jurisdiction over certain crimes committed in aircraft flying over the state, such as the possession of marijuana crime in this case).

13. The federal maritime jurisdiction as to aircraft applies only if the plane is "out of the jurisdiction of any particular State." 18 U.S.C.A. § 7(5).

14. All found in title 18 U.S.C.A.

15. Restatement (Second) of the Foreign Relations Law of the United States §§ 28, 29, 31 (1965), places power to prescribe conduct on U.S. vessels and planes under the nationality principle. But the Supreme Court speaks of a ship as part of the territory of the sovereignty whose flag it flies. See United States v. Flores, note 6 supra.

16. This principle of jurisdiction is treated more completely in § 2.9(a), as the problem arises most often in connection with state jurisdiction.

17. On possible interpretations of this when the crime is conspiracy, see note 27 infra.

18. United States v. Guiteau, 12 D.C. (1 Mackey) 498, (1882) (the murder of President James A. Garfield). By like reasoning, where a murder victim died on a military installation but the blow causing death was inflicted off the base, there is no federal jurisdiction. United States v. Parker, 622 F.2d 298 (8th Cir.1980).

19. See note 6 supra.

federal courts have no jurisdiction, because the one situs of the crime is the foreign ship where the shot takes effect.[20] A similar problem would arise if A in the street shoots and kills B in a post office, or if A in Maryland subjects B in the District of Columbia to similar treatment. Doubtless Congress could do what many states have done and provide that crimes committed partly in federal territory and partly outside are subject to federal jurisdiction without regard to the one situs of the crime.[21]

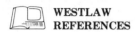

WESTLAW REFERENCES

110k97 /p power jurisdiction! /s crime criminal /s territor!

20. United States v. Davis, 25 F.Cas. 786 (No. 14932) (C.C.D.Mass.1837).

21. See Restatement (Second) of the Foreign Relations Law of the United States §§ 17, 18 (1965).

22. Blackmer v. United States, 284 U.S. 421, 52 S.Ct. 252, 76 L.Ed. 375 (1932) (criminal contempt for U.S. national in France to fail to return to U.S. to give testimony in answer to subpoena); Regina v. Azzopardi, 1 Car. & K. 203, 174 Eng.Rep. 776 (1843).

See United States v. Bowman, 260 U.S. 94, 43 S.Ct. 39, 67 L.Ed. 149 (1922). See Restatement of Conflict of Laws § 426 (1934); Restatement (Second) of the Foreign Relations Law of the United States § 30 (1965).

Of course, in the case of the United States, it is not enough to conclude that established principles of international law permit other than territorial jurisdiction. Congress must be found to have the power to assume such jurisdiction. There are at least two bases upon which Congress might exercise most, if not all, of the power recognized under principles of international law: (1) that the powers of sovereignty which England exercised in her American colonies vested in the colonies collectively upon succession and then in the United States as successor to the colonies, United States v. Curtiss-Wright Export Corp., 299 U.S. 304, 57 S.Ct. 216, 81 L.Ed. 255 (1936); and (2) that the Constitution delegates sufficiently broad powers to the Congress to cover the situation. See George, Extraterritorial Application of Penal Legislation, 64 Mich.L. Rev. 609, 614–16 (1966).

23. Restatement of Conflict of Laws § 426 (1934); United States v. Smiley, 27 F.Cas. 1132 (No. 16,317) (C.C. N.D.Cal.1864) (no federal jurisdiction without a statute over crime of plundering sunken treasure 150 feet from Mexican shore, though defendants apparently were Americans).

24. E.g., Treason against the United States committed "within the United States or elsewhere," 18 U.S.C.A. § 2381; United States v. Chandler, 72 F.Supp. 230 (D.Mass.1947).

The federal government has jurisdiction, which it exercises, to prescribe criminal law for the conduct of members of American armed forces abroad; such criminal

110k16 /p 18 +5 13 & "assimilative crimes act" /p assault battery

airspace /p jurisdiction! /p territor!

situs locus /s crime criminal /p jurisdiction /s territor!

(b) Federal Power as to Conduct Outside the States—Other Bases

(1) Nationality. A nation has the power to prescribe rules of conduct (with criminal punishment for violations) for its own nationals while they are outside its territorial limits.[22] Jurisdiction over nationals abroad depends, however, on the existence of a statute exercising that power.[23] The United States has a few such statutes expressly punishing its nationals for crimes committed abroad,[24] but

cases are tried by courts martial. It is unconstitutional to subject to this courts martial jurisdiction civilian dependents overseas with members of the armed forces, Reid v. Covert, 354 U.S. 1, 77 S.Ct. 1222, 1 L.Ed.2d 1148 (1957) (capital case); Kinsella v. United States ex rel. Singleton, 361 U.S. 234, 80 S.Ct. 297, 4 L.Ed.2d 268 (1960) (noncapital case), or overseas civilian employees of the armed forces, Grisham v. Hagan, 361 U.S. 278, 80 S.Ct. 310, 4 L.Ed.2d 279 (1960) (capital case); McElroy v. United States ex rel. Guagliardo, 361 U.S. 281, 80 S.Ct. 305, 4 L.Ed.2d 282 (1960) (noncapital case). Nor may a former member of the armed forces, now a "civilian," be subjected to courts martial jurisdiction for crimes committed overseas by him while a member of the military. United States ex rel. Toth v. Quarles, 350 U.S. 11, 76 S.Ct. 1, 100 L.Ed. 8 (1955). On the question of who is a "civilian" in this context, see Bishop, Courts-Martial Jurisdiction Over Military-Civilian Hybrids: Retired Regulars, Reservists, and Discharged Prisoners, 112 U.Pa.L.Rev. 317 (1964). It has been suggested that, in view of the holdings in the aforementioned cases, it might be desirable for Congress to enact criminal provisions applicable to such cases and to provide for trial of these cases in the United States under the usual venue rule. George, supra note 22, at 621.

The proposed new federal code deals specifically with extraterritorial jurisdiction. Some of the stated bases for jurisdiction illustrate the "protective principle," discussed infra this section, while others illustrate the nationality principle. In the latter category are instances where "the offense is committed by a federal public servant who is outside the territory of the United States because of his official duties or by a member of his household residing abroad or by a person accompanying the military forces of the United States," or "the offense is committed by or against a national of the United States outside the jurisdiction of any nation" (e.g., Antarctica, the moon). National Comm'n on Reform of Federal Criminal Laws, Final Report—Proposed New Federal Criminal Code § 208 (1971). See Epstein, The Extraterritorial Reach of the Proposed Criminal Justice Reform Act of 1975, 4 Am.J. Crim.L. 275 (1976); Feinberg, Extraterritorial Jurisdiction and the Proposed Federal Criminal Code, 72 J.Crim.L. & Crim. 385 (1981).

courts sometimes infer jurisdiction based upon nationality was conferred in light of the purposes of the particular criminal statute.[25]

While the United States government thus has the power (rather sparingly exercised) to make criminal the conduct of its own nationals abroad, there is a question whether it can go further and make criminal the conduct of aliens abroad which harms American citizens, as where an Englishman murders an American in England or France. The United

States, unlike some nations, generally claims no jurisdiction in this situation.[26]

(2) The "Protective Principle." A nation has the power to enact substantive criminal laws dealing even with the conduct of aliens in foreign territory when the conduct "threatens its security as a state or the operation of its governmental functions," as with "the counterfeiting of the state's seals and currency, and the falsification of its official documents." [27] The United States has made some

25. See United States v. Perez-Herrera, 610 F.2d 289 (5th Cir.1980) (court concludes Congress intended to exercise jurisdiction as to extraterritorial acts of U.S. citizens re crime of attempting to import marijuana into United States, given "the realities of drug smuggling"); United States v. Layton, 509 F.Supp. 212 (N.D.Cal.1981) (federal jurisdiction over killing Cong. Ryan in Guyana, as it is "reasonable to infer that Congress meant to protect its members not only while in this country, but also when outside the territorial limits of the United States, at least when the attack is by a United States citizen").

26. Restatement (Second) of the Foreign Relations Law of the United States § 30 (1965): "A state does not have jurisdiction to prescribe a rule of law attaching legal consequences to conduct of an alien outside its territory merely on the ground that the conduct affects one of its nationals." But see the 1984 amendment to 18 U.S.C.A. § 7(7), extending the jurisdiction of the federal government to any "place outside the jurisdiction of any nation with respect to any offense by or against a national of the United States."

Case of the S.S. Lotus [1927] P.C.I.J., Ser. A, No. 9, involved the validity, under international law, of a Turkish statute making it a crime for a foreigner to do an act against a Turkish subject abroad, which act is a Turkish crime when committed in Turkey. Here Turkey was undertaking to prosecute for manslaughter a French officer who had negligently let his ship run into a Turkish ship on the high seas, killing eight Turkish seamen. After the collision the French ship had proceeded to Turkey, where the officer was arrested. The Permanent Court of International Justice held (in a 7-to-6 decision) that no principle of international law forbade the prosecution; but the view that jurisdiction may be based solely on the principle of protection of nationals abroad is weakened by the Court's statement that, the Turkish ship being a bit of Turkish territory, a prosecution for manslaughter committed thereon (and manslaughter is committed "at the spot where the mortal effect is felt") "may also be justified from the point of view of the so-called territorial principle."

The proposed new federal code makes greater use of the protective principle, for extraterritorial jurisdiction is said to exist, e.g., when "the President of the United States, the President-elect" or various other described federal officials are the victim or intended victim of a crime of violence, "the offense is treason," or "the offense consists of a forgery or counterfeiting, or an uttering of forged copies or counterfeits of the seals, currency, instruments of credit, stamps, passports, or public documents issued by

the United States; or perjury or a false statement in an official proceeding of the United States; or a false statement in a matter within the jurisdiction of the government of the United States." National Comm'n on Reform of Federal Criminal Laws, Final Report—Proposed New Federal Criminal Code § 208 (1971).

27. Restatement (Second) of the Foreign Relations Law of the United States § 33 (1965). However, the power to reach nonresident aliens by use of the protective principle has sometimes been questioned: Cook, The Application of the Criminal Law of a Country to Acts Committed by Foreigners Outside the Jurisdiction, 40 W.Va.L.Q. 303 (1934); Garcia-Mora, Criminal Jurisdiction Over Foreigners for Treason and Offenses Against the Safety of the State Committed Upon Foreign Territory, 19 U.Pitt.L.Rev. 567 (1958); Woolsey, Extraterritorial Crimes, 20 Am.J. Int'l L. 757 (1926).

Aliens who have not entered the United States may sometimes be reached on another basis, namely, their connection with crimes committed within the United States. "Sometimes this is accomplished by invoking the doctrine of conspiracy and finding at least one overt act by one of the conspirators done within the United States. The primary conduct of the other conspirators is then considered to be within the ambit of federal law even though they may be citizens of other countries who never entered the United States during the course of the conspiracy. At other times judicial power is based on the vicarious responsibility of a principal for acts of his agent or of an accomplice for the conduct of the primary actor." George, supra note 22, at 619. See, e.g., Chua Han Mow v. United States, 730 F.2d 1308 (9th Cir.1984) (overt act within United States); United States v. Postal, 589 F.2d 862 (5th Cir.1978) (overt act within United States).

Quite a step beyond this are United States v. Ricardo, 619 F.2d 1124 (5th Cir.1980) (noting proof of overt act not now required under conspiracy statute and concluding it will suffice for jurisdiction that the conspiracy entered into and under way outside the country was "intended * * * to be consummated within the territorial boundaries"); and United States v. Baker, 609 F.2d 134 (5th Cir. 1980) (no conspiracy charge; jurisdiction over possession outside United States with intent to distribute within United States, reliance on "objective territorial principle"). Compare United States v. Columbia-Colella, 604 F.2d 356 (5th Cir.1979) (no United States jurisdiction over purchase in Mexico by Mexican national of vehicle stolen in United States, as no conspiracy and injury in this country complete before purchaser became involved). For an assessment of this development, see Blakesley, United

use of the protective principle, as illustrated by the federal statute which makes it a crime for either an alien or a national to commit perjury before a diplomatic or consular officer abroad,[28] but for the most part federal criminal law rests only upon the territorial basis of jurisdiction.[29]

(3) Universal Jurisdiction. The federal government (like that of any other nation) has the power to make piracy (as defined by international law) a crime wherever it occurs, even when one foreigner commits an act of piracy against another foreigner on a foreign vessel on the high seas, as a special matter of international law.[30] There may be other isolated instances of federal power to make criminal law based on a "universal" rather than on a territorial or nationality principle of jurisdiction.[31] The rule seems limited to such matters as piracy and aggressions against uncivilized persons, however; there is certainly no broad jurisdictional rule that the United States may make conduct by anyone anywhere criminal.[32]

 WESTLAW REFERENCES

crime criminal   /p   jurisdiction   /s   protective   /s principle
"universal jurisdiction" "universality principle"

(c) Federal Power as to Conduct Within the States. The federal government has the power to create statutory crimes as to conduct within the United States, without regard to federal territoriality or nationality, where the United States Constitution expressly grants Congress the power,[33] or, far more common, because the Constitution gives Congress the power to do what is "necessary and proper" to carry out the various expressly conferred powers, such as the power to regulate interstate commerce, to establish post offices, to tax, to prosecute war, and so forth.[34] The scope of

States Jurisdiction Over Extraterritorial Crime, 73 J.Crim.L. & Crim. 1109 (1982).

28. 22 U.S.C.A. § 1203 (1964). See United States v. Archer, 51 F.Supp. 708 (S.D.Cal.1943) (perjury by alien before vice consul in Mexico). See also 18 U.S.C.A. § 1546, which makes punishable the making and use of false statements to secure documents necessary for admission into the United States, applied to the making of false statements before United States consuls in several Latin American countries in United States v. Rodriguez, 182 F.Supp. 479 (S.D.Cal.1960), reversed on other grounds sub nom. Rocha v. United States, 288 F.2d 545 (9th Cir.1961).

Consider also United States v. Benitez, 741 F.2d 1312 (11th Cir.1984) (jurisdiction over assault of federal drug agent in Columbia, as "the crime certainly had a potentially adverse effect upon the security or governmental functions of the nation"); United States v. Columbia-Colella, 604 F.2d 356 (5th Cir.1979) (noting that under protective theory federal government may punish one who has defrauded its treasury, no matter where the fraudulent scheme was perpetrated); United States v. Layton, 509 F.Supp. 212 (N.D.Cal.1981) (federal jurisdiction over killing of Cong. Ryan in Guyana, as statute under which prosecution brought represents "an effort by the government to protect itself against obstructions and frauds").

29. Thus, while it is a federal offense to counterfeit in this country the currency of another nation, 18 U.S.C.A. § 482 (1958), there is no federal statute making it a crime to falsify United States currency abroad.

Some other nations have utilized the protective principle to a greater extent. See Berge, Criminal Jurisdiction and the Territorial Principle, 30 Mich.L.Rev. 238, 266–68 (1931).

30. See Restatement (Second) of the Foreign Relations Law of the United States § 34 (1965). "Piracy" is defined

in Art. 15 of the Convention on the High Seas of April 29, 1958, reproduced id. at § 34, reporters' notes.

This same definition is utilized in the proposed new federal code. See National Comm'n on Reform of Federal Criminal Laws, Final Report—Proposed New Federal Criminal Code § 212 (1971).

31. E.g., 18 U.S.C.A. § 969, punishing the sale of arms, liquor or drugs, apparently even by non-Americans, to aboriginal natives on certain Pacific islands which are not American possessions. See Levitt, Jurisdiction Over Crimes, 16 J.Crim.L. & Crim. 495, 497 (1926), dealing with aggressions against uncivilized persons.

While slave trade, traffic in women for prostitution, and traffic in narcotic drugs have been the subject of universal condemnation, the principle of universal jurisdiction has not yet been recognized as to these crimes. Restatement (Second) of the Foreign Relations Law of the United States § 34, reporters' notes (1965).

32. Of such a "universal" or "cosmopolitan" theory of jurisdiction, adopted as to some situations by some other nations, see Berge, Criminal Jurisdiction and the Territorial Principle, 30 Mich.L.Rev. 238, 268 (1931); Levitt, Jurisdiction over Crimes (pts. I & II), 16 J.Crim.L. & Crim. 316, 495 (1926). The Levitt article contains a valuable discussion of the theoretical basis of criminal jurisdiction—territorial, general security (jurisdiction of a sovereign to protect itself and its citizens from conduct outside its limits which causes harm or may cause harm to the sovereign or even its citizens), and cosmopolitan (universal).

33. E.g., U.S. Const. art. I, § 8 (power to punish counterfeiting, piracies, felonies on high seas, offenses against the law of nations); art. III, § 3 (power to punish treason).

34. On the broad scope of the "necessary and proper" clause, U.S. Const. art. I, § 8, cl. 18, see Marshall, C.J., in

federal substantive criminal law of this variety has been growing steadily since the nation was founded, so that at the present time there is a substantial amount of such federal criminal law.[35]

Federal criminal law of this type is employed, according to one observer,[36] in three different ways. First, it is used to punish anti-social conduct primarily injurious to the federal government. In this classification fall crimes like treason, espionage, bribery of federal officers, tampering with federal juries, contempt of federal courts, failure to pay federal taxes, thefts from national banks, thefts of federal property, and murder of federal law enforcement officers.

Secondly, federal criminal law is widely used to punish anti-social conduct of primarily local concern, often conduct with which the local police are unable or unwilling to cope. Thus transporting a stolen automobile (or a woman for immoral purposes, or a kidnapped person) across a state line is made a federal crime, although actually it is the car theft (or prostitution, or kidnapping)—a local matter— rather than the incidental act of transportation across a state border, which constitutes the real evil to be combatted. The federal criminal statute punishing flight across state lines to avoid prosecution for state crimes is another example. Use of the mails to defraud (or to disseminate obscene matter, or to send lottery tickets) is a federal offense; but fraud and obscenity and lotteries are matters of local concern, and the use of the mails may

well be simply incidental to, rather than an essential ingredient of, the crime. The federal taxing power has been the basis for federal control (with criminal penalties for violations) over narcotics and gambling, although admittedly these federal laws are aimed at anti-social behavior of local concern far more than at raising revenue. Since by federal income tax law most money obtained illegally in violation of local criminal laws (as by extortion, bootlegging, false pretenses, larceny and embezzlement) constitutes taxable income, many persons who have successfully escaped state prosecution for state crimes have found themselves behind federal prison bars for failure to pay their proper federal income taxes.

Thirdly, federal criminal law is utilized to secure compliance with federal administrative regulations. The so-called "administrative crime," both federal and state, is discussed elsewhere in this book.[37]

The proposed new federal criminal code takes a quite different approach to the problem of federal jurisdiction over conduct within the states. Currently, it is the practice to describe federal crimes in such a way that the jurisdictional requirements are set forth as elements of the various offenses (e.g., *use of the mails* to defraud,[38] *interstate transportation* of stolen vehicles[39]). The new code, however, defines offenses in terms of substantive misbehavior (e.g., theft), just as is done in a state code. The matter of jurisdiction is dealt with separately[40] by reference to certain bases of jurisdiction which are set out

---

McCulloch v. Maryland, 17 U.S. (4 Wheat.) 316, 4 L.Ed. 579 (1819); 1 R. Rotunda, J. Nowak, & J. Young, Treatise on Constitutional Law ch. 3 (1986).

35. Mostly found in Title 18 of U.S.C.A., but also found in other Titles. For a short history of the expansion of the federal criminal law, see Schwartz, Federal Criminal Jurisdiction and Prosecutors' Discretion, 13 Law & Contemp.Prob. 64 (1948), pointing out that this growth has quite naturally accompanied the expansion of the role of the United States government in the regulation of various aspects of public welfare—interstate transportation, communication, wholesomeness of food, marketing of securities, wages and hours of labor, wartime price regulation, etc. Almost all such federal regulation is enforced by criminal penalties. See also the consultant's report of Professor Norman Abrams, in 1 National Comm'n on

Reform of Federal Criminal Laws, Working Papers 33 (1970).

36. Schwartz, supra note 35.

37. See § 2.6.

38. 18 U.S.C.A. § 1341.

39. 18 U.S.C.A. § 2312.

40. E.g., National Comm'n on Reform of Federal Criminal Laws, Final Report—Proposed New Federal Criminal Code § 1701 (1971), first defines arson as being committed when a person "starts or maintains a fire or causes an explosion with intent to destroy * * * a building or inhabited structure of another or a vital public facility," and then states that there is federal jurisdiction over this offense under certain specified subsections of § 201, which sets forth the common jurisdictional bases.

elsewhere in the code.[41] This approach has several advantages: (1) It facilitates sound sentencing policy, for no longer "will federal sentence limits for fraud or obscenity or murder accidentally vary according to the particular federal jurisdictional base which is invoked." [42] (2) Technical issues of jurisdiction will "recede from their present prominence in federal criminal law," [43] as proof of any one jurisdictional base will suffice [44] and the government is relieved of any burden of showing that the defendant knew of the special fact which results in federal jurisdiction.[45] (3) International extradition will be facilitated "since many of the treaties require the extraditable offense to be penal in both the demanding and the surrendering state," [46] which arguably is not now the case as to such crimes as mail fraud.

Of the various bases of jurisdiction set forth in the proposed code, the most noteworthy is that "the offense is committed in the course of committing or in immediate flight from the commission of any other offense over which federal jurisdiction exists." [47] This is the so-called "piggyback" basis,[48] and is intended to permit a more rational classification of offenses. For example, the crime of impersonating a federal official is now a felony punishable by up to three years imprisonment.[49] This may be too high a maximum permissible penalty for the simple act of impersonation, which could more appropriately be viewed as only an offense of the misdemeanor variety,[50]

but it may at the same time be too low a maximum when this is the only available basis of federal jurisdiction over, say, a kidnapping which is accomplished by the impersonation. The virtue of the "piggyback" approach to federal jurisdiction would be that such crimes as impersonation of a federal officer could be classified, for sentencing purposes, in a more rational way without depriving the federal courts of the authority to deal effectively with more serious harms which arise out of these lesser offenses. This change would be most significant in the area of civil rights violations, for these prosecutions "have in the past proceeded under statutes providing limited sanctions rather than for the murder that actually occurred in connection with the civil rights offense." [51]

 WESTLAW REFERENCES

crime criminal /p "necessary and proper"
di administrative crime
di(federal /s power /p state /s power /p crime criminal /s jurisdiction)

(d) Concurrent Jurisdiction; Double Jeopardy. Particularly in the case of federal criminal jurisdiction of the auxiliary type (that is, where the federal interest is insubstantial and the offense serves primarily as a means for supplementing state law enforcement), but also with respect to other forms of federal jurisdiction as well, the federal and state government have concurrent jurisdic-

41. Id. at § 201 sets forth the common jurisdictional bases, such as that the victim was a federal public servant engaged in the performance of his official duties; that the property which is the subject of the offense was owned by or in the custody of the United States; that the offense affects interstate or foreign commerce; or that the U.S. mails or a facility in interstate or foreign commerce is used in commission or consummation of the offense.

42. National Comm'n on Reform of Federal Criminal Laws, Study Draft of a New Federal Criminal Code xxix (1970).

43. Ibid.

44. Final Report, supra note 40, at § 205 specifically so provides. Compare United States v. McRary, 665 F.2d 674 (5th Cir.1982), (though facts show maritime jurisdiction, conviction must be reversed because charge based on another theory not supported by the proof).

45. Id. at § 204 so provides. This is now the case as to some elements of federal offenses which serve as the

jurisdictional base. See United States v. Licausi, 413 F.2d 1118 (5th Cir.1969) (defendant need not know that deposits of bank he robbed were insured by FDIC); McEwen v. United States, 390 F.2d 47 (9th Cir.1968) (defendant need not know that person assaulted was federal officer); United States v. Allegrucci, 258 F.2d 70 (3d Cir.1958) (receiver of stolen goods need not know they were stolen from interstate commerce).

46. Study Draft, supra note 42, at xxix.

47. Final Report, supra note 40, at § 201(b).

48. Id. at § 201, Comment.

49. 18 U.S.C.A. § 912.

50. It is so treated in the proposed code. See Final Report, supra note 40, at § 1381.

51. Study Draft, supra note 42, at xxx.

tion over much criminal activity: the state over bank robbery, the federal over robbery of a federally-insured institution; the state over car theft, the federal over interstate transportation of a stolen vehicle; and so on. In such situations, the question arises whether the offender should or could be subjected to only state prosecution, only federal prosecution, or both state and federal prosecution.

Prosecution by both the state and federal governments is not barred by the constitutional protection against double jeopardy. In *Bartkus v. Illinois*,[52] the Supreme Court sustained a state conviction for robbery of a federally-insured bank after the defendant had been acquitted on federal charges based on the same robbery. And in the companion case of *Abbate v. United States*,[53] where the order of prosecution was reversed, the Court upheld a federal conviction for conspiracy to destroy communications facilities operated or controlled by the United States after the defendant had been convicted in the state courts for conspiracy to destroy the property of another. In both cases, the rationale was that the policies underlying the double jeopardy bar against reprosecution were inapplicable because separate sovereignties were involved. The Court expressed the fear that a contrary rule would result in a state (or federal) prosecution for a minor offense barring a subsequent federal (or state) prosecution for a seri-

ous impingement upon the interests of the latter jurisdiction.[54]

The *Bartkus* and *Abbate* cases have been soundly criticized by commentators.[55] Generally, the argument is that the evils of reprosecution—as far as the defendant is concerned—are just as great when separate sovereignties are involved and that they are not offset by the separate interests of the state and federal governments. It has also been noted that a middle ground exists between the *Bartkus-Abbate* approach and an absolute bar on reprosecution: the second prosecution could be barred except upon a showing that distinct and separate substantial governmental interests are involved in the two prosecutions.[56] This has some appeal, although it is often difficult to determine how the interests in the relevant state and federal statutes should be characterized.[57] In view of the fact that the dual sovereignties approach has now been rejected in other contexts,[58] it has sometimes been suggested that the Supreme Court might adopt that middle position.[59] However, the Court has shown no such inclination.[60]

(1) State Prosecution First. If the defendant's conduct has already been the basis for a state prosecution, there is currently no general statutory bar on the federal level to prosecution in the federal courts. As to certain specified crimes, however, Congress has expressly provided that prosecution for these

52. 359 U.S. 121, 79 S.Ct. 676, 3 L.Ed.2d 684 (1959).

53. 359 U.S. 187, 79 S.Ct. 666, 3 L.Ed.2d 729 (1959).

54. In *Bartkus*, the Court referred to Screws v. United States, 325 U.S. 91, 65 S.Ct. 1031, 89 L.Ed. 1495 (1945), where the defendants were convicted in federal court under federal statutes with maximum penalties of one and two years respectively, although the state crime involved was a capital offense. In *Abbate*, the Court noted that the defendants' conspiracy to dynamite telephone company facilities had resulted in only a three-month sentence from the state court.

55. See, e.g., Fisher, Double Jeopardy, Two Sovereignties and the Intruding Constitution, 28 U.Chi.L.Rev. 591 (1961); Pontikes, Dual Sovereignty and Double Jeopardy, 14 Wes.Res.L.Rev. 700 (1963); Notes, 44 Minn.L.Rev. 534 (1960); 80 Harv.L.Rev. 1538 (1967).

56. Pontikes, supra note 55, at 713–20; Note, 80 Harv. L.Rev. 1538, 1559–63 (1967).

57. "Bank robbery, for example, is treated here as an auxiliary offense [i.e., one which only serves to assist local

law enforcement] although an argument can be made that the offense is designed to protect a particular Federal interest—namely, funds that are Federally-insured or otherwise Federally-connected." 1 National Comm'n on Reform of Federal Criminal Laws, Working Papers 34 (1970).

58. Murphy v. Waterfront Comm'n, 378 U.S. 52, 84 S.Ct. 1594, 12 L.Ed.2d 678 (1964) (after state grant of immunity to witness, federal government may not make use of compelled testimony or its fruits); Elkins v. United States, 364 U.S. 206, 80 S.Ct. 1437, 4 L.Ed.2d 1669 (1960) (overturning "silver platter" doctrine which permitted use in federal trial of evidence unconstitutionally seized by state officers).

59. Notes, J.Crim.L.C. & P.S. 29 (1971); 66 Nw.U.L. Rev. 248 (1971).

60. United States v. Wheeler, 435 U.S. 313, 98 S.Ct. 1079, 55 L.Ed.2d 303 (1978) (relying on *Bartkus* and *Abbate* in holding double jeopardy clause did not prohibit a federal criminal prosecution of an Indian convicted of a lesser offense in a tribal court).

offenses shall not be undertaken following a state prosecution.[61] Beyond this, the matter is solely one of discretionary nonprosecution by federal prosecutors. Shortly after the *Abbate* decision, the Attorney General issued a memorandum to all U.S. attorneys directing that "no federal case should be tried when there has already been a state prosecution for substantially the same act or acts" except with the approval of an Assistant Attorney General after consultation with the Attorney General.[62] This policy has been followed by subsequent administrations and has served as the basis for dismissal of convictions on the government's motion in several cases where prosecutions were inadvertently initiated after state prosecutions.[63]

The proposed new federal criminal code would codify the existing practice, for it provides that when conduct constitutes a federal offense and an offense under the law of a state, a subsequent federal prosecution may not be undertaken in the following situations unless "the Attorney General of the United States certifies that the interests of the United States would be unduly harmed if the federal prosecution is barred": (1) where the state prosecution resulted in an acquittal or conviction and the federal prosecution is based on the same conduct or arose from the same criminal episode unless the law defining the state offense is intended to prevent a substantially different harm or evil from the law defining the federal offense, or unless the federal offense was not consummated when the state trial began; or (2) where the state prosecution was terminated in favor of the defendant in a way which necessarily required a determination inconsistent with a fact or a legal proposition which must be established for conviction of the federal of-

fense.[64] This provision, the draftsmen explain, creates a presumptive bar against successive prosecution but yet permits federal reprosecution in the exceptional case where substantial federal interests are defeated or inadequately protected by the state prosecution.[65]

(2) Federal Prosecution First. If the defendant's conduct has already been the basis for a federal prosecution, then, under the Model Penal Code view, a subsequent state prosecution should be barred in two circumstances: (1) where the federal prosecution resulted in an acquittal or conviction and the state prosecution is based on the same conduct, unless each offense requires proof of a fact not required by the other and the law defining each of the offenses is intended to prevent a substantially different harm or evil, or unless the state offense was not consummated when the federal trial began; or (2) where the federal prosecution was terminated in favor of the defendant in a manner which necessarily required a determination inconsistent with a fact which must be established for conviction of the state offense.[66] About half of the states have adopted legislation along these lines,[67] although frequently the test is stated somewhat differently. Generally, the question is whether the federal and state statutes are so much alike that a prosecution under the former bars a prosecution under the latter, which has often proved to be a difficult determination to make.[68] Also, some state constitutions have been interpreted as barring prosecution in a *Bartkus* type of case.[69]

The proposed new federal code would deal with this issue as a matter of federal law, under Congress's power to preempt a state's

---

61. See, e.g., 18 U.S.C.A. §§ 659, 660, 1992, 2117.

62. N.Y.Times, April 6, 1959, p. 1, col. 4, p. 19, cols. 1, 2.

63. See Petite v. United States, 361 U.S. 529, 80 S.Ct. 450, 4 L.Ed.2d 490 (1960); Marakar v. United States, 370 U.S. 723, 82 S.Ct. 1573, 8 L.Ed.2d 803 (1962); Orlando v. United States, 387 F.2d 348 (9th Cir.1967).

64. Final Report, supra note 40, at § 707.

65. Working Papers, supra note 57, at 346–48.

66. Model Penal Code § 1.10.

67. 3 W. LaFave & J. Israel, Criminal Procedure § 24.5(b) (1984).

68. See Bartkus v. Illinois, 359 U.S. 121, 79 S.Ct. 676, 3 L.Ed.2d 684 (1959), for a discussion of these difficulties.

69. See, e.g., People v. Cooper, 398 Mich. 450, 247 N.W.2d 866 (1976); State v. Hogg, 118 N.H. 262, 385 A.2d 844 (1978).

criminal jurisdiction.[70] A federal prosecution would constitute a bar to a subsequent state prosecution in two circumstances: (1) where the federal prosecution resulted in an acquittal or conviction and the state prosecution is based on the same conduct or arose from the same criminal episode, unless the statute defining the federal offense is intended to prevent a substantially different harm or evil from the law defining the state offense, or unless the state offense was not consummated when the federal trial began; or (2) where the federal prosecution was terminated in the defendant's favor in such a way as to necessarily require a determination inconsistent with a fact or a legal proposition which must be established for conviction of the state offense.[71]

The proposed code also attempts to ensure that a federal prosecution is not undertaken in the first instance if the matter is more appropriately one for the state authorities. Federal enforcement agencies are expressly "authorized to decline or discontinue federal enforcement efforts whenever the offense can effectively be prosecuted by nonfederal agencies and it appears that there is no substantial Federal interest in further prosecution or that the offense primarily affects state, local or foreign interests." [72] These issues "are for the prosecuting authorities alone and are not litigable." [73]

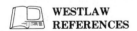
WESTLAW
REFERENCES

di concurrent jurisdiction

di double jeopardy

70. Pennsylvania v. Nelson, 350 U.S. 497, 76 S.Ct. 477, 100 L.Ed. 640 (1956).

71. Final Report, supra note 40 at § 708. This is much like the Model Penal Code test, text at note 66 supra, although the Model Penal Code also includes the requirement that the state and federal offenses each require proof of a fact not required by the other.

72. Id. at § 207, which goes on to state: "A substantial federal interest exists in the following circumstances, among others: (a) the offense is serious and state or local law enforcement is impeded by interstate aspects of the case; (b) federal enforcement is believed to be necessary to vindicate federally-protected civil rights; (c) if federal jurisdiction exists under section 201(b), the offense is closely related to the underlying offense, as to which there is a

bartkus & 79 +5 676 & "concurrent jurisdiction" "double jeopardy" & date(after 1980)

---

§ 2.9 Criminal Jurisdiction—The States

Definition of the power of a state of the United States to declare conduct criminal requires consideration of: (1) the subject matter which a state, under its police power, may regulate; and (2) the territory which its laws may encompass.

A state, unlike the federal government, may declare activities to be criminal without the necessity of finding some express or implied authority therefor in its constitution. It is commonly said that a state has regulatory power (usually termed its "police power") to regulate its internal affairs for the protection or promotion of public health, safety and morals, or—somewhat more vaguely—for the protection or promotion of the public welfare.[1] Of course, in many areas of local regulation (with criminal sanctions for violations) much of what is done in the name of promoting the public welfare is actually the result of the effective operation of pressure groups on the legislature.[2]

Assuming that a state criminal law is a proper exercise of the police power of the state, there is still the question of the territorial scope of the power of that state. Clearly California can make murder a crime. But can it punish a person (perhaps a citizen of California, perhaps not) who commits murder in Delaware, or is its power to make murder criminal limited to murders committed in California? If its power is limited to California

substantial federal interest; (d) an offense apparently limited in its impact is believed to be associated with organized criminal activities extending beyond state lines; (e) state or local law enforcement has been so corrupted as to undermine its effectiveness substantially."

73. Ibid.

§ 2.9

1. There are, of course, some limits to the scope of the police power of a state, imposed by the U.S. Constitution, federal statutes and treaties valid thereunder, and by the constitution of the particular state. On the constitutional limitations, see §§ 2.10–2.15.

2. As to the challenge of such legislation on the ground that it is beyond the police power of the state, see § 2.12.

murders, then there is the difficulty encountered in crimes committed partly in each of two states, as where *A,* standing in California, shoots across the border killing *B,* who is standing in Oregon. Another problem is the extent to which state citizenship may give that state power to apply its criminal laws to its citizens who commit crimes outside the state, or perhaps even to noncitizens who commit crimes against its citizens outside the state. Once again, as is the case with the federal government's power to create crimes, states have not always undertaken to exercise all the power which they might properly exercise.

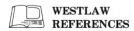 **WESTLAW REFERENCES**

di police power

(a) Common Law View of Territorial Jurisdiction. The common law adopts as the principal basis of jurisdiction a territorial theory of jurisdiction over crimes: a state has power to make conduct or the result of conduct [3] a crime if the conduct takes place or the result happens within its territorial limits.[4] Conversely, there can be no territorial jurisdiction where conduct and its results both occur outside its territory.[5]

3. Some crimes are defined so as to require, in addition to certain conduct (act or omission and state of mind), a certain result. See § 1.2.

4. The territorial limits of a sea-coast state include a strip of the border sea extending three nautical miles. People v. Stralla, 14 Cal.2d 617, 96 P.2d 941 (1939). Some states claim more than three miles. See Skiriotes v. Florida, 313 U.S. 69, 61 S.Ct. 924, 85 L.Ed. 1193 (1941). There is some authority that the territorial limits extend to planes flying over the state. Graham v. People, 134 Colo. 290, 302 P.2d 737 (1956); Marsh v. State, 95 N.M. 224, 620 P.2d 878 (1980).

5. Restatement of Conflict of Laws § 425 (1934), which, however, recognizes in § 426 (1948 Supp.) another type of jurisdiction: state jurisdiction by statute to punish its own citizens outside its territorial limits. See § 2.9(c)(2).

6. Restatement of Conflict of Laws § 428 (1934); J. Beale, Conflict of Laws § 428.5 (1935).

7. Commonwealth v. Apkins, 148 Ky. 207, 146 S.W. 431 (1912) (victim, who took defendant's poison in Ohio, died in Kentucky; *held,* Kentucky has no jurisdiction); People v. Duffield, 387 Mich. 300, 197 N.W.2d 25 (1972) (Mich. has jurisdiction where victim beaten there but died in Indiana); State v. Gessert, 21 Minn. 369 (1875) (defendant stabbed victim in Minnesota; victim died in Wisconsin;

At common law (that is, in the absence of statute) jurisdiction over crimes is limited even further than the territorial principle would seem to require, by the notion that each crime has only one situs (or locus), and that only the place of the situs has jurisdiction. In other words, the common law picked out one particular act (or omission) or result of the act (or omission) as vital for the determination of the place of commission (i.e. the situs) of each of the various crimes and gave jurisdiction to that state (and only that state) where the vital act or result occurred. Generally, it may be said that the situs of a crime at common law is the place of the act (or omission) if the crime is defined only in these terms, and the place of the result if the definition of the crime includes such a result.[6] Thus murder (for instance, where the killing is accomplished by shooting or by mailing poisoned candy) is committed at the place where the fatal force impinges upon the body of the victim (the place where the bullet strikes or the poison is consumed), rather than where the fatal force is initiated by the defendant's act (where he fires the bullet or mails the poison) or where the victim dies.[7] Bigamy is committed where the illegal marriage ceremony takes place, not where the parties thereafter cohabit.[8] The crime of

held, Minnesota has jurisdiction); State v. Carter, 27 N.J.L. 499 (1859) (defendant mortally wounded victim in New York; victim died in New Jersey; *held,* New Jersey has no jurisdiction; dictum that if shot across border, state where bullet strikes has jurisdiction); State v. Hall, 114 N.C. 909, 19 S.E. 602 (1894) (defendant in North Carolina shot across state border hitting and killing victim in Tennessee; *held,* North Carolina has no jurisdiction, since crime was committed in Tennessee); Commonwealth v. Robinson, 468 Pa. 575, 364 A.2d 665 (1976) (victim shot in Pennsylvania died out of state, Pennsylvania has jurisdiction). See also State v Rossbach, 288 N.W.2d 714 (Minn.1980) (this common law rule relied upon in holding state where victim located had jurisdiction on charge of aggravated assault).

Cases involving venue are closely analogous; once again, the county where the fatal impact takes place has venue, not where the defendant acted or death occurred. E.g. State v. Bowen, 16 Kan. 475 (1876) (defendant delivered fatal blow in Wilson County; victim died elsewhere; *held,* Wilson County has venue).

8. Johnson v. Commonwealth, 86 Ky. 122, 5 S.W. 365 (1887) (marriage in Tennessee followed by cohabitation in Kentucky; Kentucky lacks jurisdiction to prosecute for bigamy); State v. Stephens, 118 Me. 237, 107 A. 296 (1919)

false pretenses is committed where the property is obtained, not where the false pretenses are made.[9] Forgery is committed where the false instrument is made or altered, not where it is uttered; and conversely, uttering a forged instrument is committed where it is offered, not where it is made.[10] Robbery is committed where the property is taken from the victim, not where he is first seized or intimidated.[11] Receiving stolen property is committed where the goods are received, not where they were stolen.[12] Libel is committed where the defamatory matter is circulated, not where it is written.[13] The crime of abandoning the family is committed where the family lives at the time the defendant aban-

dons it, not the place to which the family later moves.[14]

There is one peculiarity in a number of states, however, occurring in connection with the crime of larceny and perhaps other forms of theft. The weight of authority as to larceny is that the crime may be prosecuted, not only at the place where the goods are stolen (where the original taking and asportation take place) but also wherever the goods may be subsequently brought, on the theory that "every asportation is a new taking." [15] Thus where goods are stolen in state *A* and brought into state *B*, the latter has jurisdiction to prosecute for the larceny.[16] A substantial mi-

(Maine has no bigamy jurisdiction where marriage took place in Canada and cohabitation in Maine, despite statute seeming to give Maine jurisdiction); State v. Ray, 151 N.C. 710, 66 S.E. 204 (1909) (statute purporting to give N.C. jurisdiction unconstitutional); Wilson v. State, 16 Okla.Cr. 471, 184 P. 603 (1919) (Oklahoma has no bigamy jurisdiction over bigamous Texas marriage followed by Oklahoma cohabitation). Many states, however, make bigamous cohabitation within the state a crime (separate from bigamy) even though the bigamous marriage took place outside the state; the state then has jurisdiction over the cohabitation crime. State v. Stewart, 194 Mo. 345, 92 S.W. 878 (1906); State v. Moon, 178 N.C. 715, 100 S.E. 614 (1919).

Similarly, incest is committed where the intercourse or marriage takes place, not where the parties later come or return. See In re May's Estate, 280 App.Div. 647, 117 N.Y.S.2d 345 (1952).

9. Updike v. People, 92 Colo. 125, 18 P.2d 472 (1933) (false pretenses made by letter mailed in Idaho; check mailed by victim in Colorado; *held,* Colorado is where defendant obtained the check, so Colorado has jurisdiction); Connor v. State, 29 Fla. 455, 10 So. 891 (1892) (Florida information quashed because no allegation that the money was obtained in Florida.)

10. Lindsey v. State, 38 Ohio St. 507 (1882) (defendant forged instrument in Missouri, then mailed it to Ohio; *held,* Ohio has jurisdiction over crime of uttering); State v. Hudson, 13 Mont. 112, 32 P. 413 (1893) (question of venue). Cf. State v. Kleen, 491 S.W.2d 244 (Mo.1973) (where check signed in Missouri but payee and amount entered in Tennessee, where it delivered, crime of making and delivering insufficient funds check did not occur in Missouri); State v. Saxton, 30 Utah 2d 456, 519 P.2d 1340 (1947) (passing bad check occurred in state where check passed, though bank on which it drawn in another state).

11. Sweat v. State, 90 Ga. 315, 17 S.E. 273 (1893) (question of venue). Contra: Thomas v. State, 262 Ark. 79, 553 S.W.2d 32 (1977) (because "one continuous threat of force").

12. People v. McGovern, 307 Ill. 373, 138 N.E. 632 (1923) (Illinois has jurisdiction over crime of receiving car stolen in a foreign state); People v. Dwyer, 397 Ill. 599, 74

N.E.2d 882 (1947) (same). It has been held, however, that receiving stolen property is also committed where the receiver may later take the goods. See note 16 infra.

13. State v. Piver, 74 Wash. 96, 132 P. 858 (1913) (California editor of California newsaper circulated it in Washington among other places; *held,* Washington has jurisdiction over the libel).

14. Jemmerson v. State, 80 Ga. 111, 5 S.E. 131 (1888) (Georgia has no jurisdiction where abandonment took place in Alabama). Compare the situation where the charge is the omission of nonsupport, discussed in note 33 infra.

15. E.g. Worthington v. State, 58 Md. 403, 409 (1882).

16. E.g., Schultz v. Lainson, 234 Iowa 606, 13 N.W.2d 326 (1944). See Annot., 156 A.L.R. 862, 865–66 (1945), noting the rule has sometimes also been applied to goods stolen in a foreign *country* and brought into a state, e.g. Wis.Stat.Ann. 939.03.

The same rule has been applied to embezzlement, Commonwealth v. Parker, 165 Mass. 526, 43 N.E. 499 (1896) (conversion of property in New York, property taken into Massachusetts; *held,* Massachusetts has jurisdiction under statute providing that whoever embezzles "shall be deemed guilty of larceny"); to the crime of receiving stolen property, State v. Pambianchi, 139 Conn. 543, 95 A.2d 695 (1953) (car stolen in New York; defendant received it there and then took it to Connecticut; *held,* Connecticut has jurisdiction, since receiving, like larceny, is a continuing crime); and to the crime of concealing stolen property. Commonwealth v. Carroll, 360 Mass. 580, 276 N.E.2d 705 (1971) (stolen money received in N.Y., but concealment continued as defendants returned to Mass. with it).

As noted in Model Penal Code § 1.03, Comment (Tent. Draft No. 5, 1956), the same result may be reached by making possession of stolen goods under specific circumstances a substantive offense. The Code, therefore, does not deal with the problem in terms of jurisdiction.

It has been held that the rule applicable to larceny does not apply to burglary and robbery. People v. McGowan, 127 Cal.App. 39, 14 P.2d 1036 (1932) (burglary in Oregon, goods carried to California; California cannot try for

nority of cases, however, hold that state *B* has no jurisdiction.[17]

Another peculiarity exists in connection with the situation of one who, outside the state, incites or encourages or hires another to commit a crime within the state. If the crime committed within the state is a felony, the absent person is at common law an accessory before the fact.[18] The common law rule is that an accessory before the fact, who commits all his accessorial acts outside the state, commits no crime within the state and so is not subject to its jurisdiction.[19] This same rule is sometimes expressed in these terms: One who, at all times outside the state, commits a crime within the state by a "guilty agent" is not subject to the jurisdiction of the state. The rule has in many jurisdictions been changed by statute.[20]

The situation just described is to be distinguished from that of one who, outside the state, commits a crime within the state by an "innocent agent." Thus where *A* in Ohio tells lies to his innocent agent in New York, who innocently repeats them in New York to

victim *B*, who in New York delivers money to the agent, who then forwards it to *A* in Ohio—here *A* commits the crime of obtaining property from *B* by false pretenses in New York, although *A* was at no time actually present in that state.[21]

Courts have experienced some difficulty in determining the situs of inchoate offenses, such as attempt and conspiracy. As to attempt, perhaps the most sensible view is that the attempt has the same situs as the completed offense would have had if the defendant were successful.[22] Thus attempted murder is committed at the place where the victim is missed, rather than where the defendant does his act.[23] However, the view has also been taken that an attempt has its situs where a substantial step was taken, even though the offense was actually completed in another jurisdiction.[24]

As to conspiracy, at least where it is defined as an agreement plus an overt act, if an agreement is entered into in state *A* to commit a crime in state *B*, and an overt act takes place in state *B*, then state *B* is the situs of

burglary, but can for larceny of the goods); see also Smith v. State, 55 Ala. 59, 60 (1876) (question of venue; "If, in the course of a robbery, larceny is committed, the offender could be convicted of the latter, not of the former offense, in any county into which he might carry the goods.")

17. E.g. Brown v. United States, 35 D.C. 548 (1910); Doane v. Commonwealth, 218 Va. 500, 237 N.E.2d 797 (1977). See Annot., 156 A.L.R. 862, 871–72 (1945).

18. With a misdemeanor all connected with it are principals, so the rule here discussed applies to felonies but not misdemeanors. See § 6.6.

19. Restatement of Conflict of Laws § 428, comment f (1934); State v. Chapin, 17 Ark. 561 (1856); Johns v. State, 19 Ind. 421 (1862); State v. Wyckoff, 31 N.J.L. 65 (1864); State v. Huginski, 139 Vt. 95, 422 A.2d 935 (1980). Consider also Linn v. State, 505 P.2d 1270 (Wyo.1973) (state law makes accessoryship a distinct crime, thus Wyoming has jurisdiction over person who aided in that state a crime committed in Nevada).

20. See notes 58 and 59 infra.

21. People v. Adams, 3 Denio 190 (N.Y.1846), aff'd 1 N.Y. 173 (1848); Lindsey v. State, 38 Ohio St. 507 (1882); State v. Devot, 66 Utah 319, 242 P. 395 (1925); Annot., 42 A.L.R. 272, 275 (1926). See Johns v. State, State v. Wyckoff, note 19 supra, distinguishing the situation of the "guilty" agent (accessory before the fact situation) from that of the "innocent" agent. The innocent agent situation is sometimes likened to the bullet which flies across the state line, the bullet being a sort of innocent agent. See People v. Adams, supra.

22. State v. Stow, 83 N.J.L. 14, 84 A. 1063 (1912) (defendant in New Jersey wrote letter to person in Pennsylvania advising him to illegally register as voter in New Jersey; held that the attempt was in Pennsylvania because the completed crime would have had its situs there).

23. Simpson v. State, 92 Ga. 41, 17 S.E. 984 (1893) (defendant in South Carolina fired at victim in Georgia and missed, the bullets landing in Georgia; *held*, Georgia has jurisdiction. Query if the bullets had come to earth on the South Carolina side. It would seem that Georgia, the place where the harm denounced by the crime of attempted murder existed, should even so be the situs.) Cf. State v. Winckler, 260 N.W.2d 356 (S.D.1977) (assault with deadly weapon of attempted battery type, jurisdiction where intended victim located).

The murder cases often speak like this: one cannot commit a crime within a state unless he is present within the state; but his presence need not be physical, it may be constructive. And one is constructively present because he constructively accompanies his bullet across the state line. Of course, this fictional talk really means: one need not be physically present within a state in order to commit a crime within the state. See Annot., 42 A.L.R. 272 (1926).

24. Commonwealth v. Neubauer, 142 Pa.Super. 528, 16 A.2d 450 (1940) (extortion case, defendant demanded money from victim in Pennsylvania, but arranged for payment in Ohio; held that attempt was in Pennsylvania although completed crime occurred in Ohio).

the conspiracy.[25] However, when no overt act is required for the commission of conspiracy, it has been held that an agreement in state *A* to commit a crime in state *B,* is a conspiracy with its situs in state *A.*[26] Also, similar to the rule noted earlier as to larceny, conspiracy has sometimes been viewed as a continuing offense which may have its situs in more than one jurisdiction; the situs may be the place of original agreement and also those states in which acts in furtherance of the agreement are undertaken.[27]

Another problem concerns crimes committed on navigable rivers which constitute boundaries between two states. It is usual for each of the two states involved to have concurrent jurisdiction (by act of Congress) over crimes committed on any part of the river without regard to the actual boundary line, which usually runs down the center of the main channel of the river.[28] Thus a state has often punished violations of its own laws oc-

curring on a part of the river within the boundaries of the neighboring state.[29] But where the defendant's conduct, although a crime by the laws of the prosecuting state, is not a crime by the laws of the neighboring state, and the conduct takes place on that part of the river within the neighbor's borders, the former does not have jurisdiction, at least over a crime which is only *malum prohibitum.*[30]

Although most crimes are committed by affirmative action, some consist of failure to act where there is a legal duty to act. "If there is a duty to act, failure to perform that duty is, for the purpose of jurisdiction, tantamount to an act."[31] Thus the state wherein the act is legally required to be performed has jurisdiction over a crime based on nonaction.[32] This means, for example, that the crime of non-support of the family is committed where the duty to support should be discharged— where the family lives.[33] But a state may

25. International Harvester Co. v. Commonwealth, 124 Ky. 543, 99 S.W. 637 (1907); State v. Faunce, 91 N.J.L. 333, 102 A. 147 (1917); State v. Hicks, 233 N.C. 511, 64 S.E.2d 871 (1951); cf. Hyde v. United States, 225 U.S. 347, 32 S.Ct. 793, 56 L.Ed. 1114 (1912). This view is sometimes expressed in a statute; see, e.g., provision discussed in Carter v. State, 418 A.2d 989 (Del.1980). As explained in Model Penal Code § 1.03. "Since conspiracy normally involves a less immediate threat than attempt and the conspiracy may be formed far from the place of the intended consummation of the crime, we deem it wise to retain the requirement of an overt act in the state." Model Penal Code § 1.03, Comment (Tent.Draft No. 5, 1956).

26. State v. Pooler, 141 Me. 274, 43 A.2d 353 (1945); State v. LaPlume, 118 R.I. 670, 375 A.2d 938 (1977).

27. State v. Davis, 203 N.C. 13, 164 S.E. 737 (1932).

28. See, e.g., State v. Nelson, 92 Wis.2d 855, 285 N.W.2d 924 (1979). "Undoubtedly one purpose, perhaps the primary purpose, in the grant of concurrent jurisdiction was to avoid any nice question as to whether a criminal act sought to be prosecuted was committed on one side or the other of the exact boundary in the channel, that boundary sometimes changing by reason of the shifting of the channel." Nielsen v. Oregon, 212 U.S. 315, 29 S.Ct. 383, 53 L.Ed. 528 (1909).

29. E.g., Lemore v. Commonwealth, 127 Ky. 480, 105 S.W. 930 (1907); for other cases see Beale, The Jurisdiction of a Sovereign State, 36 Harv.L.Rev. 241, 248 (1923). The principle applies to offenses committed on bridges spanning the boundary river. State v. LeGear, 346 N.W.2d 21 (Iowa 1984); State v. George, 60 Minn. 503, 63 N.W. 100 (1895). It applies also to a temporary sandbar in the river. State v. Rorris, 222 Iowa 1348, 271 N.W. 514 (1937).

30. Nielsen v. Oregon, 212 U.S. 315, 29 S.Ct. 383, 53 L.Ed. 528 (1909) (defendant fished with a purse net on Washington side of Columbia River pursuant to Washington license; Oregon convicted him of crime of fishing with a purse net; *held,* conviction reversed; Oregon has no jurisdiction).

31. Restatement of Conflict of Laws § 70, comment a (1934).

32. Sometimes there is uncertainty as to whether the crime can be characterized as an omission-type offense for this purpose when it is not expressly defined in terms of a failure to do something. Compare State v. Damon, 317 A.2d 459 (Me.1974) (state had jurisdiction over crime of escape while on furlough from state prison, though his departure occurred while he on furlough in another state, as offense is failure to resume physical confinement in Maine); with State v. Cochran, 96 Idaho 862, 538 P.2d 791 (1975) (mother permitted to have her children for holidays; they otherwise in custody of state department of social services; visitation rights expired while she had children in Montana, so no jurisdiction in Idaho over kidnapping).

33. Commonwealth v. Booth, 266 Mass. 80, 165 N.E. 29 (1929); State v. Beam, 181 N.C. 597, 107 S.E. 429 (1921). It would seem that the family could properly move after the abandonment, and the crime is committed in the state to which the family moves. People v. Meyer, 12 Misc. 613, 33 N.Y.S. 1123 (1895) (question of venue). But what if the defendant was never a resident in the state to which the family moves? Compare the crime of begetting an illegitimate child, which is committed where the intercourse took place, not where the child is born. Commonwealth v. Lanoue, 326 Mass. 559, 95 N.E.2d 925 (1950) (Massachusetts has no jurisdiction where intercourse in Rhode Island, though birth in Massachusetts).

have difficulty in some circumstances imposing a legal duty to act on someone outside the state [34] unless that person is a resident of the state [35] or a former resident.[36] It may be imposed on a nonresident over whom the state has jurisdiction of the person [37] or who contracted to do the act within the state.[38] If there is a legal duty to act in one state, and failure to act results in criminal consequences in another state, the latter state may have jurisdiction.[39]

Although a state does not have territorial jurisdiction over crimes committed outside the state, what if one leaves the state for the sole purpose of committing a crime against the laws of that state, as where *A* and *B*, to avoid the duelling or gambling laws of state *X*, go over the border into state *Y* and there duel or gamble? An occasional case has held that state *X* has jurisdiction over the crime thus committed outside its territory—a result deemed necessary to defeat subterfuges by criminals.[40]

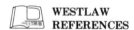 **WESTLAW REFERENCES**

topic(110) /p territor! /6 jurisdiction

(b) Statutory Extensions of Territorial Jurisdiction. Without departing from the territorial principle of jurisdiction—some conduct or result of conduct must still occur within the state—a number of states have by statute enlarged their criminal jurisdiction by

making other local conduct or results (other than the one particular act or omission or result which the common law considered vital for the determination of the situs of the crime) the basis for jurisdiction. If such conduct or its effects happen within the state,[41] that state is given jurisdiction.[42]

Thus some states by statute provide for jurisdiction to punish for conduct done within the state causing or risking a bad result to occur outside the state, even though without a statute the situs of the crime is in the latter state, which alone has jurisdiction over the crime. Many of the modern codes accomplish this with a provision essentially like that in the Model Penal Code, declaring that a state has jurisdiction as to conduct occurring within the state which "establishes complicity in the commission of, or an attempt, solicitation or conspiracy to commit, an offense in another jurisdiction which is an offense under the law of this State." [43] Under such a statute, where *A* in North Carolina shoots across the border killing *B* in Tennessee, North Carolina has jurisdiction to punish *A*.

Another type of statute provides for jurisdiction in the converse situation: conduct performed outside the state causing a bad result to occur in the state. We have already noted the common law view that, where *A* fatally wounds *B* in state *X*, but *B* dies from his wound in state *Y*, state *Y* has no jurisdiction

34. Beattie v. State, 73 Ark. 428, 84 S.W. 477 (1904) held that Arkansas could not impose a legal duty on a Missouri resident to keep his cattle fenced in in Missouri.

Model Penal Code § 1.03(1)(e) defines the limits of a state's power to impose duties on persons outside the state by requiring that the duty relate to "domicile, residence or a relationship to a person, thing or transaction in the State."

35. See Beattie v. State, note 34 supra.

36. This is the usual situation with the crime of abandoning the family. E.g. In re Gornostayoff, 113 Cal.App. 255, 298 P. 55 (1931).

37. State v. Wellman, 102 Kan. 503, 170 P. 1052 (1918) (defendant personally served by wife in Georgia divorce action, subject to Georgia criminal action for non-support, though at all times in North Carolina).

38. State v. Beam, 181 N.C. 597, 107 S.E. 429 (1921).

39. Restatement of Conflict of Laws § 70, comment a (1934). Thus in the *Beattie* case, note 34 supra, if by Missouri law a duty existed to fence in cattle in Missouri,

Arkansas could punish for his failure, causing cattle to run at large in Arkansas, just as a state may have jurisdiction over consequences in the state of affirmative action taken in another state.

40. E.g., Commonwealth v. Crass, 180 Ky. 794, 203 S.W. 708 (1918) (travel from Kentucky to Tennessee to bet on a Kentucky election).

41. A few of the modern codes have followed Model Penal Code § 1.03(5) in expressly stating that for this purpose a state "includes the land and water and airspace above such land and water with respect to which the State has legislative jurisdiction."

42. See George, Extraterritorial Application of Penal Legislation, 64 Mich.L.Rev. 609 (1966); Leflar, Choice of Law in Criminal Cases, 25 Case W.Res.L.Rev. 44 (1974); Rotenberg, Extraterritorial Legislative Jurisdiction and the State Criminal Law, 38 Texas L.Rev. 763 (1960); Note, 1956 Wis.L.Rev. 496.

43. Model Penal Code § 1.03(1).

over the homicide, since the situs of the crime is where the fatal force strikes the victim.[44] A number of states, however, provide by statute for jurisdiction over homicide where the death occurs within the state from mortal wounds inflicted outside the state.[45] Other statutes are worded more broadly, not being limited to homicide; these provide for the jurisdiction of the state over crimes commenced outside the state but consummated in the state.[46]

Many of the modern codes also address specific situations concerning out-of-state conduct, typically following the Model Penal Code format. One type of provision declares that there is jurisdiction over conduct outside the state which constitutes an attempt to commit an offense within the state.[47] Another says that there is jurisdiction over conduct outside the state which constitutes a conspiracy to commit an offense within the state, provided that an overt act in furtherance of the conspiracy occurs within the state.[48] Some statutes specifically address the troublesome failure-to-act situation by asserting jurisdiction whenever the omission amounts to a failure to perform a legal duty imposed by the state "with respect to domicile, residence or a relationship to a person, thing or transaction" in the state.[49]

A third type of statute gives jurisdiction to the state if any part of the crime (not just the one vital part which determines the one situs of the crime) occurs within the state.[50] Under such a statute, California has jurisdiction over a murder by the defendant who in California mails poisoned candy to the victim in Delaware, where the victim eats it and dies.[51] New York has jurisdiction over a defendant who makes false pretenses in New York, as a result of which he obtains property from the victim in Pennsylvania.[52] Some courts have imposed a limitation on the meaning of "part" of a crime within the state: "A crime is not committed * * * partly in this State unless the act within this State is so related to the crime that if nothing more had followed, it would amount to an attempt."[53]

Many of the modern codes contain a general provision of this type,[54] usually in the lan-

---

44. See State v. Carter note 7 supra.

45. Model Penal Code § 1.03(1)(a), (4) provides that it is sufficient that the result occurs within the state and that in homicide cases "result" means either death of or bodily impact upon the victim, and further provides that if the body is found within the state "it is presumed" that such result occurred within the state. Many of the modern codes have adopted this provision.

46. Berge, Criminal Jurisdiction and the Territorial Principle, 30 Mich.L.Rev. 238, 254 (1932).

47. As provided in Model Penal Code § 1.03(1)(b).

48. As provided in Model Penal Code § 1.03(1)(c).

49. As provided in Model Penal Code § 1.03(1)(e). Illustrative of the results under such statutes are State v. Shaw, 96 Idaho 897, 539 P.2d 250 (1975) (state has jurisdiction over Nevada resident for nonsupport of family now living in Idaho); Poole v. State, 60 Wis.2d 152, 208 N.W.2d 328 (1973) (Wisconsin has nonsupport jurisdiction over Arizona resident).

50. Berge, Criminal Jurisdiction and the Territorial Principle, 30 Mich.L.Rev. 238, 255 (1932); Note, 23 Va.L. Rev. 692 (1937); 39 Harv.L.Rev. 492 (1926). See, e.g., Lane v. State, 388 So.2d 1022 (Fla.1980) (such a statute applied to find jurisdiction in state for felony murder where felony commenced in the state but the fatal blow and death occurred elsewhere). On jurisdiction over interstate felony murder, see Comment, 50 U.Chi.L.Rev. 1431 (1984). See also Smith v. State, ___ Nev. ___, 697 P.2d 113 (1985) (where victim kidnapped in Nevada with intent of sexually assaulting and killing her, but assault and attempted murder occurred in another state, Nevada had jurisdiction over those crimes). Under such a statute there is an implied requirement that the defendant's conduct could have been a crime if committed wholly within the state. People v. Zayas, 217 N.Y. 78, 111 N.E. 465 (1916). There is no need for it to have been a crime under the law of the foreign state. Compare the Model Penal Code approach, discussed in the text following.

51. People v. Botkin, 132 Cal. 231, 64 P. 286 (1901).

52. People v. Zayas, 217 N.Y. 78, 111 N.E. 465 (1916); State v. Sheehan, 33 Idaho 553, 196 P. 532 (1921). Without such a statute only Pennsylvania has jurisdiction. See note 9 supra.

53. People v. Werblow, 241 N.Y. 55, 148 N.E. 786 (1925); People v. Buffum, 40 Cal.2d 709, 256 P.2d 317 (1953); Vincze v. Sheriff, 86 Nev. 474, 470 P.2d 427 (1970). In the *Werblow* case defendant and his confederates in New York laid plans to obtain money by false pretenses from a bank in London. The false pretenses were made and the money was obtained outside New York. It was held that, as the planning in New York did not amount to an attempt to obtain money by false pretenses, the crime of false pretenses was not committed in part in New York, which therefore had no jurisdiction under the statute.

54. Illustrative of the application of such statutes is Bright v. State, 490 A.2d 564 (Del.1985) (victim kidnapped in Delaware and thereafter raped several times along road by Del.-Md. border; *held*, Delaware has jurisdiction even if rapes in Maryland, as lack-of-consent element of the crimes began in Delaware).

guage of the Model Penal Code, whereunder it is generally sufficient if "either the conduct which is an element of the offense or the result which is such an element occurs within" the state.[55] The Model Penal Code adds two important qualifications to this general rule which, however, are seldom explicitly stated in the modern criminal codes. One is that, except when a contrary legislative intent plainly appears, there is no jurisdiction if causing or intending a certain result is an element of the crime and the result occurs or was designed or likely to occur only in another jurisdiction where such conduct would not be an offense.[56] Another is that there is no jurisdiction if causing a particular result is an element of the offense and that result would not be a crime in the other state where the conduct occurred, provided the defendant did not intentionally or knowingly cause the result within the state of its occurrence.[57]

Statutes articulating the bases of jurisdiction often eliminate the common law rule, discussed above, that one who outside the state acts as accessory before the fact is not subject to the jurisdiction of the state wherein his guilty agent (the criminal principal) commits the crime. A number of states specifically provide for jurisdiction to punish the accessory.[58] Other states reach the same jurisdictional result as a consequence of a common type of statute providing that an accessory before the fact is punishable as a principal.[59]

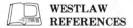

(c) Other Possible Bases of Jurisdiction.

(1) Based on the Protective Principle. While it is clear that a state has the power to legislate so as to give itself criminal jurisdiction over conduct by noncitizens occurring outside the state, which conduct produces harmful results in the state,[60] there is the question of what results qualify. For instance, suppose a Louisiana citizen in Louisiana forges title certificates to Texas land,[61] or a Virginian in Virginia counterfeits North Carolina currency.[62] Or suppose a Californian is murdered by an Oregonian in Oregon. May Texas or North Carolina or California, respectively, by statute give itself jurisdiction? The trouble is that no conduct of the defendant and no definite results of his conduct occurred in the state which wishes to prosecute. Yet should not a state be able to defend itself and perhaps even its citizens from injury intended to result from conduct without the state? There is not much authority on the point. The Texas court held that

---

55. Model Penal Code § 1.03(1)(a).

56. Model Penal Code § 1.03(2). See Hawaii Rev.Stat. § 701–106; Me.Rev.Stat.Ann. tit. 17–A, § 7 (without unless qualification); N.H.Rev.Stat.Ann. 625:4 (without unless qualification); N.J.Stat.Ann. 2C:1–3.

57. Model Penal Code § 1.03(3). Illustrative of the narrower provision, whereunder there is no jurisdiction even if defendant intended the result to occur in the other state, is State v. Luv Pharmacy, 118 N.H. 398, 388 A.2d 190 (1978), where Penthouse, a Delaware corporation doing business in New York, was charged with sale of obscene literature, and the statute said causing a result in the state gives jurisdiction if the result would be criminal where defendant acted, so that it was necessary to show that the literature would also be deemed obscene in New York.

58. Berge, Criminal Jurisdiction and the Territorial Principle, 30 Mich.L.Rev. 238, 258 (1932). See Restatement of Conflict of Laws § 428, comment (b) (1934); State v. Wolkow, 110 Kan. 722, 205 P. 639 (1922) and annotation thereto, 42 A.L.R. 272 (1926).

Model Penal Code § 1.03(1) also takes this view by providing that conduct within the state includes the defendant's "own conduct or the conduct of another for which he is legally accountable," which is the approach taken in many of the modern codes.

Consider State v. Palermo, 224 Kan. 275, 579 P.2d 718 (1978) (Morgan obtained drugs from defendant in Missouri for purpose of resale, Morgan then took the drugs to Kansas and sold them; no jurisdiction in Kansas over defendant, notwithstanding statute declaring there is jurisdiction if person outside the state "counsels, aids, abets, or conspires with another to commit a crime within this state," as that provision not applicable to situation, such as here, where person outside the state "did not intend to commit a crime within the state, and could not reasonably foresee that his act would cause, aid or abet in the commission of a crime within that state").

59. See § 6.6(e).

60. See § 2.9(b).

61. As in Hanks v. State, 13 Tex.App. 289 (1882).

62. As in State v. Knight, 1 N.C. 143 (1799).

Texas had jurisdiction,[63] but other cases have held that there can be no jurisdiction.[64] It may well be that a state, like a nation, has power to protect its governmental interests in its currency, seals and public documents from counterfeiting by non-citizens in other states, so that Texas or North Carolina in the above cases have power to make the conduct criminal.[65] On the other hand, a state, like a nation, probably has no power to protect its own citizens from conduct by non-citizens taking place in other states and resulting in harm there; thus in the above example California has no power to make punishable the murder of a Californian by an Oregonian in Oregon or elsewhere outside of California.[66]

(2) Based on Citizenship. We now depart from the territorial theory of jurisdiction, which gives jurisdiction over conduct by citizens or noncitizens to the sovereign within whose territory the conduct or the result of conduct occurs. We have already seen that a nation may by statute give itself jurisdiction over crimes committed by its nationals abroad.[67] The Supreme Court has held that a similar non-territorial principle of jurisdiction can be exercised by the states.[68] Although on its facts the case is limited to jurisdiction over a state's citizens for conduct on the high seas,[69] the same principle should be applicable to acts done on land outside the state, either abroad or in another state of the United States.[70]

(3) Universal Jurisdiction. One conceivable theory of jurisdiction is that a sovereign has power to punish anyone who commits a crime anywhere, without regard to territoriality, citizenship, or threatened or actual injury to the sovereign or its citizens. A few nations outside the Anglo-American system have claimed such jurisdiction, sometimes termed "universal" or "cosmopolitan" jurisdiction. We have seen that such a theory is given very limited application as to the United States as a sovereign.[71] No American state has purported to exercise any such wide jurisdiction.

63. Hanks v. State, note 61 supra.

64. State v. Knight, note 64 supra; People v. Merrill, 2 Parker Crim. 590 (N.Y.Sup.Ct.1855), rev'd on other grounds, 14 N.Y. 74 (1856). (N.Y. has no jurisdiction over the crime of selling in another state a Negro kidnapped from N.Y. though it could have jurisdiction over the crime of kidnapping in N.Y. with intent to sell as a slave elsewhere). Restatement of Conflict of Laws §§ 425–428 (1934), seems to agree, requiring that some "result" of an act outside the state occur within the state, in order to acquire jurisdiction by statute. It would seem that in the cases cited no "result" occurred within the state, within the meaning of the Restatement.

65. We have already noted that a nation has power to prescribe rules of conduct (with criminal punishment for violations) forbidding counterfeiting, by aliens abroad, of the nation's currency, seals and public documents, as a matter of the "protective principle" of jurisdiction. See § 2.8(b)(2). It would seem that a state should have similar power.

Thus, Model Penal Code § 1.03(1)(f) would allow a state expressly to prohibit conduct outside the state "when the conduct bears a reasonable relation to a legitimate interest of this State and the actor knows or should know that his conduct is likely to affect that interest." Some of the modern codes contain a provision along these lines.

66. Thus we have already noted that a nation may not prescribe rules of conduct governing conduct by aliens abroad simply because the conduct affects nationals of the nation outside the territory of the nation. See § 2.8. It would seem that the same rule is applicable to state jurisdiction.

67. See § 2.8(b)(1).

68. Skiriotes v. Florida, 313 U.S. 69, 61 S.Ct. 924, 85 L.Ed. 1193 (1941). In this case a Florida statute made it a crime to use diving equipment to obtain commercial sponges off the Florida coast. The Supreme Court held that Florida could properly apply this statute to a citizen of Florida outside the territorial limits of Florida, since the state had a legitimate interest in regulating the sponge industry and Congress had not preempted the field of sponge fishing on the high seas.

69. See People v. Weeren, 26 Cal.3d 654, 163 Cal.Rptr. 255, 607 P.2d 1279 (1980) (relying upon *Skiriotes* in holding California had jurisdiction over violation of fishing laws by its citizens more than 3 miles from shore); Livings v. Davis, 465 So.2d 507 (Fla.1985) (relying on *Skiriotes* in holding Florida had jurisdiction over violation of fishing laws by its citizens outside Florida's 9-mile gulf boundary).

70. Restatement of Conflict of Laws § 426 (1948 Supp.), is worded as broadly. In Commonwealth v. Gaines, 2 Va. Cas. (4 Va.) 172 (1819), Virginia exercised jurisdiction over its own citizen to punish larceny committed against another citizen in the District of Columbia. The statute so exercising jurisdiction was later repealed. See Strouther v. Commonwealth, 92 Va. 789, 22 S.E. 852 (1895). In State ex rel. Chandler v. Main, 16 Wis. 398 (1863), dealing with the constitutionality of an absentee ballot statute with criminal penalties for violations, the court said: "But the power of a state over its own citizens stands upon a still stronger ground, and it may * * * pass * * * laws which are binding and obligatory upon them everywhere, and for the violation of which they may be punished whenever the state can find them within its jurisdiction."

71. See § 2.8(b)(3) as to piracy and crimes against uncivilized people.

(d) Problems of Extradition and Double Jeopardy. From the foregoing discussion it is obvious that at times a state has jurisdiction over a crime committed by a person who was not in the state at the time of its commission. Since only that state can prosecute him, and since it can prosecute him only within its own territory, and since he must be present at his trial, the state must obtain his presence. He might voluntarily come to the state; but if he does not, the principal method of getting him there is by extradition. Originally there was a good deal of difficulty in extraditing one who committed his crime while outside the state, because of the United States Constitution's apparent requirement that the defendant "flee from justice"; [72] but modern extradition acts have done away with this requirement.[73]

It is also obvious from the foregoing that each of two states may have jurisdiction over one crime. Where A in North Carolina shoots across the border killing B in Tennessee, for instance, we saw that, while at common law only Tennessee had jurisdiction over the murder, North Carolina could also legislate jurisdiction to itself (without, of course, depriving Tennessee of jurisdiction). The majority view as to larceny, that the crime is committed in the state where the property is first taken but also in the state wherein the property is later taken by the thief, also gives each of two or more states jurisdiction over the crime. A state may by statute probably

take jurisdiction over crimes committed by its citizens in other states; thus where a citizen of Virginia commits a burglary in West Virginia, both states may have jurisdiction. Two states may have concurrent jurisdiction over crimes committed on boundary rivers. What if the defendant is tried and convicted or acquitted on the merits (not acquitted on the ground of lack of jurisdiction) in one of the two states; may the other then try him?

In the case of concurrent jurisdiction over boundary rivers, it has been said that the state "first acquiring jurisdiction of the person may prosecute the offense, and its judgment is a finality in both States, so that one convicted or acquitted in the courts of the one State cannot be prosecuted for the same offense in the courts of the other." [74] In the other situations, however, conviction or acquittal in one state is not a bar to prosecution in the other state. As explained in *Heath v. Alabama*,[75] it follows from the Supreme Court's earlier "dual sovereignty" decisions regarding state and federal prosecutions [76] that each state with concurrent jurisdiction is free to prosecute, for "their powers to undertake criminal prosecutions derive from separate and independent sources of power and authority." The Court declined the invitation "to restrict the applicability of the dual sovereignty principle to cases in which two governmental entities, having concurrent jurisdiction and pursuing quite different interests, can demonstrate that allowing only one entity

---

72. U.S.Const. art IV, § 2. Similarly, the Federal Extradition Act provides for interstate rendition of any "fugitive from justice" charged with "having committed treason, felony or other high crime." 18 U.S.C.A. § 3182.

73. The language of the Constitution and federal statute, supra note 65, has not been interpreted as precluding states from adopting more expensive extradition provisions. See cases collected in Note 38 N.D.L.Rev. 322, 324 (1962). Accordingly, 48 states have adopted the Uniform Criminal Extradition Act, which also provides for rendition of persons who might not technically be "fugitives" from the demanding state (e.g., the person who aided the commission of a crime within the demanding state through activities outside the state). See 11 U.L.A. § 6 (1974).

74. Nielsen v. Oregon, 212 U.S. 315, 29 S.Ct. 383, 53 L.Ed. 528 (1909); State v. Cunningham, 102 Miss. 237, 59 So. 76 (1912). Contra: Phillips v. People, 55 Ill. 429 (1870) (crime of assault with intent to kill committed on boat on

Mississippi River; conviction of that crime in Iowa no bar to prosecution in Illinois).

In the *Heath* case, discussed in the text following, the Court concluded that "*Nielsen* is limited to its unusual facts and has continuing relevance, if at all, only to questions of jurisdiction between two entities deriving their concurrent jurisdiction from a single source of authority."

75. ___ U.S. ___, 106 S.Ct. 433, 88 L.Ed.2d 387 (1985).

76. Under the concept of "dual sovereignty," the Supreme Court has repeatedly held that a prior state prosecution is no bar to a federal prosecution, and vice-versa. United States v. Wheeler, 435 U.S. 313, 98 S.Ct. 1079, 55 L.Ed.2d 303 (1978); Abbate v. United States, 359 U.S. 187, 79 S.Ct. 666, 3 L.Ed.2d 729 (1959); Bartkus v. Illinois, 359 U.S. 121, 79 S.Ct. 676, 3 L.Ed.2d 684 (1959); United States v. Lanza, 260 U.S. 377, 43 S.Ct. 141, 67 L.Ed. 314 (1922).

to exercise jurisdiction over the defendant will interfere with the unvindicated interests of the second entity." [77] Frequently, however, a statutory provision will prohibit a second prosecution in a concurrent jurisdiction situation. [78] Of course, the prosecuting officials may, in their discretion, decide not to prosecute where another state has prosecuted, not because they do not have the power to do so, but because in the particular case it may not be entirely fair to do so.

 WESTLAW REFERENCES

di extradition
110k97(2)

§ 2.10 Constitutional Limitations on the Power to Create Crimes

We have already seen that while the states have broad authority to create crimes, [1] the federal government has no jurisdiction to create crimes (except in federal territory) unless some provision of the United States Constitution expressly or impliedly gives Congress such power. [2] Thus Congress cannot make it a crime for a manufacturer of or dealer in gambling devices to fail to file a record of sales and deliveries of such devices, if the devices he manufactures or sells do not move in interstate commerce. [3] The federal government has succeeded, however, in accomplishing a good deal of regulation of various activities within the states (with criminal penalties for violations) because of the broad interpretation given to such constitutional provisions as the commerce clause, [4] the taxation clause, [5] and the war power clause. [6]

Both the states and the federal government, therefore, may be said to possess considerable authority (the police power [7]) to declare conduct criminal. But there are constitutional limits, other than those mentioned above, on the exercise of this power. As discussed earlier (for purposes of facilitating comparison between those statutes which are vague [8] and those which are merely ambiguous and thus subject to clarification by courts using accepted techniques of interpretation [9]), legislation creating crimes must be fairly definite. Attention has also been previously given (because of its obvious relation to problems concerning the repeal and amendment of

---

77. Two dissenters argued that the federal-state dual sovereignty doctrine "was born of the need to accommodate complementary state and federal concerns within our system of concurrent territorial jurisdictions" and thus "cannot justify successive prosecutions by different States."

78. Model Penal Code § 1.10 provides that in a case of concurrent jurisdiction, a prosecution in the other jurisdiction is a bar to a subsequent prosecution in the state if: (1) the first prosecution resulted in an acquittal or a conviction and the subsequent prosecution is based on the same conduct, unless (a) the former and present offenses each require proof of a fact not required by the other and each is intended to prevent a substantially different harm or evil, or (b) the second offense was not consummated when the former trial began; or (2) the former prosecution was terminated in a way which required a determination inconsistent with a fact which must be established for conviction of the offense for which the defendant is subsequently prosecuted. Similar provisions are to be found in some of the more recent recodifications.

§ 2.10
1. See § 2.9.

2. § 2.8(c).

3. See United States v. Five Gambling Devices, 346 U.S. 441, 74 S.Ct. 190, 98 L.Ed. 179 (1953).

4. E.g., United States v. Darby, 312 U.S. 100, 61 S.Ct. 451, 85 L.Ed. 609 (1941), upholding a federal statute mak-

ing it a crime to ship goods in interstate commerce manufactured by employees who were not paid wages within the limits set by the Fair Labor Standards Act.

5. Much of the federal regulation of intrastate dealings in narcotics, firearms, gambling, etc., has been achieved through this device. Nigro v. United States, 276 U.S. 332, 48 S.Ct. 388, 72 L.Ed. 600 (1928) (narcotics); Sonzinsky v. United States, 300 U.S. 506, 57 S.Ct. 554, 81 L.Ed. 772 (1937) (firearms); United States v. Kahriger, 345 U.S. 22, 73 S.Ct. 510, 97 L.Ed. 754 (1953) (gambling). These cases illustrate that a federal tax statute may be valid even though raising revenue is a relatively minor purpose.

6. E.g., Yakus v. United States, 321 U.S. 414, 64 S.Ct. 660, 88 L.Ed. 834 (1944), upholding a federal statute making it a crime to sell meat at more than ceiling prices set by regulations issued pursuant to the Emergency Price Control Act.

7. The federal courts have sometimes expressed the thought that, within the general range of the express or implied powers granted by the Constitution, Congress exercises a power analogous to the police power exercised by state legislatures. See Annots., 81 L.Ed. 938 (1937), 99 L.Ed. 40 (1955). Constitutional limitations on the police power apply even though Congress admittedly has power over the subject matter under the enumerated powers of the Constitution.

8. See § 2.3.

9. See § 2.2.

legislation [10]) to the ex post facto clause, which requires that penal legislation operate only prospectively.[11] In addition, the equal protection clause requires that the police power, even in areas of legitimate governmental concern, not be exercised by resort to arbitrary statutory classifications.[12] And most important, the police power is also constitutionally limited in the sense that certain activity is beyond regulation by the criminal law. Such a conclusion may be reached via the substantive due process notion that conduct may not be punished unless it bears a substantial relationship to injury to the public,[13] or by a finding that the legislation in question intrudes upon freedom protected by the Bill of Rights (such as freedom of speech).[14] (All of the above limitations flow from provisions of the United States Constitution applicable to both the federal government and the fifty states, although state courts often rely upon similar language in their respective state constitutions.) Finally, in the case of state legislation, the activity may be beyond the reach of the substantive criminal law because the federal government has preempted the area or because prohibition of the activity would impose an undue burden on interstate commerce.[15]

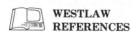
**WESTLAW
REFERENCES**

di police power

(a) Significance of a Successful Constitutional Challenge. In order to understand better the respective roles of legislatures and appellate courts in determining the actual boundaries of the substantive criminal law, it is necessary to appreciate the significance of a successful constitutional challenge on each of the bases mentioned above. In some instances, for example, it is only the means used by the legislature which gives rise to the

constitutional violation; in others the evil lies in the ends sought.

The reversal of a conviction on ex post facto grounds can hardly be viewed as a significant limitation upon the legislature's exercise of its police power, for the objection goes to the retroactive application of the statute rather than its subject matter. Indeed, in most cases such a decision can hardly be viewed as reflecting an instance of legislative overreaching, for it is unlikely that the legislature considered the retroactivity problem. The reversal leaves the statute under which the prosecution was brought intact,[16] available for use prospectively.

By contrast, a successful equal protection challenge to a criminal statute renders the challenged provisions void. Those whose conduct comes within the statute may not be made the object of penal sanctions so long as other conduct, which the legislature may not permissibly distinguish, is exempted. The vice is in the manner in which the legislature has drawn the line between criminal and noncriminal conduct, and depending upon the circumstances the problem may be either that the legislature has gone too far or that it has not gone far enough. A statute proscribing interracial marriages, for example, goes too far; it is void on equal protection grounds,[17] and the legislature can hardly react to the nullification of this statute by a broader enactment prohibiting marriage without regard to race. On the other hand, the voiding of a criminal statute prohibiting interracial cohabitation by members of the opposite sex not married to each other,[18] does not bar the subsequent enactment of a law proscribing all such cohabitation without regard to race. The outer limits of the legislature's power have not been affected, although the manner in which the legislature acted within those limits has been declared arbitrary.

---

10. See § 2.5.

11. See § 2.4.

12. See § 2.11.

13. See § 2.12.

14. See § 2.14.

15. See § 2.15.

16. This would not be so in the unlikely event that a statute proscribed only conduct occurring prior to its enactment.

17. Loving v. Virginia, 388 U.S. 1, 87 S.Ct. 1817, 18 L.Ed.2d 1010 (1967).

18. As in McLaughlin v. Florida, 379 U.S. 184, 85 S.Ct. 283, 13 L.Ed.2d 222 (1964).

That situation bears some resemblance to those cases in which a statute has been declared void for vagueness. Again, the statute in its present form has been rendered void, but the legislature is still free to enact new laws on the same subject. The court has passed only "upon the legitimacy or illegitimacy of means, invalidating a particular regulation with regard to those as to whom it is indefinite and *because* it is indefinite, and reserving judgment as to whether the end sought to be achieved is achievable through more definite regulation."[19] No decision is reached on the constitutional boundaries of the police power; indeed, the uncertainty as to precisely how far the legislature intended to go removes this question from consideration. A void-for-vagueness finding means only that the extent to which the legislature meant to exercise its power is unclear and that the court, in view of this uncertainty, will not attempt to cure the ambiguity because the matter is one appropriately for the legislature. The message to the legislature is "try again."

In sharp contrast are those cases in which the contention accepted by the appellate court is that the legislature has stepped beyond the outer limits of its power to create crimes, as where it is held that the statute proscribes conduct bearing no substantial relationship to injury to the public. If the only end the statute in question sought to accomplish is one which the legislature may not constitutionally accomplish, then the statute has been completely voided.[20] Often, however, the court will rule in such a way that the statute remains in effect but does not thereafter

reach all of the conduct clearly within its terms. Sometimes this is done by merely nullifying a part of the statute, so that some of the conduct proscribed originally is read out of the statute.[21] Or, the court may narrow the reach of the statute by in effect adding something to it, either a new element which must be proved by the prosecution[22] or a new defense which may be raised by the defendant.[23] In any event, the court has dealt with an instance of legislative overreaching, and the clear message to the legislature is "hands off." Certain activity has been insulated from legislative regulation, and the legislature will thereafter be denied access to the protected area absent a stronger showing of need.[24]

It is apparent that it is of some consequence whether the court says "hands off" or "try again." The former is a direct rejection of the legislature's judgment that certain conduct should be within the ambit of the criminal law; the latter only calls for greater care in setting forth what is proscribed. Given the sensitive nature of the relationship between legislatures and courts in developing the substantive criminal law (particularly state legislatures vis-á-vis the United States Supreme Court), courts are often reluctant to erect absolute limits to the police power and thereby foreclose experimentation with some other statutory formulation. This is reflected in the growing hesitancy of courts to circumscribe the police power on substantive due process and equal protection grounds,[25] and in their tendency to resort to a void-for-vagueness rationale instead—even when the statute in question is reasonably specific.[26]

19. Note, 109 U.Pa.L.Rev. 67, 111 (1960).

20. E.g., Talley v. California, 362 U.S. 60, 80 S.Ct. 536, 4 L.Ed.2d 559 (1960).

21. A state court, recognizing that a statute of that state is impermissibly broad, may do so, although in so doing it may render the statute void for vagueness. Winters v. New York, 333 U.S. 507, 68 S.Ct. 665, 92 L.Ed. 840 (1948). It is often unclear whether a state statute continues to have some limited validity after the United States Supreme Court has found it too broad and thus unconstitutional as applied to a particular litigant. See, e.g., NAACP v. Button, 371 U.S. 415, 83 S.Ct. 328, 9 L.Ed.2d 405 (1963).

22. E.g., Lambert v. California, 355 U.S. 225, 78 S.Ct. 240, 2 L.Ed.2d 228 (1957).

23. E.g., Haynes v. United States, 390 U.S. 85, 88 S.Ct. 722, 19 L.Ed.2d 923 (1968).

24. See Note, 109 U.Pa.L.Rev. 67, 109–15 (1960).

25. See §§ 2.11, 2.12.

26. E.g., Stromberg v. California, 283 U.S. 359, 51 S.Ct. 532, 75 L.Ed. 1117 (1931), where defendant was convicted for displaying a red flag as a symbol of opposition to organized government. The Court found the statute vague instead of ruling that such symbolic acts could not be reached by the criminal law.

WESTLAW REFERENCES

di void for vagueness
topic(92) /p "police power" /p limit!

(b) Procedures for Raising Constitutional Objections. Although primarily a matter of procedure, brief note should be taken here of the various ways in which the aforementioned constitutional objections might be raised by one who is being threatened with prosecution, one who is being prosecuted, or one who has been convicted. Even before one has engaged in the conduct proscribed by the statute in question, it may be possible to go to court for an injunction restraining prosecution under an unconstitutional statute or for a declaratory judgment that the statute is unconstitutional.[27] If he has already been charged with violating the statute, he may seek a writ of prohibition restraining the court from proceeding with the prosecution.[28] Or, when prosecuted for violating the terms of the statute, he may demur to or move to quash the indictment or information on the ground of the unconstitutionality of the statute on which the charge is based.[29] After a verdict of guilty, he may raise the issue by a motion in arrest of judgment.[30]

A question of some difficulty is whether the defendant, not having raised the question of unconstitutionality of the statute at the trial by one of the above devices, may raise the issue for the first time on appellate review.[31] The courts are not in agreement as to the answer.[32] A person who has been convicted and is serving his sentence under an unconstitutional statute may, by the weight of authority, obtain his release by habeas corpus,[33] but there are some decisions to the contrary.[34]

It should also be noted here that a person who wishes to challenge the constitutionality of a state criminal statute may be able to seek relief in the federal courts. One who is

---

27. Courts have been quite reluctant to enjoin criminal proceedings. Injunctive relief is most unlikely where there does not even exist a threat of prosecution. Bunker Hill Distributing, Inc. v. District Attorney, 376 Mass. 142, 379 N.E.2d 1095 (1978). If a criminal prosecution is pending, relief will often be denied on the theory that there exists the adequate legal remedy of interposing a defense in the criminal prosecution. Quinely v. City of Prichard, 292 Ala. 178, 291 So.2d 295 (1974). In some jurisdictions, at least, this general disinclination to interfere with a criminal prosecution is less intense when the effort is to restrain enforcement of an allegedly unconstitutional statute. See P.B.I.C., Inc. v. District Attorney, 357 Mass. 770, 258 N.E.2d 82 (1970).

There are some situations where injunctions will be granted. The clearest case for injunctive relief is where prosecution is threatened (or even begun) under a criminal statute or ordinance or administrative regulation already held unconstitutional by the court of last resort. Alexander v. Elkins, 132 Tenn. 663, 179 S.W. 310 (1915). Where the statute or ordinance or regulation is alleged (but not yet held) to be unconstitutional, some courts permit resort to injunctive relief if property rights are irreparably threatened, e.g., Bueneman v. Santa Barbara, 8 Cal.2d 405, 65 P.2d 884 (1937); and some if personal rights are threatened, as where the threat involves a multiplicity of criminal prosecutions, e.g., Kenyon v. City of Chicopee, 320 Mass. 528, 70 N.E.2d 241 (1946); while some have refused injunctive relief even under those conditions, e.g., Buffalo Gravel Corp. v. Moore, 201 App.Div. 242, 194 N.Y.S. 225, affirmed 234 N.Y. 542, 138 N.E. 439 (1922), criticized in Fleishmann, Injunctions Restraining Prosecutions Under Unconstitutional Statutes, 9 A.B.A.J. 169 (1923).

On resort to a declaratory judgment action to question the constitutionality of a criminal statute or ordinance,

see E. Borchard, Declaratory Judgments 552–60 (1934); S. Eager, The Declaratory Judgment Action ch. 4 (1971).

28. Alves v. Justice Court, 148 Cal.App.2d 419, 306 P.2d 601 (1957).

29. Some states use the demurrer to raise the question whether the charge states a criminal offense; others the motion to quash. A modern tendency is to abolish sundry pleas in abatement and in bar and motions to quash and to substitute a motion to dismiss the charge.

30. A motion for new trial would not be appropriate.

31. In general an appellate court does not pass on issues not raised at the trial, but this is not an absolute rule.

32. See Note, 33 Colum.L.Rev. 692, 695–99 (1933); and compare Valentine v. United States, 394 A.2d 1374 (D.C. App.1978); Davis v. State, 383 So.2d 620 (Fla.1980); State v. Jones, 289 N.W.2d 597 (Iowa 1980); State v. Ervin, 223 Kan. 201, 573 P.2d 600 (1977) (all holding no); with Crutchfield v. State, 627 P.2d 196 (Alaska 1980); Simmons v. State, 246 Ga. 390, 271 S.E.2d 468 (1980); People v. Lynch, 410 Mich. 343, 301 N.W.2d 796 (1981) (all holding yes on a "plain error" or similar theory).

33. Simmons v. State, 246 Ga. 390, 271 S.E.2d 468 (1980); Nelson v. Tullos, 323 So.2d 539 (Miss.1975); State ex rel. Skinkis v. Treffert, 90 Wis.2d 528, 280 N.W.2d 316 (1979). The theory of the majority view is that the court which convicted the defendant under a void statute lacked jurisdiction, so that habeas corpus lies.

34. Medley v. Warden, 214 Md. 625, 135 A.2d 422 (1957); Frisco v. Alvis, 136 N.E.2d 688 (Ohio App.1955). The theory of the minority view is that the court which convicted the defendant had jurisdiction to determine the constitutional question, and its judgment therefore cannot be attacked on habeas corpus.

threatened with state prosecution under a statute alleged to be unconstitutonal might seek federal declaratory and injunctive relief; federal abstention is the general rule here.[35] A person in state custody awaiting trial under a law claimed to violate the Constitution might also seek relief via federal habeas corpus.[36] Federal habeas corpus, however, is more likely to be a source of relief following conviction, although there are procedural hurdles to be surmounted here as well.[37]

WESTLAW REFERENCES

di prohibition
di arrest of judgement
di habeas corpus
di abstention doctrine
synopsis,digest(younger pullman /p abstain***
    abstention /p stay enjoin*** injuncti** /p
    crim**** penal)

---

§ 2.11 Constitutional Limitations— Equal Protection

The legislatures, both federal and state, in statutes dealing with civil or criminal liability often make classifications with respect to the persons covered by the statutes or the subject matter encompassed thereby. In the criminal field legislation has not infrequently singled out special groups or special types of subject matter for special treatment. Such statutes are sometimes challenged (rarely successfully)

on the ground that they violate the equal protection clause in the United States Constitution or a comparable provision in a state constitution.

WESTLAW REFERENCES

di equal protection clause

(a) Kinds of Classifications. This singling out in penal statutes is accomplished in one of three ways: (1) a statute may define as criminal certain conduct when it is engaged in by certain persons or under certain limited circumstances; (2) a statute may define certain conduct as criminal and then go on to exempt from the statute certain persons or special situations; or (3) a statute (or a number of related statutes) may make distinctions, for purposes of setting the punishment which may be imposed, depending upon the persons engaging in or the circumstances surrounding certain conduct.

Illustrative of the first category are the "joyriding" statutes to be found in a number of states. The ordinary larceny statute requires an intent to deprive the owner permanently of the property, so that taking for temporary use is not larceny, yet the "joyriding" statute covers taking for temporary use when the property taken is an automobile. Similarly, while the typical embezzlement statute requires a fraudulent conversion of

---

35. In Younger v. Harris, 401 U.S. 37, 91 S.Ct. 746, 27 L.Ed.2d 669 (1971), the Court stressed the concept of "Our Federalism," which represents "a system in which there is sensitivity to the legitimate interests of both State and National Government, and in which the National Government, anxious though it may be to vindicate and protect federal rights and federal interests, always endeavors to do so in ways that will not unduly interfere with the legitimate activities of the States." Thus, concluded the Court, "a federal court should not enjoin a state criminal prosecution begun prior to the institution of the federal suit except in very unusual situations, where necessary to prevent immediate irreparable injury," that is, only on a "showing of bad faith, harassment, or any other unusual circumstance that would call for equitable relief." Though there are in theory some narrow exceptions to the *Younger* bar, as a practical matter "the universe of bad-faith harassment claims that can be established is virtually empty." Fiss, Dombrowski, 86 Yale L.J. 1106, 1115 (1977).

Federal relief by way of a declaratory judgment is also barred when the state prosecution is pending, Samuels v.

Mackell, 401 U.S. 66, 91 S.Ct. 764, 27 L.Ed.2d 688 (1971), but not otherwise when "a federal plaintiff demonstrates a genuine threat of enforcement of a disputed state criminal statute, whether an attack is made on the constitutionality of the statute on its face or as applied." Steffel v. Thompson, 415 U.S. 452, 94 S.Ct. 1209, 39 L.Ed.2d 505 (1974). Two exceptions to *Steffel* are where that plaintiff's interests are "intertwined" with those of others against whom criminal prosecution has been commenced, or where state proceedings are begun after the federal complaint but before any proceedings of substance on the merits have taken place in federal court. Hicks v. Miranda, 422 U.S. 332, 95 S.Ct. 2281, 45 L.Ed.2d 223 (1975).

36. For a thoughtful argument in favor of greater availability of habeas corpus at this point, see Amsterdam, Criminal Prosecutions Affecting Federally Guaranteed Civil Rights: Federal Removal and Habeas Corpus Jurisdiction to Abort State Court Trials, 113 U.Pa.L.Rev. 793 (1965).

37. See R. Sokol, A Handbook of Federal Habeas Corpus (2d ed. 1969); Note, 83 Harv.L.Rev. 1038 (1970).

another's property, some states have singled out public officials for special treatment: such an official may be punished as severely as the embezzler if he converts (not "fraudulently" converts) public funds under his control. The legislature in each case has concluded that a special evil exists requiring special treatment: a determination that a more serious problem is involved in the unauthorized use of automobiles than in similar use of other types of property; or a determination that a more serious danger exists with respect to treasurers of public funds, who are not as closely watched as, for instance, corporate treasurers.

Illustrative of the second category are the common Sunday closing laws. These statutes require commercial establishments to remain closed on Sunday, but typically go on to exempt certain kinds of businesses, stores of a certain size, or sales of specifically enumerated items. For example, the legislature may exempt the sale of food and medicine on the ground that public health requires that these commodities be available every day of the week. The legislature may exempt businesses which employ only one or two employees on the ground that these establishments do not pose the same risk to tranquility as larger retail operations, such as department stores or discount centers. Or, the legislature may permit the sale of recreational items only by stores in designated recreation areas because it is thought that the public need is adequately served thereby.

The third category, which involves distinctions for purposes of punishment rather than distinctions between what is criminal and what is not, may be illustrated by a burglary statute divided into degrees: first-degree burglary is that burglary which occurs during the nighttime; and second-degree burglary, carrying a lesser penalty, is that which occurs in the daytime. Or the distinction may be found in two related statutes dealing with similar conduct but providing different penalties. For example, the taking of property from

another with fraudulent intent may be punished as larceny, but the fraudulent appropriation of property held as a bailee may be made criminal under another statute carrying different penalties. Once again, it would appear that the legislature has determined that there is something more reprehensible in burglary by night than by day, and that the technical concept of "trespass" is important for purposes of determining the seriousness of a taking of someone else's property.

Criminal statutes containing such classifications (particularly those in the first category) are sometimes challenged on the ground that they are over-inclusive, that is, that they cover more conduct than the legislature under its police power may reach. The challenge may be that there is a substantive due process violation because the statute prohibits conduct bearing no substantial relationship to injury to the public,[1] or that the statute is too broad because it infringes upon rights specifically enumerated in the constitution.[2] Although a claim of over-inclusiveness is sometimes cast in equal protection terms, the typical equal protection case is one in which it is alleged that the defect in the statute is its under-inclusiveness.[3] That is, it is acknowledged that the legislature has the power to reach the conduct covered by the statute, but it is claimed that the legislature has acted in an arbitrary fashion by not including or by specifically excluding other conduct which is not distinguishable. In brief, the argument is that since the classification does not include all who are similarly situated with respect to the purpose of the law, there is a violation of the equal protection requirement of reasonable classification.

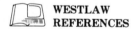 **WESTLAW REFERENCES**

di joyriding

over-inclusive under-inclusive /p "equal protection" /p classif!

1. See § 2.12.

2. See § 2.14.

3. On "over-inclusiveness" and "under-inclusiveness" in equal protection cases, see Tussman & tenBroek, The Equal Protection of the Laws, 37 Calif.L.Rev. 341 (1949).

(b) Equal Protection and the Supreme Court.[4] The United States Constitution provides that no state may deny to any person within its jurisdiction the equal protection of the laws.[5] Although there is no comparable provision applicable to the federal government,[6] the Supreme Court has taken the view that the federal government is under some equal protection kind of restraint by virtue of the due process clause.[7] These constitutional provisions bar arbitrary enforcement of laws which are fair on their face,[8] and also require that Congress and the state legislatures refrain from arbitrary classifications in legislation.[9] Only the latter limitation is considered here.[10]

Generally, it may be said that the United States Supreme Court has been quite permissive in allowing state legislatures to draw whatever classifications they choose in enacting criminal laws. This is most clearly reflected in a series of cases involving criminal statutes in the realm of economic and business regulation, where the Court has followed these propositions in testing the statutes challenged: (1) States have a wide scope of discretion in making statutory classifications, and the classifications violated the equal protection clause only when they are without any reasonable basis.[11] (2) A classification with some reasonable basis does not violate the equal protection clause merely because it is not made with mathematical nicety or because in practice it results in some inequality. (3) When a classification is called into question, if any state of facts reasonably can be

conceived that would sustain it, the existence of such facts at the time the law was enacted must be assumed. (4) One who questions a statutory classification carries the burden of showing that it does not rest upon any reasonable basis. (5) Classifications of an unusual character deserve closer scrutiny.[12]

It is apparent from these propositions why the Court has said that the claim that state legislation violates the equal protection clause is "the usual last resort of constitutional arguments," [13] for the person challenging the statute must ordinarily prove an elusive negative: that no state of facts can be conceived by which the classification can be said to have some reasonable basis. Such facts are readily assumed by the Court even in the absence of any evidence bearing on the reasons behind the legislature's classification. Thus a regulation prohibiting trucks from carrying advertisements, enacted to prevent distractions to drivers and pedestrians, does not violate the equal protection clause because it excepts advertisements of products sold by the owner of the truck; in response to the argument that the distraction would be the same no matter what the subject of the advertisement, the Court said that local authorities might have concluded that those who advertised their own wares do not present the same traffic problem.[14] Similarly, a statute making it unlawful to solicit the sale of eye glasses but exempting those who sell ready-to-wear glasses selected by the customer was upheld; the Court said it would assume that the ready-to-

---

4. See 2 R. Rotunda, J. Nowak, & J. Young, Treatise on Constitutional Law ch. 18 (1986), for a most helpful analysis of the Court's equal protection decisions.

5. U.S. Const. amend. XIV.

6. U.S. Const. amend. V contains a due process clause but no equal protection clause.

7. Bolling v. Sharpe, 347 U.S. 497, 74 S.Ct. 693, 98 L.Ed. 884 (1954).

8. Yick Wo v. Hopkins, 118 U.S. 356, 6 S.Ct. 1064, 30 L.Ed.2d 220 (1886).

9. But these constitutional provisions do not invalidate a statute merely because it could lead to discriminatory enforcement. United States v. Batchelder, 442 U.S. 114, 99 S.Ct. 2198, 60 L.Ed.2d 755 (1979).

10. On the former, see 2 W. LaFave & J. Israel, Criminal Procedure § 13.4 (1984).

11. The legislature need not have employed "the least restrictive or even the most effective or wisest means to achieve its legitimate ends." Jones v. Helms, 452 U.S. 412, 101 S.Ct. 2434, 69 L.Ed.2d 118 (1981). It is for the legislature, not the courts, to decide on the wisdom of the legislation, and thus it will be upheld if the question is "at least debatable." Minnesota v. Clover Leaf Creamery Co., 449 U.S. 456, 101 S.Ct. 715, 66 L.Ed.2d 659 (1981).

12. Although these propositions are reflected in many cases decided by the Court, they are most clearly stated in Morey v. Doud, 354 U.S. 457, 77 S.Ct. 1344, 1 L.Ed.2d 1485 (1957).

13. Buck v. Bell, 274 U.S. 200, 47 S.Ct. 584, 71 L.Ed. 1000 (1927).

14. Railway Express Agency v. New York, 336 U.S. 106, 69 S.Ct. 463, 93 L.Ed. 533 (1949).

wear business might present distinct problems of regulation.[15]

It is also important to note that the Supreme Court has taken account of the practical problems of legislating and of enforcing legislation when judging the classifications found in criminal statutes. As a result, even if it may appear that there is inequality resulting from the classification adopted by the legislature, the classification may be upheld because of these practical considerations. For example, a statute challenged as being over-inclusive for exempting some but not all conduct of the same type may be upheld because a broader exemption might create serious enforcement difficulties. Thus a Sunday closing law which permits amusement park vendors to sell selected items but which does not allow department stores to sell the same items is not objectionable, given the fact that it would be most difficult—from an enforcement standpoint—to ensure that the latter establishments so restrict their operations.[16] A statute challenged as being under-inclusive may be sustained on the ground that legislatures must be permitted to take a "piecemeal" approach and to deal with a general problem a step at a time. "The legislature may select one phase of one field and apply a remedy there, neglecting the others."[17] It has been suggested, however, that such selectivity in dealing with only part of a general problem should not be upheld when it appears that the

exclusion of other conduct from the statute was motivated by political considerations.[18]

Notwithstanding this considerable deference to the line-drawing by state legislatures between criminal and noncriminal or between various degrees of crime, some classifications have received close scrutiny by the United States Supreme Court. It would appear that when the consequences of the classification are more serious, then something more by way of justification is required. And thus while differing degrees of punishment may be permitted for various forms of theft based upon technical common-law distinctions, the legislature may not go so far as to provide for sterilization of those convicted of three felonious larcenies but not of those convicted of three felonious embezzlements.[19] Classifications by name, rather than by generic category, are permissible, but they receive closer attention because they do not afford flexibility in light of changed circumstances. For this reason, the Supreme Court declared unconstitutional a statute making it an offense to sell money orders without a license but excepting the sale of American Express money orders; although the statute was intended to afford protection to the public, and although American Express might be unique because it is a responsible institution operating on a world-wide basis, the classification did not take account of the possibility that at a later date American Express would not

15. Williamson v. Lee Optical, 348 U.S. 483, 75 S.Ct. 461, 99 L.Ed. 563 (1955).

16. McGowan v. Maryland, 366 U.S. 420, 81 S.Ct. 1101, 6 L.Ed.2d 393 (1961).

17. Williamson v. Lee Optical, 348 U.S. 483, 75 S.Ct. 461, 99 L.Ed. 563 (1955).

Thus, in response to the defendant railroad's claim that a statute making it an offense to operate a train without a "full crew" denied equal protection because other modes of transportation were not covered, the Court, in Brotherhood of Loc. Fire & Eng. v. Chicago, R. I. & P. R. Co., 393 U.S. 129, 89 S.Ct. 323, 21 L.Ed.2d 289 (1968), asserted that the legislature was not "required to investigate the various differing hazards encountered in all competing industries and then to enact additional legislation to meet these distinct problems." On similar analysis, the Court in Minnesota v. Clover Leaf Creamery Co., 449 U.S. 456, 101 S.Ct. 715, 66 L.Ed.2d 659 (1981), upheld a statute banning retail sale of milk in plastic but not other nonreturnable, nonrefillable containers.

18. Tussman & tenBroek, supra note 3. Even assuming the correctness of this view, statutes would seldom be struck down on this basis, as evidence of the true reason behind a legislature's classification will seldom be available.

Note, 90 Yale L.J. 1777, 1777–78 (1981), argues that the one-step-at-a-time principle "should be a doctrine of timebound legislature purposes" and that consequently a judicial decision based upon it "should be limited to a specific number of years."

19. Skinner v. Oklahoma ex rel. Williamson, 316 U.S. 535, 62 S.Ct. 1110, 86 L.Ed. 1655 (1942). Chief Justice Stone, concurring, believed the case should be disposed of on due process grounds, as if the legislature's assumption that criminal traits are inheritable is accepted as valid, then equal protection does not require sterilization of all criminals or none. Given the majority opinion's conclusion that marriage and procreation are "basic civil rights of man," the Court could have disposed of this case in a style similar to those discussed in § 2.14.

have these characteristics or that some competing company would have them.[20]

Very close scrutiny is given to any classifications based upon race. Given the historical fact that the central purpose of the Fourteenth Amendment was to eliminate racial discrimination emanating from official sources in the states, racial classifications are "constitutionally suspect"[21] and subject to the "most rigid scrutiny,"[22] particularly when a criminal statute is involved.[23] As a consequence, the Supreme Court has taken a markedly different approach in cases involving criminal statutes with racial classifications. Instead of the usual position that the statute will be found to violate the equal protection clause only if the person challenging it meets his burden of establishing that no state of facts can be conceived by which the classification can be said to have some reasonable basis, the Court instead places the burden of justifying the classification upon the state. That is, the statute is presumed to be unconstitutional rather than to be constitutional, and the state can overcome this presumption only by clearly establishing some overriding statutory purpose by which the classification is *necessary*—not merely rationally related—to the accomplishment of a permissible state policy.[24]

In *McLaughlin v. Florida* [25] the challenged statute provided that: "Any negro man and white woman, or any white man and negro woman, who are not married to each other, who shall habitually live in and occupy in the nighttime the same room shall each be punished by imprisonment not exceeding twelve months, or by fine not exceeding five hundred dollars." Other statutes of general application proscribed adultery and lewd cohabita-

tion, but they required proof of intercourse along with the other elements of the crime. The Supreme Court first rejected the notion in an earlier case [26] that a criminal statute with racial classifications could be justified merely on the ground that it provided for punishment of both the Negro and white participants in the forbidden conduct. A classification is not necessarily reasonable, the Court emphasized, simply because the law is applied equally to all those within the defined class. The state characterized the challenged statute as intended to prevent breaches of the basic concepts of sexual decency, but this characterization could not save the statute, as the state could not show that illicit intercourse was more likely in cases of interracial cohabitation. Similarly, in *Loving v. Virginia* [27] the Supreme Court struck down a comprehensive statutory scheme aimed at prohibiting and punishing interracial marriages. Because the statutes prohibited interracial marriages only when they involved white persons, it was apparent that they were intended to maintain white supremacy, which is not a permissible state policy.

Strict judicial scrutiny is also given to criminal statutes which draw classifications in terms of the ability to exercise some fundamental constitutional right, such as the freedom of speech. Illustrative is *Carey v. Brown*,[28] striking down a statute prohibiting residential picketing but exempting picketing of a place of employment involved in a labor dispute and declaring: "When government regulation discriminates among speech-related activities in a public forum, the Equal Protection Clause mandates that the legislation be finely tailored to serve substantial stated interests, and the justifications offered

---

20. Morey v. Doud, 354 U.S. 457, 77 S.Ct. 1344, 1 L.Ed. 2d 1485 (1957). Two of the three dissenting Justices took the view that the legislature's classification should be allowed to stand until the changed circumstances actually occurred.

21. Bolling v. Sharpe, 347 U.S. 497, 74 S.Ct. 693, 98 L.Ed. 884 (1954).

22. Korematsu v. United States, 323 U.S. 214, 65 S.Ct. 193, 89 L.Ed. 194 (1944).

23. McLaughlin v. Florida, 379 U.S. 184, 85 S.Ct. 283, 13 L.Ed.2d 222 (1964).

24. Ibid. Two members of the Court would go even farther and hold that a *criminal* statute with racial classifications always violates the equal protection clause.

25. 379 U.S. 184, 85 S.Ct. 283, 13 L.Ed.2d 222 (1964).

26. Pace v. Alabama, 106 U.S. 583, 1 S.Ct. 637, 27 L.Ed. 207 (1883).

27. 388 U.S. 1, 87 S.Ct. 1817, 18 L.Ed.2d 1010 (1967).

28. 447 U.S. 455, 100 S.Ct. 2286, 65 L.Ed.2d 263 (1980).

for any distinctions it draws must be carefully scrutinized." The Court in *Carey* stressed that it had not been established that there was a valid reason to permit labor picketing but not public protests on other issues.[29]

Gender-based classifications are not "inherently suspect" and thereby subject to "strict scrutiny" in the way that racial classifications are, but at the same time they are not treated with the deference long accorded economic regulation. Such classifications, then, are tested under a third, intermediate approach. Members of the Supreme Court have had difficulty agreeing upon how to state or apply this intermediate test, but it is sometimes said that such a classification will be upheld if it bears a "fair and substantial relationship" to legitimate state ends. Utilizing that approach, the Court in *Michael M. v. Superior Court*[30] upheld a statutory rape provision which defined the offense as unlawful sexual intercourse with a female under 18. In concluding the test had been met, the Court reasoned (i) that one interest underlying the statute is prevention of illegitimate teenage pregnancies, justifying the legislative conclusion to punish the participant who suffers fewer of the harmful consequences of such a pregnancy, and (ii) that a gender neutral statute would frustrate the state's interest in enforcement because a female would be less likely to report a violation if she was also subject to prosecution.[31]

**WESTLAW
REFERENCES**

92k250 /p "equal protection" /p crim**** penal /p (reasonabl* rational** /s basis foundation related relationship) classif!

synopsis,digest("equal protection" /s classif! /p #burden)

topic(92) /p classif! /s rac*** /p crim**** penal

(c) Equal Protection in the State Courts. State courts, of course, are more frequently called upon to adjudicate claims that some criminal statute contains an arbitrary classification and thus violates the equal protection clause of the Fourteenth Amendment. In addition, it may be claimed that the statute conflicts with an equal protection or similar guarantee in the state constitution, a matter on which the state courts have the last word. And while the cases before the United States Supreme Court have been concerned for the most part with the economic regulations, the state cases also deal with statutes more in the mainstream of the criminal law (e.g., those defining various forms of theft).

Generally, it may be said that state courts have also exercised considerable restraint; they tend to follow the philosophy expressed in the opinions of the United States Supreme Court that the legislature's classification should be sustained if any set of facts can be conceived which would give the classification a reasonable basis. Thus possession of cannabis may be punished in the same fashion as possession of addicting drugs, notwithstanding considerable evidence that it is not addicting, for the legislature may have concluded that it also presents a danger to public safety and welfare.[32] Likewise, the legislature may punish assault with intent to rape as severely as rape, for it may have concluded that one who attempts rape is as much a menace to society as one who succeeds.[33] The legislature may make any theft of livestock a felony, though other theft is graded by the value of the property taken, in order to further "the legitimate purpose of deterring a type of theft easy to commit and difficult to detect."[34] Or, the legislature may properly decide to punish theft by "servants, agents or

29. See also Police Department of the City of Chicago v. Mosley, 408 U.S. 92, 92 S.Ct. 2286, 33 L.Ed.2d 212 (1972) (same result on ordinance prohibiting school picketing having same exemption).

30. 450 U.S. 464, 101 S.Ct. 1200, 67 L.Ed.2d 437 (1981).

31. Even before *Michael M.,* most courts had rejected equal protection challenges to rape and statutory rape laws which protect only women. See Annot., 99 A.L.R.3d 129 (1980). As for prostitution laws extending only to

women, see State v. Devall, 302 So.2d 909 (La.1974) (constitutional, legislature could conclude male prostitution not a social problem of any importance).

32. People v. Stark, 157 Colo. 59, 400 P.2d 923 (1965), and cases cited therein.

33. State v. Cook, 242 Or. 509, 411 P.2d 78 (1966).

34. State v. Clark, 632 P.2d 841 (Utah 1981).

employees" more severely than theft by others.[35]

At least in some states, however, one challenging a statute on equal protection grounds may not have quite as heavy a burden of proving the absence of a rational basis for the classification as he would have before the United States Supreme Court.[36] In part this may be attributable to the fact that the state court is closer to the conditions which prevail in that state, so that it is easier to convince the court that no circumstances justifying the statutory distinction are present.[37] Or, as is also sometimes true when the claim is that the statute violates substantive due process,[38] it may be because some state courts are less willing to allow the state legislature to regulate business activity.[39] Also, some state courts are more willing to use equal protection analysis to strike down statutes which carry a considerable risk of arbitrary enforcement.[40]

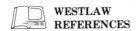 **WESTLAW REFERENCES**

people /3 stark /p "equal protection"
find 400p2d923

§ 2.12 Constitutional Limitations—Substantive Due Process

The United States Constitution forbids both the federal government and the states to de-

prive any person of life, liberty, or property without due process of law.[1] Most state constitutions also contain a due process clause in identical or similar form. Although the term "due process" might appear to refer only to matters of procedure—requiring that certain procedures be followed and prohibiting others—it is also a substantive limitation on the powers of government. This is as true in the realm of criminal law as elsewhere; the constitutional requirement of due process looms large in criminal procedure, and is also important as a limitation on the manner and extent to which conduct may be defined as criminal in the substantive criminal law. We have already seen, for example, that due process requires that the Congress and the state legislatures be reasonably definite in declaring what conduct is criminal.[2]

The concern here is with substantive due process as a constitutional limitation on the boundaries of the police power. That is, the question is: when will a criminal statute (one, it may be presumed, which is not vague, retroactive, or arbitrary in its classification of conduct) be declared unconstitutional because of the nature of the conduct it attempts to prohibit? The most obvious answer, perhaps, is that such a constitutional defect will be found to be present when the conduct in question involves the exercise of freedoms and rights protected by the Bill of Rights. For example,

---

35. People v. Finston, 214 Cal.App.2d 54, 29 Cal.Rptr. 165 (1963).

36. This is especially so if the equal protection clause in the state constitution is deemed more demanding than its federal counterpart. See, e.g., People v. Marcy, 628 P.2d 69 (Colo.1981), where the court said, regarding its application of the state provision: "Equal protection of the laws under the Fourteenth Amendment to the United States Constitution is not necessarily the limit of that responsibility."

37. In Rucker v. State, 342 S.W.2d 325 (Tex.Crim.App. 1961), the court readily accepted the defendant's claim that there was no basis for making the punishment for trespass less when the trespasser was a peddler, salesman, or solicitor.

38. See § 2.12.

39. In Mikell v. Henderson, 63 So.2d 508 (Fla.1953), the court struck down a cruelty to animals statute which contained an exception to poultry shipped on steamboats and other craft. The court was concerned with the fact that the statute would not allow the defendant to continue

his business of raising fighting cocks (unless, of course, he did so aboard a boat).

Some of the state equal protection cases in which statutory classifications have been declared unconstitutional are explainable on the ground that the real defect in the statute was that it intruded on First Amendment freedoms. See Police Comm'r v. Siegel Enterprises, 223 Md. 110, 162 A.2d 727 (1960), and cases cited therein. Compare the cases discussed in § 2.14.

40. Thus, while the Fourteenth Amendment equal protection clause does not bar enactment of statutes covering essentially the same conduct but providing different penalties, United States v. Batchelder, 442 U.S. 114, 99 S.Ct. 2198, 60 L.Ed.2d 755 (1979), some states have ruled otherwise as a matter of state constitutional law. See People v. Marcy, 628 P.2d 69 (Colo.1981), and cases cited therein.

§ 2.12

1. U.S. Const. amends. V (federal) and XIV (the states).

2. See § 2.3.

freedom of expression may not be abridged by making it an offense to distribute handbills which do not contain the names of the printer and distributor.[3] Situations of this kind are discussed in a later section.[4]

By contrast, the discussion which follows concerns those instances in which criminal statutes are invalidated without a finding that they constitute a threat to some freedom or right guaranteed by the Bill of Rights. Sometimes this is done, more likely by a state court, on the basis that the statute prohibits conduct that bears no substantial relationship to injury to the public. Or, although this same factor is likely to be present, a court sometimes will strike down a statute on the more specific ground that it does not contain one of the traditional elements of a criminal offense. The objection may be that the statute contains no *mens rea* requirement, that is, that it punishes conduct innocently engaged in without any sort of bad state of mind, or it may be that the statute punishes mere status or condition instead of requiring some specific act or omission to act.

(a) Legislation Bearing No Substantial Relationship to Injury to the Public.[5] At an earlier time, the United States Supreme Court not infrequently held legislation invalid because the Court concluded that the legislation did not have a substantial relationship to some matter of legitimate public concern. The Court's function in this regard, as it was conceived during that period, is expressed in the following quotation from an early case: "There are, of necessity, limits beyond which

legislation cannot rightfully go. * * * [T]he courts must * * * upon their own responsibility, determine whether in any particular case, these limits have been passed. * * * If, therefore, a statute purporting to have been enacted to protect the public health, the public morals, or the public safety, has no real or substantial relation to those objects, * * * it is the duty of the courts to so adjudge, and thereby give effect to the Constitution."[6] The Court carried out its duty, as thus conceived, by striking down well over a hundred statutes involving economic regulation during the first third of the twentieth century. Many of these statutes carried criminal sanctions for their violation.[7]

The decline in the Court-asserted control over legislative policy began in 1934 with *Nebbia v. New York,*[8] upholding the conviction of a grocer under a statute prohibiting the sale of milk under established prices. The change in attitude is reflected in the Court's statement in *Nebbia* "that the legislature is primarily the judge of the necessity of such an enactment, that every possible presumption is in favor of its validity, and that though the court may hold views inconsistent with the wisdom of the law, it may not be annulled unless palpably in excess of legislative power."[9] Since 1941, the Court has not once struck down economic legislation as violative of substantive due process; even when there has been no clear evidence of the legislature's purpose, the Court has been willing to reason that the legislature might have reached certain conclusions that would have

3. Talley v. California, 362 U.S. 60, 80 S.Ct. 536, 4 L.Ed.2d 559 (1960).

4. See § 2.14.

5. For a more detailed assessment of substantive due process in the Supreme Court, consult 2 R. Rotunda, J. Nowak, & J. Young, Treatise on Constitutional Law ch. 15 (1986).

6. Mugler v. Kansas, 123 U.S. 623, 8 S.Ct. 273, 31 L.Ed. 205 (1887).

7. E.g., Allgeyer v. Louisiana, 165 U.S. 578, 17 S.Ct. 427, 41 L.Ed. 832 (1897) (state criminal statute punishing taking out insurance on property within state in an out-of-state insurance company; *held,* unconstitutional as a violation of 14th Amendment due process guaranteeing right to make contracts); Lochner v. New York, 198 U.S. 45, 25 S.Ct. 539, 49 L.Ed. 937 (1905) (state criminal statute pun-

ishing employer permitting employee to work more than 60 hours a week; *held,* unconstitutional on same grounds); Coppage v. Kansas, 236 U.S. 1, 35 S.Ct. 240, 59 L.Ed. 441 (1915) (state criminal statute punishing employer who makes "yellow-dog contract" with employee; *held,* unconstitutional on same grounds); Adkins v. Children's Hospital, 261 U.S. 525, 43 S.Ct. 394, 67 L.Ed. 785 (1923) (federal criminal statute punishing District of Columbia employers who pay less than minimum wages to women employees; *held,* injunction restraining enforcement granted, as statute unconstitutional under Fifth Amendment due process guaranteeing freedom of contract).

8. 291 U.S. 502, 54 S.Ct. 505, 78 L.Ed. 940 (1934).

9. Nebbia v. New York, 291 U.S. 502, 54 S.Ct. 505, 78 L.Ed. 940 (1934).

justified enactment of the challenged criminal statute.[10] This same restraint has usually [11] been reflected in cases involving criminal statutes dealing with other than economic regulation.[12]

This is not to say, of course, that the Supreme Court has withdrawn completely from its role of passing on the constitutionality of criminal statutes. Rather, the point is that the Court is now most reluctant to strike down statutes on a ground which, in effect, necessitates passing judgment on "the wisdom, need and propriety of laws that touch economic problems, business affairs or social conditions." [13] Thus, even when a criminal statute is challenged on this basis, the Court is more likely to decide the case on void-for-vagueness [14] or equal protection grounds,[15] which usually affords the legislature some opportunity to proscribe the conduct once again on a somewhat different basis. Or, the Court may prefer to find that the challenged statute infringes upon some guarantee in the Bill of Rights,[16] even when this requires recognition of "penumbral rights" not specifically enumerated in the first ten amendments.[17] These decisions undoubtedly reflect the attitude that the Court is on more solid ground in

finding that a criminal statute conflicts with the Bill of Rights than in finding that it bears no substantial relation to the public welfare.[18] And here as well, the Court's decision is less likely to be as restrictive in terms of the continuing power of the legislature to declare certain conduct criminal. A "pure" substantive due process decision, finding that a particular criminal prohibition is not related to an injury to the public, insulates the prohibited conduct from future legislative restriction unless and until new events occur or new facts are found showing that such a prohibition does serve the public welfare. By contrast, a finding that a statute violates due process on the more specific ground that it intrudes upon the protections of the Bill of Rights, often leaves the legislature with some freedom to again prohibit the conduct, either by reaching new incidents of it or the same incidents plus others.[19]

WESTLAW REFERENCES

legislat*** /p nebbia

(b) No Substantial Relation to Injury to the Public: The State Courts. While the United States Supreme Court has all but

---

10. E.g., Ferguson v. Skrupa, 372 U.S. 726, 83 S.Ct. 1028, 10 L.Ed.2d 93 (1963); Railway Express Agency v. New York, 336 U.S. 106, 69 S.Ct. 463, 93 L.Ed. 533 (1949). For a historical review of the swing of the pendulum away from emphasis on property rights and toward a more social interpretation of due process, see Jacobson, Federalism and Property Rights, 15 N.Y.U.L.Rev. 319 (1938).

11. But see Moore v. City of East Cleveland, 431 U.S. 494, 97 S.Ct. 1932, 52 L.Ed.2d 531 (1977) (ordinance under which defendant convicted proscribed occupancy of dwelling unit except by single family, defined to include sibling grandchildren but not nonsibling grandchildren, with whom defendant resided; ordinance violates due process; plurality reasons that when government intrudes into family living arrangements the usual deference to the legislature is inappropriate, and court must examine more carefully the importance of the government interests and the extent to which they are served by the regulation).

12. In Griswold v. Connecticut, 381 U.S. 479, 85 S.Ct. 1678, 14 L.Ed. 510 (1965), involving a statute making it a crime to use contraceptives, the Court expressly rejected the argument that Lochner v. New York, supra note 7, should serve as a guide, and instead invalidated the statute by finding that it invaded the penumbral right of privacy. See § 2.14(d). Similarly, in Whalen v. Roe, 429 U.S. 589, 97 S.Ct. 869, 51 L.Ed.2d 64 (1977), the Court noted that there was a time when under Lochner the instant statute, requiring disclosure to the state of the

identification of persons obtaining certain types of drugs by prescription, would have been invalidated because of the state's failure to establish a necessity for it, but that this was no longer so because the "holding in Lochner has been implicitly rejected many times."

13. Griswold v. Connecticut, 381 U.S. 479, 85 S.Ct. 1678, 14 L.Ed.2d 510 (1965).

14. Stromberg v. California, 283 U.S. 359, 51 S.Ct. 532, 75 L.Ed. 1117 (1931).

15. Skinner v. Oklahoma ex rel. Williamson, 316 U.S. 535, 62 S.Ct. 1110, 86 L.Ed. 1655 (1942).

16. See § 2.14.

17. As in Griswold v. Connecticut, supra note 13.

18. But some have argued in favor of the Court reaching the latter issue. See Hindes, Morality Enforcement Through the Criminal Law and the Modern Doctrine of Substantive Due Process, 126 U.Pa.L.Rev. 344 (1977); Packer, The Aims of the Criminal Law Revisited: A Plea for a New Look at "Substantive Due Process," 44 So.Cal.L. Rev. 490 (1971).

19. For example, in Smith v. California, 361 U.S. 147, 80 S.Ct. 215, 4 L.Ed.2d 205 (1959), where the Court voided a strict liability statute dealing with sale of obscene literature, the legislature might respond by adding a scienter requirement.

abandoned the practice of invalidating criminal statutes on the basis that they bear no substantial relation to injury to the public, the same cannot be said for the state courts. This substantive due process basis for invalidating legislation originated in the state courts, and it is perhaps not surprising that it has continued to be used in many states after falling into disuse on the national level.[20] Sometimes the state court decisions purport to be based upon the due process clause of the Fourteenth Amendment, although it is more common for the courts to strike down statutes on the additional or alternate ground that the legislation offends the due process provisions in the state constitution. When the latter rather than the former approach is utilized, the state courts have the last word.[21]

Although the United States Supreme Court has or would find a certain state criminal statute consistent with the Fourteenth Amendment, it does not follow that the highest court of that state will necessarily reach a similar conclusion as to the statute vis-a-vis the state constitution. As one court has said: "What is permissible under the Federal Constitution in matters of State economic regulation is not necessarily permissible under state law. The Constitution of a State may guard more jealously against the exercise of the State's police power."[22] This becomes evident when one compares the state decisions with those of the United States Supreme Court. For example, the Supreme Court has upheld a state criminal statute making debt-adjusting by nonlawyers a crime,[23] but at

least one state court has found a comparable statute unconstitutional.[24] Similarly, while the Supreme Court has held that a state may bar the sale of wholesome foods (e.g., imitation skimmed milk) in order to prevent consumer confusion,[25] some state courts have reached the contrary conclusion.[26]

It is difficult to generalize concerning the concept of substantive due process in the state courts, for the various state decisions cannot be harmonized.[27] In some jurisdictions, the courts in recent years have been as reluctant as the Supreme Court to interfere with legislative policies; in others this is not so, as reflected by the fact that the courts there rely upon early Supreme Court decisions which have since been overruled or rejected.[28] To the extent that it may be said that state courts are more likely to find substantive due process defects in challenged criminal statutes, the following factors are important:

(1) In some jurisdictions, a more limited view is taken of the purposes for which the police power may be exercised. Courts in these states are likely to acknowledge that the legislature may act for the protection of public morals, health, and safety, but may balk at the notion that laws may be enacted for the more general purpose of advancing public welfare. Thus, a criminal statute may be invalidated on the ground that it was passed solely for esthetic reasons,[29] although the trend today is away from this view.[30] Or, the state court may adopt the libertarian philosophy of John Stuart Mill[31] that an individ-

---

20. See Paulsen, The Persistence of Substantive Due Process in the States, 34 Minn.L.Rev. 91, 93 (1950).

21. If a state court holds that a statute of that state violates the federal constitution, the United States Supreme Court may thereafter rule to the contrary, e.g., Olsen v. Nebraska ex rel. Western Reference & Bond Ass'n, 313 U.S. 236, 61 S.Ct. 862, 85 L.Ed. 1305 (1941), but this does not prevent the state court from then finding that the statute is invalid under the state constitution, e.g., Boomer v. Olsen, 143 Neb. 579, 10 N.W.2d 507 (1943).

22. Coffee-Rich, Inc. v. Commissioner of Public Health, 348 Mass. 414, 204 N.E.2d 281 (1965).

23. Ferguson v. Skrupa, 372 U.S. 726, 83 S.Ct. 1028, 10 L.Ed.2d 93 (1963).

24. Commonwealth v. Stone, 191 Pa.Super. 117, 155 A.2d 453 (1959).

25. Hebe Co. v. Shaw, 248 U.S. 297, 39 S.Ct. 125, 63 L.Ed. 255 (1919).

26. Coffee-Rich, Inc. v. Commissioner of Public Health, supra note 22.

27. Hetherington, State Economic Regulation and Substantive Due Process of Law, 53 Nw.U.L.Rev. 226, 241 (1958).

28. Paulsen, supra note 20, at 98–99.

29. State v. Brown, 250 N.C. 54, 108 S.E.2d 74 (1959), and cases cited therein. *Brown* involved a statute making it an offense to have a junkyard within 150 feet of a hard-surfaced highway unless concealed from view.

30. Bachman v. State, 235 Ark. 339, 359 S.W.2d 815 (1962), and cases cited therein.

31. See J. Mill, On Liberty, in Utilitarianism, Liberty and Representative Government 95–96 (Am. ed. 1951).

ual's own welfare, physical or moral, is not sufficient ground in itself to justify the state's interference with the individual's conduct. On this basis, such crimes as becoming intoxicated in private,[32] possession of intoxicants for one's own use,[33] or operating a motorcycle without a safety helmet[34] have sometimes been held to be beyond the state's police power.

(2) State courts, because they are closer to local conditions, are more likely to pass judgment on the legislative conclusion that an evil exists which calls for criminal legislation. Substantive due process cases in the United States Supreme Court for the most part are not based upon a close evaluation of the conditions within the state which might have given rise to the challenged legislation; in the absence of such information the Court is willing to speculate that the legislature might have found facts showing a need for the statute in question.[35] By contrast, the state cases are often based upon a rather extensive consideration of the conditions prevailing in the state, determined by the court through a process of judicial notice or otherwise. One consequence of this, of course, is that state courts often uphold statutes or ordinances by setting forth in some detail the actual conditions which gave rise to and thus justify their en-

actment.[36] By the same token, a state court will sometimes strike down a statute on the basis of a finding that the evil as perceived by the legislature does not exist. For example, one court invalidated a statute making it an offense to sell imitation cream, apparently enacted because of a concern that consumers would confuse it with real cream, because it concluded that the average consumer of that state would not be confused.[37]

(3) State courts, because they are closer to local conditions, are more likely to pass judgment on whether the legislature's response is an effective means of dealing with an acknowledged evil. Sometimes a state court will find that a statute violates due process on the ground that those persons at whom the statute is directed will escape detection while others, engaged in innocent pursuits, are likely to be deterred. For example, one court was confronted with a statute which made it a crime to possess cattle hide from which the ears had been removed or the brand obliterated. The court acknowledged that larceny of cattle was a serious problem in the state, and noted that cattle could be identified only by their brands or earmarks. However, the court struck down the statute because, while it would cover persons engaged in the manufacture of leather goods, it would not likely

On the judicial reaction to Mill's philosophy, see Comment, 37 U.Chi.L.Rev. 605 (1970).

32. Commonwealth v. Campbell, 133 Ky. 50, 117 S.W. 383 (1909); City of Carthage v. Block, 139 Mo.App. 386, 123 S.W. 483 (1909).

33. State v. Williams, 146 N.C. 618, 61 S.E. 61 (1908); State v. Gilman, 33 W.Va. 146, 10 S.E. 283 (1889). Compare Crane v. Campbell, 245 U.S. 304, 38 S.Ct. 98, 62 L.Ed. 304 (1917), upholding such legislation on the ground that it was an appropriate means of insuring that liquor would not become available to others.

34. People v. Fries, 42 Ill.2d 446, 250 N.E.2d 149 (1969); American Motorcycle Ass'n v. Davis, 11 Mich.App. 351, 158 N.W.2d 72 (1968). The great majority of the courts, however, have upheld motorcycle helmet statutes as a valid exercise of the police power. See cases cited in Comment, supra note 31, at 615 n. 46. But in doing so, they have frequently rejected the assumption that these statutes are solely for the benefit of the wearer. See, e.g., People v. Newhouse, 55 Misc.2d 1064, 287 N.Y.S.2d 713 (1968) (injuries might cause cyclist and his dependents to become public charges); State v. Anderson, 3 N.C.App. 124, 164 S.E.2d 48 (1968), aff'd, 275 N.C. 168, 166 S.E.2d 49 (1969) (reducing accidents holds down cost of insurance to

general public); State v. Fetterly, 254 Or. 68, 456 P.2d 996 (1969) (helmet protects wearer from stones propelled by wheels of other vehicles, and thus prevents accidents in which others might be injured).

35. E.g., Railway Express Agency v. New York, 336 U.S. 106, 69 S.Ct. 463, 93 L.Ed. 533 (1949).

36. E.g., State v. Gordon, 143 Conn. 698, 125 A.2d 477 (1956) (city ordinance barred auctions after 6 p.m.; court refers to problems of safety, health and morality which existed in that community when such auctions were held); State v. Grant, 107 N.H. 1, 216 A.2d 790 (1966) (ordinance required restaurants to close between midnight and 6 a.m.; court refers to evidence showing that drunks and undesirables were congregating in restaurants at these hours); Gundaker Central Motors v. Gassert, 23 N.J. 71, 127 A.2d 566 (1956) (law made it a crime to sell new or used cars on Sunday; court takes notice of traffic problems and long hours worked by salesmen when auto dealers were open on Sunday).

37. Coffee-Rich, Inc. v. Commissioner of Public Health, supra note 22. See also City of Shreveport v. Curry, 357 So.2d 1078 (La.1978) (ordinance prohibiting frog gigging on particular lake 11 months a year invalid, as it serves no purpose whatsoever).

result in the conviction of persons stealing cattle. A cattle thief, the court concluded, would react to the statute by simply disposing of the hide, which is of relatively minor value as compared to the carcass.[38] This approach is in sharp contrast to that of the United States Supreme Court, which refuses to look into "the adequacy or practicability of the law" challenged.[39]

(4) State courts are more willing to pass upon the wisdom of the legislature's response to an acknowledged evil by taking account of other, less restrictive means by which the public interest might be protected. While the United States Supreme Court has repeatedly said that it will not inquire into the wisdom of the legislature's choice of means for dealing with an evil,[40] state courts have not exercised the same restraint. Not infrequently, a state law is invalidated because the court believes that the legislature could have found an equally effective but less severe method of serving the public interest. For example, it has been held that a statute making it an offense to sell certain wholesome products, such as imitation ice cream, violates due process because the purpose of the law—prevention of consumer confusion and fraud—could be just as well accomplished by legislation requiring clear labelling.[41] Similarly, another court has held invalid a law proscribing the

use of large signs advertising the price of gasoline at service stations; the statute's purpose of preventing misleading advertising, said the court, could be just as well accomplished by regulating the contents rather than the size of such signs.[42]

(5) State courts, because they are closer to local conditions, are more likely to conclude that the true purpose of a statute is to serve a special interest group rather than the public. The United States Supreme Court has refused to speculate concerning the motives of the legislature when it appears that there is some legitimate purpose upon which the statute in question could be based.[43] By comparison, state courts sometimes take the view that "if the dominant purpose of the legislation be to serve private interests under the cloak of the general public good, the resulting legislation is a perversion and abuse of power and therefore unlawful."[44] This is not to say, of course, that the mere fact a statute was sponsored and drafted by a private interest group compels the conclusion that it is unconstitutional.[45] But on the other hand, even in the absence of such evidence—indeed, even in the absence of any discussion of legislative motives—it would appear that state courts sometimes strike down criminal statutes because, by their terms, they appear to be intended to aid some special interest group.[46] Some com-

38. Park v. State, 42 Nev. 386, 178 P. 389 (1919).

39. Nebbia v. New York, 291 U.S. 502, 54 S.Ct. 505, 78 L.Ed. 940 (1934).

40. See, e.g., Ferguson v. Skrupa, supra note 23.

41. State v. A.J. Bayless Markets, Inc., 86 Ariz. 193, 342 P.2d 1088 (1959).

42. State v. Redman Petroleum Corp., 77 Neb. 163, 360 P.2d 842 (1961).

43. For example, in Goesaert v. Cleary, 335 U.S. 464, 69 S.Ct. 198, 93 L.Ed. 163 (1948), the Court refused to speculate that the reason behind a statute prohibiting females from tending bar was "an unchivalrous desire of male bartenders to try to monopolize the calling." Compare McGowan v. Maryland, 366 U.S. 420, 81 S.Ct. 1101, 6 L.Ed.2d 393 (1961), where a Sunday closing law was challenged as respecting an establishment of religion, and the Court inquired into the legislature's purpose.

44. Gundaker Central Motors v. Gassert, 23 N.J. 71, 83, 127 A.2d 566, 573 (1956).

45. Ibid., where a statute barring the sale of automobiles on Sunday had its origin in a bill drafted by the New Jersey State Automotive Trade Association.

46. This consideration would appear to underly those decisions barring the sale of wholesome substitutes for other foods, e.g., State v. A.J. Bayless Markets, Inc., 86 Ariz. 193, 342 P.2d 1088 (1959); Coffee-Rich, Inc. v. Commissioner of Public Health, 348 Mass. 414, 204 N.E.2d 281 (1965); and those prohibiting effective advertisement of lower prices, e.g., State v. Redman Petroleum Corp., 77 Nev. 163, 360 P.2d 842 (1961). The above cases must be distinguished from others in which the improper purpose of the legislature is clearly the basis of decision, as with those decisions finding a violation of a constitutional provision forbidding imprisonment for debt in those criminal statutes intended to help a creditor collect his debt. E.g., Burnam v. Commonwealth, 228 Ky. 410, 15 S.W.2d 256 (1929) (bad check statute punishing obtaining goods by innocently giving check not having sufficient funds, but payment within 10 days after notice of dishonor a defense); State v. Johnson, 163 Miss. 521, 141 So. 338 (1932) (bad check statute with similar provisions). Compare Coleman v. State, 119 Fla. 653, 161 So. 89 (1935) (misdemeanor for tenant to hold over; held, constitutional; dissent on ground statute was merely to aid landlord in civil matter).

mentators have concluded that, given the pressures which are brought to bear on state legislatures, this kind of judicial interference with legislative policies is most appropriate.[47]

(6) Some state courts still subscribe to the view that the police power may not be utilized to absolutely prohibit a "legitimate" business. At one time this was the philosophy of the United States Supreme Court, which held that the due process clause forbids a state to prohibit a business which is "useful" and not "inherently immoral or dangerous to public welfare."[48]   The Supreme Court has long since abandoned that rule,[49] but it is still followed in some of the state due process cases. It has been held, for example, that a statute making it criminal to engage in the business of debt adjusting is unconstitutional; the possibility of fraud by those so engaged, the court held, could not serve as a justification for prohibiting this business.[50]

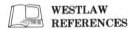

WESTLAW REFERENCES

topic(state +1 court jurisdiction) /p digest("due process")

(c) State Cases: Statutes Covering Harmless Conduct. While much of the preceding discussion has most directly concerned state criminal statutes in the realm of economic regulation, it should not be concluded that the state due process cases are limited to such statutes. Statutes directed at the more traditional problems of the criminal law have also been challenged in many cases. If these decisions are also taken account of, it may be said that the most troublesome recurring problem in the state due process cases is:

When may the legislature, in the interest of crime prevention or effective law enforcement, constitutionally enact legislation which proscribes more conduct than that which actually endangers the public? Although this issue is sometimes confused with that of when the legislature may enact strict liability offenses,[51] we are not here concerned with statutes which punish acts without regard to whether the actor intended or knew he was doing them (e.g., a statute making it an offense to sell liquor to minors without regard to whether the seller knew the buyer was a minor). Rather, the question here is when the legislature may proscribe the knowing or intentional doing of certain acts, even though all who engage in such acts are not bent upon some evil or harmful course.[52]

For example, the legislature might be concerned about street crimes committed by juveniles. Existing laws, of course, adequately cover the commission of these crimes, but they may be thought inadequate; additional legislation may be desired either as a means of preventing these crimes from happening or as a means for prosecuting those who commit but are not apprehended for these crimes. The legislative body may respond by making it an offense for *any* juvenile to be on the street after a certain time of night,[53] or by making it an offense for *any* juvenile to carry a knife or other sharp instrument.[54] Or, the legislature, concerned about the narcotics traffic and the difficulties in apprehending persons while actually in the possession of narcotics, may make it an offense for *any* person to possess certain instruments for taking narcotics (hypodermic needles and syr-

47. "In some states the judiciary is reluctant to sit idly by while minority groups capture the machinery of the state in order to secure a monopoly position. Given the short legislative session in many states and the concentrated attention which pressure groups may devote to that session, one may well sympathize with that point of view." Paulsen, supra note 20, at 117. "Judicial invalidation of such legislation may be technically anti-democratic, but it can hardly be called frustration of the popular will in any meaningful sense." Hetherington, supra note 27, at 249.

48. Adams v. Tanner, 244 U.S. 590, 37 S.Ct. 662, 61 L.Ed. 1336 (1917).

49. The Court took a contrary view starting with Olsen v. Nebraska ex rel. Western Reference & Bond Ass'n, 313

U.S. 236, 61 S.Ct. 862, 85 L.Ed. 1305 (1941), and explicitly rejected *Adams* in Ferguson v. Skrupa, 372 U.S. 726, 83 S.Ct. 1028, 10 L.Ed.2d 93 (1963).

50. Commonwealth v. Stone, 191 Pa.Super. 117, 155 A.2d 453 (1959).

51. Which is discussed in § 2.12(d).

52. Sometimes this is referred to as the absence of "criminal intent," although this term tends to result in confusion of these cases with strict liability cases.

53. Alves v. Justice Court of Chico Judicial District, 148 Cal.App.2d 419, 306 P.2d 601 (1957).

54. People v. Munoz, 9 N.Y.2d 51, 211 N.Y.S.2d 146, 172 N.E.2d 535 (1961).

inges) without a doctor's authorization.[55] Similarly, a legislative body, because of a growing fraudulent practice of returning the covers of unsold magazines for credit and then selling the coverless magazines, may make it a crime for *any* person to sell a magazine without a cover.[56] Each of these statutes is admittedly an effective way of reaching those who have engaged or intend to engage in some other conduct which the legislature may unquestionably prohibit, but they obviously also cover persons engaged in innocent pursuits.

It cannot be said that a criminal statute must always be so narrowly drafted that it only covers those persons pursuing the evil objective which is the source of legislative concern. As one court has put it, "it is within the competency of the lawgiver, in the common interest, to declare an act criminal irrespective of the * * * motive of the doer of the act. The Legislature may make the doing of the prohibited act criminal or penal, regardless of a corrupt or criminal purpose * * *. The criminal mind is not essential where the Legislature has so willed." [57] But the legislative power in this regard is not without limits, as evidenced by the fact that each of the statutes referred to above was declared unconstitutional. Generally, it may be said that the vice of these statutes is that they are too sweeping in encompassing activity which is wholly innocent.

Sometimes these statutes, although not drafted in terms of presumptions (as contrasted to a statute which, for example, says

that a person in possession of stolen property will be presumed to know that it was stolen), are dealt with in a fashion quite similar to that found when statutory presumptions are challenged.[58] That is, the question is said to be whether there is a rational connection between the fact proved and fact presumed thereby. Thus the statute on possession of hypodermic syringes and needles was invalidated because it, in effect, created "a conclusive presumption that the possession is for an illegal purpose—an unrebuttable presumption which factually runs counter to human experience." [59] In other cases, essentially the same conclusion has been reached by noting that a fairly high percentage of those engaging in the proscribed conduct would be unlikely to have any evil purpose in mind.[60] The possession cases serve as the best illustration of this point; it is one thing to bar possession of brass knuckles, which are not likely to be found on innocent persons, and quite another to prohibit any kind of knife or sharp instrument.[61] In addition to this matter of probabilities, however, it is sometimes also important to weigh the social utility of the innocent conduct which comes within the statutory prohibition. Thus, even if a statute prohibiting all loitering on the streets is unconstitutional, it does not follow that the same is true of a statute making it an offense to loiter in a school building, for there is no substantial reason for protecting the right of the general public to do so.[62]

(d) Mental State and Act as Constitutional Requirements. Criminal statutes declaring conduct criminal without regard to

---

55. State v. Birdsell, 235 La. 396, 104 So.2d 148 (1958).

56. People v. Bunis, 9 N.Y.2d 1, 210 N.Y.S.2d 505, 172 N.E.2d 273 (1961). Sometimes it appears that the breadth of the statute is not attributable to a legislative concern with crime prevention or effective law enforcement, but rather is only the result of poor drafting. Such would seem to be the case with the statute invalidated in State v. Spino, 61 Wash.2d 246, 377 P.2d 868 (1963), which defined as second-degree arson any intentional burning of property not covered by the first-degree arson statute.

57. State v. Labato, 7 N.J. 137, 80 A.2d 617 (1951).

58. See § 2.13.

59. State v. Birdsell, 235 La. 396, 104 So.2d 148 (1958).

60. See e.g., Alves v. Justice Court of Chico Judicial District, 148 Cal.App.2d 419, 306 P.2d 601 (1957), invali-

dating a juvenile curfew ordinance, where the court lists all the legitimate reasons for being about at night which were not covered by the few exceptions listed in the statute. As the court said in People v. Bunis, 9 N.Y.2d 1, 210 N.Y.S.2d 505, 172 N.E.2d 273 (1961): "The Legislature may not validly make it a crime to do something which is innocent in itself merely because it is *sometimes* done improperly, *sometimes* attended by improper motives or done as part of an illegal scheme." (Emphasis added.)

61. See the discussion in People v. Munoz, 9 N.Y.2d 51, 211 N.Y.S.2d 146, 172 N.E.2d 535 (1961).

62. People v. Johnson, 6 N.Y.2d 549, 190 N.Y.S.2d 694, 161 N.E.2d 9 (1959), distinguishing People v. Diaz, 4 N.Y.2d 469, 176 N.Y.S.2d 313, 151 N.E.2d 871 (1958).

the evil motives of the actor, discussed above, must be distinguished from strict liability statutes, which make certain acts or omissions criminal without regard to whether the actor intended for the proscribed consequences to occur or knew that they would occur. Illustrative of the latter kind of offense are: (1) a statute which makes it a crime to receive stolen property without regard to whether the receiver knew that the property was stolen;[63] (2) a statute which makes it a crime to convert another person's property to your own use without regard to whether you know that the property in question belonged to another;[64] and (3) a statute which makes it a crime to manufacture tablets or notebooks on which policy-game records are kept without regard to whether the manufacturer intended or knew that the items would be so used.[65] Each of the above statutes was declared unconstitutional as a violation of due process, although none of the three decisions provides much guidance on the question of when, if ever, the imposition of strict liability is constitutionally permissible. It is said, for example, that there exists a basic policy in this country "that a person should not be punished for a crime unless they knew they were committing a crime or intended to commit a crime,"[66] but this statement can hardly be accepted in the face of the great many court decisions upholding strict liability statutes.[67] Sometimes more traditional substantive due process language is used; it may be concluded, for example, that because the statute also covers acts done innocently it does not reasonably relate to the public welfare.[68] This at least suggests that it may be appropriate to consider, as in the evil motive cases, the degree to which persons who are *actually* innocent are likely to come within the reach of the statute. It would also permit the conclusion that there may be instances in which the public welfare is served by imposition of strict liability, as where there is reason to hold those engaged in certain business activity to the highest of standards.[69]

The United States Supreme Court has on one occasion held a strict liability law in violation of due process by a somewhat different analysis. In *Lambert v. California*,[70] the challenged provision was a Los Angeles ordinance which made punishable the failure of any convicted felon to register with the police within five days after entering the city. Defendant was convicted of violating this ordinance; there was proof of her failure to register, but her offer to prove that she was unaware of her duty to register was rejected. The Court reversed, emphasizing the unfairness of the ordinance to one in the defendant's position. Because "circumstances which might move one to inquire as to the necessity of registration are completely lacking," the result is an "absence of an opportunity either to avoid the consequences of the law or to defend any prosecuton brought under it." Three Justices dissented on the ground that the majority had improperly drawn a constitutional line between acts and omissions, with the result that none of the great many strict-liability-failure-to-act statutes could withstand challenge. Although the intended reach of the *Lambert* decision is far from clear, the dissenters' construction is not necessarily correct. Although the reasoning of *Lambert* is most likely to be applicable to omission statutes, there may well be many instances in which it is not unfair to put the burden of inquiry on the defendant.[71] Likewise, an "absence of an opportunity * * *

---

63. People v. Estreich, 272 App.Div. 698, 75 N.Y.S.2d 267 (1947).

64. State v. Prince, 52 N.M. 15, 189 P.2d 993 (1948).

65. State v. Lisbon Sales Book Co., 21 Ohio Op.2d 455, 182 N.E.2d 641 (Com.Pl.1961).

66. Id.

67. See § 3.8.

68. State v. Prince, supra note 64.

69. This reason is often given in justification of strict liability as to, for example, the manufacture and sale of food and drugs. See § 3.8.

70. 355 U.S. 225, 78 S.Ct. 240, 2 L.Ed.2d 228 (1957).

In Powell v. Texas, 392 U.S. 514, 88 S.Ct. 2145 20 L.Ed. 2d 1254 (1968), the opinion of the Court notes, referring to *Lambert*, that the "Court has never articulated a general constitutional doctrine of *mens rea*."

71. As where the failure-to-act provisions are applicable only to those engaged in certain businesses.

to avoid the consequences of the law" might well be found to exist as to some statutes imposing strict liability for certain acts.[72]

While strict liability offenses are not uncommon, legislatures have not often enacted statutes providing for punishment without proof of a voluntary act or omission by the defendant. When they have done so, these statutes have generally been held to be beyond the police power of the state. Thus, the legislature may not constitutionally make it a crime to have a reputation as a habitual criminal, as one who carries concealed weapons, or as one who associates with such persons.[73] And, although possession of something may qualify as an act, the mere unwitting possession of an item cannot be declared criminal.[74] One common expression is that "an unexecuted intent to violate the law amounts to no more than a thought, and is not punishable as a crime,"[75] although this has usually been interpreted as not barring a state from declaring criminal the existence of such unexecuted intent when accompanied by some act.[76] The United States Supreme Court has cast serious doubt upon whether a state may ever criminally punish mere "status" without proof of some irregular behavior in the jurisdiction.[77]

A more detailed consideration of the requirements of a mental state and voluntary act, including the question of what limitations thereon might be appropriate, is to be found in the next chapter.[78]

 WESTLAW REFERENCES

"strict liability" /s "due process"

(e) Taking Clause Objections Distinguished. Sometimes constitutional objections to criminal statutes have instead been grounded in that part of the Fifth Amendment which declares: "nor shall private property be taken for public use, without just compensation."[79] The claim typically is that by making certain conduct criminal which was theretofore innocent, the government has rendered certain property in the defendant's possession virtually useless, thus amounting to an unconstitutional taking of that property.

The response of the Supreme Court has been that "a prohibition simply upon the use of property for purposes that are declared, by valid legislation, to be injurious to the health, morals, or safety of the community, cannot in any sense, be deemed a taking or an appropriation of property for the public benefit."[80]

---

72. E.g., as in State v. Lisbon Sales Book Co., supra note 65. In Smith v. California, 361 U.S. 147, 80 S.Ct. 215, 4 L.Ed.2d 205 (1959), the Court held that the sale of obscene literature could not be made a strict liability offense. There was an opportunity "to avoid the consequences of the law" there, namely, by inspecting every book sold, but it was held that this burden could not be imposed upon the bookseller because it would tend to restrict the distribution of materials protected by the First Amendment.

73. People v. Belcastro, 356 Ill. 144, 190 N.E. 301 (1934): "With mere guilty intention, divorced from an overt act or outward manifestation thereof, the law does not concern itself."

74. State v. Labato, 7 N.J. 137, 80 A.2d 617 (1951).

75. Lambert v. State, 374 P.2d 783 (Okla.Crim.1962).

76. Ibid., upholding a statute making it an offense for a person without a liquor license to possess alcoholic beverages with intent to sell them. Compare the unusual result in Bolin v. State, 266 Ala. 256, 96 So.2d 582 (1957), holding that possession of the ingredients for a stink bomb for the purpose of making a stink bomb may not be made criminal because "the offense is made to stand not upon the result or effect of the act, but upon the intent with which the act is committed." In some of the cases holding

unconstitutional act-plus-unexecuted-intent statutes, the underlying concern may be that the required act is not a significant step toward execution of the intent, so that whether the intent existed is likely to be a matter of speculation. See Proctor v. State, 15 Okla.Cr. 338, 176 P. 771 (1918), holding unconstitutional the statutory crime of owning a building with intent to sell liquor therein.

77. Robinson v. California, 370 U.S. 660, 82 S.Ct. 1417, 8 L.Ed.2d 758 (1962), holding that criminal punishment for narcotic addiction constitutes cruel and unusual punishment. However, the Court did not base its decision solely upon the fact that the statute did not require proof of any antisocial behavior in the state, but also emphasized that the status being punished was an illness which might be contracted innocently or involuntarily. For discussion of *Robinson* and its interpretation in Powell v. Texas, 392 U.S. 514, 88 S.Ct. 2145, 20 L.Ed.2d 1254 (1968), see § 2.14(f).

78. See §§ 3.2–3.10.

79. U.S.Const. amend. V. See 2 R. Rotunda, J. Nowak, & J. Young, Treatise on Constitutional Law §§ 15.10–15.14 (1986); Sax, Takings and the Police Power, 74 Yale L.J. 36 (1964).

80. Mugler v. Kansas, 123 U.S. 623, 8 S.Ct. 273, 31 L.Ed. 205 (1887).

Thus a law prohibiting the manufacture or sale of intoxicating liquors is not an unconstitutional taking of a manufacturer's buildings and machinery [81] or of a stock of liquor manufactured or acquired before the law went into effect.[82]

A modern example is provided by *Andrus v. Allard,* [83] concerning the Eagle Protection Act, which makes it unlawful to "take, possess, sell, purchase, barter, offer to sell, purchase or barter, transport, export or import" bald or golden eagles or any part thereof. Possession or transport but not sale of eagles or parts acquired prior to the effective date of the Act were exempted, and the defendants were convicted of selling previously acquired Indian artifacts partly composed of feathers of such birds. In rejecting their claim that this amounted to an unconstitutional taking, the Court reasoned that "where an owner possesses a full 'bundle' of property rights, the destruction of one 'strand' of the bundle is not a taking, because the aggregate must be viewed in its entirety. * * * In this case, it is crucial that appellees retain the rights to possess and transport their property, and to donate or devise the protected birds."

**WESTLAW
REFERENCES**

andrus /5 allard /s tak***

---

§ 2.13 Constitutional Limitations—Due Process and Statutory Presumptions, Defenses, and Exceptions

As noted in the previous section, criminal statutes are sometimes drafted in broad terms and thus cover persons other than those bent upon some evil purpose, the apparent reason being that the legislature has attempted to relieve the prosecution from the burden of proving some fact which is often difficult to establish. For example, a legislative body, concerned with the fraudulent practice of returning the covers of unsold magazines for credit and then selling the coverless magazines, might make it a crime for any person to sell a magazine without a cover.[1] We have seen that such statutes are often held to violate due process because they encompass much innocent activity. What, then, of a legislative attempt to afford similar assistance to the prosecution by provisions in the substantive criminal law relating to the proof of the crime? For example, given the fact that the statute described above is unconstitutional, would it be permissible for the legislature to redefine the crime as sale of coverless magazines with intent to defraud, and then provide that the mere fact of sale shall be presumptive evidence of intent to defraud? Or, could the legislature make it a crime to sell coverless magazines, and then provide that the defendant might by way of an affirmative defense show the absence of any fraudulent intent? Or, what of a statute which made it an offense to sell a coverless magazine, and then set forth certain exceptions (e.g., where the cover had been destroyed) which the defendant might prove? Although these questions may appear to concern matters of evidence and burden of proof, and thus to be procedural in nature, they also have an important substantive dimension and thus are appropriately dealt with here.[2]

**WESTLAW
REFERENCES**

di presumption

(a) Forms of Presumptions. Courts dealing with case law, and legislatures with statute law, have frequently created presumptions in aid of one side of a legal dispute, both in the civil[3] and criminal fields of law. Given

---

81. Ibid.

82. Everard's Breweries v. Day, 265 U.S. 545, 44 S.Ct. 628, 68 L.Ed. 1174 (1924).

83. 444 U.S. 51, 100 S.Ct. 318, 62 L.Ed.2d 210 (1979).

§ 2.13

1. Held unconstitutional in People v. Bunis, 9 N.Y.2d 1, 210 N.Y.S.2d 505, 172 N.E.2d 273 (1961).

2. For the same reason, they are dealt with in the Model Penal Code. See Model Penal Code § 1.12, Comment at 188 n. 1 (1985).

3. As to judge-made presumptions in civil litigation, there are, for instance, the presumption that a letter properly addressed, stamped and mailed has been delivered to the addressee; the presumption of death from seven years absence; and the negligence presumption that is labeled "res ipsa loquitur."

the long-accepted notion that the prosecution in a criminal case must prove all elements of the charge and that it must prove its case beyond a reasonable doubt, the constitutional validity of these presumptions is most likely to be challenged on the criminal side of the law. Moreover, these challenges are most likely to be directed to presumptions created by the legislature, apparently because legislatures have been less restrictive than courts in creating rebuttable presumptions.[4]

Statutory presumptions are not uncommon in the criminal law. Thus many "bad check" statutes make it a crime to give a check, with intent to defraud, on a bank wherein the drawer has insufficient funds, and further provide that nonpayment of the check shall be prima facie evidence of the intent to defraud. Some statutes provide that it is a crime to receive stolen property knowing it to have been stolen, and that the possession of stolen goods shall create a presumption of such knowledge. Even in the absence of an expressly stated statutory presumption, courts sometimes hold that the legislature impliedly created a statutory presumption; for example, if the legislature has created a crime without using any expression (e.g., "knowingly," "willfully") requiring a bad intent, the statute may be construed as meaning that the doing of the forbidden conduct is prima facie evidence of a bad intent, which the defendant may rebut by showing he had no such intent.[5]

"Presumption" is a slippery word, but at least it means this: "a presumption is a standardized practice, under which certain facts are held to call for uniform treatment with respect to their effect as proof of other facts."[6]

But, precisely what treatment is intended is often not made clear in the statute creating the presumption. For example, what of a statute which makes it an offense for any person who has been convicted of a crime of violence or who is a fugitive from justice to receive a firearm shipped in interstate commerce, and which then provides that possession of a firearm by such a person shall give rise to a presumption that it was shipped in interstate commerce? There are at least four possibilities as to the impact of that statutory presumption:

(1) At a minimum, it must mean that the basic fact (possession) must be allowed to go to the jury as some evidence of the presumed fact (interstate shipment).[7] Such a statutory "presumption," if it can even be called that under such a limited interpretation, does not disadvantage the accused except in the unlikely event that in its absence the basic fact would not have been admissible. Thus, it need not be considered further here.

(2) It is much more likely (particularly if the statute refers to the basic fact as "presumptive evidence" or as establishing a "prima facie case") that the statutory presumption will permit an instruction to the jury that it is authorized to conclude that the presumed fact exists—and thus to convict—if it finds that the basic fact exists.[8] For example, under the statute described above, if the government proved possession and the defendant offered no counter-proof, the jury would be told that it may but need not convict. This kind of presumption, which the Supreme Court now prefers to call a "permissive inference,"[9] tends to operate to the disadvantage of the accused by persuading the jury that it

---

4. The power of courts to create presumptions is generally held to be more limited than the power of legislatures. See, e.g., State v. Scoggin, 236 N.C. 19, 72 S.E.2d 54 (1952).

5. E.g., Bradley v. People, 8 Colo. 599, 9 P. 783 (1885) (statute made it larceny to brand the animal of another; statute formerly read "willfully" brand; defendant claimed he thought he branded his own animal; held, a bad intent is required but presumed from the act of branding, defendant may show good faith); Rex v. Ewart, 25 N.Z.L.R. 709 (1905) (statute punished selling oscene matter; defendant sold newspaper containing obscene matter but claimed he did not know or have reason to

know of it; held, guilty mind still required, but doing the act is prima facie evidence of guilty mind, though defendant may show trier of fact he had no guilty mind).

6. C. McCormick, Evidence § 342 (E. Cleary ed., 3d ed. 1984).

7. For a case viewing a presumption in this way, see United States v. Ross, 92 U.S. 281, 23 L.Ed. 707 (1876).

8. For a case viewing a presumption in this way, see Luria v. United States, 231 U.S. 9, 34 S.Ct. 10, 58 L.Ed. 101 (1913).

9. Ulster County Court v. Allen, 442 U.S. 140, 99 S.Ct. 2213, 60 L.Ed.2d 777 (1979).

may convict solely upon proof of the basic fact, a conclusion the jury might not otherwise reach.

(3) Another possibility is that the presumption will be said to shift the burden of persuasion, so that defendant will now be required to go forward with evidence negativing the presumed fact.[10] Thus, under the statute described above, once the prosecution proved possession it would be incumbent upon the defendant to offer evidence tending to show the absence of interstate shipment, and if he put in no evidence of this nature the jury would be instructed, in effect, to convict. This is what the Supreme Court has characterized as a "mandatory presumption" of the "rebuttable" kind.[11] Because such foreclosure is a harsh penalty, statutory presumptions in the criminal law have seldom been given this interpretation.[12]

(4) Finally, the presumption might be viewed as removing the presumed element from the case upon proof of the facts giving rise to the presumption. Thus, under the statute described above, once the prosecution proved possession the matter of interstate shipment would no longer be a distinct matter for consideration by the factfinder. As such, it may not even seem like a presumption, but rather more like a redefinition of the crime. Yet, the Supreme Court has chosen to characterize this kind of situation as involving a "conclusive" mandatory presumption."[13]

WESTLAW REFERENCES

92k266(7) & crim**** penal /p legislat! congress! /p presum! % presumably

10. For a case viewing a presumption in this way, see Morrison v. California, 291 U.S. 82, 54 S.Ct. 281, 78 L.Ed. 664 (1934).

11. Francis v. Franklin, ___ U.S. ___, 105 S.Ct. 1965, 85 L.Ed.2d 344 (1985).

12. The Reporter for the Model Penal Code proposed the use of foreclosure, Model Penal Code § 1.12, Comment at 204 n. 59 (1985), but this view was not adopted, Model Penal Code § 1.12.

13. Francis v. Franklin, ___ U.S. ___, 105 S.Ct. 1965, 85 L.Ed.2d 344 (1985).

14. 319 U.S. 463, 63 S.Ct. 1241, 87 L.Ed. 1519 (1943).

(b) Permissive Inferences. The law with respect to the constitutionality of presumptions in criminal statutes developed out of a series of cases which, until recently, made no effort to categorize presumptions in the manner set out above. In the first of these cases, *Tot v. United States*,[14] involving the statute utilized in the above hypothetical (which the Court has only recently put into the mandatory presumption category [15]), the Court held:

> Under our decisions, a statutory presumption cannot be sustained if there be no rational connection between the fact proved and the ultimate fact presumed, if the inference of the one from proof of the other is arbitrary because of lack of connection between the two in common experience. This is not to say that a valid presumption may not be created upon a view of relation broader than that a jury might take in a specific case. But where the inference is so strained as not to have a reasonable relation to the circumstances of life as we know them, it is not competent for the legislature to create it as a rule governing the procedure of courts.

The Court later stated in *Leary v. United States*[16] that a statutory presumption is irrational "unless it can at least be said with substantial assurance that the presumed fact is more likely than not to flow from the proved fact on which it is made to depend." But when the Court a year later held the requirement that a defendant be found guilty beyond a reasonable doubt was constitutionally compelled as a matter of due process,[17] the sufficiency of the *Leary* test was put into doubt. In *Leary*, as in other statutory presumption cases before and after, the Court dealt ambiguously with the relevance of the beyond a reasonable doubt standard in this context.[18]

15. Ulster County Court v. Allen, 442 U.S. 140, 99 S.Ct. 2213, 60 L.Ed.2d 777 (1979).

16. 395 U.S. 6, 89 S.Ct. 1532, 23 L.Ed.2d 57 (1969).

17. In re Winship, 397 U.S. 358, 90 S.Ct. 1068, 25 L.Ed. 2d 368 (1970).

18. In United States v. Gainey, 380 U.S. 63, 85 S.Ct. 754, 13 L.Ed.2d 658 (1965), the Court upheld a statute authorizing conviction for carrying on the business of a distiller on the basis of the defendant's unexplained presence at an illegal still, concluding that there was a rational connection between the basic fact and the presumed fact because "strangers to the illegal business rarely penetrate the curtain of secrecy." The Court did not expressly

Then came *Ulster County Court v. Allen,*[19] in which four persons—three adult males and a 16-year-old girl—were jointly tried for illegal possession of two loaded handguns. When the vehicle in which they were riding was stopped for speeding, police saw the handguns positioned crosswise in an open handbag the girl admitted was hers. Pursuant to a presumption set out in the relevant statute, the jury was instructed that "upon proof of the presence of * * * the hand weapons, you may infer and draw a conclusion that such prohibited weapon was possessed by each of the defendants who occupied the automobile at the time when such instruments were found," but that such presumption "is effective only so long as there is no substantial evidence contradicting the conclusion flowing from the presumption." The Court classified this as a "permissive inference," that is, one which did not remove the burden of persuasion from the prosecution and left the jury free to accept or reject the inference,[20] and concluded that consequently

> it affects the application of the "beyond a reasonable doubt" standard only if, under the facts of

the case, there is no rational way the trier could make the connection permitted by the inference. For only in that situation is there any risk that an explanation of the permissible inference to a jury, or its use by a jury, has caused the presumptively rational factfinder to make an erroneous factual determination.

In other words, in testing a permissive inference it is only necessary that, considering *all* the evidence in the *particular* case, there be a rational basis for telling the jury that it may infer one fact from proof of another. Such was the case in *Allen,* the Court next concluded, for the evidence showed that the guns "were too large to be concealed in [the girl's] handbag," and "part of one of the guns was in plain view, within easy access of the driver of the car and even, perhaps, of the other two respondents who were riding in the rear seat."

The trouble with this analysis is that the "Court's heavy emphasis on the evidence adduced at trial appears to * * * transform the analysis of the instructions into a harm-

state this meant presence eliminated even a reasonable doubt of the defendant's involvement in the business, but noted that the statute did not prevent the jury from being properly instructed on the reasonable doubt standard, nor prevent the judge from considering a motion for a directed verdict.

In United States v. Romano, 382 U.S. 136, 86 S.Ct. 279, 15 L.Ed.2d 210 (1965), a statute providing that presence of the defendant at an illegal still is sufficient evidence to authorize conviction for possession of the still was held unconstitutional. *Gainey* was distinguished on the ground that while anyone present at an illegal still "is very probably connected with the illegal enterprise," he might well be involved with "supply, delivery or operational activities having nothing to do with possession." The beyond a reasonable doubt test was not mentioned.

In Leary v. United States, 395 U.S. 6, 89 S.Ct. 1532, 23 L.Ed.2d 57 (1969), a statutory provision authorizing conviction for having marijuana with knowledge it was illegally imported on the basis of unexplained possession was found unconstitutional under the more-likely-than-not test, and thus the Court noted it "need not reach the question whether a criminal presumption which passes muster when so judged must also satisfy the criminal 'reasonable doubt' standard."

Four statutory presumptions were challenged in Turner v. United States, 396 U.S. 398, 90 S.Ct. 642, 24 L.Ed.2d 610 (1970): (1) Because no heroin is produced in this country, the provision allowing conviction for having heroin with knowledge of its illegal importation on the basis of unex-

plained possession was upheld. The Court noted this statute would meet both the more-likely-than-not and the beyond-a-reasonable-doubt tests. (2) The same presumption as to cocaine is unconstitutional under the more-likely-than-not test, as the possessor is not likely to know whether his cocaine was imported or stolen from legal sources in the country. (3) Because all heroin is illegally imported and is almost always obtained by purchase, there "is no reasonable doubt that a possessor of heroin * * * did not purchase the heroin in or from the original stamped package," and thus the statutory presumption to this effect is constitutional. (4) Most significant, the Court then struck down the same presumption as to cocaine. Such a presumption might well have passed muster under the more-likely-than-not test, for the Court earlier noted that thefts of cocaine from legal sources (i.e., in stamped packages) were "considerably less than the total smuggled." The Court found this presumption unconstitutional because there was a "reasonable possibility" the defendant had stolen the cocaine or obtained it in or from a stamped package in possession of the actual thief.

19.   442 U.S. 140, 99 S.Ct. 2213, 60 L.Ed.2d 777 (1979).

20.   This description of the presumption "is certainly suspect," for the jury "might easily have understood the judge as saying that unless there was substantial evidence rebutting the presumption, it remained in effect and authorized conviction." Saltzburg, Burdens of Persuasion in Criminal Cases: Harmonizing the Views of the Justices, 20 Am.Crim.L.Rev. 393, 417 n. 134 (1983).

less error analysis,"[21] as the *Allen* dissenters complained. As one commentator put it: "The Court's look-at-all-the-evidence approach ignores the possibility of the jury's disbelieving all the other evidence and convicting only on the basis of the inference. The jury could have believed that the prosecution had proved the defendants' presence in the car, disbelieved the rest of the evidence, and yet still gone on to convict because of the inference. A harmless error standard that looks heavily to the facts in the record can permit an instruction to be upheld, and a conviction affirmed, primarily on the basis of facts that a jury did not believe beyond a reasonable doubt."[22] It has thus been cogently suggested that a safer form of jury instruction in the so-called permissive inference case, except where the specified proved fact would *alone* support a finding of the presumed fact beyond a reasonable doubt, is one which makes clearer than the instruction in *Allen* the need for the jury to consider the specified proved fact (e.g., presence in the car) with "all surrounding circumstances" [23] in drawing the inference of the presumed fact (e.g., possession of the guns). (Indeed, it may be that the majority in *Allen* was proceeding on the assumption that the instruction in that case was of this char-

acter,[24] in which case the above-stated criticism would not apply).

In a civil case context, the Supreme Court on one occasion tested the validity of a presumption on the notion that "the greater includes the lesser."[25] Under this approach, the presumption is translated into a substantive rule, and then that rule is tested by the due process limitations on the police power of the state. Thus a presumption—whether rational or not—would be permitted if the state could constitutionally enact a criminal statute which required no proof of the fact being established by resort to the statutory presumption.[26] This might suggest that a permissive inference, *even if irrational*, should be upheld if the crime could have been defined by the legislature without including the presumed fact as an element (surely not the case in *Allen*[27]). But such reasoning is unsound, for resort to an inference to prove an element presents a problem of rational jury control which total legislative elimination of the element does not. It is one thing to create an offense of carrying a firearm which does not contain any requirement that the gun be loaded. It is quite another to define the crime as the possession of a loaded gun and then provide that upon proof of some irrelevant fact

21. Allen & DeGrazia, The Constitutional Requirement of Proof Beyond a Reasonable Doubt in Criminal Cases: A Comment Upon Incipient Chaos in the Lower Courts, 20 Am.Crim.L.Rev. 1, 11 (1982).

22. Ibid.

23. Graham, Evidence and Trial Advocacy Workshop: Presumptions—More Than You Ever Wanted to Know and Yet Were Too Disinterested to Ask, 17 Crim.L.Bull. 431, 445 (1981).

24. Thus, Graham, id. at 445, says that the majority in *Allen* was "interpreting the instruction actually given as including the surrounding circumstances within the basic facts." Similarly, Saltzburg, Burdens of Persuasion in Criminal Cases: Harmonizing the Views of the Justices, 20 Am.Crim.L.Rev. 393, 418 (1983), says that in *Allen* the "majority and dissent differ more in their reading of what the trial judge did than in their approach to presumptions and inferences." He goes on to suggest that the entire Court would likely have approved an instruction stating "If you believe that the defendants were in the car and weapons were in open view, you could reason from this that the defendants were jointly in possession of the weapons; but this is not the only way to view the evidence, and the important thing is that you must believe beyond a reasonable doubt that a defendant possessed the weapons before voting to convict the defendant"; and that

all members of the Court would likely condemn an instruction that "If you believe that the defendants were in the car where weapons were found, this is sufficient for you to convict them of possession, unless there is some adequate explanation for the defendants' presence." Id. at 418–19.

25. Ferry v. Ramsey, 277 U.S. 88, 48 S.Ct. 443, 72 L.Ed. 796 (1928).

26. For example, in *Ferry* a statute imposed liability upon bank directors who, knowing of their bank's insolvency, assented to the reception of deposits, and also provided that proof of the bank's insolvency should be prima facie evidence of the directors' knowledge and assent. The Court upheld the presumption on the ground that the legislature could have adopted a statute making the directors personally liable for deposits accepted after insolvency without their knowledge thereof.

27. There, "possession of the gun was the *sine qua non* of the offense. Without proof of possession, due process or the eighth amendment, or both, should preclude punishing a person for mere presence in a car that contains a gun." Allen & DeGrazia, The Constitutional Requirement of Proof Beyond a Reasonable Doubt in Criminal Cases: A Comment Upon Incipient Chaos in the Lower Courts, 20 Am.Crim.L.Rev. 1, 15 (1982).

(e.g., that the sun was shining) the jury may infer the gun was loaded.[28]

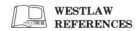

WESTLAW
REFERENCES

ulster /p "permissive inference"
franklin /p "mandatory presumption"

(c) Mandatory Rebuttable Presumptions. Under the Supreme Court's current terminology, a mandatory rebuttable presumption is one that "does not remove the presumed element from the case but nevertheless requires the jury to find the presumed element unless the defendant persuaded the jury that such a finding is unwarranted."[29] In *Allen,* the Court took pains to point out that the statutory presumption at issue there was not of this sort and that, if it were, then a more demanding test would apply: "since the prosecution bears the burden of establishing guilt, it may not rest its case entirely on a presumption unless the fact proved is sufficient to support the inference of guilt beyond a reasonable doubt."

That statutory rebuttable presumptions are subject to *at least* such a constitutional limitation is apparent from two more recent cases involving presumptions not of the statutory variety. In *Sandstrom v. Montana,*[30] where the defendant was convicted of deliberate homicide, the jury was instructed that "the law presumes that a person intends the ordinary consequences of his voluntary acts." Because the jury might have interpreted this instruction as shifting the burden of persuasion to the defendant once his voluntary actions were proved, the Court concluded it was

unconstitutional; it conflicted with the due process principle that "a State must prove every ingredient of an offense beyond a reasonable doubt, and * * * may not shift the burden of proof to the defendant."[31] Similarly, in *Francis v. Franklin,*[32] where in a murder prosecution the jury was instructed that "a person of sound mind and discretion is presumed to intend the natural and probable consequences of his acts, but the presumption may be rebutted," the Court first concluded that a reasonable juror could have understood this to mean that the burden of proof on the element of intent was shifted to defendant once the predicate acts were proved.[33] Because that was so, the Court concluded, "the challenged language undeniably created an unconstitutional burden-shifting presumption with respect to the element of intent."

Just where this leaves statutory mandatory rebuttable presumptions is not entirely clear. *Sandstrom* and *Francis* (again, neither involving presumptions set out by statute) made no inquiry as to whether the presumptions involved there met the beyond a reasonable doubt test alluded to in *Allen.* Perhaps this is only because they obviously did not meet that standard, so that "mandatory presumptions, at least those which operate to place a burden of persuasion on the defendant, will be rigidly scrutinized in accordance with a test which requires that a rational jury could find the presumed fact beyond a reasonable doubt from the basic facts."[34] But another interpretation is that since *Sandstrom* a presumption may never be used to assign a burden of persuasion to the defendant in a crimi-

---

28. It has been suggested that the rational jury control argument merely concerns a matter of judicial convenience and thus is not of constitutional stature. Note, 34 U.Chi.L.Rev. 141, 147 (1966). But if it is a violation of due process to leave jurors free to decide, without any legally fixed standards, what is prohibited and what is not in each particular case, as held in Giaccio v. Pennsylvania, 382 U.S. 399, 86 S.Ct. 518, 15 L.Ed. 447 (1966), then it may be asked why the same is not true when the jurors are instructed that certain facts are probative of other facts but common sense tells them that there is no rational connection.

29. Francis v. Franklin, ___ U.S. ___, 105 S.Ct. 1965, 85 L.Ed.2d 344 (1985).

30. 442 U.S. 510, 99 S.Ct. 2450, 61 L.Ed.2d 39 (1979).

31. Quoting Patterson v. New York, 432 U.S. 197, 97 S.Ct. 2319, 53 L.Ed.2d 281 (1977).

32. ___ U.S. ___, 105 S.Ct. 1965, 85 L.Ed.2d 344 (1985).

33. Though the state court had chosen to call the instruction only a permissive inference, to be tested under the less demanding standard of *Allen,* the Supreme Court rightly concluded the classification depended not upon the label selected by the state "but rather what a reasonable juror could have understood the charge as meaning."

34. C. McCormick, Evidence § 347 (E. Cleary ed., 3d ed. 1984), adding: "In making this assessment, the Court will not consider the other evidence in the case" as it would were only a permissible inference involved.

nal case.[35] This would mean, for example, that even if the beyond a reasonable doubt test were satisfied,[36] it would be impermissible to provide by statute that it is a crime to possess heroin with knowledge of its illegal importation and that, upon proof of possession, the knowledge will be presumed unless the defendant proves otherwise.

Some have voiced still broader concern, which is that not even the beyond a reasonable doubt test is appropriate when the legislature could have achieved essentially the same result by recasting the presumed element as an affirmative defense. Under *Patterson v. New York,*[37] when a crime may constitutionally be defined without a particular factual matter being stated as an element, then that matter may be expressed as an affirmative defense and the burden of proof as to it placed on the defendant. *Sandstrom,* which does not disapprove of *Patterson,* thus

> appears to approve of traditionally constructed affirmative defenses, but to regard as constitutionally impermissible the unorthodox method of creating affirmative defenses through presumptions. This distinction, however, is difficult to support because placing a burden of persuasion on a defendant by a presumption is the functional equivalent of creating an affirmative defense in the conventional manner. * * * To be constitutional, the state need only use the correct words in its statute. If the state makes the mistake of effectively creating an affirmative defense through the use of mandatory presumption language rather than in the manner approved in *Patterson,* then the statute is unacceptable even though there is no functional difference between the two methods.[38]

This seeming inconsistency is understandably of less concern to those who believe that imposition of a burden of proof on the defendant as to a matter can be more serious than (and thus should not be equated with) the total elimination of that matter from the legislative scheme defining and classifying crimes.[39]

 WESTLAW REFERENCES

synopsis,digest(sandstrom /p presumption /p burden /s persuasion proof)

(d) Conclusive Mandatory Presumptions. A conclusive mandatory presumption, the Supreme Court tells us, "removes the presumed element from the case once the State has proven the predicate facts giving rise to the presumption."[40] In another branch of *Sandstrom,* the Court dealt with the jury instruction there in those terms, for a reasonable juror could well have interpreted that instruction "as an irrebuttable direction by the court to find intent once convinced of the facts triggering the presumption." So viewed, the instruction was declared unconstitutional, for such a conclusive presumption "would 'conflict with the overriding presumption of innocence with which the law endows the accused and which extends to every element of the crime,' and would 'invade [the] factfinding function' which in a criminal case the law assigns solely to the jury."

This analysis has not gone unchallenged:

> If the instruction is given in every case of murder, a traditional element of the definition of the crime has been removed. If the instruction accurately describes state law, intent is not included as an element of murder; rather, the state must

35. Allen & DeGrazia, The Constitutional Requirement of Proof Beyond a Reasonable Doubt in Criminal Cases: A Comment Upon Incipient Chaos in the Lower Courts, 20 Am.Crim.L.Rev. 1, 12 (1982); Graham, Evidence and Trial Advocacy Workshop: Presumptions—More Than You Ever Wanted to Know and Yet Were Too Disinterested to Ask, 17 Crim.L.Bull. 431, 439 (1981).

36. As the Court concluded in Turner v. United States, discussed in note 18 supra.

37. 432 U.S. 197, 97 S.Ct. 2319, 53 L.Ed.2d 281 (1977).

38. Allen & DeGrazia, The Constitutional Requirement of Proof Beyond a Reasonable Doubt in Criminal Cases: A Comment Upon Incipient Chaos in the Lower Courts, 20 Am.Crim.L.Rev. 1, 13–14 (1982).

39. Sometimes the expressed concern is that selected, unpopular defendants may be denied the benefits of a defense if they must bear the burden of persuasion. Underwood, The Thumb on the Scales of Justice: Burdens of Persuasion in Criminal Cases, 86 Yale L.J. 1299, 1321–22 (1977). A more direct argument is that imposition of the burden of persuasion on the defendant by a greater-includes-the-lesser approach "must be rejected because it permits the imposition of stigma without requiring the government to prove that there is a difference between greater and lesser offenders." Saltzburg, Burdens of Persuasion in Criminal Cases: Harmonizing the Views of the Justices, 20 Am.Crim.L.Rev. 393, 407 (1983).

40. Francis v. Franklin, ___ U.S. ___, 105 S.Ct. 1965, 85 L.Ed.2d 344 (1985).

show only a voluntary act and its ordinary consequences. Alternatively, the instruction may be
read to define the crime to require either proof
of intent or proof that the defendant's act was
voluntary and that the ordinary consequences of
that act would be death. In either case, the
instruction merely provides an untraditional definition of homicide that foregoes the usual requirement of intent. This involves no burden
shifting at all; the issue has simply been removed as an absolute requirement. Consequently, neither alternative should have been objectionable to the Court on the grounds that the
reasonable doubt requirement was violated.
Montana may very well have defined homicide
in an unusual fashion, but under the Court's
theory *all* it did was define the crime. Without
a constitutional limitation on a state's definition
of crime, Montana's statute should have been
perfectly acceptable.[41]

In a case like *Sandstrom,* of course, one
wonders if the instruction *does* accurately describe state law; surely it does not reflect a
legislatively-made judgment as to what it is
that constitutes the crime of murder. But
this only points up the fact that doubts about
Sandstrom's applicability to legislatively-cre-
ated presumptions are most substantial as to
those statutory provisions which encompass a
conclusive presumption within a particular
crime definition. For example, a statute
might provide that it is bigamy for one to
remarry knowing his spouse is alive, and also
that the fact the spouse is alive shall give rise
to a conclusive presumption that he knew the
spouse was alive.[42] Such a statute really
means that as a matter of substantive law one
who actually has a spouse and who remarries
is guilty of bigamy whether or not he knows
his spouse is alive, and thus the more appropriate constitutional question is whether the

legislature may constitutionally so provide.[43]
Yet, even before *Sandstrom* some cases held
statutory conclusive presumptions unconstitutional as a violation of due process or an
infringement on the rights of the judiciary or
a denial of defendant's right to a jury trial,
even though the statute, if worded in the form
of a rule of substantive law rather than in the
fictional language of a conclusive presumption, would probably have been held constitutional.[44]

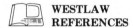 **WESTLAW
REFERENCES**

mandatory /3 presumption /s conclusive

"due process" /p presumption /s conclusive /p
    crim**** penal

(e) Affirmative Defenses. As noted
above, one point of emphasis in the administration of the criminal law has always been
that the prosecution has the burden of coming
forward with evidence and the burden of persuading the fact-finder as to the guilt of the
accused.[45] Yet, this is not a universal rule,
for there are certain excuses or justifications
allowed to the defendant which have traditionally been viewed as affirmative defenses.
Illustrative are insanity, intoxication, self-defense and similar claims of justification for
conduct that would otherwise be criminal,
and excuses such as necessity and duress. In
some jurisdictions, at least as to some of these
defenses, the defendant not only has the burden of first producing evidence but also has
the burden of persuasion.[46] Usually the burden is to establish the defense by a preponderance of the evidence, but the Supreme Court
has held that it is not a violation of due
process for a state to impose upon the defen-

41. Allen & DeGrazia, The Constitutional Requirement
of Proof Beyond a Reasonable Doubt in Criminal Cases: A
Comment Upon Incipient Chaos in the Lower Courts, 20
Am.Crim.L.Rev. 1, 13 (1982).

42. For various examples of conclusive presumptions
in criminal statutes, see Brosman, The Statutory Presumption, 5 Tul.L.Rev. 17, 18–19 (1930).

43. See § 2.12.

44. See Brosman, supra note 42 at 28–41.

45. "Throughout the web of the English Criminal Law
one golden thread is always to be seen, that it is the duty
of the prosecution to prove the prisoner's guilt." Woolm-
ington v. Director of Public Prosecutions [1935] A.C. 462,
481. The Supreme Court has held that the requirement
of proof beyond a reasonable doubt is a matter of due
process. In re Winship, 397 U.S. 358, 90 S.Ct. 1068, 25
L.Ed.2d 368 (1970).

46. See C. McCormick, Evidence § 341 (E. Cleary ed.,
3d ed. 1984).

dant the burden of proving his insanity beyond a reasonable doubt.[47]

The question of whether the previously discussed [48] *Tot* rational connection rule is applicable to affirmative defenses came before the Supreme Court in *Leland v. Oregon,* [49] involving a conviction under an Oregon statute which imposed upon the defendant the burden of proving the defense of insanity beyond a reasonable doubt. The Court distinguished *Tot* on the basis that there a presumption of guilt rested upon "proof of a fact neither criminal in itself nor an element of the crime charged," while in the instant case the prosecutor was required "to prove beyond a reasonable doubt every element of the offense charged." Because the distinction rests upon "the grammatical point that the defense rests on an exception or proviso divorced from the definition of the crime," [50] it is less than persuasive. If taken seriously, it would mean that legislatures would be free to impose substantial burdens of proof on defendants by merely re-defining crimes, taking out critical elements and fashioning them into defenses instead.[51]

A more convincing distinction might start with the observation that one of the reasons underlying the rational connection test for presumptions—rational jury control—does not arise with affirmative defenses, as no suggestion is made to the jury that it might reach a certain conclusion based upon evidence which is not probative. Once this point is reached, the affirmative defense might then be tested by two inquiries: (1) whether the defense is defined in terms of a fact so central to the nature of the offense that, in effect, the prosecution has been freed of the burden to establish that the defendant engaged in conduct with consequences of some gravity; and (2) whether the need for narrowing the issues, coupled with the relative accessibility of evidence to the defendant, justifies calling upon him to put in evidence concerning his defensive claim.[52] It would appear that most of the traditional affirmative defenses could be upheld on this basis, and this approach would also leave legislatures some room for innovation.[53]

It may also be suggested that the argument that "the greater includes the lesser" carries some force as to affirmative defenses, at least as to relatively minor crimes. For example, consider the public welfare offenses,[54] which impose strict liability as to certain activities, such as the sale of food. If it is permissible to convict a person for sale of impure food without a showing of any intent, knowledge, recklessness, or even negligence on his part, then it is difficult to see what objection could be raised to adding to such statutes an affirmative defense of some kind, such as that the defendant may show lack of knowledge of the impurity or due care in the processing of the food.[55]

47. Leland v. Oregon, 343 U.S. 790, 72 S.Ct. 1002, 96 L.Ed. 1302 (1952).

48. See § 2.13(b).

49. 343 U.S. 790, 72 S.Ct. 1002, 96 L.Ed. 1302 (1952).

50. Model Penal Code § 1.12, Comment at 194 (1985).

51. "For example, a state legislature, outraged by some shocking crime, might attempt to re-define rape by abolishing that crime and imposing a similar penalty for 'fornication' defined as extra-marital sexual intercourse, but permitting the accused to escape liability if he could prove consent." Note, 55 Colum.L.Rev. 527, 545 (1955).

52. This is essentially the approach taken by the Model Penal Code draftsmen. Model Penal Code § 1.12, Comment (1985).

53. Compare Barrett v. United States, 322 F.2d 292 (5th Cir.1963), rev'd 380 U.S. 63, 85 S.Ct. 754, 13 L.Ed.2d 658 (1965), suggesting that only the historically accepted defenses (such as insanity and self-defense) are presently constitutionally acceptable as affirmative defenses.

See § 1.8(c) for further discussion of the burden of proof for affirmative defenses, and § 4.5(e) for specific consideration of the insanity defense.

54. See Sayre, Public Welfare Offenses, 33 Colum.L. Rev. 55 (1933); and § 3.8.

55. See Note, supra note 51, at 544. Thus, the Model Penal Code position, providing for situations in which the defendant would have to establish a defense by a preponderance of the evidence, is explained this way: "These were characteristically situations where the defense did not obtain at all or as broadly under antecedent law and the Code sought to introduce a mitigation. Resistance to the mitigation, often based upon the prosecution's difficulty in obtaining evidence, would presumably be lowered if the burden of persuasion were imposed on the defendant. Where the prosecution's problem appeared genuine and there was something to be said against allowing the defense at all, shifting the burden was believed to be acceptable." Model Penal Code § 1.12, Comment at 198 (1985).

However, as discussed in more detail elsewhere herein,[56] the Supreme Court appears not to have taken such an approach. In *Patterson v. New York*,[57] defendant was charged with murder, defined as intentionally causing the death of another, and was permitted by statute to show by a preponderance of the evidence the affirmative defense that he "acted under the influence of extreme emotional disturbance for which there was a reasonable explanation or excuse," which would downgrade the offense to manslaughter. The Court upheld this allocation of the burden of persuasion, relying largely upon the pragmatic notion that were the rule otherwise legislative bodies might opt to eliminate certain defenses entirely rather than impose upon prosecutors the burden of disproving their existence on a case-by-case basis. As for the Court's prior decision in *Mullaney v. Wilbur*,[58] declaring unconstitutional a state murder statute which imposed upon defendants the burden of proving that heat-of-passion mitigation needed to reduce the crime to manslaughter, it was characterized in *Patterson* as holding only that "shifting the burden of persuasion with respect to a fact which the State deems so important that it must be either proved or presumed is impermissible under the Due Process Clause."

This appeared to mean, the dissenters objected, that (just as in *Leland*) the outcome was determined merely by labels, so that the burden of proof could be put upon the defendant whenever the legislature was ingenious enough to characterize the matter as an "affirmative defense." Not so, the *Patterson* majority objected, for "there are obviously constitutional limits beyond which the States may not go." This suggests that the only limitation here is of the greater-includes-the-lesser type; if the legislature could define a particular crime as consisting only of elements X and

Y (rather than X and Y plus Z), then and only then may the legislature instead define the crime as X and Y but allow the defendant to prove non-Z. But some find more promise in *Patterson*. It has been suggested, for example, that the Court's handling of that case reflects "an ambivalence, shared by many scholars, about the insanity defense," in that the Court treated the extreme emotional disturbance defense "as being sufficiently close to insanity to warrant the same burden of persuasion that could have been placed on the defendant to prove insanity."[59] From this, it is reasoned that *Patterson* plus *Mullaney* "require the prosecution to bear the burden of proving those elements necessary to distinguish a greater from a lesser offense among traditionally demarcated degrees of criminal activity."[60]

 WESTLAW REFERENCES

di affirmative defense

leland /p "affirmative defense"

digest,synopsis(presumption /p rational** /s connect*** relate* /p crim**** penal)

(f) Statutory Exceptions. Sometimes claims of exemption from a statutory prohibition are based upon some proviso or exception appearing in the statute, in which case courts frequently hold that the burden of coming forward with proof of the exculpatory fact is on the defendant.[61] For example, where a statute made it an offense for a carrier to possess pheasants without being qualified by law to do so, and ten different qualifications were provided by the same laws, it was held that it was for the defendant to establish the qualification he had rather than for the prosecution to prove the absence of all ten.[62]

It is apparent that in many instances these statutory exceptions could not meet the rational connection test; indeed, courts have

---

56. See § 1.8(c).

57. 432 U.S. 197, 97 S.Ct. 2319, 53 L.Ed.2d 281 (1977).

58. 421 U.S. 684, 95 S.Ct. 1881, 44 L.Ed.2d 508 (1975).

59. Saltzburg, Burdens of Persuasion in Criminal Cases: Harmonizing the Views of the Justices, 20 Am. Crim.L.Rev. 393, 409–10 (1983).

60. Id. at 411.

61. E.g., People v. Williams, 61 Colo. 11, 155 P. 323 (1916); State v. McLean, 157 Minn. 359, 196 N.W. 278 (1923); State v. Rosasco, 103 Or. 343, 205 P. 290 (1922).

62. This is the classic case of King v. Turner, 105 Eng. Rep. 1026 (K.B.1816). See G. Williams, Criminal Law: The General Part § 293 (2d ed. 1961).

always explained the placing of the burden on the defendant on a quite different basis, namely that the exculpating facts are peculiarly within the knowledge of the accused. Here again, therefore, the question arises as to whether the constitutional limitations imposed by the *Tot* decision and its progeny are applicable to these statutory exceptions. Although the courts have not given careful attention to this question, it is submitted that the reasons given above for different treatment of affirmative defenses are equally applicable to statutory exceptions. However, in light of the previously discussed [63] tension between *Patterson* and *Sandstrom,* in that the legislature cannot do by a device called a "presumption" what it can do by using the words "affirmative defense," there is admittedly somewhat greater chance that a part of a criminal statute characterized as an exception or proviso would not be deemed within *Patterson's* embrace.

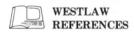 **WESTLAW REFERENCES**

digest,synopsis(statut*** law /s ex**ption /s burden /p crim**** penal)

---

§ 2.14 Constitutional Limitations—The Bill of Rights

A criminal statute may be held unconstitutional on its face or as applied to some situations within its terms because it conflicts with some guarantee of the Bill of Rights (which, when a state law is involved, requires an initial determination that the constitutional provision relied upon is applicable to the states through the Fourteenth Amendment). The conflict may be with the freedom of speech, press, assembly, religion, association, or privacy; with the right to be secure against illegal searches; with the privilege against self-incrimination; or with the prohibition on cruel and unusual punishment.

(a) Substantive Due Process and the Bill of Rights. As noted earlier,[1] the United States Supreme Court has all but abandoned its earlier practice of declaring criminal statutes unconstitutional on the ground that the proscribed conduct bears no real or substantial relation to injury to the public. Thus it would now be most unusual for the Court to hold a law invalid solely upon the basis that no reason *for* prohibiting the delineated conduct has been established. It is not at all unusual, however, for the Supreme Court to strike down a criminal statute (or, at least, to declare it unenforceable as to some fact situations within its terms) because there exists a good reason *for not* proscribing all of the conduct covered by the statute. This happens when it appears that the challenged statute attempts to prohibit conduct which is protected by the Bill of Rights of the United States Constitution. Indeed, it may be said that the latter ground for invalidating statutes has in a sense replaced the former; today the Court is likely to reject a "direct"[2] substantive due process challenge to a criminal statute in favor of a finding that the statute conflicts with the Bill of Rights, even when this result may be reached only by recognition of "penumbral rights" not specifically enumerated in the Constitution.[3]

This is not to say, however, that only the grounds for decision have changed and that the constitutional limits of penal legislation have remained fixed. The Court was once quick to strike down legislative experiments in economic and social reform but slow to assimilate freedoms guaranteed by the Bill of Rights into the due process clause of the Fourteenth Amendment, but now it is criminal statutes imposing restrictions on speech, assembly, religion and the like which are most vulnerable. While some of the reasons which have been given for this "double standard"

---

63. See § 2.13(c).

§ 2.14

1. See § 2.12(a).

2. "Direct" is used here in the sense that the claim is simply that there is a violation of due process because the law is not reasonably related to the public welfare, and is

to be distinguished from cases in which state criminal statutes are alleged to violate due process because of some provision of the Bill of Rights which is applicable to the states through the Fourteenth Amendment.

3. E.g., Griswold v. Connecticut, 381 U.S. 479, 85 S.Ct. 1678, 14 L.Ed.2d 510 (1965).

are less than satisfying,[4] there is general agreement that it is more appropriate for the Supreme Court to determine when legislative policies conflict with the Bill of Rights than to undertake a more general assessment of the wisdom of these policies.[5]

The limitations upon federal and state power flowing from the Bill of Rights are many, and this vast subject today accounts for most of the content of the typical law school course in constitutional law. Accordingly, no attempt will be made here to treat the subject exhaustively. Rather, the purpose of this section is merely to point out some of the most significant limitations on the legislative power to create crimes.

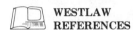 **WESTLAW REFERENCES**

di bill

(b) Freedom of Expression and Association.[6] The First Amendment provides that "Congress shall make no law * * * abridging the freedom of speech, or of the press; or the right of the people peaceably to assemble," [7] and it has long been clear that this prohibition is also applicable to the states via the due process clause of the Fourteenth Amendment.[8] A literal reading of the language quoted above might well suggest that there is absolutely no constitutional room for

a criminal statute which attempts to punish any kind of oral or written communication or any peaceable assembly, but this is not the case. The Supreme Court, by defining what lies within these freedoms and in deciding what constitutes an abridgement of them, has established that certain criminal statutes of this kind are permissible.

Not every form of communication is protected by the First Amendment. "There are certain well-defined and narrowly limited classes of speech, the prevention and punishment of which has never been thought to raise any Constitutional problem. These include the lewd and obscene, the profane, the libelous, and the insulting or 'fighting' words—those which by their very utterance inflict injury or tend to incite an immediate breach of the peace." [9] Because such communications are not an essential part of the exposition of ideas, they are deemed to be of slight social value as compared to the public interest in order and morality. As a consequence, the Supreme Court does not require a showing of need for legislation proscribing such conduct.[10]

This is not to suggest, however, that a legislature may proscribe certain speech or writing merely by the use of such labels as "obscenity" and "libel." The question of what communications lie outside the First Amend-

---

4. For a discussion of some of them, see P. Freund, The Supreme Court of the United States ch. 3 (1961).

5. For example, it has been observed that the Supreme Court is not in the best position to assess local conditions, and that local conditions are likely to justify varying local standards of economic due process but not different standards under the First Amendment. Hetherington, State Economic Regulation and Substantive Due Process of Law, 53 Nw.U.L.Rev. 226, 250 (1958).

6. For a more detailed discussion of this subject, see 3 R. Rotunda, J. Nowak, & J. Young, Treatise on Constitutional Law ch. 20 (1986).

7. U.S. Const. amend. I.

8. Gitlow v. New York, 268 U.S. 652, 45 S.Ct. 625, 69 L.Ed. 1138 (1925). In addition, these rights are expressly granted protection in many state constitutions.

9. Chaplinsky v. New Hampshire, 315 U.S. 568, 62 S.Ct. 766, 86 L.Ed. 1031 (1942). Compare Lewis v. City of New Orleans, 415 U.S. 130, 94 S.Ct. 970, 39 L.Ed.2d 214 (1974) (ordinance punishing "opprobrious" language to or with reference to a police officer while in performance of his duties overbroad, as it goes beyond "fighting words");

Gooding v. Wilson, 405 U.S. 518, 92 S.Ct. 1103, 31 L.Ed.2d 408 (1972) (statute proscribing use of opprobrious words or abusive language unconstitutional where not construed to apply only to "fighting words").

10. Thus, there has never been a need to show that the proscribed speech in these categories presents a clear and present danger. Ginsberg v. New York, 390 U.S. 629, 88 S.Ct. 1274, 20 L.Ed.2d 195 (1968) (materials obscene only to children); Roth v. United States, 354 U.S. 476, 77 S.Ct. 1304, 1 L.Ed.2d 1498 (1957) (obscene literature); Beauharnais v. Illinois, 343 U.S. 250, 72 S.Ct. 725, 96 L.Ed. 919 (1952) (group libel).

But, in Stanley v. Georgia, 394 U.S. 557, 89 S.Ct. 1243, 22 L.Ed.2d 542 (1969), where the defendant was convicted for possessing obscene materials in his own home, the Court rejected the state's contention that in light of *Roth* obscenity is entitled to no constitutional protection, and held that the states' power to regulate obscenity "does not extend to mere possession by the individual in the privacy of his own home." *Stanley* has been given a narrow interpretation. See, e.g., Paris Adult Theatre 1 v. Slayton, 413 U.S. 49, 93 S.Ct. 2628, 37 L.Ed.2d 446 (1973).

ment is itself an issue of constitutional law, and thus in the last analysis must be answered by the Supreme Court. For example, it is for the Court to decide upon the permissible reach of obscenity statutes [11] and criminal defamation laws.[12] Also, a criminal statute intended to deal with situations outside the First Amendment may not be drafted in such a way that it tends to limit access to constitutionally protected materials; and thus a strict liability statute on possession of obscene literature is unconstitutional because it would tend to influence booksellers to carry only those reading materials they had personally examined as to contents.[13]

Other forms of speech may also be prohibited by the criminal law on the basis of the danger flowing from the content of what is said. "The most stringent protection of free speech would not protect a man in falsely shouting fire in a theatre and causing a pan-

ic."[14] The test is often said to be whether there is a "clear and present danger" that the words in question will bring about evils which the legislature has a right to prevent,[15] although more recently the test has been restated in a somewhat more sophisticated form: "In each case [courts] must ask whether the gravity of the 'evil,' discounted by its improbability, justifies such invasion of free speech as is necessary to avoid the danger."[16] Under such a test, it is clear that the First Amendment does not bar the existence of such crimes as solicitation, conspiracy, or obtaining property by falsely spoken words: "There is no question but that the State may thus provide for the punishment of those who indulge in utterances which incite to violence and crime and threaten the overthrow of organized government by unlawful means."[17]

Other criminal statutes and ordinances,[18] while not attempting to proscribe speech on

---

11. The Court's test for obscenity was stated thusly in Miller v. California, 413 U.S. 15, 93 S.Ct. 2607, 37 L.Ed.2d 419 (1973): "The basic guidelines for the trier of fact must be: (a) whether 'the average person, applying contemporary community standards' would find that the work, taken as a whole, appeals to the prurient interest, (b) whether the work depicts or describes, in a patently offensive way, sexual conduct specifically defined by the applicable state law, and (c) whether the work, taken as a whole, lacks serious literary, artistic, political, or scientific value." See, e.g., New York v. Ferber, 458 U.S. 747, 102 S.Ct. 3348, 73 L.Ed.2d 1113 (1982) (upholding statute proscribing sale of child pornography); Jenkins v. Georgia, 418 U.S. 153, 94 S.Ct. 2750, 41 L.Ed.2d 642 (1974) (nudity alone not obscenity under *Miller* standard).

It is also for the Court to decide whether more general statutes may be applied to certain speech on the ground that such speech is obscene or otherwise not protected. See Cohen v. California, 403 U.S. 15, 91 S.Ct. 1780, 29 L.Ed.2d 284 (1971), holding that breach of the peace conviction of defendant who walked through courthouse wearing jacket bearing the words "Fuck the Draft" where women and children were present could not be justified on theory of state's power to prohibit obscene expression or (under the circumstances) "fighting words."

12. Garrison v. Louisiana, 379 U.S. 64, 85 S.Ct. 209, 13 L.Ed.2d 125 (1964).

13. Smith v. California, 361 U.S. 147, 80 S.Ct. 215, 4 L.Ed.2d 205 (1959).

14. This is the oft-quoted statement of Justice Holmes in Schenck v. United States, 249 U.S. 47, 39 S.Ct. 247, 63 L.Ed. 470 (1919).

15. Ibid.

16. Dennis v. United States, 341 U.S. 494, 71 S.Ct. 857, 95 L.Ed. 1137 (1951).

Thus, a statute prohibiting threats against the President, although it makes criminal a form of pure speech, is constitutional because of the national interest in protecting the chief executive, although First Amendment considerations require that the statute not be interpreted as covering more "political hyperbole." Watts v. United States, 394 U.S. 705, 89 S.Ct. 1399, 22 L.Ed.2d 664 (1969). On the other hand, a statute making it a crime to cast contempt by words on the American Flag is unconstitutional, as (1) it is not limited to words which incite others to unlawful action; (2) it is not limited to "fighting words," those likely to provoke the average person to retaliation; (3) ideas may not be suppressed merely because they are offensive to their hearers; and (4) respect for our national symbol cannot be demanded. Street v. New York, 394 U.S. 576, 89 S.Ct. 1354, 22 L.Ed.2d 572 (1969).

17. Stromberg v. California, 283 U.S. 359, 51 S.Ct. 532, 75 L.Ed. 1117 (1931). But, the state may not punish mere advocacy of the necessity or propriety of violence to accomplish political reform, as opposed to incitement to imminent action. Brandenburg v. Ohio, 395 U.S. 444, 89 S.Ct. 1827, 23 L.Ed.2d 430 (1969). See also Hess v. Indiana, 414 U.S. 105, 94 S.Ct. 326, 38 L.Ed.2d 303 (1973) (advocacy of illegal action at some indefinite future time may not be proscribed).

18. Sometimes the problem is the constitutionality, not of a state criminal statute, but of a municipal ordinance carrying penalties of fine or imprisonment or both. However, though one view is that ordinance violations are not criminal, see § 1.7(c), the principles involved in the clash between the police power of the municipality and freedom of expression are essentially the same as those involved in connection with state criminal statutes.

the basis of its content, fix limitations on the time, place, and manner of such expression. In passing upon the constitutionality of these regulations, the Court has frequently employed a balancing-of-interests test; for example, an ordinance banning the practice of summoning occupants of a residence to the door, without their prior consent, for the purpose of soliciting orders for the sale of goods was upheld on the ground that the householder's interest in privacy outweighed the commercial interests of the salesman.[19] However, the law must be narrowly drawn to proscribe only that conduct which interferes with some superior interest;[20] even assuming that the distribution of handbills may be limited to prevent defrauding of the public, this does not warrant a law requiring that handbills of any kind carry the name and address of the persons who printed them and caused them to be distributed.[21] So-called "commercial speech,"

that which is connected to the selling of a product or service,[22] although also entitled to First Amendment protection,[23] is subject to greater time, place, or manner restrictions.[24]

The expression of ideas through conduct is subject to greater regulation, as the Court has rejected the notion that the Constitution affords "the same kind of freedom to those who would communicate ideas by conduct such as patrolling, marching, and picketing on streets and highways as * * * to those who communicate ideas by pure speech."[25] Therefore, it is permissible for a legislature to proscribe that picketing which unreasonably interferes with ingress or egress to public buildings.[26] Expression by speech or conduct in public parks or streets is subject to regulation in order to protect the primary use of these facilities, but proceeding without a permit may not be punished where the law sets no

19. Breard v. City of Alexandria, 341 U.S. 622, 71 S.Ct. 920, 95 L.Ed. 1233 (1951).

20. Regan v. Time, Inc., ___ U.S. ___, 104 S.Ct. 3262, 82 L.Ed.2d 487 (1984) (statute permitting publication of illustrations of U.S. currency only for "philatelic, numismatic, educational, historical or newsworthy purposes" is not a valid time, place or manner regulation, as it discriminates on the basis of content; statute's size and color limitations, however, are valid as reasonable manner regulations to prevent counterfeiting); Clark v. Community for Creative Non-Violence, 468 U.S. 288, 104 S.Ct. 3065, 82 L.Ed.2d 221 (1984) (regulation forbidding sleeping in parks is a reasonable time, place and manner restriction serving substantial government interest of protecting national parks, and it leaves open ample alternative methods of communication); Members of City Council v. Taxpayers for Vincent, 466 U.S. 789, 104 S.Ct. 2118, 80 L.Ed.2d 772 (1984) (ordinance proscribing posting of signs on public property permissible; is content-neutral and furthers significant esthetic interests); Schad v. Mount Ephraim, 452 U.S. 61, 101 S.Ct. 2176, 68 L.Ed.2d 671 (1981) (ordinance excluding all live entertainment in commercial zone invalid; live entertainment poses no significantly different problems for other commercial uses).

21. Talley v. California, 362 U.S. 60, 80 S.Ct. 536, 4 L.Ed.2d 559 (1960).

22. In First National Bank of Boston v. Bellotti, 435 U.S. 765, 98 S.Ct. 1407, 55 L.Ed.2d 707 (1978), the Court emphasized that not all speech motivated by commercial and monetary desires is "commercial speech."

23. Bolger v. Youngs Drug Products Corp., 463 U.S. 60, 103 S.Ct. 2875, 77 L.Ed.2d 469 (1983) (offensiveness to some individuals not a proper interest to justify prohibition on the mailing of unsolicited ads for contraceptives);

Linmark Associates, Inc. v. Township of Willingboro, 431 U.S. 85, 97 S.Ct. 1614, 52 L.Ed.2d 155 (1977) (ordinance prohibiting real estate "for sale" signs to stem "white flight" invalid; restriction of free flow of truthful commercial information to achieve such objective impermissible); Bigelow v. Virginia, 421 U.S. 809, 95 S.Ct. 2222, 44 L.Ed. 2d 600 (1975) (ad for legal abortion is protected commercial speech).

24. Village of Hoffman Estates v. Flipside, Hoffman Estates, Inc., 455 U.S. 489, 102 S.Ct. 1186, 71 L.Ed.2d 362 (1982) (ordinance requiring business to obtain license if it sells items "designed or marketed for use with illegal cannabis or drugs" not facially invalid; this restriction on commercial speech does not appreciably limit the communication of information, except that directed at promoting illegal drug use).

25. Cox v. Louisiana, 379 U.S. 536, 85 S.Ct. 453, 13 L.Ed.2d 471 (1965). So too, the "symbolic speech" involved in the destruction of a draft registration card, because it also involves conduct, can be proscribed to protect the governmental interest in insuring the continuing availability of issued certificates. United States v. O'Brien, 391 U.S. 367, 88 S.Ct. 1673, 20 L.Ed.2d 672 (1968).

But compare Spence v. Washington, 418 U.S. 405, 94 S.Ct. 2727, 41 L.Ed.2d 842 (1974) (flag misuse statute unconstitutionally applied to hanging privately-owned flag upside down with peace symbol affixed; Court gives greater consideration to defendant's motivation to communicate/and communicative nature of the conduct).

26. Cameron v. Johnson, 390 U.S. 611, 88 S.Ct. 1335, 20 L.Ed.2d 182 (1968). Compare United States v. Grace, 461 U.S. 171, 103 S.Ct. 1702, 75 L.Ed.2d 736 (1983) (total prohibition on picketing on sidewalks surrounding Supreme Court invalid).

appropriate standards for the official who is to pass upon the permit application.[27]

The right of assembly is protected in much the same way,[28] as is freedom of association. While the First Amendment does not expressly mention the latter, it has been construed to include this and other penumbral rights.[29]

> ### WESTLAW
> ### REFERENCES

"fighting words" /p first /3 amendment

opprobrious /5 word language speech /p first /3 amendment

(c) Freedom of Religion.[30] The First Amendment also provides that "Congress shall make no law * * * prohibiting the free exercise" of religion,[31] and this prohibition has likewise been held applicable to the states.[32] Just as is true of the bar on abridging freedoms of speech, the press, or assembly, the language quoted above has not been interpreted as forbidding any criminal legislation touching upon the protected area.

In *Reynolds v. United States* [33] the Supreme Court applied the secular regulation rule: the First Amendment bestows protection upon religious beliefs, but not upon religious acts which contravene generally applicable legislation. Therefore, because antipolygamy stat-

utes were constitutional as generally applied, the religious practice of polygamy was not protected. Although this decision suggested that any religious belief taking the form of action was outside the First Amendment, the Court later moved to a less restrictive position. While the freedom to believe was absolute and thus subject to no regulation, the freedom to act could be restricted, provided the power to regulate was "so exercised as not, in attaining a permissible end, unduly to infringe the protected freedom." [34] This gave rise to a balancing test; criminal laws which made punishable acts done in the pursuit of religious beliefs would be upheld when so applied if the interest advanced by the statute was of greater importance than the interest in permitting the particular religious practice to continue. For example, a woman may be convicted for allowing her nine-year-old niece to sell religious literature on street corners in violation of the child labor laws, as society's interest in child welfare is more important than this particular form of religious practice.[35] By contrast, a statute permitting prosecution of parents for the failure of their children to salute the flag at school may not be enforced against Jehovah's Witnesses, for there is no genuine interest in obtaining com-

27. E.g., Shuttlesworth v. City of Birmingham, 394 U.S. 147, 89 S.Ct. 935, 22 L.Ed.2d 162 (1969) (permit for parade); Kunz v. New York, 340 U.S. 290, 71 S.Ct. 312, 95 L.Ed. 280 (1951) (permit for street meeting); Saia v. New York, 334 U.S. 558, 68 S.Ct. 1148, 92 L.Ed. 1574 (1948) (permit for use of amplifying device).

28. E.g., Coates v. City of Cincinnati, 402 U.S. 611, 91 S.Ct. 1686, 29 L.Ed.2d 214 (1971) (invalidating ordinance prohibiting assembly of three or more persons on public way "in a manner annoying to persons passing by"); DeJonge v. Oregon, 299 U.S. 353, 57 S.Ct. 255, 81 L.Ed. 278 (1937) (attendance at peaceable meeting of Communist Party where overthrow of government not advocated may not be made criminal).

29. E.g., NAACP v. Button, 371 U.S. 415, 83 S.Ct. 328, 9 L.Ed.2d 405 (1963) (statute punishing solicitation of legal business may not be applied to NAACP's activity of supplying counsel for Negro litigants); Bates v. Little Rock, 361 U.S. 516, 80 S.Ct. 412, 4 L.Ed.2d 480 (1960) (city ordinance punishing refusal to make membership lists public abridges freedom of association). On these "penumbral rights" generally, see Griswold v. Connecticut, 381 U.S. 479, 85 S.Ct. 1678, 14 L.Ed.2d 510 (1965).

Here again, reasonable regulation is permissible. See, e.g., Roberts v. United States Jaycees, ___ U.S. ___, 104

S.Ct. 3244, 82 L.Ed.2d 462 (1984) (application of statute forbidding sex discrimination to young men's civic and service organization did not abridge their freedom of intimate association or expressive association).

30. For a more detailed discussion of this subject, see 3 R. Rotunda, J. Nowak, & J. Young, Treatise on Constitutional Law ch. 21 (1986).

31. U.S. Const. amend. I.

That Amendment also provides that Congress shall make no law "respecting an establishment of religion," and thus a criminal statute may also be held unconstitutional because it is intended to promote a particular kind of religion. See Epperson v. Arkansas, 393 U.S. 97, 89 S.Ct. 266, 21 L.Ed.2d 228 (1968), holding unconstitutional a statute making it a misdemeanor to teach the theory of evolution in the public schools.

32. Cantwell v. Connecticut, 310 U.S. 296, 60 S.Ct. 900, 84 L.Ed. 1213 (1940).

33. 98 U.S. 145, 25 L.Ed. 244 (1878).

34. Cantwell v. Connecticut, 310 U.S. 296, 60 S.Ct. 900, 84 L.Ed. 1213 (1940).

35. Prince v. Massachusetts, 321 U.S. 158, 64 S.Ct. 438, 88 L.Ed. 645 (1944).

pulsory unification of opinion.[36] More recently, the Court has referred to the need to show a "compelling state interest," [37] but even without relying upon this test later held that application of the compulsory school-attendance law to Amish children who had graduated from the eighth grade would violate their rights under the free exercise clause.[38] The Court stressed that the Amish had supported their claim that such attendance would endanger the free exercise of their religious beliefs, and also that the state's admittedly strong interest would not be adversely affected by an exception for Amish children, in light of the adequacy of the Amish alternative mode of continuing informal education.

Applying one or more of the tests mentioned above, state courts have upheld convictions under statutes of general application notwithstanding the defendant's claim that he was pursuing a religious belief. For example, a father who causes the death of his child by failing to call a doctor, though he honestly believes in prayer rather than doctors as a cure, may be guilty of manslaughter.[39] Criminal laws punishing spiritualism and fortune telling have been held valid,[40] as have statutes punishing the practice of medicine without a license as applied to one who believes he is a divine healer.[41] However, a different result has been reached when the conduct in question has been found "central" to the religion; on this basis the California supreme court

held that members of the Native American Church who used peyote as the sacramental heart of their religious worship could not be convicted under statutes prohibiting the possession or use of peyote.[42]

Another troublesome kind of case is presented when the criminal statute in question does not attempt to punish acts done in the practice of religion, but instead proscribes other acts and thus makes the practice of religion more burdensome. This happens, for example, when a Sunday closing law is applied to Orthodox Jewish businessmen who because of their religion are also closed on Saturday. Confronted with such a situation, the Supreme Court upheld this application of the law, emphasizing that the burden was only indirect and that the state was pursuing a secular goal by the only reasonable method available.[43]

 **WESTLAW REFERENCES**

reynolds /12 98 +4 145 /p religio! /p first /3 amendment

(d) Freedom From Unreasonable Search and the Right of Privacy. The United States Constitution also protects "the right of the people to be secure in their persons, houses, papers and effects, against unreasonable searches and seizures," [44] and this protection is likewise granted against both the federal government and the states.[45] The freedom

36. West Virginia Board of Education v. Barnette, 319 U.S. 624, 63 S.Ct. 1178, 87 L.Ed. 1628 (1943).

37. Sherbert v. Verner, 374 U.S. 398, 83 S.Ct. 1790, 10 L.Ed.2d 965 (1963), not involving a criminal prosecution, where the Court said: "It is basic that no showing merely of a rational relationship to some colorable state interest would suffice; in this highly sensitive constitutional area, [o]nly the gravest abuses, endangering paramount interests, give occasion for permissible limitation."

38. 406 U.S. 205, 92 S.Ct. 1526, 32 L.Ed.2d 15 (1972).

39. Craig v. State, 220 Md. 590, 155 A.2d 684 (1959); Commonwealth v. Breth, 44 Pa.County Ct. 56 (1915). Of course if manslaughter requires that defendant realize the risk involved, as some states hold, see § 7.12, then honest religious conviction may negative this realization.

40. McMasters v. State, 21 Okla.Cr. 318, 207 P. 566 (1922); State v. Neitzel, 69 Wash. 567, 125 P. 939 (1912).

41. Smith v. People, 51 Colo. 270, 117 P. 612 (1911). See Cawley, Criminal Liability in Faith Healing, 39 Minn. L.Rev. 48 (1954).

42. People v. Woody, 61 Cal.2d 716, 40 Cal.Rptr. 69, 394 P.2d 813 (1964), noted in 17 Stan.L.Rev. 494 (1965). See also Native American Church v. United States, 468 F.Supp. 1247 (S.D.N.Y.1979), affirmed 633 F.2d 205 (2d Cir.1980). Compare Leary v. United States, 383 F.2d 851 (5th Cir.1967), noted in 56 Calif.L.Rev. 100 (1968), reversed on other grounds 395 U.S. 6, 89 S.Ct. 1532, 23 L.Ed.2d 57 (1969).

See also Frank v. State, 604 P.2d 1068 (Alaska 1979) (because "the utilization of moose meat at a funeral potlatch is a practice deeply rooted in the Athabascan religion," a valid religious freedom defense existed as to out-of-season killing of moose to supply meat for potlatch).

43. Braunfeld v. Brown, 366 U.S. 599, 81 S.Ct. 1144, 6 L.Ed.2d 563 (1961).

44. U.S. Const. amend. IV.

45. Mapp v. Ohio, 367 U.S. 643, 81 S.Ct. 1684, 6 L.Ed. 1081 (1961).

from unreasonable searches and seizures is of primary significance in the realm of criminal procedure, where it is protected by an exclusionary rule which bars from evidence the fruits of an invasion of that right. However, it is also a limitation on the substantive criminal law, in that the failure to permit another to intrude upon your constitutional right against unreasonable searches may not be made criminal. For example, one may not be convicted for refusing entry to a building or fire inspector who is neither acting in an emergency nor armed with a search warrant for the premises.[46]

Other criminal statutes do not attempt to punish directly an assertion of one's constitutional right against unreasonable searches, but do proscribe conduct which ordinarily would not be discovered without inquiry into the individual's most private actions. Illustrative is a law which makes it a criminal offense to use a contraceptive device, which was declared unconstitutional by the Supreme Court in *Griswold v. Connecticut*.[47] That decision is based upon the "penumbral" right of privacy,[48] not specifically mentioned in the Constitution, which the opinion of the Court declares flows from the First Amendment right of association, the Third Amendment prohibition on quartering of soldiers, the Fourth Amendment protection against unreasonable searches, the Fifth Amendment protection against self-incrimination, and the

provision in the Ninth Amendment that "the enumeration in the Constitution, of certain rights, shall not be construed to deny or disparage others retained by the people." A law forbidding use of contraceptives rather than regulating their manufacture or sale [49] is unduly broad because it invades this right. The *Griswold* Court declared: "Would we allow the police to search the sacred precincts of marital bedrooms for telltale signs of the use of contraceptives? The very idea is repulsive to the notions of privacy surrounding the marriage relationship."

The precise scope of the *Griswold* decision is not entirely clear, and thus it cannot be said with certainty whether many other criminal statutes might also be found unconstitutional as violating the penumbral right of privacy. It is undoubtedly true, as Justice Stewart noted in dissent, that "even after today a State can constitutionally still punish at least some offenses which are not committed in public." Although it has been noted that *Griswold* furnishes some support for those who argue that the state should not be able to prohibit any private sexual activity between two consenting adults,[50] a majority of the Court has taken the view that states may still forbid fornication, adultery, and homosexuality.[51] However, in light of the emphasis upon marital privacy in *Griswold,* it would appear that other laws attempting to prohibit certain kinds of sexual activity by married

---

46. Camara v. Municipal Court, 387 U.S. 523, 87 S.Ct. 1727, 18 L.Ed.2d 930 (1967); See v. City of Seattle, 387 U.S. 541, 87 S.Ct. 1737, 18 L.Ed.2d 943 (1967); LaFave, Administrative Searches and the Fourth Amendment: The Camara and See Cases, 1967 Supreme Court Rev. 1.

47. 381 U.S. 479, 85 S.Ct. 1678, 14 L.Ed.2d 510 (1965). See Symposium, 64 Mich.L.Rev. 197 (1965).

48. For more on this right, see 2 R. Rotunda, J. Nowak, and J. Young, Treatise on Constitutional Law §§ 18.26–18.30 (1986).

49. But in Carey v. Population Service International, 431 U.S. 678, 97 S.Ct. 2010, 52 L.Ed.2d 675 (1977), the Court invalidated a law allowing only pharmacists to sell nonmedicinal contraceptives to persons over 16 and prohibiting the sale of such items to those under 16. The general restriction was deemed a burden on the adult's freedom of choice not justified by a compelling state interest. The prohibition as to those under 16 was also struck down, but a majority of the Court appeared to accept that statutes strictly regulating the sexual activities of minors would be permissible.

50. Emerson, Nine Justices in Search of a Doctrine, 64 Mich.L.Rev. 219, 232 (1965); Katin, Griswold v. Connecticut: The Justices and Connecticut's "Uncommonly Silly Law," 42 Notre Dame Law 680, 702–05 (1967); Richards, Unnatural Acts and the Constitutional Right to Privacy: A Moral Theory, 45 Ford.L.Rev. 1281 (1977); Note, 1966 Duke L.J. 562, 575; Comment, 60 Nw.U.L.Rev. 813, 832 (1966).

51. This view was expressed in the concurring opinions of Justices Goldberg (joined by the Chief Justice and Justice Brennan), White and Harlan.

The Court thereafter summarily affirmed a lower court ruling that a sodomy statute could be constitutionally applied to consensual and private homosexual relations. Doe v. Commonwealth's Attorney, 425 U.S. 901, 96 S.Ct. 1489, 47 L.Ed.2d 751 (1976). The Court thereafter declined to review such a sodomy conviction. Enslin v. Bean, 436 U.S. 912, 98 S.Ct. 2252, 56 L.Ed.2d 413 (1978).

couples, such as acts of perversion, requiring a type of enforcement similar to that condemned in *Griswold*, might be successfully challenged.[52]

Griswold was relied upon by the Supreme Court in *Stanley v. Georgia*,[53] holding that the First Amendment freedom of expression [54] and the penumbral right to privacy together prohibit making private possession of obscene material a crime. However, the Court, while recognizing the defendant's "right to be free from state inquiry into the contents of his library," [55] pointed out that the holding in no way infringed upon the power of the state or federal government to make private possession of "other items, such as narcotics, firearms, or stolen goods, a crime." [56]

Griswold was again relied upon in *Roe v. Wade*,[57] where the Court overturned a statute which proscribed abortion except when necessary to save the life of the mother. The statute was held to violate due process because it unnecessarily infringed upon a woman's right to privacy, declared by the Court to be "broad enough to encompass a woman's decision whether or not to terminate her pregnancy." [58] This right was deemed "fun-

damental," and thus could be limited only in furtherance of a "compelling state interest." One such interest, that in the existence of the fetus, was held not to arise until the fetus was viable and thus then capable of "meaningful life" independent of the mother. As for the state's interest in the pregnant woman's health, it was held only to permit the establishment of medical procedures for abortions performed after the first trimester.[59]

 WESTLAW REFERENCES

griswold /p privacy /p penumbra*

(e) Privilege Against Self-Incrimination. The United States Constitution provides that no person "shall be compelled in any criminal case to be a witness against himself," [60] and this prohibition is applicable to both the federal government and the states.[61] This privilege against self-incrimination has had the greatest significance in the area of criminal procedure; its most obvious application is to allow a defendant in a criminal case a free choice as to whether to take the stand in his defense, although more recently it has been held applicable in other procedural contexts,

---

52. See Emerson, supra note 50, at 231. Thus, in Cotner v. Henry, 394 F.2d 873 (7th Cir.1968), the court granted habeas corpus relief to the defendant, convicted of engaging in sodomy with his wife, and directed the state courts to resolve the constitutional questions involved. "Under *Griswold* Indiana courts could not interpret the statute constitutionally as making private consensual physical relations between married persons a crime absent a clear showing that the state had an interest in preventing such relations, which outweighed the constitutional right to marital privacy. The Indiana courts might, however, construe the statute as being inapplicable to married couples or as outlawing such physical relations between married couples only when accomplished by force."

53. 394 U.S. 557, 89 S.Ct. 1243, 22 L.Ed.2d 542 (1969).

54. See note 10 supra.

55. *Stanley* does not immunize from seizure obscene materials possessed at a port of entry for the purpose of importation for private use, United States v. Thirty-Seven Photographs, 402 U.S. 363, 91 S.Ct. 1400, 28 L.Ed.2d 822 (1971); nor does it immunize from prosecution the seller of obscenity who uses the mails to reach willing adult recipients, United States v. Reidel, 402 U.S. 351, 91 S.Ct. 1410, 28 L.Ed.2d 813 (1971).

56. Thus, the right to privacy was not an independent ground for the decision in *Stanley*, for the Court noted that these other possession crimes do not involve First Amendment rights.

57. 410 U.S. 113, 93 S.Ct. 705, 35 L.Ed.2d 147 (1973). The Court later struck down other abortion regulations. See City of Akron v. Akron Center for Reproductive Health, 462 U.S. 416, 103 S.Ct. 2481, 76 L.Ed.2d 687 (1983); Bellotti v. Baird, 443 U.S. 622, 99 S.Ct. 3035, 61 L.Ed.2d 797 (1979); Doe v. Bolton, 410 U.S. 179, 93 S.Ct. 739, 35 L.Ed.2d 201 (1973).

58. As the Court later noted, the *Griswold-Roe* right to privacy encompasses "the interest in independence in making certain kinds of important decisions," namely, those "relating to marriage, procreation, contraception, family relationships, and child rearing and education." Whalen v. Roe, 429 U.S. 589, 97 S.Ct. 869, 51 L.Ed.2d 64 (1977). There is no right to privacy as to medical treatment generally. People v. Privitera, 23 Cal.3d 697, 153 Cal.Rptr. 431, 591 P.2d 919 (1979) (upholding statute making it a crime to sell or proscribe laetrile to cancer patients).

59. See Simopoulos v. Virginia, 462 U.S. 506, 103 S.Ct. 2532, 76 L.Ed.2d 755 (1983) (requirement that second-trimester abortions be performed in licensed outpatient clinics not unreasonable); Planned Parenthood Association v. Ashcroft, 462 U.S. 476, 103 S.Ct. 2517, 76 L.Ed.2d 733 (1983) (requiring presence of second physician during abortions after first trimester reasonable).

60. U.S. Const. amend V.

61. Malloy v. Hogan, 378 U.S. 1, 84 S.Ct. 1489, 12 L.Ed. 2d 653 (1964).

such as police interrogation. Even more recently, however, the privilege has been recognized as a limitation upon the permissible reach of the substantive criminal law.

The thrust of this substantive law aspect of the privilege against self-incrimination is that the failure to do something, such as to register or to pay a tax, may not be punished as a crime when the obligation to so act carries with it a real and appreciable hazard that the individual will thereby incriminate himself by providing information which may be used to support other criminal prosecutions. Thus one may not be convicted for willful failure to pay the wagering occupation tax or to register before engaging in the business of accepting wagers, given the facts that wagering is widely prohibited under federal and state law and that information obtained from the payment of the tax or registering is readily available to assist the efforts of state and federal authorities to enforce these other laws.[62] Similarly, one may not be convicted of knowingly possessing an unregistered firearm or of failure to register a firearm when the information

received by compliance with these requirements would readily facilitate prosecution under other sections of the National Firearms Act regarding the making or transfer of such firearms.[63] Such criminal statutes, if defined solely in terms of persons who have violated other laws (e.g., statute *A* requires everyone who has violated statute *B* to register), would undoubtedly be unconstitutional on their face.[64] In other instances, close to the same result is reached by upholding the statute but yet affording those prosecuted thereunder a full defense by merely claiming the privilege.[65]

The United States Supreme Court, relying upon the privilege against self-incrimination, has held that a person under restraint by the police has a constitutional right to remain silent.[66] One procedural consequence of this is that the prosecution may not "use at trial the fact that [the defendant] stood mute or claimed his privilege in the face of accusation." [67] It may well follow that this extension of the privilege has similar significance in terms of what is permissible in the substan-

---

62. Marchetti v. United States, 390 U.S. 39, 88 S.Ct. 697, 19 L.Ed.2d 889 (1968). Similarly, in Grosso v. United States, 390 U.S. 62, 88 S.Ct. 709, 19 L.Ed.2d 906 (1968), the Court held that in view of the fact that the state in which defendant allegedly accepted wagers had adopted a comprehensive statutory system for punishment of gambling, he could not be prosecuted for willful failure to pay the federal excise tax on wagering. But *Marchetti* and *Grosso* do not bar conviction for making false statements on the registration form; to avoid incriminating himself, the individual must instead claim the privilege. United States v. Knox, 396 U.S. 77, 90 S.Ct. 363, 24 L.Ed.2d 275 (1969).

Following *Marchetti* and *Grosso* it was held in Leary v. United States, 395 U.S. 6, 89 S.Ct. 1532, 23 L.Ed.2d 57 (1969), that one may not be convicted of being a transferee of marijuana without having paid the transfer tax where information obtained by the payment of the tax is made available to federal and state officials charged with enforcement of the marijuana laws. However, conviction for selling marijuana not pursuant to a written order on which the seller's name must appear is permissible, for there is no substantial possibility that a purchaser of marijuana would ever comply with the order requirements, in that if he were to do so he would be subject to a $100-an-ounce tax and would acknowledge a transaction which is illegal under both state and federal law. Minor v. United States, 396 U.S. 87, 90 S.Ct. 284, 24 L.Ed.2d 283 (1969).

63. Haynes v. United States, 390 U.S. 85, 88 S.Ct. 722, 19 L.Ed.2d 923 (1968).

Compare with *Haynes,* and with *Marchetti* and *Grosso,* supra note 62, California v. Byers, 402 U.S. 424, 91 S.Ct. 1535, 29 L.Ed.2d 9 (1971) (statute requiring motorist involved in accident to stop and give his name and address did not involve self-incrimination in constitutional sense, where statute was essentially regulatory and noncriminal, self-reporting was indispensable, burden was on public at large, and possibility of self-incrimination was insubstantial); United States v. Freed, 401 U.S. 601, 91 S.Ct. 1112, 28 L.Ed.2d 356 (1971) (amended National Firearms Act, providing that no information or evidence provided in compliance therewith may be used in criminal proceedings against applicant or registrant for violation of law occurring prior to or concurrently with filing of application or registration, and barring the compiling of records containing the information or evidence, does not violate the self-incrimination clause).

64. The Court in *Haynes* indicated it would have so ruled but for the fact the registration in a few uncommon situations would be required of those who had not violated other provisions of the Act (e.g., where one found a lost or abandoned firearm).

65. This was the result in the cases cited notes 62 and 63 supra.

66. Miranda v. Arizona, 384 U.S. 436, 86 S.Ct. 1602, 16 L.Ed.2d 694 (1966).

67. Ibid. Post-arrest silence may be used for impeachment purposes if not preceded by *Miranda* warnings. Fletcher v. Weir, 455 U.S. 603, 102 S.Ct. 1309, 71 L.Ed.2d 490 (1982).

tive criminal law. It has been suggested that offenses which include as an element the failure to give a reasonable or satisfactory account to a police officer may now be unconstitutional.[68] However, the Supreme Court has not as yet resolved this issue.[69]

> **WESTLAW**
> **REFERENCES**

di privilege against self-incrimination

(f) Freedom From Cruel and Unusual Punishment. The United States Constitution prohibits the federal government from imposing cruel and unusual punishment for federal crimes;[70] almost all states have similar constitutional provisions forbidding such punishment for state crimes;[71] and the due process clause of the Fourteenth Amendment also prohibits the states from inflicting such punishment for state crimes.[72] While the prohibition on cruel and unusual punishment has sometimes been the basis for challenging action taken in the process of administering the criminal law,[73] it also has considerable significance with respect to the permissible reach of the substantive criminal law. In this regard, the prohibition has three aspects: (1) it limits the methods which may be used to inflict punishment; (2) it limits the amount of punishment which may be prescribed for various offenses; and (3) it bars any and all penal sanctions in certain situations.[74]

As to the first of these, it seems clear that the Eighth Amendment bars those forms of punishment which were considered cruel at the time of its adoption, such as burning at the stake, crucifixion, breaking on the wheel,[75] quartering, the rack and thumbscrew,[76] and extreme instances of solitary confinement.[77] The scope of the amendment is not so limited, however; it "must draw its meaning from the evolving standards of decency that mark the progress of a maturing society."[78] Thus even a punishment which inflicts no physical hardship or pain may be found to be cruel and unusual, as with a deprivation of citizenship which results in the "total destruction of the individual's status in organized society."[79]

Sterilization, found constitutional by some courts,[80] has been declared cruel and unusual by others,[81] which seems more in keeping with the Supreme Court's recent emphasis on the Eighth Amendment as protecting the "dignity of man."[82] Castration constitutes cruel and unusual punishment.[83] Flogging, condemned as cruel in dicta,[84] has been up-

---

68. Amsterdam, Federal Constitutional Restrictions on the Punishment of Crimes of Status, Crimes of General Obnoxiousness, Crimes of Displeasing Police Officers, and the Like, 3 Crim.L.Bull. 205, 228 (1967).

69. The Court's decisions on such provisions are based on other grounds. See Kolender v. Lawson, 461 U.S. 352, 103 S.Ct. 1855, 75 L.Ed.2d 903 (1983) (statute which, as construed, made it an offense for a person lawfully stopped not to provide "credible and reliable" identification is void for vagueness); Brown v. Texas, 443 U.S. 47, 99 S.Ct. 2637, 61 L.Ed.2d 357 (1979) (Fourth Amendment bars conviction of a person for the offense of refusing to identify himself to the police where police did not have grounds to stop that person in order to seek identification).

70. U.S. Const. amend. VIII.

71. Nineteen states proscribe cruel "or" unusual punishment; 22 prohibit cruel "and" unusual punishment; and 6 prohibit only "cruel" punishment. S. Rubin, The Law of Criminal Correction 423 (2d ed. 1973).

72. Robinson v. California, 370 U.S. 660, 82 S.Ct. 1417, 8 L.Ed.2d 758 (1962). See Sutherland, Due Process and Cruel Punishment, 64 Harv.L.Rev. 271 (1950).

73. E.g., Louisiana ex rel. Francis v. Resweber, 329 U.S. 459, 67 S.Ct. 374, 91 L.Ed. 422 (1947) (even assuming prohibition on cruel and unusual punishment is binding on the states, this does not bar a state from executing a condemned prisoner by the electric chair after a first attempt to do so failed because of faulty mechanism).

74. For a more detailed discussion of all three, see Note, 79 Harv.L.Rev. 635 (1966).

75. In re Kemmler, 136 U.S. 436, 10 S.Ct. 930, 34 L.Ed. 519 (1880).

76. Chambers v. Florida, 309 U.S. 227, 60 S.Ct. 472, 84 L.Ed. 716 (1940).

77. In re Medley, 134 U.S. 160, 10 S.Ct. 384, 33 L.Ed. 835 (1890). There are a number of cases, however, in which solitary confinement has been held constitutional, e.g., Stroud v. Johnston, 139 F.2d 171 (9th Cir.1943).

78. Trop v. Dulles, 356 U.S. 86, 78 S.Ct. 590, 2 L.Ed.2d 630 (1958).

79. Ibid.

80. E.g., State v. Feilin, 70 Wash. 65, 126 P. 75 (1912).

81. E.g., Mickle v. Henrichs, 262 F. 687 (D.Nev.1918).

82. Trop v. Dulles, supra note 78.

83. State v. Brown, 284 S.C. 407, 326 S.E.2d 410 (1985).

84. Weems v. United States, 217 U.S. 349, 30 S.Ct. 544, 54 L.Ed. 793 (1910).

held,[85] although the fact that it is unique from all other authorized forms of punishment in that the aim is the infliction of severe pain strongly suggests the Supreme Court would declare it impermissible.

Every modern form of carrying out the death penalty—electrocution,[86] hanging,[87] shooting,[88] and lethal gas[89]—has been upheld. As for the question of whether the death penalty is inherently cruel, so as to constitute a per se violation of the Eighth Amendment, the Supreme Court answered in the negative in *Gregg v. Georgia.*[90] In reaching this conclusion, the Court emphasized three factors: (i) that the "imposition of the death penalty for the crime of murder has a long history of acceptance both in the United States and England"; (ii) that it was "now evident that a large proportion of American society continues to regard it as an appropriate and necessary criminal sanction"[91]; and (iii) that the death penalty serves "two principal social purposes: retribution and deterrence of capital crimes by prospective offenders." Regarding the concern expressed a few years earlier by the Court that the penalty of death not be imposed in an arbitrary and capricious manner,[92] the Court in *Gregg* concluded it did not require an absolute prohibition upon capital

punishment. Rather, that concern could "be met by a carefully drafted statute that ensures that the sentencing authority is given adequate information and guidance." In upholding the statutory scheme at issue in *Gregg,* the Court stressed that it (1) specified ten aggravating circumstances,[93] any one of which must be found by the jury to exist beyond a reasonable doubt before a death sentence can be imposed; (2) allowed the jury to make a binding recommendation[94] of mercy even without finding any mitigating circumstances; and (3) provided for an automatic appeal at which both the sufficiency of the jury's finding of an aggravated circumstance and whether the sentence was disproportionate compared to those sentences imposed in similar cases would be assessed.[95]

The Supreme Court later concluded that the Eighth Amendment requires that the sentencing authority "not be precluded from considering, as a mitigating factor, any aspect of a defendant's character or record and any of the circumstances of the offense that the defendant proffers as a basis for a sentence less than death."[96] This means it is unconstitutional for a state to mandate the death penalty for a certain degree or category of murder[97] or for those murders unaccompanied by

---

85. E.g., State v. Cannon, 55 Del. 587, 190 A.2d 514 (1963).

86. In re Kemmler, supra note 75.

87. Dutton v. State, 123 Md. 373, 91 A. 417 (1914).

88. Wilkerson v. Utah, 99 U.S. 130, 25 L.Ed. 345 (1879).

89. Gray v. Lucas, 710 F.2d 1048 (5th Cir.1983); People v. Daugherty, 40 Cal.2d 876, 256 P.2d 911 (1953).

90. 428 U.S. 153, 96 S.Ct. 2909, 49 L.Ed.2d 859 (1976). See also Proffit v. Florida, 428 U.S. 242, 96 S.Ct. 2960, 49 L.Ed.2d 913 (1976) (statute constitutional where trial judge, the sentencing authority, must weigh 8 specified aggravating circumstances against 7 mitigating circumstances, and decisions are reviewed by appellate court); Jurek v. Texas, 428 U.S. 262, 96 S.Ct. 2950, 49 L.Ed.2d 929 (1976) (statute constitutional, as must be finding of aggravating circumstances, defendant allowed to show any mitigating circumstance, and there is appellate review).

91. This conclusion was based upon the fact that after the Supreme Court's decision in Furman v. Georgia, 408 U.S. 238, 92 S.Ct. 2726, 33 L.Ed.2d 346 (1972), holding a particular death penalty scheme unconstitutional, the "legislatures of at least 35 States have enacted new statutes that provide for the death penalty for at least some crimes that result in the death of another person."

92. Furman v. Georgia, 408 U.S. 238, 92 S.Ct. 2726, 33 L.Ed.2d 346 (1972).

93. Where one of the statutory aggravating circumstances is invalid on vagueness grounds, this does not invalidate a death sentence that is otherwise adequately supported by other aggravating circumstances. Zant v. Stephens, 462 U.S. 862, 103 S.Ct. 2733, 77 L.Ed.2d 235 (1983).

94. However, the death penalty is not constitutionally required to be imposed by a jury. Spaziano v. Florida, ___ U.S. ___, 104 S.Ct. 3154, 82 L.Ed.2d 340 (1984).

95. It has been questioned whether appellate review is a meaningful safeguard. See Dix, Appellate Review of the Decision to Impose Death, 68 Geo.L.J. 97 (1979).

96. Lockett v. Ohio, 438 U.S. 586, 98 S.Ct. 2954, 57 L.Ed.2d 973 (1978). Lower courts have not construed this rule as being applicable to penalties other than capital punishment. Thus, for example, it is not unconstitutional for a statute to mandate the penalty of life imprisonment upon conviction for a serious offense. Terrebone v. Blackburn, 646 F.2d 997 (5th Cir.1981) (distribution of heroin); State v. Nims, 357 N.W.2d 608 (Iowa 1984) (kidnapping); Taylor v. State, 452 So.2d 441 (Miss.1984) (murder).

97. Roberts v. Louisiana, 431 U.S. 633, 97 S.Ct. 1993, 52 L.Ed.2d 637 (1977) (statute imposing mandatory death

a few specified mitigating circumstances,[98] just as it is unconstitutional for a sentencing judge to disregard as a matter of law relevant mitigating circumstances.[99] These holdings also reflect the Court's view that under the Eighth Amendment capital punishment must "be imposed fairly, and with reasonable consistency, or not at all," for "a consistency produced by ignoring individual differences is a false consistency." [100]

The prohibition on cruel and unusual punishment also bars punishment authorized by statute which is excessive, that is, out of all proportion to the offense committed.[101] A leading case is *Weems v. United States,* [102] involving a public official in the Philippines convicted of falsifying an official record, where the punishment was fifteen years of *cadena temporal* (hard and painful labor and constant enchainment, deprivation of parental authority, loss of the right to dispose of property inter vivos, and continual surveillance for life). Although the Court viewed the punishment as inherently cruel, it also condemned the penalty as excessive in relation to the crime committed, a conclusion which was based upon a comparison of the punishment imposed with the penalties authorized by various American jurisdictions for comparable offenses.

This comparative technique was substantially limited by the Court shortly after the

Weems decision,[103] which may explain why courts have seldom held that a punishment may be unconstitutionally cruel because of excessiveness.[104] Generally, it may be said that courts have shown considerable deference to the legislative judgment as to how severe a penalty should be authorized for specific classes of offenses.[105] Illustrative of the usual response to a claim of excessive punishment is *Perkins v. North Carolina,*[106] where a federal court, although shocked at the sentence of from twenty to thirty years imposed for fellatio,[107] upheld the sentence because it was within "the astounding statutory limit of 'not less than five nor more than sixty years'." While there are cases holding sentences invalid for being clearly out of proportion to the offense—for example, six years for picking flowers in a public park [108]— often these decisions have been based upon state constitutional provisions expressly prohibiting disproportionate sentences.[109]

The Supreme Court has returned to the proportionality issue in recent years, especially with respect to the death penalty. In *Gregg v. Georgia,*[110] where the contention was that capital punishment was per se invalid, the Court proceeded to consider "whether the punishment of death is disproportionate in relation to the crime for which it is imposed." The Supreme Court indicated such an inquiry is particularly appropriate as to the punish-

sentence for first-degree murder of police officer unconstitutional); Roberts v. Louisiana, 428 U.S. 325, 96 S.Ct. 3001, 49 L.Ed.2d 974 (1976) (statute imposing a mandatory death sentence for a first-degree murder in five categories, e.g., killing during perpetration of an armed robbery, is unconstitutional); Wooden v. North Carolina, 428 U.S. 280, 96 S.Ct. 2978, 49 L.Ed.2d 944 (1976) (mandatory death penalty for all first-degree murder unconstitutional).

98. Lockett v. Ohio, 438 U.S. 586, 98 S.Ct. 2954, 57 L.Ed.2d 973 (1978) (statute mandating death penalty if none of three specified mitigating circumstances found to be present is unconstitutional); Bell v. Ohio, 438 U.S. 637, 98 S.Ct. 2977, 57 L.Ed.2d 1010 (1978) (same).

99. Eddings v. Oklahoma, 455 U.S. 104, 102 S.Ct. 869, 71 L.Ed.2d 1 (1982).

100. Eddings v. Oklahoma, 455 U.S. 104, 102 S.Ct. 869, 71 L.Ed.2d 1 (1982).

101. Weems v. United States, 217 U.S. 349, 30 S.Ct. 544, 54 L.Ed. 793 (1910), cites with approval the dissent in O'Neil v. Vermont, 144 U.S. 323, 12 S.Ct. 693, 36 L.Ed. 450 (1892), which asserts that "all punishments which by their

excessive length or severity are greatly disproportioned to the offenses charged" are barred.

102. 217 U.S. 349, 30 S.Ct. 544, 54 L.Ed. 793 (1910).

103. Badders v. United States, 240 U.S. 391, 36 S.Ct. 367, 60 L.Ed. 706 (1916).

104. See D. Fellman, The Defendant's Rights Today 400–02 (1976), for a representative list of sentences which have and have not been invalidated for excessiveness.

105. See Note, 36 N.Y.U.L.Rev. 846, 852 (1961).

106. 234 F.Supp. 333 (W.D.N.C.1964).

107. Severe punishment for sex offenses is not unusual in this country. See G. Mueller, Legal Regulation of Sexual Conduct 65–158 (1961); Note, supra note 74, at 643–44.

108. State ex rel. Garvey et al. v. Whitaker, 48 La.Ann. 527, 19 So. 457 (1896). For other similar cases, see S. Rubin, supra note 71, at 439–40.

109. See Note, 48 W.Va.L.Rev. 63 (1941).

110. 428 U.S. 153, 96 S.Ct. 2909, 49 L.Ed.2d 859 (1976).

ment of death, which is "unique in its severity and irrevocability," but then concluded that because "we are concerned here only with the imposition of capital punishment for the crime of murder, and when life has been taken deliberately by the offender, we cannot say that the punishment is invariably disproportionate to the crime. It is an extreme sanction, suitable to the most extreme of crimes."

Gregg created doubt about the constitutionality of the death penalty for offenses other than murder, and soon thereafter the Court confronted that issue in *Coker v. Georgia*. [111] The plurality,[112] concluding "that death is indeed a disproportionate penalty for the crime of raping an adult woman," reasoned:

> Rape is without doubt deserving of serious punishment; but in terms of moral depravity and of the injury to the person and to the public, it does not compare with murder, which does involve the unjustified taking of human life. Although it may be accompanied by another crime, rape by definition does not include the death or even the serious injury to another person. The murderer kills; the rapist, if no more than that, does not. Life is over for the victim of the murderer; for the rape victim, life may not be nearly so happy as it was, but it is not over and normally is not beyond repair. We have the abiding conviction that the death penalty, which "is unique in its severity and irrevocability," is an excessive penalty for the rapist who, as such, does not take human life.

Coker is, to be sure, a most significant decision. "It is the first modern decision in which the Supreme Court has relied on disproportionality to invalidate a punishment under the cruel and unusual punishment clause." [113] Its scope, however, is not entirely clear, which prompted the two *Coker* dissenters to declare

that the decision "casts serious doubt upon the constitutional validity of statutes imposing the death penalty for a variety of conduct which though dangerous, may not necessarily result in any immediate death, e.g., treason, airplane hijacking, and kidnapping." One possible view of *Coker* is that it "announced a first principle of morality in law—society may not take the life of a defendant who has not taken the life of his victim." [114] If this is so, then capital punishment would also be barred in all the cases mentioned by the *Coker* dissenters. It seems unlikely, however, that the decision will be so broadly applied. In particular, "since treason, a crime against masses of people, may cause more aggregate harm than a single murder, the greater public injury may justify the imposition of the death penalty." [115]

The *Coker* proportionality inquiry, the Court later noted in *Enmund v. Florida*, [116] involved the Court looking "to the historical development of the punishment at issue, legislative judgments, international opinion, and the sentencing decisions juries have made before bringing its own judgment to bear on the matter." This same approach was taken by the *Enmund* plurality,[117] which concluded that the Eighth Amendment does not permit imposition of the death penalty on a defendant who aids and abets a felony in the course of which murder is committed by others, but who does not himself kill, attempt to kill, or intend that killing take place or that lethal force be employed. This conclusion that all those guilty of felony-murder [118] are not proper candidates for the death penalty was grounded in another part of the *Coker* analysis—that which declared the death penalty is unconstitutional unless it measurably contrib-

---

111. 433 U.S. 584, 97 S.Ct. 2861, 53 L.Ed.2d 982 (1977).

112. White, J., joined by Stewart, Blackmun and Stevens, JJ. Brennan and Marshall, JJ., concurred on the ground that the death penalty constitutes cruel and unusual punishment in all circumstances. Powell, J., concurred on the facts of the case because there was "no indication that petitioner's offense was committed with excessive brutality or that the victim sustained serious or lasting injury." Burger, C.J., and Rehnquist, J., dissented.

113. Radin, The Jurisprudence of Death: Evolving Standards for the Cruel and Unusual Punishment Clause, 126 U.Pa.L.Rev. 989, 990 (1978).

114. The Supreme Court, 1976 Term, 91 Harv.L.Rev. 70, 125 (1977).

115. Id. at 128.

116. 458 U.S. 782, 102 S.Ct. 3368, 73 L.Ed.2d 1140 (1982).

117. Four Justices dissented, while Brennan, J., concurred on the ground that the death penalty is in all circumstances cruel and unusual punishment.

118. The felony-murder rule is usually interpreted as making all participants in the felony guilty of the murder. See § 7.5(c).

utes to the goals of retribution and deterrence. As for deterrence, the *Enmund* plurality concluded "there is no basis in experience
for the notion that death so frequently occurs
in the course of a felony for which killing is
not an essential ingredient that the death
penalty should be considered as a justifiable
deterrent to the felony itself." Moreover, executing Enmund "to avenge two killings that
he did not commit and had no intention of
committing or causing does not measurably
contribute to the retributive end of ensuring
that the criminal gets his just deserts."

During the *Coker-Enmund* period, the Court
on more than one occasion declined to strike
down serious penalties other than death on
lack-of-proportionality grounds.[119] But then
came *Solem v. Helm*,[120] in which the majority[121] first concluded that the Eighth Amendment "principle that a criminal sentence
must be proportionate to the crime for which
the defendant has been convicted" was also
applicable to felony prison sentences. Proportionality analysis, the Court next cautioned,
"should be guided by objective criteria, including (i) the gravity of the offense and the
harshness of the penalty; (ii) the sentences
imposed on other criminals in the same jurisdiction; and (iii) the sentences imposed for
commission of the same crime in other jurisdictions." In the instant case, Helm was convicted of uttering a "no account" check for
$100, ordinarily punishable by a five year
maximum term, but received a sentence of
life imprisonment without parole under the

state's recidivist statute because of his prior
convictions for six felonies, all of which were
minor and nonviolent and none of which was
a crime against a person. The Court concluded:

> Applying objective criteria, we find that Helm
> has received the penultimate sentence for rela-
> tively minor criminal conduct. He has been
> treated more harshly than other criminals in the
> State who have committed more serious crimes.
> He has been treated more harshly than he would
> have been in any other jurisdiction, with the
> possible exception of a single State. We con-
> clude that his sentence is significantly dispropor-
> tionate to his crime, and is therefore prohibited
> by the Eighth Amendment.[122]

Solem is unlikely to result in the invalidation of many legislatively-determined prison
terms; as the Court cautioned, "outside the
context of capital punishment, *successful* challenges to the proportionality of particular
sentences [will be] exceedingly rare."[123] The
first of the *Solem* objective factors, the relation between the gravity of the offense and
the harshness of the penalty, is "least capable
of objective measurement,"[124] but the com-
plexity of the sentencing process is such that
reviewing courts are properly cautioned
"against injecting their value judgments into
the details of legislative sentencing
schemes."[125] And in any event, each of the
latter two *Solem* objective factors "also limits
proportionality review in a manner designed
to ensure that only objectively extreme
sentences will be invalidated."[126]

---

119. Hutto v. Davis, 454 U.S 370, 102 S.Ct. 703, 70 L.Ed.2d 556 (1982) (granting of habeas corpus relief to prisoner sentenced to 40 years for possessing less than 9 ounces of marijuana an improper intrusion into the legis- lative linedrawing process); Rummel v. Estelle, 445 U.S. 263, 100 S.Ct. 1133, 63 L.Ed.2d 382 (1980) (mandatory life sentence after third felony of obtaining $120.27 by false pretenses, based on two earlier minor felonies, not cruel and unusual punishment).

120. 463 U.S. 277, 103 S.Ct. 3001, 77 L.Ed.2d 637 (1983). The case is discussed in Note, 1984 Duke L.J. 789.

121. There were four dissenters.

122. The *Rummel* case, note 119 supra, was distin- guished because there the defendant was eligible for re- lease on parole.

123. Quoting from Rummel v. Estelle, 445 U.S. 263, 100 S.Ct. 1133, 63 L.Ed.2d 382 (1980).

124. The Supreme Court, 1982 Term, 97 Harv.L.Rev. 70, 133 (1983).

125. Ibid.

126. Id. at 134–35. "By comparing a penalty with other penalties within the jurisdiction—by asking whether a particular sentence fits in with the rest—a court focuses on the 'internal consistency' of a jurisdiction's criminal code. The intrajurisdictional comparison thus allows al- teration only of aberrations from the code, rather than of significant segments of it. Similarly, the requirement of interjurisdictional comparison of sentences precludes a court from invalidating a sentence of which numerous jurisdictions approve." Id. at 135.

Consider United States v. Gracia, 755 F.2d 984 (2d Cir. 1985) (nine-year sentence for criminal contempt for failure to testify under grant of immunity was cruel and unusual punishment, as testifying falsely punishable by 5-year maximum).

If only one punishment is provided by law and that punishment is cruel and unusual, then the whole statute is unconstitutional.[127] On the other hand, if the statute provides in the alternative for both proper punishment and cruel punishment, the statute is no doubt valid as to the proper part.[128]

The third aspect of the constitutional ban on cruel and unusual punishment is that it bars the imposition of penal sanctions of any kind under certain circumstances. As such, the Eighth Amendment not only limits what legislatures may do by way of prescribing penalties for crime, but also what is permissible in terms of defining conduct as criminal. Thus, in *Robinson v. California* [129] the United States Supreme Court held unconstitutional a statute making it a crime for a person to "be addicted to the use of narcotics." The basis of the Court's decision in *Robinson* is not entirely clear, as emphasis was placed upon three different considerations: (1) the statute created a "status" crime as it did not require proof of any antisocial conduct within the jurisdiction; (2) the statute made it a crime to suffer the "illness" of narcotics addiction; and (3) the statute made it a crime to suffer from an illness "which may be contracted innocently or involuntarily." Which of these three factors should be considered decisive is, of course, a matter of some importance in determining the implications of the *Robinson* decision.

The Court's emphasis upon the fact that the California statute permits conviction of a defendant "whether or not he has ever used or possessed any narcotics within the State, and whether or not he has been guilty of any antisocial behavior there" suggests that, at least, *Robinson* supports the proposition that crimes of status and personal condition are unconstitutional—a result which has been reached in other cases as a matter of substantive due process.[130] It may well be, therefore, that many status crimes long recognized in American law, such as the crimes of being a vagrant, common prostitute, common drunkard, and disorderly person,[131] inflict cruel and unusual punishment when interpreted to allow conviction without proof of the commission of some act.[132] On the other hand, if this is all that *Robinson* means, then the scope of that decision is quite limited; it might be held, for example, that narcotics addiction is still punishable when proof of acts is required.[133] In the later case of *Powell v. Texas*,[134] four members of the Court interpreted *Robinson* as meaning merely that "criminal penalties may be inflicted only if the accused has committed some act * * * which society has an interest in preventing," arguing that were it otherwise the Supreme Court would be "the ultimate arbiter of the standards of criminal responsibility, in diverse areas of the criminal law, throughout the country." On that interpretation of *Robinson*, they concluded that Powell, a chronic alcoholic, was consti-

127. Weems v. United States, 217 U.S. 349, 30 S.Ct. 544, 54 L.Ed. 793 (1910) (punishment for falsifying official records was mandatory 12–20 years imprisonment in chains; held, since the only authorized punishment is invalid, defendant must be discharged).

128. Thus in Trop v. Dulles, 356 U.S. 86, 78 S.Ct. 590, 2 L.Ed.2d 630 (1958), a federal statute providing for loss of nationality for native-born citizens convicted by courts-martial of wartime desertion was held unconstitutional under the Eighth Amendment, though the punishment of 3 years at hard labor and dishonorable discharge awarded by the court was not affected.

129. 370 U.S. 660, 82 S.Ct. 1417, 8 L.Ed.2d 758 (1962). See Broeder & Merson, Robinson v. California: An Abbreviated Study, 3 Am.Crim.L.Q. 203 (1965); Neibel, Implications of Robinson v. California, 1 Houston L.Rev. 1 (1963); Notes, 51 Calif.L.Rev. 219 (1963); 79 Harv.L.Rev. 635 (1966). The only previous use of the Eighth Amendment to limit the power to create crimes was in Stoutenburgh v.

Frazier, 16 D.C.App. 229 (1900) (statute making it a crime to be a "suspicious person" inflicts cruel and unusual punishment).

130. See § 2.12(d). Also, status crimes have sometimes been invalidated on void-for-vagueness grounds, e.g., Lanzetta v. New Jersey, 306 U.S. 451, 59 S.Ct. 618, 83 L.Ed. 888 (1939); In re Newbern, 53 Cal.2d 786, 3 Cal. Rptr. 364, 350 P.2d 116 (1960). See Cuomo, Mens Rea and Status Criminality, 40 So.Calif.L.Rev. 463 (1967), for a discussion of the various constitutional arguments against status criminality.

131. See Lacey, Vagrancy and Other Crimes of Personal Condition, 66 Harv.L.Rev. 1203 (1953).

132. Note, supra note 74, at 647.

133. This was the result reached in State ex rel. Blouin v. Walker, 244 La. 699, 154 So.2d 368 (1963).

134. 392 U.S. 514, 88 S.Ct. 2145, 20 L.Ed.2d 1254 (1968).

tutionally convicted of being "found in a state of intoxication in any public place."

The emphasis of the Court in *Robinson* upon the fact that narcotics addiction is an illness has broader implications. From this it would seem to follow, as a few courts have held,[135] that public intoxication cannot be punished when the defendant suffers from the illness of alcohol addiction, notwithstanding the fact that the offense requires an act of sorts—appearing in a public place while in an intoxicated condition. The Supreme Court reached a contrary result in *Powell,* although this was attributable in part to the fact that the record in the case revealed little about the defendant's drinking problem or the nature of alcoholism. As noted above, four members of the Court based the affirmance of Powell's conviction upon a narrow interpretation of *Robinson.* The four dissenting justices in *Powell,* on the other hand, saw *Robinson* as standing for this proposition: "Criminal penalties may not be inflicted upon a person for being in a condition which he is powerless to change." But lower courts have more recently held quite consistently that alcoholism is no defense to a charge of drunkenness.[136]

If the Eighth Amendment prohibits the punishment of antisocial acts which are attributable to an illness, it is apparent that it is of some importance to determine precisely what sort of connection between the illness and the conduct is necessary. For example, does *Robinson* prohibit conviction of narcotics addicts for using narcotics or for possessing narcotics for their own use? While lower courts have generally answered this question in the negative,[137] it might be argued that the "illness" rationale of *Robinson* bars conviction for that conduct which is an inevitable

consequence of the addiction.[138] This is essentially the position of the dissenters in *Powell,* for they concede that public intoxication is not merely a crime of status, but argue that the defendant, once intoxicated, could not prevent himself from appearing in public places. Concurring Justice White, although concluding there was no showing Powell was unable to prevent himself from appearing in public while intoxicated, observed that "punishing an addict for using drugs convicts for addiction under a different name."

But, if possession and use of narcotics are inevitable for the addict, why cannot it also be said that the commission of other offenses—such as larceny, robbery, burglary, and prostitution—are likewise inevitable because they supply the funds necessary for the continued use of narcotics? It is apparent that courts will be reluctant to extend the cruel and unusual punishment doctrine this far,[139] although it is difficult to articulate a principle upon which to justify not doing so if conviction for possession and use were deemed impermissible. The absence of such a principle is stressed in the opinion of the Court in *Powell,* but the dissenters argued that a constitutional bar on conviction of a chronic alcoholic for being intoxicated in public would not likewise bar conviction for such crimes as theft and robbery because they "are not part of the syndrome of the disease of chronic alcoholism."

The same difficulty is present when one considers the question of whether the *Robinson* decision does not compel the broadening of the definition of insanity to encompass all those who cannot control their behavior because of a mental disease or defect.[140] In *Powell,* four members of the court argued that

---

135. Easter v. District of Columbia, 361 F.2d 50 (D.C. Cir.1966); Driver v. Hinnant, 356 F.2d 761 (4th Cir.1966).

136. Vick v. State, 453 P.2d 342 (Alaska 1969); People v. Hoy, 380 Mich. 597, 158 N.W.2d 436 (1968); Seattle v. Hill, 72 Wn.2d 786, 435 P.2d 692 (1967).

137. United States v. Moore, 486 F.2d 1139 (D.C.Cir. 1973); State v. Herro, 120 Ariz. 604, 587 P.2d 1181 (1978); State v. Smith, 33 N.Y.2d 221, 351 N.Y.S.2d 663, 306 N.E.2d 787 (1973). See Annot., 73 A.L.R.3d 16 (1976).

138. The majority in *Robinson,* in listing the conduct which the state could prohibit, omitted use of narcotics,

which Justice White in dissent viewed as deliberate. In support of the view that addicts cannot be punished for possession or use, see Cuomo, supra note 130, at 187–93; Note, supra note 74, at 651–52.

139. This extension was rejected in People v. Borrero, 19 N.Y.2d 332, 227 N.E.2d 18, 280 N.Y.S.2d 109 (1967), but the court reached this conclusion upon the questionable assumption that *Robinson* is limited to offenses not defined in terms of conduct.

140. Courts have refused to reach this conclusion, Jackson v. Dickson, 325 F.2d 573 (9th Cir.1963); White v.

extension of *Robinson* to that case would have the unfortunate result of raising to constitutional dimension the issue of what test of insanity must be employed in the state courts.

By contrast, the third factor emphasized by the Court in *Robinson,* that addiction is an illness "which may be contracted innocently or involuntarily," probably should not be viewed as critical. It is true that reliance upon this factor would be a convenient way of limiting the reach of the *Robinson* decision. It is also true that such a limitation has some merit, at least in the sense that it identifies a class of cases in which the cruel and unusual punishment argument is most compelling: those in which the defendant was *at no time* at fault for creating his condition.[141] However, the decision in *Robinson* cannot be said to rest upon this factor, as the Court struck down the addiction statute as to all cases rather than recognize that involuntary or innocent addiction could be put forward as a valid defense.[142] None of the various views expressed in *Powell* question that conclusion.

WESTLAW REFERENCES

cruel /2 unusual /2 punishment /s death /3
    penalty sentence

110k1213 /p murder!

coker +4 georgia /12 433 +4 584 /p
    disproportion! proportion!

eight /3 amendment /p solem +4 helm /12
    103 +4 3001

§ 2.15 Other Constitutional Limitations on the States

State criminal statutes may be found to suffer from constitutional defects other than those discussed in the previous sections. For one thing, state legislation may be challenged on the ground that it violates some provision of the state constitution. Most state constitutions have provisions comparable to those in the federal constitution dealing with due process, equal protection, and the guarantee of specific rights. While state courts often give these provisions essentially the same interpretation as their counterparts in the United States Constitution, they are sometimes construed more broadly, with the result that a state statute which would have withstood challenge before the United States Supreme Court is invalidated by a state court as contrary to the state constitution. In addition, a state criminal statute may be voided because it fails to satisfy certain formal requirements imposed by the state constitution. A number of state constitutions provide that the title of a statute must describe the body of the statute, that no more than one subject may be contained in one statute, and that the legislature must follow certain procedures in enacting bills into law. Such provisions are usually held to be mandatory, with the result that, if they are violated in the case of a criminal statute, the statute will be held unconstitutional.[1] On the other hand, some relatively unimportant formal provisions (such as the rather common state constitutional provision that all statutes should be headed by the clause, "Be it enacted by [the legislature of the state]") have been held to be directory

Rhay, 64 Wash.2d 15, 390 P.2d 535 (1964). Although there are cases holding that it is a violation of substantive due process to abolish the insanity defense, e.g., Sinclair v. State, 161 Miss. 142, 132 So. 581 (1931); State v. Strasburg, 60 Wash. 106, 110 P. 1020 (1910), the Supreme Court has ruled that states are not constitutionally required to adopt any particular insanity test, Leland v. Oregon, 343 U.S. 790, 72 S.Ct. 1002, 96 L.Ed. 1302 (1952). See Note, supra note 74, at 652–54.

141. As compared to those cases in which the addiction was preceded by a conscious and deliberate decision to experiment with drugs. See Note, supra note 74, at 649.

142. If the source of the addiction was a matter of importance, then Justice Clark's objections in dissent

would be persuasive: "Nor is the conjecture relevant that petitioner may have acquired his habit under lawful circumstances. There was no suggestion by him to this effect at trial, and surely the State need not rebut all possible lawful sources of addiction as part of its prima facie case."

§ 2.15

1. E.g., State v. Haun, 61 Kan. 146, 59 P. 340 (1899) (criminal statute unconstitutional where title not descriptive of body); Acklen v. Thompson, 122 Tenn. 43, 126 S.W. 730 (1909) (criminal statute unconstitutional where title not descriptive of body of statute and body of statute embraces more than one subject).

only, so that the failure of the legislature to comply therewith does not make the statute unconstitutional.[2]

In addition, and because of the nature of our federal system, there are certain limitations in the United States Constitution which are applicable only to state legislation. For one thing, state legislatures are expressly forbidden to legislate on certain matters.[3] The Constitution also gives the Congress the authority to legislate on certain subjects[4] (e.g., "To regulate Commerce * * * among the several States"), which must be considered in connection with the provision that the constitution and laws of the United States made in pursuance thereof are the supreme law of the land, notwithstanding anything in the constitution or laws of any state.[5] This gives rise to two difficult problems: (1) Where the Constitution gives Congress a regulatory power, but says nothing about denying such power to the states, may a state regulate on such matters when the Congress has not done so? (2) Where, again, the Constitution gives such power to Congress but does not deny it to the states, but the Congress has regulated on a particular subject, may a state adopt additional regulations on the same subject?

(a) Congress Has Not Acted: The Negative Implications of the Commerce Clause.[6] As to the first of these two ques-

tions, the major battleground has been the commerce clause,[7] and the Supreme Court has on innumerable occasions had to pass upon the competing interests of state and national power in the field of commerce—between the police power of the states, on the one hand, and the power of the national government to ensure freedom of interstate commerce, on the other. Many of the Supreme Court cases in this area of the law have involved civil matters, especially the power of the state to tax; but a number of the cases have involved criminal prosecutions for violation of state statutes which, while regulating local matters, also operate as regulations of interstate commerce. The Court has struck down some of these criminal statutes as unconstitutional burdens on interstate commerce.[8]

Over the years, the Supreme Court has set forth a number of different tests for determining the validity of state laws in this context. After an early statement to the effect that the question was whether the particular subject called for uniform regulation or for diversity in regulation,[9] the Court used many other expressions, such as whether the state law was a "burden," or a "substantial" or "undue" burden on commerce; whether the effect on commerce was "direct" or "indirect"; and whether the regulation was or was not imposed "on" interstate commerce itself.[10]

---

2. E.g., City of Cape Girardeau v. Riley, 52 Mo. 424 (1873).

3. U.S.Const. art. I, § 10.

4. U.S.Const. art. I, § 8.

5. U.S.Const. art. VI.

6. See 1 R. Rotunda, J. Nowak & J. Young, Treatise on Constitutional Law ch. 11 (1986); Eule, Laying the Dormant Commerce Clause to Rest, 91 Yale L.J. 425 (1982); Maltz, How Much Regulation is Too Much—An Examination of Commerce Clause Jurisprudence, 50 Geo.Wash.L. Rev. 47 (1981).

7. U.S.Const. art. I, § 8, cl. 3.

8. E.g., Welton v. Missouri, 91 U.S. 275, 23 L.Ed. 347 (1876) (criminal prosecution for violating state licensing statute requiring peddlers of wares made outside state to obtain license); Minnesota v. Barber, 136 U.S. 313, 10 S.Ct. 862, 34 L.Ed. 455 (1890) (criminal prosecution for violating state health statute in selling for food animal slaughtered out-of-state and not inspected and certified in state, where effect of statute was to make it impossible for animals slaughtered outside state to be sold in state); Edwards v. California, 314 U.S. 160, 62 S.Ct. 164, 86 L.Ed.

119 (1941) (criminal prosecution for violating state depression-born statute forbidding importation of nonresident indigents into state); Southern Pacific Co. v. Arizona ex rel. Sullivan, 325 U.S. 761, 65 S.Ct. 1515, 89 L.Ed. 1915 (1945) (suit against interstate railroad to recover statutory penalty for violating state statute limiting length of trains in the interest of safety); Morgan v. Virginia, 328 U.S. 373, 66 S.Ct. 1050, 90 L.Ed. 1317 (1946) (criminal prosecution for violating state racial segregation statute making it a crime for interstate bus passenger to refuse to segregate); Dean Milk Co. v. City of Madison, 340 U.S. 349, 71 S.Ct. 295, 95 L.Ed. 329 (1951) (municipal health ordinance making it unlawful to sell milk not pasteurized at a plant within 5 miles of municipality; defendant was out-of-state milk company).

9. Cooley v. Board of Wardens of the Port of Philadelphia, 53 U.S. (12 How.) 299, 13 L.Ed. 996 (1851). This remains a relevant consideration. See, e.g., Ray v. Atlantic Richfield Co., 435 U.S. 151, 98 S.Ct. 988, 55 L.Ed.2d 179 (1978) (tug escort law upheld; it "not the type of regulation that demands a uniform national rule").

10. See Stern, The Problems of Yesteryear—Commerce and Due Process, 4 Vand.L.Rev. 446, 451–52 (1951).

However, recently the Court has utilized a three-part inquiry: "(1) whether the challenged statute regulates evenhandedly with only 'incidental' effects on interstate commerce, or discriminates against interstate commerce either on its face or in practical effect; (2) whether the statute serves a legitimate local purpose; and, if so, (3) whether alternate means could promote this local purpose as well without discriminating against interstate commerce.[11] The burden is on the person challenging the statute to show the discrimination against interstate commerce, and the state must then justify the local benefits and unavailability of alternatives.[12]

Illustrative of laws which discriminate against interstate commerce are those which make it an offense to engage in conduct only with respect to goods coming from out of the state [13] or only as to goods leaving the state,[14] those which have "a sweeping extraterritorial effect," [15] and those which bear disproportionately upon out-of-staters.[16] With respect to legitimacy of purpose, it is relevant that the legislation was intended as a protectionist measure [17] or that its contribution to some

legitimate objective is speculative at best [18] or minimal in relation to the burden imposed on interstate commerce.[19]   As for alternate means, it is of course particularly significant that the local interest could have been just as well protected by restrictions directed more to local activities.[20]

The case of *Edwards v. California* [21] deserves special mention here, as, unlike almost all the other cases in this area, the concern was not with the regulation of business but rather with the right of individuals to move about.   The Court reversed a conviction under a California statute which made it a misdemeanor for any person to bring "into the State any indigent person who is not a resident of the State, knowing him to be an indigent person," holding that an outright ban on immigration into a state by a class of "undesirables" is an undue burden on interstate commerce.   On the basis of the *Edwards* decision and others, the Court now speaks of a "constitutional right to travel from one State to another," [22] which appears to be derived from the commerce clause and other constitutional provisions as well,[23] and which might

11.   Hughes v. Oklahoma, 441 U.S. 322, 99 S.Ct. 1727, 60 L.Ed.2d 250 (1979).

12.   Ibid.

13.   City of Philadelphia v. New Jersey, 437 U.S. 617, 98 S.Ct. 2531, 57 L.Ed.2d 475 (1978) (law invalid which prohibited importation of most "solid or liquid waste which originated or was collected outside the territorial limits of the State").

14.   Hughes v. Oklahoma, supra note 11 (law invalid which prohibited exporting from state minnows for sale but imposed no limits on in-state disposition).

15.   Edgar v. Mite Corp., 457 U.S. 624, 102 S.Ct. 2629, 73 L.Ed.2d 269 (1982) (state statutes on business takeovers permitted Illinois official to block a nationwide tender offer).

16.   Kassel v. Consolidated Freightways Corp., 450 U.S. 662, 101 S.Ct. 1309, 67 L.Ed.2d 580 (1981) (prohibition on use of 65-ft. double-trailer trucks bears disproportionately on out-of-staters); Raymond v. Motor Transportation, Inc. v. Rice, 434 U.S. 429, 98 S.Ct. 787, 54 L.Ed.2d 664 (1978) (because many exceptions in the statute favor local industry, it cannot be assumed state's own political processes will act as a check on the regulation).

17.   Kassel v. Consolidated Freightways Corp., supra note 16 (two members of majority stress impermissible purpose shown by legislative history).

18.   Raymond Motor Transportation, Inc. v. Rice, supra note 16 (prohibited 65-ft. double trailers shown to be just as safe if not safer than permitted 55-ft. single rigs).

19.   Edgar v. Mite Corp., supra note 15.

20.   Hughes v. Oklahoma, supra note 11 (limits on instate use of minnows would more likely serve the purported objective of the statute).

21.   314 U.S. 160, 62 S.Ct. 164, 86 L.Ed. 119 (1941).

22.   United States v. Guest, 383 U.S. 745, 86 S.Ct. 1170, 16 L.Ed.2d 239 (1966) (sustaining under the federal Civil Rights Act criminal prohibition of conspiracies to injure any citizen in the exercise of "any right or privilege secured * * * by the Constitution or laws of the United States" an indictment charging conspiracy to injure Negroes in the exercise of the right to travel freely to and from the State of Georgia).

23.   Other bases may be the state privilege and immunities clause, U.S.Const. art. IV, § 2, cl. 1, the federal privileges and immunities clause, U.S.Const. amend. XIV, § 1, and the due process clauses.   "The right to travel is a part of the 'liberty' of which the citizen cannot be deprived without due process of law. * * * Freedom of movement across frontiers in either direction, and inside frontiers as well, was a part of our heritage.   Travel abroad, like travel within the country * * * may be as close to the heart of the individual as the choice of what he eats, or wears, or reads.   Freedom of movement is basic to our scheme of values." Aptheker v. Secretary of State, 378 U.S. 500, 84 S.Ct. 1659, 12 L.Ed.2d 992 (1964), quoting Kent v. Dulles, 357 U.S. 116, 78 S.Ct. 1113, 2 L.Ed.2d 1204 (1958).

well be used to strike down some current vagrancy statutes and similar criminal laws.[24]

WESTLAW
REFERENCES

("southern pacific" /4 arizona) (edwards /2
    california) (morgan /4 virginia) /p commerce /p
    crim**** penal misdemeanor felony
topic(92) /p vagran** /s statute law ordinance

(b) Congress Has Acted: The Pre-emption Doctrine.[25] A state criminal law, otherwise within the police power of the state, may be invalid because a federal law on the subject has "preempted" (or "occupied") the field to the exclusion of state law. "In the complex system of polity which prevails in this country, the powers of government may be divided into four classes: [1] Those which belong exclusively to the states; [2] Those which belong exclusively to the national government; [3] Those which may be exercised concurrently and independently by both; [4] Those which

may be exercised by the states, but only until Congress shall see fit to act upon the subject."[26] The sometimes difficult problem in this area of constitutional law is whether to place a particular state criminal statute within category 3 or category 4, when both a federal and state criminal statute deal with the same subject matter. The problem would be easier to solve if Congress expressly provided that its statute was to be exclusive or not; but it seldom does so.[27]

Not infrequently a state criminal statute exists side by side with a federal statute, both punishing identical or substantially identical conduct. The state statute has often been upheld on the theory that the two statutes do not conflict with one another, and that Congress did not intend to make its law exclusive.[28] The state statute is even more clearly valid if the conduct punished by the state and nation is parallel but not substantially identical.[29] On the other hand, some state criminal

24. See Amsterdam, Federal Constitutional Restrictions on the Punishment of Crimes of Status, Crimes of General Obnoxiousness, Crimes of Displeasing Police Officers, and the Like, 3 Crim.L.Bull. 205, 211–16 (1967).

25. See 1 R. Rotunda, J. Nowak & J. Young, Treatise on Constitutional Law §§ 12.1–12.4 (1986); Grant, The Scope and Nature of Concurrent Power, 34 Colum.L.Rev. 995 (1934); Hirsch, Toward a New View of Federal Preemption, 1972 U.Ill.L.F. 515; Hunt, State Control of Sedition: The Smith Act as the Supreme Law of the Land, 41 Minn.L.Rev. 287 (1957); Note, 12 Stan.L.Rev. 208 (1959).

26. Ex parte McNiel, 80 U.S. (13 Wall.) 236, 20 L.Ed. 624 (1872).

27. 18 U.S.C.A. § 3231 contains a general provision that Title 18 of the U.S.Code shall not impair the jurisdiction of the states. This provision, however, has not been taken to mean that the federal government cannot preempt the field in the criminal area. See, e.g., Pennsylvania v. Nelson, 350 U.S. 497, 76 S.Ct. 477, 100 L.Ed. 640 (1956).

The proposed new federal criminal code expressly provides that the "existence of federal jurisdiction over an offense shall not, in itself, prevent any state or local government from exercising jurisdiction to enforce its own laws applicable to the conduct in question." National Comm'n on Reform of Federal Criminal Laws, Final Report—Proposed New Federal Criminal Code § 206 (1971). As to the resulting risk of prosecutions on both the state and federal level, this is dealt with by (a) authorizing federal agencies "to decline or discontinue federal enforcement efforts whenever the offense can effectively be prosecuted by nonfederal agencies and it appears that there is no substantial Federal interest in further prosecution or that the offense primarily affects state, local or foreign interests," id. at § 207; (b) making a previous state prose-

cution a bar to a federal prosecution for the same conduct under certain circumstances, one exception being where the state law "is intended to prevent a substantially different harm or evil from the law defining the offense for which he is subsequently prosecuted," id. at § 707; and (c) making a prior federal prosecution a bar to a state prosecution for the same conduct under certain circumstances, an exception being where the federal law "is intended to prevent a substantially different harm or evil from the law defining the offense for which he is subsequently prosecuted," id. at § 708.

28. E.g., Sexton v. California, 189 U.S. 319, 23 S.Ct. 543, 47 L.Ed. 833 (1903) (state extortion statute punished extortion by threats to accuse victim of federal crime; federal extortion statute punished same conduct; state statute upheld); Hebert v. Louisiana, 272 U.S. 312, 47 S.Ct. 103, 71 L.Ed. 270 (1926) (state statute punished manufacture of liquor; federal Volstead Act punished the same conduct; state statute upheld); California v. Zook, 336 U.S. 725, 69 S.Ct. 841, 93 L.Ed. 1005 (1949) (state statute punished sale or arrangement of interstate transportation over state's public highways if carrier has no permit from I.C.C.; federal statute punished substantially same conduct; state statute upheld); People v. VonRosen, 13 Ill.2d 68, 147 N.E.2d 327 (1958) (federal statutes on conduct with respect to U.S. flag left room for Illinois statute making criminal the public desecration of the flag; here magazine contained picture of a young lady nude except for hat, sunglasses and a small but well-placed American flag).

29. E.g., Fox v. Ohio, 46 U.S. (5 How.) 410, 12 L.Ed. 213 (1847) (federal statute punished counterfeiting; state statute punished uttering a counterfeit coin; state statute upheld). Thus it seems clear that the federal statute punishing interstate transportation of stolen cars does not

legislation has been held unconstitutional under the supremacy clause on the theory that federal legislation has occupied the field. Thus a state perjury statute was held unconstitutional as applied to perjury committed in a federal hearing upon a contested Congressional election.[30] A state statute punishing a banker for accepting a deposit knowing the bank to be insolvent was held invalid as applied to an officer of a national bank, because federal legislation on national banks impliedly indicated an intent to occupy the field to the exclusion of the states.[31] And more recently a state sedition statute punishing advocacy of the violent overthrow of the government of the United States was held invalid in view of the specific federal statute [32] punishing such conduct.[33]

It is not always easy to distinguish the cases decided one way from those decided the other. As the Court has acknowledged, there is no "rigid formula or rule which can be used as a universal pattern to determine the meaning and purpose of every act of Congress. This Court, in considering the validity of state laws in the light of treaties or federal laws touching the same subject, has made use of the following expressions: conflicting; contrary to; occupying the field; repugnance; difference; irreconcilability; inconsistency; violation; curtailment; and interference. But none of these expressions provides an infalli-

ble constitutional test or an exclusive constitutional yardstick. In the final analysis, there can be no one crystal clear distinctly marked formula." [34] However, in *Pennsylvania v. Nelson* [35] the Supreme Court set forth three tests for determining the pre-emption issue: (1) Is the federal legislative scheme as to the subject matter in question so pervasive as to indicate that Congress must have meant the states were not to supplement the federal legislation? (2) Is the federal interest in the subject matter so dominant that Congress must have meant to preclude the states from dealing with the matter? (3) Would state enforcement in the matter present a serious danger to effective federal enforcement?

Of these three questions, the first two most directly focus upon a determination of what Congress intended. However, in many cases an inquiry into the intent of Congress is not fruitful, as often Congress enacts legislation without anticipating the problem of pre-emption. It is undoubtedly true, therefore, that the Supreme Court has often invalidated state laws on a pre-emption theory (often by resort to "intent of Congress" analysis), when in fact Congress did *not* intend to nullify the concurrent jurisdiction of the states.[36] However, although the Court has frequently been criticized on this basis,[37] it can be said that often the result reached has been sound because it

---

pre-empt the field so as to invalidate state laws on theft of cars.

30. In re Loney, 134 U.S. 372, 10 S.Ct. 584, 33 L.Ed. 950 (1890), the Court stating that the administration of justice in federal courts "would be greatly embarrassed" if the states were allowed to enter this area of law.

31. Easton v. Iowa, 188 U.S. 220, 23 S.Ct. 288, 47 L.Ed. 452 (1903), the Court emphasizing the "confusion" which would necessarily result from two sovereigns exercising concurrent control in the area of insolvent national banks.

32. 18 U.S.C.A. § 2385, the "Smith Act."

33. Pennsylvania v. Nelson, 350 U.S. 497, 76 S.Ct. 477, 100 L.Ed. 640 (1956). Note that in the absence of federal legislation the states may punish sedition against the United States. Gitlow v. New York, 268 U.S. 652, 45 S.Ct. 625, 69 L.Ed. 1138 (1925). That part of the Pennsylvania sedition statute punishing advocacy of the violent overthrow of Pennsylvania government was not necessarily invalidated. See Braden v. Commonwealth, 291 S.W.2d 843 (Ky.1956); Commonwealth v. Gilbert, 334 Mass. 71, 134 N.E.2d 13 (1956).

34. Hines v. Davidowitz, 312 U.S. 52, 61 S.Ct. 399, 85 L.Ed. 581 (1941). "The problems arise when Congress does not deal explicitly with the issue of preemption and the claim is made that particular congressional legislation precludes state regulation on the same subject. Most such issues present sui generis problems whose resolution depends on widely variant considerations, including, of course, the unique terms, history, and objectives of the relevant federal legislation." W. Lockhart, Y. Kamisar & J. Choper, Constitutional Law 346–47 (5th ed. 1980).

35. 350 U.S. 497, 76 S.Ct. 477, 100 L.Ed. 640 (1956).

36. See Note, supra note 25, at 208, for citations to various authorities to the effect that Congress did not intend, by passage of the Smith Act and related legislation, to occupy the field of sedition. Also, see id. at 217 on the point that the Court in *Nelson* found that enforcement of state sedition laws would result in conflict with federal enforcement despite the Justice Department's express disclaimer of such conflicts.

37. See authorities cited in Note, supra note 25, at 208 n. 1.

in fact rests upon a determination that the continued existence of the state law is not consistent with the general purpose of the federal statute, considering the evil Congress sought to remedy and the methods it chose for this purpose.[38]

Also, it has been pointed out that the pre-emption decisions of the United States Supreme Court can be better understood if account is taken of the fact that pre-emption has become a "preferential ground" for decision in cases posing other serious constitutional questions.[39] That is, state statutes are sometimes voided on the ground that they conflict with federal legislation when it might well be argued that, even in the absence of federal legislation, the state laws are unconstitutional. Pre-emption is often a more attractive ground for decision (in much the same way that void-for-vagueness often is[40]) because it permits the Court to avoid another very difficult constitutional issue and the necessity of erecting permanent limits on the police power of the states.[41] Thus, whether a state law will be held to be pre-empted may be influenced to some degree by the presence of other factors, such as:

(1) whether the state law may intrude into an area of exclusive national concern. As noted earlier, even when Congress has not acted, a state law may be invalidated because it intrudes upon an area of Congressional power, such as the power to regulate interstate commerce. When it appears that a substantial argument of this kind might be made, the chances are greater that the fact Congress

has legislated will result in a finding of pre-emption. Thus, such a finding is often made to rest upon facts which have long been utilized to support a finding that the state law burdens interstate commerce, such as the entire halting of the flow of commerce to enforce compliance with state laws[42] or the use of state laws to favor local economic interests.[43] Similarly, in *Hines v. Davidowitz*[44] a state alien registration law was voided on the ground that it was preempted by the federal alien registration act, but the Court placed considerable emphasis upon the fact that the subject matter appeared to be of exclusive national concern, as reflected in the constitutional provision granting Congress the power to prescribe "a uniform rule of naturalization" and the foreign relations power.[45]

(2) whether the state law may result in the unfair imposition of multiple punishment. Although the double jeopardy clause does not prevent both the federal government and a state from punishing the same act, where that act constitutes a crime against both sovereigns,[46] the thought that such double prosecution and punishment is not altogether fair may influence a finding of pre-emption. As the Court said in *Nelson*, "We are not unmindful of the risk of compounding punishments which would be created by finding concurrent state power."[47] This factor is apt to receive greater consideration when the penalties provided under the two laws are severe.[48]

(3) whether the state law may violate due process. A finding of pre-emption sometimes serves as a convenient means of striking down

---

38. A number of commentators have argued that this, rather than the intent of Congress, should be determinative. See, e.g., H. Hart & A. Sacks, The Legal Process 1410–17 (1958).

39. See Note, supra note 25, at 217–25.

40. See § 2.10(a).

41. Of course, no limit is permanent in that the Supreme Court might overrule prior decisions on the permissible reach of state police power. However, it is far less permanent if the Court merely rules that the state statute in question is void so long as Congress does not repeal or amend the relevant federal statutes.

42. E.g., Castle v. Hayes Freight Lines, Inc., 348 U.S. 61, 75 S.Ct. 191, 99 L.Ed. 68 (1954).

43. E.g., City of Chicago v. Atchison, T. & S.F. Ry., 357 U.S. 77, 78 S.Ct. 1063, 2 L.Ed.2d 1174 (1958).

44. 312 U.S. 52, 61 S.Ct. 399, 85 L.Ed. 581 (1941).

45. Sometimes the preemption and commerce clause objections will both be accepted in the same case upon very similar analysis. See Edgar v. Mite Corp., 457 U.S. 624, 102 S.Ct. 2629, 73 L.Ed.2d 269 (1982).

46. Abbate v. United States, 359 U.S. 187, 79 S.Ct. 666, 3 L.Ed.2d 729 (1959); Bartkus v. Illinois, 359 U.S. 121, 79 S.Ct. 676, 3 L.Ed.2d 684 (1959); United States v. Lanza, 260 U.S. 377, 43 S.Ct. 141, 67 L.Ed. 314 (1922).

47. Pennsylvania v. Nelson, 350 U.S. 497, 76 S.Ct. 477, 100 L.Ed. 640 (1956).

48. Compare Pennsylvania v. Nelson, supra, with California v. Zook, 336 U.S. 725, 69 S.Ct. 841, 93 L.Ed. 1005 (1949).

a statute which probably violates due process, as the Court has sometimes hinted. For example, in *Hines v. Davidowitz,* [49] holding that a state alien registration law was pre-empted, the Court stressed that "it is also of importance that this legislation deals with the rights, liberties, and personal freedoms of human beings, and is in an entirely different category from state tax laws or state pure food laws regulating the labels on cans." [50]

 WESTLAW REFERENCES

topic(110) /p pre-empt***

pennsylvania /3 nelson /p pre-empt***

hines /3 davidowitz /p pre-empt***

49. 312 U.S. 52, 61 S.Ct. 399, 85 L.Ed. 581 (1941).

50. Similarly, in Pennsylvania v. Nelson, supra note 47, the Court stressed that many state antisedition laws were vague and almost wholly without safeguards.

Chapter 3

BASIC PREMISES OF THE CRIMINAL LAW

Table of Sections

---

§ 3.1 The Basic Premises

We have already noted [1] that the substantive law of crimes consists primarily of (1) the definitions of the various specific crimes, from murder on down to such minor offenses as speeding, (2) some broader general principles of the substantive criminal law applicable to more than a single crime and so not made a part of the definitions of specific crimes,[2] and (3) some even broader propositions of law, the basic premises which underlie the whole of the Anglo-American substantive criminal law.[3] These basic premises have been of great importance in shaping the criminal law, although we shall see that they have not always been wholly accepted without exception.

The first of these basic premises concerns the requirement of an act; generally, it may be said that conduct, to be criminal, must consist of something more than a mere bad state of mind. We have already seen this requirement reflected in court decisions holding that mere status or condition cannot constitutionally be made a crime.[4] The requirement of an act is discussed further in this chapter,[5] as is the notion that the failure to carry out a legal duty may also serve as the basis of liability.[6]

Another basic premise is that conduct, to be criminal, must consist of something more than mere action (or non-action where there is a legal duty to act); some sort of bad state of mind is required as well. Again, we have already noted that this requirement has sometimes been expressed as a constitutional limitation on the power to create crimes.[7] The various mental states are discussed in more detail in the present chapter.[8] In addition, consideration is given herein to the many statutes which impose liability without fault, that is, liability without regard to the

§ 3.1

1. See § 1.2.

2. E.g., the great defense-to-liability principles of insanity, infancy, mistake of fact or law, coercion, necessity, self-defense; and the affirmative-liability principles concerning the responsibility of parties to crime (principles and accessories) and concerning liability for the inchoate crimes of attempt, conspiracy and solicitation.

3. There is no general agreement as to the terminology to be used to describe these three types of legal propositions concerning crimes. J. Hall, General Principles of Criminal Law 17 (2d ed. 1960), calls them, in the order listed in the text above: (1) "rules"; (2) "doctrines"; and (3) "principles." His valuable book deals at length with the second and third types. The excellent book by the English author, Glanville Williams, Criminal Law: The General Part (2d ed. 1961), uses the terms "general part" and "general principles" to cover both the second and third types of substantive criminal law.

In this book the expression "general principles" will be used to cover the second type (considered in chapters 4–6), and the expression "basic premises" to cover the third type (treated in this chapter).

4. See §§ 2.12(d), 2.14(f).

5. See § 3.2.

6. See § 3.3.

7. See § 2.12(d).

8. See §§ 3.4–3.7.

defendant's mental state at the time he or another engaged in the proscribed acts.[9]

A third basic premise is that the physical conduct and mental state must concur, and it is considered in this chapter.[10] Generally, it may be said that the defendant's mental state must concur with his act or omission, in the sense that the former actuates the latter. A somewhat different problem of concurrence, also discussed herein, concerns the question of whether the bad results of the defendant's conduct must coincide in type or degree with the results intended or risked. As we shall see, the better view is that one should not be convicted for causing a greater or different harm than is reflected in his mental state, although there are many exceptions to this in current law.

A fourth basic premise concerns harm; only harmful conduct should be made criminal. It is reflected in the substantive due process notion that a criminal statute is unconstitutional if it bears no reasonable relation to injury to the public.[11] As yet, however, substantive due process has not been viewed as barring criminal statutes proscribing private acts of immorality between consenting adults,[12] although the wisdom of using the

criminal law for the promotion and protection of private morality has long been a subject of debate.[13] On the one hand, it is argued that private immorality, like treason, in fact harms society by jeopardizing its existence.[14] On the other, it is contended that any infringement of individual liberty is itself a harm for which there must be justification; that there is no proof that society is harmed by private immorality; that the enforcement of laws against private sin is necessarily impracticable and unevenhanded; and that such laws serve only to present the unscrupulous with an opportunity for blackmail.[15] The subject of harm is not discussed further in the present chapter, although certain aspects of it will be treated later.[16]

Yet another basic premise is that as to those crimes which require not only some forbidden conduct but also some particular result of that conduct, the conduct must be the "legal cause" (often called "proximate cause") of the result. This premise gives rise to problems of considerable difficulty, and they are discussed in this chapter.[17]

The sixth basic premise is that a person who has engaged in criminal conduct may only be subjected to the legally prescribed

---

9. See §§ 3.8–3.10.

10. See § 3.11.

11. See § 2.12.

12. See Comment, 45 Fordham L.Rev. 553 (1976). However, the "penumbral" right of privacy may impose some limits here. See § 2.14(d); Note, 25 Wayne L.Rev. 1067 (1979).

13. A century ago John Stuart Mill, On Liberty (1863), argued, "The only purpose for which power can rightfully be exercised over any member of a civilized community against his will is to prevent harm to others. His own good, either physical or moral, is not a sufficient warrant." The great English judge and criminal law historian, Sir James Fitzjames Stephen, wrote Liberty, Equality, Fraternity (2d ed. 1874), in reply. More recently the debate was carried on, in book form, by English Lord Justice Patrick Devlin, The Enforcement of Morals (1965), holding that enforcement of morality is a proper function of the criminal law; with Oxford Professor H.L.A. Hart, Law, Liberty and Morality (1963), arguing to the contrary. The impetus for the modern debate was the conclusion, reached by the American Law Institute in its Model Penal Code and by the Wolfenden Committee in England, see Report of the Committee on Homosexual Offenses and Prostitution (1957), that homosexual conduct between consenting adults in private ought not to be criminal.

See also Dworkin, Lord Devlin and the Enforcement of Morals, 75 Yale L.J. 986 (1966); Hindes, Morality Enforcement Through the Criminal Law and the Modern Doctrine of Substantive Due Process, 126 U.Pa.L.Rev. 344 (1977); Hughes, Morals and the Criminal Law, 71 Yale L.J. 662 (1962); Rostow, The Enforcement of Morals, 1960 Cambridge L.J. 174; Wollheim, Crime, Sin and Mr. Justice Devlin, Encounter 34 (Nov.1959); Note, 18 Ariz.L.Rev. 207 (1976); Comment 14 U.C.L.A.L.Rev. 581 (1967).

On the broader issue of overcriminalization, see H. Packer, The Limits of the Criminal Sanction (1968); Kadish, More on Overcriminalization: A Reply to Professor Junker, 19 U.C.L.A.L.Rev. 719 (1972); Kadish, The Crisis of Overcriminalization, 374 Annals 157 (1967); Junker, Criminalization and Criminogenesis, 19 U.C.L.A.L.Rev. 697 (1972); Skolnick, Criminalization and Criminogenesis: A Reply to Professor Junker, 19 U.C.L.A.L.Rev. 715 (1972).

14. P. Devlin, supra note 13.

15. H. Hart, supra note 13.

16. E.g., in ch. 6, dealing with uncompleted criminal conduct, where the question is when the threat to society is great enough to justify punishment of aborted, interrupted, or abandoned criminal schemes.

17. See § 3.12.

punishment. The role of punishment has already been considered,[18] and will not be discussed in the following sections.

The final basic premise of the criminal law is that conduct is not criminal unless forbidden by law which gives advance warning that such conduct is criminal. This idea, sometimes termed "the principle of legality," is often expressed by the Latin phrase *nullum crimin sine lege, nulla poena sine lege* (no crime or punishment without law). The various areas of the criminal law in which the principal of legality operates have already been treated at some length. It is reflected in the ex post facto prohibition,[19] the rule of strict construction of criminal statutes,[20] the void-for-vagueness doctrine,[21] and the trend away from open-ended common law crimes.[22]

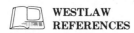 **WESTLAW REFERENCES**

di legal cause

digest(crime criminal /p eviden! proof prov*** /p conduct /p solicitat!)

---

§ 3.2   The Requirement of an Act

Bad thoughts alone cannot constitute a crime; there must be an act, or an omission to act where there is a legal duty to act. Thus the common law crimes are defined in terms of act or omission to act, and statutory crimes are unconstitutional unless so defined. A bodily movement, to qualify as an act forming the basis of criminal liability, must be voluntary.

(a) Meaning of "Act." The word "act" has been defined in many different ways, often depending upon the purpose for which the word is used. Sometimes, for example, there

are said to be both positive and negative acts, the latter referring to leaving undone something that ought to be done.[1] Similarly, the word has sometimes been defined so as to encompass both internal and external acts; internal acts are said to be "acts of the mind" which do not necessarily "realize themselves in acts of the body."[2] The view has also been taken that an act includes three constituent parts: (1) its origin, such as bodily activity; (2) certain surrounding circumstances; and (3) certain consequences.[3] For example, in a situation in which *A* shoots and kills *B*, this "act" might be said to include the muscular contraction by which the trigger was pulled, the circumstances that the weapon was loaded and that *B* was in the line of fire, and the consequence of *B*'s death.

Other theorists has subscribed to a much narrower definition; to them, acts are merely bodily movements.[4] This, of course, excludes what was referred to above as negative acts, internal acts, surrounding circumstances, and consequences. This is the modern view, as reflected in the Model Penal Code,[5] and is adopted here because it is this definition of act which is most meaningful in discussing the requirement of an act. There are analytical difficulties in calling an omission an act, and thus it is better simply to acknowledge that either an act or an omission to act contrary to a legal duty suffices. For the reasons explained later, internal acts (that is, mere thoughts) cannot constitute a crime, which means that it is better to exclude them from the definition of act.

In favor of defining acts to include the circumstances and consequences, it has been argued that this approach is desirable because

18. See § 1.5.

19. See § 2.4.

20. See § 2.2(d).

21. See § 2.3.

22. See § 2.1.

§ 3.2

1. J. Salmond, Jurisprudence 503 (9th ed. 1937).

2. Ibid.

3. Id. at 505. See also G. Williams, Criminal Law: The General Part § 11 (2d ed. 1961).

4. O. Holmes, The Common Law 54 (1881). See also Cook, Act, Intention and Motive, 26 Yale L.J. 645 (1917).

5. Model Penal Code § 1.13(2): " 'act' or 'action' means a bodily movement whether voluntary or involuntary." Similarly, Restatement, Torts (Second) § 2 (1965) provides: "The word 'act' is used throughout the Restatement of this Subject to denote an external manifestation of the actor's will and does not include any of its results, even the most direct, immediate and intended."

offenses are often defined in terms of circumstances (e.g., in perjury, that the witness is sworn; in bigamy, that the defendant is already married) and consequences (e.g., in homicide, the killing of a human being), and because a more limited view as to the meaning of the word "act" may result in a holding that no mental state is necessary as to these circumstances or consequences.[6] As to the latter, this problem may be avoided (as in the Model Penal Code) by merely recognizing certain circumstances and consequences as material elements of an offense[7] and then requiring some mental state as to each material element.[8] A definition of act which encompasses circumstances and consequences, on the other hand, presents a serious problem in determining the termination point of one's acts,[9] and also poses serious analytical difficulties in discussing "voluntary" acts.[10]

WESTLAW REFERENCES

di act

topic(110) /p defin! /5 criminal +1 act conduct

(b) Necessity for an Act. One basic premise of Anglo-American criminal law is that no crime can be committed by bad thoughts alone. Something in the way of an act, or of an omission to act where there is a legal duty to act,[11] is required too.[12] To wish an enemy dead, to contemplate the forcible ravishment of a woman, to think about taking another's wallet—such thoughts constitute none of the existing crimes (not murder or rape or larce-

ny) so long as the thoughts produce no action to bring about the wished-for results. But, while it is no crime merely to entertain an intent to commit a crime, an attempt (or an agreement with another person) to commit it may be criminal; but the reason is that an attempt (or a conspiracy) requires some activity beyond the mere entertainment of the intent.

Mere thoughts must be distinguished from speech; an act sufficient for criminal liability may consist of nothing more than the movement of the tongue so as to form spoken words.[13] Some crimes are usually committed by the act of speech, such as perjury and false pretenses and the inchoate crimes of conspiracy and solicitation. Other crimes, usually committed by other forms of activity, may nevertheless be committed by spoken words; thus one person can murder another by maneuvering him into the electric chair by giving perjured testimony at his trial for a capital crime. And, because one is guilty of a crime if he encourages or commands or hires another to commit it,[14] it would seem that practically all crimes may be committed by conduct which includes no voluntary bodily movement other than speaking.

The common law crimes all require an act or omission in addition to a bad state of mind.[15] A statute purporting to make it criminal simply to think bad thoughts would, in the United States, be held unconstitutional.[16] And a statute which is worded vaguely on the question of whether an act (or omission), in

---

6. G. Williams, supra note 3, at § 11.

7. Model Penal Code § 1.13(10).

8. Model Penal Code § 2.02(1).

9. See Cook, supra note 4.

10. For more on the theoretical problems in defining act, see H. Morris, Freedom and Responsibility ch. 3 (1961).

11. See § 3.3.

12. For a discussion of the requirement of an act or omission for criminal liability, see Hitchler, The Physical Element of Crime, 39 Dick.L.Rev. 95 (1934).

13. E.g., People v. Coleman, 350 Mich.268, 86 N.W.2d 281 (1957).

14. See § 6.7.

15. E. g., Dugdale v. Regina, 1 El. & Bl. 435, 118 Eng. Rep. 499 (1853) (indictment charging possession of obscene

matter with intent to sell, held not to charge a crime, since no act is alleged; but indictment charging procuring obscene matter with intent to sell does allege a crime).

16. E. g., In re Leroy T., 285 Md. 508, 403 A.2d 1226 (1979); Ex parte Smith, 135 Mo. 223, 36 S.W. 628 (1896). State v. Labato, 7 N.J. 137, 80 A.2d 617 (1951); Proctor v. State, 15 Okl.Cr. 338, 176 P. 771 (1918); Lambert v. State, 374 P.2d 783 (Okla.Crim.1962); Note, 30 Yale L.J. 762 (1921).

As to England, there is no express constitutional provision restricting legislative power to create crimes, but parliament has seldom, if ever, made it a crime merely to entertain a bad intent. Cf. the isolated case of Larsonneur, 24 Cr.App. 74 (1933), where defendant was convicted for being an alien "found" in the country although she was handed over to English police by officials of the Irish Free State. The case is criticized in Morris, An Australian News Letter, 1955 Crim.L.Rev. 290, 295.

addition to a state of mind, is required for criminal liability will be construed to require some act (or omission).[17]

Several reasons have been given in justification for the requirement of an act. One is that a person's thoughts are not susceptible of proof except when demonstrated by outward actions.[18] But, while this is doubtless true in most instances, it fails to take account of the possibility that one might confess or otherwise acknowledge to others the fact that he has entertained a certain intent. Another reason given is the difficulty in distinguishing a fixed intent from mere daydream and fantasy.[19] Most persuasive, however, is the notion that the criminal law should not be so broadly defined to reach those who entertain criminal schemes but never let their thoughts govern their conduct.[20]

It should also be noted that even bad thoughts plus action do not equal a particular crime if the action is not that which the definition of the crime requires. No doubt, for instance, the legislature can make it a crime to put poison in a well with intent to cause injury or death; if so, such a crime can be committed though no one comes close to taking a drink before the poison is discovered. But if the statute most nearly in point punishes "assault with intent to kill," such a statute is not violated under the above circumstances, the reason being that the action taken is not the action which the crime, by its

definition, requires.[21] Some crimes are so defined that a series of acts is required for their commission. Burglary, for instance, at common law (and by some modern statutes) requires both a "breaking" and an "entering" of a dwelling house; the defendant normally first opens a closed door or window and then walks or climbs through the open door or window. Doing the first act without the second (or the second without the first) would not satisfy such a definition of burglary.

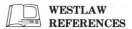

WESTLAW REFERENCES

crime criminal /p speech speak! spoke* /p false +1 pretenses

inten**** /s attempt! /s commit! commission /s crime criminal +1 act conduct

(c) Voluntary Nature of Act. The word "act" might be defined in a broad sense to include such involuntary actions as bodily movements during sleep or unconsciousness, or in a narrow sense to mean only voluntary bodily movement.[22] At all events, it is clear that criminal liability requires that the activity in question be voluntary.[23] The deterrent function of the criminal law would not be served by imposing sanctions for involuntary action, as such action cannot be deterred. Likewise, assuming revenge or retribution to be a legitimate purpose of punishment, there would appear to be no reason to impose punishment on this basis as to those whose ac-

---

17. Baender v. Barnett, 255 U.S. 224, 41 S.Ct. 271, 65 L.Ed. 597 (1921) (dealing with the constitutionality of a federal statute punishing the possession of a counterfeiting die, upheld the statute, but only after construing it to require a willing and conscious possession).

Thus a statute making it a crime to "aid and abet" another to commit a crime is construed to require some action to encourage the other, and not mere presence at the scene of the crime even if accompanied by mental approbation. E. g., Anderson v. State, 66 Okl.Cr. 291, 91 P.2d 794 (1939) (defendant, present when *A* murdered *B*, mentally approved but did nothing to encourage *A*; held, he is not guilty of aiding and abetting *A* to commit murder).

18. 4 W. Blackstone, Commentaries * 21 (1897).

19. G. Williams, supra note 3, at 2.

20. R. Perkins, Criminal Law 605 (3d ed. 1982).

21. Peebles v. State, 101 Ga. 585, 28 S.E. 920 (1897). Accord: Howard v. State, 73 Ga.App. 265, 36 S.E.2d 161 (1945) (defendant maliciously pulled his neighbor's fence

posts from the ground, causing the neighbor expense and annoyance though causing no injury to the posts; held, not guilty of the crime most nearly in point—malicious injury or destruction of property; no doubt the legislature could have made it a crime maliciously to unearth another's fence post).

It is not false pretenses to tell what is thought to be a lie, though it is actually the truth, with intent to defraud, for the crime requires, in addition to the bad state of mind, the act of telling a lie. E. g., State v. Asher, 50 Ark. 427, 8 S.W. 177 (1888).

22. See definitions in note 5 supra, and O. Holmes, The Common Law 54 (1881) (a bodily movement, to be an act, "must be willed"); Cook, supra note 4, at 647 ("a muscular movement that is willed"). See also O'Connor, The Voluntary Act, 15 Med.Sci. & Law 31 (1975), assessing various definitions.

23. Model Penal Code § 2.01(1). Most of the modern recodifications expressly state that this is so.

tions were not voluntary. Restraint or rehabilitation might be deemed appropriate, however, where individuals are likely to constitute a continuing threat to others because of their involuntary movements, but it is probably best to deal with this problem outside the criminal law.[24]

Just what is meant by the term "voluntary" has caused the theorists considerable difficulty. Sometimes a voluntary act is said to be an external manifestation of the will. Or, it may be said to be behavior which would have been otherwise if the individual had willed or chosen it to be otherwise. There are those who believe that the term is indefinable, and also those who take the view that a voluntary act must be defined in terms of conditions which render an act involuntary.[25] The Model Penal Code comes closest to the last approach, as it identifies certain movements which are deemed not to be voluntary acts: a reflex or convulsion; those during unconsciousness or sleep; those during hypnosis or resulting from hypnotic suggestion; and others which are not a product of the effort or determination of the actor, either conscious or habitual.[26]

The cases, though few in number, lend support to most of the specific classifications. It has been held, for example, that one is not guilty of murder if he killed the victim while asleep or in the clouded state between sleeping and waking.[27] Even assuming that "the conduct of a sleep-walker may be purposive (though not recollected on waking), and may be regarded as expressing unconscious desire,"[28] it is nonetheless undoubtedly sound not to impose liability for an unconscious desire which is manifested in this way. Similarly, it has been held that there is no voluntary act as to movements following unconsciousness,[29] and the defense of hypnotism has been allowed.[30] As to the latter, it should be noted that there is a difference of opinion as to whether acts during or resulting from hypnosis are actually involuntary, stemming largely from differing views on whether a hypnotized person will engage in acts that are repugnant to him.[31] The residual category in the Model Penal Code formulation also covers the classic

---

24. Model Penal Code § 2.01, Comment at 215 (1985): "People whose involuntary movements threaten harm to others may present a public health or safety problem, calling for therapy or even for custodial commitment; they do not present a problem of correction." Compare H. Silving, Constituent Elements of Crime 83 (1967): "But, obviously, such person is dangerous, and it is desirable that he be subject to measures applicable to those acquitted by reason of mental incapacity. Given constitutionality of applying measures to those acquitted by reason of insanity, it may be appropriate to inquire whether the difference, if any, between the mental state in the behavior of, for instance, a somnambulist and the mental state in the conduct of, for example, a schizophrenic affords a valid basis for differential constitutional treatment of defendants affected by such types of incapacity."

25. On these various views, see H. Morris, supra note 10, at 106.

26. Model Penal Code § 2.01(2). Most of the modern recodifications do not contain such a list. Several, however, define a voluntary act as one performed consciously as a result of effort or determination, or in similar terms. Courts interpreting such language sometimes use the Model Penal Code list. See, e. g., State v. Mishne, 427 A.2d 450 (Me.1981).

27. Fain v. Commonwealth, 78 Ky. 183, 39 Am.Rep. 213 (1879). See also Sallee v. State, 544 P.2d 902 (Okl. Crim.App.1976); Bradley v. State, 102 Tex.Cr. 41, 277 S.W. 147 (1926).

28. G. Williams, supra note 3, at 12.

29. Government of the Virgin Islands v. Smith, 278 F.2d 169 (3d Cir.1960) (defendant offered defense of unconsciousness through epilepsy when he drove his car into a fatal accident; when he introduces some evidence of this, prosecution must prove his consciousness beyond a reasonable doubt); People v. Freeman, 61 Cal.App.2d 110, 142 P.2d 435 (1943) (if defendant, after becoming unconscious through epilepsy, got in his car, drove it, and had a fatal accident he would not be guilty of negligent homicide by automobile). See also People v. Baker, 42 Cal.2d 550, 268 P.2d 705 (1954); People v. Hardy, 33 Cal.2d 52, 198 P.2d 865 (1948). Compare State v. Pettay, 216 Kan. 555, 532 P. 2d 1289 (1975) (if epileptic not in throes of an epileptic seizure at the time of the crime, he may be held criminally responsible).

Another approach is to view these cases as appropriate for exculpation on the ground of mental disease or defect, e.g., People v. Furlong, 187 N.Y. 198, 79 N.E. 978 (1907). Cf. People v. Grant, 71 Ill.2d 551, 17 Ill.Dec. 814, 377 N.E.2d 4 (1978) (where epileptic defendant received insanity defense instruction, it is not error to fail to instruct also on voluntary act requirement). But see State v. Welsh, 8 Wash.App. 719, 508 P.2d 1041 (1973) (trial judge erred in concluding defendant's psychomotor epilepsy relevant to insanity defense). For a useful assessment of the alternatives for defense of an epileptic defendant, see Note, 27 Case W.Res.L.Rev. 771 (1977).

30. People v. Marsh, 170 Cal.App.2d 284, 338 P.2d 495 (1959) (raised as a defense, but rejected by jury).

31. The authorities are cited in G. Williams, supra note 3, at § 250. See also Orne, Review of Reiter, Antiso-

case in which one person physically forces another person into bodily movement, as where A by force causes B's body to strike C; under these circumstances, there is no voluntary act by B.[32] But it does not include so-called "brainwashing," whereby attitudinal changes are produced through a process of coercive persuasion.[33]

There is general agreement that a mere reflex is not a voluntary act. It should be noted, however, that the term "reflex" does not cover all instances of bodily movement in quick response to some outside force or circumstances. A reflex is a muscular reaction "in which the mind and will have no share,"[34] such as a knee jerk or the blinking of the eyelids.[35] It does not include, for example, the case in which A, finding himself about to fall, reaches out to seize some object in order to avoid falling, for in that instance A's mind has quickly grasped the situation and dictated some action.[36]

Although a voluntary act is an absolute requirement for criminal liability, it does not follow that every act up to the moment that the harm is caused must be voluntary.[37] Thus, one may be guilty of criminal homicide (or battery) even though he is unconscious or asleep at the time of the fatal (or injurious) impact, as where A, being subject to frequent fainting spells, has such a spell while driving his car (or, after becoming aware that he is sleepy, continues to drive and falls asleep at the wheel), with the result that the car, out of control, runs into and kills (or injures) B while A is unconscious or asleep. Here A's voluntary act consists of driving the car, and if the necessary mental state can be established as of that time (e.g., finding recklessness on the basis of A's knowledge that he was very sleepy or subject to epileptic seizures), it is enough to make him guilty of a crime.[38]

cial or Criminal Acts and Hypnosis: A Case Study, 46 A.B. A.J. 81 (1960). However, the Model Penal Code view is that, even assuming that the hypnotized subject will not follow suggestions which are repugnant to him, this is "insufficient to warrant treating his conduct as voluntary; his dependency and helplessness are too pronounced." Model Penal Code § 2.01, Comment at 221 (1985).

32. Cf. Martin v. State, 31 Ala.App. 334, 17 So.2d 427 (1944) (where police took intoxicated defendant from his home out to the street, defendant not guilty of appearing in public while intoxicated, as no voluntary act); State v. Boleyn, 328 So.2d 95 (La.1976) (if defendant, while unconscious, was removed from prison area by another prisoner, defendant has not voluntarily engaged in act of escape). Compare the situation where A by threats, rather than by physical force, causes B to strike C. In such a case B has engaged in a "voluntary act", in the sense in which that term is used here, even though he would not have so acted but for A's threats. B may, however, be able to assert the defense of duress. See § 5.3. As to A's liability, see § 6.7.

33. Delgado, Ascription of Criminal States of Mind: Toward a Defense Theory for the Coercively Persuaded ("Brainwashed") Defendant, 63 Minn.L.Rev. 1, 10 n. 43 (1978) ("Unlike cases of hypnotism, * * * the acts of the coercively persuaded defendant lack the reflexive, unpremeditated, automatic quality that is required for an actus reus defense"); Dressler, Professor Delgado's "Brainwashing" Defense: Courting a Determinist Legal System, 63 Minn.L.Rev. 335, 350 (1979) ("All theories of coercive persuasion support the view that the conduct of a coercively persuaded actor is voluntary as so defined. No theory suggests that the conduct is either reflexive or committed while unconscious"). See also Alldridge, Brainwashing as a Criminal Law Defence, 1984 Crim.L. Rev. 726; Lunde & Wilson, Brainwashing as a Defense to Criminal Liability: Patty Hearst Revisited, 13 Crim.L.

Bull. 341 (1977); Comment, 44 U.Mo.K.C.L.Rev. 438 (1976).

Consult the Delgado and Dressler articles for an interesting debate on whether a separate defense based on coercive persuasion should be recognized.

34. Restatement, Torts (Second) § 2, Comment (1965).

35. In People v. Newton, 8 Cal.App.3d 359, 87 Cal.Rptr. 394 (1970), the defendant, convicted of murder of a police officer, wrested the gun from the officer and shot him after the defendant had been shot in the stomach. A doctor testified that "it is not at all uncommon for a person shot in the abdomen to lose consciousness and go into this reflex shock condition for short periods of time." The court held an unconsciousness instruction should have been given.

36. Restatement, Torts (Second) § 2, Comment (1965). But, even though there is a voluntary act in such a case, it does not necessarily follow that there will be criminal liability for the resulting injury to person or property. A may be without the required mental state, or may have the defense of necessity. See § 5.4.

37. It is to avoid such a result that Model Penal Code § 2.01(1) says that liability must be "based on conduct which includes a voluntary act."

38. Tift v. State, 17 Ga.App. 663, 88 S.E. 41 (1916); State v. Gooze, 14 N.J.Super. 277, 81 A.2d 811 (1951); People v. Decina, 2 N.Y.2d 133, 157 N.Y.S.2d 558, 138 N.E.2d 799 (1956); State v. Olsen, 108 Utah 377, 160 P.2d 427 (1945). See also Fain v. Commonwealth, supra note 27, where the court held A not guilty of murder if he shot B while asleep, but suggested that if A knew he was prone to do acts of violence when asleep, yet he went to sleep with a gun at hand, he would be subject to punishment for his recklessness. Cf. People v. Freeman, supra note 29,

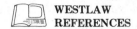

crim**** /s commit commission /s voluntary
    involuntary conscious unconscious +1 act

(d) Crimes of Personal Condition.

A few crimes—notably the crime of vagrancy—are often defined in such a way as to punish status (e.g., being a vagrant) rather than to punish specific action or omission to act.[39] Statutes creating crimes of this sort, though occasionally held invalid as creating an unreasonable restraint on personal liberty or on account of vagueness in definition, have often been upheld notwithstanding their definition of crime in terms of "being" rather than "acting." [40] There is a growing body of authority, however, that such statutes are unconstitutional, either as a violation of substantive due process [41] or on cruel and unusual punishment grounds.[42]

where the defendant became unconscious because of epilepsy before he started to drive.

Similar analysis is called for in other circumstances. See, e.g., Mason v. State, 603 P.2d 1146 (Okl.Crim.App. 1979) (defendant may be convicted of being in "actual physical control" of vehicle while intoxicated, though he unconscious when found within; defendant conscious when he started the car, and having created such a dangerous situation he cannot "later extricate himself from these self-created dangerous circumstances by being discovered while unconscious").

39. See Douglas, Vagrancy and Arrest on Suspicion, 70 Yale L.J. 1 (1960); Dubin & Robinson, The Vagrancy Concept Reconsidered, 37 N.Y.U.L.Rev. 102 (1962); Lacey, Vagrancy and Other Crimes of Personal Condition, 66 Harv.L.Rev. 1203 (1953).

40. Ibid.

41. See § 2.12(d).

42. See § 2.14(f).

43. Baender v. Barnett, 255 U.S. 224, 41 S.Ct. 271, 65 L.Ed. 597 (1921) (federal crime to possess counterfeiting dies *held* valid when construed to require willing and conscious possession); People v. Gory, 28 Cal.2d 450, 170 P.2d 433 (1946) (state statute making it a crime to possess marijuana, assumed valid, construed to require conscious possession); see dissent in People v. Cox, 91 Or. 518, 179 P. 575 (1919) (crime to possess intoxicating liquor said to include unconscious possession and as so construed is assumed to be valid). Contra: Dugdale v. Regina, supra note 15 (indictment alleging possession of obscene matter *held* to charge no crime since it charges no act).

44. E.g., South Staffordshire Water Co. v. Sharman, [1896] 2 Q.B. 44 (landowner held to possess a ring in a pool on his land, though he did not know of the ring's exis-

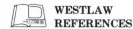

crim*** /p defin*** /s vagrant "drug addict"
    homosexual

(e) Crimes of Possession.

Some crimes are defined in terms of possession. Thus, possession of intoxicating liquor or of narcotics or of counterfeiting dies, or possession of burglar's tools with intent to commit a burglary therewith, may be made criminal. Though possession is not, strictly speaking, an act (bodily movement) or an omission to act, crimes based upon possession are generally upheld.[43] For legal purposes other than criminal law—e.g., the law of finders—one may possess something without knowing of its existence,[44] but possession in a criminal statute is usually construed to mean conscious possession.[45] So construed, knowingly receiving an item [46] or retention after awareness of control over it [47] could be considered a sufficient act or omission to serve as the proper basis for a

tence, so as to entitle him to the ring as against the person who found it when hired by landowner to clean the pool).

45. E.g., United States v. Sawyer, 294 F.2d 24 (4th Cir. 1961). See also cases cited in note 43 supra. It has been said that the legislature cannot make unconscious possession the basis of a crime, e.g., State v. Labato, 7 N.J. 137, 80 A.2d 617 (1951), but compare Note, 30 Yale L.J. 762 (1921). See also Note, 77 Colum.L.Rev. 596, 619 (1977), criticizing the majority view that possession of an unusable amount of a controlled substance is criminal, in part because knowledge of the object's presence is unlikely in such circumstances.

46. Several modern recodifications define possession as including the situation in which the defendant "knowingly procured or received the thing possessed."

47. Several modern recodifications define possession as including the instance in which the defendant "was aware of his control thereof for a sufficient period to have been able to terminate his possession."

In State v. Flaherty, 400 A.2d 363 (Me.1979), defendant was charged with theft and with unlawful possession of a firearm when another's rifle was found in his car. Defendant claimed that the owner of the rifle mistakenly put it into defendant's car and that he had just discovered it there shortly before, and the jury acquitted him of theft but convicted him of the illegal possession. The appellate court ruled defendant should have received an instruction under a statute of the type noted above, as with such an instruction "the jury might reasonably have concluded that the Defendant had not been aware of his control of the rifle for a sufficient period to have been able to terminate his possession." The court explained such a provision provides a " 'grace' period * * * designed to separate illegal possession from temporary control incidental to the lawful purpose of terminating possession.

crime.[48] This knowledge or awareness, however, concerns only the physical object and not its specific quality or properties;[49] one may be said to be in possession of narcotics even when he believes that the substance is not a narcotic, although this belief might well bar conviction because the required mental state is lacking.[50]

The word "possession" is often used in the criminal law without definition, which perhaps reflects only the fact that it is "a common term used in everyday conversation that has not acquired any artful meaning."[51] Certainly the term encompasses actual physical control,[52] although even as to this "something more than momentary control" is said to be necessary.[53] However, possession need not be exclusive in a single person; joint possession is possible in the criminal law.[54] Both statutes and court decisions [55] sometimes define

possession more expansively as covering any exercise of dominion and control over the property in question. This approach, it has been noted, "is simply not informative in any functional manner" because the "terms 'dominion' and 'control' are nothing more than labels used by courts to characterize given sets of facts."[56]

Certainly a part of the problem, as the Supreme Court noted some years ago, is that the word possession "is interchangeably used to describe actual possession and constructive possession which often so shade into one another that it is difficult to say where one ends and the other begins."[57] Constructive possession, which is simply a doctrine used to broaden the application of possession-type crimes to situations in which actual physical control cannot be directly proved,[58] is often described

Thus a 'sufficient period' is not always the absolute minimum time required to get rid of the contraband. So long as the Defendant's control of the contraband remains incidental to the lawful purpose of terminating his possession and, viewed under the circumstances, remains 'temporary,' it falls within the 'sufficient period' permitted him by" the statute.

48. Model Penal Code § 2.01(4) defines possession as an act which may form the basis of criminal liability "if the possessor knowingly procured or received the thing possessed or was aware of his control thereof for a sufficient period to have been able to terminate his possession."

49. Model Penal Code § 2.01, Comment at 224 (1985); G. Williams, supra note 3, at § 6; People v. Gory, 28 Cal. 2d 450, 170 P.2d 433 (1946).

Under this approach, if a person receives a package in the mail and the police thereafter seize that package before the recipient opens it and they find it contains narcotics, the recipient is deemed to have had possession of the narcotics by receiving the package and its contents. Commonwealth v. Lee, 331 Mass. 166, 117 N.E.2d 830 (1954). Some courts have declined to allow a conviction on such facts, reasoning that there was no possession of the contents absent knowledge of their identity. See, e.g., Commonwealth v. Rambo, 488 Pa. 334, 412 A.2d 535 (1980). Usually, however, as in *Rambo,* the court could have more logically have noted that the applicable possession statute also has a mental state element of intent or knowledge which was not satisfied upon such evidence.

50. E.g., where the statute refers to one who "knowingly possesses."

51. Kramer v. United States, 408 F.2d 837 (8th Cir. 1969).

52. People v. Garcia, 197 Colo. 550, 595 P.2d 228 (1979); State v. Ellis, 263 S.C. 12, 207 S.E.2d 408 (1974).

53. State v. Williams, 211 Neb. 650, 319 N.W.2d 748 (1982). See People v. Mijares, 6 Cal.3d 415, 99 Cal.Rptr. 139, 491 P.2d 1115 (1971) (where, when defendant's friend passed out, defendant took narcotics outfit from friend's pocket and threw it into the street before summoning aid, defendant did not have possession of the drugs, as a contrary rule "could result in manifest injustice to admittedly innocent individuals"); Tingley v. Brown, 380 So.2d 1289 (Fla.1980) (in holding statute proscribing possession of undersize crawfish is constitutional, court declares that the "mere holding of a crawfish while measuring it to determine if it is a legal size is a superficial possession and is insufficient to support a criminal prosecution for illegal possession"). Compare People v. Norris, 40 Mich.App. 45, 198 N.W.2d 430 (1972) (defendant guilty of possession of blackjack, though he took it away from guest in his home and threw it on a couch after a few minutes).

54. United States v. Morando-Alvarez, 520 F.2d 882 (9th Cir.1975); People v. Ireland, 38 Ill.App.3d 616, 348 N.E.2d 277 (1976); State v. Reeves, 209 N.W.2d 18 (Iowa 1973); Miller v. State, 579 P.2d 200 (Okl.Crim.App.1978).

55. United States v. Morando-Alvarez, 520 F.2d 882 (9th Cir.1975); State v. Reeves, 209 N.W.2d 18 (Iowa 1973); Miller v. State, 579 P.2d 200 (Okl.Crim.App.1978).

56. Whitebread & Stevens, Constructive Possession in Narcotics Cases: To Have and Have Not, 58 Va.L.Rev. 751, 759–60 (1972). See, e.g., United States v. Martorano, 709 F.2d 863 (3d Cir.1983), noting the split of authority as to whether for "dominion and control" the defendant must have had the power to dispose of the object.

57. National Safe Deposit Co. v. Stead, 232 U.S. 58, 34 S.Ct. 209, 58 L.Ed. 504 (1914).

58. State v. Florine, 303 Minn. 103, 226 N.W.2d 609 (1975).

in terms of dominion and control.[59] It is not uncommon, however, for constructive possession to be even more broadly defined to include as well circumstances in which the defendant had the ability to reduce an object to his control.[60]

WESTLAW REFERENCES

crim**** /s defin! /s possession /p know! aware!

(f) Vicarious Liability. It is a general principle of criminal law that one is not criminally liable for how someone else acts, unless of course he directs or encourages or aids the other so to act. Thus, unlike the case with torts, an employer is not generally liable for the criminal acts of his employee even though the latter does them in furtherance of his employer's business.[61] In other words, with crimes defined in terms of harmful acts and bad thoughts, the defendant himself must personally engage in the acts and personally think the bad thoughts, unless, in the case of a statutory crime, the legislature has otherwise provided.[62]

WESTLAW REFERENCES

crim**** /s defin! /s accomplice /s encourag! aid***

---

59. United States v. Martorano, 709 F.2d 863 (3d Cir. 1983); State v. Florine, 303 Minn. 103, 226 N.W.2d 609 (1975); State v. Ellis, 263 S.C. 12, 207 S.E.2d 408 (1974).

60. United States v. Martinez, 588 F.2d 495 (5th Cir. 1979); Tanksley v. State, 332 So.2d 76 (Fla.App.1976).

61. E. g., Lovelace v. State, 191 Miss. 62, 2 So.2d 796 (1941). See § 3.9. Some modern statutes, however, make the employer liable for the acts of his employees, and such statutes are generally upheld as within the police power. E. g., In re Marley, 29 Cal.2d 525, 175 P.2d 832 (1946) (statute punishing "every person who by himself or his employee or agent" sells anything at short weight).

62. See § 3.9.

§ 3.3

1. Model Penal Code § 2.01(1) states: "A person is not guilty of an offense unless his liability is based on conduct which includes a voluntary act or the omission to perform an act of which he is physically capable." The modern recodifications typically state that crimes may be committed either by an act or an omission.

For discussion of criminal liability based on omission to act, see J. Hall, General Principles of Criminal Law 190–

§ 3.3 Omission to Act

Most crimes are committed by affirmative action rather than by non-action. But there are a number of statutory crimes which are specifically defined in terms of failure to act; and other crimes which, though not specifically so defined, may be committed either by affirmative action or by failure to act under circumstances giving rise to a legal duty to act.[1]

Illustrative of the former are statutes making it a crime for a taxpayer to fail to file a tax return, for a parent to neglect to furnish medical care for his sick children,[2] for a motorist to fail to stop after involvement in an automobile accident, or for a draftee to fail to report at the appointed time and place for induction into the armed forces. Such crimes of omission give rise to little difficulty so far as criminal liability for omission is concerned. The criminal statute itself imposes the duty to act, and breach of the duty is made a crime.[3]

More difficult, however, are crimes which are not specifically defined in terms of omission to act but only in terms of cause and result. Murder and manslaughter are defined so as to require the "killing" of another person; arson so as to require a "burning" of appropriate property. Nothing in the definition of murder or manslaughter or arson af-

---

205, 208–11 (2d ed. 1960); 1 P. Robinson, Criminal Law Defenses §§ 86, 87 (1984); Williams, Criminal Law: The General Part §§ 3, 4, 11 (2d ed. 1961); Frankel, Criminal Omissions: A Legal Microcosm, 11 Wayne L.Rev. 367 (1965); Glazebrook, Criminal Omissions: The Duty Requirement in Offenses Against the Person, 76 L.Q.Rev. 386 (1960); Hughes, Criminal Omissions, 67 Yale L.J. 590 (1958); Kerchheimer, Criminal Omissions, 55 Harv.L.Rev. 615 (1942); Perkins, Negative Acts in Criminal Law, 22 Iowa L.Rev. 659 (1937); Robinson, Criminal Liability for Omissions, 29 N.Y.L.School L.Rev. 101 (1984); Snyder, Liability for Negative Conduct, 35 Va.L.Rev. 446 (1949); Woozley, A Duty to Rescue: Some Thoughts on Criminal Liability, 69 Va.L.Rev. 127 (1983).

2. On omission liability under child abuse statutes, see Annot., 1 A.L.R.4th 38 (1980).

3. It has been suggested that there is reluctance to enact such statutes because, inter alia, "a governmental demand to perform is significantly more intrusive than a command to refrain from harmful action and therefore must be justified by a significant, overriding public interest." 1 P. Robinson, supra note 1, at 86(b).

firmatively suggests that the crime may or may not be committed by omission to act. But these crimes may, in appropriate circumstances, be thus committed. So a parent who fails to call a doctor to attend his sick child may be guilty of criminal homicide if the child should die for want of medical care, though the parent does nothing of an affirmative nature to cause the child's death.

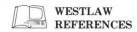

**WESTLAW
REFERENCES**

110k26

(a) Duty to Act. For criminal liability to be based upon a failure to act it must first be found that there is a duty to act—a legal duty and not simply a moral duty. As we have seen, some criminal statutes themselves impose the legal duty to act, as with the tax statute and the hit-and-run statute.[4] With other crimes the duty must be found outside the definition of the crime itself—perhaps in another statute, or in the common law, or in a contract.[5]

Generally one has no legal duty to aid another person in peril, even when that aid can be rendered without danger or inconvenience to himself.[6] He need not shout a warning to a blind man headed for a precipice or to an absent-minded one walking into a gunpowder room with a lighted candle in hand. He need not pull a neighbor's baby out of a pool of water or rescue an unconscious person stretched across the railroad tracks, though the baby is drowning or the whistle of an approaching train is heard in the distance. A doctor is not legally bound to answer a desperate call from the frantic parents of a sick child, at least if it is not one of his regular patients. A moral duty to take affirmative action is not enough to impose a legal duty to do so.[7] But there are situations which do give rise to a duty to act:[8]

(1) Duty Based Upon Relationship. The common law imposes affirmative duties upon persons standing in certain personal relationships to other persons—upon parents to aid their small children, upon husbands to aid their wives, upon ship captains to aid their crews, upon masters to aid their servants. Thus a parent may be guilty of criminal homicide for failure to call a doctor for his sick child,[9] a mother for failure to prevent the

4. Model Penal Code § 2.01(3) expressly states that liability may be based on an omission when "the omission is expressly made sufficient by the law defining the offense." Only a few of the modern codes contain such a provision. But doubtless this situation is encompassed within the broader, more common provisions cited in note 5 infra.

5. This point is expressed in various ways in the modern codes. Many of them follow Model Penal Code § 2.01(3) by stating that liability may be based upon an omission where a duty of performance is "imposed by law." Similar are those provisions which generally state that the duty must be "required by law," or that there must be a violation of a "legal duty."

6. A statute which merely permits intervention in certain circumstances without risk of tort liability, see statutes collected in Note, 7 Vt.L.Rev. 143, 182–83 (1982), does not impose a duty to do so. Pope v. State, 284 Md. 309, 396 A.2d 1054 (1979). Compare the type of statute discussed in note 70 infra.

7. Thus in State v. Ulvinen, 313 N.W.2d 425 (Minn. 1981), holding defendant was guilty of no crime in failing to warn her daughter-in-law that defendant's son was planning to kill her, though the plan was carried out, the court declared: "However morally reprehensible it may be to fail to warn someone of their impending death, our statutes do not make such an omission a criminal offense."

Perhaps the reason why there is no legal duty to act except in the exceptional circumstances discussed below is the difficulty which the law would encounter in "setting any standards of unselfish service to fellow men, and of making any workable rule to cover possible situations where fifty people might fail to rescue one," as where fifty good swimmers sit on the beach watching with interest while someone drowns a few feet off shore. W. Prosser & W. Keeton, Torts § 56 (5th ed. 1984).

8. Most of the cases have taken the position that whether a legal duty exists is a question of law to be determined by the court rather than a question of fact for the jury, e.g., State v. Walden, 306 N.C. 466, 293 S.E.2d 780 (1982); People v. Beardsley, 150 Mich. 206, 113 N.W. 1128 (1907). See Frankel, supra note 1, at 369–70.

9. As explained in Commonwealth v. Konz, 498 Pa. 639, 450 A.2d 638 (1982): "The inherent dependency of a child upon his parent to obtain medical aid, i.e., the incapacity of a child to evaluate his condition and summon aid by himself, supports imposition of such a duty upon the parent." See also Robey v. State, 54 Md.App. 60, 456 A.2d 953 (1983); State v. Crawford, 188 Neb. 378, 196 N.W.2d 915 (1972); People v. Henson, 33 N.Y.2d 63, 349 N.Y.S.2d 657, 304 N.E.2d 358 (1973); Commonwealth v. Breth, 44 Pa.County Ct. 56 (1915); Regina v. Downes, 13 Cox Crim.Cas. 111 (1875). The latter two cases were cases where the parents, believing in prayer rather than in medicine, failed to call the doctor. Cf. Regina v. Shep-

fatal beating of her baby by her lover,[10] a husband for failure to aid his imperiled wife,[11] a ship captain for failure to pick up a seaman or passenger fallen overboard,[12] and an employer for failure to aid his endangered employee.[13] Action may be required to thwart the threatened perils of nature (e.g., to combat sickness, to ward off starvation [14] or the elements); or it may be required to protect against threatened acts by third persons.[15]

Aside from the relationships mentioned above, perhaps other relationships may give rise to a duty to act. If two mountain climbers, climbing together, are off by themselves on a mountainside, and one falls into a crevass, it would seem that the nature of their joint enterprise, involving a relationship of mutual reliance, ought to impose a duty upon the one mountaineer to extricate his imperiled colleague.[16] So also if two people, though not closely related, live together under one roof, one may have a duty to act to aid the other who becomes helpless.[17]

(2) Duty Based Upon Statute. A statute (other than the criminal statute whose violation is in question) sometimes imposes a duty to act to help another in distress. Thus it is commonly provided that a driver involved in an automobile accident must stop and render whatever assistance is necessary to others who may be injured in the accident. Failure to stop after an accident would of course be a violation of the hit-and-run statute itself; but furthermore, if an injured party should die for lack of this assistance, the driver might well be criminally liable for the homicide as

hard, 9 Cox Crim.Cas. 123 (1862) (no duty to act owed by parent to emancipated child).

For other cases, see Annot., 100 A.L.R.2d 483 (1965) (homicide: failure to provide medical or surgical attention).

10. Smith v. State, ___ Ind. ___, 408 N.E.2d 614 (1980); Palmer v. State, 223 Md. 341, 164 A.2d 467 (1960). See also State v. Walden, 306 N.C. 466, 293 S.E.2d 780 (1982) (mother guilty of assault for failure to prevent beating).

11. Westrup v. Commonwealth, 123 Ky. 95, 93 S.W. 646 (1906) (husband had duty to summon medical aid for wife where "she was in a helpless state and unable to appeal elsewhere for aid"); State v. Smith, 65 Me. 257 (1876) (husband failed to provide clothing and shelter for insane wife in winter); State v. Mally, 139 Mont. 599, 366 P.2d 868 (1961) (husband had duty to get medical attention for wife where she "as helpless as the newborn"); Territory v. Manton, 8 Mont. 95, 19 P. 387 (1888) (husband left intoxicated wife out in the snow). But a man owes no duty to act to aid his mistress, as distinguished from his wife. People v. Beardsley, 150 Mich. 206, 113 N.W. 1128, 13 L.R.A. (N.S.) 1020, 121 Am.St.Rep. 617, 13 Ann.Cas. 39 (1907).

It would seem that a wife owes a similar duty to act to safeguard her husband. Commonwealth v. Konz, 498 Pa. 639, 450 A.2d 638 (1982). But the court in *Konz* found no duty in the instant case because it had been the choice of the defendant's husband to forego medical treatment for his diabetes. The court reasoned that the duty to a spouse is not the same as a duty to one's child because spouses "do not generally suffer the same incapacity as do children with respect to the ability to comprehend their states of health and obtain medical assistance. * * * The marital relationship gives rise to an expectation of reliance between spouses, and to a belief that one's spouse should be trusted to respect, rather than ignore, one's expressed preferences. That expectation would be frustrated by imposition of a broad duty to seek aid since one's spouse would then be forced to ignore the expectation that the preference to forego assistance will be honored."

12. United States v. Knowles, 26 Fed.Cas. 800 (N.D. Cal.1864). See Harris v. Pennsylvania R.R. Co., 50 F.2d 866 (4th Cir.1931) (civil case). See Annot., 91 A.L.R.2d 1032 (1963).

13. Queen v. Brown, 1 Terr.L.Rep. 475 (Can.1893). See Rex v. Smith, 2 Car. & P. 449, 172 Eng.Rep. 203 (1826).

14. Harrington v. State, 547 S.W.2d 616 and 621 (Tex. Crim.App.1977) (mother and father guilty of murder for letting 2-year-old child starve; both parents have this duty unless one of them or some other person had sole and exclusive care, custody, and control of the child). For other cases, see Annot., 61 A.L.R.3d 1207 (1975).

15. People v. Chapman, 62 Mich. 280, 28 N.W. 896 (1886) (husband, who stood by while another raped the wife, guilty of rape of his wife); Rex v. Russell, [1933] Vict. L.R. 59 (father, who stood by while his wife drowned their small children, guilty of manslaughter of the children). One who stands by without interfering while another commits a crime is not usually guilty of that crime, e.g., People v. Woodward, 45 Cal. 293 (1873); Anderson v. State, 66 Okl.Cr. 291, 91 P.2d 794 (1939). Yet the personal relationship of the bystander to the victim may give rise to a legal duty to interfere.

16. But compare People v. Beardsley, 150 Mich. 206, 113 N.W. 1128, 13 L.R.A.(N.S.) 1020, 121 Am.St.Rep. 617, 13 Ann.Cas. 39 (1907), holding that where a man and his mistress were spending the weekend in his rooms in an adulterous joint enterprise, the man owed no duty to provide medical assistance when the mistress became helpless upon taking poison. For a criticism of *Beardsley*, see Hughes, supra note 1, at 624.

17. Regina v. Instan, 17 Cox Crim.Cas. 602 (1893) (aunt, who took niece into her house and maintained her, became helpless through illness; niece did not feed her or call a doctor, so aunt died; niece *held* guilty of manslaughter).

well. Here the duty to act to preserve life is to be found in the hit-and-run statute. The same result would follow from statutes making it a criminal offense not to provide safety measures, if, as a result of such omission, someone should die.[18] Statutes sometimes impose upon a person the duty to furnish necessaries to other persons; and failure to do so may lead to criminal liability for a resulting death.[19] No doubt a duty to act may be imposed by a non-criminal statute, by an ordinance, or by an administrative regulation or order.

(3) Duty Based Upon Contract. The duty to act to aid others may arise, not out of personal relationship or out of statute, but out of contract. A lifeguard employed to watch over swimmers at the beach, and a railroad gateman hired to safeguard motorists from approaching trains, have a duty, to the public they are employed to protect, to take affirmative action in appropriate circumstances. The lifeguard cannot sit idly by while a swimmer at his beach drowns off shore; the gateman must lower the gate when a train and automobile approach his crossing on collision courses. Omission to do so may make the lifeguard or gateman liable for criminal homicide.[20] So too a nurse may be contractually obligated to act to aid her patient, and an asylum superintendent to aid those in his charge. For a duty to act, by virtue of a contract, to exist, the victim need not be one of the contracting parties.[21]

A more difficult problem concerns the duty, not of the one who is employed to safeguard the public in a particular way, but rather of his fellow employee, whose employment contract does not specifically require him to act in that way. What if, for instance, a locomotive engineer standing near a crossing sees a train and car approaching the crossing; does he owe a duty to the motorist to wake up the sleeping gateman, in view of his employment by the railroad to operate trains? It would seem that a duty to act might be imposed on him, though there is authority to the contrary.[22]

(4) Duty Based Upon Voluntary Assumption of Care. Although one might not, as an original matter, have a duty to act to rescue a stranger in peril, yet once he undertakes to help him he may have a duty to see the job through. Thus, although he may have no duty to pick an unconscious person off the railroad tracks as a train is approaching around the bend, yet if he once lifts him off the track, he cannot thereafter lay him down again in his original position; if he should do so, and the train should kill him, he would be criminally liable for the homicide. A more difficult problem is involved if he starts to aid the other but does not go so far as to improve the other's position, as where a good swimmer starts to swim out to a drowning bather but turns back on recognizing the bather as his enemy. Perhaps here he would be liable only if his conduct in starting to go to the other's rescue induced other prospective rescuers to forego action. So too if one voluntarily and gratuitously assumes responsibility for a helpless person—such as for a child or an insane

18. Cf. Commonwealth v. Welansky, 316 Mass. 383, 55 N.E.2d 902 (1944) (night club operator held to have common law affirmative duty of providing safety precautions for patrons; here failure to provide proper fire exits caused many deaths from fire; operator guilty of manslaughter).

19. See Annots., 61 A.L.R.3d 1207 (1975) (food, clothing and shelter); 100 A.L.R.2d 483 (1965) (medical attention).

20. State v. Benton, 38 Del. 1, 187 A. 609 (1936) (railroad gateman); State v. Harrison, 107 N.J.L. 213, 152 A. 867 (1931) (same). It would seem that the duty to act exists even if the beach owner who hired the lifeguard, or the railroad which employed the gateman, is not legally required to provide these safety services to the public, although a contrary inference is found in the early case of

Regina v. Smith, 11 Cox Crim.Cas. 210 (1869) (railroad gateman).

21. State v. O'Brien, 32 N.J.L. 169 (1867) (contract between railroad and switchman, but latter owes duty to the public as well as to the railroad).

22. Anderson v. State, 27 Tex.App. 177, 11 S.W. 33, 3 L.R.A. 644, 11 Am.St.Rep. 189 (1889) (brakeman has no duty to signal engineer to stop train when he sees child on the tracks.) Perhaps a distinction might be drawn, in the railroad crossing situation, between a railroad employee on duty and one off duty; and between an engineer, whose general duties include affording safety to the public, and a stenographer, whose general duties have nothing to do with safety.

or infirm person—he has a duty thereafter to act to protect the other from harm.[23]

(5) Duty Based Upon Creation of the Peril. If one person himself places another in a position of danger—either intentionally or negligently or without fault—does he have an affirmative duty to safeguard the other from that danger? The clearest case of such a duty is that in which the defendant is himself at fault in creating the danger.[24] But there may perhaps be a duty to act even if the defendant innocently creates the situation of danger,[25] as where one accidentally starts a fire in a building and then fails to take steps to rescue another person trapped therein. It has been argued, however, that one who innocently creates danger is on principle in the same position as that of a bystander who happens by when a situation of danger has developed.[26]

By way of contrast, where a duty to act to save an imperiled person otherwise exists, it is no defense to a crime based upon failure to act that the victim was at fault in negligently getting himself into his predicament, as where a seaman negligently falls overboard.[27]

(6) Duty to Control Conduct of Others. One may stand in such a personal relationship to another that he has an affirmative duty to control the latter's conduct in the interest of the public safety, so that omission to do so may give rise to criminal liability. A parent not only has a duty to act affirmatively to safeguard his children, but he also has a duty to safeguard third persons from his children; an employer has a similar duty to curb his employee while the latter is performing his employer's business. Thus a car-owner may be criminally liable to third persons injured or killed as a result of his failure to control his speeding chauffeur.[28]

(7) Duty of Landowner. A landowner may have a duty to act affirmatively to provide for the safety of those whom he invites onto his land. A night-club owner may be criminally liable, for instance, for the deaths of his pa-

---

23. Cornell v. State, 159 Fla. 687, 32 So.2d 610 (1947) (grandmother took over care of grandchild from mother, then got so drunk she let it smother to death; *held,* guilty of manslaughter); Stehr v. State, 92 Neb. 755, 139 N.W. 676 (1913) (stepfather liable for manslaughter for death of sick stepchild for whom he failed to summon doctor on time).

Compare Pope v. State, 284 Md. 309, 396 A.2d 1054 (1979), where defendant permitted a woman and 3-month-old child to stay with her temporarily because they had nowhere else to live, but did not intervene when the woman beat her child nor seek medical attention for the child thereafter. In reversing defendant's conviction for child abuse, the court held there was no duty absent a consensual transfer of responsibility from the parent to the defendant. "It would be most incongruous that acts of hospitality and kindness, made out of common decency and prompted by sincere concern for the well-being of a mother and her child, subjected the Good Samaritan to criminal prosecution for abusing the very child he sought to look after. And it would be especially ironic were such criminal prosecution to be predicated upon an obligation to take affirmative action with regard to abuse of the child by its mother, when such obligation arises solely from those acts of hospitality and kindness."

24. E.g., People v. Fowler, 178 Cal. 657, 174 P. 892 (1918) (defendant committed battery on victim, leaving him lying unconscious on the side of the road, so that he was later run over by a car and killed; *held,* defendant guilty of murder); Jones v. State, 220 Ind. 384, 43 N.E.2d 1017 (1942) (defendant raped girl, causing her such distress that she fell into creek, from which he intentionally failed to rescue her, so that she drowned; *held,* he was guilty of murder).

25. Commonwealth v. Cali, 247 Mass. 20, 141 N.E. 510 (1923) (defendant accidentally set a fire to a house, then intentionally let it burn down to collect the insurance; *held,* guilty of arson); Green v. Cross, 103 L.T.R.(N.S.) 279 (K.B.1910) (defendant found a dog caught in a vermin trap which he had lawfully laid down, but he delayed for two hours taking steps to release the dog; *held,* conviction of statutory offense of cruelty to animals could be had on such evidence). Contra: King v. Commonwealth, 285 Ky. 654, 148 S.W.2d 1044 (1941) (defendant shot and wounded X while defending his father from X's attack, and then made no effort to summon a doctor, resulting in X's death; *held,* if original shooting lawful, then no duty to seek aid).

Of course, if there is a duty to act based upon a provision of a statute, the statute may require action from someone not personally at fault; thus a hit-and-run statute may require a motorist, innocent or not, who is involved in an accident, to stop and render aid to anyone injured in the accident.

26. Kirchheimer, Criminal Omissions, 55 Harv.L.Rev. 615, 627 (1942). This seems true enough, and the different results apparently stem from a desire to extend the scope of affirmative duty to act.

27. Harris v. Pennsylvania R.R. Co., 50 F.2d 866 (4th Cir.1931).

28. Moreland v. State, 164 Ga. 467, 139 S.E. 77 (1927) (manslaughter case). Very likely a car-owner has a duty to curb the speed of any other person he permits to drive even though not an employee.

trons killed as a result of the owner's failure to provide proper fire escapes.[29]

Over the years of the development of tort and criminal law, the trend has been in the direction of creating new situations wherein an affirmative duty to act is imposed.[30] No doubt the trend will continue in the future.

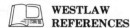 **WESTLAW REFERENCES**

110k26 /p duty oblig! fail***

285k2(1) 211k13 203k74 /p duty oblig! fail*** /p prevent provide protect care

(b) Knowledge of Legal Duty and Facts Giving Rise to Duty. Although part of the larger problem of when the imposition of strict liability should be permitted and when a mistake of fact or law should be recognized as a defense,[31] some attention should be given here to the question of whether liability may be imposed for an omission when the defendant was either unaware of the facts giving rise to the duty to act or unaware of the existence or scope of the legal duty.

Though one might otherwise be under a duty to act, so that omission to do so would ordinarily render him criminally liable, the prevailing view is that he may not be held liable if he does not know the facts indicating a duty to act. Thus, while a father normally has a duty to rescue his young child from drowning, if he does not know the child is in the water then his ignorance may relieve him from criminal responsibility for the child's death.[32] And while a parent has a duty to obtain medical attention for a seriously ill child, the parent's ignorance of the child's

condition may likewise relieve him or her of responsibility for the child's death.[33] Similarly, most courts have taken the view that one may not be convicted under a hit-and-run statute if he was unaware of the fact that an accident has occurred.[34] Of course, sometimes there may be a duty to take care to know the facts, as well as a duty to go into action when the facts are known. Thus a grandmother, who undertook the care of her infant grandchild, who did not know that the child was smothering to death because, after taking charge of the child, she had put herself into a drunken stupor, was held criminally liable for the child's death.[35]

Some courts have taken the position that the imposition of strict liability in omission cases is inappropriate. Basically, the argument is that, notwithstanding whatever reasons might be given for saying that those who engage in certain activity should be held to act at their peril (e.g., those engaged in the sale of liquor should be held strictly liable for sales to minors), it is unfair to hold individuals liable for failing to act when they were unaware of the circumstances which ought to prompt such action. As one court has put it, one cannot be said to have a duty to report something of which he has no knowledge.[36] On the other hand, the imposition of strict liability in omission cases has sometimes been justified on essentially the same basis as in other cases. This approach is reflected in one case which held that one might be convicted under a hit-and-run statute without proof that he was aware that an accident had occurred; the court viewed driving on the high-

---

29. Commonwealth v. Welansky, 316 Mass. 383, 55 N.E.2d 902 (1944) (omission is gross negligence, so guilty of manslaughter).

30. See W. Prosser & W. Keeton, Torts § 56 (5th ed. 1984), as to civil cases. The civil cases are closely analogous to criminal cases.

31. See §§ 3.8, 5.1.

32. Westrup v. Commonwealth, 123 Ky. 95, 93 S.W. 646, 6 L.R.A. (n. s.) 685 (1906): "One cannot be said in any manner to neglect or refuse to perform a duty unless he has knowledge of the condition of things which require performance at his hands." Here a husband failed to call for medical attention during his wife's childbirth.

33. Cf. Fabritz v. Traurig, 583 F.2d 697 (4th Cir.1978) (state conviction for child abuse void as a matter of due

process, as no evidence that "the mother had knowledge of the critical gravity of her daughter's condition when she deferred resort to medical advice").

34. See, e.g., State v. Tennant, ___ W.Va. ___, 319 S.E.2d 395 (1984) (citing many cases from other jurisdictions).

35. Cornell v. State, 159 Fla. 687, 32 So.2d 610 (1947) (manslaughter by gross negligence.)

36. Harding v. Price, [1948] 1 K.B. 695. Thus the court held that unawareness of the accident barred conviction notwithstanding the fact that the statute, unlike its predecessor, did not contain a "knowingly" provision.

ways as a high-risk activity which merited the imposition of liability without regard to knowledge of the specific facts, and also expressed concern over the problems of proof which would be presented if the prosecution had to establish scienter beyond a reasonable doubt in every hit-and-run case.[37]

What, then, of the case in which the defendant, though aware of the facts, was unaware of the existence or scope of the duty to act? For example, could a parent who, finding his small child drowning in the bathtub, fails to pull the child out, successfully defend on the ground that he did not know that a parent has a duty to act to protect his small children from the perils of drowning? Or, could a driver successfully defend a prosecution for failure to report an accident on the ground that he mistakenly believed that the statutory reference to "accident" was intended to cover only cases of collision and not the present instance of a passenger falling while alighting from the vehicle?[38] By application of the general principle that ignorance of the law is usually no excuse,[39] the answer would seem to be no. An exception, of course, may be where the statute only covers "wilful" or "knowing" failure to carry out a duty, for there ignorance of the existence or scope of the duty negates the required mental state, as has been held as to certain omissions covered by the Internal Revenue Code.[40]

The critical question, then, is when a legislature may impose liability for failure to perform some duty even in the absence of knowledge as to the existence or scope of that duty, which the Supreme Court confronted in *Lam-*

bert v. California.[41] The defendant was convicted because she, a convicted felon, failed to register with the Los Angeles authorities as required by ordinance, and she was not permitted to raise ignorance of the registration requirement as a defense. The Supreme Court reversed on the ground that due process requires that ignorance of a duty must be allowed as a defense when "circumstances which might move one to inquire as to the necessity of [taking certain affirmative action] are completely lacking." The dissenters, erroneously it seems, criticized the majority for drawing a distinction between acts and omissions; the distinction is actually between omissions involving duties of a highly unusual and unforeseeable nature and all other cases. The *Lambert* defense would most likely not be available when the legal duty is consistent with a strong moral duty, as in the drowning hypothetical described above. Likewise, it probably would be unavailable in the case described above involving the mistaken interpretation of the accident-reporting requirements.[42]

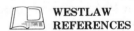 **WESTLAW REFERENCES**

48ak336 /p hit-and-run /p kn*w!

lambert /3 california /p ignoran** kn*w! /p "due process"

(c) Possibility of Performing the Act. Just as one cannot be criminally liable on account of a bodily movement which is involuntary,[43] so one cannot be criminally liable for failing to do an act which he is physically incapable of performing.[44] A father who cannot swim need not dive into deep water to

---

37. State v. McWaters, 106 W.Va. 46, 144 S.E. 718 (1928).

38. Quelch v. Phipps, [1955] 2 Q.B. 107, held no on these facts.

39. See § 5.1(d).

40. United States v. Murdock, 290 U.S. 389, 54 S.Ct. 223, 78 L.Ed. 381 (1933); Hargrove v. United States, 67 F.2d 820 (5th Cir.1933).

41. 355 U.S. 225, 78 S.Ct. 240, 2 L.Ed.2d 228 (1957).

42. As one commentator has observed, this is because "the motorist should make it his business to be informed about this kind of duty; thus, the nonculpability of ignorance is hardly a conceivable possibility. A motorcar is a lethal instrument; those who drive should ascertain the

extent of the legal obligations which this activity may impose on them, as far as reasonably practical. But the question also arises whether enough is done by official agencies to bring to motorists notice of the full range of duties which the law places upon them." Hughes, supra note 1, at 611.

For a helpful discussion of ignorance of legal duty and the facts giving rise to the duty in omission cases, see id. at 607–20.

43. See § 3.2(c).

44. United States v. Spingola, 464 F.2d 909 (7th Cir. 1972) (statute required filing of annual financial report of labor union with Secretary of Labor, defendant's conviction overturned, as he not allowed to show that "he

rescue his drowning child. But impossibility means impossibility. Thus, though a poverty-stricken parent would not be criminally liable for his child's death resulting from failure to provide food and shelter if it is impossible for him to obtain these necessaries, he would be liable if he failed to go to an available welfare agency for help.[45]

A related question concerns the amount of inconvenience and expense and risk which the rescuer must undergo in order to fulfill his duty to act. A parent must doubtless leave his companions in the middle of an interesting bridge hand to rescue his smothering baby. Must he risk his life by diving into a dangerous whirlpool to save his drowning child? Probably the amount of risk which a person must take depends to some extent upon the fact situation giving rise to the duty to act.[46] Thus a parent, to carry out his duty to aid his child, might be required to take a greater chance with his own life than would be required of a motorist who has innocently injured a stranger in an automobile accident.[47]

A somewhat different problem concerns the chance one should take with a third person's life: should a parent endanger the third person's life to save his own child; should a ship captain endanger the lives of all on board in order to pick up a seaman or passenger fallen overboard? In such a choice-of-evils situation, the omission to act may be excused because of the risk to third persons involved in acting.[48]

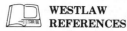

WESTLAW REFERENCES

110k26 /p impossib! possib! incapab! capab!

(d) Causation. Most of the criminal cases on omission to act deal with criminal homicide—murder or manslaughter. Homicide crimes require not only conduct (act or omission, with accompanying state of mind) but a certain result of conduct (the death of the victim). It must therefore be shown, in the homicide-by-omission cases, not only that the defendant had a duty to act, but also that his failure to act caused the death.

The problem of causation in omission cases has been a matter of real difficulty for many theorists.[49] For example, it has been claimed that when a speeding train runs over a child which the father failed to rescue, the cause of death is the train and not the forbearance of the father. However, problems of this nature disappear once it is acknowledged that the question of causation is not solely a question of mechanical connection, but rather a question of policy on imputing or denying liability.[50]

---

possessed neither the sophistication necessary to prepare it himself nor the ability to compel its timely preparation by others); Port Huron v. Jenkinson, 77 Mich. 414, 43 N.W. 923 (1889) (holding unconstitutional an ordinance purporting to impose a penalty on one who omits to do an impossible act); State v. Olson, 356 N.W.2d 110 (N.D.1984) (though hit-and-run statute imposed strict liability, defendant nonetheless may not be convicted if he "lacks the mental: or physical ability to perform the required act").

Model Penal Code § 2.01(1) provides for criminal liability for "the omission to perform an act of which [a person] is physically capable." Many modern codes contain a comparable provision.

2 P. Robinson, supra note 1, at § 87(b)(1), argues that the Model Penal Code "physically capable" term is ambiguous and that as a matter of policy this qualification should also cover the situation in which the defendant is physically able but not mentally able because of some psychological disorder.

45. Stehr v. State, 92 Neb. 755, 139 N.W. 676 (1913).

46. See Kirchheimer, Criminal Omissions, 55 Harv.L. Rev. 615, 636 (1942).

47. In State v. Walden, 306 N.C. 466, 293 S.E.2d 780 (1982), the court emphasized it was not saying "that

parents have the legal duty to place themselves in danger of death or great bodily harm in coming to the aid of their children. To require such, would require every parent to exhibit courage and heroism which, although commendable in the extreme, cannot realistically be expected or required of all people. But parents do have the duty to take every step reasonably possible under the circumstances of a given situation to prevent harm to their children." As for what must be done when another person is assaulting the child, the court said it would be for the jury to decide whether under the circumstances of the particular case physical resistance, verbal objection, or seeking help would be the necessary response.

48. United States v. Knowles, 26 F.Cas. 800 (N.D.Cal. 1864).

49. For a discussion of some of these difficulties, see J. Hall, supra note 1, at 195–97; Hughes, supra note 1, at 627–31.

50. See J. Hall, supra note 1, at 196. Thus, for example, it is not necessary to find some theory to support the conclusion that a stranger who also failed to rescue the child is not the cause of the death, for causation alone does not determine liability.

Legal or "proximate" cause, at the very least, requires a showing of "but for" causation: [51] but for the omission the victim would not have died. Failure on the part of a parent to call a doctor for a sick child may often make the parent criminally liable for the child's death; but only if the doctor could have saved it, not if it would have died in spite of medical attention. It is apparent that this is a matter which often is not susceptible of easy proof, and convictions have sometimes been reversed because of what the appellate court viewed as less than adequate proof of causation.[52] It has been argued that the courts have been somewhat too demanding in this regard, and that it should suffice if the prosecution establishes a serious sickness and a failure to summon aid.[53] This approach, it is claimed, would bring the omission-causation cases in line with the act-causation cases, where an act may be said to cause another's death notwithstanding the fact that the victim's life would have soon been taken by some other cause.[54]

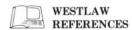

WESTLAW REFERENCES

110k26 /p caus!

(e) Crimes Which May be Committed by Omission to Act. Other than the crimes which are specifically defined in terms of omission to act (e.g., failure to file a tax return; failure to stop and aid after accident), what possible crimes may be committed by failure to act? Most of the actual cases are,

as already noted, homicide cases, wherein someone died by reason of a failure to act. The homicidal crime thus committed may be murder or manslaughter depending upon state-of-mind factors applicable generally to these crimes.[55] Thus one's failure to act to save someone toward whom he owes a duty to act is murder if he knows that failure to act will be certain or substantially certain to result in death or serious bodily injury.[56] If he does not know that death or serious injury is substantially certain to result, but the circumstances are such as to involve a high degree of risk of such death or injury if he does not act (in some jurisdictions he must, in addition, be conscious of this risk), his failure to act will afford a basis for liability for involuntary manslaughter.[57] A failure to act which, under the circumstances, amounts to no more than ordinary negligence would not, by the general rules of criminal homicide, make him liable for either murder or manslaughter. Thus it cannot accurately be said that an omission to act (assuming a duty to act) plus death equals murder, or equals manslaughter, without considering the *mens rea* requirements of those crimes.

It would seem that criminal battery may be committed by an omission to act (if there exists a duty to act), as well as by an affirmative act. If a parent, knowing that injury is substantially certain to result to his infant child unless he acts to prevent it, fails to act, and the infant is injured but not killed as a result, the parent would doubtless be guilty of

51. See § 3.12(b).

52. Bradley v. State, 79 Fla. 651, 84 So. 677 (1920); State v. Lowe, 66 Minn. 296, 68 N.W. 1094 (1896).

53. Cf. State v. Fabritz, 276 Md. 416, 348 A.2d 275 (1975) (though child abuse statute covers situation of one who happens to "cause" the child to suffer "physical injury," this includes aggravation of injury, done by another person, because parent did not obtain prompt medical attention).

54. Hughes, supra note 1, at 630. The classic case in the act-causation category is where *A* shoots *B* so that *B* is unable to board a plane which crashes with the loss of everyone on board; *A* will be held guilty of murder even though *B* does not die until after the time of the airplane crash in which he would have lost his life.

55. State v. Crawford, 188 Neb. 378, 196 N.W.2d 915 (1972) (manslaughter); Harrington v. State, 547 S.W.2d 616 (Tex.Crim.App.1977) (murder).

56. This is but an application of the murder rule that if there is such a very high degree of risk of death (in most jurisdictions, consciously realized by the defendant) as to "evince a depraved heart," failure to act to save the other would be murder. See § 7.4.

57. This is but an application of the manslaughter rule that one who recklessly causes another's death is guilty of involuntary manslaughter. See § 7.12. Professor Perkins has thought up a voluntary manslaughter case based on failure to act: a man without justification strikes a railroad gateman a hard blow; the blow reasonably provokes the gateman into a passion to kill his attacker; the assailant immediately gets into his car and drives toward the crossing as a train approaches; the gateman, still in a reasonable passion, intending to cause his assailant's death, omits to lower the gate; so that the assailant is killed. R. Perkins & R. Boyce, Criminal Law 671 (3d ed. 1982).

battery.[58] The same result should follow if his omission amounted to recklessness, though he did not intend any injury to the child.[59]

In a case already noted an omission to put out a fire accidentally started, with intent to cause the building to burn down, was held to amount to arson.[60] A father was held guilty of "abandoning and exposing" his infant child to the elements when, after his estranged wife had deposited the child, poorly clad in cold weather, on his doorstep, he carefully stepped over the child and proceeded on his way out the door.[61] A driver was said to be guilty of the crime of "ill-treating" a dog by failing to stop his car and render aid after hitting the animal.[62]

 WESTLAW REFERENCES

110k26 /p crime /s omit*** omission fail***

(f) A Broader Duty to Rescue? The traditional Anglo-American position on criminal omissions, which confines the duty to act in saving others from harm to certain narrowly-defined categories, has long been the subject of serious debate. Note has frequently been taken of the fact that many European codes adopt a much broader view, imposing a duty to rescue on anyone who could do so without danger to himself,[63] and this has led to the recommendation that duty and liability should be based upon "the defendant's clear recognition of the victim's peril plus his failure to take steps which might reasonably be taken without risk to himself to warn or protect the victim."[64] Those who subscribe to this view ask, for example, why criminal sanctions should not be imposed upon an expert swimmer who fails to come to the rescue of a drowning child.

One long-standing explanation for not expanding legal duty to conform to moral duty is that the latter notion is extremely vague. Precisely how does one define a doctor's moral duty, in terms of the effort and expense which must be undertaken, to aid one known to be in need of medical attention? Does everyone who knows of the existence of a starving person have a moral duty to give that person food? But in response to the argument that no broader rule can be formulated, it is contended that an appeal to common decency is no less specific than the standard of liability for negligent acts.[65] Another argument made against a more general duty to rescue is that it would unduly broaden the "circumstances under which the ordinary citizen will be exposed to the hazards of legal prosecution" because "omissions are so inherently ambiguous that speculation about the omitter's guilt and dangerousness is more of a threat to society than is the preventable harm by omission."[66] Others question whether this would be so, and also label as speculation the related claim that a broader duty to rescue would influence people to interfere officiously in the affairs of others.[67]

Finally, the point is made that, despite frequent avowals to the contrary, we really do

58. State v. Walden, 306 N.C. 466, 293 S.E.2d 780 (1982).

59. These hypothetical cases are but applications of the rules that battery may be committed by intention to injure or by recklessness. See § 7.15(c).

60. Commonwealth v. Cali, 247 Mass. 20, 141 N.E. 510 (1923).

61. Queen v. White, L.R. 1 C.C. 311 (1871) (if the child had died, it would have doubtless been a homicide case; but the child was saved in the nick of time by a constable).

62. Commonwealth v. Putch, 18 Pa.D. & C. 680 (1932).

63. See Dawson, Negotiorum Gestio: The Altruistic Intermeddler, 74 Harv.L.Rev. 1073, 1101 (1961); Frankel, supra note 1, at 371 n. 11; Hughes, supra note 1, at 632–34.

64. Hughes, supra note 1, at 626. He would utilize some of the existing categories (e.g., that concerning the railroad crossing guard) to impose a duty to be aware of the peril. See also Feinberg, The Moral and Legal Responsibility of the Bad Samaritan, 3 Crim.J.Ethics 56 (Winter/Spring 1984), concluding at 86 that a "sound system of social coordination would assign * * * to everyone * * * positive duties to give assistance" in "those cases of sudden and unanticipated peril to others that require immediate attention, and are such that a bystander can either make an 'easy rescue' himself or else sound the alarm to notify those whose job it is to make difficult rescues."

65. Wechsler & Michael, A Rationale of the Law of Homicide, 37 Colum.L.Rev. 701, 751 n. 175 (1937).

66. Frankel, supra note 1, at 424.

67. Hughes, supra note 1, at 634.

not view death-causing omissions in the same way as death-causing acts,[68] so that what is in fact a distinction on moral grounds is appropriately also a distinction in the criminal law. However, this does not necessarily mean that omissions outside existing legal duty categories should be ignored by the criminal law; it may only mean that such omissions should be subject to lesser sanctions than those provided for acts which bring about the same results. For example, causing the death of a stranger by failing to rescue him would not be considered homicide, and thus would not be punished as severely as affirmative acts with the same mental state and the same consequences. Some of the European "Good Samaritan laws" operate in this way,[69] and similar legislation has been adopted in a few states.[70]

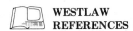

WESTLAW
REFERENCES

digest,synopsis(duty oblig!   /4   rescue*)

§ 3.4   The Mental Part—In General

It is commonly stated that a crime consists of both a physical part and a mental part; that is, both an act or omission (and sometimes also a prescribed result of action or omission, or prescribed attendant circumstances, or both) and a state of mind. This section discusses generally what is required of crimes in the way of the mental part, variously called *mens rea* ("guilty mind") or *scienter* or criminal intent. The following sections will discuss the various types of *mens rea* in greater detail.

68.   J. Hall, supra note 1, at 210.

69.   See H. Silving, Constituent Elements of Crime 90 (1967).

70.   In Minnesota, the "bill's sponsor * * * said he was moved to introduce the bill by reports of the gang rape earlier this year of a woman in a New Bedford, Mass., barroom who was hoisted onto a pool table and repeatedly assaulted while spectators stood by and some reportedly shouted 'go for it!' More recently, a 14-year-old St. Louis girl was raped last month while bystanders did nothing for 40 minutes until an 11-year-old boy called police." National L.J., Aug. 22, 1983, p. 5, col. 1.

Actually, the terms "mental part" and "*mens rea*" and "state of mind" are somewhat too narrow to be strictly accurate, for they include matters that are not really mental at all. Thus we shall see that, though many crimes do require some sort of mental fault (i.e., a bad mind), other crimes (which are commonly said to require *mens rea*) require only some sort of fault which is not mental.[1] The unadorned word "fault" is thus a more accurate word to describe what crimes generally require in addition to their physical elements.

(a) Common Law and Statutory Crimes. During the early days of the development of common law crimes, the judges often declared conduct to be criminal which did not include any bad state of mind. But in more recent times (i.e., since about 1600), the judges have generally defined common law crimes in terms which require, in addition to prescribed action or omission, some prescribed bad state of mind, although that state of mind has differed from one common law crime to another.[2] The basic premise that for criminal liability some *mens rea* is required is expressed by the Latin maxim *actus not facit reum nisi mens sit rea* (an act does not make one guilty unless his mind is guilty). The words and phrases used by the judges to express the bad mind necessary for common law crimes include "maliciously" (as in murder, arson, malicious mischief), "fraudulently" (forgery), "feloniously" (larceny), "wilfully and corruptly" (perjury), and "with intent to . . . ." (e.g., "with intent to steal," another phrase used in defining larceny; "with intent to commit a felony therein," in burglary).[3]

§ 3.4

1.   In addition, some crimes require no fault at all, mental or otherwise; these impose liability without fault. But such crimes are said not to require *mens rea.*

2.   Robinson, A Brief History of Distinctions in Criminal Culpability, 31 Hastings L.J. 815 (1980); Turner, the Mental Element in Crimes at Common Law, 6 Camb.L.J. 31 (1936).

3.   The common law did occasionally depart from the requirement of a literally bad mind. Thus manslaughter could be committed by a type of negligent conduct which, in England, did not require a subjective bad mind, though it did require objective fault. In two crimes, libel and

Most crimes today, of course, are statutory crimes. In some jurisdictions common law crimes have been abolished; in others common law crimes are sparingly used. In all jurisdictions most of the common law crimes have been stated in the form of statutory law. And of course, in modern times, new statutory crimes, unknown to the common law, far outnumber the relatively few common law crimes originally created by the judges. The "mental" aspects of statutory crimes may be roughly classified as follows as to type:

(1) Many statutes defining conduct which is criminal employ words (usually adverbs) or phrases indicating some type of bad-mind requirement: "intentionally" or "with intent to . . ."; "knowingly" or "with knowledge that . . ."; "purposely" or "for the purpose of . . ."; "fraudulently" or "with intent to defraud"; "wilfully"; "maliciously"; "corruptly"; "designedly"; "recklessly"; "wantonly"; "unlawfully"; "feloniously" and so on. (2) Some of the statutes use words or phrases indicating a requirement of fault, but not necessarily mental fault—e.g., "negligently", "carelessly", or "having reason to know . . ." (3) Some statutes define criminal conduct without any words or phrases indicating any express requirement of fault; thus "whoever does so-and-so (or: whoever omits to do so-and-so) is guilty of a crime and subject to the following punishment . . ."[4] However, although the statute may contain no adverbs or phrases indicating a requirement of fault, some fault may be inherent in a verb which the statute employs (e.g., whoever "refuses" to do something or "permits" another to do something.)

It may be said of statutory crimes that, so far as the mental element is concerned, (1) some crimes (like most of the common law crimes) require "subjective fault"—actually a

bad mind of some sort; (2) others require only "objective fault"—fault which is not a matter of the mind; and (3) others require no fault at all, either subjective (mental) or objective (non-mental), such statutes providing instead for "liability without fault."[5] To illustrate: (1) The statutory crime of receiving stolen property is generally worded in terms of receiving stolen property "knowing the property to be stolen." Such wording requires that the defendant, to be guilty, must know in his own mind (i.e., subjectively) that the property he receives is stolen. If he does not know but ought to know—that is, if a reasonable man in his position would know—that the property is stolen, his objective fault in not knowing what he should know is insufficient for guilt, since a statute so worded clearly requires subjective fault. (2) If, however, the statute reads "having reason to know" the property to be stolen, instead of "knowing" that fact, an objective standard of guilt is set up, and he is guilty, though he does not know, if a reasonable man would have known that the property is stolen. (3) And if the statute reads, "Whoever receives stolen property," without anything further about either "knowing" or "having reason to know," he is, literally at least, guilty when he receives property which is actually stolen, even if he does not know, and reasonably does not know, that the property he receives is stolen property.[6]

WESTLAW REFERENCES

110k21 /p scienter "mens rea" "criminal intent"
110k21 /p know!

(b) Ambiguity as to Requisite Mental State. Much of the difficulty involved in ascertaining what, if any, state of mind is required for a particular crime lies in the ambiguous meaning of the particular word or phrase used. Even "knowingly" is not entire-

---

nuisance, vicarious liability was imposed upon a faultless employer for the conduct of his employee.

4. Legislatures seldom if ever expressly provide that lack of fault shall be irrelevant, by any such phrase as "without regard to fault."

5. See Comment, Liability Without Fault Criminal Statutes, 1956 Wis.L.Rev. 625, for such a classification of Wisconsin criminal statutes.

6. To escape conviction under such a statute he must successfully argue (1) that, in spite of the literal wording of the statute, the legislature actually intended to require subjective knowledge or at least objective fault (negligence) in not knowing, or (2) that, if the legislature did mean what it literally said, the statute in question is unconstitutional. See § 2.12(d).

ly clear; for instance, does one know a fact (e.g., that property is stolen) when he is 95% sure of it but not completely certain? An even more ambiguous word, but one which legislatures often use in criminal statutes, is "wilfully." [7] "Maliciously" in the definitions of crimes is also a word of many meanings.[8] Least helpful of all are words like "unlawfully" and "feloniously"; statutes using such words say in effect that one is guilty of a crime if he does some defined act or omission guiltily.

Still further difficulty arises from the ambiguity which frequently exists concerning what the words or phrases in question modify. What, for instance, does "knowingly" modify in a sentence from a "blue sky" law criminal statute punishing one who "knowingly sells a security without a permit" from the securities commissioner? To be guilty must the seller of a security without a permit know only that what he is doing constitutes a sale, or must he also know that the thing he sells is a security, or must he also know that he has no permit to sell the security he sells? As a matter of grammar the statute is ambiguous; it is not at all clear how far down the sentence the word "knowingly" is intended to travel— whether it modifies "sells," or "sells a security," or "sells a security without a permit." [9]

 **WESTLAW REFERENCES**

di knowingly
di willful

(c) Basic Types of Mental State. The difficulties inherent in such a variety of ex-

pressions as to *mens rea* as is used by the common law and by statutes in defining crimes have led modern thinkers to classify the mental aspects of crime into a few general types; and to urge that, in drafting penal codes, a single expression be used to express a single type of *mens rea* culpability. The Model Penal Code has thus reduced the matter to four basic types of crimes which require fault: (1) crimes requiring *intention* (or *purpose*) to do the forbidden act (omission) or cause the forbidden result; (2) crimes requiring *knowledge* of the nature of the act (omission) or of the result which will follow therefrom or of the attendant circumstances; (3) those requiring *recklessness* in doing the act (omission) or causing the result (subjective fault in that the actor must in his own mind realize the risk which his conduct involves); and (4) those requiring only *negligence* in so doing or causing (objective fault in creating an unreasonable risk; but, since the actor need not realize the risk in order to be negligent, no subjective fault is required).[10] Most of the modern criminal codes expressly provide for these four basic types of culpability. Of course, there remains the possibility that, for some crimes or for some elements of a crime, a statute may impose strict liability.

The Model Penal Code also deals with the troublesome problem of whether a given culpability requirement applies to all elements of the offense. It provides that when the law defining the offense prescribes the kind of culpability that is sufficient without distinguishing among the material elements thereof, then it is to apply to all the material

---

7. See United States v. Adamson, 665 F.2d 649 (5th Cir.1982), noting that the term has "a statutory and common law history that is less than unequivocal" and that "as employed in diverse statutes may correspond to any of the different levels of the Model Penal Code's hierarchy of culpable states of mind (i.e., purpose, knowledge, recklessness, or negligence)." For one effort to construe the term in a particular context, see United States v. Pomponio, 429 U.S. 10, 97 S.Ct. 22, 50 L.Ed.2d 12 (1976). On use of the term in federal statutes, see Note, 51 Notre Dame Law. 786 (1976).

8. See, e.g., McGahee v. State, 170 Ga.App. 227, 316 S.E.2d 832 (1984), approving a jury instruction that "maliciously imports a wish to vex, annoy, or injure another, or an intent to do a wrongful act."

9. For another illustration, see Liparota v. United States, ___ U.S. ___, 105 S.Ct. 2084, 85 L.Ed.2d 434 (1985) (7 U.S.C.A. § 2024(b) provides that "whoever knowingly uses, transfers, acquires, alters, or possesses coupons or authorization cards in any manner not authorized by [the statute] or the regulations" is subject to fine and imprisonment; Court decides that "knowingly" mental state extends down to include the "not authorized" part of the statute).

10. Model Penal Code § 2.02(2).

See also J. Hall, General Principles of Criminal Law ch. 4 (2d ed. 1960), and G. Williams, Criminal Law—The General Part chs. 2–3 (2d ed. 1961), for a three-fold classification into crimes of intention, recklessness and negligence.

elements unless a contrary purpose plainly appears in the statute.[11]

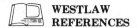

WESTLAW
REFERENCES

110k21 /p mental mind /s element aspect state

(d) Differing Mens Rea Requirements for a Single Crime. Aside from the mental element, we have seen that many crimes are made up not of one but of several physical elements, including not only an act or omission, but also some specific result of that act or omission, or some prescribed attendant circumstances, or perhaps both result and circumstances. Thus the crime of murder requires (aside from its mental ingredients) not only some act or omission (e.g., shooting a gun, wielding an axe, or failing to pull one's infant child out of a bathtub full of water) but also a particular result thereof (the death of the victim). It may properly be said also that lack of justification, such as the justification of self-defense, is a required attendant circumstance in a case where the defendant raises the issue of justification in his defense.[12]

It should be noted that the mental ingredients of a particular crime may differ with regard to the different elements of the crime.[13] Thus in the case of intent-to-kill murder, where the defendant's defense is that he killed in self-defense, the element of conduct causing death requires the intention type of *mens rea* on the part of the defendant; but the element of lack-of-self-defense-justification requires only negligence on his part (i.e., that he unreasonably believed it was necessary to kill to save himself).[14] One might imagine a carefully drafted statutory crime worded:

"Whoever sells intoxicating liquor to one whom he knows to be a policeman and whom he should know to be on duty" is guilty of a misdemeanor. Such a statute, aside from its *mens rea* aspects, covers several different physical elements—(1) the sale (2) of intoxicating liquor (3) to a policeman (4) who is on duty. As to elements (1) and (2), the statute evidently provides for liability without fault: if he in fact sells intoxicating liquor it is no defense that he either reasonably or unreasonably thinks he is making a gift rather than a sale, or thinks he is selling Coca-Cola rather than whiskey. As to element (3), however, the statute requires the seller to have actual knowledge that the purchaser is a policeman; so a reasonable or even unreasonable belief that he is a fireman would be a defense. As to the fourth element, a negligence type of fault is all that is required; a reasonable belief that the policeman is off duty is a defense, but an unreasonable belief is not.

Thus with the various crimes—whether the old common law crimes or the newer statutory crimes not known to the common law—it must be recognized that there may be different *mens rea* requirements as to the different physical elements that go to make up these crimes.

WESTLAW
REFERENCES

patterson /s 97 +4 2319 /p element /s crime /p "mens rea" intent scienter

(e) Mental State and the General Principles of Criminal Law. In two later chapters[15] we consider the various general princi-

---

11. Model Penal Code § 2.02(4). The phrase "material element" is defined in § 1.13(10) to mean an element that does not relate exclusively to the statute of limitations, jurisdiction, venue or to any other matter similarly unconnected with (i) the harm or evil, incident or conduct, sought to be prevented by the law defining the offense, or (ii) the existence of a justification or excuse for such conduct.

12. If such attendant circumstance is actually a part of the definition of the crime, then burden of proof must as a matter of due process be on the defendant. See, e.g., Mullaney v. Wilbur, 421 U.S. 684, 95 S.Ct. 1881, 44 L.Ed. 2d 508 (1975). Otherwise the burden may (but need not) be placed on the defendant. Patterson v. New York, 432 U.S. 197, 97 S.Ct. 2319, 53 L.Ed.2d 281 (1977).

13. See Robinson & Grall, Element Analysis in Defining Criminal Liability: The Model Penal Code and Beyond, 35 Stan.L.Rev. 681 (1983), critically discussing how the Model Penal Code and state codes have gone about accomplishing this.

14. See Model Penal Code § 2.02, Comment at 232 (1985). So too with the crime of rape, where the defendant must intend to have sexual intercourse with the victim; the view is often taken that a negligent mistake in believing that the woman has consented will suffice for guilt. But see Director of Public Prosecutions v. Morgan, 61 C.A. 136 (1975) (no guilt if defendant subjectively believes there was consent).

15. Chs. 4 and 5.

ples of criminal law of the defense-to-liability type: mistake of fact, mistake of law, insanity, infancy, intoxication, coercion, necessity, consent, self-defense, entrapment and the like. As we shall see, some of these principles operate, when applicable, to eliminate the mental element which a specific crime requires. Thus larceny requires, in addition to the acts of taking and carrying away another's property, a mental element termed "intent to steal." If one takes away another's coat mistakenly thinking it to be his own coat, his mistake of fact (e.g., he failed to recognize that the coat he took was not his own) or of law (e.g., he mistakenly thought that, when the coat's owner said yesterday, "I'll give you my coat tomorrow," title automatically passed to him when tomorrow arrived) as to ownership negatives the required intent to steal. His insanity or infancy or extreme intoxication, if any such matter exists, may similarly negative the existence of the necessary mental element which larceny requires.[16] Thus these chapters necessarily deal in some detail with the mental aspects of crime.

The same may be said for the affirmative-liability principles concerning the responsibility of parties to crime and concerning liability for inchoate crimes. Special problems regarding the mental state requirement are often confronted in determining whether a person is a party to a crime committed by another or whether an inchoate offense, such as an attempt, has occurred. Thus the chapter on these subjects [17] will also give attention to the mental aspects of crime.

In the chapters of this book dealing with the elements of specific crimes,[18] rather than with general principles, we shall consider what are the *mens rea* requirements for each of the crimes considered, as well as the physical requirements for those crimes.

16. On the other hand, some of the defenses of the next chapters operate on some principle other than that they negative the mental element, e.g., self-defense, consent of the victim, and perhaps coercion, necessity and entrapment.

WESTLAW REFERENCES

110k23 110k33 110k48 /p eliminate* negat! cancel*** /p (mental /s state element) intent

§ 3.5 Intent and Knowledge

The meaning of the word "intent" in the criminal law has always been rather obscure, largely as a result of its use in such phrases as "criminal intent," "general intent," "specific intent," "constructive intent," and "presumed intent." Intent has traditionally been defined to include knowledge, and thus it is usually said that one intends certain consequences when he desires that his acts cause those consequences or knows that those consequences are substantially certain to result from his acts. The modern view, however, is that it is better to draw a distinction between intent (or purpose) on the one hand and knowledge on the other.

WESTLAW REFERENCES

di intent
di knowledge

(a) The Traditional View of Intent. A crime may be defined in such a way that the defendant, to be guilty of it, must intentionally engage in specific conduct (and, perhaps also, intentionally do so under specified attendant circumstances, the intention requirement applying to the circumstances as well), or a crime may be defined in terms of an intention to produce a specified result. Illustrative of the latter are intent-to-kill murder, which requires that a person intend to kill another human being; intent-to-injure battery, which requires that he intend to do bodily injury to another; assault with intent to kill, which requires that he intend to kill the one assaulted; false pretenses, which requires that he intend to deceive his victim; and treason, which requires that he intend to aid the enemy.

17. Ch. 6.
18. Chs. 7 and 8.

The following are examples of the former type of crime: common-law burglary, which requires that the burglar intentionally engage in the conduct of breaking and entering, and perhaps also that he intend that the building thus broken into be a dwelling house; larceny, which requires that the thief intentionally engage in the conduct of taking and carrying away property; and forcible rape, which requires that the rapist intend to engage in sexual intercourse, and perhaps also that he intend to engage in it with a woman not his wife. Although it is true that burglary is not generally expressly defined as "intentionally breaking and entering," etc., larceny as "intentionally taking and carrying away," etc., or rape as "intentionally having sexual intercourse," etc., such an intention is nevertheless a requirement for each of these crimes. Sometimes it is spoken of as a "general intent" to distinguish it from the "specific intent" which a crime may specifically, by its definition, require, over and above any required intention to engage in the forbidden conduct (as burglary requires a specific intent to commit a felony, larceny a specific intent to steal).

With crimes which require that the defendant intentionally cause a specific result, what is meant by an "intention" to cause that result? Although the theorists have not always been in agreement as to the answer to this question,[1] the traditional view is that a person who acts (or omits to act) intends a result of his act (or omission) under two quite different circumstances: (1) when he consciously desires that result, whatever the likelihood of that result happening from his conduct; and (2) when he knows that that result is practically certain to follow from his con-

duct, whatever his desire may be as to that result.[2]

Thus, to take the first of these circumstances, if A shoots B at such a distance that his chances of hitting and killing him are small, but with the desire of killing him, he intends to kill him; and if by good luck the bullet hits B in a vital spot, A will be held to have intended to kill B, sufficient for guilt of murder of the intent-to-kill variety.[3] Or, if C fails to pull his infant child D off the railroad tracks, desiring to cause D's death thereby, C intends to kill D though he realizes that the chances are great that someone else will save the child or that the child will crawl away before the next train is due to arrive.

As to the second of the two circumstances listed above, this would cover the case in which E, for the purpose of killing his mother F for her life insurance, places a time bomb on a plane he knows is carrying both F and G. E has an intent to kill G because, though he may regret the necessity of killing G and thus not desire that result, he knows that the death of G is substantially certain to follow from his act.[4] Or if H, who has a legal duty to act affirmatively to aid J in peril, fails to unlock the farmhouse door upon which J is knocking during a blizzard, knowing that J is practically certain to perish in the storm if the door remains locked, H intends to kill J even though he may wish that J by some miracle survive. "Practical" or "substantial" certainty of the result rather than "absolute" certainty is all that is required; H is nonetheless guilty of J's murder (of the intent-to-kill type) though he knows there may be a slight possibility that someone else will happen by in time to rescue J, or that J can make it to another farm without perishing on the way.

§ 3.5

1. See discussion of the views of Austin, Bentham, Markby, and Salmond in Cook, Act, Intention, and Motive in the Criminal Law, 26 Yale L.J. 645, 653–58 (1917).

2. G. Williams, Criminal Law: The General Part §§ 16, 18 (2d ed. 1961); Cook, supra note 1, at 657–58; Perkins, A Rationale of Mens Rea, 52 Harv.L.Rev. 905, 910–11 (1939); Restatement, Torts (Second) § 8A (1965).

3. Studstill v. State, 7 Ga. 2 (1849) (where A carefully aims gun at B, who is so far off that it is improbable the

ball will reach its object, but the ball nevertheless carries the distance and kills B, A intended to kill B and so is guilty of murder).

4. Similarly, Restatement, Torts (Second) § 8A, Comment (1965) gives this illustration of intent: "A throws a bomb into B's office for the purpose of killing B. A knows that C, B's stenographer, is in the office. A has no desire to injure C, but knows that his act is substantially certain to do so. C is injured by the explosion. A is subject to liability to C for an intentional tort."

Although the matter has received less attention, it would appear that an intention to engage in certain conduct or to do so under certain attendant circumstances may likewise be said to exist on the basis of what one knows. A thief may be said to intentionally take and carry away property when he knowingly does so. And, assuming for the moment that burglary is viewed as requiring that the burglar intend to break and enter some building and also that he intend to do so into a dwelling house, the requirement of intention as to circumstances is satisfied if he knows the building in question to be a dwelling.[5] (Perhaps because it is more apparent that knowledge rather than desire is most significant as to attendant circumstances, it is common for statutes to be drafted in terms of knowledge of these circumstances. Thus, statutes defining the crime of receiving stolen property usually say "knowing the property to be stolen," and statutes on issuing bad checks often say "knowing he has insufficient funds on deposit in the bank" to cover the check.)

WESTLAW REFERENCES

crim**** /p common-law /p burglary /s defin! /s intent

crim**** /p common-law /p defin! /s general specific +1 intent

crime criminal /p statut*** legislat! /s define defini**** /s know! inten**** /s circumstance

(b) The Modern View: Intent and Knowledge Distinguished. As concluded

above, the word "intent" in the substantive criminal law has traditionally not been limited to the narrow, dictionary definition of purpose, aim, or design, but instead has often been viewed as encompassing much of what would ordinarily be described as knowledge. This failure to distinguish between intent (strictly defined) and knowledge is probably of little consequence in many areas of the law, as often there is good reason for imposing liability whether the defendant desired or merely knew of the practical certainty of the results.[6] Yet, because there are several areas of the criminal law in which there may be good reason for distinguishing between one's objectives and knowledge,[7] the modern approach is to define separately the mental states of knowledge and intent (sometimes referred to as purpose, most likely to avoid confusion with the word "intent" as traditionally defined).[8] This is the approach taken in the Model Penal Code.[9]

Thus, as to the results of one's conduct, the Code provides that one acts "purposely" when "it is his conscious object * * * to cause such a result,"[10] while one acts "knowingly" if "he is aware that it is practically certain that his conduct will cause such a result."[11] One is said to act "purposely" as to the nature of his conduct if "it is his conscious object to engage in conduct of that nature,"[12] and to act "knowingly" as to the nature of his conduct if "he is aware that his conduct is of that nature."[13] As to the attendant circumstances, one acts "purposely" when "he is

5. See, e.g., State v. Roufa, 241 La. 474, 129 So.2d 743 (1961) (statute makes it a crime to intentionally possess obscene literature with intent to display same; court holds this requires proof of defendant's knowledge of the obscene character of the material).

6. See Model Penal Code § 2.02, Comment at 234 (1985).

7. E.g., treason, requiring a purpose to aid the enemy, Haupt v. United States, 330 U.S. 631, 67 S.Ct. 874, 91 L.Ed. 1145 (1947), and attempts and conspiracy, where a purpose to bring about the criminal result is required, Dennis v. United States, 341 U.S. 494, 71 S.Ct. 857, 95 L.Ed. 1137 (1951); Hartzel v. United States, 322 U.S. 680, 64 S.Ct. 1233, 88 L.Ed. 1534 (1944).

8. Separate definitions of the two terms are to be found in most of the modern recodifications.

9. Model Penal Code § 2.02(2)(a) & (b).

10. Model Penal Code § 2.02(2)(a)(i). Most modern codes use a "conscious objective" formulation. A few others define the matter in terms of the defendant's purpose to cause a result, his specific intention to do so, or by reference to defendant having "actively desired" such a result.

11. Model Penal Code § 2.02(2)(b)(ii). Several, but far from all, of the modern recodifications contain such a definition.

12. Model Penal Code § 2.02(2)(a)(i). Many of the state recodifications contain such a provision. A few others define the matter in terms of the defendant's purpose to engage in such conduct, his specific intent to do so, or his specific design to do so.

13. Model Penal Code § 2.02(2)(b)(i). Most of the modern recodifications contain a provision of this type.

aware of the existence of such circumstances or he believes or hopes that they exist," [14] while one acts "knowingly" when "he is aware * * * that such circumstances exist." [15]

Although the foregoing provisions contemplate that one "knows" of present (as opposed to future) events only if he is actually aware of them, an important exception is recognized elsewhere in the Code. This exception has to do with what is commonly termed "wilful blindness," "where it can almost be said that the defendant actually knew," as when a person "has his suspicion aroused but then deliberately omits to make further inquiries, because he wishes to remain in ignorance." [16] Illustrative is *United States v. Jewell*,[17] where the evidence was that the defendant was paid $100 to drive a truck with a secret compartment into the United States from Mexico and that he deliberately refrained from looking into the compartment and ascertaining whether there were drugs inside. "Whether such cases should be viewed as instances of acting recklessly or knowingly presents a subtle but important question." [18] The notion that it is properly classified as knowledge in the hierarchy of mental states is grounded in the conclusion "that deliberate ignorance and positive knowledge are equally culpable." [19]

This conclusion is most convincing if the "wilful blindness" category is rather narrowly circumscribed. Such is the case in the Model Penal Code, which states that when "knowledge of the existence of a particular fact is an element of an offense, such knowledge is established if a person is aware of a high probability of its existence, unless he actually believes that it does not exist." [20] Very few of the modern recodifications contain a provision of this type, though it is noteworthy that even in the absence of such an enactment some courts have construed the mental state of knowledge as including such a situation.[21] The Model Penal Code requirement of awareness of a high probability of the existence of the fact serves to ensure that the purpose to avoid learning the truth is culpable.[22] As for

---

14. Model Penal Code § 2.02(2)(a)(ii). Perhaps because an intent mental state is rarely utilized as to attendant circumstances, few of the modern codes contain such a provision.

15. Model Penal Code § 2.02(2)(b)(i). Most of the modern recodifications contain a provision of this type.

16. G. Williams, Criminal Law: The General Part 157, 159 (2d ed. 1961). See also Edwards, The Criminal Degrees of Knowledge, 17 Mod.L.Rev. 294 (1954); Comment, 63 Iowa L.Rev. 466 (1977); Note, 45 Brooklyn L.Rev. 1083 (1979).

17. 532 F.2d 697 (9th Cir.1976).

18. Model Penal Code § 2.02, Comment (Tent. Draft No. 4, 1955).

19. United States v. Jewell, 532 F.2d 697 (9th Cir. 1976).

20. Model Penal Code § 2.02(7).

21. McAllister v. United States, 747 F.2d 1273 (9th Cir. 1984); United States v. Suttiswad, 696 F.2d 645 (9th Cir. 1982); United States v. Mohabir, 624 F.2d 1140 (2d Cir. 1980); United States v. Murrieta-Bejarano, 552 F.2d 1323 (9th Cir.1977); United States v. Jewell, 532 F.2d 697 (9th Cir.1976).

While the preceding cases all are rather demanding in requiring that the instruction to the jury somehow cover the Model Penal Code ingredients of this concept, in United States v. Burns, 683 F.2d 1056 (7th Cir.1982), the court upheld this instruction: "No person can intentionally avoid knowledge by closing his eyes to facts which should prompt him to investigate." See also United States v. Glick, 710 F.2d 639 (10th Cir.1983).

22. As stated by the dissenters in United States v. Jewell, 532 F.2d 697 (9th Cir.1976): "It is not culpable to form 'a conscious purpose to avoid learning the truth' unless one is aware of facts indicating a high probability of that truth. To illustrate, a child given a gift-wrapped package by his mother while in Mexico may form a conscious purpose to take it home without learning what is inside; yet his state of mind is totally innocent unless he is aware of a high probability that the package contains a controlled substance. Thus, a conscious purpose instruction is only proper when coupled with a requirement that one be aware of a high probability of the truth."

But consider Perkins, "Knowledge" as a Mental State Requirement, 29 Hastings L.J. 953, 964 (1978): "The notion that it is not culpable to form 'a conscious purpose to avoid learning the truth' unless one is aware of facts indicating a high probability of that truth results from a failure to distinguish culpability from proof. Whenever the need to investigate is recognized, culpability is established by a conscious effort to avoid learning the truth for fear of learning that contemplated action would be unlawful. But without awareness of facts indicating a high probability of unlawfulness, the need to investigate may be overlooked. And there is no conscious purpose to avoid learning the truth when the risk of unlawfulness has not been realized. In other words, without either other evidence or awareness of facts indicating a high probability of unlawfulness, there is no basis for an inference that the need to investigate had been recognized, and there could be no wilful avoidance without such recognition. Hence discussion in this area should place the emphasis on proof rather than culpability."

the Model Penal Code exception where the defendant actually believes the fact does not exist, it assures that the defendant is not convicted "on an objective theory of knowledge," for example, in *Jewell* "that a reasonable man should have inspected the car and would have discovered what was hidden inside."[23]

It should be noted, however, that the word "knowledge"—used in criminal statutes with some frequency—has not always been interpreted as having the meaning given in the Model Penal Code. Just as we have seen that the word "intent" has not been limited to its dictionary definition, it is also true that the word "knowledge" has likewise sometimes been given a broader definition. Cases have held that one has knowledge of a given fact when he has the means for obtaining such knowledge,[24] when he has notice of facts which would put one on inquiry as to the existence of that fact,[25] when he has information sufficient to generate a reasonable belief as to that fact,[26] or when the circumstances are such that a reasonable man would believe that such a fact existed.[27] Sometimes belief in the existence of an attendant circumstance is deemed sufficient,[28] sometimes it is not.[29] While these decisions, at least in some in-

stances, may have resulted in the setting of desirable limits on the mental state required for various crimes, they have led to considerable confusion because the word "knowledge" has been taken to mean many different things—all the way down to mere negligence in not knowing.[30]

 WESTLAW REFERENCES

crim**** /p defin! /s knowingly purposely /s conduct
jewell & 532 +5 697

(c) Disparity Between Intended and Actual Result. With crimes which require that the defendant intentionally cause a forbidden result, it not infrequently happens that there is a difference between the result he intends and the result he achieves, which gives rise to a question as to his criminal liability in such a case. There are four general types of cases:

(1) Unintended Victim. Perhaps the result intended (e.g., harm to the person or harm to property) is exactly as intended except that it happens to someone other than the intended victim. *A* aims his gun at his enemy *B* with intent to kill *B* but, missing, hits and kills *A*'s friend *C* instead. *A* throws a rock at *B* intended to injure *B* but, missing again, hits

---

23. United States v. Jewell, 532 F.2d 697 (9th Cir.1976) (dissent). But see note 21 supra, citing statutes not including this qualification upon the wilful blindness rule.

24. E.g., State v. Perkins, 181 La. 997, 160 So. 789 (1935).

25. E.g., State v. Young, 194 La. 1061, 195 So. 539 (1940); Commonwealth v. Rosenberg, 379 Mass. 334, 398 N.E.2d 451 (1979).

26. E.g., State v. Smith, 22 N.J. 59, 123 A.2d 369 (1956).

27. E.g., Woods v. State, 15 Ala.App. 251, 73 So. 129 (1916); State v. Sidway, 139 Vt. 480, 431 A.2d 1237 (1981). Consider also Commonwealth v. Dellamano, 393 Mass. 132, 469 N.E.2d 1254 (1984) (actual knowledge required even though statute employs "reason to know" test). Contra: United States v. Stephens, 569 F.2d 1372 (5th Cir. 1978); Kimoktoak v. State, 584 P.2d 25 (Alaska 1978).

28. E.g., State v. VanTreese, 198 Iowa 984, 200 N.W. 570 (1924) (belief that property received was stolen).

29. E.g., Montgomery v. Commonwealth, 189 Ky. 306, 224 S.W. 878 (1920) (belief that check uttered was forged); State v. Murphy, 674 P.2d 1220 (Utah 1983) (belief that purchaser of drugs would use them for illicit purpose).

30. As stated in State v. Beale, 299 A.2d 921 (Me.1973), rejecting the minority reasonable man approach to the

mental state of knowledge: "It appears to us that the minority jurisdictions which follow the 'ordinary reasonable man' test are failing to stress sufficiently the distinction between civil and criminal responsibility. In civil cases the failure of the defendant to act with the degree of care which a person of ordinary prudence would have used may be the test of his responsibility without any determination that the defendant, himself, was a person of ordinary prudence or that he had any wrongful intent. On the other hand, the very essence of this criminal offense is the intentional wrongdoing of the defendant."

In State v. Shipp, 93 Wn.2d 510, 610 P.2d 1322 (1980), concerning a statute which declared a person acts knowingly when "he has information which would lead a reasonable man in the same situation to believe that facts exist which facts are described by a statute defining an offense," the court construed this language as only allowing an inference of knowledge in such circumstances. Relying upon *Sandstrom*, discussed in the text at note 70 infra, the court concluded the statute would be unconstitutional if construed as creating a mandatory presumption. The court also declined to read the statute literally as adopting an objective negligence standard, as the state criminal code's hierarchy of mental states put knowledge above recklessness, which is a subjective standard.

and injures *D* instead. *A* aims a brick at *B*'s car with intent to damage it, but he misses again, hitting *E*'s car, parked next to *B*'s, and damaging it. Or *A* sets fire to a wheat field intending to burn *B*'s farm house, but the wind shifts and *F*'s farm house is burned instead. In these cases the problem is whether *A* is criminally liable for the murder of *C*, the battery to *D*, the malicious injury to *E*'s car, or for arson for the burning of *F*'s house.

(2) Unintended Manner. Perhaps the end result which the defendant succeeds in producing is exactly as intended, but it is achieved in an unintended manner. *A* aims a gun at *B*'s heart with intent to kill, but his aim is bad and he hits *B*'s head, killing him. Or *A* shoots *B* with intent to kill, but only wounds him; however, in his weakened condition *B* catches pneumonia and dies; or a doctor so carelessly treats the wound that an infection sets in, so that *B* dies; or *B* catches scarlet fever from a fellow patient at the hospital and dies. Or *A* shoots at *B*, with intent to kill, and misses completely; but this unnerving experience causes *B* to go the long route home, during the course of which he is run over and killed by a truck negligently operated. In each case, *A* intended to kill *B*, and the end result was *B*'s death, and *B*'s death would not have occurred but for *A*'s conduct in trying to kill *B*. But is *A* criminally liable for murder when the result happens in an unintended manner?

(3) Unintended Type of Harm. Perhaps the result achieved differs from the result intended as to type of harm, as where *A* throws a rock at *B* with intent to injure *B* but misses,

unintentionally breaking *B*'s (or *C*'s) window. Is he guilty of the malicious destruction of the window? Or he throws the rock at the window and instead hits the person. Is he guilty of a battery?

(4) Unintended Degree of Harm. Perhaps the result achieved differs from the result intended as to the degree of harm. For example, *A* strikes *B* with a stick, intending only to injure him, but the blow brings about *B*'s death. Is *A* guilty of murder? Or, the situation may be somewhat the reverse; *A* strikes *B* with intent to kill him, but the only result is bodily injury. Of what crime, if any, is *A* guilty under these circumstances?

The first of these situations is often discussed in terms of mental state: it is said that the principle of "transferred intent" applies, so that, for example, *A*'s intent to kill *B* is transferred to *C*, who was actually killed as a result of *A*'s conduct.[31] Actually, it is probably more correct to say that the crime merely requires an intent to kill another, so that there is no problem as to mental state, and no need to resort to the fiction of "transferred intent." [32] Rather, the question is whether the fact a different person was killed somehow makes it unfair to impose criminal liability for murder on *A*, a problem which is more appropriately dealt with as a matter of causation. The same is true of the second situation; the fact the intended result came about in an unexpected manner raises the policy question of whether it is therefore unfair to impose liability on *A*. Because these are matters of causation,[33] they will be dealt with in a later section of this book.[34]

31. See Perkins, supra note 2, at 927–28. This "transferred intent" terminology is frequently used in the cases. See, e.g., United States v. Montoya, 739 F.2d 1437 (9th Cir. 1984); O'Connor v. United States, 399 A.2d 21 (D.C.App. 1979); Holt v. State, 266 Ind. 586, 365 N.E.2d 1209 (1977); Gladden v. State, 273 Md. 383, 330 A.2d 176 (1974); Commonwealth v. Puleio, 394 Mass. 101, 474 N.E.2d 1078 (1985); State v. Hamilton, 89 N.M. 746, 557 P.2d 1095 (1976); Riddick v. Commonwealth, 226 Va. 244, 308 S.E.2d 117 (1983).

When, as in State v. Cates, 293 N.C. 462, 238 S.E.2d 465 (1977), there is simply a case of mistaken identity, as where the defendant shoots *C* believing him to be *B*, the requisite intent clearly can be found without resorting to the fiction of transferred intent. In such circumstances,

however, a transferred intent type of analysis is sometimes used, as in *Cates*, to attach defendant's prior premeditation and deliberation re killing *B* to the killing of *C*.

32. One court, reasoning that the "function of the transferred intent doctrine is to insure the adequate punishment of those who accidentally kill innocent bystanders, while failing to kill their intended victims," has held that the doctrine is inapplicable when both the intended victim and a bystander are killed. People v. Birreuta, 162 Cal.App.3d 454, 208 Cal.Rptr. 635 (1984).

33. They are so characterized in Model Penal Code § 2.03.

34. See § 3.12(f).

The third situation, which concerns an unintended type of harm, might also be discussed in terms of causation, although it seems better to deal with the problem as a matter of the required concurrence between the mental state and harm.[35] As we shall see, the rule is that ordinarily an intention to cause one type of harm cannot serve as a substitute for the statutory or common-law requirement of intention as to another type of harm.[36] Two notable exceptions are felony-murder and misdemeanor-manslaughter, where the commission of a certain type of felony or misdemeanor will supply the only necessary mental state to support a homicide conviction; here, problems of causation must be confronted.[37] As to the fourth situation, where the harm caused is of a different degree than intended, the issue might be discussed either in terms of concurrence of mental state and results (particularly when the harm done is greater than intended) or as a question of causation (particularly when the harm done is less than intended).[38] It is dealt with herein as a matter of concurrence.[39]

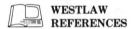

WESTLAW REFERENCES

digest("transferred intent")

synopsis(felony-murder /p mental-state inten! /p harm injury result! consequence)

35. See § 3.11(d).

36. There are also some crimes which contain, as part of their mental element, the intent to commit some other crime. For example, common law burglary requires the intent to commit a felony within the dwelling. These should not be viewed as exceptions to the rule, as the intent to commit another crime is an additional requirement and not a substitute for the required mental state as to the *actus reus* of the crime.

37. See § 3.12(h).

38. This is dealt with in terms of causation in Model Penal Code § 2.03(2)(a).

39. See § 3.11(e).

40. Cf. State v. Simonson, 298 Minn. 235, 214 N.W.2d 679 (1974) (one who receives stolen property with intent to restore it to owner only if reward paid has the requisite intent to permanently deprive).

41. Harvick v. State, 49 Ark. 514, 6 S.W. 19 (1887) (*A* broke and entered *B*'s shop at night with intent to steal all the money in the safe if there was any; in fact, there was only $6 therein; *A* held guilty of burglary; he intended to commit grand larceny, a felony, if the safe were full enough).

(d) Conditional and Multiple Intentions.

Where a crime is defined so as to require that the defendant have a particular intention in his mind—as larceny requires that he have an intention to deprive the owner permanently of his property, burglary that he have an intention to commit a felony, and assault with intent to kill that he have an intention to kill—the problem arises whether he has the required intention when his intention is conditional. Thus *A* takes and carries away *B*'s property intending to restore it to *B* if *A*'s dying aunt should leave him a fortune. *A* breaks and enters *B*'s house intending to rape Mrs. *B* if he finds her at home alone. *A* points a gun at *B* telling him he will shoot him unless he removes his overalls, and intending to kill *B* if he does not comply. Perhaps *A*'s aunt does actually leave him the fortune; and Mrs. *B* is away from home; and *B* does remove his overalls. In these cases *A* is guilty of larceny,[40] burglary,[41] and assault with intent to kill,[42] respectively.

But the condition in some circumstances may be such as to exclude liability. Thus *A* will not be guilty of larceny if his intention, when taking and carrying away *B*'s property, is to return it if it proves to be *B*'s property, but to keep it if it turns out to be *A*'s own property.[43] The Model Penal Code sums it up

42. People v. Connors, 253 Ill. 266, 97 N.E. 643 (1912) (emphasizing that condition of *B* removing overalls was one which *A* had no right to make); Commonwealth v. Richards, 363 Mass. 299, 293 N.E.2d 854 (1973) (in prosecution of defendant as accessory to assault with intent to kill, it sufficient that defendant intended to kill only if necessary to effectuate the robbery or make the escape). Compare State v. Irwin, 55 N.C.App. 305, 285 S.E.2d 345 (1982) (where defendant held knife to matron's throat in making jail escape and said he would kill her if anyone intervened, defendant not guilty of assault with intent to kill, as evidence was only of "a specific intent *not to* kill anyone if * * * the others complied with defendant's demands"); State v. Kinnemore, 34 Ohio App.2d 39, 295 N.E.2d 680 (1972) (where defendant held scissors to victim's neck and said he would kill her if not allowed to escape, no assault with intent to kill, as defendant's "objective was escape—not murder"). For other cases in the assault area, see § 7.16(c).

43. Cf. State v. Ferrel, ___ Mont. ___, 679 P.2d 224 (1984) (defendant did not violate theft statute by telling employer she would not return interest on proceeds from sale of employer's cattle until employer compensated her for value of expropriated garden, as condition negatived

by saying that where a crime requires the defendant to have a specified intention, he has the required intention although it is a conditional intention, "unless the condition negatives the harm or evil sought to be prevented by the law defining the offense." [44] For one to take another's property intending to give it back if he inherits other property involves a condition which does not negative the evil which larceny seeks to prevent; but taking it intending to restore it if it is not his own property does involve a condition which negatives that evil.

A person often acts with two or more intentions. These intentions may consist of an immediate intention (intent) and an ulterior one (motive),[45] as where the actor takes another's money intending to steal it and intending then to use it to buy food for his needy family. Sometimes the two intentions are not so distinguishable, but rather are two immediate intentions, as where a man transports a girl across the state line intending that she should on arrival at their destination work as a waitress in the daytime and as a prostitute at night. It may be said that, so long as the defendant has the intention required by the definition of the crime, it is immaterial that he may also have had some other intention.[46]

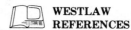

find 106 so2d 684

(e) "Criminal," "Constructive," "General," and "Specific" Intent. Much of the existing uncertainty as to the precise meaning of the word "intent" is attributable to the fact that courts have often used such phrases as "criminal intent," "general intent," "specific intent," "constructive intent," and "presumed intent." "Criminal intent," for example, is often taken to be synonymous with *mens rea,* the general notion that except for strict liability offenses some form of mental state is a prerequisite to guilt. As a result, the phrase "criminal intent" is sometimes used to refer to criminal negligence or recklessness.[47] Similarly, the notion of "constructive intent" has been used by some courts; it is first asserted that intent is required for all crimes, and then it is added that such intent may be inferred from recklessness or negligence.[48] It would make for clearer analysis if courts would merely acknowledge that for some crimes intent is not needed and that recklessness or negligence will suffice.[49]

We have already noted that, where the definition of a crime requires some forbidden act by the defendant, his bodily movement, to qualify as an act, must be voluntary.[50] To some extent, then, all crimes of affirmative action require something in the way of a

---

the harm or evil sought to be prevented by the theft statute—permanent deprivation of property).

44. Model Penal Code § 2.02(6).

45. See § 3.6.

46. O'Neal v. United States, 240 F.2d 700 (10th Cir. 1957) (interstate transportation of a girl with the intent to have her work as a waitress in the day and prostitute at night; conviction of Mann Act violation *held* affirmed, because the purpose of prostitution need not be the sole purpose of the trip). See also United States v. Snow, 507 F.2d 22 (7th Cir.1974) (other reason for transportation was so that woman could work as a dancer; defendant guilty of violating Mann Act if prostitution "an important reason," even if "not the sole, or even the most important reason"); Rex v. Gillow, 1 Moody C.C. 85, 168 Eng.Rep. 1195 (Crown Cas.Res. 1825) (defendant, illegally hunting game, was discovered by three gamekeepers; as they rushed him, he fired intending to hit them in order to prevent his apprehension; his intent to prevent apprehension, which is not an intention required for the crime of shooting with intent to do grievous bodily harm, is immaterial, and it is not necessary to seek a dominant intent;

he is guilty of the crime, since he shot with an intent to do grievous bodily harm).

Compare the situation which arises under the topic of causation in extortion or false pretenses cases when the *victim* of the threats or misrepresentation, rather than the *defendant,* acts with two intentions—as where, after the lady threatened to accuse her male victim of adultery with her, the man paid her money, partly from love for her and partly from fear of her threats: People v. Williams, 127 Cal. 212, 59 P. 581 (1899) (the fear induced by the threat must be "the operating or controlling cause" of the payment, for extortion).

47. E.g., People v. Campbell, 237 Mich. 424, 212 N.W. 97 (1927); State v. Clardy, 73 S.C. 340, 53 S.E. 493 (1906).

48. E.g., Pool v. State, 87 Ga. 526, 13 S.E. 556 (1891); Luther v. State, 177 Ind. 619, 98 N.E. 640 (1912); Woodward v. State, 164 Miss. 468, 144 So. 895 (1932).

49. See Holmes, J., in Commonwealth v. Pierce, 138 Mass. 165, 52 Am.Rep. 264 (1884).

50. See § 3.2(c).

mental element—at least an intention to make the bodily movement which constitutes the act which the crime requires. So too with crimes of omission; the defendant must ordinarily know (sometimes, should know) the facts indicating the necessity of action in order to be criminally liable for his omission.[51] To this extent, crimes of omission also ordinarily require some sort of mental element (knowledge, or negligence in not knowing). We shall later see that some of the broad defenses to criminal liability (especially insanity, infancy, and involuntary intoxication) operate, when applicable, to relieve the actor from liability because these conditions negative his mental capacity to commit any crime.[52] These notions are sometimes summed up with the expression that all crimes require a "general intent," although the phrase "general intent" is also used on occasion for other purposes as well.[53]

"General intent" is often distinguished from "specific intent," although the distinction being drawn by the use of these two terms often varies. Sometimes "general intent" is used in the same way as "criminal intent" to mean the general notion of *mens rea*, while "specific intent" is taken to mean the mental state required for a particular crime.[54] Or, "general intent" may be used to encompass all forms of the mental state requirement, while "specific intent" is limited to the one mental state of intent.[55] Another possibility is that "general intent" will be used to characterize an intent to do something on an undetermined occasion, and "specific intent" to denote an intent to do that thing at a particular time and place.[56]

However, the most common usage of "specific intent" is to designate a special mental element which is required above and beyond any mental state required with respect to the *actus reus* of the crime.[57] Common law larceny, for example, requires the taking and carrying away of the property of another, and the defendant's mental state as to this act must be established, but in addition it must be shown that there was an "intent to steal" the property.[58] Similarly, common law burglary requires a breaking and entry into the dwelling of another, but in addition to the mental state connected with these acts it must also be established that the defendant acted "with intent to commit a felony therein."[59] The same situation prevails with many statutory crimes: assault "with intent to kill" as to certain aggravated assaults;[60] confining another "for the purpose of ransom or reward" in kidnapping; making an untrue statement "designedly, with intent to defraud" in the crime of false pretenses; etc. Likewise, criminal attempts require proof of an intent to bring about the consequences set forth in the crime attempted, and this is so

---

51. See § 3.3(b).

52. These defenses apparently apply even to the liability-without-fault cases.

53. See Remington & Helstad, The Mental Element in Crime—A Legislative Problem, 1952 Wis.L.Rev. 644, 648–52, and sources cited therein.

54. This usage is criticized in J. Hall, General Principles of Criminal Law 142 (2d ed. 1960).

55. See Perkins, supra note 2, at 924; Ricketts v. State, 291 Md. 701, 436 A.2d 906 (1981) (indecent exposure is a general intent crime, including acts that are only reckless or negligent, and thus is not a crime of moral turpitude). In State v. Daniels, 236 La. 998, 109 So.2d 896 (1959), the court made the following distinction, based upon language in the Louisiana criminal code: "Specific intent is present when from the circumstances the offender must have subjectively desired the prohibited result; whereas general intent exists when from the circumstances the prohibited result may reasonably be expected to follow from the offender's voluntary act, irrespective of any subjective desire to have accomplished such result."

56. State v. Rocker, 52 Haw. 336, 475 P.2d 684 (1970) (intent required for crime of indecent exposure "is a general intent not a specific intent, i.e., it is not necessary that the exposure be made with the intent that some particular person see it"); State v. Hobbs, 252 Iowa 432, 107 N.W.2d 238 (1961) (statute making it an offense to possess burglary tools with intent to use same in a burglary construed to require only "general intent" to use tools on some undetermined occasion to commit a burglary, rather than a "specific intent" to burglarize a specific place at a particular time).

57. See discussion in State v. Huber, 356 N.W.2d 468 (S.D.1984).

58. See § 8.5.

59. See § 8.13(e).

60. Such cases require careful analysis. Because a similar intent to kill is not required for murder, it would be erroneous to charge a jury that assault with intent to kill is established where the facts, had death resulted, would suffice to establish murder. Bonfanti v. State, 2 Minn. 123 (Gil. 99) (1858).

even though no such intent is required for the completed crime.[61]

This distinction between "general intent" and "specific intent" is not without importance in the criminal law. For example, the traditional view is that the rules on when mistake of fact or mistake of law will constitute a defense differ depending upon what kind of intent is involved.[62] Also, some courts have taken the view that intent may be presumed (discussed below) only as to a general intent.[63] It has been suggested, however, that greater clarity could be accomplished by abandoning the "specific intent"-"general intent" terminology,[64] and this has been done in the Model Penal Code.[65]

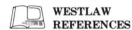 **WESTLAW REFERENCES**

di mens rea

crim**** /p assault /p general specific +1 intent /s voluntary involuntary +1 intoxication

(f) Proof of Intention ("Presumed Intent"). A maxim much used in criminal law cases states that a person is "presumed to intend the natural and probable consequences of his acts." Thus if *A* fires a gun in the vicinity of *B*, and his bullet kills *B*, it is said that *A* is presumed to have intended the killing of *B* if the circumstances are such that *B*'s death is "natural and probable." If this is taken as a rule of substantive law, it is apparent that it would in effect destroy the concept of intention and replace it entirely with negligence. This is because the defen-

dant would be held to have intended whatever a reasonable man would have foreseen as probable.[66]

In the illustration given above, it certainly will not do to conclude conclusively, from the mere fact that *A*'s bullet killed *B*, that *A* intended that result, even though such a result was the foreseeable result of shooting. *A* may actually have meant to kill *B*; but he may have intended only to wound *B*; or he may have intended to miss him completely, wishing only to scare him; or he may have been simply negligent, having no intent to kill, wound or scare. By the same token, it should not be said that the conclusion that *A* intended to kill *must* be reached in the absence of counterproof showing that *A* had no such intent; the so-called presumption of intent does not impose upon the accused any duty to produce evidence.[67] Rather, it merely means that the fact-finder *may* (but need not) conclude under those circumstances that *A* intended to kill *B*. Thus the matter is reduced to an inference (or "permissive presumption") rather than a true presumption of the mandatory sort.[68]

The Supreme Court concluded as much in *Sandstrom v. Montana*.[69] The defendant there was charged with deliberate homicide, which under Montana law consisted of purposely or knowingly causing the death of another. The jury was instructed in accordance with Montana law that the "law presumes that a person intends the ordinary consequences of his voluntary acts." The defen-

---

61. Thus, while murder may be committed without an intent to kill, attempted murder may not. Merritt v. Commonwealth, 164 Va. 653, 180 S.E. 395 (1935).

62. See § 5.1.

63. E.g., Vandiver v. State, 97 Okl.Crim. 217, 261 P.2d 617 (1953). This assumption has been challenged. Hall, supra note 55, at 143–44, points out that while rape is said to be a general intent crime and burglary a specific intent crime, "if the person who broke and entered is sober, has a kit of tools with him, and so on, there is no more need for evidence *aliunde* to establish his criminal intention than there is in forced intercourse." See Commonwealth v. Johnson, 80 Montg. 216 (Pa.Com.Pl.1962) (where defendant entered dwelling of 75-year-old spinster, he resided some distance away, the spinster did not know the defendant, the defendant offered no explanation for his presence there at night, he lurked in the bedroom in the dark for 15 minutes, and he departed by crashing through the

window; *held,* jury may infer a felonious intent from these facts).

64. Hall, supra note 54, at 142.

65. Because "the concept of 'general intent' * * * has been an abiding source of confusion and ambiguity in the penal law." Model Penal Code § 2.02, Comment at 231 n. 3 (1985).

66. G. Williams, supra note 2, at § 35.

67. 9 J. Wigmore, Evidence § 2511 (Chadbourne rev. 1981). However, the defendant may well have to put in evidence in order to bring into the case some affirmative defense, such as mistake of fact or mistake of law, which would negative the mental state.

68. Ibid.; G. Williams, supra note 2, at § 291.

69. 442 U.S. 510, 99 S.Ct. 2450, 61 L.Ed.2d 39 (1979).

dant was convicted, but his conviction was overturned by the Supreme Court on the ground that this instruction violated "the Fourteenth Amendment's requirement that the State prove every element of a criminal offense beyond a reasonable doubt." The state first argued that the instruction "merely described a permissive inference." A cautious instruction of that type would have been permissible,[70] but that clearly was not what had occurred. As the Court correctly noted, the jurors "were not told that they had a choice, or that they might infer that conclusion; they were told only that the law presumed it." The Court likewise rejected the state's claim the instruction merely placed a burden of production on the defendant, properly noting that the jurors were never told that the presumption could be rebutted.

Rather, the Court continued in *Sandstrom*, the jury might "have interpreted the instruction in either of two more stringent ways": one possibility was that the jury took the instruction as "an irrebuttable direction by the court to find intent once convinced of the facts triggering the presumption," and the other was that the jury interpreted the instruction "to find upon proof of the defendant's voluntary actions (and their 'ordinary' consequences), unless *the defendant* proved the contrary." A conclusive presumption here, the Court noted in *Sandstrom*, would be unconstitutional because it "would 'conflict with the overriding presumption of innocence with which the law endows the accused and which extends to every element of the crime,'[71] and would 'invade [the] factfinding function'[72] which in a criminal case the law assigns solely to the jury." Similarly, a presumption which shifted the burden of proof

would be unconstitutional as infringing upon the due process requirement that "a State must prove every ingredient of an offense beyond a reasonable doubt."[73]

It is not always easy to prove at a later date the state of a man's mind at that particular earlier moment when he was engaged in conduct causing or threatening harm to the interests of others. He does not often contemporaneously speak or write out his thoughts for others to hear or read. He will not generally admit later to having the intention which the crime requires. So of course his thoughts must be gathered from his words (if any) and actions in the light of all the surrounding circumstances. Naturally, what he does and what foreseeably results from his deeds have a bearing on what he may have had in his mind.

Of course, the defendant, if he elects to take the witness stand, is allowed to testify to what was in his mind at the time he engaged in his harmful conduct.[74] The jury may not believe him, however, if his words and acts in the light of all the circumstances make his explanation seem improbable. Thus, if *A*, charged with murdering *B* on the intent-to-kill theory, testifies that he intended only to scare *B*, but the evidence of bystanders and others show that he was an expert marksman, that he was standing close to *B* when he fired, that he took careful aim before firing, and that his bullets pierced *B* five times in vital areas of his body—under all the circumstances the jury might well disbelieve his testimony and conclude that he meant to kill *B*. This would be especially so if *A* had yelled, just before shooting, "I'll kill you, *B*," or, without any such words, if it were shown that he had a solid reason for wishing *B* dead.[75]

---

70. McCormick, Evidence § 348 (3d ed. Cleary ed. 1984), noting that the problems suggested by *Sandstrom* can be met by proceeding as contemplated by Uniform Rules of Evidence § 303(c): "Whenever the existence of a presumed fact is submitted to the jury, the court shall instruct the jury that it may regard the basic facts as sufficient evidence of the presumed fact but is not required to do so. In addition, if the presumed fact establishes guilt or is an element of the offense or negatives a defense, the court shall instruct the jury that its existence, on all the evidence, must be proved beyond a reasonable doubt."

71. Quoting Morissette v. United States, 342 U.S. 246, 72 S.Ct. 240, 96 L.Ed. 288 (1952).

72. Quoting United States v. United States Gypsum, 438 U.S. 422, 98 S.Ct. 2864, 57 L.Ed.2d 854 (1978).

73. Quoting Patterson v. New York, 432 U.S. 197, 97 S.Ct. 2319, 53 L.Ed.2d 281 (1977).

74. 2 J. Wigmore, Evidence § 581 (Chadbourne rev. 1979).

75. On the significance of motive in this regard, see § 3.6(a).

The legislature sometimes creates statutory presumptions to aid the prosecution in proving the mental side of the crime, including a required intention. Thus it may be provided that it is a crime to give a bad check with intent to defraud, and that nonpayment of the check for lack of funds on deposit gives rise to a presumption that the check-giver intended to defraud. Such a statute provides for more than an inference (or "permissive presumption"); it provides instead for a true presumption of the "mandatory" type,[76] discussed elsewhere herein.[77]

WESTLAW REFERENCES

sandstrom /s 442 +5 510 /p statut! legislat!

§ 3.6   Motive

A defendant's motive, if narrowly defined to exclude recognized defenses and the "specific intent" requirements of some crimes, is not relevant on the substantive side of the criminal law. On the procedural side, a motive for committing a crime is relevant in proving guilt when the evidence of guilt is circumstantial, and a good motive may result in leniency by those who administer the criminal process.

WESTLAW REFERENCES

di motive
di intent

(a) Relevance in the Substantive Criminal Law. It is often said that motive is immaterial in the substantive criminal law, and that the most laudable motive is no defense while a bad motive cannot make an otherwise innocent act criminal.[1] On the oth-

er hand, it has sometimes been claimed that the substantive law frequently takes account of good and bad motives.[2] These differing viewpoints, it would seem, are attributable to disagreement as to what is meant by the word "motive" and how it differs from "intention," a matter which has caused the theorists considerable difficulty for years.[3] Motive has been variously defined as "the desire coupled with the intention to bring about a certain consequence as an end, by means of other consequences which are also desired and intended but only as means,"[4] as "a desire viewed in its relation to a particular action, to the carrying out of which it urges or prompts,"[5] and as "ulterior intention—the intention with which an intentional act is done (or, more clearly, the intention with which an intentional consequence is brought about)."[6]

Perhaps because these definitions are less than completely satisfying, it is typical to clarify the definition with an illustration, such as that when *A* murders *B* in order to obtain *B*'s money, *A*'s intent was to kill and his motive was to get the money.[7] Such an illustration might well suggest that "intent" is limited to one's purpose to commit the proscribed act (including, as in the illustration, the proscribed consequences), and that all inquiries into why one did the proscribed act are concerned with motive. This view has sometimes been taken.[8] But, if this view is correct, then the notion that motive is immaterial in the substantive criminal law is wrong, for there are a number of instances in which this inquiry into why an act was committed is crucial in determining whether or not the defendant has committed a given crime. For example, if one evening *A* breaks into *B*'s house, it is most important to know

---

76. 9 J. Wigmore, Evidence § 2511a (Chadbourne rev. 1981).

77. See § 2.13.

§ 3.6

1. E.g., 22 C.J.S. Criminal Law § 31(1) (1961). For other sources, see Hitchler, Motive as an Essential Element of Crime, 35 Dick.L.Rev. 105 n. 1 (1931).

2. Hitchler, supra note 1; Cook, Act, Intention and Motive in the Criminal Law, 26 Yale L.J. 645 (1917).

3. See the discussion in J. Hall, General Principles of Criminal Law 83–93 (2d ed. 1960); H. Morris, Freedom

and Responsibility ch. 4 (1961); J. Salmond, Jurisprudence § 134 (9th ed. 1937); G. Williams, Criminal Law: The General Part § 21 (2d ed. 1961); Cook, supra note 2; Hitchler, supra note 1.

4. Cook, supra note 2, at 660–61.

5. Hitchler, supra note 1, at 105.

6. G. Williams, supra note 3, at 48.

7. Cook, supra note 2, at 660.

8. J. Salmond, supra note 3, at § 134.

why he did so, as it is burglary only if he did so for the purpose of committing a felony. Likewise, if *C* shoots and kills *D,* it may well be important to determine *why* he did so, for if he acted in self-defense he is not guilty of murder.

As shown by the burglary example, there are crimes which are defined in terms of certain acts or consequences plus a mental state which is concerned with something beyond the defendant's intent to do those acts or cause those consequences. These are often referred to as "specific intent" crimes which—although itself somewhat misleading—suggests that what is involved is a matter of intention and not motive. While some have taken the contrary view,[9] it is undoubtedly better, for purposes of analysis, to view such crimes as *not* being based upon proof of a bad motive. This can be accomplished by taking the view that intent relates to the means and motive to the ends, but that where the end is the means to yet another end, then the medial end may also be considered in terms of intent.[10] Thus, when *A* breaks into *B's* house in order to get money to pay his debts, it is appropriate to characterize the

purpose of taking money as the intent and the desire to pay his debts as the motive.[11]

The notion that good motives are irrelevant is more complex, although there are numerous examples in the cases where a person has been found guilty of a crime in spite of what might be viewed as a good motive in committing it.[12] A married man who, knowing that he is already married to a living wife, goes through a marriage ceremony with a second woman, is guilty of bigamy (for his conduct and state of mind fulfill the definition of bigamy), though he acts in accordance with an honest religious belief in the rightness of his second marriage.[13] One who intentionally kills another human being is guilty of murder, though he does so at the victim's request and his motive is the worthy one of terminating the victim's sufferings from an incurable and painful disease.[14] One who sends an obscene writing through the mails is guilty of the federal postal crime of depositing obscene matter in the mails, although he is activated by the beneficent motive of improving the reader's sexual habits and thereby bettering the human race.[15] One who intentionally destroys a fence around a graveyard without the owner's consent is guilty of violating the crim-

---

9. E.g., Hitchler, supra note 1, at 113.

10. G. Williams, supra note 3, at 48.

11. Even when a crime is defined in terms of "corrupt motive," it may often be concluded that what actually is involved is a form of intent. See J. Hall, supra note 3, at 90–92, pointing out that the "corrupt motive" required in Commonwealth v. McSorley, 189 Pa.Super. 223, 150 A.2d 570 (1959), involving a charge of misfeasance in office, was in fact knowledge by the defendant that he was making illegal use of funds.

12. In United States v. Badolato, 701 F.2d 915 (11th Cir.1983), where defendant Quarnstrom claimed he joined a drug conspiracy in order to gather information for a movie script, the court responded: "Seldom does anyone enter into an illegal activity without the hope of acquiring something perceived to be important. The usual goal in a drug conspiracy is financial gain. Yet a person would be just as guilty if the motive were revenge or even to obtain money for a worthy cause. It may be that one bears a grudge against the dominant drug seller in a particular area, and the only purpose in entering the conspiracy is to obtain inside knowledge of the operation for sabotage purposes. Or it may be that one wants to write a book, play or television script. Regardless of what the conspirator hopes to get out of it, conspiracy is a criminal act, and the issue properly phrased is whether Quarnstrom knowingly and intentionally entered into it."

13. Reynolds v. United States, 98 U.S. 145, 25 L.Ed. 244 (1878); Long v. State, 192 Ind. 524, 137 N.E. 49 (1922). So too one who opens his mother's grave in a dissenters' burial ground, with the motive of removing her body for a new burial in holy ground, is guilty of the crime of unlawful disinterment in spite of the pious motive underlying his action: Regina v. Sharpe, 7 Cox Crim.Cas. 214 (Ct.Crim.App.1857).

14. People v. Roberts, 211 Mich. 187, 178 N.W. 690, (1920) (wife, suffering from an incurable and painful disease, requested her husband to put her out of her misery by killing her; he intentionally put paris green, a poison, within her reach; she took it and died; husband *held* guilty of first-degree murder by poison); Rex v. Simpson, 84 L.J.K.B. (n. s.) 1893 (1915) (soldier killed his very sick son after he learned his wife was neglecting the child in favor of bringing soldiers home at night; he could not see the child suffer any longer; father *held* guilty of murder in spite of his kind motive). See Annot., 25 A.L.R. 1007 (1923).

15. United States v. Harmon, 45 F. 414 (D.Kan.1891). The court suggests, however, that if a district attorney or judge deposits in the mail the same obscene writing in connection with the prosecution or trial of the case, his act does not make him criminally liable, for such conduct must be an implied exception to the criminal statute.

inal statute on malicious mischief covering such intentional conduct, though he destroys the fence with the praiseworthy motive of building a better fence.[16] And one who, under oath on the witness stand, intentionally tells a lie concerning a material matter is guilty of perjury, although his act is prompted by a desire "to escape the importunities of 'Wall Street.' "[17]

Although it is cases such as these which are frequently cited for the proposition that good motives are no defense, others have relied upon many of the defense-to-liability general principles of criminal law to support the proposition that good motives are sometimes a defense.[18] Thus it is noted that one who commits what is otherwise a crime may have the defense of necessity if his conduct, though it literally violates the law, avoids an immediate harm greater than the harm which the criminal law in question seeks to prevent—as where he steals food because he is starving and will soon die without the food; or where he breaks out of prison, which is on fire, in violation of a statute against prison-breaking, in order to save himself from the fiery death which awaits him if he stays.[19] He has the mental state which the crime in question requires (an intent to deprive the foodowner of his property; an intent to break out of prison); nevertheless, he is not guilty of the crime because his conduct, though literally forbidden by the criminal law, is justified by the policy of the criminal law which, in the limited circumstances covered by the defense of necessity, seeks to promote a value (in the two

instances above, the value of human life) greater than the value of the literal obedience to the criminal law.[20]

At this point, it is apparent that it is somewhat difficult to square necessity and the other defenses, such as self-defense, with the proposition that good motives are no defense. Can it be said, on the one hand, that a desire to stop a relative's continued suffering is a matter of motive and thus no defense to a murder charge and, on the other hand, that a desire to obtain food to keep from starving is not a matter of motive and thus a defense to a theft charge? This sounds as if the notion that motives are irrelevant in the substantive law requires that the word "motive" be defined as those purposes, ends, and objectives which are deemed irrelevant, which brings one full circle. One might well take the position that it would be better to abandon the difficult task of trying to distinguish intent from motive and merely acknowledge that the substantive criminal law takes account of some desired ends but not others.

There is, however, at least one good reason to resist characterizing the defenses, such as necessity and self-defense, as instances in which a good motive serves as a defense. Such a characterization leads to analytical difficulties, for it suggests that these defenses are available only if the actor, in each case, had as his primary inducement the objective recognized as lawful by the defense. Although this position has sometimes been taken,[21] the better view is that the law is not concerned with motive once facts supporting

16. Phillips v. State, 29 Tex. 226 (1867).

17. People ex rel. Hegeman v. Corrigan, 195 N.Y. 1, 87 N.E. 792, 797 (1909).

18. E.g., Hitchler, supra note 1, at 114. The courts have sometimes done likewise. "The courts frequently point out that not even the highest motive, outside the well-recognized legal justifications, is a defense to proposed killing." Lebron v. United States, 229 F.2d 16 (D.C. Cir.1955).

19. See § 5.4. He also has the necessity defense if he believes (or, perhaps, reasonably believes) his conduct to be necessary to avoid the greater harm, even though in fact his belief is unfounded, as where, in the cases put in the text, rescuers with food appear unexpectedly just after he has consumed the stolen food; or the fire is put out just as it reaches the prisoner's cell.

20. Some courts, instead of talking in terms of necessity, speak of an "implied exception" in the statute when they do not wish to apply the statute literally—as where a policeman, in pursuit of a fleeing criminal, goes over the speed limit. See § 2.2(c). In one case it was held that a policeman who engaged in gambling in violation of the literal language of the statute, in order to secure evidence to convict gamblers, was not guilty of gambling because he lacked the necessary criminal intent: State v. Torphy, 78 Mo.App. 206 (1899). It would seem that the proper basis for these decisions is really, not implied exception or lack of intent, but rather necessity: law enforcement is a value greater than the value secured by literal compliance with the speeding or gambling laws.

21. Thus, Cook, supra note 2, at 662, concludes that "although there may exist all the external circumstances which would justify one in killing to prevent felony or in

the defense have been established.[22] Thus, when a person authorized to carry out a death sentence does so, he is acting lawfully whether he pursues his duties with regret, joy, or indifference.[23] Similarly, when an individual finds himself in a position where the law grants him the right to kill another in his own defense, it makes no difference whether his dominant motive is other than self-preservation.[24] This does not mean, of course, that the defense can be manufactured after the event by resort to facts not known to the actor when he engaged in the conduct. Thus, in the prison-break illustration described earlier,

the defendant would not have a defense if he escaped from prison and then later learned, to his pleasant surprise, that when he left it was on fire and that he would have been burned to death had he remained.[25] But, this limitation on the availability of this and other defenses is not based upon the notion that it is the defendant's motive which is critical; rather, it rests upon the policy that motive is not relevant once it is shown that the defendant was aware of facts which would give rise to a defense. Just as the defendant's intent to bring about certain consequences may be es-

self-defense, he would still be guilty of murder, if he should kill solely for revenge and not with the motive (desire and intention) to save hs life or to stop the commission of the felony."

22. Cf. United States v. Winston, 558 F.2d 105 (2d Cir. 1977) (if defendant had legitimate reason for discharging employee then he not guilty of violating Railway Labor Act prohibition on coercing employees in matters involving unionization; "once justification has been established, motivation is immaterial," and thus it error to instruct jury that defendant guilty if objective of coercion played "any part in the defendant's motivation").

Of course, it is appropriate to take into account the defendant's motives as evidence bearing on the question of whether the killing was necessary and thus within the scope of the right of self-defense, People v. Williams, 32 Cal. 280 (1867), just as it is appropriate (as discussed later in this section) to receive evidence of motive to prove the defendant's intent.

23. J. Hall, supra note 3, at 88–89.

24. Golden v. State, 25 Ga. 527 (1858): "Whenever the circumstances of the killing would not amount to murder, the proof even of express malice will not make it so. One may harbor the most intense hatred toward another; he may court an opportunity to take his life; may rejoice while he is imbruing his hands in his heart's blood; and yet, if, to save his own life, the facts showed that he was fully justified in slaying his adversary, his malice shall not be taken into the account. The principle is too plain to need amplification." Of course, there must be reasonable grounds to believe and actual belief as to facts giving rise to self-defense, Josey v. United States, 135 F.2d 809 (D.C. Cir.1943).

Statements apparently contrary to *Golden* have sometimes appeared in the cases. Thus, in Wortham v. State, 70 Ga. 336, 339 (1883), the court said: "It must appear that the circumstances were such as to excite the fears of a reasonable man; and it must also further appear that he acted under those fears, and not in a spirit of revenge." This may merely mean, as in the *Josey* case, that there must also be actual belief in existence of facts which give rise to a right of self-defense. See also Collett v. Commonwealth, 296 Ky. 267, 176 S.W.2d 893 (1943) (statements similar to those in *Wortham,* but court appears to rest decision on ground that defendant must have reasona-

bly believed that his life was in danger, actual danger later established being insufficient); Garcia v. State, 91 Tex.Cr.R. 9, 237 S.W. 279 (1921) (court says bad motive would negate defense even if defendant were aware of facts permitting killing to prevent theft, but decision rests upon fact defendant entered plea of guilty and thus waived the defense); Alsup v. State, 120 Tex.Cr.R. 310, 49 S.W.2d 749 (1932) (evidence tended to show that defendant persuaded others to stage bank robbery so that he could shoot them and collect reward; court at one point says that to have defense of shooting one fleeing with proceeds of robbery it must be shown that defendant was acting to prevent the fleeing with property and not upon malice, but later indicates question is whether defendant had reasonable belief deceased was carrying proceeds of robbery).

25. Thus, Model Penal Code § 3.02(1) gives the defense of necessity to one whose conduct literally constitutes a criminal offense only when he "believes" the conduct to be necessary to avoid a harm (and provided that the harm sought to be avoided is in fact greater than the harm sought to be prevented by the law defining the offense).

Similarly, while one who intentionally kills another is ordinarily guilty of murder (or, if he is reasonably provoked by the other into a passion, of manslaughter), if his conduct in killing the other is done to save himself from the other's deadly attack upon him, he has the defense of self-defense and is guilty of no crime. See § 5.7. To avail himself of the defense, however, he must have acted from a reasonable and actual belief as to facts supporting the defense. If *A* intentionally kills *B*, and this act saves *A*'s life (because *B*, when shot to death, was on the point of launching a deadly attack upon *A*), *A* does not have the defense of self-defense if he did not realize his danger; if, after killing *B* in cold blood, *A* learns that his act saved his life, he is nevertheless guilty. Trogdon v. State, 133 Ind. 1, 32 N.E. 725 (1892); Collett v. Commonwealth, 296 Ky. 267, 176 S.W.2d 893 (1943).

Likewise, when *A* kills *B* while trying to arrest him, the fact that *B* had actually committed a burglary is not admissible in justification of *A*'s killing, as whether *A* was acting lawfully in using force to effect an arrest or prevent escape depends upon his reasonable belief as of the time of the killing, not the actual facts as later determined. People v. Burt, 51 Mich. 199, 16 N.W. 378 (1883).

tablished without proof of any motive for it, so too as to a defense to liability.

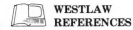
(b) Relevance in Criminal Procedure. Even though it may be concluded that "motive" (when narrowly defined not to include recognized defenses or certain required "specific intents") is not relevant in the substantive criminal law, an offender's reasons for engaging in proscribed conduct are often relevant on the procedural side of the criminal law. For one thing, the existence of a good motive on the part of the guilty person may be taken into account wherever there is room for the exercise of discretion in the proceedings against that person. The police, taking into account the motives of the offender, may decide not to invoke the criminal process. The prosecutor, for the same reason, may decide not to charge the offender with a crime, or may charge him with a less serious offense than he actually committed. The jury, if the defendant's good motive comes to its attention,[26] might exercise its uncontrolled discretion to acquit. Motives are most relevant when the trial judge sets the defendant's sentence, and it is not uncommon for a defendant to receive a minimum sentence because he was acting with good motives, or a rather high sentence because of his bad motives.

Likewise, motive may be taken into account by correctional officials.

Also, especially when the prosecution's case against the criminal defendant is circumstantial, the fact that the defendant had some motive, good or bad, for committing the crime is one of the circumstances which, together with other circumstances, may lead the factfinder to conclude that he did in fact commit the crime; whereas lack of any discernible motive is a circumstance pointing in the direction of his innocence.[27] And lack of motive, together with other circumstances, may indicate that the defendant was insane and so not criminally responsible for his actions.[28] Nevertheless, it must be emphasized again that a conviction of crime does not require any proof of motive.[29]

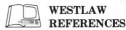
§ 3.7   Recklessness and Negligence

We have seen that some crimes require that the defendant intentionally or knowingly do an act or omit to act, or that he intentionally or knowingly cause a specified result of his act or omission. But other crimes may be committed by a reckless act or omission or by recklessly causing a specified result. Still others may be committed by negligence in acting or in omitting to act or in causing some

---

26. Otherwise inadmissible evidence of motive is not admissible for that purpose. "Jury nullification is an historical prerogative of the jury; it is not a right of the defendant." State v. Weitzman, 121 N.H. 83, 427 A.2d 3 (1981).

27. E.g., Commonwealth v. De Petro, 350 Pa. 567, 39 A.2d 838 (1944) (prosecution for arson to defraud the insurance company; proof that defendant was in financial difficulties; conviction *held* affirmed, against defendant's claim that the fire was an accident; "Proof of motive is never necessary in such cases but it is always relevant"). See also State v. Miller, 186 Conn. 654, 443 A.2d 906 (1982); Commonwealth v. Shain, 493 Pa. 360, 426 A.2d 589 (1981).

In many jurisdictions an instruction to this effect must be given upon request. State v. Hunter, 136 Ariz. 45, 664 P.2d 195 (1983); People v. Gibson, 133 Cal.App.3d 780, 184 Cal.Rptr. 378 (1982); State v. Osborne, 18 Wn.App. 318, 569 P.2d 1176 (1977).

28. See State v. Ehlers, 98 N.J.L. 236, 119 A. 15 (1922) (defendant, without motive, shot six-year-old son to death).

29. United States v. Pomponio, 429 U.S. 10, 97 S.Ct. 22, 50 L.Ed.2d 12 (1976) (on charge of willfully filing a false income tax return, conviction does not require "a finding of bad purpose or evil motive"); Schmidt v. United States, 133 F. 257 (9th Cir.1904) (evidence of guilt of perjury was direct, not circumstantial, and undisputed; there was no proof of motive; conviction of perjury *held* affirmed; in a direct-evidence case it is proper to refuse an instruction that lack of motive is a circumstance favoring innocence; "while the prosecution is never required to prove a motive for the crime, it is always permitted to do so"); State v. Ehlers, supra note 28 (prosecution evidence proved that defendant killed his six-year-old son but failed, defendant contends, to prove any motive; conviction of first-degree [premeditated and deliberate] murder *held* affirmed; motive is not an essential element; the conviction is supported by proof of an intentional killing as a result of premeditation and deliberation).

harmful result.[1] Thus, for instance, it is common to make reckless driving and careless driving crimes, without reference to any bad result of such conduct.[2] As to crimes defined in terms of specified harmful results, involuntary manslaughter (and battery) may be committed, among other ways, by reckless conduct which causes death (or bodily injury) to another human being;[3] and malicious mischief by reckless conduct causing injury or destruction to the property of another. Perhaps fewer crimes are defined in terms of negligence, as distinguished from recklessness; but in some states negligent conduct in the operation of an automobile, which causes a death, constitutes a special statutory crime (not manslaughter proper); and there are other special statutory crimes based upon bad results negligently caused.[4]

It came to be the general feeling of the judges when defining common law crimes (not always so strongly shared later by the legislatures when defining statutory crimes) that something more was required for criminal liability than the ordinary negligence which is sufficient for tort liability. The thought was this: When it comes to compensating an injured person for damages suffered, the one who has negligently injured an innocent victim ought to pay for it; but when the problem is one of whether to impose criminal punishment on the one who caused the injury, then something extra—beyond ordinary negligence—should be required. What is that "something extra" which the criminal law generally requires? It might logically be either one or both of two things: (1) Perhaps the defendant's conduct must involve a greater risk of harm to others than tort negligence requires. In other words, perhaps a "high degree of negligence," rather than "ordinary negligence," is necessary. (2) Perhaps, without requiring any riskier conduct than is necessary for ordinary negligence, the criminal law might require that the defendant consciously realize, in his own mind, the risk he is creating—a realization which is not required in the case of ordinary negligence. In other words, perhaps the difference between ordinary negligence and criminal negligence is simply that objective fault will do for the former, while subjective fault is required for the latter. (3) Perhaps the criminal law might require both (a) conduct creating a higher degree of risk than is necessary for ordinary negligence and (b) a subjective awareness that the conduct creates such a risk. The term "recklessness" is sometimes used to designate conduct which involves these two extra factors, (a) and (b), in addition to the requirements of ordinary negligence.[5] The other expression commonly used to indicate something more than ordinary negligence is "gross negligence," but that expression does not give any clue as to whether it is

§ 3.7

1. The judges when creating common law crimes (except in the very early days) did not generally go beyond recklessness in creating crimes; but the legislatures have not been so particular, and have created a number of crimes based upon negligence.

2. See, e.g., State v. Young, 371 So.2d 1029 (Fla.1979); State v. Baker, 203 N.W.2d 795 (Iowa 1973).

3. There is also a type of murder, known as "depraved-heart murder," the basis of which is causing death by a recklessness of a high degree. See § 7.4.

4. For the automobile statutes, see R. Moreland, The Law of Homicide, 246–52 (1952); Riesenfeld, Negligent Homicide, 25 Calif.L.Rev. 1 (1936); Robinson, Manslaughter by Motorist, 22 Minn.L.Rev. 755 (1938); Annot., 20 A.L.R.3d 473 (1968). Some statutes require ordinary negligence, State v. Baker, 203 N.W.2d 795 (Iowa 1973), some a higher degree of negligence or recklessness, State v. Young, 371 So.2d 1029 (Fla.1979). Statutes making certain other conduct criminal, if done with some degree of

negligence, are collected in Elliott, Degrees of Negligence, 6 So.Cal.L.Rev. 91, 132 (1933).

Though most states require, for involuntary manslaughter, greater negligence than ordinary negligence, a few states by statute have made it manslaughter, or a lower degree of manslaughter, to cause death by ordinary negligence. E.g., Thompson v. State, 554 P.2d 105 (Okl.Crim. App.1976) (is negligent homicide where there is "want of the usual and ordinary care and caution"); Njecick v. State, 178 Wis. 94, 189 N.W. 147 (1922) (manslaughter in the fourth degree requires less than gross negligence; mere inadvertence is sufficient).

5. However, usage of the term has not been consistent. Sometimes recklessness is defined to include both of these requirements, as in Model Penal Code § 2.02(2)(c); sometimes it is used simply to distinguish the requirement of subjective fault, as in J. Hall, General Principles of Criminal Law 115 (2d ed. 1960); and sometimes it is defined to cover the inadvertent creation of a high degree of risk, as in Commonwealth v. Welansky, 316 Mass. 383, 55 N.E.2d 902 (1944).

greater riskiness or subjective realization of risk or both which goes into the word "gross."

WESTLAW REFERENCES

criminal /s reckless! careless! negli! /5 act omission

(a) Negligence. Negligence, which will usually do for tort liability and which will sometimes do for criminal liability,[6] has been defined in various ways,[7] and discussed at great length;[8] but the lowest common denominator of all definitions contains these two items: (1) an expression of the required degree of risk which the defendant's conduct must create, and (2) an expression that that conduct is to be judged by an objective (reasonable man) standard.

WESTLAW REFERENCES

di negligence

negli! /s "criminal liability"

(1) Unreasonable Risk. The degree of risk which negligence requires is said to be an "unreasonable" (or "unjustifiable") risk of harm to others (either to their persons or to their property). "Unreasonable risk" is an expression which takes into account the fact that we all create some risk to others in our everyday affairs without subjecting ourselves to liability for negligence. Thus there is always some such risk involved in driving an automobile carefully; but it is not unreasonable to take this small risk in view of the social utility of driving. Driving at a high rate of

speed involves even more risk to others, but it may not be unreasonable to take this risk in order to rush a badly injured person to the hospital. The test for reasonableness in creating risk is thus said to be determined by weighing the magnitude of the risk of harm against the utility of the actor's conduct.[9] Under such a test, even a slight risk may be unreasonable. Thus it has been suggested that if there were 1000 pistols on a table, all unloaded but one, and if *A*, knowing this, should pick one at random and fire it at *B*, killing him, *A*'s conduct in creating the risk of death, though the risk is very slight (one-tenth of 1%), would be unreasonable, in view of its complete lack of social utility.[10]

Aside from the utility of the actor's conduct, another variable factor involved in the question of whether a particular risk is unreasonable is the extent of the actor's knowledge of the facts bearing upon the risk. A person may or may not create an unreasonable risk of harm to others depending upon what he knows. If *A* hands a loaded gun to *B*, who appears normal but whom *A* knows to be a madman, *A* creates an unreasonable risk of harm to those within range of the gun; but if *A* does not know *B* to be mad, the risk he creates, though identical in amount, is not unreasonable.[11]

Still another variable concerns the nature and extent of the harm which may be caused by the defendant's conduct, and the number of persons who may be harmed. It may not

6. See, e.g., State v. Jenkins, 278 S.C. 219, 294 S.E.2d 44 (1982) (crime of unlawful neglect of child requires only simple negligence).

7. Restatement, Torts (Second) § 282 (1965) defines tort negligence as "conduct which falls below the standard established by law for the protection of others against unreasonable risk of harm"; § 283 states that that standard is that of "a reasonable man under like circumstances"; § 284 defines "conduct" to include both (1) an act and (2) a failure to act where there is a duty to act.

8. E.g., W. Prosser & W. Keeton, Torts chs. 5–12 (5th ed. 1984); Restatement, Torts (Second) §§ 281–503 (1965).

9. Restatement, Torts (Second) § 291 (1965); W. Prosser & W. Keeton, Torts § 31 (5th ed. 1984).

10. G. Williams, Criminal Law: The General Part § 26 (2d ed. 1961), suggesting that the risk is so unreasonable as to create criminal liability for manslaughter and probably even murder.

11. People v. Howk, 56 Cal.2d 687, 16 Cal.Rptr. 370, 365 P.2d 426 (1961) (the defendant sold a gun to another man who recently had told him he wanted a gun to kill a certain girl; that same day the other killed the girl by shooting her with the gun; *held*, this evidence supports defendant's conviction of involuntary manslaughter on the basis of criminal negligence).

So too one who knows that he is subject to epileptic seizures without warning and who nevertheless goes driving and suffers an attack, during which attack his car runs onto the sidewalk and kills a pedestrian, is guilty of homicide by reckless driving. People v. Decina, 2 N.Y.2d 133, 157 N.Y.S.2d 558, 138 N.E.2d 799 (1956); but if he did not know, from prior experience, that he was subject to such attacks, his driving would not constitute negligence, see Government of the Virgin Islands v. Smith, 278 F.2d 169 (3d Cir.1960).

be unreasonable under some circumstances to endanger property though it would be unreasonable, under the same circumstances, to endanger bodily security. It may not be unreasonable to subject persons to the danger of slight injury to their persons, though it would be to subject them to danger of great bodily injury or death. It may not be unreasonable to endanger a single person though it would be to endanger a great many persons. Thus the railroad employee who on Saturday, erroneously thinking it to be Sunday when no trains run, pulls up the tracks for the purpose of repairing them just in time to cause the wreck of the Saturday Flyer, creates an unreasonable risk (in spite of the social utility involved in repairing the tracks) in view of the fact that the risk is of death and serious injury, not simply of slight injury or property damage, and, more than that, of the fact that it is a risk to many persons, not just to one or a few.

All of this suggests why we cannot measure the risk required for tort or for criminal liability in terms of percentages of chance of harm. The percentages of chance of harming others vary according to the social utility of the defendant's conduct, according to what he knows of the surrounding circumstances, and according to the nature and extent of possible harm resulting from his conduct.

WESTLAW REFERENCES

criminal & reasonabl! unreasonabl! justifiabl! unjustifiabl!
 /p risk! /3 harm! injur! /s (social /2 utility)
 (public /2 interest)
criminal & risk /4 harm /s knowledge extent
 nature /4 risk
criminal /3 liability & unreasonabl! /4 risk

(2) Objective Standard. While negligence thus requires that the defendant's conduct create an unreasonable risk of harm to others, he is nonetheless negligent though he

is unaware of the fact that his conduct creates any such risk. All that negligence requires is that he ought to have been aware of it (i.e., that a reasonable man would have been aware of it). Thus negligence is framed in terms of an objective (sometimes called "external") standard, rather than in terms of a subjective standard.[12]

The tort-negligence concept, just discussed, applies in only a relatively few modern statutory crimes. More often, it is a concept applicable to a defense to crime, rather than an element in the crime itself, as in the defense of self-defense.[13] But for the most part, as we have seen, something more than negligence is required for criminal liability. To progress from ordinary negligence to some greater fault (greater than negligence though less than intention or knowledge) which the criminal law ordinarily requires, the components of ordinary negligence which may be varied are the above two—(1) the unreasonable-risk component and (2) the objective-standard component. To repeat: (1) we may require that the defendant's conduct create a risk greater than simply an unreasonable risk, or (2) while requiring only an unreasonable risk, we may require that the defendant have a subjective awareness of the unreasonable risk he creates, or (3) we may require both the higher risk and an awareness of that higher risk.

Before leaving negligence as a basis for criminal liability, it should be noted that there is something of a dispute as to whether criminal liability should, on principle, ever be based upon objective negligence. It has been suggested that the threat of punishment for negligence cannot serve to deter people from negligent conduct; one who is unaware of the risk he is creating cannot be deterred from creating it by thoughts of punishment if he creates it.[14] But others have argued that the threat of punishment for risk-creating does

---

12. Another way of expressing this idea is to say that inadvertence in creating a risk will do for negligence; one is negligent though he does not "advert to" (realize) the fact that his conduct creates an unreasonable risk of harm to others.

13. Thus an intended homicide or battery may be justified on the ground of self-defense, a matter of "affirm-

ative defense" which depends on whether the defendant was free from negligence in believing that his adversary was about to attack him and that he had to kill or wound the adversary in order to protect himself. See § 5.7.

14. J. Hall, General Principles of Criminal Law 137 (2d ed. 1960); G. Williams, supra note 8, at § 43.

tend to make people think harder about the risks created by their conduct, thus tending to reduce risky conduct and so to promote public safety, the great object of the criminal law.[15]

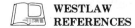

WESTLAW REFERENCES

risk /3 tak! creat! /s harm injury /s criminal crime punishment

(b) Criminal Negligence. Though the legislatures and the courts have often made it clear that criminal liability [16] generally requires more fault than the ordinary negligence which will do for tort liability, they have not so often made it plain just what is required in addition to tort negligence— greater risk, subjective awareness of the risk, or both. Statutes are sometimes worded in terms of "gross negligence" or "culpable negligence" or "criminal negligence," without any further definition of these terms. Some manslaughter statutes provide that it is manslaughter to kill another while doing a lawful act "without due caution or circumspection," an expression which literally sounds almost exactly like the term "without due care" so often used to describe tort negligence. "Wilful and wanton disregard of the safety of others" and "recklessness" are other expressions sometimes appearing in statutes—again usually without further definition.

The courts too, when describing the fault which crimes of the negligence type generally require, speak of "gross" or "culpable" or "criminal" negligence, or "wilful and wanton" conduct, or "reckless" conduct, often without pointing out specifically what these adjectives mean. The following is a typical example of a court's plain statement that criminal liability for manslaughter requires more than ordinary (tort) negligence, but making it hazy what that extra something is: "[Criminal liability is always predicated] not upon mere negligence or carelessness but upon that degree of negligence or carelessness which is denominated 'gross' and which constitutes such a departure from what would be the conduct of an ordinarily careful and prudent man under the same circumstances as to furnish evidence of that indifference to consequences which in some offenses takes the place of criminal intent." [17] A requirement of "indifference to consequences" would seem to be another way of requiring an awareness of the risk (i.e., a subjective standard). But the introductory phrase, "as to furnish evidence of," weakens this requirement by seeming to say that the defendant does not actually have to realize the risk and be indifferent to it; he is guilty of criminal negligence if his conduct is so great a departure from that of a reasonable man that the reasonable man would have realized the risk (i.e., an objective standard).

A few cases, however, have spelled out with some clarity what criminal negligence requires in addition to the requirements of ordinary negligence, though they have reached three quite different conclusions: (1) One clearly expressed view is contained in an opinion by Holmes in a manslaughter case. The defendant, not a doctor, in order to cure a sick woman, wrapped her in rags soaked in kerosene, causing burns from which she died. The defendant requested the trial court to instruct the jury that, however much risk of death to the victim his conduct entailed, he

---

15. Holmes, J., in Commonwealth v. Pierce, 138 Mass. 165, 52 Am.Rep. 264 (1884) (the leading case on applying an objective standard of negligence for manslaughter); Model Penal Code § 2.02, Comment at 243 (1985).

16. The principal crimes which may be committed by some type of negligence greater than tort negligence, though less than intention, are involuntary manslaughter and criminal battery, discussed at §§ 7.12, 7.15. Note, however, that there are types of involuntary manslaughter and battery other than the type committed by conduct amounting to criminal negligence. Thus for manslaughter there is (1) intended-bodily-harm-causing-unintended-death manslaughter, and (2) misdemeanor-manslaughter; and for battery there is (1) intended-bodily-harm battery, and (2) misdemeanor-battery.

17. Fitzgerald v. State, 112 Ala. 34, 20 So. 966 (1896) (conviction of involuntary manslaughter as a result of unintended death from a gunshot wound *held* reversed because trial judge charged jury that ordinary negligence causing death constitutes manslaughter).

For other vague cases on the degree of negligence necessary for manslaughter, see Annots., 99 A.L.R. 756, 829 (1935) (automobiles); 23 A.L.R. 1554 (1923) (firearms); 23 A.L.R.2d 1401, 1405 (1952), updated by 26 A.L.R.3d 561 (1969) (hunting); 161 A.L.R. 10 (1946) (manslaughter statutes using expression "gross", "criminal", or "culpable" negligence).

could not be guilty if he honestly believed his treatment would cure her. The defendant's defense thus was that he could not be guilty if he was subjectively unaware of the risk he created. Instead, the trial judge charged the jury in effect that the defendant would be guilty if his conduct created a great risk, whether he realized it or not. The appellate court affirmed his conviction, clearly stating that the standard to be applied in a manslaughter case is an objective standard, and urging that such a view of the law is correct on principle since it tends to make people careful.[18] The court thus required that the defendant's conduct be riskier than is required for tort negligence; but, instead of requiring that the defendant be aware of it, it required only that a reasonable man would have been aware of it.[19]

(2) On the other hand, a few cases have quite clearly spelled out that while no greater risk of harm is required for criminal than for tort liability, yet there is a difference between the two: the defendant must realize the risk for criminal law, though he need not for tort law.[20] In applying this subjective test for criminal negligence, it would seem that a person can be said to realize the risk which his conduct entails not only (a) when he directly knows it to be risky but also (b) when he knows that he does not know whether it is risky or not, and in fact it is risky.[21]

---

18. Commonwealth v. Pierce, 138 Mass. 165, 52 Am. Rep. 264 (1884). In Commonwealth v. Welansky, 316 Mass. 383, 55 N.E.2d 902 (1944), where defendant night-club owner omitted to provide proper fire escapes, so that many patrons died in a fire, the court, affirming a conviction of manslaughter, held that more than negligence was necessary (a higher risk: "grave danger to others must have been apparent"); "but even if a particular defendant is so stupid [or] so heedless * * * that in fact he did not realize the grave danger," he is guilty of manslaughter "if an ordinary normal man under the same circumstances would have realized the gravity of the danger."

Another clear case applying the objective standard is the depraved-heart murder case of Regina v. Ward, [1956] 1 Q.B. 351, wherein the Court of Criminal Appeal approved the trial court's instruction that one is guilty of murder where his conduct, which actually caused the victim's death, was likely to cause (i.e., involved a very high degree of risk of) death or serious bodily injury to the victim, if a reasonable man would have realized this likelihood, even though he himself did not realize the likelihood.

In a jurisdiction which applies an objective standard for battery, manslaughter or murder of the negligence type, the situation may arise wherein a reasonable man would not have realized the great risk which his conduct entailed; but the perceptive defendant actually did realize it, yet went ahead with his conduct anyway. Under the objective standard he should be guilty, see Commonwealth v. Welansky supra, as well, of course, as under a subjective standard.

19. Some modern negligent homicide statutes are of this type. People v. Haney, 30 N.Y.2d 328, 333 N.Y.S.2d 403, 284 N.E.2d 564 (1972); State v. Ohnstad, 357 N.W.2d 827 (N.D.1984); State v. Hallett, 619 P.2d 335 (Utah 1980). But the question is whether a reasonable man in the defendant's circumstances would have been aware, and thus account must properly be taken of the fact defendant found himself in an emergency situation not affording time for reflection. People v. Futterman, 86 A.D.2d 70, 449 N.Y.S.2d 108 (1982).

Consider also the developments in England, where recklessness has been more recently defined to include "not only deciding to ignore a risk of harmful consequences resulting from one's acts that one has recognized as existing, but also failure to give any thought to whether or not there is any such risk in circumstances where, if any thought were given to the matter, it would be obvious that there was." See the assessments of this formula in Griew, Reckless Damage and Reckless Driving: Living with Caldwell and Lawrence, 1981 Crim.L.Rev. 743; Smith, Subjective or Objective? Ups and Downs of the Test of Criminal Liability in England, 27 Vill.L.Rev. 1179 (1982); Syrota, A Radical Change in the Law of Recklessness?, 1982 Crim.L. Rev. 97; Williams, Recklessness Redefined, 40 Camb.L.J. 252 (1981). See also Duff, Recklessness, 1980 Crim.L.Rev. 282, 291, criticizing a Law Commission proposal to define recklessness as requiring realization of the risk: "Some failures of attention or realisation may manifest, not merely stupidity or 'thoughtlessness,' but the same indifference or disregard which characterises the conscious risk-taker as reckless."

20. Trujillo v. People, 133 Colo. 186, 292 P.2d 980 (1956) (manslaughter), noted in 28 Rocky Mt.L.Rev. 409 (1956).

Some cases clearly spell out a subjective test without making it clear whether in addition the degree of risk must be higher than for ordinary negligence. Thus in two manslaughter cases where the defendant, practicing as a physician, prescribed a fatal treatment or medicine for his sick patient, it was held that the defendant could not be guilty of manslaughter if he honestly believed that his treatment or medicine would cure; a subjective standard was thus required. State v. Schulz, 55 Iowa 628, 8 N.W. 469 (1881); Rice v. State, 8 Mo. 561 (1844). Cf. Commonwealth v. Pierce, supra.

21. Thus Hart, The Aims of the Criminal Law, 23 Law & Contemp.Prob. 401, 416 (1958), suggests that the defendant in Commonwealth v. Pierce, supra note 15, who wrapped kerosene rags about his patient's body may have been subjectively negligent even though he thought his treatment would cure. Though he did not directly realize the possibility of harm, he did realize (1) his own deficiency in appraising the possibility of harm (not having had the special training and knowledge of a doctor) and (2) the risk which such a deficiency created.

(3) Lastly, a few cases quite clearly spell out that criminal liability requires both greater risk and subjective realization of that risk. Thus in a case wherein the defendant, having previously suffered blackouts and having been warned by his doctor not to drive alone, was driving alone when he suffered another blackout, so that his car went out of control and killed another motorist, the defendant was held guilty of a statutory crime punishing one who causes death while driving a car "in wilful and wanton disregard for the rights or safety of others." The court stated that one is guilty of "wilful and wanton disregard" where, knowing of the existing conditions "and conscious from such knowledge that injury will likely or probably result from his conduct, and with reckless indifference to the consequences," he goes ahead with his conduct.[22]

Much of the source of the confusion in the law lies in the criminal statutes, which have used expressions like "gross" and "culpable" negligence and "wilful and wanton" disregard of safety without defining these terms. The courts thus have had to do their best with little guidance from the legislature, with va-

rying results.[23] The Model Penal Code, however, sets forth definitions for the terms "recklessness"[24] and "negligence,"[25] and in most recent recodifications the Model Penal Code approach has been substantially followed.[26]

WESTLAW REFERENCES

di involuntary manslaughter
di battery
criminal! /4 negli! /s standard /4 care
gross culpabl! /3 negli! /p wilful! wanton! /3
　　disregard! & criminal /3 negli!
fi 677 f2d 1018

(c) Violation of Statute or Ordinance.
In tort law, one who violates a statute (or ordinance) the purpose of which is to protect a certain class of persons from a certain type of harm, is, by the weight of authority, guilty of negligence *per se* if his victim is a member of that class and receives that type of harm.[27] The notion is that the legislature (or city council) has established the standard of conduct of the reasonable man, so that the violator has necessarily fallen below that standard; or, putting it another way, he has necessarily

---

22. State v. Gooze, 14 N.J.Super. 277, 81 A.2d 811 (1951) (subjective standard is apparent from word "conscious"; high risk from the expression "injury will likely or probably result"). Another such case is Bussard v. State, 233 Wis. 11, 288 N.W. 187 (1939) (though defendant was "negligent in a high degree" he is not guilty of "gross negligence" manslaughter without subjectively realizing the high degree of risk his conduct entailed), noted at 1941 Wis.L.Rev. 25, 27.

23. See, e.g., Lupro v. State, 603 P.2d 468 (Alaska 1979) (crime of negligent homicide requires "reckless disregard of consequences"); McCreary v. State, 371 So.2d 1024 (Fla. 1979) (manslaughter statute requiring "culpable negligence" means "reckless disregard," but statute using recklessness standard means a degree of negligence "more than a mere failure to use ordinary care"); Thompson v. State, 554 P.2d 105 (Okl.Crim.App.1976) (homicide in "reckless disregard of the safety of others" is established by "want of the usual and ordinary care").

24. "A person acts recklessly with respect to a material element of an offense when he consciously disregards a substantial and unjustifiable risk that the material element exists or will result from his conduct. The risk must be of such a nature and degree that, considering the nature and purpose of the actor's conduct and the circumstances known to him, its disregard involves a gross deviation from the standard of conduct that a law-abiding person would observe in the actor's situation." Model Penal Code § 2.02(2)(c). Thus, the Code defines recklessly

in terms of both greater risk and subjective awareness. For a detailed assessment of this formulation, see Treiman, Recklessness and the Model Penal Code, 9 Am.J. Crim.L. 281 (1981), which also notes at 375–86 the extent to which the Code formula has been adopted in modern codes.

25. "A person acts negligently with respect to a material element of an offense when he should be aware of a substantial and unjustifiable risk that the material element exists or will result from his conduct. The risk must be of such a nature and degree that the actor's failure to perceive it, considering the nature and purpose of his conduct and the circumstances known to him, involves a gross deviation from the standard of care that a reasonable person would observe in the actor's situation." Model Penal Code § 2.02(2)(d). Thus, the Code defines negligence in terms of greater risk and the objective standard.

26. Compare People v. Calvaresi, 188 Colo. 277, 534 P.2d 316 (1975) (where legislature departed from Model Penal Code formulation by adding "reasonably should be aware" to definition of recklessness, so both recklessness and negligence were objective standards, the distinction between the two "is not sufficiently apparent to be intelligently and uniformly applied").

27. W. Prosser & W. Keeton, Torts § 36 (5th ed. 1984). A minority view is that the violation is not negligence *per se* but rather evidence of negligence which the jury may, but need not, accept. Ibid.

created an unreasonable risk of harm to others. But violation of a statute (ordinance) does not constitute *per se* that greater negligence (whichever of the three possibilities it is) which criminal law generally requires,[28] though it does constitute some evidence of that negligence.[29] Insofar as criminal negligence is held to require subjective awareness of risk, the defendant's knowledge of the existence and contents of the statute (ordinance), and his knowing disregard of its terms, would of course be relevant.[30] If the objective standard is used, his lack of knowledge of the existence and terms of the law and of its violation is not relevant; but his conduct in committing the violation does not necessarily create that high degree of risk which crimes generally require.

WESTLAW REFERENCES

violat! /4 statute ordinance /p criminal! negli! /p protected /4 class

(d) Proof of Subjective Realization of Risk. Just as intention on the defendant's part, when intention is required for criminal liability, must often be inferred from his words and conduct in the light of the surrounding circumstances,[31] so too his subjective realization of risk (when that is a necessary requirement for liability based on criminal

negligence) must generally be inferred from his words and conduct in the light of the circumstances. Sometimes the defendant at the time of his risky conduct, or before, or after (in the form of an admission or confession) uses words, overheard by a witness, which show that he actually did realize the risk. But often there are no words to help us. If the defendant's conduct is in fact risky, and if the risk is obvious, so that a reasonable man would realize it, we might well infer that he did in fact realize it; but the inference cannot be conclusive, for we know that people are not always conscious of what reasonable people would be conscious of.[32]

Thus the defendant, if he takes the witness stand, may testify that he did not at the time realize the riskiness of his conduct; and the jury may or may not believe him. Doubtless the jury is more likely to believe him if his conduct, though it involves risk to others, also involves risk to himself or to his loved ones. The seaman aboard the wooden sailing ship, carrying a cargo of rum, who causes the vessel to burn to the waterline when, stealing rum from the hold, his candle sets the rum afire, probably does not realize the risk of burning the ship which his conduct involves, for if the ship should catch fire, he is likely to perish with the rest.[33] The driver of an auto-

---

28. Commonwealth v. Adams, 114 Mass. 323, 19 Am. Rep. 362 (1873) (*A*, speeding in violation of ordinance, struck and injured a pedestrian *B; held,* conviction of battery reversed, because of trial court's charge that violation plus injury equals battery); State v. Cope, 204 N.C. 28, 167 S.E. 456 (1933) (*A*, speeding in violation of statute, struck and killed a pedestrian *B; held,* conviction of manslaughter reversed because of trial court's charge that violation plus death equals manslaughter).

Of course, the legislature may enact a statute to the effect that causing a certain result either by negligence or by violating a special statutory provision is a crime, in which case the latter alternative might be viewed as a form of negligence per se. See, e.g., State v. Wong, 125 N.H. 610, 486 A.2d 262 (1984) (upholding statute saying it negligent homicide to cause death by negligent operation of motor vehicle or by driving under the influence).

29. Commonwealth v. Hawkins, 157 Mass. 551, 32 N.E. 862 (1893) (firing pistol within city, in violation of ordinance, is evidence of recklessness required for battery).

30. In State v. Cope, supra note 28, the court said that an intentional, willful or wanton violation of a statute or ordinance designed for the protection of human life or limb does constitute that greater negligence required by

the criminal law, and seemed to suggest that an instruction to the jury in these terms would have been permissible. An instruction along these lines has sometimes been upheld when the kind of negligence required is actual awareness of risks which suffice for tort liability even when not known. Cain v. State, 55 Ga.App. 376, 190 S.E. 371 (1937). The theory is that the violation of the statute establishes the defendant's deviation from the reasonable man standard, and that his intentional violation of the statute establishes his awareness of the risk.

31. See § 3.5(f).

32. Of course, the legislature could declare that a certain situation shall conclusively be deemed to involve recklessness, for in reality they are making it criminal to bring about that situation. See State v. Cushman, 133 Vt. 121, 329 A.2d 648 (1974) (upholding "recklessly endangering" statute which says that both recklessness and danger "shall be presumed where a person knowingly points a firearm at or in the direction of another"), rejected in State v. McLaren, 135 Vt. 291, 376 A.2d 34 (1977), only to extent statute deemed to cover unloaded or otherwise inoperative firearm.

33. Cf. Queen v. Faulkner, 11 Ir.R.C.L. 8, 13 Cox Crim. Cas. 550 (1877) (defendant not guilty of arson of the ship,

mobile carrying his children who, to cross the state line and thus prevent his arrest by the sheriff who had jumped on the running board to make the arrest, raced the car across the state-line bridge, having an accident thereon which killed the policeman, probably did not realize that his conduct involved a great risk of an accident; he would not knowingly have subjected his children to such a risk.[34] Of course, sometimes people do consciously take chances with their own lives and those of their families, so that it is not conclusive, because one's conduct endangers himself or his family, that he was not conscious of the danger involved.

Whether or not the defendant was consciously aware of the risk or simply failed to be aware is often a close question. But there are other instances in which the undisputed facts are not at all consistent with a claim of inadvertence. In the latter situation, a defendant charged with a subjective fault crime (e.g., reckless homicide) is not entitled to have the jury consider the alternative of guilt under a lesser objective fault crime (e.g., negligent homicide). Thus, in a manslaughter by recklessness case in which defendant aimed a gun at his wife and pulled the trigger, thinking but not knowing the gun was unloaded, it was proper not to submit a negligent homicide instruction to the jury.[35] But when the defendant who plunged a knife into a person during a religious ceremony testified, as did his followers, that he had performed this ritual in the past without untoward results because of his power to suspend a person's heartbeat, pulse and breathing, an instruction on negligent homicide was required.[36]

WESTLAW REFERENCES

proof evidence /s subjective! conscious! /3 realiz!
    /s risk danger harm

because he had no intent to burn it, although he had an intent to steal rum).

34. State v. Weisengoff, 85 W.Va. 271, 101 S.E. 450 (1919) (defendant not guilty of murder).

35. Boggess v. State, 655 P.2d 654 (Utah 1982) ("the evidence would not admit of a finding that he was una-

(e) Risk of What Harm? With crimes of negligence and recklessness, where a risk of harm to others is required, the type of harm involved is not necessarily the same for all such crimes. Thus the risk of harm which is required for manslaughter is risk of death or serious bodily injury; for battery, it is risk of bodily injury (something less than serious bodily injury); for malicious mischief, it is risk of property damage or destruction. A special statute making it a crime to kill another by driving a car recklessly would require a risk of death or serious bodily injury; another statute making it a crime to injure another by negligent driving while intoxicated would require, so far as risk is concerned, only a risk of bodily injury.

WESTLAW REFERENCES

di recklessness
di manslaughter
di battery
di malicious mischief

(f) Recklessness vs. Intention and Knowledge. We have seen that crimes defined so as to require that the defendant intentionally cause a forbidden bad result are usually interpreted to cover one who knows that his conduct is *substantially certain* to cause the result, whether or not he desires the result to occur.[37] "Recklessness" in causing a result exists when one is aware that his conduct *might* cause the result, though it is not substantially certain to happen. One may act recklessly if he drives fast through a thickly settled district though his chances of hitting anyone are far less that 90%, or even 50%. Indeed, if there is no social utility in doing what he is doing, one might be reckless though the chances of harm are something less than 1%. Thus, while "knowledge" and the knowing-type of "intention" require a consciousness of almost-certainty, recklessness

ware but should have been aware of a substantial and unjustifiable risk, or that he failed to perceive the nature and degree of the risk").

36. People v. Strong, 37 N.Y.2d 568, 376 N.Y.S.2d 87; 338 N.E.2d 602 (1975).

37. See § 3.5.

requires a consciousness of something far less than certainty or even probability.[38]

WESTLAW
REFERENCES

di (reckless! careless! /s define* definition)

(g) What Kind of Fault Should Criminal Liability Require? We have noted that some crimes require objective fault while others require subjective fault, and that some require the creation of an unreasonable risk of harm while others require the creation of a higher degree of risk; and we have noted also that statutes are often vague on these requirements and that courts, with so little guidance from the language of the statutes, disagree as to the requirements. Before leaving this topic we should ask: on principle, what should the criminal law require? (1) Should it require a greater risk of harm than tort law generally requires? (2) Should it require a subjective awareness of whatever risk is required, or (as with torts) should it require only that a reasonable man would have realized it?

It is clear that there is no need to choose one answer for all crimes. As to degree of risk, one would naturally expect a higher requirement for murder, with its heavier punishment, than for involuntary manslaughter, which carries a lighter penalty. Thus we shall see that "depraved-heart" murder requires more risk than does manslaughter; if manslaughter requires a "high degree of risk," as many states would say, murder (of the "depraved-heart" type) requires a "very high degree of risk." On the other hand, a state which has had a bad experience of automobile deaths on the highways might logically create a new crime of negligent-death-by-automobile (perhaps carrying a lighter pun-

ishment than manslaughter proper), imposing criminal liability on one who creates an "unreasonable risk" of death—something less than a "high degree of risk." [39]

As to the subjective-vs.-objective choice, here too there need not be one answer for all crimes. Subjective fault is greater fault than objective fault; one who consciously does risky things is morally a worse person than one who unconsciously creates risk. But, on the other hand, objective fault is greater fault than no fault at all, and some conduct (as we shall see later in more detail) [40] is criminal though it involves no fault. It is surely not so startling to punish objective fault as it is to impose criminal liability without fault. The principal policy question is whether the threat of punishment for objective fault will deter people from conducting themselves in such a way as to create risk to others. Though the matter is disputed,[41] it would seem that some people can be made to think, before they act, about the possible consequences of acting, so that the existence of objective-fault crimes does tend to reduce risky conduct.[42] Still, one would hardly wish to impose the death penalty or life imprisonment on one who unconsciously created risk. We might logically require subjective fault for murder while allowing objective fault for manslaughter; or require subjective fault for manslaughter while allowing objective fault for a special situation of danger, such as the driving of an automobile in a risky way. The point is that the legislature might, in the exercise of its police power, require subjective fault for some crimes and objective fault for other crimes. Other things being equal, of course, a lighter punishment should be provided for objective-negligence crimes than for subjective-negligence crimes.[43] Indeed, some

---

38. All of this shows that those twin words "natural and probable" so often used in describing liability for ordinary tort negligence—one is liable for the natural and probable consequences of his risky conduct—are not to be taken literally. Literally, the word "natural" requires something considerably greater than 50%; and "probable" requires at least 51%. But no such high chance of harm is required generally for ordinary negligence or criminal negligence.

39. State v. Baker, 203 N.W.2d 795 (Iowa 1973).

40. See §§ 3.8–3.10.

41. See text at notes 14–15 supra.

42. See, e.g., People v. Strong, 37 N.Y.2d 568, 376 N.Y.S.2d 87, 338 N.E.2d 602 (1975), justifying a negligent homicide statute on this basis.

43. But see State v. Lucero, 87 N.M. 242, 531 P.2d 1215 (1975) (rejecting trial judge's holding that statute making it a felony to "knowingly, intentionally or negligently" abuse a child was unconstitutional because it "makes no

state courts have held certain objective-negligence crimes invalid because of the high penalty and lack of any apparent justification in the particular circumstances for such liability.[44]

Another criticism of objective fault is that it is unjust to impose criminal sanctions absent culpability, which is surely lacking when the defendant's doing of harm was not a matter of choice by him.[45] The "moral protest involved when such liability is imposed for negligence is simply that the defendant does not deserve to be subjected to this—which is, to the added burdens of imprisonment or fine and the disgrace and stigma which invariably accompany them—unless he has made a conscious choice to do something he knew to be wrong."[46] In response, it has been argued that there is a form of culpability here—that of failing to bring one's faculties to bear so as to perceive the risks that one is taking.[47] The argument is made that "culpability functions as the touchstone of the question whether by virtue of his illegal conduct, the violator has lost his moral standing to complain of being subjected to sanctions. If his illegal conduct is unexcused, if he had a fair chance of avoiding the violation and did not, we are inclined to regard the state's imposing a sanction as justified."[48]

 WESTLAW REFERENCES

fault /s criminal /3 liability

(h) Disparity Between Foreseeable Result and Actual Result. With crimes requiring that the defendant intentionally cause a forbidden result, we saw that there was a problem of liability when an unintended victim was harmed, when the intended victim was harmed in an unintended manner, or when the resulting harm differed in either type or degree from that intended. The same sort of problem arises in crimes which require that the defendant recklessly or negligently cause the forbidden harm. Here it may arise as to the unforeseeable victim, the foreseeable victim harmed in an unforeseeable manner, an unhazarded type of harm, or an unexpected degree of harm.

(1) Unforeseeable Victim: Perhaps A recklessly or negligently creates a risk of harm to B; as it turns out, B escapes harm; but C is harmed. A recklessly drives a car in such a way as to endanger motorists and pedestrians, but he misses them all; however, a window-washer overlooking the street is so intrigued by watching A's unusual driving that he loses his footing and falls. Is A criminally liable for the window-washer's resulting injury or death?

(2) Unforeseeable Manner: Perhaps A recklessly or negligently creates a risk of a certain type of harm to B, but B is injured in an unusual manner. Thus A recklessly drives his car so as to endanger the lives of pedestrians, but he misses pedestrian B, scaring him to such an extent that he must go to a hospital, where he catches smallpox from another hospital patient and dies. Is A criminally responsible for B's death, which he has in a sense caused?

(3) Unhazarded Type of Harm: A acts recklessly toward B, foreseeably endangering his property but not his person; but, as it turns out, B's property escapes without injury, yet B is killed (or injured). Or the converse situation may occur, as where A foreseeably endangers B's person but not his property, but his property and not his person is injured or

44. Speidel v. State, 460 P.2d 77 (Alaska 1969) (holding unconstitutional a statute making negligent failure to return a rental car on time a felony punishable by 5 years imprisonment); People v. Johnson, 193 Colo. 199, 564 P.2d 116 (1977) (statute making it a felony to receive stolen goods "having reasonable cause to believe" that the goods were stolen is unconstitutional).

distinction among intentional, knowing or negligent acts and makes no provision for lesser included offenses or degrees of offense according to the degree of culpability of the defendant").

45. J. Hall, General Principles of Criminal Law 138–39 (2d ed. 1960).

46. Note, 81 Yale L.J. 949, 979 (1972).

47. Hart, Negligence, Mens Rea and Criminal Responsibility, in Punishment and Responsibility 152 (1968).

48. Fletcher, The Theory of Criminal Negligence: A Comparative Analysis, 119 U.Pa.L.Rev. 401, 417 (1971).

destroyed. What crime, if any, has *A* committed in these two instances?

(4) Unexpected Degree of Harm: A throws a small stone at *B*, giving rise to a foreseeable risk of some minor bodily injury to *B*, but *B* is a hemophiliac and bleeds to death. Is *A* guilty of involuntary manslaughter? Or, *A* recklessly creates a risk of death to *B*, but his conduct unexpectedly only injures *B*. Is *A* guilty of battery?

In the first two of these situations, the results have been essentially the same as the foreseeable harm, and thus the mental state requirement is satisfied. Whether the unexpected victim or unexpected manner should nonetheless present a bar to conviction is a matter of policy best categorized as a question of causation,[49] and it is discussed herein in that context.[50] Although the latter two situations might also be considered as presenting issues of causation,[51] the more fundamental question is whether the required mental states of recklessness and negligence should somehow be interchangeable from crime to crime, so that one who knows or should know of a particular kind of risk might on that basis be held liable when the harm which actually occurs is of an unhazarded type or unexpected degree. These situations, therefore, are discussed in the section on concurrence.[52]

49. The issue is so characterized in Model Penal Code § 2.03(3).

50. See § 3.12.

51. Model Penal Code § 2.03(3)(a) treats as a question of causation the situation where the probable injury or harm would have been more serious or more extensive than that actually caused.

52. See § 3.11.

§ 3.8

1. For a collection of common types of strict-liability criminal statutes see Sayre, Public Welfare Offenses, 33 Colum.L.Rev. 55, 84–88 (1933); Model Penal Code 141–145 (Tent. Draft No. 4, 1955). Liquor and narcotics laws, pure food laws, and traffic laws commonly impose liability without fault. See, e.g., People v. Caddy, 189 Colo. 353, 540 P.2d 1089 (1975) (speeding is strict liability crime, so defective speedometer no defense); City of Dickinson v. Mueller, 261 N.W.2d 787 (N.D.1977) (sale of liquor to minor is strict liability offense).

A statute is not of the strict liability variety simply because it permits conviction of the defendant without proof that he was aware his conduct was criminal. Al-

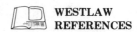

WESTLAW REFERENCES

criminal /p unforesee! /s victim result harm (degree /2 harm) manner

§ 3.8 Liability Without Fault—Strict Liability

For several centuries (at least since 1600) the different common law crimes have been so defined as to require, for guilt, that the defendant's acts or omissions be accompanied by one or more of the various types of fault (intention, knowledge, recklessness or—more rarely—negligence); a person is not guilty of a common law crime without one of these kinds of fault. But legislatures, especially in this century, have often undertaken to impose criminal liability for conduct unaccompanied by fault. A statute may simply provide that whoever does (or omits to do) so-and-so, or whoever brings about such-and-such a result, is guilty of a crime, setting forth the punishment.[1] Usually, but not always, the statutory crime-without-fault carries a relatively light penalty—generally of the misdemeanor variety. Often this statutory crime has been created in order to help the prosecution cope with a situation wherein intention, knowledge, recklessness or negligence is hard to prove, making convictions difficult to obtain unless

though a statute might be drafted in such a way that such awareness is required for conviction, see § 5.1(d), in the absence of such a requirement there usually exists a mens rea requirement that defendant intend or know what he is doing in a physical sense (apart from knowledge as to its legality). But courts sometimes confuse these matters, as in Liparota v. United States, ___ U.S. ___, 105 S.Ct. 2084, 85 L.Ed.2d 434 (1985). At issue there was the meaning of 7 U.S.C.A. § 2024(b), providing that "whoever knowingly uses, transfers, acquires, alters, or possesses [food stamp] coupons or authorization cards in any manner not authorized by" statute or regulations is guilty of a crime. To be sure, the statute was ambiguous as to whether Congress had intended by that language to require proof that a defendant was aware his acquisition or possession was unauthorized by law. However, the majority, in answering in the affirmative, mischaracterized the issue in asserting that such a result was supported by the "generally disfavored status" of strict liability offenses. As the dissenters correctly pointed out, a contrary reading of the statute would not involve "creating a strict liability offense," for it still would be true that a defendant could not be convicted if "he was unaware of the circumstances of the transaction that made it illegal."

the fault element is omitted.[2] The legislature may think it important to stamp out the harmful conduct in question at all costs, even at the cost of convicting innocent-minded and blameless people. It may expect a lot of prosecutions in a certain area of harmful activity and therefore wish to relieve the prosecuting officials of the time-consuming task of preparing evidence of fault. Doubtless with many such crimes the legislature is actually aiming at bad people and expects that the prosecuting officials, in the exercise of their broad discretion to prosecute or not to prosecute, will use the statute only against those persons of bad reputation who probably actually did have the hard-to-prove bad mind, letting others go who, from their generally good reputation, probably had no such bad mental state.[3]

It should be noted, once again, that crimes are frequently made up of several physical elements, and that a crime may be defined so as to require one type of fault as to one element, another type as to another element, and no fault at all as to a third element.[4] On the other hand, a statute may impose strict liability as to all the elements.[5]

WESTLAW REFERENCES

di fault

(a) Statutory Interpretation. It is rare if ever that the legislature states affirmatively in a statute that described conduct is a crime though done without fault. What it does is simply to omit from the wording of the statute any language ("knowingly," "fraudulently," "wilfully," "with intent to," etc.) indicating that fault is a necessary ingredient.[6] Since crimes usually do require some fault (as expressed by the old maxim *actus non facit reum nisi mens sit rea*), the defendant often argues as to a particular statutory crime of which he is accused that the legislature really meant to require some fault.

Criminal statutes which are empty of words denoting fault, but which do not affirmatively provide for liability without fault, have been dealt with in various ways by the courts. Sometimes the court holds that the statute means what it says and so imposes criminal liability without regard to fault. But sometimes the court reads into the statute some requirement of fault, the absence of which

2. The history of the criminal statute in question often discloses that the statute originally read, "whoever knowingly," ("wilfully," "fraudulently") does so-and-so; the statute was later amended to strike out the "knowingly", etc. E.g., State v. Dobry, 217 Iowa 858, 250 N.W. 702 (1933); Commonwealth v. Mixer, 207 Mass. 141, 93 N.E. 249 (1910); State v. Prince, 52 N.M. 15, 189 P.2d 993 (1948).

3. When the strict liability statute applies to a particular form of business activity and is enforced by a specialized agency having responsibility for enforcement of that statute and other regulation of that type of business activity, there may be an established and sound routine for exercising this discretion. See Comment, 1956 Wis.L. Rev. 641, noting the general policy of the Wisconsin Department of Agriculture to refrain from prosecuting inadvertent violations of the food and drug laws until a specific warning has been given the violator and he had had ample opportunity to cease the offending action or correct the offending condition.

When the statute is enforced by law enforcement agents on a more general basis, there may understandably be more concern with how the discretion is exercised. Thus Heaney, J., dissenting in United States v. Flum, 518 F.2d 39 (8th Cir.1975), holding the statute on carrying a weapon onto an aircraft was of the strict liability type, expressed concern with the "troublesome problem of selective enforcement" revealed by the fact that in a recent

year 67,710 weapons had been detected but only 1,147 arrests had been made.

4. Thus in § 3.4(d), we considered the hypothetical statute punishing the person who sells liquor to one whom he knows to be a policeman and whom he should know to be on duty. Such a statute provides for absolute liability as to the element of the sale of liquor, a requirement of knowledge as to the element of the purchaser's occupation as a policeman, and a requirement of negligence as to the element of the purchaser's duty status.

5. E.g., the blue-sky statute providing that whoever files a false statement as to financial condition with the Secretary of State is guilty of a crime, construed in State v. Dobry, supra note 2. Defendant filed what he believed to be a true statement but which was in fact false, and as the statute imposed strict liability as to this element, he was held guilty. But he would also be guilty if he wrongly believed that what he filed did not relate to financial condition, as that element too requires no fault. So too he would be guilty if he filed with the Secretary of State in the erroneous belief he was filing with the Secretary of the Treasury.

6. Or, the legislature may include such words in the statute but do so in such a manner as to make it unclear whether they extend to all the elements thereafter stated. See, e.g., Liparota v. United States, ___ U.S. ___, 105 S.Ct. 2084, 85 L.Ed.2d 434 (1985).

fault constitutes a defense;[7] the court may, however, place upon the defendant the burden of coming forward with some evidence of, or perhaps even of persuading the jury of, the absence of this fault.[8]

A number of factors may be considered of importance in deciding whether the legislature meant to impose liability without fault or, on the other hand, really meant to require fault, though it failed to spell it out clearly. (1) The legislative history of the statute or its title or context may throw some light on the matter.[9] (2) The legislature may have in some other statute provided guidance as to how a court is to determine whether strict liability was intended.[10] (3) The severity of the punishment provided for the crime is of importance. Other things being equal, the greater the possible punishment, the more likely some fault is required; and, conversely, the lighter the possible punishment, the more likely the legislature meant to impose liability without fault.[11] (4) The seriousness of harm to the public which may be expected to follow from the forbidden conduct is another factor. Other things being equal, the more serious the consequences to the public, the more likely the legislature meant to impose liability without regard to fault, and vice versa.[12] (5) The defendant's opportunity to ascertain the true facts is yet another factor which may be important in determining

---

7. See Frankfurter, J., dissenting in Lambert v. California, 355 U.S. 225, 78 S.Ct. 240, 2 L.Ed.2d 228 (1957): "Considerations of hardship often lead courts, naturally enough, to attribute to a statute the requirements of a certain mental element—some consciousness of wrongdoing and knowledge of the law's command—as a matter of statutory construction."

8. See 3.8(d).

9. See § 2.2(e)(f). See, e.g., United States v. Margraf, 483 F.2d 708 (3d Cir.1973), remanded on other grounds 414 U.S. 1106, 94 S.Ct. 833, 38 L.Ed.2d 734 (1973) (one subsection of statute without fault words deemed to impose strict liability where another subsection, enacted at same time, states intent requirement); State v. Stanfield, 105 Wis.2d 553, 314 N.W.2d 339 (1982) (legislative documents expressly state strict liability intended). In State v. Dobry, 217 Iowa 858, 250 N.W. 702 (1933), the fact that the legislature struck out the word "knowingly" formerly contained in the statute was held to show a legislative intention to impose liability without fault. On the other hand, in State v. Miller, 74 Kan. 667, 87 P. 723 (1906), a statute which was devoid of fault-words in the body of the act was held to require fault because the title contained a phrase requiring fault.

10. Compare State v. Rushing, 62 Haw. 102, 612 P.2d 103 (1980) (mere absence of fault words does not make welfare fraud statute strict liability crime; another statute says crime is strict liability only if such legislative purpose "plainly appears"); with State v. Buttrey, 293 Or. 575, 651 P.2d 1075 (1982) (driving while license suspended is strict liability crime notwithstanding statute declaring this so only when legislature "clearly indicates," as statute contains affirmative defense re ignorance of suspension in limited circumstances not applicable in this case).

Several of the modern codes have provided that a statute is not to be treated as a strict liability offense unless it "clearly indicates" or "plainly appears" that such result was intended by the legislature. Some of the provisions so provide as to offenses outside the criminal code, as does Model Penal Code § 2.05(1)(b); some so provide as to offenses both inside and outside the code, and some impose the *added* requirement that the offense be of a certain type. By contrast, it is sometimes provided that as to very minor offenses a strict liability approach is proper whenever no fault words appear in the statute.

11. Compare State v. Strong, 294 N.W.2d 319 (Minn. 1980) (crime of taking contraband into state prison, though lacking fault words, not a strict liability crime; court stresses it is a felony punishable by 3–5 years imprisonment); State v. Collova, 79 Wis.2d 473, 255 N.W.2d 581 (1977) (driving after license revoked not strict liability; imprisonment up to one year possible, and mandatory 10-day sentence); Regina v. Tolson, 23 Q.B.D. 168 (1889) (bigamy statute, empty of fault-words, *held* to require negligence fault in view of serious consequences of conviction: maximum of seven years penal servitude or two years at hard labor, plus forfeiture of goods and loss of civil rights; "such a fate seems properly reserved for those who have transgressed morally, as well as unintentionally done something prohibited by law"); People v. Clark, 242 N.Y. 313, 151 N.E. 631 (1926) (felony for public officer to receive emolument except as authorized by law, with ten years imprisonment the maximum; *held*, statute requires the defendant know the emolument he receives is not authorized), with Krueger v. Noel, 318 N.W.2d 220 (Iowa 1982) (crime of depositing substance on highway likely to injure is strict liability offense; it is a simple misdemeanor punishable by a maximum of 30 days imprisonment or a fine up to $100); Commonwealth v. Mixer, 207 Mass. 141, 93 N.E. 249, 31 L.R.A., N.S. 467 (1910) (liquor statute, empty of fault-words—having been amended to strike out "wilfully"—*held* not to require fault, the statute providing for a relatively light misdemeanor penalty).

12. Thus a federal statute, empty of fault-words, makes it a felony (1) to sell narcotics except on a form issued by the government and (2) to sell or buy narcotics without government stamps on the package. In United States v. Balint, 258 U.S. 250, 42 S.Ct. 301, 66 L.Ed. 604 (1922), the seller sold opium, but not on a government form because he thought it was sugar; *held*, he is guilty though without fault. In Nigro v. United States, 4 F.2d 781 (8th Cir.1925), the buyer bought narcotics in packages with forged stamps, though he thought them genuine; *held*, he is not guilty because of his lack of knowledge, distinguishing *Balint*. One distinction is that to sell opium as sugar may make drug addicts of innocent purchasers, a serious matter; but to buy narcotics without genuine stamps merely

whether the legislature really meant to impose liability on one who was without fault because he lacked knowledge of these facts. The harder to find out the truth, the more likely the legislature meant to require fault in not knowing; the easier to ascertain the truth, the more likely failure to know is no excuse.[13] (6) The difficulty prosecuting officials would have in proving a mental state for this type of crime. The greater the difficulty, the more likely it is that the legislature intended to relieve the prosecution of that burden so that the law could be effectively enforced.[14] (7) The number of prosecutions to be expected is another factor of some importance. The fewer the expected prosecutions, the more likely the legislature meant to re-

quire the prosecuting officials to go into the issue of fault; the greater the number of prosecutions, the more likely the legislature meant to impose liability without regard to fault.[15] All the above factors have a bearing on the question of the interpretation of the empty statute, but no single factor can be said to be controlling. Thus some statutes have been held to impose liability without fault although the possible punishment was quite severe, generally because one or more of the other factors pointed toward strict liability.[16]

When, because of the operation of one or more of the factors, the court reads into an empty statute a requirement of fault, that fault may be of the objective (negligence) type, or it may be of the subjective (mental) type.[17]

---

causes the government to lose some revenue, a relatively minor matter. See also United States v. Flum, 518 F.2d 39 (8th Cir.1975) (crime of boarding or attempting to board aircraft with weapon is strict liability; court stresses the serious problem of aircraft hijacking).

13. Thus, concerning *Balint* and *Nigro,* supra note 12, it is doubtless easier to distinguish opium from sugar (so lack of knowledge that he was selling opium is no defense) than to distinguish genuine from forged stamps (so lack of knowledge that stamps were forged is a defense). It was argued by the defendant in *Mixer,* supra note 11, that the statute (whoever transports liquor into a town is guilty of a misdemeanor) could not have been meant to apply to a carrier who transported liquor into town in sugar barrels believing the barrels to contain sugar, because a carrier cannot legally inspect the contents of packages shipped by the shipper. The court answered, however, that a carrier may properly inspect such packages. See also United States v. Erne, 576 F.2d 212 (9th Cir.1978) (failure to collect and deposit withholding and FICA taxes is strict liability; court stresses burden not great because statute excepts certain situations beyond person's control); Krueger v. Noel, 318 N.W.2d 220 (Iowa 1982) (crime of depositing on highway a substance likely to injure a person or vehicle is strict liability as to that likelihood, as it not a great burden to require one who has knowingly deposited to stop and ascertain the danger); State v. Collova, 79 Wis. 2d 473, 255 N.W.2d 581 (1977) (driving car after license revocation not strict liability crime, as driving "is a wholly routine and innocent act" which would not prompt one to inquire of the state re license status).

14. Compare United States v. Flum, 518 F.2d 39 (8th Cir.1975) (crime of attempting to board aircraft while carrying weapon is strict liability; court stresses difficulty of proving mental state as to person who appears at screening area); with State v. Strong, 294 N.W.2d 319 (Minn.1980) (crime of taking contraband into prison, though lacking fault words, not a strict liability crime; court stresses it not difficult to prove such act intentional).

15. Thus in People v. Vogel, 46 Cal.2d 798, 299 P.2d 850 (1956), where a statute made it bigamy for one already married to marry another, and the defendant married

another honestly and reasonably but erroneously believing he was divorced, the court held that his honest reasonable belief was a defense, giving as one reason for this construction of the statute that the offense was infrequently committed, so that it was unlikely the legislature meant to impose liability without fault in order to make sure the morally-guilty bigamist did not escape.

16. State v. Dobry, 217 Iowa 858, 250 N.W. 702 (1933) (blue sky law; 5 yrs. maximum); State v. Ross, 55 Or. 450, 104 P. 596 (1909) (state officer converting state funds; 15 yrs.); Pappas v. State, 135 Tenn. 499, 188 S.W. 52 (1916) (removal of mortgaged property from state; 5 years); State v. Lindberg, 125 Wash. 51, 215 P. 41 (1923) (state banking act punishing borrowing from bank by director thereof; 10 yrs.); Boyd v. State, 217 Wis. 149, 258 N.W. 330 (1935) (blue sky law; 5 yrs.). In addition, with such sex offenses as bigamy and statutory rape it is common to provide for strict liability, with severe maximum punishment, as to one who remarries or has intercourse reasonably believing that his spouse is dead or divorced, or that the girl is over age; and such statutes have not been deemed unconstitutional as violations of due process, e.g., Commonwealth v. Murphy, 165 Mass. 66, 42 N.E. 504 (1896) (statutory rape); Commonwealth v. Mash, 48 Mass. (7 Met.) 472 (1844) (bigamy to remarry honestly and reasonably believing husband dead); Williams v. North Carolina, 325 U.S. 226, 65 S.Ct. 1092, 89 L.Ed. 1577 (1945) (bigamy to remarry reasonably believing divorced).

17. Thus in Regina v. Tolson, 23 Q.B.D. 168 (1889), where the court held that a reasonable belief, but not an unreasonable belief, that the missing spouse was dead constituted a defense to bigamy, the court read into the statute a requirement of negligence as to the belief. Accord: People v. Vogel, 46 Cal.2d 798, 299 P.2d 850 (1956). But in People v. Clark, 242 N.Y. 313, 151 N.E. 631 (1926), where the court held that a belief (apparently reasonable or unreasonable so long as honestly entertained) that the emolument received was legal constituted a defense to the statute punishing public officers who received any emolument not legally authorized, the court read into the statute a requirement of mental fault, i.e., knowledge that the emolument was not so authorized.

Perhaps the stronger the factors are for requiring fault (heavier punishment, less harmful consequences, etc.), the greater the likelihood that the required fault is subjective fault, though it is often difficult to guess in advance in any case just what requirement of fault if any the court will read into the statute.

The courts which construe empty statutes as requiring some type of fault ordinarily make the prosecution allege and prove that fault in order to secure a conviction, just as if the missing words were written in the statute. But some courts have found another way of dealing with the empty statute which is construed to require fault—a method which falls midway between imposing liability without fault (the prosecution need not allege or prove any fault, and the defendant can raise no defense that he was without fault) and dealing with the statute just as if words of fault were written therein (the prosecution must allege and prove fault, just as it must prove all elements of the crime). These courts say that, though fault is required, it need not be alleged by the prosecution or proved in its presentation at the trial; rather, it is up to the defendant to put in evidence of his lack of fault during his presentation at the trial.

Thus in a bigamy case [18] the statute, devoid of any words requiring fault, provided in effect that one who, having a living spouse, marries someone else is guilty of bigamy unless then divorced. The defendant honestly and reasonably thought he was divorced when he married the second time, but he actually was not divorced. The court held that the bigamy statute requires that the defendant have reason to believe he is not divorced, so

that a reasonable belief that he is divorced is a defense. The legislature's omission of any expression of fault in the body of the statute has some effect, however; it was done "to reallocate the burden of proof on that issue [i.e., fault] in a bigamy trial. Thus, the prosecution makes a prima facie case upon proof that the second marriage was entered into while the first spouse was still living * * * and his bona fide and reasonable belief that facts existed that left the defendant free to remarry is a defense to be proved by the defendant." [19] The one point these cases do not ordinarily make clear is whether the rule requires only that the defendant go forward with some evidence of lack of the required fault in order to escape conviction, the prosecution still having the burden of persuading the jury that the defendant was at fault; or whether the defendant actually has the burden of persuading the jury by a preponderance of the evidence that he is free of fault.

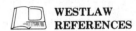 **WESTLAW REFERENCES**

digest,synopsis(strict** /4 liab! /p (mental mind /s state element intent) "mens rea")

110k21 /p strict** /4 liab!

(b) Constitutionality. As discussed earlier,[20] the United States Supreme Court has recognized that as a general matter it is constitutionally permissible to enact strict-liability criminal statutes. "There is wide latitude in the lawmakers to declare an offense and to exclude elements of knowledge and diligence from its definition." [21] The Court has on only one occasion struck down a strict-liability crime, and this was in rather unusual circum-

---

18. People v. Vogel, 46 Cal.2d 798, 299 P.2d 850 (1956).

19. 46 Cal.2d 803, 299 P.2d 850, 854 (1956). Accord: Bradley v. People, 8 Colo. 599, 9 P. 783 (1885) (statute makes it larceny to brand, or obliterate the brand on, the animal of another; the statute formerly read "wilfully", but was amended to strike out that word; defendant thought the calf he branded was his own; *held*, statute still requires bad intent, but omission of "wilfully" means the intent is presumed from the act, and defendant must show he had no bad intent); Sherras v. De Rutzen, [1895] 1 Q.B. 918 (one section of statute makes it a crime to sell liquor to policeman on duty; another section makes it a crime knowingly to permit policeman on duty to remain

on premises; defendant served liquor to policeman out of uniform; *held,* knowledge that policeman is on duty is required, but defendant must prove lack of knowledge); King v. Ewart, 25 N.Z.L.R. 709 (1905) (statute makes it a crime to sell obscene written matter; defendant sold newspaper containing obscene matter of which he was unaware; *held,* statute requires defendant have a guilty mind, but doing the act prima facie shows the existence of this mind, the absence of which defendant must prove).

20. See § 2.12(d).

21. Lambert v. California, 355 U.S. 225, 78 S.Ct. 240, 2 L.Ed.2d 228 (1957).

stances.[22] Though it has been argued that the ruling in that case should be extended to proscribe strict-liability offenses more generally,[23] this has not occurred. Rather, this decision has had very little impact.[24]

Constitutional attacks in the state courts have, in the main, been equally unsuccessful. Most of the state decisions reject the notion that there is some general constitutional bar to strict-liability crimes[25] or even that the sanction of imprisonment is constitutionally impermissible on a strict-liability basis.[26] But a few states take a somewhat narrower view of what is allowed under their state constitutions. Thus, some authority is to be found to the effect that a strict-liability criminal statute is unconstitutional if (1) the subject matter of the statute does not place it "in a narrow class of public welfare offenses,"[27] (2) the statute carries a substantial penalty of imprisonment,[28] or (3) the statute imposes an unreasonable duty in terms of a person's responsibility to ascertain the relevant facts.[29]

WESTLAW
REFERENCES

topic(92) /p strict** /4 liab!

(c) Pros and Cons of Strict-Liability Crimes. Aside from the question of constitutionality, there is the question of wisdom in providing for strict-liability crimes. The reasons for having statutes imposing criminal liability without fault are those of expediency: in some areas of conduct it is difficult to obtain convictions if the prosecution must prove fault, so enforcement requires strict liability.[30] If the conduct to be stamped out is harmful enough, or if the number of prosecutions to be expected is great enough, the legislature may thus wish to make the absence of fault no defense, in order to relieve the prosecution of the task of going into the matter.[31]

---

22. Lambert v. California, 355 U.S. 225, 78 S.Ct. 240, 2 L.Ed.2d 228 (1957), holding unconstitutional as a violation of due process a Los Angeles ordinance imposing strict liability for failure to register as a felon. *Lambert* is discussed in § 2.12(d).

23. Erlinder, Mens Rea, Due Process, and the Supreme Court: Toward a Constitutional Doctrine of Substantive Criminal Law, 9 Am.J.Crim.L. 163 (1981); Hippard, The Unconstitutionality of Criminal Liability Without Fault: An Argument for a Constitutional Doctrine of Mens Rea, 10 Houst.L.Rev. 1039 (1973); Saltman, Strict Criminal Liability and the United States Constitution: Substantive Criminal Law Due Process, 24 Wayne L.Rev. 1571 (1978).

See the strong attack upon strict-liability crimes—from the point of view both of wisdom and of constitutionality, contained in the article by Professor Henry Hart, The Aims of the Criminal Law, 23 Law & Contemp.Prob. 401 (1958). As to constitutionality, he disapproves of the *Lambert* distinction between strict-liability crimes of affirmative action and strict-liability crimes of omission and would apply the same rule of unconstitutionality to both types. He defines "crime" as used in the various constitutions, federal and state, as meaning conduct which is blameworthy; and he argues therefrom that in effect these constitutions provide that conduct lacking blameworthiness be not punished as crimes. He doubtless believes also that Fourteenth Amendment due process forbids the states to punish as crimes conduct lacking fault.

24. In Texaco, Inc. v. Short, 454 U.S. 516, 102 S.Ct. 781, 70 L.Ed.2d 738 (1982), the majority said of *Lambert:* "Its application has been limited, lending some credence to Justice Frankfurter's colorful prediction in dissent that the case would stand as 'an isolated deviation from the strong current of precedents—a derelict on the waters of the law.'"

25. E.g., Goodrow v. Perrin, 119 N.H. 483, 403 A.2d 864 (1979); State v. Stepniewski, 105 Wis.2d 261, 314 N.W.2d 98 (1982), approved in Stepniewski v. Gagnon, 732 F.2d 567 (7th Cir.1984).

26. E.g., State v. McDowell, 312 N.W.2d 301 (N.D. 1981).

27. State v. Campbell, 536 P.2d 105 (Alaska 1975) partially overruled on a totally different point Kimoktoak v. State, 584 P.2d 25 (Alaska 1978) (instant statute, dealing with failure to attempt return of lost property, not within that class).

28. Hentzner v. State, 613 P.2d 821 (Alaska 1980) (crime of selling unregistered securities, punishable by 20 years imprisonment, may not be strict liability).

29. State v. Brown, 389 So.2d 48 (La.1980) (possession of controlled substance law would be unconstitutional if construed as strict-liability crime, as it "requires little imagination to visualize a situation in which a third party hands the controlled substance to an unknowing individual who then can be charged with and subsequently convicted for violation of [this law] without even being aware of the nature of the substance he was given").

30. State v. Collova, 79 Wis.2d 473, 255 N.W.2d 581 (1977): "The usual rationale for strict liability statutes is that the public interest is so great as to warrant the imposition of an absolute standard of care—the defendant can have no excuse for disobeying the law. Because of the multitude of cases arising under these regulatory statutes, there is a need for quick, simple trials unhindered by examinations of the subjective intent of each defendant."

31. See Holmes, J., in Commonwealth v. Smith, 166 Mass. 370, 44 N.E. 503 (1896): "When according to common experience a certain fact generally is accompanied by knowledge of further elements necessary to complete what

For the most part, the commentators have been critical of strict-liability crimes. "The consensus can be summarily stated: to punish conduct without reference to the actor's state of mind is both inefficacious and unjust. It is inefficacious because conduct unaccompanied by an awareness of the factors making it criminal does not mark the actor as one who needs to be subjected to punishment in order to deter him or others from behaving similarly in the future, nor does it single him out as a socially dangerous individual who needs to be incapacitated or reformed. It is unjust because the actor is subjected to the stigma of a criminal conviction without being morally blameworthy. Consequently, on either a preventive or retributive theory of criminal punishment, the criminal sanction is inappropriate in the absence of *mens rea*." [32]

As to the argument of necessity in support of strict liability, "the answer, among others, is that (a) maximizing compliance with law, rather than successful prosecution of violators, is the primary aim of any regulatory statute; (b) the convenience of investigators and prosecutors is not, in any event, the prime consideration in determining what conduct is criminal; (c) a prosecutor, as a matter of common knowledge, always assumes a heavier burden in trying to secure a criminal conviction than a civil judgment; (d) in most situations of attempted control of mass conduct, the technique of a first warning, followed by criminal prosecution only of knowing violators, has not only obvious, but proved superiority; and (e) the common-sense advantages of using the criminal sanction only against deliberate violators is confirmed by the policies which prosecutors themselves tend always to follow when they are free to make their own selection of cases to prosecute." [33]

Dissents to some of these propositions have occasionally been registered.[34] For example, it has been suggested that a strict-liability offense may be a more efficacious deterrent than an ordinary criminal statute because "a person engaged in a certain kind of activity would be more careful precisely because he knew that this kind of activity was governed by a strict liability statute" [35] and because "the presence of strict liability offenses might have the added effect of keeping a relatively large class of persons from engaging in certain kinds of activity." [36] Also, it is contended that strict-liability offenses often do require "fault" in a restrictive sense, in that they "can be interpreted as legislative judgments that persons who intentionally engage in certain activities and occupy some peculiar or distinctive position of control are to be held accountable for the occurrence of certain consequences." [37]

Yet, it is generally agreed that conviction for strict-liability offenses should be insulated "from the type of moral condemnation that is and ought to be implicit when a sentence of imprisonment may be imposed." [38] Thus, the Model Penal Code would permit strict liability only for "offenses which constitute violations" [39]; violations under the Code are not crimes, may be punished only by a fine, forfeiture, or other civil penalty, and may not give rise to any disability or legal disadvantage based on conviction of a criminal offense.[40] Likewise, others have urged that a strict-liability crime should carry a label with less

it is the final object of the law to prevent, or even short of that, when it is very desirable that people should find out whether the further elements are there, actual knowledge being a matter difficult to prove, the law may stop at the preliminary fact, and in the pursuit of its policy may make the preliminary fact enough to constitute the crime."

32. Packer, Mens Rea and the Supreme Court, 1962 Sup.Ct.Rev. 107, 109.

33. Hart, The Aims of the Criminal Law, 23 Law & Contemp.Prob. 401, 423–24 (1958).

34. See generally Note, 75 Colum.L.Rev. 1517 (1975).

35. Wasserstrom, Strict Liability in the Criminal Law, 12 Stan.L.Rev. 731, 736 (1960). See also Note, 1970 Wis.L. Rev. 1201, 1207.

36. Wasserstrom, supra note 35, at 737. See also Brady, Strict Liability Offenses: A Justification, 8 Crim.L. Bull. 217, 223–24 (1972).

37. Wasserstrom, supra note 35, at 743. See also Note, 1970 Wis.L.Rev. 1201, 1206.

38. Model Penal Code § 2.05, Comments (Tent.Draft No. 4, 1955).

39. Model Penal Code § 2.05(1)(a).

40. Id. at § 1.04(5).

sinister connotations, such as "public tort," [41] "public welfare offense," [42] or "civil offense." [43] Reforms along these lines have seldom been adopted.[44] Consequently, as things now stand some crimes which may be committed without fault are punishable by imprisonment, and those who commit them are labelled as criminal.

WESTLAW REFERENCES

collova /p strict** absolute** /4 liab!

morissette /s (strict** absolute** /4 liab!) (liab! /4 fault) /p public /s welfare interest

(d) Alternatives to Strict Liability. In light of the criticisms which have been made of strict liability, it is appropriate to take note of possible alternative approaches. One would be only fault liability but with substantially higher penalties, on the theory that in terms of deterrent efficacy the reduced likelihood of conviction would thereby be offset by the increased magnitude of the punishment. But if the nature and circumstances of the activity in question is such that proof of fault is extremely difficult and likely to be largely a matter of chance, it might be questioned whether this would be a fairer system.[45] Assume, for example, that the choice is between convicting all 100 defendants who have sold food later shown to be impure and fining each $250, or convicting the five out of the 100 the prosecutor can show had knowledge of the impurities and fining them each $5,000. The increased penalties for the five (contrasted to no penalty at all for others known to have sold impure food but whose fault cannot be proved) might seem more unjust than the imposition of a $250 fine without regard to fault in all 100 cases.

Secondly, it has been argued that between liability based upon subjective fault and strict liability, "there is a 'half-way house': criminal liability predicated upon negligence. * * * [T]he idea of criminal responsibility based upon the actor's failure to act as carefully as he should affords an important and largely unutilized means for avoiding the tyranny of strict liability in the criminal law." [46] Doubtless there are circumstances in which the strict liability approach is now utilized where the negligence alternative would suffice, but this is not inevitably the case. As to certain forms of conduct, even the negligence standard may present insurmountable problems of proof for the prosecution.[47] Moreover, as suggested earlier, sometimes strict liability is grounded in the notion that the activity engaged in by the defendant is so hazardous to the general public that simply performing in a non-negligent fashion should not be deemed sufficient.

Another possible alternative is shifting the burden of proof. As one commentator has put it: "It is fundamentally unsound to convict a defendant for a crime involving a substantial term of imprisonment without giving him the opportunity to prove that his action was due to an honest and reasonable mistake of fact or that he acted without guilty intent. If the public danger is widespread and serious, the practical situation can be met by shifting to the shoulders of the defendant the burden of proving a lack of guilty intent." [48] To the extent that strict liability in a particular area is grounded in the prosecutor's difficulties in proving fault, this is an attractive

---

41. See Note, 35 Harv.L.Rev. 462 (1922), attributing the term to Professor Joseph H. Beale.

42. Sayre, Public Welfare Offenses, 33 Colum.L.Rev. 55 (1933).

43. Brett, Strict Responsibility: Possible Solutions, 37 Mod.L.Rev. 417, 436 (1974); Gauzewitz, Reclassification of Certain Offenses as Civil instead of Criminal, 12 Wis.L. Rev. 365 (1937); Perkins, The Civil Offense, 100 U. of Pa. L.Rev. 832 (1952).

44. A few of the modern codes follow Model Penal Code § 2.05(1)(a) by providing that strict liability within the code is limited to certain minor offenses. An even

smaller number provide, as in Model Penal Code § 2.05(2), that strict liability offenses outside the code must be treated as very minor offenses unless a mental state is actually proved.

45. Note, 75 Colum.L.Rev. 1517, 1548–50 (1975).

46. Packer, Mens Rea and the Supreme Court, 1962 Sup.Ct.Rev. 107, 109–10.

47. Note, 75 Colum.L.Rev. 1517, 1553 (1975).

48. Sayre, Public Welfare Offenses, 33 Colum.L.Rev. 55, 82 (1933).

alternative.[49] Here again, however, it is a less than satisfactory measure when the basis of the strict liability is the imposition of an absolute standard upon high-risk activity. And some object that this alternative would result in a significant loss of deterrence but yet the conviction of many blameless defendants who were unable to muster proof of their innocence.[50]

Finally, it has been suggested that strict liability could be replaced with a "prior warning method,"[51] whereby a warning is issued upon discovery by the authorities of a violation, after which any subsequent violations of the same type by the same person would be subject to prosecution on a strict liability basis. As a matter of administrative practice, this is precisely the approach now used with apparent success by various specialized enforcement agencies.[52] Whether formalizing this "one-bite" limitation into the substantive law would reduce the deterrent effect of the law is unclear. However, some feel that "under such an alternative, those merchants who believe that their fault in selling prohibited foodstuffs is unprovable, and who would be deterred by absolute liability statutes will not be deterred," meaning such a system "spares faultless individuals from punishment at the cost of increased harm to victims of undeterred, but deterrable, crime."[53]

WESTLAW REFERENCES

"criminal** negligent**" /p strict** absolut*** /4 liab!

§ 3.9 Liability Without Fault—Vicarious Liability

The last section considered one type of criminal liability based upon conduct without fault on the part of the defendant—the strict-liability crime. Now we consider another

type of such criminal liability, where the defendant, generally one conducting a business, is made liable, though without personal fault, for the bad conduct of someone else, generally his employee. As we shall see, courts have not always distinguished carefully between strict and vicarious liability, although there is clearly an important difference between these two types of liability without fault. With strict liability, there must be a showing that the defendant personally engaged in the necessary acts or omissions; only the requirement of mental fault is dispensed with altogether. By contrast, with vicarious liability it is the need for a personal *actus reus* that is dispensed with, and there remains the need for mental fault on the part of the employee. It is common, however, for a vicarious liability statute to also impose strict liability; in such an instance, there is no need to prove an act or omission by the defendant-employer (one by his employee will do), and there is no need to prove mental fault by anyone.

In the area of the civil law we are quite used to vicarious responsibility (the doctrine of respondeat superior), although in criminal law it is a departure from the basic premise of criminal justice that crime requires personal fault (once again, *actus facit reum nisi mens sit rea*). Said one court: "The distinction between respondeat superior in tort law and its application to the criminal law is obvious. In tort law, the doctrine is employed for the purpose of settling the incidence of loss upon the party who can best bear such loss. But the criminal law is supported by totally different concepts. We impose penal treatment upon those who injure or menace social interest, partly in order to reform, partly to prevent the continuation of the anti-social activity and partly to deter others. If a defendant has personally lived up to the social standards of the criminal law and has not menaced or injured anyone, why impose penal treat-

49. On when it is constitutionally permissible to shift the burden of proof, see § 1.8.

50. "Those same factors which make fault difficult to prove—lack of witnesses or lack of external criteria for establishing mental states—also make the likelihood of faultlessness difficult to prove." Note, 75 Colum.L.Rev. 1517, 1550 (1975).

51. Mueller, Mens Rea and the Law Without It, 58 W.Va.L.Rev. 34, 62–63 (1955).

52. See, e.g., Comment, 1956 Wis.L.Rev. 641, 653–55, describing the enforcement of the food and drug laws by the Wisconsin Department of Agriculture.

53. Note, 75 Colum.L.Rev. 1517, 1552 (1975).

ment?"[1] The answer, as given by the court itself, is that some crimes represent a use of the machinery of criminal justice to impose strict standards of performance on certain business activities which, if improperly conducted, pose a danger to the public. However, it is one thing to hold that the faultless employer ought to pay for the damage which his employee (often impecunious) inflicts upon third persons in the course of furthering his employer's business; it is much more drastic to visit criminal punishment and moral condemnation upon the employer who is innocent of any personal fault.[2]

 WESTLAW REFERENCES

di vicarious liability

(a) **Common Law Crimes.** The common law did not impose criminal liability upon a faultless employer for the unauthorized criminal conduct of his employee except in two isolated instances: nuisance and libel.[3] An employer was criminally liable for the criminal nuisances and libels of his employees though he did not know of or authorize the conduct and may have even forbidden it. In other areas of conduct constituting common law crimes the employer is not liable for what the employee did without his knowledge or authorization, and even the two exceptions of nuisance and libel have seldom received recognition in this country.[4]

(b) **Statutory Crimes—Interpretation.** Some criminal statutes, generally containing no language of fault,[5] specifically impose criminal liability upon the employer for the bad conduct of his employee—e.g., "whoever, by himself or by his agent, sells articles at short weight shall be punished by * * *," or "whoever sells liquor to a minor is punishable by * * * and any sale by an employee shall be deemed the act of the employer as well as the act of the employee."[6] Such statutes (generally carrying a misdemeanor penalty) are naturally construed to impose vicarious liability upon the employer though he expressly forbade his employee to engage in the forbidden conduct.[7]

Although virtually all of the statutes expressly imposing vicarious liability do so only in the context of an employer-employee relationship, this is not inevitably the case.[8] There are, for example, statutes which hold the registered owners of vehicles vicariously

§ 3.9

1. Commonwealth v. Koczwara, 397 Pa. 575, 155 A.2d 825 (1959).

2. Of course, one person, who may be an employer, may be personally at fault in the matter of another's conduct and so liable criminally for the latter's conduct, as where he hires, commands, encourages or helps the other to commit the crime. See § 6.7. An employer who authorizes his employee to do a forbidden act, or to omit to do a required act, would himself be at fault. But in this section it is assumed that the defendant is not at fault.

3. Sayre, Criminal Responsibility for the Acts of Another, 43 Harv.L.Rev. 689, 708–712 (1930).

4. An English statute changed the rule as to libel so as to allow the employer to show in his defense that he did not know of or authorize the libel, and most American courts have taken this view without a statute. Sayre, supra note 3, at 710–11. There is little authority in this country to support the view that criminal nuisance is a vicarious liability offense, and it has been suggested that the rule is to the contrary.

5. Again, this is not necessary. If a statute can impose strict liability on the employee and vicarious liability on the employer, certainly it can impose only liability with fault on the employee and then hold the employer criminally liable for these acts of the employee done with a bad state of mind. Sayre, supra note 3, at 721–22. This is

sometimes done, Restatement, Agency (Second) § 217D, Comment (1958). An act may be within the scope of employment even though it is consciously criminal. Restatement, Agency (Second) § 231 (1958).

6. The latter part of this provision merely states the generally accepted rule that the imposition of vicarious liability on the employer does not thereby free the employee of criminal liability. E.g., Beacham v. State, 289 P.2d 397 (Okl.Crim.1955).

7. In re Marley, 29 Cal.2d 525, 175 P.2d 832 (1946); State v. Lundgren, 124 Minn. 162, 144 N.W. 752 (1913); Commonwealth v. Sacks, 214 Mass. 72, 100 N.E. 1019, 45 L.R.A. (N.S.) 1 (1913); State v. Beaudry, 123 Wis.2d 40, 365 N.W.2d 593 (1985). Possibly, however, the employer is not liable if the employee did his act by mistake or for the purpose of getting his employer into trouble. In re Marley, supra. And he is not liable unless the employee is acting within the scope of his employer's business. Sayre, supra note 3, at 714; Annot., 43 L.R.A. (N.S.) 2, 30 (1913).

8. Thus, Model Penal Code § 2.06(2)(b) states generally that a person "is legally accountable for the conduct of another person when * * * he is made so accountable for the conduct of such other person by the Code or by the law defining the offense." Many modern recodifications contain such a provision.

liable for parking and similar violations involving their vehicles.[9] Occasionally a statute has attempted to impose vicarious liability upon parents for the conduct of their children.[10]

Often statutes are not that specific as to whether or not they impose vicarious liability. In such a case, if the statutory crime is worded in language requiring some type of fault ("knowingly," "wilfully," "with intent to," etc.), then it is the rule that the employer must personally know or be wilful or have the requisite intention to be liable for the criminal conduct of his employee; even though the latter is acting to further his employer's business, the employer is not criminally liable unless he knew of or authorized that action.[11] That is, if the statute requires mental fault, it will not be presumed that the legislature intended that the fault of the employee should suffice for conviction of the employer.

In between the statutes which specifically require fault and those which specifically impose criminal liability on the employer for his employee's conduct fall those statutes which

neither contain fault-words nor contain any expression that the conduct of the employee makes the employer liable. Thus a statute may simply state that "whoever employs children under 14 in a factory is guilty of a misdemeanor." The factory owner instructs his manager not to employ children under 14, but the manager disregards the instruction and does so. Is the owner liable?[12] The question is one of construction of the statute,[13] and is likely to be approached in much the same way as the question of whether statutes empty of language of fault are to be construed to impose strict liability.[14] If the authorized punishment is light—a fine or perhaps a short imprisonment—the statute is likely to be construed to impose vicarious liability on a faultless employer.[15] But if the permitted punishment is severe—a felony or a serious misdemeanor—the statute is not apt to be so construed in the absence of an express provision for vicarious responsibility.[16] A possible intermediate view is to construe the statute as requiring the employer's fault, but to impose upon him the burden of showing lack of fault rather than to impose upon the prosecu-

9. City of Chicago v. Hertz Commercial Leasing Corp., 71 Ill.2d 333, 17 Ill.Dec. 1, 375 N.E.2d 1285 (1978); Iowa City v. Nolan, 239 N.W.2d 102 (Iowa 1976); City of Kansas City v. Hertz Corp., 499 S.W.2d 449 (Mo.1973); City of Columbus v. Webster, 170 Ohio St. 327, 164 N.E.2d 734 (1960). These provisions typically state that the registered owner "shall be prima facie responsible," and the cases are not always clear as to whether the statute merely creates an inference or imposes vicarious liability. But see City of Missoula v. Shea, ___ Mont. ___, 661 P.2d 410 (1983) (provision declaring presumption owner was driving is invalid, but provision imposing vicarious liability on owner is valid).

10. See State v. Akers, 119 N.H. 161, 400 A.2d 38 (1979) (holding unconstitutional a statute imposing vicarious liability on parents for offenses of minor children re use of snowmobiles).

11. Vachon v. New Hampshire, 414 U.S. 478, 94 S.Ct. 664, 38 L.Ed.2d 666 (1974) (conviction violates due process for lack of evidence where owner of store convicted of "knowingly or wilfully" contributing to the delinquency of a child on evidence that someone at the store sold a 14-year-old girl a button inscribed "Copulation Not Masturbation"); Lovelace v. State, 191 Miss. 62, 2 So.2d 796 (1941) (statute made it a crime to give a bad check with intent to defraud; gas station owner *held* not guilty of the crime where, without his knowledge or authorization, his manager gave a bad check with intent to defraud, to further the owner's business). For other cases see Sayre, supra note 3, at 703 n. 56, and Annot., 43 L.R.A. (N.S.) 2, 23–24 (1913).

12. Compare Overland Cotton Mill Co. v. People, 32 Colo. 263, 75 P. 924 (1904) (*held,* yes); with Commonwealth v. Morakis, 208 Pa.Super. 180, 220 A.2d 900 (1966) (*held,* no).

13. In jurisdictions with statutes of the type discussed in note 8 supra, courts ought to be more reluctant to infer vicarious liability in the absence of express language making one person accountable for the conduct of another.

14. See § 3.8.

15. Hershorn v. People, 108 Colo. 43, 113 P.2d 680, 139 A.L.R. 297 (1941); State v. Beaudry, 123 Wis.2d 40, 365 N.W.2d 593 (1985); Sayre, supra note 3, at 714, citing cases both ways construing "petty misdemeanor" statutes; see also Annots., 43 L.R.A. (N.S.) 2 (1913) (general) and 139 A.L.R. 306 (1942) (liquor laws).

16. Once again, if the statute is construed to impose liability on the employer without fault, it is a defense to him that the employee was not acting within the scope of his employment. E.g., Minden v. Silverstein, 36 La.Ann. 912 (1884) (liquor store owner not guilty when *janitor* sold liquor on Sunday in violation of ordinance). Possibly also it is a defense that the employee's conduct was a mistake, e.g., Commonwealth v. Stevens, 153 Mass. 421, 26 N.E. 992 (1891), or was done to get his employer into trouble. See note 5 supra. However, a consciously criminal act may still be within the scope of employment. Restatement, Agency (Second) § 231 (1958).

tion the burden of showing the employer's knowledge or approval of the employee's conduct.[17]

In construing statutes of this type, courts often jump to the unwarranted conclusion that a statute which imposes strict liability must of necessity also impose vicarious liability.[18] A particularly outrageous example is afforded by the Supreme Court's decision in *United States v. Dotterweich*,[19] which upheld the conviction of the president of a company that shipped misbranded or adulterated products in interstate commerce notwithstanding the fact that he had nothing to do with the shipment. The case presented two distinct issues as to the meaning of the applicable statute, the Food, Drug, and Cosmetic Act: (1) whether whoever was responsible for the shipment could be held criminally liable even without mental fault (the issue of strict liability); and (2) whether the president of the company could be held criminally liable, notwithstanding his own lack of connection with the shipment (the issue of vicarious liability). The Court assumed an affirmative answer on the first issue without careful examination of this premise, and then merely concluded that because the liability was strict it was also vicarious.[20]

There is no basis for assuming that vicarious liability necessarily follows from strict liability.[21] That is, even when it is correctly decided that the legislature has intended to permit conviction of the actor even when he is without mental fault, this result does not compel the conclusion that the legislature must have also intended that it be possible to convict someone else (the actor's employer) as well.[22] It is true, of course, that when strict liability is imposed upon the employee, there is no greater severity in holding the employer liable than in holding the employee liable,[23] but this is hardly conclusive on the issue of legislative intent, which may vary depending upon the subject matter. For example, in enacting a child labor law the legislature might well impose strict liability on hiring agents in the hope of inducing them to obtain clear proof of a person's age prior to hiring that person, but yet might not wish to hold absent employers for all mistakes by their hiring agents.[24] On the other hand, when the legislature enacts criminal statutes dealing with the sale of dangerous articles, it might well wish to impose strict liability and also to bar those engaged in such hazardous enterprises from escaping liability by doing business through others.[25]

17. See Annot., 139 A.L.R. 306, 319–21 (1942). Such an intermediate position is sometimes taken in the use of statutes seeming to impose strict liability upon faultless defendants. See § 3.8.

18. E.g., People v. Travers, 52 Cal.App.3d 111, 124 Cal. Rptr. 728 (1975) (on issue of whether defendant, owner of gas station, may be held criminally liable for misrepresentations of his employee during his absence, without his knowledge and not on his instructions, court says it depends on "whether the doctrine of *mens rea* * * * applies to a case such as this").

19. 320 U.S. 277, 64 S.Ct. 134, 88 L.Ed. 48 (1943).

20. For criticism of *Dotterweich* along these lines, see Packer, Mens Rea and the Supreme Court, 1962 Sup.Ct. Rev. 107, 116–19.

21. "It will not do, therefore, to argue that because a crime does not require *mens rea*, one should be convicted for his servant's unauthorized commission of it, or *vice versa*. The dispensing with the usual requirement of *mens rea* and the imposition of criminal liability for the unauthorized acts of one's servant are parallel but disconnected results flowing from a common cause." Sayre, supra note 3, at 722.

Some courts appreciate the distinction. See, e.g., People v. Wilcox, 83 Mich.App. 654, 269 N.W.2d 256 (1978)

(though statute requiring certain recordkeeping by second-hand goods dealer is of strict liability type, it does not follow it imposes vicarious liability; legislature did not intend vicarious liability, as shown by failure to use language expressly providing, as in pawnbroker statute enacted at same session of the legislature).

22. Williams, Criminal Law: The General Part § 96 (2d ed. 1961). This confusion of strict liability and vicarious liability is also responsible for the assumption that vacarious liability can never be imposed for crimes requiring mental fault by the employee. "But this is specious reasoning. If one's criminal liability may be based upon the physical activity of his servant, why may it not equally be based upon the accompanying mental activity of his servant?" Sayre, supra note 3, at 721.

23. Model Penal Code § 2.06, Comment at 305 (1985).

24. Commonwealth v. Morakis, 208 Pa.Super. 180, 220 A.2d 900 (1966), so interpreting the state's child labor statute.

25. Groff v. State, 171 Ind. 547, 85 N.E. 769 (1908), so interpreting the state's pure food laws. See also State v. Beaudry, 123 Wis.2d 40, 365 N.W.2d 593 (1985) (statute re closing hours for taverns imposes vicarious liability, as the "state has been particularly concerned with when and to whom alcoholic beverages may be sold").

A final type of statute punishes those who "permit" or "allow" or "suffer" some forbidden thing to be done—e.g., "one who sells or permits to be sold intoxicating liquors to a minor is punishable by * * *." The better view is that an employer does not "allow" or "permit" his employee to do an act unless he knows of or authorizes it,[26] or at least is reckless in failing to know of it,[27] but some courts have construed such language so as to impose upon the employer liability without fault on account of the act of the employee.[28]

WESTLAW REFERENCES

vicarious** /s liab! responsib! /p (mental mind /s state element intent) "mens rea" fault /p crim**** penal

(c) Constitutionality. Statutes imposing criminal liability upon the innocent employer for the illegal conduct of his employee are generally upheld as constitutional.[29] The assumption is that it "is not too onerous a burden" to require the employer to "control and supervise his employees."[30] The Supreme Court has never passed directly upon the constitutional limits of vicarious liability, but it is noteworthy that in *United States v. Park*[31] the Court upheld the imposition of

liability upon a corporation president who had a "responsible relation" to the corporate conduct which was criminal and who did not show he was "powerless" to prevent the violation.

Park has been viewed by lower courts as relevant to the constitutional issue.[32] Consistent with *Park* are those cases which uphold the vicarious liability provision by reading in an "escape valve" regarding certain violations clearly beyond the defendant's control, as where a statute making the owner of a car liable for all parking violations involving that vehicle is construed as not applicable if the car was stolen.[33] By the same token, cases holding the imposition of vicarious liability unconstitutional typically stress that liability is imposed even as to persons over whom the defendant has no control[34] or even if the defendant had done everything within his power to prevent the violation.[35] Apparently a "responsible relation" can be grounded in an employment[36] or bailment[37] relationship, but not a parent-child relationship.[38]

The Pennsylvania case of *Commonwealth v. Koczwara*[39] imposes another quite proper limitation even when vicarious liability is imposed for conduct by the defendant's employ-

26. So construed in People v. Forbath, 5 Cal.App.2d 767, 42 P.2d 108 (1935); Thurman v. Adams, 82 Miss. 204, 33 So. 944 (1903).

27. See G. Williams, supra note 22, at § 60.

28. E.g., State v. Anderson, 127 La. 1041, 54 So. 344 (1911).

29. E.g., In re Marley, 29 Cal.2d 525, 175 P.2d 832 (1946) (statute making it crime to sell article at short weight himself or by his employee, *held*, no violation of due process or equal protection); see Annot., 43 L.R.A. (N.S.) 2, 36 (1913).

But see Davis v. City of Peachtree City, 251 Ga. 219, 304 S.E.2d 701 (1983) (city ordinance making liquor permit licensee responsible for the actions of an employee who sold wine to a minor violates the due process clause, as the city's "admittedly legitimate interests of deterring employers from allowing their employees to break the law and of facilitating the enforcement of these laws" did not justify imposition of the burdens placed upon the licensee upon conviction, especially because "there are other, less onerous alternatives which sufficiently promote these interests," such as resort to civil penalties).

30. People v. Travers, 52 Cal.App.3d 111, 124 Cal.Rptr. 728 (1975).

31. 421 U.S. 658, 95 S.Ct. 1903, 44 L.Ed.2d 489 (1975).

32. City of Chicago v. Hertz Commercial Leasing Corp., 71 Ill.2d 333, 17 Ill. Dec. 1, 375 N.E.2d 1285 (1978); Iowa City v. Nolan, 239 N.W.2d 102 (Iowa 1976).

33. Iowa City v. Nolan, 239 N.W.2d 102 (Iowa 1976).

34. City of Campellsburg v. Odewalt, 24 Ky.L.R. 1717, 72 S.W. 314 (1903) (ordinance providing that person in possession of premises on which liquor is dispensed in violation of law is guilty, *held* unconstitutional; court says otherwise defendant would be responsible for those who came onto his land without his authority).

35. State v. Akers, 119 N.H. 161, 400 A.2d 38 (1979) (statute making parent criminally liable for offenses of minor children in operation of snowmobile violates due process, as it applies even if the conduct had been forbidden and parent had done all he could do to prevent it).

36. E.g., In re Marley, 29 Cal.2d 525, 175 P.2d 832 (1946).

37. E.g., City of Chicago v. Hertz Commercial Leasing Corp., 71 Ill.2d 333, 17 Ill. Dec. 1, 375 N.E.2d 1285 (1978).

38. State v. Akers, 119 N.H. 161, 400 A.2d 38 (1979). See Note, 6 Val.U.L.Rev. 332 (1972). Compare parental responsibility in tort law, discussed in Note, 32 Case W.Res.L.Rev. 559 (1982).

39. 397 Pa. 575, 155 A.2d 825 (1959), noted in 5 Vill.L. Rev. 682 (1960).

ee. Koczwara, a tavern owner, was convicted of violating the liquor code on the basis of acts committed by his bartender which occurred in his absence and without his knowledge or consent. As a second offender, he received the mandatory penalty of a $500 fine and three months in jail. The court held that punishment by imprisonment in such circumstances would be a denial of due process under the state constitution. "It would be unthinkable to impose vicarious criminal responsibility in cases involving true crimes. Although to hold a principal criminally liable might possibly be an effective means of enforcing law and order, it would do violence to our more sophisticated modern-day concepts of justice. * * * A man's *liberty* cannot rest on so frail a reed as whether his employee will commit a mistake in judgment." [40]

The distinction drawn by the court between a fine and imprisonment is an appropriate one.[41] To the extent that vicarious liability can be justified in the criminal law, it should not be utilized to bring about the type of moral condemnation which is implicit when a sentence of imprisonment is imposed.[42] On the other hand, imposition of a fine is consistent with the rationale behind vicarious criminal liability. Vicarious liability is imposed because of the nature and inherent danger of certain business activities and the difficulties of establishing actual fault in the operation of such businesses. A fine, unlike imprisonment, is less personal and is more properly viewed as a penalty on the business enterprise.[43]

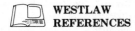 **WESTLAW REFERENCES**

topic(92) /p vicarious** /s liab! responsib!

("iowa city" /s nolan) koczwara /p (vicarious** /s liab! responsib!) "respondent superior" /p constitution! unconstitution! "due process" "equal protection"

(d) Pros and Cons of Vicarious-Liability Crimes. The reasons for enacting vicarious-liability statutory crimes, imposing liability upon innocent and careful employers for the conduct of their employees acting within the scope of their employers' business, are the same as those which underlie strict-liability crimes.[44] That the employer knew of or authorized the employee's conduct is sometimes difficult to prove, so the legislature makes the matters of knowledge and authorization irrelevant. The number of prosecutions to be expected may be such that the legislature undertakes to relieve the prosecution of the time-consuming task of proving the employer's knowledge or authority. Perhaps the legislature hopes that the prosecuting officials will use the statute only against persons who probably did know of or authorize the employee's conduct in question. Perhaps too vicarious-liability crimes tend to make employers more careful in the selection and supervision of their employees than they otherwise would be.

Yet, it must be recognized that the imposition of criminal liability for faultless conduct is contrary to the basic Anglo-American premise of criminal justice that crime requires personal fault on the part of the accused. Perhaps the answer should be the same as the answer proposed in the case of strict-liability crimes: it is proper for the legislature to single out some special areas of human activity and impose vicarious liability on employers who are without personal fault, but the matter should not be called a "crime" [45] and the

40. Cases upholding the imposition of vicarious liability often stress that only fines are involved. See, e.g., City of Chicago v. Hertz Commercial Leasing Corp., 71 Ill.2d 333, 17 Ill.Dec. 1, 375 N.E.2d 1285 (1978); State v. Beaudry, 123 Wis.2d 40, 365 N.W.2d 593 (1985). But other courts have upheld vicarious liability statutes notwithstanding the imposition of a short term of imprisonment on the employer. In re Marley, 29 Cal.2d 525, 175 P.2d 832 (1946); Hershorn v. State, 108 Colo. 43, 113 P.2d 680 (1941).

41. "Where the offense * * * is punishable by imprisonment * * * it seems clear that the doctrine of

respondeat superior must be repudiated." Sayre, supra note 3, at 717.

42. Model Penal Code § 2.06, Comment at 306 (1985).

43. This is so even though it is the operator of the business, as an individual, who is fined. On enterprise liability, see § 3.10.

44. See § 3.8(c).

45. In this sense, the *Koczwara* case, described in the text above, may not go far enough. Thus, a dissenting judge objected: "If it is wrong to send a person to jail for acts committed by another, is it not wrong to convict him

punishment should not include more than a fine or forfeiture or other civil penalty; that is, it should not include imprisonment. As the law now stands, however, in almost all jurisdictions imprisonment and the word "criminal" may be visited upon perfectly innocent employers for the sins of their employees.

If the problem is essentially one of the difficulty in proving actual fault by the person being held vicariously liable, then any assessment of the vicarious liability solution must take into account alternative means of dealing with that problem. One which has sometimes been utilized is adoption of a statutory inference or presumption which has the effect of imposing some kind of burden on the defendant to prove lack of knowledge or authorization regarding the other person's conduct. Of course, there are constitutional limits upon what may be done along these lines,[46] and some [47] but not all [48] of these statutes have been held unconstitutional. Indeed, it is sometimes said that imposition of vicarious liability is the "safe" alternative, to be preferred over burden-shifting statutes.[49] But even if this is so, the vicarious liability need not be unlimited. Consistent with the constitutional power to characterize certain matters as affirmative defenses to be proved by the defendant,[50] a vicarious liability statute might allow a defendant to avoid conviction by proving that he had exercised due diligence to prevent the crime.[51]

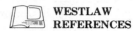

WESTLAW REFERENCES

vicarious** /s liab! responsib! /p public /s interest welfare policy

§ 3.10 Liability Without Fault—Enterprise Liability

Contrary to the early common law view, it is now generally conceded that a corporation may be held criminally liable for conduct performed by an agent of the corporation acting in its behalf within the scope of his employment. Under the better view, called the "superior agent" rule, corporate criminal liability for other than strict-liability regulatory offenses is limited to situations in which the conduct is performed or participated in by the board of directors or a high managerial agent. Partnerships and unincorporated associations may also be held criminally liable when so provided by statute, which is frequently the case as to regulatory offenses.

Enterprise officers and employees are not ordinarily held personally liable for crimes of the enterprise or of their subordinates except under usual principles of accountability. If the individual personally engaged in the criminal conduct or directed or permitted its com-

at all? There are those who value their good names to the extent that they see as much harm is a degrading criminal conviction as in a jail sentence. The laceration of a man's reputation, the blemishing of his good name, the wrecking of his prestige by a criminal court conviction may blast a person's chances for honorable success in life to such an extent that a jail sentence can hardly add much to the ruin already wrought to him by the conviction alone."

This objection would be met by limiting vicarious liability to what the Model Penal Code characterizes as an "offense," which is subject only to civil penalties and does not give rise to any disability or legal disadvantage based upon conviction of a criminal offense. Model Penal Code § 1.04(5).

46. See § 2.13.

47. E.g., City of Missoula v. Shea, ___ Mont. ___, 661 P.2d 410 (1983) (statutory presumption that registered owner of vehicle is the person who illegally parked it is invalid); Doe v. City of Trenton, 143 N.J.Super. 128, 362 A.2d 1200 (1976) (rebuttable presumption that parent "permitted or suffered" minor child to violate the law where violation occurred within year of delinquency adjudication is invalid).

48. E.g., Commonwealth v. Pauley, 368 Mass. 286, 331 N.E.2d 901 (1975) (upholding statute permitting inference that registered owner who offers no explanation is the person who was driving the car when it involved in violation of toll tunnel regulation).

49. In Commonwealth v. Pauley, supra note 48, the court observed: "It is perhaps worth mentioning that the Turnpike Authority could have avoided constitutional questions in the present situation by turning the offense into a 'public welfare' offense, in which any requirement of 'intent to evade' would be eliminated and the registered owner made liable in a stated sum for failure of anyone operating his car to pay the toll." See also City of Missoula v. Shea, supra note 47, invalidating the presumption but upholding another part of the statutory scheme utilizing a vicarious liability theory.

50. See § 1.8(c).

51. Cf. Model Penal Code § 2.07(5), allowing corporations and unincorporated associations a "due diligence" defense in certain circumstances.

mission, it is no defense that the offense was performed on behalf of the enterprise.

(a) Corporations. The early common law view was that a corporation could not be guilty of a crime: it had no mind, and thus was incapable of the criminal intent then required for all crimes; it had no body, and thus could not be imprisoned.[1] This view has changed with the growth and development of the corporate entity in the modern business world,[2] and today it is almost universally conceded that a corporation may be criminally liable for actions or omissions of its agents in its behalf.[3]

Movement away from the old common law view began, as might be expected, with strict liability welfare offenses, for there no mental state was required and the penalty (a fine) was such that it could be imposed upon a corporation. Initially, corporations were prosecuted only for acts of nonfeasance.[4] The case for corporate criminal liability was strongest in such instances, for the public duty imposed by law (e.g., to keep a railroad bridge in repair) seemed just as applicable to corporations as to others, and no individual corporate employee could be said to be in breach of this duty. This reasoning led some courts to rule that a corporation could not be convicted for misfeasance,[5] but this view has not prevailed.[6] Rather, courts abandoned the nonfeasance-misfeasance distinction on two grounds: (1) the distinction often proved to be more a matter of form than of substance, in that the same offense often could be just as easily characterized as a failure to act (e.g., failure to construct a safe bridge) as an act (e.g., construction of a bridge in an unsafe manner);[7] and (2) it seemed appropriate to punish for misfeasance when the mischief aimed at by the penal statute could just as easily be produced by a corporation.[8]

Once corporations were subjected to criminal prosecution for the *acts* of their agents, it became apparent that a form of vicarious liability was involved. But the Supreme Court decided in *New York Cent. & H.R.R. v. United States*[9] that constitutionally "the act of agent, while exercising the authority delegated to him * * * may be controlled, in the interest of public policy, by imputing his act to his employer and imposing penalties upon the corporation for which he is acting." This language has been frequently relied upon in both federal[10] and state[11] cases, so that now it is said to be "familiar law that a substantive offense committed by a corporate employee in the scope of his employment will be imputed to the corporation."[12] That language, it should be noted, makes no distinction between imputing acts and mental state, reflecting the fact that courts have now concluded that a corporate agent may also supply the intent or other mental state needed for conviction of a corporation.[13] As one court noted, it is "as easy and logical to ascribe to a

---

§ 3.10

1. H. Henn & J. Alexander, Corporations and Other Business Enterprises 184 (3d ed. 1983).

2. See Brickey, Corporate Criminal Accountability: A Brief History and an Observation, 60 Wash.U.L.Q. 393 (1982).

3. United States v. Wise, 370 U.S. 405, 82 S.Ct. 1354, 8 L.Ed.2d 590 (1962); United States v. Koppers Co., Inc., 652 F.2d 290 (2d Cir.1981); United States v. FMC Corp., 572 F.2d 902 (2d Cir.1978); W.T. Grant v. Superior Court, 23 Cal.App.3d 284, 100 Cal.Rptr. 179 (1972); Commonwealth v. Beneficial Finance Co., 360 Mass. 188, 275 N.E.2d 33 (1971); State v. Pacific Powder Co., 226 Or. 502, 360 P.2d 530 (1961).

4. E.g., New York & G. L. R. Co. v. State, 50 N.J.L. 303, 13 A. 1 (1888); People v. Clark, 8 N.Y.Cr. 169, 14 N.Y.S. 642 (1891).

5. State v. Great Works Mill & Mfg. Co., 20 Me. 41, 37 Am.Dec. 38 (1841).

6. E.g., State ex rel. Losey v. Willard, 54 So.2d 183 (Fla.1951).

7. Commonwealth v. Proprietors of New Bedford Bridge, 2 (Gray) 68 Mass. 339 (1854).

8. Commonwealth v. N.Y. Cent. & H. River R. Co., 206 Mass. 417, 92 N.E. 766 (1910).

9. 212 U.S. 481, 29 S.Ct. 304, 53 L.Ed. 613 (1909).

10. E.g., Old Monastery Co. v. United States, 147 F.2d 905 (4th Cir.1945); United States v. New York Great A. & P. Tea Co., 67 F.Supp. 626 (E.D.Ill.1946).

11. E.g., Regan v. Kroger Grocery & Baking Co., 386 Ill. 284, 54 N.E.2d 210 (1944); State v. Western Union Tel. Co., 13 N.J. 172, 80 A.2d 342 (1951).

12. United States v. Thompson-Powell Drilling Co., 196 F.Supp. 571 (N.D.Tex.1961).

13. United States v. Dye Construction Co., 510 F.2d 78 (10th Cir.1975); United States v. Carter, 311 F.2d 934 (6th Cir.1963); State v. I. & M. Amusements, Inc., 10 Ohio App. 2d 153, 226 N.E.2d 567 (1966).

corporation an evil mind as it is to impute to it a sense of contractual obligation." [14]

It does not necessarily follow, of course, that vicarious corporate liability exists with respect to all crimes. For one thing, if the statute only provides for the punishment of death or imprisonment, then a corporation is not subject to prosecution under it because of the impossibility of imposing such a sentence upon a corporation.[15] This problem is often obviated in modern codes by a special provision which permits fines on corporations in fixed amounts for offenses not otherwise carrying such a penalty,[16] and such statutes are not invalid as discriminatory where part of the punishment provided for individuals could not be applied to corporations.[17] Another limitation expressed in dicta in earlier cases is that some crimes, such as bigamy, perjury, rape or murder, are inherently human and thus not subject to commission by a corporation.[18] It is now established that a corporation may be guilty of manslaughter,[19] and it has been persuasively argued that there "is no logical reason why a corporation should not equally be able to incur criminal liability for murder." [20]

Sometimes the language of the statute must be examined in order to determine whether the legislature intended the statute also to apply to corporations. For example, it has occasionally been held that a statutory definition of homicide as "the killing of one human being by the act, procurement or omission of another" is inapplicable to a corporation because the word "another" clearly means another human being,[21] although it seems more logical to say that a corporation can (indeed, only can) kill one human by the act of another human. The word "person" is common in criminal statutes, and is sometimes defined in a general provision as including corporations unless a contrary legislative intention clearly appears in the statute.[22] In the absence of such a statutory definition, the general rule followed today by courts is that "the word 'person' in a penal statute which is intended to inhibit an act, means 'person in law' (that is, an artificial as well as a natural person), and therefore includes corporations, if they are within the spirit and purpose of the stat-

14. United States v. MacAndrews & Forbes Co., 149 F. 823 (C.C.S.D.N.Y.1906).

15. People v. Strong, 363 Ill. 602, 2 N.E.2d 942 (1936); State v. Truax, 130 Wash. 69, 226 P. 259 (1924).

If the penalty prescribed for an offense is both fine and imprisonment, the inability to punish by imprisonment does not prevent prosecution of a corporation and punishment by a fine upon conviction. United States v. Union Supply Co., 215 U.S. 50, 30 S.Ct. 15, 54 L.Ed. 87 (1909); State v. Salisbury Ice & Fuel Co., 166 N.C. 366, 81 S.E. 737 (1914); Commonwealth v. McIlwain School Bus Lines, Inc., 283 Pa.Super. 1, 423 A.2d 413 (1980).

16. E.g., Ill.—S.H.A. ch. 38, ¶ 1–7.

17. W. H. Small & Co. v. Commonwealth, 134 Ky. 272, 120 S.W. 361 (1909); People v. Schomig, 74 Cal.App. 109, 239 P. 413 (1925).

18. E.g., United States v. John Kelso Co. 86 F. 304 (N.D.Cal.1898); Stewart v. Waterloo Turn Verein, 71 Iowa 226, 32 N.W. 275 (1887).

19. See Granite Construction Co. v. Superior Court, 149 Cal.App.3d 465, 197 Cal.Rptr. 3 (1983); Commonwealth v. Fortner L.P. Gas Co., 610 S.W.2d 941 (Ky.App. 1980); State v. Lehigh Valley Ry. Co., 90 N.J.L. 372, 103 A. 685 (1917); Id. 92 N.J.L. 261, 106 A. 23 (1918), aff'd 94 N.J.L. 171, 111 A. 257 (1920); Commonwealth v. McIlwain School Bus Lines, Inc., 283 Pa.Super. 1, 423 A.2d 413 (1980).

In *Granite Construction* the corporation argued that as an economically motivated entity it could be liable only for property crimes. The court responded: "This argument is unsuccessful. It overlooks the substantial indirect economic benefit that may accrue to the corporation through crimes against the person. To get these economic benefits, corporate management may shortcut expensive safety precautions, respond forcibly to strikes, or engage in criminal anticompetitive behavior."

For further discussion of corporate criminal liability for homicide, see Maakestad, A Historical Survey of Corporate Homicide in the United States, 69 Ill.B.J. 772 (1981); Comment, 17 Cal.West.L.Rev. 465 (1981); Note, 54 Notre Dame Law. 911 (1979).

20. Mueller, Mens Rea and the Corporation, 19 U.Pitt. L.Rev. 21, 23 (1957): "Why should not a corporation be guilty of murder where, for instance, a corporate resolution sends the corporation's workmen to a dangerous place of work without protection, all officers secreting from these workmen the fact that even a brief exposure to the particular work hazards will be fatal, as was the case in the notorious Hawk's Nest venture in West Virginia, where wholesale death was attributable to silicosis?"

21. People v. Rochester Ry. & Lt. Co., 195 N.Y. 102, 88 N.E. 22 (1909).

22. Most of the modern recodifications contain such a provision.

ute." [23] The same approach has been utilized in finding that the words "any tenant," [24] "everyone," [25] "whoever," [26] and "every owner" [27] may, in the proper context, include corporations.

WESTLAW REFERENCES

"enterprise liability" /p employee agent representative
101k526 /p criminal** /s liab! responsib! /p
    employee agent representative

(b) Corporate Liability: Policy Considerations. It must be emphasized again that corporate criminal liability is a form of vicarious liability.[28] Indeed, it sometimes involves what has been termed "vicarious liability twice removed,"[29] in that the shareholders may suffer for the criminal acts of the corporate management (without regard to the shareholders' opportunity to control the management) and also for those of lesser employees (without regard to the nature of the management's efforts to control these employees). This is a substantial departure from the ordinary rule that a principal is not answerable criminally for the acts of his agent without the principal's authorization, consent or knowledge,[30] and thus corporate criminal liability continues to be a matter of vigorous debate.[31]

The following arguments have been made in favor of corporate criminal liability: (1) that the corporate business entity is so common that such liability is necessary to effectuate regulatory policy;[32] (2) that the imposition of sanctions upon the stockholders will prompt them to "see that the corporate business is so conducted as not to injure others or infringe upon public right and good order";[33] (3) that often no one other than the corporation could be convicted, either because the offense is an omission of a duty imposed only on the corporation,[34] or because "the division of responsibility within a corporation is so great that it is difficult to fix on an individual";[35] (4) that, even when an individual agent could be convicted, it may be unjust to single out one person for substantial punishment when the offense resulted from habits common to the organization as a whole;[36] (5) that the fines should be borne by those who received the fruits of the illegal enterprise so as to prevent unjust enrichment;[37] (6) that proceeding against the corporation (rather than merely against an individual) serves to link the offense with the corporation in the public mind;[38] and (7) that vicarious liability is less severe here than if imposed upon a human principal, as the individual shareholders escape the opprobrium and incidental disabilities of a personal indictment or conviction and their loss is limited to the equity held in the corporation.[39]

A number of the above contentions have been challenged with these counter-arguments: (1) that the imposition of a criminal

---

23. Overland Cotton Mill Co. v. People, 32 Colo. 263, 75 P. 924 (1904).

24. State v. Rowland Lumber Co., 153 N.C. 610, 69 S.E. 58 (1910).

25. Union Colliery Co. v. Queen, 31 Can.S.Ct. 81 (1900).

26. United States v. American Socialist Soc'y, 260 F. 885 (S.D.N.Y.1919); Commonwealth v. Graustein & Co., 209 Mass. 38, 95 N.E. 97 (1911). Contra: Parkway Cabs, Inc. v. City of Cincinnati, 52 Ohio App. 195, 3 N.E.2d 630 (1935).

27. United States v. Van Schaick, 134 F. 592 (1904).

28. See Note, 60 Harv.L.Rev. 283 (1946).

29. Mueller, supra note 20, at 42.

30. People v. Jarvis, 135 Cal.App. 288, 27 P.2d 77 (1933); State v. Burns, 215 Minn. 182, 9 N.W.2d 518 (1943).

31. See, e.g., Coffee, "No Soul to Damn; No Body to Kick": An Unscandalized Inquiry Into the Problem of Corporate Punishment, 79 Mich.L.Rev. 386 (1981); Elkins,

Corporations and the Criminal Law: An Uneasy Alliance, 65 Ky.L.Rev. 73 (1976); Fisse, Reconstructing Corporate Criminal Law: Deterrence, Retribution, Fault, and Sanctions, 56 So.Cal.L.Rev. 114 (1983); Miller, Corporate Criminal Liability: A Principle Extended to Its Limits, 38 Fed. Bar. J. 49 (1979); Developments in the Law, 92 Harv.L. Rev. 1227 (1979); Comments, 73 Calif.L.Rev. 443 (1985); 29 U.C.L.A.L.Rev. 447 (1982).

32. Model Penal Code § 2.07, Comment at 337 (1985).

33. Commonwealth v. Pulaski Co. Agr. & Mech. Ass'n, 92 Ky. 197, 17 S.W. 442 (1891).

34. G. Williams, Criminal Law: The General Part § 283 (2d ed. 1961).

35. Id.

36. Id.; Model Penal Code § 2.07, Comment (Tent. Draft No. 4, 1955).

37. Id.

38. G. Williams, supra note 34, at § 283.

39. Model Penal Code § 2.07, Comment at 337 (1985)

fine on the corporation is often ineffective as a profit-diminishing sanction, in that the economic cost of the fine may be "passed on" to the consumer by means of higher prices or rates;[40] (2) that in the "endocratic" corporation (the large publicly-held corporation whose stock is scattered in small fractions among thousands of stockholders) the stockholders simply cannot control the management, and thus should not be penalized for their failure to do so;[41] (3) that the availability of the corporation as a defendant provides a convenient "scapegoat" whereby corporate agents engaged in the wrongdoing escape the personal criminal liability which would be a greater deterrent;[42] (4) that depriving wrongdoers of their ill-gotten gains is not a function of the criminal law,[43] and that in any event fines are usually unrelated to the gains and may penalize stockholders other than those who profited from the illegal activity;[44] and (5) that the criminal prosecutions of corporations are not adequately reported to the public to result in damage to the "corporate image." [45]

Unfortunately, most of the court decisions concerning vicarious corporate criminal liability do not involve an assessment of these arguments. Rather, the tort principle of *respondeat superior* is applied without question,[46] so that the crimes of any employee—no matter what his position in the corporate hierarchy [47]—become the crimes of the corporation. And if the crimes require "intent," "knowledge," or some other mental state, it is often said that such a mental state by "subordinate, even menial, employees" suffices.[48]

 WESTLAW REFERENCES

corporat*** company /s criminal** penal /s liab! responsib! /p vicarious** "respondent superior"

corporat*** company /s criminal** penal /s liab! responsib! /p employee agent representative /p public /4 policy welfare interest

corporat*** company /p criminal** penal /s liab! responsib! /p employee agent representative /p benefi! nonbenefi!

(c) Corporate Liability: Limitations. Although it is unwise to assume that vicarious liability always automatically follows from strict liability,[49] it is fair to say that generally the imposition of criminal liability on corporations for acts of any and all employees which constitute violations of strict-liability regulatory offenses is sound. For the most part, these statutes may be said to impose a duty upon the corporation not to act in such a way as to endanger the health, safety or welfare of the general public, and thus the corporation is quite properly held for such acts by any employee. But, if the crime is one for which mens rea is required, should the mental state of any corporate employee suffice? No, it has been forcefully argued; the mind or brain of the corporation consists only of "those officers, whether elected or appointed, who direct, supervise and manage the corporation within its business sphere and policy-wise, the 'inner circle.' "[50] Under this approach, for example, the intent to steal by a minor corporate employee in taking another's property within the scope of his employment and in behalf of the corporation would not constitute the requisite corporate mens rea,

40. G. Williams, supra note 34, at § 283; Note, 71 Yale L.J. 280, 285 n. 17 (1961).

41. Id. at 281.

42. Id. at 292 n. 50.

43. G. Williams, supra note 34, at § 186.

44. Id. at § 283.

45. Note, 71 Yale L.J. 280, 287 n. 35 (1961).

46. See Lee, Corporate Criminal Liability, 28 Colum.L. Rev. 1, 181 (1928); Note, 60 Harv.L.Rev. 283 (1946).

47. United States v. Chicago Express, Inc., 273 F.2d 751 (7th Cir.1960); United States v. George F. Fish, Inc., 154 F.2d 798 (2d Cir.1946); Regan v. Kroger Grocery & Baking Co., 386 Ill. 284, 54 N.E.2d 210 (1944); Common-

wealth v. Beneficial Finance Co., 360 Mass. 188, 275 N.E.2d 33 (1971).

48. E.g., Standard Oil Co. v. United States, 307 F.2d 120 (5th Cir.1962). The prosecution need not prove that a specific person had the requisite mental state; it is sufficient to show that some agent of the corporation did. United States v. American Stevedores, Inc., 310 F.2d 47 (2d Cir.1962). Collective knowledge of several employees can provide the requisite state of mind. Inland Freight Lines v. United States, 191 F.2d 313 (10th Cir.1951); United States v. T.I.M.E.–D.C., Inc., 381 F.Supp. 730 (W.D.Va. 1974).

49. See § 3.9.

50. Mueller, supra note 20, at 41.

and thus the corporation would not be guilty of larceny.[51]

This is essentially the position taken in the Model Penal Code and reflected (to some degree at least) in several modern recodifications. Except when the offense consists of an omission to discharge a specific duty of affirmative performance imposed on the corporation by law,[52] or the offense is a violation [53] or is defined by a statute outside the Code in which a legislative purpose to impose liability on corporations plainly appears,[54] under the Model Penal Code a corporation may be convicted of the commission of an offense only if it was "authorized, requested, commanded, performed or recklessly tolerated by the board of directors or by a high managerial agent acting in behalf of the corporation within the scope of his office or employment." [55] Many modern recodifications contain a provision along these lines.[56] "High managerial agent" is defined in the Code as "an officer of a corporation or * * * any other agent of a corporation * * * having duties of such responsibility that his conduct may fairly be assumed to represent the policy of the corporation."[57] Some modern codes contain such a definition, while others include a broader definition encompassing both those who have re-

sponsibility as to the formulation of policy and those who supervise in a managerial capacity.[58]

When corporate liability is possible because the offense is a violation or is defined by a statute plainly so providing, then under the Model Penal Code "it shall be a defense if the defendant proves by a preponderance of evidence that the high managerial agent having supervisory responsibility over the subject matter of the offense employed due diligence to prevent its commission." [59] This latter provision, to be found in only a small number of modern recodifications,[60] shifts the presumption of *mens rea*, but may be justified on the ground that the prosecution's normal burden of proof would frustrate enforcement of laws specifically applicable to corporations.[61]

The Model Penal Code provision is generally consistent with those cases adopting the so-called "superior agent" rule. Under this rule, corporate criminal liability (except for strict liability offenses) is limited to situations in which the criminal conduct is performed or participated in by corporate agents sufficiently high in the hierarchy to make it reasonable to assume that their acts reflect the policy of the corporate body.[62] Most of these cases

51. People v. Canadian Fur Trappers' Corp., 248 N.Y. 159, 161 N.E. 455 (1928).

52. Model Penal Code § 2.07(1)(b) allows conviction of a corporation in such circumstances in any event, as do most of the modern recodifications.

53. Under the Code, an offense is a violation "if it is so designated in this Code or in the law defining the offense or if no other sentence than a fine, or fine and forfeiture or other civil penalty is authorized upon conviction or if it is defined by a statute other than this Code which now provides that the offense shall not constitute a crime. A violation does not constitute a crime and conviction of a violation shall not give rise to any disability or legal disadvantage based on conviction of a criminal offense." Model Penal Code § 1.04(5).

54. If the offense is of either of these types, then under the Code it is only necessary that the conduct be performed by an agent of the corporation acting in behalf of the corporation within the scope of his office or employment. Model Penal Code § 2.07(1)(a).

55. Model Penal Code § 2.07(1)(c).

56. But in most of these jurisdictions this "superior agent" requirement is not applicable in misdemeanor cases.

57. Model Penal Code § 2.07(4)(c).

58. The difference between the two definitions is highlighted by State v. Chapman Dodge Center, Inc., 428 So.2d 413 (La.1983), where a corporation was convicted of unauthorized use of property, a crime requiring fraudulent intent. The court reversed because the "record reveals no evidence of complicity by the officers or the board of directors," but the dissent objected it should suffice that the general manager, left in charge of the auto dealership and "in whom the corporation had rested the authority to manage its day-to-day business operations," committed the offense.

59. Model Penal Code § 2.07(5), which adds this qualification: "This paragraph shall not apply if it is plainly inconsistent with the legislative purpose in defining the particular offense." The qualification is criticized in Mueller, supra note 20, at 41–46.

60. For criticism of this due diligence defense, see Elkins, Corporations and the Criminal Law: An Uneasy Alliance, 65 Ky.L.Rev. 73 (1976); Comment, 29 U.C.L.A.L. Rev. 447 (1982). For defense of it, see Miller, Corporate Criminal Liability: A Principal Extended to Its Limits, 38 Fed.Bar.J. 49 (1979).

61. Mueller, supra note 20, at 43 n. 87.

62. E.g., People v. Canadian Fur Trappers' Corp., 248 N.Y. 159, 161 N.E. 455 (1928). See discussion of cases in Notes, 50 Geo.L.J. 547 (1962); 60 Harv.L.Rev. 283 (1946).

assume it would not be necessary for the prosecution to prove the necessary corporate *mens rea;* rather the corporation could rebut the presumption of responsibility by showing it had taken adequate precautions against its commission.[63]

Another limitation on vicarious corporate criminal liability should be re-emphasized here, for (unlike the "superior agent" rule) it is universally accepted: except where the law defining the offense specifically provides otherwise, the conduct giving rise to corporate liability must be "performed by an agent of the corporation acting in behalf of the corporation within the scope of his office or employment."[64] However, this does not mean that a corporation can escape liability merely by contending that criminal acts are "ultra vires" (beyond the power of the corporation, as defined by its charter or act of incorporation),[65] that the agents acts were not expressly authorized,[66] or that the agent acted contrary to instructions.[67] The criminal act must be directly related to the performance of the duties which the officer or agent has the broad authority to perform,[68] and must be done with the "intention to perform it as a part of or incident to a service on account of which he is employed."[69] It is not necessary that the criminal acts actually benefit the corporation,[70] but an agent's acts are not "in

behalf of the corporation" if undertaken solely to advance the agent's own interests or interests of parties other than the corporate employer.[71] "Thus the taking in or paying out of money by a bank teller, while certainly one of his regular functions, would hardly cast the corporation for criminal liability if in such 'handling' the faithless employee was pocketing the funds as an embezzler or handing them over to a confederate under some ruse."[72]

 **WESTLAW REFERENCES**

101k529 101k526 /p intent "mens rea" (mental mind /s element state) /p agent officer employee representative

101k529 101k526 /p (scope /s employment authority) "ultra vires" /p agent officer employee representative

(d) Partnerships and Other Unincorporated Associations. Generally, it may be said that the fact that the defendant is a partner in a business enterprise has no bearing on the question of whether he is accountable for the criminal conduct of others. The usual rules of accountability apply,[73] and thus a partner is not by virtue of his status liable for the crimes of his co-partners or employees of the partnership,[74] although he is liable for such crimes when he has authorized or participated in them.[75]

---

63. Holland Furnace Co. v. United States, 158 F.2d 2 (6th Cir.1946) (where salesman obtained fraudulent statement, corporation could show this was done contrary to directions which were "in good faith and not merely formal and colorable"); John Gund Brewing Co. v. United States, 204 F. 17, modified, 206 F. 386 (8th Cir.1913).

64. Model Penal Code § 2.07(1).

65. United States v. Mirror Lake Golf & Country Club, Inc., 232 F.Supp. 167 (W.D.Mo.1964); Louisville R. Co. v. Commonwealth, 130 Ky. 738, 114 S.W. 343 (1908).

66. United States v. American Radiator & Standard Sanitary Corp., 433 F.2d 174 (3d Cir.1970); Continental Baking Co. v. United States, 281 F.2d 137 (6th Cir.1960); Stewart v. Waterloo Turn Verein, 71 Iowa 226, 32 N.W. 275 (1887).

67. United States v. Hilton Hotels Corp., 467 F.2d 1000 (9th Cir.1972); United States v. Harry L. Young & Sons, 464 F.2d 1295 (10th Cir.1972). But, this is a relevant fact under the "superior agent" rule.

68. Continental Baking Co. v. United States, 281 F.2d 137 (6th Cir.1960).

69. Restatement (Second) of Agency § 235 (1958).

70. United States v. Carter, 311 F.2d 934 (6th Cir. 1963); Old Monastery Co. v. United States, 147 F.2d 905 (4th Cir.1945); United States v. Empire Packing Co., 174 F.2d 16 (7th Cir.1949).

71. United States v. Ridglea State Bank, 357 F.2d 495 (5th Cir.1966); Standard Oil Co. of Tex. v. United States, 307 F.2d 120 (5th Cir.1962).

72. Standard Oil Co. of Tex. v. United States, 307 F.2d 120 (5th Cir.1962).

73. See §§ 6.6–6.8.

74. Gordon v. United States, 347 U.S. 909, 74 S.Ct. 473, 98 L.Ed. 1067 (1954); United States v. Wilson, 59 F.2d 97 (W.D.Wash.1932); State v. Maurisky, 102 Conn. 634, 129 A. 714 (1925); Vostre v. State, 142 Fla. 366, 195 So. 151 (1940); People v. Wilcox, 83 Mich.App. 654, 269 N.W.2d 256 (1978); J. Crane & A. Bromberg, Partnerships § 54 (1968).

75. Levin v. United States, 5 F.2d 598 (9th Cir.1925); State v. O'Kelley, 258 Mo. 345, 167 S.W. 980 (1914); J. Crane & A. Bromberg, supra note 74 at § 54.

Of course, a particular criminal statute may be construed to impose vicarious liability on a partner, as an individual, for crimes committed by his co-partners or partnership employees. When the statute in question does not do so explicitly, the problem of determining the actual meaning of the statute is not unlike that discussed earlier.[76] Once again, courts have a tendency to find that a statute imposes vicarious liability because it imposes strict liability, so that it is sometimes said that partners are liable for those crimes committed in the operation of the business which do not require proof of any mental state.[77] However, for the reasons stated earlier,[78] vicarious liability should not automatically follow from strict liability; determination of legislative intent requires that the two questions (i.e., does the statute impose liability on the actor without requiring mental fault; does the statute impose liability on others) be separately considered. Under this approach, it may nonetheless be concluded that a given strict liability statute [79] also makes partners vicariously liable, as where it imposes a nondelegable duty on the business [80] or where it appears that a contrary result would frustrate the policy behind the statute.[81]

What, then, of criminal liability of the *partnership* as a business enterprise, as distinguished from the several partners as individuals? In the absence of a statute imposing vicarious liability, it is clear that the partnership is not criminally liable for the crimes of individual partners or employees of the partnership.[82] Even with a statute which does impose vicarious liability, the liability is usually said to be that of the partners as individuals rather than the partnership as an entity.[83] This is because of the traditional view that a partnership has no legal existence apart from its several individual partners, so that only the partners as individuals are subject to criminal proceedings.[84] There is, however, a movement away from this view, called the aggregate theory of partnership, toward the entity theory, under which the partnership can sue and be sued in its own name.[85] In a jurisdiction which has adopted the entity theory, it is possible that a court might rule that under a statute providing for vicarious liability for certain business crimes (but making no specific reference to liability of partnerships), prosecution could be brought against the partnership.

Even where the entity theory has not been adopted, there are two situations in which prosecution of the partnership is possible. One is where the offense consists of an omission to perform some act which the partnership (as opposed to the partners, as individu-

---

76. See § 3.9(b).

77. J. Crane & A. Bromberg, supra note 75, at § 54.

78. See § 3.9.

79. This is not to say that vicarious liability could not be imposed even when the actor must have mental fault. See § 3.9 n. 5. Illustrative, though liability is imposed on the partnership rather than the partners as individuals, is United States v. A. & P. Trucking Co., 358 U.S. 121, 79 S.Ct. 203, 3 L.Ed.2d 165 (1958), dealing with "knowing" violations by partnership employees.

80. E.g., City of Spokane v. Patterson, 46 Wash. 93, 89 P. 402 (1907) (partner prosecuted for violation of city ordinance proscribing blasting within city without taking safety precautions, blast was by employee who failed to follow partner's instructions; *held,* partner may be convicted, as purpose of ordinance was to impose nondelegable duty on those in quarrying business). Cf. People v. Berridge, 212 Mich. 576, 180 N.W. 381 (1920) (possession of liquor violation; *held,* liquor stored in business premises of partnership is possessed by all partners).

81. E.g., Ex parte Casperson, 69 Cal.App.2d 441, 159 P.2d 88 (1945) (partners prosecuted for violation of pure

food laws, though criminal acts—shipping inedible and mislabelled eggs—apparently done by another party; *held,* partners may be convicted, for just as sole proprietor cannot escape liability where sale by clerk, partners should not escape liability on similar showing; court also emphasizes that if only actor could be reached, then law would have a loophole, as often it cannot be established what specific person acting for the partnership was responsible).

82. United States v. Brookman Co., 229 F.Supp. 862 (N.D.Cal.1964); State v. Spears, 57 N.M. 400, 259 P.2d 356 (1953).

83. Cf. People v. Stills, 302 Ill.App. 302, 23 N.E.2d 822 (1939) (where partnership guilty of crime, partners to be indicted as individuals, not as a firm).

84. People v. Schomig, 74 Cal.App. 109, 239 P. 413 (1925); X–L Liquors v. Taylor, 17 N.J. 444, 111 A.2d 753 (1955).

85. Soursos v. Mason City, 230 Iowa 157, 296 N.W. 807 (1941); Lobato v. Paulino, 304 Mich. 668, 8 N.W.2d 873 (1943); State v. Pielsticker, 118 Neb. 419, 225 N.W. 51 (1929).

als) is required by law to perform.[86] The other is where the statute in question expressly provides for liability of the partnership for conduct performed in its behalf,[87] although whether the legislature intended such a result in face of the prevailing aggregate theory may present a difficult issue. The leading case is *United States v. A. & P. Trucking Co.*,[88] involving prosecution of partnerships for "knowingly" violating certain Interstate Commerce Commission regulations and "knowingly and willfully" violating provisions of the Motor Carrier Act. The latter Act refers to "any person,"[89] but "person" is defined therein to mean "any individual, firm, copartnership, corporation, company, association, or joint-stock association."[90] The statute concerning the violation of ICC regulations refers to "whoever,"[91] but a separate enactment dealing with the construction of statutes provides that "in determining the meaning of any Act of Congress, unless the context indicates otherwise—* * * the words 'person' and 'whoever' include corporations, companies, associations, firms, partnerships, societies, and joint stock companies, as well as individuals."[92] On the basis of these provisions, a majority of the Court concluded that partnerships could be prosecuted for the violations in question. Congress could hardly have intended otherwise, the majority argued, as both enactments have as their purpose compliance by motor carriers with safety and

other requirements, and in effectuating this policy it could hardly make any difference what kind of business form is used by the carrier. Moreover, the words "knowingly" and "willfully" in the statutes do not indicate to the contrary; partnerships cannot so act, but neither can corporations, and as to both Congress must have intended to deter such violations by providing for the imposition of monetary sanctions on the business enterprise.[93]

As a matter of policy, it would appear that the kind of vicarious liability involved in the *A. & P. Trucking* case is generally preferable to vicarious liability of the partners as individuals. For one thing, it ensures that vicarious liability will not be utilized to impose the sanction of imprisonment, for the partnership can only be fined even if the statute in question also includes imprisonment as a sanction generally available.[94] For another, prosecution of the partnership instead of the partners protects the partners, as individuals, from acquiring criminal status and the disabilities or legal disadvantages which might flow from conviction of a crime.

Generally, what has been said above about partnerships is true of the other forms of unincorporated associations. Vicarious liability on the individual members thereof or on the business entity does not exist in the absence of a statute providing to the contrary.

---

86. Model Penal Code § 2.07(3)(b) so provides as to all unincorporated associations, as do some modern recodifications. Illustrative is Brown v. State, 22 Ala.App. 31, 111 So. 760 (1927) (prosecution for failure of partnership to obtain license for vehicle, prosecution of the partnership and fine on the group instead of individual partners appropriate; reversed on other grounds).

87. See Model Penal Code § 2.07(3)(a). Some modern recodifications contain similar provisions.

88. 358 U.S. 121, 79 S.Ct. 203, 3 L.Ed.2d 165 (1958), noted in 1 B.C.Ind. & Com.L.Rev. 109 (1959); 47 Geo.L.J. 807 (1959); 8 Kan.L.Rev. 486 (1960); 33 St.John's L.Rev. 404 (1959).

89. 49 U.S.C.A. § 322(a).

90. 49 U.S.C.A. § 303(a)(1).

91. 18 U.S.C.A. § 836.

92. 1 U.S.C.A. § 1. Most modern recodifications at the state level contain a definitional provision to the effect that the word "person" includes a partnership.

93. The Court stated:

"The business entity cannot be left free to break the law merely because its owners * * * do not personally participate in the infraction. The treasury of the business may not with impunity obtain the fruits of violations which are committed knowingly by agents of the entity in the scope of their employment. Thus pressure is brought on those who own the entity to see to it that their agents abide by the law."

Four members of the Court dissented as to the construction of the statute on ICC regulation violations. Because that statute did not explicitly subject partnerships to criminal liability, they believed that the rule of strict construction of penal statutes compelled the conclusion that partnerships were not covered, particularly in light of the fact that most states adhere to the aggregate theory of partnerships.

94. The Court stated:

"As in the case of corporations, the conviction of the entity can lead only to a fine levied on the firm's assets."

However, as illustrated by the statutes in the *A. & P. Trucking* case, it is quite common for regulatory legislation on both the federal and state level to provide for the application of criminal penalties to a variety of unincorporated groups.[95] Where the offense in question is not of the strict liability variety, the better view is that the unincorporated association (as well as the corporation) should ordinarily be entitled to prove by way of defense that the appropriate supervisory official exercised due diligence to prevent its commission.[96] Finally, it should be kept in mind that the fact vicarious liability has been imposed upon an unincorporated association in no way affects the liability of the individual who actually performed the criminal acts with any required mental fault.[97]

 **WESTLAW REFERENCES**

289k175 /p agent employee representative partner
289k67 41k27
101k369
(park /s 95 +4 1903) dotterweich /p agent officer
   representative employee /p criminal** penal

(e) Corporate Officers and Employees. A corporate agent who engages in criminal conduct is personally liable notwithstanding the fact that he acted in behalf of the corporation within the scope of his office.[98] Certain problems in holding the corporate employee liable have sometimes arisen, but these can be easily solved by sound drafting. For example, when the circumstances are such that the employee is an accessory to the crime committed by the corporation as a principal, it has been held that the accessory may not be subjected to greater liability than the principal. This means that if the offense does not allow for imposition of a fine, then the corporation cannot be held criminally liable and the employee-accessory cannot either.[99] And if the offense does allow for a fine and imprisonment, the employee-accessory may only be fined because that is the only sanction which may be imposed upon the corporation.[100] The Model Penal Code includes provisions to overcome these difficulties,[101] as do most of the modern recodifications.[102]

An officer of a corporation is not personally liable for the crimes of the corporation or of corporate employees merely by virtue of the fact that he is an officer.[103] Rather, the usual principles of accountability ordinarily apply,[104] so that it must be shown that the criminal acts were done by his direction or with his permission.[105] The question of who,

95. For a representative list of statutes and decisions, see Model Penal Code § 2.07, Comment at 342–43 (1985). Most modern recodifications define "person" as including an unincorporated association.

96. This is the position taken in Model Penal Code § 2.07(5).

97. Model Penal Code § 2.07(6)(a) & (c). Moreover, if the individual has primary responsibility for carrying out a duty imposed by law on the unincorporated association, and he recklessly fails to perform the duty, Model Penal Code § 2.07(6)(b) would permit conviction of the individual on this basis.

98. United States v. Wise, 370 U.S. 405, 82 S.Ct. 1354, 8 L.Ed.2d 590 (1962); Hartson v. People, 125 Colo. 1, 240 P.2d 907 (1951); State v. Pincus, 41 N.J.Super. 454, 125 A.2d 420 (1956); People v. Sakow, 45 N.Y.2d 131, 408 N.Y.S.2d 27, 379 N.E.2d 1157 (1978).

"Nonetheless, juries have frequently found corporate defendants criminally culpable while acquitting agents who clearly committed the criminal acts. This phenomenon perhaps reflects an intuitive feeling by jurors that individuals acting within the pressures of a bureaucratic and sometimes highly diffuse corporate structure are often unwitting or even unwilling participants in an illegal transaction, and that a criminal conviction is too harsh a sanction for business misconduct that is not of a highly immoral or detestable character." Note, 31 Vand.L.Rev. 965, 968 (1978).

99. People v. Strong, 363 Ill. 602, 2 N.E.2d 942 (1936).

100. People v. Duncan, 363 Ill. 495, 2 N.E.2d 705 (1936).

101. Section 2.07(6) provides that the individual is accountable "to the same extent as if [his conduct] were performed in his own name or behalf" and that "he is subject to the sentence authorized by law when a natural person is convicted of an offense of the grade and the degree involved."

102. Virtually all of them state that a person is accountable for what he does in the name of an organization. A lesser number expressly declare that the person may be sentenced as a natural person when accountable for the conduct of an organization.

103. State v. McBride, 215 Minn. 123, 9 N.W.2d 416 (1943); People v. Matherson, 35 N.Y.2d 694, 361 N.Y.S.2d 346, 319 N.E.2d 708 (1974). McCollum v. State, 165 Tex. Cr.R. 241, 305 S.W.2d 612 (1957).

104. See §§ 6.6–6.8.

105. State v. Pincus, 41 N.J.Super. 454, 125 A.2d 420 (1956); People v. Aldrich Restaurant Corp., 53 Misc.2d 574, 279 N.Y.S.2d 624 (1967); State v. McBride, 215 Minn. 123, 9 N.W.2d 416 (1943).

if anyone, should be held personally liable for the strict-liability criminal omissions of the corporation has been particularly troublesome. Under existing law, the corporate officer generally escapes individual liability even though he is under an affirmative obligation to perform the duty in behalf of the corporation.[106] The Model Penal Code position is that the corporate agent having "primary responsibility for the discharge of the duty" imposed by law on the corporation is accountable for "a reckless omission to perform the required act to the same extent as if the duty were imposed by law directly upon himself." [107] A few of the modern recodifications contain such a provision.

The Supreme Court has on two occasions confronted the question of when a corporate officer may be held criminally liable because of the commission of a public welfare type of offense by the corporation. *United States v. Dotterweich* [108] involved a prosecution of a corporation and defendant, its president and general manager, for two interstate shipments of misbranded and adulterated drugs. Company employees had merely repackaged drugs received from the manufacturer and sent them out in response to an order from a doctor, and defendant had no personal connection with either shipment. The Supreme Court affirmed Dotterweich's conviction, holding that all persons having a "responsible share in the furtherance of the transaction which the statute outlaws" violate the Federal Food, Drug and Cosmetic Act. Stressing that the statute was enacted as a regulatory measure to protect public health and welfare and was of the strict liability type, the *Dotterweich* majority concluded it "puts the burden of acting at hazard upon a person otherwise innocent but standing in responsible relation to a public danger." Despite the criticism of the four

dissenters "that guilt is personal and that it ought not lightly be imputed to a citizen who, like the respondent, has no evil intention or consciousness of wrongdoing," the majority concluded there was sufficient evidence to hold Dotterweich responsible for the shipment. But the precise meaning of *Dotterweich* was, at best, unclear; the Court never specified what evidence was decisive and declined to elaborate upon the "responsible relation" test, which was simply left to "the good sense of prosecutors, the wise guidance of trial judges, and the ultimate judgment of juries." Notwithstanding reference in *Dotterweich* to an aiding-and-abetting theory,[109] lower courts found the requisite "responsible relation" to be present absent any evidence the charged official participated in the illegal transaction or was even present at the time it occurred.[110]

In *United States v. Park,*[111] arising under the same Act, the corporation, a national retail food chain, and Park, president and chief executive officer of the corporation, were charged with causing food to be held in a warehouse where it was exposed to rodents and thereby became contaminated. Although the three dissenters in *Park* found the trial judge's instruction to the jury to find Park guilty if he "had a responsible relation to the situation" to be "nothing more than a tautology," the majority deemed this *Dotterweich*-style instruction sufficient. But once again the Court did not indicate just what evidence sufficed to show the requisite "responsible relation." At trial there had been testimony that Park was "responsible for the entire operation of the company," including providing sanitary conditions, but that he had delegated "normal operating duties," including sanitation, to trusted subordinates. Park had earlier received notice of unsanitary conditions at

---

106. People v. Clark, 8 N.Y.Cr.R. 169, 14 N.Y.S. 642 (1891).

107. Section 2.07(6)(b).

108. 320 U.S. 277, 64 S.Ct. 134, 88 L.Ed. 48 (1943).

109. The Court stated at one point: "To speak with technical accuracy, under § 301 [of the Act] a corporation may commit an offense and all persons who aid and abet its commission are equally guilty."

110. United States v. Shapiro, 491 F.2d 335 (6th Cir. 1974); Golden Grain Macaroni Co. v. United States, 209 F.2d 166 (9th Cir.1953).

111. 421 U.S. 658, 95 S.Ct. 1903, 44 L.Ed.2d 489 (1975). For other discussion of *Park,* see Sethi & Katz, The Expanding Scope of Personal Criminal Liability of Corporate Executives, 32 Food Drug Cosm.L.J. 544 (1977); Note, 69 J.Crim.L. & C. 75 (1978).

another warehouse, but had been assured his subordinates had taken corrective action. The majority asserted that the prosecution "establishes a prima facie case when it introduces evidence sufficient to warrant a finding by the trier of the facts that the defendant had, by reason of his position in the corporation, responsibility and authority either to prevent in the first instance, or promptly to correct, the violation complained of, and that he failed to do so."

Does this mean that the *Dotterweich-Park* standard is one of absolute, strict liability upon the responsible corporate officials so that, for example, Park would be guilty of any contamination occurring at any of the corporation's 874 retail outlets or 16 warehouses? Apparently not. Though the *Park* majority did not agree with the view of the three dissenters that *Dotterweich* requires a showing the official "engaged in wrongful conduct amounting at least to common law negligence," the majority significantly did say that the "concept of 'responsible relationship' * * * imports some measure of blameworthiness." Moreover, the Court in *Park* also declared:

> The duty imposed by Congress on responsible corporate agents is, we emphasize, one that requires the highest standard of foresight and vigilance, but the Act, in its criminal aspect, does not require that which is objectively impossible. The theory upon which responsible corporate agents are held criminally accountable for "causing" violations of the Act permits a claim that a defendant was "powerless" to prevent or correct the violation to "be raised defensively at a trial on the merits." If such a claim is made, the defendant has the burden of coming forward with evidence, but this does not alter the Government's ultimate burden of proving beyond a reasonable doubt the defendant's guilt, including his power, in light of the duty imposed by the

Act, to prevent or correct the prohibited condition.

Though this language is susceptible to various interpretations,[112] it appears that "with the impossibility defense, the strict liability standard as applied to indirect actors becomes in practice a standard of extraordinary care." [113] "Under this view, all that must be proved by the government is a deviation from that standard—something certainly less than common law negligence; it can be characterized as 'very slight' or 'slight' negligence, to be distinguished from 'ordinary' negligence." [114] Application of *Park* by the lower courts generally squares with this standard-of-care interpretation of the case.[115]

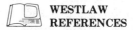

WESTLAW REFERENCES

289k175 /p agent employee representative partner
289k67 41k27
101k369
(park /s 95 +4 1903) dotterweich /p agent officer representative employee /p criminal** penal

---

§ 3.11   Concurrence of Mental Fault With Acts and Results

This section deals with two different problems concerning concurrence of the mental fault (intent, knowledge, recklessness, or negligence) with other elements of the various crimes. One problem is that of the necessary concurrence of the mental fault with the act or omission which is the basis for liability—that is, the act or omission which constitutes the "legal cause" of the bad result, when the crime in question is defined in terms of a certain bad result. This is sometimes referred to as concurrence in time, although we shall see that actually concurrence in time is neither required nor sufficient; the true meaning of the requirement that the mental

112. Compare Abrams, Criminal Liability of Corporate Officers for Strict Liability Offenses—A Comment on Dotterweich and Park, 28 U.C.L.A.L.Rev. 463 (1981); with Brickey, Criminal Liability of Corporate Officers for Strict Liability Offenses—Another View, 35 Vand.L.Rev. 1337 (1982).

113. Developments in the Law—Corporate Crime, 92 Harv.L.Rev. 1227, 1264 (1979).

114. Abrams, supra note 112, at 470.

115. See, e.g., United States v. Starr, 535 F.2d 512 (9th Cir.1976); United States v. Hata & Co., Ltd., 535 F.2d 508 (9th Cir.1976), both using language reflecting a standard-of-care approach.

fault concur with the act or omission is that the former actuate the latter.

The second problem concerns concurrence of the mental fault with the bad results, which arises as to those crimes defined in terms of bad results. This is often spoken of as the requirement of concurrence in kind and intensity, which reflects the notion that ordinarily the mental fault (intent, recklessness, etc.) must be of the same order as the harm caused. Or, to put it another way, mental states are not interchangeable between crimes; if one sets out with intent to cause the harm covered in crime A and then inadvertently causes the harm covered by crime B, neither crime A nor crime B has been committed. There are a number of important exceptions to this, however, in that some crimes are defined in terms of causing one result while having a mental state concerning another, quite different result.

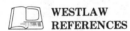

WESTLAW REFERENCES

di concurrence

(a) Concurrence of Mental Fault and Act or Omission.[1] With those crimes which require some mental fault (whether intention, knowledge, recklessness, or negligence) in addition to an act or omission, it is a basic premise of Anglo-American criminal law that the physical conduct and the state of mind must concur.[2] Although it is sometimes assumed that there cannot be such concurrence unless the mental and physical aspects exist at precisely the same moment of time,[3] the better view is that there is concurrence when the defendant's mental state actuates the physical conduct.[4] That is, mere coincidene in point of time is not necessarily sufficient, while the lack of such unity is not necessarily a bar to conviction.

The easiest cases are those in which the bad state of mind follows the physical conduct,[5] for here it is obvious that the subsequent mental state is in no sense legally related to the prior acts or omissions of the defendant.[6] Thus it is not a criminal battery for A accidentally to strike and injure his enemy B, though A, on realizing what has happened, rejoices at B's discomfiture.[7] It is not burglary for A to open the door and enter B's house at night with an innocent intention, though A later decides to steal B's property therein.[8] The crime of receiving stolen property knowing it to be stolen is not committed when A receives from B property which he does not know to be stolen, though when A later learns it is stolen he decides to keep it.[9] It is not larceny for A to take possession of and carry

---

§ 3.11

1. See Marston, Contemporaneity of Act and Intention, 86 L.Q.Rev. 208 (1970); White, The Identity and Time of the Actus Reus, 1977 Crim.L.Rev. 148 (1977).

2. State v. Snow, 383 A.2d 1385 (Me.1978). A number of states have enacted a statute expressing this basic premise in this language: "In every crime there must exist a union, or joint operation, of act or intent, or criminal negligence." See, e.g., People v. Green, 27 Cal.3d 1, 164 Cal.Rptr. 1, 609 P.2d 468 (1980), applying such a statute.

3. Sabens v. United States, 40 App.D.C. 440 (1913).

4. 1 W. Russell on Crime 54 (12th ed. J. Turner, 1964). See, e.g., Commonwealth v. Blow, 370 Mass. 401, 348 N.E.2d 794 (1976), where the jury was instructed in such terms.

5. The physical conduct might begin first but continue until the requisite state of mind occurs. See, e.g., Fagan v. Metropolitan Police Comm'r, [1969] Q.B. 439 (crime of assault where defendant parked car on officer's foot inadvertently and then, upon learning what he had done, did not move the car, as the requisite act was "continuing"). The *Cali* case, note 13 infra, might provide another basis for deciding *Fagan* adversely to the defendant.

6. However, subsequent statements by the defendant may sometimes have evidential value for purposes of determining his prior mental state. People v. Claborn, 224 Cal.App. 38, 36 Cal.Rptr. 132 (1964) (defendant made statement immediately after his car collided with that of a police officer that "I didn't kill you this way, but I will kill you now"; *held*, statement properly admitted to show defendant's prior intent).

7. See State v. Sanborn, 120 Me. 170, 113 A. 54, 56 (1921).

8. See Jackson v. State, 102 Ala. 167, 15 So. 344 (1894) (instruction that in burglary intent to steal must exist *before* the acts of breaking and entering is incorrect, for it must be *concurrent* with the acts); State v. Moore, 12 N.H. 42 (1841) (one who lawfully enters a house and then steals is not guilty of burglary unless he in fact intended to steal on entry; in criminal law his intent to steal will not "relate back" to the entry; but compare the notion of trespass *ab initio* found in tort law).

9. Cf. Arcia v. State, 26 Tex.App. 193, 9 S.W. 685 (1888).

off *B*'s property with an innocent mind, although later *A*, overcome by temptation, converts the property with an intent to steal it.[10] Similarly, it is not robbery if the act of force or intimidation by which the taking is accomplished precedes the formation of the larcenous purpose.[11] And one who expresses approval to his employee for the latter's prior crime is not held accountable for the crime, as he could have been had he directed his employee to commit the crime.[12]

With crimes committed by conduct in the form of omission to act, as well as with those committed by conduct of the affirmative-action sort, the state of mind must concur with the conduct. Thus, under a statute making it a crime (arson) to burn one's own building with intent to defraud an insurance company, one who accidentally starts a fire in his own building is not thereby guilty, for his affirmative conduct in starting the fire is unaccompanied by any intent to defraud. But his further omission-to-act conduct in departing the premises without taking steps to extinguish the fire or to sound the alarm, intending that the building should burn so as to enable him to collect the insurance money, constitutes arson, for here his criminal omission to act coincides with his intent to defraud.[13]

Of course, in some of the illustrations given above it may appear that the activity in question ought to be criminal. Often it can be and has been made criminal, without violence to the basic premise of concurrence, by redefining the crime or creating new crimes to cover other physical conduct which does concur with the defendant's mental state. This development is most evident in the area of larceny, where the offense was broadened by the courts by such doctrines as "breaking bulk" and "continuing trespass," and where such crimes as larceny by bailee and embezzlement were brought into being.[14]

What, then, of the case in which the bad state of mind exists prior to the defendant's act or omission? Certainly one who at one time has such a state of mind cannot be convicted for having it merely because at some later date the acts or results which he once intended accidentally occur. Thus if *A* forms an intent to kill *B*, then abandons that intent, but at some later date inadvertently runs over *B* and kills him, *A* can hardly be considered to be guilty of murder merely because the results of his conduct coincide with his former intent.[15] The imposition of criminal liability on this basis would be essentially the same as imposing liability for bad

---

10. See § 8.5(f). E.g., Wilson v. State, 96 Ark. 148, 131 S.W. 336 (1910) (if *A* takes *B*'s bull in good faith, thinking it to be his own, and then learns that it is *B*'s, and then sells it as his own, *A* is not guilty of larceny); State v. Hopple, 83 Ida. 55, 357 P.2d 656 (1960) (if *A* puts *B*'s trespassing sheep into *A*'s corral to prevent their trampling on *A*'s cattle feed, and *A* later decides to steal the sheep, he is not guilty of larceny; *A*'s conviction *held* reversed because trial court refused to allow *A* to give this explanation).

For the same reason it is not larceny for the finder of lost property to take possession of it with intent to return it to the owner, although later he converts it to his own use with an intent to steal, e.g., People v. Betts, 367 Ill. 499, 11 N.E.2d 942 (1937). Nor is it larceny for one, who has received an overpayment of money by mistake, innocently to pocket it and carry it off, although later, on learning of the mistake, he decides to steal it, e.g., United States v. Rogers, 289 F.2d 433 (4th Cir.1961), and cases cited therein.

11. People v. Green, 27 Cal.3d 1, 164 Cal.Rptr. 1, 609 P.2d 468 (1980) (as "when an individual kills or renders another unconscious for reasons wholly unrelated to larceny—e.g., because of anger, fear, jealousy, or revenge—and then, seeing that his victim has been rendered defenseless,

decides to take advantage of the situation by appropriating some item of value from his person").

12. Morse v. State, 6 Conn. 9 (1825) (defendant subsequently approved his bartender's crime of extending credit to a Yale student).

13. Commonwealth v. Cali, 247 Mass. 20, 141 N.E. 510 (1923) (a duty to act to put out the fire or to give the alarm arises from the fact that he accidentally started the fire).

14. See §§ 8.2, 8.6. However, if the legislature instead were to expressly provide that the act and mental state need not concur, this may be found to be beyond the legislature's power. United States v. Fox, 95 U.S. 670, 24 L.Ed. 538 (1878) (federal statute provided that whoever has bankruptcy proceedings commenced against him within three months after obtaining credit with intent to defraud is guilty of a crime; *held* "The criminal intent essential to the commission of a public offense must exist when the act complained of is done; it cannot be imputed to a party from a subsequent independent transaction.").

15. Similarly, when defendant formed intent to kill *X*, later found *X*, and *X* attacked him with an axe, to which defendant responded by killing *X* to defend himself, it was error to instruct the jury that the mere existence of the prior intent and the later act of killing was sufficient to

thoughts alone, which, for reasons we have noted earlier,[16] is not done.

One way to explain the above situation is simply to say that there is no concurrence because the mental state, being abandoned, did not actuate the physical conduct. But this may also be true when the mental state has not been abandoned. Assuming again that A forms an intent to kill B, but now that he has not abandoned that intent, and that he accidentally runs over B and kills him, the result still should be that there is no concurrence of the mental and physical elements. This is because "his moving and steering of his car were not done in order to give effect to desire to kill." [17] Even this language must be narrowly read, it would seem, to mean that the acts must be done for the actual carrying out of the intent and not merely to prepare for its execution. In the above illustration, for example, it would not appear to make any difference that, at the time of the accident, A was driving to a store to purchase a gun with which to kill B.

Consider next the case in which A decides to kill B, and then voluntarily becomes intoxicated for the purpose of nerving himself for the accomplishment of his plan, and then, while intoxicated, kills B. Assuming that A had the required mental state prior to intoxication, but then became so intoxicated as to be unable to have such a mental state,[18] is he guilty of murder? Most courts have said yes, disposing of the problem with the maxim that voluntary intoxication is not a defense under these circumstances,[19] but in one case the defendant was acquitted on the ground that

there was no concurrence of mental fault and act.[20] But, if—as suggested above—the requirement of concurrence is not one of coexistence at a particular point of time, but rather of the state of mind actuating the physical conduct, then it would appear that A may be convicted of murder if there is this latter connection between the death-causing acts and his prior mental state. Just as in the previous illustration, if the killing were inadvertent and thus not attributable to the prior mental fault there would be no murder; but if the defendant's death-causing acts were more directly [21] a consequence of the prior mental fault, then the basic premise of concurrence is satisfied.

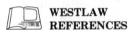 **WESTLAW REFERENCES**

crim**** /p concur! occur /s inten! motiv! mental-state state-of-mind /s conduct omission

sabens & 40 +5 440

(b) Attendant Circumstances and Results. With crimes which require physical conduct, mental fault, and attendant circumstances, the circumstances must concur with the conduct and fault. For example, it is not burglary, which requires that the dwelling broken into and entered be that of another, if one enters a house with intent to steal when, unknown to him, the former owner has just died and left the house to him. And, because the crime of rape requires that the victim not be the defendant's wife, it is not rape for one to have sexual intercourse with his wife against her will an hour before their divorce.[22]

---

establish murder. State v. Rider, 90 Mo. 54, 1 S.W. 825 (1886).

16. See § 3.2.

17. 1 W. Russell, supra note 4, at 54.

18. Perhaps not just intent, but the first degree murder requirement of premeditation and deliberation. See § 7.7(a).

19. Harris v. Commonwealth, 183 Ky. 542, 209 S.W. 509 (1919); State v. Butner, 66 Nev. 127, 206 P.2d 253 (1949); State v. Hammonds, 216 N.C. 67, 3 S.E.2d 439 (1939); State v. Robinson, 20 W.Va. 713 (1882).

20. Sabens v. United States, 40 App.D.C. 440 (1913).

21. That is, more directly than where the death of B is accidental. Where A intends to kill B and gets drunk for

this purpose and then, because of his intoxication, inadvertently runs over B, it could be said that the death was a consequence of the prior intent, as the intent led to the drinking which led to the failure to see B. But, this is not distinguishable from the case put previously where A intends to kill B and for this purpose drives to buy a gun and inadvertently hits B en route. Thus, more is required than that the death-causing acts would not have occurred but for the prior intent. Perhaps it could be said that just as there must be "legal" causation between the acts and the results, see § 3.12(c), there must also be such causation between the mental state and the acts, although the latter is commonly referred to as concurrence.

22. In some jurisdictions the crime of rape has been redefined to obviate this result. For discussion of this

With crimes defined in terms of conduct which produces a bad result (such as murder, manslaughter, and battery), there may be a time lag between the conduct and the result. In such a case it is the concurrence of the state of mind with the conduct, not with the result, which is necessary. Thus *A* may shoot *B* with intent to kill him; but if *B* lives on for a month before dying from the wound, by which time *A*, having repented of his earlier conduct, has employed some leading doctors in a vain attempt to save *B*'s life, *A* is guilty of intent-to-kill murder, for his intent to kill *B* concurred with his act of shooting *B*, and his later reformation is irrelevant on the issue of guilt.[23] Similarly, when *A* drives his car toward *B*'s car with the intent of injuring *B*, but at the last moment he changes his mind and puts on the brakes but yet skids into *B*'s car, the change of heart is no bar to conviction.[24] There was an intent to injure which concurred with the injury-causing acts, and the fact that the results occurred only after a change in intent and ineffectual acts to avoid the results is immaterial. Likewise, one may be found guilty of reckless homicide notwithstanding a last-moment attempt to avoid the accident.[25]

WESTLAW
REFERENCES

crim**** /p circumstance /s occur concur! /s result! consequence /s conduct omission

(c) What Act Must Concur With the Mental Fault? With crimes defined in terms of a mental state, act or omission, and a certain bad result, a particular kind of act or

omission is seldom required. The emphasis is upon results caused by the defendant, and any act or omission (with the prescribed state of mind) which causes that result will do. Thus, intent-to-kill murder may be committed by an infinite variety of acts, though the act must both concur with the mental fault (here intent) and be the "legal cause" of the results (here the death of another).[26] If attention is not focused upon the proper act, it may appear that the requirement of concurrence has not been met.

For example, consider the case in which the defendant, aware that he is extremely sleepy and in danger of falling asleep at the wheel of his car, drives on, then falls asleep, and then drives into the rear of another car, resulting in the death of one of the passengers. It might be contended that the awareness which makes up the mental fault existed prior to the time he went to sleep, and that the death-causing acts occurred subsequent to the time he fell asleep, so that there is not that concurrence of act and mental state needed for commission of a crime. But, we know that the acts subsequent to his falling asleep are not acts upon which criminal liability is based, as they do not even qualify as voluntary acts.[27] Rather, the act—which is the cause of death—is continuing to drive while knowing that he is very sleepy, which obviously concurs with the required mental state.[28]

The same kind of analysis can be utilized in dealing with the mistake-as-to-death cases, which have been a considerable source of difficulty to courts and commentators. The ba-

problem, see Barry, Spousal Rape: The Uncommon Law, 66 A.B.A.J. 1088 (1980); Geis, Rape-in-Marriage: Law and Law Reform in England, United States and Sweden, 6 Adelaide L.Rev. 284 (1978); Schwartz, The Spousal Exemption for Criminal Rape Prosecution, 7 Vt.L.Rev. 33 (1982); Comments, 65 Marq.L.Rev. 120 (1981); 8 San.F.U. L.Rev. 239 (1980); Notes, 18 J.Fam.L. 565 (1980); 52 N.Y. U.L.Rev. 306 (1977).

23. Compare the situation as to the inchoate offenses of attempt and conspiracy, where the intended harm has not occurred, as to which it is sometimes possible to escape liability for what would otherwise be one of these crimes by a subsequent change of heart and effective abandonment of or withdrawal from the plan. See §§ 6.3, 6.5.

24. People v. Claborn, 224 Cal.App. 38, 36 Cal.Rptr. 132 (1964).

25. State v. Stentz, 33 Wash. 444, 74 P. 588 (1903).

26. Causation is discussed in more detail in § 3.12, although some of the problems in this area must be anticipated in the discussion which immediately follows.

27. Model Penal Code § 2.01, Comment at 220 (1985).

28. Similarly, in People v. Decina, 2 N.Y.2d 133, 157 N.Y.S.2d 558, 138 N.E.2d 799 (1956), the court held there was sufficient concurrence between the act of driving and having the mental state of knowing that an epileptic seizure could strike at any time, though there was no voluntary act after a seizure did occur and defendant's car struck and killed four children.

sic facts common to all of these cases are that the defendant has engaged in two separate acts: first, an act done with intent to kill which, unknown to the defendant, does not bring about death; and second, an act done to conceal the crime or dispose of what is thought to be a dead body, which does bring about death. For example, *A* poisons *B* and then, thinking *B* dead, decapitates her; the poison was insufficient to cause death, and *B* dies from the decapitation.[29] *C* strikes *D* on the head, and then rolls what is thought to be *D*'s dead body over a cliff in order to give the appearance of an accident; *C* did not give *D* a killing blow, and *D* dies from exposure at the bottom of the cliff.[30] Numerous cases from foreign jurisdictions provide many other grisly illustrations.[31]

In all of these cases in which there was an intent to kill and an attack on the victim in furtherance of that intent, there is no question but that the defendant could be convicted of attempted murder. But, what about a charge of murder? Is it not true that a murder conviction is foreclosed because of a lack of concurrence, in that the act done with intent to kill did not kill and the act which did kill was not done with intent to kill? Some courts have so held,[32] although the weight of authority is to the contrary.[33]

The rationale of some of the cases is obscure, but convictions in such cases have been upheld on the ground that disposal of the body was part of the original plan,[34] or on the notion that the two acts were part of a single transaction with a common intention.[35] Although it has been said that "ordinary ideas

29. Jackson v. Commonwealth, 100 Ky. 239, 38 S.W. 422, 1091 (1896) (*held,* murder; court's discussion is not of the issue of concurrence, but of the related problem of jurisdiction over the crime, which was raised because the poison was administered in Ohio while the decapitation occurred in Kentucky).

30. Thabo Meli v. Regina, [1954] 1 W.L.R. 228, 1 All E.R. 393 (murder, as disposal of the body in this way was part of the original plan).

31. In each of the following cases, the first act of the defendant was done with intent to kill, and the evidence showed (or the court assumed) that the defendant mistakenly believed his victim to be dead and that death actually resulted from the defendant's second act: State v. Masilela, 1968 (2) S.A. 558 (defendant strangled victim, but victim died from carbon-monoxide poisoning as a result of defendant setting fire to bed in which victim lay; *held,* murder, as strangulation a "directly contributing cause of his death" because it made victim incapable of escaping from the fire); Regina v. Church, [1965] 2 W.L.R. 1220 (defendant choked victim, then threw her into river, trial court instructed that no murder if defendant believed victim dead, appellate court said trial judge too generous and that jury should be able to convict "if they regarded the appellant's behavior from the moment when he first struck her to the moment when he threw her into the river as a series of acts designed to cause death or grievous bodily harm."); Rex v. Shorty, 1950 Southern Rhodesia 280 (defendant struck victim, then placed body in sewer; *held,* only attempted murder, as immersion in sewer an intervening act without intent to kill); Lingraj Das v. Emperor, 24 Indian L.R. Patna Ser. 131 (1945) (defendant choked victim, then placed her on railroad tracks, train cut her in two; *held,* murder, as the series of acts are one transaction); Thavamani v. Emperor, 1943 Madras Weekly Notes 342 (defendant struck victim, then placed body in well; *held,* murder, as the two phases of the transaction were so close as to be considered one); King v. Nehal Mahto, 18 Indian L.R. Patna Ser. 485 (1939)

(defendant beat victim and then placed body on railroad tracks, victim decapitated; *held,* murder, as all one transaction); Kaliapa Goudan v. Emperor, 1933 Madras Weekly Notes 745 (defendant choked victim, then placed body on train tracks, victim decapitated; *held,* murder, though court also questions trial judge's assumption that defendant believed victim dead); Queen v. Khandu, 15 Indian L.R. Bombay Ser. 194 (1891) (defendant struck victim, then burned down hut with body in it; *held,* not murder, as no concurrence of intent and death-causing act of burning hut).

In the following cases, the defendant did not act with intent to kill, but was charged with murder on the basis of some lesser mental state, such as intent to do great bodily harm, or a high degree of recklessness; again, the evidence showed (or the court assumed) that the defendant believed his act killed the victim, and that death resulted from the defendant's second act: Regina v. Chiswibo, [1961] 2 S.Afr.L.R. 714 (defendant hit victim with axe then put him down ant-bear hole; *held,* not murder, as defendant did not intend to kill and thus disposing of body not part of original plan, distinguishing Thabo Meli supra note 30); King v. Sreenarayan, 27 Indian L.R. Patna Ser. 67 (1948) (defendant struck victim, then put body on pyre and burned same; *held,* not murder, as disposal not part of original plan, since no intent to kill, but defendant guilty of negligent homicide for mistakenly believing victim to be dead); In re Palani Goundan, 1919 Madras Weekly Notes 340 (defendant struck victim, then hanged her to give appearance of suicide, *held,* not murder, court says this not kind of case where two acts should be viewed as one transaction, apparently because of no intent to kill); Emperor v. Dalu Sardar, 18 Calcutta Weekly Notes 1279 (1914) (same).

32. See note 31 supra.

33. See note 31 supra.

34. E.g., Thabo Meli v. Regina, supra note 30.

35. E.g., Lingraj Das v. Emperor, supra note 31.

of justice and common sense require that such a case shall be treated as murder," [36] other commentators have been firmly of the view that there is no concurrence in these cases.[37] It is argued, for example, that no one would be guilty of murder when *A* strikes *B* with intent to kill and then departs erroneously believing *B* to be dead, and then *C* causes *B*'s death by mutilating what he believes to be a dead body; and that the same should be true when there is but one actor.[38]

It does seem clear that one cannot merely couple the prior intent to kill with the acts done with intent to dispose of a dead body, as the former intent did not actuate these acts, and to the extent that the cases rest upon this or similar notions they conflict with the principle of concurrence. However, there is no need to make such a connection, for there is an earlier act (*A* giving poison to *B*, and *C* striking *D*, in the illustrations given above) which clearly does concur, and if that act can be said to be the "legal" or "proximate" cause of death, then all the requirements for a crime are met. In short, the best approach to the mistake-as-to-death cases is to try to establish that the act which does concur with the intent was the legal cause of death,[39] rather than to try to establish concurrence between the intent and the subsequent act which, admittedly, could more readily be found to be the legal cause of death.

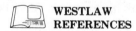 **WESTLAW REFERENCES**

crim*** /p conduct omission /p intent! motiv! /p result consequence /p legal proximate /s caus!

(d) Concurrence of Mental Fault and Results—Difference as to Type of Harm. An intention to cause one type of harm cannot serve as a substitute for the statutory or common-law requirement of intention as to another type of harm. Thus where *A* intentionally steals a gas meter out of a house, and as a result a woman is made ill by the escaping gas, it cannot be said that the intent to steal suffices also to establish the intent to injure another.[40] And where *A* throws a rock with intent to hit *B* and misses, unintentionally breaking *B*'s (or *C*'s) window, *A* is not guilty of malicious destruction of property of the intent-to-destroy type.[41] Similarly, where *A* intends to steal rum from the hold of a ship and lights a match in order to see better, causing a fire which destroys the ship, *A* is not guilty of arson of the intent-to-burn type.[42] In all of these instances, however, the fact that *A* intended another type of harm does not foreclose the possibility that he might be found to have acted recklessly or negligently (if that is the required mental state) as to the harm caused, so that he might be convicted on this basis.

As these cases illustrate, what has sometimes been referred to as "transferred intent" is applicable only within the limits of the same crime; *A*'s intent to kill *B* may suffice as to his causing the death of *C*, but *A*'s intent to steal from *C* will not suffice as to his causing the burning of *C*'s property. That is, while a defendant can be convicted when he both has the *mens rea* and commits the *actus reus* required for a given offense, he cannot be convicted if the *mens rea* relates to one crime and the *actus reus* to another. Although the courts have not carefully articulated the reasons why this is so, the basic point is that a contrary rule would disregard the requirement of an appropriate mental state.[43] The distinctions now drawn between various kinds of crimes in terms of their seriousness, as reflected by the punishments provided for them, would lose much of their significance if an intent to cause any one specific type of harm would suffice for conviction as to any other type of harm which is criminal when intentionally caused. There is no rational basis, for example, to support the conclusion

36. G. Williams, Criminal Law: The General Part 174 (2d ed. 1961).

37. J. Hall, General Principles of Criminal Law 189 (2d 1960); 1 W. Russell, supra note 4, at 56.

38. 1 W. Russell, supra note 4, at 55–56.

39. On legal cause in such cases, see § 3.12(f)(6).

40. Regina v. Cunningham, 41 Crim.App.R. 155, [1957] 3 Weekly L.R. 76.

41. Regina v. Pembliton, 12 Cox Crim.Cas. 607 (1874).

42. Regina v. Faulkner, 13 Cox Crim.Cas. 550 (1877).

43. Williams, supra note 36, at § 47.

that one who inadvertently burns a house while attempting to steal property therein should have his conduct classified in the same way as that of one who intentionally burdens the house of another.[44]

The same result should be reached when the mental state is recklessness or negligence. For example, it may happen that A acts recklessly toward B, foreseeably endangering his property but not his person; but, as it turns out, B's property escapes without injury, yet B is killed (or injured). Or the converse situation may occur, as where A foreseeably endangers B's person but not his property, but his property and not his person is injured or destroyed. It would seem that in either case A would not be criminally liable on account of the actual result, for manslaughter or battery in the first situation or for malicious mischief in the second.[45]

There are a few notable exceptions to this general rule that a mental state as to one type of harm will not suffice for a crime involving another type of harm, and they come into play when the unintended harm is the death of another. Under the felony-murder rule, one may be guilty of murder if he causes the death of another in the course of committing a felony (or, at least, one of certain dangerous felonies); and, under the misdemeanor-manslaughter rule, one may be guilty of involuntary manslaughter if he causes the death of another while committing a *malum in se* type of misdemeanor. These rules, however, are not based upon notions of "transferred intent," but rather stem from certain peculiarities in the law of homicide, which will be discussed later.[46]

It should also be noted that there are some crimes which contain, as part of their mental element, the intent to commit some other crime. Thus common-law burglary requires the intent to commit a felony within the dwelling. These crimes should not be viewed as exceptions to the rule that intent cannot be transferred between crimes, as the intent to commit another crime is an additional requirement and not a substitute for the required mental state as to the *actus reus* of the crime. In burglary, for example, intent to commit a felony is an additional element of the offense rather than an alternative to the necessary mental state for the acts of breaking and entering another's dwelling.

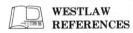 **WESTLAW REFERENCES**

di(criminal /p intent! /5 transfer!)

(e) Concurrence of Mental Fault and Results—Difference as to Degree of Harm. With many crimes which are defined so as to require some forbidden harmful result, the degree of harm, within fairly broad limits, may not be relevant to the question of criminal liability. For A intentionally to strike B without justification is a battery, and it makes no difference as to A's guilt of simple battery whether B is lightly scratched or seriously injured. So if A intends a light injury but actually inflicts a serious injury, or intends a serious injury but inflicts only a light injury, we need not worry about the difference between his intent and his achievement so far as simple battery is concerned.[47] And if one intends to kill his enemy painlessly but succeeds in inflicting pain before death, he is

---

44. Thus Model Penal Code § 2.03(2) provides that the element of purposely or knowingly causing a particular result is not established when the actual result is not within the purpose of contemplation of the actor, with limited exceptions.

45. Thus Model Penal Code § 2.03(3) provides that the element of recklessly or negligently causing a particular result is not established when the actual result is not within the risk of which the actor is or (in the case of negligence) should be aware, with limited exceptions.

Note that in the law of torts one who negligently creates a risk of bodily harm to another may be liable for property damage, and vice versa. This was not true under

Restatement, Torts § 281(b) (1935), but the rule has been changed in Restatement, Torts (Second) § 281(b) (1965), to conform to the tort cases in the field. It does not necessarily follow, of course, that criminal law, with its more drastic consequences for the defendant and its emphasis upon factors other than compensation of the injured party, should be in accord.

46. See §§ 7.5, 7.13.

Note also the felony-mayhem statute discussed in State v. Cody, 18 Or. 506, 23 P. 891 (1890). See § 7.17.

47. But see infra as to mayhem and aggravated battery.

guilty of nothing more than murder.[48] With the crime of malicious mischief, it makes no difference whether A intends to injure B's property but actually destroys it, or intends to destroy but actually only injures it.[49]

On the other hand, some crimes differ from others according to the degree of the resulting harm, as battery (requiring only bodily injury) differs from criminal homicide (requiring death), or a battery (requiring only slight injury) differs from mayhem (requiring loss of a bodily member or—today generally—disfigurement), or as a simple battery differs from statutory aggravated battery with intent to kill or maim. It is as to such crimes that the problem arises of what significance should be attributed to a difference in degree between the harm intended and the harm done. For example, A may intend to injure B but by mistake succeed in killing him, and the question is whether A is guilty of murder or manslaughter. Conversely, A may intend to kill but succeed only in wounding B; is A guilty of simple battery or aggravated battery-with-intent-to-kill? A may strike at B's jaw with his fist with intent merely to knock him down, but instead he shatters B's glasses and causes B to lose his eyesight; is A guilty of mayhem? Conversely, A aims at his glasses with intent to put out the eyes but merely succeeds in connecting with B's jaw, knocking him down but causing no permanent injury; is he then guilty of simple battery?

The easier problem is the one involved where the harm inflicted is less in degree than the harm intended. Here A is clearly guilty of the lesser crime—of simple battery (or of battery-with-intent-to-kill under a common type of statute) where he intends to kill

but only injures; of simple battery (or of statutory battery-with-intent-to-maim) where he intends to put out the eye but only bruises the victim's jaw.[50] On principle, there seems to be no reason for refusing to recognize an intention to do a greater degree of harm as an equivalent of an intention to do the amount of harm that actually resulted. Indeed, it can often be said that the latter is necessarily encompassed in the former; if one intends to do *serious* bodily harm to another, then he intends to do bodily harm to him.

Where the harm inflicted is greater in degree than that intended, and the criminal law divides the matter into two separate though related crimes according to the degree of harm, there is greater difficulty in holding A criminally liable according to the harm actually done. But it is quite well settled (though perhaps not inherently just) that if A, intending merely to inflict mild bodily harm upon B, actually but unexpectedly succeeds in killing B, he is guilty of criminal homicide—not murder, to be sure, but involuntary manslaughter. A intentionally strikes B a light blow on the mouth; unknown to A, B is a hemophiliac ("bleeder"); the doctors are unable to stop the bleeding so that B dies; A is guilty of involuntary manslaughter though he never intended to kill B and though B's death from so light a blow is entirely unforeseeable.[51] And it is equally well settled that if A, intended to do B serious bodily injury but not to kill him, actually inflicts a fatal wound, A is guilty of murder, in spite of the difference between the degree of harm intended and that achieved.[52] Similarly, if A throws a stone at B intending to strike his body, but by bad luck the stone strikes B's eye and puts it

48. In those states which make murder by torture a category of first degree murder, he is not guilty of this sort of first degree murder, since this requires that the defendant intend to cause pain. People v. Charez, 50 Cal. 2d 778, 329 P.2d 907 (1958).

49. Note that in the substantive law of torts the degree of harm actually caused by a particular tort is important, for there the amount to be recovered in damages depends upon the damage caused. But in the substantive criminal law the degree of harm caused by a particular crime may be irrelevant, though as a matter of discretion the ultimate punishment may depend somewhat on the degree of harm.

50. See Model Penal Code § 2.03(2)(a). Some of the modern codes contain such an express provision.

51. See § 7.13(d). E.g., State v. Frazier, 339 Mo. 966, 98 S.W.2d 707 (1936); Baker v. State, 30 Fla. 41, 11 So. 492 (1892) (unforeseeable heart condition). Going one step further, in Ex parte Heigho, 18 Idaho 566, 110 P. 1029, 32 L.R.A.(N.S.) 877 (1910), A struck B with his fist, which so excited a spectator, B's mother-in-law C, that C died of a heart attack; *held*, A is guilty of manslaughter of C.

52. See § 7.3.

out, *A* is guilty of the greater crime of mayhem,[53] as an intent merely to injure plus actual maiming or disfiguring will do.[54] (Some statutes, however, define mayhem as maiming or disfiguring with intent to maim or disfigure; under such a statute, of course, there must be an intent to maim or disfigure.)[55]

It has been rightly pointed out that the doctrine that when one intends a lesser crime he may be convicted of a graver offense committed inadvertently would lead to anomalous results if generally applied.[56] Actually, it appears that there is no such doctrine, and that the results described above are attributable to unique concepts which have developed as to the offenses mentioned.[57] Even as to these crimes, it would doubtless be better to abandon the notion that an intent to cause some lesser harm will suffice for conviction of the greater crime, as done in the Model Penal Code.[58] "Whether the matter is viewed in relation to the just condemnation of the actor's conduct or in relation to deterrence or correction," [59] there is no basis for imposing on a defendant either the label or the sanctions applicable to one who intentionally caused the results which the defendant fortuitously caused while intending some lesser degree of harm. In short, the better result when the actual harm exceeds the intended harm is to deal with the actor's conduct in terms of harm intended.[60]

The same issue may arise as to crimes involving recklessness and negligence, as where *A* recklessly endangers *B*'s limbs but not his life and yet succeeds in killing *B*. Thus *A*, by throwing a relatively small stone in the vicinity of *B* without any intent to hit him, creates a risk of injuring him but not of killing him; unfortunately he hits *B* and so is guilty of recklessness-battery; but *B* is quite unforeseeably a hemophiliac and bleeds to death. Is *A* guilty of involuntary manslaugh-

---

53. The usual definition of mayhem, the malicious maiming or disfiguring of another, is not as a matter of ordinary language very helpful in solving this specific problem.

54. Brown v. United States, 84 U.S.App.D.C. 222, 171 F.2d 832 (1948) (if *A* commits battery on *B* so violently as to put out eye or cause loss of leg or arm, mayhem though no specific intent to cause that result); Carpenter v. People, 31 Colo. 284, 72 P. 1072 (1903) (if *A* strikes *B*, causing *B* to lose his ear by falling against a root, *A* commits mayhem, which requires no intent to maim); Terrell v. State, 86 Tenn. 523, 8 S.W. 212, 8 Am.Cr.Rep. 532 (1888) (*A* throws brick at *B*, unintentionally putting out *B*'s eye; *held*, mayhem).

55. State v. Bloedlow, 45 Wis. 279, 2 Am.Cr.Rep. 631 (1878) (*A* threw stone at *B* putting out *B*'s eye; *held*, these facts do not warrant conviction of mayhem). So too as to simple battery vs. one type of aggravated battery (assault with intent to maim): if *A* throws a stone at *B* with intent to strike his body, and by mistake he puts out *B*'s eye, *A* is not guilty of the aggravated battery, which requires a specific intent to maim. Note the unusual statute construed in State v. Cody, 18 Or. 506, 23 P. 891 (1890), defining mayhem as "purposely and maliciously, or in the commission or attempt to commit a felony" maiming or disfiguring another—a sort of felony-mayhem akin to the more usual felony-murder.

56. Model Penal Code § 2.04, Comment at 273 (1985).

57. G. Williams, supra note 36, at 193.

58. Murder, as defined in Model Penal Code § 210.2, does not include as an alternative mental element the intention to cause grievous bodily harm. Model Penal Code § 210.2, Comment at 28 (1980), observes that this departure from the common law is based upon the conclu-

sion that such cases are best judged by the standards of recklessness and extreme recklessness, as to which the defendant's intent to injure is a relevant consideration.

Manslaughter, as defined in Model Penal Code § 210.3, does not include causing the death of another by simple battery, and Model Penal Code § 210.3, Comment at 77 (1980), observes that the prevailing law to the contrary has not been followed because it serves no proper purpose of the penal law.

The Model Penal Code does not have the crime of mayhem. It does include simple assault and the more serious offense of aggravated assault, the former dealing in part with the causing of bodily injury to another and the latter dealing in part with the causing of *serious* bodily injury to another. The latter requires purpose, knowledge, or recklessness as to the *serious* bodily injury, and thus the mental state for simple assault will not suffice to establish an aggravated assault. Model Penal Code § 211.1.

59. Model Penal Code § 210.3, Comment at 78 (1980).

60. The same may be said for a similar situation discussed in § 5.1(c). This is the case in which, because of the defendant's mistake as to certain facts, his intent is to do a lesser degree of harm (judged by the statutory penalties for the two crimes involved) than he actually accomplishes. For example, the defendant may intend to break into a store but actually break into a building being used as a dwelling. If, as is sometimes the case, breaking and entering a dwelling is a separate and more serious offense than breaking and entering a nondwelling, the appropriate result is to permit conviction for the lesser crime, even though strictly speaking the *actus reus* of that offense did not occur. This is the approach adopted in Model Penal Code § 2.04(2).

ter? Given the fact that the battery is an unlawful act, the result might well be yes, although here as well it is clear that the better policy is not to hold the defendant liable for the fortuitous fatality.[61]

 WESTLAW
REFERENCES

involuntary-manslaughter (crim**** /5 negligen! injury) (aggravated +1 assault) /p inten! uninten! /s harm consequence /s victim

---

§ 3.12   Causation

With crimes so defined as to require not merely conduct but also a specified result of conduct, the defendant's conduct must be the "legal" or "proximate" cause of the result. For one thing, it must be determined that the defendant's conduct was the cause in fact of the result, which usually (but not always) means that but for the conduct the result would not have occurred. In addition, even when cause in fact is established, it must be determined that any variation between the result intended (with intent crimes) or hazarded (with reckless or negligent crimes) and the result actually achieved is not so extraordinary that it would be unfair to hold the defendant responsible for the actual result.

(a) The Problem. We have already noted that some crimes are so defined that conduct accompanied by an intention to cause a harmful result may constitute the crime without regard to whether that result actually occurs. Thus it is perjury to tell a material lie on the witness stand with intent to mislead judge and jury, though the lie is so transparent that no one who hears it believes it and thus the outcome of the case is not affected. It is forgery to make a false writing with intent to

defraud, though no one except the writer sees it, so that no one is actually defrauded. So too reckless or negligent conduct may constitute a crime though no one is harmed, as is true of the crimes of reckless driving and careless (negligent) driving. With all such crimes there is no need to worry about causation.

On the other hand, some crimes are defined in such a way that the occurrence of a certain specific result of conduct is required for its commission. The crime (or one way to commit the crime) may require an intention to produce that result.[1] Thus the intent-to-kill type of murder requires that the defendant intend to produce a death; the intent-to-injure type of battery that the defendant intend to cause a bodily injury;[2] the intent-to-injure type of malicious mischief that the defendant intend to cause an injury to property; arson that the defendant intend to cause a burning of property; and false pretenses that the defendant intend to cause the victim to pass title to his property. Some crimes may be committed by recklessness in producing the necessary result. Manslaughter and battery, for instance, may be committed by reckless conduct which produces death or injury respectively;[3] and there is a type of murder ("depraved-heart" murder) as to which a very high degree of recklessness causing death constitutes murder. Reckless conduct which brings about property damage may constitute malicious mischief. Probably false pretenses may be committed by one who recklessly makes a false statement knowing he does not know whether the statement is true or false, on the basis of which the victim hands over his property to him. Still other crimes may be committed by negligence in causing the required result, as is the case with some mod-

---

61. Model Penal Code § 210.3 precludes liability both as to the intended-battery and recklessness-battery situations.

§ 3.12

1. Some crimes, e.g., criminal homicide, battery, malicious mischief, may be committed with alternative kinds of fault—intention or recklessness. The intention type requires an intention to produce the harmful result, the recklessness type recklessness in producing it.

2. Mayhem, a sort of aggravated battery requiring a maiming-injury or disfiguring-injury result, by its common law definition requires only an intent to injure, not to maim (disfigure); by some modern statutes a specific intent to cause a maiming (or disfiguring) injury is required. See § 7.17(d).

3. Mayhem apparently may not be committed by recklessly causing a maiming or disfiguring injury; at least an actual intent to cause bodily injury is required. See § 7.17(d).

ern statutes punishing persons who negligently cause death or injury by driving an automobile (or by driving an automobile while intoxicated).[4]

With those crimes which require that the defendant intentionally or recklessly or negligently cause a certain result, there exists the problem of causation. With these crimes it is not enough for criminal liability that the defendant conduct himself with an intention to produce the specified result, or that he conduct himself in such a manner that he recklessly or negligently creates a risk of that result. A is not liable, of course, for murder though he shoots at B intending to kill, so long as his bullet hits no one; nor for manslaughter or battery though he drives his car recklessly, if his conduct fails to harm an endangered pedestrian or motorist. For these crimes of cause-and-result we must have at the very least the required fatal or injurious consequence. Suppose, therefore, in addition to the element of A's intentional or reckless conduct, we add the element of a death or injury to B. It is still not enough for criminal liability that A so conducted himself and that B simultaneously died or was injured. Thus if A shoots at B intending to kill but misses, but at that moment B drops dead of some cause wholly unconnected with the shooting, A is not liable for the murder of B, in spite of the simultaneous existence of the two required ingredients, A's intentional conduct

and the fatal result.[5] What is missing is the necessary causal connection between the conduct[6] and the result of conduct; and causal connection requires something more than mere coincidence as to time and place.[7] It is required, for criminal liability, that the conduct of the defendant be both (1) the actual cause, and (2) the "legal" cause (often called "proximate" cause) of the result.

In brief, this ordinarily means (1) that the defendant's conduct must be the "but-for" cause (sometimes called the "cause in fact") of the forbidden result (the word "cause" in the phrase "legal cause" or "proximate cause"), and in addition (2) that the forbidden result which actually occurs must be enough similar to, and occur in a manner enough similar to, the result or manner which the defendant intended (in the case of crimes of intention), or the result or manner which his reckless or negligent conduct created a risk of happening (in the case of crimes of recklessness and negligence) that the defendant may fairly be held responsible for the actual result even though it does differ or happens in a different way from the intended or hazarded result (the word "legal" or "proximate" in the phrase "legal cause" or "proximate cause").[8]

When causing a particular result is an element of the crime charged, it must be proved by the prosecution beyond a reasonable doubt.[9] In the usual case there is no difficul-

---

4. Note that while *crimes* may or may not be defined so as to require a bad result, *torts* necessarily are so defined; for, in torts, if there is no bad result (injury to person or property), there are no damages for which to sue.

5. So too of crimes consisting of omission to act where there is a duty to act: failure to act must cause the forbidden result. See § 3.3(d).

6. The reference is to that conduct done with the intent or recklessness, not any conduct of the defendant. See State v. Rose, 112 R.I. 402, 311 A.2d 281 (1973) (manslaughter conviction reversed where it not shown whether death caused by accidental non-negligent striking of victim with vehicle or culpably negligent driving on after impact).

7. In People v. Mulcahy, 318 Ill. 332, 149 N.E. 266 (1925), A, a policeman, went into a bar and therein committed the misdemeanor of failing to arrest drunks and gamblers. While A was thus committing the misdemeanor his gun went off accidentally, killing B. It was contended that A was guilty of misdemeanor-manslaughter

on the ground that death resulted from his misdemeanor. It was held that there was no causal connection between the misdemeanor and the death, only a coincidence of time and place, so that A was not guilty of manslaughter of B.

8. For other discussions of "legal" or "proximate" cause in the criminal law, see J. Hall, General Principles of Criminal Law ch. 8 (2d ed. 1960); H. Hart & A. Honore, Causation in the Law chs. 12–14 (1959); G. Williams, Criminal Law: The General Part ch. 4 (2d ed. 1961); Kadish, Complicity, Cause and Blame: A Study in the Interpretation of Doctrine, 73 Calif.L.Rev. 323 (1985); Mueller, Causing Criminal Harm, in Essays in Criminal Science 169 (G. Mueller ed. 1961); Ryu, Causation in Criminal Law, 106 U.Pa.L.Rev. 773 (1958); Williams, Causation in Homicide, 1957 Crim.L.Rev. 429. Note, 78 Colum.L.Rev. 1249 (1978).

9. Henderson v. Kibbe, 431 U.S. 145, 97 S.Ct. 1730, 52 L.Ed.2d 203 (1977); State v. Crocker, 431 A.2d 1323 (Me. 1981); Commonwealth v. Green, 477 Pa. 170, 383 A.2d 877 (1978).

ty in showing the necessary causal connection between conduct and result. *A* with intent to kill *B* aims his gun at the heart of *B*, a person in good health, and pulls the trigger. No one else is trying to kill *B* at that moment. *A*'s aim is good and *B*, pierced through the heart, dies in a few moments. Here *A*'s conduct in fact caused *B*'s death (i.e., but for *A*'s conduct *B* would have lived), and the actual result, the death of *B* from a wound in the heart, is exactly the result intended. (Since *A* not only legally caused *B*'s death, but intended to do so, he is guilty of murder in the absence of circumstances of mitigation or justification). Or *A*, driving his car at a reckless speed, and aware that his conduct is creating a substantial and unreasonable risk of death and injury to other motorists on the road he travels, crashes his car into another car, killing its driver *B*. Here *A*'s conduct in fact caused *B*'s death and the result which occurred (*B*'s death in a car crash) is exactly the kind of result, both as to the type of victim and the type of harm to him, which falls within the risk that *A* created by his conduct. (Since *A*'s conduct legally caused *B*'s death, and was accompanied by recklessness, he is guilty of manslaughter.)

It is the unusual case—numerically in the minority, yet arising often enough to warrant considerable attention by the courts—which gives difficulty in the area of causation. Perhaps at the moment when *A* fired at *B* and hit him in the heart, *X*, acting independently, also shot at *B* and hit him in the head, either wound being sufficient by itself to kill *B*. Or (leaving out the existence of a third person)

perhaps the wound which *A* inflicted upon *B* would not have been fatal except for the fact that *B* was already weakened by sickness or prior injury. Or the wound which *A* inflicted upon *B* would not have been fatal if properly treated, but the doctor or nurse called to attend *B* so negligently treats the wound that *B* dies. Or the fatal (or non-fatal) wound is so painful to *B* that he commits suicide to escape the pain. Or *B* successfully dodges *A*'s bullet by diving into the river where, unable to swim to shore, he drowns. In another class of cases, *A* misses *B* and instead hits and kills or wounds *C*. These out-of-the ordinary cases raise the causation problem—is there in the eyes of the law a sufficient causal connection between the defendant's conduct and the result of his conduct?—and the answers are generally spelled out in the terms of "concurrent cause," "intervening cause," "superseding cause," "preexisting weakness," "transferred intent" and the like.[10]

WESTLAW REFERENCES

203k5 110k26 /p actual** legal** proximate** nexus connection /3 caus!

(b) Cause in Fact. In order that conduct be the actual cause of a particular result, it is almost always sufficient that the result would not have happened in the absence of the conduct; or, putting it another way, that "but for" the antecedent conduct the result would not have occurred.[11] So where *A* shoots at *B*, who is hit and dies, we can say that *A* caused *B*'s death, since but for *A*'s conduct *B* would not have died.[12] However, although but-for

---

10. The problem of legal (or proximate) cause arises in the area of tort law as well as in that of criminal law. Thus concerning tort liability for negligence the actor's conduct must not only be negligent, but the negligent conduct must also be the legal (proximate) cause of the injured party's harm. Restatement (Second) of Torts § 430 et seq. (1965). So too with intentional torts (e.g., battery, intentional trespass to land, intentional damage to chattels), involving an actor who intends to cause injury to another's person or property, the actor's conduct must be the legal cause of the actual harmful result. Restatement (Second) of Torts § 870 (1965).

Thus the tort-battery liability problem of *A*'s firing a gun at *B* and, missing *B*, hitting and injuring *C*, has its counterpart in the bad-aim criminal problem stated in the text above. And the tort-negligence liability problem in-

volved when *A* negligently injures *B*, whose injury is greatly increased by his doctor's negligent treatment, has its parallel in the criminal problem concerning the careless doctor posed above.

11. Model Penal Code § 2.03(1) declares that conduct "is the cause of a result when * * * it is an antecedent but for which the result in question would not have occurred." Some of the modern codes contain such a provision.

12. As previously indicated in the text supra, *A* is not necessarily criminally liable for murder or manslaughter on these bare facts; though it is clear that *A* caused *B*'s death, it must also be shown, for criminal liability, that *A* "legally" caused *B*'s death—a matter dealt with later in this section. And, of course, it must also be shown that *A*

causation explains almost all of the cases wherein it is held that the conduct in question causes the result in question, it does not explain them all.

In torts law there is the situation where A wrongfully (intentionally or negligently) starts a fire which by itself is sufficient to burn B's property, while at about the same time X (wrongfully or innocently) or lightning starts another fire also sufficient to burn B's property. The two fires meet and combine and burn B's property. Here one cannot say that but for A's conduct B's property would not have been burned. Yet A is held to have caused the injury to B's property.[13]

In the criminal law too the situation sometimes arises where two causes, each alone sufficient to bring about the harmful result, operate together to cause it. Thus A stabs B, inflicting a fatal wound; while at the same moment X, acting independently, shoots B in the head with a gun, also inflicting such a wound; and B dies from the combined effects of the two wounds. It is held that A has caused B's death (so he is guilty of murder if his conduct included an intent to kill B, manslaughter if his conduct constituted recklessness).[14] (X, of course, being in exactly the same position as A, has equally caused B's

death.) So the test for causation-in-fact is more accurately worded, not in terms of but-for cause, but rather: Was the defendant's conduct a substantial factor in bringing about the forbidden result?[15] Of course, if the result would not have occurred but for his conduct, his conduct is a substantial factor in bringing about the result; but his conduct will sometimes be a substantial factor even though not a but-for cause.[16]

What if A shoots and instantaneously kills B who, from disease or from a prior mortal wound independently inflicted by a third person X, was at death's door, with but an hour more to live, at the moment A killed him. Here we can properly say that but for A's conduct B would have lived (though only for an hour); thus A has caused B's death.[17] So one who hastens the victim's death is a cause of his death.[18]

A difficulty is presented in the situation where A inflicts a mortal wound on B, who, though dying, has an hour to live; then X, acting independently, kills B instantaneously. Can it be said that A has in fact caused B's death? (X, by substantially hastening B's death is surely a cause of B's death.[19]) Or is A saved from criminal liability because X's conduct somehow cut off A's conduct as a

---

had the requisite criminal mental fault—e.g., an intent to kill (for murder) or recklessness (for manslaughter).

13. Restatement (Second) of Torts § 432 (1965) (dealing with tort of negligence). Id. at § 431 thus phrases the question concerning causation: Was A's conduct "a *substantial factor* in bringing about the harm"?, rather than: "But for A's conduct would the result have happened?"

14. Wilson v. State, 24 S.W. 409 (Tex.Cr.1893); J. Hall, supra, note 8, at 267–68. So too, perhaps, if A and X, acting independently, each inflict on B a wound not by itself mortal, but B dies of the combined effect of the two wounds: Here it has been held that the conduct of A (and of X) has caused the death of B. Henderson v. State, 11 Ala.App. 37, 65 So. 721 (1914). But Professor Hall would not hold that A's conduct caused B's death if A acted first, B later. J. Hall, supra note 8, at 267.

A few states have provided by statute that in a concurrent cause situation the defendant is not the cause of the result if the other cause was sufficient to produce that result but defendant's conduct was not. For application of such a provision, see State v. Crocker, 431 A.2d 1323 (Me. 1981).

15. See Note, 78 Colum.L.Rev. 1249, 1265 (1978).

16. The "substantial factor" language is sometimes used in the cases. See, e.g., State v. Spates, 176 Conn. 227,

405 A.2d 656 (1978); Commonwealth v. Paquette, 451 Pa. 250, 301 A.2d 837 (1973); State v. Serebin, 119 Wis.2d 837, 350 N.W.2d 65 (1984). Consider also Holsemback v. State, 443 So.2d 1371 (Ala.Crim.App.1983) (where two defendants independently stabbed victim, who died, each could be convicted of murder "if each inflicted an injury that caused, contributed to, or accelerated" victim's death).

17. People v. Ah Fat, 48 Cal. 61 (1874).

18. Focht, Proximate Cause in the Law of Homicide, 12 So.Cal.L.Rev. 19, 27 (1938), concludes that for criminal homicide liability A must "substantially" hasten B's death. H. Hart & A. Honroe, supra note 8, at 308–09, discuss an English case in which the judge charged the jury that they might find causation lacking where a doctor, because of his treatment of a patient, shortened the patient's life but a matter of hours.

19. On the other hand, if it cannot be said to a medical certainty that B was still alive when X acted, then this causation has not been proved. People v. Dlugash, 41 N.Y.2d 725, 395 N.Y.S.2d 419, 363 N.E.2d 1155 (1977) (A shot B in chest 3 times, about 5 minutes later X shot B 5 times, wounds inflicted by A could have brought about death in 5 minutes, X thus only guilty of attempted murder).

cause of death? Some cases have held as to such a situation that *A*'s conduct is not a cause of *B*'s death,[20] but there is some authority to the contrary.[21] Although the commentators have generally approved the former view,[22] it has been questioned whether a different result is not called for on somewhat different facts, as in this situation: *A* is entering a desert; *B* secretly puts a fatal dose of poison in *A*'s water keg; *A* takes the water keg into the desert where *C* steals it; both *A* and *C* think it contains water; *A* dies of thirst.[23] It is argued that " 'causing death' normally involves the notion of shortening life and not merely determining the manner of dying," [24] so that *B* and not *C* is the cause of death.

Of course, in all these cases involving two assailants, if *A* and *X* are not acting independently, but are working together to cause *B*'s death, one is as guilty as the other on general principles concerning accomplices in crime, no matter which one actually applies the coup de grace.[25]

Finally, special mention must be made of a frequently recurring situation which might appear to be of the type previously described. It is that in which *A*'s conduct has very seriously injured *B*, ultimately resulting in *B*'s condition deteriorating to the point where his heart and breathing action can be continued only with a life support system, use of which is finally terminated by Dr. *X* because *B*'s condition is irreversible. In such circumstances, *A* will of course contend that Dr. *X* was the cause of death. Often this contention is rebuffed by use of the concept of "brain death" to conclude that *B*'s death occurred before Dr. *X* terminated the system.[26] But courts have indicated that in any event *A* is still the cause of *B*'s death, for Dr. *X*'s actions are not to be viewed as an independent intentional killing but rather as a foreseeable consequence of *B*'s medical treatment.[27]

 WESTLAW REFERENCES

203k5 /p substantial /3 factor
topic(110 203) /p fact*** actual** proximate** legal**
    /3 caus! /p foresee! predict!

(c) Legal (Proximate) Cause Generally. We have already noted that, even though *A*'s conduct may actually cause *B*'s death (or injury), his conduct is not necessarily the "legal" (or "proximate") cause of *B*'s death (injury).[28] The problems of legal causation arise when the actual result of the defendant's conduct varies from the result which the defendant intended (in the case of crimes of intention) or from the result which his conduct created a risk of happening (in the case of crimes of recklessness and negligence). The variance may be (1) as to the person or property

---

20. State v. Scates, 50 N.C. 420 (1858) ("we cannot imagine how [*A*] can be said to have killed [*B*], without involving the absurdity of saying that the deceased was killed twice"); State v. Wood, 53 Vt. 560 (1881). Of course, *A* may be guilty of attempted murder if not guilty of murder itself.

21. State v. Batiste, 410 So.2d 1055 (La.1982) (*A* shot *B* 3 times, bullet passed through lungs and heart, and then *X* shot *B* at close range in the forehead; *A* is guilty of voluntary manslaughter, as the "law will not stop, in such a case, to measure which wound is the more serious, and to speculate upon which actually caused the death"); Commonwealth v. Costly, 118 Mass. 1 (1875). If *B* dies from the combined effect of the two wounds, however, perhaps both *A* and *X* have caused the death. People v. Lewis, 124 Cal. 551, 57 P. 470 (1899). This notion is criticized in Hall, supra note 8, at 267.

22. E.g., J. Hall, supra note 8, at 267; H. Hart & A. Honore, supra note 8, at 219.

23. H. Hart & A. Honore, supra note 8, at 219.

24. H. Hart & A. Honore, supra note 8, at 220. They suggest, however, that there may be situations in which one who prolongs his victim's life might be said to have caused his death, as where *A* poisons *B* so that *B* is too ill to sail on a voyage and *B* dies of the poison a day after the ship is lost with all on board. Id. at 220 n. 1.

25. See § 6.7.

26. State v. Fierro, 124 Ariz. 182, 603 P.2d 74 (1979); Swafford v. State, 421 N.E.2d 596 (Ind.1981); State v. Shaffer, 229 Kan. 310, 624 P.2d 440 (1981); State v. Meints, 212 Neb. 410, 322 N.W.2d 809 (1982).

27. Matter of J.N., 406 A.2d 1275 (D.C.App.1979) ("a reasonable medical procedure"); Commonwealth v. Golston, 373 Mass. 249, 366 N.E.2d 744 (1977) (not reckless act so as to be superseding cause).

28. And in addition, once again, though he may both (a) actually cause and (b) legally cause *B*'s death or injury, he is not necessarily criminally liable for that result, since his conduct must (c) include the necessary mental fault— intention or recklessness or negligence—which the particular crime may require.

harmed, or (2) as to the manner in which the harm occurs, or (3) as to the type or degree of the harm.[29] Although most of the actual cases concern homicide, where the result in question was someone's death, the same principles apply to other cause-and-result crimes involving some injury or loss other than death—such as bodily injury to the person (as in criminal battery) or injury to or loss of property (as in malicious mischief, arson, false pretenses).

The problems of legal causation arise in both tort and criminal settings, and the one situation is closely analogous to the other. Although the courts have generally treated legal causation in criminal law as in tort law,[30] on principle they do not have to, for the issue is not precisely the same in the two situations.[31] In tort law, it would seem, one might logically require one who actually injured another (especially if he intended to cause an injury to another, but also even if he only negligently caused such an injury), to pay for the damage actually caused without regard to the likelihood or unlikelihood of the particular result achieved, on the theory that of the two of them he, rather than the innocent victim, should bear the cost. (The trend in tort law has, in fact, been in the direction of expanding liability, though courts still talk in terms of legal or proximate cause).

But with crimes, where the consequences of a determination of guilt are more drastic (death or imprisonment, generally accompanied by moral condemnation, as contrasted with a mere money payment) it is arguable that a closer relationship between the result achieved and that intended or hazarded should be required.[32] The most obvious difference in this regard between the two areas of law, of course, is that in tort law the defendant may be held responsible for harms different than those actually risked by his conduct,[33] while this is generally not the cause in the criminal law.[34] It is significant that it is in the limited areas of the criminal law where this is possible—felony-murder and misdemeanor-manslaughter—that there has been the greatest move away from the notion that legal cause in tort cases is controlling.[35]

There is yet another reason for taking a somewhat different view of causation in criminal law then in tort law. The requirement of causation in criminal law, more often than not, serves not to free defendants from all liability but rather to limit their punishment consistent with accepted theories of punishment.[36] It is generally accepted, for example, that these theories support the conclusion that when *A* shoots at *B* with intent to kill and misses, he should not be punished as severely as would have been appropriate had he killed *B*.[37] This being so, the same should

---

29. As to this third situation, at least when the harm is of a different type or greater degree than that covered by the defendant's mental state, the case often may be disposed of without reaching the question of causation. This is because criminal liability usually cannot be imposed when the defendant's mental state was such that he intended or knowingly or unknowingly risked a different or lesser harm. See § 3.11. The felony-murder and misdemeanor-manslaughter rules are major exceptions to this requirement of concurrence in mental state and harm, and thus these cases must be dealt with in terms of causation. They are discussed in the present section.

30. E.g., State v. McFadden, 320 N.W.2d 608 (Iowa 1982) (though different policies sometimes come into play in criminal cases, giving tort proximate cause instruction here not error in involuntary manslaughter case, as no policy difference here); State v. Harris, 194 Neb. 74, 230 N.W.2d 203 (1975) (tort proximate cause instruction proper in this felony-murder case).

31. As to causation-in-fact, the two situations are exactly alike: in torts, which necessarily require a bad result to the plaintiff, the defendant's conduct must actu-

ally cause the result; in criminal law, as to those crimes requiring a bad result, the defendant's conduct must similarly actually cause the result.

32. See J. Hall, supra note 8, at 254–57; Comment, The Use of the Tort Liability Concept of Proximate Cause in Cases of Criminal Homicide, 56 Nw.U.L.Rev. 791 (1962); Commonwealth v. Paquette, 451 Pa. 250, 301 A.2d 837 (1973).

Beale, The Proximate Consequences of an Act, 33 Harv. L.Rev. 633 (1920), deals with tort and criminal cases without distinction; and this has, until recently been the standard treatment of the subject.

33. Restatement (Second) of Torts § 281, Comment j (1965).

34. See § 3.11.

35. See § 3.12(h).

36. See § 1.5.

37. Model Penal Code § 5.05, Comment at 490 (1985); Note, 78 Colum.L.Rev. 1249, 1252–60 (1978).

be true when *B*'s death results from a series of events too extraordinary or too dependent on the acts of another to be attributed to *A*.[38] *A* should not suffer the penalty for murder, nor should he be entirely free of criminal sanctions.[39]

The problem of legal causation arises in respect to both crimes of intention and crimes of recklessness and negligence. *A* shoots at *B* with intent to kill him; perhaps he misses *B* but kills an unintended victim *C;* or perhaps he does hit *B*, who dies in quite an unintended manner (e.g., *B*, only injured, goes to the hospital, where his doctor negligently dresses the wound, a fact which leads to gangrene and death). Or *A* recklessly endangers *B*'s life; perhaps, however, it is an unexpected victim *C*, not *B*, who dies; or perhaps *B* dies but in an unexpected manner. Though the two situations are analogous, they do not necessarily call for precisely the same treatment. One might logically, it would seem, be harder on those who intend bad results, more readily holding them criminally liable for results which differ from what they intended, than on those (morally less at fault) whose conduct amounts only to reckless or negligent creation of risk of bad results.[40] For this reason, cause-and-result crimes of intention must be treated separately from those of recklessness and negligence.

 WESTLAW REFERENCES

di legal cause
topic(110 203) /p proximate** legal** /3 caus! /p natural** probabl* likely /4 consequence result

(d) Intentional Crimes—Unintended Victim ("Transferred Intent"). In the unintended-victim (or bad-aim) situation—where *A* aims at *B* but misses, hitting *C*—it is the view of the criminal law that *A* is just as guilty as if his aim had been accurate. Thus where *A* aims at *B* with a murderous intent to kill, but because of a bad aim he hits and kills *C*, *A* is uniformly held guilty of the murder of *C*.[41] And if *A* aims at *B* with a first-degree-murder state of mind, he commits first degree murder as to *C*, by the majority view.[42] So too, where *A* aims at *B* with intent to injure *B* but, missing *B*, hits and injures *C*, *A* is guilty of battery of *C*.[43] On similar principles, where *A* throws a rock at *B*'s property intending to injure or destroy it but instead hits and injures or destroys *C*'s property, *A* should be guilty of malicious mischief to *C*'s property. And if *A* sets a fire with intent to burn *B*'s property, but because of a shift in the wind the fire burns *C*'s property, *A* should be guilty of the arson of *C*'s property.

38. H. Hart & A. Honore, supra note 8, at 354–55.

39. See, e.g., People v. Dlugash, 41 N.Y.2d 725, 395 N.Y.S.2d 419, 363 N.E.2d 1155 (1977) (where it not proved victim still alive when defendant shot him, murder conviction reduced to attempted murder). Of course, there are also instances in which the defendant did not intend to kill or to do any other harm, in which case conviction for attempt will not be possible. Nonetheless, conviction of some crime is often possible, either an offense defined in terms of recklessly endangering (but not causing) certain harm, or (when the homicide prosecution was based upon the felony-murder or misdemeanor-manslaughter rules) the felony or misdemeanor which was the remote cause of death. See, e.g., People v. Stewart, 40 N.Y.2d 692, 389 N.Y.S.2d 804, 358 N.E.2d 487 (1976) (where gross medical negligence, conviction of intent-to-injure manslaughter reduced to assault).

40. Thus compare Restatement of Torts §§ 279–280 (1934) (intentional torts), with id. §§ 431 et seq. (negligent torts); and see comment to id. § 279 for the difference between legal cause in intentional torts and legal cause in negligent torts.

41. Mayweather v. State, 29 Ariz. 460, 242 P. 864 (1926) (*A* with intent to kill fired gun at enemy *B*, hitting friend *C;* held, *A* murdered *C*); Coston v. State, 144 Fla. 676, 198 So. 467 (1940) (*A* put poison in *B* 's whiskey bottle with intent to kill *B*. *B* gave the bottle to *C* who, not knowing of the poison, handed a drink to *D*, who drank and died of the poison; held, *A* murdered *D*); Gladden v. State, 273 Md. 383, 330 A.2d 176 (1974) (*A* with intent to kill fired at *B* but hit *C*; held, *A* murdered *C*). See Annot., 18 A.L.R. 917 (1922).

42. Gater v. State, 141 Ala. 10, 37 So. 692 (1904) (premeditation); State v. Gardner, 57 Del. 588, 203 A.2d 77 (1964) (express malice aforethought); State v. Payton, 90 Mo. 220, 2 S.W. 394 (1886) (lying in wait). Contra: Bratton v. State, 29 Tenn. 103, 10 Humph. 103 (1849) (only second degree murder of *C*). See cases in Focht, supra note 18, at 41 n. 111 (1938); Annot., 18 A.L.R. 914 (1922).

43. People v. Weaver, 71 Cal.App.2d 685, 163 P.2d 456 (1945) (*A* struck at *B* with a knife, which landed instead in *C* 's chest; *C* calmly told *A:* "Madam, you cut the wrong man"); Medina v. People, 133 Colo. 67, 291 P.2d 1061 (1956) (battery with a deadly weapon with intent to commit bodily harm upon the person of another). In Rex v. Lewis, 6 Car. & P. 161, 172 Eng.Rep. 1190 (1833), *A* put poison in *B* 's su-gar, but *C* ate it and became ill; held, *A* guilty of statutory crime of administering poison to *C*.

These proper conclusions of law as to criminal liability in the bad-aim situation are sometimes said to rest upon the ground of "transferred intent": To be guilty of a crime involving a harmful result to C, A must intend to do harm to C; but A's intent to harm B will be transferred to C; thus A actually did intend to harm C; so he is guilty of the crime against C. This sort of reasoning is, of course, pure fiction. A never really intended to harm C; but it is not necessary, in order to impose criminal liability upon A, to pretend that he did. What is really meant, by this round-about method of explanation, is that when one person (A) acts (or omits to act) with intent to harm another person (B), but because of a bad aim he instead [44] harms a third person (C) whom he did not intend to harm, the law considers him (as it ought) just as guilty as if he had actually harmed the intended victim.[45] In other words, criminal homicide, battery, arson and malicious mischief do not require that the defendant cause harm to the intended victim; an unintended victim will do just as well.[46]

It may be extraordinary when A takes aim on B with a gun or rock, that anyone except B should be within gunshot or rock throwing range; or, when A sets his fire, that the wind should shift so as to blow toward C's property. Thus A and B are not, as they suppose, alone on the desert; C, a tramp, is asleep nearby behind some sagebrush, and he is struck and killed by the bullet A intended for B. Is A guilty of murder? In tort law this fact makes no difference to A's liability; there is no requirement, in order to hold A liable for the harm he causes to C as a result of a bad aim at B, that the harm he causes be likely or even foreseeable.[47] It has sometimes been argued, however, that "the plain man's view of justice" requires that the notion of transferred intent in the criminal law be limited to those cases where the defendant was negligent as to the actual victim.[48]

44. In People v. Birreuta, 162 Cal.App.3d 454, 208 Cal. Rptr. 635 (1984), it was held that the doctrine does not apply if A harms both B and C, as the "function of the transferred intent doctrine is to insure the adequate punishment of those who accidentally kill innocent bystanders, while failing to kill their victims."

45. See State v. Gardner, 57 Del. 588, 203 A.2d 77 (1964): A shot at B with "express malice aforethought" but accidentally hit and killed C. Dealing with the question whether the first degree murder statute required that the "express malice" be directed toward the person killed, the court, holding no, stated: "We assume that our lawmakers have felt, as did Lord Coke and as do most authorities today, that a man's crime is no less heinous because he happens to kill a different person than he intended to kill."

In Model Penal Code § 2.03(2)(a), the situation is dealt with in terms of causation rather than transferred intent, and it is there provided that when purposely or knowingly causing a particular result is an element of an offense, that element is not established if the actual result is not within the purpose or contemplation of the actor. Certain exceptions are listed, and one is where the actual result differs only in that a different person or different property is injured or affected. Some of the modern codes have adopted such a provision.

46. Sometimes a statutory crime may be worded in such a way as to require for guilt that the intended victim and the actual victim be one and the same—e.g., "whoever with a deadly weapon commits a battery on another with intent to kill or maim *such person* is punishable . . . ." A threw a glass bomb full of sulphuric acid at B with intent to maim B, but A missed B, maiming C. It was properly held in State v. Martin, 342 Mo. 1089, 119 S.W.2d

298 (1938), that A was not guilty of a battery on C with intent to maim C; the statute (badly worded, of course) required a specific intent to maim C, and A had no such intent. (Nor, of course, was A guilty of a battery on B with intent to maim B; since he missed B, there was no battery on B.)

Compare the statute involved in Medina v. People, 133 Colo. 67, 291 P.2d 1061 (1956), making it a crime to commit an assault or battery with a deadly weapon with intent to commit "upon the person of another" a bodily injury. Here A shot at B with intent to injure B but hit C; *held* conviction affirmed.

47. See Restatement (Second) of Torts § 16, comment (b) (1965), making this same point as to battery in the bad-aim situation.

48. G. Williams, Criminal Law: The General Part 133 (2d ed. 1961). Consider also Note, 78 Colum.L.Rev. 1249, 1267–72 (1978), criticizing the transferred intent theory and concluding at 1272 that an "adequate replacement for the doctrine would be a rebuttable presumption of aggravated recklessness with respect to the death of the actual victim if it occurs while the offender is attempting to murder someone else," and, at 1285, that a "preferable approach would be * * * simply to prosecute the offender for attempting the offense with respect to the intended victim, and for causing harm, with whatever culpability he possessed, to the actual victim."

Model Penal Code § 2.03(2)(a) takes the view that it makes no difference that a different person was killed. See note 45 supra. However, it may be that the additional requirement in § 2.03(2)(b) that the actual result "is not too remote or accidental in its occurrence to have a [just] bearing on the actor's liability or on the gravity of his

Whether such a limitation is a sensible one depends upon the rationale behind what is often referred to as transferred intent. If it is simply that one who intends to kill and who does cause death is rightly viewed as a murderer, then the limitation should not be imposed. But it is questionable whether this is the rationale; at least this view has not been followed when the person the defendant intended to kill actually dies but the result is an abnormal and unforeseeable one.[49] In the bad-aim cases, the actor may be convicted of attempting to murder his intended victim, so the rationale behind transferred intent must somehow explain why a higher penalty should be permitted merely because he killed a third person. One suggestion is that while, in a moral view, one who attempts a crime is as bad as one who succeeds, the penalties are not as great for attempts because the public would not tolerate the severe punishment imposed when the harm is done (e.g., the penalty for murder) for one who did not actually bring about the harm.[50] When a third person is killed this barrier is not present, although, to complete the argument, it must be assumed that it is present when the defendant was not even negligent as to the person killed.

There are, of course, some situations where, though A intentionally kills or injures B, A is not guilty of murder or battery. Though he kills B, he may be guilty only of voluntary manslaughter (e.g., when B has provoked A into a reasonable rage to kill);[51] or he may be

guilty of no crime at all (e.g., when he is privileged to kill or injure B in self-defense, or to prevent B's commission of a felony).[52] Now suppose A shoots at B under these circumstances but, missing B, hits and kills or injures C, an innocent bystander. If A aims at his attacker B in proper self-defense, but hits C instead, he is not generally guilty of murder or battery of C. Once again, he is only as guilty as to C as he would have been had his aim been accurate enough to have hit B.[53] So too if A aims at B with intent to kill under circumstances which would make him guilty of voluntary manslaughter of B, but he hits and kills C instead, A is guilty of voluntary manslaughter of C.[54]

The situation, discussed above, concerning the unintended victim of an intentional crime—which we have referred to for short as the bad-aim situation—is to be distinguished from an entirely different unintended-victim case—the mistaken-identity situation—which is governed by a quite separate set of legal rules. Thus in the semi-darkness A shoots, with intent to kill, at a vague form he supposes to be his enemy B but who is actually another person C; his well-aimed bullet kills C.[55] Here too A is guilty of murdering C, to the same extent he would have been guilty of murdering B had he made no mistake. A intended to kill the person at whom he aimed, so there is even less difficulty in holding him guilty than in the bad-aim situation.[56] And of course A's conceivable argument that his mis-

offense" might be utilized to impose the limitation suggested by Williams.

49. E.g., Bush v. Commonwealth, 78 Ky. 268 (1880) (defendant shot victim with intent to kill, victim died of scarlet fever contracted from attending doctor, *held,* defendant not the legal cause of victim's death).

50. G. Williams, supra note 48, at § 49, based in part upon the analysis in Wechsler & Michael, A Rationale of the Law of Homicide, 37 Colum.L.Rev. 701, 1261, 1295–98 (1937).

51. See § 7.10.

52. See §§ 5.7, 5.10. Of course, A may be privileged to injure B in self-defense or in some other circumstances, even though he may have no privilege to kill B.

53. Pinder v. State, 27 Fla. 370, 8 So. 837 (1891). See Annot., 18 A.L.R. 917, 927 (1922). The same result would follow where A aims at B in other circumstances wherein he would be justified in killing or injuring B but, missing B, hits C.

Of course, the situation may be such that A ought not to shoot at B in self-defense, etc., because of the presence of bystanders like C whom A might hit instead. If there is a high degree of risk to people like C involved in A's shooting at B, A's killing of C will amount to manslaughter, Henwood v. People, 54 Colo. 188, 129 P. 1010 (1913); Annot., 18 A.L.R. 917, 928 (1922); if a substantial certainty, to murder.

54. Wheatley v. Commonwealth, 26 Ky.L.Rep. 436, 81 S.W. 687 (1904); Rex v. Gross, 23 Cox Crim.Cas. 455 (1913). See Annot., 18 A.L.R. 917, 927 (1922).

55. Or A takes C's wallet, thinking it to be B's; or burns C's house, in the belief it is B's; or rapes C thinking she is B; and so on.

56. If A tries to kill his tormenter B with a voluntary-manslaughter state of mind, but, because he has lost his glasses, he kills C mistaking him for B, he is guilty of voluntary manslaughter. White v. State, 44 Tex.Crim. 346, 72 S.W. 173 (1902).

take of fact (as to the victim's identity) somehow negatives his guilt of murder would be unavailing: his mistake does not negative his intent to kill; and on the facts as he supposes them to be A is just as guilty of murder as he is on the facts which actually exist.[57]

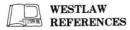

WESTLAW REFERENCES

topic(110 203) /p transfer*** /3 intent
opinion(transfer*** /3 intent /p self-defense (justif!
    /3 homicide))

(e) Reckless and Negligent Crimes—Unhazarded Victim ("Transferred Negligence"). An analogous problem exists as to crimes of recklessness or negligence. Thus suppose A recklessly creates a risk of death or bodily injury to another person B (or to a whole class of persons, including B), so that he would be liable for involuntary manslaughter (or battery) if he killed (or injured) B. But he misses B; instead, C, who was not the person foreseeably endangered or a member of a foreseeably endangered class,[58] is killed or injured. Is A guilty of involuntary manslaughter if C is killed, or of battery if C is injured? Or (if one likes to speak in fictions) is the recklessness which A directed toward B to be "transferred" to C, with the result that A was reckless with respect to C so as to afford the basis for manslaughter or battery liability? To give two illustrations: (1) A puts household poison in a whiskey bottle and

places the bottle in a locked drawer to which, as A knows, only A and B have keys, thereby recklessly endangering B; but C, a burglar breaks into the drawer by force, takes a drink and dies.[59] (2) A drives a car through town so fast that he creates a high degree of risk of death to other motorists (a class of persons), but not to people within buildings along his route. He crashes into what appears to be an ordinary pleasure vehicle but which actually is full of explosives. The resulting explosion causes a window to shatter over C, sitting near the window; the glass cuts C's artery, causing death.[60]

In these situations, the better view may be that A is not criminally liable for C's death.[61] If one accepts the argument, discussed above, that negligence to the person killed should be required in the transferred intent cases, then it seems to follow that the same result should be reached here,[62] particularly in view of the fact that a narrower view of legal causation is often taken when the defendant is a reckless or negligent wrongdoer rather than an intentional wrongdoer. To hold A criminally liable for C's death would extend the criminal law beyond tort law, where one is not liable to the "unforeseeable plaintiff."[63]

If the above view is correct, then there would be no "transferred negligence" in criminal law. The mental state for a negligence crime would encompass all those persons the defendant *should* foresee as endangered by

---

57. See § 5.1.

58. Although one ordinarily (but not necessarily) intends harm only to a single individual, it is common for one to be reckless or negligent as to a class of persons—those foreseeably endangered by his conduct.

59. This hypothetical case, involving foreseeable risk to a single person only, is presented in G. Williams, Criminal Law: The General Part § 36 (1953), which presents a more complete discussion than § 50 (2d Ed. 1961).

60. This illustration, involving foreseeable risk to a class of persons, is adapted from one in Restatement (Second) of Torts § 281, comment c (1965).

61. Such is the conclusion of Professor Williams as to illustration (1), and of the Restatement as to the analogous tort problem raised by illustration (2). See also Restatement (Second) of Torts § 430, comment b (1965).

Model Penal Code § 2.03(3)(a) provides that the element of recklessly or negligently causing a particular result is established when "the actual result differs from the proba-

ble result only in the respect that a different person or different property is injured or affected," suggesting a contrary result. Some modern codes have adopted similar provisions. However, the requirement in § 2.03(3)(b) that the actual result "is not too remote or accidental in its occurrence to have a [just] bearing on the actor's liability or on the gravity of his offense" might well support the conclusion reached above.

62. Of course, here the problem cannot be discussed in terms of the law of attempts, as the crime of attempt has not occurred because of the defendant's lack of intent. Rather, the issue is whether it is best to punish the defendant only for a reckless or negligent conduct crime which does not require bad results (and which, in all likelihood, will carry a lesser penalty).

63. This view received its principal impetus in torts from Chief Judge Cardozo's opinion in Palsgraf v. Long Island R.R., 248 N.Y. 339, 162 N.E. 99, 59 A.L.R. 1253 (1928). See also Restatement (Second) of Torts § 281, comment c (1965).

his conduct, and he would not be held to be the legal cause of the harm resulting to other persons from his conduct. There could, however be "transferred recklessness," by which the defendant's conscious awareness of the danger to one person would suffice when another person is harmed *and* the defendant was negligent as to that person. For example, A recklessly fires a gun in the general direction of B, of whose presence A is actually aware, but the shot hits C, who A did not see but should have seen. This would be an appropriate case for what some would call "transferred recklessness"; more appropriately, it might be said that here A is the legal cause of C's injury.

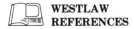

WESTLAW REFERENCES

fi 691sw2d744

(f) Intentional Crimes—Unintended Manner. It sometimes happens that the defendant successfully brings about the end result he intends (e.g., death or injury to a certain person), but he does so in a manner which he never contemplated. The variation between intended manner and actual manner may be relatively slight, as where A with intent to kill shoots at B's heart but hits him in the head, killing him. It may on the other hand be very great, as where A, shooting at B with intent to kill, misses him completely, but causing him to turn north rather than continuing south; then, while traveling north, B is struck by lightning and killed—a result which would not have happened but for A's shot at B. Or it may be somewhere in between these extremes, as where A, shooting at B with intent to kill, merely wounds B; but the doctor who tends his wounds negligently treats him, with death resulting from the infection which a careful doctor would have prevented.

We have already noted that courts are somewhat more willing to find the defendant's acts to be the legal cause of the results when the defendant actually intended those results, albeit they came about in a manner other than he intended. It does not follow, however, that the law should hold the defendant criminally liable for those results in every case in which what he intended actually came about, no matter how abnormal or unforeseeable the chain of events might be. In the second illustration given above (where B was struck by lightning), "most people would not only refuse to say that the man had caused [the] death but would recoil at the prospect of punishing him with the same severity as that reserved for murder." [64] When intended results come about in a highly unlikely manner, the defendant should not be punished for those results (as opposed to punishment for attempting to bring them about), for to do otherwise would bring the criminal law into sharp conflict with our sense of justice. Thus, the Model Penal Code appropriately deals with this situation by putting the issue squarely to the jury's sense of justice; [65] the inquiry is whether the actual result is "too remote or accidental in its occurrence to have a [just] bearing on the actor's liability or on the gravity of his offense." [66] The decided cases, discussed below, generally conform to this view, although many of them rest upon difficult distinctions between intervening, concurrent, natural, human, and other classifications of causes.

(1) Direct Cause. Where the only difference between the intended manner and the actual manner lies in the precise nature of the injury inflicted, there is no difficulty in holding the defendant liable. A is thus guilty of murdering B where he intentionally inflicts a fatal wound, or of battery if he non-fatally wounds B (whether with intent to kill or

64. H. Hart & A. Honore, supra note 8, at 354.

65. See Model Penal Code § 2.03, Comment at 262 (1985).

66. Model Penal Code § 2.03(2)(b). A few of the modern codes contain a similar provision. Del.Code tit. 11, § 261; Hawaii Rev.Stat § 702–214 ("or too dependent on another's volitional conduct"); Mont.Code Ann. 45–2–201;

N.J.Stat.Ann. 2C:2–3 ("or dependent on another's volitional act"); Pa.Cons.Stat.Ann. tit. 18, § 303. A few others utilize a different test: whether the injury which actually occurred happened "in a manner which the person knows or should know is substantially more probable by such person's conduct." Ariz.Rev.Stat. § 13–203; Ky.Rev.Stat. 501.060.

merely to injure *B*), though he hits another part of *B*'s body than the precise spot at which he aims.[67] So too if *A* should aim a rock at *B*'s right eye with intent to put it out; it would be mayhem though his aim was off and the rock struck the left eye, putting it out.[68]

(2) Pre-existing Weakness. Sometimes *A* attacks *B* with intent to kill, but succeeds only in inflicting what would be a non-fatal wound in a person of ordinary health. But *B* is in a weakened condition from disease or prior wounds or exposure or intoxication, and so he dies. (Sometimes, in addition, he would have died sooner or later anyway from this disease or other condition, but *A*'s murderous attack carries *B* off sooner than otherwise.) [69] It is held that *A* is guilty of murdering *B*, his act being a direct cause of *B*'s death.[70]

(3) Intervening Cause: Generally. The intended result achieved in an unintended manner often happens as a consequence of some intervening act (a) of the victim himself, (b) of a third person, (c) of the defendant,[71] or (d) of a non-human source. We are not concerned here with the case, discussed earlier, in which the defendant's act and some other act concur to bring about the victim's death (e.g., *A* stabs *C*, *B* shoots *C*, *C* expires by bleeding to death from both wounds). Rather, the question here is the significance of subsequent acts from any of these four sources when they are more than a concurring cause of death, as where the defendant did not inflict a fatal

wound and the victim died only from the effects of the subsequent act.

The significance of acts from each of these four sources is discussed in some detail below. As a preliminary matter, however, it is important to note in a general way how courts have dealt with these kinds of cases. As might be expected, courts have tended to distinguish cases in which the intervening act was a *coincidence* from those in which it was a *response* to the defendant's prior actions. An intervening act is a *coincidence* when the defendant's act merely put the victim at a certain place at a certain time, and because the victim was so located it was possible for him to be acted upon by the intervening cause. The case put earlier in which *B*, after being fired upon by *A*, changed his route and then was struck by lightning is an illustration of a coincidence. However, it is important to note that there may be a coincidence even when the subsequent act is that of a human agency, as where *A* shoots *B* and leaves him lying in the roadway, resulting in *B* being struck by *C*'s car; or where *A* shoots at *B* and causes him to take refuge in a park, where *B* is then attacked and killed by a gang of hoodlums.

By contrast, an intervening act may be said to be a *response* to the prior actions of the defendant when it involves reaction to the conditions created by the defendant. The most obvious illustrations are actions of the victim to avoid harm, actions of a bystander to rescue him, and actions of medical personnel in treating the victim. But, while a re-

---

67. In People v. Cobler, 2 Cal.App.2d 375, 37 P.2d 869 (1934), *A*, with intent to kill, gave *B* poison in a glass of milk, which *B* drank; *B* became dizzy and fell, receiving a brain injury; *held*, *A* murdered *B* whether *B* died of the poison or of the brain injury.

68. De Arman v. State, 33 Okl.Crim. 79, 242 P. 783 (1926) (*A* aimed blows all over *B*, causing crippling injuries).

69. We have already noted that it is murder intentionally to kill another, though the defendant's act merely hastens appreciably the inevitable death of his victim.

70. People v. Brown, 62 Cal.App. 96, 216 P. 411 (1923) (*B* weakened by prior wound); Hopkins v. Commonwealth, 117 Ky. 941, 80 S.W. 156, 25 Ky.Law Rep. 2117 (1904) (*B* weakened by consumption); State v. Jenkins, 276 S.C. 209, 277 S.E.2d 147 (1981) (*B* suffered rare, fatal reaction to dye used in arteriogram); State v. Durham, 156 W.Va.

509, 195 S.E.2d 144 (1973) (*B* had a fatty damaged liver, so drugs used in treatment triggered hepatitic death). See cases in Focht, Proximate Cause in the Law of Homicide, 12 So.Cal.L.Rev. 19, 24 (1938).

The pre-existing weakness situation arises also where *A* attacks *B* with intent only to injure, but because of his weakness *B* dies, a result *A* did not intend and which may have been quite unforeseeable. As to *A*'s liability for manslaughter, see § 3.12(h).

71. In one sense, it may seem inappropriate to speak of the defendant intervening in his own acts. The cases involve acts by the defendant, after he thinks the victim is dead, to dispose of the body or conceal the crime. As with other kinds of intervening cause, without these subsequent acts the harm for which the prosecution is commenced would not have occurred.

sponse usually involves a human agency, this is not necessarily the case; infection of a wound inflicted by the defendant may be said to be an instance of germs responding to the victim's condition.

As common sense would suggest, the perimeters of legal cause are more closely drawn when the intervening cause was a matter of coincidence rather than response. There is less reason to hold the defendant liable for the bad results when he has merely caused the victim to be at a particular place at a particular time, than when he has brought other agencies into play in response to a danger or injury. Thus—though the distinction is not carefully developed in many of the decided cases—it may be said that a coincidence will break the chain of legal cause unless it was foreseeable, while a response will do so only if it is abnormal (and, if abnormal, also unforeseeable). If A shoots B and leaves him disabled and then C runs over B with his car (coincidence), the question is whether A could not have reasonably foreseen this possibility; if A shoots B and then Dr. C gives B improper medical treatment (response), the basic question is whether the treatment was abnormal (generally, negligent medical treatment is not so viewed). If A shoots B and B is taken to the hospital, where he comes into contact with some communicable disease which causes his death (coincidence), A is not guilty of murder unless this

was foreseeable (unlikely, unless it was generally known that there had been an outbreak of this disease); if instead B's wounds became infected and he died (response), A is guilty of murder (infection not abnormal).

(4) Intervening Cause: Acts of the Victim. Suppose that A approaches B with a deadly weapon and a murderous intent to kill, so that B, in order to escape, "voluntarily" jumps out a window, or precipitates himself into a ravine, or plunges into a river, with fatal consequences to B. Here A is held guilty of murdering B.[72] Similarly, if A comes at B with an intent to injure but not to kill, causing B to jump to escape the threatened injury, A is liable for manslaughter if B is killed,[73] and battery if B is only injured. Such impulsive acts to avoid harm are quite normal, and thus A may be said to be the legal cause of the consequences. Similarly, where A, intending to kill, merely inflicts a non-fatal wound, but A in a delirium rips off the bandages and dies from the loss of blood, the involuntary intervening act of B would not cut off A's liability for murder.[74]

More difficult are cases where the victim's act is voluntary rather than instinctive,[75] as where he refuses to go to a doctor who could save his life, or refuses to submit to a lifesaving operation; and so he dies when he might have been saved. It has been held that, even here, A's act constitutes the legal cause of B's death.[76] Even where the victim's refusal is

---

72. Thornton v. State, 107 Ga. 683, 33 S.E. 673 (1899); State v. Myers, 7 N.J. 465, 81 A.2d 710 (1951); and Annot., 25 A.L.R.2d 1171 (1952), superceded in part by Annot., 47 A.L.R.2d 1072 (1956). Of course, if A's intention was to kill B by frightening him into jumping to his death, A would be guilty of murder. But even if A actually never contemplated that B would jump, A is liable, for there is a sufficient causal connection.

73. Whaley v. State, 157 Fla. 593, 26 So.2d 656 (1946); Patterson v. State, 181 Ga. 698, 184 S.E. 309 (1936).

74. Stanton's Case, 2 City Hall Rec. 164 (N.Y.1817).

75. But see United States v. Guillette, 547 F.2d 743 (2d Cir.1976), where the defendants were convicted of conspiracy to deprive X of his civil rights where "death results." X was killed when a bomb exploded upon his entry of his house. The prosecution's theory was that the defendants arranged for the bomb so that X could not testify against them at a pending trial; the defendants' was that X had set a booby trap for them and accidentally triggered it. The court concluded that "under the common law even if

[X] died from an explosion that he himself had accidentally caused, appellants would still be considered in the chain of legal causation if the immediate cause of death—setting a bomb as a booby trap—was a foreseeable protective reaction to their criminal efforts to locate and dissuade him from testifying."

76. Franklin v. State, 41 Tex.Crim. 21, 51 S.W. 951 (1899) (B refused to have his leg amputated to prevent spread of gangrene produced by bullet fired by A); Regina v. Blaue, [1975] 1 W.L.R. 1411, [1975] 3 All.E.R. 446 (C.A.), discussed in 35 Camb.L.J. 15 (1976) (B refused blood transfusion because she a Jehovah's witness; A nonetheless was the cause of death, as "those who use violence on other people must take their victims as they find them"). The same sort of problem may arise in connection with mayhem—e.g., A attacks B with intent to maim him, and succeeds in severely injuring B's eyes; though B might have his eyesight saved by an operation, he refuses to undergo the operation.

unreasonable it may nonetheless not be abnormal, as where the victim refuses to consent to amputation of a leg; there may well be instances, however, in which the refusal is so extremely foolish as to be abnormal.[77]

What, then, of suicide by the victim? If A wounds B with intent to kill, but thereafter C shoots B with intent to kill and does kill him instantly, we know that A is not the cause of B's death. If, instead, B takes his own life, we again have a deliberate act directed toward killing B which has intervened, so one might expect the same result. Such a result is certainly appropriate when B commits suicide from some motive unconnected with the fact that he is wounded, but suicide is not abnormal when B acts out of the extreme pain of wounds inflicted by A or when the wound has rendered him irresponsible.[78] Although voluntary harm-doing usually suffices to break the chain of legal cause, this should not be so when A causes B to commit suicide

(5) Intervening Cause: Acts of a Third Person. The most common case involves the negligent treatment of wounds by a doctor or nurse. A, intending to kill B, merely wounds him; but the doctor so negligently treats the wound that B dies. It is generally held that A is guilty of murdering B, i.e., that A's act legally caused B's death,[80] unless the doctor's treatment is so bad as to constitute gross negligence or intentional malpractice.[81] In short, mere negligence in medical treatment is not so abnormal that the defendant should be freed of liability. It might seem to follow that the same result would be reached when, for example, B dies in a traffic accident attributable to the negligence of the ambulance driver who is taking B to the hospital.[82] But, it is very likely that A would not be held to be the legal cause of B's death in such a case, as the death is from new injuries; the medical negligence cases have usually emphasized

In United States v. Hamilton, 182 F.Supp. 548 (D.D.C. 1960), where A wounded B nonfatally, sending him to the hospital where tubes were inserted in his nose, and 3 days later B died of asphyxiation when he pulled these tubes out, it was held that A legally caused B's death whether it was a reflex action, or a semiconscious act, or a conscious and deliberate act on B's part.

77. See Franklin v. State, supra note 76. See also H. Hart & A. Honore, supra note 8, at 318–22.

78. Stephenson v. State, 205 Ind. 141, 179 N.E. 633 (1932); State v. Angelina, 73 W.Va. 146, 80 S.E. 141 (1913). Some other cases reflect a greater willingness to find the defendant the legal cause of the victim's death notwithstanding the victim's suicide, e.g., People v. Lewis, 124 Cal. 551, 57 P. 470 (1899), criticized in J. Hall, supra note 8, at 265–67, where the court concluded that the victim died from both wounds.

79. J. Hall, supra note 8, at 274. This exception may well be significant in another kind of case where, though the manner of the harm is precisely as intended, there is a legal cause issue because of an intervening voluntary act. This is where A, with intent to bring about the death of B, urges B to commit suicide and provides the means for doing so, and B complies. Although it has been argued that A has not caused B's death, H. Hart & A. Honore, supra note 8, at 295, Hall is of the view that "there is no *a priori* reason why causation by giving an incentive should not receive wider recognition in the criminal law." J. Hall, supra note 8, at 273. See People v. Roberts, 211 Mich. 187, 178 N.W. 690 (1920) (defendant guilty of first degree murder, though suicide not criminal, on ground that he "administered" the poison); Sanders v. State, 54 Tex.Crim. 101, 112 S.W. 68 (1908) (defendant not guilty, on ground suicide not a crime and therefore urging or aiding

by creating a situation so cruel and revolting that death is preferred.[79]

another to commit suicide not criminal); Model Penal Code § 210.5, which provides that a person may be convicted of criminal homicide for causing another to commit suicide if he purposely does so by force, duress or deception.

80. People v. Fite, 627 P.2d 761 (Colo.1981) (discontinuation of antibiotic therapy not gross negligence and thus was not a superceding cause); Wright v. State, 374 A.2d 824 (Del.1977) (if wound "calculated to destroy life, negligence, mistake, or lack of skill by treating medical personnel will not be an intervening cause of death"); Johnson v. State, 64 Fla. 321, 59 So. 894 (1912); Hamblin v. State, 81 Neb. 148, 115 N.W. 850 (1908). The liability rule probably applies to negligently treated non-fatal wounds (if inflicted with an intent to kill); Focht, Proximate Cause in the Law of Homicide, 12 So.Cal.L.Rev. 19, 33–34 (1938); Downing v. State, 114 Ga. 30, 39 S.E. 927 (1901); as well as to fatal wounds so negligently treated as to produce an earlier death than otherwise.

81. As in People v. Stewart, 40 N.Y.2d 692, 389 N.Y.S.2d 804, 358 N.E.2d 487 (1976) (one view of evidence was that anesthesiologist failed to provide oxygen to patient during operation; "if this occurred it was a grave neglect, perhaps gross negligence, but in any event sufficient to break whatever causal relationship existed at the time of this incidental operation" to repair hernia, done after completion of surgery for knife wound inflicted by defendant). See also Parsons v. State, 21 Ala. 300 (1852); People v. Whithurst, 2 Labatt 178 (Cal.1858); State v. Morphy, 33 Iowa 270, 276 (1871).

82. No reported case of this kind has been found, but J. Hall, supra note 8, at 264, discusses an unreported case in which the murder charge was dismissed.

that the negligence aggravated the wound inflicted by the defendant.[83]

This kind of accident must be distinguished from a somewhat different situation, as where A, with intent to kill B, only wounds B, leaving him lying unconscious in the unlighted road on a dark night, and then C, driving along the road, runs over and kills B. Here C's act is a matter of coincidence rather than a response to what A has done, and thus the question is whether the subsequent events were foreseeable, as they undoubtedly were in the above illustration.[84]

(6) Intervening Cause: Acts of the Defendant. Assume that A, with intent to kill B, strikes B and renders him unconscious, and then, mistakenly believing B to be dead, hangs B to give the appearance of suicide; B actually dies of strangulation. As noted earlier, this kind of case has usually been thought to present a problem of concurrence in that the act done with intent to kill did not kill and the act which did kill was done without intent to kill.[85] Courts have usually responded to this issue by declaring that there was concurrence because A's actions were all part of a single transaction.[86] It may be suggested, however, that instead of resorting to this artificial device to establish concurrence, it might be better to ask whether the act which clearly concurs with the intent (A's striking of B) is

not properly viewed as the legal cause of death.

Although this act by A was not in itself sufficient to cause death, we know from the medical treatment cases that this in itself is no bar to finding legal cause.[87] What then of the defendant's mistaken belief, whether reasonable or unreasonable, that his victim is dead? While this belief bars a finding of intent to kill at the time of the acts done to avoid detection, it should not bar a finding of legal cause. Although the defendant's awareness of certain facts may extend legal cause farther than would otherwise be the case,[88] it has never been assumed that legal cause requires that death occur in a way that the defendant actually anticipated. In the negligent medical treatment cases, for example, it would appear to make no difference that the treatment was not anticipated by the defendant because he left his victim thinking him dead; legal cause would be found to exist in such a case because the medical treatment, though unanticipated, is not an abnormal response.[89] By the same token, acts by the defendant himself to dispose of the body are not abnormal and thus do not break the causal chain,[90] and this is so even though it might be acknowledged that mutilating what is thought to be a corpse, if done by another person, is such an unusual occurrence as to break the chain of causation.[91]

83. E.g., State v. Jacobs, 194 Conn. 119, 479 A.2d 226 (1984); State v. Tomassi, 137 Conn. 113, 75 A.2d 67 (1950). See Regina v. Jordan, 40 Crim.App. 152 (1956), discussed in Camp & Havard, Causation in Homicide—A Medical View, 1957 Crim.L.Rev. 576; and Williams, Causation in Homicide, 1957 Crim.L.Rev. 429 (A stabbed B, B was hospitalized and after the wound had almost healed B died of pneumonia due to the improper administration of certain medicine; held, A not the cause of death).

84. People v. Fowler, 178 Cal. 657, 174 P. 892 (1918). Perhaps if C were driving in a reckless way, A would not be liable. If A in the Fowler case had merely an intent to injure, but not to kill, A would be guilty of manslaughter; but no doubt A, having put B in an unconscious or helpless position on a dark road, has an affirmative duty to act to pull him off the road, and failure to act under the circumstances where A knows death is substantially certain to occur (or even where he realizes there is a very high risk though no certainty of such death) should make him guilty of murder of the intent to kill (or of the depraved heart) variety.

85. See § 3.11(c).

86. See cases cited § 3.11, note 31.

87. E.g., Commonwealth v. Hackett, 84 Mass. 136 (1861).

88. In Bush v. Commonwealth, 78 Ky. 268 (1880), defendant shot his victim, she was treated by a physician with scarlet fever and contracted this disease and died. This was held to be a superceding cause, but the result might well be different if the defendant had been aware that there was a scarlet fever epidemic.

89. Similarly, in Cunningham v. People, 195 Ill. 550, 63 N.E. 517 (1902), the court held that if the defendant's blows caused the victim to be so unsteady that when he tried to leave he fell and struck his head on the pavement, which brought about his death, then legal cause was established; no concern was indicated over whether the defendant believed his victim dead when he departed prior to the victim's attempt to do so.

90. H. Hart & A. Honore, supra note 8, at 298–99; 33 Harv.L.Rev. 611 (1920); 70 L.Q.Rev. 146, 147 (1954).

91. H. Hart & A. Honore, supra note 8, at 298. Cf. People v. Elder, 100 Mich. 515, 59 N.W. 237 (1894) (defen-

(7) Intervening Cause: Non-human Acts.
Assume that *A* intends to kill *B* but only
wounds him, leaving him unconscious in a
pasture, where he is kicked in the head by a
grazing horse or struck by lightning or
snowed under by a blizzard, in any event with
fatal results. This is properly labelled a coincidence, and thus if the intervening factor is
foreseeable—as if the pasture is crowded with
lively horses or if a blizzard is obviously blowing up—*A* would be liable for murder, though
the horse or the blizzard, not *A*'s bullet, applied the coup de grace to *B*. [92] On the other
hand, if the event which actually kills *B* is
quite unexpected—as if lightning strikes *B*, or
the storm or the horse-kick is highly unlikely—*A* will not be considered the legal cause of
B's death.[93]

In one well-known case *A* attacked *B* with
intent to kill, but he only wounded *B*, sending
him to the hospital for treatment; at the
hospital he caught scarlet fever from his doctor and died. It was held that *A* was not
criminally liable for *B*'s death.[94] This is the
proper result, as again, we are dealing with a
matter of coincidence, and it cannot be said
that what happened was foreseeable.[95]

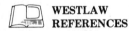

WESTLAW
REFERENCES

203k5 /p (remote accidental** indirect** accelerate*
  /s result death) "direct cause"

203k5 /p interven*** superven*** supersed*** /4
  cause

**(g) Reckless and Negligent Crimes—Un-
foreseeable Manner.** The courts have
tended to apply the same rules to recklessness
and negligence crimes as they have to intent
crimes, although the number of cases in the
former category are not great.[96] Again, it is
usual for courts to distinguish direct cause
from intervening cause cases, and, in the latter group, to separate out coincidence cases
from response cases. Nonetheless, there is
some reason to believe that where the harm
(which, it may be assumed, came about in a
somewhat out-of-the-ordinary way) was merely risked or knowingly risked, rather than
intended, courts are likely to take a more
limited view of what constitutes legal cause.

For crimes requiring proof of recklessness
or negligence by the defendant, it must be
established that the reckless or negligent conduct (not just any conduct of the defendant)
caused the prohibited result. Thus where
driver *A* struck pedestrian *B* and then drove
on, but only *A*'s conduct after impact was
culpably negligent, *B*'s manslaughter conviction was reversed for lack of proof as to
whether *B* died from the initial impact or
from being dragged by *A*'s car thereafter.[97]

(1) Direct cause: As noted earlier, where *A*
intends to shoot *B* in the heart but instead
hits *B* in the head, or where *A* intends to put
out *B*'s left eye but instead puts out his right
eye, the courts have had no difficulty in finding *A* to be the legal cause of the harm. The

dant struck victim, then bystander stepped up and kicked
victim and killed him; *held,* defendant's acts not legal
cause of death).

92. There is no substantial difference in principle between the problem posed in the text and the automobile
case, People v. Fowler, supra note 89. As stated in connection with Fowler, if *A* merely intended to injure *B*, his
crime would be manslaughter, unless a case could be made
out for murder on the basis of an omission to act where
there is a duty to act, accompanied by an intent to kill
(knowledge that death is certain from the horses or the
blizzard) or by a depraved heart (very great risk of death
or serious bodily injury from horses or blizzard, and probably *A*'s realization of this risk).

93. People v. Rockwell, 39 Mich. 503, 3 Am.Cr.Rep. 224
(1878) (kick of a horse).

94. Bush v. Commonwealth, 78 Ky. 268 (1880). Compare the situation where the wound, though not of itself
fatal, brings on a disease, e.g., pneumonia, which proves
fatal. Here *A* is responsible for *B*'s death. People v.

Love, 71 Ill.2d 74, 15 Ill.Dec. 628, 373 N.E.2d 1312 (1978)
(where defendant inflicted injuries requiring splenectomy
and victim contracted and died from pneumonia, defendant was the cause of death).

95. Unless, of course, there are additional facts showing, for example, that the defendant should have been
aware of a scarlet fever epidemic.

96. Most of the cases presenting issues of legal cause
have involved intent crimes or have arisen out of prosecutions for felony-murder or misdemeanor-manslaughter.

97. State v. Rose, 112 R.I. 402, 311 A.2d 281 (1973).
Compare State v. Southern, 304 N.W.2d 329 (Minn.1981)
(conviction affirmed upon similar facts; court admits
death might have been caused either by initial impact or
by dragging, and adds that "defendant, by her gross negligence in failing to stop and in leaving the scene, made it
impossible to determine this. Further, her conduct also
had the effect of ensuring the child's death." Compare
Southern with the *Dlugash* case in note 39 supra.

same would likely be true where the crime was one of recklessness or negligence, although the problem is unlikely to arise because the knowing or inadvertent creation of risks is not likely to be as specific as the intents mentioned above.

We have also seen that where A intends to kill B, he takes his victim as he finds him, so that if B would not have died but for some highly unusual condition (as where B is a hemophiliac) A is still the legal cause of B's death. The same result has been reached in the "constructive homicide" cases, as where A only intended to do a minor injury to B but this battery serves as a basis for a homicide conviction under the misdemeanor-manslaughter rule.[98] Such a result in the latter case is unfortunate, for it does violence to the principle of *mens rea*. [99] What then of the case in which A does not intend to kill B but only proceeds with conscious awareness of an unreasonable risk that he might do so, as where A drops a large object from a window down in the general direction of B? If the object strikes B and crushes him A is clearly guilty of recklessness-manslaughter; but what if the object causes B a very minor injury but B bleeds to death because he is a hemophiliac?

The same issue may arise when it is not the victim's unusual condition which brings about his death. Suppose that A, a stevedore loading a vessel, very carelessly handles a plank suspended over the ship's hold, thereby recklessly creating a risk that B, at work below in the hold, will be killed by virtue of being struck by the falling plank. As it turns out,

because of A's conduct the plank does fall into the hold, but it misses B; however, it causes a spark which ignites gasoline fumes (the existence of which A was reasonably unaware of) in the hold, burning B to death. Is A to be held for recklessness-manslaugher of B? [100]

Notwithstanding the fact that if in either of these cases A had intended to kill B he would be held to be the legal cause of B's death, a different result might be reached where A was only reckless or negligent and the victim was harmed in a way which was not foreseeable. Although a completely convincing basis for such a distinction probably cannot be articulated, it rests upon the notion that the issue of legal cause is largely one of "the plain man's sense of justice" [101] and that the issue should be put "to the jury's sense of justice." [102] So viewed, it would seem that legal cause is more likely to be found lacking when the defendant was only reckless or negligent and the manner of the harm was not foreseeable.[103]

(2) Intervening Cause: Most of the cases involving crimes of recklessness or negligence where the manner of achieving the actual result differs from the manner which was foreseeable are those where some factor intervenes between the defendant's conduct and the result. Thus A recklessly fires a gun in the vicinity of a rowboat on a dangerous river; B and C are in the boat; B in fright jumps overboard, capsizing the boat; and C drowns. A was held guilty of recklessness-manslaughter, for B's instinctive response to the situation was a normal consequence of A's con-

98. E.g., Rutledge v. State, 41 Ariz. 48, 15 P.2d 255 (1932); State v. Frazier, 339 Mo. 966, 98 S.W.2d 707 (1936).

99. See § 3.11; J. Hall, supra note 8, at 260.

100. This hypothetical case is derived from In re Polemis, [1921] 3 K.B. 560, 90 L.J.K.B. 1353, a tort case which held the stevedore liable for the damage to the ship resulting from the explosion. It does not necessarily follow that A should be criminally liable for B's death.

101. H. Hart & A. Honore, supra note 8, at 355.

102. Model Penal Code § 2.03, Comment at 261 n. 17 (1985). A finding of no legal cause might well be expected under Model Penal Code § 2.03(3)(b) because the jury would be told to so find if the actual result was "too remote or accidental in its occurrence to have a [just] bearing on the actor's liability or on the gravity of his

offense." (A few modern codes contain a comparable provision.) Of course, the jury would be likewise instructed when the defendant acted with intent, Model Penal Code § 2.03(2)(b), but the nature of the instruction is such that it seems likely the jury would respond by taking into account the mental state of the defendant. That is, given a certain degree of remoteness, the result is more likely to be found to have a just bearing on the actor's liability when he intended for that result to occur.

103. On the other hand, there is no hesitation in holding defendant to be the cause of death as to foreseeable events. See, e.g., Commonwealth v. Paquette, 451 Pa. 250, 301 A.2d 837 (1973) (murder by extreme recklessness; "defendant cannot escape the natural consequences of his act merely because of foreseeable complications," such as pneumonia after severe beating of infant).

duct.[104] Or *A* recklessly endangers *B*'s life, but his reckless conduct only causes a non-fatal injury; however, a doctor (or nurse) negligently treats the wound, so that *B* dies. *A* is liable for *B*'s death (i.e., he is guilty of manslaughter of the recklessness type) if the doctor's treatment is merely negligent,[105] but not if his treatment is grossly negligent or intentionally wrong.[106]

Although "one who intentionally inflicts a wound calculated to destroy life, and from which death ensues, cannot throw responsibility for the act either upon the carelessness or ignorance of his victim or upon unskillful or improper treatment which aggravated the wound and contributed to his death," [107] is the same true when the defendant merely recklessly or negligently inflicts a wound? That is, are intervening causes dealt with in precisely the same way, without regard to the nature of the defendant's mental state? Most of the cases reflect no obvious differences, and courts tend to apply the same principles whether the defendant was acting with intent to injure or kill or was merely reckless or

negligent. Of course, if there was prior negligence by both the defendant and the victim, then the jury will have to decide whether or not the latter was the sole cause of the injury.[108] But it also appears that there is a greater likelihood of the victim's subsequent acts to avoid harm being found abnormal when the defendant is only charged with acting recklessly or negligently.[109] It is less apparent that any such distinctions are drawn when the intervening act is medical treatment,[110] although it may be suggested that what has sometimes been viewed as less than gross negligence in treatment when the defendant acted with intent might not be so viewed if the defendant had only been reckless or negligent.[111] The one instance in which the cases do reflect a clear difference is where the intervening act is that of the defendant himself; subsequent acts to conceal a crime, causing the death of one the defendant believes to be dead, are considered normal only when the defendant originally acted with intent to kill.[112]

104. Letner v. State, 156 Tenn. 68, 299 S.W. 1049 (1927).

105. People v. Calvaresi, 188 Colo. 277, 534 P.2d 316 (1975); State v. Gabriella, 163 Iowa 297, 144 N.W. 9 (1913).

106. See Focht, Proximate Cause in the Law of Homicide, 12 So.Cal.L.Rev. 19, 34 (1938).

107. State v. Tomassi, 137 Conn. 113, 75 A.2d 67 (1950).

108. E.g., State v. Hallett, 619 P.2d 335 (Utah 1980) (defendant who destroyed stop sign guilty of negligent homicide of driver who drove into intersection even though driver was exceeding 25 m.p.h. speed limit, as driver could still have stopped had there been a sign). See also Palmer v. State, 451 So.2d 500 (Fla.App.1984); State v. Crace, 289 N.W.2d 54 (Minn.1979); Williams v. State, 554 P.2d 842 (Okl.Crim.App.1976); State v. Northrup, ___ R.I. ___, 486 A.2d 589 (1985). But contributory negligence is not a defense. See § 5.11(a).

109. United States v. Warner, 4 McLean 463, 28 F.Cas. 404 (C.C.Ohio 1848) (captain of ship by criminal negligence wrecked ship, some passengers abandoned ship though it was safe to remain aboard); Rex v. Story, [1931] N.Z.L.R. 417 (defendant criminally negligent in colliding with another car, driver of other car drove across road to get to an open space where, because the soil was loose, the car fell down an embankment, resulting in the driver's death). Cf. Patterson v. State, 181 Ga. 698, 184 S.E. 309 (1936) (if defendant guilty of simple assault, victim's response in jumping out of moving car must be found to be reasonable to support manslaughter conviction; if defendant guilty of felonious assault, this is murder even if victim did not act prudently).

But, even a deliberate self-inflicted harm by the victim may not break the chain of legal cause when this is precisely the risk which the defendant was aware he created. State v. Marti, 290 N.W.2d 570 (Iowa 1980) (where defendant's wife, who often talked of suicide, was intoxicated and asked defendant to load pistol for her and he did so and placed it within her reach, after which she committed suicide with it, *held,* defendant guilty of manslaughter); Persampieri v. Commonwealth, 343 Mass. 19, 175 N.E.2d 387 (1961) (where defendant's wife, who was emotionally disturbed and had been drinking, threatened to kill herself and defendant, instead of trying to bring her to her senses, taunted her, told her where gun was, loaded it for her, saw that safety was off, and told her means by which she could pull the trigger, and defendant's wife then committed suicide, *held,* defendant guilty of recklessness-manslaughter).

110. The cases are collected in Annot., 100 A.L.R.2d 769 (1965).

But see Wright v. State, 374 A.2d 824 (Del.1977), declaring that when "a wound is not dangerous or calculated to produce death, and the victim dies solely as a result of improper or negligent treatment, this will be an intervening cause of death and the defendant will not be liable for homicide."

111. E.g., Karl v. State, 144 So.2d 869 (Fla.1962) (child with skull fracture remained in emergency room of hospital for two and a half hours before receiving treatment).

112. The cases have ordinarily been thought to present an issue of concurrence of mental state and act rather than of legal cause, and thus the explanation has been

WESTLAW
REFERENCES

203k74 /p (interven*** superven*** supersed*** /4
cause) reckless! wanton!

(h) Unintended Type of Harm—Felony-Murder and Misdemeanor-Manslaughter.

Where A intends one type of harmful result, but his conduct causes quite another type of harm to the intended victim (or to an unintended victim), A has generally been held not criminally liable for the harm actually caused.[113] This is not because legal cause is lacking; indeed, often the connection between the defendant's actions and the harm is very close, as where A throws a rock at B's window and instead the rock hits C. Rather, it is the principle of *mens rea* which bars conviction. A's intent cannot be "transferred" from his actual purpose to the result—that is, from one kind of crime to another—because this would destroy the meaningful distinctions between crimes of varying seriousness carrying quite different penalties.[114]

There are the felony-murder and misdemeanor-manslaughter situations in criminal homicide, however, where liability for a caused death may result, not from the fact that the defendant intended to kill the victim, but because he had some quite different bad intention in his mind and was acting to carry out that bad intention. Thus, if A, while committing or attempting a felony such as robbery, unintentionally kills B, he may be guilty of murder; if he unintentionally kills B

in the commission of a misdemeanor (such as speeding) he may be guilty of manslaughter.[115] This is so not because of any transfer of intent to (say) rob B, bad though that intent is, to the death of B, thus leading us wrongly to conclude that A intended to kill B so as to be guilty of murder of the intent-to-kill variety. It is so because there are several types of murder in addition to intent-to-kill murder, and one type is the felony-murder.[116]

It is not sufficient that A, who has committed a felony or misdemeanor, has somehow caused B's death; the causation link must be to that conduct by A which constitutes the requisite felony or misdemeanor. Thus, if A engages in a heated argument with B and then commits a battery upon B, after which B dies from a cerebral hemorrhage, but the medical evidence cannot establish whether the hemorrhage was prompted by the battery or the excitement of the prior argument, A may not be convicted of misdemeanor-manslaughter.[117] Sometimes the point, though expressed in terms of causation, is that the nature of the offense (especially in misdemeanor-manslaughter cases) is such that the violation of it really cannot be said to have caused the resulting harm. This is particularly true as to violation of licensing requirements where the absence of the license appears not—in a "but for" sense—to have caused the bad results.[118]

It has sometimes been claimed, perhaps because the felony-murder and misdemeanor-

---

that where the initial intent was not to kill, the subsequent disposal of the body could not be viewed as part of one transaction. See cases collected in § 3.11, n. 31.

113. Unless, of course, A has been reckless or negligent as to the risk of the actual harm occurring.

114. See § 3.11.

115. For felony-murder and misdemeanor-manslaughter, see §§ 7.5, 7.13.

116. And there are several alternative ways to commit involuntary manslaughter, one type being misdemeanor-manslaughter.

117. Fine v. State, 193 Tenn. 422, 246 S.W.2d 70 (1952). Compare People v. Schreiber, 104 Ill.App.3d 618, 60 Ill. Dec. 417, 432 N.E.2d 1316 (1982) (medical evidence showed that victim's death of arteriosclerotic cardiovascular disease associated with mechanical stress attributable to his being tightly bound by the robbers); State v. Sommers, 201 Neb. 809, 272 N.W.2d 367 (1978) (though defendant's

car slid on very icy viaduct, death still caused by his driving while intoxicated, as evidence showed no attempt to control vehicle until he had traveled 370 ft. on the slick surface).

118. State v. Gerak, 169 Conn. 309, 363 A.2d 114 (1975) (no misdemeanor-manslaughter where crime was discharging firearm in city without a permit; "it cannot reasonably be said that failure to obtain a permit was the proximate cause of death"); Burns v. State, 240 Ga. 827, 242 S.E.2d 579 (1978) (no misdemeanor-manslaughter where crime was carrying pistol without license, as "no showing of a causal relationship between appellant's not having complied with the state's licensing laws * * * and the victim's death"); Frazier v. State, 289 So.2d 690 (Miss.1974) (no manslaughter where defendant driving without license when intoxicated passenger grabbed away the wheel; no proof absence of license caused the collision, especially because defendant had been driving for some years and was a capable driver).

manslaughter rules border on strict liability, that the only casual relationship which must be established in such cases is cause-in-fact, which ordinarily only requires proof that but for the defendant's acts (here the felony or misdemeanor) the harm would not have occurred. Thus it is said that if a kidnapper is carefully driving a car in which the kidnapped person is a passenger, and an accident occurs in which that person is killed, then the kidnapper is guilty of murder because kidnapping is a felony.[119] This is not so. Generally, it may be said that rules of causation are the same in felony-murder and misdemeanor-manslaughter cases as in the areas previously discussed, and thus, for example, legal cause will not be present where there intervenes (1) a coincidence that is not reasonably foreseeable (which disposes of the above case) or (2) an abnormal response.

For instance, if A sets fire to his home to collect the insurance and as a consequence someone in the building or a fireman fighting the blaze is killed, then A is clearly guilty of murder; A is the direct cause of the death of those trapped in the building, and in the case of the fireman the intervening act of firefighting could hardly be viewed as abnormal.[120] Assume no such person is killed, but instead, although the firemen have roped off the area, a foolhardy bystander B ducks under the rope and dashes into the house, disregarding the fire chief's warning cries, in order to rescue some articles for the owner, and B is killed when the fiery building collapses on top of him. It would seem that this is such an abnormal response that A would not be held to be the legal cause of B's death,[121] although

a contrary result would be reached in the case where a member of A's family, after reaching a position of safety outside the house, rushes back in to retrieve some items of property and then cannot escape from the burning building.[122] Similarly, if A sets out to rob B's store it is normal for B to try to protect his property, and if as a result there is an exchange of gunfire in which a shot from B's gun hits and kills a bystander, A is the legal cause of this death.[123] The same is true where the shot comes from the gun of a policeman;[124] appearance of the police in response to a robbery is just as normal as appearance of firemen to fight a fire. In these two cases, however, even though causation is established, a limited interpretation of the felony-murder rule might result in A not being convicted of murder.[125]

Two Pennsylvania homicide cases—one involving the felony-murder doctrine, the other the misdemeanor-manslaughter doctrine, and both imposing limitations thereon—have given rise to a good deal of discussion. In the former case, A and B, after robbing X, were fleeing the scene when policeman P appeared and, in the ensuing gunfire, justifiably shot B to death. At his trial for the felony-murder of B, A was convicted on the theory that the death of B in the manner of its occurrence was a natural and foreseeable result of the commission by A and B of the robbery of X. On appeal A's conviction was reversed, however; the court, without specifically saying that tort notions of proximate cause are inapplicable in criminal cases, stated that A could not be guilty of felony-murder of one whose death constituted a justifiable homicide by

119. Seavey, Mr. Justice Cardozo and the Law of Torts, 52 Harv.L.Rev. 372, 386 (1938).

120. E.g., State v. Glover, 330 Mo. 709, 50 S.W.2d 1049, 87 A.L.R. 400 (1932) (fireman killed).

121. An even more unforeseeable death exists if B dashes into the fiery building to commit suicide. Cf. Regina v. Horsey, 3 F. & F. 287, 176 Eng.Rep. 129 (1862).

122. State v. Leopold, 110 Conn. 55, 147 A. 118 (1929) ("the effort of a person to save property of value * * * is such a natural and ordinary course of conduct that it cannot be said to break the sequence of cause and effect").

123. Commonwealth v. Moyer, 357 Pa. 181, 53 A.2d 736 (1947).

124. Jackson v. State, 286 Md. 430, 408 A.2d 711 (1979); Commonwealth v. Almeida, 362 Pa. 596, 68 A.2d 595 (1949) (later overruled, see note 129 infra).

125. In People v. Washington, 62 Cal.2d 777, 44 Cal. Rptr. 442, 402 P.2d 130 (1965), the defendant's accomplice was killed by their robbery victim. The court seemed to acknowledge that legal cause was present, but then interpreted the "in the perpetration or attempt to perpetrate" language of the California felony-murder statute as excluding cases where the shot was fired by someone other than the felons. See also Commonwealth ex rel. Smith v. Myers, infra note 129.

P.[126] In the misdemeanor-manslaughter case, A and B raced their cars in a drag race as a result of a challenge by A accepted by B. During the 70–90 m.p.h. race B, trying to pass A's car, hit an oncoming truck driven by C and was killed. A was convicted of manslaughter of B on the theory that the death of B in the manner it occurred was a foreseeable consequence of the unlawful and reckless conduct of A and B in racing as they did. On appeal A's conviction was reversed, however, the court stating that the tort concept of proximate cause is inapplicable in criminal cases, "a more direct causal connection being required." [127] No explanation of the required "more direct causal connection" was given.[128]

It is submitted that the true reason for the holding in these two cases is the court's feeling, not clearly expressed in the two cases, that A should not, in all justice, be held for the death of B who was an equally willing and foolhardy participant in the bad conduct which caused his death. Thus, in the first case, the court suggests that perhaps A would have been held guilty of felony-murder had the policemen shot a bystander to death instead of A's co-felon B,[129] although on principles of legal causation there is no basis for this kind of distinction.[130] And, in the second case, if C, the driver of the truck which B hit, had been killed rather than B, the court might well have thought that A ought to be guilty of manslaughter of C,[131] although here again the distinction cannot be justified in terms of legal cause.[132] The two Pennsylvania cases no doubt illustrate a growing dissatisfaction with the felony-murder and misdemeanor-manslaughter doctrines, con-

126. Commonwealth v. Redline, 391 Pa. 486, 137 A.2d 472 (1958), noted in 71 Harv.L.Rev. 1565 (1958), expressly refraining from overruling Commonwealth v. Almeida, 362 Pa. 596, 68 A.2d 595, 12 A.L.R.2d 183 (1949) (A was robbing X when two policemen, P1 and P2, appeared and started firing; in the ensuing fusillade, P1 shot P2 to death; A's felony-murder conviction of P2 was affirmed). Accord: People v. Austin, 370 Mich. 12, 120 N.W.2d 766 (1963).

127. Commonwealth v. Root, 403 Pa. 571, 170 A.2d 310, 82 A.L.R.2d 452 (1961), noted in 7 Vill.L.Rev. 297 (1962). Accord: Thacker v. State, 103 Ga.App. 36, 117 S.E.2d 913 (1961); State v. Peterson, 270 Or. 166, 526 P.2d 1008 (1974). For cases contra, see note 132 infra.

In Commonwealth v. Atencio, 345 Mass. 627, 189 N.E.2d 223 (1963), noted at 21 Wash. & Lee L.Rev. 121 (1964), A, B, and C engaged in a game of "Russian roulette;" A and B pulled the trigger without firing the bullet, but, when C fired, the gun went off, killing C. The convictions of A and B of involuntary manslaughter of the criminal-negligence type were affirmed, the court distinguishing the Root case on the ground that there skill was an element, here only luck.

Atencio, like Root, involves the death of a willing participant in a dangerous and foolish game. To hold the survivor guilty in one case but not the other indicates conflicting views of the effect of this factor upon manslaughter liability.

128. Some courts have expressly rejected this analysis or at least have declined to hold that it constitutes a general prohibition upon a tort-type proximate cause instruction to the jury. See State v. McFadden, 320 N.W.2d 608 (Iowa 1982) (misdemeanor-manslaughter case); State v. Harris, 194 Neb. 74, 230 N.W.2d 203 (1975) (felony-murder case).

129. The court refrained from overruling Commonwealth v. Almeida, in which a bystander-policeman rather than a co-robber was the one killed; the robber was held guilty of felony-murder of the bystander.

However, Almeida was finally overruled in Commonwealth ex rel. Smith v. Myers, 438 Pa. 218, 261 A.2d 550 (1970). The court noted that Almeida could not be reconciled with Redline, supra note 126, in terms of proximate cause, but the decision in Smith was based upon a conclusion that the "basic premises" of the felony-murder doctrine were "shaky" and that therefore, "with so weak a foundation, it behooves us not to extend it further and indeed, to restrain it within the bounds it has always known."

130. "A distinction based on the person killed * * * would make the defendant's criminal liability turn upon the marksmanship of victims and policemen. A rule of law cannot be based on such a fortuitous circumstance." People v. Washington, 62 Cal.2d 777, 44 Cal.Rptr. 442, 402 P.2d 130 (1965). Likewise, Morris, The Felon's Responsibility for the Lethal Acts of Others, 105 U.Pa.L.Rev. 50 (1956), argues against application of the felony-murder rule whenever the fatal shot is fired by someone other than the felon, though it is acknowledged that there is legal cause no matter who fired the shot.

131. As in Jacobs v. State, 184 So.2d 711 (Fla.1966) (A and B drag racing, C is to act as timekeeper and thus attempts to pass B to get to finish line first, C strikes car of D coming from opposite direction, C and D killed; held, A, who was racing well ahead of the scene of the accident, is guilty of manslaughter).

132. This is perhaps even more obvious than in the other case. Clearly, either A is the legal cause of the collision of the vehicles of B and C or he is not, and it should make no difference which one of the two drivers (B or C) died from the collision. State v. Melcher, 15 Ariz. App. 157, 487 P.2d 3 (1971); State v. McFadden, 320 N.W.2d 608 (Iowa 1982); Campbell v. State, 285 So.2d 891 (Miss.1973). For other cases, see Annot., 13 A.L.R.3d 431 (1967).

cerning which there is a slowly-emerging trend toward legislative abolition.[133] However, to the extent that these cases rely wholly or in part upon the requirement of legal cause as a means of limiting these doctrines, they tend to distort the meaning of legal cause.[134]

As a general matter, proximate cause questions in felony-murder and misdemeanor-manslaughter cases have been worked out in much the same way as previously described. Where, for example, the injury defendant inflicted upon the victim or the surgery or treatment necessitated thereby brings on not abnormal complications resulting in the victim's death, the defendant is the proximate cause of death.[135] The same is true where the

defendant's conduct brings about the victim's death because of a pre-existing weakness of the victim.[136] Impulsive acts of the victim in an effort to escape being harmed by the defendant's conduct,[137] or self-inflicted harms attributable to the victim's weakened condition,[138] are quite normal and thus do not break the causal chain. Nor do responses of third parties which are not abnormal, such as those previously mentioned or negligent medical treatment.[139] And if the defendant's felony or misdemeanor causes the victim to be at a certain place at a time when some nonresponsive harm befalls him, proximate cause still exists if the events were foreseeable, as where a speeding driver strikes and

133. See §§ 7.5(h), 7.13(e).

134. If the prosecution's theory is neither felony murder nor misdemeanor manslaughter, but rather that defendant was reckless in creating a risk as to his confederate, then courts are much more likely to conclude that causation is present. See, e.g., State v. Pellegrino, 194 Conn. 279, 480 A.2d 537 (1984).

135. Sims v. State, 466 N.E.2d 24 (Ind.1984) (robber beat 92-year-old man with brick, requiring surgery to prevent life-threatening infection, man worsened and died after surgery); State v. Harris, 194 Neb. 74, 230 N.W.2d 203 (1975) (robber knocked down 81-year-old woman, broken hip required surgery, she died month after hip healed from effects of surgery, including pneumonia and circulatory problems); Commonwealth v. Green, 477 Pa. 170, 383 A.2d 877 (1978) (gunshot wound required removal of kidney, death from "post-operative complications"); Commonwealth v. Johnson, 445 Pa. 276, 284 A.2d 734 (1971) (arson caused extensive burns, death from pneumonia attributable to "immobilization that was required to treat those burns").

136. Armstrong v. State, 502 P.2d 440 (Alaska 1972) (manslaughter case, death by asphyxiation; deep unconsciousness, preventing reflex coughing to clear throat, brought about by combined effects of blows to head and excessive alcohol consumption); Hamrick v. People, 624 P.2d 1320 (Colo.1981) ("defendant must take his victim as he finds him" and thus is guilty of felony-murder where he "attacked an epileptic who had consumed a considerable amount of whiskey and had failed to take his prescribed medication"); State v. Spates, 176 Conn. 227, 405 A.2d 656 (1978) (pre-existing heart condition, victim had fatal heart attack during robbery); Matter of Anthony M., 63 N.Y.2d 270, 481 N.Y.S.2d 675, 471 N.E.2d 447 (1984) (elderly victim of robbery suffered heart failure 3 days later); State v. Atkinson, 298 N.C. 673, 259 S.E.2d 858 (1979) (pre-existing heart condition, fatal heart attack during robbery-beating).

This rule seems unduly harsh when the defendant was unaware of the pre-existing condition and inflicted only a light blow, but has been applied there as well. See, e.g., State v. Chavers, 294 So.2d 489 (La.1974) (misdemeanor-manslaughter conviction affirmed where a blow to jaw

triggered heart attack; "Although the holdings to this effect have received scholarly criticism, * * * they do represent the prevailing view in American decisional interpretations of the misdemeanor-manslaughter statutes").

137. State v. Casper, 192 Neb. 120, 219 N.W.2d 226 (1974) (evidence sufficient for felony-murder conviction where victim of attempted robbery, upon being threatened with castration, ran into the river and his dead body found floating downstream several days later); State v. Selby, 183 N.J.Super. 273, 443 A.2d 1076 (1981) (defendant attempted rape of hitchhiker in rear seat of moving car, she jumped out and was killed; felony-murder conviction affirmed, court approves instruction that conviction proper if "the defendant's actions and threats were such as to put a reasonably prudent person in fear of her life, serious bodily harm or an assault with intent to rape, and had impelled the deceased, acting as such a reasonably prudent person to take the steps which culminated in her death," which may have been unduly generous to defendant by virtue of being limited to a reasonable response).

Compare Commonwealth v. Bianco, 388 Mass. 358, 446 N.E.2d 1041 (1983) (defendants pulled victims from car parked with motor running on boat ramp and fought with them, victims then got back into car which defendants were damaging, car then plunged into water and victims drowned; manslaughter conviction reversed, as insufficient evidence whether victims were trying to escape from the battery or to preserve the car from further damage, and only former related to misdemeanor of battery; whether attack upon the car would be sufficient misdemeanor not decided, as case not tried on that theory).

138. Commonwealth v. Stafford, 451 Pa. 95, 301 A.2d 600 (1973) (felony-murder, defendant hit victim with crowbar, a few days later victim found unconscious by bed and later died; it makes no difference whether fall from bed the cause of death, as "the blows to the head were severe and were the direct cause of his deteriorated physical condition which, in turn, ultimately led to his collapsing on the floor").

139. Matter of J.N., 406 A.2d 1275 (D.C.App.1979) (felony-murder, felon the cause of death where "the action of such medical personnel is either reasonable or negligent").

kills an intoxicated man robbers left helpless in the middle of the road at night in a snowstorm.[140]

This is not to suggest, however, that the basic premise of legal causation might never be employed to keep the felony-murder and misdemeanor-manslaughter cases within reasonable bounds. As noted earlier, if the basic inquiry is whether the result was so unusual in its occurrence "to have a [just] bearing on the actor's liability or on the gravity of his offense," [141] it is not inappropriate to give some consideration to whether the defendant intended that result or was merely reckless or negligent as to that result. In felony-murder and misdemeanor-manslaughter cases, the defendant need not even have been reckless or negligent as to the result of death, although, to the extent that these two doctrines have any real justification, it may be that the commission of the felony or misdemeanor tends to show recklessness or negligence in this regard. Thus if, as has been suggested, a more limited view of legal cause might be taken as to reckless and negligent crimes, this may also be true as to felony-murder and misdemeanor-manslaughter cases.

For example, assume that A shoots at B with intent to kill, misses him, but B dies of fright. Since it is true that in cases where A inflicts a very minor wound and B is so weak that he dies from it, A is said to take his victim as he finds him, it is not inconceivable that A would be found to be the legal cause of B's death in the above example. However, if B were to die from fright or excitement as a consequence of A's commission of a misdemeanor in B's presence, then legal cause might well be found to be lacking.[142]

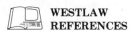 **WESTLAW
REFERENCES**

synopsis,digest(misdemeanor-manslaughter felony-murder /s (proximate** legal** /4 caus!) interven*** superven*** supersed***)

(i) Year-and-a-Day Rule in Homicide.[143] Several centuries ago, when doctors knew very little about medicine, the judges created an absolute rule of law: one cannot be guilty of murder if the victim lives for a year and a day after the blow. The difficulty in proving that the blow caused the death after so long an interval was obviously the basis of the rule. Now that doctors know infinitely more, it seems strange that the year-and-a-day rule should survive to the present, but it has done so in most of the American states, either by judicial decision or by statute.[144] Some cases and statutes even apply the rule to manslaughter as well as to murder.[145] But the modern trend is to abolish the rule.[146]

---

140. Cf. People v. Kibbe, 35 N.Y.2d 407, 362 N.Y.S.2d 848, 321 N.E.2d 773 (1974) (prosecution on extreme recklessness theory). The defendant's conviction was overturned in federal court, Kibbe v. Henderson, 534 F.2d 493 (2d Cir.1976), but that decision was reversed, Henderson v. Kibbe, 431 U.S. 145, 97 S.Ct. 1730, 52 L.Ed.2d 203 (1977).

141. Model Penal Code § 2.03(2)(b), (3)(b). A few modern codes contain such provisions.

142. Graves v. Commonwealth, 273 S.W.2d 380, 47 A.L.R.2d 1068 (Ky.1954) (A while intoxicated created a disturbance at B's house, B died from the excitement; held, A not guilty of manslaughter); Commonwealth v. Couch, 32 Ky.L.R. 638, 106 S.W. 830 (1908) (A unlawfully discharged firearm on public highway, startling B, a pregnant woman, and B later died; held, A not guilty of manslaughter). Contra: People v. Studer, 59 Cal.App. 547, 211 P. 233 (1922); In re Heigho, 18 Idaho 566, 110 P. 1029 (1910). See Annot., 47 A.L.R.2d 1072 (1956).

143. See Comment, 12 Creighton L.Rev. 683 (1979); Recent Decision, 4 U.Balt.L.Rev. 186 (1974).

144. State v. Minster, 302 Md. 240, 486 A.2d 1197 (1985) (court surveys the field and, citing authorities, concludes "the rule remains extant in twenty six states"). See Annot., 60 A.L.R.3d 1323 (1974).

145. E.g., Rex v. Dyson, [1908] 2 K.B. 454. Contra: Commonwealth v. Evaul, 5 Pa.D. & C. 105 (1925).

146. E.g., Commonwealth v. Lewis, 381 Mass. 411, 409 N.E.2d 771 (1980) ("the rule appears anachronistic upon a consideration of the advances of medical and related science in solving etiological problems as well as in sustaining or prolonging life in the face of trauma or disease"); People v. Stevenson, 416 Mich. 383, 331 N.W.2d 143 (1982) ("the old rule is simply too often demonstrably wrong to be upheld"); State v. Young, 77 N.J. 245, 390 A.2d 556 (1978) (abolished for future cases; it an anachronism not specifically required by murder statute); People v. Brengard, 265 N.Y. 100, 191 N.E. 850, 93 A.L.R. 1465 (1934) (no such rule because statute defining murder does not mention it); State v. Hefler, 310 N.C. 135, 310 S.E.2d 310 (1984) (refusing to extend the rule to involuntary manslaughter cases); Commonwealth v. Ladd, 402 Pa. 164, 166 A.2d 501 (1960) (advances in medicine have destroyed all justification for the rule).

Compare State v. Minster, 302 Md. 240, 486 A.2d 1197 (1985) (issue for legislature, which could pick from variety of solutions, such as extending the time as a few jurisdictions have done, changing the rule from an irrebuttable presumption to a rebuttable one with a higher burden of

Where the year-and-a-day rule still obtains, what if some event following the defendant's injury-causing conduct (most likely improper medical treatment) causes the victim to die before that time has run? Although defendants have claimed this breaks the causal chain, this is not correct. The defendant is not absolved from liability where death occurs within a year and a day, and this is so even if proper treatment would have kept the victim alive beyond that time.[147]

WESTLAW REFERENCES

203k6 /p year-and-a-day

(j) Absolute Liability Crimes. Assume that a strict liability statute makes it an offense to pollute rivers or streams with certain substances, which of course means that it is not necessary to conviction that the defendant be shown to have intended to do so or that he was reckless or negligent in this regard. *A* (a company which produces this substance) fills one of its own tank-cars with this substance and then arranges for shipment of this tank-car to its destination via *B* railroad. The train on which this car is carried travels for some distance along the side of a stream, during which time some of the substance leaks out of the car and into the stream.[148] Is *A* guilty of the strict-liability pollution offense?

A, of course, might show that he used due care to prevent his tank-car from leaking, but we know that such evidence does not disprove any required mental state, as none is required. What of causation? If only the but-for tests were used, it would appear that *A* is guilty, as but for *A*'s conduct in having the material shipped the pollution would not have occurred. In a tentative draft, the Model Penal Code only required that the but-for test

be met in absolute liability cases,[149] but in response to criticism [150] the following was added: "When causing a particular result is a material element of an offense for which absolute liability is imposed by law, the element is not established unless the actual result is a probable consequence of the actor's conduct." [151] This is an appropriate way in which to handle legal cause in strict liability cases, and is certainly preferable to the approach in a few such cases of dispensing with the causation requirement.[152]

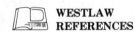

WESTLAW REFERENCES

topic(110) /p strict** absolute** /3 liab!

(k) Causation and the Jury. In *Kibbe v. Henderson*,[153] the habeas corpus petitioner had been convicted of extreme recklessness murder on evidence he left his robbery victim intoxicated and helpless at night during a snowstorm in the middle of a road, where the victim was struck and killed by a speeding car. The court held that since the Constitution requires proof beyond a reasonable doubt on every element of the crime, the failure to instruct the jury on causation created an impermissible risk that the jury had not made a finding on that element. The Supreme Court reversed,[154] noting that the jury had been read the statutory requirement that defendant "thereby cause the death" and had been told of the meaning of recklessness (including that the defendant must have been aware of and disregarded "a substantial and unjustifiable risk"), that both counsel had vigorously argued the causation issue, and that a more elaborate instruction on causation would likely have favored the prosecution on the facts of this case. The Court did not say that what was done below was sound procedure, but only that Kibbe, who had not requested a

---

proof, or abolishing the rule entirely); Elliott v. Mills, 335 P.2d 1104 (Okl.Crim.App.1959) (issue is for the legislature).

147. Matter of J.N., 406 A.2d 1275 (D.C.App.1979).

148. These were essentially the facts in Moses v. Midland Ry., 113 L.T.R. (n.s.) 451 (K.B.1915). There the question was the liability of the railroad for "causing to flow" into any waters containing salmon any poisonous matter, and the court held the railroad had not done so.

149. Model Penal Code § 2.03 (Tent.Draft No. 4, 1955).

150. H. Hart & A. Honore, supra note 8, 361.

151. Model Penal Code § 2.03(4). A few of the modern codes contain such a provision.

152. Mueller, supra note 8 at 185.

153. 534 F.2d 493 (2d Cir.1976).

154. Henderson v. Kibbe, 431 U.S. 145, 97 S.Ct. 1730, 52 L.Ed.2d 203 (1977).

causation instruction at the close of the trial, thus had failed to meet his heavy burden on this collateral attack to show prejudice.

There is state authority to the effect that, at least when a somewhat complex causation question is present in the case, it is not sufficient merely to tell the jury that they must find the defendant was the cause or the proximate cause of the results.[155] "The definition of 'proximate cause' is clearly a term which is not within the common and ordinary knowledge of a layman. Its meaning has been the subject of much lengthy litigation. It is asking too much to expect a jury, without proper definition, to understand and apply such a technical term."[156] Of course, a highly sophisticated set of instructions elaborating upon such concepts as intervening cause and superceding cause may, as a practical matter, be of little help. Noteworthy in this regard is the Model Penal Code approach of having the jury determine whether the result "is not too remote or accidental in its occurrence to have a [just] bearing on the actor's liability or on the gravity of his offense."[157] The advantage of thereby "putting the issue squarely to the jury's sense of justice is that it does not attempt to force a result which the jury may resist."[158] The disadvantage is that there may be inequality in application of this flexible standard by juries.

 WESTLAW REFERENCES

topic(110 203) /p jury /s instruct! charge* /s proximate** legal** /3 caus!

---

155. State v. Crocker, 431 A.2d 1323 (Me.1981); Williams v. State, 554 P.2d 842 (Okl.Crim.App.1976).

156. Williams v. State, 554 P.2d 842 (Okl.Crim.App. 1976).

157. Model Penal Code § 2.03(2)(b), (3)(b). However, only a few of the modern codes have adopted such a provision.

158. Model Penal Code § 2.03, Comment (Tent.Draft No. 4, 1955).

Chapter 4

RESPONSIBILITY

Table of Sections

302

§ 4.1 The Insanity Defense: Theory and Purpose

The insanity defense is quite different from other defenses in that the result, if it is successfully interposed, is not acquittal and outright release of the accused but rather a special form of verdict or finding ("not guilty by reason of insanity") which is usually followed by commitment of the defendant to a mental institution. Thus, its purpose is usually said to be that of separating from the criminal justice system those who should only be subjected to a medical-custodial disposition.

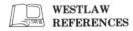
WESTLAW REFERENCES

di insanity

(a) Insanity as a Defense. "Insanity" is a word frequently encountered in legal situations quite outside the criminal law. One test for insanity for the purpose of civil commitment, for example, is whether the person sought to be committed can properly take care of himself and his affairs. A person who is insane cannot make a valid will, but here the test is whether the testator understands the nature of his property and its disposition. One who is insane cannot make a contract, or testify in court, or serve on a jury, but in each instance the test for insanity differs somewhat because of the circumstances involved. Insanity is also a ground for divorce in some jurisdictions, and here again a different test is likely to be used.

The word "insanity" is also used in different criminal law settings, and once again the meaning of the word differs depending upon the circumstances. There is, for instance, insanity as a defense to a criminal prosecution, which is the kind of insanity with which we are principally concerned in this book. Although such insanity may be defined in one of several ways, depending upon the law of the jurisdiction, none of those definitions will suffice for other uses of the word "insanity" in the criminal process, such as (1) to determine

who is incompetent to stand trial;[1] (2) to determine who is incompetent to submit to execution;[2] (3) to determine who is to be committed following a successful insanity defense;[3] or (4) to determine who is ineligible for release following such commitment.[4]

As for insanity as a defense, under the prevailing *M'Naghten* rule (sometimes referred to as the right-wrong test) the defendant cannot be convicted if, at the time he committed the act, he was laboring under such a defect of reason, from a disease of the mind, as not to know the nature and quality of the act he was doing; or, if he did know it, as not to know he was doing what was wrong. A few jurisdictions have supplemented *M'Naghten* with the unfortunately-named "irresistible impulse" test which, generally stated, recognizes insanity as a defense when the defendant had a mental disease which kept him from controlling his conduct. For several years (but no longer) the District of Columbia followed the so-called *Durham* rule (or product test), whereby the accused is not criminally responsible if his unlawful act was the product of mental disease or mental defect. And in recent years a substantial minority of states have adopted the Model Penal Code approach, which is that the defendant is not responsible if at the time of his conduct as a result of mental disease or defect he lacked substantial capacity either to appreciate the criminality of his conduct or to conform his conduct to the requirements of law. These might be said to represent four different definitions of insanity for purposes of the substantive criminal law, but, as will be noted when these tests are discussed in greater detail,[5] some believe that the practical differences between them are not great.

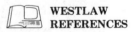
WESTLAW REFERENCES

insanity /s defense /s m*naghten

(b) Purpose of the Defense. There exist in the criminal law a number of substantive

§ 4.1

1. See § 4.4(a).

2. See § 4.4(c).

3. See § 4.6(a).

4. See § 4.6(c).

5. See §§ 4.2, 4.3.

defenses to a charge of criminal conduct.[6] These defenses are usually defined in terms of unusual circumstances which, when raised by the defendant, evidence a situation in which the purposes of the criminal law would not be served by conviction of the defendant. For example, take the defense of self-defense.[7] For A intentionally to kill B is murder, and the various purposes of the criminal law [8] are served by convicting and punishing A for his crime of taking a human life. But if A killed B to prevent B from killing him, then the defense of self-defense comes into play because the purposes of the criminal law are better served by A's acquittal; "authorizing the potential victim to kill his assailant constitutes a sanction which may be assumed to fulfill punitive, restraining, and deterrent functions in the service of the community's objective to safeguard human life." [9]

In some respects, at least, the insanity defense is like self-defense and the other defenses. Again we are dealing with an unusual situation which is ordinarily raised by the defendant and which, if it in fact existed, means the purposes of the criminal law would not be served by conviction. (The insanity defense, as it relates to these purposes, is discussed herein.) Yet, the actual consequence of a successful insanity defense is quite different than with respect to any other defense; in every other case, a successful defense results in acquittal and outright release of the defendant, but with the insanity defense the probable result is commitment of the defendant to a mental institution until he has recovered his sanity.[10] Acceptance of the defendant's insanity defense is specially noted by a jury verdict (or, in a trial without jury, a judge's finding) of "not guilty by reason of insanity," after which he will (in some jurisdictions) be automatically committed or (in others) be subjected to proceedings which are most likely to result in commitment.

It is apparent, then, that the insanity defense serves a unique purpose. Few efforts to articulate that purpose have been made, although the general assumption seems to be that the defense makes it possible to separate out for special treatment certain persons who would otherwise be subjected to the usual penal sanctions which may follow convictions:

> The problem is the drawing of a line between the use of public agencies and force (1) to condemn the offender by conviction, with resultant sanctions in which the ingredient of reprobation is present no matter how constructive one may seek to make the sentence and the process of correction, and (2) modes of disposition in which the condemnatory element is absent, even though restraint may be involved. * * * Stating the matter differently, the problem is to etch a decent working line between the areas assigned to the authorities responsible for public health and those responsible for the correction of offenders.[11]

Another view, however, is that the "real function" of the insanity defense "is to authorize the state to hold those 'who must be found not to possess the guilty mind *mens rea,*' even though the criminal law demands that no person be held criminally responsible if doubt is cast on any material element of the offense charged." [12] That is, the defense is seen as a device whereby certain persons are singled out for commitment, not as an alternative to conviction and imprisonment, but rather as an alternative to outright acquittal. Under this theory, the insanity defense is unlike the other defenses in that it does not apply only to persons against whom each of the elements of the offense charged could be established.

There is actually some truth to both views, and this is because the circumstances which give rise to a defense of insanity *sometimes* also warrant the conclusion that the defendant did not commit the acts with the mental state required for conviction of the crime

---

6. See Ch. 5.

7. See § 5.7.

8. Discussed in § 1.5.

9. Goldstein & Katz, Abolish the "Insanity Defense"— Why Not?, 72 Yale L.J. 853, 857 (1963).

10. See § 4.6.

11. Model Penal Code § 4.01, Comment at 164–65 (1985).

12. Goldstein & Katz, supra note 9, at 864.

charged. But this is not always the case,[13] for "the insanity defense is broader than the mens rea concept," [14] as evidenced by the fact that the defense would in theory even be available in a prosecution for a strict-liability crime which required no proof of the defendant's mental state.[15]

Thus, at one extreme, if the effect of the defendant's mental disease was that he did not even know what he was doing—if, to take an oft-cited example, he strangled his wife but believed that he was squeezing lemons [16]—he would certainly have a valid insanity defense under any of the insanity tests now in use. But, in a homicide prosecution which included as an element of the charge that the defendant killed his wife intentionally,[17] knowingly,[18] or recklessly (defined in subjective terms, in that the defendant was actually aware of the risk attending his actions),[19] it would also be correct to say that this defendant is simply not guilty for lack of *mens rea*. At least to the extent that courts have declined to admit evidence of mental disease except in the context of an insanity defense,[20] it could be said that in this situation the defense serves as a device for committing those who would otherwise be acquitted.

At the other extreme, if the effect of the defendant's mental disease was that he was significantly lacking in the ability to control his actions, he would again have an insanity defense under at least some of the insanity tests. But it is unlikely [21] that it could be said that this defendant, merely because of limitations upon his powers of self-control, did not act with intent (that is, with a purpose of bringing about the harmful result), knowledge (awareness that the harmful result would follow), or recklessness (awareness of a substantial risk that the harmful risk will follow), whatever the relevant mental state is for the offense charged.[22] In such a situation, the insanity defense serves as a means to bring about commitment of the defendant in lieu of conviction and imprisonment.

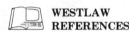 **WESTLAW REFERENCES**

"mens rea" /s insanity

(c) Theories of Punishment and the Defense. Another helpful way of looking at the defense of insanity is in relation to the various theories of punishment,[23] for the philosophical reasons for allowing the defense are tied up with these theories.[24]

(1) Prevention. One theory underlying punishment of those who commit crimes is that by subjecting them to an unpleasant experience they will be less likely to commit other crimes in the future. But, this "can be effective only with men who can understand the signals directed at them by the [criminal] code, who can respond to warnings, and who can feel the significance of the sanctions im-

---

13. Unfortunate language in some cases seems to assume that it *is* always the case. See, e.g., United States v. Currens, 290 F.2d 751 (3d Cir.1961), assuming that if the defendant has "lost the capacity to control" his actions, then "he must be found not to possess the guilty mind, the *mens rea*, necessary to constitute his prohibited act a crime." Compare State v. Ellingwood, 409 A.2d 641 (Me. 1979), correctly noting that on the facts there presented defendant's insanity excused, but did not negate, the existence of a culpable mental state.

14. Note, 112 U.Pa.L.Rev. 733, 734 (1964).

15. Ibid. But see Sayre, Public Welfare Offenses, 33 Colum.L.Rev. 55, 78 (1933), arguing that insanity should not be a defense to speeding and other traffic violations, in that lunatics who commit these minor crimes ought to be restrained by the criminal law.

16. Model Penal Code § 4.01, Comment at 166 (1985).

17. See, § 3.5(a), (b).

18. See § 3.5(a), (b).

19. See § 3.7(d).

20. See A. Goldstein, The Insanity Defense 16–18 (1967); and § 4.7.

21. At least some psychiatrists hold to the view that lack of control *does* mean that such mental states are not present. See, e.g., the testimony of Dr. Bernard L. Diamond set forth in People v. Gorshen, 51 Cal.App.2d 716, 336 P.2d 492 (1959), discussed in § 4.7, that intention requires free will and that the defendant lacked free will because he killed his foreman to avoid total disintegration.

22. See the useful discussion of the mens rea-insanity relationship in Comment, 28 Me.L.Rev. 500 (1977).

23. Discussed in more detail in § 1.5.

24. Compare with the following the arguments of the government, summarized in United States v. Torniero, 570 F.Supp. 721 (D.Conn.1983), affirmed 735 F.2d 725 (2d Cir. 1984), as to why the insanity defense is inconsistent with the theories of punishment.

posed upon violators." [25] Punishment, therefore, is not at all likely to deter the insane individual from future antisocial conduct. The insanity defense diverts these persons to what is hopefully a process of treatment directed at the causes of their actions and intended to overcome the mental disability which might bring about future harmful conduct.

(2) Restraint. Another purpose of punishment is protection of society from dangerous persons; those convicted of serious crimes are usually incarcerated for a substantial period of time, during which they cannot endanger society by more criminality. The insanity defense is quite consistent with this notion, for if the defense is successfully interposed, the defendant is not merely incarcerated for a fixed period of time but is instead committed until such time as he no longer is dangerous.[26]

(3) Rehabilitation. Under this theory, sanctions are imposed upon the convicted defendant for the purpose of altering his behavior pattern and making him a more useful citizen in the community. It is generally assumed that the rehabilitation of the insane person should be accomplished through means which differ from those which are useful for the rehabilitation of others.[27] The insanity defense diverts the insane person to a mental hospital instead of a prison so that he may receive rehabilitation through treatment.

(4) Deterrence. Punishment of those who violate the criminal laws also serves as a means of general prevention, in that the law-abiding tendencies of the general public are reinforced by the example of punishment of those who have not been law abiding. This purpose would not be served by conviction and punishment of the insane, for "the examples are likely to deter only if the person who is *not* involved in the criminal process regards the lessons as applicable to him," which he is likely to do "only if he identifies with the offender and with the offending situation." [28] It is unlikely that the sane person (or even the insane person who believes himself to be sane) will identify with the insane defendant, and thus the insane cannot be effectively used as a deterrent example to others. Or, if one accepts the argument that such identification will nonetheless occur because the public will not scrutinize that closely the characteristics of those punished, it may still be argued that the objective of deterrence should not be enhanced by punishment of the insane. "It would be widely regarded as incalculably cruel and unjust to incarcerate men who are not personally responsible in order to serve social functions." [29]

(5) Education. Yet another theory of punishment is that the process of prosecution, conviction, and imposition of sanctions serves to educate the general public by making known what conduct is prohibited by the criminal law. This function, however, is most important as to relatively minor offenses which do not involve inherently bad conduct; there is no need to educate the public about those crimes, such as murder, for which the insanity defense is most frequently interposed. Moreover, the punishment of individuals who, because of their insanity, would be viewed by the general public as not blameworthy would only blur the distinction between good and bad conduct and thus work against the education theory.

(6) Retribution. The oldest theory of punishment, that the criminal owes the community a measure of suffering because of that which he inflicted, still persists at least to some degree.[30] Assuming there is some current validity to this theory, it may nonetheless be said that the purpose of retribution would not be served by conviction and punishment of the insane. Indeed, the insanity defense developed as a means of saving from retributive punishment those individuals who

---

25. A. Goldstein, supra note 20, at 12–13.

26. On the standards for release, see § 4.6(c).

27. Note, 40 Temple L.Q. 348, 360 (1967).

28. A. Goldstein, supra note 20, at 13.

29. Ibid.

30. Note, 40 Temple L.Q. 348, 358–59 (1967).

were so different from others that they could not be blamed for what they had done.[31]

WESTLAW REFERENCES

insanity insane (mental** /3 ill****) /p punish! /s cruel /5 unusual unjust!

(d) Abolish the Insanity Defense? Yet another way of viewing the insanity defense is through consideration of the arguments which have been made over the years—pro and con—concerning whether the defense should be abolished. Of course, if the insanity defense were abolished there would have to be substituted some other mechanism to deal with the insane person who has engaged in harmful conduct, perhaps by merely taking mental condition into account after conviction in deciding what is to be done with the offender [32] (and, perhaps also by establishing and utilizing commitment procedures for those whose insanity negates the mental state needed for conviction and who thus have nonetheless been found not guilty).[33]

The following arguments have been made in favor of abolishing the insanity defense: [34]

(1) Insanity is in practice only a "rich man's defense" in that only the wealthy can afford the array of experts needed to mount a convincing defense—experts who are in short supply and whose time would be better spent in treatment of those who have been committed or imprisoned.

(2) The key terms in the various insanity tests are so vague that they "invite semantic jousting, metaphysical speculation, intuitive moral judgments in the guise of factual determinations." [35]

(3) The function of the insanity defense remains uncertain, but even accepting the common assertion that the purpose is to remove from the criminal process those who are not blameworthy, "there is just no basis in psychiatry to make a differentiation between * * * the man who is personally blameworthy for his makeup from the man who is not." [36]

(4) The crucial decision to be made concerns the proper disposition of mentally abnormal persons who commit criminal acts, and this is a matter which is better dealt with in a direct way following conviction than indirectly during trial.

(5) Persons channelled out of the criminal process following a finding of not guilty by reason of insanity are not protected against administrative abuse of their rights to the same degree that they would be if they remained within the criminal justice system.

(6) "A number of informed observers believe that it is therapeutically desirable to treat behavioral deviants as responsible for

---

31. Ibid; A. Goldstein, supra note 20, at 12.

32. Consider in this regard the "guilty but mentally ill" option discussed in § 4.5(h).

33. See Goldstein & Katz, supra note 9, at 872–76.

34. See 1 National Comm'n on Reform of Federal Criminal Laws, Working Papers 248–51 (1970) for a more detailed statement of these arguments in a consultant's report by Professor David Robinson.

See also S. Halleck, Psychiatry and the Dilemma of Crime 212–28, 341–42 (1967); H. Hart, The Morality of the Criminal Law 24–25 (1964); N. Morris, Madness and the Criminal Law 28–88 (1982); T. Szaz, Law, Liberty, and Psychiatry 123–46 (1963); W. Winslade & J. Ross, The Insanity Plea 198–226 (1983); B. Wootton, Crime and the Criminal Law 65–93 (2d ed. 1981); Gerber, The Insanity Defense Revisited, 1984 Ariz.St.L.J. 83; Goldstein, The Brawner Rule—Why? or No More Nonsense on Non Sense in the Criminal Law, Please!, 1973 Wash.U.L.Q. 126; Morris, The Criminal Responsibility of the Mentally Ill, 33 Syrac.L.Rev. 477 (1982); Morris, Psychiatry and the Dan-

gerous Criminal, 41 So.Cal.L.Rev. 514 (1968); Thomas, Breaking of the Stone Tablet: Criminal Law Without the Insanity Defense, 19 Idaho L.Rev. 239 (1983).

Compare Wexler, An Offense-Victim Approach to Insanity Defense Reform, 26 Ariz.L.Rev. 17, 22 (1984), arguing for a compromise between the abolition and retention positions, and claiming that "an 'offense-victim' limitation on the assertability of the insanity defense will disallow the defense in instances (e.g., homicides against non-family members) that may well exceed bounds of public tolerance, but will nonetheless allow the defense to be asserted for most offenses and even for a large segment of homicide cases."

35. 1 Working Papers, supra note 34, at 249. See also Thomas, supra note 34, at 247, arguing "that psychiatry cannot offer sufficient certainty to produce reasonable and consistent accuracy in resolving questions of criminal responsibility."

36. Remarks of Justice Weintraub, in Insanity as a Defense: A Panel Discussion, 37 F.R.D. 365, 372 (1964).

their conduct rather than as involuntary victims playing a sick role." [37]

(7) As a practical matter, the insanity defense is most often utilized to avoid the harshness of the death penalty. A more direct response would be to abolish the death penalty.

(8) "The insanity defense discriminates against persons who commit crimes because of influences on their personalities other than mental disease or defect." [38]

(9) The insanity defense sometimes serves as a means of facilitating detention of those who did not have the *mens rea* required and whose present dangerousness has not been determined.

In favor of retaining the insanity defense, these points have been made: [39]

(1) Efforts to keep the insanity question out of the criminal trial have been largely unsuccessful. Under the bifurcated trial system, whereby the issue of guilt is first tried and the issue of insanity is then tried separately, evidence essentially equivalent to that which would be entered for purposes of the insanity defense frequently is brought out in the first part of the trial on the issue of *mens rea*.[40] This could be avoided by eliminating *both* the *mens rea* requirement and the insanity defense, but the few efforts to do so have been held to deny due process.[41]

(2) Defendants who now go free because they lacked *mens rea* would, if the insanity defense were abolished, be more likely to be convicted on the assumption that they would be weeded out at the disposition stage, resulting in their premature labeling as an offender.

(3) "[E]liminating the insanity defense would remove from the criminal law and the public conscience the vitally important distinction between illness and evil, or would tuck it away in an administrative process." [42] So the argument goes, it is extremely important that we retain the concept of responsibility in the criminal law and "that 'blame' be retained as a spur to individual responsibility." [43] Moreover, we would rebel at the notion of labeling as criminal those who are generally conceded not to be blameworthy.[44]

(4) If the choice between sanctions, the official condemnation of conviction and punishment on the one hand and the indeterminate detention for treatment and its accompanying stigma on the other, is to be made in a way which will be acceptable to the public, then the decision must "be made by a democratically selected jury rather than by experts— because the public can identify with the former but not with the latter." [45] Moreover,

37. 1 Working Papers, supra note 34, at 251.

38. Ibid.

39. See A. Goldstein, supra note 20, at 222–25 for a more detailed statement of these arguments.

See also H. Fingarette, The Meaning of Criminal Insanity 1–15 (1972); H. Packer, The Limits of the Criminal Sanction 131–35 (1968); Arenella, Reflections on Current Proposals to Abolish or Reform the Insanity Defense, 8 Am.J.L. & Med. 271 (1982); Bonnie, The Moral Basis of the Insanity Defense, 69 A.B.A.J. 194 (1983); Brady, Abolish the Insanity Defense? No!, 8 Houst.L.Rev. 629 (1971); Dershowitz, Abolishing the Insanity Defense, 9 Crim.L. Bull. 434 (1973); Kadish, The Decline of Innocence, 26 Camb.L.J. 273 (1968); Monahan, Abolish the Insanity Defense?—Not Yet, 26 Rutgers L.Rev. 719 (1973); Morse, Excusing the Crazy: The Insanity Defense Reconsidered, 58 So.Cal.L.Rev. 777, 795–801 (1985); Reisner & Semmel, Abolishing the Insanity Defense: A Look at the Proposed Federal Criminal Code Reform Act in Light of the Swedish Experience, 62 Calif.L.Rev. 753 (1974); Robitscher & Haynes, In Defense of the Insanity Defense, 31 Emory L.J. 9 (1982); Wales, An Analysis of the Proposal to "Abolish" the Insanity Defense in S. 1: Squeezing a Lemon, 124

U.Pa.J.Rev. 687 (1976); and United States v. Torniero, 570 F.Supp. 721 (D.Conn.1983), affirmed 735 F.2d 725 (2d Cir. 1984) (rejecting prosecution's motion that the court "abolish" the insanity defense).

40. See § 4.5(g).

41. State v. Lange, 168 La. 958, 123 So. 639 (1929).

42. A. Goldstein, supra note 20, at 223.

43. Id. at 225. See also Arenella, supra note 39, at 274.

44. "Judges and juries would be forced either to return a verdict of conviction, which they would regard as morally obtuse, or to acquit the defendant in defiance of the law. They should be spared that moral embarrassment." Bonnie, supra note 39, at 195. See also the remarks of Professor Wechsler in Panel Discussion, supra note 36, at 381–383.

45. A. Goldstein, supra note 20, at 225. Monahan, supra note 39, at 738, though otherwise sympathetic with the abolitionists' position, says he is "unable, however, to answer the claims that the elimination of the insanity defense would lead to the complete acquittal of the abnormal offender, and would eventually usher in a legal sys-

the receipt of psychiatric input in a trial, subject to traditional adversary procedures, is the best approach "for exposing differences in professional judgments." [46]

A few states have by statute abolished the defense of insanity by legislation providing that evidence of mental disease or defect is admissible only to negate the mental state required for the offense charged.[47] Some case authority is to be found holding such abolition constitutional. In *State v. Korell*,[48] the court rejected the defendant's contention that the insanity defense was so firmly established in the common law at the time our Constitution was adopted that it was a fundamental right protected by the Fourteenth Amendment due process clause. The court noted that the Supreme Court, in *Powell v. Texas*,[49] characterized the defense as one of those doctrines which "have historically provided the tools for a constantly shifting adjustment of the tension between the evolving aims of the criminal law and changing religious, moral, philosophical, and medical views of the nature of man," a process always "thought to be the province of the States." Early court decisions holding abolition of the insanity defense unconstitutional [50] were distinguished because the statutes there challenged, unlike their modern counterparts, did not even permit trial testimony on mental condition to cast doubt on whether a defendant has the requisite mental state.[51]

As for the contention that abolition of the insanity defense constitutes cruel and unusual punishment under the Eighth Amend-

ment, the *Korell* court concluded this was not so because the Supreme Court's teachings in *Robinson v. California* [52] and *Powell* were merely that neither status nor illness could themselves be made criminal.[53] Some commentators support that line of reasoning,[54] but others do not. They read *Powell* as merely rejecting the notion that a particular "test of insanity is constitutionally required," [55] while indicating a willingness "to require at least some defense based on the impairment of free will." [56]

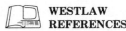

WESTLAW REFERENCES

insane insanity /5 defense /s moral!

§ 4.2 The Traditional Tests: "Right-Wrong" and "Irresistible Impulse"

In a majority of the jurisdictions in this country, what is most often referred to as the *M'Naghten* rule has long been accepted as the test to be applied for the defense of insanity. Under *M'Naghten,* an accused is not criminally responsible if, at the time of committing the act, he was laboring under such a defect of reason, from disease of the mind, as not to know the nature and quality of the act he was doing, or if he did know it that he did not know he was doing what was wrong.

A few of the jurisdictions which follow *M'Naghten* have supplemented it with another test which is unfortunately labeled the "irresistible impulse" rule. Those two words suggest limitations upon the rule which are not strictly adhered to in practice, so that the

tem based upon non-existent treatment procedures and unfounded faith in our ability to predict dangerousness, a system in which it would be impossible to define the very phenomena we wish to prohibit, and which would leave the citizen at the mercy of politically chosen 'experts.' "

46. Reisner & Semmel, supra note 39, at 787.

47. Idaho Code § 18–207; Mont.Code Ann. 46–14–102; Utah Code Ann.1953, 76–2–305.

48. ___ Mont. ___, 690 P.2d 992 (1984).

49. 392 U.S. 514, 88 S.Ct. 2145, 20 L.Ed.2d 1254 (1968).

50. See note 41 supra. For a useful discussion of those cases, see Robitscher & Haynes, supra note 39, at 51–55.

51. Compare State in Interest of Causey, 363 So.2d 472 (La.1978), relying upon those earlier decisions in holding that "the due process-fundamental fairness concepts of

our state and federal constitutions would be violated, at least in adult prosecutions for crimes requiring intent, if an accused were denied the right to plead the insanity defense." The court then concluded there was also such a right in juvenile court proceedings.

52. 370 U.S. 660, 82 S.Ct. 1417, 8 L.Ed.2d 758 (1962).

53. See § 3.2(d).

54. E.g., Morris, The Criminal Responsibility of the Mentally Ill, 33 Syrac.L.Rev. 477, 518–20 (1982).

55. Robitscher & Haynes, supra note 39, at 59.

56. Wales, supra note 39, at 704. Dicta in some cases asserts that the insanity defense is constitutionally required. See, e.g, United States v. Greene, 489 F.2d 1145 (D.C.Cir.1973); Ingles v. People, 92 Colo. 518, 22 P.2d 1109 (1933); State v. Smith, 88 Wn.2d 639, 564 P.2d 1154 (1977).

"irresistible impulse" rule may more accurately be described as a test whereby the accused is not criminally responsible if he had a mental disease which kept him from controlling his conduct.

(a) The *M'Naghten* Case. In 1843 Daniel M'Naghten shot and killed Edward Drummond, private secretary to Sir Robert Peel. M'Naghten, believing that Peel was heading a conspiracy to kill him, had intended to take Peel's life, but he instead shot Drummond because he mistakenly believed him to be Peel. At the trial of his case, M'Naghten claimed that he was insane and could not be held responsible because it had been his delusions which caused him to act. The jury agreed, and M'Naghten was found not guilty by reason of insanity.[1]

Due to the importance of both the victim and the intended victim, the decision was not a popular one. The House of Lords debated the decision and posed to the justices of the Queen's Bench five questions[2] concerning the standards for acquitting a defendant due to his insanity. The answers to these questions were appended to the report of the original case, and have come to be considered as if they were a part of that decision.

It should be noted that four of the five questions of the House of Lords referred only to the proper test and procedures for acquitting one who was "affected with insane delusions respecting one or more particular subjects or persons." Only question three, regarding what should be left for the jury to decide, did not have such a reference in it.[3]

But regardless of whether the House of Lords meant to inquire only about a specific facet of insanity, a portion of the judges' answers has come to be the most widely accepted test for the type or degree of mental disorder which will absolve a person from criminal responsibility.

The majority of the justices[4] stated: "[T]o establish a defense on the ground of insanity, it must be clearly proved that, at the time of the committing of the act, the party accused was laboring under such a defect of reason, from disease of the mind, as not to know the nature and quality of the act he was doing, or if he did know it that he did not know he was doing what was wrong." This advisory opinion soon became known as the *M'Naghten* test of insanity. It is clear, however, that the judges were merely attempting to state the law as it then existed; the right-wrong test had previously been utilized in both England and the United States.[5]

Taken literally, the *M'Naghten* rule appears to refer to a certain mental disability which must produce one of two conditions, both of which are defined in terms of lack of cognition. Thus the elements of *M'Naghten* might be distinguished in this way:

(1) (disability) that the accused have suffered a defect of reason, from a disease of the mind; *and*

(2) (result) that consequently at the time of the act he did not know

(a) the nature and quality of the act, *or*

(b) that the act was wrong.

§ 4.2

1. M'Naghten's Case, 8 Eng.Rep. 718 (1843).

2. The questions overlapped a great deal. Question I asked what the law was with respect to alleged crimes committed by persons afflicted with insane delusion, while Question IV asked if a person with an insane delusion was excused thereby. Question II asked what questions should be submitted to the jury when insanity is set up as a defense by a person alleged to be afflicted with insane delusion, and Question III inquired in what terms the question as to the person's state of mind at the time should be left to the jury. Question V dealt with the admissibility of expert testimony.

3. See note 2 supra.

4. Fourteen of the fifteen judges joined in this statement. Justice Maule, in a separate opinion, indicated

that knowledge of right and wrong was the sole test of insanity, but he objected that the judges should have asked to be excused from giving an advisory opinion.

5. See Platt & Diamond, The Origins of the "Right and Wrong" Test of Criminal Responsibility and its Subsequent Development in the United States: An Historical Survey, 54 Cal.L.Rev. 1227 (1966), documenting the facts that the "essential concept and phraseology of the rule" were already embedded in English and American law and that the right-wrong test can be traced to Hebrew law, Greek moral philosophy, Roman law, and the literature of the Church in the Middle Ages.

On the history of the law of insanity, see S. Glueck, Mental Disorder and the Criminal Law ch. 5 (1925); 1 F. Wharton & M. Stille, Medical Jurisprudence ch. 26 (5th ed.1905).

The *M'Naghten* test has become the predominant rule in the United States. It remains the test for insanity in over one-half of the American jurisdictions,[6] although it is occasionally supplemented with a test for loss of volitional control.[7] But a substantial minority of states has rejected the *M'Naghten* test, usually in favor of the Model Penal Code approach.[8]

 WESTLAW REFERENCES

m*naghten /7 rule test theory case

(b) The Meaning of *M'Naghten*. Although the *M'Naghten* rule has been one of the most widely debated topics in the criminal law,[9] there is very little explanation or clarification of the rule to be found in the case law. This is probably due to the small percentage of defendants who raise an insanity defense and the extreme rarity of appeals by these defendants.[10]

(1) "Disease of the Mind." There has never been a clear and comprehensive determination of what type of mental disease or defect

is required to satisfy the *M'Naghten* test. Some believe that only a few types of psychoses will suffice.[11] However, it would seem that any mental abnormality, be it psychosis, neurosis, organic brain disorder, or congenital intellectual deficiency (low IQ or feeblemindedness), will suffice *if* it has caused the consequences described in the second part of the test.[12] Thus, although many psychiatrists apparently believe that only a few psychoses will give rise to a successful insanity defense under the *M'Naghten* rule,[13] this is not because certain illnesses or defects are per se excluded but rather because they do not produce the lack of cognition required under *M'Naghten*.

One disorder, the psychopathic personality, would clearly appear to be excluded by the requirement that the accused have suffered from a disease of the mind. Although it is virtually impossible to define adequately a psychopathic personality,[14] it is commonly asserted that a psychopath is one who exhibits an abnormality only in the repetitious performance of antisocial or criminal acts.[15] Such a

6. Although the federal courts had theretofore followed the Model Penal Code test discussed in § 4.3, in 1984 Congress mandated a test which is essentially a restatement of the *M'Naghten* rule: "It is an affirmative defense to a prosecution under any Federal statute that, at the time of the commission of the acts constituting the offense, the defendant, as a result of a severe mental disease or defect, was unable to appreciate the nature and quality of the wrongfulness of his acts." 18 U.S.C.A. § 20.

Several states have also adopted the *M'Naghten* rule by legislation. Others have reached this result by judicial decision; see the recent applications in Gurganus v. State, 451 So.2d 817 (Fla.1984); State v. Allen, 4 Kan.App.2d 534, 609 P.2d 219 (1980); Laney v. State, 421 So.2d 1216 (Miss.1982); State v. Simants, 197 Neb. 549, 250 N.W.2d 881 (1977); Clark v. State, 95 Nev. 24, 588 P.2d 102 (1979); State v. Hartley, 90 N.M. 488, 565 P.2d 658 (1978); State v. Jackson, 302 N.C. 101, 273 S.E.2d 666 (1981); State v. Brown, 5 Ohio St.3d 133, 449 N.E.2d 449 (1983); State v. Law, 270 S.C. 664, 244 S.E.2d 302 (1978); Davis v. Commonwealth, 214 Va. 728, 204 S.E.2d 273 (1974).

7. See note 95 infra.

8. See § 4.3.

9. See § 4.2(c).

10. A. Goldstein, The Insanity Defense 23 (1967).

11. A. Goldstein, The Insanity Defense 48 (1967).

12. See, e.g., State v. Elsea, 251 S.W.2d 650 (Mo.1952) (paranoia); State v. Johnson, 233 Wis. 668, 290 N.W. 159 (1940) (feeblemindedness); State v. Hadley, 65 Utah 109, 234 P. 940 (1925) (senility). "The law makes no distinc-

tions between various forms of mental unsoundness as to the test of responsibility." H. Weihofen, Mental Disorder as a Criminal Defense 119 (1954).

Also, PTSD (the post-traumatic stress disorder, such as experienced by some Vietnam veterans) qualifies, as it is a personality disorder. Note, 9 Vt.L.Rev. 69, 99 (1984). For discussion of trials in which evidence of such a disorder produced not guilty by reason of insanity verdicts in *M'Naghten* jurisdictions, see Erlinder, Paying the Price for Vietnam: Post-Traumatic Stress Disorder and Criminal Behavior, 25 B.C.L.Rev. 305, 320–21 (1984); Ford, In Defense of the Defenders: The Vietnam Vet Syndrome, 19 Crim.L.Bull. 434 (1983).

However, PMS (the premenstrual syndrome), "a hormone deficiency disease * * * related to antisocial behavior," Taylor & Dalton, Premenstrual Syndrome: A New Criminal Defense?, 19 Cal.W.L.Rev. 269, 271, 274 (1983), does not qualify. "PMS is not a disease or defect of the mind, but a physiological disorder." Note, 59 Notre Dame Law 253, 264 (1983). "No scientific evidence indicates that PMS syndrome alone can produce psychosis; thus, there is little hope that an insanity defense based on PMS syndrome will succeed." Note, 1983 Duke L.J. 176, 177.

13. Model Penal Code § 4.01, Appendix A (1985) (statement of Dr. Guttmacher).

14. Royal Commission on Capital Punishment, 1949–53 Report § 394 (1953).

15. Id. at §§ 394–402.

person differs from others only in the quantity or types of his actions and not by the quality of his mental facilities,[16] and thus he would not have an insanity defense under *M'Naghten.* [17] But even in this situation the "disease of the mind" element of *M'Naghten* is not itself a unique limiting factor, as the psychopath likewise could not qualify under the lack-of-cognition requirement.

When a jury is instructed on the *M'Naghten* test, the usual practice is merely to recite the "disease of the mind" element to the jury. No effort is made to define or explain what qualifies as a mental disease.[18]

(2) "Know." It is the word "know" in the test which has been the source of most of the criticism of *M'Naghten.* The test has been described as unrealistic on the assumption that "know" refers only to intellectual awareness. It has been contended that few if any individuals have existed who do not have any intellectual awareness of what they are doing,[19] and that a test phrased merely in terms of such cognition is unduly restrictive.[20] It is impossible, so the argument goes, to separate a man's intellect from his will in testing his mental capabilities.[21]

Others have contended that the word "know" encompasses more than just the minimal awareness of facts or the ability to mechanically repeat what has happened.[22]

To them, "know" refers to "affective"[23] or "emotional"[24] knowledge, "so fused with affect that it becomes a human reality,"[25] knowledge which "can exist only when the accused is able to evaluate his conduct in terms of its actual impact upon himself and others and when he is able to appreciate the total setting in which he is acting."[26] That is, the person must be able to grasp the underlying significance of what he did and not just be able to register and repeat physical surroundings and the actions he took.[27] Some have even gone so far as to assert that a person must have the capacity to choose between acts in order to know what he is doing,[28] although this would seem to stretch the term beyond all limits.

As one study has shown, there is no basis for the claim that the *M'Naghten* test has been strictly applied so as to extend only to intellectual awareness. Very few appellate decisions are to be found taking that limited view,[29] and as to some of these the limitation may be of little significance because of the availability of the "irresistible impulse" control test in addition to *M'Naghten.* [30] In most of the *M'Naghten* jurisdictions the word "know" is not defined at all, leaving the jury free to determine the meaning on the basis of the expert testimony received at trial.[31] Of the lesser number of jurisdictions which have

---

16. Id. at § 401.

17. "[S]ince a psychopath would not ordinarily be held to suffer from a disease of the mind, or, except in the rare case of the moral defective, from mental deficiency, it would not be open to the courts to find them irresponsible, either under the M'Naghten Rules in their present form or if the law were amended in the way we have suggested in the preceding chapter." Id. at § 401, p. 139.

18. A. Goldstein, The Insanity Defense 48 (1967).

19. Royal Commission on Capital Punishment, 1949–53 Report § 291 (1953); G. Zilboorg, Mind, Medicine and Man 273 (1943).

20. Royal Commission on Capital Punishment, 1949–53 Report § 250 (1953).

21. 2 J. Stephen, A History of the Criminal Law of England 157 (1883); Royal Commission on Capital Punishment, 1949–53 Report §§ 191–92 (1953); Guttmacher, The Psychiatrist as an Expert Witness, 22 U.Chi.L.Rev. 325 (1955).

22. A. Goldstein, supra note 18, at 49–50; Zilboorg, Misconceptions of Legal Insanity, 9 Am.J. Orthopsychiatry 540, 552–53 (1939).

23. S. Brakel & R. Rock, The Mentally Disabled and the Law 388 (1971).

24. A. Goldstein, supra note 18, at 49.

25. Zilboorg, supra note 22, at 553.

26. A. Goldstein, supra note 18, at 49.

27. H. Weihofen, supra note 12, at 74.

28. 2 J. Stephen, supra note 21, at 170–71.

29. Illustrative of the few is State v. Everett, 110 Ariz. 429, 520 P.2d 301 (1974) (testimony defendant did not know right from wrong on an emotional level properly excluded, as *M'Naghten* "does not concern itself with the emotional state of a defendant").

30. E.g., State v. Kirkham, 7 Utah 2d 108, 319 P.2d 859 (1958), approving an instruction that the defendant must have been insane to the extent that he "did not know he had a revolver, that it may be loaded, or that, if discharged, it may injure or kill."

31. A. Goldstein, supra note 18, at 50.

addressed the question of what "know" means, the great majority have favored a broad construction of the word.[32]

(3) "Nature and Quality of the Act." Many courts feel that knowledge of "the nature and quality of the act" is the mere equivalent of the ability to know that the act was wrong.[33] Indeed, in many jurisdictions the *M'Naghten* rule is stated merely in terms of the defendant's ability to distinguish right from wrong, and there is no mention of or instruction on knowledge of the nature and quality of the act.[34] When mentioned, it is usually by mere repetition of the wording in *M'Naghten*,[35] although the phrase has also turned up in other forms, such as "nature or quality"[36] and "nature and consequences."[37]

When considered at all, the entire phrase has been typically held to mean that the defendant must have understood the physical nature and consequences of the act.[38] Thus, an accused must have known that holding a flame to a building would cause it to burn,[39] or that holding a person's head under water would cause him to die.[40] Only a few courts

have indicated that the phrase refers to something more than knowledge of physical consequences. In *State v. Esser*,[41] for example, the Wisconsin court held that the phrase implied a true insight into the nature of the conduct and that it was forbidden.[42] This, of course, is another way of reaching the result which is also possible by giving the word "know" a broad construction. "To know the quality of an act, with all its social and emotional implications, requires more than an abstract, purely intellectual knowledge. Likewise, to talk of appreciating the full significance of an act means that 'nature and quality' must be understood as including more than the physical nature of the act."[43]

It is error to instruct the jury that to be insane the defendant must not have known the nature and quality of the act *and* that it was wrong.[44] This is because a person might well be able to appreciate the physical consequences of the act and yet be incapable of understanding that it was forbidden.[45]

(4) "Wrong." If the defendant does not know the nature and quality of his act, then

32. Id. at 49. E.g., State v. Schantz, 98 Ariz. 200, 403 P.2d 521 (1965); State v. Davies, 146 Conn. 137, 148 A.2d 251 (1959); State v. Rawland, 294 Minn. 17, 199 N.W.2d 774 (1972); Thompson v. State, 159 Neb. 685, 68 N.W.2d 267 (1955). For citations to cases in eleven states, see A. Goldstein, supra note 18, at 236 n. 13.

33. E.g., Montgomery v. State, 68 Tex.Crim.App. 78, 151 S.W. 813 (1912); Jessner v. State, 202 Wis. 184, 231 N.W. 634 (1930).

34. E.g., Cochran v. State, 65 Fla. 91, 61 So. 187 (1913); State v. McGee, 361 Mo. 309, 234 S.W.2d 587 (1950).

35. E.g., People v. Wells, 33 Cal.2d 330, 202 P.2d 53 (1949); State v. Skaug, 63 Nev. 59, 161 P.2d 708 (1945).

36. State v. Williams, 96 Minn. 351, 105 N.W. 265 (1905).

37. Kobyluk v. State, 94 Okl.Crim.App. 73, 231 P.2d 388 (1951).

38. Rex v. Codere, 12 Crim.App. 21 (1916), rejecting view that "nature" and "quality" referred, respectively, to the physical and moral aspects of the act. *Codere* is followed in this country; see A. Goldstein, supra note 18, at 51, citing trial transcripts.

39. Knights v. State, 58 Neb. 225, 78 N.W. 508 (1899).

40. People v. Sherwood, 271 N.Y. 427, 3 N.E.2d 581 (1936).

41. 16 Wis.2d 567, 115 N.W.2d 505 (1962).

42. "We think, however, that including the former element (nature and quality) gives important emphasis to

one element of the realization of the wrongfulness of an act. Suppose that one vaguely realizes that particular conduct is forbidden, but lacks real insight into the conduct. He may be furtive about such conduct, but not really be able to make a normal moral judgment about it. Our study of the record in this case leads us to believe that this proposition is important. Although defendant Esser realized very soon after the fatal shot, first that it would be advisable to hide the victim's body, and later that he should report his act to the police, even referring to it as 'murder,' yet the expert testimony tends to create a reasonable doubt that he could appreciate and evaluate his act as the time he did it. Although Esser's conduct after the shooting suggests a knowledge that his acts had been wrong and therefore that he could distinguish right from wrong, the expert testimony describing his mental illness tends to show that at the time of the killing he did not understand the nature and quality of his acts and therefore could not distinguish right from wrong with respect to them." Id.

43. A. Goldstein, supra note 18, at 51.

44. E.g., Knights v. State, 58 Neb. 225, 78 N.W. 508 (1899); State v. Moeller, 50 Haw. 110, 433 P.2d 136 (1967); Price v. Commonwealth, 228 Va. 452, 323 S.E.2d 106 (1984).

45. People v. Sherwood, 271 N.Y. 427, 3 N.E.2d 581 (1936) (accused might know that death would result from holding child under water but might not have known that this was wrong; therefore a conjunctive wording is prejudicial error).

quite obviously he does not know that his act is "wrong," and this is true without regard to the interpretation given to the word "wrong." For example, a madman who believes that he is squeezing lemons when he chokes his wife to death [46] does not know the nature and quality of his act and likewise does not know that it is legally and morally wrong. On the other hand, as noted above, a defendant might know the nature and quality of his act (especially if that is taken to refer only to the physical consequences), but yet not know that it is "wrong." The extent to which such situations might arise, however, depends upon whether the *M'Naghten* test refers to legal wrong or moral wrong: "A kills B knowing that he is killing B, and knowing that it is illegal to kill B, but under an insane delusion that the salvation of the human race will be obtained by his execution for the murder of B, and that God has commanded him (A) to produce that result by those means. A's act is a crime if the word 'wrong' means illegal. It is not a crime if the word wrong means morally wrong." [47]

The *M'Naghten* judges did not make clear what construction they were giving to the word "wrong." At one point they said that a person is punishable if "he knew at the time of committing such crime that he was acting contrary to law; by which expression we * * * mean the law of the land." But at another point they observed: "If the question were to be put as to the knowledge of the accused solely and exclusively with reference to the law of the land, it might tend to confound the jury by inducing them to believe that an actual knowledge of the law of the land was essential in order to lead to a conviction; whereas the law is administered on the principle that everyone must be taken conclusively to know it, without proof that he does know it. If the accused was conscious that the act was one which he ought not to do, and if that act was at the same time contrary to the law of the land, he is punishable."

In England, *M'Naghten* is now read as requiring that the defendant know that the act was legally wrong. [48] In this country, however, the question of whether wrong means legally or morally wrong has not been clearly resolved. The issue has very seldom been raised; this part of the *M'Naghten* test is simply given to the jury without explanation. [49] In the few cases in which the matter has been put into issue, some have held that the defendant must not have known that the act was legally wrong, [50] while others have interpreted "wrong" to mean morally wrong. [51] Some courts have held that the defendant must not have realized that the act was wrong *and* punishable, but have not made it clear whether this refers to both moral and legal wrong or only one of the two. [52]

In the unlikely event that the defendant knew that his act was morally wrong but did not know that it was illegal, then it would seem that the *M'Naghten* test for insanity has not been met. In this instance, as is true generally, "knowledge of the law is presumed." [53] The concern is instead with the case in which the defendant knew that his acts were contrary to law but yet believed that they were morally correct. Some have asserted that this is also an unlikely circumstance, given the fact that "the vast majority of cases in which insanity is pleaded as a defense * * * involve acts which are universally regarded as morally wicked as well as illegal." [54] But whether this is so will depend

---

46. See Model Penal Code § 4.01, Comment at 166 (1985).

47. 2 J. Stephen, A History of the Criminal Law of England 149 (1883).

48. Regina v. Windle, 2 Q.B. 826, 2 All Eng.R. 1 (1952).

49. S. Brakel & R. Rock, supra note 23, at 387; A. Goldstein, supra note 18, at 52; H. Weihofen, supra note 12, at 78. See, e.g., State v. Abercrombie, 375 So.2d 1170 (La.1979).

50. E.g., State v. Hamann, 285 N.W.2d 180 (Iowa 1979); State v. Bean, 235 Kan. 800, 686 P.2d 160 (1984); State v.

Andrews, 187 Kan. 458, 357 P.2d 739 (1961); State v. Crenshaw, 98 Wn.2d 789, 659 P.2d 488 (1983).

51. E.g., People v. Schmidt, 216 N.Y. 324, 110 N.E. 945 (1915).

52. H. Weihofen, supra note 12, at 79.

53. Id. at 79. On ignorance of the law generally, see § 5.1(d).

54. S. Glueck, supra note 5, at 184.

upon how another ambiguity is resolved—that is, "whether 'moral wrong' is to be judged by the personal standards of the accused or by his awareness that society views the act as wrong." [55] Society's moral judgment will usually be identical with the legal standard,[56] and thus interpretation of "wrong" in the *M'Naghten* test as moral wrong will not significantly broaden the test if moral wrong is to be determined by an objective standard.[57] But interpretation of "wrong" as moral wrong has nonetheless been opposed because it "invites * * * jury nullification"[58] and conflicts with the principle that criminal sanctions are proper for "all who might be deterred." [59]

One final observation about the meaning of the word "wrong" is required. The question under *M'Naghten* is only whether (because of a disease of the mind) the defendant did not know that the act he performed was wrong. An inability to differentiate generally between right and wrong is not necessary.[60]

(5) Insane Delusions. In responding to the questions put to them by the House of Lords, the *M'Naghten* judges discussed the situation of persons who labor under "partial delusions only, and are not in other respects insane." As to such a person, he was said to be "nevertheless punishable according to the nature of the crime committed, if he knew at the time of committing such crime that he was acting contrary to law." Later, the judges explained that "he must be considered in the same situation as to responsibility as if the facts with respect to which the delusion exists were real. For example, if under the influence of his delusion he supposes another man to be in the act of attempting to take away his life, and he kills that man, as he supposes in self-defense, he would be exempt from punishment. If his delusion was that the deceased had inflicted a serious injury on his character and fortune, and he killed him in revenge for such supposed injury, he would be liable to punishment."

This has given rise to the question of whether, under the *M'Naghten* test, there is a separate and distinct rule which is to be applied in the case of a defendant suffering from insane delusions. Although some American cases might be read as if they were following somewhat different standards in such a case,[61] it is undoubtedly fair to conclude that this particular part of *M'Naghten* does not set up a unique formula differing from the right-wrong test. The significant considerations are these:

(i) The *M'Naghten* judges were merely attempting to state the law of England as it then existed. The right-wrong test had been utilized in the earlier cases, but in no prior case can there be found a separate rule for defendants suffering from delusions. Thus it would seem that the judges did not intend to state a test which was inconsistent with the right-wrong test they had set forth.[62]

---

55. A. Goldstein, supra note 18 at 52. The cases generally take the latter view. See State v. Hamann, 285 N.W.2d 180 (Iowa 1979); People v. Irwin, 166 Misc. 751, 4 N.Y.S.2d 548 (1938); State v. Crenshaw, 98 Wn.2d 789, 659 P.2d 488 (1983).

56. A. Goldstein, supra note 18, at 52.

57. This may depend, however, upon a further interpretation of the objective standard. Under one approach, for example, it might be said that one who acts upon what he believes to be a command of God knows that his acts are morally wrong if he knows that the general public would nonetheless view the act as wrong. Compare People v. Schmidt, 216 N.Y. 324, 340, 110 N.E. 945, 949 (1915) defining knowledge of "wrong" as "knowledge that, according to the accepted standards of mankind, it is * * * condemned as an offense against good morals," but yet stating that a woman would not know that her act was wrong if she killed her infant child because of an insane delusion that God ordained the sacrifice.

58. State v. Hamann, 285 N.W.2d 180 (Iowa 1979).

59. State v. Crenshaw, 98 Wn.2d 789, 659 P.2d 488 (1983).

60. In *M'Naghten* the judges noted that the question should be put "with reference to the party's knowledge of right and wrong in respect to the very act with which he is charged." No court has ever held that a defendant must be incapable of generally differentiating right from wrong and thus totally incapable of ever committing any crime.

61. E.g., Horn v. Commonwealth, 292 Ky. 587, 167 S.W.2d 58 (1942); Davis v. State, 161 Tenn. 23, 28 S.W.2d 993 (1930).

62. H. Weihofen, supra note 12, at 107–08.

(ii) The person described by the *M'Naghten* judges simply does not exist.[63] "There is not, and never has been, a person who labors under partial delusion only and is not in other respects insane." [64] This is because a delusion is not an isolated disorder, but rather a symptom of a widespread disorder.[65]

(iii) If the affirmative part of the *M'Naghten* judges' statement about insane delusions is considered alone, it is clearly compatible with the right-wrong test. If a person suffering from delusions imagines facts which, if true, would justify his acts, then it would seem that this person is not in a position to discriminate between right and wrong with respect to his acts.[66]

(iv) If the negative part of the statements in *M'Naghten* is taken as an exclusive text in delusion cases, thus barring an insanity defense if the facts regarding which the delusion exists would not constitute a defense if true, this would constitute an inroad upon the right-wrong test. But it is unlikely that any courts would so hold today.[67] Rather, the better view is that a mental disease may qualify under the right-wrong test even though its primary symptom is a delusion concerning imagined facts which, if true, would not themselves constitute a defense.[68]

 WESTLAW REFERENCES

m*naghten /p disease
digest,synopsis(mental** /3 disease defect! /p
     wrongful! /s act*** conduct***)

(c) The Criticism of *M'Naghten*. The *M'Naghten* test has long been the subject of controversy. Although the critics of *M'Naghten* have been far more vocal than the defenders,[69] at least until recently,[70] the extensive literature on the subject provides more than an adequate exploration of the issues involved. Only the major criticisms will be briefly considered here.

(1) Based Upon Outmoded Concepts. The criticism of *M'Naghten* which is most frequently heard is that it is "based on an entirely obsolete and misleading conception of the nature of insanity, since insanity does not only, or primarily, affect the cognitive or intellectual faculties, but affects the whole personality of the patient, including both the will and the emotions." [71] Typical is this statement from *Durham v. United States* [72]: "The science of psychiatry now recognizes that a man is an integrated personality and that reason, which is only one element in that personality, is not the sole determinant of his conduct. The right-wrong test, which considers knowledge or reason alone, is therefore an inadequate guide to mental responsibility for criminal behavior." Or, as the point was expressed by another court, it is an "absurdity" to determine the insanity issue by only asking the right-wrong question "when one surveys the array of symptomatology which

---

63. Id. at 109–11.

64. C. Mercier, Criminal Responsibility 198 (1926).

65. W. Overholser, The Psychiatrist and the Law 63 (1953).

66. G. Williams, Criminal Law: The General Part § 160 (2d ed. 1961).

67. H. Weihofen, supra note 12, at 112.

68. Parsons v. State, 81 Ala. 577, 2 So. 854 (1887); Ryan v. People, 60 Colo. 425, 153 P. 756 (1915).

69. A. Goldstein, supra note, 18, at 46.

70. The pro-*M'Naghten* forces now appear to be gaining strength. The Congress has adopted a *M'Naghten*-style insanity test for the federal courts, see note 6, supra, and various recent law reform proposals have been stated only in cognitive terms, albeit not in the precise language of *M'Naghten*. Thus, the 1984 Model Insanity Defense and Post-Trial Disposition Act of the National Conference

of Commissioners on Uniform State Laws states, in § 201: "An individual is not criminally responsible if at the time of the alleged offense, as a result of mental illness or defect, the individual was substantially unable to appreciate the wrongfulness of the alleged conduct." As the commentary thereto points out, that standard conforms with a "resolution adopted by the ABA House of Delegates on February 9, 1983," and has "also received the official support of the American Psychiatric Association." See Report to the House of Delegates by the Standing Committee on Association Standards for Criminal Justice of the American Bar Association and the Commission on the Mentally Retarded (1983); American Psychiatric Association Statement on the Insanity Defense, December, 1982, 140 Amer.J.Psych. 6 (1983).

71. Royal Commission on Capital Punishment, 1949–53 Report 80 (1953).

72. 214 F.2d 862 (D.C.Cir.1954).

the skilled psychiatrist employs in determining the mental condition of an individual." [73]

In response, it has been argued that this criticism is misdirected in that it erroneously assumes that *M'Naghten* is intended to provide a medical definition rather than a legal definition.[74] "[I]t is always necessary to start any discussion of *M'Naghten* by stressing that the case does not state a test of psychosis or mental illness. Rather, it lists conditions under which those who are mentally diseased will be relieved from criminal responsibility. Thus, criticism of *M'Naghten* based on the proposition that the case is premised on an outdated view of mental disease is inappropriate. The case can only be criticized justly if it is based on an outdated view of the mental conditions that ought to preclude application of criminal sanctions." [75]

(2) Inconsistent With Purposes of Criminal Law. As the immediately preceding comments suggest, a more appropriate criticism of *M'Naghten* might be that it is inadequate to the task of selecting those mentally disabled persons who ought not be subjected to punishment under our system of criminal law.[76] This criticism has also been voiced with considerable frequency. As most often stated, the concern is that the right-wrong test is not sufficient to exclude all insane nondeterrables because it only takes account of impairment of cognition and ignores impairment of volitional capacity. "Volitional ability to choose the right and avoid the wrong is as fundamental" in this regard, so the argument goes, "as is the intellectual power to discern right from wrong and understand the nature and quality of [one's] acts." [77]

Supporters of *M'Naghten,* on the other hand, argue that the objectives of the crimi-

nal law are better served by an insanity test which is concerned with cognition rather than self-control. For example, one argument is that the goal of general deterrence [78] is best served by a rule which declares irresponsible only those persons who quite clearly could not have been deterred because they could not have employed reason to restrain the act.[79] Fundamental to this view is the proposition that "it is essential to maintain the threat" of punishment "so long as there is any chance that the preventive influence [of the criminal law] may operate." [80] By starting from that point, it appears "safe" to exempt from punishment those who did not know what they were doing, for such individuals are quite clearly not deterrable and may be exculpated without diminishing the pressure on ordinary men to conform with the law. This is not true, so the argument goes, if exculpation is possible because of lack of self-control; especially because a complete inability to resist seldom exists,[81] the threat of punishment must be maintained against those who because of mental disease are strongly tempted to break the law—just as it is against those who are for other reasons under a strong compulsion to engage in criminal conduct.

Others have taken a somewhat different approach in contending that *M'Naghten* is consistent with the purposes of the criminal law. They begin with the proposition that deterrability is *not* the touchstone of responsibility; it is noted that in one sense all offenders are nondeterrable (i.e., they were not deterred). Rather, responsibility rests upon "moral blameworthiness." But, how is moral blame to be determined? Not by asking whether it was reasonable, on the facts of the individual case, to expect compliance with the law, for the criminal law frequently imposes

---

73. United States v. Currens, 290 F.2d 751 (3d Cir. 1961).

74. F. Lindman & D. McIntyre, The Mentally Disabled and the Law 337 (1961); 1 National Comm'n on Reform of Federal Criminal Laws, Working Papers 236–37 (1970).

75. Livermore & Meehl, The Virtues of M'Naghten, 51 Minn.L.Rev. 789, 800 (1967).

76. S. Brakel & R. Rock, supra note 23, at 386; M. Guttmacher & M. Weihofen, Psychiatry and the Law 420 (1952).

77. State v. Green, 78 Utah 580, 6 P.2d 177 (1931).

78. See § 1.5.

79. Model Penal Code § 4.01, Comment (Tent. Draft No. 4, 1955).

80. Wechsler, The Criteria of Criminal Responsibility, 22 U.Chi.L.Rev. 367, 374 (1955).

81. H. Weihofen, supra note 12, at 84.

moral condemnation in the absence of such an expectation.[82] Instead, moral blameworthiness "is less a quality of the offender, resting on his actual ability or inability to conform, than of the normative judgment of others that he ought to have been able to conform."[83] The *M'Naghten* test is then found an appropriate device for identifying those without moral blame, for it isolates "that group that is popularly viewed as insane" and whose "acquittal will not offend the community sense of justice."[84]

(3) Asks Questions Psychiatrist Cannot Answer. A common objection among psychiatrists to the right-wrong test is that it is directed to ethical and moralistic rather than scientific concerns. It is claimed that the question of the defendant's knowledge of right and wrong is more of a problem for a theologian and that it requires the psychiatrist to forsake his objective role and make value judgments.[85] This criticism, however, is based upon a misunderstanding of what is being asked of the experts. "We are not being asked whether a defendant acted according to our accepted standards of morality or whether his own theoretical standards were the generally accepted ones. What we are asked is whether the defendant had sufficient intellect or sufficiently clear mind at the time of the crime to know what these generally accepted standards were."[86] The psychiatrist is not being called upon to respond to the ethical question of what *is* right or wrong, but only to indicate whether the defendant was able to make moral and ethical discriminations.[87]

(4) Restricts Expert Testimony. Yet another criticism of the *M'Naghten* test is that it unjustifiably restricts expert testimony and thus keeps from the factfinder much relevant information concerning the defendant's mental condition.[88] The "true vice" of *M'Naghten* is said to be that "the ultimate deciders—the judge or the jury—will be deprived of information vital to their final judgment."[89]

This contention has been thoroughly debunked by Goldstein, who concluded after a thorough analysis of the relevant appellate opinions that there is "virtually no support in law for the view that *M'Naghten* is responsible for inhibiting the flow of testimony on the insanity issue."[90] Rather, the policy of the courts has been to admit any evidence which is probative of the defendant's mental condition,[91] and this has been so even when the evidence appears to relate solely to defendant's lack of self-control.[92] A similar conclusion was reached by the Model Penal Code draftsmen: "No American case has been found where a trial court excluded evidence or refused to charge on the defense of insanity merely because the evidence in support of the defense related to neurosis or psychopathic

---

82. Illustrative cases included: (a) conviction for taking the life of another to save one's own life in a nondefensive situation; and (b) conviction under a penal statute of which the defendant was reasonably ignorant. Livermore & Meehl, supra note 75, at 794.

83. Id. at 794–95.

84. Id. at 855.

85. Model Penal Code § 4.01, Appendix A (1985).

86. Ibid. (Views of Dr. Manfred S. Guttmacher.)

87. Allen, The Rule of the American Law Institute's Model Penal Code, 45 Marq.L.Rev. 494, 498 (1962).

88. Freedman, Guttmacher & Overholser, Mental Disease or Defect Excluding Responsibility, 1961 Wash.U.L.Q. 250, 251.

89. United States v. Freeman, 357 F.2d 606 (2d Cir. 1966).

90. A. Goldstein, supra note 18, at 53–54.

91. See, e.g., State v. Smith, 223 Kan. 203, 574 P.2d 548 (1977) (use of Model Penal Code test instead of *M'Naghten*

"would not have afforded the experts any more latitude" than was actually allowed in this case); State v. Rawland, 294 Minn. 17, 199 N.W.2d 774 (1972) ("evidence should be received freely" so that the factfinder can "take account of the entire man and his mind as a whole").

92. For example, in State v. Carlson, 5 Wis.2d 595, 93 N.W.2d 354 (1958), a medical witness was called to testify that an electroencephalograph test showed the defendant could not control his behavior. The trial judge rejected this testimony because it would not show that the defendant was unable to distinguish between right and wrong, the sole test in Wisconsin. The Wisconsin Supreme Court reversed, holding that under the right-wrong test no evidence should be excluded which reasonably tends to show the mental condition of the defendant at the time of his acts. The reason, the court said on another occasion, was that a defendant who can show lack of self-control might generate a reasonable doubt in the minds of jurors applying the *M'Naghten* test. State v. Shoffner, 31 Wis.2d 412, 143 N.W.2d 458 (1966).

personality or other mental disturbance rather than a psychosis." [93]

Goldstein also documents the conclusion that psychiatrists have not been forced to testify in terms of a definition of "know" which is limited to intellectual awareness. Based upon an analysis of numerous transcripts, he found that expert witnesses were regularly permitted to explain their interpretation of this word in *M'Naghten* and to assert that the defendant did not have the requisite knowledge because of his lack of normal emotional awareness. [94]

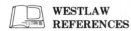 **WESTLAW REFERENCES**

durham /12 214 +4 862 /p insan*** psychiatr***

(d) The "Irresistible Impulse" Test. Of the jurisdictions in this country which still follow the *M'Naghten* rule, a few have also adopted what is commonly (but unfortunately) termed the "irresistible impulse" test. [95] Broadly stated, this rule requires a verdict of not guilty by reason of insanity if it is found that the defendant had a mental disease which kept him from controlling his conduct. Such a verdict is called for even if the defendant knew what he was doing and that it was wrong; the defendant's mental condition need not satisfy both the *M'Naghten and* "irresistible impulse" tests.

The notion that an "irresistible impulse" should qualify as an insanity defense even predates the *M'Naghten* case. Prior to the time that the *M'Naghten* judges responded to the inquiries from the House of Lords, writings in the field of medical jurisprudence emphasized that an individual might know what he was doing and that it was wrong but nonetheless be unable to control his conduct. [96] And in 1840, just a few years before *M'Naghten*, an English judge instructed the jury as follows concerning one Oxford, charged with treason for firing a pistol at Queen Victoria: "If some controlling disease was, in truth, the acting power within him which he could not resist, then he will not be responsible." [97] When the judges were later consulted about the law of insanity in *M'Naghten*, no mention was made of the test used in *Oxford*, but this is probably attributable to the fact that their answers were confined to the questions put to them in a particular case which concerned a defendant who had acted because of a delusion. [98] After *M'Naghten*, English trial judges instructed juries only in terms of the right-wrong test, and "irresistible impulse" was expressly rejected as "a most dangerous doctrine" in 1863. [99]

In the United States, a lack-of-control type of test may be traced back as far as 1834. [100] The phrase "irresistible impulse" was appar-

---

93. Model Penal Code § 4.01, Appendix A (Tent. Draft No. 4, 1955).

94. A. Goldstein, supra note 18, at 56–58.

95. One state has accomplished this by statute. Ga. Code § 26–703. Two others have done so by court decision. State v. Hartley, 90 N.M. 488, 565 P.2d 658 (1978); Davis v. Commonwealth, 214 Va. 728, 204 S.E.2d 273 (1974). At one time many other states (albeit never a majority) followed the "irresistible impulse" test as a supplement of *M'Naghten*, but most of these have since adopted the Model Penal Code test. Even a legislative adoption of the *M'Naghten* rule may be viewed as foreclosing recognition of the "irresistible impulse" supplement. State v. Craney, 347 N.W.2d 668 (Iowa 1984).

96. I. Ray, The Medical Jurisprudence of Insanity 263 (1838) (referring to persons "irresistibly impelled to the commission of criminal acts"); F. Winslow, The Plea of Insanity in Criminal Cases 74 (1843) (referring to persons "driven by an irresistible impulse").

97. Regina v. Oxford, 175 Eng.Rep. 941 (1840). S. Glueck, Mental Disorders and the Criminal Law 153 (1925) comments: "In this case the jury found the prisoner not guilty, being evidently more impressed with the gener-

al statements of the Justice as to 'controlling disease * * * which he could not resist,' than with his more specific remarks about the knowledge of right and wrong."

98. Id. at 236–37. "It is a reasonable conclusion that if, following the *Oxford* case, the Lords had asked the Judges to state the test when insanity is set up as a defense they would have responded in the language employed by Lord Denman to the jury in that case, which, as already stated, was as follows: 'If some controlling disease was, in truth, the acting power within him which he could not resist, then he will not be responsible.' It is not likely that Lord Denman, who joined in the answers of the Judges to the questions of the Lords, would have done so if he had believed the answers related to any problem of mental disease other than 'insane delusion.' " Keedy, Irresistible Impulse as a Defense in the Criminal Law, 100 U.Pa.L.Rev. 956, 961 (1952).

99. Regina v. Burton, 176 Eng.Rep. 354 (1863).

100. In State v. Thompson, Wright's Ohio Rep. 617 (1834), the judge charged the jury that "if his mind was such that he retained the power of discriminating, or to leave him conscious he was doing wrong, a state of mind in which at the time of the deed he was free to forbear, or

ently first used in 1844,[101] but the context in which it was used left it uncertain whether such a test separate and distinct from *M'Naghten* was actually being adopted.[102] A few jurisdictions accepted the test in the 1860's and 1870's, but the leading judicial exposition of the "irresistible impulse" test came in the 1887 case of *Parsons v. State.*[103] The court held that in every criminal trial where the defense of insanity is interposed the jury should receive the following inquiries:

  1. Was the defendant at the time of the commission of the alleged crime, as a matter of fact, afflicted with a *disease of the mind,* so as to be either idiotic, or otherwise insane?

  2. If such be the case, did he know right from wrong as applied to the particular act in question? If he did not have such knowledge, he is not legally responsible.

  3. If he did have such knowledge, he may nevertheless not be legally responsible if the two following conditions concur:

  (1) If, by reason of the duress of such mental disease, he had so far lost the *power to choose* between the right and wrong, and to avoid doing the act in question, as that his free agency was at the time destroyed.

  (2) and if, at the same time, the alleged crime was so connected with such mental disease, in the relation of cause and effect, as to have been the product of it *solely.*[104]

In one very important respect the *Parsons* case is representative of the test as it is used in the United States. The courts have generally stated the rule in terms of the defendant's inability to resist doing wrong or to control his acts, and the phrase "irresistible impulse" is very seldom used.[105] This means that in practice the test is broader than the misleading "irresistible impulse" language

suggests, for the jury is not ordinarily told that the defendant must have acted upon a sudden impulse or that his acts must have been totally irresistible. Rather, the jury is given the rule in terms of the capacity for self-control or free choice.[106]

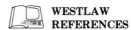

WESTLAW REFERENCES

110k50

digest,synopsis("irresistible impulse")

(e) Criticism of the "Irresistible Impulse" Test. As the "irresistible impulse" test grew in popularity, it received praise from both lawyers and psychiatrists who believed that *M'Naghten* standing alone was too restrictive because of its failure expressly to encompass the defendant who was unable to control his conduct. However, it did not escape criticism. On the one hand, as is evidenced by the fact that most *M'Naghten* jurisdictions did not also adopt a control test, the "irresistible impulse" rule was sometimes viewed as an unnecessary or unwise broadening of the criteria for determining irresponsibility. At the other extreme, there were those who came to believe that the "irresistible impulse" test was inadequate because it did not go far enough beyond *M'Naghten.* Some of the major criticisms are discussed below.

(1) "Impulse" Requirement Too Restrictive. One of the complaints about the "irresistible impulse" test is that it is too restrictive because it covers only impulsive acts. The test is described as applicable only to those crimes which "have been suddenly and impulsively committed after a sharp internal conflict," [107] and is said to give "no recognition to mental illness characterized by brooding and reflection." [108]

---

to do the act, he is responsible as a sane man." Similarly, in Clark v. State, 12 Ohio Rep. 483 (1843), the jury was asked: "Was the accused a free agent in forming the purpose to kill Cyrus Sells?"

101. Commonwealth v. Rogers, 48 Mass. 500 (1844).

102. H. Weihofen, supra note 12, at 86–87.

103. 81 Ala. 577, 2 So. 854 (1887).

104. Today most states do not require proof that the impulse was the sole cause of the act. H. Weihofen, supra note 12, at 91.

105. For a discussion of the cases, see A. Goldstein, supra note 18, at 69.

106. Id. at 71.

107. Royal Commission on Capital Punishment, 1949–53 Report 110 (1953).

108. Durham v. United States, 214 F.2d 862 (D.C.Cir. 1954).

It has been clearly established that this criticism is unfounded.[109] As noted above, the word "impulse" is only rarely used. Even if used in a jury instruction, it has not been established that jurors will take the word as requiring suddenness. The jury is *not* told that the "irresistible impulse" defense requires proof of sudden, unplanned action,[110] and any evidence tending to show loss of control because of a mental disease is freely admitted.[111]

(2) "Irresistible" Requirement Too Restrictive. Another objection which has been voiced focuses more upon the word "irresistible." It is claimed that the test is too restrictive because it requires a total impairment of volitional capacity.[112] If this is a fair statement of the limits of the test, then it is indeed restrictive, for conditions where an absolute inability to resist exists are rare,[113] and individuals in such circumstances "would in all probability be sufficiently out of touch with reality to meet" the *M'Naghten* test of irresponsibility.[114]

This criticism may also be questioned on the ground that it is based more upon the "irresistible impulse" label than upon the test as it is determined. Given the facts that juries are usually instructed in terms of loss of self-control or free choice, evidence is freely admitted, and experts are not prevented from explaining what they mean by loss of control,[115] it seems unlikely that juries are led to believe that an absolute inability to resist is

required. The requirement set forth in the *Parsons* case that the impulse must be the sole cause of the act has seldom been followed,[116] nor is there any evidence of a tendency to follow the practice of the military courts in inquiring whether the acts would not have been inhibited even by a "policeman at the elbow" of the defendant.[117]

(3) Inconsistent With Purposes of Criminal Law. Others feel that the supplementing of *M'Naghten* with the "irresistible impulse" test broadens the insanity defense too much. Their position, in brief, is that deterrence is an important objective of the criminal law and that this purpose is not served by declaring irresponsible those who—even because of a mental disease—fail to control their impulses toward wrongdoing. As one commentator observed: "The possibly resistible but abnormally compelling urge may justify a marked difference in treatment of an offender after conviction. The point here insisted upon, is that assuming deterrence to be the objective and the basis of liability, such a resistible urge can not logically exonerate from liability itself. On the contrary it is the very type of case where the will to resist most needs strengthening and development through example."[118] Similar reasoning has often been used by courts which have refused to adopt the "irresistible impulse" test.[119]

In response, it has been questioned whether conviction of a person actuated by an insane impulse would deter others from the commis-

---

109. A. Goldstein, supra note 18, at 70–75.

110. See, e.g., State v. Davies, 146 Conn. 137, 148 A.2d 251 (1959); Commonwealth v. Harrison, 342 Mass. 279, 173 N.E.2d 87 (1961). The only case which has expressly held that a planned act may not qualify is Snider v. Smyth, 187 F.Supp. 299 (E.D.Va.1960), affirmed 292 F.2d 683 (4th Cir.1961). It has been noted that this was not an appeal from a conviction but merely an opinion on a petition for habeas corpus, and that the evidence admitted was not in fact restricted to impulsive behavior. A. Goldstein, supra note 18, at 73.

111. Id. at 71.

112. Wechsler, The Criteria of Criminal Responsibility, 22 U.Chi.L.Rev. 367, 375 (1954).

113. H. Weihofen, supra note 12, at 84, where he also notes: "More common are urges that are not wholly irresistible. Most exhibitionists, for example, have enough control not to yield to their impulse in the presence of a policeman. * * * Nevertheless, these individ-

uals are the victims of urges so strong that most persons could not resist them under most circumstances."

114. Model Penal Code § 4.01, Appendix A (1985) (statement of Dr. Guttmacher).

115. A. Goldstein, supra note 18, at 71.

116. H. Weihofen, supra note 12, at 91.

117. United States v. Kunack, 17 C.M.R. 346 (1954).

118. Waite, Irresistible Impulse and Criminal Liability, 23 Mich.L.Rev. 443, 454 (1925).

119. E.g., People v. Hubert, 119 Cal. 216, 51 P. 329 (1897): "We do not know that the impulse was irresistible, but only that it was not resisted. Whether irresistible or not must depend upon the relative force of the impulse and the restraining force, and it has been well said that to grant immunity from punishment to one who retains sufficient intelligence to understand the consequences to him of a violation of the law, may be to make an impulse irresistible, which before was not."

sion of crime.[120] Experience, it is said, has shown that acceptance of the "irresistible impulse" test does not diminish the deterrent effect of the criminal law.[121] Indeed, the most compelling reason for recognizing the test is that it comports better with the objectives of the criminal law; it describes "persons who could not respond to the threat of sanction and who would readily be perceived by others as incapable of responding." [122]

(4) Presents Issue Incapable of Proof. Yet another objection to the "irresistible impulse" test, found mainly in the earlier cases rejecting the test, is that it is too vague and uncertain and thus too difficult to prove or disprove. It has been said, for example, that "the difficulty would be great, if not insuperable, of establishing by satisfactory proof whether an impulse was or was not 'uncontrollable.' " [123]

This does not appear to be an adequate reason for rejecting the "irresistible impulse" test, for a similar objection may be made about any insanity test.[124] The objection was fully considered and rejected in the *Parsons* decision, the leading case on the subject: "It is no satisfactory objection to say that the rule above announced by us is of difficult application. The rule in *M'Naghten's Case* is equally obnoxious to a like criticism. The difficulty does not lie in the rule, but is inherent in the subject of insanity itself." [125]

**WESTLAW
REFERENCES**

"irresistible impulse" /p m*naghten

---

120. Keedy, supra note 98, at 991.

121. Hoedemaker, "Irresistible Impulse" as a Defense in Criminal Law, 23 Wash.L.Rev. 1, 7 (1948).

122. A. Goldstein, supra note 18, at 67–68.

123. State v. Bundy, 24 S.C. 439 (1886).

124. H. Weihofen, supra note 12, at 97; Keedy, supra note 98, at 990.

125. Parsons v. State, 81 Ala. 577, 2 So. 854 (1887).

§ 4.3 The Modern Tests: "Product" and "Substantial Capacity"

Under what was usually referred to as the *Durham* rule, utilized by the District of Columbia Court of Appeals for nearly twenty years, an accused was not criminally responsible if his unlawful act was the product of mental disease or mental defect. As originally formulated this rule was criticized because of the ambiguity in the words "product" and "mental disease or defect." Subsequent cases defined those terms in such a way that the *Durham* rule began to resemble the American Law Institute Model Penal Code insanity test, which ultimately supplanted *Durham*.[1]

Under the Model Penal Code test, followed in a substantial minority of the states, a person is not responsible for criminal conduct if, as a result of mental disease or defect (not defined but expressly stated not to include an abnormality manifested only by repeated criminal or otherwise antisocial conduct), he lacks substantial capacity either to appreciate the criminality [wrongfulness] of his conduct or to conform his conduct to the requirements of law.

(a) The *Durham* "Product" Test. In 1871, New Hampshire became the first state to reject completely the *M'Naghten* test. Influenced by the writings of Dr. Isaac Ray, who contended that insanity "is never established by a single diagnostic symptom, but by the whole body of symptoms, no particular one of which is present in every case," [2] the court held that a defendant was to be found not guilty by reason of insanity if his crime "was the offspring or product of mental disease." [3] The New Hampshire solution was praised by some,[4] but was criticized by others on the ground that its inherent ambiguity left juries

§ 4.3

1. Until repudiated by a statutory *M'Naghten*-type rule in 1984. 18 U.S.C.A. § 20.

2. I. Ray, Medical Jurisprudence of Insanity 39 (5th ed. 1871).

3. State v. Jones, 50 N.H. 369 (1871). See also State v. Pike, 49 N.H. 399 (1869).

4. E.g., 1 J. Bishop, Criminal Law 268–69 (9th ed. 1923); 2 J. Stephen, History of the Criminal Law of England 97 (1883).

with insufficient guidance on the critical issue of responsibility.[5] Subsequent experience in New Hampshire did not afford a basis for evaluating that criticism,[6] nor did it provide any further elucidation of the "product" test.[7] For the next eighty-three years, no other American jurisdiction adopted the New Hampshire rule[8] or even gave it serious consideration.[9]

Then, in 1954, the United States Court of Appeals for the District of Columbia decided the case of *Durham v. United States*.[10] In an opinion by Judge Bazelon, the court held "that an accused is not criminally responsible if his unlawful act was the product of mental disease or defect." This broader test of criminal responsibility, the court concluded, was preferable to the tests then in use in the District—*M'Naghten* and irresistible impulse.[11] Also relying upon the writings of Dr. Ray, the court found the *M'Naghten* rule wanting "in that (a) it does not take sufficient account of psychic realities and scientific knowledge, and (b) it is based upon one symptom and so cannot validly be applied in all circumstances." As for the so-called irresistible impulse test, it was found inadequate "in that it gives no recognition to mental illness characterized by brooding and reflection." The "product" rule, on the other hand, would give psychiatrists greater leeway to put before the factfinder all relevant information concerning the character of the defendant's mental disease or defect, while leaving the jury free to perform its traditional function of applying "our inherited ideas of moral respon-

sibility"[12] to the circumstances of the individual case.

No effort was made in *Durham* to explain the meaning of the word "product" in this context, nor were mental disease and mental defect defined. "Disease" was merely distinguished from "defect"; the former, but not the latter, was a condition capable of either improving or deteriorating. Some indication of how the new rule should be applied in practice was given by this suggested jury instruction: "If you the jury believe beyond a reasonable doubt that the accused was not suffering from a diseased or defective mental condition at the time he committed the criminal act charged, you may find him guilty. If you believe he was suffering from a diseased or defective mental condition when he committed the act, but believe beyond a reasonable doubt that the act was not the product of such mental abnormality, you may find him guilty. Unless you believe beyond a reasonable doubt either that he was not suffering from a diseased or defective mental condition, or that the act was not the product of such abnormality, you must find the accused not guilty by reason of insanity. Thus your task would not be completed upon finding, if you did find, that the accused suffered from a mental disease or defect. He would still be responsible for his unlawful act if there was no causal connection between such mental abnormality and the act. These questions must be determined by you from the facts which you find to be fairly deducible from the testimony and the evidence in this case."

5. 1 F. Wharton & M. Stille, Medical Jurisprudence 180 (5th ed. 1905).

6. Later cases on the subject rarely reached the appellate level in that state, and apparently no evidence of experience at the trial level has been reported. Weihofen, The Flowering of New Hampshire, 22 U.Chi.L.Rev. 356, 357 (1955).

7. However, at the time it was adopted the court seemed to view "product" in terms of complete loss of self control: "If the defendant had an insane impulse to kill his wife, which he could not control, then mental disease produced the act. If he could have controlled it, then his will must have assented to the act, and it was not caused by disease, but by the concurrence of his will, and was therefore a crime." State v. Jones, 50 N.H. 369 (1871).

8. Montana flirted with the New Hampshire rule. State v. Peel, 23 Mont. 358, 59 P. 169 (1899); State v. Keerl, 29 Mont. 508, 75 P. 362 (1904); State v. Narich, 92 Mont. 17, 9 P.2d 477 (1932). See Note, 1 Mont.L.Rev. 69 (1940).

9. The cases are few in which the matter was even raised by defense counsel. See People v. Hubert, 119 Cal. 216, 51 P. 329 (1897); State v. Craig, 52 Wash. 66, 100 P. 167 (1909); Eckert v. State, 114 Wis. 160, 89 N.W. 826 (1902).

10. 214 F.2d 862 (D.C.Cir.1954).

11. Smith v. United States, 36 F.2d 548 (D.C.Cir.1929).

12. Quoting Holloway v. United States, 148 F.2d 665, 667 (D.C.Cir.1945).

WESTLAW REFERENCES

"model penal code" /p insan*** /3 test

(b) The Response to *Durham*. The *Durham* decision brought forth a flood of commentary from both lawyers and psychiatrists.[13] The psychiatrists, generally, applauded the decision,[14] although some were sharply critical.[15] As for the legal profession, *Durham* was usually viewed with considerable skepticism;[16] some lawyers, however, were most sympathetic to the decision.[17]

In praise of *Durham* it was said that the new rule would "expand the area of inquiry and communication of the medical expert as a witness."[18] Now a psychiatrist could present his testimony in regard to the mental condition of the accused in concepts familiar to him and which actually exist in mental life.[19] As a result, a proper allocation of the duty of determining insanity had been achieved among the judge, jury and expert psychiatric witness.[20]

The critics of *Durham* saw it as a "non-rule"[21] in that it provided the jury with no standard by which to judge the evidence and left the jury entirely dependent upon the testimony of the experts.[22] For one thing, the word "product" was not defined in *Durham*, an omission which some deemed indefensible.[23] Given the *Durham* court's rejection of the irresistible impulse test, it seemed fair to conclude that the product requirement could be satisfied by something less than total destruction of the defendant's capacity for self-control. If "product" was intended as a but-for test of causation, so that the question would be whether the accused would have committed the criminal acts if he had not suffered from a mental disease or defect, then *Durham* called for an answer that could rarely be given.[24] Moreover, a but-for test would leave the prosecution with the impossible burden of proving beyond a reasonable doubt that the defendant's acts were *not* the product of his mental disease or defect.[25] The uncertainty about the meaning of "product" made the "mental disease or defect" part of *Durham* more critical than under *M'Naghten* or the irresistible impulse test. Thus, *Durham* was also criticized because of its failure to define this phrase.[26]

The *Durham* court disapproved of *M'Naghten* and irresistible impulse as insanity tests on the ground that they made absence

---

13. Only a representative sampling can be listed here: Arnold, Due Process in Trials, 300 Annals 123 (1955); de Grazia, The Distinction of Being Mad, 22 U.Chi.L.Rev. 339 (1955); Douglas, The Durham Rule: A Meeting Ground for Lawyers and Psychiatrists, 41 Iowa L.Rev. 485 (1956); Guttmacher, The Psychiatrist as an Expert Witness, 22 U.Chi.L.Rev. 325 (1955); Hall, Psychiatry and Criminal Responsibility, 65 Yale L.J. 761 (1956); Halleck, The Insanity Defense in the District of Columbia—A Legal Lorelei, 49 Geo.L.J. 294 (1960); Hill, The Psychological Realism of Thurman Arnold, 22 U.Chi.L.Rev. 377 (1955); Katz, Law, Psychiatry, and Free Will, 22 U.Chi.L.Rev. 397 (1955); Roche, Criminality and Mental Illness—Two Faces of the Same Coin, 22 U.Chi.L.Rev. 320 (1955); Sobeloff, Insanity and the Criminal Law: From M'Naghten to Durham and Beyond, 41 A.B.A.J. 793 (1955); Szasz, Psychiatry, Ethics, and the Criminal Law, 58 Colum.L.Rev. 183 (1958); Watson, Durham Plus Five Years: Development of the Law of Criminal Responsibility in the District of Columbia, 116 Am.J.Psychiatry 289 (1959); Wechsler, The Criteria of Criminal Responsibility, 22 U.Chi.L.Rev. 367 (1955); Weihofen, The Flowering of New Hampshire, 22 U.Chi.L.Rev. 356 (1955); Wertham, Psychoauthoritarianism and the Law, 22 U.Chi.L.Rev. 336 (1955); Zilboorg, A Step Toward Enlightened Justice, 22 U.Chi.L.Rev. 331 (1955).

14. E.g., Roche, Guttmacher, and Zilboorg, all supra note 13.

15. Szasz, supra note 13, at 190 ("unadulterated nonsense"); Wertham, supra note 13, at 337 ("it gives undemocratic leeway to the partisan and/or bureaucratic expert, and, on account of its wording, lends itself to grave abuse").

16. E.g., Wechsler, supra note 13.

17. E.g., de Grazia, supra note 13.

18. Roche, supra note 13, at 324.

19. Guttmacher, supra note 13, at 329.

20. de Grazia, supra note 13, at 347.

21. A. Goldstein, The Insanity Defense 84 (1967).

22. Ibid; F. Lindman & D. McIntyre, The Mentally Disabled and the Law 342 (1961); Wertham, supra note 13, at 337.

23. Wechsler, supra note 13, at 371.

24. Ibid.

25. Acheson, McDonald v. United States: The Durham Rule Redefined, 51 Geo.L.J. 580, 583 (1963); Kuh, The Insanity Defense—An Effort to Combine Law and Reason, 110 U.Pa.L.Rev. 771 (1962).

26. Wechsler, supra note 13, at 368.

of responsibility depend upon particular symptoms of mental disease or defect (lack of cognition, lack of capacity for self-control). This, said the critics, was the "fundamental error" in *Durham,* for it rested upon the assumption that the concern is simply with mental disorder rather than with the question of when the disorder should be accorded the specific legal consequence of a defense to criminal conviction.[27] The symptoms cannot be disregarded, for it is only by reference to them that responsibility criteria can be properly limited so as to exclude only the nondeterrables from criminal sanctions. Such a limitation has been defended in these words:

> So long as there is any chance that the preventive influence may operate, it is essential to maintain the threat. If it is not maintained, the influence of the entire system is diminished upon those who have the requisite capacity, albeit that they sometimes may offend. * * * The category must be so extreme that to the ordinary man, burdened by passion and beset by large temptations, the exculpation of the irresponsibles bespeaks no weakness in the law. He does not identify himself and them; they are a world apart.[28]

The *Durham* rule did not gain acceptance in other jurisdictions. Defense counsel frequently sought approval of the "product" test in lieu of *M'Naghten* and irresistible impulse, but appellate courts uniformly declined to follow *Durham.*[29] Finally, in 1972, the *Durham* rule was abandoned even in the District of Columbia.[30] But the 18 years of experience with *Durham* remain instructive on the fundamental question of how the insanity defense should be defined.

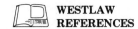 **WESTLAW REFERENCES**

durham /12 214 +4 862 /p product

(c) The *Durham* Test Defined. The *Durham* decision was far from the last word on the application of the "product" test in the District of Columbia. In the decade following *Durham,* over one hundred appellate opinions involving the sanity issue were decided by the United States Court of Appeals for the District of Columbia.[31] It became apparent that many of the criticisms of *Durham* were not without substance, and thus the court set about the task of responding to them by giving greater content to the *Durham* test. In this interval, *Durham* "traveled a remarkably circuitous path toward the conclusion that the jury needed some guidance, that words like 'mental disease' and 'product' were inadequate, and that the standard would have to incorporate somehow a description of the sorts of effects of disease that were relevant to compliance with the criminal law."[32]

(1) The Definition of "Product." In *Carter v. United States*[33] the court had occasion to explain the meaning of "product" in the *Durham* test. The trial judge's instruction in terms of "the consequence, a growth, natural result or substantive end of a mental abnormality" was held to be neither adequate nor accurate:

> When we say the defense of insanity requires that the act be a "product of" a disease, we mean that the facts on the record are such that the trier of the facts is enabled to draw a reasonable inference that the accused would not have committed the act he did commit if he had not been diseased as he was. There must be a relationship between the disease and the act, and that relationship, whatever it may be in degree, must

27. Id. at 373.

28. Id. at 374. Wechsler notes, however, that if the categories are too extreme they will be unworkable because they "call for a finding so severe that it must rest too largely on conjecture." Id. at 375.

29. See Krash, The Durham Rule and Judicial Administration of the Insanity Defense in the District of Columbia, 70 Yale L.J. 905, 906 n. 8, citing cases from twenty-two states and several federal courts of appeals.

30. United States v. Brawner, 471 F.2d 969 (D.C.Cir. 1972), adopting the Model Penal Code test, theretofore

accepted by virtually all other federal courts, in the "interest of uniformity of judicial approach and vocabulary." For a more complete assessment of that development, see Symposium, 1973 Wash.U.L.Q. 17. The Model Penal Code test has by statute been replaced by a *M'Naghten*-style formulation. 18 U.S.C.A. § 20.

31. President's Commission on Crime in the District of Columbia, Report 550 (1966).

32. A. Goldstein, supra note 21, at 86.

33. 252 F.2d 608 (D.C.Cir.1957).

be, as we have already said, critical in its effect in respect to the act. By "critical" we mean decisive, determinative, causal; we mean to convey the idea inherent in the phrases "because of," "except for," "without which," "but for," "effect of," "result of," "causative factor"; the disease made the effective or decisive difference between doing and not doing the act. The short phrases "product of" and "causal connection" are not intended to be precise, as though they were chemical formulae. They mean that the facts concerning the disease and the facts concerning the act are such as to justify reasonably the conclusion that "But for this disease the act would not have been committed."

This definition of "product" as a but-for test of causation, of course, did not still the critics, who had already said that use of a but-for test would require an answer which could seldom be given.[34] Nor did it satisfy those who believed that a test of criminal responsibility should be narrowly drawn so as to exclude from penal sanctions only non-deterrables.[35] This latter objection was also voiced from within the court:

> Apart from all other objections the product aspect of *Durham* is a fallacy in this: assuming arguendo that a criminal act can be the "product" of a "mental disease" that fact should not per se excuse the defendant; it should exculpate only if the condition described as a "mental disease" affected him so substantially that he could not appreciate the nature of the illegal act or could not control his conduct.[36]

Although the court did not abandon the but-for definition of product, the criticisms of it were overcome indirectly by the court's later

action in defining the term "mental disease and defect." [37]

Another objection which was made concerning the but-for definition was that it placed the prosecution in an impossible position because if a psychiatrist could come to a firm opinion on the product issue it would almost invariably be in the defendant's favor: "while occasionally one can say that an act *was* a product of mental disease, one can rarely if ever say that an act was *not* a product. To analogize, one can sometimes find a needle in the haystack, but one cannot find that there is *not* a needle in the haystack." [38] That this criticism had merit was clearly reflected in the cases decided under *Durham*.[39] However, that problem was largely overcome by the court's later holding that psychiatrists could no longer [40] testify whether the alleged offense was the product of mental illness:

> The term "product" has no clinical significance for psychiatrists. Thus there is no justification for permitting psychiatrists to testify on the ultimate issue. Psychiatrists should explain how defendant's disease or defect relates to his alleged offense, that is, how the development, adaptation and functioning of defendant's behavioral processes may have influenced his conduct. But psychiatrists should not speak directly in terms of "product," or even "result" or "cause." [41]

(2) The Definition of "Mental Disease or Defect." Durham was intended to enable psychiatrists to testify freely and completely without what were believed to be the eviden-

---

34. See text at note 24 supra. The court in *Carter* acknowledged the difficulty with this curious statement: "To the precise logician deduction of the foregoing inference involves a tacit assumption that if the disease had not existed the person would have been a law-abiding citizen. This latter is not necessarily factually true and can rarely, if ever, be proved, but in the ordinary conduct of these cases we make that tacit assumption. For ordinary purposes we make no mention of this logician's nicety."

35. See quote in the text at note 28 supra for a statement of this position.

36. Blocker v. United States, 288 F.2d 853 (D.C.Cir. 1961) (Burger, J., concurring).

37. See text at note 48 infra.

38. Acheson, supra note 25, at 583.

39. See, for example, Wright v. United States, 250 F.2d 4 (D.C.Cir.1957), holding that the government had not

sustained its burden of proof where, of eleven testifying psychistrists, no opinion on the product issue was elicited from five, two said they had "insufficient data to support a conclusion," one said it was "likely" there was a causal connection, another said there "could very well be" a causal connection, still another that it was "surely possible," and the last answered "yes" to a hypothetical question on the matter. The United States Attorney for the District noted that "such a state of the record is not unusual in the degree of its ambiguity on the issue." Acheson, supra note 25, at 584.

40. Previously it was the practice for counsel to question psychiatrists closely on whether they believed the defendant's acts were the product of mental disease. See, e.g., Wright v. United States, supra note 39.

41. Washington v. United States, 390 F.2d 444 (D.C. Cir.1967).

tiary limitations of the right-wrong and irresistible impulse tests. But when test cases under *Durham* arose, raising such questions as whether psychopathy or neurosis were mental diseases, "disputes about nomenclature arose which were strikingly reminiscent of those which had previously characterized trials under *M'Naghten.*"[42] Prosecution psychiatrists would classify the defendant's behavior as not psychotic; defense psychiatrists, on the other hand, would claim that it was psychotic or else the product of a lesser mental disorder claimed to qualify as a "mental disease or defect."

Illustrative of the problems which resulted is the case of *Blocker v. United States.*[43] Blocker, on trial for murder, interposed an insanity defense. Three psychiatrists on the staff of St. Elizabeth's Hospital testified on the issue; one found nothing wrong with the defendant, the other two testified that he suffered from a sociopathic personality disturbance, and all three agreed that a sociopathic personality disturbance was not considered a mental disease or defect. Less than a month after Blocker's conviction, the Assistant Superintendent of St. Elizabeth's testified in another case that he believed a sociopathic personality disturbance was a mental disease, and Blocker then sought a new trial because of this new medical evidence. The court of appeals held that he was entitled to a new trial so that he might have "the most mature expert opinion available on an issue vital to his defense." As one of the participants in that decision later acknowledged, "we tacitly conceded the power of St. Elizabeth's Hospital Staff to alter drastically the scope of a rule of law by a 'week-end' change in nomenclature

which was without any scientific basis, so far as we have any record or information."[44]

Blocker intensified the criticism that the undefined "mental disease or defect" part of *Durham* left the jury without standards to guide it and unduly dependent upon the experts' classifications of mental abnormalities. Two subsequent developments, however, substantially overcame these difficulties: (1) the court announced a judicial definition of what is included in the term "mental disease or defect"; and (2) the court developed guidelines to govern expert testimony on the issue.

In *McDonald v. United States*[45] the court agreed with the proposition, often stated theretofore by critics of *Durham*, that "what psychiatrists may consider a 'mental disease or defect' for clinical purposes, where their concern is treatment, may or may not be the same as mental disease or defect for the jury's purpose in determining criminal responsibility." Consequently, the court concluded "the jury should be told that a mental disease or defect includes any abnormal condition of the mind which substantially affects mental or emotional processes and substantially impairs behavior controls." Because under *McDonald* a mental condition had to have behavioral consequences in order to qualify as a "mental disease or defect," *Durham* was in effect limited in such a way that it was not significantly different[46] from the American Law Institute "substantial capacity" test.[47] Moreover, *McDonald* also overcame the difficulties with the "product" portion of *Durham*, for the requirement that the defendant's abnormality have behavioral consequences made relatively unimportant the second issue of whether (on a

---

42. A. Goldstein, supra note 21, at 85.

43. 274 F.2d 572 (D.C.Cir.1959).

44. Blocker v. United States, 288 F.2d 853 (D.C.Cir. 1961) (Burger, J., concurring).

45. 312 F.2d 847 (D.C.Cir.1962).

46. "Under the A.L.I. the state must prove that, despite the existence of a mental disease or defect, the defendant had the substantial capacity to choose a legal course of conduct. Under the modified Durham rule the prosecution must show a lack of connection between the

criminal act and a *disease which substantially impaired the defendant's capacity.* In both cases the substantial capacity is the main issue although arrived at from different approaches." Note, 44 Tulane L.Rev. 192, 199 (1969).

47. President's Commission on Crime in the District of Columbia, Report 533 (1966); Acheson, supra note 25, at 588; Note, supra note 46, at 197, all make reference to the similarity. When the *Durham* test was abandoned in favor of the Model Penal Code test, the court retained the *McDonald* definition of "mental disease or defect." United States v. Brawner, 471 F.2d 969 (D.C.Cir.1972).

but-for analysis) the mental disease caused the defendant's acts.[48]

In *Washington v. United States* [49] the court again noted that "the classifications [the medical profession] has developed for purposes of treatment, commitment, etc., may be inappropriate for assessing responsibility in criminal cases." This being the case, it was imperative that the roles of the psychiatrist and the jury be kept separate and distinct. Each, said the court, has "different judgments to make": the psychiatrist is concerned with "the medical-clinical concept of illness"; while the jury must decide "the legal and moral question of culpability." And thus the court provided an explanatory instruction to guide the expert, counsel, and the jury on the kind of expert testimony which was expected.[50]

 **WESTLAW REFERENCES**

blocker /12 288 +4 843 /p mental** insan***

48. "Once the jury finds that the effects of the mental disease are present which *McDonald* requires, the issue of 'product' relation with the crime will in many cases be virtually decided. If the jury finds the defendant suffering from a mental condition which impairs his control over his behavior, which is the McDonald standard, then it is an easy jump to the finding that the mental condition caused the particular behavior involved in the criminal case." Acheson, supra note 25, at 587.

49. 390 F.2d 444 (D.C.Cir.1967).

50. It is set out as an appendix to the opinion, and reads in part: "This word of caution is especially important if you give an opinion as to whether or not the defendant suffered from a 'mental disease or defect' because the clinical diagnostic meaning of this term may be different from its legal meaning. You should not be concerned with its legal meaning. Neither should you consider whether you think this defendant should be found guilty or responsible for the alleged crime. These are questions for the court and jury."

51. Legislatures have divided as to which of these alternative words to use in the insanity test. The issue is similar to that of whether "wrong" in *M'Naghten* means legal wrong or moral wrong, discussed in § 4.2(b)(5), and has often been considered in those terms. See, e.g., United States v. Sibley, 595 F.2d 1162 (9th Cir.1979); United States v. Segna, 555 F.2d 226 (9th Cir.1977). In United States v. Brawner, 471 F.2d 969 (D.C.Cir.1972), the court reasoned:

"As to the option of terminology noted in the ALI code, we adopt the formulation that exculpates a defendant whose mental condition is such that he lacks substantial capacity to appreciate the wrongfulness of his conduct.

(d) The A.L.I. "Substantial Capacity" Test. About a year following the *Durham* decision, the American Law Institute's Model Penal Code project produced yet another test for the insanity defense. Although its psychiatric advisory committee recommended adoption of *Durham,* the Institute instead approved a formulation which consisted of a modernized version of the *M'Naghten* and irresistible impulse tests:

(1) A person is not responsible for criminal conduct if at the time of such conduct as a result of mental disease or defect he lacks substantial capacity either to appreciate the criminality [wrongfulness] [51] of his conduct or to conform his conduct to the requirements of law.

(2) As used in this Article, the terms "mental disease or defect" do not include an abnormality manifested only by repeated criminal or otherwise anti-social conduct.[52]

As indicated in the accompanying commentary,[53] the Code draftsmen rejected the *Durham* rule because of the ambiguity of the

We prefer this on pragmatic grounds to 'appreciate the criminality of his conduct' since the resulting jury instruction is more like that conventionally given to and applied by the jury. While such an instruction is of course subject to the objection that it lacks complete precision, it serves the objective of calling on the jury to provide a community judgment on a combination of factors. And since the possibility of analytical differences between the two formulations is insubstantial in fact in view of the control capacity test, we are usefully guided by the pragmatic considerations pertinent to jury instructions."

52. Model Penal Code § 4.01. This differs from the 1955 tentative draft in two respects: (1) the bracketed word "wrongfulness" was inserted to indicate an option in the choice of words; and (2) the words "As used in this article" were added to avoid a misunderstanding that the Code attempts to legislate medical terminology. See Model Penal Code § 4.01 (Tent.Draft No. 4, 1955), also setting forth the following alternative formulations of paragraph (1): "(a) A person is not responsible for criminal conduct if at the time of such conduct as a result of mental disease or defect his capacity either to appreciate the criminality of his conduct or to conform his conduct to the requirements of law is so substantially impaired that he cannot justly be held responsible. (b) A person is not responsible for criminal conduct if at the time of such conduct as a result of mental disease or defect he lacks substantial capacity to appreciate the criminality of his conduct or is in such state that the prospect of conviction and punishment cannot constitute a significant restraining influence upon him."

53. Model Penal Code § 4.01, Comment at 173 (1985).

word "product." [54] *M'Naghten* and irresistible impulse, however, were not totally rejected; these two tests combined were seen as properly focusing upon impairment of cognition and impairment of volitional capacity— conditions which must be taken into account in an effort to exclude nondeterrables from penal sanctions. The result, therefore, was a broader statement of the concepts basic to the *M'Naghten* and irresistible impulse tests.

Most significant is the fact that the A.L.I. test only requires a lack of "substantial capacity." This is clearly a departure from the usual interpretation of *M'Naghten* and irresistible impulse, whereby a complete impairment of cognitive capacity and capacity for self-control is necessary.[55] Substantial capacity, the draftsmen noted, is all "that candid witnesses, called on to infer the nature of the situation at a time that they did not observe, can ever confidently say, even when they know that a disorder was extreme." [56] Moreover, even if witnesses could be more specific, it is undoubtedly true that there are many cases of advanced mental disorder in which rudimentary capacities of cognition and volition exist but which clearly present inappropriate occasions for the application of criminal sanctions.[57] The draftsmen acknowledged that the word "substantial" imputes no specific measure of degree, but concluded that identifying the degree of impairment with precision was "impossible both verbally and logically." [58]

The A.L.I. test uses the word "appreciate" instead of "know," a term which has been responsible for much of the criticism and misunderstanding of *M'Naghten*.[59] It thus seems apparent that expert testimony concerning the emotional or affective aspects of the defendant's personality is clearly relevant on this aspect of the A.L.I. formulation.[60] As to the "conform" part of the test, it avoids the implication (often drawn from the irresistible impulse test [61]) that the loss of volitional capacity can be reflected only in sudden or spontaneous acts as distinguished from those accompanied by brooding or reflection.[62]

As to paragraph (2) of the A.L.I. test, the draftsmen explained that it "is designed to exclude from the concept of 'mental disease or defect' the case of so-called 'psychopathic personality.' " [63] They noted that the psychopath differs from a normal person only quantitatively and not qualitatively, and that there is considerable difference of opinion on whether psychopathy should be called a disease. Thus the draftsmen favored "excluding a condition that is manifested only by the behavior phenomena that must, by hypothesis, be the result of disease for irresponsibility to be established," and avoiding "litigation of what is essentially a matter of terminology." [64]

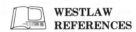 **WESTLAW REFERENCES**

"substantial capacity" /p m*naghten durham

(e) The Response to the A.L.I. Test. The Model Penal Code test (sometimes with minor variations) was adopted by virtually all of the United States Courts of Appeals,[65] only to be repudiated by Congress in 1984 in favor of a

54. At that time, *Durham* had not yet been clarified by subsequent cases, as discussed in § 4.3(c).

55. See § 4.2.

56. Model Penal Code § 4.01, Comment (Tent.Draft No. 4, 1955).

57. Allen, The Rule of the American Law Institute's Model Penal Code, 45 Marq.L.Rev. 494, 501 (1962).

58. Model Penal Code § 4.01, Comment (Tent.Draft No. 4, 1955).

59. See § 4.2(b)(2).

60. Allen, supra note 57, at 501.

61. See § 4.2(e)(1).

62. Even so, courts have not been receptive to certain claims, such as that a pathological gambler lacks substantial capacity to conform his conduct to the requirements of

law. See, e.g., United States v. Lewellyn, 723 F.2d 615 (8th Cir.1983) (embezzlement charge); United States v. Torniero, 735 F.2d 725 (2d Cir.1984) (transporting stolen property charge); United States v. Gould, 741 F.2d 45 (4th Cir.1984) (entry of bank with intent to rob charge).

63. Model Penal Code § 4.01, Comment (Tent.Draft No. 4, 1955).

64. Ibid.

65. United States v. Brawner, 471 F.2d 969 (D.C.Cir. 1972) ("wrongfulness"); United States v. Freeman, 357 F.2d 606 (2d Cir.1966) ("wrongfulness"); United States v. Currens, 290 F.2d 751 (3d Cir.1961) ("to appreciate the criminality of his conduct" omitted); United States v. Chandler, 393 F.2d 920 (4th Cir.1968); Blake v. United States, 407 F.2d 908 (5th Cir.1969) ("wrongfulness"); United States v. Smith, 404 F.2d 720 (6th Cir.1968); United

M'Naghten-style statutory formulation.[66] A significant minority of the states have accepted the A.L.I. test, usually by statute but sometimes by court decision.[67]

(1) Paragraph (1) of the Test. The "substantial capacity" test has also been criticized by some commentators. Certain critics of *M'Naghten* and irresistible impulse have asserted that the defects in those two tests are also present in the A.L.I. formulation. It is claimed, for example, that the A.L.I. test is only a "refurbishing" of the two traditional rules,[68] and that it has failed to "bridge the gap that now exists between legal and psychiatric thinking." [69]

Others have been critical of the A.L.I test on the ground that it is ambiguous. Thus, it has been asserted that the word "result" introduces the most objectionable aspects of the *Durham* "product" test.[70] Use of the words "substantial capacity" and "appreciate" has been questioned on the ground that they do not have a common, absolute meaning. These words, it is said, are bound to encourage differences among expert witnesses and also among jurors over whether the defendant's degree of impairment or depth of awareness was sufficient.[71]

In the main, however, the A.L.I. test has drawn praise from the commentators. As to the objections summarized above, it has been noted that "the *Durham* experience has taken much of the bite from such criticisms. It is now apparent that a precise definition of in-

sanity is impossible, that the effort to eliminate functional definitions deprives the jury of an essential concreteness of statement and that it is entirely sensible to leave 'mental disease' undefined, at least so long as it is modified by a statement of minimal conditions for being held to account under a system of criminal law." [72] The Model Penal Code formulation has rightly been praised as achieving the two important objectives of a test of responsibility: (1) giving expression to an intelligible principle; and (2) fully disclosing that principle to the jury.[73]

(2) Paragraph (2) of the Test. Much of the criticism of the A.L.I. proposal has been directed at paragraph (2), which excludes from the definition of "mental disease or defect" an abnormality manifested only by repeated criminal or otherwise anti-social conduct. As noted earlier, the draftsmen's purpose was to exclude the psychopath.

Such a fixed, rigid exclusion from the definition of mental disease or defect has been opposed on several grounds. One objection is that such an exclusion is unwarranted in the face of existing doubts as to whether the psychopathic personality constitutes a valid psychiatric classification.[74] Another is that psychopaths are generally not deterrable and thus are not deserving of penal sanctions.[75] Also, it has been noted that some headway is now being made in the treatment of psychopaths by psychiatric therapy and that therefore they are fit subjects for medical-custodial

States v. Shapiro, 383 F.2d 680 (7th Cir.1967) ("wrongfulness"); Pope v. United States, 372 F.2d 710 (8th Cir.1967) (exact words not important); Wade v. United States, 426 F.2d 64 (9th Cir.1970) ("wrongfulness"); Wion v. United States, 325 F.2d 420 (10th Cir.1963). The First Circuit intimated it would approve the A.L.I. test, Beltran v. United States, 302 F.2d 48 (1st Cir.1962).

66. 18 U.S.C.A. § 20.

67. Commonwealth v. Sheehan, 376 Mass. 765, 383 N.E.2d 1115 (1978); State v. Johnson, 121 R.I. 254, 399 A.2d 469 (1979); Graham v. State, 547 S.W.2d 531 (Tenn. 1977); State v. Grimm, 156 W.Va. 615, 195 S.E.2d 637 (1973).

68. H. Weihofen, The Urge to Punish 99–100 (1956). "To some it may seem that in abandoning some words and replacing them with others the Code points to the promised land. But a real change can scarcely be effected by the use of words which bear a dictionary synonymity with those erased." P. Roche, The Criminal Mind 180 (1958).

69. H. Weihofen, supra note 69, at 100.

70. Comment, 4 Catholic Law. 297, 307 (1957). This objection is effectively refuted in Cutler, Insanity as a Defense in Criminal Law, 5 Catholic Law. 44, 55 (1959).

71. Kuh, The Insanity Defense—An Effort to Combine Law and Reason, 110 U.Pa.L.Rev. 771, 797–99 (1962). See also 1 National Comm'n on Reform of Federal Criminal Laws, Working Papers 245 (1970); Roche, supra note 68, at 179; Comment, 4 Catholic Law. 297, 307 (1957). The words criticized, it should be recalled, where deliberately chosen by the draftsmen because of their imprecision. See Model Penal Code § 4.01, Comments (Tent.Draft No. 4, 1955).

72. A. Goldstein, The Insanity Defense 87 (1967).

73. Allen, supra note 57, at 500.

74. J. Biggs, The Guilty Mind 160 (1955).

75. Kuh, supra note 71, at 800; Weihofen, The Definition of Mental Illness, 21 Ohio St.L.J. 1, 7 (1960).

disposition.[76] Others have expressed approval of paragraph (2) of the A.L.I. test, arguing that such a limitation is essential to keep the defense from swallowing up virtually all of criminal liability.

Whether paragraph (2) will in fact exclude the psychopathic personality from the insanity defense is questionable. A psychiatrist is unlikely to base his diagnosis of the criminal psychopath solely upon his criminal or antisocial conduct.[77] Thus, the actual impact of paragraph (2) may be to exclude only those psychopaths who received a routine examination, but not those affluent and fortunate enough to receive a more careful diagnosis.[78]

Because of doubts about the soundness or effectiveness of paragraph (2), some courts adopted a modified form of the A.L.I. test in which there are no express exclusions from "mental disease or defect." [79] But most of the legislative enactments of the A.L.I. test include paragraph (2).

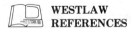

WESTLAW REFERENCES

a.l.i. /p "substantial capacity"

---

§ 4.4 Incompetency at Time of Criminal Proceedings

If a defendant is suffering from a mental disease or defect which renders him unable to understand the proceedings against him or to assist in his defense, he may not be tried, convicted, or sentenced so long as that condition persists. Rather, he is ordinarily committed to a mental institution until such time as he recovers. In practice, these commitments have to a significant respect displaced the process of trial, acquittal on grounds of insanity, and commitment following acquittal.

If a defendant sentenced to death is suffering from a mental disease or defect which renders him unable to understand the nature and purpose of the punishment about to be imposed, he may not be executed until such time as he has recovered from that condition.

(a) Incompetency to Stand Trial. For a variety of reasons, the insanity defense is raised in only a very small percentage of criminal cases.[1] In part, this is because many individuals who might raise the defense never go to trial. Some are screened out very early as a part of the discretion exercised by the police and prosecution. Persons arrested for minor crimes by the police may be diverted to the civil commitment route when it appears that their conduct resulted from mental illness.[2] Even in more serious cases, the prosecutor may decide to initiate civil commitment proceedings (or, influence the bringing of such proceedings by others) or to place the apparently mentally ill person on a form of administrative probation on the condition that he seek psychiatric assistance.[3] Also significant is the fact that of those charged, the overwhelming majority (in some jurisdictions over 90%) will plead guilty, often as a result of a process of "plea negotiations" whereby the defendant enters a guilty plea in exchange for

76. Kuh, supra note 71, at 800.

77. 1 National Comm'n on Reform of Federal Criminal Laws, Working Papers 245–46 (1970); Kozol, The Psychopath Before the Law, 44 Mass.L.Q. 106, 116 (No. 2, 1959); Kuh, A Prosecutor Considers the Model Penal Code, 63 Colum.L.Rev. 608, 626 (1963); Kuh, supra note 71, at 799.

78. Diamond, From M'Naghten to Currens, and Beyond, 50 Calif.L.Rev. 189, 194 (1962).

79. E.g., United States v. Huffman, 467 F.2d 189 (6th Cir.1972); United States v. Currens, 290 F.2d 751 (3d Cir. 1961).

§ 4.4

1. See A. Goldstein, The Insanity Defense ch. 11 (1967). Published criminal statistics seldom give any indication of the percentage of cases in which the insanity defense is raised. California is an exception; there, for example, in 1965, of 36,643 felony dispositions, only 195 cases (0.53%)

went to trial on an insanity plea. A. Matthews, Mental Disability and the Criminal Law 28 (1970). Observations in major cities indicated that the insanity defense was rarely invoked:

City	Months of Observation	Number of Cases
Chicago	4	1
Detroit	3	0
Miami	2	0
New York	3	1
San Francisco	4	1

Id. at 25–26.

2. On civil commitment procedures, see S. Brakel & R. Rock, The Mentally Disabled and the Law 17–132 (1971).

3. The latter technique is recommended in President's Comm'n on Law Enf't and Admin. of Justice, The Challenge of Crime in a Free Society 133–34 (1967).

the prosecutor's promise to seek or obtain sentencing concessions.[4] There are certain to be included in this large number of cases many in which an insanity defense might be raised with at least a reasonable chance of success.[5] And, just as some defendants plead guilty instead of defending on grounds of insanity, some go to trial without raising the defense because of a tactical decision that the risk of conviction and sentence is more appealing than the risk of indeterminate commitment to a mental institution.[6]

Of particular interest here, however, is yet another reason: because the person who was insane at the time of his conduct is likely to be incompetent at the time of trial, he may be declared incompetent to stand trial and then committed. If he does not recover, he will never be tried; if he does ultimately recover but a substantial interval of time has elapsed, the prosecutor may dismiss the prosecution either (a) because essential witnesses to or evidence of the crime are no longer available, or (b) because of a judgment that no purpose would now be served by prosecution.[7] It is precisely those individuals who are most likely to be able to make a clear showing of insanity at the time of their conduct—the persistently and obviously psychotic—who are withdrawn from the criminal process in this way.[8] Commitment for incompetency to stand trial thus appears to have displaced the insanity defense to a significant degree.[9]

This is not to suggest that the legal test of incompetency to stand trial is the precise equivalent of any of definitions of the insanity defense. Apart from the obvious fact that the concern is with the defendant's mental condition at a different point in time, the question of competency to stand trial is not concerned with the defendant's responsibility but rather with his ability to participate in the proceedings in a meaningful way. "[I]t is not enough for the * * * judge to find that 'the defendant [is] oriented to time and place and [has] some recollection of events' "; rather, "the 'test must be whether he has sufficient present ability to consult with his lawyer with a reasonable degree of rational understanding—and whether he has a rational as well as factual understanding of the proceedings against him.' "[10] This, essentially, is the common law test of competency to stand trial, which has been codified in many jurisdictions[11] and in others continues as a result of judicial interpretation of competency statutes which merely refer to the defendant's "insanity" or "unsound mind."[12]

Under this test, there are two distinct matters to be determined: (1) whether the defendant is sufficiently coherent to provide his counsel with information necessary or relevant to constructing a defense; and (2) whether he is able to comprehend the significance of the trial and his relation to it.[13] The defendant must have an "ability to confer

---

4. See D. Newman, Conviction: The Determination of Guilt or Innocence Without Trial (1966).

5. Whether such cases are appropriate for plea negotiations is a matter of dispute. Compare Enker, Perspectives on Plea Bargaining, in President's Comm'n on Law Enf't and Admin. of Justice, Task Force Report: The Courts 108, 113 (1967), with Griffiths, Ideology in Criminal Procedure, or a Third Model of the Criminal Process, 79 Yale L.J. 359, 398–99 (1970).

6. For the considerations which defense counsel is likely to take into account in deciding whether to raise an insanity defense, see § 4.5(a).

7. Model Penal Code § 4.06(2) also gives the court power to dismiss the charge when it "is of the view that so much time has elapsed since the commitment of the defendant that it would be unjust to resume the criminal proceedings."

8. A. Goldstein, supra note 1, at 24–25.

9. F. Matthews, Mental Illness and the Criminal Law 3 (1967); Comment, 59 Mich.L.Rev. 1078 (1961).

10. Dusky v. United States, 362 U.S. 402, 80 S.Ct. 788, 4 L.Ed.2d 824 (1960).

11. Most states have a statutory test at least approximating that just quoted.

12. S. Brakel & R. Rock, supra note 2, at 410; H. Weihofen, Mental Disorder as a Criminal Defense 435 (1954); Slough & Wilson, Mental Capacity to Stand Trial, 21 U.Pitt.L.Rev. 593, 595–96 (1960); Model Penal Code § 4.04, Comment at 231 (1985); Note, 81 Harv.L.Rev. 454, 457 (1967).

13. For further description and assessment of the *Dusky* test, see Mickenberg, Competency to Stand Trial and the Mentally Retarded Defendant: The Need for a Multi-Disciplinary Solution to a Multi-Disciplinary Problem, 17 Cal.W.L.Rev. 365, 380–89 (1981); Silten & Tullis, Mental Competency in Criminal Proceedings, 28 Hastings L.J. 1053, 1058–65 (1977); Annot., 23 A.L.R.4th 493 (1983).

intelligently, to testify coherently and to follow the evidence presented." [14] It is necessary that the defendant have a rational as well as a factual understanding of the proceedings. This necessitates a level of comprehension going beyond surface knowledge,[15] but does not require functioning at normal levels.[16] Sufficient competency can exist even though achieved only by compelled medication,[17] but such medication has sometimes been viewed as impermissibly infringing on the defendant's ability to establish an insanity defense.[18]

It has sometimes been suggested that the ability to consult meaningfully with counsel requires a capacity on the part of the defendant "to remember the facts surrounding the occurrence of the alleged offense." [19] Were this literally true, then in any case in which the defendant could not recall relevant events because of amnesia it would be necessary to delay the trial because of the defendant's incompetency. But this is not the case; [20] rather, the courts have held that the loss of memory due to amnesia is not alone an adequate ground upon which to base a finding of incompetency to stand trial.[21] As one court quite frankly put it: "When it is considered that the result of an order finding defendant unfit for trial in these circumstances would be outright release, assuming the amnesia is permanent and there is no other mental defect sufficient to warrant commitment, it can be more easily understood why all the courts which have passed on this question have refused to allow amnesia to be classified as the sort of mental defect causing incapacity to stand trial." [22] But trial of an amnesiac defendant can be fundamentally unfair in some circumstances, and consequently trial judges must determine, on a case-by-case basis, whether the defendant could likely receive (and, at the conclusion of the trial), whether he in fact did receive) a fair trial.[23]

The notion that a defendant who is incompetent may not be tried, which is a require-

14. Martin v. Estelle, 546 F.2d 177 (5th Cir.1977).

15. People v. Swallow, 60 Misc.2d 171, 301 N.Y.S.2d 798 (1969).

16. Feguer v. United States, 302 F.2d 214 (8th Cir. 1962).

17. United States v. Hayes, 589 F.2d 811 (5th Cir.1979); State v. Hayes, 118 N.H. 548, 389 A.2d 1379 (1978); People v. Parsons, 82 Misc.2d 1090, 371 N.Y.S.2d 840 (1975); Ake v. State, 663 P.2d 1 (Okl.Crim.App.1983); State v. Hancock, 247 Or. 21, 426 P.2d 872 (1967); State v. Stacy, 556 S.W.2d 552 (Tenn.1977).

Contra: State v. Maryott, 6 Wn.App. 96, 492 P.2d 239 (1971). Statutes in a few states also require a contrary result. Winick, Psychotropic Medication and Competency to Stand Trial, 1977 A.B.F.Res.J. 769, 772–75.

18. Commonwealth v. Louraine, 390 Mass. 28, 453 N.E.2d 437 (1983). Other courts have held it is sufficient that defendant is allowed to inform the jury of the medication and its effects upon him. State v. Jojola, 89 N.M. 489, 553 P.2d 1296 (App.1976); State v. Law, 270 S.C. 664, 244 S.E.2d 302 (1978); State v. Gwaltney, 77 Wn.2d 906, 468 P.2d 433 (1970).

19. United States v. Wilson, 263 F.Supp. 528 (D.D.C.1966), remanded 391 F.2d 460 (D.C.Cir.1968).

20. See Notes, 52 Iowa L.Rev. 339 (1966); 8 Kan.L.Rev. 132 (1959); 27 Md.L.Rev. 182 (1967); 71 Yale L.J. 109 (1961); Annot., 46 A.L.R.3d 544 (1972).

21. United States v. Mota, 598 F.2d 995 (5th Cir.1979); United States v. Stevens, 461 F.2d 317 (7th Cir.1972); Commonwealth v. Griffin, 622 S.W.2d 214 (Ky.1981); Morrow v. State, 293 Md. 247, 443 A.2d 108 (1982); Common-

wealth v. Lombardi, 378 Mass. 612, 393 N.E.2d 346 (1979); Commonwealth v. Whitt, 493 Pa. 572, 427 A.2d 623 (1981).

22. People v. Francobandera, 33 N.Y.2d 429, 354 N.Y.S.2d 609, 310 N.E.2d 292 (1974).

23. United States v. Swanson, 572 F.2d 523 (5th Cir. 1978); Wilson v. United States, 391 F.2d 460 (D.C.Cir. 1968). As stated in People v. Francabandera, supra note 22:

"In making these findings the court should consider the following factors:

"(1) The extent to which the amnesia affected the defendant's ability to consult with and assist his lawyer.

"(2) The extent to which the amnesia affected the defendant's ability to testify in his own behalf.

"(3) The extent to which the evidence in suit could be extrinsically reconstructed in view of the defendant's amnesia. Such evidence would include evidence relating to the crime itself as well as any reasonably possible alibi.

"(4) The extent to which the Government assisted the defendant and his counsel in that reconstruction.

"(5) The strength of the prosecution's case. Most important here will be whether the Government's case is such as to negate all reasonable hypotheses of innocence. If there is any substantial possibility that the accused could, but for his amnesia, establish an alibi or other defense, it should be presumed that he would have been able to do so.

"(6) Any other facts and circumstances which would indicate whether or not the defendant had a fair trial."

ment of due process,[24] has several reasons underlying it.[25] For one, it ensures the accuracy of the proceedings, as an incompetent defendant is not in a position to exercise several rights (e.g., to testify in his own behalf, to confront opposing witnesses) which are intended to accomplish that end. Second, it ensures the fairness of the proceedings, as it avoids the situation of a trial in which the defendant is unable to make certain basic decisions concerning the course of his defense. Third, it aids in maintaining the dignity of the proceedings, for an incompetent defendant is likely to conduct himself in the courtroom in a manner which would disrupt the trial. Finally, under our theory of the criminal law it is important that the defendant know why he is being punished, a comprehension which is greatly dependent upon his understanding what occurs at trial.

The issue of the defendant's competency to stand trial is usually raised at the time of arraignment, when the defendant is called upon to plead,[26] although it may be raised at

any time during the course of the trial.[27] The issue may be raised by the defendant, of course, but his failure to do so does not constitute a waiver of the due process right not to be tried when incompetent, for "it is contradictory to argue that a defendant may be incompetent, and yet knowingly or intelligently 'waive' his right to have the court determine his capacity to stand trial."[28] It may also be raised by the prosecutor[29] (which is frequently the case because in this way the prosecutor can also obtain psychiatric evidence about the defendant to rebut an insanity defense[30]) or by the court,[31] and this is so even if the defense would prefer to go to trial without an inquiry into competency[32] (an understandable desire in some instances, in that the defendant would prefer conviction and sentence to a definite term instead of indefinite commitment[33]).

The issue must be raised in such a way to create a reasonable doubt in the judge's mind concerning the defendant's present capacity to stand trial;[34] a mere unsupported sugges-

24. Drope v. Missouri, 420 U.S. 162, 95 S.Ct. 896, 43 L.Ed.2d 103 (1975); Bishop v. United States, 350 U.S. 961, 76 S.Ct. 440, 100 L.Ed. 835 (1956).

25. For a more detailed discussion of these reasons, see Note, 81 Harv.L.Rev. 454, 457–58 (1967).

26. H. Weihofen, supra note 12, at 439. If there is doubt as to defendant's competency, he may not enter a guilty plea. State v. Harris, 406 So.2d 128 (La.1981). Whether the *Dusky* standard or some higher standard applies when the defendant wishes to waive counsel or to plead guilty is a matter on which the courts are divided. See Silten & Tullis, supra note 13, at 1065–74; Note, 68 Va.L.Rev. 1139 (1982).

27. Indeed, in Pate v. Robinson, 383 U.S. 375, 86 S.Ct. 836, 15 L.Ed.2d 815 (1966), it was held that due process requires a hearing when the circumstances at trial create doubts about the defendant's competence. See also Drope v. Missouri, 420 U.S. 162, 95 S.Ct. 896, 43 L.Ed.2d 103 (1975).

Also, if after a verdict of guilty but before sentencing the defendant becomes incapable of comprehending the nature and purpose of the proceedings or of stating any reasons that may exist why sentence should not be pronounced, sentencing is stayed until he has recovered.

At the other extreme, in a few jurisdictions the issue may be raised even before indictment, possibly at the preliminary hearing or more likely at the grand jury proceedings. H. Weihofen, supra note 12, at 436–38.

28. Pate v. Robinson, supra note 27. But consider State v. Hayes, 118 N.H. 458, 389 A.2d 1379 (1978) (if defendant by his own voluntary choice, made while competent, becomes incompetent to stand trial because he

withdraws from medication, he may be deemed to have waived his right to be tried while competent). Contra: Lane v. State, 388 So.2d 1022 (Fla.1980).

29. State v. Hebert, 186 La. 308, 172 So. 167 (1937); People v. Janek, 287 Mich. 563, 283 N.W. 689 (1939).

30. A. Goldstein, supra note 1, at 37, 108.

31. White v. Commonwealth, 197 Ky. 79, 245 S.W. 892 (1922); People v. Esposito, 287 N.Y. 389, 39 N.E.2d 925 (1942).

32. Seidner v. United States, 260 F.2d 732 (D.C.Cir. 1958).

33. Note, 81 Harv.L.Rev. 454, 456 (1967).

34. Whether this is so as a constitutional matter is not entirely clear. In Pate v. Robinson, 383 U.S. 375, 86 S.Ct. 836, 15 L.Ed.2d 815 (1966), the Court noted in passing that the applicable state statute required a hearing if there was a "bona fide doubt" as to defendant's competence. In Drope v. Missouri, 420 U.S. 162, 95 S.Ct. 896, 43 L.Ed.2d 103 (1975), the Court asserted that the state's statutory procedure, which required a hearing whenever the court "has reasonable cause to believe" the defendant to be incompetent, "is, on its face, constitutionally adequate," but then later discussed the case in terms of a "reasonable doubt" standard, only to conclude that there was "sufficient doubt of his competence to stand trial so as to require further inquiry on the question." Lower courts typically use the bona fide doubt terminology, e.g., United States ex rel. Mireles v. Greer, 736 F.2d 1160 (7th Cir. 1984); Reese v. Wainwright, 600 F.2d 1085 (5th Cir.1979), but some use other formulations, such as "a substantial question of possible doubt," Rhay v. White, 385 F.2d 883

tion that defendant is insane will not suffice.[35] If a reasonable doubt does exist, then the judge must take the appropriate steps for determination of the issue.[36] In most jurisdictions there exists statutory authority for the judge to have the defendant committed while he is examined by court-appointed experts or the staff of a public hospital. At common law, the judge had discretion to determine the method to be used to try the issue; he could either decide the question himself or impanel a jury.[37] Today, the great majority of jurisdictions require that this issue be decided by the judge, though in a few states the matter may or must be determined by a jury.[38] Although the burden of proof is sometimes upon the defendant to show his incompetency,[39] this is probably not the case in practice,[40] particularly when the issue has not been raised by the defendant.[41] The preponderance-of-the-evidence standard is usually utilized,[42] but some states require clear and convincing evidence.

If the defendant is found incompetent, the criminal proceedings are suspended and he is invariably committed to a mental institution until he recovers.[43] Most states place the responsibility for determining whether a defendant has recovered with the court, although a few jurisdictions at least sometimes have the decision made by a jury or by medical personnel.

(9th Cir.1967); Commonwealth v. Hill, 375 Mass. 50, 375 N.E.2d 1168 (1978).

35. Howell v. Todhunter, 181 Ark. 250, 25 S.W.2d 21 (1930); People v. Croce, 208 Cal. 123, 280 P. 526 (1929).

36. State v. Detar, 125 Kan. 218, 263 P. 1071 (1928); State v. Folk, 56 N.M. 583, 247 P.2d 165 (1952). It is unnecessary to hold a hearing on the matter if the judge can otherwise satisfy himself that the defendant is competent. Enriquez v. Procunier, 752 F.2d 111 (5th Cir.1984).

37. Weihofen, supra note 12, at 446.

38. See, e.g., Lindsey v. State, 252 Ga. 493, 314 S.E.2d 881 (1984), appeal after remand 254 Ga. 444, 330 S.E.2d 563 (1985). There is no constitutional right to have the issue determined by a jury. White Hawk v. Solem, 693 F.2d 825 (8th Cir.1982).

39. See Spencer v. Zant, 715 F.2d 1562 (11th Cir.1983) (applying Georgia law); White v. Estelle, 669 F.2d 973 (5th Cir.1982) (applying Texas law); State v. Aumann, 265 N.W.2d 316 (Iowa 1978) (placing burden on defendant does not violate due process); State v. Lopez, 91 N.M. 779, 581 P.2d 872 (1978).

WESTLAW REFERENCES

di incompetency

digest,synopis(competen*** incompeten*** /4 trial /p insan*** mental** /p "due process")

(b) Commitment for Incompetency: The Risk of Unfairness. Although the traditional procedures described above are intended to protect the defendant's due process right not to be tried while incompetent, they do not always operate to the benefit of the individual committed. For one thing, the commitment is based upon a charge of a crime which he may not have in fact committed or for which he could not be convicted if he was afforded the opportunity to prove his innocence or to establish some defect in the prosecution's case. Secondly, he is being held for the purpose of getting him into a state of mind whereby he can be prosecuted, but the commitment might continue for years without a serious attempt at treatment or even when it is reasonably certain that his condition is untreatable. Moreover, in most jurisdictions the practice has been to institutionalize because of incompetence to stand trial without regard to whether there is really any need for custody, that is, without reference to the legal criteria for civil committability (generally, whether the person is dangerous to society or is in need of treatment and unable to care for himself[44]). Finally, the critical decisions of

40. "The weight of authority suggests that the prosecution bears the burden of proof of competency once the issue has been raised by the parties or by the judge on his own motion." Commonwealth v. Crowley, 393 Mass. 393, 471 N.E.2d 353 (1984).

41. Some statutes expressly state that the burden is on the movant.

42. See Brown v. Warden, 682 F.2d 348 (2d Cir.1982), holding "that a finding that a defendant is mentally competent to stand trial satisfies due process when the court finds that the prosecution has carried the burden of proving the defendant's competency by a preponderance of the evidence."

43. In one survey it was determined that hospitalization is mandatory in at least 42 jurisdictions, but discretionary in the rest, with some requiring hospitalization if the accused is found to be "dangerous" or a "menace." S. Brakel & R. Rock, supra note 2, at 415.

44. S. Brakel & R. Rock, supra note 2, at 36–37.

incompetency and, perhaps more important, recovery or nonrecovery have often been made without sufficient procedural safeguards to ensure their accuracy.[45] For all of these reasons, it has been said that the process "poses a very real risk of abuse and of being bent to punitive purposes."[46]

The Supreme Court addressed many of these problems in the most important decision of *Jackson v. Indiana.*[47] The case involved a mentally defective deaf mute with a mental level of a pre-school child who, after being charged with two robberies, was found incompetent to stand trial because he lacked "comprehension sufficient to understand the proceedings and make his defense." On that basis alone he was committed to a state mental hospital, and it appeared the commitment would be for life, as there was little likelihood that his condition would ever improve. Jackson challenged his commitment on both equal protection and due process grounds, and the Court held in his favor on both theories.

On the equal protection question, the Court first noted it had previously held in *Baxstrom v. Herold*[48] that a person civilly committed upon completion of his prison sentence was denied equal protection when not afforded the same procedural guarantees as others subjected to the civil commitment process. This meant the equal protection claim was, if anything, just as strong here. "If criminal conviction and imposition of sentence are insufficient to justify less procedural and substantive protection against indefinite commitment than that generally available to others, the mere filing of criminal charges surely cannot suffice." The state countered

that commitment of a defendant incompetent to stand trial is only temporary, pending his recovery, and thus need not be subject to the same limitations as indeterminate civil commitments. But the Court rejected this contention,[49] noting that the statutory scheme did not make the likelihood of improvement a relevant factor and also that the record did not suggest any possibility that Jackson would recover.

The Court in *Jackson* thus applied to this context the teaching of *Baxstrom* that "the State cannot withhold from a few the procedural protections or the substantive requirements for commitment that are available to all others." This means, for one thing, that the *procedures* for commitment of a defendant not competent to be tried must (at least if the commitment is other than "temporary") be "substantially similar" to those made available to those persons subjected to the civil commitment process.[50] (This was not a problem in *Jackson,* the Court concluded, as the procedures in the two contexts—notice, examination by two doctors, judicial hearing, representation by counsel, right to introduce evidence and to cross-examine, decision by court alone, and appellate review were essentially the same.) For another, this means that the *standards* for commitment and release must likewise be substantially the same as for other persons. Jackson had thus been denied equal protection, as he was subject "to a more lenient commitment standard and to a more stringent standard of release than those generally applicable to all others not charged with offenses."

Similar considerations underlie the *Jackson* Court's second holding that "indefinite com-

45. For example, when the question of defendant's recovery is left to the superintendent of the hospital where he is held, as is usually the case, id. at 362, "the ordinary institutional goal of restoring mental health is apt to be confused with recovery of legal competency." Note, 81 Harv.L.Rev. 454, 471 (1967).

46. A. Goldstein, supra note 1, at 185.

47. 406 U.S. 715, 92 S.Ct. 1845, 32 L.Ed.2d 435 (1972).

48. 383 U.S. 107, 86 S.Ct. 760, 15 L.Ed.2d 620 (1966).

49. Stating: "Were the State's factual premises that Jackson's commitment is only temporary a valid one, this might well be a different case."

50. Illustrative of that type of equal protection violation is the earlier case of Commonwealth v. Druken, 356 Mass. 503, 254 N.E.2d 779 (1969), where the statutory scheme for commitment on grounds of incompetency to stand trial differed in several material respects from the statutory provisions on civil commitment. For example, under the latter but not the former, the individual was to be certified as mentally ill by two doctors, neither of whom was to hold an office in the institution where the person was committed, and the individual's mental status was to be reviewed within 60 days and periodically thereafter.

mitment of a criminal defendant solely on account of his incompetency to stand trial does not square with the Fourteenth Amendment's guarantee of due process." Because "Jackson's commitment rests on proceedings that did not purport to bring into play * * * *any* of the articulated bases for exercise of Indiana's power of indefinite commitment," [51] it violated the due process requirement "that the nature and duration of commitment bear some reasonable relation to the purpose for which the individual is committed." Specifically, the Court held

> that a person charged by a State with a criminal offense who is committed solely on account of his incapacity to proceed to trial cannot be held more than the reasonable period of time necessary to determine whether there is a substantial probability that he will attain that capacity in the foreseeable future. If it is determined that this is not the case, then the State must either institute the customary civil commitment proceeding that would be required to commit indefinitely any other citizen, or release the defendant. Furthermore, even if it is determined that the defendant probably soon will be able to stand trial, his continued commitment must be justified by progress toward that goal.

The Supreme Court declined "to prescribe arbitrary time limits," but merely noted that Jackson's three and one-half years of confinement "establishes the lack of a substantial probability that he will ever be able to participate fully in a trial." It thus remains unclear exactly to what extent automatic commitment for incompetency to stand trial may still be utilized. Some states permit such commitment for up to a year [52] or 18 months,[53] while some authorize commitment for as long as three years.[54] At least one court has held that the "reasonable period" language in *Jackson* does not permit confinement for competency determination alone for a time ex-

ceeding the maximum possible sentence for the offense charged.[55]

Yet another noteworthy aspect of the *Jackson* case is the Court's pronouncement that its prior decisions on the due process requirement of a competency inquiry do not "preclude the States from allowing at a minimum, an incompetent defendant to raise certain defenses such as insufficiency of the indictment, or make certain pretrial motions, through counsel." It had theretofore been generally assumed that if the defendant is found incompetent to stand trial, then no aspect of the criminal proceedings may be pursued until he has regained his competency. The harshness of this view is clearly reflected by the decision in *United States v. Barnes.*[56] Four defendants were indicted for a murder allegedly committed over ten years earlier, and three of them successfully moved to dismiss the indictment on the ground that they had been denied a speedy trial. The fourth defendant's motion, based upon exactly the same ground, was denied because he was found to be "presently insane and so mentally incompetent as to be unable to understand the proceedings against him." The court acknowledged that there would be no need for the defendant to assist his counsel in making the speedy trial defense, but concluded that this made no difference because the test of incompetency was stated in the alternative.[57] The curious result: because this defendant was unable to understand the proceedings at which the charge against him would be dismissed, he should be committed until such time as he would be able to participate in a trial which would not occur.

Preferable to *Barnes* is the Model Penal Code approach, which would allow the unfit defendant to pursue "any legal objection to

---

51. Earlier stated by the Court to "include dangerousness to self, dangerousness to others, and the need for care or treatment or training."

52. E.g., West's Fla.Stat.Ann.R.Crim.P., Rule 3.212.

53. State ex rel. Haskins v. County Court, 62 Wis.2d 250, 214 N.W.2d 575 (1974).

54. E.g., West's Ann.Cal.Penal Code § 1370, upheld in Estate of Hofferber, 28 Cal.3d 161, 167 Cal.Rptr. 854, 616 P.2d 836 (1980).

55. United States v. DeBellis, 649 F.2d 1 (1st Cir.1981), noting that "every court to have considered this specific question in dictum has reached the same conclusion."

56. 175 F.Supp. 60 (S.D.Cal.1959).

57. The court noted that the applicable statute, 18 U.S.C.A. § 4244, refers to one who is "presently insane or otherwise so mentally incompetent as to be unable to understand the proceedings against him, *or* properly to assist in his own defense." (Emphasis added.)

the prosecution which is susceptible of fair determination prior to trial and without the personal participation of the defendant." [58] Under this view, counsel for an incompetent defendant would often be permitted to present those motions ordinarily determined at the pretrial stage, such as to quash the indictment or to suppress critical evidence.[59]

It might even be desirable to go beyond this and sometimes permit the incompetent defendant to present defenses which ordinarily are only raised at trial. For example, if the examination of the accused to determine incompetency also discloses that he has a valid insanity defense, there is much to be said for permitting the court to enter a judgment of acquittal on that ground.[60] This avoids the possibility of having to try that issue long after the event,[61] and has the added advantage that a defendant committed following such acquittal is much more likely to respond to treatment than a defendant whose status is uncertain because of an outstanding criminal charge.[62] Similarly, it makes sense to hear such defenses as alibi at this early stage,[63] for the witnesses might well be unavailable at a trial held following a substantial period of commitment for incompetency.[64]

One commentator has made yet another proposal, one which would afford the defendant a no-lose full trial in these circumstances. If the defendant were found not guilty, that would be the end of the matter; if

he were found guilty, the verdict would be set aside and he would be committed "until he is sufficiently recovered to be retried or until other appropriate disposition can be made of the case." [65] A few jurisdictions allow procedures along these lines. An even more extreme proposal contemplates

> abandonment of the traditional rule against trying incompetent defendants. Incompetency should instead be grounds for obtaining a trial continuance during which the state must provide resources to assist the defendant toward greater trial competence. If trial competence is not achieved within six months, the state should be required to dismiss the charges or proceed to a trial governed, where necessary, by procedures designed to compensate for the incompetent defendant's trial disabilities.[66]

Finally, note must be taken of the recognition in *Jackson* that the petitioner had a "substantial" claim that the charges against him should be dismissed. The Court did not reach this claim, but did take note of the bases upon which it could be grounded: "the Sixth-Fourteenth Amendment right to a speedy trial, or the denial of due process inherent in holding pending criminal charges indefinitely over the head of one who will never have a chance to prove his innocence." [67] Of course, it is also possible that dismissal of charges following a substantial period of incompetency will be permissible under state law even if not constitutionally

---

58. Model Penal Code § 4.06(3).

59. See Foote, A Comment on Pre-Trial Commitment of Criminal Defendants, 108 U.Pa.L.Rev. 832, 841 (1960).

60. Model Penal Code § 4.07(1) so provides.

61. After the passage of some time, it may be very difficult to obtain and present evidence concerning defendant's mental condition at the time of the crime. See Williams v. United States, 250 F.2d 19 (D.C.Cir.1957).

62. Comment, 59 Mich.L.Rev. 1078, 1093 (1961).

63. Foote, supra note 59, at 841.

64. Model Penal Code § 4.07, alternate subsections (3) and (4), so provide.

Compare the proposal in Foote, supra note 59, at 845–46, which would actually permit a full trial in these circumstances. If the defendant were found not guilty, that would be the end of the matter; if he were found guilty, the verdict would be set aside and he would be committed "until he is sufficiently recovered to be retried

or until other appropriate disposition can be made of the case."

65. Foote, supra note 59, at 845–46.

66. Burt & Morris, A Proposal for the Abolition of the Incompetency Plea, 40 U.Chi.L.Rev. 66, 67 (1972). As for the compensating procedures, they suggest extra pretrial discovery "that would materially assist the defendant in overcoming the disabilities under which he labors," a higher burden of proof on the prosecution upon defendant's motion for a directed verdict, and an instruction to the jury to "take into account, in the defendant's favor, the disabilities under which he went to trial." Id. at 94–95. See also the ABA Comm'n on the Mentally Disabled Report, Incompetence to Stand Trial on Criminal Charges, 2 Mental Disability L.Rep. 617, 620–34 (1978).

67. Citing United States ex rel. Wolfersdorf v. Johnston, 317 F.Supp. 66 (S.D.N.Y.1970); United States v. Jackson, 306 F.Supp. 4 (N.D.Cal.1969); People ex rel. Myers v. Briggs, 46 Ill.2d 281, 263 N.E.2d 109 (1970).

compelled.[68] In such circumstances, there remains the troublesome question of whether the charges should be dismissed with or without prejudice (that is, with or without a bar to subsequent reinstatement).[69] But because of the concern "that the dismissal of serious criminal charges against an incompetent defendant who may regain competency to stand trial in two or three years would constitute a grave public disservice," there is a disinclination to dismiss with prejudice unless it presently appears likely a fair trial would not later be possible.[70]

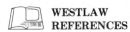

WESTLAW REFERENCES

jackson +4 indiana /12 92 +4 1845 /p
competen*** incompeten***

(c) Incompetency at Time Set for Execution. It is the rule in all jurisdictions that a sentence of execution cannot be carried out if the prisoner is insane at the time set for execution.[71] The common law was quite vague on the meaning of insane in this context, but it is usually taken to mean that the defendant cannot be executed if he is unaware of the fact that he has been convicted and that he is to be executed.[72] Stated another way, he must be so unsound mentally "as to be incapable of understanding the nature and purpose of the punishment about to be executed upon him."[73] Whether this is a correct or complete statement of the rule remains somewhat unclear because of continuing uncertainty about the reasons underlying it.[74]

One traditional explanation for the rule is that if the defendant were sane he might be in a position to urge some reason why the sentence should not be carried out.[75] The logic of this has been questioned on the ground that it is unlikely a defendant who by hypothesis was sane during trial and at the time of sentencing would thereafter think of a reason not previously considered. Even less convincing is the explanation that the prisoner's insanity is itself sufficient punishment,[76] for when he regains his sanity he is subject to execution.[77] Yet another reason is that it is a rule of humanity—a refusal to take the life of an unfortunate prisoner[78]—but this has been characterized as "inverted humanitarianism."[79] Then there is the theological rationale that a person should not be put to death while insane because he is unable to make his

---

68. State v. Gaffey, 92 N.J. 374, 456 A.2d 511 (1983).

69. See the various views expressed in State ex rel. Haskins v. County Court, 62 Wis.2d 250, 214 N.W.2d 575 (1974).

70. State v. Gaffey, 92 N.J. 374, 456 A.2d 511 (1983).

71. See, e.g., Howell v. Kincannon, 181 Ark. 58, 24 S.W.2d 953 (1930); Goode v. Wainwright, 448 So.2d 999 (Fla.1984); State v. Allen, 204 La. 513, 15 So.2d 870 (1943); State v. Vann, 84 N.C. 722 (1881); Commonwealth v. Moon, 383 Pa. 18, 117 A.2d 96 (1955); Grossi v. Long, 136 Wash. 133, 238 P. 983 (1925). Most states authorizing the death penalty have statutes specifically so providing. Note, 88 Yale L.J. 533 n. 3 (1979). For a thorough discussion of this rule and its rationale, see Hazard & Louisell, Death, the State, and the Insane; Stay of Execution, 9 U.C.L.A.L.Rev. 361 (1962).

The rule applies only to capital cases, Kelley v. State, 157 Ark. 48, 247 S.W. 381 (1923); Davidson v. Commonwealth, 174 Ky. 789, 192 S.W. 846 (1917); so that a person convicted and sentenced to prison may not raise the question of present insanity as a bar to carrying out the sentence, Kelley v. State, supra. There generally exist statutory provisions for transferring the insane prisoner to a hospital for the criminally insane. H. Weihofen, supra note 12, at 465.

72. Commonwealth v. Moon, 383 Pa. 18, 117 A.2d 96 (1955).

73. H. Weihofen, supra note 12, at 464.

74. In Comment, 23 So.Cal.L.Rev. 246, 256 (1950), it is argued: "If * * * punishment is an act of vengeance, then the prisoner's ability to appreciate his impending fate would seem to be the standard. * * * If the policy [behind the rule] is based on the right of the defendant to make his peace with God, then a realization of his original guilt should be added to the test. If the reason is that he should have an opportunity to suggest items in extenuation or make arguments for executive clemency, then the standard should probably involve intelligence factors as well as moral awareness."

75. 4 W. Blackstone, Commentaries 395*–96* (13th ed. 1800); 1 M. Hale, Pleas of the Crown 34–35 (1736).

76. M. Guttmacher & H. Weihofen, Psychiatry and the Law 434 (1952); Hazard & Louisell, supra note 71, at 383–84.

77. Ex parte Phyle, 30 Cal.2d 838, 186 P.2d 134 (1947).

78. E. Coke, Third Institute 6 (1797).

79. "Is it not an inverted humanitarianism that deplores as barbarous the capital punishment of those who have become insane after trial and conviction, but accepts the capital punishment for sane men, a curious reasoning that would free a man from capital punishment only if he is not in full possession of his senses?" Phyle v. Duffy, 34 Cal.2d 144, 208 P.2d 668 (1949) (Traynor, J., concurring).

peace with God while in that condition,[80] which is at best difficult to assess in our theologically pluralistic society.[81]

Perhaps the most acceptable explanation is "simply that it is unnecessary to put the insane prisoner to death."[82] For one thing, the insane prisoner may be spared the death penalty without weakening the deterrent effect of that penalty. Taking the life of an insane person does not serve as an example to others, for a potential offender would not consider the possibility of escaping the death penalty by becoming insane following conviction. Likewise, the retributive function of punishment is not served by execution of the insane prisoner. Viewing retribution in the sense of exacting a punishment equivalent to the harm done, it may be said that killing an insane person does not have the same moral quality as killing a sane one. Or, if retribution is taken to mean that punishment serves to give law-abiding citizens a form of release, then the answer is that this will occur only if the public is able to identify with the prisoner, which they cannot do if he is insane.[83]

There was no established procedure at common law for trying a claim that the defendant was insane and thus not subject to execution. If facts were brought to the attention of the court which sentenced the defendant raising a

reasonable doubt in the mind of the judge, then he could "take such action as, in his discretion, he deemed best"[84]; he could try the issue himself or empanel a jury to do so. Most jurisdictions have now enacted statutes on the subject. Many of these statutes permit only the warden to initiate proceedings to determine insanity for the purpose of staying execution,[85] and this has been held not to violate due process.[86] Some statutes follow the common law procedure of petition to the court, and some others allow the claim to be made to the governor.[87] Several statutes require trial of the issue after a plausible claim of insanity is raised, but others merely require examination of the prisoner by a psychiatrist, delegating the ultimate decision to the governor, warden or state hospital director.[88] Some of the statutes expressly provide for jury trial of the issue,[89] although there is no constitutional right to jury trial.[90] Notwithstanding earlier Supreme Court decisions to the contrary,[91] it would seem that a hearing on a claim of insanity is now constitutionally required.[92]

In some states, the question of recovery is judicially determined.[93] Elsewhere, the practice is merely for the superintendent of the hospital where the prisoner is held to certify that he has recovered, after which the gover-

80. Hawles, Remarks on The Trial of Mr. Charles Bateman, 11 State Trials 474, 477 (Howell ed. 1816).

81. Hazard & Louisell, supra note 71, at 388.

82. Id. at 389.

83. For the suggestion that the rule is constitutionally required under the Eighth Amendment cruel and unusual punishment prohibition, see Radin, The Jurisprudence of Death: Evolving Standards for the Cruel and Unusual Punishments Clause, 126 U.Pa.L.Rev. 989, 1027–30 (1978); Notes, 32 Stan.L.Rev. 765 (1980); 88 Yale L.J. 533, 536 (1979). The issue is discussed but not resolved in Gray v. Lucas, 710 F.2d 1048 (5th Cir.1983).

84. Nobles v. Georgia, 168 U.S. 398, 18 S.Ct. 87, 42 L.Ed. 515 (1897).

85. Note, 88 Yale L.J. 533, 538 (1979).

86. Caritativo v. California, 357 U.S. 549, 78 S.Ct. 1263, 2 L.Ed.2d 1531 (1958).

87. Note, 88 Yale L.J. 533, 538 (1979). It has been held constitutional to vest in the governor the power to decide this matter without a hearing. Solesbee v. Balkcom, 339 U.S. 9, 70 S.Ct. 457, 94 L.Ed. 694 (1950); Goode v. Wainwright, 448 So.2d 999 (Fla.1984).

88. Note, 88 Yale L.J. 533, 539 (1979).

89. Id. at 540.

90. Nobles v. Georgia, supra note 84; Solesbee v. Balkcom, 339 U.S. 9, 70 S.Ct. 457, 94 L.Ed. 604 (1950).

91. See cases in notes 86 and 90 supra.

92. As observed in Note, 88 Yale L.J. 533, 553 (1979): "In light of the constitutional principles articulated in recent due process and death penalty cases, it is apparent that Nobles, Solesbee, and Caritativo are no longer controlling. At the very least, the due process clause requires that a condemned prisoner be provided notice of when and how his insanity claim will be reviewed and a hearing in order to review that claim prior to execution. Moreover, a proper balancing of interests requires that, at a minimum, the procedural scheme provide for proper diagnosis of the prisoner's mental condition, an adequate opportunity for review, and efficient but fair control of repeated or feigned insanity claims."

But see Goode v. Wainwright, 448 So.2d 999 (Fla.1984) (decision of issue by governor, upon receipt of report of commission of three psychiatrists, as contemplated by statute, is constitutional notwithstanding lack of hearing at which defendant could challenge commission's conclusions).

93. H. Weihofen, supra note 12, at 469.

nor sets a new date for execution.[94] It is very likely, however, that the prisoner has a constitutional right to a hearing on the question of his recovery.[95]

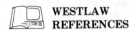
WESTLAW
REFERENCES

insan*** mental** /s death /3 penalty

§ 4.5 Procedures for Presenting the Insanity Defense

It is the defendant who usually raises the insanity defense, although it is not uncommon for the defendant deliberately not to do so for the reason that the consequences of conviction are preferred over commitment following a verdict of not guilty by reason of insanity. There is some questionable authority that in such an instance the court or prosecutor may force the insanity issue into the case. In some states the defendant must give advance warning by plea or notice of his intention to rely upon the insanity defense.

It is to the advantage of both the prosecution and defense to have the defendant examined by a psychiatrist whose orientation and examination procedures are such as will probably support their side of the case. In most states the prosecutor can obtain a court-ordered examination which is usually conducted by a psychiatrist in the employ of the state. The indigent defendant is constitutionally entitled to the services of a psychiatrist.

There is a general presumption of sanity, and thus the initial burden (called the burden of going forward) is on the defendant to introduce evidence creating a reasonable doubt of his sanity. As to the burden of convincing the jury (called the burden of persuasion), some states require the defendant to prove insanity by a preponderance of the evidence, while others require the prosecution to prove sanity beyond a reasonable doubt. At the close of all the evidence, the jury is instructed

on the insanity test and is given several verdict alternatives: guilty; not guilty; not guilty by reason of insanity; and (in a minority of jurisdictions only) guilty but mentally ill.

(a) Raising the Insanity Defense: Who and Why. Unlike other defenses which, if successful, will result in acquittal and outright release,[1] the insanity defense may not appear to be an appealing alternative to the defendant. Except for the defendant who is charged with a crime punishable by death, the disadvantages of a finding of not guilty by reason of insanity may seem just as great or even greater than those which would flow from a verdict of guilty. In the former instance the defendant is not formally condemned and may gain some satisfaction from the fact that he was not responsible for what he did and that he is now being sent to an institution which is supposed to provide treatment for his illness. "But he must weigh those advantages against the fact that his detention is for an entirely indeterminate period; that he may be kept in a hospital as long as or longer than he would have remained in prison; and that being regarded as mentally ill may bring him as much stigma, economic deprivation, family dislocation, and often as little treatment or physical comfort as being a criminal."[2]

This being the case, it is apparent that the decision of defense counsel in deciding whether or not to raise the insanity defense is likely to be influenced substantially by his assessment of the consequences of a finding of criminality as opposed to a finding of insanity. The stigma will probably appear to be just as great in one instance as the other, so that counsel will focus his attention on the matter of length of incarceration.[3] If conviction would be followed by a very long sentence, then commitment for an indefinite term may seem preferable. But, except in such a situa-

---

94. Id. at 468–69.

95. The Court found it unnecessary to pass on the issue in Phyle v. Duffy, 334 U.S. 431, 68 S.Ct. 1131, 92 L.Ed. 1494 (1948), although both the majority and concurring opinions indicated that the prisoner would have a constitutional right to a hearing on his claim.

§ 4.5

1. For a comparison of the insanity defense with other defenses, see § 4.1.

2. A. Goldstein, The Insanity Defense 20 (1967).

3. Id. at 167.

tion, the imposition of a fixed sentence within legislatively-set limits and the possibility of probation or parole is certain to seem a better course than the risk of a commitment which could last the rest of the defendant's life. Counsel is also likely to lean in the direction of a criminal disposition because he is more familiar with that process; he may be able to predict with reasonable accuracy how much time the defendant would actually have to serve if convicted of the instant crime under the known circumstances, but he may know little or nothing about whether his client's impairment could readily be corrected by treatment or whether effective treatment is available.[4] It is common, therefore, for defense counsel *not* to put the insanity question into issue notwithstanding the availability of some evidence indicating that the defense would be successful.[5]

The facts suggesting that the defendant may have a valid insanity defense may nonetheless come to the attention of the prosecutor or the court. Indeed, if the prosecutor is uncertain whether the defense will be raised at trial he will seek out such facts in order to determine whether he should be prepared to prove the defendant's sanity. He may obtain information about the circumstances surrounding the crime or of defendant's psychiatric history by police investigation, his own investigation, the subpoena of witnesses before the grand jury, or commitment of the defendant for a determination of his competence to stand trial.[6] At trial, testimony of a witness may bring to the attention of the

prosecutor and judge the possibility of an insanity defense which the defendant has already decided to forego.

In these circumstances, may the prosecutor or court interject the insanity defense into the case over the wishes of defendant and defense counsel?[7] Some decisions indicate that the answer is yes,[8] although their current status is in doubt as a result of *Lynch v. Overholser*.[9] The defendant, with a history of passing bad checks, understandably preferred to plead guilty to a bad check charge and receive a sentence which could not exceed one year, but the court refused the plea because the defendant appeared to have an insanity defense. At trial, the prosecution introduced evidence of the defendant's insanity, resulting in a verdict of not guilty by reason of insanity and, as provided for under District of Columbia law, the defendant's mandatory commitment.[10] The court of appeals approved on the ground that "society has a stake in seeing to it that a defendant who needs hospital care does not go to prison,"[11] but the Supreme Court reversed. Noting that the result was automatic commitment on the basis of merely a reasonable doubt of defendant's sanity, a doubt not raised by the defendant himself, the Court interpreted the commitment statute as not reaching such a situation.[12]

It must be emphasized that the Court in *Lynch* did not pass directly upon the question of whether the defendant is entitled to keep the insanity defense out of the case entirely. But several recent decisions have held that the defendant is so entitled,[13] and thus it

---

4. Id. at 168. See Halleck, The Insanity Defense in the District of Columbia—A Legal Lorelei, 49 Geo.L.J. 294 (1960); Krash, The Durham Rule and Judicial Administration of the Insanity Defense in the District of Columbia, 70 Yale L.J. 905 (1961).

5. Indeed, often he will recommend to the defendant that he pursue a process of plea negotiations so as to further minimize the adverse consequences of the criminal-disposition alternative. See the authorities cited in § 4.4, note 5, for the differing views on the propriety of such a course.

6. See § 4.4(a).

7. See Singer, The Imposition of the Insanity Defense on an Unwilling Defendant, 41 Ohio St.L.J. 637 (1980); Notes, 65 Minn.L.Rev. 927 (1981); 53 Tex.L.Rev. 1065 (1975).

8. E.g., Tatum v. United States, 190 F.2d 612 (D.C.Cir. 1951); followed in United States v. Wright, 627 F.2d 1300 (D.C.Cir.1980).

9. 369 U.S. 705, 82 S.Ct. 1063, 8 L.Ed.2d 211 (1962).

10. On mandatory versus discretionary commitment see § 4.6(a).

11. Overholser v. Lynch, 288 F.2d 388 (D.C.Cir.1961).

12. In later holding automatic commitment constitutional, the Court emphasized that "automatic commitment * * * follows only if the *acquittee himself* advances insanity as a defense." Jones v. United States, 463 U.S. 354, 103 S.Ct. 3043, 77 L.Ed.2d 694 (1983).

13. See, e.g., People v. Gauze, 15 Cal.3d 709, 125 Cal. Rptr. 773, 542 P.2d 1365 (1975); Labor v. Gibson, 195 Colo. 416, 578 P.2d 1059 (1978); Frendak v. United States, 408

appears that *Lynch* has emerged "as authority for the proposition that neither prosecutor nor judge can assert the insanity defense when a competent defendant, who is adequately represented, has chosen not to do so." [14] This proposition draws support from other, more recent Supreme Court decisions recognizing the importance of allowing the defendant to make strategic decisions on his own behalf.[15]

Whether such a proposition is a sensible one is a matter on which opinions differ. On the one hand, it is argued that this defense should be subject to abandonment for tactical reasons [16] in the same way as alibi or entrapment.[17] On the other, it is contended that judge and prosecutor must be allowed to raise the defense as part of their general obligation to see that justice is done—in this instance, to see that those not responsible do not go to jail and that they are not returned to society uncured.[18] The latter argument may lose some of its force if the fairness and effectiveness of the procedures for commitment, treatment, and release are in doubt.[19]

A.2d 364 (D.C.App.1979); State v. Jones, 99 Wn.2d 735, 664 P.2d 1216 (1983).

This means that whether to interpose the defense is a decision to be made by the defendant rather than his counsel, People v. Gauze, supra; that defendant can withdraw an insanity plea earlier entered, Corder v. State, 467 N.E.2d 409 (Ind.1984); and that an insanity defense instruction should not be given over defendant's objection even when the defendant introduces psychiatric testimony for the limited purpose of showing he did not have the requisite mental state, State v. Vosler, 216 Neb. 461, 345 N.W.2d 806 (1984).

14. A. Goldstein, supra note 2, at 188.

15. Faretta v. California, 422 U.S. 806, 95 S.Ct. 2525, 45 L.Ed.2d 562 (1975) (defendant has constitutional right to proceed pro se; Court stresses a particular defendant may not want an attorney, who by "law and tradition" has "the power to make binding decisions of trial strategy in many areas"); North Carolina v. Alford, 400 U.S. 25, 91 S.Ct. 160, 27 L.Ed.2d 162 (1970) (relying on *Lynch*, Court holds a defendant claiming to be innocent may be allowed to plead guilty, where "he insisted on his plea because in his view he had absolutely nothing to gain by a trial and much to gain by pleading").

16. "Defendants may not wish to disparage or deny the validity of their motives for committing a crime by pleading insanity. They may prefer a limited prison term to the indefinite commitment likely to follow an insanity acquittal, or they may object to the quality of treatment in a mental hospital. They may want to avoid the stigma that typically accompanies an adjudication of insanity—a

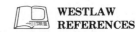

WESTLAW
REFERENCES

lynch /12 82 +4 1063 /p insan*** mental**

(b) Raising the Insanity Defense: When and How. The earliest point in the criminal process at which the insanity defense might be raised in a formal way [20] is at the preliminary hearing. At that hearing, the magistrate is to determine whether there is probable cause to believe that the defendant committed a crime, and thus it might be thought that defense counsel could challenge the existence of probable cause by attempting to show that the defendant was insane at the time of the crime. Having the issue resolved in the defendant's favor at this early stage might be supported on the notion that "persons who are blameless should not have to suffer the sanctions of the criminal process for a moment longer than necessary." [21] But in practice, the defense is seldom raised at this stage of the process. The preliminary hearing is very frequently waived,[22] and even

stigma that often surpasses that accompanying a criminal conviction. They may attempt to pressure the jury into acquitting them by not offering the jury the 'compromise' verdict of insanity, or they may prefer to use the evidence of their lack of mental responsibility not to plead insanity, but only to achieve a conviction of a lesser offense than that with which they are charged. Finally, they may be opposed to psychiatric treatment." Note, 65 Minn.L.Rev. 927, 945–46 (1981).

17. A. Goldstein, supra note 2, at 188. Model Penal Code § 4.03, Comment at 229 (1985): "Despite the view that in some cases it might be desirable to give the trial judge the power to raise the defense of irresponsibility when the defendant refuses to permit his counsel to do so, such a provision was finally omitted as being too great an interference with the conduct of the defense."

18. Note 7, Vill.L.Rev. 689, 691 (1962). As stated in United States v. Wright, 627 F.2d 1300 (D.C.Cir.1980), society has an "obligation, through the insanity defense, to withhold punishment of someone not blameworthy."

19. See § 4.6.

20. It may be raised informally by defense counsel in discussions with the prosecutor concerning whether the defendant should be charged with a crime or instead placed on "administrative probation" for purposes of private treatment. See § 4.1.

21. A. Goldstein, supra note 2, at 181.

22. F. Miller, Prosecution: The Decision to Charge a Suspect with a Crime ch. 6 (1969).

when it is not defense counsel [23] usually prefer not to expose the nature and dimensions of their defense at this early stage.[24] Considerable uncertainty currently exists as to the place of the insanity defense at the preliminary hearing,[25] as well as to the larger question of the extent to which the defendant may raise any affirmative defenses at this time.[26] Several persuasive arguments have been presented in opposition to permitting the defense to be litigated at the preliminary hearing: (1) The magistrate is unlikely to be qualified to try such an issue. (2) He ordinarily would have no authority to institute commitment procedures against a defendant who negated probable cause with an insanity defense. (3) The trial of defenses, and particularly a defense as complicated as the insanity defense, would require more refined and lengthy procedures, which in turn would frustrate the objectives of the hearing and add to trial delay.[27]

Close to a quarter of the states have enacted statutes providing that if the grand jury fails to return an indictment on the ground of insanity, then that fact is to be certified to the court and the court may (in some states, must) initiate commitment proceedings.[28] But these statutes are of little practical significance, for in almost all jurisdictions the de-

fendant is not entitled to appear before the grand jury or to present evidence to that body.[29] Because the prosecutor exercises considerable control over the business of the grand jury and its decision-making, a case is not likely to be terminated at this point on the ground of defendant's insanity unless the prosecutor desires such a disposition.[30] Moreover, an insanity determination by the grand jury which serves as the basis for a subsequent commitment is vulnerable to attack on constitutional grounds.[31]

Thus, arraignment (the time at which the defendant is called upon to enter his plea) is the earliest point at which the defendant is likely to be able to interpose the defense of insanity. In most jurisdictions, however, he is under no obligation to do so at that time; under the prevailing rule the defendant may respond to the charge against him simply with a plea of not guilty, and he need not disclose in advance the nature of the defense upon which he is going to rely. This means that the prosecutor must resort to the various means described earlier in order to determine the likelihood of the insanity defense being raised at trial and to obtain psychiatric data about the defendant for use in rebutting that defense.

23. There is a constitutional right to defense counsel at the preliminary hearing, Coleman v. Alabama, 399 U.S. 1, 90 S.Ct. 1999, 26 L.Ed.2d 387 (1970).

24. This is particularly so in view of the fact that in most jurisdictions the defendant's success at the preliminary hearing does not bar his subsequent indictment by the grand jury. 2 W. LaFave & J. Israel, Criminal Procedure § 14.3(b) (1984).

25. A. Goldstein, supra note 2, at 180.

26. "The type of evidence which may defeat a showing of probable cause has not been thoroughly explored. In the District of Columbia, alibi witnesses are considered relevant. * * * It is questionable, however, whether testimony that establishes an affirmative defense can preclude a finding of probable cause. * * * Unlike an alibi, which negates commission of the act, an affirmative defense admits commission but relies on a legally created right not to be held responsible. The legal issue of guilt is to be determined at trial and should therefore be beyond the consideration of the hearing examiner." Note, 56 Geo.L.J. 193, 193 n. 15 (1967).

27. A. Goldstein, supra note 2, at 181–82.

28. Id. at 182–84; H. Weihofen, Mental Disorder as a Criminal Defense 354–55 (1954). Most of these statutes

are unclear as to whether they refer to insanity at the time of the act or present insanity, although they seem to cover both situations. Id. at 354.

29. 2 W. LaFave & J. Israel, supra note 24, at § 15.2(b).

30. A. Goldstein, supra note 2, at 183–84, notes that the grand jury "might serve as an internal administrative procedure to assist the prosecutor in exercising his discretion when he expects the insanity defense will be raised and he wishes to be in a position to agree to it or not; or when defense counsel asks him to exercise his discretion to dismiss the criminal charge and to have the defendant committed. The grand jury's subpoena power makes it possible to conduct a full investigation. Its composition makes it more representative of the community and its decision, therefore, more acceptable. Its secrecy makes it less stigmatizing and perhaps less traumatizing."

31. Novosel v. Helgemoe, 118 N.H. 115, 384 A.2d 124 (1978) (violates state due process clause where grand jury proceedings are secret and nonadversary, examination of witnesses does not occur, and written record is not required, accused may be compelled to appear without counsel, hearsay evidence is considered, and probable cause standard is applied).

A majority of jurisdictions, in recognition of the fact that it is extremely important for the prosecution to know in advance of trial whether an insanity defense will be raised, have adopted legislation requiring the defendant to give advance notice. In some states this legislation requires a special plea of not guilty by reason of insanity as a prerequisite to raising the defense at trial. But much more common is a requirement that the defendant file a written notice at a certain time prior to trial manifesting his intention to defend on the ground of insanity.[32] Some of these statutes go on to provide that the defendant must set forth in his notice the names of his witnesses and the substance of his defenses.[33] Unless the matter is put into issue by the prosecution's evidence [34] or the defendant establishes good cause for his failure [35] to so plead or give notice,[36] the defendant may not thereafter defend on grounds of insanity.[37] These statutes usually also provide that the trial court may commit the defendant for examination after his indication of an intention to raise the insanity defense.[38]

The requirement that the defendant by plea or notice disclose in advance of trial his intention to rely upon the insanity defense has been challenged on the ground that it infringes upon the defendant's constitutional privilege against self-incrimination. The argument, in brief, is that this right frees the defendant from any obligation to provide the prosecutor with information which might be useful to the prosecution's case and, particularly, to identify the nature of the defense before the prosecution has put in its case. The claim has been consistently rejected in the state courts,[39] and this result would seem to be bolstered by the Supreme Court holding that the defendant may constitutionally be required to give advance notice of his intention to rely upon an alibi.[40] It has been argued, however, that a notice-of-insanity requirement is more vulnerable than a notice-of-alibi statute, in that the former, unlike the latter, involves an admission by the defendant that he did the acts charged.[41]

 WESTLAW REFERENCES

digest,synopsis(insan*** /s notice)

(c) Court-Ordered Psychiatric Examination. Lay testimony is unlikely to be sufficient either in effectively presenting an insanity defense or in rebutting such a defense.[42] Thus, in a case in which the issue of insanity is to be litigated both the defense and the prosecution will be interested in having the accused examined well in advance of trial.

One common complaint about the procedure for trying the insanity defense issue is that "it lacks the impartiality which should be characteristic of scientific inquiry." [43] In an attempt to eliminate the so-called "battle

---

32. Model Penal Code § 4.03(2) provides that evidence of an insanity defense is not admissible unless the defendant at the time of his plea or within 10 days thereafter (or at such later time as the court may for good cause permit) files a written notice of his purpose to rely upon the defense.

33. H. Weihofen, supra note 28, at 359. The defense must have a right to similar discovery in order to satisfy the due process requirement of reciprocity in Wardius v. Oregon, 412 U.S. 470, 93 S.Ct. 2208, 37 L.Ed.2d 82 (1973). Thus, under such provisions the prosecution must disclose the identity of psychiatrists it plans to call as witnesses on the insanity issue. State v. Curtis, 544 S.W.2d 580 (Mo. 1976).

34. State v. Wallace, 170 Or. 60, 131 P.2d 222 (1942).

35. Substantial albeit not literal compliance is sufficient, and on this point courts typically ask whether the defendant did enough so that the prosecution was not taken by surprise. Ronson v. Commissioner, 604 F.2d 176 (2d Cir.1979).

36. Taylor v. District Court, 182 Colo. 406, 514 P.2d 309 (1973); State v. Fitzgibbon, 32 Wn.2d 881, 203 P.2d 1016 (1949).

37. United States v. Winn, 577 F.2d 86 (9th Cir.1978); State v. Gunter, 208 La. 694, 23 So.2d 305 (1954).

38. H. Weihofen, supra note 28, at 358.

39. See State ex rel. Sikora v. District Court, 154 Mont. 241, 462 P.2d 897 (1969), and cases cited therein.

40. Williams v. Florida, 399 U.S. 78, 90 S.Ct. 1893, 26 L.Ed.2d 446 (1970). However, in footnote 14 the Court emphasized it was *not* deciding "whether and to what extent a State can enforce discovery rules against a defendant who fails to comply, by excluding relevant, probative evidence," characterized as "a question raising Sixth Amendment issues."

41. See the dissenting opinion in the *Sikora* case, supra note 39.

42. A. Goldstein, supra note 2, at 124.

43. H. Weihofen, supra note 28, at 329.

of the experts," [44] most jurisdictions have enacted statutes providing for examination of the defendant by a court-appointed psychiatrist.[45] Appointment under these provisions may come because the defense, prosecutor, or court has asserted that the defendant is not competent to stand trial (in which case the examination will nonetheless probably result in the psychiatrist gaining information relating to the accused's condition at the time of the alleged crime), or it may be triggered by the defendant's action of pleading or giving notice of an insanity defense. Under the most common type of procedure, the court designates a specific psychiatrist who will thereafter examine the defendant in his office or in a court clinic or the jail. Elsewhere, the defendant is temporarily committed to a mental hospital for examination by a member of the hospital staff. Under both procedures, "the examination is ordinarily made by a psychiatrist employed by the government, either because the statutes require it or because a government psychiatrist is the only one available." [46] Upon completion of the examination, a report is prepared and copies are furnished to the court, the prosecutor, and defense counsel.[47]

The report is likely to have a very significant impact upon the outcome of the case. It has been established that if there is a conflict between the conclusions reached by the so-called impartial expert and by an expert retained by one of the parties, the jury will in almost every instance accept those of the former.[48] As a result, both the prosecutor and defense counsel are influenced by his findings.[49] This would be a desirable result if the appointed expert could be counted upon to bring the "truth" into court, but this is not the case. "An impartial expert, and the added credibility he brings with him, could be justified only if there was a high degree of consensus among psychiatrists on the answers to questions likely to arise in the courtroom, on the qualifications of persons competent to present such answers and on the techniques to be used at the various stages of examination. No such consensus can be said to exist." [50] In part, the problem arises out of the fact that the statutes concerning examination by an impartial expert often do not set forth the minimum qualifications required of the examiner,[51] do not stipulate the kind of examination which is to be conducted,[52] and "give the examining expert little or no guidance as to what his report must contain." [53] But the more fundamental point is that the single expert only represents the point of view of his particular school of psychiatry.[54]

One other problem relating to court-ordered mental examinations is this: to what extent, if at all, is the defendant who is ordered to submit to such an examination protected by the constitutional privilege against self-incrimination? [55] This issue, which took on

44. A. Goldstein, supra note 2, at 131.

45. Such provisions are to be found in 31 states and the District of Columbia. For citations to the statutes, see id. at 254–55 n. 20. On the power of a court to order such an examination even absent such statutory authorization, see Annot., 17 A.L.R.4th 1274 (1982).

46. A. Goldstein, supra note 2, at 131. In 14 states the experts are staff members of the state mental hospital or mental health department and in others a government psychiatrist must be a member of any examining commission appointed. In 12 states and the federal courts any competent disinterested expert may be appointed, including a government employed psychiatrist, and Model Penal Code § 4.05 so provides. A. Goldstein, supra note 2, at 255 n. 23.

47. For a more detailed statement of these procedures, see A. Goldstein, supra note 2, at 131–36; H. Weihofen, supra note 28, at Ch. 7.

48. See Weihofen, Eliminating the Battle of Experts in Criminal Insanity Cases, 48 Mich.L.Rev. 961, 967–68 (1950).

49. A. Goldstein, supra note 2, at 132.

50. Id. at 133.

51. Id. at 131; H. Weihofen, supra note 28, at 334.

52. A. Goldstein, supra note 2, at 132. Thus, the examinations are likely to be very brief. H. Weihofen, supra note 28, at 334.

53. Model Penal Code § 4.05, Comment (Tent. Draft No. 4, 1955). Code § 4.05(3), by contrast, sets forth in detail the matters to be included within the report.

54. See note 99 infra. Thus, A. Goldstein, supra note 2, at 135, suggests that the better practice would be to provide for examination by a board of experts, one of whom is chosen by the defense, as is now the practice in a few states.

55. For a more detailed treatment of this issue, consult Aronson, Should the Privilege Against Self-Incrimination

much greater significance once the privilege was held applicable to the states [56] and interpreted as extending to pretrial questioning of a detained suspect,[57] can arise in various ways. One question is whether a defendant's incriminating admissions to the examiner tending to show that he engaged in the conduct charged (e.g., "yes, I shot him") are admissible at trial against him. (It is not unlikely that such an admission will be made, as one accepted technique of examination is to ask the defendant "about his view of the facts and the feelings which he experienced at the time of the crime." [58]) There is general agreement that the privilege extends to such admissions,[59] although courts have differed upon the means by which the privilege is to be enforced. Statutory provisions to the effect that such admissions by the defendant are not admissible at trial on the issue of guilt [60] are usually thought to be adequate,[61] and in the absence of such provisions some courts have held that the defendant may refuse to submit to the examination without penalty.[62]

But are such admissions properly admitted as a part of the basis for the expert's opinion on the defendant's sanity? The courts have quite consistently answered in the affirmative, at least where the defendant has asserted an insanity defense and introduced supporting psychiatric testimony.[63] The Supreme Court has not had occasion to rule on this precise point, but has referred to these lower court decisions with apparent approval.[64] The view which is typically taken is that consequently it suffices if, after such a statement is admitted into evidence, the jury is instructed that it is not to consider the admission on the question of guilt.[65] This view has been justly criticized on the ground that the jury is unlikely to be able to obey such an instruction.[66] Another approach is to permit such evidence to be admitted on the issue of insanity only if that issue is tried in a separate hearing following determination of the issue of guilt.[67] This bifurcated trial procedure [68] has the unique advantage that defendant's statements cannot operate to his prejudice on the issue of guilt, but yet they are brought to the attention of the factfinder as a very relevant part of the examination process.

Apply to Compelled Psychiatric Examinations?, 26 Stan.L. Rev. 55 (1973); Danforth, Death Knell for Pre-Trial Mental Examination? Privilege Against Self-Incrimination, 19 Rutgers L.Rev. 489 (1965); Griffith & Griffith, The Patient's Right to Protection Against Self-Incrimination During Psychiatric Examination, 13 Toledo L.Rev. 269 (1982); Slobogin, Estelle v. Smith: The Constitutional Contours of the Forensic Evaluation, 31 Emory L.J. 71 (1982); Notes, 50 Geo.Wash.L.Rev. 275 (1982); 83 Harv.L. Rev. 648 (1970); 18 Me.L.Rev. 96 (1966); 40 Temple L.Q. 366 (1967); Comments 11 Colum.J.L. & Soc.Prob. 403 (1975); 1969 Wis.L.Rev. 270; 1964 Wis.L.Rev. 671.

56. Malloy v. Hogan, 378 U.S. 1, 84 S.Ct. 1489, 12 L.Ed. 2d 653 (1964).

57. Miranda v. Arizona, 384 U.S. 436, 86 S.Ct. 1602, 16 L.Ed.2d 694 (1966).

58. Note, 83 Harv.L.Rev. 648, 652 (1970).

59. Gibson v. Zahradnick, 581 F.2d 75 (4th Cir.1978); United States v. Bohle, 445 F.2d 54 (7th Cir.1971); State v. Vosler, 216 Neb. 461, 345 N.W.2d 806 (1984).

60. E.g., 18 U.S.C.A. § 4244.

61. United States v. Bennett, 460 F.2d 872 (D.C.Cir. 1972); Edmunds v. United States, 260 F.2d 474 (D.C.Cir. 1958).

62. French v. District Court, 153 Colo. 10, 384 P.2d 268 (1963); People v. Wax, 75 Ill.App.2d 163, 220 N.E.2d 600 (1966); State v. Olson, 274 Minn. 225, 143 N.W.2d 69 (1966).

63. E.g., United States v. Byers, 740 F.2d 1104 (D.C.Cir. 1984); United States v. Madrid, 673 F.2d 1114 (10th Cir. 1982); United States v. Reifsteck, 535 F.2d 1030 (8th Cir. 1976).

64. Estelle v. Smith, 451 U.S. 454, 101 S.Ct. 1866, 68 L.Ed.2d 359 (1981).

65. In re Spencer, 63 Cal.2d 400, 46 Cal.Rptr. 753, 406 P.2d 33 (1965). Compare the stricter view, required by statute and discussed in Commonwealth v. Martin, 393 Mass. 781, 473 N.E.2d 1099 (1985), whereunder defendant's statement during examination is not admissible even for this purpose "if such statement constitutes a confession of guilt of the crime charged."

66. State ex rel. La Follette v. Raskin, 34 Wis.2d 607, 150 N.W.2d 318 (1967). Cf. Bruton v. United States, 391 U.S. 123, 88 S.Ct. 1620, 20 L.Ed. 476 (1968) (defendant's right of confrontation violated by admission of codefendant's confession implicating defendant notwithstanding instruction to jury to consider confession only against codefendant, as there is a substantial risk the jury would not comply with that instruction); Jackson v. Denno, 378 U.S. 368, 84 S.Ct. 1774, 12 L.Ed.2d 908 (1964) (submitting defendant's confession to jury with instructions to consider same only if jury finds confession to be voluntary is a violation of due process, as there is a substantial risk jury would not follow that instruction).

67. State ex rel. La Follette v. Raskin, supra note 66.

68. See § 4.5(f).

But the broader issue is just why it is that the entire examination process is not contrary to the defendant's privilege against self-incrimination. That is, why is it not a violation of the privilege to require the defendant to submit to an examination which may very well provide the prosecution with information which can be admitted for the purpose of defeating the defendant's insanity defense? Some courts have simply accepted without question the notion that the privilege is inapplicable in this context,[69] while other courts have offered a variety of explanations. Sometimes that conclusion has been grounded upon the proposition that the defendant's mental condition is real evidence and thus for that reason not within the privilege.[70] (In defining the scope of the privilege, the Supreme Court has held that it only protects the accused from providing "evidence of a testimonial or communicative nature," [71] and thus has upheld such practices as the taking of a blood sample,[72] placing the suspect in a lineup,[73] requiring him to speak for voice identification,[74] and requiring him to provide a handwriting exemplar.[75]) But in *Estelle v. Smith* [76] the Supreme Court rejected this argument out of hand, noting that the privilege against self-incrimination is "directly involved" when the state uses as evidence against the defendant "the substance of his disclosures during the pretrial psychiatric examination." In short, mental examinations are unlike these other practices in that "examinations impinge on values protected by the privilege." [77]

Another reason which is sometimes given for not extending the privilege to the court-ordered examination concerns the concept of "waiver." That is, the problem is sometimes resolved on the ground that the defendant has waived the protection of the privilege by raising the insanity defense or by submitting to examination without protest.[78] *Estelle* can easily be read as approving this theory, for the court went out of its way to distinguish the instant case, in which the defendant had not interposed an insanity defense or offered psychiatric evidence for any purpose, from one in which "a defendant asserts the insanity defense and introduces supporting psychiatric testimony." But the waiver theory has been severely criticized.[79] As one court put it:

> It seems to us at best a fiction to say that when the defendant introduces his expert's testimony he "waives" his Fifth Amendment rights. What occurs is surely no waiver in the ordinary sense of a known and voluntary relinquishment, but rather merely the product of the court's decree that the act entails the consequences—a decree that remains to be justified. Even if the average defendant pleading insanity were aware of this judicially prescribed consequence (an awareness that the doctrine of waiver would normally require), his acceptance of it could hardly be called unconstrained.[80]

Yet a third theory, which may be what the Supreme Court in *Estelle* was actually referring to in noting that if a state could not examine an insanity-defense defendant then it would be deprived "of the only effective means it has of controverting his proof on an issue that he interjected into the case," has to do with not giving the defendant an unfair advantage. Thus, courts which have rejected the Fifth Amendment claim in this context have not infrequently referred to the need for

---

69. E.g., State v. Coleman, 96 W.Va. 544, 123 S.E. 580 (1924).

70. E.g., United States v. Cohen, 530 F.2d 43 (5th Cir. 1976); United States v. Handy, 454 F.2d 885 (9th Cir. 1971); United States v. Baird, 414 F.2d 700 (2d Cir.1969); People v. Nelson, 92 Ill.App.3d 35, 47 Ill.Dec. 683, 415 N.E.2d 688 (1980).

71. Schmerber v. California, 384 U.S. 757, 86 S.Ct. 1826, 16 L.Ed.2d 908 (1966).

72. Ibid.

73. United States v. Wade, 388 U.S. 218, 87 S.Ct. 1926, 18 L.Ed.2d 1149 (1967).

74. Ibid.

75. Gilbert v. California, 388 U.S. 263, 87 S.Ct. 1951, 18 L.Ed.2d 1178 (1967).

76. 451 U.S. 454, 101 S.Ct. 1866, 68 L.Ed.2d 359 (1981).

77. Note, 83 Harv.L.Rev. 648, 660 (1970). For a statement of those values and their application in their context, see id. at 656–60.

78. Corder v. State, 467 N.E.2d 409 (Ind.1984); State v. Olson, supra note 62; State v. Swinburne, 324 S.W.2d 746 (Mo.1959).

79. See, e.g., Slobogin, supra note 55, at 91; Note, 50 Geo.Wash.L.Rev. 275, 289–91 (1982).

80. United States v. Byers, 740 F.2d 1104 (D.C.Cir. 1984).

a "fair state-individual balance"[81] or for "fundamental fairness"[82] or "judicial common sense"[83] in resolving the issue. These courts have thus "denied the Fifth Amendment claim primarily because of the unreasonable and debilitating effect it would have upon society's conduct of a fair inquiry into the defendant's culpability."[84] As the matter was explained by one court:

> It would be a strange situation, indeed, if, first, the government is to be compelled to afford the defense ample psychiatric service and evidence at government expense and second, if the government is to have the burden of proof, * * * and yet it is to be denied the opportunity to have its own corresponding and verifying examination, a step which perhaps is the most trustworthy means of attempting to meet that burden.[85]

Such practical considerations of what constitutes a fair but effective criminal process are rightly taken into account in determining the reach of the Fifth Amendment privilege against self incrimination.[86]

If, on the basis of one or more of the above theories, a defendant has no constitutional right not to submit to a court-ordered psychiatric examination, then of course it follows that the defendant is not exercising a constitutional right if he refuses to talk with the court-appointed psychiatrist. Sanctions are

thus permissible in the event of such noncooperation. Some courts permit the prosecutor to comment on the defendant's silence in this respect at trial.[87] But this alone is insufficient, for "it permits the defendant to present expert testimony that cannot be effectively challenged."[88] Thus the better approach is to bar the noncooperating defendant from presenting any psychiatric testimony on his own behalf.[89]

Yet another question is whether a defendant has a constitutional right to the assistance of counsel in connection with a court-ordered psychiatric examination. Some courts have held that a defendant is entitled to notice of and an opportunity to consult with counsel regarding an examination by a government psychiatrist,[90] a conclusion which finds support in the Supreme Court's decision in *Estelle v. Smith.*[91] As one court explained, counsel can render meaningful assistance prior to the interview:

> A defendant facing such an exam must make decisions with significant legal consequences and is in obvious need of counsel. * * * He may wish to refuse to submit to the government examination and risk exclusion of his own expert testimony at trial, and rely instead on lay testimony to establish insanity. * * * A defendant may need advice regarding what sort of

81. United States v. Bohle, 445 F.2d 54 (7th Cir.1971); United States v. Albright, 388 F.2d 719 (4th Cir.1968).

82. Pope v. United States, 372 F.2d 710 (8th Cir.1967), vacated on other grounds 392 U.S. 651, 88 S.Ct. 2145, 20 L.Ed.2d 1317 (1968).

83. United States v. Reifsteck, 535 F.2d 1030 (8th Cir. 1976); Alexander v. United States, 380 F.2d 33 (8th Cir. 1967).

84. United States v. Byers, 740 F.2d 1104 (D.C.Cir. 1984), following that approach.

85. Pope v. United States, 372 F.2d 710 (8th Cir.1967), vacated on other grounds 392 U.S. 651, 88 S.Ct. 2145, 20 L.Ed.2d 1317 (1968).

86. The Supreme Court has done so in concluding that a defendant may not take the stand in his own behalf and then claim immunity from cross-examination on the matters he has himself put into dispute. Brown v. United States, 356 U.S. 148, 78 S.Ct. 622, 2 L.Ed.2d 589 (1958); Fitzpatrick v. United States, 178 U.S. 304, 20 S.Ct. 944, 44 L.Ed. 1078 (1900).

87. Karstetter v. Cardwell, 526 F.2d 1144 (9th Cir. 1975); Lee v. County Court, 27 N.Y.2d 432, 318 N.Y.S.2d 705, 267 N.E.2d 452 (1971); State v. Hudson, 73 Wn.2d 660, 440 P.2d 192 (1968).

88. Slobogin, supra note 55, at 105.

89. United States v. Handy, 454 F.2d 885 (9th Cir. 1971); People v. Hayes, 421 Mich. 271, 364 N.W.2d 635 (1984); State v. Whitlow, 45 N.J. 3, 210 A.2d 763 (1965); State ex rel. Johnson v. Richardson, 276 Or. 325, 555 P.2d 202 (1976).

90. United States v. Garcia, 739 F.2d 440 (9th Cir. 1984); Spivey v. Zant, 661 F.2d 464 (5th Cir.1981); Schantz v. Eyman, 418 F.2d 11 (9th Cir.1969); United States v. Driscoll, 399 F.2d 135 (2d Cir.1968).

But see Vardas v. Estelle, 715 F.2d 206 (5th Cir.1983), concluding that when a defendant interposed a defense of insanity, a step which by state law would authorize the state to conduct its own psychiatric evaluation, defendant and his counsel had sufficient notice that such examination would occur, so that no specific notice was required as a constitutional matter.

91. 451 U.S. 454, 101 S.Ct. 1866, 68 L.Ed.2d 359 (1981), holding, as to a defendant who had not interposed an insanity defense, that defendant's right to counsel had been violated by conducting an examination of defendant without notifying counsel "that the psychiatric examination would encompass the issue of their client's future dangerousness."

questions he should expect, the need to cooperate, and the possible ramifications of his answers. He may have legitimate fifth amendment concerns regarding use of statements made in an examination * * * and may well be unaware that his statements may not be admitted for the purpose of establishing any issue except mental condition.[92]

A few courts have ruled that a defendant also has a right to have his attorney present during the psychiatric examination.[93] However, the overwhelming majority of the cases hold to the contrary.[94] These cases very often stress that the presence of counsel would limit the effectiveness of the examination,[95] which is a practical consideration of the kind the Supreme Court has acknowledged must be taken into account in determining the scope of the Sixth Amendment right to counsel.[96] Denial of counsel at the examination is also consistent with the Court's other reasoning concerning the need for assistance of counsel. In *United States v. Ash,*[97] holding there is no right to have defense counsel present at a photograph identification, the Court declared that for the Sixth Amendment to apply the defendant must find himself "confronted, just as at trial, by the procedural system, or by his expert adversary, or by both." But a defendant who was allowed to consult with counsel before the examination is not in such a situation during the examination; at that time "he

had no decisions in the nature of legal strategy or tactics to make," and the "examining psychiatrist is not an adversary, much less a professional one," in the sense in which that phrase is used in the right to counsel cases.[98]

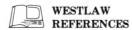 **WESTLAW REFERENCES**

psychiat! psycholog! /s indigen** /s insan***
synopsis(psychiat! psycholog! /s court /4 appoint!
     /s insan*** mental**)

(d) Examination of Defendant by Own Psychiatrist. If the defendant can afford to do so, he will be examined by a psychiatrist of his own choosing. However, the effectiveness of the examination in terms of constructing a convincing defense of insanity will be determined in large measure by the defense counsel. He must select a psychiatrist whose orientation is such as to favor the defendant's position,[99] and he must develop a close working relationship with him and adequately inform him as to the kinds of information which are needed concerning the defendant's past condition.[100]

In this respect the indigent defendant will sometimes be at a significant disadvantage.[101] Statutes in some states authorize payment of reasonable expenses related to the defense of indigent defendants,[102] which are at least sometimes construed to cover a psychiatric examination by a defense psychiatrist.[103]

---

92. United States v. Garcia, 739 F.2d 440 (9th Cir. 1984).

93. Howe v. State, 611 P.2d 16 (Alaska 1980); People v. Cerami, 33 N.Y.2d 243, 351 N.Y.S.2d 681, 306 N.E.2d 799 (1973); Shepard v. Bowe, 250 Or. 288, 442 P.2d 238 (1968).

94. E.g., United States v. Byers, 740 F.2d 1104 (D.C.Cir. 1984); United States v. Cohen, 530 F.2d 43 (5th Cir.1976); United States v. Greene, 497 F.2d 1068 (7th Cir.1974); United States v. Trapnell , 495 F.2d 22 (2d Cir.1974); Strickland v. State, 247 Ga. 219, 275 S.E.2d 29 (1981); State v. Brown, 235 Kan. 688, 681 P.2d 1071 (1984); State v. Hardy, 283 S.C. 590, 325 S.E.2d 320 (1985). For other cases, see Annot., 3 A.L.R. 4th 910 (1981).

95. United States v. Greene, 497 F.2d 1068 (7th Cir. 1974); State v. Breaux, 337 So.2d 182 (La.1976); Livingston v. State, 542 S.W.2d 655 (Tex.Crim.1976).

96. See, e.g., United States v. Wade, 388 U.S. 218, 87 S.Ct. 1926, 18 L.Ed.2d 1149 (1967), concerning the right to counsel at a lineup, where the Court felt constrained to note that "no substantial countervailing policy considerations have been advanced against the requirement of the presence of counsel."

97. 413 U.S. 300, 93 S.Ct. 2568, 37 L.Ed.2d 619 (1973).

98. United States v. Byers, 740 F.2d 1104 (D.C.Cir. 1984).

99. "The organically oriented psychiatrist will often find himself eliciting and reading a patient's history and symptoms differently from the dynamically oriented psychiatrist. What is a psychosis to one may be neurosis to another, what some call psychopathy may be interpreted by others as a failure of communication between a psychiatrist of a high social class and an offender from the lower rungs of society." A. Goldstein, supra note 2, at 134.

100. For a very useful discussion of counsel's responsibility in this regard, see id. at 124–27.

101. See Goldstein & Fine, The Indigent Accused, the Psychiatrist, and the Insanity Defense, 110 U.Pa.L.Rev. 1061 (1962).

102. See statutes collected in n. 4 of Ake v. Oklahoma, ___ U.S. ___, 105 S.Ct. 1087, 84 L.Ed.2d 53 (1985).

103. E.g., Bailey v. State, 421 So.2d 1364 (Ala.Crim. App.1982).

But, especially absent a statute clearly authorizing the granting of such assistance at state expense, courts have generally not looked with favor upon assertions that an indigent defendant is denied a fair trial of his insanity defense if he is not provided with a psychiatrist of his own choosing. Such assistance is said to be merely "collateral" and thus not something which must be provided at public expense.[104] Moreover, it is assumed to be adequate that the defendant was examined by a state psychiatrist; the state is said to have no "constitutional obligation to promote * * * a battle of experts by supplying defense counsel with funds wherewith to hunt for other experts who may be willing, as witnesses for the defense, to offer the opinion that the accused is criminally insane."[105] It has been suggested that the equal protection approach developed in *Griffin v. Illinois*[106] undercuts these cases,[107] but courts have been most reluctant to extend the *Griffin* holding to situations in which the indigent defendant requested appointment of his own psychiatrist.[108] In so doing, some argue, they have failed to recognize that substantial equality cannot be accomplished unless the indigent defendant has a psychiatrist whose orientation and preparation is such as to support the defense theory of the case.[109]

In the recent case of *Ake v. Oklahoma*,[110] the Supreme Court held "that when a defendant demonstrates to the trial judge that his sanity at the time of the offense is to be a significant factor at trial, the State must, at a minimum, assure the defendant access to a competent psychiatrist who will conduct an appropriate examination and assist in evaluation, preparation, and presentation of the defense." The Court added that it was leaving "to the States the decision on how to implement this right," but failed to indicate clearly whether implementation requires that a defendant who makes the requisite showing is inevitably entitled to a psychiatrist *of his own*. Indeed, *Ake* appears to have been written so as to be deliberately ambiguous on this point, thus leaving the issue open for future consideration, as comments supporting a move in either direction appear throughout the majority opinion in the case.

On the one hand, the reference in the above holding to a psychiatrist assisting "in evaluation, preparation, and presentation of the defense" certainly suggests that a psychiatrist serving exclusively in the defense camp is necessary.[111] This position is also bolstered by the Court's recognition that "psychiatrists disagree widely and frequently" on the various questions related to the insanity defense and that consequently juries "must resolve differences in opinion" after hearing from "the psychiatrists for each party." Also significant is the fact that the Court makes reference to existing statutes concerning provision of assistance to the defense, rather than those which merely provide for examination of the defendant by a court-appointed "neutral" psychiatrist. Finally, it is relatively clear that in the other branch of *Ake*, concerning the right to psychiatric assistance at a capital sentencing proceeding, the Court has given express recognition to the need for a separate psychiatrist on the defense side.[112]

104. United States ex rel. Smith v. Baldi, 192 F.2d 540 (3d Cir.1951), affirmed 344 U.S. 561, 73 S.Ct. 391, 97 L.Ed. 549 (1951).

105. McGarty v. O'Brien, 188 F.2d 151 (1st Cir.1951).

106. 351 U.S. 12, 76 S.Ct. 585, 100 L.Ed. 891 (1956). The Court, in holding that an indigent defendant had been denied equal protection of the laws because he was not provided with a transcript for appeal, asserted: "There can be no equal justice where the kind of trial a man gets depends on the amount of money he has."

107. A. Goldstein, supra note 2, at 140.

108. See, e.g., United States v. Naples, 307 F.2d 618 (D.C.Cir.1962); Willis v. United States, 285 F.2d 663 (D.C. Cir.1960); United States v. Bradson, 241 F.2d 107 (7th Cir. 1957).

109. A. Goldstein, supra note 2, at 140.

110. ___ U.S. ___, 105 S.Ct. 1087, 84 L.Ed.2d 53 (1985).

111. As the Court stated at another point, "without the assistance of a psychiatrist to conduct a professional examination on issues relevant to the defense, to help determine whether the insanity defense is viable, to present testimony, and to assist in preparing the cross-examination of a State's psychiatric witnesses, the risk of an inaccurate resolution of sanity issues is extremely high."

112. A state psychiatrist did testify at that proceeding regarding defendant's future dangerousness, and the Court stressed defendant's need to "offer a well-informed expert's opposing view."

On the other hand, it must be noted that the *Ake* case involved a fact situation in which there was *absolutely no* psychiatric testimony available on the insanity defense.[113] The defendant had been denied a psychiatrist of his own, and the court-ordered examination had been limited to defendant's competency to stand trial, so that even the psychiatrists at the state hospital were unable to testify about defendant's mental condition at the time of the offense. Moreover, the Court in *Ake* did caution that an indigent defendant has no "constitutional right to choose a psychiatrist of his personal liking or to receive funds to hire his own," and also restated the now-familar doctrine that a state need not "purchase for the indigent defendant all the assistance that his wealthier counterpart might buy." Finally, the Supreme Court distinguished the cases relied upon by the court below [114] by characterizing them as instances in which the defendant had been examined by "neutral psychiatrists" who "were not beholden to the prosecution," though the psychiatrists in those cases were the court's witnesses—not appointed for defendant's exclusive use and, at least in one instance, permanent employees of the state's psychiatric facility who were unlikely to view the insanity defense from a defendant's perspective.[115]

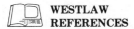 **WESTLAW REFERENCES**

307 +4 618 /p psychiat! psycholog!

(e) Burden of Proof. The phrase "burden of proof" is somewhat ambiguous and is often used for different purposes. To avoid confu-

sion, it is helpful to distinguish between (1) the initial burden of going forward with the evidence (sometimes called the production burden), and (2) the burden of persuasion. Failure of the party who has the burden of going forward to meet that burden will result in the factual matter being foreclosed adversely to him, either by a directed verdict or by an instruction to the jury. The burden of persuasion, on the other hand, involves the situation in which the factual matter is before the jury for decision; the burden is that of convincing the jury to accept the version of those facts alleged by the party bearing the burden.

On the issue of lack of responsibility because of insanity, the initial burden of going forward is everywhere placed upon the defendant.[116] This proposition is often stated in terms of a presumption of sanity; most men are sane, and thus the defendant in this particular case is presumed to be sane until some amount of evidence to the contrary is produced.[117] Were it otherwise, the prosecution would be confronted with the intolerable burden of establishing the defendant's sanity in every criminal case. The burden of going forward is usually met by testimony of lay or expert witnesses for the defense tending to show that the defendant was insane at the time of the conduct charged, although this is not of necessity so. It sometimes happens that the insanity defense will become an issue in the case because of testimony elicited by the prosecutor from his own witnesses or by

113. The Court noted, in this connection, that the jury was instructed defendant was presumed sane unless he presented evidence to raise a reasonable doubt about his sanity at the time.

114. United States ex rel. Smith v. Baldi, 344 U.S. 561, 73 S.Ct. 391, 97 L.Ed. 549 (1953), and the case discussed therein, McGarty v. O'Brien, 188 F.2d 151 (1st Cir.1951).

115. But, the Court's discussion of *Smith*, supra note 115, is itself most ambiguous. Two possible ways of now looking at *Smith* were put forward: (i) that "it suggests the proposition that there is no constitutional right to more psychiatric assistance than the defendant in *Smith* had received"; or (ii) that it "was addressed to altogether different variables, and that we are not limited by it in considering whether fundamental fairness today requires a different result."

116. For citations to cases in every jurisdiction, see Weihofen, supra note 28, at 214 n. 1. Sometimes this is stated by statute, either directly or by characterizing the defense as an "affirmative defense."

117. Davis v. United States, 160 U.S. 469, 16 S.Ct. 353, 40 L.Ed. 499 (1895).

In several jurisdictions this presumption remains in the case even after defendant has met his burden of going forward, serving as evidentiary weight countering evidence given by the defendant as to his insanity. See, e.g., Commonwealth v. Kostka, 370 Mass. 516, 350 N.E.2d 444 (1976); State v. Wilson, 85 N.M. 552, 514 P.2d 603 (1973). Such use of the presumption has been sharply criticized. See Eule, The Presumption of Sanity: Bursting the Bubble, 25 U.C.L.A.L.Rev. 637 (1978).

the defense on cross-examination of prosecution witnesses.[118]

The states are not in agreement on the quantum of evidence which is required to discharge the burden of going forward. The prevailing rule is that the evidence must raise a reasonable doubt of the defendant's mental responsibility for the criminal act.[119] A few jurisdictions, however, appear to require a lesser standard [120] which is sometimes stated as merely "some evidence," [121] "slight evidence," [122] or a "scintilla" of evidence.[123] This latter view leads to some difficult questions. For example, if the defendant meets this lesser burden but the prosecution does not thereafter produce any evidence of the defendant's insanity, should the court direct a verdict of not guilty by reason of insanity? Yes, answered one court, for once the defendant met his production burden the defendant's sanity became an essential element to be proved by the government beyond a reasonable doubt.[124] No, answered another, for a directed verdict requires not merely some evidence but rather proof sufficient to compel a reasonable juror to entertain a reasonable doubt.[125]

Once the defendant has met his burden of going forward with the evidence, it then must be determined which party has the burden of persuasion. In about half of the states, this burden rests with the prosecution; in these jurisdictions the prosecution must then proceed to prove responsibility beyond a reasonable doubt.[126] In the other states,[127] the burden of persuasion is on the defendant to convince the jury of his insanity, but only by the civil standard of a preponderance of the evidence.[128] But in the federal system, recent legislation has placed upon the defendant the burden of proving his insanity defense by "clear and convincing evidence." [129]

In those states in which the burden of persuasion rests upon the defendant, the most common explanation is that insanity is an affirmative defense rather than an element of the crime and that the presumption of insanity justifies the requirement that the defendant prove his sanity.[130] A supporting consideration is the fear that if the rule were otherwise it would be too easy for a defendant who was sane to create a reasonable doubt concerning his sanity.[131] Some, however, have questioned the propriety of placing the burden on the defendant. It is argued that the fundamental proposition that the state must prove the defendant's guilt beyond a reasonable doubt should logically extend to the issue of criminal responsibility, in that the essential element of *mens rea* is not proven unless it is shown that the defendant was capable of entertaining the requisite mens rea.[132] Another contention is that it is more equitable to place the burden on the state,

---

118. Pollard v. United States, 282 F.2d 450 (6th Cir. 1960); Douglas v. United States, 239 F.2d 52 (D.C.Cir. 1956).

119. See, e.g., People v. Redmond, 59 Ill.2d 328, 320 N.E.2d 321 (1974).

120. Which nonetheless is not met by merely filing notice of the defense. State v. Gratiot, 104 Idaho 782, 663 P.2d 1084 (1983).

121. Flowers v. State, 236 Ind. 151, 139 N.E.2d 185 (1956); Torske v. State, 123 Neb. 161, 242 N.W. 408 (1932).

122. United States v. Milne, 487 F.2d 1232 (5th Cir. 1973).

123. Tatum v. United States, 190 F.2d 612 (D.C.Cir. 1951); In re Rosenfield, 157 F.Supp. 18 (D.D.C.1957).

124. Fitts v. United States, 284 F.2d 108 (10th Cir. 1960).

125. McDonald v. United States, 312 F.2d 847 (D.C.Cir. 1962).

126. This is only occasionally provided for by statute. For citation to cases in other jurisdictions, see Hermann,

Assault on the Insanity Defense, 14 Rutgers L.Rev. 241, 267–82 (1983); Note, 22 Am.Crim.L.Rev. 49, 54–55 n. 35 (1984); Annot., 17 A.L.R.3d 146 (1968).

Model Penal Code § 4.03(1) makes insanity an affirmative defense, which means, by virtue of § 1.12(2), that once evidence supporting the defense is admitted it must be disproved by the prosecution beyond a reasonable doubt.

127. About a dozen other states have adopted this standard by case law. See cases collected in Note, 22 Am. Crim.L.Rev. 49, 54 N. 34 (1984).

128. Except for Ariz.Rev.Stat. § 13–502, which mandates a clear and convincing evidence standard.

129. 18 U.S.C.A. § 20.

130. H. Weihofen, supra note 28, at 220.

131. Ortwein v. Commonwealth, 76 Pa. 414, 18 Am. Rep. 420 (1874). See Morse, Excusing the Crazy: The Insanity Defense Reconsidered, 58 So.Cal.L.Rev. 777, 824–25 (1985).

132. S. Glueck, Mental Disorder and the Criminal Law 41 (1925).

which has resources available to obtain the necessary psychiatric evidence, than on the defendant, who is likely to be indigent.[133]

In 1952, in *Leland v. Oregon*,[134] the Supreme Court upheld a since-repealed Oregon statute which required the accused to establish his insanity beyond a reasonable doubt. The Court could see "no practical difference of such magnitude as to be significant in determining the constitutional question" between the Oregon statute and the provisions found in about half the states requiring the defendant to prove his sanity by a preponderance of the evidence. The fact the latter rule was followed in a large number of states was deemed quite relevant under the test then utilized for due process violations—whether the practice "offends some principle of justice so rooted in the traditions and conscience of our people as to be ranked as fundamental." The Supreme Court later held, relying in part upon the dissent in *Leland*, that "the Due Process Clause protects the accused against conviction except upon proof beyond a reasonable doubt of every fact necessary to constitute the crime with which he is charged."[135] Yet the Court thereafter dismissed, as not presenting a substantial federal question, an appeal claiming a state statute burdening the defendant with proving insanity by a prepon-

derance of the evidence was unconstitutional.[136] As the Court later explained in *Patterson v. New York*,[137] "once the facts constituting a crime are established beyond a reasonable doubt, based on all the evidence including the evidence of the defendant's mental state, the State may refuse to sustain the affirmative defense of insanity unless demonstrated by a preponderance of the evidence."[138] As this language suggests, special steps may be required by trial courts to ensure that shifting the burden of proving insanity to the defendant does not, as a practical matter, lessen the constitutionally-imposed burden on the prosecution to prove beyond a reasonable doubt all elements of the crime, including the requisite mental state.[139]

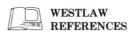

WESTLAW REFERENCES

di burden of proof
topic(110) /p insan! mental*** /p "burden of proof"

(f) Witnesses and Their Testimony. In almost every jurisdiction, a lay witness who is sufficiently acquainted with the defendant to form an intelligent opinion as to his sanity may testify to that opinion,[140] although it is common to require that the witness precede or accompany his opinion with a statement of the facts and circumstances upon which it is

---

133. S. Brakel & R. Rock, The Mentally Disabled and the Law 400 (1971).

134. 343 U.S. 790, 72 S.Ct. 1002, 96 L.Ed. 1302 (1952).

135. In re Winship, 397 U.S. 358, 90 S.Ct. 1068, 25 L.Ed.2d 368 (1970). See also Mullaney v. Wilbur, 421 U.S. 684, 95 S.Ct. 1881, 44 L.Ed.2d 508 (1975).

136. Rivera v. Delaware, 429 U.S. 877, 97 S.Ct. 226, 50 L.Ed.2d 160 (1976).

137. 432 U.S. 197, 97 S.Ct. 2319, 53 L.Ed.2d 281 (1977).

138. See, e.g., State v. McKenzie, 177 Mont. 280, 581 P.2d 1205 (1978), vacated on other grounds 443 U.S. 903, 99 S.Ct. 3094, 61 L.Ed.2d 871 (1979); Ybarra v. State, ___ Nev. ___, 679 P.2d 797 (1984); Kind v. State, 595 P.2d 960 (Wyo.1979).

139. Justice Rehnquist, concurring in Mullaney v. Wilbur, 421 U.S. 684, 95 S.Ct. 1881, 44 L.Ed.2d 508 (1975), cautioned: "The Court noted in *Leland* that the issue of insanity as a defense to a criminal charge was considered by the jury only after it had found that all elements of the offense, including the *mens rea*, if any, required by state law, had been proved beyond a reasonable doubt. * * * Although as the state court's instructions in *Leland* recognized, * * * evidence relevant to insanity as defined by

state law may also be relevant to whether the required *mens rea* was present, the existence or nonexistence of legal insanity bears no necessary relationship to the existence or nonexistence of the required mental elements of the crime. For this reason, Oregon's placement of the burden of proof of insanity on Leland, unlike Maine's redefinition of homicide in the instant case, did not effect an unconstitutional shift in the State's traditional burden of proof beyond a reasonable doubt of all necessary elements of the offense."

This comment certainly raises the question of whether the necessary separation of the mental state element, to be proved by the prosecution beyond a reasonable doubt, and the insanity defense, to be proved by the defendant, has been maintained in those jurisdictions which bar psychiatric testimony on the mental state issue on the ground that it suffices if such evidence is received on the insanity defense. See § 4.7.

140. E.g., Wise v. State, 251 Ala. 660, 38 So.2d 553 (1949); Jarrard v. State, 206 Ga. 112, 55 S.E.2d 706 (1949); State v. Conn, 286 Md. 406, 408 A.2d 700 (1979). For citations to cases in all jurisdictions, see H. Weihofen, supra note 28, at 301–02 n. 1.

founded.[141] Just how much exposure the lay witness must have had to the defendant is a matter which has caused considerable disagreement. Sometimes such testimony is permitted on the basis of a single meeting of only a few minutes duration,[142] while on other occasions such a brief observation has been held inadequate.[143] A lay witness may testify as to the defendant's sanity based upon observation of usual or normal human behavior by him, but may testify as to his insanity only if he has seen the defendant engage in irrational or abnormal behavior.[144] Although "a persuasive case is unlikely to be made on lay testimony alone,"[145] courts have not infrequently upheld verdicts based upon a jury's acceptance of lay testimony of sanity over expert testimony of insanity.[146]

As for expert testimony, the testimony of a psychiatrist is ordinarily the most useful, although even physicians in general practice are often allowed to testify as experts on the insanity question.[147] In most jurisdictions qualified clinical psychologists are also permitted to give expert testimony relating to an insanity defense.[148] The expert's opinion may be based upon (1) his personal examination of the defendant, (2) his evaluation of all the testimony in the case, or (3) a hypothetical question propounded by counsel.[149] The latter technique has been the subject of considerable criticism,[150] and it is not frequently used.

It is generally agreed that the witness may not be asked the ultimate question of whether the defendant was responsible, for this, like an inquiry into whether a person was negligent, seeks a legal conclusion and thus invades the province of the jury.[151] For a time, courts were for the same reason also inclined to hold that the witness could not be asked the "test questions," that is, that he could not be permitted to state his opinion in terms of the applicable legal test of insanity (e.g., "I believe that defendant had a disease of the mind which deprived him of knowledge of right and wrong").[152] The prevailing rule is now to the contrary.[153]

The rule permitting the asking of the test questions rests upon the assumption that the resulting testimony, particularly from a psychiatrist, will better advance the jury's inquiry.[154] It has been questioned, however, whether this is the case. "The essential vice of allowing the test questions is that they tend to supplant the factual detail upon

---

141. E.g., State v. Eisenstein, 72 Ariz. 320, 235 P.2d 1011 (1951). See H. Weihofen, supra note 28, at 308–09 n. 27, for citations to cases in all jurisdictions imposing this limitation.

142. E.g., State v. Butner, 66 Nev. 127, 206 P.2d 253 (1949) (3 to 8 minutes).

143. Winn v. State, 136 Tex.Crim. 513, 126 S.W.2d 481 (1939) (5 minutes). In view of the risk that a lay witness may misinterpret the defendant's actions on a single occasion, a very sensible rule is that adopted in People v. Cole, 382 Mich. 695, 172 N.W.2d 354 (1969): "Before a lay witness is permitted to state an opinion regarding the sanity or insanity or mental competency or incompetency of a person whose mental condition is at issue, the witness must have had ample opportunity to observe the speech, manner, habits, or conduct of the person. To render himself competent under this rule, the witness must establish he was sufficiently acquainted with the defendant or testator so as to testify to mental condition on a comparative basis and not merely to some manifested idiosyncrasy or eccentric behavior."

144. United States v. Milne, 487 F.2d 1232 (5th Cir. 1973); Alexander v. State, 358 So.2d 379 (Miss.1978).

145. A. Goldstein, supra note 2, at 124.

146. E.g., Montano v. State, 468 N.E.2d 1042 (Ind. 1984); Ice v. Commonwealth, 667 S.W.2d 671 (Ky.1984); Commonwealth v. Tyson, 485 Pa. 344, 402 A.2d 995 (1979).

147. E.g., Holt v. State, 84 Okl.Crim.App. 283, 181 P.2d 573 (1947). This conclusion is more understandable when the doctor was the defendant's attending physician or one who had occasion to examine and treat the defendant in the past.

148. United States v. Portis, 542 F.2d 414 (7th Cir. 1976); People v. Free, 94 Ill.2d 378, 69 Ill.Dec. 1, 447 N.E.2d 218 (1983).

149. For a description of each technique, see H. Weihofen, supra note 28, at 277–83.

150. Briggs, Medico-Legal Insanity and the Hypothetical Question, 14 J.Crim.L.C. & P.S. 62 (1923).

151. Bryant v. State, 191 Ga. 686, 13 S.E.2d 820 (1941).

152. E.g., State v. McCann, 329 Mo. 748, 47 S.W.2d 95 (1932).

153. E.g., Tvrz v. State, 154 Neb. 641, 48 N.W.2d 761 (1952); State v. Leland, 190 Or. 598, 227 P.2d 785 (1951). Model Penal Code § 4.07(4) permits the expert to give his opinion as to the extent, if any, to which the capacity of the defendant to appreciate the criminality of his conduct or to conform his conduct to the requirements of law was impaired as a result of mental disease or defect.

154. H. Weihofen, supra note 28, at 286.

which the decision on responsibility should ideally be based. * * * The jury is left with the impression that it must choose between the experts, because it is not told enough about the defendant's mental life to enable it to make an intelligent judgment about *him,* rather than about the psychiatric witnesses."[155]

In addition to opinion evidence, a defendant's mental condition may be proved by circumstantial evidence. This can ordinarily be done: (1) by evidence of the defendant's actions and declarations prior to, at, and subsequent to the time of the conduct charged; (2) by evidence of facts which sometimes cause or predispose one to insanity (e.g., circumstances which might cause psychic stress, hereditary insanity, the presence of substances in the body likely to affect the mind); or (3) by evidence of prior or subsequent insanity, such as civil adjudication of insanity at a time not too remote from the time of the alleged crime.[156]

 **WESTLAW REFERENCES**

110k452(2) /p witness

(g) The Bifurcated Trial.[157] In a few jurisdictions, the defense of insanity is tried separately from the other issues in the case. Under California law, for example, a defendant may plead (1) not guilty, (2) not guilty and also not guilty by reason of insanity, or (3) merely not guilty by reason of insanity. If the second form of plea is entered, the guilt-stage of the trial is first concluded without any reference to the insanity defense, after which (if defendant was found guilty) a separate proceedings takes place before the same or a different jury for purposes of trying the insanity defense. If the third form of plea is entered, this has the effect of a plea of guilty with reservation of the insanity defense, so that only the insanity issue is tried.[158] Such procedures have been upheld whether the insanity issue is determined before [159] or after [160] the main trial, and even though the insanity issue is tried before a different jury.[161]

The purpose of the mandated bifurcated trial procedure is to eliminate from the basic trial on the issue of whether the defendant engaged in the conduct a great mass of evidence having no bearing on that question and which may confuse the jury or be made the basis of appeals to the sympathy or prejudice of the jury.[162] In California, at least, this objective was not realized. As a result of the ruling in *People v. Wells* [163] that evidence of mental disease or defect was admissible on the issue of whether the defendant had the requisite mental state,[164] this mass of evidence was often heard at both the guilt-stage and insanity-stage of the trial.[165] A very few states have invalidated their bifurcated trial statutes, precisely because the legislation was deemed to bar such evidence at the guilt-stage of the trial.[166]

155. A. Goldstein, supra note 2, at 103–04. Some support for this view is developing. See, e.g., Washington v. United States, 390 F.2d 444 (D.C.Cir.1967).

156. For a thorough discussion of the uses of circumstantial evidence on the insanity issue, consult H. Weihofen, supra note 28 at 312–28.

157. See Gallivan, Insanity, Bifurcation and Due Process: Can Values Survive Doctrine, 13 Land & Water L.Rev. 515 (1978); Hermann, Assault on the Insanity Defense, 14 Rutgers L.Rev. 241, 291–310 (1983); Robitscher & Haynes, In Defense of the Insanity Defense, 31 Emory L.J. 9, 18–26 (1982); Note, 66 Nw.U.L.Rev. 327 (1971); Annot., 1 A.L.R.4th 884 (1980).

158. For a more detailed description, see Louisell & Hazard, Insanity as a Defense: The Bifurcated Trial, 49 Calif.L.Rev. 805 (1961).

159. State v. Toon, 172 La. 631, 135 So. 7 (1931).

160. People v. Hickman, 204 Cal. 470, 268 P. 909, 270 P. 1117 (1928); State v. Repp, 122 Wis.2d 246, 362 N.W.2d 415 (1985).

161. People v. Troche, 206 Cal. 35, 273 P. 767 (1928).

162. California, Commission for the Reform of Criminal Procedure, Report 16–17 (1927).

163. 33 Cal.2d 330, 202 P.2d 53 (1949).

164. See § 4.7.

165. For the full impact of *Wells* on the bifurcated trial process, see Louisell & Hazard, supra note 158. (This partial responsibility doctrine has recently been abolished, West's Ann.Cal.Penal Code § 25(a), as a result of a referendum. See Comment, 71 Calif.L.Rev. 1197 (1983).)

166. State v. Shaw, 106 Ariz. 103, 471 P.2d 715 (1970); Morgan v. State, 392 So.2d 1315 (Fla.1981); Sanchez v. State, 567 P.2d 270 (Wyo.1977). But see Muench v. Israel, 715 F.2d 1124 (7th Cir.1983), holding "that a state is not constitutionally compelled to recognize the doctrine of

A different question is whether a defendant who plans to interpose an insanity defense should be entitled to a bifurcated trial if he prefers to proceed in that fashion. On occasion it has been held that bifurcation is called for to protect the defendant's privilege against self-incrimination, as where the defendant made an inculpatory statement during a compulsory pretrial psychiatric examination.[167] Several states take the position that whether to grant the defendant's bifurcation request is a matter within the sound discretion of the judge, with bifurcation called for only when "a defendant shows that he has a substantial insanity defense and a substantial defense on the merits to any element of the charge, either of which would be prejudiced by simultaneous presentation with the other."[168] In a very few other states, a defendant may opt for a bifurcated trial as a matter of right. But it has frequently been held that failure to allow a defendant asserting an insanity defense to have a bifurcated trial does not violate his constitutional rights.[169]

 WESTLAW REFERENCES

people +4 wells /12 202 +4 53 /p insan! mental***

(h) Instructions and Verdict. At the conclusion of all the evidence, the trial judge instructs the jury on the law. Now, for the first time and *after* hearing what may be a

vast amount of evidence on the insanity issue, the jury is finally authoritatively told what the legal test for the insanity defense is and who has the burden of proving what. Particularly in those jurisdictions where there does not exist a standard "pattern" jury instruction on the insanity defense, the judge's oral instructions may be rambling, imprecise, or even downright misleading.[170]

In most jurisdictions, if the insanity issue reaches the jury then it will be given three alternative verdict forms: guilty; not guilty; or not guilty by reason of insanity.[171] If properly instructed, the jury will be told that their first order of business is to determine whether the defendant committed the acts charged and that they should reach the insanity question only if they make that initial determination in the affirmative.[172] Occasionally, however, the jury is told to reach the insanity issue first and to proceed to the issue of guilt or innocence only if the defendant is not found not guilty by reason of insanity,[173] which makes possible the curious result of commitment without a finding that the defendant had even done the acts charged.

One might think, simply as a matter of logic, that if the insanity issue is in the case the jury would be told of its significance, that is of the fact that commitment must or may[174] follow a finding of not guilty by reason of insanity. However, the view taken in

---

diminished capacity and hence a state may exclude expert testimony offered for the purpose of establishing that a criminal defendant lacked the capacity to form a specific intent."

167. State ex rel. LaFollette v. Raskin, 34 Wis.2d 607, 150 N.W.2d 318 (1967). Compare State ex rel. Johnson v. Dale, 277 Or. 359, 560 P.2d 650 (1977) (inefficient procedure of bifurcated trial unnecessary, as defendant deemed to have adequate protection of privilege against self-incrimination at unitary trial).

168. State v. Helms, 284 N.C. 508, 201 S.E.2d 850 (1974). See also Houston v. State, 602 P.2d 784 (Alaska 1979); People v. Donaldson, 65 Mich.App. 588, 237 N.W.2d 570 (1975); State v. Boyd, __ W.Va. __, 280 S.E.2d 669 (1981).

169. Vardas v. Estelle, 715 F.2d 206 (5th Cir.1983); Murphy v. Florida, 495 F.2d 553 (5th Cir.1974), affirmed on other grounds 421 U.S. 794, 95 S.Ct. 2031, 44 L.Ed.2d 589 (1975); Langworthy v. State, 284 Md. 588, 399 A.2d 578 (1979); McKenzie v. Osborne, 195 Mont. 26, 640 P.2d 368 (1981).

The Supreme Court has never addressed the issue, but likely would agree with the above decisions. Cf. McGautha v. California, 402 U.S. 183, 91 S.Ct. 1454, 28 L.Ed. 2d 711 (1971) (no constitutional right to bifurcation of guilt and death penalty determination by jury).

170. See the examples set forth in Arens & Susman, Judges, Jury Charges and Insanity, 12 How.L.J. 1 (1966).

171. H. Weihofen, supra note 28, at 363, indicates that even in jurisdictions where there is not a specific provision to this effect it is nonetheless the practice to give the jury these three alternatives.

172. Goldstein & Katz, Abolish the "Insanity Defense"—Why Not?, 72 Yale L.J. 853, 865 (1963).

173. This occurred in the second *Durham* trial. See the charge to the jury set out in R. Donnelly, J. Goldstein & R. Schwartz, Criminal Law 773–76 (1962).

174. See § 4.6(a) on mandatory versus discretionary commitment.

many jurisdictions [175] on this matter is that the jury should *not* be told of the consequences of an acquittal by reason of insanity.[176] The questionable explanation for this position is that such an instruction would distract the jury from the insanity issue and would invite compromise verdicts.[177] The better view is to the contrary, for, as explained in *Lyles v. United States,*[178] it does not make sense that a jury should be presented with three verdict choices (guilty, not guilty, and not guilty by reason of insanity) but know the consequences of only the first two.[179] Fortunately, the *Lyles* position has gained support from other courts [180] and some legislatures.

In recent years, a substantial minority of states have enacted legislation requiring that in trials involving an insanity defense a fourth alternative verdict form be provided: "Guilty but mentally ill." The jury is given both an insanity defense instruction and an instruction as to what lesser or different type of mental illness permits a GBMI verdict. If

a GBMI verdict is returned, the defendant is then sentenced just as if an unqualified guilty verdict had been returned. The only significance of the GBMI verdict is that the defendant is examined by psychiatrists before beginning his prison term and, if he is found to be in need of treatment, is transferred to a mental health facility.[181] If the defendant's mental illness persists, absent civil commitment he may be held only until his sentence expires; if the defendant regains his sanity he nonetheless serves the balance of his sentence.

Several commentators have questioned the constitutionality of these provisions.[182] However, GBMI statutes have been upheld against claims that they deny equal protection, violate due process and impose cruel and unusual punishment,[183] and also against the contention that the statutes are impermissibly vague in setting out two ambiguous and overlapping definitions of insanity.[184] These provisions have been praised in some quarters.

---

175. See Comment, 72 Ky.L.J. 207, 211–12 (1984), concluding that 19 states hold an instruction should not be given, that 18 others hold instruction is proper, and that another 6 hold that the judge may in his discretion either give or not give such an instruction. See also Annot., 11 A.L.R.3d 737 (1967).

176. Curry v. State, 271 Ark. 913, 611 S.W.2d 745 (1981); State v. Gratiot, 104 Idaho 782, 663 P.2d 1084 (1983); Montague v. State, 266 Ind. 51, 360 N.E.2d 181 (1977); State v. Hamann, 285 N.W.2d 180 (Iowa 1979); Payne v. Commonwealth, 623 S.W.2d 867 (Ky.1981); State v. McDonald, 89 Wn.2d 256, 571 P.2d 930 (1977).

Under this view, an exception exists "when the jury has been misinformed as to the disposition of the defendant" by the prosecutor. Johnson v. State, 265 Ind. 689, 359 N.E.2d 525 (1977). Accord: State v. Huber, 361 N.W.2d 236 (N.D.1985). Contra: Ice v. Commonwealth, 667 S.W.2d 671 (Ky.1984).

177. Another, put forward in People v. Goad, 421 Mich. 20, 364 N.W.2d 584 (1984), is that "because of the numerous possible contingencies under the statutory scheme" it would be necessary "to lead the jury through a labyrinth of complex statutory provisions."

178. 254 F.2d 725 (D.C.Cir.1957).

179. See Hermann, Assault on the Insanity Defense, 14 Rutgers L.Rev. 241, 282–91 (1983). Of course, the jury is not entitled to know the precise consequence of a guilty verdict (i.e., what sentence the judge will impose) or even the range of possibilities (i.e., what the statutory minimum and maximum penalties are). People v. Cole, 382 Mich. 695, 172 N.W.2d 354 (1969). But, the point made in the *Lyles* case is that the jury will know as a matter of common knowledge "that a verdict of not guilty means

that the prisoner goes free and that a verdict of guilty means that he is subject to such punishment as the court may impose."

180. Roberts v. State, 335 So.2d 285 (Fla.1976); Kuk v. State, 80 Nev. 291, 392 P.2d 630 (1964); Commonwealth v. Mulgrew, 475 Pa. 271, 380 A.2d 349 (1977); State v. Nuckolls, ___ W.Va. ___, 273 S.E.2d 87 (App.1980). But, failure to so instruct is not error if defendant did not request such an instruction. Commonwealth v. McCann, 503 Pa. 190, 469 A.2d 126 (1983). Moreover, the instruction need not "predict to the jury the likelihood that the defendant would not be released from custody at any future hearing." Commonwealth v. McColl, 375 Mass. 316, 376 N.E.2d 562 (1978).

181. A person found guilty but mentally ill, it has been noted, has "a much stronger right to treatment" claim than other prisoners. Comment, 74 J.Crim.L. & C. 428, 431 (1983).

182. Hermann & Sor, Convicting or Confining? Alternative Directions in Insanity Law Reform: Guilty But Mentally Ill vs. New Rules for Release of Insanity Acquittees, 1983 Brigham Young U.L.Rev. 499, 553–65; Sherman, Guilty But Mentally Ill: A Retreat from the Insanity Defense, 7 Am.J.L. & Med. 237, 256–60 (1981); Comment, 12 U.Mich.J.L.Ref. 188 (1978); Notes, 85 Dick. L.Rev. 289, 312–15 (1981); 8 Hofstra L.Rev. 973, 994–95 (1980); 21 Washburn L.J. 515, 546–51 (1982); 92 Yale L.J. 475 (1983).

183. Cooper v. State, 253 Ga. 736, 325 S.E.2d 137 (1985); People v. McLeod, 407 Mich. 632, 288 N.W.2d 909 (1980).

184. Worthy v. State, 253 Ga. 661, 324 S.E.2d 431 (1985); Taylor v. State, 440 N.E.2d 1109 (Ind.1982).

It is said, for example, that "the GBMI verdict provides a workable middle ground for fact-finders who must face the vagaries of conflicting psychiatric opinion."[185] But most of the commentary has been critical,[186] and deservedly so.

For one thing, the GBMI procedure is not a sensible way to go about achieving its purported purpose of determining which prisoners need psychiatric treatment:

> It surely makes no sense for commitment procedures to be triggered by a jury verdict based on evidence concerning the defendant's past rather than present mental condition and need for treatment. Decisions concerning the proper placement of incarcerated offenders should be made by correctional and mental health authorities, not by juries or trial judges.[187]

For another, the incidental effect of the GBMI procedure (doubtless intended by most of its proponents) is likely to be that of weakening the insanity defense [188] by working "to deceive juries into rejecting valid insanity pleas."[189] "Jurors faced with the GBMI alternative may be tempted to adopt it as a compromise verdict based on the assumption that dangerous offenders would be neutralized by incarceration, while still receiving psychiatric treatment."[190] Such an indirect attack upon the insanity defense has been condemned even by those who are not sympathetic to the defense.[191]

WESTLAW REFERENCES

lyles /12 254 +4 725 /p insan! mental*** /p verdict instruct***

---

185. Comment, 85 Dick.L.Rev. 289, 290 (1981).

186. See Hermann & Sor, supra note 182, at 543–83, also citing other sources; Hermann, Assault on the Insanity Defense, 14 Rutgers L.Rev. 241, 36–69 (1983); Morse, Excusing the Crazy: The Insanity Defense Reconsidered, 58 So.Cal.L.Rev. 777, 804 (1985); Note, 14 Rutgers L.Rev. 453 (1983).

187. Bonnie, The Moral Basis of the Insanity Defense, 69 A.B.A.J. 194 (1983).

188. Project, 16 U.Mich.J.L.Ref. 77, 80 (1982), concluded this had not occurred in Michigan—"that the statute has merely substituted a new name tag for certain defendants who, in the absence of the new statute, probably would have been found guilty"—but cautioned that this result was attributable to unique circumstances, so that

§ 4.6 Procedures Following Finding of Not Guilty by Reason of Insanity

After a finding that the defendant is not guilty by reason of insanity, he is usually committed to a mental institution for treatment. In some jurisdictions commitment is mandatory following such an acquittal, but the majority view is that commitment is to be ordered only if it is found (usually, by the trial judge) that the defendant's insanity continues or that he is dangerous. Because of limited resources and the emphasis upon security, the individual committed may receive little or no treatment. Some courts have recognized a "right to treatment" for those who have been committed.

In most jurisdictions the release decision is vested in the committing court or some other court, although often the court will not have occasion to consider the matter unless the patient or the authorities having custody of him seek release. Four different standards for release are now in use: (1) sanity; (2) lack of dangerousness; (3) sanity and lack of dangerousness; (4) sanity or lack of dangerousness. Considerable uncertainty exists as to the meaning of each standard. The burden of proof is usually placed upon the patient.

(a) Commitment. In a minority of states [1] and also in the federal courts,[2] statutes require automatic, mandatory commitment of a defendant who has been found not guilty by reason of insanity. The judge is left with absolutely no discretion; he has no authority to conduct an inquiry into the defendant's present mental condition,[3] nor can he fail to commit on the ground that the defendant was

there was "reason to believe that the GBMI verdict may have a different effect in other states."

189. Note, 57 Ind.L.J. 639, 640 (1982).

190. Hermann & Sor, supra note 182, at 566.

191. Morris, The Criminal Responsibility of the Mentally Ill, 33 Syracuse L.Rev. 477, 531 (1982), citing "the distaste of doing indirectly and clandestinely what should be done directly and openly."

§ 4.6

1. Automatic commitment is also provided for in Model Penal Code § 4.08(1).

2. 18 U.S.C.A. § 4243.

3. Gleason v. West Boylston, 136 Mass. 489 (1884).

recently declared sane in civil proceedings.[4] In all other jurisdictions, commitment is possible but not mandatory.[5] This is because of statutory provisions allowing commitment only upon a showing of grounds for such action.

There is considerable variation in the procedures and standards which have been prescribed. As to who makes the decision, virtually all states have given this responsibility to the trial judge, though a few have provided for a jury determination of this issue. The statutes vary somewhat as to the criterion for decision, but most of them are construed to mean "that the defendant must be insane and be dangerous to himself or others."[6] In some states the defendant has the burden of proving he should not be committed, but more often the burden is on the state. The state usually has to make its showing by clear and convincing evidence, but in some states the preponderance-of-the-evidence standard is followed, while in one jurisdiction the grounds for commitment must be shown beyond a reasonable doubt.

Whether mandatory commitment or discretionary commitment is the most sound procedure is a matter of debate. In favor of mandatory commitment it is argued that it "not only provides the public with the maximum immediate protection, but may also work to the advantage of mentally diseased or defective defendants by making the defense of irresponsibility more acceptable to the public and to the jury."[7] It is also said that mandatory commitment will deter spurious claims of insanity.[8] Discretionary commitment is thus criticized on the grounds that it may provide insufficient protection for society and that jurors will be reluctant to acquit on grounds of insanity.[9]

The objection to mandatory commitment is more fundamental. Under this practice, the operative assumption is that the trial of the insanity defense has established something about the defendant which justifies his being kept in custody. That is, he is treated as if the crime had been proved against him, as if he had been proved insane at the time of the crime, and as if the insanity continued to the time of disposition.

> In the mandatory commitment jurisdictions, these assumptions present difficult problems for legal theory. For one thing, there is ordinarily no explicit finding by the jury that the defendant would have been guilty of the crime but for the insanity. For another, in half the states, an acquittal by reason of insanity does not mean that the defendant was proved insane. It means only that there was a reasonable doubt on the question. Even in jurisdictions where the defendant must prove his insanity to win acquittal, the presumption of continuity is applied across the board without regard to whether the insanity was of the sort which is likely to have continued. The inflexibility of the assumption is made dramatically evident by the fact that the defendant who has just won his acquittal is presumably competent to stand trial and, therefore, at least superficially "sane."[10]

Because the mandatory commitment procedure is theoretically unsound, so the argument goes, it will appear to be punitive and for that reason have an adverse effect upon efforts to treat the individual committed.[11]

---

4. Hodison v. Rogers, 137 Kan. 950, 22 P.2d 491 (1933).

5. In practice, however, commitment usually follows. A. Goldstein, The Insanity Defense 145 (1967).

6. 2 P. Robinson, Criminal Law Defenses § 173(g) (1984). A danger to property is sometimes deemed sufficient. State v. Lafferty, 192 Conn. 571, 472 A.2d 1275 (1984). See also the discusson of the *Jones* case, text at note 14 infra.

7. Model Penal Code § 4.08, Comment at 256 (1985).

8. In re Rosenfield, 157 F.Supp. 18 (D.D.C.1957), remanded 262 F.2d 34 (D.C.Cir.1958).

9. Note, 112 U.Pa.L.Rev. 733, 746, 758 (1964). And of the various discretionary commitment procedures, that of giving this added decision to the criminal trial jury has been criticized as the "poorest and most cumbersome,"

Weihofen, Institutional Treatment of Persons Acquitted by Reason of Insanity, 38 Tex.L.Rev. 849, 850 (1960), and on the ground that the jury may be called upon to decide the matter notwithstanding the fact that no evidence of *present* mental condition was admitted. Comment, 56 Nw. U.L.Rev. 409, 439 (1961).

10. A. Goldstein, supra note 5, at 144. See also H. Weihofen, Mental Disorder as a Criminal Defense 300–01 (1954); German & Singer, Punishing the Not Guilty: Hospitalization of Persons Acquitted by Reason of Insanity, 29 Rutgers L.Rev. 1011 (1976); Comment, 56 Nw.U.L.Rev. 409, 423–24 (1961); Note, 94 Harv.L.Rev. 605 (1981).

11. "The prisoner can only view the decision to send him to the mental hospital as a sentence in a hospital in lieu of a prison. He sees the action as a means of substitute punishment and not benevolent action of a

Commitment procedures following a finding of not guilty by reason of insanity have frequently been challenged on constitutional grounds where, as is not uncommon, those procedures either involve mandatory commitment or otherwise differ from the procedures required in the civil commitment process. These challenges have only rarely succeeded,[12] and such a result is even more unlikely today [13] in light of *Jones v. United States*.[14] The defendant in that case was automatically committed following the not guilty by reason of insanity finding in his trial for attempted petit larceny, and under District of Columbia law could only obtain his release [15] by showing by a preponderance of the evidence that he was no longer mentally ill or dangerous. Relying principally on *Addington v. Texas*,[16] where the Supreme Court held that the government in a civil commitment proceeding is constitutionally required to demonstrate by clear and convincing evidence that the individual is mentally ill and dangerous, the defendant in *Jones* claimed the D.C. procedures were constitutionally defective as a matter of due process and equal protection. The Supreme Court did not agree.

The Court in *Jones* turned first to the question of whether a D.C. verdict of not guilty by reason of insanity, necessitating both (i) a finding beyond a reasonable doubt that defendant committed an act that constitutes a criminal offense and (ii) a finding by a preponderance of the evidence that defendant committed the act because of mental illness, "is sufficiently probative of mental illness and dangerousness to justify commitment." The Court declared that the first of the above two findings "certainly indicates dangerousness"

and is generally "at least as persuasive as any predictions about dangerousness that might be made in a civil-commitment proceeding." As for defendant's claim that this was not so in the present case because of the nature of the crime charged, the Court responded that dangerousness was not limited to acts of violence. The Court next concluded "that the insanity acquittal supports an inference of continuing mental illness" so as to justify automatic commitment. "It comports with common sense," said the *Jones* majority, "to conclude that someone whose mental illness was sufficient to lead him to commit a criminal act is likely to remain ill and in need of treatment."

As for the defendant's claim his commitment was unconstitutional because based on a preponderance of the evidence standard, while *Addington* had required proof by clear and convincing evidence, the Court responded that in "equating these situations, petitioner ignores important differences between the class of potential civil-commitment candidates and the class of insanity acquittees that justify differing standards of proof." For one thing, the insanity acquittee has himself advanced the insanity defense [17] and proved his mental illness, meaning "there is good reason for diminished concern as to the risk of error." For another, the proof he committed a criminal act eliminates the risk, as it was put in *Addington,* that he is being committed for mere "idiosyncratic behavior."

The final issue considered in *Jones* was whether the defendant "nonetheless is entitled to his release because he has been hospitalized for a period longer than he could have

concerned community. Thus, the basis for treatment which may be desirable or necessary is complicated by the issue of punishment and forced hospitalization." Hearings on the Constitutional Rights of the Mentally Ill Before the Subcomm. on Constitutional Rights of the Senate Comm. on the Judiciary, 87th Cong., 1st Sess., 625–26 (1961).

12. See, e.g., Bolton v. Harris, 395 F.2d 642 (D.C.Cir. 1968).

13. Stoneberg v. State, 106 Idaho 519, 681 P.2d 994 (1984); State v. Field, 118 Wis.2d 269, 347 N.W.2d 365 (1984). But see State v. Robb, 125 N.H. 581, 484 A.2d 1130 (1984) (under state due process clause, defendant

must be allowed to rebut the inference of dangerousness with such factors as evidence of his intervening behavior).

14. 463 U.S. 354, 103 S.Ct. 3043, 77 L.Ed.2d 694 (1983), also discussed in Comment, 68 Minn.L.Rev. 822 (1984); Note, 21 Houst.L.Rev. 421 (1984).

15. Absent certification of his recovery by the hospital chief of service.

16. 441 U.S. 418, 99 S.Ct. 1804, 60 L.Ed.2d 323 (1979).

17. Compare United States v. Henry, 600 F.2d 924 (D.C.Cir.1979) (automatic commitment procedures not available when insanity defense not put into the case by the defendant).

been incarcerated if convicted." As to this, the Court reasoned:

> A particular sentence of incarceration is chosen to reflect society's view of the proper response to commission of a particular criminal offense, based on a variety of considerations such as retribution, deterrence, and rehabilitation. * * * The State may punish a person convicted of a crime even if satisfied that he is unlikely to commit further crimes.

> Different considerations underlie commitment of an insanity acquittee. As he was not convicted, he may not be punished. His confinement rests on his continuing illness and dangerousness. * * * There simply is no necessary correlation between severity of the offense and length of time necessary for recovery. The length of the acquittee's hypothetical criminal sentence therefore is irrelevant to the purposes of his commitment.

Central to the *Jones* decision is the notion, as theretofore stated by some lower courts, that defendants acquitted on the basis of an insanity defense constitute an "exceptional class" [18] entitled to no hearing because their prior insanity is presumed to continue.[19] But such analysis is unsatisfactory for many reasons: (1) Where the burden of proof is on the prosecution to prove sanity,[20] the jury's verdict only means that there was a reasonable doubt as to sanity, and thus the only presumption is one of a continuing reasonable doubt.[21] (2) The presumption is only prima facie evidence and thus is rebuttable, but without a hearing there is no opportunity for rebuttal.[22] (3) The presumption continues only for a reasonable time, and thus should not be applicable when considerable time has passed since the occurrence giving rise to the criminal charge.[23] (4) The defendant was more recently found or presumed to be sane,

for otherwise he could not have been placed on trial.[24]

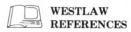
WESTLAW REFERENCES

257ak439 /p "right to treatment" (automatic! mandatory /3 commitment)

257ak439 /p discretion! /s commit!

topic(92) /p automatic mandatory /3 commit!

(b) Treatment and the "Right to Treatment". An individual who is committed following his acquittal on grounds of insanity may, nonetheless, be improperly characterized as in the "criminal insane" category and be dealt with in essentially the same way as the convicted defendant who becomes insane while serving his sentence and the charged defendant who is found incompetent to stand trial.[25] One survey showed that he would be confined in a separate ward or unit of the state mental hospital in twenty-seven states, unsegregated in the hospital in five states, held in a ward or unit of the penal institution in two states, confined in either the penal institution or state hospital in three states, and committed to a separate institution for the criminally insane in nine states.[26]

Wherever confined, he may receive little or no treatment. Most of these institutions are severely overcrowded and lack sufficient competent personnel to undertake an effective treatment program. Moreover, the administrators of these institutions find themselves confronted with the irreconcilable functions of therapy and security.

> The therapeutic ideal calls for allowing patients more and more responsibility for their own actions and judgments, with correlative diminishing restrictions and controls, which inevitably means accepting greater or less security risk. Any type of institutionalization, even in the best

---

18. Overholser v. Leach, 257 F.2d 667 (D.C.Cir.1958).

19. Ragsdale v. Overholser, 281 F.2d 943 (D.C.Cir. 1960); In re Clark, 86 Kan. 539, 121 P. 492 (1912).

20. See § 4.5(e).

21. Comment, 56 Nw.U.L.Rev. 409, 425 (1961).

22. Id. at 424.

23. Id. at 423.

24. It has been noted, id. at 419, that this is the weakest of the four contentions, in that a person could be sane under the test for competency to stand trial (see

§ 4.4) but yet insane under the test for commitment. The argument was nonetheless accepted in Long v. State, 38 Ga. 491 (1868).

25. Weihofen, Institutional Treatment of Persons Acquitted by Reason of Insanity, 38 Tex.L.Rev. 849, 850 (1960). Failure to make the distinction may be subject to challenge, at least in some respects, on equal protection grounds. See Baxstrom v. Herold, 383 U.S. 107, 86 S.Ct. 760, 15 L.Ed.2d 620 (1966).

26. Weihofen, supra note 25, at 850.

of hospitals, militates against therapy. A warmer, closer, family environment would be better. Maximum security in practice means close confinement in a cell or cell-like room, and there is little in the nature of a treatment program that can be carried on under such conditions.[27]

The conflict is usually resolved by favoring security over therapy. One reason for this is that effective therapy may appear impossible due to the rapid turnover and limited training of the professional staff. More important, perhaps, is the fear of public criticism should an insane killer or rapist escape.[28]

In recent years, increased attention has been given to the notion that an individual held in custody on grounds of insanity, particularly one committed following a finding of not guilty by reason of insanity, has a "right to treatment."[29] A leading case is *Rouse v. Cameron*,[30] in which the habeas corpus petitioner (committed upon a finding that he was not guilty by reason of insanity of carrying a dangerous weapon) objected to the district court's refusal to consider his allegation that he had received no psychiatric treatment. The court of appeals indicated that absence of treatment might render mandatory commitment unconstitutional under various theories: (1) commitment without an express finding of present insanity might violate due process if treatment were not promptly undertaken; (2) confinement longer than would have been permissible upon conviction might violate due process if no treatment was provided; (3) failure to provide treatment might constitute a denial of equal protection; and (4) indefinite

confinement without treatment may be so inhumane as to be cruel and unusual punishment. However, the right to treatment recognized by the court was based upon language in the 1964 Hospitalization of the Mentally Ill Act: "A person hospitalized in a public hospital for a mental illness shall, during his hospitalization, be entitled to medical and psychiatric care and treatment."[31]

The dimensions of the right were stated by the *Rouse* court in these terms:

> The hospital need not show that the treatment will cure or improve him but only that there is a bona fide effort to do so. This requires the hospital to show that initial and periodic inquiries are made into the needs and conditions of the patient with a view to providing suitable treatment for him, and that the program provided is suited to his particular needs.

The case was remanded for a hearing on whether petitioner was receiving adequate treatment, with instructions that if he was not the hospital should be afforded a "reasonable opportunity"[32] to initiate treatment, but the court declined "to detail the possible range of circumstances in which release would be the appropriate remedy." Elaboration is also lacking in *Youngberg v. Romero*,[33] concerning the claim of a person involuntarily committed to a state institution for the mentally retarded that he had a due process right to "habilitation." The Court did hold, however, that "the minimally adequate training required by the Constitution is such training as may be reasonable in light of respon-

---

27. Id. at 853–54.

28. Id. at 854. Moreover, because of the close confinement in separate units the facilities available to other patients may not be available. Id. at 860.

29. See Bassiouni, The Right of the Mentally Ill to Cure and Treatment: Medical Due Process, 15 DePaul L.Rev. 291 (1965); Bazelon, Implementing the Right to Treatment, 36 U.Chi.L.Rev. 742 (1969); Birnbaum, The Right to Treatment, 46 A.B.A.J. 499 (1960); Katz, The Right to Treatment—An Enchanting Legal Fiction?, 36 U.Chi.L.Rev. 755 (1969).

30. 373 F.2d 451 (D.C.Cir.1967). See also Tribby v. Cameron, 379 F.2d 104 (D.C.Cir.1967); Darnell v. Cameron, 348 F.2d 64 (D.C.Cir.1965). And, as to the defendant committed as incompetent to stand trial, see Nason v. Superintendent, 353 Mass. 604, 233 N.E.2d 908 (1968), discussed in § 4.4(b).

31. D.C.Code 1981, § 21–562.

32. The court stated: "In determining the extent to which the hospital will be given an opportunity to develop an adequate program, important considerations may be the length of time the patient has lacked adequate treatment, the length of time he has been in custody, the nature of the mental condition that caused his acquittal, and the degree of danger, resulting from the condition, that the patient would present if released." With respect to the last point, see People v. Buttes, 134 Cal.App.3d 116, 184 Cal.Rptr. 497 (1982) (inability to treat defendant's condition does not require release, as state has overriding interest in protecting the public from an insane sex offender).

33. 457 U.S. 307, 102 S.Ct. 2452, 73 L.Ed.2d 28 (1982).

dent's liberty interests in safety and freedom from unreasonable restraints."

Several commentators have expressed doubts as to whether the right to treatment concept can actually have a significant impact. It has been questioned whether many courts will be willing to recognize such a right in the face of the unavailability of sufficient medical personnel and medical health appropriations,[34] and whether legislative bodies would in any event respond with the necessary resources in light of other priorities.[35] However, litigation in the federal courts has prompted several states to overhaul their institutional mental health facilities.[36]

It has also been questioned whether the courts are in a position to define and enforce the right to treatment. Psychiatrists have objected that "the definition of treatment and the appraisal of its adequacy are matters for medical determination,"[37] while legal commentators have asserted "it would assign too great a role to litigation and to the judiciary to superintend treatment processes."[38] To this, the author of the *Rouse* decision, Judge Bazelon, has responded that courts can define and superintend treatment in the same manner that they now review other administrative action based upon special expertise.[39]

"[T]he judge must decide only whether the patient is receiving carefully chosen therapy which respectable professional opinion regards as within the range of appropriate treatment alternatives, not whether the patient is receiving the best of all possible treatment in the best of all possible mental hospitals."[40] But, as the Supreme Court cautioned in *Youngberg,* courts should not "second-guess the expert administrators on matters on which they are better informed."

WESTLAW REFERENCES

(36　+4　742) rouse　/p　"right to treatment"

(c) **Release.** In most jurisdictions, the decision whether to release a person who was committed following acquittal on grounds of insanity is vested in the committing court or some other court.[41] In some jurisdictions the matter comes up for decision as a matter of course after some period of time has passed since the commitment, while elsewhere it must be initiated by some official, usually the superintendent of the facility where the person is confined, or by the patient himself.[42] The patient may seek his release by way of a writ of habeas corpus[43] except where some similar procedure is specifically required by

---

34. Note, 42 Notre Dame Law, 573, 576 (1967).

35. Katz, supra note 37, at 781. Courts dealing with the "right to treatment" issue have generally been able to avoid a direct clash with legislative bodies by securing voluntary compliance, thus leaving unresolved the question of how compliance with a court's decree requiring additional expenditures is to be resolved when the legislature does not appropriate the necessary funds. Comment, 80 Harv.L.Rev. 1282, 1303 (1973).

36. Frug, Judicial Power of the Purse, 126 U.Pa.L.Rev. 715, 718 (1978). On the extent of court supervision of those facilities necessitated by this litigation, see Eisenberg & Yeazell, The Ordinary and Extraordinary in Institutional Litigation, 93 Harv.L.Rev. 465 (1980).

37. Council of the American Psychiatric Ass'n, Position Statement on the Question of Adequacy of Treatment, 123 Am.J.Psychiatry 1458 (1967).

38. A. Goldstein, The Insanity Defense 169 (1967). See also Notes, 80 Harv.L.Rev. 898 (1967); 77 Yale L.J. 87 (1967).

39. Bazelon, supra note 29. The analogy was pursued by the court in Tribby v. Cameron, 379 F.2d 104 (D.C. Cir.1967): "We do not suggest that the court should or can decide what particular treatment this patient requires. The court's function here resembles ours when we review

agency action. We do not decide whether the agency has made the best decision, but only make sure that it has made a permissible and reasonable decision in view of the relevant information and within a broad range of discretion."

40. Bazelon, supra note 29, at 745.

41. Jury trial is rarely required. But see State ex rel. Gebarski v. Circuit Court, 80 Wis.2d 489, 259 N.W.2d 531 (1977).

For a useful discussion of the role of the court in making this decision, see Deveau v. United States, 483 A.2d 307 (D.C.App.1984).

42. Comment, 56 Nw.U.L.Rev. 409, 449 (1961).

Model Penal Code § 4.08 provides for a court hearing upon application of the committed person or the commissioner of mental hygiene.

43. Golden, Petitioner, 341 Mass. 672, 171 N.E.2d 473 (1961) (habeas corpus available notwithstanding statutory provision that release possible only upon leave of the governor); Underwood v. People, 32 Mich. 1 (1875); In re Boyett, 136 N.C. 415, 48 S.E. 789 (1904) (habeas corpus available notwithstanding statutory requirement that hospital or penal authorities must consent to release).

statute.[44] To avoid the necessity of repeated hearings upon the same patient's claims, some jurisdictions permit challenge of the continuation of the commitment only after a specified time following the date of commitment or the time of the last hearing on the matter.[45] Such restrictions have been upheld as constitutional.[46] In a minority of jurisdictions, some other agency or person, usually the superintendent of the facility in which the patient is confined, may make the release decision.

There is disagreement on whether it is best to put the release decision (when the issue is not raised by the patient directly) in the hands of the court or in those of the administrator of the facility where the patients are confined. Some argue that the psychiatrist should be the exclusive judge of a patient's fitness for release,[47] which may be correct if it is properly assumed that only a medical question is involved.[48] However, the quality of decision-making at that level has been criticized on various grounds,[49] and at least to the extent that those criticisms are valid and in response to a practice of too liberal release practices, there is something to the notion that the judiciary must be involved to ensure that the release decision will "be made by a

politically responsible group whose concern will be for community as well as individual welfare." [50]

But since it is difficult to assess who should make the decision unless it is known what the decision involves, it is important to also consider the statutory criteria for release. The standards governing both the administrative and the judicial decisions whether to release the patient fall into four groups: (1) Is the patient sane? (2) Is the patient not dangerous? (3) Is the patient sane *and* not dangerous? (4) Is the patient sane *or* not dangerous?[51] The first of these rests upon an assumption that the basis for commitment was a therapeutic one, and the second on an assumption that commitment is a form of preventive detention.[52] The third standard serves both objectives, for an individual who has regained his sanity but is still dangerous cannot obtain release, nor can one who represents no danger if his mental illness persists.[53] The last standard is difficult to explain, for it would seem to serve neither objective adequately; the dangerous individual may be released if he has recovered his sanity, and the individual who still requires treatment to restore him to sanity may be released if he is not dangerous. Perhaps it rests upon the

---

44. Miller v. Superintendent, 198 Md. 659, 80 A.2d 898 (1951).

45. H. Weihofen, supra note 10, at 382–83. This is sound policy, as in the absence of such a restriction courts are often flooded wih repeat applications from the same patients. For example, one patient filed 50 habeas corpus petitions over a period of five years. Id. at 383.

Model Penal Code § 4.08(5) provides that the committed person may not apply for release until he has been confined for a period of not less than six months and not until at least one year has elapsed since a hearing on a previous application.

46. Application of Perkins, 165 Cal.App.2d 73, 331 P.2d 712 (1958); People v. D'Angelo, 13 Cal.2d 203, 88 P.2d 708 (1939).

47. Szasz, Civil Liberties and Mental Illness—Some Observations on the Case of Miss Edith L. Hough, 131 J. Nervous Diseases 58 (1960).

48. Note, 112 U.Pa.L.Rev. 733, 749 (1964).

49. One complaint is that the administrators are too conservative in their release decisions, either because they desire to effectuate a complete recovery or because they fear adverse publicity should a released patient thereafter commit a serious crime. A. Goldstein, supra note 38, at 152; Weihofen, Institutional Treatment of Persons Acquit-

ted by Reason of Insanity, 38 Tex.L.Rev. 847, 864 (1960); Note, 68 Yale L.J. 293, 303 (1958).

On the other hand, it is claimed that the administrators are too lenient in their release decisions, resulting in the release of dangerous persons, because of continual pressure from overcrowded facilities and shortage of trained personnel. Note, supra, at 303.

50. Note, 112 U.Pa.L.Rev. 733, 749 (1964). See also Goldstein & Katz, Dangerousness and Mental Illness, Some Observations on the Decision to Release Persons Acquitted by Reason of Insanity, 70 Yale L.J. 225, 227–30 (1960).

51. A. Goldstein, supra note 38, at 147. Model Penal Code § 4.08 follows the second position.

In about two-thirds of the states there also exist provisions for conditional release, a device which resembles parole. The tests for conditional release are stated in various ways—sometimes in terms of public safety, sometimes in terms of whether the patient is improved or whether it will serve his best interests. A. Goldstein, supra note 38, at 150. Model Penal Code § 4.08 provides for conditional release.

52. A. Goldstein, supra note 38, at 148.

53. Id. at 150.

assumption that a sane person will not be dangerous while an insane person is assumed to be if he cannot prove to the contrary, and that only a person who is both dangerous and insane can justifiably be subjected to continued confinement.[54]

The meaning of the critical words "sane" and "dangerous" in this context is somewhat obscure. As to the former, the applicable statutes differ considerably. They may put the issue in terms of whether the patient is no longer mentally ill, whether he is cured, whether he is restored to sanity, whether he is entirely and permanently recovered, whether he has recovered sufficiently to be released, whether a recurrence of insanity is improbable, or simply whether he is sane.[55] The critical terms are undefined, and thus "they are usually broad enough to allow administrators free rein in the first instance and to give reviewing courts little guidance."[56]

The dangerousness test is most often stated in terms of whether continued detention is necessary for the safety of the patient or the public,[57] but this is also ambiguous.

> Dangerous behavior might be construed to include: (1) only the crime for which the insanity defense was successfully raised; (2) all crimes; (3) only felonious crimes (as opposed to misdemeanors); (4) only crimes for which a given maximum sentence or more is authorized; (5) only crimes categorized as violent; (6) only crimes categorized as harmful, physical or psychological, reparable or irreparable, to the victim; (7) any conduct, even if not labelled criminal, categorized as violent, harmful or threatening; (8) any conduct which may provoke violent retaliatory acts; (9) any physical violence toward oneself; (10) any combination of these.[58]

It is clear that the choice which is made among these alternatives can have a very substantial impact upon release policies, par-

ticularly in those jurisdictions where automatic commitment follows acquittal on the basis of a broadly-stated definition of insanity. Under such circumstances, it may happen that the only "danger" is that the patient will again engage in conduct of a nonviolent nature. Although it has been questioned whether confinement can be justified under those circumstances,[59] release was denied upon such facts in *Overholser v. Russell*,[60] where apparently the only risk was that the patient might again write bad checks (the crime for which he was found not guilty by reason of insanity):

> The danger to the public need not be possible physical violence or a crime of violence. It is enough if there is competent evidence that he may commit any criminal act, for any such act will injure others and will expose the person to arrest, trial and conviction. There is always the additional possible danger—not to be discounted even if remote—that a nonviolent criminal act may expose the perpetrator to violent retaliatory acts by the victim of the crime.

As noted earlier,[61] the Supreme Court has recently adopted this position.[62]

The most debated issue concerning the tests for release is whether the sane but dangerous patient should be entitled to release. No, says the Model Penal Code,[63] and this position is explained in this way:

> It seemed preferable to the Institute to make dangerousness the criterion for continued custody, rather than to provide that the committed person may be discharged or released when restored to sanity as defined by the mental hygiene laws. Although his mental disease may have greatly improved, such a person may still be dangerous because of factors in his personality and background other than mental disease. Also, such a standard provides a means for the control of the occasional defendant who may be quite dangerous but who successfully feigned mental disease to gain an acquittal.[64]

---

54. Ibid.

55. Id. at 147.

56. Id. at 148.

57. Ibid.

58. Goldstein & Katz, supra note 50, at 235.

59. Ragsdale v. Overholser, 281 F.2d 943 (D.C.Cir.1960) (Fahy, J., conc.).

60. 283 F.2d 195 (D.C.Cir.1960).

61. See § 4.6(a).

62. Jones v. United States, 463 U.S. 354, 103 S.Ct. 3043, 77 L.Ed.2d 694 (1983), where the charge was attempted shoplifting.

63. Model Penal Code § 4.08(2).

64. Model Penal Code § 4.08, Comment at 259–60 (1985).

In response, it is argued that

> to hold a patient solely for potential dangerousness would snap the thin line between detention for therapy and detention for retribution. * * * Not to release such persons would in effect be to equate an undefined "dangerousness" with an undefined mental illness. Since there can be no such equation, a decision not to release solely on the basis of *potential* dangerousness would be like a decision not to discharge a tubercular patient—though no longer infectious—because he is a potential killer or checkforger.[65]

In most jurisdictions the burden of proof is on the patient, in habeas corpus or other statutory proceedings for release, to persuade the court that he meets the statutory criteria and is thus entitled to release. Sometimes the burden is a preponderance of the evidence, and sometimes it is clear and convincing evidence.[66] But in either event the burden will often be an insurmountable one. This is particularly so when his petition for release is opposed by the authoritative judgment of the hospital staff.[67] He may be no more successful, however, even when his application has the full support of the hospital authorities, for courts are often skeptical of the ability of mental health professionals to determine whether the individual is no longer dangerous.[68]

WESTLAW REFERENCES

257ak440 /p decision /s court judge judicial legal

65. Goldstein & Katz, supra note 50, at 237.

66. Under 18 U.S.C.A. § 4243(d), the person found not guilty by reason of insanity has the burden of proof "by a preponderance of the evidence," except that if the offense was one "involving bodily injury to, or serious danger to the property of, another person, or involving a substantial risk of such injury or damage," then the burden of proof is "by clear and convincing evidence."

67. Weihofen, Institutional Treatment of Persons Acquitted by Reason of Insanity, 38 Tex.L.Rev. 847, 866 (1960).

68. Taylor v. Commissioner, 481 A.2d 139 (Me.1984).

§ 4.7

1. 1 P. Robinson, Criminal Law Defenses § 64 (1984); Arenella, The Diminished Capacity and Diminished Responsibility Defenses: Two Children of a Doomed Marriage, 77 Colum.L.Rev. 827 (1977); Dix, Psychological Abnormality as a Factor in Grading Criminal Liability: Diminished Capacity, Diminished Responsibility, and the

257ak440 /p standard criteria eligib! /4 release discharge

257ak440 /p burden /2 proof proving

§ 4.7 Partial Responsibility

A defendant in a criminal case, at the time he engaged in the conduct giving rise to the charges against him, may have been suffering from an abnormal mental condition which was not of a kind or character to afford him a successful insanity defense under the right-wrong test or other standard applicable in that jurisdiction. But, while this defendant is therefore ineligible for a finding of not guilty by reason of insanity, his mental abnormality may nonetheless be a most relevant consideration in the determination of whether he is guilty of the crime charged. Under the doctrine referred to as partial responsibility, diminished responsibility, or (somewhat less accurately) partial insanity,[1] recognized in some but not all jurisdictions,[2] evidence concerning the defendant's mental condition is admissible on the question of whether the defendant had the mental state which is an element of the offense with which he is charged.

Such evidence has been most frequently received in cases requiring a determination whether the defendant acted with the premeditation and deliberation required for first degree murder. In at least some jurisdictions, however, this evidence has been held admissible on the issue of whether the defendant's

Like, 62 J.Crim.L.C. & P.S. 313 (1971); Keedy, A Problem of First Degree Murder: Fisher v. U.S., 90 U.Pa.L.Rev. 267 (1950); Lewin, Psychiatric Evidence in Criminal Cases for Purposes Other Than the Defense of Insanity, 26 Syracuse L.Rev. 1051 (1975); Taylor, Partial Insanity as Affecting the Degree of Crime—A Commentary on Fisher v. U.S., 34 Calif.L.Rev. 625 (1946); Weihofen & Overholser, Mental Disorder Affecting the Degree of the Crime, 56 Yale L.J. 959 (1947); Comments, 16 Rutgers L.Rev. 174 (1961); 33 Tex.L.Rev. 492 (1955); 18 U.C.L.A.L.Rev. 561 (1971); Notes, 46 Colum.L.Rev. 1005 (1946); 43 Cornell L.Q. 283 (1957); 41 Ky.L.J. 232 (1953); 20 So.Cal.L.Rev. 95 (1946); Annots., 16 A.L.R.4th 666 (1982); 22 A.L.R.3d 1228 (1968).

2. Lewin, supra note 1, at 1055 states that "today less than 25 states and federal jurisdictions have approved the doctrine." It has more recently been asserted that enthusiasm for the doctrine is on the wane. State v. Wilcox, 70 Ohio St.2d 182, 436 N.E.2d 523 (1982). On statutory recognition of the doctrine, see note 57 infra.

crime is murder or manslaughter and the issue of whether the defendant had the requisite mental state for other lesser offenses.

(a) Distinguished From Insanity Defense.

It must be emphasized that the notion of partial responsibility is quite separate and distinct from the defense of insanity. If a successful insanity defense is interposed, the result is a finding of not guilty by reason of insanity [3] and, usually, commitment of the defendant.[4] By contrast, an appropriate showing of partial responsibility will result in a finding of not guilty of the offense charged, although the circumstances will usually be such that conviction of some lesser offense is still possible. The ultimate result, then, is not commitment but rather a sentence of imprisonment following conviction of an offense carrying lesser penalties than the crime originally charged.

The distinction between partial responsibility and the defense of insanity is sometimes important for other reasons as well. Thus, for example, failure to give advance notice, to enter a special plea, or to take other steps required only to preserve an insanity defense [5] would not bar the introduction of evidence to show partial responsibility.[6] And, in those jurisdictions utilizing the bifurcated trial procedure, where the insanity defense is held in abeyance until the second stage of the trial following determination of the general guilt of the defendant,[7] evidence of partial repsonsibility is admissible at the first stage of the trial and only the first stage.[8]

In those jurisdictions which have rejected the doctrine of partial responsibility,[9] the rejection has usually occurred as a result of a mistaken assumption that the doctrine does not involve considerations separate and distinct from established law concerning the defense of insanity. Insanity is viewed as an all-or-nothing proposition, so that the defendant must either establish his insanity as a complete defense or else be held fully responsible for the crime charged. The insanity defense is considered to be the only means by which evidence of defendant's abnormal mental condition may be admitted, apparently on the erroneous conclusion that a defendant who did know right from wrong (or, who otherwise fails to establish a complete defense of insanity) must thereby have possessed the requisite mental state for the crime charged.[10]

On the other hand, those jurisdictions which have accepted the notion that evidence of an abnormal mental condition may be considered on the issue whether the defendant had the mental state required for the offense charged [11] have typically done so by emphasizing the difference between partial responsibility and the insanity defense. Because the various tests for insanity as a defense do not of necessity require a determination of defendant's ability to have the specific mental state defined for the offense charged,[12] there is no inconsistency in the conclusion that a defendant undeserving of a finding of not guilty by reason of insanity might nonetheless have lacked that mental state. For example, if such a defendant is charged with first degree

---

3. See § 4.5(h).

4. See § 4.6. As noted later, a tactical decision may be made by the defendant to defend by claiming partial responsibility rather than by interposing an insanity defense, in order to thereby avoid the risk of an indeterminate commitment.

5. See § 4.5(b).

6. But there has been some movement toward broadening notice provisions to cover all instances in which the defendant intends to introduce expert testimony on his mental condition. See, e.g., Fed.R.Crim.P. 12.2(b), and the provisions discussed in People v. Mangiapane, 85 Mich. App. 379, 271 N.W.2d 240 (1978); and State v. Schleigh, 210 Or. 155, 310 P.2d 341 (1957). This development is a most desirable one. See Note, 1979 Wis.L.Rev. 628, 647–49.

7. See § 4.5(g).

8. People v. Wetmore, 22 Cal.3d 318, 149 Cal.Rptr. 265, 583 P.2d 1308 (1978); People v. Wells, 33 Cal.2d 330, 202 P.2d 53 (1949).

9. See cases collected in Annot., 22 A.L.R.3d 1228, 1235 (1968).

10. E.g., Johnson v. State, 292 Md. 405, 439 A.2d 542 (1982); State v. Bouwman, 328 N.W.2d 703 (Minn.1982); State v. Holloway, 156 Mo. 222, 56 S.W. 734 (1900); State v. Flint, 142 W.Va. 509, 96 S.E.2d 677 (1957); Dean v. State, 668 P.2d 639 (Wyo.1983).

11. See cases collected in Annot., 22 A.L.R.3d 1228, 1239 (1968).

12. On this distinction, see § 4.1.

murder, thus calling for the prosecution to prove that the killing was committed with premeditation and deliberation,[13] evidence tending to show that the defendant did not premeditate or deliberate because of a mental abnormality remains most relevant.[14] Or, if such a defendant is charged with manslaughter of the recklessness type, thus calling for the prosecution to show defendant was consciously aware of the risk of death,[15] evidence tending to show that defendant was unaware because of some mental abnormality would again be most relevant.[16]

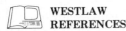

WESTLAW REFERENCES

di diminished responsibility doctrine

(b) Specific Applications. The majority of the courts which have held evidence of an abnormal mental condition admissible on the issue of mental state have been concerned with the admission of this evidence for the purpose of negating the premeditation or deliberation requisite to first degree murder. A considerably lesser number have held the evidence admissible to negate the existence of malice aforethought and thereby reduce a charge of murder to manslaughter, undoubtedly because there exists much doubt about the relevancy of subjective factors in drawing

the line between those two crimes. Finally, in a few instances the doctrine of partial responsibility has also been applied where the question was whether the defendant had the requisite mental state to be convicted of any crime.

(1) First or Second Degree Murder. In many states murder is divided into two degrees, the purpose being to limit the applicability of the more severe sanction (usually the death penalty) to only certain kinds of murder. One form of first degree murder is intent-to-kill murder accompanied by premeditation and deliberation. In the absence of premeditation and deliberation, intent-to-kill murder constitutes murder in the second degree.[17] Deliberation requires a cool mind that is capable of reflection,[18] while premeditation requires that the one with the cool mind did reflect—at least briefly—before his act of killing.

Given the obviously subjective character of the premeditation and deliberation requirements, it is perhaps not surprising that many courts have adopted the partial responsibility doctrine in cases involving a prosecution for first degree murder.[19] It has been noted, for example, that it would be grossly inconsistent to receive evidence of voluntary intoxication

---

13. See § 7.7(a).

14. State v. DiPaolo, 34 N.J. 279, 168 A.2d 401 (1961).

Indeed, the cause of defendant's lack of premeditation and deliberation might be some condition which is not a "mental disease or defect," as that term is used in the context of the insanity defense. Thus, it has been suggested that PMS (the premenstrual syndrome) might be a basis for a partial responsibility defense, especially on the issue of premeditation and deliberation. See Taylor & Dalton, Premenstrual Syndrome: A New Criminal Defense?, 19 Cal.W.L.Rev. 269, 283 (1983); Note, 1983 Duke L.J. 176, 178.

15. See § 7.12(a).

16. State v. Burge, 195 Conn. 232, 487 A.2d 532 (1985).

17. See § 7.7.

18. State v. Bowser, 214 N.C. 249, 199 S.E. 31 (1938).

19. E.g., People v. Goedecke, 65 Cal.2d 850, 56 Cal. Rptr. 625, 423 P.2d 777 (1967); Battalino v. People, 118 Colo. 587, 199 P.2d 897 (1948); State v. Donahue, 141 Conn. 656, 109 A.2d 364 (1954); Gurganus v. State, 451 So. 2d 817 (Fla.1984); State v. Santiago, 55 Haw. 162, 516 P.2d 1256 (1973); State v. Hood, 346 N.W.2d 481 (Iowa

1984); Commonwealth v. Prendergast, 385 Mass. 625, 433 N.E.2d 438 (1982); State v. Anderson, 515 S.W.2d 534 (Mo. 1974); Starkweather v. State, 167 Neb. 477, 93 N.W.2d 619 (1958); Fox v. State, 73 Nev. 241, 316 P.2d 924 (1957); State v. Vigliano, 43 N.J. 44, 202 A.2d 657 (1964); State v. Padilla, 66 N.M. 289, 347 P.2d 312 (1959); People v. Moran, 249 N.Y. 179, 163 N.E. 553 (1928); State v. Cooper, 286 N.C. 549, 213 S.E.2d 305 (1975); State v. Wallace, 170 Or. 60, 131 P.2d 222 (1942); State v. Fenik, 45 R.I. 309, 121 A. 218 (1923); Commonwealth v. Walzack, 468 Pa. 210, 360 A.2d 914 (1976); Dejarnette v. Commonwealth, 75 Va. 867 (1881); Hempton v. State, 111 Wis. 127, 86 N.W. 596 (1901); State v. Pressler, 16 Wyo. 214, 92 P. 806 (1907).

The leading case to the contrary is Fisher v. United States, 328 U.S. 463, 66 S.Ct. 1318, 90 L.Ed. 1382 (1946), interpreting the law in the District of Columbia. The Court mistakenly concluded that evidence of mental deficiencies was not admissible on the degree-of-murder issue, erroneously assuming that the rule must be the same as in earlier cases holding such evidence inadmissible on the murder-versus-manslaughter issue. *Fisher* was viewed as lacking current vitality in United States v. Brawner, 471 F.2d 969 (D.C.Cir.1972).

to disprove premeditation and deliberation,[20] and then not accept evidence of an involuntary mental condition for the same purpose.[21]

Moreover, given the fact that the premeditation and deliberation requirements are usually relevant to the critical question of which murderers may be subjected to the death penalty, it is clear that the doctrine of partial responsibility is particularly applicable here.

A heavier sanction accompanies premeditated murder, not because of the act of murder but because of the mental processes which accompany it. If the objective of this heavier sanction be deterrence, it is doubtful that a person *incapable* of premeditation and deliberation will be dissuaded from committing a premeditated murder by the higher penalty imposed for murder accompanied by these mental processes. Nor is a "fully responsible" person likely to be deterred because those who are incapable of premeditation also face the same punishment. If this differential treatment reflects a community attitude that "cold-blooded" murder is somehow more culpable than killing which springs from momentary impulses, these traditional notions are actually undermined by inflicting the penalty reserved for the "cold-blooded" on those capable only of the impulse.[22]

(2) Murder or Manslaughter. In most jurisdictions, voluntary manslaughter consists of an intentional homicide committed under certain extenuating circumstances, namely, that the defendant, when he killed the victim, was in a state of passion engendered in him by an adequate provocation (i.e., a provocation which would cause a reasonable man to lose his normal self-control).[23] It is important to note, for purposes of comparison with the

preceding discussion, that "the murder-manslaughter distinction has a wholly different history and is based on wholly different criteria from those involved in distinguishing degrees of murder. The former is of common law origin, the latter statutory; the former involves an objective test, the latter subjective." [24]

Under the traditional doctrine, then, heat-of-passion voluntary manslaughter is distinguishable from murder by resort to objective criteria. True, the defendant must have in fact been provoked and his passion must have in fact not "cooled" at the time of the killing, but in addition the circumstances must have been such that a reasonable man would have been provoked and would not have cooled.[25] This being the case, it is apparent that the concept of partial responsibility has no place in the decision whether what has been charged as murder is actually heat-of-passion voluntary manslaughter. To hold otherwise would conflict with the reasonable man standard, which by its very nature presumes a person without serious mental and emotional defects.[26]

There is a modern tendency, not yet far advanced, to add other extenuating circumstances in the category of voluntary manslaughter. For example, while a reasonable belief in the existence of circumstances requiring the use of deadly force is necessary for complete exoneration under an affirmative defense such as self-defense,[27] there is some authority that an "imperfect" defense (in the sense that the belief was not reasonable) will downgrade what would otherwise be

20. Such evidence is clearly admissible for this purpose. See, e.g., Hopt v. Utah, 104 U.S. 631, 26 L.Ed. 873 (1881).

21. "The law is not the creation of such barbarous and insensible animal nature as to extend a more lenient legal rule to the case of a drunkard, whose mental faculties are disturbed by his own will and conduct, than to the case of a poor demented creature afflicted by the hand of God." State v. Noel, 102 N.J.L. 659, 133 A. 274 (1926).

22. F. Lindman & D. McIntyre, The Mentally Disabled and the Law 356 (1961).

23. See § 7.10.

24. Weihofen & Overholser, supra note 1, at 969.

25. See § 7.10.

26. United States v. Brawner, 471 F.2d 969 (D.C.Cir. 1972); State v. McAllister, 41 N.J. 342, 196 A.2d 786 (1964). Taylor v. State, 452 So.2d 441 (Miss.1984); State v. Klimas, 94 Wis.2d 288, 288 N.W.2d 157 (App.1979). There are a few cases to the contrary, e.g., Fisher v. People, 23 Ill. 283 (1859); Davis v. State, 161 Tenn. 23, 28 S.W.2d 993 (1930); State v. Green, 78 Utah 580, 6 P.2d 177 (1931), but none of them includes a careful consideration of the significance of the holding as it relates to the long-standing objective standards applied to heat-of-passion voluntary manslaughter. The California rule, discussed infra, is not contrary, as it rests upon a conclusion that there are other kinds of manslaughter included within the applicable statute.

27. See § 5.7.

murder to voluntary manslaughter.[28] In those jurisdictions recognizing the "imperfect" defense type of voluntary manslaughter, it would be appropriate to introduce evidence of the defendant's abnormal mental condition as bearing on the question of whether he unreasonably believed that defensive measures involving deadly force were called for.[29]

It is well to keep in mind that we are here concerned with the dividing line between murder and manslaughter and that the traditional distinction between the two crimes is that murder is a killing "with malice aforethought." That phrase, however, has not been given its literal meaning.[30] Thus, it is more meaningful to say that a killing is murder if done (1) with intent to kill,[31] (2) with intent to do serious bodily harm,[32] (3) with a depraved heart (i.e., extremely negligent conduct),[33] or (4) in the commission or attempted commission of a felony,[34] subject to the qualification that an intentional homicide is only manslaughter if the killing occurred in a heat of passion (objective test) or, perhaps, in an "imperfect" defense. If this prevailing meaning of "malice aforethought" is accepted, then, as noted above, the only occasion for receiving evidence of the defendant's abnormal mental condition on the issue of malice aforethought will be when the evidence relates to a claim that the defendant believed (albeit unreasonably) that defensive deadly force was required.[35]

Evidence of the defendant's mental condition as it relates to the murder versus manslaughter issue was not so limited in California,[36] but this can only be explained on the ground that the California courts had adopted a somewhat unusual definition of malice aforethought, as explained in *People v. Conley.*[37] Conley was charged with murder because he shot and killed both a woman with whom he had been romantically involved and her husband. A defense psychiatrist testified that the defendant "was in a dissociative state at the time of the killings and because of personality fragmentation did not function with his normal personality." The trial judge refused to instruct on manslaughter, and on appeal it was held that this was prejudicial error because that testimony raised a doubt as to whether the defendant killed with malice aforethought.

Noting that manslaughter was defined by statute as "the unlawful killing of a human being without malice,"[38] the *Conley* court first concluded that the language of the statute did not require the conclusion that malice could be negated only by the usual provocation formula.[39] The court then proceeded to identify another kind of mitigating circumstance which would make the defendant's crime only manslaughter: "If because of mental defect, disease, or intoxication, * * * the defendant is unable to comprehend his duty to govern his actions in accord with the duty imposed by law, he does not act

28. See § 7.11.

29. Similar analysis was utilized in People v. Wells, 33 Cal.2d 330, 202 P.2d 53 (1949), involving an unusual statute making an assault committed by a life-term prisoner "with malice aforethought" a capital offense. The court held that evidence of the defendant's abnormal mental condition would be admissible to show that the defendant attacked the victim out of an unreasonable fear for his own safety, for such an attack would not be "with malice aforethought."

30. See § 7.1(a).

31. See § 7.2.

32. See § 7.3.

33. See § 7.4.

34. See § 7.5.

35. Unless, of course, the objective test is abandoned in the heat-of-passion cases, as a few courts seem to have done without careful consideration of the matter. See note 26 supra.

36. The partial responsibility doctrine has more recently been "abolished" in that state. West's Ann.Cal. Penal Code § 25. (This statute was brought about as a part of a sweeping reform of California criminal justice by a referendum measure, Proposition 8, denominated "the Victims' Bill of Rights." See Comment, 71 Calif.L.Rev. 1197 (1983).) However, the abolition in § 25 concerns only admitting evidence of mental illness and the like "to show or negate capacity to form the particular * * * mental state required"; per § 28 such evidence is admissible "solely on the issue of whether or not the accused actually formed the required specific intent, premeditated, deliberated, or harbored malice aforethought."

37. 64 Cal.2d 310, 40 Cal.Rptr. 815, 411 P.2d 911 (1966).

38. West's Ann.Cal.Penal Code § 192.

39. The other theretofore recognized mitigating circumstance, an "imperfect" defense, was not mentioned by the court and clearly was not present in the case.

with malice aforethought and cannot be guilty of murder * * *."

As is made even more apparent by the *Conley* court's repeated references to their earlier decision in *People v. Gorshen*,[40] this added mitigating circumstance concerns an absence of self-control such as would likely afford a complete insanity defense under any of the extant insanity tests except *M'Naghten*.[41] The *Conley* rule, then, can best be understood as a limited measure for taking account of a defendant's inability to conform his conduct to the requirements of law, adopted in a jurisdiction where *M'Naghten* was the sole test for insanity, and where departure from *M'Naghten* was believed to be a matter for the legislature.[42]

(3) Crime or No Crime. The term partial responsibility may be misleading, for it suggests that it involves a doctrine under which a defendant is partially responsible for the commission of some offense.[43] This, of course, is not true. If the defendant's mental condition was such that he did not premeditate and deliberate, then there is *no* responsibility for first degree murder but *full* responsibility for second degree murder.[44] Likewise, if it was such that he killed without malice aforethought, then there is *no* responsibility for murder but *full* responsibility for manslaughter. This suggests, of course, that there may

be instances in which the doctrine of partial responsibility might be applied so as to result in a complete acquittal, in that there is no lesser offense as to which the defendant possesses the requisite mental state.

This might even occur on a charge of murder. In *People v. Gorshen*,[45] for example, the defense psychiatrist testified that the defendant's abnormal mental condition was such that his act of killing was not intentional. The trial judge acknowledged that if he accepted the psychiatrist's testimony in toto he should acquit the defendant, and the defendant claimed on appeal from the judge's finding of guilty of murder in the second degree that he should have been acquitted.[46] Certainly conviction of voluntary manslaughter would not have been appropriate if the psychiatrist's testimony had been accepted, for voluntary manslaughter has always been defined as an *intentional* homicide under certain extenuating circumstances.[47]

The possibility of complete acquittal may be even greater as to charges outside the homicide area, for there will often be no lesser offense which remains proved in the face of evidence of defendant's abnormal mental condition.[48] Such a result could be anticipated, for example, if the evidence raised a reasonable doubt of defendant's intent to steal in a larceny case[49] or robbery case,[50] intent to

---

40. 51 Cal.2d 716, 336 P.2d 492 (1959). In *Gorshen* the defense psychiatrist testified that defendant could not have controlled his conduct even if there had been a policeman at his elbow, and the court asserted that such testimony was admissible to show "uncontrollable compulsion" similar to that which would establish an irresistible impulse insanity defense in jurisdictions (not including California) which had adopted that test of insanity.

41. See §§ 4.2, 4.3 on the other tests.

42. People v. Berry, 44 Cal.2d 426, 282 P.2d 861 (1955); People v. Daugherty, 40 Cal.2d 876, 256 P.2d 911 (1953).

43. Lewin, supra note 1, at 1060.

44. Taylor, supra note 1, at 630 n. 17.

45. 51 Cal.2d 716, 336 P.2d 492 (1959).

46. The appellate court did not dispute the defendant's analysis, but affirmed on the ground that the trial judge could have found no reasonable doubt that defendant intended to kill.

47. See §§ 7.10, 7.11. Query, however, if evidence of an abnormal mental condition, interposed other than for an insanity defense, could defeat a charge of depraved-heart murder or criminal-negligence involuntary man-

slaughter, at least where those crimes are defined by objective standards. See §§ 7.4, 7.12; and consider State v. Burge, 195 Conn. 232, 487 A.2d 532 (1985) (in reckless manslaughter prosecution, evidence on mental incapacity admissible to show absence of requisite awareness and conscious disregard of risk); Robinson v. Commonwealth, 569 S.W.2d 183 (Ky.App.1978) (in reckless homicide prosecution it error to exclude evidence of defendant's diminished capacity, as defendant not reckless if failure to perceive danger was due to mental incapacity). Compare State v. Baker, ___ Haw. ___, 691 P.2d 1166 (1984) (diminished capacity defense not available on charge of manslaughter by recklessness).

48. There is less likely to be a lesser offense of the negligence type. Compare the situation as to homicide, discussed in note 47 supra.

49. People v. Colavecchio, 11 App.Div.2d 161, 202 N.Y.S.2d 119 (1960); State v. Booth, 284 Or. 615, 588 P.2d 614 (1978).

50. People v. Wilson, 261 Cal.App.2d 12, 67 Cal.Rptr. 678 (1968); People v. Chapman, 261 Cal.App.2d 149, 67 Cal.Rptr. 601 (1968).

commit a crime within the dwelling in a burglary case,[51] intent to escape in a felonious escape case,[52] or the requisite knowledge in an income tax evasion case.[53] Some courts have nonetheless applied the partial responsibility doctrine to offenses other than homcide,[54] at least if the offense is of the specific intent variety.[55]

WESTLAW REFERENCES

partial diminished /2 responsibility insanity /p murder /s first second /2 degree

manslaughter /p partial diminished /2 responsibility insanity

(c) Policy Considerations. The logic of the partial responsibility doctrine would seem to be unassailable. The reception of evidence of the defendant's abnormal mental condition, totally apart from the defense of insanity, is certainly appropriate whenever that evidence is relevant to the issue of whether he had the

mental state which is a necessary element of the crime charged.[56] Were it otherwise, major crimes specifically requiring a certain bad state of mind would, in effect, be strict liability offenses as applied to abnormal defendants.[57]

Opposition to the doctrine has been based more upon what are thought to be practical difficulties in its use.[58] It is claimed, for example, that juries are ill equipped to handle psychiatric testimony which makes subtle distinctions, such as that a defendant's mental impairment prevented him from premeditating and deliberating but not from having an intent to kill.[59] This difficulty, some say, stems not from the partial responsibility doctrine but rather from the fact that in some jurisdictions the distinction between first and second degree murder has not been made sufficiently clear.[60] But others seriously question the trustworthiness and reliability of psychiatric testimony on the mental state issue,[61]

51. People v. Taylor, 220 Cal.App.2d 212, 33 Cal.Rptr. 654 (1963).

52. Schwickrath v. People, 159 Colo. 390, 411 P.2d 961 (1966).

53. Rhodes v. United States, 282 F.2d 59 (4th Cir.1960).

54. See, in addition to cases previously cited, Hensel v. State, 604 P.2d 222 (Alaska 1979) (receiving stolen property); Bimbow v. State, 161 Ind.App. 338, 315 N.E.2d 738 (1974) (assault with intent to kill); State v. Barney, 244 N.W.2d 316 (Iowa 1976) (assault with intent to murder); State v. Dargatz, 228 Kan. 322, 614 P.2d 430 (1980) (incitement to riot); State v. Miller, 677 P.2d 1129 (Utah 1984) (conspiracy); State v. Conklin, 79 Wn.2d 805, 489 P.2d 1130 (1971) (forgery). Contra: Stamper v. Commonwealth, 228 Va. 707, 324 S.E.2d 682 (1985) (possession of drugs with intent to distribute).

55. Compare United States v. Busic, 592 F.2d 13 (2d Cir.1978) (partial responsibility doctrine not applicable to crime of aircraft piracy, as it a general intent crime); State v. Huber, 356 N.W.2d 468 (S.D.1984) (doctrine not applicable to general intent crimes of resisting arrest and assault); with Hendershott v. People, 653 P.2d 385 (Colo. 1982) (partial responsibility doctrine applicable to crime of assault even though it not a specific intent crime). See Comment, 71 Calif.L.Rev. 1197, 1208–10 (1983), arguing that limiting the partial responsibility doctrine to specific intent crimes is unprincipled and unconstitutional.

56. As stated in United States v. Brawner, 471 F.2d 969 (D.C.Cir.1972): "Neither logic nor justice can tolerate a jurisprudence that defines the elements of an offense as requiring a mental state such that one defendant can properly argue that his voluntary drunkenness removed his capacity to form the specific intent but another defendant is inhibited from a submission of his contention that an abnormal mental condition, for which he was in no

way responsible, negated his capacity to form a particular specific intent, even though the condition did not exonerate him from all criminal responsibility."

57. See Model Penal Code § 4.02, Comment (Tent. Draft No. 4, 1955). Model Penal Code § 4.02(1) provides that evidence the defendant suffered from a mental disease or defect is admissible whenever relevant to prove he did or did not have a state of mind which is an element of the offense. But less than a third of the modern recodifications contain a provision along these lines.

58. For an excellent summary of the arguments pro and con, see S. Brakel & R. Rock, The Mentally Disabled and the Law 392–96 (1971); and Lewin, supra note 1, at 1089–99.

59. Wahrlich v. Arizona, 479 F.2d 1137 (9th Cir.1973); State v. Bouwman, 328 N.W.2d 703 (Minn.1982); State v. Wilcox, 70 Ohio St.2d 182, 436 N.E.2d 523 (1982); Commonwealth v. Hollinger, 190 Pa. 155, 42 A. 548 (1899); Note, 43 Cornell L.Q. 283, 284 (1957).

60. Weihofen & Overholser, supra note 1, at 974.

61. Bethea v. United States, 365 A.2d 64 (D.C.App. 1976) (concluding that "the notion of partial or relative insanity," unlike other recognized incapacitating circumstances, is not "susceptible to quantification or objective demonstration" or "to lay understanding").

The problems which exist here are most helpfully elaborated upon in Note, 1979 Wis.L.Rev. 628, which concludes at 659: "Serious questions have been raised, however, about the relevancy and competency of psychiatric testimony on the issue. Of critical concern, for instance, are those questioning the lack of diagnostic agreement among psychiatrists, potential psychiatric bias, the difficulty of determining a past state of mind, and the disproportionate weight given to psychiatric testimony. Serious doubts

especially in light of the "marked propensity of those who purport to have psychiatric expertise to tailor their testimony to the particular client whom they represent." [62] It has been suggested, however, that this problem may be solved through "careful administration by the trial judge," who should ordinarily "require counsel first to make a proffer of the proof to be adduced outside the presence of the jury" and "then determine whether the testimony is grounded in sufficient scientific support to warrant use in the courtroom, and whether it would aid the jury in reaching a decision on the ultimate issues." [63]

Another argument is that the doctrine will result in compromise verdicts—that a jury divided on the sufficiency of an insanity defense may agree upon the middle ground of partial responsibility and conviction for a lesser offense.[64] In response, it has been noted that many opportunities for compromise already exist [65] and that compromise is not necessarily wrong when it is the only way to the quantum of punishment appropriate under the circumstances.[66]

about the ability of many psychiatrists to handle legal issues raise the possibility of uninformed and uninformative testimony being presented to a trier of fact which has come to place great reliance on the medical profession."

One way to try to deal with this problem, reflected in a 1985 amendment to West's Ann. Cal.Penal Code § 29, is to allow the expert to testify about the defendant's mental illness, defect or disorder but not to testify directly on whether the defendant did or did not have the mental state required by the offense charged. Also, such evidence may be received only on the question of whether defendant had the requisite mental state, not as to his capacity to form such mental state. See note 36 supra.

62. Steele v. State, 97 Wis.2d 72, 294 N.W.2d 2 (1980).

63. United States v. Brawner, 471 F.2d 969 (D.C.Cir. 1972). See also Arenella, supra note 1 (suggesting at 830 that the problem is that courts in some jurisdictions admit "any evidence showing that the defendant was less capable than a normal person of entertaining the relevant mental state," and proposing at 863 that the solution is to admit "evidence only of some consciously entertained thought or emotion which directly negates or confirms the requisite state of mind. If trial judges understand how rare these cases are and reject all psychiatric testimony that evaluates a defendant's general capacity to entertain the requisite state of mind, most expert testimony will be excluded from trial"); Comment, 71 Calif.L.Rev. 1197 (1983); Note, 1979 Wis.L.Rev. 628. Consider also the recent change in California law discussed in note 61 supra.

64. Note, 43 Cornell L.Q. 283, 286 (1957).

LaFave & Scott Crim.Law 2nd Ed.HB—14

Finally, concern has been expressed that application of the partial responsibility doctrine will result in inadequate protection for the public.[67] Individuals who theretofore would have been convicted of the offense charged and subjected to a long prison term or else found not guilty by reason of insanity and committed indefinitely, it is feared, will now serve shorter sentences for lesser offenses or else be completely acquitted at trial.[68] To the extent that the doctrine is utilized only to reduce what otherwise would be murder in the first degree to either murder in the second degree or voluntary manslaughter, the risks are probably not great. The sentences for these lesser offenses are "usually long enough to keep the offender in custody until he is cured or has reached an age when the criminal tendencies of even the most dangerous are likely to have disappeared." [69] But the danger is a real one when the result will be complete acquittal [70] or conviction of a rela-

65. H. Weihofen, Mental Disorder as a Criminal Defense 186–87 (1954).

66. Weihofen & Overholser, supra note 1, at 977.

67. Commonwealth v. Rightnour, 435 Pa. 104, 253 A.2d 644 (1969).

68. Indeed, for this reason defendants may prefer to claim partial responsibility instead of defending upon grounds of insanity. See A. Goldstein, The Insanity Defense 195–96, 202 (1967).

69. Id. at 199. See State v. Correra, ___ R.I. ___, 430 A.2d 1251 (1981), emphasizing this point.

70. "The complete acquittal of such offenders would release from state control the very persons society should probably fear most—because their endowments are fewer, because they are more suggestible, more manipulable, more fearful." A. Goldstein, supra note 68, at 202.

In McCarthy v. State, 372 A.2d 180 (Del.1977), upholding the trial judge's failure to instruct on the doctrine of diminished responsibility regarding the charges of rape, attempted rape and kidnapping, all without lesser-included offenses, the court asserted that "acceptance of the doctrine requires that there be some lesser-included offense which lacks the requisite specific intent of the greater offense charged. Otherwise, the doctrine of diminished responsibility becomes an impermissible substitute test of criminal responsibility." Compare People v. Wetmore, 22 Cal.3d 318, 149 Cal.Rptr. 265, 583 P.2d 1308 (1978), rejecting such a limitation because "we do not perceive how a defendant who has in his possession evidence which rebuts an element of the crime can logically

tively minor offense,[71] at least until such time as commitment procedures equivalent to those following a finding of not guilty by reason of insanity [72] are made applicable.[73]

Doubtless underlying all of these concerns is the fear that recognition of the partial responsibility doctrine will, as a practical matter, often result in the prosecution being unable to meet its burden of proof. While the burden of proof as to the insanity defense may be placed on the defendant,[74] this is not so as to the matter of partial responsibility.[75] "Since the purpose of the diminished-capacity doctrine is to establish the absence of an essential element of the crime, the state still has the burden of overcoming this effort by proof of all the essential elements beyond a reasonable doubt." [76]

 WESTLAW REFERENCES

brawner /12 471 +4 969 /p mental*** insan!

(d) Constitutional Considerations. As several recent cases rejecting the partial responsibility doctrine have acknowledged,[77] the significance of such a rejection is that psychiatric evidence is inadmissible on the issue of whether the defendant in fact possessed the requisite mental state. This evidentiary consequence prompts the question of whether such exclusion of psychiatric evidence violates the defendant's constitutional right to present evidence in his own behalf. Some state court

decisions embracing the partial responsibility doctrine have suggested that because of this due process right they could hardly reach any other result,[78] but federal courts have generally been unreceptive to the claim that nonrecognition of the partial responsibility doctrine is unconstitutional.[79]

In *Chambers v. Mississippi,*[80] holding that strict application of the state's evidentiary rules to exclude the defendant's evidence violated due process, the Court declared: "The right of an accused in a criminal trial to due process is, in essence, the right to a fair opportunity to defend against the state's accusations. The rights to confront and cross-examine witnesses and to call witnesses in one's own behalf have long been recognized as essential to due process." As explained in Justice Harlan's concurring opinion, this right of a defendant is violated where "the State has recognized as relevant and competent the testimony of this type of witness, but has arbitrarily barred its use by the defendant." Thus, if psychiatric testimony is relevant and competent on the mental state issue and there is no good reason for barring it, then, as some have concluded,[81] exclusion of this evidence is constitutionally impermissible.

This question was confronted in *Hughes v. Matthews,*[82] holding that petitioner's rights were violated when he was not allowed to introduce psychiatric testimony to show that he lacked the specific intent required for the

---

be denied the right to present that evidence merely because it will result in his acquittal."

71. "Though the problem is less critical where there are lesser-included offenses, because the state will retain some hold on the offender, it must nevertheless be taken into account because the hold may be inadequate." A. Goldstein, supra note 68, at 202.

72. See § 4.6. In People v. Wetmore, 22 Cal.3d 318, 149 Cal.Rptr. 265, 583 P.2d 1308 (1978), the court noted that the statute on confinement of a defendant found not guilty by reason of insanity was not applicable to a defendant acquitted on partial responsibility grounds, so that if such a person could not be safely released it would be necessary to institute civil commitment proceedings.

73. See Weihofen & Overholser, supra note 1, at 980–81, suggesting this result could presently be attained in many states without additional statutory authority.

74. See § 4.5(e).

75. State v. Santiago, 55 Haw. 162, 516 P.2d 1256 (1973); State v. Gramenz, 256 Iowa 134, 126 N.W.2d 285

(1964). Contra: State v. McKenzie, 186 Mont. 481, 608 P.2d 428 (1980).

76. State v. Correra, ___ R.I. ___, 430 A.2d 1251 (1981).

77. State v. Edwards, 420 So.2d 663 (La.1982); Johnson v. State, 292 Md. 405, 439 A.2d 542 (1982); People v. Atkins, 117 Mich.App. 430, 324 N.W.2d 38 (1982); State v. Bouwman, 354 N.W.2d 1 (Minn.1984), 328 N.W.2d 703 (Minn.1982); State v. Wilcox, 70 Ohio St.2d 182, 436 N.E.2d 523 (1982).

78. People v. Wetmore, 22 Cal.3d 318, 149 Cal.Rptr. 265, 583 P.2d 1308 (1978); Hendershott v. People, 653 P.2d 385 (Colo.1982); Commonwealth v. Walzack, 468 Pa. 210, 360 A.2d 914 (1976).

79. Muench v. Israel, 715 F.2d 1124 (7th Cir.1983); Wahrlick v. Arizona, 479 F.2d 1137 (9th Cir.1973).

80. 410 U.S. 284, 93 S.Ct. 1038, 35 L.Ed.2d 297 (1973).

81. E.g., Comment, 71 Calif.L.Rev. 1197, 1202–04 (1983).

82. 576 F.2d 1250 (7th Cir.1978).

charged crime of first-degree murder.[83] Noting that evidence is relevant "when it pertains to a fact in issue and has a tendency to prove or disprove that fact," the federal court concluded that most certainly psychiatric evidence would be relevant on the issue of the defendant's capacity to form an intent to kill. As for the matter of competency, that is, whether psychiatric testimony is "trustworthy evidence of mental state," the court concluded the "best indication that Wisconsin views psychiatric testimony as competent evidence is its use in other parts of the criminal proceeding," that is, with respect to competency to stand trial and the insanity defense. Whether that must be so is perhaps the heart of the matter. Significantly, another panel of the same court later upheld a similar exclusion of psychiatric evidence,[84] doubtless influenced by the intervening state court decision in *Steele v. State*.[85] In *Steele*, the court concluded that psychiatric testimony was relevant and competent to make the "gross evaluation" of whether or not a defendant is criminally responsible under the insanity defense, but that such testimony was not relevant or competent for the "fine tuning" necessary to assess capacity to form an intent of the sort demanded by the criminal law.[86]

As for whether the defendant's right to present such evidence must bow to some competing state interest, the court in *Hughes* rejected the two justifications put forward by the state because they were unpersuasive on the facts of the particular case. One, that permitting psychiatric testimony would result in guilty persons going free, was deemed "unpersuasive in the present case where the testimony was offered only to show that a second-degree murder conviction was proper."[87] The other reason given, that exclusion of psychiat-

ric evidence on mental state "ensures the integrity of Wisconsin's bifurcated trial system," under which psychiatric testimony is received but once and not at the guilt stage, was inapplicable because the defendant in this case had not interposed an insanity defense and consequently there had been no bifurcated trial.

 WESTLAW REFERENCES

hughes /12 576 +4 1250 /p mental** insan! psycholog! psychiatr! incompeten***

§ 4.8 The XYY Chromosome Defense

Women normally have two special sex chromosomes (gonosomes) called X chromosomes (XX), while most men have an X chromosome paired with a Y chromosome (XY). Some individuals are born with chromosomal abnormalities, in that they have either too few or too many chromosomes. One of these abnormalities is the so-called "super-male" or XYY, who has an extra Y chromosome. There is evidence that XYY males are more likely than others to engage in antisocial or criminal conduct which will result in their confinement in an institution. However, the behavioral impact of this genetic abnormality has not been precisely determined, and thus an XYY defendant is unlikely to be recognized as having an insanity defense.

 WESTLAW REFERENCES

chromosom! /p defense /p mental! insan!

(a) Chromosomal Abnormalities. Chromosomes are threadlike structures of complex molecules which transmit the genetic information arranged and ordered in the cell and which determine the heredity of all plant and

---

83. In Wisconsin first-degree murder is murder "with intent to kill," Wis.Stat.Ann. 940.01, while second-degree murder is murder "by conduct imminently dangerous to another and evincing a depraved mind, regardless of human life," Wis.Stat.Ann. 940.02.

84. Muench v. Israel, 715 F.2d 1124 (7th Cir.1983).

85. 97 Wis.2d 72, 294 N.W.2d 2 (1980).

86. In State v. Flattum, 122 Wis.2d 282, 361 N.W.2d 705 (1985), the court viewed *Steele* as being based on the problem that exists "with the inconsistency between the

law's conception of intent and the psychiatrist's understanding of the term," and thus concluded that a psychiatrist could testify on whether defendant lacked the intent to kill because of voluntary intoxication, "but only if that opinion is based solely on the defendant's voluntary intoxicated conditon" and not on "defendant's mental health history."

87. The court left open the sufficiency of this justification in a case where there was no lesser offense of which the defendant could be convicted.

animal life. In human beings, the characteristic number of chromosomes found in the nucleus of each cell is 46. Egg and sperm cells contain 23 chromosomes each, but upon uniting the chromosomes are pooled so that the new individual has 46 chromosomes arranged in 23 pairs. As the fertilized ovum grows, the chromosomes divide so that each normal cell of the human body contains this same number of chromosomes. Twenty-two of the 23 pairs of chromosomes in each cell are called autosomes, while the remaining pair are referred to as gonosomes. The autosomes contain genes which determine most of the biological characteristics of the individual, but the gonosomes contain those genes which determine the person's primary sexual characteristics.

The normal female possesses two X-type gonosomes, or an XX complement, and the normal male possesses one X-type and a much smaller Y-type gonosome, or an XY structure. (The structure may be determined by a process known as karotyping, which involves culturing the cells, photographing the stained chromosomes, and rearranging the photographed chromosomes to fit a standard pattern.) It is thus obvious that it is the sperm of the father which determines the sex of the child. Because the mother's sex chromosomes are both X, each ovum must contain an X chromosome. But the father's XY pair of chromosomes divides in the formation of sperm; one sperm cell contains an X chromosome and the other a Y chromosome. The child will be male (XY) or female (XX), depending upon which sperm cell fertilizes the egg.

This process does not always work properly, and thus some individuals are born with more

or less than the normal complement of two gonosomes. Some women, for example, have only one X chromosome (referred to as XO or Turner's Syndrome); others are the so-called "super females" who possess one extra X chromosome (XXX); and even XXXX and XXXXX complements have been reported. As for males (i.e., whenever at least one Y chromosome is present), the most common chromosomal abnormality—occurring in about one of every 400 male births—is the XXY (the Klinefelter Syndrome). Others which have been described and confirmed include the XYY, XXYY, and XXXXY. Of particular interest here are those with an extra Y chromosome, the XYY's or so-called "super males." [1]

(b) **The XYY Syndrome.** The first report of an XYY male occurred in 1961,[2] but it was not until 1965 that an investigation was conducted into the possible relationship between chromosome abnormalities and antisocial behavior. That year, a team of researchers at the maximum security State Hospital at Carstairs in Kanarkshire, Scotland (for patients who require treatment in conditions of special security on account of their dangerous, violent or criminal propensities), determined that about three per cent of the 315 males tested there were XYY.[3] A year later, other researchers in England examined the chromosome complement of detained males six feet and over in height (XYY's are significantly taller than XY's) and found XYY's in 24% of those mentally subnormal and detained because of antisocial behavior, 8% of those mentally ill and detained because of antisocial behavior, and 8% of those sentenced to imprisonment for 6 months to 5 years.[4] More recent studies in the United States,[5] Austra-

§ 4.8

1. The above is based upon the descriptions in Burke, The "XYY Syndrome": Genetics, Behavior and the Law, 46 Denver L.J. 261 (1969); Fox, XYY Chromosomes and Crime, 2 Aust. & N.Z.J.Crimin. 5 (1969); Note, 22 Okla.L. Rev. 287 (1969). See those sources for citations to the medical literature.

2. Sandberg, Koepf, Ishihara, & Hauschka, An XYY Human Male, Lancet 488 (Aug. 26, 1961).

3. Jacobs, Brunton, Melville, Brittain, & McClemont, Aggressive Behavior, Mental Subnormality and the XYY Male, 208 Nature 1351 (1965).

4. Casey, Blank, Street, Segall, McDougall, McGrath, & Skinner, YY Chromosomes and Antisocial Behavior, Lancet 859 (Oct. 15, 1966).

5. Telfer, Baker, Clark & Richardson, Incidence of Gross Chromosomal Errors Among Tall Criminal American Males, 159 Science 1249 (1968).

lia,[6] and Denmark[7] have also revealed the presence of gross chromosomal errors among criminal or delinquent males in numbers that could not be accounted for by chance alone.[8] There are presently no accurate figures on the proportion of XYY constitutions in the general noncriminal male population, but the best estimates are that the figure would be about one in a thousand (0.1%) and certainly not more than two in a thousand (0.2%).[9]

While some students of the XYY male question whether enough evidence has been collected to warrant use of the term "XYY syndrome,"[10] some tentative conclusions about the XYY male have been reached on the basis of the research conducted to date. He is very likely to be extremely tall, with long limbs and facial acne. Contrary to early expectations, he is not predisposed to unusually aggressive behavior; he is much more likely to have committed a crime against property than a crime against the person. However, he is likely to begin his criminal activities at a very early age, although he is not likely to have a significant family history of crime or mental illness. He is much more resistant to conventional corrective training and treatment than other prisoners or patients.[11]

But, while it is now possible to identify some characteristics of the XYY male and to conclude that this type of chromosomal abnormality is found in small but consistent numbers of antisocial males who have been insti-

tutionalized for criminal or abnormal behavior, presently available medical evidence is unable to establish a reasonably certain causal connection between the XYY defect and criminal conduct.[12] That is, we know that there exists a strong statistical correlation between the genetic condition and antisocial behavior, but confirmation of the causal link through the demonstration of a physiological mechanism is not yet possible.[13] One theory, as yet unproven, is that the XYY condition causes a certain hormone (plasma testosterone) to be present in abnormal amounts, which in turn brings about a greater degree of "maleness" and thus aggressive behavior.[14] Others reject this theory and instead suggest that the causal connection may ultimately be made on the basis of the known fact that chromosomes are the ultimate source of the biochemical substances called enzymes which regulate all biochemical processes, which in turn are known to have an effect upon behavior.[15] Support for this theory is found in the widespread physical and mental abnormalities observable in persons affected by other chromosomal defects, such as mongolism.[16]

(c) **XYY and the Insanity Defense.** In view of the limitations on existing knowledge concerning the XYY male, an insanity defense based upon the defendant's XYY condition is unlikely to succeed.[17] The difficulties in presenting this kind of defense are illus-

6. Wiener, Sutherland, Bartholomew & Hudson, XYY Males in a Melbourne Prison, Lancet, i, 150 (1968).

7. Nielson, The XYY Syndrome in a Mental Hospital, 8 Brit.J.Crimin. 186 (1968).

8. For a more detailed description of the various studies, see Court Brown, Males With an XYY Sex Chromosome Complement, 5 J.Med.Genet. 341 (1968); Fox, supra note 1.

9. Fox, supra note 1, at 15.

10. Id. at 16.

11. For more on the XYY syndrome, see Burke, supra note 1; Fox, supra note 1; Money, Gaskin & Hull, Impulse, Aggression and Sexuality in the XYY Syndrome, 44 St. John's L.Rev. 220 (1969); Saulitis, Chromosomes and Criminality: The Legal Implications of the XYY Syndrome, 1 J.Leg.Med. 269, 269–83 (1979); Taylor, Genetically-Influenced Antisocial Conduct and the Criminal Justice System, 31 Cleve.St.L.Rev. 61, 61–65 (1982); Notes, 3 Conn.L.Rev. 484 (1971); 57 Geo.L.J. 892 (1969); 22 Okl.L. Rev. 287 (1969).

12. Note, 57 Geo.L.J. 892, 904 (1969).

13. Burke, supra note 1, at 270.

14. Note, 57 Geo.L.J. 892, 900–01 (1969).

15. Burke, supra note 1, at 270.

16. Id. at 272.

17. The only known instance in which a finding of not guilty by reason of insanity was returned following evidence of the defendant's XYY condition is the unreported Australian case of Regina v. Hannell. However, the circumstances of the trial were such "that one may not contend that the verdict was based on the 'extra Y chromosome'. One may not even say that the 'extra Y chromosome' played any part at all in the verdict. It is, in fact, quite possible that the jury would have returned the same verdict on the basis of his mental deficiency alone, his abnormal electro-encephalograph and his epilepsy alone, or both, without there being any mention of his genetic make up." Bartholomew & Sutherland, A Defense of Insanity and the Extra Y Chromosome: R. v. Hannell, 2 Aust. & N.Z.J.Crimin. 29, 36 (1969).

trated by *Millard v. State*,[18] where the defendant, on trial for robbery with a deadly weapon, interposed the insanity defense. The basis for his insanity plea, as later developed at trial, was that he had an extra Y chromosome, resulting in his lacking substantial capacity either to appreciate the criminality of his conduct or to conform his conduct to the requirements of law (Maryland follows the A.L.I. test).

The defendant's only medical witness was a professor who had engaged in considerable research in the field of genetics. He testified that he had examined the defendant and found him to be an XYY and that he had studied published reports showing that such a person is likely to have marked antisocial aggressive reactions. In response to a question, the witness stated that the defendant did have a mental defect, but when asked if the defendant lacked substantial capacity either to appreciate the criminality of his conduct or to conform his conduct to the requirement of law, he answered that he could not say because he had not examined him as a psychiatrist and had no competence in that area. Upon further questioning, he asserted the defendant had a propensity toward crime because of his genetic abnormality. On behalf of the state, a psychiatrist testified that in his opinion the defendant was not insane. He added that he had not made any study of the defendant with respect to the extra Y chromosome because, in his judgment, if such a genetic defect existed it was not a mental defect. Upon this evidence, the trial judge declined to submit the issue of the defendant's sanity to the jury, and the defendant was convicted.

The conviction was affirmed on appeal:

[T]o simply state that persons having the extra Y chromosome are prone to aggressiveness, are antisocial, and continually run afoul of the criminal laws, is hardly sufficient to rebut the presumption of sanity and show the requisite lack of

"substantial capacity" under § 9(a). Moreover, we think it entirely plain from the record that in testifying that appellant had a "mental defect," Dr. Jacobson did so only in a most general sense, without full appreciation for the meaning of the term as used in § 9(a), and particularly without an understanding that such term expressly excludes "an abnormality manifested only by repeated criminal or otherwise antisocial conduct." But even if it were accepted that appellant had a "mental defect" within the contemplation of § 9(a), Dr. Jacobson, by his own testimony, indicated an inability to meaningfully relate the effect of such defect to the "substantial capacity" requirements of the subsection. * * * In so concluding, we do not intend to hold, as a matter of law, that a defense of insanity based upon the so-called XYY genetic defect is beyond the pale of proof under § 9(a).

As one commentator has suggested, the *Millard* decision illustrates the fact that "an attorney defending an XYY individual will be required to call upon both a geneticist and a psychiatrist to give expert testimony. The geneticist's role would be to testify with respect to the individual's genetic structure, any distinguishing characteristics which are relevant to an insanity defense, and the result of family studies designated to determine the influence of genetics and environment on the development of this individual. The psychiatrist's testimony would focus upon the defendant's mental capacity or condition."[19] But in the absence of sound medical support for an XYY defense, courts are understandably unsympathetic to defense efforts to obtain such expert testimony.[20]

(d) XYY and the Insanity Tests. Assuming such testimony, and perhaps some added knowledge about the XYY in confirmation of existing theories, how will the XYY defendant fare under the various insanity tests? One problem, as illustrated by the testimony in the *Millard* case, is whether an XYY chromosomal abnormality can be said to be a mental

---

18. 8 Md.App. 419, 261 A.2d 227 (1970).

19. Note, 57 Geo.L.J. 892, 902–03 (1969).

20. People v. Tanner, 13 Cal.App.3d 596, 91 Cal.Rptr. 656 (1970) (XYY testimony barred), noted at 25 Ark.L.Rev. 346 (1971); People v. Yukl, 83 Misc.2d 364, 372 N.Y.S.2d 313 (1975) (defendant's request for a qualified

cytogeneticist to carry out chromosome tests of defendant's blood at state expense refused); State v. Roberts, 14 Wn.App. 727, 544 P.2d 754 (1976) (defendant's request for continuance to allow additional psychiatric examination for symptoms of the XYY syndrome refused). See Annot., 43 A.L.R.3d 1414 (1972).

disease or defect or, at least, evidence of such a disease or defect. Beyond that, there are questions of whether an XYY condition does have a bearing upon the cognition or control tests.

The initial question is whether an individual with an XYY chromosomal abnormality can be said to be suffering from a "disease of the mind" (under the *M'Naghten* or irresistible impulse tests) or a "mental disease or defect" (under the A.L.I. test). A precise answer cannot be given, for these terms have not been adequately defined by the courts.[21] But if these phrases are given a liberal interpretation, as many have proposed, then this initial difficulty may be overcome. It has been pursuasively argued that it should be sufficient that "the accused suffers from a disorder or disturbance of his mental functioning which goes considerably beyond the usual range of variations in excitability, impulsiveness, obtuseness or lack of self control found in ordinary persons," [22] and that such a showing may be possible as to a defendant with an XYY chromosomal abnormality.

There are also those who state flatly that the XYY individual is suffering only from "physical compulsion or physical abnormality," [23] but they nonetheless believe that the defendant's XYY condition may be admissible as evidence of his mental condition,[24] particularly if some evidence is forthcoming that the physical malady may cause a mental disturbance. Thus, it has been suggested that developments here may parallel those which occurred earlier concerning proof of epilepsy to show mental condition.[25] Courts first insisted upon proof of a link between the malady and mental disturbance,[26] but later they merely required proof of the malady and took judicial notice of the medical fact that epilepsy could have a serious effect on the defendant's mentality.[27]

There is general agreement that it is highly unlikely that a successful insanity defense can be predicated upon an XYY abnormality where the test of criminal responsibility is determined under the *M'Naghten* rules.[28] *M'Naghten* is generally assumed to be restricted to the cognitive element,[29] and existing knowledge about the XYY individual does not suggest that possession of the extra Y chromosome of itself affects a person's ability to appreciate either the nature and quality of his acts or whether they are wrong.

The chances are somewhat greater that an XYY condition may serve as the foundation for an insanity defense under the irresistible impulse test. Problems exist because of the "unwillingness of geneticists to mechanistically attribute compulsive or aggressive behavior to any single genetic defect" [30] and also because of the uncertainty over the exact meaning of this test.[31] If the word "impulse" is taken literally, as it probably should not be, to require a sudden loss of control, then it seems unlikely that the XYY defendant can qualify.[32] But a more serious hurdle exists because of the common assumption that this test requires "a complete impairment of ability to * * * control," [33] for it is unlikely that future research will find that the XYY individual has a total lack of control.[34]

In jurisdictions which follow the A.L.I. insanity test,[35] the XYY syndrome might well be significant in establishing that the defendant lacked substantial capacity to conform his conduct to the requirements of law.[36] Cer-

21. A. Goldstein, The Insanity Defense 47 (1967).
22. Fox, supra note 1, at 17.
23. Note, 22 Okl.L.Rev. 287, 299 (1969).
24. Ibid; Note, 57 Geo.L.J. 892, 906 (1969).
25. Note, 57 Geo.L.J. 892, 905 n. 55 (1969).
26. Walsh v. People, 88 N.Y. 458 (1882).
27. State v. Wright, 112 Iowa 436, 84 N.W. 541 (1900).
28. Burke, supra note 1, at 274; Fox, supra note 1, at 17; Note, 57 Geo.L.J. 892, 907 (1969); Note, 22 Okl.L.Rev. 287, 298 (1969); Note, 21 Syracuse L.Rev. 1221, 1228 (1970).
29. See § 4.2(b)(2).
30. Burke, supra note 1, at 274 n. 59.
31. See § 4.2(d).
32. Note, 57 Geo.L.J. 892, 908 (1969).
33. Model Penal Code § 4.01, Comment 171 (1985).
34. Note, 57 Geo.L.J. 892, 908 (1969).
35. See § 4.3(d).
36. Burke, supra note 1, at 276; Note, 57 Geo.L.J. 892, 911–12 (1969); Note, 52 N.D.L.Rev. 729, 736 (1976).

tainly the defendant's chances would be better than under the irresistible impulse test, for the A.L.I. test "does not demand *complete* impairment of capacity. It asks instead for *substantial* impairment." [37] But even here the changes are not substantial, as the A.L.I. test "calls for a more complete lack of mental control over one's acts than is commonly associated with XYY offenders or unusually aggressive individuals generally." [38]

Finally, it is well to note that even if insanity standards were modified so as to encompass the XYY defendant, the defense is not likely to be an attractive one to the defendant. There presently exists no treatment or cure for the XYY anomaly. Thus, an XYY defendant who successfully pleaded insanity "would find himself in a compulsory criminal commitment proceeding," and "once the disease for which he was committed is established as 'in his genes,' he can expect never to be released." [39]

§ 4.9   Automatism

A defense related to but different from the defense of insanity is that of unconsciousness, often referred to as automatism: one who engages in what would otherwise be criminal conduct is not guilty of a crime if he does so in a state of unconsciousness or semi-consciousness. Although this is sometimes explained on the ground that such a person could not have the requisite mental state for commission of the crime, the better rationale

is that the individual has not engaged in a voluntary act.

(a) Meaning of "Automatism." The term "automatism," which has appeared in the legal literature with some frequency in recent years,[1] has been defined

> as connoting the state of a person who, though capable of action, is not conscious of what he is doing. It is to be equated with unconsciousness, involuntary action [and] implies that there must be some attendant disturbance of conscious awareness. Undoubtedly automatic states exist and medically they may be defined as conditions in which the patient may perform simple or complex actions in a more or less skilled or uncoordinated fashion without having full awareness of what he is doing. * * * Clinically, automatism has been described in a wide variety of conditions. These include epileptic and post-epileptic states, clouded states of consciousness associated with organic brain disease, concussional states following head injuries and, less commonly, in some types of schizophrenic and acute emotional disturbance. Metabolic disorders such as anoxia and hypoglycemia as well as drug-induced impairment of consciousness can be manifested by automatic behavior. Finally, as is well known, automatic acts can occur during sleepwalking and hypnagogic states.[2]

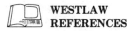 WESTLAW REFERENCES

di automatism

(b) The Automatism Defense. Although the cases in the United States are not substantial in number, they support the proposition that automatism is a defense.[3] Thus it

---

37. Model Penal Code § 4.01, Comment (Tent. Draft No. 4, 1955).

38. Saulitis, supra note 11, at 287.

39. Note, 9 Harv.J.Legis. 469, 485 (1972).

§ 4.9

1. Beck, Voluntary Conduct: Automatism, Insanity and Drunkenness, 9 Crim.L.Q. 315 (1967); Blackwell, Automatism and Amnesia, 79 S.A.L.J. 16 (1962); Campbell, Psychological Blow Automatism: A Narrow Defence, 23 Crim.L.Q. 342 (1981); Automatism and Amnesia, 79 S.A. L.J. 16 (1962); Edwards, Automatism and Social Defence, 8 Crim.L.Q. 258 (1966); Elliott, Automatism and Trial by Jury, 6 Melbourne, U.L.Rev. 53 (1967); Holland, Automatism and Criminal Responsibility, 25 Crim.L.Q. 95 (1982); Howard, Automatism and Insanity, 4 Sydney L.Rev. 36 (1962); Jennings, The Growth and Development of Automatism as a Defence in Criminal Law, 2 Osgoode Hall, L.J.

370 (1962); Kahn, Automatism, 1965 N.Z.L.J. 113; Mackay, Non-Organic Automatism—Some Recent Development, 1980 Crim.L.Rev. 350; Leigh, Automatism and Insanity, 5 Crim.L.Q. 160 (1962); Prevezer, Automatism and Involuntary Conduct, 1958 Crim.L.Rev. 361; Puxon, The Defence of Automatism, 106 Sol.J. 163 (1962); Scoble, Amnesia, Automatism and Insanity, 79 S.A.L.J. 338 (1962); Sullivan, Self Induced and Recurring Automatism, 123 New.L.J. 1093 (1973); Williams, Automatism, in Essays in Criminal Science (G. Mueller ed. 1961); Comment, 15 San Diego L.Rev. 839 (1978).

2. F. Whitlock, Criminal Responsibility and Mental Illness 119–20 (1963).

3. See, e.g., People v. Froom, 108 Cal.App.3d 820, 166 Cal.Rptr. 786 (1980); State v. Caddell, 287 N.C. 266, 215 S.E.2d 348 (1975); Commonwealth v. Crosby, 444 Pa. 17, 279 A.2d 73 (1971); Greenfield v. Commonwealth, 214 Va.

has been held that one who kills another when in a clouded state somewhere between sleep and wakefulness is not guilty of a crime.[4] Likewise, one who, while driving a car, suddenly and without warning "blacks out" so that his car runs upon the sidewalk and kills a pedestrian, is not guilty of any crime [5]—unless, of course, because of previous blackouts he is on notice that it may happen again, in which case his conduct in driving may amount to criminal negligence.[6]

Consistent with the definition of automatism set out above, American courts have recognized that an automatism defense might be made out when the defendant's condition is brought about by any one of a variety of circumstances, including epilepsy,[7] somnabulism,[8] hypnotism,[9] a concussion or some other physical trauma,[10] or even an emotional trauma.[11] While case authority is generally lacking, it has been argued that an automatism defense might be made out by a defendant who, at the time of his or her acts, was suffering from PMS (the premenstrual syndrome) [12] or PTSD (post-traumatic stress disorder).[13] But it is not enough that the defendant suffers from amnesia and thus cannot remember the events in question,[14] or that he was suffering from a multiple personality disorder.[15] Also, a person who has been "brainwashed" does not have an automatism defense.[16]

710, 204 S.E.2d 414 (1974); State v. Utter, 4 Wn.App. 137, 479 P.2d 946 (1971); Polston v. State, 685 P.2d 1 (Wyo. 1984); Fulcher v. State, 633 P.2d 142 (Wyo.1981). For other cases, see Annot., 27 A.L.R.4th 1067 (1984).

However, unconsciousness through voluntary intoxication may not qualify for this defense. See People v. Baker, 42 Cal.2d 550, 268 P.2d 705 (1954) (although voluntary intoxication can produce unconsciousness, the effect of this can only be to negative some specific intent required by the crime; it cannot be the complete defense of unconsciousness); Lewis v. State, 196 Ga. 755, 27 S.E.2d 659 (1943). For other cases, see Annot., supra, at 1083–85; and consider Mackay, Intoxication as a Factor in Automatism, 1982 Crim.L.Rev. 146, reasoning that intoxication should bar an automatism defense only if the defendant was aware his drinking might produce unconsciousness.

4. Fain v. Commonwealth, 78 Ky. 183 (1879).

5. Government of the Virgin Islands v. Smith, 278 F.2d 169 (3d Cir.1960) (unconsciousness through epilepsy); People v. Freeman, 61 Cal.App.2d 110, 142 P.2d 435 (1943) (same).

6. E.g., Tift v. State, 17 Ga.App. 663, 88 S.E. 41 (1916). See § 3.2(c).

7. People v. Higgins, 5 N.Y.2d 607, 186 N.Y.S.2d 623, 159 N.E.2d 179 (1959); State v. Welsch, 8 Wn.App. 719, 508 P.2d 1041 (1973).

8. Fain v. Commonwealth, 78 Ky. 183 (1979); Bradley v. State, 102 Tex.Crim.R. 41, 277 S.W. 147 (1926).

9. People v. Marsh, 170 Cal.App.3d 284, 338 P.2d 495 (1959); People v. Worthington, 105 Cal. 166, 38 P. 689 (1894).

10. People v. Newton, 8 Cal.App.3d 359, 87 Cal.Rptr. 394 (1970); Read v. People, 119 Colo. 506, 205 P.2d 233 (1949); Carter v. State, 376 P.2d 351 (Okl.Crim.App.1962).

11. People v. Wilson, 66 Cal.2d 749, 59 Cal.Rptr. 156, 427 P.2d 820 (1967); People v. Lisnow, 88 Cal.App.3d Supp. 21, 151 Cal.Rptr. 621 (1978).

12. PMS "is a hormone deficiency disease" which studies have shown "may be related to antisocial behavior." Taylor & Dalton, Premenstrual Syndrome: A New Criminal Defense?, Cal.W.L.Rev. 269, 271, 274 (1983). "Physio-

logical anomalies render the PMS sufferer unable to control her actions during the short time PMS symptoms surface." Note, 59 Notre Dame Law. 253, 265 (1983). But, "PMS is not a disease or defect of the mind, but a physiological disorder," and thus "might fit more appropriately within the automatism defense." Id. at 264. Impediments to recognition of such a defense "include: the difference of opinion within the medical profession; fears that criminal defendants will abuse the PMS defense; and concerns that recognition of an exclusively female defense will promote sexism." Id. at 267.

13. "Following the traumatic event, a person who suffers from PTSD may have a number of symptoms that include: self medication through substance or alcohol abuse, memory loss, loss of sleep, nightmare reliving of the original traumatic event, intrusive thoughts, exaggerated startle response, reduction in emotional response, a feeling of alienation, and 'dissassociative states" during which the original event is relived and 'the individual behaves as though experiencing the event of the moment.' " Erlinder, Paying the Price of Vietnam: Post-Traumatic Stress Disorder and Criminal Behavior, 25 B.C.L.Rev. 305, 310–11 (1984). Erlinder suggests at 329 that PTSD could be the basis of an automatism defense, and notes that in the Lisnow case, note 11 supra, it was held to be error to exclude PTSD testimony on this point.

14. State v. Gish, 87 Idaho 341, 393 P.2d 342 (1964); Lester v. State, 212 Tenn. 338, 370 S.W.2d 405 (1963); Polston v. State, 685 P.2d 1 (Wyo.1984).

15. State v. Grimsley, 3 Ohio App.3d 265, 444 N.E.2d 1071 (1982).

16. See Delgado, Ascription of Criminal States of Mind: Toward a Defense Theory for the Coercively Persuaded ("Brainwashed") Defendant, 63 Minn.L.Rev. 1, 10 (1978); and Dressler, Professor Delgado's "Brainwashing" Defense: Courting a Determinist Legal System, 63 Minn.L. Rev. 335 (1979), disputing whether there ought to be a brainwashing defense. See also Alldridge, Brainwashing as a Criminal Defense, 1984 Crim.L.Rev. 726, concluding at 737: "There are valid moral agreements to the effect that 'brainwashing' should afford an excuse to all crimes. It would be based upon the idea that a person acting when brainwashed is not properly regarded as the same person

The basis of the automatism defense is seldom made clear in the cases.[17] One may, of course, note some similarities between the insanity defense and the automatism defense, although it is clear that the latter is not merely a facet of the former; the automatism defense may be present notwithstanding the defendant's lack of the "mental disease or defect" which insanity requires.[18] Another explanation is that the automaton-defendant is not criminally liable because he lacks the mental state which the crime requires, and this appears to be the rationale most commonly hinted at in the cases.[19] However, it is undoubtedly more correct to say that such a person is not guilty of a crime because he has not engaged in an "act" (defined as a voluntary bodily movement[20]), and without an act there can be no crime.[21] This rationale, which is employed in the Model Penal Code,[22] goes well beyond the no-mental-state reasoning, for it would support an automatism defense to a charge of a strict-liability offense.[23] But under either of the latter two theories the defense, if successful, results in outright acquittal.[24]

Some authority is to be found to the effect that the defendant has the burden of proving the defense of automatism.[25] The prevailing view, however, is that the defendant need only produce evidence raising a doubt as to his consciousness at the time of the alleged crime.[26] If the defense really is concerned with whether the defendant engaged in a voluntary act, an essential element of the crime,[27] then it would seem that the burden of proof must as a constitutional matter be on the prosecution.[28]

 WESTLAW REFERENCES

automatism /s defense

(c) Automatism vs. Insanity. As noted earlier,[29] one of the purposes served by the insanity defense is that it makes possible the commitment of some persons, not as an alternative to conviction and imprisonment, but rather as an alternative to outright acquittal. That is, if the defendant did not commit the acts with the mental state required for conviction of the crime charged, but this is because he was suffering from a mental disease or defect, the result is likely to be a finding of

---

as the character occupying that body when 'unprogrammed.' "

17. "Most of the case law on this subject comes from California where * * * a statute specifically exempts unconscious action from liability, thus unfortunately obviating the need to make express the reasons for such a separate defense." Fox, Physical Disorder, Consciousness, and Criminal Liability, 63 Column.L.Rev. 645, 655 (1963). The reference is to Cal.Penal Code § 26, providing that "all persons are capable of committing crimes except those belonging to the following classes: * * * Persons who committed the act charged without being conscious thereof." Most modern recodifications expressly state that there is no criminal liability unless there is a voluntary act, and several add that an act is not voluntary unless it is performed consciously as a result of effort or determination. See statutes cited in § 3.2(c).

18. See Ellis v. United States, 274 F.2d 52 (10th Cir. 1959) (epilepsy is not unsanity); Carter v. State, 376 P.2d 351 (Okl.Crim.App.1962) (defense of unconsciousness is not the same as defense of insanity). But see Fox, supra note, 17, noting the difficulties in distinguishing this defense and that of insanity.

19. Model Penal Code § 2.01, Comment (Tent.Draft No. 4, 1955). See, e.g., State v. Welsh, 8 Wn.App. 719, 508 P.2d 1041 (1973) (testimony indicating defendant suffering from psychomotor epilepsy and had seizure when he attacked his wife goes to the issue of whether defendant had the requisite intent).

20. See, § 3.2(c).

21. See § 3.2.

22. Model Penal Code § 2.01, requiring a voluntary act (or omission) for every offense and defining voluntary acts as excluding a reflex or convulsion; a bodily movement during unconsciousness or sleep; conduct during hypnosis or resulting from hypnotic suggestion; or a bodily movement that otherwise is not a product of the effort or determination of the actor, either conscious or habitual.

23. Illustrative is the *Charlson* ease, discussed in the text following, applying the automatism defense where one of the charges was the strict-liability offense of causing grievous bodily harm.

24. See Fulcher v. State, 633 P.2d 142 (Wyo.1981) (noting that the defense is thus unlike the insanity defense, for there are no follow-up consequences after acquittal).

25. State v. Caddell, 287 N.C. 266, 215 S.E.2d 348 (1975); Fulcher v. State, 633 P.2d 142 (Wyo.1981).

26. Government of Virgin Islands v. Smith, 278 F.2d 169 (3d Cir.1960); People v. Cruz, 83 Cal.App.3d 308, 147 Cal.Rptr. 740 (1978); State v. Welsh, 8 Wn.App. 719, 508 P.2d 1041 (1973).

27. See § 3.2.

28. See § 1.8.

29. See § 4.1(b).

not guilty by reason of insanity followed by commitment rather than a mere finding of not guilty followed by release.[30] In this way, so the argument goes, society is protected from persons who might present a continuing danger to the public.

If, as just noted, the insanity defense has been utilized as if it "superceded" a no-mental-state defense for those who might pose a continuing danger because of their mental illness, it might logically be asked whether there has developed a comparable relationship between the insanity defense and the no-voluntary-act automatism defense. That is, is there here as well pressure to "make the insanity defense the exclusive avenue for bringing subjective evidence into the trial," [31] to the end that those who did not act voluntarily might be committed if there is some chance that they are still dangerous?

The American cases in this area are not particularly helpful in this regard, although they do reflect that what has been described herein as automatism has more often than not been instead labelled insanity,[32] perhaps for the reason suggested above.[33] Consider, for example, the sleepwalking cases. The leading case, *Fain v. Commonwealth*,[34] makes no mention at all of insanity, although the Kentucky court in a subsequent case asserted that it could not see "how these facts [evidence of somnambulism] would constitute any defense other than that embraced in a plea of insanity." [35] Similarly, another court charac-

terized somnambulism as "a species of insanity." [36] To the same effect are the epilepsy cases; sometimes epilepsy has been held to present an insanity defense,[37] sometimes an automatism defense.[38]

The experience in Britain, where the automatism defense has been raised with much greater frequency, is instructive. There are three cases which are worthy of brief note here: *Regina v. Charlson* [39]; *Regina v. Kemp* [40]; and *Bratty v. Attorney-General for Northern Ireland*.[41] Charlson, who struck his ten-year-old son with a mallet and then threw him out of a window, was charged with (1) causing grievous bodily harm with intent to murder; (2) causing grievous bodily harm with intent to cause such harm; and (3) causing grievous bodily harm (a strict-liability offense). There was evidence that Charlson had a cerebral tumor, because of which he would be subject to outbursts of impulsive violence over which he would have no control. He did not plead insanity, and testimony was offered that he was not suffering from any mental disease. Charlson was acquitted of all three charges by a jury which had been instructed in part as follows:

> No specific intention need be proved by the prosecution before the accused can be found guilty of the third charge * * *. You must, however, be satisfied that he was acting consciously * * *. Therefore, in considering this third charge you have to ask yourself "was the accused knowingly striking his son, or was he acting as an automaton without any control or knowledge

---

30. This is because courts often decline to admit evidence of mental disease except in the context of an insanity defense. See § 4.1(b).

31. A. Goldstein, The Insanity Defense 207 (1967).

32. The cases are collected in Annot., 27 A.L.R.4th 1067, 1076–78 (1984).

33. The inapplicability of that reason, on the other hand, may influence a court to rule that automatism is a defense separate from insanity. See Fulcher v. State, 633 P.2d 142 (Wyo.1981) (where unconsciousness resulted from concussion without permanent brain damage, so that condition is only temporary, insanity defense followed by commitment would be inappropriate, and thus separate defense of unconsciousness must be available). See also Polston v. State, 685 P.2d 1 (Wyo.1984).

34. 78 Ky. 183 (1879).

35. Tibbs v. Commonwealth, 138 Ky. 558, 128 S.W. 871 (1910).

36. Bradley v. State, 102 Tex.Cr.R. 41, 277 S.W. 147, 149 (1925).

37. E.g., People v. Higgins, 5 N.Y.2d 607, 186 N.Y.S.2d 623, 159 N.E.2d 179 (1959); People v. Furlong, 187 N.Y. 198, 79 N.E. 978 (1907). Cf. People v. Grant, 71 Ill.2d 551, 17 Ill.Dec. 814, 377 N.E.2d 4 (1978) (where defendant charged with battery on policeman claimed he had suffered an epileptic seizure , instruction on insanity fully informed the jury of the issue of defendant's volitional capacity, so that failure to instruct on involuntary conduct did not result in an unfair trial).

38. E.g., Government of the Virgin Islands v. Smith, 278 F.2d 169 (3d Cir.1960); People v. Freeman, 61 Cal. App.2d 110, 142 P.2d 435 (1943).

39. [1955] 1 All E.R. 859.

40. [1956] 3 All E.R. 249.

41. [1961] 3 All E.R. 535.

of the act which he was committing?" * * * If you are left in doubt about the matter, and you think he might well have been acting as an automaton without any real knowledge of what he was doing, then the proper verdict would be not guilty, even on the third and least serious of these alternatives.

The commentators have uniformly expressed concern over the result in *Charlson*.[42] As one writer put it, "it is difficult to accept with equanimity a state of the criminal law in which it is more than possible, it is proper, to set free someone who on his own showing is likely to be suffering from a condition which may make him repeat an irrational and savage attack on a child with whose welfare he is entrusted by law."[43] A similar concern appears to have influenced the judge in *Kemp*, where the defendant was charged with causing grievous bodily harm to his wife by striking her with a hammer. It was agreed that Kemp was suffering from arteriosclerosis and had not known what he was doing at the time. One doctor, called by the prosecution, gave as his opinion that this was due to melancholia, a disease of the mind induced by the arteriosclerosis. Two other doctors, one called by the defense and one by the prosecution, testified that the defendant's condition did not constitute a disease of the mind.

Although it was Kemp's position that he was entitled to outright acquittal on the basis of *Charlson*, the trial court instructed only on insanity on the ground that the facts of the case fit within *M'Naghten* whether one accepted the evidence of the prosecution or defense: "The hardening of the arteries is a disease which is shown on the evidence to be capable of affecting the mind in such a way as to cause a defect, temporarily or permanently, of its reasoning and understanding, and is thus a disease of the mind within the meaning of the rule." Most significant, the court made it apparent that this conclusion was not based upon any medical definition of the term "mental disease or defect" but rather upon the policy "that people who committed crimes of violence, even though they were not responsible for their actions, ought not to be allowed to go free because they might commit an act of violence again."

In *Kemp*, unlike *Charlson*, there was at least some expert testimony of mental disease, but it is generally agreed that the two cases may not be reconciled on this basis.[44] It was noted, for example, that both cases "involved organic interference with the brain," and that it "is difficult to understand why arteriosclerosis can be said to affect the powers of 'reasoning, understanding, and so on,' when a cerebral tumor cannot."[45] *Kemp* was viewed as a way of "meeting what has been accepted as a defect in the law,"[46] namely, an avenue of outright release for dangerous defendants.

The matter reached the House of Lords in the *Bratty* case, an appeal from a conviction in a murder case in which both automatism and insanity were raised as defenses. The only evidence on both defenses was Bratty's testimony that he "had some terrible feeling and then a sort of blackness" before the killing, and expert testimony that he was suffering from psychomotor epilepsy at the time he strangled his victim. The trial judge refused to instruct on automatism, and the insanity defense was rejected by the jury. The House of Lords upheld the conviction, explaining that the defendant's own testimony had not provided a basis for an automatism instruction because there was no medical evidence to support the claim of blackout, and that the evidence of psychomotor epilepsy did not provide a basis because the doctors who testified "agreed that psychomotor epilepsy * * * is a defect of reason due to disease of the mind." As stated by Lord Kilmuir, "where the only cause alleged for the unconsciousness is a defect of reason from disease of the mind, and that cause is rejected by the jury, there can be

---

42. E.g., Cross, Reflections on Bratty's Case, 78 Law W.Rev. 236, 239 (1962); Howard, supra note 1, at 40; Kahn, supra note 1, at 120; Mackay, supra note 1, at 359; Williams, supra note 1, at 353–54.

43. Howard, supra note 1, at 40.

44. Leigh, supra note 1, at 163.

45. Howard, supra note 1, at 40.

46. Edwards, Automatism and Criminal Responsibility, 21 Mod.L.Rev. 375, 386 (1958).

no room for the alternative defense of automatism."

Lord Denning's opinion in *Bratty* has received more attention. He noted that the question of whether the evidence concerning the cause of the defective consciousness establishes a disease of the mind is a policy matter to be decided by the courts rather than the medical experts.[47] As to the policy, he stated: "It seems to me that any mental disorder which has manifested itself in violence and is prone to recur is a disease of the mind. At any rate it is the sort of disease for which a person should be detained in hospital rather than be given an unqualified acquittal." Lord Denning, therefore, quite frankly acknowledged that the need for protective custody of the defendant is a major consideration in determining whether the defendant has an automatism-disease or an insanity-disease.

While *Kemp* and *Bratty* have received a sympathetic reception on the ground that it is desirable to avoid the result reached in *Charlson*,[48] it has been questioned whether "the broadening of the definition of the phrase 'disease of the mind' may not be a cure worse than the ill it is intended to remedy."[49] By this extention of the insanity defense into an area which might otherwise be occupied by the defense of automatism, medical experts are "forced into the position of making statements in court they would not make in the clinic,"[50] while a defendant who "has acted unconsciously due to a physical or organic disorder [is] faced with a verdict of insanity and committal" to an institution intended only for the treatment of mental illness.[51] It has been suggested that it would be preferable if provision were made whereby one who interposed a successful automatism defense could be detained or conditionally discharged for the purpose of his receiving the surgical or medical treatment which might be necessary to prevent a recurrence of the unconsciousness.[52]

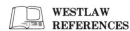 **WESTLAW REFERENCES**

automatism /s insan***
di somnambulism

§ 4.10 Intoxication

One who is charged with having committed a crime may claim in his defense that, at the time, he was intoxicated[1] (by alcohol or by narcotic drugs[2]) and so is not guilty. If the

47. This would mean that even if *all* of the expert testimony in the case is to the effect that the defendant was *not* suffering from a mental disease, the court might rule otherwise on policy grounds. Such was the result reached in Regina v. O'Brien, 56 D.L.R.2d 65 [1966], discussed in Beck, supra note 1, where the defendant without provocation and with no apparent motive attacked and severely wounded the proprietor of a grocery store. At trial defense counsel raised the defense of automatism but carefully avoided the question of insanity. The sole witness for the defense was a consultant in neurology and psychiatry who testified that there was a history of epilepsy and migraine in the accused's family and expressed the opinion based on the evidence he heard of the assault that it could have been committed by a person in an epileptic fugue. He was asked on cross-examination if the accused was suffering from a disease of the mind, to which he replied that epilepsy was an organic disease of the brain and that although epilepsy affected the mind it was not a disease of the mind. The trial judge ruled that the defense of insanity could not be submitted to the jury on this evidence and thus submitted only the defense of automatism. The jury convicted the defendant of attempted murder, and on appeal he claimed that the trial judge erred in not allowing the defense of insanity to go to the jury. Relying upon the *Bratty* case, the New Brunswick Court of Appeal held that epilepsy was a disease of the mind.

48. E.g., Beck, supra note 1, at 319; Kahn, supra note 1, at 120.

49. Cross, supra note 42, at 239.

50. Beck, supra note 1, at 319. "When the three psychiatrists who gave evidence in *Bratty* testified that psychomotor epilepsy was a mental disease, they were using that term to express the truth that the organic disease of epilepsy can affect the mind. The medical witnesses in *Bratty* realized the way the term disease of the mind is used in the criminal law and tailored their opinions to that use." Id. at 318.

51. Ibid.

52. Beck, supra note 1, at 319; Cross, supra note 42, at 240–41; Howard, supra note 1, at 40; Jennings, supra note 1, at 380–81; Kahn, supra note 1, at 120; Prevezer, supra note 1, at 440.

§ 4.10

1. See, generally, Hall, Intoxication and Criminal Responsibility, 57 Harv.L.Rev. 1045 (1944); Paulsen, Intoxication as a Defense to Crime, 1961 U.Ill.L.F. 1; Comment, 55 Colum.L.Rev. 1210 (1955); Special Project, 33 Vand.L. Rev. 1145 (1980); Annots., 73 A.L.R.3d 98 (1976); 8 A.L.R.3d 1236 (1966).

2. Although the word "intoxicate" is sometimes limited to the results of drinking alcohol, it has also been more broadly defined as to excite or stupefy "by alcoholic drinks

crime in question is that of driving while intoxicated, or of being drunk in a public place, he will not get very far with the defense, for with such crimes intoxication, far from being a defense, is an element of the crime.[3]

With crimes of which intoxication is not an element, the defendant's defense may be: I committed, while intoxicated, an act that I would not have committed when sober, so that my conduct was the result of my intoxication.[4] His claim that he would not have committed the crime had he been sober is no defense, however,[5] any more than one's claim that he would not have committed a crime of violence had he been a less excitable or pugnacious person, or a crime of theft had he been of a less acquisitive nature.

His claim, however, may be the stronger one that, as a result of his intoxication, he possessed a state of mind like that of an insane person—so that he did not know that what he was doing was wrong (in a jurisdiction applying the *M'Naghten* test) or that he

was unable to resist what he knew to be wrong (in a jurisdiction adding the irresistible impulse test)—and so he should have the same defense that an insane person would have. He is not, however, insane just because he is intoxicated, for insanity requires a "disease of the mind" (or, in modern terminology, "mental disease or defect"), a requirement which mere drunkenness cannot satisfy;[6] and therefore, being sane, he is not eligible for the defense of insanity.

Nevertheless, though intoxication is not insanity, it does have an effect upon criminal liability in some circumstances. Where the intoxication was "involuntary," it may be a defense in the same circumstances as would insanity. Or, the intoxication may negate the existence of an element of the crime.

(a) Intoxication Negativing Intention or Knowledge. Intoxication is a defense to crime if it negatives a required element of the crime;[7] and this is so whether the intoxication is voluntary or involuntary.[8] Perhaps the defendant is too intoxicated to accomplish

or a narcotic." Webster's New International Dictionary (3d ed.1981). Since the rules relating to alcoholic intoxication are the same as those relating to intoxication by narcotic substances, the term "intoxication" will be used in this book to cover both matters.

Model Penal Code § 2.08(5)(a) defines intoxication as "a disturbance of mental or physical capacities resulting from the introduction of substances into the body." Several modern recodifications define the term the same way.

3. E.g., Shelburn v. State, 446 P.2d 56 (Okl.Cr.1968) (driving under the influence); City of Seattle v. Hill, 72 Wash.2d 786, 435 P.2d 692 (1967) (public intoxication). But see § 4.10(h).

As to *in*voluntary intoxication as a defense to such crimes, see State v. Brown, 38 Kan. 390, 16 P. 259 (1888) (public intoxication); People v. Koch, 250 App.Div. 623, 294 N.Y.S. 987 (1937) (driving under the influence).

4. See Paulsen, supra note 1, at 1, 23–24, for how criminal conduct may result from intoxication by alcohol or drugs: "Drinking alcohol impairs judgment, releases inhibitions, and thus permits the drinker to engage in behavior quite different from the normal pattern. * * * Drinking 'stimulates' the drinker, but does so by 'loosening the brakes,' not by 'stepping on the gas.' * * * The effect of a narcotic drug is to make the addict less aggressive, without any great interference with mental powers. * * * 'Opiates are quieting drugs that repress hostile urges, create a passive, dreamy state and depress sexual drives. On the other hand, the opiates are valuable to criminals in other ways. They allay anxieties and, therefore, supply a kind of "dutch courage" which may be valuable to criminals in the commission of certain

acts such as petty thievery. It is particularly important to note that this "dutch courage" is achieved without any great deterioration in mental ability or manual dexterity, such as is induced by alcohol and other drugs.'"

5. Roberts v. People, 19 Mich. 401 (1870) (assault with intent to murder; voluntary intoxication is a defense if it makes one incapable of entertaining the necessary intent to kill; "If he did entertain it in fact, though but for the intoxication he would not have done so, he is responsible for the intent as well the acts."

6. Rucker v. State, 119 Ohio St. 189, 162 N.E. 802 (1928) (acute alcoholism is not the same as the unsound mind which insanity requires); Commonwealth v. Hicks, 483 Pa. 305, 396 A.2d 1183 (1979) (voluntary intoxication not a "disease of the mind" under *M'Naghten*).

7. This is so even if an applicable statute provides that voluntary intoxication is no excuse for crime, since intoxication which negatives an element is not excusing a crime which has been committed but rather negativing the commission of the crime. Brennan v. People, 37 Colo. 256, 86 P. 79 (1906) (voluntary intoxication may negative premeditation and deliberation and so reduce an intentional killing from first degree murder, though statute provides intoxication does not excuse crime).

8. Most of the modern criminal codes provide either that intoxication is a defense if it negatives a mental state or that it is admissible in evidence whenever relevant to negate an element of the offense charged. See Model Penal Code § 2.08(1).

A few of the modern recodifications are silent on the question, and a few others expressly state that voluntary

the physical act which the crime requires, as where, in a burglary situation, he is so drunk that he cannot move, much less break and enter the building in question. But generally intoxication, when it negatives an element of the crime, does so by negativing some mental element (intent or knowledge) which the crime requires.

Thus one who takes and carries away another person's property by stealth or at gunpoint is not guilty of larceny or of robbery if he is too intoxicated to be able to entertain the necessary intent to steal.[9] One cannot be guilty of burglary when, although he breaks and enters another's house, his intoxication deprives him of the capacity to intend to commit a felony therein.[10] One is not guilty of rape, or of assault with intent to rape, if he is intoxicated to such an extent that he is unable to entertain the intent to have sexual intercourse.[11] Assault with intent to murder is not committed by one too drunk to have an intent to kill.[12] The same result obtains as to all crimes with the mental state of "intent."[13]

A crime which is defined as "knowingly" (and sometimes a crime defined as "wilfully," when "wilfully" means "knowingly") doing some act may be negatived by intoxication which negatives the required knowledge.[14] A crime (like forgery or false pretenses) which requires an intent to defraud is not committed by one too drunk to have such an intent.[15]

On the same basis, intoxication which negatives the underlying felony is a defense to a charge of felony murder. Thus, a defendant, charged with first degree murder on account of a killing during the commission of a robbery, may properly defend himself from the first degree murder charge on the ground that, being too intoxicated to entertain the intent to rob, he was not guilty of the underlying felony of robbery.[16]

It is sometimes stated that intoxication can negative a "specific intent" which the crime in question may require [17] (meaning some intent in addition to the intent to do the physical act which the crime requires [18]), but it

---

intoxication is not a defense. In two states intoxication is admissible to show an absence of intent only if defendant would nonetheless be guilty of a lesser offense.

9. Heideman v. United States, 259 F.2d 943 (D.C.Cir. 1958) (robbery); Edwards v. State, 178 Miss. 696, 174 So. 57 (1937) (larceny); People v. Koerber, 244 N.Y. 147, 155 N.E. 79 (1926) (robbery); Jamison v. State, 53 Okl.Crim. 59, 7 P.2d 171 (1932) (larceny).

10. Allen v. United States, 239 F.2d 172 (6th Cir.1956) (burglary of post office); People v. Jones, 263 Ill. 564, 105 N.E. 744 (1914) (attempted burglary); People v. Eggleston, 186 Mich. 510, 152 N.W. 944 (1915) (burglary).

11. People v. Guillett, 342 Mich. 1, 69 N.W.2d 140 (1955) (assault to rape); see Director of Public Prosecutions v. Beard, [1920] A.C. 479 (a killing during forcible rape, which requires an intent to have intercourse by force; dictum that if one is so drunk that he is unable to form the intent to commit rape, he is not guilty of rape; but *held* conviction of murder restored, for on the evidence defendant was not so intoxicated as to have a defense to rape), noted at 34 Harv.L.Rev. 78 (1921). Contra: Walden v. State, 178 Tenn. 71, 156 S.W.2d 385 (1941) (since rape does not require a specific intent, it cannot be negatived by voluntary intoxication making the defendant unconscious of his acts), criticized in text infra at note 21. Compare People v. Freedman, 4 Ill.2d 414, 123 N.E.2d 317 (1954) (crime of taking indecent liberties "with the intent of gratifying sexual desires" is negatived by intoxication), with State v. Huey, 14 Wash.2d 387, 128 P.2d 314 (1942) (crime of taking indecent liberties, defined so that no particular purpose of sexual gratification is required, is not negatived by intoxication).

12. Roberts v. People, 19 Mich. 401 (1870).

13. State v. Watts, 223 N.W.2d 234 (Iowa 1974) (intent to carry concealed weapon); Commonwealth v. Kichline, 468 Pa. 265, 361 A.2d 282 (1976) (intent-to-kill variety of murder).

14. Compare Stenzel v. United States, 261 Fed. 161 (8th Cir.1919) (federal statute punishing one who "willfully" causes or attempts to cause insubordination or disloyalty in the United States military or naval forces is negatived by intoxication which prevents the defendant from being aware of what he is saying), with Embry v. State, 310 P.2d 617 (Okl.Crim.1957) (defendant guilty of "wilfully" destroying state property though so intoxicated that he is unaware of the fact that he is destroying property).

15. People v. Blake, 65 Cal. 275, 4 P. 1 (1884).

16. People v. Koerber, supra note 9. See also Director of Public Prosecutions v. Beard, supra note 11. The defendant might, of course, be guilty of murder, on some other theory of murder, though intoxicated. See § 4.10(b) for the second degree murder possibility.

17. See, e.g., United States v. Scott, 529 F.2d 338 (D.C. Cir.1975) (crime of entering bank with intent to rob); State v. Caldrain, 115 N.H. 390, 342 A.2d 628 (1975) (crime of breaking and entering with intent to rape).

18. Thus burglary requires an intent to commit a felony within the building in addition to the intent to break and enter the building; larceny an intent to steal the property in addition to the intent to take and carry away the property.

cannot negative a crime's "general intent"[19] (meaning an intent to do the physical act—or, perhaps, recklessly doing the physical act—which the crime requires).[20] Some cases therefore have held that voluntary intoxication cannot be a defense to rape even though it blots out the intent to have intercourse, since that intent is a general intent and not a specific intent.[21] But this is wrong on principle, for if intoxication does in fact negative an intention which is a required element of the crime (whether it be called specific intent or general intent), the crime has not been committed.[22] Some cases have held that intoxication cannot be a defense to battery, a crime sometimes said to require only a general intent.[23] This, however, is correct on principle, since battery can be committed not only with an intent to do the physical act of striking the other person (which intoxication can negative) but also, without any such intent to strike, by recklessly striking; and recklessness cannot,

by the weight of authority, be negatived by intoxication.[24]

A few jurisdictions, going even further astray, have held that voluntary intoxication is no defense even when it negatives the "specific intent" or knowledge which a crime may require.[25] This view is clearly wrong.

By way of conclusion, it may be said that it is better, when considering the effect of the defendant's voluntary intoxication upon his criminal liability, to stay away from those misleading concepts of general intent and specific intent.[26] Instead one should ask, first, what intent (or knowledge) if any does the crime in question require; and then, if the crime requires some intent (knowledge), did the defendant in fact entertain such an intent (or, did he in fact know what the crime requires him to know).[27]

In order for intoxication to serve as a defense to a crime by blotting out some intent or

19. See, e.g., State v. Sterline, 235 Kan. 526, 680 P.2d 301 (1984) (following general intent—specific intent distinction); People v. Langworthy, 416 Mich. 630, 331 N.W.2d 171 (1982) (following that distinction, though it recognized to be unsound, as solution lies with legislature).

This distinction is seldom followed in the modern recodifications. But see the Colo. and La. provisions cited in note 8 supra. An Indiana statute which limited the voluntary intoxication defense to crimes with the mental element stated by statute in a particular way was held unconstitutional in Terry v. State, 465 N.E.2d 1085 (Ind. 1984), stating: "Any factor which serves as a denial of the existence of *mens rea* must be considered by the trier of fact before a guilty finding is entered."

20. Thus rape requires an intent to do the physical act of accomplishing sexual intercourse with the victim; arson requires an intent to do the physical act of burning the property; battery requires an intent to cause bodily injury to another or (with no such intent) recklessness in causing such injury. For a discussion of the effect of intoxication on crimes of specific and general intent, see Comment, 55 Colum.L.Rev. 1210 (1955).

21. Abbott v. Commonwealth, 234 Ky. 423, 28 S.W.2d 486 (1930); People v. Langworthy, 416 Mich. 630, 331 N.W.2d 171 (1982); State v. Scarborough, 55 N.M. 201, 230 P.2d 235 (1951); Walden v. State, 178 Tenn. 71, 77, 156 S.W.2d 385, 387 (1941) (with rape "no intent is requisite other than that evidenced by the doing of the acts constituting the offense," so intoxication cannot be a defense).

22. See Director of Public Prosecutions v. Beard, supra note 11, for the correct proposition that great intoxication may negative the intent to have sexual intercourse which the crime requires.

23. United States v. Meeker, 527 F.2d 12 (9th Cir. 1975); Englehardt v. State, 88 Ala. 100, 7 So. 154 (1890);

Maddox v. State, 31 Ala.App. 332, 17 So.2d 283 (1944); Commonwealth v. Farrell, 322 Mass. 606, 78 N.E.2d 697 (1948).

24. See § 4.10(c). By contrast, attempted battery requires a higher mental state, and thus even voluntary intoxication is a defense to such a charge. State v. D'Amico, 136 Vt. 153, 385 A.2d 1082 (1978).

25. McDaniel v. State, 356 So.2d 1151 (Miss.1978); State v. Richardson, 495 S.W.2d 435 (Mo.1973); State v. Shipman, 354 Mo. 265, 189 S.W.2d 273 (1945) (defendant's voluntary intoxication cannot negative the specific intent to commit a felony which burglary requires); State v. Stasio, 78 N.J. 467, 396 A.2d 1129 (1979) (court adopts general principle that "voluntary intoxication will not excuse criminal conduct" because of "need to protect the public" and so that "the opportunities of false claims by defendants may be minimized"); State v. Vaughn, 268 S.C. 119, 232 S.E.2d 328 (1977) ("voluntary intoxication, where it has not produced permanent insanity, is never an excuse or a defense to crime, regardless of whether the intent involved be general or specific"); Chittum v. Commonwealth, 211 Va. 12, 174 S.E.2d 779 (1970). A few of the modern codes takes this position.

26. However, that unfortunate terminology is even used in the more recent cases. See, e.g., People v. DelGuidice, 199 Colo. 41, 606 P.2d 840 (1979); People v. Langworthy, 416 Mich. 630, 331 N.W.2d 171 (1982); Harrell v. State, 593 S.W.2d 664 (Tenn.1979); State v. Mriglot, 88 Wn.2d 573, 564 P.2d 784 (1977).

27. Once again, if the crime does not require him to intend anything, or to know anything, but instead applies if he is reckless, the principles governing the effect of intoxication upon recklessness, discussed below, apply.

knowledge which the crime requires, it is enough that the defendant, because of his intoxication, actually lacked the requisite intent or knowledge.[28] He need not be insane [29] or so intoxicated as to be unconscious or to be incapable of distinguishing between right and wrong.[30] One who, having already formed the intention to commit a crime, drinks in order to work up his nerve to commit the crime, cannot avail himself of the defense of intoxication even though, by the time he does commit the crime, he has become too intoxicated to entertain the intent which the crime requires.[31]

 WESTLAW REFERENCES

digest,synopsis(intoxica**** /p intent*** burglary)

(b) Intoxication Negativing Premeditation and Deliberation. Just as intoxication may negative some required intention or knowledge, so too it may negative the premeditation and deliberation which a common type of first degree murder statute requires. Just as one may be so emotionally upset, or in such a panic, or so mentally abnormal (though not insane), as to be incapable of premeditation and deliberation,[32] so intoxication may rob him of his capacity to premeditate and delib-

erate and thus reduce his crime from first degree to second degree murder.[33] It is generally, held, however, that intoxication cannot further reduce the homicide from second degree murder down to manslaughter.[34] This is because one may be guilty of second degree murder, in most jurisdictions which divide murder into two degrees, by killing without any intent to kill or injure but with a high degree of recklessness (the "depraved heart" type of murder),[35] and, as we shall see below, although intoxication can negative a required intention, it cannot (by the majority view) negative recklessness. Nevertheless, there is some authority for the proposition that intoxication which blots out not only the premeditation and deliberation but also the intent to kill or do serious injury will reduce a homicide down to manslaughter.[36]

Once again, for intoxication to negative premeditation and deliberation it must be so severe as to rob the defendant of his ability to premeditate and deliberate, although it need not in addition be so great as to render him unconscious or to deprive him of his normal ability to know right from wrong. Once again, too, he must not, before becoming intoxicated, have premeditated and deliberated

---

28. However, the common law view of the matter was that there must be "evidence of a state of drunkenness rendering the accused incapable of forming such an intent." Director of Public Prosecutions v. Beard, [1920] A.C. 479. Similarly demanding standards are often stated in the modern cases. See, e.g., People v. Johnson, 32 Ill. App.3d 36, 335 N.E.2d 144 (1975) ("whether the intoxication is so extreme as to entirely suspend the power of reason"); People v. Savoie, 419 Mich. 118, 349 N.W.2d 139 (1984) (rejecting position adopted earlier in People v. Crittle, 390 Mich. 367, 212 N.W.2d 196 (1973), that the jury should be instructed "in terms of whether in the light of defendant's intoxication he in fact had the required specific felonious intent"); State v. McLaughlin, 286 N.C. 597, 213 S.E.2d 238 (1975) ("intoxication to a degree precluding the ability to form a specific intent to kill").

29. State v. Smith, 260 Or. 349, 490 P.2d 1262 (1971).

30. People v. Leonardi, 143 N.Y. 360, 38 N.E. 372 (1894). Contra: Tate v. Commonwealth, 258 Ky. 685, 80 S.W.2d 817 (1935) (for voluntary intoxication to be effective it must be "so complete and of such an advanced degree as to totally deprive the defendant of his reason and to render him incapable of knowing right and wrong"). On the other hand, if he has the requisite intent or knowledge he is guilty, though his intoxication robs him of his moral sense of right and wrong: Roberts v. People, supra note 12.

31. People v. Krist, 168 N.Y. 19, 60 N.E. 1057 (1901); State v. Robinson, 20 W.Va. 713, 43 Am.Rep. 799 (1882); see Roberts v. People, 19 Mich. 401 (1870).

32. See § 7.7(a).

33. Hopt v. People, 104 U.S. 631, 26 L.Ed. 873 (1881); Aszman v. State, 123 Ind. 347, 24 N.E. 123 (1890); State v. Wilson, 234 Iowa 60, 11 N.W.2d 737 (1943). Contra: State v. Stacy, 104 Vt. 379, 160 A. 257 (1932). See Annots., 12 A.L.R. 861 (1921), 23 A.L.R. 438 (1923), 79 A.L.R. 897 (1932).

34. People v. DelGuidice, 199 Colo. 41, 606 P.2d 840 (1979); Commonwealth v. Bridge, 495 Pa. 568, 435 A.2d 151 (1981); Johnson v. Commonwealth, 135 Va. 524, 115 S.E. 673 (1923). See Annot., 8 A.L.R. 1052 (1920).

35. See § 7.4.

36. People v. Modesto, 59 Cal.2d 722, 31 Cal.Rptr. 225, 382 P.2d 33 (1963) (intoxication, if it negatives the intent to strike or injure the victim, reduces the homicide to involuntary manslaughter); Rex v. Meade [1909] 1 K.B. 895 (not murder but manslaughter where intoxication negatives intent to kill or do serious bodily injury); see State v. Braley, 224 Ore. 1, 355 P.2d 467 (1960) (dissenting opinion). See Annot., 8 A.L.R. 1052, 1057–58 (1920).

and formed an intent to kill, then drinking to get up his nerve; he is eligible for a first degree murder conviction even though by the time of the killing he may have become so intoxicated that he was no longer capable of premeditation and deliberation.[37]

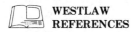 **WESTLAW REFERENCES**

digest,synopsis(intoxicat! /s premeditat*** deliberat***)

(c) Intoxication and Recklessness or Negligence. Some crimes may be committed without any sort of intention or knowledge but with some degree of criminal negligence or recklessness.[38] As we have seen,[39] the word "negligence" is often used in different ways, although under the better view negligence (in the tort sense) must be distinguished from criminal negligence or a high degree of negligence (conduct, measured by an objective standard, which creates a high degree of risk) and from recklessness (also requiring a subjective awareness of the risk).

When the defendant's actions are judged by an objective standard—whether a reasonable man would be aware of the risk—then it is beyond dispute that the defendant's intoxication is no defense. Just as in the law of torts,[40] the defendant is held to the standard of the reasonable man of ordinary prudence, so that his ignorance of the risk because of his intoxication is not relevant. Thus, when one is charged with assault upon a police officer under a statute which requires a showing that he "knows or reasonably should know that such victim is a peace officer," his intoxication may be considered by the jury in determining whether he actually knew the victim was an officer but not in determining whether he reasonably should have known.[41]

But if the crime requires what is most properly called recklessness, in that the defendant must be aware of the risk which his conduct creates, then what is the effect of his unawareness because of intoxication? There is some authority for the proposition that, where awareness is required for criminal liability, lack of awareness because of intoxication negatives the crime; that so long as he is actually unaware of the risk, it makes no difference how he came to be unaware.[42] On principle, this view might seem correct. However, the majority of cases in America support the creation of a special rule relating to intoxication, so that, if the only reason why the defendant does not realize the riskiness of his conduct is that he is too intoxicated to realize it, he is guilty of the recklessness which the crime requires.[43] The Model Penal Code

37. Aszman v. State, supra note 33.

38. Some crimes require intention or knowledge as to one element, criminal negligence as to another—e.g., for rape one must intend to have sexual intercourse with the victim but he need not intend to do it without her consent; he is guilty if he negligently but mistakenly thinks he has the lady's consent to the intercourse. United States v. Short, 4 U.S.C.M.A. 437, 16 C.M.R. 11 (1954).

39. See § 3.7.

40. W. Prosser & W. Keeton, Torts 178 (5th ed. 1984); McCoid, Intoxication and Its Effect Upon Civil Responsibility, 42 Iowa L.Rev. 38 (1956).

41. People v. Garcia, 250 Cal.App.2d 15, 58 Cal.Rptr. 186 (1967).

42. Regina v. Stones, 72 N.S.Wales Weekly Notes 465 (1955); G. Williams, Criminal Law: The General Part §§ 182, 183 (2d ed. 1961).

43. State v. Shine, 193 Conn. 632, 479 A.2d 218 (1984) (rejecting argument this approach unconstitutional); Brown v. Commonwealth, 575 S.W.2d 451 (Ky.1978) (stressing this also the Model Penal Code position); People v. Townsend, 214 Mich. 267, 183 N.W. 177 (1921) (defendant, voluntarily intoxicated, drove the car off the road, killing his passenger; he is guilty of manslaughter though he did not realize his conduct might kill another); People v. Register, 60 N.Y.2d 270, 469 N.Y.S.2d 599, 457 N.E.2d 704 (1983) (intoxication no defense to charge of depraved-heart murder, as it a variety of recklessness); State v. Trott, 190 N.C. 674, 130 S.E. 627 (1925) (defendant, intoxicated, in charge of car, allowed another, also intoxicated, to drive it; the driver drove in such a way as to imperil many lives, killing victim; conviction of depraved heart murder *held* affirmed); Embry v. State, 310 P.2d 617 (Okl. Crim.App.1957) (defendant's intoxication *held* no defense to malicious mischief, although it rendered him unaware that his conduct endangered another's property).

Cf. United States v. Short, 4 U.S.C.M.A. 437, 16 C.M.R. 11 (1954) (defendant attempted to have forcible sexual intercourse, but claimed that his intoxication rendered him unable to understand that she did not consent to his conduct; conviction of assault to rape *held* affirmed, because one may be guilty of rape if he negligently believes she consents when she does not consent).

Of course, in many situations it may be that, although the intoxicated defendant did not realize the risk to others involved in his conduct at the time he caused the injury in question, nevertheless he engaged in drinking at a time when he realized the risk to others of his getting drunk, as where he drinks just before he knows he will drive a car.

adopts the latter view [44] on the ground "that awareness of the potential consequences of excessive drinking on the capacity of human beings to gauge the risks incident to their conduct is by now so dispersed in our culture that it is not unfair to postulate a general equivalence between the risks created by the conduct of the drunken actor and the risks created by his conduct in becoming drunk." [45] Many of the modern recodifications follow the Model Penal Code in this respect.[46]

WESTLAW REFERENCES

topic(intoxication) /p negligen! reckless! /p criminal homicid** murder*** burglar!

(d) Intoxication and Self Defense. In order for one who kills or injures another to avail himself of the defense of self defense, it is necessary that he reasonably believe that his adversary intends to kill or injure him and that the only way to prevent this result is to kill or injure the adversary first. It may be that an intoxicated defendant actually believes these matters, but had he been sober he would have not believed them. At least where his intoxication is voluntary, he does not have the defense of self defense, which requires that the defendant appraise the situation as would a reasonable *sober* man.[47]

WESTLAW REFERENCES

self-defense /s intoxicat!

(e) Intoxication and Voluntary Manslaughter. One of the requirements for the reduction of an intentional homicide from murder down to voluntary manslaughter is the requirement that the defendant must have been provoked into a reasonable loss of self control by his victim's conduct.[48] It may be that a defendant, while intoxicated, is actually provoked by the other's conduct into killing him, although, had been sober, he would not have been so provoked. Thus intoxication may make the defendant more pugacious or excitable than he is when he is sober. Since the provocation which will do for voluntary manslaughter must be that which will arouse a heat of passion in a reasonable *sober* man, the defendant's voluntary intoxication which unreasonably provokes him will not do to reduce his homicide to manslaughter.[49] But, if the provocation would be adequate with respect to a sober man, then the fact of defendant's intoxication is relevant in determining whether he was in fact acting in the heat of passion.[50]

WESTLAW REFERENCES

"voluntary manslaughter" /s intoxicat!

(f) Involuntary Intoxication as a Defense. Thus far we have been considering the usual case where the defendant is "voluntarily" intoxicated (where his intoxication is "self-induced," as it is sometimes expressed). We have seen that such intoxication is a defense only if it negatives some required element of the crime in question. It is not enough that it puts the defendant in a state of mind which resembles insanity. Involuntary intoxication, on the other hand, does constitute a defense if it puts the defendant in such

In such a case he has the required awareness of the risk. Edwards v. State, 202 Tenn. 393, 304 S.W.2d 500 (1957). See People v. Decina, 2 N.Y.2d 133, 157 N.Y.S.2d 558, 138 N.E.2d 799 (1956).

44. Model Penal Code, § 2.08(2): "When recklessness establishes an element of the offense, if the actor, due to self-induced intoxication, is unaware of a risk of which he would have been aware had he been sober, such unawareness is immaterial."

45. Model Penal Code § 2.08, Comment at 359 (1985). Other considerations listed by the draftsmen are "the weight of the prevailing law" and "the impressive difficulties posed in litigating the foresight of any particular actor at the time when he imbibes and the relative rarity of cases where intoxication really does engender unawareness as distinguished from imprudence."

46. Illustrative of the application of such a statute is State v. Barrett, 408 A.2d 1273 (Me.1979) (where arson defined as starting fire "in conscious disregard of a substantial risk that his conduct will endanger any person or damage or destroy the property of another," defendant liable even if because of voluntary intoxication he unaware of that risk).

47. Springfield v. State, 96 Ala. 81, 11 So. 250 (1892); Golden v. State, 25 Ga. 527 (1858).

48. See § 7.10(b).

49. Bishop v. United States, 107 F.2d 297 (D.C.Cir. 1939); State v. Hall, 214 N.W.2d 205 (Iowa 1974); Commonwealth v. Hicks, 483 Pa. 305, 396 A.2d 1183 (1979); Regina v. McCarthy, [1954] 2 All E.R. 262.

50. People v. Rogers, 18 N.Y. 9 (1858).

a state of mind, e.g., so that he does not know the nature and quality of his act or know that his act is wrong, in a jurisdiction which has adopted the *M'Naghten* test for insanity.[51]

When is intoxication, through alcohol or drugs, properly characterized as involuntary?[52] One such case is when the intoxication has resulted from an innocent mistake by the defendant as to the character of the substance taken, as when another person has tricked him into taking the liquor or drugs.[53] Another, recognized by dicta in some cases, is intoxication under duress,[54] although the courts have been quite restrictive in determining what pressures are required to overcome the will of the actor.[55] Yet another instance of involuntary intoxication is when the substance was taken pursuant to medical advice.[56] Finally, there is pathological intoxication, which is self-induced in the sense that the defendant knew what substance he was taking, but which was "grossly excessive in degree, given the amount of the intoxicant."[57] In the latter case, the intoxication is involuntary only if the defendant was unaware that he is susceptible to an atypical reaction to the substance taken.[58] The mere fact the defendant is an alcoholic[59] or addict[60] is not sufficient to put his intoxicated or drugged condition into the involuntary category.

---

51. People v. Penman, 271 Ill. 82, 110 N.E. 894 (1915) (defendant killed victim after taking cocaine tablets thinking, because of a deception practiced upon him, that they were breath purifiers; this is involuntary intoxication, and if it made him unconscious of what he did, it is a defense, which the court calls temporary insanity); Heyward v. State, 470 N.E.2d 63 (Ind.1984) (defendant not entitled to instruction that involuntary intoxication a complete defense; "the intoxication must have at least temporarily put the accused into a state of mind which resembled insanity"); Prather v. Commonwealth, 215 Ky. 714, 287 S.W. 559 (1926) (defendant converted trust funds while under influence of morphine; he became a morphine addict as a result of an operation which caused great pain; the effect of the drug was to dull his conception of right and wrong and leave him without will power to resist the temptation to do wrong; defendant's condition was involuntary and constitutes a defense); City of Minneapolis v. Altimus, 306 Minn. 462, 238 N.W.2d 851 (1976) ("if the defendant is mentally deficient due to involuntary intoxication," then statutory standard applicable to insanity defense is to be used); Torres v. State, 585 S.W.2d 746 (Tex.Crim.App.1979) (if drugged condition involuntary, then standard applicable under insanity defense applies).

Most of the modern recodifications have a provision to this effect. Under Model Penal Code § 2.08(4), involuntary intoxication is a defense "if by reason of such intoxication the actor at the time of his conduct lacks substantial capacity either to appreciate its criminality [wrongfulness] or to conform his conduct to the requirements of law."

52. See Annot., 73 A.L.R.3d 195 (1976).

53. People v. Scott, 146 Cal.App.3d 823, 194 Cal.Rptr. 633 (1983) (defendant involuntarily intoxicated where, unknown to defendant, PCP put in punch); People v. Penman, supra note 51; Torres v. State, 585 S.W.2d 746 (Tex. Crim.App.1979) (involuntary intoxication instruction necessary on evidence that when defendant complained of headache her "friend" gave her an Alka-Seltzer in which, without her knowledge, he put drugs, as "the accused has exercised no independent judgment or volition in taking the intoxicant"). Thus, Model Penal Code § 2.08(5)(b) defines self-induced intoxication as intoxication "caused by substances which the actor knowingly introduces into his body, the tendency of which to cause intoxication he knows or ought to know." A few of the modern recodifications include such a definition.

54. Burrows v. State, supra note 51; Borland v. State, 158 Ark. 37, 249 S.W. 591 (1923); McCook v. State, 91 Ga. 740, 17 S.E. 1019 (1893); State v. Sopher, 70 Iowa 494, 30 N.W. 917 (1886); Perryman v. State, 12 Okl.Cr. 500, 159 P. 937 (1916).

55. For example, Burrows v. State, supra note 51, concerned a youth who was hitchhiking through a desert region when he was picked up by the driver of a car. The driver threatened to eject the youth from the car unless he drank intoxicating liquor. Having in consequence of this threat drunk a considerable amount of liquor, the youth, no longer able to appreciate the consequences of his act, shot the driver to death. The court held that his intoxication was not the result of duress.

Model Penal Code § 2.08(5)(b) requires that the substances be taken "under such circumstances as would afford a defense to a charge of crime," thus incorporating the principles of the choice of evils defense, id. at § 3.02, and the duress defense, id. at § 2.09.

56. Prather v. Commonwealth, supra note 51 (defendant acquired morphine habit following painful operation); City of Minneapolis v. Altimus, 306 Minn. 462, 238 N.W.2d 851 (1976) (where Valium prescribed for defendant's back problem; it necessary "that the defendant must not know, or have reason to know, that the prescribed drug is likely to have an intoxicating effect"). Cf. Johnson v. Commonwealth, 135 Va. 524, 115 S.E. 673 (1923) (defendant became intoxicated, but not on doctor's orders, to deaden the pain of a toothache; while intoxicated he killed another; his intoxication held to be voluntary, so that it constituted no defense to the crime of murder).

57. Model Penal Code § 2.08(5)(c). See Comment, 1969 Utah L.Rev. 419. Only a few of the modern codes contain a comparable provision.

58. Kane v. United States, 399 F.2d 730 (9th Cir.1968). Model Penal Code § 2.08(5)(c) includes such a requirement.

59. Evans v. State, 645 P.2d 155 (Alaska 1982); State v. Palacio, 221 Kan. 394, 559 P.2d 804 (1977).

---

60. See note 60 on page 395.

WESTLAW REFERENCES

"involuntary intoxication"

110k56

(g) Intoxication and Insanity. While, as we have seen, the defense of intoxication is quite different from the defense of insanity, yet excessive drinking may bring on actual insanity (delirium tremens); in such a case, if a defendant does not know right from wrong (in a *M'Naghten* test jurisdiction), he is not guilty of a crime because of his otherwise criminal conduct.[61] However, a temporary mental condition brought about by use of alcohol or drugs, as compared to a "settled" or "established" form of insanity, is not sufficient for a defense of insanity.[62] Conversely, excessive drinking may be behavior which

results from some forms of insanity.[63] One who is thus actually insane does not lose the defense of insanity just because, at the time he committed the act in question, he was also intoxicated.[64]

WESTLAW REFERENCES

110k829(6)

(h) Narcotics Addiction and Chronic Alcoholism.[65] The traditional defense of intoxication, discussed above, must be distinguished from the more recent concern over whether the narcotics addict and chronic alcoholic may be convicted and punished for their status or for certain acts attributable to their condition. The latter problem has often been dealt with in terms of the constitutional prohibition on cruel and unusual punishment,[66]

60. Commonwealth v. Sheehan, 376 Mass. 765, 383 N.E.2d 1115 (1978); State v. Bishop, 632 S.W.2d 255 (Mo. 1982).

61. See People v. Griggs, 17 Cal.2d 621, 110 P.2d 1031 (1941) (defendant, a chronic alcoholic, killed another; he should have been allowed to withdraw his guilty plea; insanity may come about through long continued intoxication); People v. Toner, 217 Mich. 640, 187 N.W. 386 (1922) (approving requested charge to jury that defendant would not be guilty if at the time of the alleged crime he was suffering from delirium tremens and did not know that what he was doing was wrong; but conviction affirmed because the evidence showed he did not have delirium tremens).

Similarly, mere narcotics addiction raises no issue of mental disease or defect such as would support an insanity defense, but it is otherwise as to evidence that the addiction has caused physiological damage to the defendant's brain which caused him to lack substantial capacity to conform his conduct to the requirements of law. United States v. Lyons, 731 F.2d 243 (5th Cir.1984).

62. Evans v. State, 645 P.2d 155 (Alaska 1982) ("mental disease or defect ∗ ∗ ∗ must be severe enough to constitute an insanity defense by itself without regard to the intoxicated state of the accused"); Wells v. State, 247 Ga. 792, 279 S.E.2d 213 (1981) (no insanity defense where delusional,: state produced by voluntary drugged condition; "voluntarily contracted madness is no excuse for crime"); People v. Free, 94 Ill.2d 378, 69 Ill.Dec. 1, 447 N.E.2d 218 (1983) ("voluntary intoxication or voluntary drugged condition precludes the use of the insanity defense *unless* the mental disease or defect is traceable to the habitual or chronic use of drugs or alcohol ∗ ∗ ∗ and such use results in a 'settled' or 'fixed' permanent type of insanity"); State v. Hall, 214 N.W.2d 205 (Iowa 1974) (must be "settled or established" insanity); Commonwealth v. Sheehan, 376 Mass. 765, 383 N.E.2d 1115 (1978) ("where the defendant voluntarily consumes drugs knowing that such consumption will cause a mental disease or defect, a finding of lack of criminal responsibility would

not be warranted"); State v. Preston, 673 S.W.2d 1 (Mo. 1984) (intoxication must have resulted in a psychosis); State v. Wicks, 98 Wn.2d 620, 657 P.2d 781 (1983) (must be evidence of permanent impairment of the mind, a psychotic disorder of a settled nature, such as delirium tremens); State v. Kolisnitschenko, 84 Wis.2d 492, 267 N.W.2d 321 (1978) (court "not willing to hold in this case that a temporary psychotic state which lasts only for the period of intoxication and which is brought into existence by the interaction of a stormy personality and voluntary intoxication constitutes a mental disease which is a defense to the crime charged").

63. See Paulsen, Intoxication as a Defense, 1961 U.Ill. L.F. 1, 21.

64. Greider v. Duckworth, 701 F.2d 1228 (7th Cir.1983) (insanity defense available even if source of insanity was voluntary intoxication); State v. Plummer, 117 N.H. 320, 374 A.2d 431 (1977) (chronic alcoholism a defense if it produces insanity in the form of dipsomania).

65. See Bowman, Narcotic Addiction and Criminal Responsibility Under Durham, 53 Geo.L.J. 1017 (1965); Fingarette, Addiction and Criminal Responsibility, 84 Yale L.J. 413 (1975); Frankel, Narcotic Addiction, Criminal Responsibility and Civil Commitment, 1966 Utah L.Rev. 581 (1966); Hutt & Merrill, Criminal Responsibility and the Right to Treatment for Intoxication and Alcoholism, 57 Geo.L.J. 835 (1969); Merrill, Drunkenness and Reform of the Criminal Law, 54 Va.L.Rev. 1135 (1969); Tao, Legal Problems of Alcoholism, 37 Ford.L.Rev. 405 (1969); Tao, Psychiatry and the Utility of the Traditional Criminal Law Approach to Drunkenness of Offenses, 57 Geo.L.J. 818 (1969); Wald, Alcohol, Drugs, and Criminal Responsibility, 63 Geo.L.J. 69 (1974); Symposium, Modern Trends in Handling the Chronic Alcoholic Offender, 19 S.C.L.Rev. 303 (1967); Notes, 59 Geo.J.J. 761 (1971); 61 Minn.L.Rev. 901 (1977).

66. Robinson v. California, 370 U.S. 660, 82 S.Ct. 1417, 8 L.Ed.2d 758 (1962); Driver v. Hinnant, 356 F.2d 761 (4th Cir.1966).

although courts have not infrequently referred (at least for purposes of analogy) to the voluntary act requirement [67] and to such defenses as automatism, compulsion, and involuntary intoxication.[68]

One of the leading cases is *Robinson v. California,*[69] in which the Supreme Court held unconstitutional, on cruel and unusual punishment grounds, a statute making it a criminal offense for a person to "be addicted to the use of narcotics." The basis for this holding is somewhat obscure in the *Robinson* opinion, for the Court emphasized all of these factors: (1) under the statute, conviction was possible for the mere "status" of being an addict, for it was not necessary to prove any use of narcotics or other irregular behavior within the state; (2) addiction is an illness; and (3) addiction may be contracted innocently or involuntarily (e.g., from the use of medically prescribed narcotics, or at the time of birth because of maternal addiction).

Relying in part upon the *Robinson* decision, some courts then held that it would be cruel and usual punishment to convict a chronic alcoholic—a "person who is powerless to stop drinking and whose drinking seriously alters his normal living pattern"—of the crime of public drunkenness.[70] This offense, of course, involves more than status, so *Robinson* clearly was broadly interpreted as barring conviction for a disease or for acts "which are complusive as symptomatic of the disease."[71] Some reliance was also placed upon traditional criminal law concepts; it was said that "a chronic alcoholic cannot have the *mens rea* necessary to be held responsible criminally

for being drunk in public," [72] and that he has not engaged in any voluntary act.[73]

But in *Powell v. Texas,*[74] the Supreme Court refused to adopt such a "wide-ranging new constitutional principle." One reason was the state of the record in that case; the medical testimony was that when appellant was sober, the act of taking the first drink was a "voluntary exercise of his will," but that this exercise of will was undertaken under the "exceedingly strong influence" of a "compulsion" which was "not completely overpowering." Noting that these "concepts, when juxtaposed in this fashion, have little meaning," the Court found this testimony illustrative of the fact that medical knowledge in this area had not progressed to the point where it could support "a constitutional doctrine of criminal responsibility." [75] Moreover, the Court indicated its reluctance to "constitutionalize" the whole area of criminal responsibility, and thus gave *Robinson* a narrow reading. *Robinson* was interpreted as only barring punishment of status on the ground that unless so viewed "it is difficult to see any limiting principle that would serve to prevent this Court from becoming, under the aegis of the Cruel and Unusual Punishment Clause, the ultimate arbiter of the standards of criminal responsibility, in diverse areas of the criminal law, throughout the country." This means an addict may constitutionally be convicted of possession of the drugs intended for his own use,[76] though the actual practice in some jurisdictions is to channel such offenders into a pretrial diversion program.[77]

---

67. Driver v. Hinnant, supra note 66.

68. Salzman v. United States, 405 F.2d 358 (D.C.Cir. 1968) (Wright, J., conc.).

69. 370 U.S. 660, 82 S.Ct. 1417, 8 L.Ed.2d 758 (1962), noted in 51 Calif.L.Rev. 219 (1963); 59 Nw.U.L.Rev. 271 (1964); 41 Tex.L.Rev. 444 (1963); 111 U.Pa.L.Rev. 122 (1962).

70. Driver v. Hinnant, supra note 66, at 762; Easter v. District of Columbia, 361 F.2d 50 (D.C.Cir.1966).

71. Driver v. Hinnant, supra note 66.

72. Easter v. District of Columbia, supra note 70, at 53. But the court did not discuss exactly what *mens rea*, if any, was required for this crime.

73. Driver v. Hinnant, supra note 66.

74. 392 U.S. 514, 88 S.Ct. 2145, 20 L.Ed.2d 1254 (1968), noted in 46 J.Urb.L. 110 (1968); 21 S.C.L.Rev. 111 (1968).

75. The Court was also concerned because there "is as yet no known generally effective method for treating the vast number of alcoholics in our society." Given this fact, the Court concluded that use of the criminal process against chronic alcoholics, despite its limitations, was a rational response to the problem.

76. United States v. Moore, 486 F.2d 1139 (D.C.Cir. 1973); State v. Herro, 120 Ariz. 604, 587 P.2d 1181 (1978); State v. Smith, 219 N.W.2d 655 (Iowa 1974); People v. Davis, 33 N.Y.2d 221, 351 N.Y.S.2d 663, 306 N.E.2d 787 (1973). See Annot., 73 A.L.R.3d 16 (1976).

77. See Notes, 60 Geo.L.J. 667 (1972); 26 Stan.L.Rev. 923 (1974).

Running through all of the decisions in this area is a concern for some limiting principle whereby application of the cruel and unusual punishment prohibition in some circumstances would not ultimately result in the exoneration of narcotics addicts and chronic alcoholics for all conduct (e.g., taking of property, killing or injuring people) somehow related to their condition. In *Robinson,* the Court emphasized that states were free to punish such crimes as the sale, purchase, or possession of narcotics. In the pre-*Powell* cases holding that a chronic alcoholic could not be convicted of public intoxication, it was likewise noted that such a person "would be judged as would any person not so afflicted" with respect to other behavior.[78] Clearly, neither narcotics addiction nor chronic alcoholism is per se a defense.[79]

Following *Powell,* lower courts rather consistently have held that alcoholism is no defense to a charge of drunkenness.[80] What conceivably could occur, however, in the event of somewhat greater medical knowledge about alcoholism than was displayed in *Powell,* is a broadening of the involuntary intoxication classification—heretofore limited to intoxication by mistake, duress, or medical advice.[81] If the medical evidence is not merely that the defendant is an alcoholic, or a chronic alcoholic, but that he was reached at the stage where even the taking of the first drink is not a matter of choice, his intoxication may be viewed as involuntary rather than voluntary so that the broader defense comparable to that for insanity would apply.[82] But to date most courts have been disinclined to equate alcoholism with involuntariness.[83] (The issue is confronted less often today, for most states have decriminalized drunkenness.[84])

What then of the narcotics addict who resorts to crime in order to obtain funds for drugs to prevent withdrawal symptoms? This is a more serious problem, in the sense that a great many crimes are committed under precisely these circumstances.[85] Although it certainly could be argued that such a person is in need of treatment for his addiction rather than punishment for the crime committed to support it, there is no discernible trend toward recognizing a defense in such a case.[86] Moreover, some have argued there should be

78. E.g., Driver v. Hinnant, supra note 66.

79. Nor do either necessarily qualify under the defense of insanity. Heard v. United States, 348 F.2d 43 (D.C.Cir. 1964); Johnson v. State, 43 Ala.App. 224, 187 So.2d 281 (1966).

80. Vick v. State, 453 P.2d 342 (Alaska 1969); People v. Hoy, 380 Mich. 597, 158 N.W.2d 436 (1968); Seattle v. Hill, 72 Wn.2d 786, 435 P.2d 692 (1967). But see State v. Fearon, 283 Minn. 90, 166 N.W.2d 720 (1969) (chronic alcoholic cannot be convicted under statute covering only a "person who becomes intoxicated by voluntarily drinking"); State ex rel. Harper v. Zegeer, ___ W.Va. ___, 296 S.E.2d 873 (1982) (conviction of chronic alcoholic for public drunkenness violates state constitutional protection against cruel and unusual punishment). See Annot., 40 A.L.R.3d 321 (1971).

81. See § 4.10(f).

82. In Driver v. Hinnant, supra, note 66, the court asserted in another context that the "chronic alcoholic has not drunk voluntarily, although undoubtedly he did so originally." Other courts, however, have been more cautious, indicating that some but not all chronic alcoholics would avail themselves of the involuntary intoxication rules.

"Not every person commonly called a 'chronic alcoholic' is addicted to the point where he has a physiological or psychological dependency upon alcohol and his drinking is so involuntary and compulsive that one might argue he is irresponsible for his acts. * * * If [the defendant] had

been intoxicated to the point that he could not distinguish between right and wrong in respect to the shooting [of the victim] and such intoxication was involuntary because he suffered from a type of chronic alcoholism which compels involuntary drinking to satisfy a psychological or physiological dependency thereon, [he] would have a defense." Roberts v. State, 41 Wis.2d 537, 164 N.W.2d 525 (1969).

See also Wright, J., concurring in Salzman v. United States, supra note 68, arguing that if defendant's chronic alcoholism had reached the point where it controlled his behavior, he should have the benefit of an instruction which parallels that for insanity.

83. See cases in note 80 supra.

84. As noted in State ex rel. Harper v. Zegeer, ___ W.Va. ___, 296 S.E.2d 873 (1982): "Most states have adopted the Uniform Alcoholism and Intoxication Treatment Act [9 U.L.A. 57 (1979)] that deals with alcoholism as a disease. Other stopped short of decriminalization, and instead developed diversionary systems for both alcoholics and public drunks." On decriminalization, see Notes, 94 Harv.L.Rev. 1660, 1670–74 (1981); 50 Wash.L.Rev. 755 (1975).

85. See President's Comm'n on Law Enforcement and Administration of Justice, Task Force Report: Narcotics and Drug Abuse 10–11 (1967).

86. See People v. Borrero, 19 N.Y.2d 332, 280 N.Y.S.2d 109, 227 N.E.2d 18 (1967); State v. White, 27 N.J. 158, 142 A.2d 65 (1958), both holding it no defense that the crime was committed by a narcotics addict in order to obtain

no defense here because "there is no medical foundation for adopting the general proposition at the crux of the exculpatory legal arguments, the proposition that addictive conduct is involuntary." [87]

(i) Procedure for Intoxication Defense. Where voluntary or involuntary intoxication negatives an element of the crime charged, or where involuntary intoxication puts the defendant in a state of mind resembling insanity, there is no special plea which raises the defense of intoxication; the defendant simply pleads not guilty. Nevertheless, the defense of intoxication is an "affirmative" defense in the sense that the defendant has the burden of going forward, so that he must put on some evidence of his intoxication, unless the prosecution's own proof shows the defendant's intoxication.

Once the defendant has thus introduced some evidence of his intoxication, who has the burden of persuasion? Where the claim is that involuntary intoxication put the defendant into a state of mind resembling insanity, the burden of proof (as with the insanity defense itself [88]) may constitutionally be placed upon the defendant.[89] But the same is not true when the intoxication negatives an element of the crime.[90]

---

funds for drugs. Model Penal Code § 2.08, Comment at 366 (1985), makes it clear that the Code effects no change here.

See also United States v. Sullivan, 406 F.2d 180 (2d Cir. 1969), holding it no defense that defendant "had in some five years of alcoholic addiction progressed to a panhandling stage where he was willing to take part in illegal activity to support his addiction."

87. Fingarette, Addiction and Criminal Responsibility, 84 Yale L.J. 413, 443 (1975), adding: "On the other hand, massive descriptive evidence indicates that individuals often make choices to abandon addictive conduct or abstain from drug use permanently or temporarily."

88. See § 4.5(e).

89. City of Minneapolis v. Altimus, 306 Minn. 462, 238 N.W.2d 851 (1976).

§ 4.11 Infancy

At common law, children under the age of seven are conclusively presumed to be without criminal capacity, those who have reached the age of fourteen are treated as fully responsible, while as to those between the ages of seven and fourteen there is a rebuttable presumption of criminal incapacity. Several states have made some change by statute in the age of criminal responsibility for minors. In addition, all jurisdictions have adopted juvenile court legislation providing that some or all criminal conduct by those persons under a certain age must or may be adjudicated in the juvenile court rather than in a criminal prosecution.

(a) Common Law. At the early common law infancy apparently was not a defense to a criminal prosecution, although a youthful defendant usually received a pardon.[1] In the tenth century, by statute no one under the age of fifteen could be subjected to capital punishment unless he attempted to escape or refused to give himself up.[2] Finally, by the beginning of the fourteenth century it was established that children under the age of seven were without criminal capacity.[3] Seven was the age of responsibility under the Roman Civil Law, and this probably influenced the common law through Canon Law.[4]

---

90. Greider v. Duckworth, 701 F.2d 1228 (7th Cir.1983); State v. Schulz, 102 Wis.2d 423, 307 N.W.2d 151 (1981). Compare United States ex rel. Goddard v. Vaughn, 614 F.2d 929 (3d Cir.1980). See § 1.8(b).

§ 4.11

1. Kean, The History of the Criminal Liability of Children, 53 L.Q.Rev. 364 (1937).

2. F. Attenborough, The Laws of the Earliest English Kings 169 (1922).

3. Kean, supra note 1, at 366.

4. Woodbridge, Physical and Mental Infancy in the Criminal Law, 87 U.Pa.L.Rev. 426, 435 (1939).

By 1338 infants over seven were presumed to lack the capacity to commit crime, but the presumption could be rebutted by proof of malice,[5] which in turn could be shown by concealment of the crime. At this time the age at which the presumption of incapacity no longer was applicable had not been precisely fixed, but by the seventeenth century the age of discretion had been established at fourteen.[6] The common law had thus developed to its present form: (1) children under seven had no criminal capacity; (2) children at age fourteen and over had the same criminal capacity as adults; and (3) children over seven and under fourteen were presumed to be without capacity, but this presumption could be rebutted in an individual case.[7]

The early common law infancy defense was based upon an unwillingness to punish those thought to be incapable of forming criminal intent and not of an age where the threat of punishment could serve as a deterrent.[8] The rebuttable presumption was explained on the ground that failure to punish particularly atrocious acts committed by those between the ages of seven and fourteen would encourage other children to commit them with impunity.[9] The early commentators emphasized that the presumption of incapacity could be rebutted by proof of the youthful defendant's ability to distinguish between good and evil.[10] Moreover, the weight of the presumption was said to decrease as the child approached the age of discretion,[11] and this view has also been followed in the United States.[12]

The burden of proof in overcoming the presumption is on the prosecution,[13] although there is not complete agreement on what exactly must be proved. Various phrases have been used to describe what is required: guilty knowledge of wrongdoing,[14] a mischievous inclination,[15] an "intelligent design and malice in the execution of the act,"[16] a consciousness of the wrongfulness of the act,[17] and knowledge of good from evil.[18] However, "the most modern definition of the test is simply that the surrounding circumstances must demonstrate * * * that the individual knew what he was doing and that it was wrong."[19] Some courts have taken the position that an inference of such knowledge may arise from proof of the child's general knowledge of the difference between good and evil,[20] while elsewhere proof of this general knowledge has not been deemed sufficient to show knowledge of the consequences of the particular acts engaged in.[21]

Conduct of the defendant relating to the acts charged may be most relevant in overcoming the presumption. Thus hiding the body,[22] inquiry as to the detection of poi-

---

5   Y.B. 11, 12 Edward III (Rolls Series) 626, 627 (1338).

6.   1 E. Coke, Institutes on the Laws of England 247b (1642).

7.   The age of responsibility may have earlier been fixed at twelve, 4 W. Blackstone, Commentaries on the Laws of England 23 (1769), at least for capital offenses, 1 M. Hale, Pleas of the Crown 22 (1778). Also, at an earlier time the infancy defense apparently was valid up to the age of twenty-one for misdemeanors of nonfeasance, but not for misdemeanors that required affirmative acts, such as battery and riot. Id. at 20; 4 W. Blackstone, supra, at 22.

8.   3 E. Coke, Institutes on the Laws of England 4 (1644).

9.   4 W. Blackstone, supra note 7, at 24.

10.   Id. at 23; 1 M. Hale, supra note 7, at 26.

11.   Ibid.

12.   McCormack v. State, 102 Ala. 156, 15 So. 438 (1894); Clay v. State, 143 Fla. 204, 196 So. 462 (1940).

13.   Godfrey v. State, 31 Ala. 323 (1858).

14.   Rex v. Owen, 172 Eng.Rep. 685 (1830); The Queen v. Smith, 1 Cox.Crim.Cas. 260 (1845); Watson v. Commonwealth, 247 Ky. 336, 57 S.W.2d 39 (1933).

15.   Martin v. State, 90 Ala. 602, 8 So. 858 (1891); McCormack v. State, 102 Ala. 156, 15 So. 438 (1894).

16.   Godfrey v. State, 31 Ala. 323 (1858).

17.   Regina v. Vampleu, 176 Eng.Rep. 234 (1862); Halman v. Commonwealth, 84 Ky. 457, 15 S.W. 731 (1886); Beason v. State, 96 Miss. 105, 50 So. 488 (1909); State v. Guild, 10 N.J.C. 163 (1828); State v. Aaron, 4 N.J.C. 231 (1818).

18.   Rex v. Wild, 168 Eng.Rep. 1341 (1835); Miles v. State, 99 Miss. 165, 54 So. 946 (1911).

19.   Adams v. State, 8 Md.App. 684, 688, 262 A.2d 69, 72 (1970).

20.   State v. Nickelson, 45 La.Ann. 1172, 14 So. 134 (1893); Commonwealth v. Mead, 92 Mass. 398 (1865).

21.   Willet v. Commonwealth, 76 Ky. 230 (1877); Scott v. State, 71 Tex.Crim.R. 41, 158 S.W. 814 (1913); Price v. State, 50 Tex.Crim.R. 71, 94 S.W. 901 (1906).

22.   Rex v. York, 1 Foster 70 (1748); Y.B. 11, 12, Edward III (Rolls Series) 626, 627 (1338).

son,[23] bribery of a witness,[24] or false accusation of others[25] have all been relied upon in finding capacity. In other instances, however, the gruesome nature of the crime,[26] the attempt to silence a witness,[27] and the disposal of evidence[28] have been found insufficient to rebut the presumption. The factors most often looked to are the cunning[29] and shrewdness[30] of the child.

It is the defendant's age at the time of the alleged conduct and not at the time of the proceedings which controls.[31] Also, it is the defendant's physical age rather than his "mental age" which is used to determine capacity,[32] although some have viewed this as illogical.[33]

(b) Legislation on Capacity or Lack of Jurisdiction. The question of when young persons can be convicted of crimes is now typically addressed by a statute of one kind or another. One type of statute is that which is expressed in terms of lack of capacity, to be found in a minority of the modern criminal codes. A very few of these statutes follow the common law format by utilizing, as to a specified age group, a presumption of incapacity which can be overcome only by a showing that the juvenile knew the wrongfulness of what he was doing. The other simply specify an age—usually 14 but in some instances 10, 13, 15, or 16—below which capacity is conclusively presumed to be lacking.[34] Where the absolute minimum age is below 14, the question may arise as to whether the common law

presumption of incapacity is still operative as to those between the statutory age and the common law age of 14.[35]

Even in states with modern criminal codes, the problem is more frequently addressed in terms of the allocation of jurisdiction between the criminal and juvenile courts. A typical provision of this type declares that juveniles under 14—or, under some other age, such as 10, 15, or 16—may not be subjected to criminal prosecution but only to delinquency proceedings in juvenile court. Some other statutes give exclusive jurisdiction to the juvenile court unless the juvenile was of a certain age, usually 16, but with exceptions for certain serious offenses. Still others merely declare more generally that juvenile court jurisdiction is not exclusive. Except for this last type of provision (or, for one which sets the age of exclusive juvenile court jurisdiction below 14), these jurisdiction statutes eliminate any question concerning the applicability of the common law rules in a criminal prosecution context.[36]

(c) Juvenile Court Jurisdiction. All jurisdictions have by statute or constitutional provision established a juvenile court system.[37] Juvenile courts typically deal with juvenile delinquents, juveniles otherwise in need of supervision, and neglected and dependent children. The most common statutory definition of delinquency is conduct which transgresses penal law,[38] and it is only that aspect of juvenile court jurisdiction which is

23. Regina v. Vampleu, 176 Eng.Rep. 234 (1862).

24. State v. Milholland, 89 Iowa 5, 56 N.W. 403 (1893).

25. Godfrey v. State, 31 Ala. 323 (1858).

26. State v. Vineyard, 81 W.Va. 98, 93 S.E. 1034 (1917).

27. People v. Lang, 402 Ill. 170, 83 N.E.2d 688 (1949).

28. Ibid.

29. See, e.g., State v. Guild, 10 N.J.C. 163 (1828).

30. See, e.g., State v. Bostick, 4 Del. 563 (1845).

31. Neville v. State, 148 Ala. 681, 41 So. 1011 (1906); Triplett v. State, 169 Miss. 306, 152 So. 881 (1934).

32. State v. Dillon, 93 Idaho 698, 471 P.2d 553 (1970); State v. Jackson, 346 Mo. 474, 142 S.W.2d 45 (1940).

33. See Woodbridge, Physical and Mental Infancy in the Criminal Law, 87 U.Pa.L.Rev. 426 (1939).

34. It has been noted that this approach is as a theoretical matter unsound because "chronological age is only

one pertinent fact" bearing on immaturity, but that it "is significantly easier to apply in practice." 2 P. Robinson, Criminal Law Defenses § 175(e) (1984). See Couch v. State, 253 Ga. 764, 325 S.E.2d 366 (1985) (notwithstanding 16-year-old defendant's argument that he had mental age of 10, he not covered by statute declaring a person is not guilty of a crime unless he has attained the age of 13; "The age referred to in the code section is, of course, biological age" rather than " 'mental age'—if, indeed, such a thing could even be determined").

35. See, e.g., Dove v. State, 37 Ark. 261 (1881) (yes).

36. But not necessarily in juvenile court. See § 4.11(c).

37. See § 1.7(a).

38. S. Fox, Juvenile Courts in a Nutshell § 11 (3d ed. 1984).

of concern here, for the following discussion is intended only to reflect the extent to which that jurisdiction has diminished the practical significance of common law and statutory provisions on the criminal capacity of children.

Most juvenile court acts place no lower age limit on juvenile court jurisdiction. Thus, unless the common law immunity for infants under seven is incorporated into juvenile law,[39] children under seven may be adjudged delinquent for conduct for which they lacked criminal responsibility. This issue seems not to have been confronted in the cases (perhaps indicating that it is not the practice to adjudicate as delinquent children under seven), and the commentators are not in agreement on the point. On the one hand, it is claimed that "the traditional concept of incapacity has no application" in juvenile court,[40] presumably on the ground that juvenile courts are not intended to deal with moral responsibility and are concerned only with the welfare of children. On the other, it is contended that the common law immunity should be applicable because the juvenile court serves to vindicate the public interest in the enforcement of the criminal law.[41] Even if that is so, it does not follow that a significantly higher minimum age of criminal responsibility set by statute

should be deemed equally applicable to delinquency proceedings in juvenile court.[42]

A related question is whether the common law presumption of incapacity may be asserted as a defense to juvenile court proceedings by alleged delinquents between the age of seven and fourteen. The majority view is that no such defense is available.[43] In support of this position, it is contended that "the purpose of treatment of immature offenders is solely rehabilitation" and that "rebuttable presumptions of incapacity become superfluous in the light of this treatment purpose."[44] But some courts have held that the common law defense, as codified in the state penal code, is equally applicable to delinquency proceedings in juvenile court.[45] That result has been praised on the ground "that the recent switch from treatment back to blameworthiness as the hallmark of juvenile offender law lays the basis for recognizing the infancy defense's crucial role in the new juvenile justice court."[46]

All juvenile court acts set an upper age limit upon juvenile court jurisdiction.[47] In almost all states the age is eighteen,[48] and the fact the person before the court is not older must be established by the state.[49] Laws setting the age limit for girls higher than for boys were at one time upheld against attacks

39. Cf. In re Gladys R., 1 Cal.3d 855, 83 Cal.Rptr. 671, 464 P.2d 127 (1970).

40. Model Penal Code § 4.10, Comment at 275 (1985).

41. "A toddler who is too young to distinguish 'mine' from 'thine' hardly threatens social interests in private property when he makes away with a playmate's toy." S. Fox, supra note 38, at § 8. See also Walkover, The Infancy Defense in Juvenile Court, 31 U.C.L.A.L.Rev. 503, 555–56 (1984).

42. In re Dow, 75 Ill.App.3d 1002, 31 Ill.Dec. 39, 393 N.E.2d 1346 (1979).

43. State v. D.H., 340 So.2d 1163 (Fla.1976); In re Davis, 17 Md.App. 98, 299 A.2d 856 (1973), noted in 34 Md. L.Rev. 178 (1974); In re Michael, ___ R.I. ___, 423 A.2d 1180 (1981).

44. Ludwig, Responsibility for Young Offenders, 29 Neb.L.Rev. 521, 534 (1950).

45. In re Gladys R., 1 Cal.3d 855, 83 Cal.Rptr. 671, 464 P.2d 127 (1970); Commonwealth v. Durham, 255 Pa.Super. 539, 389 A.2d 108 (1978); State v. Q.D., 102 Wn. 2d 19, 685 P.2d 557 (1984).

As to the proper avenues of inquiry on this matter of capacity, the court in *Gladys R.* suggested assessment of the child's age, experience, knowledge and conduct. "In cases since *Gladys R.*, courts making the capacity determination have looked at evidence gleaned from a variety of sources, including interviews of the child by psychologists and school personnel, police interrogation of the accused on the right/wrong issue, opinions of relatives and others as to the child's substantive knowledge of right and wrong and his capacity to make judgments concerning right and wrong, admissions of the accused to parents, conduct and circumstances surrounding the crime suggesting consciousness of guilt, and prior involvement in wrongdoing." Walkover, supra note 41, at 560–61.

46. Walkover, supra note 54, at 507. See also Fox, Responsibility in the Juvenile Court, 11 Wm. & Mary L.Rev. 659 (1970).

47. S. Fox, supra note 38, at 33.

48. Id. See, e.g., Me.Rev.Stat.Ann. tit. 17–A, § 10–A.

49. State v. Mendenhall, 21 Ohio App.2d 135, 255 N.E.2d 307 (1969); Miguel v. State, 500 S.W.2d 680 (Tex. Civ.App. 1973).

made on equal protection grounds,[50] but the more recent cases have found these provisions unconstitutional.[51]

Assuming an age limit of eighteen, what if the youth was seventeen at the time of the alleged delinquent acts but has passed his eighteenth birthday prior to the time that juvenile court proceedings are begun? Some statutes expressly provide that the juvenile court still has jurisdiction because it is the age at the time of the conduct which is determinative,[52] although many of the juvenile court acts are silent on this point. In the face of this ambiguity, most courts which have considered this issue have held that it is the age at the time of the proceedings which controls,[53] while some others have taken the position that it is the age at the time of the conduct which governs.[54]

In most states the jurisdiction of the juvenile court extends to all criminal conduct committed by those within the court's age-limit jurisdiction. Exceptions are sometimes made, however, so as to give exclusive jurisdiction to the criminal courts. Sometimes an exception to juvenile court jurisdiction is created as to certain serious offenses, either identified by name (usually murder and rape) or magnitude of punishment; and sometimes the exception goes to certain minor offenses (usually lesser traffic offenses and violations of the fish and game laws).[55] In other states and for other crimes the jurisdiction of the two courts may be concurrent. In such cases the juvenile court usually must waive its jurisdiction before the criminal courts can obtain jurisdiction over the juvenile.[56]

Certain procedures are required for an effective waiver of juvenile court jurisdiction. The Supreme Court in *Kent v. United States*,[57] construing the District of Columbia waiver statute, held that the juvenile court must afford a hearing on waiver and state reasons or considerations for the transfer sufficient to demonstrate that there has been a full investigation, and specific enough to permit meaningful review. Subsequent decisions have often viewed *Kent* as constitutionally based.[58]

The criteria to be utilized in making the waiver decision may be set forth in the juvenile court act itself or in court decisions.[59] Generally, it is fair to say that juvenile court legislation usually gives little indication of the waiver criteria; the typical reference is merely to the best interests of the public or of the child.[60] Of the court decisions setting forth the factors juvenile courts should consider before waiving jurisdiction, *Summers v. State*,[61] gives the most comprehensive summary:

> [Jurisdiction may be waived if] the offense has specific prosecutive merit in the opinion of the prosecuting attorney; or it is heinous or of an aggravated character, greater weight being given to offenses against the person than to offenses against property; or, even though less serious, if the offense is part of a repetitive pattern of juvenile offenses which would lead to a determi-

50. People v. Pardo, 47 Ill.2d 420, 265 N.E.2d 656 (1970); Lamb v. State, 475 P.2d 829 (Okl.Cr.App. 1970).

51. Lamb v. Brown, 456 F.2d 18 (10th Cir.1972); In re Patricia A., 31 N.Y.2d 83, 335 N.Y.S.2d 33, 286 N.E.2d 432 (1972).

52. Model Penal Code § 4.10, Comment at 282 (1985), referring to statutes in twenty jurisdictions. More recently enacted statutes take this position. S. Fox, supra note 38, at § 10. See People of Territory of Guam v. Quinata, 704 F.2d 1085 (9th Cir.1983).

53. E.g., State ex. rel. Koopman v. County Court Branch No. 1, 38 Wis.2d 492, 157 N.W.2d 623 (1968). When the time of the proceedings is deemed controlling, some hold the critical time to be when proceedings are instituted, e.g., State v. Fowler, 194 A.2d 558 (Del.Sup.Ct. 1963), and others when the trial commences, Sweet v. Porter, 75 Wn.2d 880, 454 P.2d 219 (1969).

54. E.g., State v. Jones, 220 Tenn. 477, 418 S.W.2d 769 (1966).

55. S. Fox, supra note 38, at § 11. Some states also provide there is no juvenile court jurisdiction if the juvenile has several prior delinquency adjudications for conduct which, if engaged in by an adult, would be a serious crime. See State v. Berard, 121 R.I. 551, 401 A.2d 448 (1979), holding such a statute constitutional.

56. See generally, Schornhorst, The Waiver of Juvenile Court Jurisdiction: Kent Revisited, 43 Ind.L.J. 583, 597 (1968).

57. 383 U.S. 541, 86 S.Ct. 1045, 16 L.Ed.2d 84 (1966).

58. E.g., United States ex rel. Turner v. Rundle, 438 F.2d 839 (3d Cir.1971); Bouge v. Reed, 254 Or. 418, 459 P.2d 869 (1969). Compare In re Bullard, 22 N.C.App. 245, 206 S.E.2d 305 (1974).

59. E.g., Lewis v. State, 86 Nev. 889, 478 P.2d 168 (1970).

60. S. Fox, supra note 38, at § 62.

61. 248 Ind. 551, 230 N.E.2d 320 (1967).

nation that the said juvenile may be beyond rehabilitation under the regular statutory juvenile procedures; or where it is found to be in the best interest of the public welfare and for the protection of the public security generally that said juvenile be required to stand as an adult offender.

Other courts have likewise emphasized the juvenile's trend toward antisocial behavior,[62] his past record,[63] and the willful nature of the act,[64] as the most important factors.

 WESTLAW REFERENCES

di infancy

kent /12 86 +4 1045 /p juvenile minor /p waiv***

---

62. Stephenson v. State, 204 Kan. 80, 460 P.2d 442 (1969).

63. Jimmy, H. v. Superior Court, 3 Cal.3d 709, 91 Cal. Rptr. 600, 478 P.2d 32 (1970).

64. Lewis v. State, 86 Nev. 889, 478 P.2d 168 (1970).

Chapter 5

JUSTIFICATION AND EXCUSE

Table of Sections

---

§ 5.1 Ignorance or Mistake

Ignorance or mistake as to a matter of fact or law is a defense if it negatives a mental state required to establish a material element of the crime, except that if the defendant would be guilty of another crime had the situation been as he believed, then he may be convicted of the offense of which he would be guilty had the situation been as he believed it to be. (A quite different kind of mistake of law, whereby the defendant believes that his conduct is not proscribed by the criminal law, is generally not a defense.)

(a) Generally. No area of the substantive criminal law has traditionally been surrounded by more confusion than that of ignorance or mistake of fact or law. It is frequently said, on the one hand, that ignorance of the law is no excuse, and, on the other, that a mistake of fact is an excuse. Neither of these propositions is precisely correct, and both are subject to numerous exceptions and qualifications.[1] Uncertainty as to the precise significance of the defendant's mistake or ignorance of the surrounding facts is attributable in part to assertions, usually unexplained, in some decisions that the error must be a reasonable one or that the defendant is subject to conviction notwithstanding the mistake. Another source of confusion is the indiscriminate use of the phrase "ignorance of the law" to encompass both the situation in which the defendant is unaware of the existence of a statute proscribing his conduct, and that where the defendant has a mistaken impression concerning the legal effect of some collateral matter and that mistake results in his misunderstanding the full significance of his conduct (as where, in a bigamy case, the defendant mistakenly believes that his prior divorce is valid). These two situations call for quite different analysis and, frequently, different results.[2]

In actuality, the basic rule is extremely simple: ignorance or mistake of fact or law is a defense when it negatives the existence of a mental state essential to the crime charged.[3] Indeed, it is so simple because, unlike the other defenses discussed in this chapter, it is merely a restatement in somewhat different form of one of the basic premises of the criminal law. Instead of speaking of ignorance or mistake of fact or law as a defense, it would be just as easy to note simply that the defendant cannot be convicted when it is shown that he does not have the mental state required by law[4] for commission of that particular offense.[5] For example, to take the classic case of the man who takes another's umbrella out of a restaurant because he mistakenly believes that the umbrella is his, it is not really necessary to say that the man, if charged with larceny, has a valid defense of mistake of fact; it would be more direct and to the point to assert that the man is not guilty because he does not have the mental state (intent to steal the property of another[6]) required for the crime of larceny. Yet, the practice has developed of dealing with such mistakes as a matter of defense,[7] perhaps because the facts showing their existence are usually brought out by the defendant,[8] and they are so classified in this book.[9]

§ 5.1

1. See J. Hall, General Principles of Criminal Law ch. 11 (2d ed. 1960).

2. See Dutile & Moore, Mistake and Impossibility: Arranging a Marriage Between Two Difficult Partners, 74 Nw.U.L.Rev. 166, 171–81 (1979).

3. Model Penal Code § 2.04(1)(a). Several modern codes contain such a provision. Surprising, however, a larger number have a provision along these lines which mentions only mistakes of fact. "This is no doubt due to the reaction of legislators who, even if laymen, are familiar with the common law maxim that 'ignorance of the law is no excuse.'" 1 P. Robinson, Criminal Law Defenses § 62(d) (1984). That is, the failure to follow the Model Penal Code formulation is probably attributable to legislative confusion of the two kinds of mistakes of law discussed herein. In these states, it is unclear at best whether a mistake of law would be recognized as a defense when because of the mistake the defendant lacks the requisite state of mind (e.g., knowledge of lack of license or privilege in the crime of trespass). Ibid.

4. See § 3.4.

5. See State v. Molin, 288 N.W.2d 232 (Minn.1979) (for this reason, defendant not entitled to an instruction on the defense of mistake where an adequate instruction on

the prosecution burden to prove intent was given). Compare State v. Freeman, 267 N.W.2d 69 (Iowa 1978) (mistake of fact is "a separate and distinct issue notwithstanding its relation to the State's duty to prove a criminal intent," and thus mistake of fact instruction was necessary).

6. See § 8.5.

7. The practice is even followed in Model Penal Code § 2.04, although it is noted that "ignorance or mistake has only evidential import; it is significant whenever it is logically relevant, and it may be logically relevant to negate the required mode of culpability or to establish a special defense." Model Penal Code § 2.04, Comment at 269 (1985).

8. "It may well be, as a practical matter, that the defendant may have to act affirmatively to raise the issue, to carry the burden of pleading, to undercut a prima facie case that the prosecution has established. But this can be true with respect to negating any other element of the offense as it is with those situations in which we speak of the defendant as having a 'mistake defense.'" 1 P. Robinson, Criminal Law Defenses § 62(b) (1984).

9. Problems of ignorance or mistake of fact or law also arise in connection with other defenses, as, for example, when the homicide defendant claims self-defense but he

Once the basic rule is understood, it is then apparent why the two different kinds of mistake of law mentioned earlier call for different results. If, instead of the mistake of fact in the umbrella hypothetical, the defendant took the chattel through a mistake of law, such as that his prior dealings had vested ownership of it in him, he would again not have the intent-to-steal mental state required for the crime of larceny.[10] By contrast, this intent to steal would be present if the defendant took the umbrella he knew was owned by another but he could honestly say that he was unaware that such a taking was proscribed by the criminal law. It is in this latter sense that it may be correctly said that ignorance of the law is no excuse, although even here, as will be discussed later, there are exceptions when the defendant reasonably believes his conduct is not proscribed by law and that belief is attributable to an official statement of the law or to the failure of the state to give fair notice of the proscription.

**WESTLAW
REFERENCES**

110k32
110k33

(b) Ignorance or Mistake Negating Mental State; Reasonableness. The rather simple rule that an honest mistake of fact or law is a defense when it negates a required mental element of the crime would appear to be fairly easy to apply to a variety of cases. One merely identifies the mental state or states required for the crime, and then inquires whether that mental state can exist in light of the defendant's ignorance or mistake of fact or law. For example, on a charge of receiving property knowing it to be stolen, the critical mental element is knowledge concerning the illegal means by which the property was obtained. If the defendant knew that the

goods were stolen, but believed them to be television sets when they were in fact radios, it would be apparent that this mistake of fact would be no defense because it does not negate the mental element of the crime. On the other hand, if the defendant by a mistake of either fact or law did not know the goods were stolen, even though the circumstances would have led a prudent man to believe they were stolen, he does not have the required mental state and thus may not be convicted of the crime.[11] Frequently, however, the cases do not proceed along this easy route, for two reasons: (1) because of uncritical acceptance of the general statement that the mistake must be reasonable; and (2) because imprecise drafting has left it uncertain what mental element is actually required for the offense in question.

Illustrative of the first point is the case of *United States v. Short*.[12] The defendant was convicted of assault with intent to commit rape, and he appealed on the ground that the court had erred in refusing a defense-requested instruction that he could not be convicted if he believed the girl had consented. The conviction was affirmed, and it was held that the requested instruction was too broad because it failed to qualify the defendant's belief by stating the belief must be reasonable. In support of this conclusion, the court noted that on a charge of rape the defendant would only be entitled to an instruction that reasonable belief as to consent was a defense.[13]

As the dissenting judge in *Short* pointed out, the notion that a mistake of fact is a defense only when reasonable is far too general and does not apply in many cases. One example cited was where the defendant is charged with knowing possession of marijuana; because such possession denotes conscious knowledge of the thing possessed, even negligent ignorance of the character of the ciga-

---

was mistaken in his belief that he was under deadly attack. These matters are considered in the following sections of this chapter.

10. State v. Sawyer, 95 Conn. 34, 110 A. 461 (1920). See also State v. Cude, 14 Utah 2d 287, 383 P.2d 399 (1963) (where statute makes it larceny to take one's own property with intent to deprive another person of his rights in it, defendant entitled to instruction that he not guilty if by

ignorance of law he unaware garageman had a mechanic's lien on defendant's car, kept at garage when defendant did not pay repair bill).

11. State v. Ebbeler, 283 Mo. 57, 222 S.W. 396 (1920).

12. 4 U.S.C.M.A. 437, 16 C.M.R. 11 (1954).

13. The court cited McQuirk v. State, 84 Ala. 435, 4 So. 775 (1888) for that proposition.

rettes would be a defense, for knowledge is a higher and different statutory requirement than negligence.[14] As for the majority's reliance upon the reasonable belief requirement under the crime of rape, the dissenting judge contended that the crime of rape was distinguishable from assault with intent to rape because the former requires only a general criminal intent while the latter requires a specific intent. As discussed earlier, the phrases "general intent" and "specific intent" only tend to cause confusion,[15] and thus the dissenting judge's point can be best related by avoiding those terms and by instead going directly to the kind of mental element required for these two crimes. First of all, at least under the case relied upon by the majority in *Short*,[16] the crime of rape must be understood as *not* including an element of knowledge of the woman's lack of consent,[17] from which it follows that not every mistake by the defendant by which he believes the woman is consenting will be a defense.[18] But, the crime of assault with intent to rape clearly sets forth a mental element; the defendant's purpose in assaulting the woman must be rape. This purpose of intercourse against the woman's will cannot be present if the defendant believes—even unreasonably—that the woman is consenting. (This fundamental

point has gone unrecognized even in some of the modern codes.[19])

The second factor mentioned earlier, uncertainty in criminal legislation as to precisely what mental state, if any, is required—has also accounted for much of the confusion in this area, as is aptly illustrated by the offense of bigamy. Many of the bigamy statutes in this country are silent on the matter of *mens rea*.[20] As a consequence, a common view of the crime of bigamy is that none of the following constitutes a valid defense: reasonable belief that the first spouse is dead [21]; reasonable belief that the first marriage was illegal [22]; reasonable belief that a decree concerning the first marriage was a divorce decree [23]; or reasonable belief that a foreign divorce would be recognized in the jurisdiction.[24] Such results have been reached through a process of statutory construction of bigamy statutes, often based upon these principles: (a) that when the legislature specified certain defenses (e.g., belief in the death of the other spouse based upon seven years absence) it intended to exclude all others; (b) that if the legislature had intended to require *mens rea* for the crime of bigamy it would have explicitly indicated this in the statute; and (c) that the statutory language justifies the assumption that the

---

14. United States v. Lampkins, 4 U.S.C.M.A. 31, 15 C.M.R. 31 (1954).

15. See § 3.5(e).

16. See n. 13 supra. Other cases also take the view that in a rape case the defendant's belief in consent must be reasonable, e.g., State v. Dizon, 47 Haw. 444, 390 P.2d 759 (1964), although it is sometimes asserted, under the moral wrong theory discussed later in this section, that even a reasonable belief would be no defense because the defendant, even under the facts as he believed them to be, would be committing an immoral act. See White v. State, 44 Ohio App. 331, 185 N.E. 64 (1933).

17. If, on the other hand, this crime is interpreted as requiring a subjective mental state as to the lack of consent, then a mistake causing defendant to believe the woman is consenting would be a defense. See People v. Mayberry, 15 Cal.3d 143, 125 Cal.Rptr. 745, 542 P.2d 1337 (1975); Director of Public Prosecutions v. Morgan, 61 C.A. 136 (1975).

18. The same is true in other contexts in which a court starts with a "general intent" characterization and then says defendant's mistake must be reasonable. See, e.g., Williams v. United States, 337 A.2d 772 (D.C.App.1975) (unauthorized use of vehicle statute is "general intent" type of crime, and thus defendant's actual but unreasona-

ble belief the car had been abandoned no defense); State v. Morse, 127 Ariz. 25, 617 P.2d 1141 (1980) (receiving stolen property charge; because "specific intent is not an element," instruction that ignorance of law no excuse proper).

19. Namely, those requiring that the defendant's mistake be reasonable. "One suspects that some jurisdictions simply do not understand the implications of such a provision, especially when a jurisdiction has conflicting provisions: one requiring recklessness as to circumstance of elements and another requiring reasonable mistakes." 1 P. Robinson, Criminal Law Defenses § 62(c)(2) (1984).

20. See Moore, Bigamy, A Crime Though Unwittingly Committed, 30 U.Cinn.L.Rev. 35, 36 (1961).

21. Commonwealth v. Mash. 48 Mass. (7 Metc.) 472 (1844), is the leading American case. See also Cornett v. Commonwealth, 134 Ky. 613, 121 S.W. 424 (1909); State v. Goonan, 89 N.H. 528, 3 A.2d 105 (1938); Manahan v. State, 188 Tenn. 394, 219 S.W.2d 900 (1949); State v. Ackerly, 79 Vt. 69, 64 A. 450 (1906).

22. People v. Hartman, 130 Cal. 487, 62 P. 823 (1900).

23. Burnely v. State, 201 Miss. 234, 29 So.2d 94 (1947).

24. State v. DeMeo, 20 N.J. 1, 118 A.2d 1 (1955).

legislature favored the policy that those who remarry do so at their peril.[25]

These three principles are highly questionable, however, and they have been rejected in the more carefully reasoned decisions. As to the notion that the enumeration of certain defenses indicates an intention to bar other defenses, it is more logical to conclude that the legislature merely intended to set forth special defenses applicable to this particular crime while at the same time permitting resort to defenses which are applicable to crimes generally.[26] Likewise, the absence of words in the statute requiring a certain mental state does not warrant the assumption that the legislature intended to impose strict liability; to the contrary, at least for an offense as serious as bigamy, it should be presumed that the legislature intended to follow the usual *mens rea* requirement "unless excluded expressly or by necessary implication." [27] The implication that the legislature favored the remarry-at-your-peril doctrine certainly is not "necessary." Indeed, consideration of the matter on policy grounds justifies the conclusion that no good purpose would be served by punishing those who remarry honestly believing their prior spouse to be dead or reasonably believing that their prior marriage was terminated by a valid divorce.[28]

Of course, if an offense is truly of the strict liability variety,[29] then the most obvious consequence of that fact is that there is no mental state to be negated and no mistake or ignorance of fact or law will suffice to exonerate. Illustrative is the offense of selling liquor to a minor or permitting him to stay upon premises licensed for the sale of liquor, which in most jurisdictions is viewed as imposing absolute liability upon those who operate establishments licensed to sell intoxicating beverages.[30] Under such a strict liability provision, it is no defense that defendant believed the minor was of age,[31] and this is true even if the minor appeared to be of age,[32] represented himself as having reached the requisite age,[33] or produced false credentials showing that he was of age.[34]

The possible harshness of the strict liability approach is made most apparent when the defendant can show that he made a reasonable mistake of fact or law. For this reason, cases in which such a mistake is in evidence have sometimes influenced appellate courts to accept such a mistake as a defense notwithstanding the regulatory nature of the offense and the absence of any *mens rea* requirement in the statutory formulation. For example, even where the statute provided that no person should sell liquor to any minor "actually or apparently, under the age of eighteen years," it was interpreted to mean "actually *and* apparently" on the ground that otherwise a businessman would be penalized for acting in good faith in selling intoxicants to one who appeared to be over the statutory age.[35] Similarly, a conviction for transporting undersized

---

25. See Moore, supra note 20, at 38–39.

26. This point is forcefully made in People v. Vogel, 46 Cal.2d 798, 299 P.2d 850 (1956); and Long v. State, 44 Del. 262, 65 A.2d 489 (1949).

27. People v. Vogel, supra. To the same effect is the leading English case, Regina v. Tolson, 23 Q.B.D. 168 (1889).

28. Long v. State, supra, note 26. For a discussion of the policy considerations, see Model Penal Code § 230.1, Comment at 384–87 (1980); Comment, 15 Mercer L.Rev. 275 (1963).

29. See § 3.8.

30. The cases are collected in Annot., 12 A.L.R.3d 991 (1967).

31. People v. Wilson, 106 Colo. 437, 106 P.2d 352 (1940); State v. Koliche, 143 Me. 281, 61 A.2d 115 (1948); State v. Parr, 129 Mont. 175, 283 P.2d 1086 (1955); Commonwealth v. Koczwara, 397 Pa. 575, 155 A.2d 825 (1959).

32. Crampton v. State, 37 Ark. 108 (1881); Duncan v. Commonwealth, 289 Ky. 231, 158 S.W.2d 396 (1942); State v. Hartfiel, 24 Wis. 60 (1869).

33. Edgar v. State, 37 Ark. 219 (1881); People v. Werner, 174 N.Y. 132, 66 N.E. 667 (1903); State v. Sasse, 6 S.D. 212, 60 N.W. 853 (1894).

34. State v. Dahnke, 244 Iowa 599, 57 N.W.2d 553 (1953); People v. Davin, 1 App.Div.2d 811, 148 N.Y.S.2d 903 (1956); West Allis v. Megna, 26 Wis.2d 545, 133 N.W.2d 252 (1965).

35. People v. Malinauskas, 202 Misc. 565, 110 N.Y.S.2d 314 (1952). See also United States v. Anton, 683 F.2d 1011 (7th Cir.1982) (8 U.S.C.A. § 1326, on reentry by deported alien, construed to require at least negligence, and thus defendant could defend on ground he reasonably believed he had the requisite consent of the Attorney General to reenter).

fish was reversed because the defendant truck driver established that he did not know the fish were undersized and the cargo was so packed that he could not have reasonably been expected to examine it.[36] These courts, in effect, have concluded that the statute is *not* an absolute liability statute but rather requires negligence, and thus their holdings do not conflict with the general principle that ignorance or mistake of fact or law is a defense only if it negates a required mental state.

 WESTLAW
REFERENCES

sell*** sold sale /s liquor alcohol beer /s minor /p mistake ignorance /s law fact

(c) The "Lesser Legal Wrong" and "Moral Wrong" Theories. It sometimes happens that because of ignorance or mistake of fact or law, the defendant is unaware of the magnitude of the wrong he is doing. That is, if the circumstances were as the defendant believed them to be, then he would be guilty of some lesser crime or else a noncriminal but (in the eyes of society) immoral act. For example, assume that the defendant, in a jurisdiction which by statute makes burglary of a dwelling a more serious offense than burglary of a store, reasonably believes that the building he has entered is a store when it is in fact a dwelling. Is he guilty of the crime of burglary of a dwelling, or of the crime of burglary of a store, or neither? Or, assume a defendant is charged with the crime of statutory rape, but he shows that he reasonably believed the girl had reached the age of consent so that, at most, he thought he was merely engaging in an immoral act. Is he, or is he not, guilty of the crime of statutory rape?

Some cases appear to support the general proposition that in such instances the mistake by the defendant may be disregarded because of the fact that he actually intended to do some legal or moral wrong. For that reason, the assumption seems to be, he is not deserving of the usual ignorance or mistake defense. Thus, in the leading English case of *Regina v. Prince*,[37] where the defendant, charged with unlawfully taking a girl under the age of sixteen out of the possession of the father against his will, acted on the reasonable belief that the girl was eighteen, it was held no defense that he "thought he was committing a different kind of a wrong from that which in fact he was committing." And in *White v. State*,[38] where the defendant was convicted of the statutory offense of abandoning a pregnant wife, it was held that his defense that he did not know his wife was pregnant was properly refused, for in any event his abandonment was "a violation of his civil duty," and thus he acted at his peril. Similar reasoning accounts in part for the nearly unanimous view that a reasonable mistake of age is not a defense to a charge of statutory rape.[39] As one court explicitly stated, even under his own understanding of the circumstances the defendant intended to commit the crime of fornication, and on that basis he may be held accountable for a crime different and more serious than he intended.[40]

Although the matter is sometimes not made entirely clear, the assumption in these cases

---

36. State v. Williams, 94 Ohio App. 249, 115 N.E.2d 36 (1952). See also United States v. Herbert, 698 F.2d 981 (9th Cir.1983) (despite the fact that generally a violation of 26 U.S.C.A. § 5861 does not require proof that defendant knew possession of certain types of weapons was against the law or that weapon he possessed was of the type required to be registered, such strict liability would not be applied to "an ordinary firearm that is internally and undetectably modified to be automatic yet legal in appearance," as surely "Congress did not intend that this statute be so draconian").

37. L.R. 2 Cr.Cas.Res. 154 (1875).

38. 44 Ohio App. 331, 185 N.E. 64 (1933).

39. See, e.g., People v. Olsen, 36 Cal.3d 638, 205 Cal. Rptr. 492, 685 P.2d 52 (1984); People v. Cash, 419 Mich.

230, 351 N.W.2d 822 (1984). The cases are collected in Annot., 8 A.L.R.3d 110 (1966).

Of course, the result may be otherwise under a modern code which particularizes the limited circumstances in which a statute may be read as imposing strict liability. See, e.g., State v. Elton, 680 P.2d 727 (Utah 1984) (because under code scheme unlawful sexual intercourse statute cannot be construed as a strict liability offense, prosecution must prove at least recklessness on the mistake as to the girl's age).

40. Commonwealth v. Murphy, 165 Mass. 66, 42 N.E. 504 (1896).

is not merely that the crimes involved are of the strict liability variety, thus barring ignorance or mistake of fact or law as a defense. Rather, they rest upon the notion that *some* varieties of ignorance or mistake should not be a defense, namely, those which indicate that the defendant still intended to do what constitutes a legal or moral wrong. (In the *Prince* case, for example, it was noted that the defendant would have a valid defense if he were to show that he mistakenly believed the girl's father had consented, for then he "would not know he was doing an act wrong in itself.") The lesser legal wrong and moral wrong theories, then, are grounded upon the proposition that a "guilty mind," in a very general sense, should suffice for the imposition of penal sanctions even when the defendant did not intentionally, knowingly, recklessly or even negligently engage in the acts described in the statute. That is, the defense of ignorance or mistake of fact or law "rests ultimately on the defendant's being able to say that he has observed the community ethic." [41]

That position is unsound, and has no place in a rational system of substantive criminal law. As noted earlier,[42] it is generally true that crimes defined in terms of causing a certain bad result require mental fault of the same kind and intensity, and mental fault sufficient for some other kind of crime will not suffice. (For example, acts done in with an intent to injure a person, if they unexpectedly result in injury to property, may not result in conviction of the actor for an intent-to-destroy-property type of crime.[43]) This is because considerations of deterrence, correction, and just condemnation of the actor's conduct all focus attention upon the harm intended rather than the harm actually caused. In the above example, the actor's

conduct deserves condemnation, he stands in need of correction, and official response to his actions is warranted as a deterrent—*not* because of the property damage, but because of the actor's intent to harm a person. Clearly, the same analysis is called for when, because of ignorance or mistake of fact or law, the defendant's mental state is not of the same kind or intensity as the bad results his conduct has brought about.

If this is true, then it obviously follows that there is no justification for failing to take account of the defendant's ignorance or mistake when as a result he thought he was doing something which at most may be labelled immoral. "Moral duties should not be identified with criminal duties," [44] and thus when fornication is itself not criminal it should not become criminal merely because the defendant has made a reasonable mistake about the age of the girl with whom he has intercourse.[45] Moreover, the moral wrong theory poses the added difficulty of determining precisely what the "community ethic" actually is, not an easy task in a heterogeneous society in which our public pronouncements about morality often are not synonymous with our private conduct.[46]

This is not to say, however, that the law should always recognize as a defense ignorance or mistake of fact or law by which the actor believes he is only committing a lesser degree of crime or merely an immoral act. There may be sound policy reasons for, in effect, imposing strict liability as to certain elements of particular crimes. Indeed, illustrations of this are to be found in the Model Penal Code, which clearly rejects the lesser legal wrong and moral wrong theories as general principles. For example, the Code position on sex offenses is that when criminality depends on a child's being below the age of 10,

---

41. P. Brett, An Inquiry Into Criminal Guilt 149 (1963).

42. See § 3.11.

43. Regina v. Pembliton, 12 Cox Crim.Cas. 607 (1874).

44. Hughes, Criminal Responsibility, 16 Stan.L.Rev. 470, 481 (1964).

45. People v. Hernandez, 61 Cal.2d 529, 39 Cal.Rptr. 361, 393 P.2d 673 (1964). See also Myers, Reasonable

Mistake of Age: A Needed Defense to Statutory Rape, 64 Mich.L.Rev. 105 (1965). As discussed in the text following, the result is different if the legislature has made statutory rape a strict liability offense. See, e.g., Goodrow v. Perrin, 119 N.H. 483, 403 A.2d 864 (1979).

46. Hughes, supra note 45, at 481.

it is then and only then no defense that the actor believed the child to be older,[47] "for no credible error regarding the age of a child in fact less than 10 years old would render the actor's conduct anything less than a dramatic departure from societal norms." [48] The point is that such judgments should be made as matters of policy on an offense-by-offense basis, as in the Code,[49] in lieu of uncritical acceptance of the more general lesser legal wrong and moral wrong theories.

When one of those exceptional situations is not present, so that ignorance or mistake of fact or law is a defense, yet the defendant would be guilty of some other crime if the facts had been as he believed them to be, there remains the question of what disposition is appropriate. To return to an earlier illustration, what if the defendant is on trial for burglary of a dwelling, but he shows by way of defense that he believed the building to be a store, and burglary of a store constitutes a lesser crime? As already concluded, conviction for burglary of a dwelling would not be possible because the mistake negates a required mental state. Moreover, conviction for burglary of a store might appear to be precluded because the required *actus reus* is

not present; and even conviction of attempted burglary of a store might be in doubt under some versions of the impossibility doctrine.[50] Under the Model Penal Code, the defendant in these circumstances may be convicted "of the offense of which he would be guilty had the situation been as he supposed." [51] Such a provision avoids some procedural difficulties,[52] and permits an appropriate result whereby the defendant is found "guilty of the lesser crime which on his own assumptions he committed." [53]

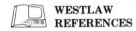 **WESTLAW REFERENCES**

guest /s 583 +5 836

(d) Belief Conduct Not Proscribed by the Criminal Law. It bears repeating here that the cause of much of the confusion concerning the significance of the defendant's ignorance or mistake of law is the failure to distinguish two quite different situations: (1) that in which the defendant consequently lacks the mental state required for commission of the crime and thus, as explained above, has a valid defense; and (2) that in which the defendant still had whatever mental state is required for commission of the crime and only claims that he was unaware

---

47. Model Penal Code § 213.6(1).

48. Model Penal Code § 213.6, Comment at 414 (1980).

49. Compare with the situation discussed in the preceding text that covered by Model Penal Code § 223.1. Though the traditional view was "that the amount actually stolen determined whether the offense was grand or petty theft," meaning a defendant's reasonable mistake as to value was no defense to a charge of grand theft, that position is rejected in the Code because the "amount involved in a theft has criminological significance only if it corresponds with what the thief expected or hoped to get." Model Penal Code § 223.1, Comment at 146 (1980).

50. See § 6.3.

51. Model Penal Code § 2.04(2). A few modern codes contain a provision essentially like the Model Penal Code formulation, which contemplates that the mistake will "reduce the grade and degree of the offense."

Another variation found in several modern codes is that mistakes are a defense when they negate a mental state, except that the defendant may be convicted of "an included offense of which he would be guilty if the fact or law were as he believed it to be." This variation has been criticized because no conviction would be permissible if defendant thought he was committing some other crime which, technically, is not included within the offense charged (e.g., charge is arson of a dwelling, other offense is

arson of a store). 1 P. Robinson, Criminal Law Defenses § 62(c)(5) (1984). As observed in Model Penal Code § 2.04, Comment (Tent. Draft No. 4, 1955), there are two schools of thought on this. One is that conviction only of an included offense should be possible, for otherwise the defendant has not received sufficient notice of the charge against him; the other is that defendant needs no such notice when he defends by avowing his effort to commit some other crime.

52. The lesser offense might not be an included offense, so that conviction of the lesser on a charge of having committed the greater offense would not be permissible. However, deviation from the principal that the requirement of fair notice to the defendant limits conviction to the offense charged or an included offense would be justified, for the defendant can hardly claim lack of fair notice when he has raised his intention to commit the lesser crime as a matter of defense. See Model Penal Code § 2.04, Comment at 273 n. 11 (1985).

53. Ibid. See, e.g., State v. Guest, 583 P.2d 836 (Alaska 1978) (adopting Model Penal Code position and holding that if defendant, charged with statutory rape, reasonable believed the girl was 16, he could not be convicted of that crime, defined in terms of girls under 16, but could be convicted of contributing to the delinquency of a minor, defined in terms of all minors under 18).

that such conduct was proscribed by the criminal law, which, as explained below, is ordinarily not a recognized defense.[54]

Except for one particular situation which is explored later in this section, it is usually an easy task to determine in which of these two categories the defendant's mistake belongs.[55] For example, the crime of larceny is not committed if the defendant, because of a mistaken understanding of the law of property, believed that the property taken belonged to him;[56] it is committed, however, if the defendant believed it was lawful to take certain kinds of property belonging to others because of the custom in the community to do so.[57] The requisite mental state (intent to steal[58]) is lacking only in the first of these two cases, for it "is not the intent to violate the law but the intentional doing the act which is a violation of law"[59] which is proscribed.

Why is it that neither ignorance of the criminal law (in the sense that the defendant is unaware of the statute proscribing his conduct) nor mistake of the criminal law (in the sense that the defendant has mistakenly concluded that the relevant statute does not

reach his conduct) is a defense? Upon the early notion that the law is "definite and knowable,"[60] one common explanation is provided by the maxim that everyone is presumed to know the law.[61] But even if there was once a time when the criminal law was so simple and limited in scope that such a presumption was justified, it is now an "obvious fiction"[62] and "so far-fetched in modern conditions as to be quixotic."[63] No person can really "know" all of the statutory and case law defining criminal conduct. Indeed, the maxim has never served to explain the full reach of the ignorance-of-the-law-is-no-excuse doctrine, for the doctrine has long been applied even when the defendant establishes beyond question that he had good reason for not knowing the applicable law.[64]

A somewhat more satisfying explanation for the doctrine is the pragmatic proposition that if all defendants were entitled to raise an ignorance-of-the-criminal-law defense, then the finders of fact in criminal cases would repeatedly be confronted with an issue which in most instances could not be readily resolved. Both commentators[65] and courts[66]

---

54. United States v. Currier, 621 F.2d 7 (1st Cir.1980); Morgan v. District of Columbia, 476 A.2d 1128 (D.C.App. 1984); State v. Clark, 346 N.W.2d 510 (Iowa 1984); State v. Weitzman, 121 N.H. 83, 427 A.2d 3 (1981).

It is possible, of course, for the legislature to provide in certain circumstances that ignorance of the law *is* an excuse. See, e.g., the cases in note 78 infra, finding such a legislative intent. But most courts are not prepared to depart from the general principle that ignorance of the law is no excuse unless such a legislative intention clearly appears. See United v. International Minerals and Chemical Corp., 402 U.S. 558, 91 S.Ct. 1697, 29 L.Ed.2d 178 (1971) (given that general principle, "knowingly violates any such regulation" language of statute construed as "a shorthand designation for specific acts or omissions which violate the Act" rather than as a requirement defendant know what the regulations proscribe).

55. Difficulties are most likely to arise when the statute is unclear as to the extent of the mental state requirement, as in Liparota v. United States, ___ U.S. ___, 105 S.Ct. 2084, 85 L.Ed.2d 434 (1985). At issue there was the meaning of 7 U.S.C.A. § 2024(b), providing that "whoever knowingly uses, transfers, acquires, alters, or possesses [food stamp] coupons or authorization cards in any manner not authorized by" statute or regulations is guilty of a crime. The Court interpreted the statute as meaning the defendant must know his acquisition or possession of food stamps was unauthorized by law. However, the majority mischaracterized the issue by asserting that it was whether the statute should be read as requiring such knowledge

or, on the other hand, as a strict liability offense. The dissent correctly pointed out that a contrary reading of the statute would not involve "creating a strict liability offense," for it still would be true that a defendant could not be convicted if "he was unaware of the circumstances of the transaction that made it illegal."

56. State v. Sawyer, 95 Conn. 34, 110 A. 461 (1920).

57. Commonwealth v. Doane, 55 Mass. 5 (1848).

58. See § 8.5.

59. State v. Downs, 116 N.C. 1064, 21 S.E. 689 (1895).

60. 1 J. Austin, Jurisprudence 497 (4th ed. 1879).

61. Weeks v. State, 24 Ala.App. 198, 132 So. 870 (1931); Satterfield v. State, 172 Neb. 275, 109 N.W.2d 415 (1961).

62. J. Hall, General Principles of Criminal Law 376 (2d ed. 1960).

63. Id. at 378.

64. In one classic case the defendant was at sea and beyond all communications when the statute was enacted and when he violated it. Rex v. Bailey, 168 Eng.Rep. 651 (1800); In another he was a foreigner recently arrived from a country where the conduct was not criminal, Rex v. Esop, 173 Eng.Rep. 203 (1836). See also People v. Bock, 69 Misc. 543, 125 N.Y. 301, affirmed 148 App.Div. 899, 132 N.Y.S. 1141 (1911); Oakland v. Carpentier, 21 Cal. 642 (1863).

65. J. Austin, supra note 60, at 498–99.

66. People v. O'Brien, 96 Cal. 171, 31 P. 45 (1892).

have argued that such a defense would become a shield for the guilty because (a) the defendant's claim of ignorance could not ordinarily be refuted, and (b) assuming the defendant was in fact ignorant, it would require a far-reaching inquiry to ascertain whether the defendant was at fault in not knowing the law. Holmes questioned whether "a man's knowledge of the law is any harder to investigate than many questions which are gone into," [67] as have others,[68] and thus it may be doubted if part (a) of the above argument is sound. The same may not be said for part (b) of the argument, however; the questions involved in pursuing an inquiry into whether or not the defendant was at fault in his ignorance would be "even more complicated than those raised by the defenses of insanity and infancy, where the justification for the defendant's failure to know of the law and mores is not in issue, being assumed to be due to mental disease or youth." [69]

Another argument in favor of the present rule is that while it may be harsh upon the individual defendant who was reasonably ignorant or mistaken concerning the penal law, "public policy sacrifices the individual to the general good." [70] The "larger interests on the other side of the scales" [71] include realization of the educational function of the criminal law. So the argument goes, conviction of defendants for violation of new or forgotten criminal laws serves to bring home to the general public the existence of these rules and aids in establishing them as the social mores of the community.[72] If individuals were acquitted because of their own unawareness of

the law, such acquittals would—if anything—only increase the public uncertainty and confusion as to what conduct has been made criminal.

A related point, on a somewhat more theoretical plane, is that it would conflict with the principle of legality to treat a defendant in a criminal case as if the law were as the defendant thought it to be. Under the principle of legality, rules of law express objective meanings which are declared by competent officials and which are then binding.[73] There "is a basic incompatibility between asserting that the law is what certain officials declare it to be after a prescribed analysis, and asserting, also, that those officials *must* declare it to be * * * what defendants or their lawyers believed it to be. A legal order implies the rejection of such contradiction. It opposes objectivity to subjectivity, judicial process to individual opinion, official to lay, and authoritative to nonauthoritative declarations of what the law is." [74]

Whatever the merit of these several arguments in support of the general rule that ignorance or mistake as to the penal law is no defense, several commentators have expressed concern with the harshness of the rule when applied to the lesser regulatory crimes involving conduct not inherently immoral.[75] The early criminal law was "well integrated with the mores of the time," so that "a defendant's mistake as to the content of the criminal law * * * would not ordinarily affect his moral guilt." [76] But the vast network of regulatory offenses which make up a large part of today's criminal law does not stem from the

---

67. O. Holmes, The Common Law 48 (1881).

68. "The fear that an issue of knowledge of the law cannot be adjudicated seems to be unfounded. If a normal adult fires at another at point-blank range, his defense that he did not intend to kill would be received with incredulity, and so would a defense that he did not know murder to be a crime. On the other hand, if he shoots another when hunting at dusk, his defense that he did not intend to kill a man might be believed; and in the same way his belief that he is entitled by law to shoot a would-be thief might be believed whether it represents the true legal position or not." G. Williams, Criminal Law: The General Part 291 (2d ed. 1961).

69. Hall and Seligman, Mistake of law and Mens Rea, 8 U.Chi.L.Rev. 641, 647 (1941).

70. O. Holmes, supra, note 67, at 48.

71. Ibid.

72. G. Williams, supra note 68 at 289; Hall and Seligman, supra note 69, at 648.

73. J. Hall, supra note 62, at 383.

74. Ibid.

75. See Cass, Ignorance of the Law: A Maxim Reexamined, 17 Wm. & Mary L.Rev. 671, 689–99 (1976); Fletcher, The Individualization of Excusing Conditions, 47 So.Cal.L. Rev. 1269, 1295–99 (1974); Seney, "When Empty Terrors Overawe"—Our Criminal Law Defenses (Part Two), 19 Wayne L.Rev. 1359, 1364–76 (1973).

76. Hall and Seligman, supra note 69, at 644.

mores of the community, and so "moral education no longer serves us as a guide as to what is prohibited." [77] Under these circumstances, where one's moral attitudes may not be relied upon to avoid the forbidden conduct, it may seem particularly severe for the law *never* to recognize ignorance or mistake of the criminal law as a defense.[78] Moreover, some would question whether it is desirable to characterize as criminal an individual who has not demonstrated any degree of social dangerousness,[79] that is, a person whose conduct is not anti-social because (i) he reasonably thought the conduct was not criminal, and (ii) the conduct is not by its nature immoral.

The United States Supreme Court was confronted with this issue in *Lambert v. California*,[80] where the defendant had been convicted under an ordinance making it unlawful for any convicted person to remain in Los Angeles for more than five days without registering with the police department. The ordinance was held to violate the notice requirements of due process when applied to a defendant "who has no actual knowledge of his duty to register," for "circumstances which might move one to inquire as to the necessity of registration are completely lacking." This language is significant, for it emphasizes that the defendant was in no way at fault in not being aware of the legal duty in question. Thus, the holding in *Lambert* would be inapplicable to a defendant who could rightly be said to be under an obligation to ascertain the legality of his conduct. For example, it would certainly be proper to hold

to the position that an individual has a "duty to keep informed about the legal regulation governing conduct in which [he] is peculiarly engaged," [81] so that one engaged in the manufacture of dairy products could not defend on the ground of his ignorance of an available statute or administrative regulation prohibiting the sale of butter without a certain percentage of fat.

It is important to note, however, that the *Lambert* decision does not require legislative tampering with the doctrine that ignorance of the criminal law is no excuse. Ignorance of the law, after all, *is* an excuse when it negatives a required mental element of the crime, so it would be fairly simple to redraft legislation of the kind condemned in *Lambert* so that guilt depends upon a knowing violation of a legal duty. Illustrative is a statute making it an offense knowingly to attempt to evade the payment of income taxes, properly interpreted in *Hargrove v. United States* [82] as not reaching a defendant who was unaware of his duty under the law to pay taxes. Analytically, this approach is to be preferred over that of creating an exception to the general rule that ignorance of the criminality of the conduct is no excuse, for neither *Lambert* nor *Hargrove* should escape conviction merely because of ignorance that their conduct was punishable under the criminal law. Rather, the important matter is ignorance of the legal duty—in *Lambert* the duty to register, and in *Hargrove* the duty to pay taxes. Awareness of that duty, just as with awareness of the immorality of the conduct for more tradition-

---

77. Mueller, On Common Law Mens Rea, 42 Minn.L. Rev. 1043, 1060 (1958).

78. Cases recognizing some sort of ignorance of law defense typically are of this type. See, e.g., Liparota v. United States, ___ U.S. ___, 105 S.Ct. 2084, 85 L.Ed.2d 434 (1985) (federal statute making it a crime to knowingly use, transfer, acquire, alter or possess food stamps in a manner not authorized by law interpreted to mean defendant must know what he did not authorized by statute or regulation, as otherwise the statute would "criminalize a broad range of apparently innocent conduct"); United States v. Simpson, 561 F.2d 53 (7th Cir.1977) (on charge of willfully broadcasting without a license, mistake of law defense recognized for defendant who claimed he thought broadcasts lawful because his estranged wife had CB license and left the transmitter in family home); United States v. Lizarra-Lizarra, 541 F.2d 826 (9th Cir.1976) (statute on

"willfully" exporting specified property from U.S. construed to allow defense that defendant did not know the law covered items he had; Congress assumed to have so intended because the statute prohibits exportation of items listed by administrative regulation, and the regulation contained an exhaustive list of items not "known generally to be controlled by government regulation"). See also the dissent in United States v. International Minerals & Chemical Corp., 402 U.S. 558, 91 S.Ct. 1697, 298 L.Ed.2d 178 (1971).

79. See Ryu and Silving, Error Juris: A Comparative Study, 24 U.Chi.L.Rev. 421, 467 (1957).

80. 355 U.S. 225, 78 S.Ct. 240, 2 L.Ed.2d 228 (1957).

81. Mueller, supra, note 77, at 1060 n. 49.

82. 67 F.2d 820 (5th Cir.1933).

al crimes, provides the element of blameworthiness which justifies even unexpected prosecution and conviction.[83]

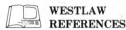
(e) Belief Conduct Not Proscribed Because of Governmental Action or Inaction. Under the better view, there are limited situations in which the defendant's belief that his conduct was not proscribed by the criminal law is a defense. These exceptions are somewhat akin to the void-for-vagueness [84] and ex post facto [85] doctrines,[86] in that the government is rightly barred from obtaining a conviction because the government (through its representatives acting in an official capacity) is responsible for the inability of the defendant to know that his conduct was proscribed.

(1) Enactment Not Reasonably Made Available. A mere claim by the defendant that the statute under which he is being prosecuted had not come to his attention prior to the time he engaged in the conduct charged is, of course, not a valid defense.[87] But, in some instances the defendant may show more— either that his conduct occurred very soon after the statute was enacted and before it

was made generally available, or that his conduct occurred later but still before the usual formalities of official publication had been fully complied with. Although the earlier decisions recognize no defense even under these circumstances,[88] the more rational position is that the defendant's belief that his conduct is not criminal is a defense when "the statute or other enactment defining the offense is not known to [him] and has not been published or otherwise reasonably made available prior to the conduct alleged." [89]

Such a situation is unlikely to arise today with respect to national or state criminal legislation; all such enactments are published, and normally these laws carry an "effective date" which affords time for publication prior to their actually becoming law.[90] The same is not necessarily true as to local legislation. Particularly in smaller communities, local ordinances may never be printed or otherwise made generally available. Nor is it often true of regulations promulgated by administrative agencies, violation of which may carry criminal sanctions.[91] While "substantive rules of general applicability" of federal administrative agencies must be published in the Federal Register,[92] many states have not attempted a systematic publication and codification of their administrative regulations.[93]

---

83. This point has so often been misunderstood, particularly in the analyses of the *Lambert* decision, that it cannot be overemphasized. Again, in *Lambert* the Supreme Court was only concerned with "knowledge of the duty to register," not knowledge of the criminality of failure to register; in *Hargrove* the court interpreted the statute only as requiring "knowledge of the existence of obligation" to pay taxes, not knowledge that failure to pay was punishable as a crime.

84. See § 2.3.

85. See § 2.4.

86. The relationship of these doctrines to the mistake-of-law area is explored in Hall and Seligman, supra note 70, at 654–55, 666–68.

87. Debardelaben v. State, 99 Tenn. 649, 42 S.W. 684 (1897).

88. State v. Click, 2 Ala. 26 (1841) (no official publication); Zakrasek v. State, 197 Ind. 249, 150 N.E. 615 (1926) (conduct 3 weeks after statute passed); Jellico Coal Co. v. Commonwealth, 96 Ky. 373, 29 S.W. 26 (1895) (conduct 6 weeks after statute passed).

89. Model Penal Code § 2.04(3)(a). A few modern codes contain such a provision, while a few others include a similar provision applicable only to "administrative reg-

ulations" and require also that defendant "could not have acquired such knowledge by the exercise of due diligence."

It has been argued that this is a constitutional requirement. "If the due process clause prevents one from being punished or losing property in litigation without prior notice, and prevents the operation of an injunction before notice of the order is provided, would it not also require notice before the effective date of the very law on which the later adjudication is based?" Murphy, The Duty of the Government to Make the Law Known, 51 Ford.L.Rev. 255, 265 (1982).

90. A number of states require publication as a precondition of effectiveness. Model Penal Code § 2.04, Comment (Tent.Draft No. 4, 1955). Compare United States v. Casson, 434 F.2d 415 (D.C.Cir.1970) (new burglary and robbery statutes for D.C. took effect immediately upon signing of legislation by President, and thus could be applied to defendant's conduct later that day).

91. See § 2.6.

92. 5 U.S.C.A. § 552.

93. "The old-time system still in effect in more than half the states is that of filing regulations in a central state office, usually that of the secretary of state. This means that a lawyer or a party may have to look to the

(2) Reasonable Reliance Upon a Statute or Judicial Decision. An individual should be able reasonably to rely upon a statute or other enactment under which his conduct would not be criminal, so that he need not fear conviction if subsequent to his conduct the statute is declared invalid.[94] A contrary rule would be inconsistent with the sound policy that the community is to be encouraged to act in compliance with legislation.[95] Thus, just as it is no defense that the defendant mistakenly believed the statute under which he was prosecuted to be unconstitutional,[96] it is a defense that he reasonably relied upon a statute permitting his conduct though it turned out to be an unconstitutional enactment.[97]

For essentially the same reason, the better view is that it is a defense that the defendant acted in reasonable reliance upon a judicial decision, opinion or judgment later determined to be invalid or erroneous.[98] The clear-est case is that in which the defendant's reliance was upon a decision of the highest court of the jurisdiction, later overruled, whether the first decision involved the constitutionality of a statute,[99] the interpretation of a statute,[100] or the meaning of the common law.[101] A contrary rule, whereby the subsequent holding would apply retroactively to the defendant's detriment, would be as unfair as ex post facto legislation.[102]

There are several decisions supporting the proposition that reasonable reliance upon a decision of a lower court is likewise a defense. Thus, if the lower court has found a repealer statute constitutional,[103] has declared the relevant criminal statute unconstitutional,[104] or has enjoined enforcement of the statute,[105] there may be a basis for reasonable reliance.[106] However, in the case of lower court decisions there is more likely to arise a question of whether the reliance is reasonable. It has been suggested, for example, that reliance

---

state capital in order to know the effective law. Even when he goes or sends to the state capital, he may find that clerks are unable or unwilling to dig out the material he seeks, for the regulations often remain unclassified or poorly classified, the indexes are often inadequate or non-existent, and piles of uncodified material may be either still effective or long superseded." 1 K. Davis, Administrative Law § 6.11 (1958).

94. Model Penal Code § 2.04(3)(b) so provides, as do several modern codes.

95. Hall and Seligman, supra note 69, at 662–63.

96. Hunter v. State, 158 Tenn. 63, 12 S.W.2d 361 (1928). The same is true when the defendant believes that the statute could not constitutionally be applied to his conduct because of the assumption, for example, that his conduct is protected by the First Amendment. Holdridge v. United States, 282 F.2d 302 (8th Cir.1960).

Distinguishable are cases in which, because of a belief in the unconstitutionality of a statute, the defendant lacks a required mental state, as in Leeman v. State, 35 Ark. 438 (1880) (defendant's belief statute taking away his right to fees was unconstitutional a defense to extortion prosecution, for it negatived corrupt intent required for guilt). And see United States v. Spock, 416 F.2d 165 (1st Cir. 1969), on the uncertainty as to the relevance of a belief that the conduct is constitutionally protected in the context of a conspiracy prosecution.

97. Brent v. State, 43 Ala. 297 (1869) (unconstitutional statute giving defendant right to carry on lottery a defense to prosecution for violation of general lottery statute); State v. Godwin, 123 N.C. 697, 31 S.E. 221 (1898) (statute relieving defendant public officials of duty a defense, though later declared unconstitutional). Contra: Swincher v. Commonwealth, 24 Ky.L.Rep. 1897, 72 S.W.

306 (1903) (unconstitutional statute permitting private police to carry weapons no defense).

While Model Penal Code § 2.04 requires "reasonable reliance" upon the statute, as generally do the cases interpreting similar provisions, e.g., Fowler v. State, 283 Ark. 325, 676 S.W.2d 725 (1984), Hall and Seligman, supra note 69, at 662, argue that "such a defense should not necessarily rest on estoppel, and the defendant ought not to be required to prove knowledge of the * * * law or his express reliance on its constitutionality."

98. Model Penal Code § 2.04(3)(b) so provides. Some modern codes contain similar provisions. Several others have provisions which are much more limited.

99. State v. O'Neil, 147 Iowa 513, 126 N.W. 454 (1910).

100. State v. Longino, 109 Miss. 125, 67 So. 902 (1915).

101. Stinnett v. Commonwealth, 55 F.2d 644 (4th Cir. 1932).

102. See § 2.4.

103. Lutwin v. State, 97 N.J.L. 67, 117 A. 164 (1922).

104. State ex rel. Williams v. Whitman, 116 Fla. 196, 156 So. 705 (1934).

105. United States v. Mancuso, 139 F.2d 90 (3d Cir. 1943); State v. Chicago, M. & St.P.R. Co., 130 Minn. 144, 153 N.W. 320 (1915); Coal & C.R. v. Conley, 67 W.Va. 129, 67 S.E. 613 (1910). Contra: State v. Keller, 8 Idaho 699, 70 P. 1051 (1902); State v. Wadhams Oil Co., 149 Wis. 58, 134 N.W. 1121 (1912).

106. The same would seem to be true if the lower court only interpreted the criminal statute as not reaching the conduct thereafter engaged in by the defendant, although a contrary result was reached in State v. Striggles, 202 Iowa 1318, 210 N.W. 137 (1926).

should not be a defense when it was known that the decision of the lower court was on appeal.[107] Some modern codes only recognize reliance upon appellate decisions.

(3) Reasonable Reliance Upon an Official Interpretation. Consistent with the above, the better view is that if a defendant reasonably relies upon an erroneous official statement of the law contained in an administrative order or grant[108] or in an official interpretation by the public officer or body responsible for interpretation, administration, or enforcement of the law defining the offense, then his belief that the conduct was not criminal is a defense.[109] This is most obviously so when the defendant is prosecuted for engaging in activity without a license, as required by state law, and he shows that upon application for such a license to the proper authority he was advised that no license was required.[110] In such a situation, the defendant has done everything which may reasonably be expected of him.

But what if the defendant, not in the context of seeking a license or permit, obtains an advisory opinion from some enforcement official, most likely the local prosecuting attorney, that his contemplated conduct would not be in violation of the criminal law? "Local prosecuting attorneys and law officers have a duty to give legal opinions to the local officials within their district, and it is only natural for private citizens as well to come to them for advice on questions of criminal lia-

bility."[111] Thus, it would seem that here as well a defense of reasonable reliance[112] should be available. But in *Hopkins v. State,*[113] the defense was rejected on the ground that otherwise the prosecutor's advice "would become paramount to the law." Such an objection is ill-founded, for the law would still be paramount; the advice would establish a defense of good faith only for the individual who received it and only so long as that individual was not authoritatively advised to the contrary.

Indeed, the result in *Hopkins* would appear to be contrary to due process, for to permit conviction of a person for conduct which he has been told by state officials is permissible "would be to sanction an indefensible sort of entrapment by the State."[114] Thus, as the Supreme Court held in *Cox v. Louisiana,*[115] demonstrators may not constitutionally be convicted of parading "near" a courthouse when they did so after the highest police officials of the city told them, in effect, that they could lawfully meet 101 feet from the courthouse steps. Similarly, due process was held to bar conviction of persons for refusing to answer questions of a state investigating commission when they relied upon assurances of the commission that they had a privilege to refuse to answer, although in fact they did not.[116]

It does not follow, of course, that one would be justified in seeking out any public official for such advice and then proceeding in reli-

---

107. Hall and Seligman, supra note 69, at 672.

108. Model Penal Code § 2.04(3)(b)(iii) so provides. To the same effect are provisions in several modern recodifications.

109. Model Penal Code § 2.04(3)(b) so provides. To the same effect see, e.g., State v. Sheedy, 125 N.H. 108, 480 A.2d 887 (1984), applying such a provision. Some statutes are more limited as to what officials may be relied upon.

110. People v. Ferguson, 134 Cal.App. 41, 24 P.2d 965 (1933). Contra: State v. Foster, 22 R.I. 163, 46 A. 833 (1900).

111. Hall and Seligman, supra note 69, at 679.

112. Just what reliance is reasonable can be a difficult issue. A rather strict view is taken in State v. Patten, 353 N.W.2d 30 (N.D.1984), where defendant, charged with removing a child from the state in violation of a custody decree, claimed the state's attorney had advised him this would not be criminal. The court held that the mistake of

law defense did not extend to "conduct that is blatantly offensive."

113. 193 Md. 489, 69 A.2d 456 (1950).

114. Cox v. Louisiana, 379 U.S. 559, 85 S.Ct. 476, 13 L.Ed.2d 487 (1965). The situation is somewhat different, however, from the usual entrapment defense. See § 5.2.

115. 379 U.S. 559, 85 S.Ct. 476, 13 L.Ed.2d 487 (1965).

116. Raley v. Ohio, 360 U.S. 423, 79 S.Ct. 1257, 3 L.Ed. 2d 1344 (1959). See also People v. Donovan, 53 Misc.2d 687, 279 N.Y.S.2d 404 (Ct.Spec.Sess.1967), holding that police action in telling defendant seated in car parked on private property to leave the property created an estoppel barring conviction for driving while intoxicated.

In United States v. Pennsylvania Industrial Chemical Corp., 411 U.S. 655, 93 S.Ct. 1804, 36 L.Ed.2d 567 (1973), holding the defendant corporation was entitled to invoke a reasonable reliance defense, the Court cited to both *Raley* and *Cox.*

ance upon the opinion received. Whether viewed in terms of the requirement that the reliance itself be reasonable or, as also provided in the Model Penal Code, that the interpretation be obtained from one "charged by law with responsibility for the interpretation, administration or enforcement of the law defining the offense," [117] such a broad interpretation of the defense is unwarranted.[118] Thus, for example, a tavern keeper could not rely upon advice from the mayor as to the meaning of the state law concerning the closing of bars on election day,[119] nor could a policeman rely upon the court clerk who administered his oath of office for an opinion about the lawfulness of the officer carrying a concealed weapon.[120] On the other hand, a chemical company could reasonably rely upon a Corps of Engineers' interpretation that the River and Harbor Act only prohibits water deposits that affect navigation, as the Corps "is the responsible administrative agency under the * * * Act." [121]

(4) Reliance upon advice of private counsel. In each of the situations heretofore described, the general objections to recognizing a mistake-of-the-criminal-law defense are inapplicable, for "the possibility of collusion is minimal, and * * * a judicial determination of the reasonableness of the belief in legality should not present substantial difficulty." [122] Is this not equally true if the defendant has reasonably relied upon a private attorney for advice? It has been argued with some persuasion that the answer is yes, at least when the defendant can show that he consulted a reputable attorney, he had a good faith belief in the legality of his conduct, and the conduct is not obviously antisocial in character.[123] Here as well, so the argument goes, the defendant has clearly shown that his actions have been entirely consistent with law-abidingness.

Yet, the cases uniformly hold that no defense is available under these circumstances,[124] and the Model Penal Code is in

117. Model Penal Code § 2.04(3)(b). See, e.g., State v. Davis, 63 Wis.2d 75, 216 N.W.2d 31 (1974) (county corporation counsel may give legal opinions on both civil and criminal matters, and thus county board member appointed as airport manager by the board had a defense to a conflict-of-interest prosecution where counsel said appointment was lawful). Some of the modern codes describe even more narrowly what officials may be relied upon.

118. "Although the courts generally do not state that the 'appropriateness' of the official controlled in deciding to allow the defense, most courts stress the position of authority of the given official and implicitly support the view that this position of authority is a crucial element of the defense." Comment, 66 Calif.L.Rev. 809, 826 (1978), collecting the cases id. at n. 74.

But in United States v. Barker, 546 F.2d 940 (D.C.Cir. 1976), where the defendants, one-time CIA operatives, were recruited to burglarize a psychiatrist's office on the representation that what was involved was a lawful investigation to obtain national security information, the court held these defendants were entitled to a mistake-of-law defense instruction even though their advice came from a person who was not in fact authorized to interpret, administer or enforce the law in question. In other words, their conduct would be excusable if based on a reasonable, good faith reliance on the apparent authority of a government official.

There exists a strong difference of opinion on the soundness of the *Barker* rule. One view is that reliance should be limited to those who are in fact the appropriate officials because such officials "are more likely than other officials to have made a careful study of the law's scope and effect" and "are in positions of accountability and

responsibility, thus significantly decreasing the opportunity for abuse of power." Comment, supra, at 830. See also Note, 77 Colum.L.Rev. 775 (1977). Another is that "if the goal is to deter reliance on careless officials, the fairer approach would seem to be to punish the officials' carelessness, not an actor's reasonable reliance upon it." 2 P. Robinson, Criminal Law Defenses § 183(e) (1984).

119. Jones v. State, 32 Tex.Crim. 533, 25 S.W. 124 (1894).

120. State v. Simmons, 143 N.C. 613, 56 S.E. 701 (1907).

121. United States v. Pennyslvania Industrial Chemical Corp., 411 U.S. 655, 93 S.Ct. 1804, 36 L.Ed.2d 567 (1973).

122. Model Penal Code § 2.04, Comment at 275 (1985).

123. Perkins, Ignorance and Mistake in Criminal Law, 88 U.Pa.L.Rev. 35, 42–43 (1939).

124. People v. McCalla, 63 Cal.App. 783, 220 P. 436 (1923); State v. Huff, 89 Me. 521, 36 A. 1000 (1897); State v. Western Union Tel. Co., 12 N.J. 468, 97 A.2d 480 (1953). It is sometimes asserted that there is a minority view that reliance upon counsel is a defense. However, the cases where this is so are of a different kind, in that the defendant's mistake of law, based upon counsel's advice, negatives a mental state required for conviction. See, e.g., United States v. Poludniak, 657 F.2d 848 (8th Cir.1981); Long v. State, 44 Del. 262, 65 A.2d 489 (1949). (Compare People v. Snyder, 32 Cal.3d 590, 186 Cal.Rptr. 485, 652 P.2d 42 (1982), holding counsel's advice defendant had been convicted only of a misdemeanor was no defense to a charge of possession of a firearm by a convicted felon, as statute is of strict liability type as to status of felon.) Even in that setting, counsel's advice the conduct is lawful

accord.[125] The principal reason for this position apparently is that the risk of collusion is greater and that those desiring to circumvent the law would shop around for bad advice.[126] "Lawyers are under enough temptations toward dishonesty already, without giving them the power to grant indulgences, for a fee, in criminal cases. Nor is the private attorney an 'officer of the state' for whose advice the state is responsible, whatever may be his status as an 'officer of the court' for other purposes." [127] It has been forcefully argued, however, that the rule should be otherwise (as it is in one jurisdiction [128]) because (i) reliance upon one's own counsel, as compared to a government official, is not inherently more blameworthy,[129] and (ii) the potential for abuse, given the necessity for reasonable reliance, is not that great and, in any event, any problems of proof "may be reduced significantly * * * by giving the defendant the burdens of production and persuasion." [130]

**WESTLAW
REFERENCES**

crim**** /p defense /p reliance belief /s judicial
   official counsel! attorney lawyer /s decision
   interpret! constru! advi*e advisory-opinion statut!

§ 5.2 Entrapment

Certain criminal offenses present the police with unique and difficult detection problems because they are committed privately between individuals who are willing participants. Consequently, in addition to employ-

ing search and seizure techniques, routine and electronic surveillance, and informants to expose such consensual crime, law enforcement officers resort to the use of encouragement. "Encouragement" is a word used to describe the activity of a police officer or agent "(a) who acts as a victim; (b) who intends, by his actions, to encourage the suspect to commit a crime; (c) who actually communicates this encouragement to the suspect; and (d) who thereby has some influence upon the commission of a crime." [1]

At the heart of the encouragement practice is the need to simulate reality. An environment is created in which the suspect is presented with an opportunity to commit a crime. The simulation of reality must be accurate enough to induce the criminal activity at the point in time when the agents are in a position to gather evidence of the crime. The tactics used vary from case to case. Some solicitations are innocuous, but since persons engaged in criminal activity are generally suspicious of strangers, government agents typically do more than simply approach a target and request the commission of a crime. Multiple requests or the formation of personal relationships with a subject may be necessary to overcome that suspicion.[2] In addition, appeals to personal considerations,[3] representations of benefits to be derived from the offense, and actual assistance in obtaining contraband or planning the details of the crime [4] are frequently employed.

---

is not inevitably a defense. It would not be, for example, if defendants "retained counsel to insure the success of their mendacious scheme, not to secure legal advice." United States v. Shewfelt, 455 F.2d 836 (9th Cir.1972).

125. Model Penal Code § 2.04. The provisions in the modern codes referred to earlier, by likewise limiting the reliance doctrine to specific situations, are also in accord.

126. State v. Downs, 116 N.C. 1064, 21 S.E. 689 (1895).

127. Hall and Seligman, supra note 69, at 652.

128. N.J.Stat.Ann. 2C:2–4 provides that belief conduct is not a crime is a defense when: "The actor otherwise diligently pursues all means available to ascertain the meaning and application of the offense to his conduct and honestly and in good faith concludes his conduct is not an offense in circumstances in which a law abiding and prudent person would also so conclude."

129. 2 P. Robinson, Criminal Law Defenses § 183(c)(1) (1984), noting it cannot be said "that a citizen who spends

a considerable sum to hire a reputable, professional tax attorney is more culpable in following that advice than a person following the advice of a seasonal I.R.S. employee hired to answer taxpayer inquiries."

130. Id. at § 183(c)(3). See also Ashworth, Excusable Mistake of Law, 1978 Crim.L.Rev. 652, 661.

§ 5.2

1. L. Tiffany, D. McIntyre, & D. Rotenberg, Detection of Crime 210 (1967).

2. See Grossman v. State, 457 P.2d 226 (Alaska 1969).

3. See, e.g., People v. Tipton, 78 Ill.2d 477, 36 Ill.Dec. 687, 401 N.E.2d 528 (1980), where government informant had previously dated the defendant; United States v. Sawyer, 210 F.2d 169 (3d Cir.1954), where investigator feigned seizure while requesting drugs.

4. See, e.g., Hampton v. United States, 425 U.S. 484, 96 S.Ct. 1646, 48 L.Ed.2d 113 (1976), where government in-

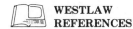

**WESTLAW
REFERENCES**

110k37(1) & encourag!

(a) Development and Scope of the Defense. The more extreme forms of encouragement activity are a matter of legitimate concern for a variety of reasons. Of central concern is the possibility that the encouragement might induce a person who otherwise would be law-abiding to engage in criminal conduct. Yet, as a historical matter, the traditional response of the law was that there were no limits upon the degree of temptation to which law enforcement officers and their agents could subject those under investigation. The attitude was that the courts would "not look to see who held out the bait, but [rather] who took it." [5]

However, there did ultimately develop, originally in the state courts, [6] a defense called "entrapment" which may be interposed in a criminal prosecution. [7] Beginning with the decision in *Sorrells v. United States* [8] in 1932, the development of the law of entrapment became largely an activity of the federal courts, with the states then adopting the doctrine thereby created. [9] The classic definition of entrapment is that articulated by Justice Roberts in *Sorrells*, the first Supreme Court decision to acknowledge the defense: "Entrapment is the conception and planning of an offense by an officer, and his procurement of its commission by one who would not have perpetrated it except for the trickery, persuasion, or fraud of the officer."

The defense of entrapment has been asserted in the context of a wide variety of criminal activity, including prostitution, [10] alcohol offenses, [11] counterfeiting, [12] price controlling, [13] and, probably most spectacularly, bribery of public officials. [14] However, the great majority of the cases in which an entrapment defense is interposed involve a charge of some drug offense. [15] There is a dearth of case authority on the question of whether the entrapment defense is available no matter what the nature of the charge brought against the defendant. But in *Sorrells* there appears a caution that the defense might be unavailable where the defendant is charged with a "hei-

---

formant supplied the drug which defendant sold; United States v. Twigg, 588 F.2d 373 (3d Cir.1978), where government informant assisted materially in setting up of a "speed" laboratory.

5. People v. Mills, 178 N.Y. 274, 70 N.E. 786 (1904). Consider also Board of Commissioners v. Backus, 29 How. Pr. 33 (N.Y.Sup.Ct.1864), where the court felt itself governed by Genesis 3:13 in which Eve, after being charged with consuming forbidden fruit, offered as a defense the fact that she had been tempted by the serpent. "That defense was overruled by the great Lawgiver, and whatever estimate we may form, or whatever judgment pass upon the character or conduct of the temptor, this plea has never since availed to shield crime or give indemnity to the culprit, and it is safe to say that under any court of civilized, not to say Christian ethics, it never will."

6. See, e.g., Michigan v. Sanders, 38 Mich. 219 (1878); O'Brian v. State, 6 Tex.App. 665 (1879). For a useful survey of the early authorities, consult Mikell, The Doctrine of Entrapment in the Federal Courts, 90 U.Pa.L.Rev. 245 (1942).

7. A number of states have also recognized entrapment as a defense to an administrative proceeding involving revocation or suspension of a license to practice a profession, trade, or business. See Petty v. Board of Medical Examiners, 9 Cal.3d 356, 107 Cal.Rptr. 473, 508 P.2d 1121 (1973), and discussion of that case in Note, 62 Calif.L.Rev. 408 (1974). Few courts have considered the issue, and the cases in which the matter is alluded to at all usually reflect nothing but the tacit assumption that the defense is available in administrative proceedings but inapplicable

to the case at bar. Roberts v. Illinois Liquor Control Commission, 58 Ill.App.2d 171, 206 N.E.2d 799 (1965); Langdon v. Board of Liquor Control, 98 Ohio App. 535, 130 N.E.2d 430 (1954). Nevertheless, extension of the entrapment defense to administrative disciplinary proceedings seems to be warranted by the policies underlying its application in criminal cases.

8. 287 U.S. 435, 53 S.Ct. 210, 77 L.Ed. 413 (1932).

9. DeFeo, Entrapment as a Defense to Criminal Responsibility: Its History, Theory and Application, 1 U.S. F.L.Rev. 243, 248 (1967). The process was not completed until 1980, when Tennessee became the last state to recognize the defense. State v. Jones, 598 S.W.2d 209 (Tenn.1980).

10. State v. McBride, 287 Or. 315, 599 P.2d 449 (1979).

11. Sorrells v. United States, 287 U.S. 435, 53 S.Ct. 210, 77 L.Ed. 413 (1932).

12. United States v. Chirella, 184 F.2d 903 (2d Cir. 1950).

13. Kott v. United States, 163 F.2d 984 (5th Cir.1933).

14. For accounts of Operation Abscam, see Time, Feb. 18, 1980, pp. 10–21; Newsweek, Feb. 18, 1980, at 32; Nation, Feb. 23, 1980, pp. 203–05.

15. According to a study of 405 federal entrapment opinions rendered between 1970 and 1975, 65% of the cases fell into the category of drug offenses excluding alcohol. Park, The Entrapment Controversy, 60 Minn.L. Rev. 163, 230 n. 223 (1976).

nous" or "revolting" crime, and the Model Penal Code formulation of the defense expressly makes it "unavailable when causing or threatening bodily injury is an element of the offense charged and the prosecution is based on conduct causing or threatening such injury to a person other than the person perpetrating the entrapment." [16] In support of this latter limitation, it is explained that one "who can be persuaded to cause such injury presents a danger that the public cannot safely disregard," and that the impropriety of the inducement will likely be dealt with by other means because the public will, "in all probability, demand the punishment of the conniving or cooperating officers." [17]

The defense of entrapment is only available when the encouragement was conducted by either personnel of law enforcement agencies or persons cooperating with law enforcement agencies, including paid informants and persons charged with crime who are cooperating in the hope of obtaining leniency. As it was put in *Sherman v. United States,*[18] the government cannot make use of an informer and then "claim disassociation through ignorance." The doctrine of entrapment does not extend to acts of inducement on the part of a private citizen who is not acting in cooperation with, or as an agent of, a law enforcement official.[19] If the entrapment defense was conceived of as being based upon the notion that a person is not culpable whenever he engages in what would otherwise be criminal conduct because of the strong inducement of another person, this limitation would be open to serious question.[20] What this limitation reflects, then, is that the "purpose of the defense is to deter misconduct in enforcing the law."[21]

 WESTLAW REFERENCES

sorrells /s 287 +5 435 /p purpose rationale reasons! /s entrapment /s defense

(b) The Subjective Approach. There are currently two major approaches to the defense of entrapment, each involving a distinct test and rationale and each with somewhat different procedural consequences. This division is reflected in the Supreme Court's decisions dealing directly with the subject of entrapment.[22] The majority view is usually referred to as the "subjective approach," although it is also called the federal approach or the *Sherman-Sorrells* doctrine, a reference to the fact that this test was adopted by a majority of the Supreme Court in the cases of *Sherman v. United States*[23] and *Sorrells v. United States.*[24] This subjective approach to entrapment has been consistently affirmed by a majority of the Supreme Court, and is adhered to by the federal courts[25] as well as a majority of the state courts.[26]

---

16. Model Penal Code § 2.13. Some of the modern codes contain such a limitation.

17. Model Penal Code § 2.13, Comment at 420 (1985).

18. 356 U.S. 369, 78 S.Ct. 819, 2 L.Ed.2d 848 (1958).

19. United States v. Mers, 701 F.2d 1321 (11th Cir. 1983). See also Henderson v. United States, 237 F.2d 169 (5th Cir.1956), collecting authorities on the private person distinction. As for the notion that a private person may be an unwitting agent when manipulated as a tool by law enforcement officials, see People v. McIntire, 23 Cal.3d 742, 153 Cal.Rptr. 237, 591 P.2d 527 (1979); and Notes, 62 B.U.L.Rev. 929 (1982); 95 Harv.L.Rev. 1122 (1982).

That notion must be distinguished from that in United States v. Valencia, 669 F.2d 37 (2d Cir.1981): "If a person is brought into a criminal scheme after being informed indirectly of conduct or statements by a government agent which could amount to inducement, then that person should be able to avail himself of the defense of entrapment just as may the person who receives the inducement." Compare United States v. Lomas, 706 F.2d 886 (9th Cir.1983): "We do not subscribe to the theory of derivative entrapment."

20. 2 P. Robinson, Criminal Law Defenses § 209(b) (1984).

21. Model Penal Code § 2.13, Comment at 419 (1985).

22. See United States v. Russell, 411 U.S. 423, 93 S.Ct. 1637, 36 L.Ed.2d 366 (1973); Masciale v. United States, 356 U.S. 386, 78 S.Ct. 827, 2 L.Ed.2d 859 (1958); Sherman v. United States, 356 U.S. 369, 78 S.Ct. 819, 2 L.Ed.2d 848 (1958); Sorrells v. United States, 287 U.S. 435, 53 S.Ct. 210, 77 L.Ed. 413 (1932).

23. 356 U.S. 369, 78 S.Ct. 819, 2 L.Ed.2d 848 (1958).

24. 287 U.S. 435, 53 S.Ct. 210, 77 L.Ed. 413 (1932).

25. See United States v. Mayo, 705 F.2d 62 (2d Cir. 1983), and cases cited therein.

26. Even as to those states which have adopted modern criminal codes, about two-thirds have retained the subjective test. Sometimes this has been done by enacting no entrapment statute at all, thus continuing the subjective test developed in the case law. See, e.g., State v. Stanley, 123 Ariz. 95, 597 P.2d 998 (App.1979); State v. Batiste, 363 So.2d 639 (La.1978); State v. McCrillis, 376 A.2d 95 (Me. 1971); State v. Grilli, 304 Minn. 80, 230 N.W.2d 445

A two-step test is used under the subjective approach: the first inquiry is whether or not the offense was induced by a government agent;[27] and the second is whether or not the defendant was predisposed to commit the type of offense charged. A defendant is considered predisposed if he is "ready and willing to commit the crimes such as are charged in the indictment, whenever opportunity was afforded."[28] If the accused is found to be predisposed, the defense of entrapment may not prevail. The predisposition test reflects an attempt to draw a line between "a trap for the unwary innocent and the trap for the unwary criminal."[29] The emphasis under the subjective approach is clearly upon the defendant's propensity to commit the offense rather than on the officer's misconduct.

The underlying rationale of the subjective approach is grounded in the substantive criminal law. The defense is explained in terms of the defendant's conduct not being criminal because the legislature intended acts instigated by the government to be excepted from the purview of the general statutory prohibition. As stated by the majority in *Sorrells:* "We are

(1975); State v. Padilla, 91 N.M. 451, 575 P.2d 960 (1978); State v. Metcalf, 60 Ohio App.2d 212, 396 N.E.2d 786 (1977); State v. Nagel, 279 N.W.2d 911 (S.D.1979); Cogdill v. Commonwealth, 219 Va. 272, 247 S.E.2d 392 (1978); Dycus v. State, 529 P.2d 979 (Wyo.1974).

Elsewhere this has been accomplished by enactment of a provision stated in subjective terms, either by merely incorporating existing case law, or by requiring that the defendant not be predisposed, that defendant would not otherwise have committed the crime, that defendant was not ready and willing to commit the offense, that defendant would not otherwise have intended to commit it, or that the defendant not have originated the criminal purpose.

27. In this connection, the Court in *Sorrells* and *Sherman* stressed that the fact government agents "merely afforded opportunities or facilities for the commission of the offense does not" constitute entrapment. Such a declaration frequently appears in the subjective-test entrapment statutes.

28. 1 E. Devitt & C. Blackmar, Federal Jury Practice and Instructions § 13.09 (3d ed. 1977). The "point of reference for ascertaining the predisposition of a defendant to commit a particular crime is the time period extending from just before the State's solicitation to just before the defendant's commission of the crime." Harrison v. State, 442 A.2d 1377 (Del.1982).

unable to conclude that it was the intention of the Congress in enacting this statute that its processes of detection and enforcement be abused by the instigation by government officials of an act on the part of persons otherwise innocent in order to lure them to its commission and to punish them."

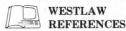

**WESTLAW
REFERENCES**

(sherman /s 356 +5 369) (sorrells /s 287 +5 435) /p entrapment /s test approach

(c) The Objective Approach. However, there is growing support for the objective approach, variously described as the "hypothetical person" approach or the Roberts-Frankfurter approach (after the writers of the concurring opinions in *Sorrells* and *Sherman*). The objective approach is favored by a majority of the commentators,[30] and is reflected in the formulation of the entrapment defense appearing in the American Law Institute's Model Penal Code.[31] Its first authoritative acceptance came by judicial decision in Alaska in 1969,[32] and now several other states

29. Sherman v. United States, 356 U.S. 369, 78 S.Ct. 819, 2 L.Ed.2d 848 (1958).

30. 1 National Comm'n on Reform of Federal Criminal Laws, Working Papers 303–28 (1970); L. Tiffany, D. McIntyre & D. Rotenberg, Detection of Crime 265–72 (1967); Donnelly, Judicial Control of Informants, Spies, Stool Pigeons and Agent Provocateurs, 60 Yale L.J. 1091 (1951); Goldstein, For Harold Lasswell: Some Reflections on Human Dignity, Entrapment, Informed Consent, and the Plea Bargain, 84 Yale L.J. 683 (1975); Williams, The Defense of Entrapment and Related Problems in Criminal Prosecution, 28 Ford.L.Rev. 399 (1959); Comments, 59 Cornell L.Rev. 546 (1974); 37 Mo.L.Rev. 633 (1972); 24 S.D.L.Rev. 510 (1979).

For defense of the subjective approach or some modified version thereof, see DeFeo, Entrapment as a Defense to Criminal Responsibility: Its History, Theory and Application, 1 U.S.F.L.Rev. 243 (1967); Park, The Entrapment Controversy, 60 Minn.L.Rev. 163 (1976); Rossum, The Entrapment Defense and the Teaching of Political Responsibility, 6 Am.J.Crim.L. 287 (1978).

31. Model Penal Code § 2.13.

32. Grossman v. State, 457 P.2d 226 (Alaska 1969).

have adopted it either by statute [33] or judicial decision.[34]

The objective approach focuses upon the inducements used by the government agents. This means that entrapment has been established if the offense was induced or encouraged by "employing methods of persuasion or inducement which create a substantial risk that such an offense will be committed by persons other than those who are ready to commit it."[35] In applying this test, it is necessary to consider the surrounding circumstances, such as evidence of the manner in which the particular criminal business is usually carried on. Though such practices as appeals to sympathy or friendship, offers of inordinate gain, or persistent offers to overcome hesitancy are suspect, courts in jurisdictions using the objective test have been reluctant to lay down absolutes.[36] Though such temptations may be impermissible in some instances, each case must be judged on its own facts.[37] Thus, it would seem that this "objective" focus upon the propriety of the police conduct leaves as much room for value judgments to be made as does the "subjective" focus upon the defendant's state of mind.

The rationale behind the objective approach is grounded in public policy considerations. Proponents of this approach reject the legisla-

tive intent argument. They believe that courts must refuse to convict an entrapped defendant not because his conduct falls outside the proscription of the statute, but rather because, even if his guilt has been established, the methods employed on behalf of the government to bring about the crime "cannot be countenanced."[38] To some extent, this reflects the notion that the courts should not become tainted by condoning law enforcement improprieties. If government agents have instigated the commission of a crime, then the courts should not in effect approve that "abhorent transaction"[39] by permitting the induced individual to be convicted. But the primary consideration is that an affirmative duty resides in the courts to control police excesses in inducing criminal behavior, and that this duty should not be limited to instances in which the defendant is otherwise "innocent."[40] So viewed, the entrapment defense appears to be a procedural device (somewhat like the Fourth Amendment and *Miranda* exclusionary rules) for deterring undesirable governmental intrusions into the lives of citizens.

As currently applied, the two approaches differ more than merely at the theoretical level. True, in *Sorrells* and *Sherman* the majority (subjective approach) and minority (objective approach) opinions agreed as to the

33. A few states have followed closely the formulation in Model Penal Code § 2.13, covering the situation in which the officer or his agent "induces or encourages another person to engage in conduct constituting such offense by either: (a) making knowingly false representations designed to induce the belief that such conduct is not prohibited; or (b) employing methods of persuasion or inducement which create a substantial risk that such an offense will be committed by persons other than those who are ready to commit it." A few others specify only the (b) portion of the Model Penal Code test.

Other provisions state it is entrapment to resort to conduct that "would persuade an average person, other than one who is ready and willing to commit the offense," that would be "likely to cause normally law-abiding persons to commit" it, that creates a "substantial risk that the acts would be committed by a person who, but for such inducement, would not have conceived of or engaged in" such conduct, that would "induce an ordinary law-abiding person" to commit the crime, or (the broadest of all if read literally) that is "likely to cause persons to commit the offense."

The fact the legislature has enacted an entrapment provision stated in objective terms is no guarantee that it

will be so interpreted by the courts. See Bailey v. People, 630 P.2d 1062 (Colo.1981); State v. Curtis, 542 P.2d 744 (Utah 1975).

34. See People v. Barraza, 23 Cal.3d 675, 153 Cal.Rptr. 459, 591 P.2d 947 (1979); State v. Wilkins, 144 Vt. 22, 473 A.2d 295 (1983); State v. Mullen, 216 N.W.2d 375 (Iowa 1974); People v. Turner, 390 Mich. 7, 210 N.W.2d 336 (1973) discussed in Note, 68 Calif.L.Rev. 946 (1980); all overruling earlier authority supporting the subjective approach.

35. Model Penal Code § 2.13.

36. However, some of the statutes which mandate an objective test set out (as commonly do the subjective-test statutes, see note 27 supra) the notion from *Sorrells* and *Sherman* that it is not entrapment merely to afford the defendant an opportunity to commit the crime.

37. Grossman v. State, 457 P.2d 226 (Alaska 1969).

38. Sherman v. United States, 356 U.S. 369, 78 S.Ct. 819, 2 L.Ed.2d 848 (1958) (Frankfurter, J., concurring).

39. Sorrells v. United States, 287 U.S. 435, 53 S.Ct. 210, 77 L.Ed. 413 (1932) (Roberts, J., concurring).

40. Model Penal Code § 2.13, Comment at 412 (1985).

result on the facts there presented.[41] But the concurring justices in *Sherman* were the dissenters in *Masciale v. United States,*[42] decided the same day. And in *United States v. Russell,*[43] the result would certainly have been different had the objective test been utilized. However, neither of the two approaches is uniformly more favorable to defendants,[44] as is reflected by this brief comparison:

> Under the [subjective approach], if *A*, an informer, makes overreaching appeals to compassion and friendship and thus moves *D* to sell narcotics, *D* has no defense if he is predisposed to narcotics peddling. Under the [objective approach] a defense would be established because the police conduct, not *D*'s predisposition, determines the issue. Under the [subjective approach], *A*'s mere offer to purchase narcotics from *D* may give rise to the defense provided *D* is not predisposed to sell. A contrary result is reached under the [objective approach]. A mere offer to buy hardly creates a serious risk of offending by the innocent.[45]

WESTLAW
REFERENCES

entrapment /s objective /s test approach

(d) Objections to the Subjective Approach. Proponents of the objective approach raise three main arguments against the subjective approach. First of all, the "legislative intent" theory is attacked as "sheer fiction."[46] It is argued that the Congress or state legislature intended to proscribe precisely the conduct in which the defendant engaged, as is reflected by the fact that the conduct is unquestionably criminal if the temptor was a private person rather than a government agent.[47] Because the prior innocence of the defendant will not sustain the defense of entrapment, then, so the argument proceeds, the public policies of deterring unlawful police conduct and preserving the purity of the courts must be controlling. Those policies, it is concluded, are not effectuated by looking to the defendant's predisposition.

A second criticism of the subjective approach is that it creates, in effect, an "anything goes" rule for use against persons who can be shown by their prior convictions or otherwise to have been predisposed to engage in criminal behavior. This is because if the trier of fact determines that a defendant was predisposed to commit the type of crime charged, then no level of police deceit, badgering or other unsavory practices will be deemed impermissible. Such a result is unsound, it is argued, because it ignores "the possibility that no matter what his past crimes and general disposition the defendant might not have committed the particular

41. In *Sherman,* a government informer met defendant at a doctor's office where he was being treated to cure his narcotics addiction, and the informer induced defendant to sell him drugs after making repeated requests and saying that he was not responding to treatment and was suffering as a consequence. The majority, applying the subjective approach, concluded that a 9-year-old sale of narcotics conviction and a 5-year-old possession conviction did not show predisposition, "particularly when we must assume from the record he was trying to overcome the narcotics habit at the time." The four concurring Justices concluded that such appeals to sympathy "can no more be tolerated when directed against a past offender than against an ordinary law-abiding citizen."

In *Sorrells,* the majority held the lower court had erred in ruling as a matter of law that there could be no entrapment, where it was shown "that the act for which defendant was prosecuted was instigated by the prohibition agent, that it was the creature of his purpose, that defendant had no previous disposition to commit it but was an industrious, law-abiding citizen, and that the agent lured defendant, otherwise innocent, to its commission by repeated and persistent solicitation in which he succeeded by taking advantage of the sentiment aroused by reminiscences of their experiences as companions in arms in the World War." Three members of the Court concurred, but relied upon the objective approach.

42. 356 U.S. 386, 78 S.Ct. 827, 2 L.Ed.2d 859 (1958). The majority, using the subjective approach, concluded the "trial court properly submitted the case to the jury"; the four dissenters, using the objective approach, concluded that the lower court "should itself have ruled on the issue of entrapment and not left it to determination by the jury."

43. 411 U.S. 423, 93 S.Ct. 1637, 36 L.Ed.2d 366 (1973). There, an undercover agent supplied an essential but difficult to obtain ingredient for defendants' operation of a "speed" laboratory. The majority ruled that "the jury finding as to predisposition was supported by the evidence" and was "fatal to his claim of entrapment." Three dissenters urged adoption of the objective test.

44. Park, supra note 30, at 199.

45. Model Penal Code § 2.10, Comment (Tent.Draft No. 9, 1959).

46. Sherman v. United States, 356 U.S. 369, 78 S.Ct. 819, 2 L.Ed.2d 848 (1958) (Frankfurter, J., concurring).

47. Ibid.

crime unless confronted with inordinate inducements."[48] Moreover, so this reasoning proceeds, this notion that the permissible police conduct may vary according to the particular defendant is inconsistent with the objective of equality under the law.

Yet a third objection to the subjective approach is that delving into the defendant's character and predisposition not only "has often obscured the important task of judging the quality of the police behavior,"[49] but also has prejudiced the defendant more generally. This is because once the entrapment defense is raised, certain usual evidentiary rules are discarded, and the defendant will be subjected to an "appropriate and searching inquiry into his own conduct and predisposition as bearing upon that issue."[50] This means a prosecutor may admit evidence of a prior criminal record, reputation evidence, acts of prior misconduct, and other information generally barred as hearsay or as being more prejudicial than probative.

 **WESTLAW REFERENCES**

entrapment /p evidence /s character

(e) Objections to the Objective Approach. Proponents of the subjective approach have likewise raised various criticisms concerning the objective approach. One of them is that defendant's predisposition, at least if known by the police when the investigation in question was conducted, has an important bearing upon the question of whether the conduct of the police and their agents was proper. For example, if it is known that a particular suspect has sold drugs in the past, then it is proper to subject that person to more persuasive inducements than would be

permissible as to an individual about whose predisposition the authorities knew nothing.[51] By like token, knowledge that a target has a weakness for a vice crime but is currently abstaining is also a fact that merits consideration when assessing an agent's conduct.[52] Thus, the objective approach is said to be inherently defective because it eliminates entirely[53] the need for considering a particular defendant's criminal predisposition. So the argument goes, "evidence of criminal proclivity ought to be taken into account when it bears on the question of whether the agent should have known that his inducement would create a substantial risk of corrupting a person not otherwise disposed to commit the offense."[54]

A second major criticism of the objective approach is that the "wrong" people end up in jail if a dangerous, chronic offender may only be offered those inducements which might have tempted a hypothetical, law-abiding person.[55] This is because, for example, the fact that the defendant in a particular case has been a shrewd, active member of a narcotics ring prior to and continuing through the incident in question is irrelevant under the objective test to a determination of the propriety of the inducements used. So the argument continues, to avoid this acquittal of "wary criminals," courts are likely to allow agents substantial leeway in determining the limits of permissible inducement, with the result that this same freedom will allow the police to lead astray the "unwary innocent."[56]

Still another criticism directed at the objective approach to entrapment is that it will foster inaccuracy in the factfinding process.

48. Ibid.

49. Model Penal Code § 2.13, Comment at 413 (1985).

50. Sorrells v. United States, 287 U.S. 435, 53 S.Ct. 210, 77 L.Ed. 413 (1932).

51. Rossum, supra note 30, at 299.

52. Park, supra note 30, at 204. Consider in this regard the facts of the *Sherman* case, summarized in note 41 supra.

53. In *Sherman,* Justice Frankfurter claimed that whether an intent originated with a defendant was "wholly irrelevant" and that all evidence which dealt with the

defendant's reputation, criminal activities, and prior disposition should be excluded. Similar statements are to be found at Model Penal Code § 2.13, Comment at 413 (1985), where the federal law of entrapment is criticized because it turns the courtroom inquiry away from the character of the police conduct to "the history of the accused and his immediate reaction to enticement."

54. Park, supra note 30, at 204.

55. Rossum, supra note 30, at 298.

56. Park, supra note 30, at 220.

It is argued that the nature of the inducement offered in secret is a factual issue less susceptible to reliable proof than the issue of predisposition.[57] This is because if a defendant claims that an inducement was improper, the agent can take the stand and rebut the allegations, resulting in a swearing match. Especially because the defense of entrapment ordinarily assumes an admission of guilt (unless inconsistent defenses are permitted), this means the factfinder will often have to make the "imponderable choice" between the testimony of an informer, often with a criminal record, and that of a defendant who has admittedly commited the criminal act.[58]

A fourth objection relates to the public policy justifications of the objective approach. It is questioned whether the "purity" of the courts is itself a sufficient justification, and whether the objective approach can be expected to serve the deterrence objective in a meaningful way. Because courts are disinclined to adopt per se rules regarding what are impermissible police inducements,[59] it is doubted whether there will actually result significant restrictions upon the types of inducements which police are entitled to utilize. Moreover, so the argument continues, even if such limitations are developed the police will still be left with the discretion to decide upon the context or target of encouragement activity. To this are added the familiar arguments against other attempts to deter the police, such as that they can be thwarted by police perjury or that they will be totally ineffective when the police are acting for objectives other than conviction. For all these reasons, this line of argument concludes, the deterrence objective should be dismissed in favor of an effort to do justice to the individual defendant in the particular case.[60]

 WESTLAW REFERENCES

92k257.5 & crim**** /p investigation

(f) Procedural Considerations. Entrapment, it has been said, is a "dangerous and judicially unpopular defense that should only be used in a few cases with ideal fact situations or in desperate circumstances where no other defense is possible."[61] This perceived danger is largely attributable to various procedural consequences which attend interposition of an entrapment defense where the majority, subjective approach is followed.

(1) Admissibility of Evidence of Defendant's Past Conduct. As the Supreme Court put it in *Sherman v. United States,*[62] under the subjective approach the prosecution may engage in a " 'searching inquiry into [defendant's] own conduct and predisposition' as bearing on his claim of innocence." In most jurisdictions this means that once entrapment has been raised as a defense, the usual evidentiary rules are no longer followed. For the purported purpose of allowing the factfinder access to all information bearing upon the "predisposition" issue, courts have allowed the receipt into evidence of defendant's prior convictions, prior arrests, and information about his "reputation" and even concerning "suspicious conduct" on his part.[63] The result, as Justice Stewart objected in *United States v. Russell,*[64] is that otherwise inadmissible "hearsay, suspicion and rumor" is brought into the case to the detriment of the defendant. The defendant, in effect, is "put on trial for his past offenses and character."[65]

Some courts are more cautious. See, e.g., State v. Batiste, 363 So.2d 639 (La.1978) (offense must be of similar character and not too remote in time); Bowser v. State, 50 Md.App. 363, 439 A.2d 1 (1981) (holding "that suspicion, rumor, secondhand reputation evidence, and other unreliable hearsay normally barred by the rules of evidence do not individually or collectively become admissible merely because the defendant has raised the defense of entrapment").

57. Id. at 221–24.

58. Id. at 224.

59. See Grossman v. State, 457 P.2d 226 (Alaska 1969).

60. Park, supra note 30, at 239.

61. Hardy, The Traps of Entrapment, 3 Am.J.Crim.L. 165 (1974).

62. 356 U.S. 369, 78 S.Ct. 819, 2 L.Ed.2d 848 (1958).

63. See Notes, 49 J.Crim.L.C. & P.S. 447, 450–52 (1959); 37 Mo.L.Rev. 633, 648–50 (1972); 1971 Utah L.Rev. 266, 269–71.

64. 411 U.S. 423, 93 S.Ct. 1637, 36 L.Ed.2d 366 (1973).

65. Grossman v. State, 457 P.2d 226 (Alaska 1969).

Although it has quite correctly been said that the "greatest fault" of the subjective approach as it developed in the federal courts "lies in the permissiveness of its ancillary rules of evidence,"[66] it is important to note that this "indiscriminate attitude toward predisposition evidence is by no means a necessary feature of the subjective test."[67] This is because less prejudicial means of determining the readiness and willingness of a defendant to engage in the criminal conduct will often be available. The most promising alternative is testimony about the defendant's actions during the negotiations leading to the charged offense, such as his ready acquiescence,[68] his expert knowledge about such criminal activity,[69] his admissions of past deeds or future plans,[70] and his ready access to the contraband.[71] Another possibility is evidence obtained in a subsequent search or otherwise which shows that the defendant was involved in a course of ongoing criminal activity.

(2) Triable by Court or Jury. Traditionally, the entrapment defense has been regarded as a matter for the jury rather than for determination by the judge. (Even where this is unquestionably the case, the judge may rule on the sufficiency of the proof to raise the issue in the first place,[72] and where uncontradicted evidence supports the conclusion that the defendant was entrapped the issue may of course be decided as a matter of law by the court.[73]) Under the majority, subjective approach to entrapment, grounded upon the im-

plied exception theory, it is apparent that "the issue of whether a defendant has been entrapped is for the jury as part of its function of determining the guilt or innocence of the accused."[74]

In support of this state of affairs, it has been argued that determining matters of credibility and assessing the subjective response to the stimulus of police encouragement are peculiarly within the ken of the jury.[75] Also, it has been observed that if the matter is placed in the hands of the jury there is an opportunity for jury nullification,[76] meaning that "the jury, if it wishes, can acquit because of the moral revulsion which the police conduct evokes in them, notwithstanding any amount of convincing evidence of the defendant's predisposition."[77] On the other hand, the argument has been made that the case for putting the matter in the hands of the court is especially strong under the subjective approach. This is because where the rules of evidence on proving predisposition are very loose, which is usually the case, "the defense can be raised only at a great price to the defendant"[78] if that evidence becomes known to the jury.[79]

Under the objective approach to entrapment, the judge-versus-jury issue "is more evenly balanced."[80] In favor of having the matter decided by the judge is the notion that it is the function of the court to preserve the purity of the court.[81] Similarly, it may be said that to the extent the objective approach

66. Park, The Entrapment Controversy, 60 Minn.L. Rev. 163, 272 (1976).

67. Ibid. Some courts do not permit proof of predisposition by character evidence. See, e.g., State v. Knight, 230 S.E.2d 732 (W.Va.1976).

68. United States v. Ortiz, 496 F.2d 705 (2d Cir.1974).

69. Whiting v. United States, 296 F.2d 512 (1st Cir. 1961).

70. People v. Caudillo, 138 Cal.App.2d 183, 291 P.2d 191 (1955).

71. United States v. Dickens, 524 F.2d 441 (5th Cir. 1975).

72. People v. Alamillo, 113 Cal.App.2d 617, 248 P.2d 421 (1952).

73. Sherman v. United States, 356 U.S. 369, 78 S.Ct. 819, 2 L.Ed.2d 848 (1958).

74. Sherman v. United States, 356 U.S. 369, 78 S.Ct. 819, 2 L.Ed.2d 848 (1958).

75. DeFeo, Entrapment as a Defense to Criminal Responsibility: Its History, Theory and Application, 1 U.S. F.L.Rev. 243, 270–71 (1967).

76. On this phenomenon, see 2 W. LaFave & J. Israel, Criminal Procedure § 21.1(g) (1984).

77. 1 National Comm'n on Reform of Federal Criminal Laws, Working Papers 324 (1970).

78. Model Penal Code § 2.13, Comment at 416 (1985).

79. On this basis, it was decided in State v. Grilli, 230 N.W.2d 445 (Minn.1975), that the defendant could elect to have a judge decide the issue of entrapment at a pretrial evidentiary hearing.

80. Model Penal Code § 2.13, Comment at 417 (1985).

81. Sorrells v. United States, 287 U.S. 435, 53 S.Ct. 210, 77 L.Ed. 413 (1932) (Roberts, J., concurring).

rests upon a deterrence-of-police rationale this function also is the proper responsibility of the court, just as it is when the court rules on suppression motions.[82] And there is the added point made by Justice Frankfurter in *Sherman,* namely,

> that a jury verdict, although it may settle the issue of entrapment in the particular case, cannot give significant guidance for official conduct for the future. Only the court, through the gradual evolution of explicit standards in accumulated precedents, can do this with the degree of certainty that the wise administration of criminal justice demands.

Also, there is a sense in which trial of the issue before the judge would be to the state's advantage; the defendant "would no longer be able to divert a jury's attention from his crime by attacking the sins of the police."[83]

However, not all of the states which have adopted the objective approach submit the issue to the judge instead of the jury.[84] In light of the above considerations, it is not entirely clear why this is so. Perhaps there is concern that taking the issue from the jury might give rise to constitutional questions about the breadth of the right to jury trial. More likely, however, is the explanation that the issue is deemed an appropriate one for the jury because the jury has "a special claim to competence"[85] on the question of what temptations would be too great for an ordinary law-abiding citizen.

(3) Inconsistent Defenses. The traditional view has been that the defense of entrapment is not available to one who denies commission of the criminal act with which he is charged, for the reason that the denial is inconsistent

with the assertion of such a defense.[86] However, a trend in the opposite direction appears to be developing,[87] and there is much to be said in favor of this latter position. For one thing, it avoids serious constitutional questions concerning whether a defendant may be required, in effect, to surrender his presumption of innocence and his privilege against self-incrimination in order to plead entrapment.[88] Also, it would seem that the adversary process is itself a sufficient restraint upon resort to positions which are truly inconsistent. In a case where two positions are unquestionably logically inconsistent, a defendant who pursued both positions would certainly be found to be lacking credibility.[89]

In any event, where the circumstances are such that there is no inherent inconsistency between claiming entrapment and yet not admitting commission of the criminal acts, certainly the defendant must be allowed to raise the defense of entrapment without admitting the crime. Thus, the inconsistency rule does not apply when the government in its own case in chief has interjected the issue of entrapment into the case.[90] And if a defendant testifies that a government agent encouraged him to commit a crime which he had never contemplated before that time and that he resisted the temptation nonetheless, there is nothing internally inconsistent in thereby claiming entrapment and that the crime did not occur.[91] Asserting the entrapment defense is not necessarily inconsistent with denial of the crime even when it is admitted that the requisite acts occurred, for the defendant might nonetheless claim that he lacked the requisite bad state of mind.[92]

---

82. Working Papers, supra note 77, at 325.

83. Model Penal Code § 2.13, Comment at 418 (1985).

84. See, e.g., People v. Barraza, 23 Cal.3d 675, 153 Cal. Rptr. 459, 591 P.2d 947 (1979).

85. Model Penal Code § 2.13, Comment at 417 (1985).

86. Groot, The Serpent Beguiled Me and I (Without Scienter) Did Eat—Denial of Crime and the Entrapment Defense, 1973 U.Ill.L.F. 254; Notes, 22 B.C.L.Rev. 911 (1981); 56 Iowa L.Rev. 686 (1971); 37 Mo.L.Rev. 633, 656 (1972). The federal cases are collected in United States v. Shameia, 464 F.2d 629 (6th Cir.1972).

87. United States v. Valencia, 669 F.2d 37 (2d Cir. 1980); United States v. Demma, 523 F.2d 981 (9th Cir.

1975); People v. Perez, 62 Cal.2d 769, 44 Cal.Rptr. 326, 401 P.2d 934 (1965); State v. McBride, 287 Or. 315, 599 P.2d 449 (1979).

88. Groot, supra note 86, at 269.

89. Id. at 263.

90. Sears v. United States, 343 F.2d 139 (5th Cir.1965).

91. State v. McBride, 287 Or. 315, 599 P.2d 449 (1979).

92. Groot, supra note 86, at 264. He describes bribery as a good example, for even though the defendant gave money to a public official, he may claim that the payment was a loan, that he lacked intent to influence official acts, or that he was merely trying to determine the honesty of

(4) Burden of Proof. In those jurisdictions which follow the majority, subjective approach to entrapment, it is generally accepted that the defendant has the burden of establishing the fact of inducement by a government agent.[93] The extent of this burden is less than clear. Some courts require a defendant to sustain a burden of persuasion by proving government inducement by a preponderance of the evidence.[94] Many courts, however, indicate that the defendant only has the burden of production, which can be met by coming forward with "some evidence" of government conduct which created a risk of persuading a nondisposed person to commit a crime.[95] In any event, once the defendant's threshold responsibility is satisfied, the burden is then on the government to negate the defense by showing beyond a reasonable doubt defendant's predisposition.[96]

In states where the objective approach is followed, the entire burden of production and persuasion is on the defendant, who must establish the impropriety of the police conduct by a preponderance of the evidence. This is a consequence of the entrapment defense under this approach being an "affirmative defense" rather than something which negatives the existence of an element of the crime charged.[97] Such an allocation of the burden of proof might be questioned on the ground that as a general matter the government is in a much better position than the defendant to obtain and preserve evidence on the question of what kinds of government inducements were utilized in the particular case. This has led to the suggestion that perhaps the real basis for placing the burden of persuasion on the defendant is that entrapment is a disfavored defense, so that factual doubts should be resolved against it.[98]

WESTLAW REFERENCES

russell /s 411 +5 423 & defendant /s
  predispos! reputation character past prior +2
  conviction arrest crim*** conduct

synopsis(entrapment /s evidence /s defendant state
  /s produc! rebut!)

(g) Due Process: Government "Overinvolvement" in a Criminal Enterprise. In *Sorrells* and *Sherman* the entrapment doctrine was explained in terms of the presumed intention of Congress rather than as a matter of constitutional law. This means, of course, that Congress may depart from the *Sorrells-Sherman* test if it wishes, and that state courts and legislatures may do likewise. In short, the law of entrapment is not itself of constitutional dimension. But there remains for consideration the question of whether certain kinds of government involvement in a criminal enterprise would warrant the conclusion that the due process rights of the person induced had been violated.

In *United States v. Russell,*[99] an undercover agent supplied the defendant and his associates with 100 grams of propanone, an essential but difficult to obtain ingredient in the manufacture of methamphetamine ("speed"); the defendants used it to produce two batches of "speed," which pursuant to agreement the agent received half of in return. The defendant, convicted of unlawfully manufacturing and selling the substance, conceded on appeal that the jury could have found him predisposed, but claimed that the agent's involvement in the enterprise was so substantial that the prosecution violated due process. In particular, he contended that prosecution should be precluded when it is shown that the criminal conduct would not have been possible had not the agent "supplied an indispensable means to the commission of the crime that could not have been obtained otherwise,

---

the official, all of which are consistent with the claim of entrapment. Id. at 266.

93. The classic statement of the burden of proof allocation is that by Learned Hand in United States v. Sherman, 200 F.2d 880 (2d Cir.1952).

94. United States v. Pugliese, 346 F.2d 861 (2d Cir. 1965).

95. United States v. Burkley, 591 F.2d 903 (D.C.Cir. 1978); State v. Jones, ___ R.I. ___, 416 A.2d 676 (1980).

96. United States v. Mosely, 496 F.2d 1012 (5th Cir. 1974).

97. Model Penal Code § 2.13, Comment at 415 (1985).

98. Park, supra note 66, at 265–67.

99. 411 U.S. 423, 93 S.Ct. 1637, 36 L.Ed.2d 366 (1973).

through legal or illegal channels." The Court in *Russell* found it unnecessary to pass on that contention because the record showed that propanone "was by no means impossible" to obtain by other sources. Though acknowledging that "we may some day be presented with a situation in which the conduct of law enforcement agents is so outrageous that due process principles would absolutely bar the government from invoking judicial processes to obtain a conviction," the majority concluded "the instant case is distinctly not of that breed" because the agent had simply supplied a legal and harmless substance to a person who had theretofore been "an active participant in an illegal drug manufacturing enterprise." Three dissenters urged adoption of the objective approach to entrapment and asserted that if propanone "had been wholly unobtainable from other sources" the agent's actions would be "conduct that constitutes entrapment under any definition."[100]

Then came *Hampton v. United States,*[101] where petitioner, convicted of distributing heroin, objected to the denial of his requested jury instruction that he must be acquitted if the narcotics he sold to government agents had earlier been supplied to him by a government informant. Three members of the Court concluded that the difference between the instant case and *Russell* was "one of degree, not of kind," in that here the government supplied an illegal substance which was the corpus delicti of petitioner's crime and thus "played a more significant role" in enabling the crime to occur. But such conduct as to a predisposed defendant was deemed not to violate due process. Significantly, two concurring Justices, while agreeing that "this case is controlled completely by *Russell,*" expressed their unwillingness "to join the plu-

rality in concluding that, no matter what the circumstances, neither due process principles nor our supervisory power could support a bar to conviction in any case where the Government is able to prove disposition." The three dissenters[102] in *Hampton* urged that conviction be "barred as a matter of law where the subject of the criminal charge is the sale of contraband provided to the defendant by a Government agent." The instant case, they contended, was different from *Russell* because (i) here the supplied substance was contraband and (ii) here the "beginning and end of this crime" coincided with the government's involvement. "The Government," they protested, "is doing nothing less than buying contraband from itself through an intermediary and jailing the intermediary."

Russell and *Hampton,* then, indicate that a majority of the Court accepts the notion that there may well be *some* circumstances in which a due process defense would be available even to a defendant found to be predisposed. However, those two cases do not provide clear guidance as to how the police conduct is to be assessed in making this judgment, though they do justify the conclusion that instances of government conduct outrageous enough to violate due process will be exceedingly rare.[103] One possibility would be an instance in which government agents induce others to engage in violence or threat of violence against innocent parties.[104] Another would be "where concern for overreaching government inducement overlaps with concern for first amendment freedoms, as where the government sends provocateurs into political organizations to suggest the commission of crimes."[105] And then of course there is the situation put by the *Russell* dissenters—supplying contraband "wholly unobtainable from

---

100. One of those dissenters also joined in another dissent by another member of the Court in which it was argued that whether the ingredient could be obtained from other sources was "quite irrelevant" and concluding: "Federal agents play a debased role when they become the instigators of the crime, or partners in its commission, or the creative brain behind the illegal scheme."

101. 425 U.S. 484, 96 S.Ct. 1646, 48 L.Ed.2d 113 (1976).

102. The ninth member of the Court, Stevens, J., took no part in the case.

103. Note, 67 Geo.L.J. 1455, 1461–62 (1979).

104. The concurring opinion in *Hampton* quoted from Judge Friendly's view in United States v. Archer, 486 F.2d 670 (2d Cir.1973), that "it would be unthinkable, for example, to permit government agents to instigate robberies and beatings merely to gather evidence to convict other members of a gang of hoodlums." See also Park, supra note 66, at 186–90.

105. Park, supra note 66, at 187.

other sources" so as to "make possible the commission of an otherwise totally impossible crime."

Special note must be taken of *United States v. Twigg*,[106] apparently the first case since *Hampton* in which a defendant has prevailed on a due process defense.[107] Neville and Twigg were convicted of conspiracy to manufacture "speed." A government informer proposed to Neville that the laboratory be established, and Neville assumed responsibility for raising the capital and arranging for distribution, while the informer supplied the equipment, raw materials and laboratory site and was in complete charge of the lab because he alone had the expertise to manufacture the drug. Distinguishing *Russell* as a case in which the defendant was an active participant before the government agent appeared on the scene, and *Hampton* as concerned with "a much more fleeting and elusive crime to detect," the majority in *Twigg* concluded that the government involvement had reached "a demonstrable level of outrageousness." In reaching that conclusion, the court stressed (i) that "the illicit plan did not originate with the criminal defendants"; (ii) that the informer's expertise was "an indispensable requisite to this criminal enterprise"; and (iii) that, "as far as the record reveals, [Neville] was lawfully and peaceably minding his own affairs" until approached by the informant.

Twigg thus suggests that a "reasonable suspicion" prerequisite may on occasion emerge

as an aspect of the due process limits upon encouragement activity. The point seems to be that overinvolvement by the government to the extent reflected in *Twigg* is permissible, if at all, only against a person who is "reasonably suspected of criminal conduct or design."[108] The other important principle recognized in *Twigg* is that "the practicalities of combating" a certain type of criminal activity must be taken into account in determining whether "more extreme methods of investigation" are constitutionally permissible. However, there is reason to question the application of that sound principle in the *Twigg* case to conclude that more extreme methods are needed to detect drug distribution than drug manufacture. It has been persuasively argued that precisely the opposite conclusion is called for, that is, that "there usually will be a greater justification for government involvement in drug manufacturing schemes than in drug sales."[109]

WESTLAW
REFERENCES

twigg /s 588 +5 373 & "due process" /p
  police (government law-enforcement +1 agent
  official involvement conduct)

---

§ 5.3 Duress

A person's unlawful threat (1) which causes the defendant reasonably to believe that the only way to avoid imminent death or serious bodily injury to himself or to another is to

---

106. 588 F.2d 373 (3d Cir.1978).

107. Subsequent cases have distinguished *Twigg* from the case at bar. See, e.g., United States v. Bocra, 623 F.2d 281 (3d Cir.1980); United States v. Nunez-Rios, 622 F.2d 1093 (2d Cir.1980). See Abramson & Lindeman, Entrapment and Due Process in the Federal Courts, 8 Am.J. Crim.L. 139 (1980).

108. As the defendant argued in his brief in *Twigg*, Note, 67 Geo.L.J. 1455, 1467 (1979).

Abscam defendants who claimed there was a "reasonable suspicion" prerequisite to proceeding with an undercover investigation were unsuccessful. See, e.g., United States v. Jannotti, 729 F.2d 213 (3d Cir.1984); United States v. Williams, 705 F.2d 603 (2d Cir.1983). Compare United States v. Kelly, 707 F.2d 1460 (D.C.Cir.1983) (issue not decided, as there was such suspicion as to this defendant).

109. This is because "a drug laboratory, which by nature is sophisticated and covert, arguably is *more* diffi-

cult to detect than the sale of drugs. Sellers of drugs need buyers and common sense suggests that the profit incentive will induce many drug dealers inadvertently to make sales to undercover agents and informants. Indeed, that the entrapment cases deal predominantly with sales of contraband by unsuspecting defendants to government agents indicates that the government frequently is able to obtain evidence of narcotics sales without having had to initiate the crime by supplying the contraband itself. On the other hand, members of a drug manufacturing ring, who already have access to the necessary materials and expertise, will likely be wary of allowing a stranger to join the conspiracy. Only when the agent is able to participate in the crime, by supplying needed materials or financing, may it be possible for him to gain the conspirators' confidence in order to obtain sufficient evidence to support a conviction on a manufacturing charge." Note, supra note 108, at 1463–64 n. 71.

engage in conduct which violates the literal terms of the criminal law, and (2) which causes the defendant to engage in that conduct, gives the defendant the defense of duress (sometimes called compulsion or coercion) to the crime in question unless that crime consists of intentionally killing an innocent third person. The rationale of the defense of duress is that, for reasons of social policy, it is better that the defendant, faced with a choice of evils, choose to do the lesser evil (violate the criminal law) in order to avoid the greater evil threatened by the other person.

(a) Nature of the Defense of Duress.[1] One who, under the pressure of an unlawful threat from another human being to harm him (or to harm a third person), commits what would otherwise be a crime may, under some circumstances, be justified in doing what he did and thus not be guilty of the crime in question. The requirement for this defense of duress is that of a threat of a human being which operates upon the defendant's mind,[2] rather than of the pressure of a human being which operates upon his body

(as where A pushes B against C, causing C to fall over the cliff where the three are standing, admiring the view).[3] The rationale of the defense is not that the defendant, faced with the unnerving threat of harm unless he does an act which violates the literal language of the criminal law, somehow loses his mental capacity to commit the crime in question.[4] Nor is it that the defendant has not engaged in a voluntary act.[5] Rather it is that, even though he has done the act the crime requires and has the mental state which the crime requires, his conduct which violates the literal language of the criminal law is justified because he has thereby avoided a harm of greater magnitude.[6] If A, armed with a gun, threatens B, a taxi driver, with death unless B drives him to the scene of a robbery planned by A, B is not guilty of the robbery which A commits at the scene, because it is better for society as a whole that B do the lesser harm (aid A in the robbery) than that B's life be lost.[7]

Some modern writers have argued concerning the defense of duress that it ought some-

§ 5.3

1. See Model Penal Code § 2.09, Comment (1985); J. Hall, General Principles of Criminal Law, Ch. 12 (2d ed. 1960); G. Williams, Criminal Law; The General Part ch. 18 (2d ed. 1961); Perkins, Compelled Perpetration Restated, 33 Hastings L.J. 403 (1981); Wasik, Duress and Criminal Responsibility, 1977 Crim.L.Rev. 453; Annot., 40 A.L.R.2d 908 (1955); Note, 9 Seton Hall L.Rev. 556 (1978).

The defense is sometimes called "compulsion" or "coercion," although the latter term is sometimes reserved for the situation where a wife is compelled by her husband to do an act which the criminal law forbids.

2. But not merely in the sense of changing the defendant's attitudes, as with so-called "brainwashing." As noted in Lunde & Wilson, Brainwashing as a Defense to Criminal Liability: Patty Hearst Revisited, 13 Crim.L. Bull. 341, 358 (1977), "a true case of coercive persuasion cannot fit under the duress rubric. The coercive aspects of the indoctrination process may occur long before the commission of the crime for which the accused stands charged. At the time of the commission of the offense * * * the defendant may be under no immediate duress."

On the question of whether the criminal law ought to recognize a separate coercive persuasion defense, compare Delgado, Ascription of Criminal States of Mind: Toward a Defense Theory for the Coercively Persuaded ("Brainwashed") Defendant, 63 Minn.L.Rev. 1 (1978); with Dressler, Professor Delgado's "Brainwashing" Defense: Courting a Determinist Legal System, 63 Minn.L.Rev. 335 (1979).

3. Here B is not guilty of a crime against C—not because he has the defense of duress, but rather because he has done no "act," defined in the criminal law as a "willed movement." See § 3.2(c).

4. If duress negatived state of mind, there would be no rule that intentional killings cannot be excused by duress—see infra—for the threat of harm would negative the defendant's capacity to intend death and so constitute a defense to murder of the intent-to-kill sort. But this point is sometimes missed. See, e.g., People v. Luther, 394 Mich. 619, 232 N.W.2d 184 (1975) (erroneous assertion that "duress overcomes the defendant's free will and his actions lack the required *mens rea* "); State v. Lucero, 98 N.M. 204, 647 P.2d 406 (1982) (by like reasoning it held "duress is not a defense to child abuse because the mental state of the defendant is not essential," as it is a strict liability crime). Were duress merely the equivalent of lack of intent, then as a constitutional matter the prosecution would have to prove lack of duress beyond a reasonable doubt. United States v. Mitchell, 725 F.2d 832 (2d Cir. 1983).

5. Sanders v. State, 466 N.E.2d 424 (Ind.1984).

6. It is similar to self defense, except that with self defense the defendant's response is an attack upon the threatening party, while the duress defense applies when the defendant saves himself by doing the threatening party's bidding by harming another. Feliciano v. State, 332 A.2d 148 (Del.1975).

7. People v. Merhige, 212 Mich. 601, 180 N.W. 418 (1920), holds that B was not guilty of bank robbery, and therefore not of murder of the felony-murder type because

times to apply even when the harm done by the defendant is greater than or equal to the threatened harm which he avoids by doing it. It has been suggested that it ought to apply, without regard to a balancing of harms done and avoided, where the unlawfully threatened harm is such that the threat of criminal punishment for doing the harmful conduct does not serve to deter the defendant;[8] so that, if *A* holds an axe over *B* 's head, threatening to kill *B* unless *B* holds *C* 's hands so that *A* can kill *C*, *B* would be justified in aiding *A* to kill *C* when the threat of criminal punishment for murder in the distant future does not in *B* 's mind offset the certainty of immediate death by means of *A* 's axe if he refuses. The Model Penal Code, however, while agreeing that there is little use in punishing when punishment cannot deter, rejects as too subjective the contention that, where the threat of punishment does not deter, one is not to be blamed for what he must choose to do. The Code instead proposes a more objective test— that one unlawfully threatened by another is justified in committing what would otherwise

be a crime if the threat which compels him to commit it is such that a person of reasonable firmness in his situation would have been unable to resist it.[9] To apply this test to the above example concerning the axe killing: *B* would be justified in helping *A* kill *C* if men of ordinary firmness (and most men are not heroes, as they are not cowards) would have done so too, to save their own lives.[10] A majority of the modern codes contain such an extension of the duress defense.

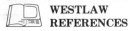

crim*** /p defin! /s duress

(b) Authorities on Duress as a Defense.
The defense of duress, like that of necessity,[11] is a common law defense, applicable in appropriate cases although no statute makes it so. But the case law in the absence of statute[12] has generally held that duress cannot justify murder[13]—or, as it is better expressed (since duress may justify the underlying felony and so justify what would otherwise be a felony murder),[14] duress cannot justify the intention-

---

of the death, during the robbery, of a bank customer shot to death by *A*.

8. G. Williams, Criminal Law: The General Part § 246 (2d ed. 1961).

9. Model Penal Code § 2.09(1). The Code limits the type of threat which will do for duress to a threat of bodily harm to the defendant or to another.

However, § 2.09(4) of the Code provides that the duress defense in that section does not preclude the choice-of-evils defense in § 3.02. Model Penal Code § 3.02 provides that conduct which the actor believes to be necessary to avoid a harm or evil to himself or to another is justifiable when (a) the harm or evil sought to be avoided by such conduct is greater than that sought to be prevented by the law defining the offense charged; and (b) neither the Code nor other law defining the offense provides exceptions or defenses dealing with the specific situation involved; and (c) a legislative purpose to exclude the justification claimed does not otherwise plainly appear. This choice-of-evils defense, also recognized by statute in several states, see § 5.4, is thus available not only for what usually has been called "necessity" (pressure from physical circumstances, such as a storm), but also for what is usually referred to as "duress" (pressure from a person). Thus, under § 3.02 a threat to destroy property unless the defendant engages in conduct causing a lesser harm or evil could be a defense.

10. But if this is a good principle for duress, when the pressure comes from human beings, why is it not a good

principle for necessity, when the pressure is from the perils of nature? If *A* and *B* are starving together in a lifeboat, with no hope of timely rescue, why may not *A* justifiably kill *B* with a knife to save himself, so long as men of reasonable firmness in the same predicament would have done the same? See Note, 75 Colum.L.Rev. 914, 923–24 (1975). Yet the Model Penal Code makes no such provision with the defense of necessity, providing instead that the defense applies only when a greater harm is avoided by the harm done, which is not the case when a life is sacrificed for a life. Model Penal Code § 3.02(1)(a).

11. "Modern cases have tended to blur the distinction between duress and necessity." United States v. Bailey, 444 U.S. 394, 100 S.Ct. 624, 62 L.Ed.2d 575 (1980).

12. For the cases, see Annot., 40 A.L.R.2d 908 (1955).

13. See Taylor v. State, 158 Miss. 505, 130 So. 502 (1930); State v. Finnell, 101 N.M. 732, 688 P.2d 769 (1984) (following common law view duress no defense to homicide charge); State v. Nargashian, 26 R.I. 299, 58 A. 953 (1904) (*A*, axe in hand, by a threat to kill *B*, got *B* to hold *C* 's hands so that *A* could kill *C*; with this help *A* killed *C* with the axe; *B* 's conviction of murder of *C held* affirmed, for *B*'s requested instruction that if *B* helped *A* kill *C* because he feared instant death from *A* was properly refused). But Model Penal Code § 2.09, Comment at 371 n. 24 (1985), which does not exclude murder from the defense, points out that duress instructions have sometimes been given in murder cases.

14. See the next paragraph infra.

al killing of [15] (or attempt to kill) [16] an innocent third person. It has been recognized, however, that duress can justify treason, though treason like murder is a capital offense [17]—an explanation of the difference between treason and murder being that treason is a continuing crime from which there may be an opportunity to escape and repair the damage done; but murder is a consummated act as to which no repairs can be effective. [18] Duress has been held a good defense to such lesser crimes as robbery, [19] burglary, [20] and malicious mischief. [21] It has been recognized that duress may be a defense to kidnaping, [22] arson, [23] prison escape, [24] and possession of a weapon. [25] When an employee hands over his employer's money to a threatening gunman who demands it, he commits what would be embezzlement (fraudulent conversion of his employer's property in his possession) but for the justification of duress. [26]

As stated above, duress is no defense to the intentional taking of life by the threatened person; but it is a defense to a killing done by another in the commission of some lesser felony participated in by the defendant under duress. Thus, if *A* compels *B* at gunpoint to drive him to the bank which *A* intends to rob, and during the ensuing robbery *A* kills a bank customer *C*, *B* is not guilty of the robbery (for he was justified by duress) and so is not guilty of felony murder of *C* in the commission of robbery. [27] The law properly recognizes that one is justified in aiding a robbery if he is

---

15. Arp v. State, 97 Ala. 5, 12 So. 301 (1893) (two men armed with shotguns threatened to kill defendant unless he killed a third person; defendant did so with an axe; duress no defense to intentional killing, especially where defendant did not seek to escape from his threateners).

16. Watson v. State, 212 Miss. 788, 55 So.2d 441 (1951) (defendant, under threats of another, shot at a third person and wounded her; conviction of assault and battery with intent to kill *held* affirmed; trial court's instruction that one is not justified by duress in attempting to kill is a proper instruction).

17. See D'Aquino v. United States, 192 F.2d 338, 358 (9th Cir.1951) (in treason trial of "Tokyo Rose," an American who broadcast from Japan to U.S. troops to lower their morale, the court's instruction covering duress limited its scope to apprehension of immediate death or serious bodily harm; instruction was correct, so conviction of treason *held* affirmed); Gillars v. United States, 182 F.2d 962, 976 (D.C.Cir.1950) (instruction that fear of concentration camp would not justify act of treason *held* not error, partly because there was no evidence that Germans threatened defendant with concentration camp).

18. See State v. Nargashian, supra note 13.

19. People v. Merhige, supra note 7; State v. St. Clair, 262 S.W.2d 25 (Mo.1953). See R.I. Recreation Center v. Aetna Cas. & Surety Co., 177 F.2d 603 (1st Cir.1949). See Annot., 1 A.L.R.4th 481 (1980).

20. Nall v. Commonwealth, 208 Ky. 700, 271 S.W. 1059 (1925) (defendant, a youth threatened by a woman with a gun, not guilty of breaking and entering with intent to steal).

21. Rex v. Crutchley, 172 Eng.Rep. 909 (1831) (defendant and others during the threshing-machine riots were forced by a mob each to give a single blow to each threshing machine; defendant escaped when he could; duress *held* a good defense to malicious destruction of the machines).

22. See State v. Ellis, 232 Or. 70, 374 P.2d 461 (1962) (though duress may justify kidnaping, here his conviction of kidnaping *held* affirmed, because his fear of death was not reasonable).

23. See Ross v. State, 169 Ind. 388, 82 N.E. 781, 782 (1907) (conviction of arson *held* affirmed, for lack of connection between threats and the burning).

24. In People v. Lovercamp, 43 Cal.App.3d 823, 118 Cal.Rptr. 110 (1974), the court stated the defense very narrowly by requiring that *all* of the following conditions exist: "(1) The prisoner is faced with a specific threat of death, forcible sexual assault or substantial bodily injury in the immediate future; (2) There is no time for a complaint to the authorities or there exists a history of futile complaints which make any result from such complaints illusory; (3) There is no time or opportunity to resort to the courts; (4) There is no evidence of force or violence used toward prison personnel or other 'innocent' persons in the escape; and (5) The prisoner immediately reports to the proper authorities when he has attained a position of safety from the immediate threat." Some other courts have taken this approach, e.g., State v. Reese, 272 N.W.2d 863 (Iowa 1978); People v. Hocquard, 64 Mich. App. 331, 236 N.W.2d 72 (1975); while others have rejected these limitations except as matters going to the weight and credibility of the defendant's testimony, e.g., Esquibel v. State, 91 N.M. 498, 576 P.2d 1129 (1978); People v. Unger, 66 Ill.2d 333, 5 Ill.Dec. 848, 362 N.E.2d 319 (1977). See Fletcher, Should Intolerable Prison Conditions Generate a Justification or an Excuse for Escape?, 26 U.C.L.A.L.Rev. 1355 (1979); Annot., 69 A.L.R.3d 678 (1976); Comments, 67 Calif.L.Rev. 1183 (1979), 127 U.Pa.L. Rev. 1142 (1979); Notes, 59 B.U.L.Rev. 334 (1979), 65 Va. L.Rev. 359 (1979).

25. United States v. Panter, 688 F.2d 268 (5th Cir.1982) (though statutes prohibited felon from possessing gun, defendant here had defense when he grabbed gun to defend himself while under attack). Compare United States v. Nolan, 700 F.2d 479 (9th Cir.1983) (*Panter* distinguished, as here defendant responsible for bringing about the confrontation).

26. State v. McGuire, 107 Mont. 341, 88 P.2d 35 (1938).

27. People v. Merhige, supra note 7; People v. Pantano, 239 N.Y. 416, 146 N.E. 646 (1925) (there was evidence that *X* and *Y* compelled the defendant, by threats to destroy him and his family, to give them information

forced by threats to do so to save his life; he should not lose the defense because his threateners unexpectedly kill someone in the course of the robbery and thus convert a mere robbery into a murder.

It is generally held that, as to those crimes which are justified by duress, the duress must consist of threatening conduct [28] which produces in the defendant (1) a reasonable fear of (2) immediate (or imminent) (3) death or serious bodily harm.[29] (Threatened *future* death or serious bodily harm, or threatened immediate *nonserious* bodily harm or property dam-

age, or a threat which produces an *unreasonable* fear of immediate death or serious bodily harm, will therefore not suffice.) Doubtless a reasonable fear of immediate death or serious bodily injury to someone other than the defendant, such as a member of his family, will do.[30] Doubtless too, the danger need not be real; it is enough if the defendant reasonably believes it to be real.[31] One threatened with immediate death or serious bodily injury may lose his defense of duress if he does not take advantage of a reasonable opportunity to escape, where that can be done without expos-

about the customary travels of bank messengers for a certain bank; thereafter *X* and *Y,* robbing the messengers, killed them; defendant's confession that he gave the information to *X* and *Y* in exchange for their promise to share with him the proceeds of robbery—which if true would make defendant guilty of murder—may have been untrue because the confession may have been coerced; so conviction of murder *held* reversed and case remanded to determine whether confession was coerced; thus the court implies that, if the defendant was forced by duress, it would not be murder). Contra: People v. Petro, 13 Cal. App.2d 245, 56 P.2d 984 (1936) (under statute limiting defense of duress to crimes not punishable with death); State v. Moretti, 66 Wash. 537, 120 P. 102 (1912) (under statute excluding murder from defense of duress).

28. In the usual case, the threat has been very precise, in the sense that the defendant has been ordered to engage in certain conduct defined as criminal or else suffer certain consequences. In People v. Richards, 269 Cal.App.2d 768, 75 Cal.Rptr. 597 (1969), defendant claimed a defense of duress to a charge of escape from prison in that he fled because of threats on his life by other inmates. The court held the defense was not available under such circumstances, as "there was no offer to show that anyone demanded or requested that the defendant escape." On principle, however, it would seem that the choice of the lesser evil should be proper whether the risk to life is by another person or by other circumstances. Compare State v. Horn, 58 Haw. 252, 566 P.2d 1378 (1977) (a "choice of evils" defense could be raised without a specific threat of death or serious bodily injury, if conditions in prison seriously exposed defendant to such harm); and the prison break cases involving necessity, § 5.4.

29. As stated in United States v. Bailey, 444 U.S. 394, 100 S.Ct. 624, 62 L.Ed.2d 575 (1980), "in the context of prison escape, the escapee is not entitled to claim a defense of duress * * * unless and until he demonstrates that, given the imminence of the threat, violation of § 751(a) was his only reasonable alternative."

See also United States v. Lee, 694 F.2d 649 (11th Cir. 1983) (no duress defense, as "there was no indication that Lee was threatened with *imminent* physical harm"); United States v. Campbell, 675 F.2d 815 (6th Cir.1982) (alleged earlier threats did not provide duress defense to bank robbery, as threat of death was not "immediately and imminently present" at time of crime); D'Aquino v. United States, supra note 18 (immediate and impending death

or serious and immediate bodily harm); Nall v. Commonwealth, supra note 20 (a threat of future injury is not enough to excuse a criminal act; the compulsion must be present, imminent and impending and of such a nature as to induce a well-grounded apprehension of death or serious bodily harm if the act is not done); State v. St. Clair, supra note 19 (same); State v. Nargashian, supra note 13 (instruction that intentional killing under threats is justified if the killer feared instant death from the threatener is wrong, because it does not require that the fear be reasonable nor take into account any opportunity to escape—aside from the fact that duress cannot justify intentional killing).

But some courts are less demanding than others as to what kind of showing of immediacy is necessary to get to the jury with the duress defense. See, e.g., Esquibel v. State, 91 N.M. 498, 576 P.2d 1129 (1978) (duress instruction required though most recent threat by prison guards was 48 to 72 hours before escape; what constitutes threat of immediate harm depends upon the circumstances of each case).

30. See United States v. Contento-Pachon, 723 F.2d 691 (9th Cir.1984) (defendant entitled to interpose duress defense where he claimed he imported drugs because of threat that wife and child would be killed); R.I. Recreation Center v. Aetna Cas. & Surety Co., supra note 19 (suit by plaintiff on a theft insurance policy which excluded thefts by employees; armed robbers held plaintiff's manager's brother and sister-in-law as hostages, threatening to kill them if the manager did not get money from plaintiff's safe for them; thus threatened he entered plaintiff's building alone and obtained money from the safe and turned it over to the robbers; judgment for insurance company *held* affirmed, for the manager committed theft, since once inside the building, he could have telephoned for help; Magruder, C.J., concurring, says: "As to fear for the bodily safety of a third person, even a close relative, there is a surprising dearth of authority; but if the question were ever presented under sufficiently strong, dramatic and convincing circumstances, I am fairly sure the courts would sanction the defense of coercion").

31. What is required is that the threatening conduct (1) "was sufficient to create in the mind of a reasonable person the fear of death or serious bodily harm," and (2) "in fact caused such fear of death or serious bodily harm in the mind of the defendant." People v. Luther, 394 Mich. 619, 232 N.W.2d 184 (1975).

ing himself unduly to death or serious bodily injury.[32] And where the offense is a continuing one, the defendant will lose his defense of duress if he fails to terminate his conduct "as soon as the claimed duress * * * had lost its coercive force." [33]

Although the great majority of the modern criminal codes provide for a duress defense, there is no uniformity in the statutory definition of this defense. Most of these statutes appear to require that there have been actual coercion which caused the defendant's conduct, for it is typically stated that the defendant must have acted "because of" the coercion or compulsion. But other provisions seem somewhat broader by declaring it sufficient that the defendant "reasonably believed" that otherwise the threatened harm would occur. As for the nature of the threatened harm, in one state only a threat of death will do, but in several others a threat of either death or serious bodily harm is sufficient. A considerable number of the statutes move beyond the common law rule in this regard by providing that threats of lesser bodily harm can sometimes suffice. Most of the duress defense statutes state that the threatened harm must be "imminent," "immediate" or "instant," but some include no such limitation. The overwhelming majority of these provisions extend to threats of harm to third parties, though a few are expressly limited to threats to injure the defendant

himself. A very distinct majority of the modern recodifications follow the Model Penal Code by requiring only that the threat be such that a person of reasonable firmness would have been unable to resist it. (Significantly, all of the statutes which extend to threats of more remote injury and to injury short of serious bodily injury are of this type.)

While a significant number of the modern provisions make the duress defense available whatever the charge against the defendant, about half of them do not allow the defense if the defendant has been charged with murder.[34] In a few jurisdictions, the exceptions are stated considerably broader. It is also generally recognized that a defendant can lose this defense by his own fault in getting into the difficulty. Thus, close to all of these statutes declare that the duress defense is unavailable if the defendant recklessly placed himself in a situation in which it was probable that he would be subjected to duress. A few go on to state that mere negligence in this regard is a bar if the defendant is charged with an offense for which negligence suffices to establish culpability.

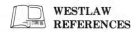 **WESTLAW REFERENCES**

defense /s duress /s murder kill! homicide

(c) Duress as a Defense: On Principle.
The case law and statutory law of duress as a defense has tended to jell into fixed rules

---

32. United States v. Lee, 694 F.2d 649 (11th Cir.1983) (no duress defense where defendant claimed he joined drug conspiracy because of threats to friend, as defendant "had numerous reasonable oportunities to inform the police"); United States v. Campbell, 675 F.2d 815 (6th Cir. 1982) (no duress defense re bank robbery because of earlier threats, as defendants never "undertook to surrender to the law"); In re Grand Jury Proceedings, 605 F.2d 750 (5th Cir.1979) (grand jury witness may not invoke duress defense to contempt charge for failure to testify, as witness who received threats must avail himself of alternative of government protection); United States v. Agard, 605 F.2d 665 (2d Cir.1979) (no duress defense to charge of weapon possession, where defendant claimed he had gun because he needed it in fight started by others, as defendant "placed himself in such a potentially dangerous situation" instead of retreating after earlier encounter); United States v. Wood, 566 F.2d 1108 (9th Cir.1977) (fear of attack provided no duress defense to carrying knife in prison, as defendant sought neither administrative detention nor transfer to another institution as means of escaping the danger); R.I. Recreation Center v. Aetna Cas. &

Surety Co., supra note 20; State v. Larrivee, 479 A.2d 347 (Me.1984); State v. St. Clair, supra note 19; State v. Nargashian, supra note 13.

33. United States v. Bailey, 444 U.S. 394, 100 S.Ct. 624, 62 L.Ed.2d 575 (1980) (even if defendants broke out of jail because of repeated beatings by guards, they were not entitled to have duress defense go to jury because they remained at large until captured after time ranging from one month to three and one-half months; two dissenters argue duress had not lost its coercive force because the "conditions that led to respondents' initial departure from the D.C. jail continue unabated"). The state cases are generally in accord. See, e.g., People v. Handy, 198 Colo. 556, 603 P.2d 941 (1979); State v. Reese, 272 N.W.2d 863 (Iowa 1978); State v. Reed, 205 Neb. 45, 286 N.W.2d 111 (1979).

34. See Thomas v. State, 246 Ga. 484, 272 S.E.2d 68 (1980) (statutory exception for "murder" applies both to killer and accomplice); State v. Rumble, 680 S.W.2d 939 (Mo.1984) (statutory exception includes felony-murder even if duress a defense to the felony alone).

which depart somewhat from the rationale underlying the rule, which, as noted above,[35] is that public policy favors the commission of a lesser harm (the commission of what would otherwise be a crime) when this will avoid a greater harm.[36] It is true that B is not justified in intentionally killing an innocent third person C, who would otherwise be safe, in order to avoid being killed himself at the hands of an armed threatener A.[37] This is because, by killing C, the harm which B avoids (death to B) is equal to but not (as it must be to justify the deed) greater than the harm which he does (death of C). On the other hand, if by killing C, B avoids death to two or more (as where A, with power to carry out the threat, threatens to kill B and Mrs. B, whom he holds as a hostage), his act ought on principle to be justified. So too, if B's act played a minor rather than a necessary part in bringing about C's death (as where A would have been able to kill C even if B had not helped), it would seem that B would be justified in doing what he did.[38]

It is not necessarily true that all acts of treason are justified by duress; some acts may be, but others are clearly not. If a prisoner of war, to save his own life, disclosed to his country's enemies military plans, which disclosure was likely to cost his country a thousand casualties, he would not be justified.[39]

It is not proper, on principle, to limit the defense of duress to situations where the instrument of coercion is a threat of death or serious bodily injury. A threat to do bodily harm less than serious bodily harm, or a threat to destroy property or reputation, ought to do where the act which the defendant does to avoid the threatened harm is relatively minor—as where A threatens to strike B with a nondeadly weapon capable of inflicting great pain unless B drives somewhat over the speed limit.[40]

On principle, the threatened harm, though perhaps it need not be "immediate," ought not to be remote in time, for until the threatened disaster is pretty close to happening, there may arise a chance both to refuse to do

---

35. See § 5.3(a).

36. We have thus eliminated, from possible theories underlying the defense, the theory that duress justifies what is otherwise criminal conduct, if the threat of criminal punishment for the crime in question does not deter him, or (as the Model Penal Code has it) if such a threat of punishment would not deter a person of reasonable firmness.

37. Note, however, that Model Penal Code § 2.09(1) would allow the defense of duress when B is coerced by A's threat to kill C to save himself from A, if A's threat is one "which a person of reasonable firmness in [B's] situation would have been unable to resist." As noted in § 5.303(a), the Model Penal Code and several states, accepting the choice-of-values rationale of the duress defense, go further and allow the defense also if the threat is such that a person of reasonable firmness in the defendant's situation could not resist it.

38. In Director of Public Prosecutions v. Lynch, [1975] 2 W.L.R. 641, the House of Lords concluded that the defense of duress could be interposed by the defendant, charged with murder, who claimed that because of threats he drove an I.R.A. gang to and from the murder of a police officer. Lord Morris commented: "Let two situations be supposed. In each let it be supposed that there is a real and effective threat of death. In one a person is required under such duress to drive a car to a place or to carry a gun to a place with knowledge that at such place it is planned that X is to be killed by those who are imposing their will. In the other situation let it be supposed that a person under such duress is told that he himself must be

there and then kill X. In either situation there is a terrible agonising choice of evils. In the former to save his life the person drives the car or carries the gun. He may cling to the hope that perhaps X will not be found at the place or that there will be a change of intention before the purpose is carried out or that in some unforeseen way the dire event of a killing will be averted. The final and fatal moment of decision has not arrived. He saves his own life at a time when the loss of another life is not a certainty. In the second (if indeed it is a situation likely to arise) the person is told that to save his life he himself must personally there and then take an innocent life. It is for him to pull the trigger or otherwise personally to do the act of killing. There, I think, before allowing duress as a defence it may be that the law will have to call a halt." Compare Thomas v. State, 246 Ga. 484, 272 S.E.2d 68 (1980) (because statute excepts "murder" from duress defense, it not available to murder accomplice). For discussion of Lynch, see Cross, Murder Under Duress, 28 U.Toronto L.J. 369 (1978); Notes, 34 Camb.L.J. 185 (1975); 38 Mod.L.Rev. 566 (1975).

The House later declined to extend Lynch to the case of a defendant charged with murder as a principal in the first degree. Abbott v. Regina, [1977] A.C. 755, criticized in Dennis, Murder and Criminal Responsibility, 96 L.Q. Rev. 208 (1980).

39. See G. Williams, Criminal Law: The General Part § 247 (2d ed. 1961).

40. Model Penal Code § 3.02 would recognize a defense here, as this choice-of-evils justification is applicable in both duress and necessity cases. See note 9 supra.

the criminal act and also to avoid the threatened harm—the opportunity to escape without undue danger which the cases recognize as enough to deprive the defendant of his defense.[41] So too, as a matter of principle, the threatened harm need not be directed at the defendant himself; it may be aimed at a member of his family or a friend (or, it would seem, even a stranger).

The present law may be right in requiring that the threat of harm produce in the defendant a reasonable ("well grounded," as the cases sometimes say) fear that the harm will be inflicted if the defendant refuses to obey.[42] A reasonable fear is generally required in analogous situations of justification, such as with the defenses of self-defense, of defense of others and of necessity;[43] and there is no reason for a different rule with duress.

The present law is right in requiring, for the defense, that the defendant be actually coerced by the threat into violating the terms of the criminal law. A taxi driver would not have the defense, for instance, if he voluntarily drove over the speed limit, only to learn later, to his surprise, that his passenger in the back seat was holding a gun pointed at the driver's head ready to order the driver to speed had he not voluntarily done so.

WESTLAW REFERENCES

defense /s duress /p threat! fear apprehension /s death injury harm

41. See supra note 32.

Just how "immediate" the threatened harm must be often poses a difficult issue. In People v. Richards, 269 Cal.App.2d 768, 75 Cal.Rptr. 597 (1969), defendant escaped from prison because he had learned that other inmates were planning to kill him. The court held the defense was not available, as there was no showing that a danger to defendant's life existed on the very afternoon of his escape. Compare the *Esquibel* case, note 30 supra.

42. E.g., United States v. Contento-Pachon, 723 F.2d 691 (9th Cir.1984); State v. Ellis, 232 Or. 70, 374 P.2d 461 (1962).

43. Model Penal Code § 2.09 does not, however, require that the fear be reasonable; nor does it with self-defense, defense of others and necessity.

44. Rizzolo v. Commonwealth, 126 Pa. 54, 17 A. 520 (1889) (instruction that, where A compels B to help A kill

(d) Mitigation of Punishment. One who commits a crime while subject to coercion, but whose situation does not come under the rules which permit justification (perhaps his crime was murder of the intent-to-kill sort; or his fear of death or serious bodily injury was not reasonable; or his fear was one of future harm), may nevertheless properly urge that his punishment, within the permissible limits of punishment for the crime in question, should be lower than it would have been if he had not been coerced.

In addition, where the defendant, coerced by another into killing a third person, is charged with murder, and by the uniform rule he was not justified in doing so, nevertheless he might successfully argue that he is not guilty of first-degree murder consisting of a deliberate and premeditated killing, since the fear generated in him by the other's threatening conduct made him incapable of premeditating and deliberating; his crime thus was only murder in the second degree.[44] The further suggestion that this fear might even render him incapable of entertaining an intent to kill, and so serve to reduce his crime to manslaughter, was rejected in one of the leading duress cases.[45] Nevertheless, a few states by statute have provided that what is otherwise murder except for duress is reduced to manslaughter;[46] and there is something rather reasonable about the view that such a crime, though not excused, at least should not be murder.[47]

C, but B does not fire the fatal shots, jury should determine whether B was coerced by fear of A so as to have no power to form the willful, deliberate and premeditated intent to kill C, *held* free from error). See § 7.7 for analogous cases.

45. State v. Nargashian, supra note 13.

46. Minn.Stat.Ann. § 609.20; N.J.Stat.Ann. 2C:2–9; Wis.Stat.Ann. 939.46. Compare People v. Gleckler, 82 Ill. 2d 145, 44 Ill.Dec. 483, 411 N.E.2d 849 (1980) (provision that murder is reduced to voluntary manslaughter where a defense is lacking because of unreasonable belief does not reduce murder upon duress to manslaughter, as even if reasonable belief as to facts, duress no defense to killing).

47. See § 7.11(c).

WESTLAW
REFERENCES

duress /p mitigat! reduc*** /s punishment sentence

(e) Guilt of the Coercer. Where *A* by threats coerces *B* to engage in criminal conduct, *A* is guilty of the crime in question although *B* may, because of the coercion, be justified and so not be guilty. In one case, where *A*, armed with a gun, forced *B*, another man, to attempt to have sexual intercourse with Mrs. *A* (*B*'s fright preventing him from being able to effect a penetration), *A* argued, on appeal from his conviction for assault with intent to rape, that he could not be guilty of the crime since *B*, because of the duress, was not guilty. The court affirmed *A*'s conviction on the erroneous ground that attempted rape cannot be justified by duress.[48] It would have been better law to affirm the conviction on the ground that, even though *B* was justified, *A* is nevertheless guilty, for one can commit a crime through means of an innocent agent, such as an underage child or an insane person.[49]

WESTLAW
REFERENCES

dowell /s 106 +5 722

(f) Coercion of Wife by Husband.[50] The common law rule was that, except for murder and treason, a married woman was not punishable for crime if she acted under the coercion of her husband; and, if she committed the criminal act in her husband's presence, there was a rebuttable presumption that he had coerced her. Something less in the way of pressure was required for a wife to be coerced than for an ordinary person to meet the requirements of the defense of duress; one early English case held that the husband's mere command would do.[51]

This special defense for wives arose at a time when married women were actually much under their husband's control; it doubtless continued because of the courts' desire to avoid the death penalty for women (who were not, until 1692, eligible for benefit of clergy) at a time when many crimes were punishable by death.[52] Today the position of married women is quite different: they may own their separate property; they may vote and serve on juries; their husbands may no longer enforce obedience with a stick the thickness of the husband's thumb; in short, their "independence * * * in political, social and economic matters rightly places upon them an increased responsibility."[53] Many of the recent state criminal codes abolish any special rule about coercion of wives by husbands and the presumption of such coercion. A number of courts, without the aid of any special statute (other than the statutes which have revolutionized the position of married women), have abolished the special common law rule and its accompanying presumption, leaving married women to the protection of the ordinary defense of duress.[54] A dwindling number of states probably still adhere to the old doctrine.[55]

WESTLAW
REFERENCES

205k108

---

48. State v. Dowell, 106 N.C. 722, 11 S.E. 525 (1890).

49. See § 6.6(a).

50. See Perkins, The Doctrine of Coercion, 19 Iowa L.Rev. 507 (1934); Model Penal Code § 2.09, Comment (Tent.Draft No. 10, 1960); Annots., 4 A.L.R. 266 (1919), 71 A.L.R. 1116 (1931).

51. See Perkins, supra note 50, at 512 n. 38.

52. Model Penal Code § 2.09, Comment at 385 (1985).

53. Conyer v. United States, 80 F.2d 292 (6th Cir.1935).

54. People v. Statley, 91 Cal.App.2d 948, 206 P.2d 76 (1949) (rejecting the common law presumption, since the basis for it has disappeared with legislation freeing wives from husband's control); State v. Renslow, 211 Iowa 642, 230 N.W. 316 (1930) (same); King v. City of Owensboro,

187 Ky. 21, 218 S.W. 297 (1920) (same); Commonwealth v. Barnes, 369 Mass. 462, 340 N.E.2d 863 (1976) (same); Commonwealth v. Santiago, 462 Pa. 216, 340 A.2d 440 (1975) (same); Morton v. State, 141 Tenn. 357, 209 S.W. 644 (1919) (same); Conyer v. United States, supra note 53 (same). See Dalton v. People, 68 Colo. 44, 189 P. 37 (1920) (husband and wife can conspire together; presumption that husband controls his wife is abandoned by legislation freeing married woman); People v. Martin, 4 Ill.2d 105, 122 N.E.2d 245 (1954) (husband and wife can conspire together, because, in part, the common law presumption of coercion is abolished by statute).

55. But many narrowly construe it. See Goodwin v. State, 506 P.2d 571 (Okl.Crim.1973) (presumption is slight and thus is rebutted by slight evidence wife acted freely).

(g) Orders of a Superior. It is no defense to a crime committed by an employee that he was only carrying out his employer's unlawful orders.[56] It is likewise no defense to a crime that it was committed by a military subordinate pursuant to an unlawful military order, as where he is ordered by his superior to shoot prisoners of war.[57] On the other hand, if he believed the unlawful order to be legal,[58] or perhaps if he reasonably believed it to be legal,[59] he is not guilty of the crime in question.

 **WESTLAW REFERENCES**

find 519 f2d 184

§ 5.4   Necessity

The pressure of natural physical forces sometimes confronts a person in an emergency with a choice of two evils: either he may violate the literal terms of the criminal law and thus produce a harmful result, or he may comply with those terms and thus produce a greater or equal or lesser amount of harm. For reasons of social policy, if the harm which will result from compliance with the law is greater than that which will result from violation of it, he is by virtue of the defense of necessity justified in violating it.

(a) Nature of the Defense of Necessity.[1] One who, under the pressure of circumstances, commits what would otherwise be a crime may be justified by "necessity" in doing as he did and so not be guilty of the crime in question. With the defense of necessity, the traditional view has been that the pressure must come from the physical forces of nature (storms, privations) rather than from other human beings.[2] (When the pressure is from human beings, the defense, if applicable, is called duress rather than necessity.)[3] However, the "modern cases have tended to blur

---

56. United States v. Decker, 304 F.2d 702 (6th Cir. 1962) ("Loyality to a superior does not provide a license for crime"). Of course, he may do some act under orders in ignorance of his employer's machinations, as where, on orders he picks up and brings to his employer another's property thinking it is his employer's; in such a case the employer, but not the innocent employee, would be guilty of larceny.

57. Axtell's Case, 84 Eng.Rep. 1060 (1660) (the soldier who commanded the guard at the execution of Charles I, on trial for murder of the King, defended on the ground of a military order which he must obey or die; *held*, that the order being traitorous, obedience to it was no defense). As to this defense in international law, see Musmanno, Are Subordinate Officials Penally Responsible for Obeying Superior Orders which Direct Commission of Crime?, 67 Dick.L.Rev. 221 (1963) (discussing Nuremberg war crimes trials).

58. Model Penal Code § 2.10 (defense that defendant "does no more than execute an order of his superior in the armed services which he does not know to be unlawful"). See Brown, Military Orders as a Defense in Civil Courts, 3 Va.L.Reg. (n.s.) 641 (1918) urging that the fact that a superior gives an order is strong evidence that the subordinate believed it to be lawful.

59. Calley v. Calloway, 519 F.2d 184 (5th Cir.1975) ("military judge properly instructed that an order to kill unresisting Vietnamese would be an illegal order, and that if Calley knew the order was illegal or should have known it was illegal, obedience to an order was not a valid defense"); United States v. Calley, 48 C.M.R. 19, 22 U.S.C.M.A. 534 (1973) (instruction proper where given in conformance with standard in Manual for Courts-Martial, i.e., whether "a man of ordinary sense and understanding" would know the order was illegal).

---

§ 5.4

1. See Model Penal Code § 3.02, Comment (1985); G. Williams, Criminal Law: The General Part ch. 17 (2d ed. 1961); J. Hall, General Principles of Criminal Law ch. 12 (2d ed. 1960); Arnolds & Garland, The Defense of Necessity in Criminal Law: The Right to Choose the Lesser Evil, 65 J.Crim.L. & C. 289 (1974); Fuller, The Case of the Speluncean Explorers, 62 Harv.L.Rev. 616 (1949); Hitchler, Necessity as a Defense in Criminal Cases, 33 Dick.L.Rev. 138 (1929); Perkins, Compelled Perpetration Restated, 33 Hastings L.J. 403 (1981); Tiffany & Anderson, Legislating the Necessity Defense in Criminal Law, 52 Denver L.J. 839 (1979); Comment, 29 U.C.L.A.L.Rev. 409 (1981).

The word "necessity" perhaps is something of a misnomer, since it is never "necessary" to avoid the greater evil by doing the lesser evil. It is not, strictly speaking, necessary for a policeman to speed after a fleeing criminal, or for A to kill B to save C and D.

2. Thus, in United States v. Contento-Pachon, 723 F.2d 691 (9th Cir.1984), the court held that defendant, who alleged he smuggled drugs into the U.S. because of threats his wife and child would otherwise be killed, could interpose a duress defense but 'not a necessity defense, as his "acts were allegedly coerced by human, not physical forces." See also Cleveland v. Municipality of Anchorage, 631 P.2d 1073 (Alaska 1981) (necessity defense limited to "physical forces of nature"; "when the threatened harm emanates from a human source," available defenses are "duress, defense of others, or crime prevention").

3. See § 3.2(c).

The typical duress case, however, has involved a situation in which A has ordered B to engage in certain conduct prohibited by the criminal law or else suffer certain consequences. It might well be argued that when

the distinction between duress and necessity." [4] More significantly, most but not all of the modern recodifications (following the Model Penal Code [5] in this respect) contain a broader choice-of-evils defense which is not limited to any particular source of danger.[6]

In any event, for a defense of necessity or choice-of-evils, the pressure must operate upon the mind of the defendant rather than upon his body. (When A and B are standing atop a precipice, and an earthquake causes A to stumble against B, throwing B over the cliff to his death, A's defense to a homicide charge is not that of necessity, for A's mind did not will his body against B's; instead, his defense is that he did no "act" (a willed movement), and one cannot be guilty of a crime of action without an act.) [7] But when A, starving to death, takes and eats B's food to save his own life, or when A in an emergency intentionally kills B to save C and D, he may be eligible for the defense of necessity.

The rationale of the necessity defense is not that a person, when faced with the pressure of circumstances of nature, lacks the mental element which the crime in question requires. Rather, it is this reason of public policy: the law ought to promote the achievement of higher values at the expense of lesser values, and sometimes the greater good for society will be accomplished by violating the literal language of the criminal law. The law for-

bids stealing and murder, for there are positive values in the right to property and the right to life; but (as in the case of the starving man) it is better to save a life than to save the property, and (in the case of the killing of B to save C and D) it is better that two lives be saved and one lost than that two be lost and one saved.

The matter is often expressed in terms of choice of evils: When the pressure of circumstances presents one with a choice of evils, the law prefers that he avoid the greater evil by bringing about the lesser evil. Thus the evil involved in violating the terms of the criminal law (taking another's property; even taking another's life) may be less than that which would result from literal compliance with the law (starving to death; two lives lost).

The defense of necessity is available only in situations wherein the legislature has not itself, in its criminal statute, made a determination of values.[8] If it has done so, its decision governs.[9] Thus the legislature might, in its abortion statute, expressly provide that the crime is not committed if the abortion is performed to save the mother's life; under such a statute there would be no need for courts to speculate about the relative value of preserving the fetus and safeguarding the mother's life.[10] Conversely the abortion statute might expressly (or by its legislative histo-

---

an individual acts to avoid a greater harm from a person who has not given such an order—e.g., see People v. Richards, 269 Cal.App.2d 768, 75 Cal.Rptr. 597 (1969), where defendant alleged he escaped from prison to avoid being killed by other inmates—the situation ought to be dealt with as a form of necessity rather than duress. In *Richards,* the court held the defense of duress was not available because "there was no offer to show that anyone demanded or requested that the defendant escape."

4. United States v. Bailey, 444 U.S. 394, 100 S.Ct. 624, 62 L.Ed.2d 575 (1980).

5. Model Penal Code § 3.02, providing that conduct believed necessary to avoid some harm is justifiable if "the harm or evil sought to be avoided by such conduct is greater than that sought to be prevented by the law defining the offense charged."

6. This is as it should be. "To restrict the scope of the lesser evils defense to instances of threats from natural forces would be to remove the justification on grounds wholly irrelevant to the question of the actor's conduct producing a net benefit." 2 P. Robinson, Criminal Law Defenses § 124(e)(1) (1984).

7. See § 3.2 for the requirement of an act. On similar principles, one cannot be guilty of a crime of omission to act if, because of pressure from the circumstances of nature, it is impossible for him to act.

8. Statutes on the necessity or choice-of-evils defense often emphasize this fact by stating, e.g., that the defense exists if "a legislative purpose to exclude the justification claimed does not otherwise plainly appear," that the defense is available "unless inconsistent with * * * some other provision of law," or that the defense is unavailable if the "law defining the offense provides exceptions or defenses dealing with the specific situation involved."

9. State v. Dorsey, 118 N.H. 844, 395 A.2d 855 (1978) (legislative determination that nuclear power plants safe enough to be permitted forecloses necessity defense based upon alleged dangers incident to generation of atomic energy). See Note, 5 Vt.L.Rev. 103 (1980).

10. Cf. Cleveland v. Municipality of Anchorage, 631 P.2d 1073 (Alaska 1981) (once legislature has defined what abortion is criminal and what is not, defendants cannot defend charge of trespass at abortion clinic on ground it necessary to save life of fetus by preventing lawful abor-

ry) [11] provide that the crime is committed even when the abortion is performed to save the mother's life; here too the legislature has made a determination of values and by its decision thereon foreclosed the possibility of the defense that the abortion was necessary to save life. But if the abortion statute (even when read in the light of its legislative history) is silent upon the matter, then the question of the defense of necessity is open, and courts can properly consider the relative merits of preserving the fetus and saving the mother.[12]

When the necessity defense applies, it justifies the defendant's conduct in violating the literal language of the criminal law and so the defendant is not guilty of the crime in question. Where the defense does not apply, and yet the defendant did act with the good motive of preserving some value, his good motive, though not a defense, may be considered in mitigation of punishment for the crime committed.[13]

One may thus be justified by necessity in violating the law and causing harm in order to avoid a greater harm by complying with the law. Perhaps he has not only a power to violate the law but a duty to do so (much as a trustee, in appropriate circumstances, has a duty, and not simply a power, to deviate from the terms of a trust). If A is confronted with a choice between (1) intentionally killing B and thus saving the population of a city and (2) letting nature run its course, thus saving B but destroying the city, he ought to be criminally liable for murder of the city population if he does nothing. The difficulty, of course, lies in the difficulty the law has in imposing an affirmative duty to act as the basis of criminal liability.[14]

 WESTLAW REFERENCES

crim**** /p defense /p necessity /p abortion
di necessity

(b) Related Defenses. The defense of necessity is, of course, clearly related to that of duress (or coercion), where the pressure on the defendant's will comes from human beings rather than from physical circumstances. Duress is generally regarded as a separate defense, but it would doubtless be possible to treat it as a branch of the law of necessity.

The defenses of self-defense and defense of others [15] are also related to the defense of necessity, justifying intentional homicide or the intentional infliction of bodily injury in cases where it is necessary to save the life of, or to prevent bodily injury to, the defendant or another. It has been said that self-defense and defense of others constitute a part of the law of necessity which has attained relatively fixed rules.[16]

 WESTLAW REFERENCES

110k38 & duress self-defense defense-of-others

tions); Gaetano v. United States, 406 A.2d 1291 (D.C.App. 1979) (even if the defendants have a "bona fide belief" that abortion terminates life, they had no necessity defense to trespass at abortion clinic, as lawfulness of abortion settled by Supreme Court in Roe v. Wade). See Note, 48 U.Cin.L.Rev. 501 (1979).

11. Perhaps the legislative history discloses a proposal by some members of the legislature to amend the abortion statute by exempting the abortion done to save the mother's life, followed by a voting down of the proposal by the whole legislature on the ground that the law ought to punish such abortions in order to preserve the fetal child.

12. Rex v. Bourne, [1939] 1 K.B. 687 (doctor performed operation upon young girl, who had been raped; continuation of pregnancy would make her a physical and mental wreck; the abortion statute punishes "unlawful" abortions but does not mention this specific defense; trial court instructed jury that the value of preserving mother's health is higher than the value of the unborn child; verdict of not guilty).

Sometimes the legislature, by its use of language in the statute defining a crime, uses language which strongly suggests the possibility of a defense of necessity but, by going no further, makes no specific value judgments. Thus a statute punishing cruelty to animals might make it a crime "unnecessarily" to beat an animal or "needlessly" to kill it or "unnecessarily" to deprive it of sustenance and protection from the elements. So too statutory adverbs like "unlawfully" may suggest, though less strongly, the possibility that conduct is not unlawful if required by necessity.—See Rex v. Bourne, supra, so construing "unlawfully" in abortion statute.

13. See § 3.6.

14. See § 3.3.

15. See §§ 5.7, 5.8.

16. G. Williams, Criminal Law: The General Part § 234 (2d ed. 1961).

(c) **Examples of the Defense.** Although the cases are not numerous, the defense of necessity has been held applicable in a number of situations.[17] The master of a ship forced by a storm to take refuge in a port in order to save the lives of those on board is not guilty of violating an embargo law forbidding entry into that port.[18] Sailors who on the high seas refuse to obey the captain's orders are not guilty of mutiny when their object is to force the captain to return the unseaworthy vessel to port for necessary repairs.[19] A doctor who performs an abortion upon a young-girl rape victim in order to prevent her from becoming a physicial and metal wreck has been held not guilty of the crime of abortion under a statute punishing one who "unlawfully" produces a miscarriage.[20] A parent who withdraws his child from school because of the child's feeble health is not guilty of violating the school law which provides for compulsory attendance unless excused by the school board.[21] A police officer speeding after a fleeing criminal, or an ambulance driver on the way to the hospital with an emergency case, is not guilty of violating the speed laws.[22] A police officer who plays a hand at cards in order, by disarming suspicion, to catch and arrest a gambler is not guilty of violating the gambling laws.[23] A glaucoma victim who shows that smoking marijuana is medically beneficial to his eye condition is not guilty of using and possessing marijuana.[24] A prisoner who departs from prison is not guilty of the crime of prison-escape if the prison, through no fault of the prisoner, is afire[25]—"for he is not to be hanged because he would not stay to be burnt."

In addition to these decided cases, the Model Penal Code commentaries suggest that the defense is available in these situations: a person intentionally kills one person in order to save two or more; a firefighter destroys some property to prevent the spread of fire to other property; a mountain climber lost in a storm takes refuge in a house and appropriates provisions; a ship (or airplane) captain jettisons cargo to preserve the ship or plane and its passenger; a druggist dispenses a drug without the required prescription to alleviate suffering in an emergency.[26]

On the other hand, the defense of necessity has been rejected in other circumstances. One who, unemployed and in great want, but not actually starving, helps himself to groceries from a grocery store is neverthelss guilty of larceny; "economic necessity" is no defense to crime, the court says.[27] A prisoner who escapes from a prison camp where the conditions are unsanitary and the treatment brutal

---

17. Occasionally the courts, holding the defendant to be innocent, do not specifically mention "necessity." Sometimes the result is based upon an "implied exception" in the statute: the legislature must have meant an exception for this situation. See § 2.2(c). And in State v. Torphy, infra note 23, the court found no intent to violate the law in the particular situation. But in both the implied-exception and the no-intent cases the real reason for the holdings seems to be justification based on necessity.

18. See The William Gray, 29 F.Cas. 1300 (No. 17,694) (C.C.N.Y.1810) (the court says that necessity excused the master of guilt; the ship therefore was *held* not subject to forfeiture).

19. United States v. Ashton, 24 F.Cas. 873 (No. 14,470) (C.C.Mass.1834) ("The law deems the lives of all persons far more valuable than any property").

20. Rex v. Bourne, supra note 12. See discussion in the text supra for possible different results in the abortion situation based upon legislative determination of values.

21. State v. Jackson, 71 N.H. 552, 53 A. 1021 (1902) (however the court speaks as though the school board impliedly excused attendance).

22. State v. Gorham, 110 Wash. 330, 188 P. 457 (1920). See Annot., 9 A.L.R. 367 (1920).

23. State v. Torphy, 78 Mo.App. 206 (1899) (the court based its holding on the ground that the police officer had no intent to gamble; it would seem, however, that he did have such an intent, and that the proper ground for the decision is justification by necessity—i.e., the value of law enforcement outweighs the value of literal adherence to the gambling laws).

24. United States v. Randall, 104 Wash.D.C.Rep. 2249 (D.C.Super.1976), discussed in Note, 46 Geo.Wash.L.Rev. 273 (1978).

25. See People v. Whipple, 100 Cal.App. 261, 279 P. 1008 (1929) (holding, however, that it is no defense to prison-escape that the prison was unsanitary and the treatment inhumane).

26. Model Penal Code § 3.02, Comment at 9–10 (1985).

27. State v. Moe, 174 Wash. 303, 24 P.2d 638 (1933) (in this case, a crowd of persons in great want helped themselves to groceries; the convictions of several members of the crowd of larceny and riot were affirmed); Rex v. Holden, 168 Eng.Rep. 607 (Cr.Cas.Res.1809) (prosecution for forgery of persons who were indigent and distressed

is nonetheless guilty of the crime of escaping from an officer.[28] One who brings whiskey to church as a precautionary measure against the possibility of a sudden heart attack is guilty of the crime of bringing intoxicating liquor to church.[29]

So too, in the area of homicide committed under the pressure of circumstances, one who intentionally kills another to save himself (as where two dying men are together without food or water or hope of timely rescue) may be guilty of murder. Two famous lifeboat cases, one English and the other American, have reached the courts. In the English case three sailors and a cabin boy, as a result of shipwreck, were adrift in an open lifeboat more than a thousand miles from land; on the twentieth day, having been nine days without food and seven days without water, two of the men killed the cabin boy with a knife; the three men fed upon his body and drank his blood; four days later the three survivors were rescued by a passing ship, although in this time they and the boy (who was in the weakest condition) would probably have died had not one of them been killed and eaten. The court held this to be murder by the two killers, not justified by the circumstances.[30] The American case involved an overloaded lifeboat after a shipwreck, with nine seamen and thirty-two passengers aboard the boat. A storm came up which threatened to sink the boat; to lighten the boat so that she might ride out the storm, some of the crew members, including the defendant, threw fourteen male passengers overboard to their certain deaths. Thus lightened the boat remained afloat. But after arrival in port, the defendant was tried for manslaughter.[31] The court instructed the jury that some of the crew members are necessary to navigate the boat; that any supernumerary seamen should be sacrificed before the passengers; and that as between people in an equal situation the determination of who are to be sacrificed for the safety of the whole group is to be determined by lot.[32] The jury's guilty verdict was upheld by the court.[33]

WESTLAW REFERENCES

crim**** /p defense /s necessity /p circumstance

(d) Requirements of the Defense. The rationale of the defense, as stated above, lies in the social advantage gained when the defendant chooses the lesser of two evils and thus, by bringing about the lesser harm, avoids the greater harm.

(1) The Harm Avoided. The harm avoided need not be physical harm (death or bodily injury). It may, for instance, be harm to property, as where a firefighter destroys some property to prevent the spread of fire which threatens to consume other property of

---

and who were tempted to engage in this activity by the necessities of the moment; they were *held* guilty of forgery and executed).

28. People v. Whipple, supra note 25 (stating, however, that escape might be justified if done to save one's life, as if the prison should catch fire); Dempsey v. United States, 283 F.2d 934 (5th Cir.1960) (defendant, a diabetes sufferer, escaped because he needed an insulin injection immediately; he did not first apply for relief to the prison authorities; conviction of prison escape *held* affirmed). For more on the prison escape cases, see authorities in § 5.3 n. 24.

29. Bice v. State, 109 Ga. 117, 34 S.E. 202 (1899).

30. Regina v. Dudley & Stephens, L.R. 14 Q.B.D. 273 (1884) (the death sentence imposed by the court was commuted by the Crown to six months imprisonment).

31. The appropriate crime, unless justified by necessity, would seem to be murder, for the killings were intentional, but the grand jury apparently refused to indict for more than manslaughter. Of course, the law might, not unsensibly, be that intentional homicide in cases of necessity is not murder, is not justified (no crime), but rather is mitigated to manslaughter. But in most jurisdictions it is murder, unless necessity justifies it, in which case it is no crime at all.

32. The court in Regina v. Dudley & Stephens, supra note 30, in a dictum rejected the notion that the two seamen would have been justified in killing the cabin boy if the four persons aboard had drawn lots to see who was to be sacrificed and the lot had fallen upon the cabin boy. But it would seem that, if the defense is to be allowed at all in such cases, lot-drawing is the fair way to determine the matter. In the Biblical story of Jonah, when a storm threatened to wreck the ship, those aboard drew lots, the lot fell upon Jonah, and he was pitched overboard; but the timely arrival of the whale prevented the development of a homicide situation which would raise the question whether, under the circumstances, including the drawing of lots, necessity justified the homicide.

33. United States v. Holmes, 26 F.Cas. 360 (No. 15,383) (C.C.E.D.Pa.1842). (The defendant was sentenced to six months solitary confinement at hard labor; the President refused to grant a pardon).

greater value. It may be harm to the defendant himself, as where he takes another's food to save his own life;[34] or it may be harm to others, as where A, in no personal danger, intentionally runs his car over B in order to avoid hitting C and D.

(2) The Harm Done. On the other side of the equation, too, the harm done is not limited to any particular type of harm. It includes intentional homicide (as where A, faced with an emergency situation wherein he must either kill B or kill C and D, kills B to save the others)[35] as well as lesser types of harm, like intentional battery or property damage (e.g., the plane commander jettisons cargo into the sea when one engine becomes disabled on an ocean passage). No doubt, in cases where there is a difference between the harm which his conduct actually causes and the harm which was necessarily to be expected from his conduct—as where A, driving a car, suddenly finds himself in a predicament where he must either run down B or hit C's house and he reasonably chooses the latter, unfortunately killing two people in the house who by bad luck happened to be just at that place inside the house where A's car struck—it is the

harm-reasonably-expected, rather than the harm-actually-caused, which governs.

(3) Intention to Avoid Harm. To have the defense of necessity, the defendant must have acted with the intention of avoiding the greater harm. Actual necessity, without the intention, is not enough. If A kills his enemy B for revenge, and he later learns to his happy surprise that by killing B he saved the lives of C and D, A has no defense to murder.[36] In other words, he must believe that his act is necessary to avoid the greater harm. An honest (and, doubtless, reasonable) belief in the necessity of his action is all that is required, however, so that he has the defense even if, unknown to him, the situation did not in fact call for the drastic action taken.[37] Thus if A kills B reasonably believing it to be necessary to save C and D, he is not guilty of murder even though, unknown to A, C and D could have been rescued without the necessity of killing B.[38]

(4) Relative Value of Harm Avoided and Harm Done. The defendant's belief as to the relative harmfulness of the harm avoided and the harm done does not control, however.[39] It is for the court, not the defendant, to weigh

34. It is sometimes mistakenly suggested, however, that it is necessary the defendant acted "to promote the general welfare." United States v. Contento-Pachon, 723 F.2d 691 (9th Cir.1984).

35. It might be argued that intentional homicide is a moral wrong, even when done to save life, so that necessity cannot justify intentional killings, yet the law does not and should not undertake to punish all acts that might be considered immoral. G. Williams, Criminal Law: The General Part § 237 (2d ed. 1961).

36. See § 3.6 for a discussion of motive in criminal law.

37. Thus, "the person's actions should be weighed against the harm reasonably foreseeable at the time, rather than the harm that actually occurs." Nelson v. State, 597 P.2d 977 (Alaska 1979).

38. A few of the modern codes expressly state that only a reasonable belief is needed for the defense of necessity. See City of Chicago v. Mayer, 56 Ill.2d 366, 308 N.E.2d 601 (1974) (under such a statute, question is whether the defendant, a third year medical student, could reasonably believe that police movement of injured person would harm him further, not whether untrained person would reasonably believe).

Note, however, that Model Penal Code § 3.02 requires only that the actor "believes" his conduct to be necessary to avoid the harm, without any requirement that the belief be reasonable; but if he is "reckless or negligent
* * * in appraising the necessity for his conduct," he

has no defense to crimes of recklessness or negligence. (This is consistent with Model Penal Code treatment of all these defenses: with crimes of intention, the belief, to justify the defendant's conduct, need not be reasonable.) Several of the modern codes adopt this position. But see State v. Kee, 398 A.2d 384 (Me.1979) using Model Penal Code language construed to require "that it be shown as a fact that such physical harm is imminently threatened").

Several others, however, if read literally, require that there be an actual necessity. This view is sometimes taken when there is no governing statute. See State v. Jacobs, 371 So.2d 801 (La.1979) (for medical necessity to be a defense to prison escape, it must be shown "prisoner was *actually* in danger"). That view is wrong, as "it denies a defense even to persons whose beliefs are reasonable but wrong" and adopts the unrealistic "position that people must act at their peril when the legislature cannot or will not establish specific standards for their guidance." Note, 75 Colum.L.Rev. 914, 927 (1975).

39. United States v. Coupez, 603 F.2d 1347 (9th Cir. 1979) (necessity defense not available for robberies and bombings even if defendant believed they needed to respond to "crimes" of the capitalist socio-economic system); Nelson v. State, 597 P.2d 977 (Alaska 1979) (no necessity defense, for, notwithstanding what defendants may have believed, court concludes harm to be avoided, danger to truck stuck in mud, not greater than that defendants caused by taking and damaging highway equipment in attempt to free truck).

the relative harmfulness of the two alternatives;[40] to allow the defense the court must conclude that the harm done by the defendant in choosing the one alternative[41] was less than [42] the harm which would have been done if he had chosen the other.[43] A person with unusual values might think it more important to preserve a valuable painting than to save a human life; but if, faced in an emergency with a choice of saving one of the two, he should choose to destroy the life to save the painting, the court would disagree as to his choice of values [44] and so reject his defense of necessity.

Sometimes, in necessity cases, the choice of values as to both alternatives concerns human lives: if some are sacrificed, the rest can be saved. Although it would perhaps be possible to assign a higher value to the life of a young person than to that of an older one,

and to the life of a virtuous person than to that of an immoral one—so that A might be justified in killing old bad B in order to save young innocent C—yet the law doubtless considers one person's life equal to that of another (as one man's vote is the equal of another's), without regard to the age, character, health or good looks of the persons involved.[45] Thus, in the example above, if the pressure of circumstances puts virtuous C in the pathway of death, and the only way to prevent C's death is for A to kill immoral B, A would not be justified in doing so.[46]

Sometimes, but not always, the situation is such that the harm threatened by the pressure of circumstances cannot be avoided by the defendant; the harm will occur whatever choice he makes. If two men in mid-ocean are on a plank which can hold only one, either one can be saved if the other is sacri-

---

40. Modern choice-of-evil and necessity statutes usually make it clear that the defendant's value system does not control on the issue of which is the greater evil. See, e.g., State v. Fee, 126 N.H. 78, 489 A.2d 606 (1985) (court concludes interest in having burglary alarm reset at pharmacy did not outweigh that of not having the pharmacist drive there while intoxicated).

Some of the statutes state that this justification may "not rest upon considerations pertaining to the morality and advisability of the statute defining the offense charged." The intent here appears to be to exclude the civil disobedience case from the necessity or choice-of-evils defense. See also note 43 infra. But this statutory language has been questioned because "the lesser evils defense *always* involves a claim that *application* of the law defining the offense *in the particular situation* would be inadvisable or even immoral." 2 P. Robinson, Criminal Law Defenses § 124(d)(2) (1984).

41. Model Penal Code § 3.02(1)(a) says that the harm threatened must outweigh that "sought to be prevented by the law defining the offense charged." Several modern codes contain the same or similar language. This language has been criticized because it "offers a puzzling elastic standard against which to measure the threatened harm" because, e.g., in an arson context it is unclear whether "the harm or evil sought to be prevented by an arson statute [is] the harm of burning an empty and isolated field or the violent destruction of a multi-million dollar building." 2 P. Robinson, Criminal Law Defenses § 124(g)(1) (1984). The proper view, of course, is that the harm *actually* caused by the defendant should be balanced against that prevented.

42. In a few jurisdictions the statutes require that the harm prevented "clearly outweigh" that caused. "It is questionable, however, whether actors should be punished for producing what society recognizes as a net benefit, simply because it was only slightly greater than the harm

averted." 2 P. Robinson, Criminal Law Defenses § 124(g)(2) (1984).

43. In this connection, courts have properly concluded that public protests about certain activities do not prevent those activities, and thus whatever harm would result from those activities may not be weighed in the balance. See, e.g., United States v. Dorrell, 758 F.2d 427 (9th Cir. 1985) (entry of military base and spray painting government property would not terminate the nuclear missile program and its alleged harmful effects); Cleveland v. Municipality of Anchorage, 631 P.2d 1073 (Alaska 1981) (trespasses at abortion clinic delayed but did not prevent abortions); State v. Marley, 54 Haw. 450, 509 P.2d 1095 (1973) (trespass at corporate offices to protest "war crimes" would not prevent those occurrences). Indeed, it may generally be said that "in most cases of civil disobedience a lesser evils defense will be barred. This is because as long as the laws or policies being protested have been lawfully adopted, they are conclusive evidence of the community's view on the issue." 2 P. Robinson, Criminal Law Defenses § 124(d)(1) (1984).

44. See United States v. Ashton, supra note 19 ("The law deems the lives of all persons far more valuable than any property").

45. It is not necessarily inconsistent with the above that a living person may be assigned a higher value than an unborn child: Rex v. Bourne, supra note 12.

46. Note, however, that in the lifeboat cases, doubtless because of the traditions of the sea, the suggestion has been made that the law should give a higher value to the lives of passengers than to those of sailors (except those sailors necessary to navigate); there was no suggestion, however, that in shipwreck cases women and children should be assigned a higher value than men—and indeed it would be hard to prove that there is a greater intrinsic value in the life of a woman over that of a man! United States v. Holmes, supra note 33.

ficed, so that if one kills the other he is not justified (unless, perhaps, they have drawn lots).[47] But if a mountain climber, one of two roped together on a mountain, falls over a ledge and dangles in space, and the other, unable to pull his companion to safety, is slowly losing his grip on the mountainside, and if the inevitable consequence, unless the rope parts, is that both will plunge to their deaths, it is not a question of which one of the two shall die to save the other; for the dangling mountaineer is doomed in any event.[48] If the other should cut the rope (no doubt in violation of the moral code of mountaineers), the law would consider that he has killed (accelerated death by a few moments) justifiably, for it is better that one be saved than that both should die.[49]

(5) Optional Courses of Action; Imminence of Disaster. The defense of necessity applies when the defendant is faced with this choice of two evils: he may either do something which violates the literal terms of the criminal law and thus produce some harm, or not do it and so produce a greater harm. If, however, there is open to him a third alternative, which will cause less harm than will be caused by violating the law, he is not justified in violating the law.[50] So in the case of the criminal statute which forbade taking intoxicating liquor to church, wherein the defendant took whiskey there for medicinal purposes, the court, rejecting his defense of necessity, pointed out the alternative of staying at home or of bringing some other kind of medicine.[51] A starving man is not justified in stealing food from a grocery if he can obtain food by presenting himself at a soup kitchen. A prisoner subjected to inhumane treatment by his jailors is not justified in breaking prison if he can bring about an improvement in conditions by other means.[52] One man in a

47. It would seem, however, that if *A* reaches the plank first, and *B* then seeks to pull him off so as to save himself, *A*, having reached a position of safety, would be entitled to keep *B* off. So too, in the lifeboat situation, those already in the boat loaded to capacity would be justified in keeping swimmers from climbing aboard by rapping them over the knuckles with an oar.

Some have questioned whether it is correct for the outcome in such cases to depend "entirely on fortuity—on whether the seamen reached the plank simultaneously or separately," and that in any event the governing consideration should be that "each succumbed to an overwhelming pressure which no ordinary individual could withstand." Note, 75 Colum.L.Rev. 914, 923–24 (1975). But the Model Penal Code and state statutes recognize that pressure as a defense only in coercion cases. See § 5.3.

48. Putting it in other words, there is no chance in such a situation to determine by lot which one shall be sacrificed to save the other.

49. So too, it is easier to justify jettisoning the cargo of an overloaded vessel in danger of foundering, for the cargo will be destroyed if the ship sinks, than it is to justify taking another's food to prevent hunger, for the food will be safe from destruction if the hungry man does not eat it.

50. Because the defense will fail "if there was a reasonable, legal alternative to violating the law," prison escape must be the only reasonable alternative. United States v. Bailey, 444 U.S. 394, 100 S.Ct. 624, 62 L.Ed.2d 575 (1980). The Court in *Bailey* added that because prison escape is a continuing offense, the defense would be available only if the defendant surrendered "as soon as the claimed * * * necessity had lost its coercive force." See, e.g., United States v. Bifield, 702 F.2d 342 (2d Cir.1983).

See also United States v. Seward, 687 F.2d 1270 (10th Cir.1982) (necessity defense not available to trespassers at nuclear plant site, as noncriminal alternative available to

deal with danger asserted by defendants); United States v. Cassidy, 616 F.2d 101 (4th Cir.1979) (even if U.S. possession of nuclear weapons illegal, no necessity defense for those who damaged the Pentagon, as noncriminal alternatives available); United States v. Richardson, 588 F.2d 1235 (9th Cir.1978) (defense of necessity not available as to smuggling of Laetrile into U.S. to treat cancer patients, as alternative of seeking legal authorization existed); United States v. Mowat, 582 F.2d 1194 (9th Cir.1978) (no necessity defense where trespass on military reservation because friends endangered by impending target bombing on island, as defendant could simply have notified officials friends were there); Nelson v. State, 597 P.2d 977 (Alaska 1979) (no necessity to take highway department equipment in order to free defendant's truck, stuck in mud, as defendants could have called a tow truck).

51. Bice v. State, supra note 29.

52. United States v. Bailey, 444 U.S. 394, 100 S.Ct. 624, 62 L.Ed.2d 575 (1980). But see People v. Whipple, supra note 25 (the prosecution argued that the prisoner who escaped was not entitled to the defense of necessity because he had not first exhausted his legal means of rectifying the intolerable conditions; the court answers: "In a remote mountain camp, far from the sheriff's office, what relief could he obtain by telling his custodian that he wanted to see the sheriff? If the defense could be admitted at all, it should not be conditioned upon the making of a plainly useless request.").

In People v. Richards, supra note 3, where the defendant claimed he escaped to avoid being killed by other inmates, the court concluded "that the principles set forth in *Whipple* should be adhered to and applied in this case. The prisoner should be denied self-help by escape, and should be relegated to relief through established administrative channels, or, that failing, through the courts."

lifeboat facing death by starvation cannot justifiably kill another to save himself (unless perhaps lots are first drawn); a fortiori he cannot do so if he can, without starving to death, wait a while longer, with a possibility of rescue during the interval of waiting.[53]

It is sometimes said that the defense of necessity does not apply except in an emergency—when the threatened harm is immediate, the threatened disaster imminent.[54] Perhaps this is but a way of saying that, until the time comes when the threatened harm is immediate, there are generally options open to the defendant, to avoid the harm, other than the option of disobeying the literal terms of the law[55]—the rescue ship may appear, the storm may pass; and so the defendant must wait until that hope of survival disappears.[56]

(6) No Fault in Bringing About the Situation. So far we have assumed that the defendant was not personally at fault in creating the situation calling for the necessity of his choosing between two evils. Thus, in the lifeboat cases, he did not cause the shipwreck or produce the shortage of sustenance or bring on the storm. If, however, he was at fault in creating the situation, he may be criminally liable in some circumstances.

One approach, taken in the Model Penal Code[57] and followed in some of the modern

codes, is to determine the level of liability on the basis of the defendant's culpability in creating the danger. Thus, if he intentionally brings on the situation, he may be guilty of a crime of intention; if he was reckless, of a crime of recklessness; if negligent, of a crime of negligence.[58] Thus if A drives recklessly and thereby creates a situation where he must either stay in the roadway and run down B and C or go on the sidewalk and strike D, and he chooses the lesser harm and hence strike and kills D, he is guilty of the recklessness type of manslaughter of D (on account of his reckless conduct in creating the situation) but not, it would seem, for the intentional murder of D. These provisions also apply when the defendant was at fault in appraising the necessity for his conduct.

A few jurisdictions go farther than this, providing that the defense of necessity or choice-of-evils simply is unavailable to one who was at fault in occasioning or developing the situation requiring choice of a lesser harm. This approach is objectionable because it does not distinguish between levels of fault. "The person who negligently starts the forest fire is not distinguished from the person who does so intentionally. Both would be convicted of the intentional offense of arson for burn-

In People v. McKnight, 626 P.2d 678 (Colo.1981), the court, citing cases from many other jurisdictions, declared "that normal conditions of confinement, as a matter of law, will not support a defense of choice of evils," particularly "where appellant made no effort to seek help through established, lawful channels."

53. The judge in Regina v. Dudley & Stephens, supra note 30, mentions the fact that the four persons in the lifeboat might possibly have been picked up the day after the killing (although in fact the rescue vessel did not appear for four days). Doubtless, the judge meant that, as of the time of the killing of the cabin boy, with no sail in sight, there was, for all the four could tell, a chance of being picked up next day, although in fact, as shown by subsequent events, there was no chance of rescue for four more days. The judge thus indicates that, where there appears to the defendant to be a possibility of rescue in time, he must wait until that possibility no longer exists.

54. G. Williams, Criminal Law: The General Part § 232 (2d ed. 1961). Many of the modern codes require that the threat be of "imminent" harm. Some make much the same point by also or instead declaring that the defendant's response must be an "emergency" measure, or

must be "immediately necessary." But Model Penal Code § 3.02 is not worded in terms of immediacy.

55. "Since the lesser evils defense already requires that the actor engage in conduct only when necessary to avoid the harm, the imminence requirement is an inappropriate and unnecessary additional limitation." 2 P. Robinson, Criminal Law Defenses § 124(f)(1) (1984).

56. State v. Warshow, 138 Vt. 22, 410 A.2d 1000 (1979) (thus, no necessity defense for trespass at site of nuclear power plant, as purported dangers were "long-range risks and dangers that do not presently threaten health and safety").

57. Model Penal Code § 3.02(2).

58. However, Model Penal Code § 3.02(2)—and, generally, the statutes just referred to—deals only with where "the actor was reckless or negligent in bringing about the situation." If literally interpreted, this produces an anomalous result: "Thus one who *intentionally* sets the forest fire receives the defense, while the defendant who only *negligently* creates the triggering conditions does not.!" 2 P. Robinson, Criminal Law Defenses § 123(c)(3) (1984).

ing the firebreak." [59] Even more objectiona-ble, however, is the provision found in one state which permits the defense only if the "situation occasioned or developed through no conduct of the actor."

WESTLAW
REFERENCES

110k38 /p imminent immediate option! avoid! alternative choice

---

§ 5.5 Public Duty

A public officer is justified in using reasona-ble force against the person of another, or in taking his property, when he acts pursuant to a valid law, or court order or process, requir-ing or authorizing him so to act. By the better view, he is justified in so acting, even if the law turns out to be unconstitutional or the process defective, if he reasonably believes the law or process to be valid.

(a) Executing a Court Order. A public officer is justified in detaining an individual, in using a reasonable amount of force against the person of another, or in taking or destroy-ing another's property, when he is acting pur-suant to a valid court order requiring him or authorizing him so to act.[1] Thus, the public executioner is not guilty of murder, though he intentionally brings about another's death, when he is carrying out the death penalty imposed by a court of competent jurisdiction which condemned the defendant to death.[2] So too an officer, executing a valid civil pro-cess, is justified in taking another's property on a writ of attachment or execution; or, executing a valid arrest warrant, in using force against another in effecting the arrest.[3] A person who is required or authorized to

assist a public officer is likewise justified in so acting.[4]

There is a question whether the justifica-tion is lost when it turns out that the legal process executed by the public officer was defective or was issued by a court lacking jurisdiction. Various positions are to be found in the modern codes: some extend the defense to situations in which the officer actu-ally believed his conduct was authorized or required by the court order [5]; some others go not so far by requiring that the belief be reasonable; and a few others define the de-fense in such a way that the particular public officer's belief appears to be irrelevant, either in the sense that the defense extends even to instances in which that officer knows the pro-cess is invalid, or in the sense that actual validity of the court order is essential to the defense.

Similarly, there is also a split of authority as to the extent of the public duty defense as to a private person who was assisting a public official. Many statutes declare it is sufficient that this person actually believed his assis-tance was required or authorized by law, while others require that the belief be a rea-sonable one. A few other provisions appear to make the private person's state of mind concerning the validity of the order or the lawfulness of the officer's conduct in carrying it out irrelevant in terms of narrowing or expanding the defense.

WESTLAW
REFERENCES

"reasonable force" & public government state county city /s offic*** /p execut! perform! exercis! /s order duty judgment

---

59. 2 P. Robinson, Criminal Law Defenses § 123(c)(2) (1984).

§ 5.5

1. Thus, many modern codes declare that it is a de-fense that the defendant's conduct was "required or autho-rized by a judicial decree," or utilize similar language.

2. In a few modern codes this situation is specifically addressed.

4 W. Blackstone, Commentaries 179 (1769), suggests, however, that if the executioner beheads one adjudged to be hanged, or vice versa, he is guilty of murder.

3. This latter subject is discussed in § 5.10(a). For the civil process, see W. Prosser & W. Keeton, Torts § 25 (5th ed. 1984).

4. Many of the public-duty-as-a-defense statutes extend to persons giving such aid. Also, statutes are to be found authorizing such assistance as to particular public duties, such as arrest.

5. This is also the view taken in Model Penal Code § 3.03(3)(a).

(b) Other Actions of Public Officials. Statutes in the modern codes dealing with the public duty defense are not limited to official action pursuant to court order, but rather extend to other exercises of public duty as well. Usually this is indicated by a broad provision covering any instance in which the actor's conduct is "required or authorized by law," though sometimes these statutes make specific mention of the performance of official duties by a public servant. These statutes do not themselves recognize any room for error (even reasonable mistake) concerning what the law actually authorizes with respect to these duties, nor do they typically[6] require that the public official's conduct be limited to the least intrusive step needed under the circumstances.[7]

WESTLAW
REFERENCES

"public duty" /s defense

(c) Military Duties. Yet another aspect of the public duty defense is where the conduct was required or authorized by "the law governing the armed services or the lawful conduct of war."[8] Several modern codes specify that situation within a more general public duty statute. This means, for example, that if a soldier intentionally kills an enemy combatant in time of war and within the rules of warfare, he is not guilty of murder; but if he

intentionally kills a prisoner of war, then he commits murder.[9]

WESTLAW
REFERENCES

di(crim**** /p military (armed +1 forces services) /p exercis! perform! execut*** /s duty) % "selective service" induction

§ 5.6 Domestic Authority; Other Special Relationships

The parent of a minor child, or one "in loco parentis" with respect to such child, is justified in using reasonable force upon the child for the purpose of promoting the child's welfare. Similarly, a schoolteacher is justified in using reasonable force upon a pupil for the purpose of enforcing school discipline. Other persons with responsibility for the care, discipline or safety of others (e.g., an asylum superintendent, prison warden, ship captain) are justified in using reasonable force upon others for the purpose of carrying out their responsibilities.

(a) Parents of a Minor Child.[1] The parent of a minor child is justified in using a reasonable amount of force upon the child for the purpose of safeguarding or promoting the child's welfare. Thus the parent may punish the child for wrongdoing and not be guilty of

---

6. Some statutes, however, refer specifically to "reasonable exercise or performance of official powers, duties or functions."

7. "In the absence of express proportionality and necessity requirements, an actor could argue that his conduct, even if unnecessary or disproportionate or both, was nonetheless justified under the circumstances, as long as it did not exceed the maximum statutory limit. This result seems clearly improper. Election officials, for example, may well be authorized to physically remove persons who disrupt the election process. Yet resort to physical removal may be unnecessary, and thus, unjustified, if undertaken before asking the disruptive voter to stop whistling a candidate's campaign song. Further, even if necessary, such removal might be unjustified as disproportionate, considering the voter's interest in voting and in freedom from personal injury." 2 P. Robinson, Criminal Law Defenses § 149(c) (1984).

8. Model Penal Code § 3.03(1)(d). This must be distinguished from the military orders defense, discussed in § 5.3(g).

9. State v. Gut, 13 Minn. 341 (Gil. 315) (1868) (warfare between the United States and the Sioux Indians; defendant aided in the lynching of a Sioux Indian prisoner lodged in a jail).

§ 5.6

1. See 2 P. Robinson, Criminal Law Defenses § 144 (1984); Levy, Criminal Liability for the Punishment of Children: An Evaluation of Means and Ends, 43 J.Crim. L.C. & P.S. 719 (1953); Annot., 89 A.L.R.2d 396 (1963).

Husband and wife. As to the right of a husband to enforce domestic discipline upon his wife, the view that a husband might justifiably beat his wife, for this purpose, with a stick no thicker than his thumb, if it ever prevailed, no longer is true; and the husband who thus beats his wife is guilty of a battery. Fulgham v. State, 46 Ala. 143 (1871); Commonwealth v. McAfee, 108 Mass. 458 (1871) (manslaughter); State v. Rhodes, 61 N.C. 453 (1868) (stating, however, that if the matter is trivial, the courts will not interfere). See Stedman, Right of Husband to Chastise Wife, 3 Va.L.Reg. (N.S.) 241 (1917).

a battery [2] or of a violation of a statute punishing cruelty to children if the punishment is inflicted for this beneficent purpose, and if the punishment thus inflicted is not excessive in view of all the circumstances (including the child's age, sex, health, his misconduct on the present occasion and in the past, the kind of punishment inflicted, and the degree of harm done to the child thereby).[3]

There is a dispute as to whether the test of liability in the case of a parent should be (1) an objective one, concerned with whether a reasonable man would consider the punishment excessive, or (2) a subjective one, concerned with whether the punisher acted with "malice," i.e., a purpose other than that of promoting the child's welfare.[4] The courts which adopt the latter view say, however, that such "malice" may be inferred from the infliction of excessive punishment, or punishment which results in serious injury to the child.[5]

The Model Penal Code combines these two views,[6] as do virtually all the statutes on this subject appearing in the recent recodifications. On the matter of the reasonableness of the force, some statutes merely say it must be reasonable, reasonable and moderate, reasonable and necessary, reasonable and appropriate, or other than deadly force. Others more wisely essentially follow the Model Penal

Code formulation, requiring the force be "not designed to cause or known to create a substantial risk of causing death, serious bodily harm, disfigurement, extreme pain or mental distress or gross degradation." As for the proper purpose, these provisions state that the parent must be acting to maintain discipline, to restrain or correct, to prevent or punish misconduct, or to promote or safeguard and promote the welfare of the child.

The parent's [7] right to use reasonable force has been extended to those, not parents, who are "in loco parentis"—such as a stepfather [8] or even a paramour living with the child's mother without benefit of matrimony,[9] a guardian,[10] or the director of an orphanage.[11] Modern statutes seldom employ the "in loco parentis" term. Rather, they typically refer to other persons responsible for or entrusted with the general care and supervision of the child,[12] and, less frequently, to persons acting at the request of a parent.[13] Such formulations may extend somewhat beyond the traditional "in loco parentis" test.[14]

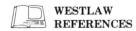 **WESTLAW REFERENCES**

di in loco parentis
parent /s punish! /s child /p reasonable! malic!

(b) School Teacher.[15] A schoolteacher may use reasonable force upon his pupil for

2. Ordinarily, when the parent's punishment kills the child, it is murder, the punishment being greatly excessive. But if the parent should use a reasonable amount of force, and unforeseeable death should ensue from the accident, the parent would not be guilty of any crime. Cf. State v. England, 220 Or. 395, 349 P.2d 668 (1960) (under statute, parent not liable for child's death as a result of administering lawful punishment negligently).

3. See State v. Thorpe, ___ R.I. ___, 429 A.2d 785 (1981), and cases cited therein.

4. See, e.g., Boyd v. State, 88 Ala. 169, 7 So. 268 (1890), favoring the latter view.

5. See, e.g., State v. Thorpe, ___ R.I. ___, 429 A.2d 785 (1981); State v. McDonie, 96 W.Va. 219, 123 S.E. 405 (1924).

6. Model Penal Code § 3.08.

7. The parent of an adopted child comes under the rule of justification: See State v. Koonse, 123 Mo.App. 655, 101 S.W. 139 (1907) (but held, the punishment was excessive).

8. Gorman v. State, 42 Tex. 221 (1875).

9. State v. Alford, 68 N.C. 322 (1873).

10. All the statutes make specific reference to a guardian.

Cf. Eitel v. State, 78 Tex.Crim. 552, 182 S.W. 318 (1916) (a guardian is not justified in punishing his ward after he has lost control over her and she has gone into the world and supported herself).

11. Richardson v. State Bd. of Control, 98 N.J.L. 690, 121 A. 457 (1923).

12. This language is also used in Model Penal Code § 3.08(1).

13. This language is used in Model Penal Code § 3.08(1).

14. Cf. State v. Pittard, 45 N.C.App. 701, 263 S.E.2d 809 (1980), review denied 300 N.C. 378, 267 S.E.2d 682 (1980) (day care center employee was not in loco parentis re child placed in the temporary care of the center, as such relationship is established only when the person intends to assume the status of a parent by taking on obligations incidental to the parental relationship, especially support and maintenance).

15. See E. Bolmeier, Legality of Student Disciplinary Practices (1976); J. Hyman & J. Wise, Corporal Punish-

the purpose of either promoting the child's education or of maintaining reasonable discipline in the school. Thus he may punish the pupil for wrongdoing, without criminal liability for battery or for violating a special statute punishing cruelty to children, if he does so to maintain discipline and does not inflict punishment which is excessive under the circumstances.[16] The privilege is not a delegation to the teacher of the parent's right to punish the child; therefore, the teacher can exercise the power to punish even if the parent disapproves or even if the parent has no such power himself.[17] The privilege of a teacher applies to the pupil's misconduct affecting school discipline which takes place off the school grounds—as where, on their way from home to school, one pupil commits a battery upon another.[18]

Here, as with punishment by parents, courts have taken two different views of the test of liability. Under the "malice" rule, the teacher is deemed to act in a quasi-judicial capacity and thus is not criminally liable because of an error in judgment or because the punishment was disproportionate, so long as the purpose was to promote discipline rather than the "malicious" purpose to inflict pain.[19] Under the reasonableness test, on the other hand, the punishment must not exceed what is reasonable under the circumstances.[20] This latter view has been characterized as "the more enlightened" one because it "refuses to

make the teacher the sole arbiter" of whether the punishment inflicted was called for.[21]

The Model Penal Code focuses upon both the reasonableness of the punishment and the purpose underlying its use,[22] as is generally the case in the statutes on this subject appearing in the modern criminal codes. The amount of force which may be used is equivalent to that authorized for parents.[23] As for the permissible purpose, it is variously stated in this legislation in terms of maintaining discipline, maintaining discipline or promoting the welfare of the child, maintaining discipline consistent with the welfare of the child, maintaining order, quelling a disturbance and removing the offending student, or restraining or correcting the student.

 WESTLAW REFERENCES

teacher schoolteacher /s punish! disciplin! /s child student /p reasonable! malic!

(c) Other Relationships. Many of the modern codes deal not only with the parent-child and teacher-student relationships, but also with other situations in which there is a special responsibility for certain persons to see to the care, discipline or safety of others. Most often addressed in this legislation is the authority of those responsible for incompetent persons. These provisions typically follow the Model Penal Code position by recognizing that nondeadly force may be used to promote the welfare of an incompetent person (includ-

---

ment in American Education (1979); Levy, supra note 1, at 730–32; Stroud, The Teacher Privilege to Use Corporal Punishment, 11 Ind.L.Rev. 349 (1978); Sweeney, Corporal Punishment in Public Schools: A Violation of Substantive Due Process, 33 Hastings L.J. 1245 (1982); Annot., supra note 1, at 442–58.

16. See Annot., supra note 1, at 442–58. In Ingraham v. Wright, 430 U.S. 651, 97 S.Ct. 1401, 51 L.Ed.2d 711 (1977), the Court held that the Eighth Amendment Prohibition on "cruel and unusual punishment" was "designed to protect those convicted of crimes" and thus "does not apply to the paddling of children as a means of maintaining discipline in public schools." The Court added that "[t]he schoolchild has little need for the protection of the Eighth Amendment," in that "[p]ublic school teachers and administrators are privileged at common law to inflict only such corporal punishment as is reasonably necessary for the proper education and discipline of the child; any punishment going beyond the privilege may result in both civil and criminal liability."

17. State v. Mizner, 45 Iowa 248 (1876) (though a parent cannot punish girl over 18, who is in Iowa no longer a minor, teacher can punish girl pupil over 18, and even one over 21 who was admitted to school as a pupil when she misrepresented her age).

18. Cleary v. Booth, [1893] 1 Q.B. 465.

19. Boyd v. State, 88 Ala. 169, 7 So. 268 (1890).

20. People v. Ball, 58 Ill.2d 36, 317 N.E.2d 54 (1974).

21. People v. Curtis, 116 Cal.App.Supp. 771, 300 P. 801 (1931).

22. Model Penal Code § 3.08(2).

23. This is accomplished by cross-reference to the section dealing with parents, by repeating the language from that section on the permissible quantum of force, or by stating the authority of parents and teachers together.

ing the prevention of his misconduct) or to maintain discipline within an institution.[24] Similarly, it is frequently provided that correctional officials are justified in using reasonable force to maintain order in and enforce the rules of a prison or jail.[25]

Even prior to the drafting of the Model Penal Code, legislation allowing those responsible for maintaining order and decorum on trains or other carriers to expel disorderly passengers was not uncommon.[26] Legislation on this subject is typically found in the modern recodifications, usually following the Model Penal Code in extending the justification to persons authorized or required to maintain order in other public places (e.g., a theatre).[27] But only a few states [28] have adopted another Model Penal Code provision expressly recognizing that a person responsible for the safety of a vessel or aircraft may use force (even deadly force if necessary) to prevent interference with operation of the vessel or aircraft.[29]

Several of the modern codes also declare that the use of force by a doctor is justified in specified circumstances.[30] Many follow the Model Penal Code formulation,[31] providing that the force must be used as part of a recognized form of treatment and with consent of the patient or one authorized to consent on the patient's behalf, except that consent is unnecessary in an emergency.[32] Even if the rules concerning civil liability are not this broad,[33] it is important that medical personnel be allowed to administer unconsented medical treatment in emergencies without

fear of criminal liability.[34] This "good Samaritan" notion doubtless accounts for yet another common statutory provision, namely, that one is justified in using force upon another to the extent reasonably believed necessary to thwart a suicide attempt.[35]

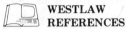 **WESTLAW REFERENCES**

reasonable! necessary /3 force /p maintain! +1 discipline order /p prison (correctional +1 institution facility) train aircraft vessel church

§ 5.7 Self Defense

One who is not the aggressor in an encounter is justified in using a reasonable amount of force against his adversary when he reasonably believes (a) that he is in immediate danger of unlawful bodily harm from his adversary and (b) that the use of such force is necessary to avoid this danger. It is never reasonable to use deadly force against his nondeadly attack. There is a dispute as to whether one threatened with a deadly attack must retreat, if he can safely do so, before resorting to deadly force, except that it is agreed that ordinarily he need not retreat from his home or place of business.

(a) Generally. It is only just that one who is unlawfully attacked by another, and who has no opportunity to resort to the law for his defense, should be able to take reasonable steps to defend himself from physical harm.[1] When the steps he takes are reasonable, he has a complete defense to such crimes against the person as murder and manslaughter, at-

---

24. Model Penal Code § 3.08(3).

25. See also Model Penal Code § 3.08(5).

26. Model Penal Code § 3.08, Comment (Tent.Draft No. 8, 1958). Under these statutes, only reasonable force was allowed. State v. Kinney, 34 Minn. 311, 25 N.W. 705 (1885) (improper for conductor to expel nonpaying passenger while train moving).

27. Model Penal Code § 3.08(7).

28. "Perhaps because this is an aspect of the law of the sea, it rarely has been put in statutory form." Model Penal Code § 3.08, Comment (Tent. Draft No. 8, 1958).

29. Model Penal Code § 3.08(6).

30. Only a few also extend to nonmedical personnel not acting under the direction of a doctor.

31. Model Penal Code § 3.08(4).

32. More particularly described in the Code as "in an emergency when the actor believes that no one competent to consent can be consulted and that a reasonable person, wishing to safeguard the welfare of the patient, would consent."

33. See, e.g., Bonner v. Moran, 126 F.2d 121 (D.C.Cir. 1941) (civil liability where doctor failed to obtain parent's consent to operation on 15-year-old boy).

34. For more on the medical authority justification, see 2 P. Robinson, Criminal Law Defenses § 145 (1984).

35. For more on this suicide prevention authority, see, 2 P. Robinson, supra note 34, at § 146.

§ 5.7

1. On self-defense, see Model Penal Code § 3.04, Comment (1985); Ashworth, Self-Defence and the Right to Life, 34 Camb.L.J. 282 (1975); Beale, Retreat from A

tempted murder, assault and battery and the aggravated forms of assault and battery.[2] His intentional infliction of (or, if he misses, his attempt to inflict) physical harm upon the other, or his threat to inflict such harm, is said to be justified when he acts in proper self-defense, so that he is not guilty of any crime.

In order that one be entitled to use force in self-defense (or in defense of others) to oppose the force of his adversary, it is necessary that the adversary's force be, or at least that the defendant reasonably believe it to be,[3] "unlawful" force—meaning, in general, that it be a crime or tort (generally assault and battery) for the adversary to use the force.[4] Thus one cannot properly defend himself against known lawful force or against the use of force to which he has consented.[5]

The law of self-defense (and of defense of others) makes a distinction between "deadly" force and "nondeadly" (or "moderate") force, holding that there are situations wherein it is reasonable to use nondeadly force but not to use deadly force. "Deadly force" may be de-

fined as force (a) which its user uses with the intent to cause death or serious bodily injury to another or (b) which he knows creates a substantial risk of death or serious bodily injury to the other.[6] One thus uses deadly force if he fires at another with intent to kill him or do him serious bodily harm,[7] though actually he misses him completely or causes him only minor bodily injury. But merely to threaten death or serious bodily harm, without any intention to carry out the threat, is not to use deadly force,[8] so that one may be justified in pointing a gun at his attacker when he would not be justified in pulling the trigger.[9]

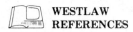 **WESTLAW REFERENCES**

203k109

(b) Amount of Force. In determining how much force one may use in self-defense, the law recognizes that the amount of force which he may justifiably use must be reasonably related to the threatened harm which he seeks to avoid. One may justifiably use [10]

Murderous Assault, 16 Harv.L.Rev. 567 (1903); Beale, Homicide in Self-Defence, 3 Colum.L.Rev. 526 (1903); Perkins, Self-Defense Re-examined, 1 U.C.L.A.L.Rev. 133 (1954). The principles of self-defense as a justification for the torts of assault and battery are very similar to those governing self-defense as a justification in the criminal law. See W. Prosser & W. Keeton, Torts § 19 (5th ed. 1984); Restatement (Second) of Torts §§ 63, 65, 67 (1965).

2. It has been suggested that self-defense is a defense to other types of crimes in appropriate cases; thus when *A* attacks *B*, *B* may in self-defense justifiably take *C*'s car in which to escape from *A*. J. Hall & G. Mueller, Criminal Law and Procedure 663 (2d ed. 1965). It is doubtless true that *B* is justified in taking *C*'s car, so he is not guilty of larceny thereof, but his defense is necessity, see § 5.4, rather than self-defense. In United States v. Panter, 688 F.2d 268 (5th Cir.1982), holding that a convicted felon in reasonable fear of his own safety who took temporary possession of a firearm for self-protection was not guilty of violating the statute prohibiting convicted felons from possessing firearms, the court noted it was unclear whether the defense should be labelled self-defense or necessity.

Self-defense might also be a defense to a criminal charge of unlawful restraint. Model Penal Code § 3.04(3) expressly recognizes, as do a few of the modern codes, that the use of confinement as protective force is permissible if it is terminated as soon as can safely be done.

3. United States v. Middleton, 690 F.2d 820 (11th Cir. 1982). State v. Beyer, 258 N.W.2d 353 (Iowa 1977).

However, Mode Penal Code § 3.04 permits the use of force in self-protection on the basis of the user's belief (as

opposed to the prevailing requirement of reasonable belief) "that such force is immediately necessary for the purpose of protecting himself against the use of unlawful force," but § 3.09(1) provides that the defense is unavailable if "the actor's belief in the unlawfulness of the force * * * is erroneous" and "his error is due to ignorance or mistake as to the provisions of the Code, any other provision of the criminal law or the law governing the legality of an arrest or search." This exception is based upon the general principle "that knowledge of illegality is not ordinarily an element of an offense." Model Penal Code § 3.04, Comment at 41 (1985).

4. See Model Penal Code § 3.11.

5. Daniel v. State, 187 Ga. 411, 1 S.E.2d 6 (1939) (defendant reached for gun to rob victim; victim properly fired at defendant but missed; defendant killed victim; held, the evidence fails to show defendant acted in proper self-defense).

6. Model Penal Code § 3.11(2).

7. State v. Clay, 297 N.C. 555, 256 S.E.2d 176 (1979). It would seem that one may commit assault (or battery) with a deadly weapon without intending death or serious bodily harm, see §§ 7.15, 7.16, so that one who engages in that conduct is not necessarily using deadly force.

8. Model Penal Code § 3.11(2).

9. United States v. Black, 692 F.2d 314 (4th Cir.1982).

10. A fortiori he may threaten to use it, without actually using it.

nondeadly force against another in self-defense if he reasonably believes that the other is about to inflict unlawful bodily harm (it need not be death or serious bodily harm) upon him [11] (and also believes that it is necessary to use such force to prevent it). That is, under such circumstances he is not guilty of assault (if he merely threatens to use the nondeadly force or if he aims that force at the other but misses) or battery (if he injuries the other by use of that force).[12] He may justifiably use *deadly* force [13] against the other in self-defense, however, only if he reasonably believes that the other is about to inflict un-

lawful death or serious bodily harm upon him (and also that it is necessary to use deadly force to prevent it).[14] Such use of deadly force is authorized in the modern codes, which typically go on to permit this amount of force in defense of serious offenses against the person.[15]

As for the rule that deadly force may only be used against what is reasonably believed to be deadly force, it may generally be said that "this requirement precludes the use of a deadly weapon against an *unarmed* assailant." [16] But this is not inevitably the case; account

11. As to the amount of force threatened by the adversary: State v. Woodward, 58 Ida. 385, 74 P.2d 92 (1937) (on a charge of assault with a deadly weapon, which defendant justified on grounds of self-defense, the court instructed the jury that, for self-defense, defendant's act must have been necessary to prevent the infliction upon him of "great bodily injury" by the other; conviction of assault with a deadly weapon held reversed, for the instruction was erroneous; it may be enough that the defendant's act was necessary to prevent "bodily harm"). But see Annot., 114 A.L.R. 634 (1938), for differing views on whether it is a defense to assault and battery that the defendant reasonably feared bodily harm less than death or serious bodily harm from his adversary.

Model Penal Code § 3.04 allows the use of nondeadly force in self-defense against an adversary's non-deadly force, as do the new criminal codes. See, statutes cited in note 24 infra.

12. If, however, he uses deadly force, though either he misses or he hits but merely injures, he ought to be guilty of statutory aggravated assault (or battery) with intent to kill, if he intended to kill; or assault or battery with intent to do serious bodily harm, if that was his intent; or perhaps assault or battery with a deadly weapon, if he intentionally used such a weapon on his adversary. E. g., Caldwell v. State, 160 Ala. 96, 49 So. 679 (1909) (instruction that, for self-defense, defendant must reasonably believe he is in imminent peril of death or great bodily harm, although proper when the charge is murder or assault or battery with intent to murder, is not applicable when the charge is assault or battery with a weapon); Jupe v. State, 86 Tex.Crim. 573, 217 S.W. 1041 (1920) (same distinction made, between charge of assault to murder and simple assault).

13. If he is justified in using deadly force, he is of course justified in threatening to use it. If he is not justified in using deadly force, he may nevertheless be justified in threatening to use it without intending to use it. See note 8 supra and text thereto.

14. Beard v. United States, 158 U.S. 550, 15 S.Ct. 962, 39 L.Ed. 1086 (1895) (defendant, on own premises, killed his advancing adversary who threatened to assault him: "the question for the jury was whether, without fleeing from his adversary, he had, at the moment he struck the deceased, reasonable grounds to believe, and in good faith believed, that he could not save his life or protect himself

from great bodily harm except by doing what he did"); People v. Johnson, 2 Ill.2d 165, 117 N.E.2d 91 (1954) (where defendant turned and began shooting upon receiving a blow to the back of the head from an unknown source, he "was not under a reasonable apprehension of death or great bodily harm"); People v. Williams, 56 Ill. App.2d 159, 205 N.E.2d 749 (1965) (where member of gang threw brick at cab driver, driver was justified in firing at the gang, as he reasonably believed the gang was about to attack him); Shorter v. People, 2 N.Y. 193, 51 Am.Dec. 286 (1849) (one may justifiably kill his adversary in self-defense if he reasonably believes that the adversary has "a design to take away his life, or do him some great bodily harm" and that the danger is imminent that such a design will be accomplished); State v. Spaulding, 298 N.C. 149, 257 S.E.2d 391 (1979) (actual show of deadly force unnecessary where, as here, other party made threats, advanced with hand in pocket, and had previously stabbed defendant).

15. Some of these provisions extend to the most extreme intrusions on freedom of the person (e.g., kidnapping and rape). Perhaps such provisions may be properly classified as primarily serving defense of the person, even though they apply even when the crime does not threaten death or serious bodily harm. State v. Philbrick, 402 A.2d 59 (Me.1979). See Fabricant, Homicide in Response to a Threat of Rape: A Theoretical Examination of the Rule of Justification, 11 Golden Gate U.L.Rev. 945, 947 (1981), noting the law deems deadly force proper "to prevent crimes which threaten harm so severe and permanent as to be incapable of repair through subsequent legal proceedings."

But those statutes which permit deadly force, when necessary, as to all forcible felonies against the person, are more properly characterized as of the prevention-of-crime variety. See § 5.10(c), and consider State v. Harris, 222 N.W.2d 462 (Iowa 1974) (deadly force permitted only as to "an atrocious, violent felony about to be or being committed"; court says that while some treat this as self-defense, better rationale is "that such crimes themselves imperil human life or involve danger of great bodily harm").

As for provisions allowing deadly force as to lesser threats to the person when they occur in the context of a burglary, they are explainable in part in defense-of-property terms. See § 5.9(b).

16. Note, 54 Wash.L.Rev. 221, 228 (1978).

must be taken of the respective sizes [17] and sex [18] of the assailant and defendant, of the presence of multiple assailants,[19] and of the especially violent nature of the unarmed attack.[20] Past violent conduct of the assailant known by the defendant is also relevant in assessing what the defendant reasonably believed was the quantum of risk to him.[21]

**WESTLAW
REFERENCES**

di("sexual assault" rape battery /p self-defense /p
  amount deadly non-deadly /s force)

wanrow /s 559 +5 548 /p self-defense

(c) Reasonable Belief in Necessity for Force. As indicated in the above statements, the case law [22] and statutory law [23] on self-defense generally require that the defendant's belief in the necessity of using force to prevent harm to himself be a reasonable one, so that one who honestly though unreasonably believes in the necessity of using force in self-protection loses the defense.[24] When his be-

lief is reasonable, however, he may be mistaken in his belief and still have the defense. Thus one may be justified in shooting to death an adversary who, having threatened to kill him, reaches for his pocket as if for a gun, though it later appears that he had no gun and that he was only reaching for his handkerchief.[25] In appraising the situation one may, under the circumstances, be reasonable though mistaken since, as Mr. Justice Holmes has put it in a famous expression: "Detached reflection cannot be demanded in the presence of an uplifted knife." [26] One who because of voluntary intoxication thinks that he is in danger of imminent attack, though a sober man would not have thought so, does not have the reasonable belief which the law requires.[27]

There is a little authority that an honest belief in the necessity of self-defense will do; it need not in addition be a reasonable belief.[28] The Model Penal Code supports this view, on the theory that there should be no

---

17. Willingham v. State, 262 Ala. 550, 80 So.2d 280 (1955); Hinson v. State, 218 So.2d 36 (Miss.1969).

18. Kress v. State, 176 Tenn. 478, 144 S.W.2d 735 (1940); State v. Wanrow, 88 Wn.2d 221, 559 P.2d 548 (1977) (thus condemning a self-defense instruction stated in the masculine gender where the defendant was a woman).

19. Allen v. United States, 157 U.S. 675, 15 S.Ct. 720, 39 L.Ed. 854 (1895); State v. Pearson, 288 N.C. 34, 215 S.E.2d 598 (1975).

20. Hinson v. State, 218 So.2d 36 (Miss.1969); Easterling v. State, 267 P.2d 185 (Okl.Crim.1954).

21. State v. Spaulding, 298 N.C. 149, 257 S.E.2d 391 (1979) (actual show of deadly force unnecessary here, as assailant who made threats and advanced with hand in pocket had stabbed defendant on prior occasion); State v. Wanrow, 88 Wn.2d 221, 559 P.2d 548 (1977) (instruction to jury to consider only acts or circumstances "at or immediately before the killing" error). Because of its emphasis on this point and on the relevance of the sex of the assailant and defendant (see note 18 supra), *Wanrow* has rightly been recognized as having an important bearing upon self-defense claims by battered wives who have killed their husbands. See Notes, 32 Hasting L.J. 895 (1981); 54 Wash.L.Rev. 221 (1978).

22. See e.g., United States v. Beard, Shorter v. People, both supra note 14, for statements requiring reasonable belief in the need to use force.

23. The modern codes typically make it explicit that the defendant must have been reasonable in his belief as to the need for force of the amount used.

24. For the possibility of reducing a homicide under these circumstances from murder to manslaughter, see § 5.7(i).

25. See Shorter v. People, 2 N.Y. 193, 197, 51 Am.Dec. 286, 287 (1849) (one is justified in killing another in self-defense when reasonably apprehending death or serious bodily harm, "although it may afterward turn out that the appearances were false, and there was *in fact* neither design to do him serious injury, nor danger that it would be done").

26. Brown v. United States, 256 U.S. 335, 41 S.Ct. 501, 65 L.Ed. 961 (1921).

27. Springfield v. State, 96 Ala. 81, 11 So. 250 (1892).

28. Grainger v. State, 13 Tenn. 459 (1830) (an overpowering bully threatened the defendant, a timid and cowardly man, with violence, intending a battery but not to kill; if the defendant thought himself in danger of great bodily harm from the bully, the killing was in self-defense); Vigil v. People, 143 Colo. 328, 353 P.2d 82 (1960) (instruction that right to self-defense is based on what reasonable persons would do under similar circumstances *held* error; animals, who cannot reason, instinctively act in self-preservation, so self-defense by mankind is not based upon the reasonable man concept); State v. Cope, 78 Ohio App. 429, 67 N.E.2d 912 (1946) (one may properly act in self-defense not only when a reasonable person would so act, but when one with the particular qualities of the defender himself would do so; a nervous, timid, easily-frightened man is not measured by the same standard as a stronger, braver man). Compare Teal v. State, 22 Ga. 75, 84 (1857) (defendant's requested instructions that "the fears of a coward would justify homicide" is erroneous; the fears must, for self-defense, be those "of a reasonable man; reasonably courageous—reasonably self-possessed").

conviction of a crime requiring intentional misconduct of one who is guilty only of negligence in making the unreasonable mistake.[29] Only a few of the modern codes have adopted this position.[30]

Of course, whether a reasonable belief is required or not, the defendant must *actually* believe in the necessity for force.[31] He has no defense when he intentionally kills his enemy in complete ignorance of the fact that his enemy, when killed, was about to launch a deadly attack upon him.[32] Nevertheless, if he acts in proper self-defense, he does not lose the defense because he acts with some less admirable motive in addition to that of defending himself, as where he enjoys using force upon his adversary because he hates him.[33]

WESTLAW REFERENCES

self-defense /p honest! /s belie*** /s necess*** /s force

(d) Imminence of Attack. Case law[34] and legislation concerning self-defense require that the defendant reasonably believe his adversary's unlawful violence to be almost immediately forthcoming. Most of the modern codes require that the defendant reasonably perceive an "imminent" use of force,[35] although other language making the same point

is sometimes to be found.[36] Very few of the self-defense provisions in the modern codes fail to address this point explicitly.

As a general matter, the requirement that the attack reasonably appear to be imminent is a sensible one. If the threatened violence is scheduled to arrive in the more distant future, there may be avenues open to the defendant to prevent it other than to kill or injure the prospective attacker; but this is not so where the attack is imminent. But the application of this requirement in some contexts has been questioned. "Suppose *A* kidnaps and confines *D* with the announced intention of killing him one week later. *D* has an opportunity to kill *A* and escape each morning as *A* brings him his daily ration. Taken literally, the *imminent* requirement would prevent *D* from using deadly force in self-defense until *A* is standing over him with a knife, but that outcome seems inappropriate. * * * The proper inquiry is not the immediacy of the threat but the immediacy of the response necessary in defense. If a threatened harm is such that it cannot be avoided if the intended victim waits until the last moment, the principle of self-defense must permit him to act earlier—as early as is required to defend himself effectively."[37]

However, the question of whether there should be an imminence-of-attack require-

---

29. Model Penal Code § 3.04(1), requiring only that the actor "believes" that the use of force is necessary. See Model Penal Code § 3.04, Comment at 36 (1985); G. Williams, Criminal Law: The General Part, § 73 at 208 (2d 1961), arguing that the defendant lacks moral guilt under such circumstances.

Model Penal Code § 3.09 provides that one who acts in unreasonable self-defense may be liable for a crime which may be committed by recklessness (e.g., manslaughter, battery) when he makes a reckless mistake as to the necessity of using force.

30. But see Coleman v. State, 320 A.2d 740 (Del.1974) ("reasonable man" test still a factor, but not controlling, under such a statute).

31. State v. Kelly, 97 N.J. 178, 478 A.2d 364 (1984) (concluding evidence on battered wife syndrome admissible for this purpose).

32. Josey v. United States, 135 F.2d 809 (D.C.Cir.1943) (instruction that force is justified if the defendant has reasonable grounds to believe that adversary's attack is imminent *held* properly refused for failure to state that, in addition, the defendant must actually believe it); Trogdon v. State, 133 Ind. 1, 32 N.E. 725 (1892).

33. Golden v. State, 25 Ga. 527 (1858).

34. E.g. see formulations in United States v. Beard, and Shorter v. People, supra note 14.

See People v. Williams, 56 Ill.App.2d 159, 205 N.E.2d 749 (1965), where a member of a gang beating an old man in the street threw a brick at a cab parked across the intersection, after which the driver fired at the gang; *held*, the danger to the driver was imminent, as the "gang was a short distance from defendant" and "had the present ability to carry out the threatened harm."

35. As noted in State v. Daniels, ___ Mont. ___, 682 P.2d 173 (1984), the word "imminent" refers to the aggressor's threatened conduct rather than the defender's response.

36. Some utilize the slightly broader requirement, taken from Model Penal Code § 3.04(1) that defensive force must be against unlawful attack "on the present occasion." Another says the defendant must believe he is "about to be injured." Some in addition or instead say that the force must be "immediately necessary."

37. 2 P. Robinson, Criminal Law Defenses § 131(c)(1) (1984).

ment and, if so, how it should be characterized, is most dramatically presented in the context of a homicide by a battered wife. It sometimes occurs that a wife who has repeatedly been subjected to serious bodily harm by her husband will take his life on a particular occasion when there was not, strictly speaking, any immediate threat of repetition of the husband's conduct,[38] though the wife knew with virtual certainty that more severe beatings were in the offing. Such a state of affairs often comes about, experts have testified,[39] because of what is known as the "battered woman syndrome" [40]: "a man physically and psychologically abuses a wife or loved one, gains her foregiveness, seeks her love and reconciliation and then repeats the cycle over and over so many times that the woman, at all times hoping the relationship will last, is reduced to a state of learned helplessness." [41] Some have argued that the "battered wife thus is literally faced with the dilemma of either waiting for her husband to kill her or striking out at him first," [42] and that consequently the "imminency" requirement should be abolished or loosely construed [43] so that on such facts the battered wife's self-defense claim will prevail.[44] Others just as fervently contend that the bat-

tered wife case shows just how essential the "imminency" requirement really is, as especially in such circumstances the law must encourage resort to alternatives other than the taking of human life.[45]

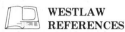

WESTLAW
REFERENCES

"battered wife syndrome"

(e) The Aggressor's Right to Self-Defense. It is generally said that one who is the aggressor in an encounter with another—i.e., one who brings about the difficulty with the other [46]—may not avail himself of the defense of self-defense.[47] Ordinarily, this is certainly a correct statement, since the aggressor's victim, defending himself against the aggressor, is using lawful, not unlawful, force; [48] and the force defended against must be unlawful force, for self-defense.[49] Nevertheless, there are two situations in which an aggressor may justifiably defend himself. (1) A nondeadly aggressor (i.e., one who begins an encounter, using only his fists or some nondeadly weapon) who is met with deadly force in defense may justifiably defend himself against the deadly attack. This is so because the aggressor's victim, by using deadly force against nondeadly aggression, uses unlawful force.

38. See Note, 24 Wayne L.Rev. 1705 (1978), describing several homicide by "battered wife" cases reported in the media over a short span of time, including some in which the husband was killed while he was asleep, was shot in the back, or was pursued for some distance and then shot.

39. Courts are divided as to whether such expert testimony should be admissible in the criminal prosecution. Compare Ibn-Tamas v. United States, 407 A.2d 626 (D.C. App.1979); State v. Kelly, 97 N.J. 178, 478 A.2d 364 (1984) (admissible); with State v. Thomas, 66 Ohio St.2d 518, 423 N.E.2d 137 (1981) (inadmissible).

40. See L. Walker, The Battered Woman (1979).

41. State v. Kelly, 33 Wn.App. 541, 655 P.2d 1202 (1982), reversed 102 Wn.2d 188, 685 P.2d 564 (1984).

42. Note, 32 Hastings L.J. 895, 928 (1981).

43. A more likely possibility, it would seem, as to statutes using the "immediately necessary" formulation. See note 36 supra.

44. Note, 32 Hastings L.J. 895, 926-30 (1981). See also Comment, 26 Vill.L.Rev. 105 (1980); Note, 10 Rutgers-Camden L.J. 643 (1979).

45. See Note, supra note 44, at 930, citing to such arguments by others. Illustrative of cases in which the battered spouse has not prevailed because of a lack of an actual or threatened assault by the husband on that

occasion are People v. Dillon, 24 Ill.2d 122, 180 N.E.2d 503 (1962); State v. Leaphart, 673 S.W.2d 870 (Tenn.Crim. 1983). See also Jahnke v. State, 682 P.2d 991 (Wyo.1984) (same result as to child abuse victim).

See Note, 34 Stan.L.Rev. 615 (1982), arguing that in such circumstances the crime should be reduced to manslaughter under the imperfect self-defense theory discussed in § 5.7(i).

46. But see People v. Townes, 391 Mich. 578, 218 N.W.2d 136 (1974) (person who merely created a threat to property, by not leaving defendant's store when ordered to do so, not an "aggressor" within this rule).

47. United States v. Nolan, 700 F.2d 479 (9th Cir.1983); United States v. Peterson, 483 F.2d 1222 (D.C.Cir.1973); McMahon v. State, 617 P.2d 494 (Alaska 1980); Townsend v. Commonwealth, 474 S.W.2d 352 (Ky.1971); State v. O'Brien, 434 A.2d 9 (Me.1981); State v. McCray, 312 N.C. 519, 324 S.E.2d 606 (1985); State v. Craig, 82 Wn.2d 777, 514 P.2d 151 (1973). Most modern codes so provide.

48. That is true, of course, only if the victim is responding to aggression on this occasion, as compared to retaliation for aggression on some prior occasion. State v. Henson, 552 S.W.2d 378 (Mo.1977).

49. See § 5.7(a).

(2) So too, an aggressor who in good faith effectively withdraws from any further encounter with his victim (and to make an effective withdrawal he must notify the victim, or at least take reasonable steps to notify him) [50] is restored to his right of self-defense.[51]

Some modern codes specify still other circumstances in which a person, by virtue of his own prior conduct, has lost the right of self-defense he would otherwise have. Most common is a provision that one who provokes the use of force against himself for the purpose of causing serious bodily harm may not defend against the force he has provoked. Some statutes expressly disallow defense against force which was the product of combat by agreement, and some declare that those involved in certain criminal activities do not during such time have any right of self-defense. A few states have provisions generally not permitting defensive force against one who is an occupier or possessor of property and is defending that property under a claim of right.[52]

**WESTLAW
REFERENCES**

self-defense /p aggressor /p withdraw*** non-deadly

(f) Necessity for Retreat. We have already noted that one may not, in self-defense, use more force than reasonably appears to be necessary to avoid his adversary's threatened

harm.[53] A difficulty arises, however, when there is one way open to avoid the threatened harm other than by injuring or killing the adversary: what if, instead of standing his ground and using force, the defender can safely (though ignominiously) run away? There is a strong policy against the unnecessary taking of human life (and a somewhat weaker policy against causing unnecessary bodily injury). On the other hand, there is a policy against making one act a cowardly and humiliating role.

It seems everywhere agreed that one who can safely retreat need not do so before using nondeadly force.[54] "If he does not resort to a deadly force, one who is assailed may hold his ground whether the attack upon him be of a deadly or some lessor [sic] character. Although it might be argued that a safe retreat should be taken if thereby the use of *any* force could be avoided, yet * * * the logic of this position never has been accepted when moderate force is used in self-defense."[55]

Thus the question of the duty to retreat is a problem only when deadly force is used in self-defense. The majority of American jurisdictions holds that the defender (who was not the original aggressor) need not retreat, even though he can do so safely, before using deadly force upon an assailant whom he reasonably believes will kill him or do him serious

50. In Rowe v. United States, 164 U.S. 546, 17 S.Ct. 172, 41 L.Ed. 547 (1896), the aggressor, after kicking at the other, stepped back and leaned against a counter, not in an attitude for personal conflict; the court held the jury should have determined whether this was intended to be, and could be reasonably interpreted to be, a withdrawal in good faith from further controversy. State v. Broadhurst, 184 Or. 178, 196 P.2d 407 (1948), says of good-faith withdrawal that an aggressor must bring home to the other his intention to withdraw "in such a way that the adversary, as a reasonable man, must have known that the assault was ended." This statement is somewhat ambiguous as to whether actual notice of withdrawal is required, or only reasonable steps to give notice. In People v. Button, 106 Cal. 628, 39 P. 1073 (1895), the aggressor's attack so dazed his victim that the latter did not realize the aggressor was withdrawing; the aggressor was held not to have effectively withdrawn. This case, then, seems to require that the notice be actual.

51. Rowe v. United States, State v. Broadhurst (holding that defendant did not notify the deceased of his

purpose to withdraw; a secret purpose will not do), both supra note 50; Annot., 55 A.L.R.3d 1000 (1973).

52. Following Model Penal Code § 3.04(2)(a)(ii). The exceptions are where the actor is a public officer performing his duty (or a person assisting him), the actor is making reentry or recapture after dispossession, or the actor believes such force is necessary to protect himself against death or serious bodily harm.

53. See 5.7(b), pointing out that, as a matter of law, it is unreasonable to use deadly force against a nondeadly attack.

54. Some of the modern recodifications expressly state that this is so.

55. State v. Abbott, 36 N.J. 63, 174 A.2d 881 (1961) (holding, however, that there is a duty to retreat before using deadly force). Accord: State v. Gough, 187 Iowa 363, 174 N.W. 279 (1919); People v. Katz, 263 App.Div. 883, 32 N.Y.S.2d 157 (1942) (intimating that an aggressor, who brought on the difficulty, when attacked by his victim, is obliged to retreat).

bodily harm.[56]   A strong minority, however, taking what might be regarded as a more civilized view,[57] holds that he must retreat ("retreat to the wall," it is sometimes said), before using deadly force, if he can do so in safety.[58]   But even in those jurisdictions which require retreat, the defender need not retreat unless he knows he can do so in complete safety;[59] and he need not retreat from his home or place of business,[60] except perhaps when the defender was the original aggressor[61] or the assailant is a co-occupant of those premises.[62]   Moreover, the retreat requirement does not apply to a police officer or a private person assisting him.[63]

If retreat is to be preferred over use of deadly force, then it might be argued that certain other alternative steps which would terminate the dangerous encounter should likewise be required in lieu of self-defense with deadly force.   Thus, the Model Penal Code expressly provides that deadly force is not permissible if the actor knows he can avoid the necessity for its use "by surrendering possession of a thing to a person asserting a claim of right thereto or by complying with a demand that he abstain from any action which he has no duty to take."[64]   A few modern codes contain such surrender-possession and comply-with-demand limits on deadly force.

56. E.g., Brown v. United States, 256 U.S. 335, 41 S.Ct. 501, 65 L.Ed. 961 (1921); People v. Gonzales, 71 Cal. 569, 12 P. 783 (1887); Runyan v. State, 57 Ind. 80, 26 Am.Rep. 52 (1877); Haynes v. State, 451 So.2d 227 (Miss.1984); Neal v. State, 604 P.2d 145 (Okla.Crim.App.1979); Voigt v. State, 53 Tex.Crim. 258, 109 S.W. 205 (1908).   For a collection of cases, see Annot., 18 A.L.R. 1279 (1922).   See also Beale's and Perkins' articles, supra note 1.

57. "It merely states the obvious conclusion that, if the actor may retreat in complete safety, then the use of defensive force is not necessary."   2 P. Robinson, Criminal Law Defenses § 131(c) (1984).

58. E.g., King v. State, 233 Ala. 198, 171 So. 254 (1936); State v. Marish, 198 Iowa 602, 200 N.W. 5 (1924); State v. Cox, 138 Me. 151, 23 A.2d 634 (1941); State v. Austin, 332 N.W.2d 21 (Minn.1983); State v. Davis, 214 S.C. 34, 51 S.E.2d 86 (1948).   Compare Gillis v. United States, 400 A.2d 311 (D.C.App.1979), purporting to adopt a middle position: there is no duty to retreat, but the failure to retreat may be considered by the jury in determining "whether a defendant, if he safely could have avoided further encounter by stepping back or walking away, was actually or apparently in imminent danger of bodily harm."

Even in jurisdictions with modern recodifications, the retreat doctrine is a minority position.   Virtually all of the statutes recognizing it explicitly state that this retreat rule is not applicable to a peace officer or a person assisting him in the performance of his duties.

59. State v. Abbott, supra note 55, quoting with approval from what is now Model Penal Code § 3.04(2)(b)(ii) (deadly force is not justifiable if "the actor knows that he can avoid the necessity of using such force with complete safety by retreating"); Commonwealth v. Palmer, 467 Pa. 476, 359 A.2d 375 (1976).

60. E.g., Beard v. United States, 158 U.S. 550, 15 S.Ct. 962, 39 L.Ed. 1086 (1895) (attacked on own land 50–60 yards from his dwelling house; but the case is not clear whether the defender need not retreat wherever he is, or need not retreat when he is on his own land); State v. Baratta, 242 Iowa 1308, 49 N.W.2d 866 (1951) (attacked in his place of business); State v. W.J.B., ___ W.Va. ___, 276

S.E.2d 550 (1981) (attacked in his own dwelling).   See Annots., 41 A.L.R.3d 584 (1972); 52 A.L.R.2d 1458 (1957).

As for application of the rule when defendant is outside his house, compare State v. Pugliese, 102 N.H. 728, 422 A.2d 1319 (1980) (statute construed to adopt common law rule, and thus no retreat needed outside house but within curtilage); with State v. Bonano, 59 N.J. 515, 284 A.2d 345 (1971) (reasoning "better rule" is to require retreat into the dwelling.   The rule has even been held applicable to attack in one's social club, State v. Marlowe, 120 S.C. 205, 112 S.E. 921 (1922); his automobile, State v. Borwick, 193 Iowa 639, 187 N.W. 460 (1922); and when a guest in another's house, Kelley v. State, 226 Ala. 80, 145 So. 816 (1933); Barton v. State, 46 Md.App. 616, 420 A.2d 1009 (1980).

61. As stated in United States v. Peterson, 483 F.2d 1222 (D.C.Cir.1973), "the law is well settled that the 'castle' doctrine can be invoked only by one who is without fault in bringing the conflict on."

62. On the ground that this exception to the retreat requirement is based upon the defender's interest in the premises and the assailant's status as an intruder upon those premises, some courts have held that there is a duty to retreat when the attack is by one who is a co-occupant of the premises.   State v. Shaw, 185 Conn. 372, 441 A.2d 561 (1981); State v. Bobbitt, 415 So.2d 724 (Fla.1982); State v. Grierson, 96 N.H. 36, 69 A.2d 851 (1949); State v. Pontery, 19 N.J. 457, 117 A.2d 473 (1955).   This does not include an attack by a mere guest.   State v. Felton, 180 N.J.Super. 361, 434 A.2d 1131 (1981); Commonwealth v. Eberle, 474 Pa. 548, 379 A.2d 90 (1977).   See Annot., 100 A.L.R.3d 532 (1980).   The majority view, however, is to the contrary.   People v. Lenkevich, 394 Mich. 117, 229 N.W.2d 298 (1975); State v. Sales, 285 S.C. 113, 328 S.E.2d 619 (1985).   The majority view is apparently based upon the notion that the status of the person attacking is not relevant and that the dominant consideration is the fact that the defender has no safer place to which to retreat.   See Annot., 26 A.L.R.3d 1296 (1969).

63. People v. Johnson, 75 Mich.App. 337, 254 N.W.2d 667 (1977).

64. Model Penal Code § 3.04(2)(b)(ii).

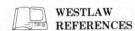

203k118

(g) Accidental Injury to Third Person.

If *A* in proper self-defense aims at his adversary *B* but misses *B* and unintentionally strikes innocent bystander *C*, he is not liable for *C*'s injury or death.[65] But the result is otherwise if under all the circumstances (including the need to defend himself) *A* was reckless with regard to *C*. In such a case he would be liable for battery if he merely injures, involuntary manslaughter if he kills, *C*.[66]

self-defense   /p   injury death "transferred intent"   /p
    bystander

(h) Resisting Unlawful Arrest.

A problem much like that of self-defense against unlawful aggression is that concerning the right to use force to resist an unlawful arrest. Here the threatened harm is not, as with self-defense, that of bodily injury or death but rather the indignity and inconvenience of undergoing arrest and its accompanying detention. In most jurisdictions the arrested person is justified in using nondeadly force,[67] but not in using deadly force,[68] to resist the arrest. (If he uses deadly force, intentionally killing the arresting person, he may, by a view, have his crime mitigated from murder to voluntary manslaughter, on the theory that the unlawful arrest is the sort of provocation which causes reasonable men to lose their self-control.) [69]

It is arguable, however, that it is not justifiable to use any force to resist an unlawful arrest by one whom the arrested person knows to be a police officer. There are remedies for release available to one unlawfully arrested,[70] and the indignity of the arrest and the inconvenience of the detention until release are relatively minor matters, goes the argument; the remedies should be used rather than force.[71] The Model Penal Code adopts a rule outlawing the use of force against a known police officer, though the arrest is unlawful.[72] Many of the modern codes include

---

65. People v. Adams, 9 Ill.App.3d 61, 291 N.E.2d 54 (1972); State v. Green, 157 W.Va. 1031, 206 S.E.2d 923 (1974).

66. See People v. Jackson, 390 Mich. 621, 212 N.W.2d 918 (1973); Model Penal Code § 3.09(3). If one *intentionally* kills an innocent third person to save himself from another's attack, he does not have the defense of self-defense. Cf. State v. Soine, 348 N.W.2d 824 (Minn.App. 1984) (self-defense did not justify defendant's threatening of innocent bystanders in an effort to "even the score"). As to the possibility of the defense of duress, see § 5.3.

67. See John Bad Elk v. United States, 177 U.S. 529, 20 S.Ct. 729, 44 L.Ed. 874 (1900) (deadly force in fact used); State v. Bowen, 118 Kan. 31, 234 P. 46 (1925); Hughes v. Commonwealth, 19 Ky.L.R. 497, 41 S.W. 294 (1897) (officer's manner of making unlawful arrest reasonably caused defendant to believe life in danger; deadly force used); People v. Cherry, 307 N.Y. 308, 121 N.E.2d 238 (1954) (nondeadly force); State v. Hooker, 17 Vt. 658 (1845) (nondeadly force).

68. State v. Perrigo, 67 Vt. 406, 31 A. 844 (1895); State v. Gum, 68 W.Va. 105, 69 S.E. 463 (1910). A few states, however, have allowed the use of deadly force: Perdue v. State, 5 Ga.App. 821, 63 S.E. 922 (1909); State v. Bethune, 112 S.C. 100, 99 S.E. 753 (1919); Cf. People v. Burt, 51 Mich. 199, 16 N.W. 378 (1883) (reduction to manslaughter). If the officer making the unlawful arrest assaults the arrested person in such a way as to cause him reasonably to fear for his life, the latter may use deadly force: Hughes v. Commonwealth, supra note 67.

69. See § 7.10(b)(4), citing cases which indicate a dispute as to whether unlawful arrest is a reasonable provocation.

70. The unlawfully arrested person may apply to a magistrate for release upon a writ of habeas corpus, but he will not be entitled to release in spite of the unlawful arrest if at the time of the hearing on the writ there is established probable cause to believe he has committed the crime. See Waite, The Law of Arrest, 24 Tex.L.Rev. 279, 281 (1946).

71. See Notes, 7 Nat.Res.J. 119 (1967); 3 Tulsa L.Rev. 40 (1966).

In People v. Curtis, 70 Cal.2d 347, 74 Cal.Rptr. 713, 450 P.2d 33 (1969), the defendant unsuccessfully argued that a statute forbidding the use of force to resist an unlawful arrest by a known police officer was unconstitutional, in that it eliminated the remedy of self-help against arrests in violation of the Fourth Amendment. See Chivigny, The Right to Resist an Unlawful Arrest, 78 Yale L.J. 1128 (1969) (arguing self-help should be permitted in certain circumstances); Lerblance, Impeding Unlawful Arrest: A Question of Authority and Criminal Liability, 61 Denver L.J. 655 (1984) (favoring "a test for criminality based on reasonableness," that is, whether the resistance was reasonable in view of the totality of the "circumstances of the encounter," depending upon whether there "was a substantial impediment" of the officer and "whether the resistance was a blameworthy act," focusing on "whether the circumstances were such as to provoke a person into defensive conduct," id. at 697–99).

72. Model Penal Code § 3.04(2)(a)(i).

such a provision,[73] and even in the absence of such an enactment some courts have abandoned the common law view.[74]

WESTLAW REFERENCES

self-defense /s resist! /s unlawful /s arrest

(i) "Imperfect" Self-Defense. We have noted that one who uses force against another with an honest but unreasonable belief that he must use force to defend himself from an imminent attack by his adversary is not, in most jurisdictions, justified in his use of force, for proper self-defense requires that the belief in the necessity for the force he uses be reasonable.[75] Although in many jurisdictions such a person is guilty of murder when he uses deadly force in such circumstances, some courts and legislatures have taken the more humane view that, while he is not innocent of crime, he is nevertheless not guilty of murder; rather, he is guilty of the in-between crime of manslaughter.[76]

WESTLAW REFERENCES

self-defense manslaughter /p honest! unreasonabl* /s belie*** /s force /s necess***

---

§ 5.8   Defense of Another

The prevailing rule is that one is justified in using reasonable force in defense of another person, even a stranger, when he reasonably believes that the other is in immediate danger of unlawful bodily harm from his adversary and that the use of such force is necessary to avoid this danger. Deadly force is reasonable force only when the attack of the adversary upon the other person reasonably appears to the defender to be a deadly attack.

(a) Relationship to Person Defended. Some early English cases suggested that force may not be used in defense of another unless the defender stands in some personal relationship to the one in need of protection (e.g., husband, wife, child, parent, relative, or employee or employer),[1] and some American statutes still on the books purport to limit the use of force in defense of others to the defense of those who bear some designated relationship to the defender.[2] Yet the modern and better rule is that there need be no such relationship, so that one is entitled in an appropriate case to use force to protect a friend or acquaintance or even a stranger from threatened harm by a third person.[3] The modern codes rather consistently take this view.

WESTLAW REFERENCES

di(defense +2 another) & relationship /s victim defendant intervenor aggressor

(b) Reasonable Belief in Necessity for Force. As with self-defense, so too with the defense of another, one is not justified in using force to protect the other unless he

---

73. Some follow the Model Penal Code in declaring there is no right to resist only if it was "known" the other party was a police officer. Some instead require that it "reasonably appears" to the defendant that the other party was a police officer.

Some statutes extend the rule to resistance of one known or reasonably believed to be assisting a peace officer. Some statutes make explicit what is surely true elsewhere as well: a person may still defend against excessive force in making the arrest.

74. See, e.g., Commonwealth v. Moreira, 388 Mass. 596, 447 N.E.2d 1224 (1983); State v. Kutchara, 350 N.W.2d 924 (Minn.1984).

75. See § 5.7(c).

76. See, e.g., People v. Flannel, 25 Cal.3d 668, 160 Cal. Rptr. 84, 603 P.2d 1 (1979); State v. Jones, 299 N.C. 103, 261 S.E.2d 1 (1980); and further discussion in § 7.11(a). This means that when the defense of self-defense is properly interposed, it will ordinarily be necessary to instruct the jury on this variety of voluntary manslaughter as well. People v. Lockett, 82 Ill.2d 546, 45 Ill.Dec. 900, 413 N.E.2d 378 (1980).

§ 5.8

1. This is no longer the English view. Denman, J., in Regina v. Prince, L.R. 2 Cr.Cas.Res. 154 (1875).

2. Model Penal Code § 3.05, Comment (Tent. Draft No. 8, 1958), lists statutes from 16 states. However, such provisions are seldom found in states with modern recodifications.

3. Williams v. State, 70 Ga.App. 10, 27 S.E.2d 109 (1943) (stranger); State v. Totman, 80 Mo.App. 125 (1899) (apparently a bystander). New Jersey, which then had a statute which limited the defense-of-others defense to protection of spouses, parent, child, brother, sister, master, mistress or servant, allowed the defense to one who was no more than a friend of the person defended: State v. Fair, 45 N.J. 77, 211 A.2d 359 (1965).

reasonably believes that the other is in immediate danger of unlawful bodily harm and
that force is necessary to prevent that harm; [4]
and even when he entertains these reasonable
beliefs, he may not use more force than he
reasonably believes necessary to relieve the
risk of harm.[5]

The courts have experienced some difficulty
in the case where the defender goes to the aid
of another reasonably believing the other is in
danger of unlawful bodily harm, but in fact
the bodily harm directed at him is lawful.
Thus B unlawfully attacks C and C defends
himself in proper self-defense (or plainclothes
policeman C tries lawfully to arrest B and
properly uses force against B in making the
arrest). A arrives on the scene and, not
knowing the true facts, reasonably concludes
that B is the innocent victim of an unlawful
attack by C; so A goes to B's rescue and uses
force against C.

One set of cases adopts what is sometimes
called the "alter ego" rule, which holds that
the right to defend another is coextensive
with the other's right to defend himself; thus
the defender A who intervenes to protect B
against C takes the risk that B is not in fact
privileged to defend himself in the manner he
employs; so that, where B is not privileged, A
is guilty of assault and battery or murder of B
in spite of his reasonable belief that B is
privileged.[6] It has been argued that, at least
in the case of the policeman in civilian
clothes, such a rule is necessary to prevent
the hampering of law enforcement.[7]

The other view is that, so long as the defendant reasonably believes that the other is
being unlawfully attacked, he is justified in
using reasonable force to defend him.[8] This
view, which has been adopted in the new state
criminal codes, is surely the preferable view.
As the New Jersey court expressed it: not
only, on a matter of justice, should one "not

4. If the harm to the third party is over, this defense
does not authorize resort to punitive or retaliatory force.
Commonwealth v. Monico, 373 Mass. 298, 366 N.E.2d 1241
(1977).

5. See § 5.7(c). Most of the statutes cited there also
encompass the defense-of-another situation.

6. E.g., People v. Young, 11 N.Y.2d 274, 229 N.Y.S.2d
1, 183 N.E.2d 319 (1962) (defendant guilty of battery for
using nondeadly force against plainclothes policeman trying to make lawful arrest); State v. Wenger, 58 Ohio St.2d
336, 390 N.E.2d 801 (1979) (no defense, as person assisted
was being lawfully arrested without unnecessary force);
Moore v. State, 25 Okl.Crim. 118, 218 P. 1102 (1923)
(defendant guilty of assault with intent to kill for using
deadly force against one who was properly defending self
against defendant's brother); State v. Gelinas, ___ R.I. ___,
417 A.2d 1381 (1980) (defendant-intervenor stands in shoes
of the other person, thus no defense unless other person
could defend because of arresting officer's excessive force);
State v. Cook, 78 S.C. 253, 59 S.E. 862 (1907) (defendants
guilty of murder for killing special policeman, apparently
in plain clothes, trying lawfully to arrest defendants'
sister); Murphy v. State, 188 Tenn. 583, 221 S.W.2d 812
(1949) (defendant guilty of voluntary manslaughter for
killing one using proper force in self-defense against defendant's son); Leeper v. State, 589 P.2d 379 (Wyo.1979)
(defendant in shoes of her husband, who had no right of
self-defense because engaging in mutual combat). See
Note, 8 Minn.L.Rev. 340 (1924).

7. This argument was advanced and rejected in State
v. Chiarello, 69 N.J.Super. 479, 174 A.2d 506 (1961).

8. E.g., Fersner v. United States, 482 A.2d 387 (D.C.
App.1984) (in murder prosecution, trial judge erred in
instructing that defendant's right to use force in defense
of another of a certain amount depended exclusively on

the perceptions of the third party); State v. Menilla, 177
Iowa 283, 158 N.W. 645 (1916) (defendant killed her husband reasonably but erroneously believing husband was
about to kill son unless she shot husband first; this is
justifiable defense of another, although son knew he was
in no danger and so could not himself have killed father in
self-defense); Alexander v. State, 52 Md.App. 171, 447
A.2d 880 (1982), affirmed 294 Md. 600, 451 A.2d 664 (1982)
(defendant, a prisoner who assaulted a correctional officer,
had a defense if it reasonably appeared to him that other
prisoner being unlawfully beaten); Commonwealth v.
Martin, 369 Mass. 640, 341 N.E.2d 885 (1976) (same);
State v. Fair, 45 N.J. 77, 211 A.2d 359 (1965) (defendant
killed in defense of another reasonably but erroneously
believing that the one he killed was trying to kill the third
person); State v. Chiarello, supra note 8 (defendant, reasonably but erroneously believing two men were trying to
murder Edwards, struck at the two with a deadly weapon;
Edwards would not have been justified in using such force
in self-defense; held, defendant not guilty of assault with
deadly weapon); State v. Robinson, 213 N.C. 273, 195 S.E.
824 (1938) (stepson, reasonably but erroneously believing
that stepfather was properly defending himself against
third party's deadly attack, killed the latter; under these
circumstances, stepson was justified in killing third party
to prevent the supposed felony); Mayhew v. State, 65 Tex.
Crim. 290, 144 S.W. 229 (1912) (in murder case, where
defendant went to aid of his son who was the aggressor
against the third party, instruction that one may act in
defense of another only if the other justified in defending
self held error; it is the defendant's own intent which
governs; and if he reasonably believes the other needs
protection, he is entitled to act on that belief, though it is
erroneous). See Notes, 8 Minn.L.Rev. 340 (1924); 35 Okla.
L.Rev. 141 (1982).

be convicted of a crime if he selflessly attempts to protect the victim of an apparently unjustified assault, but how else can we encourage bystanders to go to the aid of another who is being subject to assault?" [9] To impose liability upon the defender in these circumstances is to impose upon him liability without fault; and yet the assault and homicide crimes are crimes which require fault.

The defense of defending of others overlaps somewhat with the defense of crime prevention.[10] Thus one may be justified in defending another person in order to prevent the commission of a felony (e.g., murder, assault with intent to kill or do serious bodily injury) upon him.[11] There may be some situations where the defense of others may be justified only on the grounds of crime prevention.[12]

 WESTLAW REFERENCES

"defense of another" /p "alter ego" (reasonable! /s belie***) imminent immediate /s harm injury

(c) Necessity for Retreat. Because many jurisdictions have adopted a retreat rule with respect to the defense of self defense,[13] often in statutory provisions which also extend to defense of third parties, this rule is frequently applicable in the present context as well. It is apparent, however, that the retreat alternative must be assessed somewhat differently here. To take the most obvious case, surely the ability of the defendant to retreat without risk to himself should not control when the force is being used to protect another party who cannot retreat.

A few of the modern codes substantially follow the Model Penal Code [14] by giving special attention to when retreat is and is not

required in a defense-of-another situation. Under the Code, the defender who would be required to retreat if defending himself need not do so here unless he knows he can thereby secure the complete safety of the person being defended. If the person being defended would be required to retreat, then the defender must try to cause him to do so if the defender knows he could obtain complete safety in that way. Finally, the dwelling-workplace exception to the retreat rule applies here if the place is the dwelling or place of work of either the defender or the person defended.

 WESTLAW REFERENCES

"defense of another" /p retreat

§ 5.9 Defense of Property

One is justified in using reasonable force to protect his property from trespass or theft, when he reasonably believes that his property is in immediate danger of such an unlawful interference and that the use of such force is necessary to avoid that danger. Under the better view, deadly force is never reasonable except where the unlawful interference with property is accompanied by a threat of deadly force (in which case it is proper to use deadly force in self-defense), or where the unlawful interference involves an invasion of an occupied dwelling house under circumstances causing the defender reasonably to believe that the invader intends to commit a felony therein or to do serious bodily harm to its occupants.

(a) Generally. One whose lawful possession [1] of property is threatened by the unlaw-

9. State v. Fair, 45 N.J. 77, 211 A.2d 359, 368 (1965).

10. See § 5.10(c).

11. E.g., State v. Robinson, supra note 8.

12. Commonwealth v. Jackson, 467 Pa. 183, 355 A.2d 572 (1976) (aunt-niece relationship not sufficient to allow defense of relative, as statute lists only husband, wife, child or servant; aunt nonetheless had a defense under the more limited prevention-of-felony statute, as niece in fact subjected to felonious attack). Cf. Mitchell v. State, 43 Fla. 188, 30 So. 803 (1901) (defendant killed in defense of sister, reasonably but erroneously believing she was the subject of unlawful deadly attack; conviction of manslaughter *held* affirmed because (1) the statute on defense

of others did not list the brother-sister relationship, so this defense was unavailable; (2) the defense of crime prevention was unavailable because the applicable statute requires that a felony actually be committed—it is not enough that the defendant reasonably believed it to be committed).

13. See § 5.7(f).

14. Model Penal Code § 3.05(2).

§ 5.9

1. The cases have generally been concerned with intrusion upon the right of possession of the individual using protective force. However, some modern statutes autho-

ful conduct of another, and who has no time to resort to the law for its protection, may take reasonable steps, including the use of force,[2] to "prevent or terminate"[3] such interference with the property. The defender of property, to justify the use of force, must reasonably believe[4] (a) that his real property is in immediate danger of unlawful entry or trespass, or that his personal property is in immediate danger of an unlawful trespass or carrying away, and (b) that the use of force is necessary to avoid this danger.[5]

Even when he entertains these reasonable beliefs, however, he may not use more than reasonable force—the amount of force that reasonably appears necessary to prevent the threatened interference with the property.[6] It is not reasonable to use any force at all if the threatened danger to property can be avoided by a request to the other to desist from interfering with the property.[7] And even when it is reasonable to use some force,

it is not reasonable to use deadly force to prevent threatened harm to property, such as a mere trespass or theft, even though the harm cannot otherwise be prevented.[8] This is because the preservation of human life is more important to society than the protection of property.[9] Of course, if the defender's reasonable force in protection of his property is met with an attack upon his person, he may then respond by defending himself and then may be entitled to use deadly force.[10]

 WESTLAW REFERENCES

to("defense of property")

(b) Defense of Dwelling.[11] In the case of a mere civil trespass upon a dwelling, the rule stated above also applies, so that once again deadly force may not be used.[12] Yet, it has long been recognized that the limitations on the use of force to protect other property are not always applicable when defense of a

---

rize use of force to protect another's property. See § 5.9(e).

2. Thus, the defense is typically interposed in a prosecution for criminal homicide or battery. But this is not inevitably the case; see, e.g., State v. Gallagher, 191 Conn. 433, 465 A.2d 323 (1983) (common law right to resist unlawful entry applies to illegal entry by police officer to arrest, notwithstanding fact that defendant would not be justified in resisting the arrest itself merely because it illegal). Model Penal Code § 3.06(4) would also allow use of confinement as protective force, provided the confinement is terminated as soon as it is safe to do so. A few states have adopted such a provision.

3. Virtually all of the statutes cited herein use this language, which is significant. See, e.g., State v. Nelson, 329 N.W.2d 643 (Iowa 1983) (such language does not permit recovery of personal property wrongfully taken on an earlier occasion); State v. Farley, 225 Kan. 127, 587 P.2d 337 (1978) (such language permits defense of dwelling even after entry completed).

4. Model Penal Code § 3.06(1) requires only an honest belief; it need not in addition be reasonable. This is in accordance with its view concerning self-defense, defense of another, law enforcement, etc., that one should not be guilty of a crime of intention, like intent-to-injure battery and intent-to-kill murder, unless he has the required intent. The Code does provide for the possibility of guilt of a crime of recklessness (e.g., recklessness-manslaughter, recklessness-battery) if the mistake is a reckless one. Id. at § 3.09(2). Some modern statutes follow the Model Penal Code in this respect. The others require a reasonable belief.

5. Most modern codes contain a statute so providing.

6. Thus the use of force for the purpose of revenge after the harm to the property has occurred is not privileged. State v. Allen, 131 W.Va. 667, 49 S.E.2d 847 (1948).

7. State v. Cessna, 170 Iowa 726, 153 N.W. 194 (1915); State v. Woodward, 50 N.H. 527 (1871). See Model Penal Code § 3.06(3)(a), which requires a request before using force unless making the request would be useless or dangerous. But only a few of the defense-of-property statutes in the modern codes make this explicit.

8. State v. Metcalfe, 203 Iowa 155, 212 N.W. 382 (1927) (chicken-stealing case; in defense of property against trespass not involving force or danger to the property owner, one may not use deadly force); Commonwealth v. Beverly, 237 Ky. 35, 34 S.W.2d 941 (1931) (chicken-stealing case; in defense of his property, even against a nonviolent felony not involving invasion of the home, one may use reasonable force short of deadly force); Commonwealth v. Emmons, 157 Pa.Super. 495, 43 A.2d 568 (1945) (defendant shot from her house and seriously wounded in the street one who she believed was stealing her automobile; conviction of aggravated battery *held* affirmed, for the felony of larceny is not a felony by force, and the defendant was not defending her habitation); Montgomery v. Commonwealth, 98 Va. 840, 36 S.E. 371 (1900) (mere trespass does not justify landowner using deadly force). See Note, 18 Minn.L.Rev. 77 (1933); Annots., 25 A.L.R. 508 (1923), 32 A.L.R. 1541 (1924), 34 A.L.R. 1488 (1925).

9. Simpson v. State, 59 Ala. 1 (1877).

10. See § 5.7.

11. See Comment, 50 U.Mo.K.C.L.Rev. 64 (1981).

12. Commonwealth v. McLaughlin, 163 Pa. 651, 30 A. 216 (1894); State v. Hibler, 79 S.C. 170, 60 S.E. 438 (1907).

dwelling [13] is involved,[14] although the courts are not in agreement as to when deadly force may be used.

An early view, based upon the English notion that defense of the home that sheltered life was just as important as defense of life itself,[15] permitted the householder to use deadly force if it reasonably appeared necessary to prevent forcible entry against his will after a warning to the intruder not to enter and to desist from the use of force.[16] Subsequent decisions have for the most part rejected this rule as too broad.[17] Some courts now say that deadly force is permissible only when the defender reasonably believes that the trespasser intends to commit a felony or do harm to him or another within the house.[18] This rule, incorporated into some statutes, also attaches special importance to the dwelling as a place of security, for it permits the use of deadly force even when the anticipated attack would not result in the killing or serious injury of someone within.[19] Other courts have adopted a still narrower view, more in keeping with the right of self-defense [20] and crime prevention,[21] by holding that deadly force may be used only against an entry of a dwelling reasonably believed to be for the purpose of committing a felony (including killing or doing great bodily harm therein).[22]

Modern statutes on protection of dwellings (or, of premises generally) state that necessary deadly force may be used to prevent or terminate some specific felony, such as arson or burglary or robbery, or all forcible felonies, or all felonies. By contrast, the Model Penal Code approach,[23] adopted in a few states, is more specific in its requirement that deadly force be limited to instances in which there is a substantial risk to the person. Deadly force may be used if the defender believes that the other person is attempting to commit or consummate arson, burglary, robbery or other felonious theft or property destruction and either (1) has employed or threatened deadly force against or in the presence of the defender, or (2) the use of force other than deadly force would expose the defender or another to substantial danger of serious bodily harm.

A separate question is that of whether the householder is entitled to use deadly force to resist dispossession of a dwelling. While the old common law view on use of force in defense of a dwelling was broad enough to permit deadly force under these circumstances,[24] the same is not true of the more limited rules on deadly force which have developed in recent years. Consideration of the dispossession case as a separate issue seems not to have occurred in this country,[25] except by the draftsmen of the Model Penal Code. Noting the difficult question of policy involved,[26] they

---

13. The special rules on defense of a dwelling have occasionally been applied to places of business as well, e.g., Suell v. Derricott, 161 Ala. 259, 49 So. 895 (1909), although it is questionable whether such an extension is proper.

14. State v. Couch, 52 N.M. 127, 193 P.2d 405 (1948).

15. The English cases are discussed in State v. Patterson, 45 Vt. 308 (1873).

16. Brown v. People, 39 Ill. 407 (1866); Young v. State, 74 Neb. 346, 104 N.W. 867 (1905); State v. Conally, 3 Or. 69 (1869).

17. Likewise, the modern codes do not contain such a broad rule.

18. Falco v. State, 407 So.2d 203 (Fla.1981); Smith v. State, 106 Ga. 673, 32 S.E. 851 (1899); Armstrong v. State, 11 Okl.Cr. 159, 143 P. 870 (1914).

19. People v. Eatman, 405 Ill. 491, 91 N.E.2d 387 (1950).

20. See § 5.7.

21. See § 5.10(c).

22. Carroll v. State, 23 Ala. 28 (1853); State v. Countryman, 57 Kan. 815, 48 P. 137 (1897); Morrison v. State, 212 Tenn. 633, 371 S.W.2d 441 (1963).

23. Model Penal Code § 3.06(3)(d)(ii).

24. Model Penal Code § 3.06, Comment at 92 (1985).

25. In England it has been held that deadly force may be used to resist dispossession, even against a landlord entering under a mistaken claim of right. Rex v. Hussey, 18 Crim.App. 160 (1924).

26. "On the one hand, it is desirable to reduce to a minimum the cases where fatal force may be used by way of self-help. To kill a man is, on a dispassionate view, an evil both more serious and more irrevocable than the loss of possession of a dwelling for a period during which a court order is being obtained to recover it, at least if no special circumstances are present. On the other hand, to be illegally ousted from one's dwelling is a provocation that is not to be depreciated. The inconvenience may be aggravated by the circumstances, as where the eviction takes place in the night, or far from other habitation. Moreover, any persistent effort to break into a home is likely to arouse in the householder a reasonable fear for

have taken the position that deadly force may only be used when "the person against whom the force is used is attempting to dispossess him of his dwelling otherwise than under a claim of right to its possession." [27]

(c) Use of Mechanical Devices. Just as one cannot use deadly force to protect his property from trespass or theft, so too he cannot use a deadly spring gun or other mechanical device as a protection against trespass or theft.[28] A killing by such a device is justifiable only if the one who employs the device would in fact have been justified in taking the life of the trespasser had he been present, as where the trespasser tries to enter an occupied dwelling to do great violence to the occupants or to commit a burglary therein.[29]

The Model Penal Code rejects the latter justification, taking the view that use of a deadly mantrap is never justifiable.[30] The common law rule was properly rejected on the ground that it does not prescribe a workable standard of conduct, in that liability depends upon fortuitous circumstances—the intentions of the trespasser who happens to be

killed or seriously injured by the mechanical device.[31] Under the Code, nondeadly mechanical devices such as spiked fences may justifiably be used to protect one's property.[32]

(d) Re-entry and Recaption. If a person reasonably believes that he has been illegally dispossessed of real or personal property by another, he may resort to reasonable nondeadly force to repossess the property if he acts immediately after the dispossession or upon hot pursuit.[33] Thus, a momentary advantage obtained by the supposed wrongdoer does not alter the rules on defense of property; where force is allowed to defend property, similar force may be used to regain possession promptly after its loss.[34]

Assume, however, that an attempt at recapture of a chattel is made only after some interval has elapsed since the dispossession. The common law rule is that the use of force in recaption is then not justified;[35] the victim of the original dispossession is left to his remedy in the courts.[36] The Model Penal Code, however, permits recaption of personal property at any time if the actor believes that the person against whom he uses force has no

---

his own safety, unless he knows that the assailant is breaking in under a claim of right." Model Penal Code § 3.06, Comment at 93 (1985).

27. Model Penal Code § 3.06(3)(d)(i). Only a few jurisdictions have adopted such a special provision.

28. State v. Green, 118 S.C. 279, 110 S.E. 145 (trespass); State v. Beckham, 306 Mo. 566, 267 S.W. 817 (1924) (petty theft). See Note, 18 Minn.L.Rev. 77 (1933); Annots., 47 A.L.R.3d 646 (1973); 44 A.L.R.3d 383 (1972).

29. State v. Barr, 11 Wash. 481, 39 P. 1080 (1895) (spring gun, set to protect an empty cabin, killed the trespasser trying to enter but not to commit burglary; conviction of murder *held* affirmed; but court intimates that a spring gun might be proper to protect an occupied dwelling against burglary); see other cases cited in Annots., supra note 28.

30. Model Penal Code § 3.06(5). Some of the modern codes expressly take this position. Occasionally this conclusion has been reached by courts even in the absence of such a provision. A leading case is People v. Ceballos, 12 Cal.3d 470, 116 Cal.Rptr. 233, 526 P.2d 241 (1974).

31. Model Penal Code § 3.06, Comment at 101 (1985).

32. Model Penal Code § 3.06(5) sets forth three requirements: (a) that the device is not designed to cause or

known to create a substantial risk of causing death or serious bodily harm; (b) that use of the device is reasonable under the circumstances, as the actor believes them to be; and (c) that the device is one customarily used for this purpose or that reasonable care is taken to make its use known to probable intruders. Some states have adopted such a provision.

33. State v. Elliot, 11 N.H. 540 (1841); State v. Dooley, 121 Mo. 591, 26 S.W. 558 (1894). "The retaking is not any the less immediate because the fresh pursuit turns out to be a protracted chase." Model Penal Code § 3.06, Comment at 84 (1985).

34. Ibid. Thus, even if the original aggressor acted under a claim of right, prompt recapture is still permissible, as the property could be defended against dispossession notwithstanding the claim of right. Ibid.

35. Allen v. People, 82 Ill. 610 (1876); State v. Dooley, note 40.

36. Most of the provisions in the modern codes use the phrase "prevent or terminate," which is somewhat ambiguous on this point. Such language, however, is likely to be interpreted as following the common law view. State v. Nelson, 329 N.W.2d 643 (Iowa 1983).

claim of right to possession of the property in question.[37] This is based upon the notion that the rules of the criminal law in this area, which are not likely to be known to the general public, should correspond to the privileges which "a well-conducted person would expect to have." [38]

Almost all states have legislation making it a crime for one entitled to the possession of land to recover it by force,[39] and thus the courts have held that forcible re-entry is not justified unless made immediately upon the wrongful dispossession.[40] The theory is that because land is indestructible and buildings immovable, no harm is likely to result during the delay while the matter is determined in the courts.[41] Again, the Model Penal Code takes a broader view consistent with what is expected of the "well-conducted person": force may be used to re-enter, other than immediately after dispossession, if the actor believes (a) that the person against whom the force is used has no claim of right to possession, and (b) that the circumstances are of such urgency that it would be an exceptional hardship to postpone action until a court order could be obtained.[42]

 **WESTLAW
REFERENCES**

reasonable! necess*** /5 force /p re-entry
  re-capture recover /s land chattel property

(e) Property of Another. Although, as we have seen,[43] virtually all the modern codes have recognized the right to come to the defense of third parties who are threatened with

bodily harm, the situation is different as to defense of another's property. Some of the statutes dealing with all forms of property allow defense by anyone; others permit defense only by the person whose property is threatened or who is "in lawful possession" of the property, and still others recognize specific third-party relationships justifying property defense: where there is a legal duty to protect the property, where the owner has requested assistance, or where there is a family or similar relationship. There are also statutes dealing with certain types of property, such as dwellings [44] or non-premises, which permit defense by any third party. But many other special-category statutes are much more limited. There are protection-of-premises provisions allowing defense only by a "person in lawful possession or control" or a "person who is licensed or privileged to be therein." Some statutes dealing only with defense of dwellings permit defense only by the person whose dwelling it is [45] or by anyone within the dwelling, and some statutes on non-premises are also limited to property of the defender. And then there are a group of non-dwelling provisions which require that the property be lawfully in the possession of the defender or a member of his immediate family or belong to a person whose property he has a legal duty to protect.

The Model Penal Code approach [46] is grounded in the conclusion that there is "no adequate reason for limiting the privilege to protect property of others." [47] The narrower approach taken in the many statutes referred

37. Model Penal Code § 3.06(1)(b)(ii). Thus, for example, it would not be permissible under the Code to use force against a bona fide purchaser of the goods from the wrongdoer, even though he has not acquired title. Model Penal Code § 3.06, Comment (Tent.Draft No. 8, 1958). Only a few of the modern codes contain such a provision.

38. Model Penal Code § 3.06, Comment (Tent.Draft No. 8, 1958).

39. W. Prosser & W. Keeton, Torts § 23 (5th ed. 1984).

40. State v. Webb, 163 Mo.App. 275, 146 S.W. 805 (1912).

41. Model Penal Code § 3.06, Comment at 86 (1985).

42. Model Penal Code § 3.06(1)(b)(ii). "To give examples of situations where exceptional hardship may be found; the land may carry a mature crop that will rot if not immediately harvested; or the premises may be the

seat of a business or profession (e.g. a doctor's office or a school) that will suffer grave damage if the owner is not able to carry it on." Model Penal Code § 3.06, Comment at 87 (1985). Again, only a few of the modern codes contain such a provision.

43. See § 5.8(a).

44. See, e.g., People v. Stombaugh, 52 Ill.2d 103, 284 N.E.2d 640 (1972) (non-occupant guest may defend).

45. Such statutes are sometimes construed more broadly; see, e.g., State v. Mitcheson, 560 P.2d 1120 (Utah 1977) (person may defend his substitute habitation, as where he a guest in a hotel, motel or home of another).

46. Model Penal Code § 3.06(1).

47. Model Penal Code § 3.06, Comment at 37 (Tent. Draft No. 8, 1958).

to above appears to be based upon two policy judgments. One is that a mistake as to the respective legal rights of the disputants is more likely when property interests are involved. The other is that property interests are somewhat less deserving of protection and that consequently violence by strangers for the purpose of protecting such interests should not be encouraged.[48]

WESTLAW REFERENCES

ci(560 +5 1120)

§ 5.10 Law Enforcement (Arrest, Escape Prevention, Crime Prevention)

A police officer, or a person aiding him, is justified in using reasonable force to make a lawful arrest or to prevent the escape from custody of one already arrested. Deadly force may not be used to arrest or prevent the escape of a misdemeanant, but may be used in the case of a felon if it reasonably appears that the felon will otherwise avoid arrest or escape from custody.

One, not necessarily a police officer, is justified in using reasonable force to prevent or terminate what he reasonably believes to be the commission of a misdemeanor amounting to a breach of the peace or of a felony, but it is not reasonable to use deadly force except in the case of a "dangerous" felony.

(a) Effecting an Arrest.[1] At common law a police officer or private person may arrest without an arrest warrant for a felony or breach of the peace committed in his presence. In addition, an officer may arrest without a warrant for a felony not in his presence if he has reasonable grounds to believe (a) that a felony has been committed, and (b) that the person to be arrested committed it. A private person, however, is privileged to make such an arrest only if the felony has in fact been committed.[2]

The authority to arrest is now governed by statute in most jurisdictions. The prevailing view is that an officer may arrest under authority of an arrest warrant,[3] without a warrant on reasonable grounds to believe[4] that a felony has been committed by the person arrested,[5] or without a warrant for any offense committed in his presence.[6] The requirement of a warrant for misdemeanors out of the

---

48. For a vigorous argument against both of these reasons, see 2 P. Robinson, Criminal Law Defenses § 131(e)(2) (1984).

§ 5.10

1. See Pearson, The Right to Kill in Making Arrests, 28 Mich.L.Rev. 957 (1930); Perkins, The Law of Arrest, 25 Iowa L.Rev. 201, 265–289 (1940); Waite, The Law of Arrest, 24 Texas L.Rev. 279, 301–303 (1946).

For the converse situation of the right of one who is being arrested to use force to resist *unlawful* arrest, see § 5.7(h).

2. Bohlen & Shulman, Arrest With and Without a Warrant, 75 U.Pa.L.Rev. 485 (1927); Hall, Legal and Social Aspects of Arrest Without a Warrant, 49 Harv.L.Rev. 566 (1936); Wilgus, Arrest Without a Warrant, 22 Mich.L. Rev. 673 (1924).

3. It is common to provide by statute that the officer need not have the warrant with him at the time of arrest.

If the person arrested turns out to be someone other than the person named in the warrant, the prevailing view is that the officer is excused for the mistaken identity if he used reasonable diligence. Filer v. Smith, 96 Mich. 347, 55 N.W. 999 (1893); Wallner v. Fid. & Dep. Co., 253 Wis. 66, 33 N.W.2d 215 (1948).

4. Some state statutes on use of force by an officer to arrest state that in this context the reasonable belief must be "in facts or circumstances which if true would in law

constitute an offense," and that a mistake of law (however reasonable) will not suffice.

5. Another common statutory provision is that an officer may arrest a person who has committed a felony, which appears to mean that the arrest is valid if it turns out that the arrestee in fact did commit a felony, though the officer lacked reasonable grounds at the time of the arrest. See W. LaFave, Arrest: The Decision to Take a Suspect Into Custody 414–16 (1965); Waite, Public Policy and the Arrest of Felons, 31 Mich.L.Rev. 749 (1933). Such an arrest would not be a constitutional one under the Fourth Amendment bar against "unreasonable searches and seizures," for an arrest may not be justified on the basis of facts not known by the police at the time of the arrest. Henry v. United States, 361 U.S. 98, 80 S.Ct. 168, 4 L.Ed.2d 134 (1959).

It does not necessarily follow, however, that states may not characterize such arrests as "lawful" in the sense that reasonable force used in making them is privileged. Cf. People v. Curtis, 70 Cal.2d 347, 74 Cal.Rptr. 713, 450 P.2d 33 (1969) (statute barring use of force to resist unlawful arrest by police officer not unconstitutional on ground it eliminates remedy of self-help against arrests in violation of Fourth Amendment).

6. See 2 W. LaFave, Search and Seizure § 5.1(b) (1978). Under the better and prevailing view, the officer must have reasonable grounds to believe that an offense has been committed in his presence, and thus the arrest does

presence is sometimes too strict,[7] and thus in recent years some jurisdictions have allowed officers to arrest without warrant for misdemeanors on reasonable grounds to believe under some [8] or any circumstances. By statute, the power of private persons to arrest without warrant has typically been extended to all offenses occurring in the presence.[9]

Sometimes a police officer making a lawful arrest, with or without a warrant,[10] for a felony or misdemeanor, meets with such resistance as to make him reasonably believe that the person he is trying to arrest will immediately inflict on the officer bodily harm (or serious bodily harm or death), and that the only way to prevent it is to use moderate (or deadly) force upon the arrestee. In such a

situation, the officer's use of reasonable force is justifiable under the rules concerning the defense of self-defense,[11] except that, even in a jurisdiction which ordinarily requires a retreat, if it can be safely done, before using deadly force,[12] the officer making the arrest is not obliged to retreat.[13]

A different problem is presented when the person to be arrested, instead of resisting, flees, so that the officer is in no danger of any bodily harm. The general rule, as now commonly expressed by statute, is that the officer may utilize that degree of physical force which he reasonably believes necessary to make the arrest.[14] This is not to suggest, however, that the use [15] of deadly force is generally permissible whenever necessary.

---

not become unlawful after the fact if it turns out the person arrested committed no crime. Bursack v. Davis, 199 Wis. 115, 225 N.W. 738 (1929). See 2 W. LaFave, supra, at § 5.1(c).

7. See W. LaFave, supra note 5, at 17–21.

8. E.g., Neb.Rev.Stat. § 29–404.02, which permits an officer to arrest a person without a warrant if he "has reasonable cause to believe that such person has committed * * * a misdemeanor, and the officer has reasonable cause to believe that such person either (a) will not be apprehended unless immediately arrested; (b) may cause injury to himself or others or damage to property unless immediately arrested; (c) may destroy or conceal evidence of the commission of such misdemeanor; or (d) has committed a misdemeanor in the presence of the officer."

9. In contrast to the situation in which the arrest is by a police officer, see n. 6, supra, these statutes have usually been interpreted to mean that the offense must have in fact occurred. See Note, 65 Colum.L.Rev. 502 (1965), criticizing the rule as "inconsistent with the theory that citizen's arrests are a desirable and necessary adjunct to official law enforcement."

The power of private persons to arrest is seldom addressed in the modern substantive codes, though there are exceptions. Some permit arrest on reasonable belief of a felony in fact committed, some on reasonable belief of any offense in fact committed, one for any offense in the person's presence, and one on reasonable belief of a felony or of a misdemeanor in the presence.

10. An arrest, with or without a warrant, may not be lawful if the arresting person does not make known to the person to be arrested the purpose of the arrest, unless the latter knows very well what the purpose is. See Perkins, The Law of Arrest, 25 Iowa L.Rev. 201, 248–253 (1940). Therefore, Model Penal Code § 3.07(2)(a)(i) requires that the arresting person make known the purpose of the arrest, unless he believes that it is otherwise known by or cannot reasonably be made known to the person to be arrested. Several modern codes contain such a provison. This "notification requirement merely states what would in any case be required by the normal application of the

necessity requirement." 2 P. Robinson, Criminal Law Defenses § 142(f)(4) (1984).

11. E.g., State v. Reppert, 132 W.Va. 675, 52 S.E.2d 820 (1949) (officer making lawful arrest of misdemeanant is not justified in intentionally killing him when he forcibly resists arrest or tries to escape after arrest, unless the officer reasonably fears death or serious bodily injury); Durham v. State, 199 Ind. 567, 159 N.E. 145 (1927) (same).

Most of the modern code provisions on use of force by a police officer in making an arrest, refer in express terms to the officer's right to act in his own defense.

12. See § 5.7(f).

13. State v. Dunning, 177 N.C. 559, 98 S.E. 530 (1919) (while in an altercation between individuals one may have at times to retreat, this is not true of an officer arresting another under a warrant). Cf. People v. Ligouri, 284 N.Y. 309, 31 N.E.2d 37 (1940) (defendant, not a policeman, while trying to prevent a robbery from being committed against him, found a robber pointing a gun at him; he shot the robber, though he might have retreated safely; conviction of murder *held,* reversed; New York's retreat rule not applicable in prevention-of-felony case).

Statutes in modern codes imposing an obligation to retreat typically make it clear that this obligation does not apply to an officer or to a private person assisting an officer. Even in jurisdictions without a retreat doctrine, it is sometimes stressed that an officer attempting to arrest need not desist because of actual or threatened resistance.

14. In this context, it is not inevitably necessary that the arrest in fact be otherwise lawful. Several modern codes declare it is sufficient that the officer did not know the arrest was unlawful, that he reasonably believed it was lawful, that he actually believed it to be lawful, or that a "reasonable person would believe" it lawful.

Similar provisions dealing specifically with arrests made with a warrant are common. They provide that force may be used if the officer reasonably believed, the warrant valid, or unless he knew it was invalid.

15. As compared with a threat of such force, which some codes expressly recognize is permissible.

The common law view was that an officer may use deadly force, if he reasonably believes it necessary, to prevent the escape of a person fleeing from an arrest for a felony; but he may not use such force in the case of one fleeing from arrest for a misdemeanor, though the misdemeanant will otherwise escape.[16] This means an officer is not justified in shooting at a speeding automobile driver who does not heed his signal to stop: if he aims at the driver, he is guilty of murder when he kills; if he aims at the tires, this criminally negligent conduct should make him guilty of manslaughter for the resulting death to a motorist.[17]

The felony portion of the above rule may have made some sense in the days when all felonies were punishable by death; but it is too harsh a rule in these days of many felonies which are not subject to any such penalty.[18] Thus, while a significant minority of the modern codes follow the common law rule,

most do not.[19] Instead, they limit the use of deadly force to arrests for offenses in the forcible felony category, or for those felonies reasonably (or actually) believed to involve the use or threat of deadly force. Several of the codes add that deadly force may also be used, if necessary, where the person to be arrested is armed with a gun or it is believed that, if the arrest is delayed, there is a substantial risk that the person to be arrested will cause death or serious bodily harm.[20] But even if the officer might otherwise employ deadly force, he may not do so if it would create a substantial danger to innocent bystanders.[21]

These statutory provisions must now be construed in light of *Tennessee v. Garner,*[22] where the Court held that apprehension by the use of deadly force is a seizure subject to the reasonableness requirement of the Fourth Amendment, and that "use of deadly force to prevent the escape of all felony suspects,

16. Stinnett v. Virginia, 55 F.2d 644 (4th Cir.1932) ("That rule is that the officer has the right to use such force as under the circumstances appears reasonably necessary to effect the arrest or prevent the escape of the felon, and that, if the reasonable use of such force results in the death of the felon, the officer is not to be held criminally accountable therefor."); Durham v. State, supra note 11; State v. Smith, 127 Iowa 534, 103 N.W. 944 (1905) (an officer is not justified in killing a mere misdemeanant to effect his arrest or prevent his escape; modern notions concerning the sanctity of human life lead to the rule that it is better that the misdemeanant escape than that his life be taken; but it is otherwise with felons, though before deadly force is used on a felon there must be no other reasonably apparent method for making the arrest or preventing the escape); People v. Klein, 305 Ill. 141, 137 N.E. 145 (1922) (police officer may not shoot at automobile driver exceeding speed limit, although the officer cannot otherwise catch and arrest him; conviction of murder *held* affirmed); State v. Sigman, 106 N.C. 728, 11 S.E. 520 (1890) (same as State v. Smith, supra). If an officer properly uses nondeadly force against an arrestee resisting arrest, he is not responsible for the unexpected death of the arrestee produced by the nondeadly force. State v. Phillips, 119 Iowa 652, 94 N.W. 229 (1903) (policeman gave moderate blow on head with "billy"; arrestee had uncommonly thin skull).

17. People v. Klein, supra note 17. In some jurisdictions, by statute or case law, an officer may not use deadly force to arrest or prevent the escape of a felon, though he reasonably believes the other to be a felon and that deadly force is necessary to arrest him or prevent his escape, unless the arrestee has actually committed the felony, e.g., Commonwealth v. Duerr, 158 Pa.Super. 484, 45 A.2d 235 (1946), or unless the felony for which the arrest is made was actually committed by someone, though not necessar-

ily by the arrestee. But the right to use force to make an arrest ought to coincide with the law of arrest, which does not require for validity, in the case of arrest by a police officer, that the arrestee have actually committed the felony, or even that anyone have committed it. See note 6 supra.

18. Mogin, The Policeman's Privilege to Shoot a Fleeing Suspect: Constitutional Limits on the Use of Deadly Force, 18 Am.Crim.L.Rev. 533 (1981); Sherman, Execution Without Trial: Police Homicide and the Constitution, 33 Vand.L.Rev. 71 (1980).

19. See Day, Shooting the Fleeing Felon: State of the Law, 14 Crim.L.Bull. 285 (1978); Wukitsch, Survey of the Law Governing Police Use of Deadly Force, 55 N.Y.S.B.J. 12 (1983); Note, 12 Wm. & Mary L.Rev. 67 (1970). One study concludes that a movement away from the common law position via statute has not had a significant impact. Waegel, The Use of Lethal Force by Police: The Effect of Statutory Change, 30 Crime & Delinq. 121 (1984).

20. Some codes limit that provision to felonies, as does Model Penal Code § 3.07(2)(b), and others to felonies involving the use or threat of deadly force.

21. Model Penal Code § 3.07(2)(b). Some modern codes so state. Others instead say that the right to use force in making an arrest does not excuse reckless (and, sometimes, negligent) actions against innocent bystanders. The former type of provision has been criticized on the ground that it can sometimes "generate improper results": "even if the use of deadly force endangers an innocent bystander, the failure to use it could result in the death of many more." 2 P. Robinson, Criminal Law Defenses § 142(f)(5) (1984).

22. ___ U.S. ___, 105 S.Ct. 1694, 85 L.Ed.2d 1 (1985).

whatever the circumstances, is constitutionally unreasonable." Utilizing the Fourth Amendment "balancing process," the Court declared it had not been persuaded "that shooting nondangerous fleeing suspects" effectively served law enforcement interests which were "so vital as to outweigh the suspect's interest in his own life." As for the argument that the common law rule, "the prevailing rule at the time of the adoption of the Fourth Amendment," could hardly be unconstitutional under that Amendment, the *Garner* majority [23] responded that this was not so in light of "sweeping change in the legal and technological context": the common law rule arose when virtually all felonies were punishable by death, when all felons were relatively dangerous, and when deadly force required hand-to-hand combat and consequently risk to the arresting officer, but none of this was true today. Thus the Tennessee statute, which followed the common law approach, was deemed unconstitutional "insofar as it authorizes the use of deadly force against" an "unarmed, nondangerous suspect," such as the suspected fleeing and apparently unarmed burglar in the instant case.

As for when deadly force would be permissible, the Court explained:

> Where the officer has probable cause to believe that the suspect poses a threat of serious physical harm, either to the officer or to others, it is not constitutionally unreasonable to prevent escape by using deadly force. Thus, if the suspect threatens the officer with a weapon or there is probable cause to believe that he has committed a crime involving the infliction or threatened infliction of serious physical harm, deadly force

may be used if necessary to prevent escape, and if, where feasible some warning has been given.

Although this certainly means that a statute following the Model Penal Code formulation will pass muster, it must be emphasized that the Supreme Court did *not* expressly state (as did the court of appeals) that the Model Penal Code declares the "Fourth Amendment limitations on the use of deadly force against fleeing felons." Moreover, the Court asserted it was not adopting a rule which "requires the police to make impossible, split-second evaluations of unknowable facts." This suggests that certain types of statutes referred to earlier, such as those permitting deadly force against an *armed* felon or against a person who committed a type of felony defined in terms of actual or potential serious harm to a *person,* may also pass the *Garner* test, though they would permit use of deadly force when additional facts about the degree of actual danger in the particular case were yet lacking. Significantly, the Court refused to recognize such a general category with respect to the offense of burglary because it is only a crime against property and is rarely attended by physical violence.

A police officer is authorized to summon bystanders to assist him in effecting a lawful arrest.[24] Because the private citizen is required by law to respond to such a request,[25] he not only has the same authority as the officer to use force in making the arrest,[26] but may also be justified when the officer is not. Since the person summoned may not delay to inquire into the officer's authority to make that particular arrest, his good faith assistance is justified even if it turns out that the officer was exceeding his authority.[27]

---

23. The three dissenters objected: "A proper balancing of the interests involved suggests that use of deadly force as a last resort to apprehend a criminal suspect fleeing from the scene of a nighttime burglary is not unreasonable within the meaning of the Fourth Amendment."

24. Firestone v. Rice, 71 Mich. 377, 38 N.W. 885 (1888); McMahan v. Green, 34 Vt. 69, 80 Am.Dec. 665 (1861).

25. Babington v. Yellow Taxi Corp., 250 N.Y. 14, 164 N.E. 726 (1928); Moyer v. Meier, 205 Okl. 405, 238 P.2d 338 (1951).

26. Commonwealth v. Fields, 120 Pa.Super. 397, 183 A. 78 (1936). Modern codes typically say the private person may use the amount of force which is reasonably (or,

sometimes, actually) believed necessary to carry out the officer's directions. As for deadly force, the modern recodifications typically state it is permissible only if he was so authorized by the officer and did not know or believe that authorization to be improper.

27. Watson v. State, 83 Ala. 60, 3 So. 441 (1888).

Thus, Model Penal Code § 3.07(4)(a) provides that a private person summoned by an officer is justified in using whatever force would be proper if the arrest were lawful, provided that "he does not believe the arrest is unlawful." Many modern codes likewise say it is sufficient the private person did not know or believe the arrest was unlawful.

As to the comparatively rare situation in which a private person makes an arrest on his own, he acts at his peril in using deadly force. He is not privileged if it turns out that the person against whom the deadly force was used actually did not commit a dangerous felony.[28] The Model Penal Code takes the next logical step and bars the use of deadly force by a private person in making arrests except when that person believes he is assisting a peace officer.[29]

WESTLAW REFERENCES

find 105sct1694

felon* misdemean**** /p arrest*** /p police law-
enforcement +1 officer /p reasonabl!
unreasonable necess*** deadly non-deadly /s
force

(b) Preventing Escape From Custody by Arrested Person. One is justified in using force to prevent the escape of an already-arrested person to the same extent that he would be justified in using force to effect that person's arrest for the crime for which he is in custody.[30] Thus, since an officer is not justified in using deadly force to arrest a misdemeanant who is fleeing from arrest, so he is not justified in using such force to prevent the escape of one already arrested for a misdemeanor, though without the employment of such force the misdemeanant is sure to escape.[31]

However, most modern codes also permit a guard or policeman employed at a prison or jail to use any force, including deadly force, when reasonably believed necessary to prevent the escape of a person. This is because of the greater public interest in preventing escape by persons in institutions who are in the custody of the law and not merely of individuals.[32]

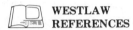

WESTLAW REFERENCES

escap*** /s detention jail custody hospital institution
/s reasonabl! unreasonabl! necess*** deadly nondeadly /s force

(c) Crime Prevention and Termination. The privilege to use force to prevent the commission of a crime about to be committed, or to prevent the consummation of a crime already underway, overlaps somewhat with two other privileges already discussed: (1) the privilege of the defense of property (in the case of a crime against property, like burglary and larceny), and (2) the privilege of self-defense or defense of another (in the case of a crime against the person, like murder, mayhem, assault and battery).[33] On the other hand, there are crimes which do not involve a threat of harm to property or to bodily security (e.g., treason, perjury, statutory rape), so that the justification, if any, for the use of force must come solely under the defense of crime prevention, which is not limited to police officers or those aiding them.

One who reasonably believes [34] that a felony, or a misdemeanor amounting to a breach

---

A requirement of an affirmative belief that the arrest is lawful was rejected as too stringent, as the person responding to the summons may not have the opportunity to reach any conclusion as to the lawfulness of the arrest. Model Penal Code § 3.07, Comment at 128 (1985).

Compare Model Penal Code § 3.07(4)(b), concerning the situations in which a private person assists another private person or, without being summoned, assists a police officer, where the person assisting in an unlawful arrest is justified in using the force permitted for a lawful arrest only if "(i) he believes the arrest is lawful, and (ii) the arrest would be lawful if the facts were as he believes them to be." Such provisions exist in a few jurisdictions.

28. Commonwealth v. Chermansky, 430 Pa. 170, 242 A.2d 237 (1968).

29. Model Penal Code § 3.07(2)(b)(ii). As originally proposed to the Institute, this provision permitted the use of deadly force by peace officers only. Model Penal Code § 3.07, Comment at 116 n. 25 (1985). Many modern codes

likewise state that the private person acting on his own may not use deadly force to arrest, but only if necessary for self defense.

30. This is typically made explicit in the modern codes.

31. Thomas v. Kinkead, 55 Ark. 502, 18 S.W. 854 (1982).

32. Model Penal Code § 3.07, Comment at 126 (1985).

33. Indeed, the great majority of the modern codes deal with crime prevention and termination within statutes concerning those two privileges. See §§ 5.7, 5.8, 5.9.

Where the privileges overlap, the defendant is entitled to the benefits of both if he acted for both purposes.

34. Model Penal Code § 3.07(5) requires only an honest belief; it need not in addition be reasonable. This is in accordance with its view concerning self-defense, defense of another, defense of property, etc., that one should not be guilty of a crime of intention, like intent-to-injure battery and intent-to-kill murder, unless he has the re-

of the peace,[35] is being committed, or is about to be committed, in his presence[36] may use reasonable force to terminate or prevent it. Thus moderate force may justifiably be used in such cases. But, as with self-defense, the law has jelled somewhat on the reasonableness of using deadly force in crime prevention.

Originally, the law was that deadly force was justifiable to prevent or terminate a felony, but was not justifiable to prevent or terminate a misdemeanor. This rule made some sense in the days when the relatively few felonies were all punishable by death anyway;[37] but with the expansion of the felony concept to many new types of conduct, and the lowering of the penalties for many felonies, it will not do today. It is a felony to file a false income tax return; but one is not justified in shooting the filer on his way to the mailbox, even though the filing cannot otherwise be prevented.

The modern rule limits the right to use deadly force to "dangerous" felonies (those felonies of the type which involve a substan-

tial risk of death or serious bodily harm)[38] or, as it is sometimes said, to "atrocious" felonies involving "violence or surprise."[39] Thus it is not justifiable to kill to prevent grand larceny[40] or adultery,[41] though these crimes cannot otherwise be prevented. It ought not to be justifiable to shoot to kill to prevent some modern statutory forms of burglary not involving the house, such as "burglary" of a hen house or telephone booth.[42] As to the dangerous (atrocious) felonies (e.g., murder, voluntary manslaughter, mayhem, kidnaping, arson, burglary of a dwelling, robbery, forcible sodomy, forcible rape), one is, of course, not justified in killing except when it reasonably appears necessary to kill to prevent the commission, or bring about the termination of the felony.[43] And the commission of the felony must appear to be imminent, rather than in the more distant future, to justify the use of such force.

There is a question, as to the dangerous felonies, whether the justification for killing should depend upon the type of felony involved, or whether it should depend on the

quired intent. The Code does provide for the possibility of guilt of a crime of recklessness (e.g. recklessness-manslaughter, recklessness-battery) if the mistake as to existence of a crime is a reckless one. Id. at § 3.09(2).

At the other extreme, some jurisdictions, generally by statute, require, for the use of deadly force to prevent felonies, more than that the actor reasonably believes that a crime (felony) is being or is about to be committed; the requirement is that the crime *actually* be committed or be about to be committed.

35. Spicer v. People, 11 Ill.App. 294 (1882) (use of force justified to prevent fighting or other breach of the peace, though only a misdemeanor). Model Penal Code § 3.07(5) allows force in crime prevention for "a crime involving or threatening bodily harm, damage to or loss of property or a breach of the peace."

36. State v. Marley, 54 Haw. 450, 509 P.2d 1095 (1973) (no defense to criminal trespass on property of major defense contractor that defendants sought to stop "war crimes," as information about those crimes received through the media did not satisfy the "in presence" requirement).

37. 4 W. Blackstone, Commentaries 182 (the law does not allow "any crime to be *prevented* by death, unless the same, if committed, would also be *punished* by death").

38. Restatement (Second) of Torts § 143(2) (1965).

39. Storey v. State, 71 Ala. 329 (1882) (not justifiable to kill to prevent felony of stealing a horse; examples of atrocious felonies: murder, robbery, house-breaking in the nighttime, rape, mayhem, any felony against the person);

Commonwealth v. Emmons, 157 Pa.Super. 495, 498, 43 A.2d 568, 569 (1945) (not justifiable to kill to prevent theft of car; "There is no right to kill in order to prevent *any* felony. To justify the killing it must be to prevent the commission of a felony which is either an atrocious crime or one attempted to be committed by force (or surprise) such as murder, arson, burglary, rape, kidnapping, sodomy or the like."); State v. Terrell, 55 Utah 314, 186 P. 108 (1919) (justifiable to shoot to kill to prevent burglary— here burglary of wire-enclosed pen holding commercially raised rabbits; this is a felony of violence or surprise); State v. Nyland, 47 Wash.2d 240, 287 P.2d 345 (1955) (not justifiable to kill to prevent adultery of wife and her male companion; adultery, though a felony, is not a felony of violence and surprise, like murder, robbery, burglary, arson, sodomy and rape).

40. Storey v. State, Commonwealth v. Emmons, both supra note 39.

41. State v. Nyland, supra note 46. Cf. Moore v. State, 91 Tex.Crim. 118, 237 S.W. 931 (1922) (justifiable to kill to prevent statutory rape).

42. Thus State v. Terrell, supra note 39, is wrong on principle.

43. E.g., Tolbert v. State, 31 Ala.App. 301, 15 So.2d 745 (1943) (requested instruction that if deceased when killed was attempting to rape defendant, defendant was justified in killing him *held* properly refused, for right to kill requires necessity to kill to prevent the rape, and the instruction did not contain this requirement).

risk encountered in the particular felony involved. Thus arson is a type of felony which generally involves a substantial risk of death or serious bodily harm; but in a particular case of arson there may be no such risk because of the arsonist's careful planning. If one kills to prevent this particular arson, is he justified because it is justifiable to kill to prevent arson, or is he not justified because this particular arson did not involve a substantial risk of death or serious bodily harm? Doubtless, the matter is generally treated in the former fashion,[44] but it would seem that the latter method is more just.[45]

In order to have the benefit of the defense of crime prevention, it is necessary that the actor act with the purpose (motive) of crime prevention. Thus he is not justified in shooting to death his enemy, though he later discovers, to his agreeable surprise, that the enemy was on the point of committing, or was in the process of committing, a dangerous felony.[46]

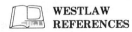 **WESTLAW REFERENCES**

203k107

(d) Other Law Enforcement Activity. Although the matter has seldom been litigated or made the subject of legislation,[47] it

would appear that in certain other circumstances the otherwise criminal conduct of a police officer, or a private person acting on behalf of an officer,[48] may be privileged because the person was pursuing law enforcement purposes at the time. Illustrative is *Lilly v. West Virginia,*[49] overturning an involuntary manslaughter conviction for a death caused by a federal agent's violation of the speeding laws while pursuing a violator. The court reasoned, in effect, that the applicable speeding prohibition contained an implied exception for "public officials engaged in the performance of a public duty where speed and the right of way are a necessity."

The question of how far this privilege extends, however, is most starkly presented as to undercover law enforcement activity by police and their agents. This undercover activity may include dealing in contraband substances,[50] and often involves providing inducement to others to engage in criminal activity. As to the latter, the inducements in some circumstances will constitute a defense, called entrapment,[51] for the person induced, and the common assumption is that when this is the case the encouraging police may be convicted of the crime in question.[52] Thus, it has been held that if game wardens, posing as fur buyers, induce some boys who would not other-

---

44. See supra, notes 38–39.

45. See Model Penal Code § 3.07(5)(a)(ii), requiring, for the use of deadly force in crime prevention (except to suppress a riot or mutiny) that the actor believe that there is a substantial risk that the person to be prevented from committing the crime will cause death or serious bodily harm to another unless the crime is prevented or terminated, and also that the use of the deadly force will not endanger innocent persons.

46. See Laws v. State, 26 Tex.Crim. 643, 10 S.W. 220 (1888) (instruction that defendant was not justified in killing victim if he killed him from a previously-formed intent to kill him, and not to prevent the theft then being committed, was properly given; but conviction of murder *held* reversed on other grounds); Regina v. Dadson, 4 Cox Crim.Cas. 358 (Ct.Crim.App.1850) (defendant shot at victim, stealing wood, a felony, but defendant did not know victim was stealing wood; conviction of shooting at another, with intent to do grievous bodily harm, *held* affirmed). Cf. Josey v. United States, 135 F.2d 809 (D.C.Cir.1943) and Trogdon v. State, 133 Ind. 1, 32 N.E. 725 (1892), both upholding the same principle in the area of self-defense.

47. But see Iowa Code Ann. § 704.11, declaring that in specified circumstances "a peace officer or person acting

as an agent of or directed by any police agency who participates in the commission of a crime by another person solely for the purpose of gathering evidence leading to the prosecution of such other person shall not be guilty of that crime or the crime of solicitation."

48. See Kohler v. Commonwealth, 492 S.W.2d 198 (Ky. 1973) (defendant entitled to instruction on his theory of defense in sale of heroin prosecution, namely, that he dealt in drugs at request of police in order to gather evidence of drug activity by others).

49. 29 F.2d 61 (4th Cir.1928).

50. Kohler v. Commonwealth, 492 S.W.2d 198 (Ky. 1973) (sale of heroin).

51. See § 5.2.

52. It is a basic principle of criminal law that one who induces another to commit a crime is himself guilty of the crime, as where *A* induces *B* to murder *C*. See § 6.7. The applicability of this principle to the entrapment situation is brought out in Mikell, The Doctrine of Entrapment in the Federal Courts, 90 U.Pa.L.Rev. 245, 264 (1942).

wise have done so to engage in forbidden beaver trapping, the boys are not to be punished, but the game wardens are guilty of illegal trapping.[53] It is doubtful, however, whether it makes sense to conclude that the officer is guilty in any instance in which the "target" was entrapped. Why should the officer's otherwise legitimate activity be punishable merely because, under the prevailing subjective theory of entrapment, it turns out that the object of the investigation was not predisposed? But the question has not received careful attention from the courts, as excessive zeal in law enforcement rarely leads to a criminal prosecution of the police.[54]

Presumably there are certain kinds of criminal conduct which are so serious that any law enforcement exception will not extend to them. "It would be unthinkable, for example, to permit government agents to instigate robberies and beatings merely to gather evidence to convict other members of a gang of hoodlums."[55] But once some other illegal activity is sanctioned for law enforcement purposes, "problems may be anticipated as to where to draw the line."[56]

Finally, it is well to note that in some circumstances the action taken for a law enforcement purpose will not be criminal simply because the required mental state was not present. Thus, as to the crime of "feloniously" (i.e., with an evil purpose) receiving stolen property, this element is not present where the purchaser obtained the property so that it

could be turned over to the authorities.[57] And one who helps another enter a store to take whiskey is not an accomplice to larceny and burglary where he intended to and immediately did summon the police, for the requisite intent to permanently deprive was not present.[58]

§ 5.11 Consent, Conduct, or Condonation by Victim

Consent of the victim is a defense only when it negatives an element of the offense or precludes infliction of the harm to be prevented by the law defining the offense. Neither the victim's guilt of a crime nor his contributory negligence is per se a defense. Likewise, the victim's subsequent condonation or ratification of the crime or acceptance of restitution is not a defense, although statutes in some jurisdictions permit the "compromise" of certain minor crimes by restitution.

(a) **Consent.** Generally, it may be said that consent by the victim is not a defense in a criminal prosecution.[1] The explanation most commonly given for this rule is that a criminal offense is a wrong affecting the general public, at least indirectly, and consequently cannot be licensed by the individual directly harmed.[2] Thus, it is no defense to a charge of murder that the victim, upon learning of the defendant's homicidal intentions, furnished the defendant with the gun and ammunition.[3] Nor is it a defense to the statu-

---

53. Reigan v. People, 120 Colo. 472, 210 P.2d 991 (1949).

54. Rather, instances of allegedly criminal conduct by those enforcing the law typically surface when another person is prosecuted and he raises an entrapment or due process defense. See, e.g., United States v. Brown, 635 F.2d 1207 (6th Cir.1980) (undercover agent participated in many burglaries); People ex rel. Difanis v. Boston, 92 Ill. App.3d 963, 48 Ill.Dec. 302, 416 N.E.2d 333 (1981) (undercover agents patronized prostitutes); State v. Pooler, 255 N.W.2d 328 (Iowa 1977) (undercover agent participated in break-in with defendant).

55. United States v. Archer, 486 F.2d 670 (2d Cir.1973) (stated, however, in context of discussion of another person's entrapment defense). The statute discussed in note 54 supra contains a proviso that the officer or agent "does not intentionally injure a nonparticipant in the crime."

56. Baucom v. Martin, 677 F.2d 1346 (11th Cir.1982) (state prosecution of FBI agent for bribery of state official

enjoined; prosecution barred under Supremacy Clause, as the agent's acts were authorized by federal law as part of his duties and he did no more than was necessary and proper for him to do).

57. Ward v. Commonwealth, 399 S.W.2d 463 (Ky.1966).

58. Wilson v. People, 103 Colo. 441, 87 P.2d 5 (1939).

§ 5.11

1. See, e.g., Harley v. United States, 373 A.2d 898 (D.C. App.1977) (crime of sodomy); State v. McFarland, 369 A.2d 227 (Me.1977) (crime of fellatio); State v. Steinbrink, 297 N.W.2d 291 (Minn.1980) (sexual conduct with person under 16).

2. State v. West, 157 Mo. 309, 57 S.W. 1071 (1900).

3. Martin v. Commonwealth, 184 Va. 1009, 37 S.E.2d 43 (1946). As for consent to life-ending procedures by a terminally ill patient, see Castel, Nature and Effects of Consent With Respect to the Right to Life and Right to Physical and Mental Integrity in the Medical Field, 16

tory offense of fraternity "hazing" that the pledges consented to the activity.[4]

Certain crimes, however, are defined in terms of the victim's lack of consent, and as to these the consent of the victim is obviously a bar to conviction.[5] Rape, for example, is typically defined as the "unlawful carnal knowledge of a woman without her consent," [6] and thus consent by the woman to sexual intercourse negatives an element of the offense.[7]

More troublesome are other crimes which, while not defined in terms of lack of consent by the victim, are concerned with the infliction of certain types of harm which may sometimes not occur if the victim has given some degree of consent.[8] Larceny, for example, requires a trespassory taking, which is

not present when the victim's consent is obtained in certain ways.[9] Likewise, the requirement of "unlawful" application of force for the crime of battery is sometimes not present because of the consent of the victim.[10] But consent to a battery is a defense only if "the bodily harm consented to or threatened by the conduct consented to is not serious." [11]

Assuming a situation in which consent is a defense, what constitutes consent? This question has been most frequently confronted, as might be expected, in cases where the charge was rape.[12] Submission to physical force [13] or to a threat of great and immediate bodily harm [14] is not consent.[15] Assent by one "who is legally incompetent" [16] or "who by reason of youth, mental disease or defect or intoxication

Alberta L.Rev. 293 (1978); Kennedy, The Legal Effect of Requests by the Terminally Ill and Aged Not to Receive Further Treatment from Doctors, 1976 Crim.L.Rev. 217.

4. People v. Lenti, 46 Misc.2d 682, 260 N.Y.S.2d 284 (1965).

5. Model Penal Code § 2.11(1) states consent is a defense "if such consent negatives an element of the offense." Some of the modern codes contain a comparable provision.

6. Adams v. Commonwealth, 219 Ky. 711, 294 S.W. 151 (1927).

7. Unless the consent is withdrawn before penetration occurs. Battle v. State, 287 Md. 675, 414 A.2d 1266 (1980).

8. Model Penal Code § 2.11(1) states consent is a defense, even if it does not negative an element, if it "precludes the infliction of the harm or evil sought to be prevented by the law defining the offense." Several of the modern codes contain such a provision. Under such a provision, for example, "the consent of a spouse should provide a defense to persistent non-support if the supported spouse neither needs nor desires support, and there are no dependent children." 1 P. Robinson, Criminal Law Defenses § 66(d) (1984).

9. See § 8.2, and Williams, Theft, Consent and Illegality, 1977 Crim.L.Rev. 127. See, e.g., Hill v. State, 253 Ark. 512, 487 S.W.2d 624 (1972) (consent of lienholder a defense to charge of disposing of property subject to lien).

10. See § 7.15. The Model Penal Code deals specifically with this situation by providing in § 2.11(2) that "when conduct is charged to constitute an offense because it causes or threatens bodily harm, consent to such conduct or to the infliction of such harm is a defense if: (a) the bodily harm consented to or threatened by the conduct consented to is not serious; or (b) the conduct and the harm are reasonably foreseeable hazards of joint participation in a lawful athletic contest or competitive sport."

11. Model Penal Code § 2.11(2)(a). Several modern codes contain such a provision.

Courts have rejected the claim that consent should be a defense even as to more serious injury if the victim was a

masochist who obtained pleasure from such severe treatment. People v. Samuels, 250 Cal.App.2d 501, 58 Cal. Rptr. 439 (1967), noted in 81 Harv.L.Rev. 1339 (1968); Commonwealth v. Appleby, 380 Mass. 296, 402 N.E.2d 1051 (1980). Compare Leigh, Sado-Masochism, Consent, and the Reform of the Criminal Law, 39 Modern L.Rev. 130 (1976), contending that if the victim consents to sadomasochistic activities there should be no criminal liability unless the conduct results in "mutilation," "disfigurement, either permanently or for an extended period," or "serious impairment of mental or physical powers either permanently or for a protracted period."

12. Where, however, the question has caused the greatest difficulty. See Note, 43 U.Chi.L.Rev. 613 (1976), contending "that the legal community has not yet developed a principled standard of effective nonconsent in rape. Instead, courts and legislatures have tried to manipulate evidence and other rules around an undefined issue, usually guided by questionable assumptions about rape complainants and rapists."

13. Almon v. State, 21 Ala.App. 466, 109 So. 371 (1926).

14. Harley v. United States, 373 A.2d 898 (D.C.App. 1977); Curtis v. State, 236 Ga. 362, 223 S.E.2d 721 (1976); State v. Rusk, 289 Md. 230, 424 A.2d 720 (1981); State v. Schuster, 282 S.W.2d 553 (Mo.1955). When there have been such threats, resistance by the victim is not required to negative consent. State v. Reinhold, 123 Ariz. 50, 597 A.2d 532 (1979).

15. The same would generally be true of other crimes where consent is a defense, although some account must be taken of the purpose of the statute in question. Thus, Model Penal Code § 2.11(3)(d) characterizes as "ineffective consent" that induced by force or duress "of a kind sought to be prevented by the law defining the offense." A few of the modern recodifications have a provision with this qualification, but more simply state without qualification that consent induced by force or duress is not consent.

16. Model Penal Code § 2.11(3)(a). Some modern codes contain such a provision. Ala.Code 1975, § 13A-2-7; Colo.Rev.Stat. 18-1-505; Del.Code tit. 11, § 453; Hawaii Rev.Stat. § 702-235; Me.Rev.Stat.Ann. tit. 17-A, § 109;

is manifestly unable or known by the actor to be unable to make a reasonable judgment as to the nature or harmfulness of the conduct charged to constitute the offense" [17] is not effective consent.[18]

As to assent by deception, the distinction which has traditionally been drawn is between fraud in the factum and fraud in the inducement. Fraud in the factum involves a form of deception which results in a misunderstanding by the victim as to the very fact of the defendant's conduct, while fraud in the inducement merely involves deception as to some collateral matter; the former cannot result in effective consent, but the latter can. For example, if a doctor engages in sexual intercourse with a female patient under circumstances in which she does not know what is occurring and believes that she is only submitting to an examination or operation, this is fraud in the factum and the woman cannot be said to have consented.[19] On the other hand, if the doctor convinces the woman that she should submit to intercourse because this would be effective treatment for her illness, the woman has given effective consent because this is only fraud in the inducement.[20] Just what is a "collateral matter" under this approach is sometimes a matter of dispute, as is reflected by the split of authority on the question of whether it is rape for a man to have intercourse with a woman by misrepresenting himself as her husband.[21] Perhaps it is more helpful to ask, as does the Model

Penal Code, whether the deception was "of a kind sought to be prevented by the law defining the offense." [22]

This same distinction between fraud in the factum and fraud in the inducement is also relevant as to other crimes defined in terms of lack of consent.[23] However, as to other offenses where consent is only sometimes a defense, such as battery, both forms of deception may be considered unlawful and thus a bar to effective consent.[24]

Because persons engaging in certain types of activities subject themselves, to some degree, to the risk of harm, the question naturally arises as to whether and to what extent the election to participate in certain activity amounts to consent to bodily harm. The issue is sometimes addressed by a statute declaring, for example, that one has consented to the "reasonably foreseeable hazards" of joint participation in a lawful athletic contest or competitive sport, of medical or scientific experimentation conducted by recognized methods, of a certain occupation or profession, or of other lawful activity. Under this test, it would appear that a participant in an athletic contest consents to that harm which is inflicted within the rules of the game and also that which occurs as a result of minor and common deviation from the rules, but not that attributable to deviations amounting to unprovoked exceedingly violent attacks.[25] As for medical or scientific experimentation, much depends upon the extent to which the

Mont.Code Ann. 45–2–211; N.H.Rev.Stat.Ann. 626:6; N.J. Stat.Ann. 2C:2–10; N.D.Cent.Code 12.1–17–08; Pa.Cons. Stat.Ann. tit. 18, § 311.

17. Model Penal Code § 2.11(3)(b). Some modern codes contain such a provision.

18. See Groce v. State, 126 Tex.Crim.R. 10, 70 S.W.2d 163 (1934) (youth); Smith v. State, 161 Ga. 421, 131 S.E. 163 (1925) (mental disease); Commonwealth v. Burke, 105 Mass. 376 (1870) (intoxication). See also Brody, Rape of the Mentally Deficient: Satisfaction of the Nonconsent Element, 15 J. Marshall L.Rev. 115 (1982).

19. Pomeroy v. State, 94 Ind. 96 (1883); State v. Ely, 114 Wash. 185, 194 P. 988 (1921).

20. Don Moran v. People, 25 Mich. 356 (1872).

21. Compare Lewis v. State, 30 Ala. 54 (1857) (not rape); with Crosswell v. People, 13 Mich. 427 (1865). See Scutt, Fraudulent Impersonation and Consent in Rape, 9 U.Queens.L.J. 59 (1975).

22. Model Penal Code § 2.11(3)(d).

23. See, e.g., People v. Cook, 228 Cal.App.2d 716, 39 Cal.Rptr. 802 (1964) (under statute prohibiting taking possession of auto from dealer without his consent, crime not committed by purchase of car with bad check, as this only fraud in the inducement).

24. Commonwealth v. Gregory, 132 Pa.Super. 507, 1 A.2d 501 (1938); Bartell v. State, 106 Wis. 342, 82 N.W. 142 (1900).

25. See DiNicola & Mendeloff, Controlling Violence in Professional Sports, 21 Duq.L.Rev. 843 (1983); Hallowell & Meshbesher, Sports Violence and the Criminal Law, Trial 26 (Jan. 1977); Hechter, Criminal Law & Violence in Sports, 19 Crim.L.Q. 425 (1977); Perelman, Violence in Professional Sports: Is It Time for Criminal Penalties?, 2 Loy.L.A.Ent.L.J. 75 (1982); Comments, 13 Am.Crim.L.Rev. 235 (1975); 1975 Wis.L.Rev. 771; Notes, 22 Ariz.L.Rev. 919 (1980); 75 Mich.L.Rev. 148 (1976).

subject has been made aware of the risks involved.[26]

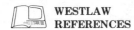

WESTLAW REFERENCES

consent /s victim /s defense /s rape

(b) Guilt of the Victim. The fact that the victim of a crime was himself engaged in criminal activity is not, in and of itself, a defense. As explained in the leading case of *State v. Mellenberger,*[27] the doctrine of particeps criminis (whereby one party to a crime may not recover in a civil suit against another party thereto) has no place in the criminal law, for the purpose of the criminal law is the suppression of crime and the punishment of criminals. Criminal prosecutions are not brought for the protection and benefit of the victim, and thus the victim's status as a criminal is not relevant.[28]

Thus, the crime of false pretenses may be committed by cheating the operators of an illegal lottery,[29] larceny by trick by inducing the victim to part with embezzled funds,[30] and robbery by taking the fruits of a burglary.[31] So too, larceny may be committed by taking items of contraband, such as bootleg liquor or slot machines, from the person who is committing a crime by possessing them.[32]

For a time, an exception to the general rule was recognized in some jurisdictions. The exception was limited to cases in which one party induced another person to join in an illegal scheme and then defrauded him of his money or property, and was based upon the assumption that the protection of the law should not extend so far as to protect those who surrender their goods in the hope of obtaining a benefit by illegal means.[33] Such reasoning is incorrect, for it would permit swindlers to operate with immunity by drawing their victims into illegal schemes. Fortunately, statutory enactments have put an end to this minority position.

Notwithstanding the rule that guilt of the victim is no defense, it must be remembered that the victim's criminal activity may give rise to circumstances whereby another may act with justification for the purpose of thwarting or terminating the criminal actions. These circumstances are described herein under the headings of self-defense,[34] defense of another,[35] defense of property,[36] and law enforcement.[37]

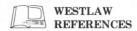

WESTLAW REFERENCES

mellenberger /s 95 +5 709 & "particeps criminis"

(c) Contributory Negligence by the Victim. In the law of torts, contributory negligence by the plaintiff is a defense to an action based upon the defendant's negligence. This defense "does not rest upon the idea that the defendant is relieved of any duty toward the plaintiff. Rather, although the defendant has violated his duty, has been negligent, and would otherwise be liable, the plaintiff is denied recovery because his own conduct disentitles him to maintain the action. In the eyes of the law both parties are at fault; and the defense is one of the plaintiff's disability, rather than the defendant's innocence."[38]

---

26. In Halushka v. University of Saskatchewan, 53 D.L.R.2d 436 (1965), where the subject of the experiment was merely told electrodes would be put on his arms, legs and head and a catheter into his arm, but in fact he was given an untested anesthetic and the catheter was advanced through the various heart chambers out into the pulmonary artery, resulting in cardiac arrest, liability in tort was upheld. On criminal liability in such a case, see Skegg, 'Informed Consent' to Medical Procedures, 15 Med. Sci. & Law 125 (1975).

27. 163 Or. 233, 95 P.2d 709 (1939).

28. Frazier v. Commonwealth, 291 Ky. 467, 165 S.W.2d 33 (1942). The point is seldom expressly stated in a criminal code.

29. Kelley v. State, 76 Nev. 65, 348 P.2d 966 (1960); State v. Mellenberger, 163 Or. 233, 95 P.2d 709 (1939).

30. Levin v. United States, 338 F.2d 265 (D.C.Cir.1964).

31. State v. Pokini, 45 Hawaii 295, 367 P.2d 499 (1961); Hall v. State, 160 Tex.Crim.R. 553, 272 S.W.2d 896 (1954).

32. People v. Odenwald, 104 Cal.App. 203, 285 P. 406 (1930); State v. Johnson, 77 Idaho 1, 287 P.2d 425 (1955).

33. McCord v. People, 46 N.Y. 470 (1871); State v. Crowley, 41 Wis. 271 (1876).

34. See § 5.7.

35. See § 5.8.

36. See § 5.9.

37. See § 5.10.

38. W. Prosser & W. Keeton, Torts § 65 (5th ed. 1984).

Given this rationale for the contributory negligence defense, it is apparent that it has no place in the criminal law. Negligence by the victim, just as with criminal conduct by the victim, "does not bar an action against another for the wrong which he has committed against the peace and dignity of the state." [39] Thus it has been frequently held, for example, that it is no defense to a charge of manslaughter or reckless homicide arising out of defendant's operation of an automobile that the deceased driver or pedestrian was also negligent. [40]

This is not to say, however, that negligence by the victim is inadmissible in a criminal prosecution. As discussed earlier, [41] such negligence may have a bearing upon the issue of whether the defendant's conduct was the proximate cause of the injury, and it is also significant in determining whether the defendant was criminally negligent. [42] For these reasons, it would be incorrect for the trial judge to instruct that the victim's negligence is totally immaterial on all aspects of the case. [43]

 WESTLAW REFERENCES

defense /p contributory! /s negligen*** /s victim decedent /s cause /s death injury /p homicide manslaughter reckless!

(d) Condonation, Ratification, and Settlement. Condonation, the forgiveness of a criminal offense by the victim, is no defense. Sometimes this is explained on the ground that condonation is after-the-fact consent by the victim and thus cannot be any more effective than before-the-fact consent. [44] This, however, might suggest that condonation is a defense in those circumstances where before-the-fact consent would bar conviction, but this is not the case. [45] While before-the-fact consent may negative an element of the offense or preclude infliction of the harm to be prevented by the law in question, this is not true of subsequent condonation. [46] Such forgiveness "has no proper place in the criminal law. The interest of the state is paramount and controls prosecutions * * * [f]or it is the public, not a complainant, that is injured by the commission of a crime." [47] Acts by the victim alleged to constitute ratification (formal sanction, not necessarily involving forgiveness) are for the same reason no defense. [48]

39. State v. Plaspohl, 239 Ind. 324, 157 N.E.2d 579 (1959). See also State v. Moore, 129 Iowa 514, 106 N.W. 16 (1906), the case most frequently cited for this rationale; State v. Crace, 289 N.W.2d 54 (Minn.1979); State v. Rotella, 196 Neb. 741, 246 N.W.2d 74 (1976); State v. Northrup, ___ R.I. ___, 486 A.2d 589 (1985). The point is seldom expressly stated in a criminal code.

By the same token, negligence by a third party—someone other than the victim—is no defense. State v. Alterio, 154 Conn. 23, 220 A.2d 451 (1966); State v. Schaub, 231 Minn. 512, 44 N.W.2d 61 (1950); State v. Romero, 69 N.M. 187, 365 P.2d 58 (1961).

40. Hanby v. State, 39 Ala.App. 392, 101 So.2d 553 (1958); State v. Plaspohl, 239 Ind. 324, 157 N.E.2d 579 (1959); Penix v. Commonwealth, 313 Ky. 587, 233 S.W.2d 89 (1950); State v. Ward, 258 N.C. 330, 128 S.E.2d 673 (1962); State v. San Antonio, 97 R.I. 48, 195 A.2d 538 (1963).

41. See § 3.12(f)(6)

42. State v. Crace, 289 N.W.2d 54 (Minn.1979); Coggins v. State, 222 Miss. 49, 75 So.2d 258 (1954); State v. Rachels, 218 S.C. 1, 61 S.E.2d 249 (1950); Fox v. State, 145 Tex.Crim.R. 71, 165 S.W.2d 733 (1942).

43. Commonwealth v. Amecca, 160 Pa.Super. 257, 50 A.2d 725 (1947). Compare State v. Northrup, ___ R.I. ___, 486 A.2d 589 (1985) (instruction victim's conduct in stand-

ing where he did had nothing to do with the case not error where no evidence introduced that victim was negligent).

44. Blount v. State, 102 Fla. 1100, 138 So. 2 (1931).

45. People v. Furrh, 146 Cal.App.2d 740, 304 P.2d 849 (1956) (consent to intercourse is "subsequent acquiescence" so far as preliminary assault is concerned, and thus is no defense); State v. Craig, 124 Kan. 340, 259 P. 802 (1927) (mother's forgiveness of son's act of burning her barn no defense, although crime of arson would not have been committed if mother's consent had been obtained before the burning).

46. Hill v. State, 253 Ark. 512, 487 S.W.2d 624 (1972) (consent of lienholder a defense to charge of selling property subject to a lien, but not if consent came after the sale); State v. Taylor, 121 N.H. 489, 431 A.2d 775 (1981) (after-the-fact consent to kidnapping or false imprisonment does not negate any element of the crime); Battle v. State, 287 Md. 675, 414 A.2d 1266 (1980) (consent after penetration no defense to charge of rape).

47. People v. Brim, 22 Misc.2d 335, 199 N.Y.S.2d 744 (1960).

48. Phillips v. State, 38 Ala.App. 632, 91 So.2d 518 (1956); Piracci v. State, 207 Md. 499, 115 A.2d 262 (1955); State v. Higgin, 257 Minn. 46, 99 N.W.2d 902 (1959); Lewallen v. State, 166 Tex.Crim.R. 287, 313 S.W.2d 293 (1958).

So too, it is no defense that the victim has been made whole by recovering a judgment in a civil action against the defendant.[49] Nor is it a defense that the defendant has voluntarily made restitution[50]; "satisfaction of a private wrong is not a bar to a criminal prosecution."[51] Once again, the dominant theme is that when a crime has been committed the principal injury, in the contemplation of the law, is that which has been suffered by the public.[52]

In some jurisdictions, condonation or settlement has by legislation been made a defense to certain crimes. Some of these enactments deal with specific offenses where the legislature has presumably made the judgment that conviction is unwise if the victim has otherwise obtained satisfaction, perhaps because the crime is in reality more private than public in nature. Thus, in some states a subsequent marriage of the parties following seduction is proof of condonation and a bar to prosecution.[53] Likewise, statutes in certain jurisdictions permit a prosecution for adultery only upon the complaint of an offended spouse, so that if the aggrieved spouse condones the offense the husband or wife may not be convicted.[54]

About ten states have much broader compromise statutes, covering most or all misdemeanors, which provide that if the injured party appears in court and acknowledges that he has received satisfaction for the injury, then the prosecution is to be terminated.[55] These statutes have been strictly construed so that, for example, it must appear that the injured party in fact appeared in court and made the necessary acknowledgment of satisfaction; mere evidence of compromise is not sufficient.[56] More important, these provisions have been construed as being applicable only to those crimes which overlap a civil remedy. Thus, compromise with a person injured in an automobile accident is no defense to a charge of leaving the scene of an accident,[57] nor is compromise with the owner of a damaged aircraft a bar to prosecution for operating an aircraft under the influence of liquor.[58]

It is undoubtedly true that there are certain crimes which are more private than public, as to which settlement is to be encouraged in lieu of prosecution. "In one class of cases, the public wrong is merged in that of the individual, and compensation to him is accepted as the adequate measure of redress. In the other, the individual grievance is swallowed up in the greater wrong done to society; and nothing but public punishment will suffice, to vindicate the violated law."[59] Yet, it may be questioned whether indiscriminate compromise statutes, covering a wide range of offenses and involving restitution by the defendant, represent sound policy.

49. People v. Alba, 46 Cal.App.2d 859, 117 P.2d 63 (1941).

50. Chick v. Wingo, 387 F.2d 330 (6th Cir.1967); Savitt v. United States, 59 F.2d 541 (3d Cir.1932); State v. Swallom, 244 N.W.2d 321 (Iowa 1976); Commonwealth v. Spiegel, 169 Pa.Super. 252, 82 A.2d 692 (1951).

But, as noted in Swallom, the defendant's restitution is admissible on a charge of passing a bad check, for it is relevant to the issue of intent to defraud.

51. Commonwealth v. Spiegel, supra.

52. Sometimes the public and private injury may appear to merge because the state is the victim of the crime. If, under those circumstances, the prosecutor promises to forego prosecution if the defendant makes restitution to the state, he may be held to his bargain. People v. Johnson, 372 Ill. 18, 22 N.E.2d 683 (1939).

53. Combs v. Commonwealth, 283 S.W.2d 714 (Ky. 1955); People v. Gould, 70 Mich. 240, 38 N.W. 232 (1888).

In Blount v. State, 102 Fla. 1100, 138 So. 2 (1931), where the court declined to reach a similar result in the absence of such a statute, the policy underlying these statutes was questioned on the ground that the defendant might resort to "the marital relation only for the selfish purpose of avoiding punishment for his crime."

54. People v. Dalrymple, 55 Mich. 519, 22 N.W. 20 (1885); State v. Ayles, 74 Or. 153, 145 P. 19 (1914).

55. For the Arizona statute, references to similar statutes in other jurisdictions, and a general discussion of the theory behind these statutes, see State v. Garoutte, 95 Ariz. 234, 388 P.2d 809 (1964).

56. People v. Trapp, 46 Misc.2d 642, 260 N.Y.S.2d 305 (1965).

57. People v. O'Rear, 220 Cal.App.2d 927, 34 Cal.Rptr. 61 (1963).

58. State ex rel. Schafer v. Fenton, 104 Ariz. 160, 449 P.2d 939 (1969).

59. Childs v. State, 118 Ga.App. 706, 165 S.E.2d 577 (1968).

For one thing, reliance upon the misdemeanor-felony distinction as a basis for deciding when compromise should be permitted is highly questionable. There is nothing inherent in the label "misdemeanor" or in the characteristics of misdemeanors generally [60] which suggest that settlement is to be preferred. This point is aptly illustrated by *State v. Garouette*,[61] where the court, after noting that it "was never thought that the taking of a human life could be paid for and forgotten," reluctantly concluded that the defendant's compliance with the misdemeanor compromise statute barred prosecution for manslaughter by motor vehicle because the crime had been changed from a felony to a misdemeanor (apparently without any legislative consideration of the significance of this change in relation to the 85-year-old compromise statute).

Even assuming there is something to the misdemeanor-felony dichotomy, it is apparent that a statutory policy of permitting compromise of most or all misdemeanors involving an "injured party" is indiscriminate. As noted in *Garouette:*

> The present state of the law has this incongruous result. If a drunk or reckless driver does not hit anyone, he may go to jail * * *. If guilty, he cannot escape punishment. There is no "injured person" or "injured party" or possible "remedy by civil action," and the compromise statute may not be invoked. But if he damages property, hits someone, or even kills them, under the compromise statute he may completely escape punishment by paying civil damages.

Finally, these statutes might be questioned on the ground that they discriminate against the indigent, who are unable to make a private settlement and in that way avoid conviction. "The law should treat rich and poor alike, and the fact that a man might be able to pay for damages due to his negligence should not save him from criminal prosecution."[62] Indeed, these compromise statutes may violate the equal protection clause of the United States Constitution.[63]

 WESTLAW REFERENCES

misdemeanor felony /s "compromise statute"

(e) Administration of the Criminal Law. Subject to the exceptions which have been noted, it may be concluded that the substantive criminal law does not recognize as a defense the victim's consent, guilt of a crime, contributory negligence, condonation or ratification of the defendant's conduct, or acceptance of a settlement. However, these factors not infrequently have a significant impact upon the administration of the criminal law.[64] Because of their presence, it sometimes occurs that the police decide not to arrest,[65] the prosecutor decides not to charge,[66] or the judge [67] or jury [68] decides not to convict.

There are undoubtedly a variety of reasons why this happens. Most likely, however, the presence of such circumstances leads the decision-maker to conclude that (a) the harm to be prevented by the statute has thus not occurred; (b) prosecution, conviction, and punishment would serve no purpose or would be harmful to the present relationship between the offender and victim; or (c) the limited resources of the criminal justice system are better devoted to other, more serious matters.

 WESTLAW REFERENCES

williams /s 399 +5 235

---

60. See § 1.6(a).

61. 95 Ariz. 234, 388 P.2d 809 (1964).

62. State v. Garouette, 95 Ariz. 234, 388 P.2d 809 (1964).

63. Cf. Williams v. Illinois, 399 U.S. 235, 90 S.Ct. 2018, 26 L.Ed.2d 586 (1970) (statute, authorizing imprisonment of those unable or unwilling to pay fines imposed in a criminal case, violation of equal protection when applied to indigent defendant so as to bring about imprisonment longer than could otherwise be imposed for the offense); Tate v. Short, 401 U.S. 395, 91 S.Ct. 668, 28 L.Ed.2d 130

(1971) (same result where statute does not otherwise authorize imprisonment).

64. See generally Hall, The Role of the Victim in the Prosecution and Disposition of a Criminal Case, 28 Vand. L.Rev. 931 (1975).

65. See W. LaFave, Arrest ch. 5 (1965).

66. See F. Miller, Prosecution chs. 9, 18 (1970).

67. See D. Newman, Conviction chs. 10, 11 (1966).

68. See H. Kalven and H. Zeisel, The American Jury chs. 17, 18 (1966).

Chapter 6

ANTICIPATORY OFFENSES;
PARTIES

Table of Sections

§ 6.1 Solicitation

Assume that *A* wishes to have his enemy *B* killed, and thus—perhaps because he lacks the nerve to do the deed himself—*A* asks *C* to kill *B*. If *C* acts upon *A*'s request and fatally shoots *B*, then both *A* and *C* are guilty of murder.[1] If, again, *C* proceeds with the plan to kill *B*, but he is unsuccessful, then both *A* and *C* are guilty of attempted murder.[2] If *C* agrees to *A*'s plan to kill *B* but the killing is not accomplished or even attempted, *A* and *C* are nonetheless guilty of the crime of conspiracy.[3] But what if *C* immediately rejects *A*'s homicidal scheme, so that there is never even any agreement between *A* and *C* with respect to the intended crime? Quite obviously, *C* has committed no crime at all. *A*, however, because of his bad state of mind in intending that *B* be killed and his bad conduct in importuning *C* to do the killing, is guilty of the crime of solicitation.[4] For the crime of solicitation to be completed, it is only necessary that the actor with intent that another person commit a crime, have enticed, advised, incited, ordered or otherwise encouraged that person to commit a crime. The crime solicited need not be committed.[5]

(a) Common Law and Statutes. Whether the offense of solicitation was known to the common law before the nineteenth century is uncertain. In one early case it was held that a man could not be indicted for simply requesting a servant to leave his master's service,[6] although the opinion states that enticing a servant to embezzle his master's goods would be indictable.[7] Shortly thereafter, however, it was held in another case that no offense was charged where it was not alleged that the servant actually took the goods.[8] Only two special types of solicitation were clearly indictable under the early cases: a solicitation to commit a forgery to be used in trial or perjury [9]; and the offering of a bribe to a public official.[10]

The 1801 case of *Rex v. Higgins* [11] was based upon an indictment charging the defendant with soliciting a servant to steal his master's goods, although the servant had ignored the request. Defense counsel examined the prior cases and concluded, except with respect to the unique situation concerning perjury, forgery, and bribery: "In none of the books is there any case or precedent to be found of an indictment for bare solicitation to commit an offense without an act in pursuance of it, and the silence of all writers on Crown law on this subject is of itself a strong argument that no such offense is known to the law." The judges unanimously ruled that the common law misdemeanor of solicitation had been charged.[12] However, the only cases cited in their opinions as precedent were those which had dealt with bribery, perjury, or forgery.

---

§ 6.1

1. *C* is quite clearly guilty of murder because he is the person who did the shooting, and it is obviously no defense that he acted at the request of another. Under either the common law concept of accessory before the fact or modern princples of accountability, *A* is also guilty of murder. See § 6.6.

2. The analysis is the same as set forth in note 1 supra concerning the completed crime of murder. On attempts, see §§ 6.2, 6.3.

3. In some jurisdictions an overt act in furtherance of the conspiracy would also be required. See § 6.4.

4. See Blackburn, Solicitation to Crimes, 40 W.Va.L. Rev. 135 (1934); Curran, Solicitation: A Substantive Crime, 17 Minn.L.Rev. 499 (1933); Hitchler, Solicitations, 41 Dick.L.Rev. 225 (1937); Wechsler, Jones & Korn, The Treatment of Inchoate Crimes in the Model Penal Code of the American Law Institute: Attempt, Solicitation, and Conspiracy, 61 Colum.L.Rev. 571, 621–28 (1961); Annots., 35 A.L.R. 961 (1925) (on common law solicitation), 77 A.L.R.3d 519 (1977), 51 A.L.R.2d 953 (1957) (both on solicitation statutes).

5. State v. Foster, 379 A.2d 1219 (Me.1977); State v. Furr, 292 N.C. 711, 235 S.E.2d 193 (1977).

But, as some statutes make clear, it is no defense to a conspiracy charge that the crime solicited *was* committed, though the defendant may not be convicted of both solicitation and the object crime. Some statutes also declare that the defendant may not be convicted of solicitation and also a conspiracy or attempt which had the same objective.

6. Regina v. Daniel, 87 Eng.Rep. 856 (1704).

7. However, the opinion is ambiguous in that it is not stated whether there would still be an offense if the servant ignored the request.

8. Regina v. Collingwood, 87 Eng.Rep. 1029 (1704).

9. Rex v. Johnson, 80 Eng.Rep. 753 (1679).

10. Rex v. Vaughan, 98 Eng.Rep. 308 (1769).

11. 102 Eng.Rep. 269 (1801).

12. The phrase "attempt to incite" was used to describe the acts, as the servant had not actually been incited to steal. This was not meant to classify the

Indeed, the opinions of the judges rest more upon the policy of finding the acts to be an offense than upon whether the offense had previously existed in the common law.[13]

Since the *Higgins* case the offense of solicitation has been recognized as a common law offense both in England [14] and the United States [15] with few exceptions.[16] The solicitation of another to commit a felony is uniformly held indictable as a misdemeanor under the common law [17] and, when the issue has presented itself, the same result has been reached as to the soliciting of another to commit a misdemeanor which would breach the peace, obstruct justice or otherwise be injurious to the public welfare.[18] There is no reported decision in this country which holds that the solicitation of *any* type of misdemeanor is a common law offense.[19]

Even in those jurisdictions with modern recodifications, it is not uncommon for there to be no statute making solicitation a crime. In those states with solicitation statutes, there is considerable variation in their coverage. Some extend to the solicitation of all crimes, some only the solicitation of felonies or particular classes of felonies, and some only the solicitation of certain specified offenses. These solicitation statutes typically provide that the solicitation constitutes a grade of crime one level below the offense which was solicited. Some, however, general-

ly authorize punishment equivalent to that which is provided for the solicited crime.

The Model Penal Code defines solicitation broadly to include requesting another to commit any offense,[20] and would generally make solicitation punishable to the same degree as authorized for the offense solicited.[21] The theory is that "to the extent that sentencing depends upon the antisocial disposition of the actor and the demonstrated need for a corrective sanction, there is likely to be little difference in the gravity of the required measures depending on the consummation or the failure of the plan." [22]

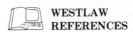 **WESTLAW REFERENCES**

crime /s solicitation /p common-law statut!

(b) Policy Considerations. As already noted, the solicitation of crimes has received varied statutory treatment in this country. In some jurisdictions, all common law crimes (including solicitation) have been abolished but no general solicitation statute has been enacted.[23] Elsewhere the statutes cover only the solicitation of certain crimes,[24] while other jurisdictions have made no statutory additions to the limited common law offense. This suggests, as does language in some of the reported cases, that there is not a uniformity of opinion on the necessity of declaring criminal the soliciting of others to commit offenses.

offense as an attempt but only to show that the solicitation was an offense though the one solicited had not acted.

13. "It would be a slander upon the law to suppose that an offense of such magnitude is not indictable." Holt, C.J. "This is a very grievous offense, and it is most important to the public that it be made known as such." Grose, J.

14. Regina v. Gregory, L.R. 1 Cr.Cas.Res. 77 (1867).

15. U.S. v. Lyles, 4 Cranch C.C. 469, Fed.Cas.No. 15, 646 (1834); Cox v. People, 82 Ill. 191 (1876); Commonwealth v. Flagg, 135 Mass. 545 (1883); State v. Beckwith, 135 Me. 423, 198 A. 739 (1938); State v. Hampton, 210 N.C. 283, 186 S.E. 251 (1936).

16. It has been held by one court that a bare solicitation is not indictable in itself, and is not a sufficient basis for a conviction for an attempt. State v. Lampe, 131 Minn. 65, 154 N.W. 737 (1915).

17. State v. Avery, 7 Conn. 266 (1828); State v. Foster, 379 A.2d 1219 (Me.1977); Commonwealth v. Flagg, 135 Mass. 545 (1883); State v. Hampton, 210 N.C. 283, 186 S.E.

251 (1936); State v. Blechman, 135 N.J.L. 99, 50 A.2d 152 (1946).

18. U.S. v. Lyles, 4 Cranch C.C. 469, Fed.Cas. No. 15, 646 (1834); Cox v. People, 82 Ill. 191 (1876); Smith v. Commonwealth, 54 Pa. 209 (1880).

19. In State v. Sullivan, 110 Mo.App. 75, 84 S.W. 105 (1904) there is dicta which might be so interpreted, but the case holds that the solicitation of a felony is always an offense and that as for solicitation of misdemeanors, the evil character of the offense solicited should be determinative.

20. Model Penal Code § 5.02.

21. Id. at § 5.05. The exception is that a solicitation to commit a capital crime or felony of the first degree is punishable as a felony of the second degree.

22. Model Penal Code § 5.05, Comment at 490 (1985).

23. See § 6.1(a).

24. Such as only felonies, particular classes of felonies or certain specified offenses.

One view is that a mere solicitation to commit a crime, not accompanied by agreement or action by the person solicited, presents no significant social danger It is argued, for example, that solicitation is not dangerous because the resisting will of an independent agent is interposed between the solicitor and commission of the crime which is his object.[25] Similarly, it is claimed that the solicitor does not constitute a menace in view of the fact that he has manifested an unwillingness to carry out the criminal scheme himself.[26] There is not the dangerous proximity to success which exists when the crime is actually attempted,[27] for, "despite the earnestness of the solicitation, the actor is merely engaging in talk which may never be taken seriously." [28]

On the other hand, it is argued "that a solicitation is, if anything, more dangerous than a direct attempt, because it may give rise to that cooperation among criminals which is a special hazard. Solicitation may, indeed, be thought of as an attempt to conspire.[29] Moreover, the solicitor, working his will through one or more agents, manifests an approach to crime more intelligent and masterful than the efforts of his hireling." [30] It is noted, for example, that the imposition of liability for criminal solicitation has proved to be an important means by which the leadership of criminal movements may be suppressed.[31]

Without regard to whether it is correct to say that solicitations are more dangerous than attempts, it is fair to conclude that the purposes of the criminal law [32] are well served by inclusion of the crime of solicitation within the substantive criminal law. Providing punishment for solicitation aids in the prevention of the harm which would result should the inducements prove successful,[33] and also aids in protecting the public from being exposed to inducements to commit or join in the commission of crimes.[34] As is true of the law of attempts, the crime of solicitation (a) provides a basis for timely law enforcement intervention to prevent the intended crime, (b) permits the criminal justice process to deal with individuals who have indicated their dangerousness, and (c) avoids inequality of treatment based upon a fortuity (here, withholding of the desired response by the person solicited) beyond the control of the actor.[35]

Objections to making solicitation a crime or to extending it to such minor crimes as adultery [36] are sometimes based upon the fear that false charges may readily be brought, either out of a misunderstanding as to what the defendant said [37] or for purposes of harass-

---

25. People v. Werblow, 241 N.Y. 55, 148 N.E. 786 (1925); Hicks v. Commonwealth, 86 Va. 223, 9 S.E. 1024 (1889).

26. State v. Davis, 319 Mo. 1222, 6 S.W.2d 609 (1928) (concurring opinion).

27. Gervin v. State, 212 Tenn. 653, 371 S.W.2d 449 (1963).

28. 1 National Comm'n on Reform of Federal Criminal Laws, Working Papers 370 (1970).

29. This is not to suggest, however, that in the absence of a solicitation statute that a prosecution based upon an attempted conspiracy theory will necessarily prevail. See State v. Sexton, 232 Kan. 539, 657 P.2d 43 (1983).

30. Wechsler, Jones & Korn, supra note 4, at 621–22. See also State v. Schleifer, 99 Conn. 432, 121 A. 805 (Dist. Ct.1923).

31. Wechsler, Jones & Korn, supra note 4, at 622, citing many cases concerning political agitation and labor agitation.

32. See § 1.5.

33. People v. Burt, 45 Cal.2d 311, 288 P.2d 503 (1955).

34. Ibid., holding on this basis that the solicitation statute covered one who solicited another within the state to commit a crime outside the state.

35. Model Penal Code art. 5, Introduction at 294 (1985). See also People v. Lubow, 29 N.Y.2d 58, 323 N.Y.S.2d 829, 272 N.E.2d 331 (1971).

36. In State v. Butler, 8 Wash. 194, 35 P. 1093 (1894), the court quotes Baron Parke in the case of Rex v. Roderick, 7 Car. & P. 795 (1837): "What expressions of the face, or double entendres of the tongue, are to be adjudged solicitation? What freedoms of manners amount to this crime? Is every cyprian who nods or winks to the married men she meets upon the sidewalk indictable for soliciting to adultery? And could the law safely undertake to decide what recognitions in the street were chaste, and what were lewd? It would be a dangerous and difficult rule of criminal law to administer."

37. "[E]ven for persons trained in the art of speech, words do not always perfectly express what is in a man's mind. Thus in cold print or even through misplaced emphasis, a rhetorical question may appear to be a solicitation. The erroneous omission of a word could turn an innocent statement into a criminal one (for example, 'You shoot the President' versus 'Should you shoot the Presi-

ment. This risk is inherent in the punishment of almost all inchoate crimes, although it is perhaps somewhat greater as to the crime of solicitation in that the crime may be committed merely by speaking. In an attempt to deal with this problem, some state statutes require corroboration of the testimony of the person allegedly solicited that the solicitation was made.[38] On occasion, even in the absence of such a statute, courts have refused to uphold convictions for solicitation-type offenses when corroboration was lacking.[39] Another statutory approach, found in one state, is to require that the solicitation take place "under circumstances which indicate unequivocally" the defendant's intent that a crime be committed.[40] Yet another state requires that the person solicited commit an overt act in response to the solicitation.[41]

When, as is usually the case, a solicitation-type statute covers only inducements to engage in criminal conduct, then it can hardly be claimed that the statute unconstitutionally proscribes free speech.[42] As one court put it, "if consummated crimes themselves are constitutional in terms of their criminality * * *, then constitutionality follows as to their incipient or inchoate phases."[43] Sometimes the converse has also been held to be true, namely, that a statute making it illegal

to solicit conduct which is not itself criminal intrudes upon protected free speech interests.[44] The contrary argument is that the criminal law may be used to protect the public from solicitations to do that which they could lawfully do—or, indeed, that which they have a constitutional right to do. Thus, it has been held that even if the constitutional right of privacy allows consenting adults to engage in sodomy in private, a statute may nonetheless proscribe "public solicitations of strangers for sodomy."[45]

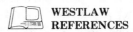 **WESTLAW REFERENCES**

crime /s solicitation /p policy corroborat*** circumstance

(c) Required Mental State and Act. Although the crime of solicitation might be defined quite simply as asking another person to commit an offense, this does not adequately reflect either the mental element or act which must exist in order for the crime to be completed.

As to the required mental state, none is explicitly stated in the usual common law definition of solicitation,[46] and likewise none is expressly set forth in several solicitation statutes.[47] However, the acts of commanding or requesting another to engage in conduct which is criminal would seem of necessity to require an accompanying intent that such

dent?').'' 1 National Comm'n on Reform of Federal Criminal Laws, Working Papers 372 (1970).

38. West's Ann.Cal.Penal Code § 653f (requiring two witnesses or one witness and corroborating circumstances).

39. Kelly v. United States, 194 F.2d 150 (D.C.Cir.1952) (conviction for unlawfully inviting another to accompany him for lewd and immoral purpose reversed, for under the circumstances the uncorroborated testimony of the police officer allegedly solicited was insufficient).

40. Wis.Stat.Ann. 939.30.

41. N.D.Cent.Code 12.1–06–03.

The proposed federal solicitation statute is also in this form. National Comm'n on Reform of Federal Criminal Laws, Final Report—Proposed New Federal Criminal Code § 1003 (1971). This makes the crime very close to conspiracy, although it is noted in the accompanying commentary that the required overt act need not establish that the solicitee is in agreement; it would be sufficient, for example, that he returned for further discussions. Compare National Comm'n on Reform of Federal Criminal Laws, Study Draft of a New Federal Criminal Code

§ 1003 (1970), which would have instead required that the solicitation occur "under circumstances strongly corroborative" of the solicitor's intent to promote or facilitate the commission of a crime.

42. See note 69 infra.

43. Cherry v. State, 18 Md.App. 252, 306 A.2d 634 (1973).

44. City of Columbia v. Scott, 47 Ohio App.2d 287, 353 N.E.2d 858 (1975).

45. United States v. Carson, 319 A.2d 329 (D.C.App. 1974).

46. E.g., Commonwealth v. Flagg, 135 Mass. 545 (1883): "It is an indictable offense at common law for one to counsel and solicit another to commit a felony or other aggravated offense, although the solicitation is of no effect, and the crime counselled is not in fact committed."

47. See statutes collected in Model Penal Code § 5.02, Appendix (Tent.Draft No. 10,1960). This is true even as to a few of the modern recodifications. West's Fla.Stat.Ann. § 777.04; Va.Code 1950, § 18.2–29.

conduct occur,[48] and there is nothing in the decided cases suggesting otherwise.[49] Virtually all of the more recently enacted solicitation statutes avoid any doubt by setting forth in specific terms the intent requirement. Some state the solicitor must intend that an offense be committed, some that he must intend to promote or facilitate its commission, and some others that he must intend that the person solicited engage in criminal conduct.

Thus, as to those crimes which are defined in terms of certain prohibited results, it is necessary that the solicitor intend to achieve that result through the participation of another. If he does not intend such a result, then the crime has not been solicited, and this is true even though the person solicited will have committed the crime if he proceeds with the requested conduct and thereby causes the prohibited result. For example, if B were to engage in criminally negligent conduct which caused the death of C, then B would be guilty of manslaughter[50]; but it would not be a criminal solicitation to commit murder or manslaughter for A to request B to engage in such conduct *unless* A did so for the purpose of causing C's death.[51]

Likewise, where the prohibited result involves special circumstances as to which a *mens rea* requirement is imposed, the solicitor cannot be said to have intended that result unless he personally had this added mental state. For example, assume a jurisdiction with the usual misdemeanor of battery[52] and also a felony of aggravated battery, defined in part as inflicting bodily harm upon a person known to be a peace officer. If A, not knowing that C was an officer, asked B to do bodily harm to C, then A has solicited a battery rather than an aggravated battery.[53]

In the usual solicitation case, it is the solicitor's intention that the criminal result be directly brought about by the person he has solicited; that is, it is his intention that the crime be committed and that the other commit it as a principal in the first degree,[54] as where A asks B to kill C. However, it would seem sufficient that A requested B to get involved in the scheme to kill C in any way which would establish B's complicity in the killing of C were that to occur.[55] Thus it would be criminal for one person to solicit another to in turn solicit a third party,[56] to solicit another to join a conspiracy,[57] or to

48. A defendant's direction to the intended killer that he also kill the intended victim's daughters if they were at home when the victim was murdered constituted solicitations of the daughters' murder notwithstanding the contingency. People v. Miley, 158 Cal.App.3d 25, 204 Cal. Rptr. 347 (1984).

49. Indeed, reference to the mental element was made in the seminal case of Rex v. Higgins, discussed in the text supra at note 11: "A solicitation or inciting of another, by whatever means it is attempted, is an act done; and that such an act done with a criminal intent is punishable by indictment has been clearly established * * *."

50. See § 7.12.

51. The issue apparently has not arisen in any reported solicitation case. Essentially the same principle is involved in the law of attempts, see § 6.2 (c), as an attempt requires an intent to achieve the prohibited result, and thus one does not attempt to commit a crime by negligently endangering another. Thacker v. Commonwealth, 134 Va. 767, 114 S.E. 504 (1922).

52. See § 7.15.

53. The distinction might be important for several reasons, depending upon the law of the jurisdiction. If only solicitation of felonies has been made criminal, then

A has not committed a criminal solicitation. If the penalties for solicitation are determined by the seriousness of the crime solicited then A will receive a lesser penalty.

54. See § 6.6(a).

55. Model Penal Code § 5.02 is explicit on this point, for it provides that one is guilty of solicitation if "with the purpose of promoting or facilitating its commission he commands, encourages or requests another person to engage in specific conduct which would constitute such crime or an attempt to commit such crime or which would establish his complicity in its commission or attempted commission." Some modern codes have adopted this "complicity in its commission" approach.

As to the reference in Model Penal Code § 5.02 to an attempt to commit a crime, it is intended to cover the case in which the actor solicits conduct which he and the person solicited believe to be the completed crime but which, because of legal impossibility, does not constitute the crime. See Model Penal Code § 5.02, Comment at 373–74 (1985).

56. People v. Bloom, 149 App.Div. 295, 133 N.Y.S. 708 (1912); King v. Bently, [1923] 1 K.B. 403 (1922).

57. Regina v. DeKromme, 66 L.T.R. (n. s.) 301 (Cr.Cas. Res.1892).

solicit another to aid and abet the commission of a crime.[58]

An evil intent cannot alone constitute a crime; there must also be an act.[59] However, the mere speaking of words is an act,[60] and that is the kind of act which most often completes the crime of solicitation, although the crime may also be committed through the written word.[61] Courts, legislatures and commentators have utilized a great variety of words to describe the required acts for solicitation, including the following and variants thereof; advises,[62] commands, counsels,[63] encourages, entices,[64] entreats,[65] importunes, incites,[66] induces, procures, requests, solicits,[67] and urges. Some of these words are doubtlessly more appropriate than others, in that

the crime of solicitation should not be extended to persons who merely express general approval of criminal acts[68] or who are otherwise legitimately exercising their rights to free speech.[69]

It is not necessary that the act of solicitation be a personal communication to a particular individual. Thus an information charging one with soliciting from a public platform a number of persons to commit the crimes of murder and robbery is sufficient.[70] However, there is some authority to the effect that it is not a criminal solicitation to make a general solicitation by publication to a large indefinable group.[71]

What if the solicitor's message never reaches the person intended to be solicited, as

58. Meyer v. State, 47 Md.App. 679, 425 A.2d 664 (1981). Contra: Kelley v. Hart, [1934] 1 West.Weekly R. 333 (Alberta Sup.Ct.App.Div.).

59. See § 3.2.

60. See § 3.2.

61. E.g., Regina v. Banks, 12 Cox Crim.Cas. 393 (1873) (but, only attempted solicitation in that defendant's letter never reached the addressee).

62. E.g., Commonwealth v. Willard, 39 Mass. 476 (22 Pick) (1839).

63. E.g., Commonwealth v. Flagg, 135 Mass. 545 (1883).

64. E.g., Commonwealth v. Willard, 39 Mass. 476 (22 Pick) (1839); W. Clark & W. Marshall, Law of Crimes 220 (7th ed. 1967).

65. E.g., National Comm'n on Reform of Federal Criminal Laws, Final Report—Proposed New Federal Criminal Code § 1003 (1971).

66. E.g., State v. Blechman, 135 N.J.L. 99, 50 A.2d 152 (1946); La.Stat.Ann.–Rev.Stat. 14:28.

67. E.g., State v. Blechman, 135 N.J.L. 99, 50 A.2d 152 (1946).

68. "While it may be true that persons who merely express approval of or even applaud the commission of a crime are antisocial, we are not prepared to say that such antisocial tendencies constitute such a threat as to be punishable." 1 National Comm'n on Reform of Federal Criminal Laws, Working Papers 371 (1970).

In Turner v. LaBelle, 251 F.Supp. 443 (D.Conn.1966), an action to restrain enforcement of a state statute alleged to chill First Amendment rights, the court was concerned with a statute which subjected to criminal penalties anyone who "advocates, encourages, justifies, praises, incites, or solicits any assault upon * * * the police force of this or any other state * * * or the killing or injuring of any class or body of persons, or of any individual * * *." By reading the questionable words "justifies" and "praises" in the same sense as "encourages," "advocates" and "incites" the court was able to uphold the statute as neither overbroad or vague.

69. "The Institute recognized that a legislative question remained whether the prohibition of solicitations should be curtailed to protect free speech. It concluded that one who uses words as a means to crime, who intends that his words should cause a criminal result, does not make a contribution to community discussion that is worthy of protection. But the main problem was not perceived as whether to protect the actor who intends that a crime will result. Rather, it was how to prevent legitimate agitation of an extreme or inflammatory nature from being misinterpreted as solicitation to crime. It would not be difficult to convince a jury that inflammatory rhetoric in behalf of an unpopular cause is in reality an invitation to violate the law rather than an effort to seek its change through legitimate criticism." Model Penal Code § 5.02, Comment at 375–76 (1985).

"The phrase preferred here is 'commands, induces, entreats or otherwise attempt to persuade.' The verb 'solicits' has been rejected because its common law history has made it too vague. Words such as 'counsels,' 'encourages,' and 'requests' have also been rejected because they suggest equivocal situations too close to casual remarks or even to free speech, although 'requests' would be a possible extension of the scope of the prohibition." 1 National Comm'n on Reform of Federal Criminal Laws, Working Papers 371 (1970).

70. State v. Schleifer, 99 Conn. 432, 121 A. 805 (Dist.Ct. 1923).

71. People v. Quentin, 58 Misc.2d 601, 296 N.Y.S.2d 443 (1968) (defendants distributed brochure containing a recipe for making a psychedelic agent; they were charged with soliciting others to possess unlawful chemical compounds). But see United States v. Galleanni, 245 F. 977 (D.Mass.1917) (solicitation by newspaper advertisement not to register for the draft); and Blackburn, supra note 4, at 146 (asserting that "solicitations of this type are more dangerous than solicitations of a special kind, for here solicitation is to a great number").

where an intermediary fails to pass on the communication or the solicitor's letter is intercepted before it reaches the addressee? The act is nonetheless criminal, although it may be that the solicitor must be prosecuted for an attempt to solicit on such facts.[72] Liability properly attaches under these circumstances, as the solicitor has manifested his dangerousness and should not escape punishment because of a fortuitous event beyond his control.[73]

 WESTLAW REFERENCES

crime /s solicitation /p inten! mental-state /s advise command counsel encourage entice entreat importune incite induce procure request solicit urge

(d) Defenses. As noted earlier, the crime of solicitation requires no agreement or action by the person solicited, and thus the solicitation is complete when the solicitor, acting with the requisite intent, makes the command or request. What then of the case in which the solicitor thereafter has a change of heart and persuades the person solicited not to commit the crime or otherwise prevents the crime from being committed? It might be argued that such a renunciation of criminal purpose should be no defense. Given the fact that a solicitation is punishable although immediately rejected by the other party,[74] it might be

thought illogical for it to be otherwise when the other party accepted the solicitation and only later was stopped from acting on it. In the latter situation the solicitation came even closer to bringing about the antisocial conduct originally intended. Also, it could be maintained that "the solicitor has engaged in irreparably harmful conduct in implanting the suggestion of criminality in the mind of another." [75]

On the other hand, it might well be argued that a voluntary renunciation of criminal purpose by the solicitor should be a defense to the crime of solicitation. One basis for the defense is that the solicitor, by his act of renunciation, has shown that he is not sufficiently dangerous to require application of the corrective processes of the law to him. Another is that by allowing the defense solicitors will be encouraged to prevent the solicited crimes from occurring because they will thereby escape liability altogether.[76]

Apparently the question of whether voluntary renunciation is a defense to a solicitation charge has never been decided one way or another by an appellate court.[77] However, voluntary renunciation [78] is currently a statutory defense in several of the modern recodifications,[79] and is also a defense to solicitation under the Model Penal Code formulation.[80]

---

72. People v. Bloom, 149 App.Div. 295, 133 N.Y.S. 708 (1912); Rex v. Krause, 66 J.P. 121 (1902); Regina v. Banks, 12 Cox Crim.Cas. 393 (1873). Model Penal Code § 5.02(2) would permit a conviction for solicitation in such circumstances, as do a few of the modern codes.

73. Model Penal Code § 5.02, Comment at 381 (1985).

74. People v. Burt, 45 Cal.2d 311, 288 P.2d 503 (1955).

75. Note, 64 Colum.L.Rev. 1469, 1515 (1964). This is consistent with the notion that one of the reasons for making solicitation criminal is to protect the public from inducements to commit crimes. People v. Burt, supra note 74.

76. The arguments in favor of allowing the defense are developed in more detail in Model Penal Code § 5.01, Comment at 359–60 (1985).

77. In Commonwealth v. Peaslee, 177 Mass. 267, 59 N.E. 55 (1901), an attempt case which included solicitation of another to burn a building, the conviction was reversed on a procedural ground because the solicitation was not alleged as one of the overt acts in the attempt, but the court suggested that on the evidence the defendant could have been convicted of solicitation or attempt notwithstanding his change of mind effectively communicated to

the person solicited. In Regina v. Banks, 12 Cox Crim. Cas. 393 (1873), it is indicated that it would be a defense to solicitation or attempted solicitation if, after mailing the soliciting letter, the defendant had intercepted it before it reached the addressee.

78. As noted in Chennault v. State, 667 S.W.2d 299 (Tex.App.1984), interpreting a statutory renunciation provision, "repetence or a change of heart is required."

79. Most accord with the Model Penal Code provision, note 80 infra, in that an unsuccessful attempt to prevent the solicited crime will never suffice. But a few merely require that the defendant have notified the person solicited and then have given timely notice to the police or otherwise made substantial effort to prevent the crime.

National Comm'n on Reform of Federal Criminal Laws, Final Report—Proposed New Federal Criminal Code § 1005 (1971) provides that it is an affirmative defense to a solicitation charge "that, under circumstances manifesting a voluntary and complete renunciation of his criminal intent, the defendant prevented the commission of the crime solicited."

80. Model Penal Code § 5.02(3), providing that "it is an affirmative defense that the actor, after soliciting another

It is not uncommon for law enforcement officers and others acting on their behalf to encourage suspects to engage in criminal conduct as a means of identifying persons who are willing to engage in certain forms of criminal activity. This practice is most prevalent as to such crimes as prostitution, gambling, and sale of narcotics, which (because they involve only "willing victims") would otherwise go undetected. If the inducements are not so extreme as to constitute entrapment,[81] then the practice is a permissible one. It does not constitute the crime of solicitation for a person, having reason to believe another is willing to commit a crime, to furnish an opportunity for the commission of the offense, if the purpose is, in good faith, to secure evidence against a guilty person and not to induce an innocent person to commit a crime.[82]

As noted at the outset of this section, it is generally true that if A solicits B to commit a crime and B then proceeds to commit the crime in response to A's solicitation, then A is liable as an accomplice for the crime which B has committed. However, there are exceptions.[83] For example, if A solicited B to commit the crime with A, and the nature of the crime is such that A's participation is inevitably incident to its commission, then it may be concluded that the legislature—by defining

the offense solely in terms of one of the two necessary parties' participation—did not intend to impose liability on a person in A's position.[84] So too, A should not be considered an accomplice to B's crime if the legislative purpose in enacting the statute violated by B was to protect persons such as A.[85]

In situations such as these, where the soliciting party would not be held guilty of the completed crime if it were committed as a result of the solicitation, the act of soliciting is itself not criminal.[86] Or, to state it another way, it is a defense to a charge of solicitation to commit a crime that if the criminal object were achieved, the solicitor would not be guilty of a crime under the law defining the offense or the law concerning accomplice liability.[87] Were the rule otherwise, the law of criminal solicitation would conflict with the policies expressed in the definitions of the substantive criminal law. This does not mean, of course, that the mere fact the solicitor was legally incapable of committing the crime directly provides him with a defense when he solicits another to do it.[88]

On the other hand, it is *not* a defense to a solicitation charge that, unknown to the solicitor, the person solicited could not commit the crime.[89] The defendant's culpability is to be measured by the circumstances as he believes

---

person to commit a crime, persuaded him not to do so or otherwise prevented the commission of the crime, under circumstances manifesting a complete and voluntary renunciation of his criminal purpose."

81. See § 5.2.

82. People v. Clark, 7 Ill.2d 163, 130 N.E.2d 195 (1955); People v. Lewis, 365 Ill. 156, 6 N.E.2d 175 (1936).

83. See § 6.8(e).

84. Thus, if a man has intercourse with a prostitute he is not an accomplice in the crime of prostitution. People v. Anonymous, 161 Misc. 379, 292 N.Y.S. 282 (1936).

85. Thus, the underage female who consents to the crime of statutory rape is not an accomplice to that crime. Regina v. Ryrrell, [1894] Q.B. 710.

86. Lott v. United States, 205 F. 28 (9th Cir.1913). But see Leffel v. Municipal Court, 54 Cal.App.3d 569, 126 Cal. Rptr. 773 (1976) (potential customer of prostitute guilty of disorderly conduct, defined by statute as soliciting an act of prostitution).

87. This is essentially the formulation used in Model Penal Code § 5.04(2). A few of the modern codes contain this formulation. A few others state it is a defense that the solicitor is a victim of the crime solicited or that the

solicitation is inevitably incident to the crime solicited. Another few recognize the defense only in the latter situation.

88. Thus, even if defendant cannot rape his own wife, he can be guilty of soliciting another to rape his wife. Some of the modern codes expressly recognize it is no defense that defendant belongs to a class of persons legally incapable of committing the offense solicited.

89. Benson v. Superior Court of Los Angeles, 57 Cal.2d 240, 18 Cal.Rptr. 516, 368 P.2d 116 (1962) (defendant solicited undercover agent to commit perjury in anticipated child custody proceedings; *held*, no defense that, unknown to defendant, there would be no such proceedings because investigator was not pregnant); Commonwealth v. Jacobs, 91 Mass. (9 Allen) 274 (1864) (defendant solicited another to leave state for purpose of entering military service elsewhere; *held*, no defense that, unknown to defendant, other person was physically unfit for military service).

Obviously, it is also no defense that the person solicited is an undercover agent and under no circumstances would have committed the crime solicited. Saienni v. State, 346 A.2d 152 (Del.1975); Meyer v. State, 47 Md.App. 679, 425

them to be.[90] Nor is it a defense that the person solicited is irresponsible or would have an immunity to prosecution or conviction for commission of the crime solicited.[91]

WESTLAW REFERENCES

crime /s solicitation /p defense repent! intercept! "change of heart" renunciat***

(e) The Scope of the Solicitation. In the law of conspiracy, the question has frequently arisen as to whether an agreement reached by several persons on a single occasion as to several objective crimes is but one conspiracy or is as many conspiracies as there were criminal objectives.[92] The generally accepted answer is that because the requisite act for conspiracy is agreement, one agreement amounts to but one conspiracy regardless of the number of objectives.[93] By analogy to that rule, it certainly might be argued that a solicitation on one occasion concerning several criminal objectives likewise involves but a single instance of the requisite act for the crime of solicitation, and consequently but one solicitation offense.

However, in what is apparently the only reported decision on this question, a different result was reached. In *Meyer v. State,*[94] the court rejected "the notion that merely because there is but one solicitor, one solicitee, and one conversation, only one solicitation can arise." Rather, the court concluded, the

number of incitements depends upon the number of separate events which were solicited, which is not inevitably determined by the number of intended victims or intended crimes. Thus, the *Meyer* court stated, "an entreaty made by a solicitor to blow up a building in the hope that two or more particular persons may be killed in the blast could be characterized as one solicitation, notwithstanding that implementation of the scheme might violate several different laws or, because of multiple victims, constitute separate violations of the same law."[95] But in the instant case, where defendant in one conversation solicited three murders to occur on separate occasions and for separate fees, the court concluded there were multiple solicitation offenses.

WESTLAW REFERENCES

ci(425 +5 664)

(f) Solicitation as an Attempt. Whether a solicitation constitutes an attempt was the subject of debate in the late nineteenth and early twentieth centuries, primarily between two scholars of the criminal law. Bishop held to the view that any solicitation to commit an offense was an attempt to commit that offense.[96] Wharton, on the other hand, asserted that a solicitation was not indictable as an attempt.[97] Of the cases cited by Bishop to support his position, only one holds a solicitor

---

A.2d 664 (1981); State v. Davis, 319 Mo. 1222, 6 S.W.2d 609 (1928).

90. Thus Model Penal Code § 5.04(1)(a) provides that it is immaterial to the liability of the solicitor that "he or the person whom he solicits * * * does not occupy a particular position or have a particular characteristic which is an element of such crime, if he believes that one of them does." A few of the modern codes contain such a provision.

91. Model Penal Code § 5.04(1)(b) so provides, as do several of the modern codes.

Some of the modern solicitation statutes also state that it is no defense that the person solicited was unaware of the criminal nature of the conduct or of defendant's criminal purpose, or that some factor precluded him from having the mental state required of the person solicited. Absent such a provision, if the solicitor withholds certain facts from the other party so that the solicited acts, under the circumstances as believed by the party solicited, would not be criminal, then a criminal solicitation has not oc-

curred. The solicitor has not incited the other person to commit a crime, but rather may have committed an attempt through his scheme to have an innocent agent act for him. G. Williams, Criminal Law: The General Part 616–17 (2d ed. 1961); Model Penal Code § 5.01, Comment at 346–47 (1985).

92. See § 6.5(d)(1).

93. Braverman v. United States, 317 U.S. 49, 63 S.Ct. 99, 87 L.Ed. 23 (1942).

94. 47 Md.App. 679, 425 A.2d 664 (1981). See Annot., 24 A.L.R.4th 1324 (1983).

95. But in People v. Hairston, 46 Ill.2d 348, 263 N.E.2d 840 (1970), where this particular issue was not presented to the appellate court, the court upheld defendant's conviction on 3 counts of solicitation because he, as a gang leader, had given an "order" to a youth to shoot 3 occupants of a nearby car.

96. 1 J. Bishop, Criminal Law § 768(c) (8th ed. 1892).

97. 1 F. Wharton, Criminal Law § 218 (12th ed. 1932).

guilty of an attempt,[98] and it involved something more than a bare solicitation.[99]

Some of the reported decisions seem to say that a solicitation constitutes a specific type of attempt, although in these cases the facts usually indicate that something more than a bare solicitation was involved.[100] Another group of cases supports the position that a mere solicitation is not an attempt, but that a solicitation accompanied by other overt acts, such as the furnishing of materials, is an attempt.[101] Yet another view is that a solicitation may become an attempt only if the overt acts have proceeded beyond what would constitute preparation if the solicitor himself planned to commit the offense.[102] Finally, there are also cases holding that the solicitor cannot be guilty of an attempt no matter what he does because it is not his purpose personally to commit the offense.[103] The trend is toward the latter two positions.[104]

Although the issue has seldom been raised in the recent appellate decisions, it continues to be of some importance. This is particularly true in those jurisdictions where there is no crime of solicitation or where the crime of solicitation does not extend to as many offenses as does the crime of attempt. And, even where the solicitation of any type of

crime is covered, the defendant may not be convicted of what is only a solicitation upon a charge of an attempt.[105]

 WESTLAW REFERENCES

solicitation /s attempt /s act step

§ 6.2   Attempt—Acts and Mental State

The crime of attempt, a relatively recent development of the common law, consists of: (1) an intent to do an act or to bring about certain consequences which would in law amount to a crime; and (2) an act in furtherance of that intent which, as it is most commonly put, goes beyond mere preparation. The primary purpose in punishing attempts is not to deter the commission of completed crimes, but rather to subject to corrective action those individuals who have sufficiently manifested their dangerousness.

(a) Development of the Crime of Attempt.[1] Although the crime of attempt did not exist in early English law,[2] in the fourteenth century courts occasionally convicted of a felony those who were guilty only of an unsuccessful attempt to commit that felony.[3] These convictions apparently were rested upon the doctrine that *voluntas reputabitur pro*

---

98. See Curran, Solicitation: A Substantive Crime, 17 Minn.L.Rev. 499, 501–02 (1933), showing that the other cases cited by Bishop only held that the solicitation was itself an offense.

99. People v. Bush, 4 Hill 133 (N.Y.1843), where the defendant solicited another to commit arson and also furnished him with a match.

100. E.g., State v. Avery, 7 Conn. 266 (1828); State v. Ames, 64 Me. 386 (1875); People v. Coleman, 350 Mich. 268, 86 N.W.2d 281 (1957); State v. Hayes, 78 Mo. 307 (1883); People v. Bloom, 149 App.Div. 295, 133 N.Y.S. 708 (1912); Rudolph v. State, 128 Wis. 222, 107 N.W. 466 (1906).

101. E.g., People v. Bush, 4 Hill 133 (N.Y.1843); State v. Bowers, 35 S.C. 262, 14 S.E. 488 (1892).

102. E.g., Braham v. State, 571 P.2d 631 (Alaska 1977); State v. Mandel, 78 Ariz. 226, 278 P.2d 413 (1954); People v. Adami, 36 Cal.App.3d 452, 111 Cal.Rptr. 544 (1973); Griffin v. State, 26 Ga. 493 (1858); State v. Otto, 102 Idaho 250, 629 P.2d 646 (1981); State v. Lowrie, 237 Minn. 240, 54 N.W.2d 265 (1952); State v. Davis, 319 Mo. 1222, 6 S.W.2d 609 (1928).

Sometimes a "substantial step" test is applied to the solicitor's conduct. See, e.g., Saienni v. State, 346 A.2d 152 (Del.1975) (defendant guilty of attempted murder

where he solicited the crime on contract, drew a diagram of the area where the crime was to occur, gave detailed instructions, and directed rehearsals).

103. E.g., People v. O'Bryan, 132 Cal.App. 496, 23 P.2d 94 (1933); State v. Schleifer, 99 Conn. 432, 121 A. 805 (Dist.Ct.1923); Cox v. People, 82 Ill. 191 (1876); State v. Blechman, 135 N.J.L. 99, 50 A.2d 152 (1946); Wiseman v. Commonwealth, 143 Va. 631, 130 S.E. 249 (1925); State v. Hudon, 103 Vt. 17, 151 A. 562 (1930).

104. Model Penal Code § 5.02, Comment at 369 (1985).

105. State v. Davis, 319 Mo. 1222, 6 S.W.2d 609 (1928).

§ 6.2

1. For more detailed accounts of the history of attempt, see J. Hall, General Principles of Criminal Law 558–74 (2d ed. 1960); 1 W. Russell, Crime 173–76 (12th ed. 1964); Meehan, The Trying Problem of Criminal Attempt—Historical Perspective, 14 U.Brit.Col.L.Rev. 137 (1979); Sayre, Criminal Attempts, 41 Harv.L.Rev. 821, 822–37 (1928).

2. The old English law "started from the principle that an attempt to do harm is no offense." 2 F. Pollack & F. Maitland, History of English Law 508 n. 4 (2d ed. 1903).

3. Sayre, supra note 1, at 826.

facto—the intention is to be taken for the deed. However, even at that time a mere intention alone would not suffice. Coke pointed out that to be liable to punishment the defendant must have manifested his intent "by some open deed tending to the execution of his intent. * * * So as if a man had compassed the death of another, and had uttered the same by words or writing, yet he should not have died for it, for there wanted an overt deed tending to the execution of his compassing. But if a man had imagined to murder, or rob another, and to that intent had become *insidiator viarum* [one who lies in wait to commit an offense], and assaulted him though he killed him not, nor took anything from him, yet was it felony, for there was an overt deed." [4] Thus, even in medieval law there was an insistence on conduct. [5]

Instances of convictions based upon the doctrine *voluntas reputabitur pro facto* were quite rare and were confined to attempts to commit the more heinous felonies; there did not exist a general conception that an attempt to commit a crime was criminal as such. [6] However, there existed other means for checking criminal conduct, including the system of frankpledge and surety for the peace, and such crimes as vagrancy, unlawful assembly, and going armed. [7]

The modern doctrine of criminal attempts is said to have had its origin in the Court of Star Chamber, [8] which had as one of its functions the correction of the manifest defects and shortcomings of the common law courts. The Chamber did deal with many cases of what we would today call attempts, and the word "attempt" was occasionally used loosely in describing these situations. [9] However, the Court of Star Chamber never formulated a general theory of criminal attempts, [10] although the principle was developed that an attempt to commit the offense of duelling was itself a distinct offense. [11]

The Court of Star Chamber was abolished in 1640, and its influence upon subsequent common law courts is a matter of dispute. [12] But it is clear that many years elapsed after its abolition before a doctrine of criminal attempt was actually formulated. "[T]he language of the common law courts after 1640 continues to reflect the early common law views and statements antedating the Star Chamber; there is not a ripple in the calm surface to indicate that a new doctrine of criminal attempts had been suggested." [13] Most likely the development of the crime of attempt was retarded by the fact that other means often existed for dealing with unsuccessful or incomplete criminal schemes. Of particular significance is the accelerated growth of the aggravated assault type of crime during this period. [14]

The modern doctrine of attempt may actually be traced back to the case of *Rex v. Scofield* [15] in 1784. The defendant was charged with having put a lighted candle and combustible material in a house he was renting with intention of setting fire to it, but there was no allegation or proof that the house was burned. On his behalf it was contended that an attempt to commit a misdemeanor was not a misdemeanor, but the court rejected that argument: "The intent may make an act, innocent in itself, criminal; nor is the completion of an act, criminal in itself, necessary to constitute criminality."

The doctrine that an attempt to commit a crime was itself a crime was thereafter crystalized in the 1801 case of *Rex v. Higgins.* [16] The defendant was indicted for soliciting a servant to steal his master's goods, but the

4. E. Coke, Third Institute 5 (1644).

5. See J. Hall, supra note 1, at 561; Sayre, supra note 1, at 822–27.

6. Sayre, supra note 1, at 827.

7. J. Hall, supra note 1, at 562.

8. 2 J. Stephen, History of Criminal Law 223–24 (1883).

9. J. Hall, supra note 1, at 567.

10. Id. at 568.

11. 1 W. Russell, supra note 1, at 173–74.

12. Compare J. Hall, supra note 1, at 569, with Sayre, supra note 1, at 829.

13. Sayre, supra note 1, at 829.

14. J. Hall, supra note 1, at 573.

15. Cald. 397 (1784).

16. 2 East 5 (1801).

indictment contained no charge that the servant stole the goods. The court, relying upon *Scofield*, affirmed the conviction: "All offenses of a public nature, that is, all such acts or attempts as tend to the prejudice of the community, are indictable." This statement was soon accepted and repeated by the commentators,[17] and the courts thereafter made it clear that it was a misdemeanor indictable at common law to attempt to commit any felony or misdemeanor, whether such felony or misdemeanor was an offense at common law or was created by statute.[18] Such is the common law rule in the United States, subject to the qualification that some decisions support the view that it is not criminal to attempt to commit a statutory misdemeanor of the *malum prohibitum* variety.[19] It has been questioned, however, whether those decisions represent the law today.[20]

Most American jurisdictions have enacted some form of general attempt statute, and with few exceptions these statutes cover an attempt to commit any felony or misdemeanor.[21] In addition, some states have adopted legislation making it an offense to attempt certain specific crimes.[22] (Omission of an offense from both the general and the specific attempt statutes provides immunity for one who attempts that offense only if the jurisdiction has abolished common law crimes.[23]) Except in the more modern recodifications, these statutes usually do not elaborate upon the term attempt, and thus courts have interpreted them by following the principles of attempt liability developed at common law.[24]

It is important to keep in mind that even with this full development of the crime of attempt, prosecution for attempt is only one of several ways in which the criminal law can reach conduct merely tending toward the doing of some harm otherwise proscribed by law. The crimes of assault[25] and burglary,[26] which served as a means of dealing with the most common forms of attempt prior to recognition of attempt as a distinct crime, are still very much with us. In addition, even the most modern codes include crimes defined in terms of conduct which is arguably of itself harmless but which has been made criminal because it is (or is very likely to be) a step toward the doing of harm. For example, one modern code includes not only a host of possession-type crimes (e.g., possession of obscene material with intent to disseminate it,[27] possession of a forged instrument with intent to issue or deliver same,[28] possession of burglary tools with intent to commit a burglary,[29] possession of explosives or incendiary devices with intent to use them in committing an offense,[30] possession of any instrument adapted for the use of narcotics by subcutaneous injection,[31] possession of weapons with intent to use same against another unlawfully,[32] possession of a gambling device[33]), but also other substantive offenses defined in terms of using certain items for a particular purpose,[34] offering to do something,[35] attracting an intended victim,[36] or even being in a certain place for a

17. E.g., 1 W. Russell, Crimes & Misdemeanors (1st ed. 1819).

18. Rex v. Roderick, 7 C. & P. 796 (1837).

19. E.g., State v. Redman, 121 S.C. 139, 113 S.E. 467 (1922); Whitesides v. State, 79 Tenn. 474 (1883).

20. Model Penal Code § 5.01, Comment at 362 (1985).

21. Model Penal Code § 5.01, Comment at 362 (1985).

22. Model Penal Code § 5.01, Comment at 299 (1985).

23. State v. Sutherlin, 228 Ind. 587, 92 N.E.2d 923 (1950).

24. Model Penal Code, § 5.01, Comment at 300 (1985).

25. See § 7.16.

26. See § 8.13.

27. Ill.—S.H.A. ch. 38, ¶ 11–20.

28. Id. at ¶ 17–3.

29. Id. at ¶ 19–2.

30. Id. at ¶ 20–2.

31. Id. at ¶ 22–50.

32. Id. at ¶ 24–1.

33. Id. at ¶ 28–1.

34. E.g., id. at ¶ 70–1, proscribing use of official stationery of the state university for private promotional scheme.

35. E.g., id. at ¶ 11–14, defining prostitution as including the act of offering or agreeing to perform an act of sexual penetration for money; id. at ¶ 29–1, on offering a bribe.

36. E.g., id. at ¶ 11–6, defining indecent solicitation of a child as including the luring or attempt to lure any child under the age of 13 into a motor vehicle with the intent to commit an indecent act.

bad purpose.[37] As will become more apparent later, many (but not all) of these statutes reach conduct which is merely preparatory in nature and which thus would not be encompassed within the general law of attempts.

Defendants prosecuted for attempting to violate such statutes have with some frequency interposed the objection that these statutes themselves define a particular kind of attempt, from which it is argued that there may be no such thing as an attempt to attempt. Thus, to take the most common case, it is claimed that one cannot be said to have attempted an assault of the attempted-battery type.[38] Although it has been noted that a charge of attempted assault might more logically be characterized as an attempted battery,[39] the courts have upheld convictions for attempted assault on the ground that the crime of assault—with its usual requirement of present ability to inflict injury—is more limited than attempted battery.[40] Similarly, courts have consistently held that it is permissible to charge and convict for an attempt to commit a crime, such as burglary, which is defined in terms of doing an act with intent to commit some other crime.[41] This is a proper result, for "if a preliminary act is prominent enough to serve as the basis of substantive liability, it should also provide a sufficient foundation for attempt liability." [42] By contrast, where a certain crime is actually defined in terms of either doing or attempting a certain crime, then the argument that there is no crime of attempting this attempt is persuasive.[43]

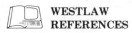
WESTLAW REFERENCES

crime /s attempt /s common-law

(b) The Rationale of Attempt. It has been noted "that the main rationale behind the practice of punishing attempts to commit serious felonies in the Star Chamber and later in the seventeenth century common law courts was preventive and that the all-embracing doctrine was formulated in the eighteenth century simply to extend this to attempts to commit any crime. * * * More bluntly, the law of attempts exists because there is just as much need to stop, deter and reform a person who has unsuccessfully attempted or is attempting to commit a crime than one who has already committed such an offense." [44]

Thus, one important function served by the crime of attempt is to provide a basis whereby law enforcement officers may intervene in time to prevent a completed crime. More precisely, attempt law makes possible preventive action by the police *before* the defendant has come dangerously close to committing the intended crime; as one court put it, the police must be allowed "a reasonable margin of safety after the intent to commit the crime was sufficiently apparent to them." [45] Of course,

---

37. E.g., id. at ¶ 11–18, making it criminal to enter or remain in a place of prostitution with intent to engage in an act of sexual penetration.

38. See § 7.16(a).

39. Model Penal Code § 5.01, Comment at 363 (1985).

40. "The mere fact that assault is viewed as preceding a battery should not preclude us from drawing a line on one side of which we require the present ability to inflict corporal injury, denominating this an assault, and on the other side conduct which falls short of a present ability, yet so advanced toward the assault that it is more than mere preparation and which we denominate an attempt." State v. Wilson, 218 Or. 575, 346 P.2d 115 (1959). See also Miller v. State, 37 Ala.App. 470, 70 So.2d 811 (1954); Allen v. State, 22 Ala.App. 74, 112 So. 177 (1927); State v. Skillings, 98 N.H. 203, 97 A.2d 202 (1953). Contra: In re M., 9 Cal.3d 517, 108 Cal.Rptr. 89, 510 P.2d 33 (1973), discussed in Comment, 14 Santa Clara L.Rev. 83 (1973).

41. E.g., DeGuidio v. State, 289 N.W.,2d 135 (Minn. 1980) (attempted burglary); People ex rel. Blumke v. Fos-

ter, 300 N.Y. 431, 91 N.E.2d 875 (1950) (attempt to possess burglary tools); People v. Bennett, 182 App.Div. 871, 170 N.Y.S. 718, affirmed 224 N.Y. 594, 120 N.E. 871 (1918) (attempt to offer a bribe).

42. Model Penal Code § 5.01, Comment at 364 (1985).

43. Milazzo v. State, 377 So.2d 1161 (Fla.1979) (no attempt crime re statute of attempted transfer of controlled substances); King v. State, 339 So.2d 172 (Fla.1976) (no attempt crime re statute on uttering forged instrument, defined to include attempt to negotiate); State v. Dyer, 388 So.2d 374 (La.1980) (no attempt crime re statute on attempted concealment of firearm).

44. Stuart, The Actus Reus in Attempts, 1970 Crim.L. Rev. 505, 511.

45. Bell v. State, 118 Ga.App. 291, 163 S.E.2d 323 (1968). Thus the court in *Bell* concluded that the act of bringing dynamite to certain premises would suffice in a prosecution for attempt to destroy premises by dynamite, for "to hold otherwise would jeopardize the safety of

law enforcement agencies could be given authority to take preventive action in other ways, including ways which do not at all involve the substantive law of crimes. Illustrative is the stop-and-frisk legislation which permits an officer to stop, frisk and question a person he suspects is "about to" commit an offense.[46] Such laws may serve a useful purpose by permitting a limited form of preventive action in ambiguous situations,[47] but it does not follow from this that stronger preventive measures (which may include prosecution and conviction) are unnecessary when the defendant's criminal purpose is apparent.[48]

The objectives of the criminal law[49] would not be sufficiently served if the only action which could be taken against an attempt were on-the-spot prevention of the crime on that particular occasion. An attempt "yields an indication that the actor is disposed toward such activity, not alone on this occasion but on others."[50] Indeed, in some circumstances a person whose criminal scheme has miscarried on a particular occasion may present a greater continuing danger than the person who succeeded. Prosecution and conviction are thus appropriate, for the individual who has engaged in an attempt should be subjected to rehabilitative measures and to restraints which adequately protect the public.

Indeed, exculpation of those who fail due to a fortuity "would involve inequality of treatment that would shock the common sense of justice."[51] Assume that A, B, C, and D all set out to murder their respective enemies. A succeeds, but the others fail: B's aim is bad; C's gun misfires; and D is intercepted by the police just as he is about to fire. Although there was a day when only A would be punished on the ground that the others had done no harm,[52] it is now accepted that "criminal attempts are harmful in a substantive sense"[53] and that consequently it would be unthinkable to consider B, C, and D immune from punishment.[54]

Finally, it is important to note that "general deterrence is at most a minor function" of the law of attempt.[55] There may be instances in which the actor has planned what he perceives to be almost the "perfect crime," so that the chance of discovery is thought to be very slight unless the plan miscarries in some way. In such a case the threat of punishment for the attempt may serve as a deterrent. However, as a general proposition it may be said that such a threat is unlikely to deter a person who is willing to risk the sanction provided for the crime which is his object.

In considering the dimensions of attempt law, the purposes served by this crime must constantly be kept in mind. These purposes have a bearing upon such questions as what mental state[56] and what acts[57] are required, whether either impossibility of success[58] or

---

would-be captors and the property which is the target of would-be dynamiters."

46. See Model Code of Pre-Arraignment Procedure § 110.2 (1975).

47. See Terry v. Ohio, 392 U.S. 1, 88 S.Ct. 1868, 20 L.Ed.2d 889 (1968), where the Court approved such action on the facts there presented. Justice Douglas dissented, but not without noting that "while arresting persons who have already committed crimes is an important task of law enforcement, an equally if not more important function is crime prevention and deterrence of would-be criminals."

48. On the relationship between attempt law and stop-and-frisk legislation, see LaFave, "Street Encounters" and the Constitution: Terry, Sibron, Peters, and Beyond, 67 Mich.L.Rev. 39, 67 n. 134 (1968); LaFave, Penal Code Revision: Considering the Problems and Practices of the Police, 45 Tex.L.Rev. 434, 453–54 (1967).

49. See § 1.5.

50. Model Penal Code art. 5, Introduction at 294 (1985).

51. Ibid.

52. "For what harm did the attempt cause, since the injury took no effect?" 2 Bracton, Legibus 337, f. 128, 13 (Twiss ed. 1878).

53. J. Hall, supra note 1, at 218, quoting many writers on this point.

54. See Ryu, Contemporary Problems of Criminal Attempts, 32 N.Y.U.L.Rev. 1170, 1171–74 (1957), noting the theoretical basis upon which the old view was abandoned in both the civil law and common law.

55. Model Penal Code art. 5, Introduction at 294 (1985).

56. See § 6.2(c).

57. See § 6.2(d).

58. See § 6.3(a).

abandonment [59] should be a defense, and what degree of punishment should be permitted.[60]

 **WESTLAW REFERENCES**

find 392 us 1

(c) The Mental State.[61]

(1) Intent to Commit a Crime. The mental state required for the crime of attempt, as it is customarily stated in the cases,[62] is an intent to commit some other crime. Some attempt statutes do not specify the requisite mental state,[63] although in the modern recodifications an intent to commit some offense is usually set forth as an element of the crime of attempt.[64] Especially precise is the language of the Wisconsin statute, which requires "that the actor have an intent to perform acts and attain a result which, if accomplished, would constitute such crime." [65] This makes it more apparent that it is the intent to do certain proscribed acts or to bring about a certain proscribed result, rather than an intent to engage in criminality, which is required. Thus, if the defendant intended to do something which he believed was against the

law but which in fact was not unlawful, then he cannot be said to have engaged in a criminal attempt.[66] So too, ignorance of the applicable criminal law [67] is no more of an excuse here than as to completed crimes, and thus it would make no difference that the defendant engaged in the attempt without knowledge that his intended result would be a crime.[68]

Some crimes, such as murder, are defined in terms of acts causing a particular result plus some mental state which need not be an intent to bring about that result. Thus, if *A, B, C* and *D* have each taken the life of another, *A* acting with intent to kill,[69] *B* with an intent to do serious bodily injury,[70] *C* with a reckless disregard of human life,[71] and *D* in the course of a dangerous felony,[72] all three are guilty of murder because the crime of murder is defined in such a way that any one of these mental states will suffice. However, if the victims do not die from their injuries, then only *A* is guilty of attempted murder;[73] on a charge of attempted murder it is not sufficient to show that the defendant intended to do serious bodily harm,[74] that he acted in reckless disregard for human life,[75] or that he

---

59. See § 6.3(b).

60. See § 6.3(c).

61. See Enker, Mens Rea and Criminal Attempt, 4 A.B.F.Res.J. 845 (1977); Sayre, Criminal Attempts, 41 Harv.L.Rev. 821, 837–42 (1928); Skilton, The Mental Element in a Criminal Attempt, 3 U.Pitt.L.Rev. 181 (1937); Smith, Two Problems in Criminal Attempts—Re-Examined–I, 1962 Crim.L.Rev. 135 (1957); Stuart, Mens Rea, Negligence and Attempts, 1968 Crim.L.Rev. 647.

62. E.g., State v. Harvill, 106 Ariz. 386, 476 P.2d 841 (1970); Bell v. State, 118 Ga.App. 291, 163 S.E.2d 323 (1968); Larsen v. State, 86 Nev. 451, 470 P.2d 417 (1970); State v. Goddard, 74 Wn.2d 848, 447 P.2d 180 (1969).

63. See Model Penal Code § 5.01, Appendix A (Tent. Draft No. 10, 1960).

64. Some follow Model Penal Code § 5.01(1) by also stating that the defendant must have been "acting with the kind of culpability otherwise required for commission of the crime." A few use this latter language without any express intent requirement. It would seem that the statutes in the latter category are most readily susceptible to the interpretation that an attempt can be reckless or negligent if the completed crime could be. Cf. People v. Krovarz, 697 P.2d 378 (Colo.1985).

65. Wis.Stat.Ann. 939.32(2).

66. Thus, in Wilson v. State, 85 Miss. 687, 38 So. 46 (1905), where the defendant raised the numbers but not the words designating the amount due on a check, it was held that he was not guilty of attempted forgery because

he did not intend to commit the crime of forgery, for forgery requires a material alteration (which the mere changing of the numbers was not).

67. See § 5.1(d).

68. G. Williams, Criminal Law: The General Part 618 (2d ed. 1961).

69. See § 7.2.

70. See § 7.3.

71. See § 7.4.

72. See § 7.5.

73. Under the approach generally taken in the modern codes, "intent" is narrowly defined to distinguish it from "knowledge." See § 3.5(a). This means the knowledge mental state, though proper for the crime of murder, should not be used in attempt murder jury instructions. State v. Brown, 479 A.2d 1317 (Me.1984).

74. People v. Harris, 72 Ill.2d 16, 17 Ill.Dec. 838, 377 N.E.2d 28 (1978); State v. Butler, 322 So.2d 189 (La.1975); Flanagan v. State, 675 S.W.2d 734 (Tex.Crim.App.1982); Rex v. Whybrow, 35 Cr.App.R. 141 (1951).

75. Thacker v. Commonwealth, 134 Va. 767, 114 S.E. 504 (1922). "[W]hile a person may be guilty of murder though there was no actual intent to kill, he cannot be guilty of an attempt to commit murder unless he has a specific intent to kill." Merritt v. Commonwealth, 164 Va. 653, 180 S.E. 395 (1935).

Contra: Gentry v. State, 437 So.2d 1097 (Fla.1983) ("logic" dictates conclusion higher mental state should not be

was committing a dangerous felony.[76] Again, this is because intent is needed for the crime of attempt, so that attempted murder requires an intent to bring about that result described by the crime of murder (i.e., the death of another).[77]

As is true generally of anticipatory offenses,[78] a clear understanding of the requisite mental state in a particular case necessitates an analysis of the elements of the crime to which the anticipatory offense relates. The crime of attempt does not exist in the abstract, but rather exists only in relation to other offenses; a defendant must be charged with an attempt to commit a specifically designated crime,[79] and it is to that crime one must look in identifying the kind of intent required. For example, if the charge is attempted theft and theft is defined as requiring an intent to permanently deprive the owner of his property, then that same intent must be established to prove the attempt.[80] It is not enough to show that the defendant intended to do some unspecified criminal act.[81]

The Model Penal Code draftsmen put the case of a defendant who intends to demolish a building and proceeds with his plan to do so notwithstanding knowledge that it is virtually

inevitable that persons within the building will be killed by the explosion.[82] If the plan does not succeed, is he guilty of attempted murder? In view of the intent requirement, it would seem not, for his intent was to destroy the building rather than to kill the inhabitants, although some doubt exists because the concept of "intent" has sometimes been thought to include consequences which the defendant knows are substantially certain to result.[83] Under the Code, the defendant would be deemed guilty of attempted murder,[84] a result which is "based on the conclusion that the manifestation of the actor's dangerousness is just as great—or very nearly as great—as in the case of purposive conduct." [85]

(2) Recklessness and Negligence. May a defendant be convicted of an attempt to commit a crime which is defined only in terms of reckless or negligent conduct? In theory at least, it is conceivable that conviction might be possible if the completed crime consists simply of reckless or negligent creation of danger *and* it was shown that the defendant actually intended to engage in conduct creating that danger. Thus, it has been suggested that if one attempts to start his car in order to drive it, knowing it has no brakes, this would warrant a conviction for attempting to

required merely because of fortuity that victim survived); People v. Castro, 657 P.2d 932 (Colo.1983) (reasoning that extreme indifference murder requires a conscious object to engage in conduct that creates a grave risk of death, and that this sufficed under attempt statute applicable to one who, "acting with the kind of culpability otherwise required for commission of an offense, * * * intentionally engages in conduct constituting a substantial step toward the commission of the offense").

76. Head v. State, 443 N.E.2d 44 (Ind.1982). Contra: Amlotte v. State, 456 So.2d 448 (Fla.1984).

77. The principle applies to other crimes as well, so that intent will be necessary as to the attempt even if unnecessary as to the completed crime. Commonwealth v. Ware, 375 Mass. 118, 375 N.E.2d 1183 (1978).

78. See § 6.1(c) and § 6.4(e).

79. People v. Urbana, 18 Ill.2d 81, 163 N.E.2d 511 (1959); State v. Beckwith, 135 Me. 423, 198 A. 739 (1938); Baker v. State, 6 Md.App. 148, 250 A.2d 677 (1969).

80. People v. Matthews, 122 Ill.App.2d 264, 258 N.E.2d 378 (1970).

81. In re Smith, 3 Cal.3d 192, 90 Cal.Rptr. 1, 474 P.2d 969 (1970) (where defendant convicted of attempted kidnapping on evidence that he grabbed woman, brandished screwdriver, and said they were going in her car, which he

attempted to open, effective counsel might well have argued that this did not show intent to kidnap as opposed to intent to rape or to steal).

Often, however, the intent can be inferred from the defendant's conduct and the surrounding circumstances. See, e.g., Larsen v. State, 86 Nev. 451, 470 P.2d 417 (1970) (where defendant with mask and simulating gun in pocket attempted to enter motel office, jury could infer that he intended to enter unlawfully with intent to commit larceny within); Hines v. State, 458 S.W.2d 666 (Tex.Cr.App. 1970) (attempted entry of dwelling at nighttime justifies inference of intent to steal just as where there is an actual breaking and entering).

82. Model Penal Code § 5.01, Comment at 305 (1985).

83. See § 3.5(a).

84. This is because it is sufficient that the defendant, acting with the kind of culpability otherwise required for the completed offense, believed that he would cause the particular result which is an element of the completed crime. Model Penal Code § 5.01(1)(b). Most of the modern codes have not adopted such a provision. One court has so construed its attempt statute even though it lacks particular language so stating. People v. Krovarz, 697 P.2d 378 (Colo.1985).

85. Model Penal Code § 5.01, Comment at 305 (1985).

drive negligently.[86] Such a result could be reached without holding that an attempt may be committed through negligence, and therefore could be distinguished from the case in which the defendant had merely been negligent in failing to discover the condition of his brakes.

The above analysis, it should be noted, cannot be applied when the completed crime consists of recklessly or negligently causing a certain result, for if there were an intent to cause such a result then the attempt would not be to commit that crime but rather the greater crime of intentionally causing such result.[87] For example, so long as the crime of attempt is deemed to require an intent-type of mental state, there can be no such thing as an attempt to commit criminal-negligence involuntary manslaughter.[88] "The consequence involved in that crime is the death of the victim and an act done with intent to achieve this, if an attempt at all, is attempted murder." [89]

It has been strongly urged, however, that recklessness or negligence should suffice for attempt liability and that therefore it *should* be possible to attempt such a crime as involuntary manslaughter. "If a pharmacist is grossly negligent in making up a prescription

and the patient dies as a result of taking the dosage on the bottle, the pharmacist is clearly guilty of manslaughter. Surely the policy considerations which dictate such a conviction apply equally if, through chance, the negligent error is discovered before any damage is done. There seems to be every reason for a verdict of attempted manslaughter."[90] It may well be that the purposes of the criminal law would be properly served by conviction of the pharmacist for his grossly negligent conduct even though it did not in fact cause harm, but it might be questioned whether this result should be reached by a redefinition of attempt law as opposed to merely making it an offense to engage in negligent or reckless conduct which endangers others.[91]

(3) Liability Without Fault. Although the issue has seldom reached the courts, it would seem to follow from the generally accepted notion that intent is required for an attempt that there is no such thing as strict liability attempt. That is, even if the completed crime may be committed without intent, knowledge, recklessness or even negligence, the same is not true of an attempt to commit that crime. An attempt to commit a strict liability offense is thus possible only if it is shown that the

86. G. Williams, supra note 68, at 619–20.

87. State v. Hembd, 197 Mont. 438, 643 P.2d 567 (1982) (no such crime as attempted arson by negligence). But see People v. Castro, discussed in note 75 supra.

88. State v. Almeda, 189 Conn. 303, 455 A.2d 1326 (1983); People v. Reagan, 99 Ill.2d 238, 75 Ill.Dec. 701, 457 N.E.2d 1260 (1983); Rhode v. State, 181 Ind.App. 265, 391 N.E.2d 666 (1979); State v. Howard, 405 A.2d 206 (Me. 1979); State v. Zupetz, 322 N.W.2d 730 (Minn.1982); Bailey v. State, ___ Nev. ___, 688 P.2d 320 (1984); People v. Foster, 19 N.Y.2d 150, 278 N.Y.S.2d 603, 225 N.E.2d 200 (1967) (but holding that negotiated plea of guilty to attempted manslaughter "should be sustained on the ground that it was sought by defendant and freely taken as part of a bargain which was struck for the defendant's benefit"); People v. Brown, 21 App.Div.2d 738, 249 N.Y.S.2d 922 (1964); State v. Melvin, 49 Wis.2d 246, 181 N.W.2d 490 (1970) (defendant on trial for attempted murder not entitled to instruction on attempted homicide by reckless conduct). Cf. State v. Grant, 418 A.2d 154 (Me.1980), noted at 34 Me.L.Rev. 479 (1982) (defendant may not be convicted of attempted fourth or fifth degree homicide, the imperfect self defense crimes requiring recklessness or negligence, respectively, as to the need for defense, as defendant cannot intend to act recklessly or negligently).

In People v. Weeks, 86 Ill.App.2d 480, 230 N.E.2d 12 (1967), the court relied upon the *Foster* and *Brown* cases in

holding that there was no such crime as an attempt to commit heat-of-passion voluntary manslaughter. The court was in error in asserting that voluntary manslaughter, because it can result only from serious provocation, cannot be committed intent to kill. See § 7.10, and compare Taylor v. State, 444 So.2d 931 (Fla.1983); State v. Crutcher, 231 Iowa 418, 1 N.W.2d 195 (1942); State v. Norman, 580 P.2d 237 (Utah 1978). In Commonwealth v. Hebert, 373 Mass. 535, 368 N.E.2d 1204 (1977), the court recognized that attempted voluntary manslaughter was logically possible but nonetheless declined to recognize such a crime because of the availability of the assault with intent to kill statute in such circumstances. See Sachs, Is Attempt to Commit Voluntary Manslaughter a Possible Crime?, 71 Ill.B.J. 166 (1982).

89. Smith, Two Problems in Criminal Attempts, 70 Harv.L.Rev. 422, 434 (1957).

90. Stuart, supra note 61 at 662. See also, Smith, supra note 89, at 432.

91. See, e.g., Model Penal Code § 211.2, providing that a person is guilty of a misdemeanor "if he recklessly engages in conduct which places or may place another person in danger of death or serious bodily injury." Many of the modern recodifications contain such a provision.

defendant acted with an intent to bring about the proscribed result.[92]

It has been argued that "if crimes of * * * strict liability are necessary and valid instruments of policy, then there is no reason for not applying this same policy in the case of attempts."[93] Thus, so the argument goes, "if it is right and necessary in the public interest that *D* should be held liable for selling adulterated milk although he did not know and had no reasonable means of knowing that the milk was adulterated, why is it not right that he should be guilty of an attempt if he tries unsuccessfully to sell the same milk in similar circumstances."[94] Others, however, have contended that there is "no reason of policy to extend the dubious notion of strict liability to the law of attempts."[95] Taking into account the rather shaky justification for strict-liability crimes,[96] the latter view is a more appealing one.

It must be noted that the above comments are applicable to the true strict-liability offense, which must be distinguished from those crimes which do require proof of an intent to bring about some result but yet do not require a showing of any state of mind as to certain attendant circumstances. As to the latter offenses, the question is whether one may likewise be said to have attempted to commit such a crime when no intent (or even knowledge) is established concerning those attendant circumstances. It has been noted that authority on this issue is lacking[97] and that it

is consequently difficult to say what the result would be under prevailing principles of attempt liability.[98] However, a persuasive argument has been made "that an attempt is so essentially connected with consequences—with that event or series of events which is the principal constituent of the crime—that the only essential intention is an intention to bring about those consequences; and that if recklessness, or negligence, or even blameless inadvertence with respect to the remaining constituents of the crime (the pure circumstances) will suffice for the substantive crime, it will suffice also for the attempt."[99] Under this view, if the crime of burglary may be committed without regard to the defendant's knowledge that he was actually acting in the nighttime, then the same is true of attempted burglary.[100] Likewise, assuming it is a federal offense to kill or injure an FBI agent and that recklessness or even negligence with respect to the victim's status will suffice, an attempt to commit that offense would also only require recklessness or negligence as to the victim's position.[101]

 WESTLAW REFERENCES

crim**** /s attempt /p intent! /p reckless! negligen!

(d) The Act.[102] One of the basic premises of the criminal law is that bad thoughts alone cannot constitute a crime.[103] This is no less true as to an attempt, and thus it is not enough that the defendant have intended to

92. Cf. Gardner v. Akeroyd, [1952] 2 Q.B. 743, holding, by analogy to the law of attempts, that the statutory offense of doing acts preparatory to the commission of the strict liability crime of selling meat above the statutory maxima was not itself a liability without fault offense.

93. Smith, Two Problems in Criminal Attempts Re-Examined–I, 1962 Crim.L.Rev. 135, 143.

94. Ibid.

95. Stuart, Mens Rea, Negligence and Attempts, 1968 Crim.L.Rev. 647, 660.

96. See § 3.8(c).

97. Smith, Two Problems in Criminal Attempts, 70 Harv.L.Rev. 422, 434 (1957).

98. Model Penal Code § 5.01, Comment (Tent.Draft No. 10, 1960).

99. Smith, supra note 97, at 434. Model Penal Code § 5.01 was drafted so as to make it clear that such should

be the result. Compare Williams, The Problem of Reckless Attempts, 1983 Crim.L.Rev. 365, 375, concluding it should be required "that the defendant was reckless as to the circumstances."

100. Smith, supra note 97, at 433.

101. Model Penal Code § 5.01, Comment at 303 n. 13 (1985).

102. See J. Hall, General Principles of Criminal Law 576–86 (2d ed. 1960); G. Williams, Criminal Law: The General Part 621–32 (2d ed. 1961); Levenbrook, Prohibiting Attempts and Preparations, 49 U.Mo.K.C.L.Rev. 41 (1980); Misner, The New Attempt Laws: Unsuspected Threat to the Fourth Amendment, 33 Stan.L.Rev. 201 (1981). Sayre, Criminal Attempts, 41 Harv.L.Rev. 821, 843–58 (1928); Skilton, The Requisite Act in a Criminal Attempt, 3 U.Pitt.L.Rev. 308 (1937); Stuart, The Actus Reus in Attempts, 1970 Crim.L.Rev. 505.

103. See § 3.2.

commit a crime. There must also be an act, and not any act will suffice.

Precisely what kind of act is required is not made very clear by the language which has traditionally been used by courts and legislatures. It is commonly stated that more than an act of preparation must occur,[104] which perhaps is of some help, although the situation is confused somewhat because courts occasionally say that preparatory acts will be enough under certain circumstances.[105] The traditional attempt statute requires an "act toward the commission of" some offense,[106] although slightly different wording is also to be found: "conduct which tends to effect the commission of" a crime; an act "in furtherance of" or "tending directly toward" or which "constitutes a substantial step toward"[107] the commission of an offense. Similarly, the courts use a wide variety of phrases: "a step toward the commission of the crime"[108]; an "act in part execution of the intent"[109]; "a direct movement toward the commission of the offense"[110]; "the commencement of the consummation"[111]; or "some appreciable fragment of the crime."[112]

The situation is further complicated by the fact that the acts in question may be committed in so many different ways because of the great number of offenses on which the crime of attempt may be overlaid. An infinite variety of situations can arise. If A, with a gun in his pocket, checks in at the airline ticket counter and takes a seat in the departure lounge, has he attempted to commit the of-

fense of boarding an aircraft while carrying a concealed weapon?[113] If B, planning to rob a bank messenger, drives around to the places where it is expected that the messenger will make deliveries but fails to locate him, has he attempted to commit the crime of robbery?[114] If C proceeds with a bunco scheme which requires that he display a large roll of fake money to another, convince the other person to withdraw his own money from the bank to prove that the bank is a safe place to keep one's funds, and then make a sleight of hand switch of the victim's money for the fake money, has he attempted to commit the crime of theft if the intended victim procures his bank book and goes to the bank but does not draw out his money?[115] The result which is reached in any one of these cases is unlikely to afford a clear indication of how the other two should be resolved.

A closer look at the decided cases on the law of attempt, however, affords some guidance as to what types of acts will be sufficient. In many instances the cases cannot be reconciled with one another, but this is because different courts have utilized somewhat different tests on this issue. It is to these tests that we now look.

(1) The Proximity Approach. Under one approach, the question is whether the defendant's act was sufficiently proximate to the intended crime. But, how proximate must the act be? The strictest approach, at least in one sense, would be to require that the defendant have engaged in the "last proximate

104. People v. Gallardo, 41 Cal.2d 57, 257 P.2d 29 (1953); State v. Bereman, 177 Kan. 141, 276 P.2d 364 (1954); Minn.Stat.Ann. § 609.17.

105. Bell v. State, 118 Ga.App. 291, 163 S.E.2d 323 (1968); Commonwealth v. Peaslee, 177 Mass. 267, 59 N.E. 55 (1901).

106. Model Penal Code § 5.01, Comment at 299 (1985). Such language appears even in some of the modern recodifications.

107. This language is used in most of the modern recodifications.

108. State v. Harvill, 106 Ariz. 386, 476 P.2d 841 (1970).

109. State v. Bereman, 177 Kan. 141, 276 P.2d 364 (1954); State v. Thomas, 438 S.W.2d 441 (Mo.1969).

110. State v. Bereman, 177 Kan. 141, 276 P.2d 364 (1954). See also Bell v. State, 118 Ga.App. 291, 163 S.E.2d

323 (1968) ("directly tending to" commission of the crime); State v. Anderson, 172 N.W.2d 597 (N.D.1969) ("tending directly toward" commission of the crime); State v. Thomas, 438 S.W.2d 441 (Mo.1969) (the act "must move directly toward" commission of the crime).

111. State v. Bereman, 177 Kan. 141, 276 P.2d 364 (1954); State v. Goddard, 74 Wash.2d 848, 447 P.2d 180 (1969).

112. People v. Buffum, 40 Cal.2d 709, 718, 256 P.2d 317, 321 (1953).

113. Yes, concluded the court in United States v. Brown, 305 F.Supp. 415 (W.D.Tex.1969).

114. No, concluded the court in People v. Rizzo, 246 N.Y. 334, 158 N.E. 888 (1927).

115. No, concluded the court in People v. Orndorff, 261 Cal.App.2d 212, 67 Cal.Rptr. 824 (1968).

act," that is, that he have done everything which he believes necessary to bring about the intended result. If this approach were taken, then it would be attempted murder if *A* shot at *B* and missed or *B* were hit but did not die, but not if *A* were just about to fire but had not done so. Similarly, an attempt at false pretenses would exist only if the defendant had done everything he needed to do prior to actual receipt of the money.[116] And any crime planned to be committed through an innocent agent would be attempted as soon as the agent were briefed on what he was to do, even though considerable time was still to elapse before the agent was to act.[117] It is generally accepted that where the actor has engaged in the "last proximate act" he has committed an attempt.[118] However, "no jurisdiction operating within the framework of Anglo-American law requires that the last proximate act occur before an attempt can be charged."[119] Although it was intimated in the famous English case of *Regina v. Eagleton*[120] that the last proximate act was necessary, that view was very promptly rejected by the same court.[121] Thus the first administration of poison in a case of intended slow poisoning by repeated doses would amount to attempted murder even though it quite obviously was not the last proximate act.[122]

Because the last act is not required, some courts have instead tried to identify an aspect of the criminal scheme which is indispensable—the notion being that there is not a proximity to success until the defendant has obtained control over that indispensable ele-

ment. This approach has been followed most frequently as to those schemes which require that the defendant induce someone else to take certain action. Thus, in the bunco scheme case described earlier,[123] it could be said that indispensable to the scheme was the victim's withdrawal of his money from the bank, so that the theft was not attempted unless the intended victim did draw out his funds. Similarly, if the scheme is to defraud an insurance company by having the named beneficiary file a false claim, it would be indispensable that the beneficiary file the claim or at least agree to file it.[124] (Consistent with this view is the generally accepted notion that a bare solicitation is not an attempt because completion of the crime requires action by the person solicited.[125]) The indispensable element approach has also been used when the scheme is such that the defendant cannot undertake the crime until he obtains some item; for example, it has been held that one cannot attempt to vote illegally until he gets a ballot[126] and that one cannot attempt an assault with a deadly weapon until he acquires the weapon.[127]

Yet another variation of the proximity approach is that which focuses upon whether the defendant's acts may be said to be physically proximate to the intended crime. The emphasis is not so much upon what the defendant has done as upon what remains to be done, and the time and place at which the intended crime is supposed to occur take on considerable importance.[128] Thus, in the case described earlier[129] in which the defendant unsuccessfully sought out the bank messen-

---

116. Regina v. Eagleton, 6 Cox Crim.Cas. 559 (1855).

117. Williams, supra note 102, at 623–24.

118. Thus, one of the alternate tests in Model Penal Code § 5.01(1) is whether the defendant has engaged in conduct with the purpose of causing a criminal result "with the belief that it will cause such result without further conduct on his part."

119. Model Penal Code § 5.01, Comment at 321 n. 97 (1985). See, e.g., People v. Bracey, 41 N.Y.2d 296, 392 N.Y.S.2d 412, 360 N.E.2d 1094 (1977) (required "dangerous proximity" need not be final act); Sizemore v. Commonwealth, 218 Va. 980, 243 S.E.2d 212 (1978) (defendant guilty of attempted murder even though he never pulled the trigger of gun).

120. 6 Cox Crim.Cas. 559 (1855).

121. Regina v. Roberts, 7 Cox Crim.Cas. 39 (1855).

122. King v. White [1910] 2 K.B. 124.

123. See text at note 115.

124. In re Schurman, 40 Kan. 533, 20 P. 277 (1889).

125. See § 6.1(f).

126. State v. Fielder, 210 Mo. 188, 109 S.W. 580 (1908).

127. State v. Wood, 19 S.D. 260, 103 N.W. 25 (1905).

128. The act must "be something more than mere preparation, remote from the time and place of the intended crime." State v. Dumas, 118 Minn. 77, 136 N.W. 311 (1912).

129. See text at note 114 supra.

ger, it was held that the robbery had not been attempted.

> [T]hese defendants had planned to commit a crime, and were looking around the city for an opportunity to commit it, but the opportunity fortunately never came. Men would not be guilty of an attempt at burglary if they had planned to break into a building and were arrested while they were hunting about the streets for the building not knowing where it was. Neither would a man be guilty of an attempt to commit murder if he armed himself and started out to find the person whom he had planned to kill but could not find him. So here these defendants were not guilty of an attempt to commit robbery in the first degree when they had not found or reached the presence of the person they intended to rob.[130]

The physical proximity test may be viewed as but a part of a broader notion that, as put by Justice Holmes, there "must be a dangerous proximity to success." [131] Under this approach, account must be taken of "the gravity of the crime, the uncertainty of the result, and the seriousness of the apprehension, coupled with the great harm likely to result." [132] Thus the "potentially and immediately dangerous circumstances" presented by the defendant's entry of a company's premises carrying dynamite with intent to destroy one of the company's buildings make that act sufficient for the crime of attempting to destroy premises by dynamite.[133] "While it might be argued that the accused should have been allowed to actually place the dynamite or even prepare to ignite it before being apprehended, again, this would be a dangerous requirement. Even if there might exist an opportunity to prevent the ignition of the explosive there still would be a chance that the perpetrator

might instead ignite it and hurl it toward or into the building in which case preventive measures would virtually be precluded." [134]

What are the merits of the proximity approach? In support of it, it has been argued that an act should not be punished except "to prevent some harm which is foreseen as likely to follow that act under the circumstances in which it is done." [135] Under this view, deterrence of the completed crime is assumed to be the function of attempt law, so that conduct does not constitute an attempt until the defendant has come dangerously close to accomplishing the completed crime. The proximity test has been questioned on the ground that it is inconsistent with the rule that impossibility of success is not necessarily a defense,[136] and on the broader principle that "the primary purpose of punishing attempts is to neutralize dangerous individuals and not to deter dangerous acts." [137] So the argument goes, whether one should be subjected to the corrective processes of the law for his actions tending toward the commission of a substantive crime is not an issue which should necessarily be determined by the extent to which that person's conduct actually created a danger.

(2) The Probable Desistance Approach. Some courts have taken the view that the act required to establish a criminal attempt must be one which in the ordinary course of events would result in the commission of the target crime except for the intervention of some extraneous factor.[138] This, it would seem, necessitates a determination of whether one who had gone that far with a criminal scheme would thereafter voluntarily desist from his efforts to commit the crime. One commentator has stated the test somewhat differently:

130. People v. Rizzo, 246 N.Y. 334, 158 N.E. 888 (1927).

131. Dissenting in Hyde v. United States, 225 U.S. 347, 32 S.Ct. 793, 56 L.Ed. 1114 (1912).

132. Commonwealth v. Kennedy, 170 Mass. 18, 48 N.E. 770 (1897). See also, O. Holmes, The Common Law 68–69 (1881).

133. Bell v. State, 118 Ga.App. 291, 163 S.E.2d 323 (1968).

134. Ibid. See also Cody v. State, 605 S.W.2d 271 (Tex. Crim.App.1980) (pouring gasoline on floor and placing wads of paper nearby sufficient; defendant need not have struck a match).

135. O. Holmes, supra note 132, at 67.

136. G. Williams, supra note 102, at 631. On when impossibility *is* a defense, see § 6.3(a).

137. Model Penal Code § 5.01, Comment at 323 (1985). See also, G. Williams, supra note 102, at 632; Stuart, supra note 102, at 508.

138. People v. Buffum, 40 Cal.2d 709, 256 P.2d 317 (1953); West v. State, 437 So.2d 1212 (Miss.1983); State v. Goddard, 74 Wash.2d 848, 447 P.2d 180 (1969); Hamiel v. State, 92 Wis.2d 656, 285 N.W.2d 639 (1979); Boyles v. State, 46 Wis.2d 473, 175 N.W.2d 277 (1970).

The defendant's conduct must pass that point where most men, holding such an intention as the defendant holds, would think better of their conduct and desist. All of us, or most of us, at some time or other harbor what may be described as a cirminal intent to effect unlawful consequences. Many of us take some steps—often slight enough in character—to bring the consequences about; but most of us, when we reach a certain point, desist, and return to our roles as law-abiding citizens. The few who do not and pass beyond that point are, if the object of their conduct is not achieved, guilty of a criminal attempt.[139]

An inquiry into whether there exists a probability of desistance or whether a normal person would thereafter desist has something to commend it, at least as compared with the proximity approach, for it does square with the function of attempt law in identifying dangerous persons. However, the probable or normal desistance approach has been criticized as a "highly artificial device" in that there exists no basis for making such judgments as when desistance is no longer probable or when the normal citizen would stop.[140] Because of the lack of an empirical basis for making such predictions, this approach as applied does not differ from the proximity test.[141]

(3) The Equivocality Approach. A totally different approach is that which is referred to as the equivocality theory[142] or the *res ipsa loquitur* test.[143] As stated by Salmond: "An attempt is an act of such a nature that it is itself evidence of the criminal intent with which it is done. A criminal attempt bears criminal intent upon its face."[144] Or, as put by Turner: "The actus reus of an attempt to commit a specific crime is constituted when the accused person does an act which is a step towards the commission of the specific crime,

and the doing of such act can have no other purpose than the commission of that specific crime."[145] This is not merely a restatement in somewhat different form of the necessity to prove the mental state, for, unlike proof of the intent itself, the defendant's confession or other representations about his intentions may not be taken into consideration. Rather, "it is as though a cinematograph film, which had so far depicted merely the accused person's acts without stating what was his intention, had been suddenly stopped, and the audience were asked to say to what end those acts were directed. If there is only one reasonable answer to this question then the accused has done what amounts to an 'attempt' to attain that end. If there is more than one reasonably possible answer, then the accused has not yet done enough."[146]

A well-known example of this approach is the New Zealand case of *Campbell & Bradley v. Ward,*[147] where the court held the evidence did not establish the necessary act for attempted theft. A car in which the two defendants and another were riding stopped and the defendants' companion got out of the car and entered a parked car, but he left and returned to the defendants when the owner of the parked car approached. Nothing in the parked car had been taken or disturbed. The defendants fled but they were later arrested and each of them confessed that they were participants in a plan whereby their companion was going to steal a battery and radio from the parked car. The court somewhat reluctantly concluded that the act of entering the car was too equivocal.

It is not at all uncommon for courts in this country to refer explicitly to the necessity for unequivocal behavior in order to prove an attempt.[148] However, it is not entirely clear

139. Skilton, supra note 102 at 309–10.

140. Stuart, supra note 102, at 509.

141. Model Penal Code § 5.01, Comment at 325 (1985).

142. G. Williams, supra note 102, at 629.

143. Model Penal Code § 5.01, Comment at 326 (1985).

144. J. Salmond, Jurisprudence 404 (7th ed.1924). See also his discussion of this theory in The King v. Barker, [1924] N.Z.L.R. 865.

145. Turner, Attempts to Commit Crimes, 5 Cambridge L.J. 230, 236 (1934).

146. Turner, quoted in G. Williams, supra note 102, at 629.

147. [1955] N.Z.L.R. 471.

148. E.g., United States v. McDowell, 714 F.2d 106 (11th Cir.1983); United States v. Everett, 700 F.2d 900 (3d Cir.1983); Lemke v. United States, 14 Alaska 587, 211 F.2d 73 (1954); State v. Mandel, 78 Ariz. 226, 278 P.2d 413

to what extent these statements reflect an acceptance of the equivocality theory as applied in *Campbell & Bradley*, as opposed to a concern with the need for adequate proof of criminal intent *in addition to* proof of the act. The situation is further confounded because a number of courts have asserted that equivocal conduct will not suffice, but then seem to qualify that somewhat with the statement that if "the design of a person to commit a crime is clearly shown, slight acts done in furtherance thereof will constitute an attempt." [149]

What can be said for the equivocality approach? In contrast to the proximity theory, it is arguably consistent with the major purpose of the crime of attempt in that equivocal acts may well reflect an equivocal purpose. Statements of intent made prior to equivocal acts or a confession of intent made subsequent thereto give no assurance of that firmness of purpose which manifests the actor's dangerousness.[150] "But once the actor must desist or perform acts that he realizes would incriminate him if all external facts were known, in all probability a firmer state of mind exists." [151]

Yet, most commentators have been critical of the equivocality approach. It is said to restrict unduly the value of confessions in attempt cases.[152] Moreover, if strictly followed it would bar conviction for attempt even when the defendant, whose intent was otherwise established, had engaged in virtually the last act required for the carrying out of his intent.[153] Putting other evidence to one

side in assessing the act itself would also lead to unfortunate results when the defendant's conduct shows *some* criminal purpose but is equivocal in the sense that it does not establish beyond a reasonable doubt the particular offense being attempted.[154]

(4) The Model Penal Code Approach. The Model Penal Code requires "an act or omission constituting a substantial step in a course of conduct planned to culminate in [the actor's] commission of the crime." [155] Moreover, conduct cannot constitute a substantial step "unless it is strongly corroborative of the actor's criminal purpose." [156] This, the draftsmen note, will broaden the scope of attempt liability in a way which is consistent with the purpose of restraining dangerous persons, as: (1) the emphasis is upon what the actor has already done rather than what remains to be done; (2) liability will be imposed only if some firmness of criminal purpose is shown; and (3) the conduct may be assessed in light of the defendant's statements.[157]

The Model Penal Code's "substantial step" language is to be found in the great majority of the attempt statutes in the modern recodifications. Even in the absence of such a statute, the courts in several jurisdictions have adopted the Model Penal Code "substantial step" approach.[158] The "substantial step" statutes referred to above more often than not also include the Model Penal Code requirement that the step must be "strongly corroborative" of the defendant's criminal purpose.

The Model Penal Code is also unique in that it sets forth several categories of conduct

---

(1954); People v. Buffum, 40 Cal.2d 709, 256 P.2d 317 (1953).

149. E.g., Larsen v. State, 86 Nev. 451, 470 P.2d 417 (1970), quoting People v. Downer, 57 Cal.2d 800, 806, 22 Cal.Rptr. 347, 372 P.2d 107 (1962).

150. G. Williams, supra note 102, at 631.

151. Model Penal Code § 5.01, Comment at 329 (1985).

152. Ibid.; J. Hall, supra note 102, at 581. It should be noted, however, that some of the cases seeming to use the equivocality approach do take confessions into account. See, e.g., United States v. Everett, 700 F.2d 900 (3d Cir. 1983); United States v. Hough, 561 F.2d 594 (5th Cir. 1977).

153. G. Williams, supra note 102, at 630 puts the case of a defendant who goes up to a haystack, fills his pipe,

and lights a match, which he says are equivocal acts but should result in attempt liability if the defendant thereafter confessed that his intent was to set fire to the stack.

154. Ibid.

155. Model Penal Code § 5.01(1)(c).

156. Model Penal Code § 5.01(2).

157. Model Penal Code § 5.01, Comment at 329–30 (1985).

158. United States v. Ivic, 700 F.2d 51 (2d Cir.1983); United States v. Joyce, 693 F.2d 838 (8th Cir.1982); United States v. Mandujano, 499 F.2d 370 (5th Cir.1974); State v. Latraverse, ___ R.I. ___, 443 A.2d 890 (1982).

which are not to be held insufficient as a matter of law if strongly corroborative of the actor's criminal purpose.[159] Although states which have followed the Code approach in other respects have for the most part declined to enumerate these categories by statute,[160] the categories are worthy of brief note here because they illustrate how the Code approach would achieve results different from the other tests:[161]

"(a) lying in wait, searching for or following the contemplated victim of the crime." By contrast, cases taking the proximity approach have sometimes found the act insufficient where the victim had not arrived at the intended crime scene[162] or where the defendant was still searching out the victim.[163]

"(b) enticing or seeking to entice the contemplated victim of the crime to go to the place contemplated for its commission." Cases utilizing other theories have sometimes found insufficient the defendant's acts of offering the intended victim a reward for going to the place where the crime was to be committed.[164]

"(c) reconnoitering the place contemplated for the commission of the crime." Whether this would suffice at common law is unclear because the cases have usually emphasized other factors as well, such as the possession of necessary equipment.[165] However, reconnoitering in advance of the time for the crime probably would not suffice where the physical proximity test is employed.[166]

"(d) unlawful entry of a structure, vehicle or enclosure in which it is contemplated that the crime will be committed." As *Campbell & Bradley* illustrates, this well might not suffice under the equivocality approach. However, such entry could be expected to be sufficient under the proximity approach, although there is some questionable authority to the contrary.[167]

"(e) possession of materials to be employed in the commission of the crime, which are specially designed for such unlawful use or which serve no lawful purpose of the actor under the circumstances." Some decisions in accord are to be found. Illustrative is the holding that possession of a still and mash are sufficient for an attempt illegally to manufacture intoxicating beverages.[168]

"(f) possession, collection or fabrication of materials to be employed in the commission of the crime, at or near the place contemplated for its commission, where such possession, collection or fabrication serves no lawful purpose of the actor under the circumstances." Again, decisions in accord are to be found, such as that the defendant's arrival with inflammables at the premises to be burned is enough,[169] although it would be otherwise under the proximity theory if the crime was to be completed later.[170]

"(g) soliciting an innocent agent to engage in conduct constituting an element of the crime." Doubtless this would also be sufficient at common law because the defendant has even taken his last step.[171]

159. Model Penal Code § 5.01(2).

160. Even when such elaboration in the statute is lacking, courts often rely upon the Model Penal Code categories in the decision of specific cases. See, e.g., People v. Terrell, 99 Ill.2d 427, 77 Ill.Dec. 88, 459 N.E.2d 1337 (1984).

161. The quoted phrases at the outset of the following paragraphs are all taken directly from Model Penal Code § 5.01(2).

162. E.g., People v. Volpe, 122 N.Y.S.2d 342 (1953).

163. E.g., People v. Rizzo, 246 N.Y. 334, 158 N.E. 888 (1927).

164. E.g., Mullins v. Commonwealth, 174 Va. 477, 5 S.E.2d 491 (1939). But see Stephens v. Sheriff, 93 Nev. 338, 565 P.2d 1007 (1977) (delivery of victim to supposed "hit men" sufficed for attempted murder).

165. E.g., People v. Gibson, 94 Cal.App.2d 468, 210 P.2d 747 (1949). See also United States v. Jackson, 560 F.2d 112 (2d Cir.1977) (reconnoitering a "substantial step" where defendant also possessed the necessary paraphernalia of guns, shells, handcuffs and masks).

166. Cf. Commonwealth v. Peaslee, 177 Mass. 267, 59 N.E. 55 (1901).

167. E.g., Kelly v. Commonwealth, 1 Grant 484 (Pa. 1858).

168. E.g., Anderson v. Commonwealth, 195 Va. 258, 77 S.E.2d 846 (1953).

169. E.g., State v. Bliss, 80 S.W.2d 162 (Mo.1935). See also United States v. Ivic, 700 F.2d 51 (2d Cir.1983) (transporting fully operational time bomb to close vicinity of where it to be placed was a "substantial step" though bomb not put in place because of lack of a parking place); People v. Terrell, 99 Ill.2d 427, 77 Ill.Dec. 88, 459 N.E.2d 1337 (1984) (hiding behind gas station until it opened, while in possession of loaded gun and stocking mask, was a "substantial step").

170. Commonwealth v. Peaslee, 177 Mass. 267, 59 N.E. 55 (1901).

171. G. Williams, supra note 102, at 623–24.

WESTLAW REFERENCES

crim**** /s attempt /p proximate desist! equivoca!

§ 6.3   Attempt—The Limits of Liability

Under the traditional approach, legal impossibility but not factual impossibility is a defense to a charge of attempt. Legal impossibility is the situation in which the defendant did everything he intended to do but yet had not committed the completed crime, while factual impossibility is that in which the defendant is unable to accomplish what he intends because of some facts unknown to him. The modern and better view is that impossibility is not a defense when the defendant's actual intent (not limited by the true facts unknown to him) was to do an act or bring about a result proscribed by law. Considerable uncertainty exists in the cases as to whether voluntary abandonment is a defense to a charge of attempt, but the better view is that it is. As with the modern view of impossibility, this follows from the fact that the purpose of the crime of attempt is to subject dangerous persons to the corrective processes of the law.

Although the crime of attempt is sometimes defined as if failure were an essential element, the modern view is that a defendant may be convicted on a charge of attempt even if it is shown that the crime was completed. Taking into account the rationale of attempt, a person who attempts a crime should be amenable to the same punishment as a person who completed the crime, subject to the qualification that extreme sanctions intended only for general deterrence should not be permitted.

(a) Impossibility. Judging from the volume of literature in this area, scholars in the field of substantive criminal law appear to be more fascinated with the subject of impossibility in attempts than with any other subject.[1] Perhaps this is not surprising, for the question of whether we should punish a person who has attempted what was not possible under the surrounding circumstances requires careful consideration of many of the fundamental notions concerning the theory and purposes of a system of substantive criminal law.

Moreover, the cases on the subject are often intriguing. Consider these fact situations, all from relatively recent reported decisions. *A* was dancing with a girl when she collapsed in his arms, after which he took her out to his car and engaged in sexual intercourse with her; *A* believed the girl was drunk but she had actually died.[2] *B* broke into a coin box with intent to take money from the box, but it turned out that the box did not contain any money.[3] *C* received certain property which he believed to be stolen, but the property had not been stolen but was only represented as such to *C* by law enforcement officers.[4] *D* was smoking what he believed to be marijuana, but he was in fact puffing on an innocuous

§ 6.3

1. Only a representative listing is possible here. See J. Hall, General Principles of Criminal Law 586–99 (2d ed. 1960); G. Williams, Criminal Law: The General Part 633–53 (2d ed. 1961); Deusner, The Doctrine of Impossibility in the Law of Criminal Attempts, 4 Crim.L.Bull. 398 (1968); Elkind, Impossibility in Criminal Attempts: A Theorist's Headache, 54 Va.L.Rev. 20 (1968); Enker, Impossibility in Criminal Attempts—Legality and the Legal Process, 53 Minn.L.Rev. 665 (1969); Hughes, One Further Footnote on Attempting the Impossible, 42 N.Y.U.L.Rev. 1005 (1967); Keedy, Criminal Attempts at Common Law, 102 U.Pa.L. Rev. 464, 476–89 (1954); Perkins, Criminal Attempt and Related Problems, 2 U.C.L.A.L.Rev. 319, 333–38 (1955); Ryu, Contemporary Problems of Criminal Attempts, 32 N.Y.U.L.Rev. 1170, 1183–91 (1957); Sayre, Criminal Attempts, 41 Harv.L.Rev. 821, 848–55 (1928); Skilton, The Requisite Act in a Criminal Attempt, 3 U.Pitt.L.Rev. 308,

315–16 (1937); Smith, Two Problems in Criminal Attempts, 70 Harv.L.Rev. 422, 435–48 (1957); Smith, Two Problems in Criminal Attempts Re-Examined—II, 1962 Crim.L.Rev. 212; Strahorn, The Effect of Impossibility on Criminal Attempts, 78 U.Pa.L.Rev. 962 (1930); Thornton, Attempting the Impossible (Again), 25 Crim.L.Q. 294 (1983); Weigand, Why Lady Eldon Should be Acquitted: The Social Harm in Attempting the Impossible, 27 DePaul L.Rev. 231 (1978); Williams, Attempting the Impossible— A Reply, 22 Crim.L.Q. 49 (1980); Notes, 4 Am.J.Crim.L. 317 (1976); 14 Wake Forest L.Rev. 243 (1978); 70 Yale L.J. 160 (1960); Annot., 37 A.L.R.3d 375 (1971).

2. United States v. Thomas, 31 U.S.C.M.A. 278, 32 C.M.R. 278 (1962).

3. Gargan v. State, 436 P.2d 968 (Alas.1968).

4. Booth v. State, 398 P.2d 863 (Okl.Crim.App.1964).

weed.[5] *E* put a gun to his wife's head and pulled the trigger twice, but the weapon did not fire, for, unknown to *E*, the gun was not loaded.[6] Query whether *A, B, C, D,* and *E* are all guilty of attempt, whether they are all not guilty, or whether on some basis only some of them are guilty.

The traditional approach in dealing with such fact situations has been to distinguish what is called "legal impossibility" from what is termed "factual impossibility." If the case is one of legal impossibility, in the sense that what the defendant set out to do is not criminal, then the defendant is not guilty of attempt. On the other hand, factual impossibility, where the intended substantive crime is impossible of accomplishment merely because of some physical impossibility unknown to the defendant, is not a defense. This in itself may appear to be a rather simple distinction, but courts have frequently experienced considerable difficulty with it.[7] Account must also be taken of what some view as a third category, perhaps best termed "inherent impossibility," where any reasonable person would have known from the outset that the means being employed could not accomplish the ends sought. In addition, the impossibility of success may sometimes be relevant in a more limited sense, for it might cast doubt upon whether the defendant was acting with the requisite mental state for the crime of attempt.

(1) Mental State. It is important to keep in mind that impossibility will sometimes have a bearing upon the issue of whether the defendant acted with the necessary mental state. This is because the impossibility may sometimes establish the lack of the requisite intent even when it is of the factual variety and thus would not otherwise be a defense. For example, impotence is not a defense to a charge of attempted rape because it merely constitutes a factual impossibility of success.[8] However, if the defendant has known for some time that he is impotent, then that evidence is certainly relevant to show a lack of intent to rape.[9] Similarly, a defendant's declared intent to kill another person may be put in doubt if he only attacks with a small switch.[10]

Of course, if the defendant is unaware of the facts which show he cannot succeed, then it would seem that those facts do not relate to his intent. There nonetheless may be cases in which it appears on the surface that the defendant was unaware of those facts, yet a more careful inquiry may show that he in fact was aware and proceeded as he did because he really did not want to do any harm. For example, consider the case of *State v. Damms,*[11] referred to earlier. The defendant, while driving with his estranged wife, pulled a gun from under the car seat while engaged in an argument with her. He threatened her life but also spoke of reconciliation. When the car stopped she fled; he pursued her, overtook her, placed the gun against her head and pulled the trigger twice, but the gun was not loaded. These acts occurred in the presence of two policemen, who arrested the defendant. The Wisconsin Supreme Court affirmed the defendant's conviction for attempted murder, concluding that it was an "extraneous factor"[12] that the gun was unloaded, while a dissenting justice concluded that the cause of failure was not extraneous because it resulted from the defendant's own conduct in not loading the gun. One commentator has pointed out that neither opinion took account of the unloaded gun as it bears upon "the potential dangerousness of the of-

---

5. United States v. Giles, 7 Crim.L.Rptr. 2259 (A.F.Ct. Mil.Rev.1970).

6. State v. Damms, 9 Wis.2d 183, 100 N.W.2d 592 (1960).

7. See, for example, the sharp conflict between the majority and dissenting opinions in United States v. Thomas, 13 U.S.C.M.A. 278, 32 C.M.R. 278 (1962), which also takes note of the conflicting authority on many of the recurring situations.

8. Waters v. State, 2 Md.App. 216, 234 A.2d 147 (1967); Preddy v. Commonwealth, 184 Va. 765, 36 S.E.2d 549 (1946). See Annot., 23 A.L.R.3d 1351 (1969).

9. State v. Ballamah, 28 N.M. 212, 210 P. 391 (1922).

10. Kunkle v. State, 32 Ind. 220 (1869) (dictum).

11. 9 Wis.2d 183, 100 N.W.2d 592 (1960).

12. Wis.Stat.Ann. 939.32(2) requires an act which demonstrates that the defendant "would commit the crime except for the intervention of another person or some other extraneous factor."

fender. The dissent, by ignoring defendant's state of mind, failed to consider the possibility that the act of omission, although directly traceable to the actor, may have been caused by a factor other than the exercise of internal control. Likewise, the majority's definition, by focusing solely upon defendant's awareness at the conscious level of the omission, did not consider the possibility that failure to load the gun might have resulted from internal control at the unconscious level." [13]

Some commentators, however, have gone well beyond that point by asserting, in effect, that a person's intent is to do what he was actually doing rather than what he thought he was doing. One of the most famous impossibility cases is *People v. Jaffe*,[14] where the defendant purchased certain goods on the mistaken belief that they were stolen. As will be discussed later,[15] the court of appeals reversed the defendant's conviction of an attempt to receive stolen goods. It has been asserted, however, that the *Jaffe* decision is "easily explainable, without reference to any conception of 'legal impossibility'" in that "the necessary intent * * * was lacking." [16] So the argument goes, the defendant's intent was to receive the very goods received, and since those goods were in fact not stolen he cannot be said to have intended to receive stolen goods. On the same basis, it has been claimed that there is no intent to kill if one strikes at a block of wood believing it to be his deadly enemy,[17] and no intent to steal if one carries away his own umbrella believing it to belong to someone else.[18] The "primary intent" is said to be that of dealing with the object at hand.[19]

Surely there is nothing about the concept of intent [20] which justifies such conclusions. It has been aptly noted that such analysis "must at the least be supported by argument before we can accept it, for it certainly is not supported by the conventions of ordinary language, which would not in the least be strained by saying, for example, that a man who forcibly has intercourse with his wife believing her to be her own twin sister intends to commit rape." [21] However, no arguments in support of that curious position have been offered. Indeed, considerations of policy lead to the contrary conclusion, for certainly one who strikes at an inanimate object thinking it to be a man is more comparable, in terms of dangerousness, to a person who actually strikes at a human being than one who is chopping wood.

(2) Factual Impossibility. All courts are in agreement that what is usually referred to as "factual impossibility" is no defense to a charge of attempt. That is, if what the defendant intends to accomplish is proscribed by the criminal law, but he is unable to bring about that result because of some circumstances unknown to him when he engaged in the attempt, then he may be convicted. On this basis, attempt convictions have been affirmed in such circumstances as these: where the defendant attempted to steal from an empty pocket,[22] an empty receptacle,[23] or an empty house [24]; where the defendant shot with intent to kill a certain person but failed because the intended victim was not where the defendant believed he was [25] or because the victim was too far away to be killed by the weapon employed [26]; where the defendant at-

---

13. Note, 70 Yale L.J. 160, 165 (1960). From the studies which have been conducted of attempted suicides, it may be concluded that in many instances the individual has subconsciously selected means which are impossible or otherwise bound to fail. See id. at 166–67 and sources cited therein.

14. 185 N.Y. 497, 78 N.E. 169 (1906).

15. See text following note 52 infra.

16. Keedy, supra note 1, at 477.

17. Id. at 482.

18. Ibid.; Perkins, supra note 1, at 331.

19. Ibid.

20. See § 3.5.

21. Hughes, supra note 1, at 1012.

22. People v. Fiegelman, 33 Cal.App.2d 100, 91 P.2d 156 (1939); State v. Wilson, 30 Conn. 500 (1862); People v. Moran, 123 N.Y. 254, 25 N.E. 412 (1890).

23. Gargan v. State, 436 P.2d 968 (Alaska 1968); State v. Meisch, 86 N.J.Super. 279, 206 A.2d 763 (1965).

24. State v. Utley, 82 N.C. 556 (1880).

25. People v. Lee Kong, 95 Cal. 666, 30 P. 800 (1892); State v. Mitchell, 170 Mo. 633, 71 S.W. 175 (1902).

26. Kunkle v. State, 32 Ind. 220 (1869).

tempted to kill with an unloaded [27] or defective [28] gun or by use of poison [29] or a bomb [30] which was incapable of producing death; where the defendant attempted rape but was impotent [31]; where the defendant attempted an abortion but the woman was not pregnant [32] or the drugs or instruments were incapable of producing an abortion [33]; where the intended victim of false pretenses had no money [34] or was not deceived [35]; where the intended victim of extortion was not put in fear [36]; and where an attempt at bribery was unsuccessful because the employee who was to offer the bribe instead went to the police [37] or because the other party was unwilling to take a bribe.[38]

In all of the above situations, it is clear as a matter of policy that no reason exists for exonerating the defendant because of facts unknown to him which made it impossible for him to succeed. In each instance the defendant's mental state was the same as that of a person guilty of the completed crime,[39] and by committing the acts in question he has demonstrated his readiness to carry out his illegal venture. He is therefore deserving of conviction and is just as much in need of restraint and corrective treatment as the defendant who did not meet with the unanticipated events which barred successful completion of the crime.

One commentator, however, has suggested a test for impossibility cases which would afford a defense in at least some of the fact situations set forth above. Under his approach, "an attempt at a particular crime, to be punishable as a relative criminal attempt, must create a substantial impairment of some interest protected by the involved prohibitions against the crime or its related attempt." [40] The assumption is that the law of attempts is intended to prevent certain lesser harms than the completed crime, so that no conviction should be permitted unless that identifiable harm has occurred. Thus, he concluded, the impotent defendant *is* guilty of attempted rape because the crime of attempted rape is intended to protect women from being put in fear of a sexual attack,[41] and the defendant who puts an unloaded gun to his intended victim's head likewise *is* guilty of attempted murder because the crime of attempted murder is intended to protect against the fear of violence,[42] but it would be otherwise when the intended victim was not even aware of the unsuccessful attempt to take his life.[43] Apart from the obvious difficulty in identifying what the interests are which are invaded by various sorts of attempts, that approach is clearly inconsistent with the modern rationale of attempt law.[44] A person whose acts and accompanying mental state show him to be dangerous is deserving of conviction of attempt without regard to whether he encroached up-

27. State v. Damms, 9 Wis.2d 183, 100 N.W.2d 592 (1960).

28. Mullen v. State, 45 Ala. 43 (1871); People v. VanBuskirk, 113 Cal.App.2d 789, 249 P.2d 49 (1952).

29. Commonwealth v. Kennedy, 170 Mass. 18, 48 N.E. 770 (1897); State v. Glover, 27 S.C. 602, 4 S.E. 564 (1888).

30. People v. Grant, 105 Cal.App.2d 347, 233 P.2d 660 (1951).

31. Waters v. State, 2 Md.App. 216, 234 A.2d 147 (1967); Preddy v. Commonwealth, 184 Va. 765, 36 S.E.2d 549 (1946).

32. People v. Cummings, 141 Cal.App.2d 193, 296 P.2d 610 (1956); People v. Huff, 339 Ill. 328, 171 N.E. 261 (1930); State v. Moretti, 52 N.J. 182, 244 A.2d 499 (1968).

33. State v. Fitzgerald, 49 Iowa 260 (1878); State v. Crews, 128 N.C. 581, 38 S.E. 293 (1901).

34. People v. Arberry, 13 Cal.App. 749, 114 P. 411 (1910).

35. People v. Camodeca, 52 Cal.2d 142, 338 P.2d 903 (1959); State v. Visco, 183 Kan. 562, 331 P.2d 318 (1958); Commonwealth v. Johnson, 312 Pa. 140, 167 A. 344 (1933).

36. People v. Fratianno, 132 Cal.App.2d 610, 282 P.2d 1002 (1955).

37. Osborn v. United States, 385 U.S. 323, 87 S.Ct. 429, 17 L.Ed.2d 394 (1966).

38. People v. Bennett, 182 App.Div. 871, 170 N.Y.S. 718 (1918).

39. Subject to the possibility, discussed in the text above at notes 11–13, that a closer look into the facts might reveal that the defendant subconsciously did not want to succeed.

40. Strahorn, supra note 1, at 971.

41. Id. at 972.

42. Id. at 974.

43. Id. at 975.

44. See § 6.2(b).

on some lesser interest of the victim than intended.[45]

(3) Legal Impossibility. The case of *Wilson v. State*,[46] mentioned earlier in the discussion of the requisite mental state for the crime of attempt,[47] deserves further consideration here because it is a case which quite clearly calls for a result different from that in the cases of factual impossibility described above. The defendant was convicted of attempt to commit forgery, in that he had tampered with a draft for two dollars and fifty cents by writing in the figure 1 so as to make what read $2 50/100 appear instead as $12 50/100. No change was made in the written out sum of "two and 50/100 dollars," nor was any attempt made to obliterate the words "Ten Dollars or Less" stamped on the document. Noting that the completed crime of forgery requires the alteration of a material part of the document, which the figures themselves were not, the Mississippi Supreme Court concluded that the defendant had not committed the crime of attempted forgery. The court held, in effect, that since the defendant had done everything which he had meant to do and had thereby not committed a completed crime, he could hardly be considered guilty of an attempt.

Despite all of the disagreement between the commentators on the subject of impossibility, it is uniformly agreed that the result in *Wilson* was correct. "It may be true that the layman and perhaps Wilson himself would be very surprised to be told that what he had done did not amount to forgery or an attempt to commit forgery, but an immoral motive to inflict some injury on one's fellows coupled with a misapprehension about the content of the criminal law are not good reasons for conviction."[48] The important point to keep in mind here is that one would not have to invent a doctrine called legal impossibility to dispose of the *Wilson* case. Rather, all that is involved is an application of the principle of legality[49]; the defendant did not intend to do anything which had been made criminal, and what is not criminal may not be turned into a crime after the fact by characterizing his acts as an attempt.[50] "The reason for not convicting him has nothing to do with the failure of the enterprise, but rather with the absence of any prohibition of the conduct whether completed or not."[51]

If *Wilson* marked the boundaries of the legal impossibility doctrine as it has been applied by the courts, then there would be no basis for criticism of it. But that has not been the case, as is illustrated by the famous case of *People v. Jaffe*.[52] The defendant there was convicted of an attempt to violate a section of the criminal code which makes it an offense for a person to buy or receive any stolen property knowing the same to have been stolen. Unknown to the defendant, the property in question had been restored to the owners and was within their control when he purchased it, and thus no longer had the character of stolen goods. The prosecution relied upon the "empty pocket" and other factual impossibility cases, but the court reversed Jaffe's conviction on the ground that "if the accused had completed the act which

---

45. For a more detailed rebuttal of the Strahorn theory, see Elkind, supra note 1, at 24–25.

46. 85 Miss. 687, 38 So. 46 (1905).

47. See § 6.2 at n. 66.

48. Hughes, supra note 1, at 1022.

49. Elkind, supra note 1, at 26.

50. In Commonwealth v. Henley, 504 Pa. 408, 474 A.2d 1115 (1984), the court, after concluding neither factual nor legal impossibility was a defense under the new code, cautioned: "Under the new Code, an intent to commit an act which is not characterized as a crime by the laws of the subject jurisdiction cannot be the basis of a criminal charge and conviction even though the actor believes or misapprehends the intended act to be proscribed by the criminal laws. An example of this is where a fisherman believes he is committing an offense in fishing on a certain lake without a license when a fishing license is, in fact, not required in the subject jurisdiction. Since the conduct here would be perfectly legal, the actor could not be held accountable for any attempted crime."

51. Hughes, supra note 1, at 1006.

The same may be said for other cases in which what the defendant intended to do has not been made criminal. See, e.g., People v. Teal, 196 N.Y. 372, 89 N.E. 1086 (1909) (defendant not guilty of attempted subornation of perjury where materiality of false testimony an essential ingredient of perjury and false testimony sought by defendant was not material); Foster v. Commonwealth, 96 Va. 306, 31 S.E. 503 (1898) (where defendant under 14 years of age and thus conclusively presumed incapable of committing rape, he cannot be convicted of attempted rape).

52. 185 N.Y. 497, 78 N.E. 169 (1906).

he attempted to do, he would not be guilty of a criminal offense." In other words, since Jaffe had done everything he had intended to do—in the sense that he had already received the goods in question—and had not thereby committed the crime of receiving stolen property, he could not be found guilty of attempting to commit that crime.

Although this sounds very much like the reasoning used in *Wilson,* it is apparent that *Jaffe* and *Wilson* are not precisely the same kind of case. In *Wilson* the defendant may have thought he was committing a crime, but if he did it was not because he intended to do something that the criminal law prohibited but rather because he was ignorant of the material alteration requirement of the crime of forgery. In *Jaffe,* on the other hand, what the defendant intended to do was a crime, and if the facts had been as the defendant believed them to be he would have been guilty of the completed crime.

Jaffe is not an aberration in the law, for defendants have prevailed with a legal impossibility type of defense in many other cases where the defendant would have been guilty if the actual facts were consistent with his belief. Thus, there are other decisions holding that one has not attempted to receive stolen property if the defendant's belief that the goods were stolen is in error.[53] In addition, it has been held: that the defendant had not attempted to take deer out of season when he shot a stuffed deer believing it to be alive[54]; that the defendant had not attempted to bribe a juror when he offered a bribe to a person he mistakenly believed to be a juror[55]; that the defendant had not attempted to illegally contract a valid debt when he believed the debt to be valid but it was unauthorized and a nullity.[56] But the *Jaffe* analysis has been rejected on other occasions in which the defendant was held properly convicted of an attempt although, in one sense, he had done everything intended but had not committed the completed crime. Attempt convictions have been affirmed where the defendant mistakenly believed that the property received was stolen,[57] that the substance sold[58] or received[59] was heroin or other illegal drugs, that the cigarette smoked contained marijuana,[60] that the girl with whom he had sexual intercourse was alive,[61] and that the man he shot was alive.[62]

These latter decisions represent the better view as to the impossibility defense, which has been criticized by many commentators[63] and rejected in the Model Penal Code[64] and in virtually all of the recent recodifications.[65]

53. Booth v. State, 398 P.2d 863 (Okl.Crim.1964). Moreover, the same result has been reached where the charge is attempted larceny but by prearrangement with the police the property owner permits his agent to hand the property over to the defendant. People v. Rollino, 37 Misc.2d 14, 233 N.Y.S.2d 580 (1962).

54. State v. Guffey, 262 S.W.2d 152 (Mo.App.1953).

55. State v. Taylor, 345 Mo. 325, 133 S.W.2d 336 (1939); State v. Porter, 125 Mont. 503, 242 P.2d 984 (1952).

56. Marley v. State, 58 N.J.L. 207, 33 A. 208 (1895).

57. People v. Rojas, 55 Cal.2d 252, 10 Cal.Rptr. 465, 358 P.2d 921 (1961); Darr v. People, 193 Colo. 445, 568 P.2d 32 (1977); Bandy v. State, 575 S.W.2d 278 (Tenn. 1979).

58. United States v. Quijada, 588 F.2d 1253 (9th Cir. 1978); State v. Lopez, 100 N.M. 291, 669 P.2d 1086 (1983).

59. State v. McElroy, 128 Ariz. 135, 625 P.2d 904 (1981). People v. Siu, 126 Cal.App.2d 41, 271 P.2d 575 (1954).

60. United States v. Giles, 7 Crim.L.Rptr. 2259 (A.F.Ct. Mil.Rev.1970).

61. United States v. Thomas, 13 U.S.C.M.A. 278, 32 C.M.R. 278 (1962).

62. People v. Dlugash, 41 N.Y.2d 725, 395 N.Y.S.2d 419, 363 N.E.2d 1155 (1977).

63. See, e.g., J. Hall, supra note 1, at 598; Elkind, supra note 1, at 27; Enker, supra note 1, at 679; Hughes, supra note 1, at 1009; Sayre, supra note 1, at 854.

64. Model Penal Code § 5.01(1) (a) ("purposely engages in conduct which would constitute the crime if the attendant circumstances were as he believes them to be").

65. Many attempt statutes use the Model Penal Code language. Some state in addition or instead that neither factual nor legal impossibility is a defense, that impossibility because of a "misapprehension of circumstances" is no defense, or that it is no defense that the circumstances were such that commission of the crime was not possible. See also National Comm'n on Reform of Federal Criminal Laws, Final Report—Proposed New Federal Criminal Code § 1001(1) (1971).

Sometimes the legislative history of a statute which does not expressly abolish the defense of impossibility in any of the above ways will clearly indicate an intention that the defense not be allowed. See, e.g., United States v. Everett, 700 F.2d 900 (3d Cir.1983).

It has been noted that courts need not await adoption of a statute such as these before rejecting the distinction

The *Jaffe* approach, concluded the Code draftsmen,

> is unsound in that it seeks to evaluate a mental attitude—"intent" or "purpose"—not by looking to the actor's mental frame of reference, but to a situation wholly at variance with the actor's beliefs. In so doing, the courts exonerate defendants in situations where attempt liability most certainly should be imposed. In all of these cases the actor's criminal purpose has been clearly demonstrated; he went as far as he could in implementing that purpose; and, as a result, his "dangerousness" is plainly manifested.[66]

This rejection of the impossibility defense, it must be emphasized, has no effect upon such cases as *Wilson,* which may still be disposed of upon the ground that the requisite intent was lacking. As noted earlier, decisions such as *Wilson* rest upon the principle of legality, and it is "perfectly consistent with the legality principle to treat, as criminal attempts, those situations in which the actor intends to violate the statute and performs an act he thinks is in furtherance of that intent."[67]

However, some commentators, while rejecting the kind of reasoning employed in *Jaffe,* have taken the position that the defense of impossibility is not totally without

merit. Part of the concern is simply with sufficient proof of the defendant's mental state, and it has been pointed out that cases of either factual or legal impossibility can arise in which doubts are raised about whether the defendant had the requisite intent. *Jaffe,* for example, is said to be a case where the defendant's purchase of property which in fact was not stolen is equivocal,[68] so that further inquiry is called for to determine if the goods were purchased at a very low price or were received under generally suspicious circumstances.[69] Likewise, it is said that similar close scrutiny on the intent issue is required when the prosecution contends that the defendant intended to kill when giving the victim a nonpoisonous substance[70] or that the defendant intended to possess narcotics when he in fact possessed an innocuous substance.[71] The perceived risk is that without an impossibility defense a much broader class of persons are potentially subject to prosecution, so that the chances of an erroneous conviction are enhanced.[72]

A slightly different objection begins with the premise that criminal conduct should be clearly defined by the legislature in advance whenever possible, with the courts being delegated rather limited power to fill in the de-

between legal and factual impossibility, as that can be accomplished under most attempt statutes now in force by simply not misapplying the principle of legality. Elkind, supra note 1, at 33. However, courts continue to follow reluctantly the legal-impossibility-is-a-defense rule while expressing the wish that the legislature would make it possible for them to do otherwise. See, e.g., People v. Rollino, 37 Misc.2d 14, 233 N.Y.S.2d 580 (1962); Booth v. State, 398 P.2d 863 (Okl.Crim.App.1964).

66. Model Penal Code § 5.01, Comment at 308–09 (1985).

67. Elkind, supra note 1, at 26.

68. Consider, in this regard, the equivocality test used by some courts in determining whether the act was sufficient. See § 6.2(d)(3).

69. Enker, supra note 1, at 679–82; Hughes, supra note 1, at 1030.

70. Id. at 1033.

71. Enker, supra note 1, at 692. Consider in this regard United States v. Oviedo, 525 F.2d 881 (5th Cir. 1976), taking this approach. In reversing defendant's conviction for attempted sale of heroin which turned out to be an uncontrolled substance, the court reasoned:

"When the defendant sells a substance which is actually heroin, it is reasonable to infer that he knew the physical

nature of the substance, and to place on him the burden of dispelling that inference. However, if we convict the defendant of attempting to sell heroin for the sale of a non-narcotic substance, we eliminate an objective element that has major evidentiary significance and we increase the risk of mistaken conclusions that the defendant believed the goods were narcotics.

"Thus, we demand that in order for a defendant to be guilty of a criminal attempt, the objective acts performed, without any reliance on the accompanying *mens rea,* mark the defendant's conduct as criminal in nature. The acts should be unique rather than so commonplace that they are engaged in by persons not in violation of the law."

72. "Assume two cases in which the sole direct evidence of the defendant's alleged belief that the goods are stolen is a confession or the testimony of an informer or an accomplice. In one case the goods possessed are in fact stolen; in the other they are not. It is reasonably clear that most of us would rest easier with a conviction in the first case than in the second although we might have a difficult time articulating reasons for this distinction. [It may be] that possession of stolen goods furnishes some evidence of belief that they are stolen while, clearly, possession of goods not in fact stolen furnishes no reason to believe that the defendant thought they were stolen." Enker, supra note 1, at 679–80.

tails. Thus, while "a crucial factor justifying legislative delegation of the power to define the act element of attempts in the preparation-attempt cases was the inability of the legislature to provide for the infinitely varying acts in advance," there are some instances in which "the legislature is perfectly capable of deciding in advance whether or not to require the particular element." [73] Put in terms of the *Jaffe* case, the impossibility issue arose in the first instance because the receiving statute required the person *know* the property to have been stolen, a problem which the legislature could very easily have avoided by instead providing that *belief* that the property was stolen is sufficient. That being the case, "analytic tools are lacking" [74] whereby a court could decide whether, on an attempt theory, belief may suffice for conviction without doing violence to the legislature's wishes. So the argument goes, the proper solution to *Jaffe* is to "attend to the statute defining the substantive crime." [75]

(4) Inherent Impossibility. Yet another type of impossibility, which understandably has seldom confronted the courts, is what might be called inherent impossibility—the situation in which the defendant employs means which a reasonable man would view as totally inappropriate to the objective sought. The matter has been frequently discussed by the commentators in relation to this example put by one judge:

> Even though a "voodoo doctor" just arrived here from Haiti actually believed that his malediction would surely bring death to the person on whom he was invoking it, I cannot conceive of an American court upholding a conviction of such a

maledicting "doctor" for attempted murder or even attempted assault and battery. Murderous maledictions might have to be punished by the law as disorderly conduct, but they could not be classed as attempted crimes unless the courts so far departed from the law of criminal attempts as to engage in legislation. A malediction arising out of a murderous intent is not such a substantial overt act that it would support a charge of attempted murder. [76]

Why should this be so? Because, some commentators have argued, the inherent impossibility of success shows that the defendant is not dangerous. "If in the point of view of a reasonable man in the same circumstances as the defendant the desired criminal consequence could not be expected to result from the defendant's acts, it cannot endanger social interests to allow the defendant to go unpunished, no matter how evil may have been his intentions." [77] Others, however, have contended that acquittal of such a defendant could be explained only on the ground that his acts do not seem to call for retribution, [78] in that he *has* manifested sufficient dangerousness to warrant corrective treatment. [79] "When a man makes a harmless attempt to commit a crime, he may well try again, perhaps more effectively. The voodoo witch doctor may use a gun next time. Thus the purposes of special deterrence and neutralization can be served by punishing even the marginal cases." [80] It has also been suggested that the "reasonable man" test is an inappropriate one because it would extend to the case in which the defendant pursued "an extremely marginal chance of successfully committing a harm." [81]

73. Id. at 685.

74. Id. at 687.

75. Id. at 696.

76. Commonwealth v. Johnson, 312 Pa. 140, 167 A. 344 (1933) (Maxey, J., dissenting). To the same effect is Pollack's opinion in Attorney General v. Sillem, 159 Eng.Rep. 178 (1863): "If a statute simply made it a felony to attempt to kill any human being, or to conspire to do so, an attempt by means of witchcraft, or a conspiracy to kill by means of charms and incantations, would not be an offense within such a statute. The poverty of language compels one to say 'an attempt to kill by means of witchcraft,' but such an attempt is really no attempt at all to kill. It is true the sin or wickedness may be as great as

an attempt or conspiracy by competent means; but human laws are made, not to punish sin, but to prevent crime and mischief."

77. Sayre, supra note 1, at 850. See also Skilton, supra note 1, at 315–16.

78. Elkind, supra note 1, at 28.

79. Id. at 33–34; Ryu, supra note 1, at 1189; Strahorn, supra note 1, at 967.

80. Elkind, supra note 1, at 33–34.

81. J. Hall, supra note 1, at 593.

Cases have arisen where one might say that on the facts known to the defendant a reasonable man would conclude that the chances of attaining the desired objective were

On the ground that even those who make unreasonable mistakes may be dangerous, the Model Penal Code eliminates the defense of impossibility even in cases of inherent impossibility.[82] However, the court would be empowered to dismiss the prosecution or impose a lower sentence than generally permitted for the crime attempted if the defendant's conduct was "so inherently unlikely to result or culminate in the commission of a crime that neither such conduct nor the actor presents a public danger." [83] Because of the absence of cases in point, it is difficult to generalize about the existing state of the law concerning inherent impossibility. The Model Penal Code approach was expressly rejected by one legislature, which recognizes impossibility as a defense when "such impossibility would have been clearly evident to a person of normal understanding." [84] Elsewhere, inherent impossibility may also continue to be a defense even in the face of statutory language which seemingly abolishes all impossibility defenses.[85]

**WESTLAW
REFERENCES**

(wilson /s 38 +5 46) (jaffe /s 78 +5 169) /p "principle of legality" (factual** legal** /s impossib!)

slight or impossible. See Dahlberg v. People, 225 Ill. 485, 80 N.E. 310 (1907), where a woman who threw red pepper in a man's eyes was held improperly convicted of attempted mayhem because the medical testimony revealed that the red pepper would not have destroyed or seriously injured the man's eyesight. Although the court seemed to think there was no attempt because of impossibility, a better approach might have been to consider whether on that evidence it was established that the defendant intended a mayhem-type result. Compare Kunkle v. State, 32 Ind. 220 (1869), where the defendant's attempt to kill another was unsuccessful because of the distance from the victim and the manner in which the shot was loaded in the shotgun, but the defendant's conviction was affirmed because the evidence showed that the defendant believed the shot would be effective at that distance.

82. Model Penal Code § 5.01, Comment at 315–16 (1985).

83. Model Penal Code § 5.05(2).

84. Minn.Stat.Ann. § 609.17.

85. Thus, Ill.—S.H.A. ch. 38, ¶ 8–4(b) states: "It shall not be a defense to a charge of attempt that because of a misapprehension of the circumstances it would have been

(b) Abandonment. [86] In one well known case [87] the facts were as follows: In October 1967, while his wife was away on a trip, one Staples, under an assumed name, rented an office on the second floor of a building directly over the mezzanine of a bank. Staples was aware of the layout of the building, and specifically of the relation of the office he rented to the bank vault. He paid rent for the period October 23–November 23, and the landlord had the 10 days before the start of that period to finish some interior repairs and painting. During the prerental period Staples brought into the office certain equipment, including drilling tools, two acetylene gas tanks, a blow torch, a blanket and a linoleum rug. Learning that no one was in the building on Saturdays, he drilled several holes part way through the floor on Saturday, October 14. He covered the holes with the rug, and at some point he locked his tools in a closet, although he left the key on the premises. Around the end of November, the landlord notified the police and turned the equipment over to them. Some time later Staples was arrested, after which he voluntarily gave a statement to the police which read in part as follows: "The actual commencement of my plan made me begin to realize that even if I were to succeed a fugitive life of living off of stolen money would not give the enjoyment of

impossible for the accused to commit the offense attempted." But the drafting committee's commentary, Tentative Final Draft of the Proposed Illinois Criminal Code of 1961, p. 212 (1960) says: "However, inherent impossibility (attempt to kill by witchcraft such as repeatedly stabbing a cloth dummy made to represent the person intended to be killed) is not intended to be excluded as a defense." See People v. Elmore, 128 Ill.App.2d 312, 261 N.E.2d 736 (1970), where the court acknowledged that inherent impossibility would be a defense, but concluded that the defendants' acts in falsely listing items as destroyed in a fire for purposes of recovering from an insurance company was not an instance of inherent impossibility, although apparently other items were destroyed up to the limit of the company's liability, because the defendants may have thought that they could not collect all of the insurance money unless they included items not in fact destroyed.

86. See Wasik, Abandoning Criminal Intent, 1980 Crim.L.Rev. 785.

87. People v. Staples, 6 Cal.App.3d 61, 85 Cal.Rptr. 589 (1970).

the life of a mathematician however humble a job I might have. * * * My wife came back and my life as bank robber seemed more and more absurd."

Is Staples guilty of attempted burglary, or is his apparent abandonment of the criminal scheme under these circumstances a valid defense? One way to approach this issue is *not* to think about the possibility of some unique doctrine that an attempt, unlike most other crimes,[88] may be abandoned after it has been committed, but rather to ask whether upon the available facts it may be said that the essential elements of an attempt are present. That is, looking at all of the facts may it be said that there existed both (1) the requisite mental state of an intent to commit a burglary,[89] and (2) an act in furtherance of that intent beyond mere preparation,[90] or on the other hand does it appear that at least one of these elements is missing so that the crime of attempt was never committed? If it is concluded that the necessary mental state and act are present, then a different approach is required; it then must be asked whether abandonment can ever be a defense to what would otherwise be a completed attempt and, if so, whether the circumstances of the abandonment in this case bring it within that defense.

(1) Mental State and Act. As to the bearing of Staples' abandonment on the question of whether he had the requisite intent, it has been suggested that "where the accused has changed his mind, it would be only just to interpret his previous intention where possible as only half-formed or provisional, and hold it to be insufficient mens rea."[91] It is undoubtedly true that under some circumstances the defendant's abandonment will create a reasonable doubt as to whether he ever

actually had the criminal intent. For example, proof of voluntary abandonment is rather strong evidence of lack of intent by a defendant, charged with attempted rape, who did not commit the rape notwithstanding the ability to do so.[92] Likewise, the failure to carry out what appears to be an attempt at suicide may show that it was not seriously intended or was subconsciously desired to fail.[93] In the *Staples* case, one might expect the defense to contend that the totality of the evidence shows that Staples was a Walter Mitty type who fantasized about the perfect crime but never really formed an intent to burglarize the bank. However, the court—properly it would seem—concluded that the defendant's intent was clearly established. "Defendant admitted in his written confession that he rented the office fully intending to burglarize the bank, that he brought in tools and equipment to accomplish this purpose, and that he began drilling into the floor with the intent of making an entry into the bank."

What is the relevance of the abandonment on the issue of whether the requisite act occurred? It has been observed that "anywhere between the conception of the intent and the overt act toward its commission, there is room for repentance; and the law in its beneficence extends the hand of forgiveness."[94] However, that language should not be taken too seriously, for if the overt act has not yet occurred there is nothing to forgive. That is, in such a case the law is not taking account of the defendant's repentance, and thus it makes no difference whether the absence of the requisite act is attributable to the defendant's change of heart or to the fact that he became aware of an increased risk of apprehension.[95] Yet, it is undoubtedly true that courts are sometimes influenced by the fact of voluntary

88. But, as to solicitation see § 6.1(d).

89. See § 6.2(c).

90. See § 6.2(d).

91. G. Williams, Criminal Law: The General Part 620–21 (2d ed. 1961).

92. Oakley v. State, 22 Wis.2d 298, 125 N.W.2d 657 (1964).

93. G. Williams, supra note 91, at 621. Compare the discussion of impossibility brought about by subconscious desire, text supra at notes 11–13.

94. State v. Hayes, 78 Mo. 307 (1883).

95. United States v. Joyce, 693 F.2d 838 (8th Cir.1982) (defendant's motive for not going through with drug sale, even if it attributable to discovery that other party was an undercover agent, is not "particularly relevant" and could not convert "what would otherwise be 'mere preparation' into an attempt").

withdrawal to the extent that they characterize the defendant's prior acts as mere preparation upon facts which would certainly justify a contrary conclusion.[96] The *Staples* case, however, does not lend itself to such a result, for, as the court noted, the defendant had quite clearly passed the stage of preparation when he commenced the drilling, for it was an unequivocal act which actually constituted a fragment of the contemplated crime. As the court put it, the drilling was "the beginning of the 'breaking' element."

(2) As a Defense. Assuming now that both the mental state and act required for the crime of attempt are found to exist, how will Staples fare if he claims to have a defense because of his abandonment? At this point we may find it useful to look more closely at all of the facts in order to determine precisely why he did not proceed with his scheme. One possibility (indeed, the possibility which the court in Staples found to be supported by the evidence) is that his self-serving statement to the police implying repentance was false and that instead the defendant ceased his efforts because he "became aware that the landlord had resumed control over the office and had turned defendant's equipment and tools over to the police." If this conclusion is correct, then quite clearly the purposes of the crimi

nal law would be ill-served by requiring acquittal. Withdrawal by one who thought his plan had been detected or who encountered more resistance than he anticipated does not negative his dangerousness,[97] and it is totally consistent with the rationale of attempt law [98] to subject such a person to the corrective processes of the law.

The cases are in agreement that what is usually referred to as involuntary abandonment is no defense. Thus, if the defendant fails because of unanticipated difficulties in carrying out the criminal plan at the precise time and place intended and then decides not to pursue the victim under these less advantageous circumstances, he is still guilty of attempt.[99] The same is true when the defendant withdraws because of a belief that the intended victim has become aware of his plans,[100] or because he thinks that his scheme has been discovered or would be thwarted by police observed in the area of the intended crime.[101]

What then if Staples' abandonment were truly voluntary in character, in that he was in no sense influenced by extrinsic circumstances but rather underwent a real change of heart? The Model Penal Code recognizes a defense under these circumstances,[102] and that view has been adopted in some of the

96. Commonwealth v. Peaslee, 177 Mass. 267, 59 N.E. 55 (1901), is most often noted in this regard. See Rotenberg, Withdrawal as a Defense to Relational Crimes, 1962 Wis.L.Rev. 596, 598; Model Penal Code § 5.01, Comment at 357 (1985). See also Griffin v. State, 26 Ga. 493, 506 (1858), where it is said that it would be only preparation if the defendant were to put poison in his victim's food and place the food on the table but repent and then withdraw it before it is eaten.

97. Rotenberg, supra note 96, at 600.

98. See § 6.2(b).

99. United States v. McDowell, 714 F.2d 106 (11th Cir. 1983) ("Refusal to purchase [drugs] because of inability to agree on price, or dissatisfaction with the quality, or lack of opportunity to inspect is not necessarily a complete and voluntary renunciation of criminal purpose"); United States v. Bussey, 507 F.2d 1096 (9th Cir.1974) (abandonment no defense where plan failed because of time lock on bank vault); Pyle v. State, 476 N.E.2d 124 (Ind.1985) (abandonment no defense where defendant, attempting murder, inflicted only superficial wound on victim but did not fire additional shots as police appeared on the scene); Barnes v. State, 269 Ind. 76, 378 N.E.2d 839 (1978) (abandonment no defense to attempted robbery where it attrib-

utable to inability to open cash register); Boyles v. State, 46 Wis.2d 473, 175 N.W.2d 277 (1970) (defendant told victim to hand over sack of money and at same time reached for gun in his pocket, when gun became caught in the pocket victim walked away and defendant did not pursue him).

100. State v. Thomas, 438 S.W.2d 441 (Mo.1969) (defendant attempted to cash check at store by pretending that he was person named thereon, but he never endorsed check and finally left the premises after the clerk repeatedly checked with the manager on whether the check could be cashed).

101. People v. VonHecht, 133 Cal.App.2d 25, 283 P.2d 764 (1955) (defendant left car at store for installation of new set of wheels and tires, indicating at that time his intention to pay for them with stolen credit card which he then produced, but upon his return said he would pay cash for them after seeing police officer in the store); Stewart v. State, 85 Nev. 388, 455 P.2d 914 (1969) (defendant pulled gun on operator of gas station and asked for his money, but then left station when he saw police car drive in).

102. Model Penal Code § 5.01(4), discussed in text infra at notes 123–124.

modern criminal codes.[103]   However, it is impossible to generalize about the current status of such a defense; one survey concluded that the issue remains an open question in most jurisdictions,[104] and in some states the cases in point cannot be reconciled.[105]

The traditional view as expressed by most commentators is that abandonment is *never* a defense to a charge of attempt if the defendant has gone so far as to engage in the requisite acts with criminal intent.[106]   The assumption seems to be that because a completed crime may not thereafter be abandoned [107] it follows that the same must be true as to the crime of attempt.   "A criminal attempt is a 'complete offense' in the sense that one who has carried a criminal effort to such a point that it is punishable, can no more wipe out his criminal guilt by an abandonment of his plan than a thief can obliterate the larceny by a restoration of the stolen chattel." [108]   Many of the cases denying the defense [109] are in fact assault cases, and it has been correctly noted that they are distinguishable because something in the way of a completed offense has been committed.[110]   In the attempt cases stating without reservation that abandonment, even due to a stricken

conscience, is not a defense, a close examination of the facts before the court will usually disclose that the defendant would not have had a defense in any event because he involuntarily withdrew.[111]

The language which is frequently used to define the crime of attempt lends itself to the interpretation that voluntary abandonment *is* a defense.   A common statutory definition of attempt is stated in terms of one who engages in acts toward the commission of a crime "but fails in the perpetration thereof or is prevented or intercepted in executing such crime. Some courts have said that an attempt requires conduct which in the ordinary course of events would result in commission of the target crime except for the intervention of some extraneous factor.[112]   Yet, the broad judicial pronouncement that no kind of abandonment is a defense has been made notwithstanding such language in the applicable statute and precedents.[113]   And while the Model Penal Code draftsmen state that the "prevailing view" is in favor of allowing voluntary desistance as a defense, the American cases cited in support [114] for the most part contain such statements in dictum or in concurring or dissenting opinions.   Cases in

---

103. See note 123 infra.   Compare Wis.Stat.Ann. 939.32(2), which does not expressly state that abandonment is a defense, but which defines attempt so as to require that the defendant engage in acts which show that he "would commit the crime except for the intervention of another person or some other extraneous factor."

104. Rotenberg, supra note 96, at 596–97.

105. E.g., compare People v. Staples, 6 Cal.App.3d 61, 85 Cal.Rptr. 589 (1970) ("it would seem that the character of the abandonment * * * is not controlling. * * * Once that attempt is found there can be no exculpatory abandonment."); with People v. VonHecht, 133 Cal.App. 2d 25, 283 P.2d 764 (1955) ("Abandonment is a defense if the attempt to commit a crime is freely and voluntarily abandoned before the act is put in process of final execution and *where there is no outside cause* prompting such abandonment.").

106. E.g., 2 J. Stephen, A History of the Criminal Law of England 226–27 (1883); Perkins, Criminal Attempt and Related Problems, 2 U.C.L.A.L.Rev. 319, 354 (1955).

107. Nor is it a defense that the defendant's repentance has led the victim to condone the crime, see § 5.11(d).

108. Perkins, supra note 106, at 354.

109. E.g., Lewis v. State, 35 Ala. 380 (1860); State v. Gill, 101 W.Va. 242, 132 S.E. 490 (1926).

110. Model Penal Code § 5.01, Comment at 358 (1985).

111. E.g., People v. Staples, 6 Cal.App.3d 61, 85 Cal. Rptr. 589 (1970) (evidence supported conclusion defendant withdrew because his plan was discovered); People v. Robinson, 180 Cal.App.2d 745, 4 Cal.Rptr. 679 (1960) (jury could have found defendant would have carried out robbery but for intervention of police); State v. Thomas, 438 S.W.2d 441 (Mo.1969) (defendant abandoned attempt to cash check when clerk became suspicious and checked again with manager of store); Stewart v. State, 85 Nev. 388, 455 P.2d 914 (1969) (defendant left gas station without taking money after police car pulled into station).

112. See § 6.2(d)(2).

113. E.g., People v. Staples, 6 Cal.App.3d 61, 85 Cal. Rptr. 589 (1970), where the court asserts that neither involuntary nor voluntary abandonment is a defense, although West's Ann.Cal.Penal Code § 664 defines an attempt in terms of one who attempts to commit a crime "but fails, or is prevented or intercepted in the perpetration thereof," and People v. Buffum, 40 Cal.2d 709, 256 P.2d 317 (1953) says that an attempt "must be in such progress that it will be consummated unless interrupted by circumstances independent of the will of the attempter."

114. Model Penal Code § 5.01, Comment at 357 n. 270 (1985).

which the defendant's claim of voluntary withdrawal was plausible enough to make failure to instruct on the defense reversible error are extremely rare.[115]

On balance, the arguments in favor of recognizing voluntary abandonment as a defense to a charge of attempt are more persuasive than the arguments against the defense. For one thing, recognition of the defense is consistent with the rationale of attempt,[116] as a complete and voluntary renunciation of criminal purpose "tends to negative dangerousness."[117] In addition, if the defense is allowed, then those who have crossed the threshhold of attempt will still be encouraged to desist and thereby escape any penalty.[118] The counter-argument is that the defense may actually embolden those considering some criminal endeavor because they will be more willing to take the first steps toward the crime when they know they can withdraw with impunity.[119] This risk, however, seems slight,[120] as does the risk that recognition of the defense will result in the acceptance of false claims of repentance.[121]

Although this subject is often discussed in terms of voluntary versus involuntary aban-

donment, the Model Penal Code requires that the defendant's abandonment occur "under circumstances manifesting a complete and voluntary renunciation of his criminal purpose."[122] The renunciation is not voluntary if "motivated, in whole or in part, by circumstances, not present or apparent at the inception of the actor's course of conduct, which increase the probability of detection or apprehension or which make more difficult the accomplishment of the criminal purpose," and is not complete if "motivated by a decision to postpone the criminal conduct until a more advantageous time or to transfer the criminal effort to another but similar objective or victim."[123] This definition of the defense appears to be somewhat broader than the usual statement (e.g., that there must be "no outside cause"[124] or "extraneous factor"[125]), a difference which may be of some importance in those cases where the defendant is dissuaded from completing the crime by the intended victim[126] or where the defendant changes his mind upon learning that the fruits of the crime would not be as great as previously expected.[127]

Assuming a defense of voluntary abandonment, does there come a point at which it is

---

115. People v. Collins, 234 N.Y. 355, 137 N.E. 753 (1922); People v. Graham, 176 App.Div. 38, 162 N.Y.S. 334 (1916).

116. See § 6.2(b).

117. Model Penal Code § 5.01, Comment at 359 (1985).

118. Ibid. Some who agree that voluntary abandonment should be a defense view this particular argument in favor as "unreal." Stuart, The Actus Reus in Attempts, 1970 Crim.L.Rev. 505, 521.

119. Skilton, The Requisite Act in a Criminal Attempt, 3 U.Pitt.L.Rev. 308, 310 n. 4 (1937).

120. "First, any consolation the actor might draw from the abandonment defense would have to be tempered with the knowledge that the defense would be unavailable if the actor's purposes were frustrated by external forces before he had an opportunity to abandon his effort. Second, the encouragement this defense might lend to the actor taking preliminary steps would be a factor only where the actor was dubious of his plans and where, consequently, the probability of continuance was not great." Model Penal Code § 5.01, Comment at 360 (1985).

121. 2 J. Stephen, A History of the Criminal Law of England 226 (1883). Model Penal Code § 5.01(4) makes renunciation of criminal purpose an affirmative defense, so the defendant must come forward first with evidence in support of the defense.

122. Model Penal Code § 5.01(4). Many of the modern recodifications contain this formulation.

123. Model Penal Code § 5.01(4). Several of the modern recodifications also contain this elaboration.

124. People v. VonHecht, 133 Cal.App.2d 25, 283 P.2d 764 (1955).

125. Wis.Stat.Ann. 939.32(2).

126. See People v. Crary, 265 Cal.App.2d 534, 71 Cal. Rptr. 457 (1968) (defendant offered owner of gas station pair of pliers in exchange for money to buy gas but owner refused; defendant then pulled gun and said it was a stickup, but owner then gave defendant "fatherly advice" against committing the holdup and said he would give him two dollars worth of gas, which he did; defendant then left pliers and departed without money he knew was in cash register); LeBarron v. State, 32 Wis.2d 294, 145 N.W. 2d 79 (1966) (defendant assaulted woman with intent to rape her, dragged her into a shack, at which point she pleaded with him to desist because she was pregnant; defendant left after noting she was in maternity clothes).

127. See Ryu, Contemporary Problems of Criminal Attempts, 32 N.Y.U.L.Rev. 1170, 1198–99 (1957), discussing a German case holding "that where a man desists from consummating an attempted larceny because he was disappointed by the smallness of the value of the property in issue, his desistance nevertheless constitutes a voluntary withdrawal."

too late for the defendant to withdraw? Obviously there must be, for it would hardly do to excuse the defendant from attempted murder after he had wounded the intended victim or, indeed, after he had fired and missed.[128] It might even be argued that it is too late whenever the defendant has taken the last proximate step, for at that point his dangerousness is not rebutted by the withdrawal. On the other hand, as the Model Penal Code draftsmen point out, recognizing withdrawal, even after the last proximate act has occurred will encourage desistance at a time when such encouragement is most important.[129]

 WESTLAW REFERENCES

attempt /p (voluntary involuntary +1 abandonment) "change of heart" renunciat***

(c) Prosecution and Punishment. Assume that A has been charged with and is on trial for the offense of burglary, but during the course of the trial the evidence develops in such a way that it appears A may have only attempted the offense of burglary. May A be convicted of attempted burglary? At one time the answer was no, for while it was generally recognized that when a charge of an offense included within it a lesser offense the defendant could be convicted of that lesser crime, this rule was subject to one important qualification: "upon an indictment for a felony, the defendant could not be convicted of a misdemeanor." [130] Thus a conviction for the common law misdemeanor of attempt could not be had upon an indictment charging the felony of burglary.

Insofar as can be determined, that exception was based upon the fact that under early English criminal procedure a defendant in a felony trial had fewer rights than a defendant on trial for a misdemeanor.[131] That quite clearly is not the case in the United States,[132] and thus there has been no reason to honor this exception in this country. The courts are in general agreement that an attempt conviction may be had on a charge of the completed crime,[133] and statutes to this effect exist in some jurisdictions.

This is not to say, however, that upon any charge of a completed crime the trier of fact will inevitably be confronted with the possibility of returning a verdict or finding of only an attempt. The judge may give an instruction on the attempt alternative only if the evidence would support such a verdict.[134] For example, if on A 's trial for burglary A merely interposes an alibi defense or admits to being within the dwelling but claims to have been acting with an innocent intent, then the only logical alternatives are guilty of burglary or not guilty. On the other hand, if A asserts that he had not yet entered at the time of his apprehension, then the third alternative of guilt of attempted burglary exists. In such a case the attempt alternative may go to the jury even over the defendant's objection.[135]

Quite obviously the reverse is not true. That is, if A had been on trial only for attempted burglary but it was shown at trial that he had actually entered the dwelling, clearly A may not be convicted of the greater uncharged offense of burglary. But, under those facts may he even be convicted of attempted burglary? The crime of attempt is often defined as if failure were an essential element,[136] and on this basis it has sometimes been held that proof of the completed crime

---

128. See People v. Corkery, 134 Cal.App. 294, 25 P.2d 257 (1933); State v. Gray, 19 Nev. 212, 8 P. 456 (1885).

129. Model Penal Code § 5.01, Comment at 360 (1985).

130. Hanna v. People, 19 Mich. 316 (1869).

131. Rex v. Westbeer, 168 Eng.Rep. 108 (1739).

132. Hanna v. People, 19 Mich. 316 (1869).

133. E.g., State v. Miller, 252 A.2d 321 (Me.1969). But even in those jurisdictions where a conviction of both conspiracy to commit a crime and actual commission of that crime is possible, see § 6.5(h), the same is not true as to attempting and completing the crime. United States v. York, 578 F.2d 1036 (5th Cir.1978). Statutes to this effect

are not uncommon. In some states the statutes also provided that there may not be a conviction for an attempt and another inchoate crime with the same objective.

134. State v. Chance, 3 N.C.App. 459, 165 S.E.2d 31 (1969).

135. People v. Miller, 28 Mich.App. 161, 184 N.W.2d 286 (1970).

136. Bell v. State, 118 Ga.App. 291, 163 S.E.2d 323 (1968) (an act "more or less directly tending to but falling short of, the commission of the crime"); Makins v. State, 6 Md.App. 466, 252 A.2d 15 (1969) (an act "falling short of

requires reversal of an attempt to commit it.[137] The assumption that failure is required may be derived from the old common law rule of merger, whereby if an act resulted in both a felony and a misdemeanor the misdemeanor was said to be absorbed into the felony.[138] (Taking that as the basis of the rule, then the problem would not arise if the completed crime would also be only a misdemeanor[139] or, in the alternative, if the completed crime would be a felony but an attempt to commit it had by statute also been made a felony.[140]

The English merger rule was laid to rest by statute in 1851,[141] and there seems no reason to follow it in this country. As one court observed, a defendant can hardly complain "where the determination of his case was more favorable to him than the evidence warranted."[142] Thus, many recent cases have held that a defendant may be convicted of the attempt even if the completed crime is proved,[143] and many jurisdictions expressly so provide by statute.

Considerable variation is to be found across the country concerning the authorized penalties for attempt. As to statutory provisions concerning the sentences which may be imposed for all or a broad class of attempts, the most common in the modern recodifications is that which declares the attempt to be a crime one degree below the object crime. Another common provision establishes categories according to the severity of the penalty for the completed crime and specifies a range of pen-

alties for attempts to commit crimes within each category. Some merely provide that the penalty for attempt may be as great as for the completed crime. As to statutes dealing with attempts to commit particular crimes, the authorized punishment is usually lower than for the completed crime, but in some instances the same or even a higher punishment is possible.[144]

Taking into account the rationale of the crime of attempt,[145] the Model Penal Code penalty provisions are most sensible. An attempt may be punished to the same extent as the completed crime, except that a lower punishment is provided for attempts to commit capital crimes or the most serious felonies.[146] "To the extent that sentencing depends upon the antisocial disposition of the actor and the demonstrated need for a corrective sanction, there is likely to be little difference in the gravity of the required measures depending on the consummation or the failure of the plan."[147] The more severe penalties designed for general deterence are withheld because the threat of punishment for the attempt would not add significantly to the deterrent efficacy of the sanction threatened for the completed crime.[148]

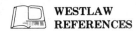 **WESTLAW REFERENCES**

convict*** /s attempt /s completed lesser +1 offense

the actual commission of the crime"); State v. Thomas, 438 S.W.2d 441 (Mo.1969) (an act "which falls short of the completion of the crime").

137. Lewis v. People, 124 Colo. 62, 235 P.2d 348 (1951); People v. Lardner, 300 Ill. 264, 133 N.E. 375 (1921). Compare Barry v. State, 90 Wis.2d 316, 280 N.W.2d 204 (1979) (notwithstanding statutory language saying it an attempt if crime would have occurred "except for the intervention of another person or some other extraneous factor," failure to consummate the crime is not an element of an attempt).

138. See G. Williams, Criminal Law: The General Part 653 (2d ed. 1961).

139. People v. Mather, 4 Wend. 229 (N.Y.1830).

140. People v. Bristol, 23 Mich. 118 (1871).

141. 14 § 15 Vict. c. 100, § 12 (1851).

142. People v. Vanderbilt, 199 Cal. 461, 249 P. 867 (1926).

143. United States v. York, 578 F.2d 1036 (5th Cir. 1978); Richardson v. State, 390 So.2d 4 (Ala.1980); State v. Moores, 396 A.2d 1010 (Me.1979); Lightfoot v. State, 278 Md. 231, 360 A.2d 426 (1976); State v. Gallegos, 193 Neb. 651, 228 N.W.2d 615 (1975).

144. See Model Penal Code § 5.05, Comment at 487 (1985).

145. See § 6.2(b).

146. Model Penal Code § 5.05(1). Section 5.05(2) permits the judge to impose a lower sentence than otherwise authorized or even to dismiss the prosecution if the conduct was "so inherently unlikely to result or culminate in the commission of a crime that neither such conduct nor the actor presents a public danger."

147. Model Penal Code § 5.05, Comment at 490 (1985).

148. Ibid.

§ 6.4 Conspiracy—Acts and Mental State

Although the crime of conspiracy is somewhat vague, which is one of many reasons why it is often asserted that the prosecution has a distinct advantage in conspiracy cases, it may be said to require: (1) an agreement between two or more persons, which constitutes the act; and (2) an intent thereby to achieve a certain objective which, under the common law definition, is the doing of either an unlawful act or a lawful act by unlawful means. The crime of conspiracy serves (like other anticipatory offenses) as a means to proceed against persons who have sufficiently manifested their disposition to criminality, and also as a device for acting against the special and continuing dangers incident to group activity.

(a) Development of the Crime of Conspiracy. [1]

The crime of conspiracy, unknown to the early common law,[2] emerged from the enactment of three statutes during the reign of Edward I.[3] These statutes were intended to correct the abuses of ancient criminal procedure, and conspiracy was accordingly defined narrowly. "Combinations only to procure false indictments or to bring false appeals or to maintain vexatious suits could constitute conspiracies."[4] Moreover, the crime of conspiracy was not complete unless the person falsely accused had been actually indicted and acquitted.[5]

The first significant expansion of conspiracy occurred with the decision by the Court of Star Chamber in 1611 of *Poulterers' Case*.[6] The defendants had confederated to bring a false accusation against one Stone, but Stone was so clearly innocent that the grand jury refused to indict him. This being so, it was the contention of the defendants that no conspiracy had occurred, but the court decided to the contrary. Thus, *Poulterers' Case* gave rise to a doctrine which survives to this day: the gist of conspiracy is the agreement, and so the agreement is punishable even if its purpose was not achieved.

Later in the seventeenth century the courts took a second step toward broadening the crime of conspiracy: an agreement to commit any offense became a punishable conspiracy.[7] During this same period, the tendency of the courts was in the direction of undertaking to punish acts which were immoral even if not in violation of express law, and thus it was not surprising that in arguments of counsel it was claimed that a combination could be criminal even if the object thereof was not criminal. With apparently but one exception,[8] this suggestion was rejected by the courts.[9]

Nonetheless, Hawkins asserted in 1716 that "there can be no doubt, but that all confederacies whatsoever, wrongfully to prejudice a third person, are highly criminal at common law," [10] and just a few years thereafter a case supporting the Hawkins doctrine was decided.[11] The vast majority of the decisions, however, continued to adhere to the long-established law that the object of the conspiracy or the means used must in fact be criminal.[12]

Then in 1832 came Lord Denman's famous epigram that a conspiracy indictment must "charge a conspiracy either to do an unlawful

§ 6.4

1. For more detailed accounts of the history of conspiracy, see P. Winfield, History of Conspiracy and Abuse of Legal Procedure (1921); R. Wright, The Law of Criminal Conspiracies and Agreements (1887); Arens, Conspiracy Revisited, 3 Buffalo L.Rev. 242 (1954); Harno, Intent in Criminal Conspiracy, 89 U.Pa.L.Rev. 624 (1941); Pollack, Common Law Conspiracy, 35 Geo.L.J. 328 (1947); Sayre, Criminal Conspiracy, 35 Harv.L.Rev. 393 (1922).

2. P. Winfield, supra note 1, at 29–37.

3. First Ordinance of Conspirators, 1292, 20 Edw. I; Second Ordinance of Conspirators, 1300, 28 Edw. I; Third Ordinance of Conspirators, 1305, 33 Edw. I.

4. Sayre, supra note 1, at 396.

5. Id. at 397.

6. 77 Eng.Rep. 813 (1611).

7. Sayre, supra note 1, at 400.

8. Starling's Case, 82 Eng.Rep. 1039 (1664).

9. Regina v. Daniell, 87 Eng.Rep. 856 (1704).

10. 1 W. Hawkins, Pleas of the Crown 348 (6th ed. 1787).

11. Rex v. Journeymen Taylors of Cambridge, 88 Eng. Rep. 9 (1721), where the court said that "a conspiracy of any kind is illegal, although the matter about which they conspired might have been lawful for them, or any of them, to do, if they had not conspired to do it."

12. Sayre, supra note 1, at 404.

act or a lawful act by unlawful means,"[13] which was "seized upon by judges laboring bewildered through the mazes of the conspiracy cases as a ready solution for all their difficulties."[14] Although Lord Denman's statement was somewaht ambiguous, in that the word "unlawful" might be interpreted to mean criminal, courts in England and the United States gave it a broad reading. Illustrative is the 1844 case of *State v. Burnham*[15]: "When it is said in the books that the means must be unlawful, it is not to be understood that those means must amount to indictable offenses, in order to make the offense of conspiracy complete. It will be enough if they are corrupt, dishonest, fraudulent, immoral, and in that sense illegal, and it is in the combination to make use of such practices that the dangers of this offense consist."

Thus the definition which persists in those jurisdictions retaining common law crimes is that conspiracy is a combination between two or more persons formed for the purpose of doing either an unlawful act or a lawful act by unlawful means.[16] (Where conspiracy is defined by statute, the common law definition is sometimes followed, elsewhere other language is used which makes it apparent that some noncriminal objectives are also covered, while some states have now limited conspiracy to criminal objectives.) Although a more precise definition of conspiracy may be difficult, it is useful to keep in mind that conspiracy, like most other offenses, requires both an act and an accompanying mental state.[17] The

agreement constitutes the act, while the intention to thereby achieve the objective is the mental state. Following a brief look at the practical consequences and theoretical justification of conspiracy prosecutions, the requisite act and mental state are discussed in this section.[18] Other limits on conspiracy liability are considered in the section which follows.

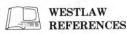 **WESTLAW REFERENCES**

di conspiracy

(b) The Prosecution's Advantage. Some years ago, Judge Learned Hand called conspiracy "the darling of the modern prosecutor's nursery,"[19] and this characterization certainly is not without justification. Wherever one might think the "balance of advantage" generally lies in the criminal process,[20] it is clear that a conspiracy charge gives the prosecution certain unique advantages and that one who must defend against such a charge bears a particularly heavy burden. This is attributable not only to the elusive quality of conspiracy as a legal concept, but also to various rules of procedure and evidence which have special application in a conspiracy context.

Conspiracy has been and certainly continues to be a most controversial subject for a variety of reasons. Prosecutors continue to rely heavily upon this particular weapon in their arsenal, and this has heightened concern about the dangers of unfairness to conspiracy defendants.[21] The controversy has

---

13. Rex v. Jones, 110 Eng.Rep. 485 (1832).

14. Sayre, supra note 1, at 405.

15. 15 N.H. 396 (1844).

16. Pettibone v. United States, 148 U.S. 197, 13 S.Ct. 542, 37 L.Ed. 419 (1893); Commonwealth v. Hunt, 4 Metc. 111 (Mass.1842).

17. See § 3.1.

18. Dividing the crime of conspiracy up into its constituent elements poses some problems, given the nature of the offense. Even separating out the act from the mental state can be troublesome given the fact that "the crime is so predominantly mental in composition." Harno, supra note 1, at 632. Herein, the agreement (including the intent to agree by the parties to it) is dealt with as the act (see § 6.4(d)), while the mental state concerns the purpose of achieving a certain result (see § 6.4(e)). Although in one sense an aspect of the necessity for an agreement,

separate attention is given herein to the "two or more persons" requirement (see § 6.5(g)) and to the breadth and length of the conspiracy (see § 6.5(d), (e)). Similarly, the question of what objectives suffice for conspiracy liability (see § 6.5(a)) is treated herein separately from the mental state requirement, although again there is clearly a close relationship. Another element of conspiracy which exists in some jurisdictions by statute is that one of the conspirators have engaged in an overt act in furtherance of the conspiracy (see § 6.5(c)).

19. Harrison v. United States, 7 F.2d 259 (2d Cir.1925).

20. See Goldstein, The State and the Accused: Balance of Advantage in Criminal Procedure, 69 Yale L.J. 1149 (1960).

21. See, e.g., Goldstein, The Krulewitch Warning: Guilt by Association, 54 Geo.L.J. 133 (1965); Klein, Conspiracy—The Prosecutor's Darling, 24 Brooklyn L.Rev. 1

been intensified because of the activities against which the law of conspiracy has been invoked. There is, of course, that sad chapter in our history when labor unions were condemned and suppressed as criminal conspiracies.[22] More recently, we have witnessed several instances in which conspiracy law has been used against those who are called "political" defendants, and here as well many see the conspiracy device as posing a serious threat to the freedom of speech and association.[23]

Although these matters cannot be fully explored here, it will be useful to take note of the principal reasons why it is so often said that conspiracy prosecutions afford the prosecution undue advantage. Some appreciation of these factors is essential to a full understanding of the significance of the remaining discussion concerning the bases of and limitations upon liability for criminal conspiracy.

(1) Vagueness. The criticism which commentators have voiced most often and most strongly is that there is an inherent vagueness in the crime of conspiracy. "In the long category of crimes there is none," wrote Dean Harno, "not excepting criminal attempt, more difficult to confine within the boundaries of definitive statement than conspiracy."[24] Professor Sayre, in his classic article on the subject, noted: "A doctrine so vague in its outlines and uncertain in its fundamental nature as criminal conspiracy lends no strength or glory to the law; it is a veritable quicksand of shifting opinion and ill-considered thought."[25] And Justice Jackson, in his oft-quoted concurring opinion in *Krulewitch v. United States,*[26] referred to conspiracy as an "elastic, sprawling and pervasive offense, * * * so vague that it almost defies definition [and also] chameleon-like [because it] takes on a special coloration from each of the many independent offenses on which it may be overlaid."

Undoubtedly the main reason for this criticism is the fact that the law of conspiracy developed in such a way that certain objectives not in themselves criminal will suffice.[27] However, the vagueness stems from other aspects of the crime as well, including the uncertainty over what is sufficient to constitute the agreement[28] and what attendant mental state must be shown.[29] These ambiguities compound the difficulties of defending against a conspiracy charge, for "it is hard to find an antidote for the poison you cannot identify."[30]

(2) Venue. The Sixth Amendment provides that in "all criminal prosecutions, the accused shall enjoy the right to a speedy and public trial, by an impartial jury of the State and district wherein the crime shall have been committed."[31] Similarly, most state constitutions also provide that a defendant in a criminal case is entitled to be tried in the county, parish, or district where the crime occurred. These venue provisions constitute an important constitutional guarantee, for they "safeguard against the unfairness and hardship involved when an accused is prosecuted in a remote place."[32]

Given the common reference to the agreement in conspiracy as the "gist" of the of-

(1957); Selz, Conspiracy Law in Theory and Practice: Federal Conspiracy Prosecutions in Chicago, 5 Am.Crim.L. 35 (1977); Weinreb, The Threat of Unfairness in Conspiracy Prosecutions: A Proposal for Procedural Reform, 2 N.Y.U.Rev.L. & Soc.Chg. 1 (1972); Note 16 Hastings L.J. 465 (1965).

22. See Cousens, Agreement as an Element in Conspiracy, 23 Va.L.Rev. 898 (1937); Pollack, Common Law Conspiracy, 35 Geo.L.J. 328 (1947); Sayre, Criminal Conspiracy, 35 Harv.L.Rev. 393 (1922).

23. See J. Mitford, The Trial of Dr. Spock (1969); Church, Conspiracy Doctrine and Speech Offenses: A Reexamination of Yates v. United States From the Perspective of United States v. Spock, 60 Cornell L.Rev. 569 (1975); Nathanson, Freedom of Association and The Quest for Internal Security: Conspiracy from *Dennis* to Dr. Spock, 65 Nw.U.L.Rev. 153 (1970); O'Brian, Loyalty Tests

and Guilt by Association, 61 Harv.L.Rev. 592 (1948); Notes, 44 Tulane L.Rev. 587 (1970); 1970 Wis.L.Rev. 191; 79 Yale L.J. 872 (1970).

24. Harno, Intent in Criminal Conspiracy, 89 U.Pa.L. Rev. 624 (1941).

25. Sayre, supra note 25, at 393.

26. 336 U.S. 440, 69 S.Ct. 716, 93 L.Ed. 790 (1949).

27. See § 6.5(a).

28. See § 6.4(d).

29. See § 6.4(e).

30. J. Mitford, supra note 23, at 61.

31. U.S. Const. amend. VI.

32. United States v. Cores, 356 U.S. 405, 78 S.Ct. 875, 2 L.Ed.2d 873 (1958).

fense,[33] it might be thought that the place of trial for conspiracy prosecutions must be the place where the agreement was made. But, while it has long been settled that a conspiracy prosecution may be brought at the place of agreement,[34] it is clear that the prosecution may also elect to have the trial in any locale where any overt act by any of the conspirators took place.[35] Although it is argued in support of this rule that if it were otherwise conspiracy prosecutions would often be impossible because of the frequent difficulty of proving the place of agreement,[36] the rule makes it possible for the prosecution to select a district inconvenient to the defendant or one in which a jury may be more disposed to convict.[37] As Justice Jackson observed:

> The leverage of a conspiracy charge lifts [the constitutional venue] limitation from the prosecution and reduces its protection to a phantom, for the crime is considered so vagrant as to have been committed in any district where any one of the conspirators did any one of the acts, however innocent, intended to accomplish its object. The Government may, and often does, compel one to defend at a great distance from any place he ever did any act because some accused confederate did some trivial and by itself innocent act in the chosen district.[38]

(3) Hearsay Exception. The general rule that hearsay is not admissible in a criminal prosecution is marked by many exceptions. One of these is the co-conspirator exception: any act or declaration by one co-conspirator

committed during and in furtherance of the conspiracy is admissible against each co-conspirator.[39] The rationale most often given for this exception is that each of the conspirators is the agent of all the others.[40]

However, the co-conspirator hearsay exception as applied often extends beyond that rationale. The requirement that the act or statement be in furtherance of the conspiracy is often applied broadly, with the result that any evidence somehow relating to the conspiracy comes in.[41] Sometimes statements are admitted into evidence notwithstanding the fact that they were made prior to the formation of the conspiracy[42] or after its termination.[43] And on the ground that the addition of a new member does not create a new conspiracy,[44] statements by one conspirator are held admissible against others who joined the group after they were made.[45]

Another requirement of the co-conspirator hearsay exception is that a statement by one conspirator is not admissible against the others unless the existence of the conspiracy has been independently established.[46] However, courts have been sympathetic to the problems of the prosecution in presenting evidence in a vast conspiracy case, and thus have admitted evidence falling under the exception, subject to an instruction to the jury that such evidence is not to be considered against the other defendants if independent proof of

---

33. E.g., People v. GemHang, 131 Cal.App.2d 69, 280 P.2d 28 (1955).

34. Hyde v. Shine, 199 U.S. 62, 25 S.Ct. 760, 50 L.Ed. 90 (1905).

35. Hyde v. United States, 225 U.S. 347, 32 S.Ct. 793, 56 L.Ed. 1114 (1912); People v. Cory, 26 Cal.App. 735, 148 P. 532 (1915).

36. Hyde v. United States, 225 U.S. 347, 32 S.Ct. 793, 56 L.Ed. 1114 (1912).

37. Developments in the Law—Criminal Conspiracy, 72 Harv.L.Rev. 920, 975–76 (1959).

38. Krulewitch v. United States, 336 U.S. 440, 69 S.Ct. 716, 93 L.Ed. 790 (1949) (Jackson, J., concurring).

39. 4 J. Wigmore, Evidence § 1079 (Chadbourne rev. 1972); Levie, Hearsay and Conspiracy, 52 Mich.L.Rev. 1159 (1954). But see Lutwak v. United States, 344 U.S. 604, 73 S.Ct. 481, 97 L.Ed. 593 (1953), holding that acts do not come within the exception.

40. Anderson v. United States, 417 U.S. 211, 94 S.Ct. 2253, 41 L.Ed.2d 20 (1974); People v. Berkowitz, 50 N.Y.2d 333, 428 N.Y.S.2d 927, 406 N.E.2d 783 (1980).

41. E.g., Allen v. United States, 4 F.2d 688 (7th Cir. 1925).

42. E.g., Ross v. State, 98 Tex.Crim. 567, 267 S.W. 499 (1925).

43. E.g., Arlington v. State, 98 Tex.Crim. 68, 263 S.W. 593 (1924).

Sometimes the conspiracy is deemed to continue into the concealment phase, so as to make the statements admissible. State v. Waterbury, 307 N.W.2d 45 (Iowa 1981).

44. Marino v. United States, 91 F.2d 691 (9th Cir.1937).

45. E.g., United States v. United States Gypsum Co., 333 U.S. 364, 68 S.Ct. 525, 92 L.Ed. 746 (1948).

46. Glasser v. United States, 315 U.S. 60, 62 S.Ct. 457, 86 L.Ed. 680 (1942).

the conspiracy is not thereafter presented.[47] As Justice Jackson saw it, "In other words, a conspiracy often is proved by evidence that is admissible only upon assumption that conspiracy existed. The naive assumption that prejudicial effects can be overcome by instructions to the jury * * * all practicing lawyers know to be unmitigated fiction." [48]

(4) Circumstantial Evidence. Most conspiracy convictions are based upon circumstantial evidence, and this evidence is often admitted under rather loose standards of relevance. As one court put it, "Wide latitude is allowed [the prosecution] in presenting evidence, and it is within the discretion of the trial court to admit evidence which even remotely tends to establish the conspiracy charged." [49] The Supreme Court has offered this explanation:

> Secrecy and concealment are essential features of successful conspiracy. The more completely they are achieved, the more successful the crime. Hence the law rightly gives room for allowing the conviction of those discovered upon showing sufficiently the essential nature of the plan and their connections with it, without requiring evidence of knowledge of all its details or of the participation of others. Otherwise the difficulties, not only of discovery, but of certainty in

proof and of correlating proof with pleading would become insuperable, and conspirators would go free by their very ingenuity.[50]

There is, to be sure, something to the point that the prosecution confronts particularly difficult problems in proving conspiracy because persons who join together for a criminal purpose resort to methods that are "devious, hidden, secret and clandestine." [51] However, it may well be that in some respects the courts are "overcompensating for the difficulties faced by the prosecution." [52] Courts are particularly vulnerable to this criticism when they confuse the agreement requirement with the evidence from which it may be inferred,[53] and when upon proof of agreement other defendants are connected with the conspiracy upon slight additional evidence.[54]

(5) Joint Trial. When several defendants have been charged as participants in a single conspiracy, they may be required to defend against the charges in a single trial.[55] Given the inherent nature of most conspiracies, this is understandable. "Only by prosecuting all the members together and by culling the sum total of their knowledge is it possible to obtain a detailed mosaic of the whole undertak-

---

47. E.g., Parente v. United States, 249 F.2d 752 (9th Cir.1957); People v. Batten, 9 Mich.App. 195, 156 N.W.2d 640 (1967).

48. Krulewitch v. United States, 336 U.S. 440, 69 S.Ct. 716, 93 L.Ed. 790 (1949) (Jackson, J., concurring).

49. Nye & Nissen v. United States, 168 F.2d 846 (9th Cir.1948). For example, in United States v. Garelle, 438 F.2d 366 (2d Cir.1970), the court held admissible the defendant's address book containing a notation "ask about Mel," an alias used at times by another alleged member of the conspiracy, noting that people whose names are associated together in writing in such a manner are somewhat more likely to be associated in other ways, acknowledging that such an inference is less than compelling, but concluding that more direct proof of association among conspirators is often difficult to produce in court. See also People v. Bailey, 60 Ill.2d 37, 322 N.E.2d 804 (1975).

50. Blumenthal v. United States, 332 U.S. 539, 68 S.Ct. 248, 92 L.Ed. 154 (1947).

51. Marrash v. United States, 93 C.C.A. 511, 168 F. 225 (1909).

52. Developments, supra note 37, at 984.

53. E.g., Davidson v. United States, 61 F.2d 250 (8th Cir.1932).

54. E.g., United States v. Elliot, 571 F.2d 880 (5th Cir. 1978); Fox v. United States, 381 F.2d 125 (9th Cir.1967); Tomplain v. United States, 42 F.2d 202 (5th Cir.1930).

In United States v. Alvarez, 548 F.2d 542 (5th Cir.1977), the court concluded: "Mature reflection has convinced us, however, that the 'slight evidence' rule is of doubtful application to the state of facts presented here, where the issue for review is whether Alvarez was connected with the demonstrated conspiracy *at all.* It being of the nature of conspiracy to conceal itself, the 'slight evidence' rule finds its proper application where persons are clearly connected to the conspiring group or are found acting in such a manner as unmistakably to forward its purposes. In such instances, given the clandestine character of such projects, slight additional evidence suffices to base an inference that one who had been shown beyond reasonable doubt to be a participant was as well a *knowing* participant. But where, as here, the question is whether a defendant was connected with the conspiracy at all, to apply such a rule is to risk convicting him of the crime itself upon 'slight evidence.' "

55. And see Schaffer v. United States, 362 U.S. 511, 80 S.Ct. 945, 4 L.Ed.2d 921 (1960), holding the joinder not prejudicial even after dismissal of the conspiracy count. However, several conspiracies may not be joined in a single trial "when the only nexus among them lies in the fact that one man participates in all." Kotteakos v. United States, 328 U.S. 750, 66 S.Ct. 1239, 90 L.Ed 1557 (1946).

ing." [56] However, a joint trial may present added disadvantages for the several defendants.

For one thing, what would otherwise be rights individual to each defendant may become, in effect, group rights which must be exercised jointly by all of the defendants. The most obvious example of this is the statutory right to challenge peremptorily prospective jurors; it is not uncommon for the several joined defendants to have in toto no more peremptory challenges than a single defendant would have if tried alone.[57] Also, certain rights which are individual in nature and which remain so even in a joint trial may be diminished in the joint-trial setting. Such is the case as to the right to counsel.[58]

The greatest danger, however, is that the probability of an individual defendant being convicted may be greatly enhanced by his association through joinder with the others. This is particularly true when there is a long, complicated trial involving many defendants, where the jury may have great difficulty in keeping the evidence [59] and jury instructions [60] straight as they apply to particular defendants. But even when the alleged conspirators are few in number, the individual defendant "occupies an uneasy seat. There generally will be evidence of wrongdoing by somebody. It is difficult for the individual to make his own case stand on its own merits in the minds of jurors who are ready to believe that birds of a feather are flocked together. If he is silent, he is taken to admit it and if, as often happens, codefendants can be prodded

into accusing or contradicting each other, they convict each other." [61]

**WESTLAW
REFERENCES**

crim**** /s conspiracy /p venue

(c) The Rationale of Conspiracy. However, even those who have voiced such criticisms have acknowledged that "the basic conspiracy principle has some place in modern criminal law." [62] The crime of conspiracy, which exists in virtually all jurisdictions,[63] serves two important but different functions: (1) as with solicitation and attempt, it is a means for preventive intervention against persons who manifest a disposition to criminality; and (2) it is also a means of striking against the special danger incident to group activity.[64]

Viewing conspiracy solely as an anticipatory offense, it is useful to compare conspiracy with attempt. As we have seen,[65] under attempt law it must be shown that the defendant has taken what is sometimes referred to as a "substantial step" toward commission of the crime; earlier acts of preparation will not suffice. Conspiracy law, however, attacks inchoate crime at a far more incipient stage—the crime of conspiracy is complete at the time of the agreement or (in some jurisdictions) at the time of the first overt act in pursuance of the conspiracy by any party thereto.[66] How can this earlier legal intervention be justified?

This question can best be answered by noting once again two significant considerations which are properly taken into account in

---

56. Note, 48 Yale L.J. 1447, 1450 (1939).

57. Developments, supra note 37, at 979–80.

58. Id. at 980.

59. See, e.g., United States v. Central Supply Ass'n, 6 F.R.D. 526 (N.D.Ohio 1947) (102 defendants, 1616 exhibits).

60. See, e.g., United States v. Liss, 137 F.2d 995 (2d Cir. 1943).

61. Krulewitch v. United States, 336 U.S. 440, 69 S.Ct. 716, 93 L.Ed. 790 (1949) (Jackson, J., concurring).

62. Krulewitch v. United States, 336 U.S. 440, 69 S.Ct. 716, 93 L.Ed. 790 (1949) (Jackson, J., concurring).

But see Johnson, The Unnecessary Crime of Conspiracy, 61 Calif.L.Rev. 1137, 1164 (1973), concluding that while the crime of conspiracy filled a gap when the law of

attempts was dominated by the proximity approach, see § 6.2(d)(1), "insofar as conspiracy adds anything to the attempt provisions of the reform codes under discussion, it adds only overly broad criminal liability."

63. Of the modern recodifications, only Alaska's is without a crime of conspiracy.

64. Model Penal Code § 5.03, Comment at 387 (1985). See also Dennis, The Rationale of Criminal Conspiracy, 93 L.Q.Rev. 39 (1977); Developments in the Law—Criminal Conspiracy, 72 Harv.L.Rev. 920, 923–25 (1959), where these two functions are respectively referred to as the "specific object" and "general danger" rationales.

65. See § 6.2(d).

66. See § 6.5(c), noting that any act in pursuance of the conspiracy, however insignificant, will suffice.

marking the boundaries of inchoate offenses: (a) the need to permit law enforcement intervention before the defendant's activities come dangerously close to bringing about the criminal result; and (b) the need to subject to corrective treatment those who have clearly indicated their criminal disposition.[67] Thus, the attempt cases on what constitutes a "substantial step" reflect a concern with whether the actor was close to success [68] and whether the actor's conduct is so unequivocal as to make certain his intentions.[69]

These points are reached earlier when the defendant has chosen to combine with others. In theory at least, the act of reaching agreement with one or more other persons on an unlawful purpose is a clearer manifestation of intent than, say, such acts by one person as purchasing a gun. It is less likely that the defendant will turn back, for "a conspirator who has committed himself to support his associates may be less likely to violate this commitment than he would be to revise a purely private decision." [70] Even if the defendant does have a change of heart, he no longer has control of the situation; his fellow conspirators may finish what he started. The agreement also increases the danger to society, for by a division of labor the group is more likely to be able to bring about the criminal result. This is particularly true when the objects of the conspiracy are ambitious and elaborate.[71]

But, as suggested above, conspiracy cannot be viewed solely as an inchoate crime. If it were, then it would hardly make sense to say that it "is an offense of the gravest character, sometimes quite outweighing, in injury to the public, the mere commission of the contemplated crime," [72] nor would it be sensible to allow punishment for both the conspiracy and its criminal object.[73] The other function of conspiracy is as a sanction against group activity. "The antisocial potentialities of a conspiracy, unlike those of an attempt, are not confined to the objects specifically contemplated at any given time. The existence of a grouping for criminal purposes provides a continuing focal point for further crimes either related or unrelated to those immediately envisaged." [74]

 **WESTLAW REFERENCES**

conspiracy /p 72 +5 920

(d) The Agreement.[75] As noted earlier, an essential element of every crime is an act (or omission).[76] The crime of conspiracy might appear to be an exception to this general rule, however, in that a conspiracy may be found to exist by virtue of the fact that the parties thereto have entered into an agreement. But conspiracy is not an exception, for the agreement itself is the requisite act.[77] As one court observed: "When two agree to carry [an unlawful design] into effect, the very plot is an

---

67. Model Penal Code art. 5, Introduction at 294 (1985).

68. E.g., Commonwealth v. Peaslee, 177 Mass. 267, 59 N.E. 55 (1901); Commonwealth v. Kelley, 162 Pa.Super. 526, 58 A.2d 375 (1948).

69. E.g., Lemke v. United States, 14 Alaska 587, 211 F.2d 73 (1954); People v. Lyles, 156 Cal.App.2d 482, 319 P.2d 745 (1957).

70. Developments, supra note 64, at 924.

71. "The advantages of division of labor and complex organization characteristic of modern economic society have their counterparts in many forms of criminal activity. Manufacture or importation and distribution of contraband goods, for example, often demands a complicated organization. The interrelations of the parties in schemes to defraud may be highly complex." Note, 62 Harv.L.Rev. 276, 283–84 (1948).

72. United States v. Rabinowich, 238 U.S. 78, 35 S.Ct. 682, 59 L.Ed. 1211 (1915).

73. See § 6.5(h).

74. Developments, supra note 64, at 924–25. This point has often been stressed by the courts, e.g., Iannelli v. United States, 420 U.S. 770, 95 S.Ct. 1284, 43 L.Ed.2d 616 (1975); Callanan v. United States, 364 U.S. 587, 81 S.Ct. 321, 5 L.Ed.2d 312 (1961) ("concerted action ∗ ∗ ∗ decreases the probability that the individuals involved will depart from their path of criminality"); United States v. Rabinowich, 238 U.S. 78, 35 S.Ct. 682, 59 L.Ed. 1211 (1915) (conspiracy "involves deliberate plotting to subvert the laws, educating and preparing the conspirators for further and habitual criminal practices").

75. See Marcus, Conspiracy: The Criminal Agreement in Theory and Practice, 65 Geo.J.J. 925 (1977); Orchard, "Agreement" in Criminal Conspiracy, 1974 Crim.L.Rev. 292, 335.

76. See § 3.2.

77. This is made clear in most of the modern recodifications, which specify that an agreement is necessary. Some in addition or instead say that what is necessary is that the defendant "combine," or "plans with another."

act in itself * * *. The agreement is an advancement of the intention which each has conceived in his mind; the mind proceeds from a secret intention to the overt act of mutual consultation and agreement." [78]

The agreement is all-important in conspiracy, for one must look to the nature of the agreement to decide several critical issues, such as whether the requisite mental state is also present,[79] whether the requisite plurality is present,[80] and whether there is more than one conspiracy.[81] As courts have so often said, the agreement is the "essence" [82] or "gist" [83] of the crime of conspiracy.

One might suppose that the agreement necessary for conspiracy is essentially like the agreement or "meeting of the minds" which is critical to a contract, but this is not the case.[84] Although there continues to exist some uncertainty as to the precise meaning of the word in the context of conspiracy,[85] it is clear that the definition in this setting is somewhat more lax than elsewhere. A mere tacit understanding will suffice,[86] and there need not be any written statement or even a speaking of words which expressly communicates agreement.[87] As the Supreme Court has put it: "The agreement need not be shown to

have been explicit. It can instead be inferred from the facts and circumstances of the case." [88] It is possible for various persons to be parties to a single agreement (and thus one conspiracy) even though they have no direct dealings with one another [89] or do not know the identify of one another,[90] and even though they are not all aware of the details of the plan of operation [91] or were not all in on the scheme from the beginning.[92]

Because most conspiracies are clandestine in nature, the prosecution is seldom able to present direct evidence of the agreement. Courts have been sympathetic to this problem, and it is thus well established that the prosecution may "rely on inferences drawn from the course of conduct of the alleged conspirators." [93] This notion has been traced back [94] to an oft-quoted instruction in an 1837 English case, where the judge told the jury: "If you find that these two persons pursued by their acts the same object, often by the same means, one performing one part of an act and the other another part of the same act, so as to complete it, with a view to the attainment of the object which they were pursuing, you will be at liberty to draw the conclusion that they have been engaged in a conspiracy to

---

78. State v. Carbone, 10 N.J. 329, 91 A.2d 571 (1952).

79. See § 6.4(e).

80. See § 6.5(g).

81. See § 6.5(d).

82. E.g., Iannelli v. United States, 420 U.S. 770, 95 S.Ct. 1284, 43 L.Ed.2d 616 (1975).

83. E.g., People v. GemHang, 131 Cal.App.2d 69, 280 P.2d 28 (1955).

84. G. Williams, Criminal Law: The General Part 666 (2d ed. 1961).

85. "It is universally conceded that an agreement need not be express, although whether the idea of an implied agreement connotes only an unspoken, actual consensus or has broader, fictional components is by no means clear." Model Penal Code § 5.03, Comment at 419 (1985).

86. United States v. Hartley, 678 F.2d 961 (11th Cir. 1982); O'Neil v. State, 237 Wis. 391, 296 N.W. 96 (1941).

87. American Tobacco Co. v. United States, 328 U.S. 781, 66 S.Ct. 1125, 90 L.Ed. 1575 (1946); State v. Gillespie, 336 S.W.2d 677 (Mo.1960).

88. Iannelli v. United States, 420 U.S. 770, 95 S.Ct. 1284, 43 L.Ed.2d 616 (1975).

89. United States v. Fincher, 723 F.2d 862 (11th Cir. 1984), noting also that it makes no difference that a non-conspirator government undercover agent is the go-between linking the conspirators.

90. Blumenthal v. United States, 332 U.S. 539, 68 S.Ct. 248, 92 L.Ed. 154 (1947); United States v. Watson, 594 F.2d 1330 (10th Cir.1979); People v. Moran, 166 Cal.App. 2d 410, 333 P.2d 243 (1958).

91. Blumenthal v. United States, 332 U.S. 539, 68 S.Ct. 248, 92 L.Ed. 154 (1947); United States v. Michelena-Orovia, 702 F.2d 496 (5th Cir.1983), on rehearing 719 F.2d 738 (5th Cir.1983).

92. United States v. Burchinal, 657 F.2d 985 (8th Cir. 1981).

93. Interstate Circuit v. United States, 306 U.S. 208, 59 S.Ct. 467, 83 L.Ed. 610 (1939). There are limits, of course, as to what inferences may be drawn. See, e.g., McBrady v. State, 460 N.E.2d 1222 (Ind.1984) (fact that A, hours after stealing B's car, sold it to C, did not permit inference of pre-existing conspiracy to commit theft by A and C).

94. See Cousens, Agreement as an Element of Conspiracy, 23 Va.L.Rev. 989 (1937), describing the importation and acceptance of this instruction in the United States.

effect that object." [95] Such language, it has been noted, might be erroneously interpreted as meaning that there need be only a concurrence of wills rather than concurrence resulting from agreement,[96] and may in practice have resulted in "neglect of the fundamental fact that there is an agreement to be proved." [97]

Assume that A wants to burglarize a store and thus approaches B to solicit his assistance in the commission of the crime, that upon hearing A's plan B manifests his complete concurrence in the scheme and expresses his willingness to participate, but that B secretly intends not to go through with the plan and has merely feigned agreement because he wishes to trap A. Is there a conspiracy under these circumstances? No is the answer traditionally given by the courts.[98] B quite clearly is not guilty of conspiracy, if for no other reason because he does not have the intent-to-burglarize mental state [99]; A does have the requisite mental state, but yet may not be convicted of conspiracy because there has been no agreement and thus no criminal

act.[100] Although it has been suggested that A might appropriately be convicted of attempted conspiracy on those facts,[101] the Model Penal Code unilateral approach to conspiracy [102] (generally followed in modern recodifications [103]) instead makes it possible for A to be convicted of conspiracy.[104] There is something to be said for that result: A's culpability is hardly decreased by B's secret intention, and, while the chances of the scheme succeeding may be minimal under these circumstances, A has nonetheless engaged in conduct which provides unequivocal evidence of his firm purpose to commit a crime.[105]

Although it is generally true that an act is not required when there is instead an omission which constitutes the failure to perform a legal duty,[106] there would not appear to be any set of circumstances in which a failure to agree instead of an agreement would suffice for the crime of conspiracy. For example, a conspiracy not to pay certain taxes is not established by the absence of any agreement

---

95. Regina v. Murphy, 172 Eng.Rep. 502 (1837). This language persists in the cases even today. See, e.g., Griffin v. State, 248 Ark. 1223, 455 S.W.2d 882 (1970).

96. Williams, supra note 84, at 667. The same danger exists, it has been observed, because "courts have commonly referred to agreement or combination, in the alternative." Model Penal Code § 5.03, Comment at 419 (1985). Such language is also to be found in some of the more recent recodifications.

97. Cousens, supra note 94, at 910.

98. United States v. DeBright, 742 F.2d 1196 (9th Cir. 1984); People v. Foster, 99 Ill.2d 48, 75 Ill.Dec. 411, 457 N.E.2d 405 (1983); Moore v. State, 290 So.2d 603 (Miss. 1974); DeLaney v. State, 164 Tenn. 432, 51 S.W.2d 485 (1932); Williams v. State, 646 S.W.2d 221 (Tex.Crim.App. 1983); Regina v. O'Brien, [1955] 2 D.L.R. 311 (1954).

99. See 6.4(e).

100. Because this is the reason, it thus follows that if A, B and C had joined together and indicated agreement with each other on a common criminal scheme, but only B secretly intended not to pursue the plan, A and C could still be convicted of conspiracy because there would be an agreement between them. Jung Quey v. United States, 138 C.C.A. 314, 222 F. 766 (1915).

101. Developments in the Law—Criminal Conspiracy, 72 Harv.L.Rev. 920, 927 n. 35 (1959). But courts have not been sympathetic to this view, at least when there were alternative means of reaching A's conduct. See Hutchinson v. State, 315 So.2d 546 (Fla.App.1975) (attempted conspiracy theory rejected, court notes defendant could be

convicted of solicitation); State v. St. Christopher, 305 Minn. 226, 232 N.W.2d 798 (1975) (attempted conspiracy theory rejected, but Model Penal Code unilateral approach accepted).

102. Model Penal Code § 5.03(1) is stated in terms of what is required to establish liability with respect to any given actor, in contrast to the traditional approach of requiring agreement between two or more persons.

103. Most modern codes, as does the Model Penal Code, define conspiracy in terms of a single actor agreeing with another, rather than as an agreement between two or more persons. But this is no guarantee that each of these statutes will be interpreted as embracing the unilateral approach. See, e.g., People v. Foster, 99 Ill.2d 48, 75 Ill. Dec. 411, 457 N.E.2d 405 (1983).

104. See, e.g., Saienni v. State, 346 A.2d 152 (Del.1975); Garcia v. State, 271 Ind. 510, 394 N.E.2d 106 (1979); State v. St. Christopher, 305 Minn. 226, 232 N.W.2d 798 (1975).

105. Model Penal Code § 5.03, Comment at 400 (1985). "[S]uch an approach is justified in that a man who believes that he is conspiring to commit a crime and wishes to conspire to commit a crime has a guilty mind and has done all in his power to plot the commission of an unlawful purpose." Friedman, Mens Rea in Conspiracy, 19 Modern L.Rev. 276, 283 (1956). Compare Burgman, Unilateral Conspiracy: Three Critical Perspectives, 29 DePaul L.Rev. 75 (1979), criticizing the Model Penal Code approach.

106. See § 3.3.

to pay those taxes.[107] However, conduct of an individual which constitutes a failure to perform a legal duty, such as the failure of a law enforcement official to enforce the law against a certain group, is relevant as some evidence that the individual had entered into an agreement with the group.[108]

Is it possible for a person to become a party to the crime of conspiracy even in the absence of any agreement on his part? The question is deliberately stated in this way, for the inquiry is whether the principles applicable in determining whether one is a party to a substantive crime [109] are also applicable to conspiracy. As we shall see,[110] it is possible for one to become a party to a crime directly committed by another without there being any agreement or communication of any kind between the two persons. For example, A is an accomplice to murder if, knowing that B and C have set out to kill D, he prevents a warning from reaching D, and this is so even though A's actions were not by preconcert with B and C and did not become known to B and C prior to the killing.[111] This is because A has actually aided in the murder of D and rendered the aid with the intent that D be killed. But, on these facts may it be concluded by like analysis that A is a member of a conspiracy with B and C because A knew of the conspiracy and intentionally gave aid to the conspiratorial objective?

The Supreme Court has assumed without deciding the issue that the answer is yes,[112] and other courts have taken the position that aiding a conspiracy with knowledge of its purposes suffices to make one a party to the conspiracy.[113] In support of that view, it has been argued that one who aids what is known to be a conspiracy is deserving of punishment, for he has the requisite evil intent and also has taken some action to bring that intent to fruition.[114] Although he has not increased the danger to the community in the same way as other conspirators by enhancing the chances of the objective being achieved through mutual support and encouragement, he has added to the danger by giving aid which makes it more probable that the criminal objective will be achieved.[115] Moreover, if giving aid to a known conspiracy is recognized as an independent ground for conviction of conspiracy, then "the impetus to derive a fictional consensus to support the liability would be diminished." [116]

On the other hand, it has been objected that the aiding and abetting theory is not applicable in the circumstances stated above. "A

107. Jones v. United States, 251 F.2d 288 (10th Cir. 1958).

108. Jezewski v. United States, 13 F.2d 599 (6th Cir. 1926). But see Weniger v. United States, 47 F.2d 692 (9th Cir.1931) (fact that county sheriff did not enforce prohibition laws not sufficient to show that he had joined conspiracy of village officials to permit sale of liquor upon payment of certain fees to the village).

109. See §§ 6.6–6.8.

110. See § 6.7(a).

111. State ex rel. Attorney General v. Talley, 102 Ala. 25, 15 So. 722 (1894).

112. The government relied upon this theory in United States v. Falcone, 311 U.S. 205, 61 S.Ct. 204, 85 L.Ed. 128 (1940), thus claiming that those who supplied the operators of illicit stills with sugar, yeast and cans were in a conspiracy with the operators. The Court responded: "The argument, the merits of which we do not consider, overlooks the fact that the opinion below [109 F.2d 579 (2d Cir.1940)] proceeds on the assumption that the evidence * * * fell short of showing respondents' participation in the conspiracy or that they knew of it." However, on a later occasion the Court asserted that the Falcone decision "comes down merely to this, that one does not become a party to a conspiracy by aiding and abetting it, through

sales of supplies or otherwise, unless he knows of the conspiracy; and the inference of such knowledge cannot be drawn merely from knowledge the buyer will use the goods illegally." Direct Sales Co. v. United States, 319 U.S. 703, 63 S.Ct. 1265, 87 L.Ed. 1674 (1943).

As to what will suffice to show such knowledge, it has been suggested that knowledge may sometimes be inferred from awareness that the objective could not be achieved except by cooperative efforts, in much the same way as knowledge of the nature of the operation will support the conclusion that a defendant was in a conspiracy with other parties he did not know but whose existence would be essential to the contemplated scheme. Comment, 16 U.C.L.A.L.Rev. 155, 159 n. 21 (1968).

113. United States v. Kasvin, 757 F.2d 887 (7th Cir. 1985); United States v. Galiffa, 734 F.2d 306 (7th Cir. 1984); Duke v. United States, 233 F.2d 897 (5th Cir.1956); Luteran v. United States, 93 F.2d 395 (8th Cir.1937); Pattis v. United States, 17 F.2d 562 (9th Cir.1927); Simpson v. United States, 11 F.2d 591 (4th Cir.1926).

114. Comment, supra note 112, at 171; Model Penal Code § 5.03, Comment at 420 (1985).

115. Comment, supra note 112, at 172.

116. Model Penal Code § 5.03, Comment at 420 (1985).

person does not aid and abet a conspiracy by helping the 'conspiracy' to commit a substantive offense, for the crime of conspiracy is separate from the offense which is its object. It is necessary to help the 'conspiracy' in the commission of the crime of conspiracy, that is, in the commission of the act of agreement." [117] Thus, so the argument goes, one may become a conspirator without agreement by giving aid only if the assistance is that of bringing two or more persons together with the intention that they reach an agreement to commit a crime.[118] On a more practical level, taking into account the several disadvantages which may flow from being a conspiracy defendant,[119] there is the contention that one who aids a conspiracy should be subjected to prosecution and punishment on some theory other than that he has become a member of the conspiracy.[120] On this basis, the Model Penal Code characterizes such activity as an attempt.[121]

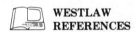

**WESTLAW
REFERENCES**

to(91) /p conspiracy /s agreement /s essence gist

(e) The Mental State. [122] Although the crime of conspiracy is "predominantly mental

in composition," [123] there has nonetheless always existed considerable confusion and uncertainty about precisely what mental state is required for this crime. The traditional definition of conspiracy does not focus upon the requisite state of mind,[124] and the matter has often been dealt with ambiguously by the courts [125] and has been largely ignored by the commentators.[126] As we shall see, this is undoubtedly attributable to two factors: (1) it is conceptually difficult to separate the mental state requirement from the agreement which constitutes the act [127]; and (2) as with all inchoate crimes, it is necessary to take into account the elements of the crime which is the objective.[128]

(1) Intent to Agree Distinguished. At the outset, it is useful to note that there are really two intents required for the crime of conspiracy.[129] Every conspiracy involves an agreement, so it must be established that the several parties intended to agree. But such an intent is "without moral content," [130] and thus it is also necessary to determine what objective the parties intended to achieve by their agreement. Only if there is a common purpose to attain an objective covered by the law of conspiracy [131] is there liability.

---

117. Developments, supra note 101, at 934.

118. As occurred in People v. Strauch, 240 Ill. 60, 88 N.E. 155 (1909), where the father introduced his son to another with the intent that they should enter into a conspiracy, which they did, and the court held that "if any two of the defendants charged entered into such conspiracy, and the third aided, assisted, and encouraged the making of such unlawful agreement, such third party would be equally guilty with those who actively participate in the unlawful agreement."

119. See § 6.4(b).

120. Model Penal Code § 5.03, Comment at 420–21 (1985).

121. Model Penal Code § 5.01(3). That position has been criticized on the ground that "it would seem more appropriate to punish the aider and abettor * * * with the penalties attaching to conspiracy rather than the penalties attaching to attempting the substantive object of the conspiracy. After all, the complicitous party is not only increasing the chances that the substantive offense will be consummated, he is facilitating the realization of the greater potential harm inherent in conspiracy." Comment, supra note 112, at 174.

122. See Elliott, Lynch & Smith, Mens Rea in Statutory Conspiracy, 1978 Crim.L.Rev. 202; Marcus, Criminal Conspiracy: The State of Mind Crime—Intent, Proving Intent, and Anti-Federal Intent, 1976 U.Ill.L.F. 627.

123. Harno, Intent in Criminal Conspiracy, 89 U.Pa.L. Rev. 624, 632 (1941).

124. "The traditional definition said nothing about the actor's state of mind except insofar as the concept of agreement itself carries certain implications about his attitude toward the crime." Model Penal Code § 5.03, Comment at 403 (1985).

125. "The verbalisms of the courts describing the intent in conspiracy are well-nigh terrifying. The decisions abound in statements that the intent must be 'evil,' 'wicked,' or 'corrupt'; that the federation must be 'corrupt,' and that the 'motives' of the actors must be 'evil' or 'corrupt.'" Harno, supra note 123, at 636.

126. "It is a curious fact that in all that has been written about criminal conspiracy there is scant mention of intent." Id. at 629.

127. See § 6.4(d).

128. As stated by Justice Jackson, concurring in Krulewitch v. United States, 336 U.S. 440, 69 S.Ct. 716, 93 L.Ed. 790 (1949), conspiracy, "chameleon-like, takes on a special coloration from each of the many independent offenses on which it may be overlaid."

129. See Harno, supra note 123, at 631.

130. Developments in the Law—Criminal Conspiracy, 72 Harv.L.Rev. 920, 936 (1959).

131. See, § 6.5(a).

One of these intents may exist without the other. Quite clearly there may be an intent to agree without there also being a common intent to achieve an unlawful objective, as where A and B agree to burn certain property and A knows the property belongs to C but B (perhaps because he has been misled by A) believes that the property belongs to A. On the other hand, two persons may share an unlawful objective without having reached an agreement; A and B might both want C's property burned and yet have reached no agreement in that regard—even if they had communicated their intentions to one another.[132]

The intent to agree is so intimately tied up with the agreement (the act part of the crime) that it is best dealt with in that context. Indeed, it may even be said that such intent is not really part of the *mens rea* of conspiracy; as one court put it, the state of mind in conspiracy "does not refer to the act of conspiring, but to the fruits of the conspiracy."[133] Thus, the concern in what follows is not with the intent to agree but rather with the additional mental state which is required in order to make the agreement a criminal conspiracy.

(2) Intent to Achieve Objective. Although there may be some uncertainty in existing law on the requisite state of mind because of the varied phrases used by the courts[134] and the occasional assertion that liability is based upon "joining" or "adhering" to a group,[135] it may generally be said that the mental state required is an intent to achieve a particular result which is criminal[136] or which though noncriminal is nonetheless covered by the law of conspiracy.[137] (As is considered in more detail later,[138] certain noncriminal objectives are included within the common law definition and also in some statutory formulations of the crime.) This has been characterized as a specific intent,[139] although it has also been said that it would be difficult "to conceive of any crime in which the intent is less specific"[140] because of the many different objectives which might be intended. Doubtless we would be better off if the phrase "specific intent" were abandoned because of the confusion which it has caused,[141] but to the extent that it has meaning it is fair to say that conspiracy is a specific intent crime.[142]

Confusion is most likely to arise in those cases where the objective of the conspiracy, if achieved, is itself a crime, for under such circumstances the mental state for that crime must also be taken into account. Clearly, a "conspiracy to commit a particular substantive offense cannot exist without *at least* the degree of criminal intent necessary for the substantive offense itself."[143] If A and B

---

132. Thus, in State v. King, 104 Iowa 727, 74 N.W. 691 (1898), A told B that if he would whip C someone would pay his fine, to which B replied that he did not want anyone to pay his fine because he had a grievance of his own against C. Thereafter, B beat C severely, after which A indicated his satisfaction with what B had done. The court held that there had been no agreement between A and B and thus no conspiracy.

133. Elkin v. People, 28 N.Y. 177, 179 (1863).

134. See note 125 supra.

135. E.g., Laska v. United States, 82 F.2d 672 (10th Cir. 1936); Burkhardt v. United States, 13 F.2d 841 (6th Cir. 1926).

136. This intent need not be so particular that the conspirator has in mind a particular time, place, victim, etc., but at least must relate to a particular type of criminal activity. See, e.g., United States v. Gallishaw, 428 F.2d 760 (2d Cir.1970) (jury instruction which, in effect, said defendant who supplied gun could be convicted if he knew generally that the others would "use the gun to violate the law" was reversible error).

137. The Model Penal Code, which requires a criminal objective for conspiracy, uses the phrase "with the purpose

of promoting or facilitating its commission." Model Penal Code § 5.03(1).

Most of the modern codes specifically state that an "intent" or "purpose" to commit a crime is required.

138. See § 6.5(a).

139. Harno, supra note 123, at 636.

140. Developments, supra note 130, at 935.

141. See § 3.5(e).

142. Thus, if specific intent is taken to mean an intent which goes beyond the required acts (e.g., in burglary, where the acts are breaking and entering a dwelling, and the intent is to commit a felony therein, see § 8.13), then conspiracy is a special intent crime because the intent is more than the intent to agree. Also, the notion that a specific intent must be proved and may not be presumed from the commission of the acts has been applied in conspiracy cases. See Harno, supra note 123, at 637–39.

143. Developments, supra note 130, at 939. See also United States v. Lichenstein, 610 F.2d 1272 (5th Cir.1980) (applying this rule, it necessary that conspiracy to submit false statement to U.S. Customs include the intent to deceive needed for the completed crime); McDonald v.

agree to take *C*'s property, for example, this is not a conspiracy to commit the crime of larceny unless *A* and *B* had the intent to permanently deprive required for commission of larceny.[144] Likewise, where *D* and *E* agree to conceal *F*, this is not a conspiracy to violate the statute making it an offense to conceal a person against whom it is known a federal warrant has issued unless *D* and *E* had that knowledge.[145]

On the other hand, the fact that conspiracy requires an intent to achive a certain objective means that individuals who have together committed a certain crime have not necessarily participated in a conspiracy to commit that crime. To take the example given by the Model Penal Code draftsmen,[146] assume that two persons plan to destroy a building by detonating a bomb, though they know and believe that there are inhabitants in the building who will be killed by the explosion. If they do destroy the building and persons are killed, they are guilty of murder, but this is because murder may be committed other than with an intent-to-kill mental state.[147] Their plan constitutes a conspiracy to destroy the building, but not a conspiracy to kill the inhabitants, for they did not intend the latter result. It follows, therefore, that there is no such thing as a conspiracy to commit a crime which is defined in terms of recklessly or negligently causing a result.[148]

A somewhat different problem is that presented in *People v. Horn*,[149] where the defendants were convicted of conspiracy to commit murder. There was evidence that the defendants had been so intoxicated as to lack the capacity to entertain malice aforethought, meaning their scheme, if carried out, would have been only voluntary manslaughter. The trial judge's refusal to instruct on the lesser offense of conspiracy to commit voluntary manslaughter was held to be reversible error. A dissent in *Horn* cogently pointed out that concepts of diminished capacity and the like, applicable to determine the level of a criminal homicide, did not carry over to conspiracy, where only an intent mental state (unadorned by further malice aforethought or premeditation-deliberation distinctions) need be proved. The failure of the *Horn* majority to accept that reasoning is doubtless attributable to a desire to afford conspiracy defendants the same sentence-mitigating benefits they would have as to the object crime. Such a concern is especially legitimate in *Horn*, where, as the majority emphasized, "the punishment for conspiracy to commit a homicide is the same as the punishment for the conspired felony."

(3) Providing Goods or Services.[150] One problem in this area which has continued to perplex the courts is that of determining under what circumstances the supplier of goods or services to a known criminal undertaking becomes a party to the conspiracy. If the notion "that a conspiracy is a partnership in criminal purposes and that all are guilty who join it with knowledge of such purposes"[151]

State, 454 So.2d 488 (Miss.1984) (though defendant participated in possession and transportation of marijuana, he did so in effort to extricate his brother and a good friend from involvement in the activity, and thus was not a member of a conspiracy to possess with intent to distribute).

144. There remains, of course, the possibility that the absence of the intent required for the other crime will not bar conviction for conspiracy if the intent is nonetheless wrongful. See, e.g., Rex v. Ripsal, 97 Eng.Rep. 852 (1762), where an indictment for conspiracy to extort failed to allege the mental state required for extortion, but was deemed sufficient on the ground that there had been a conspiracy to injure the victim.

145. Fulbright v. United States, 91 F.2d 210 (8th Cir. 1937).

146. Model Penal Code § 5.03, Comment at 407–08 (1985).

147. See § 7.4.

148. This must be distinguished from an offense such as reckless driving which is defined only in terms of conduct creating a risk of harm, where there might be a conspiracy to commit that crime if the intent is to create that risk—as by urging the driver of a car to go faster. Model Penal Code § 5.03, Comment at 408 (1985).

149. 12 Cal.3d 290, 115 Cal.Rptr. 516, 524 P.2d 1300 (1974).

150. See Note, 53 Colum.L.Rev. 228 (1953), dealing with such situations in terms of conspiracy liability and also accessory liability for the completed crime. On the latter situation, see § 6.7(d).

151. Scales v. United States, 227 F.2d 581 (4th Cir. 1955), rev'd 355 U.S. 1, 78 S.Ct. 9, 2 L.Ed.2d 19 (1957). See also Bender v. State, 253 A.2d 686 (Del.1969): "If a person understands the unlawful nature of the acts taking place, and nevertheless assists in any manner in the carrying out of the common scheme, he thereupon becomes a conspirator to commit the offense."

was generally accepted as the basis of conspiracy liability, then it might be said that all such suppliers are conspirators. But, as we have seen, it is intent rather than knowledge which is usually required, and thus the question is when the circumstances will suffice to show that the supplier shared the intent to achieve the criminal objective. The two leading cases on this point are *United States v. Falcone* [152] and *Direct Sales Co. v. United States.* [153]

In *Falcone,* a group of distillers and others who supplied them with sugar, yeast and cans were convicted of a conspiracy to operate illicit stills. The Court of Appeals reversed as to the suppliers, holding that the seller of innocent goods does not become a conspirator merely because of his knowledge that the buyer plans to use them in the commission of a crime. "[I]n prosecutions for conspiracy * * * his attitude towards the forbidden undertaking must be more positive. It is not enough that he does not forego a normally lawful activity, of the fruits of which he knows that others will make an unlawful use; he must in some sense promote their venture himself, make it his own, have a stake in its outcome." Before the Supreme Court, the government attempted to avoid that result by shifting to a theory that the suppliers had aided and abetted a conspiracy, but they did not succeed because the evidence did not show the suppliers knew that a conspiracy existed between others.

In *Direct Sales,* the defendant company, a registered drug manufacturer and wholesaler, was convicted of conspiracy to violate the narcotics laws upon a showing that the corporation "sold morphine sulphate to Dr. Tate in such quantities, so frequently and over so long a period it must have been known he could dispense the amounts received in lawful practice and was therefore distributing the drug illegally." The defendant contended that such a result was inconsistent with the rationale of *Falcone,* but the Supreme Court held that *Falcone* was not controlling because the "commodities sold there were articles of free commerce" while in the instant case they were "restricted commodities, incapable of further legal use except by compliance with rigid regulations." The Court noted that the character of the goods in the present case was important for two reasons: (1) to show that the defendant knew the illegal use to which they were being put by the buyer; and (2) to show that the defendant had taken "the step from knowledge to intent and agreement." Although declining to state that a "stake in the venture" would be essential, the Court found sufficient evidence of the defendant's intent from the fact that it actively stimulated repeated sales of unlimited quantities of a restricted commodity and thus received profits which it was known could only come from its encouragement of the illegal operation.

Lower courts have also placed reliance upon the factors stressed in *Direct Sales:* the quantity of the sales [154]; the continuity of the relationship between seller and buyer [155]; the seller's initiative or encouragement [156]; and the nature of the goods.[157] The failure of the seller to submit sales reports required by government regulations has also been considered relevant,[158] as has the failure to keep the usual business records or other secretive techniques.[159] Intent may also be inferred from the fact that the seller has made inflated

152. 109 F.2d 579 (2d Cir.1940), affirmed 311 U.S. 205, 61 S.Ct. 204, 85 L.Ed. 128 (1940).

153. 319 U.S. 703, 63 S.Ct. 1265, 87 L.Ed. 1674 (1943).

154. E.g., Eley v. United States, 117 F.2d 526 (6th Cir. 1941).

155. E.g., United States v. Michelana-Orovia, 702 F.2d 496 (5th Cir.1983), on rehearing 719 F.2d 738 (5th Cir. 1983) (thus crew member on ship headed for U.S. with 12 tons of marijuana was member of conspiracy to import marijuana, but not conspiracy to distribute marijuana in U.S.).

156. E.g., Bartoli v. United States, 192 F.2d 130 (4th Cir.1951); United States v. Cusimano, 123 F.2d 611 (7th Cir.1941).

157. E.g., United States v. Tramaglino, 197 F.2d 928 (2d Cir.1952); United States v. Kertess, 139 F.2d 923 (2d Cir.1944).

158. E.g., United States v. Tramaglino, 197 F.2d 928 (2d Cir.1952); United States v. Loew, 145 F.2d 332 (2d Cir. 1944).

159. E.g., United States v. Loew, 145 F.2d 332 (2d Cir. 1944); Bacon v. United States, 127 F.2d 985 (10th Cir. 1942).

charges,[160] that he has supplied goods or services which have no legitimate use,[161] or that the sales to the illegal operation have become the dominant proportion of the seller's business.[162]

Dictum in one case suggests that

> a supplier who furnishes equipment which he *knows* will be used to commit a serious crime may be deemed from that knowledge alone to have intended to produce the result. * * * For instance, we think the operator of a telephone answering service with positive knowledge that his service was being used to facilitate the extortion of ransom, the distribution of heroin, or the passing of counterfeit money who continued to furnish the service with knowledge of its use, might be chargeable on knowledge alone with participation in a scheme to extort money, to distribute narcotics, or to pass counterfeit money. The same result would follow the seller of gasoline who knew the buyer was using his product to make Molotov cocktails for terroristic use.[163]

There do not appear to be any decisions reaching such a result,[164] although it certainly could be argued that taking account of the seriousness of the criminal objective is appropriate in striking a balance between the "conflicting interests * * * of the vendors in freedom to engage in gainful and otherwise lawful activities without policing their vend-

ees, and that of the community in preventing behavior that facilitates the commission of crimes." [165]

(4) Liability Without Fault. Although the question has seldom been confronted in the cases, it seems clear that there is no such thing as liability without fault conspiracy. "While one may, for instance, be guilty of running past a traffic light of whose existence one is ignorant, one cannot be guilty of conspiring to run past such a light, for one cannot agree to run past a light unless one supposes that there is a light to run past." [166] Thus, even if what was done under an agreement has been made unlawful on a liability without fault basis, there can be no conviction for conspiracy unless it is shown that the parties actually intended to achieve what was done.[167] This is as it should be, for the fact that a statute has made the doing of a certain act an offense without regard to mental fault can hardly be said to have a worked a change in the mental element of the distinct crime of conspiracy.[168]

The offense which is a liability without fault crime in all respects must be distinguished from the offense which does require a certain mental state as to some elements of the crime but not as to others. This is the case as to several federal statutes in which

160. People v. Lauria, 251 Cal.App.2d 471, 59 Cal.Rptr. 628 (1967) (dictum).

161. Ibid., citing as a leading case People v. McLaughlin, 111 Cal.App.2d 781, 245 P.2d 1076 (1952), where the court upheld a conviction of the suppliers of horse racing information by wire for conspiracy to promote bookmaking, when it was established that the wire-service information had no other use.

162. People v. Lauria, 251 Cal.App.2d 471, 59 Cal.Rptr. 628 (1967) (dictum), noting that in *Direct Sales* the Court found significant the fact that the defendant had attracted as customers a disproportionately large group of physicians who had been convicted of violating the narcotics laws.

163. Ibid.

164. Rather, the cases continue to emphasize that knowing aid is not sufficient. See, e.g., United States v. Alvarez, 610 F.2d 1250 (5th Cir.1980), on rehearing 625 F.2d 1196 (5th Cir.1980) (unloading illegal cargo of plane does not make one a member of the known conspiracy).

The court in *Lauria* cited no conspiracy cases for this proposition, but instead relied upon Regina v. Bainbridge, [1959] 3 W.L.R. 656 (holding supplier of oxygen-cutting equipment to one known to intend to use it to break into

bank an accessory to the crime); and Sykes v. Director of Public Prosecutions, [1962] A.C. 528 (holding one having knowledge of theft of pistols, submachine guns, and ammunition guilty of misprision of felony for failure to disclose theft to authorities).

165. Model Penal Code § 5.03, Comment at 404 (1985).

Given the several disadvantages which flow from being a defendant in a conspiracy case, see § 6.4(b), others have indicated that knowing facilitation should not be sufficient for conspiracy liability even if it is recognized as a basis of liability for the completed crime as an accessory. Ibid.; Note, supra note 150, at 241.

166. United States v. Crimmins, 123 F.2d 271 (2d Cir. 1941).

167. Churchill v. Walton, [1967] 1 All E.R. 467, noted in 83 L.Q.Rev. 325 (1967).

168. G. Williams, Criminal Law: The General Part § 84 (2d ed. 1961), also noting "that the idea that conspiracy may be a crime of absolute responsibility is fundamentally inconsistent with the rule, now quite firmly established, that secondary parties to a crime cannot be convicted in the absence of knowledge of all the facts." On strict liability as to accomplices, see § 6.7(f).

the attendant circumstances affording a basis for federal jurisdiction are made an element of the crime.[169] Although strict liability is often imposed as to these circumstance elements, for a time some federal courts held that knowledge of those circumstances was essential for a conspiracy to violate such statutes.[170] The better view, however, is that when one "sets out with the purpose of engaging in the proscribed conduct or producing the undesirable result with the lesser culpability concerning attendant circumstances that suffices for commission of the crime, and his preparation progresses to the point of a conspiracy or attempt, the reasons for reaching his behavior as an inchoate crime are in no way decreased by such lesser culpability concerning the circumstances."[171] The Supreme Court has now adopted this position as to the federal conspiracy statute.[172] The Court explained that a contrary result, requiring that the conspirators be aware of the facts giving rise to federal jurisdiction, would not serve the policies underlying the crime of conspiracy.[173] This means, for example, that a conspiracy to transport stolen goods in interstate commerce does not require knowledge by the conspirators that the stolen goods are to be transported across state lines, for such awareness would be unnecessary on a transportation charge.[174]

(5) The "Corrupt Motive" Doctrine. In *People v. Powell,*[175] the defendants were prosecuted for conspiracy to violate a statute requiring municipal officers to advertise for bids before purchasing supplies, and they asserted as a defense that they had acted in good faith because they were unaware of the existence of the statute. The court ruled in their favor, holding it was "implied in the meaning of the word conspiracy" that the agreement "must have been entered into with an evil purpose, as distinguished from a purpose to do the act prohibited, in ignorance of the prohibition." Under what has since become known as the corrupt motive doctrine, it has similarly been held, for example, that election officials may defend against a charge of conspiracy to violate the election laws by showing they were ignorant of those laws,[176] and that druggists could defend against a charge of conspiracy to violate the prohibition laws by establishing that they had erroneously interpreted those

---

169. Such would no longer be the case under the proposed new federal code, which gives distinct treatment to the jurisdictional and behavioral content of the law. National Comm'n on Reform of Federal Criminal Laws, Final Report—Proposed New Federal Criminal Code § 201 (1971).

170. Thus, it was held that while one may be convicted of transporting stolen goods through interstate commerce even without knowledge of the interstate element, a conspirator must be aware of the past or contemplate the future passage of the goods through interstate commerce. E.g., United States v. Tannuzzo, 174 F.2d 177 (2d Cir. 1949). Similarly, it was held that though one may be convicted of using the mails to defraud merely upon a showing that the mails were in fact used, for a conspiracy it must be established that use of the mails was contemplated. E.g., United States v. Taylor, 217 F.2d 397 (2d Cir. 1954).

171. Model Penal Code § 5.03, Comment at 409 (1985).

172. United States v. Feola, 420 U.S. 671, 95 S.Ct. 1255, 43 L.Ed.2d 541 (1975) (because assault of federal officer crime does not require knowledge of victim's status, conspiracy to commit such an assault does not either); United States v. Freed, 401 U.S. 601, 91 S.Ct. 1112, 28 L.Ed.2d 356 (1971) (conspiracy to possess unregistered firearms does not require knowledge of lack of registration, as such mental state not required for the possession crime). See Berger, Conspiracy and Federal Jurisdiction: From Crimmins to Feola, 22 Vill.L.Rev. 554 (1977).

173. The Court explained that knowledge by the conspirators "that their planned joint venture violates federal as well as state law seems totally irrelevant to that purpose of conspiracy law which seeks to protect society from the dangers of concerted criminal activity," and also to that purpose of allowing intervention of the criminal law when "the likelihood of a commission of an act is sufficiently great and the criminal intent sufficiently well formed."

174. United States v. Franklin, 586 F.2d 560 (5th Cir. 1978). Compare United States v. Prince, 529 F.2d 1108 (6th Cir.1976) (defendant not a member of conspiracy to violate Travel Act, involving travel in interstate commerce with intent to engage in, e.g., prostitution, unless defendant, a madam in a house of prostitution, knew of interstate transportation of girls working for her).

See also United States v. Sorrow, 732 F.2d 176 (11th Cir. 1984) (conspiracy to defraud the United States, an offense under 18 U.S.C.A. § 371, does not require anti-federal intent under the *Feola* rationale, as "whether persons who plan to defraud the United States in fact realize that federal dollars are the object of their scheme is irrelevant to the goal of safeguarding federal fiscal resources").

175. 63 N.Y. 88 (1875).

176. Commonwealth v. Gormley, 77 Pa.Super. 298 (1921).

laws as not being applicable to their selling methods.[177]

Some courts have rejected the corrupt motive doctrine,[178] usually by resort to the general rule that ignorance of the criminality of one's conduct is no defense.[179] Several other courts which have considered the issue have accepted the *Powell* rule in one form or another. Because it was noted in *Powell* that the offense was "innocent in itself," many jurisdictions utilize the *malum in se-malum prohibitum* distinction[180] here and thus recognize a claim of good faith only if the criminal objective of the conspiracy was not inherently wrong.[181] Assuming circumstances in which the defense may be presented, some courts have taken the view that it is sufficient that the defendants were unaware of the statute prohibiting their objective,[182] while others require the absence of a corrupt or evil motive in a more general sense.[183]

The decisions accepting the corrupt motive doctrine usually give no explanation for it beyond the notion expressed in *Powell* that such a result is implied by the word conspiracy. That reasoning is hardly convincing,[184] and it has been questioned whether any other reason exists for making an exception to the general principle that ignorance of the law is no excuse.[185] Some commentators have suggested, however, that the corrupt motive doc-

trine is consistent with the rationale underlying the crime of conspiracy.[186] Thus, taking note of the fact that conspiracy reaches farther back than attempt to a point where immediate achievement of the objective is less likely, it is argued that "the danger arising from the mere act of agreement is less when the defendants are actuated by no 'criminal intent,' and so may be expected to desist if, before committing the act, they discover its illegality."[187] Similarly, it has been suggested that a group which combines to achieve an objective not inherently wrong and not known by them to be illegal poses no threat of continued wrongdoing because they are unlikely to undertake similar schemes after learning that the objective is against the law.[188] On the other hand, it has been observed that the corrupt motive doctrine has created much confusion concerning the *mens rea* requirements of conspiracy, and that the question of whether unawareness of regulatory offenses should be a defense is better resolved without regard to whether there was group activity.[189]

(6) Plurality of Intent. Although some of the decisions seem to suggest that when a person joins a group enterprise he is by that fact alone shown to have the same intention as the others,[190] it must be remembered that the question of whether the requisite intent was present must be separately considered as

177. Landen v. United States, 299 F. 75 (6th Cir.1924).

178. E.g., People v. McLaughlin, 111 Cal.App.2d 781, 245 P.2d 1076 (1952); People v. Cohn, 358 Ill. 326, 193 N.E. 150 (1934). Also, in some of the decisions relying upon *Powell* it appears that the defendants were in addition or instead ignorant of certain factual matters which would have afforded them a defense without resort to the corrupt motives rule. See, e.g., State v. Burns, 215 Minn. 182, 9 N.W.2d 518 (1943).

179. See § 5.1(d). It would seem that such a result could be expected under most of the modern recodifications, for they accept this general principle and do not, in their conspiracy provisions, give any express recognition to the corrupt motive doctrine.

180. See § 1.6(b).

181. E.g., Commonwealth v. Benesch, 290 Mass. 125, 194 N.E. 905 (1935).

182. E.g., Mitchell v. State, 248 Ala. 169, 27 So.2d 36 (1946); Commonwealth v. Benesch, 290 Mass. 125, 194 N.E. 905 (1935).

183. E.g., Cruz v. United States, 106 F.2d 828 (10th Cir. 1939).

184. "We demur to the notion that there is anything particularly wicked attached to the word 'conspiracy.' No doubt in common speech 'conspiracy' has a melodramatic and sinister implication, but it has been pointed out that it carries no such implication in law. The definition of it is simply an agreement to do an unlawful act—an act prohibited by statutory provisions—or a lawful act by unlawful means. It does not matter how prosaic the unlawful act may be or how ignorant the conspirators may be of the fact that the act is prohibited by the statutory provision." Rex v. Clayton, 33 Crim.App.R. 113 (1943).

185. United States v. Mack, 112 F.2d 290 (2d Cir.1940).

186. See subhead § 6.4(c).

187. Note, 38 Harv.L.Rev. 96, 99 (1924).

188. Developments, supra note 134, at 936.

189. Model Penal Code § 5.03, Comment at 417–18 (1985).

190. E.g., United States v. Patten, 226 U.S. 525, 33 S.Ct. 141, 57 L.Ed. 333 (1913): "[T]he conspirators must be held to have intended the necessary and direct consequences of their acts and cannot be heard to say the

to each individual who is alleged to be a member of the conspiracy. If, for example, *A*, *B*, and *C* agree to take *D*'s property, and *A* and *B* thereby intend to permanently deprive *D* of the property but *C* does not have that intent, then it is not correct to conclude that *C* is part of a conspiracy to commit larceny. Likewise, where the corrupt motive doctrine prevails, if *E*, *F*, and *G* agree to do a certain act which is not inherently wrong but which is proscribed by a statute of which only *E* and *F* are aware, then it may not be said that *G* was a member of a conspiracy to violate that statute.

Moreover, because of the plurality requirement [191] it must be shown that the requisite intent existed as to at least two persons. That is, there must be a common design, so that if only one party to the agreement has the necessary mental state then even that person may not be convicted of conspiracy.[192] This result has been questioned on the ground that there still exists a need to proceed against that person because of his criminal disposition,[193] and under the unilateral approach of the Model Penal Code [194] the one party to the agreement with the necessary mental state could be convicted.

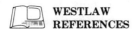

WESTLAW REFERENCES

conspiracy /p "corrupt motive" (powell /s 63 +5 88) "evil purpose"

---

§ 6.5 Conspiracy—The Limits of Liability

Under the modern view, conspiracy statutes are limited to criminal objectives. Impossibility of success is not a defense, as criminal combinations are dangerous apart from the danger of attaining the particular objective. Most states have by statute added to the defi-

nition of conspiracy the requirement of an overt act, but this is not a significant change because virtually any act in furtherance of the objective will suffice.

An agreement to commit several crimes is but one conspiracy. Several persons may be parties to a single conspiracy even if they have never directly communicated with one another; the question is whether they are aware of each other's participation in a general way and have a community of interest. Conspiracy is an offense which continues up to the point of abandonment or success. The traditional rule is that withdrawal by one conspirator after the conspiracy has been formed does not give him a defense to a charge of conspiracy, although there is good reason to question that rule.

In most jurisdictions an acquittal or similar disposition of one conspirator bars conviction of a single remaining co-conspirator. A person may be guilty of a conspiracy to commit a crime he could not personally commit (e.g., a woman may conspire to rape), but one who is in a legislatively protected class and thus could not even be guilty as an accessory of the crime which is the objective is likewise not guilty of conspiracy to commit that crime. That must be distinguished from the oft-criticized Wharton rule, whereby a conspiracy is said to require the participation of more persons than are logically necessary to commit the completed crime.

If the conspiracy is successful, under the prevailing rule a conspirator may be subject to conviction for both the conspiracy and the completed crime. Cumulative sentences are permissible in most jurisdictions, though this has been criticized when the conspiracy is to do no more than that crime.

---

contrary. In other words by purposely engaging in a conspiracy which necessarily and directly produces the result which the statute is designed to prevent, they are in legal contemplation, chargeable with intending that result."

191. See § 6.5(g).

192. Regle v. State, 9 Md.App. 346, 264 A.2d 119 (1970) (only other person insane); Commonwealth v. Benesch,

290 Mass. 125, 194 N.E. 905 (1935) (only one person had corrupt motive).

193. Developments, supra note 130, at 940.

194. Model Penal Code § 5.03, Comment at 398–402 (1985).

(a) The Conspiratorial Objective.[1] The generally accepted common law definition of conspiracy is "a combination of two or more persons * * * to accomplish some criminal or unlawful purpose, or to accomplish some purpose, not in itself criminal or unlawful, by criminal or unlawful means."[2] Not every unlawful purpose is criminal[3] and thus acts lawful when performed by an individual may become criminal when the object of an agreement by many to perform them.[4] Although the common law rule is based on what is probably an incorrect reading of the early cases,[5] it has survived except when changed by statute. Most states provide that the object of a criminal conspiracy must be some crime[6] or some felony.[7]

Only conspiracies to falsely accuse others of felonies were criminal in the early seventeenth century.[8] A loosely reasoned assertion by Hawkins that "there can be no doubt, but that all confederacies whatsoever, wrongfully to prejudice a third person, are highly criminal at common law"[9] helped extend the law of conspiracy to cover non-criminal objects.

This extension is usually justified on the grounds that the means to perpetrate the wrong are particularly dangerous to the public,[10] because the conspirators will draw new courage and be less likely to refrain from the act than an individual,[11] or that the moral fibre of the community is weakened by concerted wrongdoing.[12] As stated in an early case: "An unlawful act may not prove injurious * * * when attempted by an individual, and may be readily prevented; the same act attempted by the confederation of two or more may become dangerous to the public peace and to the security of persons and property, and harmful to public morals by the very weight and power of numbers."[13]

Thus in England it was held to be a criminal conspiracy to combine to falsely accuse one of fathering a bastard,[14] to indenture a girl at prostitution,[15] to marry off a pauper so as to charge another parish with his support,[16] or to raise workmen's wages.[17] Lord Edenborough refused to extend the doctrine to civil trespass,[18] but was later overruled.[19]

§ 6.5

1. See Notes, 75 Colum.L.Rev. 1122, 1129–35 (1975); 68 Harv.L.Rev. 1056 (1955).

2. Commonwealth v. Hunt, 45 Mass. (4 Metc.) 111 (1842); King v. Jones, 110 Eng.Rep. 485 (1832).

3. "We use the terms criminal or unlawful, because it is manifest that many acts are unlawful, which are not punishable by indictment or other public prosecution, and yet there is no doubt * * * that a combination by numbers, to do them would be an unlawful conspiracy and punishable by indictment * * * but yet it is clear that it is not every combination to do unlawful acts to the prejudice of another, which is punishable as conspiracy." Commonwealth v. Hunt, 45 Mass. (4 Metc.) 111 (1842).

4. See, e.g., State v. Blackledge, 216 Iowa 199, 243 N.W. 534 (1932) (diverting trust funds of Lodge).

5. See Sayre, Criminal Conspiracy, 35 Harv.L.Rev. 393 (1922).

6. This is the position taken in the great majority of the modern recodifications. There is some authority that one may conspire to violate a statutory provision defined in terms of attempting a certain crime. See, e.g., United States v. Dearmore, 672 F.2d 738 (9th Cir.1982). But see United States v. Meachum, 626 F.2d 503 (5th Cir.1980).

7. Only a few of the modern recodifications are so limited. Some statutes are limited in other ways, such as by specifying the crimes which will suffice as objectives, or by including all felonies and higher misdemeanors.

8. 3 E. Coke, Institutes 143 (1644).

9. 1 W. Hawkins, Pleas of the Crown 348 (6th ed. 1787).

10. Commonwealth v. Waterman, 122 Mass. 43 (1877).

11. State v. Dalton, 134 Mo.App. 517, 114 S.W. 1132 (1908).

12. United States v. Lancaster, 44 F. 896 (C.C.W.D.Ga. 1891).

13. Fimara v. Garner, 86 Conn. 434, 85 A. 670 (1913). Cf. United States v. Rabinowich, 238 U.S. 78, 35 S.Ct. 682, 59 L.Ed. 1211 (1915).

14. Child v. North & Timberly, 83 Eng.Rep. 900 (1661); King v. Tymberly, 83 Eng.Rep. 930 (1662); King v. Armstrong, 86 Eng.Rep. 196 (1677); Queen v. Best, 87 Eng.Rep. 941 (1705). These four cases all mention possible civil liability (false suit) of the putative father and exortion motives as well as violations of spiritual law. Therefore their precedential value for extending the law of conspiracy is weak.

15. Rex v. Delaval, 97 Eng.Rep. 913 (1763).

16. King v. Edwards, 88 Eng.Rep. 229 (1725).

17. King v. Journeymen-Taylors, 88 Eng.Rep. 9 (1791). This case, however, seems to have been statutorily based as it was a crime to attempt to raise the wages of workingmen. 7 Geo. I c. 13, 2 & 3 Edw. VI, c. 15.

18. King v. Turner, 104 Eng.Rep. 357 (1811). Lord Ellenborough stated: "I should be sorry that the cases in conspiracy against individuals * * * should be pushed still further."

Conspiracies to defraud by acts not criminal by one person have been consistently held to be punishable. Beginning with a conspiracy by London hewers to deprive the tax men of their revenue,[20] combinations to defraud the government have been declared criminal conspiracies.[21] Today practically any scheme to affect the government may be indicted as a conspiracy to defraud.[22] Schemes to defraud individuals[23] or corporations[24] are generally held to be criminal conspiracies, and were punishable as conspiracies before the fraud became a substantive crime.[25]

In the United States the cases have occasionally held that no indictment for criminal conspiracy lies if the object is merely *malum prohibitum*.[26] Generally, however, combinations are prohibited where either the object or means are mischievous to the public[27] or oppressive to individuals.[28] Thus combinations to commit fornication,[29] to interfere with the "social intercourse" of a picnic,[30] or to use a car without the owner's permission have been punished as conspiracies.[31] Most states require only a nominal showing of harm to the public from conspiracies,[32] but others require a strong probability of public injury[33] or that the object benefit the conspirators to the necessary prejudice of the public.[34] The wide sweep of the present substantive criminal law, however, has made criminal many acts formerly only unlawful, and thus most combinations today are to commit crimes[35] or to defraud.[36]

The breadth of the law of conspiracy makes it subject to prosecutorial[37] and judicial abuse.[38] Statutes which make criminal combinations to commit acts injurious to the pub-

---

19. Reg. v. Rowlands, 177 Eng.Rep. 1439 (1851). This case contained aggravating circumstances not present in the one it overruled and thus was not a proper vehicle for that task.

20. King v. Sterline, 83 Eng.Rep. 331 (1663). Hawkins based his argument in large part upon this case.

21. E.g., United States v. Terranova, 7 F.Supp. 989 (N.D.Cal.1934).

22. Goldstein, Conspiracy to Defraud the United States, 68 Yale L.J. 405 (1959).

23. State v. Parker, 114 Conn. 354, 158 A. 797 (1932); State v. Gannon, 75 Conn. 206, 52 A. 727 (1902); State v. Roberts, 34 Me. 320 (1851).

24. State v. Fleming, 243 S.C. 265, 133 S.E.2d 800 (1963).

25. State v. Bacon, 27 R.I. 252, 61 A. 653 (1905).

26. People v. Dorman, 415 Ill. 385, 114 N.E.2d 404 (1953).

27. R. Wright, The Law of Criminal Conspiracies and Agreements 115–19 (1887); Developments in the Law—Criminal Conspiracy, 72 Harv.L.Rev. 920, 942 (1959); Note, 68 Harv.L.Rev. 1056, 1061–64 (1955).

28. R. Wright, supra note 27, at 119–29; Note, supra note 27, at 1064, 65.

29. Baker v. Commonwealth, 204 Ky. 420, 264 S.W. 1069 (1924); State v. Chevencek, 127 N.J.L. 476, 23 A.2d 176 (1941).

30. State v. Ameker, 73 S.C. 330, 53 S.E. 484 (1906).

31. State v. Davis, 88 S.C. 229, 70 S.E. 811 (1911). The defendants were sentenced to five years for conspiracy although their civil liability was limited to the cost of gas and wear and tear on the car.

32. State v. Hardin, 144 Iowa 264, 120 N.W. 470 (1909) (peaceably removing a witness from the jurisdiction); State v.LaFera, 61 N.J.Super. 489, 161 A.2d 303, reversed in part 35 N.J. 75, 171 A.2d 311 (1960) (state contract bidding violation); State v. DeWitt, 2 Hill (S.C.) 282 (1834) (destroying a will).

33. Commonwealth v. Bessette, 351 Mass. 148, 217 N.E.2d 893 (1966) (no harm shown by violation of law forbidding assignment of state contracts); Commonwealth v. Bessette, 351 Mass. 157, 217 N.E.2d 899 (1966) (no harm in approving extra payment on state contract unless work not done or unnecessary). But see Commonwealth v. Kelley, 358 Mass. 43, 260 N.E.2d 691 (1970) (use of authority as Turnpike Authority Chairman to make illegal payments).

34. Heard v. Rizzo, 281 F.Supp. 720 (E.D.Pa.), affirmed 392 U.S. 646, 88 S.Ct. 2307, 20 L.Ed.2d 1358 (1968); State v. Dibella, 157 Conn. 330, 254 A.2d 477 (1968) (conspiracy to bribe). But see State v. Rexroad, 147 W.Va. 819, 131 S.E.2d 709 (1963) (not criminal conspiracy to combine to allow man to die from beating).

35. State v. Guthrie, 265 N.C. 659, 144 S.E.2d 891 (1965) (interfering with public school); State v. Goldberg, 261 N.C. 181, 134 S.E.2d 334 (1964) (bribing an athlete). But see Macias v. People, 161 Colo. 233, 421 P.2d 116 (1966) (no conspiracy to combine to burglarize a phone booth, since a phone booth could not be burglarized). This decision depends on the provision that only crimes can be the subject of a criminal conspiracy, a result Colorado reached by judicial interpretation of its broadly drawn conspiracy statute. Lipschitz v. People, 25 Colo. 261, 53 P. 1111 (1898). Cf. Commonwealth v. Engleman, 336 Mass. 66, 142 N.E.2d 406 (1957) (trade secrets not the subject of larceny).

36. E.g., People v. Tierney, 253 Cal.App.2d 1, 61 Cal. Rptr. 164 (1967) (misrepresenting innocent pictures as obscene).

37. Krulewitch v. United States, 336 U.S. 440, 69 S.Ct. 716, 93 L.Ed. 790 (1949) (Jackson, J., concurring).

38. Professor Sayre thought the rule concerning unlawful rather than criminal conduct was devised for "cases where the actual deeds were of doubtful criminali-

lic health or morals or to trade or commerce or for the perversion or obstruction of justice or the due administration of the laws are particularly objectionable. The Supreme Court has recognized this possible abuse and has held that such conspiracy statutes may be unconstitutionally vague because they do not give adequate notice of what conduct will be considered criminal.[39] Specifically, the Court held that a statute proscribing conspiracies to commit acts injurious to the public morals would be vague unless the state court construed it narrowly. On remand, the Utah Supreme Court held the provision vague and violative of due process.[40]

However, other state courts have upheld their rather broad conspiracy statutes in the face of similar due process objections. Statutes making combinations "to pervert or obstruct justice, or the due administration of the laws" have been upheld because such acts were defined at common law and in the statutes.[41] Similarly, a statute prohibiting conspiracies to injure trade or commerce has been held not to be vague,[42] and the same result has been reached as to legislation proscribing conspiracies to perform any act injurious to the public health[43] and conspiracies to commit acts injurious to public health, morals or to obstruct justice.[44]

Notwithstanding such decisions, it is undoubtedly a fair conclusion that "most such provisions failed to provide a sufficiently definite standard of conduct to have any place in a penal code."[45] It is far better to limit the general conspiracy statute to objectives which are themselves criminal, as has been done in the most recent recodifications. To the extent that broader conspiracy statutes and common law conspiracy made it possible to reach group activity directed toward acts which one person could do with impunity because of the "frustrating technicalities"[46] of certain areas of substantive criminal law, the solution is reform in those areas. And if it is true that there are some activities which should be criminal only if engaged in by groups, these should be specifically identified in special conspiracy provisions "no less precise than penal provisions generally."[47]

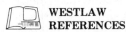 **WESTLAW REFERENCES**

conspiracy /s agreement /s object*** /s lawful unlawful criminal

(b) Impossibility. Is it a defense to a charge of conspiracy that it is impossible for the conspirators to achieve their objective? For example, in a jurisdiction where an essential element of the crime of abortion is that the woman be pregnant, are *A* and *B* guilty of a conspiracy to commit abortion if their plan was to commit an abortion on *C*, a police agent who falsely represented to *A* and *B* that she was pregnant?[48]

Before discussing that question, it is useful to review briefly how the issue of impossibility has been dealt with in the law of attempts, where it has arisen with much greater frequency.[49] As to attempts, the traditional approach has been to distinguish between factual and legal impossibility. Factual impossibility is not a defense, and thus, to take the classic case, one is guilty if he at-

---

ty, [to save] the judges from the often embarrassing necessity of having to spell out the crime." Sayre, supra note 5, at 406. See also People v. Beasley, 370 Mich. 242, 121 N.W.2d 457 (1963), for a criticism of the breadth and severity of conspiracy law.

39. Musser v. Utah, 333 U.S. 95, 68 S.Ct. 397, 92 L.Ed. 562 (1948).

40. State v. Musser, 118 Utah 537, 223 P.2d 193 (1950).

41. Calhoun v. Superior Court, 46 Cal.2d 18, 291 P.2d 474 (1955); Lorenson v. Superior Court, 35 Cal.2d 49, 216 P.2d 859 (1950); People v. Sullivan, 113 Cal.App.2d 510, 248 P.2d 520 (1952); State v. Nielsen, 19 Utah 2d 66, 426 P.2d 13 (1967). Cf. Davis v. Superior Court, 175 Cal.App. 2d 8, 345 P.2d 513 (1959) which questions but follows the California rule.

42. McKinnie v. State, 214 Tenn. 195, 379 S.W.2d 214 (1964), reversed on other grounds 380 U.S. 449, 85 S.Ct. 1101, 14 L.Ed.2d 151 (1965).

43. People v. Rehman, 253 Cal.App.2d 119, 61 Cal. Rptr. 65 (1967).

44. People ex rel. Hannon v. Ryan, 34 A.D.2d 393, 312 N.Y.S.2d 706 (1970).

45. Model Penal Code § 5.03, Comment at 396 (1985).

46. Developments, supra note 27, at 944.

47. Model Penal Code § 5.03, Comment at 396 (1985).

48. These were the facts in State v. Moretti, 52 N.J. 182, 244 A.2d 499 (1968), holding the defendants are guilty.

49. See § 6.3(a).

tempted to steal from an empty pocket.[50] On the other hand, what is called legal impossibility *is* a defense, so that one who received goods believed to have been stolen but which were not then stolen goods is not guilty of an attempt to receive stolen goods.[51] It is often not a simple matter to determine whether a given set of facts should be characterized as factual or legal impossibility, as is reflected in the many decided cases on the subject.[52]

Although the defense of impossibility in the law of attempts serves several functions,[53] one important consideration has been "the view that the criminal law need not take notice of conduct that is innocuous, the element of impossibility preventing any dangerous proximity to the completed crime."[54] Courts have tended to assume that the sole purpose of the law of attempts is to deal with conduct which creates a risk of immediate harmful consequences, and on that assumption have concluded that there is no need for the law to intervene if the actor's conduct presented no such risk because it was legally impossible for him to complete the crime. (Only recently has this assumption been challenged; the modern view, in contrast to the traditional view, is that the law of attempts also serves as a means for proceeding against those who have sufficiently manifested their dangerousness, so that legal impossibility is not a defense because it is not a useful guide in determining whether the actor "is disposed toward such activity, not alone on this occasion but on others."[55])

Courts have generally taken a broader view of the purposes of the law of conspiracy.

"The antisocial potentialities of a conspiracy, unlike those of an attempt, are not confined to the objects specifically contemplated at any given time. The existence of a grouping for criminal purposes provides a continuing focal point for further crimes either related or unrelated to those immediately envisaged. Moreover, the uneasiness produced by the consciousness that such groupings exist is in itself an important antisocial effect. Consequently, the state has an interest in stamping out conspiracy above and beyond its interest in preventing the commission of any specific substantive offense."[56]

It is not surprising, therefore, that courts have not been as receptive to the impossibility defense when the charge is conspiracy rather than attempt. As noted in one decision:

The case has been argued as though, for purposes of the defense of impossibility, a conspiracy charge is the same as a charge of attempting to commit a crime. It seems that such an equation could not be sustained, however, because * * * a conspiracy charge focuses primarily on the *intent* of the defendants, while in an attempt case the primary inquiry centers on the defendants' *conduct* tending toward the commission of the substantive crime. The crime of conspiracy is complete once the conspirators, having formed the intent to commit a crime, take any step in preparation[57]; mere preparation, however, is an inadequate basis for an attempt conviction regardless of the intent. * * * Thus, the impossibility that the defendants' conduct will result in the consummation of the contemplated crime is not as pertinent in a conspiracy case as it might be in an attempt prosecution.[58]

---

50. People v. Fiegelman, 33 Cal.App.2d 100, 91 P.2d 156 (1939); People v. Jones, 46 Mich. 441, 9 N.W. 486 (1881); People v. Moran, 123 N.Y. 254, 25 N.E. 412 (1890).

51. People v. Jaffe, 185 N.Y. 497, 78 N.E. 169 (1906).

52. For a useful survey of the cases, see United States v. Thomas, 13 U.S.C.M.A. 278, 32 C.M.R. 278 (1962).

53. "First, it has been used to verify criminal purpose; if the means selected were absurd, there is good ground for doubting that the actor really planned to commit a crime. * * * A second function that the defense of impossibility seems to have served in some cases is to supplement the defense of entrapment. In situations in which the technical entrapment rules do not exonerate the defendant, there is a temptation to find that the presence of traps and decoys makes the actor's endeavors

impossible." Model Penal Code § 5.01, Comment at 315 (1985).

54. Ibid.

55. Model Penal Code art. 5, Introduction at 294 (1985).

56. Developments in the Law—Criminal Conspiracy, 72 Harv.L.Rev. 920, 924–25 (1959).

57. The reference here is to the over-act requirement added in some jurisdictions by statute, see § 6.5(c).

58. State v. Moretti, 52 N.J. 182, 244 A.2d 499 (1968). See also Comment, 15 Wash. & Lee L. Rev. 122, 125–26 (1958); and the dissent of Judge Ferguson in United States v. Thomas, 13 U.S.C.M.A. 278, 32 C.M.R. 278 (1962). Viewing the situation as one of legal impossibility, he

As a result, while the attempt cases are notable for their lengthy explorations of the distinction between factual and legal impossibility, the conspiracy cases have usually gone the simple route of holding that impossibility of any kind is not a defense.[59] It has been held, for example: that there may be a conspiracy to commit abortion even when, unknown to the conspirators, the woman was not pregnant[60]; that there may be a conspiracy to commit rape on a woman believed to be unconscious although she was in fact dead[61]; that there may be a conspiracy to defraud the United States notwithstanding the fact that the fraud was impossible of commission because the government was aware of the scheme[62] or because the forged bonds were not witnessed by the proper official[63]; that there may be a conspiracy to smuggle liquor in violation of the customs law even though, unknown to the conspirators, the liquor was of domestic origin[64]; and that there may be a

conspiracy to obstruct justice even if the scheme of having certain individuals called as jurors could not have been accomplished by the conspirators.[65]

A few decisions are to be found holding that impossibility is a defense upon a charge of conspiracy. In one instance the result is attributable in part to the erroneous premise that the impossibility-in-attempt cases are controlling,[66] while in another the holding appears to have been influenced by the fact that the alleged conspirators were entrapped.[67]

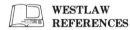

WESTLAW REFERENCES

conspiracy /s impossibility

(c) The Overt Act Requirement.[68] At common law a conspiracy was punishable even though no act was done beyond the mere making of the agreement.[69] This is still the rule in the absence of a statute providing

---

strongly disagreed with the majority's conclusion that the defendants were properly convicted of attempted rape because of their intercourse with a dead woman thought to be only unconscious, but then added: "Despite my position with respect to the charge of attempted rape, I would affirm the conviction of conspiracy to commit rape. Unlike criminal attempts, legal impossibility is not recognized as a defense to a charge of conspiracy. * * * Although both crimes are, in a sense, inchoate offenses, their development has been somewhat different. At common law, conspiracy consisted only of the agreement to do an unlawful act or a lawful act in an unlawful manner. * * * Here, the accused agreed to have intercourse with an unconscious girl against her will and while she was unable to resist. * * * As what these two men thus subjectively agreed to be their objective constitutes in law the offense of rape, * * * guilt of conspiracy is made out."

59. See, e.g., United States v. Giordano, 693 F.2d 245 (2d Cir.1982); United States v. Pietri, 683 F.2d 877 (5th Cir.1982). For other cases, see Annot., 37 A.L.R.3d 325 (1971).

The modern recodifications seldom address this issue one way or the other. But the fact a code is silent on this issue, while expressly declaring impossibility is no defense to an attempt charge, is not to be taken to mean that impossibility *is* a defense to conspiracy. State v. Bird, 285 N.W.2d 481 (Minn.1979).

60. Ibid. Contra: People v. Tinskey, 394 Mich. 108, 228 N.W.2d 782 (1975).

61. United States v. Thomas, 13 U.S.C.M.A. 278, 32 C.M.R. 278 (1962).

62. United States v. Everett, 692 F.2d 596 (9th Cir. 1982).

63. Beddow v. United States, 70 F.2d 674 (8th Cir. 1934).

64. Craven v. United States, 22 F.2d 605 (1st Cir.1927).

65. Gallagher v. People, 211 Ill. 158, 71 N.E. 842 (1904).

66. Ventimiglia v. United States, 242 F.2d 620 (4th Cir. 1957), criticized in Comment, 15 Wash. & Lee L.Rev. 122 (1958). In *Ventimiglia*, the court held that it was a defense to a charge of conspiring to violate a section of the Taft-Hartley Act forbidding the payment of money by an employer to any representative of any of his employees, that the person to whom payment was made in fact was not such a representative. However, *Ventimiglia* may not really be an impossibility case but rather a no-mental-state case, in that the court also notes that the defendants did not actually believe that the recipient of the money was their employees' representative.

O'Kelley v. United States, 116 F.2d 966 (8th Cir.1941), may be distinguished on the same basis. The court in that case held that the defendants could not be convicted of a conspiracy to take goods from interstate commerce where the evidence showed that at the time the goods were taken they had already been delivered and thus were no longer in interstate commerce, but there is no indication that it was the defendants' intention to take the goods from interstate commerce.

67. Woo Wai v. United States, 223 F. 412 (9th Cir. 1915). On the relationship between the impossibility and entrapment defenses, see note 53 supra.

68. See Developments in the Law—Criminal Conspiracy, 72 Harv.L.Rev. 920, 945–48 (1959); Note, 75 Colum.L. Rev. 1122, 1153–58 (1975).

69. King v. Gill, 106 Eng.Rep. 341 (1818); Poulterers' Case, 77 Eng.Rep. 813 (1611). Thompson v. State, 106 Ala.

otherwise,[70] but most of the states now require that an overt act in furtherance of the plan be proven for all [71] or specified conspiratorial objectives. In a few states this overt act must be a "substantial step" toward commission of the crime.

The statutes uniformly require an overt act by only one of the conspirators,[72] and the act need not be criminal or unlawful in itself.[73] If the defendant charged with committing the only overt act is acquitted, then the other alleged members of the conspiracy must also be acquitted.[74]

The overt act provisions in the conspiracy statutes raise the issue whether the act is a part of the offense or merely an element of proof. A few statutes make this clear, but most are open to both constructions. The Supreme Court currently regards the overt act merely as evidence of the offense,[75] but this has not always been the rule.[76] The problem is rarely important except for purposes of the statute of limitations,[77] jurisdiction [78] or venue.[79]

"The function of the overt act in a conspiracy prosecution is simply to manifest 'that the conspiracy is at work,' * * * and is neither a project still resting solely in the minds of the conspirators nor a fully completed operation no longer in existence." [80] Thus the overt act may be the substantive offense which was the object of the conspiracy,[81] but may not be simply a part of the act of agreement.[82]

Courts have said that the overt act must be a step towards the execution of the conspiracy,[83] an act to effect the object of the conspiracy,[84] or a step in preparation for effecting the object.[85] However, these definitions have sometimes led to confusion of the overt act with the object of the conspiracy. Thus it has sometimes been required that the overt act be the commencement of the consummation,[86] criminal,[87] or an element of the offense which is the object of the conspiracy.[88] These decisions are incorrect,[89] for they are inconsistent

67, 17 So. 512 (1895); Garland v. State, 112 Md. 83, 75 A. 631 (1910).

70. State v. D'Ingianni, 217 La. 945, 47 So.2d 731 (1950); Martin v. State, 197 Miss. 96, 19 So.2d 488 (1944). A few of the modern recodifications follow the common law rule that no overt act need be proven.

71. This is the position taken in virtually all of the modern recodifications.

72. See Blumenthal v. United States, 332 U.S. 539, 68 S.Ct. 248, 92 L.Ed. 154 (1947). United States v. Rabinowich, 238 U.S. 78, 35 S.Ct. 682, 59 L.Ed. 1211 (1915).

73. Braverman v. United States, 317 U.S. 49, 63 S.Ct. 99, 87 L.Ed. 23 (1942).

74. DeWess v. State, 216 Tenn. 104, 390 S.W.2d 241 (1965). See § 6.5(g)(1).

75. Yates v. United States, 354 U.S. 298, 77 S.Ct. 1064, 1 L.Ed.2d 1356 (1957).

76. Hyde v. United States, 225 U.S. 347, 32 S.Ct. 793, 56 L.Ed. 1114 (1912). The majority and dissenting opinions in this case give a good exposition of the two positions. See also Note, 37 Harv.L.Rev. 1121 (1924).

77. One overt act must be proven within the period of limitations, Grunewald v. United States, 353 U.S. 391, 77 S.Ct. 963, 1 L.Ed.2d 931 (1957). Merely keeping the conspiracy secret after the object is accomplished is no overt act, ibid., but this exception is narrowly construed. United States v. Nowak, 448 F.2d 134 (7th Cir.1971) (false answers to FSLIC examinee after loan fraudulently obtained). See Developments in the Law—Criminal Conspiracy, 72 Harv.L.Rev. 920, 948 (1959); Note, 70 Yale L.J. 1311 (1961).

78. See Developments, supra note 77 at 947–48.

79. Venue lies in any district where an overt act is committed or where the agreement is made. Hyde v. United States, 225 U.S. 347, 32 S.Ct. 793, 56 L.Ed. 1114 (1912). See generally Abrams, Conspiracy and Multi-Venue in Federal Criminal Prosecutions: The Crime Committed Formula, 9 U.C.L.A.L.Rev. 751 (1962).

80. Yates v. United States, 354 U.S. 298, 77 S.Ct. 1064, 1 L.Ed.2d 1356 (1957).

81. United States v. Hayutin, 398 F.2d 944 (2d Cir. 1968); State v. Erwin, 101 Utah 365, 120 P.2d 285 (1941).

82. People ex rel. Conte v. Flood, 53 Misc.2d 109, 277 N.Y.S.2d 697 (1966).

83. State v. Sullivan, 68 Ariz. 81, 200 P.2d 346 (1948).

84. Williams v. State, 16 Okl.Crim. 217, 182 P. 718 (1919).

85. State v. Moretti, 52 N.J. 182, 244 A.2d 499 (1968). One court, probably incorrectly, has said the overt act must be done openly. Commonwealth v. Cohen, 203 Pa. Super. 34, 199 A.2d 139 (1964).

86. Hall v. United States, 109 F.2d 976 (10th Cir.1940).

87. State v. Heron, 94 Ariz. 81, 381 P.2d 764 (1963).

88. People v. Bauer, 32 A.D.2d 463, 305 N.Y.S.2d 42 (1969).

89. Thus, for example, a defendant may be convicted of a conspiracy to violate the wire fraud and mail fraud statutes where neither he nor his co-conspirator used the mails or other communications media, as the overt act need not be the objective and can be perfectly innocent in itself. United States v. Donahue, 539 F.2d 1131 (8th Cir.

with the function of the overt act requirement as stated above.[90]

If the agreement has been established but the object has not been attained,[91] virtually any act will satisfy the overt act requirement. Thus unexplained possession of a large quantity of dynamite,[92] an interview with a lawyer,[93] attending a lawful meeting,[94] picking a lock,[95] making a phone call,[96] delivering goods without the proper invoices,[97] distributing handbills in violation of an injunction,[98] and giving a co-conspirator money to deliver to another [99] have all been held to be overt acts in the context of the criminal object alleged. The overt act requirement may be satisfied by an omission,[100] and it may be the commission of some crime other than the object of the conspiracy.[101]

The overt act requirement may be said to be a legislative determination that mere agreement to commit the offense is insufficient to warrant criminal prosecution.[102] It has been suggested, however, that an overt act should not be required if the contemplated crime is serious, likely of completion, or likely to encourage future criminal activity.[103] The Model Penal Code excepts conspiracies to commit felonies of the first or second degree from the overt act requirement [104] on the ground that in such instances "the importance of preventive intervention is *pro tanto* greater than in dealing with less serious offenses." [105] However, this exception has not been generally adopted in the recent codes, including those which in other respects have tended to follow the Model Penal Code approach.[106]

WESTLAW REFERENCES

di(conspiracy /s "overt act" /s evidence proof)

(d) The Scope of the Conspiracy. [107] The agreement which is an essential element of every conspiracy [108] has two dimensions: the persons privy thereto, and the objectives encompassed therein. Even when it is clear that every defendant is a conspirator, it may be extremely important to determine precisely what the object dimension and party dimension of the agreement are, for that in turn will decide the critical question of whether more than one conspiracy exists.

This question may be an extremely important one for a variety of reasons.[109] Assume, for example, that *A* agrees with *B* that *A* will retail for *B* any narcotics delivered to him by *B*, and that some time later *B* makes contact with wholesaler *C* in another part of the

---

1976). See also State v. Johns, 213 Neb. 76, 328 N.W.2d 181 (1982).

90. See text at note 80 supra. One court has even stated that an overt act was required at common law. State v. Gladstone, 78 Wn.2d 306, 474 P.2d 274 (1970).

91. Rose v. St. Clair, 28 F.2d 189 (W.D.Va.1928).

92. Cline v. State, 204 Tenn. 251, 319 S.W.2d 227 (1958) (conspiracy to blow up school building).

93. Kaplan v. United States, 7 F.2d 594 (2d Cir.1925).

94. Bary v. United States, 248 F.2d 201 (10th Cir.1957) (conspiracy to overthrow the government).

95. People v. Siebelo, 61 Cal.App. 92, 214 P. 462 (1923).

96. United States v. Fellabaum, 408 F.2d 220 (7th Cir. 1969); Singer v. United States, 208 F.2d 477 (6th Cir.1953); Bartoli v. United States, 192 F.2d 130 (4th Cir.1951); Smith v. United States, 92 F.2d 460 (9th Cir.1937).

97. United States v. Harris, 409 F.2d 77 (4th Cir.1969).

98. People v. Makvirta, 224 App.Div. 419, 231 N.Y.S. 279 (1928).

99. People v. Wolff, 24 A.D.2d 828, 264 N.Y.S.2d 40 (1965). A payment to a co-conspirator is not an overt act, but merely seals the agreement. People v. Hines, 168 Misc. 453, 6 N.Y.S.2d 2 (1938).

100. Gerson v. United States, 25 F.2d 49 (10th Cir. 1928) (failure to list assets in bankruptcy).

101. Commonwealth v. Byrd, 490 Pa. 544, 417 A.2d 173 (1980); State v. Sinnott, 72 S.D. 100, 30 N.W.2d 455 (1947).

102. People v. George, 74 Cal.App. 440, 241 P. 97 (1925).

103. Developments, supra note 77, at 948.

104. Model Penal Code § 5.03(5).

105. Model Penal Code § 5.03, Comment at 453 (1985).

106. But a few excluded certain criminal objections.

107. See Note, 75 Colum.L.Rev. 1122, 1158–64 (1975).

108. See § 6.4(d).

109. It has been noted that the reason the question is asked in a particular case may influence how it is answered. For example, it has been suggested that the courts which have readily found one large conspiracy in response to a claim of a variance between charge and proof would not necessarily reach the same result on the same facts if the question were, for example, one conspirator's liability for the crimes of another conspirator. Model Penal Code § 5.03, Comment at 424 (1985).

country and enters into an arrangement to obtain narcotics from *C,* after which *C* takes some steps toward making the delivery but is apprehended by police who heard *C* make some statements about the plan. If it is concluded that *A, B,* and *C* are all parties to a single conspiracy, then: *A, B* and *C* may be tried in a single prosecution; *A* may be required to stand trial across the country at the place of *C's* acts; *C's* statements will be admissible against *A; C's* recent acts will foreclose any claim by *A* that the statute of limitations had run; if there is a statutory overt act requirement,[110] *C's* act will suffice as against *A*; and middleman *B* will be subject to prosecution and punishment for one conspiracy instead of two.

(1) The Object Dimension. One way in which the problem can arise is when the same group has planned or committed several crimes, simultaneous or successive violations of either the same statute or several different statutes. At one time, there was a split of authority in the federal courts on the approach to be taken in analyzing such a situation. Some courts applied the "same evidence" test, which meant that it was very easy to establish the existence of more than one conspiracy by showing that if the various objectives were accomplished their proof would be based upon different facts.[111] Others focused upon the agreement rather than the acts done or to be done in pursuance of it, holding that there was but one conspiracy if the several objectives were part of a single agreement.[112]

The issue was finally resolved in *Braverman v. United States.*[113] The defendants there were engaged in the illegal manufacture, transportation and distribution of liquor in violation of a number of internal revenue laws, for which they were charged and convicted on seven counts. Each count charged a conspiracy to violate a different internal revenue law, although the government conceded that only a single agreement had been proved. The Court reversed on this analysis:

> [T]he precise nature and extent of the conspiracy must be determined by reference to the agreement which embraces and defines its objects. Whether the object of a single agreement is to commit one or many crimes, it is in either case that agreement which constitutes the conspiracy which the statute punishes. The one agreement cannot be taken to be several agreements and hence several conspiracies because it envisages the violation of several statutes rather than one.

The Court emphasized that the same evidence test, an appropriate guide in other circumstances,[114] was not applicable to conspiracy: "Since the single continuing agreement, which is the conspiracy here, thus embraces its criminal objects, it differs from successive acts which violate a single penal statute and from a single act which violates two statutes." Other courts have reached the same result where the conspiracy was to violate the same statute on successive occasions[115] or to violate more than one statute by a single course of action.[116] But *Braverman* is not applicable to a single agreement to violate separate conspiracy statutes.[117]

110. See § 6.5(c).

111. E.g., Meyers v. United States, 94 F.2d 433 (6th Cir.1938) (conspiracies to possess an unregistered still and to make mash); Beddow v. United States, 70 F.2d 674 (8th Cir.1934) (conspiracies to forge and to utter endorsements on government bonds); Vlassis v. United States, 3 F.2d 905 (9th Cir.1925) (conspiracies to import, to deal in, and to sell unregistered cocaine).

112. E.g., United States v. Anderson, 101 F.2d 325 (7th Cir.1939) (conspiracy to obstruct interstate transportation of coal and to obstruct the mails); United States v. Mazzochi, 75 F.2d 497 (2d Cir.1935) (conspiracy to sell heroin to *A* and opium to *B* at same time and place); Miller v. United States, 4 F.2d 228 (7th Cir.1925) (conspiracy to steal and to transport alcohol).

113. 317 U.S. 49, 63 S.Ct. 99, 87 L.Ed. 23 (1942).

114. See Blockburger v. United States, 284 U.S. 299, 52 S.Ct. 180, 76 L.Ed. 306 (1932).

115. United States v. Samuel Dunkel & Co., 184 F.2d 894 (2d Cir.1950); State v. Moritz, 293 N.W.2d 235 (Iowa 1980).

116. United States v. Anderson, 101 F.2d 325 (7th Cir. 1939); Mason v. State, 302 Md. 434, 488 A.2d 955 (1985).

117. Albernaz v. United States, 450 U.S. 333, 101 S.Ct. 1137, 67 L.Ed.2d 275 (1981) (because *Braverman* distinguished the case where there is "a single act which violates two statutes," it is not applicable here, where defendants convicted of violation of 21 U.S.C.A. § 963, proscribing conspiracy to import marijuana, and violation of 21 U.S.C.A. § 846, proscribing conspiracy to distribute marijuana). See also American Tobacco Co. v. United States, 328 U.S. 781, 66 S.Ct. 1125, 90 L.Ed. 1575 (1946).

Although *Braverman* might be objected to on the ground that an agreement to commit several crimes should be treated as a number of anticipatory offenses in the same way as an attempt to commit several crimes, this objection is not convincing. There are at least two reasons for dealing with the conspiracy situation differently: (1) conspiracy, unlike attempt, is defined in terms of agreement; and (2) conspiracy, in contrast to attempt, reaches farther back into preparatory conduct.[118] However, *Braverman* has also been criticized on other grounds. It has been noted that "inquiry into the precise time at which each objective was conceived * * * is unrealistic" because of the difficulty in making that determination,[119] and that, in any event, the *Braverman* rule "tends to place a premium upon foresight in crime."[120] So the argument goes, if the second object was agreed to before attainment of the first, then no new grouping has been created and thus there does not exist an added danger justifying a finding of more than one conspiracy.[121] Thus, the Model Penal Code provides that there is but one conspiracy if the multiple crimes are the object of the same agreement *or* continuous conspiratorial relationship.[122] This view has been adopted by statute in some states, and it has been suggested that courts elsewhere are inclined to reach the same result by "finding that the original agreement subsequently came to 'embrace' additional objects."[123]

(2) The Party Dimension.[124] Somewhat more difficult is the situation in which there is a question as to the number of parties in a particular conspiracy because of the absence of evidence showing direct communication or cooperation between all of the defendants.[125] In dealing with this issue, it is useful to distinguish two different structures: (1) the so-called "wheel" or "circle" conspiracy, in which there is a single person or group (the "hub") dealing individually with two or more other persons or groups (the "spokes"); and (2) the "chain" conspiracy, usually involving the distribution of narcotics or other contraband, in which there is successive communication and cooperation in much the same way as with legitimate business operations between manufacturer and wholesaler, then wholesaler and retailer, and then retailer and consumer.

United States v. Bruno[126] involved both types of relationships, although the concern presently is solely with the chain relationship. Some 88 defendants were indicted for a conspiracy to import, sell and possess narcotics, and the proof established the existence of a vast and continuing operation which involved smugglers who brought the narcotics into New York, middlemen who paid the smugglers and distributed to retailers, a group of retailers operating in New York, and another group of retailers operating in Texas and Louisiana. The evidence did not show any cooperation or communication between the smugglers and either group of retailers, yet the court held there was a smuggler-middleman-retailer "chain" conspiracy because the parties' knowledge of the existence and importance of the remote links could be inferred from the nature of the enterprise: "the smugglers knew that the middlemen must sell to retailers, and the retailers knew that the middlemen must buy of importers of one sort or another. Thus the conspirators at one end of the chain knew that the unlawful business would not, and could not, stop with their buyers; and those at the other end knew that it had not begun with their sellers." Thus, the court concluded, the evidence was

---

118. Model Penal Code § 5.03, Comment at 437 (1985).

119. Model Penal Code § 5.03, Comment at 439 (1985).

120. Developments in the Law—Criminal Conspiracy, 72 Harv.L.Rev. 920, 930 (1959).

121. Ibid.

122. Model Penal Code § 5.03(3).

123. Model Penal Code § 5.03, Comment at 439 (1985).

124. See Note, 57 Colum.L.Rev. 387, 388–93 (1957).

125. Model Penal Code § 5.03(2) provides that if a person guilty of conspiracy "knows that a person with whom he conspires to commit a crime has conspired with another person or persons to commit the same crime, he is guilty of conspiring with such other person or persons, whether or not he knows their identity, to commit such crime." Several of the modern recodifications have such a provision.

126. 105 F.2d 921 (2d Cir.1939), reversed 308 U.S. 287, 60 S.Ct. 198, 84 L.Ed. 257.

sufficient to show that community of interest between all of the defendants which makes for but one conspiracy, as each member knew "that the success of that part with which he was immediately concerned, was dependent upon the success of the whole." [127]

The *Bruno* court distinguished the case of *United States v. Peoni,* [128] also involving a "chain." Peoni sold counterfeit money to Regno, Regno sold it to Dorsey, and Dorsey then passed it on to innocent persons. Peoni was held not to be a co-conspirator with Dorsey because the evidence did not establish "a concert of purpose" between the two; Peoni knew that Regno *might* turn the bills over to another person for ultimate disposal, but it really made no difference to him whether Regno passed the bills himself or sold them to a second passer. This conclusion appears justified, for it was not shown that Peoni planned further sales [129] or that the one sale was of such a large amount that Regno could not have disposed of the entire amount himself. *Peoni* is thus different from the usual one-conspiracy "chain" involving an ongoing scheme from which it may be concluded that the defendants had "knowledge of its essential features and broad scope." [130]

A "wheel" or "circle" arrangement, on the other hand, is by its nature less likely to support the conclusion that the parties had a community of interest. For example, reconsider the *Bruno* case, this time focusing upon the "wheel" part of the organization. Granting the existence of a single smuggler-middle-man-retailer "chain" conspiracy because of the clear interdependence of the parties, may it also be said that the New York group of retailers are in the *same* conspiracy as the Texas-Louisiana retailers, between whom there was no cooperation or communication? It would seem doubtful, at least in the absence of any evidence showing some form of interdependence between the two groups, but the *Bruno* court answered in the affirmative. Any retailer, said the court, "knew that he was a necessary link in a scheme of distribution, and the others, whom he knew to be convenient to its execution, were as much parts of a single undertaking or enterprise as two salesmen in the same shop." The notion seems to be that if the hub views his dealings with each spoke as a part of a single large enterprise, but each spoke is concerned only with his own transactions with the hub, the knowledge of the spoke that there are other spokes will nonetheless justify the conclusion that the spoke was aware of and consented to the plan as envisaged by the hub.[131]

Compare the Supreme Court's treatment of the issue in *Kotteakos v. United States,* [132] where Brown, the hub, made fraudulent applications for loans under the National Housing Act at different times on behalf of several

---

127. Thus, it is now clear that "the large scale heroin-cocaine traffic cases which involved the vertical chain of importation, purchase, adulteration, packaging, distribution and eventual street pushing [are] properly encompassed in an indictment charging a single conspiracy." United States v. Moten, 564 F.2d 620 (2d Cir.1977). See, e.g., United States v. Martino, 664 F.2d 860 (2d Cir.1981); United States v. Prieskorn, 658 F.2d 631 (8th Cir.1981).

128. 100 F.2d 401 (2d Cir.1938).

129. "Had the prosecution established that the 'chain' had been created for more than a single sale, the resulting inference that Peoni knew that further sales were being made would seem strong enough to sustain his conviction." Note, supra note 124, at 391.

130. Blumenthal v. United States, 332 U.S. 539, 68 S.Ct. 248, 92 L.Ed. 154 (1947). The defendants in *Blumenthal* were convicted of conspiring to sell whiskey at illegal prices. Two of them operated a company which received the whiskey from an unidentified owner and the other three sold the whiskey for the company to tavern owners. The defendants unsuccessfully claimed that there were two conspiracies, one between the owner and company

operators, another between the company operators and salesmen. "The scheme was in fact the same scheme; the salesmen knew or must have known that others unknown to them were sharing in so large a project; and it hardly can be sufficient to relieve them that they did not know, when they joined the scheme, who those people were or exactly the parts they were playing in carrying out the common design and object of all. By their separate agreements, if such they were, they became parties to the larger common plan, joined together by their knowledge of its essential features and broad scope, though not of its exact limits, and by their common single goal."

131. Note, supra note 124, at 388–89. The court later expressed some doubt about this aspect of *Bruno*: "[I]t is not so clear why the New York and Texas groups of retailers were not in a 'spoke' relation with the smugglers and the middleman, so that there would be two conspiracies unless the evidence permitted the inference that each group of retailers must have known the operation to be so large as to require the other as an outlet." United States v. Borelli, 336 F.2d 376 (2d Cir.1964).

132. 328 U.S. 750, 66 S.Ct. 1239, 90 L.Ed. 1557 (1946).

persons, many of whom had no connection with one another. The Court held this was not one conspiracy—that the similarity of purpose by the various spokes was not the same as a common purpose—and later elaborated upon the rationale of *Kotteakos* in these terms:

> Each loan was an end in itself, separate from all others, although all were alike in having similar illegal objects. Except for Brown, the common figure, no conspirator was interested in whether any loan except his own went through. And none aided in any way, by agreement or otherwise, in procuring another's loan. The conspiracies therefore were distinct and disconnected, not parts of a larger general scheme, both in the phase of agreement with Brown and also in the absence of any aid given to others as well as in specific object and result. There was no drawing of all together in a single, over-all, comprehensive plan.[133]

Even under this reasoning, however, some wheel arrangements, may properly be found to be a single conspiracy.[134] For example, where the feasibility of an illegal horse racing wire service depends upon there being several customers paying high rates, subscribers aware of this situation are properly considered co-conspirators.[135] So too, a state-wide attempt to unionize coal fields, centered in three separate areas but directed from a central headquarters, constitutes but one conspiracy because the effectiveness of the strike would depend upon the activities undertaken at all three locations.[136] As with the chain arrangement, a wheel is more likely to be characterized as a single conspiracy if continuing relationships are involved.[137]

Some courts have taken to examining the "totality of the circumstances" in determining whether a particular course of conduct constitutes one or several conspiracies.[138] The factors usually considered in this connection are: (1) the number of alleged overt acts in common; (2) the overlap in personnel; (3) the time period during which the alleged acts took place; (4) the similarity in the methods of operation; (5) the locations in which the alleged acts took place; (6) the extent to which purported conspiracies share a common objective; and (7) the degree of interdependence needed for the overall operation to succeed.[139]

(3) RICO Conspiracies. Under the Racketeer Influence and Corrupt Organizations Act of 1970 (RICO),[140] it is "unlawful for any person employed by or associated with any enterprise engaged in, or the activities of which affect, interstate or foreign commerce, to conduct or participate, directly or indirectly, in the conduct of such enterprise's affairs through a pattern of racketeering activity or collection of unlawful debt."[141] ("Racketeering activity" includes a great variety of serious criminal conduct, including murder, kidnapping, arson, robbery, bribery, extortion and drug dealing,[142] and for there to be a "pattern" there must be at least two such acts

---

133. Blumenthal v. United States, 332 U.S. 539, 68 S.Ct. 248, 92 L.Ed. 154 (1947).

134. What is necessary is that the prosecution "supply proof that the spokes are bound by a 'rim'; that is, the circumstances must lead to an inference that some form of overall agreement exists." United States v. Kenny, 645 F.2d 1323 (9th Cir.1981). See, e.g., United States v. McMurray, 680 F.2d 695 (10th Cir.1981); People v. Quintana, 189 Colo. 330, 540 P.2d 1097 (1975).

135. State v. McLaughlin, 132 Conn. 325, 44 A.2d 116 (1945).

136. United States v. Anderson, 101 F.2d 325 (7th Cir. 1939).

137. Cf. Anderson v. Superior Court, 78 Cal.App.2d 22, 177 P.2d 315 (1947).

138. See, e.g., United States v. Tercero, 580 F.2d 312 (8th Cir.1978). "In determining whether there is a common design the nature and effect of the scheme is not to be judged by dismembering it but rather by looking at it as a whole." United States v. Cole, 704 F.2d 554 (11th Cir. 1983) (holding one conspiracy where women associated with Outlaw Motorcycle Club in Florida were dispatched by particular male members with which they associated to Mississippi brothel to work as prostitutes and, though each woman wired money back to her associated male, some man-woman pairs changed membership and other pairs floated in and out of the ongoing operation).

139. Note, 65 Minn.L.Rev. 295, 310–11 (1981), citing cases applying each of these factors.

140. 18 U.S.C.A. § 1961 et seq.

141. 18 U.S.C.A. § 1962(c).

142. 18 U.S.C.A. § 1961(1).

within a 10 year span.[143]) This RICO statute has its own conspiracy provision.[144]

In *United States v. Elliott*,[145] it was held that a single conspiracy may exist under this conspiracy statute even when, applying pre-RICO concepts applicable to the general federal conspiracy statute,[146] the circumstances would indicate there were multiple conspiracies. The latter conclusion would otherwise be reached because a single agreement or common objective could not be inferred from the commission of highly diverse crimes by apparently unrelated individuals. But, as stated in *Elliott*,

> RICO helps to eliminate this problem by creating a substantive offense which ties together these diverse parties and crimes. Thus, the object of a RICO conspiracy is to violate a substantive RICO provision—here, to conduct or participate in the affairs of an enterprise through a pattern of racketeering activity—and not merely to commit each of the predicate crimes necessary to demonstrate a pattern of racketeering activity. The gravamen of the conspiracy charge in this case is not that each defendant agreed to commit arson, to steal goods from interstate commerce, to obstruct justice, and to sell narcotics; rather, it is that each agreed to participate, directly and indirectly, in the affairs of the enterprise by committing two or more predicate crimes.

That is, under the *Elliott* interpretation of the RICO statute it is irrelevant that each defendant participated in the enterprise's affairs through different, even unrelated crimes, if each crime was intended to further the enterprise's affairs.

143. 18 U.S.C.A. § 1961(5).

144. 18 U.S.C.A. § 1962(d).

145. 571 F.2d 880 (5th Cir.1978).

146. 18 U.S.C.A. § 371.

147. Bradley, Racketeers, Congress and the Courts: An Analysis of RICO, 65 Iowa L.Rev. 837, 376–79 (1980); Holderman, Reconciling RICO's Conspiracy and "Group" Enterprise Concepts with Traditional Conspiracy Doctrine, 52 U.Cin.L.Rev. 385 (1983); Note, 65 Va.L.Rev. 109 (1979).

148. Note, 65 Va.L.Rev. 109, 127 (1979).

149. E.g., United States v. Lee Stoler Enterprises, 652 F.2d 1313 (7th Cir.1981); United States v. Barton, 647 F.2d 224 (2d Cir.1981).

150. Holderman, supra note 152, at 385. See, e.g., United States v. Griffin, 660 F.2d 996 (4th Cir.1981);

The *Elliott* approach has been sharply criticized by legal commentators,[147] and understandably so. "RICO did not change conspiracy law; it merely made conducting the affairs of an enterprise in certain ways that Congress judges harmful a new substantive offense, separate from and in addition to the underlying illegal racketeering activity. The requirement remains that the activities making up a multiple criminal conspiracy must be connected, and the term 'enterprise' as applied by *Elliott* does not supply that connection."[148] Thus, while initially a few other courts accepted the *Elliott* approach,[149] the more recent "trend rejects the ideas espoused in *Elliott* and returns to traditional conspiracy principles in determining complicity in multidefendant RICO prosecutions."[150]

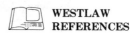 **WESTLAW REFERENCES**

conspiracy /p scope (elliott /s 571 +5 880) /p rico

(e) The Duration of the Conspiracy.[151] The temporal dimensions of a conspiracy is a matter of considerable importance for a number of reasons. The longer a conspiracy is deemed to continue, the greater the chances that additional persons will be found to have joined it.[152] Also, as the conspiracy continues there may occur new overt acts at different locations which will afford the prosecution new choices for the place of trial.[153] If the conspiracy has not yet ended, then the hearsay acts and declarations of one conspirator will be admissible against the other conspira-

United States v. Errico, 635 F.2d 152 (2d Cir.1980); United States v. Anderson, 626 F.2d 1358 (8th Cir.1980).

151. See Note, 75 Colum.L.Rev. 1122, 1164–67 (1975).

152. See, e.g., McDonald v. United States, 89 F.2d 128 (8th Cir.1937); Laska v. United States, 82 F.2d 672 (10th Cir.1936); Skelly v. United States, 76 F.2d 483 (10th Cir. 1935), where defendants were convicted of conspiracy to kidnap notwithstanding the fact that their association with the kidnappers began after the kidnap victim had been exchanged for ransom.

153. See Brown v. Elliott, 225 U.S. 392, 32 S.Ct. 812, 56 L.Ed. 1136 (1912), holding that each overt act gave the government another choice of venue under the Sixth Amendment.

tors,[154] and one conspirator may be held liable for substantive crimes committed by other members of the conspiracy.[155] Most important, however, is the fact that the statute of limitations for the crime of conspiracy does not begin to run at the time of the agreement or (when required by statute [156]) the overt act, but only from the point at which the conspiracy is terminated.[157] For this purpose, "the conspiracy continues up to the abandonment or success." [158]

As to abandonment by all the parties,[159] the generally accepted view is that abandonment is presumed if no party to the conspiracy has done any overt act to further its objective during the applicable period of limitations.[160] For example, where the applicable statute of limitations specified three years, and the indictment was returned on October 25, 1954, it must be shown that "at least one overt act in furtherance of the conspiracy was performed after" October 25, 1951.[161]

As to the success of the conspiracy, it is important to keep in mind that "success" has not necessarily been accomplished at the point in time when the crime which was the objective of the conspiracy has been completed, in the sense that enough has been done to support a conviction for that crime. For example, a conspiracy to commit a theft, a burglary, or a robbery is not ended upon the completion of those crimes if the fruits thereof are still to be divided among the conspirators.[162] "Kidnappers in hiding, waiting for ransom, commit acts of concealment in furtherance of the objectives of the conspiracy itself, just as repainting a stolen car would be in furtherance of a conspiracy to steal; in both cases the successful accomplishment of the crime necessitates concealment." [163] But it is at precisely this point that the problem becomes complicated [164]; as reflected in a series of Supreme Court decisions, it is not easy to determine what acts of concealment will

---

154. E.g., Fiswick v. United States, 329 U.S. 211, 67 S.Ct. 224, 91 L.Ed. 196 (1946).

155. However, under the better view membership in the conspiracy is not per se sufficient to make one a party to a crime committed by one of the other conspirators. See § 6.8(a).

156. See § 6.5(c).

157. The earlier cases took the view that the statute of limitations ran from the *first* overt act, e.g., United States v. Owen, 32 F. 534 (D.Or.1887), or that each successive overt act gave rise to a separate conspiracy on which the statute ran independently, e.g., Jones v. United States, 162 F. 417 (9th Cir.1908). Apparently if the statute required no overt act, then the time commenced running from the date of the agreement. Model Penal Code § 5.03, Comment at 461 (1985).

The Supreme Court ruled otherwise in United States v. Kissel, 218 U.S. 601, 31 S.Ct. 124, 54 L.Ed. 1168 (1910): "It is true that the unlawful agreement satisfies the definition of the crime, but it does not exhaust it. It also is true, of course, that the mere continuance of the result of a crime does not continue the crime. * * * But when the plot contemplates bringing to pass a continuous result that will not continue without the continuous cooperation of the conspirators to keep it up, and there is such continuous cooperation, it is a perversion of natural thought and of natural language to call such continuous cooperation a cinematographic series of distinct conspiracies, rather than to call it a single one."

158. United States v. Kissel, 218 U.S. 601, 31 S.Ct. 124, 54 L.Ed. 1168 (1910). Model Penal Code § 5.03(7) so provides, and such a provision is to be found in several of the modern recodifications.

159. As to abandonment of the conspiracy by one party, see § 6.5(f).

160. Lonabaugh v. United States, 179 F. 476 (10th Cir. 1910); Cooke v. People, 231 Ill. 9, 82 N.E. 863 (1907); People v. Hines, 284 N.Y. 93, 29 N.E.2d 483 (1940). This is expressly stated in some of the modern recodifications.

It has been suggested that this rule might be limited to situations where the crime of conspiracy is defined to require an overt act, Developments in the Law—Criminal Conspiracy, 72 Harv.L.Rev. 920, 960–62 (1959), but Model Penal Code § 5.03(7) makes this the applicable test whether or not allegation and proof of an overt act is required.

161. Grunewald v. United States, 353 U.S. 391, 77 S.Ct. 963, 1 L.Ed.2d 931 (1957).

162. E.g., United States v. Girard, 744 F.2d 1170 (5th Cir.1984); United States v. Mennuti, 679 F.2d 1032 (2d Cir.1982); United States v. Walker, 653 F.2d 1343 (9th Cir. 1981); People v. Lewis, 222 Cal.App.2d 136, 35 Cal.Rptr. 1 (1963); Shetsky v. State, 290 P.2d 158 (Okl.Crim.App. 1955). Consider also United States v. Helmich, 704 F.2d 547 (11th Cir.1983) (for purposes of statute of limitations, a 1981 indictment for conspiracy to commit espionage not barred by fact that transmittal of defense information occurred in 1964, as defendant traveled to Russia to collect his payment in 1980).

163. Grunewald v. United States, 353 U.S. 391, 77 S.Ct. 963, 1 L.Ed.2d 931 (1957).

164. For a very useful analysis of this problem, see Note, 70 Yale L.J. 1311 (1961).

suffice to establish a continuation of the conspiracy.

In *Krulewitch v. United States*,[165] Krulewitch and another were convicted of conspiracy to transport a woman in interstate commerce for purposes of prostitution. A month and a half after the trip in question, Krulewitch's female co-conspirator made a statement attempting to conceal his role in the crime, and this conversation was admitted at trial on the ground that it fell within an exception to the hearsay rule because it was made in furtherance of the conspiracy. Before the Supreme Court, the petitioners contended that the conspiracy was at an end when the transportation was completed, while the government, relying upon lower court cases,[166] asserted that the declarations were admissible as being in furtherance of an "implied but uncharged conspiracy aimed at preventing detection and punishment." Justice Jackson, in his oft-quoted concurring opinion, noted that acceptance of the government's position would "result in an indeterminate extension of the statute of limitations," for if "the law implies an agreement to cooperate in defeating prosecution, it must imply that it continues as long as prosecution is a possibility, and prosecution is a possibility as long as the conspiracy to defeat it is implied to continue." The majority, however, rejected the government's contention by merely noting that hearsay statements, to be admissible against the other conspirators, "must be made in furtherance of the conspiracy charged."

Apparently with *Krulewitch* in mind, the government proceeded more cautiously in *Lutwak v. United States*,[167] a prosecution for conspiring to violate those statutes making it a crime for an alien to obtain entry by misrepresentation or concealment of a material fact.[168] Again the question was the admissibility against other conspirators of acts and statements occurring after the date of the substantive offenses, but this time the government had expressly charged in the indictment that integral to the conspiracy were concealment and other acts [169] extending beyond that date. Notwithstanding "the government's seemingly well-founded contention that the [subsequent acts] were not a mere retrospective concealment of a consummated scheme to obtain entry, but an integral part of the plan Lutwak originally devised," [170] the Court ruled in favor of the defendants. The holding was rested upon the questionable [171] conclusion that there was "no statement in the indictment of a single overt act of concealment that was committed after [the date of entry], and no substantial evidence of any," and thus the ultimate question of whether acts of concealment could ever extend the life of a conspiracy remained unanswered.

Then came *Grunewald v. United States*,[172] a case involving convictions for conspiracy to defraud the government by fixing income tax cases. The defendants had used improper influence to obtain "no prosecution" rulings for certain taxpayers in 1948 and 1949, dates outside the three-year statute of limitations, but had engaged in acts of concealment [173] up

---

165. 336 U.S. 440, 69 S.Ct. 716, 93 L.Ed. 790 (1949).

166. Most in point was Lew Moy v. United States, 237 F. 50 (10th Cir.1916), a prosecution for conspiracy to violate the immigration laws by bringing into the country certain aliens not entitled to entry, where the court held: "Successfully to consummate the unlawful introduction of the prohibited aliens required more than the mere bringing of them across the line. It was necessary to evade the immigration officials by transporting them into the interior and concealing their identity."

167. 344 U.S. 604, 73 S.Ct. 481, 97 L.Ed. 593 (1953).

168. The prosecution was related to the War Brides Act, which provided that alien spouses of honorably discharged veterans could come into the country, notwithstanding any immigration quotas to the contrary. The scheme involved the sending of three honorably discharged veterans to France to marry Lutwak's relatives

and bring them into the United States, after which the couples would sever their marital ties.

169. The subsequent separation and divorce allegedly contemplated by the original agreement, see note 168 supra.

170. Note, supra note 164, at 1322.

171. It has been noted that reliance upon the indictment was not justified in that only one overt act need be pleaded and that the government may nonetheless then prove other acts, which was done in this case. Id. at 1323 n. 62.

172. 353 U.S. 391, 77 S.Ct. 963, 1 L.Ed.2d 931 (1957).

173. One of the conspirators had a carpenter build a hiding place for secret papers, another misled revenue agents as to the nature of expenses listed on their books, numerous instructions were passed among those involved

to 1954, the time of indictment. In response to the defense claim that the prosecution was barred by the statute of limitations, the government contended that an actual rather than an implied agreement to conceal existed and had been an express part of the original conspiracy. This attempt to distinguish *Krulewitch* and *Lutwak* was unsuccessful, for the Court found on the record before it that "the distinction between 'actual' and 'implied' conspiracies to conceal, as urged upon us by the Government, is no more than a verbal tour de force":

> The crucial teaching of *Krulewitch* and *Lutwak* is that after the central criminal purposes of a conspiracy have been attained, a subsidiary conspiracy to conceal may not be implied from circumstantial evidence showing merely that the conspiracy was kept a secret and that the conspirators took care to cover up their crime in order to escape detection and punishment. As was there stated, allowing such a conspiracy to conceal to be inferred or implied from mere overt acts of concealment would result in a great widening of the scope of conspiracy prosecutions, since it would extend the life of a conspiracy indefinitely. Acts of covering up, even though done in the context of a mutually understood need for secrecy, cannot themselves constitute proof that concealment of the crime after its commission was part of the initial agreement among the conspirators. For every conspiracy is by its very nature secret; a case can hardly be supposed where men concert together for crime and advertise their purpose to the world. And again, every conspiracy will inevita-

bly be followed by actions taken to cover the conspirators' traces.[174]

The Court in *Grunewald,* therefore, appears to have accepted the notion that a subsidiary agreement to conceal may be a basis for finding that a conspiracy continues beyond commission of the substantive offenses which are its object. However, the Court made it clear that the prosecution bears a heavy burden in proving such a subsidiary agreement, much more than has been "demanded to infer conspiratorial agreements for non-concealment objectives."[175] Mere proof of the "elements which will be present in virtually every conspiracy case, that is, secrecy plus overt acts of concealment," will not suffice. Rather, what appears to be required is that which the Court found lacking in *Grunewald:* "direct evidence [of] an express original agreement among the conspirators to continue to act in concert in order to cover up, for their own self-protection, traces of the crime after its commission."[176] This test, it has been aptly noted, makes proof of a subsidiary conspiracy to conceal virtually impossible, for it will be the most unusual case in which the prosecution will be able to obtain direct evidence of an explicit agreement to conceal.[177]

However, there remains another avenue open to the prosecution: it may be shown that the conspiracy was to commit a crime of such a nature that acts of concealment were actually part of the commission of the substantive crime. This was the alternate argument urged by the government in *Grunewald.*[178]

not to tell the grand jury anything, and one conspirator warned a secretary to tell any inquirer that she did not remember. Note, supra note 169, at 1325–26.

174. Grunewald v. United States, 353 U.S. 391, 77 S.Ct. 963, 1 L.Ed.2d 931 (1957).

175. Note, supra note 164, at 1327. On proof of the agreement by circumstantial evidence, see § 6.4(d).

176. Some lower court cases appear to have departed from, e.g., United States v. Hickey, 360 F.2d 127 (7th Cir. 1966), or circumvented, e.g., United States v. Nowak, 448 F.2d 134 (7th Cir.1971), this direct evidence requirement. For criticism of that trend, see Note, 17 Ga.L.Rev. 539 (1983).

177. Developments, supra note 160, at 963. Of course, the situation may be somewhat different as to state conspiracy charges, as the state courts have not been as demanding. The Court in *Krulewitch* noted that the

government's contentions were supported by some state decisions. See Hooper v. State, 187 Ark. 88, 58 S.W.2d 434 (1933); Baldwin v. State, 46 Fla. 115, 35 So. 220 (1903); Carter v. State, 106 Ga. 372, 32 S.E. 345 (1899); State v. Emory, 116 Kan. 381, 226 P. 754 (1924); Commonwealth v. Smith, 151 Mass. 491, 24 N.E. 677 (1890); People v. Mol, 137 Mich. 692, 100 N.W. 913 (1904); Watson v. State, 166 Miss. 194, 146 So. 122 (1933); State v. Gauthier, 113 Or. 297, 231 P. 141 (1924). However, the more recent state cases have tended to follow the reasoning of *Krulewitch, Lutwak,* and *Grunewald;* see, e.g., State v. Yslas, 139 Ariz. 60, 676 P.2d 1118 (1984); *People v. Hardeman,* 244 Cal. App.2d 1, 53 Cal.Rptr. 168 (1966); Commonwealth v. Pass, 468 Pa. 36, 360 A.2d 167 (1976).

178. "That two different characterizations of the conspiratorial objective were possible in *Grunewald* is due to the fact that the prosecution was brought under the broad 'conspiracy to defraud the United States' provision, a

The conspiracy's objective, it was contended, was not merely to obtain the "no prosecution" rulings for the taxpayers in 1948 and 1949, but rather to assure them complete immunity from tax prosecution, an objective which could not be realized until 1952, when the six-year statute of limitations would run out as against the taxpayers. The Supreme Court accepted this theory, but remanded the case for a new trial because the jury had not been instructed that it could convict only upon this basis. To the same effect is *Forman v. United States*,[179] holding that the defendants could be tried on the theory that the conspiracy did not end with the filing of tax returns concealing certain income, but rather continued "until action thereon is barred and the evasion permanently effected."[180]

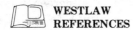

WESTLAW REFERENCES

conspiracy /s conceal! /p (grunewald /s 353 +5 391)

(f) Withdrawal.[181] Whether a particular individual has withdrawn from a conspiracy may be an important issue for several reasons. For one thing, a defendant may attempt to establish his withdrawal as a defense in a prosecution for substantive crimes subse-

quently committed by the other conspirators.[182] Or, the defendant, if charged only with conspiracy, may want to prove his withdrawal so as to show that as to him the statute of limitations has run.[183] Another possibility is that the defendant will rely upon his withdrawal as a means of limiting the admissibility against him of the subsequent acts and declarations of the other conspirators.[184] It may also be significant whether a person other than the defendant has withdrawn from the conspiracy. The defendant, on the one hand, may wish to show that an overt act or a substantive crime was committed by a former co-conspirator only after that conspirator had withdrawn,[185] or, on the other, may try to show that a fellow conspirator did not withdraw so as to gain the benefit of the rule in some jurisdictions that testimony of one co-conspirator against another must be corroborated.[186]

In all of the above contexts, virtually all courts have dealt with the issue in the same way, applying exactly the same test as to whether an effective withdrawal occurred.[187] What is required is an "affirmative act bringing home the fact of his withdrawal to his confederates,"[188] made in time for his com-

statute which permits great flexibility in describing the particular manner in which the 'fraud' upon the Government would be effected." Model Penal Code § 5.03, Comment at 467–68 (1985).

179. 361 U.S. 416, 80 S.Ct. 481, 4 L.Ed.2d 412 (1960).

180. If the agreement was "to block collection of the tax," as stated by the court of appeals, 261 F.2d 181 (9th Cir.1958), then the conspiracy could continue indefinitely, for there is no statute of limitations on a government action to collect taxes in the case of a false or fraudulent return. See Note, supra note 164, at 1330.

181. See Note, 75 Colum.L.Rev. 1122, 1168–79 (1975).

182. E.g., Loser v. Superior Court, 78 Cal.App.2d 30, 177 P.2d 320 (1947); State v. Peterson, 213 Minn. 56, 4 N.W.2d 826 (1942). On this defense, see § 6.8(d).

183. At one time it was necessary for the prosecution to show that the defendant had not withdrawn before the statutory period preceding the indictment, Ware v. United States, 154 F. 577 (8th Cir.1907), although the rule now is that the defendant must show that he had withdrawn from the conspiracy. Hyde v. United States, 225 U.S. 347, 32 S.Ct. 793, 56 L.Ed. 1114 (1912).

But see United States v. Read, 658 F.2d 1225 (7th Cir. 1981), construing *Hyde* to mean "that the burden of going forward with evidence of withdrawal and with evidence that he withdrew prior to the statute of limitations re-

mains on the defendant. However, once he advances sufficient evidence, the burden of persuasion is on the prosecution to disprove the defense of withdrawal beyond a reasonable doubt." *Read* is criticized in Comment, 4 Cardozo L.Rev. 151 (1982), but approved in Note, 51 Geo. Wash.L.Rev. 420 (1983).

184. E.g., United States v. Keenan, 267 F.2d 118 (7th Cir.1959).

185. E.g., Marino v. United States, 91 F.2d 691 (9th Cir.1937).

186. E.g., Rex v. Whitehouse, [1941] 1 D.L.R. 683 (1940).

187. Model Penal Code § 5.03, Comment at 472 (1985); Developments in the Law—Criminal Conspiracy, 72 Harv. L.Rev. 920, 959 (1959).

188. Loser v. Superior Court, 78 Cal.App.2d 30, 177 P.2d 320 (1947).

In United States v. United States Gypsum Co., 438 U.S. 422, 98 S.Ct. 2864, 57 L.Ed.2d 854 (1978), appeal after remand 600 F.2d 414 (3d Cir.1979), the Court disapproved an instruction stating defendant could withdraw only by notifying each conspirator he would no longer participate or by disclosing the scheme to law enforcement officials, stating: "Affirmative acts inconsistent with the object of the conspiracy and communicated in a manner reasonably calculated to reach co-conspirators have generally been

panions to effectively abandon the conspiracy [189] and in a way which would be sufficient to inform a reasonable man of the withdrawal.[190] The notice is insufficient unless it is given to all of the other conspirators.[191] One court has used a more stringent test, requiring that the defendant also successfully persuade his co-conspirators not to pursue the conspiracy any further,[192] arguably a proper result upon the unique facts there presented.[193] The Model Penal Code, on the other hand, provides that withdrawal by an individual occurs "only if and when he advises those with whom he conspired of his abandonment or he informs the law enforcement authorities of the existence of the conspiracy and of his participation therein."[194]

A quite different matter is the question of whether withdrawal is an affirmative defense to the crime of conspiracy.[195] The traditional rule here "is strict and inflexible: since the crime is complete with the agreement, no subsequent action can exonerate the conspirator of that crime."[196] In those jurisdictions which have added by statute an overt act requirement,[197] the defendant is not punishable as a member of the conspiracy only if he withdraws before the overt act has been committed,[198] but as a practical matter this is not significantly different from the common law rule.[199]

Some commentators have expressed disagreement with the rule that withdrawal is not an affirmative defense to conspiracy, although there is no agreement on what would be a better rule. It has been suggested, for example, that withdrawal should be permitted, except when the "agreement is dangerous enough at its formation to warrant punishment,"[200] until "a significant act has taken place betraying the positive disposition of the group to accomplish its object."[201] It has also been argued that both prevention of the ultimate crime and permanent renunciation are called for, to be accomplished by requiring "the withdrawer to seasonably notify and assist police officials in the arrest of the co-

regarded as sufficient to establish withdrawal or abandonment."

189. Rex v. Whitehouse, [1941] 1 D.L.R. 683 (1940).

190. State v. Allen, 47 Conn. 121 (1879).

191. Loser v. Superior Court, 78 Cal.App.2d 30, 177 P.2d 320 (1947). This position has been criticized on the ground that "the courts have gone beyond the rationale of notification. It appears sufficient that the defendant reasonably expected his withdrawal to be communicated to the rest of his associates by those whom he informed; to require him personally to contact all members seems too harsh." Developments, supra note 187, at 958.

192. Eldredge v. United States, 62 F.2d 449 (10th Cir. 1932).

193. The defendant, a member of a conspiracy to embezzle bank funds and conceal the theft by false bookkeeping methods, eventually advised his coconspirators he would no longer act to conceal the deficit. He then relied upon this "withdrawal" to show that the statute of limitations on the conspiracy charge had run as to him, notwithstanding the continued actions of concealment by the others. The court's holding appears to be based upon the notion that this defendant should not be able to escape on the statute of limitations argument in view of the fact that the embezzlement had occurred prior to his withdrawal and that he knew that his associates would continue to act to prevent discovery of that crime.

The *Eldredge* result has been criticized for the "injustice involved in making the defendant's liability contingent upon the acts of others." Developments, supra note 187, at 959.

194. Model Penal Code § 5.03(7)(c). Several of the modern recodifications contain such a provision.

195. This is similar to the questions of whether withdrawal is a defense to solicitation, see § 6.1(d), or attempt, see § 6.3(b), and must be distinguished from the defense to conspiracy that because of withdrawal the statute of limitations has run.

196. Model Penal Code § 5.03, Comment at 457 (1985). See, e.g., Orear v. United States, 261 F. 257 (5th Cir.1919); Dill v. State, 35 Tex.Crim.R. 240, 33 S.W. 126 (1895).

197. See § 6.5(c).

198. United States v. Britton, 108 U.S. 199, 2 S.Ct. 531, 27 L.Ed. 698 (1883); United States v. Jiminez, 622 F.2d 753 (5th Cir.1980). This result may have been reached not out of any policy considerations, but only as an incidental result of the terms used in conspiracy statutes to define the overt act requirement. Developments, supra note 187, at 957 n. 257.

199. "The common dictum in jurisdictions requiring an overt act that the first such act affords a *locus poenitentiae* does not seriously alter the common law rule * * * in view of the insignificant nature of the act that suffices, and research has unearthed no case in which this *locus poenitentiae* actually operated to exonerate a conspirator." Model Penal Code § 5.03, Comment at 457 (1985).

200. Developments, supra note 187, at 957.

201. Ibid.

conspirators before the ultimate crime is committed." [202]

The Model Penal Code recognizes withdrawal as an affirmative defense to a conspiracy charge, but requires that the defendant must have "thwarted the success of the conspiracy, under circumstances manifesting a complete and voluntary renunciation of his criminal purpose." [203] This provision is based upon two most sensible propositions: (1) the act of agreement is not of itself sufficiently undesirable and indicative of the defendant's dangerousness to warrant punishment in spite of subsequent withdrawal; and (2) it is proper to require a thwarting of the conspiracy because the objective of a conspiracy will generally be pursued in spite of renunciation by one conspirator.[204] Most of the modern recodifications take this position, though some instead provide that it is sufficient the defendant gave a timely warning to the authorities or otherwise made a substantial effort to prevent the crime. (In each event the renunciation must be complete and voluntary; some of the statutes elaborate that it must not have been motivated by a presumed increased difficulty in committing the crime or increased likelihood of detection or apprehension, or by a decision to postpone the crime to another time or transfer the effort to another victim or place or similar objective.) A few of these statutes permit renunciation only prior to the occurrence of an overt act.

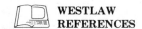 **WESTLAW REFERENCES**

(g) The Plurality Requirement. To constitute a conspiracy, there "must be a combination of two or more persons." [205] This plurality requirement has given rise to several issues, including the following: (1) whether one conspirator may lawfully be convicted if his sole alleged co-conspirator has been acquitted; (2) whether there may be a conspiracy consisting solely of a man and his wife; (3) whether there may be a conspiracy consisting solely of a corporation and a corporate agent; and (4) whether there may be a conspiracy when no more persons are involved than are necessary to commit the offense which is the objective of the conspiracy.

(1) Acquittal or Similar Disposition of Co-conspirator.[206] The requirement of two or more persons referred to above might be restated in terms of at least two guilty parties, for the traditional view is that acquittal of all persons with whom the defendant is alleged to have conspired precludes his conviction.[207] Thus, if *A* and *B* are jointly charged with a conspiracy not alleged to involve any other parties [208] and the jury returns a verdict of guilty as to *A* and not guilty as to *B, A's* conviction may not stand.[209] This, of course, might be explained on the ground that internal consistency should be required in the verdicts returned by a single jury.[210] However,

---

202. Rotenberg, Withdrawal as a Defense to Relational Crimes, 1962 Wis.L.Rev. 596, 605.

203. Model Penal Code § 5.03(6). Thus, the Code position is that a more stringent test should be applied with regard to withdrawal as a defense to conspiracy than for withdrawal to avoid liability as an accomplice to a substantive offense, for the latter only requires that the defendant terminate his complicity prior to commission of the offense *either* by wholly depriving it of its effectiveness *or* by giving timely warning to law enforcement authorities or other proper effort to prevent commission of the crime. Model Penal Code § 2.06(6)(c).

204. Model Penal Code § 5.03, Comment at 458 (1985).

205. Commonwealth v. Hunt, 45 Mass. (4 Metc.) 111 (1842).

206. See Annot., 19 A.L.R.4th 192 (1983).

207. United States v. Sheikh, 654 F.2d 1057 (5th Cir. 1981); United States v. Masiello, 235 F.2d 279 (2d Cir.

1956); Martinez v. People, 129 Colo. 94, 267 P.2d 654 (1954); State v. Raper, 204 N.C. 503, 168 S.E. 831 (1933).

208. If the indictment does allege others were involved, even "others unknown," then acquittal of *B* has no effect on *A's* conviction if the evidence at trial was sufficient to show that others were involved in the conspiracy. United States v. Sheikh, 654 F.2d 1057 (5th Cir.1981).

209. State v. Valladares, 99 Wn.2d 663, 664 P.2d 508 (1983). And thus, as held in Martinez v. People, 129 Colo. 94, 267 P.2d 654 (1954), where two persons are jointly charged with conspiracy and it is not alleged that others were also involved, it is permissible for the trial court to submit but one verdict form to the jury whereby both defendants must be jointly found guilty or not guilty.

210. On the comparable issue in the area of parties to crime, where the question is whether one defendant may be convicted as an accomplice when the alleged principal was acquitted, see § 6.6(d)(3).

the rule in conspiracy cases sometimes is extended beyond this, so that if *A* had been tried alone and convicted, after which *B* was separately tried and acquitted,[211] it would still be true that *A*'s conviction will be overturned.[212] This rule, it has been suggested, "rather than based solely on logic, reflects the community sense of a just outcome." [213] But it is not constitutionally compelled,[214] and a growing number of courts treat the rule as limited to inconsistent verdicts and thus inapplicable where the acquittal was in a separate trial.[215]

It has similarly been held that the grant of a new trial to one of only two conspirators requires similar action as to the other,[216] although this result has been questioned when the reversal is based upon error prejudicial to only one of them.[217] As to the entry of a *nolle prosequi* as to all except one of the defendants to a charge of conspiracy, some courts view the *nolle prosequi* as equivalent to an acquittal and thus consider it a bar to conviction of

the remaining conspirator.[218] The better view, however, based upon the fact that a *nolle* is merely a declaration by the prosecution that it will not presently pursue the charge further,[219] is that entry of a *nolle prosequi* as to all except one conspiracy defendant will not vitiate his conviction.[220] There is actually no inconsistency in result in such a case, and this is also true when the only other conspirator has been granted immunity in exchange for his testimony [221] or is otherwise immune from prosecution on some basis which is unrelated to his alleged involvement in the conspiracy.[222]

Although this might not seem to square completely with the above, it is clear that one conspirator may be convicted even if his sole co-conspirator has not been brought to justice.[223] Thus, if it is alleged that the conspiracy involved only *A* and *B*, *A* may be tried and convicted even though *B* is dead,[224] has not been apprehended,[225] or even if *B* is only a

211. As compared with when *B* simply obtains a dismissal of the charges, which does not affect *A*'s conviction. People v. Chapman, 36 Cal.3d 98, 201 Cal.Rptr. 628, 679 P.2d 62 (1984).

212. E.g., Sherman v. State, 113 Neb. 173, 202 N.W. 413 (1925).

213. Developments in the Law—Criminal Conspiracy, 72 Harv.L.Rev. 920, 974 (1959).

214. See, e.g., People v. Berkowitz, 50 N.Y.2d 333, 428 N.Y.S.2d 927, 406 N.E.2d 783 (1980) noting the Supreme Court's due process collateral estoppel rule of Ashe v. Swenson, 397 U.S. 436, 90 S.Ct. 1189, 25 L.Ed.2d 469 (1970), is not applicable where the defendant was not a party to the prior prosecution.

215. See, e.g., United States v. Roark, 753 F.2d 991 (11th Cir.1985); Smith v. State, 250 Ga. 264, 297 S.E.2d 273 (1982); Gardner v. State, 286 Md. 520, 408 A.2d 1317 (1979); Commonwealth v. Brown, 473 Pa. 458, 375 A.2d 331 (1977).

See also United States v. Espinosa-Cerpa, 630 F.2d 328 (5th Cir.1980), reaching the same result by reliance upon Standefer v. United States, 447 U.S. 10, 100 S.Ct. 1999, 64 L.Ed.2d 689 (1980), rejecting the applicability of nonmutual collateral estoppel to criminal cases and specifically holding that the prior acquittal of one party could not be invoked to bar the government's subsequent relitigation of the fact of that party's criminal conduct as an element in the prosecution of a second defendant.

216. Feder v. United States, 257 F. 694 (2d Cir.1919); People v. James, 189 Cal.App.2d 14, 10 Cal.Rptr. 809 (1961).

217. Developments, supra note 213 at 973. In such a case, it may be argued that the reversal as to the other defendant (assuming a remand for new trial) is just as if

the other defendant had not been tried, a circumstance (as discussed below) which does not bar conviction of the other conspirator.

218. E.g., State v. Jackson, 7 S.C. 283 (1876).

219. United States v. Rossi, 39 F.2d 432 (9th Cir.1930); Commonwealth v. McLaughlin, 293 Pa. 218, 142 A. 213 (1928).

220. United States v. Fox, 130 F.2d 56 (3d Cir.1942); Cline v. State, 204 Tenn. 251, 319 S.W.2d 227 (1958); State v. Lloyd, 152 Wis. 24, 139 N.W. 514 (1913). Some modern recodifications expressly state that it is no defense that the other conspirators have not been prosecuted or convicted.

221. People v. Gilbert, 26 Cal.App.2d 1, 78 P.2d 770 (1938); People v. Bryant, 409 Ill. 467, 100 N.E.2d 598 (1951); Hurwitz v. State, 200 Md. 578, 92 A.2d 575 (1952).

222. Farnsworth v. Zerbst, 98 F.2d 541 (5th Cir.1938) (diplomatic immunity). Some modern recodifications expressly state it is no defense that the co-conspirators are immune from prosecution.

223. Some modern recodifications expressly state it is no defense that the co-conspirators are not amenable to justice.

224. Joyce v. United States 153 F.2d 364 (8th Cir.1946); State v. Alridge, 206 N.C. 850, 175 S.E. 191 (1934); State v. Davenport, 227 N.C. 475, 42 S.E.2d 686 (1947).

225. Rosenthal v. United States, 45 F.2d 1000 (8th Cir. 1930); Commonwealth v. MacKenzie, 211 Mass. 578, 98 N.E. 598 (1912). Even if the alleged co-conspirator has been apprehended but his case has been severed and not yet tried, the defendant's conviction will still stand. United States v. Koritan, 283 F.2d 516 (3d Cir.1960); State v. Salimone, 19 N.J.Super. 600, 89 A.2d 56 (1952). Compare

"person unknown." [226]   In all such cases, of course, it remains a part of the prosecution's case at A's trial to establish A's agreement with another.[227]

It must be emphasized that an acquittal or similar disposition of a co-conspirator is a bar *only* if there then remains but one conspirator.   Where two or more defendants have been lawfully convicted, for example, it makes no difference that others also alleged to be a part of the conspiracy have not been convicted,[228] and this is so even when the person alleged to be the "head" of the conspiracy has not been convicted.[229]   However, in a jurisdiction which has adopted the overt act requirement, acquittal of the one defendant who allegedly engaged in the requisite overt act is a bar to conviction of the others.[230]

The general rule that conviction of only one defendant in a conspiracy prosecution will not be upheld when all the other alleged conspirators have been acquitted or similarily disposed of, even in separate trials, has not escaped criticism.   It has been said to be "founded upon a false premise, for a not guilty verdict is not necessarily a declaration of innocence by the jury, but simply an indication of lack of proof of guilt beyond reasonable doubt." [231]   And it has been noted that there are circumstances in which there clearly is no basis for finding an inconsistency in the verdicts, as where conspirator A is tried and acquitted for lack of evidence, after which

conspirator B is apprehended and convicted in part on the basis of A's testimony, or where A is convicted on the basis of the testimony of a certain witness who dies before the trial of B.[232]

The Model Penal Code departs from the traditional view of conspiracy as an entirely bilateral or multilateral relationship in favor of a unilateral approach.   That is, the Code definition of conspiracy requires agreement by the defendant but not agreement between two or more persons,[233] and one consequence of this is that an inconsistent disposition or verdict in a different trial [234] will not affect a defendant's liability.   "This result ＊ ＊ ＊ recognizes that inequalities in the administration of the law are, to some extent, inevitable, that they may reflect unavoidable differences in proof, and that, in any event, they are a lesser evil than granting immunity to one criminal because justice may have miscarried in dealing with another." [235]

A substantial minority of the modern recodifications expressly provide that it is no defense that the co-conspirators have been either acquitted or convicted of a different offense.   A greater number instead or in addition state that it is not a defense that the co-conspirator lacked capacity.   A few others specify it is not a defense that the co-conspirator lacked certain requisite characteristics, that he only feigned agreement, or that he

---

People v. Levy, 299 Ill.App. 453, 20 N.E.2d 171 (1939), holding that judgment should not be entered upon the verdict of guilty until the indicted co-conspirator had been tried and convicted.

226.   Prichard v. United States, 181 F.2d 326 (6th Cir. 1950); People v. Sagehorn, 140 Cal.App.2d 138, 294 P.2d 1062 (1956); State v. Caldwell, 249 N.C. 56, 105 S.E.2d 189 (1958).

227.   Worthington v. United States, 64 F.2d 936 (7th Cir.1933); Commonwealth v. Avrach, 110 Pa.Super. 438, 168 A. 531 (1933).

228.   Burton v. United States, 175 F.2d 960 (5th Cir. 1949); State v. Caldwell, 249 N.C. 56, 105 S.E.2d 189 (1958); State v. Edwards, 89 R.I. 378, 153 A.2d 153 (1959). This means that if only A and B are on trial, but the charge and proof was that C was also a participant in the conspiracy, then it is permissible for A to be found guilty and B not guilty. Rosencrans v. United States, 378 F.2d 561 (5th Cir.1967); State v. Papalos, 150 Me. 370, 113 A.2d 624 (1955).

229.   Belvin v. United States, 12 F.2d 548 (4th Cir. 1926).

230.   Herman v. United States, 289 F.2d 362 (5th Cir. 1961).

231.   United States v. Fox, 130 F.2d 56 (3d Cir.1942).

232.   Developments, supra note 213, at 974.

233.   Model Penal Code § 5.03(1). As noted earlier, most of the modern recodifications define conspiracy in the manner of the Model Penal Code, but this has not always resulted in these provisions being interpreted as adopting the unilateral approach. See § 6.4(d).

234.   However, "no position is taken with respect to the validity of an inconsistent verdict in a joint trial," on the ground that a jurisdiction should deal with this issue as a facet of the general problem of inconsistent verdicts. Model Penal Code § 5.03, Comment at 402 (1985).

235.   Ibid. See also Commonwealth v. Byrd, 490 Pa. 544, 417 A.2d 173 (1980), discussing the Model Penal Code position.

was unaware of the criminal intent or criminal nature of the conduct.

(2) Husband and Wife.[236] It was established at early common law that a husband and wife could not make up the two parties necessary to constitute a conspiracy,[237] and this rule was accepted in the United States as a part of the common law.[238] It was based primarily on the old notion that husband and wife became by marriage one person,[239] although occasionally a court would also suggest that the rule was merely an extension of the ancient doctrine that the wife was not liable for the substantive offenses committed jointly with her husband because she was presumably under his control.[240] In any event, the rule was always limited to instances in which husband and wife were the sole conspirators; a husband and wife could be convicted as co-conspirators if there were one or more other parties to the conspiracy.[241]

In recent years, virtually every jurisdiction which has had occasion to consider the issue has rejected the common law rule.[242] Taking into account the fact that husband and wife are no longer considered one in other fields of law and also that the old presumption of coercion no longer obtains,[243] it has been concluded that there remains no valid reason for the rule. A husband-wife combination results in the same mutual encouragement as other conspiratorial combinations, thereby increasing the likelihood that the unlawful object will be achieved, and also manifests at least

the same degree of continuing danger as do other groups.[244]

However, there is not complete agreement that the old common law rule should be abolished merely because the reasons originally given for it are no longer applicable. As recently as 1960 four Justices of the Supreme Court took the contrary view:

> It is not necessary to be wedded to fictions to approve the husband-wife conspiracy doctrine, for one of the dangers which that doctrine averts is the prosecution and conviction of persons for "conspiracies" which Congress never meant to be included within the statute. A wife, simply by virtue of the intimate life she shares with her husband, might easily perform acts that would technically be sufficient to involve her in a criminal conspiracy with him, but which might be far removed from the arms-length agreement typical of that crime. It is not a medieval mental quirk or an attitude "unnourished by sense" to believe that husbands and wives should not be subjected to such a risk, or that such a possibility should not be permitted to endanger the confidentiality of the marriage relationship.[245]

(3) Corporations.[246] Although it is clear that a corporation may be indicted as a conspirator,[247] problems may arise in determining the existence of the plurality necessary for a conspiracy. No problem exists when two corporations and an officer of each are indicted,[248] or when a corporation is indicted with one of its officers and a third party,[249] for in such situations it is clear (without regard to whether the corporation and its agent are

---

236. See Annot., 74 A.L.R.3d 838 (1976).

237. 1 W. Hawkins, Pleas of the Crown 351 (6th ed. 1787).

238. Dawson v. United States, 10 F.2d 106 (9th Cir. 1926); People v. Miller, 82 Cal. 107, 22 P. 934 (1889); State v. Clark, 9 Houst. 536, 33 A. 310 (1891).

239. 3 W. Holdsworth, A History of English Law 520–33 (3d ed. 1923).

240. E.g., State v. Clark, 9 Houst. 536, 33 A. 310 (1891).

241. People v. Gilbert, 26 Cal.App.2d 1, 78 P.2d 770 (1938); People v. Estep, 346 Ill.App. 132, 104 N.E.2d 562.

242. United States v. Dege, 364 U.S. 51, 80 S.Ct. 1589, 4 L.Ed.2d 1563 (1960); People v. Pierce, 61 Cal.2d 879, 40 Cal.Rptr. 845, 395 P.2d 893 (1964); People v. Martin, 4 Ill. 2d 105, 122 N.E.2d 245 (1954); Commonwealth v. Lawson, 454 Pa. 23, 309 A.2d 391 (1973). See Annot., 74 A.L.R.3d 838 (1976).

243. See § 5.3(f).

244. Developments, supra note 213, at 950, concluding that those arguments are more compelling than the contention "that the margin of increased danger to society when the wife proceeds from tacit support to active participation with her husband is sufficiently small not to permit merit special punishment as conspiracy."

245. United States v. Dege, 364 U.S. 51, 80 S.Ct. 1589, 4 L.Ed.2d 1563 (1960).

246. See Welling, Intercorporate Plurality in Criminal Conspiracy Law, 33 Hasting L.J. 1155 (1982); Comment, 72 Ky.L.J. 225 (1983).

247. E.g., United States v. General Motors Corp., 121 F.2d 376 (7th Cir.1941). See Annot., 52 A.L.R.3d 1274 (1973).

248. United States v. MacAndrews & Forbes, Co., 149 F. 823 (S.D.N.Y.1906).

249. People v. Dunbar Contracting Co., 165 App.Div. 59, 151 N.Y.S. 164 (1914).

one) that there are at least two distinct participants in the conspiracy. However, plurality has been found to be lacking when the corporate entity and a single agent are the only parties,[250] and also when two corporations and one person acting as the agent of both were the only alleged conspirators.[251] This is a logical result, for if only one human actor is involved then mutual encouragement is lacking and the risk of the object of the scheme being attained has not been enhanced.[252]

Some courts have gone one step farther by holding that the requisite plurality does not exist when two or more agents of the same corporation have conspired together.[253] The premise apparently is that such collective action for a corporate principal produces no greater antisocial effects than similar action taken by a single corporate agent.[254] Other cases have reached a contrary result,[255] and it may be significant that in these cases the agents were acting chiefly for their own benefit.[256] It has been cogently argued, however, that the necessry plurality is present whenever two or more agents of the same corporation are involved: "When a corporation acts through more than one person to accomplish an antisocial end, the increased likelihood of success, potentially more serious effects of the contemplated offense, and the danger of further unlawful conduct which are the essence of conspiracy rationales are present to the same extent as if the same persons combined their resources without incorporation." [257]

(4) The Wharton Rule and Related Problems. Crimes are often defined in such a way

that they may be directly committed only by a person who has a particular characteristic or occupies a particular position, as with adultery, which can be committed only by a married person.[258] This, however, has not prevented courts from concluding that others outside the legislative class may be guilty of these crimes on an accomplice theory,[259] or that other persons may likewise be guilty of a conspiracy to commit such crimes. Thus, for example, an unmarried man may be convicted of conspiring with a married man that the latter commit adultery [260]; a person not bankrupt may be convicted of conspiring with a bankrupt to conceal the latter's property from the trustee, an offense defined only in terms of a bankrupt's actions [261]; and the giver of a bribe may be convicted of conspiring with a public official to commit the crime of receiving a bribe, defined as receiving by a public officer.[262] This is as it should be. "The substantive offense seems more likely to be accomplished once the agreement is made, and in any event, a combination dangerous in itself, no matter who is liable for the substantive offense, introduces the normal general dangers of conspiracy.[263]

The above situation must be distinguished from that in which the person is a member of a legislatively protected class. Again the situation is comparable to that which obtains as to accomplice liability; one who may not be deemed an accomplice to a crime because a contrary holding would conflict with the legislative purpose [264] may likewise not be found to be a member of a conspiracy to commit that crime. The leading case is *Gebardi v. United*

---

250. Union Pac. Coal Co. v. United States, 173 F. 737 (8th Cir.1909).

251. United States v. Santa Rita Store Co., 16 N.M. 3, 113 P. 620 (1911).

252. Developments, supra note 213, at 952.

253. E.g., Nelson Radio & Supply Co. v. Motorola, 200 F.2d 911 (5th Cir.1952) (civil case).

254. Developments, supra note 213, at 953.

255. United States v. Hartley, 678 F.2d 961 (11th Cir. 1982); Novotny v. Great American Federal Savings and Loan Ass'n, 584 F.2d 1235 (3d Cir.1978), vacated on other grounds 442 U.S. 366, 99 S.Ct. 2345, 60 L.Ed.2d 957 (1979); Mininsohn v. United States, 101 F.2d 477 (3d Cir.1939); State v. Parker, 114 Conn. 354, 158 A. 797 (1932).

256. Developments, supra note 213, at 953.

257. Ibid.

258. State v. Martin, 199 Iowa 643, 200 N.W. 213 (1924).

259. See § 6.8(e).

260. State v. Martin, 199 Iowa 643, 200 N.W. 213 (1924).

261. Tapack v. United States, 220 F. 445 (3d Cir.1915).

262. State v. Myers, 36 Idaho 396, 211 P. 440 (1922).

263. Developments, supra note 213, at 954.

264. See § 6.8(e).

States,[265] where a man and a woman were convicted of a conspiracy to violate the Mann Act in that the man transported the woman from one state to another for immoral purposes. Both convictions were reversed:

> [W]e perceive in the failure of the Mann Act to condemn the woman's participation in those transportations which are effected with her mere consent, evidence of an affirmative legislative policy to leave her acquiescence unpunished. We think it a necessary implication of that policy that when the Mann Act and the conspiracy statute came to be construed together, as they necessarily would be, the same participation which the former contemplates as an inseparable incident of all cases in which the woman is a voluntary agent at all, but does not punish, was not automatically to be made punishable under the latter. It would contravene that policy to hold that the very passage of the Mann Act effected a withdrawal by the conspiracy statute of that immunity which the Mann Act itself confers.

This kind of legislative-intent reasoning must in turn be distinguished from what has come to be known as the Wharton rule.[266] As stated by the commentator whose name it bears, "when to the idea of an offense plurality of agents is logically necessary, conspiracy, which assumes the voluntary accession of a person to a crime of such a nature that it is aggravated by a plurality of agents, cannot be maintained."[267] The classic cases are duel-ing, bigamy, adultery, and incest,[268] to which may be added such other offenses as pandering,[269] gambling,[270] the buying and selling of contraband goods,[271] and the giving and receiving of bribes.[272] The rule does not apply when the offense could be committed by one of the conspirators alone,[273] nor even when cooperation was a practical but not logical necessity.[274]

Although there is some authority to the contrary,[275] the prevailing view is that the Wharton rule does not apply when the number of conspirators exceeds the essential participants in the contemplated crime.[276] Thus, while it is not a conspiracy for *A* and *B* to agree to the commission of adultery involving only themselves, if *C* conspires with *A* and *B* for the commission of adultery by the latter two then all three are guilty of conspiracy.[277] So too, there is no conspiracy if *D* agrees with *F* to give *F* a bribe, but it is otherwise if *D* and *E* agreed to bribe *F*.[278]

A somewhat different limitation on the Wharton rule is this: if the law defining the substantive offense does not specify any punishment for one of the necessary participants, then it is no bar to a conspiracy conviction that only the essential participants were involved. That is, the rule applies only if the statute defining the criminal objective "requires the culpable participation of two per-

---

265. 287 U.S. 112, 53 S.Ct. 35, 77 L.Ed. 206 (1932).

266. That it is distinguishable is illustrated by the *Gebardi* case just discussed. The Wharton rule applied only when a plurality of agents is logically necessary, and thus the Supreme Court found it to be inapplicable in *Gebardi* because "criminal transportation under the Mann Act may be effected without the woman's consent as in cases of intimidation or force."

267. 2 F. Wharton, Criminal Law § 1604 (12th ed. 1932).

268. Ibid.

269. Stewart v. Commonwealth, 225 Va. 473, 303 S.E.2d 877 (1983).

270. People v. Purcell, 304 Ill.App. 215, 26 N.E.2d 153 (1940).

271. United States v. Katz, 271 U.S. 354, 46 S.Ct. 513, 70 L.Ed. 986 (1926).

272. People v. Wettengel, 98 Colo. 193, 58 P.2d 279 (1935).

273. E.g., United States v. Davis, 578 F.2d 277 (10th Cir.1978) (introduction of contraband into penitentiary).

This means that the rule does not apply merely because a defendant is also charged with the object crime on an aiding and abetting theory, for that only shows there was in fact a concert of action. People v. Carter, 415 Mich. 558, 330 N.W.2d 314 (1982).

274. Lisansky v. United States, 31 F.2d 846 (4th Cir. 1929); State ex rel. Durner v. Huegin, 110 Wis. 189, 85 N.W. 1046 (1901).

275. E.g., United States v. Sager, 49 F.2d 725 (2d Cir. 1931) (three persons bribing one juror); People v. Wettengel, 98 Colo. 193, 58 P.2d 279 (1935) (two persons bribing district attorney).

276. Baker v. United States, 393 F.2d 604 (9th Cir. 1968); People v. Bloom, 195 Colo. 246, 577 P.2d 288 (1978); State v. Campbell, 217 Kan. 756, 539 P.2d 329 (1975); State v. Lennon, 3 N.J. 337, 70 A.2d 154 (1949).

277. State v. Clemenson, 123 Iowa 524, 99 N.W. 139 (1904).

278. United States v. Burke, 221 F. 1014 (D.N.Y.1915).

sons for its violation." [279] For example, if *A* agrees with *B* to give him an illegal rebate, but the applicable statute imposes a penalty only on the giver of the rebate, then *A* and *B* may be convicted of conspiracy.[280] Or, if *C* agrees to make an illegal sale of liquor to *D*, but the statute penalizes only the seller, *C* and *D* are guilty of conspiracy.[281]

By taking into account these two limitations, the apparent rationale of the Wharton rule may be seen more clearly. The notion seems to be that if all the necessary participants would be subject to punishment for the completed substantive crime and if only the necessary participants are parties to the agreement, then the agreement presents no danger beyond that inherent in the crime planned. Put somewhat differently, under the circumstances just stated it may be said that the legislature took into account the dangers of the combination in setting the penalties for the substantive offense, so that it would be inconsistent to permit a separate punishment for the same combination on a conspiracy theory.

As the Supreme Court emphasized in *Iannelli v. United States*,[282] "the broadly formulated Wharton's Rule does not rest on principles of double jeopardy," but instead "has current vitality only as a judicial presumption, to be applied in the absence of legislative intent to the contrary." The issue in *Iannelli* was whether the rule applied so as to bar

prosecution for conspiracy to violate a federal statute [283] making it a crime for five or more persons to conduct, finance, manage, supervise, direct, or own a gambling business prohibited by state law. In answering in the negative, the Court noted that the classic Wharton's Rule offenses listed above are those in which the consequences of the crime "rest on the parties themselves rather than society at large" and in which the agreement poses no distinct threat in the sense that it is likely to lead to "agreements to engage in a more general pattern of criminal conduct." By contrast, the criminal objective of the conspiracy charge in the instant case both involved "the participation of additional persons—the bettors—who are parties neither to the conspiracy nor to the substantive offense that resulted from it," and was "likely to generate additional agreements to engage in other criminal endeavors." Those distinctions and the legislative history of the statute [284] all supported the conclusion reached by the Court, namely, that Congress did not intend to foreclose prosecution for conspiracy to violate that statute. Employing similar reasoning, lower courts have held the Wharton rule inapplicable as to various other criminal objectives which threaten the interests of those other than the immediate participants in the conspiracy.[285]

To the extent that it avoids cumulative punishment for conspiracy and the completed

---

279. United States v. Previte, 648 F.2d 73 (1st Cir. 1981).

280. United States v. Grand Trunk R.R., 225 F. 283 (W.D.N.Y.1915). See also United States v. Previte, 648 F.2d 73 (1st Cir.1981) (conspiracy charge against bribe giver and receiver lawful as to object offenses of 18 U.S. C.A. § 201(f) & (g), covering, respectively, person who gives thing of value to public official for performing official acts and public official who asks to receive same, for "each of them allows conviction in this instance of only *one* of the two persons involved"). Compare People v. Davis, 408 Mich. 255, 290 N.W.2d 366 (1980) (Wharton rule *does* apply to conspiracy to bribe even if both parties not culpable under object crime where, as here, both parties culpable for giving and receiving bribe under separate statutes).

281. Vannata v. United States, 289 F. 424 (2d Cir. 1923).

282. 420 U.S. 770, 95 S.Ct. 1284, 43 L.Ed.2d 616 (1975), discussed in Comment, 71 Nw.U.L.Rev. 548 (1976).

283. 18 U.S.C.A. § 1955.

284. Especially, that the offense was carefully drafted "in a manner that fails specifically to invoke the concerns which underlie the law of conspiracy," and that the "five or more persons" limitation "was designed to restrict federal intervention to cases in which federal interests are substantially implicated."

285. E.g., United States v. Foster, 566 F.2d 1045 (6th Cir.1977) (Wharton rule not applicable to conspiracy to violate banking laws, as a bank failure can have wide economic repercussions); United States v. Bommarito, 524 F.2d 140 (2d Cir.1975) (Wharton rule not applicable to conspiracy to violate the Comprehensive Drug Abuse Prevention and Control Act, 21 U.S.C.A. § 801 et seq., as drug distribution schemes "involve grave dangers to persons who are not parties to the substantive offense").

offense,[286] the Wharton rule makes sense. However, when it is applied in circumstances where the object of the conspiratorial agreement has not been achieved,[287] the rule and its rationale are then properly subject to the criticism that they "completely overlook the functions of conspiracy as an inchoate crime. That an offense inevitably requires concert is no reason to immunize criminal preparation to commit it," [288] for even in such a case there should exist "a basis for preventive intervention by the agencies of law enforcement and for the corrective treatment of persons who reveal that they are disposed to criminality." [289] For this reason, the Wharton rule is rejected in the Model Penal Code, which instead provides only that a person who could not be convicted of the substantive offense as an accomplice may likewise not be convicted of conspiracy to commit that offense.[290] Consistent with the unilateral approach of the Code, such person's immunity does not bar a conspiracy conviction of the other party to the agreement.[291]

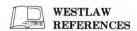

WESTLAW REFERENCES

"wharton rule"

(h) Punishment.[292] At common law, all conspiracies—except conspiracy to commit

treason—were misdemeanors.[293] Because of the significant procedural differences between the trial of felonies and the trial of misdemeanors, if a felony was committed in furtherance of the conspiracy the misdemeanor of conspiracy was said to merge into that felony. This, of course, meant that in such a case punishment could not be imposed for both the conspiracy and the felony, but it also meant that proof of the felony would bar conviction even for the conspiracy.[294] The problem did not exist if the completed offense was a misdemeanor [295] or conspiracy was by statute made a felony.[296]

Because the original justification for the merger doctrine no longer exists, it has now been abandoned.[297] It is thus clear that the conspiracy and the crime which was its object are separate and distinct offenses. This means that a conspiracy conviction may not be obtained on a charge of the completed crime,[298] and that acquittal of the crime which was the object of the conspiracy is no bar to conviction for the conspiracy to commit it.[299] Most significant, however, is the fact that with rejection of the merger doctrine it is now possible for a defendant to be convicted and punished for both the conspiracy and the substantive offense.[300]

---

286. See § 6.5(h).

287. Wharton indicated that the rule should apply only when the crime intended was not perpetrated, 2 F. Wharton, Criminal Law § 1604 (12th ed. 1932), a limitation which others have criticized, e.g., R. Perkins & R. Boyce, Criminal Law, 690 (3d ed. 1982), and which was not recognized in the cases from the very beginning, Shannon v. Commonwealth, 14 Pa. 226 (1850).

288. Model Penal Code § 5.04, Comment at 483 (1985).

289. Model Penal Code § 5.03, Comment at 388 (1985).

290. Model Penal Code § 5.04(2). This provision appears in a few of the modern recodifications. A few others, by contrast, have adopted the Wharton rule.

The other aspect of the Wharton rule is dealt with more directly by the Code provision that one may not be convicted of both the substantive crime and a conspiracy to commit it, § 1.07(1) (b).

291. Model Penal Code § 5.04(1). This has significance beyond those situations which would otherwise be governed by the Wharton rule. Thus, while in *Gebardi*, discussed in the text at note 265 supra, the Court ruled that neither party could be convicted of conspiracy, under the Code approach the conviction of the man for conspiracy would stand.

292. See Note, 75 Colum.L.Rev. 1122, 1183–88 (1975).

293. Commonwealth v. Donoghue, 250 Ky. 343, 63 S.W.2d 3 (1933); People v. Richards, 1 Mich. 216 (1849).

294. Commonwealth v. Kingsbury, 5 Mass. 106 (1809).

295. People v. Mather, 4 Wend. 229 (N.Y.1830).

296. State v. Mayberry, 48 Me. 218 (1859).

297. Pinkerton v. United States, 328 U.S. 640, 66 S.Ct. 1180, 90 L.Ed. 1489 (1946).

298. Braverman v. United States, 317 U.S. 49, 63 S.Ct. 99, 87 L.Ed. 23 (1942).

299. People v. Robinson, 43 Cal.2d 132, 271 P.2d 865 (1954).

300. Pinkerton v. United States, 328 U.S. 640, 66 S.Ct. 1180, 90 L.Ed. 1489 (1946); Elmore v. State, 269 Ind. 532, 382 N.E.2d 893 (1978); State v. Williams, 395 A.2d 1158 (Me.1978); People v. Carter, 415 Mich. 558, 330 N.W.2d 314 (1982); Commonwealth v. Shea, 323 Mass. 406, 82 N.E.2d 511 (1948); Bell v. Commonwealth, 220 Va. 87, 255 S.E.2d 498 (1979); Keith v. Leverette, 163 W.Va. 98, 254 S.E.2d 700 (1979).

The rationale behind permitting cumulative sentences was stated this way in *Callanan v. United States*:[301]

This settled principle derives from the reason of things in dealing with socially reprehensible conduct: collective criminal agreement—partnership in crime—presents a greater potential threat to the public than individual delicts. Concerted action both increases the likelihood that the criminal object will be successfully attained and decreased the probability that the individuals involved will depart from their path of criminality. Group association for criminal purposes often, if not normally, makes possible the attainment of ends more complex than those which one criminal could accomplish. Nor is the danger of a conspiratorial group limited to the particular end toward which it has embarked. Combination in crime makes more likely the commission of crimes unrelated to the original purpose for which the group was formed. In sum, the danger which a conspiracy generates is not confined to the substantive offense which is the immediate aim of the enterprise.

This reasoning was rejected by the draftsmen of the Model Penal Code: "When a conspiracy is declared criminal because its object is a crime, it is entirely meaningless to say that the preliminary combination is more dangerous than the forbidden consummation; the measure of its danger is the risk of such a culmination. On the other hand, the combination may and often does have criminal objectives that transcend any particular offenses that have been committed in pursuance of its goals. In the latter case, cumula-tive sentences for conspiracy and substantive offenses ought to be permissible."[302] The Code so provides,[303] but this view is taken only in a minority of the modern recodifications.[304]

Most jurisdictions have now enacted general conspiracy statutes with express penalty provisions, but these provisions vary considerably from state to state.[305] Some statutes provide that conspiracy is a misdemeanor regardless of its object, some that the permissible maximum sentence is the same regardless of the objective, and some provide different maxima depending upon whether the objective was a felony or misdemeanor.[306] If the statute does not set the maximum sentence in terms of an equivalent or fraction of the maximum permitted for the criminal objective, it may happen that the penalty for the conspiracy is greater than the permissible penalty for the crime which was its object.[307] The Model Penal Code authorizes penalties for conspiracy equivalent to those permitted for the most serious offense which was an object of the conspiracy.[308] The theory is that the rehabilitative needs of the defendant will be essentially the same whether or not the plan is consummated, and that no added general deterrence would be gained by permitting punishment beyond that authorized for the crime which was his object.[309] Many of the modern recodifications take that position, though about as many provide that the conspiracy crime is one class lower than the object crime.

---

301. 364 U.S. 587, 81 S.Ct. 321, 5 L.Ed.2d 312 (1961).

302. Model Penal Code § 5.03, Comment at 390 (1985). See also Developments in the Law—Criminal Conspiracy, 72 Harv.L.Rev. 920, 970 (1959), suggesting that when the specific danger of the conspiracy has been punished by imposition of the penalty for the substantive offense, then the "sentence for the conspiracy should be varied according to the propensity of the particular combination to produce further unlawful activity," taking into account "the number of persons involved in the conspiracy, the number and gravity of the offenses contemplated, the continuing or temporary nature of the organization, and the past criminal behavior of the conspirators."

303. Model Penal Code § 1.07(1)(b).

304. Some modern codes also expressly state that the defendant may not be convicted both of conspiracy and some other inchoate offense with the same objective.

305. See Model Penal Code § 5.05, Comment at 488 (1985).

306. Model Penal Code § 5.05, Comment at 488–89 (1985). Several of the modern recodifications take the latter approach.

307. E.g., Clune v. United States, 159 U.S. 590, 16 S.Ct. 125, 40 L.Ed. 269 (1895) (sentence of two years upheld over objection that crime which was object of conspiracy could be punished only by $100 fine).

308. Model Penal Code § 5.05(1), with the exception that a conspiracy to commit a capital offense or a felony of the first degree is a felony of the second degree.

309. Model Penal Code § 5.05, Comment at 490 (1985).

**WESTLAW
REFERENCES**

(callanan /s 364 +5 587) merge* /p conspiracy
/s crime offense /s separate distinct

---

§ 6.6   Parties to Crime

In the commission of each criminal offense there may be several persons or groups which play distinct roles before, during and after the offense. Collectively these persons or groups are termed the parties to the crime. The common law classification of parties to a felony consisted of four categories: (1) principal in the first degree; (2) principal in the second degree; (3) accessory before the fact; and (4) accessory after the fact.

This classification scheme gave rise to many procedural difficulties,[1] but if they were overcome a person in any one of the four categories could be convicted and subjected to the penalties authorized for commission of the felony. It was later recognized that the accessory after the fact, by virtue of his involvement only after the felony was completed, was not truly an accomplice in the felony. This category has thus remained distinct from the others, and today the accessory after the fact is not deemed a participant in the felony but rather one who has obstructed justice, subjecting him to different and lesser penalties. The distinctions between the other three categories, however, have now been largely abrogated, although some statutes resort to the common law terminology in defining the scope of complicity.[2] It thus remains important to understand what is collectively encompassed within these three categories.

The common law classification scheme described above existed only as to felonies. When treason was committed, those who

would be included within any of the four felony categories were all classified as principals.[3] As to misdemeanors, all parties were again held to be principals,[4] although conduct which would constitute one an accessory after the fact to a felony was not criminal when the post-crime aid was to a misdemeanant.[5]

In this section, the principal in the first degree, principal in the second degree, and accessory before the fact classifications will be described, with emphasis upon the distinctions between them. (Because the accessory after the fact is not truly a "party" to the crime, this category will be discussed later with related forms of post-crime aid.[6]) Note will be taken of the procedural technicalities which developed out of this classification scheme, and of the ways in which these difficulties have now been largely overcome by statute. A closer look at accomplice liability will be undertaken in a later section,[7] where more specific treatment is given to the questions of what acts or omissions with what mental state are required to establish complicity in an offense directly committed by another.

**WESTLAW
REFERENCES**

110k59 /p "common law"

(a) Principal in the First Degree. A principal in the first degree may simply be defined as the criminal actor. He is the one who, with the requisite mental state,[8] engages in the act[9] or omission[10] concurring[11] with the mental state which causes[12] the criminal result.[13] In each section of this book which deals with a substantive offense, the elements are defined in terms of what an actor, or first degree principal, must do to be guilty of that offense.

---

§ 6.6

1. See § 6.6(d).

2. E.g., Va.Code 1950, § 18.2–18.

3. 4 W. Blackstone, Commentaries on the Laws of England* 35 (1765).

4. State v. Nowell, 60 N.H. 199 (1880); State v. Hunter, 79 S.C. 73, 60 S.E. 240 (1908).

5. Sturgis v. State, 2 Okl.Crim. 362, 102 P. 57 (1909).

6. See § 6.9(a).

7. See § 6.7.

8. See §§ 3.4–3.7.

9. See § 3.2.

10. See § 3.3.

11. See § 3.11.

12. See § 3.12.

13. State v. Bailey, 63 W.Va. 668, 60 S.E. 785 (1908).

One who uses an intermediary to commit a crime is not ordinarily a principal in the first degree.[14] It is otherwise, however, when the crime is accomplished by the use of an innocent or irresponsible agent, as where the defendant causes a child [15] or mentally incompetent [16] or one without a criminal state of mind [17] (most likely because the defendant has misled or withheld facts from him) to engage in conduct. In such a case the intermediary is regarded as a mere instrument and the originating actor is the principal in the first degree. The principal is accountable for the acts or omissions of the innocent or irresponsible person, and the principal's liability is determined on the basis of that conduct [18] and the principal's own mental state.[19] Thus, if *A*, with intent to bring about *B*'s death, causes *C* (a child) to take *B*'s life, *A* is guilty of intent-to-kill murder. But because the crime of obtaining property by false pretenses requires an actual intent to defraud,[20]

A has not committed that crime by negligently causing *B* to make false statements to *C*.[21]

There can be more than one principal in the first degree.[22] This occurs when more than one actor participates in the actual commission of the offense. Thus, when one man beats a victim and another shoots him, both may be principals in first degree to murder.[23] And when two persons forge separate parts of the same instrument, they are both principals in the first degree to the forgery.[24] While there may be more than one principal in the first degree, there must always be at least one for a crime to have taken place.[25]

Although it has been said that a principal in the first degree must be present at the commission of the offense, this is not literally so. He may be "constructively" present when some instrument which he left or guided caused the criminal result.[26] Thus, when an actor leaves poison for another who later

---

14. Such actions would fit into the classification of accessory before the fact or principal in the second degree. Regina v. Manley, 1 Cox Crim.Cas. 104 (1844).

15. Maxey v. United States, 30 App.D.C. 63 (1907) (child given funds and directed to obtain abortion); Commonwealth v. Hill, 11 Mass. 136 (1841) (child used to pass counterfeit check); Regina v. Michael, 2 Moody 120 (1840) (poison administered by child).

16. Johnson v. State, 142 Ala. 70, 38 So. 182 (1904) (insane person incited to kill); People v. Monks, 133 Cal. App. 440, 24 P.2d 508 (1933) (incompetent induced to draw check against insufficient funds).

17. United States v. Bryan, 483 F.2d 88 (3d Cir.1973) (defendant a principal in the first degree if he engineered theft of a shipment of whiskey by using innocent dupe); Boushea v. United States, 173 F.2d 131 (8th Cir.1949) (innocent party induced to submit false claim); People v. Mutchler, 309 Ill. 207, 140 N.E. 820 (1923) (fraudulent check cashed by innocent agent).

The "innocent agent" theory has also been used where the agent is innocent because of the defendant's duress. State v. Thomas, 619 S.W.2d 513 (Tenn.1981).

18. Dusenbery v. Commonwealth, 220 Va. 770, 263 S.E.2d 392 (1980) (defendant not guilty of rape by "innocent agent" he forced to engage in intercourse with another, a penetration by agent did not occur).

19. Where the crime can be committed only by a certain type of individual (e.g., a certain type of employee), must the principal be that type of person, or does it suffice that the "innocent agent" is that type of person? Some courts have reached the latter conclusion, United States v. Tobin-Builes, 706 F.2d 1092 (11th Cir.1983); United States v. Ruffin, 613 F.2d 408 (2d Cir.1979), reasoning that such an approach is essential to reach those persons operating behind the scenes. See Annot., 52 A.L.R.Fed. 769 (1981).

The issue is a difficult one, and surely this result does not inevitably follow from the fact that when a theory of accomplice liability is used it suffices that the person aided was of the special character required by the statute. See § 6.8(e).

20. See § 8.7(f).

21. Such, it is noted in Model Penal Code § 2.06, Comment at 303 (1985), "probably has been the law; even more clearly, it should be the law." Model Penal Code § 2.06(2)(a) provides that a person is legally accountable for the conduct of another when, "acting with the kind of culpability that is sufficient for the commission of the offense, he causes an innocent or irresponsible person to engage in such conduct." A number of the modern recodifications contain such a provision.

This is an improvement over the statutory treatment of the subject (to be found in relatively few states), providing for the liability of a person who counsels, advises, or encourages a child or lunatic to commit a crime. "It is paradoxical to speak of counseling or encouraging irresponsible persons to commit a crime, since by hypothesis their conduct is not criminal, and this is even clearer in the case of innocent, responsible agents." Model Penal Code § 2.06, Comment at 301 (1985).

22. State v. Adams, 105 La. 737, 30 So. 101 (1901).

23. Roney v. State, 76 Ga. 731 (1886); and see Smith v. People, 1 Colo. 121 (1869).

24. Rex v. Bingley, 168 Eng.Rep. 890 (1821).

25. United States v. Rodgers, 419 F.2d 1315 (10th Cir. 1969). This is for the obvious reason that without one there can be no criminal act. 1 J. Bishop, Criminal Law § 649 (9th ed. 1923).

26. Id. at § 653.

drinks it, he is a first degree principal,[27] as is the person whose unwitting agent acts for him in his absence.[28]

digest(principal /3 "first degree" /p agent child incompetent)

(b) Principal in the Second Degree. To be a principal in the second degree, one must be present at the commission of a criminal offense and aid, counsel, command, or encourage the principal in the first degree in the commission of that offense.[29] This requirement of presence may be fulfilled by constructive presence. A person is constructively present when he is physically absent from the situs of the crime but aids and abets the principal in the first degree at the time of the offense from some distance.[30] This may happen when one stands watch for the primary actor,[31] signals to the principal from a distance that the victim is coming,[32] or stands ready (though out of sight) to render aid to the principal if needed.[33] However, one must be close enough to render aid if needed.[34]

The assistance rendered by the principal in the second degree has traditionally been referred to as "aiding and abetting."[35] The term "abet" is an appropriate one, for it contemplates aid combined with *mens rea*,[36] while the term "aid" standing alone is insufficient in that it does not suggest the necessity for a mental state in addition to conduct.[37] As is true in the criminal law generally, one can be guilty as a principal in the second degree only if the requisite acts (or omissions) and accompanying mental state are both present. These requirements will be discussed later.[38]

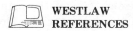

digest(principal /3 "second degree" /p "constructive** presen**")

(c) Accessory Before the Fact. An accessory before the fact is one who orders, counsels, encourages, or otherwise aids and abets another to comit a felony and who is not present at the commission of the offense.[39] The primary distinction between the accessory before the fact and the principal in the second degree is presence. If a person was actually or constructively present at the offense, due to his participation he is a principal in the second degree; if he was not present, he is an accessory before the fact.[40] Through prior counseling followed by appear-

27. Rex v. Harley, 172 Eng.Rep. 744 (1830).

28. See cases cited in notes 15–17 supra.

29. Commonwealth v. Lowrey, 158 Mass. 18, 32 N.E. 940 (1893).

30. Mulligan v. Commonwealth, 84 Ky. 229, 1 S.W. 417 (1886); McCarney v. People, 83 N.Y. 408 (1881).

31. Mitchell v. Commonwealth, 33 Va. 845 (1879).

32. State v. Hamilton, 13 Nev. 386 (1878).

33. 1 J. Bishop, supra note 25, at § 653. In Sutton v. Commonwealth, 228 Va. 654, 324 S.E.2d 665 (1985), a girl living with her aunt and uncle was coerced into having sexual intercourse with the uncle. The aunt played a part in this coercion over a period of time, but at the precise time the rape was occurring the aunt was in bed in another room. The majority concluded this was enough for constructive presence because "her malevolent, intimidating influence on her niece was present and continued unabated." A concurring opinion asserted this reasoning was in error but that the result was correct because of a statute declaring accessories before the fact are punishable as principals. A dissenting justice correctly noted that the majority's analysis extended beyond the common law constructive presence doctrine, as the aunt was not standing watch or otherwise available to give assistance at that time and was in all probability asleep when the rape occurred.

34. Rex v. Soares, 186 Eng.Rep. 664 (1802). But see United States v. Peichev, 500 F.2d 917 (9th Cir.1974) (though aiding and abetting statute interpreted as requiring status of common law principal in second degree, court utilizes broad view of "constructive presence," holding that it sufficed that by prearrangement defendant was in Canada en route to airstrip pursuant to plan to assist escape of those who were then hijacking a plane in San Francisco; it sufficient defendant "assumes a station with the knowledge of the perpetrators where he may be able to assist either in the commission of the crime or in the escape").

35. 4 W. Blackstone, supra note 3, at 34.

36. People v. Williams, 179 Cal.App.2d 487, 3 Cal.Rptr. 782 (1960).

37. People v. Dole, 122 Cal. 486, 55 P. 581 (1898); State v. Allen, 34 Mont. 403, 87 P. 177 (1906).

38. See § 6.7.

39. 1 J. Bishop, supra note 25, at §§ 660–63; 4 W. Blackstone, supra note 3, at 36.

40. 1 F. Wharton. Criminal Law 351–52 (12th ed. 1932). See, e.g., Moehring v. Commonwealth, 223 Va. 564, 290 S.E.2d 891 (1982) (defendant, who arranged for another to kill his wife, but who was not actually or constructively present at killing, is accessory before the fact).

ance at the scene of the crime to aid the primary actor, one may become both an accessory before the fact and also a principal in the second degree.[41]

The aid or counsel may be far removed in time from the commission of the offense,[42] although it must be shown to have retained some relationship to it by causing, encouraging, or assisting the offense.[43] If one contributes specific material aid, he will still be an accessory though it is not used in the offense.[44] The exact time of the commission of the offense is also immaterial. One may intend to aid a crime which is to occur on a certain date but which in fact occurs later, and he will still be an accessory before the fact to the crime.[45] The quantity of the aid is immaterial,[46] and it may come through some intermediary.[47] More will be said later [48] about precisely what conduct and mental state are required.

Although the accessory before the fact is often the originator of the offense, this need not be the case. Indeed, if one is enlisted by another to lend aid toward the commission of the offense and the aid is given, the person giving the assistance may thereby become an accessory before the fact.[49]

 **WESTLAW REFERENCES**

110k70 /p presen** participat***
110k73

(d) Problems of Procedure. The common law distinction between principals and accessories in felony cases gave rise to several procedural difficulties. There developed several technical and not altogether logical rules which tended to shield accessories from punishment notwithstanding overwhelming evidence of their criminal assistance. This is undoubtedly another instance of resort to procedural niceties in order to limit the application of the death penalty, which at early common law was the penalty for all parties to any felony.

(1) Criminal Jurisdiction. Under the common law territorial theory of jurisdiction, a state's criminal law reaches only those wrongs which are deemed to have their situs in that state.[50] Generally, it may be said that the situs of a crime is the place of the act (or omission) if the crime is defined only in these terms, and the place of the result if the definition of the crime includes such a result. The crime of murder, which is quite obviously defined in the terms of a result, thus has its situs where the fatal force impinges upon the body of the victim. For example, if *A* fires a shot at *B* and hits and kills *B*, and *A* was then standing in state *X* but *B* was standing over the border in state *Y*, state *Y* would have jurisdiction over this crime.[51]

What if, in the above example, *A* had as his accessory one *C*, who, at all times in state *X*, commanded or encouraged *A* to commit the crime or perhaps assisted *A* before the crime by supplying him with the gun or ammunition? As a matter of logic, one might well conclude that *C* is likewise subject to prosecution in state *Y*, for *C* is a party to a crime which had its result in that state. However, the common law rule was otherwise; an accessory could only be tried where the acts of accessoryship occurred, rather than where the ultimate crime took place.[52] Therefore *C* would be punishable only in state *X* and not in state *Y*, the jurisdiction which might well be most interested in his prosecution.

41. Regina v. Hilton, 8 Cox Crim.Cas. 87 (1858).

42. Workman v. State, 216 Ind. 68, 21 N.E.2d 712 (1939).

43. 4 W. Blackstone, supra note 3, at 37; 1 F. Wharton, supra note 40, at 354.

44. State v. Tazwell, 30 La.Ann. 884 (1878).

45. Commonwealth v. Balakin, 356 Mass. 547, 254 N.E.2d 422 (1969); McGhee v. Commonwealth, 221 Va. 422, 270 S.E.2d 729 (1980).

46. 1 F. Wharton, supra note 40, at 362.

47. People v. Wright, 26 Cal.App.2d 197, 79 P.2d 102 (1938).

48. See § 6.7.

49. Keithler v. State, 10 Miss. 192 (1848).

50. See § 2.9.

51. E.g., State v. Hall, 114 N.C. 909, 19 S.E. 602 (1894).

52. State v. Chapin, 17 Ark. 561 (1856); People v. Hodges, 27 Cal. 340 (1865); Linn v. State, 505 P.2d 1270 (Wyo.1973).

No comparable difficulty existed if the aid was given under circumstances which placed the accomplice in the category of principal in the second degree. If, in the example given above, *C* had been present at the time of the shooting giving aid or encouragement to *A* as they both stood in state *X,* then state *Y* would have jurisdiction over both *A* and *C.* One court will have jurisdiction over all principals,[53] for by definition a principal in the second degree abets the crime at the time and place that it is committed by the principal in the first degree.

(2) Variance Between Charge and Proof. Under the common law rules of pleading, it was not necessary for the defendant to be charged specifically as a principal in the first degree or principal in the second degree; a general allegation that the defendant was a principal would suffice.[54] If the indictment did specify either that the defendant actually committed the felony or that he was present aiding and abetting, it did not matter that the proof placed the defendant in the other principal category. Thus, where *A* was charged as a principal in the first degree and *B* as a principal in the second degree, both *A* and *B* could be convicted notwithstanding proof that their roles were reversed.[55]

The same was not true, however, when the variance between charge and proof was spread over the principal and accessory categories. If the defendant were charged as a principal, he could not be convicted upon proof that he was an accessory.[56] Likewise, one charged only as an accessory could not be convicted if the evidence established that he

was instead a principal.[57] As a result, it was possible for an accomplice to escape altogether because of uncertainty as to whether he had been actually or constructively present at the time the offense was committed by the principal in the first degree.

(3) Conviction of Principal Required. The most significant procedural limitation on conviction of an accessory at common law was that conviction of the principal was an absolute prerequisite. An accessory could not be placed on trial in advance of the principal,[58] and this was so even if the principal was not amenable to prosecution because he could not be apprehended or had died.[59] A principal and accessory could be jointly charged and tried,[60] although in such a case the finder of fact was required first to determine the guilt of the principal. The accessory could not be convicted unless the principal was found guilty,[61] and this was also the case when the accessory was tried separately at a later time.[62] If the principal's conviction was later reversed on appeal [63] or he was pardoned,[64] then the conviction of the accessory could not stand.

Once again, the same limitations did not apply with respect to the prosecution of one who was a principal in the second degree. A second degree principal could be tried and convicted even though the person who actually committed the crime had not yet been tried.[65] Indeed, the principal in the second degree could be convicted notwithstanding the prior acquittal of the principal in the first degree.[66]

---

53. State v. Hamilton, 13 Nev. 386 (1878).

54. Nelson v. State, 187 Ga. 576, 1 S.E.2d 641 (1939); State v. Ochoa, 41 N.M. 589, 72 P.2d 609 (1937).

55. Neumann v. State, 116 Fla. 98, 156 So. 237 (1934); Reed v. Commonwealth, 125 Ky. 126, 100 S.W. 856 (1907).

56. Smith v. State, 37 Ark. 274 (1881); Shelton v. Commonwealth, 261 Ky. 18, 86 S.W.2d 1054 (1935); State v. Fitch, 164 W.Va. 337, 263 S.E.2d 889 (1980) (urging legislature to remedy this situation).

57. Agresti v. State, 2 Md.App. 278, 234 A.2d 284 (1967).

58. State v. Graham, 190 La. 669, 182 So. 711 (1938). See also Lewis v. State, 285 Md. 705, 404 A.2d 1073 (1979), discussing and rejecting this common law view.

59. Commonwealth v. Phillips, 16 Mass. 423 (1820).

60. State v. Duncan, 28 N.C. 98 (1845).

61. And could not be convicted of a higher degree of the crime than the principal. State v. Ward, 284 Md. 189, 396 A.2d 1041 (1978).

62. Bowen v. State, 25 Fla. 645, 6 So. 459 (1889).

63. Ray v. State, 13 Neb. 55, 13 N.W. 2 (1882) (accessory after the fact).

64. State v. Duncan, 28 N.C. 98 (1845).

65. McCall v. State, 120 Fla. 707, 163 So. 38 (1935).

66. Rooney v. United States, 203 F. 928 (9th Cir.1913); Christie v. Commonwealth, 193 Ky. 799, 237 S.W. 660

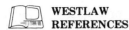
(e) Legislative Reform. The problems discussed above have been largely overcome by legislation. In 1861, for example, an English statute provided that an accessory before the fact could be "indicted, tried, convicted and punished as if he were a principal felon" and that he may be "indicted and convicted of a substantive felony, whether the principal felon shall or shall not have been previously convicted, or shall or shall not be amenable to justice."[67]

Virtually all states have now expressly abrogated the distinction between principals and accessories before the fact. One form of legislation [68] declares that accessories before the fact are now principals,[69] although substantially the same result has been reached by providing that those who would have been accessories before the fact may be prosecuted, tried and punished as if they were principals.[70] Some statutes, following the English model, declare that an accessory before the fact may be punished for a "substantive felony" whether or not the principal has been convicted,[71] while others maintain the common law classifications but provide that conviction of the principal is not a pre-condition to the prosecution of an accessory before the fact.[72]

Indeed, whether or not the common law terminology is retained, the modern codes usually address specifically the troublesome question of whether nonconviction of the principal for one reason or another bars conviction of an accomplice. Most common are those provisions declaring that the accomplice may be convicted even if the principal has not been prosecuted, has not been convicted, has immunity to prosecution or conviction, has been acquitted, or has been convicted of a different offense or degree of offense. Some statutes also state that it is no barrier to conviction of an accomplice that the principal has not been charged or is not amenable to justice. Certain other provisions, by contrast, appear to be directed at the "innocent agent" situation.

By virtue of such legislation, the procedural problems discussed earlier have been obviated in most jurisdictions. Relying upon these statutes, courts have held that an accessory acting elsewhere may be tried in the jurisdiction where the felony occurred,[73] that the charge need not specify whether the defendant was an accessory or principal,[74] that if the charge does specify it is not a fatal variance if the proof puts the case in the other category,[75] and that an accessory may be prosecuted even though the principal has not yet been convicted,[76] or has been previously acquitted,[77] or has been previously convicted only of a lesser offense.[78]

It must be emphasized, however, that not all of these changes have occurred in all jurisdictions. Even in the recent decisions it is possible to find, for example, the view that conviction of an accessory cannot stand if the

(1922); State v. Thompkins, 220 S.C. 523, 68 S.E.2d 465 (1951).

67. The Accessories and Abettors Act, 24 & 25 Vict. c. 94 (1861).

68. This approach is only rarely taken in the modern recodifications.

69. See Model Penal Code § 2.04, Appendix (Tent. Draft No. 1, 1953), citing statutes from twenty-two states.

70. Ibid., citing statutes from twelve states. A few of the modern codes deal with the problem this way.

71. Model Penal Code § 2.04, Appendix (Tent.Draft No. 1, 1953), citing statutes from six states.

72. Ibid., citing statutes from six states.

73. State v. Wolkow, 110 Kan. 722, 205 P. 639 (1922).

74. State v. Williamson, 282 Md. 100, 382 A.2d 588 (1978); Johnson v. State, 453 P.2d 390 (Okl.1969); State v. Frazier, 76 Wash.2d 373, 456 P.2d 352 (1969).

75. United States v. Bryan, 483 F.2d 88 (3d Cir.1973).

76. Howard v. People, 97 Colo. 550, 51 P.2d 594 (1935); Schmidt v. State, 255 Ind. 443, 265 N.E.2d 219 (1970).

77. Standefer v. United States, 447 U.S. 10, 100 S.Ct. 1999, 64 L.Ed.2d 689 (1980) (noting also that only four states now "clearly retain the common law bar"); Kott v. State, 678 P.2d 386 (Alaska 1984); State v. Spillman, 105 Ariz. 523, 468 P.2d 376 (1970); See Annot., 9 A.L.R. 4th 972 (1981).

78. Potts v. State, 430 So.2d 900 (Fla.1982).

principal is acquitted in a separate trial,[79] that the charge must specify whether the defendant is an accessory or a principal,[80] and that the charge and proof must be consistent as to whether the defendant was an accessory or a principal.[81] Interpretation of the statutes described above is varied, and a particular statute may well be found not to have overcome *all* of the procedural difficulties of yesteryear. For example, legislation providing that an accessory may be tried although the principal has not been "arrested and tried" may be held not to permit trial of an accessory before a principal who is in custody awaiting trial.[82] Or, a statute authorizing trial of an accessory even though the principal has not theretofore been convicted may be interpreted not to permit trial of an accessory if his principal was previously acquitted.[83] Also, the rule requiring internal consistency in a verdict may bar acquittal of the principal and conviction of an accessory in a single trial.[84]

Although it is now generally true that conviction of the principal is no longer a prerequisite to prosecution and conviction of an accessory, it is of course still necessary for the prosecution to show on trial of the accessory that the crime was committed, as well as whom and how the defendant aided in its commission.[85] It is generaly accepted, however, that the prior conviction of the principal is *not* admissible at the accessory's trial to es-

tablish that the crime was committed.[86] This is because of "the right of every defendant to stand or fall with the proof of the charge made against him, not somebody else."[87] Indeed, it may well be that admission of the conviction is a denial of the accessory's constitutional right to confront the witnesses against him.[88]

A much more modern approach to the entire subject of parties to crime is to abandon completely the old common law terminology and simply provide that a person is legally accountable for the conduct of another when he is an accomplice of the other person in the commission of the crime. Such is the view taken in the Model Penal Code,[89] which provides that a person is an accomplice of another person in the commission of an offense if, with the purpose of promoting or facilitating the commission of the offense, he solicits the other person to commit it, or aids or agrees or attempts to aid the other person in planning or committing it, or (having a legal duty to prevent the crime) fails to make proper effort to prevent it.[90] A similar approach has been taken in many of the recent recodifications.[91]

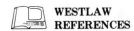

WESTLAW REFERENCES

legislat*** "model penal code" /p accessory accomplice /s principal /s charge* convict*** acquit***

---

79. People v. Taylor, 12 Cal.3d 686, 117 Cal.Rptr. 70, 527 P.2d 622 (1974), extending the doctrine of collateral estoppel to such a situation notwithstanding the absence of the usual identity of parties requirement.

80. State v. Bennett, 157 W.Va. 702, 203 S.E.2d 699 (1974).

81. State v. Fitch, 164 W.Va. 337, 263 S.E.2d 889 (1980), promptly overruled, however, in State v. Petry, ___ W.Va. ___, 273 S.E.2d 346 (1980).

82. Feaster v. State, 175 Ark. 165, 299 S.W. 737 (1927).

83. People v. Wyherk, 347 Ill. 28, 178 N.E. 890 (1931).

84. The prevailing view is to require acquittal of the accomplice if a simultaneous verdict acquits the person charged with the actual commission of the crime. See People v. Allsip, 268 Cal.App.2d 830, 74 Cal.Rptr. 550 (1969); State v. Hess, 233 Wis. 4, 288 N.W. 275 (1939).

85. Roth v. United States, 339 F.2d 863 (10th Cir.1964).

86. United States v. Miranda, 593 F.2d 590 (5th Cir. 1979); People v. Sullivan, 72 Ill.2d 36, 17 Ill.Dec. 827, 377

N.E.2d 17 (1978); State v. Stefanelli, 78 N.J. 418, 396 A.2d 1105 (1979).

87. United States v. Toner, 173 F.2d 140 (3d Cir.1949).

88. State v. Jackson, 270 N.C. 773, 155 S.E.2d 236 (1967).

89. Model Penal Code § 2.06(2)(c).

90. Model Penal Code § 2.06(3), subject to the exceptions set forth in § 2.06(6). Also, § 2.06(7) expressly provides that it is not a bar that "the person claimed to have committed the offense has not been prosecuted or convicted or has been convicted of a different offense or degree of offense or has an immunity to prosecution or conviction or has been acquitted."

91. This approach is also taken in the proposed new federal code. National Comm'n on Reform of Federal Criminal Laws, Final Report—Proposed New Federal Criminal Code § 401 (1971).

§ 6.7 Accomplice Liability—Acts and Mental State

This and the following section are concerned with the general principles governing accomplice liability. Because these principles are applicable to those who come within the common law classifications of principal in the second degree and accessory before the fact,[1] no attempt will be made to distinguish between these two classifications or to identify the accomplices in those terms. Rather, consistent with the modern approach,[2] the word "accomplice" is used herein to describe all persons who are accountable for crimes committed by another,[3] without regard to whether they were or were not actually or constructively present at the time the crimes were committed.

As we have seen, in the process of determining whether a person has committed a crime it is useful to give separate consideration to whether that person engaged in the requisite acts[4] (or omissions[5]) and to whether he had the requisite mental state.[6] This same approach is used herein in determining the limits of accomplice liability. It may generally be said that one is liable as an accomplice to the crime of another if he (a) gave assistance or encouragement or failed to perform a legal duty to prevent it (b) with the intent thereby to promote or facilitate commission of the crime. There is a split of authority as to whether some lesser mental state will suffice for accomplice liability, such as mere knowledge that one is aiding a crime or knowledge that one is aiding reckless or negligent conduct which may produce a criminal result.

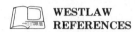

**WESTLAW
REFERENCES**

di accomplice

(a) Acts or Omissions. Several terms have been employed by courts and legislatures in describing the kinds of acts which will suffice for accomplice liability. The most common are "aid," "abet," "advise," "assist," "cause," "command," "counsel," "encourage," "hire," "induce," and "procure." Although there is very little difference between the meaning of several of these words, the following comments must be read with the caveat that the results in some cases may depend upon the precise combination of terms included within the applicable accessory statute.[7]

Such terms as "advise," "command," "counsel," "encourage," "induce," and "procure" suggest that one may become an accomplice without actually rendering physical aid to the endeavor.[8] This is the case.[9] One may become an accomplice by acting to induce an-

---

§ 6.7

1. The person who uses an innocent or irresponsible agent is considered to be a principal in the first degree, and thus that situation is not considered herein. See § 6.6(a). Likewise, the accessory after the fact is not considered herein, as under the modern view he is not truly an accomplice in the crime. See § 6.9(a).

2. The term "accomplice" is used in Model Penal Code § 2.06. It "is employed as the broadest and least technical [term] available to denote criminal complicity. Unlike 'accessory' it has no special meanings under either common law or modern legislation." Model Penal Code § 2.06, Comment at 306 (1985).

3. Except for those special cases in which vicarious liability without fault is imposed. See § 3.9.

4. See § 3.2.

5. See § 3.3.

6. See §§ 3.4–3.7.

7. For example, in Commonwealth v. Perry, 149 Mass. 357, 256 N.E.2d 745 (1970), defendant, at the suggestion of another, agreed to participate in a robbery and traveled with the others to the scene of the robbery, but then departed without participating out of a fear that he might be recognized by his former neighbors. The court reversed his conviction as an accomplice without considering the possibility that he had made an effective withdrawal, see § 6.8(d), by concluding that his acts did not come within the statutory definition of an accomplice as one who "aids" in the commission of a crime or is an accessory by "counseling, hiring, or otherwise procuring" the crime. Assuming no effective withdrawal, such a result might not be reached under other formulations, such as Model Penal Code § 2.06 ("aids or agrees or attempts to aid").

8. Accomplice liability statutes in the modern recodifications contain various words conveying this point. One approach is to say that solicitation of the crime is enough. Another, less common, is to say that conspiring with the other to commit the crime suffices.

Some of these statutes state generally that encouragement of the crime is sufficient. Others specify certain kinds or degrees of encouragement, such as "procures or hires," "induces or coerces," "counsels or advises," or "requests or importunes," likewise, no actual physical aid is necessary under those provisions stating that an agreement to aid or attempt to aid is enough.

9. McMahan v. State, 168 Ala. 70, 53 So. 89 (1910); People v. Chapman, 62 Mich. 280, 28 N.W. 896 (1886).

other through threats or promises,[10] by words or gestures of encouragement,[11] or by providing others with the plan for the crime.[12] The encouragement may come long before the time the crime was committed,[13] and may be communicated to the principal through an intermediary.[14] It is sufficient encouragement that the accomplice is standing by at the scene of the crime ready to give some aid if needed,[15] although in such a case it is necessary that the principal actually be aware of the accomplice's intentions.[16] An undisclosed intention to render aid if needed will not suffice, for it cannot encourage the principal in his commission of the crime.[17] Quite clearly, mere presence at the scene of the crime is not enough,[18] nor is mental approval of the actor's conduct.[19] Also, in the absence of unique circumstances giving rise to a duty to do so, one does not become an accomplice by refusing to intervene in the commission of a crime.[20]

Because this is so, courts have experienced considerable difficulty in cases where the defendant was present at the time of the crime and the circumstances of his presence suggest that he might be there pursuant to a prior agreement to give aid if needed. Depending upon the facts, the circumstantial evidence may be sufficient to permit the jury to find that such an agreement did exist. The mere fact that the alleged accomplice was a prior acquaintance of the actor will not support an inference of guilt,[21] although silence in the face of a friend's crime will sometimes suffice when the immediate proximity of the bystander is such that he could be expected to voice some opposition or surprise if he were not a party to the crime.[22] Mere presence plus flight has often been held insufficient,[23] the reasoning being that this is equivocal conduct because an innocent man may flee out of a fear of being wrongfully accused of guilt or from an unwillingness to appear as a witness.[24] Flight may be taken into account with other facts, however, such as that the bystander positioned himself very close to the victim.[25]

Somewhat easier, as a class, are those cases in which the liability of the accomplice is based upon the fact that he actually did "aid," "abet," or "assist" in the commission of the

---

10. State v. Scott, 80 Conn. 317, 68 A.2d 258 (1907).

11. Alonzi v. People, 198 Colo. 160, 597 P.2d 560 (1979); State v. Wilson, 39 N.M. 284, 46 P.2d 57 (1935); McGhee v. Commonwealth, 221 Va. 422, 270 S.E.2d 729 (1980).

12. State v. Haddad, 189 Conn. 383, 456 A.2d 316 (1983); Commonwealth v. Richards, 363 Mass. 299, 293 N.E.2d 854 (1973).

13. Workman v. State, 216 Ind. 68, 21 N.E.2d 712 (1939).

14. People v. Wright, 26 Cal.App.2d 197, 79 P.2d 102 (1938).

15. Commonwealth v. Morrow, 363 Mass. 601, 296 N.E.2d 468 (1973); Skidmore v. State, 80 Neb. 698, 115 N.W. 288 (1908); State v. Chastain, 104 N.C. 900, 10 S.E. 519 (1889).

16. Hicks v. United States, 150 U.S. 442, 14 S.Ct. 144, 37 L.Ed. 1137 (1893).

17. Ibid.

18. United States v. Minieri, 303 F.2d 550 (2d Cir. 1962); State v. Gomez, 102 Ariz. 432, 432 P.2d 444 (1967); McGill v. State, 252 Ind. 293, 247 N.E.2d 514 (1969); State v. Irby, 423 S.W.2d 800 (Mo.1968). State v. Scott, 289 N.C. 712, 224 S.E.2d 185 (1976); Commonwealth v. Flowers, 479 Pa. 153, 387 A.2d 1268 (1978); State v. Grazerro, ___ R.I. ___, 420 A.2d 816 (1980).

19. White v. People, 81 Ill. 333 (1876); State v. Horner, 248 N.C. 342, 103 S.E.2d 694 (1958). Nor is it sufficient that the defendant thereafter derive some benefit from the actor's conduct, Dalton v. State, 252 A.2d 104 (Del. 1969) (defendant observed his companion break into liquor store, after which defendant took advantage of the breaking by entering the store and taking liquor).

20. State v. Powell, 168 N.C. 134, 83 S.E. 310 (1914).

21. Bailey v. United States, 416 F.2d 1110 (D.C.Cir. 1969); People v. Lopez, 72 Ill.App.3d 713, 28 Ill.Dec. 906, 391 N.E.2d 105 (1979).

22. Compare State v. Parker, 282 Minn. 343, 164 N.W.2d 633 (1969) (where victim gave persons acquainted with one another a ride and one of them beat and robbed victim-driver, defendant's remaining in the car without disapproving or opposing these crimes supports his conviction), with Pace v. State, 248 Ind. 146, 224 N.E.2d 312 (1967) (defendant was driver of car, his friend in back seat robbed hitchhiker also seated in back, defendant's failure to object not sufficient to support his conviction).

23. E.g., Jones v. Commonwealth, 208 Va. 370, 157 S.E.2d 907 (1967).

24. Bailey v. United States, 416 F.2d 1110 (D.C.Cir. 1969).

25. People v. Thomas, 104 Ill.App.2d 56, 243 N.E.2d 611 (1968); Murray v. Commonwealth, 210 Va. 282, 170 S.E.2d 3 (1969).

crime.[26] The assistance may be rendered in a variety of ways. The accomplice may furnish guns,[27] money,[28] supplies[29] or instrumentalities[30] to be used in committing the crime, or he may act as a lookout[31] or man the getaway car[32] while the crime is committed. He might signal the approach of the victim,[33] send the victim to the actor,[34] prevent a warning from reaching the victim,[35] or facilitate the crime by getting the victim[36] or possible witness[37] away from the scene. The aid may be supplied through an intermediary,[38] and it is not necessary that the principal actor be aware of the assistance that was given.[39]

As noted earlier, it is generally true that liability will not flow merely from a failure to intervene.[40] But, under the general principle that an omission in violation of a legal duty will suffice,[41] one may become an accomplice by not preventing a crime which he has a duty to prevent.[42] Thus, a conductor on a train might become an accomplice in the knowing transportation of liquor on his train for his failure to take steps to prevent the offense.[43] Or, even in the absence of positive encouragement, the owner of a car who sat beside the driver might become an accomplice to the driver's crime of driving at a dangerous speed.[44]

To what extent is it necessary that the aid or encouragement have played a part in the commission of the crime? For example, if A prevented the delivery to B of a warning that C was seeking to kill him and B is thereafter killed by C, must it be shown that the murder would not have been accomplished but for A's aid? No, said one court confronted with these facts:

> The assistance given * * * need not contribute to the criminal result in the sense that but for it the result would not have ensued. It is quite sufficient if it facilitated a result that would have transpired without it. It is quite enough if the aid merely renders it easier for the principal actor to accomplish the end intended by him and the aider and abetter, though in all human probability the end would have been attained without it. If the aid in homicide can be shown to have put the deceased at a disadvantage, to have deprived him of a single chance of life, which but for it he would have had, he who furnished such aid is guilty though it can not be known or shown that the dead man, in the absence thereof, would have availed himself of that chance. As where one counsels murder he is guilty as an accessory before the fact, though it appears to be probable that murder would have been done without his counsel.[45]

26. Accomplice liability provisions in modern codes, by using such words, make it clear that such actual aid suffices.

27. Commonwealth v. Richards, 363 Mass. 299, 293 N.E.2d 854 (1973); State v. Williams, 189 S.C. 19, 199 S.E. 906 (1938).

28. Malatakofski v. United States, 179 F.2d 905 (1st Cir.1950) (supplying money for bribe).

29. Bacon v. United States, 127 F.2d 985 (10th Cir. 1942) (sale of liquor to illegal importer).

30. United States v. Eberhardt, 417 F.2d 1009 (4th Cir. 1969) (provided own blood to be poured on selective service files).

31. State v. Berger, 121 Iowa 581, 96 N.W. 1094 (1903); Clark v. Commonwealth, 269 Ky. 833, 108 S.W.2d 1036 (1937).

32. People v. Silva, 143 Cal.App.2d 162, 300 P.2d 25 (1956).

33. State v. Hamilton, 13 Nev. 386 (1878).

34. United States v. Winston, 687 F.2d 832 (6th Cir. 1982); State v. Gladstone, 78 Wash.2d 306, 474 P.2d 274 (1970) (defendant sent customer to narcotics seller; actions sufficient but no showing of purpose to facilitate crime thereby).

35. State ex rel. Attorney General v. Talley, 102 Ala. 25, 15 So. 722 (1894).

36. Breese v. State, 12 Ohio St. 146 (1861).

37. Middleton v. State, 86 Tex.Crim. 307, 217 S.W. 1046 (1920).

38. Commonwealth v. Stout, 356 Mass. 237, 249 N.E.2d 12 (1969).

39. State v. Lord, 42 N.M. 638, 84 P.2d 80 (1938); Espy v. State, 54 Wyo. 291, 92 P.2d 549 (1939).

40. State v. Powell, 168 N.C. 134, 83 S.E. 310 (1914).

41. See § 3.3(a).

42. This is often not explictly stated in accomplice liability statutes. Model Penal Code § 2.06(3), however, includes "having a legal duty to prevent the commission of the offense, fails to make proper effort to do so." Some of the modern codes contain such a provision.

43. Powell v. United States, 2 F.2d 47 (4th Cir.1924).

44. DuCros v. Lambourne, [1907] 1 K.B. 70.

45. State ex rel. Attorney General v. Talley, 102 Ala. 25, 15 So. 722 (1894).

More difficult are those cases involving, at best, encouragement of the crime. See State v. Ulvinen, 313 N.W.2d 425 (Minn.1981) (fact defendant told her son it would be

What, then, of attempted aid? For instance, in the example given above, what if *A* had been unsuccessful in his efforts to stop the delivery of the warning to *B* but *B* was killed nonetheless? At least where the attempted aid is known to the actor, it may make no difference that the aid was unsuccessful or was not utilized, as it may qualify as an encouragement. On this basis it is correct to conclude that an accessory who provides instrumentalities to a burglar for use in a particular burglary should not escape liability as an accomplice merely because the burglar found and used other instrumentalities at the crime scene.[46] On the other hand, where preconcert is lacking and there was only an attempt to aid, it might be argued that this is analogous to the uncommunicated intent to give aid if needed, so that there would be no liability. The Model Penal Code, however, covers all attempts to aid [47] on the ground that "attempted complicity ought to be criminal, and to distinguish it from effective complicity appears unnecessary where the crime has been committed."[48] Several modern codes have adopted this innovation.

 WESTLAW
REFERENCES

accomplice accessory /s act omission /s aid***
　　abet**** advise assist cause command encourage
　　hire induce procure /p communicat! participat!
　　presen** prevent! circumstance

(b) Mental State Generally. Considerable confusion exists as to what the accomplice's mental state must be in order to hold him accountable for an offense committed by another. In part, this may be attributable to some uncertainty as to whether the law should be concerned with the mental state relating to his own acts of assistance or encouragement,[49] to his awareness of the principal's mental state, to the fault requirements for the substantive offense involved, or some combination of the above.

This uncertainty is reflected in the considerable variation in the language used by courts and legislatures on this point. Some cases speak in terms of the accomplice's knowledge or reason to know of the principal's mental state,[50] some as to the accomplice's sharing the criminal intent of the actor,[51] and some about the accomplice's intent to aid or encourage.[52] Likewise, the statutes on accomplice liability may require that one "intentionally" or "knowingly" assist or encourage a crime, that one assist or encourage a crime "with the intent to promote or facilitate such commission," or that the aid and encouragement be given by one "acting with the mental state required for commission of an offense." Although to some extent these may represent different ways of stating the same mental state requirement, it is undoubtedly true that some rather subtle differences exist between them and that therefore what follows is not in all respects applicable in every jurisdiction.

Generally, it may be said that accomplice liability exists when the accomplice intentionally encourages or assists, in the sense that

---

better if he killed his wife did not make her an accomplice; remarks were not active encouragement or instigation, as they had no provable influence on his decision).

46. State v. Tazwell, 30 La.Ann. 884 (1878). See also State v. Doody, 434 A.2d 523 (Me.1981) (defendant encouraged killing by promising to make car available for that purpose, accomplice liability notwithstanding fact it turned out defendant's aid not needed).

47. Model Penal Code § 2.06(3)(a)(ii) ("aids or agrees or attempts to aid such other person in planning or committing" the offense).

48. Model Penal Code § 2.06, Comment at 314 (1985). The Code also deals with the attempted aid situation in which the crime intended is not thereafter committed or attempted, providing that in such a case the accomplice is guilty of an attempt to commit the crime. Model Penal Code § 5.01(3). To explain the applicability of this section, the draftsmen pose yet another variation of the case

discussed in the text above, namely, that *A* is unsuccessful in his efforts to stop delivery of the warning and *B* thus escapes. Model Penal Code § 5.01, Comment at 355 (1985). Model Penal Code § 5.01(3) has been adopted in several of the modern recodifications.

49. These terms are used herein as a shorthand reference to the various kinds of expressions which are used to describe the acts which will suffice for accomplice liability. See text at note 7 supra.

50. E.g., Mowery v. State, 132 Tex.Cr.R. 408, 105 S. W.2d 239 (1937).

51. E.g., United States v. Hewitt, 663 F.2d 1381 (11th Cir.1981); State v. Kendrick, 9 N.C.App. 688, 177 S.E.2d 345 (1970).

52. E.g., State v. Harrison, 178 Conn. 689, 425 A.2d 111 (1979). State v. Grebe, 461 S.W.2d 265 (Mo.1970).

his purpose is to encourage or assist another in the commission of a crime as to which the accomplice has the requisite mental state.[53] Beyond this, the situation is much less certain. There is some authority to the effect that one may become an accomplice by giving encouragement or assistance with knowledge that it will promote or facilitate a crime, although liability has seldom been imposed on this basis. Also, there is considerable diversity in the cases on the subject of whether accomplice liability may rest upon knowing aid to reckless or negligent conduct if that conduct produces a criminal result. It does seem clear, however, that liability without fault does not obtain in this area.

 **WESTLAW REFERENCES**

110k59 /p mental-state inten! know! /p purpose**

(c) Intentional Assistance or Encouragement. Under the usual requirement that the accomplice must intentionally assist or encourage, it is not sufficient that he intentionally engaged in acts which, as it turned out, did give assistance or encouragement to the principal. Rather, the accomplice must intend that his acts have the effect of assisting or encouraging another. For example, assume that A shoots and kills B while C was standing by shouting and gesturing. Is it sufficient, for purposes of accomplice liability to the crime of murder, to show that A took C's words and actions to be a manifestation of encouragement, if in fact C was attempting to dissuade A from killing B? Quite obviously not.[54] Thus, even if knowledge of the actor's intent (as opposed to sharing that intent) is otherwise sufficient, the accomplice must have intended to give the aid or encouragement.[55]

In other instances, it may be clear that the alleged accomplice intended to give aid or encouragement to another, but he will still not be liable as an accomplice. For example, assume that A and B go to C's house, that A removes the screen so as to permit B to enter, that B enters through the window and comes back out with several items of C's personal property, which A then helps B carry away from the scene. Is A an accomplice with B in the crimes of burglary and larceny if B misled A into believing that C had given B permission to borrow the property taken? Clearly not,[56] for these facts show that A was unaware that he was aiding criminal conduct. (This is not to suggest, however, that an accomplice can escape liability by showing he did not intend to aid a crime in the sense that he was unaware that the criminal law covered the conduct of the person he aided.

---

53. Even this generalization is sometimes difficult to apply because of uncertainty as to what circumstances of the crime are mental state related and thus must be within the intention of the accomplice. Compare United States v. Jones, 592 F.2d 1038 (9th Cir.1979) (defendant, who by driving getaway car of bank robber was an accomplice to crime of bank robbery, was not also an accomplice to the crime of robbery of a bank with a deadly weapon, absent proof defendant "knew that [his accomplice] was armed and intended to use the weapon, and intended to aid him in that respect"); with United States v. Gregg, 612 F.2d 43 (2d Cir.1979) (defendant could be convicted as accomplice to crime of embezzlement by one who "a president, director, officer, or manager" of an interstate common carrier, without regard to whether defendant knew person aided was such an individual, as status of embezzler was merely the "jurisdictional predicate" as to which no state of mind necessary); State v. Davis, 101 Wn.2d 654, 682 P.2d 883 (1984) (accomplice in robbery need not have known principal was armed in order to be guilty of first degree robbery—i.e., robbery while armed with a deadly weapon—as what is required is "general knowledge of crime" rather than "specific knowledge of the elements of the participant's crime"); State v. Ivy, 119 Wis.2d 591,

350 N.W.2d 622 (1984) ("if an armed robbery is found to be a natural and probable consequence of a robbery, the aider and abettor need not have had actual knowledge that the principals would be armed with a dangerous weapon").

54. Hicks v. United States, 150 U.S. 442, 14 S.Ct. 144, 37 L.Ed. 1137 (1893).

55. People v. Beeman, 35 Cal.2d 547, 199 Cal.Rptr. 60, 674 P.2d 1318 (1984). Thus, in State v. Grebe, 461 S.W.2d 265 (Mo.1970), where the jury was instructed that they could convict if they found beyond a reasonable doubt that the defendant, present at the time of the killing, and knowing the unlawful intent of the principal in the first degree, aided, abetted, helped and assisted the principal in the first degree in the commission of the act, the appellate court held this instruction reversible error in that the defendant was entitled to an instruction that she should be convicted only if she intentionally aided, abetted, helped and assisted the principal.

56. Cf. People v. Molano, 253 Cal.App.2d 841, 61 Cal. Rptr. 821 (1967), holding on similar facts that it was error to instruct that A could be convicted if either A or B entered the house with intent to commit theft.

Such is not the case,[57] for here as well the general principle that ignorance of the law is no excuse prevails.[58])

Although one might conclude from the above example that what the law *does* require is that the accomplice intend to aid or encourage what he knows is criminal conduct by another, this is an overstatement. The prevailing view is that the accomplice must also have the mental state required for the crime of which he is to be convicted on an accomplice theory. Thus, if A and B go to C's store pursuant to their prior discussion about stealing liquor from the store and A boosts B through the transom and thereafter receives the liquor as it is handed out by B, all of which was done by A to settle a score with B, and A notifies the police while B is inside, A is not an accomplice to B's crimes of burglary and larceny, for A did not intend to permanently deprive C of his goods.[59]

The notion that the accomplice may be convicted, on an accomplice liability theory, only for those crimes as to which he personally has the requisite mental state,[60] is applicable in a variety of circumstances. It means, for example, that one may not be held as an accomplice to the crime of assault with intent to kill if that intent was not shared by the accomplice.[61] But this limitation has proved most significant in the homicide area, where the precise state of mind of the defendant has great significance in determining the degree

of the offense. To determine the kind of homicide of which the accomplice is guilty, it is necessary to look to his state of mind; it may have been different from the state of mind of the principal and they thus may be guilty of different offenses.[62] Thus, because first degree murder requires a deliberate and premeditated killing,[63] an accomplice is not guilty of this degree of murder unless he acted with premeditation and deliberation.[64] And, because a killing in a heat of passion is manslaughter and not murder,[65] an accomplice who aids while in such a state is guilty only of manslaughter even though the killer is himself guilty of murder.[66] Likewise, it is equally possible that the killer is guilty only of manslaughter because of his heat of passion but that the accomplice, aiding in a state of cool blood, is guilty of murder.[67]

Brief mention should also be made here of the somewhat unique results as to accomplice liability which may flow from application of the felony-murder and misdemeanor-manslaughter rules.[68] Under these doctrines, the actor in committing a felony or dangerous misdemeanor is liable for a killing which occurs in the execution of such crimes, and there is no requirement that he have intended the homicide or have even negligently brought it about. This being the case, it is not surprising that one who intentionally aids or encourages the actor in the underlying crime may likewise be convicted of felony-murder[69] or misdemeanor-manslaughter[70]

57. Johnson v. Youden, [1950] 1 K.B. 544.

58. See § 5.1(d).

59. Wilson v. People, 103 Colo. 441, 87 P.2d 5 (1939).

60. The expression by some courts that it is sufficient that the accomplice either had the intent or was aware of the principal's intent, see note 48 supra, may not be directly contrary. In some instances, the circumstances of the aid plus the accomplice's knowledge of the principal's intent would certainly justify the conclusion that the accomplice shared that intent.

61. State v. Taylor, 70 Vt. 1, 39 A. 447 (1898). Similarly, where the crime of mayhem requires an intent to maim, defendant, by merely intending to aid a battery which, as it turns out, results in maiming is not an accomplice to mayhem. Commonwealth v. Hogan, 379 Mass. 190, 396 N.E.2d 978 (1979).

62. Commonwealth v. Bachert, 499 Pa. 398, 453 A.2d 931 (1982). Thus, a jury instruction that an accomplice may be convicted of intent-to-kill aggravated murder if

either he or his principal had the requisite mental state is in error. Clark v. Jago, 676 F.2d 1099 (6th Cir.1982).

Some difficulty in this regard was experienced under the old common law view of parties, for an accessory before the fact could not be convicted of a higher crime than his principal. 4 W. Blackstone, Commentaries on the Laws of England* 36 (1765).

63. See § 7.7(a).

64. Leavine v. State, 109 Fla. 447, 147 So. 897 (1933).

65. See § 7.10.

66. Dorsey v. Commonwealth, 13 Ky.L.R. 359, 17 S.W. 183 (1891); Moore v. Lowe, 116 W.Va. 165, 180 S.E. 1 (1935).

67. Parker v. Commonwealth, 180 Ky. 102, 201 S.W. 475 (1918); State v. McAllister, 366 So.2d 1340 (La.1978).

68. See §§ 7.5, 7.13.

69. People v. Cabaltero, 31 Cal.App.2d 52, 87 P.2d 364 (1939); People v. Michalow, 229 N.Y. 325, 128 N.E. 228

notwithstanding his lack of intent that death result.

**WESTLAW
REFERENCES**

accomplice accessory /s inten! /s assist! encourag!
/s manslaughter murder homicide

(d) Knowing Assistance or Encouragement.[71] In many cases the facts will make it clear that the accessory actually intended to promote the criminal venture, in the sense that he was personally interested in its success. Such is the case, for example, when one supplies guns for use in a bank robbery on the understanding that he will receive part of proceeds of the illegal venture,[72] or when one induces a public official to take unlawful fees so that he may also be paid for the benefit to be granted in exchange.[73] The accomplice's interest, of course, need not be financial;[74] there may be many reasons why he shares in the hope for success.[75]

But there are many other instances in which the alleged accomplice's actions will qualify only as knowing assistance, in that he is lending assistance or encouragement to a criminal scheme toward which he is indifferent.

A lessor rents with knowledge that the premises will be used to establish a bordello. A vendor sells with knowledge that the subject of the sale will be used in commission of a crime. A doctor counsels against an abortion during the third trimester but, at the patient's insistence, refers her to a competent abortionist. A utility provides telephone or telegraph service, knowing it is used for bookmaking. An employee puts through a shipment in the course of his employment though he knows the shipment is illegal. A farm boy clears the ground for setting up a still, knowing that the venture is illicit.[76]

Should such knowing assistance or encouragement suffice as a basis for accomplice liability?[77]

The earlier decisions generally held that aid with knowledge was enough,[78] and it has been forcefully argued that such a view is consistent with the preventive objectives of the criminal law. As stated in *Backun v. United States* [79]:

The seller may not ignore the purpose for which the purchase is made if he is advised of that purpose, or wash his hands of the aid that he has given the perpetrator of a felony by the plea that he has merely made a sale of merchandise. One who sells a gun to another knowing that he is buying it to commit a murder, would hardly escape conviction as an accessory to the murder by showing that he received full price for the gun.

The leading case to the contrary is *United States v. Peoni,* [80] where the court took the position that the traditional definitions of accomplice liability [81] "have nothing whatever to do with the probability that the forbidden result would follow upon the accessory's conduct; and that they all demand that he in some sort associate himself with the venture, that he participate in it as something that he wishes to bring about, that he seek by his

---

own blood, signed a press release, and stood by as others poured blood onto selective service files.

(1920); State v. Carothers, 84 Wn.2d 256, 525 P.2d 731 (1974).

70. Black v. State, 103 Ohio St. 434, 133 N.E. 795 (1921); Wade v. State, 174 Tenn. 248, 124 S.W.2d 710 (1939).

71. See Westerfield, The Mens Rea Requirement of Accomplice Liability in American Criminal Law—Knowledge or Intent, 51 Miss.L.J. 155 (1980).

72. Commonwealth v. Stout, 356 Mass. 237, 249 N.E.2d 12 (1969).

73. People v. Morhouse, 21 N.Y.2d 66, 286 N.Y.S.2d 657, 233 N.E.2d 705 (1967).

74. United States v. Hewitt, 663 F.2d 1381 (11th Cir. 1981); United States v. Harris, 441 F.2d 1333 (10th Cir. 1971).

75. See, e.g., United States v. Eberhardt, 417 F.2d 1009 (4th Cir.1969), where the accomplice provided some of his

76. Model Penal Code § 2.06, Comment at 316 (1985).

77. This is quite similar to the question of whether knowing aid should suffice for conspiracy liability. See § 6.4. This is not to suggest that the two questions must of necessity be answered in the same way. Particularly where conspiracy may not be punished to the same degree as the crime or crimes which served as the object of the conspiracy, knowing aid might arguably be considered sufficient only for conspiracy liability.

78. E.g., Jindra v. United States, 69 F.2d 429 (5th Cir. 1934); Vukich v. United States, 28 F.2d 666 (9th Cir.1928).

79. 112 F.2d 635 (4th Cir.1940).

80. 100 F.2d 401 (1938).

81. See the words quoted in text at note 7 supra.

action to make it succeed. All the words used—even the most colorless, 'abet'—carry an implication of purposive attitude towards it." Other courts have tended to accept the *Peoni* limitation on accomplice liability,[82] although dictum to the contrary still persists.[83]

Various compromises between the views expressed in *Backun* and *Peoni* have been suggested. One is that knowing aid should be deemed sufficient when the criminal scheme is serious in nature.[84] Some of the decided cases may be reconciled on this basis; this would explain, for example, why liability has been imposed for knowing aid to a group planning the overthrow of the government[85] or to one planning to burglarize a bank,[86] but not for knowing aid to such crimes as gambling,[87] prostitution,[88] and unlawful sale of liquor.[89] Taking into account the seriousness of the crime aided makes some sense, for it may be argued that in such a case the "inconvenience to legitimate trade of requiring a merchant to concern himself with the affairs of his customers"[90] is a lesser consideration than the prevention of major crimes.

Another approach is to take into account the degree to which the accomplice knowingly aided in the criminal scheme. This was the recommendation of the draftsmen of the Model Penal Code, who proposed accomplice liability for a person if, "acting with knowledge that such other person was committing or had the purpose of committing the crime, he knowingly, substantially facilitated its commission."[91] This, they explained, would avoid the imposition of liability upon the vendor who supplies materials readily available on the open market and the minor employee who minds his own business to keep his job, but at the same time provide a basis for conviction of those who were aware that they were giving subtantial aid.[92] The conflicting interests would be balanced by subordinating the "freedom to forego concern about the criminal purposes of others" to the interest in crime prevention when the supplier is aware

82. E.g., United States v. Winston, 687 F.2d 832 (6th Cir.1982); Clark v. United States, 293 F.2d 445 (5th Cir. 1961); Morei v. United States, 127 F.2d 827 (6th Cir.1942); State v. Ramsey, 368 S.W.2d 413 (Mo.1963); State v. Gladstone, 78 Wash.2d 306, 474 P.2d 274 (1970).

This *Peoni* limitation must be distinguished from the so-called procuring agent defense, recognized in some jurisdictions, whereunder the defendant may not be convicted of being an accessory to a sale of narcotics when acting as an agent of the purchaser. United States v. Barcella, 432 F.2d 570 (1st Cir.1970); Commonwealth v. Harvard, 356 Mass. 452, 253 N.E.2d 346 (1969); Jones v. State, 481 P.2d 169 (Okla.Crim.1971). Court sometimes explain such a result in *Peoni* terms, Commonwealth v. Flowers, 479 Pa. 153, 387 A.2d 1268 (1978), but it must be remembered that "whether the defendant acted as an agent of the purchaser is irrelevant, if at the same time the defendant in fact aided the seller with the intent of facilitating the sale." State v. Mansir, 440 A.2d 6 (Me.1982).

Whether the procuring agent defense is available often depends upon the nature of the statute under which the charge was brought. See, e.g., State v. Ageht, 116 Wis.2d 605, 342 N.W.2d 721 (1984) (not a defense where statute makes no distinction between buying and selling and covers possession with intent to deliver).

83. E.g., in the *Eberhardt* case, discussed in note 75 supra, where the court asserted unnecessarily considering the facts of the case: "Mengel's mere giving of blood with the knowledge that it would be used for an unlawful purpose would be enough to convict him as an aider and abetter. Just as one may not supply a weapon to another with knowledge that it will be used to commit a crime, here the appellant could not with impunity give his blood knowing the unlawful purpose to which it would be put."

Had those been the only facts, liability could still have been established on an intent-to-aid theory, for "often, if not usually, aid rendered with guilty knowledge implies purpose since it has no other motivation." Model Penal Code § 2.06, Comment at 316 (1985).

84. "For instance, we think the operator of a telephone answering service with positive knowledge that his service was being used to facilitate the extortion of ransom, the distribution of heroin, or the passing of counterfeit money who continued to furnish the service with knowledge of its use, might be chargeable on knowledge alone with participation in a scheme to extort money, to distribute narcotics, or to pass counterfeit money. The same result would follow the seller of gasoline who knew the buyer was using his product to make Molotov cocktails for terroristic use." People v. Lauria, 251 Cal.App.2d 471, 59 Cal.Rptr. 628 (1967).

85. Hanauer v. Doane, 79 U.S. 342, 20 L.Ed. 439 (1870).

86. Regina v. Bainbridge, 3 W.L.R. 656 (1959) (supplier of oxygen-cutting equipment to one known to intend to use it to break into bank an accessory).

87. State ex rel. Dooley v. Coleman, 126 Fla. 203, 170 So. 722 (1936).

88. Bowry v. Bennett, 170 Eng.Rep. 981 (1808).

89. Graves v. Johnson, 179 Mass. 53, 60 N.E. 383 (1901).

90. G. Williams, Criminal Law: The General Part 369 (2d ed. 1961).

91. Model Penal Code § 2.04(3)(b) (Tent.Draft No. 1, 1953).

92. Model Penal Code § 2.06, Comment at 318 n. 58 (1985).

that his contribution to the criminal enterprise would be a substantial one.[93] However, this recommendation was voted down by the American Law Institute, perhaps because of its vagueness,[94] and the Code thus limits accomplice liability to instances in which there exists "the purpose of promoting or facilitating the commission of an offense." [95]

A somewhat different solution is to deal with knowing assistance or encouragement as a distinct criminal offense rather than as a basis for accomplice liability for the crime aided. This would have the advantage of providing means whereby such persons, clearly less culpable than those directly participating in the crime, could be subjected to lesser and different penalties, just has long been the case for the accessory after the fact. This is the solution adopted in a few of the modern codes by adding "criminal facilitation" to the usual list of anticipatory crimes.[96]

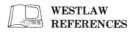 **WESTLAW
REFERENCES**

peoni /s 100 +5 401

(e) Assistance or Encouragement to Reckless or Negligent Conduct. Assume that *A*, the owner of a car, permits *B*, who *A* knows is intoxicated, to operate his car on the public highways, and that as a consequence *B* is involved in an accident which causes the death of *C*. Under principles of accomplice liability, may *A* be viewed as an accomplice to *B*'s criminal-negligence involuntary manslaughter? [97] In considering this question, it is useful to take account once again of the

teaching of *United States v. Peoni* [98] that the traditional definitions of accomplice liability [99] "have nothing whatever to do with the probability that the forbidden result would follow upon the accessory's conduct; and that they all demand that he in some sort associate himself with the venture, that he participate in it as something that he wishes to bring about, that he seek by his action to make it succeed."

As we have seen, the *Peoni* rule is today generally accepted to mean that one does not become an accomplice by an intentional act of assistance or encouragement merely because he knows that such act will facilitate a crime. If this is so, then does it not follow that one also does not become an accomplice by an intentional act of assistance or encouragement merely because he knows that such act *might* facilitate a crime? That is, in the example given above, how can *A* be an accomplice as to *C*'s death when *A* did not give the aid or encouragement with an intent that such a result ensue?

The cases in this area are generally in a state of confusion,[100] and the matter is further confounded by the fact that the problem just stated does not exist when the involuntary manslaughter is of the unlawful-act type [101] rather than the criminal-negligence type.[102] However, it has been held with some frequency that accomplice liability exists under the circumstances stated. The most common case has been like the example given above in that a car owner has permitted a person known to

---

93. Ibid.

94. Deemed unavoidable by the draftsmen. Ibid.

95. Model Penal Code § 2.06(3)(a).

96. Similarly, National Comm'n on Reform of Federal Criminal Laws, Final Report—Proposed New Federal Criminal Code § 1002 (1971), defines criminal facilitation as requiring: (1) knowing substantial assistance to a person intending to commit a felony; (2) that the other person commit the contemplated crime or a like or related felony; and (3) that the assistance provided be in fact employed in committing the crime.

97. See § 7.12.

98. 100 F.2d 401 (1938).

99. See the words quoted in text at note 7 supra.

100. See Annot., 95 A.L.R.2d 175 (1964).

101. See § 7.13.

102. This is because, as noted earlier, see text at note 68, supra, in such a case the accomplice's intent to assist in the commission of the unlawful act is sufficient also to establish complicity for the resulting death. Thus, in Regina v. Creamer, [1965] 3 All E.R. 257, where the defendant had arranged for a woman to have an abortion and was charged as an accessory before the fact to manslaughter resulting from the abortion, his counsel objected that "it is of the essence of counselling and procuring that you intend the result which you counsel or procure" and that one "cannot procure what he cannot intend, and he cannot intend an accidental killing." The court replied that the defendant had counselled the unlawful act of abortion and thus was an accessory to unlawful-act manslaughter.

be intoxicated to operate his vehicle,[103] but the same result has been reached on quite different facts.[104] Although the rationale of these decisions is seldom made explicit, the assumption apparently is that giving assistance or encouragement to one it is known will thereby engage in conduct dangerous to life should suffice for accomplice liability as to crimes defined in terms of recklessness or negligence. This conclusion, permitted under some accomplice liability statutes,[105] it might be argued, is not inconsistent with the *Peoni* rule holding knowing facilitation insufficient, for *Peoni* has been applied so as to avoid holding one as an accomplice upon a lesser mental state than would be required for conviction of the principal in the first degree.

This theory of accomplice liability has been rejected by some courts,[106] and it would seem inapplicable under many of the modern accomplice statutes requiring an actual intent to assist the commission of a crime.[107] This is not to say, however, to return to the example of *A* permitting intoxicated *B* to drive his car, that *A* will necessarily escape liability. *A* could well be found guilty of criminal-negligence involuntary manslaughter without being declared an accomplice of *B*.

To understand how this might be so, it is important to reconsider why and when accom-

---

103. Story v. United States, 16 F.2d 342 (D.C.Cir.1926); Lewis v. State, 220 Ark. 914, 251 S.W.2d 490 (1952); Ex parte Liotard, 47 Nev. 169, 217 P. 960 (1923); Eager v. State, 205 Tenn. 156, 325 S.W.2d 815 (1959). To the same effect is Stacy v. State, 228 Ark. 260, 306 S.W.2d 852 (1957), where, unlike the other cases, the owner of the vehicle was not riding with the driver but was following him in another car. But in People v. Marshall, 362 Mich. 170, 106 N.W.2d 842 (1961), where the defendant was home in bed at the time of the accident, the court held he was not an accomplice because "the killing ＊ ＊ ＊ was not counselled by him, accomplished by another acting jointly with him, nor did it occur in the attempted achievement of some common enterprise."

104. State v. DiLorenzo, 138 Conn. 281, 83 A.2d 479 (1951) (defendant aided others in installation of still for manufacture of liquor in wooden house in such a way as to create substantial risk of fire from operation of still, fire started while another was in charge of still and residents on upper floor killed; in response to defendant's claim that he could not be an aider and abetter to manslaughter when he was not present, court held that "one who engages with others in a common purpose to carry on an activity in a reckless manner or with wanton disregard for the safety of others is guilty of involuntary manslaughter, if the death of another is caused thereby"); People v. Turner, 125 Mich.App. 8, 336 N.W.2d 217 (1983) (where defendant supplied gun without safety catch and directed aiming of it and gun fired, killing another, defendant an aider and abettor of involuntary manslaughter); State v. McVay, 47 R.I. 292, 132 A. 436 (1926) (boiler burst on steamship and many lives lost, defendant was not on board but gave instructions to proceed knowing of condition of boilers; in response to defendant's claim that he could not be an aider or abettor to manslaughter when he was not present, court held he could because he, "with full knowledge of the possible danger to human life, recklessly and willfully advised, counseled, and commanded the captain and engineer to take a chance by negligent action or failure to act.").

105. Model Penal Code § 2.06(4) states: "When causing a particular result is an element of an offense, an accomplice in the conduct causing such result is an accomplice in the commission of that offense, if he acts with the kind of culpability, if any, with respect to that result that

is sufficient for the commission of the offense." This means that one "who urges a driver to increase his speed, stands in the same position as the driver if a homicide or injury occurs, unless, of course, the driver had some unshared special knowledge that has bearing on his liability." Model Penal Code § 2.04, Comment (Tent. Draft No. 1, 1953). Only a few of the modern codes contain a provision like Model Penal Code § 2.06(4).

106. People v. Marshall, 362 Mich. 170, 106 N.W.2d 842 (1961) (discussed note 103 supra); State v. Gartland, 304 Mo. 87, 263 S.W. 165 (1924) (defendant and another policeman were chasing car believed to contain bootleggers, both fired shots at car and one shot killed a passenger; held defendant could not be convicted on theory he and fellow officer were engaged in a common design and purpose, as there "could be no common design to commit a negligent act"); State v. Etzweiler, 125 N.H. 57, 480 A.2d 870 (1984) (extended discussion of the issue in several opinions).

In some other cases the court appears to have disapproved of charges or instructions based upon an accomplice theory without requiring reversal because the evidence showed that the defendant was liable for the death on the basis of his own conduct, the theory discussed in the text following. See People v. Kemp, 150 Cal.App.2d 654, 310 P.2d 680 (1957) (defendant may be held on basis of his own acts which were the proximate cause of the deaths, instructions on aiding and abetting not "sufficiently prejudicial to justify reversal"); State v. Hopkins, 147 Wash. 198, 265 P. 481 (1928) (charge was in terms of aiding and abetting, but court says defendant accountable because of her own negligence).

107. See text following note 52 supra. But see Menez v. State, 575 S.W.2d 36 (Tex.Crim.App.1979) (though accomplice statute requires that one act "with intent to promote or assist the commission of the offense," defendant deemed accomplice of person who defendant joined on drunken shooting spree, where accomplice fired shots at random and killed occupant of house, and defendant thus guilty of involuntary manslaughter of recklessness type; court relies upon unlawful act manslaughter cases without recognizing the difference between them and instant case).

plice liability is needed. It is required to establish liability as to one who did not himself engage in the conduct required for commission of the crime, and this becomes most critical when the relevant statute speaks of a specific kind of conduct. For example, the crime of burglary requires (among other things) a breaking and entering,[108] and thus if *A* breaks and enters by using a ladder supplied by *B* and held by *C* while *D* keeps a lookout, *B*, *C* and *D* are accountable for the crime of burglary only if they are accomplices of *A*, for only *A* has done the requisite breaking and entering. But certain crimes are defined quite differently, in that specific acts are not enumerated; rather, it is only required that the unspecified conduct cause a certain specified result. Such is the case as to criminal-negligence involuntary manslaughter.[109] And this is why, if *A* gives his car to intoxicated *B* and *B* runs down and kills *C*, it is not necessary to find that *A* is an accomplice to *B*'s crime; if *A*'s own conduct in turning over the car to one known to be intoxicated is itself criminally negligent and if that conduct is found to be the legal cause of the death, then *A* is guilty of manslaughter on that basis.[110] Indeed, this approach is to be much preferred over the accomplice liability theory, for the latter is not limited by the legal cause requirement[111] and thus could easily be extended to all forms of assistance or encouragement to negligent or reckless conduct.[112]

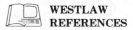 **WESTLAW REFERENCES**

accomplice /p (negligen! /s conduct) reckless! involuntary-manslaughter

(f) Liability Without Fault. Under the general principles applicable to accomplice liability, there is no such thing as liability without fault. Thus, it is not enough that the alleged accomplice's acts in fact assisted or encouraged the person who committed the crime.[113] One does not become an accomplice to a murder merely because the murderer misinterpreted his words and gestures as encouragement.[114]

A somewhat different situation is that in which the alleged accomplice is aiding another with intent to do so, but the aid is given without knowledge of the facts which make the principal's conduct a crime. It has been argued that in such a case the accomplice may be held on a liability-without-fault basis if the crime committed by the principal is of the strict liability variety, but this argument has been rejected.[115] The argument is not sound, for the special circumstances which justify the imposition of liability without fault on certain persons who themselves engage in the proscribed conduct[116] are not likely to exist as to those rendering aid.[117] For example, as a matter of policy it may be sound to

108. See § 8.13(a), (b).

109. See § 7.12.

110. "It was not the act of the driver at the time the brakes failed nor the failure of the defendant to protest her actions at that time that amounted to criminal negligence. His permitting her to drive while intoxicated is the act that constituted criminal negligence on his part, especially when he knew the brakes on the car were defective." Freeman v. State, 211 Tenn. 27, 362 S.W.2d 251 (1962). And see the *Kemp* and *Hopkins* cases, discussed in note 106 supra.

Of course, this alternate theory is not available when the crime is defined in specific terms, such as in Ex parte Liotard, 47 Nev. 169, 217 P. 960 (1923), where the defendant was convicted on an accomplice theory of the statutory crime of causing death by negligently operating a vehicle while intoxicated.

111. That is, it is not necessary to show that the crime would not have happened but for the assistance or encouragement. See text at note 45 supra.

112. Thus, the dissenting judge in Jacobs v. State, 184 So.2d 711 (Fla.1966), noted that "by the extension of such reasoning the spectators lined up along the road to watch [a drag race] might be legally tried and convicted as aiders and abetters to the manslaughter [resulting therefrom], simply because the collision might not have occurred if they had not congregated and encouraged the racing."

113. Hicks v. United States, 150 U.S. 442, 14 S.Ct. 144, 37 L.Ed. 1137 (1893).

114. Ibid.

115. Johnson v. Youden, [1950] 1 K.B. 544 (lawyers who aided builder sell house at price in excess of that permitted by law, a strict liability offense, are not accomplices to the crime where they were unaware that their client was charging an unlawful price).

116. See § 3.8(c).

117. See G. Williams, Criminal Law: The General Part 395 (2d ed. 1961).

make the filing of a false financial statement with a state official a strict liability offense, so that the person filing the statement may not defend on the ground that he believed the statement to be true.[118] It does not follow from this, however, that one who assists in the filing should likewise be held liable on this basis.

The above comments, it must be emphasized, refer only to accomplice liability as it exists under common law and statutes, where mental fault is an absolute requirement.[119] One who is not truly an accomplice may nonetheless be held responsibile for the conduct of another by virtue of special statutory provisions,[120] and such legislation may indeed impose that variety of liability without fault which is referred to as vicarious liability.[121]

 WESTLAW REFERENCES

accomplice /p "liability without fault" "strict liability"

§ 6.8   The Limits of Accomplice Liability

Under the better view, one is not an accomplice to a crime merely because that crime was committed in furtherance of a conspiracy of which he is a member, or because that crime was a natural and probable consequence of another offense as to which he is an accomplice. While guilt of the principal is ordinarily a prerequisite to accomplice liability, it may be otherwise when the principal has a defense which is personal to him or when the accomplice has attempted to aid or encourge another.

One may be an accomplice in a crime which, by its definition, he could not commit personally. However, one is not an accomplice to a crime if (a) he is a victim of the crime; (b) the offense is defined so as to make his conduct inevitably incident thereto; or (c) he takes sufficient steps to make a timely withdrawal of his aid or encouragement.

(a) Complicity and Conspiracy Distinguished. One source of continuing confusion in this area is whether the doctrines concerning complicity and conspiracy are essentially the same, so that liability as a conspirator and as an accomplice may be based upon essentially the same facts. Is one who is a member of a conspiracy of necessity a party to any crime committed in the course of the conspiracy? Is one who qualifies as an accomplice to a crime of necessity part of a conspiracy to commit that crime? Under the better view, both of these questions must be answered in the negative.

The leading case for the proposition that membership in a conspiracy is sufficient for criminal liability not only as a conspirator but also for all specified offenses committed in furtherance of the consiracy is *Pinkerton v. United States.*[1] Pinkerton was indicted both for conspiring with his brother to evade taxes and also for specific tax evasions committed by his brother while Pinkerton was in jail. Although the evidence in the case tended to show that Pinkerton actually played a part in the planning of the specific offenses notwithstanding his incarceration, the trial court instructed the jury that it could convict on the substantive counts if it found that the defendant had been engaged in a conspiracy and that the offenses charged were in furtherance of the conspiracy. The Supreme Court affirmed, holding in effect that evidence of direct participation in the commission of the substantive offenses was not necessary, although it was indicated that the result might be otherwise if the crimes were not reasona-

---

118. State v. Dobry, 217 Iowa 858, 250 N.W. 702 (1933).

119. "[T]he responsibility of secondary parties exists at common law, and is therefore subject to the common-law requirement of *mens rea*. Those statutes that enact the responsibility merely declare the common law." G. Williams, supra note 117, at 395.

120. Such a person is not properly labeled an accomplice. Thus, Model Penal Code § 2.06 does not use that

word to describe one who "is made accountable for the conduct of such other person by the Code or by the law defining the offense."

121. See § 3.9.

§ 6.8

1. 328 U.S. 640, 66 S.Ct. 1180, 90 L.Ed. 1489 (1946).

bly foreseeable as a natural consequence of the unlawful agreement.[2]

The notion that one is responsible for the substantive crimes of fellow conspirators in furtherance of the conspiracy has often been expressed in the cases,[3] although such statements have been most frequently made in decisions involving only a conspiracy charge.[4] When this "rule" has been relied upon in connection with a charge of specific offenses, the facts have often shown sufficient counseling or aiding of those offenses to make unnecessary reliance upon the conspiracy as a basis for establishing complicity.[5] But this is not to suggest that what might be called the *Pinkerton* rule has not had an impact upon the law of accomplice liability. The *Pinkerton* approach has been used from time to time by courts in establishing a basis for finding that the defendant was accountable for crimes directly committed by another. For example, in one case the defendant's conduct in referring women to an abortionist was held to make her a part of a larger conspiracy whereby she might be convicted of twenty-six individual abortions, including many performed on women not known by this defendant and referred to the abortionist by others.[6] And in another case the defendant's acts in introducing the head of the conspiracy to check-cashing agencies was deemed sufficient to make him a member of the general conspiracy and thereby liable for 131 separate forging and uttering offenses.[7] The *Pinkerton* rule also appears to have been included within some statutes defining accomplice liability.

Any assessment of the *Pinkerton* rule involves a reconsideration of the question considered at the outset of the preceding section: to what extent must the defendant's acts have

played a part in inducing or aiding the crime in order to justify holding him accountable for it as an accomplice? In support of the *Pinkerton* rule, this question might be answered in this way:

> Criminal acts done in furtherance of a conspiracy may be sufficiently dependent upon the encouragement and material support of the group as a whole to warrant treating each member as a causal agent to each act. Under this view, which of the conspirators committed the substantive offense would be less significant in determining the defendant's liability than the fact that the crime was performed as a part of a larger division of labor to which the defendant had also contributed his efforts. * * * If a defendant can be convicted as an accomplice for advising or counseling the perpetrator, it likewise seems fair to impose vicarious liability upon one who, in alliance with others, has declared his allegiance to a particular common object, has implicitly assented to the commission of foreseeable crimes in furtherance of this object, and has himself collaborated or agreed to collaborate with his associates, since these acts necessarily give support to the other members of the conspiracy. Perhaps the underlying theme of this argument is that the strict concepts of causality and intent embodied in the traditional doctrine of complicity are inadequate to cope with the phenomenon of modern-day organized crime.[8]

The better view, however, is that "aiding should mean something more than the attenuated connection resulting solely from membership in a conspiracy and the objective standard of what is reasonably foreseeable."[9] As the draftsmen of the Model Penal Code have pointed out, "law would lose all sense of just proportion" if one might, by virtue of his one crime of conspiracy, be "held accountable for thousands of additional offenses of which he was completely unaware and which he did not

---

2. This qualification was stated in dictum and was not mentioned by the Court in the discussion of *Pinkerton* in the later case of Nye & Nisen v. United States, 336 U.S. 613, 69 S.Ct. 766, 93 L.Ed. 919 (1949).

3. E.g., Pollack v. State, 215 Wis. 200, 253 N.W. 560 (1934).

4. E.g., Baker v. United States, 21 F.2d 903 (4th Cir. 1927).

5. As noted earlier, this was true in the *Pinkerton* case. See also Miller v. State, 25 Wis. 384 (1870), where the court spoke of the defendant's liability as that of a con-

spirator although she was presently supporting her husband in his homicide.

6. Anderson v. Superior Court, 78 Cal.App.2d 22, 177 P.2d 315 (1947).

7. People v. Cohen, 68 N.Y.S.2d 140 (1947).

8. Developments in the Law—Criminal Conspiracy, 72 Harv.L.Rev. 920, 998–99 (1959), but rejecting the argument.

9. 1 National Comm'n on Reform of Federal Criminal Laws, Working Papers 156 (1970).

influence at all." [10] If the *Pinkerton* rule were adhered to, each prostitute or runner in a large commercialized vice ring could be held liable for an untold number of acts of prostitution by persons unknown to them and not directly aided by them.[11] Each retailer in an extensive narcotics ring could be held accountable as an accomplice to every sale of narcotics made by every other retailer in that vast conspiracy.[12] Such liability might be justified for those who are at the top directing and controlling the entire operation, but it is clearly inappropriate to visit the same results upon the lesser participants in the conspiracy.[13]

Although the *Pinkerton* rule never gained broad acceptance, the opposition to it has grown significantly in recent years. It was rejected by the draftsmen of the Model Penal Code [14] and of the proposed new federal criminal code.[15] Most of the state statutes on accomplice liability require more than membership in the conspiracy,[16] and the language in these statutes has been relied upon by courts in rejecting the conclusion that complicity is coextensive with conspiracy.[17] The rule continues to exist in the federal system, though the courts "are mindful of the potential due process limitations on the *Pinkerton* doctrine in cases involving attenuated relationships between the conspirator and the substantive crime." [18]

A much simpler question is whether one must be guilty of engaging in a conspiracy with the principal in the first degree in order to be his accomplice. The answer is no, for while an agreement is an essential element of the crime of conspiracy,[19] aid sufficient for accomplice liability may be given without any

---

10. Model Penal Code § 2.06, Comment at 307 (1985).

11. Cf. People v. Luciano, 277 N.Y. 348, 14 N.E.2d 433 (1938), where the leaders of the ring were convicted of 62 counts of compulsory prostitution.

12. Cf. United States v. Bruno, 105 F.2d 921 (2d Cir. 1939), reversed on other grounds, 308 U.S. 287, 60 S.Ct. 198, 84 L.Ed. 257 (1939), involving 88 defendants in a narcotics conspiracy.

13. Also, "the *Pinkerton* doctrine could be the source of otherwise avoidable problems: (a) is the coconspirator liable for crimes committed before he joined the conspiracy, as he is for overt acts (a principle which serves another purpose)? (b) do different rules of evidence apply to his liability for conspiracy and his liability for the specific offense? (c) can he be acquitted for conspiracy and retried for the specific offense? (d) should the test of withdrawal from the conspiracy be the same as for terminating liability for the specific offense?" 1 National Comm'n on Reform of Federal Criminal Laws, Working Papers 157 (1970).

14. Model Penal Code § 2.06, Comment at 307–09 (1985).

15. 1 National Comm'n on Reform of Federal Criminal Laws, Working Papers 155–57 (1970). National Comm'n on Reform of Federal Criminal Laws, Final Report— Proposed New Federal Criminal Code § 401 (1971) expressly provides that if one is a co-conspirator he is also liable as an accomplice only if the usual requirements are met.

16. A very few, however, specifically include conspiracy as a basis for accomplice liability.

17. E.g., People v. McGhee, 49 N.Y.2d 48, 424 N.Y.S.2d 157, 399 N.E.2d 1177 (1979). A somewhat unusual case, in that it did not involve a conspiracy with several crimes as its object, is Commonwealth v. Perry, 357 Mass. 149, 256 N.E.2d 745 (1970). Defendant, at the suggestion of anoth-

er, agreed to participate in the robbery of a liquor store. He accompanied the others to the general area, but then left because he had formerly lived in the area and feared he might be recognized. There was no agreement that he stand by to give aid or to assist in the escape, and he gave no such aid. He was nonetheless convicted of assault with intent to rob, but his conviction was reversed on appeal. The court, after noting that the statute on accomplice liability covers only one who "aids in the commission of a felony, or is an accessory thereto before the fact by counseling, hiring or otherwise procuring such felony to be committed," concluded: "If the defendant agreed with the other persons to commit the crimes of robbery and assault and did nothing more, he is guilty of criminal conspiracy; but he was not charged with that crime. That alone does not make him an accessory before the fact or a principal to the substantive crime which was the objective of the conspiracy."

18. United States v. Alvarez, 755 F.2d 830 (11th Cir. 1985), upholding murder convictions based upon participation in a drug conspiracy. The court reasoned that "based on the amount of drugs and money involved, the jury was entitled to infer that, at the time the cocaine sale was arranged, the conspirators must have been aware of the likelihood (1) that at least some of their number would be carrying weapons, and (2) that deadly force would be used, if necessary, to protect the conspirators' interests." But the court cautioned that it had "not found, nor has the government cited, any authority for the proposition that all conspirators, regardless of individual culpability, may be held responsible under *Pinkerton* for reasonably foreseeable but originally unintended substantive crimes" and emphasized that in the instant case the defendants "were more than 'minor' participants in the drug conspiracy" and "had actual knowledge of at least some of the circumstances leading up to the murder."

19. See § 6.4.

agreement between the parties.[20] Indeed, it is even possible for *A* to encourage *B* to commit a crime so as to be liable as an accomplice without the facts also supporting the conclusion that *A* and *B* were co-conspirators.[21]

(b) Foreseeability of Other Crimes. The question considered above as to whether liability for the conspiracy also suffices for accomplice liability with regard to any crimes committed in pursuance of the conspiracy is, as was suggested, a means for testing the outer limits of the act requirement for accomplice liability. A somewhat similar question is whether, on an accomplice liability theory, one may be held accountable for a crime because it was a natural and probable consequence of the crime which that person intended to aid or encourage. This tests the outer limits of the mental state requirement for accomplice liability, for it asks, in effect, whether an intent with respect to one offense should suffice as to another offense which was the consequence of the one intended.

The established rule, as it is usually stated by courts and commentators, is that accomplice liability extends to acts of the principal in the first degree which were a "natural and probable consequence" of the criminal scheme the accomplice encouraged or aided.[22] Some accomplice liability statutes, even in recent recodifications,[23] expressly adopt this position. Under this approach, if *A* counsels or aids *B*

in the commission of a burglary or a robbery of *C*, and *B* encounters resistance from *C* and thus shoots at him in the course of the burglary or robbery, *A* is an accomplice to attempted murder.[24] On the other hand, if *A* is an accomplice in a scheme to steal a safe from a building, and one of the other parties, *B*, takes it upon himself while alone to also rob the watchman in the building, *A* is not an accomplice to the robbery.[25]

The "natural and probable consequence" rule of accomplice liability, if viewed as a broad generalization, is inconsistent with more fundamental principles of our system of criminal law. It would permit liability to be predicated upon negligence even when the crime involved requires a different state of mind.[26] Such is not possible as to one who has personally committed a crime, and should likewise not be the case as to those who have given aid or counsel.

For example, we have already established that an intent to commit one crime cannot be substituted for an intent to commit another, nor can the commission of one offense be the basis of guilt for another crime requiring a different mental state merely because the harm required for the latter offense flowed from the first crime.[27] Thus, if *A* steals a gas meter and as a result *B* is harmed by the escaping gas, *A*'s intent to steal is not of itself a basis for holding him liable for the harm to *B*; rather *A* is liable for the harm to *B* only upon a finding that he had the mental state (intent, recklessness, or whatever) required under the applicable statute on causing physi-

---

20. Harris v. State, 177 Ala. 17, 59 So. 205 (1912); State v. Anderberg, 89 S.D. 75, 228 N.W.2d 631 (1975); Espy v. State, 54 Wyo. 291, 92 P.2d 549 (1939).

21. In State v. King, 104 Iowa 727, 74 N.W. 691 (1898), *A* told *B* that if *B* would whip *C* his fine would be paid, but *B* responded that he did not want anyone to pay his fine, as he had a grievance of his own against *C*, and *B* thereafter whipped *C*. *A* was acquitted of conspiracy on the ground that there was no "concert of action," no agreement to cooperate. It seems possible that *A* might be held as an accomplice. See text in § 6.7 at note 45.

22. See W. Clark & W. Marshall, Law of Crimes 529 (7th ed. 1967); 1 Wharton, Criminal Law 181 (14th ed. C. Torcia 1978); Sayre, Criminal Responsibility for the Acts of Another, 43 Harv.L.Rev. 689, 702–06 (1930), and cases cited therein.

23. For an application of such a statute, see State v. Goodall, 407 A.2d 268 (Me.1979).

24. Some accomplice liability statutes which do *not* so provide have been construed to produce this same result. See, e.g., People v. Kessler, 57 Ill.2d 493, 315 N.E.2d 29 (1974).

25. State v. Lucas, 55 Iowa 321, 7 N.W. 583 (1880).

26. "Probabilities have an important evidential bearing on these issues; to make them independently sufficient is to predicate the liability on negligence when, for good reason, more is normally required before liability is found." Model Penal Code § 2.06, Comment at 312 (1985).

27. See § 3.11(d).

cal harm to a person.[28] Similarly, if C lights a candle to aid in a theft, resulting in a burning of the premises, C's intent to steal does not justify his conviction for arson; again, C must also be shown to have the mental state required for the crime of arson.[29] Were it otherwise, the legislative classification of offenses and punishments would lose all meaning.

For the same reason, general application of the "natural and probable consequence" rule of accomplice liability is unwarranted. A's guilt as an accomplice to one crime should not per se be a basis for holding A accountable for a related crime merely because the latter offense was carried out by A's principal, for this as well would result in A's guilt of a crime as to which he did not have the requisite mental state. Some courts have recognized this point.[30] A, an accomplice in B's crime of falsifying corporate books, is not for that reason also accountable for B's related crime of filing a false tax return based upon the false entries.[31] Similarly, C, by virtue of his accomplice liability in D's embezzlement of city funds, is not necessarily also guilty of D's related crime of filing false reports concerning those funds.[32]

Indeed, the most that can be said for the "natural and probable consequence" rule of accomplice liability is that it has usually been applied to unique situations in which unusual principles of liability obtain. Two striking

exceptions to the general rules discussed above are felony-murder[33] and misdemeanor-manslaughter,[34] for they do permit conviction for a homicide occurring in the execution of a felony or dangerous misdemeanor without any showing that the defendant intentionally, knowingly, recklessly, or even negligently caused the death. If A commits a felony or dangerous misdemeanor and in the process even accidentally causes B's death, A is guilty of murder or manslaughter because of his commission of the felony or misdemeanor. This being the case, it is appropriate that complicity in the underlying felony or misdemeanor should likewise suffice to establish guilt of the murder or manslaughter. That is, if, in the above example, C was an accomplice to A in his commission of the felony or misdemeanor, C is equally guilty with A of the homicide of B.[35] If the "natural and probable consequence" rule of accomplice liability is limited to such cases it is not objectionable—or, at least is no more objectionable than other applications of the felony-murder and misdemeanor-manslaughter rules.[36]

 **WESTLAW REFERENCES**

accomplice accessory (aid*** +2 abet****) /p natural probable /s consequence

(c) Crime by the Principal. Subject to the inconsistent verdict problem when the principal in the first degree and an accomplice are jointly tried,[37] it is now generally

28. Regina v. Cunningham, 41 Crim.App. 155 (1957).

29. Regina v. Faulknor, 13 Cox Crim.Cas. 550 (1877).

30. E.g., United States v. Greer, 467 F.2d 1064 (7th Cir. 1972) (defendant convicted of aiding theft from interstate shipment may not also be convicted of aiding interstate transportation of the stolen goods merely because it is a "foreseeable consequence of the theft, as that would base criminal liability upon negligence rather than criminal intent).

31. People v. Weiss, 256 App.Div. 162, 9 N.Y.S.2d 1 (1939), aff'd 280 N.Y. 718, 21 N.E.2d 212 (1939), noting there was no evidence the defendant "contemplated" the filing of the returns.

32. People v. Little, 41 Cal.App.2d 797, 107 P.2d 634, 108 P.2d 63 (1941), but noting absence of evidence that defendant "knew or should have known" the false reports were being filed.

33. See § 7.5.

34. See § 7.13.

35. E.g., People v. Cabaltero, 31 Cal.App.2d 52, 87 P.2d 364 (1939); People v. Michalow, 229 N.Y. 325, 128 N.E. 228 (1920). The Model Penal Code, while rejecting the broad principle of accomplice liability for "natural and probable" consequences, is consistent with the theory underlying these decisions in that § 2.06(4) provides that when causing a certain result is an element of an offense, then the accomplice in the conduct causing such a result is an accomplice in the commission of that offense if he acts with the culpability that is sufficient for the commission of the offense.

36. The objections which have been made concerning these two rules, see § 7.5(h) and § 7.13(e), are generally applicable whether one is concerned with liability of the principal in the first degree or accomplices.

37. The prevailing view is to require acquittal of the accomplice if a simultaneous verdict acquits the person charged with the actual commission of the crime. See People v. Allsip, 268 Cal.App.2d 830, 74 Cal.Rptr. 550 (1969); State v. Hess, 233 Wis. 4, 288 N.W. 275 (1939).

accepted that an accomplice may be convicted notwithstanding the fact that the principal in the first degree has been acquitted or has not yet been tried.[38] But in such situations, or even when the principal has theretofore been convicted, the guilt of the principal must be established at the trial of the accomplice as a part of the proof on the charge against the accomplice.[39] If the acts of the principal in the first degree are found not to be criminal, then the accomplice may not be convicted.[40] Ordinarily, the proof will be of completed criminal conduct by the principal, although it would seem theoretically possible for one to be an accomplice to an attempt [41] or a conspiracy.[42]

One question which has not been resolved is whether the various defenses available to the principal in the first degree are likewise available to the accomplice in the sense that the accomplice may establish the defense and thus show that no crime was committed by the principal. For example, what if A shot and killed B upon a reasonable but mistaken belief that such deadly force was necessary in his own defense. This is clearly a defense to A,[43] but should accomplice C, who aids A without such a belief, thereby go free? If, as we are assuming, C gave aid with the intent that A kill B, it would seem that C should not escape liability. Just as an accomplice may not benefit from a principal's heat of passion so as to downgrade his own liability to volun-

tary manslaughter,[44] it would seem equally true that the accomplice may not defend upon the basis of the principal's own beliefs.[45]

A similar problem was dealt with in the recent case of *United States v. Azadian.*[46] The defendant was charged with having aided and abetted a draft board employee in soliciting the receipt of money in return for using her influence in her official capacity. He was convicted, although in the same action the employee was found not guilty because of entrapment by a government informant. On appeal, the court concluded that because the defendant had not been entrapped he could not escape conviction because of the entrapment of the principal. This result was rested upon the following characterization of the entrapment defense: "It is made available not because inducement negatives criminal intent and thus establishes the fact of innocence; but because Government agents should not be permitted to act in such a fashion. The defense does not so much establish innocence as grant immunity from prosecution for criminal acts concededly committed."[47] If this is a proper characterization of entrapment,[48] then the result may be correct.[49]

Another question which deserves consideration is whether one acting in the role of an accomplice should escape liability because, unknown to him, the individual in the role of principal in the first degree is not really committing a crime because he (unlike the accom-

---

38. See § 6.6(e).

39. Miller v. People, 98 Colo. 249, 55 P.2d 320 (1936). This must be established beyond a reasonable doubt, just as if the principal were himself on trial. Aston v. State, 136 Tex.Cr.R. 12, 122 S.W.2d 1073 (1939). It is not necessary, however, that the identity of the principal be established. State v. Kern, 307 N.W.2d 29 (Iowa 1981).

40. Patton v. State, 62 Tex.Cr.R. 71, 126 S.W. 459 (1911).

41. People v. Berger, 131 Cal.App.2d 127, 280 P.2d 136 (1955).

42. As noted in Direct Sales Co. v. United States, 319 U.S. 703, 63 S.Ct. 1265, 87 L.Ed. 1674 (1943), this was the theory in United States v. Falcone, 311 U.S. 205, 61 S.Ct. 204, 85 L.Ed. 128 (1949), which failed because there was no showing that the aider was aware of the conspiracy.

43. See § 5.7.

44. Parker v. Commonwealth, 180 Ky. 102, 201 S.W. 475 (1918).

45. The same would be true of other defenses personal to the principal. See, e.g., People v. Jones, 184 Colo. 96, 518 P.2d 819 (1974) (accessory guilty even if principal not by virtue of insanity defense).

46. 436 F.2d 81 (9th Cir.1971).

47. Quoting from Carbajal-Portillo v. United States, 396 F.2d 944 (9th Cir.1968).

48. Compare, however, the somewhat different characterization by the Supreme Court, discussed in § 5.2(b).

49. The dissenting judge in *Azadian* objected that the result was inconsistent with the doctrine that there must be a guilty principal before there can be an aider or abettor, and that in any event the instant case was distinguishable from Carbajal-Portillo v. United States, 396 F.2d 944 (9th Cir.1968), relied upon by the majority, in that there the entrapper had nothing to do with the decision of the defendant to aid the illegal scheme.

plice) does not have the mental state required for commission of the offense. An excellent example is afforded by the case of *State v. Hayes.*[50] *A* proposed to *B* that they burglarize *C*'s store, and *B* feigned agreement in order to obtain *A*'s arrest. They arrived at the store together, and *A* raised the window and assisted *B* in climbing into the window. *B* handed out some food to *A*. On these facts it was held that *A* could not be convicted of burglary. *A* was not the principal in the first degree, as he did not himself enter the premises, and thus he could be held for the burglary only as an accessory to *B*. *B*, however, did not commit a burglary, for he lacked the intent to permanently deprive *C* of the food. Thus, concluded the court, *A* could not be held as an accessory to *B*'s burglary, for *B* committed no burglary. If the roles of *A* and *B* had been reversed, then *A* would quite clearly be guilty of burglary, which raises the question of whether the fortuitous event of who entered the premises should actually have a bearing on *A*'s criminality.[51] Perhaps *A* should be subject to conviction on the ground that he attempted to aid another in the commission of a crime.[52]

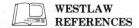 **WESTLAW REFERENCES**

azadian /s 436 +5 81

50. 105 Mo. 76, 16 S.W. 514 (1891).

51. S. Kadish, S. Schulhofer & M. Paulsen, Criminal Law and Its Processes 635 (4th ed. 1983).

52. Ibid. But see State v. Davis, 319 Mo. 1222, 6 S.W.2d 609 (1928), reversing an attempted murder conviction where the defendant solicited a police agent to kill another and the agent, without intent to kill, went to the intended victim's home according to the defendant's plan but did not kill the victim. The court held that a substantial step had not been taken toward commission of the crime.

Model Penal Code § 5.01(3) provides that a person who engages in conduct designed to aid another to commit a crime under circumstances which would make him a party if the crime were committed by the other person is guilty of an attempt to commit the crime even though the crime is not committed or attempted by such other person.

53. People v. Rybka, 16 Ill.2d 394, 158 N.E.2d 17 (1959).

54. State v. Forsha, 190 Mo. 296, 88 S.W. 746 (1905).

55. State v. Allen, 47 Conn. 121 (1879).

(d) Withdrawal From the Crime. One who has given aid or counsel to a criminal scheme sufficient to otherwise be liable for the offense as an accomplice may sometimes escape liability by withdrawing from the crime. A mere change of heart,[53] flight from the crime scene,[54] or an uncommunicated decision not to carry out his part of the scheme [55] will not suffice. Rather, it is necessary that he (1) repudiate his prior aid,[56] or (2) do all that is possible to countermand his prior aid or counsel,[57] and (3) do so before the chain of events has become unstoppable.[58] If the prior aid consisted of supplying materials to be used in commission of the offense, effective withdrawal may require that these materials be reacquired so as to prevent their use by the principal.[59] On the other hand, if one's prior efforts were limited to requesting or encouraging commission of the crime, then an intention to withdraw communicated to the others will be sufficient.[60] In the alternative, in either case an effective withdrawal might also be possible by timely warning to the police or similar actions directed toward preventing the others from committing the crime.[61] It is not necessary that the crime actually have been prevented.[62]

The issue of when withdrawal is a bar to accomplice liability is dealt with in most of the recent recodifications.[63] Some of these statutes impose added requirements, such as

56. This must be communicated repudiation. Karnes v. State, 159 Ark. 240, 252 S.W. 1 (1923); People v. Rybka, 16 Ill.2d 394, 158 N.E.2d 17 (1959); State v. Guptill, 481 A.2d 772 (Me.1984).

57. 1 F. Wharton, Criminal Law 357 (12th ed. 1932).

58. People v. Brown, 26 Ill.2d 308, 186 N.E.2d 321 (1962).

59. Model Penal Code § 2.06, Comment at 326 (1985).

60. State v. Allen, 47 Conn. 121 (1879); State v. Peterson, 213 Minn. 56, 4 N.W.2d 826 (1942); State v. Thomas, 140 N.J.Super. 429, 356 A.2d 433 (1976); Galan v. State, 44 Ohio App. 192, 184 N.E. 40 (1932).

61. Model Penal Code § 2.06, Comment at 326 (1985).

62. State v. Allen, 47 Conn. 121 (1879).

63. Some of these statutes follow Model Penal Code § 2.06(c) by providing that one is not an accomplice if he "(i) wholly deprives [his complicity] of effectiveness in the commission of the offense; or (ii) gives timely warning to the law enforcement authorities or otherwise makes proper effort to prevent the commission of the offense." Some are similar to the Model Penal Code provision, but with

that the withdrawal must not be motivated by a belief that the circumstances increase the probability of detection or apprehension or render accomplishment of the crime more difficult, or by a decision to postpone the crime to another time or transfer the effort to another victim or objective.

Permitting withdrawal under the circumstances stated above so as to avert liability is certainly appropriate. One of the objectives of the criminal law is to prevent crime, and thus it is desirable to provide an inducement to those who have counseled and aided a criminal scheme to take steps to deprive their complicity of effectiveness. Whether the added requirements imposed by some statutes concerning the person's motives are desirable is debatable. In support, it may certainly be contended that one who withdraws merely because of a belief that the chances of apprehension have increased has not truly reformed and that he is still a proper object of criminal sanctions. On the other hand, it may be argued that even one acting under such a motive should be induced to take action directed toward prevention of the crime.

One who has participated in a criminal scheme to a degree sufficient for accomplice liability may also have engaged in conduct which brings him within the definition of conspiracy or solicitation. Whether his withdrawal is a defense to those crimes is a separate matter.[64]

WESTLAW REFERENCES

accomplice accessory (aid*** +2 abet****) /s repent! "change of heart" (withdrawal abandonment /s crime)

(e) Exceptions to Accomplice Liability. Some crimes are so defined by statute or common law that they may be committed only by certain persons or classes of persons. For example, the statutory offense of concealing the death of a bastard typically refers specifically to concealment only by the mother. By definition, the crime of incest covers only those related to the victim in certain ways. And the crime of rape requires that the unconsented sexual intercourse be by a male,[65] excluding the woman's husband[66] and (in some jurisdictions) any boy under the age of fourteen.[67] As to such crimes, may a person who could not directly commit the offense become criminally liable by acting as an accomplice to another who is within the scope of the definition? The courts have consistently answered this in the affirmative.[68]

Thus, as to the crimes mentioned above, liability as an accomplice will extend to the individual who aids the mother in concealing a bastard's death,[69] to one not related to any other party who lends encouragement to an act of incest,[70] and to another woman[71] or a boy under fourteen[72] or the victim's husband[73] who procures or assists another to commit rape. Many other illustrations are to be found in the cases. For example, on an accomplice theory: one not the owner of the destroyed premises may be guilty under a statute making it an offense for the owner of property to burn it with intent to defraud the insurer[74]; one not a public officer may be

---

significant variations. Some do not follow the Model Penal Code approach.

64. See § 6.1(d) and § 6.5(f).

65. State v. Huffman, 141 W.Va. 55, 87 S.E.2d 541 (1955).

66. Ibid.

67. Preddy v. Commonwealth, 184 Va. 765, 36 S.E.2d 549 (1946).

68. E.g., Gibbs v. State, 37 Ariz. 273, 293 P. 976 (1930); Mills v. State, 53 Neb. 263, 73 N.W. 761 (1898); Cody v. State, 361 P.2d 307 (Okl.Crim.App.1961). See Annots., 5 A.L.R. 782 (1920); 74 A.L.R. 1110 (1931); 131 A.L.R. 1322 (1941).

69. State v. Sprague, 4 R.I. 257 (1856); Nichols v. State, 35 Wis. 308 (1874).

70. Cf. Whittaker v. Commonwealth, 95 Ky. 632, 27 S.W. 83 (1894).

71. People v. Haywood, 131 Cal.App.2d 259, 280 P.2d 180 (1955); People v. Trumbley, 252 Ill. 29, 96 N.E. 573 (1911).

72. Law v. Commonwealth, 75 Va. 885 (1881).

73. People v. Chapman, 62 Mich. 280, 28 N.W. 896 (1886); Bohanon v. State, 289 P.2d 400 (Okl.Crim.App. 1955); Rozell v. State, 502 S.W.2d 16 (Tex.Crim.App.1973).

74. Haas v. State, 103 Ohio St. 1, 132 N.E. 158 (1921).

guilty of improperly keeping state records [75] or of misconduct in public office [76]; one not a fiduciary [77] or public officer [78] may be guilty of the crime of embezzlement by such persons; one not the mortgagor may be guilty of the unlawful disposition of mortgaged property [79]; one not a minor may be guilty of illegal possession of alcoholic beverages by a minor [80]; and one not the driver of the car may be guilty of a traffic violation concerning operation of the vehicle.[81]

Such results as these are in no sense inconsistent with the terms of the offenses involved. While the applicable statutes state that these crimes may be committed only by certain persons or classes of persons, it must be remembered that an individual within the scope of the definition *did* commit the crime as a principal in the first degree. The evil or harm with which the legislature was concerned has thus occurred,[82] and the purposes of the criminal law [83] are well served by also holding accountable those persons not covered by the statute who assisted in bringing about the proscribed result.[84]

There are, however, some exceptions to the general principle that a person who assists or encourages a crime is also guilty as an accomplice. For one, the victim of the crime may not be held as an accomplice even though his conduct in a significant sense has assisted in the commission of the crime. "The businessman who yields to the extortion of a racketeer, the parent who pays ransom to the kidnapper, may be unwise or even may be thought immoral; to view them as involved in the commission of the crime confounds the policy embodied in the prohibition." [85] Where the statute in question was enacted for the protection of certain defined persons thought to be in need of special protection, it would clearly be contrary to the legislative purpose to impose accomplice liability upon such a person.[86] Thus the consenting victim may not become a party to statutory rape [87] or a violation of the Mann Act.[88]

Another exception is where the crime is so defined that participation by another is inevitably incident to its commission. It is justified on the ground that the legislature, by specifying the kind of individual who was guilty when involved in a transaction necessarily involving two or more parties, must have intended to leave the participation by the others unpunished.[89] A secondary consideration, equally applicable to the victim ex-

---

75. Brown, State ex rel. v. Thompson, 149 W.Va. 649, 142 S.E.2d 711 (1965).

76. State v. Tronca, 84 Wis.2d 68, 267 N.W.2d 216 (1978).

77. Gibbs v. State, 37 Ariz. 273, 293 P. 976 (1930).

78. Hutchman v. State, 61 Okl.Crim. 117, 66 P.2d 99 (1937).

79. State v. Elliott, 61 Kan. 518, 59 P. 1047 (1900).

80. State v. Norman, 193 Neb. 719, 229 N.W.2d 55 (1975).

81. People v. Hoaglin, 262 Mich. 162, 247 N.W. 141 (1933).

82. Similar reasoning has been used to explain why one can be guilty as an accomplice to an aggravated type of crime without personally engaging in the aggravating factor. See Schroeder v. State, 96 Wis.2d 1, 291 N.W.2d 460 (1980) (unmasked accomplice of masked robber is guilty of robbery while masked); Nicholas v. State, 49 Wis.2d 683, 183 N.W.2d 11 (1971) (unarmed accomplice of armed robber is guilty of armed robbery).

83. See § 1.5.

84. Some of the recent recodifications include an express provision on this subject providing it is no defense that the offense, as defined, can be committed only by a particular class or classes of persons and the accomplice does not belong to such class or classes. See also National Comm'n on Reform of Federal Criminal Laws, Final Report—Proposed New Federal Criminal Code § 401(2)(a) (1971).

85. Model Penal Code § 2.06, Comment at 323–24 (1985).

86. State v. Hayes, 351 N.W.2d 654 (Minn.App.1984) (minor who was furnished liquor not an accomplice to crime of furnishing liquor to minor); Regina v. Tyrell, 17 Cox Crim.Cas. 716 (1893).

87. Ibid.

88. Gebardi v. United States, 287 U.S. 112, 53 S.Ct. 35, 77 L.Ed. 206 (1932). Compare United States v. Southard, 700 F.2d 1 (1st Cir.1983) (a gambler-accomplice of those violating statute covering persons "engaged in the business of betting or wagering" was neither victim nor person for whose protection this statute was passed, and thus did not come within this exception).

89. Ex parte Cooper, 162 Cal. 81, 121 P. 318 (1912). Or, if such an exception is included in a new code, it may be justified as follows: "If legislators know that buyers will not be viewed as accomplices in sales unless the statute indicates that this behavior is included in the prohibition, they will focus on the problem as they frame the definition of the crime. And since the exception is confined to behavior 'inevitably incident to' the commis-

ception, is that if the law were otherwise convictions would be more difficult to obtain in those jurisdictions requiring corroboration of an accomplice's testimony.[90] Thus, under this exception one having intercourse with a prostitute is not liable as a party to the crime of prostitution,[91] a purchaser is not a party to the crime of illegal sale,[92] an unmarried man is not guilty as a party to the crime of adultery where the legislature has only specified punishment for the married participant,[93] and a female welfare recipient is not guilty as a party to a male's offense of receiving subsistence from such a person.[94]

The Model Penal Code gives express recognition to these two exceptions to accomplice liability,[95] as do many of the recent recodifications.[96]

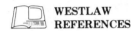

WESTLAW
REFERENCES

find 700f2d1

§ 6.9 Post-Crime Aid: Accessory After the Fact, Misprision and Compounding

At common law, one not himself a principal in the commission of a felony was an accessory after the fact if a completed felony had theretofore been committed by another; he knew of the commission of the felony by the other person; and he gave aid to the felon personally for the purpose of hindering the

felon's apprehension, conviction, or punishment. Unlike the principal in the second degree and accessory before the fact, the accessory after the fact is generally not treated as a party to the felony nor subject to the same punishment prescribed for the felony.

Misprision of felony, consisting of concealment of a known felony by one who was not a principal or accessory before the fact to the felony, is no longer an offense in most jurisdictions. The offense of compounding crime consists of the receipt of some consideration in return for an agreement not to prosecute or inform on another who is known to have committed an offense.

(a) Accessory After the Fact. At common law accessories after the fact existed only in relation to felonies. When treason was committed, all such accessories were considered to be principals,[1] although the situation may be otherwise in the United States because of the constitutional description of the elements of treason.[2] In the absence of a specific statutory provision to the contrary, one does not become an accessory after the fact by giving aid to a misdemeanant.[3]

There are three basic requirements which must be met to constitute one an accessory after the fact. The first of these is that a completed felony must have been committed.[4] It is not enough that the aider had a mistaken belief that the other person committed a felo-

---

sion of the crime, the problem, we repeat inescapably presents itself in defining the crime." Model Penal Code § 2.06, Comment at 325 (1985).

90. Id. at 324–25 n. 81, noting that the corroboration requirement exists by statute in at least 18 states.

91. People v. Anonymous, 161 Misc. 379, 292 N.Y.S. 282 (1936).

92. United States v. Farrar, 281 U.S. 624, 50 S.Ct. 425, 74 L.Ed. 1078 (1930); Wilson v. State, 130 Ark. 204, 196 S.W. 921 (1917); Wakeman v. Chambers, 69 Iowa 169, 28 N.W. 498 (1886).

93. Ex parte Cooper, 162 Cal. 81, 121 P. 318 (1912).

94. State v. Bearcub, 1 Or.App. 579, 465 P.2d 252 (1970).

95. Model Penal Code § 2.06(6).

96. National Comm'n on Reform of Federal Criminal Laws, Final Report—Proposed New Federal Criminal Code § 401 (1971), however, takes a more limited approach: "A person is not liable under this subsection for the conduct of another person when he is either expressly

or by implication made not accountable for such conduct by the statute defining the offense or related provisions, because he is a victim of the offense or otherwise." The Model Penal Code criteria were rejected "because they may impose too great a limitation on all Federal regulatory legislation, which is frequently enacted without careful regard for principles of criminal liability." 1 National Comm'n on Reform of Federal Criminal Laws, Working Papers 158 (1970).

§ 6.9

1. 4 W. Blackstone, Commentaries on the Laws of England* 35 (1765).

2. U.S. Const. art. III, § 3 specifies what acts will constitute treason. This is an exclusive definition. See United States v. Burr, 8 U.S. (4 Cranch) 455 (1808).

3. 1 J. Bishop, Criminal Law § 705 (9th ed. 1923).

4. Harrel v. State, 39 Miss. 702 (1861); State v. Price, 278 S.C. 266, 294 S.E.2d 426 (1982); State v. Tollett, 173 Tenn. 477, 121 S.W.2d 525 (1938); 4 W. Blackstone, supra note 1, at 38.

ny,[5] nor is it sufficient that the person assisted had theretofore been accused of a felony.[6] But if the felony has been committed prior to the aid, it is not also necessary that the felon have been already charged with the crime.[7] Because the felony must be complete at the time the assistance is rendered, a person cannot be convicted as an accessory after the fact to a murder because of aid given after the murderer's acts but before the victim's death.[8]

The second requirement is that the person giving aid must have known of the perpetration of the felony by the one he aids.[9] Mere suspicion is not enough.[10]

Finally, the aid must have been given to the felon personally for the purpose of hindering the felon's apprehension, conviction or punishment.[11] Because the aid must be to the felon personally, one does not become an accessory after the fact by, for example, receiving and concealing what are known to be stolen goods.[12] There must be, in the mind of

the aider, the objective of impeding law enforcement, and thus it is not sufficient that the felon was actually aided if the assistance was given out of charity or for some similar motive.[13]

As to what acts constitute the prohibited aid, some early writers seem to have assumed that any assistance would suffice. Blackstone, for example, asserted that "any assistance whatever given to the felon, to hinder his being apprehended, tried or suffering punishment, makes the assistor an accessory." [14] However, the mere failure to report the felony or to arrest the felon will not suffice.[15] Illustrative of the acts which qualify, assuming the presence of the other requirements, are harboring and concealing the felon,[16] aiding the felon in making his escape,[17] concealing, destroying or altering evidence,[18] inducing a witness to absent himself [19] or to remain silent,[20] giving false testimony at an official

5. People v. Hardin, 207 Cal.App.2d 336, 24 Cal.Rptr. 563 (1962).

6. Poston v. State, 12 Tex.App. 408 (1882).

7. Howard v. People, 97 Colo. 550, 51 P.2d 594 (1935); Heyen v. State, 114 Neb. 783, 210 N.W. 165 (1926).

8. Harrel v. State, 39 Miss. 702 (1861); State v. Williams, 229 N.C. 348, 49 S.E.2d 617 (1848). But under such circumstances, as suggested in these decisions, the aider may be found to be an accessory after the fact to the felonious assault.

9. Commonwealth v. Devlin, 366 Mass. 132, 314 N.E.2d 897 (1974); Commonwealth v. Holiday, 349 Mass. 126, 206 N.E.2d 691 (1965); Regina v. Butterfield, 1 Cox Crim.Cas. 93 (1845). Such knowledge must be personal rather than constructive, State v. Rider, 229 Kan. 394, 625 P.2d 425 (1981), but may be inferred from the facts. White v. People, 81 Ill. 333 (1875).

10. Harrel v. State, 39 Miss. 702 (1861); State v. Empey, 79 Iowa 460, 44 N.W. 707 (1890).

11. Lowe v. People, 135 Colo. 209, 209 P.2d 601 (1957); Loyd v. State, 42 Ga. 221 (1871); Maddox v. Commonwealth, 349 S.W.2d 686 (Ky.1960).

Thus, if the defendant lied to the police when they asked if he had seen the felon, but did so in his own interest rather than to aid the felon, he is not guilty. State v. Clifford, 263 Or. 436, 502 P.2d 1371 (1972). But, the intent to aid need not be the sole intent. State v. Kelley, 120 N.H. 14, 413 A.2d 300 (1980).

12. Loyd v. State, 42 Ga. 221 (1871); State v. Jackson, 344 So.2d 961 (La.1977); Wren v. Commonwealth, 67 Va. 952 (1875). The requirement of personal assistance is sometimes used so as to avoid making criminal certain

kinds of assistance which perhaps, as a matter of policy, should not be forbidden. See State v. Doty, 57 Kan. 835, 48 P. 145 (1897), holding that a mother who persuades her daughter to lie to police to protect the girl's stepfather from prosecution for criminal intercourse with the daughter does not "aid," since there was no personal assistance.

13. Hearn v. State, 43 Fla. 151, 29 So. 433 (1901) (proof did not show that whiskey and money sent to prisoner were intended to be used to bribe jailers in an escape); State v. Jett, 69 Kan. 788, 77 P. 546 (1904) (taking rape victim out of state to have her child found to be motivated by desire to protect girl's reputation rather than conceal rapist's crime).

14. 4 W. Blackstone, supra note 1, at 37.

15. Satterfield v. State, 252 Ark. 747, 483 S.W.2d 171 (1972); Levering v. Commonwealth, 132 Ky. 666, 117 S.W. 253 (1909); State v. Brown, 197 Neb. 131, 247 N.W.2d 616 (1976); Wren v. Commonwealth, 67 Va. 952 (1875).

16. United States v. Thornton, 178 F.Supp. 42 (E.D. N.Y.1959). However, mere passive refusal to consent to an unconstitutional search for the fugitive may not provide the basis for conviction. United States v. Prescott, 581 F.2d 1343 (9th Cir.1978).

17. United States v. Balano, 618 F.2d 624 (10th Cir. 1979).

18. United States v. Elkins, 732 F.2d 1280 (6th Cir. 1984); People v. Farmer, 196 N.Y. 65, 89 N.E. 462 (1909). Contra: Heath v. State, 160 Ga. 678, 128 S.E. 913 (1924).

19. Harrison v. State, 69 Tex.Cr.R. 291, 153 S.W. 139 (1912).

20. Fields v. State, 213 Ark. 899, 214 S.W.2d 230 (1948).

inquiry into the crime,[21] and giving false information to the police in order to divert suspicion away from the felon.[22] (Where, as is often true in modern legislation, certain types of aid are specified by statute,[23] all of the foregoing may not suffice.[24])

A principal in either the first or second degree may not also become an accessory after the fact by his subsequent acts.[25] However, it has been held that one who was only an accessory before the fact may also be an accessory after the fact.[26] If one does not render aid or encouragement before or during the offense, although he was present at the offense, and later gives aid, he will be liable only as an accessory after the fact.[27]

At common law, only one class was excused from liability for being accessories after the fact. Wives did not become accessories by aiding their husbands.[28] No other relationship, including that of husband to wife, would suffice.[29] But many states broadened the exemption to cover other close relatives.[30] The exemption provisions range from those exculpating husbands, wives, parents, and children to broad exclusions of ascendants, descendants and even servants.[31] Such broadening of the exemption is grounded in the assumption that it is unrealistic to expect persons to be

deterred from giving aid to their close relations.[32]

Originally, all principals and accessories were felons and thus all were punishable with death,[33] although this was soon modified by granting accessories after the fact the benefit of clergy.[34] Accessories after the fact were again subject to the same punishment as their principals when benefit of clergy became obsolete.[35] This was later changed by statute in England so that one who renders aid after a crime is guilty of a separate, lesser offense.[36] Almost all American jurisdictions prescribed penalties for the accessory after the fact without reference to the penalty attached to the principal offense.[37]

This development whereby the accessory after the fact is dealt with in a distinct way is a most appropriate one and does not conflict at all with the modern tendency to abolish the distinctions between principals in the first degree, principals in the second degree, and accessories before the fact. The latter three types of offenders have all played a part in the commission of the crime and are quite appropriately held accountable for its commission. The accessory after the fact, on the other hand, had no part in causing the crime; his offense is instead that of interfering with

---

21. Blakeley v. State, 24 Tex.Cr.R. 616, 7 S.W. 233 (1888).

22. People v. Duty, 269 Cal.App.2d 97, 74 Cal.Rptr. 606 (1969); Commonwealth v. Wood, 302 Mass. 265, 19 N.E.2d 320 (1939). Certain lies, such as about not having recently seen the felon, are sometimes deemed insufficient. State v. Clifford, 263 Or. 436, 502 P.2d 1371 (1972).

23. See text following note 49 infra.

24. See, e.g., United States v. Magness, 456 F.2d 976 (9th Cir.1972) (statute proscribes "harboring or concealing" wanted person not violated by defendant's false statement to authorities that he had not seen that person for many years).

25. Crosby v. State, 179 Miss. 149, 175 So. 180 (1937).

26. State v. Butler, 17 Vt. 145 (1845).

27. Smith v. United States, 306 F.2d 286 (D.C.Cir.1962); White v. People, 81 Ill. 333 (1876).

28. 4 W. Blackstone, supra note 1, at 38–39.

29. Ibid.

30. Model Penal Code § 242.3, Comment at 231 (1980).

31. Morse, A Survey of Accessory After the Fact Exemptions, 54 Dick.L.Rev. 324 (1950). See State v. Williams, 142 Vt. 81, 451 A.2d 1142 (1982) (statute excepts aid

to spouse, parents, grandparents, children, grandchildren, or siblings; defendant not guilty where he gave aid which helped both principals, one his brother and one not related).

32. Contra is Model Penal Code § 242.3, Comment at 237 (1980), noting that section "does not contain a statutory exemption, in part on the ground that this is a factor that can be taken into account at sentencing. It is hard to justify any particular limitation on an exemption provision. Furthermore, exemption rules create trial difficulties if the government bears the burden of proving that none of the specified relations exist." See, e.g., Orr v. State, 129 Fla. 398, 176 So. 510 (1937), holding the burden is on the state to disprove an asserted common law marriage.

33. 2 J. Stephen, History, of the Criminal Law of England 231 (1883).

34. Id. at 232. Any man who could read was allowed to plead benefit of clergy and thereby avoid capital punishment. 1 J. Stephen, History of the Criminal Law of England 461 (1883).

35. This occurred in England in 1827. Id. at 472.

36. 11 & 12 Vict., c. 46, § 1 (1848).

37. Model Penal Code § 242.3, Comment at 238 (1980).

the processes of justice and is best dealt with in those terms.[38]

Because the original view was that one who helped a felon avoid justice was an accomplice in the felony, the procedural problems described earlier concerning the accessory before the fact [39] also existed with respect to the accessory after the fact. Most significant of these problems was that an accessory after the fact could not be tried until after the principal was found guilty.[40] This meant that the accessory was immune from prosecution if the principal had been acquitted or had not been prosecuted because of his death or escape. But most jurisdictions now only require that the fact of the completed felony be proved in the trial of the accessory after the fact.[41]

This is not to suggest that all of the procedural reforms concerning the law of parties to crime are or should be equally applicable to the accessory after the fact. Unlike the principals in the first and second degree and the accessory before the fact, he has not actually had a part in causing the crime. Thus, while it is now generally accepted that a defendant may be charged as if a principal and convicted on proof that he aided another,[42] a conviction as an accessory after the fact cannot be sustained upon an indictment charging the principal crime.[43] This is as it should be, for a charge alleging the defendant's guilt of the principal crime only places him on notice that he must defend against accountability for the crime as a principal or accessory before the

fact, not that he must be prepared to meet evidence that he aided the perpetrator after the crime had been committed.[44]

Today, the accessory after the fact situation is dealt with by statute in most jurisdictions. Even in states with modern recodifications, the "accessory after the fact" terminology is still occasionally used. But in the great majority of these states the offense is characterized as "hindering" apprehension or prosecution, or is otherwise described to reflect its true character as a crime involving interference with the processes of government.[45] Most of these statutes cover aid to both felons and misdemeanants,[46] although several are limited to those who aid felons.

As for the required mental state, virtually all of the statutes in the modern recodifications substantially conform to the Model Penal Code approach [47] by requiring an intent or purpose to hinder apprehension, prosecution, conviction or punishment. In a few states, however, the mental element has been broadened to include the situation in which the intent is "to assist a person in profiting or benefiting from the commission" of a felony or any crime. One significant aspect of the common intent-to-hinder formulation is that it can usually be construed to "have dispensed with the necessity that it be shown that the putative offender actually committed a crime and that the person rendering assistance was aware of that fact." [48] But some of these statutes adhere to the common law approach by requiring that the defendant have known

38. This is not to say, however, that the nature of the crime committed by the principal is not a relevant consideration in determining what punishment is appropriate for the accessory after the fact, especially where aiding misdemeanors is also criminal. "The more serious the underlying crime involved, the greater the importance to the community of successful pursuit of the putative offender." Model Penal Code § 242.3, Comment at 239 (1980).

39. See § 6.6(d).

40. 1 F. Wharton, Criminal Law 372 (12th ed. 1932).

41. Maddox v. Commonwealth, 349 S.W.2d 686 (Ky. 1960); Lewis v. State, 285 Md. 705, 404 A.2d 1073 (1979); State ex rel. Brown v. Thompson, 149 W.Va. 649, 142 S.E.2d 711 (1965).

42. Johnson v. State, 453 P.2d 390 (Okl.1969); State v. Frazier, 76 Wn.2d 373, 456 P.2d 352 (1969).

43. State v. Townsend, 201 Kan. 122, 439 P.2d 70 (1968); State v. Cole, 502 S.W.2d 443 (Mo.App.1973); State v. Stevenson, 2 Or.App. 38, 465 P.2d 720 (1970).

44. At least in some jurisdictions, the prosecutor as a consequence is allowed to charge in the alternative and go to trial on the inconsistent theories that defendant was a party to the crime and was an accessory after the fact. Thomas v. State, 275 Ind. 499, 417 N.E.2d 1124 (1981).

45. Sometimes the offense is called "obstructing" justice or prosecution or "tampering" with evidence, sometimes it is characterized as "assisting," "aiding," or "harboring," a felon or criminal.

46. A few, however, exclude certain minor misdemeanors.

47. Model Penal Code § 242.3.

48. Model Penal Code § 242.3, Comment at 229 (1980).

of the guilt of the person aided, and some others appear to require that such guilt in fact exist. In contrast to these are a few other provisions which expressly state that it is sufficient that the defendant believed or reasonably believed the person aided was guilty.

The great majority of the provisions in the modern codes specify the kinds of aid which are proscribed. This is as it should be, for experience has shown that a "general prohibition of any 'aid' is likely to lead courts to haphazardly narrowing interpretations or perhaps to excess coverage." [49] Although the description of the specifics varies somewhat from state to state, it is nonetheless possible to generalize about the kinds of aid that will often or sometimes suffice. Five kinds of aid usually are proscribed: (1) harboring or concealing the criminal; (2) providing him with certain means (e.g., a weapon, transportation, a disguise) of avoiding apprehension; (3) concealing, destroying or tampering with evidence; (4) warning the criminal of his impending discovery or apprehension [50]; and (5) using force, deception or intimidation to prevent or obstruct the criminal's discovery or apprehension. To this list, a few jurisdictions have added the giving of false information in certain circumstances. Some other states include aid in the nature of securing the proceeds of the crime, while several other states instead follow the Model Penal Code approach [51] by making activity of that general type the separate offense of aiding consummation of crime.

The great majority of these statutes do not give special attention to aid given to a family member. Some, however, recognize an exception in the case of aid given to a relative. A few others strike a compromise by providing that the fact the person aided was a relative reduces the grade of the aider's offense.

 **WESTLAW REFERENCES**

110k82

(b) Misprision of Felony. [52] Misprision of felony consisted of a failure to report or prosecute a known felon. [53] It was sometimes said also to include a failure to prevent the commission of a felony, [54] although this view appears to be erroneous. [55] One was not guilty of this common law misdemeanor if he was accountable for the felony as either a principal or accessory before the fact. [56]

It is doubtful whether this offense ever had a meaningful existence beyond the textbook writers. [57] The offense was said to be "practically obsolete" in England almost a century ago, [58] and the few prosecutions in that country in recent years have been limited to the most extreme situations. [59] Doubt has been expressed as to whether this offense was ever inherited by the United States as a part of the common law. [60] While "it may be the duty of

---

49. Model Penal Code § 242.3, Comment at 233 (1980).

50. Some but not all of these provisions exclude a warning given in an effort to bring the other person into compliance with the law.

51. Model Penal Code § 242.4.

52. See Allen, Misprision, 78 L.Q.Rev. 40 (1962); Glazebrook, Misprision of Felony—Shadow or Phantom?, 8 Am.J.Legal Hist. 189, 283 (1964); Glazebrook, How Long Then is the Arm of the Law to Be?, 25 Mod.L.Rev. 301 (1962); Goldberg, Misprision of Felony: An Old Concept in New Context, 52 A.B.A.J. 148 (1966); Howard, Misprisions, Compoundings and Compromises, 1959 Crim.L.Rev. 750 (1959); Yahuda, Misprision of Felony, 106 Sol.J. 124 (1962); Comment, 28 U.Fla.L.Rev. 199 (1975).

53. 1 J. Bishop, Criminal Law § 717 (9th ed. 1923). Pope v. State, 38 Md.App. 520, 382 A.2d 880 (1978), affirmed in part, reversed in part 284 Md. 309, 396 A.2d 1054 (1979), states that for a misprision conviction the necessary elements are: (1) knowledge of the felony; (2) a reasonable opportunity to disclose without risk of harm;

and (3) concealment of the felony, but that prior conviction of the felon is unnecessary.

54. 1 J. Bishop, Criminal Law § 717 (9th ed. 1923).

55. G. Williams, Criminal Law: The General Part 422 (2d ed. 1961).

56. 1 J. Bishop, Criminal Law § 717 (9th ed. 1923). Cf. State v. Carson, 274 S.C. 316, 262 S.E.2d 918 (1980) (no self-incrimination defense to misprision charge unless defendant was an accessory to or principal in the felony concealed).

57. Glazebrook, supra note 52.

58. 2 J. Stephen, History of the Criminal Law of England 238 (1883).

59. E.g., Sykes v. Director of Public Prosecutions, [1961] 3 All E.R. 33, involving the failure to disclose knowledge of the theft of pistols, submachine guns and ammunition.

60. Marbury v. Brooks, 20 U.S. 556, 5 L.Ed. 522 (1822) (dictum); Holland v. State, 302 So.2d 806 (Fla.App.1974);

a citizen to accuse every offender, and to proclaim every offense which comes to his knowledge, * * * the law which would punish him in every case for not performing this duty is too harsh for man." [61]

In virtually all of the modern recodifications, a misprision statute has not been included. There is a misprision of felony statute in the United States Code,[62] but it is not a true misprision statute in that it requires an act of concealment in addition to failure to disclose.[63] Even this statute has fallen into disuse,[64] and would be eliminated from the proposed new federal criminal code in favor of the more common hindering of law enforcement offense.[65]

 WESTLAW REFERENCES

misprision +2 felon*

(c) Compounding Crime. Compounding crime consists of the receipt of some property or other consideration in return for an agreement not to prosecute or inform on one who has committed a crime.[66] There are three elements to this offense at common law and under the typical compounding statute: (1) the agreement not to prosecute; (2) knowl-

edge of the actual commission of a crime; and (3) the receipt of some consideration.

The agreement is essential.[67] Thus, if a criminal returns or gives property to the victim or another merely in the hope that the other person will not commence prosecution, there is no compounding.[68] Modern statutes vary as to what kind of agreement is necessary. An agreement not to seek or initiate prosecution will usually suffice, but some of the statutes in the modern recodifications recognize other possibilities as well. Among them are agreements to abandon a prosecution, to refrain from aiding a prosecution, to withhold evidence or procure the absence of witnesses, to conceal the offense, or to not report the crime.

That a crime has actually been committed is usually held to be an element of the offense.[69] However, some courts, under the language of individual statutes, have held that the showing of an actual offense is not required.[70]

There must also be some consideration.[71] This includes money or anything of value or advantage.[72] The consideration may pass to

---

Pope v. State, 284 Md. 309, 396 A.2d 1054 (1979); People v. Lefkovitz, 294 Mich. 263, 293 N.W. 642 (1940); 54 Harv. L.Rev. 506 (1941). But see State v. Carson, 274 S.C. 316, 262 S.E.2d 918 (1980) (common law offense of misprision of felony exists in the state).

61. Marbury v. Brooks, 20 U.S. 556, 5 L.Ed. 522 (1822).

62. 18 U.S.C.A. § 4.

63. United States v. Ciambrone, 750 F.2d 1416 (9th Cir. 1984) (thus this crime not committed by defendant when he disclosed some knowledge about counterfeiting operation, but withheld additional information because the government would not pay him for the information); United States v. Davila, 698 F.2d 715 (5th Cir.1983); United States v. Johnson, 546 F.2d 1225 (5th Cir.1977).

In United States v. Daddano, 432 F.2d 1119 (7th Cir. 1970), the court thus rejected the defendants' contention that the statute could not be applied to them because it would compel them to be witnesses against themselves in that if they reported their information about the bank robbery they could reasonably fear that the information could lead to their own conviction of being accessories after the fact.

Compare United States v. Kuh, 541 F.2d 672 (7th Cir. 1976), holding that defendants who knowingly received stolen money following its concealment could not be charged under the misprision statute for failure to disclose the underlying robbery, as the object of the Fifth Amend-

ment privilege against self-incrimination is that a person "not be compelled to give information which might tend to show he himself has committed a crime."

64. 1 National Comm'n on Reform of Federal Criminal Laws, Working Papers 530 n. 5 (1970).

65. National Comm'n on Reform of Federal Criminal Laws, Final Report—Proposed New Federal Criminal Code § 1303 (1971).

66. 4 W. Blackstone, supra note 1, at 133.

67. Austin v. Feron, 289 Ill.App. 528, 7 N.E.2d 476 (1937).

68. Fidelity & Deposit Co. v. Grand National Bank, 69 F.2d 177 (8th Cir.1934).

69. E.g., Davidson v. State, 29 Okl.Crim. 46, 232 P. 120 (1925).

70. Sheppard v. State, 151 Ga. 27, 105 S.E. 601 (1921); Fribly v. State, 42 Ohio St. 205 (1864).

71. Commonwealth v. Pease, 16 Mass. 91 (1819). "Absent consideration, a mere promise to refrain from reporting a crime did not fall within the compounding offense, no matter how serious the crime." Model Penal Code § 242.5, Comment at 246 (1980).

72. Commonwealth v. Pease, 16 Mass. 91 (1819); State v. Jackson, 344 So.2d 961 (La.1977).

another, as in a third-party beneficiary contract.[73]

Only the party who receives the consideration is criminally liable; the former criminal is not guilty of compounding by virtue of his act in giving the consideration.[74] But some modern statutes also cover the person who pays or offers to pay the consideration. A compounder need not, however, be the victim of the former criminal act.[75] At common law the compounding of any crime was itself an offense,[76] and this also is true of the compounding statutes found in most modern codes. But some states limit the offense to the compounding of felonies. This is a questionable basis for distinction, however, in that the more logical basis for barring compromise is "the likelihood that [the offender] will repeat his aggressions against others."[77] Some statutes even allow the compromise of felonies by victims, although this often is permitted only with judicial approval.[78]

It certainly makes sense to exclude from the crime of compounding the receipt of a benefit which the victim of the crime "believes to be due as restitution or indemnification for harm caused by the offense,"[79] as some states do. As explained by the draftsmen of the Model Penal Code:

In general, our society does not use penal sanctions to compel reporting of crime. [A] victim of crime who refrains from reporting the offense because his loss has been made good is no more derelict in his societal duty than one who, out of indifference or affection for the offender, fails to report known criminal conduct.

* * * In a variety of ways, current practice impugns the application of penal sanctions to the victim who agrees to forego prosecution in return for restitution. First, liability for compounding is easily evaded by accepting indemnification without explicit agreement to prosecution in return for restitution. * * *

Furthermore, many laws and practices of enforcement openly tolerate and sometimes actively encourage private compromise of criminal liability. [P]rosecutors themselves are often content to drop criminal proceedings when the alleged offender agrees to make appropriate restitution to the victim.[80]

Judicial approval, it has been argued, should not be a requirement under such circumstances.[81] It seldom is under modern compounding statutes.[82]

 WESTLAW REFERENCES

(compounding /1 crime felony) (fail*** +s report +s crime)

---

73. Hays v. State, 15 Ga.App. 386, 83 S.E. 502 (1914); State v. Ruthven, 58 Iowa 121, 12 N.W. 235 (1882); State v. Ash, 33 Or. 86, 54 P. 184 (1898).

74. Aikman v. Wheeling, 120 W.Va. 46, 195 S.E. 667 (1939); Note, 55 Dick.L.Rev. 356, 359 (1951).

75. "Some prosecutions are against witnesses or bystanders who accept money for a promise not to report or testify about criminal conduct with which they have no private concern as victim." Model Penal Code § 242.5, Comment at 251–52 (1980).

76. State v. Carver, 69 N.H. 216, 39 A. 973 (1898), noting however that compromise of a misdemeanor "of a very low grade" is not criminal.

77. Model Penal Code § 242.5, Comment at 250 (1980), noting that there are aggressive recidivist misdemeanants and also felons who do not present a continuing danger.

78. See § 5.11(d).

79. This is an affirmative defense under Model Penal Code § 242.5.

80. Model Penal Code § 242.5, Comment at 251–52 (1980).

81. Model Penal Code § 242.5, Comment at 253 (1980), arguing that a requirement of approval as to reported offenses would be contrary to the offender's desire to avoid public exposure, official inquiry and the chance of prosecution, and that a requirement of approval as to unreported offenses is unnecessary in that the prosecutor's discretion then governs.

82. Exceptions are Ariz.Rev.Stat. § 13–2405; Ga.Code § 26–2504; Vernon's Tex.Code Ann., Penal Code § 38.06 (requires that the settlement must be the "result of an agreement negotiated with the assistance or acquiescence of an attorney for the state").

Chapter 7

CRIMES AGAINST THE PERSON

Table of Sections

---

§ 7.1   Murder—"Malice Aforethought" and "Living Human Being"

Murder is a common law crime whose complete development required several centuries. Though murder is frequently defined as the unlawful killing of another "living human being" with "malice aforethought," in modern times the latter phrase does not even approximate its literal meaning. Hence it is preferable not to rely upon that misleading expression for an understanding of murder but rather to consider the various types of murder (typed according to the mental element) which the common law came to recognize and which exist today in most jurisdictions: (1) intent-to-kill murder; (2) intent-to-do-serious-bodily-injury murder; (3) depraved-heart murder; and (4) felony murder. A comparatively modern statutory innovation divides murder into degrees of murder for purposes of awarding punishment.

(a) "Malice Aforethought, Express or Implied". Murder [1] is a common law crime—that is, it was created by the English judges rather than by the English legislature. Though it was first recognized many centuries ago, its exact boundaries were not determined all at once, but rather were worked out by the

judges over several centuries of time as a parade of cases, involving different fact situations, came before the judges for decision. At first the judges thought in terms of two broad categories—felonious homicide (without as yet any subdivision into murder and manslaughter) and non-felonious homicide.[2] As time went on, felonious homicide was divided (with some help from the legislature) into murder and manslaughter, and murder was defined as the unlawful killing of another human being "with malice aforethought." What, in these early days, did "malice aforethought" mean? Literally, "malice" in the murder setting required at least an intent to kill, plus perhaps an element of hatred, spite or ill-will; "aforethought" required that the intent to kill be thought out in advance of the killing. At first the judges in fact did require for murder that the defendant actually have a previously thought-out (i.e., premeditated) intent to kill, though probably the spite, etc., was never actually necessary.[3] Later (about 1550), English statutes made it murder intentionally to kill another by poisoning or by lying in wait; but these two situations would seem to be no more than typical cases involving a premeditated intent to kill, the almost

---

1. The leading general discussions of murder and manslaughter are: G. Fletcher, Rethinking Criminal Law chs. 4 & 5 (1978); R. Moreland, The Law of Homicide (1952); Wechsler & Michael, A Rationale of the Law of Homicide, 37 Colum.L.Rev. 701, 1261 (1937); Perkins, The Law of Homicide, 36 J.Crim.L. & Crim. 391 (1946). See also Model Penal Code §§ 210.1, 210.2, 210.3, Comments (1980).

2. Non-felonious homicide was itself divided into excusable homicide (a crime, though not a felony, which was pardonable, and which as a matter of practice was always pardoned) and justifiable homicide (no crime at all).

3. E.g., *A*, according to his preconceived plan, kills *B* in order to take his money, or to put him out of his misery, not in order to satisfy any feeling of ill-will against *B*. This would be a killing with malice aforethought.

literal meaning of "malice aforethought." So
at this time in the history of criminal homicide there was only one type of murder: unlawfully killing another with a premeditated
intent to kill.

Thereafter the judges started to invent
some new types of murder where there existed no premeditated intent to kill. First of all,
when the defendant intentionally killed his
victim in a heat of passion aroused in him by
the conduct of the victim—the issue being
whether the defendant should be guilty of
murder or of voluntary manslaughter—the
judges decided that manslaughter required
that the defendant's passion be reasonable. If
he was unreasonably provoked, or if a reasonable man would have cooled off in the interval between the provocation and the defendant's fatal blow, then the defendant, though
actually in a passion and hence unable to
premeditate, would be guilty of murder. No
longer then did murder require malice aforethought in the literal sense of premeditated
intent to kill. Moreover, as time went by the
requirement of premeditation, in situations
other than that involving unreasonable passion, was dropped, so that in all situations an
unpremeditated intent to kill would do for
murder.[4]

Secondly, when the defendant unintentionally killed another person in the commission
of a felony—as where A set fire to B's house
(arson) and accidentally B or a member of his
family was burned to death—the judges held
this to be murder ("felony murder"), though
the defendant did not intend to kill at all and
a fortiori did not premeditate a killing.

Thirdly, when the defendant unintentionally killed another person while conducting
himself in an extremely negligent way
("evincing a depraved heart," as this sort of
conduct was generally described)—as where

A, a workman constructing a tall building,
without looking tossed a large stone from the
roof onto the busy roadway below, thereby
killing B, a pedestrian—the judges held such
conduct to be murder ("depraved-heart murder"), though the stone-thrower did not intend
to kill anyone.

Lastly, the judges took one more step toward the destruction of the idea that premedi-
tated-intent-to-kill murder is the sole type of
murder: it was decided that an intent to do
serious bodily injury short of death would do
for murder.

The judges still continued to say that murder is committed by one who unlawfully kills
another "with malice aforethought," now
however adding the phrase "express or implied," the word "implied" covering the four
situations just described wherein literally
there exists no premeditated intent to kill.
Modern courts and legislatures occasionally
define murder in terms of "malice aforethought, express or implied," by which they
mean the same types of murder as those
which the English judges ultimately recognized, including felony murder, depraved-
heart murder, intent-to-do-serious-bodily-injury murder and murder committed in an unreasonable passion.[5]

The moral to be drawn from this short
history of murder is that it will not solve
modern homicide cases to say simply that
murder is the unlawful killing of another
with malice aforethought, that manslaughter
is the unlawful killing of another without
malice aforethought, and that no crime is
committed if the killing is lawful. For an
understanding of the crime of murder, it is
necessary to consider, one by one, the various
types of murder which the judges created and
which, in general, remain to this day, and to
note those statutory or case-law changes to

4. Although premeditation is no longer necessary for
murder, in modern times in the United States the existence or absence of premeditation accompanying the murderer's intent to kill serves, in most states, to distinguish
between first-degree and second-degree murder. See
§ 7.7(a).

5. The foregoing history is contained in N.Y. State Law
Revision Commission, Communication to the Legislature,

Legislative Doc. No. 65, 536–540 (1937), reprinted in L.
Hall & S. Glueck, Criminal Law & Its Enforcement 37–39
(2d ed. 1958). See also R. Moreland, The Law of Homicide
chs. 1–3 (1952); 1 J. Stephen, A History of the Criminal
Law of England (1883).

these types which legislatures or courts have made in modern times.[6]

To sum up these various modern types of murder, they are: (1) intent-to-kill murder; (2) intent-to-do-serious-bodily-injury murder; (3) felony murder; (4) depraved-heart murder. We shall also consider whether there is a fifth type: (5) resisting-lawful-arrest murder. In addition to the problem of what constitutes murder—a matter developed by the common law with very little statutory intervention—there is the problem in many jurisdictions in America of how murder is divided into degrees of murder—an entirely statutory matter, since the judges themselves never undertook to divide murder into degrees. This book will deal first with murder in general, then with the ways in which murder is divided into degrees.

WESTLAW REFERENCES

synopsis,digest("malice aforethought" /s express implied /s intent! unintent!)

(b) Statutory Definitions of Murder. Several states have statutes which punish murder but which do not undertake to define murder and which thus adopt the common law definition of murder, including its various types. A typical statute of this type provides that "murder" committed in this way or that way constitutes first-degree murder; all other "murder" is second-degree murder.[7] Most of the modern recodifications, however, contain

statutes which define murder in terms of "killing" or "causing death" and which therefore do not necessarily come out with the same types of murder as common-law murder.[8] The following sections which discuss the common-law types of murder must be read with this fact in mind.

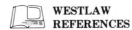

WESTLAW REFERENCES

topic(203) /p murder /3 define* definition

(c) When Does Life Begin? It is a general requirement of the law of homicide that the victim be a living human being. Shooting a dead body is not homicide, although it may be another crime.[9] The question of life arises most frequently in the cases involving destruction of the human fetus. At early common law the fetus was considered alive thirty to eighty days after conception.[10] By the mid-seventeenth century, however, it was no crime to abort, with the consent of the mother, a fetus which had not "quickened," an event that occurs four to five months after conception.[11] Even then, the killing of a fetus was not homicide unless the fetus had been "born alive." Being "born alive" required that the fetus be totally expelled from the mother and show a clear sign of independent vitality, such as respiration, although respiration was not strictly required.[12]

In the United States the "born alive" requirement[13] has come to mean that the fetus

---

6. See People v. Woods, 416 Mich. 581, 331 N.W.2d 707 (1982), holding that the word "malice" should no longer be used in jury instructions in homicide cases and that instead jurors should be told specifically what states of mind will suffice.

7. Only a few of the modern codes have taken this approach.

8. Thus in some states there is no such thing as intent-to-do-serious-bodily-injury murder. The definition of murder in Model Penal Code § 210.2 also excludes that type of common law murder on the ground that such cases are better dealt with by taking account of the defendant's purpose to injure in determining whether he committed the homicide by extreme recklessness. Model Penal Code § 210.2, Comment at 28 (1980).

9. State v. Simpson, 244 N.C. 325, 93 S.E.2d 425 (1956).

10. Means, The Law of New York Concerning Abortion and the Status of the Fetus, 1664–1968: A Case of Cessation of Constitutionality, 14 N.Y.L.F. 411, 412 (1968).

11. Id. at 420.

12. Atkinson, Life, Birth and Live-Birth, 20 L.Q.Rev. 134, 135 (1904).

13. This requirement is generally followed in the modern cases. See, e.g., People v. Greer, 79 Ill.2d 103, 37 Ill. Dec. 313, 402 N.E.2d 203 (1980); Hollis v. Commonwealth, 652 S.W.2d 61 (Ky.1983); State v. Gyles, 313 So.2d 799 (La. 1975); Commonwealth v. Edelin, 371 Mass. 497, 359 N.E.2d 4 (1976); State v. Amaro, ___ R.I. ___, 448 A.2d 1257 (1982). But see Commonwealth v. Cass, 392 Mass. 799, 467 N.E.2d 1324 (1984) (as a matter of common law development, word "person" in vehicular homicide statute construed to include a viable fetus); State v. Horne, 282 S.C. 444, 319 S.E.2d 703 (1984) (as a matter of common law development, court rules homicide prosecution may be maintained as to killing of viable fetus). See Annot., 40 A.L.R.3d 444 (1971).

Some of the modern codes define a "person," for purposes of the law of homicide, as meaning a human being

be fully brought forth [14] and establish an "independent circulation" [15] before it can be considered a human being. Proof of live birth and death by criminal agency are required beyond a reasonable doubt to sustain a homicide conviction.[16] "Independent circulation" can be established by evidence of the fetus having breathed,[17] but such proof usually is not conclusive [18] in the absence of the evidence of life,[19] such as crying.[20] Some courts have required that the umbilical cord be severed before an independent circulation can be established.[21] Severance of the cord probably is no longer required if the fetus is brought forth fully.[22]

A pathologist's opinion on live birth usually is not conclusive,[23] but it will sustain a conviction when corroborated by other evidence.[24] Where respiration alone is sufficient to establish a live birth, a pathologist's opinion on live birth will sustain a conviction even in the absence of other evidence.[25] The grossness of the crime [26] and circumstantial evidence such as preparation for the care of the baby [27] are irrelevant factors that are sometimes considered in the determination of live birth.

People v. Chavez [28] rejected the "born alive" test of earlier infanticide cases. The court in

Chavez held that since it was the typical human experience that babies are born alive, it was a legal fiction to say a fetus was not human until completely born.[29] Although a baby is dependent on its mother before birth, in another sense it has reached a state of independent existence when it reaches a stage from which it will normally grow into a living human being given the proper care. The court then held that a fetus killed during the course of birth would be considered a human being under the homicide statute if in the natural course of events the birth would be successfully completed. Nonfeasance by the mother immediately following childbirth in the care for her child might not, however, support a conviction under the *Chavez* theory.[30]

The Supreme Court of California refused to extend the *Chavez* rule to the assault of a pregnant woman resulting in the killing of an unborn but viable fetus not in the process of birth.[31] The court held that the common law homicide requirement that the fetus be in the process of birth was not changed by medical advances which might keep a fetus alive upon premature birth.[32] Furthermore, any civil law remedies available to a fetus are based on

---

who has been born and was alive at the time of the homicidal act. This is also the definition in Model Penal Code § 210.0(1). But in State v. Brown, 378 So.2d 916 (La. 1979), the legislature's revision of the definition of the word "person" in the criminal code to include "a human being from the moment of fertilization and implantation" was held not to make the killing of a fetus murder. The court stressed that other jurisdictions which had made the killing of a fetus homicide "have done so by separate enactments." See note 33 infra.

14. Jackson v. Commonwealth, 265 Ky. 295, 96 S.W.2d 1014 (1936).

15. State v. Winthrop, 43 Iowa 519 (1876).

16. Shedd v. State, 178 Ga. 653, 173 S.E. 847 (1934); Annot., 65 A.L.R.3d 413 (1975). But there may be some other crime, such as concealing a dead body which requires neither.

17. In Heubner v. State, 131 Wis. 162, 111 N.W. 63 (1907), it appears that independent circulation was established by breathing alone.

18. Morgan v. State, 148 Tenn. 417, 256 S.W.2d 433 (1923); Lane v. Commonwealth, 219 Va. 509, 248 S.E.2d 781 (1978).

19. Jackson v. Commonwealth, 265 Ky. 295, 96 S.W.2d 1014 (1936).

20. People v. Ryan, 9 Ill.2d 467, 138 N.E.2d 516 (1956).

21. Morgan v. State, 148 Tenn. 417, 256 S.W. 433 (1923).

22. Jackson v. Commonwealth, 265 Ky. 295, 96 S.W.2d 1014 (1936).

23. Montgomery v. State, 202 Ga. 678, 44 S.E.2d 242 (1947); People v. Hayner, 300 N.Y. 171, 90 N.E.2d 23 (1949).

24. People v. Ryan, 9 Ill.2d 467, 138 N.E.2d 516 (1956).

25. Bennett v. State, 377 P.2d 634 (Wyo.1963).

26. See Note, 17 Wyo.L.J. 237 (1963).

27. People v. Ryan, 9 Ill.2d 467, 138 N.E.2d 516 (1956).

28. 77 Cal.App.2d 621, 176 P.2d 92 (1947).

29. See also Evans v. State, 48 Tex.Crim. 589, 89 S.W. 974 (1905) (evidence must show fetus born alive or alive at inception of birth to sustain homicide conviction).

30. Singleton v. State, 33 Ala.App. 536, 35 So.2d 375 (1948). The same result may be reached under the traditional "born alive" theory. State v. Osmus, 73 Wyo. 183, 276 P.2d 469 (1954).

31. Keeler v. Superior Ct. v. Amador County, 2 Cal.3d 619, 87 Cal.Rptr. 481, 470 P.2d 617 (1970), reversing 80 Cal.Rptr. 865 (Cal.App.1969).

32. Keeler v. Superior Ct. of Amador County, 2 Cal.3d 619, 87 Cal.Rptr. 481, 470 P.2d 617 (1970).

different considerations than criminal liability and are inapplicable.[33] A similar conclusion was reached by the Ohio Court of Appeals in a homicide by vehicle situation.[34] The defendant's car collided with a vehicle in which a seven-month pregnant woman was riding. Before the collision the baby was viable and capable of sustaining life outside the womb. The mother aborted shortly thereafter and the injuries received by the fetus in the crash were the cause of death. In reversing the conviction, the court held that civil remedies afforded the fetus and medical advances did not justify changing the common law homicide requirement of live birth. It is clear, however, that a conviction for vehicular homicide against a fetus would be sustained under a feticide statute.[35] Furthermore, inflicting injury upon a fetus before birth may be homicide if the fetus dies after being born alive.[36]

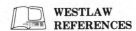 **WESTLAW REFERENCES**

topic(110 203) /p fetus /s life alive living viab!

(d) When Does Life End? As one court has noted: "Until recently, the definition of death was both medically and legally a rela-

tively simple matter. When the heart stopped beating and the lungs stopped breathing, the individual was dead according to physicians and according to the law. The traditional definition did not include the criterion of lack of brain activity because no method existed for diagnosing brain death. Moreover, until recently, no mechanical means have been available to maintain heart and lung action; and respiration, heart action, and brain function are so closely related that without artificial support, the cessation of any one of them will bring the other two to a halt within a very few minutes."[37] But the situation has now changed dramatically. By resort to modern resuscitative and supportive measures, it is possible to "restore life as judged by the ancient standards of persistent respiration and continuing heart beat. This can be the case even when there is not the remotest possibility of an individual recovering consciousness following massive brain damage."[38]

In tandem with this development[39] has come the "virtually universal acceptance in the medical profession"[40] of the concept of "brain death,"[41] the permanent cessation of all brain functions which, absent mechanical

---

33. For contrary views see Keeler v. Superior Ct. of Amador County, 80 Cal.Rptr. 865 (Cal.App.1969); Comment, 56 Iowa L.Rev. 658, 666–74 (1971); and Recent Decision, 19 Cath.U.L.Rev. 372, 382 (1970). As a consequence of the *Keeler* case, California passed a feticide statute. West's Ann.Cal.Penal Code § 187. The statute itself is anomalous in that conviction under it may be for murder or assault only and not manslaughter. Furthermore, the statute exempts the mother from its operation. Comment, 2 Pac.L.J. 170, 181, 184 (1971). There is a trend away from feticide statutes. Keeler v. Superior Ct. of Amador County, 2 Cal.3d 619, 87 Cal.Rptr. 481, 470 P.2d 617 (1970). They are to be found, however, even in some of the modern codes.

34. State v. Dickinson, 23 Ohio App.2d 259, 263 N.E.2d 253 (1970), reversing 47 Ohio Op.2d 373, 248 N.E.2d 458 (C.P. Stark County 1969).

35. Tiner v. State, 239 Ark. 819, 394 S.W.2d 608 (1965).

36. Illustrative is People v. Bolar, 109 Ill.App.3d 384, 64 Ill.Dec. 919, 440 N.E.2d 639 (1982) (victim, a newborn infant who, at the time of delivery by cesarean section made necessary by defendant's reckless conduct, exhibited only a few heartbeats which declined in rate and then terminated within minutes, was born alive and thus was an "individual" within the meaning of the homicide statutes). See also Clarke v. State, 117 Ala. 1, 23 So. 671 (1898); Ranger v. State, 249 Ga. 315, 290 S.E.2d 63 (1982);

State v. Anderson, 135 N.J.Super. 423, 343 A.2d 505 (1975). Contra: Cordes v. State, 54 Tex.Crim. 204, 112 S.W. 943 (1908).

37. In re Bowman, 94 Wn.2d 407, 617 P.2d 731 (1980).

38. Ad Hoc Committee of the Harvard Medical School to Examine the Definition of Brain Death, A Definition of Irreversible Coma, 205 J.A.M.A. 337 (1968). See also R. Beatch, Death, Dying, and the Biological Revolution 2 (1976).

39. And with another which also has a bearing here: "the possibility of transplanting organs from dead donors and the necessity of doing so before necrosis of the organ tissue," which has "prompted physicians to try to make an irrevocable determination of death fairly early in the process." Model Penal Code § 210.1, Comment at 10 (1980).

40. Swafford v. State, 421 N.E.2d 596 (Ind.1981).

41. See, e.g., Conway, Medical and Legal Views of Death: Confrontation and Reconciliation, 19 St. Louis U.L.J. 172 (1974); Horan, Definition of Death: An Emerging Consensus, 16 Trial 22 (Dec. 1980); Rodgers, Brain Death Concept Gaining Acceptance, 66 A.B.A.J. 272 (1980); Victor, Brain Death: An Overview, 27 Med.Trial Tech.Q. 55 (1980). But see Houts, Brain Death: The Issues Are Not Settled Yet, 22 Trauma 1 (1980).

support, would result in the cessation of other body functions as well. As for the criteria utilized in the medical community to determine brain death, they are: (1) a total lack of responsivity to externally applied stimuli (e.g., pinching) and inner need; (2) no spontaneous muscular movements or respiration; and (3) no reflexes, as measured by a fixed, dilated pupil and lack of ocular, pharyngeal, and muscle-tendon reflexes.[42] It has also been emphasized that a flat or isoelectric electroencephalogram (EEG) reading has great confirmatory value,[43] although more recent studies have deemphasized reliance upon the EEG and emphasized the absence of spinal reflexes.[44]

The traditional legal definition of death was just like the traditional medical definition: so long as the heart remains beating and there is breathing, death has not occurred.[45] But in light of the developments in medical science noted above, should this continue to be the legal definition in homicide cases? [46] This is an issue of some importance, as can be seen from a recitation of the facts of a recent case.[47] The defendant shot the victim in the head, and the victim was then taken to the hospital where it was preliminarily determined that he had suffered brain death. The victim was maintained on life support systems for the next three days, during which

time follow-up studies confirmed that conclusion. A doctor then terminated the support measures, and defendant was thereafter charged with murder. Given the fact that certain forms of improper medical treatment constitute an intervening and supervening cause barring a homicide conviction of the person who inflicted the original injury,[48] it is important to know just when the victim's death occurred. If as a legal matter brain death is sufficient, the the victim's death occurred before the doctor "pulled the plug," meaning no cause intervened between the defendant's conduct and the victim's death; if, on the other hand, brain death is not a proper legal test, then there is at least a chance the doctor's conduct would bar conviction.[49]

On the above facts and in similar situations there also exists the question of the criminal liability of the doctor.[50] The time of death as a legal matter is, if anything, even more important here, for it has long been accepted that it is homicide to kill one already dying,[51] to accelerate one's death,[52] to kill one condemned to be executed the next day,[53] or to kill a "worthless" victim.[54] Thus, a doctor who "pulls the plug" or removes an organ from the victim could find himself subject to criminal liability [55] if the traditional heart-lungs legal test of death were utilized.

42. Ad Hoc Committee, supra note 38.

43. Victor, supra note 41, at 56–58.

44. Task Force on Death and Dying of the Institute of Society, Ethics, and the Life Sciences, Refinements in Criteria for the Determination of Death: An Appraisal, 221 J.A.M.A. 48 (1972).

45. See Halley & Harvey, Medical vs. Legal Definitions of Death, 204 J.A.M.A. 423 (1968). The issue did not ordinarily arise in a criminal law context, but rather with respect to, e.g., determination of simultaneous death for purposes of inheritance, where the definition was cessation of heartbeat and respiration. See, e.g., Smith v. Smith, 229 Ark. 579, 317 S.W.2d 275 (1958) (circulation, respiration, pulsation); Thomas v. Anderson, 96 Cal.App. 2d 371, 215 P.2d 478 (1950) (heart and respiration stoppage).

46. The matter is put this way because the proper legal definition of death might vary depending upon the context. See generally Dworkin, Death in Context, 48 Ind.L.Rev. 623 (1973).

47. State v. Fierro, 124 Ariz. 182, 603 P.2d 74 (1979).

48. See § 3.12(f)(5), (g)(2).

49. See Guthrie, Brain Death and Criminal Liability, 15 Crim.L.Bull. 40, 50–55 (1979).

50. Id. at 58–61.

51. People v. Cione, 293 Ill. 321, 127 N.E. 646 (1920) (suffocating one dying from an assault).

52. State v. Be Bee, 113 Utah 398, 195 P.2d 746 (1948) (shooting a dying victim).

53. Commonwealth v. Bowen, 13 Mass. 356 (1816).

54. State v. Goettina, 61 Wyo. 420, 158 P.2d 865 (1945). Even though slaves were not considered human, it was homicide for a master to kill his own slave. State v. Hoover, 20 N.C. 500 (1839).

55. "The effect of the definition of death on the criminal liability of a physician acting in his professional capacity must be discussed in the theoretical realm, for to date there has been no criminal case centered on the legality of a doctor's having adopted brain death as death." Guthrie, supra note 49, at 58.

A decision reported at 4 Med., Sci. & The Law 59 (1964) is the only one dealing with the problem. A man from Newcastle upon Tyne was severely assaulted and stopped breathing 14 hours later. His heart and lungs were kept

As a policy matter, use of the brain death test as a sufficient legal definition of death in homicide cases makes great sense if, as would seem to be the case, "the harm associated with the loss of psyche is seen as the equivalent to, or even greater than, the harm associated with 'death' itself." [56] On this and like reasoning, the commentators have rather consistently concluded that the brain death test should be applied in fact situations like that described above to ensure that the person causing the original harm can be held accountable for the homicide and to ensure also that the doctor's conduct is not a basis for a homicide prosecution.[57] Certainly most—perhaps all—jurisdictions would reach that conclusion today. There is no doubt whatsoever in those many states which by statute have adopted brain death as an acceptable (though perhaps not the exclusive) legal standard.[58] But it is noteworthy that in cases arising in states lacking any statutory definition of death clearly applicable to homicide cases, the courts have consistently opted for the brain death test as the applicable legal standard.[59]

WESTLAW REFERENCES

topic(110 203) /p "brain dea**"

(e) Year-and-a-Day Rule. We have already noted, in discussing the topic of causation (a vital subject in the case of those crimes, including murder, defined so as to require both conduct and a specified result of conduct), that the English judges centuries ago required for murder (and later required for manslaughter) that the victim's death must occur within a year and a day after the fatal blow was delivered.[60] In a sense, the judges were saying that, in the case of a longer interval, the blow could not have caused the death. The year-and-a-day rule made some sense in the days of its birth, when there was little medical knowledge; but it seems strange that it should exist today. Yet the year-and-a-day rule crossed the Atlantic with the colonists and still exists in many states today.[61]

WESTLAW REFERENCES

topic(110 203) /p year-and-a-day

(f) Elements of Murder. It may be useful to summarize briefly here the required elements of murder: (1) There must be some conduct (affirmative act, or omission to act where there is a duty to act) on the part of the defendant. (2) He must have an accompanying "malicious" state of mind (intent to kill or do serious bodily injury; a depraved heart; an intent to commit a felony). (3) His conduct must "legally cause" the death of a living-human-being victim. And (4), in many jurisdictions, this death must occur within a year and a day after the defendant's conduct thus caused the victim's fatal injury.

WESTLAW REFERENCES

203k308 /p murder /s elements

---

functioning for 24 hours until his kidney could be transplanted. At this time the life support system was stopped. The hospital pathologist testified that death occurred when natural breathing stopped. The coroner testified only that he thought the kidney was to be removed upon death of the donor. The doctors were not tried, but the assailant of the donor was convicted only of assault and not manslaughter, suggesting the conclusion that the acts of the doctors were an intervening cause of death. 4 Med., Sci. & The Law 77, 78 (1964).

56. Guthrie, supra note 49, at 57.

57. Dworkin, supra note 46, at 632; Guthrie, supra note 49, at 55–57; Kennedy, Switching Off Life Support Machines: The Legal Implications, 1977 Crim.L.Rev. 443; Comment, 11 Wake Forest L.Rev. 253, 265–66 (1975).

58. See Swafford v. State, 421 N.E.2d 596 (Ind.1981), citing statutes from 25 states. Several of these states

have adopted the Uniform Determination of Death Act, 12 U.L.A. (Supp.1984), which provides: "An individual who has sustained either (1) irreversible cessation of circulation and respiratory functions, or (2) irreversible cessation of all functions of the entire brain, including the brain stem, is dead. A determination of death must be made in accordance with accepted medical standards."

59. State v. Fierro, 124 Ariz. 182, 603 P.2d 74 (1979); Swafford v. State, 421 N.E.2d 596 (Ind.1981); State v. Shaffer, 229 Kan. 310, 624 P.2d 440 (1981); Commonwealth v. Golston, 373 Mass. 249, 366 N.E.2d 744 (1977); State v. Meints, 212 Neb. 410, 322 N.W.2d 809 (1982); People v. Eulo, 63 N.Y.2d 341, 482 N.Y.S.2d 436, 472 N.E.2d 286 (1984); State v. Johnson, 56 Ohio St.2d 35, 381 N.E.2d 637 (1978).

60. See § 3.12(i).

61. See Annot., 60 A.L.R.3d 1323 (1974).

§ 7.2   Intent-To-Kill Murder

Conduct, accompanied by an intent to kill, which legally causes another's death constitutes murder, unless the circumstances surrounding the homicide are such that the crime is reduced to voluntary manslaughter [1] or such that the intentional killing is justifiable or excusable and so constitutes no crime at all.[2]   Intentional death may be produced by affirmative action involving a variety of possible weapons, or even without weapons, as by hands or feet or simply spoken words.   Intended death may likewise be produced by omission to act; but for murder liability the omission to act must be accompanied by a duty to act.[3]

(a) **Intention.** The commonest type of murder, of course, is the intent-to-kill type, where A, with an intent to kill B, by his conduct succeeds in killing B.   Usually where A's conduct causes a death his aim is good: he aims his deadly missile at B with intent to kill B, and hits B and kills B.   But sometimes his aim is bad, and he misses B but hits and kills C.   He is, of course, nonetheless guilty of murdering C.[4]

Under the traditional view, one intends to cause a certain result under two different circumstances: (1) when he desires that result, whatever the likelihood of that result occurring; and (2) when he knows that that result is substantially certain to occur, whatever his desire concerning that result.[5]   Thus (1) A has an intent to kill B when he fires his gun at B desiring to cause his death, though A's hand may be so unsteady or B so far away that A's chances of hitting B are small.   And (2) A has an intent to kill B when he fires a bullet from a high-powered rifle at his enemy C, who is holding B in front of him as a human shield; for, though he may not desire B's death (he may even be fond of B, though of course his actions demonstrate that he does not like B as much as he hates C), he knows that B is substantially certain to be killed. (So in either case, if B is actually killed, we would say that, since A intended to kill him, A is guilty of intent-to-kill murder.)

The modern view is to limit "intent" to instances where it is the actor's purpose to cause the harmful result, and the word "knowledge" is used to cover instances in which the actor knows that the harmful result is substantially certain to occur.[6]   In a criminal code utilizing such definitions, what is here called intent-to-kill murder may be described as intentionally or knowingly killing another.   Apart from the question of when capital punishment should be permitted, there is "no basis in principle for separating purposeful from knowing homicide." [7]   Many of the modern codes do not distinguish between them, although a majority do appear to require intent rather than knowledge or, at least, to classify intentional and knowing killings differently.

We have seen that, historically, in the beginning an intent to kill was not of itself enough of a bad intent for murder; the intent to kill had to be "aforethought"—i.e., thought-out in advance, premeditated.   But as time went on, the premeditation requirement was dropped, so that an unpremeditated intent to kill would do.[8]   So today an unpremeditated intent to kill is enough for the intent-to-kill type of murder.[9]

   **WESTLAW REFERENCES**

topic(203) /p murder /p intent-to-kill /p kn*w!

§ 7.2

1. See § 7.10.

2. See ch. 5.

3. For more discussion, see § 7.2(c).

4. See § 3.12(d).

5. See § 3.5(a), giving illustrations from the law of homicide.

6. See § 3.5(b).

7. Model Penal Code § 210.2, Comment (1980).

8. See § 7.1.

9. We shall see, § 7.7, that when murder is divided into degrees, an intentional, premeditated, deliberate killing is the most common form of first degree murder; whereas a plain intentional killing (minus the premeditation and deliberation) constitutes second degree murder. With or without the premeditation and deliberation, however, an intentional killing is murder (unless the special circumstances of the case reduce it part-way down to voluntary manslaughter or all the way down to no crime).

(b) Deadly-Weapon Doctrine.[10] One who intentionally kills another does not often announce to bystanders, "I have in my mind an intent to kill" at the moment, or just before or after, he kills.[11] If there are witnesses to the killing, he often acts without speaking at all or at least without speaking so specifically about his intent; and of course he often kills in secret, so that there are no witnesses. How then can the prosecution prove beyond a reasonable doubt that when he killed he intended to kill? Obviously this intent must be gathered from all the circumstances of the killing—the killer's actions and his words (if any) in the light of the surrounding circumstances.

It is commonly said in civil and in criminal cases (not just murder cases) that one is presumed to intend the natural and probable consequences of his acts.[12] Thus if one carefully aims a gun at his enemy and pulls the trigger, and the bullet strikes the enemy in the heart and kills him, we ought logically to conclude, in the absence of some other facts, that he intended to kill, though he spoke no words of intent at the time. A special application of the presumption that one intends to produce the natural results of his actions is found in the deadly-weapon doctrine applicable to homicide cases: one who intentionally uses a deadly weapon on another human being and thereby kills him presumably intends to kill him.[13]

As a constitutional matter, it is necessary to express the idea, not in terms of a mandatory presumption, but in terms of a permissive inference:[14] it may properly be inferred (i.e., the conclusion *may* be drawn, rather than *must* be drawn, in the absence of counter proof) from the fact that the killer intentionally[15] used a deadly weapon upon the deceased that he intended to kill the deceased.[16] Note that the deadly-weapon doctrine is not a category of murder separate from the intent-to-kill category; there must be an intent to kill,[17] but the intentional use

---

10. For the history of the deadly-weapon doctrine, and a consideration of the presumption—or inference—problem discussed below, see Oberer, The Deadly Weapon Doctrine—Common Law Origin, 75 Harv.L.Rev. 1565 (1962).

11. In State v. Jensen, 120 Utah 531, 236 P.2d 445 (1951), where defendant killed the victim with his fists, after having threatened to kill him, defendant, convicted of murder on the ground that he intended to kill, urged on appeal that his threat to kill was only "big talk"; *held* conviction affirmed. "There could hardly be more direct or certain evidence of the defendant's intent than for him to declare before, during and after the attack, his intention to kill." The jury was entitled to believe it was not just "big talk".

12. The matter cannot be put to the jury in that fashion, for it would amount to an unconstitutional shifting of the burden of proof. Sandstrom v. Montana, 442 U.S. 510, 99 S.Ct. 2450, 61 L.Ed.2d 39 (1979). Rather, the jury should be told that it may, but is not required to, infer that defendant intended the natural and probable consequences of his acts. See C. McCormick, Evidence § 348 (E. Cleary ed. 3d ed. 1984).

13. See, e.g., Hardy v. State, 242 Ga. 702, 251 S.E.2d 289 (1978); Commonwealth v. Boyd, 461 Pa. 17, 334 A.2d 610 (1975); Cullin v. State, 565 P.2d 445 (Wyo.1977). "Therefore, when one person assails another violently with a dangerous weapon, likely to kill and which does in fact destroy the life of the party assailed, the natural presumption is, that he intended death or other great bodily harm * * *." Shaw, C.J., in Commonwealth v. Webster, 59 Mass. (5 Cush.) 295, 52 Am.Dec. 711 (1850).

Perkins, A Re-examination of Malice Aforethought, 43 Yale L.J. 537, 550 (1934), points out that many cases, e.g.,

People v. Crenshaw, 298 Ill. 412, 131 N.E. 576 (1921), use the word "presumption" in describing the deadly-weapon doctrine, when they should be talking about an "inference."

14. See note 12 supra.

15. For the deadly-weapon doctrine to apply, the defendant must *intentionally*—not just recklessly or negligently—use the deadly weapon. One cannot otherwise properly draw the inference of an intent to kill. Thus in Bantum v. State, 46 Del. 487, 85 A.2d 741 (1952), the court says: "[T]he intentional use of a deadly weapon upon the body of another is evidence of an intention to kill or do great bodily harm in the absence of evidence to the contrary." But consider People v. Haack, 396 Mich. 367, 240 N.W.2d 704 (1976) (intent to kill may be inferred where defendant pointed loaded pistol at deceased and intentionally pulled trigger, despite his claim he thought cylinder rotated clockwise so that hammer would strike empty chamber, as natural tendency of defendant's behavior was to cause death or great bodily harm). Of course, the unintentional use of a deadly weapon upon another human being may involve such a high degree of recklessness as to serve as a basis for depraved-heart murder; or of manslaughter where there is recklessness of a lesser degree.

16. See, e.g., Commonwealth v. Murray, 460 Pa. 605, 334 A.2d 255 (1975). For strong arguments in favor of "inference" over "presumption," see Oberer, supra note 10, at 1573–76; Perkins, supra note 16, at 550. See also Note, Criminal Law—Deadly Weapon Doctrine, 34 Ky.L.J. 320 (1946).

17. Or, as we shall see, an intent to do serious bodily injury, as to which the deadly-weapon doctrine has an equally close bearing.

of a deadly weapon authorizes the drawing of an inference that the user intends to kill. It cannot be said that the intentional use of a deadly weapon which produces death is necessarily murder; we still allow the user a chance to convince the trier-of-fact [18] (generally the jury) that in spite of his intentional use of a deadly weapon he actually did not intend to kill—as where he intentionally shot toward his victim intending merely to scare or to inflict a non-fatal wound.[19]

What weapon is a "deadly weapon" for purposes of the deadly-weapon doctrine in homicide cases? [20] "[A] deadly weapon [is] one which, from the manner used, is calculated or likely to produce death or serious bodily injury." [21] Thus whether a weapon is deadly depends upon two factors: (1) what it intrinsically is and (2) how it is used. If almost anyone can kill with it, it is a deadly weapon when used in a manner calculated to kill. Thus the following items have been held to be deadly weapons in view of the circumstances of their use: loaded guns, daggers, swords, axes, iron bars, baseball bats, bricks, rocks, ice picks, automobiles, and pistols used as bludgeons.[22] Some cases have spoken of loaded guns, daggers, axes and heavy iron bars as deadly weapons *per se,* without regard to their use, perhaps with the thought that they are of such a nature that they cannot be used gently. However, while it is true that almost anyone can kill with a heavy iron bar, yet if the defendant actually used it to tap the victim lightly on the head, the deadly-weapon doctrine ought not to apply so as to authorize an inference that he intended to kill, even though the victim unfortunately had such an uncommonly thin skull that he died from the tap.[23]

There are some weapons with which the ordinary person could not kill; it takes something of an expert to kill another with a pen knife or a pin. Yet such weapons, intentionally used in an artistic way by an expert, do constitute deadly weapons.[24]

Lastly, there is the problem of death produced solely by the intentional use of the hands or feet, where there is no "weapon" at all to serve as a basis for a finding of a "deadly weapon," [25] and where, of course, it would often be ridiculous to infer an intent to kill from their use.[26] Yet in appropriate cases, generally involving big men attacking

18. On principle, he need not introduce any evidence of lack of intent to kill, for in the absence of such evidence the trier-of-fact is not bound to conclude that he intended to kill. But it is often safer for him to introduce some evidence. If he does, then on principle this evidence does not have to convince the jury by a preponderance of the evidence; all it need do is to raise in the jury's mind a reasonable doubt concerning his intent to kill.

19. Compare, however, Holmes, J., in Commonwealth v. Pierce, 138 Mass. 165, 52 Am.Rep. 264 (1884), where in a dictum he treats the deadly-weapon doctrine as conclusively proving an intent to kill: "When the jury are asked whether a stick of a certain size was a deadly weapon, they are not asked further whether the defendant knew that it was so. It is enough that he used and saw it such as it was."

20. The term must also be defined for purposes of construing a common type of aggravated battery statute, "assault with a deadly [sometimes: dangerous] weapon," or an aggravated robbery statute, "robbery when armed with a deadly weapon." "Deadly weapon" has the same meaning in all of these connections.

21. Wilson v. State, 37 Tex.Crim. 156, 38 S.W. 1013 (1897). See also Annot., 21 L.R.A. (n.s.) 497 (1909).

22. See cases cited in Notes, 34 Ky.L.J. 320 (1946); 24 N.C.L.Rev. 60 (1945). Note that a death-dealing instrument need not, like a gun, be designed for killing in order to be a "weapon." Though an automobile is not meant for killing in its ordinary use, yet when one intentionally runs his automobile into a pedestrian it may properly be called a "weapon."

23. So too of guns aimed at legs, or the flat side of swords used to strike blows. But the firing of a gun in the general area in which vital organs are located is sufficient; it need not be shown that the bullet entered a vital organ. Commonwealth v. Padgett, 465 Pa. 1, 348 A.2d 87 (1975).

The defendant would, of course, be guilty of murder in the thin-skull case if he knew of the thin skull and actually intended to kill by administering the tap. Without an intent to kill, however, he would be guilty of manslaughter of the battery-plus-death type. See § 7.13(d).

24. State v. Roan, 122 Iowa 136, 97 N.W. 997 (1904) (Case 2) (pen knife); State v. Norwood, 115 N.C. 789, 20 S.E. 712 (1894) (mother pushed pins down throat of infant child; held, murder because intent to kill shown).

25. Sometimes courts have spoken of hands and feet as "weapons," and so "deadly weapons" when used in a manner calculated to kill or do serious bodily injury. E.g., Vogg v. Commonwealth, 308 Ky. 212, 214 S.W.2d 86 (1948).

26. Even if no intent to kill can be inferred from death resulting from battery with fists, yet such a situation

small, frail men or women or children, and generally involving the repeated use of hands and feet, an inference of an intent to kill may properly be drawn.[27]

In order to get the benefit of the inference, the prosecution must show not only that a weapon actually killed but also that the weapon used was a deadly weapon. With those weapons (guns, swords, axes, iron bars, daggers) with which anyone can kill, there is probably no need to introduce the weapon into evidence or to describe the weapon to the jury; but with rocks (which may be large or small) and walking canes (which may be thick or thin) a verdict of murder may not be supportable without evidence of the weapon or a description of its size and shape.[28]

 **WESTLAW REFERENCES**

topic(203) /p murder /p "intent to kill" /p deadly
    /2 weapon % assault
topic(203 110) /p "deadly weapon" /s define*
    definition

(c) Means of Producing Intentional Death. While the method of producing an intentional death is usually some weapon in the hands of the murderer, and less frequent-

ly his hands and feet without a weapon, sometimes more subtle means are used. Thus the act of opening, on a cold winter day, a window next to the bed of a helpless sick person, who must remain warm to recover, would be murderous conduct by one who intended thereby to kill. One ingenious fellow with a flair for the picturesque caused his wife to be bitten by a rattlesnake and then, to make doubly sure, placed her face down in a fish pond.[29] Words alone may be used to produce an intentional death, as where one perjures an innocent man into the electric chair;[30] or nags another, whom he knows to have heart trouble, into some death-producing exertion;[31] or, seeing a blind man at the edge of a precipice, advises him that it is all clear ahead. Words may be used intentionally to produce death through fright or shock, as when one shouts "boo" at a person leaning precariously over the rim of the Grand Canyon or the balustrade atop the Empire State Building;[32] or where he falsely shouts, "Your son is dead" into the ears of a woman he knows to have a heart condition.[33]

So far, we have discussed deaths intentionally produced by affirmative action, including that mild form of affirmative action involved in speaking words.[34] We have already noted,

---

constitutes manslaughter of the battery-plus-death type. See § 7.13(d).

27. Commonwealth v. Buzard, 365 Pa. 511, 76 A.2d 394 (1950) (large man killed small, weak, prone man by violent and repeated use of fists; held, murder conviction affirmed, although "no deadly weapon, in the ordinary sense, was employed.") For other cases, see Annot., 22 A.L.R.2d 854 (1952). There is less difficulty in the case of the use by strong men of bare hands to strangle weaker victims to death or to push them down the stairs.

28. Cf. Greenway v. State, 59 Ga.App. 461, 1 S.E.2d 217 (1939) (conviction of voluntary manslaughter reversed).

29. Lisenba v. California, 314 U.S. 219, 62 S.Ct. 280, 86 L.Ed. 166 (1941).

30. A few states so provide by statute but even without such a statute it should constitute murder as surely as if he had fired a gun into his victim.

31. Cf. Vesey v. Vesey, 237 Minn. 295, 54 N.W.2d 385 (1952) (wife nagged husband, who had serious heart condition but did not know it, into walking through deep snow on a wintry day, knowing of his condition and desiring thereby to kill him; held, felonious homicide, so that she held the property she inherited from him at his death on constructive trust for his children by a prior marriage; note that the case arose on demurrer; doubtless the fact that she intended to kill by this method would be difficult to prove).

32. State v. Myers, 7 N.J. 465, 81 A.2d 710 (1951) (defendant commanded wife to jump into river before he threw her in; she entered water, was carried away by the current and drowned; held, jury could find defendant intended to cause her death). Most of the cases of this kind, however, have not concerned intent-to-kill murder, but rather felony-murder because the words were spoken in the commission of a felony. See Annot., 25 A.L.R.2d 710 (1952) (homicide by causing one, by threats or fright, to leap or fall to death).

33. No doubt it is sometimes difficult to prove that the victim actually died of physical injury produced by fright or shock, and even more difficult to prove that the defendant intended to kill by this method. See Annot., 47 A.L.R.2d 1072 (1956) (homicide by fright and shock). Most of the actual cases involve involuntary manslaughter prosecutions for deaths unintentionally caused by conduct producing heart failure. See § 7.13.

34. Of course, the death may be the result of action both by the defendant and by the victim; thus where A mails poisoned candy to B with intent to kill B, B in one sense applies the final coup de grace by his own act in eating the candy; A, of course, is none the less guilty of murdering B. Here we would say that B's intervening act is not only foreseeable but was actually intended, so that A's conduct clearly "legally caused" B's death. See § 3.12.

however, that intentional death may be effectively brought about by an omission to act. One is not guilty of murder for intentionally killing by failure to act, however, unless the circumstances are such that there is a duty to act.[35]

WESTLAW
REFERENCES

topic(203) /p encourage* hasten** accelerate* /3 death

vesey /p homicide murder /p coerc*** persua! (hasten** encourage* accelerate* /3 death)

(d) Causation. For one to be guilty of murder of the intent-to-kill (or any other) variety, his conduct (act or omission) must be the "legal cause" of the death of the person killed. In the realm of murder, this means (1) that his conduct must be a substantial factor in bringing about the death;[36] and (2) that in addition the actual result (death of the victim) cannot be brought about in a manner too greatly different from the intended manner. These matters have been discussed elsewhere in this book.[37]

WESTLAW
REFERENCES

topic(203) /p inten! /s murder kill /s legal** proximate** +3 caus!

---

35. See § 3.3. A typical example of a duty to act is the duty of a parent to rescue his imperilled infant, such as one who is drowning face-down in the bathtub, lacking the ability to extricate itself from its difficulty. Failure to rescue would be murder if the parent intends to kill the child, either by desiring the death or, without wishing for death, by knowing that death is substantially sure to result from failure to rescue.

36. See § 3.12(b).

37. See § 3.12(f). The bad-aim situation—where *A* aims at *B* with intent to kill, but, missing *B*, kills *C*—is also a matter of causation involving the situation of divergence between actual victim and intended victim, and is discussed in § 3.12(d).

§ 7.3

1. E.g., Holloway's Case, 79 Eng.Rep. 715 (K.B.1628) (defendant tied boy to horse's tail and caused the horse to run, breaking boy's shoulder and killing him); Errington and Other's Case, 168 Eng.Rep. 1133 (Sp.Assiz.1838) (defendants covered a sleeping drunk with straw, then threw hot cinders on the straw, which caught fire and burned him to death; instruction that it was murder if they intended to do him "serious injury" though not to kill him, manslaughter if intended only to frighten him in sport; verdict of manslaughter).

§ 7.3 Intent-To-Do-Serious-Bodily-Injury Murder

We have already seen that the English judges came to hold that one who intended to do serious bodily injury short of death, but who actually succeeded in killing, was guilty of murder in spite of his lack of an intent to kill,[1] in the absence of circumstances which mitigated the offense to voluntary manslaughter or which justified or excused it. This type of common-law murder became a part of the law of murder in America.[2]

On principle, it may seem quite proper to make it murder for one to kill another with an intent to do serious bodily injury though not to kill. Such conduct may appear at least as dangerous to life as that required for depraved-heart murder; so that if the latter conduct constitutes murder (as is almost everywhere recognized), so should the conduct here under discussion.[3] It has been suggested, however, that there is no need for the separate category of intent-to-do-serious-bodily-injury murder, and that such cases are properly encompassed within the depraved-heart murder and recklessness manslaughter categories, depending upon the facts of the particular case.[4] Most modern codes define

2. Bantum v. State, 46 Del. 487, 85 A.2d 741 (1952) ("intention to kill or to do great bodily harm"); State v. Calabrese, 107 N.J.L. 115, 151 A. 781 (Ct.Err. & App.1930) ("when one deliberately shoots another it is murder, regardless of the intent with which such killing is perpetrated"); Commonwealth v. Marshall, 287 Pa. 512, 135 A. 301 (1926) (defendant choked victim intending to do her "great bodily harm" though not to kill her; *held,* murder); State v. Jensen, 120 Utah 531, 236 P.2d 445 (1951) (intent to do "great bodily harm" will do for murder).

3. See R. Moreland, Law of Homicide 19 (1952).

4. Model Penal Code § 210.2, Comment at 28 (1980): "The deletion of intent to injure as an independently sufficient culpability for murder rests on the judgment that it is preferable to handle such cases under the standards of extreme recklessness and recklessness contained in [the murder and manslaughter provisions, respectively]. That the actor intends to cause injury of a particular nature or gravity is, of course, a relevant consideration in determining whether he acted with 'extreme indifference to the value of human life' under [the murder provision] or 'recklessly' with respect to death of another under [the manslaughter provision]. Most traditional illustrations of murder based on intent to injure will fall within the recklessness category." Thus Model Penal Code § 210.2 defines murder only as causing death "purposely or know-

murder as not including the intent-to-do-serious-bodily-injury type.[5]

"Serious bodily injury" (or "great" or "grievous bodily harm," as it is often called) is something more than plain "bodily injury";[6] it means something close to, though of course less than, death.[7] As with intent-to-kill murder, the intent to do serious bodily harm must be gathered from the defendant's conduct (including his words, if any) in the light of the surrounding circumstances; and, once again, his intentional use of a deadly weapon (one which, from the manner used, is calculated to cause death or serious bodily injury) upon another human being will properly give rise to an inference of an intent to kill or at least to do serious bodily injury.[8] And such an inference can also be properly drawn where the only "weapon" used is the defendant's hands or feet, in an appropriate case.[9]

Just as murder may be committed by an omission to act, in violation of a duty to act, when accompanied by an intent to kill, so also may it be committed where the omission is accompanied by an intent to do serious bodily injury. Thus if A fails to warn or rescue B, to whom he owes a duty, desiring to cause him serious bodily injury, or (without such a desire) knowing that such an injury is substantially sure to follow, and death to B results, A is guilty of the murder of B.

The same problems of causation arise here as with intent-to-kill murder, as where A aims at B with intent to do him serious bodily harm short of death but, missing B, strikes and kills C (i.e., an unintended victim); or where A strikes B with intent to do serious bodily harm but he inflicts only a plain bodily injury, which, however, is so negligently treated by the doctor that B dies (i.e., an unintended manner of producing the forbidden harm).

It would doubtless be quite possible to combine the two types of murder treated so far— (1) intent-to-kill murder and (2) intent-to-do-serious-bodily-injury murder—into a single type of murder called intent-to-kill-or-do-serious-bodily-injury murder. For historical reasons, and because most modern statutory treatments of murder do not seem to recognize intent-to-do-serious-bodily-injury murder, the two notions have been treated separately in this book.

 **WESTLAW REFERENCES**

topic(203) /p inten**** /s bodily /s harm injur* % "self defense"

§ 7.4   Depraved-Heart Murder

Extremely negligent conduct, which creates what a reasonable man would realize to be not only an unjustifiable but also a very high degree of risk of death or serious bodily injury to another or to others—though unaccompanied by any intent to kill or do serious bodily injury—and which actually causes the death of another, may constitute murder. There is a dispute as to whether, in addition to creating this great risk, the defendant himself must subjectively be aware of the great risk

ingly" or "recklessly under circumstances manifesting extreme indifference to the value of human life."

5. Some other codes include this type of murder. Still others appear to do so by virtue of a general "all other murder" provision for some lesser degree of murder.

6. Wellar v. People, 30 Mich. 16, (1874) ("Every assault involves bodily harm. But any doctrine which would hold every assailant as a murderer where death follows his act, would be barbarous and unreasonable").

7. Intent to do plain bodily harm plus unintended death equals involuntary manslaughter, however. See § 7.13(d).

8. Bantum v. State, 46 Del. 487, 85 A.2d 741 (1952) ("intent to kill or to do great bodily harm * * * was inferable from the intentional use of a deadly weapon [here a gun] upon the body of the deceased").

9. Bishop v. People, 165 Colo. 423, 439 P.2d 342 (1968): "It is probably true, as a general rule, that where death ensues from an attack made with the hands or feet on a person of mature years, who is in good health, malice cannot be implied. Ordinarily, death would not be caused by such means. However, this general rule does not apply where such an assault with hands or feet is committed on an infant of tender years or a person enfeebled by old age or disease."

But see State v. Jensen, 120 Utah 531, 236 P.2d 445 (1951) (large man repeatedly beat small man with fists, after having threatened to kill him; held, intent-to-kill murder; court also states that murder may be committed with an intent to do great bodily harm).

which his conduct creates, in order to be guilty of murder.

(a) Creation of Risk. Conduct which creates an unreasonable risk of injury to other persons or to their property is generally termed "ordinary negligence", a type of fault which will generally serve as the basis for tort liability and occasionally for criminal liability.[1] Conduct which creates not only an unreasonable risk but also a "high degree" of risk (something more than mere "unreasonable" risk) may be termed "gross negligence," and if in addition the one who creates such a risk realizes that he does so, his conduct may be called "recklessness."[2] Grossly negligent conduct, or reckless conduct, which results in death may serve as the basis for manslaughter liability,[3] but it will not do for murder.

For murder the degree of risk of death or serious bodily injury must be more than a mere unreasonable risk, more even than a high degree of risk. Perhaps the required danger may be designated a "very high degree" of risk to distinguish it from those lesser degrees of risk which will suffice for other crimes.[4] Such a designation of conduct at all events is more accurately descriptive than that flowery expression found in the old cases and occasionally incorporated into some modern statutes [5]—i.e., conduct "evincing a depraved heart, devoid of social duty, and fatally bent on mischief." Although "very high degree of risk" means something quite substantial, it is still something far less [6] than certainty or substantial certainty.[7]

The distinctions between an unreasonable risk and a high degree of risk and a very high degree of risk are, of course, matters of degree, and there is no exact boundary line between each category; they shade gradually like a spectrum from one group to another.[8] Some have thus questioned whether this is a sound basis upon which to make the important distinction between murder and manslaughter.[9] More appealing is the Model Penal Code approach, whereunder a reckless killing is murder only if done "under circumstances manifesting extreme indifference to the value of human life." [10] This language, which better serves the "purpose of communicating to jurors in ordinary language the task expected of them," [11] has been substantially followed in many but not all of the modern codes. (A very significant minority of the modern codes do not recognize this type of murder at all.)

It should be noted, however, that for depraved-heart murder it is not a great amount of risk in the abstract which is decisive. The risk is exactly the same when one fires his rifle into the window of what appears to be an abandoned cabin in a deserted mining town as when one shoots the same bullet into the window of a well-kept city home, when in fact in each case one person occupies the room into which the shot is fired. In the deserted cabin situation it may not be, while in the occupied home situation it may be, murder when the occupant is killed. This illustrates that it is what the defendant should realize to

---

§ 7.4

1. See § 3.7(a).

2. See § 3.7(b).

3. See § 7.12.

4. See State v. Joy, 452 A.2d 408 (Me.1982).

5. See State v. Crocker, 435 A.2d 58 (Me.1981) (applying statute covering one who "engages in conduct which manifests a depraved indifference to the value of human life," causing death); State v. Thompson, 88 Wn.2d 18, 558 P.2d 202 (1977) (applying statute covering killing "by an act imminently dangerous to others and evincing a depraved mind, regardless of human life"). See Annot., 25 A.L.R. 4th 311 (1983).

6. See Commonwealth v. Ashburn, 459 Pa. 625, 331 A.2d 167 (1975), approving the trial judge's correction of defense counsel's assertion that for the crime to be murder death must be at least 60% certain.

7. We have already noted in § 3.5 that one who knows that a result is certain or substantially certain to occur as a result of his conduct may be said to *intend* that result.

8. "I have heard it suggested that the difference is one of degree. I am the last man in the world to quarrel with a distinction simply because it is one of degree. Most distinctions, in my opinion, are of that sort, and are none the worse for it." Haddock v. Haddock, 201 U.S. 562, 26 S.Ct. 525, 50 L.Ed. 867 (1906) (Holmes, J., dissenting).

9. Elliott, Offences Against the Person—Murder, 1977 Crim.L.Rev. 70; Smith, A Case of Reckless Murder, 123 New L.J. 792 (1973); Note, 71 Calif.L.Rev. 1298 (1983).

10. Model Penal Code § 210.2(1)(b).

11. Model Penal Code § 210.2, Comment (1980). This language is not unconstitutionally vague. See State v. Dow, 126 N.H. 205, 489 A.2d 650 (1985), and cases from other jurisdictions cited therein.

be the degree of risk, in the light of the surrounding circumstances which he knows, which is important, rather than the amount of risk as an abstract proposition of the mathematics of chance.

Another matter to be noted is that the risk must not only be very high, as the defendant ought to realize in the light of what he knows; it must also under the circumstances be unjustifiable for him to take the risk. The motives for the defendant's risky conduct thus become relevant; or, to express the thought in another way, the social utility of his conduct is a factor to be considered. If he speeds through crowded streets, thereby endangering other motorists and pedestrians, in order to rush a passenger to the hospital for an emergency operation, he may not be guilty of murder if he unintentionally kills, though the same conduct done solely for the purpose of experiencing the thrill of fast driving may be enough for murder.[12] Since the amount of risk which will do for depraved-heart murder varies with these two variable factors—the

extent of the defendant's knowledge of the surrounding circumstances and the social utility of his conduct [13]—the mathematical chances of producing death required for murder cannot be measured in terms of percentages.[14]

The following types of conduct have been held, under the circumstances, to involve the very high degree of unjustifiable homicidal danger which will do for depraved-heart murder: firing a bullet into a room occupied, as the defendant knows, by several people;[15] starting a fire at the front door of an occupied dwelling;[16] shooting into the caboose of a passing train[17] or into a moving automobile,[18] necessarily occupied by human beings; throwing a beer glass at one who is carrying a lighted oil lamp;[19] playing a game of "Russian roulette" with another person;[20] shooting at a point near, but not aiming directly at, another person;[21] driving a car at very high speeds along a main street;[22] shaking an infant so long and so vigorously that it cannot

12. It may even be justifiable *intentionally* to kill—not merely to create a danger of death—under some circumstances, as where a driver intentionally runs down a single pedestrian in order to avoid running into a group of schoolchildren.

13. See § 3.7(a)(1).

14. In Commonwealth v. Ashburn, discussed in note 6 supra, the court declared that depraved-heart murder "does not depend on any precise mathematical calculation of the probable consequences of the defendant's acts."

Thus it would be nice, but not possible, to create a table of homicidal risk for purposes of distinguishing among homicidal crimes along some such lines as these:

Below 1% chance of death—no homicide crime

1%–5% chance of death—manslaughter

Over 5% chance of death—murder.

But see Ill.—S.H.A. ch. 38, ¶ 9–1, which defines the crime in terms of when the defendant "knows that such acts create a strong probability of death or great bodily harm," and thus seems incorrectly to focus exclusively upon the degree of risk.

When defendant fired two bullets into the caboose of a passing train, thereby killing a brakeman, the chances were doubtless much greater that he would not kill than that he would kill. Perhaps the chances of killing were no more than 5%, taking into account the area of the side of the caboose in relationship to the space taken up by the vital parts of its occupants. In view of the lack of social utility in shooting into the side of the caboose, the risk of 5% was held enough for murder in that case. Banks v. State, 85 Tex.Crim. 165, 211 S.W. 217 (1919).

15. People v. Jernatowski, 238 N.Y. 188, 144 N.E. 497 (1924).

16. State v. Joy, 452 A.2d 408 (Me.1982); Hyam v. Director of Public Prosecutions, [1975] A.C. 55 (1974).

17. Banks v. State, 85 Tex.Crim. 165, 211 S.W. 217 (1919).

18. Wiley v. State, 19 Ariz. 346, 170 P. 869 (1918); see Hill v. Commonwealth, 239 Ky. 646, 40 S.W.2d 261 (1931).

19. Mayes v. People, 106 Ill. 306, 46 Am.Rep. 698 (1883).

20. Commonwealth v. Malone, 354 Pa. 180, 47 A.2d 445 (1946). Cf. Commonwealth v. Atencio, 345 Mass. 627, 189 N.E.2d 223 (1963) (surviving participant in game of Russian roulette convicted of involuntary manslaughter; conviction *held* affirmed).

21. Brinkley v. State, 233 A.2d 56 (Del.1967) (defendant fired twice from eight feet away in general direction of victim while both in small room, and he "must have known that bullets ricochet in unpredictable directions upon hitting hard substances"); Myrick v. State, 199 Ga. 244, 34 S.E.2d 36 (1945).

22. State v. Trott, 190 N.C. 674, 130 S.E. 627 (1925). See also State v. Ibn Omar-Muhammad, 102 N.M. 274, 694 P.2d 922 (1985) (driving at high speed through police roadblock); State v. Snyder, 311 N.C. 391, 317 S.E.2d 394 (1984) (driving while intoxicated into intersection against light and at speed of 60–70 m.p.h.); Commonwealth v. Taylor, 461 Pa. 557, 337 A.2d 545 (1975) (traveling at great speed near playground).

Compare Sheriff v. LaMotte, ___ Nev. ___, 680 P.2d 333 (1984) (erratic driving causing death not sufficient); Essex

breathe; [23] selling "pure" (i.e., undiluted) heroin.[24] Other sorts of extremely risky conduct may be imagined; throwing stones from the roof of a tall building onto the busy street below; piloting a speedboat through a group of swimmers; swooping an airplane so low over a traveling automobile as to risk the decapitation of the motorist. In any such case, if death actually results to an endangered person, and occurs in a foreseeable way, the defendant's conduct makes him an eligible candidate for a murder conviction.[25]

For murder of the depraved-heart type the above cases show that the required risk may be risk to a group of persons, as in the case of the shots fired into the caboose or into the room containing several persons; or it may be risk only to a single person, as in the case of the thrown beer glass or the shaken baby.[26] Of course, the situation may be such that the risk of death is too slight for murder where only one person is endangered by defendant's conduct, whereas the risk is sufficient where several are thus hazarded; thus it may not be murder for a hunter to shoot at a deer with one lone hunting companion nearby, though unluckily the companion is killed; whereas the same conduct in a wooded area filled with hunters (one of whom is killed) may amount to murder.

WESTLAW REFERENCES

topic(203) /p depraved /s murder /p risk

(b) Realization of the Risk. Assuming that the defendant's conduct creates what a reasonable man would know to be an unrea-

sonable and very high degree of risk of death or serious bodily injury to another person or to several others, there remains the question of whether he is guilty of murder if he is not aware of the risk created by his conduct. He may, for instance, be too absent-minded or to feeble-minded (though not insane) or too drunk to realize the seriousness of the risk.

Most of the cases are ambiguous on the matter; they tend to speak of conduct which "evinces" or "manifests" or "shows" a depraved heart, without spelling out whether he must actually possess this depraved heart (i.e., have a subjective realization of the risk) or whether it is enough that a reasonable man would have realized the risk and so would have had a depraved heart. The same is true of many statutes, even those found in modern codes. But some of the recent recodifications follow the Model Penal Code [27] in expressly stating that the subjective state of mind of recklessness is required, while a few others express some other mental state.

The English judge and criminal law historian Stephen took the view that one should not be guilty of murder of this type unless he was subjectively aware of the risk.[28] Justice Holmes, on the other hand, thought that he should be guilty of murder if a reasonable man would have realized the risk, regardless of whether he himself actually realized it.[29] A few cases have specifically taken sides on the issue. Thus an English case, following the Holmes view, approved the trial court's instruction to the jury that if the defendant's conduct (shaking a baby, thus suffocating it to death) was such that a reasonable man would

---

v. Commonwealth, 228 Va. 273, 322 S.E.2d 216 (1984) (driving recklessly while intoxicated insufficient, can be only involuntary manslaughter); with People v. Watson, 30 Cal.3d 290, 179 Cal.Rptr. 43, 637 P.2d 279 (1981), criticized in Note, 71 Calif.L.Rev. 1298 (1983) (driving recklessly while intoxicated is murder).

23. Regina v. Ward, [1956] 1 Q.B. 351.

24. State v. Randolph, 676 S.W.2d 943 (Tenn.1984).

25. As we saw when discussing causation in connection with crimes of recklessness and negligence, the defendant may not be liable criminally for injurious consequences to unhazarded victims or to hazarded victims injured in an extraordinary fashion. See § 3.12(e), (g).

26. Under a now-superceded New York statute defining murder as including "killing * * * by an act immi-

nently dangerous to others, and evincing a depraved mind, regardless of human life," it was held that, because of the word "others," the risk must be to more than one person. People v. Ludkowitz, 266 N.Y. 233, 194 N.E. 688 (1935). Contra: Alvarez v. State, 41 Fla. 532, 27 So. 40 (1899); Hogan v. State, 36 Wis. 226 (1874), under similar statutes.

27. Model Penal Code § 210.02.

28. 3 J. Stephen, History of the Criminal Law of England, 22 (1883).

29. O. Holmes, The Common Law 53–54 (1881); Commonwealth v. Chance, 174 Mass. 245, 252, 54 N.E. 551, 554 (1899).

have realized that death or serious bodily injury was likely to result, the defendant would be guilty of murder.[30] On the other hand, some cases have considered the defendant's conduct after the fatal blow as relevant on the issue of liability for murder, thus in effect recognizing the Stephen view of the subjective nature of depraved-heart murder. So when the defendant, by driving his car in a way which created great risk, struck and fatally injured a pedestrian, his conduct in stopping and taking the victim to the hospital was held to "negative the idea of wickedness of disposition and hardness of heart" required for depraved-heart murder.[31]

No doubt most depraved-heart murder cases do not require a determination of the issue of whether the defendant actually was aware of the risk entailed by his conduct; his conduct was very risky and he himself was reasonable enough to know it to be so. It is only the unusual case which raises the issue—where the defendant is more absent-minded, stupid or intoxicated than the reasonable man.

In the unusual case where the defendant is not aware of the risk, which view is preferable, Holmes' objective view or Stephen's subjective one? It is a question of how much fault should be required for murder; for one who consciously creates risk is morally a worse person than one who unconsciously

does so, though each of the two persons may constitute an equal danger to his fellow man. On balance, it would seem that, to convict of murder, with its drastic penal consequences, subjective realization should be required.[32] One who is too absent-minded or feeble-minded to think of the risk ought not to be held guilty of murder, though it does not follow that he should escape all criminal liability, such as a conviction of manslaughter or of some other crime of negligent homicide.

The real difficulty concerns the intoxicated person who conducts himself in a very risky way but, because of his drunkenness, fails to realize it. If his conduct causes death, should he escape murder liability? The person who unconsciously creates risk because he is voluntarily drunk is perhaps morally worse than one who does so because he is sober but mentally deficient. At all events, the cases generally hold that drunkenness does not negative a depraved heart by blotting out consciousness of risk,[33] and the Model Penal Code, which generally requires awareness of the risk for depraved-heart murder (and for recklessness manslaughter), so provides.[34]

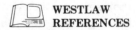
WESTLAW REFERENCES

topic(203) /p depraved /s murder /p aware! kn*w! realiz!

---

30. Regina v. Ward, [1956] 1 Q.B. 351. The word "likely" (in the requirement that death or serious injury be likely to result), which literally requires a greater-than-50% chance of the happening of one of those results, is not to be taken literally. It is better to speak in terms of a "risk" of those results.

The same position is taken in some American cases. See, e.g., State v. LaGasse, 410 A.2d 537 (Me.1980) (statute covers conduct which, objectively viewed, creates such a very high tendency to produce death that the law attributes blameworthiness to the defendant).

31. Commonwealth v. McLaughlin, 293 Pa. 218, 142 A. 213 (1928).

32. In deciding the matter, one should give some attention to the various theories of punishment, see § 1.5. If the dominant theory is revenge or retribution, the moral wrongfulness involved in subjective realization should be required for murder. As to the theory of deterrence, one may wonder whether stupid or absent-minded people can be changed into intelligent or alert-minded people by warning them that they may some day become guilty of murder if they do not make the change. (Insofar as people cannot be thus changed, subjective realization

should be required for murder.) On the other hand, if the disablement theory is dominant, the unaware (stupid and absent-minded) risk-creators should be disabled (by execution or long imprisonment), for they are as dangerous to society as those who are aware of the riskiness of their conduct.

33. E.g., Hamilton v. Commonwealth, 560 S.W.2d 539 (Ky.1977); People v. Langworthy, 416 Mich. 630, 331 N.W.2d 171 (1982). See Annot., 12 A.L.R. 861, 894 (1921), supplemented by 79 A.L.R. 897, 906 (1932). Contra: Langford v. State, 354 So.2d 313 (Ala.1977) (statute requires that some mental operation have taken place to "evidence a depraved mind," which did not occur here where defendant because of intoxication did not realize the likelihood of a death-producing collision).

34. Model Penal Code § 2.08(2): "When recklessness establishes an element of the offense, if the actor, due to self-induced intoxication, is unaware of a risk of which he would have been aware had he been sober, such unawareness is immaterial." The arguments for and against a special rule in regard to the effect of intoxication on the awareness aspects of recklessness crimes are set out in Model Penal Code § 2–08, Comment at 358–59 (1985).

```
topic(203)  /p  depraved  /s  murder  /p  insan!
   intoxicat!  incapacitat!  (mental**  /2  state  disability
   disabled)
```

§ 7.5 Felony Murder

At the early common law one whose conduct brought about an unintended death in the commission or attempted commission of a felony was guilty of murder. Today the law of felony murder varies substantially throughout the country, largely as a result of efforts to limit the scope of the felony-murder rule. American jurisdictions have limited the rule in one or more of the following ways: (1) by permitting its use only as to certain types of felonies; (2) by more strict interpretation of the requirement of proximate or legal cause; (3) by a narrower construction of the time period during which the felony is in the process of commission; (4) by requiring that the underlying felony be independent of the homicide.

(a) History of the Felony-Murder Doctrine. At one time the English common law felony-murder rule was that one who, in the commission or attempted commission of a felony, caused another's death,[1] was guilty of murder,[2] without regard to the dangerous nature of the felony involved or to the likelihood

that death might result from the defendant's manner of committing or attempting the felony.[3] Later, as the number of felonies multiplied so as to include a great number of relatively minor offenses, many of which involved no great danger to life or limb, it became necessary, in order to alleviate the harshness of the rule, to limit it in some fashion.[4] Thus, suppose a statute makes it a felony to sell intoxicating liquor; yet if the purchaser should drink so much as to fall asleep in a blizzard on the way home and die of exposure, the seller ought not to be deemed a murderer, even though the felony actually caused the death in the sense that, but for the felony, the death would not have occurred.[5] It is a felony to make a false tax return; but if the revenue agent investigating the taxpayer's return should slip on the taxpayer's front steps and break his neck, the taxpayer ought not to be guilty of murder, though his act in filing a false return may have been an actual cause of death.

In England the courts came to limit the felony-murder doctrine in one of two ways: (1) by requiring that the defendant's conduct in committing the felony involve an act of violence in carrying out a felony of violence,[6] or (2) by requiring that the death be the natural and probable consequence of the defendant's

§ 7.5

1. It has never been enough for felony murder that *while* the defendant was committing the felony someone nearby died. Thus, while *A* breaks and enters *B*'s house downstairs, *B*, knowing nothing of the burglary, suffers a heart attack upstairs; there is no causal connection between *A*'s felony and *B*'s death even in the "but-for" sense, but rather a mere coincidence of time and place. The requirement that the defendant, by his conduct in committing or attempting the felony, must actually *cause* the death is implicit in the words "in the commission or attempted commission of" which appear in the felony-murder formula. See § 7.5(f).

2. The courts sometimes explain felony murder by stating that the felon's intent to commit the felony supplies the intent to kill, so that the felon intended to kill, resulting in a plain case of intent-to-kill murder. E.g., People v. Olsen, 80 Cal. 122, 22 P. 125 (1889); Simpson v. Commonwealth, 293 Ky. 831, 170 S.W.2d 869 (1943). This sort of talk is pure fiction, and it is better to recognize felony murder as a category of murder separate from intent-to-kill murder. See People v. Root, 524 F.2d 196 (9th Cir.1975) (concluding that consequently the felony-murder statute does not involve an unconstitutional irrational presumption of intent). Various other constitution-

al attacks have likewise been rejected by the courts. See, e.g., State v. Crump, 232 Kan. 265, 654 P.2d 922 (1982).

3. R. Moreland, The Law of Homicide 42 (1952); Model Penal Code § 210.2, Comment at 30–31 (1980).

4. At the time the felony-murder rule developed, all felonies were punishable by death, so it made little difference whether the felon was hanged for the felony or for the murder. Today most felonies are punishable by penalties much less severe than those imposed for murder, so, once again, the situation is different from what it was at common law, and the need for a limitation on the felony-murder rule exists. See Powers v. Commonwealth, 110 Ky. 386, 61 S.W. 735 (1901).

5. People v. Pavlic, 227 Mich. 562, 199 N.W. 373 (1924).

6. Regina v. Serné, 16 Cox Crim.Cas. 311 (1887) (defendant committed arson of building to collect insurance and sleeping boy accidentally burned to death; "any act known to be dangerous to life, and likely in itself to cause death done for the purpose of committing a felony which caused death, should be murder"); Director of Public Prosecutions v. Beard, [1920] A.C. 479 (defendant raped victim, accidentally smothering her to prevent outcry, "an act of violence in the course or in the furtherance of rape, a felony involving violence").

conduct in committing the felony.[7] In America some cases state the felony-murder rule in the language of the unlimited common law statement, although in fact the felony involved is generally a dangerous kind of felony and the manner of its commission generally involves a risk that in the normal course of events someone might be killed.[8] The better cases, however, expressly add some limitation to the rule, most often requiring that the defendant's conduct be the proximate or legal cause of the victim's death or that the felony attempted or committed be dangerous to life. Some jurisdictions have limited the rule in other ways, such as by requiring that the felony be independent of the homicide or by a strict interpretation of the requirement that the death occur in the commission or attempted commission of a felony.[9]

 WESTLAW REFERENCES

topic(203) /p "felony murder" /s natural probable likely /s consequence result

(b) Limitation to Certain Felonies. In many states, the felony-murder rule has been limited in scope by a requirement that the felony attempted or committed by the defendant must be dangerous to life.[10] Similarly, other courts have required that the felony be one of the few which were felonies at common law (i.e., rape, sodomy, robbery, burglary, arson, mayhem, larceny),[11] or that the felony in question be *malum in se* rather than *malum prohibitum.*[12] The latter two limitations are quite similar to the first: with the exceptions of larceny and consensual sodomy, all the common-law felonies (and especially robbery, arson and rape) involve a danger to life; and

---

7. Regina v. Horsey, 176 Eng.Rep. 129 (Assiz.1862) (defendant commited arson of a barn, accidentally burning a tramp to death; jury was instructed to convict of murder only if death was the natural and probable consequence of the defendant's act in setting the fire; and if the tramp entered the barn after the fire was set, his death was not the natural and probable consequence).

8. People v. De La Roi, 36 Cal.App.2d 287, 97 P.2d 836 (Dist.Ct.App.1939) (defendant, committing mayhem, accidentally killed victim; "Whenever one, in doing an act with the design of committing a felony, takes the life of another, even accidentally, this is murder"); People v. Rye, 33 Cal.2d 688, 203 P.2d 748 (1949) (defendant, after committing robbery, beat victim to prevent his attracting attention, causing victim's death by heart attack; "Inasmuch as the homicide, was committed in the perpetration of the robbery, it is not even necessary that there be an intent to kill"); Witt v. State, 205 Ind. 499, 185 N.E. 645 (1933) (court approved instruction that arson which causes death by burning is murder, without limitation); Simpson v. Commonwealth, 293 Ky. 831, 170 S.W.2d 869 (1943) (defendant, committing robbery, accidentally fractured victim's skull; "The intent to perpetrate a different felony, during the commission of which a person is killed, supplies the elements of malice and intent to murder although the death is actually against the original intention of the party"); Jackson v. State, 286 Md. 430, 408 A.2d 711 (1979) (felony murder where officer shot defendant's hostage; "at common law, homicide arising in the perpetration of, or in the attempt to perpetrate, a felony is murder whether death was intended or not, the fact that the person was engaged in such perpetration or attempt being sufficient to supply the element of malice"); State v. Sims, 162 W.Va. 212, 248 S.E.2d 834 (1978) (statute construed to follow common law rule, and thus felony-murder crime extends to accidental killings). See R. Moreland, The Law of Homicide 48 (1952); Model Penal Code § 210.2, Comment at 30 (1980).

One California case seems to impose a novel limitation upon the felony-murder doctrine. In People v. Sears, 62

Cal.2d 737, 44 Cal.Rptr. 330, 401 P.2d 938 (1965), defendant, intending bodily injury but not a mayhem type of injury or death, inflicted a mayhem type of injury from which the victim died. The court said that even if mayhem may be committed with an intent to injure but without an intent to maim, murder in the perpetration of a mayhem requires an intent to maim. Doubtless the California court is searching for a way to limit the felony-murder doctrine.

9. As will be seen in the discussion which follows, some of these limitations have been brought about in the recodification process. See generally Alderstein, Felony-Murder in the New Codes, 4 Am.J.Crim.L. 249 (1976); Fletcher, Reflections on Felony-Murder, 12 Sw.U.L.Rev. 413 (1981); Note, 23 Cath.Law. 133 (1978); Annot., 50 A.L.R.3d 397 (1973).

10. See People v. Pavlic, 227 Mich. 562, 199 N.W. 373 (1924) (defendant sold liquor, a felony; buyer drank it, became drunk, died of exposure and acute alcoholism; not felony murder because sale of liquor, though a felony, "is an act not itself directly and naturally dangerous to life"); People v. Washington, 62 Cal.2d 777, 44 Cal.Rptr. 442, 402 P.2d 130 (1965) ("The felony-murder doctrine ascribes malice aforethought to the felon who kills in the perpetration of an inherently dangerous felony").

11. Commonwealth v. Exler, 243 Pa. 155, 89 A. 968 (1914) (unintended death from shock resulting from commission of statutory rape is not murder, since statutory rape, though a felony, is not a common-law felony); see People v. Pavlic, supra note 5 (sale of liquor, though a felony, "is only criminal because prohibited by statute. It is not a common-law felony").

12. Reddick v. Commonwealth, 17 Ky.L.Rptr. 1020, 33 S.W. 416 (Ct.App.1895) (arson is *malum in se*, so arson of hotel causing unintended death to a resident thereof constitutes murder); see People v. Pavlic, supra note 5 (sale of liquor "is not inherently criminal [i.e., is not *malum in se*] * * * is what the law terms an act *malum prohibitum* ").

generally the felonies which are designated *malum in se* as distinguished from those *malum prohibitum* likewise involve this danger to life. The limitation is best worded, however, in language of dangerousness rather than in terms of common-law felonies [13] or of felonies which are *mala in se*.[14]

The requirement that the felony be dangerous to life has been stated in two different ways. Under one approach, the question is whether on the facts of the particular case, including the circumstances under which the felony was committed, there was a foreseeable danger to human life.[15] Thus, while it may be said as an abstract proposition that the theft felonies (larceny, embezzlement and false pretenses) do not involve danger to life, a thief may commit his theft crime in a way which does create a foreseeable danger to life; under this first view it would be felony murder if death did result under these circumstances.[16] The other approach limits the felony-murder doctrine to those felonies which are "inherently dangerous," that is, the peril to human life must be determined from the elements of the felony in the abstract rather than from the facts of the particular case.[17] Under this view, false pretenses is not a dangerous felony even when committed by inducing a person to forego a life-prolonging operation.[18]

On principle, the latter approach is incorrect, for if the purpose of the felony-murder doctrine is to hold felons accountable for unintended deaths caused by their dangerous conduct, then it would seem to make little difference whether the felony committed was dangerous by its very nature or merely dangerous as committed in the particular case. If the armed robber is to be held guilty of felony murder because of a death occurring from the accidental firing of his gun, it seems no more harsh to apply the felony-murder doctrine to the thief whose fraudulent scheme

---

13. First, the common-law felony of larceny is not ordinarily a dangerous felony; if death should occur in an extraordinary, unforeseeable fashion, it ought not to be murder. Second, there are some statutory felonies which may be committed in a manner where death is foreseeable (i.e., which involve danger)—e.g., abortion, kidnaping—where if death does result it ought to be murder.

14. See § 1.6(b), for the difficulties in giving exact meaning to the expressions "malum prohibitum" and "malum in se." Furthermore, there may be felonies *mala in se* which do not involve the danger of death, and felonies *mala prohibita* which do involve such danger.

15. Jenkins v. State, 230 A.2d 262 (Del.1967) (felony was fourth degree burglary, defined by statute as the breaking and entering of a building other than a dwelling; *held*, error to instruct that this felony sufficient under all circumstances, as whether it is "foreseeably dangerous to human life" depends "upon whether someone may be reasonably expected to be present in the building, and upon other circumstances of the case"); State v. Wallace, 333 A.2d 72 (Me.1975) (it sufficient that the felony, in "the manner or method of its commission, or attempted commission, presents a serious threat to human life or is likely to cause serious bodily harm," that covers present case in which felony of sodomy was forcible); Commonwealth v. Matchett, 386 Mass. 492, 436 N.E.2d 400 (1982) (attempted extortion could suffice if jury required to "find that the extortion involved circumstances demonstrating the defendant's conscious disregard of the risk to human life"); State v. Harrison, 90 N.M. 439, 564 P.2d 1321 (1977) (felony of false imprisonment suffices if dangerous in manner of commission); Wade v. State, 581 P.2d 914 (Okl. Crim.App.1978) (it sufficient that felony "potentially dangerous in light of the facts and circumstances surrounding both the felony and the homicide").

16. E.g., People v. Olsen, 80 Cal. 122, 22 P. 125 (1889) (defendants, while stealing horses in the victim's possession, killed the victim, perhaps accidentally—perhaps the horses ran over the victim, though the evidence does not disclose the manner of death; conviction of felony murder *held* affirmed).

17. See, e.g., State v. Lashley, 233 Kan. 620, 664 P.2d 1358 (1983) (but concluding that while most forms of theft are not inherently dangerous, the offense of theft by threat is); State v. Underwood, 228 Kan. 294, 615 P.2d 153 (1980) (crime of possession of firearm by drunkard, addict or ex-felon not sufficient; felony must be inherently dangerous to square with theory of felony murder; "that the malicious and premeditated intent of committing the inherently dangerous collateral felony is transferred to the homicide to supply the elements of malice and premeditation").

The issue is often put in terms of whether the legislature viewed the particular felony as dangerous. See People v. Cline, 270 Cal.App.2d 328, 75 Cal.Rptr. 459 (1969) (felony of giving away certain drugs is "inherently dangerous," as legislature has characterized those drugs as dangerous and has defined dangerous drugs as those which are unsafe for self-medication, as these drugs are).

18. People v. Phillips, 64 Cal.2d 574, 51 Cal.Rptr. 225, 414 P.2d 353 (1966) (doctor of chiropractic advised parents of 8-year-old girl not to have her submit to operation for eye cancer but instead to have her treated by him; she died as a result, while operation would have cured her or at least prolonged her life; held, doctor's grand theft not "inherently dangerous," and thus this not felony murder). See also People v. Burroughs, 35 Cal.3d 824, 201 Cal.Rptr. 319, 678 P.2d 894 (1984) (*Phillips* followed; practicing medicine without a license not an inherently dangerous felony which can be predicate for felony murder).

includes inducing the victim to forego a life-prolonging operation.[19] The requirement that the felony be "inherently dangerous" is more understandable, however, if viewed as an attempt by some courts to limit what they believe to be "a highly artificial concept that deserves no extension beyond its required application."[20]

In the modern criminal codes, the question of what kind of felony will suffice is ordinarily addressed in the felony murder statute. Some of these statutes state without qualification that any felony will do, but it is always possible a court will conclude this language must be construed in light of the history of felony murder rather than literally, so that one of the limitations previously discussed will be read into the statute.[21] Some other of the modern statutes describe a general category of felonies which will suffice; these categories in one way or another relate to the dangerousness of the felony and, depending upon the exact language used, might give rise to the inherent-vs.-in-this-case question previously discussed. But most modern felony murder statutes limit the crime to a list of specific felonies—usually rape, robbery, kidnapping, arson and burglary—which involve a significant prospect of violence. Where these lists are found in a statute called first-degree murder and another statute of some lesser degree states it encompasses "all other murder," then it is possible that unlisted felonies will

be held to suffice for felony murder of that lesser degree.[22] But a court which views the felony murder rule with some disfavor may hold that the "all other" language is not sufficient to preserve otherwise-abolished common law crimes.[23]

WESTLAW REFERENCES

topic(203) /p "felony murder" /s (danger! /3 life) "malum in se"

(c) Vicarious Responsibility of Co-felons. Many of the felony-murder cases involve co-felons, only one of whom accidentally or intentionally fires the fatal shot. That person is of course liable for intent-to-kill murder if the shot is fired with intent to kill or of felony murder if it is fired accidentally in the commission of the felony and death is foreseeable. Are his co-felons also liable? This is not so much a matter of felony murder as a matter of parties to crime [24]—the problem of the responsibility of one criminal (A) for the conduct of a fellow-criminal (B) who, in the process of committing or attempting the agreed-upon crime, commits another crime.[25]

If A and B have agreed to rob X by killing him, or by killing him if he resists or if he recognizes his robbers or if necessary to effect an escape, A is of course guilty though B is the one who actually fires the fatal shot. Even though the two have made no such

---

19. See Ludwig, Foreseeable Death in Felony Murder, 18 U.Pitt.L.Rev. 51, 63 (1956).

20. People v. Phillips, supra note 18. The *Phillips* court, it should be added, did not hold that the doctor could not be convicted of murder. Rather, the court only objected to use of the felony-murder concept as a substitute for proof of depraved-heart murder.

See also State v. Underwood, 228 Kan. 294, 615 P.2d 153 (1980) (stressing that illogical results can occur under the broader rule, such as that a defendant is guilty of felony murder, where possession of a gun by an ex-felon is a felony, if he has a prior conviction for writing bad checks and accidentally dropped a firearm, killing a guest in his home).

21. See, e.g., State v. Underwood, 228 Kan. 294, 615 P.2d 153 (1980).

22. See Commonwealth v. Matchett, 386 Mass. 492, 436 N.E.2d 400 (1982), concluding that extortion, not listed in the first degree murder statute, could suffice for second degree felony murder.

23. State v. Dixon, 109 Ariz. 441, 511 P.2d 623 (1973) (consequently no felony murder where defendant sold narcotics to another who died from taking them).

24. However, so that there is no doubt on the matter, some modern felony-murder statutes expressly state that the killing need be done only by one of the participants in the felony. But the absence of such language has not produced a different result, as courts utilize accomplice liability statutes in conjunction with the felony-murder statutes to reach other co-felons, Commonwealth v. Allen, 475 Pa. 165, 379 A.2d 1335 (1977) ("abolition of the application of the felony-murder rule to co-felons who do not, in fact, cause the death would have constituted a startling departure from established Pennsylvania law and is not the type of change that would be expected to be made without comment"), even those not present at the scene of the killing. State v. Lowery, 419 So.2d 621 (Fla.1982).

25. See § 6.6 for a discussion of parties to crime. On the liability of parties in the felony-murder situation, see Annots., 22 A.L.R. 850 (1923), 108 A.L.R. 847 (1937).

agreement, if in the process of robbing or attempting to rob *X B*'s gun goes off accidentally, killing *X, A* would be guilty of the felony murder of *X* as much as *B* would be, under the rule concerning parties to crime that all parties are guilty for deviations from the common plan which are the foreseeable consequences of carrying out the plan (an accidental shooting during an armed robbery being a typical example of a foreseeable deviation from the plan to rob).[26] Doubtless too if *A, B* and *C* undertake to rob *X* and *B* accidentally shoots *C* to death during the robbery, *A* is as guilty as *B* of the felony murder of *C*.[27]

What if *B*, angry perhaps at *C*'s inept manner of assisting in the robbery of *X*, should intentionally shoot *C; B* would be liable for *C*'s murder, of course, of the intent-to-kill type; but would *A* be liable for intent-to-kill murder or felony murder? *B*'s intentional shooting of *C* is so far removed from the common plan as not to make *A* responsible for *B*'s intent-to-kill murder; and *B*'s act should not be considered a felony-murder by *A* because *B*'s conduct had nothing to do with furthering the robbery, the only connection between the robbery and the shooting being a mere coincidence of time and place.[28]

There may be instances, however, in which the killing by *B* is more closely related to the felony but yet was not a reasonably foreseeable consequence of the plan of *A* and *B*

because, for example, the plan as conceived did not contemplate the use or even the carrying of a weapon or other dangerous instrument. In such a case, it is less apparent that unqualified application of parties-to-crime principles, making *A* guilty of the murder by *B* merely because he is a party to the felony by *B*, is just.[29] Because of the realization that rigid application of the felony-murder doctrine in such circumstances can be unduly harsh, a substantial minority of the modern codes provide that if the defendant was not the only participant in the underlying crime, then it is an affirmative defense that the defendant: (a) did not commit the homicidal act or in any way solicit, request, command, importune, cause or aid the commission thereof; and (b) was not armed with a deadly weapon or dangerous instrument; and (c) had no reasonable ground to believe any other participant was armed with such a weapon or instrument; and (d) had no reasonable ground to believe that any other participant intended to engage in conduct likely to result in death or serious physical injury.

 WESTLAW REFERENCES

"felony murder" /s vicarious** /3 responsib! liab!

(d) The "Proximate" or "Legal" Cause Limitation. The requirement in some jurisdictions that the felony be inherently danger-

---

26. For example, in United States v. Carter, 445 F.2d 669 (D.C.Cir.1971), defendant and Whiteside robbed a cab driver. Defendant sat beside the driver and put a choke hold on him, after which Whiteside, seated in the back seat, shot the driver twice in the head. Defendant later voiced objection to another about Whiteside's senseless acts in shooting. Defendant's conviction of felony murder, on an instruction that "if two or more persons acting together and jointly are perpetrating a robbery or are attempting to perpetrate a robbery, and one or more of them, in the course of the robbery or attempted robbery, kills another person, then all the persons involved in the robbery or attempted robbery are guilty of murder in the first degree," was affirmed on appeal. A dissenting judge argued: "Possibly the homicide was the independent act of appellant's co-felon, committed to the dismay of appellant. This is not to say that appellant could not be found guilty of murder. The problem is that his guilt of that offense was not submitted to the jury in terms which would allow but not require, the jury to find that he aided and abetted the commission of the homicide. The proper test in such a case in my opinion should be, not whether the homicide was within the scope of the robbery, but

whether it was in furtherance of a common design or purpose."

27. See Rex v. Plummer, 84 Eng.Rep. 1103 (K.B.1700).

28. Rex v. Plummer, 84 Eng.Rep. 1103 (K.B.1700). (*B* shot *C* to death when the police appeared, in a rage because he thought *C* had led the others into a trap). See also Commonwealth v. Waters, 491 Pa. 85, 418 A.2d 312 (1980) (defendant was entitled to an instruction that his co-felon's shooting must have been in furtherance of the felony, for were "it otherwise, an accomplice to a robbery would be guilty of felony-murder if one of his co-felons during the course of the robbery looked out a window, saw a passerby down the street, and shot and killed him even though the passerby had no connection to the robbery whatsoever"). Contra: People v. Cabaltero, 31 Cal.App.2d 52, 87 P.2d 364 (Dist.Ct.App.1939), criticized by Morris, The Felon's Responsibility for the Lethal Acts of Others, 105 U.Pa.L.Rev. 50, 71–74 (1956).

29. But, it has been held not to be a violation of due process to convict the felony accomplice of murder. Connor v. State, 362 N.W.2d 449 (Iowa 1985).

ous to life (that is, that death be *a* foreseeable consequence of the felony), must be distinguished from the additional requirement of "proximate" or "legal" cause. A given category of felony may be inherently dangerous, but it may still be that the death which actually occurred has come about in such an extraordinary way that as a matter of causation the defendant should not be held accountable for the death. For example, as an abstract proposition arson is a crime which involves danger to life, for death sometimes results from arson. In a given case, however, the victim's conduct in exposing himself to the danger of the fire may be so abnormal and unforeseeable that it cannot be said that his death was legally caused by the defendant's felonious conduct.

The requirement of causation, as applicable to felony-murder cases as well as other cases, is discussed in detail elsewhere in this book.[30] The subject of causation is briefly reconsidered here for the purpose of showing how it has sometimes been used to limit the harshness of the felony-murder rule.

In felony-murder cases as well as other homicide cases, it is often said that the death must have been the "natural and probable consequence" of the defendant's conduct. When death has occurred only as a consequence of some intervening act following the defendant's conduct (as is frequently the case in the felony-murder context), the issue is frequently put in terms of whether the intervening cause was "foreseeable" (as distinguished from actually "foreseen").[31]

As noted earlier,[32] however, courts have drawn the perimeters of legal cause more closely when the intervening cause was a mere *coincidence* (i.e., where the defendant's act merely put the victim at a certain place at a certain time, and because the victim was so located it was possible for him to be acted upon by the intervening cause) than when it was a *response* to the defendant's prior actions (i.e., a reaction to conditions created by the defendant). Foreseeability is required as to the former, but in the latter instance the question is whether the intervening act was abnormal—that is, whether, looking at the matter with hindsight, it seems extraordinary.[33]

On the basis of these principles, it is clear that if *A* sets fire to *B*'s occupied house it is felony-murder if *B* or a member of his household[34] or a fireman fighting the blaze[35] is burned to death. While the chances may be all in favor of no one's death by fire, these deaths are neither unforeseeable nor the result of abnormal happenings. Firemen usually put out house fires without getting killed, but the death of a fireman fighting such a blaze happens often enough that its occurrence does not greatly surprise us. So too we would not view it as abnormal if a brave stranger were to rush into the house in an attempt to save a trapped member of *B*'s household crying for help at an upstairs window, and if the stranger died in the fire this

---

30. See § 3.12.

31. Thus in a leading felony-murder case, State v. Glover, 330 Mo. 709, 50 S.W.2d 1049 (1932), where defendant set fire to a drug store to collect the insurance, and a fireman was killed fighting the blaze, the court *held* the defendant guilty of murder on the felony-plus-foreseeable-death test, on the basis that he "had reason to think members of the fire department ∗ ∗ ∗ would congregate at the drug store to fight the fire, and thus would place themselves within perilous range of the flames," so that "the ensuing homicide was a natural and probable consequence of the arson." The court stated that the defendant himself realized that people would be attracted to the fire; but did not base its decision on this ground. In Commonwealth v. Moyer, 357 Pa. 181, 53 A.2d 736 (1947), *A*, armed, attempted to rob *X* and *Y*; *X* pulled a gun; *A* shot

at *X*; *X* shot at *A* but hit and killed *Y*; *held, A* guilty of murder of *Y* because his attempted robbery set in motion "a chain of events which were or should have been within his contemplation."

32. See § 3.12.

33. In the great majority of cases, the same result might be reached whether a foresight or hindsight approach is used. The distinction is occasionally of real importance, however. See § 3.12.

34. E.g., State v. Leopold, 110 Conn. 55, 147 A. 118 (1929).

35. Cf. State v. Glover, 330 Mo. 709, 50 S.W.2d 1049 (1932). Here defendant set fire to a drug store to collect insurance; the fireman was burned to death when an explosion pinned him in the ruins.

would also be felony murder.[36] On the other hand, it seems unlikely that the arsonist would be held guilty of felony murder if a looter entered the blazing building to steal whatever he could find [37] or if a fireman were to fall off the fire truck on its way back to the fire station after putting out the conflagration.[38]

Robberies by armed robbers no doubt are even more likely to result in unintended deaths than are arsons. Often it is the victim of the robbery who is accidentally killed. The armed robber committing or attempting a robbery whose loaded gun, pointed at his victim, goes off accidentally,[39] or is discharged accidentally when the robber and his victim are struggling for the gun,[40] is guilty of felony murder when the robbery victim is thus killed. And if the robber should hit his victim hard with a bludgeon, not intending to kill him but only to facilitate the robbery by disabling him temporarily, but thereby crushing his skull and causing death, the robber again would be guilty of felony murder.[41]

In the robbery situation it sometimes happens that someone other than the robbery victim is killed by the robber's gun. If the robber, in the commission or attempted commission of the crime, should, even accidentally, kill an interfering policeman or bystander at whom the robber points his gun or with whom the robber struggles, this is felony-murder. The same may sometimes be true even when a confederate robber is accidental-

ly killed by the robber's gun. Thus in one case A and B attempted to rob X, a pedestrian, on the street; while B, in front of X, held a knife in X's ribs, A, behind X, struck him over the head with the butt of his loaded pistol; the shock of the blow discharged the gun; and the bullet killed B. A was held guilty of the felony murder of B.[42]

In the robbery cases it may also happen that someone (the robbery victim, an interceding policeman, an innocent bystander, a fellow robber) is killed by a bullet fired from the gun of someone other than the robber. A series of cases, principally from Pennsylvania, raises the issue of the robber's liability under various alternative circumstances: [43] In one case A attempted to rob X and Y; X reached for his gun to frustrate the robbery; A shot at X; X returned the fire, aiming at A but accidentally killing Y. Under these circumstances A was held guilty of the murder of Y, because his actions in attempting the robbery set in motion "a chain of events which were or should have been within his contemplation." [44] In another case three robbers were preparing to flee after a robbery when two policemen, X and Y, appeared on the scene; the robbers fired at the policemen, who fired back; X's bullet struck and killed Y. It was held that the robbers were guilty of murdering Y, since their conduct in firing at the policemen, knowing that their fire would be returned, was the "proximate cause" of Y's death.[45] In a third case A and B, after rob-

---

36. In State v. Glover, supra note 40, the court speaks of arson creating a danger that firemen "and citizens generally would congregate at the drug store to fight the fire."

37. In Regina v. Horsey, 176 Eng.Rep. 129 (Assiz. 1862), the defendant committed arson of an empty barn by firing a haystack next to the barn, and a tramp who entered the barn after the fire was set was burned to death; held, defendant not liable for murder since, under the circumstances, death was not the natural and probable consequence of setting the fire.

38. An alternative reason for not holding the arsonist guilty of murder might be that the death occurred after, not "in the commission of," the arson. See § 7.5(f).

39. E.g., Rex v. Elnick, 33 Can.Crim.Cas. 174, 53 D.L.R. 298 (1920).

40. E.g., People v. Manriquez, 188 Cal. 602, 206 P. 63 (1922); Commonwealth v. Lessner, 274 Pa. 108, 118 A. 24 (1922).

41. Cf. Commonwealth v. Stelma, 327 Pa. 317, 192 A. 906 (1937) (defendant knocked victim over head with rock, not intending to kill and not at that time intending to rob; then defendant took his money from victim; later victim died of head injury; held murder in commission of robbery).

42. Robbins v. People, 142 Colo. 254, 350 P.2d 818 (1960).

43. See Annot., 56 A.L.R.3d 239 (1974); Hitchler, The Killer and His Victim in Felony-Murder Cases, 53 Dick.L. Rev. 3 (1948); Note, 28 Temp.L.Q. 453 (1955).

44. Commonwealth v. Moyer, 357 Pa. 181, 53 A.2d 736 (1947). Accord: People v. Payne, 359 Ill. 246, 194 N.E. 539 (1935) ("It reasonably might be anticipated that an attempted robbery would meet with resistance during which the victim might be shot * * * by * * * some one else in attempting to prevent the robbery").

45. Commonwealth v. Almeida, 362 Pa. 596, 68 A.2d 595 (1949). Accord: People v. Podolski, 332 Mich. 508, 52

bing X, started to flee; X grabbed his gun and fired at the robbers, his bullet killing B. A was held guilty of the murder of B on the theory that the death of B, though unintended by A, was the foreseeable consequence of A's conduct in joining in the robbery of X.[46] Three years later, in a case (the well-known *Redline* case) involving substantially the same facts (the only difference being that an interceding policeman, rather than the robbery victim, shot one of the two robbers to death), the last of the above cases was overruled. The court stated that murder cannot be based upon a shooting which constitutes a justifia-

ble homicide (e.g., where the policeman or felony victim shoots the felon to prevent the commission of the felony or to prevent the felon's escape).[47]

Although it is now generally accepted [48] that there is no felony-murder liability when one of the felons is shot and killed by the victim,[49] a police officer,[50] or a bystander,[51] it is not easy to explain why this is so. It cannot be correct, as the *Redline* court at one point indicated, that the felon is never liable where the death in question constitutes lawful homicide.[52] Nor can it be correct to say, as the court at another point says, rather

---

N.W.2d 201 (1952) (quoting from Commonwealth v. Moyer, supra). Contra: Commonwealth v. Moore, 121 Ky. 97, 88 S.W. 1085 (1905) (*A*, robbing *X*, was resisted by *X*, who shot at *A*, killing innocent bystander *Y*; to hold *A* guilty of felony murder "would be carrying the rule of criminal responsibility for the acts of others beyond all reason"). *Almeida* was later overruled. Commonwealth ex rel. Smith v. Myers, 438 Pa. 218, 261 A.2d 550 (1970).

Compare with the situation in which the police are returning the fire of the felon, the case in which one police officer shoots another without any prior shooting by the felon. See State v. Andreu, 222 So.2d 449 (Fla.App. 1969) (unknown to burglars, police staked out premises in advance; contrary to prearranged plan, one officer moved in darkness in direction to be covered by another officer, who shot and killed him on the mistaken belief that he was one of the burglars).

In People v. Wood, 8 N.Y.2d 48, 167 N.E.2d 736, 201 N.Y.S.2d 328 (1960), the defendant committed the felony of shooting in a gun fight in a tavern; when the police arrived, the defendant tried to escape; the police justifiably fired at the defendant but missed, killing two innocent bystanders. The defendant was held not guilty of felony murder under the unusually-worded New York statute punishing as murder an unjustifiable and inexcusable "killing * * * committed * * * by a person engaged in the commission of, or in the attempt to commit, a felony;" for (1) this language requires that the death-producing act of killing be the act of the felon (or of a confederate for whose acts the felon is responsible), and (2) the language requires the death to be unjustifiable and inexcusable, and here it was excusable homicide (from the policeman's point of view).

46. Commonwealth v. Thomas, 382 Pa. 639, 117 A.2d 204 (1955). See also State v. Baker, 607 S.W.2d 153 (Mo. 1980).

In Commonwealth v. Bolish, 381 Pa. 500, 113 A.2d 464 (1955) (reversed on other grounds), *A* hired *B* to commit arson; *B* unintentionally burned himself to death; the court said *A* committed murder of *B* for death to *B* was a foreseeable consequence of *A*'s conduct in causing the arson. Contra: People v. Ferlin, 203 Cal. 587, 265 P. 230 (1928) (arson).

47. Commonwealth v. Redline, 391 Pa. 486, 137 A.2d 472 (1958), noted in 71 Harv.L.Rev. 1565 (1958). A concur-

ring judge would overrule the *Almeida* and *Bolish* cases too; a dissenting judge would uphold *Almeida*, *Bolish* and *Thomas*, and he accused the majority of "coddling * * * murderers, communists and criminals."

48. But see People v. Caldwell, 36 Cal.3d 210, 203 Cal. Rptr. 433, 681 P.2d 274 (1984) (defendant's acts in confronting police with gun and preparing to shoot it out proximate cause of co-felon's killing by police); State v. Baker, 607 S.W.2d 153 (Mo.1980) (felony murder liability, as the "significant factor is whether the death was the natural and proximate result of the acts of the appellant or of an accomplice").

49. People v. Washington, 62 Cal.2d 777, 44 Cal.Rptr. 442, 402 P.2d 130 (1965); Weick v. State, 420 A.2d 159 (Del.1980); State v. Crane, 247 Ga. 779, 279 S.E.2d 695 (1981); Campbell v. State, 293 Md. 438, 444 A.2d 1034 (1982); People v. Austin, 370 Mich. 12, 120 N.W.2d 766 (1963); Sheriff v. Hicks, 89 Nev. 78, 506 P.2d 766 (1973); State v. Canola, 73 N.J. 206, 374 A.2d 20 (1977); Jackson v. State, 92 N.M. 461, 589 P.2d 1052 (1979); Wooden v. Commonwealth, 222 Va. 758, 284 S.E.2d 811 (1981).

50. People v. Antick, 15 Cal.3d 79, 123 Cal.Rptr. 475, 539 P.2d 43 (1975); People v. Gilbert, 63 Cal.2d 690, 47 Cal.Rptr. 909, 408 P.2d 365 (1965); Campbell v. State, 293 Md. 438, 444 A.2d 1034 (1982); Commonwealth v. Redline, 391 Pa. 486, 137 A.2d 472 (1958).

51. People v. Wood, 8 N.Y.2d 48, 201 N.Y.S.2d 328, 167 N.E.2d 736 (1960).

52. "How can anyone * * * have a criminal charge lodged against him for the consequences of the lawful conduct of another person? The mere statement of the question carries with it its own answer." Commonwealth v. Redline, 391 Pa. 486, 137 A.2d 472 (1958). But it is not true that one can never be guilty of murder when the act of killing constitutes a lawful homicide. It is justifiable homicide, for instance, for the public executioner to execute the death penalty on a condemned prisoner pursuant to a court judgment. But if *A* perjures an innocent man *B* into the electric chair, and the executioner *X* pulls the switch which electrocutes *B* to death, *A* can not escape criminal liability for *B*'s murder. Furthermore, in *Almeida* and *Moyer*, where bystanders rather than fellow-robbers were shot, the killings constituted lawful homicides as much as the killing in *Redline*, see § 3.12(d); yet the court in *Redline* refused to overrule those cases.

apologetically, that the felon is never liable when the death is lawful because "justifiable," though he can be when it is lawful because "excusable."[53] It has been suggested that, though it may be foreseeable that someone (robbery victim, policeman, bystander) might be killed by a robber's gun during the robbery, it is not foreseeable that anyone would be slain by another's gun.[54] It would seem, however, that robbery triggers armed resistance from robbery victims and policemen often enough that it is neither unforeseeable nor abnormal that lethal bullets might fly from guns other than those of the robbers.[55]

A more plausible explanation, it is submitted, is the feeling that it is not justice (though it may be poetic justice) to hold the felon liable for murder on account of the death, which the felon did not intend, of a co-felon willingly participating in the risky venture.[56] It is true that it is no defense to intentional homicide crimes that the victim voluntarily placed himself in danger of death at the hands of the defendant, or even that he consented to his own death: a mercy killing constitutes murder; and aiding suicide is murder unless special legislation reduces it to manslaughter.[57] But with unintended killings it would seem proper to take the victim's

willing participation into account, especially if one is not altogether enamored of the felony-murder doctrine.[58] That notion is quite clearly reflected in the provision to be found in several of the modern criminal codes: felony murder liability is expressly limited to the killing of one other than a participant in the underlying felony.

It occasionally happens that one of several co-felons accidentally kills himself while committing or attempting the felony, and the question arises as to the murder liability of his fellow-criminals for the death. Thus A and B together commit arson, or A hires B to commit an arson, and B, who starts the blaze, accidentally burns himself to death; is A guilty of the arson-murder of B? It would seem that the death of B, caused in such a way, is no more unforeseeable or abnormal than a fireman's death would be, so that A might be held liable for the felony murder of B.[59] On the other hand, if one accepts the *Redline* limitation on murder liability for a co-felon's death, on the theory that it is not right to hold him for the death of a willing participant in the risky criminal venture, there should be a similar limitation for the death of a co-felon who manages accidentally to kill himself while voluntarily engaging in the risky criminal enterprise.

53. It may be that in *Redline* the shooting of the co-felon by a policeman is "justifiable" homicide, while in *Almeida* the shooting of a bystander by a bullet aimed at the felon is, because the particular death was accidental, "excusable." There may be a semantic difference between the two words, but on principle there should be no difference in consequences. See Note, 71 Harv.L.Rev. 1565 (1958). The Pennsylvania Supreme Court has more recently abandoned the distinction. See Commonwealth ex rel. Smith v. Myers, 438 Pa. 218, 261 A.2d 550 (1970).

54. Morris, The Felon's Responsibility for the Lethal Acts of Others, 105 U.Pa.L.Rev. 50 (1956).

55. The court in *Redline*, distinguishing between (co-policeman killed by policeman) and *Almeida* (co-policeman killed by policeman) cannot, of course, mean that it is less foreseeable that a co-robber be killed by a police bullet than a co-policeman. The opposite is in fact true, for it is more foreseeable that a bullet will hit the person aimed at than that it will hit another person not aimed at. This was later acknowledged by the Pennsylvania Supreme Court when it overruled *Almeida*. See Commonwealth ex rel. Smith v. Myers, 438 Pa. 218, 261 A.2d 550 (1970).

And see People v. Washington, 62 Cal.2d 777, 44 Cal. Rptr. 442, 402 P.2d 130 (1965): Where robbery victim,

resisting the robbery, shoots and kills someone, the robber is not guilty of felony murder, but not because the death is not a foreseeable consequence of the robbery. "It is not enough that the killing was a risk reasonably to be foreseen and that the robbery might therefore be regarded as a proximate cause of the killing."

56. Unless perhaps it is the felon's own weapon which kills his colleague, as in Robbins v. People, 142 Colo. 254, 350 P.2d 818 (1960).

57. See § 7.8(c).

58. It is arguable that the felony-murder doctrine should be abolished, not merely limited. See § 7.5(h).

59. Scott v. State, 252 Ga. 251, 313 S.E.2d 87 (1984); Commonwealth v. Bolish, 381 Pa. 500, 113 A.2d 464 (1955); In re Leon, 122 R.I. 548, 410 A.2d 121 (1980). Contra: People v. Ferlin, 203 Cal. 587, 265 P. 230 (1928), where the court said the death of B "was not in furtherance of the conspiracy" between A and B to commit arson, "but was entirely opposed to it." But so is the accidental death in the commission of any felony "entirely opposed to" the felony. The cases are discussed in Morris, The Felon's Responsibility for the Lethal Acts of Others, 105 U.Pa.L. Rev. 50, 78–81 (1956).

Most of the more recent cases involving the killing of a co-felon, however, do not purport to rest upon this latter theory. Rather, it is more generally said that whenever a death is caused by a shot fired by someone other than one of the felons, the killing "can hardly be considered to be 'in furtherance' of the commission or attempted commission of a felony," [60] and does not satisfy "the 'agency' theory of felony murder." [61] Liability in any such case is declared to be "discordant with rational and enlightened views of criminal culpability and liability," [62] especially inasmuch as "the purpose of deterring felons from killing by holding them strictly responsible for killings they or their co-felons commit is not effectuated by punishing them for killings committed by persons not acting in furtherance of the felony." [63] Such reasoning logically leads to the conclusion, which several courts have reached, that the felony-murder rule is equally inapplicable when the killing by another is of the victim,[64] a police officer,[65] or a bystander.[66]

As the cases rejecting that conclusion [67] emphasize, such results cannot be explained on the ground that proximate cause is lacking.[68] Sometimes this is forthrightly acknowledged. When the California Supreme Court narrowed the felony-murder rule in that state so that it did not extend to shootings by nonfelons, the court did not purport to rest its position upon principles of causation at all; rather, it forthrightly explained that its limitation of the felony-murder doctrine was based upon a dissatisfaction with its strict liability aspect. The court thus made it clear that if a felon initiates a gun battle "the victim's self-defensive killing or the police officer's killing in the performance of his duty cannot be considered an independent intervening cause for which the defendant is not liable." [69] Causation is thus established, but malice will not be implied under the felony-murder doctrine. Rather malice must be proved under the depraved-heart theory of murder.[70] Reliance upon that theory, of course, increases the prosecution's problems of proof,[71] and in most jurisdictions reduces the penalty which may be imposed upon conviction.[72]

60. Weick v. State, 420 A.2d 159 (Del.1980).

61. Campbell v. State, 293 Md. 438, 444 A.2d 1034 (1982).

62. State v. Canole, 73 N.J. 206, 374 A.2d 20 (1977).

63. Campbell v. State, 293 Md. 438, 444 A.2d 1034 (1982).

64. Alvarez v. District Court, 186 Colo. 37, 525 P.2d 1131 (1974); Commonwealth v. Balliro, 349 Mass. 505, 209 N.E.2d 308 (1965).

65. Commonwealth ex rel. Smith v. Myers, 438 Pa. 218, 261 A.2d 550 (1970).

66. Commonwealth v. Moore, 121 Ky. 97, 88 S.W. 1085 (1905); State v. Oxendine, 187 N.C. 658, 122 S.E. 568 (1924).

67. People v. Hickman, 59 Ill.2d 89, 319 N.E.2d 511 (1974); Jackson v. State, 286 Md. 430, 408 A.2d 711 (1979); State v. Moore, 580 S.W.2d 747 (Mo.1979); Blansett v. State, 556 S.W.2d 322 (Tex.Crim.App.1977); Miers v. State, 157 Tex.Crim.R. 572, 251 S.W.2d 404 (1952).

68. Thus in State v. Moore, 580 S.W.2d 747 (Mo.1979), where the victim shot at the felon and hit a bystander, the court reasoned it "was reasonably foreseeable that the robbery attempt would meet resistance," so that the bystander's death was "the natural and proximate result of the acts of the appellant or of an accomplice."

69. People v. Gilbert, 63 Cal.2d 690, 47 Cal.Rptr. 909, 408 P.2d 365 (1965).

70. Ibid.; People v. Washington, 62 Cal.2d 777, 44 Cal. Rptr. 442, 402 P.2d 130 (1965). While *Gilbert* and *Washington* seemed to indicate that for depraved-heart murder the felons would have to fire the first shot, a broader rule was later adopted in Taylor v. Superior Court, 3 Cal.3d 578, 91 Cal.Rptr. 275, 477 P.2d 131 (1970) ("the central inquiry in determining criminal liability for a killing committed by a resisting victim or police officer is whether the *conduct* of a defendant or his accomplices was sufficiently provocative of lethal resistance to support a finding of implied malice," so that, "depending upon the circumstances, a gun battle can be initiated by acts of provocation falling short of firing the first shot"). For a rejection of even the *Taylor* depraved-heart type of liability on similar facts, see Sheriff v. Hicks, 89 Nev. 78, 506 P.2d 766 (1973). In People v. Antick, 15 Cal.3d 79, 123 Cal.Rptr. 475, 539 P.2d 43 (1975), where the co-felon shot at a police officer, who fired back and killed the co-felon, the court ruled the surviving felon could not be convicted of depraved-heart murder "based upon his vicarious liability for the crimes of his accomplice," for the accomplice did not kill "another human being" and thus did not himself commit murder.

71. On depraved-heart murder, see § 7.4. On the differences in the two theories, see § 7.5(e).

72. This is because where murder is divided into degrees, as it usually is, typically most felony murder is first degree murder while depraved-heart murder is only murder in the second degree. However, under the California approach, it was held that even if the vicarious liability/

Special mention must be made of one circumstance in which courts *have* generally been willing to impose felony-murder liability even though the shooting was by a person other than one of the felons. This is in the so-called "shield" situation,[73] where courts have reasoned "that a felon's act in using a victim as a shield or in compelling a victim to occupy a place or position of danger constitutes a direct lethal act against the victim."[74] This direct lethal act is deemed to establish a sufficiently close and direct causal connection to justify felony-murder liability.

 WESTLAW REFERENCES

topic(203) /p "felony murder" /s proximate** legal** /3 caus!

topic(203) /p "felony murder" /s predict! foresee!

"felony murder" /s interven*** superven*** supersed*** /3 caus!

redline /p "felony murder" /p lawful** justif! /s homicide kill***

(e) Felony Murder vs. Depraved-Heart Murder. Both depraved-heart murder and felony murder (with its dangerous felony and causation limitations) may convict a defendant for an unintended death; both require that the defendant's conduct involve a risk of death to another or to others. That being so, does the fact that the defendant causes the accidental death in the commission of a felony, rather than causing it while not committing any felony, add anything to his liability? It does do so in one, perhaps two, ways. First, the risk of death may be much less for felony murder than is required for depraved-heart murder, just as less risk is needed for ordinary negligence than is needed for recklessness-manslaughter and less for manslaughter than for that great amount of negligence which "evinces a depraved heart" as is required for murder. Perhaps an arson which creates a 1% chance of killing some fireman will do for murder if a fireman is in fact killed; but if the defendant, instead of committing arson, merely burns his trash in such a careless way as to create the same danger to firemen, he would not have created enough risk for depraved-heart murder or perhaps even recklessness-manslaughter. Secondly, we saw that some authorities require for depraved-heart murder that the defendant be subjectively aware of the (great) risk he creates, but that for felony murder he need not subjectively foresee the (lesser) risk he creates.

All this points up the fact that the somewhat primitive rationale of the felony-murder doctrine is that the defendant, because he is committing a felony, is by hypothesis a bad person, so that we should not worry too much about the difference between the bad results he intends and the bad results he brings about.

 WESTLAW REFERENCES

"felony murder" /p depraved

(f) "In the Commission or Attempted Commission of" the Felony. The common law felony-murder rule requires that the killing occur "in the commission or attempted commission of" the felony. The typical modern statute make it murder to cause a death, accidentally or intentionally, "in the commis-

---

implied malice doctrine is used instead of the felony-murder rule, the nature of the felony (i.e., whether or not it is listed in the first degree murder statute) nonetheless determines the degree of the crime. People v. Gilbert, 63 Cal.2d 690, 47 Cal.Rptr. 909, 408 P.2d 365 (1965). For an interesting exchange as to the soundness of that position, see Pizano v. Superior Court, 21 Cal.3d 128, 145 Cal.Rptr. 524, 577 P.2d 659 (1978).

Consider in this regard the unusual statutory provision in West's Fla.Stat.Ann. § 782.04. Felony murder is first degree murder when the killing was "by a person engaged in the perpetration of, or in the attempt to perpetrate," the felony; it is second degree murder where the killing is by "a person other than the person engaged in the perpetration of or in the attempt to perpetrate such felony." See, e.g., Mikenas v. State, 367 So.2d 606 (Fla.1978) (police officer shot co-felon, surviving felon guilty of second degree murder).

73. Johnson v. State, 252 Ark. 1113, 482 S.W.2d 600 (1972); Wilson v. State, 188 Ark. 846, 68 S.W.2d 100 (1934); Jackson v. State, 286 Md. 430, 408 A.2d 711 (1979); Keaton v. State, 41 Tex.Crim. 621, 57 S.W. 1125 (1900); Taylor v. State, 41 Tex.Crim. 564, 55 S.W. 961 (1900).

See also Pizano v. Superior Court, 21 Cal.3d 128, 145 Cal.Rptr. 524, 577 P.2d 659 (1978) (though on such facts felony-murder doctrine inapplicable under People v. Washington, note 70, using the person as a shield justifies a finding of implied malice sufficient for a first degree murder conviction).

74. Campbell v. State, 293 Md. 438, 444 A.2d 1034 (1982).

sion [or perpetration] or attempted commission [perpetration] of" certain named felonies.
Another common type of felony-murder statute says the killing must happen "in the
course of and in furtherance of" specified
felonies, and yet another declares the killing
must occur "while" specified felonies are being committed or attempted. What is the
scope of these rather vague expressions?

First of all, it is not enough that a killing
occur "during" the felony or its attempt or
"while" it is committed or attempted; something more is required than mere coincidence
of time and place.[75] Thus if, while the defendant was robbing the teller at the bank, a
customer standing in the lobby but unaware
of the robbery should, from natural causes,
suffer a fatal heart attack, the mere fact that
a death occurred at the time of and at the
place of the robbery would not make the
defendant a murderer. There must be some
causal relationship between the felony and
the death,[76] a factor which would doubtless be
present if the customer, with a weak heart,
died of a heart seizure brought on by fright at
witnessing the robbery.

Secondly, if this causal connection does exist, the killing may take place at some time
before or after, as distinguished from during,
the felony, and nevertheless qualify for a killing "in the commission or attempted commission of" the felony. How long before or after
the felony? Consider the following hypothetical situations. A conceives the idea of robbing X's gasoline station, five miles away.
He gets into his car to drive toward X's
station. Four miles (or one mile or one block)

from the station, his mind so taken up with
his thoughts concerning the robbery that he
fails to notice a pedestrian Y, he accidentally
runs over Y and kills him. Is Y's death "in
the commission or attempted commission of"
a robbery? Suppose he runs over pedestrian
Y when turning into the station? A good deal
depends upon the question concerning the
point at which mere preparation for a crime
becomes an attempt to commit it,[77] since for
felony murder A must commit or at least
attempt to commit the felony.[78] Suppose A
does get close enough for an attempt (or else
actually commits the crime)—as where he
pulls out his gun and tells X to stick up his
hands, at which point the gun goes off (accidentally or on purpose) killing X. Here the
homicide is actually accomplished "during"
the commission or attempted commission of
the robbery; such a homicide is surely "in the
commission or attempted commission of" the
felony.[79]

Suppose A, however, does not thus shoot X;
he either takes X's money at gunpoint (i.e.,
commits robbery) or is frightened away without the money after saying "stick 'em up," by
X's armed resistance or by the arrival of a
policeman P at the scene (i.e., A commits only
attempted robbery); he accidentally or intentionally shoots X or P to death on the gas
station premises while making good his escape. Or suppose X or P pursues him for two
blocks (or two miles), at which point A, to
elude pursuit, shoots X or P to death. Or
suppose, after his robbery or attempted robbery, he succeeds in effecting his escape; but
two weeks later, driving his car and thinking

75. United States v. Heinlein, 490 F.2d 725 (D.C.Cir. 1973); Commonwealth v. Waters, 491 Pa. 85, 418 A.2d 312 (1980). This is most apparent in those statutes expressly requiring that the killing also be "in furtherance" of the felony.

76. Thus the court in State v. Harrison, 90 N.M. 439, 564 P.2d 1321 (1977), concluded that its statement in earlier cases that there is felony murder whenever "the homicide is within the res gestae of the initial crime" was insufficient. The court added the requirement of causa-tion, "those acts of defendant or his accomplice initiating and leading to the homicide without an independent force intervening."

77. See § 6.2. No doubt A has not gone so far as to attempt to commit robbery in any of the above situations.

78. Thus, in United States v. Bolden, 514 F.2d 1301 (D.C.Cir.1975), where apparently the death occurred when the defendants first arrived at the store to be robbed, the court stated: "Even if appellants were 'casing' the store preparatory to a later attempt to rob, the requisite intent to rob would not yet have arisen since it is necessary that the felony (robbery here) have progressed beyond mere preparation to an indictable attempt before the homicide occurs."

79. If the mortal wound is inflicted at this point, but X lingers for a few days before he dies, at which time A, having fled the scene, is many states distant, the homicide is nevertheless in the commission of the robbery; it is the infliction of the fatal wound, not the actual death, which must occur in the commission of the felony.

about the robbery instead of the road, he accidentally runs down *Y,* a pedestrian. In all these various situations is the death "in the commission or attempted commission of" the robbery? The same sort of problems arise in connection with the other felonies commonly involved in felony-murder cases, e.g., arson, rape, burglary. The difficulty in giving exact answers lies in the inherent vagueness of the term "in the commission of."

It is sometimes said that the killing must occur in the *res gestae* of the felony or attempted felony; [80] but that, without some further explanation, is not particularly helpful. In a leading case on the scope of the term "in the commission of," [81] *A* and *B* were in the process of burglarizing *X*'s gas station at night when a policeman *P* arrived at the scene. The burglars dropped their booty and took to the near-by woods. *P* followed them for a distance from the station of several hundred feet, *B* then shot *P* to death, no doubt intentionally. *B,* and *A* as well on the basis of general principles relating to parties to crime, were guilty of intent-to-kill murder (not necessarily constituting first degree murder), but were they guilty of first degree murder (murder "in the commission of" the burglary)? The court held that they were. The homicide must be within the *res gestae* of the burglary; this means that the homicide and the burglary must be "closely connected in point of time, place and causal relation." [82] Applying these factors to the case, the court found the homicide to be in the commission of

the burglary, the time between the burglary and the fatal shot being a few minutes, the place being a few hundred feet distant, and the causal connection being that *B* fired the shot to prevent arrest on account of the burglary. At least the case tells us what to look for in construing the scope of the expression "in the commission of": (1) time, (2) place, (3) causal connection. [83]

(1) Time. For purposes of comparing the time of the commission of the felony with the time of the homicide, [84] when is the time of the felony? Robbery is first committed when the defendant takes possession of and moves (i.e., the caption and the asportation of) the victim's property, but it continues as long as he continues to carry it. [85] Burglary is committed when the defendant breaks and enters the building with the appropriate intent; nothing further, like the caption and asportation necessary for robbery, is required for burglary. Arson is committed when the building first catches fire; the further consumption of the building by fire adds nothing further to the arson already committed. Rape is committed upon the first penetration; further sexual activity by the defendant after this initial connection adds nothing to the crime of rape already committed.

Yet for purposes of the time connection implicit in the expression "in the commission of," the crimes of arson, burglary and rape may be considered to continue while the building burns, while the burglars search the building and while the sexual connection is

---

80. See, e.g., Grigsby v. State, 260 Ark. 499, 542 S.W.2d 275 (1976); State v. Hearron, 228 Kan. 693, 619 P.2d 1157 (1980); State v. Wayne, ___ W.Va. ___, 289 S.E.2d 480 (1982).

81. State v. Adams, 339 Mo. 926, 98 S.W.2d 632 (1936).

82. These three factors are frequently stressed in the cases. See, e.g., State v. Hearron, 228 Kan. 693, 619 P.2d 1157 (1980); Haskell v. Commonwealth, 218 Va. 1033, 243 S.E.2d 477 (1978); State v. Wayne, ___ W.Va. ___, 289 S.E.2d 480 (1982). See Annot., 58 A.L.R.3d 851 (1974).

83. In Bizup v. People, 150 Colo. 214, 371 P.2d 786 (1962), the defendant, a passenger in the victim's taxicab, robbed the victim at gunpoint, made him drive down a lonely road, conversed with him a while, then shot him to death. He was held guilty of first-degree murder in the perpetration of the robbery, over his objection that the homicide occurred after the robbery. The court, affirming his conviction, found the robbery and the killing to be

"closely connected in point of time, place and continuity of action;" the killing was done to complete the crime and escape detection.

84. The "time of the homicide" is the time of the infliction of the mortal blow, not necessarily the time of death. See note 79 supra.

85. Stroud v. State, 272 Ind. 12, 395 N.E.2d 770 (1979).

Time is but one factor, however, and thus the mere fact an offense of this kind is a continuing one while the stolen property is held does not mean that any killing during that interval is felony murder. See, e.g., Doane v. Commonwealth, 218 Va. 500, 237 S.E.2d 797 (1977) (defendant ran stop sign and killed a person while driving car he stole the day before; held, while the fiction of larceny as a continuing offense is proper for venue purposes, it alone cannot be used to make this killing felony murder; a showing of a nexus is also needed.

maintained. Thus in the case of the drug store arson which killed the fireman [86] the defendant argued that, even if the death was the foreseeable consequence of the defendant's conduct in committing arson, yet the death did not occur "in the perpetration of" the arson; the arson was complete the moment the fire he set was communicated to the building, and the death occurred much later. The court, however, took the view that the arson continued while the building burned, for purposes of construing the phrase "in the perpetration of" the arson.

But even if it is clear beyond question that the crime was completed before the killing, the felony-murder rule might still apply. The most common case is that in which the killing occurs during the defendant's flight. A great many of the modern statutes contain language—typically the phrase "or in immediate flight therefrom"—making this absolutely clear. But even statutes without such language have rather consistently been construed to extend to immediate flight situations.[87] In assessing what flight is sufficiently immediate, courts require that there have been "no break in the chain of events," [88] as to which a most important consideration is whether the fleeing felon has reached a "place of temporary safety." [89]

(2) Causal Connection. We have seen that the homicide must have some causal connection with the felony in order to qualify for felony murder; more than a mere coincidence of time and place is necessary. In most jurisdictions even more than a but-for causal relationship is required, the usual rule being that the death must be the foreseeable or natural result of the felony.[90] Aside from these matters, however, the term "in the commission of" implies a more or less close causal connection between felony and homicide.[91] A robber who, in flight from the scene, shoots a policeman who threatens to capture him may easily be found to have caused a death in the commission of the robbery; [92] but if, during his flight, he should happen to spot his enemy and shoot him, this death, though equal to the policeman's death in point of time and place, would lack the causal connection which existed in the policeman's case.

So too of accidental, rather than intentional, killings. A robber fleeing at high speed in his getaway car from the scene of his crime who accidentally runs over and kills a pedestrian stands on a different footing from the robber who, after his robbery and successful flight, speeds (and accidentally runs over the pedestrian) from other motives.[93] The fact that the defendant, having committed a robbery or burglary, is carrying away the booty

86. State v. Glover, 330 Mo. 709, 50 S.W.2d 1049 (1932), discussed supra note 35 in connection with the foreseeability of death resulting from the arson.

87. People v. Hickman, 59 Ill.2d 89, 319 N.E.2d 511 (1974); State v. Hearron, 228 Kan. 693, 619 P.2d 1157 (1980).

88. State v. Hutchins, 303 N.C. 321, 279 S.E.2d 788 (1981); Commonwealth v. Kichline, 468 Pa. 265, 361 A.2d 282 (1976).

89. People v. Salas, 7 Cal.3d 812, 103 Cal.Rptr. 431, 500 P.2d 7 (1972); People v. Gladman, 41 N.Y.2d 123, 359 N.E.2d 420 (1976); State v. Squire, 292 N.C. 494, 234 S.E.2d 563 (1977). See also People v. Johnson, 55 Ill.2d 62, 302 N.E.2d 20 (1973) (without qualifying word "temporary").

90. See § 7.5(d).

91. But see Christian v. United States, 394 A.2d 1 (D.C. App.1978) (though coincidence of time and place not enough, "in the course of the felony" jury instruction sufficient in lieu of an "in furtherance" instruction, where defense counsel was free to argue killing outside the scope of the original plan or design).

92. Illustrative of cases stressing the causal connection are State v. Hearron, 228 Kan. 693, 619 P.2d 1157 (1980) (victim's husband, who approached and accused defendant of the felony, then shot by him); State v. Hutchins, 303 N.C. 321, 279 S.E.2d 788 (1981) (defendant shot police so that he "could avoid identification and arrest" for the earlier felony); Commonwealth v. Kichline, 468 Pa. 265, 361 A.2d 282 (1976) (killing was of abducted robbery victim); Haskell v. Commonwealth, 218 Va. 1033, 243 S.E.2d 477 (1978) (victim shot so defendant could escape without identification); State v. Wayne, __ W.Va. __, 289 S.E.2d 480 (1982) (prison escapee shot driver in order to seize getaway car).

93. Whitman v. People, 161 Colo. 110, 420 P.2d 416 (1966) ("The 'perpetration of a robbery' does not come to an end the split second the victim surrenders his money to the gunman and most certainly the 'robbery' continues where, as in the instant case, the robbers are trying desperately to avoid arrest by police officers who are in extremely hot pursuit.").

at the time of the homicide is not so much relevant as to the matter of time [94] as it is as a matter of causal relation. One who carries booty is often more in need of a homicide to effect an escape than one who does not. Thus where a robber, carrying in his car the fruits of his robbery, is stopped by a policeman for speeding some time after and some distance away from the place of robbery and he shoots the policeman to death to prevent his discovery of the stolen goods, the causal connection between the robbery and the homicide is quite close.[95] A similar shooting by a robbery without booty would lack the causal connection necessary to place the homicide "in the commission of" the robbery.

In short, whether there is a sufficient causal connection between the felony and the homicide depends on whether the defendant's felony dictated his conduct which led to the homicide. If it did, and the matters of time and place are not too remote, the homicide may be "in the commission of" the felony; but if it did not, it may not be.

(3) Differing Views on Scope. Though the scope of the phrase "in the commission or attempted commission of" is properly a matter of time, place and causal connection, the question remains how much time, how much space, how much causal connection is close enough, how much too remote? The cases from different jurisdictions differ considerably in this regard. At one extreme are cases like the following: *A* and *B* attempted to rob *X* at his store but were interrupted by a passerby and ran out the door. *X* grabbed *B* on the sidewalk in front of the next store; *A* shot *X* dead. Though time (a few moments), place (a few feet) and causal relation (*A* shot *X* to prevent his arrest for the attempted robbery) were all very close, they were held to be not close enough for the killing to be considered in the attempt to commit robbery, because *A* and *B* had desisted from the attempt and were running away.[96] At the other extreme is the case wherein *A* and *B* robbed *X* in Philadelphia at 2 a.m., stole a car, drove to New Jersey, stopped for something to eat at a diner, sped on their way, were stopped in New Brunswick, N.J., by a policeman *P* for speeding, whereupon *A* shot *P* to death at 4 a.m. Though time (two hours), place (many miles away) and causal relation (perhaps the robbers feared that *P* was stopping them for the robbery, perhaps they feared *P* might notice the booty in the car) were rather remote, the court held that the jury could properly find that the killing occurred in the commission of the robbery.[97] Most of the cases take a view somewhere between these extremes.[98]

Is it preferable to take a narrow or broad or in-between view of the scope of the expression "in the commission or attempted commission of"? No doubt the narrow view indicates an

---

94. See § 7.5(f)(1). Some cases, however, treat the matter of carrying the booty as a more vital factor than it should be. E.g., People v. Marwig, 227 N.Y. 382, 125 N.E. 535 (1919) (attempted robbers got no booty; shooting in flight *held* not in commission of robbery). Cf. Commonwealth v. Doris, 287 Pa. 547, 135 A. 313 (1926) (robbers dropped booty and fled; shooting during flight *held* in the commission of robbery). See Recent Case, 40 Harv.L.Rev. 651 (1927). See also People v. Salas, 7 Cal.3d 812, 103 Cal. Rptr. 431, 500 P.2d 7 (1972) (if defendant has not yet reached a "place of temporary safety," it is not necessary that there also be "scrambling possession" of the booty).

95. State v. Metalski, 116 N.J.L. 543, 185 A. 351 (Ct. Err. & App.1936), held the killing to be "in the perpetration of" the robbery.

96. People v. Marwig, 227 N.Y. 382, 125 N.E. 535 (1919). Accord: State v. Opher, 38 Del. 93, 188 A. 257 (1936) (*A* attempted to rape *B*, who ran, telling *A* she would tell her mother; *A* shot *B*; *held* homicide was not first-degree murder because death was not in the commission of attempted rape). Such a result is unlikely today, especially in those jurisdictions with statutes containing

"or in immediate flight therefrom" language. See People v. Gladman, 41 N.Y.2d 123, 390 N.Y.S.2d 912, 359 N.E.2d 420 (1976), rejecting the *Marwig* approach because of such a statute.

97. State v. Metalski, 116 N.J.L. 543, 185 A. 351 (Ct. Err. & App.1936).

98. E.g., Bizup v. People, supra note 92; State v. Adams, supra note 90; Commonwealth v. Osman, 284 Mass. 421, 188 N.E. 226 (1933) (*A* raped *B*, then killed her to conceal the crime; *held*, homicide in commission of rape); MacAvoy v. State, 144 Neb. 827, 15 N.W.2d 45 (1944), (same); Commonwealth v. Doris, 287 Pa. 547, 135 A. 313 (1926), noted at 40 Harv.L.Rev. 651 (1927) (*A* and *B* robbed *X* Bank, then jumped into car to escape; gunfire disabled car and *A* was captured; *B* fled in a horse-drawn milk wagon pursued by policeman *P* and *B* shot to death; *held*, *A* guilty of murder, since the homicide was in the perpetration of the robbery). The issue of whether a killing is in the commission or attempted commission of a felony is generally a jury question, except where the homicide clearly is or is not in the commission as a matter of law.

antipathy to the whole notion of the felony-murder doctrine.

(4) Homicide Followed by Felony. A problem arises concerning felony murder if the death-blow precedes the felony or the attempt, after which the defendant continues on and commits the felony or its attempt. Of course, if the defendant knocks his intended robbery victim on the head to disable him from resistance, thereby intentionally or accidentally injuring him fatally, and thereafter he takes his victim's money, the homicide occurs in the commission of the felony and so constitutes murder (and under most statutes first-degree murder).[99] But what if the robber thus injures him in a fight, with no thoughts of robbing him, and only later seeing his adversary helpless, decides to rob him? There is a split of authority as to whether this constitutes a homicide in the commission of robbery.[100] It would seem that the homicide, done without thought of a felony, could not be "in the commission of" the felony.

WESTLAW REFERENCES

synopsis,digest("felony murder" /p causel /3 relation! connection)

topic(203 110) /p "felony murder" /s (continu*** /2 offense transaction) nexus

"felony murder" /p afterthought (precede /3 murder killing homicide)

99. E.g., United States v. Butler, 455 F.2d 1338 (D.C. Cir.1971); State v. Nelson, 65 N.M. 403, 338 P.2d 301 (1959). See also People v. Goodridge, 70 Cal.2d 824, 76 Cal.Rptr. 421, 452 P.2d 637 (1969); State v. Little, 249 Or. 297, 431 P.2d 810 (1967) (evidence in both cases that defendant had intercourse with girl after her death, but felony murder convictions affirmed on evidence of attempted rape before the death).

100. Compare Commonwealth v. Stelma, 327 Pa. 317, 192 A. 906 (1937) (defendant struck victim fatally with a rock without any intent to rob; then he conceived an intent to rob and took victim's money; *held,* first-degree murder, homicide in the perpetration of robbery), criticized in Note, 42 Dick.L.Rev. 85 (1938), with People v. Hardy, 33 Cal.2d 52, 198 P.2d 865 (1948) ("a determination to steal McLain's automobile, formed after the killing, would be insufficient to justify a conviction that the murder was committed in the perpetration of a robbery").

Although the prevailing view today is that there is no felony murder where the felony was only an afterthought following the killing, see, e.g., United States v. Mack, 466 F.2d 333 (D.C.Cir.1972); Grigsby v. State, 260 Ark. 499,

(g) Manslaughter and Aggravated Batteries as Felonies. Voluntary and involuntary manslaughter are generally felonies; and though simple battery is generally only a misdemeanor, aggravated batteries (e.g., battery with a deadly weapon, battery to prevent arrest, battery which causes great bodily harm) usually constitute felonies. What if *A* commits an act which constitutes the felony of manslaughter or aggravated battery toward *B*, from which act *B* dies; is *A* guilty of the felony-murder of *B*?

(1) Manslaughter. Suppose *A* recklessly operates his car, unintentionally killing *B,* and thus committing involuntary manslaughter, a felony.[101] Has not *A* committed a foreseeable homicide in the commission of a felony, and therefore is he not guilty of murder rather than of manslaughter? If so, manslaughter has ceased to exist as a separate crime; all manslaughters automatically ride up an escalator to become felony-murders. This is not so, of course; manslaughter will not thus serve as a felony for purposes of the felony-murder doctrine.[102]

(2) Aggravated Battery. Suppose *A* commits a battery on *B* with a deadly weapon but not intending to kill, and *B* unforeseeably dies therefrom, e.g., *A,* with a knife, cuts *B* in the arm and *B,* a hemophiliac, bleeds to death.

542 S.W.2d 275 (1976) (concluding, however, that the jury was not bound to accept the defendant's testimony that this was what occurred); Pennsylvania still firmly adheres to the minority position. See Commonwealth v. Tomlinson, 446 Pa. 241, 284 A.2d 687 (1971).

101. Or suppose *A,* in a reasonable rage, intentionally shoots *B* to death, thus committing voluntary manslaughter, a felony. Manslaughter is discussed in §§ 7.9–7.13.

102. See State v. Fisher, 120 Kan. 226, 243 P. 291 (1926) (the "same act cannot be made the basis, first, of some other felony, as manslaughter, and then that felony used as an element of murder"). So too *A* cannot murder *B* in a second-degree murder manner, e.g., without premeditation and deliberation, thus killing *B* in the commission of the felony of murder and thus committing first-degree murder in a state which makes it first-degree murder to kill in the commission of "any felony"; otherwise premeditation and deliberation are effectively stricken from the statute. See People v. Moran, 246 N.Y. 100, 158 N.E. 35 (1927). In the modern codes the issue is often avoided by a statutory listing (excluding manslaughter) of what felonies will suffice.

This constitutes manslaughter, not murder.[103] But is it not death in the commission of the felony of aggravated battery and hence murder after all? Some cases have held that the collateral felony must be a felony which is "independent" of the conduct which kills; it must involve conduct separate from the acts of personal violence which constitute a necessary part of the homicide itself. Thus, although rape, arson, robbery and burglary are sufficiently independent of the homicide, manslaughter and aggravated battery toward the deceased will not do for felony murder.[104]

What about mayhem, a special type of aggravated battery, as where *A* intentionally cuts off *B*'s arm, not intending to kill, and *B* bleeds to death? Under the rule which requires the collateral felony to be independent, perhaps mayhem will not qualify for felony-murder. It would seem, however, that many

jurisdictions would consider this to be felony murder.[105] Where the aggravated-battery felony in question is battery with intent to rape or maim, and the battery causes death, there would be little difficulty in applying the felony-murder rule.[106] Where it is battery with intent to kill or do serious bodily harm, and death results from the battery, the homicide constitutes murder of the intent-to-kill or intent-to-do-serious-bodily-harm types, with no need to resort to felony murder.

What then of a burglary committed with intent to engage in an aggravated battery? One court has concluded that such a felony will not suffice either, reasoning that "the same bootstrapping" is involved here because the offense—practically speaking, a battery occurring inside a dwelling—was still "an integral part of the homicide."[107] But the majority view is to the contrary.[108] As one court

103. See § 7.13(d) for rule that battery plus unintended death equals manslaughter.

104. In People v. Ireland, 70 Cal.2d 522, 75 Cal.Rptr. 188, 450 P.2d 580 (1969), the court reversed a felony-murder conviction based upon the felony of assault with a deadly weapon: "We have concluded that the utilization of the felony-murder rule in circumstances such as those before us extends the operation of that rule 'beyond any rational function that it is designed to serve.' * * * To allow such use of the felony-murder rule would effectively preclude the jury from considering the issue of malice aforethought in all cases wherein homicide has been committed as a result of a felonious assault—a category which includes the great majority of homicides. This kind of bootstrapping finds support neither in logic nor in law." *Ireland* was followed in People v. Smith, 35 Cal.3d 798, 201 Cal.Rptr. 311, 678 P.2d 886 (1984), where the felony was child abuse.

See also State v. Essman, 98 Ariz. 228, 403 P.2d 540 (1965); State v. Rueckert, 221 Kan. 727, 561 P.2d 850 (1977); People v. Hüter, 184 N.Y. 237, 77 N.E. 6 (1906); State v. Branch, 244 Or. 97, 415 P.2d 766 (1966); Garrett v. State, 573 S.W.2d 543 (Tex.Crim.App.1978).

Some courts have declined to follow the *Ireland* approach, e.g., State v. Jackson, 346 N.W.2d 634 (Minn.1984); State v. Wall, 304 N.C. 609, 286 S.E.2d 68 (1982), usually on the ground that the particular statutory scheme indicates a contrary legislative intent. See State v. Wanrow, 91 Wn.2d 301, 588 P.2d 1320 (1978); State v. Thompson, 88 Wn.2d 13, 558 P.2d 202 (1977), criticized in Comment, 13 Gonzaga L.Rev. 268 (1977). Thus it was held in People v. Viser, 62 Ill.2d 568, 343 N.E.2d 903 (1975), that aggravated battery was a sufficient felony for felony murder because the statute expressly covered all forcible felonies other than manslaughter. Compare Garrett v. State, 573 S.W.2d 543 (Tex.Crim.App.1978), reaching a contrary result notwithstanding such a statute: "Most voluntary manslaughter offenses are initiated as aggravated as-

saults. If a felony murder may be predicated on the underlying aggravated assault, the statutory restriction on the scope of the doctrine that prohibits basing a felony murder prosecution on voluntary manslaughter could be regularly circumvented."

105. Compare People v. Arnett, 239 Mich. 123, 214 N.W. 231 (1927), where the defendant accidentally killed a policeman while resisting arrest, a felony, with People v. Hüter, supra note 104. The *Arnett* case held the defendant guilty of felony murder, though the battery was not "independent" of the homicide. As to mayhem, note that some states have statutes providing that murder in the commission of mayhem is first-degree murder. Aside from felony murder it might be that the hypothetical case in the text would constitute murder of the intent-to-do-serious-bodily-harm or depraved-heart types.

106. The rape or mayhem, committed or attempted, would supply the collateral felony.

107. People v. Wilson, 1 Cal.3d 431, 82 Cal.Rptr. 494, 462 P.2d 22 (1969). It has been argued that under this analysis "neither forcible rape nor armed robbery—two other felonies enumerated in the first degree felony-murder statute—will support the application of the felony-murder rule" because each of those offenses consists of two distinct elements, one of which is the assault element. Note, 22 Stan.L.Rev. 1059, 1067 (1970). But the court did not go that far; see People v. Burton, 6 Cal.3d 375, 99 Cal. Rptr. 1, 491 P.2d 793 (1971) (armed robbery resulting in death is felony murder).

108. State v. Miller, 110 Ariz. 489, 520 P.2d 1113 (1974); Blango v. United States, 373 A.2d 885 (D.C.App. 1977); State v. Foy, 224 Kan. 558, 582 P.2d 281 (1978); People v. Miller, 32 N.Y.2d 157, 344 N.Y.S.2d 342, 297 N.E.2d 85 (1973); State v. Reams, 292 Or. 1, 636 P.2d 913 (1981). See also Annot., 40 A.L.R.3d 1341 (1971); Comment, 13 Wake Forest L.Rev. 369, 388–94 (1977).

explained, the rationale of felony murder, "to reduce the disproportionate number of accidental homicides which occur during the commission" of felonies, applies more forcefully in the burglary case than in the aggravated battery case because the fact the battery takes place inside a dwelling significantly increases the likelihood that death will result from the battery.[109]

(3) Double Jeopardy Distinguished. The principles discussed above should not be confused with the broader double jeopardy doctrine concerning whether a defendant may be prosecuted and punished for both felony murder and the underlying felony. One double jeopardy issue concerns when multiple prosecutions may be undertaken, as to which the Supreme Court in *Brown v. Ohio*[110] adopted the longstanding *Blockburger* test,[111] which originated as a device for determining congressional intent as to cumulative sentencing: "The applicable rule is that where the same act or transaction constitutes a violation of two distinct statutory provisions, the test to be applied to determine whether there are two offenses or only one, is whether each provision requires proof of an additional fact which the other does not." This means, as the Supreme Court later held in *Harris v. Oklahoma,*[112] that except in extraordinary circumstances[113] a defendant may not constitutionally be separately tried for felony murder and the underlying felony.

What then of prosecution, conviction and cumulative punishment for both felony murder and the underlying felony in a single prosecution? Here, the Supreme Court held in *Albernaz v. United States,*[114] *Blockburger* is merely a method for ascertaining legislative intent when nothing more concrete is available. Once the legislative intent is ascertained by that or other means, that is the end of the matter, for "the question of what punishments are constitutionally permissible is not different from the question of what punishment the Legislative Branch intended to be imposed." Thus, as the Court later made clear in *Missouri v. Hunter,*[115] where "a legislature specifically authorizes cumulative punishment under two statutes, regardless of whether those two statutes proscribe the 'same' conduct under *Blockburger,* a court's task of statutory construction is at an end and the prosecutor may seek and the trial court or jury may impose cumulative punishment under such statutes in a single trial." In some states, the courts have concluded that the legislature has authorized cumulative punishments for the felony murder and underlying felony.[116] More frequently, however, such authority has been held to be lacking.[117]

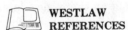 **WESTLAW REFERENCES**

digest("felony murder" /s "double jeopardy")
"felony murder" /s "double jeopardy" /p harris /s
    97 +4 2912

109. People v. Miller, 32 N.Y.2d 157, 344 N.Y.S.2d 342, 297 N.E.2d 85 (1973), explaining: "When the assault takes place within the domicile, the victim may be more likely to resist the assault; the victim is also less likely to be able to avoid the consequences of the assault, since his paths of retreat and escape may be barred or severely restricted by furniture, walls and other obstructions incidental to buildings. Further, it is also more likely that when the assault occurs in the victim's domicile, there will be present family or close friends who will come to the victim's aid and be killed."

110. 432 U.S. 161, 97 S.Ct. 2221, 53 L.Ed.2d 187 (1977).

111. Blockburger v. United States, 284 U.S. 299, 52 S.Ct. 180, 76 L.Ed. 306 (1932).

112. 433 U.S. 682, 97 S.Ct. 2912, 53 L.Ed.2d 1054 (1977).

113. The Court in *Brown* noted an exception "may exist where the State is unable to proceed on the more serious charge at the outset because the additional facts necessary to sustain that charge have not occurred or have not been discovered despite due diligence." The Court cited Diaz v. United States, 223 U.S. 442, 32 S.Ct. 250, 56 L.Ed.2d 500 (1942), where the victim died after the defendant was convicted of assault and battery.

114. 450 U.S. 333, 101 S.Ct. 1137, 67 L.Ed.2d 275 (1981).

115. 459 U.S. 359, 103 S.Ct. 673, 74 L.Ed.2d 535 (1983).

116. State v. Crump, 232 Kan. 265, 654 P.2d 922 (1982); State v. Chambers, 524 S.W.2d 826 (Mo.1975); People v. Berzupa, 49 N.Y.2d 417, 426 N.Y.S.2d 253, 402 N.E.2d 1155 (1980).

117. See People v. Wilder, 411 Mich. 328, 308 N.W.2d 112 (1981), and cases cited therein.

(h) The Future of the Felony-Murder Doctrine. Although most jurisdictions accept the felony-murder doctrine, generally with one or more of the limitations discussed above, it is arguable that there should be no such separate category of murder. The rationale of the doctrine is that one who commits a felony is a bad person with a bad state of mind, and he has caused a bad result, so that we should not worry too much about the fact that the fatal result he accomplished was quite different and a good deal worse than the bad result he intended. Yet it is a general principle of criminal law that one is not ordinarily criminally liable for bad results which differ greatly from intended results.[118] Nor, as suggested earlier,[119] can the felony-murder doctrine be justified as the approximate equivalent of depraved-heart murder, where the defendant's conduct carries with it a very high risk of death.[120] What statistics are available demonstrate that accidental killings do not occur disproportionately often even in connection with the so-called "inherently dangerous" felonies.[121]

Long ago Holmes, in his book *The Common Law,* discussing the felony-murder doctrine, supposed the case of one who, to steal some chickens, shoots at them, accidentally killing a man in the chickenhouse whose presence could not have been suspected. Holmes suggests that the fact that the defendant happened to be committing a felony when he shot is an illogical thing to fasten onto to make the accidental killing a murder, for the fact that the shooting is felonious does not increase the likelihood of killing people. "If the object of the [felony-murder] rule is to prevent such accidents, it should make accidental killing with firearms murder, not accidental killing in the effort to steal; while if its object is to prevent stealing, it would do better to hang one thief in every thousand by lot."[122]

Such criticisms have, as we have seen, resulted in the narrowing of the felony-murder doctrine in various ways in many jurisdictions. This has often been accomplished by legislative action in the context of recodification, though courts have often played an important role as well by recognizing that "the felony-murder doctrine expresses a highly artificial concept that deserves no extension beyond its required application."[123]

In other respects, however, the felony-murder doctrine is well entrenched in American law. In England, where for some years felony murder was disparagingly referred to as "constructive murder,"[124] the doctrine was abolished in 1957.[125] But in this country, despite the fact that two-thirds of the states have adopted modern codes, only two of those jurisdictions have totally abolished the felony-murder rule. (In one other state, abolition was accomplished by court decision.[126]) A few others have accomplished essentially the same result by requiring that some additional mental state be proved, such as that the death have occurred "under circumstances manifesting extreme indifference to the value of human life" or as a result of recklessness or

---

118. See § 3.11; and Schulhofer, Harm and Punishment: A Critique of Emphasis on the Results of Conduct in the Criminal Law, 122 U.Pa.L.Rev. 1497 (1974), criticizing the felony-murder rule on this basis.

119. See § 7.5(e).

120. See § 7.4.

121. On the basis of statistics from Philadelphia for the years 1948–1952, the percentage of certain felonies accompanied by homicide was calculated: robbery, .50%; rape, .35%; burglary, .0036%; auto theft, .019%. These statistics, of course, do not even reflect how many of the homicides were committed purposely, knowingly or recklessly (which would clearly be subject to prosecution without the felony-murder rule) and how many were negligent or accidental. Model Penal Code § 210.2, Comment at 38 n. 96 (1980).

122. O. Holmes, The Common Law 58 (1881).

123. People v. Phillips, 64 Cal.2d 574, 51 Cal.Rptr. 225, 414 P.2d 353 (1966).

124. The implication from this terminology is that there is something wrong with this sort of murder; it is all right to punish regular murder, but it is not quite right to pretend that something is murder which is not.

125. English Homicide Act of 1957, 5 & 6 Eliz. 2, c. 11, § 1 (one who "kills another in the course or furtherance of some other offense" is not guilty of murder "unless done with the same malice aforethought (express or implied) as is required for a killing to amount to murder when not done in the course or furtherance of another offense"). But see Murder (Abolition of Death Penalty) Act, 1965, 13 & 14 Eliz. 2, c. 71.

126. People v. Aaron, 409 Mich. 672, 299 N.W.2d 304 (1980), discussed in Notes, 28 Wayne L.Rev. 215 (1981); 50 U.M.K.C.L.Rev. 112 (1981). See also Annot., 13 A.L.R. 4th 1226 (1982).

criminal negligence. Only one state [127] has adopted the Model Penal Code rebuttable presumption formulation, whereunder "recklessness and indifference are presumed" if the killing occurred in the commission of certain specified felonies,[128] facilitating conviction for murder of the grossly reckless type.

This experience stands in sharp contrast to what has occurred with respect to the somewhat analogous misdemeanor-manslaughter rule, which very frequently has been abolished in the recodification process.[129] Consequently, there is reason to believe that the felony-murder doctrine will continue to exist (albeit in a somewhat limited form) for many years to come.

 WESTLAW REFERENCES

"felony murder" /2 doctrine rule /s critici***

* censur** disfavor**

§ 7.6 Resisting-Lawful-Arrest Murder

The old writers—e.g., Hale and Blackstone—announced the flat rule that a homicide caused by conduct in resisting a lawful arrest is murder, without regard to whether the resister had an intent to kill or do serious bodily harm, or did an act in a depraved-heart manner, or by such resistance he was committing a felony so as to come under the felony-murder rule. In other words, these writers stated there was a separate type of murder, in addition to the several types discussed in the preceding sections of this book. Some cases have faithfully reiterated this old rule,[1] but in fact these cases could have been decided on the basis of one of the other types of murder.[2]

In the few cases which actually have raised the issue of whether this separate category of murder exists, the courts have held that it does not.[3] Thus in one case an officer, with a warrant for the defendant's arrest, jumped on the running board of the defendant's car (in which he and his children were riding) to arrest him. The defendant, to prevent arrest by crossing the state line, drove toward the bridge which spanned the river constituting the boundary. The officer grabbed the steering wheel; the car, out of control, hit the bridge; and the officer was killed. It was quite obvious that the defendant did not intentionally crash into the bridge and thus endanger himself and his children as well as the officer. The trial judge, however, charged the jury that it was murder for the defendant to kill while resisting a lawful arrest, even though he did not intend to kill or do violent injury.

On appeal the conviction for murder was reversed, the court stating that it could find no case holding that death while resisting lawful arrest constituted murder where the defendant did not intentionally kill or do serious injury or do an act inherently dangerous.[4] The holding thus negatives the existence of homicide-while-resisting-lawful-arrest murder as a separate kind of murder. And on princi-

---

127. N.H.Rev.Stat.Ann. 630:1–b. "Of all the reforms proposed by the Model Penal Code, perhaps none has been less influential than the Model Penal Code's recommendation on the perennial problem of felony-murder." Fletcher, Reflections on Felony-Murder, 12 Sw.U.L.Rev. 413 (1981).

128. Model Penal Code § 210.2.

129. See § 7.13(e).

§ 7.6

1. E.g., Donehy v. Commonwealth, 170 Ky. 474, 186 S.W. 161 (1916) ("where an officer is killed while attempting to make an arrest by one knowing him to be an officer, it is not necessary to constitute [the crime of murder] that the slayer should have had any particular malice"); Regina v. Porter, 12 Cox Crim.Cas. 444 (1873) (court instructed jury that intentional blow upon one making lawful arrest is murder, though intent is only to resist arrest and not to inflict grievous bodily harm).

2. Thus in Donehy v. Commonwealth, supra note 1, the defendant, resisting arrest, filled the policeman's body with six bullets, indicating an intent to kill by the intentional use of a deadly weapon. See Dickey, Culpable Homicide in Resisting Arrest, 18 Cornell L.Q. 373, 376 (1933).

3. State v. Weisengoff, 85 W.Va. 271, 101 S.E. 450 (1919) (discussed in text below).

Cf. Regina v. Porter, supra note 1 (defendant, when being lawfully arrested, kicked out with his foot, hitting a private person assisting policeman and killing him; the court instructed the jury that if he intended to kick him as part of an intent to resist arrest, it is murder; but if he accidentally kicked him, not intending to resist arrest, it is manslaughter; verdict of manslaughter).

4. State v. Weisengoff, supra note 3.

ple there should not be this separate category.[5]

There remains the possibility that an unintended death caused by resisting lawful arrest might come under the felony-murder rule, if it is a statutory felony to resist lawful arrest and (in most jurisdictions) if death is the foreseeable result of the resister's manner of resisting arrest. In most jurisdictions the crime of resisting arrest is a misdemeanor only.[6] In one state, where it was a statutory felony to resist lawful arrest, the defendant was held guilty of murder on the felony-murder theory;[7] but another state held that the crime of battery-to-prevent-arrest, though a felony, was not a felony independent of the homicide and so could not support a felony-murder conviction.[8]

Finally, there is also the possibility that a murder statute will expressly cover the resisting-lawful-arrest situation. Although such provisions are not common, they are to be found even in a few of the modern recodifications.

WESTLAW REFERENCES

topic(203) /p resist*** prevent*** avoid*** /2 arrest /s murder homicide kill***

topic(203 110) /p resist*** /2 arrest /s misdemeanor felony

---

5. Dickey, Culpable Homicide in Resisting Arrest, 18 Cornell L.Q. 373, 378 (1933). We have seen that the felony-murder rule, even as limited in various ways, goes quite far enough in imposing murder liability for unintended death. The supposed rule of murder covering homicide in resisting lawful arrest goes considerably farther, for it does not require that the resistance amount to a felony and is not otherwise limited as is the felony-murder doctrine.

The English Homicide Act of 1957, § 1, abolishing the felony-murder doctrine, goes on to provide that a killing done in resisting lawful arrest does not, for that reason alone, constitute murder. But see Murder (Abolition of Death Penalty) Act, 1965, 13 & 14 Eliz. 2. See § 7.5 supra, note 135.

6. See Dickey, supra, note 5 at 388, collecting the statutes.

7. People v. Arnett, 239 Mich. 123, 214 N.W. 231 (1927). Michigan later by statute reduced the crime of resisting arrest to a misdemeanor.

§ 7.7 Degrees of Murder

Although the English judges created the crime of murder, including the four separate types of murder discussed in the preceding sections, they never divided murder into degrees. That development has come about through legislation. In England and in a minority of American states there is no division of murder into degrees. But in most states murder is thus divided, usually into two (sometimes into three) degrees.[1] The purpose of doing so is to limit the more severe punishments (usually but not always including the death penalty) to first degree murder, with less severe penalties (generally including life imprisonment, but not the death penalty)[2] for second degree murder.[3]

Almost all American jurisdictions which divide murder into degrees include the following two murder situations in the category of first degree murder: (1) intent-to-kill murder where there exists (in addition to the intent to kill) the elements of premeditation and deliberation, and (2) felony murder where the felony in question is one of five or six listed felonies, generally including rape, robbery, kidnapping, arson and burglary. Some states instead or in addition have other kinds of first degree murder.

(a) Premeditated, Deliberate, Intentional Killing. To be guilty of this form of first degree murder the defendant must not only intend to kill but in addition he must premed-

---

8. People v. Hüter, 184 N.Y. 237, 77 N.E. 6 (1906). See § 7.5(g).

§ 7.7

1. Even in the modern codes, only seldom is such a division lacking.

2. See Model Penal Code § 210.2, Comment at 42–43 (1980), on the penalty provisions of the modern codes applicable to second degree murder.

3. It is, however, possible to separate capital murders from non-capital murders without dividing murder into degrees. Thus the English Homicide Act of 1957 provided that murder done in certain ways is punishable by the death penalty; all other murder is punishable by life imprisonment. See also Model Penal Code § 210.2.

When murder is divided into more than one offense, usually the crimes are called first degree murder and second degree murder, but sometimes one of them is called aggravated or capital murder to distinguish it from just murder.

itate the killing and deliberate about it. It is not easy to give a meaningful definition of the words "premeditate" and "deliberate" as they are used in connection with first degree murder.[4] Perhaps the best that can be said of "deliberation" is that it requires a cool mind that is capable of reflection,[5] and of "premeditation" that it requires that the one with the cool mind did in fact reflect, at least for a short period of time before his act of killing.

It is often said that premeditation and deliberation require only a "brief moment of thought"[6] or a "matter of seconds,"[7] and convictions for first degree murder have frequently been affirmed where such short periods of time were involved.[8] The better view, however, is that to "speak of premeditation and deliberation which are instantaneous, or which take no appreciable time, * * * destroys the statutory distinction between first and second degree murder,"[9] and (in much the same fashion that the felony-murder rule

is being increasingly limited) this view is growing in popularity.[10] This is not to say, however, that premeditation and deliberation cannot exist when the act of killing follows immediately after the formation of the intent. The intention may be finally formed only as a conclusion of prior premeditation and deliberation,[11] while in other cases the intention may be formed without prior thought so that premeditation and deliberation occurs only with the passage of additional time for "further thought, and a turning over in the mind."[12]

It is not enough that the defendant is shown to have had time to premeditate and deliberate.[13] One must actually premeditate and deliberate, as well as actually intend to kill, to be guilty of this sort of first degree murder. A killer may, in a particular situation, be incapable of that cool reflection called for by the requirement of premeditation and deliberation,[14] as where his capacity to premeditate and deliberate is prevented by emo-

---

4. It has been suggested that for premeditation the killer asks himself the question, "Shall I kill him?". The intent to kill aspect of the crime is found in the answer, "Yes, I shall." The deliberation part of the crime requires a thought like, "Wait, what about the consequences? Well, I'll do it anyway."

5. See State v. Bowser, 214 N.C. 249, 199 S.E. 31 (1938) ("Deliberation means the act is done in a cool state of the blood"). See also notes 14–18 infra and accompanying text; and Annot., 18 A.L.R. 4th 961 (1982).

6. Government of the Virgin Islands v. Lake, 362 F.2d 770 (3d Cir.1966).

7. State v. Stewart, 176 Ohio St. 156, 198 N.E.2d 439 (1964). See also State v. Jones, 217 Neb. 435, 350 N.W.2d 11 (1984): "No particular length of time for premeditation is required, however, provided that the intent to kill is formed before the act and is not merely simultaneously with the act which caused the death."

8. People v. Donnelly, 190 Cal. 57, 210 P. 523 (1922) (defendant aided the killer who killed in a sudden quarrel with the victim; conviction of first-degree murder *held* affirmed; there need be no appreciable space of time between the intention to kill and the act of killing; they may be as instantaneous as successive thoughts of the mind); Sandoval v. People, 117 Colo. 588, 192 P.2d 423 (1948) (to establish premeditation and deliberation, "it matters not how short the interval between the determination to kill and infliction of the mortal wound, if the time was sufficient for one thought to follow another"; conviction of first-degree murder *held* affirmed); Commonwealth v. Scott, 284 Pa. 159, 130 A. 317 (1925) (after short conversation, defendant shot and killed a policeman who suspected him of carrying "moonshine"; trial court instructed jury that, in spite of lack of evidence of previ-

ous ill-will, jury should find first degree murder if defendant formed a conscious purpose to kill during the brief conversation; conviction of first degree murder *held* affirmed, for "it is the fully formed purpose, not the time, which constitutes the higher degree" of murder).

9. Bullock v. United States, 122 F.2d 213 (D.C.Cir. 1941). See also United States v. Shaw, 701 F.2d 367 (5th Cir.1983) (must be some appreciable time for reflection and consideration before execution); People v. Sneed, 183 Colo. 96, 514 P.2d 776 (1973) (design to kill must precede the killing by an appreciable length of time).

Consider also State v. Cotton, 56 Ohio St.2d 8, 381 N.E.2d 190 (1978), interpreting a somewhat different statutory formulation, requiring "prior calculation and design," as more demanding than the premeditation-deliberation formula and necessitating more than a few moments of deliberation.

10. As in the felony-murder area, the attempt is to limit the reach of the death penalty sanction.

11. People v. Bender, 27 Cal.2d 164, 163 P.2d 8 (1945); State v. Schrader, ___ W.Va. ___, 302 S.E.2d 70 (1982); State v. Hatfield, ___ W.Va. ___, 286 S.E.2d 402 (1982).

12. Austin v. United States, 382 F.2d 129 (D.C.Cir. 1967).

13. Hemphill v. United States, 402 F.2d 187 (D.C.Cir. 1968); People v. Caruso, 246 N.Y. 437, 159 N.E. 390 (1927).

14. If there was cool reflection when the intent was formed, it makes no difference that defendant was in a passion when the design was executed. Baxter v. State, 503 S.W.2d 226 (Tenn.1973). But if the intent was formed while defendant was in a passion, he must have committed the act after the passion subsided. State v. Bullington, 532 S.W.2d 556 (Tenn.1976).

tional upset,[15] by intoxication,[16] by feebleness of intellect short of insanity,[17] or by terror.[18] In such cases he can generally be held guilty of second degree murder, however, on the theory that, though he could not premeditate and deliberate, he could and did at least have an intent to kill (as shown, in most cases, by his intentional use of a deadly weapon upon the victim).

Premeditation and deliberation, like intent to kill, are subjective states of mind. Often there is no witness to the killing; and even if there is a witness, the killer does not always speak aloud what is in his mind. So existence of the facts of premeditation and deliberation must be determined from the defendant's conduct (so far as we can learn of it, usually from circumstantial evidence) in the light of the surrounding circumstances. There is no presumption that the murder is first degree murder; for the higher degree there must be some affirmative evidence to support a finding that the defendant in fact did premeditate and deliberate.[19]

On the basis of events before and at the time of the killing, the trier of fact will sometimes be entitled to infer that the defendant actually premeditated and deliberated his intentional killing. Three categories of evidence are important for this purpose: (1) facts about how and what the defendant did prior to the actual killing which show he was engaged in activity directed toward the killing, that is, *planning activity;* (2) facts about the defendant's prior relationship and conduct with the victim from which *motive* may be inferred; and (3) facts about the *nature of the killing* from which it may be inferred that the manner of killing was so particular and exacting that the defendant must have intentionally killed according to a preconceived design.[20] Illustrative of the first category are such acts by the defendant as prior possession of the murder weapon,[21] surreptitious approach of

---

15. People v. Caruso, 246 N.Y. 437, 159 N.E. 390 (1927) (defendant, an illiterate foreign-born, had an unreasonable belief that his child's death was due to the doctor's malpractice; he also unreasonably believed that the doctor laughed when he learned of the child's death; in a rage defendant first choked, then stabbed the doctor to death; conviction of first degree murder of the premeditation-deliberation type *held* reversed, because the evidence showed time, but not capacity, to premeditate and deliberate). See also State v. Christenson, 129 Ariz. 32, 628 P.2d 580 (1981) (evidence that defendant had difficulty dealing with stress thus admissible).

Contra: State v. Gounagias, 88 Wash. 304, 153 P. 9 (1915) (unreasonable rage will not reduce from first degree murder by negativing capacity to premeditate and deliberate), a case which is wrongly decided.

16. E.g., Aszman v. State, 123 Ind. 347, 24 N.E. 123 (1890). See § 4.10.

17. E.g., People v. Wolff, 61 Cal.2d 795, 40 Cal.Rptr. 271, 394 P.2d 959 (1964) (a combination of youthfulness and mental illness robbed defendant, age 15, of capacity to deliberate and premeditate, though he did intend to kill). See Annot., 22 A.L.R.3d 1228 (1968). Contra: Fisher v. United States, 328 U.S. 463, 66 S.Ct. 1318, 90 L.Ed. 1382 (1946), a case wrongly decided.

18. Commonwealth v. Stewart, 461 Pa. 274, 336 A.2d 282 (1975) (terror-stricken panic may negate deliberation). Cf. State v. Nargashian, 26 R.I. 299, 58 A. 953 (1904) (*A*, axe in hand threatened to kill *B* unless *B* helped *A* kill *C;* so *B* held *C*'s hands while *A* killed *C; B*'s conviction of murder *held* affirmed, for coercion is no defense to murder; the court rejected *B*'s contention that the crime was voluntary manslaughter because fear like passion can arouse a heat of passion, since *C* did nothing to arouse *B*'s fears; although panic might reduce or excuse an unlawful

act, this is not a proper case to apply such a doctrine). It would seem that fear might operate, like intoxication and passion, to negative premeditation and deliberation, in an appropriate case.

19. E.g., People v. Belencia, 21 Cal. 544 (1863) ("Presumptively, every killing is a murder; but so far as the degree is concerned, no presumption arises from the mere fact of killing"); State v. Hamric, 151 W.Va. 1, 151 S.E.2d 252 (1966) ("where a deadly weapon is used in a homicide there is a presumption of second degree murder and * * * the state has the burden of proving that such killing was deliberate and premeditated").

20. See People v. Anderson, 70 Cal.2d 15, 73 Cal.Rptr. 550, 447 P.2d 942 (1968), for an extended discussion of these three categories and their application to a series of California cases. See also Annot., 96 A.L.R.2d 1435 (1964).

21. United States v. Blue Thunder, 604 F.2d 550 (8th Cir.1979) (murder weapon, a knife, brought to scene of murder); Belton v. United States, 382 F.2d 150 (D.C.Cir. 1967) (testimony that defendant "entered the apartment with a loaded gun" permits "inference that [he] arrived on the scene already possessed of a calmly planned and calculated intent to kill"). In Hemphill v. United States, 402 F.2d 187 (D.C.Cir.1968), defendant, a social visitor at the home of another, killed a 10-year-old boy with several blows to the head with a hammer; the prosecution did not prove that he brought the hammer with him, and thus the first degree murder conviction must be reversed, for it would not be proper to permit the inference that a hammer could not have been available at the place of the killing.

The fact the defendant brought the murder weapon with him is not relevant if the nature of the weapon is such that it would be regularly carried for another purpose. Austin v. United States, 382 F.2d 129 (D.C.Cir.1967)

the victim,[22] or taking the prospective victim to a place where others are unlikely to intrude.[23] In the second category are prior threats by the defendant to do violence to the victim,[24] plans or desires of the defendant which would be facilitated by the death of the victim,[25] and prior conduct of the victim known to have angered the defendant.[26] As to the third category, the manner of killing, what is required is evidence (usually based upon examination of the victim's body) showing that the wounds were deliberately placed at vital areas of the body.[27] The mere fact that the killing was attended by much violence or that a great many wounds were inflicted is not relevant in this regard, as such a killing is just as likely (or perhaps more likely) to have been on impulse.[28] Conduct by the defendant *after* the killing in an effort to avoid detection and punishment is obviously not relevant for purposes of showing premeditation and deliberation, as it only goes to show the defendant's state of mind at the time and not before or during the killing.[29]

In dealing with the subject of causation in the criminal law, and in particular the problem of the bad aim, we noted that where A

unjustifiably aims a lethal blow at *B* with intent to kill *B*, but the blow misses *B* and kills *C*, *A* is guilty of the murder of *C* though he never intended harm to *C*. On the same principle, if *A* without justification aims at *B* with a premeditated and deliberate intent to kill *B* (so that if he should kill *B* he would be guilty of first degree murder) but, missing *B*, he accidentally hits and kills *C*, *A* is, by the great weight of authority, guilty of the first degree murder of *C*.[30]

Judge (later Justice) Cardozo suggested that the distinction between first and second degree murder based upon the existence or nonexistence of premeditation and deliberation is too vague and obscure for any jury to understand, and that it should not be continued in the law.[31] The Model Penal Code does not utilize the degree device, but instead lists several mitigating and aggravating factors which are to be taken into account at the time of sentencing.[32] As the draftsmen point out, the premeditation-deliberation formula is not a sound basis upon which to determine the severity of the sanction to be imposed upon the murder defendant; there are cases in which extreme depravity is revealed by a

N.C. 162, 321 S.E.2d 837 (1984) (victim had bragged about knocking defendant out in prior fight).

(defendant habitually carried murder weapon, a pocket knife, to trim his fingernails).

22. People v. Kemp, 55 Cal.3d 458, 11 Cal.Rptr. 361, 359 P.2d 913 (1961) (defendant entered victim's apartment through window).

23. People v. Hillery, 62 Cal.2d 692, 44 Cal.Rptr. 30, 401 P.2d 382 (1965) (defendant tied up victim and dragged her to nearby irrigation ditch before killing); Commonwealth v. Blaikie, 375 Mass. 601, 378 N.E.2d 1361 (1978) (victim lured to defendant's house).

24. United States v. Brown, 518 F.2d 821 (7th Cir. 1975); People v. Slaughter, 9 Ill.2d 384, 194 N.E.2d 193 (1963); Strickland v. State, 265 Ind. 664, 359 N.E.2d 244 (1977); State v. Whitley, 311 N.C. 656, 319 S.E.2d 584 (1984).

25. People v. Cole, 47 Cal.2d 99, 301 P.2d 854 (1956) (defendant lived with impecunious woman—his victim—and desired to marry well-to-do woman); State v. Blair, 347 N.W.2d 416 (Iowa 1984) (defendant desired to take victim's car).

26. United States v. Blue Thunder, 604 F.2d 550 (8th Cir.1979) (brief and unstable marriage to defendant); People v. Cartier, 54 Cal.2d 300, 5 Cal.Rptr. 573, 353 P.2d 53 (1960) (victim, defendant's wife, talked to sailor in bar, which made defendant angry); Commonwealth v. Blaikie, 375 Mass. 601, 378 N.E.2d 1361 (1978) (victim pressing defendant for repayment of loan); State v. Hamlet, 312

27. United States v. Blue Thunder, 604 F.2d 550 (8th Cir.1979) (knife thrust into center of victim's back with such force as to pierce his heart); People v. Stroble, 36 Cal.2d 615, 226 P.2d 330 (1951) (deliberately placed fatal blows with hammer, ice pick, axe, and knife); People v. Cartier, note 26 supra (defendant, with experience as butcher, cut out victim's heart); People v. Hillery, note 23 supra (plunging of knife into victim's chest); Commonwealth v. Blaikie, 375 Mass. 601, 378 N.E.2d 1361 (1978) (single shot in back of skull).

28. Austin v. United States, note 12 supra; People v. Caldwell, 43 Cal.2d 864, 279 P.2d 539 (1955); People v. Hoffmeister, 394 Mich. 155, 229 N.W.2d 305 (1975).

29. Austin v. United States, note 12 supra; People v. Anderson, note 20 supra. But, flight after the crime is strong evidence of premeditation where it is shown this flight was planned before the killing. Territory of Guam v. Atoique, 508 F.2d 680 (9th Cir.1974) (defendant had removed his clothing from his temporary residence before the killing).

30. See § 3.12(d). For a collection of cases, see Annot., 18 A.L.R. 917 (1922).

31. B. Cardozo, Law and Literature and Other Essays, 99–100 (1931).

32. Model Penal Code § 210.6.

murder on impulse, just as there are so-called premeditated murders (e.g., mercy killings, suicide pacts) which are "far more the product of extraordinary circumstances than a true reflection of the actor's normal character." [33]   But most of the recent state criminal codes have retained the distinction, and thus it still must be grappled with.

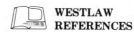

WESTLAW REFERENCES

topic(203) /p "first degree" /2 murder /s premeditat! /s deliberat! /s inten!
topic(203) /p "first degree" /2 murder /s plan!
  motive (nature manner type method /3 kill***)

(b) In the Commission of Listed Felonies. A killing (even an unintended killing) in the commission or attempted commission of a felony may be murder; [34] if it is, and if the felony in question is one listed in the first degree murder statute (e.g., rape, robbery, kidnapping, arson and burglary) then the murder will be murder in the first degree. [35]

Often we find an intentional killing committed during one of these listed felonies dealt with as a first degree murder of the

felony-murder sort, rather than of the deliberate and premeditated intent-to-kill sort. [36] This is because the prosecuting attorney may, in a particular case, find it easier to obtain a first degree murder conviction in the felony murder situation—for here he need not prove those vague concepts premeditation and deliberation in addition to the intent to kill. [37]

WESTLAW REFERENCES

203k289 /p "first degree" /2 murder /s felony

(c) Lying in Wait; Poison; Torture. Although such language is almost never found in the modern codes, at one time it was common for first degree murder statutes also to cover those murders done by poison, lying in wait, or torture. [38] "Lying in wait" is generally held to require a watching and waiting in a concealed position with an intent to kill or do serious bodily injury to another; [39] it does not, of course, require that the one "lying" in wait be in a prone, rather than a sitting or standing, position. [40] Thus it is not lying in wait to wait for the victim, at the invitation of his family, in his living room, [41] or to follow close

---

33. Model Penal Code § 210.6, Comment at 127 (1980).

34. See § 7.5. Premeditation and deliberation need not be proved for a first degree murder conviction based on felony-murder. State v. Hutchins, 303 N.C. 321, 279 S.E.2d 788 (1981); State v. Sims, 162 W.Va. 212, 248 S.E.2d 834 (1978).

35. Most of the modern codes which divide murder into degrees put at least some (occasionally all) of felony-murder into the first degree category. A few make all felony-murder second degree murder.

36. E.g., State v. Adams, 339 Mo. 926, 98 S.W.2d 632 (1936) (defendant, after burglary, fled with his confederates to nearby woods with policemen in pursuit; one of the confederates shot and killed a policeman; conviction of first degree murder *held* affirmed, for evidence supports jury's finding of killing in the commission of the burglary); State v. Metalski, 116 N.J.L. 543, 185 A. 351 (Ct.Err. & App.1936) (defendant, escaping after robbery in Philadelphia, intentionally shot policeman who stopped his car for speeding in New Brunswick, N.J.; trial court instructed jury that it might convict of first degree murder if it found the defendant killed either with premeditation or in the perpetration of the robbery; conviction of first degree murder *held* affirmed); Commonwealth v. Doris, 287 Pa. 547, 135 A. 313 (1926) (defendant and confederates fled after robbery; a confederate intentionally killed a pursuing policeman; defendant's conviction of first degree murder *held* affirmed, for the evidence supports jury's finding of killing in the commission of the robbery).

37. An indictment or information charging first degree murder need not be so specific as to charge a particular type of first degree murder. A conviction of murder in the first degree is supportable by evidence proving any of the alternative types. Often the proof will tend to support two types, in which case the trial court properly instructs the jury it may find the defendant guilty of first degree murder if it finds proof of either type. E.g., State v. Metalski, supra note 36 (proof of both premeditated and deliberate intent-to-kill murder, and of murder in commission of robbery); Commonwealth v. Bartolini, 299 Mass. 503, 13 N.E.2d 382, (1938) (proof of both deliberately premeditated intent-to-kill murder, and of murder committed with extreme atrocity or cruelty).

38. See Model Penal Code, pp. 115–20 (Tent.Draft No. 9, 1959).

39. United States v. Shaw, 701 F.2d 367 (5th Cir.1983); People v. Ward, 27 Cal.App.3d 218, 103 Cal.Rptr. 671 (1972).

Some courts appear to require an intent to kill, e.g., State v. Gause, 227 N.C. 26, 40 S.E.2d 463 (1946), while at the other extreme it has been held that "where a murder is shown to have been committed by 'lying in wait' a showing of intent is unnecessary to fix the degree." People v. Thomas, 41 Cal.2d 470, 261 P.2d 1 (1953).

40. For a collection of cases construing the phrase, see Annot., 89 A.L.R.2d 1140 (1963).

41. People v. Kahn, 198 Cal.App.2d 326, 17 Cal.Rptr. 793 (1961).

behind the victim on the street, approaching him when the victim pauses; [42] for in each case the element of concealment is missing.

It is not necessarily murder by poison to kill another person with poison, as where one administered poison innocently and for a lawful purpose and yet produces a death.[43] The homicide must first amount to murder, either because the defendant had an intent to kill or do serious bodily injury, or because his conduct evinced a depraved heart, or because the death by poison resulted from the defendant's commission or attempted commission of a felony.[44] A poison[45] is not necessarily something administered internally; it may be inhaled[46] or injected.[47]

Murder by torture requires something in the way of pain endured over a period of time. It is not enough, however, that the defendant, in murdering his victim, cause him such pain; the defendant must intend to inflict the pain.[48] The following forms of killing, among others, have been held to constitute torture when accompanied by the necessary intent to cause pain: burning,[49] beating,[50] and failure to call medical aid after inflicting a beating.[51] It has been held that the act which causes the pain must be the act which causes the death.[52]

**WESTLAW
REFERENCES**

topic(203) /p "first degree" /2 murder /s "lying in wait" poison** torture*

42. Commonwealth v. Gibson, 275 Pa. 338, 119 A. 403 (1923). See also State v. Brooks, 103 Ariz. 472, 445 P.2d 831 (1968) (not lying in wait to stand outside building with shotgun in hand waiting for victim); People v. Merkouris, 46 Cal.2d 540, 297 P.2d 999 (1956) (not lying in wait to sit in parked car across street from victim's shop for several days prior to shooting).

43. See cases cited infra note 44. If the administration is done for a lawful purpose but carelessly, the crime may be manslaughter of the criminal-negligence type.

44. State v. Wells, 61 Iowa 629, 17 N.W. 90 (1883) (defendant, to escape from jail, administered chloroform to his guard, unintentionally killing him; jury found chloroform a poison and convicted of first degree murder by poison; conviction *held* affirmed, the court stating that unlawful administration of poison causing death is murder); State v. Wagner, 78 Mo. 644, 47 Am.Rep. 131 (1883) (defendant, intending to stupefy the victim's faculties so as to get his property, and not intending to kill him, administered laudanum to him and killed him; conviction of first degree murder by poison *held* affirmed, since the defendant acted for an unlawful purpose and knew his conduct was dangerous to life); Rupe v. State, 42 Tex.Crim. 477, 61 S.W. 929 (1901) (defendant administered morphine and chloral to victim for purpose of robbing him but not to kill him; it killed him; conviction of first degree murder by poison *held* affirmed; it was murder unintentionally to kill in attempting robbery, and thus first degree murder because of the poison). Compare Bechtelheimer v. State, 54 Ind. 128 (1876) (defendant administered poison to girl intending to create in her an uncontrollable desire for sexual intercourse, which desire he meant to satisfy; instead the poison killed her; conviction of first degree murder *held* reversed, for Indiana statute requires a purpose to kill by poison).

45. State v. Jeffers, 135 Ariz. 404, 661 P.2d 1105 (1983), holds that "poison," meaning any substance introduced into the body by any means which by its chemical action is capable of causing death, includes heroin.

46. State v. Wells, supra note 44 (jury found chloroform to be a poison); State v. Baldwin, 36 Kan. 1, 12 P. 318 (1886) (same).

47. See State v. Phinney, 13 Idaho 307, 89 P. 634 (1907) (injection of morphine by hypodermic needle; although evidence may have established first degree murder, yet jury's verdict of manslaughter must stand).

48. People v. Steger, 16 Cal.3d 539, 128 Cal.Rptr. 161, 546 P.2d 665 (1976) (requirement is a willful, deliberate and premeditated intent to inflict extreme and prolonged pain). See People v. Caldwell, 43 Cal.2d 864, 279 P.2d 539 (1955) (defendant strangled wife to death; conviction of first degree murder *held* affirmed, not because there was any evidence of torture, but because there was evidence that the killing was intentional, premeditated and deliberate). Compare Townsend v. People, 107 Colo. 258, 111 P.2d 236 (1941) (defendant severely beat his wife, causing intercranial hemorrhage, which resulted in her death; the court instructed the jury that atrocity and cruelty is torture for purpose of first degree murder; conviction of first degree murder *held* reversed, for even if cruelty means the infliction of severe pain, a further essential torture, the infliction of pain "as a means of persuasion, punishment or in revenge," is missing). See Annot., 83 A.L.R.3d 1228 (1978).

49. People v. Martinez, 38 Cal.2d 556, 241 P.2d 224 (1952) (defendant doused his wife with gasoline and lit a match; she died three days later).

50. People v. Daugherty, 40 Cal.2d 876, 256 P.2d 911 (1953) (defendant stabbed wife over a period of time, dragged her over the ground, tore off her nightgown, struck her in the face, and, while she was still alive, kicked her).

51. People v. Cardoza, 57 Cal.App.2d 49, 134 P.2d 877 (1943) (defendant severely beat his wife with an ax handle, did not call for medical attention until she became unconscious; she died of shock and hemorrhage).

52. State v. Folk, 78 Ariz. 205, 277 P.2d 1016 (1954) (defendant burned victim with a burning torch, causing pain but not inflicting fatal burns; then he raped and strangled her; it was error to instruct the jury on murder by torture because of absence of evidence that death was caused by torture; but first degree murder conviction *held* affirmed on a felony-murder theory).

(d) Other First Degree Murder. Even in the modern codes, certain other types of murder are sometimes put into the first degree category. On occasion this is done by reference to some other manner of killing, such as by bombing or by procuring execution by perjury. More common are statutes putting a murder into the first degree bracket because of the status of the victim. A few statutes identify certain other aggravating characteristics, such as that the murder was committed for pay, that it involved the killing of more than one person, or that it was committed by a person with a prior murder conviction. As a consequence of rejecting the oft-criticized premeditation-deliberation distinction,[53] some jurisdictions have put all intentional killings into the first degree murder category. Less defensible is placing even depraved heart murder into this category, as a few states have done.

(e) Second Degree Murder. At one time, the typical statute dividing murder into degrees provided that a premeditated, deliberate, intentional killing, and murder in the perpetration or attempted perpetration of five or six named felonies, was first degree murder (often adding murder by lying in wait, by poison, or by torture); and that all other murder was second degree murder.[54] Under such a statute, still to be found in some states, what murder is left over for second degree murder to encompass?

First, intent-to-kill murder without the added ingredients of premeditation and deliberation is second degree murder. Second, intent-to-do-serious-bodily-injury murder (whether this intent is premeditated and deliberated or not) is second degree murder.[55] Third, depraved-heart murder falls into the second degree murder category.[56] Lastly, felony-murder, where the felony in question is not a listed one (e.g., abortion, larceny), comes under the second degree category,[57] unless the defendant's conduct is covered by some other part of the first degree murder statute, as where in the felony's commission he intentionally kills with premeditation and deliberation. Thus where a statute makes it a felony to destroy or remove a navigational marker, if a defendant should cut adrift the bell buoy marking the Inchcape Rock, as a consequence of which a vessel should strike the rock and a sailor drown, the defendant would be guilty of felony murder, for death to a mariner is the foreseeable consequence of such conduct; but the murder would be that of the second degree, for malicious mischief is not a listed felony.

Although the kind of statute just discussed does not undertake to define the crime of murder which it thus divides into degrees ("murder" committed in certain ways is first degree murder; all other "murder" is second degree murder),[58] most murder statutes in the recent criminal codes define murder and its various degrees in terms of "killing" or "causing death" under certain described conditions. Such statutes often make changes in the scope of the common law crime of murder;[59] and, not fitting into the pattern of the statute above described, the particular statute must be consulted as to the degree of murder as well as referred to as to the scope of murder.

---

53. See § 7.7(a).

54. Pennsylvania, in 1794, enacted the original statute thus dividing murder into two degrees. Most other states followed the Pennsylvania formula, with some modifications.

55. Commonwealth v. Marshall, 287 Pa. 512, 135 A. 301 (1926) (defendant intended to do great harm, but he had no intent to kill; death resulted; this is second degree murder).

56. State v. Lacquey, 117 Ariz. 231, 571 P.2d 1027 (1977). In a few states, depraved-heart murder is first degree murder.

57. People v. Poindexter, 51 Cal.2d 142, 330 P.2d 763 (1958) (defendant furnished narcotics to minor, a felony;

minor died of narcotics poisoning; taking heroin is dangerous to life; conviction of second degree murder *held* affirmed, over defendant's contention his crime was manslaughter. See People v. Olsen, 80 Cal. 122, 22 P. 125 (1889) (where the killing results from the commission or attempted commission of a felony, whether the felony is a felony listed in the first degree murder statute or not, it is murder); State v. Wanrow, 91 Wn.2d 301, 588 P.2d 1320 (1978) (felony murder by assault is second degree murder).

58. Since "murder" is not defined, the common law must be looked to.

59. Thus, as noted in § 7.3, the great majority of the modern codes do not recognize murder of the intent-to-do-serious-bodily-injury type.

§ 7.8 Aiding and Attempting Suicide

Suicide—the intentional destruction of himself by one who is sane and who has reached the age of discretion—was a common law crime (a felony) in England, punishable by burial in the highway with a stake through the suicide's body and by forfeiture of all his goods to the crown.[1] Though the matter is not entirely clear, probably suicide was considered a form of murder rather than a crime separate from murder.[2] In America today the forfeiture-of-goods and ignominious-burial forms of punishment have been abolished, so that no penalty attaches to a successful suicide. When common law crimes have been retained,[3] suicide has been characterized as a "criminal" or "unlawful" act though, not being punishable, not strictly-speaking a crime.[4]

The modern criminal law problems relating to suicide concern the criminal liability of (1) one who unsuccessfully attempts to commit suicide, causing harm to no one else; (2) one whose unsuccessful attempt kills or injures someone else—a would-be rescuer or innocent bystander; and (3) one who persuades or aids or forces another to commit a successful suicide.[5]

(a) Attempted Suicide.[6] In some states attempted suicide, which was a common law misdemeanor,[7] was at one time a crime,[8] but the prevailing view has long been otherwise.[9] None of the modern codifications treats attempted suicide as a crime.[10] Attempted suicide which harms no one but the attempter himself was rarely prosecuted.

Doubless it is better policy not to make such conduct criminal. Certainly one bent upon a successful suicide will not be deterred by thoughts of possible punishment. Moreover, "intrusion of the criminal law into such tragedies is an abuse. There is a certain moral extravagance in imposing criminal punishment on a person who has sought his own self-destruction * * * and who more properly requires medical or psychiatric attention."[11]

§ 7.8

1. Hales v. Petit, 1 Plowd. 253, 75 Eng.Rep. 387 (C.B.1565); Burnett v. People, 204 Ill. 208, 68 N.E. 505 (1903).

2. See Mikell, Is Suicide Murder?, 3 Colum.L.Rev. 379 (1903), answering that suicide is murder.

3. In states which have abolished common law crimes, see § 2.1, suicide can be no crime in the absence of a statute making it so: State v. Campbell, 217 Iowa 848, 251 N.W. 717 (1933). No state has a statute making successful suicide a crime. See, e.g., State v. Marti, 290 N.W.2d 570 (Iowa 1980); State v. Fuller, 203 Neb. 233, 278 N.W.2d 756 (1979).

4. E.g., Commonwealth v. Mink, 123 Mass. 422, 25 Am. Rep. 109 (1877) (when her fiancé broke his engagement to marry her, defendant attempted suicide with a gun, which the man tried to prevent; but the gun went off accidentally killing him; conviction of manslaughter *held* affirmed; suicide, not being punishable, is not technically a felony, but it is still "unlawful and criminal" and *malum in se*; the court suggests that the crime might have been murder, rather than merely manslaughter).

Cf. State v. Campbell, supra note 3 (on substantially the same facts, in a state which has abolished common-law crimes, conviction of murder *held* reversed, for suicide is neither a crime nor an unlawful act).

5. See Larremore, Suicide and the Law, 17 Harv.L.Rev. 331 (1904); Mikell, supra note 2; Comments, 39 Dick.L. Rev. 42 (1934); 105 U.Pa.L.Rev. 391 (1957); 1 Vill.L.Rev. 316 (1956).

6. See Annot., 92 A.L.R. 1180, 1182–84 (1934). On the related question of whether the attempted suicide of an accused person constitutes evidence of his guilt, see Comment, 1964 Wash.U.L.Q. 204.

7. Rex v. Mann, [1914] 2 K.B. 107. See May v. Pennell, 101 Me. 516, 64 A. 885 (1906); Commonwealth v. Dennis, 105 Mass. 162 (1870).

8. State v. LaFayette, 15 N.J.Misc. 115, 188 A. 918 (Ct. Com.Pl.1937); State v. Willis, 255 N.C. 473, 121 S.E.2d 854 (1961), noted at 40 N.C.L.Rev. 323 (1962). Six states once made attempted suicide a crime by statute. See Note, 40 N.C.L.Rev. 323, 326 (1962).

9. Thus, in those states which do not recognize common law crimes, see § 2.1, and which have no statute punishing it, attempted suicide is no crime; Wallace v. State, 232 Ind. 700, 116 N.E.2d 100 (1953); State v. Campbell, supra note 3. England, by the Suicide Act 1961, provided that suicide and attempted suicide should no longer be criminal.

10. Model Penal Code § 210.5, Comment at n. 10 (1980).

11. Model Penal Code § 210.5, Comment (1980).

(b) Attempted Suicide Which Harms Another.[12] One attempting suicide sometimes accidentally kills another [13] while failing to kill himself; the other is usually a person who, seeing the defendant bent on self-destruction, acts to restrain him, perhaps by struggling with him for possession of his gun. Such conduct producing such a result has been held to be murder,[14] manslaughter,[15] and no crime at all in the absence of recklessness.[16] In most cases the proper solution is probably involuntary manslaughter: if the suicide attempt is made with bystanders and potential rescuers nearby, the suicide's conduct can generally be found to be reckless as to one or more persons' lives so as to support a conviction of involuntary manslaughter of the recklessness type.[17]

12. See Annot., supra note 6, at 1184–85.

13. He may accidentally injure him, rather than kill him; in which case the question is his liability for battery, rather than for murder or manslaughter.

14. State v. Levelle, 34 S.C. 120, 13 S.E. 319 (1891) (judge's instruction that one who with a deadly weapon tries to take his own life commits an unlawful act, and if he kills an innocent person he is guilty of murder *held* correct).

See Commonwealth v. Mink, supra note 4 (conviction of manslaughter *held* affirmed, but court states crime was probably murder); Rex v. Hopwood, 8 Crim.App. 143 (1913) (murder because he intended to kill victim but it would have been murder if he had instead intended suicide). The theory for murder liability might be that suicide is a form of murder and if one intends to kill *A* but misses and kills *B* he is guilty of murder of *B*. See § 3.12(d). Or it might be that suicide is a felony, see State v. Levelle, supra, or an unlawful act of the felony-grade even if not punishable, see Commonwealth v. Mink, supra, so that the felony-murder doctrine applies.

15. Commonwealth v. Mink, supra note 4 (attempted suicide is an unlawful act, though not technically a crime, so that the unlawful-act of involuntary manslaughter is applicable). In Wallace v. State, supra note 9, defendant's conviction (the case does not say whether of murder or manslaughter) for killing a good Samaritan who intervened to prevent his suicide was affirmed, the court holding that the trial court properly refused a request to instruct that attempted suicide, being no crime, is not an unlawful act. See § 7.13.

16. State v. Campbell, supra note 3 (attempted suicide is no crime, so it cannot be an unlawful act, so it cannot be murder or, it would seem, unlawful-act manslaughter).

17. In State v. Campbell, supra note 3, the court suggests a manslaughter or murder solution if the defendant is reckless or extremely reckless. The misdemeanor-manslaughter doctrine, which in some jurisdictions is broad enough to include "unlawful" conduct which is not strictly

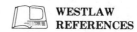

WESTLAW REFERENCES

mink (levelle /s 13 +4 319) /p suicide /3 attempt***

(c) Inducing, Aiding, Forcing Another to Commit Suicide.[18] If, *A*, by resort to force or duress, were purposely to cause *B* to commit suicide, then there is no doubt that in all jurisdictions *A* would be held to have committed the crime of murder.[19] Likewise, *A* is guilty of murder if he is actually the agent of *B*'s death, notwithstanding the fact that he acted at *B*'s request—as where *A* shoots and kills *B* upon *B*'s insistence that he wants to die now rather than continue to suffer from a serious illness.[20]

Under appropriate circumstances, one who causes another to commit suicide may be

speaking "criminal," would also cover the attempted suicide conduct; there is apparent, however, a trend to abolish unlawful-act manslaughter as a separate form of involuntary manslaughter leaving the field to recklessness manslaughter. See 7.13(e). Of course, one who attempts suicide in a dramatic way knowing that others are substantially certain to be killed, or even that there is a very high degree of risk that they will be killed, would be guilty of intent-to-kill or depraved-heart, murder if he should survive while others die.

18. See Annot., 13 A.L.R. 1259 (1921).

19. Model Penal Code § 210.5 provides that a person may be convicted of criminal homicide for causing another to commit suicide if he purposely causes such suicide by force, duress or deception. "It is only where the actor actively participates in inducing the suicide of another, as by the use of force, duress, or deception, that criminal penalties seem warranted. * * * [F]or example, the party who breaks off relations with a distraught lover may well hope or intend that the suicide of the lover will result. As morally distasteful as such conduct might be, it still seems plain that conviction of murder would not be warranted in such a case." Model Penal Code § 210.5, Comment at 99 (1980).

20. State v. Cobb, 229 Kan. 522, 625 P.2d 1133 (1981) (at request of victim the defendant injected him with fatal dose of cocaine and then shot him in head; she properly convicted of first degree murder); State v. Fuller, 203 Neb. 233, 278 N.W.2d 756 (1979) (at request of cellmate, defendant inserted needle in his arm and then collapsed bag to which it attached, killing him; defendant properly convicted of first degree murder); Turner v. State, 119 Tenn. 663, 108 S.W. 1139 (1908) (defendant paramour shot his mistress, a married woman, pursuant to a suicide pact; then, losing his nerve, he failed to shoot himself; conviction of murder *held* affirmed).

It is, of course, no defense to murder that the victim consented to be killed, as is often the case with mercy killings. See § 5.11(a).

guilty of murder even though he did not intend for the other person to take his own life. Thus if *A*, with intent to kill *B*, mortally wounds *B* and inflicts so much grief or pain upon *B* that *B* commits suicide, *A* is guilty of murder of the intent-to-kill sort.[21] Or, if *A*, in raping *B*, inflicts such serious wounds that *B*, overcome by pain and shame, kills herself, *A* is guilty of murder of the felony-murder type.[22]

There are three different views about the criminal liability of one who, whether pursu-

ant to a suicide pact[23] or not, solicits (by talk) or aids (as by providing the means of self-destruction[24]) another to commit suicide. Occasionally aiding or soliciting suicide has been held to be no crime at all on the ground that suicide is not criminal.[25] That view is most certainly unsound.[26] At one time many jurisdictions held it to be murder,[27] but a great many states now deal specifically with causing[28] or aiding[29] suicide by statute, treating it either as a form of manslaughter or as a

21. Cf. People v. Lewis, 124 Cal. 551, 57 P. 470 (1899) (manslaughter conviction affirmed, on the ground that the victim died from the combined effect of the gunshot wound in the abdomen inflicted by the defendant and the self-inflicted knife wound in his throat). This case involves a question of causation, when the defendant intends a certain result (here death) and he produces that result but in an unintended manner. See § 3.12(f).

22. Stephenson v. State, 205 Ind. 141, 179 N.E. 633 (1933). This case too involves a question of causation, especially of the foreseeability of the suicide death from the defendant's manner of committing rape. See § 3.12(h).

23. As in McMahan v. State, Burnett v. People, Regina v. Alison, infra note 27.

It has been argued that in the case of the survivor of a suicide pact, all of the arguments against treating attempted suicide as criminal apply. Because the survivor wanted to end his own life, punishing him "can serve no deterrent purpose, may hinder medical treatment, and is merely useless cruelty," which "can do no more than strengthen the will to succeed in the act of self-destruction." G. Williams, The Sanctity of Life and the Criminal Law 305 (1957). But while "there is some logic in assimilating the double suicide attempt to the case of the single attempt, there is an unavoidable danger of abuse in differentiating genuine from spurious agreements." Model Penal Code, § 210.5, Comment at 105 (1980).

24. Thus in People v. Roberts, 211 Mich. 187, 178 N.W. 690 (1920), the defendant, at his incurably-ill wife's request, mixed Paris green, a poison, and placed it within her reach; she took it and died.

25. Aven v. State, 102 Tex.Crim. 478, 277 S.W. 1080 (1925) (furnishing the means for committing suicide is no crime); see Sanders v. State, 54 Tex.Crim. 101, 112 S.W. 68 (1908). But compare Blackburn v. State, infra note 27 (though suicide is not a crime, furnishing poison to another with intent that the other kill himself is murder when the other does so).

26. "Although the distinction between aiding and abetting suicide and homicide based on the same conduct is somewhat paradoxical, we believe it has merit. The criminal is held to answer for his conduct because it constitutes murder or manslaughter, not because it coincidentally helped someone to die who wanted to die anyway. Our law makes no distinctions as to the identity of the victim in determining culpability for homicide. The only reason we view suicide noncriminal is that we consider inappropriate punishing the suicide victim or attempted

suicide victim, not that we are concerned about that person's life any less than others' lives." State v. Marti, 290 N.W.2d 570 (Iowa 1980).

27. McMahan v. State, 168 Ala. 70, 53 So. 89 (1910) (pursuant to suicide pact, deceased shot himself in defendant's presence, but defendant did not shoot himself; since suicide is self-murder, defendant, who encouraged and was present, is guilty of murder as principal); Burnett v. People, supra note 1 (paramour, in stupified condition, admitted that he and his mistress both took poison as a result of a suicide pact; mistress died but he survived; the court indicates that this would be murder on his part, but conviction *held* reversed for lack of proof of guilt, his admissions when stupified being inadmissible); Commonwealth v. Hicks, 118 Ky. 637, 82 S.W. 265 (1904) (although it is murder to aid another to commit suicide, as by furnishing him the poison, though the furnisher is not present when the suicide kills himself, here trial court properly directed verdict of acquittal, for there was no evidence of defendant's aiding suicide except his own uncorroborated confession); Commonwealth v. Bowen, 13 Mass. 356, 7 Am.Dec. 154 (1816) (defendant, a prison inmate, advised a fellow prisoner, who was to be executed next day by the state for murder to commit suicide and thus disappoint the executioner and those who planned to witness the execution; the supreme judicial court instructed the jury that if the advice persuaded the fellow-prisoner it would be murder; the jury, however, found the defendant not guilty, probably from a doubt as to whether the advice was the procuring cause of the other's death); People v. Roberts, supra note 23; Blackburn v. State, 23 Ohio St. 146 (1872) (furnishing poison to a suicide with intent that she should take it, by one who agrees but fails to join in the suicide, is murder, though suicide, is no crime; but conviction is reversed for exclusion of admissible evidence favorable to defendant); State v. Jones, 86 S.C. 17, 67 S.E. 160 (1910) (approving instruction that one who persuades another to commit suicide is guilty of murder, if the persuasion is an inducing cause of the suicide; conviction of murder *held* affirmed); Regina v. Alison, 8 Car. & P. 418, 173 Eng.Rep. 557 (1838) (lovers, in desperate want, took poison pursuant to suicide pact; she died but he survived; verdict of guilty of murder).

28. In the modern codes, many statutes cover one who "causes" a suicide. Under this type of statute, it is unclear what it takes to amount to causation. See Brenner, Undue Influence in the Criminal Law: A Proposed

---

29. See note 29 on page 652.

separate crime.[30] Such statutes typically do "not contemplate active participation by one in the overt act directly causing death," [31] and thus their existence is no barrier to a murder conviction in such circumstances.[32] Where the defendant did not intend for the other person to commit suicide, the providing of dangerous instrumentalities to one foreseeably bent on suicide is, if suicide results, a basis for a negligent homicide conviction.[33]

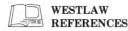

**WESTLAW
REFERENCES**

topic(203 110) /p suicide /4 aid*** abet! forc*** induc*** solicit*** assist!

§ 7.9 Manslaughter—Classification

It is sometimes stated in statutes and judicial decisions which undertake to define manslaughter that manslaughter is "the unlawful killing of another human being without malice aforethought." But as "malice aforethought" in connection with the law of homicide is not to be taken literally,[1] this definition is of small help in solving particular cases. It is more helpful to recognize at the outset that manslaughter is an intermediate crime which lies half-way between the more serious crime of murder, at the one extreme, and, at the other extreme, justifiable or excusable homicide, which is not criminal at all.[2] Thus manslaughter constitutes a sort of catch-all category which includes homicides which are not bad enough to be murder but which are too bad to be no crime whatever.[3]

Although the common law drew a distinction between voluntary manslaughter and involuntary manslaughter on the basis of the different types of conduct involved, it did not do so for any purpose of providing different punishments. Today many American jurisdictions maintain the old distinction between voluntary and involuntary manslaughter, usually awarding a less severe punishment for involuntary than for voluntary manslaughter. Some modern American statutes, however, have discarded the adjectives (voluntary and involuntary) and instead divide manslaughter into degrees, reserving a higher penalty for first degree manslaughter. But the modern trend, reflected in a majority of recent recodifications, is for these to be but one single manslaughter crime.[4]

A few modern statutes place within the manslaughter category certain homicides which constituted murder rather than manslaughter at common law. Thus, in some jurisdictions the crime of manslaughter is defined to include killings of the intent-to-do-serious-bodily-injury, depraved heart, and felony murder varieties. But whether or not that is so, manslaughter is a crime which is separate and distinct from, rather than merely a degree of, the crime of murder.[5]

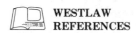

**WESTLAW
REFERENCES**

203k35 /p manslaughter /s malice

203k35 /p manslaughter /s murder

Analysis of the Criminal Offense of "Causing Suicide," 47 Albany L.Rev. 62 (1982) (proposing "undue influence" test).

29. Many modern statutes cover only one who "aids" in a suicide. Model Penal Code § 210.5(2) makes it a separate crime to aid or solicit another to commit suicide; it is a felony if the conduct causes a suicide or attempted suicide, a misdemeanor if it does not.

30. See Forden v. Joseph G., 34 Cal.3d 429, 194 Cal. Rptr. 163, 667 P.2d 1176 (1983) (defendant who drove car containing self and friend over cliff to carry out suicide pact is guilty of aiding and abetting suicide rather than murder).

31. State v. Bouse, 199 Or. 676, 264 P.2d 800 (1953).

32. State v. Cobb, 229 Kan. 522, 625 P.2d 1133 (1981) (where defendant pushed the plunger which injected co-

caine into another's veins and then shot him, she not entitled to assisting suicide instruction); State v. Bouse, 199 Or. 676, 264 P.2d 800 (1953) (even if defendant acted at other's request, it murder rather than assisting suicide).

33. State v. Bier, 181 Mont. 27, 591 P.2d 1115 (1979).

§ **7.9**

1. See § 7.1(a).

2. See ch. 5.

3. But in modern codes it is not uncommon for there to be a lesser degree of criminal homicide, often called negligent homicide. See § 7.12(e).

4. This is also the approach in Model Penal Code § 210.3.

5. State v. Brown, 22 N.J. 405, 126 A.2d 161 (1956).

§ 7.10 Heat-of-Passion Voluntary Manslaughter

Voluntary manslaughter in most jurisdictions consists of an intentional homicide committed under extenuating circumstances which mitigate, though they do not justify or excuse, the killing. The principal extenuating circumstance is the fact that the defendant, when he killed the victim, was in a state of passion engendered in him by an adequate provocation (i.e., a provocation which would cause a reasonable man to lose his normal self-control).[1]

(a) The State of Mind. Although the killing of another person—when accompanied by an intent to kill, or by an intent to do serious bodily injury short of death, or when resulting from such unreasonable and highly reckless conduct as to "evince a depraved heart"—often amounts to murder, yet it may under certain circumstances amount only to voluntary manslaughter.[2] Most killings which constitute voluntary manslaughter are of the intent-to-kill sort—so much so that voluntary manslaughter is often defined in the cases[3] (and, sometimes, by statute) as if intent to kill were a required ingredient. But, theoretical-

ly at least, they might be of the intent-to-do-serious-bodily-injury, or of the depraved-heart, types. Thus—to take the most common sort of voluntary manslaughter, a killing while in a reasonable "heat of passion"—in most cases the defendant intentionally kills the one who has aroused this passion in him. But if, in the throes of such a passion, he should intend instead to do his tormentor serious bodily injury short of death, or if he should, without intending to kill him, endanger his life by very reckless (depraved heart) conduct, the resulting death ought equally to be voluntary manslaughter rather than murder or no crime.[4] Thus, the great majority of modern statutes, either by a reference to all cases which would otherwise be murder or by similar general language, take this broad view.

The usual view of voluntary manslaughter thus presupposes an intent to kill (or perhaps an intent to do serious injury or to engage in very reckless conduct), holding that in spite of the existence of this bad intent the circumstances may reduce the homicide to manslaughter. But there is a minority view, expressed in an occasional case[5] and in a few manslaughter statutes, to the effect that the

---

§ 7.10

1. Of the modern codes, only West's Rev.Code Wash.Ann. 9A.32.060 clearly does not have this type of manslaughter. But some voluntary manslaughter statutes, by their form, leave the matter unclear at best.

The crime of voluntary manslaughter as defined by statutes in most jurisdictions covers other situations as well, but in some of the modern codes the crime is limited only to the present situation.

2. Such killings, of course, under still other circumstances (e.g., self-defense, prevention of felony) may amount to no crime whatsoever. See ch. 5.

3. E.g., Smith v. State, 83 Ala. 26, 3 So. 551 (1888) (homicide in heat of passion reasonably provoked is manslaughter, not because the law supposes that the passion "stripped the act of killing of an intent to commit it, but because it presumes that the passion disturbed the sway of reason"); People v. Brubaker, 53 Cal.2d 37, 346 P.2d 8 (1959) ("Voluntary manslaughter is * * * characterized by the presence of an intent to kill"); State v. Laswell, 78 Ohio App. 202, 66 N.E.2d 555 (1946) ("Voluntary manslaughter is the unlawful and intentional killing of another" in a reasonable passion); Wheatley v. Commonwealth, 26 Ky.L.Rptr. 436, 81 S.W. 687 (Ct.App.1904) (Case 3) (killing must be willful or intentional); Commonwealth v. Colandro, 231 Pa. 343, 80 A. 571 (1911) ("Voluntary manslaughter is a homicide intentionally committed under the influence of passion"); State v. Barker, 128 W.Va. 744, 38

S.E.2d 346 (1946) ("voluntary manslaughter, an essential element of which is intent to kill").

4. See State v. Adams, 210 La. 782, 28 So.2d 269 (1946) ("an actual intention to kill or to inflict great bodily harm is an essential element in the crime of voluntary manslaughter"); Commonwealth v. Mason, 474 Pa. 308, 378 A.2d 807 (1977) (intent to kill or to seriously injure; concurring opinion adds depraved heart category); Commonwealth v. Moore, 398 Pa. 198, 157 A.2d 65 (1959) (intent to inflict serious bodily injury).

The felony-murder analogy could hardly arise in a voluntary manslaughter situation. A loss of self-control may be the reasonable consequence of some provocations. But although the formation of an intent to kill or to do serious injury or to engage in highly dangerous conduct might be an understandable (though unreasonable) reaction to the provocation, a decision to commit robbery or rape or other felony could hardly be so.

5. E.g., Johnson v. State, 129 Wis. 146, 108 N.W. 55 (1906) (the provocation must be such as to suspend the reasonable man's ordinary judgment, making his mind "deaf to the voice of reason; make him incapable of forming and executing that distinct intent to take human life essential to murder"); Holmes v. Director of Public Prosecutions, [1946] A.C. 588 (the provocation which will do for voluntary manslaughter must cause "a sudden and temporary loss of self-control whereby malice, which is the

passion must be so great as to destroy the intent to kill, in order to accomplish the reduction of the homicide to voluntary manslaughter. Such a stringent view doubtless makes it more difficult for a defendant to obtain a reduction of his homicide to voluntary manslaughter; for he must show that his passion went so far as to rob him of his normal capacity to entertain murderous thoughts, rather than that it merely made him lose the normal self-control which enables him to resist any temptation to slay another person.

The usual type of voluntary manslaughter involves the intentional killing of another while under the influence of a reasonably-induced emotional disturbance (in earlier terminology, while in a "heat of passion") causing a temporary loss of normal self-control. Except for this reasonable emotional condition, the intentional killing would be murder.[6] The term traditionally used [7] to describe that condition—"heat of passion"—is very often used in modern manslaughter statutes, either alone or with some additional language. (But some modern statutes seek to define this mitigating circumstance more broadly and thus do not utilize the "heat of passion" term.[8]) The "passion" (emotional disturbance) involved in the crime of voluntary manslaughter is generally rage (great anger); but some cases have pointed out that other intense emotions—such as fright or terror [9] or "wild desperation" [10]—will do. A "passion for revenge," of course, will not do.[11]

There are four obstacles for the defendant to overcome before he can have his intention-

al killing reduced from murder to voluntary manslaughter: (1) There must have been a reasonable provocation. (2) The defendant must have been in fact provoked. (3) A reasonable man so provoked would not have cooled off in the interval of time between the provocation and the delivery of the fatal blow. And (4), the defendant must not in fact have cooled off during that interval.

WESTLAW REFERENCES

topic(203) /p voluntary /2 manslaughter /s intent! /s murder

203k35 /p voluntary /2 manslaughter

(b) Reasonable Provocation.[12] It is sometimes stated that, in order to reduce an intentional killing to voluntary manslaughter, the provocation involved must be such as to cause a reasonable man to kill.[13] Yet the reasonable man, however greatly provoked he may be, does not kill. The law recognizes this fact, by holding that the one who thus kills is guilty of the crime of voluntary manslaughter, while at the same time, the law considers that one who really acts reasonably in killing another (as in proper self-defense) is guilty of no crime. What is really meant by "reasonable provocation" is provocation which causes a reasonable man to lose his normal self-control; and, although a reasonable man who has thus lost control over himself would not kill, yet his homicidal reaction to the provocation is at least understandable. Therefore, one who reacts to the provocation by killing his provoker should not be guilty of murder. But neither should he be guilty of no crime at

---

formation of an intention to kill or to inflict grievous bodily harm, is negatived").

6. In Commonwealth v. Flax, 331 Pa. 145, 200 A. 632 (1938), it is said: "The law regards with some tolerance an unlawful act impelled by a justifiably passionate heart, but has no toleration whatever for an unlawful act impelled by a malicious heart."

7. See Annot., 5 L.R.A. (n.s.) 809 (1906) (heat of passion which will mitigate or reduce the degree of homicide).

8. See discussion in § 7.10(b).

9. Commonwealth v. Colandro, 231 Pa. 343, 80 A. 571 (1911).

10. People v. Borchers, 50 Cal.2d 321, 325 P.2d 97 (1958).

11. People v. Borchers, supra note 10.

12. For a full discussion of this factor, see Comment, Manslaughter and the Adequacy of Provocation: The Reasonableness of the Reasonable Man, 106 U.Pa.L.Rev. 1021 (1958).

13. Language to this effect is to be found in many of the modern statutes. About the same number of the modern manslaughter statutes utilize language which clearly does *not* contemplate a reasonable man approach. Several other statutes, if read literally, would seem to take a purely subjective approach. But such an interpretation is most unlikely, given the common law antecedents of the statutes.

all. So his conduct falls into the intermediate category of voluntary manslaughter.

There has been a tendency for the law to jell concerning what conduct does or does not constitute a reasonable provocation for purposes of voluntary manslaughter. Thus it is often held that a reasonable man may be provoked into a passion when he (or a close relative) is hurt by violent physical blows, or is unlawfully arrested or discovers his spouse in the act of adultery; but that he can never be provoked by mere words or by trespasses to his property. In modern times, however, there seems to be a growing realization that what might or might not cause a loss of self-control in a reasonable Englishman of a century ago might not necessarily produce the same reaction in the reasonable Anglo-American of today.[14] As a consequence of this realization there may be a future trend away from the usual practice of placing the various types of provocatory conduct into pigeon-holes. At all events the following is a list of provocations which have traditionally been considered, almost as a matter of law, to be reasonable or unreasonable and which, in general, influence our legal thinking today.[15]

(1) Battery. A light blow, though it may constitute a battery, can not constitute a reasonable provocation;[16] but a violent, painful blow, with fist or weapon, ordinarily will do so.[17] Even in the case where the defendant kills in response to a violent blow, however, he may not have his homicide reduced to voluntary manslaughter if he himself by his own prior conduct (as by vigorously starting the fracas) was responsible for that violent blow.[18] Something too may depend upon a comparison of the weapon used by the victim to inflict the blow upon the killer and the weapon which the latter "used in retort,"[19] as where a dagger is used in retaliation for a blow with a fist,[20] or five lethal slashes with a straight razor for one wifely blow on the head with a small fireplace poker.[21]

(2) Mutual Combat. Where two persons willingly engage in mutual combat,[22] and during the fight one kills the other as the result of an intention to do so formed during the struggle,[23] the homicide has long been held to be manslaughter, and not murder,[24] the no-

14. See Holmes v. Director of Public Prosecutions, [1946] A.C. 588, for a suggestion that notions of what constitutes a reasonable provocation may change with the evolution of society from one age to the next. England followed up this suggestion by its Homicide Act of 1957, § 3, providing that the jury should, in every case of a killing while actually provoked, determine whether the provocation was under the particular circumstances reasonable.

15. This remains true because even modern manslaughter statutes make little or no effort to specify what constitutes reasonable provocation.

16. Commonwealth v. Rembiszewski, 363 Mass. 311, 293 N.E.2d 919 (1973) (scratches on defendant's face insufficient provocation for killing with deadly instrument); Commonwealth v. Cisneros, 381 Pa. 447, 113 A.2d 293 (1955).

17. People v. Harris, 8 Ill.2d 431, 134 N.E.2d 315 (1956) (victim beat defendant severely with night stick); State v. Ponce, 124 W.Va. 126, 19 S.E.2d 221 (1942) (victim hit or shoved defendant into a rock pile).

18. State v. Ferguson, 2 Hill (S.C.) 619, 27 Am.Dec. 412 (1835) (victim, trying to stop quarrel started by defendant, threw defendant against wall; defendant killed victim with knife). Cf. State v. Hill, 20 N.C. 629, 34 Am.Dec. 396 (1839) (defendant's light blow upon victim led victim to inflict painful knife wound on defendant, who reacted by killing victim with a knife; held, victim's conduct constituted reasonable provocation).

19. See Holmes v. Director of Public Prosecutions, [1946] A.C. 588.

Likewise, it is relevant to consider whether the killer, in responding, actually intended to kill or only intended to do serious bodily harm. State v. Hoyt, 13 Minn. 132 (1868).

20. Mancini v. Director of Public Prosecutions, [1942] A.C. 1.

21. Commonwealth v. Webb, 252 Pa. 187, 97 A. 189 (1916).

22. This does not cover all cases in which a fight ensues. Thus, if one person uses lawful force on another to prevent a trespass and the individuals then begin to fight, culminating in a killing by the latter person, this is not manslaughter. State v. Smith, 123 N.H. 46, 455 A.2d 1041 (1983) ("the acts which have resulted in sufficient provocation in mutual combat cases have generally been unlawful in themselves"; "a lawful act cannot provide sufficient provocation").

23. It is not necessary that the defendant have been acting out of passion when the fight started. State v. Inger, 292 N.W.2d 119 (Iowa 1980).

24. See, e.g., People v. Leonard, 83 Ill.2d 411, 47 Ill. Dec. 353, 415 N.E.2d 358 (1981). E. Coke, Third Institute 57 (6th ed. 1680), refer to this as the killing of a man by "chance-medley."

tion being that the suddenness of the occasion,[25] rather than some provocation by the victim, mitigates the intentional killing to something less than murder. A study of this type of voluntary manslaughter concludes that cases of intentional killings in mutual combat are generally treated on the basis of provocation involved in batteries,[26] the type of provocation discussed immediately above.

(3) Assault. Where one attempts but fails to commit a violent battery upon another (thereby committing a criminal assault), there is a disagreement in the cases as to whether the ssault can arouse in a reasonable man that passion which will mitigate to manslaughter an intentional killing of the assaulter by the one assaulted.[27] The better view, however, is that an attack upon the defendant which was unsuccessful may constitute adequate provocation in extreme cases, as where the attacker fires a pistol at him.[28]

(4) Illegal Arrest.[29] The cases are in dispute concerning the effect of an illegal arrest upon the passions of a reasonable man—some taking the view that such an arrest might reasonably arouse a heat of passion in him,[30] others the view that a reasonable man could not be so aroused.[31] If an illegal arrest may be a reasonable provocation in some circumstances, it would seem that these circumstances should include the fact that the defendant knew or at least believed that his arrest was illegal; and perhaps that the defendant knew or believed he was innocent of the crime for which he was arrested, since an innocent man would more reasonably be provoked by an illegal arrest than a guilty one.[32] In any event, a *lawful* arrest cannot constitute sufficient provocation.[33]

(5) Adultery.[34] It is the law practically everywhere that a husband who discovers his wife in the act of committing adultery is reasonably provoked, so that when, in his passion, he intentionally kills either his wife or her lover (or both), his crime is voluntary manslaughter rather than murder.[35] So too a wife may be reasonably provoked into a heat of passion upon finding her husband in the act of adultery with another woman.[36] The modern tendency is to extend the rule of

25. Some modern statutes specifically mention "sudden quarrel" as a type of adequate provocation.

26. Comment, Manslaughter and the Adequacy of Provocation: The Reasonableness of the Reasonable Man, 106 U.Pa.L.Rev. 1021, 1031–32 (1958).

27. Compare State v. Kizer, 360 Mo. 744, 230 S.W.2d 690 (1950) (victim assaulted defendant with axe but did not strike him; held, not a reasonable provocation), with Sikes v. Commonwealth, 304 Ky. 429, 200 S.W.2d 956 (1947) (defendant entitled to voluntary manslaughter instruction after testifying that defendant did not strike him but was "acting like he was going to").

28. Stevenson v. United States, 162 U.S. 313, 16 S.Ct. 839, 40 L.Ed. 980 (1896).

29. For a fuller discussion, see Dickey, Culpable Homicide in Resisting Arrest, 18 Cornell L.Q. 373, 375–76 (1933); Moreland, The Use of Force in Effecting or Resisting Arrest, 33 Neb.L.Rev. 408 (1954); Annot., 66 L.R.A. 353 (1905).

30. John Bad Elk v. United States, 177 U.S. 529, 20 S.Ct. 729, 44 L.Ed. 874 (1900) (when arrested person kills an arresting officer, that which might be murder if the arrest is lawful might be nothing more than manslaughter if the arrest is unlawful, and in some circumstances, like self-defense, might be no crime); People v. White, 333 Ill. 512, 165 N.E. 168 (1929); State v. Burnett, 354 Mo. 45, 188 S.W.2d 51 (1945); Regina v. Chapman, 12 Cox Crim.Cas. 4 (1871).

31. People v. Bradley, 23 Cal.App. 44, 136 P. 955 (Dist. Ct.App.1913); Alsop v. Commonwealth, 4 Ky.L.Rptr. 547

(1882). The notion here is that a reasonable man would submit to the illegal arrest and then take legal means to secure his release, rather than resort to killing.

32. As to the latter point, see Note, 106 U.Pa.L.Rev. 1021, 1029 (1958).

33. State v. Madden, 61 N.J. 377, 294 A.2d 609 (1972).

34. See Note, 86 Just.P. 617 (1922) (English cases).

35. Manning's Case, Raym. Sir T. 212, 83 Eng.Rep. 112 (23 Chas. II); Rowland v. State, 83 Miss. 483, 35 So. 826 (1904) (Case 2) (manslaughter when husband, upon discovery of wife committing adultery with lover, shot at lover and, missing, killed wife); Gonzales v. State, 546 S.W.2d 617 (Tex.Crim.1977) (manslaughter where husband shot lover found in bed with his wife).

Compare Palmore v. State, 253 Ala. 183, 43 So.2d 399 (1949) (husband killed wife, but held murder because a reasonable husband would have cooled); Reed v. State, 62 Miss. 405 (1884) (husband killed paramour, but held murder because of cooling time). See also Burger v. State, 238 Ga. 171, 231 S.E.2d 769 (1977) (husband's testimony he went blank upon finding wife with lover not sufficient evidence his killing of them was manslaughter).

36. Scroggs v. State, 94 Ga.App. 28, 93 S.E.2d 583 (1956) (wife killed the other woman). Holmes v. Director of Public Prosecutions, [1946] A.C. 588, discussing the situation where a husband kills his wife upon her confession of adultery, makes the point that the rule concerning voluntary manslaughter "must apply to either spouse alike, for we have left behind us the age when the wife's

mitigation beyond the narrow situation where one spouse actually catches the other in the act of committing adultery. Thus it has been held that a reasonable though erroneous belief on the part of the husband that his wife is committing adultery will do.[37] Some cases have held that a reasonable man may be provoked upon suddenly being told of his wife's infidelity.[38] One case holds that the sudden sight of his wife's paramour in his mother-in-law's home might reasonably cause the husband, who knew his wife had been having an affair with the man, to lose his ordinary self-control, mitigating his killing to manslaughter.[39]

The rule of mitigation does not, however, extend beyond the marital relationship so as to include engaged persons, divorced couples and unmarried lovers—as where a man is enraged at the discovery of his mistress in the sexual embrace of another man.[40] This limitation seems questionable, however, at least in cases where there existed a longstanding relationship comparable to that of husband and wife.[41]

In the adultery situation there is a popular belief that it is not the crime of voluntary manslaughter, but rather no crime at all, for the enraged husband to kill his wife's paramour. A few states by statute [42] and one by court decision [43] once made this conduct a form of justifiable homicide, but this is no longer the case.[44] The criminal law does not recognize the existence of the so-called "unwritten law" by which a man who finds his wife in adultery becomes temporarily "insane" just long enough to enable him to kill her lover.[45] Nevertheless, juries no doubt sometimes disregard the judge's instructions in these cases and take the law into their own hands, finding the husband not guilty of any crime when, legally speaking, they ought to find him guilty of voluntary manslaughter.[46]

(6) Words.[47] The formerly well-established rule that words alone (or words plus gestures) will never do for reducing an intentional killing to voluntary manslaughter [48] has in many jurisdictions changed[49] into a rule that words alone will sometimes do,[50] at least if the words are informational (conveying information of a

---

subjection to her husband was regarded by the law as the basis of the marital relation."

37. State v. Yanz, 74 Conn. 177, 50 A. 37 (1901); Maher v. People, 10 Mich. 212, 81 Am.Dec. 781 (1862). Compare Commonwealth v. Benjamin, 369 Mass. 770, 343 N.E.2d 402 (1976) (mere suspicion of adultery insufficient).

38. See § 7.10(b)(6).

39. People v. Bridgehouse, 47 Cal.2d 406, 303 P.2d 1018 (1956).

40. Rex v. Palmer, [1913] 2 K.B. 29 (engaged couple); Rex v. Greening, [1913] 3 K.B. 846, 23 Cox Crim.Cas. 601 (1913) (couple living together as husband and wife).

See also People v. Pecora, 107 Ill.App.2d 283, 246 N.E.2d 865 (1969) (defendant's ex-wife told him she had been intimate with other men: *held,* not adequate provocation even if he "had not psychologically disengaged himself from the marital relationship since the divorce").

41. But in People v. McDonald, 63 Ill.App.2d 475, 212 N.E.2d 299 (1965), where defendant had lived with the woman he killed for some 25 years, the court ruled it would not apply the "exculpatory features of *crime passionel* to the killing of a mistress, regardless of the duration of the relationship."

42. New Mexico, Texas, Utah.

43. See Campbell v. State, 204 Ga. 399, 49 S.E.2d 867 (1948) (justifiable homicide when husband kills paramour to prevent the beginning or completion of adultery).

44. As stated in Burger v. State, 238 Ga. 171, 231 S.E.2d 769 (1977): "In this day of no-fault, on-demand

divorce when adultery is merely a misdemeanor, and when there is a debate raging in the country about whether capital punishment even for the most heinous crimes is proper, any idea that a spouse is ever justified in taking the life of another—adulterous spouse or illicit lover—to prevent adultery is uncivilized."

45. State v. Kelly, 131 Kan. 357, 291 P. 945 (1930) (approving an instruction that debauchery of a man's wife does not justify or excuse the killing of her paramour, for the doctrine of the "unwritten law" does not obtain in this state).

46. Roberts, The Unwritten Law, 10 Ky.L.J. 45 (1922); Comment, Recognition of the Honor Defense under the Insanity Plea, 43 Yale L.J. 809 (1934).

47. See Annot., 2 A.L.R.3d 1292 (1965).

48. People v. Lopez, 93 Ill.App.2d 426, 235 N.E.2d 652 (1968) (deceased called defendant dirty names and cursed his parents); Commonwealth v. Cisneros, 381 Pa. 447, 113 A.2d 293 (1955) (white wife told Mexican-Puerto Rican husband she would not live with him because their children would be black); Pennsylvania v. Bell, Addison, 156, 1 Am.Dec. 298 (Pa.1793) (words of ridicule); Freddo v. State, 127 Tenn. 376, 155 S.W. 170 (1913) (deceased called the peculiarly sensitive defendant "a son of a bitch").

49. The change cannot be attributed to legislation, as rarely do manslaughter statutes speak to the point one way or the other.

50. E.g., People v. Valentine, 28 Cal.2d 121, 169 P.2d 1 (1946) (violent argument). The court there found it impossible to reconcile the two following comments upon this

fact which constitutes a reasonable provocation when that fact is observed) rather than merely insulting or abusive words.[51] Thus a sudden confession of adultery by a wife, or information from a third person that a wife has been unfaithful, has sometimes been held to constitute a provocation to the husband of the same sort as if he had made an "ocular observation" of his wife's adultery.[52]

(7) Injuries to Third Persons. Just as a reasonable man may be provoked by some sorts of conduct which inflict injury upon himself, so too he may be provoked by the same sorts of conduct which causes injury to his close relatives.[53] It has been held that the rule does not extend beyond close relatives to more distant relatives and friends,[54] but in

view of the modern tendency to leave questions of the reasonableness of a provocation to the jury, there ought not to be any absolute rule that injuries, however grievous, to friends, however close, can never constitute a reasonable provocation.[55]

(8) Miscellaneous. Aside from the commonly-urged provocations discussed above, various defendants have from time to time tried out novel ones, generally without success—e.g., the fact that the wife, in a property settlement, actually made off with more property than had been agreed upon with her husband,[56] that a judge, in a non-support case instituted by a wife against her husband, may have erroneously ruled against the hus-

---

aspect of the law contained in prior opinions: "[1] Nothing is more surely calculated to arouse the blood of some men to a heat of passion than grievous words of reproach, yet [2] no words are sufficient provocation to reduce an offense from murder to manslaughter."

See also Lang v. State, 6 Md.App. 128, 250 A.2d 276 (1969) (deceased called defendant a chump and a chicken, shook fist at him, and dared him to fight; *held,* not adequate provocation, as while words plus conduct may constitute adequate provocation when they indicate a present intention and ability to cause bodily harm, such not the case here; defendant was in apartment, deceased was outside and made no effort to enter).

51. See Sells v. State, 98 N.M. 786, 653 P.2d 162 (1982); Commonwealth v. Berry, 461 Pa. 233, 336 A.2d 262 (1975) (defendant's mother told him she had been assaulted by man defendant then killed).

Compare State v. Butler, 277 S.C. 452, 290 S.E.2d 1 (1982) (fact woman with whom defendant had voluntary intercourse said she would "cry rape" not sufficient provocation, as such words would not be).

52. Raines v. State, 247 Ga. 504, 277 S.E.2d 47 (1981) (defendant discovered wife carrying letter to her boyfriend, she admitted and taunted him with her adultery; Haley v. State, 123 Miss. 87, 85 So. 129 (1920) (defendant's wife's sudden confession of adultery caused defendant to kill her paramour; *held,* conviction of voluntary manslaughter affirmed); State v. Flory, 40 Wyo. 184, 276 P. 458 (1929) (defendant's father-in-law raped his daughter, defendant's wife; wife told defendant about it; defendant, on seeing father-in-law a day later killed him; *held,* jury could find voluntary manslaughter).

Contra: Holmes v. Director of Public Prosecutions, [1946] A.C. 588 (when wife told husband she had committed adultery, he killed her; *held,* murder, because a confession of adultery without more is never sufficient to reduce an offense which would otherwise be murder to manslaughter), which states a rule which has since been changed by English statute, Homicide Act of 1957, 5 & 6 Eliz. 2, c. II, § 3 (jury in each case to determine whether defendant was actually provoked, by things done or things

said or both together, to lose his self-control). See Annot., 93 A.L.R.3d 925 (1979) (wife's confession of adultery as affecting degree of homicide in killing her paramour).

53. People v. Rice, 351 Ill. 604, 184 N.E. 894 (1933) (evidence that victim slapped defendant's child and later quarreled with defendant *held* to support conviction of voluntary manslaughter); State v. Grugin, 147 Mo. 39, 47 S.W. 1058 (1898) (father, on learning that his son-in-law had ravished his young unmarried daughter, asked son-in-law why he did it and received reply, "I'll do as I damn please"; father killed son-in-law; *held,* a jury question whether this is reasonable provocation for voluntary manslaughter); State v. Jones, 299 N.C. 103, 261 S.E.2d 1 (1980) (manslaughter instruction required where defendant shot man trying to break into house of and threatening to defendant's mother and siblings); State v. Flory, 40 Wyo. 184, 276 P. 458 (1929) (son-in-law, on learning that the father of his wife had raped her, killed him; *held,* jury could find this to be voluntary manslaughter). See Annot., 17 L.R.A. (n.s.) 795 (1909).

54. State v. Madden, 61 N.J. 377, 294 A.2d 609 (1972) (police officer's use of excessive force on another not basis for manslaughter verdict where, as here, the other person not a close relative of the defendant); Commonwealth v. Paese, 220 Pa. 371, 69 A. 891 (1908) (victim, in defendant's presence, severely beat defendant's friend; defendant's requested instruction that this was manslaughter if the attack aroused defendant's passion so as to destroy his self-control *held* properly refused, for the provocation rule does not extend to friends of the defendant). See Annot., 17 L.R.A. (n.s.) 795 (1909).

55. Note too that in some circumstances one is justified in using force in defense of others, and the modern trend is to extend the rule beyond close relatives so as to include friends as well. See § 5.8.

56. Zenou v. State, 4 Wis.2d 655, 91 N.W.2d 208 (1958) (this fact *held* not to reduce husband's killing his wife to voluntary manslaughter; note, however, that Wisconsin's statute requires for voluntary manslaughter that the passion negative intent to kill).

band;[57] or that a job supervisor gave an unfavorable rating likely to result in termination of employment.[58] Yet, courts have on occasion extended the notion of reasonable provocation to other situations.[59]

(9) Mistake as to Provocation. Sometimes the defendant intentionally kills another in a reasonable, but erroneous, belief that the victim has injured him—as where the circumstances of the provocation are such that the defendant reasonably concludes that his wife is committing adultery, when in fact she is not. It would seem that the provocation is adequate to reduce the homicide to voluntary manslaughter if the killer reasonably believes that the injury to him exists, though actually he has not been injured.[60] In other words, a man's passion directed against another person suffices for manslaughter if (1) he reasonably believes that he has been injured by the other, and (2) a reasonable man who actually has suffered such an injury would be put in a passion directed against the other.[61] But this issue is rarely addressed even in modern manslaughter statutes.

(10) The Reasonable Man. Some cases have considered whether the law should take into account, in measuring the adequacy of

the provocation, the fact that the defendant possesses some peculiar mental or physical characteristic, not possessed by the ordinary person, which caused him, in the particular case, to lose his self-control. It is quite uniformly held that the defendant's special mental qualities—as where, because of a sunstroke or head injury,[62] he is particularly excitable—are not to be considered.[63] Even more clearly, he does not qualify for the voluntary manslaughter treatment where, because of intoxication, he easily loses his self-control; that is to say, he is to be judged by the standard of the reasonable sober man.[64] In a case involving a defendant who killed a prostitute, the fact that the defendant, who was sexually impotent, was jeered at by the prostitute for his impotency was held not to constitute a reasonable provocation, the defendant's physical abnormality being irrelevant; the test is how the victim's conduct affects a reasonable man, not how it affects a man with the defendant's physical characteristics.[65]

There has, however, been some recent discussion of the fairness of the strictly objective reasonable-man test for determining the ade-

57. Commonwealth ex rel. Haines v. Banmiller, 393 Pa. 439, 143 A.2d 661 (1958) (upon hearing the judge's decision, husband killed wife's attorney and wounded the judge; judge's decision *held* no justification for murder, for even if it was wrong, the defendant had his remedy by appeal; under no circumstances could it justify a shooting).

58. United States v. Collins, 690 F.2d 431 (5th Cir. 1982).

59. See, e.g., State v. Harwood, 110 Ariz. 375, 519 P.2d 177 (1974) (manslaughter instruction necessary where jealous woman threatened to follow defendant everywhere and to create a commotion at his home); Patterson v. State, 566 P.2d 855 (Okl.Crim.App.1977) (manslaughter instruction necessary where deceased had repeatedly burglarized defendant's home and otherwise harassed him).

60. State v. Yanz, 74 Conn. 177, 50 A. 37 (1901) (husband shot suspected adulterer, claiming wife's adultery in mitigation; instruction that "if, in fact, no adultery was going on, and the husband is mistaken as to the fact, though the circumstances were such as to justify a belief, even, of adultery, the offense would not be reduced to manslaughter" *held* reversible error).

61. With the analogous problem of self-defense to homicide, one is entitled to the defense if he reasonably, but erroneously, believes (1) that the other is on the point of launching a deadly attack upon him and (2) that the

only way to prevent being killed is to kill the other. See § 5.7.

62. People v. Golsh, 63 Cal.App. 609, 219 P. 456 (1923) (sunstroke); State v. Nevares, 36 N.M. 41, 7 P.2d 933 (1932) (head injury).

63. State v. Little, 123 N.H. 433, 462 A.2d 117 (1983) (defendant not entitled to instruction that reasonable man standard not applicable "if you find that the defendant is shown to have some peculiar weakness of mind or emotion not arising from wickedness of heart"); Jacobs v. Commonwealth, 121 Pa. 586, 15 A. 465 (1888) (defendant's proffered evidence that he had an excitable temperament *held* properly excluded); Mancini v. Director of Public Prosecutions [1942] A.C. 1 (1941) (an unusually excitable or pugnacious individual is not entitled to rely on a provocation which would not have provoked an ordinary person).

See also People v. Pecora, supra note 40, holding that defendant's "special traits," including his "religious beliefs" and "mental disturbance," are not to be considered.

64. Bishop v. United States, 107 F.2d 297 (D.C.Cir. 1939); Warner v. State, 56 N.J.L. 686, 29 A. 505 (Ct.Err. & App.1894); Keenan v. Commonwealth, 44 Pa. 55, 84 Am. Dec. 414 (1862).

65. Bedder v. Director of Public Prosecutions, [1954] 2 All E.R. 801 (H.L.).

quacy of the provocation.[66] It has been persuasively argued that at least some individual pecularities should be taken into account "because they bear upon the inference as to the actor's character that it is fair to draw upon the basis of his act."[67] In some recent decisions courts have shown a greater willingness to consider subjective factors while still giving lip service to the reasonable man requirement.[68]

The Model Penal Code introduces a certain amount of subjectivity in its proposed test, under which a homicide otherwise murder is only manslaughter if "committed under the influence of extreme mental or emotional disturbance for which there is reasonable explanation or excuse," the reasonableness of which is to be "determined from the viewpoint of a person in the actor's situation under the circumstances as he believes them to be."[69] This provision states a middle ground between a standard which ignores all individual peculiarities and one which makes emotional distress decisive regardless of the nature of its cause. The actor's "situation" takes into account his "personal handicaps and some external circumstances," such as "blindness, shock from traumatic injury, and extreme grief," but not his "idiosyncratic moral values."[70] The ultimate question is "whether the actor's loss of self-control can be understood in terms that arouse sympathy in the ordinary citizen."[71]

A substantial minority of the modern criminal codes contain a provision along these lines.[72] Some of them, however, either by leaving out the language about the actor's situation or by use of certain other language seem less subjective than the Model Penal Code provision. A few also require that the defendant not have been at fault in bringing about the provoking events.

WESTLAW REFERENCES

203k43 /p voluntary /2 manslaughter

203k48 203k44 /p voluntary /2 manslaughter

topic(203) /p voluntary /2 manslaughter /s adulter***

topic(203) /p voluntary /2 manslaughter /2 insult*** (word /3 abus*** provocation provok***)

topic(203) /p voluntary /2 manslaughter /s reasonable /2 person man woman /s provocation provok***

(c) Actual Provocation. Assuming that the provocation was such as to cause a reasonable man to lose his self-control, there remains the question of whether the defendant was in fact provoked by the victim's conduct. If, because he is of a cooler temperament than the reasonable man, he was not actually provoked (and therefore he killed his victim in cold blood), he is guilty of murder and cannot

---

66. See Report of the Royal Commission on Capital Punishment 52–53 (1953), concluding, however, not to recommend any change in the existing law. The problem is much the same as that of whether to apply a subjective or an objective standard in the case of involuntary manslaughter based upon reckless conduct: can some people be made to act more carefully if the threat of punishment for careless conduct is hanging over their heads? See § 7.12. With voluntary manslaughter the question might be: can the threat of punishment held make some people control themselves? If so, perhaps, from a deterrence viewpoint, the test should remain an objective one. It is, of course, true that one who kills in an actual but unreasonable rage is not as bad a person as one who kills in cold blood. The law does make a distinction here, however, the latter killer being a first-degree murderer, the former one in the second degree. See § 7.10(f).

As noted earlier, see note 13 supra, some modern statutes do not expressly state that the provocation must be sufficient to excite a reasonable man.

67. Model Penal Code § 201.3, Comment (Tent.Draft No. 9, 1959).

68. E.g., Ferrin v. People, 164 Colo. 130, 433 P.2d 108 (1967) (*Held:* voluntary manslaughter instruction should have been given where psychiatric testimony was that 15-year-old defendant killed younger brother because of "pent-up anger and emotion" from being depantsed by playmates, from being teased by brother and others about losing on pinball machine and failing in school, and from actions of superiority by younger brother).

69. Model Penal Code § 210.3.

70. Model Penal Code § 210.3, Comment at 62 (1980).

71. Id. at 63.

72. For application of the statutes, see, e.g., State v. Elliott, 177 Conn. 1, 411 A.2d 3 (1979); State v. Gratzer, __ Mont., __, 682 P.2d 141 (1984); People v. Patterson, 39 N.Y.2d 288, 383 N.Y.S.2d 573, 347 N.E.2d 898 (1976); State v. Ott, 293 Or. 375, 686 P.2d 1001 (1984).

have his intentional killing reduced to voluntary manslaughter.[73]

WESTLAW REFERENCES

203k41 (topic(203) /p actual** /2 provok*** provocation)

(d) Reasonable Time to Cool Off. Assuming that the victim's conduct actually provokes, and reasonably provokes, the defendant into a passion which robs him of his normal capacity for self-control, there still remains a problem of reasonable time for the passion to subside whenever there is a time lag between provocation and infliction of the fatal wound. By the majority view, a provoked defendant cannot have his homicide reduced to voluntary manslaughter where the time elapsing between the provocation and the death blow is such that a reasonable man thus provoked would have cooled; [74] and this is so even though the defendant, being slower to cool off than the ordinary person, has not in fact cooled off by the time he delivers the lethal blow.[75] A minority view, however, eliminates the reasonable-time test, stating that if there is a reasonable and actual provocation, the defendant's crime is manslaughter if in fact, because of his peculiar temperament, he has not cooled off, though a reasonable man's passion would have subsided.[76]

What constitutes a reasonable cooling time in a particular case depends upon the nature of the provocation and the circumstances surrounding its occurrence—[77] a matter to be

---

73. People v. Gingell, 211 Cal. 532, 296 P. 70 (1931) (defendant, suspecting wife of adultery, decided to kill her, then found her in bed with paramour, then killed them both; *held,* murder, not manslaughter); State v. Robinson, 353 Mo. 934, 185 S.W.2d 636 (1945) (defendant, struck violently by victim, got a gun and stalked victim in a methodical and cold-blooded way; since there was nothing in defendant's movements to indicate any heat of passion, defendant *held* not entitled to manslaughter instruction); State v. Agnes, 92 N.J.L. 53, 104 A. 299 (Sup.Ct.1918) (defendant, knowing of wife's adulterous relations with paramour, armed self with deadly weapon and went seeking the paramour, hoping to find him in the act; when he did, he killed paramour; *held,* murder, not manslaughter); Fossett v. State, 41 Tex.Crim. 400, 55 S.W. 497 (1900) (victim insulted defendant's wife, which led to a fight in which defendant killed victim; instruction that it is manslaughter if defendant was so angered as to be incapable of cool reflection, but murder if he was capable, *held* proper; conviction of murder affirmed); Davidson v. Commonwealth, 167 Va. 451, 187 S.E. 437 (1936) (defendant, struck violently by victim, chased and stabbed him to death, then told a friend "Take my knife, I used it on him, and believe me, by God, I used it"; defendant testified that he acted in self-defense and was not thrown into a passion by the blow he received; conviction of murder *held* affirmed; this case indicates that one who claims he killed in self-defense and loses cannot well succeed in showing that he killed in a transport of passion).

74. Some of the modern statutes clearly state that this is the case. Many others, however, are ambiguous at best on this point.

75. Sheppard v. State, 243 Ala. 498, 10 So.2d 822 (1942) (husband learned of wife's adultery, several days later killed her; *held,* conviction of first-degree murder affirmed); LaLonde v. State, 614 P.2d 808 (Alaska 1980) (even if defendant had not cooled, no manslaughter here because reasonable man would have cooled in the passage of several hours); In re Fraley, 3 Okl.Crim. 719, 109 P. 295 (1910) (victim killed defendant's son, was tried and acquitted; several months later defendant killed victim; *held,* a case of murder, so on habeas corpus defendant not entitled

to release on bail); State v. Gounagias, 88 Wash. 304, 153 P. 9 (1915) (victim committed sodomy upon defendant when latter was unconscious and later circulated the news that defendant had engaged in sodomy; this caused those who heard the news to ridicule defendant with insulting remarks and gestures; two weeks after the sodomy incident the defendant, when thus insulted, lost control and killed victim; *held,* conviction of first-degree murder affirmed).

76. State v. Hazlett, 16 N.D. 426, 113 N.W. 374 (1907) (the question of "whether there was sufficient cooling time for the passion to subside and reason to resume its sway, should be governed, not by the standard of an ideal, reasonable man" but rather "from the standpoint of the defendant in the light of all the facts and circumstances"; conviction of murder held reversed because of instruction on manslaughter requiring for cooling time the time in which an ordinary man in like circumstances would have cooled); State v. McCants, 1 Speers 384 (S.C.1843) (defendant, beaten by victim in a fight, thereafter killed him and was convicted of murder; conviction *held* affirmed; fact that defendant cooled off slowly because intoxicated irrelevant; dictum that, in determining reasonable cooling time, not only the nature of the provocation, but also "the prisoner's physical and mental constitution, his condition in life and peculiar situation at the time of the affair, his education and habits," among other things, may be considered); Davis v. State, 161 Tenn. 23, 28 S.W.2d 993 (1930) (defendant's insane delusion that victim had committed adultery with defendant's wife prevented defendant from cooling off; conviction of murder *held* reversed).

It would seem that, on principle, if a reasonable-man standard (without regard to defendant's mental and physical peculiarities) is required for provocation (see supra, this section), the same standard is equally applicable for cooling-off purposes.

77. People v. Harris, 8 Ill.2d 431, 134 N.E.2d 315 (1956) ("what constitutes a sufficient 'cooling-off period' depends upon the extent to which the passions have been aroused and the nature of the act which caused the provocation * * * and, for that reason, no yardstick of time can be

determined by the jury as a question of fact,[78] unless the time is so short or so long that the court may hold that, as a matter of law, it was reasonable or unreasonable.[79]

Not infrequently there is a considerable time interval between the victim's act of provocation and the defendant's fatal conduct— time enough for passion to subside. In the meantime, however, some event occurs which rekindles the defendant's passion. If this new occurrence is such as to trigger the passion of a reasonable man,[80] the cooling-off period should start with the new occurrence—[81] a fact which the cases have not always recognized.[82]

The typical heat-of-passion manslaughter case is that in which one specific event (of one of the kinds previously discussed) immediately produces a rage in the defendant. This may account for the fact that modern codes

usually [83] state that defendant's passion must be "sudden." However, a more realistic appraisal of how human emotions work compels the conclusion—which some courts have reached [84]—that a reasonable provocation can be produced by a series of events occurring over a considerable span of time. When that is the case, then of course the measurement of the cooling time should commence with the occurrence of the last provocative event.[85]

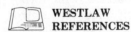 **WESTLAW REFERENCES**

203k40   /p   sufficient reasonable adequate enough   /3 time period

(e) Actual Cooling Off. One more bridge remains for the defendant to cross: although (1) he is reasonably provoked and (2) he is actually provoked and (3) a reasonable man would not have cooled off, yet he cannot have his homicide reduced to voluntary manslaugh-

---

used by the court to measure a reasonable period of passion but it must vary as do the facts of every case").

78. In a few jurisdictions, however, reasonable cooling time is held to be a matter of law for the court to decide, e.g., Brewer v. State, 160 Ala. 66, 49 So. 336 (1909). In other areas of the law, of course, the jury generally determines reasonableness of things—a matter which the jurors, all being reasonable men, are quite fitted to do!

79. State v. Ramirez, 116 Ariz. 259, 569 P.2d 201 (1977) (denial of manslaughter instruction proper where over four and a half hours passed since defendant learned of wife's adultery and his actions in interim showed cool state of mind); In re Fraley, 3 Okl.Crim. 719, 109 P. 295 (1910) (victim shot and killed defendant's son; as a matter of law passion would cool in several months); State v. Williford, 103 Wis.2d 98, 307 N.W.2d 277 (1981) (no manslaughter instruction necessary where various provoking events occurred two weeks to four years earlier).

80. An event which, standing alone, would not suffice to act as such a trigger may nonetheless suffice to rekindle an earlier passion. See, e.g., People v. Berry, 18 Cal.3d 509, 134 Cal.Rptr. 415, 556 P.2d 777 (1976) (only event immediately before killing was wife's screaming, which sufficient to rekindle passion regarding her earlier confession of adultery).

81. State v. Flory, 40 Wyo. 184, 276 P. 458 (1929) (victim, who was defendant's father-in-law, raped defendant's wife; when defendant learned of it, he was in a reasonable passion, but he cooled off; next day he saw victim, who told him "I will keep the girl"; defendant killed victim; murder conviction *held* reversed, for jury is to determine reasonable cooling time; here "a situation arose by which past facts were clearly recalled").

See also State v. Grugin, 147 Mo. 39, 47 S.W. 1058 (1898) (victim, who was defendant's son-in-law, committed adultery with defendant's young daughter; when defendant learned of it, he asked victim what possessed him to rape

her; victim replied, "I'll do as I damn please about it"; conviction of murder *held* reversed because, among other things, a jury question whether the insulting words constituted fresh provocation).

82. E.g., State v. Gounagias, 88 Wash 304, 153 P. 9 (1915) (victim committed sodomy on defendant when latter was unconscious and then circulated the story among defendant's acquaintances, who ridiculed defendant and subjected him to insulting words and gestures; later, when defendant entered a coffee house, the ten men present began to make suggestive remarks and gestures, which caused defendant to rush off and kill the victim; conviction of first-degree murder *held* affirmed, this evidence being inadmissible to reduce the homicide to voluntary manslaughter). In In re Fraley, 3 Okl.Crim. 719, 109 P. 295 (1910), defendant, who killed victim who had several months earlier killed defendant's son, argued without success that, upon seeing the victim, the recollection of the old wrong engendered in the defendant a new passion which overwhelmed him.

But cf. Whitsett v. State, 201 Tenn. 317, 299 S.W.2d 2 (1957), where sudden sight of the author of the wrongs to the defendant, without words as in the *Flory* and *Grugin* cases supra, seems to have reasonably rekindled the passions of the defendant against his wife's paramour.

83. See text at note 7 supra.

84. E.g., People v. Berry, 18 Cal.3d 509, 134 Cal.Rptr. 415, 556 P.2d 777 (1976) (defendant's rage produced by an "accumulative series of provocations" from July 13 to July 26, during which time his wife "continually provoked defendant with sexual taunts and incitements, alternating acceptance and rejection of him," all "accompanied by repeated references to her involvement with another man").

85. People v. Borchers, 50 Cal.2d 321, 325 P.2d 97 (1958); Ferrin v. People, 164 Colo. 130, 433 P.2d 108 (1967).

slaughter.[90] In each instance *A*'s purpose has been to act against the individual thought to be responsible for his outrage, and thus there are mitigating circumstances which should be taken into account even if *A* was negligent in determining the source of the provocation or in causing danger to bystanders.[91] But a few of the modern codes appear to foreclose such a result.

More difficult is the situation in which *A*, actually and reasonably provoked by *B*, in his passion strikes out at and kills *C*, known by *A* to be only an innocent bystander. The courts have quite consistently held that the killing of *C* does not qualify as manslaughter,[92] apparently upon the assumption that a reasonable man would never be so greatly provoked as to strike out in blind anger at an innocent person. The Model Penal Code, however, does not so limit provocation,[93] on the ground that there may be some such cases in which "the cause and the intensity of the actor's emotion * * * [are] less indicative of moral depravity than would be a homicidal response to a blow to one's person."[94]

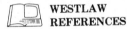 **WESTLAW REFERENCES**

203k60

fi 503sw2d921

(h) Rationale of Voluntary Manslaughter. Why is it that there exists such a crime as voluntary manslaughter to aid one who kills when provoked into a passion, yet there is no crime like, say, voluntary theft or voluntary mayhem to aid others who, reasonably provoked into a passion, steal from or maim their tormentors?[95] The answer is historical. With most crimes other than murder the English court came to have discretion as to the punishment and so could take extenuating circumstances into account in the sentencing process; but with murder the penalty remained fixed at death, without the possibility of making any allowance for the extenuating fact that the victim provoked the defendant into a reasonable passion.[96] "The rule of law that provocation may, within narrow bounds, reduce murder to manslaughter, represents an attempt by the courts to reconcile the preservation of the fixed penalty for murder with a limited concession to natural human weakness."[97]

This, of course, "fails to explain the doctrine's continued viability,"[98] and courts have by and large failed to articulate a modern rationale. It has been suggested, however, that the present rationale for heat-of-passion manslaughter is that when

> the provocation is so great that the ordinary law abiding person would be expected to lose self-

90. Wheatley v. Commonwealth, 26 Ky.L.Rep. 436, 81 S.W. 687 (Ct.App.1904) (Case 2); State v. Griego, 61 N.M. 42, 294 P.2d 282 (1956); Rex v. Gross, 23 Cox Crim.Cas. 455 (1913). This is but one aspect of the causation problem, discussed in § 3.12(d), where the bad result actually caused differs from the bad result intended; here the courts often speak in terms of the fiction "transferred intent."

91. Of course, *A* may have been more than negligent; he may have been reckless in his mistaken assumption concerning the source of the provocation or (more likely) in creating a risk to third persons in attempting to kill the provoker.

92. Dow v. State, 77 Ark. 464, 92 S.W. 28 (1906); State v. Vinso, 171 Mo. 576, 71 S.W. 1034 (1903); State v. Tilson, 503 S.W.2d 921 (Tenn.1974) (nor does it make any difference that the victim was a friend of the provoker, as a contrary rule would intolerably extend the "mutual combat" rule to any bystander who could be characterized as "on the side" of the provoker; White v. State, 44 Tex. Crim. 346, 72 S.W. 173 (1902) (second-degree murder); R. v. Scriva (No. 2), [1951] Vict.L.R. 298 (not manslaughter where defendant saw his child hit by car, attempted to attack driver, and then turned on bystander who tried to

stop him and killed bystander); Rex v. Simpson, 84 L.J. K.B. 1893, 31 T.L.R. 560 (Ct.Crim.App.1915) (defendant-father's child was sick; mother refused to come home; father in anger at mother killed child; *held*, murder, not voluntary manslaughter).

93. Model Penal Code § 210.3.

94. Model Penal Code § 210.3, Comment at 61 (1980).

95. Cf. Sensobaugh v. State, 92 Tex.Crim. 417, 244 S.W. 379 (1922) (although Texas makes it justifiable homicide to kill wife's paramour caught in adultery, husband is not justified in cutting off paramour's sex organ with a razor).

96. Of course, this is not true today in most of the United States, for there is some leeway with the punishment for murder in most states. No doubt the leeway would have to be greater if there were no separate crime of voluntary manslaughter.

97. Report of the Royal Commission on Capital Punishment 52–53 (1953), concluding that, in measuring the scope of this concession, the reasonable-man, objective, standard for provocation and cooling time should remain.

98. Dressler, Rethinking Heat of Passion: A Defense in Search of a Rationale, 73 J.Crim.L. & C. 421, 423 (1982).

ter if, because his passions subside more quickly than those of the ordinary person, he has actually cooled off by the time he commits his deadly act.[86] One who, in full possession of his faculties, kills another without justification or excuse commits murder; and it is no help to his cause that an ordinary man would not have held his emotions under control.

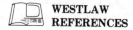

203k40 /p reasonable /2 person man woman

(f) Classification. Thus it may be seen that there are three intent-to-kill homicide situations, each calling for a different conclusion: (1) One who successfully surmounts all four hurdles—i.e., one who is reasonably and actually provoked and who reasonably and actually does not cool off—is guilty of voluntary manslaughter. (2) One who stumbles on hurdles 1 or 3—i.e., one who, though actually in a passion when he kills, is unreasonably so, either because a reasonable men would not have been provoked in the first place or because a reasonable man so provoked would have cooled—is a candidate for second-degree murder in most jurisdictions, for though he intended to kill he lacked the premeditation and deliberation which distinguishes first from second degree murder in most jurisdictions.[87] (3) One who trips up on hurdles 2 or 4—i.e., one who, although he receives a reasonable provocation and although a reasona-

ble man would not have cooled off, either is not provoked or actually cools off—kills in cold blood, with time and capacity to premeditate and deliberate, and so may be convicted of first-degree murder.[88]

topic(203) /p voluntary /2 manslaughter /p provok*** provocation /p cool***

(g) Provocation From One Other Than Person Killed. It sometimes happens that the source of the provocation is a person other than the individual killed by the defendant while in a heat of passion. This may happen (1) because the defendant is mistaken as to the person responsible for the acts of provocation; (2) because the defendant attempts to kill his provoker but instead kills an innocent bystander; or (3) because the defendant strikes out in a rage at a third party.

If A has been reasonably provoked and believes that B is the person (or, one of the persons) responsible for the provoking conduct, then his killing of B in a heat of passion is manslaughter even if it turns out that C and not B was actually the provoking party.[89] Likewise, if A, who has been reasonably and actually provoked by B into a passion to kill B, shoots at B but instead hits and kills innocent-bystander C, A 's crime is voluntary man-

86. See In re Fraley, 3 Okl.Crim. 719, 109 P. 295 (1910) ("If, in fact, the defendant's passion did cool, which may be shown by circumstances, such as the transaction of other business in the meantime, rational conversations upon other subjects, evidence of preparation for the killing, etc." then it is not necessary to inquire as to cooling time, for the homicide is murder when actually done in cold blood). But see Whitsett v. State, 201 Tenn. 317, 299 S.W.2d 2 (1957) (casual and calm conversation between provocation and killing does not necessarily show cool blood, for it may be suppressed anger; and, in the alternative, passion can be triggered by sight of the provoker; therefore, murder conviction reduced on appeal to voluntary manslaughter).

87. People v. Caruso, 246 N.Y. 437, 159 N.E. 390 (1927) (defendant, unreasonably provoked by victim, killed victim while in a rage; conviction of first-degree murder *held* reversed as not sustained by the evidence, which clearly showed no capacity to deliberate and premeditate; and intent to kill without deliberation and premeditation is only second-degree murder).

LaFave & Scott Crim.Law 2nd Ed.HB—23

Contra: State v. Gounagias, 88 Wash. 304, 153 P. 9 (1915) (defendant, at a time so long after the provocation that a reasonable man would have cooled off, but while in an actual passion induced by the provocation, killed the victim; conviction of first-degree murder *held* affirmed, under a first-degree murder statute calling for premeditation but not mentioning deliberation).

Conceivably the law might have developed in such a way that an actual rage, though not a reasonable rage, would do to reduce an intentional killing to voluntary manslaughter. Many statutes, if read literally, would produce that result; see note 20 supra. But notwithstanding such provisions, it is almost universally required that, for voluntary manslaughter, the defendant's passion be reasonable as well as actual.

88. E.g., People v. Gingell, 211 Cal. 532, 296 P. 70 (1931) (defendant first decided to kill his wife and her paramour; then, happily finding them together in bed, he shot them both).

89. State v. Michael, 74 W.Va. 613, 82 S.E. 611 (1914); Rex v. Manchuk, [1937] 4 D.L.R. 737 (Can.S.Ct.).

control so that he could not help but act violently, yet he would still have sufficient self-control so that he could avoid using force likely to cause death or great bodily harm in response to the provocation, then * * * the actor's moral blameworthiness is found not in his violent response, but in his *homicidal* violent response. He did not control himself as much as he *should* have, or as much as common experience tells us he *could* have, nor as much as the ordinary law abiding person *would* have.[99]

§ 7.11   Other-Extenuating-Circumstances Voluntary Manslaughter

The reasoning set forth at the conclusion of the last section leads to the question of whether the crime of voluntary manslaughter is not a big enough receptacle to include other intentional homicides which, by reason of other extenuating features (i.e., other than the one feature of passion induced by reasonable provocation), ought to be less than murder yet more than no crime at all. In some states such a view, however desirable, is made difficult (though not apparently impossible)[1] by narrow statutes defining voluntary manslaughter solely in terms of heat of passion. In those states which do not define voluntary manslaughter by statute, however, it has been easier to open up the crime to include other homicides.[2] But in recent years, such expansion of the concept of voluntary manslaughter has often occurred by legislation.

(a) "Imperfect" Right of Self-Defense. In order for a killer to have a "perfect" de-

fense of self-defense to homicide, (1) he must be free from fault in bringing on the difficulty with his adversary; and (2) he must reasonably believe (though he need not correctly believe) both (a) that his adversary will, unless forcibly prevented, immediately inflict upon him a fatal or serious bodily injury, and (b) that he must use deadly force upon the adversary to prevent him from inflicting such an injury. If one who is not the aggressor kills his adversary with these two actual and reasonable beliefs in his mind, his homicide is justified, and he is guilty of no crime—not murder, not manslaughter, but no crime.[3]

What if a defendant who did not initiate the difficulty honestly but unreasonably believes either that he is in danger of the injury or that killing is the only way to prevent it; or, even though he reasonably believes these things, he was at fault in bringing about the difficulty? He cannot have the defense of self-defense, for that requires both freedom from fault in the inception of the difficulty and the entertainment of beliefs which are reasonable. But is murder the only alternative? Or should the matter fall into the category of manslaughter, consisting of those homicides which lie in between murder and no crime. Some cases so hold, whether the reason for the "imperfection" of the defense is the defendant's own fault in bringing on the difficulty[4] or the unreasonableness of the honest but erroneous beliefs which he entertains.[5] On principle, the same rule should

---

99. Id. at 466–67.

§ 7.11

1. Some of the cases cited infra, taking a broad view of the scope of voluntary manslaughter, come from the various jurisdictions which have narrow statutes.

2. See Comment, 36 Ky.L.J. 443 (1948).

3. See § 5.7.

4. Reed v. State, 11 Tex.Ct.App.R. 509, 40 Am.R. 795 (1892) (defendant, caught by the deceased in the act of committing adultery with deceased's wife, shot and killed deceased to save his own life; conviction of manslaughter *held* affirmed); State v. Flory, 40 Wyo. 184, 276 P. 458 (1929) (defendant went to deceased's home angry, armed and intending to have an altercation and so produced the difficulty which caused him to kill deceased to save own life; conviction of murder *held* reduced to manslaughter); see Wallace v. United States, 162 U.S. 466, 16 S.Ct. 859, 40 L.Ed. 1039 (1896).

5. Commonwealth v. Colandro, 231 Pa. 343, 80 A. 571 (1911) (since evidence might support finding that defendant shot deceased in actual but unreasonable fear for his life, defendant was entitled to manslaughter instruction; and so conviction of murder *held* reversed); see Allison v. State, 74 Ark. 444, 86 S.W. 409 (1905); People v. Flannel, 25 Cal.3d 668, 160 Cal.Rptr. 84, 603 P.2d 1 (1979); State v. Thomas, 184 N.C. 757, 114 S.E. 834 (1922).

In the cases the word "manslaughter" is not generally modified by the adjective "voluntary," but this is the proper classification. See United States v. Skinner, 667 F.2d 1306 (9th Cir.1982) (imperfect self-defense theory does not entitle defendant to jury instruction on involuntary manslaughter, as a "killing committed in self-defense is, nevertheless, an intentional killing").

Because the "mitigating effect of imperfect self-defense is to negate malice," it "applies also to the felony of assault with intent to murder," which is thereby reduced to simple assault and battery. Faulkner v. State, 54 Md.

apply to a killing done in the case of a homicide under an "imperfect" right to defend others, as applies in the case of the homicide under an "imperfect" right of self-defense. The manslaughter provisions of some of the modern comprehensive criminal codes recognize the existence of this imperfect-right-of-self-defense or defense-of-others type of voluntary manslaughter.[6]

Where this "imperfect" right of self-defense is recognized, it is generally the case that whenever the facts would entitle the defendant to an instruction on self-defense regarding a murder charge, an instruction on this variety of manslaughter should also be given.[7] Indeed, even if a jury could not find defendant's belief reasonable (so that no self-defense instruction is necessary), the facts might still support a manslaughter instruction because the jury could find there was an actual but unreasonable belief.[8]

WESTLAW REFERENCES

topic(203) /p unreasonabl* /4 belie*** /s "self defense" /s voluntary /2 manslaughter

(b) "Imperfect" Right to Prevent Felony. Under some circumstances one has a right intentionally to kill another person to prevent or terminate the commission of a felony or to prevent the escape or effect the arrest of the felon; the tendency today is to apply this rule of justifiable homicide not to all felonies but only to dangerous or violent felonies. As with the justification of self-

defense, the defendant need not be correct in his beliefs that the other is committing such a felony or that he is such a felon; once again reasonable beliefs are all he needs.[9]

What if the defendant has an unreasonable, though honest, incorrect belief that the other is committing or attempting a felony or that the other is a felon trying to escape? Or, though the defendant is correct in his belief that the other is committing a crime or trying to escape, what if the crime in question being of a peaceful sort (like larceny) or being a mere misdemeanor, does not amount to a dangerous or violent felony? Here again, the defendant's intentional killing is not justifiable; but should it not be manslaughter rather than murder, even though it does not involve the "heat of passion" which one ordinarily associates with voluntary manslaughter? Some cases so hold;[10] and some of the most recent state criminal codes agree.[11]

WESTLAW REFERENCES

digest,synopsis(reasonabl* unreasonabl* erroneous** /4 belie*** /s felony /s manslaughter justifiabl*)

(c) "Imperfect" Defense of Coercion or Necessity. One who is coerced by another person, or forced by the pressure of natural physical circumstances (e.g., thirst, starvation) into committing what is otherwise a crime, may have in some circumstances a complete defense to the crime, but not if the crime in question consists of intentionally killing another human being.[12] Thus one

---

App. 113, 458 A.2d 81 (1983), affirmed 301 Md. 482, 483 A.2d 759 (1984).

6. Model Penal Code § 210.3 does not treat homicide in imperfect self-defense as a form of (voluntary) manslaughter, but rather, under § 3.09(2), as a problem of (involuntary) reckless manslaughter, or of negligent homicide, depending upon whether the defendant's belief as to the necessity of the homicide was reckless or negligent. Only a few of the modern codes have taken this position.

7. People v. Lockett, 82 Ill.2d 546, 45 Ill.Dec. 900, 413 N.E.2d 378 (1980); Faulkner v. State, 54 Md.App. 113, 458 A.2d 81 (1983), affirmed 301 Md. 482, 483 A.2d 759 (1984).

8. State v. Mendoza, 80 Wis.2d 122, 258 N.W.2d 260 (1977).

9. See § 5.10.

10. Bloom v. State, 155 Ind. 292, 58 N.E. 81 (1900) (defendant shot victim to prevent petit larceny, not burglary; *held,* conviction of voluntary manslaughter af-

firmed); Howard v. Commonwealth, 198 Ky. 453, 248 S.W. 1059 (1923) (defendant shot victim to prevent a petit larceny, not a robbery; conviction of manslaughter *held* affirmed); Commonwealth v. Beverly, 237 Ky. 35, 34 S.W.2d 941 (1931) (defendant killed victim to prevent petit larceny; the court certified the law to be that such homicide is manslaughter of the same sort as manslaughter by the reckless use of deadly weapons).

11. Model Penal Code §§ 3.09(2), 210.3, while not specifically providing that intentional killing in an imperfect right to prevent a felony is manslaughter, does provide that recklessness or negligence as to beliefs concerning justifiability makes the killer eligible for conviction of the crime of manslaughter (recklessness) or negligent homicide (negligence). Commonwealth v. Beverly, supra note 10, also takes this point of view. Only a few of the modern codes have followed the Model Penal Code on this point.

12. See §§ 5.3, 5.4.

who, not in self-defense or defense of another, kills an innocent third person to save himself or to save another is guilty of a crime. But it is arguable that his crime should be manslaughter rather than murder, on the theory that the pressure upon him, although not enough to justify his act, should serve at least to mitigate it to something less than murder.[13] Some of the latest state criminal codes so provide.[14]

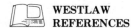

WESTLAW REFERENCES

203k126 /p duress coerc*** compel*** compulsion /s murder manslaughter

(d) Miscellaneous Intentional Killings. There are other situations too in which an intentional killing might be thought to be bad enough to be criminal yet not bad enough to be murder. It has been suggested that mental disorder not amounting to insanity might reduce the killing to manslaughter.[15] Most cases, however, have rejected this position;[16] they go only so far as to reduce the

homicide from first-degree murder to second-degree murder, the theory being that the mental defect may serve to negative the killer's capacity to deliberate and premeditate but not his malice.[17] A few cases have rejected even this moderate reduction, holding the crime to be first-degree murder.[18]

So too, a few cases have held that voluntary intoxication may reduce a homicide to manslaughter if the intoxication is so extreme as to negative the defendant's intent to kill.[19] Most of the cases, however, hold that, while voluntary intoxication may be so great as to negative premeditation and deliberation, this fact serves only to reduce the homicide from first degree to second degree murder.[20] We have already noted, in discussing voluntary manslaughter of the "heat of passion" type, that one who, because of his intoxication, is more easily provoked or slower to cool off than the reasonable man, is not eligible for voluntary manslaughter treatment, which

---

13. Contra: State v. Nargashian, 26 R.I. 299, 58 A. 953 (1904), in which *B* intentionally killed *C* because *A* with axe in hand threatened to kill *B* unless *B* killed *C*; it was *held* that *B* was guilty of murder, the court rejecting *B*'s argument "that fear, like passion, may so cloud the mind as to eliminate malice."

14. Model Penal Code, § 210.3, makes it manslaughter to kill when under a reasonable and extreme mental or emotional disturbance, a formulation somewhat broader than the traditional "heat of passion" and broad enough perhaps to include an intentional killing growing out of coercion or necessity. The Model Penal Code position is followed in but a few states.

15. See H. Weihofen, Mental Disorder as a Criminal Defense 189–92 (1954). Compare S. Glueck, Mental Disorder and the Criminal Law 484 (1925), arguing for a verdict of "partially insane and semi-responsible offender" for whom a reduced punishment may be given.

See People v. Conley, 64 Cal.2d 310, 411 P.2d 911 (1966) (mental disorder not amounting to legal insanity may preclude malice aforethought); Fisher v. People, 23 Ill. 283 (1859) (if mental disorder caused unreasonable provocation, crime would be manslaughter); Davis v. State, 161 Tenn. 23, 28 S.W.2d 993 (1930) (insane delusion can prevent cooling, so that homicide is without malice and thus only manslaughter); State v. Green, 78 Utah 580, 6 P.2d 177 (1931) (evidence that defendant had mental disorder falling short of insanity, and that he was in a heat of passion when he killed, entitled defendant to voluntary manslaughter instruction, though there was no reasonable provocation). See § 4.7 for a more detailed discussion of these and other cases.

16. See § 7.10(b)(10) for the usual view that, for purposes of voluntary manslaughter, one who, because of some peculiar mental characteristic, is more easily provoked or slower to cool than the reasonable man, is still to be judged by the reasonable-man-of-ordinary-mentality standard.

17. People v. Caruso, 246 N.Y. 437, 159 N.E. 390 (1927) (defendant, an illiterate immigrant, was unreasonably provoked into a rage to kill the doctor who had unsuccessfully treated defendant's child; conviction of first degree murder *held* reversed, because defendant's emotional upset robbed him of capacity to deliberate and premeditate), is a leading case on how factors negativing ability to premeditate and deliberate reduce homicides from first to second degree murder.

H. Weihofen, Mental Disorder as a Criminal Defense 184 (1954), lists decisions from ten states and dicta from two more, supporting the view that mental disease short of insanity will reduce to second degree murder.

18. Fisher v. United States, 328 U.S. 463, 66 S.Ct. 1318, 90 L.Ed. 1382 (1946). H. Weihofen, supra note 17, at 185, lists cases from six states.

19. E.g., King v. State, 90 Ala. 612, 8 So. 856 (1891); State v. Rumble, 81 Kan. 16, 105 P. 1 (1909); Cheadle v. State, 11 Okl.Crim. 566, 149 P. 919 (1915). Cf. Director of Public Prosecutions v. Beard, [1920] A.C. 479, 12 A.L.R. 846 (voluntary intoxication may negative intent to rape and hence felony-murder).

20. E.g., Aszman v. State, 123 Ind. 347, 24 N.E. 123 (1890).

See Annots., 12 A.L.R. 861 (1921); 79 A.L.R. 897 (1932).

serves to benefit only the reasonable sober man.[21]

Although the usual Anglo-American view is that on who commits a mercy killing, either by directly causing the other's death (as by poisoning the food of an unsuspecting victim) or by assisting [22] him to commit suicide (as by placing poison within the suicide's reach, at his request) is guilty of murder rather than manslaughter,[23] yet several modern codes provide by statute that assisting a successful suicide is manslaughter or is a separate crime less than murder.[24]

 WESTLAW REFERENCES

topic(203) /p mental /2 capacity disorder defect /s manslaughter

§ 7.12 Criminal–Negligence Involuntary Manslaughter

Manslaughter, like murder, originated as a common law crime, created by the judges rather than by the legislature. At first the courts did not distinguish between murder and manslaughter. Later murder and manslaughter became separate crimes,[1] and manslaughter itself was subdivided into two branches—voluntary manslaughter (intended homicide in a heat of passion upon adequate provocation) and involuntary manslaughter (unintended homicide under certain circumstances discussed below).[2] Involuntary manslaughter itself may be divided into two separate types,[3] whose scope has been and is still undergoing slow change, and which may be labeled (1) "criminal-negligence" manslaughter and (2) "unlawful-act" manslaughter.

All American jurisdictions undertake to punish involuntary manslaughter, though some of them either do not define it or define it rather vaguely in common law terms. A statute of the latter sort, used in some states, defines involuntary manslaughter as an unlawful killing in the commission of an unlawful act not amounting to a felony (the "unlawful-act" type of manslaughter mentioned above) or in the commission of a lawful act without due caution or circumspection (the "criminal-negligence" type). Another type of statute found in some other states uses the terms "culpable negligence" or "criminal negligence" or "gross negligence" in setting out the negligence branch of involuntary manslaughter, without, however, defining those terms. But modern statutes, to be discussed below, undertake to spell out with some particularity the requirements for involuntary manslaughter.

Statutes in a number of states divide manslaughter into two or more degrees, utilizing the common-law concepts of voluntary and involuntary manslaughter, though not using those terms. In many states, but not all, voluntary manslaughter is considered a more

---

21. See § 7.10(b)(10).

22. The most common statutory term is "aids." Other similar words are "assists," "encouraging," "solicits," and "abets."

23. E.g., People v. Roberts, 211 Mich. 187, 178 N.W. 690 (1920) (at request of his wife, who was incurably ill with multiple sclerosis, husband mixed poison and put it within her reach, thus enabling her to commit suicide; *held*, husband guilty of first-degree murder by poison).

See Annot., 25 A.L.R. 1007 (1923).

24. Model Penal Code § 210.5(2) provides that aiding suicide is a crime less than murder.

In England the survivor of a suicide pact is, by statute, guilty of manslaughter rather than of murder. Homicide Act of 1957, 5 & 6 Eliz. 2, c. II, § 4; Suicide Act of 1961, 9 & 10 Eliz. 2, c. 60, §§ 2, 3, schedule 2 (manslaughter to kill another pursuant to suicide pact, maximum of life imprisonment; aiding, abetting, counseling or procuring suicide of another is a separate crime maximum of 14 years imprisonment).

§ 7.12

1. The distinction between murder and manslaughter was said to lie in the presence or absence of malice, murder consisting of an unlawful killing *with* malice aforethought, manslaughter of an unlawful killing *without* malice aforethought. But, as pointed out in § 7.1(a), "malice" does not mean "hatred, spite or ill will," nor does "aforethought" mean "thought out in advance," in any literal sense.

2. In some states today voluntary and involuntary manslaughter receive the same punishment. In these states it might perhaps be considered that voluntary and involuntary manslaughter constitute two methods of committing a single crime, rather than two separate crimes. In states wherein the two manslaughters carry different penalties, they must be considered to be two separate but related crimes.

3. These two certainly constitute two different types of a single crime, rather than two separate crimes.

serious crime than involuntary manslaughter, carrying a heavier punishment.[4]

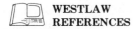
WESTLAW REFERENCES

topic(203) /p "involuntary manslaughter" /s criminal** /2 negligen**

(a) Criminal Negligence.[5] Although a few states have held that ordinary (tort) negligence [6] will suffice for involuntary manslaughter,[7] the great weight of authority requires something more in the way of negligence than ordinary negligence.[8] Most of the cases which state that more than ordinary negligence is needed for manslaughter do not clearly articulate what the extra something is; [9] but on principle it must be either

one or both of these two things: (1) the defendant's conduct, under the circumstances known to him,[10] must involve a high degree of risk of death or serious bodily injury, in addition to the unreasonable risk required for ordinary negligence; and (2) whatever the degree of risk required (merely unreasonable, or both unreasonable and high), the defendant must be aware of the fact that his conduct creates this risk.[11] (If both are required, then "recklessness" is a more appropriate term than negligence.[12])

A few cases have made it plain that manslaughter is committed when the defendant's death-producing conduct involves an unreasonable and high degree of risk of death, though the defendant does not realize it.[13]

---

4. See § 7.9.

5. See R. Moreland, The Law of Homicide ch. 10 (1952); R. Moreland, A Rationale of Criminal Negligence (1944); Annot., 161 A.L.R. 10 (1946).

6. See § 3.7 for a discussion of ordinary negligence— consisting of conduct on the part of a person which, in the light of the facts which he knows, creates an unreasonable risk of harm (bodily harm, harm involving property, etc.) to others. So far as manslaughter is concerned, the risk involved must be a risk of death or of serious bodily injury, not a risk of minor bodily injury or of injury to property. Ibid. See also § 3.12 for a discussion of the causation requirements.

7. E. g., State v. Hedges, 8 Wn.2d 652, 113 P.2d 530 (1941) (defendant shot companion while deer hunting; ordinary negligence supports conviction of manslaughter; gross negligence is not required). See Comment, 27 Ky. L.J. 111 (1939).

Compare State v. Tucker, 86 S.C. 211, 68 S.E. 523 (1910) (ordinary negligence in handling guns will do for manslaughter), with State v. Davis, 128 S.C. 265, 122 S.E. 770 (1924) (ordinary negligence in a situation not involving guns will not do for manslaughter).

8. E. g., State v. Goetz, 83 Conn. 437, 76 A. 1000 (1910) ("criminal negligence" for manslaughter is "recklessness of conduct, gross or wanton carelessness or negligence"); Ducking v. State, 259 So.2d 686 (Miss.1972) (simple negligence in failing to watch children leaving school bus does not warrant conviction for manslaughter); Commonwealth v. Aurick, 342 Pa. 382, 19 A.2d 920 (1941) (for manslaughter the negligence must be "something more than the slight negligence which will support a civil action for damages based on negligence"); Andrews v. Director of Public Prosecutions, [1937] A.C. 576 (the negligence for manslaughter must go "beyond a mere matter of compensation between subjects," i.e., beyond tort negligence; a "very high degree of negligence" is required).

9. Thus in Smith v. State, 197 Miss. 802, 20 So.2d 701 (1945), the court states that the criminal negligence required for manslaughter "must be wanton or reckless under circumstances implying danger to human life," and

"must be of a gross or flagrant character, such as would show wantonness or recklessness, or would evince a reckless disregard of human life or the safety of others, or indifference to consequences, equivalent to criminal intent," and "negligence so wanton or reckless as to be incompatible with a proper regard for human life." Whether this language means that the defendant's conduct must involve a higher degree of risk of death or serious injury to others than is required for tort negligence, or that the defendant must subjectively realize that his conduct creates an unreasonable risk (a realization not required for tort negligence), or both, is not at all plain.

10. As stated in United States v. Escamilla, 467 F.2d 341 (4th Cir.1972): "Gross negligence or even simple negligence is to be determined by all of the facts and circumstances surrounding an act which is asserted to be either." Thus the court concluded that whether defendant was negligent in handling a rifle when and as he did required consideration of the fact that the events occurred on an island of glacial ice, "a place where no recognized means of law enforcement exist and each man must look to himself for the immediate enforcement of his rights."

11. See § 3.7. Conceivably, it might be required for manslaughter liability of the criminal-negligence type that the victim's death must be more than just foreseeable; i. e., to go from tort negligence to criminal negligence we should vary (either instead of, or in addition to, the degree of risk and subjective realization possibilities discussed in the text above) the "proximate cause" ("legal cause") requirement, requiring something stricter for criminal liability than for torts.

See Commonwealth v. Root, 403 Pa. 571, 170 A.2d 310 (1961) (tort concept of proximate cause is inapplicable in manslaughter case; more direct cause is necessary), discussed infra notes 43, 44 and 46 and accompanying text.

12. See § 3.7(d).

13. E.g., Commonwealth v. Pierce, 138 Mass. 165, 52 Am.R. 264 (1884) (defendant, practicing as a physician, kept his patient wrapped with kerosene-soaked rags, causing her death); Commonwealth v. Welansky, 316 Mass. 383, 55 N.E.2d 902 (1944) (defendant, nightclub owner,

On the other hand, a few other cases have made it clear that manslaughter is not committed, even though the defendant's death-inflicting conduct involves such a risk, unless the defendant in fact was conscious of the danger.[14] Doubtless in most cases one whose conduct is highly risky is actually aware of that fact; but occasionally a particular defendant may be so absent-minded or stupid or intoxicated as not to realize the risk. One who consciously takes a chance with other people's lives—whose attitude is, I may kill someone but I'll risk it—is, of course, morally much worse than one who unconsciously does so.

It would seem that with the quite serious crime of involuntary manslaughter, a felony in most jurisdictions, actual awareness of risk should be required,[15] excepting perhaps, for reasons of policy, the case where the defendant's only reason for not being aware of the

risk is his state of voluntary intoxication.[16] In the converse case of the person who is more perceptive or knowledgeable than a reasonable man and who conducts himself in a risky manner, with full realization of the risk, although a reasonable man would not have realized it, such a person is guilty of manslaughter for the resulting death in all jurisdictions, even in those which do not require realization.[17]

The modern view, evidenced by the position taken in most of the recent comprehensive criminal codes, is to require for involuntary manslaughter a consciousness of risk—i.e., "recklessness," as does the Model Penal Code.[18] But some of these codes provide no clear definition of the standard or else utilize a standard which at least appears to be somewhat different than that in the Model Penal Code. The modern codes sometimes single out special situations for criminal condemna-

---

failed to provide proper fire escapes, causing deaths of 490 persons in a fire; manslaughter conviction proper because of the "grave danger" to others; "even if a particular defendant is so stupid [or] so heedless * * * that in fact he did not realize the grave danger, he cannot escape [criminal liability] if an ordinary normal man under the same circumstances would have realized the gravity of the danger"); Palmer v. State, 223 Md. 341, 164 A.2d 467 (1960) (defendant, mother of a small child, left the child in an environment of physical danger to the child wherein defendant's paramour frequently beat the child, finally killing it; it is not necessary that the defendant foresee death to the child; it is enough that a reasonable man would have foreseen it).

14. E. g., Bussard v. State, 233 Wis. 11, 288 N.W. 187 (1939) (under manslaughter statute requiring "gross negligence" a defendant, though his death-causing conduct in driving his car without looking ahead was "negligent in a high degree," was not guilty of manslaughter, because he was not aware of the risk his conduct entailed; his conduct after the accident in helping the victims negatives the notion that he consciously took a chance).

Some cases holding a defendant guilty emphasize that he was conscious of the risk, e.g., People v. Decina, 2 N.Y.2d 133, 157 N.Y.S.2d 558, 138 N.E.2d 799 (1956) (defendant, who knew he was subject to epileptic seizures, suffered an attack while driving his car, which thereupon ran up on the sidewalk and killed four children; defendant is guilty of statutory felony of causing death by reckless or culpably negligent driving, because, knowing of the danger, "he deliberately took a chance by making a conscious choice of a course of action, in disregard of the consequences which he knew might follow from his conscious act").

15. See § 3.7. It is there suggested that there may be the in-between case of the man who does not know that what he does is risky, but he does know that he does not

know whether it is risky or not and in fact it is risky. Perhaps this was the position of the "physician" who wrapped his patient in kerosene rags in Commonwealth v. Pierce, supra note 13. He ought to be eligible for a manslaughter conviction.

16. People v. Townsend, 214 Mich. 267, 183 N.W. 177 (1921) (defendant, convicted of involuntary manslaughter for killing a passenger by driving his car when intoxicated, claimed that he could not be guilty because he was too drunk to appreciate the danger; *held* conviction affirmed); State v. Alls, 55 N.M. 168, 228 P.2d 952 (1951) (same). See also State v. Trott, 190 N.C. 674, 130 S.E. 627 (1925) (conviction of depraved-heart murder affirmed). In Edwards v. State, 202 Tenn. 393, 304 S.W.2d 500 (1957), the issue was avoided by holding that one who, before he is yet drunk, drinks knowing that he is going to drive, is consciously creating a risk, although later when he does drive he may be so drunk as not then to appreciate the danger.

Model Penal Code § 2.08(2) provides that where recklessness (defined in terms of conscious risk-taking) is an element of the crime, unconsciousness of the risk solely due to self-induced intoxication does not negative recklessness; the comment recognizes that the reason for this special rule is one not of logic but of public policy, and that the rule is fortified by prevailing American case law. Model Penal Code § 2.08, Comment at 359 (1985).

17. See Commonwealth v. Welansky, 316 Mass. 383, 55 N.E.2d 902 (1944): "If the grave danger was in fact realized by the defendant, his subsequent voluntary act or omission which caused the harm amounts to wanton or reckless conduct, no matter whether the ordinary man would have realized the gravity of the danger or not."

18. Model Penal Code § 210.3. Section 2.02(c) defines "recklessly" as consciously disregarding a substantial and unjustifiable risk.

tion where no such consciousness exists.[19] And then there are the negligent homicide statutes to be found in many states, which do not require realization of the risk.

There is a question of manslaughter law as to whether the conduct of a person with mental or physical defects is to be judged by the standard of the hypothetical reasonable man (who is without such defects) or by the standard of a reasonable man who is endowed with the defendant's peculiar characteristics. So far as a physical deficiency—e.g., near-sightedness, deafness, epilepsy—is concerned, the defect is generally considered a "circumstance" to be considered when asking whether the defendant, "under the circumstances," acted as a reasonable man would have acted.[20] The law makes less allowance for a mental defect not amounting to insanity—e.g., ab-

sent-mindedness or stupidity[21]—although, as we have seen, the defect may operate to negative awareness of the risk where awareness is required for manslaughter.

The factual situations which have given rise to involuntary manslaughter liability on account of deaths resulting from criminal negligence or recklessness are, of course, very numerous, though those involving the operation of motor vehicles and the handling of firearms lead the list.[22] A number of reported cases have concerned criminal negligence or recklessness in omitting [23] to furnish medical care for helpless, sick or injured persons to whom the defendant owes a duty of care.[24] Other cases involve such diverse situations of criminal negligence or recklessness as: permitting overcrowded conditions in, and failing to provide adequate fire exits for, a place of

---

19. See § 7.12(e).

20. E. g., Tift v. State, 17 Ga.App. 663, 88 S.E. 41 (1916) (the conduct of one who, knowing he is subject to sudden attacks of vertigo, yet drives a car constitutes criminal negligence); State v. Gooze, 14 N.J.Super. 277, 81 A.2d 811 (App.Div.1951) ("driving his automobile alone on a through state highway with knowledge that he might at any time suddenly, without warning, lose consciousness or suffer a dizzy spell, and having been cautioned not to drive alone, constituted an act of wantonness"); People v. Decina, 2 N.Y.2d 133, 157 N.Y.S.2d 558, 138 N.E.2d 799 (1956) (the conduct of one who, knowing he is subject to sudden seizures of epilepsy, yet drives a car, constitutes criminal negligence). See R. Moreland, A Rationale of Criminal Negligence 88–90 (1944).

21. R. Moreland, supra note 20 at 90.

22. See cases cited in Annots., 5 A.L.R. 603 (1920) and 23 A.L.R. 1554 (1923) (homicide through negligent use of firearms); 99 A.L.R. 756 (1935) (homicide or battery in connection with negligent or unlawful operation of automobile); 63 A.L.R.2d 983 (1959) (sleep or drowsiness of automobile operator as affecting charge of negligent homicide); 23 A.L.R.2d 1401 (1952) (criminal responsibility for injury or death from hunting accident).

23. See § 3.3 for a general discussion of criminal liability based upon omission to act rather than upon affirmative action.

24. See Craig v. State, 220 Md. 590, 155 A.2d 684 (1959) (parents, relying on prayer, omitted to call doctors and child died; parents convicted of manslaughter; held, conviction reversed and remanded for new trial on proximate cause; but if parents' omission showed wanton and reckless disregard for child's life by failing to give medical aid at a time when such aid would have saved child, failure would constitute proximate cause of death, so as to constitute manslaughter); Commonwealth v. Breth, 44 Pa.Coun-

ty Ct. 56 (1915) (father, who relied upon prayer, omitted to call doctor; held, guilty of manslaughter); Cf. Bradley v. State, 79 Fla. 651, 84 So. 677 (1920) (father, relying on prayer, failed to call doctor; held, conviction of manslaughter reversed because no "culpable negligence" shown).

See Annot., 100 A.L.R.2d 483 (1965); Trescher & O'Neill, Medical Care for Dependent Children: Manslaughter Liability of the Christian Scientist, 109 U.Pa.L. Rev. 203 (1960) (dealing primarily with the defense of religious belief).

Whether one is liable for involuntary manslaughter for failure to provide medical care for a sick or injured helpless person depends on whether there is a duty to do so; and whether, if affirmative action had been taken, the life which was lost could have been saved. As for the defense of religious belief, it is no interference with one's freedom of religion to convict of manslaughter one who, for religious reasons, fails to call a doctor when to fail to do so constitutes criminal negligence. Yet an honest religious belief that prayer is a better cure than medicine, that Providence can heal better than doctors, might serve to negative the awareness of risk which is required for manslaughter in those states which use a subjective test of criminal negligence.

What if the defendant, who has a duty of care, believes in prayer but not in medicine and so does not call a doctor; and then he does not pray! In State v. Sanford, 99 Me. 441, 59 A. 597 (1905), the court instructed the jury that an honest belief that doctors do not cure excuses his failure to call a doctor; but they might convict of manslaughter if a failure to pray caused the death. The conviction was reversed; it is improper to leave to a jury the question of whether failure to pray caused the death, since the answer must vary according to the religious beliefs of the jury members in question.

entertainment;[25] prescribing improper medical remedies for disease or injury;[26] permitting one's baby to remain in an environment which endangered her life;[27] conducting dangerous blasting operations;[28] and taking up railroad tracks for repair just before a passenger train is due.[29]

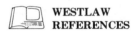

WESTLAW REFERENCES

topic(203) /p "involuntary manslaughter" /s risk*
   danger /s aware kn*w! conscious!
topic(203) /p "involuntary manslaughter" /s
   reasonable prudent /2 person man woman

(b) Omission. Manslaughter liability has not infrequently been based upon criminal negligence or recklessness in omitting to act— for example, the failure of a parent to provide medical attention for his sick child [30] or that of a railroad switchman to throw the switch.[31] For omission to act to give rise to criminal liability for a homicide resulting from the omission, it must first be shown that the one who failed to act had a duty to act—as a parent has a duty, based upon the family relationship, to act to rescue his minor child (or as a railroad switchman has a duty, based upon his contract of employment, to act to save his railroad's crew and passengers) from the perils of serious illness (or of derailment, in the case of the switchman). Thus failure

to act where there is a duty to act is the equivalent of affirmative action.[32]

But an omission to act where there is a duty to act, although death results, is not necessarily a crime at all, for murder and manslaughter liability require some sort of fault in addition to conduct which causes death. If the defendant knows that death is certain (or substantially certain) to result from his omission, he intends to kill and so is guilty of murder.[33] If under the circumstances his omission amounts to criminal negligence (or, where required, recklessness), or if his omission is an unlawful act, then he is guilty of involuntary manslaughter.[34] If his omission is not accompanied by an intent to kill and does not amount either to criminal negligence or to an unlawful act, he is not guilty of either murder or manslaughter.

WESTLAW REFERENCES

203k75

(c) Causation. With manslaughter, as with other crimes defined in terms of cause and result,[35] the defendant's conduct (whether affirmative act, or omission to act when there is a duty to act) must be the "legal cause" of the death. As treated more fully in that part of this book which deals with the basic princi-

---

25. Commonwealth v. Welansky, 316 Mass. 383, 55 N.E.2d 902 (1944) (*held*, owner liable for involuntary manslaughter when fire in nightclub caused 490 deaths).

26. Commonwealth v. Pierce, 138 Mass. 165, 52 Am.R. 264 (1884) (one undertaking to prescribe for sick patient *held* liable for involuntary manslaughter for death to patient resulting from burns caused by his wrapping her in kerosene-soaked rags); Barrow v. State, 17 Okl.Crim. 340, 188 P. 351 (1920) (prescription for pneumonia: hog's hoof brew, headache powder and prayer). See Annot., 45 A.L.R.3d 114 (1972) (homicide: improper treatment of disease).

27. Palmer v. State, 223 Md. 341, 164 A.2d 467 (1960) (mother, living with paramour, let her child remain in house with him though he constantly beat her; finally his beatings killed her).

28. People v. Clemente, 146 App.Div. 109, 130 N.Y.S. 612 (1911).

29. Reg. v. Benge, 4 F. & F. 504, 176 Eng.Rep. 665 (1865). In this case, as in the *Welansky* case, the fact that the defendant's conduct endangered many persons, not just one, doubtless is a factor which relates to criminal negligence: other things being equal, the greater the

number of persons endangered, the greater the degree of negligence. See § 3.7.

30. See note 24 supra. Another possibility is that the parent will withhold food, clothing, or shelter. See cases collected in Annot., 61 A.L.R.3d 1207 (1975).

31. State v. O'Brien, 32 N.J.L. 169 (Sup.Ct.1867) (passenger killed in the resulting passenger train derailment).

32. See § 3.3.

33. So too if there is a very high degree of risk of death from omission—at least if he is aware of this risk—and there are no circumstances which justify taking the risk, then his conduct "evinces a depraved heart," and so he is guilty of murder.

34. State v. O'Brien, 32 N.J.L. 169 (Sup.Ct.1867), spells out this distinction between murder and manslaughter through omission to act. In People v. Nelson, 309 N.Y. 231, 128 N.E.2d 391 (1955), the defendant was held guilty of manslaughter when death resulted from his failure to equip his tenement building with fire safety devices, a criminal offense.

35. See § 1.2, listing such crimes as murder, battery, mayhem, arson, malicious mischief, false pretenses.

ple of causation in criminal law,[36] this means, in connection with crimes based upon some form of negligence, not only (1) that the defendant's negligent conduct must be the "cause in fact" of the victim's death;[37] but also (2) that the victim be the person foreseeably endangered,[38] or a member of the class of persons foreseeably endangered,[39] by the defendant's negligent conduct;[40] (3) that the victim be harmed in a manner which is foreseeable;[41] and (4) that the type and degree of harm suffered by the victim be foreseeable.[42] In this connection, "foreseeable" means something less than probable or likely but more than possible; perhaps it is best described as something which, as one looks back on the event, does not strike him as extraordinary. Applying these basic principles to a case of manslaughter from death arising out of criminally negligent conduct, the defendant's conduct (which, as we have seen, must entail an unjustifiable and high degree of risk of death or serious bodily injury to another or to others, a fact of which perhaps the defendant must be aware) must in fact cause the death of a person who is foreseeably endangered by the conduct and whose death occurs in a foreseeable way. If it seems quite extraordinary that this victim was killed in the way he was killed, the defendant is not liable for manslaughter.

A Pennsylvania case, however, suggests that a defendant whose criminally-negligent conduct causes a foreseeable death should not always be guilty of manslaughter. Here A and B were drag-racing at a reckless speed; B, trying to pass A on a hill, hit C's truck headon and was killed. Is A guilty of manslaughter on account of B's death? A's conduct in thus racing B was certainly conduct involving an unreasonable and high degree of deadly risk; A doubtless was conscious of the risk, if such consciousness is required; and surely it is foreseeable that one of the participants in the race be killed. Nevertheless, the court held that A was not guilty, saying, somewhat vaguely, that tort concepts of proximate cause are inapplicable to criminal cases, and that a more direct cause is required for criminal liability.[43]

What the court really means, it appears, is that one whose criminally-negligent conduct kills another, justly should not be liable for the unintended death (even though it be a foreseeable death) of a willing participant in the same criminally-negligent conduct.[44] If C, the truck driver, or D, a pedestrian walking along the road, had been killed, A (and B) would have been liable.[45] Whether A would be liable, on this theory, for the death of E, a passenger in B's car, would depend, it would seem, upon whether E was a willing participant in B's conduct.

Although the Pennsylvania view, thus explained, has much to recommend it, a more recent Massachusetts case refused to follow it. In this case A, B and C played "Russian roulette"; as part of the game A and then B

---

36. See § 3.12.

37. See § 3.12(b).

38. The manslaughter situation may be such that only one person's life is endangered by the defendant's negligent conduct, as where A negligently handles a gun in an area wherein only B is present within gunshot range.

39. The situation may be such that a number of people of a single class are foreseeably endangered, as where A is hunting in a forest heavily populated with hunters; the ten hunters within range of A's gun, including hunter B who is killed by A's negligent shooting, form a class of endangered persons.

Or the situation may be such that a number of persons, belonging to two or more distinct classes, are endangered, as where A drives his car negligently, endangering his own passengers, motorists in other cars and pedestrians.

40. See § 3.12(e).

41. See § 3.12(g).

42. See § 3.11(e).

43. Commonwealth v. Root, 403 Pa. 571, 170 A.2d 310 (1961) (it is not clear whether the basis for the defendant's manslaughter conviction was his criminal negligence or his unlawful act of speeding; the court's rationale on proximate cause is applicable in either case).

Accord: Thacker v. State, 103 Ga.App. 36, 117 S.E.2d 913 (1961) (indictment alleged that A drag raced B; B lost control of his car and suffered fatal injuries; indictment of A for manslaughter of B held bad for lack of proximate cause).

44. This limitation on manslaughter liability is consistent with that imposed on felony-murder liability by the same court in the case of Commonwealth v. Redline, 391 Pa. 486, 137 A.2d 472 (1958), involving the foreseeable death of a cofelon during a robbery. This case is discussed in § 7.5 at note 55 and accompanying text.

45. Jacobs v. State, 184 So.2d 711 (Fla.App.1966).

each aimed the pistol at his own head and pulled the trigger without ill effect; but when *C*'s turn came, he shot himself to death. *A* and *B* were prosecuted for manslaughter on the theory that the game involved an unreasonable and high degree of risk of death, so that the conduct of each participant, encouraging the others to endanger their lives, constituted criminal negligence. *A* and *B* urged the adoption of the Pennsylvania view: they should not be liable for the death of a willing participant in the highly risky conduct. The court nevertheless upheld their convictions of manslaughter.[46]

WESTLAW REFERENCES

topic(203) /p "involuntary manslaughter" /s (proximate** legal** fact*** /3 caus!) (foresee! predict! /4 consequence result)

(d) Contributory Negligence. Another part of this book contains a discussion of the effect upon the defendant's criminal liability of the victim's contributory negligence, in connection with those crimes (including involuntary manslaughter) in which some form of negligence constitutes the required element of fault.[47] Contributory negligence is no defense to manslaughter of the criminal-negligence type.[48] But the victim's unusual conduct is nevertheless relevant to the question of the

defendant's liability for manslaughter, for it is a factor to be considered in determining whether the defendant's conduct, under all the circumstances, amounted to criminal negligence.[49]

WESTLAW REFERENCES

topic(203 110) /p "involuntary manslaughter" /s contribut!

(e) Modern Statutory Variations. In many American jurisdictions the automobile has been singled out for special statutory treatment, in an endeavor to reduce the number of highway fatalities. Because of difficulties experienced in obtaining juries willing to convict the death driver of manslaughter (in this area juries are apt to think, "There, but for the grace of God, go I"), a number of states have enacted statutes creating the new crime of homicide by automobile (which is related to the crime of manslaughter but is not manslaughter proper), generally punishable less severely than manslaughter.[50] These statutes often reduce the requirement from the criminal negligence or recklessness necessary for manslaughter liability to some lesser degree of negligence (although sometimes not so plainly as to avoid the need for judicial interpretation [51]), differing, however, as to the

---

46. Commonwealth v. Atencio, 345 Mass. 627, 189 N.E.2d 223 (1963). Although the Massachusetts court purported to distinguish the *Root* case on the ground that drag-racing is a game of skill while Russian roulette is one of luck, this is surely an unlikely sort of distinction; and the cases are really inconsistent rather than distinguishable.

47. See § 3.7(a).

48. United States v. Schmidt, 626 F.2d 616 (8th Cir. 1980); State v. McIver, 175 N.C. 761, 94 S.E. 682 (1917).

49. Held v. Commonwealth, 183 Ky. 209, 208 S.W. 772 (1919) (possible contributory negligence of boy on bicycle in turning first one way, then another, as defendant's car bore down on him, is no defense to manslaughter if defendant driver, racing another car, was driving recklessly, but it is relevant to the question of the defendant's recklessness); People v. Campbell, 237 Mich. 424, 212 N.W. 97 (1927) (possible contributory negligence of pedestrians in walking in the street with their backs to oncoming cars is no defense to manslaughter-like crime of negligent homicide by automobile; but their conduct is relevant to the question of whether defendant was negligent, i.e., whether he should have foreseen pedestrians so conducting themselves); State v. Ramser, 17 Wash.2d 581,

136 P.2d 1013 (1943) (defendant was moving building along highway at night without proper warning lights; victim's car struck the building, killing victim; victim's possible contributory negligence is no defense to manslaughter, but victim's conduct is relevant to the question of defendant's criminal negligence). See Annots., 67 A.L.R. 922 (1930), 99 A.L.R. 756, 833 (1935) on contributory negligence and homicide.

50. See Robinson, Manslaughter by Motorists, 22 Minn.L.Rev. 755 (1938); Riesenfeld, Negligent Homicide— A Study in Statutory Interpretation, 25 Calif.L.Rev. 1 (1936).

51. E. g., the statutes construed in Bentley v. State, 252 Ark. 642, 480 S.W.2d 346 (1972) (involuntary manslaughter and negligent homicide by vehicle statutes both require "reckless or wanton disregard of the safety of others," former also requires a "wilful disregard of the safety of others"); McCreary v. State, 371 So.2d 1024 (Fla. 1979) (court says the "reckless" conduct required in the vehicular homicide statute differs from the "culpable" conduct required in the manslaughter statute, which must be of a "gross or flagrant character, evincing reckless disregard of human life"). See Annot., 20 A.L.R.3d 473 (1968).

degree of negligence necessary for guilt—sometimes requiring only ordinary negligence,[52] sometimes negligence of a higher degree.[53] Another type of statute inflicts punishment (generally more severely than for manslaughter proper) on one who causes a death while driving a car while under the influence.[54]

A few states have separated out other limited homicide situations for special nonmanslaughter treatment, such as the negligent use of firearms or vicious animals. The Model Penal Code creates a new crime, less severely punished than manslaughter (which in the Code is defined in terms of high risk of death or serious harm subjectively realized), called "negligent homicide", requiring only inadvertence to risk and not limited to motor vehicles or any other special situation of danger of death or serious bodily injury.[55] Many modern codes treat negligent homicide as a criminal offense.

WESTLAW
REFERENCES

48ak344 topic(203) /p "involuntary manslaughter" /p vehic!

§ 7.13 Unlawful-Act Involuntary Manslaughter

Centuries ago it was stated to be the law that an unintended homicide in the commission of an unlawful act constituted criminal homicide;[1] and later, when criminal homicide was subdivided into the separate crimes of murder and manslaughter, this type of criminal homicide was assigned to the (involuntary) manslaughter category. As time passed it came to be considered too harsh a rule, and the courts began to place limitations upon it.

The trend today is to abolish altogether this type of involuntary manslaughter, leaving the field of involuntary manslaughter occupied only by the criminal-negligence type already discussed. Thus, about two-thirds of the modern codes do not contain a manslaughter or comparable crime grounded in defendant's death-causing unlawful act. But there is still a good deal of vitality left in the unlawful-act type, so that the problems discussed below continue to exist. The remaining modern codes have such a crime, and unlawful-act manslaughter also exists in most of the jurisdictions which have not enacted revised codes.[2]

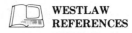

WESTLAW
REFERENCES

203k68

(a) **Meaning of "Unlawful".** "Unlawful act" is a vague expression, and literally it may be broad enough to include not only an act which is punishable as a crime (felony, misdemeanor, and perhaps ordinance violation[3]) but also noncriminal conduct such as a

---

52. E. g., the statute construed in People v. Campbell, 237 Mich. 424, 212 N.W. 97 (1927) (statute punishing, less severely than manslaughter proper, one who, by operating a vehicle "in a careless, reckless or negligent manner, but not wilfully or wantonly," causes another's death, construed to require only ordinary negligence).

53. E. g., the statute construed in People v. Young, 20 Cal.2d 832, 129 P.2d 353 (1942) (statute punishing for negligent homicide one who, by operating a vehicle "with reckless disregard of, or wilful indifference to, the safety of others," causes another's death within a year, construed to require a high degree of negligence, though the opinion is not clear as to whether the driver must also realize the risk involved in his driving).

54. E. g., statute construed in Espinoza v. People, 142 Colo. 96, 349 P.2d 689 (1960) (statute punishing, more severely than manslaughter proper, one who, while under the influence, by operating a vehicle "in a reckless, negligent or careless manner, or with a wanton or reckless disregard of human life or safety," causes another's death, construed to require only ordinary negligence if the infor-

mation charges only ordinary negligence); Utah statute construed in State v. Twitchell, 8 Utah 2d 314, 333 P.2d 1075 (1959) (statute like Colorado's upheld as constitutional against attack (1) that it singles out motorists for special treatment, (2) that it substitutes status of intoxication for criminal intent).

55. Model Penal Code § 210.4.

§ 7.13

1. Bracton, De Legibus et Consuetudinibus Angliae, written about 1260.

2. Model Penal Code § 210.3, Comment at 77–78 n. 94 (1980).

3. Some statutes specifically refer to any "public offense" other than that which suffices for felony murder. Some make it clear that they cover all or many statutes *and* ordinance violations.

On the propriety of basing a manslaughter conviction on violation of a local ordinance or regulation not dealing with motor vehicles, see Annot., 85 A.L.R.3d 1072 (1978).

trespass or other civil wrong, and in fact any conduct which the court making the determination does not like. Misdemeanors are certainly included, so much so that the unlawful-act type of manslaughter is often referred to, somewhat loosely, as the "misdemeanor-manslaughter doctrine," a sort of junior-grade counterpart of the "felony-murder doctrine." Although the misdemeanor involved is commonly a traffic offense (e.g., speeding, drunk driving), another common type of misdemeanor causing death is simple battery, as where the defendant hits the victim a light blow, intending to inflict only minor harm, but actually causing a quite unexpected death.[4]

"Unlawful act" is a phrase, however, which also includes criminal acts other than misdemeanors. Thus a felony which for some reason will not suffice for felony-murder[5] may do for unlawful-act manslaughter.[6] Local ordinance violations (which in some jurisdictions are considered crimes, in others mere "civil wrongs"[7]) may qualify as unlawful acts to

the same extent as violation of state criminal laws.[8] And going clearly outside the area of criminal conduct, it has been held that attempted suicide, though not a crime, is an unlawful act for manslaughter purposes;[9] and the sale of liquor to one already intoxicated,[10] and attempting to drive through a tollgate without paying the toll,[11] though not criminal offenses, were said to be unlawful acts for manslaughter purposes.[12]

There is a dispute as to whether a reckless act which is not a crime is an unlawful act for purposes of manslaughter liability.[13] On the other hand, in a case wherein the defendant picked up a box lying on a pier and threw it into the sea, hitting and killing a swimmer beneath the pier, it was held that the trespass to the box, a civil wrong against its owner, was not an unlawful act which would support a manslaughter conviction.[14] The word "act" in the phrase "unlawful act," though somewhat vague, includes an omission to act

---

4. See § 7.13(d).

5. See § 7.5.

6. In People v. Pavlic, 227 Mich. 562, 199 N.W. 373 (1924), the court treated a statutory felony (selling liquor) as an unlawful act for purposes of possible manslaughter liability, although it held that, in view of certain modern limitations upon unlawful-act manslaughter, this felony would not suffice. In some jurisdictions, however, statutes define manslaughter as an unintended killing in the commission of an unlawful act "not amounting to a felony."

7. See § 1.7(c).

8. Hayes v. State, 11 Ga.App. 371, 75 S.E. 523 (1912) (an "unlawful act" for purposes of involuntary manslaughter "is an act prohibited by law; that is to say, an act condemned by some statute or valid municipal ordinance of this state").

Contra: State v. Ginsberg, 15 Wn.App. 244, 548 P.2d 329 (1976) (violation of municipal housing code not sufficient; guilt should not depend on happenstance of where within the state the acts occurred). For other cases, see Annot., 85 A.L.R.3d 1072 (1978).

9. Commonwealth v. Mink, 123 Mass. 422, 25 Am.R. 109 (1877) (defendant, attempting suicide, accidentally killed her fiancé who was interfering to prevent it; *held,* defendant guilty of manslaughter, for attempted suicide, though no crime, is an unlawful act, *malum in se*). Wallace v. State, 232 Ind. 700, 116 N.E.2d 100 (1953) (attempted suicide, though not a crime, is an unlawful act). Contra: State v. Campbell, 217 Iowa 848, 251 N.W. 717 (1933) (attempted suicide, no crime, is therefore not an unlawful act).

See also Wilson v. Commonwealth, 22 Ky.L.Rptr. 1251, 60 S.W. 400 (Ct.App.1901) (defendant used instruments to

procure an abortion upon a woman who may not have been pregnant; if she were not pregnant, it is no crime; the court instructed the jury to convict of voluntary manslaughter for the woman's death if he believed her to be pregnant; *held,* conviction affirmed). (In most jurisdictions this type of manslaughter is involuntary manslaughter.)

10. State v. Reitze, 86 N.J.L. 407, 92 A. 576 (Sup.Ct. 1914), termed this conduct (which by statute involved forfeiture of liquor license but not fine or imprisonment) a "wrongful act," but only *malum prohibitum,* so defendant not liable for manslaughter when the victim, drunk, fell and killed himself while trying to climb into his wagon.

11. Estell v. State, 51 N.J.L. 182, 17 A. 118 (Sup.Ct. 1889), held this to be an unlawful act, but only *malum prohibitum,* so defendant not liable for manslaughter when horses ran over and killed gatekeeper.

12. But compare Redding v. State, 165 Neb. 307, 85 N.W.2d 647 (1957) (a statute made it a misdemeanor, but provided no penalty, for one in charge of insane person to mistreat him; defendant, in charge of insane person, mistreated him, and the insane person died; there can be no conviction of "unlawful act" manslaughter, since the misdemeanor statute, without a penalty, created no crime and therefore no unlawful act).

13. Compare Minardo v. State, 204 Ind. 422, 183 N.E. 548 (1932) (reckless driving of car an "unlawful act"), with Johnson v. State, 66 Ohio St. 59, 63 N.E. 607 (1902) (reckless bicycling not an "unlawful act").

14. Reg. v. Franklin, 15 Cox Crim.Cas. 163 (1883). The defendant was found guilty of manslaughter of the criminal-negligence type, however.

where there is a duty to act.[15] Thus "unlawful conduct" (the word "conduct" including omissions as well as affirmative acts) would be a more accurate term than "unlawful act," the more commonly used expression.

There remains the question of whether an innocent-minded violation can be an "unlawful act," as where the criminal statute which punishes certain conduct is of the strict-liability sort. Thus suppose it is a misdemeanor to drive at night without lights or at any time without brakes; suddenly, without any fault on the defendant's part, the lights go out or the brakes fail; and, before the car can be brought to a stop, a pedestrian or motorist is struck and killed. On principle, this sort of violation should not aid in any way in establishing the defendant's guilt of manslaughter,[16] as some cases have recognized.[17] On the other hand, for the defendant's condut to be "unlawful" for purposes of manslaughter liability it is not necessary that he know that

some law forbids it (in the case of an act) or commands it (in the case of an omission);[18] in other words, there is no requirement of a specific intent to violate the law which makes his conduct unlawful.

 WESTLAW REFERENCES

203k62 203k68   /p   manslaughter   /s   "unlawful act"
203k62 203k68   /p   manslaughter   /s   intent

(b) Required Causal Connection. Assuming that, while the defendant is committing an "unlawful act," a death occurs near the defendant, still the defendant is not guilty of manslaughter unless the unlawful act causes the death. Mere coincidence of time and place will not do.[19] Yet closeness of time and place does have relevance, for it seems clear that, in addition to the necessary causal connection, the requirement that the homicide be committed "in the commission of" the unlawful act necessitates, on analogy to felo-

---

15. E.g., People v. Nelson, 309 N.Y. 231, 128 N.E.2d 391 (1955) (misdemeanor statute punished failure to equip tenements with fire protection devices; defendant's failure to install them resulted in death of two tenants from fire; *held*, defendant guilty of manslaughter for "committing" a misdemeanor affecting the persons killed).

16. If the justification for unlawful-act manslaughter as a separate type is that the defendant is already doing something bad (committing an unlawful act), so a lesser degree of negligence is needed to convict him of manslaughter than the criminal negligence necessary when he is not committing any unlawful act, then the defendant's faultless act, though unlawful under strict-liability criminal statute, should not be considered "already doing something bad."

17. People v. Stuart, 47 Cal.2d 167, 302 P.2d 5 (1956) (defendant druggist, without negligence or intent to mislabel, prepared a drug and mislabeled it; a statute makes it a strict-liability crime to prepare and mislabel a drug; the purchaser of the drug gave it to a child, who died from the drug; defendant *held* not guilty of "unlawful act" manslaughter, for only intentional or criminally negligent mislabeling is an "unlawful act" for manslaughter purposes). See People v. Fitzsimmons, 11 Cr.R. 391, 69 St.R. 191, 34 N.Y.S. 1102, 1109 (Ct.Sess.1895) (boxer Bob Fitzsimmons, prize fighting in violation of misdemeanor statute, struck his sparring partner a blow, killing him; charge to the jury stated that, for manslaughter, although the defendant need not know there is a law forbidding the unlawful conduct, yet he must intentionally do the act which constitutes the unlawful conduct; verdict: not guilty of manslaughter); State v. Kotapish, 171 Ohio St. 349, 352, 171 N.E.2d 505, 507 (1960) (truck driver was driving without an emergency brake, in violation of misdemeanor statute requiring it, when the foot brake failed,

and the truck, unable to stop, killed a pedestrian; conviction of manslaughter *held* affirmed, but court indicates there would have been no liability for footbrake failure, though a criminal statute requires foot brakes, except for the misdemeanor violation with respect to the emergency brake). In People v. Nelson, 309 N.Y. 231, 128 N.E.2d 391 (1955), the defendant operated a tenement house without proper fire protection, in violation of a misdemeanor statute; a fire killed two tenants. The defendant argued that he did not know of the existence of the conditions which violated the statute. His conviction was upheld, however, because the record showed he did know of the conditions (and there was no need that he know that the conditions violated the criminal law).

18. People v. Nelson, supra note 17 (no defense that defendant, having recently bought tenement, did not know of the law requiring installation of fire protection devices).

19. People v. Mulcahy, 318 Ill. 332, 149 N.E. 266 (1925) (while policeman was committing an unlawful act by failing to arrest drunks and gamblers who were disturbing the peace and gambling in his presence in a cabaret, his gun accidentally went off, killing the hatcheck girl; *held*, conviction of involuntary manslaughter reversed for lack of any causal connection between the unlawful act and the death; causing death "while" committing an unlawful act is not enough); Commonwealth v. Williams, 133 Pa.Super. 104, 1 A.2d 812 (1938) (defendant, who had had a license to drive for several years before 1936, failed to renew it in 1936; in 1936, while driving carefully, an approaching automobile caused him to swerve into a telephone pole; his passenger was killed; conviction of manslaughter of the unlawful-act type *held* reversed, for the unlawful act did not cause the death, i.e., the death was not the result of the unlawful act).

ny-murder,[20] a somewhat close connection in point of time and place, as well as causal relation, between the unlawful act and the infliction of the death-causing injury.[21]

(c) Limitations Upon Unlawful-Act Manslaughter. Just as the felony-murder doctrine has been circumscribed by limitations (and perhaps in the end will be abolished), so too the counterpart misdemeanor-manslaughter doctrine has been subjected to limitations. "Unlawful acts" are in many (but not all) jurisdictions divided into those which are *mala in se* and those which are only *mala prohibita*.[22] As to unlawful conduct *malum*

in se, the usual rule is that where a defendant, in the commission or attempted commission of such conduct, unintentionally causes another's death, he is guilty of involuntary manslaughter, without regard either to the foreseeability of the victim's death or to the existence of any causal connection between the "unlawful excess" portion of the defendant's conduct and the victim's death.[23] But if the defendant unintentionally kills another in the commission or attempted commission of an unlawful act which is *malum prohibitum,* he is not necessarily guilty of manslaughter. In this situation three different views have been taken by the courts:

View (1): He is not guilty unless [24] the death which occurs is the foreseeable or natural consequence of the defendant's unlawful conduct.[25] It is unnecessary under this view

---

20. See § 7.5(f).

21. See People v. Mulcahy, supra note 19 (death must occur within res gestae of the unlawful act). For instance, a defendant, having committed the misdemeanor of speeding, slows down to a lawful speed, and a few minutes later, while driving at a proper speed, hits and kills a pedestrian. Though it may be true that, had it not been for the speeding violation he would not have been at the spot where the accident occurred (and so it may be said that but for the speeding, death would not have resulted), yet the fact that the accident took place at some distance from the place of the commission of the misdemeanor, and some time later, may take the matter out of the "in the commission" requirement.

22. See § 1.6(b) for cases assigning particular crimes (and noncriminal conduct constituting unlawful acts) to one category or the other.

23. State v. Davis, 196 N.W.2d 885 (Iowa 1972) (defendant, driving car while intoxicated, caused a death; conviction of manslaughter *held* affirmed; driving while intoxicated is *malum in se,* so that to cause death by drunken driving is manslaughter); Keller v. State, 155 Tenn. 633, 299 S.W. 803 (1927), noted at 41 Harv.L.Rev. 669 (1928) (defendant, driving car while under the influence of alcohol, hit and killed pedestrian who was crossing the street in the middle of the block and who could not have been avoided by a sober driver; *held,* manslaughter conviction affirmed). See also State v. Gerak, 169 Conn. 309, 363 A.2d 114 (1975) (stressing this effect of *malum in se-malum prohibitum* distinction); State v. Budge, 126 Me. 223, 137 A. 244 (1927) ("the rule is, that where involuntary homicide happens while engaged in an unlawful act, if the unlawful act is *malum in se,* misadventure does not excuse, and the offense is manslaughter," but if it is *malum prohibitum,* the unlawful act must be shown to be the proximate cause of the homicide; Dixon v. State, 104 Miss. 410, 61 So. 423, (1913) (where defendant commits a misdemeanor *malum prohibitum,* he is not guilty of manslaughter unless the death is the natural or necessary

result of its commission; but where he commits a misdemeanor *malum in se* it is manslaughter regardless).

A few of the cases, cited below as illustrative of viewpoints (1) and (2) concerning limitations on manslaughter liability in the case of unlawful conduct *malum prohibitum,* do not actually designate the unlawful act in question to be *malum prohibitum* (though the act in each case is of the sort that would be so classified in most jurisdictions which make the classification). E.g., view (1): Potter v. State, (carrying concealed weapon), Commonwealth v. Williams (driving after license expired), both infra note 25. E.g., view (2): People v. Penny, infra note 31 (practicing cosmetology without a license). Because of the absence of designation, these cases may be considered to stand for the proposition that there is no manslaughter liability for any unlawful act, even one *malum in se,* unless death is foreseeable (view no. 1) or unless the unlawful excess caused the death (view no. 2).

24. An alternative way of expressing this same view is: He is not guilty unless the unlawful act is the proximate cause of the death. State v. Hupf, 48 Del. 254, 101 A.2d 355 (1953) (requiring proximate cause in all cases of unlawful act, without regard to distinction between *malum in se* and *malum prohibitum*).

25. Potter v. State, 162 Ind. 213, 70 N.E. 129 (1904) (defendant, while committing the misdemeanor of carrying a concealed weapon, was having a friendly scuffle with another when the gun accidentally discharged, killing the other; conviction for manslaughter *held* reversed, because for manslaughter liability the homicide must be "the natural or necessary result of the act of appellant in carrying the revolver in violation of the statute"); Dixon v. State, 104 Miss. 410, 61 So. 423 (1913) (defendant, while committing three misdemeanors all *mala prohibita*—carrying a concealed weapon, drunk in a public place, shooting on a public highway—fired into the ground; the bullet ricocheted and struck and killed a woman nearby; defendant was convicted of manslaughter on the theory that unintended death in the commission of any misdemeanor

that the defendant himself subjectively fore-see the possibility of death; the word "fore-seeable" itself implies that it is enough that a reasonable man would have foreseen. Again, as with criminal-negligence manslaughter, it is not necessary that death to this particular victim, occurring in this particular manner, be foreseeable; it is enough that the victim be a member of an endangered class, and that his death come about in a foreseeable, rather than an extraordinary, way. And, once again, though contributory negligence is no defense to unlawful-act manslaughter where foreseeability of death is a requirement for guilt, the victim's careless conduct may be considered in dealing with the question whether a reasonable man would foresee that death might result from the defendant's un-lawful conduct.[26]

Finally, comparing criminal-negligence manslaughter, on the one hand, with unlaw-ful-act manslaughter with the foreseeability limitation, on the other: (a) Where one, not doing any unlawful act, unintentionally kills another, his conduct must involve not only an unreasonable but also a high degree of risk of

death or serious bodily injury (and perhaps in addition he must be conscious of this risk); whereas (b) where he is already doing an unlawful act, his conduct need involve only an unreasonable risk of death or serious bodi-ly injury, and he need not subjectively realize the risk. The notion (illogical though it may be) seems to be: if he is doing something bad (other than creating risk) at the time he unin-tentionally inflicts the fatal injury, it should be easier to attach manslaughter liability to him than if he is not doing something bad.[27]

It has already been noted that, for man-slaughter liability of the criminal-negligence sort, perhaps one is not liable for an unin-tended death which happens to a willing par-ticipant in the defendant's criminally negli-gent conduct.[28] If this limitation upon liability is valid as to the criminal negligence sort of manslaughter, it is, on principle, equal-ly so as to the unlawful-act-causing-foresee-able-death type of manslaughter;[29] if it is unjust to punish a person for the death of his willingly participating colleague in the one situation, it is equally unjust to do so in the other.[30]

A much higher degree of risk of death or serious injury is required in the former situation, involving no felonious bad conduct, than is required in the latter situation, where the defendant is already doing something bad.

But just as there is a trend to abolish the felony-murder doctrine, even as limited by the foreseeability require-ment, there is also a trend to abolish the unlawful-act manslaughter doctrine as limited by the foreseeability requirement. See § 7.13(e).

is manslaughter; *held,* conviction reversed, because, where the misdemeanor is *malum prohibitum,* death must be "the natural or necessary result" of its commission); Commonwealth v. Williams, 133 Pa.Super. 104, 1 A.2d 812 (1938) (defendant, while committing the misdemeanor of driving a car without a license—a crime which neither is a felony nor tends to cause death or serious bodily harm—struck and killed the victim; conviction of manslaughter *held* reversed as not supported by the evidence, because for manslaughter liability "the death must be the natural result or probable consequence of the unlawful act"); Holder v. State, 152 Tenn. 390, 277 S.W. 900 (1925) (no manslaughter liability for accidental death while defen-dant committed misdemeanor or *malum prohibitum* of carrying gun, unless he handled it in such a way "as to make the killing of the deceased a natural or probable result of such conduct").

26. Cf. Commonwealth v. Aurick, 138 Pa.Super. 180, 10 A.2d 22 (1939) (in unlawful-act manslaughter case the trial court's instruction to the jury, that "it does not make any difference if the girl, who was fatally injured, did not exercise due care," *held* reversible error because it "failed to inform the jury that they might also consider the conduct of deceased as bearing upon the cause of her death, in the event that it resulted not from appellant's rashness or recklessness, but from his commission of an unlawful act").

27. See § 7.5(e) for the same notion with respect to depraved-heart murder, on the one hand, and felony-murder with a foreseeable-death limitation, on the other.

28. Compare Commonwealth v. Root, 403 Pa. 571, 170 A.2d 310 (1961) (*A* and *B* engage in a drag-race; *B* is killed; *A* is not liable for manslaughter of *B*), with Com-monwealth v. Atencio, 345 Mass. 627, 189 N.E.2d 223 (1963) (*A*, *B* and *C* play Russian roulette; *C* is killed; *A* and *B* are liable for manslaughter of *C*).

29. State v. Light, 577 S.W.2d 134 (Mo.1979) (since felony-murder rule not applicable when co-felon killed by outside agency which thwarted the felony, same rule should apply here; defendant not liable for manslaughter where coparticipant in misdemeanor electrocuted while climbing telephone pole to steal wire).

It is not actually clear, from the *Root* case, supra note 28, whether the basis for the defendant's manslaughter conviction was his criminal negligence or his unlawful act of speeding.

30. The same may be said concerning view (2) immedi-ately below, which deals with the unlawful-act-whose-unlawful-excess-causes-the-death type of manslaughter: if an unintended death happens to a willing participant in

View (2): He is not guilty unless the death which occurs is in fact caused by his conduct's "unlawful excess," i.e., that portion of the defendant's whole conduct which makes the conduct unlawful.[31] The defendant's whole unlawful conduct can be in most cases divided up into two portions: the lawful part and the unlawful excess. Thus where the defendant drives at 35 m.p.h. in a zone in which the speed limit is 25 m.p.h., the first 25 m.p.h. is lawful, and only the excess 10 m.p.h. is unlawful. With the crime of driving under the influence of liquor, the driving portion of his act is lawful, but the fact that the driver is under the influence constitutes the unlawful excess. So too of hunting on Sunday, or without permission of the landowner, or without a license, where such conduct is unlawful: hunting is the lawful part; it is only the Sunday or the no-permission or the no-license feature which is unlawful.

Where the defendant, while committing an unlawful act *malum prohibitum,* unintentionally kills another, the question, under this view, is: did the unlawful excess cause the death, or would it have happened even if the defendant had been acting lawfully? Thus if the defendant, hunting without permission, in violation of a statute forbidding hunting without permission of the landowner, shoots and kills another person by accident, the question is whether the fact that he had no permission caused the death, or would the death have occurred even if he had had permission.[32] If the defendant, speeding at 35 miles per hour

in a 25 mile zone, strikes and kills a pedestrian, the question is whether the death would have occurred even if the driver had been going only 25: if he could not have stopped in time at 25 m.p.h., the unlawful excess 10 m.p.h. did not cause the death; if he could have, the extra 10 m.p.h. did cause the death.

Comparing these two views, both of which serve to limit manslaughter liability for a death resulting from the defendant's unlawful conduct: under view (1) we look at the defendant's whole conduct (e.g., driving at 35 m.p.h.) and ask whether, under all the circumstances, the victim's death was the foreseeable result of this conduct; whereas under view (2) we divide his whole conduct into its two parts, the lawful portion (the first 25 m.p.h.) and the unlawful excess (the 10 m.p.h. from 25 to 35), and ask whether the extra 10 m.p.h. in fact caused the death. Often the answer will be the same under either view, but under some circumstances the answer may differ depending upon which view is taken. Suppose, for instance, that while the defendant is driving at 35 m.p.h. in a 25-mile zone, his car strikes and kills a pedestrian who suddenly steps off the curb in the middle of the block, although the defendant instantly applies the brakes. It may be that, under all the circumstances (including the victim's careless act), the death was the unforeseeable result of the defendant's conduct in driving as he did. Yet it may also be that, if the defendant had been travelling at 25 m.p.h., he could have stopped in time to avoid hitting

the defendant's unlawful conduct, the latter is not liable, even if the unlawful excess be the cause of the death.

31. People v. Penny, 44 Cal.2d 861, 285 P.2d 926 (1955) (unlicensed cosmetologist gave face-lifting treatment which poisoned victim and caused her death; practicing cosmetology without a license is a misdemeanor; *held,* no manslaughter liability based on lack-of-license misdemeanor, for "it is extremely dubious that defendant's lack of a license had any causal connection with Mrs. Stanley's death"); State v. Budge, 126 Me. 223, 137 A. 244 (1927) (driver, while speeding and driving either under the influence or while intoxicated, all misdemeanors, struck and killed a pedestrian; instruction that the homicide was manslaughter if the defendant was doing an unlawful act *held* reversible error; speeding and driving under the influence are *mala prohibita,* and defendant is not liable unless "the excess" contributed to the accident).

32. Though it might seem, on first thoughts, that lack of permission could not have caused the death, the situation may have been such that, if the hunter had asked for permission, the landowner would have granted it only if his property were empty of people; if so, it could truly be said that the lack of permission caused the death. Thus in Commonwealth v. Samson, 130 Pa.Super. 65, 196 A. 564 (1938), the defendant operated a tenement house without a license in violation of a criminal law forbidding it. The tenement house collapsed, caught fire, and seven occupants were killed. Although the defendant argued that the same thing would have happened even if he had had a license, the court said no, because the licensing authority would not have given him a license if he had applied without fixing up the tenement house so as to make it safe for occupancy.

the careless pedestrian; if so the extra 10 m.p.h. in fact caused the death.[33]

View (3): He is not guilty unless his unlawful conduct *malum prohibitum* amounts to criminal negligence.[34] In other words, the fact that the defendant commits a misdemeanor (or other unlawful act) *malum prohibitum* adds nothing to the defendant's liability for manslaughter; if he is to be found guilty of manslaughter, it must be under the criminal-negligence branch. Of course, the fact that the defendant violated a criminal statute (or ordinance) may be some evidence of criminal negligence, especially in the case of a statute (e.g., punishing driving under the influence, or firing a gun in a public place) [35] aimed at protecting the general public from the possibility of death or serious bodily injury; but the violation is not conclusive evidence (or evidence *per se*) of criminal negligence.[36]

 **WESTLAW REFERENCES**

topic(203 110 48a) /p manslaughter /s "malum prohibitum"

(d) Assault or Battery Causing Death. An intentional battery is an unlawful act and one which is assignable to the *malum in se* category of unlawful acts. Therefore, it is almost universally held, as a specific instance of unlawful-act manslaughter, that one is guilty of involuntary manslaughter who intentionally inflicts bodily harm upon another person, as by a moderate blow with his fist, thereby causing an unintended and unforeseeable death to the victim (who, unknown to his attacker, may have a weak heart or a thin skull or a blood deficiency).[37] A criminal as-

33. Conversely, it may, under all the circumstances, be foreseeable that death may result from driving 35 in a 25-mile zone. Yet it may also be true in a particular case that the defendant could not have stopped in time even if he had been going at the lawful speed of 25 m.p.h.; if so the extra 10 m.p.h. did not cause the death.

34. People v. Pavlic, 227 Mich. 562, 199 N.W. 373 (1924) (defendant, by selling whiskey to victim, committed an unlawful act, a felony; victim drank it and on his way home fell asleep and died of acute alcoholism and exposure; conviction of manslaughter *held* reversed; this crime is not "inherently criminal"—i.e., is only *malum prohibitum*—and such an unlawful act is not enough for manslaughter liability unless done with recklessness); State v. Kellison, 233 Iowa 1274, 11 N.W.2d 371 (1943) (death resulting from violation of speed statute or rule of the road is not manslaughter unless defendant's conduct recklessly endangers others; but this rule is not applicable to drunken driving, which is *malum in se*); State v. Horton, 139 N.C. 588, 51 S.E. 945 (1905) (defendant, by hunting on lands without the landowner's consent, committed an unlawful act, a misdemeanor *malum prohibitum;* he shot at and killed the victim, thinking he was shooting at a wild turkey; conviction of manslaughter *held* reversed, since defendant's act was "not in itself dangerous to human life and negatived all idea of negligence"); Bartlett v. State, 569 P.2d 1235 (Wyo.1977) (speeding statute violation only *malum prohibitum*, so showing of criminal negligence required). See Annot., 29 A.L.R.4th 1230 (1984).

35. Compare a statute punishing intoxication in a public place—which is perhaps designed more for aesthetic than for safety purposes.

36. Commonwealth v. Hawkins, 157 Mass. 551, 32 N.E. 862 (1893) (battery prosecution on account of injury inflicted upon innocent bystander when defendant, in violation of ordinance, fired a pistol to scare boys who were annoy-

ing him; judge charged jury, on criminal-negligence battery, that violation of ordinance is not criminal negligence *per se*, but it was a circumstance to be considered by the jury in determining the question of criminal negligence; conviction of battery *held* affirmed).

37. Williams v. United States, 267 F.2d 625 (D.C.Cir. 1959) (case 1) (defendant hit victim with his fist; victim fell to the sidewalk, his head striking the concrete; he died from his head injuries; conviction of manslaughter *held* affirmed); State v. Bell, 38 Del. 328, 192 A. 553 (1937) (fair fist fight, willingly entered into by both parties, is unlawful act, and resulting death to one participant, though it was "not intended and was entirely unexpected," makes the survivor guilty of manslaughter); People v. Crenshaw, 298 Ill. 412, 131 N.E. 576 (1921) (defendant struck victim with fist, unintentionally and unexpectedly causing death; conviction of murder *held* reversed, for the crime was manslaughter, not murder); State v. Johnson, 102 Ind. 247, 1 N.E. 377 (1885) (defendant threw victim through saloon's screen door, cutting his thumb, which became infected, causing death from tetanus; battery being an unlawful act *malum in se*, the defendant is guilty of manslaughter); State v. Chavers, 294 So.2d 489 (La. 1974) (where assault caused death by aggravating pre-existing weakness, defendant guilty of manslaughter); Commonwealth v. McAfee, 108 Mass. 458, 11 Am.R. 383 (1871) (defendant hit drunken wife a blow with his open hand, causing her death; conviction of manslaughter *held* affirmed, for wife-beating, even of drunken wife, is an unlawful act); State v. Frazier, 339 Mo. 966, 98 S.W.2d 707 (1936) (defendant hit victim a moderate blow on the jaw, causing a slight cut which, because the victim was, unknown to the defendant, a hemophiliac, or "bleeder," caused his death; conviction of manslaughter *held* affirmed; battery is an unlawful act, and resulting death, though unintended and unlikely, is manslaughter.)

sault,[38] like a criminal battery, is an unlawful act *malum in se*. Therefore, if the defendant approaches close to another person intending to strike him but not to kill him, and the latter, who unknown to the defendant possesses a weak heart, has a heart seizure and dies as a result of fright produced by the threatened attack, the defendant is guilty of manslaughter, though he never touched the victim.[39]

The assault-and-battery kind of unlawful-act manslaughter has been singled out for criticism on the ground of its harshness [40] and on the ground of the lack of any rational theory-of-punishment basis for it.[41] If the modern trend away from "constructive crime" (including unlawful-act manslaughter as well as felony murder) continues, it should eventually sweep away this type of manslaughter from the Anglo-American criminal law.

38. See § 7.16 for the definition of a criminal assault. In almost all jurisdictions an attempted battery which misses the victim is a criminal assault; in a majority of jurisdictions intentionally causing mental apprehension in the victim constitutes an additional type of criminal assault.

39. Regina v. Dugal, 4 Que.L.R. 350 (Q.B.1878) (defendant, advancing on his father intending to strike him was prevented from doing so by bystanders; father, however, suffered fatal heart attack; conviction of manslaughter *held* affirmed).

In many jurisdictions it is a criminal assault intentionally to scare another though without any intent to injure him—as by pointing an unloaded gun at him in a threatening manner. In such a jurisdiction, if the victim, so threatened, should unforeseeably die of fright, from a weak heart, this would seem to be manslaughter of the assault-plus-death type: see Kwaku Mensah v. The King, [1946] A.C. 83, 90–91 (P.C.1945) (W.Afr.) (defendant claimed he pointed at victim what he thought was an unloaded gun, intending only to scare; the gun went off accidentally, killing victim; if defendant's claim is true, it is still manslaughter, the assault being an unlawful act).

Cf. In re Heigho, 18 Idaho 566, 110 P. 1029 (1910) (defendant struck another in the face with his fist; the latter's mother-in-law, witnessing the event, suffered a heart attack and died; on pre-trial habeas corpus to secure defendant's release for lack of probable cause of manslaughter, the above evidence *held* sufficient, so writ of habeas corpus denied).

No doubt it is often difficult to prove that defendant's conduct, not involving any physical blow, in fact caused the victim's death through fright, e.g., Hubbard v. Commonwealth, 304 Ky. 818, 202 S.W.2d 634 (1947) (conviction reversed for lack of proof of causal connection); but the

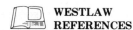 **WESTLAW REFERENCES**

203k58 203k36 203k63 /p manslaughter /s assault battery

(e) The Future of Unlawful-Act Manslaughter. As pointed out earlier in this book,[42] the traditional but vague distinction between an unlawful act which is *malum in se* and one which is *malum prohibitum*, with quite different criminal-law consequences flowing from this distinction, ought to be abandoned. Some courts, in fact, seem to get on very well without making the distinction. Some cases, as noted above, while recognizing the existence of a separate branch of involuntary manslaughter in the commission of an unlawful act, seem to apply the same rule in the case of all unlawful acts without regard to whether they are in the one category or the other.[43] Other cases, while acknowledging the existence of unlawful-act manslaughter, suggest making the more specific distinction

modern trend, at least in the torts field, is to recognize liability for death or bodily harm resulting from severe emotional distress intentionally or recklessly caused, see Prosser, Insult and Outrage, 44 Calif.L.Rev. 40 (1956).

An assault causing death would be murder, of course, if the defendant intended to kill the other, as where, knowing of the other's weak heart, he intentionally scares him to death. See § 7.2.

40. J. Hall, General Principles of Criminal Law 259–60 (2d ed. 1960) (cases expounding the rule termed "glaring examples of the dominance of constructive criminal homicide in the United States").

41. Model Penal Code § 210.3 abolishes from the manslaughter concept the entire field of unlawful-act manslaughter, including manslaughter based on assaults and batteries, stating, as to the latter, that neither the deterrence nor correction (rehabilitation) theories of punishment (see § 1.5) requires such a harsh rule. See Model Penal Code § 210.3, Comment at 77 (1980).

42. See § 1.6(b).

43. State v. Hupf, 48 Del. 254, 101 A.2d 355 (1953) ("Such a distinction has never been recognized in our cases, and we see no reason to adopt it. To do so would be to introduce confusion and uncertainty into a rule of law now plain and understandable."); See also the *Potter, Williams* and *Penny* cases, supra notes 25, 31. Under such a view, an unintended death resulting from an unlawful act (without regard to the unlawful act's classification) is manslaughter only if death is the foreseeable or natural consequence of the defendant's conduct in committing the unlawful act, or only if the death is caused by the "unlawful excess" which makes otherwise lawful conduct unlawful, according to the views considered above.

between an unlawful act in violation of a criminal law designed to protect persons against death or serious injury, on the one hand, and designed for other purposes (e.g., to protect property), on the other, rather than drawing the uncertain line between an act *malum in se* and one *malum prohibitum.* [44] The unlawful-act manslaughter statutes themselves sometimes draw a distinction along these lines. But even where the distinction is made between criminal statutes (or ordinances) which are designed to protect against death or serious bodily injury and statutes (ordinances) with other purposes, still the question ought to be not whether the crime is generally dangerous, but whether the defendant's conduct in the particular death-causing situation was under the circumstances dangerous.[45]

A modern tendency, however, is to go further and, by statute, to abandon the whole concept of involuntary manslaughter based upon unlawful conduct alone, leaving the field occupied solely by involuntary manslaughter based upon criminal negligence or recklessness (although of course the fact of the defendant's unlawful conduct may generally be looked to as evidence of criminal negligence). There is no logical reason for inflicting manslaughter punishment on one who unintentionally kills another simply because he is committing a traffic violation, unless it makes sense to punish the one-in-a-thousand traffic violation, which by bad luck produces an unexpected death, far more severely than the nine hundred and ninety-nine violations which happily do not produce any such devastating result. As Holmes suggested in discussing an analogous hypothetical case involv-

ing felony-murder (a one-in-a-thousand death resulting from a shot fired at another's chickens in an endeavor to steal them): the act of shooting at chickens knowing them to belong to another is no more or less blameworthy because an unexpected accident (the bullet hits and kills a person whose presence could not have been suspected) results, and if the object of the felony-murder rule in a larceny case "is to prevent stealing, it would do better to hang one thief in every thousand by lot." [46]

It is true that, in the case of crimes defined in terms of bad results, it is often something of an accident whether the specified result occurs or not. Where one seriously wounds another by shooting at him with intent to kill, or severely but unintentionally injures him by reckless driving, chance often takes a hand in deciding whether the victim dies or recovers, and thus whether the defendant receives a greater or lesser punishment. If the bad result which happens is actually intended, or if it is recklessly produced (especially by one conscious of the risk), it does not seem too harsh to make the severity of his punishment depend somewhat on the actual result, however accidental. Where, however, the result is both unintended and produced without any consciousness of the risk of producing it, it seems too harsh and illogical.[47] Involuntary manslaughter, therefore, ought, on principle, to be limited to the situation of unintended homicide by criminal negligence. The modern trend is properly in this direction.

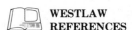

WESTLAW REFERENCES

"involuntary manslaughter" /p ("unlawful act" /s critic!) (pray /s 378 +4 1322)

---

44. See State v. McIver, 175 N.C. 761, 94 S.E. 682 (1917); State v. McNichols, 188 Kan. 582, 363 P.2d 467 (1961).

45. Compare United States v. Walker, 380 A.2d 1388 (D.C.App.1977) (crime defined as killing with "the intent to commit a misdemeanor dangerous in itself," carrying pistol without a license suffices because it is inherently dangerous).

46. O. Holmes, The Common Law 58 (1881).

47. See R. Moreland, The Law of Homicide 195 (1952), criticizing the misdemeanor-manslaughter doctrine; and consider State v. Pray, 378 A.2d 1322 (Me.1977): "The

flaw in the concept is that a person may be convicted of unlawful-act manslaughter even though the person's conduct does not create a perceptible risk of death. Thus, a person is punished for the fortuitous result, the death, although the jury never has to determine whether the person was at fault with respect to the death. The concept violates the important principle that a person's criminal liability for an act should be proportioned to his or her moral culpability for that act. The wrongdoer should be punished for the unlawful act and for homicide if he or she is at fault with respect to the death, but should not be punished for a fortuitous result merely because the act was unlawful."

"involuntary manslaughter" /p malum +2 se
    prohibitum /s distinction distinguish**

---

§ 7.14 Assault and Battery—Classification

Assault and battery,[1] which were common-law misdemeanors, today exist as statutory crimes in all American jurisdictions.[2] Simple assault and simple battery are punishable (generally as misdemeanors) under all the American criminal codes, although in some states the appropriate statute contains no definition of these crimes, leaving the matter to be determined by reference to the common law.

(a) Assault and Battery Distinguished. Although the word "assault" is sometimes used loosely to include a battery, and the whole expression "assault and battery" to mean battery,[3] it is more accurate to distinguish between the two separate crimes, assault and battery, on the basis of the existence or non-existence of physical injury or offensive touching. *Battery* requires such an injury or touching. *Assault,* on the other hand, needs no such physical contact; it might almost be said that it affirmatively requires an absence of contact.[4] Battery, like murder and manslaughter, malicious mischief and arson, thus is a crime defined in terms of conduct which produces a specified harmful result (injury or offensive touching). Assault, as we shall see, may in some jurisdictions be committed in either one of two ways—attempted battery or intentional frightening—the former requiring no harmful physical result but the latter requiring the result, not of physical contact as with battery, but rather of mental apprehension in the mind of the victim.

 WESTLAW REFERENCES

37k48 /p battery /s injury touching violence

37k48 37k49 /p battery /s intent "mens rea"
    (mental mind /3 state)

37k48 /p assault /s apprehensi** fear** frighten**

(b) Aggravated Assault or Battery. Although the common law created the twin crimes (misdemeanors) of assault and battery, in modern times legislatures have added the more serious crimes (felonies) of aggravated assaults and batteries (e.g., assault, battery with intent to kill, rob, rape; assault, battery with a dangerous weapon). It is nevertheless true that the common law did recognize the existence of a few aggravated batteries, such as mayhem (which required not merely a bodily injury but in addition a dismemberment type of injury) and rape (involving physical contact of a narrow, specialized sort); and the common law crime of robbery (the unlawful taking of another's property by violence amounting to a battery or by threat amounting to an assault) might be considered an aggravated type of assault and battery.[5]

---

§ 7.14

1. See generally Perkins, Non-Homicide Offenses Against the Person, 26 B.U.L.Rev. 119 (1946).

2. This is not to suggest, however, that every jurisdiction has statutory crimes labelled both "assault" and "battery" or that the statutory crimes so labelled necessarily coincide with the common law definitions. In some jurisdictions, the attempted-battery type of assault is prosecuted simply as an attempt to commit the crime of battery, and there is either no crime called assault or else the crime of assault is limited to the placing of the victim in apprehension of a battery.

In some jurisdictions there is no statutory crime of battery, but (as in Model Penal Code § 211.1) the crime of assault is defined to include what is usually classified as battery.

3. Model Penal Code § 211.1 defines "assault" to include both assault (attempted battery and attempted scaring) and battery.

4. It is sometimes said, somewhat inaccurately, that every battery necessarily includes an assault. But note two things: (1) If *A* intentionally shoots at *B* with a loaded gun, the bullet hitting and injuring him, *A*'s attempt to hit *B* constitutes an assault and his success in hitting *B* amounts to a battery. *A* cannot, however, be convicted of both assault and battery and sentenced consecutively for each, for his assault blends with, and is not a crime separate from, his battery. (This is but a part of the general principle that one who attempts to commit any crime, and succeeds in his attempt, cannot be convicted of both the attempt and the completed crime. See § 6.3). (2) A battery of the criminal-negligence type, as where motorist *A* by reckless driving unintentionally injures pedestrian *B*, does not include an assault, which requires an intent to injure or (alternately, in many jurisdictions) to frighten. So at most it can properly be said only that every *intentional* battery necessarily includes an assault.

5. Mayhem (see § 7.13) is generally treated, like assault and battery, as a crime against the person; but rape

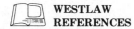

**WESTLAW
REFERENCES**

37k54 37k55 37k56 /p (intent*** /s kill murder rob!
   steal rape) (battery /s weapon)

---

§ 7.15   Battery

Criminal battery, sometimes defined briefly as the unlawful application of force to the person of another, may be divided into its three basic elements: (1) the defendant's conduct (act or omission); (2) his "mental state," which may be an intent to kill or injure, or criminal negligence, or perhaps the doing of an unlawful act; and (3) the harmful result to the victim, which may be either a bodily injury or an offensive touching. What might otherwise be a battery may be justified; and the consent of the victim may under some circumstances constitute a defense.

(a) The Harmful Result: Bodily Injury and Offensive Touching. As indicated above,[1] battery is a crime which is defined, like murder and manslaughter, in terms not only of conduct but also of a specified result of conduct. The required result for battery might be termed "bodily injury" so as to include such obvious matters as wounds caused by bullets or knives, and broken limbs or bruises inflicted by sticks, stones, feet or fists.[2] A temporarily painful blow will suffice, though afterward there is no wound or bruise or even pain to show for it. But, in addition

to these more obvious bodily injuries, offensive touchings (as where a man puts his hands upon a girl's body or kisses a woman against her will,[3] or where one person spits into another's face [4]) will also suffice for battery under the traditional view.

The modern approach, as reflected in the Model Penal Code,[5] is to limit battery to instances of physical injury and cover unwanted sexual advances by other statutes. This is the prevailing view in those jurisdictions with new criminal codes, as reflected in the use of such statutory terms as "physical injury," "bodily injury," "bodily harm," "physical harm," "force or violence upon the person," or, occasionally, "serious bodily injury." A minority of these codes follow a much broader view, sometimes extending the crime to any touching or physical contact,[6] but more often requiring that the contact be "offensive," "insulting or provoking," or done "in a rude, insolent, or angry manner."

**WESTLAW
REFERENCES**

37k48 /p battery /s physical** bodily /3 harm**
   injur**

(b) The Wrongful Conduct. The force used need not be applied directly to the body of the victim, as in the usual case where one shoots at another or strikes him with knife, club or fist. It may also be indirectly applied to the victim, as where one whips the horse

---

is usually classified as a sex crime, and robbery (see § 8.11) as a property crime.

§ 7.15

1. See § 7.14(a).

2. Thus, battery is not a lesser included offense of an attempted murder where defendant shot at but missed the victim. State v. Dauzat, 392 So.2d 393 (La.1980).

3. E.g., Wood v. Commonwealth, 149 Va. 401, 140 S.E. 114 (1927) (defendant storekeeper put hands on the bosom of a 14-year-old girl when she came to his store); Lynch v. Commonwealth, 131 Va. 762, 109 S.E. 427 (1921) (defendant, a black, told white woman he'd like to kiss her, and when she refused the invitation, he touched her, said he meant no insult, and left); Weaver v. State, 66 Tex.Crim. R. 366, 146 S.W. 927 (1912) (defendant storekeeper kissing pretty shopper commits battery if he does it against her will but not if her conduct while being kissed indicates she finds it to be aggreeable).

4. See Commonwealth v. McKie, 67 Mass. 61, 61 Am. Dec. 410 (1854) (victim spat in defendant's face, which led

defendant to beat victim with a dangerous weapon; the court terms the spitting an "assault"); Regina v. Cotesworth, 6 Mod. 172, 87 Eng.Rep. 928 (1705).

5. Model Penal Code § 211.1 covers only causing "bodily injury," on the ground that "offensive touching is not sufficiently serious to be made criminal, except in the case of sexual assaults as provided" elsewhere in the Code. Model Penal Code § 211.1, Comment at 185 (1980). But see United States v. Eades, 615 F.2d 617 (4th Cir.1980) (Maryland third degree sexual offense of unwanted touching of genital or anal area causing fear is a special form of battery, and thus is encompassed within coverage of federal battery statute).

6. N.H.Rev.Stat.Ann. 631:2–a.

Similarly, the federal statute defining battery as merely a "striking" of the victim has been construed to require no injury at all. United States v. Gan, 636 F.2d 28 (2d Cir. 1980); United States v. Martin, 536 F.2d 535 (2d Cir.1976). What is required is physical contact. United States v. Iron Shell, 633 F.2d 77 (8th Cir.1980).

on which the victim is riding, causing the horse to bolt and throw his rider,[7] or where one compels another to touch him in a way offensive to the other.[8] So too a battery may be committed by administering a poison or by infecting with a disease.[9]

As with other cause-and-result crimes, battery may be committed, if the other elements of the crime are present, by creating a situation under which the victim injures himself, as by telling a blind man walking toward a precipice that all is clear ahead, thus intentionally or recklessly causing him to fall and hurt himself,[10] or even by a simple omission to act where there is a duty to act, as where a hospital attendant fails to warn his blind patient that he is headed for an open window, thereby intentionally or recklessly causing him to fall to the ground. And, as is true of all cause-and-result crimes, one may be guilty of battery though his aim at *A* is bad and he hits *B*, the wrong person.[11]

 WESTLAW REFERENCES

37k48 /p battery /s "physical contact" (cause* /2 harm injury)

(c) The Mental Element: Intent, Negligence, Unlawfulness. There are three dis-

tinct ways of committing a battery, distinguishable from each other on the basis of the mental element with which the defendant conducts himself: (1) where the defendant acts (or omits to act) with intent to injure; (2) where he acts with criminal negligence but has no intent to injure; (3) where his conduct, though it does not amount to criminal negligence, is nevertheless unlawful, but he has no intent to injure. When his conduct, under these conditions, actually causes injury to another person, he is clearly guilty of battery under the first circumstance and (in most jurisdictions) under the second; his guilt is not so clear under the third.[12]

(1) Intent-to-Injure Battery: The most common type of battery is the intentional injury (or offensive touching).[13] One who, with intent to injure, does an act (or omits to do an act when he has a duty to act) which is the legal cause of an injury, is guilty of a criminal battery.[14] All intentional injuries and touchings are not, however, necessarily batteries, for they may be justified;[15] thus it is no battery for one to pull a drowning swimmer out of the river by the hair of his head,[16] or

---

7. Cf. People v. Moore, 50 Hun 356, 3 N.Y.S. 159 (Sup. Ct.1888) (defendant without justification took the lines of a horse-drawn sleigh in which victim was riding and turned it about; conviction of battery *held* affirmed, though defendant did not ever touch the victim).

8. E.g., Beausoliel v. United States, 107 F.2d 292 (D.C. Cir.1939) (taxi driver exposed a private organ and persuaded 6-year-old girl to hold it; conviction of battery *held* affirmed, though she touched him rather than vice versa).

9. State v. Monroe, 121 N.C. 677, 28 S.E. 547 (1897) (poison in candy); State v. Lankford, 29 Del. 594, 102 A. 63 (1917) (disease).

Model Penal Code § 211.1 defines the crime in terms of causing "bodily injury," defined in § 210.0(2) as "physical pain, illness or any impairment of physical condition." This includes that "caused indirectly, as, for example, by exposing another to inclement weather or by non-therapeutic administration of a drug or narcotic," meaning it is "unnecessary to make special provision for occasioning these harms, as some existing statutes have done." Model Penal Code § 211.1, Comment at 187–88 (1980).

10. Cf. Regina v. Martin, L.R. 8 Q.B.D. 54 (1881) (just as play at theatre ended and just before theatre patrons started to leave, defendant shut off gaslights on stairway and blocked exit with iron bar, causing a crush which injured two patrons; conviction of battery *held* affirmed).

11. See § 3.12(d).

12. Note at the outset the close relationship between criminal homicide (especially involuntary manslaughter) and battery with respect to the mental element. Intentional killing, of course, generally constitutes murder; killing by criminal negligence is manslaughter; and killing by unlawful-act conduct is manslaughter in most jurisdictions, though there is a trend toward abolishing it as a seperate type of manslaughter.

13. This type of battery is included within virtually all of the modern codes. Some statutes, though not specifically mentioning intent-to-injure, recognize the lesser mental state of recklessness as sufficient, in which case surely a conviction on proof of intent may be had.

14. Of course, if his intent is not merely to injure but rather to kill, but his aim is not quite true and he succeeds only in causing an injury, he is guilty of a battery. See § 3.11(e).

Under some forms of battery statutes, an intent to strike the victim without intending injury is sufficient. United States v. Gran, 636 F.2d 28 (2d Cir.1980).

15. See § 7.15(e).

16. See State v. Beck, 1 Hill, 363, 26 Am.Dec. 190 (S.C.1833).

for a man to lay hands upon a young lady to prevent her from heading into danger.[17]

(2) Criminal-Negligence Battery: In most jurisdictions today battery may be committed by conduct amounting to criminal negligence which legally causes an injury.[18] Some of the cases so holding have spoken in fictional language—generally to the effect that for battery one must intend to injure, but that criminal negligence supplies the intent.[19] Now that the principle of battery based upon criminal negligence is well established, it is more accurate to stop using the fiction and recognize this as a separate type of battery from the intent-to-injure type.[20]

There remains the question of the meaning of "criminal negligence" in connection with the crime of battery. It means something more than ordinary (tort) negligence, which exists when one's conduct creates an unreasonable risk of harm to others.[21] Doubtless, the defendant's conduct must involve not only an unreasonable risk of bodily injury to another person or to other persons; it must also involve a high degree of such a risk.[22] When

the point has not been specifically addressed by statute, the cases have typically not made it clear whether, in addition to this requirement of risk-creation, the defendant must subjectively realize the risk, in order to be guilty of a criminal battery.[23]

In the modern codes, a substantial majority of the battery-type statutes expressly state that the crime may be committed by recklessness—that is, where there is subjective awareness of the high risk of physical injury.[24] None of these codes recognizes mere negligence as an across-the-board basis of liability for battery. The Model Penal Code generally requires that the bodily injury be done "purposely, knowingly or recklessly" (i.e., with consciousness of the risk), but negligence is sufficient where the harm is caused "with a deadly weapon."[25] This exception to the subjective requirement for this offense is "justified on the ground that any use of an instrument or substance known for its capability of causing death should be accompanied by special care and restraint."[26] Most of the new codes have adopted this position.

17. State v. Hemphill, 162 N.C. 632, 78 S.E. 167 (1913) (under one view of the evidence: at request of girl's grandmother, her natural guardian, defendant intervened to prevent the girl being "led astray"). See Annot., 45 L.R.A. (n.s.) 455 (1913).

18. See Perkins, Non-Homicide Offenses Against the Person, 26 B.U.L.Rev. 119, 125–26 (1946); L. Hall, Assault and Battery by the Reckless Motorist, 31 J.Crim.L. & C. 133 (1940); Comment, 22 Mich.L.Rev. 717 (1924).

19. E.g., Fish v. Michigan, 62 F.2d 659 (6th Cir.1933) (if one recklessly injures another, it is a battery, for the law "holds him to have intended" the injury and "treats him as if he had done an intended wrong"); State v. Anania, 340 A.2d 207 (Me.1975) (criminal intent established by intentional doing of acts which have the inherent potential of doing bodily harm and doing them negligently, as with intentional firing of gun at close range); Brimhall v. State, 31 Ariz. 522, 255 P. 165 (1927) (reckless driving); Woodward v. State, 164 Miss. 468, 144 So. 895 (1932) (reckless driving); State v. Schutte, 87 N.J.L. 15, 93 A. 112 (Sup.Ct.1915) (reckless driving).

Perhaps the reason why the fiction is used is that with the tort of battery an intention to injure or touch offensively is needed; there is no tort battery of the negligence type; but this is not because negligently-caused injuries are not covered in tort law, but rather because such injuries are torts of another name—the tort of negligence.

20. Commonwealth v. Hawkins, 157 Mass. 551, 32 N.E. 862 (1893) (reckless shooting; "the better opinion is that nothing more is required than an intentional doing of an

action which, by reason of its wanton or grossly negligent character, exposes another to personal injury, and causes such injury").

21. Radley v. State, 197 Ind. 200, 150 N.E. 97 (1926) (conviction of battery based on negligent driving *held* reversed; for criminal liability there must be "such wanton and reckless disregard of probable harmful consequences to others as to imply the infliction of a willful, intentional injury"); People v. Waxman, 232 App.Div. 90, 249 N.Y.S. 180 (Sup.Ct. 1931) (inexperienced driver hit and injured boy on sidewalk trying to avoid child on street; conviction of battery *held* reversed, for evidence shows only ordinary negligence, not recklessness); Woodward v. State, 164 Miss. 468, 144 So. 895 (1932) ("mere negligence would not impute an intent" to injure necessary for battery).

22. Negligence of this sort might be called "gross negligence" or "negligence of a high degree," to distinguish it from "recklessness," which involves a subjectiveness which "gross negligence" does not. See § 3.7.

23. Hall, Assault and Battery by the Reckless Motorist, 31 J.Crim.L. & C. 133, 149 (1940), suggests that the problem is seldom acute because "most sober men will not drive in a reckless manner without being conscious of the risk they are creating."

24. See § 3.7(a), (b) for a discussion of the distinction between recklessness and negligence.

25. Model Penal Code § 211.1(1).

26. Model Penal Code § 211.1, Comment at 191 (1980).

(3) Unlawful-Act Battery: Absent a controlling statutory definition of battery, the law is not so clear as to whether one is guilty of a battery where he injures another as a result of his commission of an unlawful act (e.g., a misdemeanor or ordinance violation), where he intends no injury and his conduct does not amount to criminal negligence. Some cases have held that, if the defendant's wrongful conduct is *malum in se,* any injury resulting therefrom is necessarily a battery; [27] whereas, if it is only *malum prohibitum,* the defendant, to be guilty, must be found to intend injury or to be criminally negligent. [28] Some cases, however, have held the defendant guilty of battery where bodily injury results from an unlawful act, without regard to any distinction between *malum prohibitum* and *malum in se.* [29] Conversely, others have held, also without regard to this same distinction, that there is no liability for injury resulting from an unlawful act, without an intent to injure or criminal negligence. [30] It has already been suggested, in connection with the unlawful-act type of manslaughter, that there should be no such separate category of involuntary manslaughter; [31] and the suggestion is equally valid with respect to the crime of battery. With few exceptions, this type of battery is not included in the modern codes.

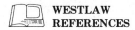

WESTLAW REFERENCES

topic(37) /p battery /s (inten! /3 injur** harm***)
topic(37) /p battery /s (criminal** /2 negligen**)

(d) Aggravated Battery. All jurisdictions have statutes, variously worded, which define aggravated batteries and punish them as felonies. [32] Traditionally, the most common statute of this type was one covering "assault [33] with intent to murder" (or to kill, or to do great bodily injury, or to rape, rob, or commit mayhem).

The crime of "assault with intent to murder" or "to kill" or "to inflict great bodily harm" cannot, it seems clear, be committed by a battery of the criminal negligence type. It is not enough for such a crime that the defendant's conduct create a high degree of risk of death, or of great bodily harm; he must actually intend to cause the specific result required by the statute. [34] Occasionally, however, a court has apparently been misled

27. King v. State, 157 Tenn. 635, 11 S.W.2d 904 (1928) (defendant, driving while intoxicated, struck and injured the victim; conviction of battery held affirmed, because driving while intoxicated is *malum in se*); Commonwealth v. Smith, 312 Mass. 557, 45 N.E.2d 742 (1942) (defendant, attempting suicide—a matter of which Massachusetts in Commonwealth v. Mink, 123 Mass. 422 (1877), had held to be *malum in se* for purposes for unlawful-act manslaughter—unintentionally shot her lover who intervened to prevent the suicide, *held,* battery, citing *Mink* case.)

Compare Commonwealth v. Adams, 114 Mass. 323, 19 Am.R. 362 (1873) (defendant, speeding in sleigh in violation of ordinance, struck pedestrian; conviction of battery *held* reversed, because speeding is *malum prohibitum* and not *malum in se*).

28. Commonwealth v. Adams, supra note 27. Under this view, then, the fact that the defendant was committing an unlawful act *malum prohibitum* adds nothing to his guilt of battery, except insofar as the violation is some evidence of criminal negligence; e.g., Commonwealth v. Hawkins, 157 Mass. 551, 32 N.E. 862 (1893).

29. State v. Lehman, 131 Minn. 427, 155 N.W. 399 (1915) (defendant intentionally fired gun in public place to frighten boys, accidentally striking victim; conviction of battery upheld on ground of unlawful act, without, however, labeling the crime of firing gun in public place as either *malum in se* or *malum prohibitum*).

30. State v. Agnew, 202 N.C. 755, 164 S.E. 578 (1932) (to convict of battery for injuries resulting from automo-

bile accident involving breach of statute, injury must be intended or proximate result of criminal negligence).

31. See § 7.13(e).

32. In addition to the possibilities discussed in the text following, there is, for example, "atrocious assault and battery," construed in State v. Crumedy, 76 N.J. 319, 387 A.2d 357 (1978), to cover doing a minor injury by an outrageous act, such as the defendant's conduct in telling the victims they had cancer and that he had legal authority to examine them.

33. The word "assault" in this connection means both assault and battery.

34. Scott v. State, 49 Ark. 156, 4 S.W. 750 (1887) (defendant with extreme recklessness fired both barrels of gun loaded with shot into room in which a group of persons sat, hitting some but killing no one; conviction of assault with intent to kill *held* reversed; extreme recklessness without intent to kill is not enough); State v. Richardson, 179 Iowa 770, 162 N.W. 28 (1917) (defendant, by driving in a criminally negligent manner, struck and badly injured the victim; conviction of assault with intent to inflict great bodily injury *held* reversed); People v. Hopper, 69 Colo. 124, 169 P. 152 (1917) (defendant, by driving recklessly, injured victim; on charge of assault with a deadly weapon with an intent to inflict upon the person of another bodily injury, *held* that trial court properly directed verdict of acquittal of this aggravated battery).

by its love for fictions to reach the opposite result.[35] The existence of the required intent to kill or murder [36] is often inferred from the defendant's use of a deadly weapon upon the body of his victim,[37] although such use is not conclusive of the intent to kill.[38] On similar principles, an assault "with intent to maim" requires a specific intent to disfigure or dismember; it is not enough recklessly or unlawfully to cause such an injury.[39]

These battery-with-intent-to statutes originated "to cure the disparity between the drastic penalties authorized for serious offenses such as murder and rape and the relatively trivial sanctions applied to an attempt to commit those offenses." [40] They persist in jurisdictions which have not recently revised their criminal codes,[41] but virtually all modern codes have eliminated this form of aggravated battery because the problem has been resolved by grading the crime of attempt according to the seriousness of the objective crime.

Modern codes do, however, with rare exception, define various types of aggravated batteries. Often the specified aggravating factor is the means used to commit the battery, such as by any weapon or, much more commonly, by what is variously called a "deadly weapon," "dangerous weapon," "dangerous instrumentality," or "deadly weapon or dangerous instrumentality." Certain other means have also been occasionally particularized as aggravating, such as using poison, entering a home, or wearing a mask.

With reference to the crime of assault with a deadly (or dangerous) weapon, the word "weapon" is not limited to man-made articles whose purpose is to kill, like guns and knives; it includes such miscellaneous articles as rocks, tree limbs and automobiles; and any such weapon is "deadly" or "dangerous" when

35. Easley v. State, 49 Ga.App. 275, 175 S.E. 23 (1934) (defendant drove recklessly and under the influence, injuring the victim; conviction of assault with intent to kill *held* affirmed, for recklessness and unlawfulness supply the intent to kill). And note People v. Benson, 321 Ill. 605, 152 N.E. 514 (1926) (defendant by reckless driving injured victim; conviction of assault with a deadly weapon with intent to inflict upon the person of another bodily injury *held* affirmed, with no consideration given to the failure of proof of a specific intent to injure).

36. Some aggravated-assault statutes are worded "with intent to murder," others "with intent to kill." The former wording, like the latter, requires a specific intent to kill; this is so even though murder itself may be committed without an intent to kill, as with murder with intent to do serious bodily harm, depraved-heart murder and felony murder. See Brosman, J., in United States v. Short, 4 U.S.C.M.A. 437, 16 C.M.R. 11 (1954) (rape, but not assault with intent to rape, may be committed without an intent to overcome the woman's resistance, as where he unreasonably and mistakenly believes she consents; this "anomaly is no greater than that involved in holding that an assault with intent to murder requires a specific intent to kill, whereas the crime of murder may be made out with a lesser intent").

But, assault "with intent to kill" covers those cases in which there is no malice, that is, where there is intent to kill but also some provocation, justification or excuse which would reduce the crime to manslaughter had death occurred. See Logan v. United States, 483 A.2d 664 (D.C. App.1984) (collecting cases). Assault "with intent to murder" does not cover conduct which, if death occurred, would be only manslaughter. State v. Faulkner, 301 Md. 482, 483 A.2d 759 (1984).

37. Nunley v. State, 223 Ark. 838, 270 S.W.2d 904 (1954) (defendant shot six bullets at ex-wife's new husband, wounding him in the wrist, arm and both hips; conviction of assault with intent to kill *held* affirmed, for intent to kill may be inferred from circumstances like the use of a deadly weapon); Wimbush v. State, 224 Md. 488, 168 A.2d 500 (1961), noted at 21 Md.L.Rev. 254 (1961) (defendant shot his mistress, who had acquired a new lover in the face, arm and hand; conviction of assault with intent to murder *held* affirmed, an intent to kill being inferable from use of deadly weapon; as to defendant's defense that he was an excellent marksman who could have killed if he wished, the court added—wrongly—that no intent to kill need be shown).

Cf. Scroggins v. State, 119 Tex.Crim.R. 32, 45 S.W.2d 983 (1932) (defendant hit victim so hard with pistol butt and knucks as to render him insane; conviction of assault with intent to murder *held* reversed for insufficient evidence of intent to kill; if defendant intended to kill, why did he not shoot?).

38. Colbert v. State, 84 Ga.App. 632, 66 S.E.2d 836 (1951) (conviction of assault with intent to kill *held* reversed, because jury was improperly instructed in effect that the use of deadly weapon necessarily shows intent to kill).

39. Banovitch v. Commonwealth, 196 Va. 210, 83 S.E.2d 369 (1954), noted at 14 Okla.L.Rev. 44 (1961) (defendant, practicing as a doctor, prescribed zinc chloride for cancer of the nose; victim, who had no cancer, lost the nose; conviction of assault with intent to maim *held* reversed).

40. Model Penal Code § 211.1, Comment at 181–82 (1980).

41. See statutes cited id. at n. 39.

used in a manner calculated to produce death or serious bodily injury.[42] A loaded gun fired recklessly is a dangerous weapon,[43] but an unloaded gun, not used as a bludgeon, ought not to be considered a dangerous or deadly weapon [44] for purposes of aggravated battery.

The Model Penal Code departed from prior statutory law in dispensing with the grading of batteries based upon the status of the victim. Such grading was deemed "unnecessary in view of the ample severity of penalties against murder and all serious attacks upon the person, regardless of the identity of the victim." [45] Yet, status of the victim is very frequently recognized as an aggravating factor even in the modern codes. Most common are provisions making it aggravated battery to commit battery against a police officer, but the same approach has sometimes been taken as to firemen, jailers, teachers, bus drivers, state officials generally, participants in court proceedings, and those who are youthful, elderly or pregnant. Statutes of this general type raise questions (not always resolved by the specific language used) concerning whether the offense is of the strict liability type as to the victim's status or whether instead the defendant must have known (or, perhaps, should have known) of that status, and whether the victim must have been involved (again, either with or without the defendant's knowl-

edge) in a certain way in his official activities at the time of the battery.[46]

Yet another very common aggravating circumstance specified in modern battery-type statutes has to do with the consequences. Virtually all of these provisions state that it is a higher degree of battery if the defendant inflicts serious bodily injury. Most of the provisions of this general type require also that this higher level of harm have been intentionally or knowingly done, but some appear not to require any such higher mental state. Then there also exist in a few states provisions essentially the reverse of this latter type: the crime is aggravated battery because of the defendant's intent to do more serious injury, even though the more serious harm did not actually occur.

WESTLAW REFERENCES

topic(37) /p "aggravated battery" /s inten! /3 kill murder maim injure harm rape

(e) Defenses to Battery. What would otherwise be a battery may be justified, as where one intentionally touches or injures his adversary in self-defense or defense of others, or to prevent the commission of a crime, or even, in an appropriate case, to save his property from harm.[47] A parent may use moderate force to spank his child, and a schoolmaster his pupil, in order to enforce discipline, without entitling the child to begin a criminal prosecution

---

42. Acers v. United States, 164 U.S. 388, 17 S.Ct. 91, 41 L.Ed. 481 (1896) (defendant struck victim hard with heavy stone, fracturing his skull; this was *held* to be a deadly weapon, from which jury might find an intent to kill); Thomas v. State, 524 P.2d 664 (Alaska 1974) (telephone a deadly weapon, given manner of use); People v. Benson, 321 Ill. 605, 152 N.E. 514 (1926) (automobile driven recklessly is deadly weapon); State v. Sudderth, 184 N.C. 753, 114 S.E. 828 (1922) (automobile driven recklessly is deadly weapon); State v. Hill, 298 Or. 270, 692 P.2d 100 (1984) (automobile driven recklessly is a deadly weapon). See also Annots., 8 A.L.R.4th 1268 (1981) (parts of body); 8 A.L.R.4th 842 (1981) (walking cane); 7 A.L.R.4th 607 (1981) (dog).

Many modern codes substantially follow Model Penal Code § 210.0(4), defining "deadly weapon" as "any firearm, or other weapon, device, instrument, material or substance, whether animate or inanimate, which in the manner it is used or is intended to be used is known to be capable of producing death or serious bodily injury."

43. Commonwealth v. Hawkins, 157 Mass. 551, 32 N.E. 862 (1893) (conviction of assault with a dangerous weapon *held* affirmed).

44. Luitze v. State, 204 Wis. 78, 234 N.W. 382 (1931); Contra: People v. Egan, 77 Cal.App. 279, 246 P. 337 (1926). See Annot., 79 A.L.R.2d 1412, 1423–26 (1961) for other cases on the subject.

45. Model Penal Code § 211.1, Comment at 185 (1980).

46. Such questions also arise when a battery-type statute is defined so as to apply only in specified circumstances, as is true on the federal level. See, e.g., United States v. Boone, 738 F.2d 763 (6th Cir.1984) (prosecution of defendant, who pushed woman pedestrian down and took her purse, under 18 U.S.C.A. § 111 for assaulting a federal official "while engaged in or on account of the performance of his official duties"; *held,* per United States v. Feola, 420 U.S. 671, 95 S.Ct. 1255, 43 L.Ed.2d 541 (1975), defendant need not know woman was a federal judge, and statute applied because she was "walking to the federal courthouse to do legal research").

47. See ch. 5.

for battery.[48] The old view which allowed a husband to beat his wife to enforce domestic discipline seems, however, to have vanished from the law as an accompaniment of the emancipation of the wife in property and other matters.

What is the effect of the victim's consent to the defendant's touch or injury?[49] Consent is a defense to what otherwise would be a minor sort of offensive touching, such as a kiss or caress;[50] and pretended consent in order to induce the other to commit the touching is also a defense.[51] Consent of the patient is a defense to a doctor who performs an operation; consent of a participant in sports, such as football and boxing, is a defense to tackles and blows, not likely to kill or seriously injure, delivered in accordance with the rules of the game.[52] Other things being equal, consent is more effective for offensive touchings and insignificant bodily injuries than for hard blows and more serious injuries.[53]

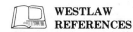 **WESTLAW REFERENCES**

37k65
37k64   /p   parent teacher

§ 7.16   Assault

The crime of assault is defined by statute in various ways. At one time, it was very common to find statutes stating assault was "an unlawful attempt, coupled with a present ability," to commit a battery,[1] but this definition is rarely found in the modern codes. In a few of these codes the offense is defined only [2] as an attempted battery; in a few more only as placing another in reasonable apprehension of a battery; and more frequently as either of the foregoing actions. A few assault-type statutes do not define the offense at all, while a good many others either have no assault statute whatsoever or else have a statute with the "assault" offense label which covers only that conduct which has traditionally been called battery.[3] In these states, the assault of the attempted-battery type is covered by the general law of attempts.[4] As for the intent-to-frighten type of assault, these jurisdictions in almost all instances cover such conduct by some other statute, usually called "threatening" or "menacing."

The principal question concerning the crime of assault has been whether it is to be limited to the situation of the attempted battery (requiring an actual intent to cause a physical injury, not just an apprehension of such an injury); or whether it should include, in addition, the civil-assault situation of the intentionally-caused apprehension of injury. A typical fact situation which raises the problem is that in which *A* points an unloaded gun at *B*, intending to make, and succeeding

48. But see Annots., 25 A.L.R.Fed. 431 (1975); 89 A.L.R.2d 396 (1963); 37 A.L.R. 704 (1925), concerning excessive punishment of child by parent or one in loco parentis.

49. For the effect of consent, generally, in criminal law, see § 5.11(a). For consent in the assault and battery area, see Puttkammer, Consent in Criminal Assault, 19 Ill.L.Rev. 617 (1925); Annot., 58 A.L.R.3d 662 (1974).

50. Thibault v. Lalumiere, 318 Mass. 72, 60 N.E.2d 349 (1945) (civil case).

51. Guarro v. United States, 237 F.2d 578 (D.C.Cir. 1956) (policeman's manner invited defendant, whom he suspected of homosexuality, to touch him).

52. See People v. Fitzsimmons, 34 N.Y.Supp. 1102 (1895) (boxing match).

Cf. Regina v. Coney, L.R. 8 Q.B.D. 534 (1882) (mutual combat in breach of the peace; combatant's consent *held* no defense to battery upon each other).

53. Compare the *Thibault* and *Guarro* cases, supra notes 87 and 88 with Commonwealth v. Collberg, 119 Mass. 350 (1876) (voluntary fist fight before large crowd;

both participants *held* guilty of battery); and Rex v. Donovan, [1934] 2 K.B. 498, 30 Cox Crim.Cas. 187 (defendant, a sex pervert, persuaded girl to let him beat her with a cane in circumstances of indecency; conviction of battery *held* affirmed, for her consent is no defense to severe blows).

Model Penal Code § 211.1 provides that simple assault (purposely, knowingly or recklessly causing bodily injury—but not purposely, knowingly, or recklessly causing serious bodily injury, which is aggravated assault, "is a misdemeanor unless committed in a fight or scuffle entered into by mutual consent, in which case it is a petty misdemeanor."

§ 7.16

1. Model Penal Code § 211.1, Comment at 176–77 (1980).

2. Of course, a statute labelled "assault" may in addition cover conduct of the battery type, as discussed in § 7.15.

3. See § 7.15.

4. See § 6.2.

in making, *B* think he is about to be shot. The weight of authority, fortified by the modern trend, is to include the latter situation as well as the former in the scope of the crime of assault.

(a) Assault as Attempted Battery. An attempt to commit any crime requires a specific intent to commit that crime;[5] and so assault of the attempted-battery sort requires an intent to commit a battery, i.e., an intent to cause physical injury to the victim. Thus in those jurisdictions where an assault is limited to an attempted battery, an intent merely to frighten, though accompanied by some fear-producing act like pointing an unloaded gun at the victim, will not suffice.[6] And since an intent to injure is required for an attempted battery, recklessness or negligence which comes close to causing injury—as where *A*, driving his car recklessly, just misses striking *B*—will not do for an assault. But, following the lead of the Model Penal Code,[7] most of the modern codes make it a separate offense recklessly to place another person in danger of death or serious bodily harm.

An attempt to commit any crime requires that the attempting party come pretty close to committing it;[8] and thus assault of the attempted-battery type is committed only when

the defendant gets near to committing a battery.[9] In some states by statute[10] or case law[11] there is the additional requirement for assault (i.e., in addition to the requirement of an attempted battery) that the assaulter have a "present ability" to commit a battery. Under a definition of assault containing such an added requirement, an attempted battery is not always an assault.[12] Under the general principle applicable to attempts one may be guilty of an attempt to commit a crime though it is impossible, for want of present ability, that the crime will result from his conduct.[13] Doubtless it is an attempted battery for *A*, with intent to hit (not simply to scare) *B*, to point his gun at *B* and pull the trigger, though unknown to *A* the gun is unloaded or lacks an effective firing pin, so that *A*'s act in pulling the trigger cannot cause a battery. But, under these circumstances, *A* lacks any "present ability" to commit a battery.[14]

An assault of the attempted-battery sort may be committed though the victim is unaware of his danger, as where *A* throws a rock at, but misses, *B* who is asleep, or where *A* shoots from the south at *B* who is facing north.[15]

5. See § 6.2.

6. Chapman v. State, 78 Ala. 463, 56 Am.R. 42 (1885).

7. Model Penal Code § 211.2.

8. See § 6.2(d).

9. People v. Lilley, 43 Mich. 521, 5 N.W. 982 (1880) (defendant, angry at victim, took knife from pocket and advanced two steps toward victim when bystanders grabbed him 10–15 feet from victim; instruction that assault is committed by intent to injure, accompanied by acts which if not interrupted will cause injury, *held* error.) But there is some authority that "a stringent concept of * * * attempt is not required when deadly weapons are involved." State v. Gordon, 120 Ariz. 172, 584 P.2d 1163 (1978) ("when a person holds a deadly weapon in a position so that it could immediately be used to physically injure another, he need go no further"; it sufficient here that defendant held knife to victim's neck).

As to whether, assault being itself a specially-named crime of attempt, there can be such a crime as attempted assault, committed when one, trying to commit a battery, fails to get close enough to the completed battery to be guilty of assault, see Annot., 79 A.L.R.2d 597 (1961).

10. E.g., statute discussed in State v. Gordon, 120 Ariz. 172, 584 P.2d 1163 (1978).

11. E.g., People v. Lilley, supra note 9.

12. State v. Wilson, 218 Or. 575, 346 P.2d 115 (1959) (one can attempt a battery without present ability, but assault requires ability in addition to attempt).

13. See § 6.3.

14. People v. Sylva, 143 Cal. 62, 76 P. 814 (1904) (*A*, who thought the gun loaded, tried to fire an unloaded gun at *B*; *held*, no assault under statute requiring a "present ability" to commit a battery).

Compare Marthall v. State, 34 Tex.Crim. 22, 36 S.W. 1062 (1894) (*D* chased *V* to rape her but could not catch her; *held*, no assault, for no ability), with People v. Jesus Yslas, 27 Cal. 630 (1865) (*D* chased *V* with upraised hatchet into room where *V* locked door on *D*; *held*, assault; *D* had "present ability" though retreat saved *V*).

15. See United States v. Dupree, 544 F.2d 1050 (9th Cir.1976); People v. Pape, 66 Cal. 366, 5 P. 621 (1885) it is no defense [to assault] that the attack is made upon an unconscious person; United States v. Bell, 505 F.2d 539 (7th Cir.1974) (victim's inability to form reasonable apprehension because of mental disease no bar to conviction for attempted-battery type of assault).

In those states where (because intent merely to scare will not suffice) it is a defense to assault that the gun was unloaded—either because this indicates the defendant intended only to scare or because, though he intended to shoot, this shows he had no present ability to shoot—there is the evidence question of which side has the burden of proof that the gun was loaded or unloaded; there is a split of opinion on the matter,[16] but the jury has been allowed to infer, from the defendant's conduct in aiming the gun and threatening to shoot, that the gun was in fact loaded.[17]

An attempted battery may, of course, involve any number of weapons besides guns—even including such a subtle weapon as the spoken word, as where A tells B, a blind man headed for a precipice, that it is all clear ahead and B almost, but not quite, falls over the edge.

 WESTLAW REFERENCES

37k48 /p assault /s attempt** /3 battery

37k48 37k49 /p assault /s inten! /4 harm injur*

37k48 37k50 /p assault /s ability

16. See Annot., 15 L.R.A. (n. s.) 1272, 1274 (1908).

17. E.g., State v. Patton, 208 Or. 610, 303 P.2d 513 (1956) (prosecution's evidence was that D in robbing V threatened V at close range with gun but did not fire it; instruction that jury may infer gun was loaded was proper, so conviction of armed robbery held affirmed).

18. The word "scare" or "frighten" is sometimes used loosely herein as a short term for the more cumbersome but more accurate expression "causing reasonable apprehension of immediate bodily harm." See W. Prosser & W. Keeton, Torts § 10 (5th ed. 1984), speaking of the requirement of apprehension of immediate bodily harm required for a civil assault: "Apprehension is not the same thing as fear, and the plaintiff is not deprived of his action merely because he is too courageous to be frightened or intimidated."

19. See Price v. United States, 85 C.C.A. 247, 156 F. 950 (1907) (A pointed unloaded gun at B who, thinking it loaded, got under a table for safety); Commonwealth v. White, 110 Mass. 407 (1872) (A pointed unloaded gun at B, intended to cause apprehension of battery but not to injure); People v. Gardner, 402 Mich. 460, 265 N.W.2d 1 (1978) (victim need not be in fear for attempted-battery type of assault). Blankenship v. State, 130 Miss. 725, 95 So. 81 (1923) (if A points gun at B and gun is unloaded or is loaded but A intends not to shoot, and B reasonably believes A will shoot, A is guilty of assault on B); People v. Wood, 10 App.Div.2d 231, 199 N.Y.S.2d 342 (1960)

(b) Assault as Intentional Scaring.[18] As we have seen, many jurisdictions have extended the scope of the crime of assault to include, *in addition to* (not as an alternative to) the attempted-battery type of assault, the tort concept of the civil assault, which is committed when one, with intent to cause a reasonable apprehension of immediate bodily harm (though not to inflict such harm), does some act which causes such apprehension.[19] For this type of assault, a present ability to inflict injury is clearly unnecessary.[20]

It is sometimes stated that this type of assault is committed by an act (or by an unlawful act) which reasonably causes another to fear immediate bodily harm.[21] This statement is not quite accurate, however, for one cannot (in those jurisdictions which have extended the tort concept of assault to criminal assault) commit a criminal assault by negligently or even recklessly or illegally acting in such a way (as with a gun or a car) as to cause another person to become apprehensive of being struck. There must be an actual intention to cause apprehension, unless there exists the morally worse intention to cause

(pointing unloaded shotgun is simple assault but not assault with weapon likely to produce grievous bodily harm); State v. Baker, 20 R.I. 275, 38 A. 653 (1897) (A fires gun toward B intending to miss B but scare him and succeeding in missing but scaring; held, assault with dangerous weapon); State v. Wiley, 52 S.D. 110, 216 N.W. 866 (1927) (A aimed unloaded gun at B; assault statute speaks of "attempt or offer" to commit a battery); State v. Deso, 110 Vt. 1, 1 A.2d 710 (1938) (A aimed unloaded gun at B); Burgess v. Commonwealth, 136 Va. 697, 118 S.E. 273 (1923) (A shot loaded gun toward B, intending to terrify but not to hit B); State v. Shaffer, 120 Wash. 345, 207 P. 229 (1922) (unloaded gun).

As noted earlier, most modern codes either include physical menacing in the crime of assault or else create a separate crime of "menacing" or "threatening" covering such conduct. See, e.g., statutes discussed in State v. Silas, 595 P.2d 651 (Alaska 1979) (either intent to injure or to cause apprehension of injury will suffice); People v. Johnson, 407 Mich. 196, 284 N.W.2d 718 (1979) (A pointed gun at B but did not fire, is assault if A intended to put B in fear and B was in reasonable apprehension).

20. Williamson v. United States, 445 A.2d 975 (D.C. App.1982); State v. Riley, 141 Vt. 29, 442 A.2d 1297 (1982).

21. E.g., Model Penal Code § 211.1, Comment at 177–78 (1980) ("an intentional subjection of another to reasonable apprehension of receiving a battery").

bodily harm.[22] It is not enough, of course, to intend to scare the other without succeeding; if the other fails to notice the threatened battery, the threatener, not having succeeded in his plan, cannot be held guilty of assault.[23] Thus criminal assault of the intent-to-scare-which-succeeds sort, like murder, manslaughter, battery and arson, requires a specified bad result, in this case mental apprehension.[24]

Criminal assault of the type under discussion needs, in addition to (1) the intent-to-scare mental element and (2) the apprehension result element, (3) the further requirement of some conduct by the defendant, conduct of the sort to arouse a reasonable apprehension of bodily harm. Thus it is not enough to constitute an assault to give another a fierce look intended to frighten, though the other is actually frightened by the look.[25] So, too, threatening words alone, without any overt act to carry out the threat,[26] or indecent proposals by a man to a woman, not accompanied by any attempt to carry them out without her consent,[27] will not do. Nevertheless, it would seem that there are situations where

informational words, without overt acts, might do.[28]

The question arises: on principle, should criminal assault be defined in terms of attempted battery, or of intentional successful frightening, or of both? One who fires at another with intent to hit him, though he misses, is, of course, a far more dangerous person than his milder counterpart who goes about intending only to frighten and not to injure.[29] Therefore, the criminal law properly first singles out for punishment the man of violence who attempts a battery. Of course, the person who successfully frightens others, though not so bad a person as the unsuccessful attacker, is not altogether admirable—so that the view of the majority of states, which include him in the net comprising the crime of assault, is not necessarily wrong, though the minority view is to leave such minor bad conduct to the civil law to discourage.[30] The Model Penal Code strikes an appropriate compromise by requiring that the defendant attempt to put another in fear of *serious* bodily injury.[31] But that limitation has been rejected in most of the modern criminal codes.

22. W. Prosser & W. Keeton, Torts § 10 (5th ed. 1984), defines the tort of assault in terms of conduct *intended* to result either in bodily harm or the apprehension of bodily harm, which conduct actually causes such apprehension.

23. State v. Barry, 45 Mont. 598, 124 P. 775, 41 L.R.A., (n.s.) 181 (1912) (*A* pointed unloaded gun at *B*, but *B* was unaware of it; *held,* no assault).

24. Doubtless if *A* intends, by pointing an unloaded gun at *B*, to scare *B*, but *C*, who is in the vicinity of the place where the gun is aimed, is the one actually scared, *A* is guilty of assault on *C*, on the bad-aim principles discussed in § 3.12(d).

25. State v. Ingram, 237 N.C. 197, 74 S.E.2d 532 (1953), noted at 29 N.Y.U.L.Q. 219 (1954) ("assault by leer").

26. State v. Smith, 309 N.W.2d 454 (Iowa 1981) (assault not a lesser included offense of terrorism by threatening a felony, as assault requires an overt act); State v. Daniel, 136 N.C. 571, 48 S.E. 544 (1904) (defendant, without a show of force, cursed victim and scared him; *held,* no assault).

Cf. State v. Hazen, 160 Kan. 733, 165 P.2d 234 (1946) (defendant with fists clenched threatened to hit and stomp victim, frightening him; assault is committed by threatening injury, without actually doing injury, "as by lifting the first or a cane in a threatening manner," although there is no intent or present ability to do the injury threatened, if the victim is reasonably apprehensive of injury).

27. Loid v. State, 55 Tex.Crim. 403, 116 S.W. 807 (1909) (defendant entered girl's room at midnight soliciting her

to sexual intercourse; she exited by the window, cut herself going over a fence to a neighbor's house; *held,* no assault).

Contra: State v. McIver, 231 N.C. 313, 56 S.E.2d 604 (1949) (black man made obscene proposals on several occasions on the street to a white woman, without stopping or otherwise attempting to follow up his proposals; it frightened her; *held,* an assault). See Annot., 12 A.L.R.2d 971 (1950).

28. See Williams, Assaults and Words, [1957] Crim.L. Rev. 219, suggesting that threatening words spoken in the darkness or when the other's back is turned should do for assault of the intent-to-scare sort, though no weapon is actually in the hands of the threatener.

29. Thus such language as appears in Blankenship v. State, 130 Miss. 725, 95 So. 81 (1923) (dealing with the harm done to one who is frightened by a defendant who points an unloaded gun at him with intent to scare), "His rights are as much violated * * * as if the actual intent to take his life existed," is not really true.

30. An attempted battery of which the victim is unaware cannot be a tort, which requires the accomplishment of harm for which to award damages. On the other hand, the intentional causing of apprehension does constitute a tort (called assault), for harm (mental, not physical) has been accomplished, for which damages can be given.

31. Model Penal Code § 211.1(1)(c). Serious bodily injury "means bodily injury which creates a substantial risk of death or which causes serious, permanent disfigure-

**WESTLAW
REFERENCES**

37k48 /p assault /s apprehensi** fear** frighten**
    /s inten!

37k48 /p assault /s apprehensi** fear** frighten**
    /s harm injur**

37k48 /p assault /s threat!

(c) Conditional Assault. With assault defined in terms of attempted battery, one may point a loaded gun at another, or flourish a knife in his face, with a threat, which he intends to carry out, to injure the other unless the latter does something he is not legally obliged to do or refrains from doing something he is legally entitled to do—as where *A*, with loaded gun pointed, tells *B*, "I'll shoot if you say that again" or "I'll fire if you don't raise your hands." It is no defense to assault of the attempted-battery sort that the victim can and does avoid injury by acceding to the other's unlawful condition;[32] or, putting it another way, the required intent to injure is not negatived by such a condition which accompanies the defendant's act and threat.[33] A fortiori the same may be said of assault of the intent-to-cause-apprehension type: where the defendant points an unloaded gun at the victim with intent to frighten but not in any event to shoot him, it is no defense to assault

that the threat, which he intends not to carry out, is to shoot only if the victim fails to comply with an unlawful demand.

The conditional intent dealt with above (to injure if an unlawful condition is not complied with) is to be distinguished from a statement, accompanying a threatening gesture, which informs the listener that no harm will in fact befall him. Thus, although an "if" clause is used in both cases, there is an important difference between, "If it were not assize time, I would not take such language from you,"[34] and "If you say so again, I will knock you down."[35]

**WESTLAW
REFERENCES**

37k48 37k49 /p assault /s condition**

(d) Aggravated Assault. In all jurisdictions statutes punish, more severely than simple assault, such aggravated assaults as "assault with intent to murder" (or to kill or rob or rape)[36] and "assault with a dangerous [or deadly] weapon."[37] It seems clear that one who, with a loaded or unloaded gun, intends only to frighten his victim without shooting him has no "intent to murder" or "intent to kill," though, as we have seen, in most juris-

---

ment, or protracted loss or impairment of the function of any bodily member or organ." Model Penal Code § 210.0(3).

32. State v. Gordon, 120 Ariz. 172, 584 P.2d 1163 (1978) (*A* held knife to *B's* neck and ordered *B* to move); People v. Thompson, 93 Cal.App.2d 780, 209 P.2d 819 (1949) (*A* pointed loaded gun at *B*, policeman investigating complaint by *A's* wife, saying, "Raise your hands," with which order *B* complied; conviction of assault with deadly weapon *held* affirmed); People v. Henry, 356 Ill. 141, 190 N.E. 361 (1934) (*A* pointed gun at *B*, theatre cashier, threatening to shoot unless *B* handed over money; *B* complied; conviction of assault with intent to rob *held* affirmed); People v. Connors, 253 Ill. 266, 97 N.E. 643 (1912) (*A*, a union striker, pointed gun at *B*, member of another union, during strike, threatening and intending to shoot if *B* did not take off his overalls; *B* complied; conviction of assault with intent to murder *held* affirmed); State v. Mitchell, 139 Iowa 455, 116 N.W. 808 (1908) (conviction of assault with intent to commit great bodily injury *held* affirmed, though the victim escaped injury by complying with the defendant's demands); Gregory v. State, 628 P.2d 384 (Okla.Crim.1981).

Cf. Hairston v. State, 54 Miss. 689, 28 Am.R. 392, 3 Am. Crim.R. 6 (1877) (*A* pointed loaded gun at *B* threatening to shoot if *B* did not comply with a *lawful* demand; conviction of assault with intent to murder *held* reversed; dic-

tum that by threatening excessive force simple assault was here committed).

33. See § 3.5(d), for a discussion of the general principle of criminal law that, with all crimes requiring a specific intent, the defendant intends to do the forbidden thing, for purposes of criminal law, though he intends to do it only if the victim fails to comply with a condition the defendant has no legal right to impose.

34. The famous tort case of Tuberville v. Savage, 1 Mod. 3, 86 Eng.Rep. 684 (1669), held this language to negative the notion of a civil assault, though spoken by one with sword in hand.

35. United States v. Myers, 27 F.Cas. 43, (No. 15,845) (C.C.D.C.1806) (when these words spoken by one with clenched fist and menacing posture, *held* assault).

36. Aggravated assault of this type is rarely included in the modern codes.

Assault with intent to murder is not the same as attempted murder, though "the two crimes have a significant overlap," as "an overt act can qualify as an attempt and yet not rise to the level of an assault." Hardy v. State, 301 Md. 124, 482 A.2d 474 (1984).

37. The current statutory pattern is similar to that for aggravated batteries, discussed in § 7.15(d).

dictions he is guilty of simple assault if he succeeds in frightening the other. One who, in such a jurisdiction, aims an unloaded gun with intent to frighten is guilty of simple assault if he succeeds in causing apprehension, but not of aggravated assault "with a dangerous weapon," the gun being unloaded.[38]

 WESTLAW REFERENCES

37k54 37k55 /p assault /3 aggravated /s murder kill rob! rape (severe great /3 injury harm)

37k56 /p assault /3 aggravated /s "deadly weapon"

(e) Defenses to Assault. The defenses which are applicable to the crime of battery[39] are generally applicable also to assault. One who is justified in wounding or killing his adversary in self-defense, or in using force to prevent the commission of a felony, can be no worse off criminally if, instead of hitting the other, he misses him completely.

 WESTLAW REFERENCES

37k63 37k65 /p assault /s defense

---

§ 7.17 Mayhem

Mayhem at common law required a type of injury which permanently rendered the victim less able to fight offensively or defensively; it might be accomplished either by the removal of (*dismemberment*), or by the *disablement* of, some bodily member useful in fighting. Today, by statute, permanent *disfigurement* has been added; and as to dismemberment and disablement, there is no longer a requirement that the member have military significance.

38. Cf. People v. Stevens, 409 Mich. 564, 297 N.W.2d 120 (1980) (inoperable gun not a dangerous weapon within meaning of felonious assault statute); State v. Baker, 20 R.I. 275, 38 A. 653 (1897) (*A* fired a *loaded* pistol at *B* with intent to miss but to scare; the bullet misses but scares *B*; conviction of assault "with a dangerous weapon" *held* affirmed, for "a loaded pistol is a dangerous weapon"). But see State v. Ott, 189 N.W.2d 377 (Minn.1971) (unloaded shotgun is a "dangerous weapon" under aggravated assault statute, as term defined to included unloaded firearm).

39. See § 7.15(e).

Concerning the required state of mind, some statutes require a specific intent to maim, others merely an intent to do bodily injury. Recklessness or negligence will not do. An unintended maiming in the commission of an unlawful act will not do, except in the very few states which have created a kind of felony-mayhem doctrine.

 WESTLAW REFERENCES

di mayhem

(a) Common-Law Mayhem. Blackstone defines mayhem, an ancient common-law crime, as "the violently depriving another of the use of such of his members as may render him the less able in fighting, either to defend himself, or to annoy his adversary," the rationale being to preserve the King's right to the military services of his subjects. Blackstone lists, by way of example, cutting off or permanently disabling a hand or finger, and striking out an eye or front tooth, and castration; he distinguishes the cutting off of an ear or nose, which conduct disfigures but does not impair the victim's fighting ability.[1] It should be noted that permanent disablement of an appropriate bodily member, as well as its dismemberment is covered; thus it is common-law mayhem permanently to disable a leg as well as to cut it off.[2] The punishment originally imposed upon one convicted of mayhem—the loss of the same member of which he had deprived his victim—was abolished long before Blackstone's day,[3] being succeeded by the more ordinary punishments of imprisonment or (in the case of some mayhems) of death. By a series of early English statutes (in 1403, 1545, 1670), mayhem was broadened

§ 7.17

1. 4 W. Blackstone, Commentaries* 205–06 (1769).

2. State v. McDonie, 89 W.Va. 185, 109 S.E. 710 (1921) (one who unlawfully scalds foot of another so toes grow together commits common-law mayhem), citing Blackstone.

3. 4 W. Blackstone, Commentaries* 206 (1769), explaining that the reason for this change was partly because of the inadequacy of retaliation as a rule of punishment, partly "because upon a repetition of the offense the punishment could not be repeated."

to include cutting out or disabling the tongue, severing the ear, and slitting the nose or lip.[4]

WESTLAW REFERENCES

topic(256)   /p   common-law

(b) Mayhem Under American Statutes. Mayhem (or "maim" or "maiming" as it is sometimes called)[5] was at one time a separate crime (almost always a felony) in the criminal codes of practically every state. But this is no longer the case. Only a few of the modern codes contain such a crime, although some others define a certain variety of aggravated battery in terms which are very similar.[6]

Although the statutes vary considerably in wording, they are all alike in abolishing the military significance of the injury inflicted upon the victim, by making it mayhem unlawfully to disfigure as well as to dismember and disable. Some list specifically such bodily components as the eyes, ears, tongue, nose and lips. Thus the modern rationale of the crime may be said to be the preservation of the natural completeness and normal appearance of the human face and body,[7] and not, as originally, the preservation of the sovereign's right to the effective military assistance of his subjects.

---

4. The last of these statutes is "called the Coventry Act, being occasioned by an assault on Sir John Coventry in the street, and slitting his nose, in revenge (as was supposed) for some obnoxious words uttered by him in parliament." Id. at 207.

5. State v. Johnson, 58 Ohio St. 417, 51 N.E. 40 (1898), states: "There is no question, we think, but that 'maim' as a noun, and 'mayhem' are equivalent words, or that 'maim' is but a newer form of the word 'mayhem' . . ."

6. Model Penal Code § 211.1 makes it a second-degree felony (1–10 years imprisonment) called "aggravated assault" to inflict "serious bodily injury" (defined to include permanent disfigurement or dismemberment) purposely or knowingly or with extreme recklessness.

7. On this development, see Perkins v. United States, 446 A.2d 19 (D.C.App. 1982), approving an instruction: "To be permanently disfigured means that the person is appreciably less attractive or that a part of his body is to some appreciable degree less useful or functional than it was before the injury."

8. See Annots., 16 A.L.R. 955 (1922); 58 A.L.R. 1320 (1929).

9. Thus it may, theoretically at least, like other crimes defined in terms of cause-and-result, be committed by omission to act where there is a duty to act, as well as by

WESTLAW REFERENCES

topic(256)   /p   dismember! disfigur! disable*

(c) The Injury—Type and Extent.[8] Mayhem, like murder, manslaughter and battery, is a cause-and-result crime;[9] and it is not committed unless the defendant's conduct causes[10] the required bad result—dismemberment, disablement or disfigurement. The removal of or permanent disablement of an arm, hand, finger, leg, foot or toe will do for mayhem. So too removal of the eye or the destruction or serious impairment of eyesight will suffice. A front tooth, but not a jaw tooth, is a bodily member within the definition of mayhem.[11] Castration is an injury which will do for mayhem.[12] As indicated above, mayhem now covers the cutting off or slitting of the ear, nose or lips.[13] On the other hand, it is not mayhem to cut a throat with a knife or to break a jaw or fracture a skull with a bludgeon.[14]

There have been questions concerning the required extent and permanency of the injury. It has been held mayhem to cut off a part of an ear or a nose, so long as the net result is an impairment of natural comeliness;[15] or a part of a finger, so long as its owner is there-

---

affirmative action, if maiming results from the omission and the defendant has the proper state of mind.

10. More accurately, "legally causes," since it is not always enough, in criminal law, that the defendant's conduct cause the injury in a "but for" sense. For a discussion of "legal cause" in criminal law, see § 3.12(c).

11. Keith v. State, 89 Tex.Crim. 264, 232 S.W. 321 (1921).

12. State v. Sheldon, 54 Mont. 185, 169 P. 37 (1917). And under modern statutes punishing dismemberment, cutting off a man's penis will do. See Cole v. State, 62 Tex.Crim. 270, 138 S.W. 109 (1911).

13. People v. Caldwell, 153 Cal.App.3d 947, 200 Cal. Rptr. 508 (1984).

14. Rex v. Lee, 1 Leach 51, 168 Eng.Rep. 128 (1763) (defendant slit wife's throat while she slept); Commonwealth v. Lester, 2 Va.Cas. 198 (1820) (defendant broke victim's jawbone with a heavy stick); Foster v. People, 50 N.Y. 598 (1872) (a blow intentionally aimed at the head with intent to fracture the skull is not assault and battery with intent to maim).

15. Key v. State, 71 Tex.Crim. 642, 161 S.W. 121 (1913) (defendant bit off one-third of victim's ear, impairing comeliness); State v. Catsampas, 62 Wash. 70, 112 P. 1116 (1911) (defendant bit off end of victim's nose).

by substantially deprived of its use.[16] It is mayhem unlawfully to render an eye practically useless, though the victim may still be able to distinguish light from darkness and notice movements immediately before the eye.[17] It is a requirement for mayhem that the disabling injury be permanent,[18] so that the temporary disablement of a finger, arm, eye, or other member will not do.[19] But there "have long been indications that the infliction of an injury forbidden by a mayhem-type statute may constitute an offense notwithstanding the possibility that alleviation of the injury is medically possible."[20]

A variety of weapons has been successfully used to commit mayhem, including guns, knives, explosives, razors and clubs. Many an ear has been bitten off. A modern weapon of some potency is acid thrown at the victim's face or body.[21]

WESTLAW
REFERENCES

mayhem /s extent kind nature type /4 injury harm

(d) The State of Mind.[22] The mental element required for mayhem can not be quite so exactly stated. (1) Of course, one who (without justification) intends a specific injury of the mayhem type, and who accomplishes that exact injury, is guilty, as where A with a knife intentionally cuts off B's left ear. However, (2) one may intend one sort of mayhem-

injury and achieve another sort, as where A, swinging his axe at B's right hand with intent to sever it, misses that hand but cuts off B's left hand or leg or puts out an eye. Or (3) one may intend bodily injury but not have in mind any mayhem type of injury; thus A intentionally knocks down B who, to A's surprise, falls against a root and loses an ear. Progressing further down the road leading from greater fault to lesser fault, one encounters the situations of the person who (4) recklessly or negligently or (5) in the commission (or attempted commission) of an unlawful act causes another to suffer an unintended injury of the mayhem type—as where A, by reckless driving, or by driving on the wrong side of the road in violation of statute or ordinance, runs his car against motorist B, inflicting injuries so severe that B requires the amputation of his leg or suffers the loss of his eyesight.

The answer in these situations depends to a great extent upon the wording of the mayhem statute. If the statute punishes one who "unlawfully" or "maliciously" dismembers or disfigures, then one is guilty in situation (3) above, i.e., where he intentionally injures another, thereby unintentionally causing an injury of the mayhem type.[23] On the other hand, a statute of the modern type punishing one who, "with intent to disable or disfigure another," successfully disables or disfigures

16. Bowers v. State, 24 Tex.App. 542, 7 S.W. 247 (1888) (defendant bit off portion of victim's thumb; this is not mayhem unless "the member was so injured as to substantially deprive the injured party of it").

17. People v. Nunes, 47 Cal.App. 346, 190 P. 486 (1920). And this is so even though there is evidence of a slight possibility that a future eye operation might improve eyesight.

18. See 3 W. Blackstone, Commentaries* 121 (1769) (mayhem is a battery whereby the victim "is forever disabled from making so good a defense against future external injuries as he otherwise might have done").

19. See State v. Briley, 8 Port. 472, 474 (Ala.1839). In Baker v. State, 4 Ark. 56 (1842), where the proof was that the victim, shot in the thigh, was unable to walk at time of defendant's trial, this evidence was held sufficient to support the verdict of mayhem, since, in the absence of contrary evidence, the continuation of the disability would be presumed.

20. Perkins v. United States, 446 A.2d 19 (D.C.App. 1982), quoting United States v. Cook, 462 F.2d 301 (D.C. Cir.1972).

21. Hiller v. State, 116 Neb. 582, 218 N.W. 386 (1928) (defendant procured agent to throw sulphuric acid at girl, causing burns which left permanent scar on leg and might result in running sore later in life). See Annot., 58 A.L.R. 1328 (1929).

22. See Annot., 1916E L.R.A. 494.

23. Carpenter v. People, 31 Colo. 284, 72 P. 1072 (1903) (defendant either bit off the victim's ear or threw him to the ground causing him to lose his ear by striking it against a root; under statute defining mayhem as "unlawfully" depriving, etc., it is mayhem in either event, a specific intent to maim not being necessary; but conviction *held* reversed on other grounds); Terrell v. State, 86 Tenn. 523, 8 S.W. 212 (1888) (defendant threw a piece of brick at victim intending to injure but not to maim; the missile put out victim's eye; under statute making it mayhem "unlawfully and maliciously" to put out another's eye, conviction *held* affirmed, no intent to maim being required); Keith v. State, 89 Tex.Crim. 264, 232 S.W. 321 (1921) (defendant, intending to injure but not to maim, knocked out the victim's front tooth; under statute using the words "wilfully and maliciously," conviction of maim-

him is not violated by one with such an indefinite state of mind; this statute would require the mental element involved in situation (2) above—i.e., an intent to maim, though not necessarily to cause the specific maiming injury actually inflicted.[24] As to the states of mind referred to in situations (4) and (5) above—involving reckless or unlawful conduct by the defendant—it seems quite clear that mayhem is not committed under these circumstances, in the absence of some special wording in the mayhem statute.[25]

 WESTLAW REFERENCES

topic(256) /p inten! /s injur** harm maim disfigur! dismember

(e) Defenses. It is a defense to mayhem that the defendant's conduct which causes the victim's maiming injury is done in necessary self-defense against an attack which threatens death or serious bodily injury.[26] On the other hand, it is no defense to mayhem that the victim consented to be maimed.[27] And one who is "reasonably provoked" into a rage to maim by the victim's conduct cannot use the provocation as a defense.[28]

 WESTLAW REFERENCES

256k2

---

ing *held* affirmed, no specific intent or premeditated design to maim being required).

Compare Perkins v. United States, 446 A.2d 19 (D.C. App.1982) (statute covering "mayhem or * * * maliciously disfiguring"; mere intent to injure sufficient for former but not the latter, as mayhem "is so egregious that sufficient intent justifiably may be inferred from malicious and wilful commission of the act. * * * In contrast, disfigurement can result from a relatively minor assault. The specific intent requirement accordingly serves to separate the less serious, though criminal, act which results in a permanent injury from the calculated and truly heinous act of mayhem").

24. Cf. State v. Hatley, 72 N.M. 377, 384 P.2d 252 (1963) (defendant deliberately struck victim, unintentionally putting out his eye; conviction of mayhem under statute requiring intent to maim or disfigure *held* affirmed; his intent to do wrong in causing the battery suffices), a case which erroneously makes use of a fiction to misconstrue a statute.

What if A, intending to murder B but not to maim him, strikes at B's heart with a knife but, missing the heart, severs an ear; or, intending to blow B to bits with an explosive, succeeds only in blowing off B's arm? Under a statute reading "with intent to commit a felony, or to disfigure or disable" or "with intent to murder, maim, or disfigure," or "in the commission or attempted commission of a felony", A is clearly guilty. In Rex v. Woodburne and Coke, XVI State Trials 54 (Howell ed. 1812), under a statute providing, "with intent to maim or disfigure," A, who had hacked away at B with a hedge bill intending to murder but succeeding only in wounding him badly, including the slitting of his nose, defended on the ground he intended to murder, which was not within the statute, and did not intend to maim or disfigure, which was within the statute; but the court left to the jury whether the defendant intended to murder by disfiguring; and the defendant was convicted and executed. Of course, in many American jurisdictions the defendant would be guilty, under these circumstances, of assault with intent to kill or

to murder, a crime more or less comparable in punishment to mayhem.

25. Thus, as to situation (5), the Oregon statute considered in State v. Vowels, 4 Or. 324 (1873), punishes one who purposely or "in the commission or attempt to commit a felony" dismembers or disfigures; and the Washington statute dealt with in State v. Catsampas, 62 Wash. 70, 112 P. 1116 (1911), punishes one who "with intent to commit a felony," or to disfigure or disable, disfigures or disables. Under these statutes, if A sets fire to B's house (arson), trapping B inside, and a beam falls on B's leg, requiring its amputation, it would seem that A is guilty of mayhem, though he did not intend to maim or even to injure B, who he thought would escape the fire unscathed. These statutes create a sort of felony-mayhem doctrine.

26. See People v. Wright, 93 Cal. 564, 29 P. 240 (1892) (it is mayhem to dismember or disfigure in a fight pursuant to an intent formed during the conflict, unless the act is done "in necessary self-defense * * * in order to prevent the infliction, or attempted infliction, of some great bodily harm by the party injured").

27. Wright's Case, Co. Lit. 127a (1604) (defendant, at companion's request, cut off latter's left hand to give him "more colour to begge"); State v. Bass, 255 N.C. 42, 120 S.E.2d 580 (1961) (defendant, who administered anesthetic to victim's hand to enable victim to cut off his fingers to obtain insurance money, *held* properly convicted of being accessory before the fact of mayhem, in spite of victim's consent to removal of fingers). Of course, a physician is not guilty of mayhem when, to save his patient's life, he amputates a gangrenous limb or bodily member.

28. Sensobaugh v. State, 92 Tex.Crim. 417, 244 S.W. 379 (1922) (husband, catching his wife in adultery with her paramour, cut off latter's sex organ with razor); and see 4 Blackstone, Commentaries,* 206 (1769). See § 7.10 for the proposition that there is no such crime as "voluntary theft" or "voluntary mayhem", comparable to "voluntary manslaughter," to aid one who is reasonably provoked into doing other things than kill those who provoke him.

Chapter 8
CRIMES RELATING TO PROPERTY

Table of Sections

§ 8.1 Theft—Historical Development

In order fully to understand the fine distinctions between modern theft crimes—principally larceny, embezzlement and false pretenses—it is necessary to look backward into legal history to see how these crimes came into existence.[1]

(a) Development and Expansion of Larceny. First came larceny, a common-law crime (invented by the English judges rather than by Parliament) committed when one person misappropriated another's property by means of taking it from his possession without his consent. The principal factor which limited the scope of larceny was the requirement that the thief must take it from the victim's possession; larceny requires a "trespass in the taking," as the matter is often stated. The judges who determined the scope of larceny (including its limitations) apparently considered larceny to be a crime designed to prevent breaches of the peace rather than aimed at protecting property from wrongful appropriation. The unauthorized taking of

§ 8.1

1. For more on this history, see G. Fletcher, Rethinking Criminal Law chs. 1–2 (1978); J. Hall, Theft, Law and Society chs. 1–4 (2d ed. 1952); Brickey, The Jurisprudence of Larceny: An Historical Inquiry and Interest Analysis, 33 Vand.L.Rev. 1101 (1980); Fletcher, Manifest Criminali-

ty, Criminal Intent and the Metamorphosis of Lloyd Weinreb, 90 Yale L.J. 319 (1980); Fletcher, Metamorphosis of Larceny, 89 Harv.L.Rev. 469 (1976); Weinreb, Manifest Criminality, Criminal Intent, and the "Metamorphosis of Larceny," 90 Yale L.J. 294 (1980).

property, even by stealth,[2] from the owner's possession is apt to produce an altercation if the owner discovers the property moving out of his possession in the hands of the thief. But when the wrongdoer already has the owner's property in his possession at the time he misappropriates it (today's embezzlement) or when he obtains the property from the owner by telling him lies (now the crime of false pretenses) there is not the same danger of an immediate breach of the peace. Upon learning how he has been wronged the owner may be as angry at the wrongdoer in these two situations as he is at the thief caught in the act of taking his property by stealth, but the malefactor in these two cases is generally less available for retaliatory measures than when the owner discovers him in the process of taking the property out of his possession.

As time went on, and especially during the time of the growth of manufacturing and the expansion of trade and business in England, the judges felt the need to broaden larceny in order to protect the owner's property from various sorts of misappropriation. They did not do this directly, by abolishing the requirement of a "trespass in the taking," but rather by discovering a trespass in at least three situations where in reality it is most difficult to find any trespass:

(1) A bailee in possession of another's packaged goods who "broke bulk" by breaking open the bales and misappropriating the contents was held guilty of larceny. Some of the judges thought that the bailee by wrongfully opening the bale terminated his possession, which thereupon flew back to the bailor, though he might be many miles away. Others considered that only the outside wrapper was possessed by the bailee; the bailor, though perhaps miles distant, still possessed

the contents.[3] It was all make-believe, of course, for the bailee actually had possession of the contents in the real sense of power to control and intent to control; but the judges felt it necessary to protect the mercantile trade, which was then growing apace in England.

(2) The judges also invented something called "constructive possession" where possession in the real sense of the word was not present. Whenever one comes across that favorite legal adjective—"constructive"—he may as well get himself ready to pretend that something exists which does not in fact exist—whether it be "constructive fraud" where there is no actual fraud, "constructive knowledge" or "notice" where there has been no knowledge or notice in fact, "constructive eviction" where the landlord has not in reality thrown his tenant out of occupancy of the premises, or "constructive trust" where no real trust has been created. "Constructive possession," no exception to the rule, was discovered to exist in these three principal situations: (a) A master (employer) delivers his property to his servant (employee) to use or to keep or to deliver for the master. One would think that, while the property was in the servant's hands, he has possession of it; his dominion over the property looks, feels, smells and tastes exactly like possession. But the judges, perceiving a need to protect masters against the depredations of their servants, came to decide that the servant had something called "custody" only, while the master still had "constructive possession." Thus, when the servant misappropriated the property, he took it from his master's possession, so that there was a "trespass in the taking," and hence the servant was guilty of larceny.[4] (b) The owner of property loses it or

---

2. Model Penal Code § 223.1, Comment at 128 (1980), says, about the legal history of the theft crimes, that the crime of robbery—the taking of property by *force* from the possession of another—was created before the crime of larceny, involving the taking by *stealth* rather than by force.

3. Carrier's Case, Y.B. 13 Edw. IV, f. 9, pl. 5 (Star Chamber and Exchequer Chamber, 1473), discussed at length in J. Hall, Theft, Law and Society ch. 1 (2d ed. 1952). Here the defendant, a carrier, employed to carry

bales to Southampton, carried them to another place, broke open the bales, took the contents and converted them to his own use; this was held to be larceny.

4. This development took some time. At first the servant was considered to have possession, so that his misappropriation could not be larceny. Reporter's Note, Y.B. 3 Hen. VII, f. 12, pl. 9 (Common Pleas, 1487). Later the servant was considered to acquire custody but not possession of property handed to him by his master to use or keep in the master's house, though he got actual

mislays it. While the actual possession is vacant (the owner is too far away from his property to exercise any dominion over it; moreover, in the case of lost property, he does not even know where it is), the owner is considered to have "constructive possession" of the property. Thus when a finder picks it up and, seeing earmarks of ownership thereon, nevertheless then decides to misappropriate it, he takes it from the owner's possession and is therefore guilty of larceny.[5]   (c) A property owner delivers the property to another person as part of a transaction to be completed in the owner's presence, as where he hands a storekeeper a large bill to pay for a small purchase, or hands a jeweler his watch to be appraised while he waits. The owner is said to have "constructive possession," while the other person has mere custody, so that, if the latter runs off with it, he takes it from the owner's possession and so is eligible for a conviction of larceny.[6]

The development of the notion of construction possession where no actual possession existed thus had the effect of broadening the scope of larceny; for a wrongful interference with this make-believe possession constituted just as much a "trespass in the taking" as a similar interference with real possession.

(3) A wrongdoer obtains possession of (but not title to) another's property by telling him lies, intending to misappropriate the property

and, at the earliest opportunity, doing so. In the leading case, the defendant hired a mare to go to Sutton, intending, however, to go to another place and sell the mare and abscond with the proceeds. He went to Smithfield and sold the mare. Since the owner had voluntarily delivered the mare to the defendant, it is somewhat difficult to find a "trespass in the taking" so as to make the misappropriation larceny. But the judges held it to be larceny,[7] a majority of them indulging in the fiction that the owner of the mare retained possession until the time of its sale by the defendant. The expression "larceny by trick" is often used to identify this type of larceny, but it is the crime of larceny and not a separate crime.

WESTLAW REFERENCES

topic(236) /p common-law
topic(236) /p "constructive possession"

(b) Creation of Embezzlement and False Pretenses. The three situations in which the judges by using fictions enlarged the notion of possession—i.e., where a bailee of property breaks bulk, where a possessor of property loses actual possession but retains "constructive" possession, and where a possessor of property is induced by lies to give up his possession—[8] thus had the effect of enlarging the scope of larceny. But the English judges

---

possession and not mere custody of such property if it was to be taken from the house. Reporter's Note, Y.B. 21 Hen. VII, f. 14, pl. 21 (K.B. 1506); Rex v. Watson, 2 East P.C. 562 (Cr.Cas.Res.1788). Still later it was held that the servant acquired mere custody of property handed him by the master to take outside the house, at least if he had no discretion but to deliver the property to someone. Rex v. Lavender, 2 East P.C. 566 (Cr.Cas.Res.1793). Then it was held that property delivered to the servant for the master by a third person was in the servant's possession, so as to preclude a larceny conviction for his misappropriation. Bazeley's Case, 2 East P.C. 571 (Cr.Cas.Res.1799). Today the principle applies as well to business employees—store clerks, bank tellers, caretakers—as to household servants. See Annot., 125 A.L.R. 367 (1940).

5. See § 8.2(f).

6. E.g., Hildebrand v. People, 56 N.Y. 394 (1874) (*A* handed *B* a $50 bill to pay for a 10 cent soda; *B* threw him out of the saloon and kept the bill; *B* held guilty of larceny).

7. Rex v. Pear, 168 Eng.Rep. 208 (1779). The then English statute on false pretenses, 30 Geo. II, c. 24 (1757),

was over twenty years old, and Pear's conduct falls literally within its terms. Why was Pear not convicted of false pretenses rather than larceny? J. Hall, Theft, Law and Society 47 (2d ed. 1952), explains the matter thus: it was not until several years after *Pear's Case* was decided that spoken words were held to constitute "false pretenses" within the meaning of the statute; at the time of *Pear's Case* something tangible (a false token or counterfeit letter) was assumed to be necessary.

8. Perhaps the first and third situations may also be considered to be "constructive possession" situations: one who bails packaged property to a carrier or other bailee has constructive possession of the contents, or at least, when the bale is broken open, constructive possession flies back to him; and one who hands over possession of his property as a result of another's lies nevertheless retains constructive possession. It makes as much sense to talk constructive possession in the breaking-bulk and larceny-by-trick cases as it does in the master-servant and lost-property cases, though actually the expression seems little used in explaining the former.

stopped short at this point. Thus in a 1799 case a bank clerk, employed by a banker, received from a depositor money for deposit in the bank; he put the money in his pocket instead of in the cash drawer, intending to misappropriate it. One might think that, as long as the judges had been pretending that, when an employer hands property to his employee, he still keeps possession, they might as easily pretend that, as soon as the depositor handed the money to the employee, possession (of the "constructive" sort) immediately lodged in the employer, the employee acquiring mere "custody," so that his misappropriation would amount to larceny. But the court held that the constructive-possession idea did not apply to property coming to a servant for his master from a third person, until the employee hands the property to the employer or puts it in a receptacle (such as a cash drawer) provided by the employer for its safe-keeping. The result was that the bank clerk was not guilty of larceny (and there was then no other crime which covered his conduct).[9] It was of course necessary, for the protection of property in an age when shops and banks were growing into something more than a one-man or one-family operation, to make such conduct criminal; if the courts would not do it, the legislature must. Accordingly, in the very year of the court's decision in the case of the bank clerk, Parliament enacted the first of a long line of embezzlement statutes.[10]

So too in the area of misappropriation of property by spoken lies, the judges stopped short of enlarging larceny to cover it, except, as noted above, where possession of, but not title to the property was obtained by the lies (i.e., larceny by trick). Parliament stepped in here too, creating the new crime of obtaining property by false pretenses.[11]

It may be wondered why the English judges, who did not hesitate, in the face of need, to invent murder and manslaughter, burglary and arson, robbery and larceny and other crimes, hesitated during the late 1700's to expand larceny to include the areas of embezzlement and false pretenses. The commentary to the Model Penal Code explains the matter in a nutshell as follows:

At this point in the chronology of the law of theft, about the end of the 18th century, a combination of circumstances caused the initiative in the further development of the criminal law to pass from the courts to the legislature. Among these circumstances were the general advance in the prestige and power of parliament and the conversion of the idea of "natural law" from an instrument for judicial defiance of monarchy to a restraining philosophy envisioning judges as interpreters of immemorial custom rather than framers of policy. Perhaps the most direct influence of all was a revulsion against capital punishment, which was the penalty for all theft offenses except petty larceny during much of the 18th century. The severity of this penalty not only made the judges reluctant to enlarge felonious larceny, but also may account for the host of artificial limitations that they engrafted on the offense, e.g., the exclusion of growing crops, fixtures, deeds, and dogs.[12]

It was noted above that when the English Parliament plugged the loopholes in larceny left by the judges' refusal to expand that crime, it did not do so by enlarging the definition of larceny to fill in the gaps, as it might have done. Common-law burglary, as defined by the judges, consists of a night-time breaking and entering of another's dwelling house with intent to commit a felony therein. A modern legislature may wish to stretch burglary to include similar daytime misconduct, or to include entering without a breaking, or buildings other than dwellings, or an intention to commit a misdemeanor as well as a

9. Bazeley's Case, 2 East P.C. 571 (Cr.Cas.Res.1799).

10. 39 Geo. III, c. 85 (1799), provided that an employee who receives, by virtue of his employment, money or goods for his employer and who fraudulently converts the same is guilty of embezzlement. Later English embezzlement statutes covered other persons who lawfully received possession of other people's property: brokers, attorneys, agents, factors, trustees, corporate directors and officers, partners and the like.

11. 30 Geo. II, c. 24 (1757). A much earlier statute, 33 Hen. VIII, c. 1 (1541), had made it a crime to obtain property by means of something more tangible than spoken lies, a "false Token or counterfeit Letter made in any other Man's Name" being required.

12. Model Penal Code § 223.1, Comment at 128–29 (1980).

felony. It often does so, not by creating some brand new crime, but by altering the definition of the old crime of burglary so as to cover the new areas.[13] But Parliament elected to create the two new crimes of embezzlement and false pretenses, assigning to the new crimes a less severe punishment than that for larceny (although today in most Anglo-American jurisdictions the punishment is the same for all three types of theft). And, since the new crimes were created to fill gaps in the law of larceny, they were considered not to overlap the crime of larceny, although as to some situations their language seemed broad enough to do so. As we now look back on history, matters would have been simpler for us in the United States today if Parliament had stretched larceny rather than creating new crimes, for here in America we have generally adopted England's tripartite scheme of things, with the three separate theft crimes, larceny, embezzlement and false pretenses. We shall see, in the sections which follow, how thin and technical are the dividing lines between the three crimes and how often, as a result, difficulties stand in the way of successful prosecution of thieves. We shall conclude with a discussion of how many Anglo-American jurisdictions have, with greater or less success, dealt with the problem.

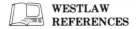 **WESTLAW REFERENCES**

topic(146) /p common-law

topic(170) /p common-law

topic(170) /p larceny /2 trick

---

13. See § 8.13.

§ 8.2

1. However, most modern codes do not take that approach, but instead include a comprehensive theft statute. See § 8.8.

2. See § 8.1(a).

3. As we have seen, the crime of embezzlement was created to punish many instances of such wrongdoing. See § 8.1(b).

4. Commonwealth v. Tluchak, 166 Pa.Super. 16, 70 A.2d 657 (1950) (defendants sold their home, including

§ 8.2 Larceny—The Trespass

Larceny at common law may be defined as the (1) trespassory (2) taking and (3) carrying away of the (4) personal property (5) of another (6) with intent to steal it. American statutes dealing with larceny as a discrete offense[1] have generally left the six elements of the crime unchanged, except that there has been considerable enlargement of the kinds of property which can be the subject of larceny.

Over the years, courts have limited the significance of the first of these elements—trespass—by declaring "constructive possession" to exist in several situations, as where an employer delivers property to his employee; the owner delivers property to another for a transaction to be completed in his presence; a bailee breaks bulk; a wrongdoer obtains possession of (but not title to) the property by lies; a wrongdoer finds lost or mislaid property; or property is delivered to a wrongdoer by mistake.

(a) Factors Negating Trespass. We have already noted in the historical survey of theft that larceny requires that there be a "trespass in the taking," i.e., that the thief take the property out of the possession of its possessor,[2] who is generally, but not always, the owner of the property in question. If the wrongdoer fraudulently converts property already properly in his possession, he does not take it from anyone's possession and so cannot be guilty of larceny.[3] Thus one who sells property to another and who then fails to deliver it cannot be guilty of larceny;[4] nor can a repairman, who properly receives an article to be repaired, be guilty of larceny when he later carries it off with intent to steal it.[5] Finders of lost or mislaid property,

fixtures and shrubbery; when purchasers took possession, they found the defendants had taken away, among other things, a commode and thirty peach trees; conviction of larceny *held* reversed; dictum that it might be fraudulent conversion).

5. Regina v. Thristle, 169 Eng.Rep. 347 (Crim.App. 1849).

But compare the situation where the owner, instead of leaving it to be repaired, stands by while the repairman repairs it. See § 8.2(c).

and those to whom property is delivered by mistake, who pick up the property or accept its delivery with an innocent intention (e.g., with lost or misdelivered property, an intention to return the property to the owner; or, with misdelivered property, a lack of knowledge of the mistake) do not commit a trespass and so cannot be guilty of larceny, even if later they succumb to the temptation of keeping the property for themselves.[6]

There is, of course, no trespass in the taking, and hence no larceny, if the owner of property actually consents to the defendant's taking his property.[7] A problem arises when the owner of property learns in advance that a thief is planning to steal his property and (often with the cooperation of the police) si-

lently lies in wait in order to catch him in the act, perhaps even smoothing the thief's way somewhat, as by leaving the door open or the key in the lock. Does the owner's lying-in-wait state of mind amount to consent so as to preclude a conviction for larceny? It is held not to constitute consent,[8] unless, according to some cases, the owner, himself or through directions to his employees, goes so far as actually to hand the property over to the thief.[9]

Where two persons both have an interest in property—as in the case of partners and co-owners (for instance, tenants in common and joint tenants)—difficulties have arisen in larceny prosecutions. Suppose a partner or co-owner fraudulently misappropriates partner-

---

6. E.g., Calhoun v. State, 191 Miss. 82, 2 So.2d 802 (1941) (defendant picked up lost article intending to return it, but later decided to steal it; conviction of larceny *held* reversed; "if the original taking is lawful and bona fide, a subsequent conversion is not larceny, because there is no trespass"). One who picks up lost property, or one on whom possession of another's property is thrust by misdelivery, is justified in taking possession and so cannot be guilty of trespass to the chattel, defined in W. Prosser & W. Keeton, Torts § 14 (5th ed. 1984), as an intentional interference with the possession or physical condition of a chattel in the possession of another, *without justification*. On the other hand, a finder, and one who receives a misdelivery, with intent to steal is guilty of a trespass in receiving the property. (So too, one who innocently picks up another's property, wrongly thinking the property is his own or that the other has consented, is guilty of a trespass, for he intends to interfere with the other's possession. W. Prosser & W. Keeton, Torts § 14 (5d ed. 1984). He is not necessarily guilty of larceny, however, for he may lack the intent to steal.)

Most of the cases involving finders and recipients of misdelivered property (including over-payments of money), who originally have innocent minds but later decide to steal, hold the defendants to be not guilty of larceny because of the lack of coincidence of the taking and the intent to steal, without mention, as in the *Calhoun* case supra, of the lack of a trespass. See § 8.5(f).

7. See § 8.1(a), where it was noted, however, that it is nevertheless larceny ("by trick") for the defendant, after obtaining from the owner possession, but not title, by lies, to convert the property with intent to steal it. E.g., Hufstetler v. State, 37 Ala.App. 71, 63 So.2d 730 (1953) (defendant, after getting gasoline station owner to fill the gasoline tank of his car, suddenly drove off without paying; conviction of larceny by trick *held* affirmed; defendant got possession but not title; the fraud vitiated the owner's consent).

8. Smith v. United States, 291 F.2d 220 (9th Cir.1961) (defendant approached bank teller with plan to rob the bank; teller pretended to agree but told bank manager; manager told teller to hand defendant a bag when defen-

dant "held him up"; defendant was arrested with the bag in his possession; conviction of bank robbery *held* affirmed; the bank did not consent to the taking in a trespass sense, but merely smoothed the way for the crime's commission); Jarrott v. State, 108 Tex.Crim.R. 427, 1 S.W.2d 619 (1927) (a policeman, learning that defendant was stealing cars, left his own car with the key in the switch and hid in the back seat; defendant got in and drove off; conviction of larceny *held* affirmed, for the owner did not consent where his actions were solely to apprehend the thief).

9. Edmondson v. State, 18 Ga.App. 233, 89 S.E. 189 (1916) (owner of valuable papers in a safe, knowing that defendant desired to steal them, asked a friend who shared an office with him and who knew the combination to the safe to get the papers and hand them to the defendant; the friend did so; conviction of larceny *held* reversed, for there is no trespass); People v. Rollino, 37 Misc.2d 14, 233 N.Y.S.2d 580 (1962) (employer, learning from employee that defendant had asked him to steal employer's property for defendant, got employee to hand package to defendant in feigned cooperation; *held* not to be larceny); Topolewski v. State, 130 Wis. 244, 109 N.W. 1037 (1906) (meat packing company's employee was asked by defendant to load meat on defendant's wagon so that defendant could steal it; employee did so after informing his employer, who instructed him to feign cooperation; conviction of larceny *held* reversed, for the element of trespass is wanting); Rex v. Turvey, [1946] 2 All E.R. 60 (owner of property instructed employee to cooperate with would-be thief by handing him the property; employee did so; appeal against larceny conviction *held* allowed). See also People v. Rollino, supra, for the proposition that it is not even *attempted* larceny in these circumstances.) But compare Smith v. United States, supra note 8, where the bank teller, on instructions from the bank manager, handed the money bag to the defendant; a conviction of bank robbery was affirmed on the ground the bank did not consent to the taking. Of course, if a policeman, rather than the owner, persuades the defendant to commit a larceny, the defense of entrapment, not that of the owner's consent, is applicable. See § 5.2.

ship or co-ownership property. The cases denying that such misappropriation constitutes larceny may be explained on the ground that there is no trespass in taking what one has a right to possess, or in the alternative on the ground that property which is partly one's own is not the property "of another." [10] The theft statutes in the modern codes usually contain an express provision to the contrary.[11]

Similar difficulties have arisen when one spouse makes off with the separate property of the other. At common law this was considered not to be larceny,[12] the usual explanation being the rule of unity which existed between husband and wife (for, as it was sometimes said, the husband and wife were one, and the husband was that one).[13] Later, larceny convictions were sometimes allowed in the exceptional case when the thieving married partner was leaving or had already separated from his mate.[14] Modern statutes allowing a married woman to own her separate property free from her husband's control, thus abrogating the unity rule, have generally been held

to authorize larceny convictions of either husband or wife.[15] A few modern criminal codes expressly state that taking property from a spouse is not a theft, while a few others have adopted the Model Penal Code position that it "is no defense that the theft was from the actor's spouse, except that misappropriation of household and personal effects, or other property normally accessible to both spouses, is theft only if it occurs after the parties have ceased living together." [16]

Switching now from various situations which, because they may involve factors which negative a trespass, tend to hinder or prevent larceny prosecutions [17] to other situations where a trespass, though perhaps difficult for the uninitiated to discover, nevertheless exists: we have already noted briefly that servants, bailees who break bulk, persons who obtain possession by lies, finders, those who receive or pick up others' property by mistake or who are erroneously overpaid are all eligible, in proper cases, for larceny convictions.[18]

---

10. State v. Elsbury, 63 Nev. 463, 175 P.2d 430 (1946) (partnership property is not "property of another," so partner who converts partnership property cannot be guilty of larceny); State v. Eberhart, 106 Wash. 222, 179 P. 853 (1919) (same). The modern trend by statute is to make misappropriation by partners a type of embezzlement.

11. See § 8.4(c).

12. See Note, 61 Colum.L.Rev. 73, 79–81 (1961).

13. Ibid., pointing out, however, that the rule that the husband owned his wife's property, though she did not own his, stands in the way of convicting a husband of stealing his wife's property but does not preclude conviction of the wife for stealing her husband's property. Her immunity, it is suggested in somewhat flowery fashion, may have been based on "an implicit judicial conclusion that it would be both inappropriate and unwise to allow the drastic sanctions of the criminal law to become a pawn in an intimate and volatile relationship." Id. at 80.

14. Ibid.

15. Whitson v. State, 65 Ariz. 395, 181 P.2d 822 (1947) (husband convicted of larceny of wife's separate property; conviction reversed on other grounds); State v. Herndon, 158 Fla. 115, 27 So.2d 833 (1946) (trial court improperly quashed information charging husband with larceny of $5,000 of wife's separate property; a man can steal from his wife); Beasley v. State, 138 Ind. 552, 38 N.E. 35 (1894) (husband indicted for larceny of wife's property, committed when they lived together; his motion to quash the indictment *held* properly denied); State v. Koontz, 124 Kan. 216, 257 P. 944 (1927) (wife gave her husband sleep-

ing powders and then disappeared with his car, trunk, all his clothing, watch, guns, diamond ring, and $66 cash; she gave some of this to another man; conviction of larceny *held* affirmed); People v. Morton, 308 N.Y. 96, 123 N.E.2d 790 (1954) (husband convicted of larceny of wife's separate property).

Of the above cases, State v. Herndon suggests that it is not larceny for one spouse to use the other's funds for food, clothing or family necessities, and People v. Morton states that "the good sense and careful judgment of prosecutors and police, judges and juries, must be relied on not to turn into larcenies petty disagreements over personal property."

16. Model Penal Code § 223.1(4).

17. As a matter of moral quality, the wrongdoing of some of those who escape larceny liability for lack of a trespass in the taking is just as bad as if their wrongdoing had involved such a trespass. A finder who picks up lost property with intent to return it and who later decides to steal it is no better morally than one who intends to steal when he picks it up. The same may be said for one who by a mistake receives delivery of another's property (including an overpayment): he is morally no better a person if he decides later to steal than if he decides to steal at the outset. Any proper criminal code should punish the wrongdoer who thus has a delayed reaction about as severely as his more precipitous counterpart, either by making his conduct a crime other than larceny, or (a better solution) by expanding larceny to take him in. See § 8.8.

18. See § 8.1.

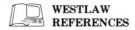

**WESTLAW
REFERENCES**

topic(234) /p trespass /2 taking

234k26

234k7 herndon /p larceny /s spouse wife husband

(b) Master and Servant. Thus we have seen that where the master (in more modern terminology, employer) puts his servant (employee) in charge of his property, the master still has possession ("constructive possession") while the servant has mere custody.[19] But if the property comes to the servant from a third person for the master, the servant has possession until he puts it in some receptacle (such as a cash drawer) designated by the master for its reception.[20] As to the first proposition, the cases draw a distinction between a caretaker or other minor sort of employee, who has custody only,[21] and one to whom the employer has delegated considera-

bly more authority, who has possession.[22] The second proposition [23] has led to some borderline distinctions.[24]

**WESTLAW
REFERENCES**

234k15 /p larceny /s employ** master servant
topic(234) /p larceny /s employ** master servant /
   s custody

(c) Transaction to be Completed in the Owner's Presence. A property owner who delivers his property to another in connection with a transaction to be completed in the owner's presence—as where he hands the other a large bill to be changed or counted or for an inexpensive purchase, or where he delivers him property to be inspected or appraised or worked upon while the owner waits—retains constructive possession, as we have seen;[25] so that, when the other misappropriates it, he is guilty of larceny; there is a trespass in the

---

19. E.g., United States v. Mafnas, 701 F.2d 83 (9th Cir. 1983) (where employee of armored car service removed money from moneybags, this larceny, as he had mere custody of the bags); Crocheron v. State, 86 Ala. 64, 5 So. 649 (1889) (field hand, furnished with a mule by his employer to plow the field, absconded with it; his conviction of larceny *held* affirmed, for he had mere custody, not possession).

20. See § 8.1.

21. Fitch v. State, 135 Fla. 361, 185 So. 435 (1938) (night watchman of a bar took money from cash register; conviction of larceny *held* affirmed, as he had custody of the property in the bar while proprietor had possession); Warren v. State, 223 Ind. 552, 62 N.E.2d 624 (1945) (member of maintenance crew working under a foreman had a key to a storage building belonging to his employer; he misappropriated property from the building; conviction of larceny *held* affirmed over his contention that his crime was properly embezzlement).

22. Morgan v. Commonwealth, 242 Ky. 713, 47 S.W.2d 543 (1932) (the office manager of a Western Union office, who had the combination to the safe, the only other combination being in a sealed envelope at the company's main office, abstracted money from the safe; conviction of larceny *held* reversed; since he had possession of the contents of the safe, his crime was not larceny but embezzlement); Bismarck v. State, 45 Tex.Crim.R. 54, 73 S.W. 965 (1903) (employee in charge of store belonging to another, with authority to sell goods, receive money, draw checks, possessed the key and knew the combination to safe; he took goods from store and delivered them to defendant; such an employee has possession, not custody, so his crime is not larceny, so defendant's conviction of receiving stolen property *held* reversed). See Annot., 125 A.L.R. 367, 371–81 (1940).

23. The original case is Bazeley's Case, § 8.1 at n. 4. See also Nolan v. State, 213 Md. 298, 131 A.2d 851 (1957)

(loan company employee took from the cash drawer money which had been placed there after being received from customers, falsifying the daily report of receipts; his conviction of embezzlement *held* reversed; his crime was larceny, not embezzlement, because the money had been put in the cash drawer before the misappropriation by the defendant); Regina v. Reed, 169 Eng.Rep. 717 (Cr.Cas.Res. 1854) (servant, sent by master to railroad station for coals to be brought back to the master's house, placed them in the master's cart; on the way home he fraudulently converted some of the coals; his conviction of larceny *held* affirmed; his placing the coals in the master's cart gave the master constructive possession; it would not have been larceny if he had carried off the coal before placing it in the cart).

24. E.g., Commonwealth v. Ryan, 155 Mass. 523, 30 N.E. 364 (1892) (employee in store sold employer's goods, received cash therefor, put the cash in the drawer of the cash register without registering the sale, and a minute or two later took the money from the drawer; conviction of embezzlement *held* affirmed, over defendant's contention that his crime was larceny; where employee intends to steal when he receives the money, putting it in the cash drawer for a short time for convenience, immediately thereafter taking it out, the crime is embezzlement, just as if he had never put the money, or had accidentally dropped it, in the drawer).

Once again, on principle it is nonsense to have to distinguish between a store manager and a minor clerk who abstracts his employer's money or goods; or between an employee who, receiving cash on behalf of his employer, pockets it at once, or after he has put it in the till for two minutes, or after he has left it there for a longer period. Morally, his offense is the same in these alternative situations.

25. See § 8.1.

taking, for, in taking it, he has removed it from the owner's (constructive) possession.[26]

(d) Bailee Who Breaks Bale or Breaks Bulk. We have seen that, as a protection for England's growing trade and commerce, the English courts in the 15th century held it to be larceny for a bailee, in rightful possession of another's baled (packaged) goods to break open the bale and misappropriate a part or all of the contents,[27] although if he misappropriated the entire bale, without breaking it open, it was not larceny.[28] Although the rule originated in the case of a bailee for purposes of transportation, it was extended to apply to other types of bailees as well.[29] The original

rule that it is larceny under these circumstances to break open a bale ("breaking bale")[30] was broadened to cover cases of misappropriation of a part (though not all) of unbaled goods shipped in bulk ("breaking bulk"),[31] and even of packaged goods so shipped, where part (but not all) of the packages are taken, though none is broken open.[32] In the United States today the situation of the misappropriating bailee who either does or does not break bale or break bulk is variously treated. In some states, it is larceny if there is such a breaking, embezzlement if not. In others there are statutes which make it larceny, or embezzlement, or a new crime (separate from larceny and embezzlement) called "larceny by bailee," or a larger new crime (encompassing both larceny and embezzle-

---

26. Atkinson v. United States, 289 F. 935 (D.C.Cir. 1923) (owner of diamond ring, asked by defendant if he might inspect it, handed it to defendant, who carried it off; conviction of embezzlement *held* reversed, because the crime was larceny); Commonwealth v. O'Malley, 97 Mass. 584 (1867) (owner, not able to read or write, handed defendant her money to count it in her presence; he ran off with it; conviction of embezzlement *held* reversed; defendant had custody but not possession, so his crime was larceny, not embezzlement); Hildebrand v. People, 56 N.Y. 394 (1874) (owner of $50 bill gave it to bartender for a 10¢ soda, expecting $49.90 in change; the bartender took the owner by the neck, shoved him out the door and kept the money; his conviction of larceny *held* affirmed; since it was an incomplete transaction, to be consummated in the presence and under the personal control of the [owner], possession did not pass from the owner to the bartender but remained in the owner); Dignowitty v. State, 17 Tex. 521 (1856) (owner of contract handed it to defendant, a party thereto, to inspect in her presence; defendant, who at first intended only to inspect, destroyed it, his conviction of larceny held affirmed).

Where the owner of money hands money to the other to go out and make change, i.e., the transaction not to be entirely consummated in the owner's presence, there is a dispute as to whether the misappropriation is larceny. Compare Regina v. Reynolds, 2 Cox Crim.Cas. 170 (1847) (not larceny, for owner parted with possession); with Justices of Court of Special Sessions of New York County v. People ex rel. Henderson, 90 N.Y. 12 (1882) (larceny, for owner retained possession).

27. See § 8.1, especially Carrier's Case, note 3 therein.

28. Often, of course, the bailed goods are not wrapped in bales which can be broken open, as where one hires or borrows a horse and buggy; if he later converts it, it is not larceny (unless there is the additional fact that he acquired possession by lies with intent to misappropriate it, thus making it a case of larceny by trick). E.g., Hill v. State, 57 Wis. 377, 15 N.W. 445 (1883) (if defendant hires

or borrows property in good faith, and later converts it, it is not larceny). See Annot., 125 A.L.R. 367, 381–84 (1940). As to unbaled goods shipped by bulk, see text immediately below.

29. E.g., Robinson v. State, 41 Tenn. 120 (1860) (bailee of trunk left in his charge for safekeeping).

30. The rule is followed in America, of course. E.g., United States v. Mafnas, 701 F.2d 83 (9th Cir.1983) (armored car service employee who opened moneybags and took money from them guilty of larceny, as he broke bulk); State v. Fairclough, 29 Conn. 47 (1860) (defendant who broke open package and converted its contents was guilty of larceny; but if he had converted the entire package, he would not have been guilty of larceny); State v. Ruffin, 164 N.C. 416, 79 S.E. 417 (1913) (defendant, given a letter to mail, opened the envelope and misappropriated money therefrom; conviction of larceny *held* affirmed).

31. Rex v. Howell, 173 Eng.Rep. 145 (1837) (defendant boatowner, employed to carry a load of wooden staves, took home one stave; charge to jury that this is larceny if defendant had an intent to convert, for separating one from the rest is breaking bulk; verdict, not guilty); Nichols v. People, 17 N.Y. 114 (1858) (defendant, owner of canal boat, took aboard 34 tons of pig iron in 100 lb. bars; on the passage he fraudulently converted 100 bars, later delivering the rest; conviction of embezzlement *held* reversed, because defendant, a bailee who had broken bulk, was guilty of larceny; the principle applies not only when one breaks a bale or package, but when one separates a part from the whole of goods shipped in bulk; it would have been different if this had been a shipment of 680 bars rather than 34 tons).

See Annot., 125 A.L.R. 367, 386–87 (1940).

32. Commonwealth v. Brown, 4 Mass. 580 (1808) (defendant wagoner, carrying a wagon load of packaged goods, misappropriated one package, but did not break it open; conviction of larceny *held* affirmed).

ment) called "theft," without regard to whether there is such a breaking.

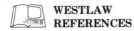

WESTLAW REFERENCES

fi 701f2d83

(e) Larceny by Trick. In our look into the history of the theft crimes we learned that one who obtains possession of, but not title to, another's property by lies, then intending fraudulently to convert the property and later doing so, is guilty of larceny.[33] The distinction between obtaining possession and obtaining title—the principal dividing line, not always easy to draw, between larceny by trick and the separate crime of false pretenses—is discussed at some length below.[34] The lies which will suffice for larceny by trick may be written or spoken; they are generally misrepresentations of some present or past fact, but there is authority that for larceny by

trick, as distinguished from false pretenses under the majority view, a false promise (i.e., a promise which the promisor, at the time he makes it, does not intend to keep) will do.[35] There is a question whether the defendant must intend, at the moment he obtains possession of the property by lies, to convert it, or whether a subsequently-formed intent to convert it will do.[36] At all events, he must, in fact, later convert it.[37]

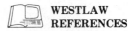

WESTLAW REFERENCES

234k14 /p possession /s trick

(f) Finders.[38] The owner of lost property or of mislaid property (with mislaid property, the owner has intentionally placed it somewhere and then forgotten it) has "constructive possession" of it as long as the actual possession is vacant;[39] therefore, a finder who picks up the lost or mislaid property intending to

---

33. See 8.1, especially Rex v. Pear, at note 7 therein. Although known as "larceny by trick," the crime is larceny, not a crime separate from larceny. This is not always the case with the crime which exists in England and some states—the separate crime, discussed immediately above, called "larceny by bailee."

34. See § 8.7(d). Briefly, the distinction is between buying property, on the one hand, and borrowong or hiring property, on the other, by the use of lies.

35. Thus in the leading larceny-by-trick case of People v. Miller, 169 N.Y. 339, 62 N.E. 418 (1902), wherein the defendant obtained the victim's money by means of various false promises, the court worked hard to find that the victim parted with possession and not title to the money, in order to affirm a larceny conviction, stating that otherwise it was "very doubtful" that the defendant could be convicted of anything, for false promises will not do for false pretenses.

36. In support of the former view, see Skantze v. United States, 288 F.2d 416 (D.C.Cir.1961) ("intending at the time to convert the money, and actually converting it, to his own use"); State v. Harrison, 347 Mo. 1230, 152 S. W.2d 161 (1941) (defendant obtained check by fraud with intent to convert it; he later converted it; conviction of larceny *held* affirmed, over defendant's contention that his crime was embezzlement; if defendant honestly receives possession of property and later fraudulently converts it, it is embezzlement, "but if possession of the property is obtained by fraud, with an intent on the part of the defendant at the time he receives it, to convert the same to his own use, and the person parting therewith intends only to surrender his possession, but not his title, the offense is larceny"). But the cases on "continuing trespass," see § 8.5(f), hold, to the contrary, that to obtain possession by lies, though without an intent to steal, is a trespass which continues, so that a later formed intent to steal, followed by an actual conversion, equals larceny.

State v. Coombs, 55 Me. 477 (1868); Commonwealth v. White, 65 Mass. (11 Cush.) 483 (1853).

37. Skantze v. United States, supra note 36 ("and actually converting it, to his own use"); Stewart v. United States, 151 F.2d 386 (8th Cir.1945) (defendant by lies got car owner to lend him his car, the defendant at the time intending to convert it, "as he actually did"; conviction of transporting stolen car in interstate commerce *held* affirmed); Blackburn v. Commonwealth, 28 Ky.L.R. 96, 89 S.W. 160 (1905) (for larceny by trick it is "as essential to show a conversion of the property" as to show that, at the time of obtaining possession of it, he had the fraudulent intent to convert; a pledge of a horse for $2 is not a conversion of the horse if the defendant has the intention to redeem the pledge and return the horse, and has an ability to do so). With ordinary forms of larceny an asportation is the necessary element, but an asportation may well not constitute a conversion. Larceny by trick, therefore, requires something more than other forms of larceny.

As to what conduct constitutes a conversion, see § 8.6(b), dealing with this required element for embezzlement. "Conversion" means the same thing in larceny by trick, embezzlement, and the tort of conversion.

38. See Riesman, Possession and the Law of Finders, 52 Harv.L.Rev. 1105, 1130–33 (1939); Annot., 36 A.L.R. 372 (1925).

39. See § 8.1. E.g., United States v. Sellers, 670 F.2d 853 (9th Cir.1982) (where bank teller placed cashed check on counter and then forgot it was there, after which customer who had already cashed it carried it off and cashed it again at another bank, the check was taken from the constructive possession of the bank); State v. Courtsol, 89 Conn. 564, 94 A. 973 (1915) (mislaid property left in trolley car; "the owner is treated as still constructively in possession of it, although its custody may be in another in whose shop or car it has been left"); Foulke v. New York

misappropriate it may be viewed as taking it by a trespass from the owner's possession, so that his conduct constitutes the necessary trespass in the taking for larceny.[40] To be guilty of larceny, however, more than a trespass is required: the finder must, at the time of the finding, (1) intend to steal it and (2) either know who the owner is or have reason to believe (from earmarkings on the property or from the circumstances of the finding)[41] that he can find out the owner's identity.[42] It is not larceny, therefore, for a finder to pick up property with knowledge of or means of discovering its ownership, intending to return it to the owner, or to pick up property with no knowledge of or means of discovering the owner, intending to keep it for himself, even though later, with full knowledge of the ownership, the finder converts it to his own use.[43] And he is not guilty of larceny if he picks up another's lost property, with no knowledge or means of discovering the owner, with intent to convert it, because later he may not use proper diligence in trying to discover the owner.[44] Modern theft statutes, it should be noted, typically deal with the theft-by-finders case in a quite different manner.[45]

WESTLAW REFERENCES

234k16 234k10

Consol. R. Co., 228 N.Y. 269, 127 N.E. 237 (1920) (mislaid property left on seat in subway car; "the owner was still constructively in possession of it"); Brooks v. State, 35 Ohio St. 46 (1878) (property lost on the street; "the title to the property, and its constructive possession, still remains in the owner; and the finder, if he takes possession of it for his own use, and not for the benefit of the owner, would be guilty of trespass").

Historically, at one time a distinction was made between the owner of lost property (who lost possession) and that of mislaid property (who kept constructive possession). E.g., Rex v. Pierce, 6 Cox Crim.Cas. 117 (1852). Today, no such distinction is made.

40. If, instead of intending to misappropriate, he intends to locate the owner and return it, there is no trespass, for one is justified in taking possession of lost or mislaid property for such a purpose.

41. With mislaid property, it is easier than with lost property to find that the circumstances disclose the ownership; the fact that property is mislaid rather than lost "implies that means are at hand to know or learn who the owner is." State v. Courtsol, supra note 39.

42. Penny v. State, 109 Ark. 343, 159 S.W. 1127 (1913) (finder of lost property, perhaps without earmarks of ownership, which had been lost in the roadway, was told by his son, who had seen the schoolteacher pass by earlier, that he thought it was the teacher's; nevertheless finder pocketed it with intent to convert it; conviction of larceny *held* affirmed; rule is that if finder "does know, or has the immediate means of ascertaining, who the owner is," and yet picks it up intending to steal it, it is larceny; here he did not know but he knew of facts, through his son, which gave him the means of ascertaining the owner); State v. Courtsol, supra note 41 (mislaid property; finder who picks it up with intent to steal, "knowing or having the means of ascertaining the owner" is guilty of larceny); People v. Betts, 367 Ill. 499, 11 N.E.2d 942 (1937) (lost property; it is larceny "if the finder, at the time of finding, intends to deprive the owner permanently of his property, and if he knows or has a reasonable clue as to who the owner is"; where there is no knowledge or clue, finder is "under no duty to advertise or to make inquiry for the owner as far as the crime of larceny is concerned"); Brooks v. State, supra note 39 (lost property; it is "larceny

by the finder when, at the time he finds it, he has reasonable ground to believe, from the nature of the property or the circumstances under which it is found, that if he does not conceal it but deals honestly with it, the owner will appear or be ascertained"); Regina v. Thurborn, 169 Eng.Rep. 293 (Cr.Cas.Res.1848) (lost property; it is not larceny if the finder, with intent to take the entire dominion over the property, really believes, when he takes the property, that the owner cannot be found; it is larceny if, with like intent, he reasonably believes the owner can be found).

See Annot., 36 A.L.R. 372 (1925).

43. See People v. Betts, Regina v. Thurborn, supra note 42. No doubt such a person is morally as bad as the finder who immediately decides to steal. Whether the crime of embezzlement or larceny by bailee applies to the situation depends upon whether fraudulently-converting finders in rightful possession are covered by the embezzlement or larceny-by-bailee statutes.

44. People v. Betts, supra note 42 (a finder is "under no duty to advertise or to make inquiry for the owner as far as the crime of larceny is concerned"); State v. Dean, 49 Iowa 73 (1878) (a finder who, because he is ignorant of the owner, picks up lost property lawfully, is not later made guilty of larceny because he omits to use reasonable diligence to discover the owner).

45. Model Penal Code § 223.5 makes the finder guilty if, coming into control of property he knows to be lost or mislaid, he fails, with intent to deprive the owner thereof, to take reasonable steps to restore the property to the owner. Under the Code he does not escape liability by his lack of knowledge of or means of ascertaining ownership existing at the time he picks it up, or (if he does not so lack knowledge or means) by his postponing his intent to steal until some time after the pick-up. On the other hand, he is not guilty (even if he does know the owner or has the means to steal) when he intends to steal at time of pick-up, if he later changes his mind and takes reasonable steps to find the owner.

Statutes along these lines appear in most of the modern codes. See, e.g., State v. Kaufman, 310 N.W.2d 709 (N.D.1981), discussing such a statute.

topic(234)   /p   "constructive possession"

(g) Delivery of Property by Mistake. Property belonging to one person may be delivered to another under a mistake as to the nature of the property (such as, delivery of gold pieces in the belief that they are nickels[46] or a trunk containing money or clothes although thought to be empty),[47] or as to the amount of the property (as where one, cashing a check for $36, is paid $4,328),[48] or as to the identity of the recipient (as where mailed property intended for one James Mucklow is delivered by the postman to another James Mucklow).[49] It is well settled that the recipient of the mistaken delivery who appropriates the property commits a trespass in the taking, and so is guilty of larceny, if, realizing the mistake at the moment he takes delivery, he then forms an intent to steal the property.[50] On the other hand, if, when he takes delivery, either (1) he does not realize the mistake and so cannot then have an intent to steal, or (2) he does realize the mistake but intends to return the property, he cannot be guilty of larceny even though he may later decide to steal,[51] for two reasons: (1) as to the original taking of delivery, there is no trespass, for he took it with an innocent mind, and (2) as to the later intent to steal, it did not coincide with the taking.

The principal difficulty in applying the rule arises in the cases of delivery of goods or money enclosed in a package or envelope or other container, so that the defendant first receives the container without knowledge of the contents and therefore without any dishonest intent to steal anything; later (perhaps a minute, perhaps several days) he opens the container, discovers the mistake and immediately decides to steal. The cases are split between the view that he is guilty of larceny because he intends to steal when he takes the property, for he does not "take" the property until he discovers its existence,[52] and the view that he is not guilty of larceny, for he "takes" the property enclosed in the container when he takes delivery of the container, so that his later intent to steal that property does not coincide with the taking.[53] As with finders, doubtless the defendant is about as bad moral-

46. Cooper v. Commonwealth, 110 Ky. 123, 60 S.W. 938 (1901) (defendant asked bank cashier for change for $2, received two half dollars and a roll of coins wrapped in paper thought to contain 20 nickels but in fact containing 20 $5 gold pieces); Regina v. Ashwell, 16 Cox Crim.Cas. 1 (Cr.Cas.Res.1885) (owner, intending to lend defendant a shilling, handed defendant a sovereign, both thinking it was a shilling).

47. Merry v. Green, 151 Eng.Rep. 916 (1841) (defendant purchased a secretary at auction, later discovered a secret drawer containing money and valuables); Robinson v. State, 11 Tex.Ct.App.R. 403 (1882) (defendant bought a trunk, later found to contain clothing).

48. Sapp v. State, 157 Fla. 605, 26 So.2d 646 (1946) (bank cashier misread figures on the check, which stated it was an order on the bank for the payment of $36 in payment of compensation benefits which totalled $4328 to date). See also United States v. Rogers, 289 F.2d 433 (4th Cir.1961) (inexperienced bank teller cashed a check for $97, dated 12 06 59, misreading it to be a check for $1,206.59, handing defendant $1,126.59 and crediting his account by $80); State v. Hector, 121 R.I. 685, 402 A.2d 595 (1979) (defendant overpaid $7,200 by teller who misread the check).

49. Rex v. Mucklow, 168 Eng.Rep. 1225 (Cr.Cas.Res. 1827); Rex v. Hudson, [1943] K.B. 458 (Ministry of Food owed money to one Hutson, mistakenly mailed the check to defendant Hudson).

50. For an explanation of the trespass element in the mistaken-delivery cases, see United States v. Rogers, 289 F.2d 433 (4th Cir.1961): For larceny there must be a

trespassory taking. "It has long been recognized, however, that when the transferor acts under a unilateral mistake of fact, his delivery of a chattel may be ineffective to transfer title or his right to possession. If the transferee, knowing of the transferor's mistake, receives the goods with the intention of appropriating them, his receipt and removal of them is a trespass and his offense is larceny." It is immaterial that the defendant had no prior plan to steal. State v. Hector, 121 R.I. 685, 402 A.2d 595 (1979).

51. See § 8.5(f). See Annot., 14 A.L.R. 894 (1921).

52. Robinson v. State, 11 Tex.Ct.App.R. 403 (1882) (merchant sold trunk, supposedly empty, but actually containing clothing, to defendant, who took it home, opened it, discovered the mistake, and decided to steal; conviction of larceny *held* affirmed); Rex v. Hudson, [1943] K.B. 458 (defendant received envelope addressed to him, inside of which was a check belonging to someone else; he did not open the envelope for several days; when he did and learned of the mistake, he decided to steal; appeal from conviction of larceny *held* dismissed); Merry v. Green, 151 Eng.Rep. 916 (1841) (defendant bought bureau at auction, afterward found a secret drawer containing valuables, which he immediately decided to steal; the court *held* the rule to be that if he bought the bureau without the contents, he was guilty of larceny).

53. Cooper v. Commonwealth, 110 Ky. 123, 60 S.W. 938 (1901) (as change for $1, defendant received wrapped roll of $5 gold pieces which both parties thought to be nickels; defendant discovered the mistake some time later upon unwrapping the roll; conviction of larceny *held* reversed); Rex v. Mucklow, 168 Eng.Rep. 1225 (1827) (defendant

ly when the urge to steal comes over him late, so that the distinctions in the law of larceny which depend upon the time when he becomes dishonest do not make much sense.[54] Such distinctions very often (but not always) have been abandoned in the modern criminal codes.

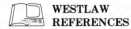

topic(234) /p mistake*** /s deliver** g*ve* receive*

(h) Property Picked up by Mistake. In what seems to be a situation analogous to that of mistaken delivery, one person picks up and carries off another person's property by mistake—as where A's lamb (or bull) is placed with or wanders into B's flock of sheep (or herd of cattle) and B, not noticing the addition, takes it away with the rest,[55] or where B, mistakenly thinking he is authorized by A to do so, carries off A 's property for some lawful purpose.[56] In a variant of this situation, B picks up A 's property, not with an innocent mind, but with a bad yet not criminal purpose—as where he intends to use it and re-

turn it.[57] Under either situation, what may happen to give rise to a larceny problem is that B later decides to steal and does so. The difficulty in holding B for larceny is not that there is no trespass in the taking, for it is clearly a trespass to pick up another person's property without legal right even if innocently done.[58] The difficulty lies in finding a coincidence of intent to steal and trespassory taking, a requirement discussed below.[59]

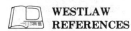

234k71(4) 234k78 /p mistake*

(i) Removal From Owner's Premises or Presence. One may be said to have taken another's property by a trespass though he has not removed it from the other's premises[60] or from his presence.[61]

234k17 /p control conceal hid! (leav*** left /4 store building shop)

---

received in the mail an envelope containing check belonging to another person of the same name; he later opened it, discovered the mistake and decided to steal it; conviction of larceny *held* wrong, and a pardon recommended).

54. Model Penal Code § 223.5 makes the transferee of property delivered by mistake (like the finder of property) guilty of theft if, with the purpose of depriving the owner thereof, he fails to take reasonable steps to restore the property to the person entitled to it. Thus nothing depends upon when he discovers the mistake or when he decides to misappropriate the property. If he does not learn of the mistake until after he takes delivery, or (if he learns on delivery) if he postpones his decision to steal, he is nonetheless guilty when he fails to take reasonable steps to restore the property. On the other hand, if he realizes the mistake and decides to steal at the moment he takes delivery, he is not guilty if he thereafter has a change of heart and takes reasonable steps.

55. Wilson v. State, 96 Ark. 148, 131 S.W. 336 (1910) (defendant took another's bull from the range, believing it to be his own); Regina v. Riley, 169 Eng.Rep. 674 (1853) (owner of lamb put him into land-owner's field, where he mingled with defendant's flock; defendant drove his flock and the additional lamb away).

56. Harvey v. State, 78 Nev. 417, 375 P.2d 225 (1962) (defendant took away owner's jewels mistakenly believing he had the owner's authority to do so to find a purchaser).

57. Commonwealth v. White, 65 Mass. (11 Cush.) 483 (1853).

58. Restatement (Second) of Torts § 221 (1965). This is different from the mistaken-delivery and finder cases,

where the original receipt by the deliveree, or pick-up by the finder, constitutes no trespass.

59. See § 8.5(f), for a discussion of "continuing trespass," which if applicable enables one to find the coincidence.

60. People v. Lardner, 300 Ill. 264, 133 N.E. 375 (1921) (defendant took goods from store's show case, put them in pockets of an overcoat he was carrying on his arm; becoming alarmed, he left the store, leaving his overcoat behind on a counter six feet from the show case; conviction of attempted larceny *held* reversed, for evidence shows completed crime of larceny); People v. Bradovich, 305 Mich. 329, 9 N.W.2d 560 (1943) (defendants took clothing from rack in store, concealed it, then noticed policemen and put the clothing on a table at another part of the same floor of the store; conviction of larceny *held* affirmed); People v. Olivio, 52 N.Y.2d 309, 438 N.Y.S.2d 242, 420 N.E.2d 40 (1981) (sufficient taking by shoplifter who has not left store if he has exercised control wholly inconsistent with the owner's rights, which may be demonstrated by, e.g., concealing the goods under clothing or in a container); State v. Moultrie, 283 S.C. 352, 322 S.E.2d 663 (1984) (larceny complete where defendant moved 3 tires 33 ft. from rack in tire store). See Annots., 19 A.L.R. 724, 726–27 (1922); 144 A.L.R. 1383, 1384–5 (1943).

61. Jarrott v. State, 108 Tex.Crim.R. 427, 1 S.W.2d 619 (1927) (policeman who owned a car, suspecting that defendant was stealing cars, left keys in the switch and hid in the back of the car; defendant drove the car away, after which the policeman got out of the back and arrested him; conviction of larceny *held* affirmed).

§ 8.3   Larceny—Taking and Carrying Away

Commission of the crime of larceny requires a taking (caption) and carring away (asportation) of another's property.[1] A taking occurs when the offender secures dominion over the property, while a carrying away requires some slight movement away of the property.

(a) Taking (Caption). The defendant does not commit larceny of another's property unless he "takes" it in the sense of securing dominion over it.[2] There is no "caption," as the taking element is sometimes called, if the defendant, in an attempt to steal another's property, strikes the latter's hand, causing him to drop the property on the ground where, because of the darkness, the defendant cannot find it.[3] So too property which, unknown to the defendant when he first tries to carry it off, is chained in such a way that, although it can be moved, it cannot be taken away, cannot be "taken."[4] On the other hand, one may "take" the property of another, although he personally does not acquire dominion over it, if he sells it as his own to an innocent third person, who then takes possession of it.[5]

As we shall see, there is a question concerning the *time* of taking of another's property, which, unknown to the defendant, has been deposited within a container of some sort.[6] Also, one can take another's property without removing it from the latter's premises or from his presence.[7]

 WESTLAW REFERENCES

234k12 /p caption tak***

(b) Carrying Away (Asportation).[8] The word "carrying" in the expression "carrying away" (the common law requirement of an asportation) is not to be taken literally, for one can be guilty of larceny of property which he cannot pick up in his hands, as by riding away a horse, leading away a cow, driving off in an automobile or pulling or pushing a heavy object along the ground or floor.[9] The distance "away" which the property must be moved need not be substantial—a slight distance will do.[10] But every part of the proper-

---

§ 8.3.

1. A modern theft statute, of course, may require neither. See, e.g., State v. Genova, 77 Wis.2d 141, 252 N.W.2d 380 (1977) (so concluding as to statute covering one who intentionally "takes and carries away, uses, transfers, conceals, or retains possession of movable property of another").

2. Modern theft statutes often make this clear by referring to the requisite conduct in terms of exercising control, as does Model Penal Code § 223.2. Some, however, adhere to the more traditional terminology.

3. Thompson v. State, 94 Ala. 535, 10 So. 520 (1892) ("There must be such a caption that the accused acquires dominion over the property.").

4. People v. Meyer, 75 Cal. 383, 17 P. 431 (1888) (coat chained to a dummy which prevented its removal; there is not such a taking as would amount to larceny); Clark v. State, 59 Tex.Crim. 246, 128 S.W. 131 (1910) (dress attached to dummy in such a way as to prevent its removal; not theft because defendant "had not reduced the dress to his control so as to constitute a taking").

This sort of case has been explained on the ground that there was no asportation, e.g., Annot., 19 A.L.R. 724, 729 (1922), but that explanation will not do for Clark v. State, supra, as the applicable statute did not require any asportation.

5. See a discussion of this larceny situation, and cases cited, infra in § 8.3(b). The problem has generally been worded in terms of whether there was a sufficient asportation by the defendant when the innocent third person,

having bought the property, takes possession and carries it away. The cases which hold the defendant guilty of larceny necessarily find a caption as well as an asportation.

6. See § 8.5(f), pointing out that some cases find that he takes it when he receives the container, others when he discovers the property which the container holds.

7. See § 8.2(i).

8. See Annots., 19 A.L.R. 724 (1922), 144 A.L.R. 1383 (1943).

9. E.g., State v. Rozeboom, 145 Iowa 620, 124 N.W. 783 (1910) ("it is entirely immaterial whether he accomplished the removal by lifting and carrying the tubs in his arms, or by rolling or pushing or pulling them along" without lifting them from the floor). On asportation of a motor vehicle, see Annot., 70 A.L.R.3d 1202 (1976).

10. Smith v. United States, 291 F.2d 220 (9th Cir.1961) (defendant put hands on bag containing money and started to pull it toward him, moving it two or three inches according to one witness, four to six inches according to another; conviction of larceny *held* affirmed, for "the least removing of the thing taken from the place it was before" is enough); Adams v. Commonwealth, 153 Ky. 88, 154 S.W. 381 (1913) (defendant put hands in victim's pocket, grasped a roll of money, pulled it to near the top of the pocket, when victim caught defendant's hand; conviction of larceny *held* affirmed); Harrison v. People, 50 N.Y. 518 (1872) (defendant put hand in victim's pocket, grasped his pocketbook, lifted it three inches from the bottom of the pocket, when its owner discovered him, seizing the

ty must be moved; it is not enough, for instance, to turn a barrel, standing on its head, onto its side, in order to get a better grip on it.[11] The movement must be a "carrying away" movement; it is not enough, for instance, merely to shoot an animal for purpose of stealing it, though it moves from a standing to a prone position when shot.[12] As already noted, so long as the defendant moves every part of it, it is not necessary to move it away from the owner's premises or from his presence.[13]

One difficult fact situation concerning the asportation element in larceny is where A, falsely pretending to be the owner of B's property, sells it to C, an innocent purchaser, who after the sale takes it and carries it off. Since A never touched it, how can it be said that he took and carried it away? The majority and better view is that C is A's innocent agent for the purpose of the caption and asportation requirements, so that C's taking and carrying away is attributable to A,[14] but there is authority to the contrary, refusing to attribute C's caption and asportation to A, on the ground that, under ordinary agency principles, the purchaser is not the seller's agent.[15] There has been less difficulty in finding an asportation by an innocent agent

in the case where A switches tags on B's baggage, so that the carrier C, following the directions on the false tag, carries the baggage to A instead of to B. Here, although A has not personally moved the baggage, the asportation of C, A's innocent agent, is held to be attributable to A.[16]

There are in some jurisdictions special larceny statutes which provide a greater punishment than for ordinary larceny where the larceny in question is "from the person" (popularly called pickpocketing) or (less frequently) "from the house" (or "dwelling house," or "building"). For larceny from the person it is not enough to move the property within the pocket; it must be moved out of the pocket.[17] So also, the crime of larceny from the house is not committed when the only asportation occurs within the house; to be guilty the defendant must have carried the property out of the house.[18]

We have already noted that for that special type of larceny called "larceny by trick," something more than a mere asportation is required; the defendant must actually convert the property.[19]

The common law asportation requirement is generally of no significance today, as theft

pocketbook and thrusting it back into the pocket; conviction of larceny *held* affirmed); State v. Carswell, 296 N.C. 101, 249 S.E.2d 427 (1978) (act of picking air conditioner up from its stand and laying it on floor sufficient asportation).

11. State v. Jones, 65 N.C. 395 (1871); Cherry's Case, 1 Leach C.C. 236 note (1781). This fine distinction, which makes not a bit of sense today, has been described as the distinction between rotating a doughnut (every part moves, as is required for larceny) and rotating a pie (the exact center portion, infinitely small, does not move).

12. Molton v. State, 105 Ala. 18, 16 So. 795 (1895); State v. Butler, 65 N.C. 309 (1871). Contra: Driggers v. State, 96 Fla. 232, 118 So. 20 (1928).

13. See § 8.2(i); also Adams v. Commonwealth, and Harrison v. People, supra note 10.

14. Smith v. State, 11 Ga.App. 197, 74 S.E. 1093 (1912) (conviction of larceny *held* affirmed; "the purchaser takes as his innocent agent, and the act of the purchaser amounts to a taking by the seller"); State v. Patton, 364 Mo. 1044, 271 S.W.2d 560 (1954). See Annots. 19 A.L.R. 724, 725–26 (1922), 144 A.L.R. 1383, 1384–85 (1943). Of course, one can commit a crime through an innocent agent, as where Fagin forces Oliver Twist, who is too young to be guilty of crime or has the defense of coercion thereto, to steal for him.

15. State v. Laborde, 202 La. 59, 11 So.2d 404 (1942), pointing out that A, who received money from C, doubtless committed the crime of false pretenses. For other cases, see Annots., 19 A.L.R. 724, 725–26 (1922), 144 A.L.R. 1383, 1384–85 (1943). When one speaks of a criminal committing a crime through means of an innocent agent, one is not necessarily talking strictly in terms of principal and agents; one may be an agent for this purpose, for instance, without being employed in a fiduciary capacity, as where A hypnotizes B into killing C. Thus the *Laborde* case is wrong in holding that a seller cannot be the agent of the principal for larceny's caption and asportation requirements.

16. Aldrich v. People, 224 Ill. 622, 79 N.E. 964 (1906); State v. Rozeboom, 145 Iowa 620, 124 N.W. 783 (1910); Commonwealth v. Barry, 125 Mass. 390 (1878).

17. Rex v. Taylor, [1911] 1 K.B. 674 (1910) (conviction of larceny from the person reduced to common law larceny).

Compare Adams v. Commonwealth and Harrison v. People, supra note 10, holding it to be ordinary larceny to move property within a pocket, though the thief is discovered before he can get it from the pocket.

18. Hicks v. State, 101 Ga. 581, 28 S.E. 917 (1897).

19. See § 8.2(e).

offenses in the modern codes are usually defined without resort to that concept.[20] In this respect, these statutes follow the Model Penal Code.[21] While this abandonment of the asportation requirement has sometimes been criticized,[22] the Code position is sound. If the defendant has taken control of the property, then it is of no penological significance whether or not he has in any sense engaged in a carrying away of that property.

**WESTLAW
REFERENCES**

234k17   /p   control***
234k17   /p   carry*** mov*** remov***
234k19

§ 8.4   Larceny—Personal Property of Another

Although common law larceny was limited to the taking of tangible personal property, modern statutes have generally covered other kinds of property as well. Most jurisdictions distinguish between grand and petit larceny, depending upon the value of the property. The property must be "of another," which excludes such items as abandoned property and wild animals.

(a) Nature of the Property. At common law, larceny was limited to misappropriations of goods and chattels—i.e., tangible personal property. It could not be larceny to carry away real property. As to those items of real property—such as trees, crops, minerals and fixtures—which become personal property after severance from the realty, the common law view was that it is not larceny to sever the property and carry it away in one continuous act,[1] but if the severance and asportation constitute two separate acts (as where the trespasser left the premises, or a substantial period of time intervened between these two events), it is larceny.[2] At common law one could not steal intangible personal property, including such substantial choses in action as stocks, bonds, checks or promissory notes, all of which are in the form of documents.[3] Written documents were considered, for purposes of larceny, to be merged into the things which they represented—so that a deed, representing real estate, or a contract, representing an intangible right to performance, could not be stolen.[4]

Modern statutes in all jurisdictions have broadened the scope of larceny to include such intangible personal property as written instruments embodying choses in action or other intangible rights.[5] In addition, a number of states have statutes making it larceny to steal such specific items savoring of real

20. See, e.g., State v. Victor, 368 So.2d 711 (La.1979) (statute requires only taking, not asportation, and thus larceny complete when shoplifter concealed store's goods in box); People v. Alamo, 34 N.Y.2d 453, 358 N.Y.S.2d 375, 315 N.E.2d 446 (1974) (crime defined as wrongful obtaining, and thus asportation not required, so jury instruction correct that crime could be committed by entering and starting car, though car did not move); Commonwealth v. Adams, 479 Pa. 508, 388 A.2d 1046 (1978) (statute requires only "taking or exercise of unlawful control," and thus larceny occurred when defendant started another's car and offered to sell it).

21. Model Penal Code § 223.2.

22. Hall, Theft, Law and Society, 54 A.B.A.J. 960, 962 (1968): " 'Asportation' is an extremely precise test to differentiate the attempt from the consummated crime; and although the difference between attempt and mere preparation is not a precise one, common law formulas and case law provide much help in determining that question."

§ 8.4

1. State v. Jackson, 218 N.C. 373, 11 S.E.2d 149 (1940) defendant severed tombstone from ground and carried it away; conviction of larceny *held* reversed); State v. Col-

lins, 188 S.C. 338, 199 S.E. 303 (1938) (defendant cut down trees, cut them into logs, put logs into truck, and hauled them off; conviction of larceny *held* reversed); Hyden v. State, 136 Tenn. 294, 189 S.W. 369 (1916) (defendant cut copper wire connecting trolley rails, put wire in a sack and carried it off; conviction of larceny *held* reversed).

See Annot., 131 A.L.R. 146 (1941).

2. Stansbury v. Luttrell, 152 Md. 553, 137 A. 339 (1927) (*A* cut *B*'s trees down, cut them into logs, left them on *B*'s premises for a while; then removed them; *held*, this constitutes larceny); State v. Gemma, 60 R.I. 382, 198 A. 784 (1938) (defendant ripped up railroad ties from ground, left them on the ground for various periods of time before carrying them off; conviction of larceny *held* affirmed).

3. State v. Dill, 75 N.C. 257 (1876) (indictment charging larceny of "one bill of fractional currency of the value," etc., *held* defective to charge common law larceny).

4. See Regina v. Powell, 169 Eng.Rep. 557 (1852) (deed); Hoskins v. Tarrence, 5 Blackf. 417 (Ind.1840) (deed); Regina v. Watts, 169 Eng.Rep. 747 (1854) (contract).

5. Tillery v. State, 44 Ala.App. 369, 209 So.2d 432 (1968); People v. Allen, 167 Colo. 158, 446 P.2d 223 (1968).

property as minerals, trees, crops and fixtures,[6] with no requirement of two separate acts of severance and asportation.[7] The trend of the modern criminal codes is to include any sort of property of value which can be moved.[8]

Gas and electricity are commonly held, without the aid of special statutes, to be property which can be stolen, the usual method being to run a gas pipe or electrical wire around the meter.[9] Property which is contraband may nevertheless be stolen.[10] On the other hand, in the absence of a specific statutory provision, it has been held not to be larceny to make use of the factory, or of the labor and services, of another.[11] Modern statutes, however, make it theft to steal labor or services or the use of property.[12]

WESTLAW REFERENCES

topic(234) /p property estate /3 tangible intangible real

234k5 /p mineral land ore timber trees gas electricity labor service

6. A few modern statutes cover only severed real estate. Most, however, define the "property" which may be the subject of theft as including *all* real estate. This latter approach has been criticized because of "the possibility of theft prosecutions in cases of holdover or eviction in a landlord-tenant relationship" and "the problem * * * of distinguishing between theft and criminal trespass." Model Penal Code § 223.2, Comment at 173–74 (1980). The Model Penal Code § 223.2 uses more cautious language so as to avoid such results, and a few states have followed that approach.

7. See Annot., 131 A.L.R. 146, 154–57 (1941). A modern case, Stephens v. Commonwealth, 304 Ky. 38, 199 S.W.2d 719 (1947), speaks of a trend, without aid of statutes, toward the view that severed real estate becomes personal property as soon as severed, so that it can be stolen by immediately carrying it off, even though severance and asportation be one continuous act.

8. Or, even property which cannot be moved. See note 6 supra.

Even such broad definitions, however, do not always suffice. See, e.g., Commonwealth v. Yourawski, 384 Mass. 386, 425 N.E.2d 298 (1981) (images and sounds of movie "Star Wars," captured on cassette tapes, not "property" within statute defining what may be subject of larceny). On theft of computer programs, see Annot., 18 A.L.R.3d 1121 (1968).

9. Commonwealth v. Shaw, 86 Mass. (4 Allen) 308 (1862) (gas); People v. Menagas, 367 Ill. 330, 11 N.E.2d 403 (1937) (electricity). See Annot., 113 A.L.R. 1282 (1938).

10. People v. Otis, 235 N.Y. 421, 139 N.E. 562 (1923) (illegal liquor); State v. Clementi, 224 Wis. 145, 272 N.W. 29 (1937) (illegal gambling device).

(b) Value of the Property: Grand Larceny vs. Petit Larceny.

Following the English precedent, practically all American jurisdictions by statute divide larceny (and, usually, theft more generally) into categories, depending upon the amount stolen. There is considerable variation in the number of categories utilized. Most common are two-, three- and four-tier arrangements, but even five- and six-tier classifications are to be found. There is likewise no agreement as to what amount should escalate the crime into the felony category. The range is from $2,000 to $50, with the most common being $100.

There are some legal questions concerned with valuation of stolen property. Property value is not necessarily its cost; rather it is its market value (a matter of buying and selling) at the time and place stolen, if there is a market for it.[13] It is the value of the property in its whole condition and in its proper place, rather than its value after re-

Model Penal Code § 223.0(7) specifically includes contraband in the definition of property which can be stolen.

11. Chappell v. United States, 270 F.2d 274 (9th Cir. 1959) (Air Force master-sergeant used airmen under his command, during duty hours, to paint three dwellings owned by him; conviction of knowingly converting any thing of value of the United States *held* reversed, for to convert there must be property, not services); State v. Gisclair, 382 So.2d 914 (La.1980) (county assessor, who used employees of his office to renovate his camp, could not be convicted of theft of services).

People v. Ashworth, 220 App.Div. 498, 222 N.Y.S. 24 (1927) (defendants used the factory and labor of *A–O* Co. to spin *X* 's wool, charging *X* 20¢ a pound; conviction of larceny of the money and of the use of the factory *held* reversed; the right to use property is not the subject of larceny).

12. Model Penal Code § 223.7 covers theft of services, defined to include "labor, professional services, transportation, telephone or other public service, accommodation in hotels, restaurants or elsewhere, admission to exhibitions, use of vehicles or other movable property." Most modern codes take an equally broad approach. Some, however, refer only to particular services, have a less broad definition, or provide no definition.

13. Modern statutes usually state that market value is to be the ordinary method of valuation. In some of the modern codes, however, the statutes are silent on this point.

Market value may be less than cost: People v. Fognini, 374 Ill. 161, 28 N.E.2d 95 (1940) (larceny from clothing store of merchandise with a substantial cost but which had remained unsold on the racks for more than three

moval, which controls.[14] In the case of property of intrinsically small value which represents a contract or property right of much greater value (as where an automobile license plate made of $1 worth of metal costs the motorist $20 to obtain; or as a check, written on paper worth a cent, represents a right to receive $100), it is the latter value which is important in larceny cases,[15] unless perhaps the owner can at a smaller cost replace the property and thereby save his right.[16] As the statutes are generally worded, it is the value of the property taken, not the thief's estimate of its worth, which governs.[17]

A thief may steal different articles from different victims at different times and places, and such takings cannot be aggregated for the purpose of making one grand larceny out of several petit larcenies.[18] Conversely, different articles stolen at one time and place from the same victim (e.g., theft of his wallet containing three twenty dollar bills; or theft of his money and his watch) can be aggregated (so that, in the case of the wallet with the three twenties, it is one sixty-dollar larceny

rather than three twenty-dollar larcenies). Cases falling in between these two extremes give more difficulty.

In the case of the thief who takes small amounts from the same victim over a period of time before his peculations are discovered, the small thefts are aggregated into one large theft if (as is generally the case) the successive takings are pursuant to a single scheme.[19] So too in the case of one who takes several small amounts (in the aggregate comprising a large total) from different victims at one time and place (as where, during a tea party downstairs, the thief searches the bedroom where several ladies' purses have been stowed, taking ten dollars from each of ten purses), the takings may, by the great weight of authority, be aggregated; it might be said that such takings are necessarily part of one scheme.[20]

Of course, there are instances when the aggregation of larcenies is a benefit, not a detriment, to the defendant, as where he has taken several items of property each of sufficient value for grand larceny: it is generally better for the defendant to be guilty of one

---

years; conviction of grand larceny *held* reversed). Conversely, it may be more than cost: State v. Barker, ___ Mont. ___, 685 P.2d 357 (1984) (market value of boots stolen from store not limited to wholesale price merchant paid); Sadler v. State, 84 Okla.Crim. 97, 179 P.2d 479 (1947) (larceny in 1944 of a rifle bought in 1942; war conditions increased the market value of firearms above original cost; conviction of grand larceny *held* affirmed). The market value is at the time and place of the theft. People v. Herring, 396 Ill. 364, 71 N.E.2d 682 (1947). The burden is on the prosecution to show that there is no market for the item and that consequently some other test should be used. State v. Jacquith, 272 N.W.2d 90 (S.D.1978). Property which has no market value may be valued by its worth to the owner. Commonwealth v. Cabot, 241 Mass. 131, 135 N.E. 465 (1922) (larceny of papers of no intrinsic value but of value to owner because they involved his reputation; conviction of larceny *held* affirmed). Another approach is to use a replacement value less depreciation test when there is no market value. State v. Jacquith, supra.

14. Eaton v. Commonwealth, 235 Ky. 466, 31 S.W.2d 718 (1930) (thief cut and removed copper wire from a mine; wire was valued at $40, exclusive of cost of installation, in the mine, less than $20 after removal; conviction of grand larceny *held* affirmed).

15. Cowan v. State, 171 Ark. 1018, 287 S.W. 201 (1926) (license plate); State v. McClellan, 82 Vt. 361, 73 A. 993 (1909) (unindorsed check). Modern theft statutes often state that it is the face value which is determinative as to negotiable instruments.

16. Thus, with respect to a stolen deed to real estate, the value is the replacement cost of drafting, executing and acknowledging a duplicate: Roberts v. State, 61 Tex. Crim. 434, 135 S.W. 144 (1911).

17. This works both ways. One who steals a piece of glass, believing it to be a diamond, is not guilty of grand larceny (though he may be guilty of attempted grand larceny); but one who steals a valuable necklace, believing it to be costume jewelry, is guilty of grand larceny.

18. Monoughan v. People, 24 Ill. 340 (1860) (thief stole four sheep from the separate yards of three different owners, all in one night; *held*, there can be no aggravation into grand larceny).

19. People v. Cox, 286 N.Y. 137, 36 N.E.2d 84 (1941) (subway employees stole subway fares, about $25 at a time, over a period of months, totaling $1500; each time one carried off the coins while the other turned back the numbers on the turnstile register; the two later divided the loot; conviction of grand larceny *held* affirmed, for the small takings were part of a single scheme).

See Annot., 53 A.L.R.3d 398 (1973). A few cases have held that there was no showing of a single scheme, so that the several larcenies were not to be aggregated. Ibid.

20. Ackerman v. State, 7 Wyo. 504, 54 P. 228 (1898) (thief took two articles belonging to two different owners from one wagon at the same time; this was *held* to be one grand larceny, not two petit larcenies).

See Annot., 37 A.L.R.3d 1407 (1971).

grand larceny of $1000 than of ten separate $100 grand larcenies. The question of whether several related takings constitute one big larceny or several smaller larcenies arises in criminal-law settings other than with respect to the grand-petit larceny distinction.[21] And the question of aggregation arises in connection with theft crimes other than larceny (e.g., embezzlement, false pretenses, receiving stolen property) which commonly draw the same line between the grand and petit varieties.[22]

It should be noted also that in practically all jurisdictions there are by statute some kinds of larceny which are felonies without regard to the value of the property taken. Such is often the case as to larceny from the person ("pickpocketing"). Then too statutes frequently make it felonious larceny to steal certain types of property regardless of value, such as automobiles and firearms. And, of course, that aggravated type of larceny called robbery is a felony which carries a severe penalty, once again without regard to the value of the property taken.

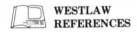

WESTLAW REFERENCES

234k23 /p cost market replacement /s valu!

234k6 /p cost market replacement /s valu!
234k6 234k23 /p aggregat!

(c) Of Another. For larceny the property must be "of another." For this reason wild animals, even though on another's land, cannot be the subject of larceny;[23] nor can property, once owned, which has been abandoned by its former owner.[24]

The common law view of larceny is that one co-owner (e.g., a partner, tenant in common, joint tenant) cannot steal from the other co-owner.[25] The modern trend is to provide by statute that it is no defense to larceny that the thief has an interest in the property taken, so long as the other has an interest therein to which the thief is not entitled.[26]

Sometimes the property which A owns is in the lawful possession of B, who has a pledge or lien interest in the property to secure a debt which A owes B. From A's viewpoint such property is considered the "property of another" for purposes of larceny, so that if A takes it from B's possession with intent to deprive him of his pledge or lien interest therein, A is guilty of larceny.[27] Similarly, if A should bail his property to B and then stealthily take it, intending to charge B with

---

21. E.g., with respect to double jeopardy: does acquittal or conviction of one taking bar prosecution for another? And with respect to the indictment or information: may the several takings all be charged in one count (as they may if they constitute one larceny) or must they be charged in separate counts?

22. As to theft generally, Model Penal Code § 223.1(2)(c) provides that the amounts involved are to be aggregated as to "thefts committed pursuant to one scheme or course of conduct, whether from the same person or several persons." Some modern codes take the same approach, while the others are silent on the question.

23. People v. Hutchinson, 169 Misc. 724, 9 N.Y.S.2d 656 (1938) (the honey of wild bees, located on another's land, cannot be the subject-matter of larceny). At common law even some domesticated animals—e.g., dogs— were not capable of being stolen, but today dogs may be the subject of larceny, either by statutes which mention dogs in particular or animals in general or under statutes which refer broadly to personal property of all kinds.

24. United States v. Smiley, 27 F.Cas. 1132 (No. 16,317) (N.D.Cal., 1864) (treasure aboard sunken steamer, abandoned by owners, is "abandoned property, which could be acquired by anyone who might have the energy and enterprise to seek its recovery"; therefore, demurrer to larceny indictment *held* sustained). As we shall see in § 8.5(a), even one who honestly but mistakenly believes the property to be abandoned is not guilty of larceny thereof. See

Morissette v. United States, 342 U.S. 246, 72 S.Ct. 240, 96 L.Ed. 288 (1952) (one who carries away property which he honestly but mistakenly believes to be abandoned property does not "steal" or "knowingly convert" it under federal theft statute).

25. E.g., State v. Elsbury, 63 Nev. 463, 175 P.2d 430 (1946) (partnership property is not "property of another," so partner cannot be guilty of larceny of such property); State v. Eberhart, 106 Wash. 222, 179 P. 853 (1919) (same).

See Dethlefsen v. Stull, 86 Cal.App.2d 499, 195 P.2d 56 (1948) (although partner cannot be guilty of larceny or embezzlement of partnership property, it may be libel to charge him with misappropriating such property). See Annot., 82 A.L.R.3d 822 (1978). The non-liability for larceny might be put, in the alternative, on the ground of a lack of trespass in the taking when one has a right to possess the property by virtue of his joint ownership.

26. Model Penal Code § 223.0(7) defines "property of another" as property in which another person has an interest which the actor is not privileged to infringe, even though the actor also has an interest in the property. This position is taken in most of the modern codes. A few, however, are to the contrary.

27. Henry v. State, 110 Ga. 750, 36 S.E. 55 (1900) (defendant, having delivered his suit and bicycle to his landlady as security for board and lodging, for which he had not paid, left taking this property with him; convic-

the value of the property, *A* would be guilty of larceny of his own property.[28]

For larceny the thief need not take the property from its owner. A second thief is guilty of larceny even though he steals the property from the first thief.[29] Many modern codes expressly provide, as does the Model Penal Code,[30] that property may be the subject of theft even though the "victim" is a person whose interest in the property is unlawful. This is as it should be. "It is inconsistent with the objectives of the criminal law of theft to permit one who wrongfully appropriates wealth to escape from liability merely because the victim of the misappropriation has also incurred criminal liability of forfeiture of his rights with respect to the property." [31]

 **WESTLAW REFERENCES**

topic(234) /p (tenant owner! /2 joint common) co-owner co-tenant

tion of larceny *held* affirmed); State v. Hubbard, 126 Kan. 129, 266 P. 939 (1928) (defendant, having delivered his $1000 car to another as a pledge to secure a $120 debt, took the car away without the pledgee's knowledge or consent; conviction of larceny of car valued at $1000 *held* affirmed); State v. Cohen, 196 Minn. 39, 263 N.W. 922 (1935) (defendant took fur coat to furrier for repairs and alterations; at a time when furrier had possessory lien for $50 services, defendant took the coat without paying the $50; conviction of larceny *held* affirmed).

See Annot., 58 A.L.R. 330 (1929). It would seem, on principle, that, for purposes of distinguishing between petit and grand larceny, the value of the pledge interest (e.g., $120 in State v. Hubbard, supra), rather than the value of the property ($1000 in Hubbard) should govern in these cases.

What of the converse case, where *A* has his "own" property rightfully in his possession, but *B* has a security interest therein, such as that of a conditional seller or a chattel mortgagee? If *A* should misappropriate the property, his crime would not be larceny, since there is no trespass in the taking. Is an embezzlement conviction precluded by the fact that it is *A* 's own property? See § 8.6(d). It is not uncommonly specifically provided that a chattel mortgagor or conditional vendee who deprives the mortgagee or vendor of his interest contrary to the terms of the mortgage or contract is guilty of a crime (perhaps called larceny). Cf. Model Penal Code § 223.0(7) (property in possession of the actor is not "property of another" who has only a security interest therein, even if legal title is in the creditor under a conditional sales contract or other security agreement).

234k9

§ 8.5   Larceny—Intent to Steal

For larceny there must be an intent to steal (or, as stated in the Latin form, *animus furandi*).[1] It is, of course, not very helpful to say that to be guilty of stealing property one must have an intent to steal the property. It is more helpful to state (as it is sometimes put) that, for larceny, one must intend to deprive the owner of the possession of his property either permanently or for an unreasonable length of time, or intend to use it in such a way that the owner will probably be thus deprived of his property. Note that the matter is stated in terms of the owner's deprivation rather than of the thief's gain, in recognition of the majority view that, for larceny, there need be no intent on the part of the thief to gain a benefit for himself (or, again to use the Latin phrase, for larceny there need

28. See Macdaniel's Case, 168 Eng.Rep. 60 (1755) ("under some circumstances a man may be guilty of larceny in stealing his own goods. * * * *A* delivereth goods to *B* to keep for him, and then stealeth them, with intent to charge *B* with the value of them; this would be felony in *A.*")

29. See King v. State, 43 Tex. 351 (1875). This is simply one aspect of the broad principle that the culpability of the victim is no defense to crime. See § 5.11(b).

30. Model Penal Code § 223.0(7).

31. Model Penal Code § 223.2, Comment at 171 (1980).

§ 8.5

1. Proof of the intent to steal, where no eyewitness can be produced, is often shown by evidence that the defendant was found in *exclusive* and *unexplained* possession of *recently* stolen property; such evidence will give rise to an inference (the jury *may* infer, though it need not), not a mandatory presumption (where the jury *must* conclude, in the absence of counterproof), that the defendant stole the property with the required intent to steal. E.g., Barfield v. United States, 229 F.2d 936 (5th Cir.1956) (prosecution for interstate transportation of stolen car knowing it to be stolen; instruction that possession of recently stolen car gives rise to presumption of guilty knowledge held reversible error; word should be *inference* not *presumption*). Moreover the jury may infer a larceny of the whole from the recent, exclusive, unexplained possession of part of the stolen property. People v. Roman, 12 N.Y.2d 220, 238 N.Y.S.2d 665, 188 N.E.2d 904 (1963), noted at 14 Syracuse L.Rev. 672 (1963).

be no *lucri causa* —"on account of pecuniary gain").[2]

Precisely what kind of intent is needed is usually addressed in rather specific terms in modern statutes dealing with theft. By far the most common approach is to follow the Model Penal Code, which defines the word "deprive" (theft requires a "purpose to deprive") as "(a) to withhold property of another permanently or for so extended a period as to appropriate a major portion of its economic value, or with intent to restore only upon payment of reward or other compensation; or (b) to dispose of the property so as to make it unlikely that the owner will recover it."[3] Some other states use the Model Penal Code formulation without the intent-to-restore part, while a few other statutes declare either that nothing short of permanent deprivation will suffice or, on the other hand, that mere temporary deprivation is enough.

Perhaps the best way to understand the meaning of "intent to steal" is to see how the courts have handled the following types of

---

2. Delk v. State, 64 Miss. 77, 1 So. 9 (1886) (defendant took owner's jackass from its stable, led it 20 feet and killed it, leaving it lying there; conviction of larceny *held* affirmed); McIntosh v. State, 105 Neb. 328, 180 N.W. 573 (1920) (defendant, convicted of larceny of a steer, objected to instruction that for larceny the intent must be to deprive the owner of his property, without adding "and with intent to convert the stolen property to the taker's own use"; conviction of larceny *held* affirmed); State v. Slingerland, 19 Nev. 135, 7 P. 280 (1885) (larceny, although defendant took owner's property only for revenge, not to obtain a benefit).

See Annot., 12 A.L.R. 804 (1921).

3. Model Penal Code § 223.0(1).

4. Model Penal Code § 223.1(3)(a) expressly provides it is an affirmative defense that the defendant "was unaware that the property or service was that of another," and many of the modern codes contain a comparable provision.

5. People v. Rosen, 11 Cal.2d 147, 78 P.2d 727 (1938) (defendant used a pistol to recapture money which he had lost by illegal gambling, honestly believing the money belonged to him; no statute gave him a right to recover money lost at gambling, however; conviction of larceny *held* reversed for lack of intent to steal); Commonwealth v. Stebbins, 74 Mass. (8 Gray) 492 (1857) (instruction that it is not larceny for defendant to take another's property under an honest belief that she had a legal right to do so, although in fact she had no such right, *held* to be a correct instruction); People v. Shaunding, 268 Mich. 218, 255 N.W. 770 (1934) (trial court's exclusion of defendant's evidence

---

situations which have a bearing on the problem.

WESTLAW REFERENCES

234k3(4) /p headnote(inten! /s depriv!)

(a) Claim of Right. One may take the property of another honestly but mistakenly believing (1) that it is his own property, or (2) that it is no one's property,[4] or (3) (though he knows it is another's property) that the owner has given him permission to take it as he did. In any such event, he lacks the intent to steal required for larceny,[5] even though his mistaken but honest belief was unreasonable.[6] As to how the defendant can prove his claim that he actually had such an honest belief, it has been pointed out that the openness of the taking, as well as the reasonableness of the belief, though not conclusive, will buttress his claim of good faith.[7]

WESTLAW REFERENCES

234k3(3) /p intent
234k3 /p mistake***

as to his belief that he had a right to take the property of another from the place from which he took it *held* reversible error, for such a belief negatives the intent to steal); West v. State, 119 Neb. 633, 230 N.W. 504 (1930) (defendant took car belonging to decedent's executor, honestly but mistakenly believing decedent had given it to her; conviction of larceny *held* reversed); Jordan v. State, 107 Tex.Crim.R. 414, 296 S.W. 585 (1927) (defendant took parts from car which had burned and been left 15 days beside the road; defendant honestly but mistakenly believed the owner had abandoned it; refusal of instruction that honest belief of abandonment is a defense to larceny *held* reversible error).

6. Rex v. Nundah, 16 N.S.W. 482 (1916) (defendant took another's property honestly believing it was his own; instruction that it was larceny unless the defendant's belief was reasonable *held* error; honest belief, not reasonable belief, is the test). Of course, the more unreasonable is the belief the defendant claims to have had at the time when he took another's property, the less apt is the jury to believe him.

7. People v. Devine, 95 Cal. 227, 30 P. 378 (1892) (property taken without secrecy or concealment); West v. State, supra note 5 (open taking after consulting attorney, with letter to owner); Stanley v. State, 61 Okl.Crim. 382, 69 P.2d 398 (1937) (taking done openly in presence of owner's representative); Thomas v. Kessler, 334 Pa. 7, 5 A.2d 187 (1939) (property taken openly and in daylight when owner's employees were present; "it is obvious that no larceny was committed").

234k3 /p "good faith" (honest** reasonable* /3 belie***)

(b) Intent to Return the Very Property Taken.

One who takes another's property intending at the time he takes it to use it temporarily and then to return it unconditionally within a reasonable time—and having a substantial ability to do so—lacks the intent to steal required for larceny.[8] It should be noted that it is the intent to return the property, not its actual return, which constitutes the defense to larceny: one who takes another's property intending at the time of taking to deprive the owner permanently is nevertheless guilty of larceny, though he later (becoming frightened, or his better nature prevailing) decides to return it and does so.[9]

Conversely, an intent to return is a defense though some unexpected obstacle prevents an actual return.[10] An intent to return, to be a defense, need not be an intent to return it to the exact spot from which it was taken if the intent is to return it to a place sufficiently near so that the owner is substantially certain to find it or get it back.[11] The intent to return, however, must be unconditional. Thus it is no defense to larceny that the taker intended to return it only if he should receive a reward for its return,[12] or only upon some other condition which he has no right to impose.[13]

8. Impson v. State, 47 Ariz. 573, 58 P.2d 523 (1936) (defendant convicted of larceny of car over his defense that he intended to use it and return it; conviction *held* reversed, for intent to use temporarily and return is a defense); People v. Brown, 105 Cal. 66, 38 P. 518 (1894) (defendant convicted of burglary after taking another boy's bicycle from a building, his defense being that he took it to get even with the other boy, intending to return it; instruction that temporary taking will do for larceny *held* reversible error, for one must "intend to permanently deprive the owner of his property"); Schenectady Varnish Co. v. Automobile Ins. Co. of Hartford, Conn., 127 Misc. 751, 217 N.Y.S. 504 (Sup.Ct. 1926) (action on theft insurance policy, the issue being whether insured's car was taken by larceny by insured's chauffeur who took it openly but without permission intending to take friends on picnic; after picnic, heading for insured's home, the car was wrecked; *held,* no recovery because not larceny for one without permission to take another's goods "intending *and having the power* to restore them"); Mitchell v. Territory, 7 Okl. 527, 54 P. 782 (1898) (defendants convicted of larceny of mules; they were entitled to have presented to the jury their defense of intent to keep the property a short time and then to return it to the owner; conviction of larceny *held* reversed); Wilson v. State, 18 Tex.Ct.App. R. 270 (1885) (defendant convicted of burglary after breaking into blacksmith's shop with intent to take a tool to use temporarily in a safe burglary and then to abandon it; conviction of burglary *held* reversed for failure to instruct that such an intent is a defense).

9. Brennon v. Commonwealth, 169 Ky. 815, 185 S.W. 489 (1916) (if defendant intends to steal when he takes another's property, his later decision to abandon it would not change his crime from larceny). This is but an aspect of the broad principle of criminal law that a subsequent wish on the part of the criminal that he had not committed his crime constitutes no defense.

10. E.g., Schenectady Varnish Co. v. Automobile Ins. Co., supra note 8 (car wreck prevented its actual return); Saferite v. State, 67 Okl.Crim. 229, 93 P.2d 762 (1939) (same). As to an intent to return followed by an intent to keep, see the next to last paragraph under this subhead.

11. In re Mutchler, 55 Kan. 164, 40 P. 283 (1895) (defendant took another's horse and buggy, drove to town 15 miles away, left this property in a stable, wrote a letter to a friend asking him to inform the owner which, in time, the friend did; conviction of larceny *held* reversed); State v. Ryan, 12 Nev. 401 (1877) (defendant convicted of burglary for breaking into building owned by railroad, taking a railroad handcar, placing it on the railroad tracks, propelling it 12 miles, then leaving it beside the tracks; conviction of burglary *held* reversed, for it was not larceny to take the handcar); Wilson v. State, 18 Tex.Ct.App.R. 270 (1885) (defendant convicted of burglary for breaking into blacksmith shop, taking a brace, using it in a safe burglary in nearby store, abandoning it near the store, where the blacksmith found it next day; conviction of burglary *held* reversed for failure to instruct on defense of intent to use temporarily).

12. Slaughter v. State, 113 Ga. 284, 38 S.E. 854 (1901) (defendant, a private detective, took another's watch, then returned it to its owner claiming a reward; conviction of larceny *held* affirmed), criticized in Note, 15 Harv.L.Rev. 492 (1901) (defendant intended to return "hoping" for a reward rather than "on condition" he get a reward); Commonwealth v. Mason, 105 Mass. 163 (1870) (defendant took another's horse with intent to hide it until owner offered a reward and then to return it and claim the reward; conviction of larceny *held* affirmed).

13. State v. Hauptmann, 115 N.J.L. 412, 180 A. 809 (1935) (defendant carried away Lindbergh baby in its nightdress with intent to return the nightdress if Lindbergh negotiated with him for payment for the baby's return; conviction of murder in the commission of larceny *held* affirmed, for it was larceny to take the nightdress with the intent to return it only on condition of negotiation); Commonwealth v. Deibert, 106 Pa.Super. 497, 163 A. 68 (1932) (defendant sold bus to another, payment to be made later; before payment was due defendant took away the bus, saying he would not return it till payment was made; conviction of larceny *held* affirmed); Regina v. Beecham, 5 Cox Crim.Cas. 181 (1851) (defendant, a railroad porter, carried off three railroad tickets, intending to return them to the railroad at the end of the trip; the

As noted above, it is not a defense to larceny merely to have an intent to return the property; in addition one must, at the time of taking, have a substantial ability to do so (even though, as events turn out, it may later become impossible to do so). Thus if one takes another's property intending to use it recklessly and then abandon it, the obstacles to its safe return to the owner are such that the taker possesses the required intent to steal.[14] Even without the intent to use recklessly, an intent to abandon, accompanied by a not-too-well founded hope that the property will find its way back to its owner does not negative the intent to steal.[15] So too, an intent to pawn the property, accompanied by an intent later to redeem the property and return it to its owner, is a defense only if the taker's financial situation is such that he has an ability to redeem it.[16]

An intent to return the property taken, in order to qualify as a defense to larceny, must be an intent to return within a reasonable time.[17] In determining what is a reasonable time, much depends upon the nature of the property and its expected useful life, for to deprive the owner of the property for so long a time that he has lost a "major portion of its economic value"[18] is to deprive him for an unreasonable time. It is one thing to take another's fresh strawberries with intent to return them two weeks later, another thing to take his diamond ring with a like intention.

As we shall see in the discussion of the notion of "continuing trespass," one who takes another's property intending only to use it temporarily before restoring it unconditionally to its owner (i.e., one who normally is found not to have an intent to steal) may nevertheless be guilty of larceny if he later changes his mind and decides not to return the property after all.[19]

A large number of states have singled out the motor vehicle for special treatment, making it a crime (generally called "joyriding," a crime somewhat less serious than larceny) to

trial court instructed the jury that the intent to return the tickets is no defense; verdict of not guilty).

Compare Fort v. State, 82 Ala. 50, 2 So. 477 (1887) (defendant, farm laborer, hired to pick cotton at certain price per 100 lbs., took from a building some cotton already weighed intending to put it in with cotton he had picked but which had not yet been weighed; conviction of burglary held affirmed, for he intended to steal the cotton taken from the building), with Regina v. Holloway, 169 Eng.Rep. 285 (1848) (defendant, employed to dress skins on a piecework basis, took some dressed skins and put them on his work bench, intending to turn them in as if he had dressed them and received payment therefor, conviction of larceny held reversed).

If one intends to return property upon a condition which he has a right to impose, it is not larceny, however. E.g., State v. Sawyer, 95 Conn. 34, 110 A. 461 (1920) (evidence that tenant spilled dye upon landlady's wall; landlady took tenant's bag, intending to return it after tenant paid $5 damages; conviction of larceny held reversed for failure of evidence to support it).

14. State v. Davis, 38 N.J.L. 176 (1875) (defendants, Princeton students, took a professor's horse and buggy, drove it recklessly, finally abandoning it, leaving it to chance whether the professor ever got it back; conviction of larceny held affirmed); see ed. note to Regina v. Holloway, 169 Eng.Rep. 285 (1848) (intent to use another's goods "in a reckless, wanton, or injurious manner, and then to leave it to mere chance whether the owner ever recovered them or no, and if he recovered them at all would probably recover them in a damaged or altered condition" is an intent to deprive the owner wholly of his property, which describes the mental state required for larceny.

15. State v. Ward, 19 Nev. 297, 10 P. 133 (1886) (defendant took another's horses, abandoning them 12 miles away with the hope they would find their way back to the owner's ranch, which hope was realized; conviction of larceny held affirmed).

16. Regina v. Medland, 5 Cox Crim.Cas. 292 (1851) (tenant took landlord's property and pawned it; instruction to jury stated that an intent to redeem and return the property is no defense where the ability to do so is very improbable; verdict of guilty); see People v. Atwater, 229 N.Y. 303, 128 N.E. 196 (1920) (defendant broker pledged another's securities as his own, doubtless intending later to redeem the pledge and restore the securities; conviction of statutory felony of hypothecating securities without the owner's consent held affirmed; dictum stresses the "vanity of such hopes" to lift the pledge and restore and the consequent loss to innocent persons, from conduct like defendant's).

17. See State v. South, 28 N.J.L. 28 (1859), quoting from the ed. note to Regina v. Holloway, 169 Eng.Rep. 285 (1848) (an intent to take temporarily "intending however to keep them for a very unreasonable time * * * would seem in common sense to be ample evidence of an intent wholly to deprive the owner of his property," i.e. the intent to steal which larceny requires).

18. See Model Penal Code § 223.0(1).

19. E.g., Commonwealth v. White, 65 Mass. (11 Cush.) 483 (1853) (the taking with intent to return is nevertheless a trespass, although not then a larcenous trespass; the trespass continues as long as he possesses the property; his later intent to steal thus coincides with the trespass, so that he is guilty of larceny).

take such a vehicle with intent to use it and return it.[20]   An important federal statute makes it a felony to transport a stolen motor vehicle, with knowledge that it is stolen, across state lines.[21]

WESTLAW REFERENCES

topic(234) /p inten! /3 return

topic(234) /p depriv! /s time /3 length period

topic(234) /p joy-rid***

(c) Intent to Return the Equivalent. It is not so clear that one who takes another's property intending, and having the financial ability, to pay for it or otherwise to restore the equivalent (rather than to restore the property itself) has a defense to a charge of larceny. Doubtless where the property taken is property which the owner has offered for sale, such an intent, with such an ability, does constitute a defense.[22] If the property is not for sale, however, perhaps an intent to pay (with ability) is not a defense; although even here if the intended payment is clearly the equivalent of (or more than) the property taken, it might be considered that the defendant lacks the intent to steal.[23] If the property is unique, for which there is no monetary equivalent, or if the owner has been made an offer

which he has rejected, it is quite clear that an intent to pay for it is no defense.[24] As noted above, the intent to pay for the property taken or otherwise to restore its equivalent is never a good defense unless there is a substantial ability to do so; a mere hope, under circumstances disclosing little foundation for optimism, that one can replace or pay for the property will not do.[25] Of course, an intent to pay for the property with a bogus check is no defense to larceny.[26]

WESTLAW REFERENCES

topic(234) /p inten! /3 pay***

(d) Intent to Collect a Debt or Satisfy a Claim. The traditional view is that it is a defense to larceny and robbery (an aggravated form of larceny), because negativing the intent to steal, that the defendant who takes another's money (by stealth or by force) intends to collect a debt which the other owes him or (even if no debt is actually owed) which he honestly believes the other owes him.[27] The matter is somewhat more difficult if he takes the other's property, rather than his money, in satisfaction of the debt, as where he takes a cow in satisfaction of a $300 debt; or where he takes money in satisfaction

---

20.   But see State v. Dunmann, 427 So.2d 166 (Fla.1983) (because omnibus theft statute's intent-to-steal element need not be intent to permanently deprive, enactment of that statute repealed by implication the joyriding statute).

For a useful discussion of these statutes, see Model Penal Code § 223.9, Comment (1980).

21.   18 U.S.C. § 2312 (Dyer Act).

22.   Mason v. State, 32 Ark. 238 (1877) (evidence showed that defendants took 30 cents worth of beer after owner, who had beer for sale, had gone to bed and refused to get up and serve them; next day defendants offered to pay $3 for the beer; owner demanded $30, which defendants refused to pay; evidence *held* insufficient to support verdict of larceny of the beer).

23.   Pylee v. State, 62 Tex.Crim.L. 49, 136 S.W. 464 (1911) (defendant took oats for his horses from owner's field, intending to pay the owner but not stopping to do so because of a skittish team; this if true is a defense to larceny; it does not appear that the oats in the field were offered for sale).

24.   Model Penal Code § 223.1(3)(c) limits the defense of intent to pay to the situation where the actor "took property exposed for sale, intending to purchase and pay for it promptly, or reasonably believing that the owner, if present, would have consented." A few of the modern codes contain such a provision.

25.   Rex v. Williams [1953] 1 All E.R. 1068 (post-mistress ran a shop which found itself in financial difficulties; she took post office money, intending to repay it out of her post office salary and shop sales; the jury found she intended to repay and honestly beieved she could; conviction of larceny *held* affirmed).

26.   Neal v. State, 355 P.2d 1071 (Okl.Crim.1960).

27.   People v. Gallegos, 130 Colo. 232, 274 P.2d 608 (1954) (employee collected wages he believed owing to him at gunpoint; conviction of robbery *held* reversed for lack of intent to steal); Barton v. State, 88 Tex.Crim.R. 368, 227 S.W. 317 (1921) (defendant pointed gun and threatened to kill the other if he did not pay debt defendant claimed was owing; conviction of assault with intent to rob *held* reversed, for trial court erred in refusing to charge that if defendant was trying to collect a debt he honestly believed owing he was not guilty).

But there is a growing body of authority taking the contrary position. See State v. Russell, 217 Kan. 481, 536 P.2d 1392 (1975); State v. Pierce, 208 Kan. 19, 490 P.2d 584 (1971); State v. Ortiz, 124 N.J.Super. 189, 305 A.2d 800 (1973); Commonwealth v. Dombrauskas, 274 Pa. Super. 452, 418 A.2d 493 (1980); Edwards v. State, 49 Wis. 2d 105, 181 N.W.2d 383 (1970).

See Annots., 88 A.L.R.3d 1309 (1978); 77 A.L.R.3d 1363 (1977); 116 A.L.R. 997 (1938).

of an unliquidated claim for damages. The trouble is that, although money is fungible, property is not so clearly the equivalent of money, or money the equal of an unliquidated claim.[28] Even so, where the property or money taken is clearly less in value than the amount of the debt or claim, it ought not to be larceny. There is, of course, no difficulty in giving the defense if the property or money is taken for security, rather than in satisfaction of, the debt or claim.[29]

The Model Penal Code position, reflected in many of the modern criminal codes, is that it is an affirmative defense that the defendant "acted under an honest claim of right to the property or service involved or that he had a right to acquire or dispose of it as he did."[30] The wisdom of this position is, at best, debatable. In support, it is contended that those "who take only property to which they believe themselves entitled constitute no significant threat to the property system and manifest no character trait worse than ignorance."[31] On the other side, it is claimed that such a rule is "but one step short of accepting lawless reprisal as an appropriate means of redressing grievances, real or fancied,"[32] and that disputed claims "are better resolved in a court of law than by violence or stealth."[33]

 WESTLAW REFERENCES

234k3 234k26 342k14 /p debt

(e) Miscellaneous Defenses. As with other crimes requiring intent, the intent to steal may be negatived by intoxication (even voluntary intoxication) which is so great as to rob the defendant of his capacity to entertain such an intent.[34]

The defenses of insanity, infancy and compulsion [35] are available, in appropriate fact situations, in larceny as in other cases. Mistakes of fact or of law constitute defenses to larceny when the mistake in question negatives the intent to steal—as shown by the cases, discussed above (though not specifically in terms of mistakes) which held it a good defense to larceny that the defendant takes under a bona fide claim of right.[36]

 WESTLAW REFERENCES

topic(234) /p intoxicat*** insan*** infan** compel** compulsion /s intent

---

28. Thomas v. State, 165 Miss. 897, 148 So. 225 (1933) (defendant, with an unliquidated claim against the other for having killed defendant's dog, forced the other at gunpoint to hand over an unliquidated cow and yearling; conviction of larceny *held* affirmed); Tipton v. State, 23 Okl.Crim. 86, 212 P. 612 (1923) (victim having assaulted defendant's wife, defendant put a liquidated price of $2000 upon his unliquidated damages and relieved victim of $1000 cash and his $1000 automobile at gunpoint; conviction of robbery *held* affirmed).

29. In re Bayles, 47 Cal.App. 517, 190 P. 1034 (1920) (landlord, with a $3 claim against tenant for a cleaning bill which tenant may not have owed him, took tenant's property worth $225 as security; since this could not be larceny, defendant *held* discharged on habeas corpus); State v. Sawyer, 95 Conn. 34, 110 A. 461 (1920) (landlady, with a $5 claim against a lodger for spilling dye on the wallpaper, took her handbag and refused to surrender it until paid $5; conviction of larceny *held* reversed).

30. Model Penal Code § 223.1(3)(b).

31. Model Penal Code § 223.1, Comment at 157 (1980).

32. State v. Ortiz, 124 N.J.Super. 189, 305 A.2d 800 (1973).

33. Commonwealth v. Dombraskas, 274 Pa.Super. 452, 418 A.2d 493 (1980).

34. See § 4.10. E.g., Wood v. State, 34 Ark. 341 (1879) (defendant when intoxicated took another's property; refusal to instruct jury that intoxication may negative abili-

ty to intend to steal *held* error); Edwards v. State, 178 Miss. 696, 174 So. 57 (1937) (defendant when intoxicated took another's taxicab; instruction that voluntary intoxication is no defense to larceny *held* error).

35. Query whether compulsion, when it constitutes a defense to a crime, is one because it negatives the mental element of the crime, or because of some reason of public policy. See § 5.3. In United States v. Durkee, 25 F.Cas. 941 (No. 15009) (C.C.N.D.Cal.1856), the defendant for self-protection took away the other's gun so as to disarm him; this was held not to be larceny because *lucri causa* is required for larceny; a better reason would be that, although *lucri causa* is not required, compulsion is a defense to larceny. For other cases on the possibility of a coercion defense in a larceny prosecution, see Annot., 1 A.L.R. 4th 481 (1980).

36. Thus, for instance, in West v. State, supra note 5, where defendant, erroneously thinking she owned a car actually owned by the former deceased owner's administrator, may have made a mistake of *fact* as to what the former owner said (she mistakenly thought he said, "I give you this car"), or she may have made a mistake of *law* as to the legal effect of what he said (she thought that, when he told her, "this car is to be yours at my death," it did become hers at his death, though he made no such provision in his will). In either event, her mistake, by making her honestly believe the car to be hers, negatives her intent to steal it.

(f) Concurrence of Larcenous Conduct and Intent to Steal. With larceny, as with other crimes requiring both specified physical conduct and a specified state of mind, the defendant's conduct and his mental state must coincide.[37] So the taking and carrying away (the physical conduct in larceny) and the intent to steal (larceny's state of mind) must concur.[38] Thus one who finds lost or mislaid property and picks it up intending to return it to the owner, but who later decides to steal it, cannot be guilty of larceny; for the taking and asportation, on the one hand, and the intent to steal, on the other, do not coincide.[39] So also, for the same reason, one who,

because of a mistake on the part of the deliverer, receives a misdelivery of property (including an overpayment of money) is not guilty of larceny when he receives it with an innocent mind (not then realizing the mistake), though he later, on learning of the mistake, decides to steal it.[40] There is some minority authority, however, for the proposition that, in the case of a misdelivery of property or overpayment of money enclosed within a container (e.g., a check within an envelope, a roll of coins within a paper wrapping, clothing within a trunk), the recipient of the container takes the enclosed property from the deliverer's possession only when he

37. For this basic premise of the criminal law, see § 3.11.

38. This applies not only to ordinary larceny by stealth but also to that specialized form of larceny called larceny by trick. E.g., Ennis v. State, 13 Okl.Crim. 675, 167 P. 229 (1917) (defendant undertook to sell another's corn for him and account for the price less a commission; he then intended to do so; he sold the corn and then decided to convert the proceeds; conviction of larceny *held* reversed, for the intent to steal did not exist at the time possession was obtained; dictum that the crime was embezzlement). But, unlike in the *Ennis* case, if the defendant obtains possession by lies, intending to return the property but not to steal it, his taking is a trespass which continues, so that a later intent to steal will coincide with the continuing trespass. See the discussion of continuing trespass *infra*, and especially State v. Coombs, 55 Me. 477 (1868) and Commonwealth v. White, 65 Mass. (11 Cush.) 483 (1853), cited infra note 44.

39. People v. Betts, 367 Ill. 499, 11 N.E.2d 942 (1937) (defendant found another's heifers in his pasture and later, not knowing who the owner was, allowed them to be sold; the court said, "Assuming that he later sold them and that the sale showed such an intent [to convert them] formed subsequent to the finding of the animals in his pasture, such an intent will not relate back to the finding so as to constitute the crime of larceny"); State v. Dean, 49 Iowa 73 (1878) (finder found lost property and took it home; the court instructed the jury, "The intention of a party committing a larceny at first may not be felonious, but if the property is wrongfully used or converted it is larceny;" *held* reversible error, so conviction of larceny reversed; where the original taking is lawful, as where the finder is ignorant of the owner, a later conversion is not larceny); Calhoun v. State, 191 Miss. 82, 2 So.2d 802 (1941) (defendant found lost article and picked it up, intending to return it to owner; later he decided to steal it; conviction of larceny *held* reversed; "if the original taking is lawful and bona fide, a subsequent conversion is not larceny, because there is no trespass"); State v. Belt, 125 S.C. 473, 119 S.E. 576 (1923) (in a case of misappropriation of lost property by finder *held* reversible error to instruct the jury that if one comes in possession of goods not his own, and keeps in possession or puts them to his own use, it is larceny); Regina v. Thurborn, 169 Eng.Rep.

293 (1848) (defendant found bank note without clues as to ownership and decided to appropriate it; later, on learning of the owner, he converted it; conviction of larceny *held* reversed; it was not larceny when he picked it up, for there were no clues; it was not larceny later, for by then he had lawful possession, so there was no trespass); see Long v. State, 33 Ala.App. 334, 33 So.2d 382 (1948) (for finder to be guilty of larceny of lost goods, "the intent to convert them absolutely to his own use must co-exist with the act of finding. If such intent does not exist at the time of the finding, a subsequent concealment or fraudulent appropriation does not constitute larceny").

Cf. State v. Courtsol, 89 Conn. 564, 94 A. 973 (1915) (defendant in trolley car picked up mislaid package belonging to another thinking it her own; when she discovered her mistake, she immediately decided to steal it; conviction of larceny *held* affirmed). Under the *Courtsol* case it would probably not have been held larceny if, when she discovered the package belonged to another, she first decided to return it and only later decided to steal it.

40. (1) *Property delivered by mistake:* Rex v. Mucklow, 1 Moody C.C. 160 (Cr.Cas.Res.1827) (letter containing check made out to James Mucklow was sent to the wrong James Mucklow, the defendant, who did not form an intent to steal it until after he received it; conviction of larceny *held* wrong and a pardon recommended); Moynes v. Coopper, [1956] 1 Q.B. 439 (same); (2) *Overpayment of money by mistake:* Cooper v. Commonwealth, 110 Ky. 123, 60 S.W. 938 (1901) (defendant, asking for change for $1 at bank, received a roll of 20 $5 gold pieces instead of 20 nickels; defendant some time later unwrapped the coins, discovered the error, and decided to misappropriate; conviction of larceny *held* reversed, for the intent to steal arose after the defendant took possession); Mitchell v. State, 78 Tex.Crim.R. 79, 180 S.W. 115 (1915) (defendant sold goods to buyer, who paid defendant $31 when he meant to pay $13; defendant did not realize the mistake until buyer later sent him a message requesting a return of the excess; defendant then decided to steal; conviction of larceny *held* reversed); Regina v. Ashwell, 16 Cox Crim. Cas. 1 (1885) (victim paid defendant a sovereign, both believing it to be a shilling; defendant, on later learning the truth, decided to steal it; *held*, not larceny, for he got possession of the coin innocently).

learns of its existence within the container, so that, if he then decides to steal, the taking and the intent to steal do coincide for larceny purposes.[41]

As an aid in finding that the taking-and-asportation and the intent to steal coincide, the law of larceny under some circumstances makes use of the fictional notion of *continuing trespass,* under which the original trespassory taking, although not coinciding with an intent to steal (for the taker originally has no such intent), continues until the taker does form such an intent. At that moment the taking (and, as soon as he moves the property, the asportation) and the intent to steal do coincide, so that the taker is guilty of larceny. What are the circumstances giving rise to a continuing trespass?

First, there must, of course, be a trespass in the original taking. As we have seen, the finder of another's lost or mislaid property, or the one upon whom another's property is thrust by a misdelivery, who takes the property with an innocent mind, is not guilty of a trespass at all. But it is a different matter in the case of one who innocently picks up another's property erroneously believing it to be his own, or mistakenly thinking the other has

authorized him to take possession. He is guilty of a trespass.[42] And, even more clearly, one who takes another's property knowing it is not his own and that the other has not authorized the taking (e.g., one who takes it intending to use it carefully and return it soon) commits a trespass. But he is not, in either case, guilty of larceny yet, for he has not yet formed an intent to steal.

Suppose that he does later decide to steal; does the trespass continue so as to produce the necessary coincidence of trespassory taking and intent to steal? The second requirement for continuing trespass (in America, at least) is that the original trespass be of a mentally-bad (though not necessarily criminal) type rather than an innocent-minded sort. Thus to pick up another's property mistakenly believing it to be one's own or that the taking is authorized, though a trespass, does not constitute a trespass which continues (so that, when the taker later decides to steal, he is not guilty of larceny);[43] whereas to take it, wrongfully, intending to use it and return it, is a trespass which does continue (so as to render the taker who later decides to steal guilty of larceny).[44]

41. Robinson v. State, 11 Tex.Ct.App. 403 (1882) (merchant sold trunk supposed to be empty, to defendant, who took it home, where he opened it and discovered that it contained clothing; upon this discovery, defendant decided to steal; conviction of larceny *held* affirmed, on the ground that the criminal intent coexisted with the finding); Rex v. Hudson, [1943] K.B. 458 (defendant received letter containing check belonging to someone else; he did not open letter for several days; when he did, he discovered the check and then decided to steal; appeal from conviction of larceny of the check *held* dismissed, for defendant's intent to steal coincided with his taking it, which took place when he learned of it). The matter is discussed further in § 8.2(g).

42. W. Prosser & W. Keeton, Torts § 15 (5th ed. 1984): for trespass, "intent" to interfere with another's possession of a chattel "requires no wrongful motive; it is no defense that the defendant believed the goods to be his own, so long as he voluntarily did the act which constituted the trespass."

43. Wilson v. State, 96 Ark. 148, 131 S.W. 336 (1910) (defendant took another's bull from the range, believing it to be his own; later, when the owner appeared, defendant refused to give it up; conviction of larceny *held* reversed, for the intent to steal did not exist at the time of the taking); Harvey v. State, 78 Nev. 417, 375 P.2d 225 (1962) (defendant, without authority, carried off another's jewel-

ry intending to try to sell it for the owner; later after the owner told him to return the jewelry, defendant, intending to steal, absconded; conviction of larceny *held* reversed, for the trespassory taking and the intent to steal did not coincide).

Contra: Regina v. Riley, 169 Eng.Rep. 674 (1853) (defendant, who had 29 sheep in a field, drove 30 sheep away to sell them, not realizing he took another's lamb with his own; later he counted them, discovered the extra lamb and sold it; conviction of larceny *held* affirmed; the original taking was a trespass but not larceny, but the trespass continued up to the time of the appropriation, so that there was larceny's requirement of coincidence of trespassory taking and intent to steal).

44. State v. Coombs, 55 Me. 477 (1868) (defendant obtained possession of horse and sleigh, lying as to his intended destination and length of absence but intending to return the property and not to steal it; later, deciding to steal it, he sold it; conviction of larceny *held* affirmed, for the wrongful taking was continuous); Commonwealth v. White, 65 Mass. (11 Cush.) 483 (1853) (substantially the same facts as in State v. Coombs; conviction of larceny *held* affirmed); Ruse v. Read, [1949] 1 All E.R. 398 (K.B.) (defendant while so drunk as to lack intent to steal rode off on another's bicycle; later he decided to steal it; dismissal of information charging larceny of bicycle *held* wrong, for defendant should have been convicted).

In the modern criminal codes, however, it is generally true that a later-formed intent to steal will suffice without regard to whether this fictitious continuing trespass is present. Sometimes this is accomplished by an express statement that the intent to deprive may occur either when the property is obtained or later. But other statutes appear to accomplish the same result either by use of such words as "retains" or "withholds" in defining the requisite acts, or by attaching the intent-to-deprive element to the failure to take reasonable measures to restore the property. The change, in any event, represents sound policy, for the "objective in this area is not to prevent initial appropriation but to compel subsequent acts to restore the owner."[45]

 WESTLAW REFERENCES

234k3(2)
larceny /p continu*** /3 trespass

§ 8.6 Embezzlement

Embezzlement, a statutory crime, is defined somewhat differently in different jurisdictions, so that it is impossible to define it authoritatively in a single way. But in general it may be defined as: (1) the fraudulent (2) conversion of (3) the property (4) of another (5) by one who is already in lawful possession of it.

(a) Need for Crime of Embezzlement. As we have already noted in connection with the historical development of the theft crimes,[1] there was a large gap in larceny caused by larceny's requirement of a trespass in the taking. Thus one, already in lawful possession of another's property, who converted it to his own use with intent to deprive the owner of it, committed no trespass in the taking and so could not be guilty of larceny. (And there was then no other crime which covered this type of misappropriation.) So the English legislature created the new crime of embezzlement to fill this loophole. It did

so by listing various kinds of persons who might have lawful possession of another's property—e.g., store clerks, bank employees, agents, attorneys, brokers, factors, trustees, bankers, merchants, corporate officers, partners, bailees—and by providing that any such person entrusted with another's property who fraudulently converted it was guilty of embezzlement.

In America the English pattern was for many years generally followed, although in a few states, instead of listing the various types of persons (and perhaps omitting some who should be included) who commit embezzlement when they fraudulently convert, the statutes simply provided that one in lawful possession of (or entrusted with) another's property who fraudulently converts it is guilty. This latter approach now prevails, especially in those jurisdictions with modern codes consolidating embezzlement with other forms of theft.[2] Such consolidation, resulting in a rather broadly-defined crime of "theft," has obviated many of the problems (discussed herein) which had arisen under the earlier embezzlement statutes adhering to the English model.

One further thing should be noted at the outset: embezzlement and false pretenses were new crimes created by the legislature for the specific purpose of plugging loopholes left by the narrowness of the crime of larceny. That being so, the courts have generally held or assumed that these crimes do not overlap, that they are mutually exclusive. Yet there may be some small areas where because of the wording of the embezzlement statute, embezzlement does overlap with larceny.

 WESTLAW REFERENCES

topic(146) /p "common law"

(b) Conversion. Although ordinary larceny requires, so far as the act is concerned, only a taking and an asportation, embezzlement requires something more: a conversion.[3]

---

45. Model Penal Code § 223.5, Comment at 228 (1980).

§ 8.6

1. See § 8.1.

2. See § 8.8.

3. A conversion is, however, a requirement for larceny by trick. See § 8.2(e).

Conversion for embezzlement purposes is not different from conversion for tort purposes.[4] A conversion of property requires a serious act of interference with the owner's rights. Thus the mere act of moving it a short distance (the asportation for larceny), or of using it casually, or of damaging it slightly, will not do. On the other hand, using it up, selling it, pledging it, giving it away, delivering it to one not entitled to it, inflicting serious damage to it, claiming it against the owner, unreasonably withholding possession of it from the owner—[5] each of these acts seriously interferes with the owner's rights and so constitutes a conversion. One is not a converter unless his acts are intentional (as distinguished from merely negligent [6]); but one can be a converter though innocent-minded, as where he is a bona fide purchaser of stolen goods. (Yet an innocent-minded converter is not guilty of embezzlement, for the crime, unlike the tort, requires a fraudulent intent in addition to the conversion.[7])

Embezzlement statutes sometimes are worded in terms of the wrongdoer's conversion "to his own use." These words are not to be taken literally, however, for it is not a requirement for a conversion that the converter gain a personal benefit from his dealing with the property.[8] Thus one might convert another's property though what he does is to benefit the corporation of which he is an officer or stockholder, or to benefit his wife or son.[9]

There is a dispute as to whether it is a conversion for one in possession of another's property to secrete it with an intent to misappropriate it at a later, more convenient time.[10] A large number of embezzlement statutes take care of the matter by specifically providing that the crime may be committed by secreting another's property with an intent to embezzle it.[11]

WESTLAW REFERENCES

146k11 146k4   /p   conversion convert   /s   inten!
146k11 146k4   /p   conversion convert   /s   "own use"

(c) Property. Embezzlement statutes are sometimes worded in terms of "property which may be the subject of larceny," or words to that effect, thus incorporating by reference all the learning, discussed above, concerning the property which will qualify for

---

4. For the tort of conversion—for which the owner of the property converted recovers, not simply damages for the harm done as is the case with the tort of trespass), but rather the full value of the property converted—see Restatement (Second) of Torts §§ 223–242 (1965); and W. Prosser & W. Keeton, Torts § 15 (5th ed. 1984).

5. A mere failure for a long time to return the property to the owner, in the absence of a demand by the owner, may not be a conversion as required for embezzlement: State v. Britt, 278 Mo. 510, 213 S.W. 425 (1919).

6. United States v. Williams, 478 F.2d 369 (4th Cir. 1973) (instruction that defendant guilty of embezzlement if he "knew or should have known" he issued cashier's check reversible error, as government must show "the acts were done wilfully and intentionally, not by inadvertence or carelessness").

7. Cf. Morissette v. United States, 342 U.S. 246, 72 S.Ct. 240, 96 L.Ed. 288 (1952) (under federal statute punishing "knowing" conversion, rather than the more usual "fraudulent" conversion, the court noted that there are differences between conversion, knowing conversion and fraudulent conversion); State v. Ross, 55 Or. 450, 104 P. 596 (1909), affirmed sub nom. Ross v. Oregon, 227 U.S. 150, 33 S.Ct. 220, 57 L.Ed. 458 (1913) (under special state statute punishing "conversion" of state moneys by one in possession, innocent-minded conversion will suffice).

8. State v. Pratt, 114 Kan. 660, 220 P. 505 (1923) (defendant, in possession of the bonds of another, sold

them for purposes of relieving the hard-pressed bank of which he was president; conviction of embezzlement *held* affirmed; "he directed its disposition and thereby applied it to his own use"); State v. Doolittle, 153 Kan. 608, 113 P.2d 94 (1941) (embezzlement conviction *held* affirmed, though defendant received no personal benefit); State v. Ross, 55 Or. 450, 104 P. 596 (1909), affirmed sub nom. Ross v. Oregon, 227 U.S. 150, 33 S.Ct. 220, 57 L.Ed. 458 (1913) (defendant deposited state funds in a bank which failed; conviction under special embezzlement statute which punishes a state official who converts state money "to his own use" *held* affirmed, though the defendant received no personal advantage).

9. But see United States v. Williams, 478 F.2d 369 (4th Cir.1973), adhering strictly to the "to his own use" language of the statute in holding that conversion to the use of a third person will not suffice.

10. Compare State v. Holley, 115 W.Va. 464, 177 S.E. 302 (1934) (defendant, in possession of flour belonging to the Red Cross, secreted it in a compartment of his building and told the Red Cross he did not have it; Red Cross found it after a search; this was *held* to be a conversion of the flour), with McAleer v. State, 46 Neb. 116, 64 N.W. 358 (1895) (secretion of another's money with intent to misappropriate it later said not to be an "actual appropriation" as required for embezzlement).

11. See Note, 39 Colum.L.Rev. 1004, 1013 (1939), listing statutes from many states.

larceny. As we have seen,[12] larceny, originally limited to tangible personal property, has been everywhere expanded to cover such intangible personal property as specialty choses in action like negotiable instruments (checks, promissory notes, bonds, stocks) and written documents (deeds, contracts) representing intangible rights; and to include such items savoring of real estate as minerals, trees, crops and fixtures. The modern trend in larceny, in fact, is in the direction of covering all sorts of property which have value and can be moved. On the other hand, the traditional view is that use of another's property [13] or the use of the labor or services of another,[14] not being property, cannot be stolen. Modern theft statutes, however, very often cover both property and services.[15]

In some states, however, embezzlement is defined, as to the property requirement, more broadly than is the case with larceny. The statute may punish the embezzlement of real as well as of personal property.[16] On principle, it seems clear that, although one cannot commit larceny of a plot of real estate (for it cannot be moved, as larceny requires),[17] yet one (e.g., a trustee, agent, guardian) who has

power to sell or mortgage another's real estate, and who deprives the other of it by fraudulently transferring it to a bona fide purchaser or mortgagee, ought to be guilty of embezzlement.[18]

The situation of the agent, with authority to draw checks upon his principal's bank account, who makes unauthorized use of the bank account for his private gain, has given rise to some problems. Thus a corporate treasurer or secretary, having authority to draw checks upon his principal's bank account to carry on his principal's business, may make out a check (a) payable to himself (or to cash) and then indorse and cash it; or (b) payable to an innocent third person and then forge the latter's indorsement and cash it; or (c) payable to a confederate third person who then indorses and cashes it and splits the proceeds with the agent; or (d) payable to his own private creditor, to whom he delivers the check in payment of his debt and who indorses it and cashes it.[19]

In the first three situations there is not too much difficulty in holding the agent liable for embezzlement of the cash,[20] for he took his principal's cash into his hands and then

---

12. See § 8.4(a).

13. Regina v. Cullum, 12 Cox Crim.Cas. 469 (1873), involved an employee, employed to navigate a barge, who made money for himself by the unauthorized use of his employer's barge to carry goods for others; his conviction of embezzlement was reversed; using his employer's property dishonestly does not constitute embezzlement.

14. Chappell v. United States, 270 F.2d 274 (9th Cir. 1959), concerned a federal statute making it a crime to embezzle or knowingly convert anything of value belonging to the United States; defendant, a master-sergeant, had an airman under his command, during duty hours, paint three houses which the sergeant owned; conviction of knowing conversion *held* reversed, because a conversion necessary for embezzlement refers to personal property, and services will not do.

15. See § 8.4(a).

16. Thus in People v. Roland, 134 Cal.App. 675, 26 P.2d 517 (1933), where an agent refused to convey real estate to his principal on demand, falsely claiming to be the owner, it was held that real property, under the California statute, could be embezzled, so that the agent's conviction of embezzlement was affirmed.

Compare Manning v. State, 175 Ga. 875, 166 S.E. 658 (1932), under a statute punishing the embezzlement of "any thing of value"; the defendant, a trustee of real estate, fraudulently sold it to an innocent purchaser; his conviction of embezzlement was *held* reversed, for "thing

of value" does not include real property. The two cases are discussed in Snyder, Word-Magic and the Embezzlement of Real Property, 28 J.Crim.L. & Crim. 164 (1937), urging that the fraudulent conversion of real estate should be embezzlement, without being hampered by the historical notion that real estate could not be embezzled.

See also State v. Clark, 60 Ohio App. 367, 21 N.E.2d 484 (1938), noted at 6 Ohio St.L.J. 68 (1939), holding it not to be embezzlement, under a statute with the words "every other thing of value," fraudulently to convert real estate.

17. It has been pointed out that this obstacle to a larceny prosecution makes sense, for "the immobility and relative indestructibility of real estate makes unlawful occupancy of land a relatively minor harm for which civil remedies supplemented by mild sanctions for trespass should be adequate." Model Penal Code § 223.2, Comment at 172 (1980).

18. Model Penal Code § 223.2(2) therefore provides: "A person is guilty of theft if he unlawfully transfers immovable property of another or any interest therein with purpose to benefit himself or another not entitled thereto." As for the treatment of this issue in the modern codes, see § 8.4(a).

19. In each case, instead of cashing it, he may deposit it and then withdraw from his deposit.

20. The agent by simply making out the check in one of these ways, with intent to defraud, cannot be said to have embezzled anything, for a check which has not been

fraudulently converted it to his own use.[21] The fourth situation is more difficult, however. It has been held that this is not embezzlement: all that the agent has control over is an intangible chose in action (the claim against the bank), which is not the sort of property which can be embezzled; and the agent never had within his possession or control the specific money actually paid to the agent's creditor.[22] The weight of authority, however, finds an embezzlement, by stretching things to the extent of finding that the agent did have control over the money itself.[23]

 **WESTLAW
REFERENCES**

146k6

tauscher /p 360 +4 764 /p embezzl! property
  theft

indorsed and delivered is nothing more than a piece of paper worth perhaps a tenth of a cent.

21. Situation (a): State v. Lockie, 43 Ida. 580, 253 P. 618 (1927) (bookkeeper, with authority to draw checks for the purchase of office supplies, drew them payable to cash, cashed them and converted the proceeds; conviction of embezzlement *held* affirmed); State v. Peterson, 167 Minn. 216, 208 N.W. 761 (1926) (company president by debit slip withdrew company money in the form of a cashier's check and used it to pay private debt; conviction of embezzlement *held* affirmed).

Situation (b): Simmons v. State, 165 Miss. 732, 141 So. 288 (1932) (treasurer of a loan association, with authority to draw checks payable to borrowers from the association, made check payable to a borrower, forged the latter's signature as indorsee, and deposited the check in his own bank account from which he withdrew the proceeds for his own purposes; conviction of embezzlement of association's money held affirmed).

Situation (c): State v. Krug, 12 Wash. 288, 41 P. 126 (1895) (city treasurer drew check payable to confederate who presented the check and eventually got the money; conviction of embezzlement—defined as use of city money for private profit—*held* affirmed); Regina v. Davenport, [1954] 1 All E.R. 602 (corporate secretary drew checks payable to confederate, who cashed them and paid proceeds to the secretary; judgment of conviction of embezzlement *held* substituted for that of larceny).

22. State v. Tauscher, 227 Or. 1, 360 P.2d 764 (1961) (indictment charged that executive secretary of charitable corporation, authorized to draw checks for corporation, made check payable to her personal creditor, who cashed the check at the bank; demurrer to the indictment sustained; *held* affirmed).

23. E.g., People v. Keller, 79 Cal.App. 612, 250 P. 585 (1926) (corporate agent drew check on principal's account payable to his private creditor, who deposited it in his bank; when the check was presented for payment, the money paid "became, for an instant of time at least, however short, the property of the depositor," the corpora-

(d) Of Another. One cannot be guilty of embezzlement if he converts his own property; the property converted must be that "of another." [24] For this reason one who borrows money and then converts the borrowed sum to his own use is not guilty of embezzlement, even though, when the time comes to repay the loan, he is unable to do so.[25] On the same principle, an employer who, by agreement with his employee, deducts a sum of money from his employee's wages, agreeing to pay that sum to a third person, is not guilty of embezzlement when he fails to pay the third person; the money which the employer deducts, not being segregated from his other funds, is not the employee's money.[26] So too a building contractor who receives from the landowner an advance payment on the con-

tion; presumably the agent, for that moment, got possession or control of the money and converted it); Bartley v. State, 53 Neb. 310, 73 N.W. 744 (1898) (state treasurer drew check on state bank account payable to a third person, who cashed it; the effect of the transaction was the same as if the treasurer presented the check, the teller placed the money on the counter and paid it at the treasurer's direction to the third person).

See Annot., 88 A.L.R.2d 688 (1963). The Annotation also points out that, aside from the difficulty of finding that a bank account is "property" which can be embezzled, there is the difficulty of finding the agent "possesses" the bank account. But many states have statutes which refer to property "in his possession *or under his care;*" and a bank account can be considered under the agent's care.

24. Though the sole stockholder of a corporation is the beneficial owner of the assets of the corporation, the corporation is considered an entity separate from its stockholder for purposes of embezzlement of the property "of another." State v. Harris, 147 Conn. 589, 164 A.2d 399 (1960); and Annot., 83 A.L.R.2d 791 (1962).

25. Commonwealth v. Stahl, 183 Pa.Super. 49, 127 A.2d 786 (1956).

So too of "borrowed"—not bailed—property where the borrower is to use the property for his own purposes, being liable later to transfer to the "lender" other property: People v. Wildeman, 325 Ill. 99, 156 N.E. 257 (1927). If there is the added fact that the borrower induced the lender by false representations to lend him the money, intending not to repay but rather to defraud the lender, the borrower may be guilty of larceny by trick (if the money is to be used for a specific purpose, so that possession of the money but not its title passes) or false pretenses (if title passes), although, as to the latter crime, a false promise to repay may not be held a misrepresentation of a past or present fact. See § 8.7(d).

26. Commonwealth v. Mitchneck, 130 Pa.Super. 433, 198 A. 463 (1938) (mine operator agreed with his employees to deduct a portion of their wages and to use the sum deducted to pay their debts to the town grocer; he failed

tract and who thereafter spends the money for his own purposes and does not fulfill the contract, is not guilty of embezzlement,[27] unless the money is earmarked to be used only for a construction purpose.[28]

Another embezzlement problem [29] concerns co-owners of property (joint tenants, tenants in common, partners): if one co-owner in possession of the jointly-owned property misappropriates the whole of such property for his own bad purposes, can he be guilty of embezzlement; is it not his own property rather than property "of another" which he is appropriating? In the absence of some statutory provision expressly covering such co-owners,[30]

the cases generally hold that there is no embezzlement.[31] Another situation, which has given rise to a split of authority in the absence of a specific statutory provision, is that of the agent,[32] authorized to collect money due his principal and to keep a certain portion of the amount collected as his commission, who misappropriates the whole amount.[33] A chattel mortgagor and one who purchases under a conditional sales contract, who misappropriates the property in his possession with intent to defraud the chattel mortgagee or conditional seller, may not be misappropriating the property "of another"; but statutes in a number of states make this misconduct a form of embezzlement.[34] On principle, a co-owner, or

to pay the grocer; conviction of embezzlement *held* reversed).

27. People v. Christenson, 412 Mich. 81, 312 N.W.2d 618 (1981) (contractor used partial payments for work at certain place for purposes other than to pay debts incurred in that construction; *held,* no embezzlement, as there was no agreement that defendant apply those specific funds to pay the workers and materialmen); Lawson v. State, 125 Miss. 754, 88 So. 325 (1921) (contractor, having contracted to build church for $6800, a price which included all labor and material, obtained an advance payment of $2100 cash to use to purchase lumber; instead of purchasing lumber he absconded; conviction of embezzlement *held* reversed, for it was his own money). This case suggests that the contractor, who lied about his intended use of the money, might be guilty of another crime; the trouble with false pretenses is in finding a misrepresentation of a present or past fact when he falsely says he intends to use the money to buy lumber; perhaps larceny by trick, which may be committed by false promises, will do, on the added theory that, the money being given for a specific purpose, title to it did not pass.

28. It would seem that such an earmarking, thus making the money a trust fund, might have been found in Lawson v. State, supra note 27, where the $2100 was to be used for the particular purpose of purchasing lumber for the church, not for any purpose which the contractor might desire. Cf. People v. Yannett, 49 N.Y.2d 296, 425 N.Y.S.2d 300, 401 N.E.2d 410 (1980) (though nursing home residents had contractual right to receive medicare refunds equal to amount they previously paid defendant, the money he was paid belonged to him and thus the failure to make the refunds was not embezzlement; result would be different if the money had "been turned over to defendant to hold in trust for the residents"); May v. State, 240 Miss. 361, 127 So.2d 423 (1961) (fraudulent conversion by promoter of preincorporation subscription for stock shares is embezzlement, for promoter is agent and not debtor; he holds the money for the specific purpose of purchasing stock shares). A few states provide that an advance payment to a contractor intended for laborers or materialmen constitutes a trust fund. See Note, 39 Colum.L.Rev. 1004, 1011 n. 50 (1939).

29. See § 8.4(c) for the analogous larceny problems.

30. Modern theft statutes, covering also embezzlement, typically do contain such a provision. See § 8.4(c).

31. As to partners, see Annot., 17 A.L.R. 982 (1922); 82 A.L.R.2d 822 (1978).

Compare State v. Kusnick, 45 Ohio St. 535, 15 N.E. 481 (1888) (under an embezzlement statute which omits the phrase "property of another," a partner is guilty), with O'Marrow v. State, 66 Tex.Crim. 416, 147 S.W. 252 (1912) (dictum that partner, having the right to use partnership property, who misappropriates the property, is not guilty of embezzlement).

32. Some cases have held an independent collection agent not to be an "agent" within the meaning of embezzlement statutes punishing agents who fraudulently convert their principals' property in their possession. E.g., Commonwealth v. Libbey, 52 Mass. (11 Metc.) 64 (1846).

Contra: People v. Riggins, 8 Ill.2d 78, 132 N.E.2d 519 (1956). Many states, however, specifically add to the class of persons who can embezzle: attorneys, factors, collection agents, commission merchants, auctioneers. See Note, 39 Colum.L.Rev. 1004, 1006 n. 13 (1939).

33. Not guilty of embezzlement: State v. Kent, 22 Minn. 41 (1875) (collector of rents for 5% commission not guilty of embezzlement for misappropriating the whole; since he had a 1/20 interest in the rents collected, it was not entirely the property of another, as embezzlement requires).

Contra: State v. January, 353 Mo. 324, 182 S.W.2d 323 (1944) (attorney, employed by client to collect a debt and keep a part for compensation, collected the debt and then converted the whole; conviction of embezzlement *held* affirmed; the entire fund "belongs to the principal until the agent exercises his right and appropriates his commission"); Commonwealth v. Hutchins, 232 Mass. 285, 122 N.E. 275 (1919) (agent to collect legacies for a commission converted the whole; conviction of larceny by embezzlement *held* affirmed on the same theory as in the *January* case).

See Annot., 56 A.L.R.2d 1156 (1957).

34. However, Model Penal Code § 223.0(7) specifically excludes from "property of another" property in the actor's possession when the other "has only a security inter-

an agent working on a commission basis, who misappropriates that part of the property in his possession which belongs to his co-owner or principal ought to be guilty of embezzlement of the other's interest in the whole.

We have seen that, although at common law one spouse could not be guilty of larceny of the other spouse's separate property, modern statutes allowing a married woman to own her separate property free from her husband's control have generally been held to authorize larceny convictions of either husband or wife.[35] The crime of embezzlement has undergone the same evolution.[36]

**WESTLAW
REFERENCES**

harris /p 164 +4 399 /p embezzl!
146k8

(e) By One in Lawful Possession. This element is the one which principally distinguishes larceny and embezzlement. For larceny there must be a trespass in the taking: the thief must take the property out of the victim's possession, which means that he cannot already have it in his possession. For embezzlement, on the other hand, the property must already be in the embezzler's lawful possession when he misappropriates it.

Yet it may be that not every case of fraudulent conversion of another's property already in one's lawful possession is covered by the particular embezzlement statute. Following the lead of the English embezzlement statutes, most American states at one time listed

the various types of persons who may have another's property in their rightful possession—employees, agents, bailees, attorneys, guardians, executors and administrators, factors, bankers and the like.[37] One trouble with undertaking to make a list is the danger of omitting someone who ought to be included.[38] As previously noted, the modern view is to make it embezzlement (or, a form of the broader crime of theft[39]) fraudulently to convert another's property in one's possession. Some statutes limit the scope of embezzlement by requiring that the property be "entrusted" or "delivered" to the embezzler with the result that he must acquire his possession of the property by being entrusted with it or by receiving delivery of it.[40] The following are some of the situations which have given rise to some difficulty:

(1) Employees. We have already noted that the master (employer) who hands his property to his servant (employee) retains possession of it, the servant having mere custody, so that the servant who misappropriates the property is guilty of larceny; but if the property comes to the servant for his master from a third person, the servant acquires possession, and his misappropriation, before he transfers possession to the master, is not larceny.[41] The crime of embezzlement was created to plug the loophole left by this gap in larceny. A typical statute on embezzlement by servants punishes a servant, clerk or agent employed by a person, partnership or corporation who misappropriates his employer's property in

est therein, even if legal title is in the creditor pursuant to a conditional sales contract or other security agreement." A similar exclusion is to be found in most modern codes. Some others, however, appear to define property so broadly as to produce a contrary result.

35. See § 8.2.

36. See Comment, 61 Colum.L.Rev. 73, 81 (1961).
Compare Golden v. State, 22 Tex.App. 1, 2 S.W. 531 (1886) (upholding instruction that husband can not be guilty of larceny or embezzlement by taking or converting wife's money); with People v. Graff, 59 Cal.App. 706, 211 P. 829 (1922) (under modern statutes, a wife can embezzle husband's separate property), noted at 11 Calif.L.Rev. 282 (1923).

37. See Note, 39 Colum.L.Rev. 1004 (1939).

38. E.g., State v. Whitehurst, 212 N.C. 300, 193 S.E. 657 (1937) (receiver of insolvent corporation not covered by embezzlement statutes). In some states the list of specific fiduciaries is followed by the catchall phrase "or other fiduciary" or the like. See Annot., 41 A.L.R. 474 (1926); See Note, 39 Colum.L.Rev. 1004, 1009 n. 31 (1939).

39. See § 8.8.

40. See State v. Frasher, 164 W.Va. 572, 265 S.E.2d 43 (1980), declaring that "the hallmark of embezzlement is the trust relationship," in that "it is necessary that the property embezzled should come lawfully into the hands of the party embezzling, and by virtue of the position of trust he occupies to the person whose property he takes."

41. See § 8.2(b).

his possession.[42] Under such statutes, misappropriating employees who have possession of their employer's property are guilty of embezzlement, those with custody are not (being guilty of larceny instead).

Sometimes it is not easy to determine whether the employee has received the property from his employer (and so has custody) or from a third person (so as to have possession)—as where the employer hands his employee a large bill with instructions to get it changed, and after getting the change the employee absconds with it.[43] Sometimes there is difficulty in deciding whether the employee, by placing the property received from a third person in a receptacle, has transferred possession to the master and thus reduced his own possession to custody.[44] Many cases draw a distinction between minor employees (caretakers, janitors, night watchmen)

who are generally considered as having mere custody of the property (and so guilty of larceny when they steal)[45] and those employees who have been delegated greater authority, who have possession (so as to be guilty of embezzlement when they fraudulently convert).[46]

A common type of embezzlement-by-servant statute, however, punishes an employee who fraudulently converts his employer's property "in his possession or under his care." Under such a statute, the crime is embezzlement without regard to the subtle distinction between custody and possession.[47] Under such statutes there is thus some overlapping between larceny and embezzlement.

(2) Finders. We have already noted that a finder of lost or mislaid property having earmarks of ownership who picks it up with intent to steal it is guilty of larceny; but he is

42. See Note, 39 Colum.L.Rev. 1004, 1004–5 (1939). A number of servant statutes, discussed below in this paragraph of the text, say "in his possession or under his care."

43. Rex. v. Sullens, 168 Eng.Rep. 1212 (1826), reversed a conviction of larceny of the change on the ground that the employee, not the employer, had possession of the change.

44. Commonwealth v. Ryan, 155 Mass. 523, 30 N.E. 364 (1892) (store clerk placed cash received from customer in cash drawer for a minute or two, then took the money out and converted it; conviction of embezzlement *held* affirmed, since he did not transfer possession for he put it in the drawer only for convenience in misappropriating it).

45. Government of Virgin Islands v. Leonard, 548 F.2d 478 (3d Cir.1977) (employee who was not authorized to place items in or remove them from storeroom, but who knew where keys to storeroom kept, took items from storeroom at night; this crime not embezzlement but larceny, as it "was similar to that of a janitor, entrusted with the key to an office, who takes an item left lying on a desk"); Fitch v. State, 135 Fla. 361, 185 So. 435 (1938); Warren v. State, discussed § 8.2 at note 23.

46. United States v. Whitlock, 663 F.2d 1094 (D.C.Cir. 1980) (distinguishing *Leonard* case, note 45 supra, court holds defendant who took money from bank vault committed embezzlement, as she "in a high position of trust * * * as an assistant cashier and assistant manager with the special trust powers that gave her access to the keys, the combination and the money"); Morgan v. Commonwealth, 242 Ky. 713, 47 S.W.2d 543 (1932) (office manager of a branch telegraph office, who had the combination of the safe, the only other combination being in a sealed envelope at the company's main office, abstracted money from the safe; his crime was embezzlement, not larceny); Bismarck v. State, 45 Tex.Crim. 54, 73 S.W. 965

(1903) (store manager took goods from the store and delivered them to the defendant; since store manager had possession, his crime is not larceny but embezzlement, so the defendant is not guilty of receiving stolen property). For other cases drawing the distinction between employees with "custody" and those with "possession," see Annot., 146 A.L.R. 532, 573–79 (1943).

47. Grin v. Shine, 187 U.S. 181, 23 S.Ct. 98, 47 L.Ed. 130 (1902) (a clerk, handed check by his employer to deliver to a third person, fraudulently converted it; the clerk argued that it was not embezzlement because he had custody only, not possession; but *held* this was embezzlement under California statute using the phrase "control or care"); Gill v. People, 139 Colo. 401, 339 P.2d 1000 (1959) (employee, hired by newspaper to sell advertising, was perhaps not authorized to collect cash for what he sold; he did receive cash and fraudulently converted it; he argued his crime was larceny, not embezzlement, because he was not authorized to accept cash, so that he had custody and not possession; conviction of embezzlement *held* affirmed, for statute says "in his possession or under his care"); State v. Lockie, 43 Ida. 580, 253 P. 618 (1927) (bookkeeper, with authority to draw checks on his employer's bank account for office supplies, drew checks payable to cash and fraudulently converted the cash; he argued his crime was larceny because he did not possess the bank account; conviction of embezzlement *held* affirmed, because the employer's property, its credit with the bank, was under his care and control within the meaning of the statute); Ker v. People, 110 Ill. 627 (1884), affirmed sub nom. Ker v. Illinois, 119 U.S. 436, 7 S.Ct. 225, 30 L.Ed. 421 (1886) (clerk took property from employer's vaults and fraudulently converted it; he contended that, as he did not possess the property, his crime was larceny and not embezzlement; conviction of embezzlement *held* affirmed under statute worded "in his possession or under his care"). For other cases, see Annot., 146 A.L.R. 532, 581–85 (1943).

not guilty of larceny if he picks it up with intent to restore it to the owner, though he later changes his mind and decides to steal it.[48] In the latter case is he guilty of embezzlement? He is in lawful possession of another's property, to be sure; but the embezzlement statutes of the state may not specifically cover finders. Statutes which limit embezzlement to property "entrusted" to or "delivered" to the wrongdoer do not cover the finder who properly picks up property. Perhaps a finder may be considered in a sense a bailee, so that if the embezzlement statute covers bailees, then finders may be covered.[49]

(3) Transferees of Property Delivered by Mistake. When considering larceny we noted that one to whom property is mistakenly delivered [50] is guilty of larceny if, realizing the mistake at once, he then intends to steal; but if he originally intends to return the property—or if he does not at the time of taking delivery realize the mistake—and only later decides to steal, he is not guilty of larceny.[51] In the latter situation, is he guilty of embezzlement? Once again, there may be difficul-

ty [52] in finding an embezzlement statute which covers such a misappropriation.[53]

 WESTLAW REFERENCES

topic(146) /p lawful /2 possession
146k13
146k9 /p employee servant agent clerk

(f) Fraudulent. The mental state required for embezzlement generally appears in the statutes in the form of the adverb "fraudulently" modifying the verb "converts." (If the statute should instead punish one who "embezzles," it would not signify anything different, for "embezzles" means "fraudulently converts.") As with larceny, the principal mental-element questions concern the conversion of another's property done under a bona fide claim of right; or done with intent to return the very property taken; or with intent to restore equivalent property; or with intent to collect a debt.[54]

(1) Claim of Right. One who converts the property of another which is in his lawful possession is not guilty of embezzlement (for his conversion is not fraudulent) if, when he

---

48. See §§ 8.2(f), 8.5(f).

49. Neal v. State, 55 Fla. 140, 46 So. 845 (1908) (finder of property first decided to restore, then decided to steal; conviction of embezzlement *held* affirmed, for she held the property in "bailment, so to speak"); see Burns v. State, 145 Wis. 373, 128 N.W. 987 (1910) (finder is a bailee). Once again, however, the bailee statute may be limited to a bailee of property "entrusted" or "delivered" to him. And see Commonwealth v. Hays, 80 Mass. (14 Gray) 62 (1859) (fraudulent conversion of money paid by mistake is not embezzlement by bailee, for the notion of bailment involves an element of trust and confidence not involved in delivery by mistake).

50. This may involve a mistake (1) as to the nature of the property delivered, as where $5 gold pieces are delivered instead of intended five cent pieces; or (2) as to the amount of the property delivered, as where a bank teller, cashing a $10 check, pays out $100; or (3) as to the identity of recipient, as where a package addressed to one John Jones is delivered to another John Jones.

51. See §§ 8.2(g), 8.5(f). There is a minority view, discussed in § 8.5(f), that, as to property misdelivered in a container, it is larceny if he intends to steal when he opens the container and learns of the mistake, though this act takes place some time after his receipt of the container.

52. Absent enactment of a modern all-encompassing theft statute, which is likely to solve this problem and many of the others addressed in this section. See § 8.8.

53. There is a dispute as to whether statutes covering bailees will do. Commonwealth v. Hays, 80 Mass. (14 Gray) 62 (1859) (fraudulent conversion of mistaken overpayment of money is not embezzlement under statute covering conversion by one to whom property has been delivered, for the statute was meant to cover bailees, and bailment involves an element of trust or confidence); Fulcher v. State, 32 Tex.Crim. 621, 25 S.W. 625 (1894) (fraudulent conversion of mistaken overpayment of money is not embezzlement under statute punishing conversion by one in possession of another's property as a bailee; money paid by mistake is not a bailment). But compare State v. Cavanaugh, 214 Iowa 457, 236 N.W. 96 (1931) (creditor assigned his claim to assignee for value; thereafter debtor in ignorance of the assignment paid debt to the assignor, who fraudulently converted the money; this is embezzlement by one to whom money is delivered, for assignor here was a bailee covered by the statute); Burns v. State, 145 Wis. 373, 128 N.W. 987 (1910) (finder of property who picks it up is a bailee though there is no contract of bailment).

See Annot., 14 A.L.R. 894, 899–901 (1921).

54. As to the counterpart questions in larceny, see § 8.5. Consult that earlier material for a discussion of how these issues are addressed in modern theft statutes encompassing embezzlement.

converts, he honestly believes the property is his own [55] or is nobody's,[56] or he otherwise honestly believes he is authorized to convert it. It should make no difference whether this bona fide claim of right is the result of a mistake of fact or a mistake of law, nor whether the mistake is reasonable or unreasonable [57] so long as it is real, for in any such event he lacks an intent to defraud.[58]

(2) Intent to Return the Very Property Taken. One who, with another's property in his rightful possession, converts it, intending, however, to return the specific property (and having a substantial ability to return it) in its original condition, after a period of time,[59] is not guilty of embezzlement, for he lacks the fraudulent intent which embezzlement requires.[60] It is the intent at the time of conversion which is important; one who converts

with a fraudulent intent is none the less guilty of embezzlement although he later decides to return the property and does so.[61]

(3) Intent to Restore Equivalent Property. A person in lawful possession of another's property may convert it in such a way that he cannot return the specific property; but he may intend to return the equivalent of the converted property to the owner, and he may have a substantial ability to do so. Commonly the property involved is money: the wrongdoer spends the money for pressing purposes of his own, intending to put back other money at a later date, and sometimes having enough private resources to be able to do so and even succeeding in doing so before his misconduct is discovered. It is uniformly held that the intent to restore the equivalent property even

---

55. People v. LaPique, 120 Cal. 25, 52 P. 40 (1898) (real estate agent, authorized to sell homeowner's house for $1,150, sold it for $1,450; honestly though mistakenly believing he was entitled to a commission of all over $1,150, he converted $300; conviction of embezzlement *held* reversed, for his bona fide claim of title negatives the mental requirement); see Lewis v. People, 99 Colo. 102, 60 P.2d 1089 (1936) (employee who honestly though mistakenly and even unreasonably believes he is entitled to a commission from a fund he holds for his employer, who converts the amount of the supposed commission, is not guilty of embezzlement, for the conversion is not fraudulent).

56. Morissette v. United States, 342 U.S. 246, 72 S.Ct. 240, 96 L.Ed. 288 (1952) (under federal statute punishing one who "knowingly converts" government property, one who honestly believes the property he converts—here rusty practice bomb casings lying on military reservation—to be abandoned is not guilty; a fortiori he would not be guilty of "fraudulently" converting the property).

57. In United States v. Williams, 478 F.2d 369 (4th Cir. 1973), the court noted that this crime cannot be committed by negligence and that consequently the court should not have instructed the jury that defendant could be convicted if he "should have known" the relevant facts.

58. In Hunter v. State, 158 Tenn. 63, 12 S.W.2d 361 (1928), the defendant converted another's property in his possession honestly believing, as a result of advice of counsel, that the statute which took ownership away from him and put it in the other was unconstitutional; he was held guilty of embezzlement. This view is properly criticized in Model Penal Code § 223.1, Comment (1980). Of course, one who converts what he knows to be another's property in ignorance of the law which punishes embezzlement is nevertheless guilty thereof, for ignorance of the law which one violates is no defense. But a mistake of law which negatives the mental element which the crime requires is a defense.

59. If the period of time is so long as to "appropriate a major portion of its economic value"—perhaps three days for fresh strawberries, six months for a racehorse, fifteen years for a diamond—intent to return the property would be no defense. See Model Penal Code § 223.0(1).

60. Conley v. State, 69 Ark. 454, 64 S.W. 218 (1901) (defendant hired a team to go on a short trip, returning the next day; instead he kept the team six weeks, travelling from place to place, but writing the owner from time to time promising to return the team; he was arrested 100 miles away; conviction of embezzlement *held* reversed, for intent to return the specific property is a defense). In some states, however, a statute provides that an intent to return embezzled property is no defense unless the property is returned before an information is filed: e.g., People v. Jackson, 138 Cal. 462, 71 P. 566 (1903). Of course, if the defendant's conversion of property consists of its destruction, damage, or sale, he will not be able to return it in its original state. The problem of intent to return as a defense to embezzlement is therefore limited to using the property gently for a period of time long enough to amount to a conversion but not long enough to be a fraudulent conversion. Perhaps the problem encompasses the situation of one who *pledges* the other's property, intending, to lift the pledge and return the property within a reasonable time. But see Spalding v. People, 172 Ill. 40, 49 N.E. 993 (1898) (treasurer of university pledged university's bonds as security for private debt he owed, intending to pay off the debt and restore the bonds; this was said to be embezzlement, just as if he had sold the bonds intending to repurchase them and restore them to the university). These may be held to be conversions, but not fraudulent conversions.

61. No doubt his change of heart, especially if brought about by twinges of conscience rather than by the fear of being caught, is entitled to be considered in mitigation of punishment by the sentencing authority.

under these conditions is no defense to embezzlement.[62]

We earlier noted with respect to larceny that intent and ability to restore the equivalent (generally, to pay for the property taken) may be a defense to that crime, especially if the property taken is property offered for sale. Perhaps the reason why such an intent with such an ability is no defense to the companion crime of embezzlement is the fact that in most embezzlement cases there is in fact no substantial ability to restore; the converter generally uses the money to gamble, play the stock market, or to keep his mistress in appropriate style.

(4) Intent to Collect a Debt. Just as it is generally held a defense to larceny that the taker takes the other's money honestly believing the latter owes him that amount,[63] so too it is a defense to embezzlement of money that the converter thereof believes that the money converted is the amount owed to him by the owner.[64]

(5) Miscellaneous Defenses. Embezzlement requires a specific intent to defraud. As with other crimes requiring some specific intent, intoxication which is such as to negative the

intent to defraud, and mistake of fact or of law which negatives such intent, are defenses to embezzlement.[65] In addition, the substantive-law defenses of infancy, insanity and compulsion apply to embezzlement as they do to other crimes.

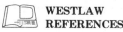

WESTLAW REFERENCES

topic(146) /p "good faith" "claim of right" (honest** /2 belie***)

146k5 /p fraud!

topic(146) /p inten! /3 return restore replace restitution

(g) Embezzlement by Public Officials. Many states have singled out state and local government officials who have public funds in their possession for special embezzlement treatment, sometimes watering down the mental element of the crime (perhaps punishing the public official who "converts" public funds, or who fails to pay them over on demand, rather than "fraudulently converts" the funds), sometimes increasing the possible punishment—all in recognition of the fact that public officials are not generally as closely watched by the public as employees or

---

62. United States v. Titus, 64 F.Supp. 55 (D.N.J.1946) (army post exchange employee took cigarettes belonging to government, sold them to a civilian at a high price, and deposited the low post exchange sales price in the post exchange cash register, keeping the overage; intent to pay and actual payment *held* no defense to embezzlement); State v. MacCullough, 115 Conn. 306, 161 A. 512 (1932) (agent sold principal's stock for cash, which he spent for own purposes, intending at the time he sold it to replace it; conviction of embezzlement *held* affirmed; the "fact that he intended, and might be able, to replace the stock entrusted to him with other stock of the same corporation would not absolve him from guilt"); State v. Pratt, 114 Kan. 660, 220 P. 505 (1923) (loan association treasurer sold bonds in his possession belonging to his employer intending to replace them or their value; conviction of embezzlement *held* affirmed); Commonwealth v. Tuckerman, 76 Mass. (10 Gray) 173 (1857) (corporate treasurer took employer's cash and spent it on pressing purposes of his own; instruction that he was guilty of embezzlement even though he intended to restore and had resources sufficient to enable him to restore other money *held* proper instruction affirming the conviction for embezzlement); Matter of Wilson, 81 N.J. 451, 409 A.2d 1153 (1979) (lawyer who made restitution of client's money he earlier converted to own use could still be disbarred, as it no less a crime that there was such intent to return); State v. Baxter, 89 Ohio St. 269, 104 N.E. 331 (1914) (state official used state funds for private purposes; before his wrongdo-

ing was known, he restored other money; conviction of embezzlement *held* affirmed).

Compare Nelson v. Rex, [1902] A.C. 250, which allowed the defense of intent to restore the equivalent, accompanied by assets four times the amount converted, to the embezzlement-like crime of fraudulent appropriation of bank money, not the crime of embezzlement proper.

63. See § 8.5(d).

64. Brannon v. State, 97 Fla. 488, 121 So. 793 (1929) (agent, claiming that his principal owed him over $500, withheld $500 of his principal's money and refused to pay it over; conviction of embezzlement *held* reversed). For other cases, see Annot., 13 A.L.R. 142, 145–47 (1921), 116 A.L.R. 997, 999–1002 (1938). Doubtless if the agent's claim is unliquidated or if the property converted is unliquidated, or if both the claim and the property are unliquidated—as if the agent converts his principal's car in satisfaction of a claim for damages arising out of an automobile accident—the difficulties which were discussed under larceny apply equally to embezzlement.

65. The claim-of-right defense, discussed above, is an application of the mistake-as-a-defense rule: one who, because of a mistake of fact or of law, honestly believes the property which he converts is his own, or is no one's, or that he is authorized to convert it, is not guilty of embezzlement.

agents of private persons or corporations are watched by their employers or principals.[66]

WESTLAW REFERENCES

146k21 146k11(2) /p official officer /s city state local public federal government /s fund money account

(h) Grand vs. Petit Embezzlement. Just as with larceny, embezzlement statutes commonly divide the crime into grand embezzlement (a felony) and petit embezzlement (a misdemeanor), depending upon the value of the property embezzled.[67] As with larceny, a series of fraudulent conversions of small amounts of property, belonging to one owner, over a period of time, all pursuant to a single scheme, may be aggregated so as to make one larger embezzlement out of several smaller ones.[68]

WESTLAW REFERENCES

topic(146) /p petit grand /3 embezz!
fi 32p2d593

---

§ 8.7   False Pretenses

False pretenses, a statutory crime, although defined in slightly different ways in the various jurisdictions, consists in most jurisdictions of these five elements: (1) a false representation of a material present or past fact (2) which causes the victim (3) to pass title to (4) his property to the wrongdoer, (5) who (a) knows his representation to be false and (b) intends thereby to defraud the victim.

(a) Need for Crime of False Pretenses. We have already noted, in connection with the historical development of the theft crimes,[1] that the modern crime of obtaining property by false pretenses (often called by the shorter term "false pretenses") was created by Parliament in 1757 to plug a loophole left by larceny. Although one who, with intent to steal, obtained possession but not title to another's property by false representations, and then converted it, was guilty of larceny (this type of larceny being called "larceny by trick"), one who obtained the title to the property was not guilty of larceny; and no other crime existed to fill the gap except in limited circumstances.[2] The 1757 English statute punished one who "knowingly and designedly, by false pretence or pretences, shall obtain from any person or persons, money, goods, wares or merchandises, with intent to cheat or defraud any person or persons of the same." [3]

Most American states enacted a statute similar to the original English statute.[4] Generally speaking, there was greater uniformity among the American false pretenses statutes

---

66. See Note, 39 Colum.L.Rev. 1004, 1008 (1939).

In State v. Ross, 55 Or. 450, 104 P. 596 (1909), affirmed sub nom. Ross v. Oregon, 227 U.S. 150, 33 S.Ct. 220, 57 L.Ed. 458 (1913), the statute punished one in possession of state moneys who "converts" such moneys with a maximum of fifteen years, while the ordinary embezzlement statutes punished fraudulent conversion by private persons with a maximum of ten years imprisonment. The defendant, honestly but wrongly, believing it to be proper, deposited state moneys in a bank; and the bank failed. His conviction under the special statute was affirmed, for the statute does not require that the conversion be fraudulent.

67. Modern theft statutes, dealing with embezzlement and all other forms of theft, usually make such gradings. For a survey of these statutes, see § 8.4(b).

68. E.g., People v. Fleming, 220 Cal. 601, 32 P.2d 593 (1934) (two conversions of two payments made at different times by owner to defendant under a single contract may be aggregated, to make one grand embezzlement instead of two petit embezzlements; there was "one design, one purpose, one impulse," so "they are a single act, without regard to time"). For several cases distinguishing one

larger embezzlement from several smaller ones, see Annot., 53 A.L.R.3d 398 (1973).

§ 8.7

1. See § 8.1.

2. The early English common law crime of cheats covered obtaining another's property by false weights and measures. A later English statute, 33 Hen. VIII, c. 1 (1541), covered obtaining his property by means of a "false Token or counterfeit Letter made in any other Man's Name"—under which the false representation had to consist of something more tangible than spoken words.

3. 30 Geo. II, c. 24 (1757).

4. The English statute, being dated 1757, is not part of the American common law (where common law crimes are recognized) in those states which take the view that the English common law, and statutes in aid thereof, must have been in effect in 1607 (founding of Jamestown) in order to be received as part of the state's common law. But in some states, which make the crucial date 1775, false pretenses may be a common law crime. Thus in State v. McMahon, 49 R.I. 107, 140 A. 359 (1928), it was

than among the American embezzlement statutes. Today, virtually all of the modern codes contain a comprehensive crime of theft,[5] which includes what was traditionally viewed as false pretenses (discussed herein) and often much related conduct as well. Many of the problems discussed below have been obviated by such legislation.

 WESTLAW REFERENCES

topic(170) /p "common law"

(b) False Representation of Material Present or Past Fact.

(1) False. For one to be guilty of false pretenses his representation must, first of all, be false. If he states a fact which he believes to be untrue but which is actually true, he is not guilty. If he represents to be gold a brick which he believes to be made of brass but which, he later learns to his surprise, is actually made of gold, he has made no false representation as the crime requires.[6] Even when the representation is false when made, if because of changed circumstances it becomes true by the time when the victim, relying thereon passes title to the other, the crime is not committed, for the falsity of the representation and the obtaining of the property must coincide.[7]

(2) Representation. The representation in false pretenses may be made orally or it may be made in writing. It may even be the result of unwritten and unspoken conduct, as where the wrongdoer, by wearing the cap and gown of an Oxford student, purposely produces the false impression that he is such a student and, on the basis of that false impression, obtains property from a tradesman on credit.[8] The representation of one fact may be implied from words which literally say something quite different: thus one who, to induce purchasers to buy land, falsely states that the state is about to build a hospital on the land, or that the federal government is about to construct a canal thereon, impliedly represents that the state or federal government has already taken affirmative action according to existing plans to construct the hospital or canal.[9] In some but not all jurisdictions the drawing and delivery of a check not postdated and without disclosure of insufficiency of funds, which states, "To the *X* Bank: Pay to the order of John Jones $50," is held to be an implied representation that the drawer has $50 in the *X* Bank to cover the check.[10]

(3) Nondisclosure. A misrepresentation for false pretenses generally requires some affirmative conduct—ordinarily the speaking or writing of words, although sometimes affirma-

held that the English statute was part of the common law of the state.

On the federal level, of course, false pretenses is criminal only when made so by statute. However, statutes on the federal level have been rather generously construed in order to conclude that they extend beyond the common-law larceny situation. See, e.g., Bell v. United States, 462 U.S. 356, 103 S.Ct. 2398, 76 L.Ed.2d 638 (1983) (federal Bank Robbery Act, covering whoever "takes and carries away, with intent to steal or purloin, any property or money or any other thing of value exceeding $100 belonging to, or in the care, custody, control, management, or possession of any bank, credit union, or any savings and loan association," *held* not limited to common-law larceny and proscribes obtaining money by false pretenses).

5. See § 8.8.

6. State v. Asher, 50 Ark. 427, 8 S.W. 177 (1887) (defendant, owner of real estate subject to a mortgage, represents that there is no existing mortgage and thereby induces the victim, on taking a mortgage upon the real estate, to part with his property; in fact there is an existing mortgage; but he makes this no-mortgage representation at the instigation of the existing mortgagee, who thus is estopped to set up his mortgage against the victim;

this it not false pretenses, for the representation is true, not false); State v. Garris, 98 N.C. 733, 4 S.E. 633 (1887) (defendant, owner of a crop, obtains property from victim by giving a mortgage on the crop after representing there is no prior mortgage on the crop; in fact there is a prior mortgage but it is invalid for failure to specify in writing the land upon which the crop grew; this is not false pretenses, for the representation of no mortgage was in fact true).

7. State v. Hendon, 170 La. 488, 128 So. 286 (1930) (on April 27 defendant bought goods from victim falsely representing he had money in the bank; on April 30, when victim delivered the goods, defendant did have money in the bank; the defendant is not guilty of false pretenses under these facts).

8. Rex v. Barnard, 173 Eng.Rep. 342 (1837).

9. People v. Sloane, 254 App.Div. 780, 4 N.Y.S.2d 784 (1938), affirmed mem. 279 N.Y. 724, 18 N.E.2d 679 (1939). If *A*, hastily thrusting a $5 bill at a bank teller, should say, "Quick, give me two 10's for a 5," and thereby obtain $20, he might be held to have impliedly misrepresented that 10 plus 10 equals 5!

10. See § 8.9(a).

tive conduct (like the wearing of the cap and gown of Oxford) not involving words. No doubt affirmative statements which reinforce false impressions which the defendant did not create, or affirmative conduct in suppressing the truth—e.g., the defendant actually hides information and so prevents the victim from learning the truth—will do as well.[11] Mere silence, however, will generally not suffice, even though the silent one realizes that the other is acting under a mistaken impression.[12] Under special circumstances there may, nevertheless, be a duty to speak to correct a misapprehension (thus making silence the basis of liability)—as where the defendant has, even though innocently, previously created the misapprehension by something he said or did,[13] or where he stands in a fiduciary relationship to the other.[14]

(4) Material. The false representation, to suffice for false pretenses, must be as to a material fact. One who obtains money from another by subletting his apartment to him for three months falsely representing that the lease has two years to run, is not guilty of false pretenses, though he intends to defraud, where under the applicable rent laws, though not under the lease itself, he has the right to possession beyond the three months period.[15]

(5) Present or Past Fact. Under the traditional view, to qualify for the crime of false pretenses the false representation must relate to a present or past fact; a false representation as to a future fact will not do.[16] It should be remembered, however, that it may be possible to find, in a statement relating to something that is to happen in the future, an implied representation that something has happened in the past.[17]

11. In the modern criminal codes, this is often expressly stated. However, some statutes fail to address the issue one way or the other.

12. Stumpff v. People, 51 Colo. 202, 117 P. 134 (1911) (defendant sold property to victim not disclosing chattel mortgage thereon; the prosecution argued that silence as to the mortgage is a representation that there was no mortgage; conviction of false pretenses *held* reversed; even if silence might do, here the information alleged a positive misrepresentation which cannot be supported by proof of silence); People v. Johnson, 87 Misc. 89, 150 N.Y.S. 331 (Sup.Ct., 1914) (since defendant made no representations, motion for directed verdict *held* granted; "mere silence or suppression of the truth, a mere withholding or knowledge upon which another may act, is not sufficient to constitute false pretenses. * * * There must be active, affirmative, false representations").

13. See § 3.3(a)(5), for how a duty to act to save a person or property in peril may arise out of the fact that the defendant's own conduct created the peril, though he may have created it innocently.

14. Model Penal Code § 223.3 includes as forms of deception: preventing the victim from acquiring information; failing to correct a false impression the deceiver previously created or which he knows to be influencing the victim to whom he stands in a fiduciary or confidential relationship; failing to disclose a known lien or adverse claim on the property he conveys to the victim. Although some modern codes do not address the question of what kind of nondisclosure will suffice, most do, usually in the same fashion as the Model Penal Code.

15. People v. Noblett, 244 N.Y. 355, 155 N.E. 670 (1927) ("the false representation, even if made, was not material").

In State v. Asher, 50 Ark. 427, 8 S.W. 177 (1888), the defendant obtained property from the victim on the false representation that there was no existing mortgage upon

property he owned; there was an existing mortgage but the mortgagee of that mortgage, having induced the defendant to lie, was estopped to assert it against the victim; the court held this not to be false pretenses because the representation was true. It would seem better analysis to base the defendant's non-liability on the ground that the representation was false but that it was not material, since the victim got exactly what he expected to get.

Model Penal Code § 223.3, concerning theft by deception, provides that deception does not include falsity as to matters having no pecuniary significance—as where a salesman lies to his purchaser about his lodge affiliations. Several of the modern codes contain such a provision.

16. Early American cases are McKenzie v. State, 11 Ark. 594 (1851); State v. Magee, 11 Ind. 154 (1858); Dillingham v. State, 5 Ohio St. 280 (1855). Pearce, Theft by False Promises, 101 U.Pa.L.Rev. 967 (1953), argues that this view first became embedded in the law by mistake. It has since become well settled, nevertheless: People v. Widmayer, 265 Mich. 547, 251 N.W. 540 (1933) (defendant sold real estate lot to the victim, falsely representing that a cemetery would be moved onto the lot and that the defendant would then sell the lot for the victim for $1200; these representations as to what would happen in the future will not do for false pretenses); State v. Allison, 194 Mo.App. 634, 186 S.W. 958 (1916) (defendant obtained money from victim by stating he would give victim injections which would cure him; this will not suffice for false pretenses); State v. Phifer, 65 N.C. 321 (1871) (defendant obtained a diamond ring by giving a check on P. Phifer & Co. and falsely stating to the victim, "I am the son of P. Phifer, and this check will be paid on presentation;" the former statement, but not the latter, will suffice for false pretenses).

17. See People v. Sloane, supra note 9, wherein the statements that the government was going to construct a hospital and a canal on certain lands were held to be

It is quite possible to view a false statement of intention—for example, a false promise (one which the promisor, at the time he makes his promise, intends not to keep)—[18] as a misrepresentation of existing fact, for he is falsely representing his present state of mind.[19] And a clever criminal can defraud his victim about as well with a false promise as with other types of false statement of fact.[20] Nevertheless, the traditional view was that false promises will not suffice for false pretenses.[21] The argument supporting this position that one cannot ever be sure whether a borrower has made a false promise or whether he has simply later changed his mind about the use of borrowed money; and that therefore there is a grave danger that honest businessmen who do not pay their debts will go to jail—[22] has been countered by

the argument that the mental state involved in a false promise is as easily discoverable as many other states of mind recognized by the criminal and civil law,[23] and by studies showing that in those minority jurisdictions which recognize false promises as false pretenses the jails are not flooded with unfortunate but honest businessmen.[24] The modern prevailing view, by case law [25] and especially by comprehensive theft legislation,[26] is in the direction of allowing false statements of intention—including false promises—to qualify as false representation for the crime of false pretenses.[27] (And, for some illogical reason, although in a particular jurisdiction a false promise will not do for the crime of false pretenses, it may do for the companion crime of larceny by trick.[28])

implied statements, sufficient for false pretenses, that the government had taken affirmative steps to formulate and carry out an existing plan to construct a hospital and canal on those lands.

18. A false promise is to be distinguished from a broken promise, i.e., a promise which the promisor originally intends to keep but which he later decides to break. One who makes a false promise can be properly said to be guilty of fraud; but one who breaks a promise he meant to keep, though not altogether admirable, cannot properly be termed fraudulent.

19. See Edgerton, J., dissenting, in Chaplin v. United States, 157 F.2d 697, 700 (D.C.Cir.1946) ("Intention is a fact and present intention is a present fact. A promise made without an intention to perform is therefore a false statement about a present fact").

20. See Curtiss, A State of Mind: Fact or Fancy, 33 Corn.L.Q. 351 (1948).

21. Thus in Chaplin v. United States, supra note 19, the defendant told the victim that he was a liquor dealer (true) and owned liquor which he could not sell without first affixing tax stamps (true) and that if the victim would advance $1075 to him, he would buy stamps, sell the liquor and repay the money advanced (false). His intent not to carry out these promises was evidenced by the fact that, after he got the money, he never used it to buy the stamps and never repaid the $1075. The court held, in a 2 to 1 decision, that he was not guilty of false pretenses, for false promises will not do.

Chaplin v. United States, supra, note 19 is the leading case. See Annot., 19 A.L.R.4th 959 (1983); Pearce, Theft by False Promises, 101 U.Pa.L.Rev. 967 (1953).

22. See Chaplin v. United States, supra note 19; People v. Cage, 410 Mich. 401, 301 N.W.2d 819 (1981).

23. See Edgerton, J., dissenting, in Chaplin v. United States, supra note 19. Pearce, Theft by False Pretenses, 101 U.Pa.L.Rev. 967 (1953); Curtiss, A State of Mind: Fact or Fancy, 33 Corn.L.Q. 351 (1948).

24. See Model Penal Code § 223.2, Comment at 189 (1980).

25. People v. Ashley, 42 Cal.2d 246, 267 P.2d 271 (1954) (defendant, who was agent for a corporation near insolvency, obtained $25,000 loan by representing that he would build a theatre; he used the borrowed money to pay the corporation's operating expenses; conviction of false pretenses *held* affirmed, for a promise made without intent to perform is a false representation of present fact and so a false pretense); Commonwealth v. Green, 326 Mass. 344, 94 N.E.2d 260 (1950) (defendant obtained money by falsely stating money was to be invested in forming an investment trust; no such trust was ever contemplated; conviction of false pretenses *held* affirmed, for false statement as to intention is false statement of fact).

26. Model Penal Code § 223.3(1) provides that one who purposely creates a false impression as to intention deceives so as to be eligible for theft by deception if he thereby obtains another's property; but goes on to caution that a mere failure to perform a promise shall not give rise to an inference that the promisor never intended to perform his promise. Many of the modern statutes contain the same caution.

Courts not infrequently emphasize that under such statutes the proof of the present intention not to keep the promise must be very strong so as to ensure against convicting for a mere breach of contract. See, e.g., People v. Churchill, 47 N.Y.2d 151, 417 N.Y.S.2d 221, 390 N.E.2d 1146 (1979).

27. Under the analogous federal statute punishing the use of the mails to defraud, 18 U.S.C.A. § 1341, one who uses the mails to defraud by means of false promises is guilty: Durland v. United States, 161 U.S. 306, 16 S.Ct. 508, 40 L.Ed. 709 (1896).

28. E.g., People v. Miller, 169 N.Y. 339, 62 N.E. 418 (1902) (defendant obtained money from victim by falsely stating his intention to invest it on the stock market, to pay 10% a week interest, and to return the money on demand; the defendant's conviction of larceny by trick

It is sometimes stated that an exaggerated expression of opinion, which generally concerns the value of property—e.g., "This land is worth $12,000" or "That stock is virtually worthless"—is "seller's talk" or "puffing wares" and not a misrepresentation of fact which will qualify for false pretenses.[29] On the other hand, it has been recognized that, under appropritae circumstances, a dishonest expression of opinion may be a misrepresentation of fact suitable for false pretenses,[30] especially where the opinion relates to a matter peculiarly within the knowledge of the one who expresses the opinion.[31]

There is a split of authority as to whether a false statement of law (rather than of fact) will do for false pretenses—as where one induces another to buy stock by making the representation, which he knows to be false, that the stock is not subject to assessment.[32] No doubt a clever criminal can accomplish a fraud as well by misrepresenting the law as by misrepresenting a fact; so that the better view is that intentional misrepresentations of law, done with intent to defraud, will do for the crime of false pretenses.[33]

A statement which though literally true is nonetheless misleading because it omits nec-

was affirmed on the ground that title to the money did not pass to the defendant and on the implicit assumption that false promises will do; the court answered the defendant's argument that his crime was false pretenses, not larceny, by stating that false promises will not do for false pretenses).

With another analogous crime—confidence game—it has with equal lack of logic been held that a false promise will do though it will not do for false pretenses: People v. Keyes, 269 Ill. 173, 109 N.E. 684 (1915). Contra: Bevins v. People, 138 Colo. 123, 330 P.2d 709 (1958) (false promise will not do for confidence game).

29. Carr v. State, 60 Ga.App. 590, 4 S.E.2d 500 (1939) (indictment charged defendant with false pretenses by obtaining $1200 loan by falsely stating that his used cars, given as security for the loan, were worth $1900 at a forced sale; held, defendant's demurrer should have been sustained by trial court, for a mere opinion, as distinguished from a fact, is not a pretense); Commonwealth v. Quinn, 222 Mass. 504, 111 N.E. 405 (1916) (defendant induced the victim to sell a farm, giving a note secured by real property concerning which defendant stated, "I have received a $42,000 offer for this property," which statement was false; this statement being "seller's talk" and not enough for false pretenses, defendant's conviction of false pretenses held reversed).

Model Penal Code § 223.3 excludes "puffing by statements unlikely to deceive ordinary persons in the group addressed," and several of the modern codes contain similar language.

30. Model Penal Code § 223.3(1) takes the broad view that it is theft by deception to create a false impression as to "intention or other state of mind," which is the position accepted in many of the modern codes. Those codes which merely use the word "impression," likely permit the same result. Some other statutes are even more ambiguous on the point, while others require that the misrepresentation be as to a fact (or, in some instances, a promise).

31. State v. Nash, 110 Kan. 550, 204 P. 736 (1922) (defendant stockbroker induced victim to sell him valuable stock by stating that the stock was very nearly worthless; conviction of false pretenses held affirmed, for under the circumstances here the representation of value was made with the purpose that it should be accepted and acted upon by the victim as a statement of fact); Williams v.

State, 77 Ohio St. 468, 83 N.E. 802 (1908) (defendant, knowing real property to be worth $330 at the most, sold it to victim for $7,700 by representing that it was worth $11,000; conviction of false pretenses held affirmed, for here the statement of value was given as a fact, not as an opinion; this is so especially where the opinion relates to a fact peculiarly within the knowledge of the one expressing the opinion).

See United States v. Rowe, 56 F.2d 747 (2d Cir.1932) (L. Hand, J., on mail fraud: "it is no longer law that declarations of value can never be a fraud. Like other words, they get their color from their setting, and mean one thing when exchanged between traders, and another when uttered by a broker to his customer. Values are facts as much as anything else").

See Annot., 14 L.R.A. (n.s.) 1191 (1908).

32. State v. Edwards, 178 Minn. 446, 227 N.W. 495 (1929), noted at 15 Corn.L.Q. 464 (1930), holds this not to be a false representation; since ignorance of the law is no excuse, the victim cannot claim to have been deceived.

Contra: Ryan v. State, 104 Ga. 78, 30 S.E. 678 (1898) (indictment charged that defendant, falsely stating the law to be that as the victim of a burglary he had the power to compromise the crime, thereby induced the wife of the man charged with burglary to pay him $50 to settle the prosecution for burglary; trial court's action overruling the demurrer to the indictment held affirmed; the maxim, ignorance of the law is no excuse, is inapplicable, and knowledge of the law will not be imputed to the burglar's wife, who did not in fact know the law). For a collection of cases both ways, see Note, 15 Corn.L.Q. 464 (1930).

33. Model Penal Code § 223.3(a) provides that a person deceives, for purposes of theft by deception, if he purposely misrepresents the law. Note, 15 Corn.L.Q. 464 (1930), concludes that a misrepresentation as to law should suffice for false pretenses.

Many modern codes expressly take this position. Some others, by use of the general word "impression," appear to permit the same result. Still others are even more ambiguous, while some appear to foreclose conviction in such a case by requiring that the misrepresentation be of a "fact" (or, sometimes, fact or promise).

essary qualifications—the half-truth which can operate to deceive quite as effectively as the outright lie—constitutes a form of misrepresentation which, when done to deceive, ought to qualify as a false pretense.[34]

Sometimes a clever swindler, after making oral misrepresentations to deceive his victim, gets the latter to sign a written contract which not only omits the offensive representations but contains a "merger clause" stating that the written contract is the entire agreement between the parties and that no representation has been made which is not set forth in the written contract. Such a merger clause, however, has been held ineffective to shield the swindler from a conviction for false pretenses.[35]

 WESTLAW REFERENCES

170k7(2) (170k7 /p implied** imply nonverbal unspoken unwritten)

topic(170) /p (fail*** /3 disclos***) nondisclos***

170k7(5) /p opinion estimate

(c) Cause and Result (The Element of Reliance). For false pretenses it is necessary that the swindler's misrepresentation *cause* the victim to pass title to his property or money to the swindler.[36] Looking at the mat-

ter from the point of view of the victim, the same thought may be expressed thus: for false pretenses it is required that the victim pass title to his property *in reliance upon* the swindler's misrepresentation.

Thus if the victim, although he passes title, does not believe the misrepresentations, the crime is not committed. He may pass title, though knowing the defendant to be lying, in order to be able to prosecute him for the crime; but the prosecution for the completed crime (though not for the attempt) must fail for lack of the element of reliance.[37] Or he may pass title, though he knows the defendant to be lying, because he nevertheless wants what the defendant offers—i.e., he would have passed title even if the defendant had told the truth. The defendant is not then guilty of false pretenses.[38]

Often the defendant, in order to induce the victim to part with his money or other property, makes several representations, some true but one false, which, operating together upon the victim's mind, cause the victim to hand over his money or other property. It has been held that if the one false representation is "one of the material matters relied upon,"[39] or is a "controlling inducement" for

34. Rex v. Kylsant, [1932] 1 K.B. 442 (Ct.Crim.App.) (prosecution for violation of a statute punishing a corporate officer who makes a statement in a prospectus knowing it to be false; defendant's statements, in a prospectus concerning a new issue of securities, about past dividends, though literally true, were as a whole misleading as to the soundness of the corporation's financial condition; appeal from conviction *held* dismissed), noted at 45 Harv.L.Rev. 1078 (1932).

35. State v. Cooke, 59 Wash.2d 804, 371 P.2d 39 (1962) (defendant salesman sold what he orally said were exclusive dealerships to four persons; the written contract, however, made no mention of the exclusiveness of the dealerships; conviction of false pretenses *held* affirmed).

36. Thus false pretenses, like murder and manslaughter and arson but unlike perjury and forgery and reckless driving, is a crime which requires that the defendant's bad conduct cause a bad result. See § 1.2(c).

37. State v. Finch, 223 Kan. 398, 573 P.2d 1048 (1978) (no false pretenses where defendant bought dress at lower price by switching sale tag from another garment, as security guard alerted cashier this had occurred); Hughes v. State, 326 So.2d 469 (Miss.1976) (no false pretenses where defendant sold deputy bottle of alleged arthritis-curing oil, as victim did not rely on misrepresentation that oil would cure arthritis); Commonwealth v. Johnson,

312 Pa. 140, 167 A. 344 (1933) (victim, though not believing defendant's lies, handed him marked money; although this is not the crime of false pretenses, defendant's conviction of attempted false pretenses *held* affirmed).

Compare the situation where the victim, not knowing that the defendant was lying, had only a "strong suspicion" that he was, and he bought in order to find out: State v. Ice & Fuel Co., 166 N.C. 366, 81 S.E. 737 (1914) (conviction of false pretenses for selling 1750 pounds of coke as one ton to a competitor who strongly suspected the defendant of selling at short weight). Consider also State v. Swoyer, 228 Kan. 799, 619 P.2d 1166 (1980) (although store security guard suspected defendant's scheme, false pretenses crime nonetheless occurred because defendant deceived cashier so as to get more merchandise than he paid for).

38. Sometimes the defendant uses a false name, but there is nothing particularly creditable about the false name or discreditable about the true name, so that the victim would have behaved exactly the same whatever name the defendant had used: People v. Whiteman, 72 App.Div. 90, 76 N.Y.S. 211 (1902); State v. Bingham, 51 Wash. 616, 99 P. 735 (1909)—both reversing convictions for false pretenses.

39. Whitmore v. State, 238 Wis. 79, 298 N.W. 194 (1941) (victim sold goods to defendant relying upon both

the transfer of property,[40] or "substantially contributed" thereto,[41] even though not the sole inducement, the victim has relied upon it, for purposes of the reliance element of false pretenses. For this reason it has been held that, even if the victim has so little faith in the defendant's representation that he undertakes to investigate its truth, without however discovering its falsity, he nevertheless has relied upon the misrepresentation for purposes of false pretenses.[42]

 WESTLAW REFERENCES

170k9 /p caus! rely relied

(d) Title Passing. The wording of the typical false pretenses statute—requiring that the defendant "obtain" property by false pretenses—is quite ambiguous on the issue of whether he must obtain title to, or possession of, the property, or whether he must obtain both title and possession. As we have already

noted, however, the crime of false pretenses requires that the defendant, by his lies, obtain *title* to the victim's property.[43] If he obtains *possession* without title by means of his lies, his crime is larceny.[44]

Whether title to property delivered to the defendant passes to him usually depends upon whether the victim *intends* to transfer title to him—so much so that the rule for false pretenses is sometimes erroneously expressed in terms of the victim's intent.[45] But there are cases wherein the victim, intending to transfer title, fails to do so—as, for instance, where the victim ships goods to the defendant who has ordered them by mail, fraudulently using the name of another person.[46] In such cases, the true distinction is not the victim's intention but the actual transfer of title, so that, since title does not in fact pass, the defendant's crime is larceny rather than false pretenses.[47]

(1) a conditional sales contract embodying defendant's promise to pay and (2) a bad check given in down payment; conviction of false pretenses *held* affirmed).

40. Woodbury v. State, 69 Ala. 242, 44 Am.Rep. 515 (1881) (explaining "controlling inducement" in terms of "but-for" inducement: "in the absence of the false pretense, he would not have parted with his property").

41. Rex v. Patmoy, 45 S.R. (N.S.W.) 127, 62 W.N. 10 (1944) (victim gave money to defendant for a diamond relying (1) on latter's misrepresentation that the diamond was a 7½ carat stone and (2) on his false promise that, if the stone was less than 7½ carats, he would give him his money back; defendant's appeal from conviction *held* dismissed).

42. State v. Foot, 100 Mont. 33, 48 P.2d 1113 (1935); State v. Cooke, 59 Wn.2d 804, 371 P.2d 39 (1962) ("It is well settled that the victim of fraud need not have relied solely upon the false representation in parting with his money, but only that he relied materially upon it").

Compare Ashford v. State, 410 S.W.2d 433 (Tex.Crim. 1967), holding that where the victim consulted his banker and lawyer and also the banker of the guarantor of notes before accepting the notes, his reliance was on those he consulted and not upon the representations of the defendant.

43. Thus, when defendant presented a stolen credit card to pay for the gas just put into the tank of his car, he was attempting false pretenses, as he only had possession of and was trying to obtain title to the gas by using the card. Blackledge v. United States, 447 A.2d 46 (D.C.App. 1982).

44. See § 8.2(e), where it is pointed out that for larceny by trick the defendant must also intend, when he obtains possession, to convert the property in question, and he must actually later convert it. It was there noted that

larceny by trick is simply one way of committing the crime of larceny; it is not a crime separate from larceny.

45. E.g., State v. Robington, 137 Conn. 140, 75 A.2d 394 (1950) (larceny by trick is committed by obtaining possession by fraud, but " 'if the owner intends to part with the title to the property as well as possession, whatever other crime may have been committed, it will not be theft' "); People v. Long, 409 Mich. 346, 294 N.W.2d 197 (1980) (defendant, who by distracting cashiers and asking for various amounts of change received $10 more than he had given, was guilty of false pretenses rather than larceny, as cashier intended to transfer both possession and title); Wilkinson v. State, 215 Miss. 327, 60 So.2d 786 (1952) ("The distinction, a rather fine one, between the crimes of obtaining property by false pretenses and that of larceny through obtaining possession by fraud seems to rest in the intention with which the owner parts with possession"); People v. Stiller, 255 App.Div. 480, 7 N.Y.S.2d 865 (1938), affirmed mem., 280 N.Y. 519, 19 N.E.2d 923 (1939) ("There is often a vary narrow distinction between a case of larceny, and one where the property is obtained by false pretenses. The character of the crime depends on the intention of the parties and that intention determines the nature of the offense").

46. In English v. State, 80 Fla. 70, 85 So. 150 (1920), English, fraudulently representing himself to be Jones, sent a telegram to the victim requesting a remittance by wire. The victim sent the remittance addressed to Jones intending to pass title to *Jones.* English's conviction of larceny *held* affirmed, for English got possession but not title. For other instances where the victim intends to pass title but does not succeed, see Note, 9 Iowa L.Bull. 204, 209–10 (1924).

47. English v. State, supra note 46; Regina v. Stewart, 1 Cox Crim.Cas. 174 (1845) (victim's servant delivered goods to defendant in violation of instructions not to

The defendant who, in committing the crime of false pretenses, obtains title to the victim's property by lies usually obtains possession from the victim as well. Indeed, delivery of possession is generally, though not always, a requirement for title to pass. What of the rare case in which the defendant obtains title but not possession? If he fails to acquire possession from the victim only because he is already in possession, he qualifies for false pretenses.[48] But even if, when obtaining title, he never has or gets possession— as where title passes by delivery of a deed of transfer without actual delivery of the property, which remains in the victim's possession— he would seem to be eligible for a false pretenses conviction. Although some cases have language which seems to require, for the crime, that the defendant obtain possession in addition to title,[49] what is really meant is that, where it takes delivery of possession of property to complete the transfer of title, obtaining possession is required; but if no such delivery is necessary, obtaining possession is not necessary for the crime.[50] On principle, it should be enough that the defendant obtains title even though, in acquiring title, he does not also acquire possession.

Normally the victim of the crime of false pretenses had the complete title to the property in question, but there may arise instances in which he has something less—such as the interest of a pledgee in possession to secure a debt, or of a purchaser in possession under a conditional sales contract with purchase payments still to be made. Under these circumstances the defendant may not be able to acquire, by his lies, the complete title, but only such title as the pledgee or conditional-sale purchaser had. Nevertheless, he may be guilty of false pretenses.[51] On the other hand, if the victim has no interest in the property other than its possession—as is the case with the finder of lost property—the defendant by fraud can obtain only possession, and the crime must be larceny by trick.[52]

Generally, of course, the defendant, by his misrepresentations, induces the victim to transfer title to the property to himself; but if

---

deliver until paid cash; defendant paid with bad check; though servant intended to pass title, title did not pass; conviction of larceny by trick *held* affirmed); Rex. v. Tideswell, [1905] 2 K.B. 273 (victim's agent, in collusion with defendant, sold property to defendant at short weight; defendant's conviction of larceny by trick *held* affirmed, because agent had no authority to pass title).

See Note, 9 Iowa L.Bull. 204, 210 (1924): "[T]he true ground for distinguishing between larceny by trick and obtaining property by false pretenses, is not, whether or not the owner delivered the goods with intent to pass title, but whether or not, as a matter of law, title did pass to the defendant."

48. Commonwealth v. Schwartz, 92 Ky. 510, 18 S.W. 775 (1892) (defendant banker, who had collected and was in possession of customer's money, induced her by lies concerning bank's solvency to lend the money to bank; conviction of obtaining money by false pretenses *held* affirmed; the general rule that the victim must obtain both possession and title is not applicable where it does not take delivery to pass title); Allen v. State, 21 Ohio App. 403, 153 N.E. 218 (1926) (defendant, already in possession of victim's money as agent, obtained title to it by false representations; conviction of false pretenses *held* affirmed).

49. See Allen v. State, 21 Ohio App. 403, 153 N.E. 218 (1926) ("As the statute provides for punishing whoever 'obtains' anything of value by false and fraudulent pretenses, it is insisted that the conviction could not be had for obtaining money of which the accused already had the possession, and, no doubt, as a general proposition, that is true").

50. Commonwealth v. Schwartz, supra note 48 (concerning defendant's argument that false pretenses "is not made out unless both possession and title are obtained by the false pretense," the court answered that, although that is true as a general principle, it "only applies where it takes the delivery of the possession to complete the transfer of the title to the property").

51. In Queen v. Martin, 112 Eng.Rep. 921 (1838), an indictment for false pretenses was held defective, necessitating reversal of a conviction, for failure to allege that the goods obtained by the defendant belonged to anyone; the prosecution argued that the indictment was good, because a person can obtain his own property by false pretenses; the court, while recognizing this to be true (e.g., one by lies obtains his own goods from a carrier with intent to defraud the carrier) since what is required is that the property be "of another" in a legal sense, yet held that the indictment must allege ownership of goods (e.g., the goods of the carrier, in the case supposed).

See State v. Samaha, 92 N.J.L. 125, 104 A. 305 (1918), discussing false pretenses: "'Actual ownership' of the money or goods by the person on whom the cheat is practiced is not essential. It is sufficient if he had lawful possession and dominion of the same."

For the analogous situation in larceny, see § 8.4(c).

52. Wilkinson v. State, 215 Miss. 327, 60 So.2d 786 (1952) (victim found stray cattle owned by *X;* defendant falsely represented that he owned the cattle, so victim handed over possession to defendant, who drove them off and sold them; defendant's conviction of larceny *held* affirmed, for victim did not intend to pass title).

instead he should get the victim to pass title to a member of the defendant's family, or to the corporation of which he is an officer, or substantial stockholder, the crime is nevertheless committed.[53]

Although it is easy enough to state the rule that false pretenses involves obtaining title, while larceny by trick involves obtaining possession, it is not always so easy to determine whether that which the defendant actually obtained was possession only, or possession plus title. It may be helpful, in discussing the matter, to divide the problems into these two situations: (1) where the property obtained is other than money and (2) where it is money:

(1) Concerning Property Other Than Money. One who induces another by lies to *sell* him his property obtains title thereto, so as to qualify for false pretenses, whereas if his lies induce the other to *lend* or *lease* him the property, his crime is larceny by trick.[54] One who, by the use of lies, induces the victim to sell him property on conditional sale, making a small down payment and promising to pay further instalments, does not obtain the complete title, for the conditional seller keeps the "security title"—the legal title, with the right to repossess the property if the future payments are not made as promised. And yet the purchaser has obtained something more than mere possession, since he has the right to complete ownership upon completing his payments, and since meanwhile the risk of loss falls on, and chance of gain enures to, him.[55] It has been held that, in this situation where the aspects of "title" are thus split between seller and buyer, the buyer gets enough of the title to qualify for the crime of false pretenses.[56] A cash-sale "buyer" who takes delivery of property upon giving a check instead of giving cash is generally held not to get title until the check is cashed;[57] so that, if the check proves worthless, title has not passed, and (assuming a worthless check is a misrepresentation of fact, or that other such misrepresentations were made) the "buyer's" crime is larceny rather than false pretenses.[58]

---

53. Commonwealth v. Langley, 169 Mass. 89, 47 N.E. 511 (1897) (corporate officer guilty of false pretenses for selling worthless stock in the corporation, though title to the money obtained passed to the corporation rather than to the officer himself; "it was not necessary * * * that he got the property on his own account, or that he derived or expected to derive personally any gain"). In the analogous situation of embezzlement, although the statute may literally require a conversion "to his own use," it is enough if the defendant converts the property in a way which benefits his son, or his corporation, rather than himself. See § 8.6(b).

54. Rex v. Pear, 2 East P.C. 685 (1779) (defendant *hired* a horse to go to place *X*, intending to steal it; he rode it to place *Y* and sold it; this was held to be larceny by trick); Hand v. United States, 227 F.2d 794 (10th Cir.1955) (defendants, telling used car salesman in California they wished to show car to their wives before buying, were permitted, on leaving a $20 deposit, to drive it off for that purpose; intending from the outset to steal, they drove the car to Denver via Reno, and Salt Lake City; their conviction of transporting a "stolen" automobile in interstate commerce *held* affirmed, for their crime was larceny, not false pretenses; the $20 deposit did not make the transaction a sale).

55. See R. Nordstrom, Sales § 131 (1970).

56. Whitmore v. State, 238 Wis. 79, 298 N.W. 194 (1941) (defendant bought goods on conditional sale, giving a worthless check as down payment; his conviction of false pretenses *held* affirmed; on a conditional sale "the legal title is merely retained for purposes of security" and "the vendee gets a sufficient property interest to support a conviction of obtaining money by false pretenses provided

the other requisites of the offense are present;" a conditional vendee "is regarded for most purposes as owner of the property covered by the conditional sales contract").

See Chappell v. State, 216 Ind. 666, 25 N.E.2d 999 (1940) (defendant, who obtained a watch on conditional sale by lies told by a confederate concerning the defendant's employment, was charged with conspiracy with the other to commit a felony; conviction affirmed on the ground that the felony was false pretenses, since most aspects of the title to the watch passed to defendant; but conviction must be affirmed even if the felony is larceny instead of false pretenses). But see Braswell v. State, 389 P.2d 998 (Okl.Cr.1964) (dictum that, in case of conditional sale, crime is properly larceny rather than false pretenses).

A conditional-sale agreement is to be distinguished from a "sale or return" arrangement under which the prospective purchaser is allowed to take possession of the property to try out for a short period, at the end of which he is either to return it or pay for it. Since title does not pass, the purchaser who lies is guilty of larceny by trick rather than of false pretenses: Hand v. United States, 227 F.2d 794 (10th Cir.1955), discussed supra note 54; State v. Robington, 137 Conn. 140, 75 A.2d 394 (1950).

57. R. Nordstrom, Sales § 166 (1970), stating that in such a case "the seller has a choice of remedies. He may sue for the price, bring suit on the check, or replevy the goods from the buyer. The buyer's right to *retain* the goods is conditional upon his making the payment due."

58. Riley v. State, 64 Okl.Cr. 183, 78 P.2d 712 (1938) (defendant, misrepresenting that he had money in the bank and that he was employed by a certain company, "bought" an automobile by giving a bogus check; convic-

(2) Concerning Money. In most cases one who hands over money to another never expects to get that very money back; and so it might be thought that in most cases of money obtained by fraud the wrongdoer obtains title, making his crime false pretenses rather than larceny by trick. It is, of course, possible to pledge money as security, or to bail money for safekeeping, to the wrongdoer, in which case title does not pass, so that the crime, if any, falls into the larceny-by-trick category.[59] What if the money is not pledged as security or bailed for safekeeping, but handed over to the the wrongdoer to do something particular with it, something which when performed precludes any chance of the return of the identical money? It is generally held that where the victim hands money to the wrongdoer with the understanding that the latter is to spend it only for a particular purpose (thus creating an agency or trust, it would seem)

title does not pass to the wrongdoer;[60] he has only a power to pass title by spending it for the specified purpose. Thus where the victim hands money to the wrongdoer to be invested on the stock market, or to purchase specified property, or to bribe a particular official, and the wrongdoer, instead of thus dealing with the money, absconds with it, the crime is larceny by trick rather than false pretenses, the wrongdoer never having acquired title.[61]

On the other hand, it is possible that the victim should agree or understand that the money, though desired for a particular purpose, might be used for any purpose—i.e., the defendant's lie about his need for money induces the defendant to make a loan rather than to create an agency or trust—in which case title to the money does pass to the defendant, so that his crime if any is false pretenses rather than larceny by trick.[62] One who obtains money from the victim by cheat-

---

tion of larceny *held* affirmed, over defendant's contention that his crime was false pretenses or embezzlement). Riley v. State was, however, explained in Braswell v. State, 389 P.2d 998 (Okl.Crim.1964), as a case of a conditional sale, where title did not pass, so the crime was larceny. As to title passing in the case of a sale made with the expectation of an immediate cash payment (not generally involving a worthless check), see Annot., 83 A.L.R. 441 (1933): since title does not pass, the crime is generally held to be larceny and not false pretenses.

59. Courtney v. State, 174 Miss. 147, 164 So. 227 (1935) (two defendants, pretending to find a pocketbook containing $1600, offered to divide the contents with the victim if he would pledge them $100 to show his good faith, the $100 to be returned when the $1600 should later be divided among the three; the victim handed over $100; the defendants, failing to show up to divide the $1600, kept the $100; defendants' conviction of obtaining $100 by false pretenses *held* reversed, for they never got title to the victim's $100, since the money was to be returned to him). Doubtless a pledge or bailment of money, without passage of title thereto, is possible even though the very money is not to be returned, for money, like wheat, is fungible. Cf. Shoemaker v. Hinze, 53 Wis. 116, 10 N.W. 86 (1881) (employer, asked by employee to take care of $40 for him, put the $40 in his wallet, mingling it with his own money, as employee saw; the wallet with its contents was thereafter stolen without the employer's fault; since the very bills were not to be returned, the transaction was *held* a debt rather than a bailment, so that the employer as debtor is not excused by the loss without fault).

60. Although a trustee has the legal title to trust property, the beneficial ownership—which is what should count for purposes of the larceny-false pretenses distinction—is in the trust beneficiary.

61. Graham v. United States, 187 F.2d 87 (D.C.Cir. 1950) (victim, at defendant's suggestion, paid defendant,

an attorney, $2000 to bribe the police; defendant never intended to use the money in this way but intended to keep it for his own use, and he converted it; conviction of larceny *held* affirmed); Commonwealth v. Barry, 124 Mass. 325 (1878) (victim at girl's request handed $20 bill to the girl to use to purchase a bottle of brandy for $3 and to return the $17 change; the girl absconded with the $20 bill; trial court charged the girl was guilty of larceny if she intended to steal when she took the $20 bill; conviction of larceny *held* affirmed, for the victim parted with possession but not title); State v. Scott, 301 Mo. 409, 256 S.W. 745 (1923) (victim handed defendant $35 to go to the store and buy a suit of clothes for victim at half price; defendant returned with a bundle for victim who, on later opening the bundle, found that it contained old rags; conviction of larceny *held* affirmed, over defendant's contention that the crime was false pretenses; victim "had no intention to part with title to the money until it had been exchanged for a suit of clothes—until the seller of the clothes received the money"); People v. Miller, 169 N.Y. 339, 62 N.E. 418 (1902) (victim handed money to defendant on the basis of his representations that he would invest it in the stock market; defendant never intended to invest the money and instead absconded with it; conviction of larceny by trick *held* affirmed; jury could have found that victim did not intend to part with title, though she may have intended that he could give title to some third person by investing it as he agreed); People v. Stiller, 255 App. Div. 480, 7 N.Y.S.2d 865 (1938), aff'd mem., 280 N.Y. 519, 19 N.E.2d 923 (1939) (victim handed money to defendant to be used to purchase controlling interest in a corporation, the defendant never intending to use it for such purpose; conviction of larceny by trick *held* affirmed, since victim parted with possession but not title to the money).

62. Kellogg v. State, 26 Ohio St. 15 (1874) (victim, induced by defendant's lie about his need for money, lent

ing at cards or by other forms of fraudulent betting is almost always held guilty of larceny by trick rather than of false pretenses, on the theory that possession but not title passes to the wrongdoer,[63] although it is somewhat difficult to see why title as well as possession does not in fact pass under these circumstances.[64]

**WESTLAW
REFERENCES**

topic(170) /p title /s possess***
topic(170) /p condition** /3 sale sell sold

(e) Property. The original English false pretenses statute covered only "money, goods, wares or merchandises," and thus was limited to tangible personal property and money. Modern statutes, although not uniform in language, have generally expanded this list to include "anything which can be the subject of larceny" or by adding, at the end, "or other valuable thing," "or other property" or "or anything of value." Such provisions general-

ly are construed to include written instruments representing choses in action (stocks and bonds, checks and promissory notes, savings-bank deposit books, insurance policies)[65] and other documents representing intangible rights (deeds, tickets, stamps). While the asportation element of larceny requires that larceny be limited to property which can be moved, false pretenses (like embezzlement) need not be so limited, there being no asportation element in false pretenses (or embezzlement). Thus one who defrauds another of title to real property should, on principle, be guilty of false pretenses; but the statutes which speak of obtaining "property" or a "valuable thing" are perhaps somewhat ambiguous, at least when read in the light of the early limitation of false pretenses to personal property; so that the cases on real property are in conflict.[66] There are similar conflicts concerning board and lodging[67] and labor or services.[68] It is generally held that one who

---

him $280, taking some false gold pieces as security; victim never expected to get the same money back; conviction of larceny *held* reversed; this is a loan and not a bailment, since the same money was not to be returned). As pointed out in note 59 supra, the court is not quite correct in thinking it must necessarily be a loan rather than a bailment if the same money is not to be returned, money being fungible.

Cf. People v. Noblett, 244 N.Y. 355, 155 N.E. 670 (1927) (defendant induced victim to pay advance rent on an apartment but never let the victim into possession; conviction of larceny by trick *held* reversed because the understanding was that defendant could spend the money as he liked, and therefore title passed as well as possession).

Perhaps this may explain why the leading case of Chaplin v. United States, 157 F.2d 697 (D.C.Cir.1946), did not even consider the possibility of larceny by trick under these facts: defendant told victim that, if she would advance him money, he would purchase liquor stamps and would return the money; defendant never intended to keep these promises; his conviction of false pretenses was reversed for lack of misrepresentation other than a false promise. But why is not the defendant guilty of larceny by trick (a false promise being a sufficient misrepresentation for that crime)? Was not money handed to the defendant for the particular purpose of buying liquor stamps? It must be that the money was handed over as a loan (with no strings attached to its use) rather than as a bailment or agency or trust.

63. Paine v. United States, 7 F.2d 263 (9th Cir.1925) (cheating at cards; larceny by trick), noted at 10 Minn.L. Rev. 253 (1926); State v. Skilbrick, 25 Wash. 555, 66 P. 53,

87 Am.St.Rep. 784 (1901) (cheating at cards; larceny by trick), noted at 15 Harv.L.Rev. 317 (1901).

64. State v. Anglin, 222 S.W. 776 (Mo.1920) (betting on matching coins; the report assumes rather than states that the defendant cheated; false pretenses, not larceny).

65. As to checks and promissory notes, see Annot., 141 A.L.R. 210, 211–216 (1942).

66. Real estate not covered: State v. Eno, 131 Iowa 619, 109 N.W. 119, 9 Ann.Cas. 856 (1906) (statute worded: money, goods "or other property"); State v. Klinkenberg, 76 Wash. 466, 136 P. 692 (1913) (statute provided: "any property, money or any check"). Real estate is covered: State v. Toney, 81 Ohio St. 130, 90 N.E. 142 (1909) (under statute which added "anything of value" to former statute, which was limited to property subject to larceny).

As is true in Model Penal Code § 223.0(6), most of the modern codes define "property" for theft purposes broadly enough to cover real property obtained by fraud. See § 8.4(a).

67. Compare Rex v. Bagley, 17 Cr.App.R. 162 (1932) (lodging is not a "chattel, money or valuable security" whch can be obtained by false pretenses); with State v. Snyder, 66 Ind. 203 (1879) (board and lodging a "thing of value" within false pretenses statute).

68. Compare State v. Ball, 114 Miss. 505, 75 So. 373 (1917) (physician's services constitute "any valuable thing" within false pretenses statute); and Stokes v. State, 366 P.2d 425 (Okl.Crim.1961) (telephone service is a "valuable thing" within false pretenses statute); with State v. Smith, 195 La. 783, 197 So. 429 (1940) (services of highway employee do not constitute "any property" within false pretenses statute). Some states have enacted special legis-

obtains the renewal of a loan,[69] or the satisfaction of a prior debt,[70] does not obtain property or a "valuable thing" within the false pretenses statutes. So too, a signature upon a document with business or pecuniary significance is usually held not to be "property" within such statutes.[71]

Although it is sometimes said that, for false pretenses as for larceny, the property obtained must be the property "of another," [72] this does not mean that the wrongdoer may not have an interest in, or even have legal title to, the property obtained, so long as the victim has an interest (for instance, a pledge or lien interest) in the property of which the wrongdoer has no right to deprive him.[73]

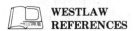 **WESTLAW REFERENCES**

170k11 /p (property estate /3 real tangible intangible) loan service land

(f) State of Mind. The typical modern false pretenses statute, like its original English ancestor, contains two words or phrases bearing on the mental state required: (a) "knowingly" (or, as some statutes word it, "designedly") and (b) "with intent to defraud."

(1) "Knowingly" ("Designedly"). To be guilty of the crime of false pretenses, one must "knowingly" ("designedly") [74] by false pretenses obtain property from another. The word "knowingly" modifies the phrase "false pretenses" so that the defendant, to be guilty, must know that his representation is false.[75] We have already noted that one who says what is in fact true, though he believes it to be false, is not guilty of false pretenses, for the pretense must, to qualify, be actually false.[76] Now we are concerned with the statement which is in fact false, and the question is: When does the wrongdoer "know" it to be false within the requirements of the statute? The following may be said to be the various states of mind which he may have when he states something to be a fact:

(i) He knows that the fact is untrue.

(ii) He believes but does not know the fact to be untrue.

(iii) He knows he does not know whether it is true or false.

(iv) He unreasonably believes the fact to be true.

(v) He reasonably believes the fact to be true.

Clearly, one who believes a false fact to be true does not know it to be false, and so, if his belief is honest, be it reasonable or unreasonable, he is not guilty.[77] At the other extreme, one who knows or (since one hardly ever

lation making it a crime, though not the crime of false pretenses, to obtain labor or services by false misrepresentation. See Note, 53 Harv.L.Rev. 893 (1940).

69. State v. Tower, 122 Kan. 165, 251 P. 401 (1926) (renewal of loan is not within false pretenses statute covering "money, personal property, right in action, or any other valuable thing").

70. Jones v. State, 9 Okla.Crim. 621, 132 P. 914 (1913) (defendant bought goods on credit, later paid for them by a bad check; conviction of false pretenses *held* reversed).

71. State v. Miller, 192 Or. 188, 233 P.2d 786 (1951) (defendant by lies induced victim to guarantee his indebtedness to *X;* conviction of false pretenses under statute covering "any money or property whatever" *held* reversed). In many states it is made a crime, not necessarily the crime of false pretenses, fraudulently to obtain a signature on a document having pecuniary significance. See Annot., 141 A.L.R. 210, 226 (1942).

72. See Queen v. Martin, 8 Ad. & E. 481, 112 Eng.Rep. 921 (1838).

73. Thus in Queen v. Martin, supra note 72, the court states that an owner of property who by lies obtains his own property from a carrier without paying the shipping charges may be guilty of false pretenses.

Instead of explaining the matter on the basis that the property obtained must be "of another" in a legal sense, it might equally well be explained on the basis that, although the defendant must in false pretenses obtain title from the victim, the word "title" does not require that the victim have the complete ownership of the property. See discussion of instances when the victim has something less than full ownership in § 8.7(d).

74. "Designedly" means the same thing as "knowingly": State v. Pickus, 63 S.D. 209, 257 N.W. 284 (1934) (" 'designedly' false means in substance willfully, knowingly and intentionally false and a false pretense is designedly made when it is made with knowledge on the part of the maker that it is in fact false").

75. See State v. Pickus, supra note 74.

76. See § 8.7(b)(1).

77. People v. Marsh, 58 Cal.2d 732, 26 Cal.Rptr. 300, 376 P.2d 300 (1962) (defendants sold electric machines to sick and neurotic people on representation that they could cure almost any illness; their offer to prove that they thought the machines would cure was denied; the prosecution's proof was that they would not cure; conviction of false pretenses *held* reversed, for an honest and reasonable belief in truth is a defense); State v. Pickus, 63 S.D.

"knows" anything in the sense of being 100% certain) believes a false fact to be false "knowingly" makes a false representation, and so is guilty of false pretenses if the other elements of the crime are present.[78] More difficult is the in-between case—number (iii) in the above list—of the one who states as a fact something which is actually contrary to fact, knowing that he does not know one way or the other whether it is true or false.[79] Such a state of mind, on principle, ought to do for false pretenses,[80] just as it will do for false pretenses' civil counterpart, the tort of deceit.[81]

(2) "Intent to Defraud." To be guilty of false pretenses (under the typical statute) it is not enough that the wrongdoer tells what he knows or believes to be false or what he knows he does not know to be true; in addition he must have an intent to defraud. Although one does not ordinarily obtain property from another by telling an intentional lie unless he does intend to defraud, it does not necessarily follow from his use of the intentional lie that he intends to defraud.[82] As with the analogous theft crimes, larceny and embezzlement, one who tells intentional lies nevertheless is not guilty of false pretenses, because he lacks the intent to defraud, if (1) he honestly but erroneously believes the property obtained is his own property or is otherwise property to which he has a lawful right;[83] or (2) he intends to restore the very property obtained, unconditionally and within a reasonable time, and has a substantial ability to do so;[84] or (3) he obtains it in satisfaction

209, 257 N.W. 284 (1934) (conviction of false pretenses *held* reversed because the trial court's instruction, authorizing conviction if the defendant made a false statement "recklessly without information to justify a belief in its truth," stated the mental element for false pretenses incorrectly; it erroneously authorized the conviction of one who negligently but honestly believed what he said was true). Although the *Marsh* case supra, and Stone v. United States, 113 F.2d 70 (6th Cir.1940) (mail fraud), state the matter in terms of an honest *and reasonable* belief, reasonableness of the belief should not be necessary in order to negative "knowingly." Of course, the jury is not as likely to be convinced by one who purports to have had a belief which was unreasonable as by one whose purported belief was reasonable.

78. See Commonwealth v. Green, 326 Mass. 344, 94 N.E.2d 260 (1950) (false pretenses requires false statement of fact "known or believed" by the defendant to be false); State v. Pickus, 63 S.D. 209, 257 N.W. 284 (1934) ("The word 'designedly' * * * covers the case only of affirmative evil intent; that is the man who knew or believed that his representation was false; possibly the man who knew he had no belief whatever concerning it when he made it").

79. State v. Pickus, supra note 78, states that the crime of false pretenses covers one who made a misrepresentation knowing or believing that he was making a false representation, and in addition "possibly the man who knew he had no belief whatever concerning it when he made it."

80. Knickerbocker Merchandising Co. v. United States, 13 F.2d 544 (2d Cir.1926) (per L. Hand, J., dealing with mail fraud based on false promises: defendants obtained money by making promises which they hoped to perform but could not perform; conviction of using the mails to defraud *held* affirmed; "it is not necessary to prove that the promisor intended not to perform; it is enough if he had no intention at all on the matter, or if he had no belief whether or not he could perform").

See also People v. Marsh, 58 Cal.2d 732, 26 Cal.Rptr. 300, 376 P.2d 300 (1962), for the proposition that one who

makes a false representation recklessly, without information justifying a belief that it is true, knows it to be false. This view would seem to cover not only the one who knows he does not know whether his representation is true or false (who should qualify for false pretenses) but also the one who honestly but unreasonably believes it to be true (who should not qualify). See also Model Penal Code § 223.3, Comment at 181–82 (1980): "If he creates the impression that he believes something to be true when in fact he has no belief on the subject, he has purposely deceived" for purposes of theft by deception, which covers what is false pretenses in most jurisdictions.

81. W. Prosser & W. Keeton, Torts § 105 (5th ed. 1984): one intends to deceive when he makes a representation which is in fact false "without any belief as to its truth, or with reckless disregard whether it be true or false. Further, than this, it appears that all courts have extended it to include representations made by one who is conscious that he has no sufficient basis of information to justify them. A defendant who asserts a fact as of his own knowledge * * * under circumstances where he is aware that he will be so understood when he knows that he does not in fact know whether what he says is true, is found to have the intent to deceive, not so much as to the fact itself, but rather as to the extent of his information."

82. State v. Hicks, 77 S.C. 289, 57 S.E. 842 (1907) (instruction that if defendant knew he was telling a lie he had the intent to defraud *held* error, requiring reversal of conviction; making a false representation is criminal "only when knowingly made, and, further than that, when made with an intention of defrauding thereby").

83. As to larceny, see § 8.5(a). As to embezzlement, see § 8.6(f). As to false pretenses, there may arise cases where one who believes himself the owner of property in another's hands finds he cannot get the property from the other without telling him lies. He may knowingly tell a lie but he has no intent to defraud.

84. Cf. Regina v. Boulton, 169 Eng.Rep. 349 (Cr.Cas. Res.1849) (defendant obtained a railroad ticket from the railroad by lies, intending to return the ticket to the railroad at the end of the journey; conviction of false

of a debt which the other actually owes [85] (or, it would seem, a debt which he honestly but erroneously believes the other to owe him).[86]

In order for one who misrepresents a fact to have an intent to defraud, it is necessary that he intend the victim to rely upon his misrepresentation,[87] an intention which generally can be inferred from the fact that the defendant actually obtained another's property or money by telling lies.

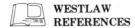
WESTLAW REFERENCES

170k8

topic(170) /p reasonabl* unreasonabl* honest** /3 belie***

170k5 /p defraud cheat

(g) Concurrence of Conduct and State of Mind.[88] In the light of the basic criminal-law principle that the mental and physical elements of the crime must coincide,[89] the knowledge of the falsity of the statement and the intent to defraud must coincide with the obtaining of the title to the property.[90] One who states what he believes to be true but which he later—before the victim, in reliance on the statement, passes title—learns to be false, has a duty to correct the misapprehension which his innocent statement has engendered, so that, if he takes title without disclos-

ing the truth, he is guilty of false pretenses (so long as the other elements of the crime are present).[91]

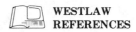
WESTLAW REFERENCES

170k5 /p time

(h) Grand vs. Petit False Pretenses. As with larceny and embezzlement, most jurisdictions draw a distinction between grand false pretenses, generally a felony, and petit false pretenses, generally a misdemeanor.

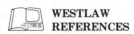
WESTLAW REFERENCES

topic(170) /p grand /s petit

(i) Possible Defenses to False Pretenses. Those charged with false pretenses have sometimes urged the following matters as defenses to liability, generally without success:

(1) The Victim's Gullibility. The defendant sometimes urges that, although the victim was actually deceived by the lies (exactly as the defendant intended), the victim was foolish to let himself be deceived; or the victim was negligent in not checking on the truth of the defendant's statement. Although at one time there was some authority that, for false pretenses, the lie had to be one calculated to

---

pretenses *held* affirmed; he intended to return the ticket on condition that he got a ride). An intent to pay for the property obtained, or otherwise to return the equivalent but not the very property, although it may be accompanied by an ability to do so, does not negative the intent to defraud and hence does not constitute a defense to false pretenses: People v. Weiger, 100 Cal. 352, 34 P. 826 (1893) (defendant intended to pay for goods obtained and felt sure he had the ability to do so; conviction of false pretenses *held* affirmed); Odom v. State, 130 Miss. 643, 94 So. 233 (1922), aff'd on rehearing, 132 Miss. 3, 95 So. 253 (1923) (defendant intended to repay and had actually repaid a considerable portion before charges were brought; conviction of false pretenses *held* affirmed).

85. State v. Hurst, 11 W.Va. 54 (1877); State v. Williams, 68 W.Va. 86, 69 S.E. 474 (1910) (defendant, with a judgment for $50 against the victim, by lies got the victim to sell him a cow for $28, then refused to pay; conviction of false pretenses *held* reversed), noted at 24 Harv.L.Rev. 403 (1911).

See Annot., 20 A.L.R.2d 1266 (1951). If what the defendant obtained is in excess of the amount due, or if the amount due is owing upon an unliquidated claim, or if the property obtained is not liquidated by an agreement be-

tween defendant and victim as to its value, perhaps the intent-to-collect-a-debt defense does not apply.

86. Thus it is a defense to larceny and to robbery that the defendant took the victim's money in payment of a debt, whether a debt was actually owing or the defendant merely believed it to be owing. See § 8.5(d).

87. See Commonwealth v. Green, 326 Mass. 344, 94 N.E.2d 260 (1950) (for false pretenses, "it must appear that there was a false statement of fact known or believed by the [speaker] to be false made with the intent that the person to whom it was made should rely upon its truth").

88. We have already noted that the falsity of the representation and the passage of title from victim to wrongdoer must coincide in point of time, for the crime of false pretenses, so that if a statement, false when made, becomes true by the time the defendant obtains title, he is not guilty. See § 8.7(b)(1).

89. See § 3.11.

90. Clarke v. People, 64 Colo. 164, 171 P. 69 (1918) (intent to defraud must exist at time of obtaining the property, but need not exist at time of making the misrepresentation).

91. See § 8.7(b)(3).

deceive a reasonable man,[92] the almost-universal modern rule is that the gullibility or carelessness of the defendant is no defense, since the criminal law aims to protect those who cannot protect themselves.[93] This rule is analogous to that which holds that the victim's contributory negligence is no defense to crimes based upon some degree of negligence (such as depraved-heart murder and recklessness manslaughter or battery), and to that which states that the victim's carelessness (as in leaving his front door unlocked or the keys in his car's ignition) is no defense to burglary of the house or larceny of the car.[94]

(2) Illegality of Victim's Conduct. One charged with false pretenses sometimes argues in his defense that the victim himself was involved in illegal conduct, as where the defendant obtains punchboard prize money from the punchboard operator by presenting a number which he has falsely altered to resemble the winning number; and by way of defense he points out that the victim was committing a crime by operating the punchboard [95] or where the defendant obtains money from the victim by falsely representing himself to be a smuggler in need of funds to

purchase a boat for smuggling purposes. The almost universal rule quite properly holds that the victim's illegal conduct is no defense to the crime of false pretenses.[96] This rule is but a part of the broader principle that the victim's badness is no defense to crimes committed against him.[97]

(3) No Pecuniary Loss to Victim. The defendant sometimes urges in his defense that, when the transaction which his misrepresentations brought about was over, the victim had suffered no pecuniary loss. The defendant induces the victim to buy stock in a silver-mining property by representing that a certain vein of silver ore is located near the property; though this representation is false, the stock in fact is worth what the victim pays for it, or more.[98] (On these facts, the stock may nevertheless not be worth what it would have been worth if the representation had been true. Yet it is possible that it may be worth as much, as would be the case if the silver-mining property was weak in silver ore but contained valuable deposits of high grade gold ore.) Of course, a civil suit would not lie against the defendant when the victim suffered no damage, at least if the victim made

---

92. Commonwealth v. Norton, 93 Mass. (11 Allen) 266 (1865) (defendant told victim this lie: "A few days ago I gave you $5 for a 20¢ purchase, but you forgot to give me the $4.80 change"; victim, believing the lie, handed him $4.80; judgment of conviction of false pretenses *held* arrested, because victim could ascertain the falsity of the representation as well as the defendant).

93. Clarke v. People, 64 Colo. 164, 171 P. 69 (1918) (instruction that "any pretense which deceives the person designed to be deceived thereby is sufficient, although it would not deceive a person of ordinary prudence" *held* approved); Lefler v. State, 153 Ind. 82, 54 N.E. 439 (1899) (victim's gullibility no defense, for "the object and purpose of the law is to protect not only the man of ordinary care and prudence, but also the weak and credulous against the strong, the ignorant, inexperienced, and unsuspecting against the experienced and unscrupulous"); State v. Nash, 110 Kan. 550, 204 P. 736 (1922) (although the absurdity of the defendant's statements may be considered on the question of whether the victim was in fact deceived, yet if he was deceived, the absurdity is no defense); State v. Foot, 100 Mont. 33, 48 P.2d 1113 (1935) (defendant's requested instruction that it is false pretenses only when the misrepresentation is of a character against which a man of ordinary caution could not have guarded himself *held* properly refused; the crime of false pretenses is meant to protect the ignorant, credulous and foolish as well as the wary and prudent).

94. See § 5.11(c).

95. State v. Mellenberger, 163 Or. 233, 95 P.2d 709 (1939).

96. State v. Foster, 38 N.M. 540, 37 P.2d 541 (1934) (defendant sold victim at a low price cigarettes which victim understood were stolen; defendant delivered boxes containing cottonseed instead of cigarettes; defendant's conviction of false pretenses *held* affirmed); State v. Mellenberger, 163 Or. 233, 95 P.2d 709 (1939) (facts stated supra note 92 and text; conviction of false pretenses *held* affirmed, overruling an earlier case holding that the victim's illegal conduct was a defense). See § 8.4(a), noting that modern theft statutes define property broadly enough to cover such situations.

Contra: State v. Donohue, 84 N.J.Super. 226, 201 A.2d 413 (1964) (indictment charged that victim paid defendant $4,200 because defendant falsely represented he could obtain victim's admission to Louisiana bar without his taking the bar examination; defendant's motion to dismiss indictment *held* granted).

See Annots., 95 A.L.R. 1249 (1935), 128 A.L.R. 1520 (1940).

97. See § 5.11(b), pointing out that one can murder a gangster, steal from a thief, or rape a prostitute.

98. State v. Sargent, 2 Wn.2d 190, 97 P.2d 692 (1940).

out as well financially as he bargained for.[99] But on the criminal side, it is generally held that the lack of financial loss is no defense to false pretenses.[100]

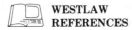

WESTLAW REFERENCES

170k22 /p negligen** careless!

170k14 /p less

(j) Crimes Related to False Pretenses. We have noted above the relationship between the crimes of larceny (by trick) and false pretenses.[101] A list of other crimes which relate to false pretenses follows:

(1) Bad Checks. There is some difficulty in making the crime of false pretenses apply to one who, with intent to defraud, obtains property or money by means of an insufficient-fund or no-account check. All jurisdictions have enacted criminal bad-check statutes, although they are not all worded uniformly. These are discussed in a separate section below.[102]

(2) Confidence Game. Several states have a separate crime (a sort of aggravated false pretenses), called confidence game, generally

carrying a punishment more severe than that which applies to false pretenses, and usually, unlike false pretenses, making no distinction between the grand and petit varieties. The rather vague definition of this crime covers obtaining money or property by any "means, instrument or device, commonly called confidence games." There is a split of authority concerning whether the crime requires that the false representation made to deceive the victim be made with some tangible device, or whether the simple spoken word will suffice.[103] There is a split too on whether a false promise will suffice for the required misrepresentation.[104] It is generally agreed, however, that the crime requires something extra (i.e., more than is required for false pretenses) in the way of acquiring or taking advantage of the victim's confidence.[105] The trouble with this distinction between the crime of confidence game and that of false pretenses is that, in the false pretenses situation too, the victim necessarily reposes confidence in the defendant and in the truth of his representations, and the defendant necessarily takes advantage of this. The modern trend is to abolish

---

99. W. Prosser & W. Keeton, Torts § 110 (5th ed. 1984).

100. Clemons v. United States, 400 A.2d 1048 (D.C. App.1979) (fact party who cashed paycheck for which payment had been stopped because the defendant had gotten and cashed a replacement check suffered no pecuniary loss no defense); State v. Sargent, 2 Wn.2d 190, 97 P.2d 692 (1940). In the analogous mail fraud situation too, financial loss to the victim is not a requirement: United States v. Rowe, 56 F.2d 747 (2d Cir.1932) (per L. Hand, J.: "A man is none the less cheated out of his property, when he is induced to part with it by fraud, because he gets a quid pro quo of equal value. It may be impossible to measure his loss by the gross scales available to a court, but he has suffered a wrong; he has lost his chance to bargain with the facts before him.").

The problem of the possible no-financial-loss defense arises frequently when the defendant obtains a loan of money, or purchases property on credit, from the victim by falsely stating that property which he puts up as security is free of encumbrances; in fact it is encumbered, but the defendant nevertheless has a sufficient equity in it to cover the amount of his debt to the victim. It is generally, but not always, held that the defendant is nevertheless guilty of false pretenses, though the victim, being adequately secured, has suffered no loss: Nelson v. United States, 227 F.2d 21 (D.C.Cir.1955); People v. Talbott, 65 Cal.App.2d 654, 151 P.2d 317 (1944).

See Annot., 53 A.L.R.2d 1215 (1957), for cases both ways.

101. See § 8.7(d). Larceny by trick is more fully discussed in § 8.2(e).

102. See § 8.9.

103. Spoken words alone are not sufficient: Davis v. People, 96 Colo. 212, 40 P.2d 968 (1935); State ex rel. Labuwi v. Hathaway, 168 Wis. 518, 170 N.W. 654 (1919). Spoken words *will* suffice: People v. Weil, 243 Ill. 208, 90 N.E. 731 (1909). See Note 7 U.Chi.L.Rev. 724 (1940), on the vague distinction between false pretenses and confidence games.

104. Compare Bevins v. People, 138 Colo. 123, 330 P.2d 709 (1958) (false promise will not suffice), with People v. Keyes, 269 Ill. 173, 109 N.E. 684 (1915) (false promise will suffice).

105. Olde v. People, 112 Colo. 15, 145 P.2d 100 (1944) (confidence of victim honestly obtained by defendant through course of regular business dealings; conviction of confidence game *held* reversed; dictum that the defendant may have been guilty of false pretenses); People v. Bimbo, 369 Ill. 618, 17 N.E.2d 573 (1938) (defendant, dressed as gypsy, prophesized victim's imminent death but told him she could save him if he brought a large sum of money wrapped in a handkerchief to a ritual; after the ritual she returned the handkerchief to him filled with waste paper rather than the money; conviction of confidence game *held* affirmed).

confidence game as a crime separate from false pretenses.[106]

(3) Mail Fraud. An important federal statute makes it a federal crime to use the mails to carry out a scheme to defraud a victim of his money or other property.[107] Unlike the crime of false pretenses it is not required that the scheme succeed in defrauding the victim; it is enough that the defendant devise the scheme and make use of the mails to carry it out. As noted above, under this statute a scheme which involves only the making of a false promise will do; whereas under the majority view a false promise alone will not do for false pretenses.[108]

(4) Securities-Registration Laws. Federal and state statutes (the federal Securities Exchange Act; state "blue sky laws") requiring the registration of securities before they can be sold provide that the promoters furnish information to the federal or state officials who must give their approval to the sale. The officials must act on the basis of information concerning the proposed venture, and the statutes require that this information be furnished by the promoters. The statutes generally make it a criminal offense knowingly to furnish false information in connection with the registration of securities.[109] Such statutes may be viewed as a sort of abbreviated false pretenses statutes, requiring a known misrepresentation of fact but not the bad result

(action by the deceived victim in reliance) needed for false pretenses.[110]

(5) Forgery.[111] Forgery is a crime aimed primarily at safeguarding confidence in the genuineness of documents relied upon in commercial and business activity.[112] Though a forgery, like false pretenses, requires a lie, it must be a lie about the document itself: the lie must relate to the genuineness of the document. A foreman who pads the time-roll by crediting himself with working more hours than he actually has worked does not commit forgery, since his lie relates to something other than the genuineness of the time-roll.[113] If, because of his misrepresentation, he successfully obtains money which he has not earned, he has committed false pretenses; if his plan does not deceive, his crime is probably attempted false pretenses.

Forgery, like false pretenses, requires an intent to defraud, but, unlike false pretenses, it does not require that anyone be actually defrauded of his money or property. One who has never had a chance to pass his forged document, or whose forgery is spotted when he tries to pass it, is nevertheless guilty of forgery. If he is successful in passing the forged document, receiving property or money for it, he is no doubt guilty of the crime of false pretenses in addition to that of forgery,[114] much as one who breaks and enters a dwelling house with intent to steal, and then

---

106. Thus the modern codes, in defining the new consolidated and comprehensive crime of "theft," see § 8.8, make theft by deception a form of theft, but make no special provision for deception through a device called a confidence game.

107. 18 U.S.C.A. § 1341.

108. See § 8.7(b)(5).

109. The statutes may be worded so that the defendant must know the facts to be false, or perhaps state untrue facts recklessly. The federal statute, 15 U.S.C.A. § 78ff, in a none-too-clear provision, punishes one who "wilfully and knowingly makes * * * any statement * * * which statement was false or misleading with respect to any material fact." Blue sky laws generally punish one who "wilfully" or "knowingly" makes a false statement. The state statute which punishes one who makes a false statement (no "wilfully" or "knowingly" in the statute) was held in State v. Dobry, 217 Iowa 858, 250 N.W. 702 (1933), to apply to one who states what is contrary to fact though he honestly believes it to be true. It may, however, be possible to interpret "false" as "known to be contra-

ry to fact" and not simply "contrary to fact": see State v. Johnston, 149 S.C. 195, 146 S.E. 657 (1929).

110. For various situations wherein the knowingly giving of false information is by statute made criminal, without regard to whether in fact the recipient of the information relied thereon, see Note, 38 Column.L.Rev. 624, 628–640 (1938), covering, in addition to securities regulation, false financial statements made to secure credit, and false statements in advertising.

111. The crime of forgery is to be found in the modern criminal codes. For further discussion of this legislation, see Model Penal Code § 224.1, Comment (1980).

112. Mack v. State, 93 Wis.2d 287, 286 N.W.2d 563 (1980).

113. De Rose v. People, 64 Colo. 332, 171 P. 359 (1918).

114. Loughridge v. State, 63 Okla.Crim. 33, 72 P.2d 513 (1937) (defendant, who knowingly presented a forged check to a bank and obtained money thereon, was *held* properly convicted of obtaining money by false pretenses; "the fact that the defendant might have been charged

does steal, is guilty of both burglary and larceny.

(6) Credit-Card Legislation. One who obtains property (and perhaps services) by misuse of a credit card may be guilty of false pretenses in two-party credit-card situations, i.e., those where the card-issuer is also the seller (or the performer of services). The defendant obtains something from the issuer by using a forged or stolen card, or a cancelled or revoked card, or he otherwise uses another's card without the latter's authority. Presenting the card doubtless is an implied representation that he is the person named on the card or that he has authority to use it.[115]

Much of the proper credit-card use today involves three parties: the credit-card issuer, the credit-card user (the purchaser or person for whom services are performed) and the creditor (seller or furnisher of services). The usual three-party arrangement is that the creditor collects from the credit-card issuer, who assumes the risk of misuse of credit cards so as to encourage creditors to honor cards promptly. Under these circumstances it is difficult to convict the misuser of a credit card of the crime of false pretenses, for the person deceived (the creditor) loses nothing, and the person who loses something (the issuer) is not the one deceived.

Therefore, special credit-card legislation has been enacted in a number of states [116] making it a new crime, generally a misdemeanor, to obtain property or services by means of a stolen, forged, cancelled or revoked credit card, or a card whose use is for any reason unauthorized.[117] Whether such special legislation concerning credit-cards impliedly repeals the general legislation covering false pretenses and forgery with respect to credit-card transactions, in situations where those crimes were formerly applicable, is not entirely settled.[118]

**WESTLAW
REFERENCES**

170k16 /p headnote("confidence game" /s false /2 pretense representation)

topic(170) /p credit-card

§ 8.8 Theft Crimes: Consolidation

We have seen that English legal history explains the fact that in American jurisdictions the wrongful appropriation of another's property was covered by three related but separate, non-overlapping [1] crimes—larceny, embezzlement and false pretenses. This fact, together with the fact (discussed below) that the borderlines between the three crimes are thin and often difficult to draw, gave rise to a

with forgery is no reason for his not being charged" with false pretenses).

See State v. Grider, 74 Wyo. 88, 288 P.2d 766 (1955) (dictum that, although defendant might have been prosecuted for false pretenses, that fact would not prevent his prosecution for forgery). But Model Penal Code § 224.1, Comment at 285 (1980), speaks of the potentiality of unfairness in cumulating convictions for forgery and for fraud based on forgery.

115. People v. Robertson, 167 Cal.App.2d 571, 334 P.2d 938 (1959) (defendant opened charge account at store by telling lies, then charged merchandise; false pretenses); Stokes v. State, 366 P.2d 425 (Okl.Crim.1961) (defendant obtained long-distance telephone call by unauthorized use of credit-card number issued by telephone company; false pretenses). Often the user of another's card must sign an invoice, and he signs the name of the other person. This has been held forgery: Shriver v. Graham, 366 P.2d 774 (Okl.Crim.1961) (also holding credit-card statute did not by implication repeal crime of forgery in connection with credit cards).

Cf. People v. Swann, 213 Cal.App.2d 447, 28 Cal.Rptr. 830 (1963) (state credit-card statute impliedly repeals forgery with respect to credit cards).

See Comments, 7 St.L.U.L.J. 158 (1962); 57 Nw.U.L.Rev. 207 (1962).

116. Such a statute is usually found in modern criminal codes. In a few jurisdictions credit card fraud is dealt with within a general theft statute. For discussion of these statutes, see Model Penal Code § 224.6, Comment (1980); Annot., 24 A.L.R.3d 986 (1969).

117. An alternative statutory form punishes one who presents such a card for the purpose of obtaining property or services; this form does not require that the seller or services-renderer be deceived or lose anything.

118. As to forgery, compare Shriver v. Graham (no repeal) with People v. Swann (repeal), both supra note 115. The problem is similar to that raised by special legislation on bad checks, which is generally but not always held not to repeal by implication the general crime of false pretenses when committed by means of bad checks. See § 8.9(b).

§ 8.8

1. There is some overlapping of larceny and embezzlement under embezzlement-by-servant statutes punishing an employee who fraudulently converts property "in his possession or under his care." See § 8.6(e)(1).

favorite indoor sport played for high stakes in our appellate courts: A defendant, convicted of one of the three crimes, claimed on appeal that, though he is guilty of a crime, his crime is one of the other two.[2] Sometimes this pleasant game was carried to extremes: A defendant, charged with larceny, is acquitted by the trial court (generally on the defendant's motion for a directed verdict of acquittal) on the ground that the evidence shows him guilty of embezzlement. Subsequently tried for embezzlement, he is convicted; but he appeals on the ground that the evidence proves larceny rather than embezzlement. The appellate court agrees and reverses the conviction.[3]

(a) Technical Distinctions Between the Three Crimes. As three rival nations which face each other across common borders often experience difficulty in maintaining friendly relations, so have the technical distinctions between the three theft crimes created unfriendly difficulties in at least two common-border areas: (1) larceny (including larceny by trick) versus embezzlement; and (2) larceny by trick versus false pretenses:

(1) Larceny vs. Embezzlement.[4] The misappropriation by an employee has created problems requiring for solution the drawing of a line between the employee's custody (the basis for larceny) and his possession (embezzlement) of his employer's property. Minor employees, such as caretakers and night watchmen, may have only custody, while employees of higher rank, like office managers, may have possession;[5] it is not always easy to draw the dividing line between minor employees with custody and those who rank high enough to have possession.[6] An employee who puts the money he receives from a customer directly in his pocket commits embezzlement, because the employer never has possession; but if he puts the money first in the till and later in his pocket, he commits larceny, since placing the money in the till gives the employer possession—unless he merely drops it in the till by mistake or places it there for only a minute or two before pocketing it.[7] An employee who receives his employer's property from the employer acquires custody only, so his misappropriation is larceny; but if he receives it from a third person to give to his master, it is embezzlement.[8]

How is it when the employer hands his employee a five-pound note to go out and get change; the employee gets the change, saying that it is for his employer; and then he absconds with the change? In a way, this is property which was handed him by the employer, and so his misappropriation constitutes larceny. But, in another way, it is property coming from a third person, so that the misappropriation is embezzlement.[9] As a matter of good sense the prosecutor, to convict, should not have to put it in one pigeonhole or the other. Some states have embezzlement-by-employee statutes which cover an employee who fraudulently converts the employer's property "in his possession or under

---

2. If the defendant is originally charged with two crimes by a district attorney uncertain as to which of the two the defendant's conduct falls within; and if the prosecution, before the case goes to the jury, elects to go to the jury on one of the two; and if the appellate court reverses the conviction based on that one on the ground the crime proved was the other; then a double jeopardy question is presented: may the defendant be retried for the other crime? See Scott, Larceny, Embezzlement and False Pretenses in Colorado—A Need for Consolidation, 23 Rocky Mt.L.Rev. 446 (1951) at n. 4 for a yes answer, citing Joy v. State, 14 Ind. 139 (1860) (prosecution elected after trial court granted defendant's motion to elect); and State v. Balsley, 159 Ind. 395, 65 N.E. 185 (1902) (trial court left both counts to the jury, which convicted of the wrong crime and acquitted of the right crime).

3. Commonwealth v. O'Malley, 97 Mass. 584 (1867) (*A*, having agreed to lend *B* $1, handed *B* a roll of money containing $38 to count and take therefrom $1; *B*, after counting the money, carried all $38 away against A's will); Nichols v. People, 17 N.Y. 114 (1858) (*A* shipped on *B's* Erie Canal boat at Albany 34 tons of pig iron, consisting of 680 bars each weighing 100 pounds; when forty miles from Albany, *B* removed 100 bars from the boat with intent to misappropriate them, later delivering the remaining 580 bars at Buffalo).

4. See Annot., 146 A.L.R. 532 (1943).

5. See § 8.2(b).

6. See Annots., 146 A.L.R. 532, 573–79 (1943); 125 A.L.R. 367 (1940).

7. See § 8.2(b).

8. Ibid.

9. In Rex v. Sullens, 168 Eng.Rep. 1212 (Cr.Cas.Res. 1826), the employee's conviction of larceny of the change was reversed, for the employer never had possession of the change; the crime is embezzlement.

his care" (or "control"); embezzlement under such a statute is generally held to overlap larceny, so as to warrant a conviction of embezzlement by an employee with custody only, though a conviction of larceny would also be upheld.[10]

The bailee (e.g., a carrier or warehouseman) of property which is made up into a bale (for transportation or storage), who breaks open the bale and misappropriates the contents is guilty of larceny. If, however, he misappropriates the whole bale without breaking it open, his crime in most jurisdictions is not larceny but embezzlement.[11] What if goods are shipped or stored in bulk but without wrapper or rope—for instance, 32 tons of pig iron, consisting of 640 bars each weighing 100 pounds? This might be viewed as one big bale without a wrapper, so that the carrier who separates 100 bars and sells them as his own breaks bulk and so commits larceny. Or it might be looked upon as the shipment of 640 separate bales, so that the conversion of 100 bars by the carrier constitutes embezzlement. It is a pretty even matter.[12]

In addition to the above difficulties which the *law* experiences in pigeon-holing borderline misappropriations into the larceny or embezzlement categories, there are situations where the proper pigeon-hole depends on what is the *fact* of the defendant's intent, a matter concerning which the prosecution can often only guess. One who finds another's lost or mislaid property bearing the earmarks of ownership, or who by mistake receives an overpayment or misdelivery of property be-

longing to another, and who intends to steal when he first takes possession of the property is guilty of larceny, for his trespassory taking and intent to steal coincide. But, if, when he first takes possession, he intends to restore the property and only later decides to misappropriate it, or if he does not until later realize the mistake and so only later decides to misappropriate it, his crime is not larceny; whether it is embezzlement depends on whether the embezzlement statute is broad enough to cover finders and persons who receive overpayments and misdeliveries by mistake.[13] In a state which has the broad embezzlement statute, the prosecuting attorney, not knowing whether the evidence will show an intent to steal instantly formed, or one which overcame the wrongdoer later, will generally charge both crimes; so that the trial court can leave it to the jury to find the defendant guilty of larceny if it finds that he formed the intent to steal at once, but of embezzlement if its finding is that he later decided to steal.

Similarly, it is not always easy to tell in advance whether the proof will show larceny by trick or embezzlement. Thus, the evidence may show that the defendant, who fraudulently converted another's property, obtained possession of (but not title to) the victim's property by lies, intending from the beginning to misappropriate it (larceny by trick), or it may show that he obtained the possession honestly and only later decided to misappropriate it (embezzlement). Evidence of one crime will not support a conviction of the other.[14]

10. See § 8.6(e)(1).

11. See § 8.2(d).

12. The distinction is between shipment by weight and shipment by number of bars; see ibid. In some states a crime called "larceny by bailee"—which where it exists is generally held to be a fourth crime in addition to larceny, embezzlement and false pretenses—covers the bailee who fraudulently converts bailed property, whether or not he breaks bulk. E.g., Bergman v. People, 177 Ill. 244, 52 N.E. 363 (1898) (distinguishing between larceny and larceny by bailee).

13. For larceny, see § 8.5(f). For embezzlement see § 8.6(e)(2), (3).

14. Ennis v. State, 13 Okl.Crim. 675, 167 P. 229 (1917) (defendant offered to sell victim's corn and account for the price; he sold the corn and fraudulently converted the

proceeds; conviction of larceny *held* reversed, since the evidence showed he originally meant to sell and account and only later decided to misappropriate; his crime is embezzlement, not larceny).

See Finlayson v. State, 46 Fla. 81, 35 So. 203 (1903) (defendant induced victims to leave their money with him overnight; conviction of larceny *held* affirmed because evidence showed fraudulent intent to convert at the outset); State v. Harrison, 347 Mo. 1230, 152 S.W.2d 161 (1941) (defendant, state official, obtained $1,500 state money stating a need to set up a state fund; he converted the money; his conviction of larceny by trick was *held* affirmed over his contention that his crime was embezzlement, for the evidence showed he obtained the money with intent to convert it at the outset). For other cases, see Annot., 146 A.L.R. 532, 549–560 (1943).

(2) Larceny by Trick vs. False Pretenses. One who obtains only possession of another's property by lies and then fraudulently converts it is a candidate for a larceny-by-trick conviction. If by lying he obtains title along with possession, his crime is false pretenses. Though this distinction is easily stated, it is not always so easy to determine whether what the defendant got from the victim was possession only, or title as well—as where the victim sells property to the defendant on conditional sale or at a cash sale where the defendant gives a bad check; or where the victim hands the defendant money to be used for one particular purpose.[15]

It is thus apparent that to retain these technical distinctions between the three crimes serves mainly to present a guilty defendant with an opportunity to postpone and perhaps altogether to escape his proper punishment. Yet, as Cardozo once expressed the matter when speaking of the difference between larceny and embezzlement, "The distinction, now largely obsolete, did not ever correspond to any essential difference in the character of the acts or in their effect upon the victim. The crimes are one today in the common speech of men, as they are in moral quality."[16] The fact that the statutory punishment is almost always the same for false pretenses and embezzlement as it is for larceny supports the notion that there is no moral difference between the activities of the thief, the embezzler and the swindler. And it can hardly make a difference to the victim whether he loses his property by another's stealth, or by his fraudulent conversion or through his falsehoods.

WESTLAW REFERENCES

digest(larceny /s embezzl! /s employee)

digest(larceny /s embezzl! /s differ distinct***
    difference)

digest(larceny /s embezzl! /s intent (state /2
    mind))

digest((larceny /2 trick) /s (false /2 pretense
    representation))

(b) Some Possible Remedies. In an attempt to deal with these problems, the embezzlement and false pretenses statutes of some American states provide in effect that one who embezzles, or one who obtains property by false pretenses, "shall be deemed guilty of larceny and punished accordingly." It might be thought that, under such statutes, if the charge is larceny but the proof shows embezzlement (or false pretenses) there may properly be a conviction of larceny, for embezzlement (or false pretenses) *is* larceny. Though a few courts so held,[17] most courts held that the statute does not make embezzlement (false pretenses) larceny but merely provides that the punishment shall be the same as for larceny.[18]

Another technique has occasionally been used to sustain a conviction where the defendant is charged with one of the three crimes but the proof shows another. "Where a defendant, by his own criminal acts, has placed himself in such a position that the evidence will support a conviction on either one of two theories, such as embezzlement by agent, or obtaining money by false pretenses, it should not be the duty of the court to draw fine hairsplitting distinctions. * * * The embezzlement statutes were enacted to remedy a defect in the common law. The courts should not, by strained constructions, add to the difficulties of the state in such prosecutions."[19]

The fact that the prosecuting attorney may join several counts in one indictment or information is helpful, especially where the law concerning the dividing line is clear enough but it is uncertain what facts, putting the case on one side of the line or the other, the proof will disclose. Thus, if uncertain whether the proof in a borderline case will show larceny or embezzlement, the prosecution may include two counts, one for each crime. The defen-

---

15. See § 8.7(d).

16. Van Vechten v. American Eagle Fire Insurance Co., 239 N.Y. 303, 146 N.E. 432 (1925).

17. Anable v. Commonwealth, 65 Va. 563 (1873); State v. De Berry, 75 W.Va. 632, 84 S.E. 508 (1915).

18. Compton v. State, 102 Ark. 213, 143 S.W. 897 (1911); State v. Burks, 159 Mo. 568, 60 S.W. 1100 (1901); State v. Sweet, 2 Or. 127 (1865).

19. State v. Gould, 329 Mo. 828, 46 S.W.2d 886 (1932).

dant may move, when the evidence is in, to have the prosecution elect upon which count he will go to the jury. Although it is often loosely stated that the grant or denial of the motion to elect is within the trial court's discretion, the situation here (the evidence relates to but one transaction, and the difficulty is whether the disputed facts require the transaction to be pigeon-holed in one category or the other) is the one situation where the motion should be denied.[20] Yet, because of the requirement that the jury by its verdict specify which of the two different crimes the defendant is guilty of,[21] there is still the danger (especially where the difficulty is that the law concerning the location of the borderline is uncertain) that the jury will select the wrong one, so that the defendant, on appeal, can show that the evidence proves the other one, and thus he can secure a reversal of his conviction.

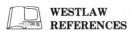 **WESTLAW REFERENCES**

topic(210) /p ˈheadnote(larceny /s embezzl! "false pretense")

(c) Consolidation of the Three Crimes into One. We have already suggested that many of the modern American difficulties in the area of misappropriation of property would have been avoided if in the beginning the English Parliament, instead of creating the new statutory crimes of embezzlement and false pretenses to plug the loopholes discovered in the law of larceny, had by statute simply extended larceny to cover the new situations which needed to be covered. American states generally followed the English

lead, recognizing the three separate crimes. But in recent years, and particularly in those jurisdictions which have enacted new criminal codes, these separate crimes have been abolished in favor of a single crime usually called "theft." [22]

Convictions under such statutes have been upheld against the contention that the statutes are unconstitutional because the defendant, charged with the consolidated crime of "larceny" or "theft," is not sufficiently informed of the nature of the crime charged unless he is accused of a particular one of the three former crimes. That is, the prosecuting attorney who charges "larceny" or "theft" need not elect a particular one of the three former crimes; if the evidence shows any one of the three, the defendant may be found guilty and the conviction will be upheld.[23] But it has occasionally been held that, in spite of the consolidation, an information or indictment which sounds like one of the former three will not support a conviction on evidence which shows another one of the former three.[24] The former view is the correct one: a defendant is entitled to notice in the indictment or information of the charge against him, but this means notification of the basic facts upon which the charge is based; he is not entitled in addition to a charge that "makes a noise" like one of the three formerly separate, but now consolidated, crimes. And thus it is quite proper to provide by statute, as is commonly done in jurisdictions with a more comprehensive crime of "theft" described in its various manifestations in several statutes, that a conviction may be had

20. Means v. United States, 65 F.2d 206 (D.C.Cir.1933) (larceny and embezzlement); Smaldone v. People, 102 Colo. 500, 81 P.2d 385 (1938) (larceny and receiving stolen property); Griffith v. State, 36 Ind. 406 (1871) (larceny and embezzlement); State v. Comer, 176 Wash. 257, 28 P.2d 1027 (1934) (larceny and false pretenses).

21. L. Orfield, Criminal Procedure from Arrest to Appeal 475 (1947).

22. Virtually all of these statutes sensibly use this neutral word, which can be applied more readily to all three forms of misappropriation than the word "larceny," which in ordinary usage refers to but one form.

23. Cameron v. Hauck, 383 F.2d 966 (5th Cir.1967); People v. Fewkes, 214 Cal. 142, 4 P.2d 538 (1931); State v.

Pete, 206 La. 1078, 20 So.2d 368 (1944); Commonwealth v. Kelley, 184 Mass. 320, 68 N.E. 346 (1903).

24. In People v. Dumar, 106 N.Y. 502, 13 N.E. 325 (1887), the indictment alleged that the defendant was guilty of "stealing, taking and carrying away" (sounding like former larceny) the victim's property; the proof showed the defendant obtained it by what was formerly false pretenses; the defendant's conviction was reversed, because in spite of the consolidation, the charge was larceny but the proof false pretenses. (This result would no longer obtain, as N.Y.—McKinney's Penal Law § 155.45 provides to the contrary.) See also State v. Dickinson, 21 Mont. 595, 55 P. 539 (1898); State v. Smith, 2 Wn.2d 118, 98 P.2d 647 (1939).

upon proof that the theft was committed in any of these various ways.

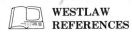

WESTLAW
REFERENCES

digest(larceny /s embezzl! /s "false pretense" /s theft)

(d) The Model Penal Code Consolidation. The Model Penal Code provides for an ambitious plan of consolidation of smaller separate crimes into one larger crime called "theft." Theft in the Code covers not only larceny, embezzlement and false pretenses, but also receiving stolen property and blackmail or extortion. Thus "theft by unlawful taking or disposition" covers what was formerly larceny and embezzlement; "theft by deception," what was formerly false pretenses and larceny by trick; "theft by extortion," what was formerly blackmail or extortion; and "theft by receiving," what was formerly receiving stolen property.[25] Many states follow essentially this approach.

The desirability of consolidating extortion (or blackmail)[26] with false pretenses is illustrated by a federal case involving these facts: An English woman wrote movie star Clark Gable a letter informing him that he was the father of her child, conceived in England in September, 1922; her intent in writing him was to induce him to pay her money. Gable had not in fact been in England in 1922 or 1923, and he had never met the lady, so that the letter contained misrepresentations of fact. The lady was charged with using the United States mails to defraud, a federal crime, and she was convicted upon the above evidence. On appeal, however, her conviction was reversed, for, since she intended to frighten, not to mislead, Gable by her lies, she used the mails to extort rather than to defraud.[27] Extortion (blackmail) may be thought of as simply another way—in addition to the ways encompassed by the three crimes of larceny, embezzlement and false pretenses—in which one person can misappropriate another's property.

It is often difficult for the police and prosecuting attorney, who find the defendant in exclusive possession of property recently stolen from the owner, to know whether he actually stole it or whether he received it from another who did the stealing. This gives a defendant, charged with larceny, a chance to urge that he received it; or, if charged with receiving, to claim that he stole it. Once again, in moral quality the two crimes, larceny and receiving, are alike, as the generally-similar statutory provisions for punishment recognize. The two crimes may be thought of as simply two ways of misappropriating another's property. Thus the Model Penal Code brackets them together as merely two ways among several ways of committing the single crime of theft.[28]

Robbery is a crime related to theft; indeed, it should be considered to be a sort of aggravated theft. Since it involves a danger to the person in addition to a danger to property, it is morally a worse crime than the other

25. Model Penal Code § 223.2 (unlawful taking or disposition), § 223.3 (deception), § 223.4 (extortion), § 223.6 (receiving stolen property). Id., § 223.1(1), provides that theft is a single offense embracing the formerly separate offenses of larceny, embezzlement, false pretenses, extortion or blackmail, receiving stolen property and the like. An accusation of theft may be supported by evidence showing that it was committed in any of these various ways, notwithstanding the specification of a different manner in the indictment or information; but the court may grant a continuance or other relief if the defendant is prejudiced by lack of fair notice or by surprise.

This latter provision is now found in many state codes.

26. *Extortion* originally was limited to the situation of a public official who corruptly obtains a fee, to which he is not entitled, for doing his official duty. In some jurisdictions extortion has been expanded to include anyone who obtains money or property from another by threats (or, in some jurisdictions, who makes threats to another with intent to obtain his money or property) to expose the other's failings or to inflict future injury on him or his family or his property. In other jurisdictions extortion is not expanded beyond its original scope, but the new crime of *blackmail* covers the added area of misconduct. See § 8.12.

27. Norton v. United States, 92 F.2d 753 (9th Cir.1937).

Similarly, in Jackson v. State, 118 Ga. 125, 44 S.E. 833 (1903), the defendant, falsely pretending to be a police officer, arrested the victim for a liquor violation, threatened to prosecute him, but offered to settle for $8, which the victim paid him. The defendant's conviction of false pretenses was reversed, for the evidence showed extortion (blackmail).

28. Model Penal Code § 223.1(1). Receiving is a form of theft under many of the modern codes.

crimes which the Model Penal Code collects together under "theft." The Code therefore treats robbery not as a form of theft but as a separate crime related to theft.[29]

WESTLAW
REFERENCES

theft /s "model penal code" /s larceny embezzl! "false pretense"

§ 8.9 Bad Checks

The difficulty in applying the crime of false pretenses to the situation where property is obtained by means of a no-account or insufficient-funds check has led all jurisdictions to enact bad-check legislation creating a new statutory crime separate from, and generally with penalties less severe than that provided for, the crime of false pretenses. There is much variety among the various jurisdictions as to the required elements of the bad-check crime, especially as to the required state of mind and as to whether there is a requirement that property be obtained as a result of issuing the bad check.

(a) Obtaining Property by Bad Checks as Crime of False Pretenses. Is one who obtains money or property in exchange for an insufficient-funds or no-account check guilty of obtaining property by false pretenses, assuming that, knowing his funds at the drawee bank to be insufficient or that he has no account there, he intends to defraud? There

are several difficulties in the way of relying altogether on the crime of false pretenses to combat the problem created by the worthless check: [1]

1. A check, addressed by the drawer to the drawee bank, states, "Pay to the order of" a named person a stated sum of money. If the drawer of the check in presenting it to the payee makes no extrinsic representation [2] concerning the check, where is the misrepresentation of present or past fact? Most, but not all, jurisdictions find that the giving of the check is an implied representation that the drawer has credit at the drawee bank sufficient to cover the amount of the check.[3] (Under the minority view, where the mere giving of the check is not a sufficient representation, the giver's extrinsic representations to the payee may contain a misrepresentation of present or past fact which will suffice for false pretenses.) [4] If, however, the check is postdated, or if the giver of the check states that he has not enough money in the bank to cover it though he expects to have by the time the check is presented for payment, there can be no implied representation that there is now enough on deposit to cover the check.[5] Although there may be a misrepresentation of fact, yet if the bad check is given by a debtor to a creditor in payment of a past due debt, the crime of false pretenses is not committed, for the debtor has obtained nothing (he owed his creditor before he gave the

---

29. Model Penal Code § 222.1. However, some jurisdictions have a crime called "theft from the person," as to which there is a split of authority concerning whether the taking must be from the body of the victim or merely from his presence or control. See State v. Tramble, 144 Ariz. 48, 695 P.2d 737 (1985); Annot., 74 A.L.R.3d 271 (1976).

§ 8.9

1. See Annot., 35 A.L.R. 344 (1925), 174 A.L.R. 173 (1948). Under Model Penal Code § 223.3 obtaining property by a worthless check is a form of "theft by deception," since a false promise will suffice for "deception" under the Code.

2. An extrinsic representation is a representation other than the representations which may appear in the check itself. Thus one may give a check and orally state, "I have money at the bank to cover this check," or "This check will be paid when you present it for payment," or "I am employed as foreman at the Steel Co. plant."

---

3. State v. Larsen, 76 Ida. 528, 286 P.2d 646 (1955); State v. Foxton, 166 Iowa 181, 147 N.W. 347 (1914)—both holding a bad check to be an implied representation sufficient for false pretenses. For cases both ways, see Annots. 35 A.L.R. 344, 348 (1925); 174 A.L.R. 173, 176 (1948).

4. Compare State v. Mullins, 292 Mo. 44, 237 S.W. 502 (1922) ("This check will be paid" will not do for false pretenses, since it relates to the future); with Smith v. People, 47 N.Y. 330 (1872) ("I have money on deposit in the bank" will do for false pretenses, since it relates to the present).

5. State v. Ferris, 171 Ind. 562, 86 N.E. 993 (1909) (postdated check; not false pretenses); Hatcher v. Commonwealth, 224 Ky. 131, 5 S.W.2d 882 (1928) (disclosure of insufficient funds not false pretenses). See Annots., 35 A.L.R. 344, 351–53 (1925); 174 A.L.R. 173, 180–81 (1948).

check and he still owes him) by his misrepresentation.[6]

2. Another difficulty in finding false pretenses arises in the situation in which a bad check is given by a buyer to a seller in a cash sale: the usual American rule of the law of sales holds that, unless the buyer's check is taken by the seller in absolute payment, title does not pass until the check is cashed.[7] Thus, when the check proves to be worthless, title never passes; and so the buyer is not guilty of false pretenses.[8]

3. Finally, the crime of false pretenses does not cover the situation of one who obtains property by giving a check, who actually has sufficient funds on deposit to cover the check, but who intends to, and does, stop payment or draw out his money before the payee of the check can cash it. If by giving the check he impliedly represents that he has money on deposit at the bank to cover the check, his representation is true. If he impliedly represents that he will do nothing (like stopping payment or closing out his account) to interfere with the payee's collection, his representation relates to the future, not to the present or past. So he is not guilty of false pretenses.[9]

Of course, the mere giving of a worthless check, though known by the giver to be worthless and given with intent to defraud, cannot ever constitute the crime of false pretenses, for the giver must *obtain* something

for it. False pretenses, in other words, is a crime which requires not only appropriate misconduct and bad state of mind, but a specified bad result as well.

 WESTLAW REFERENCES

topic(170) /p (bad worthless /2 check) /s "false pretense"

topic(170) /p post-date* /2 check

(b) Bad Check Statutes. Partly because of the difficulties, chronicled above, standing in the way of protecting property owners against property loss by using the crime of false pretenses in bad-check situations, and partly to safeguard public confidence in the check as a medium of payment in commercial activity,[10] most if not all American jurisdictions have enacted special bad-check legislation creating a new crime (concerning what is variously called bad checks, worthless checks, cold checks, false of bogus checks), generally with a penalty less severe than that awarded for the crime of obtaining property by false pretenses. The bad check statutes of the various states differ among themselves as to the necessary elements: [11] (1) Most, but not all, statutes do not require that anything be obtained from the victim as a result of giving the bad check; it is enough to give the bad check with the appropriate bad state of mind.[12] (2) Some statutes require that the check-giver have an intent to defraud,[13] but many more require only knowledge of the

---

6. United States v. Pearce, 7 Alaska 246 (1924). So too it is not false pretenses where the check is given for something which is not property or money or a thing of value: Currlin v. State, 110 Tex.Crim.R. 18, 6 S.W.2d 767 (1928) (bad check given for rent).

7. R. Nordstrom, Sales § 170 (1970), noting, however, that the fraudulent buyer has power to transfer a good title to a good faith purchaser.

8. Riley v. State, 64 Okl.Crim. 183, 78 P.2d 712 (1938) (defendant, making extrinsic representation that he had money in the bank and had a certain employment, "bought" a car by giving a bad check; conviction of larceny by trick *held* affirmed, over defendant's contention that his crime was false pretenses). For a criticism of some of the language used in the opinion, see Braswell v. State, 389 P.2d 998 (Okl.Crim.1964).

9. People v. Orris, 52 Colo. 244, 121 P. 163 (1912); State v. Alick, 62 S.D. 220, 252 N.W. 644 (1934).

10. See State v. Yarboro, 194 N.C. 498, 140 S.E. 216 (1927), expressing this purpose.

11. See Annots., 35 A.L.R. 375 (1925); 43 A.L.R. 49 (1926); 95 A.L.R. 486 (1935).

12. This, of course, differs from the crime of false pretenses, where the obtaining of property as a result of the misrepresentations is a necessary element. See State v. Foley, 140 Vt. 643, 443 A.2d 452 (1982), concluding that consequently enactment of a bad check statute did not repeal by implication the false pretenses statute.

13. See, e.g., State v. Kock, 207 Neb. 731, 300 N.W.2d 824 (1981). This is like the mental state required for false pretenses, where the defendant must both (a) know his representation to be untrue and (b) intend to defraud.

The giving of a post-dated check may be held not to violate such a statute in that it impliedly gives notice that there are no present funds and amounts to an extension of credit, State v. Stout, 8 Ariz.App. 545, 448 P.2d 115 (1968), although a contrary result has been reached where the defendant neither called the payee's attention to the fact that the check was post-dated nor arranged for him to

insufficient funds without the intent to defraud.[14] Whatever the required state of mind, it is common to provide in these statutes that the facts that (a) payment is refused by the bank for insufficient funds and (b) the check-giver fails to make good within ten days of notice of the bank's refusal is prima facie evidence of the required state of mind.[15] (3) Those statutes which do not require the obtaining of property[16] but yet do require an intent to defraud are generally held not to be violated by one who gives a bad check in payment of a pre-existing debt.[17] Nevertheless, a number of bad check statutes, changing the intent-to-defraud requirement, do cover the giving of a bad check in payment of past due debt.[18] (4) Some provide that the offense is no higher than a misdemeanor in all circumstances. This is also the position of the Model Penal Code,[19] on the ground it is "unlikely that felony sanctions will afford any particular advantage in dealing with bad-check situations."[20] But most of the statutes do recognize a felony variety of the offense in some circumstances, as where the face value of the check was a certain amount or where the defendant is a prior violator of the statute.

The problems which arise under these statutes, in addition to the problem of the check given for the pre-existing debt, are similar to those which concern the crime of false pretenses committed with bad checks: is a check-issuer guilty if he has sufficient funds on deposit when he issues the check but withdraws or stops payment before the payee can present it; what if the issuer postdates his check or discloses the fact of insufficient funds; what if, though he knows his account is insufficient, he has a hope of making a deposit before the payee presents the check? As with the check given for the past debt, the answers depend mainly upon the particular wording of the applicable bad-check statute.[21]

Since in the typical American state the statute on false pretenses antedates the bad-check statute, a problem exists as to whether the latter impliedly repeals the former when property is obtained by means of a bad check (assuming that the false pretenses statute otherwise covers this situation). In a state where the bad check statute provides for guilt without reference to obtaining anything there is no repeal;[22] but it may be that, if both crimes require obtaining property, the two conflict to such an extent that, in the area of property

hold the check, State v. Ramsbottom, 89 Idaho 1, 402 P.2d 384 (1965).

14. The statute of one state went further, requiring neither knowledge nor intent to defraud; the crime consisted of obtaining property by giving a check on the bank, not having sufficient funds therein to pay the check, unless the check-giver paid it within ten days after notice of dishonor. The statute was held unconstitutional in Burnam v. Commonwealth, 228 Ky. 410, 15 S.W.2d 256 (1929). As to the constitutionality of bad check statutes, see Annot., 16 A.L.R.4th 631 (1982).

15. As for the constitutionality of such a provision, see § 2.13(b). As for a statute which goes further and makes timely payment an affirmative defense, see State v. Carpenter, 301 N.W.2d 106 (N.D.1980) (violates equal protection clause by discriminating against indigent).

16. A fortiori, a statute which requires that the check-giver obtain something is not violated when the check is given for a pre-existing debt, since the giver obtains nothing by his check; he owed his creditor before he gave the check, and he still owes him. State v. Jarman, 84 Nev. 187, 438 P.2d 250 (1968); State v. Stout, 142 W.Va. 182, 95 S.E.2d 639 (1956).

17. Moore v. People, 124 Colo. 197, 235 P.2d 798 (1951) (the victim was not defrauded, "because his financial condition did not change on the strength of the check"). See Annot., 59 A.L.R.2d 1159 (1958).

18. This may be done specifically by providing for the guilt of one who, "to procure any property, or for the payment of a past due debt" gives a bad check knowing the funds to be insufficient; or of one who gives a bad check, with intent "to defraud or deceive," for the payment of "wages, salary, rent, property or other valuable thing."

19. Model Penal Code § 224.6.

20. Model Penal Code § 224.6, Comment at 318–19 (1980). See F. Beutel, Some Potentialities of Experimental Jurisprudence as a New Branch of Social Science 353, 410–11 (1957).

21. See Annots., 35 A.L.R. 375 (1925); 43 A.L.R. 49 (1926); 95 A.L.R. 486 (1935); 9 A.L.R.3d 719 (1966); 52 A.L.R.3d 464 (1973).

22. State v. Roderick, 85 Idaho 80, 375 P.2d 1005 (1962) (holding that the legislature intended the two crimes to fit together: if property is obtained by a bad check, the greater crime of false pretenses is committed; if not, the lesser crime of bad check is committed); State v. Foley, 140 Vt. 643, 443 A.2d 452 (1982).

obtained by bad checks, the bad-check statute supersedes the false pretenses statute.[23]

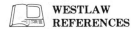

WESTLAW REFERENCES

bad worthless /2 check /2 statute law /s "false pretense"

(c) Incidence of Bad Check Crimes. A thorough study of bad check crimes in the state of Nebraska [24] disclosed that one-half of one per cent of all checks written in Nebraska were bad checks in the broad sense of forgeries, no-account checks and insufficient-funds checks. Of these bad checks, 90% were insufficient-fund checks, 9% were no-account checks, and only 1% were forgeries. What is true in Nebraska is doubtless indicative of the situation elsewhere in America: forgery of checks is a far less important factor in the disruption of commercial activity than other forms of criminal conduct relating to checks.

§ 8.10   Receiving Stolen Property

Receiving stolen property—a statutory crime separate from the crime involved in the stealing of the property—is defined in the typical statute as the receiving of stolen property knowing that it is stolen. Although most statutes do not specifically mention, it, the receiver must, in addition to knowing the property is stolen, intend to deprive the owner of his property. Some jurisdictions have by statute made changes in the elements found in the typical statute, so as to broaden the scope of the crime and thus make the receiver's conviction easier.

(a) Historical Development.[1] The ordinary thief steals in order to sell the stolen property, not to use it. Yet he cannot, by himself, successfully deal with the ultimate consumer. He must operate through a middleman, the professional receiver of stolen property. Without such receivers, theft ceases to be profitable. It is obvious that the receiver must be a principal target of any society anxious to stamp out theft in its various forms.[2]

Until the Nineteenth Century there was in England no separate substantive crime of receiving stolen property knowing it to be stolen.[3] At first the receiver with knowledge could not even be convicted of being an accessory after the fact to the larceny, for such an accessory must harbor the thief rather than his stolen property.[4] In 1692, however, an English statute provided that one who bought or received stolen property knowing the property to be stolen should be deemed an accessory after the fact to the theft.[5]

This did not, however, provide a very satisfactory weapon to use against the receiver, because of the procedural rule then in force that an accessory could not be convicted until after the principal had first been convicted of the crime; and the thief might avoid a conviction for larceny by dying, by not getting caught, or by winning an erroneous acquittal.[6] In 1701 an English statute provided that a receiver could be punished as an accessory though the thief had not already been convicted.[7] Finally, in 1827, receiving stolen property knowing it to be stolen was removed from

---

23. State v. Marshall, 202 Iowa 954, 211 N.W. 252 (1926).

24. See F. Beutel, Some Potentialities of Experimental Jurisprudence as a New Branch of Social Science (1957).

§ 8.10

1. See J. Hall, Theft, Law and Society 52–60 (2d ed. 1952).

2. See J. Hall, Theft, Law and Society ch. 5 (2d ed. 1952); Chamberlain, Anti-fence Legislation, 14 A.B.A.J. 517 (1928); Blakey & Goldsmith, Criminal Redistribution of Stolen Property: The Need for Law Reform, 74 Mich.L. Rev. 1511 (1976) (discussing the sophisticated fencing systems now in operation and what changes in the substantive law are necessary to deal with them effectively).

3. In Dawson's Case, 80 Eng.Rep. 4 (1602), it was held that the spoken words, "Thou art an arrant knave, for

thou hast bought stolen swine, and a stolen cow, knowing them to be stolen," do not constitute actionable slander, for there is no separate crime of receiving stolen property knowing it to be stolen; and one who thus receives stolen property is not an accessory to the theft, which requires that he receive the thief rather than his booty.

4. Dawson's Case, supra note 3; 1 M. Hale, Pleas of the Crown 619–20 (1736).

5. 3 & 4 W. & M. c. 9, § 4 (1692).

6. See § 6.6. Furthermore, the receiver of property from a thief, who was thereafter convicted of petit larceny, was not an accessory after the fact; it was no crime thus to aid one guilty of a mere misdemeanor.

7. 1 Anne, c. 9 (1701). Five years later this was superseded by 5 Anne, c. 31 (1706), changing the wording "although the principal felon be not before convicted" to

its position as an appendage of the theft and elevated to the dignity of a separate substantive crime.[8]

American jurisdictions, following the English lead, made receiving stolen property[9] knowing it to be stolen a separate substantive crime. In modern times there has been a trend to broaden the scope of the crime by requiring something less than actual knowledge of the stolen character of the property, by including conduct like concealing and withholding stolen property with knowledge in addition to receiving it with knowledge, and by covering property obtained by embezzlement and false pretenses as well as property obtained by larceny.[10] In most jurisdictions the punishment for receiving is the same as for larceny, embezzlement and false pretenses. The American Law Institute proposes that the crime of receiving stolen property be consolidated, along with larceny, embezzlement and false pretenses, into one large crime called theft.[11]

Although there is some variation in the statutes of the various states, the usual definition of the crime requires (1) the receiving of (2) stolen property, (3) knowing it to be stolen property, and (4) done with intent to deprive the owner of his property. These four elements—two physical and two mental—will be discussed below in the numerical order set forth above, together with a consideration of some of the modern statutory variations in the elements.

 WESTLAW REFERENCES

stolen /2 property /s receiv*** buy*** purchas***
    /s "common law"
topic(234) /p "common law"

(b) Receiving. When does one "receive" stolen property? The plainest sort of receipt occurs when one personally takes actual manual possession of the property. He also receives it when, pursuant to a prior arrangement with his employee, the latter takes possession of it.[12] Actual manual possession is not required, however, for one may receive property when he exercises control over it, though he does not lay hands, or even lay eyes, upon it—as where he has the thief deposit the stolen property in a place which he designates,[13] or, acting as a sort of broker, he earns a commission by introducing the thief to a purchaser.[14] Sometimes the negotiations between thief and would-be receiver are interrupted, generally by the police, before their transaction has been completed by a transfer of possession and the payment of money. A prospective receiver who, knowing of the theft, admits the thief, together with his stolen property, into his home or place of business for the purpose of negotiating concerning the buying of the property has not yet re-

---

"if the principal felon cannot be taken." Still later, 22 Geo. III, c. 58 (1782), provided that the receiver can be prosecuted for receiving regardless of whether the thief can be taken; and that a receiver from a petit thief can be prosecuted as an accessory.

8. 7 & 8 Geo. IV, c. 29, § 54 (1827).

9. Many of these statutes, from the very beginning, broadly encompassed "any property" or "anything of value." Model Penal Code § 223.6 covers only "movable property" on the theory that civil remedies are adequate as to immovable real estate. But most of the modern codes use language broad enough to cover both real and personal property. See Model Penal Code § 223.6, Comment n. 10 (1980).

10. The word "stolen" is ambiguous. In a narrow sense it means obtained by common-law larceny, e.g., Riley v. State, 64 Okla.Crim. 183, 78 P.2d 712 (1938); in a broader sense, it is not limited to a taking which constitutes common-law larceny, but includes obtaining by embezzlement and false pretenses as well, e.g., United States v. Turley, 352 U.S. 407, 77 S.Ct. 397, 1 L.Ed.2d 430 (1957).

11. Model Penal Code § 223.6.

12. Price v. State, 9 Okl.Crim. 359, 131 P. 1102 (1913).

13. La Fanti v. United States, 259 F. 460 (3d Cir.1919) (defendant saloonkeeper told thieves, who had brought their stolen goods to him at his saloon, that, as the place was being watched, they should take the goods to the "dumps"; they drove there and, on a signal from defendant who drove there in another car, dropped the goods in some bushes; the defendant, without stopping, returned to the saloon and was later arrested at his home; his conviction of receiving *held* affirmed; though he never had manual possession of the stolen goods, he did get "constructive" possession thereof).

14. Commonwealth v. Kuperstein, 207 Mass. 25, 92 N.E. 1008 (1910) ("It was not necessary to prove that the defendant had a physical and corporal holding of the articles alleged to have been stolen. It was enough if they were constructively in his keeping"). For more on what constitutes sufficient "constructive" possession, see Annot., 30 A.L.R.4th 488 (1984).

ceived it,[15] unless possibly the parties agree that there will be a sale, the negotiations being limited solely to the question of the price.[16] Although generally the receiver of stolen property receives it from the hands of the thief, he may be guilty though he receives it from someone else,[17] as where one, with knowledge, receives stolen goods from a receiver of the stolen goods.

Statutes on receiving stolen property have sometimes covered one who "buys or receives" stolen property with knowledge of its stolen character. Although one may receive stolen property without buying it [18] probably one who buys stolen property necessarily receives it, by exercising control over it if not by actually taking possesion of it;[19] if so, the word "buys" adds nothing to the receiver's liability. A few modern receiving statutes use "obtains control" terminology, perhaps obviating thereby problems of the kind mentioned above attributable to the seemingly narrower "receiving" concept. Other modern statutes instead or in addition use the word "possesses" or "conceals," or else a series of

verbs identical or similar to those in the Model Penal Code [20]: "receives, retains, or disposes." This wording subjects to liability one who received stolen property without knowledge of its stolen character but who, on later learning the truth, hides it from its owner or otherwise refuses to deliver it up.[21]

WESTLAW REFERENCES

324k4 /p control custody conceal hide hidden "constructiv*** possess***"

(c) Stolen. A statute punishing the receiving of "stolen" property, knowing it to be "stolen," most clearly covers property obtained by the crime of larceny. In its narrower sense the word "steal" means to obtain by larceny.[22] Even when limited to larceny, however, the crime of receiving stolen property encompasses property obtained by robbery [23] or obtained in a burglary.[24] A more difficult question concerns property obtained by embezzlement and false pretenses: has such property been "stolen"? Under the narrow meaning of "stolen"[25] these crimes are

---

15. Regina v. Wiley, 4 Cox Crim.Cas. 412 (Cr.Cas.Res. 1850) (defendant, on being arrested as a receiver, said he did not think he would have bought the property).

16. Compare Ogburn v. State, 132 Tex.Crim.R. 19, 101 S.W.2d 574 (1936) (defendant and thief drove to place where thief had hidden three stolen articles; defendant agreed on the price of one item; the thief put a second item, though no price was fixed, in defendant's car; the third item was still on the ground; defendant received the first item, possibly the second, but not the third; although it is not necessary for receipt that the purchase be consummated, still the property must come under receiver's control); with Rex v. Gleed, 12 Crim.App. 32 (1916) (thief drove van with stolen cask containing 60 gallons of gin to receiver's place, where receiver helped him lower it from the van to the ground; although possession during this maneuver was joint, the receiver had enough control over the stolen goods to have received it, so appeal from conviction held dismissed).

17. See People v. Marino, 271 N.Y. 317, 3 N.E.2d 439 (1936) ("it is not necessary that he receive it from the thief or know the thief who stole it").

18. See Ogburn v. State, supra note 16 ("it is not necessary to show that a purchase by him of the stolen property has been consummated"). One may, of course, receive stolen property by accepting it as a gift from the thief, or by hiding it for the thief, as well as by buying it from him. E.g., People ex rel. Briggs v. Hanley, 226 N.Y. 453, 123 N.E. 663 (1919) (gift of stolen property made to his mistress by the thief); Daniel v. State, 212 Miss. 223, 54 So.2d 272 (1951) (hiding it).

19. Thus Model Penal Code § 223.6 defines "receiving" to include "acquiring * * * title." Actually, of course, one who "buys" from a thief generally acquires no title. So "buys" in connection with the crime of receiving means "purports to buy," much as "marries" in a bigamy statute really means "goes through a marriage ceremony."

20. In Model Penal Code § 223.6 "receiving" is defined broadly as "acquiring possession, control or title, or lending on the security of the property."

21. Commonwealth v. Kelly, 300 Pa.Super. 451, 446 A.2d 941 (1982) (liability in such a situation, as statute includes one who "retains" with guilty knowledge).

22. See Black's Law Dictionary 1267 (5th ed. 1979). Thus property obtained by "joyriding" (taking a car for temporary use, intending to return it)—a crime separate from larceny and one generally punishable less severely than larceny—is not "stolen" property. Daugherty v. Thomas, 174 Mich. 371, 140 N.W. 615 (1913) (construing statute making car owner liable for injury caused by negligence of the driver, unless the car has been "stolen").

23. Marco v. State, 188 Ind. 540, 125 N.E. 34 (1919) ("every robbery includes a larceny").

24. It is burglary at common law to break and enter a dwelling house at night with intent to commit the felony of larceny. If after entry the burglar actually commits larceny, he has committed two successive crimes, burglary and larceny. The property obtained by the larceny is of course "stolen" property.

25. The rule of statutory interpretation which calls for a strict construction of criminal statutes, see § 2.2(d), is, of

not covered.[26] Sometimes, however, "stolen" has been construed to mean obtained by any one of the three principal forms of theft—by embezzlement and false pretenses as well as by larceny,[27] and the new codes "have unanimously so provided."[28] No doubt it ought on principle to be a crime knowingly to receive property obtained by embezzlement or false pretenses.[29]

Conduct which constitutes larceny (or, under the broader receiving statutes, embezzlement or false pretenses) when done by adults, is commonly juvenile delinquency (no crime at all) when done by children of certain ages.[30] Yet it has been held that the receiver who, knowing of the child's conduct in acquiring the property, nevertheless receives it from the child, is guilty of receiving "stolen" property.[31] It is different, however, if he receives property acquired by a child so young as not to be responsible (under seven years, at com-

mon law) or by a person, of whatever age, who acquired it while insane.[32]

Sometimes the owner, or a policeman acting on the owner's behalf, catches the thief with the stolen property before he has had time to pass it on to his receiver. In order to be able to prosecute the receiver, the owner or policeman may return the property to the thief who, cooperating with his captors in order to reduce his own punishment, then sells the property to the receiver. In such a case the receiver is not guilty of receiving "stolen" property, for the property in question was not "stolen" at the moment he received it; it lost its character as stolen property once it has been recovered by the owner or the policeman.[33] But under those modern statutes following the Model Penal Code view [34] that it suffices the defendant believed the property probably had been stolen, the receiver in this and similar circumstances could be convicted. In support of this result, it may be

course, an argument for construing "stolen" in the narrower way.

26. State v. George, 263 Mo. 686, 173 S.W. 1077 (1915) (conviction of receiving stolen goods *held* reversed, because the evidence proved the different crime of receiving embezzled goods); Regina v. Prince, 11 Cox Crim.Cas. 193 (Cr.Cas.Res.1868) (conviction of receiving stolen money *held* reversed, because the evidence proved the money was obtained by false pretenses rather than by larceny).

27. Thus in United States v. Turley, 352 U.S. 407, 77 S.Ct. 397, 1 L.Ed.2d 430 (1957), the word "stolen" in the National Motor Vehicle Theft Act, punishing the interstate transportation of a stolen car knowing it to be stolen, was held to cover an embezzled car, and said to cover a car obtained by false pretenses. This broad construction was based on the notion that the word "steal" is not as a matter of dictionary meaning necessarily limited to the larceny situation, and the evil which the Act was meant to cure covers wrongful transportation of cars obtained by any of the various types of theft.

28. Model Penal Code § 223.6, Comment at 241 (1980).

29. Surely "it is inappropriate to make the liability of the receiver turn on the method by which the original thief acquired the property." Id.

30. See § 4.11.

31. McCoy v. State, 241 Ind. 104, 170 N.E.2d 43 (1960) (mother received property taken by son aged eleven; conviction of receiving "stolen" property *held* affirmed, for "stolen" applies to property unlawfully taken by minors subject to the juvenile laws); People v. Pollak, 154 App. Div. 716, 139 N.Y.S. 831 (1913), affirmed 209 N.Y. 541, 102 N.E. 1109 (1913) (defendant received property taken by 15-year-old boys; conviction of receiving "stolen" property *held* affirmed; the juvenile delinquency laws, applying to

those under sixteen, do not make the boys wholly irresponsible for their acts; compare the situation of infants and insane persons).

32. Walters v. Lunt, [1951] 2 All E.R. 645 (K.B.Div.) (goods taken by child of seven; a child under eight is not capable of committing any offense; one who receives such goods cannot be convicted of receiving "stolen" goods).

See People v. Pollak, supra note 31, as to property taken by infants and lunatics or idiots.

Under the old law a wife could not be guilty of larceny of her husband's property. See § 8.2 at note 13. In Regina v. Kenny, 13 Cox Crim.Cas. 397 (Ct.Crim.App. 1877), a wife took her husband's property and delivered it to her adulterer; he was held not to be guilty of receiving "stolen" property. Today one spouse can steal from another.

33. Regina v. Dolan, 6 Cox Crim.Cas. 449 (Ct.Crim.App. 1855); Regina v. Schmidt, 10 Cox Crim.Cas. 172 (Ct.Crim. App.1866); State v. Sterling, 230 Kan, 790, 640 P.2d 1264 (1982); State v. Nguyen, 367 So.2d 342 (La.1979) (defendant, employed by owner to recover the property, could not be convicted when he accomplished his mission). See also People v. Jaffe, 185 N.Y. 497, 78 N.E. 169 (1906) (conviction of attempted receiving *held* reversed). The problem of whether the receiver is guilty of an attempt to receive stolen property is discussed § 6.3.

Compare the situation where the owner or policeman, on discovering the thief, does not interrupt him but watches to see what he does with it; such property is still stolen, and the thief's receiver can be convicted of receiving stolen property. Copertino v. United States, 256 F. 519 (3d Cir.1919).

34. Model Penal Code § 223.6.

said that the defendant in such a case is just as culpable as one who actually receives what he knows to be stolen property.[35]

There is a question as to whether the receiver to be guilty must receive the very property stolen, or whether it is enough that he receive the proceeds of the stolen property. In one case the thief stole money, deposited it in a bank, withdrew money from the bank account and paid his mistress, who knew of these transactions; the mistress was held guilty of receiving although she did not receive the very bills stolen.[36]

 WESTLAW REFERENCES

topic(234) & jaffe (booth /p 398 +4 863) /p stolen /2 property goods

(d) Knowing it is Stolen. Under the wording of the original English and some modern American receiving statutes, one must receive the stolen property "knowing," at the time he receives it, that it is stolen property. As a matter of language, the word "knowing" literally imports something pretty close to 100% certainty; "believing," some-

thing less than certainty; and "suspecting," something less certain than "believing." If the word "knowing" in receiving statutes required absolute certainty, there would be few convictions, for one seldom knows anything to a certainty, and the receiver in particular is careful not to learn the truth.[37] But it is everywhere held that positive knowledge is not required. In most jurisdictions a belief on the part of the receiver that the property is stolen property is all that is necessary.[38] On the other hand, a mere suspicion, not rising to the dignity of a belief, ought not to be enough.[39] For one to know property to be stolen (under the test of belief) he need not have any belief concerning the facts relating to the theft;[40] he need not, for instance, have a belief as to the identity of the thief or of his victim.[41] In most modern codes these problems have been resolved by a statutory provision to the effect that it is sufficient that the person believed the property probably was stolen.[42]

Most jurisdictions properly hold that an actual belief that the property is stolen is

---

35. But, there is the concern that conviction will be based upon speculation about the defendant's belief without the corroboration provided when the property is in fact stolen. See Model Penal Code § 223.6, Comment n. 21 (1980).

36. People ex rel. Briggs v. Hanley, 226 N.Y. 453, 123 N.E. 663 (1919). See Note, 19 Colum.L.Rev. 229 (1919). Liability is clearer if only the form of the stolen property is changed, as where a live lamb is changed into meat or gold dust fashioned into a golden goblet.

37. See United States v. Werner, 160 F.2d 438 (2d Cir. 1947), per L. Hand, J.: "The receivers of stolen goods almost never 'know' that they have been stolen, in the sense that they could testify to it in a court room. * * * Nor are we to suppose that the thieves will ordinarily admit their theft to the receivers: that would much impair their bargaining power."

38. United States v. Werner, 160 F.2d 438 (2d Cir.1947) ("believes to have probably been stolen"); People v. Rife, 382 Ill. 588, 48 N.E.2d 367 (1943) ("The knowledge need not be that actual or positive knowledge which one acquires from personal observation of the fact, but it is sufficient if the circumstances accompanying the transaction be such as to make the accused believe the goods had been stolen"); Commonwealth v. Boris, 317 Mass. 309, 58 N.E.2d 8 (1944) ("it was enough if the circumstances attending the receipt of the goods generated an actual belief in him that the property had been stolen"); Camp v. State, 66 Okl.Crim. 20, 89 P.2d 378 (1939) ("actual belief that the property was stolen"); State v. Alpert, 88 Vt. 191,

92 A. 32 (1914) ("believe" the property to have been stolen).

39. Compare Commonwealth v. Baker, 115 Pa.Super. 183, 175 A. 438 (1934) (instruction that defendant is guilty of receiving stolen property if the circumstances were such as would lead a reasonable man to suspect the property was stolen *held* reversible error, because (a) actual knowledge not ought-to-have knowledge, is required, and (b) "the question for the jury was whether this defendant *knew*—not suspected,—that the goods were stolen"); and State v. Goldman, 65 N.J.L. 394, 47 A. 641 (1900) (instruction that what one ought to have suspected he must be regarded as having suspected *held* reversible error; "the proof must be that the defendant had knowledge, not that he had suspicions"); with Henze v. State, 154 Md. 332, 140 A. 218 (1928) (defendant bookmaker, who had won large bet from a bank clerk at gambling, received from clerk in payment of the debt money which clerk had stolen; defendant had guilty knowledge because under circumstances he "believed, or reasonably suspected," the money was stolen; conviction of receiving *held* affirmed).

40. Commonwealth v. Boris, supra note 38.

41. People v. Marino, 271 N.Y. 317, 3 N.E.2d 439 (1936) (one may be guilty "although he may never know who is the thief or from whom the property was stolen").

42. Applying such a provision, the court in State v. Gabriel, 192 Conn. 405, 473 A.2d 300 (1984), held that defendant could be convicted if he knew or believed it was "more probable than not" that the property was stolen.

required for guilt.[43] This is but an application of the general principle that a mistake of fact, whether reasonable or unreasonable, which negatives the state of mind which a crime requires blots out guilt.[44] One cannot be held to have believed what he did not in fact believe just because he ought to have believed it.[45] Of course, the fact that a reasonable man would have believed property to be stolen is some evidence that the receiver did in fact believe it stolen;[46] but although one may properly infer a guilty belief from that fact, he is not bound to do so.

One who receives stolen property under a bona fide claim of right—as where he honestly believes it to be his own property or to be no one's property—cannot have an actual belief that the property is stolen, and so cannot be guilty of the crime.[47]

In most cases there is no direct testimony of the receiver's actual belief. Proof thereof must therefore be inferred from the circumstances surrounding his receipt of the stolen property. His exclusive possession of recently stolen property, if unexplained or falsely explained, justifies the inference that he received it with guilty knowledge, according to the majority view.[48] The circumstance that the buyer paid an inadequate price for the goods, that the seller was irresponsible, that the transaction between them was secret—these factors all point toward the buyer's guilty knowledge.[49] Even the buyer's post-receipt conduct indicating guilty knowledge may relate back so as to show guilty knowl-

---

43. State v. Melina, 297 Minn. 342, 210 N.W.2d 855 (1973) (it insufficient that defendant had reason to know or should have known); Commonwealth v. Baker, 115 Pa. Super. 183, 175 A. 438 (1934) (instruction requiring conviction if reasonable man would have suspected the goods to be stolen *held* reversible error for two reasons: (a) the question is whether the defendant himself knew, not whether a reasonable man would have known, and (b) the question is whether the defendant knows, not whether he suspects); State v. Alpert, 88 Vt. 191, 92 A. 32 (1914) (instruction that jury should find that defendant believed goods to be stolen if a reasonable man would have so believed *held* reversible error; the question is whether the defendant, not some other person believed the goods stolen).

See L. Hand, J., in United States v. Werner, 160 F.2d 438 (2d Cir.1947) ("[S]ome decisions even go so far as to hold that it is enough [to prove knowledge] if a reasonable man in the receiver's position would have supposed that the goods were stolen. That we think is wrong; and the better law is otherwise").

See Annot., 147 A.L.R. 1058 (1943).

44. See § 5.1.

45. Some statutes unwisely permit conviction based on mere negligence because they extend to instances in which there were "reasonable grounds to believe" the stolen goods were stolen. See, e.g., Farzley v. State, 231 Ala. 60, 163 So. 394 (1935) (under such a statute, these words provide a substitute for actual belief, so as to authorize conviction of one who did not believe, if a reasonable man would have believed).

46. State v. Gargare, 88 N.J.L. 389, 95 A. 625 (1915) (instruction that if the jury finds the circumstances of the defendant's purchase of stolen goods to be such as to lead a reasonable man to believe the goods were stolen, then the circumstances may be sufficient to justify a guilty verdict, *held* proper, so conviction affirmed).

See United States v. Werner, 160 F.2d 438 (2d Cir.1947). See Annot., 147 A.L.R. 1058 (1943).

47. State v. Caveness, 78 N.C. 484 (1878) (approving an instruction on bona fide claim of right).

48. Wertheimer v. State, 201 Ind. 572, 169 N.E. 40 (1929); State v. DiRienzo, 53 N.J. 360, 251 A.2d 99 (1969); Annot., 89 A.L.R.3d 1202 (1979).

In Barnes v. United States, 412 U.S. 837, 93 S.Ct. 2357, 37 L.Ed.2d 380 (1973), the Supreme Court held that this "traditional common-law inference deeply rooted in our law * * * comports with due process."

See Annot., 68 A.L.R. 187 (1930), pointing out that most of the cases which accept the majority view nevertheless hold that this one circumstance, unaided by other proof, is not sufficient for a conviction. No inference should be drawn, however, if the possession is "constructive" rather than real: United States v. Russo, 123 F.2d 420 (3d Cir. 1941) (stolen goods found in truck owned by defendant but at all times stored in a garage principally occupied by another). A minority view is that the recent-exclusive-unexplained-possession rule, because it is applicable to larceny, cannot also be applicable to receiving since one cannot be both the thief and the receiver. People v. Harris, 394 Ill. 325, 68 N.E.2d 728 (1946).

49. See United States v. Werner, 160 F.2d 438 (2d Cir. 1947) ("In prosecutions for receiving stolen property for obvious reasons one of the most telling indices of guilt is a low price paid by the receiver"); Huggins v. People, 135 Ill. 243, 25 N.E. 1002 (1890) (circumstances from which guilty knowledge may be inferred: "that the purchase was for much less than the real value; that the defendant denied that the property was in his possession, or concealed it; his failure to make reasonable explanation; the evil reputation of the person from whom purchased or received, and the like"); State v. Ham, 104 S.W.2d 232 (Mo.1937) ("The more frequent factors from which guilty knowledge has been inferred is inadequacy of price, irresponsibility of the vendor or depositor, and secrecy of the transaction").

edge at the time of the receipt.[50] The fact that he knowingly received other stolen property from the same (or even from another) thief at nearly the same time as the receipt of the stolen property in question is evidence from which it may be inferred that he had a guilty knowledge that the property in question was stolen.[51]

Some jurisdictions, while purporting to keep the requirement of knowledge, provide that the existence of certain circumstances under which one receives stolen property is prima facie evidence of (or creates a presumption of)[52] the fact that he knew the property was stolen.[53] An occasional statute which has gone all the way—abolishing the requirement of knowledge altogether, and imposing liability on one who simply receives stolen property, without regard to whether he knew or ought to have known, or failed to make reasonable inquiry—has been struck down as unconstitutional.[54] Statutes which have altered the

mental requirement of knowledge in some way have generally done so as to certain types of receivers (such as junk dealers) or as to certain types of sellers (e.g., children under 18), or as to certain types of property (e.g., used automobile parts), leaving the requirement of actual knowledge for the ordinary person who receives ordinary property from an ordinary seller.[55]

 WESTLAW REFERENCES

324k3 /p belie*** /s reason! probabl* likely

(e) With Intent to Deprive the Owner. It is not enough for guilt that one receives stolen property with knowledge that it is stolen. Otherwise, the policeman who catches a thief in possession of stolen property and who takes the booty from him in order to return it to its owner would be guilty. Some sort of a bad state of mind, in addition to the guilty knowledge, is required.[56] This is so although

---

50. Thus in United States v. Werner, 160 F.2d 438 (2d Cir.1947), the defendant, when the police started to investigate his receipt of stolen property, suggested to his seller that they should falsify a bill of sale; the court said that, as nothing had happened after receipt to open the defendant's eyes, this evidence of guilty knowledge might relate back to the time of receipt.

51. People v. Marino, 271 N.Y. 317, 3 N.E.2d 439 (1936) (defendant automobile dealer is charged with receiving a stolen automobile knowing it to be stolen; evidence admitted of the receipt and sale of other automobiles at or near the time of receipt of the automobile in question, though it was not shown that the others were received from the same thief; conviction of receiving *held* affirmed; the evidence of the other crimes was admissible to show guilty mind). See Annot. 105 A.L.R. 1288 (1936).

52. The terms prima facie evidence and presumption in these statutes may well mean not that it *may* be inferred, but rather that, in the absence of counterproof, it *must* be concluded, that the receiver knew. On the constitutionality of such provisions, see § 2.13(c).

53. Model Penal Code § 223.6 provides that the required knowledge is presumed in the case of a dealer who "(a) is found in possession or control of property stolen from two or more persons on separate occasions; or (b) has received stolen property in another transaction within the year preceding the transaction charged; or (c) being a dealer in property of the sort received, acquires it for a consideration which he knows is far below its reasonable value." Most modern codes "also contain presumptions designed to aid the proof of culpability in prosecutions for receiving stolen property." Model Penal Code § 223.6, Comment at 245 (1980).

A statute of this type providing that the fact that one receives stolen property from one under 18 creates a

rebuttable presumption that the receiver knows it to be stolen was held unconstitutional in People v. Stevenson, 58 Cal.2d 794, 26 Cal.Rptr. 297, 376 P.2d 297 (1962), for lack of a rational connection between the fact proved and the fact presumed; the statute covers receiving as well as buying, and baseballs and bicycles as well as things like fur coats which young people are not apt to own.

54. People v. Estreich, 272 App.Div. 698, 75 N.Y.S.2d 267 (1947), affirmed mem. 297 N.Y. 910, 79 N.E.2d 742 (1948) (statute punished junk dealers who receive stolen machinery equipment; with other receivers and other property knowledge or lack of diligence is required; statute *held* unconstitutional under the U.S. Constitution's fourteenth amendment due process clause); Kilbourne v. State, 84 Ohio St. 247, 95 N.E. 824 (1911) (statute punishing anyone who receives railroad part which has been unlawfully removed from railroad car and which is necessary to its operation and whose removal might endanger life *held* unconstitutional).

55. A strong plea for criminal statutes which distinguish between the professional receiver and the lay receiver is found in J. Hall, Theft, Law & Society ch. 5 (2d ed. 1952). Nevertheless, few jurisdictions make the distinction which Professor Hall recommends.

56. Arcia v. State, 26 Tex.App. 193, 9 S.W. 685 (1888) (conviction of receiving *held* reversed for trial court's error in refusing to instruct as to the intent which is required, in addition to the guilty knowledge). But see United States v. Mavrick, 601 F.2d 921 (7th Cir.1979) (receiving stolen property statute, 18 U.S.C.A. § 659, construed not to have intent-to-deprive element, but because of "the policy of not punishing innocent conduct" the defendant may raise as an affirmative defense "that his possession of the stolen goods was innocent even though he knew the goods to be stolen").

this requirement is not generally spelled out in the statute defining the offense of receiving stolen property.[57]

The necessary intent, as in the related crime of larceny, is an intent to deprive the owner of his property. The receiver's purpose is generally, of course, to deprive the owner by benefiting himself. But he is equally guilty though his purpose is to deprive the owner, not by benefiting himself but rather by aiding the thief, as by hiding the stolen property for him.[58]

No doubt if he received it only to destroy it (perhaps because he wanted to do harm to the owner though he did not seek any benefit for himself), he would have the necessary intent to deprive the owner.[59] Although one who receives what he knows to be stolen property with the intent to restore it unconditionally to its owner does not have the requisite intent for the crime, his intention to restore it for a reward does (as in larceny) constitute an intent to deprive the owner.[60]

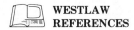

WESTLAW REFERENCES

324k3 /p depriv!

digest(stolen /2 property goods /s receiv*** buy*** purchas*** /s depriv!

(f) Concurrence of Conduct, Knowledge and Intent. We have already noted that the

stolen character of the property and the receiver's receipt of the property must coincide in point of time, so that if the property, once stolen, has been recovered by the owner before it is received by the receiver, the latter can not be guilty.[61] It only remains to note that the two mental elements of the crime (knowledge of the property's stolen character, and intent to deprive the owner) must likewise coincide with the receiver's receipt thereof.[62] One who innocently receives stolen property is not guilty if, when he later learns of the stolen nature thereof, he conceals it from the owner or refuses to deliver it up, unless, as is the case in some states,[63] the crime is defined in terms of the knowing concealment or withholding of stolen property in addition to the knowing receipt thereof.

WESTLAW REFERENCES

324k3 /p time

(g) Grand vs. Petit Receiving. Receiving-stolen-property statutes, like statutes dealing with other theft crimes, commonly draw a dividing line between the felony and the misdemeanor of receiving. Thus it may be provided that to receive property of a value of fifty dollars or less is a misdemeanor, more than fifty dollars is a felony.[64]

---

57. Hensel v. State, 604 P.2d 222 (Alaska 1979) (intent-to-deprive-owner element read into statute).

Where an element of the crime does not appear in the statute defining the crime, it may be held that the prosecution need not allege and prove it; rather, it is up to the defendant to raise the absence of the element as a matter of defense under his not-guilty plea. Cf. State v. Smith, 88 Iowa 1, 55 N.W. 16 (1893) (for the crime of receiving an intent, in addition to knowledge, "is not, by our statute, a necessary fact to be averred or proven"; the court may be saying, however, that, in spite of what other states hold, in this state intent is not an element).

58. Daniel v. State, 212 Miss. 223, 54 So.2d 272 (1951); Rex v. Richardson, 172 Eng.Rep. 1265 (1834).

See Arcia v. State, 26 Tex.App. 193, 9 S.W. 685 (1888) (the receiving "must be accompanied by a criminal intent, an intent to aid the thief, or to obtain a reward for restoring the property to the owner, or an intent to in some way derive profit from the act").

59. In the analogous crime of larceny, one need not act *lucri causa* (on account of gain). See § 8.5.

60. People v. Wiley, 3 Hill 194 (N.Y.Sup.Ct.1842); People v. O'Reilly, 153 App.Div. 854, 138 N.Y.S. 776 (1912)—

both cases involving a go-between who, acting on behalf of the thief, received possession of the stolen property from the thief in order to restore it to the owner for a fraction of its value.

See also State v. Simonson, 298 Minn. 235, 214 N.W.2d 679 (1974).

61. See § 8.10(c).

62. State v. Caveness, 78 N.C. 484 (1878) ("To be guilty, he must have known at the moment of receiving it that it had been stolen, and he must at that time have also received it with a felonious intent").

See Camp v. State, 66 Okl.Crim. 20, 89 P.2d 378 (1939) ("it is necessary to show that the party receiving the property had knowledge at the time the property was received that it had been stolen").

63. See § 8.10(b).

64. Just as taking at different times and places cannot be aggregated into one grand larceny, see § 8.4(b), a receiving at different times cannot be aggregated into grand receiving. But see State v. Post, 286 N.W.2d 195 (Iowa 1979) (contrary result where crime defined to cover one who "exercises control over stolen property").

As noted above, a few states single out some kinds of receivers (e.g., junk dealers) for special receiving-stolen-property treatment, either by increasing the punishment of such persons, generally the professional receivers, who receive stolen property, or by authorizing their conviction on proof that they should have known rather than that they actually knew, the property to be stolen.[65]

 WESTLAW REFERENCES

topic(234) /p aggregat***

(h) The Thief as Receiver. It is clear that the person who actually steals the property (i.e., what the common law referred to as a principal in the first degree) cannot be convicted of receiving (or, if the statute provides, of concealing or withholding) that stolen property.[66] Conversely, it is generally (but not universally) held that the person who instigated or encouraged the thief to commit the theft (i.e., the accessory before the fact, at common law, though modern statutes in

many jurisdictions make him guilty as a principal) can be convicted of receiving, in accordance with a prearranged plan, the property which the thief steals pursuant to the other's inducement or encouragement.[67] In the middle stands the aider and abettor, the person who was present and aiding at the time of the theft but did not himself do the caption and asportation necessary for larceny (i.e., what the common law called a principal in the second degree). There is a split of authority as to whether he can be guilty of receiving stolen property.[68]

If under the above rules the instigator or aider of the actual thief can be convicted of receiving, there remains the question of whether he can be convicted both of the theft and of the receiving, with the possibility of consecutive sentences for each. Some courts have indicated that such a double conviction is proper;[69] but a United States Supreme Court decision construed a federal law as permitting conviction of one or the other but not of both.[70]

---

65. As to the various regulations imposed upon junk dealers, with an eye to preventing them from receiving stolen property, see Annots., 30 A.L.R. 1427, 1436–40 (1924), 45 A.L.R.2d 1391, 1421–25 (1956).

66. See United States v. Gardis, 424 U.S. 544, 96 S.Ct. 1023, 47 L.Ed.2d 222 (1976) (bank robber may not be convicted of receiving proceeds of the robbery); Leon v. State, 21 Ariz. 418, 189 P. 433 (1920) ("The rule seems to be well settled that, where a larceny has been committed, the principal thief—that is, the one who is guilty of the actual caption and asportation of the property—cannot be adjudged guilty of criminally receiving the thing stolen, for the reason that he cannot receive from himself"); People v. Taylor, 4 Cal.App.2d 214, 40 P.2d 870 (1935) ("The actual thief cannot receive from himself the fruits of his larceny"); State v. Bleau, 139 Vt. 305, 428 A.2d 1097 (1981) (same); State v. Hall, ___ W.Va. ___, 298 S.E.2d 246 (1982) (same); Annots., 43 A.L.R.Fed. 847 (1979), 136 A.L.R. 1087, 1088–92 (1942).

67. Leon v. State, 21 Ariz. 418, 189 P. 433 (1920) (defendant induced girl to search for her grandmother's money hidden in the house and when found to take it to defendant; defendant's conviction of receiving *held* affirmed, as defendant had no part in the caption and asportation); People v. Spinuzza, 99 Colo. 303, 62 P.2d 471 (1936) (defendant advised and encouraged thief to commit burglary and steal; he later received fruits of the theft; his conviction of receiving *held* affirmed).

Contra: Byrd v. State, 117 Tex.Crim.R. 489, 38 S.W.2d 332 (1931), noted at 27 Ill.L.Rev. 207 (1932) (defendant, according to prior arrangement with thief, received stolen property from thief and sold it, keeping a commission for himself; conviction of receiving *held* reversed).

See Annot., 136 A.L.R. 1087, 1095–1101 (1942).

68. Compare Metcalf v. State, 98 Fla. 457, 124 So. 427 (1929) (defendant waited outside building to receive goods taken from the building by the principal thief; defendant's conviction of receiving *held* affirmed); and Milanovich v. United States, 365 U.S. 551, 81 S.Ct. 728, 5 L.Ed. 2d 773 (1961) (defendant wife transported thieves to building; they entered and stole money and later handed money to defendant; conviction of both larceny and receiving *held* improper, but the Court states that the evidence supported defendant's conviction of either larceny or receiving; with Snider v. State, 119 Tex.Crim.R. 584, 44 S.W.2d 998 (1931), 119 Tex.Crim.R. 635, 44 S.W.2d 997 (1931) (companion cases) (defendant drove thief to the place of the theft, was present at the theft, drove the thief away and received part of the stolen property as his share of the loot; conviction of receiving *held* reversed since evidence proved him a thief). See Annot., 136 A.L.R. 1087, 1101–03 (1942).

69. See People v. Feinberg, 237 Ill. 348, 86 N.E. 584 (1908) (the two crimes are distinct, so that one does not merge in the other, "nor [is] the defendant's conviction of one * * * incompatible with conviction of the other").

70. Milanovich v. United States, 365 U.S. 551, 81 S.Ct. 728, 5 L.Ed.2d 773 (1961) (so decided as a matter "of statutory construction, not of common law distinctions"; Congress by creating the crime of receiving stolen property meant to reach a new group of wrongdoers and did not mean to multiply the offense of the thief himself; defendant-wife's conviction of both larceny and receiving *held* reversed).

**WESTLAW
REFERENCES**

324k6 /p headnote(steal*** stole* /s receiv***)

gaddis /p steal*** stole* /s receiv***

(i) Defenses. The general principles of defense which are applicable to other crimes apply to the crime of receiving. As noted above, one who honestly though mistakenly (because of a mistake of fact) believes the property he receives is not stolen cannot be found guilty of knowing it to be stolen.[71] Likewise, intoxication may be so severe as to negative the existence of the receiver's knowledge, though had he been sober he would have known the property to be stolen. Insanity and infancy are good defenses to this as to all other crimes. Doubtless under appropriate circumstances one can be coerced into doing the act of receiving.[72] The defense of entrapment does not apply in the situation wherein the police, having caught the thief with his booty, gives it back to him with instructions to take the property to the receiver, for, as noted above,[73] the receiver cannot be guilty in view of the fact that the property has in this situation lost its character as stolen property.

**WESTLAW
REFERENCES**

324k5

See State v. Webber, 112 Mont. 284, 116 P.2d 679 (1941) (one who, without participating in the actual theft, has encouraged the thief to commit the larceny, and who afterwards receives the stolen property, is guilty of larceny and may, at the prosecution's option, be prosecuted either for the larceny or for the receiving; defendant's conviction of receiving *held* affirmed).

Where the defendant has committed either larceny or receiving but not both, the prosecution may not know in advance which crime the evidence may prove; thus where the evidence is that the defendant has been found in exclusive possession of recently stolen property, the prosecution may not be able to tell which crime the jury will find. It is then proper to charge on two counts both larceny and receiving, with appropriate instructions given to the jury at the end of the evidence distinguishing the two crimes, and letting the jury find which one (but not both) of the two crimes the defendant has committed. People v. Taylor, 4 Cal.App.2d 214, 40 P.2d 870 (1935).

71. See § 8.10d).

72. Cf. State v. Renslow, 211 Iowa 642, 230 N.W. 316 (1930) (wife, prosecuted for receiving stolen property from her husband, requested an instruction that she presumably acted under her husband's coercion; instruction re-

(j) Federal Crimes Involving Receiving Stolen Property. Aside from the federal crime of receiving stolen property in places within the maritime (as on American ships upon or planes flying over the high seas) or territorial (e.g., in the District of Columbia, at army posts, navy yards, post offices) jurisdiction of the United States,[74] there are several federal statutes, backing up the state statutes on receiving, making it a federal crime to receive, with knowledge, stolen motor vehicles, securities, money or other property, provided that the property in question moves as, or is a part of, or constitutes interstate commerce.[75]

**WESTLAW
REFERENCES**

digest(18 +4 2315 /p receiv*** /s steal*** stole*
    /s kn*w!)

corey /p int**state /2 commerce /p stole*
    steal***

(k) Thief as Accomplice. Many jurisdictions have a case-law or statutory rule which either bars a conviction of crime upon the uncorroborated testimony of an accomplice or, though it does not absolutely bar the conviction, requires that the jury be instructed to look with caution upon an accomplice's testimony.[76] The question arises: is the thief an "accomplice" of the receiver within this rule?

fused; her conviction *held* affirmed, for the common law presumption of coercion of wife by husband when she commits crime in his presence has been abrogated by statutes removing disabilities of married women).

73. See § 8.10(c).

74. 18 U.S.C.A. § 662.

75. 18 U.S.C.A. §§ 2311–17. See Hall, Federal Anti-Theft Legislation, 1 Law & Contemp.Prob. 424 (1934). As noted in § 8.10(c), the word "stolen" in these statutes encompasses larceny, embezzlement and false pretenses: United States v. Turley, 352 U.S. 407, 77 S.Ct. 397, 1 L.Ed. 2d 430 (1957). Although, to be guilty, the receiver must know the property to be stolen (in the sense of actual belief), he need not also know that the goods which he received were or had been in interstate commerce: Corey v. United States, 305 F.2d 232 (9th Cir.1962). As to what is meant by "moving as, or is a part of, or constitutes interstate commerce," see Annot., 56 A.L.R.2d 1309, 1327–28 (1957).

76. E.g., State v. Sheldon, 91 Ariz. 73, 369 P.2d 917 (1962) (per statute, corroboration of accomplice's testimony required); People v. Niemoth, 409 Ill. 111, 98 N.E.2d

There is a split of authority on the point, the majority view being that the thief is not an accomplice,[77] unless perhaps the receiver and the thief conspired before the theft to have the thief steal and deliver the stolen property to the receiver.[78]

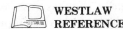

WESTLAW REFERENCES

thief /s accomplice /s receiver

(*l*) Jurisdiction and Venue. Property stolen in a foreign country or another state may be received in the state to which the stolen property is brought and delivered to the receiver. The latter state has jurisdiction over the crime of receiving.[79] When the theft is in one county and the receiving in another, venue is in latter county.[80]

WESTLAW REFERENCES

topic(324) /p jurisdiction venue

733 (1951) ("testimony of an accomplice * * * is to be received with suspicion and acted upon with caution").

77. Compare Leon v. State, 21 Ariz. 418, 189 P. 433 (1920) (thief is not an accomplice); People v. Kupperschmidt, 237 N.Y. 463, 143 N.E. 256 (1924) (thief is an accomplice), criticized as "an unfortunate decision" in J. Hall, Theft, Law and Society 182 (2d ed. 1952). For a list of cases both ways, see Annot., 53 A.L.R.2d 817, 826–38 (1957). On whether the *receiver* is an accomplice of the thief for corroboration purposes, see 74 A.L.R.3d 560 (1976).

78. Stephenson v. United States, 211 F.2d 702 (9th Cir. 1954) (though the thief is not normally an accomplice of the receiver, he is an accomplice in the case of prior conspiracy; trial court's refusal to give cautionary instruction *held* reversible error). See Annot., 53 A.L.R.2d 817, 838–46 (1957).

Consider also the exception recognized in People v. Kyllonen, 402 Mich. 135, 262 N.W.2d 2 (1978) (statute covering those who "aid in the concealment" does not reach thief who merely supplies the goods, but does reach thief who helps with concealment after the transfer was completed).

79. State v. Rutledge, 232 S.C. 223, 101 S.E.2d 289 (1957) (defendant within state received goods some of which were stolen in another state; conviction of receiving *held* affirmed).

See Annot., 67 A.L.R.2d 752 (1959), pointing out the reasons advanced for this result: (1) the larceny itself, though originally committed in another state or country, becomes a fresh larceny in any place where the stolen goods are brought; (2) receiving being an independent crime, it matters not where the larceny occurred. The

(m) Consolidation of Receiving With Other Theft Crimes. It has been suggested that the crime of receiving stolen property be consolidated with larceny, embezzlement and false pretenses into a single crime called "theft."[81] Many states have taken this step. Under such a consolidation, one against whom the evidence was that he was found in possession of recently stolen property, who was charged with larceny of the property, could not defend upon the ground that his offense was receiving; and, if charged with receiving, could not defend on the ground that he was the thief.[82]

WESTLAW REFERENCES

receiv*** /2 stolen /s consolidat*** /s theft /s larceny embezzl! "false pretense"

§ 8.11 Robbery

Robbery, a common-law felony,[1] and today everywhere a statutory felony regardless of

receiving statutes of some states expressly apply to property stolen in another state.

80. This is so even under a statute which provides that where a crime is committed partly in one county, partly in another, venue is in either county. See Annot., 30 A.L.R.2d 1265, 1293–95 (1953).

81. See Model Penal Code § 223.6, making receiving stolen property a form of theft. See § 8.8(d). See also Scurlock, The Element of Trespass in Larceny, 22 Temp. L.Q. 253, 286 (1949).

But see Comment, 48 Nw.U.L.Rev. 198, 238 (1953) (there should be no consolidation, because professional receivers should be punished more severely than lay receivers).

82. Where the two crimes are separate, and the evidence is equivocal, the prosecutor may charge both offenses, leaving it to the jury to determine which of the two the evidence proves. See § 8.10(h), especially People v. Taylor, supra note 76.

§ 8.11

1. The crime of robbery was created before that of larceny. See Model Penal Code § 223.1, Comment at 128 (1980), dealing with the "long history of expansion of the role of the criminal law in protecting property. That history begins with a concern for crimes of violence—in the present context, the taking of property by force from the possession of another, i.e., robbery. The criminal law then expanded, via the ancient quasi-criminal writ of trespass, to cover all taking of another's property from his possession without his consent, even though no force was used. This misconduct was punished as larceny." The scope of robbery grew gradually: "formerly the offense seems to have been confined to cases of actual violence to the person; but in later times it has been extended to

the amount taken, may be thought of as aggravated larceny [2]—misappropriation of property under circumstances involving a danger to the person as well [3] as a danger to property—and thus deserving of a greater punishment than that provided for larceny.[4] Robbery consists of all six elements of larceny [5]— a (1) trespassory (2) taking and (3) carrying away of the (4) personal property (5) of another (6) with intent to steal it—plus two additional requirements: (7) that the property be taken from the person or presence of the other and (8) that the taking be accomplished by means of force or putting in fear.[6] These eight elements, the last two in particular, are discussed immediately below:

(a) Trespassory Taking and Carrying Away the Property of Another.

(1) Trespassory. As with larceny, robbery requires that there be a trespass in the taking. Although the victim's consent to the taking of his property will negative the trespass—as where, to catch a suspected robbery, the victim actually induces the defendant to rob him—the fact that the victim, acting as a decoy, voluntarily enters the robber's den, and is robbed there, does not constitute such consent as vitiates the trespass.[7]

The trespass requirement for robbery is in actuality more stringent than that needed for larceny, for the seventh element of robbery is that the property be taken, not merely from the victim's possession (actual or "construc-

---

constructive violence by putting in fear, and not only to cases where property has been taken or delivered under a threat of bodily violence to the party robbed, or some other person, but also where the fear has resulted from apprehension of violence to the habitation and property, or has been occasioned by threats of preferring a charge of an infamous crime [i.e., sodomy or attempted sodomy]." Commissioners on Criminal Law, Fourth Report lxvii (1839), quoted in J. Michael & H. Wechsler, Criminal Law and its Administration 383–84 (1940).

2. Larceny is a lesser included crime within the crime of robbery, so that one charged with robbery can be convicted of larceny: Government of Virgin Islands v. Jarvis, 653 F.2d 762 (3d Cir.1981); People v. Nelson, 56 Cal. 77 (1880); State v. Kobylasz, 242 Iowa 1161, 47 N.W. 2d 167 (1951); State v. Davis, 242 N.C. 476, 87 S.E.2d 906 (1955); State v. Neider, ___ W.Va. ___, 295 S.E.2d 902 (1982).

3. The modern trend is to consider robbery as an offense against the person rather than against property, which sometimes is more than a theoretical matter. See Mitchell v. State, 281 Ark. 112, 661 S.W.2d 390 (1983) (consequently when defendant took from restaurant employee money of the business and also personal effects, this only one robbery).

4. Robbery may be considered a greater crime than the sum of the two lesser crimes of larceny and assault (or battery). As stated in Model Penal Code § 222.1, Comment at 98 (1980): "The violent petty thief operating in the streets and alleys of our big cities—the 'mugger'—is one of the main sources of insecurity and concern of the population at large. There is a special element of terror in this kind of depredation. The ordinary citizen does not feel particularly threatened by surreptitious larceny, embezzlement or fraud. But there is understandable abhorrence of the robber who accosts on the streets and who menaces his victims with actual or threatened violence against which there is a general sense of helplessness. In proportion as the ordinary person fears and detests such behavior, the offender exhibits himself as seriously deviated from community norms, thus justifying more serious

sanctions. In addition, the robber may be distinguished from the stealthy thief by the hardihood that enables him to carry out his purpose in the presence of his victim and over his opposition—obstacles that might deter ordinary sneak thieves and that justify the feeling of special danger evoked by robbery."

5. See § 8.2.

6. American statutes do not generally spell out the eight elements; they define the crime of robbery in different ways, often in the somewhat undetailed language used by Blackstone, Hawkins, Hale and East in defining common-law robbery, e.g., "the felonious and violent taking of goods or money from the person of another by force or intimidation." Some statutes specify a taking from the person of another "or in his presence." Some states, especially those which have recently enacted comprehensive criminal codes, add more detail—e.g., concerning the type of fear that will suffice. At the other extreme, a number of statutes punish robbery without defining it, leaving the definition to the common law. Almost all states distinguish between simple robbery and aggravated robbery (e.g., armed robbery), the latter carrying a heavier penalty upon conviction.

7. Tones v. State, 48 Tex.Crim. 363, 88 S.W. 217 (1905).

Some definitions of robbery, found in case law or legislation, contain a requirement that the taking be "against the will" of the victim; but where the defendant's conduct causes the victim to lose his will, as where the defendant drugs the victim into unconsciousness and then takes his property from his person or presence, he nevertheless commits robbery. State v. Snyder, 41 Nev. 453, 172 P. 364 (1918).

Compare the situation where the defendant comes upon one already unconscious, e.g., voluntarily drunk or drugged, and helps himself to the property on his person or in his presence; this is not robbery. People v. O'Connor, 310 Ill. 403, 141 N.E. 748 (1923), noted at 6 Ill. L.Q. 236 (1924). See further discussion in § 8.11(d). Of course, consent obtained at the point of a gun, as in the ordinary case of robbery, does not negative the trespass.

tive") as larceny requires, but from his person or presence as well.[8]

(2) Taking and Carrying Away. Just as larceny requires that the thief both "take" (secure dominion over) and "carry away" (move slightly) the property in question, so too robbery under the traditional view requires both a taking [9] and an asportation (in the sense of at least a slight movement) [10] of the property. Modern statutes, however, are frequently less demanding, often reflecting the Model Penal Code position [11] that asportation is not required for the underlying theft and, indeed, that it suffices that the theft was merely attempted. Some of these statutes do require at least a taking, while others extend also to the attempted theft situation.[12] This latter broadening of the law of robbery is sound, for the "same dangers are posed by the actor who is interrupted or who is foiled by an empty pocket as by the actor who succeeds in effecting the theft." [13]

8. See § 8.11(c).

9. See People v. Clark, 70 Cal.App.2d 132, 160 P.2d 553 (1945) (robbery is complete when the defendant "gains possession" of the property "and reduces it to his manual possession"); Mason v. Commonwealth, 200 Va. 253, 105 S.E.2d 149 (1958) (defendant took victim's television set in his arms and was handing it to his confederate when owner struck him with a board; defendant then threw a radio at owner and fired his gun at him; conviction of robbery *held* reversed, for the "taking" and "asportation" elements of robbery did not coincide with the "violence or intimidation" element).

10. People v. Clark, 70 Cal.App.2d 132, 160 P.2d 553 (1945) (defendant, convicted of robbery, appealed on the ground that the evidence did not prove asportation; conviction *held* affirmed; "whether appellant conveyed the money one yard or one mile from the presence of his victim is immaterial in so far as the element of asportation is concerned. * * * His escape with the loot is not necessary to complete the crime").

11. Model Penal Code § 222.1.

12. Elsewhere, the prosecution on such facts must be for attempted robbery, which is likely to carry a significantly lower penalty.

13. Model Penal Code § 222.1, Comment at 99–100 (1980).

14. The property need not be valuable. State v. Gomez, 234 Kan. 447, 673 P.2d 1160 (1983) (it robbery to take $180 bill known as "funny money").

Some modern robbery statutes, however, are not limited to personalty. See, e.g., People v. Dillon, 34 Cal.3d 441, 194 Cal.Rptr. 390, 668 P.2d 697 (1983) (statute covers robbery of standing crop of marijuana).

(3) Property of Another. Property (including money) which can be taken by larceny can be taken by robbery;[14] and, conversely, items which cannot be stolen (e.g., labor or services, in most jurisdictions) cannot be the subject of robbery. Just as with larceny the thief need not steal from the owner, so too, for robbery, the robber may rob one who has possession or custody of property, though he is not the owner of it.[15]

 **WESTLAW REFERENCES**

342k10
topic(342) /p tak*** /s asportation "carry*** away"

(b) Intent to Steal. The intent to steal (the *animus furandi,* to use the Latin term) required for larceny is the same intent to steal (or, as it is sometimes called, intent to rob) needed for robbery.[16] Thus the same factors which negative the intent to steal in larceny will negative the intent to rob in robbery—as where the taking is under an

15. Victim has possession: People v. Madas, 201 N.Y. 349, 94 N.E. 857 (1911) (defendant robbed victim, cashier and office manager of money belonging to private banker; conviction of murder in commission of robbery *held* affirmed; to prove robbery it is unnecessary to show that the money belonged to the victim). Victim has custody: O'Donnell v. People, 224 Ill. 218, 79 N.E. 639, 8 Ann.Cas. 123 (1906) (defendant grabbed watchman in charge of a railroad station, intending to blow open the railroad's safe in the station; conviction of assault with intent to rob *held* affirmed).

16. People v. Ford, 60 Cal.2d 772, 36 Cal.Rptr. 620, 388 P.2d 892 (1964) ("one of the essential elements of robbery is a specific intent to steal"; conviction of robbery *held* reversed for failure of court to instruct the jury to that effect, although defendant made no request to instruct); Moyers v. State, 186 Ga. 446, 197 S.E. 846 (1938) (although the statute's definition of robbery does not expressly say so, it "implies an intent to steal"); State v. Hollway, 41 Iowa 200, 20 Am.R. 586 (1875) ("In robbery, as in larceny, it is essential that the taking of the goods be *animo furandi*"); People v. Koerber, 244 N.Y. 147, 155 N.E. 79 (1926) ("The gist of robbery is larceny by force from the person * * * and * * * the gist of larceny is the taking and carrying away of the personal property of another with the specific intent to steal such property"); Barton v. State, 88 Tex.Crim. 368, 227 S.W. 317 (1921) ("The *animo furandi* is an element of robbery as it is of theft"). The term "intent to rob" may be used with robbery, without meaning anything different from the more usual term "intent to steal": People v. Koerber, supra.

Traxler v. State, 96 Okl.Crim. 231, 251 P.2d 815 (1952), holds that an intent to return the property taken—here an automobile taken at gunpoint for the purpose of escap-

honest, though mistaken, claim of ownership of, or claim of a lawful right to possess, the property; [17] or where he takes from the victim what he honestly, although mistakenly, believes the latter owes him (even though he may not further believe that violence or in-

timidation is a proper method of collecting debts); [18] or where he takes the victim's property intending (and having a substantial ability) to return the very property within a reasonable time; [19] or where he is too intoxicated to entertain the specific intent to rob; [20] or

ing police capture—is no defense to robbery under a statute defining robbery as the "wrongful" taking, rather than "felonious" taking, and thus, the court holds, eliminating any requirement of an intent to steal. The court is surely wrong about the intent-to-steal requirement, although it is right in the result it reaches, for the obstacles to the car's safe return when taken for such a purpose were so great that the intent to return, without an ability to do so, would not negative the intent to steal.

17. Rugless v. State, 97 Ark. 152, 133 S.W. 600 (1911) (defendant, putting another in fear, took his horse from him claiming ownership; charged with robbery he was convicted of larceny; conviction of larceny *held* reversed); State v. Hicks, 102 Wn.2d 182, 683 P.2d 186 (1984) (failure to instruct on good faith claim of title defense was prejudicial error).

See Moyers v. State, 186 Ga. 446, 197 S.E. 846 (1938) (dictum that the taking of property under a "fair claim of right," believing it to be legally one's own, or that he has a legal right to its possession, is not larceny or robbery; but conviction of robbery for collecting a debt by force or fear *held* affirmed).

As with larceny, the mistaken claim may be the result of a mistake of fact—as where the defendant mistakenly thought the owner had used words of gift when handing him the property to use; or a mistake of law—as where he heard the words right but mistook their legal consequences, mistakenly believing that title passed.

There is a question as to whether one who, having lost money at illegal gambling, retakes his lost money from the winner by stealth, or by force or fear, is guilty of larceny or robbery. If, by applicable law, the money still belongs to him, he is not guilty; but even if he wrongly though honestly believes it is still his money, he lacks the intent to steal necessary for larceny or robbery. People v. Rosen, 11 Cal.2d 147, 78 P.2d 727 (1938), noted at 27 Calif. L.Rev. 211 (1939).

But there has been some movement away from this arguably outdated rule. See Cates v. State, 21 Md.App. 363, 320 A.2d 75 (1974): "In a bucolic western scene or in the woody atmosphere of the frontier in the nineteenth century, the six-shooter may have been an acceptable device for do-it-yourself debt collection. If the law permitted a might-makes-right doctrine in that milieu, it is of dubious adaptability to urban society in this final third of the twentieth century."

See also Comment, 41 J.Crim.L. & C. 467 (1950); Annot., 77 A.L.R.3d 1363 (1977).

18. People v. Gallegos, 130 Colo. 232, 274 P.2d 608 (1954) (defendant took money at gunpoint from his employer for wages he honestly believed owing to him; acquittal of defendant on his motion *held* affirmed, on state's appeal, for "the intent to steal is absent"); State v. Hollyway, 41 Iowa 200 (1875) (same); Barton v. State, 88

Tex.Crim. 368, 227 S.W. 317 (1921) (conviction of assault with intent to rob *held* reversed).

Contra: Moyers v. State, 186 Ga. 446, 197 S.E. 846 (1938) (conviction of robbery *held* affirmed, for a creditor has no right to collect a debt by violence or intimidation).

See Annot., 88 A.L.R.3d 1309 (1978).

As with larceny, one who (by force or fear) takes another's property in satisfaction of an unliquidated claim may be guilty of robbery: Thomas v. State, 165 Miss. 897, 148 So. 225 (1933), noted at 6 Miss.L.J. 431 (1934) (after victim killed defendant's dog, defendant, with a shotgun, took victim's cattle as damages; conviction of robbery *held* affirmed); Tipton v. State, 23 Okla.Crim. 86, 212 P. 612 (1923) (after victim had assaulted defendant's wife, defendant took victim's money at gunpoint; conviction of robbery *held* affirmed; one cannot thus collect unliquidated damages); Henderson v. State, 149 Tex.Crim. 167, 192 S.W.2d 446 (1946) (after victim damaged defendant's car, defendant forcibly took $5 as damages; conviction of robbery *held* affirmed, for creditor cannot collect unliquidated damages by taking with force or fear).

So too, as with larceny, one who (by force or fear) takes more than the amount of the debt may be guilty of robbery: Bass v. State, 151 Tex.Crim. 172, 206 S.W.2d 599 (1947) (defendant, with a claim for $3.85, collected $20 at knife-point; conviction of robbery *held* affirmed).

As with larceny, one who by force or fear collects an unliquidated claim or collects an amount in excess of his claim, but does it as security for, rather than in payment of, the debt, ought not to be guilty of robbery.

19. As with larceny, robbery requires an intent to deprive the owner permanently (or for an unreasonable length of time) of his property. And, as with larceny, intent and ability to pay for the property taken—i.e., to restore equivalent property rather than the very property taken—may be a defense. Of course, an actual return of the property, of itself, is no defense. See Annot., 135 Am. St.R. 474, 497 (1911).

But see United States v. Lewis, 628 F.2d 1276 (10th Cir. 1980) (18 U.S.C.A. 2113, proscribing entry of federally insured bank with intent to commit bank robbery, construed to mean "that an individual who enters a bank with the intention of taking money by intimidating employees of the bank" is guilty even if he intends "that the bank was to be deprived of the funds only temporarily").

20. People v. Koerber, 244 N.Y. 147, 155 N.E. 79 (1926) (prosecution for felony-murder for a homicide in commission of robbery; conviction *held* reversed for trial court's failure, in view of the evidence to instruct that intoxication might negative defendant's intent to rob); State v. Byers, 136 Wash. 620, 241 P. 9 (1925) (conviction of robbery *held* reversed for erroneous instruction that voluntary intoxication is no defense to robbery).

where he is perpetrating a practical joke.[21] Of course, one who collects debts or borrows property or perpetrates jokes by use of violence or intimidation, though he is not guilty of robbery, need not go free: for he is guilty of at least simple battery if he uses force, and of simple assault if he uses intimidation,[22] and of aggravated assault or battery (e.g., assault with a deadly weapon) under appropriate circumstances.[23] Coercion is a defense to robbery as it is to most other crimes.[24]

An intent to steal need not include an intention to convert the property to one's own use; it is sufficient that there is an intention to permanently deprive the owner of the property.[25]

 **WESTLAW REFERENCES**

342k3 /p "animus furandi" (intent /2 steal rob)
topic(342) /p intoxicat*** /s intent

(c) From the Person or Presence of the Victim. Robbery, like larceny, requires that the thief commit a trespass in his taking of the property of another—i.e., the taking must be from the victim's possession, actual or constructive.[26] But under the traditional view robbery requires something more than simply a trespassory taking: the taking must be from the person or presence of the victim [27] as well as from his possession.

Property is on the victim's person if it is in his hand, the pocket of the clothing he wears, or is otherwise attached to his body or his clothing (e.g., an earring or watch chain).[28] One case raises the question of whether a deceased person can be a "person" for purposes of robbery. A, after an argument with B, during which B hit A on the head with a bicycle pump, stabbed B, killing her (thus committing the crime of manslaughter), and then, erroneously believing B to be unconscious but alive, took money from B's dress. The court affirmed A's conviction of robbery, holding that a homicide victim is still a "person" within the meaning of the robbery statute, at least when the interval of time between the infliction of the fatal blow and the taking of the property is short.[29]

21. Commonwealth v. White, 133 Pa. 182, 19 A. 350 (1890) (defendant took a pinch of tobacco from victim by force as a practical joke; conviction of robbery *held* reversed; dictum that it might be battery).

22. See People v. Rosen, 11 Cal.2d 147, 78 P.2d 727 (1938) (defendant collected gambling loss at gunpoint; "not robbery, although the act may be punishable as an unlawful assault or trespass"); Commonwealth v. White, 133 Pa. 182, 19 A. 350 (1890) (defendant took pinch of tobacco by force, an act which "might fairly have subjected him to a prosecution for assault and battery").

23. It cannot, however, be the aggravated assault of assault with intent to rob (or, with intent to commit robbery) since the intent to rob is, as already noted, missing.

24. People v. Merhige, 212 Mich. 601, 180 N.W. 418 (1920) (defendant pleaded guilty to robbery after trial judge told him he had no defense to robbery though compelled by robbers at gunpoint to drive his taxi to the bank which they robbed; motion to change plea to not guilty *held* granted in view of this erroneous statement of the law). Perhaps, however, coercion is a defense, not because it negatives the required intent, but rather because public policy favors preserving greater values at the expense of lesser ones. See § 5.3; Annot., 1 A.L.R.4th 481 (1981).

25. People v. Green, 27 Cal.3d 1, 164 Cal.Rptr. 1, 609 P.2d 468 (1980) (thus robbery where defendant by force had victim remove her clothes because he wanted to destroy them and prevent their use as evidence).

26. See § 8.11(a).

27. Some of the case-law and statutory definitions of robbery speak of the requirement that the taking be "from the person of another" without adding "or in his presence." Yet, even under the narrower wording, a taking in the presence of the victim will do. E.g., People v. Braverman, 340 Ill. 525, 173 N.E. 55 (1930) (defendant at gunpoint forced store manager to open safe, then locked him in a room, then took money from the safe; the robbery statute's language was "from the person of another" without mention of "presence"; conviction of robbery *held* affirmed; "the words 'taking from the person of another,' as used in the common law definition of robbery, * * * included within their meaning the taking * * * from the presence of the person assaulted, of property which either belonged to him or was under his personal control and protection"); State v. Deso, 110 Vt. 1, 1 A.2d 710 (1938) (statutory provision punishing a taking "from the person" is satisfied by a taking from the presence).

28. It is not enough that property elsewhere was acquired by using what was taken from the victim's person. Government of Virgin Islands v. Jarvis, 653 F.2d 762 (3d Cir.1981) (charge was that money taken from victim's person, proof insufficient where it shown defendant took car keys from victim's person and then used keys to steal his car and contents, including money).

29. Carey v. United States, 296 F.2d 422 (D.C.Cir.1961), noted at 8 Wayne L.Rev. 438 (1962). See also Stebbing v. State, 299 Md. 331, 473 A.2d 903 (1984), to the same effect. Doubtless it would have been even easier to hold it to be robbery if A had killed B for the very purpose of taking his money or property. Conversely, it would be more difficult to find robbery if A had killed B accidently. Of

The phrase "from the presence" or "in the presence" has been construed in a number of cases. "Presence" in this connection is not so much a matter of eyesight as it is one of proximity and control: the property taken in the robbery must be close enough to the victim and sufficiently under his control that, had the latter not been subjected to violence or intimidation by the robber, he could have prevented the taking.[30] Thus the robber takes property from the victim's presence if he locks or ties the victim up in one room of a building and then helps himself to valuables located in another room of the same building; and this is so even though, because of the walls, one cannot see from the one room into the other.[31] Conversely, it would not be robbery to use force or fear to immobilize a property owner at one place while a confederate takes the owner's property from a place several miles away, even though, by using a spy glass, one might see from the one place to the other; for the distance between the owner and his property is such that the owner could

not have prevented the taking even if he had been free to try to interfere.[32]

Some robbery statutes define robbery to require a taking "from," rather than "in," the victim's presence. The difference in wording does not signify any difference in meaning, however. Under the former statutes, it is not necessary that the robber carry the property so far that, by the time he drops it or is apprehended, he has taken it completely away from the victim's presence.[33]

While some of the modern robbery statutes contain this "person or presence" requirement, most of them do not. These latter provisions follow the Model Penal Code on this point,[34] and thus encompass some other situations which ought to be included within the crime of robbery.[35]

WESTLAW REFERENCES

cobert /p deceased dea** expire* /s rob robbery

topic(342) /p presence /s control

course, it is not robbery to steal money or property from the body of a deceased person for whose death the thief was in no way responsible—not so much because the deceased is not a "person" as because the requirement that the defendant use force or fear on the victim is missing.

30. E.g., People v. Braverman, 340 Ill. 525, 173 N.E. 55 (1930) (defendants at gunpoint forced store manager to open safe, then locked manager in a small room, then took money from the safe; conviction of robbery *held* affirmed; the "presence" requirement is "that the property should be in the possession or under the control of the individual robbed in such a way or to such an extent that violence or putting in fear was the means used by the robber to take it"); Commonwealth v. Stewart, 365 Mass. 99, 309 N.E.2d 470 (1974) (defendant properly convicted of robbing supermarket's meatcutter by taking money from safe, though night manager and not meatcutter responsible for the safe, as it was the meatcutter who was intimidated, and he could have prevented the taking if not intimidated); Commonwealth v. Homer, 235 Mass. 526, 127 N.E. 517 (1920) (defendant got victim into his hotel room and then at gunpoint forced her to telephone her maid to instruct maid to bring and deliver victim's jewelry to defendant; maid later delivered jewelry to defendant, who had forced victim to go into bathroom; this evidence proves robbery, though conviction *held* reversed on other grounds; "A thing is in the presence of a person, in respect to robbery, which is so within his reach, inspection, observation or control, that he could, if not overcome by violence or prevented by fear, retain his possession of it").

31. People v. Braverman, supra note 30; State v. Calhoun, 72 Iowa 432, 34 N.W. 194 (1887) (defendant entered

victim's home, choked her, tied her up, forced her to tell him where she had hidden her money, and then went into another room and took the money from its hiding place; conviction of robbery *held* affirmed). See also State v. Mosley, 102 Wis.2d 636, 307 N.W.2d 200 (1981) ("presence" requirement met where money and jewelry taken from one room unbeknownst to victim, held at gunpoint by accomplice in adjoining room).

32. Model Penal Code § 222.1 defines robbery in terms of the use of force or fear in the course of committing a theft, without any stated requirement that the taking be from the person or presence of the victim. Thus the hypothetical spyglass case above would seem to be robbery under the Model Penal Code, for fear was used in the course of committing a theft.

33. State v. Hitchcock, 87 Ariz. 277, 350 P.2d 681 (1960) (defendant at gunpoint took victim's property at latter's office, then forced victim to accompany defendant outside to victim's car; a struggle ensued, during which the defendant shot victim before being subdued; defendant's conviction of felony-murder during a robbery *held* affirmed).

34. Model Penal Code § 222.1.

35. "For example, an offender might threaten to shoot the victim in order to compel him to telephone directions for the disposition of property located elsewhere or the threat may be to one person in order to secure property from another who is not then present." Model Penal Code § 222.1, Comment at 112 (1980).

(d) By Means of Violence or Intimidation. Robbery requires that the taking be done by means of violence or intimidation.[36] Larceny from the person or presence of the victim is not robbery without this added element of force or fear.

(1) Violence.[37] The line between robbery and larceny from the person (between violence and lack of violence) is not always easy to draw. The "snatching" cases, for instance, have given rise to some dispute. The great weight of authority, however, supports the view that there is not sufficient force to constitute robbery when the thief snatches property from the owner's grasp so suddenly that the owner cannot offer any resistance to the taking.[38] On the other hand, when the owner, aware of an impending snatching, resists it, or when, the thief's first attempt being

ineffective to separate the owner from his property, a struggle for the property is necessary before the thief can get possession thereof, there is enough force to make the taking robbery.[39] Taking the owner's property by stealthily picking his pocket is not taking by force and so is not robbery;[40] but if the pickpocket or his confederate jostles the owner,[41] or if the owner, catching the pickpocket in the act, struggles unsuccessfully to keep possession,[42] the pickpocket's crime becomes robbery. To remove an article of value, attached to the owner's person or clothing, by a sudden snatching or by stealth is not robbery unless the article in question (e.g., an earring, pin or watch) is so attached to the person or his clothes as to require some force to effect its removal.[43]

36. This does not mean that the victim must be aware that the violence or intimidation had such consequences. Thus, it is robbery even if the violence or intimidation was employed for the very purpose of making the victim unaware of the taking. People v. Bartowsheski, 661 P.2d 235 (Colo.1983).

37. See Note, 23 J.Crim.L. & Crim. 113 (1932); Annots., 57 L.R.A. 432 (1903); 46 L.R.A. (n.s.) 1149 (1913); 1918E L.R.A. 937 (1918).

38. Lear v. State, 39 Ariz. 313, 6 P.2d 426 (1931), noted at 23 J.Crim.L. & Crim. 113 (1932) (defendant grabbed bag of silver from owner's grasp and ran off; no robbery); People v. Patton, 76 Ill.2d 45, 27 Ill.Dec. 766, 389 N.E.2d 1174 (1979) (defendant grabbing purse threw victim's arm back "a little bit," but purse gone before victim realized what happened; no robbery); Ellis v. State, 38 Okl.Crim. 243, 260 P. 93 (1927) (defendant grabbed promissory note from owner's hands; no robbery); Annot., 42 A.L.R.3d 1381 (1972).

(In most jurisdictions which follow this majority view against robbery such a snatching constitutes larceny from the person, a crime less serious than robbery but more serious than ordinary larceny. See § 8.3.)

Contra: Jones v. Commonwealth, 112 Ky. 689, 66 S.W. 633 (1902) (defendant snatched pocketbook from hands of owner so quickly that owner had no chance to resist; robbery); Commonwealth v. Jones, 362 Mass. 83, 283 N.E.2d 840 (1972) (following *Jones* over majority view, which "wrongly emphasizes the victim's opportunity to defend himself over the willingness of the purse snatcher to use violence if necessary"). In a few jurisdictions—e.g., Ga.—the robbery statute specifically provides that sudden snatching is a form of robbery.

39. McDow v. State, 110 Ga. 293, 34 S.E. 1019 (1900) (defendant, after owner refused his demand for property in the owner's hands, snatched it and ran off with it; conviction of robbery *held* affirmed); State v. Moore, 106 Mo. 480, 17 S.W. 658 (1891) (defendant grabbed at owner's pocketbook lying on top of packages she was carrying;

owner at the same moment caught hold of it, defendant then struck her and wrested it from her grasp; conviction of robbery *held* affirmed). See Lear v. State, 39 Ariz. 313, 6 P.2d 426 (1931) (while merely snatching is not a taking by force, "if there be a struggle to keep it, or any violence, or disruption, the taking is robbery").

40. Hall v. People, 171 Ill. 540, 49 N.E. 495 (1898) (defendant unbuttoned the vest, and removed the pocketbook, of an owner too drunk, from voluntary drinking, to realize his loss; conviction of robbery *held* reversed); Brennon v. State, 25 Ind. 403 (1865) (substantially the same). The crime is, instead, the lesser crime of larceny from the person. See § 8.3.

41. Snyder v. Commonwealth, 21 Ky.L.Rptr. 1538, 55 S.W. 679 (Ct.App.1900) (defendant shoved victim to divert his attention); State v. Gorham, 55 N.H. 152 (1875) (defendant put arms around victim ostensibly to whisper, and then picked his pocket); Mahoney v. People, 3 Hun (N.Y.) 202 (Sup.Ct.1874) (an accomplice jostled and crowded the victim while the defendant picked his pocket).

42. Bauer v. State, 45 Ariz. 358, 43 P.2d 203 (1935) (after defendant, a "sporting woman," pulled a purse from the victim's pocket, the victim took hold of it; there was a struggle for possession, which defendant, with the help of a confederate, won, tearing victim's coat in the process).

Cf.: People v. Jones, 290 Ill. 603, 125 N.E. 256 (1919) (victim, quite drunk, realized that defendant had picked his pocket, accused him of doing so after the taking was complete; there was no struggle to prevent the taking; defendant resented the accusation by hitting victim; conviction of robbery *held* reversed).

43. People v. Campbell, 234 Ill. 391, 84 N.E. 1035 (1908) (defendant pulled at owner's diamond pin attached to his shirt by a spiral fastener; owner felt the jerk and, seeing defendant with the pin in his hand, grabbed the hand and recovered the pin; defendant's conviction of robbery *held* affirmed); State v. Broderick, 59 Mo. 318 (1875) (defendant grabbed owner's watch chain, fastened to a watch and a button hole, and broke it loose and ran;

On the ground that the law should not make such fine distinctions and that the law of robbery is more properly directed at conduct placing the victim in serious fear, the Model Penal Code position is that only an infliction of "serious bodily injury" will suffice.[44] However, the modern codes have consistently rejected such a limitation.

One may commit robbery by striking his victim with fist or weapon and then, having thus rendered the victim unconscious or dazed or unwilling to risk another blow, taking his property away from him.[45] One may also render one's victim helpless by more subtle means, as by administering intoxicating liquors or drugs in order to produce a state of unconsciousness or stupefaction; to act in this way is to use force for purposes of robbery.[46] But for one to hypnotize his victim and then

to make her hand over her property to him has been held not to involve the use of force or fear necessary for robbery.[47]

As for the relationship of the force to the taking,[48] various positions are to be found in the modern codes. Some require that the taking be by force, which perhaps covers the case where the force facilitated the taking but was used before any intent to take was formed [49]: some require that the force be used for the purpose of the taking [50]; while a third group merely requires that the force occur "in the course of" the theft (or, perhaps, an attempted theft or flight thereafter).

(2) Intimidation.[51] The elements of force and fear—of violence or intimidation—are alternatives: [52] if there is force, there need be no fear, and *vice versa.*[53] (Thus, all modern codes define robbery in terms of actual or

conviction of robbery *held* affirmed); Rex v. Lapier, 168 Eng.Rep. 263 (Cr.Cas.Res.1784) (defendant grabbed a lady's earring, tearing her ear; conviction of robbery *held* approved); Rex v. Mason, 168 Eng.Rep. 876 (Cr.Cas.Res. 1820) (defendant grabbed owner's watch, gave several pulls and broke the watch's chain, thus securing possession; conviction of robbery *held* approved).

Cf. Model Penal Code § 222.1, Comment at 108 (1980): "Any taking from the person will involve some use of 'force' and perhaps 'fear' in some general sense of being startled. But it is force or threat of force directed at placing the victim in serious fear for his safety that justifies the escalated penalties of the robbery offense."

Note, 23 J.Crim.L. & Crim. 113 (1932), suggests that the line now drawn in snatching and pickpocket cases between larceny from the person and robbery serves to "put a premium on criminal skill and adroitness, and to punish the less practiced and unprofessional thief for his lack of ability in committing a felony that is no more dangerous or heinous than when committed by one clever and nimble enough to be guilty of mere larceny."

44. Model Penal Code § 222.1.

45. It is robbery even if the blow is not accompanied by any intent to steal, such an intent coming into the defendant's mind only when he discovers the victim helpless to resist the taking of his property. See 8.11(e).

46. People v. Dreas, 153 Cal.App.3d 623, 200 Cal.Rptr. 586 (1984) (drugs used to overcome victim's resistance, constitutes robbery); State v. Snyder, 41 Nev. 453, 172 P. 364 (1918) (defendant administered drug to saloon-keeper to produce unconsciousness, doubtless so as to be able to steal without resistance, and then, while the latter was unconscious, took money from the cash register; conviction of robbery *held* affirmed), noted at 28 Yale L.J. 284 (1919).

Since it is a battery to administer a drug to an unsuspecting victim, e.g., Johnson v. State, 92 Ga. 36, 17 S.E. 974 (1893), it seems clear that such conduct is "force" which will do for robbery.

On analogy to the cases which uphold the robbery conviction of one who fights with another with no intent to steal and then, having rendered his opponent helpless, does steal, it would seem that it is robbery to steal from the person or presence of the victim after administering drugs or liquor to him for some purpose other than a purpose to steal. It is not robbery, however, to steal from the person or presence of one for whose helplessness through drugs or drink the thief was not responsible, e.g., Hall v. People, 171 Ill. 540, 49 N.E. 495 (1898) (victim voluntarily drunk).

47. Louis v. State, 24 Ala.App. 120, 130 So. 904 (1930), noted at 22 J.Crim.L. & Crim. 279 (1931). The Note criticizes the holding on the ground that, since one is guilty of seduction of a girl whom he hypnotizes into having intercourse, he should equally be guilty of robbery when he hypnotizes her into handing over her property. But the analogy between seduction and robbery is not altogether apt: seduction does not require force but only a lack of consent, whereas robbery requires force in addition to a lack of consent.

48. See § 8.11(e) for further discussion.

49. See cases in note 79 infra.

50. Applying such a provision, it was held in Harris v. State, 451 So.2d 406 (Ala.Crim.1984), that there was no robbery where defendant's force came later in resisting arrest.

51. See Note, 24 Minn.L.Rev. 708 (1940).

52. Of course, there is often both force and fear, the two factors operating together to enable the robber to take the victim's property. E.g., Sweat v. State, 90 Ga. 315, 17 S.E. 273 (1893) (defendants pretended to arrest victim, who had money in his coat; they handcuffed him and carried him off; they threatened him with vague but dire consequences if he did not consent to their taking the money; they took it when he, frightened by their talk, consented; conviction of robbery *held* affirmed).

53. And thus the purse-snatching cases discussed earlier must be distinguished from the situation in State v.

threatened injury). The commonest sort of fear in robbery, of course, is the fear, engendered by the robber's intentional threat,[54] of immediate bodily injury [55] or death to the property owner himself, as where the robber points a gun, loaded or unloaded,[56] at the owner with a threat to shoot unless the latter hands over his property. But the threat of immediate bodily injury or death need not be directed at the owner himself; it may be made to a member of his family, or other relative, or even to someone in his company, though there be no threat to do harm to the owner himself.[57]

The traditional view is that the threat must be of immediate harm, rather than of future harm.[58] Some modern statutes are somewhat ambiguous on this point, but most of them expressly state that the threat must be as to "immediate" or "imminent" harm. This is as it should be, for it is the immediacy of the threats that escalates the theft from extortion [59] to robbery.[60]

It is sometimes loosely said that the threat may be of injury to the property, rather than to the person, of the owner (or of his family or of a person in his company),[61] but doubtless this aspect of robbery is limited to a threat to destroy a dwelling house.[62] A mere threat,

Witherspoon, 648 S.W.2d 279 (Tenn.1983) (no struggle over purse, but this robbery nonetheless because defendant's action in blocking the open door of her car made her apprehensive for her own safety, and thus she did not physically resist him taking of the purse from the car). It is sometimes stated that there is no robbery without violence, but that "constructive" violence will do as well as "actual" violence, and that "constructive" violence covers intimidation. E.g., Clary v. State, 33 Ark. 561 (1878) ("The principle, indeed, of robbery is violence, but it has been often holden, that actual violence is not the only means by which a robbery may be effected, but that it may also be effected by fear, which the law considers as constructive violence"). This fiction was doubtless helpful in the historical development of robbery from a requirement of actual violence to the alternative requirement of intimidation. For a very brief history of robbery, see supra note 1. Today, however, there is no need to talk in fictions.

54. Though, at least under some statutes, a reckless infliction of harm will suffice, this is not so as to a threat. "The term 'threaten' implies purposeful behavior." Model Penal Code § 222.1, Comment at 114 (1980).

55. It need not be a fear of *serious* bodily injury. Though Model Penal Code § 222.1 requires such a fear, that position has been consistently rejected in the modern codes.

56. Even a toy gun, or a finger in the pocket to simulate a gun, will do for robbery if, because it looks real, the robbery victim fears for his personal safety. See Annot., 61 A.L.R.2d 996 (1958).

57. See Reane's Case, 168 Eng.Rep. 410 (Cr.Cas.Res. 1794), wherein it was said to be robbery to obtain money from the owner by taking the latter's child, holding it over the river and threatening to throw it in unless the money be paid.

See also Lear v. State, 39 Ariz. 313, 6 P.2d 426 (1931) ("The fear may be either of an unlawful injury to the person or property of the person robbed, or of a relative or member of his family; or of an immediate and unlawful injury to the person or property of any one in the company of the person robbed at the time of the robbery"); Breckinridge v. Commonwealth, 97 Ky. 267, 30 S.W. 634 (1895) (robbery has "been extended so as not only to include fear of personal violence, but fear of the loss of his

property; fear that his child in possession of the persons intending the robbery may be killed"); Manson v. State, 101 Wis.2d 413, 304 N.W.2d 729 (1981) (threat to others present suffices).

Model Penal Code § 223.4, Comment at 207 (1980), makes the excellent point that, while many jurisdictions require that the threat be to harm the victim or a member of his family, on principle it should be enough to threaten to harm anyone, for there "is no justification for providing as a matter of law that threat of injury to a third party can never intimidate or that the provisions on extortion can be evaded by finding a victim who will respond to such threats." The modern robbery statutes generally follow the Model Penal Code position on this matter.

58. "Immediate" does not mean "instantaneous," however. In Tipton v. State, 23 Okl.Crim. 86, 212 P. 612 (1923), the defendant, after getting the victim to come to his home, pointed a gun at him and frightened him into going to the bank—the defendant following some distance behind—which the victim entered alone, procuring a $1000 cashier's check, meeting the defendant outside and handing him the check. The defendant argued these facts did not prove robbery since, once alone, the victim was no longer in fear of immediate personal violence. The defendant's conviction of robbery was affirmed, the court stating that "we see no reason why a short separation of the accused and the person robbed, who was still laboring under apprehension and fear of personal violence, should make the case any different from one where there was no such separation." Obtaining property by threat of future harm may come under the heading of extortion or blackmail. See § 8.12.

Though the threat must be of immediate use of physical force, that threat can occur without use of any words, and thus if words are used they need not expressly declare the harm would be immediate. People v. Woods, 41 N.Y.2d 279, 392 N.Y.S.2d 400, 360 N.E.2d 1082 (1977).

59. See § 8.12.

60. Model Penal Code § 222.1, Comment (1980).

61. See Lear v. State, Breckinridge v. Commonwealth, both quoted supra note 57.

62. Rex v. Simons, 2 East P.C. 731 (1773); Brown's Case, 2 East P.C. 731 (1780). This is not the case, however, in the modern statutes.

unaccompanied by physical force, to accuse the property owner of the crime of sodomy (but not of other crimes) has been held a sufficient threat for robbery.[63] There must be a causal connection between the defendant's threat of harm and his acquisition of the victim's property—that is, the threat must induce the victim to part with his property.[64] Thus a defendant who obtains property from a victim who, knowing the gun to be unloaded, hands over the property in order to be able to prosecute the defendant for robbery would not qualify for the crime.[65]

As in the analogous crime of assault, the word "fear" in connection with robbery does not so much mean "fright" as it means "apprehension"; one too brave to be frightened may yet be apprehensive of bodily harm.[66] The victim who is not apprehensive of harm from the robber so long as he does what the robber tells him to do, though he does expect harm if he refuses, is nevertheless "put in fear" for purposes of robbery.[67]

The statement is sometimes made (and some cases even hold) that the threat of harm, for robbery, must be such as would, under the circumstances, arouse in the victim a reasonable fear of harm, or cause a reasonable man to be apprehensive of harm, or induce a reasonable person to part with his property.[68] Of

---

63. See Montsdoca v. State, 84 Fla. 82, 93 So. 157 (1922) ("Threat of prosecution is generally regarded as insufficient to create fear [required for robbery], upon the theory that a man in the hands of the law is not legally presumed to be in danger of bodily harm. The one exception grafted upon the doctrine by the English cases is a threat to bring against the victim the charge of sodomy").

See Annot., 27 A.L.R. 1299 (1923).

The reason why sodomy is singled out for special treatment is described in Britt v. State, 26 Tenn. 45 (1846), as turning upon "the overwhelming and withering character of the charge and its damning infamy, so well calculated to unman and subdue the will and alarm the fears of the falsely accused"! Montsdoca v. State, supra, cites Bishop's criticism of the sodomy rule to the effect that "there is clearly no foundation of principle for the exception. It is an excrescence on the law." This exception is not recognized in the modern robbery statutes. A few of them, however, include within robbery the commission or threat of a serious felony during the course of committing a theft. This position is also taken in Model Penal Code § 222.1.

Obtaining property from the owner by threat to accuse the owner of crime, where this conduct does not come under the heading of robbery, falls into the blackmail-extortion category, discussed § 8.12.

64. See Montsdoca v. State, 84 Fla. 82, 93 So. 157 (1922) (it is robbery to create in the victim a reasonable apprehension of violence "to avoid which he parts with the thing"); State v. Parsons, 44 Wash. 299, 87 P. 349 (1906) (it is enough for robbery that the putting in fear employed "is the moving cause inducing him to part unwillingly with his property").

The requirement of a causal connection between the threat and the property-acquisition in robbery is analogous to the requirement of a causal connection between the misrepresentation and the property-acquisition in false pretenses. See § 8.7(c).

65. Perhaps this is not so under those modern statutes which merely speak of a threat being made "in the course of" the robbery.

66. See § 7.16(b). See W. Prosser & W. Keeton, Torts § 10 (5th ed. 1984), speaking of the requirement of the apprehension of immediate bodily harm which a civil assault requires: "Apprehension is not the same thing as fear, and the plaintiff is not deprived of his action merely because he is too courageous to be frightened or intimidated."

67. Ross v. State, 31 Okl.Crim. 143, 237 P. 469 (1925) (bank cashier, when approached by armed bank robbers who pointed a gun at her and said "stick 'em up," displayed great poise and coolness, and was not afraid of the robbers so long as she did what they told her; she realized, however, that if she attempted to resist, violence sufficient to overcome her resistance would be used; conviction of robbery *held* affirmed).

68. E.g., Montsdoca v. State, 84 Fla. 82, 93 So. 157 (1922) (it is robbery to create in the victim "a reasonable apprehension of violence" to avoid which he parts with his property); Long v. State, 12 Ga. 293 (1852) ("The rule is this: if the fact be attended with such circumstances of terror—such threatening by word or gesture, as in common experience, are likely to create an apprehension of danger, and induce a man to part with his property for the safety of his person; it is a case of robbery"); Steward v. People, 224 Ill. 434, 79 N.E. 636 (1906) (for robbery by intimidation the fear "must be of such a character that the injured party is put in fear of such a nature as in reason and common experience is likely to induce a person to part with his property"); Parnell v. State, 389 P.2d 370 (Okl.Crim.1964) (defendant, having orally agreed to fix victim's attic for $25, and having worked a few hours in the attic and used $12 worth of lumber, then, in the company of another man, demanded $600 of the victim, and 84–year–old woman who was alone in the house; the demand put her in a state of shock and fear, so she paid him $300, and the two men left; conviction of robbery *held* reversed, for the demand for $600, under the circumstances, without some further threat of injury, would not have made a reasonable person so fearful that he would part with this property); Peebles v. State, 138 Tex.Crim. 55, 134 S.W.2d 298 (1939) (defendant a man, told victim, a woman, on a busy sidewalk to give him her money, threatening, if she refused, to "leave her like he left a woman the night before"; she then let him take her money; conviction of robbery *held* reversed, for the defendant's words, under the circumstances, were not "reasonably calculated" to put her in fear; "it appears unreasonable

course, if the circumstances are such that a reasonable person would not be scared, a jury might properly infer that the victim, in spite of his testimony to the contrary, was not in fact scared (though it is a little hard to see what other reason he might have had to give up his property, if he was not in fact in a state of fear).[69] But if the victim is actually frightened by the defendant into parting with his property, the defendant's crime, on principle, is robbery, even though an ordinary person, with more fortitude than the victim, would not have been thus frightened.[70]

WESTLAW REFERENCES

342k6 342k7   /p   resist!

342k6 342k7   /p   snatch*** grab!

342k6 342k7   /p   force /s fear

that the [defendant's] language * * * would have engendered in her fear of such a nature 'as in reason and common experience is likely to induce her to part with her money against her will' "), criticized at 24 Minn.L.Rev. 708 (1940).

69. Conversely, if a reasonable man would be scared, the victim's testimony that he was scared is likely to be believed. See Long v. State, 12 Ga. 293 (1852) ("The law * * * will presume fear where there appears to be just ground for it").

70. The correct test is properly stated in State v. Parsons, 44 Wash. 299, 87 P. 349 (1906): it is robbery by intimidation, "no matter how slight * * * the cause creating the fear may be, nor by what other circumstances the taking may be accompanied. It is enough that * * * the putting in fear employed is sufficient to overcome resistance on the part of the person from whom the property is taken, and is the moving cause inducing him to part unwillingly with his property."

In State v. Carr, 43 Iowa 418 (1876), where the defendant was convicted of robbing a Bohemian by putting him in fear, the court, affirming the conviction, upheld the trial court's instruction that "it is not necessary that the means used to put a party in fear should be such as to put in fear a man used to the ways of the world," it being enough if the defendant's treatment of the Bohemian "was calculated to put such a man as he in fear."

In Williams v. State, 51 Neb. 711, 71 N.W. 729 (1897), where the victim was an inexperienced youth, the evidence of the defendant's conduct scaring the victim was said to sustain the defendant's guilt of robbery (though the conviction was reversed for some inadmissible evidence), citing State v. Carr, supra, for the proposition that the test is whether the defendant's conduct is calculated to put in fear "such a man as he."

See Note, 24 Minn.L.Rev. 708 (1940), for a discussion of the dispute as to whether to apply an objective or subjective test in the putting-in-fear aspect of robbery.

topic(342) /p immediate imminent /2 harm injury /s threat!

(e) Concurrence of Conduct and State of Mind. It is a general principle of criminal law—applicable to robbery as it is to other crimes—that the defendant's conduct and his state of mind must concur.[71] For robbery this means, among other things, that the defendant's larcenous conduct (his taking of the victim's property) and his violence-or-intimidation conduct must concur. Thus, under the traditional view it is not robbery to steal property without violence or intimidation (e.g., to obtain it by stealth or fraud or sudden snatching), although the thief later, in order to retain the stolen property or make good his escape, uses violence or intimidation upon the property owner.[72] The defendant's acts of violence or intimidation must occur either *before*

In the analogous theft crime of false pretenses, where property is obtained by misrepresentations rather than by intimidation, the defendant is guilty if his misrepresentations in fact induce the victim to part with his property, although a reasonable person would never have believed the defendant's lies. See § 8.7(i)(1). The cases of Parnell v. State and Peebles v. State, supra note 68, which applied the test of the effect the threats would have on a reasonable man, thus were wrongly decided.

In the converse case, where the victim is less fearful than the reasonable man, and is not made apprehensive by defendant's conduct though a reasonable man would have been, the defendant's crime would not be robbery, which requires that the victim actually be put in fear (in the absence of violence).

71. See § 3.11.

72. Thompson v. State, 24 Ala.App. 300, 134 So. 679 (1931) (during a card game one player suddenly snatched money from the victim player's coat, and another player held the victim while the first one escaped; conviction of robbery *held* reversed); People v. Jones, 290 Ill. 603, 125 N.E. 256 (1919) (defendant stealthily took pocketbook from drunken victim's pocket and put it in his own pocket; when victim accused him of taking it, defendant struck him and knocked him out; conviction of robbery *held* reversed, for the defendant's actions "were those of a pickpocket and not of a highwayman"); State v. Holmes, 317 Mo. 9, 295 S.W. 71 (1927) (defendant, handed diamonds by owner for inspection, displayed a gun, locked up the owner, and escaped with the diamonds; conviction of robbery *held* reversed), noted at 27 Colum.L.Rev. 999 (1927); Mason v. Commonwealth, 200 Va. 253, 105 S.E.2d 149 (1958) (defendant by stealth took television set from store and handed it to a confederate; store owner appeared and swung a board at defendant; defendant then threw a radio at and fired a gun at store owner; conviction of robbery *held* reversed). See Annot., 93 A.L.R.3d 643 (1979).

the taking (though continuing to have an operative effect until the time of the taking) or *at* the time of the taking.[73]

But a different result is often possible today because of the language used in the modern codes, such as that it is sufficient the force or intimidation was used to "retain possession" or to "carry away" the property, or in "resisting apprehension." Most common, however, are provisions following the Model Penal Code view[74] that it suffices these acts occurred "in flight" thereafter. This is a desirable change from common law notions. "The thief's willingness to use force against those who would restrain him in flight suggests that he would have employed force to effect the theft had the need arisen."[75]

Concerning the required concurrence of the defendant's conduct and state of mind, there is a question as to the robbery liability of one who strikes another, perhaps intentionally but with no intent to steal (or who intimidates another, though without an intent to steal), and who then, seeing his adversary helpless, takes the latter's property from his person or his presence. In other words, does robbery require that the defendant's violence-or-intimidation acts be done for the very purpose of taking the victim's property, or is it enough that he takes advantage of a situation which he created for some other purpose? The great weight of authority in the earlier cases favors the latter view, holding that under the circumstances it is robbery;[76] but it can be argued that on principle it ought not to be

Compare State v. Holmes, supra, with Roberts v. State, 49 Okl.Crim. 181, 292 P. 1043 (1930). Here the defendant, who owed 95 cents for gasoline, told the gas station attendant he had a $20 bill; the attendant handed the defendant $19.05; the defendant, who had no such bill, pulled a gun and escaped with the $19.05. The defendant's conviction of robbery was *held* affirmed, over his contention that the taking preceded the intimidation, on the ground that the attendant, having handed the money to the defendant in an uncompleted transaction to be completed in his presence, had kept ("constructive") possession (i.e., he gave the defendant only custody); the defendant then obtained possession by intimidation, which is enough for robbery. Consider also State v. Long, 234 Kan. 580, 675 P.2d 832 (1984) (just as defendant took money from box inside building and stuffed it into his shirt, victim appeared and tried to block the doorway, but defendant pushed her aside; *held*, taking—obtaining dominion and control—is not complete where it "immediately resisted by the owner before the thief can remove it from the premises or from the owner's presence").

73. See the cases cited in note 82 supra. Occasionally this view is expressed by statute.

74. Model Penal Code § 222.1.

75. Model Penal Code § 222.1, Comment at 104 (1980).

76. Carey v. United States, 296 F.2d 422 (D.C.Cir.1961) (defendant, after an argument with his landlady in which she emphasized her point by striking him on the head with a bicycle pump, stabbed her to death—in such a way that he was later convicted of manslaughter—and then, believing her unconscious, took money from her dress; conviction of robbery *held* affirmed; it does not matter that his intent to steal arose after the victim had died); People v. Jordan, 303 Ill. 316, 135 N.E. 729 (1922) (defendant knocked victim down in a fight, then took his money; conviction of robbery *held* affirmed, even on the assumption that the intent to steal arose after the fight began); Commonwealth v. Stelma, 327 Pa. 317, 192 A. 906 (1937) (defendant, perhaps not then intending to steal knocked victim down and struck him on the head with a brick, inflicting fatal injuries; then defendant may for the first

time have decided to steal money from the victim's pocket; later the victim died; defendant's conviction of felony-murder, in the perpetration of a robbery, *held* affirmed; defendant committed robbery, for "it is immaterial when the design to rob was conceived"), noted at 42 Dick.L.Rev. 85 (1938); Turner v. State, 150 Tex.Crim. 90, 198 S.W.2d 890 (1946) (defendant, claiming victim had backed his car into defendant's car, fought with him, knocked him down, and took money from him; conviction of robbery *held* affirmed, over defendant's contention that the intent to steal arose after the violence was inflicted); Rex v. Blackham, 2 East P.C. 711 (1787) (defendant threatened female victim in order to have sexual intercourse with her; without any demand on his part she paid him money; this is robbery, though defendant instilled fear in the victim for a purpose other than to obtain her money).

Perhaps contra: See People v. Sanchez, 30 Cal.2d 560, 184 P.2d 673 (1947) (defendant claimed he killed victim in self-defense and, only later deciding to steal, took the victim's property from his person; the jury, disbelieving this defense, found him guilty of murder in the commission of robbery; conviction *held* affirmed, the court stating that the instructions made it clear that for such a conviction, "the killer must *at the time of the killing*, have had the purpose to rob" (emphasis added).

In the above cases the defendant's conduct in striking or intimidating the victim constituted criminal conduct, e.g., assault, battery, manslaughter. But it has been held that even if the defendant renders the victim helpless in proper self-defense, with no intent to steal, and then decides to and does steal, it is nevertheless robbery. Diaz v. State, 147 Tex.Crim. 560, 182 S.W.2d 805 (1944), noted at 49 Dick.L.Rev. 119 (1945). Doubtless the same result would follow if the defendant accidentally struck the victim.

Of course, if the defendant is not in any way responsible for the victim's helplessness, as where he discovers him run over by a car driven by another, the defendant who does not himself use violence or intimidation in taking the victim's property from his person or presence is not guilty of robbery but only of larceny. See Note, 49 Dick.L.Rev. 119, 122 (1945).

robbery, being only larceny (plus, if the circumstances warrant it, assault or battery or whatever other crime the defendant may have committed before his theft).[77]

Under many of the modern codes, there would not be a robbery under the circumstances just described. Certainly this is true under those robbery statutes which expressly state that the force must be used for the purpose of committing the theft. And it is likewise true under those statutes requiring no such mental state but taking (as does the Model Penal Code[78]) the position that a reckless infliction of harm will suffice, provided the harm occurs "in the course of" the theft (or, perhaps, of an attempt to commit it or flight thereafter). Less certain is what the result must be under a third group of modern statutes which say that the taking must be by force, though these statutes certainly lend themselves to interpretation in accordance with the traditional view that these facts constitute robbery.[79]

 **WESTLAW
REFERENCES**

342k3 342k6 /p time coincide concomitant

77. Ibid. Insofar as the rationale of robbery, as an aggravated form of theft, is the hardihood which enables the robber to carry out his theft in the face of the victim's opposition, thus displaying a trait which requires a longer period of incapacitation and rehabilitation, see note 4 supra, it may be said that the thief who simply takes advantage of the victim's helpless condition, even though the defendant may be somehow responsible therefor, does not evidence the same hardihood.

78. Model Penal Code § 222.1. In justification, it is said: "When injury is actually inflicted, even though recklessly, the willingness of the actor to expose the victim to serious harm is sufficiently demonstrated." Model Penal Code § 222.1, Comment at 114 (1980).

79. State v. Myers, 230 Kan. 697, 640 P.2d 1245 (1982) (where aggravated robbery requires taking by force or threat of force while armed, it sufficient that defendant shot victim and then returned 3 hours later to take victim's wallet, as there was a continuous chain of events and the prior force made it possible to take the property without resistance); State v. Mason, 403 So.2d 701 (La. 1981) (it sufficient that taking of purse accomplished as a result of earlier acts of pushing victim onto bed and pulling her clothes; acts of violence need not have been for purpose of taking the property).

80. See § 8.4(b).

Special types of larceny, such as "larceny from the person" (pickpocketing, sudden snatching), however, do not make the value distinction.

(f) Aggravated Robbery. Larceny statutes generally differentiate between the misdemeanor of petty larceny and the felony of grand larceny according to the value of the property taken.[80] This is not true of robbery statutes, however; the value of the property taken in the robbery does not matter, so long as the property has some value.[81]

Most robbery statutes nevertheless distinguish, for purposes of punishment, between simple robbery and aggravated robbery.[82] The most common aggravating factors are: (a) that the robber was armed with a "dangerous" (or "deadly") weapon; (or, sometimes, that he exhibited the weapon or that he represented that he had a gun); (b) that the robber used a dangerous instrumentality; (c) that the robber actually inflicted serious bodily injury;[83] and (d) that the robber had an accomplice.

Armed robbery statutes (i.e., statutes involving factor (a) above) have required some interpretation, especially concerning the words "dangerous" or "deadly."[84] The great weight of authority holds that an unloaded pistol, not used as a bludgeon, is nevertheless

81. However, the fact that the property has very little value may show it was taken as a practical joke rather than with an intent to steal it. Commonwealth v. White, 133 Pa. 182, 19 A. 350 (1890) (defendant took a pinch of tobacco from victim by force; conviction of robbery *held* reversed).

82. In a few states the latter is called first-degree robbery, the former second-degree robbery.

83. In a few states it is sufficient that the robber attempted such injury.

84. Perhaps, as a matter of language, "deadly" might be considered a narrower word than "dangerous;" it may be that "deadly" requires a risk of death or serious bodily harm; whereas "dangerous" might include a risk of bodily harm less than serious bodily harm or death. Cf. Tatum v. United States, 110 F.2d 555 (D.C.Cir.1940) (dictum that an assault with a dangerous weapon need not be an assault with a deadly weapon, apparently because "deadly" means likely to kill and "dangerous" means likely to kill or do serious bodily harm). But "dangerous weapon" and "deadly weapon" are both generally defined as a weapon which, as used or attempted to be used, may endanger life or inflict great bodily harm, e.g., see Price v. United States, 85 C.C.A. 247, 156 F. 950 (9th Cir.1907) ("dangerous" weapon); Floyd v. Commonwealth, 191 Va. 674, 62 S.E.2d 6 (1950) ("deadly" weapon).

a dangerous or deadly weapon for armed-robbery purposes.[85] (Some jurisdictions even hold that a toy pistol is such a weapon.)[86] The majority view seems wrong, however: intimidation by some means is a necessary ingredient of simple robbery without violence; something additional in the way of dangerousness is needed for aggravated robbery; but the robber's use of an unloaded (or toy) gun adds nothing extra to the bare fact that he intimidated the victim.[87] Aside from the problem of fire arms, there are many cases

which deal with the dangerous or deadly character of knives, blackjacks, iron pipes, rakes, books and fists and a variety of other weapons.[88]

Another armed-robbery problem concerns the robber who obtains the victim's property while unarmed but who later arms himself and makes use of his newly acquired arms to retain his booty or to make his escape. Once more there is a split of authority on the point, the answer depending, to some extent, upon the wording of the statute.[89]

85. People v. Egan, 77 Cal.App. 279, 246 P. 337 (1926); Hayes v. State, 211 Md. 111, 126 A.2d 576 (1956), noted at 17 Md.L.Rev. 257 (1957); Commonwealth v. Cody, 165 Mass. 133, 42 N.E. 575 (1895); Contra: Luitze v. State, 204 Wis. 78, 234 N.W. 382 (1931). See also People v. Ellis, 94 Ill.App.3d 777, 50 Ill.Dec. 619, 419 N.E.2d 727 (1981) (loaded but inoperable gun is a "dangerous weapon" because it *could* be used as bludgeon). If the view is taken that an unloaded gun is not a dangerous or deadly weapon, it is possible to place on the defendant the burden of proving that the gun, with which he threatened the victim was unloaded. E.g., Campbell v. People, 124 Colo. 8, 232 P.2d 738 (1951). Without going so far as to "presume" the gun to be loaded from the fact that the defendant pointed a gun at the victim within firing range and threatened to fire it, at least such conduct can give rise to an "inference" that it was loaded. State v. Lanegan, 192 Or. 691, 236 P.2d 438 (1951) (in Oregon an assault requires pointing loaded gun; conviction of assault with intent to rob *held* affirmed, because jury could infer gun was loaded, though there was no direct proof it was actually loaded).

For other cases, see Annot., 79 A.L.R.2d 1412, 1426–30 (1961).

86. People v. Coleman, 53 Cal.App.2d 18, 127 P.2d 309 (1942); People ex rel. Griffin v. Hunt, 267 N.Y. 597, 196 N.E. 598 (1935).

Contra: People v. Skelton, 83 Ill.2d 58, 46 Ill.Dec. 571, 414 N.E.2d 455 (1980) (noting it even too light to use as bludgeon); Cooper v. State, 201 Tenn. 149, 297 S.W.2d 75 (1956).

See Annot., 81 A.L.R.3d 1006, 1035–43 (1977). Most cases hold that it is not armed robbery to rob with the aid of a simulated gun consisting of a hand in the pocket. Id. at 1002–04.

87. See Note, 17 Md.L.Rev. 257 (1957). Perhaps another way to express the matter is this: the greater punishment is awarded for armed robbery so as to deter the dangerous person who is actually capable of inflicting death or serious bodily harm. The robber with the unloaded or toy gun is not nice—is guilty in fact of (simple) robbery—but he is not the dangerous type for whom the greater penalty is reserved. See also State v. Franklin, 130 Ariz. 291, 635 P.2d 1213 (1981) (no armed robbery where defendant merely made motion inside coat pocket as if he had gun, even if victim reasonably believed there was a gun); State v. Butler, 89 N.J. 220, 445 A.2d 399 (1982) (no armed robbery where defendant merely placed hand in pocket and pretended to have gun).

88. E.g., People v. Dozie, 224 Cal.App.2d 474, 36 Cal. Rptr. 728 (1964) (defendants, having beaten victim into unconsciousness with their fists, took his property; conviction of first-degree robbery *held* reversed, for one equipped with his naked hands or fists is not armed with a "dangerous or deadly weapon"); People v. Bennett, 208 Cal.App. 2d 317, 25 Cal.Rptr. 257 (1962) (defendant, having used a shod foot to kick victim into unconsciousness, from which the victim did not regain consciousness for nine days, took his property from his person or presence; conviction of first-degree robbery, while armed with a "dangerous or deadly weapon," *held* affirmed); Commonwealth v. Tarrant, 367 Mass. 411, 326 N.E.2d 710 (1975) (where defendant's German shepherd responded to defendant's commands and moved in close proximity of victim, dog was a "dangerous weapon"; where the instrumentality is not per se harm-inducing, its potential danger must be measured by objective standards and not by the victim's apprehension).

See also Annots., 8 A.L.R.4th 1268 (1981) (parts of human body); 8 A.L.R.4th 842 (1981) (walking cane); 7 A.L.R.4th 607 (1981) (dog); 100 A.L.R.3d 287 (1980) (pocket knife).

89. One point of view is that this does not constitute armed robbery. See People v. DePompeis, 410 Ill. 587, 102 N.E.2d 813 (1951) (under statute defining armed robbery as robbery by a person "if he is armed with a dangerous weapon," the court states that "the gist of the offense of armed robbery is the force and intimidation used in taking the property"). Some armed-robbery statutes seem to require this result by requiring that the taking be *by means of* a dangerous or deadly weapon.

Contra: People v. Pond, 169 Cal.App.2d 547, 337 P.2d 877 (1959) (defendant, having obtained victim's wallet in an unarmed robbery in victim's home, got a knife from the kitchen and used it to threaten victim in an attempt to persuade him to disclose the location of his wall safe; defendant also used knife to threaten child in a vain attempt to avoid capture by police; conviction of first-degree robbery *held* affirmed under statute providing that "all robbery which is perpetrated * * * by a person being armed with a dangerous or deadly weapon is robbery in the first degree"; "perpetration" includes the escape phase, the court citing the felony-murder analogy), noted at 46 Iowa L.Rev. 151 (1960). Cf. State v. Mirault, 92 N.J. 492, 457 A.2d 455 (1983) (where aggravating element was inflicting or attempting to inflict serious bodily harm, it sufficed that such force directed at arresting

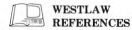

342k11 /p aggravat*** /2 robbery /s dangerous
    lethal deadly /2 weapon

topic(342) /p aggravat*** /2 robbery /s harm
    injury

tarrant /p "german shepherd" dog doberman

(g) Federal Robbery Statutes. Aside from the federal statute punishing robbery when committed within the maritime (e.g., on a United States vessel on the high seas) or territorial (e.g., on an army post or in a federal court house) jurisdiction of the United States,[90] there are these important federal robbery statutes: (a) the Federal Bank Robbery Act (punishing robbery of property in the custody or possession of any national bank or of any bank which is insured by the federal government);[91] (b) two provisions punishing robbery where the property taken is mail matter, or is property or money belonging to the federal government;[92] and (c) the Hobbs Act, punishing the obstruction of interstate commerce by robbery (or by extortion).[93]

topic(342) /p 18 +4 2112 2114

officer at scene, as statute covers such conduct while making escape).

It was noted above, see 8.11(e), that it is generally held not to be robbery, but only larceny, to obtain the victim's property by stealth, although later the robber, to retain the stolen property or to make good his escape, uses violence or intimidation upon the victim. (The Model Penal Code, however, suggests that, on principle, this should be robbery.) On analogy to that prevailing view, it would seem that it is not armed robbery to obtain the victim's property by unarmed robbery although arms are later used to retain the stolen property or effect an escape. (But if, as the Model Penal Code suggests, it is robbery in the analogous situation, it should be armed robbery here.)

90. 18 U.S.C.A. § 2111.

91. 18 U.S.C.A. § 2113. See Annot., 59 A.L.R.2d 946 (1958). This statute has been interpreted to include not only the usual type of robbery, but also other means of acquiring the property or money of banks, such as by false pretenses. Bell v. United States, 462 U.S. 356, 103 S.Ct. 2398, 76 L.Ed.2d 638 (1983).

92. 18 U.S.C.A. §§ 2112, 2114.

§ 8.12 Extortion or Blackmail

The common-law misdemeanor of extortion consists of the corrupt taking of a fee by a public officer, under color of his office, where no fee is due, or not so large a fee is due, or the fee is not yet due.[1] Modern statutes continue to make such conduct by public officials criminal, generally under the name of "extortion";[2] the crime is generally classified as a crime against the administration of justice or against the conduct of government, rather than as a crime against property.

topic(165) /p "common law"

(a) Statutory Extortion or Blackmail. We have seen, in the discussion of robbery, that to obtain another's property by means of a threat of immediate bodily harm to the victim (or to someone in his company) is robbery; and robbery is held to embrace also a threat to destroy the victim's home or a threat to accuse him of sodomy. That was, however, as far as robbery by threats went—doubtless because the severe penalty for robbery, long a capital offense, restrained the courts from expanding robbery to include the acquisition of property by means of other effective threats—such as a threat to inflict future rather than immediate bodily harm, or to destroy the victim's property other than his

93. 18 U.S.C.A. § 1951. See Note, 12 Vand.L.Rev. 495 (1959).

§ 8.12.

1. W. Hawkins, Pleas of the Crown, 418 (1787); Commonwealth v. Bagley, 24 Mass. (7 Pick.) 279 (1828) (officer demanded and received a fee not yet due, though in all probability it would soon become due; verdict of guilty of extortion; *held*, judgment entered upon the verdict). There is a dispute as to whether an officer is guilty (i.e., whether his intention is "corrupt") if he takes a fee not due, honestly though mistakenly (by a mistake of fact or of law) believing it to be due. Compare State v. Dickens, 2 N.C. 406 (1796) (mistake no defense); with State v. Cutter, 36 N.J.L. 125 (1873) (mistake is a defense).

2. See United States v. Dozier, 672 F.2d 531 (5th Cir. 1982); United States v. Williams, 621 F.2d 123 (5th Cir. 1980), discussing that part of the Hobbs Act, 18 U.S.C.A. § 1951ff, which covers such conduct and, like the common law crime, does not require proof of threat, fear or duress. On the state level, modern criminal codes typically include as one kind of prohibited threat the threat to take or withhold official action.

house, or to accuse him of some crime other than sodomy, or to expose his failings or secrets or otherwise to damage his good name or business reputation. To fill this vacuum practically all states have enacted statutes[3] creating what is in effect a new crime—in some states called statutory extortion, in others blackmail, and generally carrying a penalty less severe than for robbery. These statutes vary greatly in their wording[4] and therefore in their coverage:

(1) Many statutes require that the defendant actually acquire the victim's property by reason of his threat;[5] but some require only that the defendant make a threat with intent thereby to acquire the victim's property. Under the former type of statute—the type which requires not just bad conduct but also a bad result of that conduct—the defendant is not guilty of extortion (blackmail) if the victim, threatened with harm by the defendant, pays the latter not because he fears his threats but in order to be able to prosecute him for the crime.[6] Moreover, under a statute of that type, it has been held that the victim's fear created by the defendant's threat must be the "operating or controlling" cause of the victim's parting with his property.[7] Under the latter type of statute, of course, there is no need to inquire about the causal relationship between the threat and the payment.[8]

(2) Some statutes require that the threats be written; but in most states the threats may be either written or oral.

(3) All statutes cover the demand for (or acquisition of) money; many statutes add the word "property"[9] or "chattel"; a few, worded more broadly, speak of "pecuniary advantage" or "anything of value" and the like. A number of statutes leave the realm of property altogether and cover threats made to induce the defendant to do "any act against his will"—as where the defendant by threats induces the victim to sign a statement admitting an illicit love affair with the defendant's wife.[10]

(4) Practically all the statutes cover threats to injure (i.e., to cause bodily harm to the person or to injure the property of) the victim or some other person. Thus a threat to kill the victim in the future, unless money is paid to the threatener, constitutes the crime of extortion (or blackmail). A threat to cause economic harm to another may under some circumstances be a threat to injure another's property, as where a corrupt labor leader threatens to call a strike of employees unless the employer pays a monetary tribute to the labor leader personally.[11] Some of the statutes specifically mention threats to unlawfully detain. Practically all the statutes cover threats to accuse the victim of a crime; and it

---

3. Comment, 44 Mich.L.Rev. 461, 466 (1945), cites statutes from virtually all states.

4. Comments, 44 Mich.L.Rev. 461 (1945); 54 Colum.L. Rev. 84 (1954), discuss the differences in these statutes.

5. If the property is not actually obtained, then there must be a prosecution for attempted extortion.

6. See People v. Gardner, 144 N.Y. 119, 38 N.E. 1003 (1894) (this is not extortion, but the defendant may be convicted of attempted extortion).

7. People v. Williams, 127 Cal. 212, 59 P. 581 (1899) (defendant threatened to accuse victim of adultery with her; he handed her money; the court gave an instruction that, although the victim may have been motivated in part by love for the defendant or by their past relationship, if her threat and his fear to any extent induced him to pay her the money, she is guilty of extortion; conviction of extortion *held* reversed, for the fear must be "the operating or controlling cause"). This requirement is analogous to the causation requirement in false pretenses, where the defendant's misrepresentations (rather than, in extortion, his threats) must be a "controlling" or a "material" or "substantial" inducement for the victim's transfer

of title of property to the defendant. See § 8.7(c). Perhaps, on the basis of the false pretenses analogy, "the controlling cause" is too strong language; "a substantial cause" ought to do, even though some other cause operated on the victim's mind with equal strength.

8. There may, however, be a requirement that the threat cause the victim to fear. Compare State v. Brownlee, 84 Iowa 473, 51 N.W. 25 (1892) (the threat must operate on the mind of the victim, to some extent, so as to induce fear); with State v. McGee, 80 Conn. 614, 69 A. 1059 (1908) (the threat need not actually induce fear, so long as a reasonable man would have been put in fear).

9. On the meaning of the word "property" in this context, see Annot., 67 A.L.R.3d 1021 (1975).

10. Furlotte v. State, 209 Tenn. 122, 350 S.W.2d 72 (1961), noted in 29 Tenn.L.Rev. 462 (1962), and in 15 Vand.L.Rev. at 862 (1962).

11. United States v. Compagna, 146 F.2d 524 (2d Cir. 1944) (under federal statute punishing obstruction of commerce by extortion); People v. Bolanos, 49 Cal.App.2d 308, 121 P.2d 753 (1942).

does not matter whether the threat is to file a formal complaint charging the victim with the crime or simply to publicize the fact that he has committed a crime. Most of the statutes include threats to expose some disgraceful defect or secret of the victim which, when known, would subject him to public ridicule or disgrace.[12] A smaller number of statutes specifically include threats to publish defamatory matter about the victim or to injure his personal character or business reputation.

It is, of course, no defense to extortion (blackmail) that the victim in fact is guilty of the crime, or possessor of the defect, which the defendant threatens to expose.[13] One may be privileged, or even be under a duty, to disclose the matter; but he must not use this as a means of acquiring money for himself from the other. There is a dispute concerning how far one who has in fact been injured by another's crime—for instance, the victim of the other's embezzlement or malicious mischief—can go in threatening to expose the wrongdoer's guilt of this very crime unless the latter makes reasonable restitution for the harm he has done. (Of course, he may not demand more than the damage done). Some courts find that in these circumstances

there is no "intent to extort or gain" as required by their statutes.[14] Other courts, dealing with statutes which do not specifically require an intent to gain, have found the threatener guilty under these same circumstances.[15] However, some modern statutes include a defense covering such circumstances.

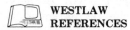

(b) Relationship to Other Crimes. Statutory extortion (or blackmail) is, of course, closely related to the crime of robbery, having in fact been created in order to plug a loophole in the robbery law by covering sundry threats which will not do for robbery. Besides differences in the necessary types of threats, the two crimes differ in these ways: (a) robbery by intimidation requires that the defendant acquire the victim's property as a result of his threat, whereas with statutory extortion most (but not all) statutes do not require this result; and (b) robbery requires that the property be taken from the person or

---

12. For cases interpreting such provisions, see Annot., 74 A.L.R.3d 1255 (1976).

13. People v. Eichler, 75 Hun 26, 26 N.Y.Supp. 998 (1894), appeal dismissed mem. 142 N.Y. 642, 37 N.E. 567 (1894).

14. Mann v. State, 47 Ohio St. 556, 26 N.E. 226 (1890); State v. Burns, 161 Wash. 362, 297 P. 212 (1931). Under this view, it would seem that an honest though mistaken belief that one has been damaged by another's criminal conduct would be a defense. The statement in *Burns,* supra, "If [the threatened person] embezzled no money, then appellants are guilty of extortion of the most dire type," apparently refers to a threatener who knows the other has not committed embezzlement. Possibly under this theory one who threatens to expose a crime in order to collect a debt not arising out of the crime itself would not be guilty of extortion, although no cases seem to go so far.

15. People v. Fichtner, 281 App.Div. 159, 118 N.Y.S.2d 392 (1952), affirmed mem. 305 N.Y. 864, 114 N.E.2d 212 (1953) (statute defines extortion as obtaining another's property through "a wrongful use of fear"; the court held that "the law does not authorize the collection of just debts by threatening to accuse the debtor of crime, even though the complainant is in fact guilty of the crime," and that "it makes no difference whether the indebtedness for which a defendant demands repayment is one arising out

of the crime for the prosecution of which he threatens the complainant, or is entirely independent and having no connection with the crime"); In re Sherin, 27 S.D. 232, 130 N.W. 761 (1911), modified on rehearing at 28 S.D. 420, 133 N.W. 701 (1911) (statute defines extortion as obtaining another's property through wrongful use of fear; defendant argued that the word "extort" implies a requirement of gain; the court, however, held that "one can extort that to which he is rightfully entitled, as well as that to which he is not entitled").

For a more complete collection of cases under the various statutes, see Annot., 135 A.L.R. 728 (1941), concluding that the weight of authority denies the defense to extortion that the threatener believed the money or property due him and believed the debtor guilty of the crime for which exposure is threatened.

One who collects a debt or supposed debt at gunpoint is not generally held guilty of robbery, at least if the debt is liquidated and the creditor takes no more than is owed him. See § 8.11(b). Why then should debt-collection by threats other than that of immediate bodily harm be treated differently? Perhaps a reason can be found in the fact that the former type of debt-collector can at least be found guilty of simple or aggravated assault in most states, while the latter type must generally be guilty of extortion or of nothing, for assault is not an available compromise.

presence of the victim, while extortion (even under those statutes which call for the defendant's acquisition of property) has no such limitation. It is sometimes said that robbery differs from statutory extortion in those states which require property acquisition in that in the former the taking of property must be "against the will" of the victim, while in the latter the taking must be "with the consent" of the victim, induced by the other's unlawful threat;[16] but, in spite of the different expressions, there is no difference here, for both crimes equally require that the defendant's threats induce the victim to give up his property, something which he would not otherwise have done.

Some cases involve a threat of harm of the extortion type (e.g., to accuse of a crime other than sodomy), backed up by a threat of immediate bodily injury, unless a payment be made. If the threatener by his multiple threats induces the victim to make the payment, he may be guilty of robbery.[17]

Statutory extortion is a crime related to false pretenses, the principal difference being that the former involves threats while the latter involves lies. False pretenses, of course, requires that property be obtained as a result of the lies; similarly, statutory extortion in some states requires that property be obtained as a result of the threats (though in most states it is enough to make the threats with intent to acquire the property). Some cases involve both lies and threats, as where a person, falsely representing himself to be a policeman, threatens to arrest and prosecute a violator for his crime. Such conduct has been held to constitute extortion rather than false pretenses, the lie being told merely to render the threat more effective.[18]

16. The words "against his will" and "without his consent, induced by a wrongful use of fear" often appear in robbery and extortion statutes respectively.

17. People v. Bodkin, 304 Ill. 124, 136 N.E. 494 (1922) (defendants, falsely claiming to be federal policemen, showed a gun and threatened to arrest victim for liquor violations unless paid money; victim, even after learning they were not in fact policemen, paid them; conviction of robbery *held* affirmed, for the victim's "impelling motive" in making the payment was the fear of bodily harm).

The fact that statutory extortion and false pretenses are closely related has led to the suggestion, discussed elsewhere in this book,[19] that extortion be consolidated, along with larceny, embezzlement, false pretenses and some other property crimes, into one large property crime called "theft."

WESTLAW REFERENCES

topic(165 342) /p robbery /s extortion

(c) Federal Extortion Statutes. Federal statutes punish extortion by federal government employees, blackmail by threatening to inform about federal crimes, the mailing of extortion letters, and extortions which interfere with interstate commerce, among other matters.

WESTLAW REFERENCES

topic(165) /p "interstate commerce"

§ 8.13 Burglary

Burglary was defined by the common law to be the breaking and entering of the dwelling house of another in the nighttime with the intent to commit a felony.[1] The offense was comprised of narrowly defined elements in order to meet the specific needs and reasons for the offense. Across the intervening centuries these elements have been expanded or discarded to such an extent that the modern-day offense commonly known as burglary bears little relation to its common-law ancestor.

WESTLAW REFERENCES

67k2 /p "common law"

18. Jackson v. State, 118 Ga. 125, 44 S.E. 833 (1903) (conviction of false pretenses *held* reversed, for the evidence showed blackmail).

19. See § 8.8.

§ 8.13

1. 4 W. Blackstone, Commentaries on the Laws of England* 224 (1769); 3 E. Coke, Institutes of the Laws of England 63 (1644); 2 E. East, Pleas of the Crown 484 (1803); 1 M. Hale, Pleas of the Crown 549 (1736).

(a) **Breaking.** In order to constitute a breaking at common law, there had to be the creation of a breach or opening; a mere trespass at law was insufficient.[2] If the occupant of the dwelling had created the opening, it was felt that he had not entitled himself to the protection of the law, as he had not properly secured his dwelling. Thus, it was uniformly held that entry through a pre-existing opening, such as an open door or window, did not constitute a breaking.[3] Similarly, it was held that if a door or window were partially open, the further opening of it was not a breaking.[4] The rationale was demonstrated in the exception made for entry through a chimney, which was held to be a breaking though it was through an existing opening because the occupants had rendered the structure as closed as possible and the opening could not be considered as inviting an offense.[5]

In requiring a breaking the law was not asking that the occupants of a dwelling turn their home into a fortress, but only that they not leave openings which would "invite" another to enter. For this reason the breaking need not involve force or violence, for once the house was closed the law protected it. Thus, the opening of a door or window which was closed but not locked in any way was a sufficient breaking.[6]

The law was not ready to punish one who had been "invited" in any way to enter the dwelling. The law sought only to keep out intruders, and thus anyone given authority to come into the house could not be committing a breaking when he so entered.[7] When the authority granted was restricted to certain portions of the structure or times of the day, there was a breaking when the structure was opened in violation of these restrictions.[8] Thus when a servant entered a section of a house without permission there was a breaking,[9] as the master had closed off the section and not invited him in; and when the servant opened the dwelling to a conspirator there was a breaking,[10] for the master could do no more to keep the intruder out. However, there could be no common-law breaking when the place was open to the public for then the owner had invited everyone in.[11]

When entry was gained by fraud[12] or threat of force,[13] a constructive breaking was deemed to have occurred.[14] Although this

---

2. 3 E. Coke, supra note 1, at 63.

3. 2 E. East, supra note 1, at 485; Rex v. Lewis, 2 C. & P. 628 (Oxford Cir.1827). See also State v. Dunbar, 282 S.C. 169, 318 S.E.2d 16 (1984), taking the same view as to the "breaking" element in a housebreaking statute.

4. 3 E. Coke, supra note 1, at 64; 4 W. Blackstone, supra note 1, at 226; 7 N. Dane, Abridgment of American Law 133–4 (1824). However, several jurisdictions in this country have held such to be a breaking. This view first appeared in Murmutt v. State, 67 S.W. 508 (Tex.Crim. 1902); and State v Sorenson, 157 Iowa 534, 138 N.W. 411 (1912), follows this view but admits that all earlier authority was against it. See Annot., 70 A.L.R.3d 881 (1976).

5. Rex v. Brice, [1821] R. & R. 450; 4 W. Blackstone, supra note 1, at 226; 1 W. Hawkins, Pleas of the Crown 160–61 (1787).

6. Rex v. Callen, [1809] Russ. & R. 157; Rex v. Hall, [1818] Russ. & R. 355; Rex v. Haines, [1821] Russ. & R. 451; State v. Boon, 35 N.C. (13 Ired.) 244 (1852).

7. 4 W. Blackstone, supra note 1, at 226–7; Turner v. State, 24 Tex.App. 12, 5 S.W. 511 (1887). If two share a dwelling neither can ordinarily commit a breaking, Clarke v. Commonwealth, 25 Grat. 908 (Va.1874). For a modern illustration of the same point, see State v. Steinbach, 101 Wn.2d 460, 679 P.2d 369 (1984) (14-year-old girl removed from mother's home by court order not guilty of burglary when she broke in, as neither the court order nor her mother prohibited her from returning home).

8. State v. Corcoran, 82 Wash. 44, 143 P. 453 (1914). For modern applications, see State v. Cochran, 191 Conn. 180, 463 A.2d 618 (1983) (invited guest in portion of single family home guilty of burglarizing bedroom therein); State v. McDonald, 346 N.W.2d 351 (Minn.1984) (though defendant had consent to enter public area of drug store during business hours, entry of nonpublic areas to steal drugs was burglary).

9. 1 M. Hale, supra note 1, at 554; Hild v. State, 67 Ala. 39 (1880); Lowder v. State, 63 Ala. 143 (1879).

10. 4 W. Blackstone, supra note 1, at 227; 1 M. Hale, supra note 1, at 553; Alexander v. State, 89 S.W. 642 (Tex. Crim.R.1906).

11. State v. Stephens, 150 La. 944, 91 So. 349 (1922); Love v. State, 52 Tex.Crim.R. 84, 105 S.W. 791 (1907); State v. Newbegin, 25 Me. 500 (1846).

12. Thieves who tricked a maid into opening a door by asking to speak with the master had committed a breaking, Le Mott's Case, 84 Eng.Rep. 1073 (1650). See also, Ann Hawkin's Case (1704), 2 E. East, supra note 1, at 485.

13. If the owner so opens his door to the offenders, there is a breaking, 1 W. Hawkins, supra note 5, at 161; but if he merely throws his money out to them there is none, 2 E. East, supra note 1, at 486.

14. There is also authority that a constructive breaking has occurred whenever a confederate within opens the

would seem an exception to the basic common-law rule, it is only an extension of its rationale. In this situation the occupant of the dwelling had not invited the offender into his home by a grant of authority or through his negligence. The intruder had indeed caused the opening of the structure. If the occupant had a reasonable chance to close the opening procured in this manner, then no breaking would have occurred,[15] as it would have been the owner who allowed the opening to invite an intrusion.

It was disputed whether one who gained entry without a breaking, but committed a breaking in order to leave, was guilty of burglary.[16] The correct view was that of Hale, who explained that the burglary indictment charged "fregit intravit" (breaking and entering), so that "fregit & excivit" (breaking and leaving) would not suffice.[17] This would also be in accord with the rationale for requiring a breaking as a part of the offense. If no breaking had occurred until the leaving, any intrusion that had occurred was due to the occupant's negligence or granting of authority. In England the question was settled by a statute making the breaking to leave a sufficient breaking for commission of the offense.[18] In this country, courts have continued to follow the original distinction in defining what constitutes a sufficient breaking.[19]

A breaking occurs if a part of the house was opened even though the original entry into the structure was gained without a breaking.[20] The opening of an article which was not a part of the structure would not suffice as a breaking.[21]

In the modern American criminal codes, only seldom is there a requirement of a breaking. This is not to suggest, however, that elimination of this requirement has left the "entry" element unadorned, so that any type of entry will suffice. Rather, at least *some* of what was encompassed within the common law "breaking" element is reflected by other terms describing what kind of entry is necessary. The most common statutory term is "unlawfully," but some jurisdictions use other language, such as "unauthorized," by "trespass," "without authority," "without consent," or "without privilege."

Though these statutory formulae are not in all respects identical, they generally require that the entry be unprivileged. A more precise way of describing this situation is by excluding those entries of premises when they are open to the public or by a person licensed or privileged to enter.[22] This is a sound approach. It "retains the core of the common-law conception" of breaking but yet excludes those situations which "involve no surreptitious intrusion" and "no element of aggravation of the crime that the actor proposes to carry out."[23] But these statutes have not always been interpreted in this way.[24]

---

door to admit the defendant. State v. Smith, 311 N.C. 145, 316 S.E.2d 75 (1984).

15. State v. Henry, 31 N.C. (9 Ired.) 463 (1849). However, this requirement is not mentioned in the early authorities.

16. 4 W. Blackstone, supra note 1, at 227.

17. 1 M. Hale, supra note 1, at 554.

18. 12 Anne c. 7 (1713).

19. Rolland v. Commonwealth, 82 Pa. 306 (1876); Adkinson v. State, 64 Tenn. 569 (1875). Contra: State v. Ward, 43 Conn. 489 (1876), which held the belief that the statute was only declaratory of the common law.

20. Marshall v. State, 94 Ga. 589, 20 S.E. 432 (1894); 1 W. Hawkins, supra note 5, at 161; 7 N. Dane, Abridgment of the American Law 135 (1824).

21. State v. Wilson, 1 N.J.L. 439 (1793); 2 M. Bacon Abridgment of the Law 134 (1854); 1 M. Hale, supra note 1, at 554. Whether the opening of a cabinet or closet

constituted a breaking depended upon whether it was a part of the structure, Allen v. State, 28 Okl.Crim. 373, 231 P. 96 (1924); See also State v. Wilson, 1 N.J.L. 439 (1793).

22. Model Penal Code § 221.1 takes this approach, which has been followed in some states.

23. Model Penal Code § 221.1, Comment at 69 (1980), describing the excluded situations as where "a servant enters his employer's house as he normally is privileged to do, intending on the occasion to steal some silver; a shoplifter enters a department store during business hours to steal from the counters; a litigant enters the courthouse with intent to commit perjury; a fireman called on to put out a fire resolves, as he breaks down the door of the burning house, to misappropriate some of the householder's belongings."

24. See, e.g., State v. Baker, 183 Neb. 499, 161 N.W.2d 864 (1968) (though defendant had consent to enter store to do custodial work, his entry still "unlawful" because of his intent to steal existing at the time of entry).

WESTLAW REFERENCES

67k9 /p trespass***

67k9 /p "constructive breaking" (creat*** exist*** /2 opening)

(b) Entry. Following the breaking there had to be an entry by the actor. It was sufficient if any part of the actor's person intruded, even momentarily, into the structure.[25] Thus it has been held that the intrusion of a part of a hand in opening a window,[26] or the momentary intrusion of part of a foot in kicking out a window,[27] constituted the requisite entry.

If the actor instead used some instrument which protruded into the structure, no entry occurred unless he was simultaneously using the instrument to achieve his felonious purpose.[28] Thus there was no entry where an instrument was used to open the building, even though it protruded into the structure;[29] but if the actor was also using the instrument to reach some property therein, then it constituted an entry.[30]

A constructive entry occurred when a person sent one incapable of committing an offense or one under his control into the building to achieve his felonious purpose. Thus, when an adult sent a child through an opening or a husband ordered his wife into the building, this sufficed; the person so ordered was only a tool being used by the actor.[31]

There must be a causal connection between the breaking and entering to fulfill the requirement. Thus if one gained admittance

without a breaking but committed a breaking once inside, there could be no burglary unless there was an entry through this breaking.[32] However, the entry may be separate in time from the breaking. If a man causes a breaking on one night and returns the next and enters through the breach he previously created, then there would be a sufficient breaking and entering to sustain the offense.[33]

The requirement of an entry appears almost uniformly in modern burglary statutes. While under some of these statutes only an "entry" of the requisite type[34] will suffice, far more common today is the burglary statute which covers one who either enters or remains in the premises. This means, of course, that the requisite intent to commit a crime within need only exist at the time the defendant unlawfully remained within.[35]

This common statutory expansion in the definition of burglary makes great sense. A lawful entry does not foreclose the kind of intrusion burglary is designed to reach, as is illustrated by the case of a bank customer who hides in the bank until it closes and then takes the bank's money. Moreover, this expansion forecloses any argument by a defendant found in premises then closed that he had entered earlier when they were open.[36] But for this expansion not also to cover certain other situations in which the unlawful remaining ought not be treated as burglary,[37] it is best to limit the remaining-within alternative to where that conduct is done surreptitiously.[38]

25. 2 E. East, supra note 1, at 490. See People v. King, 61 N.Y.2d 550, 475 N.Y.S.2d 260, 463 N.E.2d 601 (1984), concluding "entry" element in statute has this common law meaning.

26. Rex v. Bailey, [1818] Russ. & R. 341.

27. People v. Roldan, 100 Ill.App.2d 81, 241 N.E.2d 591 (1968).

28. Neither Coke, Blackstone, nor Hale make the distinction, though it might be implied from their examples. 1 W. Hawkins, supra note 5, at 161–62, queries whether this is not the proper distinction, and 2 E. East, supra note 1, at 490, states that such is the law though it was not mentioned in the earlier writings.

29. Mattox v. State, 179 Ind. 575, 101 N.E. 1009 (1913).

30. Walker v. State, 63 Ala. 49 (1873); 1 Hale, supra note 1, at 555.

31. 1 M. Hale, supra note 1, at 555–6.

32. Regina v. Davis, 6 Cox Crim.Cas. 369 (1854).

33. Rex v. Smith, Russ. & R. 417, 168 Eng.Rep. 874 (1820).

34. See § 8.13(a) on the qualifying terms used in modern burglary statutes.

35. See § 8.13(e).

36. See Model Penal Code § 221.1, Comment (1980).

37. For example, where a visitor in one's home becomes involved in an argument with his host, threatens to punch him in the nose and is asked to leave, and then after he does not leave continues his threats. Id.

38. As in Model Penal Code § 221.1. Some states have followed this approach.

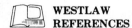

67k9   /p   intru!
67k9(3)

(c) Dwelling of Another. The third and fourth requirements of the offense, that the invaded structure be the dwelling house of another, were essential because common-law burglary found its theoretical basis in the protection of man's right of habitation. Blackstone wrote that burglary was a heinous offense because of its invasion of this right, which each man could punish with death and which, in a civilized society, the law would punish similarly.[39] Indeed, the very term "burglar" indicates a "house-thief" when broken down to its original components.[40] It was, therefore, of prime importance to determine what structures would qualify as dwelling houses under the common law.

The original term used in defining burglary was "mansion house,"[41] but from its introduction the term was understood to include all dwellings, regardless of their size or worth.[42] Because the basis of the crime was invasion of the right of habitation, the structure need only be a dwelling, that is, a place of human habitation, and occupancy rather than ownership was determinative.[43]

If the place is one of human habitation, there is no requirement that a person be present therein at the time of the offense. If

the residents are away, be it for a short time or for extended portions of the year,[44] it will still suffice as a dwelling house. However, an unfinished house will not so qualify,[45] even if a workman constantly sleeps therein for the purpose of protection.[46] A place of business may be the subject of burglary if it is usually slept in by the proprietor or one of his employees.[47] A place of business used only during the day will not so qualify,[48] but if it is attached to a residence it will.[49]

When several persons resided in the same structure, the charge was to be a burglary of the mansion house of the proprietor.[50] This distinction later became irrelevant, as it went only to the form of the indictment. A hotel room or an apartment [51] may be the subject of a burglary, as they are places of residence.

Buildings not used for habitation (such as barns, stables, and other outhouses) might still be the subject of burglary if they were part of the messuage or curtilage of the mansion house.[52] They were included under the term mansion house because such a residence was usually surrounded by such buildings.[53] The question was whether they were spacially close enough to the dwelling to be deemed part of the curtilage.[54] The curtilage originally signified a fenced-in area,[55] and it would seem that the buildings need be close enough to the residence to have been included in a

39. 4 W. Blackstone, supra note 1, at 223.

40. 3 E. Coke, supra note 1, at 63.

41. The offense had to be charged as having occurred in a mansion house, 1 W. Hawkins, supra note 5, at 162.

42. 3 E. Coke, supra note 1, at 64.

43. Ibid.

44. J. Kelyng, Cases in the Reign of Charles II 52 (1708). See also State v. Albert, 426 A.2d 1370 (Me.1981) (reaching the same result as to the statutory term "dwelling place," used to define a more serious grade of burglary); Commonwealth v. Kingsbury, 378 Mass. 751, 393 N.E.2d 391 (1979) (statutory term "dwelling house" covers apartment with no furniture or personal effects, where tenants had taken possession); State v. Ervin, 96 N.M. 366, 630 P.2d 765 (1981) (statutory term "dwelling house" includes house unoccupied over a year, absent evidence occupant had abandoned the house. Compare State v. Ferebee, 273 S.C. 403, 257 S.E.2d 154 (1979) (where former tenant abandoned the premises, there was no new tenant, and owner never occupied the apartment, it not a dwelling).

45. Rex v. Lyons, 1 Leech's Cr.Cas. 185 (1778).

46. Fuller's Case, 1 Leech's Cr.Cas. 186 (1782).

47. 1 M. Hale, supra note 1, at 557.

48. 1 W. Hawkins, supra note 5, at 164.

49. Rex v. Gibson, Multon, & Wiggs, 1 Leech's Cr.Cas. 357 (1785). See Minneman v. State, 466 N.E.2d 438 (Ind. 1984), following this view in construing the word "dwelling" in a burglary statute.

50. 2 E. East, supra note 1, at 502; 1 M. Hale, supra note 1, at 557.

51. People v. Carr, 225 Ill. 203, 99 N.E. 357 (1912); see also 3 E. Coke, supra note 1, at 65. But see Robinson v. State, 364 So.2d 1131 (Miss.1978).

52. 4 W. Blackstone, supra note 1, at 225.

53. 1 M. Hale, supra note 1, at 558.

54. 2 M. Bacon, Abridgment of the Law 136 (1854); 1 M. Hale, supra note 1, at 558–9.

55. 2 E. East, supra note 1, at 493; see also State v. Brooks, 4 Conn. 446 (1823).

reasonable fencing,[56] but the breaking of the curtilage itself was not an offense.[57] At common law, there was no requirement that the buildings be connected to the residence;[58] however, the English have since changed this by statute.[59]

The fourth requirement was that the dwelling house be that of another. Therefore it had to be determined whose dwelling was invaded, for one could not commit a burglary against his own dwelling.[60] As it was the right of habitation and not the ownership of property that was being protected, occupancy controlled the question of whether the dwelling was that of another.[61]

If several people occupy the same dwelling, none may commit a burglary thereto as it is not the property of another.[62] However, if a portion of the structure has been set aside for one resident, as in letting an apartment, any of the others (including the owner) could commit a burglary into that portion of the dwelling.[63] Some commentators said this was so only if there was a separate entrance to that portion,[64] but the proper common-law view was that the rooms may have been so set aside regardless of the exits or entrances.[65]

A transient guest or lodger does not have such an interest in the dwelling that the burglary could be charged as against his habitation.[66] A burglary would still have occurred, but at common law it had to be charged as one against the mansion house of the landlord.[67] There would be a burglary if the structure was used as a dwelling by agents of the state [68] or of a corporation,[69] and this is so although no one individual has occupied it in such a way as to be deemed a possessor or occupant of the structure.

There is no jurisdiction which retains the common-law requirement that the offense take place against a dwelling house or building within its curtilage for all degrees of the offense, though some require that the offense be against a dwelling house for a higher grade of the offense. Modern statutes instead typically describe the place as a "building" or "structure," and these terms are often broadly construed.[70] Some burglary statutes also extend to still other places,[71] such as all or some types of vehicles.[72]

The requirement that the structure be that of another has virtually disappeared from the wording of modern burglary statutes. Under

56. State v. Bugg, 66 Kan. 668, 72 P. 236 (1903); 2 E. East, supra note 1, at 493; Hale felt the buildings must be within a "bow shot" of the mansion house, 1 M. Hale, supra note 1, at 559; separation by a road is conclusive of not being within the curtilage, Rex v. Westwood, Russ. & R. 495, 168 Eng.Rep. 915 (1822).

57. This was apparently connected with a more ancient form of the offense, 4 Blackstone, supra note 1, at 226; 3 Holdsworth A., History of English Law 369 (3d ed.1923).

58. 4 W. Blackstone, supra note 1, at 225; 3 E. Coke, supra note 1, at 65.

59. 7 & 8 Geo. IV c. 29, § 13 (1827).

60. 2 E. East, supra note 1, at 507.

61. White v. State, 49 Ala. 344 (1873); State v. Williams, 12 Mo.App. 591 (1882); State v. Harold, 312 N.C. 787, 325 S.E.2d 219 (1985).

Application of this principle under modern burglary laws has resulted in the holding that an estranged husband can commit burglary of the former family home in which he no longer lives. State v. Herrin, 6 Ohio App.3d 68, 453 N.E.2d 1104 (1982); Knox v. Commonwealth, 225 Va. 504, 304 S.E.2d 4 (1983).

62. Clarke v. Commonwealth, 66 Va. (25 Grat.) 908 (1874).

63. 2 E. East, supra note 1, at 504; 1 W. Hawkins, supra note 5, at 163.

64. 2 E. East, supra note 1, at 505; J. Kelyng, Cases in the Reign of Charles II 84 (1708).

65. 1 M. Hale, supra note 1, at 556–7; 1 W. Hawkins, supra note 5, at 163.

66. 1 M. Hale, supra note 1, at 557; 4 W. Blackstone, supra note 1, at 556–7, might be interpreted as holding the opposite.

67. 1 M. Hale, supra note 1, at 557.

68. Id. at 522.

69. 4 W. Blackstone, supra note 1, at 225; 2 E. East, supra note 1, at 501.

70. See, e.g., State v. Bronson, 259 N.W.2d 465 (Minn. 1977) (statutory term "building" covers site used for basketball being converted to ice arena and presently without one wall). But there are limits; see, e.g., State v. Fisher, 232 Kan. 760, 658 P.2d 1021 (1983) (open-air, free-standing low-fenced hog pens not "structures" within meaning of burglary statute).

71. Even telephone booths have been found to receive the extra protection of a burglary statute. Sanchez v. People, 142 Colo. 58, 349 P.2d 561 (1960).

72. This may make sense in some circumstances, as where the vehicle is a motor home (as specified in the Wis. statute), but many of these provisions have been broadly interpreted to extend to situations which ought not be treated as burglary. See, e.g., State v. Pierre, 320 So.2d

the language of these statues it might seem that a man could be convicted of burglary for entering his own home if he intends to beat his wife or file a fraudulent tax return. But this problem is generally taken care of by the usual requirement that the entry be un-privileged.[73] In some circumstances, however, determining what that means may involve problems not unlike those which arose because of the "of another" element.[74]

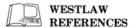

WESTLAW REFERENCES

topic(67) /p dwell*** /s abandoned unoccupied (not +2 occupied) incomplete unfinished empty /3 house home building premises residence

topic(67) /p dwelling premises residence /p estranged wife ex-husband ex-spouse

(d) Nighttime. Although the requirement that the acts be committed in the night may not have been required in the ancient common law,[75] by the time of Lord Coke it was an essential element of the offense.[76] Indeed, this element became one of the theoretical bases for the offense, as the night was considered the time when honest men might fall prey to criminals.[77]

The distinction between day and night was whether the countenance of a man could be discerned by natural light even though the sun may have set.[78] Artificial light or moonlight, regardless of their intensity, would not suffice.[79] Some have thought that the distinction rested merely on whether the act was committed after sunset and before sunrise, but this view is clearly erroneous. As far

back as the time of Coke the question was determined by the visibility of a man's countenance,[80] and before this there was only the ancient crime of Hamsoaken which need not have been committed at night.[81]

While the acts had to take place during the night, there was no requirement that they be done during the same night. If the breaking occurred one night and the entry the next, this would be sufficient.[82]

There is no jurisdiction which presently requires for all grades of the offense that the acts be done in the night. It has been retained as a required element for higher degrees of the offense in some jurisdictions, while it has been entirely discarded in the remaining jurisdictions. Of those retaining it for some degrees, one defines it to be the period between sunset and sunrise, while the others declare it to be from thirty minutes past sunset to thirty minutes before sunrise. No jurisdiction has yet taken the English statutory approach of setting specific times to define the nighttime.[83]

WESTLAW REFERENCES

67k8 /p "common law"

67k8 /p night! light*** daylight twilight

(e) Intent to Commit a Felony. To have committed the offense of burglary at common law, one must have intended to commit a felony while fulfilling the other requirements.[84] If the actor when he was breaking and entering only intended to commit a sim-

---

185 (La.1975) (simple burglary committed by opening hood of car and taking battery).

73. See § 8.13(a).

74. See, e.g., Cladd v. State, 398 So.2d 442 (Fla.1981) (where husband physically but not legally separated from wife, he may be convicted of burglary based on entry of home then possessed only by wife; husband's consortium rights do not require different result).

75. 3 W. Holdsworth, History of the Common Law 369 (1923).

76. 3 E. Coke, supra note 1, at 63.

77. 4 W. Blackstone, supra note 1, at 224.

78. 4 W. Blackstone, supra note 1, at 224; 3 E. Coke, supra note 1, at 63; 1 M. Hale, supra note 1, at 550–51.

79. 2 M. Bacon, Abridgment of the Law 135 (1854); 4 W. Blackstone, supra note 1, at 224; 7 N. Dane, Abridgment of American Law 134 (1824).

80. 3 E. Coke, supra note 1, at 63.

81. 3 W. Holdsworth, History of the Common Law 369 (1923).

82. 1 M. Hale, supra note 1, at 551.

83. 6 & 7 Geo. V, c. 50 § 46 (9 p.m. to 6 a.m.)

84. 3 E. Coke, supra note 1, at 65. Otherwise the offense "is only a trespass," 4 W. Blackstone, supra note 1, at 227.

Thus the intent must exist at the time of the entry, People v. Hill, 67 Cal.2d 105, 60 Cal.Rptr. 234, 429 P.2d 586 (1967), although this may not be the case as to those statutes, cited note 44 supra, under which either entry or unlawfully remaining within suffices.

ple trespass, he was not guilty of a burglary although he in fact committed a felony after entering.[85] If he broke and entered the house of another in the nighttime with only the intent to strike someone therein, it would not be burglary even if the victim died from the blow.[86] However, if the intent to commit a felony existed at the time, it made no difference that this purpose was not achieved.[87]

There was doubt expressed as to whether the intent to commit a statutory felony rather than a common-law felony would suffice.[88] The accepted common-law view was that the intent to commit either fulfilled the requirement.[89] It should also be noted that simply charging the defendant with the "intent to steal" was sufficient, as all larceny was a felony at common law.[90]

The intent must be to commit a felony within the dwelling house.[91] Thus it would not be a burglary to pass through a dwelling as a matter of choice on the way to an offense elsewhere, although it would be if the route was necessary to reach the object or situs of the intended crime.[92]

This final requirement has also been revised by modern statutory schemes. Virtually no jurisdictions require an intent to commit a felony for all forms of the offense. Not at all uncommon, however, are statutes requiring that the actor have an intent to commit a felony or some form of theft within the structure. This is not a significant change, as

the common-law definition also included theft.[93] But the prevailing view in the modern codes is that an intent to commit any offense will do. This is a sound position, as "an intrusion for any criminal purpose creates elements of alarm and danger to persons who may be present in a place where they should be entitled to freedom from intrusion."[94]

One jurisdiction, perhaps to obviate the problems of proof concerning whether the defendant's intent was formed before or after the unlawful entry or remaining, has expressly provided that actual commission of the offense within is an alternative basis for conviction. Of course, if the prosecution cannot prove the requisite intent and even if the crime never occurred, the defendant's conduct will in many jurisdictions fall within a lesser offense, usually denominated criminal trespass.

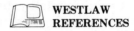

WESTLAW REFERENCES

67k3 /p intent*** /4 felony /s time

(f) Aggravated Burglary. In the modern criminal codes, it is quite common for there to exist statutory definitions of different types of burglary of varying levels of seriousness (and, consequently, subject to varying levels of punishment). Sometimes this is accomplished by a series of statutes called burglary in the first, second and (perhaps) third degree; sometimes

---

85. 4 W. Blackstone, supra note 1, at 227; 7 N. Dane, Abridgment of the American Law 137 (1824).

86. 3 E. Coke, supra note 1, at 65; 2 E. East, supra note 1, at 513.

87. 4 W. Blackstone, supra note 1, at 227; 3 E. Coke, supra note 1, at 65.

88. 1 M. Hale, supra note 1, at 562.

89. 2 M. Bacon, Abridgment of the Law 139 (1854); 7 N. Dane, Abridgment of American Law 137 (1824); 1 W. Hawkins, supra note 5, at 164.

90. 1 M. Hale, supra note 1, at 561.

91. 3 E. Coke, supra note 1, at 63.

92. People v. Wright, 206 Cal.App.2d 184, 23 Cal.Rptr. 734 (1945). Consider also Robles v. State, 664 S.W.2d 91 (Tex.Crim.App.1984) (where defendant forced his way into bank president's home, intending to take president to bank and then steal money there, conviction of burglary proper, as statute does not require that intent to steal be re property within premises entered).

Compare State v. O'Rourke, 121 R.I. 434, 399 A.2d 1237 (1979) (statutory "felony therein" language barred conviction for burglary of apartment where it entered with purpose of breaking through common wall to adjoining drug store).

93. 1 M. Hale, supra note 1, at 561.

94. Model Penal Code § 221.1, Comment at 75 (1980). As further noted therein: "Their perception of alarm and danger, moreover, will not depend on the particular purpose of the intruder. The fact that he may be contemplating a minor offense will be no solace to those who may reasonably fear the worst and who may react with measures that may well escalate the criminal purposes of the intruder." Also, if the statute extends to an intent to commit any crime, difficult problems of proof regarding exactly what kind of crime was intended can be avoided. See note 126 infra.

by statutes with other varying offense labels; and sometimes within a single statute which identifies certain aggravating circumstances which escalate the crime up to a higher level. As to what constitutes the requisite aggravating circumstances, we have already noted two common factors: that the place entered was a dwelling; and that the offense occurred in the nighttime. Even more common as legislatively-defined aggravating circumstances are that the defendant was armed in some way while committing the burglary or that he injured (or perhaps, only threatened to injure) a person in the premises. Some jurisdictions have adopted the view that the burglary is of the more serious kind whenever there was a person inside the place entered.

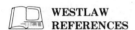
WESTLAW REFERENCES

67k10 /p aggravated /3 burglary

(g) Critique. The statutory revision of the offense, when viewed in totality, has resulted in a modern crime which has little in common with its common-law ancestor except for the title of burglary.[95] The modern offense cannot be justified from its history. It cannot be rationalized as giving a recognized protection to citizens who have secured themselves in their homes, as was its ancestor, for the requirements of a breaking and entering of a dwelling house have been eroded. it cannot be justified any longer as protecting helpless citizens from the brigands who roam in the night, as the requirement that the acts occur in the nighttime is also vanishing. Nor is

protection from serious crime a justification for the offense, for the intent requirement itself is beginning to be eroded.

Burglary is in fact a rather unique type of attempt law, as all the required elements merely comprise a step taken toward the commission of some other offense. While such an approach might have filled a void in the law of attempts during an earlier period,[96] it is doubtful that the offense is any longer required to punish or deter such preliminary conduct. An expanded law of attempts is now available to reach such conduct.[97]

The one feature of burglary which separates it from other attempts and from theft crimes generally is the punishment inflicted upon the offender. Unlike the usual attempt, burglary is generally held not to merge into a completed offense, thus allowing punishment for the offense committed and also for attempting to commit it in this particular way.[98] The punishment for the burglary itself [99] is usually far greater than for most of the offenses which might actually be committed within the structure. This might suggest that the best way to deal with the offense of burglary would be to abolish it. So the argument goes, modern laws of attempt would better serve in punishing the conduct, as this would better ensure a punishment rationally connected to the grievousness of the offense which was being attempted; an attempted petty theft would no longer be punishable as severely as an attempted murder.[100]

---

95. For other surveys of this development, see Notes, 51 Colum.L.Rev. 1009 (1951); 100 U.Pa.L.Rev. 411 (1951).

96. See Model Penal Code § 221.1, Comment at 63 (1980).

97. See §§ 6.2, 6.3. But there remains one difficult problem: "It is not uncommon for surreptitious entry to occur under circumstances where law enforcement officials are hard pressed to establish precisely what crime the actor contemplated within the premises. * * * An attempt prosecution would require just such specific proof, whereas prosecution under a burglary statute requires only that it be established that the intrusion was made as a conscious step toward the accomplishment of one of a number of possible criminal objectives." Model Penal Code § 221.1, Comment at 67–68 (1980).

98. Such double punishment is currently allowed in most states, e.g., State v. Arnold, 115 Ariz. 421, 565 P.2d

1282 (1977); People v. Manning, 71 Ill.2d 132, 15 Ill.Dec. 765, 374 N.E.2d 200 (1978); State v. Davis, 613 S.W.2d 218 (Tenn.1981). Sometimes statutes specifically declare that a person may be convicted of both burglary and the object offense. There is no statute which forbids such a double punishment generally, but in a few jurisdictions it is allowed only where the offense committed was a felony.

99. The very high maximum penalties traditionally found in burglary statutes "have been continued under the most aggravated forms of burglary defined in recently drafted codes." Model Penal Code § 221.1, Comment at 78 n. 56 (1980).

100. Burglarious intrusion might nonetheless be made an element of aggravation in grading certain crimes. See Model Penal Code § 221.1, Comment at 66–67 (1980).

A second approach is demonstrated by the Model Penal Code. The draftsmen expressed the desire to abolish the offense, but realized that it was so imbedded in the laws and minds of legislatures that this would be impossible.[101] The Model Penal Code approach is thus to narrow the offense considerably in order to bring its coverage back more closely to that of its common-law ancestor.[102] Because the common-law requirement of "breaking" had given rise to absurd distinctions, it is not included; but the "core of the common-law conception," [103] entry without privilege, is retained so as to avoid such bizarre results as convicting a shoplifter of burglary when his intent to steal existed prior to walking into the store.[104] The Code provision covers entry of a "building or occupied structure" [105] which has not been abandoned,[106] thus eliminating the prospect of a burglary conviction for such acts as stealing from an unoccupied phone booth,[107] car,[108] or cave.[109] The purpose to

commit any crime is sufficient under the Code, but this is rationalized on the ground that (a) the offense is otherwise limited, as explained above; (b) the offense carried moderate penalties except in circumstances of special danger; [110] and (c) it comports better with the realities of law enforcement, in that when the burglar is apprehended his precise criminal purpose may be unclear.[111] The "dwelling of another" and "nighttime" elements of the common law are utilized for grading purposes.[112] Finally, conviction for burglary and also for the crime intended upon entry or for an attempt to commit that crime is barred except where the intended crime is a most serious one.[113]

WESTLAW REFERENCES

burglary /s "model penal code"
burglary /p (51 +4 1009) (100 +4 411)

101. Model Penal Code § 221.1, Comment at 67 (1980).

102. Model Penal Code § 221.1.

103. Model Penal Code § 221.1, Comment at 69 (1980).

104. See People v. Sine, 277 App.Div. 908, 98 N.Y.S.2d 588 (1950); noted in 19 Ford.L.Rev. 323 (1950); 2 Syracuse L.Rev. 193 (1950).

105. The latter is defined in Code § 221.0(2) as "any structure, vehicle or place adapted for overnight accommodation of persons, or for carrying on business therein, whether or not a person is actually present."

106. That the building or structure was abandoned is an affirmative defense. Model Penal Code § 221.1(1).

107. People v. Clemison, 105 Cal.App.2d 679, 233 P.2d 924 (1951); People v. Miller, 95 Cal.App.2d 631, 213 P.2d 534 (1950).

108. People v. Chambers, 102 Cal.App.2d 696, 228 P.2d 93 (1951).

109. People v. Buyle, 22 Cal.App.2d 143, 70 P.2d 955 (1937).

110. Burglary is a felony of the third degree (punishable by imprisonment for a term with a minimum of one to

two years and a maximum of five years, Model Penal Code § 6.06) except when it is perpetrated in the dwelling of another at night or if, in the course of committing the offense, the actor purposely, knowingly, or recklessly inflicts or attempts to inflict bodily injury on anyone, or he is armed with explosives or a deadly weapon, in which case it is a felony of the second degree (punishable by imprisonment for a term with a minimum of one to three years and a maximum of ten years, ibid). Model Penal Code § 221.1(2).

111. Model Penal Code § 221.1, Comment at 75 (1980).

112. See note 110 supra. "Night" is defined as the period between thirty minutes past sunset and thirty minutes before sunrise. Model Penal Code § 221.0(2).

113. Conviction for both is permitted only when the additional offense constitutes a felony of the first or second degree, Model Penal Code § 221.1(3), which under the Code means only such crimes as murder, manslaughter, kidnapping, rape, arson, and robbery. Some jurisdictions follow essentially this approach. See, e.g., State v. Cloutier, 286 Or. 579, 596 P.2d 1278 (1979).

*

Appendix A
WESTLAW REFERENCES

Analysis

Introduction

This informational appendix is designed to aid the reader in the general use of the WESTLAW system and more specifically to demonstrate how WESTLAW can be used in conjunction with this text to help make research in the area of substantive criminal law swift and complete.

The WESTLAW System

WESTLAW is a computer-assisted legal research service of West Publishing Company. It is accessible through a number of different types of computer terminals. The materials available through WESTLAW are contained in databases stored at the central computer in St. Paul, Minnesota.

To use the WESTLAW service a "query" or search request is typed into the terminal and sent to the central computer. There it is processed and all of the documents that satisfy the search request are identified. The text of each of these documents is then stored on magnetic disks and transmitted to the user via a telecommunication network. This data then appears on the user's terminal, where it may be reviewed and evaluated. The user must then decide if the displayed documents are pertinent or if further research is desired. If further research is necessary, the query may be recalled for editing, or an entirely new query may be sent. Documents displayed on the terminal may be printed or, on some terminals, the text may be stored on its own magnetic disks.

Improving Legal Research with WESTLAW

The WESTLAW system is designed for use in conjunction with the more traditional tools of legal research. In principle, WESTLAW works as an index to primary and secondary legal materials. Yet it differs from traditional digests and indices in that more terms can be researched, and more documents retrieved.

Through WESTLAW it is possible to index, or search for any significant term or combination of terms in an almost infinite variety of grammatical relationships by formulating a query composed of those terms. Unlike manual systems of secondary legal sources that reference only a few key terms in each document, WESTLAW is capable of indexing every key word. This enables documents to be located using terms not even listed in manual reference systems.

In addition to its expanded search term capabilities, WESTLAW, through its numerous databases, enables the user to research issues in any and every jurisdiction quickly and efficiently. The queries found in this text are primarily designed to access WESTLAW's federal and state case law databases. However, WESTLAW provides access to many specialized libraries as well. For example, WESTLAW contains separate topical databases for areas of federal and state law such as tax, securities, energy, and government contracts.

WESTLAW also includes the text of the United States Code and the Code of Federal Regulations, the Federal Register, West's INSTA–CITE ™, Shepard's ® Citations, *Black's Law Dictionary* and many other legal sources. Furthermore, because new cases are continuously being added to the WESTLAW databases as they are decided by the courts, the documents retrieved will include the most current law available on any given issue.

In addition, WESTLAW queries augment the customary role of footnotes to text by directing the user to a wider range of supporting authorities. Readers may use the preformulated queries supplied in this edition "as is" or formulate their own queries in order to retrieve cases relevant to the points of law discussed in the text.

Query Formulation: (a) General Principles

The art of query formulation is the heart of WESTLAW research. Although the researcher can gain technical skills by using the terminal, there is no strictly mechanical procedure for formulating queries. One must first comprehend the meaning of the legal issue to be researched before beginning a search on WESTLAW. Then the user will need to supply imagination, insight, and legal comprehension with knowledge of the capabilities of WESTLAW to formulate a useful query. Effective query formulation requires an alternative way of thinking about the legal research process.

Using WESTLAW is a constant balancing between generating too many documents and missing important documents. In general, it is better to look through a reasonable number of irrelevant documents than it is to be too restrictive and miss important material. The researcher should take into consideration at the initial query formulation stage what he or she will do if too many, or not enough documents are retrieved. Thought should be given as to how the query might be narrowed or the search broadened, and what can be done if the initial search retrieves zero documents.

Some issues by their very nature will require more lengthy queries than others; however, it is best to strive for efficiency in structuring the query. Look for unique search terms that will eliminate the need for a lengthy query. Keep in mind that WESTLAW is literal. Consider all possible alternative terms. Especially consider inherent limitations of the computer. It doesn't think, create, or make analogies. The researcher must do that for the computer. The computer is designed to look for the terms in the documents in relationships specified by the query. The researcher should know what he or she is looking for, at least to the extent of knowing how the terms are likely to show up in relevant documents. Always keep in mind the parameters of the system as to date and database content.

The WESTLAW Reference Manual should be consulted for more information on query formulation and WESTLAW commands. The Reference Manual is updated periodically to reflect new enhancements of WESTLAW. It provides detailed and comprehensive instructions on all aspects of the WESTLAW system and offers numerous illustrative examples on the proper format for various types of queries. Material contained in the Reference Manual enables the user to benefit from all of the system's capabilities in an effective and efficient manner.

Query Formulation: (b) The WESTLAW Query Defined

The query is a message to WESTLAW. It instructs the computer to retrieve documents containing terms in the grammatical relationships specified by the query. The terms in a query are made up of words and/or numbers that pinpoint the legal issue to be researched.

An example of the kind of preformulated queries that appear in this publication is reproduced below. The queries corresponding to each section of the text appear at the end of the section.

The query appearing below is taken from Chapter 3, Section 3.10(b) and appears at the end of this section of the text.

```
corporat*** company  /s  criminal** penal  /s  liab!
responsib!  /p  employee agent representative  /p
public  /4  policy welfare interest
```

This query instructs WESTLAW to retrieve documents containing a form of the root CORPORAT or the word COMPANY within the same sentence as either a form of the root CRIMINAL or the word PENAL, all within the same sentence as either a form of the root LIAB or a form of the root RESPONSIB, all within the same paragraph as EMPLOYEE or AGENT or REPRESENTATIVE, all within the same paragraph as PUBLIC, which must

be within four words of POLICY or WELFARE or INTEREST.

This query illustrates what a standard request to WESTLAW looks like—words or numbers describing an issue, tied together by connectors. These connectors tell WESTLAW in what relationships the terms must appear. WESTLAW will retrieve all documents from the database that contain the terms appearing in those relationships.

The material that follows explains the methods by which WESTLAW queries are formulated, and shows how users of *Criminal Law* can employ the preformulated queries in this publication in their research of substantive criminal law. In addition, there are instructions that will enable readers to modify their queries to fit the particular needs of their research.

Query Formulation: (c) Selection of Terms

After determining the legal issue that is to be researched, the first step in query formulation is to select the key terms from the issue that will be used as search terms in the query. Words, numbers, and various other symbols may be used as search terms.

The goal in choosing search terms is to select the most unique terms for the issue. In selecting such terms it is frequently helpful to imagine how the terms might appear in the language of the documents that will be searched by the query. Moreover, it is necessary to consider the grammatical and editorial structure of the document. This involves a consideration of how the writer of the document (i.e., judge or headnote and synopsis writer) has worded both the factual and legal components of the issue involved in the case.

Although traditional book research generally starts with a consideration of the general legal concepts under which particular problems are subsumed, WESTLAW research starts with a consideration of specific terms that are likely to appear in documents that have addressed those problems. This is so because documents are retrieved from WESTLAW on the basis of the terms they contain. The more precise the terms, the more relevant the search results will be. For example, in researching obscenity and the Twenty-First Amendment, inclusion of the unique terms "Twenty-First Amendment" or "equal protection," rather than the common term "constitution," would retrieve more specific, and hopefully more pertinent documents.

Once the initial search terms have been selected for a query, it is important to consider synonyms, antonyms, and other alternatives for the search terms. A space left between each of these alternative terms will be read as an "or" in WESTLAW. (See Section e: Query Formulation: Proximity Connectors.) The nature of the legal issue will determine which alternative terms are desirable.

Query Formulation: (d) The Format of Search Terms

Once the key search terms have been selected, it is necessary to consider the proper form in which the term should appear in the query. As WESTLAW is literal in its search for terms, and as a term may appear in a variety of ways, derivative forms of each search term must be considered. There are two devices available on WESTLAW for automatically generating alternative forms of search terms in a query. The first of these is the Unlimited Root Expander, the symbol (!). Placement of the ! symbol at the end of the root term generates other forms containing the same root. For example, adding the ! symbol to the root REALIZ in the following query:

    realiz! /s risk

instructs the computer to generate the words REALIZE, REALIZES, REALIZED, REALIZING, REALIZATION, and REALIZABLE as search terms for the query. Yet time and space are saved by not having to include each of these alternatives in the query.

The second device used to automatically general alternative forms of search terms is the Universal Character, the symbol (*). This symbol permits the generation of all possible characters by placing one or more asterisks at the location in the term where the universal character is desired. For example, placing

three asterisks on the root MURDER in the following query:

    murder***   /s manslaughter

instructs the computer to generate all forms of the root term with up to three additional characters. Thus, the terms MURDER, MURDERING, MURDERED, MURDERS, MURDERER, MURDEROUS, and MURDERESS would be generated by this query. (Note, however, that words with more than three letters following the root, other than plurals, will not be generated. Thus, the above query would not generate MURDEROUSLY or MURDEROUSNESS.) The symbol * may also be embedded inside of a term as in the following query:

    int**state   /s   crime

This will generate the alternative terms INTERSTATE and INTRASTATE without the need to enter both terms. As WESTLAW automatically generates plural forms for search terms (e.g., the endings -s -es and -ies) it is generally unnecessary to use the root expansion devices to obtain plural forms of search terms.

Query Formulation: (e) Proximity Connectors

Once the search terms and alternate search terms have been selected the next consideration is how these terms may be ordered so as to retrieve the most relevant documents. The connectors and their meanings appear below.

Space (or). A space between search terms is read as an "or" by WESTLAW. For example, leaving a space between the query terms MURDER and HOMICIDE:

    murder homicide

instructs the computer to retrieve documents that contain either the word MURDER or the word HOMICIDE or both.

(&) Ampersand. The symbol & means "and." Placing it between two terms instructs the computer to retrieve documents that contain both of the terms without regard to word order. For example, inserting the & between the terms MURDER and PUNISHMENT:

    murder & punishment

commands the computer to retrieve documents that contain both the term MURDER and the term PUNISHMENT anywhere in the text. The ampersand may also be placed between groups of alternative terms. By placing an & between MURDER or HOMICIDE and PUNISHMENT or SENTENCE.

murder homicide & punishment sentence

documents containing the terms MURDER and/or HOMICIDE and the terms PUNISHMENT and/or SENTENCE may be retrieved.

/p (same paragraph). The /p symbol means "within the same paragraph." It requests that the terms to the left of the /p appear within the same paragraph as the terms to the right of the connector. For example, placing the /p between CRIME and PUNISHMENT:

crime /p punishment

instructs the computer to retrieve documents in which both the terms CRIME and PUNISHMENT appear in the same paragraph. The terms on each side of the /p connector may appear in the document in any order within the paragraph. As with the & connector the /p may be placed between groups of alternative terms. Thus, the query

crime felony /p punishment sentence

will succeed in retrieving all documents in which the terms CRIME and/or FELONY appear in the same paragraph as PUNISHMENT and/or SENTENCE.

/s (same sentence). The /s symbol requires that the search terms so connected occur within the same sentence. A /s placed between MENTAL and STATE

mental /s state

will retrieve documents that contain the words MENTAL and STATE in the same sentence, without regard to which of these terms occur first in the sentence. As with the previous connectors, the /s may be placed between groups of alternative terms. Inserting the /s between the terms MENTAL or MIND and STATE or ELEMENT

mental mind /s state element

instructs the computer to retrieve documents with the terms MENTAL and/or MIND and

the terms STATE and/or ELEMENT regardless of which terms appear first.

+s (precedes within sentence). The +s symbol requires that the term to the left of the +s connector precede the terms to the right of the connector within the same sentence. The query

former +s government

instructs the computer to retrieve all documents in which the word FORMER precedes the word GOVERNMENT where both words appear in the same sentence. This connector may also be used between groups of alternative terms. Thus, the query

former previous +s government agency

commands the computer to retrieve all documents in which the terms FORMER and/or PREVIOUS precede the terms GOVERNMENT and/or AGENCY in the same sentence.

/n (numerical proximity—within n words). The /n symbol means "within n words," where n represents any whole number between 1 and 255, inclusive. It requests that the term to the left of the /n appear within the designated number of words as terms to the right of the connector. For example, in the following query:

vicarious /3 liability

the computer is structed to retrieve all documents in which the term VICARIOUS appears within 3 words of the term LIABILITY, without regard to word order. In addition, the + symbol may be used to require that the terms to the left of the numerical proximity connector precede the terms to the right of the connector. Thus, the query above could be altered to require that VICARIOUS precede LIABILITY by no more than 3 words by replacing the /3 connector with the +3 connector.

vicarious +3 liability

Both the /n and the +n connectors may also be used between groups of alternative search terms. For example:

vicarious strict +3 liability

instructs the computer to retrieve all documents in which the words VICARIOUS or

STRICT occur within the three words preceding the words LIABILITY.

" " (quotation marks). The " " (quotation marks) symbol is the most restrictive grammatical connector. When used to enclose search terms it requires that the computer retrieve only those documents in which enclosed terms appear exactly as they do within the quotation marks. For example, placing the following words within quotation marks

''criminal law''

commands the computer to retrieve all documents in which the terms CRIMINAL and LAW occur in precisely the same order as they do within the quotation marks.

The quotation marks symbol is especially effective when searching for legal terms of art, legal concepts, or legal entities that occur together as multiple terms. Some examples are:

''felony murder'' ''animus furandi'' ''mens rea''

% (exclusion/but not). The % symbol may be translated as "but not." It instructs the computer to exclude documents that contain terms appearing after the percentage symbol. For example, to retrieve documents containing the term RIGHT within the three words of COUNSEL but not the term CIVIL, the following query would be used:

right /3 counsel % civil

Any document containing the word CIVIL would automatically be excluded in the document search.

The connectors described above may be used in a variety of combinations, enabling the user to fine-tune a query to meet his or her specific research needs.

Advanced Search Techniques: (a) The Field Search

Within any given database a more specialized search may be conducted. Rather than searching the entire text of a case for a designated query term, the search may be limited to specific portions of the case by conducting a "field search." A search may be restricted to a particular field (or portion) of a document by incorporating the field name into the que-

ry, followed by the field search terms enclosed in parentheses.

The fields available for WESTLAW case law databases are described below.

Title Field: The title field may be used to retrieve a particular case on WESTLAW. The ampersand, rather than the v. is used between the names of the parties. Thus, to retrieve the case entitled *Russell M. Polston v. The State of Wyoming* the following query would be used:

title (polston & wyoming)

Citation Field: The citation field may be used for any document for which a citation exists in the WESTLAW databases. The proper database must first be selected. A numerical proximity connector is then used instead of the publication name to separate volume and page number. For example, to retrieve the case appearing at 685 P.2d 1, the Pacific database must be selected. The following query may then be used:

citation (685 +5 1)

Court Field: The court field permits searches for case law to be restricted to particular states, districts, or courts. The correct database in which to conduct the search must be chosen. For example, to restrict a search to cases appearing in the Atlantic Reporter from the District of Columbia and Maryland, the following query could be used in the "atl" database:

court (dc md) & 110k21

Judge Field: A search may be limited to the individual or majority opinion of a particular judge. To retrieve all cases in which Justice Powell has authored an opinion the following query would be used:

judge (powell)

Synopsis Field: The synopsis field consists of the editorially prepared summary of the case found immediately after the title. By reading the synopsis it may be determined if the decision generally encompasses the legal issue being researched without reading the entire decision.

The synopsis field search can be especially useful in focusing broad queries which might retrieve too many cases if the entire case was searched. For example, the following query would limit retrieval to cases in which the enterprise liability was a key element:

> synopsis ("enterprise liability")

Topic Field: The topic field contains the West topics and Key Numbers assigned to the headnotes in a case. A search in this field may be conducted by using either the West topic name or by using the West topic number designated for that topic. For example, the West digest topic of Criminal Law has been given the number 110. Thus, in order to retrieve cases classified under the digest topic criminal law either of these two queries could be used:

> topic ("criminal law") /p strict** absolute** /4 liab!

or

> topic (110) /p strict** absolute** /4 liab!

Digest Field: The digest field contains digest paragraphs prepared by West editors. It includes headnotes, corresponding digest topics and Key Numbers, the title and citation of the case, courts, and year of decision. The digest field can be used to search for terms which are not among the West topic headings. For example, the following query may be used to research felony murder cases even though this is not one of the West topic headings.

> digest ("felony murder" /s constitution! unconstitution!)

Headnote Field: A headnote search limits the search to the language of the headnote, exclusive of the digest topic and Key Number lines and case identification information. Thus, the headnote field is useful in conducting a search where exclusion of the topic name, the key number or the title of the case is necessary to retrieve only the most pertinent cases. For example, if the query includes statute or rule numbers the digest field can be helpful to exclude unwanted citation and key numbers. The query found below is an illustration of this function. The search, run in the United States Court of Appeals database will retrieve cases discussing rob-

bery under the Hobbs Act, 18 U.S.C.A. § 1951.

> headnote (18 +5 1951 /p robbery)

Opinion Field: The opinion field contains the text of the case, court and docket numbers, and the names of the attorneys and judges participating. The opinion field search is useful in retrieving cases in which a particular attorney, judge or witness has been involved. The following format can be used to retrieve this information:

> opinion (percy +3 foreman)

NOTE: Terms may be searched for in clusters of fields by joining any number of field names by commas. This technique is illustrated below:

> synopsis,digest(strict** /4 liab! /p "mens rea")

With this query, documents containing the terms STRICT**, LIAB!, and MENS REA in either the synopsis or digest portions of the case will be retrieved.

Advanced Search Techniques: (b) Field Browsing

The WESTLAW fields listed above may be used in yet another way. This second method, known as field browsing, may be used with any query. Once a search has been completed, the documents retrieved may be scanned by entering the "f" command. A list of fields available for browsing is then displayed. Once a field has been selected, WESTLAW will display only the specified field(s).

The WESTLAW Reference Manual should be consulted for further instruction on using WESTLAW fields for searching or browsing.

Advanced Search Techniques: (c) Date Restrictions

WESTLAW may be instructed to retrieve documents appearing before, after or on a specified date, as well as within a range of dates. To use the date restriction the term DATE, followed in parentheses by the words BEFORE and/or AFTER, or the abbreviations BEF and/or AFT, or the symbols <and> must be included in the query. Note that the month, day and year may be included to further restrict the search. Date restrictions should be placed at the beginning or end of the query and connected to the query by an ampersand. The following are examples of how the date restriction may be used within a query:

```
    date (after 1965) & "criminal** negligen**"  /p
strict**  /4  liab!
    date (aft 1965) & "criminal** negligen**"  /p
strict**  /4  liab!
    "criminal negligen** "  /p  strict**  /4  liab!  &
date (bef 1975)
    "criminal negligen** "  /p  strict**  /4  liab!  &
date (aft may 10, 1965 and bef feb 21, 1981)
```

Advanced Search Techniques: (d) Key Number Searching

Searches may be performed using West Digest Topic and Key Numbers as search terms. When using this search technique, the query consists of the West Digest Topic Number followed by the letter k (or the symbol available on WALT keyboards) and then the Key Number classified as a subheading under the Digest Topic and Key Number. For example, to retrieve cases under the Digest Topic classification of Criminal Law (Digest Topic number 110), and under its subsection or Key Number for Merger of Offenses, (Key Number 30), the following queries would be used:

```
    110k30 or 110 30
```

A complete list of Digest Topics and their numerical equivalents appears in the WESTLAW Reference Manual and is also available on-line in the WESTLAW database directory.

Advanced Search Techniques: (e) The Find Command

The FIND command may be used at any point in a search to retrieve a particular case from WESTLAW. No matter what the database, a case may be displayed by typing FIND followed by the case citation. For example:

```
    find 239 nw2d 102
```

will retrieve the case of *Iowa City v. Nolan* no matter what the database. To return to the original screen, the GOBACK command is then entered.

Advanced Search Techniques: (f) The Locate Command

The LOCATE command may be used when viewing documents retrieved by a search query, to find documents within the search results which contain certain words. To locate a term, LOCATE or LOC is typed followed by the ENTER key. On the screen which follows the LOCATE terms are then typed. The terms may or may not be words contained in the query. WESTLAW will then search the documents retrieved by the query to find the LOCATE terms. For example, to search the documents retrieved by the query:

```
    "criminal** negligen** "  /p  strict** absolute**   /4
liab!
```

for those documents containing the term "mens rea" type LOCATE followed by the term "MENS REA." Documents containing the term will then be displayed.

Citation Research with WESTLAW: (a) Shepard's® Citations on WESTLAW

From any point in WESTLAW, case citations may be entered to retrieve Shepard's listings for those citations. To enter a citation to be Shepardized, the following format is used:

```
    sh 239 nw2d 102
```
or
```
    sh 239 n.w.2d 102
```
or
```
    sh 239nw2d102
```

When the citation is entered, Shepard's listings for the citation will be displayed. To shepardize a citation it is not necessary to be in the same database as that of the citation. For example, a Supreme Court citation may be entered from the Pacific Reporter database.

Citation Research with WESTLAW: (b) WESTLAW as a Citator

It is possible to retrieve new cases citing previous decisions by using WESTLAW itself as a citator. Using WESTLAW as a citator complements Shepard's Citations by retrieving very recent decisions not yet included in Shepard's. Because citation styles are not always uniform, special care must be taken to identify variant forms of citations.

Retrieving Cases that Cite Other Court Decisions

WESTLAW can be used as a citator of other court decisions if the title of the decision, its citation, or both, are known. When only the title of the case is known, use the following format:

    morissette   /7 "united states"

This query instructs the computer to retrieve all documents citing the case of *Morissette v. United States*. The /7 numerical connector requires that the term MORISSETTE occur within seven words of the term "UNITED STATES."

If the citation of the case is known, it may be added to the query to retrieve only those documents citing the correct case name and case citation. For example, to retrieve cases that have referred to the *Morissette* decision by its citation, 72 S.Ct. 240, the following format may be used:

    72 +7 240

If both the citation and the case title are known, one or both of the case name terms may be used to retrieve all documents citing this case. The queries below illustrate this format.

    morissette /7 "united states" 15 72 +7 240

or

    morissette /15 72 +7 240

or

    "united states" /15 72 +7 240

West's INSTA–CITE®

INSTA–CITE, West Publishing Company's case history system, allows users quickly to verify the accuracy of case citations and the validity of decisions. It contains prior and subsequent case histories in sequential listings, parallel citations and precedential treatment.

Some examples of the kind of direct case history provided by INSTA–CITE are: "affirmed," "certiorari denied," "decision reversed and remanded," and "judgment vacat-

ed." A complete list of INSTA–CITE case history and precedential treatment notations appears in the WESTLAW Reference Manual.

The format for entering a case citation into Insta-Cite consists of the letters IC followed by the citation, with or without spaces and periods:

    342 u.s. 246

or

    342 us 246

or

    342us246

Special Features: (a) Black's Law Dictionary

WESTLAW contains an on-line version of Black's Law Dictionary. The dictionary incorporates definitions of terms and phrases of English and American law.

The dictionary may be accessed at any point while using WESTLAW by typing DI followed by the term to be defined:

    di

To obtain definitions of a phrase, enter the command DI followed by the phrase without quotation marks:

    di judge pro tempore

If the precise spelling of a term to be defined is not known, or a list of dictionary terms is desired, a truncated form of the words may be entered with the root expansion symbol (!) attached to it:

    di bar!

This example will produce a list of dictionary terms beginning with the root BAR. From the list of terms a number corresponding to the desired term can be entered to obtain the appropriate definition of BARRISTER.

WESTLAW Queries: (a) Query Format

The queries that appear in this publication are intended to be illustrative. They are approximately as general as the material in the text to which they correspond.

Although all of the queries in this publication reflect proper format for use with WESTLAW, there is seldom only one "correct" way to formulate a query for a particular problem. The queries reflect a wide range of alternative ways that queries may be structured for effective research. Such variance in query style reflects the great flexibility that the WESTLAW system affords its users in formulating search strategies.

For some research problems, it may be necessary to make a series of refinements to the queries such as the addition of search terms or the substitution of different grammatical connectors, adequately to fit the particular needs of the individual researcher's problem. The responsibility remains with the researcher to "fine-tune" the WESTLAW queries in accordance with his or her own research requirements. The primary usefulness of the preformulated queries is in providing users with a foundation upon which further query construction can be built.

Individual queries may retrieve from one to over a hundred cases, depending on the database to which they are addressed. If a query does not retrieve any cases in a given database, it is because there are no documents in that database which satisfy the proximity requirements of the query. In this situation, to search another database with the same query, enter the letter S followed by the initials DB, followed by the new database identifier. Thus, if a query was initially addressed to the District Courts (dct) database, but retrieved no documents, the user could then search the Courts of Appeals (cta) database with the same query by entering the following command:

    s db cta

The maximum number of cases retrieved by a query in any given database will vary, depending on a variety of factors, including the relative generality of the search terms and proximity connectors, the frequency of litigation or discussion of the issue in the courts and administrative bodies, and the number of documents comprising the database.

WESTLAW Queries: (b) Textual Illustrations

Examples from the text of this edition have been selected to illustrate how the queries provided in this treatise may be expanded, restricted, or altered to meet the specific needs of the reader's research in the area of substantive criminal law. A portion of Chapter 7 section 7.12(a) of this text appears below. The footnotes have been omitted for purposes of brevity.

Involuntary Manslaughter

A few cases have made it plain that manslaughter is committed when the defendant's death-producing conduct involves an unreasonable and high degree of risk of death, though the defendant does not realize it. On the other hand, a few other cases have made it clear that manslaughter is not committed, even though the defendant's death-inflicting conduct involves such a risk, unless the defendant in fact was conscious of the danger. Doubtless in most cases one whose conduct is highly risky is actually aware of that fact; but occasionally a particular defendant may be so absent-minded or stupid or intoxicated as not to realize the risk. One who consciously takes a chance with other people's lives—whose attitude is, I may kill someone but I'll risk it—is, of course, morally much worse than one who unconsciously does so.

This excerpt discusses a defendant's awareness of risk in involuntary manslaughter cases. In order to retrieve documents discussing this point of law, the following preformulated query is given as a suggested search strategy on WESTLAW.

    topic (203) /p "involuntary manslaughter" /s risk
    danger /s aware! kn*w! conscious

In the text of a case retrieved by the query, the paragraph below appears.

    R 1 OF 3   P 3 OF 15   NW   T
    364 N.W.2d 310
    (2)
    203k74
    HOMICIDE
    k. Negligence in performance of lawful act.
    Mich.App. 1985.
    Gross negligence for purpose of **involuntary manslaughter** does not require that defendant be personally **aware** of **danger** or that he **knowingly** and **consciously** created **danger**, but only that **danger** be

apparent to ordinary mind; personal **knowledge** is not part of the test. M.C.L.A. § 750.321.

People v. Jackson

364 N.W.2d 310

The query can be altered in a number of ways to tailor it to the needs of the individual researcher. For example, to research involuntary manslaughter cases involving the "reasonable person" standard of care, the following query could be used:

topic (203) /p "involuntary manslaughter" /s reasonable prudent /2 person man woman

By adding REASONABLE or PRUDENT within two words of PERSON, MAN or WOMAN, and deleting RISK, DANGER, AWARE!, KN*W! and CONSCIOUS!, the query retrieves documents which discuss the "reasonable person" standard in the context of a Homicide topic paragraph. One such document retrieved from the Northeastern (ne) database is shown below.

R   2   OF   12   P   22   OF   43   NE   T

408 N.E.2d 614

203k74

HOMICIDE

k.   Negligence in performance of lawful act.

Ind.App. 1980.

Defendant, who was convicted of neglect of a dependent and **involuntary manslaughter** of her son after he died due to injuries inflicted by defendant's boyfriend while he was living with her, was not entitled to relief on appeal on basis of contention that defendant had not committed any intentional or negligent acts resulting in son's death; the standard of care was what a **reasonable person** would do or not do under the circumstances, and defendant had a duty to not place son in situation which might endanger his life or health and she further had a duty to remove child from any situation of danger. IC 35–42–1–4, 35–46–1–4 (1980 Supp.).

Smith v. State

408 N.E.2d 614

Just how a query is altered will depend upon the research objectives of the individual.

Ranking Documents Retrieved on WESTLAW: Age and Term Options

Documents retrieved by a query can be ordered in either of two ways. One way is to order documents by their dates, with the most recent documents displayed first. This is ranking by AGE. Using the AGE option is suggested when the user's highest priority is to retrieve the most recent decisions from a search.

Alternatively, documents can be ranked by the frequency of appearance of query terms. This is ranking by TERMS. When a search is performed with the TERMS option, the cases containing the greatest number of different search terms will be displayed first.

When a database is accessed by entering a database identifier, WESTLAW responds with a screen requesting that the query be entered. At this point the user may select which type of ranking, AGE or TERMS, is desired.

The queries offered in this text were formulated and tested for relevancy with use of the TERMS option. Accordingly, in certain instances use of the AGE option with the preformulated queries may display less relevant, yet more recent cases, first.

Conclusion

This appendix has demonstrated methods that can be used to obtain the most effective research results in the area of substantive criminal law. The addition of WESTLAW references at the end of each section of the text opens the door to a powerful and easily accessed computerized law library.

The queries may be used as provided or they may be tailored to meet the needs of researcher's specific problems. The power and flexibility of WESTLAW affords users of this publication a unique opportunity to greatly enhance their access to and understanding of substantive criminal law.

*

Table of Cases

A., In re Patricia, 31 N.Y.2d 83, 335 N.Y.S.2d 33, 286 N.E.2d 432 (1972)—§ **4.11 n. 51, 64.**

A. & P. Trucking Co., United States v., 358 U.S. 121, 79 S.Ct. 203, 3 L.Ed.2d 165 (1958)—§ **3.10**; § **3.10 n. 79, 88.**

Aaron, People v., 409 Mich. 672, 299 N.W.2d 304 (1980)—§ **7.5 n. 126.**

Aaron, State v., 4 N.J.C. 231 (1818)—§ **4.11 n. 17.**

Abbate v. United States, 359 U.S. 187, 79 S.Ct. 666, 3 L.Ed. 2d 729 (1959)—§ **2.8**; § **2.8 n. 53, 54, 60**; § **2.9 n. 76**; § **2.15 n. 46.**

Abbott v. Commonwealth, 234 Ky. 423, 28 S.W.2d 486 (1930)—§ **4.10 n. 21.**

Abbott v. Regina, (1977) A.C. 755—§ **5.3 n. 38.**

Abbott, State v., 36 N.J. 63, 174 A.2d 881 (1961)—§ **5.7 n. 55, 65.**

Abercrombie, State v., 375 So.2d 1170 (La.1979)—§ **4.2 n. 49.**

Acers v. United States, 164 U.S. 388, 17 S.Ct. 91, 41 L.Ed. 481 (1896)—§ **7.15 n. 42.**

Ackerly, State v., 79 Vt. 69, 64 A. 450 (1906)—§ **5.1 n. 21.**

Ackerman v. State, 7 Wyo. 504, 54 P. 228 (1898)—§ **8.4 n. 20.**

Acklen v. Thompson, 122 Tenn. 43, 126 S.W. 730 (1909)—§ **2.15 n. 1.**

Acunia v. United States, 404 F.2d 140 (9th Cir.1968)—§ **1.2 n. 13.**

Adami, People v., 36 Cal.App.3d 452, 111 Cal.Rptr. 544 (1973)—§ **6.1 n. 102.**

Adams v. Commonwealth, 219 Ky. 711, 294 S.W. 151 (1927)—§ **5.11 n. 6.**

Adams v. Commonwealth, 153 Ky. 88, 154 S.W. 381 (1913)—§ **8.3 n. 10, 13, 17.**

Adams v. State, 8 Md.App. 684, 262 A.2d 69 (1970)—§ **4.11 n. 19.**

Adams v. Tanner, 244 U.S. 590, 37 S.Ct. 662, 61 L.Ed. 1336 (1917)—§ **2.12 n. 48, 49.**

Adams, Commonwealth v., 479 Pa. 508, 388 A.2d 1046 (1978)—§ **8.3 n. 20.**

Adams, Commonwealth v., 114 Mass. 323, 19 Am.Rep. 362 (1873)—§ **1.6 n. 36**; § **3.7 n. 28**; § **7.15 n. 27, 28.**

Adams, People v., 9 Ill.App.3d 61, 291 N.E.2d 54 (1972)—§ **5.7 n. 65.**

Adams, People v., 3 Denio 190 (N.Y.1846)—§ **2.9 n. 21.**

Adams, State v., 210 La. 782, 28 So.2d 269 (1946)—§ **7.10 n. 4.**

Adams, State v., 339 Mo. 926, 98 S.W.2d 632 (1936)—§ **7.5 n. 81, 98**; § **7.7 n. 36.**

Adams, State v., 105 La. 737, 30 So. 101 (1901)—§ **6.6 n. 22.**

Adamson, United States v., 665 F.2d 649 (5th Cir.1982)—§ **3.4 n. 7.**

Addington v. Texas, 441 U.S. 418, 99 S.Ct. 1804, 60 L.Ed. 2d 323 (1979)—§ **4.6**; § **4.6 n. 16.**

Adkins v. Bordenkircher, 674 F.2d 279 (4th Cir.1982)—§ **1.8 n. 44.**

Adkins v. Children's Hospital, 261 U.S. 525, 43 S.Ct. 394, 67 L.Ed. 785 (1923)—§ **2.12 n. 7.**

Adkinson v. State, 64 Tenn. 569 (1875)—§ **8.13 n. 19.**

Aetna Ins. Co. v. Commonwealth, 106 Ky. 864, 51 S.W. 624 (1899)—§ **2.1 n. 60.**

Agard, United States v., 605 F.2d 665 (2d Cir.1979)—§ **5.3 n. 32.**

Ageht, State v., 116 Wis.2d 605, 342 N.W.2d 721 (1984)—§ **6.7 n. 82.**

Agnes, State v., 92 N.J.L. 53, 104 A. 299 (Sup.Ct.1918)—§ **7.10 n. 73.**

Agnew, State v., 202 N.C. 755, 164 S.E. 578 (1932)—§ **7.15 n. 30.**

Agresti v. State, 2 Md.App. 278, 234 A.2d 284 (1967)—§ **6.6 n. 57.**

Agrillo-Ladlad, United States v., 675 F.2d 905 (7th Cir. 1982)—§ **2.2 n. 4.**

Ah Fat, People v., 48 Cal. 61 (1874)—§ **3.12 n. 17.**

Aikman v. Wheeling, 120 W.Va. 46, 195 S.E.2d 667 (1939)—§ **6.9 n. 74.**

Ake v. Oklahoma, ___ U.S. ___, 105 S.Ct. 1087, 84 L.Ed.2d 53 (1985)—§ **4.5**; § **4.5 n. 102, 110.**

Ake v. State, 663 P.2d 1 (Okl.Crim.App.1983)—§ **4.4 n. 17.**

Akers, State v., 119 N.H. 161, 400 A.2d 38 (1979)—§ **3.9 n. 10, 35, 38.**

Akron, City of v. Akron Center for Reproductive Health, 462 U.S. 416, 103 S.Ct. 2481, 76 L.Ed.2d 687 (1983)—§ **2.14 n. 57.**

Akron, City of v. Sabol, 2 Ohio App.2d 109, 206 N.E.2d 575 (1965)—§ **1.7 n. 36.**

Alamillo, People v., 113 Cal.App.2d 617, 248 P.2d 421 (1952)—§ **5.2 n. 72.**

Alamo, People v., 34 N.Y.2d 453, 358 N.Y.S.2d 375, 315 N.E.2d 446 (1974)—§ **8.3 n. 20.**

Alba, People v., 46 Cal.App.2d 859, 117 P.2d 63 (1941)—§ **5.11 n. 49.**

Albernaz v. United States, 450 U.S. 333, 101 S.Ct. 1137, 67 L.Ed.2d 275 (1981)—§ **6.5 n. 117**; § **7.5 n. 114.**

Albert, State v., 426 A.2d 1370 (Me.1981)—§ **8.13 n. 44.**

Albrecht, People v., 145 Colo. 202, 358 P.2d 4 (1960)—§ **1.8 n. 55, 58.**

Albright, United States v., 388 F.2d 719 (4th Cir.1968)—§ **4.5 n. 81.**

Aldrich v. People, 224 Ill. 622, 79 N.E. 964 (1906)—§ **8.3 n. 16.**

Aldrich Restaurant Corp., People v., 53 Misc.2d 574, 279 N.Y.S.2d 624 (1967)—§ **3.10 n. 105.**

Alexander v. Elkins, 132 Tenn. 663, 179 S.W. 310 (1915)—§ **2.10 n. 27.**

Alexander v. State, 52 Md.App. 171, 447 A.2d 880 (1982)—§ **5.8 n. 8.**

Alexander v. State, 358 So.2d 379 (Miss.1978)—§ **4.5 n. 144.**

Alexander v. State, 89 S.W. 642 (Tex.Crim.R.1906)—§ **8.13 n. 10.**

Alexander v. United States, 380 F.2d 33 (8th Cir.1967)—§ **4.5 n. 83.**

Alexander, State v., 76 Or. 329, 148 P. 1136 (1915)—§ **2.2 n. 100.**

Alford, State v., 68 N.C. 322 (1873)—§ **5.6 n. 9.**

Bachert, Commonwealth v., 499 Pa. 398, 453 A.2d 931 (1982)—§ **6.7 n. 62.**

Bachman v. State, 235 Ark. 339, 359 S.W.2d 815 (1962)—§ **2.12 n. 30.**

Backun v. United States, 112 F.2d 635 (4th Cir.1940)—§ **6.7; § 6.7 n. 79.**

Bacon v. United States, 127 F.2d 985 (10th Cir.1942)—§ **6.4 n. 159; § 6.7 n. 29.**

Bacon, State v., 27 R.I. 252, 61 A. 653 (1905)—§ **6.5 n. 25.**

Bad Elk, John, United States v., 177 U.S. 529, 20 S.Ct. 729, 44 L.Ed. 874 (1900)—§ **5.7 n. 67; § 7.10 n. 30.**

Badders v. United States, 240 U.S. 391, 36 S.Ct. 367, 60 L.Ed. 706 (1916)—§ **2.14 n. 103.**

Badolato, United States v., 701 F.2d 915 (11th Cir.1983)—§ **3.6 n. 12.**

Baender v. Barnett, 255 U.S. 224, 41 S.Ct. 271, 65 L.Ed. 597 (1921)—§ **3.2 n. 17, 43.**

Bagley, Commonwealth v., 24 Mass. (7 Pick.) 279 (1828)—§ **8.12 n. 1.**

Bagley, Rex v., 17 Cr.App.R. 162 (1932)—§ **8.7 n. 67.**

Bailey v. People, 630 P.2d 1062 (1981)—§ **5.2 n. 33.**

Bailey v. State, ___ Nev. ___, 688 P.2d 320 (1984)—§ **6.2 n. 88.**

Bailey v. State, 421 So.2d 1364 (Ala.Crim.App.1982)—§ **4.5 n. 103.**

Bailey v. United States, 416 F.2d 1110 (D.C.Cir.1969)—§ **6.7 n. 21, 24.**

Bailey, People v., 60 Ill.2d 37, 322 N.E.2d 804 (1975)—§ **6.4 n. 49.**

Bailey, Rex v., Russ. & R. 341 (1818)—§ **8.13 n. 26.**

Bailey, Rex v., 168 Eng.Rep. 651 (1800)—§ **5.1 n. 64.**

Bailey, State v., 63 W.Va. 668, 60 S.E. 785 (1908)—§ **6.6 n. 13.**

Bailey, United States v., 444 U.S. 394, 100 S.Ct. 624, 62 L.Ed.2d 575 (1980)—§ **1.8 n. 27; § 5.3 n. 11, 29, 33; § 5.4 n. 4, 50, 52.**

Bainbridge, Regina v., 3 W.L.R. 656 (1959)—§ **6.4 n. 168; § 6.7 n. 86.**

Baird, United States v., 414 F.2d 700 (2d Cir.1969)—§ **4.5 n. 70.**

Baker v. Commonwealth, 204 Ky. 420, 264 S.W. 1069 (1924)—§ **6.5 n. 29.**

Baker v. Muncy, 619 F.2d 327 (4th Cir.1980)—§ **1.8 n. 41.**

Baker v. State, 377 So.2d 17 (Fla.1979)—§ **1.6 n. 31.**

Baker v. State, 6 Md.App. 148, 250 A.2d 677 (1969)—§ **6.2 n. 79.**

Baker v. State, 30 Fla. 41, 11 So. 492 (1892)—§ **3.11 n. 51.**

Baker v. State, 4 Ark. 56 (1842)—§ **7.17 n. 19.**

Baker v. United States, 393 F.2d 604 (9th Cir.1968)—§ **6.5 n. 276.**

Baker v. United States, 21 F.2d 903 (4th Cir.1927)—§ **6.8 n. 4.**

Baker, Commonwealth v., 115 Pa.Super. 183, 175 A. 438 (1934)—§ **8.10 n. 39, 43.**

Baker, People v., 42 Cal.2d 550, 268 P.2d 705 (1954)—§ **3.2 n. 29; § 4.9 n. 3.**

Baker, State v., ___ Haw. ___, 691 P.2d 1166 (1984)—§ **4.7 n. 47.**

Baker, State v., 607 S.W.2d 153 (Mo.1980)—§ **7.5 n. 46, 48.**

Baker, State v., 203 N.W.2d 795 (Iowa 1973)—§ **3.7 n. 2, 4, 39.**

Baker, State v., 183 Neb. 499, 161 N.W.2d 864 (1968)—§ **8.13 n. 24.**

Baker, State v., 246 Iowa 215, 66 N.W.2d 303 (1954)—§ **1.8 n. 28.**

Baker, State v., 20 R.I. 275, 38 A. 653 (1897)—§ **7.16 n. 19, 38.**

Baker, State ex rel. Sherburne v., 50 La.Ann. 1247, 24 So. 240 (1898)—§ **2.4 n. 40.**

Baker, United States v., 609 F.2d 134 (5th Cir.1980)—§ **2.8 n. 27.**

Balakin, Commonwealth v., 356 Mass. 547, 254 N.E.2d 422 (1969)—§ **6.6 n. 45.**

Balano, United States v., 618 F.2d 624 (10th Cir.1979)—§ **6.9 n. 17.**

Baldi, United States ex rel. Smith v., 192 F.2d 540 (3d Cir. 1951)—§ **4.5 n. 105.**

Baldwin v. New York, 399 U.S. 66, 90 S.Ct. 1886, 26 L.Ed. 2d 437 (1970)—§ **1.6 n. 68; § 1.7 n. 107.**

Baldwin v. State, 46 Fla. 115, 35 So. 220 (1903)—§ **6.5 n. 177.**

Baldwin, State v., 305 A.2d 555 (Me.1973)—§ **2.7 n. 10, 12, 14.**

Baldwin, State v., 36 Kan. 1, 12 P. 318 (1886)—§ **7.7 n. 46.**

Balint, United States v., 258 U.S. 250, 42 S.Ct. 301, 66 L.Ed. 604 (1922)—§ **3.8 n. 12, 13.**

Ball, People v., 58 Ill.2d 36, 317 N.E.2d 54 (1974)—§ **5.6 n. 20.**

Ball, State v., 114 Miss. 505, 75 So. 373 (1917)—§ **8.7 n. 68.**

Ballamah, State v., 28 N.M. 212, 210 P. 391 (1922)—§ **6.3 n. 9.**

Balliro, Commonwealth v., 349 Mass. 505, 209 N.E.2d 308 (1965)—§ **7.5 n. 64.**

Balsley, State v., 159 Ind. 395, 65 N.E. 185 (1902)—§ **8.8 n. 2.**

Bandy v. State, 575 S.W.2d 278 (Tenn.1979)—§ **6.3 n. 57.**

Banks v. State, 85 Tex.Crim. 165, 211 S.W. 217 (1919)—§ **7.4 n. 14, 17.**

Banks, Regina v., 12 Cox Crim.Cas. 393 (1873)—§ **6.1 n. 61, 72, 77.**

Banmiller, Commonwealth ex rel. Haines v., 393 Pa. 439, 143 A.2d 661 (1958)—§ **7.10 n. 57.**

Banovitch v. Commonwealth, 196 Va. 210, 83 S.E.2d 369 (1954)—§ **7.15 n. 39.**

Bantum v. State, 46 Del. 487, 85 A.2d 741 (1952)—§ **7.2 n. 15; § 7.3 n. 2, 8.**

Barasch, People ex rel. Chicago Bar Association v., 211 Ill. 2d 407, 173 N.E.2d 417 (1961)—§ **1.7 n. 50.**

Baratta, State v., 242 Iowa 1308, 49 N.W.2d 866 (1951)—§ **5.7 n. 60.**

Barcella, United States v., 432 F.2d 570 (1st Cir.1970)—§ **6.7 n. 82.**

Barfield v. United States, 229 F.2d 936 (5th Cir.1956)—§ **1.8 n. 64; § 8.5 n. 1.**

Barilleau, State v., 128 La. 1033, 55 So. 664 (1911)—§ **1.7 n. 7.**

Barker, King v., (1924) N.Z.L.R. 865—§ **6.2 n. 144.**

Barker, State v., ___ Mont. ___, 685 P.2d 357 (1984)—§ **8.4 n. 13.**

Barker, State v., 128 W.Va. 744, 38 S.E.2d 346 (1946)—§ **7.10 n. 3.**

Barker, United States v., 546 F.2d 940 (D.C.Cir.1976)—§ **5.1 n. 118.**

Barnard, Rex v., 173 Eng.Rep. 342 (1837)—§ **8.7 n. 8.**

Barnes v. State, 269 Ind. 76, 378 N.E.2d 839 (1978)—§ **6.3 n. 99.**

Barnes v. United States, 412 U.S. 837, 93 S.Ct. 2357, 37 L.Ed.2d 380 (1973)—§ **2.2 n. 55; § 8.10 n. 48.**

Barnes, Commonwealth v., 369 Mass. 462, 340 N.E.2d 863 (1976)—§ **5.3 n. 54.**

Barnes, United States v., 175 F.Supp. 60 (S.D.Cal.1959)—§ **4.4; § 4.4 n. 56.**

Barnett, United States v., 376 U.S. 681, 84 S.Ct. 984, 12 L.Ed.2d 23 (1965)—§ **1.7 n. 103.**

Barney, State v., 244 N.W.2d 316 (Iowa 1976)—§ **4.6 n. 54.**

Barr, State v., 11 Wash. 481, 39 P. 1080 (1895)—§ **5.9 n. 29.**

Barraza, People v., 23 Cal.3d 675, 153 Cal.Rptr. 459, 591 P.2d 947 (1979)—§ **5.2 n. 34, 84.**

Barrett v. United States, 423 U.S. 212, 96 S.Ct. 498, 46 L.Ed.2d 450 (1976)—§ **2.2 n. 29.**

Barrett v. United States, 322 F.2d 292 (5th Cir.1963)—§ **2.13 n. 53.**

Barrett, State v., 408 A.2d 1273 (Me.1979)—§ **4.10 n. 46.**

Barron, United States v., 594 F.2d 1345 (10th Cir.1979)—§ **2.6 n. 7, 9.**

Barrow v. State, 17 Okl.Crim. 340, 188 P. 351 (1920)—§ **7.12 n. 26.**

Barry v. State, 90 Wis.2d 316, 280 N.W.2d 204 (1979)—§ **6.3 n. 137.**

Barry, Commonwealth v., 125 Mass. 390 (1878)—§ **8.3 n. 16.**

Barry, Commonwealth v., 124 Mass. 325 (1878)—§ **8.7 n. 61.**

Barry, State v., 45 Mont. 598, 124 P. 775, 41 L.R.A., (N.S.) 181 (1912)—§ **7.16 n. 23.**

Barstrom v. Herold, 383 U.S. 107, 86 S.Ct. 760, 15 L.Ed.2d 620 (1966)—§ **4.6 n. 33.**

Bartell v. State, 106 Wis. 342, 82 N.W. 142 (1900)—§ **5.11 n. 24.**

Bartkus v. Illinois, 359 U.S. 121, 79 S.Ct. 676, 3 L.Ed.2d 684 (1959)—§ **2.8;** § **2.8 n. 52, 54, 60, 68;** § **2.9 n. 76;** § **2.15 n. 46.**

Bartlett v. State, 569 P.2d 1235 (Wyo.1977)—§ **7.13 n. 34.**

Bartley v. State, 53 Neb. 310, 73 N.W. 744 (1898)—§ **8.6 n. 23.**

Bartoli v. United States, 192 F.2d 130 (4th Cir.1951)—§ **6.4 n. 156;** § **6.5 n. 96.**

Bartolini, Commonwealth v., 299 Mass. 503, 13 N.E.2d 382 (1938)—§ **7.7 n. 37.**

Barton v. State, 46 Md.App. 616, 420 A.2d 1009 (1980)—§ **5.7 n. 60.**

Barton, State v., 88 Tex.Crim. 368, 227 S.W. 317 (1921)—§ **8.5 n. 27;** § **8.11 n. 16, 18.**

Barton, United States v., 647 F.2d 224 (2d Cir.1981)—§ **6.5 n. 149.**

Bartowsheski, People v., 661 P.2d 235 (Colo.1983)—§ **8.11 n. 36.**

Bary v. United States, 248 F.2d 201 (10th Cir.1957)—§ **6.5 n. 94.**

Bass v. State, 151 Tex.Crim. 172, 206 S.W.2d 599 (1947)—§ **8.11 n. 18.**

Bass, State v., 255 N.C. 42, 120 S.E.2d 580 (1961)—§ **7.17 n. 27.**

Bass, United States v., 404 U.S. 336, 92 S.Ct. 515, 30 L.Ed. 2d 488 (1971)—§ **2.2 n. 25, 26, 27.**

Batchelder, United States v., 442 U.S. 114, 99 S.Ct. 2198, 60 L.Ed.2d 755 (1979)—§ **2.3 n. 8, 52;** § **2.11 n. 9, 40.**

Batdorf, State v., 293 N.C. 486, 238 S.E.2d 497 (1977)—§ **2.7 n. 10, 13.**

Bates v. Little Rock, 361 U.S. 516, 80 S.Ct. 412, 4 L.Ed.2d 480 (1960)—§ **2.14 n. 29.**

Batiste, State v., 410 So.2d 1055 (La.1982)—§ **3.12 n. 21.**

Batiste, State v., 363 So.2d 639 (La.1978)—§ **5.2 n. 26, 63.**

Battalino v. People, 118 Colo. 587, 199 P.2d 897 (1948)—§ **4.7 n. 19.**

Batten, People v., 9 Mich.App. 195, 156 N.W.2d 640 (1967)—§ **6.4 n. 47.**

Battle v. State, 287 Md. 675, 414 A.2d 1266 (1980)—§ **5.11 n. 7, 46.**

Baucom v. Martin, 677 F.2d 1346 (11th Cir.1982)—§ **5.10 n. 56.**

Bauer v. State, 45 Ariz. 358, 43 P.2d 203 (1935)—§ **8.11 n. 42.**

Bauer, People v., 32 A.D.2d 463, 305 N.Y.S.2d 42 (1969)—§ **6.5 n. 88.**

Baxstrom v. Herold, 383 U.S. 107, 86 S.Ct. 760, 15 L.Ed.2d 620 (1966)—§ **4.4;** § **4.4 n. 48;** § **4.6 n. 25.**

Baxter v. State, 503 S.W.2d 226 (Tenn.1973)—§ **7.7 n. 14.**

Baxter, State v., 89 Ohio St. 269, 104 N.E. 331 (1914)—§ **8.6 n. 62.**

Bayles, In re, 47 Cal.App. 517, 190 P. 1034 (1920)—§ **8.5 n. 29.**

Bayless Markets, Inc., A.J., State v., 86 Ariz. 193, 342 P.2d 1088 (1959)—§ **2.11 n. 46;** § **2.12 n. 41, 46.**

Bazeley's Case, 2 East P.C. 571 (Cr.Cas.Res.1799)—§ **8.1 n. 4, 9;** § **8.2 n. 23.**

Be Bee, State v., 113 Utah 398, 195 P.2d 746 (1948)—§ **7.1 n. 52.**

Beacham v. State, 289 P.2d 397 (Okl.Crim.1955)—§ **3.9 n. 6.**

Beale, State v., 229 A.2d 921 (Me.1973)—§ **3.5 n. 30.**

Beam, State v., 181 N.C. 597, 107 S.E. 429 (1921)—§ **2.9 n. 33, 38.**

Bean, State v., 235 Kan. 800, 686 P.2d 160 (1984)—§ **4.2 n. 50.**

Bearcub, State v., 1 Or.App. 579, 465 P.2d 252 (1970)—§ **6.8 n. 94.**

Beard v. United States, 158 U.S. 550, 15 S.Ct. 962, 39 L.Ed. 1086 (1895)—§ **5.7 n. 14, 22, 34, 60.**

Beardsley, People v., 150 Mich. 206, 113 N.W. 1128, 13 L.R.A. (N.S.) 1020, 121 Am.St.Rep. 617, 13 Ann.Cas. 39 (1907)—§ **3.3 n. 8, 11, 16.**

Beasley v. State, 138 Ind. 552, 38 N.E. 35 (1894)—§ **8.2 n. 15.**

Beasley, People v., 370 Mich. 242, 121 N.W.2d 457 (1963)—§ **6.5 n. 38.**

Beason v. State, 96 Miss. 105, 50 So. 488 (1909)—§ **4.10 n. 17.**

Beattie v. State, 73 Ark. 428, 84 S.W. 477 (1904)—§ **2.9 n. 34, 35, 39.**

Beaudry, State v., 123 Wis.2d 40, 365 N.W.2d 593 (1985)—§ **3.9 n. 7, 15, 25, 40.**

Beauharnais v. Illinois, 343 U.S. 250, 72 S.Ct. 725, 96 L.Ed. 919 (1952)—§ **2.14 n. 10.**

Beausoliel v. United States, 107 F.2d 292 (D.C.Cir.1939)—§ **7.15 n. 8.**

Beazell v. Ohio, 269 U.S. 167, 46 S.Ct. 68, 70 L.Ed. 216 (1925)—§ **2.4 n. 10, 37.**

Bechtelheimer v. State, 54 Ind. 128 (1876)—§ **7.7 n. 44.**

Beck, State v., 1 Hill, 363, 26 Am.Dec. 190 (S.C.1833)—§ **7.15 n. 16.**

Beckham, State v., 306 Mo. 566, 267 S.W. 817 (1924)—§ **5.9 n. 28.**

Beckwith, State v., 135 Me. 423, 198 A. 739 (1938)—§ **6.1 n. 15;** § **6.2 n. 79.**

Bedder v. Director of Public Prosecutions, [1954] 2 All E.R. 801 (H.L.)—§ **7.10 n. 65.**

Beddow v. United States, 70 F.2d 674 (8th Cir.1934)—§ **6.5 n. 63, 111.**

Beebe v. Phelps, 650 F.2d 774 (5th Cir.1981)—§ **2.4 n. 26.**

Beecham, Regina v., 5 Cox Crim.Cas. 181 (1851)—§ **8.5 n. 13.**

Beeman, People v., 35 Cal.2d 547, 199 Cal.Rptr. 60, 674 P.2d 1318 (1984)—§ **6.7 n. 55.**

Beilke, State v., 267 Minn. 526, 127 N.W.2d 516 (1964)—§ **7.12 n. 21.**

Bird, State v., 285 N.W.2d 481 (Minn.1979)—§ **6.5 n. 59, 60.**

Birdsell, State v., 235 La. 396, 104 So.2d 148 (1958)— § **2.12 n. 55, 59.**

Birreuta, People v., 162 Cal.App.3d 454, 208 Cal.Rptr. 635 (1984)—§ **3.5 n. 33;** § **3.12 n. 32.**

Bishop v. People, 165 Colo. 423, 439 P.2d 342 (1968)—§ **7.3 n. 9.**

Bishop v. United States, 350 U.S. 961, 76 S.Ct. 440, 100 L.Ed. 835 (1956)—§ **4.4 n. 24.**

Bishop v. United States, 107 F.2d 297 (D.C.Cir.1939)— § **4.10 n. 49;** § **7.10 n. 64.**

Bishop, State v., 228 N.C. 371, 45 S.E.2d 858 (1947)—§ **1.2 n. 15;** § **4.10 n. 60.**

Bismarck v. State, 45 Tex.Crim.R. 54, 73 S.W. 965 (1903)— § **8.2 n. 22;** § **8.6 n. 46.**

Bissing, State ex rel. Sanborn v., 210 Kan. 389, 502 P.2d 630 (1972)—§ **1.7 n. 102.**

Bizup v. People, 150 Colo. 214, 371 P.2d 786 (1962)—§ **7.5 n. 83, 98.**

Black v. State, 103 Ohio St. 434, 133 N.E. 795 (1921)— § **6.7 n. 70.**

Black v. State, 59 Wis. 471, 18 N.W. 457 (1884)—§ **1.8 n. 89.**

Black, United States v., 692 F.2d 314 (4th Cir.1982)—§ **5.7 n. 9.**

Blackburn v. Commonwealth, 28 Ky.L.R. 96, 89 S.W. 160 (1905)—§ **8.2 n. 37.**

Blackburn v. State, 23 Ohio St. 146 (1872)—§ **7.8 n. 25, 27.**

Blackham, Rex v., 2 East P.C. 711 (1787)—§ **8.11 n. 76.**

Blackledge v. United States, 447 A.2d 46 (D.C.App.1982)— § **8.7 n. 43.**

Blackledge, State v., 216 Iowa 199, 243 N.W. 534 (1932)— § **6.5 n. 4.**

Blackmer v. United States, 284 U.S. 421, 52 S.Ct. 252, 76 L.Ed. 375 (1932)—§ **2.8 n. 22.**

Blaikie, Commonwealth v., 375 Mass. 601, 378 N.E.2d 1361 (1978)—§ **7.7 n. 23, 26, 27.**

Blair, State v., 347 N.W.2d 416 (Iowa 1984)—§ **7.7 n. 25.**

Blake v. United States, 407 F.2d 908 (5th Cir.1969)—§ **4.3 n. 65.**

Blake, People v., 65 Cal. 275, 4 P. 1 (1884)—§ **4.10 n. 15.**

Blakeley v. State, 24 Tex.Cr.R. 616, 7 S.W. 23 (1888)— § **6.9 n. 21.**

Blango v. United States, 373 A.2d 885 (D.C.App.1977)— § **7.5 n. 108.**

Blankenburg v. Commonwealth, 272 Mass. 25, 172 N.E. 209 (1930)—§ **1.7 n. 58.**

Blankenship v. State, 130 Miss. 725, 95 So. 81 (1923)— § **7.16 n. 19, 29.**

Blansett v. State, 556 S.W.2d 322 (Tex.Crim.App.1977)— § **7.5 n. 67.**

Blau v. United States, 340 U.S. 159, 71 S.Ct. 223, 95 L.Ed. 170 (1950)—§ **1.7 n. 66.**

Blaue, Regina v., (1975) 1 W.L.R. 1411, (1975) 3 All E.R. 446 (C.A.)—§ **3.12 n. 76.**

Bleau, State v., 139 Vt. 305, 428 A.2d 1097 (1981)—§ **8.10 n. 72.**

Blechman, State v., 135 N.J.L. 99, 50 A.2d 152 (1946)— § **6.1 n. 17, 66, 67, 103.**

Bliss, State v., 80 S.W.2d 162 (Mo.1935)—§ **6.2 n. 169.**

Blockburger v. United States, 284 U.S. 299, 52 S.Ct. 180, 76 L.Ed. 306 (1932)—§ **6.5 n. 114;** § **7.5;** § **7.5 n. 111.**

Blocker v. United States, 288 F.2d 853 (D.C.Cir.1961)— § **4.3 n. 36, 44.**

Blocker v. United States, 274 F.2d 572 (D.C.Cir.1959)— § **4.3;** § **4.3 n. 43.**

Bloedlow, State v., 45 Wis. 279, 2 Am.Cr.Rep. 631 (1878)— § **3.11 n. 55.**

Bloemer v. Turner, 281 Ky. 832, 137 S.W.2d 387 (1939)— § **2.6 n. 23.**

Bloom v. Illinois, 391 U.S. 194, 88 S.Ct. 1477, 20 L.Ed.2d 522 (1968)—§ **1.7;** § **1.7 n. 68, 81, 105, 107.**

Bloom v. State, 155 Ind. 292, 58 N.E. 81 (1900)—§ **7.11 n. 10.**

Bloom, People v., 195 Colo. 246, 577 P.2d 288 (1978)—§ **6.5 n. 276.**

Bloom, People v., 149 App.Div. 295, 133 N.Y.S. 708 (1912)—§ **6.1 n. 56, 72, 100.**

Blouin, State ex rel. v. Walker, 244 La. 699, 154 So.2d 368 (1963)—§ **2.14 n. 133.**

Blount v. State, 102 Fla. 1100, 138 So. 2 (1931)—§ **5.11 n. 44, 53.**

Blow, Commonwealth v., 370 Mass. 401, 348 N.E.2d 794 (1976)—§ **3.11 n. 4.**

Blue, State v., 225 Kan. 576, 592 P.2d 897 (1979)—§ **1.8 n. 92.**

Blue Thunder, United States v., 604 F.2d 550 (8th Cir. 1979)—§ **7.7 n. 21, 26, 27.**

Blumenthal v. United States, 332 U.S. 539, 68 S.Ct. 248, 92 L.Ed. 154 (1947)—§ **6.4 n. 50, 90, 91;** § **6.5 n. 72, 130, 133.**

Blumke, People ex rel. v. Foster, 300 N.Y. 431, 91 N.E.2d 875 (1950)—§ **6.2 n. 41.**

Board of Commissioners v. Backus, 29 How.Pr. 33 (N.Y. Sup.Ct.1864)—§ **5.2 n. 5.**

Boasberg, Petition of, 286 App.Div. 951, 143 N.Y.S.2d 272 (1955)—§ **1.7 n. 87.**

Bobbitt, State v., 415 So.2d 724 (Fla.1982)—§ **5.7 n. 62.**

Bock, People v., 69 Misc. 543, 125 N.Y. 301 (1911)—§ **5.1 n. 64.**

Bocra, United States v., 623 F.2d 281 (3d Cir.1980)—§ **5.2 n. 107.**

Bodkin, People v., 304 Ill. 124, 136 N.E. 494 (1922)—§ **8.12 n. 17.**

Boggess v. State, 655 P.2d 654 (Utah 1982)—§ **3.7 n. 35.**

Bohanon v. State, 289 P.2d 400 (Okl.Crim.App.1955)— § **6.8 n. 73.**

Bohle, United States v., 445 F.2d 54 (7th Cir.1971)—§ **4.5 n. 59, 81.**

Bolanos, People v., 49 Cal.App.2d 308, 121 P.2d 753 (1942)—§ **8.12 n. 11.**

Bolar, People v., 109 Ill.App.3d 384, 64 Ill.Dec. 919, 440 N.E.2d 639 (1982)—§ **7.1 n. 36.**

Bolden, United States v., 514 F.2d 1301 (D.C.Cir.1975)— § **7.5 n. 78.**

Boleyn, State v., 328 So.2d 95 (La.1976)—§ **3.2 n. 32.**

Bolger v. Youngs Drug Products Corp., 463 U.S. 60, 103 S.Ct. 2875, 77 L.Ed.2d 469 (1983)—§ **2.14 n. 23.**

Bolin v. State, 266 Ala. 256, 96 So.2d 582 (1957)—§ **2.12 n. 76.**

Bolish, Commonwealth v., 381 Pa. 500, 113 A.2d 464 (1955)—§ **7.5 n. 46, 47, 59.**

Bolling v. Sharpe, 347 U.S. 497, 74 S.Ct. 693, 98 L.Ed. 884 (1954)—§ **2.11 n. 7, 21.**

Bolton v. Harris, 395 F.2d 642 (D.C.Cir.1968)—§ **4.6 n. 12.**

Bommarito, United States v., 524 F.2d 140 (2d Cir.1975)— § **6.5 n. 285.**

Bonano, State v., 59 N.J. 515, 284 A.2d 345 (1971)—§ **5.7 n. 60.**

Bonfanti v. State, 2 Minn. 123 (Gil. 99) (1858)—§ **3.5 n. 60.**

Bonner v. Moran, 126 F.2d 121 (D.C.Cir.1941)—§ **5.6 n. 33.**

Boomer v. Olsen, 143 Neb. 579, 10 N.W.2d 507 (1943)— § **2.12 n. 21.**

Boon, State v., 35 N.C. (13 Ired.) 244 (1852)—§ **8.13 n. 6.**

Boone, United States v., 738 F.2d 763 (6th Cir.1984)—§ **7.15 n. 80.**

Booth v. State, 398 P.2d 863 (Okl.Crim.App.1964)—§ **6.3 n. 4, 53, 65.**

Booth, Commonwealth v., 266 Mass. 80, 165 N.E. 29 (1929)—§ **2.9 n. 33.**

Booth, State v., 284 Or. 615, 588 P.2d 614 (1978)—§ **4.6 n. 49.**

Borchers, People v., 50 Cal.2d 321, 325 P.2d 97 (1958)—§ **7.10 n. 10, 11, 85.**

Bordenkircher, State ex rel. Miller v., ___ W.Va. ___, 272 S.E.2d 676 (1980)—§ **2.5 n. 13.**

Borelli, United States v., 336 F.2d 376 (2d Cir.1964)—§ **6.5 n. 131.**

Boris, Commonwealth v., 317 Mass. 309, 58 N.E.2d 8 (1944)—§ **8.10 n. 38, 40.**

Borland v. State, 158 Ark. 37, 249 S.W. 591 (1923)—§ **4.10 n. 54.**

Borrero, People v., 19 N.Y.2d 332, 280 N.Y.S.2d 109, 227 N.E.2d 18 (1967)—§ **2.14 n. 139; § 4.10 n. 86.**

Borwick, State v., 193 Iowa 639, 187 N.W. 460 (1922)—§ **5.7 n. 60.**

Bostick, State v., 4 Del. 563 (1845)—§ **4.10 n. 30.**

Boston, People ex rel. Difanis v., 92 Ill.App.3d 963, 48 Ill. Dec. 302, 416 N.E.2d 333 (1981)—§ **5.10 n. 61.**

Botkin, People v., 132 Cal. 231, 64 P. 286 (1901)—§ **2.9 n. 51.**

Bouge v. Reed, 254 Or. 418, 459 P.2d 869 (1969)—§ **4.10 n. 71; § 4.11 n. 58.**

Bouie v. City of Columbia, 378 U.S. 347, 84 S.Ct. 1697, 12 L.Ed.2d 894 (1964)—§ **2.4 n. 57, 62, 67, 69, 72, 74, 77, 78.**

Boulton, Regina v., 169 Eng.Rep. 349 (Cr.Cas.Res.1849)—§ **8.7 n. 84.**

Bourne, Rex v., (1939) 1 K.B. 687—§ **5.4 n. 12, 20, 45.**

Bouse, State v., 199 Or. 676, 264 P.2d 800 (1953)—§ **7.8 n. 31, 32.**

Boushea v. United States, 173 F.2d 131 (8th Cir.1949)—§ **6.6 n. 17.**

Bouwman, State v., 354 N.W.2d 1 (Minn.1984)—§ **4.6 n. 77.**

Bouwman, State v., 328 N.W.2d 703 (Minn.1982)—§ **4.6 n. 59, 77; § 4.7 n. 10.**

Bowen v. State, 25 Fla. 645, 6 So. 459 (1889)—§ **6.6 n. 62.**

Bowen, Commonwealth v., 13 Mass. 356, 7 Am.Dec. 154 (1816)—§ **7.1 n. 53; § 7.8 n. 27.**

Bowen, State v., 118 Kan. 31, 234 P. 46 (1925)—§ **5.7 n. 67.**

Bowen, State v., 16 Kan. 475 (1876)—§ **2.9 n. 8.**

Bowers v. State, 24 Tex.App. 542, 7 S.W. 247 (1888)—§ **7.17 n. 16.**

Bowers, State v., 35 S.C. 262, 14 S.E. 488 (1892)—§ **6.1 n. 101.**

Bowman, In re, 94 Wn.2d 407, 617 P.2d 731 (1980)—§ **7.1 n. 37.**

Bowman, United States v., 260 U.S. 94, 43 S.Ct. 39, 67 L.Ed. 149 (1922)—§ **2.8 n. 22.**

Bowry v. Bennett, 170 Eng.Rep. 981 (1808)—§ **6.7 n. 88.**

Bowser v. State, 50 Md.App. 363, 439 A.2d 1 (1981)—§ **5.2 n. 63.**

Bowser, State v., 214 N.C. 249, 199 S.E. 31 (1938)—§ **4.7 n. 18; § 7.7 n. 5.**

Boxer, People v., 24 N.Y.S.2d 628 (Sp.Sess.1940)—§ **1.6 n. 48.**

Boyajian, State v., 344 A.2d 410 (Me.1975)—§ **2.6 n. 15.**

Boyce Motor Lines, Inc. v. United States, 342 U.S. 337, 72 S.Ct. 329, 96 L.Ed. 367 (1952)—§ **2.3 n. 34, 35; § 2.6 n. 21.**

Boyd v. State, 217 Wis. 149, 258 N.W. 330 (1935)—§ **3.8 n. 16.**

Boyd v. State, 88 Ala. 169, 7 So. 268 (1890)—§ **5.6 n. 4, 19.**

Boyd, Commonwealth v., 461 Pa. 17, 334 A.2d 610 (1975)—§ **7.2 n. 13.**

Boyd, State v., ___ W.Va. ___, 280 S.E.2d 669 (1981)—§ **4.5 n. 168.**

Boyett, In re, 136 N.C. 415, 48 S.E. 789 (1904)—§ **4.6 n. 51.**

Boyles v. State, 46 Wis.2d 473, 175 N.W.2d 277 (1970)—§ **6.1 n. 141; § 6.2 n. 138; § 6.3 n. 99.**

Bracey, People v., 41 N.Y.2d 296, 392 N.Y.S.2d 412, 360 N.E.2d 1094 (1977)—§ **6.1 n. 119.**

Bradbury, State v., 136 Me. 347, 9 A.2d 657 (1939)—§ **2.1 n. 27, 65.**

Braden v. Commonwealth, 291 S.W.2d 843 (Ky.1956)—§ **2.15 n. 33.**

Bradley v. People, 8 Colo. 599, 9 P. 783 (1885)—§ **2.13 n. 5; § 3.8 n. 19.**

Bradley v. State, 102 Tex.Cr. 41, 277 S.W. 147 (1925)—§ **3.2 n. 27; § 4.9 n. 8, 36.**

Bradley v. State, 79 Fla. 651, 84 So. 677 (1920)—§ **3.3 n. 52; § 7.12 n. 24.**

Bradley, People v., 23 Cal.App. 44, 136 P. 955 (Dist.Ct.App. 1913)—§ **7.10 n. 31.**

Bradley, State v., 215 Kan. 642, 527 P.2d 988 (1974)—§ **2.2 n. 68.**

Bradovich, People v., 305 Mich. 329, 9 N.W.2d 560 (1943)—§ **8.2 n. 60.**

Bradson, United States v., 241 F.2d 107 (7th Cir.1957)—§ **4.5 n. 108.**

Braham v. State, 571 P.2d 631 (Alaska 1977)—§ **6.1 n. 102.**

Braley, State v., 224 Or. 1, 355 P.2d 467 (1960)—§ **4.10 n. 36.**

Branch, State v., 244 Or. 97, 415 P.2d 766 (1966)—§ **7.5 n. 104.**

Brandenburg v. Ohio, 395 U.S. 444, 89 S.Ct. 1827, 23 L.Ed. 2d 430 (1969)—§ **2.14 n. 17.**

Brannon v. State, 97 Fla. 488, 121 So. 793 (1929)—§ **8.6 n. 64.**

Braswell v. State, 389 P.2d 998 (Okl.Crim.1964)—§ **8.7 n. 56, 58; § 8.9 n. 8.**

Bratton v. State, 29 Tenn. 103, 10 Humph. 103 (1849)—§ **3.12 n. 42.**

Bratty v. Attorney-General for Northern Ireland, (1961), 3 All E.R. 535—§ **4.9; § 4.9 n. 41.**

Braunfeld v. Brown, 366 U.S. 599, 81 S.Ct. 1144, 6 L.Ed.2d 563 (1961)—§ **2.14 n. 43.**

Braverman v. United States, 317 U.S. 49, 63 S.Ct. 99, 87 L.Ed. 23 (1942)—§ **6.1 n. 93; § 6.5; § 6.5 n. 73, 113, 117, 298.**

Braverman, People v., 340 Ill. 525, 173 N.E. 55 (1930)—§ **8.11 n. 27, 30, 31.**

Brawner, United States v., 471 F.2d 969 (D.C.Cir.1972)—§ **1.1 n. 18; § 4.3 n. 30, 47, 51, 65; § 4.6 n. 56, 63; § 4.7 n. 19, 26.**

Breard v. City of Alexandria, 341 U.S. 622, 71 S.Ct. 920, 95 L.Ed. 1233 (1951)—§ **2.14 n. 19.**

Breaux, State v., 337 So.2d 182 (La.1976)—§ **4.5 n. 95.**

Breckinridge v. Commonwealth, 97 Ky. 267, 30 S.W. 634 (1895)—§ **8.11 n. 57, 61.**

Breese v. State, 12 Ohio St. 146 (1861)—§ **6.7 n. 36.**

Brengard, People v., 265 N.Y. 100, 191 N.E. 850 (1934)—§ **2.1 n. 81; § 3.12 n. 146.**

Brennan v. People, 37 Colo. 256, 86 P. 79 (1906)—§ **4.10 n. 7.**

Brennan, People v., 229 App.Div. 378, 242 N.Y.S. 692 (1930)—§ **1.8 n. 18.**

Brennon v. Commonwealth, 169 Ky. 815, 185 S.W. 489 (1916)—§ **8.5 n. 9.**

Brennon v. State, 25 Ind. 403 (1865)—§ **8.11 n. 40.**

Brent v. State, 43 Ala. 297 (1869)—§ **5.1 n. 97.**

Breth, Commonwealth v., 44 Pa.County Ct. 56 (1915)— § **2.14 n. 39;** § **3.3 n. 9;** § **7.12 n. 24.**

Brewer v. State, 160 Ala. 66, 49 So. 336 (1909)—§ **7.10 n. 78.**

Brewer, United States v., 139 U.S. 278, 11 S.Ct. 538, 35 L.Ed. 190 (1891)—§ **2.3 n. 1.**

Brice, Rex v., (1821) R. & R. 450—§ **8.13 n. 5.**

Bridge, Commonwealth v., 495 Pa. 568, 435 A.2d 151 (1981)—§ **4.10 n. 34.**

Bridgehouse, People v., 47 Cal.2d 406, 303 P.2d 1018 (1956)—§ **7.10 n. 39.**

Briggs, People ex rel. v. Hanley, 226 N.Y. 453, 123 N.E. 663 (1919)—§ **8.10 n. 18, 36.**

Briggs, People ex rel. Myers v., 46 Ill.2d 281, 263 N.E.2d 109 (1970)—§ **4.4 n. 74.**

Bright v. State, 490 A.2d 564 (Del.1985)—§ **2.9 n. 54.**

Briley, State v., 8 Port. 472 (Ala.1839)—§ **7.17 n. 19.**

Brim, People v., 22 Misc.2d 335, 199 N.Y.S.2d 744 (1960)— § **5.11 n. 47.**

Brimhall v. State, 31 Ariz. 522, 255 P. 165 (1927)—§ **7.15 n. 19.**

Brinegar v. United States, 338 U.S. 160, 69 S.Ct. 1302, 93 L.Ed. 1879 (1949)—§ **1.4 n. 10.**

Brinkley v. State, 233 A.2d 56 (Del.1967)—§ **7.4 n. 21.**

Bristol, People v., 23 Mich. 118 (1871)—§ **6.3 n. 140.**

Britt v. State, 26 Tenn. 45 (1846)—§ **8.11 n. 63.**

Britt, State v., 278 Mo. 510, 213 S.W. 425 (1919)—§ **8.6 n. 5.**

Britton, United States v., 108 U.S. 199, 2 S.Ct. 531, 27 L.Ed. 698 (1883)—§ **6.5 n. 198.**

Broadhurst, State v., 184 Or. 178, 196 P.2d 407 (1948)— § **5.7 n. 50, 54.**

Broderick, State v., 59 Mo. 318 (1875)—§ **8.11 n. 43.**

Bronson, State v., 259 N.W.2d 465 (Minn.1977)—§ **8.13 n. 70.**

Brookings, City of v. Thomsen, 84 S.D. 651, 176 N.W.2d 46 (1970)—§ **1.7 n. 31.**

Brookman Co., United States v., 229 F.Supp. 862 (N.D.Cal. 1964)—§ **3.10 n. 82.**

Brooks v. State, 35 Ohio St. 46 (1878)—§ **8.2 n. 39, 42.**

Brooks, People v., 334 Ill. 549, 166 N.E. 35 (1929)—§ **1.4 n. 25.**

Brooks, State v., 103 Ariz. 472, 445 P.2d 831 (1968)—§ **7.7 n. 42.**

Brooks, State v., 4 Conn. 446 (1823)—§ **8.13 n. 55.**

Brotherhood of Loc. Fire & Eng. v. Chicago, R.I. & P.R. Co., 393 U.S. 129, 89 S.Ct. 323, 21 L.Ed.2d 289 (1968)— § **2.11 n. 17.**

Browder, State v., 486 P.2d 925 (Alaska 1971)—§ **1.7 n. 97, 106.**

Brown v. Commonwealth, 575 S.W.2d 451 (Ky.1978)— § **4.10 n. 43.**

Brown v. Elliot, 225 U.S. 392, 32 S.Ct. 812, 56 L.Ed. 1136 (1912)—§ **6.5 n. 153.**

Brown v. Ohio, 432 U.S. 161, 97 S.Ct. 2221, 53 L.Ed.2d 187 (1977)—§ **7.5;** § **7.5 n. 110, 113.**

Brown v. People, 39 Ill. 407 (1866)—§ **5.9 n. 16.**

Brown v. State, 22 Ala.App. 31, 111 So. 760 (1927)—§ **3.10 n. 87.**

Brown v. Texas, 443 U.S. 47, 99 S.Ct. 2637, 61 L.Ed.2d 357 (1979)—§ **2.14 n. 69.**

Brown v. United States, 356 U.S. 148, 78 S.Ct. 622, 2 L.Ed. 2d 589 (1958)—§ **4.5 n. 86.**

Brown v. United States, 84 U.S.App.D.C. 222, 171 F.2d 832 (1948)—§ **3.11 n. 54.**

Brown v. United States, 256 U.S. 335, 41 S.Ct. 501, 65 L.Ed. 961 (1921)—§ **5.7 n. 26, 56.**

Brown v. United States, 35 D.C. 548 (1910)—§ **2.9 n. 17.**

Brown v. Warden, 682 F.2d 348 (2d Cir.1982)—§ **4.4 n. 4.**

Brown, Commonwealth v., 473 Pa. 458, 375 A.2d 331 (1977)—§ **6.5 n. 215.**

Brown, Commonwealth v., 4 Mass. 580 (1808)—§ **8.2 n. 32.**

Brown, People v., 21 App.Div.2d 738, 249 N.Y.S.2d 922 (1964)—§ **6.2 n. 88.**

Brown, People v., 26 Ill.2d 308, 186 N.E.2d 321 (1962)— § **6.8 n. 58.**

Brown, People v., 62 Cal.App. 96, 216 P. 411 (1923)— § **3.12 n. 70.**

Brown, People v., 105 Cal. 66, 38 P. 518 (1894)—§ **8.5 n. 8.**

Brown, Queen v., 1 Terr.L.Rep. 475 (Can.1893)—§ **3.3 n. 13.**

Brown, State v., 284 S.C. 407, 326 S.E.2d 410 (1985)— § **2.14 n. 83.**

Brown, State v., 235 Kan. 688, 681 P.2d 1071 (1984)—§ **4.5 n. 94.**

Brown, State v., 479 A.2d 1317 (Me.1984)—§ **6.2 n. 73.**

Brown, State v., 5 Ohio St.3d 133, 449 N.E.2d 449 (1983)— § **4.2 n. 6.**

Brown, State v., 389 So.2d 48 (La.1980)—§ **3.8 n. 29.**

Brown, State v., 378 So.2d 916 (La.1979)—§ **7.1 n. 13.**

Brown, State v., 197 Neb. 131, 247 N.W.2d 616 (1976)— § **6.9 n. 15.**

Brown, State v., 250 N.C. 54, 108 S.E.2d 74 (1959)—§ **2.12 n. 29.**

Brown, State v., 22 N.J. 405, 126 A.2d 161 (1956)—§ **7.9 n. 5.**

Brown, State v., 38 Kan. 390, 16 P. 259 (1888)—§ **4.10 n. 3.**

Brown, State ex rel. v. Thompson, 149 W.Va. 649, 142 S.E.2d 711 (1965)—§ **6.8 n. 75;** § **6.9 n. 41.**

Brown, United States v., 635 F.2d 1207 (6th Cir.1980)— § **5.10 n. 54.**

Brown, United States v., 518 F.2d 821 (7th Cir.1975)— § **7.7 n. 24.**

Brown, United States v., 305 F.Supp. 415 (W.D.Tex.1969)— § **6.2 n. 113.**

Brown, United States v., 381 U.S. 437, 85 S.Ct. 1707, 14 L.Ed.2d 484 (1965)—§ **2.4 n. 85, 86, 89, 90.**

Brownlee, State v., 84 Iowa 473, 51 N.W. 25 (1892)—§ **8.12 n. 8.**

Brown's Cases 2 East P.C. 731 (1780)—§ **8.11 n. 62.**

Brubaker, People v., 53 Cal.2d 37, 346 P.2d 8 (1959)— § **7.10 n. 3.**

Bruce v. State, 268 Ind. 180, 375 N.E.2d 1042 (1978)—§ **2.8 n. 3.**

Bruno, United States v., 105 F.2d 921 (2d Cir.1939)—§ **6.5;** § **6.5 n. 126, 131;** § **6.8 n. 12.**

Brunson, State v., 2 Bailey 149 (S.C.1831)—§ **2.1 n. 43.**

Bruton v. United States, 391 U.S. 123, 88 S.Ct. 1620, 20 L.Ed. 476 (1968)—§ **4.5 n. 66.**

Bryan, United States v., 483 F.2d 88 (3d Cir.1973)—§ **6.6 n. 17, 75.**

Bryant v. State, 191 Ga. 686, 13 S.E.2d 820 (1941)—§ **4.5 n. 151.**

Bryant, People v., 409 Ill. 467, 100 N.E.2d 598 (1951)— § **6.5 n. 221.**

Buck v. Bell, 274 U.S. 200, 47 S.Ct. 584, 71 L.Ed. 1000 (1927)—§ **2.11 n. 13.**

Buck, State v., 275 N.W.2d 194 (Iowa 1979)—§ **2.5 n. 22.**

Conley v. State, 69 Ark. 454, 64 S.W. 218 (1901)—§ **8.6 n. 60.**

Conley, People v., 64 Cal.2d 310, 40 Cal.Rptr. 815, 411 P.2d 911 (1966)—§ **4.6; § 4.6 n. 37; § 7.11 n. 15.**

Conn, State v., 286 Md. 405, 408 A.2d 700 (1979)—§ **4.5 n. 140.**

Connally v. General Constr. Co., 269 U.S. 385, 46 S.Ct. 126, 70 L.Ed. 322 (1926)—§ **2.2 n. 46; § 2.3 n. 5, 23, 25.**

Connolly v. Commonwealth, 377 Mass. 527, 387 N.E.2d 519 (1979)—§ **1.8 n. 42.**

Connor v. State, 362 N.W.2d 449 (Iowa 1985)—§ **7.5 n. 29.**

Connor v. State, 29 Fla. 455, 10 So. 891 (1892)—§ **2.9 n. 9.**

Connors, People v., 253 Ill. 266, 97 N.E. 643 (1912)—§ **3.5 n. 42; § 7.16 n. 32.**

Consolidated Laundries Corp., United States v., 291 F.2d 563 (2d Cir.1961)—§ **1.8 n. 100.**

Conte, People ex rel. v. Flood, 53 Misc.2d 109, 277 N.Y.S.2d 697 (1966)—§ **6.5 n. 82.**

Contento-Pachon, United States v., 723 F.2d 691 (9th Cir. 1984)—§ **5.3 n. 30, 42; § 5.4 n. 2, 34.**

Continental Baking Co. v. United States, 281 F.2d 137 (6th Cir.1960)—§ **3.10 n. 67, 68.**

Conyer v. United States, 80 F.2d 292 (6th Cir.1935)—§ **5.3 n. 53, 54.**

Cook v. United States, 138 U.S. 157, 11 S.Ct. 268, 34 L.Ed. 906 (1891)—§ **2.4 n. 46.**

Cook, People v., 228 Cal.App.2d 716, 39 Cal.Rptr. 802 (1964)—§ **5.11 n. 23.**

Cook, State v., 242 Or. 509, 411 P.2d 78 (1966)—§ **2.11 n. 33.**

Cook, State v., 78 S.C. 253, 59 S.E. 862 (1907)—§ **5.8 n. 6.**

Cook, United States v., 462 F.2d 301 (D.C.Cir.1972)—§ **7.17 n. 20.**

Cooke v. People, 231 Ill. 9, 82 N.E. 863 (1907)—§ **6.5 n. 160.**

Cooke v. United States, 267 U.S. 517, 45 S.Ct. 390, 69 L.Ed. 767 (1925)—§ **1.7 n. 94, 96, 98.**

Cooke, State v., 59 Wash.2d 804, 371 P.2d 39 (1962)—§ **8.7 n. 35, 42.**

Cooley v. Board of Wardens of the Port of Philadelphia, 53 U.S. (12 How.) 299, 13 L.Ed. 996 (1851)—§ **2.15 n. 9.**

Coolidge, United States v., 14 U.S. (1 Wheat.) 415, 4 L.Ed. 124 (1816)—§ **2.1 n. 17.**

Coombs, State v., 55 Me. 477 (1868)—§ **8.2 n. 36; § 8.5 n. 38, 44.**

Cooper, Ex parte, 162 Cal. 81, 121 P. 318 (1912)—§ **6.8 n. 89, 93.**

Cooper v. Commonwealth, 110 Ky. 123, 60 S.W. 938 (1901)—§ **8.2 n. 46, 53; § 8.5 n. 40.**

Cooper v. People ex rel. Wyatt, 13 Colo. 337, 22 P. 790 (1889)—§ **1.7 n. 73.**

Cooper v. State, 253 Ga. 736, 325 S.E.2d 137 (1985)—§ **4.5 n. 183.**

Cooper v. State, 201 Tenn. 149, 297 S.W.2d 75 (1956)—§ **8.11 n. 86.**

Cooper, People v., 398 Mich. 450, 247 N.W.2d 866 (1976)—§ **2.8 n. 69.**

Cooper, State v., 286 N.C. 549, 213 S.E.2d 305 (1975)—§ **4.7 n. 19.**

Cope, State v., 78 Ohio App. 429, 67 N.E.2d 912 (1946)—§ **5.7 n. 28.**

Cope, State v., 204 N.C. 28, 167 S.E. 456 (1933)—§ **3.7 n. 28, 30.**

Copertino v. United States, 256 F. 519 (3d Cir.1919)—§ **8.10 n. 33.**

Coppage v. Kansas, 236 U.S. 1, 35 S.Ct. 240, 59 L.Ed. 441 (1915)—§ **2.12 n. 7.**

Corcoran, State v., 82 Wash. 44, 143 P. 453 (1914)—§ **8.13 n. 8.**

Corder v. State, 467 N.E.2d 409 (Ind.1984)—§ **4.5 n. 13, 78.**

Cordes v. State, 54 Tex.Crim. 204, 112 S.W. 943 (1908)—§ **7.1 n. 36.**

Cordova, United States v., 89 F.Supp. 298 (E.D.N.Y. 1950)—§ **2.8 n. 5.**

Cordoza, People v., 57 Cal.App.2d 49, 134 P.2d 877 (1943)—§ **7.7 n. 51.**

Cores, United States v., 356 U.S. 405, 78 S.Ct. 875, 2 L.Ed. 2d 873 (1958)—§ **6.4 n. 32.**

Corey v. United States, 305 F.2d 232 (9th Cir.1962)—§ **8.10 n. 75.**

Corkery, People v., 134 Cal.App. 294, 25 P.2d 257 (1933)—§ **6.3 n. 128.**

Cornell v. State, 159 Fla. 687, 32 So.2d 610 (1947)—§ **3.3 n. 23, 35.**

Cornett v. Commonwealth, 134 Ky. 613, 121 S.W. 424 (1909)—§ **5.1 n. 21.**

Correra, State v., ___ R.I. ___, 430 A.2d 1251 (1981)—§ **4.6 n. 69, 76.**

Corrigan, People ex rel. Hegeman v., 195 N.Y. 1, 87 N.E. 792 (1909)—§ **3.6 n. 17.**

Cory, People v., 26 Cal.App. 735, 148 P. 532 (1915)—§ **6.4 n. 35.**

Costello, Commonwealth v., 392 Mass. 393, 467 N.E.2d 811 (1984)—§ **1.8 n. 39.**

Costly, Commonwealth v., 188 Mass. 1 (1875)—§ **3.12 n. 21.**

Coston v. State, 144 Fla. 676, 198 So. 467 (1940)—§ **3.12 n. 41.**

Cotesworth, Regina v., 6 Mod. 172, 87 Eng.Rep. 928 (1705)—§ **7.15 n. 4.**

Cotner v. Henry, 394 F.2d 873 (7th Cir.1968)—§ **2.14 n. 52.**

Cotton, State v., 56 Ohio St.2d 8, 381 N.E.2d 190 (1978)—§ **7.7 n. 9.**

Couch v. State, 253 Ga. 764, 325 S.E.2d 366 (1985)—§ **4.10 n. 40.**

Couch, Commonwealth v., 32 Ky.L.R. 638, 106 S.W. 830 (1908)—§ **3.12 n. 142.**

Couch, State v., 52 N.M. 127, 193 P.2d 405 (1948)—§ **5.9 n. 14.**

Countryman, State v., 57 Kan. 815, 48 P. 137 (1897)—§ **5.9 n. 22.**

County Court, State v., 70 Wis.2d 230, 234 N.W.2d 283 (1975)—§ **1.7 n. 27.**

County Court, State ex rel. Haskins v., 62 Wis.2d 250, 214 N.W.2d 575 (1974)—§ **4.4 n. 59, 76.**

County Court Branch No. 1, State ex rel. Koopman v., 38 Wis.2d 492, 157 N.W.2d 623 (1968)—§ **4.10 n. 66.**

County Court of Ulster County v. Allen, 442 U.S. 140, 99 S.Ct. 2213, 60 L.Ed.2d 777 (1979)—§ **1.8 n. 65.**

Coupez, United States v., 603 F.2d 1347 (9th Cir.1979)—§ **5.4 n. 39.**

Courtney v. State, 174 Miss. 147, 164 So. 227 (1935)—§ **8.7 n. 59.**

Courtsol, State v., 89 Conn. 564, 94 A. 973 (1915)—§ **8.2 n. 39, 41, 42; § 8.5 n. 39.**

Cowan v. State, 171 Ark. 1018, 287 S.W. 201 (1926)—§ **8.4 n. 15.**

Cox v. Louisiana, 379 U.S. 559, 85 S.Ct. 476, 13 L.Ed.2d 487 (1965)—§ **5.1; § 5.1 n. 114, 115, 116.**

Cox v. Louisiana, 379 U.S. 536, 85 S.Ct. 453, 13 L.Ed.2d 471 (1965)—§ **2.14 n. 25.**

Cox v. People, 82 Ill. 191 (1876)—§ **6.1 n. 12, 15, 18, 103.**

Cox v. United States, 332 U.S. 442, 68 S.Ct. 115, 92 L.Ed. 59 (1947)—§ **2.6 n. 37.**

Dahnke, State v., 244 Iowa 599, 57 N.W.2d 553 (1953)—§ **5.1 n. 34.**

Dailey, State v., 191 Ind. 678, 134 N.E. 481 (1922)—§ **2.1 n. 21.**

Dale, State ex rel. Johnson v., 277 Or. 359, 560 P.2d 650 (1977)—§ **4.5 n. 169.**

D'Alemberte v. Anderson, 349 So.2d 164 (Fla.1977)—§ **2.6 n. 12.**

Dalrymple, People v., 55 Mich. 519, 22 N.W. 20 (1885)—§ **5.11 n. 54.**

Dalton v. People, 68 Colo. 44, 189 P. 37 (1920)—§ **5.3 n. 54.**

Dalton v. State, 252 A.2d 104 (Del.1969)—§ **6.7 n. 19.**

Dalton, State v., 168 N.C. 204, 83 S.E. 693 (1914)—§ **2.1 n. 23, 49.**

Dalton, State v., 134 Mo.App. 517, 114 S.W. 1132 (1908)—§ **2.1 n. 50, 51;** § **6.5 n. 11.**

D'Amico, State v., 136 Vt. 153, 385 A.2d 1082 (1978)—§ **4.10 n. 24.**

Damms, State v., 9 Wis.2d 183, 100 N.W.2d 592 (1960)—§ **6.3;** § **6.3 n. 6, 11, 27.**

Damon, State v., 317 A.2d 459 (Me.1974)—§ **2.9 n. 32.**

D'Angelo, People v., 13 Cal.2d 203, 88 P.2d 708 (1939)—§ **4.6 n. 46.**

Daniel v. State, 212 Miss. 223, 54 So.2d 272 (1951)—§ **8.10 n. 18, 58.**

Daniel v. State, 187 Ga. 411, 1 S.E.2d 6 (1939)—§ **5.7 n. 5.**

Daniel, Regina v., 87 Eng.Rep. 856 (1704)—§ **6.1 n. 6, 9.**

Daniel, State v., 136 N.C. 571, 48 S.E. 544 (1904)—§ **7.16 n. 26.**

Daniels, State v., ___ Mont. ___, 682 P.2d 173 (1984)—§ **5.7 n. 35.**

Daniels, State v., 236 La. 998, 109 So.2d 896 (1959)—§ **3.5 n. 55.**

Danville, City of v. Clark, 63 Ill.2d 408, 348 N.E.2d 844 (1976)—§ **1.7 n. 38.**

D'Aquino v. United States, 192 F.2d 338 (9th Cir.1951)—§ **5.3 n. 17, 29.**

Darby, United States v., 312 U.S. 100, 61 S.Ct. 451, 85 L.Ed. 609 (1941)—§ **2.10 n. 4.**

Darchuck, State v., 117 Mont. 15, 156 P.2d 173 (1945)—§ **1.6 n. 31.**

Dargatz, State v., 228 Kan. 322, 614 P.2d 430 (1980)—§ **4.6 n. 54.**

Darnell v. Cameron, 348 F.2d 64 (D.C.Cir.1965)—§ **4.6 n. 30.**

Darr v. People, 193 Colo. 445, 568 P.2d 32 (1977)—§ **6.3 n. 57.**

Daugherty v. Thomas, 174 Mich. 371, 140 N.W. 615 (1913)—§ **8.10 n. 22.**

Daugherty, People v., 40 Cal.2d 876, 256 P.2d 911 (1953)—§ **2.14 n. 89;** § **4.6 n. 42;** § **7.7 n. 50.**

Dauzat, State v., 392 So.2d 393 (La.1980)—§ **7.15 n. 2.**

Davenport, Regina v., 1 All E.R. 602 [1954]—§ **8.6 n. 21.**

Davenport, State v., 227 N.C. 475, 42 S.E.2d 686 (1947)—§ **6.5 n. 224.**

Davidson v. Commonwealth, 167 Va. 451, 187 S.E. 437 (1936)—§ **7.10 n. 73.**

Davidson v. Commonwealth, 174 Ky. 789, 192 S.W. 846 (1917)—§ **4.4 n. 71.**

Davidson v. State, 29 Okl.Crim. 46, 232 P. 120 (1925)—§ **6.9 n. 69.**

Davidson v. United States, 61 F.2d 250 (8th Cir.1932)—§ **6.4 n. 53.**

Davies, State v., 146 Conn. 137, 148 A.2d 251 (1959)—§ **4.2 n. 32, 110.**

Davila, United States v., 698 F.2d 715 (5th Cir.1983)—§ **6.9 n. 63.**

Davin, People v., 1 App.Div.2d 811, 148 N.Y.S.2d 903 (1956)—§ **5.1 n. 34.**

Davis, In re, 17 Md.App. 98, 299 A.2d 956 (1973)—§ **4.11 n. 43.**

Davis v. City of Peachtree City, 251 Ga. 219, 304 S.E.2d 701 (1983)—§ **3.9 n. 29.**

Davis v. Commonwealth, 214 Va. 728, 204 S.E.2d 273 (1974)—§ **4.2 n. 6, 95.**

Davis v. People, 96 Colo. 212, 40 P.2d 968 (1935)—§ **8.7 n. 103.**

Davis v. State, 383 So.2d 620 (Fla.1980)—§ **2.10 n. 32.**

Davis v. State, 161 Tenn. 23, 28 S.W.2d 993 (1930)—§ **4.2 n. 61;** § **4.7 n. 26;** § **7.10 n. 76;** § **7.11 n. 15.**

Davis v. Superior Court, 175 Cal.App.2d 8, 345 P.2d 513 (1959)—§ **6.5 n. 41.**

Davis v. United States, 160 U.S. 469, 16 S.Ct. 353, 40 L.Ed. 499 (1895)—§ **1.8 n. 15, 24, 25, 26, 29;** § **4.5 n. 117.**

Davis, Commonwealth v., 75 Ky. (12 Bush.) 240 (1876)—§ **2.2 n. 35.**

Davis, People v., 408 Mich. 255, 290 N.W.2d 366 (1980)—§ **6.5 n. 280.**

Davis, People v., 33 N.Y.2d 221, 351 N.Y.S.2d 663, 306 N.E.2d 787 (1973)—§ **4.10 n. 76.**

Davis, Regina v., 6 Cox Crim.Cas. 369 (1854)—§ **8.13 n. 32.**

Davis, State v., 101 Wn.2d 654, 682 P.2d 883 (1984)—§ **6.7 n. 53.**

Davis, State v., 8 Ohio App.3d 205, 456 N.E.2d 1256 (1982)—§ **1.8 n. 41.**

Davis, State v., 613 S.W.2d 218 (Tenn.1981)—§ **8.13 n. 98.**

Davis, State v., 63 Wis.2d 75, 216 N.W.2d 31 (1974)—§ **5.1 n. 117.**

Davis, State v., 196 N.W.2d 885 (Iowa 1972)—§ **7.13 n. 23.**

Davis, State v., 242 N.C. 476, 87 S.E.2d 906 (1955)—§ **8.11 n. 2.**

Davis, State v., 203 N.C. 13, 164 S.E. 737 (1932)—§ **2.9 n. 27.**

Davis, State v., 214 S.C. 34, 51 S.E.2d 86 (1948)—§ **5.7 n. 58.**

Davis, State v., 319 Mo. 1222, 6 S.W.2d 609 (1928)—§ **6.1 n. 26, 89, 102, 105;** § **6.8 n. 52.**

Davis, State v., 128 S.C. 265, 122 S.E. 770 (1924)—§ **7.12 n. 7.**

Davis, State v., 88 S.C. 229, 70 S.E. 811 (1911)—§ **6.5 n. 31.**

Davis, State v., 38 N.J.L. 176 (1875)—§ **8.5 n. 14.**

Davis, United States v., 578 F.2d 277 (10th Cir.1978)—§ **6.5 n. 273.**

Davis, United States v., 167 F.2d 228 (D.C.Cir.1948)—§ **2.1 n. 18, 31.**

Davis, United States v., 25 F.Cas. 786 (No. 14932) (C.C.D. Mass.1837)—§ **2.8 n. 20.**

Dawson, United States v., 10 F.2d 106 (9th Cir.1926)—§ **6.5 n. 238.**

Dawson Case, 80 Eng.Rep. 4 (1602)—§ **8.10 n. 3, 4.**

De Arman v. State, 33 Okl.Crim. 79, 242 P. 783 (1926)—§ **3.12 n. 68.**

De Berry, State v., 75 W.Va. 632, 84 S.E. 508 (1915)—§ **8.8 n. 17.**

De Grange, Commonwealth v., 97 Pa.Super. 181 (1929)—§ **2.1 n. 37.**

De La Roi, People v., 36 Cal.App.2d 287, 97 P.2d 836 (Dist. Ct.App.1939)—§ **7.5 n. 8.**

De Petro, Commonwealth v., 350 Pa. 567, 39 A.2d 838 (1944)—§ **3.6 n. 27.**

De Rose v. People, 64 Colo. 332, 171 P. 359 (1918)—§ **8.7 n. 113.**

De Wolfe, State v., 67 Neb. 321, 93 N.W. 746 (1903)—§ **2.1 n. 21.**

Director of Public Prosecutions v. Lynch, 2 W.L.R. 641 (1975)—§ **5.3 n. 38.**

Director of Public Prosecutions v. Morgan, 61 C.A. 136 (1975)—§ **3.4 n. 14; § 5.1 n. 17.**

DiRienzo, State v., 53 N.J. 360, 251 A.2d 99 (1969)—§ **8.10 n. 48.**

District of Columbia v. Colts, 282 U.S. 63, 51 S.Ct. 52, 75 L.Ed. 177 (1930)—§ **1.6 n. 31.**

District of Columbia v. John R. Thompson Co., 346 U.S. 100, 73 S.Ct. 1007, 97 L.Ed. 1480 (1953)—§ **1.4 n. 43; § 2.2 n. 83.**

Dixon v. State, 104 Miss. 410, 61 So. 423 (1913)—§ **1.6 n. 26, 32, 41, 45, 46, 50; § 7.13 n. 23, 25.**

Dixon, State v., 109 Ariz. 441, 511 P.2d 623 (1973)—§ **7.5 n. 23.**

Dizon, State v., 47 Haw. 444, 390 P.2d 759 (1964)—§ **5.1 n. 16.**

Dlugash, People v., 41 N.Y.2d 725, 395 N.Y.S.2d 419, 363 N.E.2d 1155 (1977)—§ **3.12 n. 19, 39, 97; § 6.3 n. 62.**

Doane v. Commonwealth, 218 Va. 500, 237 N.E.2d 797 (1977)—§ **2.9 n. 17; § 7.5 n. 85.**

Doane, Commonwealth v., 55 Mass. 5 (1848)—§ **5.1 n. 57.**

Dobbert v. Florida, 432 U.S. 282, 97 S.Ct. 2290, 53 L.Ed.2d 344 (1977)—§ **2.4; § 2.4 n. 15, 18, 27.**

Dobry, State v., 217 Iowa 858, 250 N.W. 702 (1933)—§ **2.1 n. 68; § 2.2 n. 66, 68; § 3.8 n. 2, 5, 9, 16; § 6.7 n. 118; § 8.7 n. 109.**

Dockerty v. People, 96 Colo. 338, 44 P.2d 1013 (1935)—§ **1.7 n. 84.**

Doe, In re, 120 R.I. 732, 390 A.2d 920 (1978)—§ **1.8 n. 45.**

Doe v. Bolton, 410 U.S. 179, 93 S.Ct. 739, 35 L.Ed.2d 201 (1973)—§ **2.14 n. 57.**

Doe v. City of Trenton, 143 N.J.Super. 128, 362 A.2d 1200 (1976)—§ **3.9 n. 47.**

Doe v. Commonwealth's Attorney, 425 U.S. 901, 96 S.Ct. 1489, 47 L.Ed.2d 751 (1976)—§ **2.14 n. 51.**

Dolan, Regina v., 6 Cox Crim.Cas. 449 (Ct.Crim.App. 1855)—§ **8.10 n. 33.**

Dole, People v., 122 Cal. 486, 55 P. 581 (1898)—§ **6.6 n. 37.**

Dolph, People v., 124 Colo. 553, 239 P.2d 312 (1951)—§ **2.1 n. 24, 59.**

Dombrauskas, Commonwealth v., 274 Pa.Super. 452, 418 A.2d 493 (1980)—§ **8.5 n. 27, 33.**

Dombrowski v. Pfister, 380 U.S. 479, 85 S.Ct. 1116, 14 L.Ed.2d 22 (1965)—§ **2.3 n. 42, 65.**

Donahey v. City of Montgomery, 43 Ala.App. 20, 178 So.2d 832 (1965)—§ **1.7 n. 38.**

Donahue, State v., 141 Conn. 656, 109 A.2d 364 (1954)—§ **4.7 n. 19.**

Donahue, United States v., 539 F.2d 1131 (8th Cir.1976)—§ **6.5 n. 89.**

Donaldson, People v., 65 Mich.App. 588, 237 N.W.2d 570 (1975)—§ **4.5 n. 168.**

Donehy v. Commonwealth, 170 Ky. 474, 186 S.W. 161 (1916)—§ **7.6 n. 1, 2.**

Donnelly, People v., 190 Cal. 57, 210 P. 523 (1922)—§ **7.7 n. 8.**

Donoghue, Commonwealth v., 250 Ky. 343, 63 S.W.2d 3 (1933)—§ **6.5 n. 293.**

Donohue, State v., 84 N.J.Super. 226, 201 A.2d 413 (1964)—§ **8.7 n. 96.**

Donough, Commonwealth v., 377 Pa. 46, 103 A.2d 694 (1954)—§ **1.8 n. 22, 28.**

Donovan, People v., 53 Misc.2d 687, 279 N.Y.S.2d 404 (Ct. Spec.Sess.1967)—§ **5.1 n. 116.**

Donovan, Rex v., 2 K.B. 498, 30 Cox Crim.Cas. 187 (1934)—§ **7.15 n. 53.**

Doody, State v., 434 A.2d 523 (Me.1981)—§ **6.7 n. 46.**

Dooley, State v., 121 Mo. 591, 26 S.W. 558 (1894)—§ **5.9 n. 33, 35, 41.**

Dooley, State ex rel. v. Coleman, 126 Fla. 203, 170 So. 722 (1936)—§ **6.7 n. 87.**

Doolittle, State v., 153 Kan. 608, 113 P.2d 94 (1941)—§ **8.6 n. 8.**

Doris, Commonwealth v., 287 Pa. 547, 135 A. 313 (1926)—§ **7.5 n. 94, 98; § 7.7 n. 36.**

Dorman, People v., 415 Ill. 385, 114 N.E.2d 404 (1953)—§ **6.5 n. 26.**

Dorrell, United States v., 758 F.2d 427 (9th Cir.1985)—§ **5.4 n. 43.**

Dorsey v. Commonwealth, 13 Ky.L.R. 359, 17 S.W. 183 (1891)—§ **6.7 n. 66.**

Dorsey, State v., 118 N.H. 844, 395 A.2d 855 (1978)—§ **5.4 n. 11.**

Dortort, Commonwealth v., 202 Pa.Super. 211, 208 A.2d 797 (1965)—§ **1.7 n. 27.**

Dosztal, State v., 135 Ariz. 485, 662 P.2d 450 (1983)—§ **2.5 n. 26.**

Dotterweich, United States v., 320 U.S. 277, 64 S.Ct. 134, 88 L.Ed. 48 (1943)—§ **3.9; § 3.9 n. 19, 20; § 3.10; § 3.10 n. 108.**

Doty, State v., 57 Kan. 835, 48 P. 145 (1897)—§ **6.9 n. 12.**

Dougherty, United States v., 473 F.2d 1113 (D.C.Cir. 1972)—§ **1.8 n. 78.**

Douglas v. United States, 239 F.2d 52 (D.C.Cir.1956)—§ **4.5 n. 118.**

Dove v. State, 37 Ark. 261 (1881)—§ **4.10 n. 35, 41.**

Dover v. State, ___ Wyo. ___, 664 P.2d 536 (1983)—§ **2.2 n. 30, 31.**

Dow, In re, 75 Ill.App.3d 1002, 31 Ill.Dec. 39, 393 N.E.2d 1346 (1979)—§ **4.11 n. 42.**

Dow v. State, 77 Ark. 464, 92 S.W. 28 (1906)—§ **7.10 n. 104.**

Dow, State v., 126 N.H. 205, 489 A.2d 650 (1985)—§ **7.4 n. 11.**

Dowell, State v., 106 N.C. 722, 11 S.E. 525 (1890)—§ **5.3 n. 48.**

Downer, People v., 57 Cal.2d 800, 22 Cal.Rptr. 347, 372 P.2d 107 (1962)—§ **6.2 n. 149.**

Downes, Regina v., 13 Cox Crim.Cas. 111 (1875)—§ **3.3 n. 9.**

Downing v. State, 114 Ga. 30, 39 S.E. 927 (1901)—§ **3.12 n. 80.**

Downs, State v., 116 N.C. 1064, 21 S.E. 689 (1895)—§ **5.1 n. 59, 126.**

Dozie, People v., 224 Cal.App.2d 474, 36 Cal.Rptr. 728 (1964)—§ **8.11 n. 88.**

Dozier, United States v., 672 F.2d 531 (5th Cir.1982)—§ **8.12 n. 2.**

Draper v. United States, 358 U.S. 307, 79 S.Ct. 329, 3 L.Ed. 2d 327 (1959)—§ **1.4 n. 3.**

Dreas, People v., 153 Cal.App.3d 623, 200 Cal.Rptr. 586 (1984)—§ **8.11 n. 46.**

Driggers v. State, 96 Fla. 232, 118 So. 20 (1928)—§ **8.3 n. 12.**

Driscoll, United States v., 399 F.2d 135 (2d Cir.1968)—§ **4.5 n. 90.**

Driver v. Hinnant, 356 F.2d 761 (4th Cir.1966)—§ **2.14 n. 135; § 4.10 n. 66, 67, 70, 73, 78, 82.**

Drope v. Missouri, 420 U.S. 162, 95 S.Ct. 896, 43 L.Ed.2d 103 (1975)—§ **4.4 n. 24, 27, 34.**

Druken, Commonwealth v., 356 Mass. 503, 254 N.E.2d 779 (1969)—§ **4.4 n. 50.**

Dube, State v., 409 A.2d 1102 (Me.1979)—§ **2.6 n. 6.**

Duckling v. State, 259 So.2d 686 (Miss.1972)—§ **7.12 n. 8.**

DuCros v. Lambourne, (1907) 1 K.B. 70—§ **6.7 n. 44.**

Dudley & Stephens, Regina v., L.R. 14 Q.B.D. 273 (1884)—§ **5.4 n. 30, 32, 53.**

Duerr, Commonwealth v., 158 Pa.Super. 484, 45 A.2d 235 (1946)—§ **5.10 n. 17.**

Duffield, People v., 387 Mich. 300, 197 N.W.2d 25 (1972)—§ **2.9 n. 7.**

Dugal, Regina v., 4 Que.L.R. 350 (Q.B.1878)—§ **7.13 n. 39.**

Dugdale v. Regina, 1 El. & Bl. 435, 118 Eng.Rep. 499 (1853)—§ **3.2 n. 15, 43.**

Duke v. United States, 233 F.2d 897 (5th Cir.1956)—§ **6.4 n. 113.**

Dumar, People v., 106 N.Y. 502, 13 N.E. 325 (1887)—§ **8.8 n. 24.**

Dumas, State v., 118 Minn. 77, 136 N.W. 311 (1912)—§ **6.2 n. 128.**

Dunbar, State v., 282 S.C. 169, 318 S.E.2d 16 (1984)—§ **8.13 n. 3.**

Dunbar Contracting Co., People v., 165 App.Div. 59, 151 N.Y.S. 164 (1914)—§ **6.5 n. 249.**

Duncan v. Commonwealth, 289 Ky. 231, 158 S.W.2d 396 (1942)—§ **1.6 n. 24, § 5.1 n. 32.**

Duncan v. Louisiana, 391 U.S. 145, 88 S.Ct. 1444, 20 L.Ed. 2d 491 (1968)—§ **1.6 n. 68.**

Duncan v. Missouri, 152 U.S. 377, 14 S.Ct. 570, 38 L.Ed. 485 (1894)—§ **2.4 n. 47.**

Duncan, People v., 363 Ill. 495, 2 N.E.2d 705 (1936)—§ **3.10 n. 100.**

Duncan, State v., 28 N.C. 98 (1845)—§ **6.6 n. 60, 64.**

Dunkel & Co., Samuel, United States v., 184 F.2d 894 (2d Cir.1950)—§ **6.5 n. 115.**

Dunmann, State v., 427 So.2d 166 (Fla.1983)—§ **8.5 n. 20.**

Dunn v. Mayor and Council of Wilmington, 59 Del. 287, 219 A.2d 153 (1966)—§ **1.7 n. 19.**

Dunning, State v., 177 N.C. 559, 98 S.E. 530 (1919)—§ **5.10 n. 13.**

Dupree, United States v., 544 F.2d 1050 (9th Cir.1976)—§ **7.16 n. 15.**

Duran v. District Court, 190 Colo. 272, 545 P.2d 1365 (1976)—§ **1.7 n. 52.**

Durham v. State, 199 Ind. 567, 159 N.E. 145 (1927)—§ **5.10 n. 11, 18.**

Durham v. United States, 214 F.2d 862 (D.C.Cir.1954)—§ **2.2 n. 102, 105; § 4.2 n. 72, 108; § 4.3; § 4.3 n. 10, 29, 39, 47, 54; § 4.5 n. 173.**

Durham, Commonwealth v., 255 Pa.Super. 539, 389 A.2d 108 (1978)—§ **4.11 n. 45.**

Durham, State v., 156 W.Va. 509, 195 S.E.2d 144 (1973)—§ **3.12 n. 70.**

Durkee, United States v., 25 F.Cas. 941 (No. 15009) (C.C. N.D.Cal.1856)—§ **8.5 n. 35.**

Durland v. United States, 161 U.S. 306, 16 S.Ct. 508, 40 L.Ed. 709 (1896)—§ **8.7 n. 27.**

Durner, State ex rel. v. Huegin, 110 Wis. 189, 85 N.W. 1046 (1901)—§ **6.5 n. 274.**

Dusablon, People v., 16 N.Y.2d 9, 261 N.Y.S.2d 38, 209 N.E.2d 90 (1965)—§ **2.4 n. 42.**

Dusenbery v. Commonwealth, 220 Va. 770, 263 S.E.2d 392 (1980)—§ **6.6 n. 18.**

Dusky v. United States, 362 U.S. 402, 80 S.Ct. 788, 4 L.Ed. 2d 824 (1960)—§ **4.4 n. 10, 13, 26.**

Dutton v. State, 123 Md. 373, 91 A. 417 (1914)—§ **2.14 n. 87.**

Duty, People v., 269 Cal.App.2d 97, 74 Cal.Rptr. 606 (1969)—§ **6.9 n. 22.**

Dwyer, People v., 397 Ill. 599, 74 N.E.2d 882—§ **2.9 n. 12.**

Dycus v. State, 529 P.2d 979 (Wyo.1974)—§ **5.2 n. 26.**

Dye Construction Co., United States v., 510 F.2d 78 (10th Cir.1975)—§ **3.10 n. 13.**

Dyer, State v., 388 So.2d 374 (La.1980)—§ **6.2 n. 43.**

Dyer, State v., 289 A.2d 693 (Me.1972)—§ **1.6 n. 38.**

Dyke v. Taylor Implement Mfg. Co., 391 U.S. 216, 88 S.Ct. 1472, 20 L.Ed.2d 538 (1968)—§ **1.7 n. 68.**

Dyson, Rex v., 2 K.B. 454 (1908)—§ **3.12 n. 145.**

Eades, United States v., 615 F.2d 617 (4th Cir.1980)—§ **7.15 n. 5.**

Eager v. State, 205 Tenn. 156, 325 S.W.2d 815 (1959)—§ **6.7 n. 103.**

Eagleton, (Regina v., 6 Cox Crim.Cas. 559 (1855)—§ **6.1; § 6.1 n. 116, 120.**

Early v. United States, 394 F.2d 117 (10th Cir.1968)—§ **1.8 n. 104.**

Easley v. State, 49 Ga.App. 275, 175 S.E. 23 (1934)—§ **7.15 n. 35.**

Easter v. District of Columbia, 361 F.2d 50 (D.C.Cir. 1966)—§ **2.14 n. 135; § 4.10 n. 72.**

Easterling v. State, 267 P.2d 185 (Okl.Crim.1954)—§ **5.7 n. 20.**

Easton v. Iowa, 188 U.S. 220, 23 S.Ct. 288, 47 L.Ed. 452 (1903)—§ **2.15 n. 31.**

Eatman, People v., 405 Ill. 491, 91 N.E.2d 387 (1950)—§ **5.9 n. 19.**

Eaton v. Commonwealth, 235 Ky. 466, 31 S.W.2d 718 (1930)—§ **8.4 n. 14.**

Eaton, United States v., 144 U.S. 677, 12 S.Ct. 764, 36 L.Ed. 591 (1892)—§ **2.6 n. 23.**

Ebbeler, State v., 283 Mo. 57, 222 S.W. 396 (1920)—§ **5.1 n. 11.**

Eberhardt, United States v., 417 F.2d 1009 (4th Cir. 1969)—§ **6.7 n. 30, 75, 83.**

Eberhart, State v., 106 Wash. 222, 179 P. 853 (1919)—§ **8.2 n. 10, § 8.4 n. 25.**

Eberle, Commonwealth v., 474 Pa. 548, 379 A.2d 90 (1977)—§ **5.7 n. 62.**

Eckert v. State, 114 Wis. 160, 89 N.W. 826 (1902)—§ **4.3 n. 9.**

Eddings v. Oklahoma, 455 U.S. 104, 102 S.Ct. 869, 71 L.Ed. 2d 1 (1982)—§ **2.14 n. 99, 100.**

Edelin, Commonwealth v., 371 Mass. 497, 359 N.E.2d 4 (1976)—§ **7.1 n. 13.**

Edenburg, People v., 88 Cal.App. 558, 263 P. 857 (1928)—§ **2.4 n. 4, 37.**

Edgar v. Mite Corp., 457 U.S. 624, 102 S.Ct. 2629, 73 L.Ed. 2d 269 (1982)—§ **2.15 n. 15, 19, 45.**

Edgar v. State, 37 Ark. 219 (1881)—§ **5.1 n. 33.**

Edmondson v. State, 18 Ga.App. 233, 89 S.E. 189 (1916)—§ **8.2 n. 9.**

Edmunds v. United States, 260 F.2d 474 (D.C.Cir.1958)—§ **4.5 n. 61.**

Edwards v. California, 314 U.S. 160, 62 S.Ct. 164, 86 L.Ed. 119 (1941)—§ **2.15; § 2.15 n. 8, 21.**

Edwards v. State, 49 Wis.2d 105, 181 N.W.2d 383 (1970)—§ **8.5 n. 27.**

Edwards v. State, 202 Tenn. 393, 304 S.W.2d 500 (1957)—§ **4.10 n. 43; § 7.12 n. 16.**

Edwards v. State, 178 Miss. 696, 174 So. 57 (1937)—§ **4.10 n. 9; § 8.5 n. 34.**

Edwards, King v., 88 Eng.Rep. 229 (1725)—§ **6.5 n. 16.**

Edwards, State v., 420 So.2d 663 (La.1982)—§ **4.6 n. 77.**

Edwards, State v., 89 R.I. 378, 153 A.2d 153 (1959)—§ **6.5 n. 228.**

Green v. United States, 356 U.S. 165, 78 S.Ct. 632, 2 L.Ed. 2d 672 (1958)—§ **1.7 n. 67, 90, 95.**

Green, Commonwealth v., 477 Pa. 170, 383 A.2d 877 (1978)—§ **3.12 n. 9, 135.**

Green, Commonwealth v., 326 Mass. 344, 94 N.E.2d 260 (1950)—§ **8.7 n. 25, 78, 87.**

Green, People v., 27 Cal.3d 1, 164 Cal.Rptr. 1, 609 P.2d 468 (1980)—§ **3.11 n. 2, 11, 26; § 8.11 n. 25.**

Green, State v., 157 W.Va. 1031, 206 S.E.2d 923 (1974)— § **5.7 n. 65.**

Green, State v., 78 Utah 580, 6 P.2d 177 (1931)—§ **4.2 n. 77; § 4.7 n. 26; § 7.11 n. 15.**

Green, State v., 118 S.C. 279, 110 S.E. 145—§ **5.9 n. 28.**

Green, State ex rel. Sweezer v., 360 Mo. 1249, 232 S.W.2d 897 (1950)—§ **2.4 n. 9.**

Greene, In re, 52 Fed. 104 (C.C.S.D.Ohio 1892)—§ **2.1 n. 21.**

Greene, United States v., 497 F.2d 1068 (7th Cir.1974)— § **4.5 n. 94, 95.**

Greene, United States v., 489 F.2d 1145 (D.C.Cir.1973)— § **4.1 n. 56.**

Greenfield v. Commonwealth, 214 Va. 710, 204 S.E.2d 414 (1974)—§ **4.9 n. 3.**

Greening, Rex v., [1913] 3 K.B. 846, 23 Cox Crim.Cas. 601 (1913)—§ **7.10 n. 40.**

Greenough, In re, 116 Vt. 277, 75 A.2d 569 (1950)—§ **2.7 n. 2.**

Greenway v. State, 59 Ga.App. 461, 1 S.E.2d 217 (1939)— § **7.2 n. 28.**

Greenwood Village, City of v. Fleming, 643 P.2d 511 (Colo. 1982)—§ **1.7 n. 37.**

Greer, People v., 79 Ill.2d 103, 37 Ill.Dec. 313, 402 N.E.2d 203 (1980)—§ **7.1 n. 13.**

Greer, United States v., 467 F.2d 1064 (7th Cir.1972)— § **6.8 n. 30.**

Gregg v. Georgia, 428 U.S. 153, 96 S.Ct. 2909, 49 L.Ed.2d 859 (1976)—§ **2.14; § 2.14 n. 90, 110.**

Gregg, United States v., 612 F.2d 43 (2d Cir.1979)—§ **6.7 n. 53.**

Gregory v. State, 628 P.2d 384 (Okla.Crim.1981)—§ **7.16 n. 32.**

Gregory v. State, 259 Ind. 652, 291 N.E.2d 67 (1973)—§ **1.6 n. 28.**

Gregory, Commonwealth v., 132 Pa.Super. 507, 1 A.2d 501 (1938)—§ **5.11 n. 24.**

Gregory, Regina v., L.R. 1 Cr.Cas.Res. 77 (1867)—§ **6.1 n. 14.**

Greider v. Duckworth, 701 F.2d 1228 (7th Cir.1983)— § **4.10 n. 64, 90.**

Grider, State v., 74 Wyo. 88, 288 P.2d 766 (1955)—§ **8.7 n. 114.**

Griego, State v., 61 N.M. 42, 294 P.2d 282 (1956)—§ **7.10 n. 90.**

Grierson, State v., 96 N.H. 36, 69 A.2d 851 (1949)—§ **5.7 n. 62.**

Griffin, In re, 63 Cal.2d 757, 408 P.2d 959, 48 Cal.Rptr. 183 (1965)—§ **2.4 n. 24.**

Griffin v. Illinois, 351 U.S. 12, 76 S.Ct. 585, 100 L.Ed. 891 (1956)—§ **4.5; § 4.5 n. 106.**

Griffin v. State, 248 Ark. 1223, 455 S.W.2d 882 (1970)— § **6.4 n. 95.**

Griffin v. State, 26 Ga. 493 (1858)—§ **6.1 n. 102; § 6.3 n. 96.**

Griffin, Commonwealth v., 622 S.W.2d 214 (Ky.1981)— § **4.4 n. 28.**

Griffin, People ex rel. v. Hunt, 267 N.Y. 597, 196 N.E. 598 (1935)—§ **8.11 n. 86.**

Griffin, United States v., 660 F.2d 996 (4th Cir.1981)— § **6.5 n. 150.**

Griffith v. State, 36 Ind. 406 (1871)—§ **8.8 n. 20.**

Griggs, People v., 17 Cal.2d 621, 110 P.2d 1061 (1941)— § **4.10 n. 61.**

Grigsby v. State, 260 Ark. 499, 542 S.W.2d 275 (1976)— § **7.5 n. 80, 100.**

Grilli, State v., 304 Minn. 80, 230 N.W.2d 445 (1975)— § **5.2 n. 26, 79.**

Grimaud, United States v., 220 U.S. 506, 31 S.Ct. 480, 55 L.Ed. 563 (1911)—§ **2.6; § 2.6 n. 3, 17, 25.**

Grimm, State v., 156 W.Va. 615, 195 S.E.2d 637 (1973)— § **4.3 n. 67.**

Grimsley, State v., 3 Ohio App.3d 265, 444 N.E.2d 1071 (1982)—§ **4.9 n. 15.**

Grin v. Shine, 187 U.S. 181, 23 S.Ct. 98, 47 L.Ed. 130 (1902)—§ **8.6 n. 47.**

Grindstaff v. State, 214 Tenn. 58, 377 S.W.2d 921 (1964)— § **1.6 n. 31.**

Grisham v. Hagan, 361 U.S. 278, 80 S.Ct. 310, 4 L.Ed.2d 279 (1960)—§ **2.8 n. 24.**

Grisham v. State, 10 Tenn. 589 (1831)—§ **2.1 n. 43.**

Griswold v. Connecticut, 381 U.S. 479, 85 S.Ct. 1678, 14 L.Ed. 510 (1965)—§ **2.12 n. 12, 13, 17; § 2.14; § 2.14 n. 3, 29, 47, 58.**

Groce v. State, 126 Tex.Crim.R. 10, 70 S.W.2d 163 (1934)— § **5.11 n. 18.**

Groff v. State, 171 Ind. 547, 85 N.E. 769 (1908)—§ **3.9 n. 25.**

Gross, Rex v., 23 Cox Crim.Cas. 455 (1913)—§ **3.12 n. 54; § 7.10 n. 90.**

Grossi v. Long, 136 Wash. 133, 238 P. 983 (1925)—§ **4.4 n. 71.**

Grossman v. State, 457 P.2d 226 (Alaska 1969)—§ **5.2 n. 2, 32, 37, 59, 65.**

Grosso v. United States, 390 U.S. 62, 88 S.Ct. 709, 19 L.Ed. 2d 906 (1968)—§ **2.14 n. 62, 63.**

Grugin, State v., 147 Mo. 39, 47 S.W. 1058 (1898)—§ **7.10 n. 53, 81, 82.**

Grunewald v. United States, 353 U.S. 391, 77 S.Ct. 963, 1 L.Ed.2d 931 (1957)—§ **6.5; § 6.5 n. 77, 161, 163, 172, 174, 177, 178.**

Guarro v. United States, 237 F.2d 578 (D.C.Cir.1956)— § **7.15 n. 51, 53.**

Guest, State v., 583 P.2d 836 (Alaska 1978)—§ **5.1 n. 53.**

Guest, United States v., 383 U.S. 745, 86 S.Ct. 1170, 16 L.Ed.2d 239 (1966)—§ **2.15 n. 22.**

Guffey, State v., 262 S.W.2d 152 (Mo.App.1953)—§ **6.3 n. 54.**

Guild, State v., 10 N.J.C. 163 (1828)—§ **4.10 n. 17, 29.**

Guillett, People v., 342 Mich. 1, 69 N.W.2d 140 (1955)— § **4.10 n. 11.**

Guillette, United States v., 547 F.2d 743 (2d Cir.1976)— § **3.12 n. 75.**

Guiteau, United States v., 12 D.C. (1 Mackey) 498 (1882)— § **2.8 n. 18.**

Gum, State v., 68 W.Va. 105, 69 S.E. 463 (1910)—§ **5.7 n. 68.**

Gund Brewing Co., John v. United States, 204 F. 17, modified 206 F. 386 (8th Cir.1913)—§ **3.10 n. 63.**

Gundaker Central Motors v. Gassert, 23 N.J. 71, 127 A.2d 566 (1956)—§ **2.12 n. 36, 44, 45.**

Gunter v. State, 499 S.W.2d 954 (Tenn.1973)—§ **1.6 n. 27.**

Gunter, State v., 208 La. 694, 23 So.2d 305 (1954)—§ **4.5 n. 37.**

Guptill, State v., 481 A.2d 772 (Me.1984)—§ **6.8 n. 56.**

Harley v. United States, 373 A.2d 898 (D.C.App.1977)—§ **5.11 n. 1, 14.**

Harley, Rex v., 172 Eng.Rep. 744 (1830)—§ **6.6 n. 27.**

Harmon, United States v., 45 F. 414 (D.Kan.1891)—§ **3.6 n. 15.**

Harold, State v., 312 N.C. 787, 325 S.E.2d 219 (1985)—§ **8.13 n. 61.**

Harper, State ex rel. v. Zegeer, —— W.Va. ——, 296 S.E.2d 873 (1982)—§ **4.10 n. 80, 84.**

Harrel v. State, 39 Miss. 702 (1861)—§ **6.9 n. 4, 8, 10.**

Harrell v. State, 593 S.W.2d 664 (Tenn.1979)—§ **4.10 n. 26.**

Harrington v. State, 547 S.W.2d 616 (Tex.Crim.App. 1977)—§ **3.3 n. 14, 55.**

Harris v. Commonwealth, 183 Ky. 542, 209 S.W. 509 (1919)—§ **3.11 n. 19.**

Harris v. Oklahoma, 433 U.S. 682, 97 S.Ct. 2912, 53 L.Ed. 2d 1054 (1977)—§ **7.5; § 7.5 n. 112.**

Harris v. Pennsylvania R.R. Co., 50 F.2d 866 (4th Cir. 1931)—§ **3.3 n. 12, 27.**

Harris v. State, 451 So.2d 406 (Ala.Crim.1984)—§ **8.11 n. 50.**

Harris v. State, 177 Ala. 17, 59 So. 205 (1912)—§ **6.8 n. 20.**

Harris, People v., 72 Ill.2d 16, 17 Ill.Dec. 838, 377 N.E.2d 28 (1978)—§ **6.2 n. 74.**

Harris, People v., 8 Ill.2d 431, 134 N.E.2d 315 (1956)—§ **7.10 n. 17, 77.**

Harris, People v., 394 Ill. 325, 68 N.E.2d 728 (1946)—§ **8.10 n. 48.**

Harris, State v., 406 So.2d 128 (La.1981)—§ **4.4 n. 26.**

Harris, State v., 194 Neb. 74, 230 N.W.2d 203 (1975)—§ **3.12 n. 30, 128, 135.**

Harris, State v., 222 N.W.2d 462 (Iowa 1974)—§ **5.7 n. 15.**

Harris, State v., 147 Conn. 589, 164 A.2d 399 (1960)—§ **8.6 n. 24.**

Harris, United States v., 441 F.2d 1333 (10th Cir.1971)—§ **6.7 n. 74.**

Harris, United States v., 409 F.2d 77 (4th Cir.1969)—§ **6.5 n. 97.**

Harrison v. People, 50 N.Y. 518 (1872)—§ **8.3 n. 10, 13, 17.**

Harrison v. State, 442 A.2d 1377 (Del.1958)—§ **5.2 n. 28.**

Harrison v. State, 69 Tex.Cr.R. 291, 153 S.W. 139 (1912)—§ **6.9 n. 19.**

Harrison v. United States, 7 F.2d 259 (2d Cir.1925)—§ **6.4 n. 19.**

Harrison, Commonwealth v., 342 Mass. 279, 173 N.E.2d 87 (1961)—§ **4.2 n. 110.**

Harrison, State v., 178 Conn. 689, 425 A.2d 111 (1979)—§ **6.7 n. 52.**

Harrison, State v., 90 N.M. 439, 564 P.2d 1321 (1977)—§ **7.5 n. 15, 76.**

Harrison, State v., 347 Mo. 1230, 152 S.W.2d 161 (1941)—§ **8.2 n. 36; § 8.8 n. 14.**

Harrison, State v., 107 N.J.L. 213, 152 A. 867 (1931)—§ **3.3 n. 20.**

Harriss, United States v., 347 U.S. 612, 74 S.Ct. 808, 98 L.Ed. 989 (1954)—§ **2.3 n. 18.**

Hartfiel, State v., 24 Wis. 60 (1869)—§ **5.1 n. 32.**

Hartley, State v., 90 N.M. 488, 565 P.2d 658 (1978)—§ **4.2 n. 6, 95.**

Hartley, United States v., 678 F.2d 961 (11th Cir.1982)—§ **6.4 n. 86; § 6.5 n. 255.**

Hartman, People v., 130 Cal. 487, 62 P. 823 (1900)—§ **5.1 n. 22.**

Hartson v. People, 125 Colo. 1, 240 P.2d 907 (1951)—§ **3.10 n. 98.**

Hartzel v. United States, 322 U.S. 680, 64 S.Ct. 1233, 88 L.Ed. 1534 (1944)—§ **3.5 n. 7.**

Hartzog, State v., 26 Wn.App. 576, 615 P.2d 480 (1980)—§ **1.6 n. 33.**

Harvard, Commonwealth v., 356 Mass. 452, 253 N.E.2d 346 (1969)—§ **6.7 n. 82.**

Harvey v. State, 78 Nev. 417, 375 P.2d 225 (1962)—§ **8.2 n. 56; § 8.5 n. 43.**

Harvick v. State, 49 Ark. 514, 6 S.W. 19 (1887)—§ **3.5 n. 41.**

Harvill, State v., 106 Ariz. 386, 476 P.2d 841 (1970)—§ **6.2 n. 62, 108.**

Harwood, State v., 110 Ariz. 375, 519 P.2d 177 (1974)—§ **7.10 n. 59.**

Haskell v. Commonwealth, 218 Va. 1033, 243 S.E.2d 477 (1978)—§ **7.5 n. 82, 92.**

Haskell, United States v., 169 F. 449 (E.D.Okl.1909)—§ **2.4 n. 50.**

Haskins, State ex rel. v. County Court, 62 Wis.2d 250, 214 N.W.2d 575 (1974)—§ **4.4 n. 53, 69.**

Hata & Co., Ltd., United States v., 535 F.2d 508 (9th Cir. 1976)—§ **3.10 n. 117.**

Hatcher v. Commonwealth, 224 Ky. 131, 5 S.W.2d 882 (1928)—§ **8.9 n. 5.**

Hatfield, State v., —— W.Va. ——, 286 S.E.2d 402 (1982)—§ **7.7 n. 11.**

Hathaway, State ex rel. Labuwi v., 168 Wis. 518, 170 N.W. 654 (1919)—§ **8.7 n. 103.**

Hatley, State v., 72 N.M. 377, 384 P.2d 252 (1963)—§ **7.17 n. 24.**

Haun, State v., 61 Kan. 146, 59 P. 340 (1899)—§ **2.15 n. 1.**

Haupt v. United States, 330 U.S. 631, 67 S.Ct. 874, 91 L.Ed. 1145 (1947)—§ **3.5 n. 7.**

Hauptmann, State v., 115 N.J.L. 412, 180 A. 809 (1935)—§ **8.5 n. 13.**

Hawes v. Dinkler, 224 Ga. 785, 164 S.E.2d 799 (1968)—§ **1.7 n. 22.**

Hawkin, Ann, (1704) 2 E. East—§ **8.13 n. 12.**

Hawkins, Commonwealth v., 157 Mass. 551, 32 N.E. 862 (1893)—§ **3.7 n. 29; § 7.13 n. 36; § 7.15 n. 20, 28, 43.**

Haworth v. Chapman, 113 Fla. 591, 152 So. 663 (1933)—§ **2.2 n. 21.**

Hayes v. State, 211 Md. 111, 126 A.2d 576 (1956)—§ **8.11 n. 85.**

Hayes v. State, 11 Ga.App. 371, 75 S.E. 523 (1912)—§ **7.13 n. 8.**

Hayes, People v., 421 Mich. 271, 364 N.W.2d 635 (1984)—§ **4.5 n. 89.**

Hayes, State v., 351 N.W.2d 654 (Minn.App.1984)—§ **6.8 n. 86, 87.**

Hayes, State v., 118 N.H. 548, 389 A.2d 1379 (1978)—§ **4.4 n. 17.**

Hayes, State v., 105 Mo. 76, 16 S.W. 514 (1891)—§ **6.8; § 6.8 n. 50.**

Hayes, State v., 78 Mo. 307 (1883)—§ **6.1 n. 100; § 6.3 n. 94.**

Hayes, United States v., 589 F.2d 811 (5th Cir.1979)—§ **4.4 n. 17.**

Hayner, People v., 300 N.Y. 171, 90 N.E.2d 23 (1949)—§ **7.1 n. 23.**

Haynes v. State, 451 So.2d 227 (Miss.1984)—§ **5.7 n. 56.**

Haynes v. United States, 390 U.S. 85, 88 S.Ct. 722, 19 L.Ed.2d 923 (1968)—§ **2.10 n. 23; § 2.14 n. 63, 64.**

Haynes, United States v., 81 F.Supp. 63 (W.D.Pa.1948)—§ **1.6 n. 40.**

Hays v. State, 15 Ga.App. 386, 83 S.E. 502 (1914)—§ **6.9 n. 73.**

Hunt, Commonwealth v., 45 Mass. (4 Metc.) 111 (1842)—§ 6.4 n. 16; § 6.5 n. 2, 3, 205.

Hunt, People ex rel. Griffin v., 267 N.Y. 597, 196 N.E. 598 (1935)—§ 8.11 n. 86.

Hunter v. State, 158 Tenn. 63, 12 S.W.2d 361 (1928)—§ 5.1 n. 96; § 8.6 n. 58.

Hunter, State v., 136 Ariz. 45, 664 P.2d 195 (1983)—§ 3.6 n. 27.

Hunter, State v., 79 S.C. 73, 60 S.E. 240 (1908)—§ 6.6 n. 4.

Hupf, State v., 48 Del. 254, 101 A.2d 355 (1953)—§ 7.13 n. 24, 43.

Hurst, State v., 11 W.Va. 54 (1877)—§ 8.7 n. 85.

Hurt v. State, 184 Tenn. 608, 201 S.W.2d 988 (1947)—§ 1.6 n. 36.

Hurtado v. California, 110 U.S. 516, 4 S.Ct. 111, 28 L.Ed. 232 (1884)—§ 1.4 n. 6.

Hurwitz v. State, 200 Md. 578, 92 A.2d 575 (1952)—§ 6.5 n. 221.

Hussey, Rex v., 18 Crim.App. 160 (1924)—§ 5.9 n. 25.

Hutchins, Commonwealth v., 232 Mass. 285, 122 N.E. 275 (1919)—§ 8.6 n. 33.

Hutchins, State v., 303 N.C. 321, 279 S.E.2d 788 (1981)—§ 7.5 n. 88, 92; § 7.7 n. 34.

Hutchinson v. State, 315 So.2d 546 (Fla.App.1975)—§ 6.4 n. 101.

Hutchinson, People v., 169 Misc. 724, 9 N.Y.S.2d 656 (1938)—§ 8.4 n. 23.

Hutchinson, State ex rel. Trotchy v., 224 Ind. 443, 68 N.E.2d 649 (1946)—§ 1.7 n. 83.

Hutchman v. State, 61 Okl.Crim. 117, 66 P.2d 99 (1937)—§ 6.8 n. 78.

Hüter, People v., 184 N.Y. 237, 77 N.E. 6 (1906)—§ 7.5 n. 104; § 7.6 n. 8.

Hutto v. Davis, 454 U.S. 370, 102 S.Ct. 703, 70 L.Ed.2d 556 (1982)—§ 2.14 n. 119.

Hutton v. Superior Court, 147 Cal. 156, 81 P. 409 (1905)—§ 1.7 n. 82.

Hyam v. Director of Public Prosecutions, [1975] A.C. 55 (1974)—§ 7.4 n. 16.

Hyde v. Shine, 199 U.S. 62, 25 S.Ct. 760, 50 L.Ed. 90 (1905)—§ 6.4 n. 34.

Hyde v. United States, 225 U.S. 347, 32 S.Ct. 793, 56 L.Ed. 1114 (1912)—§ 2.9 n. 25; § 6.2 n. 131; § 6.4 n. 35, 36; § 6.5 n. 76, 79, 183.

Hyden v. State, 136 Tenn. 294, 189 S.W. 369 (1916)—§ 8.4 n. 1.

Hygrade Provision Co. v. Sherman, 266 U.S. 497, 45 S.Ct. 141, 69 L.Ed. 402 (1925)—§ 2.3 n. 28, 30.

Hynes v. Mayor and Council of Borough of Oradell, 425 U.S. 610, 96 S.Ct. 1755, 48 L.Ed.2d 243 (1976)—§ 2.3 n. 61.

I. & M. Amusements, Inc., State v., 10 Ohio App.2d 153, 226 N.E.2d 567 (1966)—§ 3.10 n. 13.

Iannelli v. United States, 420 U.S. 770, 95 S.Ct. 1284, 43 L.Ed.2d 616 (1975)—§ 6.4 n. 74, 82, 88; § 6.5; § 6.5 n. 282.

Ibn Omar-Muhammad, State v., 102 N.M. 274, 694 P.2d 922 (1985)—§ 7.4 n. 22.

Ibn-Tamas v. United States, 407 A.2d 626 (D.C.App. 1979)—§ 5.7 n. 39.

Ice v. Commonwealth, 667 S.W.2d 671 (Ky.1984)—§ 4.5 n. 146, 176.

Ice & Fuel Co., State v., 166 N.C. 366, 81 S.E. 737 (1914)—§ 8.7 n. 37.

Impson v. State, 47 Ariz. 573, 58 P.2d 523 (1936)—§ 8.5 n. 8.

In re (see name of party)

Inger, State v., 292 N.W.2d 119 (Iowa 1980)—§ 7.10 n. 23.

Ingles v. People, 92 Colo. 518, 22 P.2d 1109 (1933)—§ 4.1 n. 56.

Ingraham v. Wright, 430 U.S. 651, 97 S.Ct. 1401, 51 L.Ed. 2d 711 (1977)—§ 5.6 n. 16.

Ingram, State v., 237 N.C. 197, 74 S.E.2d 532 (1953)—§ 7.16 n. 25.

Inland Freight Lines v. United States, 191 F.2d 313 (10th Cir.1951)—§ 3.10 n. 48.

Instan, Regina v., 17 Cox Crim.Cas. 602 (1893)—§ 3.3 n. 17.

International Harvester Co. v. Commonwealth, 124 Ky. 543, 99 S.W. 637 (1907)—§ 2.9 n. 25.

International Minerals & Chemical Corp., United States v., 402 U.S. 558, 91 S.Ct. 1697, 29 L.Ed.2d 178 (1971)—§ 2.2 n. 55, 57; § 2.6 n. 1; § 5.1 n. 54, 78.

Interstate Circuit v. United States, 306 U.S. 208, 59 S.Ct. 467, 83 L.Ed. 610 (1939)—§ 6.4 n. 93.

Interstate Circuit, Inc. v. City of Dallas, 390 U.S. 676, 88 S.Ct. 1298, 20 L.Ed.2d 225 (1968)—§ 2.3 n. 7, 47, 61.

Iowa City v. Nolan, 239 N.W.2d 102 (Iowa 1976)—§ 3.9 n. 9, 32, 33.

Irby, State v., 423 S.W.2d 800 (Mo.1968)—§ 6.7 n. 18.

Ireland, People v., 38 Ill.App.3d 616, 348 N.E.2d 277 (1976)—§ 3.2 n. 54.

Ireland, People v., 70 Cal.2d 522, 75 Cal.Rptr. 188, 450 P.2d 580 (1969)—§ 7.5 n. 104.

Iron Shell, United States v., 633 F.2d 77 (8th Cir.1980)—§ 7.15 n. 13.

Irwin, People v., 166 Misc. 751, 4 N.Y.S.2d 548 (1938)—§ 4.2 n. 55.

Irwin, State v., 55 N.C.App. 305, 285 S.E.2d 345 (1982)—§ 3.5 n. 42.

Isbell v. United States, 227 F. 788 (10th Cir.1915)—§ 1.8 n. 97.

Ivic, United States v., 700 F.2d 51 (2d Cir.1983)—§ 6.2; § 6.2 n. 158, 169.

Ivy, State v., 119 Wis.2d 591, 350 N.W.2d 622 (1984)—§ 6.7 n. 53.

J.N., Matter of, 406 A.2d 1275 (D.C.App.1979)—§ 3.12 n. 27, 139, 147.

Jackson v. Bishop, 404 F.2d 571 (8th Cir.1968)—§ 1.2 n. 10.

Jackson v. Commonwealth, 265 Ky. 295, 96 S.W.2d 1014 (1936)—§ 7.1 n. 14, 19, 22.

Jackson v. Commonwealth, 100 Ky. 239, 38 S.W. 422 (1896)—§ 3.11 n. 29.

Jackson v. Denno, 378 U.S. 368, 84 S.Ct. 1774, 12 L.Ed.2d 908 (1964)—§ 4.5 n. 66.

Jackson v. Dickson, 325 F.2d 573 (9th Cir.1963)—§ 2.14 n. 140.

Jackson v. Indiana, 406 U.S. 715, 92 S.Ct. 1845, 32 L.Ed.2d 435 (1972)—§ 4.4; § 4.4 n. 47.

Jackson v. State, 286 Md. 430, 408 A.2d 711 (1979)—§ 3.12 n. 124; § 7.5 n. 8, 67, 73.

Jackson v. State, 92 N.M. 461, 589 P.2d 1052 (1979)—§ 7.5 n. 49.

Jackson v. State, 118 Ga. 125, 44 S.E. 833 (1903)—§ 8.8 n. 27; § 8.12 n. 18.

Jackson v. State, 102 Ala. 167, 15 So. 344 (1894)—§ 3.11 n. 8.

Jackson v. Virginia, 443 U.S. 307, 99 S.Ct. 2781, 61 L.Ed. 2d 560 (1979)—§ 1.8 n. 84, 102.

Jackson, Commonwealth v., 467 Pa. 183, 355 A.2d 572 (1976)—§ 5.8 n. 12.

Johnson, People v., 193 Colo. 199, 564 P.2d 116 (1977)—§ **3.7 n. 44.**

Johnson, People v., 75 Mich.App. 337, 254 N.W.2d 667 (1977)—§ **5.7 n. 63.**

Johnson, People v., 32 Ill.App.3d 36, 335 N.E.2d 144 (1975)—§ **4.10 n. 28.**

Johnson, People v., 55 Ill.2d 62, 302 N.E.2d 20 (1973)—§ **7.5 n. 89.**

Johnson, People v., 6 N.Y.2d 549, 190 N.Y.2d 694, 161 N.E.2d 9 (1959)—§ **2.12 n. 62.**

Johnson, People v., 2 Ill.2d 165, 117 N.E.2d 91 (1954)—§ **5.7 n. 14.**

Johnson, People v., 372 Ill. 18, 22 N.E.2d 683 (1939)—§ **5.11 n. 52.**

Johnson, People v., 87 Misc. 89, 150 N.Y.S. 331 (Sup.Ct. 1914)—§ **8.7 n. 12.**

Johnson, Rex v., 80 Eng.Rep. 753 (1679)—§ **6.1 n. 9.**

Johnson, State v., 121 R.I. 254, 399 A.2d 469 (1979)—§ **4.3 n. 67.**

Johnson, State v., 56 Ohio St.2d 35, 381 N.E.2d 637 (1978)—§ **7.1 n. 59.**

Johnson, State v., 77 Idaho 1, 287 P.2d 425 (1955)—§ **5.11 n. 32.**

Johnson, State v., 233 Wis. 668, 290 N.W. 159 (1940)—§ **4.2 n. 12.**

Johnson, State v., 163 Miss. 521, 141 So. 338 (1932)—§ **2.12 n. 46.**

Johnson, State v., 58 Ohio St. 417, 51 N.E. 40 (1898)—§ **7.17 n. 5.**

Johnson, State v., 102 Ind. 247, 1 N.E. 377 (1885)—§ **7.13 n. 37.**

Johnson, State v., 12 Minn. 476, 12 Gilf. 378 (1867)—§ **2.4 n. 33.**

Johnson, State ex rel. v. Dale, 277 Or. 359, 560 P.2d 650 (1977)—§ **4.5 n. 167.**

Johnson, State ex rel. v. Richardson, 276 Or. 325, 555 P.2d 202 (1976)—§ **4.5 n. 89.**

Johnson, United States v., 718 F.2d 1317 (5th Cir.1983)—§ **1.8 n. 77.**

Johnson, United States v., 457 U.S. 537, 102 S.Ct. 2579, 73 L.Ed.2d 202 (1982)—§ **2.2 n. 102.**

Johnson, United States v., 546 F.2d 1225 (5th Cir.1977)—§ **6.9 n. 63.**

Johnston v. Bloomington, 61 Ill.App.3d 209, 18 Ill.Dec. 538, 377 N.E.2d 1174 (1978)—§ **1.7 n. 27.**

Johnston v. State, 100 Ala. 32, 14 So. 629 (1894)—§ **1.2 n. 13.**

Johnston, State v., 149 S.C. 195, 146 S.E. 657 (1929)—§ **2.1 n. 66; § 8.7 n. 109.**

Johnston, United States ex rel. Wolfersdorf v., 317 F.Supp. 66 (S.D.N.Y.1970)—§ **4.4 n. 74.**

Jojola, State v., 89 N.M. 489, 553 P.2d 1296 (App.1976)—§ **4.4 n. 18.**

Jones v. Commonwealth, 208 Va. 370, 157 S.E.2d 907 (1967)—§ **6.7 n. 23.**

Jones v. Commonwealth, 112 Ky. 689, 66 S.W. 633 (1902)—§ **8.11 n. 38.**

Jones v. Helms, 452 U.S. 412, 101 S.Ct. 2434, 69 L.Ed.2d 118 (1981)—§ **2.11 n. 11.**

Jones v. Slick, 56 So.2d 459 (Fla.1952)—§ **2.4 n. 87.**

Jones v. State, 481 P.2d 169 (Okla.Crim.1971)—§ **6.7 n. 82.**

Jones v. State, 220 Ind. 384, 43 N.E.2d 1017 (1942)—§ **3.3 n. 24.**

Jones v. State, 9 Okla.Crim. 621, 132 P. 914 (1913)—§ **8.7 n. 70.**

Jones v. State, 32 Tex.Crim. 533, 25 S.W. 124 (1894)—§ **5.1 n. 119.**

Jones v. United States, 463 U.S. 354, 103 S.Ct. 3043, 77 L.Ed.2d 694 (1983)—§ **4.5 n. 12; § 4.6; § 4.6 n. 9, 14, 62.**

Jones v. United States, 362 U.S. 257, 80 S.Ct. 725, 4 L.Ed. 2d 697 (1960)—§ **1.4 n. 4.**

Jones v. United States, 251 F.2d 288 (10th Cir.1958)—§ **6.4 n. 107.**

Jones v. United States, 162 F. 417 (9th Cir.1908)—§ **6.5 n. 157.**

Jones, Commonwealth v., 362 Mass. 83, 283 N.E.2d 840 (1972)—§ **8.11 n. 38.**

Jones, King v., 110 Eng.Rep. 485 (1832)—§ **6.5 n. 2.**

Jones, People v., 184 Colo. 96, 518 P.2d 819 (1974)—§ **6.8 n. 45.**

Jones, People v., 329 Ill.App. 503, 69 N.E.2d 522 (1946)—§ **2.4 n. 54.**

Jones, People v., 263 Ill. 564, 105 N.E. 744 (1941)—§ **4.10 n. 10.**

Jones, People v., 290 Ill. 603, 125 N.E. 256 (1919)—§ **8.11 n. 42, 72.**

Jones, People v., 46 Mich. 441, 9 N.W. 486 (1881)—§ **6.5 n. 50.**

Jones, Rex v., 110 Eng.Rep. 485 (1832)—§ **6.4 n. 13.**

Jones, State v., 217 Neb. 435, 350 N.W.2d 11 (1984)—§ **7.7 n. 7.**

Jones, State v., 289 N.W.2d 597 (Iowa 1980)—§ **2.10 n. 32.**

Jones, State v., 598 S.W.2d 209 (Tenn.1980)—§ **5.2 n. 9.**

Jones, State v., —— R.I. ——, 416 A.2d 676 (1980)—§ **5.2 n. 95.**

Jones, State v., 299 N.C. 103, 261 S.E.2d 1 (1980)—§ **5.7 n. 76; § 7.10 n. 53.**

Jones, State v., 220 Tenn. 477, 418 S.W.2d 769 (1966)—§ **4.10 n. 54.**

Jones, State v., 44 N.M. 623, 107 P.2d 324 (1940)—§ **2.2 n. 102; § 2.4 n. 61, 66.**

Jones, State v., 86 S.C. 17, 67 S.E. 160 (1910)—§ **7.8 n. 27.**

Jones, State v., 50 N.H. 369 (1871)—§ **4.3 n. 3, 7; § 4.5 n. 13.**

Jones, State v., 65 N.C. 395 (1871)—§ **8.3 n. 11.**

Jones, United States v., 592 F.2d 1038 (9th Cir.1979)—§ **6.7 n. 53.**

Jordan v. De George, 341 U.S. 223, 71 S.Ct. 703, 95 L.Ed. 886 (1951)—§ **1.6 n. 61.**

Jordan v. State, 107 Tex.Crim.R. 414, 296 S.W. 585 (1927)—§ **8.5 n. 5.**

Jordan, People v., 303 Ill. 316, 135 N.E. 729 (1922)—§ **8.11 n. 76.**

Jordan, Regina v., 40 Crim.App. 152 (1956)—§ **3.12 n. 83.**

Josey v. United States, 135 F.2d 809 (D.C.Cir.1943)—§ **3.6 n. 24; § 5.7 n. 32; § 5.10 n. 46.**

Journeymen Taylors of Cambridge, Rex v., 88 Eng.Rep. 9 (1721)—§ **6.4 n. 11; § 6.5 n. 17.**

Joy v. State, 14 Ind. 139 (1860)—§ **8.8 n. 2.**

Joy, State v., 452 A.2d 408 (Me.1982)—§ **7.4 n. 4, 16.**

Joyce v. United States, 153 F.2d 364 (8th Cir.1946)—§ **6.5 n. 224.**

Joyce, United States v., 693 F.2d 838 (8th Cir.1982)—§ **6.2 n. 158; § 6.3 n. 95.**

Jung Quey v. United States, 138 C.C.A. 314, 222 F. 766 (1915)—§ **6.4 n. 100.**

Jupe v. State, 86 Tex.Crim. 573, 217 S.W. 1041 (1920)—§ **5.7 n. 12.**

Jurek v. Texas, 428 U.S. 262, 96 S.Ct. 2950, 49 L.Ed.2d 929 (1976)—§ **2.14 n. 90.**

Justices of Court of Special Sessions of New York County v. People ex rel. Henderson, 90 N.Y. 12 (1882)—§ **8.2 n. 26.**

Kibbe, People v., 35 N.Y.2d 407, 362 N.Y.S.2d 848, 321 N.E.2d 773 (1974)—§ **3.12 n. 140.**

Kichline, Commonwealth v., 468 Pa. 265, 361 A.2d 282 (1976)—§ **4.10 n. 13; § 7.5 n. 88, 92.**

Kidwell v. State, 249 Ind. 430, 230 N.E.2d 590 (1967)—§ **2.2 n. 70.**

Kilbourne v. State, 84 Ohio St. 247, 95 N.E. 824 (1911)—§ **8.10 n. 54.**

Kimoktoak v. State, 584 P.2d 25 (Alaska 1978)—§ **3.5 n. 27; § 3.8 n. 27.**

Kind v. State, 595 P.2d 960 (Wyo.1979)—§ **4.5 n. 138.**

King v. _____ (see opposing party)

King v. City of Owensboro, 187 Ky. 21, 218 S.W. 297 (1920)—§ **5.3 n. 54.**

King v. Commonwealth, 285 Ky. 654, 148 S.W.2d 1044 (1941)—§ **3.3 n. 25.**

King v. Ewart, 25 N.Z.L.R. 709 (1905)—§ **3.8 n. 19.**

King v. Nehal Mahto, 18 Indian L.R. Patna Ser. 485 (1939)—§ **3.11 n. 31.**

King v. Sreenarayan, 27 Indian L.R. Patna Ser. 67 (1948)—§ **3.11 n. 31.**

King v. State, 339 So.2d 172 (Fla.1976)—§ **6.2 n. 43.**

King v. State, 233 Ala. 198, 171 So. 254 (1936)—§ **5.7 n. 58.**

King v. State, 157 Tenn. 635, 11 S.W.2d 904 (1928)—§ **1.6 n. 31; § 7.15 n. 27.**

King v. State, 90 Ala. 612, 8 So. 856 (1891)—§ **7.11 n. 19.**

King v. State, 43 Tex. 351 (1875)—§ **8.4 n. 29.**

King, People v., 61 N.Y.2d 550, 475 N.Y.S.2d 260, 463 N.E.2d 601 (1984)—§ **8.13 n. 25.**

King, State v., 82 Wis.2d 124, 262 N.W.2d 80 (1978)—§ **1.7 n. 50, 53.**

King, State v., 257 N.W.2d 693 (Minn.1977)—§ **2.6 n. 6, 14, 16.**

King, State v., 104 Iowa 727, 74 N.W. 691 (1898)—§ **6.4 n. 132; § 6.8 n. 21.**

Kingsbury, Commonwealth v., 378 Mass. 751, 393 N.E.2d 391 (1979)—§ **8.13 n. 44.**

Kingsbury, Commonwealth v., 5 Mass. 106 (1809)—§ **6.5 n. 294.**

Kinkead, Thomas v., 55 Ark. 502, 18 S.W. 854 (1982)—§ **5.10 n. 31.**

Kinnemore, State v., 34 Ohio App.2d 39, 295 N.E.2d 680 (1972)—§ **3.5 n. 42.**

Kinney, State v., 34 Minn. 311, 25 N.W. 705 (1885)—§ **5.6 n. 26.**

Kinsella v. United States ex rel. Singleton, 361 U.S. 234, 80 S.Ct. 297, 4 L.Ed.2d 268 (1960)—§ **2.8 n. 24.**

Kirby, United States v., 74 U.S. (7 Wall.) 482, 19 L.Ed. 278 (1869)—§ **2.2 n. 13.**

Kirkham, State v., 7 Utah 2d 108, 319 P.2d 859 (1958)—§ **4.2 n. 30.**

Kissel, United States v., 218 U.S. 601, 31 S.Ct. 124, 54 L.Ed. 1168 (1910)—§ **6.5 n. 157, 158.**

Kizer, State v., 360 Mo. 744, 230 S.W.2d 690 (1950)—§ **7.10 n. 27.**

Kleen, State v., 491 S.W.2d 244 (Mo.1973)—§ **2.9 n. 10.**

Klein, People v., 305 Ill. 141, 137 N.E. 145 (1922)—§ **5.10 n. 16, 17.**

Klimas, State v., 94 Wis.2d 288, 288 N.W.2d 157 (App. 1979)—§ **4.7 n. 26.**

Klinkenberg, State v., 76 Wash. 466, 136 P. 692 (1913)—§ **8.7 n. 66.**

Knickerbocker Merchandising Co. v. United States, 13 F.2d 544 (2d Cir.1926)—§ **8.7 n. 80.**

Knight, State v., 230 S.E.2d 732 (W.Va.1976)—§ **5.2 n. 67.**

Knight, State v., 1 N.C. 143 (1799)—§ **2.9 n. 62, 64.**

Knights v. State, 58 Neb. 225, 78 N.W. 508 (1899)—§ **4.2 n. 39, 44.**

Knowles, United States v., 26 Fed.Cas. 800 (N.D.Cal. 1864)—§ **3.3 n. 12, 48.**

Knox v. Commonwealth, 225 Va. 504, 304 S.E.2d 4 (1983)—§ **8.13 n. 61.**

Knox v. Municipal Court, 185 N.W.2d 705 (Iowa 1971)—§ **1.7 n. 71, 73, 75, 82, 85.**

Knox, United States v., 396 U.S. 77, 90 S.Ct. 363, 24 L.Ed. 2d 275 (1969)—§ **2.14 n. 62.**

Kobyluk v. State, 94 Okl.Crim.App. 73, 231 P.2d 388 (1951)—§ **4.2 n. 37.**

Koch, People v., 250 App.Div. 623, 294 N.Y.S. 987 (1937)—§ **4.10 n. 3.**

Kock, State v., 207 Neb. 731, 300 N.W.2d 824 (1981)—§ **8.9 n. 13.**

Koczwara, Commonwealth v., 397 Pa. 575, 155 A.2d 825 (1959)—§ **3.9; § 3.9 n. 1, 39, 45; § 5.1 n. 31.**

Koerber, People v., 244 N.Y. 147, 155 N.E. 79 (1926)—§ **4.10 n. 9, 16; § 8.11 n. 16, 20.**

Kohler v. Commonwealth, 492 S.W.2d 198 (Ky.1973)—§ **5.10 n. 48, 50.**

Kolender v. Lawson, 461 U.S. 352, 103 S.Ct. 1855, 75 L.Ed. 2d 903 (1983)—§ **2.3 n. 24, 48, 49; § 2.14 n. 69.**

Koliche, State v., 143 Me. 281, 61 A.2d 115 (1948)—§ **5.1 n. 31.**

Kolisnitschenko, State v., 84 Wis.2d 492, 267 N.W.2d 321 (1978)—§ **4.10 n. 62.**

Konz, Commonwealth v., 498 Pa. 639, 450 A.2d 638 (1982)—§ **3.3 n. 9, 11.**

Koonse, State v., 123 Mo.App. 655, 101 S.W. 139 (1907)—§ **5.6 n. 7.**

Koontz, State v., 124 Kan. 216, 257 P. 944 (1927)—§ **8.2 n. 15.**

Koopman, State ex rel. v. County Court Branch No. 1, 38 Wis.2d 492, 157 N.W.2d 623 (1968)—§ **4.11 n. 53.**

Koppers Co., United States v., 652 F.2d 290 (2d Cir.1981)—§ **3.10 n. 3.**

Korell, State v., ___ Mont. ___, 690 P.2d 992 (1984)—§ **4.1; § 4.1 n. 48.**

Korematsu v. United States, 323 U.S. 214, 65 S.Ct. 193, 89 L.Ed. 194 (1944)—§ **2.11 n. 22.**

Koritan, United States v., 283 F.2d 516 (3d Cir.1960)—§ **6.5 n. 225.**

Korpan, United States v., 354 U.S. 271, 77 S.Ct. 1099, 1 L.Ed.2d 1337 (1957)—§ **2.3 n. 31.**

Kostka, Commonwealth v., 370 Mass. 516, 350 N.E.2d 444 (1976)—§ **4.5 n. 117.**

Kotapish, State v., 171 Ohio St. 349, 171 N.E.2d 505 (1960)—§ **7.13 n. 17.**

Kott v. State, 678 P.2d 386 (Alaska 1984)—§ **6.6 n. 77.**

Kott v. United States, 163 F.2d 984 (5th Cir.1933)—§ **5.2 n. 13.**

Kotteakos v. United States, 328 U.S. 750, 66 S.Ct. 1239, 90 L.Ed. 1557 (1946)—§ **6.4 n. 55; § 6.5; § 6.5 n. 132.**

Kramer v. United States, 408 F.2d 837 (8th Cir.1969)—§ **3.2 n. 51.**

Kraus & Bros., M. v. United States, 327 U.S. 614, 66 S.Ct. 705, 90 L.Ed. 894 (1946)—§ **2.3 n. 11; § 2.6 n. 22.**

Krause, Rex v., 66 J.P. 121 (1902)—§ **6.1 n. 72.**

Kress v. State, 176 Tenn. 478, 144 S.W.2d 735 (1940)—§ **5.7 n. 18.**

Kring v. Missouri, 107 U.S. 221, 2 S.Ct. 443, 27 L.Ed. 506 (1883)—§ **2.4 n. 37.**

Krist, People v., 168 N.Y. 19, 60 N.E. 1057 (1901)—§ **4.10 n. 31.**

Kroger Grocery & Baking Co., United States ex rel. Porter v., 163 F.2d 168 (7th Cir.1947)—§ **1.7 n. 87.**

Krovarz, People v., 697 P.2d 378 (Colo.1985)—§ **6.2 n. 64, 84.**

Krueger v. Noel, 318 N.W.2d 220 (Iowa 1982)—§ **3.8 n. 11, 13.**

Krug v. Washington, 164 U.S. 704, 17 S.Ct. 995, 41 L.Ed. 1183 (1896)—§ **8.6 n. 21.**

Krug, State v., 12 Wash. 288, 41 P. 126 (1895)—§ **8.6 n. 21.**

Krulewitch v. United States, 336 U.S. 440, 69 S.Ct. 716, 93 L.Ed. 790 (1949)—§ **6.4;** § **6.4 n. 26, 38, 48, 61, 62, 128;** § **6.5;** § **6.5 n. 37, 170, 177.**

Kuh, United States v., 541 F.2d 672 (7th Cir.1976)—§ **6.9 n. 63.**

Kuk v. State, 80 Nev. 291, 392 P.2d 630 (1964)—§ **4.5 n. 180.**

Kunack, United States v., 17 C.M.R. 346 (1954)—§ **4.2 n. 117.**

Kunkle v. State, 32 Ind. 220 (1869)—§ **6.3 n. 10, 26, 81.**

Kunz v. New York, 340 U.S. 290, 71 S.Ct. 312, 95 L.Ed. 280 (1951)—§ **2.14 n. 27.**

Kuperstein, Commonwealth v., 207 Mass. 25, 92 N.E. 1008 (1910)—§ **8.10 n. 14.**

Kupperschmidt, People v., 237 N.Y. 463, 143 N.E. 256 (1924)—§ **8.10 n. 77.**

Kusnick, State v., 45 Ohio St. 535, 15 N.E. 481 (1888)—§ **8.6 n. 31.**

Kutchara, State v., 350 N.W.2d 924 (Minn.1984)—§ **5.7 n. 74.**

Kwaku Mensah v. The King, [1946] A.C. 83 (P.C.1945) (W.Afr.)—§ **7.13 n. 39.**

Kyle v. State, 208 Tenn. 170, 344 S.W.2d 537 (1961)—§ **1.4 n. 22.**

Kyllonen, People v., 402 Mich. 135, 262 N.W.2d 2 (1978)—§ **8.10 n. 78.**

Kylsant, Rex v., (1932) 1 K.B. 442 (Ct.Crim.App.)—§ **8.7 n. 34.**

La Fanti v. United States, 259 F. 460 (3d Cir.1919)—§ **8.10 n. 13.**

La Follette, State ex rel. v. Raskin, 34 Wis.2d 607, 150 N.W.2d 318 (1967)—§ **4.5 n. 66, 67, 167.**

LaBarge v. State, 74 Wis.2d 327, 246 N.W.2d 794 (1976)—§ **2.2 n. 55, 74, 97.**

Labato, State v., 7 N.J. 137, 80 A.2d 617 (1951)—§ **2.12 n. 57, 74;** § **3.2 n. 16, 45.**

Labor v. Gibson, 195 Colo. 416, 578 P.2d 1059 (1978)—§ **4.5 n. 13.**

Laborde, State v., 202 La. 59, 11 So.2d 404 (1942)—§ **8.3 n. 15.**

Labuwi, State ex rel. v. Hathaway, 168 Wis. 518, 170 N.W. 654 (1919)—§ **8.7 n. 103.**

Lacquey, State v., 117 Ariz. 231, 571 P.2d 1027 (1977)—§ **7.7 n. 56.**

Ladd, Commonwealth v., 402 Pa. 164, 166 A.2d 501 (1960)—§ **3.12 n. 146.**

LaFayette, State v., 15 N.J.Misc. 115, 188 A. 918 (Ct.Com. Pl.1937)—§ **2.1 n. 24;** § **7.8 n. 8.**

LaFera, State v., 61 N.J.Super. 489, 161 A.2d 303—§ **6.5 n. 32.**

Lafferty, State v., 192 Conn. 571, 472 A.2d 1275 (1984)—§ **4.6 n. 9.**

LaGasse, State v., 410 A.2d 537 (Me.1980)—§ **7.4 n. 30.**

LaLonde v. State, 614 P.2d 808 (Alaska 1980)—§ **7.10 n. 75.**

Lamb v. Brown, 456 F.2d 18 (10th Cir.1972)—§ **4.10 n. 64;** § **4.11 n. 51.**

Lamb v. State, 475 P.2d 829 (Okl.Cr.App.1970)—§ **4.10 n. 50.**

Lambert v. California, 355 U.S. 225, 78 S.Ct. 240, 2 L.Ed. 2d 228 (1957)—§ **2.10 n. 22;** § **3.3;** § **3.3 n. 41;** § **3.8 n. 7, 21, 22, 23, 24;** § **5.1;** § **5.1 n. 80, 83.**

Lambert v. State, 374 P.2d 783 (Okla.Crim.1962)—§ **2.12 n. 75, 76;** § **3.2 n. 16.**

Lampe, State v., 131 Minn. 65, 154 N.W. 737 (1915)—§ **6.1 n. 16.**

Lampkins, United States v., 4 U.S.C.M.A. 31, 15 C.M.R. 31 (1954)—§ **5.1 n. 14.**

Lancaster v. Municipal Court, 6 Cal.3d 805, 100 Cal.Rptr. 609, 494 P.2d 681 (1972)—§ **1.7 n. 21.**

Lancaster, State v., 506 S.W.2d 403 (Mo.1974)—§ **2.2 n. 71.**

Lancaster, United States v., 44 F. 896 (C.C.W.D.Ga.1891)—§ **6.5 n. 12.**

Landen v. United States, 299 F. 75 (6th Cir.1924)—§ **6.4 n. 177.**

Lane v. Commonwealth, 219 Va. 509, 248 S.E.2d 781 (1978)—§ **7.1 n. 18.**

Lane v. State, 388 So.2d 1022 (Fla.1980)—§ **2.9 n. 50;** § **4.4 n. 28.**

Lanegan, State v., 192 Or. 691, 236 P.2d 438 (1951)—§ **8.11 n. 85.**

Laney v. State, 421 So.2d 1216 (Miss.1982)—§ **4.2 n. 6.**

Lang v. State, 6 Md.App. 128, 250 A.2d 276 (1969)—§ **7.10 n. 50.**

Lang, People v., 402 Ill. 170, 83 N.E.2d 688 (1949)—§ **4.11 n. 27.**

Langdon v. Board of Liquor Control, 98 Ohio App. 535, 130 N.E.2d 430 (1954)—§ **5.2 n. 7.**

Lange, State v., 168 La. 958, 123 So. 639 (1929)—§ **4.1 n. 41.**

Langford v. State, 354 So.2d 313 (Ala.1977)—§ **7.4 n. 33.**

Langley, Commonwealth v., 169 Mass. 89, 47 N.E. 511 (1897)—§ **8.7 n. 53.**

Langworthy v. State, 284 Md. 588, 399 A.2d 578 (1979)—§ **4.5 n. 169.**

Langworthy, People v., 416 Mich. 630, 331 N.W.2d 171 (1982)—§ **4.10 n. 19, 21, 26;** § **7.4 n. 33.**

Lankford, State v., 29 Del. 594, 102 A. 63 (1917)—§ **7.15 n. 19.**

Lanoue, Commonwealth v., 326 Mass. 559, 95 N.E.2d 925 (1950)—§ **2.9 n. 33.**

Lanza, United States v., 260 U.S. 377, 43 S.Ct. 141, 67 L.Ed. 314 (1922)—§ **2.9 n. 76;** § **2.15 n. 46.**

Lanzetta v. New Jersey, 306 U.S. 451, 59 S.Ct. 618, 83 L.Ed. 888 (1939)—§ **2.3 n. 6, 14, 21;** § **2.14 n. 130.**

Lapier, Rex v., 168 Eng.Rep. 263 (Cr.Cas.Res.1784)—§ **8.11 n. 43.**

LaPique, People v., 120 Cal. 25, 52 P. 40 (1898)—§ **8.6 n. 55.**

LaPlume, State v., 118 R.I. 670, 375 A.2d 938 (1977)—§ **2.9 n. 26.**

Lardner, People v., 300 Ill. 264, 133 N.E. 375 (1921)—§ **6.3 n. 137; 8.2 n. 60.**

Larrivee, State v., 479 A.2d 347 (Me.1984)—§ **5.3 n. 32.**

Larsen v. State, 86 Nev. 451, 470 P.2d 417 (1970)—§ **6.2 n. 62, 81, 149.**

Larsen, State v., 76 Idaho 528, 286 P.2d 646 (1955)—§ **8.9 n. 3.**

Larsonneur, 24 Cr.App. 74 (1933)—§ **3.2 n. 16.**

Lashley, State v., 233 Kan. 620, 664 P.2d 1358 (1983)—§ **7.5 n. 17.**

Laska v. United States, 82 F.2d 672 (10th Cir.1936)—§ **6.4 n. 135;** § **6.5 n. 152.**

Laswell, State v., 78 Ohio App. 202, 66 N.E.2d 555 (1946)—§ **7.10 n. 3.**

Latham, United States v., 385 F.Supp. 57 (E.D.Ill.1974)—§ **1.6 n. 4.**

Latraverse, State v., ___ R.I. ___, 443 A.2d 890 (1982)—§ **6.1 n. 158.**

Lauria, People v., 251 Cal.App.2d 471, 59 Cal.Rptr. 628 (1967)—§ **6.4 n. 160, 162, 163, 164;** § **6.7 n. 84.**

Lauritsen, State v., 178 Neb. 230, 132 N.W.2d 379 (1965)—**2.2 n. 37.**

Lavender, Rex v., 2 East P.C. 566 (Cr.Cas.Res.1793)—§ **8.1 n. 4.**

Law v. Commonwealth, 75 Va. 885 (1881)—§ **6.8 n. 72.**

Law, State v., 270 S.C. 664, 244 S.E.2d 302 (1978)—§ **4.2 n. 6;** § **4.4 n. 18.**

Laws v. State, 26 Tex.Crim. 643, 10 S.W. 220 (1888)—§ **5.10 n. 46.**

Lawson v. State, 125 Miss. 754, 88 So. 325 (1921)—§ **8.6 n. 27, 28.**

Lawson, Commonwealth v., 454 Pa. 23, 309 A.2d 391 (1973)—§ **6.5 n. 242.**

Layton, United States v., 509 F.Supp. 212 (N.D.Cal.1981)—§ **2.8 n. 25, 28.**

Le Mott's Case, 84 Eng.Rep. 1073 (1650)—§ **8.13 n. 11, 12.**

Leaphart, State v., 673 S.W.2d 870 (Tenn.Crim.1983)—§ **5.7 n. 45.**

Lear v. State, 39 Ariz. 313, 6 P.2d 426 (1931)—§ **8.11 n. 38, 39, 57, 61.**

Leary v. United States, 395 U.S. 6, 89 S.Ct. 1532, 23 L.Ed.2d 57 (1969)—§ **2.13;** § **2.13 n. 16, 18;** § **2.14 n. 62.**

Leary v. United States, 383 F.2d 851 (5th Cir.1967)—§ **2.14 n. 42.**

Leavine v. State, 109 Fla. 447, 147 So. 897 (1933)—§ **6.7 n. 64.**

LeBarron v. State, 32 Wis.2d 294, 145 N.W.2d 79 (1966)—§ **6.3 n. 126.**

Lebron v. United States, 229 F.2d 16 (D.C.Cir.1955)—§ **3.6 n. 18.**

Lee v. County Court, 27 N.Y.2d 432, 318 N.Y.S.2d 705, 267 N.E.2d 452 (1971)—§ **4.5 n. 87, 94.**

Lee, Commonwealth v., 331 Mass. 166, 117 N.E.2d 830 (1954)—§ **3.2 n. 49.**

Lee, Rex v., 1 Leach 51, 168 Eng.Rep. 128 (1763)—§ **7.17 n. 14.**

Lee, United States v., 694 F.2d 649 (11th Cir.1983)—§ **5.3 n. 29, 32.**

Lee Kong, People v., 95 Cal. 666, 30 P. 800 (1892)—§ **6.3 n. 25.**

Leeman v. State, 35 Ark. 438 (1880)—§ **5.1 n. 96.**

Leeper v. State, 589 P.2d 379 (Wyo.1979)—§ **5.8 n. 6.**

Leffel v. Municipal Court, 54 Cal.App.3d 569, 126 Cal. Rptr. 773 (1976)—§ **6.1 n. 86.**

Lefkovitz, People v., 294 Mich. 263, 293 N.W. 642 (1940)—§ **6.9 n. 60.**

Lefler v. State, 153 Ind. 82, 54 N.E. 439 (1899)—§ **8.7 n. 93.**

LeGear, State v., 346 N.W.2d 21 (Iowa 1984)—§ **2.9 n. 29.**

Lehigh Valley Ry. Co., State v., 92 N.J.L. 261, 106 A. 23 (1918)—§ **3.10 n. 19.**

Lehigh Valley Ry. Co., State v., 90 N.J.L. 372, 103 A. 685 (1917)—§ **3.10 n. 19.**

Lehman, State v., 131 Minn. 427, 155 N.W. 399 (1915)—§ **7.15 n. 29.**

Leick v. People, 131 Colo. 353, 281 P.2d 806 (1955)—§ **4.5 n. 167.**

Leland v. Oregon, 343 U.S. 790, 72 S.Ct. 1002, 96 L.Ed. 1302 (1952)—§ **1.8 n. 28;** § **2.13;** § **2.13 n. 47, 49;** § **2.14 n. 140;** § **4.5;** § **4.5 n. 134, 140.**

Leland, State v., 190 Or. 598, 227 P.2d 785 (1951)—§ **4.5;** § **4.5 n. 153.**

Lemke v. United States, 14 Alaska 587, 211 F.2d 73 (1954)—§ **6.2 n. 148;** § **6.4 n. 69.**

Lemore v. Commonwealth, 127 Ky. 480, 105 S.W. 930 (1907)—§ **2.9 n. 29.**

Lenkevich, People v., 394 Mich. 117, 229 N.W.2d 298 (1975)—§ **5.7 n. 62.**

Lennon, State v., 3 N.J. 337, 70 A.2d 154 (1949)—§ **6.5 n. 276.**

Lenti, People v., 46 Misc.2d 682, 260 N.Y.S.2d 284 (1965)—§ **5.11 n. 4.**

Leon, In re, 122 R.I. 548, 410 A.2d 121 (1980)—§ **7.5 n. 59.**

Leon v. State, 21 Ariz. 418, 189 P. 433 (1920)—§ **8.10 n. 66, 67, 77.**

Leonard, People v., 83 Ill.2d 411, 47 Ill.Dec. 353, 415 N.E.2d 358 (1981)—§ **7.10 n. 24.**

Leonardi, People v., 143 N.Y. 360, 38 N.E. 372 (1894)—§ **4.10 n. 10.**

Leopold, State v., 110 Conn. 55, 147 A. 118 (1929)—§ **3.12 n. 122;** § **7.5 n. 34.**

Lessner, Commonwealth v., 274 Pa. 108, 118 A. 24 (1922)—§ **7.5 n. 40.**

Lester v. State, 212 Tenn. 338, 370 S.W.2d 405 (1963)—§ **4.9 n. 14;** § **7.17 n. 14.**

Lester, Commonwealth v., 2 Va.Cas. 198 (1820)—§ **7.17 n. 16.**

Letner v. State, 156 Tenn. 68, 299 S.W. 1049 (1927)—§ **3.12 n. 104.**

Lett, People v., 61 Ill.App.3d 467, 18 Ill.Dec. 744, 378 N.E.2d 208 (1978)—§ **1.4 n. 26.**

Levelle, State v., 34 S.C. 120, 13 S.E. 319 (1891)—§ **7.8 n. 14.**

Levering v. Commonwealth, 132 Ky. 666, 117 S.W. 253 (1909)—§ **6.9 n. 15.**

Levin v. United States, 338 F.2d 265 (D.C.Cir.1964)—§ **5.11 n. 30.**

Levin v. United States, 5 F.2d 598 (9th Cir.1925)—§ **3.10 n. 76.**

Levy, People v., 299 Ill.App. 453, 20 N.E.2d 171 (1939)—§ **6.5 n. 225.**

Lew Moy v. United States, 237 F. 50 (10th Cir.1916)—§ **6.5 n. 166.**

Lewallen v. State, 166 Tex.Crim.R. 287, 313 S.W.2d 293 (1958)—§ **5.11 n. 48.**

Lewellyn, United States v., 723 F.2d 615 (8th Cir.1983)—§ **4.3 n. 62.**

Lewis v. City of New Orleans, 415 U.S. 130, 94 S.Ct. 970, 39 L.Ed.2d 214 (1974)—§ **2.14 n. 9.**

Lewis v. Commonwealth, 184 Va. 69, 34 S.E.2d 389 (1945)—§ **2.1 n. 56.**

Lewis v. People, 124 Colo. 62, 235 P.2d 348 (1951)—§ **6.3 n. 137.**

Lewis v. People, 99 Colo. 102, 60 P.2d 1089 (1936)—§ **8.6 n. 55.**

Lewis v. State, 285 Md. 705, 404 A.2d 1073 (1979)—§ **6.6 n. 58;** § **6.9 n. 41.**

Lewis v. State, 86 Nev. 889, 478 P.2d 168 (1970)—§ **4.11 n. 59, 64.**

Lewis v. State, 220 Ark. 914, 251 S.W.2d 490 (1952)—§ **6.7 n. 103.**

Lewis v. State, 196 Ga. 755, 27 S.E.2d 659 (1943)—§ **4.9 n. 3.**

Lewis v. State, 35 Ala. 380 (1860)—§ **6.3 n. 109.**

Nolan, United States v., 700 F.2d 479 (9th Cir.1983)—§ **5.3 n. 25**; § **5.7 n. 47.**

Norman, State v., 580 P.2d 237 (Utah 1978)—§ **6.2 n. 88.**

Norman, State v., 193 Neb. 719, 229 N.W.2d 55 (1975)— § **6.8 n. 80.**

Norris, People v., 40 Mich.App. 45, 198 N.W.2d 430 (1972)—§ **3.2 n. 53.**

North American Van Lines v. United States, 243 F.2d 693 (6th Cir.1957)—§ **2.2 n. 2.**

North Carolina v. Alford, 400 U.S. 25, 91 S.Ct. 160, 27 L.Ed.2d 162 (1970)—§ **4.5 n. 15.**

Northrup, State v., ___ R.I. ___, 486 A.2d 589 (1985)— § **3.12 n. 108**; § **5.11 n. 39, 43.**

Norton v. United States, 92 F.2d 753 (9th Cir.1937)—§ **8.8 n. 27.**

Norton, Commonwealth v., 93 Mass. (11 Allen) 266 (1865)—§ **8.7 n. 92.**

Norwood, State v., 115 N.C. 789, 20 S.E. 712 (1894)—§ **7.2 n. 24.**

Novosel v. Helgemoe, 118 N.H. 115, 384 A.2d 124 (1978)— § **4.5 n. 31.**

Novotny v. Great American Federal Savings and Loan Ass'n, 584 F.2d 1235 (3d Cir.1978)—§ **6.5 n. 255.**

Nowak, United States v., 448 F.2d 134 (7th Cir.1971)— § **6.5 n. 77, 176.**

Nowell, State v., 60 N.H. 199 (1880)—§ **6.6 n. 4.**

Nuckolls, State v., ___ W.Va. ___, 273 S.E.2d 87 (App. 1980)—§ **4.5 n. 180.**

Nundah, Rex v., 16 N.S.W. 482 (1916)—§ **8.5 n. 6.**

Nunes, People v., 47 Cal.App. 346, 190 P. 486 (1920)— § **7.17 n. 17.**

Nunez-Rios, United States v., 622 F.2d 1093 (2d Cir. 1980)—§ **5.2 n. 107.**

Nunley v. State, 233 Ark. 838, 270 S.W.2d 904 (1954)— § **7.15 n. 37.**

Nye & Nissen v. United States, 168 F.2d 846 (9th Cir. 1948)—§ **6.4 n. 49.**

Nye & Nissen v. United States, 336 U.S. 613, 69 S.Ct. 766, 93 L.Ed. 919 (1949)—§ **6.8 n. 2.**

Nyland, State v., 47 Wash.2d 240. 287 P.2d 345 (1955)— § **5.10 n. 39, 41.**

Oakland v. Carpentier, 21 Cal. 642 (1863)—§ **5.1 n. 64.**

Oakley v. State, 22 Wis.2d 298, 125 N.W.2d 657 (1964)— § **6.3 n. 92.**

O'Brian v. State, 6 Tex.App. 665 (1879)—§ **5.3 n. 6.**

O'Brien, People v., 96 Cal. 171, 31 P. 45 (1892)—§ **5.1 n. 66.**

O'Brien, Regina v., 56 D.L.R.2d 65 (1966)—§ **4.9 n. 47.**

O'Brien, Regina v., 2 D.L.R. 311 (1954)—§ **6.4 n. 98.**

O'Brien, State v., 434 A.2d 9 (Me.1981)—§ **5.7 n. 47.**

O'Brien, State v., 32 N.J.L. 169 (Sup.Ct.1867)—§ **3.3 n. 21**; § **7.1 n. 38**; § **7.12 n. 31, 34.**

O'Brien, United States v., 391 U.S. 367, 88 S.Ct. 1673, 20 L.Ed.2d 672 (1968)—§ **2.14 n. 25.**

O'Bryan, People v., 132 Cal.App. 496, 23 P.2d 94 (1933)— § **6.1 n. 12, 103.**

Obstein, State v., 52 N.J. 516, 247 A.2d 5 (1968)—§ **4.5 n. 90.**

Ocampo v. United States, 234 U.S. 91, 34 S.Ct. 712, 58 L.Ed. 1231 (1914)—§ **1.4 n. 5.**

Oceanic Steam Navigation Co. v. Stranahan, 214 U.S. 320, 29 S.Ct. 671, 53 L.Ed. 1013 (1909)—§ **2.6 n. 33.**

Ochoa, State v., 41 N.M. 589, 72 P.2d 609 (1937)—§ **6.6 n. 54.**

O'Connor v. United States, 399 A.2d 21 (D.C.App.1979)— § **2.1 n. 18**; § **3.5 n. 31.**

O'Connor, People v., 310 Ill. 403, 141 N.E. 748 (1923)— § **8.11 n. 7.**

Odenwald, People v., 104 Cal.App. 203, 285 P. 406 (1930)— § **5.11 n. 32.**

Odom v. State, 130 Miss. 643, 94 So. 233 (1922)—§ **8.7 n. 84.**

O'Donnell v. People, 224 Ill. 218, 79 N.E. 639, 8 Ann.Cas. 123 (1906)—§ **8.11 n. 15.**

Ogburn v. State, 132 Tex.Crim.R. 19, 101 S.W.2d 574 (1936)—§ **8.10 n. 16, 18.**

Ogull, United States v., 149 F.Supp. 272 (S.D.N.Y.1957)— § **2.4 n. 52.**

O'Haver v. Montgomery, 120 Tenn. 448, 111 S.W. 449 (1908)—§ **1.7 n. 35.**

Ohnstad, State v., 357 N.W.2d 827 (N.D.1984)—§ **3.7 n. 19.**

O'Kelley v. United States, 116 F.2d 966 (8th Cir.1941)— § **6.5 n. 66.**

O'Kelley, State v., 258 Mo. 345, 167 S.W. 980 (1914)— § **3.10 n. 75.**

Old Monastery Co. v. United States, 147 F.2d 905 (4th Cir. 1945)—§ **3.10 n. 10, 70.**

Olde v. People, 122 Colo. 15, 145 P.2d 100 (1944)—§ **8.7 n. 105.**

O'Leary v. State, 604 P.2d 1099 (Alaska 1979)—§ **4.10 n. 62.**

Olinyk v. People, 642 P.2d 490 (Colo.1982)—§ **1.2 n. 13.**

Oliver, People v., 1 N.Y.2d 152, 151 N.Y.S.2d 367, 134 N.E.2d 197 (1956)—§ **2.5 n. 28.**

Olivio, People v., 52 N.Y.2d 309, 438 N.Y.S.2d 242, 420 N.E.2d 40 (1981)—§ **8.2 n. 60.**

Olmstead, People v., 32 Ill.2d 306, 205 N.E.2d 625 (1965)— § **1.7 n. 14.**

Olsen v. Nebraska ex rel. Western Reference & Bond Ass'n, 313 U.S. 236, 61 S.Ct. 862, 85 L.Ed. 1305 (1941)— § **2.12 n. 21, 49.**

Olsen, People v., 36 Cal.3d 638, 205 Cal.Rptr. 492, 685 P.2d 52 (1984)—§ **5.1 n. 39.**

Olsen, People v., 80 Cal. 122, 22 P. 125 (1889)—§ **7.5 n. 2, 16**; § **7.7 n. 57.**

Olsen, State v., 108 Utah 377, 160 P.2d 427 (1945)—§ **3.2 n. 38.**

Olson, State v., 356 N.W.2d 110 (N.D.1984)—§ **3.3 n. 44.**

Olson, State v., 274 Minn. 225, 143 N.W.2d 69 (1966)— § **4.5 n. 62, 78.**

Omaechevarria v. Idaho, 246 U.S. 343, 38 S.Ct. 323, 62 L.Ed. 763 (1918)—§ **2.3 n. 26, 34.**

O'Malley, Commonwealth v., 97 Mass. 584 (1867)—§ **8.2 n. 26**; § **8.8 n. 3.**

O'Marrow v. State, 66 Tex.Crim. 416, 147 S.W. 252 (1912)—§ **8.6 n. 31.**

O'Neal v. United States, 240 P.2d 700 (10th Cir.1957)— § **3.5 n. 46.**

O'Neil v. State, 237 Wis. 391, 296 N.W. 96 (1941)—§ **6.4 n. 86.**

O'Neil v. Vermont, 144 U.S. 323, 12 S.Ct. 693, 36 L.Ed. 450 (1892)—§ **2.14 n. 101.**

O'Neil, State v., 147 Iowa 513, 126 N.W. 454 (1910)—§ **2.2 n. 103**; § **2.4 n. 59, 68**; § **5.1 n. 99.**

Opher, State v., 38 Del. 93, 188 A. 257 (1936)—§ **7.5 n. 96.**

Orear v. United States, 261 F. 257 (5th Cir.1919)—§ **6.5 n. 196.**

O'Rear, People v., 220 Cal.App.2d 927, 34 Cal.Rptr. 61 (1963)—§ **5.11 n. 57.**

O'Reilly, People v., 153 App.Div. 854, 138 N.Y.S. 776 (1912)—§ **8.10 n. 60.**

Orlando v. United States, 387 F.2d 348 (9th Cir.1967)— § **2.8 n. 63.**

Robinson, People v., 43 Cal.2d 132, 271 P.2d 865 (1954)—§ **6.5 n. 299.**

Robinson, State v., 353 Mo. 934, 185 S.W.2d 636 (1945)—§ **7.10 n. 73.**

Robinson, State v., 213 N.C. 273, 195 S.E. 824 (1938)—§ **5.8 n. 8.**

Robinson, State v., 20 W.Va. 713, 43 Am.Rep. 799 (1882)—§ **3.11 n. 19;** § **4.10 n. 31;** § **5.8 n. 10.**

Robles v. State, 664 S.W.2d 91 (Tex.Crim.App.1984)—§ **8.13 n. 92.**

Rocha v. United States, 288 F.2d 545 (9th Cir.1961)—§ **2.8 n. 28.**

Rochester Ry. & Lt. Co., People v., 195 N.Y. 102, 88 N.E. 22 (1909)—§ **3.10 n. 21.**

Rocker, State v., 52 Haw. 336, 475 P.2d 684 (1970)—§ **3.5 n. 56.**

Rockwell, People v., 39 Mich. 503, 3 Am.Cr.Rep. 224 (1878)—§ **3.12 n. 93.**

Roderick, Rex v., 7 Car. & P. 795 (1837)—§ **6.1 n. 18, 36.**

Roderick, State v., 85 Idaho 80, 375 P.2d 1005 (1962)—§ **8.9 n. 22.**

Rodgers, United States v., 419 F.2d 1315 (10th Cir.1969)—§ **6.6 n. 25.**

Rodgers, United States v., 150 U.S. 249, 14 S.Ct. 109, 37 L.Ed. 1071 (1893)—§ **2.8 n. 6.**

Rodriguez, United States v., 182 F.Supp. 479 (S.D.Cal. 1960)—§ **2.8 n. 28.**

Roe v. Wade, 410 U.S. 113, 93 S.Ct. 705, 35 L.Ed.2d 147 (1973)—§ **2.14;** § **2.14 n. 57;** § **5.4 n. 12.**

Rogers, Commonwealth v., 48 Mass. 500 (1844)—§ **4.2 n. 101.**

Rogers, People v., 18 N.Y. 9 (1858)—§ **4.10 n. 50.**

Rogers, United States v., 289 F.2d 433 (4th Cir.1961)—§ **3.11 n. 10;** § **8.2 n. 48, 50.**

Rojas, People v., 55 Cal.2d 252, 10 Cal.Rptr. 465, 358 P.2d 921 (1961)—§ **6.3 n. 57.**

Roland, People v., 134 Cal.App. 675, 26 P.2d 517 (1933)—§ **8.6 n. 16.**

Roldan, People v., 100 Ill.App.2d 81, 241 N.E.2d 591 (1968)—§ **8.13 n. 27.**

Rolland v. Commonwealth, 82 Pa. 306 (1876)—§ **8.13 n. 19.**

Rollerson, United States v., 308 F.Supp. 1014 (D.D.C. 1970)—§ **1.7 n. 91.**

Rollino, People v., 37 Misc.2d 14, 233 N.Y.S.2d 580 (1962)—§ **6.3 n. 53, 65;** § **8.2 n. 9.**

Roman, People v., 12 N.Y.2d 220, 238 N.Y.S.2d 665, 188 N.E.2d 904 (1963)—§ **8.5 n. 1.**

Romano, United States v., 382 U.S. 136, 86 S.Ct. 279, 15 L.Ed.2d 210 (1965)—§ **2.13 n. 18.**

Romero, State v., 69 N.M. 187, 365 P.2d 58 (1961)—§ **5.11 n. 39.**

Romero-Galue, United States v., 757 F.2d 1147 (11th Cir. 1985)—§ **2.8 n. 8.**

Roney v. State, 76 Ga. 731 (1886)—§ **6.6 n. 23.**

Ronson v. Commissioner, 604 F.2d 175 (2d Cir.1979)—§ **4.5 n. 35.**

Rooney v. North Dakota, 196 U.S. 319, 25 S.Ct. 264, 49 L.Ed. 494 (1905)—§ **2.4 n. 21.**

Rooney v. United States, 203 F. 928 (9th Cir.1913)—§ **6.6 n. 66.**

Root, Commonwealth v., 403 Pa. 571, 170 A.2d 310, 82 A.L.R.2d 452 (1961)—§ **3.12 n. 127;** § **7.12 n. 11, 43, 46;** § **7.13 n. 28, 29.**

Root, People v., 524 F.2d 196 (9th Cir.1975)—§ **7.5 n. 2.**

Rorris, State v., 222 Iowa 1348, 271 N.W. 514 (1937)—§ **2.9 n. 29.**

Rosasco, State v., 103 Or. 343, 205 P. 290 (1922)—§ **1.8 n. 24;** § **2.13 n. 61.**

Rose v. Locke, 423 U.S. 48, 96 S.Ct. 243, 46 L.Ed.2d 185 (1975)—§ **2.3 n. 30, 41;** § **2.4 n. 77, 78.**

Rose v. St. Clair, 28 F.2d 189 (W.D.Va.1928)—§ **6.5 n. 91.**

Rose v. United States, 149 F.2d 755 (9th Cir.1945)—§ **1.8 n. 79, 80.**

Rose, State v., 112 R.I. 402, 311 A.2d 281 (1973)—§ **3.12 n. 6, 97.**

Rosen, People v., 11 Cal.2d 147, 78 P.2d 727 (1938)—§ **8.5 n. 5;** § **8.11 n. 17, 22.**

Rosenberg, Commonwealth v., 379 Mass. 334, 398 N.E.2d 451 (1979)—§ **3.5 n. 25.**

Rosencrans v. United States, 378 F.2d 561 (5th Cir.1967)—§ **6.5 n. 228.**

Rosenfield, In re, 157 F.Supp. 18 (D.D.C.1957)—§ **4.5 n. 123;** § **4.6 n. 8.**

Rosenthal v. United States, 45 F.2d 1000 (8th Cir.1930)—§ **6.5 n. 225.**

Rosenthal, People v., 370 Ill. 244, 18 N.E.2d 450 (1938)—§ **1.7 n. 62.**

Ross v. Oregon, 227 U.S. 150, 33 S.Ct. 220, 57 L.Ed. 458 (1913)—§ **2.4 n. 8, 55;** § **8.6 n. 7, 8, 66.**

Ross v. State, 98 Tex.Crim. 567, 267 S.W. 499 (1925)—§ **6.4 n. 42.**

Ross v. State, 31 Okl.Crim. 143, 237 P. 469 (1925)—§ **8.11 n. 67.**

Ross v. State, 169 Ind. 388, 82 N.E. 781 (1907)—§ **5.3 n. 23.**

Ross, State v., 55 Or. 450, 104 P. 596 (1909)—§ **3.8 n. 16;** § **8.6 n. 7, 8, 66.**

Ross, United States v., 92 U.S. 281, 23 L.Ed. 707 (1876)—§ **2.13 n. 7.**

Ross-Lewin v. Johnson, 39 N.Y.Sup.Ct. 408 (1884)—§ **1.6 n. 40.**

Rossbach, State v., 288 N.W.2d 714 (Minn.1980)—§ **2.9 n. 7.**

Rossi v. United States, 289 U.S. 89, 53 S.Ct. 532, 77 L.Ed. 1051 (1933)—§ **1.8 n. 11.**

Rossi, People v., 18 Cal.3d 295, 134 Cal.Rptr. 64, 555 P.2d 1313 (1976)—§ **2.5 n. 30.**

Rossi, United States v., 39 F.2d 432 (9th Cir.1930)—§ **6.5 n. 219.**

Rotella, State v., 196 Neb. 741, 246 N.W.2d 74 (1976)—§ **5.11 n. 39.**

Roth v. United States, 339 F.2d 863 (10th Cir.1964)—§ **2.4 n. 78;** § **6.6 n. 85.**

Roth v. United States, 354 U.S. 476, 77 S.Ct. 1304, 1 L.Ed. 2d 1498 (1957)—§ **2.14 n. 10.**

Roufa, State v., 241 La. 474, 129 So.2d 743 (1961)—§ **3.5 n. 5.**

Rouse v. Cameron, App.D.C., 373 F.2d 451 (D.C.Cir.1967)—§ **4.6;** § **4.6 n. 38.**

Rowan v. People, 93 Colo. 473, 26 P.2d 1066 (1933)—§ **1.8 n. 75.**

Rowe v. United States, 164 U.S. 546, 17 S.Ct. 172, 41 L.Ed. 547 (1896)—§ **5.7 n. 50, 51.**

Rowe, United States v., 56 F.2d 747 (2d Cir.1932)—§ **8.7 n. 31, 100.**

Rowland v. State, 83 Miss. 483, 35 So. 826 (1904)—§ **7.10 n. 35.**

Rowland Lumber Co., State v., 153 N.C. 610, 69 S.E. 58 (1910)—§ **3.10 n. 24.**

Rowlands, Reg. v., 177 Eng.Rep. 1439 (1851)—§ **6.5 n. 19.**

Rozeboom, State v., 145 Iowa 620, 124 N.W. 783 (1910)—§ **8.3 n. 9, 16.**

Rozell v. State, 502 S.W.2d 16 (Tex.Crim.App.1973)—§ **6.8 n. 73.**

Scott, People v., 251 Mich. 640, 232 N.W. 349 (1930)—§ **2.5 n. 1.**

Scott, State v., 289 N.C. 712, 224 S.E.2d 185 (1976)—§ **6.7 n. 18.**

Scott, State v., 301 Mo. 409, 256 S.W. 745 (1923)—§ **8.7 n. 61.**

Scott, State v., 80 Conn. 317, 68 A.2d 258 (1907)—§ **6.7 n. 10.**

Scott, United States v., 578 F.2d 1186 (6th Cir.1978)—§ **1.8 n. 104.**

Scott, United States v., 529 F.2d 338 (D.C.Cir.1975)—§ **4.10 n. 17.**

Screws v. United States, 325 U.S. 91, 65 S.Ct. 1031, 89 L.Ed. 1495 (1945)—§ **2.3 n. 34; § 2.8 n. 54.**

Scroggins v. State, 119 Tex.Crim.R. 32, 45 S.W.2d 983 (1932)—§ **7.15 n. 37.**

Scroggs v. State, 94 Ga.App. 28, 93 S.E.2d 583 (1956)—§ **7.10 n. 36.**

Sears v. United States, 343 F.2d 139 (5th Cir.1965)—§ **5.2 n. 90.**

Sears, People v., 62 Cal.2d 737, 44 Cal.Rptr. 330, 401 P.2d 938 (1965)—§ **7.5 n. 8.**

Seattle, City of v. Hill, 72 Wn.2d 786, 435 P.2d 692 (1967)—§ **2.14 n. 136; § 4.10 n. 3, 80.**

SEC v. Robert Collier & Co., 76 F.2d 939 (2d Cir.1935)—§ **2.2 n. 51, 67.**

See v. City of Seattle, 387 U.S. 541, 87 S.Ct. 1737, 18 L.Ed.2d 943 (1967)—§ **2.14 n. 46.**

Segna, United States v., 555 F.2d 226 (9th Cir.1977)—§ **4.3 n. 51.**

Seidner v. United States, 260 F.2d 732 (D.C.Cir.1958)—§ **4.4 n. 32.**

Sekt v. Justice's Court, 26 Cal.2d 297, 159 P.2d 17 (1945)—§ **2.5 n. 10, 11.**

Selby, State v., 183 N.J.Super. 273, 443 A.2d 1076 (1981)—§ **3.12 n. 137.**

Sellers, United States v., 670 F.2d 853 (9th Cir.1982)—§ **8.2 n. 39.**

Sells v. State, 98 N.M. 786, 653 P.2d 162 (1982)—§ **7.10 n. 51.**

Sensobaugh v. State, 92 Tex.Crim. 417, 244 S.W. 379 (1922)—§ **7.10 n. 95; § 7.17 n. 28.**

Serebin, State v., 119 Wis.2d 837, 350 N.W.2d 65 (1984)—§ **3.12 n. 16.**

Serné, Regina v., 16 Cox Crim.Cas. 311 (1887)—§ **7.5 n. 6.**

Seward, United States v., 687 F.2d 1270 (10th Cir.1982)—§ **5.4 n. 50.**

Sexton v. California, 189 U.S. 319, 23 S.Ct. 543, 47 L.Ed. 833 (1903)—§ **2.15 n. 28.**

Sexton, State v., 232 Kan. 539, 657 P.2d 43 (1983)—§ **6.1 n. 29.**

Shackelford, United States v., 180 F.Supp. 857 (S.D.N.Y. 1957)—§ **2.4 n. 52.**

Shackford, State v., 262 A.2d 359 (Me.1970)—§ **4.6 n. 80; § 4.7 n. 79.**

Shaffer, Commonwealth v., 367 Mass. 508, 326 N.E.2d 880 (1975)—§ **5.7 n. 66.**

Shaffer, State v., 229 Kan. 310, 624 P.2d 440 (1981)—§ **3.12 n. 26; § 7.1 n. 59.**

Shaffer, State v., 120 Wash. 345, 207 P. 229 (1922)—§ **7.16 n. 19.**

Shain, Commonwealth v., 493 Pa. 360, 426 A.2d 589 (1981)—§ **3.6 n. 27.**

Shameia, United States v., 464 F.2d 629 (6th Cir.1972)—§ **5.2 n. 86.**

Shanon v. Commonwealth, 14 Pa. 226 (1850)—§ **6.5 n. 287.**

Shapiro, United States v., 491 F.2d 335 (6th Cir.1974)—§ **3.10 n. 110.**

Shapiro, United States v., 383 F.2d 680 (7th Cir.1967)—§ **4.3 n. 65.**

Sharon v. Hill, 24 F. 726 (C.C.Cal.1885)—§ **1.7 n. 57.**

Sharpe, Regina v., 7 Cox Crim.Cas. 214 (Ct.Crim.App. 1857)—§ **3.6 n. 13.**

Sharpnack, United States v., 355 U.S. 286, 78 S.Ct. 291, 2 L.Ed.2d 282 (1958)—§ **2.8 n. 4.**

Shaunding, People v., 268 Mich. 218, 255 N.W. 770 (1934)—§ **8.5 n. 5.**

Shaw v. Director of Public Prosecutions, A.C. 220 (1962)—§ **1.2 n. 13.**

Shaw, Commonwealth v., 86 Mass. (4 Allen) 308 (1862)—§ **8.4 n. 9.**

Shaw, State v., 185 Conn. 372, 441 A.2d 561 (1981)—§ **5.7 n. 62.**

Shaw, State v., 96 Idaho 897, 539 P.2d 250 (1975)—§ **2.9 n. 49.**

Shaw, State v., 106 Ariz. 103, 471 P.2d 715 (1970)—§ **4.5 n. 166.**

Shaw, United States v., 701 F.2d 367 (5th Cir.1983)—§ **7.7 n. 9, 39.**

Shea, Commonwealth v., 324 Mass. 710, 88 N.E.2d 645 (1949)—§ **1.8 n. 97.**

Shea, Commonwealth v., 323 Mass. 406, 82 N.E.2d 511 (1948)—§ **6.5 n. 300.**

Shedd v. State, 178 Ga. 653, 173 S.E. 847 (1934)—§ **7.1 n. 16.**

Sheedy, State v., 125 N.H. 108, 480 A.2d 887 (1984)—§ **5.1 n. 111.**

Sheehan, Commonwealth v., 376 Mass. 765, 383 N.E.2d 1115 (1978)—§ **4.3 n. 67; § 4.10 n. 60, 62.**

Sheehan, State v., 33 Idaho 553, 196 P. 532 (1921)—§ **2.9 n. 52.**

Sheikh, United States v., 654 F.2d 1057 (5th Cir.1981)—§ **6.5 n. 207, 208.**

Shelburn v. State, 446 P.2d 56 (Okl.Cr.1968)—§ **4.10 n. 3.**

Sheldon, State v., 91 Ariz. 73, 369 P.2d 917 (1962)—§ **8.10 n. 76.**

Sheldon, State v., 54 Mont. 185, 169 P. 37 (1917)—§ **7.17 n. 12.**

Shelton v. Commonwealth, 261 Ky. 18, 86 S.W.2d 1054 (1935)—§ **6.6 n. 56.**

Shepard v. Bowe, 250 Or. 288, 442 P.2d 238 (1968)—§ **4.5 n. 93.**

Shepard, Regina v., 9 Cox.Crim.Cas. 123 (1862)—§ **3.3 n. 9.**

Shepherd v. People, 25 N.Y. 406 (1862)—§ **2.4 n. 17.**

Sheppard v. State, 243 Ala. 498, 10 So.2d 822 (1942)—§ **7.10 n. 75.**

Sheppard v. State, 151 Ga. 27, 105 S.E. 601 (1921)—§ **6.9 n. 70.**

Sherbert v. Verner, 374 U.S. 398, 83 S.Ct. 1790, 10 L.Ed.2d 965 (1963)—§ **2.14 n. 37.**

Sherburne, State ex rel. v. Baker, 50 La.Ann. 1247, 24 So. 240 (1898)—§ **2.4 n. 40.**

Sheriff v. Hicks, 89 Nev. 78, 506 P.2d 766 (1973)—§ **7.5 n. 49, 70.**

Sheriff v. LaMotte, ___ Nev. ___, 680 P.2d 333 (1984)—§ **7.4 n. 22.**

Sheriff, Clark County v. Luqman, ___ Nev. ___, 697 P.2d 107 (1985)—§ **2.6 n. 16.**

Sherin, In re, 27 S.D. 232, 130 N.W. 761 (1911)—§ **8.12 n. 15.**

Sherman v. State, 113 Neb. 173, 202 N.W. 413 (1925)—§ **6.5 n. 212.**

Thomas, Commonwealth v., 382 Pa. 639, 117 A.2d 204 (1955)—§ **7.5 n. 46, 47.**

Thomas, People v., 104 Ill.App.2d 56, 243 N.E.2d 611 (1968)—§ **6.7 n. 25.**

Thomas, People v., 41 Cal.2d 470, 261 P.2d 1 (1953)—§ **7.7 n. 39.**

Thomas, State v., 66 Ohio St.2d 518, 423 N.E.2d 137 (1981)—§ **5.7 n. 39.**

Thomas, State v., 619 S.W.2d 513 (Tenn.1981)—§ **6.6 n. 17.**

Thomas, State v., 140 N.J.Super. 429, 356 A.2d 433 (1976)—§ **6.8 n. 60.**

Thomas, State v., 438 S.W.2d 441 (Mo.1969)—§ **6.2 n. 109, 110; § 6.3 n. 100, 111, 136.**

Thomas, State v., 58 Wash.2d 746, 364 P.2d 930 (1961)—§ **1.8 n. 63.**

Thomas, State v., 184 N.C. 757, 114 S.E. 834 (1922)—§ **7.10 n. 5.**

Thomas, United States v., 13 U.S.C.M.A. 278, 32 C.M.R. 278 (1962)—§ **6.3 n. 2, 7, 61; § 6.5 n. 52, 58, 61.**

Thompkins, State v., 220 S.C. 523, 68 S.E.2d 465 (1951)—§ **6.6 n. 66.**

Thompson v. Missouri, 171 U.S. 380, 18 S.Ct. 922, 43 L.Ed. 204 (1898)—§ **2.4 n. 31, 34.**

Thompson v. State, 554 P.2d 105 (Okl.Crim.App.1976)—§ **3.7 n. 4, 23.**

Thompson v. State, 159 Neb. 685, 68 N.W.2d 267 (1955)—§ **4.2 n. 32.**

Thompson v. State, 24 Ala.App. 300, 134 So. 679 (1931)—§ **8.11 n. 72.**

Thompson v. State, 106 Ala. 67, 17 So. 512 (1895)—§ **6.5 n. 69.**

Thompson v. State, 94 Ala. 535, 10 So. 520 (1892)—§ **8.3 n. 3.**

Thompson v. Utah, 170 U.S. 343, 18 S.Ct. 620, 42 L.Ed. 1061 (1898)—§ **2.4 n. 38.**

Thompson v. Whitman, 85 U.S. (18 Wall.) 457, 21 L.Ed. 897 (1873)—§ **2.7 n. 15.**

Thompson, People v., 93 Cal.App.2d 780, 209 P.2d 819 (1949)—§ **7.16 n. 32.**

Thompson, State v., 88 Wn.2d 18, 558 P.2d 202 (1977)—§ **7.4 n. 5; § 7.5 n. 104.**

Thompson, State v., Wright's Ohio Rep. 617 (1834)—§ **4.2 n. 100.**

Thompson, State ex rel. Brown v., 149 W.Va. 649, 142 S.E.2d 711 (1965)—§ **6.8 n. 79; § 6.9 n. 41.**

Thompson-Powell Drilling Co., United States v., 196 F.Supp. 571 (N.D.Tex.1961)—§ **3.10 n. 12.**

Thornhill v. Alabama, 310 U.S. 88, 60 S.Ct. 736, 84 L.Ed. 1093 (1940)—§ **2.3 n. 50, 65, 66.**

Thornton v. State, 107 Ga. 683, 33 S.E. 673 (1899)—§ **3.12 n. 72.**

Thornton, United States v., 178 F.Supp. 42 (E.D.N.Y. 1959)—§ **6.9 n. 16.**

Thorpe, State v., ___ R.I. ___, 429 A.2d 785 (1981)—§ **5.6 n. 3, 5.**

Thristle, Regina v., 169 Eng.Rep. 347 (Crim.App.1849)—§ **8.2 n. 5.**

Thurborn, Regina v., 169 Eng.Rep. 293 (Cr.Cas.Res.1848)—§ **8.2 n. 42, 43; § 8.5 n. 39.**

Thurman v. Adams, 82 Miss. 204, 33 So. 944 (1903)—§ **3.9 n. 26.**

Tibbs v. Commonwealth, 138 Ky. 558, 128 S.W. 871 (1910)—§ **4.9 n. 35.**

Tideswell, Rex v., (1905) 2 K.B. 273—§ **8.7 n. 47.**

Tierney, People v., 253 Cal.App.2d 1, 61 Cal.Rptr. 164 (1967)—§ **6.5 n. 36.**

Tift v. State, 17 Ga.App. 663, 88 S.E. 41 (1916)—§ **3.2 n. 38; § 4.9 n. 6; § 7.12 n. 20.**

Tillery v. State, 44 Ala.App. 369, 209 So.2d 432 (1968)—§ **8.4 n. 5.**

Tilson, State v., 503 S.W.2d 921 (Tenn.1974)—§ **7.10 n. 92.**

Tiner v. State, 239 Ark. 819, 394 S.W.2d 608 (1965)—§ **7.1 n. 35.**

Tingley v. Brown, 380 So.2d 1289 (Fla.1980)—§ **3.2 n. 53.**

Tinskey, People v., 394 Mich. 108, 228 N.W.2d 782 (1975)—§ **6.5 n. 60.**

Tipton v. State, 23 Okl.Crim. 86, 212 P. 612 (1923)—§ **8.5 n. 28; § 8.11 n. 19, 58.**

Tipton, People v., 78 Ill.2d 477, 36 Ill.Dec. 687, 401 N.E.2d 528 (1980)—§ **5.2 n. 3.**

Tite v. State Tax Comm'n, 89 Utah 404, 57 P.2d 734 (1936)—§ **2.6 n. 33.**

Titus, United States v., 64 F.Supp. 55 (D.N.J.1946)—§ **8.6 n. 62.**

Tluchak, Commonwealth v., 166 Pa.Super. 16, 70 A.2d 657 (1950)—§ **8.2 n. 4.**

Tobin-Builes, United States v., 706 F.2d 1092 (11th Cir. 1983)—§ **6.6 n. 19.**

Tolbert v. State, 31 Ala.App. 301, 15 So.2d 745 (1943)—§ **5.10 n. 43.**

Tollett, State v., 173 Tenn. 477, 121 S.W.2d 525 (1938)—§ **6.9 n. 4.**

Tolson, Regina v., 23 Q.B.D. 168 (1889)—§ **2.1 n. 83; § 2.2 n. 76; § 3.8 n. 11, 17; § 5.1 n. 27.**

Tomassi, State v., 137 Conn. 113, 75 A.2d 67 (1950)—§ **3.12 n. 83, 107.**

Tomlinson, Commonwealth v., 446 Pa. 241, 284 A.2d 687 (1971)—§ **7.5 n. 100.**

Tompkins, People v., 186 N.Y. 413, 79 N.E. 326 (1906)—§ **2.2 n. 99.**

Tomplain v. United States, 42 F.2d 202 (5th Cir.1930)—§ **6.4 n. 54.**

Toner, People v., 217 Mich. 640, 187 N.W. 386 (1922)—§ **4.10 n. 61.**

Toner, United States v., 173 F.2d 140 (3d Cir.1949)—§ **6.6 n. 87.**

Tones v. State, 48 Tex.Crim. 363, 88 S.W. 217 (1905)—§ **8.11 n. 7.**

Toney, State v., 81 Ohio St. 130, 90 N.E. 142 (1909)—§ **8.7 n. 66.**

Toon, State v., 172 La. 631, 135 So. 7 (1931)—§ **4.5 n. 159.**

Topolewski v. State, 130 Wis. 244, 109 N.W. 1037 (1906)—§ **8.2 n. 9.**

Tores v. State, 585 S.W.2d 746 (Tex.Crim.App.1979)—§ **4.10 n. 53.**

Torniero, United States v., 735 F.2d 725 (2d Cir.1984)—§ **4.3 n. 62.**

Torniero, United States v., 570 F.Supp. 721 (D.Conn. 1983)—§ **4.1 n. 24.**

Torphy, State v., 78 Mo.App. 206 (1899)—§ **3.6 n. 20; § 5.4 n. 17, 23.**

Torres v. State, 585 S.W.2d 746 (Tex.Crim.App.1979)—§ **4.10 n. 51.**

Torske v. State, 123 Neb. 161, 242 N.W. 408 (1932)—§ **4.5 n. 121.**

Toscano, State v., 74 N.J. 421, 378 A.2d 755 (1977)—§ **1.1 n. 18.**

Tot v. United States, 319 U.S. 463, 63 S.Ct. 1241, 87 L.Ed. 1519 (1943)—§ **2.13; § 2.13 n. 14.**

Toth, United States ex rel. v. Quarles, 350 U.S. 11, 76 S.Ct. 1, 100 L.Ed. 8 (1955)—§ **2.8 n. 24.**

Totman, State v., 80 Mo.App. 125 (1899)—§ **5.8 n. 3.**

Wiley v. State, 19 Ariz. 346, 170 P. 869 (1918)—§ **7.4 n. 18.**

Wiley, People v., 3 Hill 194 (N.Y.Sup.Ct.1842)—§ **8.10 n. 60.**

Wiley, Regina v., 4 Cox Crim.Cas. 412 (Cr.Cas.Res.1850)—§ **8.10 n. 15.**

Wiley, State v., 52 S.D. 110, 216 N.W. 866 (1927)—§ **7.16 n. 19.**

Wilkerson v. Utah, 99 U.S. 130, 25 L.Ed. 345 (1879)—§ **2.14 n. 88.**

Wilkins, State v., 144 Vt. 22, 473 A.2d 295 (1983)—§ **5.2 n. 34.**

Wilkinson v. State, 215 Miss. 327, 60 So.2d 786 (1952)—§ **8.7 n. 45, 52.**

Willard v. State, 174 Tenn. 642, 130 S.W.2d 99 (1939)—§ **2.1 n. 33.**

Willard, Commonwealth v., 39 Mass. 476 (22 Pick.) (1839)—§ **6.1 n. 62, 64.**

Willard, State ex rel. Losey v., 54 So.2d 183 (Fla.1951)—§ **3.10; § 3.10 n. 6.**

Willet v. Commonwealth, 76 Ky. 230 (1877)—§ **4.10 n. 21.**

Williams v. Director, Patuxent Institution, 276 Md. 272, 347 A.2d 179 (1975)—§ **1.7 n. 12.**

Williams v. Florida, 399 U.S. 78, 90 S.Ct. 1893, 26 L.Ed.2d 446 (1970)—§ **4.5 n. 40.**

Williams v. Illinois, 399 U.S. 235, 90 S.Ct. 2018, 26 L.Ed.2d 586 (1970)—§ **5.11 n. 63.**

Williams v. New York, 337 U.S. 241, 69 S.Ct. 1079, 93 L.Ed. 1337 (1949)—§ **1.5 n. 56.**

Williams v. North Carolina, 325 U.S. 226, 65 S.Ct. 1092, 89 L.Ed. 1577 (1945)—§ **3.8 n. 16.**

Williams v. State, 646 S.W.2d 221 (Tex.Crim.App.1983)—§ **6.4 n. 98.**

Williams v. State, 554 P.2d 842 (Okl.Crim.App.1976)—§ **3.12 n. 108, 155, 156.**

Williams v. State, 70 Ga.App. 10, 27 S.E.2d 109 (1943)—§ **5.8 n. 3.**

Williams v. State, 16 Okl.Crim. 217, 182 P. 718 (1919)—§ **6.5 n. 84.**

Williams v. State, 77 Ohio St. 468, 83 N.E. 802 (1908)—§ **8.7 n. 31.**

Williams v. State, 51 Neb. 711, 71 N.W. 729 (1897)—§ **8.11 n. 70.**

Williams v. United States, 337 A.2d 772 (D.C.App.1975)—§ **5.1 n. 18.**

Williams v. United States, 267 F.2d 625 (D.C.Cir.1959)—§ **7.13 n. 37.**

Williams v. United States, 250 F.2d 19 (D.C.Cir.1957)—§ **4.4 n. 61.**

Williams, Commonwealth v., 133 Pa.Super. 104, 1 A.2d 812 (1938)—§ **7.13 n. 19, 23, 25, 43.**

Williams, People v., 56 Ill.App.2d 159, 205 N.E.2d 749 (1965)—§ **5.7 n. 14, 34.**

Williams, People v., 179 Cal.App.2d 487, 3 Cal.Rptr. 782 (1960)—§ **6.6 n. 36.**

Williams, People v., 61 Colo. 11, 155 P. 323 (1916)—§ **2.13 n. 61.**

Williams, People v., 127 Cal. 212, 59 P. 581 (1899)—§ **3.5 n. 46; § 8.12 n. 7.**

Williams, People v., 32 Cal. 280 (1867)—§ **3.6 n. 22.**

Williams, Rex v., 1 All E.R. 1068 [1953]—§ **8.5 n. 25.**

Williams, State v., 211 Neb. 650, 319 N.W.2d 748 (1982)—§ **3.2 n. 53.**

Williams, State v., 142 Vt. 81, 451 A.2d 1142 (1982)—§ **6.9 n. 31.**

Williams, State v., 358 So.2d 943 (La.1978)—§ **2.4 n. 29.**

Williams, State v., 395 A.2d 1158 (Me.1978)—§ **6.5 n. 300.**

Williams, State v., 94 Ohio App. 249, 115 N.E.2d 36 (1952)—§ **5.1 n. 36.**

Williams, State v., 189 S.C. 19, 199 S.E. 906 (1938)—§ **6.7 n. 27.**

Williams, State v., 68 W.Va. 86, 69 S.E. 474 (1910)—§ **8.7 n. 85.**

Williams, State v., 146 N.C. 618, 61 S.E. 61 (1908)—§ **2.12 n. 33.**

Williams, State v., 96 Minn. 351, 105 N.W. 265 (1905)—§ **4.2 n. 36.**

Williams, State v., 12 Mo.App. 591 (1882)—§ **8.13 n. 61.**

Williams, State v., 229 N.C. 348, 49 S.E.2d 617 (1848)—§ **6.9 n. 8.**

Williams, State v., 2 Tenn. Over. 108 (1808)—§ **2.1 n. 40.**

Williams, State ex rel. v. Whitman, 116 Fla. 196, 156 So. 705 (1934)—§ **5.1 n. 104.**

Williams, United States v., 705 F.2d 603 (2d Cir.1983)—§ **5.2 n. 108.**

Williams, United States v., 621 F.2d 123 (5th Cir.1980)—§ **8.12 n. 2.**

Williamson v. Lee Optical, 348 U.S. 483, 75 S.Ct. 461, 99 L.Ed. 563 (1955)—§ **2.11 n. 15, 17.**

Williamson v. United States, 445 A.2d 975 (D.C.App. 1982)—§ **7.16 n. 20.**

Williamson, State v., 282 Md. 100, 382 A.2d 588 (1978)—§ **6.6 n. 74.**

Willie, State v., 360 So.2d 813 (La.1978)—§ **4.5 n. 139.**

Williford, State v., 103 Wis.2d 98, 307 N.W.2d 277 (1981)—§ **7.10 n. 79.**

Willingham v. State, 262 Ala. 550, 80 So.2d 280 (1955)—§ **5.7 n. 17.**

Willis v. United States, 285 F.2d 663 (D.C.Cir.1960)—§ **4.5 n. 108.**

Willis, State v., 255 N.C. 473, 121 S.E.2d 854 (1961)—§ **7.8 n. 8.**

Wilson, Ex parte, 114 U.S. 417, 5 S.Ct. 935, 29 L.Ed. 89 (1885)—§ **1.6 n. 64.**

Wilson, Matter of, 81 N.J. 451, 409 A.2d 1153 (1979)—§ **8.6 n. 62.**

Wilson v. Commonwealth, 22 Ky.L.Rptr. 1251, 60 S.W. 400 (Ct.App.1901)—§ **7.13 n. 9.**

Wilson v. People, 103 Colo. 441, 87 P.2d 5 (1939)—§ **5.10 n. 58; § 6.7 n. 59.**

Wilson v. State, 188 Ark. 846, 68 S.W.2d 100 (1934)—§ **7.5 n. 73.**

Wilson v. State, 16 Okla.Cr. 471, 184 P. 603 (1919)—§ **2.9 n. 8.**

Wilson v. State, 130 Ark. 204, 196 S.W. 921 (1917)—§ **6.8 n. 92.**

Wilson v. State, 96 Ark. 148, 131 S.W. 336 (1910)—§ **3.11 n. 10; § 8.2 n. 55; § 8.5 n. 43.**

Wilson v. State, 85 Miss. 687, 38 So. 46 (1905)—§ **6.2 n. 66; § 6.3; § 6.3 n. 46.**

Wilson v. State, 37 Tex.Crim. 156, 38 S.W. 1013 (1897)—§ **7.2 n. 21.**

Wilson v. State, 24 S.W. 409 (Tex.Cr.1893)—§ **3.12 n. 14.**

Wilson v. State, 18 Tex.Ct.App.R. 270 (1885)—§ **8.5 n. 8, 11.**

Wilson v. United States, 391 F.2d 460 (D.C.Cir.1968)—§ **4.4 n. 23.**

Wilson, People v., 1 Cal.3d 431, 82 Cal.Rptr. 494, 462 P.2d 22 (1969)—§ **7.5 n. 107.**

Wilson, People v., 261 Cal.App.2d 12, 67 Cal.Rptr. 678 (1968)—§ **4.6 n. 50.**

Wilson, People v., 66 Cal.2d 749, 59 Cal.Rptr. 156, 427 P.2d 820 (1967)—§ **4.9 n. 11.**

*

Table of Statutes and Model Penal Code References

ARKANSAS
Statutes

Sec.	This Work Sec.	Note
41–2206 (Cont'd)	8.10	88
41–2302	8.7	111
41–2308	8.7	116

CALIFORNIA
West's Annotated Penal Code

Sec.	This Work Sec.	Note
653f	6.1	38
664	6.3	113

COLORADO
Revised Statutes

Sec.	This Work Sec.	Note
18	1.1	15
18–1–13	2.5	16
18–1–501	3.2	47
	3.3	5
18–1–606	3.10	52
	3.10	56
	3.10	59
18–1–607	3.10	103

CONNECTICUT
General Statutes Annotated

Sec.	This Work Sec.	Note
53a–11	1.1	15
	3.10	103
53a–19	5.7	36
53–20	5.9	59

DELAWARE
Code

Tit.	This Work Sec.	Note
11	1.1	15
11, § 42	8.2	47
11, § 222	3.10	22
11, § 452	5.11	11
11, § 453	5.11	16
11, § 1247	6.9	111

DISTRICT OF COLUMBIA
Code

Sec.	This Work Sec.	Note
49–301	2.1	20

FLORIDA
West's Statutes Annotated

Sec.	This Work Sec.	Note
45	1.1	15

FLORIDA
West's Statutes Annotated

Sec.	This Work Sec.	Note
776.051	5.10	33
782.04	7.5	72
812.011 through 812.081	8.8	22

GEORGIA
Code

Sec.	This Work Sec.	Note
26	1.1	15
26–401	3.10	22
26–703	4.2	95
26–802	6.6	79
26–1801 thru 26–1817	8.8	22
26–2504	6.9	82

HAWAII
Revised Statutes

Sec.	This Work Sec.	Note
701–118	3.10	22
	3.10	96
705–520	6.5	130

IDAHO
Code

Sec.	This Work Sec.	Note
18–207	4.1	47

ILLINOIS
Revised Statutes

Ch.	This Work Sec.	Note
38	1.1	15
38, ¶ 11–6	6.2	36
38, ¶ 11–14	6.2	35
38, ¶ 11–18	6.2	37
38, ¶ 11–20	6.2	27
38, ¶ 20–2	6.2	30
38, ¶ 22–50	6.2	31
38, ¶ 24–1	6.2	32
38, ¶ 28–1	6.2	33
38, ¶ 29–1	6.2	35
38, ¶ 34–3	2.5	16
38, ¶ 70–1	6.2	34
38, ¶ 1005–8–1	1.2	11
38, ¶ 1005–8–3	1.2	11

INDIANA
West's Annotated Code

Sec.	This Work Sec.	Note
35	1.1	15
35–41–1–22	3.10	22
35–42–5–1	8.11	12
	8.11	35

IOWA
Code Annotated

Sec.	This Work Sec.	Note
704.6	5.7	57
704.11	5.10	47
706.1	6.4	96
715.2	8.7	111

KANSAS
Statutes Annotated

Sec.	This Work Sec.	Note
21–3303	6.1	76

KENTUCKY
Revised Statutes

Sec.	This Work Sec.	Note
500.080	3.10	22
502.050	3.10	52
	3.10	56
	3.10	58
502.060	3.10	103
503.080	5.9	5
504.020	4.3	67
504.070	4.5	33
504.130	4.5	185
505.010	5.2	26
506.010	6.3	65
506.030	6.1	76

LOUISIANA
Revised Statutes Annotated

Art.	This Work Sec.	Note
14:1 et seq.	1.1	13
14:2	3.10	22
	8.4	6
14:7	2.1	1
14:10	3.5	10
14:13	4.11	36
14:26	6.4	96
14:28	6.1	80

MAINE
Revised Statutes Annotated

Tit.	This Work Sec.	Note
17–A	1.1	15
17–A, § 2	3.10	22

MINNESOTA
Statutes Annotated

Sec.	This Work Sec.	Note
609	1.1	15
609.17	6.2	104
	6.3	84
	6.3	123

MINNESOTA
Statutes Annotated

Sec.	This Work Sec.	Note
609.20	5.3	46
609.245	8.11	101
	8.11	103

MISSOURI
Vernon's Annotated Statutes

Sec.	This Work Sec.	Note
546.011	6.3	147
560.110	8.13	127
562.041	6.7	8
562.061	3.10	103

MONTANA
Code Annotated

Sec.	This Work Sec.	Note
45–2–202	3.3	5
	3.3	44
45–2–211	5.11	16
45–6–302	8.10	20

NEBRASKA
Revised Statutes

Sec.	This Work Sec.	Note
28–202	6.5	72
28–509	8.10	24
28–1412	5.10	42

NEW JERSEY
Statutes Annotated

Sec.	This Work Sec.	Note
2C	1.1	15
2C:2–9	5.3	46
2C:5–4	6.7	8
	6.7	49
	6.8	100
2C:20–7	8.10	88
2C:103	2.9	47
	2.9	56
	2.9	59
	2.9	60
2C:204	5.1	19
2C:307	5.10	27
2C:501	6.2	161

NEW MEXICO
Statutes Annotated

Sec.	This Work Sec.	Note
30–1–12	3.10	22
	6.7	8
	6.7	42
30–1–14	8.4	6

NEW YORK

McKinney's Penal Law

Sec.	This Work Sec.	Note
1.07	3.10	22
40.20	2.9	80
40.30	2.9	80
100.20	6.1	105
115.05	6.7	101
155.45	8.8	25

NORTH DAKOTA

Century Code

Sec.	This Work Sec.	Note
12.1–01	8.8	27

OHIO

Revised Code

Sec.	This Work Sec.	Note
2923.01	6.5	59
	6.5	61

OKLAHOMA

Statutes Annotated

Tit.	This Work Sec.	Note
21, § 423	6.5	78

OREGON

Revised Statutes

Sec.	This Work Sec.	Note
161.170	3.10	52
	3.10	56
	3.10	59
161.175	3.10	103
161.205	5.8	4
	5.8	10

PENNSYLVANIA

Consolidated Statutes Annotated

Tit.	This Work Sec.	Note
18, § 904	6.5	34

SOUTH DAKOTA

Codified Laws

Sec.	This Work Sec.	Note
22–3–9	2.9	49
	2.9	56

TEXAS

Penal Code

Sec.	This Work Sec.	Note
7.22	3.10	56
	3.10	58

UTAH

Code Annotated

Sec.	This Work Sec.	Note
76–2–401	5.6	44

VIRGINIA

Code

Sec.	This Work Sec.	Note
18.2–16	2.1	18
18.2–18	6.6	2
18.2–29	6.1	47

WASHINGTON

West's Revised Code Annotated

Sec.	This Work Sec.	Note
9A.04.020	2.2	34
9A.04.050	4.10	34
9A.04.110	3.10	22
	8.4	6
9A.16.020	5.7	2

WISCONSIN

Statutes Annotated

Sec.	This Work Sec.	Note
939.01 et seq.	1.1	14
939.03	2.9	17
939.23	3.5	12
	3.5	15
939.30	6.1	40
	6.1	73
	6.4	100
	6.4	107
	6.4	141
	6.5	6
	6.5	72
939.32(2)	6.2	65
	6.3	12
	6.3	103
	6.3	125

WYOMING

Statutes

Sec.	This Work Sec.	Note
6–1–104	3.10	22

Index

References are to Sections

CHRONIC ALCOHOLISM
Defense, § 4.10(h).

CITIZENSHIP
Jurisdiction basis, § 2.9(c)(2).

CIVIL LAW
Interaction with criminal law, § 1.3(c).

COERCION
See Duress.

COMBINATION
See Conspiracy.

COMMERCE CLAUSE
As limitation on states, § 2.15(b).

COMMITMENT
Incompetent to stand trial, § 4.4(b).
Not guilty by reason of insanity, § 4.6(a).

COMMON LAW CRIMES
England, § 2.1(b).
Pros and cons of, § 2.1(f).
United States, § 2.1(c).
Where abolished, § 2.1(d).
Where retained, § 2.1(e).

COMPETENCY AT TIME OF TRIAL
See Incompetency at Time of Proceedings.

COMPOUNDING CRIME
Common law, § 6.9(c).
Statutes covering, § 6.9(c).

COMPROMISE STATUTES
Bar to prosecution, § 5.11(d).

COMPULSION
See Duress.

CONCLUSIVE PRESUMPTIONS
Constitutionality, § 2.13(d).

CONCURRENCE
Acts and circumstances, § 3.11(b).
Acts and mental state, § 3.11(c).
Acts and results, § 3.11(d), (e).
As basic premise, § 3.1.
Conduct and intent in larceny, § 8.5(f).
Conduct and mental state in false pretenses, § 8.7(g).
Conduct and mental state in receiving stolen property, § 8.10(f).
Conduct and mental state in robbery, § 8.11(e).
Mental state and act or omission, § 3.11(a).
Mental state and circumstances, § 3.11(b).
Mental state and results,
  Difference as to degree of harm, § 3.11(e).
  Difference as to type of harm, § 3.11(d).

CONCURRENT JURISDICTION
Federal then state prosecution, § 2.8(d)(2).
State then federal prosecution, § 2.8(d)(1).
Two states prosecute, § 2.9(d).

CONDITIONAL ASSAULT
Generally, § 7.16(c).

CONDITIONAL INTENT
Generally, § 3.5(d).

CONDONATION BY VICTIM
Factor in criminal justice administration, § 5.11(e).
When a defense, § 5.11(d).

CONDUCT
Defined, § 1.2.

CONFIDENCE GAME
False pretenses and, § 8.7(j)(2).

CONSENT OF VICTIM
Battery, § 7.15(e).
Factor in criminal justice administration, § 5.11(e).
What constitutes consent, § 5.11(a).
When a defense, § 5.11(a).

CONSPIRACY
Accomplice liability distinguished, § 6.8(a).
Agreement, § 6.4(d).
Aiding and abetting of, § 6.4(d).
Common law, § 6.4(a).
Defense that conspirator would not be guilty of completed crime, § 6.5(g)(4).
Development of the crime, § 6.4(a).
Duration of, § 6.5(e).
Impossibility no defense, § 6.5(b).
Mental state,
  "Corrupt motive" doctrine, § 6.4(e)(5).
  Intent to achieve objective, § 6.4(e)(2).
  Intent to agree, § 6.4(e)(1).
  Liability without fault, § 6.4(e)(4).
  Plurality of intent, § 6.4(e)(6).
  Providing goods or services, § 6.4(e)(3).
Objective of, § 6.5(a).
Overt act requirement, § 6.5(c).
Plurality requirement,
  Acquittal of co-conspirator, § 6.5(g)(1).
  Corporations, § 6.5(g)(3).
  Husband and wife, § 6.5(g)(2).
  Wharton rule, § 6.5(g)(4).
Prosecutor's advantage,
  Circumstantial evidence, § 6.4(b)(4).
  Hearsay exception, § 6.4(b)(3).
  Joint trial, § 6.4(b)(5).
  Vagueness, § 6.4(b)(1).
  Venue, § 6.4(b)(2).
Punishment of, § 6.5(h).
Rationale of the crime, § 6.4(c).
RICO conspiracies, § 6.5(d)(3).
Scope of,
  Object dimension, § 6.5(d)(1).
  Party dimension, § 6.5(d)(2).
  RICO conspiracies, § 6.5(d)(3).
Statutes covering, § 6.4(a).
Withdrawal from, § 6.5(f).

CONSTITUTIONAL LIMITATIONS
  See also Bill of Rights; Bills of Attainder; Commerce Clause; Due Process; Equal Protection; Ex Post Facto Laws; Pre-emption Doctrine; Void-for-Vagueness Doctrine.
Power to create crimes,
  Procedures for raising, § 2.10(b).
  Successful challenge of, § 2.10(a).

CONSTRUCTIVE INTENT
Defined, § 3.5(e).

CONSTRUCTIVE POSSESSION
Meaning, § 3.2(e).

CONTEMPT OF COURT
Proceedings, § 1.7(e).

CONTRACT DUTIES
Omission to act, § 3.3(a)(3).

CONTRIBUTORY NEGLIGENCE
Factor in criminal justice administration, § 5.11(e).
Not a defense, § 5.11(c).
Relevant to causation issue, § 3.12(f)(6).
Relevant to issue of defendant's negligence, §§ 5.11(c), 7.12(d).

CONVERSION
Embezzlement, § 8.6(b).

CONVULSION
Automatism, § 4.9(a).
Involuntary act, § 3.2(c).

COOLING TIME
Manslaughter, § 7.10(d).

CORPORATE AGENT
Liability of, § 3.10(e).

CORPORATE OFFICER
Liability of, § 3.10(e).

CORPORATIONS
See also Enterprise Liability.
As conspirators, § 6.5(g)(3).

CORPUS DELICTI
Proof of, § 1.4(b).

CORRUPT MOTIVE DOCTRINE
Conspiracy, § 6.4(e)(5).

COUNTY ORDINANCES
Proceedings for violation of, § 1.7(c).

CREATION OF PERIL
Omission to act, § 3.3(a)(5).

CREDIT CARD LEGISLATION
False pretenses and, § 8.7(j)(6).

CRIME PREVENTION
Imperfect defense causing death as manslaughter, § 7.11(b).
Use of force in, § 5.10(c).

CRIME TERMINATION
Use of force in, § 5.10(c).

CRIMES
See also Administrative Crimes; Common Law Crimes.
Administrative, § 2.6.
Classification of, § 1.6.
Common law, §§ 1.6(f), 2.1.
Felony, § 1.6(a).

CRIMES—Cont'd
Infamous, § 1.6(d).
Involving moral turpitude, § 1.6(c).
Malum in se, § 1.6(b).
Malum prohibitum, § 1.6(b).
Misdemeanor, § 1.6(a).
Petty offenses, § 1.6(e)
Statutory, § 1.6(f).
Torts distinguished, § 1.3(b).

CRIMES AGAINST THE PERSON
See Assault; Battery; Manslaughter; Mayhem; Murder.

CRIMES RELATING TO PROPERTY
See Bad Checks; Blackmail; Burglary; Embezzlement; Extortion; False Pretenses; Larceny; Receiving Stolen Property; Robbery; Theft.

CRIMINAL ATTEMPT
See Attempt.

CRIMINAL INTENT
See Intent; Mental State.

CRIMINAL JURISDICTION
See Jurisdiction.

CRIMINAL NEGLIGENCE MANSLAUGHTER
Generally, § 7.12.

CRIMINAL PROCEDURE
Characteristics of, § 1.4.
Discretion in, § 1.4(c).
Evidentiary tests in, § 1.4(a).
Use of part of process, § 1.4(d).

CRIMINAL PROCEEDINGS
Contempt proceedings distinguished, § 1.7(e).
Juvenile delinquency proceedings distinguished, § 1.7(a).
Ordinance violation proceedings distinguished, § 1.7(c).
Sexual psychopathy proceedings distinguished, § 1.7(b).
Statutory penalty proceedings distinguished, § 1.7(d).

CRIMINAL STATUTES
See Statutory Interpretation.

CRUEL AND UNUSUAL PUNISHMENT
Generally, § 2.14(f).
Chronic alcoholism, § 4.10(h).
Death penalty, § 2.14(f).
Insanity defense abolition, § 4.1(d).
Narcotics addiction, § 4.10(h).

DEATH PENALTY
Constitutionality, § 2.14(f).
Cruel and unusual punishment, § 2.14(f).

DEFENSE OF ANOTHER
Alter ego rule, § 5.8(b).
Imperfect defense causing death as manslaughter, § 7.11(a).
Mistaken belief of need for, § 5.8(b).
Necessity of force, § 5.8(b).
Person defended, § 5.8(a).
Property of another, § 5.9(e).
Relationship, § 5.8(a).
Retreat, § 5.8(c).

INVOLUNTARY MANSLAUGHTER—Cont'd
Unlawful act, § 7.13.

IRRESISTIBLE IMPULSE TEST
Criticism of, § 4.2(e).
Stated, § 4.2(d).

JOINT POSSESSION
Meaning, § 3.2(e).

JOINT TRIAL
Conspiracy, § 6.4(b)(5).

JURISDICTION
Generally, § 2.7.
Defined, § 2.7(a).
Federal, § 2.8.
Concurrent with state, § 2.8(d).
Conduct within states, § 2.8(c).
Double jeopardy, § 2.8(d).
Federal prosecution first, § 2.8(d)(2).
State prosecution first, § 2.8(d)(1).
Nationality, § 2.8(b)(1).
"Protective principle," § 2.8(b)(2).
Territorial, § 2.8(a).
Aircraft, § 2.8(a)(3).
Enclaves, § 2.8(a)(2).
Ships, § 2.8(a)(3).
Situs of crime, § 2.8(a)(4).
Territories, § 2.8(a)(1).
Universal, § 2.8(b)(3).
Power to create crimes, § 2.7(a).
Proof of, § 2.7(b).
State, § 2.9.
Citizenship, § 2.9(c)(2).
Double jeopardy, § 2.9(d).
Extradition, § 2.9(d).
Omission to act, § 2.9(a).
Protective principle, § 2.9(c)(1).
Situs of crime, § 2.9(a).
Statutory extensions of, § 2.9(b).
Territorial, § 2.9(a).
Universal, § 2.9(c)(3).

JURY
Causation determination, § 3.12(k).

JUSTIFICATION AND EXCUSE
See Arrest; Condonation by Victim; Consent of Victim;
Contributory Negligence; Crime Prevention; Defense
of Another; Defense of Property; Domestic Authority;
Duress; Entrapment; Escape Prevention; Guilt of
Victim; Ignorance or Mistake; Necessity; Public Du-
ty; Ratification by Victim; Self Defense; Settlement
with Victim.

JUVENILE COURTS
See Infancy; Juvenile Delinquency.

JUVENILE DELINQUENCY
See also Infancy.
Juvenile court jurisdiction, § 4.11(c).
Proceedings, § 1.7(a).

"KNOWINGLY"
See Knowledge.

KNOWLEDGE
See also Ignorance or Mistake.
Defined, § 3.5(b).
Intent distinguished, § 3.5(b).
Intoxication negativing, § 4.10(a).
Recklessness distinguished, § 3.7(f).
"Wilful blindness" as, § 3.5(b).

KNOWLEDGE OF DUTY
Omission to act, § 3.3(b).

LANDOWNER
Omission to act, § 3.3(a)(7).

LARCENY
Asportation, § 8.3(b).
Caption, § 8.3(a).
Carrying away, § 8.3(b).
Conduct must concur with intent, § 8.5(f).
Embezzlement distinguished, §§ 8.1(b), 8.8(a)(1).
False pretenses distinguished, §§ 8.1(b), 8.8(a)(2).
Grand, § 8.4(b).
Historical development of theft crimes, § 8.1.
Intent to steal,
Generally, § 8.5.
Claim of right, § 8.5(a).
Concurrence with conduct, § 8.5(f).
Intent to collect debt, § 8.5(d).
Intent to return equivalent, § 8.5(c).
Intent to return property taken, § 8.5(b).
Intent to satisfy claim, § 8.5(d).
Miscellaneous defenses, § 8.5(e).
Petit, § 8.4(b).
Property,
Nature of, § 8.4(a).
Of another, § 8.4(c).
Value of, § 8.4(b).
Taking, § 8.3(a).
Trespass,
Generally, § 8.2.
Bailee who breaks bale or bulk, § 8.2(d).
Delivery by mistake, § 8.2(g).
Finders, § 8.2(f).
Larceny by trick, § 8.2(e).
Master and servant, § 8.2(b).
Property picked up by mistake, § 8.2(h).
Removal from owner's premises or presence, § 8.2(i).
Transaction in owner's presence, § 8.2(c).

LAW ENFORCEMENT
See Arrest; Crime Prevention; Escape Prevention.

LEGAL CAUSE
Causation, § 3.12(c).

LEGAL IMPOSSIBILITY
Attempt, § 6.3(a)(3).

LEGALITY
As basic premise, § 3.1.

LEGISLATION
Recodification, § 1.1(b).

LEGISLATIVE HISTORY
Statutory interpretation, § 2.2(e).

LESSER LEGAL WRONG THEORY
Ignorance or mistake, § 5.1(c).

LIABILITY WITHOUT FAULT
See Enterprise Liability; Strict Liability; Vicarious Liability.

LIVING HUMAN BEING
Beginning of life, § 7.1(c).
End of life, § 7.1(d).

LYING IN WAIT
Murder, § 7.7(c).

MADNESS
See Insanity.

MAIL FRAUD
False pretenses and, § 8.7(j)(3).

MAIM
See Mayhem.

MALICE AFORETHOUGHT
Murder, § 7.1(a).

MALUM IN SE
Defined, § 1.6(b).

MALUM PROHIBITUM
Defined, § 1.6(b).

MANSLAUGHTER
Classification, § 7.9.
Committed by omission to act, § 3.3(e).
Criminal negligence,
　Causation, § 7.12(c).
　Contributory negligence, § 7.12(d).
　History, § 7.12(a).
　Omission, § 7.12(b).
　Reasonable man, § 7.12(a).
　Requirement of awareness of risk, § 7.12(a).
　Requirement of high risk, § 7.12(a).
　Statutory variations, § 7.12(e).
Felony for felony murder, § 7.5(g)(1).
Heat-of-passion,
　Actual cooling off, § 7.10(e).
　Actual provocation, § 7.10(c).
　Compared to first and second degree murder, § 7.10(f).
　Mental state, § 7.10(a).
　Provocation from other than person killed, § 7.10(g).
　Rationale, § 7.10(h).
　Reasonable provocation,
　　Generally, § 7.10(b).
　　Adultery, § 7.10(b)(5).
　　Assault, § 7.10(b)(3).
　　Battery, § 7.10(b)(1).
　　Illegal arrest, § 7.10(b)(4).
　　Injury to third persons, § 7.10(b)(7).
　　Miscellaneous, § 7.10(b)(8).
　　Mistake as to provocation, § 7.10(b)(9).
　　Mutual combat, § 7.10(b)(2).
　　Reasonable man, § 7.10(b)(10).
　　Words, § 7.10(b)(6).
　Reasonable time to cool off, § 7.10(d).
Intoxication and, § 4.10(e).

MANSLAUGHTER—Cont'd
Other-extenuating-circumstances,
　Aiding suicide, § 7.11(d).
　Imperfect arrest defense, § 7.11(b).
　Imperfect crime prevention defense, § 7.11(b).
　Imperfect defense of others, § 7.11(a).
　Imperfect duress defense, § 7.11(c).
　Imperfect escape prevention defense, § 7.11(b).
　Imperfect necessity defense, § 7.11(c).
　Imperfect self defense, § 7.11(a).
　Intoxication, § 7.11(d).
　Mental disorder, § 7.11(d).
Partial responsibility, § 4.7(b)(2).
Unlawful-act,
　Assault or battery causing death, § 7.12(d).
　Causation, §§ 3.12(h), 7.13(b).
　Future of, § 7.13(e).
　Limitations upon, § 7.13(c).
　Meaning of "unlawful," § 7.13(a).

MAYHEM
Common law, § 7.17(a).
Defenses to, § 7.17(e).
Mental state, § 7.17(d).
Statutory coverage, § 7.17(b).
Type and extent of injury, § 7.17(c).

MECHANICAL DEVICES
Defense of property by, § 5.9(c).

MENS REA
See Intent; Knowledge; Mental State; Negligence; Recklessness.

MENTAL DISEASE OR DEFECT
See Insanity.

MENTAL STATE
　See also Ignorance or Mistake; Intent; Knowledge; Negligence; Partial Responsibility; Recklessness.
　Generally, § 3.4.
Accomplice liability, § 6.7(b).
Ambiguity as to, § 3.4(b).
As basic premise, § 3.1.
Attempts, § 6.2(c).
Basic types, § 3.4(c).
Common law crimes, § 3.4(a).
Concurrence with act, § 3.11.
Conspiracy, § 6.4(e).
Due process requirement, § 2.12(d).
General principles and, § 3.4(e).
Single crime, differing, § 3.4(d).
Solicitation, § 6.1(c).
Statutory crimes, § 3.4(a).

MILITARY DUTIES
Defense, § 5.5(c).

MISDEMEANOR
Defined, § 1.6(a).

MISPRISION OF FELONY
Generally, § 6.9(b).

MISTAKE OF FACT
See Ignorance or Mistake.

MURDER—Cont'd
Co-felon kills self, § 7.5(d).
Conviction of felony also, § 7.5(g)(3).
Depraved-heart murder compared, § 7.5(e).
Duress defense, § 5.3(b).
First degree, § 7.7(b).
Future of the doctrine, § 7.5(h).
History of, § 7.5(a).
"In the commission of" felony,
  Generally, § 7.5(f).
  Causal connection, § 7.5(f)(2).
  Differing views on scope, § 7.5(f)(3).
  Homicide followed by felony, § 7.5(f)(4).
  Time, § 7.5(f)(1).
Limited to certain felonies, § 7.5(b).
Manslaughter as felony, § 7.5(g)(1).
Vicarious responsibility of co-felons, § 7.5(c).
First degree,
  In commission of listed felonies, § 7.7(b).
  Lying in wait, § 7.7(c).
  Other, § 7.7(d).
  Poison, § 7.7(c).
  Premeditation and deliberation, § 7.7(a).
  Torture, § 7.7(c).
Intent-to-do-serious-bodily-injury murder, § 7.3.
Intent-to-kill murder,
  Generally, § 7.2.
  Causation, § 7.2(d).
  Intention, § 7.2(a).
  Deadly weapon doctrine, § 7.2(b).
  Means of producing intentional death, § 7.2(c).
Living human being requirement,
  When life begins, § 7.1(c).
  When life ends, § 7.1(d).
Malice aforethought, § 7.1(a).
Partial responsibility, § 4.7(b)(2).
Premeditation and deliberation, § 7.7(a).
  Intoxication negativing, § 4.10(b).
Resisting-lawful-arrest murder, § 7.6.
Second degree, § 7.7(e).
Statutory definitions of, § 7.1(b).
Year-and-a-day rule, § 7.1(e).

NARCOTICS ADDICTION
See also Intoxication.
Crime, constitutionality, §§ 2.14(f), 4.10(h).

NATIONALITY
Jurisdiction, § 2.8(b)(1).

NECESSITY
Defined for particular offenses, § 5.4(a).
Examples of defense, § 5.4(c).
Imperfect defense causing death as manslaughter, § 7.11(c).
Nature of defense, § 5.4(a).
Rationale of defense, § 5.4(a).
Relationship to other defenses, § 5.4(b).
Requirements of defense,
  Harm avoided, § 5.4(d)(1).
  Harm done, § 5.4(d)(2).
  Intention to avoid harm, § 5.4(d)(3).
  Optional courses of action, § 5.4(d)(5).
  Relative value of harm avoided and harm done, § 5.4(d)(4).
Where defendant at fault in creating situation, § 5.4(d)(6).

NEGATIVE ACT
See Omission to Act.

NEGLIGENCE
See also Criminal Negligence Manslaughter; Ignorance or Mistake; Manslaughter.
"Constructive intent" including, § 3.5(e).
Criminal, § 3.7(b).
"Criminal intent" including, § 3.5(e).
Criminal law vs. tort law, § 3.7(a).
Disparity between foreseeable and actual result,
  Unexpected degree of harm, § 3.7(h)(4).
  Unforeseeable manner, § 3.7(h)(2).
  Unforeseeable victim, § 3.7(h)(1).
  Unhazarded type of harm, § 3.7(h)(3).
Gross, § 3.7(b).
High degree of, § 3.7(b).
Intoxication and, § 4.10(c).
Objective standard, § 3.7(a)(2).
Objective vs. subjective fault, § 3.7(g).
Proof of realization of risk, § 3.7(d).
Recklessness compared as basis for liability, § 3.7(g).
Recklessness distinguished, § 3.7(b).
Subjective vs. objective fault, § 3.7(g).
Tort law vs. criminal law, § 3.7(a).
Transferred, § 3.12(e).
Unreasonable risk, § 3.7(a)(1).
Violation of statute or ordinance, § 3.7(c).

NEGLIGENCE MANSLAUGHTER
Generally, § 7.12.

NIGHTTIME
Burglary, § 8.13(d).

NO-ACCOUNT CHECKS
See Bad Checks.

NO RETREAT RULE
Self defense, § 5.7(f).

NONPERFORMANCE
See Omission to Act.

NOT GUILTY BY REASON OF INSANITY
Verdict, § 4.5(h).

OBJECTIVE FAULT
Negligence, § 3.7(a)(2), (g).

OMISSION TO ACT
Causation, § 3.3(d).
Concurrence with mental state, § 3.11(a).
Crimes which may be committed by, § 3.3(e).
Duty to act,
  Generally, § 3.3(a).
  Based upon assumption of care, § 3.3(a)(4).
  Based upon contract, § 3.3(a)(3).
  Based upon creation of peril, § 3.3(a)(5).
  Based upon relationship, § 3.3(a)(1).
  Based upon responsibility to control others, § 3.3(a)(6).
  Based upon statute, § 3.3(a)(2).
  Landowner, § 3.3(a)(7).
  Moral duty compared, § 3.3(f).
In definition of crime, § 3.3(a).
Jurisdiction over, § 2.9(b).
Knowledge of duty, § 3.3(b).

OMISSION TO ACT—Cont'd
Knowledge of facts giving rise to duty, § 3.3(b).
Not in definition of crime, § 3.3(a).
Possibility of performing act, § 3.3(c).

ORDINARY NEGLIGENCE
See Negligence.

OVERT ACT
Conspiracy, § 6.5(c).

PARENTS
Discipline of children, § 5.6(a).

PARTIAL INSANITY
See Partial Responsibility.

PARTIAL RESPONSIBILITY
Constitutional considerations, § 4.7(d).
Crime or no crime, § 4.7(b)(3).
First or second degree murder, § 4.7(b)(1).
Insanity defense distinguished, § 4.7(a).
Murder or manslaughter, § 4.7(b)(2).
Policy considerations, § 4.7(c).

PARTIES TO CRIME
Abandonment of common law terminology, § 6.6(e).
Accessory before the fact, § 6.6(c).
Accomplice liability,
  Acts or omissions, § 6.7(a).
  Conspiracy distinguished, § 6.8(a).
  Crime by principal required, § 6.8(c).
  Exceptions to, § 6.8(e).
  Foreseeability of other crimes, § 6.8(b).
  Mental state,
      Generally, § 6.7(b).
    Assistance or encouragement to reckless or negligent
        conduct, § 6.7(e).
    Intentional assistance or encouragement, § 6.7(c).
    Knowing assistance or encouragement, § 6.7(d).
    Liability without fault, § 6.7(f).
  Withdrawal as a defense, § 6.8(d).
Aiding suicide, § 7.8(c).
Conspiracy, § 6.4(d).
Felony murder,
  Accomplice liability, § 7.5(c).
Principal in first degree, § 6.6(a).
Principal in second degree, § 6.6(b).
Procedural problems,
  Conviction of principal required, § 6.6(d)(3).
  Jurisdiction, § 6.6(d)(1).
  Solved by legislative reform, § 6.6(e).
  Variance between charge and proof, § 6.6(d)(2).
Thief as accomplice to receiving stolen property, § 8.10(h).

PARTNERSHIPS
See Enterprise Liability.

PERSON, CRIMES AGAINST
See Assault; Battery; Manslaughter; Mayhem; Murder.

PETIT EMBEZZLEMENT
Defined, § 8.6(h).

PETIT FALSE PRETENSES
Defined, § 8.7(h).

PETIT LARCENY
Defined, § 8.4(b).

PETTY OFFENSES
Defined, § 1.6(e).

PLAIN MEANING RULE
Statutory interpretation, § 2.2(b).

PLURALITY REQUIREMENT
Conspiracy, § 6.5(g).

POISON
Murder by, § 7.7(c).

POSITIVE ACT
See Act.

POSSESSION
See Act; Embezzlement; False Pretenses; Larceny.

POST-TRAUMATIC STRESS DISORDER
Automatism, § 4.9(a).
Mental disease, § 4.2(b)(1).

PRE-EMPTION DOCTRINE
As limitation on municipalities, § 1.7(c).
As limitation on states, § 2.15(b).

PREMEDITATION AND DELIBERATION
Murder, § 7.7(a).

PREMENSTRUAL SYNDROME
Automatism, § 4.9(a).
Not mental disease, § 4.2(b)(1).

PRESUMED INTENT
Proof of intention, § 3.5(f).

PRESUMPTION OF INNOCENCE
Meaning of, § 1.8(f).

PRESUMPTIONS
Conclusive presumptions, § 2.13(d).
Forms of, § 2.13(a).
Inferences distinguished, § 2.13(b).
Mandatory presumptions, § 2.13(c).

PREVENTION
Punishment theory, § 1.5(a)(1).

PRINCIPAL IN THE FIRST DEGREE
Party to crime, § 6.6(a).

PRINCIPAL IN THE SECOND DEGREE
Party to crime, § 6.6(b).

PRIVILEGE AGAINST SELF-INCRIMINATION
Insanity defense, § 4.5(c).
Substantive law limitation, § 2.14(e).

"PROBABLE CAUSE"
Indictment, § 1.4(a).
Preliminary hearing, § 1.4(a).

PROBABLE DESISTANCE THEORY
Attempt act, § 6.2(d)(2).

PROCURING AGENT DEFENSE
Defined, § 6.7(d).

PROPERTY CRIMES
See Bad Checks; Blackmail; Burglary; Embezzlement; Extortion; False Pretenses; Larceny; Receiving Stolen Property; Robbery; Theft.

PROPERTY DEFENSE
See Defense of Property.

PROPORTIONALITY
Cruel and unusual punishment, § 2.14(f).

"PROTECTIVE PRINCIPLE"
Jurisdiction, § 2.8(b)(2).

PROVOCATION
Manslaughter, § 7.10(b), (c).

PROXIMATE CAUSE
Causation, § 3.12(c).

PROXIMITY THEORY
Attempt act, § 6.2(d)(1).

PUBLIC DUTY
Executing court order, § 5.5(a).
Military duties, § 5.5(c).
Public official's actions, § 5.5(b).

PUNISHMENT
Accessory after the fact, § 6.9(a).
As basic premise, § 3.1.
Attempt, § 6.3(c).
Capital, § 2.14(f).
Conspiracy, § 6.5(h).
Cruel and unusual, § 2.14(f).
Duress as mitigating, § 5.3(d).
Necessarily prescribed, § 1.2(d).
Proportionality, § 2.14(f).
Theories of,
  Conflict between, § 1.5(b).
  Correction, § 1.5(a)(3).
  Deterrence, § 1.5(a)(4).
  Disablement, § 1.5(a)(2).
  Education, § 1.5(a)(5).
  General prevention, § 1.5(a)(4).
  Incapacitation, § 1.5(a)(2).
  Insanity defense and, § 4.1(c).
  Intimidation, § 1.5(a)(1).
  "Just deserts," § 1.5(a)(6).
  Particular deterrence, § 1.5(a)(1).
  Prevention, § 1.5(a)(1).
  Reformation, § 1.5(a)(3).
  Rehabilitation, § 1.5(a)(3).
  Restraint, § 1.5(a)(2).
  Retaliation, § 1.5(a)(6).
  Retribution, § 1.5(a)(6).
  Revenge, § 1.5(a)(6).
  Trends in, § 1.5(b).

PURPOSE
  See also Intent.
Criminal law, §§ 1.2(e), 1.5.

RATIFICATION BY VICTIM
Factor in criminal justice administration, § 5.11(e).
When a defense, § 5.11(d).

"REASONABLE GROUNDS TO BELIEVE"
Test for arrest, § 1.4(a).

"REASONABLE GROUNDS TO SUSPECT"
Test for stopping and questioning, § 1.4(a).

REBUTTABLE PRESUMPTIONS
Burden of proof, § 1.8(e).
Constitutionality, § 2.13(c).

RECEIVING STOLEN PROPERTY
Concurrence of conduct and mental state, § 8.10(f).
Consolidation with other theft crimes, § 8.10(m).
Defenses, § 8.10(i).
Federal crimes involving, § 8.10(j).
Grand receiving, § 8.10(g).
Historical development, § 8.10(a).
Jurisdiction, § 8.10(l).
Knowing it stolen, § 8.10(d).
Petit receiving, § 8.10(g).
Receiving, § 8.10(b).
Stolen, § 8.10(c).
Thief as accomplice, § 8.10(h).
Thief as receiver, § 8.10(h).
Venue, § 8.10(l).
With intent to deprive owner, § 8.10(e).

RECKLESSNESS
  See also Criminal Negligence Manslaughter; Ignorance or Mistake; Manslaughter; Negligence.
"Constructive intent" including, § 3.5(e).
"Criminal intent" including, § 3.5(e).
Defined, § 3.7(b).
Intent distinguished, § 3.7(f).
Intoxication negativing, § 4.10(c).
Knowledge distinguished, § 3.7(f).
Negligence compared as basis for liability, § 3.7(g).
Negligence distinguished, § 3.7(b).

RECODIFICATION
Federal efforts, § 1.1(b).
States undertaking, § 1.1(b).

REFLEX
Involuntary act, § 3.2(c).

REHABILITATION
Punishment theory, § 1.5(a)(3).

RENUNCIATION
Solicitation defense, § 6.1(d).

RESISTING ARREST
Defense of, § 5.7(h).
Force against, § 5.10(a).
Murder by, § 7.6.

RESPONDEAT SUPERIOR
See Enterprise Liability.

VICARIOUS LIABILITY
Act requirement, § 3.2(f).
Common law crimes, § 3.9(a).
Constitutionality of, § 3.9(c).
Interpretation of statute as imposing, § 3.9(b).
Pros and cons of, § 3.9(d).
Statutory crimes, § 3.9(b).
Strict liability distinguished, § 3.9(b).

VOID-FOR-VAGUENESS DOCTRINE
Generally, § 2.3(a).
Arbitrary enforcement test, § 2.3(c).
Fair warning test, § 2.3(b).
First amendment rights test, § 2.3(d).

VOLUNTARY ACT
Nature of, § 3.2(c).

VOLUNTARY MANSLAUGHTER
Generally, §§ 7.10, 7.11.

WHARTON RULE
Conspiracy, § 6.5(g)(4).

WIFE
Coercion of by husband, § 5.3(f).
Conspiracy with husband, § 6.5(g)(2).

"WILFUL BLINDNESS"
As knowledge, § 3.5(b).

WITHDRAWAL
Conspiracy, § 6.5(f).

XYY CHROMOSOME DEFENSE
A.L.I. test, § 4.8(d).
Chromosomal abnormalities, § 4.8(a).
Insanity defense and, § 4.8(c).
Irresistible impulse test, § 4.8(d).
M'Naghten test, § 4.8(d).
Mental disease or defect, § 4.8(d).
XYY syndrome, § 4.8(b).

YEAR-AND-A-DAY RULE
Causation, §§ 3.12(i), 7.1(e).

†